W9-CTW-229

Nineteenth-Century Literature Criticism

Volume 3

Nineteenth-Century Literature Criticism

Excerpts from Criticism of the
Works of Novelists, Poets, Playwrights,
Short Story Writers, and Other Creative Writers
Who Lived between 1800 and 1900,
from the First Published Critical
Appraisals to Current Evaluations

Laurie Lanzen Harris
Editor

Sheila Fitzgerald
Associate Editor

Gale Research Inc. · DETROIT · LONDON

STAFF

Laurie Lanzen Harris, *Editor*

Sheila Fitzgerald, *Associate Editor*

Emily Wade Barrett and Anna C. Wallbillich, *Senior Assistant Editors*

Cherie D. Abbey, Laura L. Britton, Denise Michlewicz, Robert Bruce Young, Jr., *Assistant Editors*

Phyllis Carmel Mendelson and Mark Scott, *Contributing Editors*

Carolyn Bancroft, *Production Supervisor*
Lizbeth A. Purdy, *Production Coordinator*

Eric F. Berger, Frank James Borovsky, Paula J. DiSante, Denise B. Grove, Serita Lanette Lockard, Brenda Marshall, Marie M. Mazur, Janet S. Mullane, Gloria A. Williams, *Editorial Assistants*

Robert J. Elster, *Research Coordinator*
Jeannine Schiffman Davidson, Ann Marie Dadah, Kathleen Gensley, Barbara L. Hammond, Robert Hill, James A. MacEachern, Carol Angela Thomas, *Research Assistants*

Linda Marcella Pugliese, *Manuscript Coordinator*
Donna D. Craft, *Assistant Manuscript Coordinator*
Colleen M. Crane, Maureen A. Puhl, Rosetta Irene Simms, *Manuscript Assistants*

L. Elizabeth Hardin, *Permissions Supervisor*
Filomena Sgambati, *Permissions Coordinator*
Janice M. Mach, *Assistant Permissions Coordinator*
Patricia A. Seefelt, *Photo Permissions*
Anna Maria DiNello, Mary P. McGrane, Susan D. Nobles, *Permissions Assistants*
Elizabeth Babini, Margaret Chamberlain, Virgie T. Leavens, Joan B. Weber, *Permissions Clerks*

The paper used in this publication meets the minimum requirements
of American National Standard for Information Sciences—Permanence
Paper for Printed Library Materials, ANSI Z39.48-1984.

Printed in the United States of America.
Published simultaneously in the United Kingdom
by Gale Research International Limited
(An affiliated company of Gale Research Inc.)

CONTENTS

5

PREFACE

The nineteenth century was a time of tremendous growth in human endeavor: in science, in social history, and particularly in literature. The era saw the development of the novel, witnessed radical changes from classicism to romanticism to realism, and contained intellectual and artistic ideas that continue to inspire authors of our own century. The importance of the writers of the nineteenth century is twofold, for they provide insight into their own time as well as into the universal nature of human experience.

The literary criticism of an era can also give us insight into the moral and intellectual atmosphere of the past, for the criteria by which a work of art is judged reflect current philosophical and social attitudes. Literary criticism takes many forms: the traditional essay, the book or play review, even the parodic poem. Criticism can also be of several kinds: normative, descriptive, interpretive, textual, appreciative, generic. Collectively, the range of critical response helps us to understand a work of art, an author, an era.

The Scope of the Work

The success of Gale's two current literary series, *Contemporary Literary Criticism (CLC)* and *Twentieth-Century Literary Criticism (TCLC),* which excerpt criticism of creative writing from the twentieth century, suggested an equivalent need among students and teachers of literature of the nineteenth century. Moreover, since the critical analysis of this literature spans almost two hundred years, a vast amount of critical material confronts the student.

Nineteenth-Century Literature Criticism (NCLC) presents significant passages from published criticism on authors who died between 1800 and 1900. Those customers who ordered the series from the sample or from early promotional material will note a small but significant change in the title of *NCLC*. In order to accurately reflect the content of *NCLC* the title was changed from *Nineteenth-Century Literary Criticism* to *Nineteenth-Century Literature Criticism,* thus indicating that it is the *literature* and the *authors* of the nineteenth century and not the *literary criticism* of that century alone with which we are concerned. Indeed, to indicate the full range of critical response to the authors covered in the series, we must draw upon the criticism of the eighteenth, nineteenth, and twentieth centuries.

The author list for each volume of *NCLC* is carefully compiled to represent a variety of genres and nationalities and to cover authors who are currently regarded as the most important writers of an era as well as those whose contribution to literature and literary history is significant. The truly great writers are rare, and in the intervals between them lesser but genuine artists, as well as writers who enjoyed immense popularity in their own time and in their own countries, are important to the study of nineteenth-century literature. The length of each author's entry is intended to represent the author's critical reception in English. Articles and books that have not been translated into English are excluded. Each author entry represents a historical overview of the critical response to the author's work: early criticism is presented to indicate initial responses, later selections represent any rise or decline in the author's literary reputation. We have also attempted to identify and include excerpts from the seminal essays on each author, and to include recent critical comment providing modern perspectives on the writer. Thus, *NCLC* is designed to serve as an introduction for the student of nineteenth-century literature to the authors of that period and to the most significant commentators on these authors.

NCLC entries are intended to be definitive overviews. Approximately 30 authors are included in each 600-page volume, compared to about 75 authors in a *CLC* volume of similar size. Because of the great quantity of critical material available on many authors, and because of the resurgence of criticism generated by events such as an author's centennial or anniversary celebration, the republication of an author's works, or publication of a newly translated work or volume of letters, an author may appear more than once.

7

The Organization of the Book

An author section consists of the following elements: author heading, biocritical introduction, principal works, excerpts of criticism (each followed by a citation), and an annotated bibliography of additional reading.

- The *author heading* consists of the author's full name, followed by birth and death dates. The unbracketed portion of the name denotes the form under which the author most commonly wrote. If an author wrote consistently under a pseudonym, the pseudonym will be listed in the author heading and the real name given in parentheses on the first line of the biocritical introduction. Also located at the beginning of the biocritical introduction are any name variations under which an author wrote, including transliterated forms for authors whose languages use nonroman alphabets. Uncertainty as to a birth or death date is indicated by a question mark.

- The *biocritical introduction* contains biographical and other background information that elucidates the author's creative output.

- The list of *principal works* is chronological by date of first publication and identifies genres. In those instances where the first publication was in other than the English language, the title and date of the first English-language edition is given in brackets. Unless otherwise indicated, dramas are dated by the first performance, rather than first publication.

- *Criticism* is arranged chronologically in each author section to provide a perspective on any changes in critical evaluation over the years. In the text of each author entry, titles by the author are printed in boldface type. This allows the reader to ascertain without difficulty the works discussed. For purposes of easier identification, the critic's name and the publication date of the essay are given at the beginning of each piece of criticism. Unsigned criticism is preceded by the title of the journal in which it appeared. For an anonymous essay later attributed to a critic, the critic's name appears in brackets in the heading and in the citation.

- A complete *bibliographical citation* designed to facilitate the location of the original essay or book follows each piece of criticism. An asterisk (*) at the end of the citation indicates that the essay is on more than one author.

- The *annotated bibliography* appearing at the end of each author section suggests further reading on the author. In some cases it includes essays for which the editors could not obtain reprint rights. An asterisk (*) at the end of a citation indicates that the essay is on more than one author.

Each volume of *NCLC* includes a cumulative index to critics. Under each critic's name are listed the authors on whom the critic has written and the volume and page where the criticism appears. *NCLC* also includes a cumulative index to authors with the volume number in which the author appears.

An appendix is included which lists the sources from which material in the volume is reprinted. It does not, however, list every book or periodical consulted for the volume.

Acknowledgments

No work of this scope can be accomplished without the cooperation of many people. The editors especially wish to thank the copyright holders of the excerpts included in this volume, the permissions managers of the book and magazine publishing companies for assisting us in securing reprint rights, and the staffs of the Detroit Public Library, University of Michigan Library, and Wayne State University Library for making their resources available to us. We are also grateful to Michael F. Wiedl III for his assistance with copyright research and Norma J. Merry for her editorial assistance.

Suggestions Are Welcome

The editors welcome the comments and suggestions of readers to expand the coverage and enhance the usefulness of the series.

AUTHORS TO APPEAR IN FUTURE VOLUMES

ABOUT, Edmond François 1828-1885
AGUILÓ I FUSTER, Mariá 1825-1897
AINSWORTH, William Harrison 1805-1882
AKSAKOV, Konstantin 1817-1860
ALCOTT, Louisa May 1832-1888
ALEARDI, Aleadro 1812-1878
ALECSANDRI, Vasile 1821-1890
ALENCAR, José 1829-1877
ALFIERI, Vittorio 1749-1803
ALGER, Horatio 1834-1899
ALLINGHAM, William 1824-1889
ALMQUIST, Carl Jonas Love 1793-1866
ALORNA, Leonor de Almeida 1750-1839
ALSOP, Richard 1761-1815
ALTIMIRANO, Ignacio Manuel 1834-1893
ALVARENGA, Manuel Inácio da Silva 1749-1814
ALVARES DE AZEVEDO, Manuel Antônio 1831-1852
ANDERSEN, Hans Christian 1805-1875
ANZENGRUBER, Ludvig 1839-1889
ARANY, János 1817-1882
ARENE, Paul 1843-1893
ARJONA DE CUBAS, Manuel Mariá de 1771-1820
ARNIM, Achim von 1781-1831
ARNIM, Bettina von 1785-1859
ARNOLD, Matthew 1822-1888
ASACHI, Gheorghe 1788-1869
ASBJÖRNSEN, Peter Christen 1812-1885
ASCASUBI, Hilario 1807-1875
ASNYK, Adam 1838-1897
ATTERBOM, Per Daniel Amadeus 1790-1855
AUERBACH, Berthold 1812-1882
AUGIER, Guillaume V.E. 1820-1889
AZEGLIO, Massimo D' 1798-1866
AZEVEDO, Guilherme de 1839-1882
BAKIN (pseud. of Takizawa Okikani) 1767-1848
BALZAC, Honoré de 1799-1850
BANVILLE, Théodore de 1823-1891
BARNES, William 1801-1886
BARONIAN, Hagop 1842-1891
BAUDELAIRE, Charles Pierre 1821-1867
BEATTIE, James 1735-1803
BECKFORD, William 1760-1844
BÉCQUER, Gustavo Adolfo 1836-1870
BELINSKY, Vissarion Grigor'ye vich 1811-1848
BELLAMY, Edward 1850-1898
BELLO, Andrés 1781-1865
BENTHAM, Jeremy 1748-1832
BÉRANGER, Jean-Pierre de 1780-1857
BERCHET, Giovanni 1783-1851

BERZSENYI, Dániel 1776-1836
BILDERDYK, Willem 1756-1831
BLACK, William 1841-1898
BLAIR, Hugh 1718-1800
BLAKE, William 1757-1827
BLICHER, Steen Steensen 1782-1848
BOCAGE, Manuel Maria Barbosa du 1765-1805
BODTCHER, Ludvig 1793-1874
BORATYNSKY, Yevgeny 1800-1844
BOREL, Pétrus 1809-1859
BOREMAN, Yokutiel 1825-1890
BORROW, George 1803-1881
BOSBOOM-TOUSSAINT, Anna L.G. 1812-1886
BOTEV, Hristo 1778-1842
BRACKENRIDGE, Hugh Henry 1748-1816
BREMER, Fredrika 1801-1865
BRINCKMAN, John 1814-1870
BRONTE, Anne 1820-1849
BRONTE, Emily 1812-1848
BROWN, Charles Brockden 1777-1810
BROWNING, Robert 1812-1889
BRYANT, William Cullen 1794-1878
BÜCHNER, Georg 1813-1837
BURNEY, Fanney 1752-1840
CABALLERO, Fernan 1796-1877
CALVERLEY, Charles Stuart 1831-1884
CAMPBELL, James Edwin 1867-1895
CAMPBELL, Thomas 1777-1844
CARLYLE, Thomas 1795-1881
CASTELO BRANCO, Camilo 1825-1890
CASTRO ALVES, Antônio de 1847-1871
CHAMISSO, Adalbert von 1781-1838
CHANNING, William Ellery 1780-1842
CHATTERJE, Bankin Chanda 1838-1894
CLARE, John 1793-1864
CLAUDIUS, Matthais 1740-1815
CLOUGH, Arthur Hugh 1819-1861
COBBETT, William 1762-1835
COLENSO, John William 1814-1883
COLERIDGE, Hartley 1796-1849
COLERIDGE, Samuel T. 1772-1834
COLLETT, Camilla 1813-1895
CONRAD, Robert T. 1810-1858
CONSCIENCE, Hendrik 1812-1883
CONSTANT, Benjamin 1767-1830
COOKE, John Esten 1830-1886
CORBIÈRE, Edouard 1845-1875
COWPER, William 1731-1800
CRABBE, George 1754-1832
CRAWFORD, Isabella Valancy 1850-1886
CRUZ E SOUSA, João da 1861-1898
DE QUINCEY, Thomas 1785-1859
DESBORDES-VALMORE, Marceline 1786-1859

DESCHAMPS, Antony 1800-1869
DESCHAMPS, Emile 1791-1871
DICKINSON, Emily 1830-1886
DEUS, Joao de 1830-1896
DINIS, Júlio 1839-1871
DINSMOOR, Robert 1757-1836
DOBROLYUBOV, Nikolay Aleksandrovich 1836-1861
DRENNAN, John Swanick 1809-1893
DUMAS, Alexandre (père) 1802-1870
DUMAS, Alexandre (fils) 1824-1895
DU MAURIER, George 1834-1896
DWIGHT, Timothy 1752-1817
ECHEVERRIA, Esteban 1805-1851
EICHENDORFF, Joseph von 1788-1857
ELIOT, George 1819-1880
EMINESCY, Mihai 1850-1889
ERBEN, Karel Jaromír 1811-1870
ERTER, Isaac 1792-1851
ESPRONCEDA, José 1808-1842
ETTINGER, Solomon 1799-1855
EUCHEL, Issac 1756-1804
FERGUSON, Samuel 1810-1886
FERNANDEZ DE LIZARDI, José Joaquín 1776-1827
FERNANDEZ DE MORATÍN, Leandro 1760-1828
FET, Afanasy 1820-1892
FEUILLET, Octave 1821-1890
FITZGERALD, Edward 1809-1883
FONTANE, Theodor 1819-1898
FORSTER, John 1812-1876
FOSCOLO, Ugo 1778-1827
FREDERIC, Harold 1856-1898
FREDRO, Aleksander 1793-1876
FREYTAG, Gustav 1816-1895
FULLER, Sarah Margaret 1810-1850
GABORIAU, Emile 1835-1873
GANIVET, Angel 1865-1898
GARRETT, Almeida 1799-1854
GARSHIN, Vsevolod Mikhaylovich 1855-1888
GASKELL, E.C. 1810-1865
GEZELLE, Guido 1830-1899
GHÁLIB, Asadullah Khán 1797-1869
GODWIN, William 1756-1836
GOETHE, Johann Wolfgang von 1749-1832
GOGOL, Nikolay Vasilievich 1809-1852
GOLDSCHMIDT, Meir Aron 1819-1887
GOMEZ DE AVELLANEDA, Gertrudis 1814-1873
GONÇALVES DIAS, Antonio 1823-1864
GONCOURT, Edmond 1822-1896
GONCOURT, Jules 1830-1870
GORDON, Yehuda Leib 1812-1891
GOZZI, Carlo 1720-1806
GRIBOYEDOV, Aleksander Sergeyevich 1795-1829
GRIGOR'YEV, Appolon Aleksandrovich 1822-1864

GROSSI, Tommaso 1790-1853
GROTH, Klaus 1819-1899
GRÜN, Anastasius (pseud. of Anton Alexander Graf von Auersperg) 1806-1876
GUERRAZZI, Francesco Domenico 1804-1873
GUTIERREZ NAJERA, Manuel 1859-1895
HA-KOHEN, Shalom 1772-1845
HALLECK, Fitz-Greene 1790-1867
HAMMON, Jupiter 1711-1800
HARRIS, George Washington 1814-1869
HAYNE, Paul Hamilton 1830-1886
HAZLITT, William 1778-1830
HEBBEL, Christian Friedrich 1813-1863
HEBEL, Johann Peter 1760-1826
HEGEL, Georg Wilhelm Friedrich 1770-1831
HEIBERG, Johan Ludvig 1813-1863
HEINE, Heinrich 1797-1856
HERCULANO, Alexandre 1810-1866
HERDER, Johann Gottfried 1744-1803
HERNANDEZ, José 1834-1886
HERTZ, Henrik 1798-1870
HERWEGH, Georg 1817-1875
HERZEN, Alexander Ivanovich 1812-1870
HOFFMAN, Charles Fenno 1806-1884
HOFFMANOWA, Klementyna 1798-1845
HOGG, James 1770-1835
HÖLDERLIN, Friedrich 1770-1843
HOLMES, Oliver Wendell 1809-1894
HOOD, Thomas 1799-1845
HOPKINS, Gerard Manley 1844-1889
HUGHES, Thomas 1822-1896
IMLAY, Gilbert 1754?-1828?
IMMERMANN, Karl Lebrecht 1796-1840
IRWIN, Thomas Caulfield 1823-1892
ISSACS, Jorge 1837-1895
JACOBSEN, Jens Peter 1847-1885
JEAN PAUL (pseud. of Johann Paul Friedrich Richter) 1763-1825
JIPPENSHA, Ikku 1765-1831
KARADŽIĆ, Vuk Stefanovic 1787-1864
KEATS, John 1759-1821
KEBLE, John 1792-1866
KHOMYAKOV, Alexey S. 1804-1860
KIERKEGAARD, Søren 1813-1855
KINGLAKE, Alexander W. 1809-1891
KINGSLEY, Charles 1819-1875
KIVI, Alexis 1834-1872
KLOPSTOCK, Friedrich Gottlieb 1724-1803
KOLLÁR, Jan 1793-1852

9

KOLTSOV, Alexey Vasilyevich 1809-1842

KOTZEBUE, August von 1761-1819

KRASIĆKI, Ignacy 1735-1801

KRASIŃSKI, Zygmunt 1812-1859

KRASZEWSKI, Josef Ignacy 1812-1887

KREUTZWALD, Friedrich Reinhold 1803-1882

KROCHMAL, Nahman 1785-1840

LACLOS, Pierre Choderlos de 1741-1803

LAFORGUE, Jules 1860-1887

LAMARTINE, Alphonse 1790-1869

LAMB, Charles 1775-1834

LAMPMAN, Archibald 1861-1899

LANDON, Letitia Elizabeth 1802-1838

LANDOR, Walter Savage 1775-1864

LANIER, Sidney 1842-1881

LARMINIE, William 1850-1899

LARRA Y SANCHEZ DE CASTRO, Mariano 1809-1837

LAUTRÉAMONT (pseud. of Isodore Ducasse) 1846-1870

LEBENSOHN, Micah Joseph 1828-1852

LECONTE DE LISLE, Charles-Marie-René 1818-1894

LE FANU, Joseph Sheridan 1814-1873

LENAU, Nikolaus 1802-1850

LEONTYEV, Konstantin 1831-1891

LEOPARDI, Giacoma 1798-1837

LERMONTOV, Mikhail 1814-1841

LESKOV, Nikolai 1831-1895

LEVER, Charles James 1806-1872

LEVISOHN, Solomon 1789-1822

LEWIS, Matthew Gregory 1775-1810

LEYDEN, John 1775-1811

LONGSTREET, Augustus Baldwin 1790-1870

LÓPEZ DE AYOLA Y HERRERA, Adelardo 1819-1871

LOVER, Samuel 1797-1868

LUZZATTO, Samuel David 1800-1865

MACEDO, Joaquim Manuel de 1820-1882

MÁCHA, Karel Hynek 1810-1836

MACKENZIE, Henry 1745-1831

MAGALHÃES, Domingos José 1811-1882

MAIMON, Solomon 1754-1800

MALLARMÉ, Stéphane 1842-1898

MANGAN, James Clarence 1803-1849

MANZONI, Alessandro 1785-1873

MAPU, Abraham 1808-1868

MARII, José 1853-1895

MARKOVIC, Sv. 1846-1875

MARTINEZ DE LA ROSA, Francisco 1787-1862

MATHEWS, Cornelius 1817-1889

MATURIN, Charles Robert 1780-1824

McCULLOCH, Thomas 1776-1843

MERIMÉE, Prosper 1803-1870

MERRIMAN, Brian 1747-1805

MEYER, Conrad Ferdinand 1825-1898

MILES, George H. 1824-1871

MITFORD, Mary Russell 1787-1855

MOE, Jörgen Ingebretsen 1813-1882

MONTAGU, Elizabeth 1720-1800

MONTGOMERY, James 1771-1854

MOODIE, Susanna 1803-1885

MOORE, Thomas 1779-1852

MÖRIKE, Eduard 1804-1875

MORRIS, William 1834-1898

MORTON, Sarah Wentworth 1759-1846

MOTOORI, Noringa 1730-1801

MÜLLER, Friedrich 1749-1825

MULTATULE (pseud. of E.D. Dekker) 1820-1887

MURGER, Henri 1822-1861

MUSSET, Alfred de 1810-1857

NEKRASOV, Nikolai 1821-1877

NEMCOVÁ, Božena 1820-1862

NERUDA, Jan 1834-1891

NESTROY, Johann 1801-1862

NEWMAN, John Henry 1801-1890

NICCOLINI, Giambattista 1782-1861

NIEVO, Ippolito 1831-1861

NJEGOŠ, Petar 1813-1851

NODIER, Charles 1780-1844

NORTH, Christopher (pseud. of John Wilson) 1785-1854

NORWID, Cyprian 1821-1883

NOVALIS (pseud. of Friedrich von Hardenberg) 1772-1801

OBRADOVIĆ, Dositej 1742-1811

OEHLENSCHLÄGER, Adam 1779-1850

OLIPHANT, Margaret 1828-1897

O'NEDDY, Philothée (pseud. of Théophile Dondey) 1811-1875

O'SHAUGHNESSY, Arthur William Edgar 1844-1881

OSTROVSKY, Alexander 1823-1886

PAINE, Thomas 1737-1809

PALSSON, Gestur 1852-1891

PALUDAN-MILLER, Frederick 1809-1876

PARKMAN, Francis 1823-1893

PATER, Walter 1839-1894

PATMORE, Coventry Kersey Dighton 1823-1896

PEACOCK, Thomas Love 1785-1866

PERK, Jacques 1859-1881

PISEMSKY, Alexey F. 1820-1881

PLATEN-HALLERMÜNDE, August 1796-1835

POMPÉIA, Raul D'Avila 1863-1895

POPOVIC, Jovan Sterija 1806-1856

POTGEITER, Everardus Johannes 1808-1875

PRAED, Winthrop Mackworth 1802-1839

PRATI, Giovanni 1814-1884

PRERADOVIĆ, Petar 1818-1872

PREŠEREN, France 1800-1849

PRINGLE, Thomas 1789-1834

PYE, Henry James 1745-1813

QUENTAL, Antero Tarquínio de 1842-1891

QUINTANA, Manuel José 1772-1857

RADCLIFFE, Ann 1764-1823

RADISHCHEV, Aleksander 1749-1802

RAFTERY, Anthony 1784-1835

RAIMUND, Ferdinand 1790-1836

REID, Mayne 1818-1883

RENAN, Ernest 1823-1892

REUTER, Fritz 1810-1874

RIMBAUD, Arthur 1854-1891

ROGERS, Samuel 1763-1855

ROSSETTI, Dante 1828-1882

RÜCKERT, Friedrich 1788-1866

RUNEBERG, Johan 1804-1877

RYDBERG, Viktor 1828-1895

RYUTEI, Tanehiko 1783-1842

SAAVEDRA Y RAMIREZ DE BOQUEDANO, Angel de 1791-1865

SAINTE-BEUVE, Charles 1804-1869

SALTYKOV-SHCHEDRIN, Mikhail 1826-1892

SANTO KYODEN 1761-1816

SATANOV, Isaac 1732-1805

SCHILLER, Friedrich 1759-1805

SCHLEGEL, August 1767-1845

SCHLEGEL, Karl 1772-1829

SCOTT, Sir Walter 1771-1832

SCRIBE, Augustin Eugene 1791-1861

SENOA, August 1838-1881

SHELLEY, Mary W. 1797-1851

SHELLEY, Percy Bysshe 1792-1822

SHERIDAN, Richard 1751-1816

SHEVCHENKO, Taras 1814-1861

SHULMAN, Kalman 1819-1899

SILVA, José Asunción 1865-1896

SLAVEYKOV, Petko 1828-1895

SLOWACKI, Juliusz 1809-1848

SMITH, Richard Penn 1799-1854

SMOLENSKIN, Peretz 1842-1885

SOARES DE PASSOS, Antonio Augusto de 1826-1860

SOGA, Tiyo 1829-1871

SOLOMOS, Dionysios 1798-1857

SOUTHEY, Robert 1774-1843

STAGNELIUS, Erik Johan 1793-1823

STARING, Antonie Christiaan Wynand 1767-1840

STENDHAL (pseud. of Henri Beyle) 1783-1842

STEVENSON, Robert Louis 1850-1894

STIFTER, Adalbert 1805-1868

STONE, John Augustus 1801-1834

STUR, L'udovít 1815-1856

SURTEES, Robert Smith 1803-1894

SYROKOMLA, Wladyslaw (pseud. of Ludwik Kondratowicz) 1823-1862

TAUNAY, Alfredo d' Ecragnole 1843-1899

TAYLOR, Bayard 1825-1878

TENNYSON, Alfred, Lord 1809-1892

TERRY, Lucy (Lucy Terry Prince) 1730-1821

THACKERAY, William 1811-1863

THOMPSON, Daniel Pierce 1795-1868

THOMPSON, Samuel 1766-1816

THOMSON, James 1834-1882

THOREAU, Henry David 1817-1862

TIECK, Ludwig 1773-1853

TIEDGE, Christoph August 1752-1841

TIMROD, Henry 1828-1867

TOLENTINO DE ALMEIDA, Nicolau 1740-1811

TOMMASEO, Nicolo 1802-1874

TOMPA, Mihály 1817-1888

TOPELIUS, Zachris 1818-1898

TOPSØE, Vilhelm 1840-1881

TROLLOPE, Anthony 1815-1882

TURGENEV, Ivan 1818-1883

TYUTCHEV, Fedor I. 1803-1873

UHLAND, Ludvig 1787-1862

VAJDA, János 1827-1899

VALAORITIS, Aristotelis 1824-1879

VALLES, Jules 1832-1885

VERDE, Cesário 1855-1886

VERY, Jones 1813-1880

VIGNY, Alfred Victor de 1797-1863

VILLAVERDE, Cirilio 1812-1894

VINJE, Aasmund Olavsson 1818-1870

VON FALLERSLEBEN, August Heinrich (pseud. of August Heinrich Hoffmann) 1798-1874

VÖRÖSMARTY, Mihaly 1800-1855

WAGNER, Richard 1813-1883

WARREN, Mercy Otis 1728-1814

WEISSE, Christian Felix 1726-1804

WELHAVEN, Johan S. 1807-1873

WERGELAND, Henrik Arnold 1808-1845

WERNER, Zacharius 1768-1823

WESCOTT, Edward Noyes 1846-1898

WESSELY, Nattali Herz 1725-1805

WHITMAN, Sarah Helen 1803-1878

WHITMAN, Walt 1819-1892

WHITTIER, John Greenleaf 1807-1892

WIELAND, Christoph Martin 1733-1813

WOOLSON, Constance Fenimore 1840-1894

WORDSWORTH, William 1770-1850

ZHUKOVSKY, Vasily 1783-1852

ZORRILLA Y MORAL, José 1817-1893

Henri Becque

1837-1899

French dramatist, critic, and journalist.

Becque is considered the first French dramatist of the naturalist school. His outstanding plays, *Les corbeaux (The Vultures)* and *La Parisienne (The Woman of Paris)*, marked a turning point in French drama. The works introduced a new genre, the *comédie rosse*, or bitter comedy, which often centered on the hypocrisy of contemporary mores. Becque strove for a more natural rendering of character and dialogue in his plays and this places his work in vivid contrast to the sentimental and melodramatic drama which was popular in his time.

Becque's life was marked by personal and financial difficulties and is reflected in the misanthropic and cynical tone of his work. The son of a government clerk, Becque grew up in Paris, where he graduated from the Lycée Bonaparte. He first worked in a railway office but, bored with his position, he turned to work in the theater. In 1865, Becque became the secretary to a Polish nobleman through whom he met Victorien de Joncières, a young composer. Becque's first literary work was the libretto to Joncières' opera, *Sardanapale*, based on Lord Byron's drama, *Sardanapalus*. He worked for a short time as drama critic for the journal *Le Peuple* and wrote his first play, *L'enfant prodigue*. Its moderate success inspired Becque to turn to literature for his livelihood, but much of his later work did not meet with popular approval. Becque was unwilling to compromise with managers and producers and he decided to produce his own plays. However, audiences found Becque's work more curious than dramatically innovative and Becque withdrew from the theater for several years.

He served in the Franco-Prussian war and later worked as a stockbroker, but eventually returned to playwriting, and spent what he termed "the happiest year of my life" writing *The Vultures*. However, it took five years to find a producer willing to stage the work as he had written it. The first production proved a triumphant success and was acclaimed by a group of young playwrights, who saw in Becque's work an important movement toward a modern approach to drama. The sobering realism of Becque's next play, *The Woman of Paris*, stood even more sharply in contrast to the superficial nature of most Parisian drama produced at the time. It was not until André Antoine founded the Théâtre Libre, a theatrical group which rejected the banality and artificiality of contemporary French drama, that Becque's work found a sympathetic home.

Success came to Becque too late to inspire subsequent works of the calibre of *The Vultures* and *The Woman of Paris*, and in his last years he wrote only a few short sketches. An important exception, the unfinished *Les Polichinelles*, was to have been his masterpiece. *Les Polichinelles* is a mordant satire of the world of finance, reflecting Becque's own unhappy tenure as a stockbroker. Scenes from the fragment have been produced, but critics generally dismiss the work for its lack of unity.

In 1886, Becque was awarded the Legion of Honor and later traveled through Italy, where he was lionized as a brilliant

The Granger Collection

dramatist. However, at home he lived in poverty and solitude, receiving little income from his writing.

Becque's perceptive analysis of social mores informs his finest work and although his plays are rarely performed today, he holds a place of importance in the development of French drama.

PRINCIPAL WORKS

Sardanapale (libretto) 1867
L'enfant prodigue (drama) 1868
Michel Pauper (drama) 1870
La navette (drama) 1878
  [*The Merry-Go-Round*, 1913]
Les corbeaux (drama) 1882
  [*The Crows*, 1912; also published as *The Vultures*, 1913]
La Parisienne (drama) 1885
  [*The Woman of Paris*, 1913]
Les Polichinelles [first publication] (unfinished drama) 1910

A. B. WALKLEY (essay date 1901)

To say that *La Parisienne* is a clever piece would be true but inadequate. It is diabolically clever. It purports to have been written by the late M. Henry Becque, single-handed, but I suspect Old Nick to have been at his elbow, an unseen collaborator. At least, there must have been brimstone in M. Becque's inkpot. No one with the slightest sense of humour can see the piece without laughing, or rather, I fear it must be admitted, without sniggering. But that is only the superficial effect. The play cuts deep. Its irony bites like vitriol. And the ultimate impression is of something grim, cruel, malignant. It tends to make us loathe ourselves, or, at any rate, our next-door neighbours. This is a strange impression to receive from a comedy, from Mme. Réjane's face of impish mischief, her ravishing gowns. It is a strange blend, this whiff of sulphur combined with *odeur de femme*. But, then, *La Parisienne* is a strange piece.

It begins with one of the most complete hoaxes ever devised by a playwright. . . . It is the familiar scene of jealous husband and teazing wife. . . . And, lo! we find that our quarrelling couple, so conjugal in every detail of their quarrel, are not husband and wife, after all, but lover and mistress. How, then, comes it that the jealous gentleman is so like a husband? That is the point, or a point, of the play. Lafont, the lover, has assumed by usage and temperament and the inevitable tendency of things, *quasi*-marital qualities. . . . If anyone is shocked by the situation it is certainly not Clotilde. She does not see the irony of it, for she cannot see herself as she is. No more does Lafont, for the same reason. No more does Du Mesnil, for Du Mesnil sees nothing at all, not even when it passes under his very nose.

But the irony is there, and its teeth drive sharp into our poor human flesh. It consists in the spectacle of two people carrying on irregular relations with precisely the same set of feelings and prejudices which would be operative were their relations regular. The "immoral" is shown to labour under the same conditions as the "moral." (pp. 283-85)

Clotilde, with all her irregularity of conduct, is entirely conventional in her ideas. She declares herself a Conservative in politics, because she inclines to the party of social "order." She is indignant at the thought that her lover might leave her for another mistress who is "without religious principles." As a matter of fact, she has no moral sense whatever. She is absolutely without conscience. Things are for her merely pleasant or unpleasant, conduct is merely expedient or inexpedient. She is a Nietzschean, a Nietzschean without knowing it, a Nietzschean in frills and furbelows of the most fashionable cut. She has lovers, but no passions, hardly even appetites, only caprices. A monster, then, something merely perverse and noxious? Yes—and No. Yes, according to any accepted standard of ethics. No, by virtue of her reality. There is a great deal of ordinary human nature in Clotilde. She desires to hurt no one, she merely means to "have a good time." She is good-humoured, patient, reasonable, tactful. Mark that she is a capable woman—indeed, the one capable member of the triangular household. She gets her fool of a husband into a good post. It would be ungenerous to inquire too closely into the means; the point is that she can do for her husband what he cannot do for himself. If Lafont were not so tiresomely jealous, she could get on excellently with him, too. This, after all, is an eminently companionable sort of monster. And, tough she has a wonderful gift of fiction, she does not tell unnecessary lies. (pp. 285-86)

Nor is she without her little chastening experience. When she has dismissed Lafont she tries another lover, who bores her to death and then leaves her in the lurch. The lesson is not thrown away. . . . Do you not hear a chuckle as the curtain descends? It must be M. Becque's unseen collaborator. Evidently on this occasion there is no need, with the charitable lady in the Scotch anecdote, to "pity the puir deil." He has had it all his own way. (p. 286)

A. B. Walkley, "'La Parisienne'" (originally published in The Times, *June, 1901), in his* Drama and Life, *Methuen & Co., 1907, pp. 283-86.*

JOHN OLIVER HOBBES (essay date 1904)

Henry Becque—the author of **"La Parisienne"**—saw life as Flaubert saw it, but he had, what Flaubert lacked, the dramatic instinct. The construction of **"La Parisienne"** is perfect in its rhythm; from the first line until the last there is not a word which does not illuminate the whole, which is not indispensable to the whole, which is not living and which is not true. The plot is better than any of the tortured inventions which pass for problems—it is a common case presented by a man who was as fearless as Molière in his exposition of the human heart. He knew, as Molière knew, and Flaubert knew, and Fielding knew, that there are no problems, and that, till death intervenes in the affairs of all the parties concerned, there is no last act on earth for any set of situations. **"La Parisienne,"** briefly, is the given sum total of all the plays and novels which have misinformed the inexperienced of the Christian world for the last hundred years or so. . . .

There are critics who, mistaking the situation for the philosophy, have called this piece immoral. One would as soon call "Georges Dandin" or "Tom Jones" immoral. A true book and a true play cannot be otherwise than moral. It is the false picture—no matter how pretty—which makes for immorality. (p. 17)

John Oliver Hobbes, "Letters from a Silent Study," in The Academy and Literature, *Vol. LXVII, No. 1678, July 2, 1904, pp. 17-18.*

JAMES HUNEKER (essay date 1905)

[What] is this naturalistic formula of Becque's that escaped the notice of the zealous Zola and set the pace for nearly all the younger men? Is it not the absence of a formula of the tricks of construction . . .? The taint of the artificial, of the sawdust, is missing in Becque's masterpieces; yet with all their large rhythms, unconventional act-ends, and freedom from the *cliché*, there is no raggedness in detail; indeed, close study reveals the presence of a delicate, intricate mechanism, so shielded by the art of the dramatist as to illude us into believing that we are in the presence of unreasoned reality. . . . He saw the mad futility of the literary men who invaded the theatre full of arrogant belief in their formulas, in their newer conventions that would have supplanted older ones. A practical playwright, our author had no patience with those who attempted to dispense with the frame of the footlights, who would turn the playhouse into a literary farm through which would gambol all sorts of incompetents masquerading as original dramatic thinkers.

Becque's major quality is his gift of lifelike characterization. Character with him is of prime importance. He did not tear down the structure of the drama but merely removed much of the scaffolding which time had allowed to disfigure its façade. While Zola and the rest were devising methods for doing away with the formal drama, Becque sat reading Molière. Molière is his real master—Molière and life. . . . In his endeavour to put before us his people in a simple, direct way he did smash several conventions. He usually lands his audience in the middle of the action, omitting the old-fashioned exposition act, careful preparation, and sometimes development, as we know it in the well-regulated drama. But search for his reasons and they are not long concealed. . . . The logic of Becque's events must retire before the logic of his characters, that is all. Humanity, then, is his chief concern. He cares little for literary style. He is not a stylist, though he has style—the stark, individual style of Henry Becque.

Complications, catastrophe, dénouement, all these are attenuated in the Becque plays. Atmosphere supplies the exposition, character painting, action. The impersonality of the dramatist is profound. (pp. 169-71)

Positivism, rather than naked realism, is Becque's note. The cold-blooded pessimism that pervades so unpleasantly many of his comedies was the resultant of a temperament sorely tried by experience, and one steeped in the materialism of the Second Empire.

So we get from him the psychology of the crowd, instead of the hero ego of earlier dramatists. He contrives a dense atmosphere, into which he plunges his puppets, and often his people appear cold, heartless, cynical. He is a surgeon, more like Ibsen than he would ever acknowledge, in his calm exposure of social maladies. And what a storehouse have been his studies of character for the generation succeeding him! Becque forged the formula, the others but developed it. (p. 172)

["L'Enfant Prodigue"] is Becque at his wittiest, merriest best. In an unpremeditated manner it displays a mastery of intrigue that is amazing. For a man who despised mere technical display, this piece is a shining exemplar of virtuosity. Let those who would throw stones at Becque's nihilism in the matter of conventional craftsmanship read "The Prodigal Son" and marvel at its swiftness of action, its stripping the vessel of all unnecessary canvas, and scudding along under bare poles! The comedy is unfailing, the characterization rich in those cunning touches which are like salt applied to a smarting wound. The plot is slight, the adventures of several provincials who visit Paris and there become entangled in the toils of a shrewd adventuress. The underplot is woven skilfully into the main texture. Hypocrisy is scourged. A father and a son discover that they are trapped by the same woman. There is *genre* painting that is Dutch in its admirable minuteness and truth; a specimen is the scene at the *concierge's* dinner. Wicked in the quality called *l'esprit gaulois*, this farce is inimitable—and also a trifle old-fashioned. (p. 173)

[While **"Michel Pauper"**] contains in solution all of Becque, it may be confessed that the outcome is rather an indigestible mess. The brutality of the opening scenes is undeniable. Michel is a clumsy fellow, who does not always retain our sympathy or respect. His courtship has all the delicacy of a peasant at pasture. But he is alive, his is a salient character. . . . The ending has a suspicion of the "arranged," even of the violent melodramatic. And how shocking is the fall of Hélène! She is the first of the Becque cerebral female monsters, though she has at least more blood than some of his later creations. She loves the Count—the shadow of an excuse for her destruction of her noble-minded husband. However, one does not read Michel Pauper for amusement.

It is in **"L'Enlèvement"** that we find Becque managing with consummate address a genuine problem. (pp. 173-74)

Terse in dialogue, compact in construction, **"L'Enlèvement"** contains some of the best of Becque. Ibsen and Dumas are writ large in the general plan and dénouement, though the character drawing is wholly Becque's. Despite his economy of action and speech, he seldom gives one the feeling of abruptness in transitional passages. His scenes melt one into the other without a jar, and only after you have read or watched one of his plays do you realize the labour involved to produce such an illusion of life while disguising the controlling mechanism. All the familiar *points de repères*, the little tricks so dear to the average playmaker, are absent. Becque conceals his technical processes, and in that sense he has great art; though often seeming quite artless. And **"L'Enlèvement"** is more than a picture of manners; it is as definitely a problem play as "A Doll's House." (pp. 175-76)

With **"La Parisienne,"** Becque is once more on his own ground. Paris and its cynical view of the relations of the sexes is embodied in this diabolically adroit and disconcernting comedy. . . . The play is full of a *blague* now slightly outmoded, but the types remain eternally true—those of the Parisian triangle. Only this three-cornered, even four-cornered, arrangement (for there are two "dear friends") is played with amazing variations. (pp. 176-77)

Throughout, these lovers quarrel like married folk. The social balance is upset, domestic virtues topsy-turvied. And yet the merciless stripping of the conventional romance,—the deluded husband, unhappy wife, and charming consoler of the afflicted,—these old properties of Gallic comedy are cast into the dust-bin. It is safe to say that since **"La Parisienne"** no French dramatic author has had the courage to revive the sentimental triangle as it was before this comedy was written. If he ventured to, he would be laughed off the stage. And for suppressing the sentimental married harlot let us be thankful to the memory of Becque.

"Les Corbeaux" is unique in modern comedy. Never played, to my knowledge, in English, its ideas, its characterization, its ground-plan, have been often ruthlessly appropriated. The verb "to steal" is never conjugated in theatreland. Yet this play's simplicity is appealing. A loving father of a family, a good-tempered bourgeois, dies suddenly. His affairs turn out badly. His widow and three daughters fall into the hands of the ravens, the partner of their father, his lawyer, his architect, and a motley crew of tradespeople. Ungrateful matter this for dramatic purposes. Scene by scene Becque exposes the outer and inner life of these defenceless women and their secret and malign persecutors. Every character is an elaborate portrait. . . . If you tell me that the theme is not a pleasant or suitable one for the drama, I shall recommend you to the spirit of the late Henry Becque for answer. **"Les Corbeaux"** is the bible of the dramatic realists. (pp. 178-80)

Becque's touch is light in comedy, rather clumsy in set drama. He is, as a rule, without charm, and he never indulges in mock pathos or cheap poetic flights. He excelled in depicting manners, and his dramatic method, as I have endeavoured to show, was direct and free from antique rhetoric and romantic turgidities. He has been superseded by a more comprehensive synthesis; France is become weary of the cynical sinners—yet that does not invalidate the high ranking of this man of genius. Whatever may be his deficiencies in the purely spiritual, Henry Becque will ever remain a commanding figure in the battalion of brilliant French dramatists. (p. 181)

James Huneker, "Henry Becque," in his Icono-clasts: A Book of Dramatists, *Charles Scribner's Sons, 1905, pp. 163-81.*

ARNOLD BENNETT (essay date 1910)

["**Les Corbeaux**"] has bits of soliloquies and other dodges of technique now demoded. But the first act was not half over before the extreme modernness of the play forced itself upon you. Tchehkoff is not more modern. The picture of family life presented in the first act was simply delightful. All the bitterness was reserved for the other acts. And what superb bitterness! No one can be so cruel as Becque to a "sympathetic" character. He exposes every foolishness of the ruined widow; he never spares her for an instant; and yet one's sympathy is not alienated. This is truth. This is a play. I had not read the thing with sufficient imagination, with the result that for me it "acted" much better than it had "read." Its sheer beauty, truth, power, and wit justified even the great length of the last act. I thought Becque had continued to add scenes to the play after it was essentially finished. But it was I who was mistaken, not he. (pp. 258-59)

Arnold Bennett, "Henry Becque" (1910), in his Books and Persons: Being Comments on a Past Epoch, 1908-1911 *(copyright, 1917, by George H. Doran Company; copyright renewed © 1945 by Marie Marguerite Bennett), Doran, 1917, pp. 255-62.*

THE SATURDAY REVIEW (essay date 1911)

Whatever the opinion of Paris, I am sure that in London [Henry Becque] would never have had the smallest chance of success. For he has the supreme virtue, hateful to the British hedonist, of a pitiless moral honesty. Every good French author has it. . . . In the modern French play adultery, at any rate, is adultery: the subject is treated honestly and frankly. The attitude of the author may be morally censorious, which is rare; or it may be absolutely non-moral and analytic. But there is no shirking the facts of the situation. The British variety, on the other hand, is smeared with suggestion. The ugliness never shows. The treatment is in the furtive manner of one who tells a story behind his hand.

In the English version of "**La Parisienne**" . . . there is little regard shown for the type of person who sniggers for a hundred nights at the exploits and perplexities of "Dear Old Charlie". The dry air of Paris is still dry; and the honest, clear reality of Henry Becque's play in the French is preserved in the English. There is no rose-and-water glamour about the wicked, faithless wife; the husband is neither more nor less ridiculous than the lover; there is none of the British stage assumption that stolen fruit is sweeter than fruit which may be lawfully eaten. Henry Becque wrote faithfully and without illusion of the ménage à trois. He does not suggest that this ménage is an exceptional or wicked arrangement; he simply portrays it as it is. The fundamental ugliness is there; the incidental humour; the discomfort; the passion. In the passion there is nothing glorious, nor romantic, nor poetic; no fine talk of heart and soul, dragged irrelevantly in to arouse an illegitimate sympathy. La Parisienne is simply the coquette without a lure beyond that of her sex—a lying, betraying, faithless, uncomfortable woman. She enjoys herself; invariably gets her own way; and does her best for everyone. She is not drawn for sympathy: she is drawn to be observed. It is a delight to observe her with Henry Becque—a delight purely of the head. She is not, as she would be if

bowdlerised for the British stage, an aphrodisiac: rather she is an antidote. No one would wish actually to be to the observer what her lover is in this play. One would even prefer to be her husband.

La Parisienne has two lovers as well as a husband. It is a pretty picture. Husband and first lover are the dearest comrades. Indeed, as La Parisienne observes in perfect sincerity, she and this lover of hers are her husband's only two faithful friends in the world. This is not an ironic epigram of Henry Becque put into the mouth of his creature. It is the plain truth of the situation—truth faithfully observed, without any elaborate or conscious cynicism on the author's part. . . . [The] humour is all of the characters and what they are: never a mere epigram of the author delivered by one of his people. The humour is dry; cruel, only as the actual ironies of life are cruel; flowing naturally from a situation every phase of which has the naïvest air of reality. Except that the husband gets his post, and that the second lover gets tired and goes away, there is no plot to the play. It is exposition merely—a piece of life observed and presented without artifice or garnishing of the theatre. I might dwell at some length on the excellences of the play from the point of view of a critic writing in Paris—on the characteristics, that is, which distinguish it from other good modern French work; but I prefer to insist to the end on the quality which is most valuable and striking from the particular English point of view. There is all through a refusal to play suggestively with sex discreetly veiling the reality. If you laugh at "**La Parisienne**" you must laugh with Molière, and every clear-seeing observer who pierces through to the inner comedy of things. You are not permitted the smoking-room chuckle, loose, cowardly, furtive. You may not turn the face aside from the qualities in misdoing which offend. You are not permitted to think romantically of loose living as a thing of champagne and oysters, all gallantry and fine devilment. The message of Henry Becque to the British playgoer is a simple negation of the West End stage-notion of a play from the French. Briefly his message is that vice is prosaic and uncomfortable, which is precisely the hedonist's idea of virtue. (pp. 11-12)

P.J., "An Honest Play from Paris," in The Saturday Review, *London, Vol. 112, No. 2905, July 1, 1911, pp. 11-12.*

THE NATION (essay date 1914)

Unquestionably, Becque, going to the masses for his subjects, was an innovator when compared with such writers as Augier, Feuillet, Sardou, and the younger Dumas, and was, in one sense, more of a realist than any of them. But he was essentially either a melodramatist or a *farceur,* and was inferior to his rivals in constructive skill, imagination, the composition of emotional climaxes, and polished dialogue. He had wit, a good sense of situation, an honest indignation against public abuses, and the courage of his convictions, but in his illustrations he was not much nearer to the truth of nature than the romanticists themselves.

This is the reason why "**The Vultures**" ("**Les Corbeaux**"), instead of being an effective satire upon an iniquitous system and professional rascality, becomes a diffuse and conventional melodrama of no particular significance. The subject—the opportunities afforded by then existing French regulations to greedy and unscrupulous practitioners to rob the widow and orphan under the cover of legal technicalities—is a good one, and it need not be doubted that, in selecting it, M. Becque was animated by sincere and philanthropic purpose. But he spoils a strong case by the extravagance and manifest artificiality of his premises and the complete theatricality of his personages. All the conditions of his story are prescribed, transparently, to insure a predestined issue, and would therefore be impotent as a demonstration, even if they could be regarded as fairly typical. His lewd and usurious old financier, his grasping and scoundrelly lawyer, his speculative architect, his dishonest tradesman, and the lesser vultures who batten upon the unfortunate Vigneron family, are one and all ancient puppets of the melodramatic stage. . . . None of the characters, with the exception of the faithful old nurse, conveys the impression of an actual living human being. (pp. 644-45)

[**"The Woman of Paris" ("La Parisienne")**] is written with a certain cleverness and vivacity, but is no way brilliant either in form or in psychological analysis. It is a simple variation of a formula upon which hundreds of farcical comedies have been built . . . . The construction is arbitrary rather than plausible or ingenious, and the use of prolonged soliloquies is excessive. Theatrically it is inferior, in sparkle, point, and essential veracity, to scores of pieces of a similar character, while as literature or drama it is of infinitesimal value. . . . [**"The Merry-Go-Round" ("La Navette")**] is a cynical trifle which skilled French comedians doubtless could make fairly amusing, but why it should be thought worthy of translation into English as a choice example of modern drama, French or other, passes comprehension. (p. 645)

> *"The Stage of Henri Becque," in* The Nation *(copyright 1914 The Nation magazine, The Nation Associates, Inc.), Vol. 98, No. 2552, May 28, 1914, pp. 644-45.*

LUDWIG LEWISOHN   (essay date 1915)

[The talent of Henri Becque] was slow to mature and even in its maturity hard, dry, and far from copious. His work is not engaging. His mind had neither a touch of ingenuity (the strong point of the older playwrights), nor of that almost silent poetry wrung from life itself which distinguishes the later naturalists. His chief gift is that of a Molièrian irony—the irony that results from the unconscious self-revelation of base or corrupt characters. "You have been surrounded by rascals, my dear, ever since your father's death," Teissier, the most brutal of these rascals, says to Marie at the end of *Les Corbeaux*. . . . "You wouldn't want a mistress who is not religious! That would be dreadful!" Clotilde (*La Parisienne*) . . . exclaims to her lover. The ironic revelation of a confusion of all moral values could scarcely be more succinct and telling. Yet Becque makes no display of these passages; he does not emphasise them or set them off by the modelling of his dialogue. Their power and meaning are gradually revealed.

His first play *L'Enfant prodigue* . . . is a lively comedy of no great interest or originality. But very doggedly during these years Becque was feeling his way, quite careless of the contemporary fashions of the stage. He had not yet found that way in *Michel Pauper*. . . . The plot is violent and crude; the dialogue stilted and sentimental; and Paris laughed the play to scorn. The first period of his activity may be said to close with a one-act play *La Navette*. . . . Here, however, amid a conventional plot conveyed through a conventional technique there are hints of the ironic manner of his best passages.

In 1880 Becque produced a robust and keen-witted little comedy in one act: *Les Honnêtes Femmes*. He had evidently now

settled down to the close and sober study of character. Through Mme. Chevalier he seeks to reveal woman's genuine attitude to motherhood and marriage. There are almost Shavian hints in her self-revelation. But these are quite unconscious on Becque's part. He had gained the impersonality of the naturalistic drama and, again, two years later, gave the public his masterpiece, *Les Corbeaux*.

The play is a study in character and in social conditions. It is wholly free from polemic intention of any kind. A piece of human life unfolds itself. The technique has not yet the plain and bare nobility attained by Hauptmann or Hirschfeld or Galsworthy at their best. But there is neither trickery nor mechanical interference. The illusion of the rhythm of life is maintained throughout. (pp. 39-41)

The dialogue is not polished nor is it particularly racy. The structure is, at times, almost crude. Yet the simple facts of life and their meaning are stamped upon the memory by Becque's dramatic irony. The play, with all its imperfections, is a masterpiece, foreshadowing the long line of works that forms the chief distinction of the modern drama.

La Parisienne is more closely-knit structurally and far better written than *Les Corbeaux*. The unity of place is maintained and the movement is both swift and nimble. Here the dramatist's whole art is concentrated upon the ironic self-revelation of a single character. (p. 43)

About the whole career of Becque there is something poverty-stricken and frustrated. Admirable as are his best plays, they seem wrung from a soul without passion or spiritual fervour. But their importance in the history of the drama is quite secure. (pp. 43-4)

> *Ludwig Lewisohn, "The Foundations of the Modern Drama," in his* The Modern Drama: An Essay in Interpretation *(copyright, 1915, by Ludwig Lewisohn; copyright renewed 1942 by Ludwig Lewisohn; reprinted by permission of Viking Penguin Inc.), B. W. Huebsch, 1915, pp. 1-46.**

ASHLEY DUKES   (essay date 1923)

Becque was a fine if not a great dramatist. He was interested first of all in people and afterwards in the symmetrical grouping of people. *La Parisienne* is a fine comedy because it is a symmetrical comedy. The author's touch is firm; his characters are never out of hand. No superfluous word is spoken; all the witticisms are *mots de situation* rather than *mots d'auteur*. On the other hand (and this is the important point) every necessary word is spoken—the subject is fully explored. Although no "thinker" Becque was logical, and his logic was rich in humour. . . . [The] famous line at the opening of the play, "Prenez garde; voilà mon mari!" [comes] at the moment when you have made up your mind that the quarrelsome pair are husband and wife. Such flashes proves that Becque was a good dramatist. He understood how to bring off a *coup de théâtre* with the greatest effect, and yet there was nothing meretricious in his work. It was in the motive behind the *coup*—the revelation of character—that he showed genius.

It is strange to think that this play was first performed six years after Ibsen's *Doll's House*, and two years before the foundation of Antoine's Théâtre Libre. The French have never taken kindly to Ibsen. One reason, perhaps, is that they have always possessed a conception of social equality between the sexes; so that Ibsen's women brought them nothing new, but only a restatement of an old idea in foreign terms. With Becque the conception of social equality was instinctive. All his women are a match for their men; Clotilde in *La Parisienne*, the group in *Les Corbeaux*, the heroines of *La Navette* and *L'Enlèvement*. They are not independent in the English way, or in the Norwegian way, but in a way of their own. It does not occur to them to talk of freedom, because they are unconscious of being oppressed. And they have saving graces. If they are moral, it is not from inclination; if they are immoral, it is not on principle. (pp. 12-14)

Becque was a native dramatist with something of the spirit of Molière. He returned to an old and fine tradition of the stage at a period when most of his contemporaries were seeking to establish a new tradition. He had nothing to say about social movements or currents of thought (being possibly even sceptical of their value), but he had a good deal to say about husbands, wives, lovers and other simple phenomena of human nature, and said it with distinction. Now that a generation has passed, we can see that he was a great artist. His eternal triangle, being equilateral, pleases the eye. His irony, born of deep feeling, touches a true sense of comedy. His writing, terse and audacious, restores a standard of dramatic dialogue. His masterly technique forms a link between the old theatre and the new. (p. 14)

> *Ashley Dukes, "Forerunners," in his* The Youngest Drama: Studies of Fifty Dramatists *(reprinted by permission of the Literary Estate of Ashley Dukes), Ernest Benn, Limited, 1923, pp. 9-60.**

SAMUEL MONTEFIORE WAXMAN   (essay date 1926)

That Becque began his dramatic career with a libretto for an opera, *Sardanapole,* was a pure accident. Its only importance lies in the fact that it was a determining factor in his life. It made a dramatist of a possible business man. It shows not the slightest promise, and we must ignore it just as Becque did himself. *L'Enfant prodigue* is a typical vaudeville of the eighteen-sixties, gay, lively, and witty, neither better nor worse than a thousand and one plays of the same French genre. (p. 39)

In *Michel Pauper,* Becque begins to show his power as a dramatist, although his play is clumsy and rhetorical. . . . It is a curious mixture of brutal realism and extreme romanticism, full of melodramatic touches. It is an abortive effort to show the power of love and money on humanity, and has strong socialistic leanings. . . . *Michel Pauper,* with its sudden gusts of passion, its long tirades, its violent brutality, reminds one strongly of the melodramatic plays of Balzac. . . . Michel is a superman who would conquer his place in this world and make it better, but the female monster, Hélène, drives him to madness and death.

In *L'Enlèvement* there is again a social preoccupation on the part of Becque; he would free the wronged wife from the chains of a brutal rake. The romantic and melodramatic elements of *Michel Pauper* more or less disguise the social problem, or rather problems, but *L'Enlèvement* is an out-and-out thesis play much in the manner of Dumas fils. In later years Becque expresses utter scorn for the thesis play, which is made by "patching up old bits of dramatic art, divorce, and illegitimate children. . . . I have a horror for thesis plays, which are almost always bad theses." (pp. 39-40)

Les Honnêtes Femmes is interesting mainly because it is entirely different from anything else that Becque has done, and it proves

that he could have written plays that pleased the public, had he so desired. In *La Navette* lies the germ of *La Parisienne*. Antonia is an unmarried Clotilde who plays the game of shuttlecock with her three lovers just as Clotilde does later with her husband and two lovers. They are the only two plays of Becque which show the slightest resemblance in theme. *La Navette* is an Aristophanesque farce with a cynical twist to it, an excellent example of modern *esprit gaulois.* (p. 41)

[With *Les Corbeaux* Becque] had at last turned the trick. He had succeeded in doing what Balzac, Flaubert, the Goncourts, and Zola had failed to do: he had written a play that was a dramatic masterpiece and yet was not in conformity with the conventions of the well-made play. . . . There is nothing of Balzac nor of Musset nor of Dumas in *Les Corbeaux;* it is pure Becque. It is the study of the effects of the sudden death of a father on a family. *Les Corbeaux* are the ravens who swoop down upon a family bereft of its head. "When a man dies," says Rosalie, the faithful family servant, "and the creditors knock at the door, we can very well say, 'Here come the ravens, they leave only what they cannot carry off.'"

The first act might well have been called a prologue. The happy Vignerons are about to celebrate the betrothal of the youngest of the three daughters, when an unbidden guest, in the form of a doctor, arrives and announces the sudden death of the father. The merriment of this first act stands out in sharp contrast with the gradually increasing wretchedness of the last three acts, in which the four women are left to the mercy of the ravens, and Becque, with a refinement of cruelty, makes every man of the play a raven. (pp. 41-2)

There is very little plot to the *Corbeaux.* The first act develops a situation whose effects on the characters of the play are analyzed in the succeeding acts. Becque resorts only once to a conventional device in the first act, where he makes Madame Vigneron give a long account of the business relations between her husband and Tessier, in the bosom of her family, where these facts must have been an old story. But this is carping criticism. Throughout the last three acts the dialogue is constructed with consummate skill and each character reveals himself by his words. And the words of the ravens are cruel, sometimes needlessly cruel. They reflect Becque's black view of life. On several occasions they mar rather than help the characterization. Not all scoundrels put into words their villainous thoughts. For instance Mme. de St. Genis would most likely have broken off her son's engagement by letter instead of subjecting poor Blanche to the torture of a painful interview, calling her to her face a *fille perdue*, because she had not waited for her marriage vows. (p. 43)

Yet, unlike many of the *rosse* plays that were written in imitation of Becque's manner, the helpless victims of the ravens awaken our sympathies. The most beautiful sentiment of *Les Corbeaux* is the closeness with which the mother, daughters, and faithful servant cling to each other in their unequal battle with the ravens. Becque had been employed many years at the Bourse, and his experiences there had led him to believe that money was the most powerful factor in men's lives, and marriage a purely business affair. His unfinished *Polichinelles* was to have been a picture of the sordid lives of a group of financiers. Becque himself despised money and the compromises that men make in the acquisition of money. He believed himself to be a victim of the ravens of the theatres and he poured all the bitterness of his soul upon the ravens that fell upon the hapless Vigneron women. (pp. 43-4)

La Parisienne represents Becque's high-water mark technically. In it he carried his simplicity of plot still further than in *Les Corbeaux,* and in it he excluded all sentiment. It is one of the most impersonal plays ever written. In *La Parisienne* there is but a semblance of plot, no exposition, and no dénouement. It is one of the most perfect examples of the *tranche de vie* in modern French drama. French critics have taken exception to the title, *La Parisienne;* Becque should have generalized less and called his play *Une Parisienne.* (p. 44)

The lover Lafont is a parody of the *genus homo* so frequently found in modern French drama. He is the polished, well-groomed man of the world, who seems to have no other occupation in life than the Donjuanic pursuit of other men's wives. Whether he is a complacent cuckold or a naïve victim of misplaced confidence, Du Mesnil is blissfully happy; it is Lafont who is wretchedly unhappy, consumed with jealousy and suspicion. (p. 46)

If the men are parodies, Clotilde is not. She is the modern, perverted society woman, who has nothing serious to keep her occupied. She is frivolous, extravagant, and full of expedients. She has more charm than Flaubert's Emma Bovary. There is nothing of the animal in her. She sins because she is bored by the humdrum occupations of the housewife. She is the acme of feminine finesse and is as finished a product as is the work in which she figures. Clotilde is coldly and deliberately calculating, she is full of worldly wisdom and is a social climber. Although she is unfaithful to her husband, she is extremely solicitous about his personal comforts and his professional success. She is deeply concerned with covering up her tracks, and is most anxious about preserving all the earmarks of respectability. She is a product of our ultra-civilized world, a neurotic, constantly in search of new titillations. Clotilde Du Mesnil is one of the most superbly portrayed characters in contemporary French literature.

Yet she is not a monster. In spite of her immorality, she has moments of remorse. When she is parting from her second lover, Simpson, again a parody, this time of the sporting man who collects mistresses as one collects butterflies, she sheds a real tear. . . . Dumas would have depicted this adulteress as a vile creature, and his mouthpiece would have dissected her character, instead of allowing her to lay her own heart bare. And so Dumas will be remembered chiefly as a moralist and a reformer, whereas Becque will live as a playwright. *La Parisienne* is the *Don Quixote* of the triangle play. (pp. 47-8)

Samuel Montefiore Waxman, "Henry Becque ('And the Caravan Passes')," in his Antoine and the Thé-âtre-Libre *(copyright © 1926 by the President and Fellows of Harvard College; excerpted by permission), Cambridge, Mass.: Harvard University Press, 1926, pp. 37-52.*

MARTIN LAMM   (essay date 1948)

In his own day and afterwards, Becque was hailed as the greatest playwright in France. He was compared with Molière, but he only wrote two plays of any significance, and these two did not meet with immediate success in the theatre; only after a time was their reputation established. In many ways they were old-fashioned for their day, particularly in construction. In order to keep the reader acquainted with the situation, Becque makes excessive use of long monologues, descriptions and asides, at a time when other dramatists of the Second Empire had already abandoned this practice. Nor does he move out of

the setting with which they were familiar. It is Augier's domestic scenes that we meet in his plays, and his characters come from the middle classes and the aristocracy of the *ancien régime.* Becque was a shrewd psychologist with none of the blurred outlines which characterized the work of his predecessors. His dialogue is heavy and clumsy, lacking their wit but also their rhetoric. Sometimes his sober objectivity seems too good to be true, but on other occasions his lines throw a cold and harsh light on a situation. It is in dealing with action that he differs most from the traditional school. The plot advances by leaps and bounds, and practically every turn of events is unexpected. In *The Vultures* we have a plot from a novel treated in a way which older dramatists regarded as indefensible. In *The Woman of Paris* we come nearer to the traditional plot, but it is a very much simplified one. In both plays it is apparent that the plot itself is only of minor importance; the main problem is the presentation of characters and the pointing of a moral.

In Becque's drama there is a strong moral sense, though it is never expressed in pious sentiments, as in the typical finale of the old school, in which virtue is triumphantly rewarded. On the contrary, it is wickedness that triumphs, but not the deliberate wickedness of Dumas' or Augier's conspirators. Becque's two chief characters, Teissier in *The Vultures* and Clotilde in *The Woman of Paris* act according to their consciences and appear to be quite satisfied with what they are doing and with the success they achieve. The author does not disturb their complacency with any moral reflections, nor does he give their victims the redeeming grandeur of tragedy. It is through the deeply moving quality of these final scenes and the way they conflict with every human sense of justice, that the author reveals the dominant note in his character, a bitter and fierce irony. Becque's sense of humour is not French, but dry and sober. (pp. 59-61)

Becque was quite ready to observe the unity of place—in *The Woman of Paris* there is one setting throughout, and in *The Vultures* only a single change of scene—but he does not seem to have done so for any particular reason, for he attacked directly the general principle of the three unities. The setting of his plays had evidently far less significance for him than it had for Zola, for his stage décor was the usual one, with a door at the back and two side entrances. His characters are different from those of his predecessors, rather because he looked at them in a different way than because he chose different types or described them differently. The action is different too, though not necessarily more true to reality, or even striving to be so. It is not concerned with theatrical effects, and still less with the desire of an audience for excitement and change. On the other hand it does not run free or seem like a piece of real life. Becque might be called a classical writer as properly as a naturalistic one. Of all the 19th century writers who have been compared with Molière, it is he who best stands up to that comparison. There is something of Molière's greatness in his grasp of the subject, but it is a Molière who is petrified and has never developed his talents, a Molière without imagination or fantasy, without lightness or grace. (p. 61)

Martin Lamm, "The Rise of Naturalism in France," in his Modern Drama, *translated by Karin Elliott (originally published as* Det moderna dramat, *A Bonnier, 1948), Basil Blackwell, 1952, pp. 52-72.**

JOHN GASSNER   (essay date 1954)

To remember Becque is to recall how difficult it has been and still is to maintain playwriting on the high level to which it was raised by him and others in the eighteen-eighties.

In remembering Becque, moreover, we are forced to give some thought to the entire question of salvation for the theatre through departures from realism. Blame for the pinchbeck nature of much dramatic writing is often placed on the triumph of the realistic technique, whereas Becque's plays, perhaps even more than Ibsen's and less only than Strindberg's, would expose the absurdity of the charge. It was precisely against meretricious theatricality that modern realism ranged its heaviest batteries, and the vacuity of much that passes for realistic drama here and abroad is the very antithesis of Becque's work as well as that of the pioneers who were his contemporaries. The proposal to discard realism so often voiced by faithhealers of the stage incorporates one fallacy: The imaginative or poetic style of drama with which they intend to displace realism can also play us false, and humbug is humbug no matter whether it wears the trappings of poetry or the sack-suit of prose, the homburg of fancy or the straw hat of suburban realism. When the play is dramaturgically unsound or unconvincing, the deception does not succeed for all the prestidigitation of fanciful and stylized playwriting. (p. 114)

[The victory Becque] gained for objective revelation, without tasting more than thin slivers of its fruits himself, had to be won all over again in spite of the recent appearance of a few good plays by Tennessee Williams and Arthur Miller.

It was Henry Becque's ironic destiny to be neglected while he was laying the foundations of French dramatic realism and then to be unable to complete a single long play when the theatre finally caught up with his art. (p. 115)

The Vultures resolves itself as if Becque had dispassionately observed a law of nature working itself out in the decline and restoration of the Vignerons' fortunes. Yet nothing could be more ironic in tone and more devastatingly satiric than this exposé of how "social Darwinists" act and think. And the more indifferent Becque is to the amorality of his characters the more thoroughly he exposes them as the vultures they are.

Becque's virtuosity in refraining from virtuosity is even more remarkable in his second masterwork *La Parisienne*. This comedy does not even have a "resolution," for Clotilde Du Mesnil, who has been betraying her husband at the beginning of the play, simply continues to betray him at the end. Nor does *La Parisienne* actually possess a "crisis." . . . [The] point of Becque's comedy is precisely that nobody is capable of intense emotion in this Parisian *milieu*. Nobody, that is, except the first lover Lafont, and he is merely ridiculous, since he claims the proprietary rights of a husband to her fidelity. Without a real crisis and resolution, with hardly any exposition, and without inserting a single bout of wit or a single prurient line Becque managed to write one of the most brilliant—and amoral—comedies of all time.

La Parisienne is full of irony, unconscious in the case of the characters; but the most ironical thing about it is that Becque's aloof observation of life should make the play pass for one of the most cleverly written pieces of the theatre. . . . [The] hoax is life's trick on the characters, for the comic and realistic point of the illicit relationship is that usage has made it indistinguishable from the unromantic state of marriage. As a romance, prolonged adultery is a highly overrated experience, and the jealousy of her lover proves as boring to Clotilde as would have been the jealousy of her husband. Becque's main achievement . . . was that his tenacious veracity should make Clotilde

so monstrously immoral without turning her into a monster (she is patient, reasonable, considerate, and congenial), and so amusing without giving her an ounce of humor to flaunt before the public. Like Joyce's Molly Bloom, she is nature unadulterated by the sense of right and wrong.

Becque needed a theatre capable of giving life to his characters instead of dipping them into greasepaint and thrusting them out into the footlight area in order that they might hurl their lines into the auditorium. The entire point of the dramatic treatment in both *The Vultures* and *La Parisienne* was, after all, the revelation of moral turpitude in the society of his time through the natural conduct of his characters. They are drawn as people who consider their questionable morals above reproach, they regard their conduct and sentiments as norms of the social level on which they thrive. Both the humor and the indictment in Becque's two masterpieces arise entirely from the discrepancy between what his characters think of themselves and our judgment of them. (pp. 117-19)

To let the actor play up to the audience and address his remarks to it instead of to other characters, to push him out of the scenery that frames the room in which the action is supposed to take place, to allow him to declaim his lines with exaggerated gestures—these were the unpardonable sins that the conventional theatre committed against Becque and other realistic dramatists. (p. 119)

All that Becque intended to do was to set down reality without distorting it for the sake of theatrical expediency. In confining himself to a segment of life, he seemed to say, "Make what you will of it, this is how people behave in our time and place, this is how they think and this is how they speak." He dispensed with tricks of the trade, such as artificially emotional or scintillating "big" scenes and act-endings that brought the curtain down with a bang at the expense of naturalness. Like Strindberg, when the Scandinavian playwright came to write his remarkably compact one-act dramas, *Miss Julie* and *The Creditors,* Becque pruned his plays of all inessentials at a time when witty conversations, *ex cathedra* preachments, and declamations were considered the indispensable machinery of any theatre that expected to attract an audience; against this kind of dramaturgy, Becque declared that drama was the art of elimination. He endeavored, moreover, to release a natural flow of action which would make it impossible for the parts of a play to be differentiated mechanically as "exposition," "climax," and "dénouement." In a play like *The Vultures,* which suffers from some prolixity, and in the more brilliantly executed, if more narrowly Parisian, comedy *La Parisienne,* it is Becque's sharp observation that stands foremost. Unlike Ibsen, he did not quite rid his work of occasional asides or soliloquies, but these do not materially detract from his realism. It is the integrity of the conception and the writing of both plays that has preserved them, and it is integrity, for which there has never been too much regard in the theatre, that explains the influence this dour playwright exerted on the formative modern dramas. From the ideal that he set for dramatists, there have been, regrettably, more descents than ascents, and this is as good a reason as any for remembering him half a century after his death.

At this time, especially in the American theatre, there is, however, an equally good reason for giving some attention to his two masterpieces, and that reason must strike us as a paradox if we still adhere to a naïve view of realism as a mere transcription of life. Becque had the gift of making a transcript look like a travesty, or if you will, a travesty look like a transcript. The "naturalness" of his dramaturgy and writing, which made it possible for him to set down reality in such a matter-of-fact manner, was in his case an instrument of satiric comedy. To treat the behavior and thought-processes of his vultures and amoralists as perfectly "natural" was the most powerful method he could have adopted to outrage us and make us consider them monstrous. The result is travesty achieved by naturalness. That is, the logic or consistency of these characters makes them exaggerations or caricatures. Conversely, for Becque to present such monsters of iniquity as perfectly natural specimens of the human species and of society is tantamount to directing his satire at the species and society. What, in other words, are we to think of the human race and of human society if Becque's amoralists are to be regarded as normal people! (pp. 120-22)

[He] was not the slave but the master of the realistic mode of playwriting coming into vogue in his day. He was a creator when he adopted the role of a transcriber, whereas many a playwright who succeeded him was a transcriber while adopting the role of a creator. Becque brought a distinctive, tart, and quizzical temperament and a nimble mind to the modern theatre. . . . With these qualities he gave a unique comic style to naturalism, a style simultaneously "natural" and grotesque. One might call it a sort of expressionistic naturalism, without expressionistic fantasy and structure. . . .

[The] maturity of Becque's mind and the tempered steel of his spirit will remain a challenge to playwrights and a reminder that naturalistic playwriting can become a thoroughly creative act. (p. 122)

> John Gassner, "Henry Becque: The Mordant Virtuoso," in his The Theatre in Our Times: A Survey of the Men, Materials and Movements in the Modern Theatre *(copyright, 1954, by John Gassner; used by permission of Crown Publishers, Inc.), Crown, 1954, pp. 114-22.*

CARL W. WOOTON (essay date 1961)

[*The Vultures*] is a slice-of-life, a realistic play. To stop with this analysis, however, is to fall short of the mark, short of Henry Becque's intent and artistry. *The Vultures* presents a group of characters who are both products and producers of their society. Becque examines their code and their manners by presenting them without commentary. Any condemnation of their behavior is implicit, inferred from the disparity between the characters' evaluation of themselves and their society and the audience's opinion of them. In addition to employing these realistic techniques, Becque indirectly assists the audience in forming its opinion by satirizing the characters' manners with a heavy irony and a grim humor, unlikely to provoke laughter. Becque thus seems to have created a realistic play, in which the techniques of the comedy of manners are used for moralizing purposes. (p. 73)

The first act opens with an idyllic scene of family singing and fun-making. Yet, the untenable basis of the Vigneron world and its moral code is immediately suggested by their concern with propriety and with the place and function of money. In the first conversation between Blanche and her mother, Becque intimates the tenuous source of the Vignerons' standards. Blanche questions whether the placing of a menu at each plate will add anything to the dinner. When Mrs. Vigneron replies that it will not detract from it, Blanche is immediately concerned with the question of its propriety, regardless of the effect. Mrs. Vig-

neron is "absolutely sure" it is the proper thing to do because she "saw it in the *Ladies' Home Companion*." The satire is immediately aimed at society's subscription to an artificial code. (p. 74)

Blanche is depicted as a romantic, and Becque uses her to expose the shortcomings of the Vigneron society's defintion of sexual purity and of the nature of marriage. Her mother describes Blanche as "a child, as modest and innocent—the dear little girl—as can be." But Blanche's innocence is seen, after the economic collapse of the family, as ironic and, moreover, strangely dependent upon the family's social status. . . . Becque exposes the economic nature of marriage in a materialistic society in two interviews between Blanche and Mrs. de Saint-Genis, George's mother. Blanche admits her imprudence to Marie after Mrs. de Saint-Genis warns her that the marriage might not take place if the Vignerons' economic status is drastically altered. Blanche, the romantic, continues to believe in the certainty of her marriage to George de Saint-Genis until her second, and final, interview with Mrs. de Saint-Genis. When it becomes obvious that Mrs. de Saint-Genis is likely to succeed in her efforts to prevent the marriage, Blanche suffers the humiliation of admitting her mistake a second time. Her appearance of innocence and naïveté is disproved, but even with her purity negated, her guilt is a matter of question in the light of Mrs. de Saint-Genis' standards. . . . However, Blanche's guilt does not lie in her fall from virginity; her guilt is not a moral guilt. The crime of Blanche was to fall from her previous economic status; her guilt lies in the failure of her father to provide for his family in the event of his death and in her inability to fulfill the dowry agreement. Her ensuing breakdown results from her inability to recognize the dichotomy of the two types of guilt, one moral and the other social and amoral, and from her inability to cope with the problems posed by the change in her social position.

Mr. Vigneron defines the position and function of money in his family's world and emphasizes the importance of propriety. In his only reliance on a mechanical convention, Becque has Mrs. Vigneron tell the story of Mr. Vigneron's rise from struggling respectability to upper-middle-class properness. . . . This creates the question, what are her standards? Ironically, they collapse with the loss of her economically determined position. Becque hints at the hypocrisy of bourgeois social values when he reveals Vigneron's ignorance of music. It is proper to listen to music, but it is not necessary to have a sound knowledge of the subject. . . . In a society based on money, the future can be ensured only by economic gains, and the very "right" to rest is bought, not really earned. Vigneron has no opportunity to know that in the event of such an accident as his death, the same perverted emphasis on money that effected his family's rise will be the cause of his family's downfall.

The family's fall from status affects Judith and Gaston as much as it affects Blanche. . . . Gaston and Judith, like Blanche, have not been prepared to cope with the reality of their society. Wealth permitted them to see only appearances, the lip service paid to traditional morals and sentimental values. Poverty forces them to realize that they possess neither charm, nor talent, nor position if they do not possess money.

The more obvious "vultures," Bourdon and Teissier, recognize the nature of their society, subscribe to its relative code and utilize the code to maintain their acquired position. To Bourdon, the Lawyers' Club is "meant to be a protection for us—not for the public." The club's standards must benefit those subscribing to them and protect the members in their pursuit of wealth. Standards are no longer established by comparison with an absolute scale of good and evil; utility alone validates them. (pp. 74-7)

Teissier needs to operate only at the level of reality. His wealth and position are secure enough to make respectability irrelevant. He does not see his parents anymore because they ask for money. "They are starving," he admits. When he sees Marie, he is attracted to her. He first wants to keep her as his mistress, and, when she refuses those terms, he offers her marriage. Marriage is the price she sets, and he is willing to pay it. People are justified by their usefulness in the same manner as codes and standards.

Since the Vigneron family is no longer useful to Marie, Teissier cannot understand why she is not willing to let her "family stay in the ditch and go out and do something" for her own account. Her refusal to be his mistress to escape poverty is motivated by her family loyalty, not by an absolute moral standard. Family loyalty is a human virtue, normally to be commended. However, in the perverted society of *The Vultures,* it is the instrument which brings Marie to sell herself. (p. 77)

Becque's play employs such realistic techniques as realistic dialogue and settings. Its action is based upon a realistic concept, a slice-of-life, a series of accidents which affect the Vigneron family. However, Becque's approach is classical rather than realistic. He is not satisfied to represent life; he holds up vices for condemnation. But unlike his master, Molière, he offers no corrective. Molière's solution was temperance: learning is all right for women, in moderation; caring for one's health is all right, in moderation; frankness is all right, in moderation. Such a solution was possible for Molière because he lived in a stable, hierarchical society which recognized absolute moral values. Becque's society is flexible and dislocated; its code is utilitarian and relative. He does not reject the utilitarian code, but he dislikes it. His moralistic intent distinguishes him from the true realists.

His intent is to reveal a society composed entirely of "vultures." Some of the "vultures" are obvious, such as Bourdon and Teissier. Others, such as Marie, seem to become "vultures" in order to survive. When Teissier says to Marie, "Child, since your father died you've been surrounded by a lot of scoundrels," Marie seems to be victimized by the "vultures," while, in fact, she, by accepting Teissier's terms, has joined their ranks. In fact, Becque suggests that by being a part of this society she has always been a "vulture." The Vignerons owed their fortune to Teissier and his ruthless methods, as Vigneron acknowledges: "I reckon it's Teissier and his factory that have made me what I am." In a corrupt society, only those willing to accept the perverted standard and basis of that society can achieve success. In *The Vultures,* Becque reveals that what appeared in the beginning to be an ideal home, and later became a group of economic relationships, had actually never been anything but a group of economic relationships. In this exposition of society and manners, however, Becque has created a comedy of manners based upon a realistic concept; he has not presented "life as it is," the goal of the realistic playwright, but life as the satirist sees "it ought not to be"— the goal of the classical comic dramatist. (pp. 78-9)

Carl W. Wooton, " 'The Vultures': Becque's Realistic Comedy of Manners," in Modern Drama *(copyright © 1961, University of Toronto, Graduate Centre for Study of Drama; with the permission of* Modern Drama*), Vol. 4, No. 1, May, 1961, pp. 72-9.*

S. I. LOCKERBIE (essay date 1962)

In contrasting Romantic belief in *imagination* with the *vérité* which he himself is aiming at, Becque is rejecting everything which, in literature, comes under the heading of the 'marvellous' in favour of normal life and real people. As against plays of lyrical expansion set in the colourful past, he wants his theatre to be a picture of contemporary life, true to observation and everyday experience. (pp. 24-5)

To achieve a compellingly probable picture of contemporary life Becque felt that a certain style and technique were necessary. In distinguishing between *esprit* and *vérité* he was, in effect, demonstrating that these were not to be found in the kind of plays written by Augier and Dumas. . . . [Becque] stresses the need for an undeviating and searching study. His ideal is a true and representative account of life, but he realises that to reach the truth a study in depth is necessary.

Simplicity of style means for him . . . prose which is close to natural speech. There are severe limits set on the development of a personal style for a realist; if he is to mirror the actual behaviour of people in life he is led fairly strictly to take ordinary conversation as his model. Becque defined his own conception of dramatic language as one which would represent "la limite exacte entre le langage parlé et le langage écrit" [the exact limit between spoken and written language]. . . . Characters, in general, are not given a greater *range* of thought and expression than their counterparts could have in life, but their speech is given more force and organisation. Similarly, devices such as the soliloquy, the *aparte* and the *tirade,* which are frankly conventional and clash with the method of objectively presented conversation, tend to be abandoned by Becque; the realist playwright is implicitly debarred from the degree of direct communication with the audience which these devices allow. So whereas the effort of many dramatists to find a style has been a matter of enlarging the resonance of dramatic speech by means of imagery, rhythm, or use of meditative monologues, Becque's is a matter of finding the most economical and the most typical form of ordinary speech for any given character in any given situation. The particular aim of such a realistic style is always to catch and isolate the exact inflection of everyday intercourse, and thus to clarify and illumine human behaviour in a way impossible in the chaotic and muddled movement of day to day living. It does not attempt to go beyond this clarification to present a personal vision. It is in his attitude towards dramatic language, especially, therefore that Becque shows himself to be a realist, aiming at the most sensitive observation of life as a sufficient form of art for him.

Finally, a realist position such as Becque adopts leads almost inevitably to the self-effacement of the dramatist. He reacted against both the didacticism of eighteenth-century *drame* and the thesis play of Dumas, and demanded that the playwright should be disinterested in the presentation of his subject. In this he was merely returning to the oblique approach to the subject that most great dramatists have, in fact, employed. But his reasons for doing so were particularly logical. . . . He denied, for example, that in Molière any personal thought or philosophy could be found; one could find only "la connaissance désintéressée des choses humaines" . . . [the disinterested knowledge of human things]. (pp. 25-8)

Becque is essentially a man of the 1850s, in terms of literary history nearer the moderate, relatively conservative Realist School than the bolder Naturalists. The natural boundary of his interests and his art did not extend to the new subject matter which the Naturalists introduced into literature, and which seemed to him to defy all the conventional decencies. In the evolution of realism, then, Becque represents a point where it is a much more coherent concept than it was in the mind of Diderot and others in the eighteenth and early nineteenth centuries, but where it is not yet inclined to attempt a study of society reaching down to the lowest social levels. (p. 29)

Les Corbeaux has something of the rigorous progression of a classical tragedy, but, on the other hand, Becque's completely different conception of literature leads him to cast his play in a different mould from that of seventeenth-century tragedy. His whole aim as a realist, after all, is to combine catastrophe with close resemblance to life, and, therefore, to prevent his crisis from reaching that degree of extremity and abstraction that it reaches in the classical theatre. He adapts the design of the play accordingly. Whereas the classical plot plunges us straight into a tragic situation with an abruptness and compression of detail that is electrifying from the start, Becque devotes a whole act to showing us the family life of the Vignerons while there is still no cloud on the horizon. The characters do ordinary things, converse in ordinary tones. The play does not appear to go forward because it is Becque's first concern to establish completely particularised and credible characters. To this he sacrifices dramatic tautness and urgency. His intention is to create the illusion of life precisely by the gradualness of our introduction to characters presented as entirely ordinary. . . . The dramatic curve of *Les Corbeaux* is thus much longer and shallower than that of a classical tragedy; it never sweeps up to sublime heights and precipitated passions; it achieves its artistic effect rather by being firmly and uncompromisingly sustained.

The principal characters are in harmony with the design and the intentions of the play. The Vignerons are not the exalted characters of classical tragedy, but troubled, uncertain, limited people, who grope towards their decisions with no great conviction, and who are quite incapable of seeing through the designs of the 'vultures' who surround them. On innumerable occasions we see them together or separately being swayed by specious arguments, or failing to understand the meaning of their situation, or hesitating over the correct course of action. (pp. 31-2)

If the chief problem of the realist playwright is to achieve expressiveness through characters who retain ordinary life-like dimensions, it can be seen that Becque's choice of the family group as a kind of character greater than all the others is an effective solution. The whole play is made more cohesive. While it has the advantage of variety of effect, since the daughters and their mother are all presented as distinct in personality, the characters are so well subordinated to the central theme that we never lose sight, either, of the larger statement that is being made. . . . It is not even necessary for Becque to round off each character fully. Marie's situation is resolved sufficiently to give the play a finished shape, but we leave Blanche abruptly with the threat of madness hanging over her, and Judith's rôle is not brought to a conclusion at all. Since it is the group which is the vehicle of the play's meaning, rather than the individuals, Becque can allow himself liberties of this kind. Such 'loose ends' do not obscure the main statement, while contributing to the general impression that we are seeing people as they are, people whose lives are not arranged in a neat pattern rising to an ordered climax.

This is not a drama of people with intense lives of their own, then, but for the play to be successful at all the individual characters have to be convincing as far as they go. The Vig-

nerons have to be credible to draw our sympathy, and we need to feel, also, that the threat weighing on them is genuinely possible. Becque achieves this credibility by the same simplicity in his character construction that he reveals in the other aspects of his stagecraft. He makes no attempt to give his characters a wide range of distinguishing characteristics, or mannerisms, but reduces them to the essential features required by the subject. . . . [The] fact that there should be so many ''corbeaux'' waiting to pounce on the Vignerons is, as we have seen, a heightening of the situation, but Bourdon, Teissier and Mme de Saint-Genis are in themselves presented without exaggeration. Here again they are not stage villains because Becque concentrates on the essential. The essential, in this case, is that they are all plotting to take advantage of the Vignerons, and in their arguing and scheming Becque lends them his own shrewdness and dialectical ability. This is probably the secret of his characterisation. He gives us not leisurely character-portraits, but characters in action, tightly associated with the whole movement of the play. All are convincing because they act exactly as their rôle demands—we know nothing of them outside this limited situation, nor do we need to.

With the dramatic method that Becque has adopted language need not be employed throughout its full range of meaning and poetic resonance. The principle of juxtaposition of episodes can be applied to speech as well and we find that a great deal of the dialogue of *Les Corbeaux,* while remaining the fairly close imitation of ordinary speech that Becque was committed to as a realist, takes on special overtones because it is arranged in a significant order. . . . The central idea of vultures closing in on their weakening prey is beautifully conveyed at the end of Act II by juxtaposing three creditors' letters, which, taken singly, would hardly have had any suggestive force. Implications are created by means of the significant arrangement: phrases that in themselves are merely commercial jargon are transformed into the most heartless expressions of greed. (pp. 33-6)

In addition, the language acquires expressiveness from the episodic technique itself, even when no formal pattern is constructed. As we become aware of the trend of thought behind a given succession of episodes, so we become aware of hidden but calculated meanings in ostensibly ordinary language. For example, what holds the first Act together and makes it relevant to the rest of the play is a steadily increasing sense of uneasiness as the characters surrounding the Vigneron family reveal themselves to be rather sinister self-seekers instead of true friends. (p. 36)

Becque, therefore, was successful on the whole in striking a balance between *la langue parlée* and *la langue écrite*. There are some lapses, mainly in the expository parts of the first Act. The realist playwright invariably finds it difficult to inform his audience of all it needs to know in the manner and tone of ordinary conversation. He has, therefore, to plant rather clumsy 'signposts' as best he can. . . . [However,] the language on the whole is handled with skill. It has the basic quality that all dramatic language must have: constant movement. The real 'action' of the play is carried on in speech which probes, analyses, and exposes character, and follows every twist and turn in the changing relationships between different persons. The finest scenes are those which can trace an inner struggle or a clash between two or more characters through their various, finely graded stages. . . . The public of Becque's day expected the play to end with the announcement of marriage, but Becque was not interested in this kind of conventional climax. The very conception of a climax is foreign to a play like *Les Corbeaux*. We readily exchange the kind of uplift we would have derived from a trumpets and heavenly chorus type of ending in return for this penetrating analysis of a petty crook burning his fingers and making a retreat. There is no caricature in this final scene: the reactions are all highly typical, and they shade into each other almost imperceptibly as gradually Dupuis begins to get the worst of the argument. The effect of a scene of this kind at the final curtain is to end the play on the same note of sober, controlled realism that it has had throughout. It suggests life as it is, and life going on as before, with its difficulties to be tackled and solved, like this unpleasant incident, but possibly for the Vigneron family, augmented by Teissier, slightly less bleak than otherwise it might have been. (pp. 37-9)

Many playwrights succeeded in imitating the surface appearance of life; but none could condense or construct like Becque, nor give their language the unrelenting analytical edge that his has at its best. . . . [Art] such as Becque's, by its shape and organisation, leads to greater awareness; both feeling and understanding in the spectator are raised to new heights. Certainly art can go further than it does in *Les Corbeaux;* everybody would agree that the really great dramatists are those who consciously transfigure reality, and set on the stage a purely imaginative world. The really great dramatists, however, are rare; and in the long intervals between them lesser but genuine artists like Becque are valuable. Realism, moreover, is the form of artistic experience most accessible to the general public of our century. If realism has failed to conquer the heights of art, as its advocates in the nineteenth century hoped, it has certainly established itself on the broad middle ground, in the novel, theatre, cinema and television. One could not wish more of this mass of creative work than that it should reach the degree of sensitivity and artistic elaboration manifest in *Les Corbeaux.* (pp. 39-40)

> *S. I. Lockerbie, "Introduction" (© S. I. Lockerbie 1962), in* Les Corbeaux *by Henry Becque, edited by S. I. Lockerbie, George G. Harrap & Co. Ltd, 1962, pp. 7-40.*

ADDITIONAL BIBLIOGRAPHY

Antoine, André. *Memories of the Théâtre-Libre*. Edited by H.D. Albright. Translated by Marvin A. Carlson. Coral Gables, Fla.: University of Miami Press, 1964, 239 p.*
    Personal recollections of Becque's early productions by the founder of the Théâtre-Libre.

Chandler, Frank Wadleigh. "Family Studies." In his *Aspects of Modern Drama*, pp. 210-32. New York: The Macmillan Co., 1939.*
    Brief textual analysis of *Les Corbeaux*.

Clark, Barrett H. "Henry Becque: *The Vultures*." In his *A Study of the Modern Drama: A Handbook for the Study and Appreciation of Typical Plays, European, English, and American, of the Last Three-Quarters of a Century*, rev. ed., pp. 119-26. New York: D. Appleton Century Co., 1938.*
    A general study of *Les Corbeaux*.

Dimnet, Ernest. "Henry Becque's Posthumous Play." *The Saturday Review* 110, No. 2871 (5 November 1910): 575-76.
    A review of Becque's *Les Polichinelles*. Dimnet states that the dramatic formula successfully used by Becque in *Les corbeaux* and *La Parisienne* is less effective in *Les Polichinelles*.

Gassner, John. "Realism and Naturalism: Henry Becque." In his *A Treasury of the Theatre, Vol. II: Modern European Drama from Henrik Ibsen to Jean-Paul Sartre*, rev. ed., edited by John Gassner, pp. 95-7. New York: Simon and Schuster, 1963.
    A critical look at Becque's career.

Smith, Hugh Allison. "Henri Becque and the Theatre Libre." In his *Main Currents of Modern French Drama*, pp. 189-207. New York: Holt, Rinehart, and Winston, 1925.
    An analysis of *Les corbeaux* and *La Parisienne* as examples of the *comédie rosse*. Smith acknowledges Becque's ability as a dramatist of the Naturalist school, but finds little value in his consistently negative scenarios.

Spiers, A.G.H. "Becque and Mérimée at the Vieux Colombier." *The Nation* 105, No. 2737 (13 December 1917): 674-75.*
    Praises *La navette* and calls Becque a dramatist who has "given a new direction to the development of the French drama."

Thomas Lovell Beddoes

1803-1849

English poet and dramatist.

Called ''The Last Elizabethan'' by Lytton Strachey, Beddoes is chiefly remembered for his evocative poetic vision. Although his works are few, he was an important figure in the Elizabethan literary revival of the nineteenth century. His work skillfully combines macabre imagery, passages of haunting beauty, and elements of the supernatural.

Beddoes's father was a celebrated physician of outstanding literary, as well as scientific, talent. Although he died when his son was young, he instilled in the boy an interest in literature and the sciences. Maria Edgeworth, Beddoes's aunt, was another important figure in his life, and encouraged his writing. Beddoes was a brilliant child who won prizes for essays in Latin and Greek and published poetry in *The Morning Post* before entering college. However, he was also beset with emotional problems. As a young man, Beddoes began to experience the severe melancholy that would plague him all of his life. His depression found expression not only in his personal life, but in the themes and characters of his works as well.

The Improvisatore, in Three Fyttes, with Other Poems, which Beddoes wrote during his first year at Pembroke College, Oxford, reflects the influence of William Shakespeare and Percy Bysshe Shelley, the idols of his youth. Dissatisfied with the work, Beddoes destroyed most of the copies. The following year, he wrote *The Brides' Tragedy*, a verse drama based on a college murder. The work was praised by such prominent critics as Bryan Waller Procter and George Darley, and established Beddoes as a writer of merit. The obsession with death and the grotesque imagery of the piece were to recur in much of his later verse.

After receiving his B.A. and M.A. from Pembroke, Beddoes traveled to Germany to attend medical school at Göttingen University. Soon after enrolling, he began working on *Death's Jest Book; or, The Fool's Tragedy*, which he described as an example of ''the florid Gothic.'' Although it contains brilliant passages and demonstrates definite lyrical talent, *Death's Jest Book* never satisfied Beddoes; he altered it repeatedly, and it was not published in his lifetime. Beddoes was soon expelled from the university for drunk and disorderly behavior and for attempting suicide. He went on to Würzburg to earn a medical degree, but was still dissatisfied with his achievements, and his outlook became increasingly morbid. John Heath-Stubbs attributed Beddoes's melancholy to latent homosexuality, which, according to Heath-Stubbs, he expressed in his works through the themes of death and self-destruction. In an effort to relieve his inner restlessness, Beddoes became involved with radical political activities.

He traveled to Zürich, where he continued to work on *Death's Jest Book*, and wrote several short pieces, later collected in *Poems Posthumous and Collected of Thomas Lovell Beddoes*. As the political climate in Europe became more intense, so did Beddoes's interest in revolutionary politics. In Germany, he delivered lectures for the liberal cause and became involved with the *Freie Reichstadt*, a German revolutionary group. Bed-

does was deported for his activities by the King of Bavaria, and from that time on, wandered aimlessly throughout Europe, never settling long in one place. He had isolated himself from English society and his family, and in a state of complete despair, committed suicide in Basel.

Although Beddoes had a remarkable capacity for lyrical, imaginative poetry, he was a poet of uneven gifts. H. W. Donner, his most recent biographer, said of him: ''His real experience forced its own expression in lyrical poetry. His poems of the last twenty years of his life possess the rich associative power which reproduces the experience out of which it was created, mostly sorrowful, but often lightened up by wit and humor, ranging from grief unutterable, to exuberant joy, varied in mood from the elegaic to the burlesque, but always complex and always genuine.'' Beddoes remains a compelling minor figure in English literature.

PRINCIPAL WORKS

The Improvisatore, in Three Fyttes, with Other Poems (poetry) 1821
*The Brides' Tragedy [first publication] (drama) 1822
Death's Jest Book; or, The Fool's Tragedy (drama) 1850

Poems Posthumous and Collected of Thomas Lovell Beddoes
　　(poetry and drama)　1851
The Letters of Thomas Lovell Beddoes　(letters)　1894

THOMAS LOVELL BEDDOES　(essay date 1822)

Leaving many other doubtful passages to the discretion, taste and temper of the reader, it is my confession that [*The Brides' Tragedy*] offends grievously in the dispensation of occurrences. The only great law for the conduct of a tragedy, which the student of Shakspeare recognizes—and he who has not studied that incarnation of nature, and read the sciences of the affections and passions in the living universe of that infinite mind, cannot be any more than contemptible in dramatic or poetical criticism: such may close this page and open another—in the opinion of him who has lived in Shakspeare methinks the only canon which [has any] right to regulate the distribution of this artificial or dramatic providence will run thus;—that from first to last the events shall arise from, or their good and evil consequences depend on the passions or passionate actions of the simulated beings—forming, actions on passions, incident on deed.

Thus alone can Tragedy reflect the moral and the method of life; thus imperfectly resemble a brief and mutilated abstract from that great and only volume, in whose pages, to be unfolded on the cloudless sky of the completing day, lies the map of all the world's lives, are traced the gradual and innumerous streams of human will, crossing each other inextricably as the lines of Gothic tracery on a Cathedral roof, of one consent, birth and end, as the complex strains from voice and instrument which float and curl innumerably individual, and under its vaults, by many roads of sound, through its arches, to that one silence out of which they were created. (pp. 529-30)

> *Thomas Lovell Beddoes, in his preface to his* The Brides' Tragedy, *F. C. & J. Rivington, 1822 (and reprinted in "Prefaces, 1821-31," in his* The Works of Thomas Lovell Beddoes, *edited by H. W. Donner, Oxford University Press, London, 1935, pp. 529-30).*

THE MONTHLY REVIEW　(essay date 1823)

[Thomas Beddoes] possesses many of the essential qualities of a true poet;—a warm, rich, and brilliant imagination; a great play of fancy; and an ear susceptible of harmony. Occasionally, too, he displays deep and tender feeling. With all these advantages, however, he is in great danger of throwing away his chance of a reputation which in all probability would prove highly honorable to him, by yielding to the sin of affectation. He *affects* to write not as nature and his genius prompt him, but as our elder dramatists wrote, and as the pseudo Mr. Barry Cornwall has *attempted* to write. We would earnestly exhort Mr. B. not to be led away by this spirit of imitation; but, if he *will* follow our old writers, let him endeavor to resemble them in their glorious conceptions and subtle discrimination of character, in the power of their feelings, and the grasp of their thought; not in the turn of their expressions, the quaintness of their antique phraseology, and the conceits and perversions in which they often indulged. By far too much *ingenuity* is visible in [*The Brides' Tragedy*]: the images and illusions are too recondite; and the feelings have scarcely ever fair play. As a

pure tragedy, it has few claims to our attention; and it betrays all those marks of a juvenile hand, which we might expect when the author informs us that he is yet a minor. (p. 96)

We presume Mr. *Lovell Beddoes* to be sprung from a family of genius on both sides, and we therefore trust in his improvement. (p. 97)

> *"Poetry and the Drama: 'The Brides' Tragedy','' in* The Monthly Review, *Vol. C, January, 1823, pp. 96-7.*

[BRYAN WALLER PROCTER]　(essay date 1823)

[*The Brides' Tragedy*] is undoubtedly one of the most promising performances of this "poetical age." There are, indeed, few things which, *as mere poetry,* surpass it. It has plenty of faults, and so much the better. It has plenty of beauties too,—many delicacies, sometimes great power of expression, sometimes originality, and seldom or never common place. (p. 169)

[Mr. Beddoes] is a poet. He is one of great hope and of very considerable performance. But he has faults; and we will tell him of them as frankly as we speak of his merits. In the first place, there is a want of earnestness very often in his play. He *toys* with his subject too much; and this . . . is destructive to a tale of midnight murder. The writer of a drama must *often* sacrifice poetry to passion, and fine phrase to the general purpose of his story. On the contrary, our author frequently makes his huntsmen and servants talk good courtly (or if he pleases poetical) language. (p. 170)

Of this play, the first three acts are decidedly the best. And the reason is this; that, after the end of the third act, we have nothing to learn except that the murderer dies. The interest runs up to the part in which Floribel (the girl) is murdered by her lover and husband, Hesperus, and then it falls. He marries again (also in the third act) but it must be owned that he is less interesting afterwards.—There is not much attempt at character in the play. Both Floribel and Olivia are gentle girls—Hesperus is a person swayed by circumstances and his own passions—Claudio is a sort of joker—and the rest have no very distinguishing traits.

We have heard it said (in reply to our strongly expressed admiration of this play) that it wants interest, and character, and unity of purpose, &c. This is true to a certain extent. But a great part of the interest of a play arises from the *mechanical* construction of it; and this Mr. Beddoes will easily acquire. . . . Let him try to fix his scenes closely, one within the other—to *"dovetail"* them, as cabinet makers would say, and he will find that the appearance of his dramas will be materially better. It is to be recollected, however, that the *first* plays of all authors have failed in the mechanism. . . . Let us pardon our author, therefore, on account of his failures in the joiner's part of tragedy (he will soon amend that), and look only to his delightful poetry. (p. 171)

[The] beauties of Mr. Beddoes's writing are so scattered over his play, that we cannot very well, by extracts, unless they were very long, do him justice. He wants, as we have said, earnestness sometimes, and but too often trifles a little with his subject; but there are marks of great and undoubted talent in his play; and the whole is clothed in a more poetical dress (a rare thing—though we *do* call ours "a poetical age,") than we have for a very long time seen displayed to the public. We hope that the public will appreciate it. (p. 172)

[*Bryan Waller Procter,*] *"Review: 'The Brides' Tragedy',"* in London Magazine (© London Magazine *1823), Vol. 7, February, 1823, pp. 169-72.*

[CHRISTOPHER NORTH (pseudonym of John Wilson)]
(essay date 1823)

The Brides' Tragedy is the work of a Minor—and, although no doubt there have been many instances of Minors writing better than they ever did after they became Majors, nevertheless we admit the plea of nonage—an old head has no business on old shoulders; and an extremely wise, rational, sober, pretty-behaved and judicious springald, is not, to our taste, a commendable specimen of human nature. Now, Mr. Beddoes is very far indeed from being a boy-wiseacre. He is often as silly as may be,—trifling to a degree that is "quite refreshing,"— as childish as his best friends could desire to see him in a summer's day,—fantastic and capricious as any Miss-in-her-teens,—and pathetic to an excess that absolutely merits the strappado. Why not? all so much the better. He is a fine, open-hearted, ingenuous, accomplished and gentlemanly youth; and we . . . pronounce him a promising poet,—we tie a wreath of laurel round his forehead,—and may it remain there till displaced to make room for a bolder branch of the sacred Tree.

The subject of the Drama is a good one, deeply, terribly tragic— "a tale of tears, a rueful story,"—a murder strange and overwhelming to the imagination, yet such a murder as the mind can image and believe in its wild and haunted moods. Mr. Beddoes deserves praise for choosing such a subject—for all true Tragedy must possess its strength in a spirit of terror. . . . We sup full of horrors, but there are some gay and fantastic garnishings and adornments of the repast, disposed quite in the manner and spirit of those great old masters. Joy and sorrow, peace and despair, innocence and guilt, saintliness and sin, sit all together at one banquet; and we scarcely distinguish the guests from each other, till something interrupts the flow of the feast, and they start up in their proper character. Yes, there is a dark and troubled, guilt-like and death-like gloom flung over this first work of a truly poetical mind, sometimes alternating with an air of ethereal tenderness and beauty, sometimes slowly and in a ghastly guise encroaching upon and stifling it, and sometimes breaking up and departing from it, in black masses, like clouds from a lovely valley on a tempestuous and uncertain day. Dip into the Poem, here and there, and you cannot tell what it is about—you see dim imagery, and indistinct figures, and fear that the author has written a very so so performance. But give it a reading from the beginning, and you will give it a reading to the end, for our young poet writes in the power of nature, and when at any time you get wearied or disappointed with his failure in passion or in plot, you are pleased—nay, delighted, with the luxuriance of his fancy, and with a strain of imaginative feeling that supplies the place of a profounder interest, and also prepares the mind to give way to that profound interest, when, by and by, it unexpectedly and strongly arrives. (pp. 723-24)

[His language] is elegant, and his versification constructed on a good principle. It is dramatic. He has no mean talents, keen perceptions, and fine feelings. He has evidently never once attempted to make his different characters speak naturally; they all declaim, harangue, spout, and poetize with equal ease and elegance; and when they go mad, which, towards the end, they almost all do, man, woman, and child, they merely become a little more figurative and metaphorical; but the train of their thoughts and feelings proceeds much the same as when they

were in their sober senses. But to point out the faults of this composition would be absurd indeed, for they are innumerable and glaring, and the deuce is in it, if Mr. Beddoes does not wonder at himself and his play, before he is three-and-twenty. Wonder he may and will, but he need never to be ashamed of it, for with all its extravagancies, and even sillinesses and follies, it shews far more than glimpses of a true poetical genius, much tender and deep feeling, a wantoning sense of beauty, a sort of light, airy, and graceful delicacy of imagination, extremely delightful, and withal a power over the darker and more terrible passions, which, when taught and strengthened by knowledge and experience of human life, will, we hope, and almost trust, enable Mr. Beddoes to write a *bonâ fide* good English tragedy. (p. 729)

[*Christopher North (pseudonym of John Wilson),*] *"Notices of the Modern British Dramatists: No. II; Beddoes,"* in Blackwood's Edinburgh Magazine, *Vol. XIV, No. LXXXIII, December, 1823, pp. 723-29.*

JOHN LACY [pseudonym of George Darley]   (essay date 1823)

The Brides' Tragedy transcends, in the quality of its rhythm and metrical harmony, the Dogs of Venice and Mirandola; just as much as it does Fazio, and the other dramas which conform to the rules of genuine English heroic verse, in the energy of its language, the power of its sentiments, and the boldness of its imagery—that is, incalculably. The impassioned sublimity of [the] speech of Hesperus (after he has murdered Floribel), is a nearer approach to the vein of our dramatic school of tragedy, than I can recognize in either the rhetoric or poetic. . . . (p. 647)

There is a good deal of extravagance [in the *Brides' Tragedy*], a good deal of hyperbolical rambling; the luxuriant growth of a fancy which maturer judgment will restrain. The author appears, also, to be making too evident a set at sublimity in [some passages; for they begin] too designedly in the established form of solemnific invocation, and [run] too long a gauntlet or second-person pronouns, the rhapsodist's right-hand monosyllable, time immemorial. Nevertheless, [they betray] a mind in which the rudiments of tragic power are, to my eyes, eminently conspicuous,—tragic power of the very highest order. I have frequently mentioned the *os magna sonans;* this is the first great qualification for a tragedist, and this qualification the Author of the *Brides' Tragedy* most undeniably possesses. Nay, more: considering the *os magna* as a quality as well as a qualification, there is one species of it *only* which is peculiar to tragedy; that which is proper to epic poetry is essentially different from this. But the *rara avis* among dramatists, is he who possesses the tragic species, and not the epic; for any one conversant with the English stage, from Shakspeare downwards, will easily perceive that almost all our dramatic writers mistake the *epic* for the *tragic* vein of magniloquence; now, the Author of the *Brides' Tragedy* is a *rara avis* of this kind. . . . [Beddoes's] tragedy is certainly a most singular and unexpected production, for this age; exhibiting, as it does, this peculiar knack in the author for the genuine *os* of the stage. After all the abuse my conscience has compelled me to pour forth on the plotlessness, still-life, puling effutiation, poetry, and prose-poetry of modern plays, it is grateful to my heart to acknowledge that this first great quality of legitimate drama is broad upon the surface of the *Brides' Tragedy.* I am almost tempted to confess after the perusal of our Minor's poem, that I have been premature in pronouncing the decline of English poetry from the Byronian epoch: and to express my confidence that tragedy has again put forth a scion worthy of the stock from which Shakspeare and Marlow sprung. But whilst I pay this cordial tribute of admiration to our author's genius, and indulge in this prospect of his eventual success as a dramatist, I cannot help avowing my fears that he is deficient in some qualifications, which, although not as splendid, are just as necessary to complete a tragedist, as that *one* which I have unreservedly allowed him. The *os magna,* alone, will not do; even that which is not epic or lyric, but strictly dramatic. He exhibits no skill in dialogue. He displays no power whatever in delineation of character. If it were possible, speaking of works of this kind, to make a distinction between the *vis tragica* and the *vis dramatica,* I should say that he possessed much of the former, but little of the latter. The energy, passion, terribility, and sublime eloquence of the stage, he appears perfectly competent to: his facilities in the artful development of story, the contrastment and individualization of characters, the composition of effective dialogue, the management of incidents, scenes, and situations, &c. are as yet *under the bushel,* if their non-appearance in his tragedy be not a proof-presumptive of their non-existence in his mind. In a word, the **Brides' Tragedy** does not exhibit any faculty in the author of representing or imitating human life in a connected series of well-ordered scenes, characters, and dialogues; but it exhibits that qualification of mind, which, if it informed such a ready-made series, would render it not only a mere work of genius, but a work of legitimate dramatic genius, an effective tragedy. We must, however, take off the edge of these exceptions to our author's flexibility of genius, by the recollection of two facts. First, that his tragedy was written premeditatedly for the closet, and not for the stage; hence poetic tragedy, more than dramatic, was his object. Secondly, he is a ''Minor.'' With the hope that he *will* devote himself to the stage, and with the expectation that increasing years will multiply his dramatic powers which are now apparently confined to one, I conclude my observations on his work. (pp. 647-48)

> *John Lacy [pseudonym of George Darley], ''A Sixth Letter to the Dramatists of the Day,'' in* London Magazine *(© London Magazine 1823), Vol. 8, December, 1823, pp. 645-52.*

THOMAS LOVELL BEDDOES   (essay date 1828?)

[**Death's Jest Book**] is undoubtedly a very faulty [poem], nor is it intended to be otherwise; it is offered as a specimen of what might be called the florid Gothic in poetry, which the author desires to leave alone and hopes therefore, probably quite superfluously, that it will meet with no imitators. It is written for those who can find entertainment in it—and in the humble hope that the greater number of critics (or, to speak more properly) reviewers will be kind enough to find it guilty of almost every literary offence according to their critical judgement; and thus assure the otherwise inconsolable author that he has succeeded in producing something which has at least the merit of being at variance with their taste. Only one thing he begs of these gentlemen, to spare him the vexation of being eulogized by them, and to avoid any such misfortune engages to deliver gratuitously to the dealers in reviews an article on and by himself replete with the choicest flowers of obloquy, depreciation of the style, hints of plagiarism, and especially (as the forlorn hope) appeals to the classical taste of the polished world, who have learned the Odes of Horace by heart at Eton &ᶜ, differing therefore materially from the tone in which certain writers in a great Review are in the habit of holding inquest

on their own works. The reader will therefore recognise directly the hand which produces the most violent attack, and with this warning hint the writer bids him farewell, and defiance to such of his reviewers as shall venture to praise him. (pp. 534-35)

> *Thomas Lovell Beddoes, ''Preface'' (1828?), in his* Death's Jest Book, *William Pickering, 1850 (and reprinted in his* The Works of Thomas Lovell Beddoes, *edited by H. W. Donner, Oxford University Press, London, 1935, pp. 530-35).*

T.F. KELSALL   (essay date 1833)

We are not in the habit of lending the shelter of our columns to the hasty & imperfect conceptions of either friend or stranger, not deeming the public to be exactly the mistress whom we should approach in gown & slippers. If in publishing the Scenes [of **''The Second Brother''**] which immediately follow or which may appear in succeeding numbers we shall have deviated from our accustomed strictness of decorum, it must be our best & only apology that we are hurried away by unaffected admiration of the Power & Beauty which they display & by the wish to impart no ordinary gratification to our readers. In offering also detached portions of this *unfinished drama* (which has been submitted to us & entrusted for publicity under peculiar circumstances) we experience the less hesitation, inasmuch that their excellence will be found to consist, not so much in the masterly development of story, or even in the delineation & Retsch-like continuity of character, as in the rich and imaginative mind, teeming with the very spirit of poetic life, which everywhere bursts thro' the language & clothes the whole surface of its creation with imagery of luxuriant or solemn-shaded thoughts. No one, we are inclined to prophesy, will rise from a persual of these gifted fragments, without regretting, with ourselves, that they are but fragments. The writer's name we are not yet at liberty to disclose, tho' by one former more open trial of his strength, he has already shewn himself capable to bend the Ulyssean bow of strenuous British Tragedy. Stimulated by public acclaim, may he, *at length* be roused to the achievement of further and still loftier flights! (pp. 23-4)

> *T. F. Kelsall, ''Introduction to Scenes from 'The Second Brother' '' (1833), in* The Browning Box; or, The Life and Works of Thomas Lovell Beddoes as Reflected in Letters by His Friends and Admirers, *edited by H. W. Donner, Oxford University Press, London, 1935, pp. 23-4.*

E. HOWARD   (essay date 1835)

I find [**''The Second Brother''**] one of the crudest & most ill-digested pieces of writing that was ever submitted to me. The labour after effect is so apparent in every line that the sensation of reading the Scene is something like that of viewing a man labouring hard at a hand-mill. It is also full of all manner of discrepancies, & contains situations not only absurd but impossible. But with all this, do not suppose that I do not think that it contains germs of great merit: there is that intensity of thought & feeling about it, that is the true characteristic of real genius. The author wants the salutary advice of a cool head & much self-discipline in order that he may cut away redundancies & learn not to follow every light that bursts upon his path. . . .

> *E. Howard, in his letter to Thomas Forbes Kelsall on January 2, 1835, in* The Browning Box or the Life and Works of Thomas Lovell Beddoes as Re-

flected in Letters by His Friends and Admirers, *edited by H. W. Donner (reprinted by permission of Oxford University Press), Oxford University Press, London, 1935, p. 25.*

THE SPECTATOR   (essay date 1850)

[*Death's Jest Book; or, The Fool's Tragedy*] turns out to be, as we anticipated, an imitation of the more extravagant dramatists of the Elizabethan age, with that unnaturalness which always attends upon conventional imitation even if the outlines of the copy be softened and refined. . . .

The author of *The Fool's Tragedy* has studied the older dramatists till they stand to him in place of records and reality. His ideas of human conduct, his views of human life, and that mode of uttering human language which we call style, are all reflections of what was extreme and partial when new, with the further disadvantage of being deficient in the boldness and consistency of an original. His plot is a conglomeration of crime; his denouement, of deaths; and all is set in motion for purposes now at least insufficient to men's minds. . . .

Stated simply, [the action of the drama] sounds like the conception of a bedlamite, or the *oegri somnia*; yet so thoroughly has the author possessed himself with the trick of his originals, that the events as presented in the drama, and surrounded by their circumstances, look not worse than in the olden tragedies. The merit of *The Fool's Tragedy*, however, is in the execution. There is more in the writer than vulgar imitation can ever reach. He has the fulness of matter, the depth of thought, the strength of expression, and the poetical feeling, that distinguished his prototypes; as well as that scornful regard to the present system of things, less sceptical than defiant, which possessed some of them. There are also touches of those dark metaphysics in which their criminals speculated when meditating crime. (p. 643)

> *"'Death's Jest-Book, or The Fool's Tragedy'," in* The Spectator *(© 1850 by The Spectator), No. 1149, July 6, 1850, pp. 643-44.*

THE ATHENAEUM   (essay date 1850)

['**Death's Jest-Book**'] has no common claims. Besides its own peculiar merits, it possesses the adventitious interest belonging to the posthumous work of one who, though he all his life produced little, was credited with great powers and lively fancies by some of our most powerful and picturesque imaginative creators. They naturally had more intimate sympathies for the author of '**The Brides' Tragedy**' than the crowd without the Temple—than the average lovers of poetry and thinkers about poetry could be ever brought to entertain. They could soar into his extravagances and hide with him in his dimnesses; and with him find no contrast too harsh to be reconciled—no combination too fearful to be dwelt on—under the influence of that quick and living Spirit the voice of which they could hear, the presence of which they could see, even though both were hidden from the uninitiated as by seven veils. (p. 1115)

'**Death's Jest-Book**' contains the fullest answer to those who, among other lamentations over the decline of drama, cite the silence of Mr. Beddoes for lack of encouragement as an instance not to be put aside. Under no dispensation could one so richly yet perversely gifted have hoped for stage success, if even he could have obtained stage hearing. . . . His ambition seems to have been to reproduce the manner of Ford, Webster, and Marlowe. Their pathos, their poetry, with its delicious

haunting tenderness . . . were emulated by him, and not unsuccessfully; but a taste, also, for what is monstrous, and harrowing, and unearthly . . . seems also to have passed into his mind. If he did not affect the horrible, he toyed with it. It need only be said, in proof of this assertion, that during the principal and most important part of this drama—the latter acts, where the action precipitates and the passion quickens—a leading personage is one raised from the dead by a process of antique sorcery. (pp. 1115-16)

[Perhaps] the real spell and charm of '**Death's Jest-Book**' lie in the lyrics that are scattered among the grisly shapes with which its pages are peopled. . . .

In grotesque ditties the author of '**Death's Jest-Book**' is less happy. With him, . . . that which is meant to be mirthful is merely uncouth: . . . its vivacity rather more dismal than lamentation or than silence. . . .

There is no closing such a book as this—such a strange composition of all that is most repulsive with all that is most fascinating—without a feeling of more than common melancholy. Thwarted, perverted, perverse Genius—in itself unhappy, by others but imperfectly recognized—conscious of powers, yet little less conscious that those powers will never find adequate utterance—is one of the saddest sights which the world of realities and dreams can show. And we have rarely, if ever, met with so full an illustration and expression of it as in this posthumous work of one not unjustly credited with every good gift which marks a poet and makes a poet's fame. (p. 1116)

> *"'Death's Jest-Book; or, the Fool's Tragedy'," in* The Athenaeum, *No. 1200, October 26, 1850, pp. 1115-16.*

THE CRITIC   (essay date 1851)

The posthumous work of a man scarcely known to the public as an author, but reputed a true poet among poets and some select readers, *Death's Jest Book*, possesses a peculiar interest. We must seek here an explanation for the one, and a justification for the other; and shall find both.

We had never been able fully to enter into the esteem in which Mr. Beddoes's drama, *The Brides' Tragedy*, was held, or to understand why so much was expected of its author by those best in a position to know the man, and to judge the poet. We now recognise how rich was the material for hope; how well-founded the perception of large and original capabilities; how easy for personal knowledge to account for defects of performance without mistrusting the power to perform. That the faculties acknowledged of Mr. Beddoes were in him to the fullest extent asserted, and even more, there is no doubt; and this leads us to inquire why they were so seldom displayed, and known within so restricted a circle?

There is one sufficient answer to the question, present at once, before passing on to a consideration of his special defects and singularities—he did not walk with his age. Poetry has ceased to be merely descriptive or pictorial—it has become representative. The public is not content with hearing what the poet has imagined; they must know what peculiar qualities of mind have induced him to adopt this treatment, and not another; must have matter for speculating as to what events or influences of his life he has desired to shadow forth. They must guess why his thought has arrayed itself thus to their eyes, and see the motions of the loom which wove the robe. . . . (pp. 12-13)

In *Death's Jest Book,* the characters and actions are more than singular, they are eccentric; and, as such, deeply marked as the conceptions of an individual mind. They would not be, but for Mr. Beddoes: yet Mr. Beddoes himself never speaks. He was a thorough Elizabethan; and shows the brave dramatic impartiality of his models. He has their love of images daring to hyperbole; of characters intense to atrocity: of strange events, huge, sudden, and inconsistent. With them he shares too, that sense of nobility (one of the most emphatic proofs of a true gift in poetry), so acutely and earnestly perceived by Emerson as distinctive of their works. He draws his personages cordially and with a free hand. All are men of mark sitting above the dais by right—if not of their virtues, then of their passions, ambition, or crimes. . . .

Mr. Beddoes, although free to a now unusual extent from the anti-dramatic propensity peculiar to the age, had not the power of dramatic construction. It has been matter of some reproach, we believe, that he was never allowed a hearing on the stage: not, however, justly. *The Brides' Tragedy* showed no special fitness for representation: and *Death's Jest Book* would not, probably, be tolerated beyond a single night, even if reduced, as would be indispensable, to half its present length. Several characters are boldly conceived, some combinations of incident are exciting, and, with all its glaring faults, we cannot deny that the plot possesses a degree of interest. But the mutual relations of the personages, the *deus ex machinâ* system which prevails throughout, with the undramatic and inconsequent nature of the *dénouement,* betray a strange and anomalous incompleteness. . . .

But the intense poetry of the work, its sense of beauty, and force of thought and language, more than compensate even for all this. There is as much of that something which defies analysis, and for which no better name than "essential poetry" can be found, in *Death's Jest Book,* as in perhaps any single work of the generation. . . .

Apart from the unaccountable defects of its construction—defects which seem to belong to nothing less than a peculiar natural inaptitude—the blemish of Mr. Beddoes's drama is excess. There is a tendency to the horrible which lapses into the grotesque; and even more decidedly pronounced, a love of the grotesque proper, for its own sake, quite extraordinary. . . . The passion verges on delirium, the ambition on insanity, the images sometimes on monstrosity; and the whole purport of the work seems to stagger blind and demented. But it is a staggering of great strides, blindness faces intense light, and the wildness utters words of long echo: and we know that a poet has been among us. (p. 13)

> *"Poetry and the Drama: 'Death's Jest Book, or, The Fool's Tragedy',"* in The Critic, London, *Vol. X, No. 234, January 1, 1851, pp. 12-13.*

THE CRITIC (essay date 1851)

[We] have scanty information concerning the late Thomas Lovell Beddoes, and the growth of that wonderful poetic luxuriance which lies everywhere about him. What little we know of him shows how strongly he was marked with a genius which the Germans call "manysided," for the profundity and ardour of his physiological and anatomical studies would seem to indicate no disposition and no power in the student to track the fanciful footsteps of the muse. Yet he followed her triumphantly into the deepest recesses of her sanctuary, returning, with unwearied brain and unabated energy, to scientific researches. The mental elasticity he displayed has few parallels in modern times, therefore are we the more surprised at the little that is known of his poetic character. . . .

Mr. Beddoes had great natural advantages; he was in full posession of that which cannot make a strictly angular mind poetical, but which fills a flexile brain with living images by which it can repeople the universe. His first poem, *The Improvisatore,* shows that at the time of its publication nature had not asserted her supremacy. Byron, Moore, and others, stood between his imitative talent and his unimitative genius. He was dazzled by the brilliant obstruction, and would not, or could not, strike it aside; hence, *The Improvisatore* sprung into sudden life to die suddenly like an echo. . . .

The Improvisatore appeared in 1821, and about a year afterwards Mr. Beddoes produced *The Brides' Tragedy,* which at once called forth high praise. . . . It was a work unmistakeably rich in imagination and richer in promise—the "all hail hereafter." Even now, after the flight of more than a quarter of a century, it stands creditably by the side of the more matured works of the author. It is the first link, and certainly an important one, in that remarkable chain of exuberant fancy by which Mr. Beddoes embraced the world of spirits and mortals. *The Brides' Tragedy* is the starting point of a gifted mind, and we are very reluctant to retrack the silent footsteps of thirty years in order to show the shadow on the dial. . . . The favourable reception of *The Brides' Tragedy* at once let free the waywardness and daring of the author's genius. He gave himself up to the full rush of composition. In the following two years most of the poetry contained in [*Poems*], besides much destroyed and lost, was struck off from his eager and muscular mind. Under his touch, language assumed a complication of figures and forms. . . . From him, and around him, fell a shower of bright sparks, the blazing fragments, as it were, of a mind which from first to last was purely fragmentary. Still he worked in silence and in solitude. The public, whose attention had been arrested by his first brilliant movement—a comet flaming though the orbit of Shelly and Keats—looked in vain for the return of the erratic visitor. He came not. He had written in secret and loneliness until it produced an indifference to fame. (p. 514)

It was evident that the author of *Death's Jest-book* found life not quite a jest. This in him was no new feeling, it was rather the full development of the old. . . .

[Mr. Beddoes] underrated his power, and lost his self-reliance, without which a poet never worked his way to eminence; yet if he has not done as much as he ought, he has yet done enough to place him in the first class of poets. Whether we look at *Death's Jest-book* published last year, or at the two unfinished dramas, fragments, and minor poems now given to the world, everywhere we see the same colossal grandeur and the same gigantic gloom; the same lyrical sweetness, dramatic strength, and imaginative resources. He squandered more wealth on a page than is contained in the brain of half the poets of the day. He might, and should, have been the Napoleon of literature, but he lacked the Corsican's courage and his indomitable will. . . . But by-gones are by-gones, and all our regrets are unavailing. Let us rather turn to the actual production of the poet. We have no idea that Mr. Beddoes' works will be highly popular. His characters are too exaggerated to "catch the nearest way" to our sympathies. Experience does not acknowledge them as it does the characters of Shakspeare. They are passions and mental idealisms, not men and women. There is little characterization and little individuality, dramatically speaking. . . .

Taking the works as poems, and not as dramas, setting aside their personality and condition, we could select passages which, for richness of beauty, could hardly be surpassed. They are as many jewels set in an imperfect casket, but they are nevertheless jewels of the rarest order. (p. 515)

It has been objected to Mr. Beddoes' works, that they are filled with an unnatural amount of gloom; and it is too true that they are overcharged with spectral fancies. . . . Mr. Beddoes did not do this to excite "vulgar admiration." It was an unconquerable failing—a weakness growing out of his excessive strength. The age itself fostered his mental habitude. . . . We throw out this as merely suggestive, at the same time regretting that such a lofty intellect should have been so eager in hunting flowers among sepulchres, skulls, and the saddest wrecks of humanity. Physically and socially, it is better to hear birds sing, than, through a moody fancy, to hear the "grave-worms hiss." Unfortunately this gloom in Mr. Beddoes is perpetual; whereas everything else about him is broken and incomplete. *The Second Brother,* and *Torrismond,* two unfinished dramas, will remain as splendid monuments, recording the impetuous and capricious mind of the gifted author. (p. 516)

> *"Poetry and the Drama: 'Poems',"* in The Critic, *Vol. X, No. 254, November 1, 1851, pp. 514-16.*

FRASER'S MAGAZINE FOR TOWN AND COUNTRY
(essay date 1851)

[In Mr. Thomas Lovell Beddoes] is the strange phenomenon of a man, modest, simple, highly educated at every point, appreciating and studying the best models, possessed of untiring energy, and fancy such as does not fall to the lot of one in ten thousand, devoting himself, with single mind and lofty purpose, to the production of works of pure art, simply for their own sake, without care for praise or pay—and failing. The simple cause of his failure being, as it seems to us, that he has trusted to this very scientific aesthetic; and fancied throughout that he could make poetry consciously and deliberately, by rule and measure, according to the school of Marlowe and his contemporaries. Thoughts and images grow up in his mind in rare profusion, and he says to himself, 'I must put these together, and make something out of them, according to the best model I know.' And he does make something out of them, gorgeous and forcible enough; but, it is made—put together: you can see the joints and nail-holes. (p. 623)

[Mr. Beddoes' characters are inhuman as a class]. Their pathos excites no sympathy; their sins make you disgusted with them, not indignant against sin, for, indeed, it is not sin; they are not moral and accountable souls, but puppets who leap from one extreme of passion to the other, without any step between. There is no inner unity in each of them, and therefore there cannot be any in the dramas which are made up out of their sayings and doings.

The truth is, Mr. Beddoes has little or no imagination, only a fancy, enormous in every sense of the word. The faculty which suggests, compares, alludes, is present in a rare degree. That which sees into things, and feels for and with them, and puts the poet at every turn in the place of that which he sees, be it a character or a flower, enabling his soul to live every day through a whole cycle of transmigrations—of that, the true dramatic faculty, Mr. Beddoes has little or none. Here and

there, as must happen with such fancy and such labour, we find a brilliant flash of scenic imagination, like that passage in the *Brides' Tragedy,* where Leonora is watching her daughter's corpse. . . . (p. 624)

It is this same want of true imagination which has tempted Mr. Beddoes, as it tempts so many, to create their own plots, instead of giving human life to one already known. . . . [Thence arises] in Mr. Beddoes a longing after the more violent kind of action. The poet does not see the insides of men and things, and the boundless depth of wonders which is in them even in their calmest and most common-place moods, but only the outsides of them, and therefore he finds it necessary to make that outside as striking and showy as possible. . . . Hence inflated language, overloaded with imagery, a growing fondness for the horrible; while the stock of really healthy human incident and character with which the poet has started, is more and more used up, because it has not been replaced as fast as employed, by that daily observation of mankind and history, loving, tolerant, and patient, which alone can keep imagination alive, and which, if anything can, will give it, in greater or less degree, where it is originally defective. And thus we have to say, sadly, of Mr. Beddoes, that his first drama, written when he was a minor, is really his best; that the notes and thoughts which he lays by, to be worked in when wanted, become, as he grows older, less and less human, more and more of mere soulless extravagant concetti, till we have at last the sad spectacle of a man of talent and education, and lofty principle, fancying in mature age that it was poetic, or even decent, to be talking everlastingly of spectres, and grave-worms, and hell, and demons, and madness, and murder, murder, murder. . . . (pp. 625-26)

But [Beddoes] is gone . . . and wasted, as too many are. We should not have dwelt so long upon the artistic faults of a worthy man deceased, were it not for the great harm to young poets, especially self-educated ones among the middle and working classes, which these poems are likely to do, recommended as they are by the charm of their power and richness. . . . Mr. Beddoes wants the spirit of love and hope. Man, his sorrows, his destinies, are nothing to him. He seems, from his biography, never to have had it kept alive in him. . . . Another great might-have-been, in a world so sadly in need. . . . (p. 626)

> *"This Year's Song-Crop,"* in Fraser's Magazine for Town and Country, *Vol. XLIV, No. CCLXIV, December, 1851, pp. 618-34.**

MR. BUTTLE (essay date 1856)

Death's Jest-Book [which I was inclined to consider more appropriately named by its second title, *The Fool's Tragedy,*] is a play of the most impossible construction. Talk of ghosts in a country churchyard!—talk of ghouls in the *Arabian Nights!* There are more hideous apparitions and revolting incidents in this drama than in the wildest imaginings of superstition or romance. There are people who die—apparently as dead as the deadest of door-nails—in the middle of an act; and in some succeeding scene, when nobody expects anything but a jolly celebration of their funeral obsequies, their bodies, borrowed for a while from the grave, come boldly upon the stage, and gibber and gloom, and utter hollow sounds, till the hairs of your head—those of them that don't fly out of your skull in the first burst of your terror—dress up like "frightful porcupines," and you have no breath left in you even to laugh. There is Wolfram, a knight—and Isbrand, the court-fool, who is his brother—and a Duke of Munsterberg—and Ziba, an Egyptian slave—and Homunculus Mandrake, a Zany. This latter is not the author of the play; nor is he, indeed, in any respect, a greater zany than any of the other personages, and might be left out altogether without any perceptible diminution of the absurdity of the whole thing. What has happened before the curtain rises we find it difficult to discover; but this is the plot: Wolfram—no, Isbrand—no, somebody else—has been in love with somebody; and she—no, the Duke—or, let me see, is it Ziba the Egyptian? The fact is, it is a little difficult to make out what it is all about. But the Duke slays Wolfram, and Ziba brings him to life again. Then there seems to be a considerable amount of enmity, as might be expected, between the dead man and his murderer. Then two or three other people die, and Death *in propria personâ* comes in and dances a kind of saraband; funeral processions cross the stage, and Isbrand, the fool, says a few comic verses, and at the end Wolfram, who begins to be tired of the upper air, gives the Duke his arm, and the last stage direction is, "Exit with the Duke into the sepulchre." These are mere dreams of lunacy and infatuation—full of sound and fury, signifying nothing. Wait a little before you throw the book out of the window and consign the author to Hanwell. In this mad and plotless play there are finer passages than any living dramatist has composed. There is grandeur, tenderness, and a power of description totally unequalled by the second-hand Elizabethans. (pp. 447-48)

Mr. Buttle, "Mr. Buttle's Reviews: 'Death's Jest-Book'," in Blackwood's Edinburgh Magazine, *Vol. LXXX, No. CCCCXCII, October, 1856, pp. 447-49.*

THOMAS F. KELSALL   (essay date 1872)

The interest and influence of *Death's Jest Book* do not in any manner depend on philosophic delineations of its *dramatis personae,* and nice gradations in their development, and consequently suffer little of that injury from breaches of continuity in the narrative, which would doubtless be inseparable from any similar liberties taken with Hamlet and Macbeth, and even Wallenstein, whose characters are gradually built up before our eyes. It is otherwise, indeed, with the construction of its story, which is powerfully and graphically unfolded, presenting novel, daring, and impressive effects, through the dark and winding labyrinth of which is ever heard that tread of the approaching Nemesis which is so essential an element in all high tragedy. The same cause that prompts, and should justify, this design, cannot but favour its execution, viz., the passionate and intense character of every verse Beddoes wrote, giving to it, however isolated or fragmentary, a distinctive excellence of its own. In all his poetry—dramatic, lyrical, or whatever else its form—we stand beside an exuberant spring of imaginative thought, that ever rises up in novel, vivid, and startling conceptions; "and has" (to adopt his own pregnant words)—

> the caverns of its inspirations
> More true than Delphian underneath our being.

And it is this profounder influence, of which our minds are conscious, that gives to his verse, despite its blemishes of turbulence and excess, an especial distinction, apart and almost unique in our literature. Beddoes invented the plots of his dramas, and in shaping these, he doubtless cared less for the harmonious proportions of the structure, than for its capability for the reception and display of those rich and varied fancies which his creative mind poured forth in such abundance. . . .

Every real poet has a style of his own, and this is not the less true of Beddoes, because in his case it is from its very excellence less obvious to direct notice. It is altogether free from mannerism; its characteristic being an expression so transparent that it seems to be a very portion of the idea which it reveals. The creations of Beddoes have no haze about them; and they stand before us with the fulness of sculpture. Neither is there any taint of rhetoric in his lines, no painful mosaic, no impasting of colours. His diction is not a parti-coloured raiment prepared to cover the naked new-born idea, and often only attracting notice to its own unfitness: it is always congenital with the thought, and as much a part of it as the skin is of the living animal. The poetry of Beddoes has been happily defined as *"essential* poetry;" its constituent elements being so intimately blended and inseparable that they are indistinguishable by sight, and . . . "transparent as a glass of poisoned water," while the clearness of the draught but intensifies its subtlety and strength. The poet's magic is in the web of his verse, and penetrating every portion of its texture, it makes its presence felt in his most fragmentary compositions, in single lines, and often in mere epithets. (pp. 57-9)

[*Death's Jest Book; or, The Fool's Tragedy* is] singular in its plot, its characters, its accessories, and, above all, singular in the felicities and vigour of its composition. It may not be a suitable pillow for the head that would court only placid dreams, but those who turn habitually to poetry as "chief nourisher in life's feast" of some of their noblest faculties, will find such congenial aliment in the imaginative thoughts that crowd this little volume.

The limits of an article have restricted the present election to a single work of its author. . . . All his other productions, however, are broadly marked with the same originality and power as *Death's Jest Book,* and will not fail, as and when, either here or elsewhere, they find audience, to make good a claim to the like rescue from obscurity and oblivion. (p. 75)

Thomas F. Kelsall, "Thomas Lovell Beddoes," in The Fortnightly Review *(reprinted by permission of Contemporary Review Company Limited), Vol. 18, July 1, 1872, pp. 51-75.*

KATE HILLARD   (essay date 1873)

[It] is by his songs that [Beddoes'] name is kept in the minds of men to-day—exquisite snatches of melody, full of the peculiar charm of that Elizabethan age to which they properly belong. (p. 551)

Beddoes' great fault as a dramatist he was quite aware of himself, and had pointed out to the friend who was continually urging him to write: "The power of drawing character and humor—two things absolutely indispensable for a good dramatist—are the first two articles in my deficiencies; and even the imaginative poetry I think you will find in all my verse always harping on the same two or three principles; for which plain and satisfactory reasons I have no business to expect any great distinction as a writer." He could draw types of character, but not individuals: the power of making the creations of the mind seem as real as "our dear intimates and chamber-fellows" was denied him. But he was not wholly destitute of humor, though he was possessed of but one kind—that grim, sardonic quality which we find so often among the Elizabethans—that mocking irony most like the grin upon a skull. His fools are his best characters, so far as strength and originality go. (pp. 553-54)

It is unnecessary to try to describe the plot of [*Death's Jest-Book*], if plot it may be called. The poem rather resembles the old bridge at Lucerne with the gloomy figures of the Dance of Death painted along its wormeaten sides, while over its old timbers roll the current of busy life, and the laughter of children echoes from its roof. With the exception of Isbrand, the characters of the play are pale and shadowy enough, but the poetry that they speak is wonderful. The gloom and tender beauty of the verse are inextricably united, as in the plays of Webster, whose "intellectual twin" Beddoes might have been. (p. 554)

But the greatest beauty of this singular poem, with its wild medley of jesters and spirits, knights and fiends, Deaths and tender women, "like flowers on a grave," is the wonderful perfection of its songs. There are no less than thirteen in this play, some of them the wild mockery of the jesters, but many of them very beautiful; and there are three more in *The Brides' Tragedy*. Since the days of Elizabeth we have had nothing to compare with them. They have that delicate poise of beauty, like the lighting of a butterfly on a bending flower, that adds to our delight the keen sense of its transitoriness. (pp. 554-55)

More simple and coherent in plot and construction than the other drama, [*The Brides' Tragedy*] has more sweetness and less strength. It is full of the innocence of love, and rich with that prodigality of beauty with which youthful genius loves to make itself splendid. . . . There are beautiful scenes and passages all through the play, the passion and the terror smacking somewhat of youth, perhaps, that loves to pile up agonies, but the poetry still so fine that one continually forgets to say, This is the work of a boy of nineteen. There is no need to say it, in fact: it is a work of genius, and demands no extenuation. (p. 555)

For imaginative power of a very high order, for the true tragic spirit, for exquisitely melodious versification, for that faculty of song which is the flower of the lyric genius, Beddoes was pre-eminently distinguished. Nor for these alone. His style is based upon the rich vocabulary of the old dramatists, and is terse, pregnant and quaint, without any trace of affectation. There was a sturdy genuineness about the man that forbade him to assume, and his phraseology was the natural outgrowth of his mind and his early education. He has not gone to work, like so many of our modern pre-Raphaelite painters, to imitate crudeness of form in the vain hope of acquiring thereby earnestness and innocence of spirit; but he has studied the best tragic models in a reverent spirit, and allowed his muse to work out her own salvation. That grim ironical humor which infuses such bitter strength into the speeches of Isbrand was always scoffing at his own verses, and nipping the blossoms of his genius in the bud. "I believe I might have met with some success as a retailer of small coal," he writes to Mr. Kelsall, "or a writer of long-bottomed tracts, but doubt of my aptitude for any higher literary or commercial occupation."

His greatest weakness as a writer of tragedy has already been mentioned as one of which he was himself but too well aware—his inability to create characters that should have any more individual existence than as the mouthpieces of various sentiments. While holding that the proper aim of the dramatic writer should be to write for the stage, his dramas are nevertheless fitted only for the closet. . . . As the beauties of his style—and they are many—recall to us the Shakespearian writers and the matchless riches of their verse, so do its faults—which are few—remind us of their faults. A turgid inflation in the tragic passages, a tendency to bombast, even more apparent in the man of forty-six than in the boy of nineteen, mar the calm strength of many of his scenes. The cloying sweetness that overloaded the verses of his juvenile work he left behind him as he grew older, but the Marlowe-like extravagance that rioted in the soliloquies of *Hesperus* still comes to the surface occasionally in the pages of *Death's Jest-Book*. It is the extravagance of strength, however, not of weakness. (pp. 556-57)

There are few left, besides Browning and Proctor and John Forster, of his original admirers, and his name seems to be another on the long list of those who have failed, as the world counts failure. But the poets know better, and among their undying brotherhood space will always be kept for this strayed singer. (p. 557)

Kate Hillard, "A Strayed Singer," in Lippincott's Magazine of Popular Literature and Science, *Vol. XII, No. 33, November, 1873, pp. 550-57.*

THE ATHENÆUM (essay date 1890)

[It] is only as a picture of Nature, coloured and distorted with some subtle allegorical intent, that '**Death's Jest-Book**' claims from the critic any serious attention. . . . In saying that the name '**Death's Jest-Book**' was a "striking name" [Beddoes] was right enough. But it is striking because it suggests some new and subtle reading of the mystery of death. (p. 879)

[No] sooner does Beddoes find himself at work upon his play than every incident arising in the development of the story, instead of being rigidly used and then rigidly cast aside, is allowed to run away with the dramatist. The *idée mère* that he started with becomes lost amid conflicting motives. Like an untrained terrier in a rat-hunt, the helpless dramatist allows his attention to be so divided between the members of the quarry swarming around him that he stands doing nothing. The agent upon whom the working out of the tragic mischief devolves is lost in the confusion; his function is shifted from one to another until at last it settles upon an entity that is neither man, woman, nor spirit, but a dead body conjured up from the tomb by a magician. . . . (pp. 879-80)

Well would it have been for Beddoes if he could have developed a story from a distinct *idée mère* as clearly and as firmly as Mrs. Shelley has done in that remarkable exercise of fancy ['Frankenstein'], the conception of which . . . is developed by every sentence in the book. And yet the chief desire of Beddoes's life was to produce imaginative work on the lines of Shakspeare, Webster, and Marlowe. His failure was egregious, and this it is that makes him so interesting as a man. . . . Beddoes tried manfully to write lyrics like Shelley, and succeeded in producing some of the most unmetrical verses in the language. He tried manfully to write tragedies in the style of Webster, and succeeded in producing a play in the style of Monk Lewis's 'Castle Spectre,' save that, while Lewis's drama is one of the most ingenious constructions among English plays, Beddoes's masterpiece is—'**Death's Jest-Book**'! (p. 880)

If Beddoes was misled into producing bad work, so was many another, but none was so far misled as he. (p. 881)

"Literature: 'The Poetical Works of Thomas Lovell Beddoes'," in The Athenaeum, *No. 3296, December 27, 1890, pp. 879-81.*

EDMUND GOSSE (essay date 1890)

It is not in the fragments that Beddoes has left behind him that we can look for the work of a full-orbed and serene poetical genius. It would be a narrow definition indeed of the word "poet" which should exclude him, but he belongs to the secondary order of makers. He is not one of those whose song flows unbidden from their lips, those born warblers whom neither poverty, nor want of training, nor ignorance, can restrain from tuneful utterance. He belongs to the tribe of scholar-poets, to the educated artists in verse. In every line that he wrote we can trace the influence of existing verse upon his mind. He is intellectual rather than spontaneous. Nor, even within this lower range, does his work extend far on either hand. He cultivates a narrow field, and his impressions of life and feeling are curiously limited and monotonous. At the feast of the Muses he appears bearing little except one small savoury dish, some cold preparation, we may say, of olives and anchovies, the strangeness of which has to make up for its lack of importance. Not every palate enjoys this *hors d'oeuvre,* and when that is the case, Beddoes retires; he has nothing else to give. He appeals to a few literary epicures, who, however, would deplore the absence of this oddly flavoured dish as much as that of any more important *pièce de resistance.*

As a poet, the great defect of Beddoes has already been alluded to,—his want of sustained invention, his powerlessness in evolution. He was poor just where, two hundred years earlier, almost every playwright in the street had been strong, namely, in the ability to conduct an interesting story to a thrilling and appropriate close. From this point of view his boyish play, **"The Brides' Tragedy,"** is his only success. In this case a story was developed with tolerable skill to a dramatic ending. But, with one exception, he never again could contrive to drag a play beyond a certain point; in the second or third act its wings would droop, and it would expire, do what its master would. These unfinished tragedies were like those children of Polynesian dynasties, anxiously trained, one after another, in the warm Pacific air, yet ever doomed to fall, on the borders of manhood, by the breath of the same mysterious disease. **"Death's Jest-Book"** is but an apparent exception. This does indeed appear in the guise of a finished five-act play; but its completion was due to the violent determination of its author, and not to legitimate inspiration. . . . [No] play in literature was less of a spontaneous creation, or was further from achieving the ideal of growing like a tree.

From what Beddoes was not, however, it is time to pass to what he was. In several respects, then, he was a poetical artist of consummate ability. Of all the myriad poets and poeticules who have tried to recover the lost magic of the tragic blank verse of the Elizabethans, Beddoes has come nearest to success. If it were less indifferent to human interests of every ordinary kind, the beauty of his dramatic verse would not fail to fascinate. To see how strong it is, how picturesque, how admirably fashioned, we have only to compare it with what others have done in the same style. . . . But Beddoes is what he himself has called "a creeper into worm-holes." He attempts nothing personal; he follows the very tricks of Marston and Cyril Tourneur like a devoted disciple. The passions with which he invariably deals are remote and unfamiliar; we may go further, and say that they are positively obsolete. . . . He dedicates himself to the service of Death, not with a brooding sense of the terror and shame of mortality, but from a love of the picturesque pageantry of it, the majesty and sombre beauty, the swift, theatrical transitions, the combined elegance and horror that wait upon the sudden decease of monarchs. . . . His attitude, however, though cold and cynical, was always distinguished, and in his wildest flights of humour he escapes vul-

garity. . . . Beddoes often lacks inspiration, but distinction he can never be said to lack.

As a lyrist he appears, on the whole, to rank higher than as a dramatist. Several of his songs, artificial as they are, must always live, and take a high place in the literature of artifice. . . . [The] song in **"Torrismond"** is perhaps the sweetest and the most ingenious; **"Dream-Pedlary"** the most exquisite. The **"Song of the Stygian Naiades"** and **"Old Adam, the Carrion Crow"** are instances of fancy combined with grisly humour, of a class in which Beddoes has no English competitor. The Harpagus ballad in the fourth act of **"Death's Jest-Book,"** and **"Lord Alcohol"** . . . are less known, but no less vivid and extraordinary. Beddoes possesses great sense of verbal melody, a fastidious ear, and considerable, though far from faultless, skill in metrical architecture. His boyish volume, called **"The Improvisatore,"** . . . shows, despite its crudity, that these gifts were early developed. (pp. xxxv-xxxix)

> *Edmund Gosse, in his introduction to* The Poetical Works of Thomas Lovell Beddoes, Vol. 1 *by Thomas Lovell Beddoes, J. M. Dent and Co., 1890, pp. xvii-xxxix.*

ARTHUR SYMONS (essay date 1891)

Beddoes has been rashly called a great poet. I do not think he was a great poet, but he was, in every sense of the word, an astonishing one. . . . How much [his poetry] has of the old, splendid audacity of the Elizabethans! How unlike timid modern verse! Beddoes is always large, impressive; the greatness of his aim gives him a certain claim on respectful consideration. That his talent achieved itself, or ever could have achieved itself, he himself would have been the last to affirm. But he is a monumental failure, more interesting than many facile triumphs.

The one important work which Beddoes actually completed, *Death's Jest-Book,* is nominally a drama in five acts. All the rest of his work, except a few lyrics and occasional poems, is also nominally dramatic. But there never was anything less dramatic in substance than this mass of admirable poetry in dialogue. Beddoes' genius was essentially lyrical: he had imagination, the gift of style, the mastery of rhythm, a strange choiceness and curiosity of phrase. But of really dramatic power he had nothing. . . . Constantly you find the most beautiful poetry where it is absolutely inappropriate, but never do you find one of those brief and memorable phrases—words from the heart—for which one would give much beautiful poetry. . . .

In senses which aim at being passionate, one sees the same inability to be natural. What we get is always literature; it is never less than that, nor more than that. It is never frank, uncompromising nature. The fact is, that Beddoes wrote from the head, collectively, and without emotion, or without inspiration, save in literature. All Beddoes' characters speak precisely the same language, express the same desires; all in the same way startle us by their ghostly remoteness from flesh and blood. . . . Beddoes may be said to have grown tired of humanity before he ever came to understand it.

Looked at from the normal standpoint, Beddoes' idea of the drama was something wildly amateurish. As a practical playwright he would be beneath contempt; as a writer of the regulation poetic drama he cannot be considered successful. But what he aimed at was something peculiar to himself—a sort of spectral dramatic fantasia. . . . *Death's Jest-Book* is perhaps the most morbid poem in our literature. There is not a page without its sad, grotesque, gay, or abhorrent imagery of the tomb. . . . Beddoes has written a new Dance of Death, in poetry; has become the chronicler of the praise and ridicule of Death. "Tired of being merely human," he has peopled a play with confessed phantoms. . . .

I have said already that the genius of Beddoes is not dramatic, but lyrical. What was really most spontaneous in him—nothing was quite spontaneous—was the impulse of song-writing. And it seems to me that he is really most successful, not in the delirious burlesque of **"The Median Supper,"** but in sweet and graceful lyrics. . . .

A beautiful lyrist, a writer of charming, morbid, and magnificent poetry in dramatic form, Beddoes will survive to students, not to readers, of English poetry, somewhere in the neighbourhood of Ebenezer Jones and Charles Wells. Charles Wells was certainly more of a dramatist, a writer of more sustained and Shakesperean blank verse; Ebenezer Jones had certainly a more personal passion to express in his rough and tumultuous way; but Beddoes, not less certainly, had more of actual poetical genius than either. And in the end only one thing counts—actual poetical genius. (p. 129)

> *Arthur Symons, "'The Poetical Works of Thomas Lovell Beddoes'" (reprinted by permission of the Literary Estate of Arthur Symons), in* The Academy, *No. 1006, August 15, 1891, pp. 128-29.*

BARNETTE MILLER (essay date 1903)

It is when one takes up Beddoes's productions in detail that one marvels most at his originality and early signs of talent. His first attempt, written while at the Charterhouse, was a novel called **"Cynthio and Bugboo,"** now lost. Mr. Bevan says that it was modeled on a work of Fielding's, and had "all the coarseness, little of the wit, and none of the truth of the original."

Beddoes's second poem (as far as it has been possible to ascertain) was **"Alfarabi."** . . . From every standpoint it is a most remarkable production for a boy of sixteen. Mr. Gosse says that this "rhapsody displays a very singular adroitness in the manufacture of easy blank verse, and precocious tendency to a species of mocking metaphysics." A few lines are of real beauty, and the poem as a whole shows an unusual appreciation of Nature and a rare discrimination in word shades. . . . (p. 312)

There is much doggerel in the poem, but as a whole it gives high promise of things to come. Curiously enough, it contains nearly all the traits of his later writings, wonderful imaginative faculty, delicate fancy, and a love of the ghastly picturesque. . . .

The most interesting fact in connection with this poem is the unmistakable influence of Milton, both in the choice of polysyllabic words and in the free use of the caesura; a few lines . . . have the full echo of the majestic swing and cadence of Milton's blank verse. (p. 313)

While the verse [in **"The Improvisatore"**] is not without defect, it shows metrical skill and sense of melody. The tone of the whole poem is morbid. . . .

Beddoes depicts Nature in her serener aspects with as much sane ease as he describes her in sterner moods; and with equal facility he describes dainty details of feminine beauty and flow-

ers, or the horrible features of a charnel-house and great battlefield. . . .

While Beddoes's scientific studies probably increased his tendency to dwell on gruesome subjects, and his natural tendency to gloom was aggravated by long association with Death, yet **"The Improvisatore,"** written before he began scientific investigation, proves beyond a doubt that these qualities were innate. (p. 314)

In marked contrast to such horrible pictures, the pastoral love scenes in **"Albert and Emily,"** and the lyric songs in **"Rudolph,"** are very refreshing. Beddoes strikes a reflective note in the poem, unusual with him. . . .

The last stanza of **"Leopold,"** where doom is represented as advancing, is quite dramatic. . . . The poem, though crude and immature in many respects, gives great promise of things to come, a promise, unfortunately, never fulfilled. (p. 315)

[**"The Brides' Tragedy"**] is written in easy blank verse. . . . [There are many passages] marked with delicate, ethereal fancy and Elizabethan conceits. . . . (p. 316)

[The murder scene] is very dramatic, as are the majority of the passages dealing with sin and crime. Beddoes strikes the chord of the darker passions with an almost master hand.

The plot of the drama is fit material for high tragedy, and Beddoes has handled it well. It is the only one of his dramas that has a central motive, and the only one possessing organic unity. Had Beddoes fulfilled with increasing years the promise that his play gave, he would have been a great dramatist, but instead he seems to have retrograded. **"Death's Jest Book,"** the work of his maturer years, is a more polished production, but it has far less dramatic power, and no unity.

"The Brides' Tragedy," notwithstanding its vagueness of characterization and general haziness, has many good points. The horror of the tragedy and the superabundance of evil motives is relieved by scenes of tenderness and beauty, adorned with luxuriance of fancy. As the production of a youth of eighteen, one marvels at the excellencies and condones the defects. (p. 318)

The drama [**"The Second Brother"**] shows no advance over **"The Brides' Tragedy,"** is less promising in the evolution of a coherent plot, and has less lyrical beauty than the other dramas.

"Torrismond" belongs to the same period of production as **"The Second Brother,"** and is still less near completion, consisting of only one act, but that act contains a song which is one of the most famous of Beddoes's lyrical productions. . . . Like the Elizabethans, one phrase expands into another, until there are explanatory clauses within explanatory clauses. (pp. 320-21)

[**"Death's Jest Book"**] as a whole presents a motley mixture. . . . [It] seems but the overflow, the excrescence of unassimilated knowledge, and not the natural development of a genius. It is apparent that Beddoes did not improve or develop beyond the **"Brides' Tragedy,"** with the exception of greater perfection of meter and lyric grace. In dramatic power he had declined. Yet the drama is not without interest or merit; the originality, the startling conception, and the beauty of isolated passages make it worth the reading; as a unit, it is a deplorable failure. . . . [But] it is certainly, from any view-point, a most remarkable production, on account of the originality of its subject-matter and the great beauty and power of many passages. . . . [Beddoes produced] a literary structure of loosely strung parts, some of exaggerated power and beauty, and some of diminutive dimension, the whole presenting an inharmonious effect. The beauty of some parts does not atone for the ugliness of others.

It is upon Beddoes's lyrics that his claim to fame rests; it is in these that he displays most gift for melody, harmony, and technical skill. But for the inevitable sinister note that mars the lyrical feeling, these lyrics could be called almost the consummate art of verse-making. (pp. 327-28)

The **"Ballad of Human Life,"** three stanzas representing the three stages of life, boy and girl, lad and lass, man and wife, is very human. There are a number of other lyrics, such as **"The Swallow Leaves Her Nest," "If Thou Wilt Ease Thine Heart," "Love in Idleness," "Song by Siegfried,"** and **"Aho, Aho, Love's Horn Doth Blow,"** especially the first two, that are excellent and deserve to be better known. While it must be acknowledged that there is a monotony about them, showing that as a lyrist Beddoes was of a high order, but not of wide range, yet the most prejudiced critic could not but conclude that the **"Love Song"** from **"Torrismond," "Dream Pedlary,"** and **"The Swallow Leaves Her Nest"** are exquisite, and rank among the best of their kind in the language.

In striking contrast to these poems, there is a second class which Mr. Gosse has classified as the poems of "Grisly Humour" [see excerpt above]. **"Song of the Stygian Naiades," "Lord Alcohol," "Adam, the Carrion Crow," "Song of Isbrand,"** from **"Death's Jest Book," "Harpagus' Ballad,"** and the **"Dance of Death"** are instances which vie with each other in grotesque and repulsive fancy. . . . They are too gruesome for enjoyment, but are rather to be wondered at as objects in a museum, and to be preserved for their variety of species rather than on account of their literary excellence.

"The Boding Dreams" and **"From the German"** show the effect of German mysticism and metaphysics. The **"Romance of the Lily"** and **"The Ghost's Moonshine,"** belong to the same category, and, judging from their tone, were probably written after Beddoes went to Germany. They fairly repel one with their ghastliness and uncanniness of conception.

In addition to his gift as a lyrist, Beddoes shows great facility as a prose writer in his letters. . . . (pp. 330-31)

The letters contain many passages of [Beddoes's] character, bits of gossip, much sarcastic humor, and many sallies of wit; all perfectly free from the melancholy and cynicism of his poetry. It would be difficult to find more racy, living expression of thought, with deep appreciation of all things beautiful in literature and art, than in these letters. (p. 332)

Beddoes had vast power of conception and mastery of rhythm, combined with "a delicate fancy and a strange choiceness of phrase," but he lacked universal sympathy and the power to express the vital emotions. **"The Brides' Tragedy,"** one of his earliest productions, shows more knowledge of human nature than any of his succeeding dramas, which, probably on account of his solitary life, have less and less sympathy with humanity. His writings were of the head and not the heart; he studied literature not life. (p. 333)

> *Barnette Miller, "Thomas Lovell Beddoes," in The Sewanee Review, Vol. XI, No. 3, July, 1903, pp. 306-36.*

LYTTON STRACHEY   (essay date 1907)

For some reason or another, this extraordinary poet [Thomas Lovell Beddoes] has not only never received the recognition which is his due, but has failed almost entirely to receive any recognition whatever. If his name is known at all, it is known in virtue of the one or two of his lyrics which have crept into some of the current anthologies. But Beddoes' highest claim to distinction does not rest upon his lyrical achievements, consummate as those achievements are; it rests upon his extraordinary eminence as a master of dramatic blank verse. Perhaps his greatest misfortune was that he was born at the beginning of the nineteenth century, and not at the end of the sixteenth. His proper place was among that noble band of Elizabethans, whose strong and splendid spirit gave to England, in one miraculous generation, the most glorious heritage of drama that the world has known. . . . As it happened, however, he came as a strange and isolated phenomenon, a star which had wandered from its constellation, and was lost among alien lights. . . . We must take him on his own merits, "unmixed with seconds": we must discover and appraise his peculiar quality for its own sake.

> He hath skill in language;
> And knowledge is in him, root, flower, and fruit,
> A palm with winged imagination in it,
> Whose roots stretch even underneath the grave;
> And on them hangs a lamp of magic science
> In his soul's deepest mine, where folded thoughts
> Lie sleeping on the tombs of magi dead.
>
> (pp. 274-75)

[*The Brides' Tragedy*] was written on the Elizabethan model, and, as a play, it is disfigured by Beddoes' most characteristic faults: the construction is weak, the interest fluctuates from character to character, and the motives and actions of the characters themselves are for the most part curiously remote from the realities of life. Yet, though the merit of the tragedy depends almost entirely upon the verse, there are signs in it that, while Beddoes lacked the gift of construction, he nevertheless possessed one important dramatic faculty—the power of creating detached scenes of interest and beauty. The scene in which the half-crazed Leonora imagines to herself, beside the couch on which her dead daughter lies, that the child is really living after all, is dramatic in the highest sense of the word; the situation, with all its capabilities of pathetic irony, is conceived and developed with consummate art and absolute restraint. (pp. 280-81)

[The] impress of a fresh and vital intelligence is stamped unmistakably upon all that is best in [Beddoes'] work. His mature blank verse is perfect. It is not an artificial concoction galvanized into the semblance of life; it simply lives. And, with Beddoes, maturity was precocious, for he obtained complete mastery over the most difficult and dangerous of metres at a wonderfully early age. . . . Beddoes had mastered [blank verse] at an age when most poets are still mouthing ineffectual wheats and barleys. . . . [His] thoughts filled and moved and animated his blank verse as easily and familiarly as a hand in a glove. . . . The effect is, of course, partly produced by the diction; but the diction, fine as it is, would be useless without the phrasing—that art by which the two forces of the metre and the sense are made at once to combat, to combine with, and to heighten each other. . . . [It] may be noticed that in his mastery of phrasing—as in so much besides—he was a true Elizabethan. (pp. 288-89)

Beddoes' power of creating scenes of intense dramatic force, which had already begun to show itself in *The Brides' Tragedy,* reached its full development in his subsequent work. The opening act of *The Second Brother*—the most nearly complete of his unfinished tragedies—is a striking example of a powerful and original theme treated in such a way that, while the whole of it is steeped in imaginative poetry, yet not one ounce of its dramatic effectiveness is lost. . . . [The] acts are crowded with beautiful passages, with vivid situations, with surprising developments, but the central plot vanishes away into nothing, like a great river dissipating itself among a thousand streams. It is, indeed, clear enough that Beddoes was embarrassed with his riches, that his fertile mind conceived too easily, and that he could never resist the temptation of giving life to his imaginations, even at the cost of killing his play. (pp. 289, 291-92)

[Perhaps] the ordinary reader finds Beddoes' lack of construction a less distasteful quality than his disregard of the common realities of existence. Not only is the subject-matter of the greater part of his poetry remote and dubious; his very characters themselves seem to be infected by their creator's delight in the mysterious, the strange, and the unreal. They have no healthy activity; or, if they have, they invariably lose it in the second act; in the end, they are all hypochondriac philosophers, puzzling over eternity and dissecting the attributes of Death. The central idea of *Death's Jest Book*—the resurrection of a ghost—fails to be truly effective, because it is difficult to see any clear distinction between the phantom and the rest of the characters. (p. 293)

If a poet must be a critic of life, Beddoes was certainly no poet. He belongs to the class of writers of which, in English literature, Spenser, Keats, and Milton are the dominant figures—the writers who are great merely because of their art. . . . [It] is in his expression that his greatness lies. His verse is an instrument of many modulations, of exquisite delicacy, of strange suggestiveness, of amazing power. Playing on it, he can give utterance to the subtlest visions. . . . Or he can evoke sensations of pure loveliness. . . . Or he can put into a single line all the long memories of adoration. . . . Or he can pass in a moment from tiny sweetness to colossal turmoil. . . . He can express alike the beautiful tenderness of love, and the hectic, dizzy, and appalling frenzy of extreme rage. . . . But, to find Beddoes in his most characteristic mood, one must watch him weaving his mysterious imagination upon the woof of mortality. One must wander with him through the pages of *Death's Jest Book,* one must grow accustomed to the dissolution of reality, and the opening of the nettled lips of graves; one must learn that "the dead are most and merriest," one must ask—"Are the ghosts eaves-dropping?"—one must realise that "murder is full of holes." (pp. 294-97)

In private intercourse Beddoes was the least morbid of human beings. His mind was like one of those Gothic cathedrals of which he was so fond—mysterious within, and filled with a light at once richer and less real than the light of day; on the outside, firm, and towering, and immediately impressive; and embellished, both inside and out, with grinning gargoyles. His conversation . . . was full of humour and vitality, and untouched by any trace of egoism or affectation. He loved discussion, plunging into it with fire, and carrying it onward with high dexterity and good-humoured force. His letters are excellent: simple, spirited, spicy, and as original as his verse; flavoured with that vein of rattling open-air humour which had produced his school-boy novel in the style of Fielding. He was

a man whom it would have been a rare delight to know. His character, so eminently English, compact of courage, of originality, of imagination, and with something coarse in it as well, puts one in mind of Hamlet: not the melodramatic sentimentalist of the stage; but the real Hamlet, Horatio's Hamlet, who called his father's ghost old truepenny, who forged his uncle's signature, who fought Laertes, and ranted in a grave, and lugged the guts into the neighbour room. His tragedy, like Hamlet's, was the tragedy of an over-powerful will—a will so strong as to recoil upon itself, and fall into indecision. It is easy for a weak man to be decided—there is so much to make him so; but a strong man, who can do anything, sometimes leaves everything undone. Fortunately Beddoes, though he did far less than he might have done, possessed so rich a genius that what he did, though small in quantity, is in quality beyond price. "I might have been, among other things, a good poet," were his last words. "Among other things"! Aye, there's the rub. But, in spite of his own "might have been," a good poet he was. Perhaps for him, after all, there was very little to regret; his life was full of high nobility; and what other way of death would have befitted the poet of death? There is a thought constantly recurring throughout his writings—in his childish as in his most mature work—the thought of the beauty and the supernal happiness of soft and quiet death. He had visions of "rosily dying," of "turning to daisies gently in the grave," of a "pink reclining death," of death coming like a summer cloud over the soul. "Let her deathly life pass into death," says one of his earliest characters, "like music on the night wind." And, in *Death's Jest Book,* Sibylla has the same thoughts. . . . Did his mind, obsessed and overwhelmed by images of death, crave at last for the one thing stranger than all these—the experience of it? It is easy to believe so, and that, ill, wretched, and abandoned by [his friends] . . . , he should seek relief in the gradual dissolution which attends upon loss of blood. And then, when he had recovered, when he was almost happy once again, the old thoughts, perhaps, came crowding back upon him—thoughts of the futility of life, and the supremacy of death and the mystical whirlpool of the unknown, and the long quietude of the grave. In the end, Death had grown to be something more than Death to him—it was, mysteriously and transcendentally, Love as well. (pp. 297-99)

Lytton Strachey, "The Last Elizabethan" (1907), in his Literary Essays *(reprinted by permission of The Society of Authors, as agents for the Strachey Estate), Harcourt Brace and Company, 1949 (and reprinted in* A Century of the Essay: British and American, *edited by David Daiches, Harcourt Brace and Company, 1951, pp. 274-300).*

ROYALL H. SNOW (essay date 1928)

Two initial contrasts face one in any effort to form a general judgment of *The Brides' Tragedy.* It was youthful charm which won the first reviewers, and still is one of the play's great virtues. . . . [But readers] of today who are won by the play's ingenuousness to read it through, will carry away echoing in their minds as great scenes only those which belong to [a] "dark and troubled" gloom. And the second contrast is between a very clear and powerful dramatic sense, and a complete flouting of the necessities of the theatre. *The Brides' Tragedy* and *Death's Jest-Book* both flare off at so many tangents, multiply needless scenes, and drop dramatic dialogue for poetry in dramatic form to an extent which makes them impossible for the stage. And yet the effectiveness of parts of these plays is unquestionable. Beddoes had a sense of the theatrical. . . .

[But the theatrical scenes are] dependent upon pure situation. Beddoes had also a sense of the true dramatic—which is a fusion of situation with character, as striking as the merely theatrical and far more deeply moving.

So there are the initial difficulties: a play whose first appeal is youthful charm and whose best scenes are gloomy; a play unfit for the stage, with a higher percentage of effective stage scenes than many which have succeeded on the boards—just what is the summing up phrase to be? It is not to be, I fancy; the paradoxes are merely to be pointed out.

The Brides' Tragedy possesses a gracefulness none other of Beddoes' work has. . . . It is a matter of tone entirely, a suffused lyricism and gentle sentimentality clothing in soft silk the harshness of the action. (pp. 45-6)

Beddoes is not an imitator in the sense that he takes a model and follows a pattern. He has simply exercised the right of every artist to absorb what is congenial to him in the work of his predecessors—without in any way ceasing to be himself. And the Beddoes of this time was in his "leafy" period, a short bright spring whose autumn was to be bitter of fruit. There was always in him a fundamental bitterness. (pp. 46-7)

The Brides' Tragedy has the distinction of being the only play [Beddoes] ever brought to real completeness. His early life is strewn with unfinished fragments, and the twenty odd years he spent abroad were not enough in which really to complete *Death's Jest-Book*—this last is compressed, rather than rounded, into a semblance of form. But in *The Brides' Tragedy* Beddoes clearly had control of his conclusion while he was at work upon his opening and middle scenes. He indulges in tangents and poetizing but he has kept his scheme of development in hand. Some of the best of his scenes precede the murder, and the interest slackens somewhat after the interruption of the bridal feast in the fourth act, yet he is far from weak in his last act. And this ability to contol his subject to the end Beddoes had shown even at school in the writing of *The Improvisatore*. Oddly enough, after *The Brides' Tragedy* he never exhibited the power again. (pp. 48-9)

The dramatic fragments, most of which belong to the two or three years following the publication of *The Brides' Tragedy*, are difficult to treat in any orderly fashion because of their variety and incompleteness. (p. 51)

The briefer and isolated bits are by no means despicable in themselves as poetry. With neither a past nor a future, they often enough have power to conquer a momentary completeness, to be poems dreadful or delightful in themselves, and out of all context. They are glittering bits: a description, a flash of metaphor, an angry comment of life and human impotency. Sometimes they are a preliminary (or variant) sketch of a passage in the completed plays; again, they are a portion which has been dropped in some revision. But the fact they have been dropped is no test of their merit—had there been place for them in the final form of the text, several of them might well have been favoured quotations from *Death's Jest-Book*.

The variety included in these fragments is considerable and gives a clue to the range possible to Beddoes' verse. . . . Directness and simplicity could not well go farther in blank verse and yet the picture is vivid and telling. (pp. 52-3)

The one act of [*Torrismond*] contains some excellent things, among others perhaps the daintiest lyric Beddoes ever wrote, but it left Beddoes with his psychological study still on his hands. He tried again with *The Second Brother,* and the change

of approach to his thesis shows a very acute sense of why the first effort had failed, and what had to be done to succeed. Depth was needed, and he got it simply enough by maturing his hero. . . . The plot, as always with Beddoes, is complicated. . . . [Contrast] is emphasized to heighten dramatic effect. . . . (p. 56)

Sharp and powerful the contrasts are, and, at some points, effective. Unfortunately, however, Beddoes the dramatist could resist everything except temptation. . . . Beddoes tried to interweave . . . two stories, but the themes were each too powerful to fuse, and the play ends abruptly with the unfinished first scene of Act IV,—the melancholy ruin of a play with promise to it. (pp. 57-8)

It is in *Death's Jest-Book* that Beddoes' spectacular and morbid genius comes to its final flowering; and it is upon this play, together with a handful of scattered lyrics, that his fame must rest. . . . *Fool's Tragedy* is something that comes from the fringes, at least, of delirium and despair. (p. 99)

[Through all of *Death's Jest-Book*] there is an incandescence of fierce language, and the daring metaphors blaze with the sparkle of black stars before the bright glow of hell. In the orderly sequence of the history of literature the play has no place; it belongs to no school and no period. Written in the nineteenth century its language has, by right divine and not artifice, the fine unexpectedness of the days of Elizabeth. Possessed of the verve of such robust and healthy times, it is saturated with the grotesque and pessimistic diabolism of the Germany of E. T. A. Hoffman. From its debris the disciples of Freud might quarry unmentionable images. And, combining such elements, it was written by an Englishman who died in the reign of Victoria. It is unique.

But also, as a play, it has certain clearly marked limitations. Its brilliance is akin to that of a diamond crushed under a piledriver—scattered, chaotic, begrimed, but still there and sparkling. Yet, despite all the diamond dust that is in it, the play suffers from an excess of plain plaster. It is patched and built, and the final edifice is a rickety one. Tediums encroach upon intensities, a growth of rhetoric chokes the poetic, the plot often eddies rather than flows; beside men firm of intent are others merely gesticulatory, and women who do nothing but simper. So that in the last analysis, Beddoes, who in individual scenes may take rank with Webster as a master of sombre intensities, has written a play which is chaotic and ineffectual. (pp. 100-01)

[The action] is erratic and confused, and in the end such greatness as the play may have rests mainly upon two scenes and its wild fool. There have been plays enough of revenge and horror. Beddoes, however, brings into this alien atmosphere a tart cynicism and a dash of metaphysics, so that the conventional murder play keeps slanting off in unexpected directions. The result is vivid. (p. 101)

The power of the abnormal is [in the play], and not an abnormal which is lurking and sly, but one which is robust and powerful, which occupies the foreground rather than lurks in the shadows of his mind. But there is also the sting of an astringent and cynical mind behind it. The familiar paraphernalia of death Beddoes uses, but in a fashion peculiar to himself. The trappings and terror of death, ruined churches, sepulchres, and ghosts have been often enough employed for the sake of the emotional pressure they put upon the living. It is only in Beddoes that the dead become the living, only in Beddoes that a scene of sombre association is used, not to depress, but to bring out the reckless and distorted gaiety of a principal character. (pp. 103-04)

Death's Jest-Book is a mad play because behind it there is [Beddoes'] despairing intellect. What is of consequence, of course, is the tone. That a dramatic character speaks for his creator, and that the young Shakespeare woos Ann Hathaway with Romeo, is an illusion so silly it scarcely deserves comment. But it is equally true that no writer can escape his own mind—he is guiltless of words and actions, but the mood, the prevailing impression left by a work of art, is the colour it takes from its creator and reflects him. (p. 113)

> *Royall H. Snow, in his* Thomas Lovell Beddoes: Eccentric & Poet *(copyright 1928 by Covici, Friede Inc.; used by permission of Crown Publishers, Inc.), Covici, Friede, 1928, 227 p.*

JOHN HEATH-STUBBS (essay date 1950)

Compared with that of [his] Romantic predecessors there is a morbidity, a love of the strange and grotesque, above all a harshness in [Beddoes'] imagery and conceptions, which is repellent to normal minds. (p. 23)

It is unfortunate that Beddoes is one of those writers to whom a label has become attached. He has been called "the Last Elizabethan" [see excerpt above]. The phrase has stuck, and has influenced most modern criticism of this poet. The mistake could only by made by a reader who studied the later Elizabethan dramatists superficially, with an eye to their more sensational imagery, rather than to the view of life which lay behind it. There is little that is really Elizabethan in Beddoes, except the outward trappings of his dramas. It is true that he handles dramatic blank verse with a technical mastery, and possesses, perhaps, something of that "unified sensibility" which Mr. Eliot has detected in the Elizabethans, to a degree rarely found in poets who wrote since the seventeenth century. But his blank verse is written with a self-conscious artistry foreign to the early dramatists, and the quality of his poetic thought is entirely different from theirs. Both Beddoes and the later Elizabethan (or, more properly, Jacobean) dramatists are obsessed by the idea of Death; but it is precisely here that their attitude and his differ most fundamentally. (p. 37)

Beddoes passes beyond the "easeful death", which could be called "soft names in many a mused rhyme" of Keats—that ceasing "upon the midnight with no pain", the Death which is "life's high mead"—to a fuller realization of that state of merging, in dissolution, with the beauty of the natural universe which Shelley envisaged in *Adonais*. He enters a region of thought and feeling not often explored in English poetry; though it is one with which the German poets, from Novalis to Rilke, have been familiar.

In one form or other, the death-wish pervades the poetry of Beddoes; now a shadow, moving grotesquely, as a skeleton, or in the misformed and dwarfish shapes of his clowns; now striding forth in images of strange and terrible power. Sometimes Death is seen as a state of mystical and transcendental union with the Universe; now it woos the poet's soul, gently, like a lover. . . . (p. 39)

[Beddoes'] imagery is at once more intensely sensuous and more intellectual than Poe's. It arises from a far deeper conflict within the soul. He is the most Germanized of English poets, and voices that longing for extinction itself, at once passionate and abstract, which seems, in Germany, a country which has

been first divided physically within itself, and then more tragically given over to the despotic leadership of men themselves neurotic, to have penetrated deeply into the communal consciousness. (p. 40)

[*The Last Man,* and *Cupid's Arrow Poisoned*], though consisting only of disconnected fragments, nevertheless comprising some of his finest work. His range is, of course, narrow, and he has no contact with the emotions of common experience as they are normally understood. In his pursuit of grotesque and novel effects he is not secure from self-conscious sensationalism. But at his best, these faults are outweighed by the vividness and intellectual suggestiveness of his images. . . . (pp. 40-1)

Moreover, though his dramas are all but unreadable as wholes, his technical mastery of blank verse is remarkable, and he could also write lyrics matchless in design and melody. . . . (p. 41)

A very strange man; yet there is a queer consistency about his life, as about his work, for which a psychological explanation should not be impossible. Beddoes's letters combine faculty of acute comment on the life and literature of his time, a fantastic, self-tormenting humour, and a curious reserve. He is more sparing of expressions of affection for his friends than almost any other writer of the time. In his personal manner he is said to have been cynical and positively misanthropic; he describes himself as a "non-conductor of friendship . . . a not-very-likeable person". Yet this character, the life-long duration of the few friendships he did make, the loyalty of Kelsall, his literary executor, the passages of an almost feminine tenderness which sometimes shine out amid the dark and cruel texture of his plays, belie. It seems to me a likely supposition that Beddoes was, in fact, always acutely aware of a homosexual temperament and proclivities. He was, at the same time, possessed of a powerful capacity for intellectual self-analysis and a strong emotional reserve. This would have checked and distorted his acute physical sensibilities, and deflected his passions, denied a normal outlet, towards the contemplation of death for its own sake.

To such a man the human body, image of his own physical limitations, would be an object at once fascinating and horrible; the means whereby, through the senses, he became cognizant of the universe, and a persistent clog and prison to the aspiring intellect. Such a hypothesis explains the continual juxtaposition of images of beauty with those of physical horror in Beddoes's poetry, and the remarkable manner in which his sensuous and intellectual perceptions are unified. (pp. 44-5)

In the work of Beddoes, as in that of many other homosexual writers, we detect an element of extreme subjectivism—an inability to describe normal situations and emotions as well as a quality of "unnaturalness" about the imagery. These are the result of an imperfectly integrated personality and of the lack of a fully adult sense of the reality of the external world. Yet Beddoes's work is cast almost entirely in dramatic mould, and the drama is of all forms of art the most objective, and that requiring the firmest grip upon external realities. (pp. 46-7)

Beddoes's plays, as plays, are failures. They are not easy reading, on the whole, even as closed dramas, and no one would dream of attempting to put them on the stage. They contain, I dare say, not one single character or situation to which the normal spectator could give his credence. . . . Beddoes merely succeeds in reviving the trappings of the later Elizabethan drama, wherewith to clothe the projections of his own inner and distorted vision. (p. 47)

John Heath-Stubbs, "The Defeat of Romanticism," in his The Darkling Plain: A Study of the Later Fortunes of Romanticism in English Poetry from George Darley to W. B. Yeats *(reprinted by permission of David Higham Associates Limited, as agents for the author), Eyre & Spottiswoode, 1950, pp. 21-61.*

H. W. DONNER (essay date 1950)

Beddoes is above all others the poet of death. Nobody has arrayed her . . . in such alluring beauty, nobody has clad physical corruption in such unspeakable horror, nobody spoken with such nostalgic longing of the death he was himself to seek so persistently. Out of their security the Victorians regarded his preoccupation as morbid, but we are gradually learning, in the school of devastating world wars, that

> Life's a single pilgrim,
> Fighting unarmed amongst a thousand soldiers.

And the throbbing presence of facts spiritual in his verse forbids any facile condemnation. . . . There is an almost threatening note in his latest fragments, as if he meant to say: Beware, the spirit will yet get the better of you. His self-inflicted death, whatever momentary misery may have been the direct cause, was the triumphant close of a career devoted to the discovery of proofs physical and spiritual of man's survival in another sphere. (p. xii)

[*The Improvisatore, In Three Fyttes, with Other Poems* is] as full of death and horror as ever *Scaroni,* but also of a beauty of imagery and loveliness of fancy, a poetical richness, that in a poet not yet eighteen necessarily foreshadowed better things to come. His feeling for nature is conspicuous, and many passages of great beauty evince his familiarity with the evening sky. His descriptive power was better developed than the narrative, and the lyrical poems at the end of the volume are full of happy conceits, woven into arabesque patterns. (p. xix)

[In Beddoes's early work there is that rare richness] of poetic imagery, flowing with the abundance of a soul steeped in poetry, such as Shakespeare had, and Spenser, Marlowe, Shelley. There is imaginative power of the first order, a power to give life to objects dead to ordinary people, a visualization of the abstract, a spiritualization of the concrete, entirely out of the common reach even of poets. He can see 'a pale soul Fluttering in rocky hell' with such vividness that the image goes to illustrate the less immaterial but perhaps more exotic sight of a trochilus picking the teeth of a crocodile. He can compress the universe in a living image, seeing new-born stars bouncing like 'light deer Down a hill'. . . . On the other hand, he can give immensity to the aspirations of man, and describe the feelings of frustration. . . . There is already that quality in his verse of a fluttering bird beating its wings against the mirror of eternity. (pp. xxvi-xxvii)

Nowhere is his power more obvious than in . . . fragments [from *The Last Man* and *Love's Arrow Poisoned*], nowhere the imagery bolder or loftier. But what he lacked in dramatic composition was the faculty of sustained creation, the ability to concentrate on essentials in unfolding the story, of making characters credible in a natural situation, and of making them speak like human beings. They are all too Beddoesian, skating as it were on the thinnest of ice, 'that glassy interval 'twixt us and nothing', to use his own phrase. . . . And the plots are crowded with incident until the outlines become confused, each detail being worked out with all the intensity and passion at the command of this singularly gifted poet, but the whole

broken irreparably to bits by the very strength of the single scenes. To that intensity of feeling we owe one of his finest achievements, *Torrismond,* . . . in which all the poet's pent-up passion had to vent itself in the first act, and he was unable to continue. We may say it was a mercy that the fragment was brought to a close before the whole parade of banquets and masques, conjuring and incest, murder and suicide was unrolled, but such was not Beddoes' intention. In *The Second Brother,* . . . the full riot is let loose. There is plenty of grand rhetoric, poetry of the most exalted brand, a nervous energy almost unique, plenty of what used to be called 'tragic passion', but of human feeling not an inkling. Neither brother has one word of regret, much less of sorrow, for the death of his own brother; the succession to a petty throne is all that matters. But Beddoes himself knew full well the futility of thrones and was striving after something very much more important. Hence one after the other of his elaborately artificial plots was discarded and abandoned. Nothing but the perfect would satisfy him, and in his constant grappling with the stubborn material of his plots, he did achieve perfection in the creation of a dramatic blank verse, unequalled since the days of Shakespeare. Hence he could sacrifice without regret the unsuccessful plots which had served his apprenticeship. That a great mass of irrecoverable poetry was thrown on the fire at the same time he did not give one thought, for he was looking forward to pour his whole soul into a play of a power sufficient to regenerate the British stage, and he felt himself step by step accumulating that power. (pp. xxvii-xxviii)

It is true that in all his early poems there are corpses and charnelhouses, and even more characteristically loving embraces bestowed on the bodies of the dead. Literary fashion encouraged scenes of horror, and they need be taken no more seriously than Beddoes seems to have taken them himself, except perhaps that the particular incident, so often repeated in his youthful work, of a child literally poking death in the eye may have had something to do with his father's dissections of animals for the highly laudable purpose of famalizing his children with natural phenomena and the zoological process of generation. It would seem as if Beddoes had become a little too familiar with such scenes. But there is nothing but enjoyment of them in his early verse, and from a different aspect he had viewed delightedly the dead bodies

> Turning to daisies gently in the grave.

(p. xxxi)

[The belief in a spirit of man all powerful and even more potent than reason, which in the preceeding ages had made man lord of all creation, was] the theme which principally occupied him in the plays and poems [of his later writing career.] We need but scratch the surface of his verse to find beneath it the palpitations of his heart, the longings of his spirit to transcend merely physical limitations, the utter loneliness and the yearnings of humanity for love and friendship

> In this December world, with men of ice,
> Cold sirs and madams.

We can see the raw flesh bleeding in a way we could not, if the poet had succeeded in endowing his dramatic characters with an existence of their own, independent and objective. But he was too self-involved to make them speak any other language than his own, and so every line becomes, however imaginary the situation, a revelation of his own striving self.

The discarding of so many partly worked-out plots and unfinished plays is in itself a sign of his development. Most of the early stories he invented are sufficiently alike to justify one in regarding them as little more than variations on a single theme. We see it outlined in the draft for *Love's Arrow Poisoned*, the complications and double-crossings, misunderstandings and retributions, a complexity of weft beyond the power of any but the most consummate stage-hand to unravel and under any circumstances too involved for any audience to grasp, culminating, in true Elizabethan fashion, in a scene of weird melodrama, the return of the departed, mummery and carnage. . . . [Beddoes ends] with a grand masque in which the hero must act the part of his own murdered self, until the moment of retribution arrives and he can plant his dagger in the usurper's breast. But Beddoes' is no mere historical review. . . . In Romantic fashion it is preceded by an incantation, the purpose of which is to make the spectre discover where his treasures are hidden. In Romantic fashion, again, the conjuring is a fake, and instead of a ghost the real man appears, for while believed to have fallen to his death, he has actually been miraculously saved halfway down the precipice. . . . The scene was sufficiently melodramatic not to be easily forgone by its youthful contriver, and so it appears again and again in various modifications. This, I feel convinced, is how *Torrismond* was planned to end; this was to be the end of *The Second Brother* also. . . . [While] Beddoes was grappling with the technical problem of plot-construction, his mind was at the same time occupied with a totally different problem of a spirtual nature, the relationship of mind and matter, a question which, as fas as I can understand, he had already tackled in *The Last Man,* although he had found his powers so far insufficient to provide a solution. The temptation must have been strong to unite the theme of his imagination with the plot of his fancy, and in *The Second Brother* we can see him at work. (pp. xxxii-xxxiv)

The death of *The Second Brother* was the birth of *Death's Jest-Book,* for Beddoes had come to realize that a mere stage-trick, employed for the temporary advancement and final overthrow of a diabolical design, could furnish no adequate illustration of his most cherished notions; and as soon as this became clear to him he abandoned his play in the middle of the fourth act. There was to be conjuring in *Death's Jest-Book* also, but no faked resurrection this time. It was to be a raising into real life of one truly dead, and the play was to prove beyond any shadow of a doubt the immortality of the soul and the power of the mind over matter. (p. xxxv)

Death's Jest-Book was not what [the critics] had a right to expect from the literary progeny whose début more than six years before had been proclaimed superior to that of Chatterton and Keats. . . . The faults of Beddoes' performance were glaring enough. The plot was as complicated and confused as ever. The dialogue as impossible. All the characters seem to declaim into the void, and none answer the others. There is no individualization, and this was the reason why Beddoes had been able seemingly without effort to incorporate parts of older plays. It was all his own drama, his own wrestling with the problems of the spirit, problems unsolved. For Beddoes himself had not noticed that his idea remained at cross-purposes with the action of the play, his elaborate Elizabethan plot at war with the central theme. He had failed to find, in Mr. Eliot's phrase, 'the objective correlative' of his thought. Nor can the 'Romantic irony' borrowed from the Germans have recommended itself to his English critics. It provided no solution, but on the contrary went to spoil one of his finest creations. . . . It is undeniable that Beddoes' sense of fun, too, fed on queer food sometimes and is not even yet always recognized by critics except under the name of the grotesque, for from his earliest

infancy his mind had so familiarized itself with skulls and crossbones that he derived infinite amusement from tossing them about like custard pies in a slap-stick comedy. His daring naturalism of language, entirely modern in its unavoidance of the homely and vigorous, was in complete contrast with his age. And to the faults apparent to his contemporaries we might add yet another. Although set in a defined historical milieu the whole spirit of the play is a product of its period and so essentially anachronistic. . . . The same applies to the details. But the play had merits also surpassing anything produced by his contemporaries.

The very plot has a primitive directness commonly avoided in Romantic drama. Whereas contemporary practice ruled that murder could only be committed in a fit of sudden lunacy, a dislocation in the brain—and Beddoes had fallen into this error himself in his more youthful compositions—in *Death's Jest-Book* there is no shirking of the issue. But the plot and all its action is of course only a pretext for the poetry, yet a necessary pretext. In the dialogue arising out of the artificially contrived situations Beddoes could express that drama of the spirit to which the plot had failed to accommodate itself. In the songs sung by the dramatic characters their inmost essence is expressed. In others an epitome of the action and situation is given. In the blank verse of his play he had found the true objective correlative of his thought, and the poetical dialogue embodies the struggles of his mind, oscillating between life and death, time and eternity. It is Beddoes' very self. (pp. xl-xli)

If the 'loved longlost boy' of the *Dream Pedlary* is to be identified with him, it seems that he must have died. Beddoes certainly henceforth did 'consecrate [his] being'

> To that divinest hope, which none can know of
> Who have not laid their dearest in the grave.

This is only one instance of the new tragic strain which [in Würzburg] forced its entrance into Beddoes' poetry and was to recur again and again until he himself was at last ready to enter the 'loved one's home'. Some of his most beautiful poetry was written at Würzburg. The quantity is minute, but the quality beyond prize. (pp. xlv-xlvi)

In the congenial surroundings of Zürich and Switzerland and in 'the pleasant translunary moods' into which he rowed and walked himself, there blossomed once more the flowers of poetry. By 1837 he had accumulated enough material to contemplate the publication of a volume of prose and poetry, *The Ivory Gate,* including of course the inevitable *Death's Jest-Book*. Nothing came of the publication. The prose tales, alas! have perished. The lyrics are among his finest and, almost without exception, among the pearls of English poetry, some gay, some burlesque, some not a little vulgar, others beautifully melancholy, and some sad and sorrowful beyond description. A great many went into *Death's Jest-Book* which Beddoes now started revising in earnest. (p. lviii)

A good and true poet [Beddoes] had been, but he had long since passed beyond mere worldly ambitions. There was poetry in his soul still, but he sought what he conceived as the source of all poetry.

The irony that is ever on the watch in our lives would so have it that even at his death he was still remembered as the author of *The Brides' Tragedy*, a work of unique promise, some would say only partly fulfilled. . . . But as in life he fulfilled his destiny, so in his poetry also he gave permanent expression to the longing in his heart for a love greater than worldly love and a truth deeper than the transitory truth of mortal life. (pp. lxviii-lxix)

H. W. Donner, in his introduction to Plays and Poems of Thomas Lovell Beddoes *by Thomas Lovell Beddoes, edited by H. W. Donner, Routledge and Kegan Paul Ltd, 1950, pp. xi-lxix.*

LOUIS O. COXE (essay date 1953)

The poetry of Thomas Lovell Beddoes should find in our time a place denied it in its own if only because we are today interested in deviation for its own sake. . . . [His] is a poetry of a sort that seems to me to offer a way out for the modern writer while it exists in its own world as a strange, viable creation.

Beddoes wished to be a dramatist. His major work, ***Death's Jest-Book,*** shows at once the limitations, potentialities and achieved merits of his dramatic verse. Its texture derives from morality and symbol, from poetic language, and these are the vehicles of the drama as exciting theater. A packed, metaphorical idiom, bristling with allusion and learning, a boisterous humor that moves deliberately into the grotesque, a sense of terror before the omnipresence of death: such is the element of the extraordinary play in the composition of which Beddoes spent the most productive years of his life. (p. 252)

Death's Jest-Book may at times become pastiche on the one hand and chaos on the other. Brought up on a diet of the Elizabethan and Jacobean playwrights, Beddoes, like all his contemporaries who tried "dramaturgy", never got free of the influence. Yet in this instance it is a happy fault, for no other of the romantic playwrights caught the idiom they echoed as fully as he did, and none had the sense of drama in the very feel of the verse to anything like the extent notable in the best parts of ***Death's Jest-Book.***

The play's plot is, "God save us, a thing of naught", or rather, of a great deal too much, most of it confused. (pp. 252-53)

To call such a congeries of implausibilities absurd is only proper; the action is eccentric; one cannot find a tragic hero or a single conflict. Beddoes alters his scheme and his intent more than once; the sub-plotting is at best irrelevant and at worst confusing as well as dull. The dramatic and poetic excitement resides in the by-play, and that for the most part concerns Isbrand, the demonic fool of Death, in whose actions and speeches we can find the essence of Beddoes' poetic gift and an adumbration at least of a form of tragedy.

Here excess is the key. Excess, calculated or at times merely chaotic, crowds into action, structure and metaphor. It is in this respect above all that Beddoes is a poet worthy of our attention, for he did not fear a risk, in particular that most dangerous of all risks: being caught out in a generalization or a cliché. . . . [His] best dramatic verse is exciting, in language, metaphor and movement. He had grasped what too few dramatists today believe, that the vehicle of a play is not character but language, a particular language that is theatrical in that it conveys the immediate action while it points ahead to impending tragedy. (p. 253)

We must not look to ***Death's Jest-Book*** for originality of motive or plot; if there is a particular view of the action it would appear to be a double one. We are to see the events as deviations from a norm of moral behaviour and consequently to condemn them, but we are not to empathize automatically. One part of the mind must be reserved to participate in the poetic and dramatic processes, to judge of what allows one to be moved, and simultaneously to say: "That was a fine touch."

What is new about this? It is so old that revival of the attitude in the theater today would create an effect of extreme novelty that no experiment with gadgetry could rival. Beddoes found in the Jacobean drama certain habits of mind that corresponded to his own. . . . (pp. 254-55)

Beddoes is no playable dramatist. . . . Beddoes had no stage craft, knew nothing at all about the theatre, his head full of Schiller and Goethe's *Goetz von Berlichingen,* of ideas about the stage that would make a modern producer shudder. And with reason. However promising the work of the inexperienced playwright may prove, it is only that. Beddoes had no chance to use a stage or to see his work performed; how could he have learned? Yet despite this, he had an attribute that is equally indispensable: he knew that language can be dramatic of itself and was able to make it so. No small measure of his success with dramatic language comes from his preoccupation with extremes, of subject and of expression. At times this becomes almost surrealist . . . , the driving to an extreme of fancy a conceit or an insight. . . . (pp. 255-56)

[It] is the tone of mockery and excess that makes the poem wholly remarkable—unique in English verse. Poetry as play, serious and grim play but play none the less. One dares not label as nonsense a poem that explores with humor and learning the notion of man's free will, however idiosyncratically expressed. (p. 259)

Much of ***Death's Jest-Book*** is fragmentary and suggestive. Occasionally there are prolepses of other poets. . . . [Sometimes] a packed parenthesis will suddenly lift the tone of a passage or take the reader, by powerful suggestion, into another dimension. . . . When he is going about his business properly, Beddoes is an economical writer in that he depends on verbs and strong verbal forms to do the heavy work. . . . At other moments he will give us poetic passages that are gently descriptive. . . . Beddoes has left out ***Death's Jest-Book*** much that modern readers want to find if they are to feel at home, for the play frankly explores other realities, taking risks of a sort we either do not approve or can not see.

Still, the failure (and it is a failure) of ***Death's Jest-Book*** derives not from the incomplete application of a technique, nor from a lack of talent, but from a spiritual malaise which, if nothing else, we share with Beddoes. . . . The weaknesses and the pathos of [the] "heroes" are known, but many writers would prefer to be committed to the sins rather than to the literature, to the personality rather than the talent, for these are public and they pay off in fame, success. Pastiche, rather than eclecticism, determines such lives and works; we are closer to romantic *mal du siècle* than we like to think. . . . We somehow want genius to be less upsetting, tidier: the American writer is so accustomed to keeping his tongue in his cheek that he has trouble talking, and he who risks a direct high tone finds the shortest shrift. Yet it may be that we are ready for another kind of writing, another way of observing. . . . Whether we accept the way of parody or not, we ought to like Beddoes; he was a man for our time a century too soon, and his work defines certain excesses we may commit, certain risks we can take, if we would wrench out of the bog. (pp. 264-65)

Louis O. Coxe, "Beddoes: The Mask of Parody" (reprinted by permission of the author), in The Hudson Review, *Vol. VI, No. 2, Summer, 1953, pp. 252-65.*

HAROLD BLOOM (essay date 1971)

Beddoes should have been a great poet, but failed for want of a subject. As a poet of death he is equal to the Shelley he imitated, the poet of *The Cenci* and *The Sensitive Plant*. Only death met the desire of his imagination, but a poet cannot demonstrate his creative exuberance in a celebration of death alone. Beddoes' "death" is as lively as it can be, and yet does not afford him much opportunity to redress the poverty of life. . . .

[Beddoes] left in manuscript his enormous and unfinished major work, *Death's Jest-Book,* a poem of Romantic apocalypticism barely disguised by its form of Jacobean revenge-drama. Scattered through the blank-verse scenes of this endless play are dozens of songs, many of them very beautiful. Beddoes' imagination is a grotesque version of his master Shelley's, and lacks Shelley's range and sanity, though it possesses an intensity hardly short of Shelley's own. The plot of *Death's Jest-Book* is not worth paraphrase, but the obsessive themes of the drama and Beddoes' other works are interesting for their own power and as evidences of the dying phase of the movement of imagination that Blake and Wordsworth had so greatly begun. (p. 439)

The emptiness of [*Death's Jest-Book*] is redeemed only in the self-parody of its songs, the best of which are triumphs of Romantic irony. . . . The finest of these lyrics, the *Song of the Stygian Naiades,* retells the story of Proserpine, involuntary queen of Hell, who wanders "red with anger, pale with fears" as her amorous king, Pluto, nightly comes home with yet another earthly maiden. The poem's content and its delicate, complex metrical form are deliberately inconsonant, which is typical of Beddoes' work. Beddoes, in despair of his time and of himself, chose to waste his genius on a theme that baffled his own imagination. The postulate of Beddoes' poetry is a world in which every metaphor resolves itself as another figure of death. For Beddoes the separation between subject and object is bridged not by any imaginative act, as in Blake, Wordsworth, and Shelley, but by dying. Memory conquers death for life in Wordsworth, while Blake and the Shelley of *Prometheus* tried to see death as only another dimension of life, as Stevens did after them. But Beddoes abandoned hope in earth's renewal. In him the apocalyptic impulse of Romanticism degenerated into the most ironic of its identifications, and death and the imagination became one. (pp. 443-44)

> *Harold Bloom, "Beddoes, Clare, Darley, and Others," in his* The Visionary Company: A Reading of English Romantic Poetry *(copyright © 1961 by Harold Bloom; copyright © 1971 by Cornell University;*

used with the permission of the publisher, Cornell University Press), revised edition, Cornell University Press, 1971, pp. 438-70.

ADDITIONAL BIBLIOGRAPHY

Donner, H. W. *Thomas Lovell Beddoes: The Making of a Poet.* Oxford: B. Blackwell, 1935, 403 p.
> The standard biography, by Beddoes's most recent editor and biographer.

Meynell, Alice. "Thomas Lovell Beddoes." In her *The Second Person Singular and Other Essays,* pp. 75-81. Oxford: Oxford University Press, 1922.
> Criticizes Beddoes's "poetry of madness," and comments on how his verse lacks a proper place in English literature.

Pierce, Frederick E. "Beddoes and Continental Romanticists." *Philological Quarterly* VI, No. 2 (April 1927): 123-32.
> Explores the influence the German Romantics might have had on *Death's Jest Book.*

Potter, G. R. "Did Thomas Beddoes Believe in the Evolution of Species?" *Modern Philology* XXI, No. 1 (August 1923): 89-100.
> Finds Beddoes both a poet and scientist, who skillfully combined both interests in poetic form.

[Procter, Bryan Waller]. "Art. IX: *The Brides' Tragedy.*" *Edinburgh Review* 38, No. LXXV (February 1823): 177-208.*
> Critical review of *The Brides' Tragedy* by Beddoes's close friend and staunch supporter.

Reeves, James. "Commentary and Notes: Thomas Lovell Beddoes." In his *Five Late Romantic Poets: George Darley, Hartley Coleridge, Thomas Hood, Thomas Lovell Beddoes, Emily Brontë,* edited by James Reeves, pp. 153-60. London: Heinemann, 1974.
> An overview of the principal criticism Beddoes received during his time and after his death. Such prominent critics and biographers as Robert Browning, Lytton Strachey, Edmund Blunden, David Daiches, and John Heath-Stubbs are cited.

"The Poems of Thomas Lovell Beddoes." *The Saturday Review (London)* 70, No. 1,831 (November 1890): 620-21.
> Unfavorable criticism citing Beddoes's lack of creativity and genius.

Wagner, Geoffrey. "Beddoes, Centennial of a Suicide." In *The Golden Horizon,* edited by Cyril Connolly, pp. 543-61. London: Weidenfeld & Nicolson, 1953.
> An account of Beddoes's life, acquaintances, and influences, explicating the use of these experiences in his verse.

Wood, Henry. "T. L. Beddoes, a Survival in Style." *American Journal of Philology* IV, No. 16 (1883): 445-55.
> A detailed investigation of Beddoes's works, attempting to show that "his style is Germanic (Anglo-Saxon, Teutonic), that it is Shakspearian, and . . . that it contains the chief elements of the historical English style."

Charlotte Brontë

1816-1855

(Also wrote under the pseudonym of Currer Bell) English novelist and poet.

The author of vivid, skillfully constructed novels, Brontë broke the traditional, nineteenth-century fictional stereotype of a woman as submissive, dependent, beautiful, but ignorant. Her highly-acclaimed *Jane Eyre; an Autobiography* best demonstrates these attitudes: its heroine is a plain woman who possesses intelligence, self-confidence, a will of her own, and moral righteousness. For her originality in form and content, Brontë is hailed as a precursor of feminist novelists, and regarded as an author whose talents were highly superior to some of her female Victorian contemporaries.

The eldest surviving daughter in a motherless family of six, Brontë helped an aunt who had been called in to rear her remaining brother, Branwell, and two sisters, Emily and Anne. Her father, a strict Yorkshire clergyman, believed firmly in the values of self-education and forbade his family from socializing with other children. In addition to their Biblical readings, he encouraged them to read William Shakespeare, William Wordsworth, Lord Byron, and Sir Walter Scott, thus he stimulated an interest in literature and intellectual activity. Charlotte and Branwell created the imaginary world of Angria, for which they invented characters, scenes, stories, and poems. Charlotte's contribution to these tales, which were collected and published posthumously as *Legends of Angria,* served as a catalyst for her mature works, and marked the beginning of her interest in writing.

For many years Brontë concealed her writing from her family. After the accidental discovery that Emily, too, secretly wrote verse, and that Anne shared their interest, the three published, at their own expense, *Poems by Currer, Ellis and Acton Bell.* Although *Poems* sold only two copies, Charlotte continued to write. Her first novel, *The Professor,* was rejected by six publishers, but her next work, *Jane Eyre,* was accepted immediately and was her first published novel. The work received lavish attention, was praised by Queen Victoria and George Eliot, and brought Brontë into popular literary circles, where she met William Makepeace Thackeray (to whom she dedicated the second edition of *Jane Eyre*), Mrs. Gaskell, Matthew Arnold, and Harriet Martineau. Some critics have attributed *Jane Eyre*'s success to the timing of its literary arrival, since it appeared between two great literary eras: the early nineteenth century, dominated by the works of Scott and Jane Austen, and the rise of the novel during the Victorian age. Brontë was consistently concerned with male and female equality, and maintained that love created the "pairing of these equals." Although she did not feel intellectually or spiritually inferior to her male contemporaries, it was necessary to write as Currer Bell, for as a pseudonymous male Brontë could enjoy an authorial freedom not granted to women in the 1840s and could be more assured of publication.

Brontë is often criticized for the didactic content of her works, as well as for her inability to create settings and topics other than those of her own experience. Her novels often illustrate these points. The setting for Lowood in *Jane Eyre* is based on

her childhood years at Cowan's Bridge school (a strict school for daughters of poor clergymen), and on her years as a teacher and governess. The sombre tone of her second published novel, *Shirley,* reflects her grief following the deaths of her brother and two sisters. The heroine of the book, modeled after Emily, is a stoic figure whose courage serves as both a tribute to Brontë's sister and a lesson to the reader. Brontë's travels to Brussels and her passionate attachment to Constantin Héger, a married schoolmaster in whose home she lived, are recreated in the student-teacher relationships and in the male characters of *The Professor* and *Villette.*

For many years, Charlotte was considered the outstanding literary figure of the Brontë family. However, David Cecil's essay, published in the early 1930s, proclaimed Emily the greater writer and marked a temporary end of Charlotte's critical superiority in the eyes of some critics. Influenced by Cecil's article, they compared Charlotte's works to those of Emily, disputing the originality and intellectual quality of Charlotte's novels. Many studies are focused more on the life of Charlotte Brontë than on her works.

Despite the largely autobiographical content of her novels and her changing literary reputation, critics still find much to praise in Brontë's works. She transmitted suspense and enjoyment to her reading audience, demonstrated remarkable imaginative force, and transcended time and place with what she called her "accents of persuasion." Recent feminist literary criticism has given new impetus to a revaluation of the significance of Brontë's attempts to depict through her fiction some of the problems of women in the nineteenth century.

PRINCIPAL WORKS

Poems by Currer, Ellis and Acton Bell [as Currer Bell, with Ellis and Acton Bell (pseudonyms of Emily and Anne Brontë)] (poems) 1846

Jane Eyre; an Autobiography [as Currer Bell] (novel) 1847

Shirley [as Currer Bell] (novel) 1849

Villette [as Currer Bell] (novel) 1853

The Professor [as Currer Bell] 1857

Emma (unfinished novel) 1860

*The Brontës' Life and Letters (letters) 1908

Legends of Angria (juvenilia) 1933

Five Novelettes: Passing Events, Julia, Mina Laury, Henry Hastings, Caroline Vernon (novellas) 1971

*This work includes letters written by Charlotte, Emily, and Anne Brontë.

ROBERT SOUTHEY (essay date 1837)

It is not my advice that you have asked as to the direction of your talents, but my opinion of them, and yet the opinion may be worth little, and the advice much. You evidently possess, and in no inconsiderable degree, what Wordsworth calls the 'faculty of verse.' I am not depreciating it when I say that in these times it is not rare. Many volumes of poems are now published every year without attracting public attention, any one of which, if it had appeared half a century ago, would have obtained a high reputation for its author. Whoever, therefore, is ambitious of distinction in this way ought to be prepared for disappointment.

But it is not with a view to distinction that you should cultivate this talent, if you consult your own happiness. I, who have made literature my profession, and devoted my life to it, and have never for a moment repented of the deliberate choice, think myself, nevertheless, bound in duty to caution every young man who applies as an aspirant to me for encouragement and advice, against taking so perilous a course. You will say that a woman has no need of such a caution; there can be no peril in it for her. In a certain sense this is true; but there is a danger of which I would, with all kindness and all earnestness, warn you. The day dreams in which you habitually indulge are likely to induce a distempered state of mind; and in proportion as all the ordinary uses of the world seem to you flat and unprofitable, you will be unfitted for them without becoming fitted for anything else. Literature cannot be the business of a woman's life, and it ought not to be. The more she is engaged in her proper duties, the less leisure will she have for it, even as an accomplishment and a recreation. To those duties you have not yet been called, and when you are you will be less eager for celebrity. You will not seek in imagination for excitement, of which the vicissitudes of this life, and the anxieties from which you must not hope to be exempted, be your state what it may, will bring with them but too much.

But do not suppose that I disparage the gift which you possess; nor that I would discourage you from exercising it. I only exhort you so to think of it, and so to use it, as to render it conducive to your own permanent good. Write poetry for its own sake; not in a spirit of emulation, and not with a view to celebrity; the less you aim at that the more likely you will be to deserve and finally to obtain it. So written, it is wholesome both for the heart and soul; it may be made the surest means, next to religion, of soothing the mind and elevating it. You may embody in it your best thoughts and your wisest feelings, and in so doing discipline and strengthen them.

Farewell, madam. It is not because I have forgotten that I was once young myself, that I write to you in this strain; but because I remember it. You will neither doubt my sincerity nor my good will; and however ill what has here been said may accord with your present views and temper, the longer you live the more reasonable it will appear to you. (pp. 102-03)

> *Robert Southey, in his letter to Charlotte Brontë in March, 1837, in* The Life of Charlotte Brontë *by E. C. Gaskell (reprinted by permission of the publisher, E. P. Dutton, Inc.), Dutton, 1957, pp. 102-03.*

THE ATHENAEUM (essay date 1846)

[*Poems by Currer, Ellis and Acton Bell* furnishes an] example of a family in whom appears to run the instinct of song. It is shared, however, by the three brothers—as we suppose them to be—in very unequal proportions; requiring, in the case of Acton Bell, the indulgences of affection to which we have alluded, to make it music,—and rising, in that of Ellis, into an inspiration, which may yet find an audience in the outer world. A fine quaint spirit has the latter, which may have things to speak that men will be glad to hear,—and an evident power of wing that may reach heights not here attempted. . . .

The Muse of Currer Bell walks half way betwixt the level of Acton's and the elevation attained by Ellis. It is rarely that the whole of one of his poems is up to the scale registered by parts. (p. 682)

> *"Poetry of the Million," in* The Athenaeum, *No. 975, July 4, 1846, pp. 682-83.*✳

[G. H. LEWES] (essay date 1847)

[*Jane Eyre: An Autobiography*] is a book after our own heart; and, if its merits have not forced it into notice by the time this paper comes before our readers, let us, in all earnestness, bid them lose not a day in sending for it. The writer is evidently a woman, and, unless we are deceived, new in the world of literature. But, man or woman, young or old, be that as it may, no such book has gladdened our eyes for a long while. Almost all that we require in a novelist she has: perception of character, and power of delineating it; picturesqueness; passion; and knowledge of life. The story is not only of singular interest, naturally evolved, unflagging to the last, but it fastens itself upon your attention, and will not leave you. The book closed, the enchantment continues. With the disentanglement of the plot, and the final release of the heroine from her difficulties, your interest does not cease. You go back again in memory to the various scenes in which she has figured; you linger on the way, and muse upon the several incidents in the life which has just been unrolled before you, affected by them as if they were the austere instructions drawn from a sorrowing existence, and not merely the cunning devices of an author's craft. Reality—deep, significant reality—is the great characteristic of the book. It *is* an autobiography,—not, perhaps, in the naked facts and circumstances, but in the actual suffering and experience. The form may be changed, and here and there some incidents invented; but the spirit remains such as it was. The machinery of the story may have been borrowed, but by means of this machinery the authoress is unquestionably setting forth her own experience. This gives the book its charm: it is soul speaking to soul; it is an utterance from the depths of a struggling, suffering, much-enduring spirit: *suspiria de profundis!* (p. 691)

There are some defects in [*Jane Eyre*]—defects which the excellence of the rest only brings into stronger relief. There is, indeed, too much melodrama and improbability, which smack of the circulating-library,—we allude particularly to the mad wife and all that relates to her, and to the wanderings of Jane when she quits Thornfield; yet even those parts are powerfully executed. But the earlier parts—all those relating to Jane's childhood and her residence at Lowood, with much of the strange love story—are written with remarkable beauty and truth. The characters are few, and drawn with unusual mastery: even those that are but sketched—such as Mr. Brockelhurst, Miss Temple, Mrs. Fairfax, Rosamond, and Blanche—are sketched with a vividness which betrays the cunning hand: a few strokes, and the figure rises before you. Jane herself is a creation. The delicate handling of this figure alone implies a dramatic genius of no common order. We never lose sight of her plainness; no effort is made to throw romance about her—no extraordinary goodness or cleverness appeals to your admiration; but you admire, you love her,—love her for the strong will, honest mind, loving heart, and peculiar but fascinating person. A creature of flesh and blood, with very fleshly infirmities, and very mortal excellencies; a woman, not a pattern: that is the Jane Eyre here represented. Mr. Rochester is also well drawn, and from the life; but it is the portrait of a man drawn by a woman, and is not comparable to the portrait of Jane. The way in which the authoress contrives to keep our interest in this imperfect character is a lesson to novelists. St. John Rivers, the missionary, has a touch of the circulating-library, but not enough to spoil the truth of the delineation; there is both art and artifice in the handling, and, although true in the main, and very powerful in parts, one feels a certain misgiving about him: it is another example of the woman's pencil. Helen Burns is lovely and loveable; true, we believe, even in her exalted spirituality and her religious fervour: a character at once eminently ideal and accurately real.

The story is so simple in its outlines, yet so filled out—not spun out—with details, that we shall not do it the injustice of here setting down the mere plot. It is confined to few characters, and is easily, naturally evolved . . . , carrying the reader on with it to the end. We have spoken of the reality stamped upon almost every part; and that reality is not confined to the characters and incidents, but is also striking in the descriptions of the various aspects of Nature, and of the houses, rooms, and furniture. The pictures stand out distinctly before you: they *are* pictures, and not mere bits of "fine writing." The writer is evidently painting by words a picture that she has in her mind, not "making-up" from vague remembrances, and with the consecrated phrases of "poetical prose." (p. 692)

In her delineation of country-houses and good society there is the ease and accuracy of one who has well known what she describes. We noticed but one slip of the pen, and that was giving to the door of Thornfield Hall a knocker; all the rest is not only accurate, but accurate in being represented from the governess point of view.

This faculty for objective representation is also united to a strange power of subjective representation. We do not simply mean the power over the passions—the psychological intuition of the artist, but the power also of connecting external appearances with internal effects—of representing the psychological interpretation of material phenomena. This is shewn in many a fine description. . . . (pp. 692-93)

[To the authoress] we emphatically say, Persevere; keep reality distinctly before you, and paint it as accurately as you can: invention will never equal the effect of truth.

The style of *Jane Eyre* is peculiar; but, except that she admits too many Scotch or North-country phrases, we have no objection to make to it, and for this reason: although by no means a fine style, it has the capital point of all great styles in being *personal,*—the written speech of an individual, not the artificial language made up from all sorts of books.

In philosophical remark she is sparing, and justly. It is what few women ever succeed in. . . . (p. 693)

[G. H. Lewes,] *"Recent Novels: French and English,"* in Fraser's Magazine for Town and Country, *Vol. XXXVI, No. CCXVI, December, 1847, pp. 690-95.**

THE WESTMINSTER REVIEW (essay date 1848)

[*Jane Eyre: An Autobiography* is decidedly] the best novel of the season; and one, moreover, from the natural tone pervading the narrative, and the originality and freshness of its style, possessing the merit so rarely met with now-a-days in works of this class, of amply repaying a second perusal. Whoever may be the author, we hope to see more such books from *her* pen; for that these volumes are from the pen of a lady, and a clever one too, we have not the shadow of a doubt: nor can there be any question as to the *reality* of many of the scenes and personages so artistically depicted; the characters are too life-like to be the mere creations of fancy, and sketchy as some of them are, they are wondrous *telling:* several of them we almost feel persuaded we have met with in real life. The Rev. Mr. Brocklehurst, with his "straight, narrow, sable-clad shape, standing erect on the rug; the grim face at the top being like a carved mask, placed above the shaft by way of capital;" the lady-like Miss Temple; sweet Helen Burns, whose death-scene is so touchingly narrated; the neat and prim little Mrs. Fairfax, and the eccentric Mr. Rochester, whom with all his faults and eccentricities one can't help getting to like; are but a few of the characters in the drama, though essential ones, and cleverly struck off. (p. 581)

[There are many passages we would gladly quote]: unfortunately, however, they are not to be easily separated from the context without spoiling them; indeed to be thoroughly appreciated and enjoyed, the whole three volumes must be regularly read through: no skipping—no peeping to see how Jane goes on a few leaves forward, or whether she gets married, or how her property comes to her. And thus perused, we venture to say no one will regret having followed our advice to *read Jane Eyre.* (p. 584)

"Critical and Miscellaneous Notices: 'Jane Eyre: An Autobiography'," in The Westminster Review, *Vol. XLVIII, No. II, January, 1848, pp. 581-84.*

[ELIZABETH RIGBY] (essay date 1848)

['**Jane Eyre: An Autobiography**'] as a work, and one of equal popularity, is, in almost every respect, a total contrast to [Thackeray's] 'Vanity Fair.' The characters and events, though some of them masterly in conception, are coined expressly for the purpose of bringing out great effects. The hero and heroine are beings both so singularly unattractive that the reader feels they can have no vocation in the novel but to be brought together; and they do things which, though not impossible, lie utterly beyond the bounds of probability. . . . Jane Eyre is merely another Pamela [from Richardson's 'Pamela'], who, by the force of her character and the strength of her principles, is carried victoriously through great trials and temptations from the man she loves. Nor is she even a Pamela adapted and refined to modern notions; for though the story is conducted without those derelictions of decorum which we are to believe had their excuse in the manners of Richardson's time, yet it is stamped with a coarseness of language and laxity of tone which have certainly no excuse in ours. It is a very remarkable book: we have no remembrance of another combining such genuine power with such horrid taste. Both together have equally assisted to gain the great popularity it has enjoyed; for in these days of extravagant adoration of all that bears the stamp of novelty and originality, sheer rudeness and vulgarity have come in for a most mistaken worship. (p. 87)

[This is] a tale in which, combined with great materials for power and feeling, the reader may trace gross inconsistencies and improbabilities, and chief and foremost that highest moral offence a novel writer can commit, that of making an unworthy character interesting in the eyes of the reader. . . . Mr. Rochester's character is tolerably consistent. He is made as coarse and as brutal as can in all conscience be required to keep our sympathies at a distance. In point of literary consistency the hero is at all events impugnable, though we cannot say as much for the heroine.

As to Jane's character—there is none of that harmonious unity about it which made little Becky [in 'Vanity Fair'] so grateful a subject of analysis—nor are the discrepancies of that kind which have their excuse and their response in our nature. The inconsistencies of Jane's character lie mainly not in her own imperfections, though of course she has her share, but in the author's. There is that confusion in the relations between cause and effect, which is not so much untrue to human nature as to human art. The error in Jane Eyre is, not that her character is this or that, but that she is made one thing in the eyes of her imaginary companions, and another in that of the actual reader. There is a perpetual disparity between the account she herself gives of the effect she produces, and the means shown us by which she brings that effect about. We hear nothing but self-eulogiums on the perfect tact and wondrous penetration with which she is gifted, and yet almost every word she utters offends us, not only with the absence of these qualities, but with the positive contrasts of them, in either her pedantry, stupidity, or gross vulgarity. She is one of those ladies who put us in the unpleasant predicament of undervaluing their very virtues for dislike of the person in whom they are represented. One feels provoked as Jane Eyre stands before us—for in the wonderful reality of her thoughts and descriptions, she seems accountable for all done in her name—with principles you must approve in the main, and yet with language and manners that offend you in every particular. Even in that *chef-d'oeuvre* of brilliant retrospective sketching, the description of her early life, it is the childhood and not the child that interests you. The little Jane, with her sharp eyes and dogmatic speeches, is

a being you neither could fondle nor love. There is a hardness in her infantine earnestness, and a spiteful precocity in her reasoning, which repulses all our sympathy. One sees that she is of a nature to dwell upon and treasure up every slight and unkindness, real or fancied, and such natures we know are surer than any other to meet with plenty of this sort of thing. As the child, so also the woman—an uninteresting, sententious, pedantic thing; with no experience of the world, and yet with no simplicity of freshness in its stead. What are her first answers to Mr. Rochester but such as would have quenched all interest, even for a prettier woman, in any man of common knowledge of what was nature—and especially in a *blasé* monster like him? A more affected governessy effusion we never read. (pp. 89-90)

Jane Eyre is throughout [the book] the personification of an unregenerate and undisciplined spirit, the more dangerous to exhibit from that prestige of principle and self-control which is liable to dazzle the eye too much for it to observe the inefficient and unsound foundation on which it rests. It is true Jane does right, and exerts great moral strength, but it is the strength of a mere heathen mind which is a law unto itself. No Christian grace is perceptible upon her. She has inherited in fullest measure the worst sin of our fallen nature—the sin of pride. Jane Eyre is proud, and therefore she is ungrateful too. It pleased God to make her an orphan, friendless, and penniless—yet she thanks nobody, and least of all Him, for the food and raiment, the friends, companions, and instructors of her helpless youth—for the care and education vouchsafed to her till she was capable in mind as fitted in years to provide for herself. On the contrary, she looks upon all that has been done for her not only as her undoubted right, but as falling far short of it. The doctrine of humility is not more foreign to her mind than it is repudiated by her heart. It is by her own talents, virtues, and courage, that she is made to attain the summit of human happiness, and, as far as Jane Eyre's own statement is concerned, no one would think that she owed anything either to God above or to man below. She flees from Mr. Rochester, and has not a being to turn to. . . . Of course it suited the author's end to represent the heroine as utterly destitute of the common means of assistance, in order to exhibit both her trials and her powers of self-support—the whole book rests on this assumption—but it is one which, under the circumstances, is very unnatural and very unjust.

Altogether the autobiography of Jane Eyre is pre-eminently an anti-Christian composition. There is throughout it a murmuring against the comforts of the rich and against the privations of the poor, which, as far as each individual is concerned, is a murmuring against God's appointment—there is a proud and perpetual assertion of the rights of man, for which we find no authority either in God's word or in God's providence—there is that pervading tone of ungodly discontent which is at once the most prominent and the most subtle evil which the law and the pulpit, which all civilized society in fact, has at the present day to contend with. We do not hesitate to say that the tone of mind and thought which has overthrown authority and violated every code human and divine abroad, and fostered Chartism and rebellion at home, is the same which has also written Jane Eyre.

Still we say again this is a very remarkable book. We are painfully alive to the moral, religious, and literary deficiencies of the picture, and such passages of beauty and power as [are contained in '**Jane Eyre**'] cannot redeem it, but it is impossible not to be spellbound with the freedom of the touch. It would be mere hackneyed courtesy to call it 'fine writing.' It bears no impress of being written at all, but is poured out rather in the heat and hurry of an instinct, which flows ungovernably on to its object, indifferent by what means it reaches it, and unconscious too. As regards the author's chief object, however, it is a failure—that, namely, of making a plain, odd woman, destitute of all the conventional features of feminine attraction, interesting in our sight. We deny that he has succeeded in this. Jane Eyre, in spite of some grand things about her, is a being totally uncongenial to our feelings from beginning to end. We acknowledge her firmness—we respect her determination—we feel for her struggles; but, for all that, and setting aside higher considerations, the impression she leaves on our mind is that of a decidedly vulgar-minded woman—one whom we should not care for as an acquaintance, whom we should not seek as a friend, whom we should not desire for a relation, and whom we should scrupulously avoid for a governess. (pp. 92-3)

[Whoever Currer Bell may be], it is a person who, with great mental powers, combines a total ignorance of the habits of society, a great coarseness of taste, and a heathenish doctrine of religion. And as these characteristics appear more or less in the writings of all three, Currer, Acton, and Ellis [Bell], alike, for their poems differ less in degree of power than in kind, we are ready to accept the fact of their identity or of their relationship with equal satisfaction. . . . [The question of authorship] can deserve a moment's curiosity only as far as **'Jane Eyre'** is concerned, and though we cannot pronounce that it appertains to a real Mr. Currer Bell and to no other, yet that it appertains to a man, and not, as many assert, to a woman, we are strongly inclined to affirm. Without entering into the question whether the power of the writing be above her, or the vulgarity below her, there are, we believe, minutiae of circumstantial evidence which at once acquit the feminine hand. No woman—a lady friend, whom we are always happy to consult, assures us—makes mistakes in her own *metier*—no woman *trusses game* and garnishes dessert-dishes with the same hands, or talks of so doing in the same breath. Above all, no woman attires another in such fancy dresses as Jane's ladies assume—Miss Ingram coming down, irresistible, 'in a *morning* robe of sky-blue crape, a gauze azure scarf twisted in her hair!!' No lady, we understand, when suddenly roused in the night, would think of hurrying on *'a frock.'* They have garments more convenient for such occasions, and more becoming too. This evidence seems incontrovertible. Even granting that these incongruities were purposely assumed, for the sake of disguising the female pen, there is nothing gained; for if we ascribe the book to a woman at all, we have no alternative but to ascribe it to one who has, for some sufficient reason, long forfeited the society of her own sex.

And if by no woman, it is certainly also by no artist. . . . There is not more disparity between the art of drawing Jane assumes and her evident total ignorance of its first principles, than between the report she gives of her own character and the conclusions we form for ourselves. Not but what, in another sense, the author may be classed as an artist of very high grade. Let him describe the simplest things in nature—a rainy landscape, a cloudy sky, or a bare moorside, and he shows the hand of a master; but the moment he talks of the art itself, it is obvious that he is a complete ignoramus.

We cannot help feeling that this work must be far from beneficial to that class of ladies whose cause it affects to advocate. Jane Eyre is not precisely the mouthpiece one would select to plead the cause of governesses, and it is therefore the greater pity that she has chosen it: for there is none we are convinced which, at the present time, more deserves and demands an earnest and judicious befriending. (pp. 93-4)

[Elizabeth Rigby,] "'Vanity Fair'—and 'Jane Eyre'," in The London Quarterly Review, No. CLXVII, December, 1848, pp. 82-99.*

THE TIMES   (essay date 1849)

With all its faults *Jane Eyre* was a remarkable production. The volumes were disfigured by coarseness; in the final development of the plot the craft of the bookmaker was more commendable than the subtle and fine working of the master; after the story had been told, pages and pages of unnecessary matter were forced upon the reader to complete three imperfect volumes, and to spoil two which could hardly be improved; yet, in spite of these and other obvious imperfections, *Jane Eyre* had as good a claim as any work of fiction to the esteem and approval of the novel-reading public of 1848. Freshness and originality, truth and passion, singular felicity in the description of natural scenery and in the analyzation of human thought, enabled this tale to stand boldly out from the mass of such compositions, and to assume its own place in the bright, but at the best evanescent, field of romantic literature. The early scenes of *Jane Eyre* are not to be surpassed: her struggles in the school, the whole picture of that academy, are drawn from the life, and we are bold to say are to this hour impressed upon the reader's mind with all the vivid force that belongs to reality, touched and adorned by the hand of genius. The fierce and gloomy nature of Rochester, pierced and shaken in the first instance by his impassioned and tender love of the poor schoolgirl—whose best recommendations are her simple nature, her tranquil devotion, and her perfect virtue—and finally overcome and beaten down by protracted physical suffering and mental torture, is a grand and solemn vision not to be mistaken or resisted. . . .

Struck, however, as we could not but be by the raciness and ability of the work, by the independent sway of a thoroughly original and unworn pen, by the masculine current of noble thoughts, and the unflinching dissection of dark yet truthful character, we perused the last words of the story with the conviction that the second effort of the author would not surpass the first. Indeed, it was not difficult to arrive at that conclusion, since the writer herself, even in *Jane Eyre*, had contrived to reveal the fact that she had been impelled to her labour by a desire to disburden her soul of the results of personal observation or actual experience, and that, with that feat accomplished, her vacation was at an end. . . . [Of the latest novel, *Shirley*,] we are fully prepared to receive, to wit, a novel made up of third volumes, a book to be read upon the strength of the book that was formerly devoured, a tale invented, concocted, and written to be sold to a crowd of customers waiting to purchase, not evoked from the brain by the spirit that gives no rest to the intellect ripe to deliver up its fruits.

Shirley is very clever, as a matter of course. It could not be otherwise. The pencil that sketched Jane Eyre and filled up the broad outlines of Rochester's fine form, could not be worn down to the stump by one vigorous performance. The faculty of graphic description, the strong imagination, the fervid and masculine diction, the analytic skill, all remain as visible as before, but are thrown away upon a structure that bears no likeness to actual life, and affords no satisfaction or pleasure to those who survey it. The story of *Shirley* may be told in a couple of pages, yet a more artificial and unnatural history cannot be conceived; and what is true of the plot is even more applicable to the *dramatis personae*. The characters, from Miss Shirley Keeldar down to the smallest boy in the narrative, are manufactured for the occasion. As for Miss Shirley, her metaphysical acumen and argumentative prowess are beyond all praise, whilst the dialectics of the precocious 12-year old would do honour to John Stuart Mill himself. . . .

[It] would be unjust to the fair authoress—for lady she is, let who will say to the contrary—if we did not allow that at times the talk is worthy of her genius and that gems of rare thought and glorious passion shine here and there throughout her volumes. But the infrequent brilliancy seems but to make more evident and unsightly the surrounding gloom. *Shirley* is not a picture of real life; it is not a work that contains the elements of popularity, that will grapple with the heart of mankind and compel its homage. It is a mental exercise that can bring its author no profit, and will not extend by the measure of an inch her previous well-deserved success. Millions understood her before—she may count by units those who will appreciate her now. *Jane Eyre* was not a pure romance. *Shirley* is at once the most high-flown and the stalest of fictions.

> *"'Shirley,'—By the Author of 'Jane Eyre',"* in The Times, *No. 20353, December 7, 1849, p. 3.*

EDINBURGH REVIEW (essay date 1850)

[We] take Currer Bell to be one of the most remarkable of *female* writers; and believe is is now scarcely a secret that Currer Bell is the pseudonyme of a woman. An eminent contemporary, indeed, has employed the sharp vivacity of a female pen to prove 'upon irresistible evidence' that **'Jane Eyre'** *must be* the work of a man! But all that 'irresistible evidence' is set aside by the simple fact that Currer Bell *is* a woman. We never, for our own parts, had a moment's doubt on the subject. That Jane herself was drawn by a woman's delicate hand, and that Rochester equally betrayed the sex of the artist, was to our minds so obvious, as absolutely to shut our ears to all the evidence which could be adduced by the erudition even of a *marchande des modes;* and that simply because we knew that there were women profoundly ignorant of the mysteries of the toilette, and the terminology of fashion (independent of the obvious solution, that such ignorance might be counterfeited, to mislead), and felt that there was no man who *could so* have delineated a woman—or *would so* have delineated a man. The fair and ingenious critic was misled by her own acuteness in the perception of details; and misled also in some other way, and more uncharitably, in concluding that the *author* of **'Jane Eyre'** was a heathen educated among heathens,—the *fact* being, that the *authoress* is the daughter of a clergyman! . . .

[It] is certain that, for many years, there had been no work of such power, piquancy, and originality. Its very faults were faults on the side of vigour; and its beauties were all original. The grand secret of its success, however,—as of all genuine and lasting success,—was its *reality*. From out the depths of a sorrowing experience, here was a voice speaking to the experience of thousands. The aspects of external nature, too, were painted with equal fidelity,—the long cheerless winter days, chilled with rolling mists occasionally gathering into the strength of rains,—the bright spring mornings,—the clear solemn nights,—were all painted to your *soul* as well as to your eye, by a pencil dipped into a soul's experience for its colours. Faults enough the book has undoubtedly: faults of conception,

faults of taste, faults of ignorance, but in spite of all, it remains a book of singular fascination. (p. 158)

A pleasant book, indeed, we are not sure that we can style ['**Shirley**']. Power it has unquestionably, and interest too, of a peculiar sort; but not the agreeableness of a work of art. Through its pages we are carried as over a wild and desolate heath, with a sharp east wind blowing the hair into our eyes, and making the blood tingle in our veins: There is health perhaps in the drive; but not much pleasantness. Nature speaks to us distinctly enough, but she does not speak sweetly. She is in her stern and sombre mood, and we see only her dreary aspects.

'**Shirley**' is inferior to '**Jane Eyre**' in several important points. It is not quite so true; and it is not so fascinating. It does not so rivet the reader's attention nor hurry him through all obstacles of improbability, with so keen a sympathy in its reality. It is even coarser in texture, too, and not unfrequently flippant; while the characters are almost all disagreeable, and exhibit intolerable rudeness of manner. In '**Jane Eyre**' life was viewed from the standing point of individual experience; in '**Shirley**' that standing point is frequently abandoned, and the artist paints only a panorama of which she, as well as you, are but spectators. Hence the unity of '**Jane Eyre**' in spite of its clumsy and improbable contrivances, was great and effective: the fire of one passion fused the discordant materials into one mould. But in '**Shirley**' all unity, in consequence of defective art, is wanting. There is no passionate link; nor is there any artistic fusion, or intergrowth, by which one part evolves itself from another. Hence its falling-off in interest, coherent movement, and life. The book may be laid down at any chapter, and almost any chapter might be omitted. The various scenes are gathered up into three volumes,—they have not grown into a work. The characters often need a justification for their introduction; as in the case of the three Curates, who are offensive, uninstructive, and unamusing. That they are not *inventions,* however, we feel persuaded. For nothing but a strong sense of their reality could have seduced the authoress into such a mistake as admitting them at all. We are confident she has seen them, known them, despised them; and *therefore* she paints them! although they have no relation with the story, have no interest in themselves, and cannot be accepted as types of a class,—for they are not *Curates* but *boors:* and although not inventions, we must be permitted to say that they are *not true.* . . . [Though] the portraits may be like the oddities from whom they are copied, they are faulty as works of art, if they strike all who never met with these oddities, as unnatural. . . . It is the same with incidents.

Again we say that '**Shirley**' cannot be received as a work of art. It is not a picture; but a portfolio of random sketches for one or more pictures. The authoress never seems distinctly to have made up her mind as to what she was to do. . . . All are by turns attempted and abandoned; and the book consequently moves slowly, and by starts—leaving behind it no distinct or satisfactory impression. Power is stamped on various parts of it; power unmistakeable, but often misapplied. Currer Bell has much yet to learn,—and, especially, the discipline of her tumultuous energies. She must learn also to sacrifice a little of her Yorkshire roughness to the demands of good taste: neither saturating her writings with such rudeness and offensive harshness, nor suffering her style to wander into such vulgarities as would be inexcusable—even in a man. . . . And while touching on this minor, yet not trivial point, we may also venture a word of quiet remonstrance against a most inappropriate obtrusion of French phrases. . . . A French word or two may be introduced now and then on account of some peculiar fitness, but Currer Bell's use of the language is little better than that of the 'fashionable' novelists. (pp. 159-61)

We scarcely know what to say to the impertinence which has been allowed to mingle so largely with the manners, even of the favourite actors in this drama. Their frequent harshness and rudeness is something which startles on a first reading, and, on a second, is quite inexplicable. . . . [We] must in that case strongly protest against Currer Bell's portraits being understood to be resemblances; for they are, one and all, given to break out and misbehave themselves upon very small provocation. The manner and language of Shirley towards her guardian passes all permission. Even the gentle, timid, shrinking Caroline enters the lists with the odious Mrs. Yorke, and the two *ladies* talk at each other, in a style which, to southern ears, sounds both marvellous and alarming. But, to quit this tone of remonstrance,—which after all is a compliment, for it shows how seriously we treat the great talents of the writer,—let us cordially praise the real freshness, vividness, and fidelity, with which most of the characters and scenes are depicted. There is, perhaps, no single picture representing one broad aspect of nature which can be hung beside two or three in **'Jane Eyre;'** but the same piercing and loving eye, and the same bold and poetic imagery, are here exhibited. (pp. 161-62)

The two heroes of the book . . .—for there are two—are not agreeable characters; nor are they felicitously drawn. They have both something sordid in their minds, and repulsive in their demeanour. Louis Moore is talked about as if he were something greater than our ordinary humanity; but, when he shows himself, turns out to be a very small person indeed. Robert, more energetic, and more decisively standing out from the canvas, is disgraced by a sordid love of money, and a shameless setting aside of an affection for Caroline in favour of the rich heiress. *He* will be universally condemned: for all our better instincts rebel against him. The authoress will appeal in vain here to *the truth* of such sordidness—the truth of thus discarding a real passion in favour of an ambitious project. True it is: *true of many men;* but *not true of noble natures*—not true of an ideal of manhood. In a subordinate character such a lapse from the elevation of moral rectitude, might have been pardoned; but in a hero—in the man for whom our sympathies and admiration are almost exclusively claimed—to imagine it possible, is a decided blunder in art—as well as an inconsistency in nature. A hero may be faulty, erring, imperfect; but he must not be sordid, mean, wanting in the statelier virtues of our kind. Rochester was far more to be respected than this Robert Moore! Nor is Louis Moore much better. (pp. 163-64)

The heroines are more loveable. Shirley, if she did not occasionally use language one would rather not hear from the lips of a lady, and did not occasionally display something in her behaviour, which, with every allowance for Yorkshire plainness, does imply want of breeding,—Shirley, we say, would be irresistible. So buoyant, free, airy, and healthy in her nature, so fascinating in her manner, she is prettily enough described by her lover as a 'Peri too mutinous for heaven, too innocent for hell.' But if Shirley is, on the whole, a happy creation, Caroline Helstone, though sometimes remarkably sweet and engaging, is—if we may venture to say so—a failure. Currer Bell is exceedingly scornful on the chapter of heroines drawn by men. The cleverest and acutest of our sex, she says, are often under the strangest illusions about women—we do not read them in their true light; we constantly misapprehend them,

both for good and evil. Very possibly. But we suspect that female artists are by no means exempt from mistakes quite as egregious when *they* delineate their sex; nay, we venture to say, that Mrs. Pryor and Caroline Helstone are as untrue to the universal laws of our common nature as if they had been drawn by the clumsy hand of a male: though we willingly admit that in both there are little touches which at once betray the more exquisite workmanship of woman's lighter pencil. (p. 164)

Not quite so glaring, and yet very glaring, is the want of truth in Caroline. There are traits about this character quite charming; and we doubt not she will be a favourite with the majority of readers. But any one examining **'Shirley'** as a work of art, must be struck with want of keeping in making the gentle, shy, not highly cultivated Caroline *talk* from time to time in the strain of Currer Bell herself rather than in the strain of Helstone's little niece. (p. 165)

This, however, is but one point in the faulty treatment of the character. A graver error,—one implying greater forgetfulness of dramatic reality and probability,—is the conduct of Caroline in her love for Moore. The mystery kept up between the two girls is the trick of a vulgar novelist. . . . [Unless] we are to be put out of court as men, and consequently incompetent to apprehend the true nature of woman, we should say that [the] entire absence of jealous feelings on Caroline's part, is an omission, which, conscious or unconscious, we cannot reconcile with any thing we have ever seen, heard, or read of about the sex. (p. 166)

We have been more than once disturbed by what looked like wilful departures from probability in this novel. We are by no means rigorous in expecting that the story is to move along the highway of every-day life. On the contrary, we are willing to allow the imagination full sweep; but we demand, that into whatever region it carry us, it must be at least consistent: if we are to travel into fairy land, it must be in a fairy equipage, *not* in a Hansom's cab. Now there are many regions in **'Shirley'** where we are glad enough to find ourselves; it is against this method by which we are transported to them that we protest. Thus in the second volume there is a really remarkable tirade about Milton's Eve: as an eloquent rhapsody we can scarcely admire it too much; but to be asked to believe that it was uttered in a quiet conversation between two young ladies, destroys half our pleasure. (pp. 166-67)

Then, again, there is Louis Moore writing long narratives in his note-book. *What* he writes is often striking; and had the authoress only thought of making him keep a journal, probability would have been sufficiently saved. But, instead of that, she obliges him to sit down in Shirley's room, draw out a note-book, and proceed to write very circumstantially, for our benefit, what every one feels he would never have *written* at all. . . . It is remarkable, too, that nothing whatever is gained by telling the story in this way. All that Louis Moore writes might have been better told by the authoress, without subterfuge. We may make the same remark as to Robert Moore's confession of his scene with Shirley. Its effect would be far truer. The attack on the Mill, too, instead of being described in the natural course of the narrative, is told us in snatches of dialogue between the two girls; who, in utter defiance of all *vraisemblance,* are calm spectators of that which they could not have seen. It is scarcely worth while to point out the several details in this scene, which betray a female and inexperienced hand. Incident is not the *forte* of Currer Bell. If her invention were in any degree equal to her powers of execution, (with a little more judgment and practice,) she would stand alone among novelists; but in invention she is as yet only an artisan, not an artist.

As a proof of this poverty of invention we may refer . . . to the singular awkwardness of making Moore confess to Yorke the interview he had had with Shirley, and the terms on which he had offered to marry her. The scene is unquestionably very powerful; but it loses much of its power by the mode in which it is presented. Had it been narrated in the due course of the story, as in any other writer's hands it would have been, it would have been, perhaps, the most striking scene in the book. (pp. 168-69)

[The scene between Mother and Daughter is] in its simple, humble, thrilling naturalness one of the most touching and *feminine* scenes in our literature; or that wild, imaginative, and original picture of the Mermaid, which shows the writer to have the true poetic power—the power, namely, of creating new life out of old materials. Surely at the present day one would think there was nothing more to be said about mermaids; yet we venture to say that mermaids never were so beautiful, so ghastly, so living, as in ['**Shirley**']. (p. 172)

[Currer Bell] has genius enough to create a great name for herself; and if we seem to have insisted too gravely on her faults, it is only because we are ourselves sufficiently her admirers to be most desirous to see her remove these blemishes from her writings, and take the rank within her reach. She has extraordinary power—but let her remember that *'on tombe du côté où l'on penche!'* (p. 173)

"Currer Bell's 'Shirley'," in Edinburgh Review, Vol. XCI, No. CLXXXIII, January, 1850, pp. 153-73.

THE ATHENAEUM   (essay date 1853)

So curious a novel as '**Villette**' seldom comes before us,—and rarely one offering so much matter for remark. Its very outset exhibits an indifference to certain precepts of Art, singular in one who by artistic management alone interests us in an unpromising subject. . . . During a considerable portion of the story we are led to expect that the old well-thumbed case of conscience is going to be tried again,—and that, having dealt with a Calvinistic missionary in '**Jane Eyre**,' Currer Bell is about to draw a full-length picture of a disciple of Loyola in '**Villette**.' But the idea is suggested—not fulfilled. Our authoress is superior to the nonsense and narrowness that call themselves religious controversy. She allows the peril of the position to be felt,—without entering on the covert rancour, the imperfect logic, and the inconclusive catastrophe which distinguish such polemics when they are made the theme of fiction.—We fancied, again, from certain indications, that something of supernatural awe and terror were to be evoked:—but as a sequel to these, Currer Bell has fairly turned round upon herself with a mockery little short of sarcasm.—The tale is merely one of the affections. It may be found in some places tedious, in some of its incidents trivial,—but it is remarkable as a picture of manners. A burning heart glows throughout it, and one brilliantly distinct character keeps it alive. (p. 186)

'**Villette**' is a book which will please much those whom it pleases at all. Allowing for some superfluity of rhetoric used in a manner which reminds us of the elder Miss Jewsbury—and for one or two rhapsodies, which might have been "toned down" with advantage,—this tale is much better written than '**Shirley**,' the preceding one by its authoress. (p. 188)

"'Villette'," in The Athenaeum, No. 1320, February 12, 1853, pp. 186-88.

THE EDINBURGH REVIEW   (essay date 1853)

'**Villette**,' by the author of '**Jane Eyre**,' is a most remarkable work—a production altogether *sui generis*. Fulness and vigour of thought mark almost every sentence, and there is a sort of easy power pervading the whole narrative, such as we have rarely met. There is little of plot or incident in the story; nearly the whole of it is confined to the four walls of a *Pensionnat* at Brussels; but the characters introduced are sketched with a bold and free pencil, and their individuality is sustained with a degree of consistency, which marks a master's hand. The descriptions, too, whether the subjects of them be solemn, ludicrous, or pathetic, are wonderfully graphic and pictorial. It is clear at a glance that the groundwork and many of the details of the story are autobiographic; and we never read a literary production which so betrays at every line the individual character of the writer. Her life has evidently been irradiated by but scanty sunshine, and she is besides disposed to look rather pertinaciously on the shady side of every landscape. With an almost painful and unceasing consciousness of possessing few personal or circumstantial advantages; with spirits naturally the reverse of buoyant; with feelings the reverse of demonstrative; with affections strong rather than warm, and injured by too habitual repression; a keen, shrewd, sagacious, sarcastic, observer of life, rather than a genial partaker in its interests; gifted with intuitive insight into character, and reading it often with too cold and critical an eye; full of sympathy where love and admiration call it forth, but able by long discipline to dispense with it herself; always somewhat too rigidly strung up for the hard struggle of life, but fighting sternly and gallantly its gloomy battle,—the character which Lucy Snowe has here drawn of herself presents rather an interesting study than an attraction or a charm. (p. 387)

"Recent Novels: 'Villette'," in The Edinburgh Review, *Vol. XCVII, No. CXCVIII, April, 1853, pp. 387-90.*

THE CRITIC   (essay date 1857)

[*The Professor*] now makes its first appearance before the public, at a time when general curiosity is sufficiently excited towards everything that appertains to Charlotte Brontë to render acceptable anything that has proceeded from her pen. We do not know that her reputation will gain anything by the publication of *The Professor;* indeed, we are inclined to believe that a contrary result is possible; but, at the same time, we admit that it is interesting as a stage in the development of a very extraordinary mind. Now that the work is before us, we are not at all surprised at the unanimity with which the publishers decided upon its merits. It is crude, unequal, and unnatural to a fault; it has all the unripe qualities of a bad first work: and if it contains symptoms of future power, they are hidden and metamorphosed by much that (had the book preceded "**Jane Eyre**") would have decided many into pronouncing against the possibility of a high degree of merit. It is therefore very fortunate that Charlotte Brontë did not make her *début* in *The Professor,* but that the good taste of the publishers compelled to postpone her appearance until she could present herself in the full splendour of her genius and powers.

We are by no means sorry, however, that the work has been put forward at this juncture. Anything which throws light upon the growth and composition of such a mind cannot be otherwise than interesting as a subject of study. In *The Professor* we may discover the germs of many trains of thinking which afterwards came to be enlarged and illustrated to a fuller degree in subsequent and more perfect works. The hero, William Crimsworth, is a Jane Eyre in petticoats; Yorke Hunsden is an undeveloped Rochester; and the experiences of Brussels and the *pension* are all here given in a less skilful and artistic form than that under which we were already acquainted with them in **"Villette."** The character of Edward Crimsworth seems scarcely natural, though it is quite possible that such a personage *may* have existed. Upon this we cannot speak positively; but we are quite sure that he is not an agreeable personage. (p. 271)

> "Fiction: 'The Professor: A Tale'," in The Critic, Vol. XVI, No. 389, June 15, 1857, pp. 271-72.

THE DUBLIN UNIVERSITY MAGAZINE   (essay date 1857)

[*The Professor*] exhibits many of the beauties and some of the defects of this gifted writer; taking its tone, as it does, principally from those experiences of a schoolteacher's life, which seem more or less strongly to have formed her mind and tinged her writings from first to last. (p. 94)

In the photographic accuracy of delineating detail—the minutest *accessoires* of the portrait [Charlotte Brontë] stands unrivalled. She produces general effects by small hints; and opens soul and character through the space between the fringes of a half-closed eye. (p. 99)

[*The Professor*] teaches that the true and healthy road to success, taken in its best sense, is steady principle and equally steady effort. That discipline, from within and from without, prepares for and heralds happiness. That love has its holiest development in the chastenings of adversity, and the agonisms of labour. We likewise learn, as the author has herself told us in a preface prepared for the work when she had an intention of publishing it in her later years, that it was an object to prevent any good which befel the hero from being more than commensurate with the means made use of to attain it—in short, to avoid *exaggeration* either as regards character or scene, and to keep events within their proper and unromantic limits of *results*.

Into this quiet and unambitious tale some faults have crept which we do not mean to extenuate. . . . But beauties have likewise found their way; the beauties of poetical expression which run like wild flowers through the hedge, clipped and pruned as it is. (pp. 99-100)

It will, we are convinced, be read by others with the same painful interest as it was by us, emanating as it does from one on whose forehead the star of Fame, thus glowingly described, rested so short an instant before it was quenched in the damps of death. (p. 100)

> "Currer Bell's 'Professor'," in The Dublin University Magazine, Vol. L, No. CCXCV, July, 1857, pp. 88-100.

[WILLIAM MAKEPEACE THACKERAY]   (essay date 1860)

Of the multitude that has read [Charlotte Brontë's] books, who has not known and deplored the tragedy of her family, her own most sad and untimely fate? Which of her readers has not become her friend? Who that has known her books has not

admired the artist's noble English, the burning love of truth, the bravery, the simplicity, the indignation at wrong, the eager sympathy, the pious love and reverence, the passionate honour, so to speak, of the woman? What a story is that of that family of poets in their solitude yonder on the gloomy northern moors! (p. 486)

As I read this little fragmentary sketch [*Emma*], I think of the rest. Is it? And where is it? Will not the leaf be turned some day, and the story be told? Shall the deviser of the tale somewhere perfect the history of little Emma's griefs and troubles? . . .

How well I remember the delight, and wonder, and pleasure with which I read *Jane Eyre,* sent to me by an author whose name and sex were then alike unknown to me; the strange fascinations of the book; and how with my own work pressing upon me, I could not, having taken the volumes up, lay them down until they were read through! Hundreds of those who, like myself, recognized and admired that master-work of a great genius, will look with a mournful interest and regard and curiosity upon this, the last fragmentary sketch from the noble hand which wrote *Jane Eyre.* (p. 487)

> [William Makepeace Thackeray,] "The Last Sketch," in The Cornhill Magazine, Vol. I, April, 1860, pp. 485-87.

WILLIAM CALDWELL ROSCOE   (essay date 1860)

[In Charlotte Brontë's] novels, it is not so much the whole story as the separate scenes and detached incidents that delight us; and it is not the characters themselves so much as the mode in which they display themselves under particular circumstances. She is perfectly master of the art of narration; her events are linked in so easy and continuous a succession, that the reader loses the sense of the exquisite art by which it is done; and the wonderful thing is, that there are no dull places. Long she is sometimes, but never dull. A certain sinewy vigour gives interest to every paragraph. Character is her favourite study; but, like most people who deliberately study character, she never thoroughly comprehends it. True perception of character seems to be something intuitive. It requires, at any rate, a nature of very extended though not necessarily deep sympathies, which finds something in itself answering to all hints, and ready to gather up all clues. Miss Brontë had nothing of this. She studies the manifestations, the workings of character; and it is these alone, for the most part, that she is enabled to reproduce. She does this with all her might. In *Shirley,* for instance, with intent and resolute eyes she sits gazing into the human heart. Darkness shades its penetralia; but her keen vision *shall* pierce the veil; she *will* compel its secrets to the light. She reads as if she set the characters in her story down before her, and set herself, not to develop them, but to write down what she sees in them. It is not a creation, but a vivisection. The anatomical process pleases us; or, if this does not interest all, there are always for such the lively details, the stirring events, the expression of feeling, the clash of passions, accompanied by an intellectual byplay of the author's own. But the concrete characters, the persons, do not interest us much. (pp. 340-41)

Miss Brontë never deals with mere abstractions; all her people have body, reality, definiteness. But they are too singular. The greatest poets have always been those who have done the greatest things with the old every-day materials; and who have never, however special may have been their web, omitted to work up with it those threads which connect it with universal interests. Miss Brontë is apt to exclude too much common sympathies and everyday knowledge. Of many of her characters we can scarcely say whether they are truthful or not, they are so different from what we have seen, known, and experienced, either in Lancashire, Yorkshire, or elsewhere. Something Jane Eyre, and Lewis Moore, and Madame Beck, have in common with us, no doubt; but no doubt also much of the charm of Currer Bell's works, and their great popularity, is due to this very thing—the minuteness and accuracy with which she has described unfamiliar scenes and characters; and to the thorough air of novelty which pervades both her subject-matter and her treatment. But this, though the most popular of attractions, is not the most lasting. (pp. 341-42)

Another thing which adds both to the singularity and the want of permanent interest of Miss Brontë's works is, that they have a world of manners of their own. Not a soul in them is represented under the ordinary conditions of propriety of demeanour. . . . It is just in acquainting Miss Brontë with the forms of social intercourse, and the ordinary modes of expression, that observation would have been of most use as the handmaid of her genius; but the opportunity of such observation she never commanded. Her school of manners,—we use the word in its wide sense,—is an imaginary one, drawn out of her own head; a very ably drawn one it is, and admirably it is made to subserve her characters and her incidents; but it is one strange to the experience of her readers. (pp. 342-43)

In her love for the study of character, she is apt to be led too far. Her sketches, in which observation alone worked, are admirable. Her Mrs. Reeds, her Miss Temple, her Miss Marchmont, her M. Pelet, are sharp and characteristic; but in her more elaborate efforts she attempts too much. No artist can delineate the whole of the character of a human being; the most successful have been those who, having taken up their creations from a certain point of view, always look at them steadily from thence, throw the light on some side they wish to be prominent, and let the rest fade off into an obscurity which the eye of the reader rounds dimly off, partly by the aid of his own imagination. They indicate a character, and dwell on one side of it. This gives the reader peace; he has time to gather a distinct image, which gains new clearness as he gazes at it. But Miss Brontë gives him no peace, she must always see the reverse side, she is anxious if possible to see both sides at once; she is always making new discoveries in her characters, we never know when we have them. Yet, as we have before said, she never represents them in course of change, never paints development of character; and she is so absorbed with what is before her, so much taken up with the scene immediately in hand, that she is apt insensibly to mould her personages so as to suit it, and give it the highest effect. She forgets what they are, in thinking of what they are doing, and hence they are sometimes different people at different times. Jane Eyre is one person as a child, another with Mr. Rochester, and a third with the St. Johns. In *Villette*, Graham is one person, Dr. John a second, Dr. Bretton a third. Perhaps he affords the most marked instance of discontinuity of general character in all these novels, and the author herself became sensible of it. (pp. 343-44)

To eke out facts by the suggestions of imagination, or to conceal them by a varnish of fancy, is a very deceptive and unsatisfactory process. And this is what Currer Bell does with her characters. She selects either an actual living person she has seen, or collects traits of one she has not seen—generally the former, and *modifies* this person to make another. Of course,

all imagined forms must have some basis of reality, and our words may seem to import a censure on such creations as Schiller's Joan of Arc, or Kingsley's Elizabeth. In both these, and such as these, there is a very large basis of fact; but the difference between them and Mr. Yorke, and Madame Beck, lies in the fact that in one case the imagination uses the facts as materials for a new creation, in the other it is employed to modify, disguise, and fill up a real figure. Miss Brontë herself was scarcely aware how faithfully she drew from the life; but her close adherence to the matter of her own limited experience is shown by the circumstance that her pictures were recognised as portraits. Hence arose not only defects in her workmanship, but a gross infraction of social rights, and an unpardonable infringement of private confidence; to the wrongfulness of which she seems to have been singularly blind, and unhappily her biographer is equally so. It is true Miss Brontë's portraits were not exact, but this only did the greater mischief. With one single exception, perhaps, that of the picture of her sister Emily as Shirley, they certainly were not flattering; they were sufficient to identify those who were unfortunate enough to have become the subjects of her keen examination; and the variation did only the further injustice of conveying a false impression of them. (pp. 344-45)

Currer Bell's novels did not do more, however, than hang up the individuals she chose as her subjects for the comment or ridicule of those who were their immediate neighbours, and penetrating enough to discover them. . . . (p. 346)

The Professor throws no new light on the characteristics of Miss Brontë's genius; no new ground is broken. . . . Miss Brontë was a great upholder of the privileges of her sex, yet no writer in the world has ever so uniformly represented women at so great a disadvantage. They invariably fall victims to the man of strong intellect, and generally muscular frame, who lures them on with affected indifference and simulated harshness; by various ingenious trials assures himself they are worthy of him, and, when his own time has fully come, raises them with a bashaw-like air from their prostrate condition, presses them triumphantly to his heart, or seats them on his knee, as the case may be, and indulges in a condescending burst of passionate emotion. All these men are in their attachments utterly and undisguisedly selfish, and we must say we grudge them their easily won victories over the inexperienced placid little girls they lay siege to. It is not thus that generous men make their advances, or that women, worthy of the name, are won. One such case might pass; but it is Miss Brontë's standing idea of a romantic courtship.

The Professor contains some very unsparing and outspoken expressions, especially in the sketches of two or three young ladies who occupied prominent places in the Brussels school described. Miss Brontë had had no opportunity of learning what in England is considered proper to be said, and naturally, from her foreign experience, adopted some touch of continental freedom of speech. (pp. 349-50)

Charlotte Brontë's works are far from being "otherwise so entirely noble;" they have defects in abundance: but there never were books more free from the stain here so quietly assumed, and so feelingly lamented as unavoidable. Rochester does *not* talk without reticence to Jane Eyre. The writer never *did* touch pitch: she might paint it; but it was in the safety of her own innocency, and we lose patience at being told, with all this array of exculpation, that she needed "purifying." Coarse materials, indeed, she too much deals with; and her own style has something rude and uncompromising in it, not always in accordance with customary ideas of what is becoming in a female writer; but it would be scarcely possible to name a writer who, in handling such difficult subject-matter, carried the reader so safely through by the unseen guardianship and unconsciously exercised influence of her stainless purity and unblemished rectitude. The conventional proprieties of speech and subject-matter she disregards, indeed; her delicacy lost some of its bloom abroad, and she may be said with justice to want refinement; but even that is the conventional refinement rather than the real one. It has been well said, and every reader perceives it, or ought to do so, that her plain speaking is itself the result of her purity.

What she has that jars on us often in her writings is not so much these things as a certain harshness, a love of the naked fact too unsparing, and a tendency to believe that what is attractive scarcely can be true. In the school of ladylike refined writing, true in its own sphere, enlivening, softening, and elevating, which deals gently with weak mortality, and, reversing the saying which dissuades us from breaking a butterfly on a wheel, punishes vice with a knitting-needle,—which compels into courtly phrases the swelling form and native hideousness of crime, and throws over the stern precipices and gloom-shrouded abysses of life—remorse and terror and madness—frail bridges of happy fancies and spirit-consoling hopes,—in this school we have many proficients. . . . Her graceful fictions have power to beguile us, to cheer us, to instruct us; and if with too silver a voice she echoes the dread undertones of the mystery of sin and suffering and death, we remember that reality has more sides than one, that each side has its truth,—and welcome the genius which instinctively turns to that aspect where beauty predominates, and whose darkest shades are error and frailties and penitence. But Miss Brontë had a different call: her feet were rougher shod to walk through both life and art; and if she does not lead us through the dark caverns of life, at least she does not attempt to measure their depths with a silken thread, or hang pale lights of fancy in their mouths. As she passes over the lesser evils of life, she describes them in their native ruggedness; through the depths she steals, in general, in the silence of fortitude; and only now and then some brief cry of personal anguish rings sharp and sudden through the darkness. (pp. 351-52)

William Caldwell Roscoe, "The Miss Brontës," in his Poems and Essays, Vol. II, *edited by Richard Holt Hutton, Chapman and Hall, 1860, pp. 309-53.**

SUSAN M. WARING   (essay date 1866)

[The] keen, incisive reader who looks to the core of things, and who knows by instinct a creation palpitating with heart-life from one galvanized into a semblance of being, will feel that the Brontë has distilled into [Lucy Snowe in **"Villette"**] a meaning more profound and far-reaching, a pathos more personal than will readily be found within the range of modern art.

Out of the four women therefore—Jane Eyre, Shirley, Caroline Helstone, and Lucy Snowe—the essential heroines of her novels, that with a touch unrivaled for sweep, matchless for delicacy, were patiently chiseled into being by those small child-fingers which Shakspeare himself would not disdain to clasp in his majestic palm, I choose the woman—Lucy Snowe, and entreat your attention.

I choose her for several reasons. Because she has never been truly recognized by any critic; because she represents a type

of woman before unknown to the realms of novel-land; because she is most minutely informed with Charlotte Brontë's own experience, and is therefore the fittest exponent of her consummate genius. . . .

[Brontë's] intense nature had with touching patience striven to find expression through the medium of the pencil, and the pilgrim to the heaths of Haworth will find hanging upon the wall of the small stone parsonage copies of engravings wrought out line by line with minute fidelity. But the pencil proved too slow and tame—therefore she would make verses next. But poetry was with this unique nature a bird of too wild a wing to bear imprisonment in any cage of rhyme—it would break bounds and be lost in illimitable space, or dash itself to death in the endeavor.

The book **"Jane Eyre,"** therefore, was the first adequate expression of the feeling which wrestled within her, and the heart of Charlotte Brontë found in words only, uncontrolled by any rules of rhythm, the joy of expression, the right of recognition. It is therefore that **"Jane Eyre"** may not be too strictly judged, for it was an outburst, a great surging heart bursting its bounds and finding outlet for its accumulated passion.

In **"Shirley"** we have the second style, rarely apt to be the best. The author says of it, with childlike humility: "I took great pains with **'Shirley,'** I did not hurry, I tried to do my best." But weariness and watching had diminished the spontaneity of the ardent nature, the fire of inspiration burned less brightly, tears had quenched it, and its loss had yet scarcely been replaced by the serene light of that crowning grace which is the final reward of those who wrestle faithfully for great prizes. It therefore chances that **"Shirley,"** full as it is of grand philosophy and pure religion, does not awaken the sympathy so entirely, or move to such fond liking as the first-born . . . of Charlotte Brontë's genius.

"Villette" shows us the third style of the master-genius. In the Brontë case at all events it is the perfected development of ripened power. Patience has wrought her "perfect work," suffering terrible and almost unremitting fulfilled her divinest mission, and calm with the repose of power, majestic almost to austerity, yet with a trembling about the mouth which tells of tears that are ended, **"Villette"** stands upon its pedestal the master-piece of its author. . . .

In cool, quiet phrases intended to give the reader the impression that she is rather a narrator of than an actor in the scenes about to transpire, Lucy Snowe opens the book. The reader—especially if he be superficial—takes her at her word, and becomes absorbed in the quaint childhood of Polly Home, intertwining itself with the boyhood of Graham Bretton. Suddenly the *dramatis personae* are swept from the boards, and we are left alone with Lucy Snowe. . . .

The fourth chapter opens with two paragraphs which for terse bitterness and condensed description are both amazing and admirable, and these comprise all we are to know of Lucy Snowe's antecedents. (p. 368)

Lucy Snowe led two lives, the outer one neutral-tinted, divested of saliency for the "common gaze;" the other surging, yearning, wild with ungratified longings and clamorous desires for sustenance withheld.

As a foil to this struggling two-sided existence walks on the stage Miss Ginevra Fanshawe, a creature so tiny of soul, so infinitesimal of heart, that fingers possessing the microscopic delicacy of the Brontës alone could ever have taken her to bits. . . .

Lucy Snowe, starving for recognition, sympathy, affection, circumscribed to arid wastes where flowers are forbidden to bloom, sees this bit of feminity, yclept Ginevra Fanshawe, embowered in delights, fed on sweetest flatteries, the treasure of a "good man's love" laid at her feet, and all these gifts of fortune vouchsafed because this waft of thistledown possesses the—comparatively—trivial gift of beauty. In the mean time the "little man," M. Paul, careers occasionally across the field of vision—eccentric, meteoric, evoking what is best of Charlotte Brontë's humor.

This humor of hers is by no means her least peculiar and individual gift. Its irony is scathing, its sarcasm more intense than that of Thackeray, because more impulsive, less studied— an accident, and not a specialty of style—a blade keen and fine, yet wielded only when truth calls upon its earnest champion. Indeed, sincerity stamps its signet upon every word ever written by the Brontë. . . . She alone, of all [her brilliant contemporaries] is always and inevitably sincere. This humor of Brontë's is at times infiltrated by something which we can not call wit, for this quality, in its usual and superficial acceptation, she certainly had not. The diamond of wit *adamantine,* "unconquerable" as it may be, fused beneath the rays of a genius so intense, yet is it not lost. It sparkles in the quick, trenchant sentences, its white light penetrates into unexplored recesses of the heart, its vivid flashes render the opaque luminous; so that which we are wont to term wit doffs its usual garb and becomes a character of style.

This humor, however, generally kept in abeyance, or else apt to reveal itself as almost pure sarcasm, whatever its qualities on other occasions, shows all its possesses of sweet and genial whenever it is brought into contact with M. Paul. And so magical does it render the atmosphere surrounding him that of all the Brontë's creations scarce one takes the fancy more irresistibly or touches the heart more nearly than this "magnificent-minded, grand-hearted, dear, faulty little man—Paul Carlos David Emanuel." He, in common with Rochester, shares a wonderful gift—a gift that makes any man or woman great however faulty besides. I mean the power of piercing beneath surfaces, sweeping away externals and conventionalities, and estimating the soul beneath them at its intrinsic value. That this highest instinct of character, this invaluable touchstone for all things, is possessed but by the few only renders it the more precious and desirable.

Opposed to M. Paul in vivid contrast—for the Brontë had a nice eye here—Michael Angelo, Reubens, Rembrandt, no painter of them all a keener vision—is Graham Bretton, who figures in the scenes of Madame Beck's pensionnat as "Dr. John;" also, as Isidore, the lover of that "dear angel," Ginevra Fanshawe. He who is "in visage, in shape, in hue, as unlike the dark, acerb, and caustic little Professor as the fruit of the Hesperides might be unlike the sloe in the wild thicket." (p. 369)

It would seem that Charlotte Brontë had been entreated to make fate more propitious to Lucy Snowe, to which she returns answer—a sad meaning underlying the words—"From the beginning I never meant to appoint her lines in pleasant places." So she gives her a "cold name on the *lucus a non lucendo* principle, for she has about her an external coldness" and relentlessly sends her forth. But we are not to be cheated by anything "external," so we recognize the fiery soul, the exquisite power of sympathy, veiled beneath indifference, and will dearly like and fondly cherish her in spite of all.

Little Polly Home—now transformed into Paulina De Bassompierre and a countess—by means of an accident requiring the medical services of "Dr. John," reappears, and the group with which the book opens is complete. Of this "airy fairy thing" Paulina, that "pleases almost to pain," Charlotte Brontë thus speaks: "I felt that this character lacked substance; I fear the reader will feel the same."

It is true that Paulina lacks the strong flavor of our common humanity with which the rest are impregnated. But what matters it when the conception is consistent with itself from beginning to end? Does not the very daintiness and ideality of "little Polly" enhance the vivid reality of the others and throw it out in stronger relief? And does not the rose-leaf-lined existence of the little countess, side by side with the tortured life of Lucy Snowe, invest this last with a most appealing pathos? and was not this a part of the original design? (pp. 370-71)

Finally, the cobwebs of machination woven by Madame Beck and her coadjutor, Père Silas, are swept away, and we learn that Lucy Snowe loves and is loved by that "guileless Napoleon," Paul Emanuel. Not with the love "born of beauty," of which she is "sensitively jealous," but with the love that touches the most "inner springs of life."

Ere this consummation is reached, however, her hour of triumph with the reader is arrived. In the whirl of that description, showing the keen anguish of a faithful heart riven by suspense, we know that Paulina, "Dr. John," and the rest are inconsequent, and we realize at last that Lucy Snowe is the book. . . .

The wonderful tale is told, the unprecedented book, full of human nature as any play of Shakspeare's, ended. Take it, search it thoroughly, it was meant to bear close and stern inspection. Hold it in the strongest light, try it by the severest tests, and know this **"Villette"** of Charlotte Brontë's is, as far as human art can make it, a diamond without a flaw, one entire and perfect chrysolite. May no other woman ever write so well, may none other ever suffer so acutely!

I lay this flower, O Charlotte Brontë! upon the altar of your memory. I know it's scarce worthy of so high a resting-place, and that blooms richer and fairer a thousand times shall shame it there. But I claim it pure rosemary at least—the flower of loving memory, and its breath is fragrant. So whomever may disdain, your deep heart would not despise it. (p. 371)

*Susan M. Waring, "Charlotte Brontë's Lucy Snowe,"
in* Harper's New Monthly Magazine, *Vol. XXXII,
No. CLXXXIX, February, 1866, pp. 368-71.*

G. B. SMITH (essay date 1873)

The novels of Charlotte Brontë were totally dissimilar in style to all which had been previously given to the world, and their quality was not such as to be at the first moment attractive. Masculine in their strength, and very largely so in the cast of thought, there could be no wonder that the public should assume Currer Bell to be of the sterner sex, and even persist in its delusion after the most express assurance to the contrary. Certainly one can sympathise with the feeling of astonishment that *Jane Eyre* should have been written by a woman. What vigour there is in it compared with the novels of another great artist, Miss Austen! For sheer force she has even eclipsed her own chief of novel-writers, Sir Walter Scott, whilst Balzac, who, as Currer Bell said, "always left a nasty taste in her mouth," is also outstripped in the delineation of passion. Many readers were doubtless repulsed from a fair and candid perusal of the works of Charlotte Brontë by certain adverse criticisms which had pronounced them extremely coarse. . . . Faithful transcripts of the life she had witnessed they certainly were; distorted they were not. Speaking of fiction, the author of *The Curiosities of Literature* has said—''Novels, as they were long *manufactured,* form a library of illiterate authors for illiterate readers; but as they are *created* by genius, are precious to the philosopher. They paint the character of an individual or the manners of the age more perfectly than any other species of composition: it is in novels we observe, as it were passing under our own eyes, the refined frivolity of the French, the gloomy and disordered sensibility of the German; and the petty intrigues of the modern Italian in some Venetian novels.'' We accept this as a tolerably substantial appraisement of the *rôle* of the novelist; but in order to be strengthened in our opinion, let us look at what the eminent philosopher Adam Smith said of the true novelist, and surely no higher praise could be desired by our story-writers. ''The poets and romance-writers who,'' he says, ''best paint the refinements and delicacies of love and friendship, and of all other private and domestic affections, Racine and Voltaire, Richardson, Marivaux, and Riccoboni, are in this case much better instructors than Zeno, Chrysippus, or Epictetus.'' But surely we need not stay to argue here that the novel, when in the hands of a true genius, can be made one of the best instructors of the human race. It is so because there is nothing of the abstract about it—which the mind of mankind generally abhors; it is a record of the concrete existence of individuals like ourselves, and must therefore be profitable both for amusement, interest, and guidance. A good novelist can scarcely be appreciated too highly. In this class we place Charlotte Brontë; she fulfils the requirements glanced at already in the words of Mr. D'Israeli, and is in every respect a faithful delineator of the scenes and persons she professes to describe. How faithful, indeed, few can scarcely tell, but the mass can darkly feel it on close acquaintance with her. The charge of coarseness brought against her works she herself indignantly repelled, but the base notion of such a charge must have cruelly wounded her spirit, which, though strong and brave as a lion, was yet pure and tender as that of a child. . . . Mrs. Gaskell goes so far as to admit that there are passages in the writings of Currer Bell which are coarse; for ourselves, we can scarcely understand what is meant. Roughness there is, but indecency none, and coarseness seems to us to imply a little more than mere roughness. Several of the characters she has drawn are reproductions in type of the wildest natures, and the over-refined sensibilities of some readers are possibly shocked by their extreme naturalness. Charlotte Brontë simply thought of painting them as they appeared, never thinking for a moment there could be harm in laying in deep shadows where deep shadows were required. Fielding was coarse, Wycherley and some of the other dramatists more so, but their examples show that coarseness is an unfortunate epithet to apply to the writings of Currer Bell. If applicable to them, it is totally inapplicable to her. Her coarseness—if such quality exist at all—was undetachable from her subjects. She would have ceased to be the true delineator and the real artist she aspired to be, had she swerved from the outlines of character she undertook to fill in. In truth, we need only turn to *Shirley* and *Jane Eyre* to prove the position that Charlotte Brontë was far beyond the common novelist. In the former story we have characters which for sweetness have been rarely excelled, whilst in the latter we have a Jupiter of rugged strength and passion. The novelist has power to go out of herself—that attribute of the great artist. It is genius which impels, and she must obey. If the characters are occasionally coarse, she is unconscious of it; she is only

aware of their truth. No need for her to lop off the distorted branches in the human forest of her delineations in order to secure a level growth of mediocrity. She could not if she would, and is too intent on the manifestations of nature to do so if she could. Such creations as please the ordinary romance-monger would be an abhorrence to her; it is because she exalted Art that she could not depart from the True, with which the former, when real, is ever in unison. (pp. 57-9)

[*The Professor*] exhibits a great amount of conscious power, but also an inability on the part of the writer to give herself free scope. A comparison between this and succeeding works will show how she was cramped in its composition. The story is good, nevertheless, though numerous publishers to whom it was submitted decided otherwise. . . . [The] novel-readers of the day demanded something which should exhibit more of the romantic and the heroic. Battling well, however, with materials which were in the outset obstructive, Currer Bell achieved a substantial success. . . . There is much in the work which is characteristic of its author as she appears in her later novels, and the drawing of at least one of the characters, Mr. Hunsden, is masterly. Some of the materials, we are told, were afterwards used in *Villette;* but if so they are carefully disguised, and the world could very well afford to welcome the two. Passages occur in *The Professor* which are almost startling in their strength of passion and eloquence, and which alone would have given to Currer Bell the stamp of originality. All the toilsome way by which the person who gives the title to the volume is led, is marked by the intensest sympathy on the part of the author, and although the reader may not be able to feel much personal enthusiasm in the various characters, he must at once yield the point that he is perusing the thoughts of no common mind. The valuable knowledge which the author acquired abroad is utilised with considerable skill, whilst she is equally at home when she comes to delineate the Yorkshire family of the Crimsworths. Her ideas of love and marriage, afterwards so fully developed in her other novels, are here touched upon. . . . Love without the union of souls, the author again and again insists, is a delusion, the sheen of a summer's day, and quite as fleeting. Altogether the idea of *The Professor* was new, and as an indication of the grooves in which its author's genius was afterwards to run, we would not willingly have lost it. As a psychological study alone it was well worthy of preservation.

But better and more remarkable works followed. The reading world has very seldom been startled by such a genuine and powerful piece of originality as *Jane Eyre*. . . . *Jane Eyre* is an autobiography, and its intention is to present a plain, unbiassed narrative of a woman's life from its commencement to a period when it is supposed to have ceased to possess interest to mankind generally. It is told fearlessly, and with a burning pen. But there is no *suppressio veri;* that, its author would have scorned: perhaps it would have been better for its reception in some quarters—limited in range we are happy to think—if the narrator of the story had glossed over some portions of her heroine's history. She has chosen, however, to adhere to stern reality, and there it is finally for us, unpleasant and rough though it be in some of its recorded experiences. The book shows the most opposite qualities—light, darkness; beauty, deformity; strength, tenderness. Its pathos is of the finest quality, stirring most deeply because it is simple and unforced. The situations are very vivid; several scenes being depicted which it would be impossible to eradicate from the memory after the most extensive reading of serial literature. Even those who regard it as coarse must admit its strange fascination. . . . Although chiefly remarkable for its prominent delineation of the passion of love is strong and impulsive natures, there are many other points which are noticeable about it, and should therefore be mentioned. The keen observation of the writer is manifest on almost every page. Intense realism is its chief characteristic. The pictures are as vivid and bold as though etched by a Rembrandt, or drawn by a Salvator Rosa. Dickens has been almost equalled by the description of the school at Lowood, to which Miss Eyre was sent, and which might well be described as Dothegirls' Hall. . . . As the story progresses it becomes most thrilling, and we are introduced to a character which is frequently regarded, and not without reason, as Currer Bell's masterpiece of powerful drawing, viz. Mr. Rochester. Strong and yet weak, a very thunderbolt for strength and explosiveness, and yet a bundle of ordinary human weaknesses, this individual stands forth as real and living a portrait as is to be found existing in word-painting. (pp. 59-62)

There can be no doubt that the first and greatest cause of the extreme vividness of the writings of Charlotte Brontë . . . is the fact that most of the characters depicted are as faithful copies from real life as though an artist had sat down and limned their features. More so: for the artist has nothing to do with psychological characteristics, which, in the case of the [author, is] as accurately described as the features. Having fixed upon [her] subjects for analysis, [she] clung to them like a shadow or a second self, and the very isolation by which [she was] surrounded lent strength to [her] conceptions. The characters are true to their respective natures, and their final ends are fearlessly worked out. Having spoken of the book which made the fame of Charlotte Brontë, let us glance at her next most important work, and the one which we like best of all—*Shirley*. It opens with a chapter in which a vein of humour unsuspected in Charlotte Brontë is manifested, and we know of no other author whose sketches so much remind us of George Eliot as this delineation of the three curates. The writer has completely unbent, relaxed from the severity which so greatly predominates in her other works, and given play to a quiet and yet quaint drollery which is positively irresistible. A little further on, however, we come to more serious business; and the terrible machinery riots which so disastrously retarded commercial progress at the period at which this history is fixed, afford excellent scope for those graphic descriptions in which Currer Bell stands almost unrivalled. . . . Though the book is singularly strong in individualities, there is, further, more general merit in its writing. Its scenic effects are beautiful; the deep love of nature which possessed the soul of Currer Bell is more observable here than elsewhere. It is what we should describe as a novel good "all round." It has no weak side; it is the most perfect piece of writing the author has left behind her. There is not the terrible sweep of passion we see in *Jane Eyre;* the roughnesses of life are smoothed down a little, and it seems altogether more humanised and humanising. The most opposite events are touched upon skilfully. . . . A little further on we get another sample of power, occurring in the description of a female character. "Nature made her in the mood in which she makes her briars and thorns; whereas for the creation of some women she reserves the May morning hours, when with light and dew she wooes the primrose from the turf, and the lily from the woodmoss." Again, we find in this novel that although Currer Bell was not a great poetess through the usual medium of measured cadence, she could write fine, genuine poetry in a prose setting. (pp. 62-4)

To the ordinary English reader [*Villette*] is probably the most uninteresting of all the works of Miss Brontë, as page after page is composed mostly of French, and that sometimes dif-

ficult and idiomatic. This doubtless operated to some extent against its popularity with the mass of novel-readers, though the book seems to have earned the most lavish encomiums from the critics. It exhibits, however, the genius neither of *Jane Eyre* nor of *Shirley*: it is, in truth, superior to the fiction of ninety per cent of novelists, but it scarcely warranted the extravagant terms of praise which were showered upon it by the reviewers. These valuable individuals, however, were, as is too often the case unfortunately, wise after the event—that is, they found it tolerably safe to eulogise a new work from the hand of one who had already established her position as amongst the most original writers of the age. One or two of the *dramatis personae* evoke sentiments of approval on account of their originality, conspicuous amongst them being Mr. Paul Emanuel and Miss de Bassompierre; but on the whole, the book is disappointing, for there is no one character whose fortunes we are anxious to follow; and a novel which fails to beget a personal interest must be said to have lost its chief charm. (p. 65)

[Whilst] Charlotte Brontë infinitely eclipses novelists of the highest reputation in isolated qualities—such as those we have already endeavoured to point out—it must be confessed that when we speak of her as the artist it cannot be as pertaining to the very highest rank. Her genius is intense, but not broad, and it is breadth alone which distinguishes the loftiest minds. But if she fails to attain the standard of the few writers who have been uplifted by common consent to the highest pinnacle of fame, she is the equal of any authors of the second rank. It is not too much to predict, in fact, that many meretricious works which have been commended for public admiration will lose in popularity, while those of which we have been speaking will increase. It is impossible for two of the works of Charlotte Brontë to fall out of our literature. They have been stamped as genuine gold and will keep continually in circulation. Works which fail to pass this ordeal are those which are either weak or false; these are both strong and true. We obtain from the author of *Jane Eyre* no multitude of characters, but those we do get we become closely familiar with—and one being of veritable flesh and blood is worth a thousand insubstantial imitations. The novels deal with no particular forms of religious belief, or social questions, which the author would doubtless but have regarded as accidents of which she cared to take no account; and hence we may affirm that after the lapse of fifty years her works would read as freshly as when they first made their appearance. It was humanity she strove to produce; not its creeds, crotchets, or peculiarities; and it is for this reason that the labour will triumphantly stand the test of time. The inner life of a soul is very much the same in all ages. Its hopes, its fears, and its joys do not change with the changing seasons and the revolving years. Ages pass away, and those writers and writings which have only appealed to transient phases of thought or particular changes of society are swept away as by a resistless current, whilst those who defy the potency of the waves are the gifted few who have shown the genuine power of interpreting nature, or of dealing with the passions of the human heart. (pp. 70-1)

> *G. B. Smith, "The Brontës," in* The Cornhill Magazine, *Vol. XXVIII, No. 164, July, 1873, pp. 54-71.**

[LESLIE STEPHEN]   (essay date 1877)

[The comparative eclipse]—if eclipse there be—of Charlotte Brontë's fame does not imply want of power, but want of comprehensiveness. There is a certain *primâ facie* presumption against a writer who appeals only to a few, though it may be amply rebutted by showing that the few are also fit. The two problems must go together; why is the charm so powerful, and why is it so limited? Any intense personality has so far a kind of double-edged influence. (p. 724)

Miss Brontë, as her warmest admirers would grant, was not and did not in the least affect to be a philosophical thinker. And because a great writer, to whom she has been gratuitously compared, is strong just where she is weak, her friends have an injudicious desire to make out that the matter is of no importance, and that her comparative poverty of thought is no injury to her work. There is no difficulty in following them so far as to admit that her work is none the worse for containing no theological or philosophical disquisitions, or for showing no familiarity with the technicalities of modern science and metaphysics. But the admission by no means follows that her work does not suffer very materially by the comparative narrowness of the circle of ideas in which her mind habitually revolved. Perhaps if she had been familiar with Hegel or Sir W. Hamilton, she would have intruded undigested lumps of metaphysics, and introduced vexatious allusions to the philosophy of identity or to the principle of the excluded middle. But it is possible, also, that her conceptions of life and the world would have been enriched and harmonised, and that, without giving us more scientific dogmas, her characters would have embodied more fully the dominating ideas of the time. There is no province of inquiry—historical, scientific, or philosophical—from which the artist may not derive useful material; the sole question is whether it has been properly assimilated and transformed by the action of the poetic imagination. By attempting to define how far Miss Brontë's powers were in fact thus bounded, we shall approximately decide her place in the great hierarchy of imaginative thinkers. That it was a very high one, I take to be undeniable. Putting aside living writers, the only female novelist whom one can put distinctly above her is George Sand; for Miss Austen, whom some fanatics place upon a still higher level, differs so widely in every way that "comparison" is absurd. It is almost silly to draw a parallel between writers when every great quality in one is "conspicuous by its absence" in the other.

The most obvious of all remarks about Miss Brontë is the close connection between her life and her writings. Nobody ever put so much of themselves into their work. She is the heroine of her two most powerful novels; for Lucy Snowe is avowedly her own likeness, and Lucy Snowe differs only by accidents from Jane Eyre; whilst her sister is the heroine of the third. All the minor characters, with scarcely an exception, are simply portraits, and the more successful in proportion to their fidelity. The scenery and even the incidents are, for the most part, equally direct transcripts from reality. And, as this is almost too palpable a peculiarity to be expressly mentioned, it seems to be an identical proposition that the study of her life is the study of her novels. More or less true of all imaginable writers, this must be pre-eminently true of Miss Brontë. Her experience, we would say, has been scarcely transformed in passing through her mind. She has written down not only her feelings, but the more superficial accidents of her life. She has simply given fictitious names and dates, with a more or less imaginary thread of narrative, to her own experience at school, as a governess, at home and in Brussels. *Shirley* contains a continuous series of photographs of Haworth and its neighbourhood; as *Villette* does of Brussels: and if *Jane Eyre* is not so literal, except in the opening account of the school-life, much of it is almost as strictly autobiographical. . . . The amazing vividness of her

portrait-painting is the quality which more than any other makes her work unique amongst modern fiction. Her realism is something peculiar to herself; and only the crudest of critics would depreciate its merits on the ground of its fidelity to facts. The hardest of all feats is to see what is before our eyes. What is called the creative power of genius is much more the power of insight into commonplace things and characters. . . . The specific peculiarity of Miss Brontë seems to be the power of revealing to us the potentiality of intense passions lurking behind the scenery of everyday life. Except in the most melodramatic—which is also the weakest—part of *Jane Eyre,* we have lives almost as uneventful as those of Miss Austen, and yet charged to the utmost with latent power. . . . [Miss Brontë] may display characters capable of shaking empires and discovering new worlds. The whole machinery is in a state of the highest electric tension, though there is no display of thunder and lightning to amaze us.

The power of producing this effect without stepping one hand's-breadth beyond the most literal and unmistakable fidelity to ordinary facts is explicable, one would say, so far as genius is explicable at all, only in one way. A mind of extraordinary activity within a narrow sphere has been brooding constantly upon a small stock of materials, and a sensitive nature has been enforced to an unusual pressure from the hard facts of life. The surroundings must surely have been exceptional, and the receptive faculties impressible even to morbidness, to produce so startling a result. . . . It is one more exemplification of the common theory, that great art is produced by taking an exceptionally delicate nature and mangling it slowly under the grinding wheels of the world. (pp. 725-28)

Miss Brontë, with all her genius, was still a young lady. Her mind, with its exceptional powers in certain directions, never broke the fetters by which the parson's daughter of the last generation was restricted. Trifling indications of this are common in her novels. The idealised portrait of Emily, the daring and unconventional Shirley, shows her utmost courage by hinting a slight reluctance to repeat certain clauses in the Athanasian Creed; and the energy with which the unlucky curates are satirised shows the state of mind to which even a young clergyman is still invested with more or less superhuman attributes. . . . And, in the next place, it seems that, even in writing to her best friends, Miss Brontë habitually dreaded any vivid expression of feeling, and perhaps observed that her sentiments when spread upon letter-paper had a morbid appearance. There are many people who can confide in the public more freely than in the most intimate friends. The mask of anonymous authorship and fictitious personages has a delusive appearance of security. The most sacred emotions are for ourselves or for the invisible public rather than for the intermediate sphere of concrete spectators. (p. 729)

Miss Brontë has as little sense of humour as Milton or Wordsworth; but her nearest approach to it is in some of those shrewd, bitter sayings which are rather more of a gibe than a compliment. When one remembers that the originals of the Yorkes [in *The Professor*] were amongst her most cherished and cultivated friends, and that they are admittedly painted to the life, one may fancy that she had received a good many of those left-handed compliments which seem to have done duty for pleasant jests in the district.

The soliloquies in which her heroines indulge proceed upon the same plan. Jane Eyre sits in judgment upon herself, and listens to the evidence of Memory and Reason, accusing her of rejecting the real and "rabidly devouring the ideal." And she decides in accordance with her witnesses. "Listen, Jane Eyre, to your sentence; to-morrow place the glass before you and draw in chalk your own picture, faithfully, without softening one defect; omit no harsh line; smooth away no displeasing irregularity: write under it, 'Portrait of a governess, disconnected, poor, and plain!'"

Similar passages occur in *Shirley* and *Villette,* and obviously represent a familiar mood. The original of this portrait was frequently engaged, it would seem, in forcing herself to hear such unpalatable truths. When other people snubbed her, after the fashion of the Yorkes, she might be vexed by their harshness, but her own thoughts echoed their opinion. Lucy Snowe is rather gratified than otherwise when Miss Fanshawe treats her to one of these pleasing fits of frank thinking aloud. She pardons the want of feeling for the sake of the honesty. (pp. 730-31)

[Paul Emanuel of *Villette* has been compared] with the famous heroes of fiction, Don Quixote, Uncle Toby, and Colonel Newcome. Don Quixote admittedly stands apart as one of the greatest creations of poetic imagination. Of Colonel Newcome I will not speak; but the comparison with Uncle Toby is enough to suggest what is the great secret both of Miss Brontë's success and its limitations. In one sense Paul Emanuel is superior even to such characters as these. He is more real: he is so real that we feel at once that he must have been drawn from a living model, though we may leave some indefinable margin of idealisation. If the merit of fiction were simply its approach to producing illusion, we might infer that Paul Emanuel was one of the first characters in the world of fiction. But such a test implies an erroneous theory of art; and, in fact, the intense individuality of Paul Emanuel is, in a different sense, the most serious objection to him. He is a real human being who gave lectures at a particular date in a *pension* at Brussels. We are as much convinced of that fact as we are of the reality of Miss Brontë herself; but the fact is also a presumption that he is not one of those great typical characters, the creation of which is the highest triumph of the dramatist or novelist. There is too much of the temporary and accidental—too little of the permanent and essential. (p. 733)

The most obvious contrast is that M. Emanuel is no humourist himself, nor even a product of humour. The imperfections, the lovable absurdities, of Uncle Toby are imbedded in the structure of character. His whims and oddities always leave us in the appropriate mood of blended smiles and tears. Many people, especially "earnest" young ladies, will prefer M. Paul Emanuel, who, like his creator, is always in deadly earnest. At bottom he is always (like all ladies' heroes) a true woman, simple, pure, heroic, and loving—a real Joan of Arc. . . . He attaches extravagant importance to trifles, indeed, for his irascible and impetuous temperament is always converting him into an Æolus of the duck-pond. So far there is, we may admit, a kind of pseudo-humorous element in his composition; but the humour, such as it is, lies entirely on the surface. He is perfectly sane and sensible, though a trifle choleric. Give him a larger sphere of action, and his impetuosity will be imposing instead of absurd. It is the mere accident of situation which gives, even for a moment, a ludicrous tinge to his proceedings. (p. 734)

Now M. Paul Emanuel, admirable and amiable as he is, never carries us into the higher regions of thought. We are told, even ostentatiously, of the narrow prejudices which he shares, though they do not make him harsh and uncharitable. The prejudices were obvious in this case to the creator, because her own

happened to be of a different kind. The "Tory and clergyman's daughter" was rather puzzled by finding that a bigoted Papist with a Jesuit education might still be a good man, and points out conscientiously the defects which she ascribes to his early training. But the mere fact of the narrowness, the want of familiarity with a wider sphere of thought, the acceptance of a narrow code of belief and morality, does not strike her as in itself having either a comic or a melancholy side. M. Paul has the wrong set of prejudices, but is not as wrong as prejudiced; and therefore we feel that a Sterne, or, say, a George Sand, whilst doing equal justice to M. Emanuel's excellent qualities, would have had a feeling (which in her was altogether wanting) of his limitation and his incongruity with the great system of the world. Seen from an intellectual point of view, placed in his due relation to the great currents of thought and feeling of the time, we should have been made to feel the pathetic and humorous aspects of M. Emanuel's character, and he might have been equally a living individual and yet a type of some more general idea. The philosopher might ask, for example, what is the exact value of unselfish heroism guided by narrow theories or employed on unworthy tasks; and the philosophic humourist or artist might embody the answer in a portrait of M. Emanuel considered from a cosmic or a cosmopolitan point of view. From the lower standpoint accessible to Miss Brontë he is still most attractive; but we see only his relations to the little scholastic circle, and have no such perception as the greatest writers would give us of his relations to the universe, or, as the next order would give, of his relations to the great world without.

Although the secret of Miss Brontë's power lies, to a great extent, in the singular force with which she can reproduce acute observations of character from without, her most esoteric teaching, the most accurate reflex from her familiar idiosyncrasy, is of course to be found in the characters painted from within. We may infer her personality more or less accurately from the mode in which she contemplates her neighbours, but it is directly manifested in various avatars of her own spirit. Among the characters who are more or less mouthpieces of her peculiar sentiment we may reckon not only Lucy Snowe and Jane Eyre, but, to some extent, Shirley, and, even more decidedly, Rochester. When they speak we are really listening to her own voice, though it is more or less disguised in conformity to dramatic necessity. There are great differences between them; but they are such differences as would exist between members of the same family, or might be explained by change of health or internal circumstances. Jane Eyre has not had such bitter experience as Lucy Snowe; Shirley is generally Jane Eyre in high spirits, and freed from harassing anxiety; and Rochester is really a spirited sister of Shirley's, though he does his very best to be a man, and even an unusually masculine specimen of his sex.

Mr. Rochester, indeed, has imposed upon a good many people; and he is probably responsible in part for some of the muscular heroes who have appeared since his time in the world of fiction. I must, however, admit that, in spite of some opposing authority, he does not appear to me to be a real character at all, except as a reflection of a certain side of his creator. He is in reality the personification of a true woman's longing (may one say it now?) for a strong master. But the knowledge is wanting. He is a very bold but necessarily unsuccessful attempt at an impossibility. The parson's daughter did not really know anything about the class of which he is supposed to be a type, and he remains vague and inconsistent in spite of all his vigour. He is intended to be a person who has surfeited from the fruit of the tree of knowledge, and addresses the inexperienced governess from the height—or depth—of his worldly wisdom. And he really knows just as little of the world as she does. . . . There is not a trace of real cynicism—of the strong nature turned sour by experience—in his whole conversation. He is supposed to be specially simple and masculine, and yet he is as self-conscious as a young lady on her first appearance in society, and can do nothing but discourse about his feelings, and his looks, and his phrenological symptoms, to his admiring hearer. Set him beside any man's character of a man, and one feels at once that he has no real solidity or vitality in him. He has, of course, strong nerves and muscles, but they are articles which can be supplied in unlimited quantities with little expense to the imagination. (pp. 734-36)

This is by far the worst blot in Miss Brontë's work, and may partly explain, though it cannot justify, the harsh criticisms made at the time. It is easy now to win a cheap reputation for generosity by trampling upon the dead bodies of the luckless critics who blundered so hopelessly. The time for anger is past; and mere oblivion is the fittest doom for such offenders. Inexperience, and consequently inadequate appreciation of the demands of the situation, was Miss Brontë's chief fault in this matter, and most certainly not any want of true purity and moral elevation. But the fact that she, in whom an instinctive nobility of spirit is, perhaps, the most marked characteristic, should have given scandal to the respectable, is suggestive of another inference. What, in fact, is the true significance of this singular strain of thought and feeling, which puts on various and yet closely allied forms in the three remarkable novels we have been considering? It displays itself at one moment in some vivid description, or—for "description" seems too faint a word—some forcible presentation to our mind's eye of a fragment of moorland scenery; at another, it appears as an ardently sympathetic portrayal of some trait of character at once vigorous and tender; then it utters itself in a passionate soliloquy, which establishes the fact that its author possessed the proverbial claim to knowledge of the heavenly powers; or again, it produces one of those singular little prose-poems—such as Shirley's description of Eve—which, with all their force, have just enough flavour of the "devoirs" at M. Heger's establishment to suggest that they are the work of an inspired school-girl. To gather up into a single formula the meaning of such a character as Lucy Snowe, or in other words, of Charlotte Brontë, is, of course, impossible. But at least such utterances always give us the impression of a fiery soul and imprisoned in too narrow and too frail a tenement. The fire is pure and intense. It is kindled in a nature intensely emotional, and yet aided by a heroic sense of duty. The imprisonment is not merely that of a feeble body in uncongenial regions, but that of a narrow circle of thought, and consequently of a mind which has never worked itself clear by reflection, or developed a harmonious and consistent view of life. There is a certain feverish disquiet which is marked by the peculiar mannerism of the style. At its best, we have admirable flashes of vivid expression, where the material of language is the incarnation of keen intuitive thought. At its worst, it is strangely contorted, crowded by rather awkward personifications, and degenerates towards a rather unpleasant Ossianesque. More severity of taste would increase the power by restraining the abuse. We feel an aspiration after more than can be accomplished, an unsatisfied yearning for potent excitement, which is sometimes more fretful than forcible.

The symptoms are significant of the pervading flaw in otherwise most effective workmanship. They imply what, in a sci-

entific sense, would be an inconsistent theory, and, in an aesthetic sense, an inharmonious representation of life. One great aim of the writing, explained in the preface to the second edition of *Jane Eyre,* is a protest against conventionality. But the protest is combined with a most unflinching adherence to the proper conventions of society; and we are left in great doubt as to where the line ought to be drawn. Where does the unlawful pressure of society upon the individual begin, and what are the demands which it may rightfully make upon our respect? At one moment in *Jane Eyre* we seem to be drifting towards the solution that strong passion is the one really good thing in the world, and that all human conventions which oppose it should be disregarded. This was the tendency which shocked the respectable reviewers of the time. Of course they should have seen that the strongest sympathy of the author goes with the heroic self-conquest of the heroine under temptation. She triumphs at the cost of a determined self-sacrifice, and undoubtedly we are meant to sympathise with the martyr. Yet it is also true that we are left with the sense of an unsolved discord. Sheer stoical regard for duty is represented as something repulsive, however imposing, in the figure of St. John Rivers; and virtue is rewarded by the arbitrary removal of the obstacles which made it unpleasant. What would Jane Eyre have done, and what would our sympathies have been, had she found that Mrs. Rochester had not been burnt in the fire at Thornfield? That is rather an awkward question. Duty is supreme, seems to be the moral of the story; but duty sometimes involves a strain almost too hard for mortal faculties.

If in the conflict between duty and passion, the good so often borders upon the impracticable, the greatest blessing in the world should be a will powerful enough to be an inflexible law for itself under all pressure of circumstances. Even a will directed to evil purposes has a kind of royal prerogative, and we may rightly do it homage. . . . Charlotte's mode of conceiving the problem is given most fully in *Villette,* the book of which one can hardly say, with a recent critic, that it represents her "ripest wisdom," but which seems to give her best solution of the great problem of life. Wisdom, in fact, is not the word to apply to a state of mind which seems to be radically inconsistent and tentative. The spontaneous and intense affection of kindred and noble natures is the one really precious thing in life, it seems to say; and, so far, the thought is true or a partial aspect of the truth, and the high feeling undeniable. But then, the author seems to add, such happiness is all but chimerical. It falls to the lot only of a few exceptional people, upon whom fortune or Providence has delighted to shower its gifts. . . . Mortify your affections, scourge yourself with rods, and sit in sackcloth and ashes; stamp vigorously upon the cruel thorns that strew your pathway, and learn not to shrink when they lacerate the most tender flesh. Be an ascetic, in brief, and yet without the true aim of the ascetic. For, unlike him, you must admit that these affections are precisely the best part of you, and that the offers of the Church, which proposes to wean you from the world, and reward you by a loftier prize, are a delusion and a snare. They are the lessons of a designing priesthood, and imply a blasphemy against the most divine instincts of human nature.

This is the unhappy discord which runs through Miss Brontë's conceptions of life, and, whilst it gives an indescribable pathos to many pages, leaves us with a sense of something morbid and unsatisfactory. She seems to be turning for relief alternately to different teachers, to the promptings of her own heart, to the precepts of those whom she has been taught to revere, and occasionally, though timidly and tentatively, to alien schools of thought. The attitude of mind is, indeed, best indicated by the story (a true story, like most of her incidents) of her visit to the confessional in Brussels. Had she been a Catholic, or a Positivist, or a rebel against all the creeds, she might have reached some consistency of doctrine, and therefore some harmony of design. As it is, she seems to be under a desire which makes her restless and unhappy, because her best impulses are continually warring against each other. She is between the opposite poles of duty and happiness, and cannot see how to reconcile their claims, or even—for perhaps no one can solve that, or any other great problem exhaustively—how distinctly to state the question at issue. She pursues one path energetically, till she feels her self to be in danger, and then shrinks with a kind of instinctive dread, and resolves not only that life is a mystery, but that happiness must be sought by courting misery. Undoubtedly such a position speaks of a mind diseased, and a more powerful intellect would even under her conditions have worked out some more comprehensible and harmonious solution.

For us, however, it is allowable to interpret her complaints in our own fashion, whatever it may be. We may give our own answer to the dark problem, or at least indicate the path by which an answer must be reached. For a poor soul so grievously beset within and without by troubles in which we all have a share, we can but feel the strongest sympathy. We cannot sit at her feet as a great teacher, nor admit that her view of life is satisfactory or even intelligible. But we feel for her as for a fellow-sufferer who has at least felt with extraordinary keenness the sorrows and disappointments which torture most cruelly the most noble virtues, and has clung throughout her troubles to beliefs which must in some form or other be the guiding lights of all worthy actions. She is not in the highest rank amongst those who have fought their way to a clearer atmosphere, and can help us to clearer conceptions; but she is amongst the first of those who have felt the necessity of consolation, and therefore stimulated to more successful efforts. (pp. 736-39)

> [Leslie Stephen,] *"Hours in a Library: Charlotte Brontë," in* The Cornhill Magazine, *Vol. XXXVI, No. 216, December, 1877, pp. 723-39.*

GEORGE SAINTSBURY   (essay date 1896)

Perhaps the most interesting way of looking at Charlotte Brontë, who, as has been said, has been violently attacked, and who has also been extravagantly praised (though not so extravagantly as her sister Emily), is to look at her in the light of a precursor or transition-novelist, representing the time when the followers of Scott had wearied the public with second-rate romances, when Thackeray had not arisen, or had only just arisen, and when the modern domestic novel in its various kinds, from the religious to the problematic, was for the most part in embryo, or in very early stages. [*Shirley*] she in fact anticipated in many of its kinds, and partly to the fact of this anticipation, partly to the vividness which her representation of personal experiences gave to her work, may the popularity which it at first had, and such of it as has survived, be assigned. In this latter point, however, lay danger as well as safety. It seems very improbable that if Charlotte Brontë had lived, and if she had continued to write, her stock of experiences would have sufficed her; and it would not appear that she had much else. She is indeed credited with inventing the "ugly hero" in the Mr. Rochester of *Jane Eyre,* but in the long-run ugliness palls almost as much as beauty, perhaps sooner. Except in

touches probably due to suggestions from Emily, the "weirdness" of the younger sister was not exhibited by the elder. The more melodramatic parts of the book would not have borne repetition, and its main appeal now lies in the Lowood scenes and the character of Jane herself, which are both admittedly autobiographical. So also Shirley is her sister Emily . . . , and *Villette* is little more than an embroidered version of the Brussels sojourn. How successful an appeal of this kind is, the experience of Byron and many others has shown; how dangerous it is, could not be better shown than by the same experience. It was Charlotte Brontë's good fortune that she died before she had utterly exhausted her vein, though those who fail to regard Paul Emanuel with the affection which he seems to inspire in some, may think that she went perilously near it. But fate was kind to her: some interesting biographies and brilliant essays at different periods have revived and championed her fame: and her books—at least *Jane Eyre* almost as a whole and parts of the others—will always be simply interesting to the novel-reader, and interesting in a more indirect fashion to the critic. For this last will perceive that, thin and crude as they are, they are original, they belong to their own present and future, not to their past, and that so they hold in the history of literature a greater place than many books of greater accomplishment which are simply worked on already projected and accepted lines. (pp. 319-20)

> *George Saintsbury, "The Novel Since 1850," in his* A History of Nineteenth Century Literature (1780-1895) *(copyright 1896; reprinted by permission of Macmillan, London and Basingstoke), Macmillan, 1896, pp. 317-41.**

WILLIAM DEAN HOWELLS   (essay date 1900)

[No] heroine of Thackeray's except Becky Sharp seems to me quite so alive as the Jane Eyre of Charlotte Brontë, whom I do not class with him intellectually, any more than I class her artistically with the great novelists. . . . She was the first English novelist to present the impassioned heroine; impassioned not in man's sense but woman's sense, in which love purifies itself of sensuousness without losing fervor.

From the beginning to the ending of her story, Jane Eyre moves a living and consistent soul; from the child we know grow the girl and woman we know, vivid, energic, passionate, as well as good, conscientious, devoted. It was a figure which might well have astonished and alarmed the little fastidious world of fifty years ago, far more smug and complacent than the larger world of to-day, and far more intolerant of any question of religious or social convention; and it is no wonder that the young author should have been attainted of immorality and infidelity, not to name that blacker crime, impropriety. In fact it must be allowed that **"Jane Eyre"** does go rather far in a region where women's imaginations are politely supposed not to wander; and the frank recognition of the rights of love as love, and its claims in Rochester as paramount to those of righteous self-will in St. John, is still a little startling. It is never pretended that Rochester is a good man, or that he is in any accepted sense worthy of the girl who listens so fearlessly to his account of the dubious life he has led. The most that can be said for him is that he truly values and loves her, and this is his best, his sole defence in his attempt to marry her while he still has a wife living under his own roof, a hopeless and horrible maniac. When the attempt is frustrated at the altar, and nothing remains for Jane Eyre but to be his on the only possible terms, or to fly, it is not feigned that she is not for a moment tempted. She loves him and she *is* tempted, but only for a moment, and then she chooses the right, owning that the wrong has allured her, with a courage that was once very novel, but without a suggestion of the pruriency which has often characterized later fiction (especially the fiction of women) in dealing with like situations.

In this as in other essentials **"Jane Eyre"** is unsparingly human, and when Jane has got away from Rochester, and finds herself unexpectedly among her kindred, and even rich and independent, she does not prefer a loveless marriage, hallowed by the most exalted motives, with her cousin St. John, but elects rather to go back and seek out the man she loves, and when she has found him opportunely widowed by the disaster that has maimed and blinded him, to marry him. She offers no defence, and one must confess that the close of the story is not ideal. No part of the story, in fact, is so good as the beginning, where the hapless little orphan substantiates herself to us in the hard keeping of her cruel aunt and cousins; and in my second reading of the novel I have not been so much moved by the love-making between Jane and Rochester as I must have been when I first read it fifty years ago. (pp. 2096-2098)

Old-fashioned, I have suggested; but now, after reading [the scene in which Rochester's mad wife makes her first appearance], I find that hardly the word. It is old-fashioned only in the sense of being very simple, and of a quaint sincerity. The fact is presented, the tremendous means are used, with almost childlike artlessness; but the result is of high novelty. Few would have had the courage to deal so frankly with the situation, to chance its turning ludicrous, or would have had the skill to unfold its fine implications of tenderness, and keep them undamaged by the matter-of-fact details. But Charlotte Brontë did all this, and did it out of the resources of her own unique experience of life, which never presented itself in the light of common day, but came to her through strange glooms, and in alternations of native solitude and alien multitude, at Haworth and in Brussels. The whole story, so deeply of nature, is steeped in the supernatural; and just as paradoxically the character of Jane Eyre lacks that final projection from the author which is the supreme effect of art, only because she feels it so intensely that she cannot detach it from herself. (p. 2100)

William Dean Howells, "Heroines of Nineteenth-Century Fiction," in Harper's Bazaar, *Vol. XXXIII, No. 50, December 15, 1900, pp. 2094-100.**

AUGUSTUS RALLI   (essay date 1913)

[*The Professor,*] in spite of its many rejections and tardy birth, is a book that still gives pleasure to read, independent of its mighty successors. It sounds no great depth of human character, and is not fervid with passion; but it is not exclusively the chrysalis whence emerged in later years the brilliant butterfly of *Villette*. Except passion, we have all the constituents of the style that subsequently underwent development rather than change; but the faults of construction, never entirely eliminated, are at their worst. The interest is well sustained because of the writer's sincerity, but threads are dropped and resumed at random, contrasts, as between Crimsworth and his brutal brother, are too glaring, and the episodes are out of proportion. The surroundings of X—(Huddersfield) and Crimsworth Hall are so admirably depicted that we are loth to part with them for good in the course of a few pages; and although incidents succeed without pause, they do not at once dissipate the regrets in the reader's mind. The theme is one that Charlotte Brontë

was afterwards to treat with greater power: that of an individual without friends or fortune who must fight his way to happiness through a hostile world. But the interest centres less in individual character than in the contrast of the Belgian type with the English, and the observation of Belgian school life through English eyes. It is the writer's conviction of the truth of this observation that gives the book its permanent value. (p. 526)

In *Jane Eyre* the quality of passion appears. In the *Professor* the words returned no echoes, the interval between the striking of the notes was not filled by the pedal-music of passion. There was the same difference as between the classical school of Pope and the romantic school of Wordsworth. In one the object is seen clearly against a clean sky; in the other it is transfigured by haze or cloud or distance. In the first there is beauty; in the second, beauty and strangeness.

This quality of strangeness springs from the union of passion and imagination, which transfigure the ordinary scenes of life, and we listen to her in gathering awe as to the traveller from whose lips fall tidings of unknown lands. In a book such as the *Pilgrim's Progress* our fear is of the burning pit; in the *Faerie Queene* of dragons and enchanters; but in *Jane Eyre* it is of something vague and unformed. . . . [The] industry which has identified all the places mentioned in the Brontë novels with their originals is, from the literary point of view, misplaced. (p. 527)

Charlotte Brontë is more akin to the poets of the romantic revival than to the other leading English novelists, all of whom have one thing in common that she has not. They are profoundly concerned with the things of this world; while with her we feel that the earth is but one point with an "unfathomed gulf" on each side, that all the rest is "formless cloud and vacant depth," and we shudder "at the thought of tottering and plunging amid that chaos." A book like *Jane Eyre* belongs to no epoch or state of society; it is simply a story told by a lonely human being. The action of Fielding, of Scott, of Miss Austen, of George Eliot, takes place on the sunlit plain: with Charlotte Brontë it is fought out on inaccessible mountains, among sharp peaks, or in deep valleys where the shadows lie thickest. (pp. 527-28)

The charge of faulty construction is frequently brought against Charlotte Brontë's novels; indeed, the least critical reader must suffer at times from having his interest in old scenes violently uprooted and transferred. If something is conceded to the requirements of autobiography, the residue can only be explained as the defects of Charlotte Brontë's qualities. . . . The episodes are successive catastrophes whence she alone escapes to tell the tale. It is the predominance of soul-history that causes this periodical quenching of the interest: the abrupt dismissal from the circle of the narrative of those whose work in stimulating the emotions of the central figure is done. (p. 529)

All Charlotte Brontë's best work had a basis of reality, and perhaps she never wrote anything more poignant than the description of Lowood and the character of Helen Burns. In homely but graphic words she speaks of physical hardships and privations; not the least distressing of her pictures is that of the pale thin girls herded in the garden verandah, during the hour of recreation, where the sound of a hollow cough was not infrequent. (pp. 529-30)

Shirley is the table-land between the peaks of *Jane Eyre* and *Villette*. It is founded on observation and hearsay rather than inner experience; only at times, as we traverse its broad spaces, do we light upon autobiographical rock. . . . But Charlotte

Brontë leavened the historical characters with many of her own generation. And *Shirley* may be described as her most social book because the interest is diffused among a score of persons, not centred in one. . . . *Shirley* is her most persistent attempt at a novel of manners, and to bring into artistic focus characters of independent interests.

There are structural faults in *Shirley;* the groups of characters lack fusion, and are not tributaries of one main narrative stream. The action is slow-moving, incident arises chiefly from the shocks of antagonistic characters. And, despite the extraordinary vividness with which these characters start up on her pages, they hardly satisfy the requirements of a novel of manners in being typical. But these are defects of Charlotte Brontë's qualities. She had, as Swinburne said, "the very rarest of all powers or faculties of imagination applied to actual life and individual character." . . . [Charlotte Brontë links her] subjects, with all their personal idiosyncrasies, to the ideas of which they are the symbols, and so discovers a path into the infinite. (pp. 530-31)

Yet, with all their vividness, the figures in *Shirley* are seen rather in low relief than rounded completeness. For Charlotte Brontë lacked that higher kind of humour which can view shocks of temperament with an indulgent if melancholy smile. She saw matter for tears rather than smiles in the seemingly-small imperfections by which happiness is just missed both for self and others, and at those sharp angles of character which intercept the sunlight from neighbouring spirits. And her method of satirising the foibles she deemed most harmful proved her range of sympathies to be but narrow. The words "subjective" and "objective" have fallen into ill repute, yet they do contain a meaning expressed by no others. All classification is arbitrary, but there does exist a point, below which when the mind narrows, and above which when it broadens, communications may not pass. And Charlotte Brontë's place is on the subjective side. (pp. 531-32)

[There is a certain unkindness in Charlotte Brontë's] satire, there is "the keenness of home criticism" directed against a world she viewed with the detachment of a spectator. She has also the spirit of reprisal; she hits back because she has been hit. The shortcomings on which she lays her finger are those which must have jarred the sensitiveness of the recluse who at rare intervals ventures into the world. (p. 532)

Shirley was Charlotte Brontë's most social book; there is a joyousness in it which, although not persistent, breaks out at intervals through the whole, despite the triple catastrophe that suspended its making. . . . A ramble through the *Shirley* country would be of endless profit to the Brontë enthusiast. The reverse of this was said about *Jane Eyre;* and although *Villette* is in part a novel of manners, at any moment mists may roll down the mountains to blot out the villages at their base and make us wanderers in the strange country of the soul. (pp. 533-34)

> *Augustus Ralli, "Charlotte Brontë," in* The Fortnightly Review *(reprinted by permission of Contemporary Review Company Limited), Vol. XCIV, September 1, 1913, pp. 524-38.*

MARY A. WARD (essay date 1917)

The detail of the country house scenes in *Jane Eyre* is extravagant and absurd—a little vulgar besides. The clerical detail of *Shirley* leaves me uncomfortable and unconvinced. I wish that Charlotte had not . . . photographed the three curates from the life. They have the faults of photography, in its cruder stages. They are not transmuted; they remain raw and clumsy. And that being so, the magic of art having failed them, the moral question raises its head, the question of justification. . . . (p. 27)

[Imagination] with its head in the clouds, its heart on fire, its hands full of treasures gathered from the common earth, and its feet walking in and loving the wilder, lonelier paths of life—it is so we must conceive Charlotte's greatest gift. She is a dreamer who observes, who is always observing; and she lives precisely because of the mingling of these two strains in her—the power of poetry and the power of bringing the poetic faculty to bear on the truth nearest her, the facts of her own daily life. "I have seen so little," she complains once or twice. But what she has made of that little! Beside *Villette,* a novel of a girls' school, how poor and ephemeral—already—do the novels look which are half journalism—that is, either rhetoric, or information, poured out for other ends than the creative, the poetic end . . . ; or the novels which rest on an elaborate "documentation," like Zola's *Lourdes.* Poetry, truth, feeling; and a passion which is of the heart, not of the senses—these are Charlotte's secrets. They are simple, but they are not to be had by everybody for the asking. (p. 29)

> *Mary A. Ward, "Some Thoughts on Charlotte Brontë" (originally an address delivered to the Brontë Society, Bradford, England, on March 30, 1917), in* Charlotte Brontë, 1816-1916: A Centenary Memorial, *edited by Butler Wood (reprinted by permission of the publisher, E. P. Dutton, Inc.), Dutton, 1918, pp. 13-38.*

EDMUND GOSSE (essay date 1918)

Among the disadvantages of Charlotte I place very high the puritanism which surrounded her from her cradle, and which entered into her very bones. It made her uselessly and contentiously austere, and it darkened her outlook upon life. That artificial deepening of the shadows may render her work more picturesque, but it deprives it of harmony. It gives a certain aspect of the dried or shrivelled to Charlotte's books when we compare them with the serene fulness, the rich and harmonious suavity, the ripeness, of the masterpieces of her supreme contemporary, George Sand.

The imagination of Charlotte Brontë, despite its prodigious vitality, was a little puerile. When she trusted to her own ears and eyes she was excellent, but the narrow range within which observation was possible for her leaves us to the last with an impression of her as a wonderful young person who never quite grew up. She has the impatience, the unreasonable angers and revolts, of an unappreciated adolescent. When she seems most certainly adult she has still her rebellious air of enduring tribulation with an angry fortitude. Her ignorance sets traps for her, and she falls into them without a struggle. (pp. 42-3)

[We must admit] that she had faults—faults of knowledge, of temper, of social experience. But her errors included none against high feeling. What she endured, what she perceived, she reproduced with the purest intensity, an intensity which transfers itself to the reader, who admits that he is thrilled, in her own splendid phrase, "to the finest fibre of my being, sir!" To this expression of concentrated emotion she brought a faculty of power in which her work is unique. She has a spell by means of which she holds us enchanted, while she lays before us the distresses and the exasperations of humanity. Her great gift, no doubt, lay in the unconscious courage with which she broke up the stereotyped complacency of the age. Her passion swept over the pools of Early Victorian fiction and roused them to storm; the undulations that it set in motion have been vibrating in our literature ever since, and perhaps the most wonderful fact about Charlotte Brontë is that the emancipation of English fiction from the chains of conventionality should have been brought about, against her own will, by this little provincial Puritan. She was, in her own words, "furnace-tried by pain, stamped by constancy," and out of her fires she rose, a Phoenix of poetic fancy, crude yet without a rival, and now, in spite of all imperfections, to live for ever in the forefront of creative English genius. (pp. 44-5)

> *Edmund Gosse, "A Word on Charlotte Brontë," in* Charlotte Brontë, 1816-1916: A Centenary Memorial, *edited by Butler Wood (reprinted by permission of the publisher, E. P. Dutton, Inc.), Dutton, 1918, pp. 39-46.*

CHAUNCEY BREWSTER TINKER   (essay date 1925)

Few novelists of the nineteenth century, that great classic era of fiction, have been so laden with praise [as the Brontës]. . . .

Well, it is all very strange, this devotion to the recluses of Yorkshire, the drab, shy girls with the flaming hearts and teeming imaginations. The theme is romantic enough, in all conscience—the governess racked with heroic passion, a sort of female counterpart of Ruy Blas, the lackey who loved a queen. Some writers seem to feel that romanticism is dead; but the Brontës, who are as romantic as Byron, seem to give the lie to such a notion. The Brontës are not dead, or even ailing. They are, perhaps, more alive than their books. . . . (p. 441)

But the day will come at last when the old unhappy tale of the Brontës must be forgotten, and the literary work of the three sisters judged on its merits and not merely prized for the light it throws upon their biography. Time knows no chivalries. Literary achievement, not romantic biography, must, in the long run, be the basis of an enduring place in literature. Their novels, which are likely to be read long after it has been forgotten that they were one and all quarried out of their biography, will of course be their chief claim to remembrance, stories as powerful as they are strange and crude, yet revealing the splendid paradox of humanity that out of weakness we may be made strong. And among the readers of these stories there will ever be many who turn from their prose to their verse, to see if in their lyrics there may perchance exist an expression of their genius free from the extravagance and rawness that mark their fictions.

It is never to be forgotten that their first appearance in the world of letters was as poetesses—or rather as poets—Currer, Ellis, and Acton Bell. The grey-green little volume of *Poems* . . . was shifted from one publisher to another . . . , and was unregarded by the public. But there is nothing surprising in the failure of the book, for it is always difficult to detect the half dozen poems of permanent value in the confusion caused by several scores of poems issuing suddenly out of the unknown. In this instance the confusion was worse because of the triple authorship and the assumption of masculine names by authors obviously female. But though the volume lacked readers in 1846, it has won them since. . . . Whether it be wholly wise to print every scrap of verse that escaped the waste-

paper basket will seem to the Brontesque disciples an insolent query; but it is a doubt sure to rise in the minds of the critical and irreverent. The menace to the poetical reputation of the Brontës has always been that of suffocation. A few of their poems are of very high quality indeed; others have real value, though marred by blemishes and discords; others contain stanzas or lines which ought to survive; but others—many others—might be permanently spared from English literature. . . . (pp. 441-42)

The lack which is common to the work of all three is of course that of discipline. These young ladies are disinclined to wait, to reconsider, to prune, to reject. . . . In the poems, as in the novels, emotion is everywhere astir, but it is always plunging into language, wreaking itself upon expression, set down hurriedly in all its rawness, never, by any chance, "recollected in tranquility." When the Brontës experience an emotion they express it. They consume no smoke. Now to say all this is, in truth, but to assert that they were young. It is in their fervid youthfulness that half their charm consists; and yet, after reading them for a time, one cannot help longing for the professional touch again. . . . Charlotte's poems, **"He saw my heart's woe,"** might come straight from the most lurid pages of **"Jane Eyre:"**

> Idolator I kneeled to an idol cut in rock,
>   I might have slashed my flesh and drawn my heart's
>   best blood,
> The Granite God had felt no tenderness, no shock,
>   My Baal had not seen nor heard nor understood.

This is like the hysteria which flows from the pen of Jane Eyre; you may find it in your heart to wish it all keyed down, but you cannot deny its passion—and then, suddenly all sinks into prose and pathos:

> Now Heaven heal the wound which I still deeply feel,
>   Thy glorious hosts look not in scorn on our poor race;
> The King eternal doth not iron judgment deal
>   On suffering worms who seek forgiveness, comfort,
>   grace.

The sincerity of this is beyond doubt, but so is the sincerity of an inarticulate cry of pain or pleasure, yet we do not call it artistic. A whole step in the creative process is lacking, and that step is the reconsideration by the artist of his first intensities, a tendency to temper and restrain in the interests of technique and an accepted mode of expression. . . .

[The present writer is] inclined to cavil at the Brontës for their lack of self-discipline and their uncertain technique. This primitive note, the speed and simplicity of the natural voice, is almost never found without plenteous imperfections; but it has beauties of its own. (p. 442)

> *Chauncey Brewster Tinker, "The Poetry of the Brontës," in* The Saturday Review of Literature *(copyright © 1925 by Saturday Review; all rights reserved; reprinted by permission), Vol. 1, No. 24, January 10, 1925, pp. 441-42.**

VIRGINIA WOOLF   (essay date 1925)

As we open *Jane Eyre* once more we cannot stifle the suspicion that we shall find [Charlotte Brontë's] world of imagination as antiquated, mid-Victorian, and out of date as the parsonage on the moor [her childhood home in Yorkshire], a place only to be visited by the curious, only preserved by the pious. So we open *Jane Eyre,* and in two pages every doubt is swept clean from our minds.

Folds of scarlet drapery shut in my view to the right hand; to the left were the clear panes of glass, protecting, but not separating me from the drear November day. At intervals, while turning over the leaves of my book, I studied the aspect of that winter afternoon. Afar, it offered a pale blank of mist and cloud; near, a scene of wet lawn and storm-beat shrub, with ceaseless rain sweeping away wildly before a long and lamentable blast.

There is nothing there more perishable than the moor itself, or more subject to the sway of fashion than the "long and lamentable blast". Nor is this exhilaration short-lived. It rushes us through the entire volume, without giving us time to think, without letting us lift our eyes from the page. So intense is our absorption that if some one moves in the room the movement seems to take place not there but up in Yorkshire. The writer has us by the hand, forces us along her road, makes us see what she sees, never leaves us for a moment or allows us to forget her. At the end we are steeped through and through with the genius, the vehemence, the indignation of Charlotte Brontë. Remarkable faces, figures of strong outline and gnarled feature have flashed upon us in passing; but it is through her eyes that we have seen them. Once she is gone, we seek for them in vain. Think of Rochester and we have to think of Jane Eyre. Think of the moor, and again, there is Jane Eyre. Think of the drawing-room, even, those "white carpets on which seemed laid brilliant garlands of flowers", that "pale Parian mantelpiece" with its Bohemia glass of "ruby red" and the "general blending of snow and fire"—what is all that except Jane Eyre?

The drawbacks of being Jane Eyre are not far to seek. Always to be a governess and always to be in love is a serious limitation in a world which is full, after all, of people who are neither one nor the other. The characters of a Jane Austen or of a Tolstoi have a million facets compared with these. They live and are complex by means of their effect upon many different people who serve to mirror them in the round. They move hither and thither whether their creators watch them or not, and the world in which they live seems to us an independent world which we can visit, now that they have created it, by ourselves. Thomas Hardy is more akin to Charlotte Brontë in the power of his personality and the narrowness of his vision. But the differences are vast. As we read *Jude the Obscure* we are not rushed to a finish; we brood and ponder and drift away from the text in plethoric trains of thought which build up round the characters an atmosphere of question and suggestion of which they are themselves, as often as not, unconscious. Simple peasants as they are, we are forced to confront them with destinies and questionings of the hugest import, so that often it seems as if the most important characters in a Hardy novel are those which have no names. Of this power, of this speculative curiosity, Charlotte Brontë has no trace. She does not attempt to solve the problems of human life; she is even unaware that such problems exist; all her force, and it is the more tremendous for being constricted, goes into the assertion, "I love", "I hate", "I suffer". (pp. 220-22)

Both Hardy and Charlotte Brontë appear to have founded their styles upon a stiff and decorous journalism. The staple of their prose is awkward and unyielding. But both with labour and the most obstinate integrity by thinking every thought until it has subdued words to itself, have forged for themselves a prose which takes the mould of their minds entire; which has, into the bargain, a beauty, a power, a swiftness of its own. Charlotte Brontë, at least, owed nothing to the reading of many books. She never learnt the smoothness of the professional writer, or acquired his ability to stuff and sway his language as he chooses. . . . [It] is the red and fitful glow of the heart's fire which illumines her page. In other words, we read Charlotte Brontë not for exquisite observation of character—her characters are vigorous and elementary; not for comedy—hers is grim and crude; not for a philosophic view of life—hers is that of a country parson's daughter; but for her poetry. . . . [Both Emily and Charlotte Brontë] are always invoking the help of nature. They both feel the need of some more powerful symbol of the vast and slumbering passions in human nature than words or actions can convey. It is with a description of a storm that Charlotte ends her finest novel *Villette*. . . . So she calls in nature to describe a state of mind which could not otherwise be expressed. But neither of the sisters observed nature accurately as Dorothy Wordsworth observed it, or painted it minutely as Tennyson painted it. They seized those aspects of the earth which were most akin to what they themselves felt or imputed to their characters, and so their storms, their moors, their lovely spaces of summer weather are not ornaments applied to decorate a dull page or display the writer's powers of observation—they carry on the emotion and light up the meaning of the book. (pp. 222-24)

> *Virginia Woolf, "Jane Eyre and Wuthering Heights," in her* The Common Reader *(copyright 1925 by Harcourt Brace Jovanovich, Inc.; copyright 1953 by Leonard Woolf; reprinted by permission of the publisher), Harcourt Brace Jovanovich, 1925, pp. 219-227.*

DAVID CECIL (essay date 1932)

Charlotte Brontë, in one of the formidable compliments which she paid to the few among her contemporaries who managed to win her esteem, once congratulated Thackeray on his power of revealing the painful realities that underlie the pleasing exterior of human society. He deserved such praise. But it was odd that she should have thought so. For to judge by their books no two writers had more different ideas of reality. The Victorian novelists are individualists, in nothing more alike than in their unlikeness to one another; and this is never more noticeable than when we shut up *Pendennis* and open *Jane Eyre*. Gone is the busy prosaic urban world with its complicated structure and its trivial motives, silenced the accents of everyday chatter, vanished are newspapers, fashions, business houses, duchesses, footmen and snobs. Instead the gale rages under the elemental sky, while indoors, their faces rugged in the fierce firelight, austere figures of no clearly defined class or period declare eternal love and hate to one another in phrases of stilted eloquence and staggering candour. (p. 119)

[With Charlotte Brontë] we return to the characteristic type of Victorian novelist, untutored, unequal, inspired. . . . Of course, she is not so great a novelist as Dickens; apart from anything else she had a narrower range. For—and in this she is not a typical Victorian—not only do her books cover nothing of the religious, the intellectual, and the purely animal sides of life; they also cover none of that vast area of everyday life which was the subject of Dickens and Thackeray and Trollope. Like them she does not write about prophets or prostitutes; but unlike them she does not write about Mr. and Mrs. Smith in the next street either. Her range is confined to the inner life, the private passions. Her books are before all things the record of a personal vision. So, of course, in a sense are all great novels; if they were not they would not be great novels at all. But the personality of Charlotte Brontë's predecessors appears in their books implicitly. (p. 120)

With [Charlotte Brontë] the hero or more frequently the heroine for the first time steps forward and takes a dominating position on the stage; and the story is presented, not through the eyes of impersonal truth, but openly through her own. Except in *Shirley,* she actually tells it herself: and even in *Shirley* the principal characters tell a great deal of the story for themselves in journals. Charlotte Brontë's imagination is stimulated to create by certain aspects of man's inner life as that of Dickens or Thackeray by certain aspects of his external life. As Thackeray was the first English writer to make the novel the vehicle of a conscious criticism of life, so she is the first to make it the vehicle of personal revelation. She is our first subjective novelist, the ancestor of Proust and Mr. James Joyce and all the rest of the historians of the private consciousness. And like theirs her range is limited to those aspects of experience which stimulate to significance and activity the private consciousness of their various heroes and heroines. (p. 121)

[Charlotte Brontë's] heroines do not try to disentangle the chaos of their consciousness, they do not analyse their emotions or motives. Indeed, they do not analyse anything. They only feel very strongly about everything. And the sole purpose of their torrential autobiographies is to express their feelings. *Jane Eyre, Villette, The Professor,* the best parts of *Shirley,* are not exercises of the mind, but cries of the heart; not a deliberate self-diagnosis, but an involuntary self-revelation.

Further, they are all revelations of the same self. It might be thought that since they are about different people her books had different imaginative ranges. But they have not; and inevitably. You can learn about the external life of many different sorts of people by observation: but no amount of observation can teach you about the inner life of anyone but yourself. All subjective novelists write about themselves. Nor was Charlotte Brontë an exception. Fundamentally, her principal characters are all the same person; and that is Charlotte Brontë. Her range is confined, not only to a direct expression of an individual's emotions and impressions, but to a direct expression of Charlotte Brontë's emotions and impressions. In this, her final limitation, we come indeed to the distinguishing fact of her character as a novelist. The world she creates is the world of her own inner life; she is her own subject.

This does not mean, of course, that she never writes about anything but her own character. She is a storyteller, and a story shows character in action, character, that is, as it appears in contact with the world of external event and personality. Only the relation of Charlotte Brontë's imagination to this world is different from that of most novelists. Theirs, inspired as it is by some aspect of human life outside their own, works, as it were, objectively. . . . Charlotte Brontë's picture of the external world is a picture of her own reactions to the external world. . . . And similarly her secondary characters are presented only as they appear to Jane Eyre or Lucy Snowe. We see as much of them as they saw of them: and what we do see is coloured by the intervening painted glass of Lucy Snowe's or Jane Eyre's temperament. At the best they are the barest sketches compared with the elaborately-finished portrait of the character through whose eyes we look at them. (pp. 121-23)

Charlotte Brontë is very far from being a consistent artist. She has all the Victorian inequality. She is even more startlingly unequal than Dickens. Her faults may not be worse faults—in

point of fact she is never, as he is, vulgar—but she had less art to conceal them. She was a very naïve writer, her faults have the naked crudeness of a child's faults; and in consequence we pass with a sharper jolt from her good passages to her bad. For example, like Dickens', her books are badly constructed. But this does not mean, as it does with him, that the structure is conventional, that the emphasis of the interest falls in a different place from the emphasis of the plot. There is not enough structure in her books to be conventional; their plots are too indeterminate to have an emphasis. Her books—and this is true of no other English novelist of comparable merit—are, but for the continued presence of certain figures, incoherent. Nor is this because they are like *Pickwick,* a succession of adventures only connected by a hero. No, each is a drama: but not one drama. Charlotte Brontë will embark on a dramatic action and then, when it is half finished, without warning abandon it for another, equally dramatic, but without bearing on what has come before or will follow after. . . . However, *Jane Eyre* does maintain a continuous interest in one central figure. *Villette* and *Shirley* do not even possess this frail principle of unity. . . . In *Shirley* Charlotte Brontë does attempt a more regular scheme. But the result of her effort is only to show her disastrous inability to sustain it. Not only is the story cumbered up with a number of minor characters like the Yorke family and Mrs. Pryor, who have no contribution to make to the main action; but that action is itself split into two independent parts. . . . Once fully launched on her surging flood of self-revelation, Charlotte Brontë is far above pausing to attend to so paltry a consideration as artistic unity.

She does not pause to consider probability either. Charlotte Brontë's incapacity to make a book coherent as a whole is only equalled by her incapacity to construct a plausible machinery of action for its component parts. Her plots are not dull; but they have every other defect that a plot could have; they are at once conventional, confusing and unlikely. *The Professor,* indeed, save in the affair of Mr. Vandenhuten, palpably introduced to establish Crimsworth in the comfortable circumstances necessary to give the book a happy ending, is credible enough; while *Shirley,* though its plot is mildly unconvincing all through, is marred only by one gross improbability, the conduct of Mrs. Pryor. But the stories of her masterpieces, *Jane Eyre* and *Villette,* are, if regarded in a rational aspect, unbelievable from start to finish.

Jane Eyre, and here too Charlotte Brontë shows herself like Dickens, is a roaring melodrama. But the melodrama of *Bleak House* itself seems sober compared with that of *Jane Eyre.* Not one of the main incidents on which its action turns but is incredible. (pp. 124-26)

Villette has not a melodramatic plot. But by a majestic feat of literary perversity Charlotte Brontë manages to make this quiet chronicle of a school teacher as bristling with improbability as *Jane Eyre.* She stretches the long arm of coincidence till it becomes positively dislocated. (p. 127)

Nor are her faults of form her only faults. Her imagination did not know the meaning of the word restraint. This does not appear so much in her narrative, for there imagination is confined to its proper function of creating atmosphere and suggesting the stress of passion. But now and again she allows herself an interval in which to give it free rein: Caroline has a dream, Jane Eyre is inspired to paint a symbolic picture, Shirley Keeldar indulges in a flight of visionary meditation. And then across the page surges a seething cataract of Gothic romanticism and personification, spectres, demons, bleeding swords, angelic countenances, made noisy with all the ejaculation, reiteration, and apostrophe that a turgid rhetoric can supply. Even if such passages were good in themselves they put the rest of the book out of focus. . . . (p. 128)

[Charlotte Brontë] can be ridiculous. And this brings us to another of her defects—her lack of humour. Not that she is wholly without it. Like all the great Victorian novelists, she has a real and delightful vein of her own. But she does not strike this vein often: and when she does not she shows herself as little humorous as it is possible to be. . . . Charlotte Brontë was about as well-equipped to be a satirist as she was to be a ballet-dancer. Satire demands acute observation and a light touch. Charlotte Brontë, indifferent to the outside world and generally in a state of tension, observes little, and never speaks lightly of anything. In consequence her satirical darts fall wide of the mark and as ponderous as lead. Painstakingly she tunes her throbbing accents to a facetious tone, conscientiously she contorts her austere countenance to a humorous grimace. (pp. 128-29)

But though her lack of humour prevents her amusing us when she means to, it often amuses us very much when she does not. Her crudeness, her lack of restraint, and the extreme seriousness with which she envisages life, combine to deprive her of any sense of ironic proportion. (p. 129)

[However], unconscious humour is not her worst fault; if it is a fault at all. It springs from the very nature of her work, from the fact that she presents life from an individual point of view: to remove the absurdity would be to remove the individuality at the same time. Moreover, it is possible to describe a scene vividly without seeing its funny side. . . . The play in *Villette*, Rochester's proposal, are among the most memorable scenes in Charlotte Brontë's books; and we enjoy them whole-heartedly. Only, our enjoyment is enriched by an ironic amusement which it could hardly have been her intention to stimulate.

But her chief defect cannot be so lightly dismissed. Charlotte Brontë fails, and fails often, over the most important part of a novelist's work—over character. Even at her best she is not among the greatest drawers of character. Her secondary figures do not move before us with the solid reality of Jane Austen's: seen as they are through the narrow lens of her heroines' temperament, it is impossible that they should. And the heroines themselves are presented too subjectively for us to see them in the round as we see Maggie Tulliver or Emma Bovary. Nor is her failure solely due to the limitations imposed by her angle of approach. Since she feels rather than understands, she cannot penetrate to the inner structure of a character to discover its basic elements. Most of her characters are only presented fragmentarily as they happen to catch the eye of her heroine; but in the one book, *Shirley,* in which she does try to present them objectively, they are equally fragmentary. And sometimes they are not only fragmentary, they are lifeless. Her satirical, realistic figures, of course, are especially lifeless. The curates in *Shirley,* the house-party in *Jane Eyre,* these are as garishly unreal as the cardboard puppets in a toy theatre. . . . Lady Ingram is not original: she is extremely conventional, the conventional silly grande dame of third-rate farce. Charlotte Brontë, unacquainted with such a character herself, has just copied it from the crude type which she found in the commonplace fiction of the time. And her lack of technical skill has made her copy even cruder than its model.

She can fail over serious character too; particularly male character. Serious male characters are always a problem for a woman

novelist. And for Charlotte Brontë, exclusively concentrated as she was on the reactions of her highly feminine temperament, they were especially a problem. Nor did she solve it. She does not usually err by making them too feminine; her heroes are not all sisters under their skins. . . . [As] a rule Charlotte Brontë errs in the other extreme. Ignorant what men are like, but convinced that at any rate they must be unlike women, she endows them only with those characteristics she looks on as particularly male: and accentuates these to such a degree that they cease to be human at all. . . . Charlotte Brontë's more orthodox heroes . . . have not even got imaginative life; they are mere tedious aggregations of good qualities, painted figureheads of virtue like the heroes of Scott. Only in Paul Emanuel has Charlotte Brontë drawn a hero who is also a living man. And he is deliberately presented on unheroic lines. (pp. 131-34)

Charlotte Brontë's hand does not only falter over her heroes. In Caroline and Shirley, her two objectively conceived heroines, it is equally uncertain. Both are departures from her usual type. Caroline is described as gentle, sweet and charming, Shirley as charming, brilliant and high-spirited. In company they sustain their rôles convincingly enough. But the moment they are alone they change, they become like each other and unlike either of the characters in which they first appear. . . . (pp. 134-35)

Formless, improbable, humourless, exaggerated, uncertain in their handling of character—there is assuredly a great deal to be said against Charlotte Brontë's novels. So much, indeed, that one may well wonder if she is a good novelist at all. All the same she is; she is even great. Her books are as living today as those of Dickens; and for the same reason. They have creative imagination; and creative imagination of the most powerful kind, able to assimilate to its purpose the strongest feelings, the most momentous experiences. Nor is it intermittent in its action. Charlotte Brontë, and here again she is like Dickens, is, even at her worst, imaginative. . . . Every page of Charlotte Brontë's novels burns and breathes with vitality. Out of her improbabilities and her absurdities, she constructed an original vision of life; from the scattered, distorted fragments of experience which managed to penetrate her huge self-absorption, she created a world.

But her limitations make it very unlike the life of any other novelists' world. For, unhelped as she is by any great power of observation and analysis, her world is almost exclusively an imaginary world. Its character and energy derive nothing important from the character and energy of the world she purports to describe; they are the character and energy of her own personality. (pp. 135-36)

Charlotte Brontë could express love and passion and despair, she could also express guilt and moral aspiration. Her pages throb with an unquenchable zest for life; only it is life conceived, not as a garden of pleasure, but as a tense and sublime battle.

Finally, her ingenuousness is an ingredient in her unique flavour. For one thing, it disinfects her imagination; blows away the smoke and sulphur which its ardent heat might be expected to generate, so that its flame burns pure and clear. Further, it breathes round it an atmosphere, not usually associated with its other outstanding characteristics, an atmosphere of artless freshness, a candid virginal charm. Nor does this diminish its force. The fact that we feel Charlotte Brontë's imagination to be in some degree the imagination of a child, with a child's hopeful credulity, a child's eager, unselfconscious responsiveness, so far from weakening its intensity, rather invests it with a sincerity irresistibly touching and winning.

Her imagination illuminates the whole of Charlotte Brontë's achievement. But there are certain aspects in which it shines especially bright. The characters, first of all: it is true that some of them, like Miss Ingram, are so preposterously conceived that no imagination could make them convincing; it is also true that we never see Charlotte Brontë's characters in the round as we see Tolstoy's or Jane Austen's, but only as they happen to cross her line of vision. Still, it is possible to see a man vividly in one line of vision; and, if it is Lucy Snowe's or Jane Eyre's, very vividly indeed. Not Henry James himself can convey the impact of a personality more forcibly than Charlotte Brontë at her best. . . . Charlotte Brontë is always at her best in describing children; and best of all when she is describing them from the inside, when, in the person of little Jane Eyre or fifteen-year-old Lucy Snowe, she is speaking as a child herself. Indeed her vision of life, like that of Dickens, appears most convincing from the eye of a child. For, like his, it has a child's intensity, a child's crudeness; the first quarter of *Jane Eyre,* with the first quarter of *David Copperfield,* is the most profoundly-studied portrait of childhood in English.

Her imagination shows itself in her settings as much as in her characters. . . . Nor are her interiors less memorable. (pp. 143-45)

[The] power of creating a scene associates itself with Charlotte Brontë's power of suggesting the eerie. She never actually brings in the supernatural. Indeed her lack of imaginative restraint would probably have made her fail if she had. . . . Charlotte Brontë's plots are full of sinister secrets and inexplicable happenings. And the lurid light of her vision does invest these with a weirdness beyond that of ordinary mundane horror. (p. 145)

Love, indeed, is the central theme of her stories: for it was inevitably the main preoccupation of so passionate a temperament. Her power to describe it is, of course, conditioned by the nature of her genius. She cannot dissect the workings of passion, nor can she illuminate its effect on character. What she can do is to convey its actual present throb. And this she does as it had never been done before in English fiction. Naturally she was too much of a Victorian and too much of a Puritan to do more than hint at its animal side. But her hints are quite enough to prevent the emotion seeming disembodied and unreal. . . . Hers is a frustrated love.

And writing as she does of the emotions of her own unsatisfied heart, Charlotte Brontë is most characteristically concerned to describe frustrated love: Jane Eyre's love for Rochester, so hopelessly, as it would seem, out of her reach; Lucy Snowe's for Dr. John, absorbed already in Ginevra Fanshawe. But the fact that it is frustrated does not make the love of Charlotte Brontë's heroines less intense. Indeed it makes it more of an obsession. Moreover, Charlotte Brontë can describe happy love equally well, if her story gives her a chance. As a matter of fact love is the occasion of her few successful flights of humour. Jane Eyre teasing Rochester, Lucy Snowe sparring with Paul Emanuel—in these she achieves real comedy. It is a little stiff and shy; it is also enchantingly demure and delicate; a sort of Puritan comedy of the sexes, unlike anything else in English literature. And she can rise higher.

In addition to love's gaieties she can describe love's ecstasy. Like most of the other novelists of her school, she is a poet;

and her poetry is the pure lyrical poetry of passion. It connects itself with her sensibility to landscape. The special emotion of her love-scenes swells to assimilate to itself the emotional quality of the scenery amid which they take place. (pp. 146-47)

Even more characteristic are Charlotte Brontë's moments of *solitary* emotion, the gusts of inexplicable anguish, yearning, exultation, which sweep across the spirit, unprovoked by any actively dramatic incident. And they are most vivid when some abnormal physical circumstance has heated them to a morbid intensity; the agony of the starving Jane Eyre, lost a whole burning July day on the Yorkshire moors; Caroline Helstone's delirious broodings that mingle tumultuously with raging wind and brilliant winter moonlight, as she tosses on her sick bed; Lucy Snowe's tormented loneliness rising to hallucination, during her three months' sojourn in the deserted school; the strange exaltation induced by drugs that compels her from her sickbed to wander through festal Villette. These scenes, indeed, are the peak of Charlotte Brontë's achievement; for in them, as in no others, her imagination finds the perfect field for its expression. Her pictures of love and character, though they reveal her powers, reveal also her defects. But solitary obsession, while it offers equal scope to her intensity and more to her imaginative strangeness, makes no demands on her she cannot satisfy. No power of psychological penetration or accurate observation is needed to communicate the impressions of the senses in an abnormal nervous state; while to be dreamlike and unrestrained is characteristic of such impressions. For once Charlotte Brontë is true not only to imagination, but to fact.

Her technical ability is akin to the rest of her genius. In certain ways she is hardly a craftsman at all. As we have seen, she cannot construct a plausible or even a coherent plot; the fabric of her books is woven with irrelevancies, frayed with loose threads. But she was a born story-teller: continuously from her first sentence to her last she engages our interest. It is partly due to the fire of her personality; like the Ancient Mariner she holds us with her glittering eye. It is also due to an exceptional mastery of the art of awaking suspense. (pp. 147-49)

Her style is similarly unequal, similarly inspired; indeed it is the mirror and microcosm of her achievement. It is an odd style, with its mixture of grandeur and provinciality, of slovenly colloquial grammar and stilted archaic phraseology, of abrupt paragraphs and rolling sentences. And in some ways it is a very bad style. Even at its best it flows turbid and irregular. It never exhibits the exact translucency of the true stylist, that sensibility to the quality and capacity of language which marks the writing of Thackeray, for instance. It is deformed by all Charlotte Brontë's customary clumsiness, all her customary lack of restraint. The words tend perpetually to get in the way of the meaning. For not only is she incapable of expressing herself briefly and smoothly, she further disfigures her plainest piece of narrative by plastering it with rhetoric; a rhetoric, too, which, undisciplined as it is by an educated taste, is as often as not extremely bad, bedizened with imagery, spasmodic with ejaculation, a compound of the commonplace and the grotesque.

All the same, Charlotte Brontë's writing is a powerful agent in her effect. For she manages to infuse her personality into it. Cliché, rhetoric and bad grammar alike are pulsing with her intensity, fresh with her charm. Moreover, her strange imagination expresses itself in her actual choice of words. There is hardly a page where we do not meet, sandwiched between commonplace and absurdity, some evocative image, some haunting, throbbing cadence. . . . [At] every turn of its furious course Charlotte Brontë's imagination throws off some such glinting spark of phrase. And now and again the sparks blaze up into a sustained passage of De Quinceyish prose poetry. (pp. 149-50)

She was a genius. She had, that is, that creative imagination which is the distinguishing quality of the artist, in the very highest intensity. No writer has ever been able to infuse his material with a stronger and a more individual vitality. No writer's work is more obviously of the stuff of which great art is made. But imagination, though it can make an artist, cannot make a craftsman. This needs other qualifications, and of these, except her turn for telling a story, Charlotte Brontë had none at all. No other English novelist of her power sat down to his task so glaringly deficient in some of the essential qualities which it required. She had no gift of form, no restraint, little power of observation, no power of analysis. And her novels suffer from it. They are badly constructed, they are improbable, they are often ridiculous. Moreover, her lack of critical capacity meant that, like those of Dickens, her books often involved themes and characters outside her imaginative range, the range of her personal impressions. The result of all this is that in spite of her genius she never wrote a wholly satisfying book. *Shirley* is her greatest failure, for there she set out to tell the story of two normal girls in the first place, and in the second to give a picture of the industrial revolution in Northern England. *Jane Eyre* is more personal and therefore better. Indeed, its first quarter is the most sustained expression of her genius. But it is marred by a grotesque plot and two full-length male portraits. *Villette*, with little regular plot, and concerned only with personal life, is her most consistently successful book. But it, too, is disfigured by unnecessary and improbable incidents; and it is nearly incoherent.

This makes her achievement almost impossible finally to estimate. . . . She cannot be placed with the great painters of human character, the Shakespeares, the Scotts, the Jane Austens; her faults are too glaring, her inspiration too eccentric. But equally she cannot be dismissed to a minor rank, to the Fanny Burneys, the Charles Reades; for unlike them she rises at times to the greatest heights. She is predestined to hover restlessly and for ever, now at the head now at the foot of the procession of letters, among the unplaceable anomalies, the freak geniuses; along with Ford and Tourneur and Herman Melville and D. H. Lawrence. Such writers never achieve a universally accepted reputation. The considerable body of people who set a paramount importance on craftsmanship and verisimilitude will never admire them. But their strange flame, lit as it is at the central white hot fire of creative inspiration, will in every age find them followers. And on these they exercise a unique, a thrilling, a perennial fascination. (pp. 152-54)

> *David Cecil, "Charlotte Brontë" (originally a lecture delivered at Oxford University between 1931-1932), in his* Early Victorian Novelists: Essays in Revaluation *(copyright 1935 by The Bobbs-Merrill Company, Inc.; copyright renewed © 1962 by David Cecil; used by permission of the publisher, The Bobbs-Merrill Company, Inc.; in Canada by Constable & Company Limited), Constable, 1934 (and reprinted by The Bobbs-Merrill Company, 1935), pp. 119-54.*

M. H. SCARGILL (essay date 1950)

From the day of its first appearance *Jane Eyre* has been credited with adding something new to the tradition of the English novel, though just what this is, and whether it is desirable, continues to puzzle the critics. To some the new quality is the voice of a woman who speaks with perfect frankness about herself; to others it is "passion," though the nature of this "passion" is left undefined. To all, *Jane Eyre* is remarkable for its intensity, and this intensity is usually taken as sufficient to counteract what critics regard as a sensational and poorly constructed plot. The cause of this intensity remains uncertain. Some have suggested that it is love; some even go so far as to suggest that it is the memory of a real love which Charlotte Brontë herself had experienced, that is that the novel is some kind of autobiography and, if we take this view to its logical conclusion, not a novel at all. (p. 120)

With the publication of *Jane Eyre,* the English novel, which had already absorbed elements from the essay, the "character," and the drama, turned away from the external towards the expression of an experience exclusively personal. This experience is not necessarily factual, but it is none the less real, and it is important, as much poetry is important, for the intensity of its feeling and the adequacy of its expression. It is intensity of feeling which has attracted readers to *Jane Eyre;* it is the origin and nature of this feeling and its means of expression, adequate or inadequate, that have puzzled them.

To many readers passion is synonymous with love, and to these it is as a love story that *Jane Eyre* appeals, a love story told with great frankness by a woman who, as [W. L. Cross] would put it, is "a realist of the feelings." To others passion is an admirable but indescribable feeling, which appeals simply because it is a feeling—by no means a foolish value to attract one to a book and infinitely superior to that which leads to admiration of *Jane Eyre* as a kind of real "confession." Intensity of feeling *Jane Eyre* has, but it is not centred exclusively upon love; in fact, in the total impact of *Jane Eyre* religious ecstasy plays a part as important as love for a person.

The greatness of a work of art is commensurate with the greatness of its inspiration and the adequacy of its means of communication. Now, the story of a woman in love would be interesting but not necessarily great; the story of a woman's fight to express her own personality in love would be even more interesting but yet not necessarily great. *Jane Eyre* is great because it is these things and also something more. It is a love story; it is a fight for the free expression of personality in love; but it is also a record of the eternal conflict between the flesh and the spirit, a conflict which is solved satisfactorily when all passion is spent. *Jane Eyre* may speak for many women, but it speaks also for all humanity, and it speaks in unmistakable terms. *Jane Eyre* is the record of an intense spiritual experience, as powerful in its way as King Lear's ordeal of purgation, and it ends nobly on a note of calm.

The expression of such an experience in terms of the novel creates considerable difficulty. The poet, for an identical purpose, takes the means of communication which is to hand, the language of his day, and has permission to put new life into it. The closer he can fashion it to his purpose, the more he is admired. . . . (p. 121)

We make no demands of probability on the poet. All we ask is that he shall symbolize his experience, recreate it for us, by whatever means he thinks best. But of the novelist we seem inclined to demand probability, a reproduction of life, regardless of the novelist's purpose. Charlotte Brontë had experienced an emotion which one would expect her to express through the medium of poetry. But she used the conventional elements of the novel, the medium she understood best. It seems logical to suppose that such a use, conscious or unconscious, of the elements of fiction would produce a new type of novel. And this is precisely the case with *Jane Eyre*. The conventions have become symbols: the fictional lover has become The Lover; the mad woman of the Gothic novel has been put to an allegorical use. *Jane Eyre* contains the elements of fiction used as a poet employs language and imagery—to impose belief, even though it be by irrational means. (p. 122)

[*Jane Eyre,* as it appears to me, is] a new contribution to English fiction, a novel which must not be criticized in the spirit in which we criticize *Vanity Fair* or *Tom Jones*. . . .

If *Jane Eyre* is to be blamed, because it doesn't do what *Tom Jones* and *Vanity Fair* do, then literary criticism is at fault. We must be willing to accept *Jane Eyre* as a profound, spiritual experience, expressed in the most adequate symbolism, a symbolism which, if divorced from its emotion, is as improbable as all poetic symbols. That way lies a truer appreciation of *Jane Eyre*. We have felt its greatness: we have often excused its means of expression. Let us now admit that in *Jane Eyre* fiction has become poetry, and let us enlarge our idea of fiction accordingly. (p. 125)

> *M. H. Scargill, "'All Passion Spent': A Revaluation of 'Jane Eyre',"* in University of Toronto Quarterly *(reprinted by permission of University of Toronto Press), Vol. XIX, No. 2, January, 1950, pp. 120-25.*

KATHLEEN TILLOTSON   (essay date 1954)

[*Jane Eyre* is not a novel of contemporary life, nor is it] a novel of a recent and specific past, impinging on the present. . . . It is both in purpose and effect primarily a novel of the inner life, not of man in his social relations; it maps a private world. Private, but not eccentric. . . . A love-story, a Cinderella fable, a Bluebeard mystery, an autobiography from forlorn childhood to happy marriage: this novel makes its appeal first and last to 'the unchanging human heart'. (pp. 257-58)

The influence of *Jane Eyre,* both social and literary, . . . bespeaks its importance in its own time; on the lower level, it started a vogue for plain heroines and ugly masterful heroes; on the higher, it affected the autobiographic children in Dickens's later novels, and at least smoothed the path for Mrs. Gaskell, Trollope, and George Eliot. The profounder explorations of *Jane Eyre* were new indeed to the novel; not before in fiction had such continuous shafts of light penetrated the 'unlit gulf of the self'—that solitary self hitherto the preserve of the poets. (pp. 260-61)

The Professor is a single-track novel . . . , masquerading as a more complex unity, and with raw edges broken off from Angrian stories. The relation between the Crimsworth brothers raises interest, but leads nowhere, is dropped after seven chapters, and never recurs; it is a vestigial appendix from the rivalries of Angrian characters. The early chapters also introduce a further false lead—more damaging to the novel because it does recur, but quite ineffectively—in Yorke Hunsden, a sharply etched character with a misleading semblance of function; and even at Brussels, M. Pelet is a too transparent device for setting the main action in motion. The fault of the novel is that the real story occupies barely half its space; the rest is an awkward prologue. Here alone, in Crimsworth's wooing of Frances Henri, the devious delicate pursuit of one solitary by another, the first

of Charlotte's many explorations of the master-pupil relation, is the growing-point of her first novel. Indeed the love-story in the first person is here already perfected. The concentration on a single view, the gradual explication of a mysterious character, the emotional suspense, of this part of the novel, she equalled but never surpassed; not even in *Villette,* where so much of the outer material is reworked. But these chapters, while perfect in scale and tone, are too slight for a novel; their context nearly destroys them, for the reader, hungering for recurrence and symmetry, is haunted by the expectation of something to develop from the incidents and characters introduced in the first half of the novel. All that those first twelve chapters achieve—the establishing of William Crimsworth as solitary, misfit, and rebel—could have been done in one chapter; even two years later she thought them 'very feeble'.

Because of its structural weakness, directly deducible to the unwillingness to give up Angrian characters entirely and the inability to combine them with the rest, *The Professor* represents an imperfect victory over 'the world below'. Charlotte was perhaps deceived into thinking it complete because of her strenuous and indeed successful effort to avoid extravagance in situation and style, to lower the social tone into congruity with the scenes and characters she knew at first hand. . . . [The] whole tone of *The Professor* show the completeness of her moral emancipation from the world of Angria, where 'romantic domestic treachery' was the norm. The emphasis upon the 'farewell' to the 'burning clime' may be at times aggressive; but the convinced preference for the 'shores of Reality' to 'illusive, void dreams' has been exemplified as well as asserted. It remained to discover the structure, the unity, which a whole novel demands; and, now safely anchored upon those shores, to rediscover the realm of dream. *The Professor* was a necessary stage; it set up a bare framework of 'working one's way through life' with a 'rational mind', a framework unknown to Angria, and from which none of her later narratives seriously departs; but it perhaps sacrificed too much to down-to-earth truthfulness in its conscientious avoidance of sudden turns of fortune and extremes of feeling. (pp. 282-85)

Jane Eyre is the completion of her victory; writing it, she was able to accept and keep in due subordination material from her fantasy world. There, Angria has become a positive value; for she has asserted her dominion, and the reader of this novel has never any doubt that she, and not any of her creatures, is in control. (p. 286)

When the Angrian plot-material in *Jane Eyre* is recognized, its subordination is seen to be a triumph of structure and emphasis. Had the story begun with the nodal situation, we should have been on a distant island . . . and have seen Rochester's father and elder brother entrapping him into marriage with a vicious lunatic. Instead, this situation is embedded in the main story, revealed retrospectively only at its climax; it is there not for its sensational sake, but as precisely that situation which will make Rochester's deception most nearly excusable, and Jane's resistance most difficult, producing the maximum of conflict between conscience and compassion and holding the reader's sympathies in true balance. By holding its revelation in reserve the author keeps the two rising lines of suspense in the middle chapters ironically parallel; Jane draws nearer and nearer to the mystery of Thornfield, unaware that it holds the destruction of her growing love. More incidental Angrian material is usually distanced in time or space, even as Spanish Town, Madeira, and India lie out on the edges of the novel's world. It is disinfected of feverish emotion: Rochester's mistresses are recollected with moderate tranquillity, and Adèle, the dancer's illegitimate child, is almost visibly stripped of glamour. Only in Blanche Ingram and Rochester's deliberate use of her as a means of tormenting Jane is there any approximation to the Angrian tone. Elsewhere, radical differences belie a superficial similiarity; a girl's arrival at a strange house, with an absent and mysterious master, is recurrent in Angria . . . , but is not there accompanied by a solidly reassuring Mrs. Fairfax, nor by the heroine's rationality and courage and her concern to earn an honest competence. Mr. Rochester looms up at first like Zamorna; but, unlike him, he can be mocked, has wit, intellect, and a conscience dormant, not dead. He is at worst an outlaw, where Zamorna was despot of a lawless world. Jane, the steady centre of the narrative, represents what no Angrian heroine ever had: an incorruptible heart. Angria storms behind locked doors; the walls between chaos and the world are thin, but they will stand.

'The first duty of an author is, I conceive, a faithful allegiance to Truth and Nature.' The statement, coming from Charlotte Brontë in 1848, is no truism; for her, that allegiance was hard-won. And it was natural also for her to place second to it the duty of a 'conscientious study of Art'; that came second in order for her, and *Jane Eyre* is her first work to show it. *The Professor* contains art, but is not a total work of art; in design and control, thanks to the backward drag of Angria, it is a broken-backed whole. (pp. 286-88)

Kathleen Tillotson, "'Jane Eyre'" (a revision of a lecture delivered at the University of London in 1949), in her Novels of the Eighteen-Forties *(reprinted by permission of Oxford University Press), Oxford University Press, Oxford, 1954, pp. 257-313.*

JACOB KORG (essay date 1957)

To contemporary reviewers Currer Bell's second published novel, *Shirley,* seemed inferior to her first, not only because it lacked the intensity and authenticity of *Jane Eyre,* but also because it seemed to have no unity. Primarily a love story, it pursues long threads of digressive narrative among rebellious workmen, affected curates, provincial families, and lonely maiden ladies, while the main plot develops so slowly that the heroine is introduced only after the first third of the novel is over and her lover appears for the first time in the last volume of the three-volume Victorian format. The result, said G. H. Lewes, was "a portfolio of sketches" so lacking in unity that whole chapters could be omitted without destroying the story [see excerpts above]. Modern critics have agreed unanimously with this view. "It attempts enormously too much," says Laura L. Hinkley. "*Shirley* concerns history, economics, ecclesiasticism, provincial society in its humors, stresses and tragedies, personal fortunes of much variety and personal passions of great intensity, incessant exposition of character, and the writer's own convictions and emotions. All these get horribly in each other's way. It is a wilderness in which the forest constantly disappears among the trees." "Once fully launched on her surging flood of self-revelation," says Lord David Cecil, "Charlotte Brontë is far above pausing to attend to so paltry a consideration as artistic unity" [see excerpt above]. (p. 125)

Although *Shirley* certainly does not have the singleness of effect which the first-person narrative of its vivid heroine gives *Jane Eyre,* its scattered parts do offer the retrospective eye a kind of design. Further, it becomes clear that this design is a way of expressing the novel's meaning. (p. 126)

Shirley lacks the strong story line and suspenseful plot development which are found in both *Jane Eyre* and *Villette.* In spite of its occasional bursts of violent action, it makes a static impression, for nearly all the significant facts of the novel are already established when it opens. The two pairs of lovers are already in love; the mill owner and his workers are already at odds. The most exciting actions, like the battle at the mill or Shirley's clash with her uncle, do not develop the plot but simply reveal character or attitudes. Revelation rather than narration is, in fact, the method of *Shirley;* the primary importance of its events is not that they alter situations but that they lead the characters to grasp more clearly situations which already exist. The characters themselves, with the exception of Caroline Helstone, are fully formed when they appear, and undergo little change.

The narrative interest is almost entirely restricted to Caroline and her destiny, for she is the only figure who faces the task of choosing her way of life. (p. 135)

But Caroline Helstone's development is only one of the means through which Charlotte Brontë attempted, in *Shirley,* to express a comprehensive romanticism. It is, as G. H. Lewes said, a "panoramic" work rather than a personal one, but Charlotte Brontë's limited experience offered her little material for constructing a broad picture of society. *Shirley* is the only novel in which she attempted anything of the sort, and it compelled her to patch together the most diverse materials. . . . Charlotte Brontë bravely tried, in *Shirley,* to go outside the narrow interpersonal sphere of *Jane Eyre* and *Villette* and to apply the romantic myth to the world of social realities. When used as an instrument of criticism, her passionate belief in nature and individualism took the form of a peculiar religion. Drawn from a mystic source, the reveries in which Shirley and Caroline undergo the experience of communion with the absolute, it is extended into everyday life to provide standards of conduct. *Shirley* is an attempt to show that the romantic view offers enlightenment for the peasantry, a corrective for the insincerity of convention-ridden upper classes, and a justification for judging people on their own merits rather than according to class distinctions. . . . Essentially, *Shirley* is a philosophical novel; its philosophy often seems to encumber it seriously, but it does serve to pull the novel's parts together into a single fabric. (pp. 135-36)

*Jacob Korg, "The Problem of Unity in 'Shirley',"
in* Nineteenth-Century Fiction *(© 1957 by the Regents of the University of California), Vol. 12, No. 1, June, 1957, pp. 125-36.*

ROBERT B. HEILMAN (essay date 1958)

[Charlotte Brontë's *The Professor*] is conventional; formally she is for "reason" and "real life"; but her characters keep escaping to glorify "feeling" and "Imagination." Feeling is there in the story—evading repression, in author or in character; ranging from nervous excitement to emotional absorption; often tense and peremptory; sexuality, hate, irrational impulse, grasped, given life, not merely named and pigeonholed. This is Charlotte's version of Gothic: in her later novels an extraordinary thing. . . . [The] vital feeling moves toward an intensity, a freedom, and even an abandon virtually nonexistent in historical Gothic and rarely approached in Richardson. From Angria on, Charlotte's women vibrate with passions that the fictional conventions only partly constrict or gloss over—in the center an almost violent devotedness that has in it at once a fire of independence, a spiritual energy, a vivid sexual responsive-ness, and, along with this, self-righteousness, a sense of power, sometimes self-pity and envious competitiveness. To an extent the heroines are "unheroined," unsweetened. Into them there has come a new sense of the dark side of feeling and person-ality.

The Professor ventures a little into the psychic darkness on which *Villette* draws heavily. . . . Charlotte draws on sex im-ages that recall the note of sexuality subtly present in other episodes: ". . . I had entertained her at bed and board . . . she lay with me, . . . taking me entirely to her death-cold bosom, and holding me with arms of bone." The climax is: "I repulsed her as one would a dreaded and ghastly concubine coming to embitter a husband's heart toward his young bride . . . ," This is Gothic, yet there is an integrity of feeling that greatly deepens the convention. (pp. 97-8)

In both *Villette* and *Jane Eyre* Gothic is used but characteris-tically is undercut.

Jane Eyre hears a "tragic . . . preternatural . . . laugh," but this is at "high noon" and there is "no circumstance of ghost-liness"; Grace Poole, the supposed laugher, is a plain person, than whom no "apparition less romantic or less ghostly could . . . be conceived"; Charlotte apologizes ironically to the "ro-mantic reader" for telling "the plain truth" that Grace gen-erally bears a "pot of porter." Charlotte almost habitually revises "old Gothic," the relatively crude mechanisms of fear, with an infusion of the anti-Gothic. When Mrs. Rochester first tried to destroy Rochester by fire, Jane "baptized" Rochester's bed and heard Rochester "fulminating strange anathemas at finding himself lying in a pool of water." The introduction of comedy as a palliative of straight Gothic occurs on a large scale when almost seventy-five pages are given to the visit of the Ingram-Eshton party to mysterious Thornfield; here Charlotte, as often in her novels, falls into the manner of the Jane Austen whom she despised. When Mrs. Rochester breaks loose again and attacks Mason, the presence of guests lets Charlotte play the nocturnal alarum for at least a touch of comedy: Rochester orders the frantic women not to "pull me down or strangle me"; and "the two dowagers, in vast white wrappers, were bearing down on him like ships in full sail."

The symbolic also modifies the Gothic, for it demands of the reader a more mature and complicated response than the rel-atively simple thrill or momentary intensity of feeling sought by primitive Gothic. (p. 98)

[In] various ways Charlotte manages to make the patently Gothic more than a stereotype. But more important is that she instinc-tively finds new ways to achieve the ends served by old Gothic—the discovery and release of new patterns of feeling, the in-tensification of feeling. . . . Charlotte leads away from stan-dardized characterization toward new levels of human reality, and hence from stock responses toward a new kind of pas-sionate engagement.

Charlotte moves toward depth in various ways that have an immediate impact like that of Gothic. Jane's strange, fearful symbolic dreams are not mere thrillers but reflect the tensions of the engagement period, the stress of the wedding-day debate with Rochester, and the longing for Rochester after she has left him. The final Thornfield dream, with its vivid image of a hand coming through a cloud in place of the expected moon, is in the surrealistic vein that appears most sharply in the ex-traordinary pictures that Jane draws at Thornfield: here Char-lotte is plumbing the psyche, not inventing a weird *décor*. . . .

In her flair for the surreal, in her plunging into feeling that is without status in the ordinary world of the novel, Charlotte discovers a new dimension of Gothic.

She does this most thoroughly in her portrayal of characters and of the relations between them. If in Rochester we see only an Angrian-Byronic hero and a Charlotte wish-fulfillment fig-ure (the two identifications which to some readers seem entirely to place him), we miss what is more significant, the exploration of personality that opens up new areas of feeling in intersexual relationships. Beyond the "grim," the "harsh," the eccentric, the almost histrionically cynical that superficially distinguish Rochester from conventional heroes, there is something almost Lawrentian: Rochester is "neither tall nor graceful"; his eyes can be "dark, irate, and piercing"; his strong features "took my feelings from my own power and fettered them in his." Without using the vocabulary common to us, Charlotte is pre-senting maleness and physicality, to which Jane responds di-rectly. (pp. 99-100)

Aside from partial sterilization of banal Gothic by dry factuality and humor, Charlotte goes on to make a much more impor-tant—indeed, a radical—revision of the mode: in *Jane Eyre* and in the other novels . . . that discovery of passion, that rehabilitation of the extra-rational, which is the historical office of Gothic, is no longer oriented in marvelous circumstance but moves deeply into the lesser known realities of human life. This change I describe as the change from "old Gothic" to "new Gothic." The kind of appeal is the same; the fictional method is utterly different.

When Charlotte went on from *Jane Eyre* to *Shirley,* she pro-duced a book that for the student of the Gothic theme is in-teresting precisely because on the face of things it would be expected to be a barren field. It is the result of Charlotte's one deliberate venture from private intensities into public exten-sities: Orders in Council, the Luddites, technological unem-ployment in 1811 and 1812, a social portraiture which develops Charlotte's largest cast of characters. Yet Charlotte cannot keep it a social novel. Unlike Warren, who in the somewhat similar *Night Rider* chose to reflect the historical economic crisis in the private crisis of the hero, Miss Brontë loses interest in the public and slides over into the private.

The formal irregularities of *Shirley*—the stop-and-start, zig-zag movement, plunging periodically into different perspec-tives—light up the divergent impulses in Charlotte herself: the desire to make a story from observed outer life, and the inability to escape from inner urgencies that with centrifugal force un-wind outward into story almost autonomously. Passion alters plan: the story of industrial crisis is repeatedly swarmed over by the love stories. But the ultimate complication is that Char-lotte's duality of impulse is reflected not only in the narrative material but in two different ways of telling each part of the story. On the one hand she tells a rather conventional, open, predictable tale; on the other she lets go with a highly charged private sentiency that may subvert the former or at least sur-round it with an atmosphere of unfamiliarity or positive strange-ness: the Gothic impulse.

For Charlotte it is typically the "pattern" versus the "strange." She describes "two pattern young ladies, in pattern attire, with pattern deportment"—a "respectable society" in which "Shir-ley had the air of a black swan, or a white crow. . . ." When, in singing, Shirley "poured round the passion, force," the young ladies thought this "strange" and concluded: "What was *strange* must be *wrong*. . . ." True, Charlotte's characters live within the established "patterns" of life; but their impulse is to vitalize forms with unpatterned feeling, and Charlotte's to give play to unpatterned feeling in all its forms. (pp. 101-02)

True to convention, the love stories end happily. But special feelings, a new pathos of love, come through. . . . There is that peculiarly tense vivacity of talk between lovers (the Jane-Rochester style), who discover a heightened, at times stagey, yet highly communicative rhetoric, drawing now on fantasy, now on moral conviction, verging now on titillating revelation, now on battle; a crafty game of love, flirting with an undefined risk, betraying a withheld avowal, savoring the approach to consummation, as if the erotic energy which in another social order might find a physical outlet were forcing itself into an electric language that is decorous but intimately exploratory. (p. 103)

Though *Shirley* is not pulled together formally as well as *Jane Eyre* or even the more sprawling *Villette,* and though the characters are as wholes less fully realized, still it accommodates the widest ranging of an extraordinarily free sensibility. Constantly, in many different directions, it is in flight from the ordinary rational surface of things against which old Gothic was the first rebel in fiction; it abundantly contains and evokes, to adapt Charlotte's own metaphor, "unpatterned feeling." It turns up unexpected elements in personality: resentfulness, malice, love of power; precocities and perversities of response; the multiple tensions of love between highly individualized lovers; psychic disturbances. And in accepting a dark magnetic energy as a central virtue in personality, Charlotte simply reverses the status of men who were the villains in the sentimental and old Gothic modes.

Of the four novels, *Villette* is most heavily saturated with Gothic—with certain of its traditional manifestations (old Gothic), with the undercutting of these that is for Charlotte no less instinctive than the use of them (anti-Gothic), and with an original, intense exploration of feeling that increases the range and depth of fiction (new Gothic). (pp. 104-05)

In *The Professor* the tensions in the author's contemplation of her own experience come into play; in *Shirley* various undercurrents of personality push up into the social surfaces of life; in *Jane Eyre* moral feeling is subjected to the remolding pressures of a newly vivid consciousness of the diverse impulses of sexuality; and in *Villette* the feeling responses to existence are pursued into sufferings that edge over into disorder. The psychology of rejection and alienation, first applied to Polly, becomes the key to Lucy, who, finding no catharsis for a sense of desolation, generates a serious inner turmoil. (p. 106)

These strains prepare us for the high point in Charlotte's new Gothic—the study of Lucy's emotional collapse and near breakdown when vacation comes and she is left alone at the school with "a poor deformed and imbecile pupil." "My heart almos died within me; . . . My spirits had long been gradually sinking; now that the prop of employment was withdrawn, they went down fast." . . .

From now on, overtly or implicitly, hypochondria and anxiety keep coming into the story—the enemies from whose grip Lucy must gradually free herself. (p. 107)

There is not room to trace Lucy's recovery, especially in the important phase, the love affair with Paul which is related to our theme by compelling, as do the Jane-Rochester and Louis Moore-Shirley relationships in quite different ways, a radical revision of the feelings exacted by stereotyped romance. What is finally noteworthy is that Charlotte, having chosen in Lucy a heroine with the least durable emotional equipment, with the most conspicuous neurotic element in her temperament, goes on through the history of Lucy's emotional maturing to surmount the need for romantic fulfillment and to develop the aesthetic courage for a final disaster—the only one in her four novels.

Some years ago Edmund Wilson complained of writers of Gothic who "fail to lay hold on the terrors that lie deep in the human soul and that cause man to fear himself" and proposed an anthology of horror stories that probe "psychological caverns" and find "disquieting obsessions." This is precisely the direction in which Charlotte Brontë moved, especially in Lucy Snowe and somewhat also in Caroline Helstone and Shirley Keeldar; this was one aspect of her following human emotions where they took her, into many depths and intensities that as yet hardly had a place in the novel. This was the finest achievement of Gothic. (pp. 107-08)

The first Gothic writers took the easy way: the excitement of mysterious scene and happening, which I call old Gothic. Of this Charlotte Brontë made some direct use, while at the same time tending toward humorous modifications (anti-Gothic); but what really counts is its indirect usefulness to her: it released her from the patterns of the novel of society and therefore permitted the flowering of her real talent—the talent for finding and giving dramatic form to impulses and feelings which, because of their depth or mysteriousness or intensity or ambiguity, or of their ignoring or transcending everyday norms of propriety or reason, increase wonderfully the sense of reality in the novel. To note the emergence of this "new Gothic" in Charlotte Brontë is not, I think, to pursue an old mode into dusty corners but rather to identify historically the distinguishing, and distinguished, element in her work. (pp. 108-09)

Robert B. Heilman, "Charlotte Brontë's 'New' Gothic", in From Austen to Conrad, *edited by R. C. Rathburn and M. Steinmann, University of Minnesota Press, Minneapolis, 1958 (and reprinted in* The Brontës: A Collection of Critical Essays, *edited by Ian Gregor, Prentice-Hall, Inc., 1970, pp. 96-109).*

DONALD W. CROMPTON (essay date 1960)

[It] has always seemed to me that many books can be found to be better than they are by by-passing the main issues and concentrating on playing hunt-the-slipper with theme and symbol. Take, for instance, *Jane Eyre.* The more one goes into *Jane Eyre* the richer the structural unity of the book becomes. Leaving aside the more obvious technical devices—the supernatural signs, the dream omens, the weather symbolism which enacts the theme at every point—one still has left a character pattern, built up on a series of parallels and antitheses, which if it lacks the finesse of a Jane Austen, nevertheless is very effective in developing that 'concentration of the area of action' which Edwin Muir saw as the essence of the dramatic novel. At the lowest level it reveals itself as a physical separating out into the opposing camps of dark and light—where light represents conventional beauty of face and form and dark the reverse. . . . This opposition is made explicit in Jane's remark about having a theoretical reverence for beauty but shunning anything 'bright but antipathetic'. The reason for it is clear. Conventional beauty in *Jane Eyre* invariably connotes either the empty head or, more frequently, the hard, shrivelled heart incapable of feeling, and it is appropriate that the eyes (the windows of the soul) should be used symbolically to suggest it. . . . This opposition is further reinforced in the general characterisation. (pp. 360-61)

At a deeper level, this antithesis between surface and depth is associated with a more fundamental contrasting of the Classical and the Romantic point of view. Throughout the novel this opposition also has been suggested in the description of the central characters. . . . A stream of images suggests the violence of the author's rejection of the Classic ideal which, to her, is synonymous with coldness, hardness and emptiness. (p. 362)

Even if this analysis is allowed, however, its value as an approach to *Jane Eyre* is relatively very slight. Perhaps it might be used to support the view that Charlotte, like Emily, could manipulate the melodramatic framework in such a way that it corresponded with her own intense vision of life. Having made the point, however, one is still left with the fact . . . that *Wuthering Heights* is a great book and that *Jane Eyre*—whatever its structure—is relatively immature in conception and execution and yields little more from sustained consideration than it does from a single reading. In some ways, of course, it is a remarkable novel, but one feels that the major qualities it has lie outside anything which might be described as the scheme of the novel. In fact, the whole point of this digression has been to suggest that the pursuit of what is interesting but essentially minor can lead to a distortion which neglects both major vice and major virtue. (pp. 362-63)

> *Donald W. Crompton, "The New Criticism: A Caveat," in* Essays in Criticism, *Vol. X, No. 3, July, 1960, pp. 359-64.**

ROBERT A. COLBY   (essay date 1960)

In the last century *Villette* was something of a fashionable shocker. . . . The reputation of the book seems for the most part to have been preserved by Miss Brontë's sister novelists of various generations—Mrs. Gaskell, George Eliot, Mrs. Ward, May Sinclair, Virginia Woolf—so that the pressed flower fragrance of the "woman's novel" has tended to cling to it. . . .

In our time, as it was in Charlotte Brontë's, *Villette* is thought of mainly as "by the author of *Jane Eyre.*" To be sure, there are good reasons why *Jane Eyre* should have edged out its successor in popularity. By comparison with the steady excitement of *Jane Eyre, Villette* may seem to some readers loosely woven and desultory in pace, not so carefully plotted. There is no mysterious manor house here, nor any hidden mad wife. The romance around which *Villette* principally turns is between two outwardly rather unattractive people, and nothing much (practically speaking) comes of it. Yet it may still be argued that in many ways Miss Brontë's last novel was her most profound accomplishment. To read *Villette* as carefully as it deserves to be read is to follow the curve of Charlotte Brontë's literary development to its completion—and at the same time to follow the direction of the nineteenth-century novel. . . .

Villette is most fruitfully approached as Charlotte Brontë's literary, not her literal, autobiography. Lucy Snowe's turbulent emotional experiences may be taken as an analogue of Charlotte Brontë's creative life, in that her achievement of mastery over her morbidly introverted imagination parallels Miss Brontë's own emancipation from the dream world she had envisaged in the Angrian legends of her youth. (p. 410)

The Professor will always be of interest to readers of *Villette* since Miss Brontë undertook the writing of her last novel after another unsuccessful attempt to publish the first. However, the relationship between the two novels is elusive. *The Professor* is not really an underdone *Villette* as it is sometimes said to be. The germ of *Villette* is contained not in what Miss Brontë tried and failed to do in *The Professor,* but in what she deliberately tried *not* to do there. (pp. 410-11)

[The] superiority of *Villette* over *The Professor* does not lie merely in its greater power. What Miss Brontë tried to repress in *The Professor* re-asserts itself in *Villette,* it is true, but with a sense of proportion. While throughout the novel passion and rationality, art and nature, romance and reality continuously exert their rival claims on Lucy's imagination, in the end these tensions are resolved. Greater richness is produced also by the contrast between the tragedy of Lucy Snowe and the happier fates of the lesser heroines Polly Home and Ginevra Fanshawe.

Many readers may feel that of the three stories developed in *Villette,* the only one that is really "done," as Henry James might have put it, is the romance between Lucy Snowe and Monsieur Paul. Had Miss Brontë succeeded in penetrating the other two romances with equal insight perhaps she would have produced a masterpiece on the order and scale of, say, *Middlemarch,* instead of the erratic and uneven masterpiece that *Villette* admittedly is. However, the superficial treatment of the secondary characters actually serves a purpose in the scheme of the novel. . . .

The characters are contrasted not only by their sensibilities. Significant differences in the descriptions of the three pairs of lovers indicate something also of the Brontëan scale of values with respect to nature and art. . . .

[The] subtle interpenetration of nature and art really informs the entire novel, binding together the loosely woven first two-thirds of the story with the more taut and tense latter portion. A good part of *Villette,* particularly its early sections, is taken up with literature and the other arts, both explicitly and by allusion. In this novel, on the whole, the arts are associated with passivity and escapism, nature with the active mind and reality. (p. 412)

[In] the very framework of *Villette* and in the point of view from which it is told, there is embedded that circularity of life and literature, romance and reality that envelops its incidents, characters, and thought. "I used to think what a delight it would be for one who loved him better than he loved himself to gather and store up those handfuls of gold dust, so recklessly flung to heaven's reckless winds," Lucy recalls in connection with one of the sylvan story hours. So she writes a book about a man who didn't write books. *Villette* then is one of those special novels that we have become more used to in our century which have a novelist writing a novel at their center. Lucy is really observing herself in the process of composing, creating characters and re-creating herself, and one understands therefore why she is so preoccupied with the workings of the mind and the imagination.

In this respect *Villette* can be contrasted with *Jane Eyre*. Where Lucy's impulse is to take up the pen, Jane's is to reach for the crayon. Jane feels that she has 'pinned down' a character when she has managed to sketch his lineaments at the drawing board. Lucy, on the other hand, is every minute the writer. . . . Jane characteristically is interested in the *features* of the people she meets, to the extent that they reveal character. That is to say, Jane is an amateur phrenologist, as are other Brontë characters.

Lucy, it is true, makes some use also of "Gall's Science" but on the whole phrenology plays a lesser part in the characterization of the personages of *Villette* than in that of the other three novels of Charlotte Brontë. (p. 415)

Much went into the moulding of *Villette;* more, undoubtedly, than we can hope to trace. Coming as it does in mid-century, Miss Brontë's final novel, more than is generally realized, is a meeting place of the streams of early nineteenth-century fiction. As an *éducation sentimentale* it links the continent with England, the sensibility of Romanticism with mid-Victorian realism. One wishes he knew more exactly just what French novels Miss Brontë steeped herself in during the 1830's and 1840's. We know she admired Balzac's *Modeste Mignon* and *Illusions Perdues* for their "analysis of motives" and "subtle perception of the most obscure and secret workings of the mind." The early chapters of *Consuelo,* her favorite novel of George Sand, anticipate the master-pupil relationship of *Villette.* (p. 417)

If a certain phase of Miss Brontë's imagination moves back to the late eighteenth century, another is lodged in a period more within her actual recall. Woven through the fabric of *Villette* are threads of various modes of fiction that flourished during her youth—here given a new twist. . . .

[Charlotte Brontë] deflates the glamorous and rationalizes the ghostly, thereby integrating the "wild, wonder and thrilling" with the "plain and homely." Her treatment of terror in particular reminds us that readers in the early nineteenth century were beset on one hand by a spate of Gothic novels and on the other by the plethora of fictions that proclaimed "A Tale Founded on Facts" on the title pages. In her wry way Miss Brontë seems to be giving us something of both worlds. We know already the good use to which she put the tale of the concealed wife in a castle, which has its origin in Mrs. Radcliffe's *A Sicilian Romance.* She may well have been recalling at this time a later romance of Mrs. Radcliffe's called *The Italian; or, the Confessional of the Black Penitents,* for in the schemes of the Marchesa Vivaldi and her confessor Schedoni, we suspect, lies the germ of the situation towards the end of *Villette* where Mme. Beck and her confessor Père Silas also plot to separate two lovers. However, this is as far as Miss Brontë permits herself to carry the situation. The pair who momentarily appear to Lucy as "a secret junta" plan no assassination, as they would if they were Radcliffean characters, but merely send Paul off to the West Indies to claim some real estate. Thus they achieve their dire ends by quite ordinary means. (p. 418)

With the nun, as with other characters in *Villette,* Charlotte Brontë distorted outmoded literary conventions in a pointedly perverse way. Making the source of the ghost stem from the comic side of the novel—in a prank played by Ginevra's foppish lover de Hamal—is surely the author's way of mocking the tradition that once had teased her own fevered fancy. This, her last word on the Gothic novel, is a laugh at it—and a laugh that liberates. Lucy Snowe, destroying the empty vestments of the nun, is the heroine of the "new" realistic novel sloughing off the trappings of the shadowy heroine of the "old" romantic novel. As Lucy Snowe clears her mind of the phantoms from the past that have haunted it, so Charlotte Brontë exorcises the Gothic novel that once fired her imagination, even as Miss Austen had exorcised it earlier in the century. . . .

One likes to think that the genius that first found itself in *Jane Eyre* ultimately fulfilled itself in *Villette.* In the history of the novel *Villette* may be said to look simultaneously backwards and forwards. It is at once a retrospect and a prospect. Certainly Miss Brontë has here anticipated some of our present-day literary techniques: the probing into the sub-conscious and the unconscious mind, even if with an archaic faculty psychology rather than with the benefit of Freudian apparatus; the exposing of instinctual passion, though imaged in poetical symbolism, rather than set forth in the blunter language to which we have grown accustomed; and, through the burning, prismatic sensibility of Lucy Snowe, the venturing into the "stream of consciousness," though Lucy calls it simply the "flow of time." Through this melange of diary, memoir, and devoir, wrung from the anguished heart of Lucy Snowe, reverberates much that in the English novel was past, and passing, and to come. (p. 419)

Robert A. Colby, " 'Villette' and the Life of the Mind," in PMLA, 75 (copyright © 1960 by the Modern Language Association of America; reprinted by permission of the Modern Language Association of America), Vol. LXXV, No. 4, September, 1960, pp. 410-19.

ERIC SOLOMON (essay date 1963)

A proper understanding of Charlotte Brontë's achievement in *Jane Eyre* should be based on the symbolic form of the novel. While any perceptive reading of the book must grant the author's artistic excesses—the improbabilities, the stilted dialogue, the lack of restraint, the flat secondary characters—still, the argument for *Jane Eyre*'s continuing fascination must go beyond the usual commonplaces about Charlotte Brontë's forcefulness, her powerful imagination, the vitality of her passionate heroine. I would argue that *Jane Eyre* is not formless "romantic" art. The novel makes up for a certain flabbiness of plot by a hard coherence of thematic and symbolic pattern. (p. 215)

Charlotte Brontë uses [several] structural methods to make her supposedly rambling novel cohere. There are parallel scenes—Jane's isolation in the red room and, later, in the room with the wounded Mason, for example; or the attempted seductions by Rochester and Rivers. The novel also sets contrasts of character—Rochester and Rivers are opposites, as are Blanche and Rosamund, the Reed sisters and the Rivers sisters. There is considerable foreshadowing: Rochester must lean on Jane when he first meets her and when they come together at the end. The book has a general thematic unity; as the hymn at the start of the novel indicates and as Helen's death makes clear, a motif is the orphan Jane's search for a home (a motif basic to Victorian fiction). By stressing the tensions in each section of the novel between spirit and flesh, order and emotion, submission and revolt, restraint and excitement, conscience and passion, and, finally, love and sin, Charlotte Brontë brings her heroine through a series of temptations, each one starting in isolation and ending in a triumph of integrity.

Much of the imagery of *Jane Eyre* is obvious—the chestnut tree, the grim landscapes, the red room that is like Hell. But two images are so pervasive that they serve as a substructure for the entire novel: fire and water—and their extremes, the flames of lust and the ice of indifference. The fire is in Jane's spirit and in Rochester's eyes. Jane desires "life, fire, feeling" . . . ; Rochester has "strange fire in his look." . . . If these two are fire, St. John Rivers (note the last name) contains the icy waters that would put out fire, destroy passion. His nature is frozen over with an "ice of reserve" . . . ; when he tells

Jane, "I am cold: no fervour infects me," her reply is, "Whereas I am hot, and fire dissolves ice." . . .

From the start of the novel, Charlotte Brontë's fire and water imagery indicates the essential idea. The fiery passion of Jane, and, later, Rochester, must be quenched by the cold waters of self-control—but not destroyed by the ice of repression. If their bodies burn, their minds must dampen the fires. Jane warns herself that secret love might "kindle" within her life an *"ignis fatuus."* . . . Yet it is Rochester who is all-fire: when, disguised as a gypsy, he has his interview with Jane, she feels his powerful attraction and says, "Don't keep me long; the fire scorches me." Rochester, for his part, realizes Jane's double quality; she has the fire of bodily love, "The flame flickers in the eye," but also the cool control of the soul, "the eye shines like dew." . . . Earlier, Rochester insists that Jane is cold because she is alone: "no contact strikes the fire from you that is within you." . . .

When Bertha, Rochester's old passionate flame, sets his bed on fire, Jane saves him by dousing the bed with water. Miss Brontë's imagery is precise and explains the relationship between the central characters. Bertha represents the flames of hellfire that have already scorched Rochester. Jane, fiery though she is, has sufficient control to water down these fires. Jane "brought my own water jug, baptized the couch afresh, and, by God's aid, succeeded in extinguishing the flames which were devouring it." . . . She will save them both from hellfire by refusing the passionate advances of Rochester. After she learns of his previous marriage, she finally gains release from her burning agony and imagines herself laid down in the dried-up bed of a great river, and "I heard a flood loosened in remote mountains, and felt the torrent come. . . ." . . . Religion— true religion, not the frigid religion that will characterize Rivers—is described in terms of water: "'the waters came into my soul . . . I came into deep waters; the floods overflowed me'." . . . And this water in Jane's spirit enables her to withstand what Rochester calls the "pure, powerful flame" . . . that fuses them. Despite the "hand of fiery iron [that] grasped my vitals," . . . despite her "veins running fire," despite Rochester's "flaming glance" which is likened to the "glow of a furnace," . . . Jane flees to the "wet turf" and sheds "stormy, scalding, heart-wrung tears." . . . (p. 216)

Although Jane is soaked with rain in her wanderings, her emotional fires still burn, ready to be re-awakened when the dangers of Rochester's appeals have passed. Rochester alone must be purged by the fires he long ago lit between himself and Bertha. This time there is no Jane to keep him from the searing, mutilating flames that destroy Bertha and Thornfield, and, ironically, put out the fiery gleam in his eyes. But Jane, meanwhile, is guarding her own flame from the freezing heartlessness of St. John Rivers. His "ice kisses" cannot reach her. She cannot forever "keep the fires of my nature continually low, to compel it to burn inwardly and never utter a cry, though the imprisoned flame consumed vital after vital." . . . She escapes from Rivers' chilling grasp and returns to the scorched ruin of Rochester where she can "kindle the lustre" of his "lamp" which has been "quenched." . . . Soon she reawakens the glow of their love, and their two natures join in a steady flame that burns neither as wildly as the lightning that destroyed the chestnut, nor as dimly as the setting sun of St. John Rivers' religious dream. The fire-water image underscores the basic idea of *Jane Eyre:* just as love must find a middle way between the flames of passion and the waters of pure reason, so Jane must find a golden mean between egocentric rage and Christlike submis-

sion, between Aunt Reed and Helen Burns, between the wild, Byronic Rochester and the tempered, controlled Rivers. Jane Eyre achieves this successful median in her own character and in her future life with the chastened Rochester. Image and idea join in a novel that not only shows the wildly passionate appeal of romantic art but also operates under the concept of formal control. (p. 217)

Eric Solomon, "'Jane Eyre': Fire and Water" (copyright © 1963 by the National Council of Teachers of English; reprinted by permission of the publisher and the author), in College English, *Vol. 25, No. 3, December, 1963, pp. 215-17.*

ROBERT BERNARD MARTIN   (essay date 1966)

[It seems] in spite of her preface that Miss Brontë was violating her own most deeply held convictions when in writing **The Professor** she 'restrained imagination, eschewed romance, repressed excitement,' avoided 'over-bright colouring,' and 'sought to produce something which should be soft, grave, and true'. . . . What is most important about this transgression against her own instincts is that it indicates a good part of the reason the novel lacks the artistic unity of the later works. When Miss Brontë eschewed imagination in her sense of the word, with its connotations of excess, exaggeration, and improbability, she failed to fulfil the claims of the Imagination, as Coleridge used the term. The true unity of a work of art eluded her at the very time she sought to find it by emphasis on a single aspect of perception. Paradoxically, it was when she was most eclectic in her choice of material that her work was most unified in effect, and the more literally improbable those materials the greater the sense of reality she achieved. (p. 28)

The world of Charlotte Brontë's novels is, to be sure, a circumscribed one when compared to the worlds of Shakespeare or Chaucer or Milton or even that of her admired master, Thackeray, but the breadth of the world the artist dreams has little relationship to our sense of fulfilment in it. Completeness is all. The horizons may be narrow, but one must have a sense of the artist's having explored them. In spite of **Shirley,** one does not go to Charlotte Brontë for an understanding of Victorian history or politics; the wise man repairs to her novels for an exploration of her own confined world, and it is only when one feels that she has attempted to close a curtain over half that world, as in **The Professor**, that one feels its cramping limits. (p. 29)

It has been customary to say of the novel, taking the lead from Miss Brontë's husband's postscript to her preface, that it is a kind of preliminary sketch for **Villette.** True, the two novels are set in Brussels, there is a professor-student relationship that develops into love, and the inhabitants of the Pension Héger have been reworked into fictional being in both novels; but these are mere surface resemblances, and in reality the first novel has less likeness to **Villette** than has **Jane Eyre.** What is most interesting about it as a first novel is the introduction of themes that characterize the rest of the novels. All too often, however, the techniques were not yet developed for giving life to these themes. (pp. 29-30)

The obvious crudities of **The Professor** are many, both stylistic and structural. For example, the book is riddled with the insecurity of syntax that always bedevilled Miss Brontë, and with her misguided insertions of schoolgirl French. Occasionally, she is so misled by her enthusiasm for her second language that she translates expressions she has already given in English, as when she writes of the closing of 'the school-year (l'année scolaire).' . . . (p. 37)

The linear movement of the plot saves Miss Brontë from gross errors of construction, although one can hardly avoid irritation at such awkward devices as the letter that opens the book, outlining the necessary background material to a correspondent known only as 'Charles', who is never again mentioned. There are other maladroit touches in Miss Brontë's descriptions when she appears unable to decide whether to speak in the voice of Crimsworth recounting a simple history or with the detached, reflective tones of the novelist consciously considering the craft of fiction while exploiting a position of uninvolvement with the action. There have been notable novels (most often with novelists as protagonists) in which the problem of turning experience into fiction becomes part of the novel itself, but they have a considerably more complex viewpoint than Miss Brontë is attempting in this novel. Rather, she occasionally slides awkwardly from first person narrator into the part of omniscient narrator, with no consequent gain in effect. . . . In *Jane Eyre* and *Villette* Miss Brontë is more subtle in her exposition, and is content to let the reader share the discoveries of her narrator without calling attention to the fact that direct information is being given. (p. 38)

The choice of Crimsworth as narrator is a serious handicap to the book, for Miss Brontë was unable to impart a believable virility to her masculine mouthpiece, while the point of view of the novel denies her the opportunity of entering the mind of the chief feminine character to carry out the detailed investigation of the feminine psyche at which she was to excel. It is true that Rochester, the brothers Moore, and even M. Paul are in part quite as unbelievable as Crimsworth, but they do not fail as characters, since they are men as seen through a woman's eyes; in the three last novels it is the credibility of the feminine central consciousness (even in *Shirley,* ostensibly told in the third-person) that matters, not that of the men it perceives. When the credibility of the central consciousness is open to question, as it is with Crimsworth, the reader is unable to accept the validity of his perceptions. At the same time it is clear that Miss Brontë does not intend the awareness of the narrator to be different from that of herself or of the reader.

Were it to serve a point, the list of flaws in the novel might be greatly extended, for it is so full of minor faults that it is doubtful that it would attract many modern readers if it were not the first published work of a great writer. Perhaps even greater flaws, however, are some of the very aspects that make the novel fascinating to lovers of the later books: the subjects that so absorbed Charlotte Brontë that she was unable to leave them out, in spite of not yet knowing how to integrate them into the plot and the themes of the novel. Awkward, intrusive, they are unassimilated diversions that impede the course of the central narrative but show clearly and naïvely the preoccupations that she was subsequently to handle with assurance. (pp. 39-40)

The importance of the sexual relationship in *The Professor* scarcely needs underlining. . . . The major theme of all the novels is the study of the adjustment between the reason and the passions, and the plot embodying that theme is always a love story, resulting in the marriage of the main characters in three of the novels; in *Villette* there is no wedding, but the stage is set for it, the characters prepared, the conflicts resolved, and all that remains is for the fates to be propitious. It is this insistence on a love match (but one far removed from those in the novels of her contemporaries) that makes the works

of Miss Brontë seem so feminine that today it is difficult to see how any of her original readers could have thought Currer Bell a man. For her love was indeed woman's whole existence. (p. 40)

An almost Puritan contempt for physical beauty, whether feminine or masculine, permeates the novels. Only in *Shirley* do the central characters possess striking good looks. (p. 45)

Rather more interestingly, Miss Brontë used particular kinds of beauty as shorthand to character description, in the same way that she used phrenology. In *The Professor* she first introduced the three major categories of feminine beauty that she was to use to such effect in the later novels. . . . The overstuffed young ladies of [the] physical type Miss Brontë portrays as vain, silly, vacuous, and affected, but not vicious; occasionally, they are even affectionate after their own blowzy fashion.

The natural complement to these large, blonde women of wax are the sensual, Oriental temptresses of the books. . . . (pp. 46-7)

The third major group of beautiful women, with all the attendant defects of loveliness, is by far the most interesting of the lot, since they are the most credible, but they are also the most difficult to classify. Probably the epitome of the type is Pauline Home de Bassompierre. She is tiny, graceful, perfectly formed on an almost infantile scale, well bred, and with a charming, regular face; she is not unintelligent, and she is affectionate, but her lisp and the tininess of her figure are indicative of the immaturity of her mind and the shallowness of her emotions. . . . In *The Professor* the type has not yet completely emerged, but there are hints of it in Mrs. Edward Crimsworth, who is described as 'young, tall, and well shaped', with 'good animal spirits', 'a good complexion and features sufficiently marked but agreeable.' . . . Her insipidity is indicated by her voice. . . . Mrs. Crimsworth is larger and less attractive than her sister-beauties, but the patent vacuity of her personality is not far removed from the basic frivolity of theirs.

In a somewhat more expected manner, great masculine beauty fares ill in Miss Brontë's works. The only two really handsome male characters of any importance are St. John Rivers and Dr. John. (p. 48)

Miss Brontë's first novel is probably her least overtly religious, but there is a strong feeling of the self-reliant Protestant ethic that so dominated her thinking. (p. 49)

The roots of Charlotte Brontë's religious faith are not far to seek, of course, since she was the daughter of a clergyman and lived most of her life under his roof, next the parish church. Unlike Emily, whose religion seems to have had pantheistic beliefs added to Christian doctrine, Charlotte Brontë seldom varied far from the conventional Evangelical position of her father, who had been educated at Cambridge when that University was the stronghold of Evangelicalism. (p. 50)

With two notable exceptions, Miss Brontë was probably as tolerant of other forms of Christianity as most of her contemporaries were. Her treatment of the two exceptions is one of the least attractive aspects of her writing, both because it reveals a stubborn intolerance and because the strength of that intolerance flashes out in *The Professor* to help ruin the unity of the novel. (p. 52)

As in *The Professor,* Miss Brontë's formal allegiance [in *Shirley*] is to a disciplined novel, with both her own emotions and those of her characters kept in firm check; it is no surprise that her absorption with the non-rational aspects of life threatens to wreck the unity of the novel by fighting against the rational impulses that she is avowedly supporting. (p. 109)

The setting is that of a Gothic novel, but when we are taken inside, we find that instead of developing the air of mystery the narrator treats us to a disquisition on the difficulties of spring-cleaning the panelling in this 'gothic old barrack.' . . . (p. 110)

Since all of Miss Brontë's novels are at least partly autobiographical, the problem of the relationship between fact and fiction was one that frequently occupied her, and it is a problem to which she never found a satisfactory, or even constant, answer. [Passages in *Shirley* show] her belief in a non-rational reality that transcends fact, but her creation of character sometimes seems a contradiction of this belief. . . .

Subsidiary characters and events may serve any of several functions in a novel: they may be necessary to move the action, and they may provide analogues to the main characters and events or a viewpoint from which to consider them. They may also . . . exist simply for the pleasure they provide in themselves. (p. 112)

As characters they hardly exist, for they neither contribute to the major themes and actions of the book nor provide pleasure in themselves. Miss Brontë has mistaken the literal for the significant. The Yorkes might stand in small for all the characters and actions in the novel that seem put in to fill out a panorama rather than because of their importance. The digressions are primarily responsible for the feeling of the reader that the book is too long for its contents. This irrelevant material is particularly noticeable because *Shirley* falls between *Jane Eyre* and *Villette,* in both of which Miss Brontë pruned extraneous matter and managed to give significance to the autobiographical matter that she employed. (pp. 113-14)

Shirley marks a watershed in Miss Brontë's novels. It has been customary to group *The Professor* and *Shirley* as examples of an attempt at realism in the novel, with *Jane Eyre* and *Villette* as triumphs of the imagination. It would be equally valid to speak of her first two novels as exemplifying Miss Brontë's early optimism and hope, with *Shirley* showing her growing doubt and pessimism, followed by the autumnal resignation of earthly hope in *Villette.* The distinct darkening in her outlook is probably responsible for the general preference of readers for *The Professor* to *Shirley,* and the greater popularity of *Jane Eyre* over that of *Villette,* although the latter novel in each pair is the more skilful technically. (p. 118)

[In] *Shirley,* Miss Brontë made her only full-length attempt at narration primarily in the third person; as a method, it is considerably less successful than the first-person narrations of the central characters of the other novels. (p. 120)

In *Shirley,* Miss Brontë is seldom detached from the reactions of her characters, and her intention is certainly not comic, even in the broadest meaning of that term, save perhaps in the case of Caroline, who is clearly intended to be viewed objectively in her over-romantic reactions to the neglect of Robert Moore. Since there is no particular use made of a discrepancy between the viewpoint of the author and that of the characters, the occasional reminder of the narrator's presence serves more as a distraction than as a guide to the meaning of the novel. . . . Miss Brontë's role as narrator is negligible and no clear impression of the narrator's personality emerges.

Probably at one moment only in the novel does Miss Brontë use the point of view of the narrator clearly and forcefully. (p. 121)

In *Jane Eyre* the character of Jane herself, capricious, changeable, and sometimes inconsistent, helps maintain a unity of tone as the action is filtered through her mind, her imagination and memory. The sensibility of the novel is Jane's own, and what might be jarring contradictions are resolved as disparate aspects of her humanly variable perceptions. Too much reliance on rationality, for instance, is as much a part of the formation of her character as is the over-dependence upon emotion. In *Shirley,* Miss Brontë is once more concerned with the old tug-of-war between rationality and the emotions, but almost as if she were aware of the difficulties of presenting this kind of divided sensibility except as it is embodied in separate characters, she splits the consciousness that Jane represents into two parts, assigning that of the too-romantic young girl to Caroline, that of the tougher, more rational woman to Shirley. (p. 122)

The emancipation of woman from mere conventionality is a theme that occupies Miss Brontë in all her novels, but nowhere else is it so important as in *Shirley.* . . . The contrast between the modern woman and the womanly woman is made continuously throughout the novel. . . . (p. 129)

In [*Shirley*] Miss Brontë is deliberately broadening her canvas, but in so doing she reverses the usual process of the social novel of her day. . . . [The] Luddite riots, the Orders in Council, the opposing interests of Tory and Whig are employed to throw light on the intensely personal conflicts that lie at the core of the novel, acting almost as metaphors to extend the significance of those conflicts. The horizons are broader, but the focus of attention remains as confined as ever it was in *Jane Eyre* or *The Professor.* The concentration of the novel remains steadfastly on the individual not the nation, and we should be thankful that Miss Brontë realized that her talents were not for the full-scale social novel; the Romantic muse is not always at ease when her attention shifts from the particular to the general. (p. 136)

Shirley is a long novel, indeed, but the ending is curiously huddled and cramped. This effect is no doubt due in part to there being . . . no real resolution; the strings of the puppets are jerked, they pair off, and the stage is cleared. The effect has its most unfortunate result in the character of Louis Moore, who is introduced late in the book. Clearly, he is intended as a model for the other characters in the novel, but like Shirley he is not given an opportunity to exercise his own character, and he remains passive throughout almost all the action in which he is concerned. (p. 139)

In many ways *Shirley* is Miss Brontë's most ambitious novel, but it is a long way from being her most successful. The reason for her failure is not, I think, the generally accepted one that she knew too little of social history to deal with the situation of 1812, but rather that she attempted to split her sensibility in too many directions, divided it among too many characters, tried to encompass too many viewpoints, and to see them all objectively. She was no Jane Austen, capable of detachment, nor was she a George Eliot, able to give full emotional validity to several points of view; the result is a series of fragments, many of them splendid. Fortunately, in her last completed novel she returned to the single point of view that had worked so well in *Jane Eyre.* (p. 141)

Robert Bernard Martin, in his The Accents of Persuasion: Charlotte Brontë's Novels *(reprinted by per-*

mission of W. W. Norton & Company, Inc.; in Canada by Faber and Faber Ltd.; copyright © 1966 by Robert Bernard Martin), Norton, 1966, Faber and Faber, 1966, 188 p.

ISABEL QUIGLY (essay date 1967)

[As most good letter-writers,] Charlotte first considered the person she was writing to, and altered tone and personality as well as matter and manner to suit whoever was at the other end.

Strong and outspoken though the letters often were, they never 'imposed' Charlotte's presence by presuming sympathy and interest: a painful, proud humility runs through them all, that reaches its highest point in the pathetic yet never craven appeals for some sign of life from the silent M. Héger: 'One suffers in silence so long as one has the strength so to do, and when that strength gives out one speaks without too carefully measuring one's words.'

But most of the letters are nothing like as explicit. Charlotte could be brisk, sometimes amusing, and she was never afraid to speak out, however unfashionably; on *In Memoriam* she wrote: 'It is beautiful; it is mournful; it is monotonous'; on *Pride and Prejudice:* 'An accurate daguerrotyped portrait of a commonplace face.' Children, the governess's *raison d'être*, she seems mostly to have disliked: 'desperate little dunces . . . excessively indulged,' 'more riotous, perverse, unmanageable cubs never grew,' 'singularly cold, selfish, animal and inferior.' In fact, Charlotte's letters are autobiography and self-portraiture. . . .

Isabel Quigly, "Strong and Outspoken," in The Spectator *(© 1967 by* The Spectator; *reprinted by permission of* The Spectator), *No. 7229, January 13, 1967, p. 49.*

BRIGID BROPHY, MICHAEL LEVEY, AND CHARLES OSBORNE (essay date 1967)

Jane Eyre is blatantly such stuff as daydreams are made on. . . . Charlotte Brontë belongs somewhere near Corvo in the sweetmeat shop, though on a broader and more accessible shelf. . . . [Reading] *Jane Eyre* is like gobbling a jar-full of schoolgirl stickjaw. So naive a work, even though it is likely to give one a pain in the belly, provokes no serious quarrel in its own right. . . .

To be precise, *Jane Eyre* is such stuff as two daydreams are made on. The first concerns the put-upon child who eventually gets her own back on everyone. (p. 65)

[However, Jane] cannot refrain from leaking little dribbles of her triumph in advance. Cruelly and unjustly punished by the adults, she or her creator can't wait till she becomes adult herself; the infant Jane must enjoy her daydream vindication there and then: she must fall grievously ill on the spot and as a direct result of adult unkindness, the doctor must be called and the adults must be shown up and shamed in his sight.

Time and again this impatience to anticipate the daydream dénouement spoils the dramatic effect. Jane Eyre as narrator vigorously, if not subtly, builds up the character of Mr Brocklehurst through his own dialogue. 'Oh, shocking!' he exclaims when he learns of Jane's indifference to the Psalms. 'I have a little boy, younger than you, who knows six Psalms by heart: and when you ask him which he would rather have, a ginger-bread-nut to eat, or a verse of a Psalm to learn, he says: "Oh! the verse of a Psalm! angels sing Psalms"', says he.' So far so good, if crude; and the crudity may be justified as straight reporting. But the narrator is then betrayed by her own indignation. She cannot wait to show Mr Brocklehurst for an ass by oblique methods. She insists he condemn himself on the spot and out of his own mouth; and she makes him continue his speech not merely with an implausibly naked self-revelation but in the very sardonic accents that would be used by, and could be used only by, a third person commenting adversely on him. Mr Brocklehurst goes on to relate that his little boy 'then gets two nuts in recompense for his infant piety'. The error is repeated when Mr Brocklehurst visits the school where Jane is now a pupil. Mr Brocklehurst is in the act of declaiming that the pupils must be taught 'to clothe themselves with shame-facedness and sobriety, not with braided hair and costly apparel' when the impatient narrator has him interrupted by the entrance of his own wife and daughters 'splendidly attired in velvet, silk, and furs'. An ironist makes his readers hold their breath until the echo is returned. Charlotte Brontë dissipates what might have been irony in mere invective.

The second daydream in *Jane Eyre* is sexual and belongs to a different period of the daydreamer's life. Some of the awkwardness of patching the two ages and the two fantasies together is probably reflected in the clumsy bridge-passage that begins Chapter 10 of the novel (whose sub-title is 'an autobiography'): 'Hitherto I have recorded in detail the events of my insignificant existence: to the first ten years of my life I have given almost as many chapters. But this is not to be a regular autobiography . . . I now pass a space of eight years almost in silence.' (pp. 66-7)

But not all this second fantasy belongs to adult life. Its core is the Oedipus situation, with Mr Rochester playing father-figure. . . . Charlotte Brontë's daydreams had clearly been formed by the Oedipal stress. The little girl can escape the guilt of her erotic relation to her father if her father is castrated: before Jane Eyre can marry her father-figure, he is mutilated in the fire that destroys his house. He loses an arm and almost all his sight—an emphatic symbolic castration, betokened twice over, by the direct loss of a limb and by the blinding that is the symbol used in the Oedipus story itself. (Mr Rochester is phallicized and castrated yet again by being likened to a tree—whose blasting by lightning forecasts, according to Mrs Leavis, his mutilation.) (pp. 67-8)

Jane Eyre essentially recites these two fantasies one after the other, with only a cursory gesture towards slotting the end of the first into the working-out of the second. . . .

The most Charlotte Brontë does to unite the two fantasies is to withhold the final vindication of the child, the £20,000, until after the adolescent with her Oedipus fixation has been foiled in her first attempt to marry Mr Rochester. This involves her, however, in perhaps the most outrageous coincidence in the repertory of melodramatic plot making. (p. 68)

When her male cousin proposes marriage to her, Jane runs away again, this time back to Mr Rochester. By perhaps the most outrageous coincidence in the repertory of happy endings, the fire which, by maiming him, has removed the unconscious psychological impediment to their marriage, has conveniently destroyed also the legal impediment, his wife.

As well as defying the laws of chance, *Jane Eyre* gives a good tossing to the laws of nature by way of much symbolic weather and a premonitory dream or two, and at last finally infringes nature with a supernatural event. Tempted to marry her cousin, Jane hears a disembodied voice cry 'Jane! Jane!' and shouts back 'I am coming! Wait for me! . . . Where are you?' She then sets off to find where he (Mr Rochester, of course) is. He has been a thirty-six-hour coach journey distant from her all along. Yet, he relates to her when they meet, 'As I exclaimed, "Jane! Jane! Jane!" a voice—I cannot tell whence the voice came, but I know whose voice it was—replied "I am coming; wait for me"; and a moment after, went whispering on the wind the words, "Where are you?"' As narrator, Jane Eyre solemnly adds 'Reader, it was on Monday night—near midnight—that I too had received the mysterious summons; those were the very words . . .', etc. (pp. 68-9)

[Perhaps] Charlotte Brontë had simply read this bit of *Moll Flanders*: 'I fell into a vehement fit of crying, every now and then calling him by his name . . . "O Jemmy!" said I, "come back, come back" . . . thus I passed the afternoon, till about seven o'clock . . . when, to my unspeakable surprise, he comes back . . . I told him . . . how loud I had called upon him . . . He told me he heard me very plain upon Delamere Forest, at a place about twelve miles off . . . "Why", said I, "what did I say?"—for I had not named the words to him. "You called aloud", says he, "and said, 'O Jemmy! O Jemmy! come back, come back.'"' (p. 69)

> *Brigid Brophy, Michael Levey, and Charles Osborne, "'Jane Eyre'," in their* Fifty Works of English Literature We Could Do Without *(copyright © 1967 Brigid Brophy, Michael Levey, Charles Osborne; reprinted with permission of Stein and Day Publishers), Stein and Day, 1968, pp. 65-9.*

JENNIFER GRIBBLE (essay date 1968)

Charlotte Brontë's first successful novel [*Jane Eyre*] is all too clearly self-projective, both in its account of the workings of the imagination and in its concern with social demands and tensions. . . . Charlotte Brontë shares with her heroine the tremendous energy of an imagination pressing at the confines of a governess's social context and a nervously retiring personality. Her letters refer again and again to the compensatory and vicarious role of "the faculty of imagination" in her own dreary life. . . . Jane, like Charlotte Brontë, is sustained by imaginative activity of various kinds; they have a common tendency to render their experience by extended images, frequently images drawn from the creative process itself. The intense and varied imagining is at times undisciplined, unrelated to the novel's real imaginative logic: in this, as in other ways, the distinction between the narrator and the heroine begins to blur.

Charlotte Brontë's tendency to an uncritical identification with her heroine, and in particular her fascinated interest in Jane's imaginative powers, suggest why the novel can so easily be dismissed as "subjective," or as "romantic" in the pejorative sense. The presence of what look like very conventional romantic elements—the mad wife, the bogus wedding, the visionary dreams and coincidences—seems to provide further symptoms of such a romanticism. (pp. 279-80)

It seems to me that Charlotte Brontë's romanticism is of a more exploratory and interesting kind than has generally been acknowledged: that in *Jane Eyre* she is attempting, if not always consistently and successfully, to examine the workings of the creative imagination. *Jane Eyre* is a portrait of the artist in a less explicit way, perhaps, than most other novels of the kind,

though it is clearly a near portrait of Charlotte Brontë as a young woman. . . . [In Jane] we see the functioning of the primary imagination, or basic acts of perception involved in the most normal contacts of the mind with "nature." But further, the novel presents and emphasizes the contrast between the more sophisticated organizing activities—the fancy, by which Jane ties the elements of her experience into uneasy and arbitrary synthesis, and the secondary imagination, which, like poetry, fuses the disparates of experience into profound and meaningful order. In Jane's responses to events, in her drawings and her dreams, we see a mind actively creating its experience. (pp. 280-81)

Far from envisaging the imagination as an escape from the realities of life, Charlotte Brontë must surely have agreed with G. H. Lewes [see excerpt above] that it is only through the imagination that "reality" can fully be explored and understood. In fact, the source of the debates between Reason and Fancy that recur in her letters and the novels is a purposeful effort to explore the relationship between "inner" and "outer" worlds. The impulse behind her first novel, *The Professor,* had been a determined adherence to "the real," a repressing of the fantastic romances of Angria, the dream kingdom she had shared in childhood with her brother. "Nature and Truth," the two great neoclassical deities, were to be her guides. But the insistent claims of her own inspiration, her own invention, proved too strong to be repressed. . . . Charlotte Brontë is attempting, from *Jane Eyre* onwards, to balance the claims of an objective, shared world of phenomena of which she must give faithful account, and a belief in the transforming, organic power of the imagination. *Jane Eyre* questions the kind of dichotomy between inner experience and outer world that she (and also G. H. Lewes) had once believed necessary. . . . In no abstract theoretic way, but in the very terms of the imaginative activity itself, it reveals how shifting is the sense of "reality," or that which the mind plays upon, how uncanny is the power of the imagination to anticipate and transform the stuff of experience, to forge its own version of the facts, to find in the natural world that complex sense of relatedness that the romantic poets find.

Such a concern makes difficult demands of the novelist, however, especially one with a predilection for autobiographical form. In *Jane Eyre* there is the need constantly to distinguish between Jane's imagination and Charlotte Brontë's, and the two are not always distinguishable. Further, despite her "romanticism," Charlotte Brontë is not writing a form of romance but attempting to register the claims of the imagination within the conventions of the nineteenth-century novel. Her novel is as firmly committed to the evaluation of Jane as a social being, to the ways in which her social experience forms her, as it is to what her imagination discovers about that experience. Such a balance of claims is not easily maintained. Charlotte Brontë's attempt to show, through Jane, the power of the imagination to anticipate, organize, and even transform the stuff of experience, is in danger of succeeding too well, that is, of lapsing into wish-fulfillment. . . . Charlotte Brontë has set herself the task of showing that her heroine's imagination is necessarily limited as well as extraordinarily powerful. It is only by confronting Jane with those aspects of society and identity that resist the controlling, synthesizing activity of the observing and perceiving mind that she can represent the power of her own imagination to tell a tale that comprehends more than Jane's, and, as well, the validity of other versions of the facts. That is, of course, essentially the meaning of our demand for "objectivity" in the novel—that the total view we absorb from its pages should take its bearings from more than one mind's view, that against any central character's integrity of vision should be ranged the other possible visions (including the author's) that make up the complexities of our composite experience. In other words, while Charlotte Brontë may explore, through Jane's experience, the interaction and fusion of internal and external, individual and society, thought and nature, she must represent as objectively as possible the facts on which Jane's imagination works, and also that which is intractable, which challenges Jane's sense of herself, her desires, her imaginative domination. (pp. 281-83)

For all the force and insight of Jane's imagination . . . , we are still aware that it here subserves as well as renders Charlotte Brontë's controlling insight, and that the essential distance between creature and creator is preserved. (p. 285)

The relationship with Rochester is the obvious danger point for Charlotte Brontë's tendency to be overinvolved in Jane's success. Jane's life as governess at Thornfield Hall, even before she meets its master, encourages her in the kind of escapist dream quoted at the outset. Her dreams are of movement—busyness, people, towns—the qualities Charlotte Brontë found lacking in the novels of Jane Austen. . . . The "stormy seas" and violent motions of which she dreams on the night she saves Rochester from the fire, and her strange prophetic drawings, have the melodramatic coloring of conventional romanticism, a coloring of which Charlotte Brontë is usually aware. But . . . Jane's visions, swinging free of any "objective" facts the novel might provide, become the substance of the novel.

There are, I think, two points at which one must agree that Charlotte Brontë is not securely in control of her heroine's imaginings—where an unqualified conventional romanticism is offered and endorsed. (p. 287)

These points of weakness, however, surely do not vitiate Charlotte Brontë's purpose in the novel as a whole. That Jane's dreams and drawings are highly colored and girlishly romantic the author does indeed see and know as part of a girlhood she had herself lived through. It is the intent of this novel to show that the heroine, in her development from daydream to maturity, hovers between fancy and real insight. The interest is not primarily in the quality of Jane's imaginative activity, but in its relationship with the context in which it works. (p. 288)

[This] remarkable novel does not merely map a private world. It attempts, though not always successfully, something quite original. In probing the relationship between one mind's world and the larger world of social relations it demonstrates the insights of romanticism within the conventions of the nineteenth-century English novel. (p. 293)

> Jennifer Gribble, "Jane Eyre's Imagination," in Nineteenth-Century Fiction (© 1968 by the Regents of the University of California), Vol. 23, No. 3, December, 1968, pp. 279-93.

NORMAN SHERRY (essay date 1969)

The Professor was rejected because it was a bad novel, and it was a bad novel for several reasons. In the first place, it is the work of a writer who is yet unskilled in certain technical matters such as plotting and character development. In the second place, in dealing with what she thought was 'real', Charlotte was in effect dealing with what were economic concerns. Thus the concern with earning a living and achieving economic independence tends to take the place of the pressures of suffering,

aspiration, passion. In the third place, Charlotte was unfair to herself in imposing unnatural limits on her genius by cutting herself off entirely from the romantic imagination.

The structure of the novel is imperfect and irritating. We begin with a quite uncalled-for letter from Crimsworth to an old school friend telling him how, after he left Eton, he turned to his brother for help. The letter was 'sent a year since', and the copy is now found by Crimsworth accidentally. 'To this letter I never got an answer,' he records, but 'The leisure time I have at command, and which I intended to employ for his private benefit, I shall now dedicate to that of the public at large . . . The above letter will serve as an introduction. I now proceed.' As the first chapter of a novel, this is extraordinarily maladroit. It lacks integration with the rest of the novel, there is no sense of anything dynamic in subject or style, indeed the reader is almost discouraged from proceeding.

Within the general pattern, the emphases fall haphazard. There is rarely a sense of building up to a significant scene, rarely a sense of conflict of any kind where there is any doubt as to the outcome, rarely a sense of true personalities in contact.

The story is told as a first person narrative by the hero, William Crimsworth. First person narrative was to prove to be Charlotte Brontë's strength in *Jane Eyre*, but she makes the mistake here of having a male instead of a female narrator. Her attempt to portray a man's mentality and a man's world is unsuccessful. Primarily, between man and man, she adopts a brusque, abrupt method of communication which rarely varies, and which reflects back on all the male characters in a kind of limited harshness. . . . The use of oaths—'Confound it'; of abrupt phrases and rhetorical questions; of crude images—'shovel up broth'; of colloquial terms—'lad', represents Charlotte's attempt to render male conversation, when no ladies are present. That she found it a strain is indicated, I think, by the amount of conversation that is carried on in terms of fairly far-fetched imagery, and the lack of real bite beneath. The struggle between Hunsden and Crimsworth, after the former has met Frances, is reminiscent of the behaviour of two schoolboys and has an uncomfortable and contrived air. . . . But the inept dialogue extends throughout the book, and some of the love scenes are particularly painful to read as a result.

Crimsworth's smugness and self-sufficiency must be apparent from [several passages throughout the book]. He does not develop through vicissitude or fortune. He is given to such reflections as:, 'There you cannot dream, you cannot speculate and theorise—there you shall out and work!'; '. . . at least, ere I deviate, I will advance far enough to see whither my career tends'; '. . . the idea of marrying a doll or a fool was always abhorrent to me.' (pp. 47-9)

As a result of the slackness of narrative, certain stylistic habits of Charlotte Brontë's—irritating at any time—now stand out in an uncomfortable relief. There is her habit of addressing the reader, for example. . . . Invariably, [these instances] come at a time of lessened emotional interest, draw attention to themselves, and break the sense of a fictional world. Often they reveal themselves as a half-disguised form of Charlotte thinking about her narrative technique. (p. 49)

Charlotte Brontë's habit of presenting mental or emotional conflict in character by means of personification—a stilted proceeding at any time—here stands out embarrassingly given the lack of emotional conviction behind it: '. . . all at once spoke Conscience—"Down, stupid tormentors!" cried she; "the man has done his duty; you shall not bait him thus . . ."'

At times, the use of personification becomes comic: 'When I left Ostend on a mild February morning, and found myself on the road to Brussels, nothing could look vapid for me . . . Liberty I clasped in my arms for the first time, and the influence of her smile and embrace revived my life like the sun and the west wind.'

Charlotte's experiment at taking 'truth and nature' for her guides may not have been successful, but the working over her Brussels experience in a realistic form was to prove a useful exercise when she came to write *Villette*. (pp. 49-50)

> *Norman Sherry, " 'The Professor'," in his* Charlotte and Emily Brontë *(copyright © Norman Sherry, 1969, 1970), Evans Brothers, 1969 (and reprinted by Arco Publishing Company, Inc., 1970, pp. 41-50).*

BERNARD JONES　(essay date 1971)

[The Angrian world which Charlotte shared with her brother Branwell] is still part of the imaginative world in the *Five Novelettes* . . . , and it is markworthy that although they are the work of Charlotte some of them are told by a fictional character called Charles Townsend whose speech must be near to Branwell's. As in childhood, Charlotte still found it helpful to speak through a mask.

[The *Novelettes*] cannot fairly be placed among Charlotte's juvenilia. . . .

Although Charlotte was already 20 years old when she began the stories, they still move forward on the basis of the home lore cultivated by [her father,] Patrick Brontë. . . . Remembering how often marriages were contrived to make 19th-century novels end happily, one is struck by the absence of marriages in the *Novelettes* which, if they are not juvenilia, are equally not fully grown works of art. Some of the leading characters are married and there are mistresses. However, Charlotte was less concerned with propriety than with personal faithfulness to attachments of all kinds. . . . [In the *Novelettes*] the probabilities of daily life are not allowed to challenge the sway of a bold imagination, and whereas [in *Jane Eyre*] parts of Rochester's make-up are unreal in the context of real 19th century society, Zamorna [in the *Novelettes*] is portrayed inexorably and lives beyond criticism in a world apart. When Charlotte addressed the 'Reader', as she often did, she had in mind such a reader as Branwell, who had created much of her geography and politics, and even some of her characters. For part of the time at least she wrote with closed eyes so that she could see the more clearly what she wanted to show. How near she came to automatic writing is hard to say, but she did write compulsively. What she saw behind closed lids was made up of the whole wealth of an imaginative home life. (p. 12)

[In the novelette *Julia*] there is an outrageous and outrageously funny description of methodists which is worthy of Hardy. This . . . , in *Caroline Vernon,* is pure Branwell. Branwell had become Charlotte's mask and her work was to owe more to him than we can ever know. . . .

[The editor] thinks that in these *Novelettes* Charlotte can be seen moving towards the maturity of outlook which she was to show in her novels. Here and there may be found readers who will count the cost of such maturity. The 19th-century novelist wasted so much time on social detail that such readers may be allowed to enjoy the wanton handling of it in the *Novelettes*. When one can be swept up into the reality of the feeling neat, only a dull head seeks to have all things plotted

as parts of a chain of mere cause and effect. Zamorna is splendid because he is always himself. But poor Rochester, being accountable for mistresses, becomes sordid. (p. 13)

> *Bernard Jones, "Brontë Novelties" (© copyright Bernard Jones 1971; reprinted with permission), in* Books and Bookmen, *Vol. 17, No. 2, November, 1971, pp. 10-13.*

ADDITIONAL BIBLIOGRAPHY

Benson, E. F. *Charlotte Brontë.* New York: Longmans, Green and Co., 1932, 313 p.
　An in-depth look at Brontë's life, including her background, religious, and political convictions, response to critics, romances, interests, and careers.

Blom, M. A. "*Jane Eyre:* Mind as Law unto Itself." *Criticism* XV, No. 4 (Fall 1973): 350-64.
　Examines Brontë's attitudes and ideals, and their influence upon the characters, incidents, and scenery of *Jane Eyre.*

Brammer, M. M. "The Manuscript of *The Professor.*" *The Review of English Studies* XI, No. 42 (1960): 157-70.
　Close comparison of Brontë's manuscript of *The Professor* and the published version, which appeared posthumously. The critic contends that Brontë's careful craftsmanship was obscured by distorted punctuation and capitalization, and by textual misreadings.

Burkhart, Charles. "Brontë's *Villette.*" *The Explicator* XXI, No. 1 (September 1962): 15-16.
　A study of Brontë's effective use of moon imagery in *Villette.*

Burns, Wayne. "Critical Relevance of Freudianism." *The Western Review* 20, No. 4 (Summer 1956): 301-14.*
　Attempts to define Brontë's Freudian methods of symbolizing emotional expression and repression in *Jane Eyre.*

Chesterton, G. K. "Charlotte Brontë As a Romantic." In *Charlotte Brontë, 1816-1916: A Centenary Memorial,* edited by Butler Wood, pp. 49-54. New York: E. P. Dutton, 1918.
　Discusses the contrast between realism and romance in *Jane Eyre.* Chesterton calls the novel "one of the finest detective stories in the world."

Chesterton, G. K. "Charlotte Brontë." In his *Varied Types,* pp. 3-12. New York: Dodd, Mead and Co., 1921.
　States that *Jane Eyre* is "the truest book ever written." Chesterton argues that Brontë's truth is emotional, signifying youth's enduring spirit.

Day, Martin S. "Brontë's *Jane Eyre.*" *The Explicator* IX, No. 6 (April 1951): 7, 9.
　Analyzes the symbols and characters in *Jane Eyre.*

Eagleton, Terry. "Class, Power and Charlotte Brontë." *Critical Quarterly* 14, No. 3 (Autumn 1972): 225-35.
　A commentary on the political attitudes found in Brontë's work. Eagleton states that her novels occupy "a middle-ground between reverence and rebellion."

Eliot, George. *The George Eliot Letters: 1836-1851, Vol. I,* edited by Gordon S. Haight. New Haven: Yale University Press, 1954, 378 p.*
　Includes, on pages 268 and 269, a letter to Charles Bray, dated 1848, in which George Eliot comments briefly on *Jane Eyre.*

Falconer, J. A. "*The Professor* and *Villette:* A Study of Development." *English Studies* 9, Nos. 1-6 (1927): 33-7.
　Traces the development of Brontë's literary career through the comparison of her first work, *The Professor,* with her last, *Villette.*

Gaskell, E. C. *The Life of Charlotte Brontë.* London: E. P. Dutton & Co., 1908, 411 p.

Biographical novel. In the introduction to this book, May Sinclair states that *The Life of Charlotte Brontë* is "a classic in its kind," and praises the book as "the finest, tenderest portrait of a woman that a woman ever drew."

Gerin, Winifred. *The Brontës: The Formative Years*. Essex: Longman Group, 1973, 68 p.*
Discusses the writings of the Brontës prior to their published works.

Gilbert, Sandra M. and Gubar, Susan. "The Spectral Selves of Charlotte Brontë." In their *The Madwoman in the Attic,* pp. 309-440. New Haven: Yale University Press, 1970.
A feminist approach to the writings of Charlotte Brontë. This book praises Brontë as "a powerful precursor for all the women who have been strengthened by the haunted and haunting beauty of her art."

Hagan, John. "Enemies of Freedom in *Jane Eyre*." *Criticism* 13 (Winter 1971): 351-76.
Analyzes the obstacles Brontë faced in her personal life, and how she portrayed herself through the character of Jane Eyre.

Hardy, Barbara. *"Jane Eyre": Charlotte Brontë*. Oxford: Basil Blackwell, 1964, 95 p.
Studies the mixture of fantasy and realism in *Jane Eyre*.

Kinkead-Weekes, Mark. "The Place of Love in *Jane Eyre* and *Wuthering Heights*." *The Brontës: A Collection of Critical Essays,* edited by Ian Gregor, pp. 76-95. Englewood Cliffs, N.J.: Prentice-Hall, Inc., 1970.*
Discusses Brontë's metaphorical treatment of love in *Jane Eyre,* and how she portrayed the "life of the heart" through characters, scenes, and actions. This essay compares Charlotte to her contemporaries, particularly her sister Emily.

Langford, Thomas. "The Three Pictures in *Jane Eyre*." *The Victorian Newsletter* No. 31 (Spring 1967): 47-8.
A discussion of the three pictures Jane shows Rochester in Chapter 13 of *Jane Eyre*, which represent, according to Langford, "the

intricate nature of the novel's unity, in contrast with the view of some that the work has a rather broken, merely episodic structure."

Lodge, David. "Fire and Eyre: Charlotte Brontë's War of Earthly Elements." In his *Language of Fiction: Essays in Criticism and Verbal Analysis of the English Novel,* pp. 114-43. London: Routledge and Kegan Paul, 1966.
Detailed investigation of the elemental imagery in *Jane Eyre,* particularly the metaphorical importance of fire in the novel.

[Nussey, Ellen.] "Reminiscences of Charlotte Brontë." *Scribner's Monthly* II, No. 1 (May 1871): 18-31.
Biography of Charlotte Brontë by one of her schoolmates and close friends.

Prescott, Joseph. "*Jane Eyre*: A Romantic Exemplum with a Difference." In *Twelve Original Essays: On Great English Novelists,* edited by Charles Shapiro, pp. 87-102. Detroit: Wayne State University Press, 1960.
Discusses the obviously female voice of *Jane Eyre*.

Rosengarten, Herbert J. "Charlotte Brontë's *Shirley* and the *Leeds Mercury*." *Studies in English Literature 1500-1900* XVI, No. 4 (Autumn 1976): 591-600.
Reveals the source of *Shirley*.

Saintsbury, George. "Three Mid-Century Novelists: Charlotte Brontë. George Eliot. Anthony Trollope." In his *The Collected Essays and Papers of George Saintsbury: 1875-1920, Vol. II,* pp. 276-87. London: J. M. Dent & Sons, 1923.*
Discusses Brontë's weakness in characterization.

Wagner, Geoffrey. "*Jane Eyre*, with a Commentary on Catherine Earnshaw: Beyond Biology." In his *Five For Freedom: A Study of Feminism in Fiction,* pp. 103-37. London: George Allen & Unwin, 1972.*
Discusses the intertwinings of sex and religion in *Jane Eyre*. Wagner considers the novel to be "a profoundly and healthily sado-masochistic fiction."

William Carleton

1794-1869

Irish short story writer, novelist, poet, and essayist.

Carleton is best known for his depiction of the Irish peasants and their culture as they existed before the Great Famine of 1847. His work deals primarily with subjects important to the peasants, who were then an emerging political group with shared concerns: education, religion, violence, and land. *Traits and Stories of the Irish Peasantry,* a collection of short stories, is considered his best work and was praised for presenting the Irish mind and culture to the world.

Carleton, the son of a peasant farmer, grew up in County Tyrone in Northern Ireland. His father was a *shenachie* (storyteller) and his mother was a singer of old Irish songs. Thus Carleton learned from birth the Gaelic oral tradition. He was expected to enter the priesthood, but his education was haphazard and he never completed his studies. When the family lost their land after his father's death, Carleton became a wanderer, gathering impressions that he would later incorporate into his stories.

After a year on the road, Carleton arrived in Dublin and converted to Protestantism, the first of many changes in his religious, political, and literary sympathies. An earlier pilgrimage to Lough Dearg, a shrine to St. Patrick, had left him disenchanted with Catholicism and his new religious convictions inspired his writing career. In Dublin he met Caesar Otway, editor of an anti-Catholic journal entitled *The Christian Examiner and Church of Ireland Magazine,* who encouraged Carleton to write a story about the experiences which led to his conversion. "The Pilgrimage to Patrick's Purgatory," later published as "The Lough Dearg Pilgrim," attracted both strong censure and praise for its intimate and detailed portrait of the Irish people, its powerful prose, and its fierce bigotry. He seemed now to despise the class and the religion to which he had been born.

Religion, politics, and social issues played a large role in Carleton's life and in his writing. As a peasant transplanted to Dublin, unwilling to earn a living with his hands but unable to fully support his family with his writing, he wrote for whomever would pay him and tailored his stories to suit their views. During the course of his career Carleton effectively alienated readers and critics of all viewpoints with his harsh and bitter attacks. In later years, he revised some of his work, deleting the most strident passages. Thus, Carleton's first critically acclaimed collection of stories represents a radical departure from the views presented in his earlier work. *Traits and Stories* consists of accurate, sympathetic portraits of the people whom he had previously criticized. Although *Traits and Stories* is still considered to be Carleton's greatest work, the peasants that it lovingly portrays were already embittered by his stories that had appeared in *The Christian Examiner* and were later collected in *Tales of Ireland.*

Carleton's stories feature outstanding descriptions of the Irish peasantry. He had mourned at their wakes and danced at their weddings, studied at their hedge-schools and drunk at their *shebeens* (drinking houses), and he recreated all of these experiences in his stories. He accurately captured the Irish char-

Portrait by John Slattery; courtesy of the National Gallery of Ireland

acter, using both pathos and humor to illuminate its weaknesses and strengths. He is often praised for his use of language and his feeling for words. He faithfully recreated the dialect of his people, and was one of the first authors to translate the colorful Gaelic speech of the peasants into English.

Carleton's novels were not as successful as his stories. Critics agree that his talents were better suited to the shorter form. Many praise *The Black Prophet: A Tale of Irish Famine* for its chilling atmosphere of horror, but conclude that the story cannot sustain the tragic theme of famine. Like his early novels, it was criticized for its inadequate and disorganized plot. Carleton attempted to rectify this fault in his later novels, but only succeeded in stringing together an abundance of complicated, disconnected events and scenes. He created several great characters, notably the miser Fardorougha and his wife Honor in *Fardorougha the Miser; or, The Convicts of Lisnamona,* but his only credible characters were peasants. His attempts to portray the gentry produced caricatures, such as those who appear in *Willy Reilly and His Dear Coleen Bawn. Willy Reilly,* like his other late novels, was dismissed by critics as sentimental and melodramatic, yet it was Carleton's most popular novel, running through at least forty editions. Many critics agree that Carleton's greatest fault lay in his incorporation of politics in his writing. His novels contain lengthy asides that lecture the reader on land rights, education, violence, superstition, and other topics which are only marginally related to his story. These polemical passages offended his contemporaries, and critics feel they diminish the quality of his work.

Carleton's work, lacking thematic unity and consistent literary quality, is great only in fragments. Critics agree that his vacillating viewpoint and his treatment of political subjects detract from his fiction and that his work could have been strengthened if his exhortatory excesses had been curtailed. However, despite these flaws, Carleton's stories continue to entertain and inform readers through their recreation of the language and culture of the Irish peasant.

PRINCIPAL WORKS

Father Butler. The Lough Dearg Pilgrim   (short stories) 1829
Traits and Stories of the Irish Peasantry   (short stories) 1830
Traits and Stories of the Irish Peasantry, second series (short stories) 1833
Tales of Ireland   (short stories) 1834
Fardorougha the Miser; or, The Convicts of Lisnamona (novel) 1839
Valentine M'Clutchy, the Irish Agent; or, Chronicles of the Castle Cumber Property   (novel) 1845
The Black Prophet: A Tale of Irish Famine   (novel) 1847
The Emigrants of Ahadarra   (novel) 1848
The Tithe Proctor: Being a Tale of the Tithe Rebellion in Ireland   (novel) 1849
The Squanders of Castle Squander   (novel) 1852
Willy Reilly and His Dear Coleen Bawn   (novel) 1855
The Life of William Carleton: Being His Autobiography and Letters; and an Account of His Life and Writings, from the Point at Which the Autobiography Breaks Off, Vol. I   (unfinished autobiography and letters) 1896

MONTHLY REVIEW   (essay date 1839)

[Before the publication of his new novel, **"Fardorougha the Miser; or, The Convicts of Lisnamona,"**] Mr. Carleton was already favourably known to the public, through the medium of his **"Tales of Ireland," "Father Butler," "Traits and Stories of the Irish Peasantry,"** &c. . . . ; and we may safely add, that the novel under notice will not inconsiderably enhance a well-merited reputation. We are sincere admirers of those patriots, who feel and prove that the honour of their native land is as much to be held up by arts and literature as by arms and gallant deeds; and foremost in the phalanx of Ireland's literary heroes . . . stands William Carleton. This author moreover possesses a peculiar talent . . .—the art of maintaining the Irish *patois* throughout the various conversations of a long book, without fatiguing the reader. This is an essential recommendation to an Irish work that is professedly popular; indeed, it is a merit which the public cannot too fully appreciate. . . . On the whole, his work is the production of decided talent, and the result of deep observation and perception with regard to the character of the Irish. There are many touches of pathos, and others of broad humour, which would not shame the most celebrated writers of the day; and the entire book is

characterised by a tone of feeling which proves that its author possesses a good heart. (pp. 550-51)

[We] have only to observe, that an attentive perusal will well repay the reader; and that of all the novels which have issued from the British or Irish press during the last season, **"Fardorougha"** is decidedly one of the best. (p. 564)

> *"'Fardorougha, the Miser; or, the Convicts of Lisnamona',"* in Monthly Review, *Vol. II, No. IV, August, 1839, pp. 550-64.*

THE ATHENAEUM   (essay date 1845)

[*Valentine M'Clutchy, the Irish Agent*] has been looked for with some interest in Ireland, having been the subject of a curious controversy while it was yet unpublished. In a remarkable letter, attacking the *Nation* for having given utterance to uncatholic sentiments, the praise bestowed on Carleton, in a review of his **'Traits and Stories,'** was quoted as a flagrant example of delinquency. In reply, the Editor of the *Nation* declared that Carleton had repented of his attacks on the Catholic priests and the Catholic religion, and that his forthcoming novel was designed as a kind of recantation and atonement. Knowing Carleton only by his writings, we have long expected such a termination to his career. From his first essays, in the *Dublin Christian Examiner,* to his more finished novels, we found in him always a hearty sympathy for the peasant order, to which he belongs, not less by birth than by strength and character of feeling; and we have noticed in several of his tales, particularly in the **'Poor Scholar,'** an earnest desire to expose the social evils which have arisen from the tenure of land in Ireland. It is no business of ours to inquire what editorial supervision or censorship of patronage prevented him from earlier fulfilling an intention which we believe him long to have cherished: we neither know, nor wish to know, the circumstances of his connexion with what are called the Conservative Evangelicals of Dublin; but we do know that he long shaped his fictions to flatter their prejudices and advance their party; and, we must add, that most of the tales written for that purpose were superior to this, which is intended as an antidote.

The purpose of the tale is to illustrate the misdeeds of Irish land-agents, in the person of Valentine M'Clutchy; to expose the absurdity of that exploded delusion "the New Reformation;" to illustrate the pernicious tendencies of the Orange system, by its deplorable results; to exhibit the delinquencies of the Irish squirearchy, and of the system of promotion in the Irish church; and last, though not least, to aid the cause of Repeal. . . .

Carleton is not formed to succeed as a controversialist either in religion or politics: he shows too plainly that he is acting the part of an advocate; but his sketches of Irish life are equally truthful and vigorous. (p. 38)

[*Valentine M'Clutchy* contains] many passages and isolated sketches worthy of Mr. Carleton's powers and established fame; the scenes in the Orange lodge and the county grand jury room, though unnecessarily offensive in their details, are descriptions which we wish we could believe exaggerated; the death-bed of Deaker is a frightful picture, to which the author has given the darkest of his colouring. But the story, as a whole, does not please us; the letters, which occupy more than half the work, are not characteristic or natural, and the *dénouement* is hurried on in the style of the worst modern melodrama. But the most grievous fault of the work is, that it is obviously the production of a partisan, and written for a purpose beyond and independent of the story. (p. 39)

"Reviews: 'Valentine M'Clutchy, the Irish Agent',"
in The Athenaeum, *No. 898, January 11, 1845, pp.*
38-9.

THOMAS DAVIS   (essay date 1845)

[In **"Tales and Sketches Illustrating the Irish Peasantry,"**] Carleton is the historian of the peasantry rather than a dramatist. The fiddler and piper, the seanachie and seer, the matchmaker and the dancing-master, and a hundred characters beside, are here brought before you moving, acting, playing, plotting, and gossiping! You are never wearied by an inventory of wardrobes, as in short English descriptive fictions; yet you see how every one is dressed. . . .

But even in these sketches, his power of external description is not his greatest merit. (p. 357)

[Carleton has represented the people's] love and generosity, their wrath and negligence, their crimes and virtues, as a hearty peasant—not a note-taking critic.

In others of his works he has created ideal characters that give him a higher rank as a poet . . . ; but here he is a genuine Seanachie, and brings you to dance and wake, to wedding and christening—makes you romp with the girls, and race with the boys—tremble at the ghosts, and frolic with the fairies of the whole parish. (pp. 357-58)

Thomas Davis, "The Irish Peasantry" (originally
published in The Nation, *July 12, 1845), in his* Essays Literary and Historical, *W. Tempest, Dundalgan*
Press, 1914, pp. 356-58.

[PATRICK JOSEPH MURRAY]   (essay date 1852)

Mr. Carleton's works are of very unequal merit. To begin with his defects. Some of his scenes and stories are utterly flat and spiritless from beginning to end; and there are here and there, in the collection of his writings, little deposits of unsavoury rubbish, which remind us of certain adjuncts such as he has himself described to be sometimes perceived, by more senses than one, beside the habitations of a particular class of his countrymen. He is now and then coarse and vulgar; even his most happy efforts are not always free from this serious drawback. Nor is the fault palliated, for it could not be excused, by an over rigid adherence to actual nature: it is generally found in those scenes where his caricatures and exaggerations are most excessive. His failures begin on his seeking to come out as a colloquial humourist or describer of outlandish incidents, on his own account; as often as he ceases to copy the real language and manners of the people, and to paint events most likely to occur among them. Of attempts at the smart or facetious not true to the usages of Irish speech, and of adventures not true to Irish life, we do not remember a single occasion in which he does not depart as widely from the common principles of good taste as from the duties of a faithful observer of men and things. Several of his dull passages are open to an opposite objection. They are indeed true copies, but copies of scenes not worth copying.

There is another fault, which a few mere strokes of the pen would cancel from all future editions. He at times breaks in upon the narrative with a little lecture on the relations of landlord and tenant, the importance of education, the duty of fore-

thought and economy, and the like. We do not mean to insinuate that these topics are not of the first importance, or that his strictures are not just and valuable; but they are out of place. . . . One of the merits of Mr. Carleton's best tales is, that they convey their own lessons, and require no gloss. When he epitomises himself into a lecture, it is like the exquisite singing of a beautiful song followed by a drawling recitation of the words. After all, the faults we have noticed are but occasional, so loosely connected with the structure of the sounder and better parts, that their removal might be easily accomplished without leaving any scar behind.

It is among the peasantry that Mr. Carleton is truly at home. He tries other characters, rarely, however, and not unsuccessfully. But the Irish peasant is his strong point: here he is unrivalled, and writes like one who has had nothing to look out for, to collect by study, to select, to mould; who merely utters what comes spontaneously into his thoughts; from whom the language and sentiments flow as easily and naturally as articulate sounds from the human lips or music from the skylark. . . . Upon the whole, he paints [the Irish peasantry] with an impartial hand: their excellent qualities he brings out fully, their general defects and the blacker vices which characterise certain individuals, he neither hides nor softens down. . . . Neither his good nor his evil persons are ideal; but it is in the delineation of the former that he appears to most advantage. In portraying scenes of true and pure affection, of generous self-sacrifice, of tender sympathy, of silent and devout resignation, of humble domestic love and happiness, his heart is poured forth in strains too simple and natural not to impress his readers with the belief that he is but recalling a past reality, and describing what he had once seen and perhaps acted and felt himself. (pp. 385-86)

The primary and essential value of Mr. Carleton's sketches of Irish peasant life and character unquestionably consists in this— that they are true, and *so* true to nature. . . . [Their value is also enhanced by the fact that the] living originals are disappearing, some of them have already disappeared. In Ireland, since our author's youth, changes rapid and deep have taken place. . . . (p. 387)

To Mr. Carleton thus belongs the great merit of perpetuating a true and living image of so much of what is already, or, ere long, will be lost. So far as our acquaintance with this sort of literature extends, no other writer has approached him in the freshness and reality of his pictures. He is not only Irish, but thoroughly Irish, intensely Irish, exclusively Irish. . . . [He] stands alone as the exhibiter of the inward and external, the constitutional and the accidental, the life, the feelings, the ways, the customs, and the language of the Irish peasant. . . . Unless another master hand should soon appear, like his, or abler than his, it is in his pages, and in his alone, that future generations must look for the truest and fullest—though still far from complete—picture of those, who will ere long have passed away from that troubled land, from the records of history, and from the memory of men for ever.

We have alluded to Mr. Carleton's peculiar success in portraying the workings of the nobler and more tender passions in the heart of the Irish peasant. His country stands not a little indebted to him for having dwelt on this part of his theme at such length, and with so much fondness. . . . The poor Irishman used to be constantly represented as an impersonation of eccentricity, knavery, recklessness, and most ludicrous absurdity in speech, manner, and costume. (pp. 388-90)

It is of the better class [of the peasantry] that Mr. Carleton's more engaging characters may be taken as fair specimens. It is among them that the scenes of deep pathos, disinterested and enduring affection, the poetic language of grief and joy are chiefly found. . . . (p. 391)

Carleton's story of **'The Poor Scholar'** [from **'Traits and Stories of the Irish Peasantry'**] is, we think, the best that has ever been written on an Irish subject by himself, or by any other. . . . The story itself, as a mere story, is extremely touching; but it is the fidelity throughout to characters and manners that makes it so delightful to all who, having been once familiarly acquainted with those characters and manners, can therefore fully appreciate so true a portrait of them. (pp. 396-97)

The stories of **'Peter Connell'** and **'Tubher Dag, or the Red Well,'** belong, in a great measure, to the class to which we have referred the **'Poor Scholar;'** and, though inferior, are yet excellent, and in some scenes exquisitely touched. **'Valentine M'Clutchy'**—bating the coarse passages and the *sermonising*—and **'Fardorougha, or the Miser,'** are the best among Mr. Carleton's longer and more ambitious, but, we think, not more successful, productions. Very little, if at all, below these in merit, are **'The Black Prophet'** and **'The Tithe Proctor.'** We, as has been already intimated, contemplate the merits of these tales and novels principally by the standard of fidelity to Irish character and Irish manners. (p. 402)

[**'The Squanders, of Castle Squander'**] contains more of the faults already pointed out, and fewer of the characteristic excellences, than any one of [Mr. Carleton's] preceding works. The incidents are little else than a rehearsal of portions of **'Valentine M'Clutchy,'** and of some of his **'Traits and Stories.'** Several of the more interesting characters, too, are old acquaintances, and we see very little of them—they are so completely kept in the back ground by the thick heavy folds that hang over the front of the stage. We get a brief glimpse here and there of true Irish life: the rest is all about tenant-right and a multitude of other topics connected with politics and political economy. . . . [The sermons] are neither very well written nor very well seasoned, and they swarm with small inaccuracies in statements of fact. Why will Mr. Carleton persist in spoiling his stories—to say nothing of the *needless* offence given to a large portion of his readers—by dissertations on topics which any fourth-rate newspaper correspondent would handle much better than he has done, leaving that field in which he stands without an equal among the living or the dead? We write in sorrow, not in anger. He is himself a true Squander of Castle Squander, neglecting the fine gifts with which nature has endowed him, and feeding on garbage and offal. We trust that this is the last of the prodigal: for there can be nobody, who will rejoice more heartily than we ourselves in seeing him return from the lecture room and the debating club to his true home in the heart and soul and every day life of the Irish peasant. We hope to meet him soon, reclaimed and 'himself again.' (p. 403)

[Patrick Joseph Murray,] "Traits of the Irish Peasantry," in Edinburgh Review, Vol. XCVI, No. CXCVI, October, 1852, pp. 384-403.

W. B. YEATS   (essay date 1889)

William Carleton was a great Irish historian. The history of a nation is not in parliaments and battle-fields, but in what the people say to each other on fair-days and high days, and in how they farm, and quarrel, and go on pilgrimage. These things has Carleton recorded.

He is the great novelist of Ireland, by right of the most Celtic eyes that ever gazed from under the brows of storyteller. His equals in gloomy and tragic power, Michael and John Banim, had nothing of his Celtic humour. One man alone stands near him there—Charles Kickham, of Tipperary. . . . But, then, he had not Carleton's intensity. (pp. xvi-xvii)

[There] is no wistfulness in the works of Carleton. I find there, especially in his longer novels, a kind of clay-cold melancholy. One is not surpised to hear, great humorist though he was, that his conversation was more mournful than humorous. He seems, like the animals in Milton, half emerged only from the earth and its brooding. When I read any portion of the **"Black Prophet,"** or the scenes with Raymond the Madman in **"Valentine M'Clutchy,"** I seem to be looking out at the wild, torn storm-clouds that lie in heaps at sundown along the western seas of Ireland; all nature, and not merely man's nature, seems to pour out for me its inbred fatalism. (p. xvii)

W.B. Yeats, "Introduction" (reprinted by permission of Michael and Anne Yeats), Stories from Carleton by William Carleton, edited by Ernest Rhys, Walter Scott, 1889 (and reprinted by Lemma Publishing Corporation, 1973, pp. ix-xvii).

W. B. YEATS   (essay date 1891)

[When Carleton began writing, the] true peasant was at last speaking, stammeringly, illogically, bitterly, but nonetheless with the deep and mournful accent of the people. Ireland had produced her second great novelist. Beside Miss [Maria] Edgeworth's well-finished four-square house of the intelligence, Carleton raised his rough clay 'rath' of humour and passion. Miss Edgeworth has outdone writers like [Samuel] Lover and [Charles] Lever because of her fine judgment, her serene culture, her well-balanced mind. Carleton, on the other hand, with no conscious art at all, and living a half-blind, groping sort of life, drinking and borrowing, has, I believe, outdone not only them but her also by the sheer force of his powerful nature. (p. 28)

As time went on, his work grew deeper in nature, and in the second series [of **'Traits and Stories of the Irish Peasantry'**] he gave all his heart to **'The Poor Scholar'**, **'Tubber Derg'**, and **'Wildgoose Lodge'**. The humorist found his conscience, and, without throwing away laughter, became the historian of his class. It was not, however, until a true national public had arisen . . . that Carleton ventured the creation of a great single character and wrote **'Fardorougha the Miser'**. In **'Fardorougha'** and the two or three novels that followed he was at his finest. Then came decadence—ruinous, complete. (p. 29)

[Carleton's novels dealing with the life of the gentry] are almost worthless, except when he touches incidentally on peasant life, as in the jury-room scene in **'Willy Reilly'**. . . . In these novels landlords, agents, and their class are described as falsely as peasants are in the books of Lover and [Thomas Crofton] Croker. In **'Valentine McClutchy'**, the first novel of his decadence, there is no lack of misdirected power. The land-agent Orangeman, the hypocrite-solicitor, and the old blaspheming landlord who dies in the arms of his drunken mistress, are figures of unforgettable horror. They are the peasant's notion of that splendid laughing world of Lever's. The peasant stands at the roadside, cap in hand, his mouth full of 'your honours' and 'my ladies', his whole voice softened by the courtesy of the powerless, but men like Carleton show the thing that is in his heart. He is not appeased because the foot that passes over him is shod with laughter. (pp. 29-30)

> *W. B. Yeats, "Introduction" (reprinted by permission of Michael and Anne Yeats),* Representative Irish Tales *(originally published, 1891), edited by W. B. Yeats (and reprinted by Humanities Press, 1979, pp. 25-32).**

DAVID J. O'DONOGHUE   (essay date 1896)

It is an easy task to define Carleton's position in Irish literature. He is unquestionably supreme so far as fiction is concerned. But his position in literature generally is not easy to define. Judging him by his best work only—by his wonderful knowledge of human nature, and not by his style—he should occupy one of the proudest places in the whole gallery of masters who have made a study of the human heart. . . . [But], to be perfectly candid, no writer has given to the world work more essentially unfit to live than are Carleton's weakest efforts. (p. 350)

His style is not remarkable for excellence, but in a painter of manners, one may be permitted to say, style is not everything. (p. 351)

His habitual over-emphasis, so much less noticeable in his earlier works, becomes in after life his most marked defect: his later novels are much defaced by this. He will not let the actions of his characters suggest their motives, but insists upon labelling them as dangerous or angelic, as the case may be. They must speak, too, not only for themselves, but for their author.

His best work is not quite free from this vice, and therefore we are brought to the conclusion that he was not a great artist. . . . But if he was not an artist, he was a poet, and a notable one. Only a true poet could have shown such feeling for nature as we recognize over and over again in the "Traits and Stories." These sketches are, for the most part, worthy of all praise, as vigorously painted canvases, where every figure is boldly and energetically drawn, with few strokes and no tricks. (pp. 352-53)

In the present meaning of the word Carleton was not a first-rate novelist. He was not a good novelist in this sense, that he did not possess the skill to construct a first-rate plot. His more ambitious works, issued as novels, are badly put together. . . . Carleton tries to depend upon the characters rather than upon the incidents in his (so-called) novels proper. (p. 353)

In each of the "Traits and Stories" there is surprising knowledge of the peasantry, but they are not notable on that account alone. The extraordinary narrative power displayed in several of them, and the immortal pathos and humour of others, justify what may seem to be the extravagant praise of those who know them well. By his insistence on the nobler qualities of his countrymen, Carleton has done them an indelible service. There is, however, a touch of caricature here and there, and especially in "Phil Purcel, the Pig-driver." . . . The manner in which the sketch comes to an end is not satisfactory. In fact, Carleton's conclusions are too often most impotent. In his "Hedge School" and "Phelim O'Toole's Courtship" we are irritated by an intended moral so incongruous and absurd as almost to destroy the pleasure derived from the sketches. . . . [The very "lame conclusions"] might be removed not only without injury but with positive advantage to the sketches in question. No

novelist with the artistic instinct would have endangered his reputation by permitting such tags to remain, and it is to be regretted that Carleton, when in subsequent editions he performed some necessary revision, did not do a little more pruning. No writer more urgently required a judicious editor.

Despite the faults already suggested, and others which it would be futile to ignore, the "Traits and Stories" are still the greatest collection of stories in Irish literature. . . . With humour equal to that of Molière, and tenderness, passion, and sympathy almost unsurpassable, he has illustrated all phases of Irish life and types of Irish character as no one else has ever done. (pp. 354-56)

If "Valentine McClutchy" had been rigorously revised by Carleton, it would have been a great novel. As it is, it is too diffuse and too strongly coloured to rank as a masterpiece, although Carleton has put into it something of his best. It bears evidence of haste, and was undoubtedly written against time. . . . There are scenes of great power and interest in the novel, but it badly needs compression. Darby O'Drive, Solomon McSlime and old Deaker, who dies drinking "the immortal memory," are wonderful creations; but Valentine McClutchy and his son are too diabolical for humanity. (pp. 358-59)

[In "The Tithe Proctor"] Carleton used his literary position unscrupulously and with needless offensiveness, and as in the analogous instance of "The Squanders of Castle Squander," few Irishmen will read the book without resentment. Carleton's mistakes or delinquencies of this description must be admitted. . . . [But] it would be criminal to deny that in some of his aberrations he has put forward an entirely slanderous, because partisan view, of the motives and actions of the people from whom he sprung. (p. 360)

Those who have read, or who shall read, the works particularly referred to, will admit the necessity of some severe criticism on a few of them. . . . [But if readers] measure Carleton's merits by "The Tithe Proctor," "The Squanders of Castle Squander," "The Evil Eye," or "The Black Baronet," *et hoc,* they are doing him and Irish literature a grave injustice. (pp. 360-61)

> *David J. O'Donoghue, in his* The Life of William Carleton: Being His Autobiography and Letters; and an Account of His Life and Writings, from the Point at which the Autobiography Breaks Off, Vol. II, *Downey & Co., 1896, 362 p.*

G. BARNETT SMITH   (essay date 1897)

All the characteristics of the Irish race seem to have been blended in William Carleton, who has not inaptly been designated "the Walter Scott of Ireland." He was brilliant and wayward, tearful and whimsical, strong in his affections, and passionately attached to his family and the homeland. If it be true what Shelley says of the poets, that "they learn in suffering what they teach in song," it is equally true of the life and writings of Carleton. The intense and full-veined humanity which permeates his works is in a large measure the outcome of his sympathetic heart. The Irish peasant never had a more tender and compassionate interpreter of his complex nature, with all its moods—moods now jocund and sunny as the spring, and now sombre and pathetic as the autumn. . . .

There was nothing classic in his writings; occasionally, indeed, there was an independence of grammar calculated to disturb the shade of [the grammarian] Lindley Murray. But if his language was not always correct, it was *living* to a degree. There was nothing of the Dryasdust element about it. His sentences were warm, vivid, palpitating with energy and emotion. Although he might not be able to turn a period with men like Matthew Arnold or Sainte-Beuve, neither could such wielders of a model diction emulate his Titanic rendering of the passions, or his bursts of rugged and perfervid eloquence. (p. 104)

As a novelist, Carleton was superior in one respect to either Dickens or Thackeray. He could draw women better. So far as I remember there is not a weak creation among all his female characters. They are living, breathing, loving, creatures—women capable of inspiring a deep affection, and at the same time worthy of it. Where is there a nobler being in fiction than Helen Folliard, the heroine of **Willy Reilly**? The way she cheers her lover in all his difficulties, remains true to him through unexampled trials, and finally testifies in his favour when he is tried for his life, has something truly sublime in it. Similar praise is due for the way in which he draws many other heroines.

I find in all Carleton's writings something of the forceful energy and dramatic intensity which characterize the novels of Charlotte and Emily Brontë. His people palpitate with life. From the moment they appear to the last glimpses we have of them we see real men and women, and not phantoms. Look at **Fardorougha, the Miser,** one of the most powerful works of fiction ever penned. The struggle depicted in the breast of Fardorougha is absolutely Titanic. The passion for gold, and the equally strong passion for his son Connor, the child of his old age, contend for the mastery, and the strength of the conflicting elements is terrible to behold. . . . The story would be unbearable for its gloomy burden of sorrow were it not for the two women characters in it. The beautiful love passages between Nora O'Brien and Connor are scarcely to be matched anywhere, while the noble devotion of Honor O'Donovan, the wife of the miser, stands almost unique. (p. 114)

Valentine M'Clutchy is another of Carleton's novels which no other man could have written. The sharp contrasts between virtue and vice are very striking, and there are some scenes which are overwhelmingly painful. . . . The eviction carried out in the cabin of the O'Regans, when the dying husband is besought by his agonized wife to give up his last breath before the myrmidons of the law enter, is, so far as I know, unexampled for its sadness and pathos. (p. 115)

Undoubtedly one of Carleton's leading claims to permanent remembrance is that he gave faithful representations of an Irish peasantry which is now fast dying out. . . . But beyond and above this there is the ineffaceable stamp of genius upon his writings. The Irish peasant appears in his habit as he lived. Every character that he has drawn is strong, distinct, individual. It is this or that man or woman and no other. Not Rembrandt could put in deeper lights or shadows when required, nor Teniers more minute or life-like touches. For this reason the best of his works at least must prove abiding. They deserve to be treasured as a precious memory, not only by all Irishmen, but by the whole of the Anglo-Saxon race. (p. 116)

> *G. Barnett Smith, "A Brilliant Irish Novelist," in* The Fortnightly Review *(reprinted by permission of Contemporary Review Company Limited), n.s. Vol. LXI, January 1, 1897, pp. 104-16.*

STEPHEN GWYNN   (essay date 1936)

Carleton attempted instinctively what Synge, nearly a century later, was to do by study with a finished literary art; he tried

to bring from [the Irish] language into the [English language] the form and colour of the Irish mind. The content of that mind, Irish feeling and Irish thought, Ireland's sense of her own past and hopes for her future could be expressed, and were expressed, in English far better by other pens than Carleton's. Neither Irish history nor Irish legend took hold on him; his interest was only in the life that lay about him, that he had taken part in with lusty vigour, and that could be turned to picturesque and popular account. (p. 63)

The most notable thing about Carleton is that one feels him to be writing for Ireland, not for England. He is telling stories of his own people to a different class of Irishmen. Yet, even so, he feels it necessary to explain, as Maria Edgeworth did not explain in *Castle Rackrent*. What is worse, however, just because he feels himself to be addressing the class who have his people in their power, he is deplorably prone to harangue—especially on the Land Laws. **"The Poor Scholar"** is spoilt by the digression which describes how an absentee landlord was induced to look into his agent's doings. This change of heart is the poor scholar's work, but we lose sight of the poor scholar for much too long. In **"Tubber Derg"** such digressions have more justification, since the whole is the history of a decent farmer family driven out to beg on the roads; a case only too common. (pp. 68-9)

For the tenderness of his work one would turn above all to **"The Poor Scholar"** and to the last passage in **"Tubber Derg."** But nothing stands out with such original force as the study of the peasant miser in **"Fardorogha,"** which, if the writer's art had matched his power of conception, might rank with Turgeniev's "King Lear of the Steppes." And in that same story the character of the miser's wife deserves to be noted for its portraiture of what is best in the Christian religion as expressed through the person of a Catholic Irish peasant woman.

But the art is at every point sadly to seek. Carleton never filled a really large canvas; and even in his short tales he is always redundant. He encumbers the essential utterance with a burden of superfluous words. He was, more is the pity, a thoroughly uneducated writer. He had a strong power for visual imagery; when he describes a landscape, it is clearly present to the mind's eye; and he had a natural feeling for the rhythmic beauty of words. (p. 70)

> *Stephen Gwynn, "Miss Edgeworth's Successors," in his* Irish Literature and Drama in the English Language: A Short History *(copyright Thomas Nelson & Sons Ltd.), Thomas Nelson, 1936, pp. 61-79.**

THOMAS FLANAGAN   (essay date 1958)

[William Carleton's] was the richest talent in nineteenth-century Ireland and the most prodigally wasted. For the critic he is a continuous torment, joy, and puzzle. . . . His best work lies in parts and fragments; scenes of unmatched power and wit are buried in trumpery plots and harsh polemic. (p. 255)

Before his career was run he had written for every shade of Irish opinion—stern Evangelical tracts for Caesar Otway; denunciations of the landlords for Thomas Davis; patronizing sketches for *The Dublin University Magazine;* unctuous Catholic piety for James Duffy; a few sketches for Richard Pigott, the sinister mock-Fenian who was to forge the famous Parnell correspondence. By the eighteen forties he was the most celebrated of Irish writers; ten years later he was written-out, a hack whose pen was for hire in Dublin's ugly literary wars.

He had but one subject, the days of his youth and the world in which he had lived them. This is the subject which haunted him and drove his pen; to this subject he was faithful, and to nothing else. (p. 256)

[Every critic of Carleton must try to account] for the contradictions in the man: the fierce sense of justice and wrong which existed beside a callous political conservatism; the love and detestation of Catholicism, felt with equal passion; the conflicting emotions of affection, scorn, and anger out of which his stories were created; the confused, groping speculations. . . .

Carleton's religious sense, like his sense of politics, shows little development—only random, ceaseless change and return. He cut his cloth to suit his odd assortment of employers, and had a chameleon ability to believe, for the moment, whatever he wrote. He was immersed in the troubled and at times bloody politics of a country which he loved and loathed. (p. 257)

Carleton's strongest single claim upon the attention of his contemporaries and his successors [was his ability to depict the heart and center of Irish life]. There can be little doubt that Carleton rendered the life of a peasant Ireland with a fullness, a passion, and an accuracy which no other writer has approached. Only to a man who himself had lived that life was such intimacy possible, and the sheer fact that Carleton came from the world of the cabins lent an accidental, dramatic charm to his character and to his work. (p. 262)

But it is this very general notion of Carleton as "the historian of the peasantry" which has worked against an understanding of all that was hard and unique in the man; in like measure, it has contributed to the sense of confusion and contradiction which he excites in most readers. For Carleton was a "spoiled priest" as well as a "peasant"—no more than in Rabelais, whom in several ways he resembled, should this be overlooked. . . . (p. 263)

[Carleton's] attitude toward his life in Gaelic Ireland was deeply ambivalent, and from this ambivalence issues the best of his work. Toward his material he directed at all times the artist's eye, which is at once loving and skeptical. In many ways his transformation from Billy Carleton, the poor scholar on the road, to Mr. William Carleton of Dublin was an escape from the crushing power not merely of material things but of his own heritage, from the haunted past, the obsessions, hatreds, and dark isolation of his own people. No mere convert's zeal, nor desire to please, can account for the extraordinary power with which *The Lough Derg Pilgrim,* his introduction to print, is written. (p. 275)

The narrator of "The Lough Derg Pilgrim" has two voices. One is a fair imitation of Caesar Otway, which is to say that it is not a human voice. The other voice, unexpected and spontaneous, is that of a man remembering his magical, preposterous youth, when the pleasure of life was asserted not by allegorical lakes, but by the randy folk whom one met along the road, like Nell M'Collum, the tinker's widow, who lent Carleton a cloak and then picked his pocket. The first voice tells us of how Carleton endured his three days of physical and spiritual torment among the penitents of Station Island; of how, during the midnight watches, it was given him to perceive the dark terrors and superstitions into which his soul had been thrust by the priests; and of "that solemn, humble, and heartfelt sense of God's presence which Christian prayer demands."

But there is nothing very grand or very terrible in the experiences of the second voice. It is the voice of a gawky and

conceited seminarian who delights in being mistaken for a priest and convinces himself that his spirit is chastened thereby—"Pride, I trample you under my foot." (pp. 282-83)

"The Lough Derg Pilgrim" suggests that Carleton's break with the instinctual life of his people liberated his powers and clarified his vision, yet exacted its own penalties. Those grisly punishments and moans of lamentation beneath the leaden Donegal sky tell us of some dark, debasing medieval world in which the Irish peasant continued to dwell, but say nothing of its bright, heraldic colors. (p. 284)

[The stories collected in *Tales of Ireland*] are slight and are marred by the insistent purposes of controversy. Occasionally they have a bright, fitful life, which characteristically is irrelevant to the stated theme. "The Priest's Funeral," for example, deals with the way in which a priest's dying wish to be received into the Protestant Church is frustrated by his fellow clergy, who are anxious not only for his soul but for the property which earlier he had willed to them. But the story is dominated by two outrageously comic figures, a bishop and a Dominican monk who sit outside the death-room bickering over appointments, obscure points of theology, ecclesiastical scandals, and the old dispute between regular and secular clergy. In genre scenes of this sort, painted with a satirical and affectionate brush, his talent was searching out its true direction. (p. 284)

["Denis O'Shaughnessy Going to Maynooth," from *Traits and Stories of the Irish Peasantry,*] is one of the very best of his comedies. At its center stands the incomparable Denis himself, at once touching, ludicrous, and insufferable. (p. 285)

Denis is all language and appetite; he revels in words which are as hard and dazzling as diamonds, and he has a lapidary's sense of their arrangement. . . . (p. 286)

[Carleton belatedly comes to a sense of his duty, however, and spoils his effect by a long account at the end of the story] of Denis's change of heart. "Ambition loses much of its fictitious glitter" for Denis and he comes to recognize the harsh and overbearing way in which he has used his family. But the reader has come to entertain a high affection for the old, overbearing Denis. . . . The new Denis has lost all traces of [his] brilliantly comic language. (pp. 289-90)

"Going to Maynooth" has been so finely wrought that [the] wretched epilogue does little to harm it. Of Carleton, as of Denis himself, it might be said that he lived by language and appetite. Though there is a widely held legend to the contrary, the Irish have rarely displayed, at least in their literature, a very rich vein of high comedy, but Carleton is a genuinely witty and humane writer. His appetite for sights and sounds was, of course, immense. . . . [Indeed], at a distance the *Traits and Stories* seems a boundless sea of murmurous voices. Each story, however, is carefully controlled by Carleton's selective intelligence. He makes use of a dozen fledgling priests, and all of them speak the inflated, quasi-theological language of the hedge schools, yet each exists in his own being. (p. 290)

[Carleton's preface to the first series of *Traits and Stories*] sounds very much like rhetoric of the loose, rhapsodic sort in which Irish literature unhappily abounds, and which seeks to link the peasantry, for good or ill, to the primal, mindless forces of nature. It speaks quite accurately, however, to Carleton's imaginative apprehension of his theme. "The red and rapid gush of their mountain streams," here mentioned in passing, is one of his controlling images. . . . In Carleton's stories the crystal clarity of lake, stream, and spring suggests an unreal, often a delusive purity of spirit and purpose, while dark, troubled water, stained to the color of blood, has the reality of experience itself. (p. 291)

[There] are two springs in **"Tubber Derg,"** one of his most powerful stories—one is a spring of "delicious crystal" but crimson oozes from the other, and a man walking near it seems "to track his way in blood." . . . In the early Carleton these contrasting waters often symbolized a simple, Manichaean dichotomy. One stream "stood for" the Irish capacity for love, affection, and sacrifice; the other stream "stood for" an inclination, equal in strength, toward violence, savagery, and superstition. And this was admirably adapted to the service of the various causes in which his pen was enlisted. But at the root of Carleton's vision lies what Yeats has called a "clay-cold melancholy" [see excerpt above]; he came to believe that his people were stained with saintliness and blood. He could never explain, to himself least of all, what meaning he attached to this, though he availed himself of the glib generalities of the day, which spoke of the "Celtic soul" and its commingling of innocence and crime. But his truest instincts, as Yeats perhaps guessed, were pantheistic and pagan, and his comparison of his people to the moorlands and meadows on which they lived is something more than metaphor.

Carleton's first notion was that the *Traits and Stories* should be a series of tales told about the kitchen fire of Ned M'Keown's mountain *shebeen*. The earliest stories—**"The Three Tasks,"** **"Shane Fadh's Wedding,"** and **"Larry M'Farland's Wake"**—fall within this scheme, and are pleasant enough stories in Crofton Croker's exuberant and trivial vein. But the convention, which even then was stiff and a bit faded, is in every way alien to his talents. (pp. 291-92)

The fourth story, **"The Battle of the Factions,"** begins as another of these tales told in the inglenook. Then, very suddenly—one can almost mark the line—Carleton drops the device. It has come time for the schoolmaster, Pat Frayne, to tell his story, since each of the rustics, in accordance with this tiresome convention, has his representative trade and his quirk of character. (p. 292)

Carleton, hearing in his mind the voice of Pat Frayne at the school of Findramore, and perhaps the voice of Billy Carleton telling his stories on the roads of Louth, had found what he needed. It is a full-cadenced voice, susceptible of infinite modulation, moving without effort from the sardonic to the tragic, and intelligent as though on instinct. (p. 293)

These stories are given life by language, by Carleton's discovery of the explosive energies of the word. His characters are realized more vividly through speech than through action. Of his plots it is often possible to say little more than that they are serviceable. . . . [Yet **"Neal Malone,"** **"Going to Maynooth,"** **"The Hedge School,"** **"The Midnight Mass,"**] and the other stories by which his reputation must stand or fall are as searching and as moving as any which the nineteenth century produced.

The later Carleton was overconcerned with plot. . . . *The Squanders of Castle Squander* and *The Black Baronet,* his late novels, are ambitious attempts at a theme which from the first had attracted Anglo-Irish writers—the decline of the Big House. But he worked very clumsily with such material. His true subject was a people emerging painfully from the submerged, broken world of Gaelic Ireland. In his attempt to record that

life he was well served by his first models—his father's long, rambling anecdotes and the loose picaresque of Le Sage.

It was a world to which not merely English forms and customs but the English language itself was alien. And yet, perhaps paradoxically, the people of whom he wrote were obsessed by language, and made drunk by the power of words. . . . Ireland's three languages—English, Gaelic, and Latin—are the knotted veins and sinews of Carleton's prose.

This sensuous delight in the thing said is what Carleton would call a "trait" of Irish character. But his feelings toward it are double and opposite, for he connects this energy and grace of speech with much that was morally ugly in Irish life. . . . Half a century before John Synge put his ear to a Wicklow floor to catch the talk of servant girls, Carleton had caught every turn and nuance of Irish speech. Unlike Synge, he judged, moralized, interrupted himself with sermons and imprecations. And he is, by this measure, the better writer, for he knew that language has moral sources and moral consequences. (pp. 294-96)

[There is much to] be said of Carleton's broken career and faulty art, his excesses, his foolishness, and his abysmal lapses of taste. Yet the Carleton of *Traits and Stories* remains, for each reader, a discovery, a writer so fine that the reader begins to doubt his own judgment. From the broken land of gunmen and gallows, of bent men upon bitter soil and lovers "scattered like nosegays" across the meadows, came a writer so gifted that he could show us everything at once. (p. 299)

Carleton wrote cheerfully for all of [the periodicals that appeared in Dublin during the 1830's], out of the abundance of stories which he had yet to tell. . . . Those early stories have the freshness and wonder of a recent past upon them, and they are written with all the energy generated by his discovery of a way to describe the life which he had left. (p. 301)

It seemed to the Carleton of those years that he had left the roads at last, save for those occasions when he walked them for pleasure, as a gentleman might, in the company of a poet. He had learned how to do one kind of story supremely well, and his inherent indolence, his constant need to make money in the surest way, his desire for literary respectability, all prompted him to keep on writing that story. The variety of his work, within this limit, is impressive. In one brilliant sketch, **"Barney Brady's Goose,"** he achieved with careless ease the effect of wild Hibernian hilarity which Samuel Lover worked at through long, strained pages. (p. 304)

It is not easy to define the power of [*Valentine M'Clutchy,* the] awkward, ill-constructed novel which Yeats so admired and which Benedict Kiely has called "the most important book of the Irish nineteenth century." Scenes of wild comedy and heartbreaking pathos are placed beside each other without regard for effect. At times the narrative gives way to sermonizing, vituperation, and sulphurous prophecies. The central figures are given allegorical names and perform allegorical functions—Valentine M'Clutchy, the agent; Darby O'Drive, the bailiff; the Reverend Phineas Lucre, the absentee clergyman; Solomon M'Slime, "the religious attorney." Judged simply as a political tract, the book is murky and ambiguous. (p. 313)

"A linked embodiment" [Carleton's own phrase] is an admirable description of the way in which the world of Carleton's early fiction is peopled. The stories themselves reinforce each other, creating the cumulative effect of a swarming, tumultuous countryside. . . . He was by instinct an artist, and dealt in the politics of the spirit. For this reason, it did not matter what he wrote, nor for whom, nor what "lessons" he tacked on to his narratives.

But for this reason, too, he had avoided the special burden which pressed upon the other writers—the need to come to terms with contemporary Ireland and the issues which confronted it. He picked up his ideas about politics from his employers or out of the Dublin air. Often they ran counter to the true thrust and power of his stories. . . . (pp. 313-14)

Valentine M'Clutchy is Carleton's *Castle Rackrent*. It is his attempt to define once and for all the tragic center of Irish life. He intended the comparison: his novel has as its subtitle *The Chronicles of Castle Cumber*. It fails in the way that all of his later novels fail; it is great only in fragments. Carleton lacked the discipline which is necessary to sustain a novel through three long volumes, and the skill which gives thematic unity to diverse material. But it succeeds in the way that the best of the *Traits and Stories* do. He could look steadily at an isolated scene and draw forth the whole of its meaning. He was not afraid of contradiction or paradox or complexity. (p. 315)

For Carleton famine was the Irish situation *in extremis*. His first story, **"The Lough Derg Pilgrim,"** had been the extended image of a terrestial hell—sufferers moving mechanically along circles of jagged stone beneath a black sky. . . . The tragic scenes which burn themselves upon the reader's memory are so much of a kind that we may give a name to them: they seem fragments of a *danse macabre* contrived by a lurid but powerful imagination.

Yet this was not contrivance. Carleton's brooding, terrible talent had seized and given shape to the substance of experience. Famine, plague, and blood always lay beyond the bend of the next year's harvest. In 1818 and again in 1822 he had walked along the roads dotted with plague huts and had seen the wasted bodies tumbled into their shallow graves. Now, in 1846, he set out to describe what he had seen, to remark upon its causes and its dangers, and to prescribe its remedies. *The Black Prophet* was to be his "big" novel, his final, summarizing statement of the moral and social ills which beset Irish society.

The vividness and clarity with which it reveals a countryside lying under sentence of death give the forcefulness of observed fact to the novel. Its background is supplied by a people struggling with dazed incomprehension against starvation and pestilence. (pp. 318-19)

But this background, thick with misery and despair, Carleton knew was insufficient to the demands of a novel. There must be lengthy, didactic, and not particularly wise discussions of the economic causes of famine. There must also be a conventional plot, rich with conspiracy, murder, and retributive justice. The plot is inadequate to Carleton's theme, for Skindacre, his land-hungry villain, possesses neither full existence as a character nor stature as an allegorical figure. The atmosphere, the incidental scenes, the pervasive tone of calamitous horror seek to enlarge the novel, but it remains constricted by the mechanical plot.

Carleton's imagination was most firmly engaged by the figure who gives the novel its title, however, and Donnel Dhu, the "prophecy-man," is the strongest link between the plot and the rich possibilities of the theme. Carleton had always had a sense of the dramatic value of this singular Irish type. (p. 319)

Larger and more portentous than the uneven story in which he appears, [Donnel Dhu] carries the weight of apprehensions which Carleton cannot formulate. To Carleton, Patrick Murray would write, had fallen the task of recording the life of "those who ere long will have passed away from that troubled land, from the records of history, and from the memory of man forever" [see excerpt above]. In the pages of *The Black Prophet,* Carleton seems to come to a startled half-recognition that this is indeed the task which fate has assigned to him. . . . For Carleton, as for Donnel Dhu, the Irish earth was a page of prophecy which he could almost read. (pp. 320-21)

The Emigrants of Ahadarra and *The Tithe-Proctor* display the divisions of his feeling [about an armed revolt]. *The Emigrants,* which was written after a visit to his own depopulated valley, is suffused by a feeling of deep and troubled sympathy for the peasants who were being wrenched away from their homesteads and packed aboard "coffin-ships." . . .

The Tithe-Proctor is so harsh and uncompromising an attack upon insurrectionists that he was never quite forgiven for it. . . . The tone at times is raging and sulphurous, but Carleton's anger is directed against rebels and landlords alike. (p. 322)

The Tithe-Proctor was the last of Carleton's novels to be written with his old fire and zest. *The Squanders of Castle Squander* has its moments, but the machinery creaks. From that book he moved, in his fitful if prolific fashion, to the sheer incompetence of his final years. (pp. 326-27)

[After the Rising of 1847, Carleton wrote *The Squanders of Castle Squander, The Black Baronet,* and *Willy Reilly and His Dear Colleen Bawn.*] They are painfully inferior to any of his earlier work. (p. 327)

[Carleton] continued to write until his death a decade later, but what he wrote has no proper place in literary history. (p. 329)

In his late, broken years Carleton boasted that no writer would succeed him until fifty years had passed. There was much vanity in this, but more truth, for the nineteenth-century Irish novel established no tradition. Between Carleton's death and the beginning of the new century Ireland produced no prose writer of real stature. (p. 333)

> *Thomas Flanagan, in his* The Irish Novelists: 1800-1850 *(originally a thesis presented at Columbia University, 1958; copyright © 1958 Columbia University Press; reprinted by permission of the publisher),* Columbia University Press, 1959, 362 p.*

RICHARD MORRISON   (essay date 1965)

Certainly Carleton knew nothing of Chaucer or the *Canterbury Tales,* yet his first sketch, *The Pilgrimage to Lough Derg,* is permeated with the same mixture of ribald humor and piety found in Chaucer. He surely knew nothing of Boccaccio, yet the device of swapping tales around the fire in Ned McKeown's Inn in *Shane Fadh's Wedding* is very similar to that of the Italian. Although most of Carleton's writing is decidedly on the gloomy side, no story or sketch is bare of the inimitable Irish humor of which he was a master. . . .

The Poor Scholar, one of Carleton's finest works, might be considered as a complement to Maria Edgeworth's *The Absentee,* for while she very ably indicates the suffering of the Irish serf from the landlord's point of view, Carleton recreates the relationship from the point of view of the peasant, taking the reader into the hearts of the people and the hovels they called home. Merciless in his characterization, Carleton exposed the peasants' shortcomings—their brutal murders, their drunkenness, treachery, and cunning—with the same bold strokes he used in depicting their unswerving loyalties, affection, charity, and other virtues. Like a scientist examining specimens objectively under a microscope, he never erred, and his delineations were so palpably true that few took offense. (p. 221)

Carleton may not have been a great novelist, but he was a true poet, and even the poorest and most melodramatic of his writings are spotted with effective poetic expressions. His fiction, though brimming with the most powerful pathos, is too often cluttered with sickening-sweet passages that are difficult to accept in our time, yet the beauty of the peculiarly Irish expressions of affectionate endearment cannot be shrugged away. (p. 222)

Carleton knew little about English gentlemen except from an Irish peasant's position, and whenever he attempted to portray the upper classes, his portraits were failures. Still, he may have estimated Dickens' qualities more accurately than the cult of Dickens will admit, for a comparison of the two men demonstrates Carleton to have been a better humorist, with a greater understanding of his subject than Dickens. True, Carleton was more limited—he was out of his depth when away from the Irish peasant—yet within this acknowledged limitation his characters appear in the full-round, believable, true to life and to logical development. (p. 224)

It is impossible to fit Carleton's writings into any broad category of his time. The poorest of his novels, *Jane Sinclair,* was praised by both Thackeray and Dickens as his best work. Its oversweet sentiment and melodramatic pathos represented a goal to strive for during that period. The brutal naturalism portrayed in the unbelievably cruel murders in *Wild Goose Lodge* is, however, horrifying in the extreme, and the subsequent aftermath, as recounted by Carleton in his autobiography, has few parallels in literature equalling the stark portrayal of the punished murderers. (p. 225)

It has been noted that Carleton's earlier characters have a good bit of Carleton himself in them. [The lead characters from *Denis O'Shaughnessy Going to Maynooth* and *Phelim O'Toole's Courtship*] are both Carleton, laughing at himself. In his later stories his characters reflect his own personality in a more vitiated form; yet all of his characters that spring from the peasantry are not only true to Irish life, but are universal. They are appreciated and understood in France, Italy, Germany, and America. (p. 226)

> Richard Morrison, "A Note on William Carleton" (copyright 1965 The Curators of the University of Missouri; reprinted by permission of the author), in University Review, Vol. XXXI, No. 3, March, 1965, pp. 219-26.

FRANK O'CONNOR   (essay date 1967)

[Carleton's] English is leaden, his judgement is dull, and he simply has no ear for speech. For Carleton there are not as many languages as there are people. There are only two languages—correct English and peasant English. Peasant English is further subdivided into honest peasant English and Babu— 'sesquipedalian and stilted nonsense', as he describes it himself in a rare flash of style. Peasant English, like correct English, is capable of what he would probably have called 'tender' passages, but Babu is purely comic in its effect. In this Carleton was wrong, as he was bound to be in any matter concerning

language, because it is the stilted and artificial quality of Babu that most often gives us the poetic shock in the hymns and songs of the country people. . . .

Because of this deafness to living speech, Carleton found it difficult to keep on one plane even for a page or two. [In **'Denis O'Shaughnessy Going to Maynooth'**] . . . he uses Babu with excellent comic effect. But when Denis has to separate forever from his beloved Susan, Babu is not enough. She must be made love to in 'correct' English. (p. 148)

> *Frank O'Connor, "The Beginnings of Modern Literature," in his* A Short History of Irish Literature: A Backward Look *(copyright © by Harriet R. O'Donovan 1967; reprinted by permission of Joan Daves), G. P. Putnam's Sons, 1967, pp. 143-53.*

MARGARET CHESNUTT   (essay date 1976)

[Carleton] wrote almost exclusively about the peasantry and drew his subject-matter from their lives, but his writings were by no means disinterested: he did his best to promote religious and later social reform, and he wrote for many parties and shades of opinion. It would be a mistake, however, to suppose that he had no consistent view of his own, for underlying his varying analyses of the roots of distress in Ireland and his varying remedies for its relief is a strong conviction that mutual respect and good will and moral behaviour on the part of all classes would cure the ills of the country. (pp. 136-37)

Many of his stories are openly didactic, and as well as intruding in his own person to point a moral Carleton very often inserts long digressions which break the flow of events. But his didacticism does not merely manifest itself in digressive passages or moral comments: it lies in the very spirit of his work. Characterization, plot, setting and atmosphere are all directed towards exemplifying the spirit and form of life of the Irish people. Though the entertainment value of his work should not be ignored, to Carleton the short story and the novel were vehicles for the discussion of social and moral issues; he was not at all preoccupied with fiction as "art" and it is quite evident that content interested him more than form. (p. 140)

[In] terms of overall structure [Carleton's stories] may be divided broadly speaking into those stories which aim directly at teaching peasant or landlord in Ireland how to attain the good life spiritually and socially, and those which teach the reading public more about the Irish peasantry. (p. 141)

In the early stories aimed directly at gentry or peasantry an interesting mechanism is discernible. These tales are built around the usual structure of introduction, exposition and resolution, but what sets them apart is the nature of the change which leads to the resolution and the agent of that change. (pp. 141-42)

[In these stories, collected in *Traits and Stories of the Irish Peasantry* and *Tales of Ireland*,] the narrator, who is one of the protagonists, is an outside agent in contrast to the narrators of the later stories, who purport to come from the community. These stories present the reader with the phenomenon of a narrator entering the community from the outside, analyzing it and bearing witness to the event which changes it in some way. It can be observed that the community does not possess within itself the means of change, and to Carleton change is imperative if the peasantry (and Irish society as a whole) are to improve. (p. 142)

[In Carleton's] *Christian Examiner* stories, especially in the overtly propagandistic stories of "**The Broken Oath**", "**Father Butler**", "**The Death of a Devotee**" and "**The Priest's Funeral**", change comes about through adversity and the agent of change is the Bible; the nature of the change is therefore a moral and/or spiritual one, and the narrator is a Protestant gentleman far enough removed from the other protagonists to be able to judge them "objectively". Each story bears witness to the conversion of an individual from Roman Catholicism to the Protestant religion, and in each story a tragic event is the catalyst. (p. 143)

The narrators of these stories play a passive part in the events and make no direct attempt to convert the main protagonists. . . . In all these stories the narrator is on the side of the saved, observing their difficulties and final salvation as a kindly friend. Through this structure [these] stories inexorably build up a damning body of evidence against the Church of Rome and, through the qualitative difference apparent between the saved and the lost, demonstrate the beneficial effects of Protestantism on the individual and on society at large.

The confessional stories of "**A Pilgrimage to Patrick's Purgatory**" and "**Confessions of a Reformed Ribbonman**" are also structured around more or less cathartic events which cause a basic change in the protagonists' way of life and thought. In both stories the protagonist makes a journey to the place where he is to have a horrific experience. He is by no means passive. . . . The narrators of these stories, who come from the ranks of the peasantry, can be seen by their language and attitudes to have risen to the rank of gentleman, and they both look back at the turning point in their lives. The didactic structure of these stories is similar: the reader is conducted step by step through the motions of what Carleton claims to be the two great evils of the country, superstitious Roman Catholic practices and violent agitation. (pp. 144-45)

In all the stories so far referred to it can be observed that the change which comes about in the protagonists is a moral one, and while it leads to a better way of life it also sets them apart from the community at large—they become different but better men. The moral implication here is that the pathway to salvation is lonely but rewarding.

"**The Battle of the Factions**" and "**The Funeral and Party Fight**" are interesting exceptions from a structural point of view to the group of stories which are openly didactic. Violent action takes place but the characteristic linear progression is lacking inasmuch as no change can be seen in the community before and after the battles. This society is incapable of healing itself; thus the structure of the stories reflects the structure of the communities. (p. 145)

In the stories directly concerned with social issues, notably "**Tubber Derg or the Red Well**" and "**The Poor Scholar**", the didactic element is uppermost. The narrator of these stories breaks continually into the flow of events with long, digressive interpolations. . . . Both stories are structured around journeys of discovery and both are circular in form in the sense that after a long struggle the families concerned regain their previous happiness; but there is a contrast with the stories of violence in that a positive conclusion is reached. . . . In both stories the nature of the change is a rise to prosperity, but it is significant that the effort which brings this change about is an individual one. The virtues of self-help are therefore another aspect of the underlying didacticism, while the necessity of perseverance and of patience in adversity is underlined at the

same time. It must nevertheless be emphasized that while Carleton saw the possibility of change for the better coming about through the personal efforts of individual peasants he despaired of the capacity of the peasant community as a whole for moral, civil or spiritual self-renewal. He did, however, realize that all these elements were interrelated and chose the element of morals as the most important of all. (pp. 146-47)

The second didactic group of tales, those aimed primarily at teaching the wider reading public more about the people, differ significantly in narrative structure from the stories of religion, social evils and violence. No significant change occurs in the course of the narrative and no outside agent enters either to precipitate a change or to observe the protagonists. These are stories which characterize the Irish peasantry by describing their life and customs. They may be subdivided into stories which are more or less openly didactic and stories of fantasy or near fantasy which are didactic only in terms of Carleton's overall aims.

"**Ned M'Keown**", "**The Three Tasks**", "**Shane Fadh's Wedding**", "**Larry M'Farland's Wake**" and "**The Battle of the Factions**" form a separate unit within [*Traits and Stories of the Irish Peasantry*], in which most of the tales belonging to this group appeared. "**Ned M'Keown**" acts as a prologue: the narrative framework is provided by members of the village community sitting round the fire drinking in Ned's public house and telling stories to one another. The atmosphere is one of comfort, nostalgia and satisfaction. . . . There is little or no authorial intrusion—the community speaks for itself.

That this was originally to have been the structure of *Traits and Stories* as a whole is clear from Carleton's parenthetic comments at the end of "**The Battle of the Factions**". . . . [By] the time he came to "**The Battle of the Factions**" he had found his self-imposed structure too limiting. . . . Authorial description and observation certainly result from the abandonment of Carleton's original design: the stories which follow "**The Battle of the Factions**" are also wider in scope, ranging outside of the village community to deal with current Irish problems, and the point of view shifts from that of the peasants themselves to that of the middle and upper classes.

Elements which differentiate the stories told around Ned's fireside from the rest of *Traits and Stories* are: the absence of an omniscient narrator and the consequent absence of "improving" digressions; the cosy atmosphere where the reader is aware of the cold night outside, the fire and drink, the feeling of "community"; and the story being told to other people, a convention which is reinforced by the comments made by the hearers on what they are told. The stories are therefore both the tale which is told and the environment in which it is told. These stories illustrate, as intended by Carleton, "Irish life, feeling, and manners" in an immediate way not achieved by the more openly "directed" stories of this group. (pp. 147-48)

The remainder of the second group of didactic tales are differentiated by the role of the narrator. . . . By intruding to point to a moral or to expand a particular theme Carleton is returning to his practice in [his earlier stories]. . . . However, the narrator is now sympathetic to the people, their character and living conditions, and he very often emphasizes that he himself comes from a peasant environment and can therefore pronounce authoritatively upon it. And in contrast to the five stories at the beginning of *Traits and Stories,* which are nostalgic vignettes of communal life, these remaining stories deal more specifically with peasant character and with current conditions. (p. 152)

[Whereas the stories in *Tales of Ireland*] arc propagandist and unsympathetic to the Irish people the stories in *Traits and Stories* try to analyze their character and living conditions in a more constructive manner. This difference can be seen in characterization, in the role played by the narrator and also in the nature of the digressions. (p. 153)

True to his declared aim of portraying the Irish peasantry in all their complexity Carleton operates with a limited number of types acting in typical situations. In his efforts to be objective he presents both the good and the bad qualities of the group, and the priests young and old, the hedge schoolmaster, the ne'er-do-well, the yeoman farmer and the active and passive woman types may be said to provide a representative cross-section of the peasantry. (p. 156)

As well as being an entertaining story, **"Denis O'Shaughnessy"** demonstrates the character of the typical young priest and describes his social status. To fulfil this purpose the character of the young priest in question must be credible, and for this reason Carleton does not confine his account merely to describing and illustrating the typical characteristics of such a personage. Denis' character is traced from the time when he was the young son chosen for the priesthood until the eve of his departure for Maynooth. The story thus treats of character development rather than static, "typical" character alone, and Carleton exhibits in the course of the story both the distinctive young priestly characteristics and the social reasons for their development. (p. 157)

As a typical young priest, Denis' character is represented as ludicrous by Carleton's standard, the standard which he expects his readers to share. . . . The final section of the story, ending with Denis' departure from Maynooth to marry Susan, is integral to its very nature, and the vein of rich, high comedy which runs through it serves to counterbalance its more serious aims.

The hedge schoolmaster is a vital part of the rural community and many such schoolmasters appear in Carleton's stories. Mat Kavanagh of **"The Hedge School"** is perhaps the most fully treated in terms of characterization but even he is not as fully rounded as Denis O'Shaughnessy, the young priest. With the exception of Mr. O'Connor, the schoolmaster in **"Neal Malone"** . . . , all of Carleton's schoolmasters share similar characteristics. This lack of individual characterization is interesting in itself and underlines Carleton's presentation of typical rather than individual character in his stories of Irish life. (pp. 161-62)

The hedge schoolmaster is . . . a learned pedant who enjoys a great deal of respect on account of his position and performs extra-scholarly functions necessary to the community. He is usually fond of whiskey, often extremely cruel, but always gregarious and greedy. By keeping an ironic distance from his schoolmasters Carleton is able to detail all the facets of their characters without condemning them outright.

Having examined Carleton's characterization of the young priest and the hedge schoolmaster, those links with the "higher life", we must now turn to the peasantry themselves. Owen M'Carthy and Larry M'Farland are representative of two very different types of men to be found among the peasantry, while Ellish Connell and Rose O'Hallaghan represent two contrasting types of women. (pp. 165-66)

The burden of Carleton's characterization of Owen M'Carthy is that he is first and foremost a good Christian subjected to unjust treatment. (p. 167)

With his characterization of Owen M'Carthy, presented in his usual didactic manner and exploiting the full range of literary sentiment, Carleton wishes to demonstrate that such men are honest and industrious and entirely undeserving of their bitter fate. . . . Owen is in fact Carleton's image of the ideal Irish peasant, noble in sentiment, generous, honest and God-fearing, and he writes of him in a reverential tone bordering at times on nostalgic sentimentality.

Very different is the attitude adopted to Phelim O'Toole or Larry M'Farland, both of whom are characterized as harum-scarum ne'er-do-wells, talented and clever but without the moral fibre necessary to succeed in adversity. . . . [While] he respects their efforts Carleton allows himself to be ironic at their expense. They can get drunk, be shrewd and cunning and find themselves in ludicrous situations, whereas these elements of behaviour never appear in connection with the M'Carthy's or the M'Evoy's, whose sterling qualities and simple character are eulogized and idealized and serve to heighten the pathos and injustice of their fate. (pp. 168-69)

Carleton presents the reader with two types of peasant women, the shrewd, hard-working farmer's wife and the beautiful, innocent young girl. There are of course shades in between, but generally speaking peasant women in *Traits and Stories* approximate either to the active Ellish Connell or the passive Rose O'Hallaghan type of **"The Geography of an Irish Oath"** and **"The Battle of the Factions"** respectively. Women rarely occupy such a prominent place as men in the stories and in this respect Ellish Connell is unique. Her history is traced from the time she marries Peter Connell through her growing prosperity to her death. She is by no means a tender little flower—she is plain and homely—but what she lacks in beauty she compensates for in energy, and she makes the fortunes of the family. . . . [However, in] all her busy life of money-making Ellish has no time for religion, and she dies before she can attend to her soul. This circumstance, in addition to her extremely materialistic nature, makes her less than an ideal woman for Carleton albeit she is a pattern of industry. He admires her energy and good sense but censures her neglect of God, which is not a pleasing thing in a woman. . . . [Carleton's industrious, vigorous women] are all to be admired but not adored. It is significant that Carleton allows himself to portray them with humour, kindly and ironic, while never a whiff of laughter enters his depiction of such women as Rose O'Hallaghan.

This other predominant type of woman in Carleton's stories has much in common with Dickens' more nauseating heroines. Like Dickens and unlike Thackeray, Carleton could not be ironic about the archetypal "good little woman". In keeping with her character, she never takes a prominent part in any of the stories but modestly and shyly occupies her place in the background. . . . He admires Ellish Connell for her cleverness but never waxes lyrical about her. It is indicative that she is plain—the ideal woman cannot be both pretty and clever. (pp. 172-74)

Rose O'Hallaghan's beauty, meekness, modesty and virginity are all attributes of Carleton's ideal woman. . . . [Such] women unquestioningly accept the decisions of their menfolk and live for them alone. Though there are great differences between active and passive women—of whom it is evident that the latter are regarded as being the more "feminine"—none of them attempt to stray outside the confines of the home. (pp. 174-75)

Either because of his lack of artistic sense or because of his eagerness to instruct, Carleton never permits the reader to draw his own conclusions about the characters in question. He tells, shows and tells again in the manner of a sympathetic journalist or social historian rather than a writer of fiction. Denis O'Shaughnessy is his most successful portrait; but even there the didactic intention appears to outweigh literary considerations. (p. 175)

> *Margaret Chesnutt, in her* Studies in the Short Stories of William Carleton *(© Margaret Chesnutt 1976; reprinted by permission of the author), Acta Universitatis Gothoburgensis, 1976, 213 p.*

EILEEN SULLIVAN   (essay date 1977)

[William Carleton's *Traits and Stories of The Irish Peasantry* and novels like *Fardorougha, The Miser, Valentine M'Clutchy, The Black Prophet,* and *The Emigrants of Ahadarra*] signal the beginning of a modern Irish prose literature. These beginnings, furthermore, are realistic statements of Ireland's social history that disclose the Irish social herarchy from Carleton's viewpoint. Carleton, from rural Ireland, records the true-to-life events of that forgotten world. He captures its reality, and he can do so because he shares that reality.

Reality, used here in a particular sense, is everything external to Carleton's inner life: for instance, the material world, society, and the past Celtic history. This reality, the present and past worlds of the Irish peasantry, limits Carleton, but its very limitation forms the mold for his individual genius. . . . Reality, then, for this discussion consists of two worlds: one actual, and one ancient, Carleton reports the reality—the actual and ancient world as it pertains to him and the Irish farmers—by relating his inner or spiritual world to that reality. Born into a world hidden to all but the native Irish, Carleton is subject to that reality. Were it not so, his poetic imagination would create a new reality, but fortunately for the unimaginative and prosaic population, Carleton must confront what he finds about him and create his works of art within that milieu. . . . The mundane and the mysterious are communicated to us by Carleton. His works, therefore, are a montage of the dual aspects of reality. And Carleton's inventive power determines the way in which he perceives the tangible and intangible worlds and how he records his perceptions. . . . His gifted way with words recaptures the Irish idiom of his class, caught between the English-speaking world and the Irish-speaking world, and immortalizes that class. . . . (pp. 130-31)

Although [his background qualifies him] to write about the rural life, Carleton cannot do so without genius and a measure of literary skill. His genius, above and beyond his literary skill, places Carleton in the reality about him like a wave pounding upon the Ulster shore and creating a misty spray. Carleton sprays a mist over his reality. He has in some way changed it, and this is acceptable because reality is subject to change, as are the waves and the shore. The extent of the change depends upon the intensity of the wave as it beats upon the shore, and often Carleton pounds with great ferocity. His mist, however, falls gently upon his suffering people. . . . His works are raw substances shorn clean of sophisticated urbanites. In addition, enjoyment does not end with the closing of his books; on the contrary, it increases to encompass the human spirit. The communication of this totality and the consistency of the

assuaging mist are the elements of Carleton's genius. The study of Carleton's literary merit, then, focuses on his ability to assimilate compatibly the ancient Irish world with the actual world of his Ireland. There is no conflict between the two worlds for either Carleton or his people. Had there been, his portraits might have been caricatures. Every bit as superstitious as his characters, Carleton naturally relates to the preternatural world, and at the bottom of this relationship lie the ancient literary traditions of Ireland.

Carleton employs his skill to express his genius. The tripartite nature of his literary skill consists of: a knowledge of literary tradition coupled with a memory for detail; an acute power of observation of his external world; and his awareness of word power and the mystery of language. He has knowledge of old Irish literary traditions which involve the art of storytelling. . . . Moreover, Carleton is not unlike the ancient artists whose dual function was to praise and satirize society. . . . Although these ancient artists create heroic themes, the inner life of the aristocracy, their emotions and religious experiences, are not subjects for their art. Actions are suitable for their descriptive powers, and scenes are more important than the narrative. This is so in Carleton's art. While the only way he can convey events is through narration, which he usually changes in some way, Carleton's emphasis is on the scenes. Naturally, he has to change characters too, substituting peasants for princes, but heroic action remains.

Carleton's knowledge of old Irish tales relates to his acute power of observation, which clarifies his attitude toward reality. He records simply what he sees; he is faithful to geography, time, living persons, and things. That is to say, Carleton accurately records the actual world as he sees it. . . . This fidelity to the external world is also found in his retelling of the personal history of his region, its people and property suitably related. Carleton, enchanted by his own existence, reproduces it so he can communicate with reality. While the enchantment lasts, he uses his powers of observation to record events, but after the Famine the enchantment disappears. (pp. 134-35)

The final measure of Carleton's skill rests in his recognition of the mystery of language. He is early attracted to letters and words and senses that he can manipulate them to influence his readers. (p. 135)

Carleton, through his personality and skill, reproduces the reality of the Irish country people. But he relates to that reality in four different ways: he refuses to accept it; he fails to idealize it; he exiles himself from it; and he revolts against it.

Carleton's refusal to accept reality involves his own quest for fame. The rural world is not the object of his deep and scrutinizing glances. The vision before his eyes . . . is unacceptable. Carleton's vision of life differs essentially from that of his family and his friends, for his imaginative mind sees this world with impatience because he cannot work out his destiny within its boundaries. He reviews, one by one, all the virtuous aspects of his world that he values most, and he accepts these values, which his novels describe in detail, but he refuses to accept the miseries. . . . In the final analysis of Carleton's refusal to accept the reality of the actual world of the rural poor, it is evident that the ancient world, the other part of its dualistic reality, is never rejected. Carleton's refusal, then, is superficial; he still belongs to the invisible world; his refusal is not total. (pp. 136-37)

Carleton's failure to idealize reality can be explained through Carleton's own personality. He cannot idealize because his inner life depends on his external existence: life is action, living is participation in the action, and writing is the recollecting of these participations. His forte, scenic description, depends upon actuality. He is unable to represent something as it is not; this means he cannot make something perfect. The capacity to idealize rests in minds of more intellectual and abstract nature; neither of these characteristics is found in Carleton. (p. 137)

The third facet of reality, which places Carleton solidly in the Irish literary tradition, is his self-imposed exile from the reality which generates his genius. . . . [He] does not idealize the actual world of the rural poor to make it compatible to his taste. When Carleton exiles himself to Dublin to escape the wretched aspects of his home, he begins to write about people from home, attending to their virtues, which he values, and their faults, which he rejects. Paradoxically, exile sharpens his focus. . . . In exile, and only in exile, can Carleton justly praise his people.

Another aspect of Carleton's literary stance is his rebellion against his reality. Carleton lacks political judgment. He writes according to his temper, not the temper of the times. . . . Carleton does not lack revolutionary tendencies, for he revolts against the inhumanity of his age. He longs to decode the enigma of the reality about him: why is it that such noble people live such ignoble lives? Carleton's generous spirit does not accept the tyranny of the peasant's life. He does not meekly submit to the peasant's reality, but feels there is something better beyond that limited world. . . . In *Valentine M'Clutchy* he fights against evils responsible for the wretchedness of the poor tenants. In *The Black Prophet*, he fights the enemies of the poor and demonstrates that inhumanity makes him choose sides. (pp. 137-39)

Consequently, his rebellion exalts the humanity of the people, and their own everyday speech carries the force of rebellion. The distinction between their language and literary language is so great that the battle would have been lost but for Carleton's genius. There is no question but that, without his dedication to his class, his novels would fall flat. Furthermore, Carleton, to express his humanity, uses the farmers' language without condescension. This speech, English in an Irish idiom, suggests that Carleton's rebellion against the reality of the peasantry is superficial. . . . [As a moralist] Carleton defines life's battle as a conflict between virtue and vice. Simply and directly, he juxtaposes the moral and the immoral characters; there is no question, either, to which character he pledges allegiance. (p. 139)

I do not believe that England, or any country dedicated to the preservation of human dignity, can afford to forget Carleton's works. His humanism—his attempts to understand human experience through his imaginative and intellectual faculties—demands a wider audience that must accept Carleton on his terms and in the light of his reality. It may never be a wide audience. But for those who interpret [what Yeats termed] the "fiery shorthand," the experiences are like trips to hell and heaven and back. (p. 140)

Eileen Sullivan, "William Carleton: Artist of Reality," in Éire-Ireland *(copyright Irish American Cultural Institute), Vol. XII, No. 1, 1977, pp. 130-40.*

MAURICE HARMON (essay date 1977)

Frank O'Connor has pointed out that [George Moore's] *The Untilled Field* established some of the recurrent themes of

modern Irish literature—rural insufficiency, anti-clericalism, and emigration. But these are also part of Carleton's response, whose treatment of peasant society, while lacking Moore's greater literary awareness and sense of form, was nevertheless more profound and intimate. (p. 133)

[Carleton] is the only Irish writer of his century to present his material in the kind of confident and complete manner that indicates the literary imagination in a fully creative relationship with its material. Again the contrast with Moore is instructive. Moore's stories are filtered through a defining and controlling intellect so that a basic idea holds the material together. Carleton writes in several voices and, while not all of these are successful and while the rational control is often weak, the emotional range and imaginative force are considerably greater than in Moore. We readily praise Carleton for his verisimilitude, for his realistic portrayal of the lives of the people, for the insight which he gives to their secret and often chaotic lives . . . ; on these levels his work is a record of the actual and the concrete. But his greatest claim to fame from the literary point of view, as distinct from the interest his work has for the historian and the folklorist, lies in those stories and those places in his best novels where he speaks out in mature control of his material.

An example of this may be found in "Going to Maynooth," which is a portrait of the artist as a young pedant and, like Joyce's later semiautobiographical novel, is written with an ironic and amused detachment even as it deals compassionately with a subject that is personal and painful. . . . By use of the mock-serious tone Carleton achieves a degree of distancing through which he can freely reveal his own family background and his experiences as a young clerical scholar. The control comes from the mocking tone that enables Carleton to commemorate and judge at the same time, and to use the philomath [schoolmaster's] English of the hedgeschool for the same dual purpose. (pp. 133-34)

"The Battle of the Factions" is a story in a different vein. Here the mockery of "Going to Maynooth" is replaced by another persona and a different tone. By presenting this material through the authoritative and exuberant figure of the teacher, Pat Frayne, Carleton achieves distance and subtly allows the confident and sympathetic relationship of narrator and story to be undermined by the actuality of his narrative. . . . The result of [the] rich freight of incident, detail, narrative, and tone is a powerful story of love and death, custom adhered to with stupid principle, and family and social life disrupted. All come naturally within the memory of Pat Frayne, who, like the old soldier with no more wars to fight, still hears the sounds of combat above the cries of loss that also escape from his story. At the same time his tale, being appropriate to the teller, reveals his own richly humorous, extravert, and passionate nature. (p. 136)

Frayne happily commemorates scenes and deeds of appalling violence with good-humored and appreciative equanimity, but events overtake him and the tragic center of the narrative becomes increasingly evident. (p. 138)

[The concept of the satanic element in man] is endemic in Carleton, just as violence and anarchy seem to be endemic in all those nineteenth-century Irish novels that try to deal realistically with Irish peasant society. It might be conjectured that violence and anarchy are not so much realistic accounts of social reality as modes of moral judgment, metaphors of the moral imagination conceived in the face of a huge unmanageable evil. . . . The real subject of these novels is not their visible world of savage murders and reprisals, nor the deceit, greed, and indifference to the landlords and their agents, but the predicament of a race so inhumanely denied a place in society or any glimmer of hope for the future.

Carleton's near obsession with the satanic individual, seen in **"Wildgoose Lodge," "The Midnight Mass,"** and **"The Lianhan Shee,"** becomes more pronounced in the novels. In *The Black Prophet,* O'Donnell the prophecy man is almost totally evil, a murderer pursued by nightmare, plotting evil, cruel, a man who has fallen from innocence. Solomon M'Slime and Valentine M'Clutchy in the novel *Valentine M'Clutchy* are Carleton's most obnoxious villains, utterly devoid of moral feeling, intent on their own greedy, cunning, and hypocritical exploitation of the people. Both of these powerful, if badly organized, novels are jagged acts of wrath against the system that denies and oppresses the people. Each is a succession of metaphors of action, characterization, and landscape for the amoral chaos to which Irish life had been reduced in the years leading to the Famine. (pp. 141-42)

But the extent and hopelessness of the calamity facing his people must have made the novelist's task virtually impossible. At his best in the short form, Carleton loses control frequently in the novels, where he works with a too-complicated plot, lurches into melodrama, and speaks directly to the landlord and the reader in lengthy asides that appeal for sanity, understanding, and justice. Flawed as works of art, the novels speak from the abyss to which his people have been driven and with a tone of utter hopelessness. . . . There was no light and no redress, except in those unacceptable fictive solutions, those happy endings so dear to Carleton, at the end of *Valentine M'Clutchy,* at the end of **"Tubber Derg,"** and at the end of *The Emigrants of Ahadarra.* In such fairytale endings wrongs are righted, the good are rewarded, and the kind landlord personally restores the land to the evicted. One wonders if Carleton knew how hollow the words sound at the end of *The Emigrants:*

> "M'Mahon," said Chevydale, "give me your hand. I am sorry that either you or your son have suffered anything on my account. I am come now to render you an act of justice—to compensate both you and him, as far as I can, for the anxiety you have endured. Consider yourselves both, therefore, as restored to your farms at the terms you proposed originally. I shall have leases prepared—give up the notion of emigration—the country cannot spare such men as you and your admirable son." . . .

One ought to be able to read this as a savagely ironic comment, but Carleton lacks Swift's toughness of mind and temperament. Coming right after M'Mahon's sorrowful farewell to his buried wife, the landlord's words arc stiff and lifeless. The true conclusion to these novels comes in the words of the prophet's daughter, a doomed protest made on an individual level but applicable to the whole people: "I tried to be good, but I'm only a cobweb before the wind—everything is against me, an' I think I'm like some one that never had a guardian angel to take care of them." (pp. 143-44)

> *Maurice Harmon, "Cobwebs before the Wind: Aspects of the Peasantry in Irish Literature from 1800 to 1916,"* in Views of the Irish Peasantry: 1800-1916, *edited by Daniel J. Casey and Robert E. Rhodes (© Daniel J. Casey and Robert E. Rhodes 1977),*

> *Archon Books (The Shoe String Press, Inc.), Hamden, Connecticut, 1977, pp. 129-59.**

ANDRÉ BOUÉ (essay date 1979)

[Carleton's] imagination, though remarkably alert, was more reproductive than creative. A swarming life fills his pages, but scenes, plots and characters are little more than kaleidoscopic reflections of the reality which he has actually seen. . . . [What] inspires this close relation of his work to past experience is much less duration than affective intensity. He longs to re-create and perpetuate the happy days of his adolescence, so that his vision is inevitably subjective. His ever-present personality manifests itself in the recurrence of themes and situations as well as in digressions or veiled confidences. Yet autobiography remains accessory in his fiction. . . .

The panoramic view he wants to present to his readers he builds up by accumulation. Each particular subject he selects is suggested by some remembered individual, event or narrative, and developed so as to illustrate some characteristic aspect of Irish life. Each of his stories, however funny or moving, is deliberately descriptive and furnished with a great wealth of detail. (p. 84)

However primitive this patchwork technique may seem, it goes far towards creating the illusion of life, and the precious counterpart of its disorder is constant variety. Carleton was a spontaneous writer who took little care of form. . . . [He] made no sustained effort to improve on the model of amorphous narrative he had received from tradition, and it would be vain to look in him for the artistic sophistication of the modern short story.

Curiously enough, he made his closest approach to it, apparently by pure instinct, in **"Wildgoose Lodge",** one of his early productions. . . . In the abrupt beginning, he exceptionally discards the once-upon-a-time convention of folk tradition. Attention is focused throughout on the narrator's emotions. The mysterious summons he receives, the anxiety and misgivings he feels, the cold darkness of the rainy winter night, the late meeting of the conspirators in the lonely chapel, the diabolical cruelty of the leader, gradually create suspense and quite naturally lead to the horror of the final scene. A strong impression of truth is here artistically produced by suggestiveness of detail, rapidity of action and relative terseness of style. But such compression is rare in Carleton. (pp. 85-6)

Fiction to him is chiefly the means of dealing attractively with actual truth. Consequently, he gives little autonomy to the imaginary world he invents. Characters born of his fancy are rarely brought together with a view to an objective study of their reactions and development, but are as a rule guided along a predetermined course. He is thus led to sacrifice the plots of his novels as well as the simpler but all the more delicately balanced anecdotal basis of his stories, making them, not carefully elaborated aesthetic constructions, but mere supports for his subjects.

The perfect verisimilitude of characters and situations drawn from life cannot fully redeem the faulty structure and lack of unity of some of his best stories. . . . Unconcerned with literary technique, he pours out the rich flow of his memories into his pages. Yet he always holds his reader's attention. The artistic imperfections of his work never obliterate its peculiar charm.

His humour, to which his prose largely owes its distinctive flavour, is fundamentally that of the country-people among whom he lived. It is at once rude, exuberant and serious. It is eminently national, since its main elements, fantasy, the macabre and verbal play, are characteristic of the Gaelic tradition and obviously derived from it. . . . Carleton freely indulges in farce, but never makes it humiliating for the Irish, never makes it suggestive of social or racial inferiority. However brutal his polemics, however dogmatic his moral preaching may be, his amused perception of human oddities is always indulgent. Far better than his contemporaries, he has expressed the singular mixture of mirth and melancholy which distinguishes the Irish character. (pp. 86-7)

His rugged style itself paradoxically contributes to his excellence, because it is quite appropriate to his subject-matter. The naturalness of his dialogue is all the more striking as it includes a skilful representation of dialect. His picturesque imagery illustrates the vividness of popular imagination. . . .

[Carleton's] lack of discipline, his bent for polemics, the limited scope of his observation, are less apparent or less prejudicial in his stories than in his novels. In these stories, his deep understanding of human nature, his dramatic gift, his humour and pathos, appear in their full maturity. In them, he realized his ambition to be the historian of his people. (p. 88)

> *André Boué, "William Carleton As a Short-Story Writer," in* The Irish Short Story, *edited by Patrick Rafroidi and Terence Brown (copyright © 1979, by Presses Universitaires de Lille (C.E.R.I.U.L.) and Colin Smythe Ltd.), Colin Smythe Ltd., 1979, pp. 81-90.*

ADDITIONAL BIBLIOGRAPHY

Brown, Terence. "The Death of William Carleton: 1869." *Hermathena*, CX (1970): 81-5.
    Examines Carleton's conversion to Protestantism and his religious convictions at the time of his death.

Chesnutt, Margaret. "An Introduction to William Carleton." *Moderna Språk* LXXI, No. 1 (1977): 25-36.
    Discusses the political, religious, and social issues of Carleton's time, and their depiction in his stories.

Cronin, John. "William Carleton: *The Black Prophet* (1847)." In his *The Anglo-Irish Novel: The Nineteenth Century, Vol. I*, pp. 83-98. Totowa, N.J.: Barnes & Noble, 1980.
    A review of Carleton criticism and a discussion of *The Black Prophet*. The essay contends that the inadequate, melodramatic plot undermines the theme of famine and diminishes the power of the novel.

Ibarra, Eileen. "William Carleton: An Introduction." *Eire-Ireland* V, No. 1 (Spring 1970): 81-6.
    A survey of critical reaction to Carleton's works, including the opinions of his contemporaries.

Kiely, Benedict. *Poor Scholar: A Study of the Works and Days of William Carleton (1794-1869)*. New York: Sheed & Ward, 1948, 198 p.
    A sympathetic and colorful account of Carleton's life and the influences on his work.

Sullivan, Eileen. "William Carleton: Ulster's Contribution to Early Nineteenth-Century Irish Fiction." *Tennessee Folklore Society Bulletin* XLI, No. 1 (March 1975): 25-31.
    Traces the influence of Northern Ireland on Carleton's work, notably in his depiction of the peasantry and the countryside.

Rosalía de Castro

1837-1885

Spanish poet and novelist.

An acknowledged master of Spanish poetry, Castro wrote intimate, musical verse. Born in the Spanish province of Galicia, she composed chiefly in her native Galician (a dialect similar to Portuguese), and incorporated the folk themes, political problems, and longings of her people in her poetry. Castro added to these her own deep nostalgia, love of nature, and a pervasive melancholy. Her poetry, therefore, while simple in form, is mystical, religious, and highly symbolic in content. As an examination of the human soul, it is universal, despite its regional concerns.

Castro was the illegitimate daughter of a Spanish noblewoman. Raised by an aunt to age 11, she spent her teens in her grandparents' home, where she was educated in languages and the arts. Despite her talent in music, art and writing (she composed her first poem at age 12), Castro was an unhappy girl. Many critics attribute her melancholy, which deepened year by year, to the illegitimacy which forced her to be separated from her mother.

At age 19, Castro moved to Madrid, where she became involved with literary circles and published *La flor*, an inconsequential collection of poems in Spanish. The following year, she married Manuel Murguria, a historian and a champion of the Galician literary renaissance. Although their marriage was troubled by financial difficulties, ill health, and the deaths of two of their six children, Marguria always encouraged his wife's writing. It was through his prompting that Castro agreed to publish *Cantares gallegos*, the Galician verses that brought her acclaim as an important poet. Her skill increased in *Follas novas*, another book on Galician themes, which is tinged with a darker and more personal tone than *Cantares gallegos*. With *En las orillas del Sar (Beside the River Sar)*, written in Spanish rather than Galician, she won national attention, but for Castro the Castilian language was not as fluid or expressive as her native tongue, and proved a less effective medium for her passionate voice. This collection, composed when Castro was suffering from cancer, reflects a despair which is barely soothed by her fervent religious faith.

While her contemporaries adhered to a rigid poetic structure in their works, Castro sought a lilting, fluid metrical style. Her simple, musical prosody, emotional themes, and natural symbols and motifs are seen by critics as influences on the work of such modern poets as Rubén Dario, Amado Nervo, and Federico García Lorca. Although she wrote several novels, she is remembered for her verse. Gerald Brenan stated: "Had she written in Castilian rather than in her native Galician dialect, she would, I feel sure, be recognized as the greatest woman poet of modern times."

PRINCIPAL WORKS

La flor (poetry) 1857
La hija del mar (novel) 1859
Flavio (novel) 1861
A mi madre (poetry) 1863

Cantares gallegos (poetry) 1863
El caballero de las botas azules (novel) 1867
Follas novas (poetry) 1880
El primer loco (novel) 1881
En las orillas del Sar (poetry) 1884
 [*Beside the River Sar*, 1937]
Poems: Rosalía de Castro (poetry) 1964

AUBREY F. G. BELL (essay date 1922)

In her preface to *Cantares Gallegos* [Rosalía de Castro] wrote: 'I have taken much care to reproduce the true spirit of our people.' That she succeeded in this all critics are agreed. A favourite method in the *Cantares Gallegos* is to take a popular quatrain and develop it at some length, as, for instance, in the beautiful variations on the lines *Airiños, airiños, aires, Airiños da miña terra, Airiños, airiños, aires, Airiños, levaime á ela* [translated in a footnote: O winds of my country blowing softly together, Winds, winds, gentle winds, O carry me thither!]. Here, as throughout the book, there is such yearning passionate sadness that we may say, in her own words, *non canta que chora*. The sadness is of *soedade* [homesickness] and brooding over her country's plight. She has felt all the peasants' sorrows, the longing of the emigrant for his country, the fate of the women at home who find no rest from toil but in the grave, above all the neglect and poverty in which those sorrows centre— with the result of sons torn from their families and scattered abroad to Castile and Portugal and across the seas in search of bread. Her themes are thus often homely; their treatment is always plaintive and musical. The metres used are very various. The book opens with a chain of *muiñeiras* singing *Galicia frorida,* and the rhythmical beat of the *muiñeira* constantly recurs throughout. Nothing could serve better to express, as she so marvellously expresses, the very soul of the Galician peasantry in its gentle, dreaming wistfulness and tearful humour. Her style is so thin and delicate, yet so flowing and natural, that it is more akin, almost, to music than to language. Few writers have attained such perfection without a trace of artifice. It is Galician . . . seen at its best, clear, soft, and pliant, rising in protest or reproach to a silvery eloquence. In *Follas Novas* the melancholy note is accentuated, without becoming morbid: the new leaves are autumnal. The music of her sad and exquisite poetry had been forged in the crucible of her own not imaginary suffering and grief, and in these lyrics she utters her *inmortales deseios* (immortal longings) as well as the woes of the peasant women of Galicia, 'widows of the living and widows of the dead'. New metres are introduced, the old skill and perfection of form is maintained. A few poems in the second half even succeed in repeating that identification between the poet and the genius of the people which makes much of *Cantares Gallegos* almost anonymous and assures its immortality. (pp. 349-50)

> *Aubrey F. G. Bell, "The Galician Revival," in* Portuguese Literature *(reprinted by permission of Oxford University Press), Oxford University Press, 1922 (and reprinted by Oxford University Press, London, 1970, pp. 347-57).**

L. A. WARREN   (essay date 1929)

[Rosalia de Castro] in my opinion is the greatest of modern Spanish poets, Bécquer being the only alternative, and ranks level with the two greatest mystical lyrical poets of the golden century, Fray Luis de León and San Juan de la Cruz. (pp. 407-08)

Rosalia is the most musical of Spanish poets; her Castilian more lyrical than that of any other author. Her Galician is softer, more languorous and lyrical than her Castilian, her Castilian more expressive of deep anguish. This is not because of a difference in the two languages, but because she wrote her Castilian poems in mature years when she felt deeply pain and sorrowful destiny. Although intensity of feeling is the greatest quality of poetry, and the actual meaning of the words of her Castilian poems expresses more than the actual meaning of the words of her Galician poems, yet, such is the musical charm of the Gallegan poems and to such an extent do the actual sounds of the Gallegan words express in rhythm a sobbing, a sighing, a moaning, that the Gallegan lyrics are the most beautiful.

Her contemporaries wrote in splendid symmetrical metre, regular and mechanical in sound, deficient in emotion. Rosalia, a lyrical poet, overflowing with an intensity of sad emotion, broke up the regular and sweeping verse, and introduced *vers libre* before the modernists. Her verse is infinitely broken, irregular and varied, moving at different paces. Technically it

is admirable, but her technique is not achieved like the modernists by a refined and calculating intellectual sense, but by spontaneous lyrical genius.

Modernistic melancholy is an exotic, subtle, intellectual way of feeling, refined and exquisite, having only the thin and narrow gamut of expression of a group of artificial, intellectual aesthetes; it appeals only to the fancy of the passing day, and but to a small group. Rosalia's lyrics come forth after long brooding from deep emotional feeling. (pp. 408-09)

The vagueness, mistiness, lack of the definite, natural to Galicia, is of the essence of Rosalia's lyric. That which the modernists try to achieve by intellectual and technical devices, comes to Rosalia as a natural gift. One notes the lack of concrete themes. She never tells us clearly what her agony is, and the reason is because it is not clear to herself; dark and formless clouds of gloom and sadness sweep through her personality, she feels more than any other author a longing and a yearning, and more than any other she feels the remorseless passage of time with death at the end swallowing up everything. "To die that is the certain and all the rest is lie and smoke." This is the great theme of her subjective poems. The great theme of her objective poems is the intense home-sickness and longing of Galicians in exile for their beautiful country and its simple ways of life, or the excessive distress of soul of emigrants as time brings ever nearer the moment of departure for exile. . . . (pp. 410-11)

[Rosalia] is impressionistic; her selection of a small number of details calls up the picture, while leaving scope for the imagination of the reader. Her favourite atmosphere is grey and misty, she has a taste for pale moonlight with clouds, trees are often thick and heavy, dense shrubs give shade and mystery; she dwells on nothing long, things come and go: now a murmur of fountains, then a tolling of church bells heard across the distance, the lap of water, the rustling of the wind, the passage of heavy grey clouds, the dripping of rain, light upon the sea, the twittering of birds, the wailing of bagpipes. Strong colours are avoided, she runs her tints one into another, they are not sharply marked off. . . . (p. 414)

There is nothing narrative or dramatic in Rosalia's poems; reflective and meditative, they are lyrical expressions of the distresses of her mind. "¡Pero qué aprisa en este mundo triste todas las cosas van!" "How quickly in this sad world all things pass away!" And there is a setting of landscape to match the sad thought, for no one has better fused impressions of landscape with feelings of the mind. . . . (p. 415)

[Whereas] early Galician poetry consists mainly of love lyrics, later Galician poetry consists of landscape lyrics, expressing melancholy brooding. Very few of Rosalia's poems deal with passionate love at all; her references to love are in a vague, grey, indefinite melancholy,—to the momentary happiness of love enjoyed, and then its subsequent vanishing, leaving the heart hopeless and desolate; or to heavy shadows and the veils of black night keeping lovers apart. Religion, though devoutly believed in, seems to bring but little consolation to her afflicted spirit, for her pessimism comes from the melancholy of the Galician temperament, not from religious doubt. (p. 418)

[Rosalia] is the most immaterial of poets; the play of forces through her is formless, will-o'-the-wisp-like. Her verse is like the wailing of bagpipes, but sweeter, sadder, more distressing, overflowing with sorrowful emotion. Her images are simple, full of Galician sights and sounds, and reflect her longing for she knows not what, for a past beyond recall. . . . (p. 419)

L. A. Warren, "Rosalia de Castro," in his Modern Spanish Literature: A Comprehensive Survey of the Novelists, Poets, Dramatists and Essayists from the Eighteenth Century to the Present Day, *Vol. II,* Brentano's Ltd, 1929, pp. 407-20.

GERALD BRENAN (essay date 1951)

[Rosalía Castro] had a life of poverty, bitterness and disillusion. But her verse has an extraordinary lyrical and musical appeal and, had she written in Castilian rather than in her native Galician dialect, she would, I feel sure, be recognized as the greatest woman poet of modern times. (pp. 349-50)

All the poems contained in [*Cantares Gallegos*] are in Galician. Since the *jograles* of the thirteenth century had made their songs, no poet of consequence had written in this language, and their verses were unknown to her because the *Cancioneros* that contained them were still sleeping on the shelves of Italian libraries. Rosalía's poetry was therefore founded upon her native folk-songs in which [as a child in Santiago de Compostella] she had had such exceptional opportunities for saturating herself. When . . . we turn to these folk-songs, we are likely, so far as the words go, to feel some disappointment. . . . However, the tone of these songs was the important thing; as Rosalía said, 'Galician poetry is all music and vagueness, all complaints and sighs and gentle smiles'. For this reason these little verses had sometimes retained traces of that peculiar movement, the bringing forward to the beginning of a new verse of an echo of the last, which, under the name of *leixa-pren,* had been the special feature of the *cantigas de amigo.* It is a mark of Rosalía Castro's amazing sensitiveness to the spirit of her native muse that she was able, from such slight indications as were provided by a few *coplas* and *muiñeiras,* to reproduce this pattern in her poetry.

Here is an example: it is one of a series of six interconnecting poems written on the theme of a *cantar de pandeiro:*

> Campanas de Bastabales
> Cando vos oyo tocar,
> Mórrome de soidades.

Bells of Bastabales, when I hear you ring I die of longings.

One will observe how the form of the little popular ditty has been expanded to make a poem in *tercetos* of a kind entirely new to Spanish poetry.

> Cada estrela, o seu diamante;
> Cada nube, branca pruma,
> Trist'a lua marcha diante.

> Diante marcha crarexando
> Veigas, prados, montes, ríos,
> Dond'o día vai faltando.

> Falta o día, a noite escura
> Baixa, baixa, pouco á pouco,
> Por montañas de verdura.

> De verdura e de follaxe,
> Salpicada de fontiñas
> Baixo a sombra d'o ramaxe.

> D'o ramaxe, donde cantan
> Paxariños piadores,
> Que c'á aurora se levantan.

> Que c'á noite s'adormecen
> Para que canten os grilos
> Que co'as sombras aparecen.

Every star its diamond, every cloud its white plume, sadly the moon marches on.

Onward marches while it lights up fields, hills, meadows, rivers, where the day is failing.

Fails the day, the dark night falls, falls, little by little, over the green mountains.

Green and leafy, sprinkled with rivulets, beneath the shade of the branches.

Branches where sing the twittering birds that rise with the first light.

Which all night sleep that the crickets may come out and trill among the shadows.

Rosalía de Castro's more usual procedure, however, is to start with a popular *copla* and then to develop it in a lyrical *romance,* somewhat as the Castilian poets of the Middle Ages had done with the *estribillo* of a *villancico,* only in a looser and less formal manner. The most wonderful example of this is the poem *Airiños, airiños, aires,* which she wrote when she was only twenty. It is a poem of nostalgia for her native country put into the mouth of an emigrant, a lyrical musical complaint evoking the life of the Galician countryside with its trees and waters and gentle rain, its country dances and its shady cemeteries, and moving with a hurry and passion that calls to mind the torrent of notes poured out by a misselthrush when it is singing on a tree top during a storm. It is, I think, one of the most entrancing lyrics ever written by a Spaniard and, just as Galician poetry had provided an essential element in the formation of the Castilian lyric of the fifteenth and sixteenth centuries, so this poem was to have an influence in the great revival of Spanish poetry that began thirty years after her death. In particular, the *Romancero Gitano* of García Lorca, with its richly musical idiom, its continual repetitions and allusions to folk-poetry and to popular themes, owes much to it. (pp. 351-53)

Rosalía Castro found no difficulty in being at the same time a mature and civilized poet, living in her own age, and an interpreter, in their own forms and idiom, of the feelings of the Galician peasantry. So close is she to the popular sensibility that, as her fellow countrywoman, Emilia Pardo Bazán, has said, within twenty years of the appearance of her book, verses written by her were believed to have a popular origin, whilst others, which were genuinely popular, were attributed to the poetess. When we compare her work to that of Thomas Hardy and William Barnes, who were attempting the same sort of thing at approximately the same time, we can see how much of the clumsiness of these poets was due to their having no genuinely popular forms or poetic traditions to write in. The English agricultural labourers and industrial workers have long been inarticulate. (p. 354)

[Rosalía Castro's next book of poetry, *Follas Novas,*] belongs, as she said in her preface, to a different inspiration from that of the *Cantares.* That is to say, most of the poems in it are subjective and personal. The first part consists of a series of short pieces written in a variety of metres, all expressing deep despair and melancholy. In a poem to the moon, for example, she begs to be carried body and soul to a place, neither in this world nor in 'the heights', where she may remember nothing. Many of these pieces show a strong influence of [Gustavo Adolfo] Bécquer, whose collected verse had been published in 1871, but she was not by nature a concentrated poet and her subjective poems lack as a rule those poignant rhythms which inject the little versicles of her contemporary under the skin of the reader. Other longer poems follow on a variety of subjects, but all in the same melancholy strain, the most notable being two on the cathedral of Santiago, *N-a Catredal* and *Amigos Vellos,* one beginning *Aquel romor de cántigas e risas* and one entitled *Adiós.* In these pieces Rosalía shows her powers as a sophisticated poet, surprising one by the beauty of her descriptions, by her continual and often daring experiments in form and metre and by the floods of feeling that from time to time seem to carry her verse away. All the same I think that Emilia Pardo Bazán is right in saying that it is in the poems in which she developed folk-song themes that she shows her lyrical gifts at their best. (pp. 354-55)

Rosalía Castro's last book of poems, *En las orillas del Sar,* came out just before her death. It was written in Spanish. Like *Follas Novas,* its inspiration was personal and subjective and, as she was suffering from the slow but painful cancer that carried her off, in great straits for money and anxious about the future of her children, it is, if possible, even more pessimistic and despairing than her previous volume. The principal theme is the longing for a life beyond death. Although it contains several notable poems, one feels that the dry, clear language of Castile did not suit her so well as the soft, caressing idiom which she had learned as a child. In Galician she is usually warm and tender: in Castilian her coldness and aloofness chill one.

Rosalía Castro is above all the poet of nostalgia: most of her best poems were written when she was away from her country, in the stone and brick wilderness of Madrid or on the treeless plains around Simancas: her longing for her native land, which she shared with so many Galician emigrants, provided her with a rich and varied subject. But under her home-sickness—*soidade, morriña*—there lay a deep, indescribable dread and horror that became more pressing as she advanced in years: as her husband observed, she seemed to have sucked in from her mother all the secret terrors she had felt when she held her in her womb. These fears, being less related to the outer world, offered a poorer material for poetry. (p. 356)

There is one other feature of Rosalía's poetry to which I must draw attention, and that is her preoccupation with the condition of the poor. In her prologue to *Follas Novas* she tells us that these poems had been written to express the endless sufferings of the Galician peasants and sailors, *soya e verdadeira xente d'o traballo n-o noso país,* which we may translate as 'the only people in our country who do any real work'. She constantly puts her poems of *soidade* into the mouths of Galician emigrants and day-labourers—Galicia, like Ireland, is a country where the land cannot support the population—and shows a special sympathy for the women, on whom, in the absence of their men-folk, the brunt of poverty chiefly falls. It is true that this feeling was at first associated with her passionate love of her own countrymen and her almost equally passionate hatred of their oppressors, the people of Castile. When, for example, in one of her poems she asks how God could have made anything so ugly as the plain of Simancas, the reply comes pat—that he made it for the Castilians. But in her later years she was equally outspoken in her scorn for the hypocrisy of the middle-class Gallegos, who spent so much of their time praying

yet remained callous and hard-hearted, and in her *romances* she treats the theme of poverty realistically, but with an almost excessive warmth and bitterness.

Now this, it must be observed, is a note that had not been heard in Spanish poetry since the time of the Archpriest of Hita. Before Rosalía, poetry in Spain lacked the sentiment of pity—or rather banished it to religious topics such as the Crucifixion—because it avoided subjects that had a social content. But she lived in a circle of people who held extreme federal and left wing sympathies. . . . Although there are no allusions to politics in [Rosalía's] work, for Spanish women at that time took no part in public affairs, there can be little doubt as to where her sympathies lay. And by associating her own troubles with those of the poor—'those accustomed to unhappiness', she wrote, 'come to feel the afflictions of others as their own'— she greatly strengthened the appeal of her work.

If the object of lyric poetry is to enchant, to enrapture, to lift the reader out of his surroundings, then Rosalía Castro is a fine lyric poet. By their repetitions, their *Ai Ai's,* their caressing diminutives, by the way in which the lines follow one another in a cataract of emotion, her poems carry one away in a sort of musical flight. Her best lyrics produce on the mind the effect of an impassioned aria sung by Galli-Curci: the impression is more immediately overpowering than is the case with most poetry. But there are some things that these poems—written as they apparently were without effort—do not give. When in Burns—who is not, I think, so fine a lyric poet, though he was a richer human being—we come on the line 'The dance ga'ed thro' the lighted ha'' we are arrested by its beauty as we are never arrested by any fragment of Rosalía's. Her poetry, pure and idiomatic though its language is, and smelling, as Emilia Pardo Bazán said, of the village (it has no trace of the sultry overtones and plush surface of Christina Rosetti), never condenses into a single epithet or phrase, but flows on from line to line in a single sequence. Nor does it show any sense of that special and peculiar relation of word to word that came in at the Renaissance from Latin poetry. Under the wind of lyric feeling that blows through them, all the words in her poems lean in one direction. There is no pause, no measure, no restraint in this exuberantly passionate verse and there is sometimes, it must be said, a displeasing note of hysteria. (pp. 357-58)

Gerald Brenan, "Nineteenth-Century Poetry and Poetic Drama," in his The Literature of the Spanish People from Roman Times to the Present Day, *Cambridge at the University Press, 1951, pp. 338-76.**

ROBERT G. HAVARD (essay date 1974)

En las orillas del Sar [is] a most passionate document of a personal tragedy, but it does not necessarily reveal Rosalía's special qualities as a poetess. Like many Romantics, Rosalía suffers at times from over-exposure, from too frank a disclosure of intimacies, so that some poems may be demeaned virtually as cathartic confessions. In the majority of poems, however, a fine balance is maintained, and it is particularly when she relies upon imagistic expression that we are led more meaningfully into her confidence, as well as into a rich poetic experience.

Turning to those poems which recall her amorous experience we find Rosalía continually in a state of emotional flux, at times eager to relive moments of erotic excitement, and at other times, more commonly, brooding with an irreparable sense of guilt. In this connection two separate patterns of imagery are prominent and are often instrumental in constructing poetic tension. The first of these concerns the highly traditional imagery of darkness and shadow, so much in evidence that a characteristic setting of *En las orillas del Sar* is the nocturnal. One of the best poems on the theme of illicit love is **"Margarita"** . . . , where we have a graphic picture of a woman tormented at night by sexual desire. The insidious aspect of her passion is well evoked in the opening stanza with its references to animals. . . . The mood of the poem is one of guilt . . . though with the persona presented as a victim, subjected to a fatalistic passion. . . . [For Rosalía] the experience of love is essentially ambiguous and deceitful. Paradox is also found in Rosalía's use of lunar imagery, an important feature of her nocturnal landscapes. The moon can either stir her passion ("despierta en mi memoria / Yo no sé qué fantasmas y quimeras") or chastise her with its purity. . . . [In many of her poems Rosalía deliberately constructed] an unorthodox and anti-heroic persona, and this is in fact very much in the literary spirit of her time. Mario Praz [in his *The Romantic Agony*] has shown how the theme of tainted or corrupted beauty was fundamental to the Romantic movement. In the pertinent chapter, "The beauty of Medusa," Praz incorporates the *morena* theme, reminding us of the *Song of Solomon* ("I am dark but comely"), and relates it to his main argument that the Romantics looked for a degree of ugliness, whether moral or physical, in all beauty, and that they found pure beauty insipid. (pp. 397-400)

[The images of light and dark used in many of her poems] compress an ambivalent psychic experience, a chain of contradictions which shapes Rosalía's dilemma. First, we perceive that "sol dorado" [the golden sun] (which may be understood as an ideal, pure or even Christian love) has been superseded by another force ("otra luz," "otro calor") [another light, another warmth], which is altogether more attractive and more penetrating. This second force, or love, which is erotic and almost certainly clandestine. . . , has the effect of relieving the persona's manifest grief. However, the word "dolor" is ambivalent; for we remember in **"Margarita"** that it constituted the person's very weakness before sexual temptation. . . . The tragic argument in [the poem beginning "Cuido que una planta bella"] is that erotic love is the narcotic which momentarily relieves pain but essentially induces pain once the immediate sensory experience is exhausted. The whole poem is another instance of submission before the "fatal power" of the flesh, and this, as with the general concept of the supremacy of evil over virtue. . . , again situates that essential Romanticism in Rosalía's poetry, corresponding to Mario Praz's examination of literary morality from De Sade to Baudelaire.

A second major aspect of Rosalía's technique is found in her use of liquid imagery, a Galician specialty. Here the recurring images of clouds, rain and sea, evoke lush Atlantic seascapes that contrast dramatically with the arid plains of Castile. Inevitably, Rosalía associates these liquid elements with her desires. Her frustration is correlated in terms of aridity. . . . The complementary notion of thirst is dominant and is often rendered in images of the sea shore. . . . (pp. 401-02)

[Rosalía's] other potent desire, that of religious salvation, is also rendered in this image pattern: "La sed del beodo es insaciable, y la del alma lo es aun más" [the thirst of the drunkard is insatiable, and that of the soul is even greater]. . . . As we know, both religious and sexual themes have a long tradition of association with liquid imagery. In Rosalía's case

the multiple association is dynamic for her sense of remorse and guilt in sexual behavior is inversely proportionate to her need for salvation. When Rosalía broods on the notion of sin, the religious and the sexual are assimilated in the one image. . . . Clearly [Rosalía's] verse takes its strength from the discordant and typically Romantic complex of religious and erotic motifs, conceived in terms of a liquid rite, and from the final implication that the two are incompatible. Here then, is a vivid insight into a woman desperate for love, both worldly and divine, whose very desires combine negatively to result in comprehensive frustration. (pp. 403-04)

In focusing upon her own weakness, and in presenting her character very often as one undermined by sensuality, the implication arises that eroticism itself is at odds with [Rosalía's] faith; and consequently, that she has been disinherited of God's love, as she feels so pungently . . . , because her very nature is alien to the Christian ideal. This point of distinction is important in terms of appreciating the integral thematic cohesion of *En las orillas del Sar,* and specifically for the understanding of that key motif of self-disapprobation that extends beyond the love-theme. The volume, after all, is constructed as an expression of an entire persona, and in stressing eroticism or sensuality in its broadest connotation as being a most significant feature of the persona, we are in a better position to appreciate the relationship of the love theme with other major concerns, as for example, her treatment of nature.

As a complement to the pattern of liquid imagery, there may be added a further vital pattern which centers upon the image of the tree. Now in this image erotic sentiment is never explicit, and it should not be considered as an example of conscious phallic symbolism, but rather as a distinctive feature in Rosalía's technique of endowing her landscapes with virile connotations. . . . In many poems the value of the tree is compounded with that of liquid imagery. . . . One of the most successful combinations of the two image patterns is found in [the poem beginning "Los unos altísimos, / Los otros menores"]. . . . Here there is a great sense of animation in the landscape, constructed out of the meeting of sea and pines. The syntax, with its muscular and almost Gongoresque inversion, enhances the motif of a triumphant ascendance in the pines, and the whole stanza suggests a primeval and procreative force in nature rising from the sea. The onlooker, "viajero rendido" [tired traveller], who is introduced in the third and last stanza, wishes only to become immersed in this timeless rhythm. . . . The poem sustains its orientation towards primitive and physical matters until the end, and reference in the second stanza to the ancient "Castro" further relates the poem's sentiment to pagan rather than Christian motifs. This dynamic animation of nature is a constant feature in Rosalía's poetry. . . . The process of animating nature is . . . another aspect of Rosalía's fundamental Romanticism, but it is also a traditional quality in Galician poetry and a phenomenon natural to Celtic poetry in general. . . . For the purpose of developing the connection with Rosalía along literary channels, much could be made of the chthonic or earth orientation of Celtic poetry in the past, which appears to have derived from primitive cults; it is probably more germane, however, to attempt a comparison with a modern Celt, the Welsh poet Dylan Thomas, whose poetry also displays that distinctive feature of conscious atavism. Rosalía's awareness of energy in nature, as in "verde y pujante crecerá la hierba" [green and powerful will grow the grass] . . . , is equally apparent in Thomas, as in his famous "The force that through the green fuse drives the flower." Other poems by Thomas, such as "Especially when the October wind,'' (with its ''vowelled beaches,'' ''oaken voices,'' ''spider-tongued and loud hill of Wales'' and ''dark-vowelled birds'') which creates an impression that nature itself is articulate, may be closely related to Rosalía's kinship with nature as seen . . . in ''Dicen que no hablan las plantas . . .'' [They say that the plants do not speak].

The ethnic affinity of Rosalía and Thomas, though stemming from a remote past, only attains reality in the present in terms of their mutual aspiration towards and quest for identity, which may be negatively defined as a process of conscious alienation from the dominant people, Castilian and English, in their respective countries. In many poems in which Rosalía takes us on a reflective journey through nature it is evident that her search or her retrospection is not only for her youth or for that lost, ideal love, but that it is also for something far more distant and elusive: her Celtic heritage. The ''camino antiguo'' [old path] . . . of **''En las orillas del Sar''** leads us through a landscape in which contours are marked by ancient place names (''Trabanca,'' ''Presa,'' ''Fondons,'' ''La Torre,'' ''Miranda''); the poem resounds to the theme of ''un eco perdido,'' [a lost echo], while the persona, like her environment, is steeped in the past. . . . (pp. 404-08)

Above all, however, it is in connection with the tree image, particularly the oaks, that Rosalía develops her identification with the *patria* and with her Celtic heritage. . . . In the very important poem **''Los robles,''** the tree itself is a symbol of Galician identity, ''árbol patrio'' [tree of the homeland] . . . , and the felling of trees is understood as a wilful destruction of that identity, leaving Galicia as barren as the plains of Castile. The trees . . . contain ''dulce misterio'' [sweet mystery] . . . a mystery which is irrevocably centered upon the remote past. When, in this poem, Rosalía evokes the image of the tree, she at last comes very near to creating a comprehensive pictorial correlative for her multiple aspiration. . . . [The] imagery firstly commingles Rosalía's love for her homeland with her fundamentally passionate and sensual temperament, evidenced in the landscape's virile connotations, and secondly, harmonizes both these features with her transcendental sentiment, which is again in this instance manifestly pagan or pantheistic. (p. 409)

We can appreciate that in happiest moments Rosalía's evocation of nature is easy and uninhibited, with her landscapes seldom failing to communicate an impression of fertility. Rosalía, like Dylan Thomas, and in the true tradition of Celtic poetry, is as attentive to the inherent power of nature as she is to its correlative function when converted into an image form. Ultimately, there is no significant distinction, for nature's autonomous energy, with all its mysterious properties, is the very substratum of Rosalía's personal identity inherited from such a remote past. Hence, all natural description contributes in some way towards the poetic presentation of the persona. Wandering along those familiar paths, her spirit engrossed and responding intuitively to the timeless and interior potency of the landscape, Rosalía appears as her most authentic self. Similarly, her tendency to personify natural elements is much more than a poetical device to help invigorate her landscape, it is rather an invocation of the living spirit of times past, and, as such, a colloquy of identity. . . . (p. 410)

Rosalía recalls her people's heritage in a Romantic and ideal spirit; it is a plaintive cry, for the semi-legendary Celtic age, as Rosalía knows well, is as irretrievable as her illegitimate birth. . . . The magical and folkloric world of her ancestors may serve Rosalía as a retreat from Christian orthodoxy and its inevitable reminders of moral rectitude; but primarily, relationship with the homeland is again realized in the nebulous terms of nostalgia, and it thus composes another feature of Rosalía's unrequited love affair with reality. The remoteness of her heritage is perhaps itself the very essence of its attraction, as all her aspirations are incited by their intrinsic factor of elusiveness; we remember the painful 'Te amo, porque me odias'' [I love you, because you hate me]. . . . This necessity to confront the elusive and the negative is a quality Rosalía shares with Bécquer, and it provides *En las orillas del Sar,* as it does [Bécquer's] *Rimas,* with a thematic continuity of challenge and quest, though this is offset more forcibly in Rosalía by varying degrees of psychic masochism. Rosalía's volume too, unlike that of her contemporary, has little sense of structural development; nor is there such an extensive use of parallelism and strict rhythm patterns as a means of corporalizing the tenuous subject-matter. While Rosalía's poetry follows established literary patterns common to Romanticism, as we have seen particularly in her treatment of nature and in the notion of a fatal sensual weakness, it is nevertheless apparent that these are essentially subjective features arrived at instinctively rather than consciously grafted, for it may be argued that her native background and the events of her life have contrived to produce a being who coincides perfectly with the Romantic persona. *En las orillas del Sar,* both in its mood and form, remains true to Rosalía's own very special temperament: it is amorphous, unfolding to the whims of her feminine intuition, at once passionate and perplexed, the authentic expression of a vagabond spirit. (pp. 410-11)

Robert G. Havard, ''Image and Persona in Rosalía de Castro's 'En las orillas del Sar','' in Hispanic Review, *Vol. 42, No. 4, Autumn, 1974, pp. 393-411.*

KATHLEEN KULP-HILL   (essay date 1977)

Although the style is unformed, the sentiments over-emoted, and many of the ideas and expressions familiar Romantic commonplaces, the poems of *La flor* are not trite and vacuous. They cannot be dismissed as a precocious tour de force or mere pastiche of Romantic influences. The reader is struck by the emotional intensity and depth of comprehension of this young woman. The content might be attributed, on the one hand, to the assimilation of Romantic modes, wherein youths of twenty summers sing of the ''autumn'' of life and prepare to hurl themselves into the abyss of nothingness because of disappointed love or lost illusions. On the other hand, it might reflect the predilections of an impressionable girl for the dramatic and tragic. Nonetheless, much of Rosalía herself and a kernel of lived experience can be sensed. It is possible that the poems refer to an unhappy amorous experience of her own. The betrayal and abandonment of her mother, which Rosalía must have felt deeply, would also have given her insight into the pleasures and deception of love. Most of the poems are stated in the first person, using fictitious feminine personages—Argelina and Inés—which might be taken as masks for herself or her mother. The full extent of confessional material in the book is impossible to determine, although it is definitely personal in tone. Its significance in Rosalía's total poetic development is indisputable. To trace the trajectory of a writer, it is necessary to read backwards, in search of roots and seeds. Already present in this first, immature effort are the dark themes of nothingness, death, solitude, sorrow, rejection by society, and religious doubt. Some of the images used to convey these themes will characterize her later works: the shadow or phantom, fallen tree of faith, sea of sorrows, withered flower of hope, abyss of nothingness, thorns, desert, weary journey. The germs of Rosalía's deepest poetry can be found here; she has already begun to select from her literary and vital experience the meaningful elements. The anguished subjectivity of *La flor* will culminate in *Follas novas (New Leaves)* and *En las orillas del Sar (On the Banks of the River Sar)*. (pp. 36-7)

The death of [Rosalía's] beloved mother Doña Teresa de Castro y Abadía, in 1862 occasioned the publication of a small private edition [*A mi madre (To My Mother)*]. The poems are, as could be expected, emotional and elegiac, with a personal intensity lent by the immediate experience with grief and Rosalía's deep affection for her mother. Thematically, the poet progresses from personal, specific sentiments to meditations on the universal experience of death, sorrow, brevity of life, abandonment, and desolation. Her grief is embittered by feelings of remorse for her ingratitude and failure to fully appreciate her mother's love and suffering in life. Although the poems are of limited literary importance, they reveal the characteristic tendency of Rosalía to release her intimate feelings through lyrical outlets. (p. 37)

[Of all the patriotic Galican poems of her time, Rosalía's] must certainly stand out as the most memorable. In [*Cantares gallegos (Galician Songs)*], the interpenetration of writer and folk is so nearly perfect that the esthetic distance is barely perceptible. She was a truly successful regionalist, in whose work her subjects could recognize themselves, and a wider audience could see and comprehend the Galicians, as well as respond to universal themes and sentiments. (p. 39)

[Rosalía] does not set out to be a bard, as did Enrique Pondal, but rather a minstrel, personified in the *"meniña gaitera"* or bagpipe girl. Her songs are not grandly heroic; they attempt to recount the humble epic of simple people. Although accurately representing the people, *Cantares* is not just a collection of folk songs. The contribution of the poet is apparent throughout. It is theirs and hers. The subjective content is admitted by the author in the prologue, where she states that the songs were "gathered by my heart as my own heritage" (*"recollidos pó-lo meu coraçón como harencia propia"* . . .). Her selection and interpretations are guided by her emotions and memory. The glosses or elaborations, while keeping to the theme and spirit of the refrain, allow her a certain artistic freedom. The perennial universality and freshness of the folk and the lyrical sensitivity of the author combine to make these poems accessible and moving to a far wider audience than a few regional enthusiasts. (p. 40)

Each poem [in *Galician Songs*] incorporates in some way a popular motif. The usual pattern is to begin with a quote from the folk repertoire, which is followed by an original variation or gloss. This may be a little story or drama or may contain personal reflections. The poetic forms come, for the most part, from the popular tradition, and have had a long and pervasive influence on the poetry of the Iberian Peninsula. They are singable, danceable cadences which adapt to—or derive from—the language itself. (p. 42)

The total stylistic effect of *Cantares* is not that Rosalía did research on prosody or painstakingly counted syllables and consulted rhyming dictionaries, but rather that she followed easily and without selfconsciousness the simple, traditional devices of repetition and coincidence of sounds and ideas. She captures the poetic qualities of the Galician language, with its colorful turns of phrase, capacity for contraction and prolon-gation, caressing diminutives, and onomatopoeic possibilities. (p. 44)

What Rosalía has done most beautifully in *Cantares* is to capture the luminous treasure of a refined popular poetry and filter it through her own exquisite sensibility. Her temperament and fervor infuse these unforgettable lyrics with shimmering intensity. (p. 51)

Whereas [*Cantares gallegos*] had the springlike quality of hope, youth, and innocence, [*Follas novas (New Leaves)*] was written in physical and spiritual exile, and the light which illumines it is crepuscular and autumnal. Galicia is no longer the object and animating force, but rather the circumstance and the backdrop. *New Leaves* does not treat the quaint, picturesque, and festive aspects, but focuses on the suffering of Galicia, particularly of the Galician women, fused with the poet's own suffering. The source are, to a certain extent, Galician life and lore, but the poems for the most part derive from her own intimate experiences. *New Leaves* contains some of Rosalía's most significant poetry and represents an important contribution to the literature of the peninsula. It has escaped more widespread attention not only because of the language, but because of the content as well. Like any really significant artistic landmark, it was not recognized until its time had come. It is not primarily a regional work, but a truly universal poetic achievement and harbinger of a new introspective age. (p. 54)

The Galician language is used in *Follas* but no longer for the sake of the folk who will not read the verses written "because of them but not to them." . . .

In *Cantares* Galician was the naturally suited vehicle to reproduce the popular motifs and provide continuity between them and the poet's glosses. The verbal portrait of the people was painted in the colors of their own speech. In *New Leaves* the language must accomplish quite a different task; it must convey the subjective and meditative content of the poet's deepest spiritual and intellectual experiences. *Cantares* retained the oral quality of song and speech; *Follas* is meant to be read and reflected upon. In Rosalía's hands, Galician proves to be an effective literary instrument—musical, suggestive, intimate, and powerful. If it once expressed the highest lyrical sentiments of the peninsula, it does so again in Rosalía's poems and becomes a truly modern tongue. (p. 55)

[*Follas novas*] includes many compositions of traditional nature and continues some of the forms found in *Cantares*. In this book, however, Rosalía is not restricted to popular models, and utilizes all the forms of the Hispanic tradition—particularly the effortless, fluid, serene lines of the *romance* (eight syllables) and the *silva* (eleven and seven syllables). There is no strict adherence to set forms, however, for she often gives these basic meters her individual touch. A tendency begins to appear toward the use of the longer meters, such as *arte mayor* (twelve syllables), which is sometimes combined with its hemistych in a *pie quebrado* ("broken foot") form, and *alejandrinos* (Alexandrine or fourteen-syllable lines). What is unusual in *Follas* is the use of varying line lengths for metrical combinations generally considered unsuitable and unharmonious, such as eight with ten or eleven syllables or eight with fourteen. The effect is striking, and follows shifts of emotion and fluctuations of thought, reflecting reality which is not stable or predictable. The syntax does not adhere to the simple patterns of oral clarity and folksong cadence, but is rearranged in a more literary manner.

The innovations in versifications with which Rosalía has been credited are not calculated experiments in an effort to be original or daring (as were those of Darío and the Modernists); hers are the result of emotions seeking rhythmic expression. Content begets form; form enhances and is an integral part of content. In this, Rosalía coincides with the Symbolists' and Modernists' search for freedom of expression, the desire to reproduce an "ideal melody" unhampered by prosody. There is also a noticeable affinity with the Symbolists in fluidity and musical suggestivity of her verse. (p. 56)

New Leaves is the testimony of a troubled soul . . . the unfolding of a deep psychological drama. In the evolution of Rosalía's poetic work, this second volume represents a phase of disintegration, struggle, and despair. In the language of the mystics, it would parallel the "dark night of the soul," the anguished experience of terror and nothingness which the mystic suffers in his quest for enlightenment and ecstasy. In psychological terms, it corresponds to the suffering of the distrubed psyche, the painful exploration of the unconscious in search of the self and spiritual wholeness. (p. 61)

In many poems of this collection, the world of established values is confused and chaotic; reality is shifting and unstable. Besides influencing verbal content, this is reflected stylistically in the irregular rhythms of the lines, the frequency of questions and negations, and the use of ellipses which trail off into silence. There is a paradoxical reversal of values: hope is a "mortal enemy" . . . ; the light and beauty of nature contrast with the darkness of the poet's soul . . . ; happiness is fearful. . . . (p. 62)

[In *En las orillas del Sar (On the Banks of the River Sar)*, Rosalía] writes in the literary language of Spain, addressing herself to the wider audience of the cultured Spanish-speaking world. The Castilian she commands is a conscious, poetic language, dignified and literary. It is natural, but not colloquial, a more formal artistic medium in keeping with the profound and universal message it contains. (p. 78)

The metric devices in *Orillas* are not new, most having appeared in the previous collection, but they have evolved and matured as the adequate vessel for the more serene and detached mood of the poems. Detectable differences in rhythm and syntax are due to the varying exigencies and possibilities of Castilian. She continues to employ unusual combinations of lines and broken rhythms. There is a noticeable tendency to longer lines—slow, meditative, almost proselike. She frequently employs the twelve-and fourteen-syllable lines already seen in *Follas,* and some even longer, of sixteen and eighteen syllables. For the more song-like compositions, the fluid traditional meters of the *romance* (eight syllables) and the *silva* (seven and eleven syllables) are used. Rhyme is predominantly assonant, in flexible combinations, although there is a tendency to more use of consonant rhyme, and some free verse occurs. Syntax has come 180 degrees from the imitation of oral patterns in *Cantares;* sentence arrangement now obeys the convoluted order of artistic design. The result is a sensitive, flexible, and highly developed poetic instrument.

In this volume, as in its predecessor, content seeks form and form enhances content. In this respect, Rosalía's proximity to the modern poets is evident, as César Barja notes: "She is a very modern poet, the most modern of Spanish poets of the nineteenth century because never did her technique of versification dominate poetry. True modern poetry, whose law may be said to consist of the total subordination of verse to poetry, to inner rhythm, to music, begins with Rosalía de Castro. . . ." (pp. 78-9)

There is great continuity between *Follas novas* and *En las orillas del Sar*. Like movements of a musical composition, they are linked by themes, varied by tempo and interpretations. *The Sar* grows out of the previous work, but the subtle yet significant change in the inward structure of the latter makes it impossible to outline them in exactly the same way.

The Sar represents further maturation of style and ideas. It is permeated with trouble and sorrow, yet is more restrained, with flashes of hope. There is an intellectual and philosophical detachment, a relinquishing of life, a quiet preparation to die. (p. 79)

The stylistic elements of *The Sar,* as compared to *New Leaves,* offer less indication of turbulence and confusion. The rhythms are more ordered, the diction more controlled. Colors are muted, or reduced to shades of light and dark, as in the earlier collection, but with less darkness and more luminosity. The themes from *New Leaves* continued in *Orillas* may modulate to greater intensity or diminish in importance, while characteristic images and symbols also evolve in their significance. . . . (p. 80)

The Sar contains some of the most beautiful nature poetry in Spanish literature, wherein nature is described not for its own sake, but forms the whole fabric of imagery. It is the source of recognizable symbols through which inner realities are communicated. (p. 81)

Nature images are used in a traditional sense, expressing the timeless human truth of the eternal involvement of nature with human life and destiny. The rotation of the seasons; water in its various forms of rain, fog, snow, streams, and the sea; trees, flowers and paths; all have the expected associations. The images are not trite, however, for they have the original freshness of lived experience, while evoking sympathetic recognition in the reader of all times and places by touching on universal experience. The result is that profound and complex themes are uttered in a limpid and accessible idiom. (pp. 81-2)

[Rosalía's first novel,] *La hija del mar (Child from the Sea)* is a lengthy and rambling novel of twenty chapters, which are given titles such as "Emotions," "Torments," "The Madwoman," "Surprise," "Crisis," and the like. Each chapter bears an epigraph, giving an indication of Rosalía's literary enthusiasms at that time. These include Ossian, George Sand, Byron, San Juan, Goethe, Góngora, José Zorrilla, and Bernardin de Saint-Pierre, among many others. (pp. 103-04)

[The plot is] complicated and disjointed, yet it can be reduced to some sort of coherency. It consists of a double ring of seduction and abandonment perpetrated by the fascinating and malevolent Alberto. The first cycle involves Candora ("Innocence"), the next, Teresa. The rings are connected by Esperanza ("Hope"), who is the child of Alberto and Candora, abducted by her father and abandoned, adopted by Teresa, Alberto's other wife, and again carried off by Alberto. The sea is the fate or destiny which operates in all their lives: it claims the child of Alberto and Teresa, the little boy lost in the storm; Esperanza, the miraculous child of the title, appears from the sea and eventually returns to it; Esperanza's beloved Fausto is buried in the sea; Alberto, the pirate, rides the sea and consigns two people to it—Daniel, whom he drowns, and Fausto, who dies as a consequence of Alberto's abduction of Esperanza. The sea is both love and death, which is not incompatible with its role as fate.

The central and best-delineated character is Teresa, a star-crossed heroine, exceptional and alienated from society. Her destiny is loneliness; she is illegitimate, orphaned, abandoned by her husband, and bereft of her children. Her external appearance reveals her unusual inner qualities; she is described as having a somber beauty, too aristocratic in mein and manner for her rude surroundings. Furthermore, she is a poet, possessed of those higher sensibilities which doom her to restlessness and suffering. Consequently, she is "mad," obsessed and visionary. Her talents are lost because of her isolation; her mind and behavior strange because of her imagination and dreaminess.

Rosalía put a great deal of her inner self into this character. She develops at length the independent and poetic temperament of Teresa and the solitude and moral suffering to which she is subjected, which are the mad poet's lot. The name Teresa is that of Rosalía's mother, and the preoccupation with passionate and unhappy love, abandonment, and illegitimacy may derive from circumstances in her own life. The novel may be said to be spiritually autobiographical in certain respects. (pp. 106-07)

The style of [*Child from the Sea*] is diffuse and immature. The author assumes the omniscient point of view, revealing to the reader the characters' appearance and actions, as well as their inner thoughts and feelings. She occasionally inserts personal comments expressing her views on the evils of superstition (in connection with the burial of Fausto), the inequities of society (the hovels of peasants in contrast to Alberto's palace), and men's oppression of women. (pp. 107-08)

Child from the Sea is a novel difficult to classify, either as to movement or genre. It has many obvious elements of Romanticism: sustained emotional intensity, improbable situations and events, focus on the exceptional in character, extremes of good and evil, fantasy and lore. Its author was, after all, twenty-two years old and steeped in the Romanticism of her formative years. . . . It is not a historical novel; the setting is contemporary and part of the action takes place in a specific part of Galicia. It is, rather, a novel of adventure and sentiment, set somewhere outside time and place. The ways of the folk and the effects of love and tragedy are timeless, and much of the action unfolds in a realm of fantasy. There are touches of *costumbrismo*—descriptions of the life and activities of the fishermen, allusion to folk practices and beliefs, and incorporation of colloquial expressions in the characters' speech. For the most part the diction is refined and even stilted and the Galician touches are vivid, but incidental rather than integral to the story. (p. 108)

Themes which are to become characteristic of Rosalía's work appear in the novel. The story and the characters (Teresa in particular) are sorrowful, and the word *dolor* occurs frequently; there is preoccupation with solitude, madness, and the poetic temperament. The image of the *sombra* also appears—the vision of her lost child Esperanza which leads Teresa in her desperate search. . . . In spite of its many defects as a novel, *Child from the Sea* represents a considerable achievement for its youthful author. It shows skill and inventiveness in spinning out a narrative, a certain psychological profundity in its characters and themes, and great sensitivity and verbal command in lyrical and descriptive passages. (p. 109)

Flavio, like [*The Child from the Sea,*] cannot be strictly classified. There are many Romantic elements—the temperaments of the principal characters, indifference to the exigencies of everyday life, fantastic or dreamlike settings. Yet the author takes a knowledgeable point of view toward this very Roman-

ticism, and reveals an awareness of transition, in herself as well as in the times and literary trends. It could best be termed psychological, for its characters offer a complex study of emotions and motives, presented with psychological depth and veracity. Much of the book is devoted to introspective analyses on the part of Flavio and Mara. These two characters are multifaceted, changeable, and enigmatic, which is to say they are people rather than types or symbols. Society is perhaps the real villain, with its restraints, false values, artificial behavior, concern for propriety, and malicious gossip. In this respect, *Flavio* resembles the Realistic novel.

Rosalía explores some of her favorite themes in this novel: the contrary nature of human love, the inner realities of poets and poetry, individual liberty, aversion to hypocrisy, and the position of women. The novel, in its study of two anguished characters, can be seen to represent the drama of conflicting elements within Rosalía herself—rebellious individualism and soaring idealism in opposition to a rational and analytical comprehension of the world. (p. 112)

[*El caballero de las botas azules (The Gentleman of the Blue Boots)*] is prefaced by a dialogue, **"A Man and a Muse"** (*"Un hombre y una musa"*), which is one of Rosalía's most interesting critical statements. It might be considered a work in its own right, but is thematically related to *El caballero,* so a presentation of it belongs here.

In an unusual variation on an old theme, the poet summons his muse, who turns out not to be the sweet, feminine ideal he is expecting. From behind the dark cloud which hides her, the muse berates the aspirant writer for his enslavement to tradition and trite subjects. She is critical, contentious, and insulting. Finally she reveals herself, and emerges from the cloud of mist—a grotesque figure in strange attire: tall and stately, dressed in a tunic, boots, and widebrimmed hat. The writer is appalled and calls her monstrous and evil. He asks her name and she replies *"Novedad"* (*"The New"*); her message is: "Shake off silly scruples and break once and for all with preoccupations of the past." (*"Déjate de vanos escrúpulos y rompe de una vez con las pasadas preoccupaciones."* . . .) This statement anticipates the declarations of Rubén Darío and other Modernists. The writer finally comprehends and sets out "with new and satirical spirit" to look ironically and penetratingly at his age. As she departs, the Muse tells him: "What greater ambition can a man have in this century of caricatures than to create his own and that of others before an appreciative audience?" . . . In the spirit of the Muse's words, the novel . . . *The Gentleman of the Blue Boots* sets out to caricature its age and protest the bad literature currently in vogue. (p. 113)

The characters of this book are, for the most part, cardboard cutouts or puppets—intentionally so, and in line with the purport of the book. The unity is provided by the character of the duke, moral and intellectual gadfly, mysterious and multifaceted. (p. 116)

The Gentleman is not a Realistic novel in the strict sense of adhering to the objective portrayal of contemporary problems and manners, but it is definitely attuned to its times. It is specifically set in Madrid in the present, and is a scathing (albeit humorous) criticism of customs, institutions, and attitudes. Barbs are levelled primarily at the middle and upper classes and their false pursuits. Fashion, education, writers, publishers, women, marriage customs, and esthetic tastes are exposed. The one great evil—here as elsewhere in Rosalía's works—is hypocrisy. Fantasy is an effective vehicle for satire (as in *Gul-*

liver's Travels), allowing the author to discuss real issues while remaining free from the limits of logic and everyday reality in order to manipulate situations and characters at will. The connection with real life is metaphorical.

Literature is her principal target. She speaks of "the pernicious fecundity" of certain poets; "terribly Spanish-historical" novels; and "pages which are flimsily written, but perfectly imprinted." She deplores the sentimental drivel dispensed in serial form under such titles as "The Honorable Woman," "Poverty without Stain," and "Love Sacrificed." She even criticizes herself. During a literary discussion, one of her characters remarks: " . . . I was incensed by my recent reading of an unknown novel which bears the title *The Gentleman of the Blue Boots*. In it, a certain sly humor, as Cervantes would say, pretensions which trail off into infinity, inconceivable audacity, and thought, if indeed it contains any, which no one can figure out, mingle woefully with an absolute lack of talent. I have read half of it and I still don't know in what chapter it begins, since it seems to begin everywhere at once. . . ." . . . (pp. 116-17)

Rosalía last novel, *El primer loco (The First Madman)* . . . is also subtitled "Strange Tale" (*"Cuento extraño"*), as was *El caballero de las botas azules*. It is indeed a strange story, not extroverted, entertaining, and socially conscious like *El caballero,* but meditative and introspective, a study of poetic temperament and madness. (p. 117)

El primer loco bears a strong resemblance in themes and characters to the earlier novels. Luis is reminiscent of Flavio as a study of the Romantic temperament which cannot come to terms with logical reality. He is more visionary and philosophical, and the book is devoted to his search for reality beyond reason. None of the women characters have the individuality of Mara in *Flavio*. Berenice is seen only through the eyes of others; the reader never directly knows her.

The author assumes the third person point of view in this novel and remains totally apart from the action. There is extensive use of dialogue, and a large part of the text is first person narrative by Luis, which at times approaches a stream of consciousness technique. Coming chronologically as it does after *El caballero de las botas azules,* so different in character, it might seem to be a regression to an earlier period, but its controlled style would indicate that it is a later and more mature work. The time, although taken to be contemporary, is vague and irrelevant; the settings are sylvan and pastoral. *El primer loco* takes place in that favorite realm of Rosalía, where illusion and reality, sanity and madness, blend and are confused. (p. 119)

Rosalía's prose does not equal her poetry in artistic qualities, yet it is not without its merits and presents some interesting aspects to the modern reader. . . .

It is her prose that Rosalía can be seen to be a woman of her times, an aspect of her identity which alters the usual image of her as the melancholic recluse or dreamer. It is in prose that she enunciates her impatience with the status quo and pleads for change. Her overt statements of protest against attitudes toward women and incisive views on contemporary literature are found in her novels, articles, and prefaces. (p. 125)

As Modernism and the Generation of 1898 emerged at the end of the nineteenth century and beginning of the twentieth, the young poets who were breaking away from Realism and reacting against their immediate predecessors retained their admiration for Bécquer and Rosalía. They held *Cantares gallegos* in high esteem for its interpenetration of author and region, its effortless rendition of traditional poetic forms, and its authentic expression of a facet of the soul of Spain. The solitary and tragic aura which surrounded Rosalía was also compatible with their own temperaments. That part of her work which most nearly resembled their own—*Follas novas* and *En las orillas del Sar*—did not directly influence them in their formative years. For a time the splendor of Rubén Darío and French and other foreign currents dominated the literary scene. When the Modernist tumult had subsided and more interiorized directions became established, the new generation of writers recognized its affinities to Rosalía and she came into her own. Many similarities can be noted in themes, techniques, and imagery between the works of Rosalía and those of Unamuno, Antonio Machado, Azorín, Juan Ramón Jiménez, Valle-Inclán, and Fernando Pessoa, yet these later writers are not her offspring but rather her siblings. (pp. 130-31)

> *Kathleen Kulp-Hill, in her* Rosalía de Castro *(copyright © 1977 by Twayne Publishers, Inc.; reprinted with the permission of Twayne Publishers, a Division of G. K. Hall & Co., Boston), Twayne, 1977, 147 p.*

ADDITIONAL BIBLIOGRAPHY

Balbontin, Jose Antonio. "Rosalia de Castro." In his *Three Spanish Poets: Rosalia de Castro, Federico Garcia Lorca, Antonio Machado,* pp. 15-56. London: Alvin Redman, 1961.
> Briefly explores Castro's poetic diction, imagery, and themes. Balbontin comments that while Rosalia did not always write with a new meter or new imagery, hers was a new mode of expression, because she spoke "of the most sublime problems in a language which everybody can understand."

Machado de Rosa, Alberto. "Heine in Spain (1856-67): Relations with Rosalía de Castro." *Monatshefte für Deutscher Unterricht* XLIX, No. 1 (January 1957): 65-82.*
> Examines artistic connections between the German poet and novelle writer Heinrich Heine and Castro, and closely contrasts several of their poems.

François René de Chateaubriand

1768-1848

French novelist, essayist, memoirist, translator, and biographer.

With his resonant style and what Charles Augustin Sainte-Beuve termed "Catholic Epicureanism," Chateaubriand helped lead the movement from classicism to Romanticism in French literature. Works such as *Atala; ou, Les amours de deux sauvages dans le désert (Atala; or, The Amours of Two Indians, in the Wilds of America)* evince his classical regard for form and Romantic emphasis on emotion and ego. While critics often find him extravagant and illogical, they consistently praise his style. Rich and descriptive, his prose won Chateaubriand the name of "enchanter."

Chateaubriand lived a life worthy of a Romantic hero. As he explained in the preface to his *Mémoires d'outre-tombe (Memoirs of François René, Vicomte de Chateaubriand, Sometime Ambassador to England):* "A traveler, soldier, poet, publicist, it is among forests that I have sung the forest, aboard ship that I have depicted the sea, in camp that I have spoken of arms, in exile that I have learnt to know exile, in courts, in affairs of the state, in Parliament that I have studied princes, politics, law and history." He was raised at his famlly's medieval chateau, where his beloved sister, Lucile, encouraged his creative pursuits. After briefly studying for the Roman Catholic priesthood and serving in the army, Chateaubriand sailed for America, purportedly to discover the Northwest Passage. The untamed landscapes and Indians that he encountered during his travels through the Northeast and Midwest inspired a Rousseauistic reverence for nature and the "noble savage" that colored all his writings. He returned to Europe in 1791 to join the royalist *armées des émigrés,* but was badly wounded, and he later escaped to England. There Chateaubriand began his literary career as a translator and writer.

The first work to win Chateaubriand recognition was *Atala,* which he published soon after his return to France in 1800. Praised especially for its descriptive power, the novel was extremely popular. *Le génie du christianisme; ou, Beautés de la religion chrétienne (Genius of Christianity; or, The Spirit and Beauties of the Christian Religion),* a work of Christian apologetics which coincided with the resurgence of Roman Catholicism in France, was an even greater success. Although the theological argument given is generally regarded as unconvincing, the work is considered a brilliant example of Chateaubriand's prose style. Incorporated into this work is *René,* an autobiographical fictional narrative detailing a melancholy youth's love for his sister. This work was later published separately. *Le génie du christianisme* attracted the attention of Napoleon, who appointed Chateaubriand secretary to the Rome Legation. For the next thirty years he was a prominent political figure who held many governmental posts, in France and abroad, and who swayed public opinion through newspaper articles and pamphlets. He continued to write, traveled extensively, and carried on numerous love affairs.

After 1830, Chateaubriand retired from public life, and devoted himself to writing. His most absorbing project was *Mémoires d'outre-tombe,* which does not only recount his varied

adventures, but embraces his dreams, memories, and convictions. Though parts are exaggerated, and many consider the work disjointed and egotistical, the memoirs reveal Chateaubriand's best traits. Stylistically sweeping and grand and elegiac in tone, they are regarded as his masterpiece. In them, and all his works, Chateaubriand expressed the *mal du siècle* that set the tone of the Romantic movement.

PRINCIPAL WORKS

Essai historique, politique et moral sur les révolutions anciennes et modernes considérées dans leurs rapports avec la révolution française (essay) 1797
Atala; ou, Les amours de deux sauvages dans le désert (novel) 1801
  [*Atala; or, The Amours of Two Indians, in the Wilds of America,* 1802]
Le génie du christianisme; ou, Beautés de la religion chrétienne (essay) 1802
  [*The Beauties of Christianity,* 1813; also published as *Genius of Christianity; or, The Spirit and Beauties of the Christian Religion,* 1854]
René (novel) 1805
  [*René,* 1813]

Les martyrs; ou, Le triomphe de la religion chrétienne
   (novel)   1809
   [*The Martyrs; or, The Triumph of the Christian Religion*,
      1812; also published as *The Two Martyrs*, 1819]
*Itinéraire de Paris à Jérusalem et de Jérusalem à Paris, en
   allant par la Grèce, et revenant par l'Egypte, la
   Barbarie, et l'Espagne*   (travel essay)   1811
   [*Travels in Greece, Palestine, Egypt and Barbary, during
      the Years 1806 and 1807*, 1811]
*De Buonaparte, des Bourbon, et de la nécessité de se
   raillier à nos princes légitimes, pour le bonheur de la
   France et celui de l'Europe*   (essay)   1814
   [*On Buonaparte and the Bourbons, and the Necessity of
      Rallying Around Our Legitimate Princes, for the Safety
      of France and of Europe* published in journal *The
      Pamphleteer*, 1814]
**Essai historique, politique et moral sur les révolutions
   anciennes et modernes*   (essay)   1815
   [*An Historical, Political and Moral Essay on Revolutions,
      Ancient and Modern*, 1815]
De la monarchie selon la charte   (essay)   1816
   [*The Monarchy According to the Charter*, 1816]
Aventures du dernier Abencérages   (novella)   1826
   [*Aben-Hamet, The Last of the Abencerages*, 1826; also
      published as *The Adventures of the Last Abencerage*,
      1870]
Les Natchez: Roman indien   (novel)   1826
   [*The Natchez: An Indian Tale*, 1827]
Voyage en Amérique   (travel essays)   1827
   [*Travels in America*, 1969]
*Essai sur la littérature anglaise et considérations sur le
   génie des hommes, des temps et des révolutions*
   (criticism)   1836
   [*Sketches of English Literature: With Considerations on
      the Spirit of the Times, Men, and Revolutions*, 1836]
Le paradis perdu [translator]   (poetry)   1836
Vie de Rancé   (biography)   1844
Mémoires d'outre-tombe   (memoirs)   1849-59
   [*Memoirs of François René, Vicomte de Chateaubriand,
      Sometime Ambassador to England*, 1902]

**This work is a revision of the earlier Essai historique, politique et
moral sur les révolutions anciennes et modernes considérées dans
leurs rapports avec la révolution française.*

F. A. CHATEAUBRIAND   (essay date 1801)

I was still very young when I conceived the idea of achieving
the epic of the natural man or of painting the manners of the
savages by connecting them with some familiar event. After
the discovery of America, I saw no subject more interesting,
especially for the French, than the massacre of the Natchez
colony in Louisiana in 1727. All the Indian tribes, after two
centuries of oppression, conspiring to restore liberty in the New
World seemed to me to offer almost as good a subject as the
conquest of Mexico. I put a few fragments of that work on
paper, but I soon saw that I lacked the true colors, and that if
I wished to present a real likeness, it would be necessary to
follow Homer's example and visit the peoples whom I wanted
to paint. (p. 105)

Of all my manuscripts concerning America, I saved only some
portions, *Atala* in particular, which in itself was only an episode
of *Les Natchez*. *Atala* was written in the desert, and under the
huts of the savages. I do not know whether the public will
enjoy this story, which departs from all the beaten paths and
presents scenes of nature and customs that are altogether foreign to Europe. There is no adventure at all in *Atala*. It is a
sort of poem, half descriptive, half dramatic. [Chateaubriand
states in a footnote:

In a time when everything in literature is corrupted I am obliged
to give warning that if I make use of the word "poem" here,
it is because I am unable to make myself understood otherwise.
I am not one of those barbarians who confuse prose and verse.
The poet, whatever may be said about this, is always *par
excellence* the superior of other men, and whole volumes of
descriptive prose are not worth fifty beautiful verses by Homer,
Virgil, or Racine.]

[The] whole thing consists of the painting of two lovers who
walk and talk in solitude; all lies in the picture of the turmoil
of love in the midst of the calm of the wilderness and the calm
of religion. I gave the most ancient forms to this work; it is
divided into prologue, recital, and epilogue. The principal parts
of the recital bear a name, such as "The Hunter," "The Hus-
bandman," etc.; and it was thus that in the first ages of Greece
the rhapsodists sang under various titles the fragments of the
Iliad and the *Odyssey*.

I will not conceal that I have sought extreme simplicity of
subject-matter and style, save for the descriptive portion, and
yet it is true that in description itself there is a way of being
both pompous and simple at the same time. Telling what I
attempted is not telling what I have accomplished. For a long
time I have read only the Bible and Homer, happy if the fact
is noticed, and I have blended with the tones of the wilderness
the feelings peculiar to my own heart and the colors of these
two great and eternal models of the beautiful and true. I will
also say that my goal was not to wring out many tears. This
seems to me a dangerous error advanced by M. de Voltaire,
that good words are those which cause the most weeping. There
is a sort of drama whose authorship would be disclaimed by
anyone which wrings the heart in a different way than does
the *Iliad*. Because you torture the soul you are not a great
writer. True tears are those caused to flow by beautiful poetry,
as much admiration as grief must mingle therein. (pp. 106-08)

I am not at all enthusiastic about the savages, like M. Rousseau,
and although I have perhaps as much ground to complain of
society as that philosopher had to be thoroughly satisfied with
it, I do not believe at all that "pure nature" is the most beautiful
thing in the world. I have always found it very ugly wherever
I have had occasion to see it. Far from entertaining the opinion
that the man who thinks is a "depraved animal," I believe
that thought makes man. All has been lost with this word
"nature." . . . Let us paint nature, but beautiful nature; art
should not concern itself with the imitation of monsters. (pp.
108-09)

Atala, like *Philoctetes*, has only three characters. Perhaps a
rather new kind of character will be found in the woman that
I have sought to paint. The contradictions of the human heart
are things which perhaps have not been sufficiently set forth,
yet they should deserve examination all the more in that they
are connected with the ancient tradition of an original fall of
man, and in consequence they open deep vistas on everything
great and mysterious in man and his story.

Chactas, Atala's lover, is a savage who is supposed to be born with genius and who is more than half civilized, since he knows not only the modern languages but also the dead languages of Europe. He must therefore express himself in a mixed style, in conformity with the line along which he moves, the border between society and nature. This gave me great advantages, by making him speak like a savage in the painting of customs and as a European in the drama and the narrative. Without this the work would have had to be given up; had I always made use of the Indian style, *Atala* would have been Hebrew for the reader.

Concerning the missionary, I believe that I have noticed that those who have brought a priest on the scene, up to the present, have either made him a criminal or a sort of *philosophe*. Father Aubry is nothing of that kind. He is a simple Christian who speaks of "the Cross, of the blood of his divine Master, of the corruption of the flesh," etc., without blushing; in a word, he is the priest as he is. I know that it is difficult to paint such a character without arousing thoughts of ridicule in the minds of certain readers. If I move no one, I shall cause laughter; this is to be discovered.

After all, if one examines what I have introduced into so small a frame; if one thinks that there is not a single interesting circumstance of the manners of the savages on which I have not dwelt, not one beautiful effect of nature and not one fine site in New France which I have not described; if one notes that I placed beside the race of hunters a complete picture of an agricultural people to show the advantages of social life over the life of the savage; if attention be paid to the difficulties which I must have met in sustaining the dramatic interest with only two characters during a long presentation of customs and many descriptions of landscapes; if, finally, it is observed that in the catastrophe itself I relied on no helps and did not try to sustain myself except by the force of the dialogue, as did the ancients; these two considerations will provoke some indulgence for me on the part of the reader. Once again, I do not flatter myself that I have succeeded; but one should always be grateful to a writer who strives to bring literature back to that ancient flavor which is too often forgotten in our times. (pp. 109-10)

> *F. A. Chateaubriand, "Chateaubriand's Preface,"*
> *translated by William Leonard Schwartz (originally*
> *a letter to the editor of* Journal des débats, *March*
> *31, 1801), in* Atala: Or the Love and Constancy of
> Two Strangers in the Desert, *edited by William Leon-*
> *ard Schwartz, translated by Caleb Bingham (with the*
> *permission of the publishers, Stanford University*
> *Press; copyright 1930 by the Board of Trustees of*
> *the Leland Stanford Junior University; renewed 1958*
> *by Anstrice B. Schwartz), Stanford University Press,*
> *1930, pp. 104-12.*

[STENDHAL (pseudonym of Henri Beyle)] (essay date 1825)

The best of [French] prose writers has the advantage, if such it be, of being the most finished hypocrite in France. Viscount Chateaubriand does not, probably, in the course of a year write a single phrase which is free from a fallacy either in reasoning or sentiment; so much so that while reading him you are incessantly tempted to cry out "Just Heavens! how false all this is! but how well it is written!" A few years ago M. Chateaubriand was a poor and unknown writer, until the thought struck him of bringing religion into fashion [in his *Genie du Christianisme*], and rendering piety agreeable to "ears polite." In

this he succeeded; and the result to him has been a blue riband and the department for foreign affairs during two years. . . . The masterpiece, as to style, of M. Chateaubriand, is the first seventy or eighty pages of a pamphlet entitled *De la Monarchie selon la Charte*. His *chef-d'oeuvre*, in a purely literary point of view, is a little romance yet unpublished, called *Les Abencerrages*. A short time after his disgrace (as they call in France dismissal from office) a noble duke, one of his friends, asked him when he should publish the *Abencerrages;* to which he replied, "When I have a great deal of leisure, and not a crown in my pocket." His *Genie du Christianisme—Itineraire à Jerusalem—*and *Martyrs,* are still purchased, but not read. This clever writer is a hypocrite only while holding the pen or speaking in his public capacity, as a peer or a minister. In society he is a highly intellectual man, of the very best *ton,* and who would repel the imputation of being devout as a slur upon his rank and acquirements; and in the confidence of familiar intercourse he does not hesitate to make free with the pretensions of priests and princes. M. Chateaubriand was not intended by Nature for a statesman. He has too much of the generosity, prodigality, and recklessness of genius. . . . (pp. 582-83)

> *[Stendhal (pseudonym of Henri Beyle),] "Present*
> *French Prose Literature," in* The New Monthly
> Magazine, *Vol. XIII, No. LIV, 1825, pp. 581-87.**

AMERICAN QUARTERLY REVIEW (essay date 1827)

[In general, the first section of *Génie du Christianisme*] is the least interesting division of the work.

In the second and third parts, which comprehend more than half of the entire work, and for which the whole was written, he is more successful. They are devoted to what Christianity has done for poetry, the fine arts, philosophy, history, eloquence, and the kindred subjects. Poetry is naturally, with [Mons. de Chateaubriand], the principal; and, certainly, the views he has taken of it are often new and striking, and exhibited with much happiness of illustration. . . . [He] considers the effects of Christianity upon poetical machinery, comparing the mythology of the Greeks, with the inventions of recent poetry; and drawing his illustrations from Homer, Virgil, Dante, Tasso, and Milton: the whole of his inquiry into the superiority of Christianity, for poetical purposes, over every other religion, being aptly prefaced by an examination of the principal epics, ancient and modern, and finished by a comparison of the Bible and Homer. The whole of this is very striking, and generally seems new; and though a good deal of it is glittering rather than rich, and some of it false, still it can hardly be read but with a strong interest. The same is true of what follows, on the fine arts, philosophy, history, and eloquence; though he has treated these subjects less amply. (pp. 472-73)

The most interesting part of [the fourth] division is, undoubtedly, his sketch of the romantic missions, undertaken by a few religious orders, to the Levant, to China, and to Paraguay, which are to be numbered among the most astonishing enterprises of human enthusiasm, and to which Mons. de Chateaubriand's eloquence has given their full poetical effect. (p. 473)

[At the time of the appearance of *Génie du Christianisme*,] it was easily perceived, that with all the accuracy and formality of its divisions into parts, books, and chapters, it was really very little connected; and that few of its subjects were either thoroughly or satisfactorily discussed; that on many, as on Dante and Ossian, he seemed to be singularly deficient in his knowledge, and wrong in his opinions; and that on others, as on chivalry and the monastic orders, he had a wrong system, which misled him even when he possessed the facts on which to found his reasoning. And, besides all this, it was no less easily seen, that, through the whole work, there was a confusion of metaphysics and poetry, of history and romance, which can properly belong to no subject, and no form of discussion; while, at the same time, the very scope and argument of the work seemed wrong, since it cannot be necessary that Christianity should be the most poetical of religions, in order to be true and good: or, even if it be so, it is not very logical to found a metaphysical proof of its truth and excellence upon its poetical beauties; so that, after all, in reading the whole work, and considering it as one effort, it seemed hard to determine whether it were a metaphysical treatise, or a discussion of what is most beautiful in ancient and modern times, or a long review, or fragments of all of them, mingled together in strange and brilliant confusion.

But then, on the other hand, there was such a deep and sincere feeling of religion running through it; such a touching melancholy, which his character seemed to have preserved from the dreadful sufferings through which he had passed; such an abstraction from the feelings of the world; such a self-devotion, which seemed to consider the past and the future without a thought of the present, and to look for hope only in the grave, and for the value of this life only in the world beyond it, that it was impossible not to be deeply moved, and feel not only sincerely, but seriously interested by it. But besides this prevalent tone, which, after all, gives something like unity to the work, it contains separate and disconnected passages of great power and eloquence. . . . When we lay down the book, they remain in our imaginations and recollections, in a bold relief, which is the surest witness to their power. (pp. 474-75)

[The initial success of *Génie du Christianisme*] cannot be said yet to have deserted it, though undoubtedly it has been gradually diminishing, until Mons. de Chateaubriand himself can no longer feel sure that posterity will admit its pretensions to be ranked among the classics of the nation's literature; though he must still feel persuaded, that, in the intellectual and religious history of the country, it will be always remembered among the most remarkable books that have been produced by the convulsions of the last forty years. (p. 475)

[The subject of *Les Martyrs, ou le Triomphe de la Religion Chrétienne*] is something entirely new, and marks not a little boldness in its author's talent. The Christians of the third century, he supposes, had so far fallen off from the purity of their religion, that a second atonement for them was become necessary; and this atonement was to be made by two mortals, one of whom, chosen from among the Idolaters, and the other from among the Christians, were to become the expiatory sacrifices both of the faithful and the Gentiles. These two victims, therefore, Eudorus, a Christian, descended from Philopoemen, the last of the Greeks, and himself an orator and soldier of no mean name, and Cymodocee, descended from Homer, and daughter of a priest of the Muses, are the hero and heroine of the poem, the martyrs in the persecutions of Dioclesian, and the unconscious subjects of the strange glory Chateaubriand has imputed to them,—that of being vicarious sufferers to complete an atonement for which the blood of the first sufferer had not proved sufficient. This is the point on which the whole of the Christian machinery of the poem rests; and on which the indispensable connexion between the human and superhuman portions, between those parts of the action that pass on earth, in heaven, in purgatory, and in hell, is established. (p. 478)

From this sketch of the singular imagination on which the poem is founded, and the extraordinary story which constitutes its action, it will not seem surprising that it has a marked character both in its defects and beauties; though certainly it seems to us that the first are the most prominent and obtrusive.

To begin, then, with its defects;—its most striking, though not, perhaps, its deepest and most serious fault, is, that it is neither poetry nor prose in its style, but a kind of eloquent and exaggerated declamation, far removed from the simplicity and grace of Fenelon's *Telemachus,* and rendered still more unpleasant by a great number of imitations and translations from other poets, especially Homer and Milton, which are sometimes perceptible for pages together, and awaken the most discordant associations.

The second considerable fault of the *Martyrs* is, we think, that it is written on a system; that it is an attempt to support and carry through a theory. The consequence of this is, that Mons. de Chateaubriand is continually making an effort to bring the machinery of Christianity into successful opposition with that of the Greek, Roman, and Druidical superstitions; and, therefore, instead of giving himself up to the free and unhesitating influence of poetry, and thus drawing us after him by an enthusiasm we cannot refuse to share, we are continually involved in the conflicts of saints and demigods, until we sometimes hardly know whether we are not reading alternately passages from Ovid's *Metamorphoses* and the *Traditions of the Church.*

Perhaps, however, after all, the chief fault of the *Martyrs* is, that it is too much encumbered with history. Chateaubriand, indeed, tells us plainly that it was an essential part of his plan to give a complete sketch of Christianity, as it existed in the time of Dioclesian; so that, before we get through, besides being made familiar with all the martyrs the Acta Sanctorum could afford him, and all the miracles and traditions he could gather from the obscure annals of the Church's sufferings in Africa, Italy, and the East, we have five books. . . . We are completely wearied as we are dragged through this wandering series of unimportant events and forgotten personages, who can interest us no more than the list of the Greek ships in Homer; so that, when we have finished the whole work, we come away, perhaps, with stronger impressions of it as a romance, containing a collection of sketches of manners in the third century, and of the early history of Christian martyrs, than as an epic of the full length and the most exact proportions, founded on the strange doctrine of a second vicarious atonement.

But though the faults of the *Martyrs* are prominent and obtrusive, we are far from thinking it is without beauties. Several of the characters are finely drawn and supported, especially that of Velleda, the Druidess, which is, in some respects, taken from Virgil's Dido; that of Demodocus, the priest of the Muses . . . ; and that of Cymodocee, the heroine, who, though perhaps too romantic for the age in which she is placed, and the work she is destined to illustrate, is a delightful union of the characters of the ancient mythology, in which she was educated, and the purer religion to which she had been converted; often confounding the language and worship of both, but never mistaking the heavenly spirit of that to which she freely offers up her life.

Besides the characters, however, there is often a high degree of eloquence in the *Martyrs*. It is true, the transparent and unpretending simplicity, which alone can give a classical value to works of this doubtful species, is wanting; but whenever a fair opportunity is afforded, for that style of powerful and striking declamation, in which no small part of M. de Chateaubriand's force resides, he is, we think, eminently successful. (pp. 479-80)

On the whole then, it seems to us, that this last and greatest of M. de Chateaubriand's literary efforts, is not destined to final success. It is, on the one hand, too much encumbered with learning, to be generally interesting, and on the other hand, too theological and systematic, to entertain much of the free and fearless spirit of poetry. It will, therefore, probably fail of the distinction to which it aspires; that, we mean, of being placed at the side of the *Télémaque,* as an enduring monument to the poetical glories of Christianity: and, regarding it as a failure, notwithstanding the grace and romantic interest of some of its characters, the eloquence of some of its declamations, and the touching beauty and truth of almost all its descriptions, it will hardly be able, we think, long to escape the oblivion, which, with a single exception, has already overtaken all its predecessors among the French prose epics. (p. 481)

[That the works of M. de Chateaubriand] show much originality, much talent, much force of personal character, is admitted; but these high qualities, it cannot be forgotten, are mingled with not a little extravagance, and even a fantastic extravagance, in the language, conception, and feelings, of almost all he has written; and, in many cases, with a gloomy and incongruous misanthropy and superstition, which may, sometimes, indeed, have their poetical side; but are oftener dark, threatening, and offensive. Thus, after all, though *Atala* may save its author's name, and though some passages of the *Genius of Christianity* and the *Martyrs,* will not soon or easily be forgotten, yet we cannot, for ourselves, think that M. de Chateaubriand and his works, are destined to that wide and popular immortality, to which they so openly and so proudly lay claim. (pp. 481-82)

> *"Works of Chateaubriand,"* in American Quarterly Review, *Vol. II, No. 4, December, 1827, pp. 458-82.*

THE NORTH AMERICAN REVIEW (essay date 1828)

[Châteaubriand's *Essay on Revolutions*] is a curious specimen of the wild extravagance of youthful genius, full of life and power, but not yet taught or tamed by wholesome experience, bursting with imaginary stores of intellectual wealth, and, that no time may be lost in communicating them, despatching with a few dashes of the pen an encyclopedia of the greatest questions in politics, morals, and literature. The plan of the work is essentially vicious, and the details extravagant often to absurdity. It also abounds in false principles, and, to a less extent, in marks of false taste in style; and it is written throughout in an amusing tone of self-sufficiency and dogmatism. That a person capable of producing such a work should be compelled, by any chance, to vegetate unknown and unthought of in a garret, was, of course, in his opinion, a fact sufficient of itself to demonstrate the utter rottenness of the existing condition of society, which he accordingly qualifies in no very favorable terms. 'I figure to myself the world,' he remarks, in one of the passages in which he treats this subject, 'I figure to myself the world as a vast forest, and the human race as a band of robbers, who lie in wait in it, to rob and murder each other.' A charming illustration of the principles and forms of social intercourse! But with all its defects, the style and substance of

the *Essay* argue powers of the highest order, and extensive research through the whole field of knowledge. (p. 230)

[The character of the *Genius of Christianity*] is rather poetical than philosophical; and it was doubtless on this account so much the better fitted to effect its object. Its popularity was much increased by the insertion, in the body of it, of the tales entitled *Atalá* and *René,* originally intended as episodes in the romance of the *Natchez.* Considered as works of art, these novels are perhaps conceived on false principles of taste, and are not unexceptionable even in a moral point of view; but they both display great power of execution, and they recommended the work to a class of readers, for whom it would otherwise have had less attraction.

The opinion of competent judges has been a good deal divided, respecting the literary character of the *Genius of Christianity;* but we incline to believe, that it will be viewed hereafter as one of the remarkable productions of the age. It possesses indeed the singular merit of being the only defence of our religion yet published, which has had an extensive vogue as a merely literary work, independently of its substantial or scientific value. It has also the advantage of being in a great measure clear of controversial topics, and consequently nearly equally interesting to Christians of all denominations. But whatever its positive merit may be, it certainly produced, from the peculiar circumstances under which it was published, a greater and happier effect, than almost any book of modern times. It was one of the most powerful, immediate agents in counteracting the current of opinion, that had set so strongly in France for many years preceding, in favor of loose doctrines in religion and morals. (pp. 231-32)

The return of the Bourbons gave a new direction to [Châteaubriand's] literary talent, which has since been exclusively and indefatigably employed on political topics. He announced and welcomed the new order of events in a powerful pamphlet, which had the effect of recommending to the affection of the people their almost forgotten, legitimate monarch. Upon Bonaparte's return from Elba, he accompanied the king to Ghent, and acted there as his principal minister. The ascendency acquired by the liberal party, soon after the second restoration of Louis the Eighth, to which we have already alluded, threw him, with the other determined royalists, into the ranks of opposition. The first fruit of his efforts, under these new circumstances, was the work entitled the *Monarchy according to the Charter,* the largest and most elaborate of his mature political essays, in which he first analyzes the nature of representative government in general, and then examines and endeavors to invalidate the grounds on which the adoption of a liberal system of administration by the king was commonly defended. With all the respect which we feel for the intellect of M. de Châteaubriand, we conceive that it is essentially a poetical, and not a philosophical one; and that his talent lies in expressing his opinions, whatever they may be, in powerful and beautiful language, rather than in forming them with extraordinary sagacity, coolness, and precision. We find him indeed adopting, at different times, with equally apparent and, we doubt not, real conviction, the most opposite theories in religion and politics, and expressing them both with the same force and fervor, without always deeming it necessary to account distinctly for the change. Hence the charge of inconsistency, which has been urged against him with considerable plausibility, and to which we shall advert more particularly hereafter.

The *Monarchy according to the Charter* does not, in our opinion, in its purely theoretical part, exhaust the great question of representative government, or even furnish any decidedly original and striking views on the subject. It is rarely indeed, if ever, that there is any real value in discussions of general principles, brought forward in the heat of controversy, for the purpose of effecting the decision of points in dispute between political parties. In the work now alluded to, there were two or three passages which the ministers affected to consider as personally disrespectful to the king, and under this pretence they struck off the name of the author from the roll of counsellors of state. This proceeding did not tend, of course, to conciliate his feelings; and, pursuing with augmented zeal his course of opposition, he undertook, with the aid of a number of friends, the publication of the *Conservateur*. . . . (pp. 233-34)

It is indeed to [Châteaubriand's] labors in the *Conservateur,* that the triumph of the royalists, as far as it was the effect of exertion, has been universally ascribed by friends and foes. Never before, with perhaps the single exception of the writings of Burke on the French revolution, was a political controversy sustained, through the channel of the press, with equal ability. The author is now upon his true ground. He loses no time in a cool investigation of facts or impartial settlement of philosophical principles, but takes for granted, that he is fighting the battles of God and the king, or according to the chosen motto of the work, *le Roi, la Charte, et les honnêtes gens,* against the efforts of a new incarnation of the principle of evil in the form of revolution. The vice in his reasoning lies in this assumption; but admitting his principles, the fearful conclusions which he drew from them followed of course; and being announced with such splendid and impressive eloquence, they struck terror into every heart. His articles, like every thing else that proceeds from his pen, are a series of poems, and in stern sublimity of spirit, as well as bold imagery and rich oriental coloring of language, resemble the terrible denunciations of the ancient Hebrew prophets, rather than the petty sparring that forms the staple of common newspaper controversy. Social order, with all its dependent charities and blessings, laws, morals, the sacred name of religion, every principle that good men regard as dear and valuable, is invoked to lend its aid in this holy war. Having firmly enchained his readers by the magic of his eloquence, he transports them successively to the scenes of all the horrors that disgraced the revolution; the groves of La Vendeé sanctified by the blood of a host of martyrs; the violated sepulchres of Henry the Fourth and St. Louis; the prisons of the reign of terror; the scaffold of Louis the Sixteenth; and finally the death-bed of the duke of Berry, from which, as a starting post, he leads on the last and most furious onset against the obnoxious favorite.

Such was the battery, which the Viscount de Châteaubriand opened upon the administration of M. de Cases and his adherents. Nothing could sustain its tremendous fire. The smaller craft of ordinary newspapers and pamphlets sunk under it like a fleet of gun-boats, under the broadside of a seventy-four. . . . The prodigious effect that had already been produced, aided by the imprudence of the liberalists, and by the fatal catastrophe of the duke of Berry, finally unsettled the administration, and threw it into royalist hands. The change in the public opinion of the country was not less complete. The liberal party were defeated at the following elections in all quarters, and instead of commanding, as they had done before, nearly half the votes in the house, and at times a majority, found themselves reduced in the new parliament, summoned on the accession of Charles the Tenth, to an insignificant fraction of some twelve or fourteen persons. Such were the wonders achieved, in the course

of two or three years, by a single pen. The result evidently proved that, although the public taste does not always accurately estimate the nice distinctions between the personal qualities of different competitors for influence, there are some talents of so transcendent a kind, that they cannot be overlooked, and if at all aided by circumstances, infallibly produce effect. (pp. 234-36)

> *"Politics of Europe," in* The North American Review, *Vol. XXVII, No. LX, July, 1828, pp. 215-68.**

BLACKWOOD'S EDINBURGH MAGAZINE   (essay date 1832)   ·

Few are aware that [Chateaubriand] is, without one single exception, the most eloquent writer of the present age; that independent of politics, he has produced many works on morals, religion, and history, destined for immortal endurance; that his writings combine the strongest love of rational freedom, with the warmest inspiration of Christian devotion; that he is, as it were, the link between the feudal and the revolutionary ages; retaining from the former its generous and elevated feeling, and inhaling from the latter its acute and fearless investigation. The last pilgrim, with devout feelings, to the holy sepulchre, he was the first supporter of constitutional freedom in France; discarding thus from former times their bigoted fury, and from modern, their infidel spirit, blending all that was noble in the ardour of the Crusades, with all that is generous in the enthusiasm of freedom. . . .

The greatest work of this writer is his **"Genie du Christianisme,"** a work of consummate ability and splendid eloquence, in which he has enlisted in the cause of religion all the treasures of knowledge and all the experience of ages, and sought to captivate the infidel generation in which he wrote, not only by the force of argument, but the grace of imagination. To us who live in a comparatively religious atmosphere, and who have not yet witnessed the subversion of the altar, by the storms which overthrew the [French] throne, it is difficult to estimate the importance of a work of this description, which insinuated itself into the mind of the most obdurate infidels by the charms of literary composition, and subdued thousands inaccessible to any other species of influence by the sway it acquired over the fancy. . . .

["**Itineraire de Paris à Jerusalem**"] is not so much a book of travels as memoirs of the feelings and impressions of the author during a journey over the shores of the Mediterranean; the cradle, as Dr Johnson observed, of all that dignifies and has blest human nature, of our laws, our religion, and our civilisation. It may readily be anticipated that the observations of such a man, in such scenes, must contain much that is interesting and delightful: our readers may prepare themselves for a high gratification; it is seldom that they have such an intellectual feast laid before them. (p. 554)

His journey into the Holy Land awakened a new . . . train of ideas, throughout the whole of which we recognise the peculiar features of M. de Chateaubriand's mind: a strong and poetical sense of the beauties of nature, a memory fraught with historical recollections; a deep sense of religion, illustrated, however, rather as it affects the imagination and the passions, than the judgment. It is a mere chimera to suppose that such aids are to be rejected by the friends of Christianity, or that truth may with safety discard the aid of fancy, either in subduing the passions or affecting the heart. On the contrary, every day's experience must convince us, that for one who can understand an argument, hundreds can enjoy a romance; and that truth, to affect multitudes, must condescend to wear the garb of fancy. (p. 559)

Chateaubriand is not only an eloquent and beautiful writer, he is also a profound scholar, and an enlightened thinker. His knowledge of history and classical literature is equalled only by his intimate acquaintance with the early annals of the church, and the fathers of the Catholic faith; while in his speeches delivered in the Chamber of Peers since the restoration, will be found not only the most eloquent but the most complete and satisfactory dissertations on the political state of France during that period, which is anywhere to be met with. . . .

The last of his considerable publications is the **"Etudes Historiques,"** a work eminently characteristic of that superiority in historical composition, which we have allowed to the French modern writers over their contemporaries in this country; and which, we fear, another generation, instructed when too late by the blood and the tears of a Revolution, will be alone able fully to appreciate. (p. 565)

> *"Chateaubriand,"* in Blackwood's Edinburgh Magazine, *Vol. XXXI, No. CXCII, March, 1832, pp. 553-65.*

[T. H. LISTER]   (essay date 1832)

Among the celebrated men of France M. de Chateaubriand holds a conspicuous station, distinguished alike by the brilliancy of his talents, and by their scope and versatility. Minister, diplomatist, orator, poet, traveller, theologian, novelist, pamphleteer—he has appeared in all these various capacities, and so appeared as invariably to ensure attention, and frequently to command admiration and respect. Yet with all this variety, there has been little inconsistency—with all this change of style and subject there has been little change of tone and feeling. Through all the manifold productions of his fertile pen [collected in his *Oeuvres Complètes*], we still see the same rash, ardent, eloquent, imaginative Chateaubriand. (p. 297)

There are two of our countrymen, one of them still living, to whom M. de Chateaubriand, in the quality of his mind, seems to have a strong resemblance: we allude to Mr. Southey—and to one still greater—to Mr. Burke. We do not mean to say that M. de Chateaubriand is as brilliant an orator, as powerful a political writer, as the latter—or that he is as good a poet as Mr. Southey—but that his mind exhibits many of those characteristics which have been displayed by each. We find in him the same predominance of imagination over judgment, the same disposition to resolve matters of speculation into matters of feeling, and to broach as his opinions what are merely his tastes; the same disposition to treat religion and politics as if they were among the fine arts, and to judge of a creed or a constitution as he would of a picture. Like Burke, he would have expatiated on the beautiful vision of Marie Antoinette as a palliation of the enormities of the "ancien régime." Like Mr. Southey, he would have directed our attention to the superior picturesqueness of the embowered cottage of the agricultural labourer over the naked row of manufacturing dwellings, as a proof that agriculture is better than manufactures. He is, however, very inferior to Burke in the mental vigour wherewith that distinguished man could array in the choicest armour of reason whatever theory his feelings and imagination might have led him to adopt. M. de Chateaubriand bears a closer resemblance to Mr. Southey; and he resembles him not only in the manner in which he employs the large resources of his gifted mind, but even in the direction of many of his

tastes. He is not only, like him, enthusiastic,—but enthusiastic upon similar subjects. There is in the minds of each the same disposition to look with peculiar fondness upon monachism and all its accessories. Pilgrimages and missions similarly affect their imaginations; and there is a mental excursiveness and love of the exciting wonders of foreign travel, alike perceptible in both. In politics the resemblance would probably have been greater, if M. de Chateaubriand had lived only a life of speculation, and had never entered into the turbulent arena of political existence, and rubbed off a little of his theoretical sentimentality by actual collision with practical statesmen. But there is much resemblance still. M. de Chateaubriand is a French High Tory, but a Tory by imagination rather than by principle; smitten with the imposing grandeur of arbitrary power, and the venerableness of prescriptive rights; commending the benignity of paternal governments, yet not unwilling to admit how beautiful is liberty. He cannot even now forget that abstract liberty was the idol of his youth; but the horrors of the French Revolution scared him from his blind devotion; and, like disappointed votaries, he has visited upon the object of his adoration that mortification which his own excessive zeal had prepared for him.

M. de Chateaubriand's earliest work is his *Essai Historique Politique et Moral sur les Révolutions anciennes et modernes, considerées dans leurs rapports avec la Révolution Française de nos jours.* . . . It is a very faulty production, full of the errors of youthful precipitance. (pp. 298-300)

In this youthful work he appears to have set out with a mania for discovering coincidences. Whatever had strongly affected his imagination among the events of modern times, and especially those connected with the French Revolution, must have its parallel in ancient history. France must be like Greece. Robespierre was like Pisistratus!—yet the epitaph on Marat must be like the ode to Harmodius, who slew the descendant of Pisistratus! and, moreover, the Jacobins resembled, not the Athenians, but the Spartans! (p. 300)

One of M. de Chateaubriand's greatest works is his *Génie du Christianisme,* a work of eminent eloquence and much research, yet one of the most unequal and unsatisfactory productions of genius that has been witnessed in modern times; full of brilliant beauties and glaring defects—passages which all must admire, and errors that might be detected by a child—excellent in intention, yet so executed as to draw down the reprobation even of those who are most zealous in the cause the writer has undertaken to defend. The illogical character of the author's mind is conspicuous in almost every portion of this splendid failure. It is conspicuous in the very outline of the work, and it is still more evident in the details. He takes up arms against objections which are not worthy of his attacks, and he combats them with arguments which he ought to have seen were inadequate to his purpose. (pp. 301-02)

[His] *intention* was certainly excellent. He saw that Deism in France was captivating its proselytes with the classical beauties of heathen fable—that both in literature and in the fine arts no models were acknowledged except those of Greece and Rome. . . . He wished to counteract the poison by teaching them to discover beauties in the Christian creed, and if he did not convince their reason, at least to captivate their tastes. In adopting this course, M. de Chateaubriand seems never to have considered what very humble ground he was condescending to occupy. He seems never to have asked himself whether such a line of defence was not derogatory to the great cause he was undertaking to advocate, and whether it was really advantageous to religion to treat it as if it was one of the fine arts. Nay more, he seems to have forgotten that the utmost success in establishing his position would profit him nothing with those whom he addressed. The deistical admirers of Greece and Rome, who thought the Heathen mythology the most beautiful, the most poetical of all mythologies, did not on that account believe in it. Their imagination did not controul their judgment; their tastes were not connected with their creed. If, therefore, the eloquence of the *Génie du Christianisme* could have succeeded in inducing them to discard their classical models of excellence, could have wrought an entire revolution in their tastes, and led them to draw thenceforth only from Holy Writ their subjects for poetry or for painting: this would no more necessarily have made them Christians, than their veneration for classical models had proved them to be worshippers of Jupiter and Minerva. The utmost success of his line of argument could have scarcely tended to do more than just to raise Christianity above the absurd and vicious mythology of Greece and Rome. (pp. 302-03)

If M. de Chateaubriand . . . had compared contemporary religions, and results of real importance to the condition of man, which are plainly deducible from each, he would have done more wisely—though even then it could not have been said that he had established his argument on lofty ground. But M. de Chateaubriand does nothing of all this: he does not compare contemporary religions: he compares the works of modern Christianity with the productions of ancient Paganism: he brings forward on either side, not results which are directly and unquestionably to be attributed to the influence of religion, but which cannot be proved to have sprung from that source, and which can only be said to have co-existed with it. He has moreover adduced circumstances, which, whether derivable from a religious creed or not, are, instead of being vitally important to the temporal welfare of man, denounced by some as absolutely worthless, and classed even by their admirers rather among the ornaments and luxuries of civilized existence, than among those great principles on which depend either our welfare in this world or our hopes of happiness in another. . . .

M. de Chateaubriand, for a devout man, seems strangely insensible to the immense inequality between the substantial importance of religion, and the value of the trappings which he summons to support it. Even to the undevout, religion will appear the most powerful engine that ever influenced the condition of man; and to commend it because ornamental arts have flourished under its mighty shadow, would appear to him trifling and absurd. (p. 304)

[M. de Chateaubriand] becomes a weak and even a dangerous advocate, through the want of a just appreciation of the points he insists upon, and a clear and comprehensive view of the principal bearings of the question before him.

But if this defect of the reasoning faculty is perceptible even in the plan and outline of his work, it is still more manifest in his management of the details. He seems to have no idea that mere assertion will not stand in the place of proof; that it is necessary to say more than that thus he feels and thinks, and that his opinions on various questionable matters are not the universal opinions of mankind. . . . [Below is] an error which shows his strange inability to perceive the consequences of his own propositions, and his blindness to the danger of attempting to prove too much.

> "Au reste," he says "c'est la religion qui, dans tous les siècles et dans tous les pays, a été la source de l'éloquence. Si Démosthène et Ciceron ont été de grands orateurs, c'est qu'avant tout ils étoient religieux." And he adds in a note: "Ils ont sans cesse le nom des dieux à la bouche.' . . .

> [It is religion that in every century and country, was the source of eloquence. If Demosthenes and Cicero were great orators, it is only because above all, they were religious. The names of their deities were continually in their mouths.]

Demosthenes and Cicero were eloquent because they were religious! and we are referred for an example to Cicero's castigation of Verres, for having appropriated statues of Mercury, of Hercules, and of Cupid,—deities assuredly little calculated to have excited religious veneration even in the most besotted of their superstitious worshippers, and in whom we know, from his own writings, the enlightened orator did not believe. "The names of their deities were continually in their mouths!" What deities? There is scarcely a schoolboy who does not know that they were little better than personified vices, and that the history of their adventures is grossly impure; yet to worship them was to be "religious!", and the eloquence of Demosthenes and Cicero sprung principally from this degraded source! But what is more, if the assertion were true, (which whoever studies the lives and writings of these great men will utterly deny,) it would militate against that very line of argument which M. de Chateaubriand is attempting to support. If Demosthenes and Cicero were eloquent, principally because they were religious, and if a false religion could produce such marvels, surely a true religion ought to have produced examples of eloquence infinitely more striking. The superiority of Christian over Heathen eloquence ought to have stood on unquestionable ground, instead of being a superiority which to many seems doubtful, and by some is utterly denied. To those who deny the superiority of Christian eloquence, M. de Chateaubriand has afforded a plea for preferring to Christianity the mythology of the Greeks; while those to whom the superiority seems doubtful are excused for placing the two religions on the same level.

It is difficult to collect from a writer who expresses his ideas with so little precision, what sort of instrumentality in the promotion of literature and the arts M. de Chateaubriand means to attribute to religion, and to what extent the cause of religion is supposed to be benefited by the connection. Religion with him sometimes seems to mean a vague abstract feeling of veneration for a superior being. Sometimes it is a belief in a particular creed. Sometimes it influences the sentiments; sometimes it merely furnishes a subject for, or enters into the machinery of a poem. The eloquence of Cicero is said to have been inspired by religion, though he pleaded for the worship of divinities, in whom, we know, he had no belief. It is adduced as one of the triumphs of our faith, that it furnished good subjects for the pen of Voltaire, the bitterest scoffer at its truths. The false and the true creed, the believer and the sceptic, are so heterogeneously mingled, that at times we scarcely know to what conclusion our author is intending to lead us. The poetical use to which Voltaire, an unbeliever, was able to apply the Christian creed, seems to prove, if any thing, the absolute futility of the line of argument pursued by M. de Chateaubriand. (pp. 306-08)

M. de Chateaubriand enters into long comparisons between the literature of ancient times and that subsequent to the introduction of Christianity. He compares Homer with Milton and Dante, Virgil with Racine. Characters and descriptions are balanced against each other; Priam is compared with Lusignan, Penelope with Eve, Dido with Rousseau's Julie and Richardson's Clementina. All this is very agreeably written, and capable of affording much amusement, but we cannot perceive its utility, we cannot perceive that it leads us to any satisfactory result. . . . It was desirable in the outset to have proved two things, before M. de Chateaubriand could proceed with his argument; one, that the chief poetical merits of Christian writers are to be traced solely to their religious sentiments; the other, that no high degree of poetical excellence can exist independent of or in opposition to true religion. Now, neither of these positions is susceptible of proof. Even in a religious epic, like that of Dante, it cannot be said that some of the most remarkable beauties are in any degree attributable to the Christian faith of the author. The masterly description of Ugolino and his children might have been written by a Heathen poet, and the strange manner in which he has interwoven Catholic legends with Pagan mythology in his visit to the Inferno, under the guidance of Virgil, render him a very bad example for M. de Chateaubriand's purpose. . . . Neither, we fear, can it be shown that poetical beauties of a very high order are not compatible with immorality and absence of all religious feeling. The works of Lord Byron and of Shelley contain examples too strong to be resisted. It is useless to contend that poetry, of which the tendency is immoral or irreligious, is not, *as poetry,* to be considered good. . . . It would be as useless to say that immoral verse is necessarily unpoetical, as that an immodest woman is necessarily ugly. If any one, in his zeal for female virtue, were to endeavour to maintain this untenable proposition, and would try to prove an inseparable connection between moral excellence and personal beauty, he would scarcely be acting more unwisely than, in our opinion, does M. de Chateaubriand in attempting to establish an intimate connection between poetical beauty and religious faith. (pp. 308-09)

M. de Chateaubriand frequently writes as if he did not know what "a proof" is. With him any circumstance that co-exists with another, or illustrates it, or can be connected with it in his imagination, is readily accepted as a proof. We do not require that any writer should now undertake to prove to us the immortality of the soul. But if it is still thought advisable to prove what, we trust, hardly any rational mind denies, we should be glad to have something more sound and cogent than M. de Chateaubriand has afforded us. We would suggest that the fifth commandment is in no respect applicable to the question, and that in the opinion of the best theologians the promised reward of long life refers only to existence in this world. But says M. de Chateaubriand, "il y a une autre preuve morale de l'immortalité de l'ame, sur laquelle il faut insister, *c'est la vénération des hommes pour les tombeaux* [there is another moral proof of the immortality of the soul, which must be insisted upon; it is mankind's respect for graves]." Now whether this vague expression be intended to imply our wish to be commemorated by a visible memorial after death, or our respect for the tombs of others, it is equally incapable of affording any proof of the immortality of the soul. (p. 310)

It is truly lamentable to see such a question discussed in so puerile a manner. So worse than puerile, so dangerously weak are the arguments brought forward, that if any one is so unfortunate as to doubt that he is an immortal being, we earnestly conjure him not to have recourse for his conversion to M. de Chateaubriand's *proofs.*

M. de Chateaubriand, as sometimes happens where the reasoning faculty is not predominant, still loves the appearance

of method and arrangement. He attends very laudably to those contrivances which conduce much to ensure clearness and make a subject seem easy and palatable to its readers. He carefully distributes the portions of his theme; is minutely observant of subdivisions; and, whatever may be found in the body of his work, the most lucid order generally reigns in his table of contents. There is also a very imposing appearance of logical precision in the concise and *tranchant* manner in which he sometimes states a question, or sums up the result of an inquiry. (pp. 313-14)

At the conclusion of the *Génie du Christianisme,* we find, concisely drawn up in the form of a logical deduction, what he calls "le resultat de cet ouvrage." It runs as follows:—

> Le Christianisme est parfait: les hommes sont imparfaits.
> Or, une conséquence parfaite ne peut sortir d'un principe imparfait.
> Le Christianisme n'est done pas venu des hommes.
> S'il n'est pas venu des hommes, il ne peut être venu que de Dieu.
> S'il est venu de Dieu, les hommes n'ont pu le connaitre que par révélation.
> Donc, le Christianisme est une religion révelée.

[Christianity is perfect: Man is imperfect. A perfect consequence can not come from an imperfect principle. Christianity, therefore, did not proceed from man. If it did not proceed from man, it can only come from God. If it came from God, men only know it by revelation. Therefore, Christianity is a revealed religion].

This at the first glance looks logical enough; but when we examine it, what do we find? An inversion of the true order of reasoning—an assumption of contested principles as if they were undeniable axioms. His second step requires proof. It is not as certain as an axiom of Euclid, that instruments imperfect in their general nature may not produce a perfect result. His fourth and fifth steps contain extensive grounds for cavil. "Whatever does not proceed from man," he tells us in the fourth "must come from God." Now the agency of man does not, as this passage would imply, exclude the superintending agency of God. This passage can therefore properly refer only to that which it neglects to specify—the *direct* and *visible* agency of the Deity. But, must every thing have proceeded either from man or from the direct interposition of God? We will not enter into that difficult and extensive subject—the origin of evil; but we would ask M. de Chateaubriand, if he means to reject those portions of Scripture which mention the existence of evil spirits? and if he recollects through whose assistance the unbelieving Jews chose to maintain that our Saviour cast out devils? He next assumes that whatever comes from God can be known to man only by revelation. He should have told us what he means by "revelation." We presume he means a direct intimation communicated otherwise than by the ordinary course of nature. His proposition therefore amounts to this; that the Deity *could not* convey to mankind the knowledge of a religious dispensation without a perceptible departure from the ordinary course of nature. These, be it remembered, are M. de Chateaubriand's *axioms*! But what is most remarkable is the inutility of the whole argument. He takes as premise what an opponent would contest just as much as the conclusion, and what, moreover, is less susceptible of proof. The Christian admits both premise and conclusion—both that Christianity is perfect, and that it was revealed; but he admits the former less as the proof than as the consequence of the latter. The sceptic admits neither. The argument is useless if addressed to the believer; and it is equally useless if addressed to the unbeliever, for he rejects the foundation on which the whole is made to rest. Yet we may presume that M. de Chateaubriand considered this passage a masterpiece of effective logic, inasmuch as he has employed it by way of a corollary to a very extensive and elaborate work.

As a critic, M. de Chateaubriand is not entitled to much praise. His opinions and views in literature are not liberal and comprehensive. He looks at the extrinsic more than at the intrinsic, and has not profited by the advancement of the age. He is of the school of Rollin, Bossu, and La Harpe, and is moreover a very Frenchman in his judgment on the literature of other nations. ''Si nous jugeons avec *impartialité*,'' says he, ''les ouvrages étrangers et les nôtres, nous trouverons toujours *une immense supériorité* du côté de la littérature Française [If we impartially judge foreign works and ours, we will always find an immense superiority on the part of French literature].'' This amusing specimen of impartiality occurs in a dissertation upon Young, whose Night Thoughts he does not think sufficiently pensive—mistranslates a few of his weakest passages, and compares them with sundry melancholy extracts from other writers, in which, after all, we must confess our inability to discern that superiority which is so apparent to M. de Chateaubriand. (pp. 315-16)

M. de Chateaubriand has written five novels—*Atala, René, Les Natchez, Le Dernier Abencerrage,* and *Les Martyrs*—all similar in tone, and apparently composed in exemplification of the principle maintained in his *Génie du Christianisme,* namely, the applicability of Christianity to the purposes of poetical or fictitious narration. . . . *Atala, René,* and *Les Natchez,* are parts of one long tale . . . , all treating alike of savage life in the forests of North America. Our author's view of savage life seems to correspond nearly with that of Rousseau, whose writings made an impression which even actual experience was not sufficient to subdue. . . . Of these three tales, *Atala,* though faulty, is perhaps the best. It is a short tale of simple structure, containing no complication of plot or diversity of incident and character, few events, and only three prominent personages. . . . This tale defeats its object. M. de Chateaubriand, both in this and other of his writings, intends to advocate religious vows, and holds celibacy in especial reverence. But if he had meant to write against such vows, he could hardly have constructed a tale better calculated for such a purpose than the story of Atala. But for this vow all might have been well. Now example is better than precept, and a few sentences laudatory of celibacy in the mouth of the missionary will weigh little with the majority of readers against a practical illustration of its evil consequences. Atala is the most interesting character in the work, and we are taught to regard her as a Christian heroine; but the good effect of the religious sentiments which are put into her mouth is completely neutralized by the termination of her life in suicide. In *René* we find religious vows again interwoven with the story. The sister of Réné the hero of the tale, flies to a convent and takes the veil, as a means of effectual separation from her brother, for whom she had conceived an unhallowed passion. This is ill-imagined. Unnatural love is revolting to our feelings; nor can it place a convent in a favourable light to represent it as an asylum for the worst of criminals. Besides, if resistance to a temptation be meritorious (as who can doubt), it must be still more meritorious when effected without the forced interposition of doors

and walls. *Atala* and *Réné* have each a merit which *Les Natchez* wants—brevity. We mean only that their length is less, not that they exhibit greater terseness and compression of style. In these requisites they are alike deficient; and, short as they are, we cannot help wishing that the small portion of incident they contain had been less elaborately beaten out. But if this is felt in *Atala* and *Réné,* still more is it felt in *Les Natchez,* which is long, heavy and ill-constructed, deficient in unity of style and skilful conduct of plot, and offensive to good taste, both in the absurd jumble of its *machinery,* and the aggravated horrors of its tragical termination. (pp. 318-20)

We should have expected . . . from the tone of [the final] passage, that we were to be made to sympathize with the oppressed Indians in their attempts at liberation: but the author's nationality struggles successfully with his admiration of ''l'homme de la nature'' [the man of nature]. He cannot resolve to take part decidedly either with French or with Indians; and the result is a degree of impartiality very detrimental to the interest of the story. (p. 320)

We wish we could say of the machinery in *Les Natchez* that it is merely ridiculous; but it is worse. As long as M. de Chateaubriand chose to confine himself to ''headstrong'' allegories and Pagan mythology, we could smile complacently at the use he made of them; but when he renders Christianity burlesque, and would bring on the scene even the persons of the Trinity, our disapprobation must assume a different tone. There is no writer whom we are less willing to charge with *intentional* impiety than M. de Chateaubriand; but we must deeply grieve for that strange perversion of judgment which could lead him to commit a fault which we are persuaded he would himself be foremost to censure. The whole of the [fourth book] of *Les Natchez* is more or less objectionable, and the concluding part of it cannot be read without pain by any right-minded person. (p. 322)

Les Martyrs, which is very superior to *Les Natchez,* has more decidedly the character of a prose epic, and the elevation of its style is more in keeping with the antiquity and dignity of its subject. . . . It abounds, perhaps, more than any other of his works, in eloquent passages and brilliant specimens of descriptive talent, but as a story it is ill constructed. It contains numerous episodes and recitals, which, though good in themselves, impede the progress of the action, allow the interest of the tale to cool, and in no way contribute to the furtherance of the plot. This want of skill in the conduct of a story is visible alike in all M. de Chateaubriand's novels, and is one of the chief impediments to his success in this department of literature. By him the art of making every circumstance converge to one common centre of interest is comparatively disregarded. Even where the tale is short, and the action simple, he cannot abstain from frequent digression. The bent of his genius is meditative and descriptive, but not at all dramatic. With him the novel is not so much an exposition of human character and actions, as a receptacle for the introduction of sentiments and descriptions. It is a convenient framework, wherein he may place some of the most brilliant extracts from his diary and common-place book. His novels, his travels, and his *Génie du Christianisme,* may, in truth, almost be considered as portions of one extensive work. Each is enriched in turn by contributions from the other; and, though the form is different, one tone and aim predominate in all. We have said that his genius is not dramatic: this is true, not only as regards his conduct of a plot, but as regards his deficiency in that quality which is still more essential to dramatic effect—the power of exhibiting character, and placing personages vividly before us. This M. de Chateaubriand does not do. He cannot individualize his personages: they are mere vehicles for abstract sentiments, imaginary mouthpieces for rendering to the world the opinions and feelings of the author. We never seem to know them; for never can we imagine them alive and actually before us. Their words may be eloquent and well-chosen, but they do not seem to lead us to the knowledge of any mind save that of M. de Chateaubriand. Even the local colouring which he throws around them serves little to impress upon us any sense of their reality. Chactas, in his native woods, wearing his native dress, seems to us not an Indian, but a Rousseau-like creation, compounded of ideal attributes—an exemplification of the sentimental philosophism of Europe travestied in a savage garb. Compare Chateaubriand's savages with those of Cooper, and we feel at once the difference. The former may describe as correctly their habiliments and their ceremonies; but Cooper's Indians are living men, and we understand them as though we had known them; while Chateaubriand's seem never to have lived but in the flowery pages which narrate their deeds.

The peculiar *forte* of M. de Chateaubriand is description. It is this which constitutes a large part of the merit of his novels: it is this, too, which renders his Travels, in spite of their inaccuracy, peculiarly agreeable. Modern literature contains few things superior to his description of the Dead Sea, in the *Itinéraire de Paris à Jérusalem.* We may also cite the descriptions of the first view of the Holy Land, of Jerusalem, of Alexandria, of Athens, of Sunium, of the desolation of the Piraeus, and of the mode of travelling in Greece. (pp. 323-25)

[Without] considering whether any of his expressions be or be not academically correct, we will confess that for us the style of Chateaubriand has a peculiar charm. We could almost read nonsense from his pen with more pleasure than sense from the pens of many others. There is a brilliancy, a clearness, and frequently a vigour in his language, which highly merit to be admired and emulated. Though confused in his reasonings, he is never confused in the exposition of his sentiments. Nothing can be more lucidly delivered than his no-reasons and false inferences; and however much we may dissent, we are seldom doubtful of his meaning. M. de Chateaubriand has distinctly a manner of his own; but still there is not much originality in his style, as will be evident to those who are conversant with the works of Fénélon, Rousseau, Buffon, Florian, and Bernardin de St. Pierre. The resemblance is not sufficiently close to warrant a charge of direct imitation, but at least it may be said that (except perhaps in his political writings) his style has been influenced by theirs. It may be said too of his prose, as of that of Rousseau, Buffon, and St. Pierre, that it is more truly poetical than any French verse, and especially more than the verse of M. de Chateaubriand himself. He, together with sundry other French writers, seems, like Antaeus, to lose his strength when lifted up from the solid ground of level prose. (pp. 326-27)

M. de Chateaubriand's active career is, we trust, still far from its close. We trust he is still destined to adorn the literature of his country with works more solidly advantageous, more permanently redounding to his own fame, than any he has yet produced. We are justified in this expectation by observing that, without any concomitant decrease of imaginative power, judgment and good taste have progressively exercised a more decided influence from the earliest period of his authorship. His is a mind of which the reasoning faculties have been overshadowed and hidden by the vast luxuriance of his fancy;

and in proportion as the latter has been pruned and repressed, the former have been more effectually developed. We should hail with pleasure, what we trust is possible, another edition of his "Oeuvres Complètes," enriched with the added fruits of his matured experience, and unencumbered with those gaudy weeds, which, with an unfortunate excess of parental indulgence, he has forborne to pluck out from the one now before us. (p. 334)

> *[T. H. Lister,] "Chateaubriand's 'Works'," in* The Foreign Quarterly Review, *Vol. X, No. XX, October, 1832, pp. 297-334.*

FRANÇOIS RENÉ de CHATEAUBRIAND   (essay date 1833)

As it is not possible for me to foresee the moment of my end; as at my age the days accorded to man are but days of grace, or rather of reprieve, I propose, lest I be taken by surprise, to make an explanation touching a work [*Mémoires d'outre-tombe*] with which I intend to cheat the tedium of those last forlorn hours which we neither desire, nor know how to employ. (p. xxi)

[Our] writers have been men leading detached lives, and their talents have perchance expressed the spirit but not the deeds of their age. If I were destined to live, I should represent in my person, as represented in my *Memoirs,* the principles, the ideas, the events, the catastrophes, the idylls of my time, the more in that I have seen a world end and a world commence, and that the conflicting characters of that ending and that commencement lie intermingled in my opinions. I have found myself caught between two ages as in the conflux of two rivers, and I have plunged into their waters, turning regretfully from the old bank upon which I was born, yet swimming hopefully towards the unknown shore at which the new generations are to land.

These *Memoirs,* divided into books and parts, have been written at different times and in different places: each section naturally entails a kind of prologue which recalls the occurrences that have arisen since the last date and describes the place in which I resume the thread of my narrative. In this way the various events and the changeful circumstances of my life enter one into the other; it happens that, in moments of prosperity, I have to tell of times of penury, and that, in days of tribulation, I retrace my days of happiness. The diverse opinions formed in diverse periods of my life, my youth penetrating into my old age, the gravity of my years of experience casting a shadow over my lighter years, the rays of my sun, from its rise to its setting, intercrossing and commingling like the scattered reflections of my existence, all these give a sort of indefinable unity to my work; my cradle bears the mark of my tomb, my tomb of my cradle; my hardships become pleasures, my pleasures sorrows, and one no longer knows whether these *Memoirs* proceed from a dark or a hoary head.

I do not say this in self-praise, for I do not know that it is good; I say what is the fact, what happened without reflection on my part, through the very fickleness of the tempests loosed against my bark, which often have left me but the rock that caused my shipwreck upon which to write this or that fragment of my life.

I have applied to the writing of these *Memoirs* a really paternal predilection; I would wish to be able to rise at the ghostly hour to correct the proofs: the dead go fast. (pp. xxiv-xxv)

A year or two of solitude spent in some corner of the earth would suffice to enable me to complete my **Memoirs;** but the only period of rest that I have known was the nine months during which I slept in my mother's womb: it is probable that I shall not recover this antenatal rest until I lie in the entrails of our common mother after death.

Several of my friends have urged me to publish a portion of my story now: I could not bring myself to accede to their wish. In the first place, I should be less candid and less veracious, in spite of myself; and then, I have always imagined myself to be writing seated in my grave. From this my work has assumed a certain religious character, which I could not remove without impairing its merit; it would be painful to me to stifle the distant voice which issues from the tomb, and which makes itself heard throughout the course of this narrative. None will be surprised that I should preserve certain weaknesses, that I should be concerned for the fate of the poor orphan destined to survive me upon earth. Should Minos judge that I had suffered enough in this world to become at least a happy Shade in the next, a little light thrown from the Elysian Fields to illumine my last picture would serve to make the defects of the painter less prominent. Life does not suit me; perhaps death will become me better. (p. xxv)

> *François René de Chateaubriand, in his* The Memoirs of François René, Vicomte de Chateaubriand, Sometime Ambassador to England, Vol. I, *translated by Alexander Teixeira de Mattos, G. P. Putnam's Sons, 1902, 262 p.*

THE NEW MONTHLY MAGAZINE AND LITERARY JOURNAL
(essay date 1836)

[In his *Essai sur la littérature anglaise,*] Chateaubriand says, in an admirable spirit of candour, "In living literature no person is a competent judge but of works written in his own language. I have expressed my opinion concerning a number of English writers; it is very possible that I may be mistaken, that my admiration and my censure may be equally misplaced, and that my conclusions may appear impertinent and ridiculous on the other side of the Channel." They can appear neither ridiculous nor impertinent; we may, and we do differ from many of these conclusions, but we feel that they have been drawn by a clever man, and drawn, too, in a spirit of candour. If any man be entitled to form a judgment, that man is Chateaubriand. A poet himself, his whole life has been a poet's education, and he has studied our literature next to his own. But there is something in the French and the English character so essentially opposed, that it is impossible for them to understand each other. . . . There is a curious little instance of the mistakes inevitable to foreign critics: Chateaubriand quotes, as a charming specimen of our simple ballad poetry, a stanza of a song:—

> Where tarries my love,
> Where tarries my love,
> Where tarries my true love from me?
> Come hither my dove,
> I will write to my love,
> And send him a letter by thee.

He appears perfectly ignorant that the song is a burlesque. (pp. 62-3)

The genius of Chateaubriand is best characterized by the word—picturesque. In the North, he dwells with delight on the massive cathedrals, where painted windows shed

A dim, religious light;

and on the fallen castles, where the ivy is now the only banner. In the South, he is impressed with the cedar rising like a natural temple, and with the stately relics of

The marble wastes of Tadmor.

He was the first who introduced into French literature that feeling for the beauty of nature, and that tendency to reverie, which are of Scandinavian origin. But we shall give the more accurate idea of a very remarkable work, by selecting portions for examination. We shall therefore pass in review the observations on [Shakspeare and Milton]. . . . (p. 64)

The great fault of Chateaubriand's remarks on Shakspeare is, that they address themselves to a by-gone school of criticism; Dr. Johnson's is very far from being the national opinion; and the alterations and adaptations made in Charles the Second's time are held anything but orthodox in the present day. But we shall not enter into the question of preference between the rival queens of the French and the English stage: the foreign critic does not and cannot understand us. But what does our author mean by saying that "all Shakspeare's young female characters are formed on one model?" He might as well say that the rose and the violet resemble each other because they are both sweet. Take, for example, two placed in similar situations—namely, disguised in male attire; and yet what can be more essentially different than the characters of Rosalind and Viola? The last, whose heart

> Tender thought clothes like a dove,
> With the wings of care,

dreaming, devoted, silent, but dying of her silence. The first, on the contrary, is "a gay creature of the element"; a coquette, who delights in teasing the lover, whose danger yet sends the blood from her cheek—witty, sarcastic, with her deeper feelings shrouded as it were in sunshine. What have she and Viola in common? (p. 65)

But Shakspeare has always been a point for dispute between ours and foreign critics. We confess that the present article appears to us a complete Border-land of debatable questions. But what shall we say of the opinion on the sonnets?—"There is more of poetry, imagination and melancholy, than sensibility, passion and depth. Shakspeare loved; but he believed no more in love than he believed in any thing else. A woman was to him a bird, a zephyr, a flower which charms and passes away."

We will not enter on the spirit of the sonnets, because this has already been done in so masterly a manner. . . . But we protest against the light assertion that "Shakspeare no more believed in love, than he believed in anything else!" Why, the very element of poetry is faith—faith in the beautiful, the divine, and the true. No one was ever great in any pursuit without earnestness,—and who can be in earnest without belief? It was from his own heart that Shakspeare drew his glorious and his touching creations, of which all nature attest the truth. . . .

[To Milton] Chateaubriand has brought all his enthusiasm; and his estimate of Milton is infinitely more English—we might say more true, than his estimate of Shakspeare. We should say this arises from having no standard of comparison by which to try the merits of "Paradise Lost." There is nothing like it in French literature, and the critic has no preconceived notions to whose test the foreign work must submit. . . . Thus has been produced a fine and elaborate criticism, written in the noblest spirit of appreciation. (p. 66)

L.E.L., "The Criticism of Chateaubriand," in The New Monthly Magazine and Literary Journal, *Vol. XLVIII, No. CLXXXIX, September, 1836, pp. 62-8.*

ALEXANDER SERGEYEVICH PUSHKIN (essay date 1837)

For a long time the French disregarded their neighbour's literatures. . . . The translators who tried to acquaint them with great foreign authors never dared to be faithful to their originals; but carefully transformed them and in their translations tried to make them appear as absolute Frenchmen. (pp. 452-53)

Now (an unheard-of precedent) the leading writer in France translates Milton *word for word* and announces that line-by-line translation would have been the consummation of his art, had he been able to achieve it! Such humility in a French writer, the prime master of his trade, must have greatly astonished the champions of *improved translations* and will probably have an important influence on literature. (p. 453)

There is no doubt that in attempting to render Milton *word for word* Chateaubriand could not in his version preserve accurately both the meaning and the idiomatic turns of phrase. A literal translation can never be true to its original. (p. 460)

If even the Russian language, which is so flexible and rich in idioms and locutions, so derivative and adaptable in its relations with foreign languages, is not suitable for line-by-line or word-for-word translations, how can French, so cautious in its habits, so jealous of its traditions, so unfriendly even to those languages which belong to the same family, endure such a test? This is especially true in a tussle with Milton's language—a poet at once refined and naïve, sombre, obscure, expressive, independent and audacious to the point of absurdity.

The translation of *Paradise Lost* is a commercial venture. Chateaubriand, a leading contemporary French writer, the teacher of all the writers of the present generation, having been at one time a prime minister, and several times an ambassador, translated Milton in his old age *for a crust of bread*. Whatever the standard of the work thus undertaken, the work itself and its purpose does credit to the famous old man. . . . Chateaubriand stands in no need of indulgence: he has appended to his translation two volumes [*Essai sur la littérature anglaise*] as brilliant as all his former works, and critics can be as stern as they like about its shortcomings, its indisputable beauties, the pages worthy of the great writer's best period, will save this book from the neglect of readers, in spite of all its shortcomings.

English critics were stern in their censure of the *Essai sur la littérature anglaise*. They found it to be too superficial, too incomplete; taking the title on trust they expected to find in Chateaubriand both learned criticism and an absolute knowledge of subjects with which they themselves are closely familiar, but that is not at all what one should have looked for in this brilliant survey. In the field of learned criticism Chateaubriand lacks firmness, he is timid and quite unlike his usual self; he speaks of writers he never read; in his judgements he skims over the surface of his subjects, treating of them at second hand, and somehow scrambles through the dull task of the bibliographer; but inspired pages constantly flow from his pen, he is for ever forgetting his critical researches and freely develops his ideas on the great epochs of history, comparing them with those of which he himself was a witness. There is much sincerity, much heartfelt eloquence, much simplicity (at times

childish, but always winning) in these fragments, having no connection with the history of English literature, but forming the most valuable part of the *Essai*. (pp. 460-61)

Alexander Sergeyevich Pushkin, in an extract from "The 'Sovremennik'" (originally published under a different title in Sovremennik, *Vol. 6, 1837), in his* Pushkin on Literature, *edited and translated by Tatiana Wolff (translation © 1971 by Tatiana Wolff), Methuen & Co Ltd, 1971, pp. 452-63.**

BLACKWOOD'S EDINBURGH MAGAZINE (essay date 1849)

[Chateaubriand's style is less pictorial than that of Lamartine] but more statesmanlike. The French of all shades of political opinion agree in placing him at the head of the writers of the last age. This high position, however, is owing rather to the detached passages than the general tenor of his writings, for their average style is hardly equal to such an encomium. He is not less vain than Lamartine, and still more egotistical,—a defect which . . . he shares with nearly all the writers of autobiography in France, but which appears peculiarly extraordinary and lamentable in a man of such talents and acquirements. His life abounded with strange and romantic adventures, and its vicissitudes would have furnished a rich field for biography even to a writer of less imaginative powers. (p. 302)

Such a life of such a man cannot be other than interesting, for it unites the greatest possible range and variety of events with the reflections of a mind of great power, ardent imagination, and extensive erudition. His autobiography, or *Mémoires d' Outre Tombe*, as it is called, was accordingly looked for with great interest. . . . The three first volumes certainly disappointed us: chiefly from the perpetual and offensive vanity which they exhibited, and the number of details, many of them of a puerile or trifling character, which they contained. The fourth volume, however, . . . exhibits Chateaubriand, in many places, in his original vigour; and if the succeeding ones are of the same stamp, we propose to return to them. (p. 304)

"Autobiography-Chateaubriand's Memoirs," in Blackwood's Edinburgh Magazine, *Vol. LXVI, No. CCCCVII, September, 1849, pp. 292-304.*

C. A. SAINTE-BEUVE (essay date 1850)

I have not said anything like all I had to say on M. de Chateaubriand's [*Mémoires d'Outre-Tombe*]. Their success has been greatly revived the last few months, or at least the impression they have made, of whatever nature it may have been, has been very strong. . . . M. de Chateaubriand's pen is like Roland's sword, which sends forth flashes of light; but here, on the matters of 1830, it is the sword of the *mad* Roland (*Orlando furioso*), which strikes at random in the frenzy of its vanity, in its rage at not having been everything under the rule of the Bourbons, at feeling that, from motives of honour, it can and should not be anything under the new reign, in his desire that this world, to which he no longer belongs, should not be worth living in after him. . . . This singular rage, at times laughable and pitiful, at times sublime in its Juvenal-like outbursts, often restores to his literary genius all its colouring and all its temper. But I shall return to discuss more thoroughly this amazing character of the politician . . . : to-day I only wish to speak of Chateaubriand the romancer, the romantic and amorous Chateaubriand.

That, too, is a very essential side of Chateaubriand, a vein which is bound up with the depths of his nature and his talent. Long ago I defined Chateaubriand to myself as *an Epicurean with a Catholic imagination*. But this demands an explanation and an unravelling. (pp. 116-17)

Now, as all who have known M. de Chateaubriand know that [his *amours*] occupied a great place in his life, it follows that these **Memoirs,** which tell so many truths to all the world and about himself, do not, however, contain everything about him, unless they are supplemented by a commentary. We, in our turn, will be very discreet, only endeavouring to define well that fundamental chord as it concerns the soul and the talent of the great writer. (p. 118)

Only in his reminiscences of childhood, perhaps, has, the author dared or tried to say a little more [than the minimum]. But still, charming and real as the Lucile of the **Mémoires d'Outre-Tombe** is in certain respects, there is less said about her perhaps and her hidden wound, than in the few pages in which the Amélie of **René** was described. As to the other emotions of his young years, M. de Chateaubriand was contented to obscure them poetically behind a cloud, and to enter them in a mass to the account of a certain *Sylphide*, who is brought in to figure in an ideal way the little errors of adolescence or of youth which others would no doubt have complacently described, and which M. de Chateaubriand preferred to cover with a vague and blushing vapour. We do not blame him for it, we merely remark it.

The only episode in which the author of the **Memoirs** has exhibited himself with the greatest appearance of truth and artlessness, is that which concerns Charlotte, a fresh picture of a natural and domestic romance, which stands out from the narrative of his exile. . . . [The story is] told with charm, poetry and truth, with the exception, however, of two or three touches which disfigure the graceful picture. Thus, beside the young Miss Ives, there is too much mention of the mother, *almost as beautiful* as her daughter, that mother who, when she is about to confide to the young man the secret she has wrung from her child's heart, becomes confused, drops her eyes and blushes: 'There is no feeling that she herself, so fascinating in her confusion, could not have aroused'. It is an indelicacy to insist so much on this pretty *Mamma*, We ask ourselves what idea was crossing the mind of the narrator, at that moment which should have been entirely devoted to the chaste and painful memory. Supposing that such an idea entered his head, he should never have written it. This betrays, by the way, the licentious tastes which the noble author indeed had, as those assure us who knew him well, but which he concealed so magnificently in his early writings: as he grew older, his pen could no longer restrain itself.

In the case of Charlotte's mother, it is both a piece of bad taste and the sign of a heart that was indifferently touched. The end of the Charlotte episode is spoiled by other touches of bad taste and fatuity. He wonders what would have become of him if he had married the young English girl, if he had become a *gentleman* sportsman: 'Would my country have lost much by my disappearance?' The reply to such a question might be an interesting one to discuss; one might support reasons for and against; one might trifle agreeably on the subject, and, if one became entirely eloquent and serious, the reply might not be very amusing, and might even be terrible, for him who challenges it.

When M. de Chateaubriand tries to describe the grief he felt at the time, after he had broken Charlotte's heart, he hardly

succeeds in convincing us; some false tones reveal the romancer who is arranging his picture, and the writer speaking in set phrases: 'Attached to my steps by thought, Charlotte, graceful, tender-hearted, followed me, purifying them, through the paths of the *Sylphide* . . .' and so on. Can you not feel, indeed, the literary and poetic phrase that tries to feign an accent of emotion? The scene in London, when he sees her again twenty-seven years later, he as an ambassador, she as the widow of Admiral Sulton, and presenting his two children to him, might have been beautiful and touching if it had not been disfigured by a few not less offensive touches. He makes Lady Sulton say to him: 'I do not find you at all changed, *not even older* . . .'. . . . Even in this scene which aims at being pathetic, we can see that double fatuity which never leaves him, the conceit of the lady-killer who wants to be thought young, and of the literary personage who cannot help being vain-glorious. (pp. 119-22)

What M. de Chateaubriand desired in love, was not so much the affection of such or such a woman in particular as the occasion for emotion and reverie, it was not so much the person that he sought as the regret, the memory, the eternal dream, the worship of his own youth, the adoration of which he felt himself the object, the renewal or the illusion of a cherished situation. What has been called *an egotism confined to two* was with him an egotism confined to one. He thought more of disturbing and consuming than of loving. . . . He has depicted himself with his philtres and his magic, as also with his ardours, his violent desires and his tempests, in the Atala and the Velléda episodes, but nowhere more openly than in a letter, a sort of testament of René, that we read in **Les Natchez.** (pp. 122-23)

René, who thinks he is in danger of death, writes to Céluta, his young Indian wife, a letter in which he reveals to her the secret of his nature and the mystery of his destiny. He says to her: . . .

> 'Céluta, there are existences so tempestuous that they seem to accuse Providence and *would cure one of the mania of being*. From the beginning of my life I have not ceased to nourish sorrows; I carried the germs of them in myself as the tree bears the germ of its fruit. An unknown poison mingled with all my feelings. . . .
>
> 'I suppose, Céluta, that René's heart now opens before thee: dost thou see the extraordinary world it contains? *From this heart rise flames which lack food, which would devour creation without being satiated, which would devour thyself . . .'*

That is very good, and he defines in a masterly manner that flame without heat, that irradiation without fire, which only desires to dazzle and kindle, but which also devastates and sterilizes. (p. 123)

[Chateaubriand represents himself, in another passage which is] too strong to be quoted, as if struggling, in solitude, with a phantom which mingles the idea of death with that of pleasure: 'Let us mingle our sensual pleasures with death! let heaven's vault fall upon and conceal us!' That is the eternal cry which is repeated in the mouths of Atala and Velléda; thus has he given to passion a new accent, a new, fatal, mad, cruel but singularly poetic note: he always introduces a wish, an ardent desire for the destruction and ruin of the world. (p. 124)

These divers sentiments which we find expressed in René's letter in **Les Natchez,** we might, by investigating them a little closely, verify in M. de Chateaubriand's other writings and in his life. As a poet, by giving to passion a more penetrating and sometimes sublime expression he has above all employed that method which consists of mingling the idea of death and destruction, a certain satanic rage, with the more natural and usually more tranquil feeling of pleasure; and here I must better define that sort of *Epicureanism* which is his, and of which I have spoken. (pp. 125-26)

Horace, Petronius, even Solomon, who already was a decadent, all love to mingle the idea of the one through the other. They will make their mistress sing at the hour of feasting, a funereal song to remind them of the flight of years, of the brevity of life. But here, in René, it is more than an acute melancholy, it is a kind of rage; the idea of eternity mingles with it; he would like to swallow up eternity in a moment. Christianity has come, which, when it does not bring peace, brings agitation and leaves the sword in the heart, and acute pain. Perverted Christianity revives an Epicureanism which is not the same after as it was before, and which feels the effect of its great fall. It is the Epicureanism of the Archangel. Even thou, O gentle Lamartine, in thy Fallen Angel, wast not free from it! Such is also the Epicureanism of René, of the dying Atala, when, speaking to Chactas, she exclaims: 'Now I should have wished to be with thee the only living creature on earth; now, feeling a Divinity which arrested me in my horrible transports, I could have wished that Divinity to become annihilated, provided that, locked in thy arms, I had rolled from abyss to abyss *with the ruins of God and the world!*' There we touch upon the new and distinctive tone that characterizes Chateaubriand in the feeling and the cry of passion. He was unable entirely to refrain from it, even in his story of Charlotte, which in other respects was purer and more moderate. He betrays himself quite at the end, and, in the odious supposition that he might have seduced her on seeing her again after twenty-seven years, he exclaims: 'Well! if I had clasped in my arms as wife and mother, her who was destined for me as virgin and wife, it would have been *with a kind of rage . . .*'. Was it not thus again that René wrote, in that well-known letter to Céluta: 'I have held you on my heart in the midst of the desert . . . I should like to have stabbed you to fix the happiness in your bosom, and to punish myself for having given you that happiness!' Ah! why that perpetual rage of vanity even in love? Even when priding himself on loving, this man, it seems, would like to destroy the world, to absorb it in himself rather than reproduce and perpetuate it; he would like to kindle it with his breath, to make a hymeneal torch, and involve it, to his own honour, in a universal conflagration.

What a long way from that insane and almost sanguinary voluptuousness, to Milton, to those chaste scenes that he, Chateaubriand himself, has so well translated! Milton, however, gave him a beautiful and pure lesson. Let us quickly compare that divine picture of Eve still in a state of innocence with the somewhat infernal flames that we find under René's false Christianity:

> So spake our general mother; and with eyes
> Of conjugal attraction unreproved,
> And meek surrender, half-embracing lean'd
> On our first father; half her swelling breast
> Naked met his, under the flowing gold
> Of her loose tresses hid: he in delight
> Both of her beauty and submissive charms,

> Smiled with superior love, as Jupiter
> On Juno smiles, when he impregns the clouds
> That shed May flowers; and pressed her matron lip
> With kisses pure: aside the devil turn'd
> For envy . . .

This Devil, has boastful Lucifer, is he not the same who, with all the charms of seduction and under an appearance of idle ennui, stealing again under the tree of Eden, took his revenge in more than one passage of Chateaubriand's disturbing scenes. (pp. 126-27)

> *C. A. Sainte-Beuve, "Chateaubriand as Romancer and Lover" (1850), in his* Causeries du Lundi *(April, 1850—July, 1850), Vol. II, translated by E. J. Trechmann, George Routledge & Sons, Limited, 1911, pp. 116-31.*

MATTHEW ARNOLD (essay date 1864)

As to Chateaubriand . . . , the common English judgment, which stamps him as a mere shallow rhetorician, all froth and vanity, is certainly wrong, one may even wonder that we English should judge Chateaubriand so wrongly, for his power goes far beyond beauty of diction; it is a power, as well, of passion and sentiment, and this sort of power the English can perfectly well appreciate. One production of Chateaubriand's, *René,* is akin to the most popular productions of Byron,—to the *Childe Harold* or *Manfred,*—in spirit, equal to them in power, superior to them in form. But this work, we hardly know why, is almost unread in England. And only let us consider this criticism of Chateaubriand's on the true pathetic: "It is a dangerous mistake, sanctioned, like so many other dangerous mistakes, by Voltaire, to suppose that the best works of imagination are those which draw most tears. . . . The true tears are those which are called forth by the *beauty* of poetry; there must be as much admiration in them as sorrow" [see excerpt above]. . . . Who does not feel that the man who wrote that was no shallow rhetorician, but a born man of genius, with the true instinct of genius for what is really admirable? Nay, take these words of Chateaubriand, an old man of eighty, dying, amidst the noise and bustle of the ignoble revolution of February 1848: "Mon Dieu, mon Dieu, quand donc, quand donc serai-je délivré de tout ce monde, ce bruit; quand donc, quand donc cela finira-t-il?" [My God, my God, when then, when then will I be delivered of this world, this noise; when then, when then will it all be finished?] Who, with any ear, does not feel that those are not the accents of a trumpery rhetorician, but of a rich and puissant nature,—the cry of the dying lion? We repeat it, Chateaubriand is most ignorantly underrated in England; and the English are capable of rating him far more correctly if they knew him better. Still Chateaubriand has such real and great faults, he falls so decidedly beneath the rank of the truly greatest authors, that the depreciatory judgment passed on him in England, though ignorant and wrong, can hardly be said to transgress the limits of permissible ignorance; it is not a *jugement saugrenu.* (pp. 154-55)

> *Matthew Arnold, "Joubert; or a French Coleridge" (originally published in* National Review, *Vol. 18, No. XXXV, January, 1864), in his* Essays Literary & Critical, *E. P. Dutton & Co., 1906, pp. 146-73.**

GEORGE BRANDES (essay date 1872)

We have [in René] an exceptional character encountering an exceptional destiny. And it is from this character that the melancholy and misanthropy of the new literature may be said to emanate. This melancholy and this misanthropy differ from any previously known. Molière's Alceste, for instance, the finest and most profound of his masculine characters, is only misanthropical in so far that he is troubled to the depths of his being by the meanness, the servility, the frivolous or cowardly duplicity which prevail at a corrupt and worldly court; but he is not melancholy, there is nothing morbid in his temperament, he does not bear the mark of Cain upon his brow.

The melancholy of the early nineteenth century partakes of the nature of a disease; and it is not a disease which attacks a single individual or a single nation only, it is an epidemic which spreads from people to people, in the manner of those religious manias which so often spread over Europe in the Middle Ages. René's is merely the first and most marked case of the disease in the form in which it attacked the most gifted intellects. (p. 32)

René bears that mark of Cain already alluded to, which is, withal, the mark of the ruler. The seal of genius, invisible to himself, has been set on his brow. Behind the mournful self-accusations of which his confession consists, lies the proud feeling of superiority which filled the writer's breast. (p. 33)

René's sufferings are the birth-throes of genius in the modern soul. He is the moment in which the chosen spirit, like the Hebrew prophet of old, hears the voice that calls him, and timidly draws back, shrinking despairingly from the task, and saying: "Choose not me, O Lord; choose another, my brother; I am too weak, too slow of speech." René is this first stage, the stage of unrest, of election. The chosen waits to see another follow the call; he looks around but sees none arise. . . . [As] he can discover no helper, no guide, it must be because it is he himself who is destined to be the guide and support of weaker souls. At last he follows the call; he sees that the time for dreaming and doubting is past, that the time to act has come. The crisis leaves him, not, like Werther, prepared to commit suicide, but with a firm resolve and a higher opinion of himself. Genius, however, is always a curse as well as a blessing. Even the greatest and most harmoniously constituted natures have, all their lives, been aware of the curse it carries with it. In René, Chateaubriand has shown us the curse alone. His own nature and the position in which he stood to the ideas of his time caused genius, as *he* knew it, to seem merely a source of lonely suffering, or of wild, egotistical pleasure, marred by the feeling of its emptiness and worthlessness.

Chateaubriand, the inaugurator of the religious reaction of the nineteenth century, himself possessed no faith, no enthusiasm, no real devotion to an idea. The ideas of the eighteenth century were beginning to suffer an eclipse, to look like fallacies; the great ideas of the nineteenth had not as yet taken scientific shape, and, placed and constituted as he was, Chateaubriand was incapable of anticipating them. Hence he became the leader of the reaction, the champion of Catholicism and the Bourbons. With the genius's instinctive inclination to seize on the great principle of the new age, but without the genius's infallible prevision of its real nature and faith in its final victory, he took hold of the ideas which a temporary revulsion in men's mood and sympathies had brought to light, and championed them with obstinacy, with magnificent but often hollow eloquence, with great talent but without warmth, without that conviction which permeates the whole individual and makes of him the enthusiastic, indefatigable organ of the idea. . . . Chateaubriand was consumed by ennui, incredulity, and cynicism. In one direction only, namely as a poet, and more especially a

colourist, did he break new ground; and hence it was only his youthful poetical efforts that satisfied and inwardly rewarded him. But of all his creations, René, the picture of the intellectual type to which he himself belonged, was the most successful. (pp. 33-4)

René's despondency, his egotism, his outward coldness and suppressed inward fire, are to be found independently . . . in many of the gifted authors of that period, and in a number of their best-known characters—Tieck's *William Lovell*, Frederick Schlegel's *Julius*, Byron's *Corsair*, Kierkegaard's *Johannes Forföreren*, and Lermontov's *Hero of our Own Time*. They constitute the European hall-mark with which the heroes of literature are stamped in the early years of the nineteenth century.

But what marks **René** as being more especially a product of the nascent reaction is the aim of the story—an aim which it has in common with only one of the above-mentioned works, Kierkegaard's *Johannes Forföreren*. Forming part of a greater whole which has a distinctly moral and religious tendency, it professes to be written for the express purpose of warning against the mental condition it portrays, of showing the glory and the indispensability of Christianity as a refuge for the disordered soul, and more particularly of proving by means of Amélie's example that the re-establishment of convents is imperative, because salvation from certain errors is only to be found in the cloister. The pious intention of the book and its very profane matter conflict in a manner which is not particularly edifying. But this too is a typical trait of the reaction; we find it again, for instance, in the first parts of Kierkegaard's *Enten-Eller* and *Stadier*. The prevailing tone is a wild longing of genius for enjoyment, which satisfies itself by mingling the idea of death and destruction, a sort of Satanic frenzy, with what would otherwise be mild and natural feelings of enjoyment and happiness. It avails little that this work, like **Atala**, has an avowedly Catholic, even clerical, tendency; its undercurrent is anything but Christian, is not even religious. (pp. 38-9)

George Brandes, "René" in his Main Currents in Nineteenth Century Literature: The Emigrant Literature, *Vol. I (originally published as* Hovedstremninger i det 19de Aarhundredes Litteratur: Emigrantlitteraturen, *Kjebenhavn, 1872), W. Heinemann Ltd., 1923, pp. 29-42.*

THE MONITOR   (essay date 1879)

French poetic prose dates from the appearance of the "Atala" of Chateaubriand. He was the first who introduced *couleur locale* into French descriptive writing. In order to draw, intellectual sight is alone requisite, but to colour one must feel. Chateaubriand had the gift of poetic observation to paint the object and the emotion it elicits. There are occasional falsetto notes in his eloquent descriptions, but his manner is frequently original and grand. (pp. 398-99)

Chateaubriand's prose is far more poetic than the French poetry of his period; it is more so than that of Lamartine and Hugo—more delicately emotional, coloured, efflorescent. Some of his choicest passages are to be found in "René." . . . "René" is a melodious dream of a soul placed amid the harmonies of the universe. It is vaguely ideal, full of mysterious beauty. Among its lovely passages is that which depicts the impression made on the mind by hearing the village bells of a Sabbath in a wood, that primitive green temple. Leaning against the trunk of a beech-tree, René listens in silence to the sacred sounds undulating on the air, and gently stirring the leaves with their vibrations. They recall the simplicity of rural manners, the innocence of early days, their affections and fancies, and, in the calm solitude, the holy feelings of religion, family, country—bells that rang when the infant was born, which recall the joys of the father, the pains and joys of the mother; bells which rang amid the silence of death, and whose voice is associated alike with the cradle and the tomb. If we were to seek for a physical image to represent the lofty, tender and ideal genius of Chateaubriand, we should somehow select a beautiful chestnut tree, full of broad leaves and brown fruit—leaves which, green or richly hued with autumn, respond the varying music to each wind of heaven—through whose branches we obtain vistas of the great fresh new world in the sunset beyond the grey ocean, and of the old, sacred, lonely world toward the dawn—a tree, too, which shelters an altar raised to God, where the soul can pray, and dream of the divine. (p. 400)

N.W., "Chateaubriand," in The Monitor, *Vol. II, No. XI, November, 1879, pp. 395-400.*

MACMILLAN'S MAGAZINE (essay date 1894)

[Fame,] after all, is a "history of variations," and Chateaubriand has not escaped the fate of greater and lesser men. Yesterday he was idolised by the many; to-day they have ceased to remember him, amid the excitement caused by the appearance of a new mediocrity in literature. Nevertheless, let us hope that the man of letters has kept a niche for the author of *René* and *The Martyrs.* He at any rate, the man of letters, should maintain something of that Olympian calm which we are told was the gift of Pericles. (p. 390)

A man of letters of the rank of Voltaire, Chateaubriand certainly was not. Yet he was a great writer, and a great power in literature. (p. 393)

The Genius of Christianity was published at a time when the soul of France, after so much revolutionary bombast, was ready to listen to a human voice that had reverence in its accents. After the mockery of Voltaire and the grim burlesque of Robespierre, how beautiful, how healing were the words of Chateaubriand! This we must remember if we would give to *The Genius of Christianity* its true place in the history of religion; it may also be said to have had a considerable political significance, since it furthered so much the designs of the First Consul. . . . We may justly ascribe to the work all the political importance which the author claims for it [in his preface to the edition of 1828 (see excerpt above)].

Would it be equally important to a literary critic who, in disregard of the historical method, should apply an absolute standard to such things? Neither by the manner of its evolution nor by its style (we by no means say this distinction is ever absolute) can it be said to merit a place among things eternal. There is in the book too much of the poetry of nature and art, and too little of the poetry of the human soul. It is with a preconceived idea that he describes nature and man. He sets out with the purpose of discovering the mark of Providence in the world, and he sees it wherever he wishes to see it. . . . Would a severe thinker like Spinoza have done thus? Would Chateaubriand himself have done it, if he had not been so deficient in humour? The beauties of nature make a moral appeal to him; the quiet landscape has its voice of thanksgiving, and when the cedar of Lebanon waves in the night air it is uttering a psalm. The correct thinker has to make himself see that man

has an aesthetic side which must not be confounded with his moral nature; it is to this aesthetic side that all beautiful things, whether in nature or art, make their appeal. There is in nature no food for the religious sense; it exists only in the heart and conscience of humanity, and there alone can it find its proper nourishment. Pascal saw this; but Chateaubriand did not see it, because he was not an accurate thinker. Yet one great truth he did see with clearness, which some thinkers more powerful than Chateaubriand have failed to grasp. He saw that the moralist has no secure ground apart from a religious idea, that indeed the moral idea without God is delusive and illogical. The theologian may be a logician: even the poor hedonist in his way may be a logician; but the moralist who builds up his scheme within the limits of consciousness, and without reference to anything beyond it, is a blundering reasoner. (pp. 397-98)

It is Chateaubriand's thesis to prove that the Christian religion is superior to all other forms of religion. To this end he is not content to confine himself to its doctrines and ritual; he endeavours also to show the superiority of Christian literature and art. In this of course he gives away his case, for in literature and in art the Greeks, after all these centuries, are still supreme. Religion satisfies an inner need, and gives completeness to man's life. It is no more compelled to explain itself than the maternal instinct or the instinct of admiration; for, if it cannot fully explain itself, it can give as certain proof of its existence as any fact vouched for by science. Every European who loves order and chastity is more or less a Christian, for no man can escape utterly from the spiritual cycle into which he was born. We think Chateaubriand would have been wise if he had been content to develop such simple ideas as these. We do not, however, agree with Madame de Staël, who, on the first publication of *The Genius of Christianity,* said that it contained neither Christianity nor genius. . . . It contains a great deal of genius; and much Christianity also, though it is the sensuous side of it rather than the spiritual. It is too much on one level; it is too highly coloured, and lacks repose and unity. But, with these and other drawbacks, it is the work of a great writer.

Probably De Quincey had *The Genius of Christianity* in mind when he said that Chateaubriand had written "the most florid prose the modern taste will bear." . . . Chateaubriand's greatest fault of style is his super-eloquence; yet his prose by its construction is classical, while it is perhaps the most rhythmical prose of modern times. Rousseau's harmony of sentence speaks rather of the musician than the poet. Chateaubriand is a poet who, working in the medium of prose, is true to his medium. (p. 398)

René bears the impress of genius as strongly as any production of the modern world; it has indeed the accent of the great masters. It is easy to urge against it that in the "borderland dim 'twixt vice and virtue" the author is disposed to play a conjurer's part; equally easy is it to say, and in accordance with the experience of ages, that the artist who does this is sure to lose his balance. It is not the less true that *René* is one of the works of our century likely to interest the centuries to come. (p. 399)

[In *The Martyrs*] Chateaubriand no doubt meant the story of the Christian virgin to reflect the higher character of Christianity. It is good morals but bad art, for Velléda is the more human, the more pathetic figure. *Atala* is one of those stories which have a great charm for us at twenty-five; "good taste in literature," as Joubert says, "is a faculty of slow growth," and the years lessen the charm a little. When one is older, the graces which are chaste and mellow become more and more attractive; and thus at length the descriptions of nature and of human passion in *Atala* seem too luxuriant. We should not care to read it as often as we have read *The Last Abencerage,* a little story by Chateaubriand which we never weary of; yet *Atala* is still pleasant to read, for, though its charm has lessened, it has by no means vanished.

The thesis which Chateaubriand had expounded at such length in *The Genius of Christianity* he was bold enough to apply in *The Martyrs.* Here we have men and women whose lives shall prove the hollowness of Paganism, the satisfying beauty and inward peace of Christianity. The thesis is good; the application is open to question. A strong piece of polemics *The Martyrs* is not, but it is a noble piece of literature. It is the fate of the writers of stories dealing with the early Christian times either to paint the Pagans too black or to make them more interesting than the Christians. (pp. 399-400)

Chateaubriand calls *The Martyrs* an epic poem, and quotes Aristotle and Dionysius of Halicarnassus to show that such a poem may be written in prose as well as verse. We might have been glad to agree with these accomplished critics, if Chateaubriand by his own example had not proved that the feat is at least extremely difficult. An epic poem, says Chateaubriand, requires some kind of supernatural machinery, so he gives us angels and demons after the Miltonic fashion. A demon who talks in stately verse may be sufferable; one who talks in prose is always wearisome. Chateaubriand's angels and demons, like their author, are lacking in humour. The work has other defects, which the reader may easily discover. Yet it is the great work of a great writer; its diction is in many places perfect, by its fitness to the subject, by its rhythm, its classical construction and refinement. We are acquainted with no writing which gives so vivid a picture of civilised and uncivilised Europe in the early Christian ages. There is in the work enough genius to fit out a colony of literary men.

Chateaubriand's limitations are easily seen, and we have certainly not closed our eyes to them. We trust, however, we have not failed to convey the idea that in spite of these limitations he is a great enchanter. (p. 400)

> *"Some Thoughts on Chateaubriand," in* Macmillan's Magazine, *Vol. LXX, No. 419, September, 1894, pp. 390-400.*

BENJAMIN W. WELLS (essay date 1897)

The novel of the romantic school [in France] was to be lyric in its style, personal in its appeal. Herein lies the cardinal importance of Chateaubriand to the development of French fiction. He took up the torch of Rousseau that was already burning low and fanned it in a serener air, to a fuller flame.

The century in fiction opens with the publication of his [*Atala,* followed by *René*], both short stories but of far reaching influence and most characteristic of the mood of the next generation and of this author who was its most eloquent representative. (p. 385)

Atala purports to be a story told at the close of the seventeenth century to a melancholy young Frenchman, René, in whom the author intends that we shall see himself. It is narrated by the old indian Chactas who has been in France in the *grand siècle,* has talked with Fénelon, listened to Bossuet and to Ninon, seen the tragedies of Racine and acquired enough of civilization to combine an Homeric simplicity of picturesque

imagery with the dainty refinements of the Hôtel Rambouillet. All of which is ridiculous enough, but it serves Chateaubriand's purpose which is to bring civilization and the "state of nature" into more effective contrast than Rousseau or Bernardin had done. For Chastas, knowing the best that culture has to offer, deliberately prefers the wilderness, as does René himself and, as Chateaubriand gives us to understand, he would do also were it not that a weary condescending charity forbids him to deprive society of his presence. Both Chactas and René have had experiences somewhat similar to that of Chateaubriand and [his sister] Lucile. René loves his sister, Chactas a young indian girl who has sworn perpetual virginity. He is a captive among her nation. She saves him and to save herself they are forced to fly together. . . . As Joubert said, the passions here are "covered with long white veils." If it be urged that to the pure all things are pure, it may be replied that we know Chateaubriand is not in that category. . . . [Atala] is a martyr to a romantic and therefore false conception of duty, but this while it might detract now from the interest of the story, added greatly to its charm in 1800, in a generation already predisposed to that *maladie du siècle* of which Chateaubriand was in part the first talented exponent and in part the cause.

This is even more clearly the central point of the interest of *René.* . . . The hero of this tale, as the name implies, is the person to whom *Atala* had been related, namely Chateaubriand himself, as he aspired to be or to be thought at twenty-three. He is a young Werther, full of discouraged world-pain such as was forced on many men of genius, first by the revolt against the dry rot of eighteenth century philosophy, then by the lie direct given to the utopian dreams of the reformers by the bloody saturnalia of the revolution. Where men a decade before had felt full of hope and strength, they felt now, at last those of more delicate organization, for it is they alone who had literary genius at this time, helpless and hopeless. From this results an anxious introspection and an eager utterance of egoism that had begun with Rousseau and culminates in Chateaubriand and in Byron. Chateaubriand like all the victims of the *maladie du siècle* are prisoned in themselves. All their invention consists of creating a new environment for their individuality. Hence the growing predominance in fiction of local color. As Brunetière says "wherever the poet sets up the scenery of his work he is and remains its centre." (pp. 389-90)

[Whatever] may have been the ancestry of *René* the posterity is neither scanty nor doubtful and, though the influence was almost wholly evil and obviously so, yet its influence was so great and it so sums up and characterizes the morbid virus of romanticism that it is well to let *René* tell his story, as far as may be in his own words as he sits with his old friend the now blind Chactas and the good but stern mission-priest Souel by the banks of the Mississippi, regarding the world with indifference and his wife and child near by with a weary ennui of which we may read particulars in the Natchez quite worthy to rank with the rankest *fleurs du mal* of Baudelaire.

René is a character with whom it is hard to feel respect or patience, a man of brilliant genius who becomes the spendthrift of his talent through a complete lack of even a rudimentary sense of social duty or self-control. He has an utter lack of will, being indeed a monstrosity of egoism, . . . so self-absorbed that nothing outside himself seems worth desire or contemplation. (pp. 391-92)

At Paris René found he was only "belittling his life to bring it to a level with society," in the country he was "fatigued by the repetition of the same scenes and ideas." No wonder that after amusing himself by throwing leaves into a brook he reflects: "See to what a degree of puerility our proud reason can descend." René had reached this point in his mental and moral degeneration when he began to feel the desire of sharing it with another. His feelings, here too, are a curious perversion of mingled christianity and paganism. "Oh, God," René exclaims "if thou hadst given me a wife after my desire, if as to our first parent so to me thou hadst brought an Eve drawn from myself! Heavenly beauty, I should have prostrated myself before thee, then taking thee in my arms, I should have prayed the eternal to give thee the rest of my life."

This is Chateaubriand's ideal of romantic love. As Sainte-Beuve says, . . . "what he sought in love was less the affection of such and such a woman than an occasion of agitation and fantasy, it was less the person that he sought, than the regret, the recollection, an eternal dream, the cult of his own youth, the adoration of which he felt himself the object, the renewal or the illusion of a cherished situation" [see excerpt above]. This appears in the relation of Chactas to Atala, it reappears in the Velléda episode of the *Martyrs,* and especially in the astonishing later "relation," for it would be hardly just to speak of *love* in connection with René or with Chateaubriand, that unites René to [his wife] Céluta. (pp. 393-94)

[René] assures his long-suffering wife that the trials of his life, which seem to us to be mere figments of a morbid fancy, are such that "they might win a man from the mania of life." He would like he says "to embrace and stab her at the same instant, to fix the happiness in your bosom and to punish myself for having given it to you," precisely as Atala had desired "that the divinity might be annihilated, if only pressed in thy arms I might have rolled from abyss to abyss with the debris of God and of the world." All of which is much more suggestive of the Marquis de Sade than of the Sermon on the Mount. Again in another place René exclaims "Let us mingle sensuous joys (*voluptés*) with death, and let the vault of heaven hide us as it falls." Which again suggests a certain chapter in the *Wandering Jew* far more than any chapter of any gospel. . . . [In writing thus, Chateaubriand] only reproduced a phase of mediaeval satanism, and if satanism is poetic our sanity can only protest that that is so much the worse for poetry. (p. 396)

René and the *Natchez* are . . . as melancholy a travesty of christian feeling as *Atala.* They are wholly morbid and essentially immoral, but also essentially autobiographical in their psychology. Their charm and their popularity depended on their morbidity, which flattered an exceptional state of the public mind, and on their imagination and style to which we shall recur after speaking of the second group of Chateaubriand's fiction, the stories that resulted from his visit to Palestine. These are *The Last of the Abencerrages* and *The Martyrs.* Both may be briefly dismissed. The former is more plaintively morbid than the American stories. The young christian girl Bianca de Bivar and the gallant Moor Aben-Hamet love one another, but associations, parents, religion, combine to frustrate their love and he finally seeks a vain consolation in a pilgrimage to Mecca. Essentially then the situation is the same as in *Atala* and *René,* namely, the conflict of passion with duty or superstition or convention. All are elegies of self-torture, of which the chief cause was lack of common sense. And the same may be said for *The Martyrs* where the two episodes that give it its character as a novel, the unrequited love and suicide of the druidess Velléda and the unfulfilled loves of the virgin Cymodocée and Eudore, are characterized by the same teasing sentimental toying with sensuality. (pp. 397-98)

[*The Martyrs*], with *Atala, René* the *Abencerrages* and the *Natchez,* but on a broader field than they, is intended to bring two modes of life or of ethical conception into juxtaposition and contrast. As there it had been the civilized and the savage or the Christian and the Moorish, so here it is the *épopée* of rising christianity and sinking paganism that he sings in rhythmic prose. Indeed *The Martyrs* is *The Genius of Christianity* in action. The time is that of Diocletian. The real subject is the contrast between the christian and the pagan morality, and, what is more interesting to Chateaubriand, between the ways in which this morality manifests itself in ceremonial and sacrificial worship. For it is much less important to him that the faith he advocates should be true to salvation than that it should furnish occasion for aesthetic pleasure and pathetic emotions, that it should afford him what he describes in Atala as "the secret and ineffable pleasures of a soul enjoying itself." (p. 398)

Clearly the nearest antetype of *The Martyrs* is Fénelon's *Télémaque.* Like that work it is made the vehicle of much chronology and geography, we are carried from the Netherlands to Greece, from Rome to Egypt, we are introduced to nearly all the prominent characters of the Antenicene church and, by a daring anticipation, to some of the *philosophes* of the eighteenth century also. But the great fault of the book is its rhythmic style that hovers between prose and poetry in a way most exasperating to the modern reader. Chateaubriand may have meant to show us "the language of Genesis beside that of the Odyssey." As a matter of fact his invocations to the Muse, his scenes in heaven and hell and his spice of the marvellous, supposed to be necessary to the making of an epic *ragout,* seem singularly flat to modern taste, while on the other hand it must be admitted that certain passages, especially the *Chants de la patrie* . . . give us perhaps the high water mark of Chateaubriand's prose style.

It is this style, this art of language that is Chateaubriand's chief title to literary remembrance. His thought was very largely morbid. It is hardly worth while to enquire how far he was sincere or capable of sincerity. In society and in ethics he was a *poseur* whose fatuous conceit is endurable now only to those who have ceased to take him seriously. But he was an incomparable artist in words. And if he fell sometimes on the side to which he inclined and erred by excess of ornament, his genius was guided, guarded, saved from itself by two critical friends, Fontanes and Joubert, whose delicate taste he trusted and whose discreet counsels he gladly accepted, much to the gain of his artistic reputation. His remarkable gifts of vivid description and eloquent appeal, thus restrained from too obvious excess, produced a style of which the effect can be felt throughout the century. . . . Chateaubriand is the essential prelude not only to Thierry but to Lamartine and Vigny, to the young Hugo, to George Sand, to Michelet, to Flaubert, to Loti and to many others. It was the example of his daring that taught men to break boldly, perhaps too boldly sometimes, with literary tradition. He is the source not of beauties alone but of faults, of those exaggerations of language in pursuit of emotional effect that mar the writing even of such romantic masters as Hugo. For there was an affectation even of simplicity in Chateaubriand, that was the very antithesis of classic restraint, though this last had itself become a mannerism during the eighteenth century. As M. Faguet has happily put it, "he insisted that this indefinite imitation should cease, that France should have a literature of her own, not a borrowed one, that since she was not pagan she should drop mythology in poetry, that since she was modern she should not have an ancient literature." And that was to invite a reaction from the sixteenth century as well as the seventeenth, from Rousard as well as from Racine. (pp. 399-400)

It may be admitted that the limitations of his genius were almost as striking as that genius itself. His imagination gave a wonderful utterance to the feelings of his own and the following generations. It did little or nothing to direct or develop their thought. But yet his novels are a cardinal point in the evolution of the French literary spirit and of French fiction. They mark, perhaps, the most important date since the renascence. For, as Madame de Stael prepared the way for the romantic school in the realm of thought, philosophy, and criticism, so Chateaubriand became its master in the realm of art and of creative imagination. (p. 401)

> *Benjamin W. Wells, "The Novels of Chateaubriand," in* The Sewanee Review *(© 1897 by The University of the South), Vol. V, No. 4, October, 1897, pp. 385-401.*

FRANCIS THOMPSON   (essay date 1902)

We should hesitate to call [*Mémoires d'outre-tombe*] a masterpiece. It defies proportion and symmetry, it riots in digressions and the most prolix *minutiae* on every topic started; not a town nor a country, scarce an island, can the author visit but you must be told its history, its features, its topography; the narrative flags and is interrupted in shameless fashion: yet withal it is supremely interesting. For it is at once the relation of a very full life and of an imaginative temperament throughout its process of development. It is history, it is psychology. And it is told with fidelity, with charm, with the romancer's eye for romance. It is coloured with the writer's strong individuality. It is morbid (for Chateaubriand was morbid), particularly in the boyish details. . . . But it is vastly more. It is the life of a great imaginative writer whose wanderings, vicissitudes, misfortunes, and glories make those of Byron pale. . . . Yet this man moans that his life has been a disaster and a tragic search for happiness. All these things likewise are vanity.

Chateaubriand would have been unhappy in a serpentless Eden, where apples were licenced. He would have wept, and said the Snake was just the one thing missing: a superior person like himself could not taste the flavour of apples without it. . . . Such a man should have been a great saint or a great sinner: he was only a great writer—and modern France makes question of that. He never seized the hour, for he was always dreaming of the hour to follow or the hour past. (pp. 378-79)

. . . . .

The latter volumes of the *Memoirs* progressively decline in attraction for the general reader. Chateaubriand the statesman is less interesting than Chateaubriand the writer and wanderer: stars and orders are less brilliant than young ardours. The *Memoirs* grow like other memoirs, the anecdotes like other anecdotes, the padding bursts through the pages. Much is sheer history of the July revolution and the like, in which the writer himself plays small part. And it is small history; the last Bourbons and the men of July are poor creatures, impermissibly dull. Here a touch and there a character shows the old keenness: but on the whole Chateaubriand old is the dregs of Chateaubriand young. . . . [These] volumes impress by the man in his vigour; vaunting religion and ogling the world, vaunting indifference and vain to the point of embroidery, fascinating though one doubts whether one emotion be wholly unsophis-

ticated, and displaying in his memoirs the gifts of a novelist which he never displayed in his novels. (pp. 386-87)

> *Francis Thompson, "French Literature and Frenchmen: The Early Days of Chateaubriand" (originally published as "The Early Days of Chateaubriand," in* The Academy, *September 13, 1902), and "French Literature and Frenchmen: The Later Years of Chateaubriand" (originally published as "The Later Years of Chateaubriand," in* The Academy, *October 11, 1902), in his* Literary Criticisms: Newly Discovered and Collected, *edited by Rev. Terrence L. Connolly, S.J., E. P. Dutton and Company, Inc., 1948, pp. 377-82, 382-87.*

IRVING BABBITT   (essay date 1912)

The English writer with whom Chateaubriand is most often compared, with whom indeed he compares himself, is Byron. The influence of Byron in England, however, was slight as compared with his influence on the continent, whereas the influence of Chateaubriand, negligible outside of France, dominates the whole of modern French literature. "Chateaubriand," M. Faguet wrote some time ago, "is the greatest date in the literary history of France since the Pléiade. He ends a literary evolution of nearly three centuries and a new evolution taking its rise in him still endures and will long continue. . . . He is the man who renewed the French imagination." Nowadays we should perhaps be more inclined to date the evolution of which M. Faguet speaks from Rousseau, and to look on Chateaubriand himself as merely the eldest son of Jean-Jacques.

The relationship to Rousseau is the common bond between Chateaubriand and Byron. They both exhibit differences from Rousseau due in large measure to an aristocratic rather than a plebeian origin. They also differ from one another in that Chateaubriand championed the Middle Ages, monarchy, and Catholicism, whereas Byron waged war on authority and tradition. Yet their resemblance to each other and to their common literary ancestor is manifest in their solitary communings with nature, and in the way each is "possessed by the demon of his heart." In both men we have Rousseauism with an added touch of wildness and misanthropy. (pp. 60-1)

"The taste of Chateaubriand," says M. Merlet, "was of a different school from his talent. He defended tradition by his doctrines, at the same time that he corrupted or renewed it by his example." In much the same fashion Byron exalted Pope in theory while he was actually overthrowing the school of Pope by his practice. . . . With Byron in [his] consciously critical vein we may compare Chateaubriand as he appears in a passage like the following: "Furthermore I am not like Rousseau an enthusiast over savages and, although I have perhaps as much ground to complain of society as this philosopher had to be satisfied with it, I do not think that *pure nature* is the most beautiful thing in the world." . . . Chateaubriand has the assurance to write this in the preface to **"Atala"** [see excerpt above], a work in which he betrays on every page his passion for the primitive, and in which, so far from avoiding the monstrous in the name of *la belle nature,* he shows, as Sainte-Beuve points out, a special predilection for crocodiles! (pp. 61-2)

[Chateaubriand] stood for the clear-cut type (*la distinction des genres est née de la nature même*), and yet by his own style was encouraging one of the most fundamental of confusions, that between prose and poetry. He did more than any one else to popularize local color and at the same time pointed out its futility. "The genius of Racine borrows nothing from the cut of the clothes. . . . People imitate arm-chairs and velvet when they no longer know how to portray the character of the man seated on this velvet and in these arm-chairs." René mocks at the malady of René. "Lord Byron," he says [in his **"Essai sur la littérature anglaise"**], "has founded a deplorable school. I presume that he has been as much afflicted at the Childe Harolds to whom he has given birth as I am at the Renés who are dreaming about me. If '**René**' did not exist I should not write it again." (p. 63)

Chateaubriand attributes to the classical influence of Fontanes the fact that he had avoided the "roughness" of his romantic followers. Much, however, of Chateaubriand's disparagement of Rousseau, on the one hand, and of the romanticists, on the other, is itself a romantic trait: he is so filled with the sense of his own uniqueness that he would acknowledge neither master nor disciples.

The contradiction between theory and practice is even more flagrant in Chateaubriand than in Byron. For Byron's laudation of the old literary order actually corresponds to something in his creative writing: he is creative in such poems as the "Vision of Judgment" as well as in the outgoings of his spirit to the mountains and the sea; he is in short a far less romantic personage than Chateaubriand. He shows himself less aloof from society than the Frenchman, even in his satire of it. Chateaubriand is thoroughly creative only when uttering his own nostalgia and nympholeptic longings, or when rendering suggestively the aspects of outer nature (these moods are of course often blended). There was, in Joubert's phrase, a "talisman" that clung to his fingers, and he used this gift of glamour, not for intellectual ends, but to enrich and deepen the life of the senses. . . . On the creative side he has far less intellectual breadth than Byron, but is far superior to him as a critic. As soon as Byron reflected, says Goethe, he was a child; and then, too, he did not have at his side such "guardian angels" as Fontanes and Joubert. . . . Now Chateaubriand also had his pseudo-classical side which unfortunately overflows at times into what should have been his creative writing. He says in one of his romantic moods that he knew a Breton folk-song one line of which was worth more than all the twelve cantos of the "Henriade." Yet a large portion of his own **"Martyrs"** is at least as artificial as the "Henriade," and precisely in the same manner. He substitutes, in fact, a literary Christianity for a literary paganism, and in such a way as to justify Boileau's warning against the use of religious mysteries as vain literary ornaments. He has as implicit a faith in poetic "machines" as Father Le Bossu, and in few pseudo-epics is the creaking of the pullies with which this "machinery" is managed so painfully audible as in the **"Martyrs."**

But along with this pseudo-classicism Chateaubriand had a genuinely classical side, in other words a genuine perception of form. He would not have been capable like Byron of comparing Pope to a Greek temple. He can speak admirably on occasion of the "antique symmetry." His protest against the sentimentality of the eighteenth century has often been cited [his preface to *Atala* (see excerpt above)]. . . . (pp. 63-6)

We have then in Chateaubriand a somewhat baffling interplay of classical, pseudo-classical, and romantic elements. The only element that counts, from the point of view of his influence even in criticism, is the romantic. What men received from him was a certain type of imaginative and emotional stimulus, an initiation into the new passion and the new revery and the new suggestiveness. What they listened to was not his plea for selectiveness and "good taste," but his plea for sympathy and enthusiasm. His saying that the time had come "to substitute for the petty criticism of faults the great and fruitful criticism of beauties," a saying that only echoed Madame de Staël, was taken up by Hugo and became a favorite formula for that *critique admirative* so dear to the romanticist, the criticism that is aesthetic rather than judicial. Chateaubriand's own application of the aesthetic point of view in the **"Génie du Christianisme"** is above all a reaction from the eighteenth century; or it would be better to say a continuation of the quarrel of the eighteenth century of Rousseau with the eighteenth century of the *philosophes* and Voltaire. . . . [The transition from] aesthetic deism to aesthetic Catholicism is evidently easy. In Chateaubriand the rays of the rising sun, in addition to falling upon a glorious landscape, also fall upon the consecrated wafer which Father Aubry was at that moment lifting in the air; whereupon the narrator exclaims, "O charm of religion! O magnificence of the Christian cult!" The right title for the **"Génie du Christianisme,"** as has been pointed out, would be the Beauties of Christianity. Chateaubriand would view everything aesthetically—even hell. (pp. 66-8)

Chateaubriand boasted that by [**"Génie du Christianisme"**] he had definitively discredited the eighteenth century. "Why," he asks, "is this century so inferior to the seventeenth?" . . . Chateaubriand's explanation of this inferiority is, of course, that the eighteenth century was irreligious, and irreligious because it was unimaginative, and unimaginative because it was over-analytical. . . . "The spirit of reasoning by destroying the imagination saps the foundations of the fine arts." The sciences always bring on ages of irreligion, which are followed in close sequence by ages of destruction.

These are themes the equivalent of which we can find developed in a thousand forms by French, German, and English romanticists at the beginning of the nineteenth century. Unfortunately, the fact that a person protests against analysis and appeals from intellect and analysis to the "imagination" or the "heart" or the "soul," or, like Madame de Staël to "enthusiasm," does not tell us all that it might regarding his ultimate point of view. Joubert uttered a similar protest against "the man who has become so anatomical that he has ceased to be a man and sees in the noblest and most touching gait only a play of muscles, like an organ manufacturer who should hear in the most beautiful music only the little clicks of the keyboard." But is the "soul" that Joubert opposes to this analytical excess the "soul" opposed to it by the romanticist? That is the crucial question. The same ambiguity clings to the word "soul" as to the words "heart" and "intuition." . . . The "soul" of Chateaubriand is plainly a Rousseauistic and not, like that of Joubert, a Platonic "soul." Formulae of this kind must, of course, be applied with great caution to the mysterious unity of a living spirit—especially when the spirit is that of a man of genius like Chateaubriand. I for one should not deny him greatness of soul in any sense. Yet he is in the main intuitive of the Many and not of the One, and what he has to offer us therefore is not wisdom, but aesthetic perceptiveness.

Now aesthetic perceptiveness is in itself a precious thing, but to claim that because you are aesthetically perceptive you are therefore religious is to fall into the underlying romantic error, which may be defined as trying to make the things that are below the intellect do duty for those that are above it. "Incredulity," says Chateaubriand, "is the principal cause of the decadence of taste and genius." We recognize here the central thesis of Ruskin. It is already a dangerous confusion to refer art and religion to a common source. . . . Sensible people feel a peculiar exasperation when romantic aesthetes like Rousseau and Ruskin and Chateaubriand set themselves up as religious teachers. They feel instinctively that something is wrong, even when unable to trace clearly the nature of the error. To lack true inwardness like Chateaubriand and at the same time to become the champion of religion is simply to substitute a pose for reality. "He never questions himself," says Joubert . . . , "unless it be to find out whether the exterior parts of his soul, I mean his taste and imagination, are content, whether his thought is harmoniously rounded and his phrases musical, whether his images are vivid, etc.; caring little whether it is all intrinsically good: that is his smallest concern." And therefore we may say with Sainte-Beuve, that we are not in the year 1800 at the dawn of a great literary age, but merely of one of the most brilliant periods of decline.

Chateaubriand's slight regard for the truth of Christianity as compared with its aesthetic charm is one of the commonplaces of criticism. He has been charged with preferring beauty to truth, but it might be less misleading to say illusion to reality, since beauty after all is more than mere aestheticism. His aim, as he tells us, is less to convince our intellects than to enchant our imaginations. To the meagreness of the intellectual as compared with the aesthetic appeal of the **"Génie du Christianisme"** is due, no doubt, the fact that it has so largely ceased to interest. (pp. 68-71)

If we trace the influence of Chateaubriand we find at the beginning aesthetic and mediaeval Christians, then aesthetic mediaevalists, and finally aesthetes who are neither mediaevalists nor Christians. The essential element from the start was the aestheticism. Though he failed to convert French writers as a class to Catholicism, even aesthetic Catholicism, he did lure them into the tower of ivory. He encouraged them to cultivate their sensorium and neglect their intellect. The heart and head of the century were thus put into opposition with each other. It is partly due to Chateaubriand that M. Faguet was enabled to write his studies of modern French writers in two series—the men of imagination in one series and the thinkers in another. (p. 72)

Chateaubriand appears to far better advantage when he is dealing with Christianity not in itself, but in its relation to art and literature. Parts II and III of the **"Génie du Christianisme"** which treat of this relation, exhibit the somewhat baffling interplay I have already noted between classic, pseudo-classic, and romantic elements; and for this reason, no doubt, they have been somewhat variously judged, though on the whole more favorably than the other parts of the work. Sainte-Beuve seems especially conscious of the classic note. He discovers in Chateaubriand a native instinct for literary excellence that has been fortified and enriched by humanistic memories; and so, though making sharp reservations as to the general thesis, he accords hearty praise to the details. "All that portion of the work," says Sainte-Beuve [in his *Chateaubriand et son groupe littéraire*], "in which the author compares the natural characters in antiquity and among the moderns" (e.g. the comparison of husband and wife in Milton's Adam and Eve with the Ulysses and Penelope of Homer) . . . "abounds in delicate beauties and exquisite shadings: it is literary criticism in the grand manner." . . . Chateaubriand for his part, who was of course the very last person to underestimate his own merits, observes in the **"Mémoires d'Outre-Tombe"**: "The paragraphs in which I deal with the influence of our religion in our manner of seeing and painting . . . the chapters which I devote to investigating

the new feelings introduced into the dramatic characters of antiquity, contain the germs of the new criticism." (pp. 73-4)

[He] shows—"a thing that had not been at all understood previously—that with the same names and under somewhat similar outer forms the characters of Racine and Euripides express entirely different sentiments. Phaedra in Racine is no longer a pagan but an erring Christian wife," etc. I believe that Chateaubriand puts us on the track here of his real influence as a critic. The lesson the new criticism took to heart was that it should penetrate beyond the mere form of a work of art to the soul.

But here again it is necessary to remember that the word "soul" is in itself ambiguous. Behind the mere outer form of a work of art there may be two "souls" (both only to be apprehended intuitively), a soul in virtue of which it has a general and representative value, and a soul in virtue of which it is unique. Both kinds of soul appear vitally fused in the work of art that is completely beautiful—one making itself felt as symmetry and repose, as inner form we may say, the other as individual life and expression. Stated Platonically the complete work of art suggests to us through the medium of the imagination the presence of the One in the Many. Now the soul that Chateaubriand instinctively seizes upon and renders is not the soul that makes for form and symmetry, but the soul that makes for expression (though he leans less one-sidedly towards expression than, for instance, Ruskin).

Moreover, he not only responds aesthetically to the present object and renders it in its uniqueness but he also has the gift, closely associated in its origins with romantic nostalgia, of journeying imaginatively in time and space, and then conveying vividly what is either temporally or spatially remote. For example, he does not give us an adequate idea of the Christianity of the period he has treated in his **"Martyrs"**—that would have required more insight into the permanent element in human nature than he possessed. He is, in fact, more at home with the paganism of the period, because behind his façade of aesthetic Catholicism, he himself lived more on the pagan than on the Christian level. What he does do at his best is to conjure up before our inner eye a vision of what was peculiar to the period, of its individual expression, of the precise picturesque details by which it differed from all other periods. This art of local color evidently concerns the historian at least as much as the literary critic; and Chateaubriand counts among the important initiators into the new historical spirit. (pp. 75-7)

We thus see history [in Chateaubriand] ceasing to be abstract and colorless and becoming concrete and expressive; we see it getting rid of its old artificial unity and cultivating instead a sense of the variable in human nature—a sense that is not tempered by any new and vital perception of unity. . . . Chateaubriand posed as a champion of the old order and the fixed standards it implied, by the actual force of his example he helped forward to an important extent the main movement of the century in both history and literary criticism from the absolute to the relative. (p. 78)

Irving Babbitt, "Chateaubriand," in his The Masters of Modern French Criticism *(copyright © 1912 by Irving Babbitt; renewal copyright © 1940 by Edward S. Babbitt and Edward S. Babbitt, Jr.; reprinted by permission of Edward Babbitt), Constable & Co., 1913 (and reprinted by Farrar, Straus and Giroux, 1963, pp. 60-78).*

MARCEL PROUST   (essay date 1919)

[*The following epigraph (in italics) is an excerpt from Chateaubriand's* Mémoires d'outre-tombe.]

> *Shadowy figures, what are we beside these famous men? We vanish past recall. You, wild sweet-william, lying on my table beside this sheet of paper, whose belated little flower I gathered on the heath, you will grow up again; but we, we shall have no second spring with the fragrant recluse who beguiled me from myself.*

(p. 367)

I love reading Chateaubriand because when on every second or third page I hear him sounding (as on a summer night after an interval of silence one hears the two notes, always the same two notes, that make up a barn-owl's cry) what is his own personal cry, just as monotonous, just as inimitable, I feel sure this is a poet. He tells us that there is nothing lasting on earth, that soon he will die and oblivion bear him away; we feel he speaks truly, since he is a man like other men; but all of a sudden, by the secret power within him, he has discovered among these events and ideas that poetry which he peculiarly seeks for, and behold! the thought which by rights should sadden us, enchants us, and proves, not that he will die, but that he is alive, that he is something of a higher order than things and events and the years. . . . And when Chateaubriand while bemoaning Chateaubriand slips the jesses of that marvellous and transcendent person who is himself, we sigh for pleasure, since at the moment when he declares himself annihilated, he makes his escape and enters upon a life where there is no such thing as dying.

To be sure, he has not always been that person. Often, and above all when he sets out to be witty, sprightly, Voltairean, though we may admire we do not recognise him. But gradually, by force of sincerity, he has become it; and then, when it is that person speaking, even when it is to convince us by every possible argument that he is but dust, he inspires an exactly contrary opinion because we feel he is alive; and we sigh for pleasure. . . . We are sure that this person is a poet, a *rara avis,* since what he says is always identical, and does not borrow any grandeur, any authenticity, from any of the things he relates, which do not alter it, whereas quite suddenly, whether it is a matter of the great Condé or of a little flower gathered at Chantilly, one feels that beneath his sentence there lies another reality, which shows through from beneath it and whose physiognomy is made apparent, beneath the several clauses of the sentence, by their lineaments which correspond to it.

It is not possible to say why this reality is of a higher order than the reality of quite another kind which makes for the historical importance of events—higher than the intellectual validity of ideas, even, or the realities of death and annihilation. And yet there is something in it which surpasses events, since when he has just spoken of the fall of empires and of the mote he is in that whirlwind, the way he speaks of a little flower gathered at Chantilly—a way which ravishes us and is identical with that by which he ravishes us on other occasions—gives us the feeling of being something which, if not outlasting empires, in this sense of still retaining a personality, is at any rate so superior to time that even if one had known that the page was to be burned as soon as one had written it, one would have gone on writing in the same ecstasy, and relinquishing all else for it, so strong would be one's feeling of having given life to something real and of a reality inherently incapable of

death; from which it follows that . . . it is of a higher order than the realities of death. And as I said, it is also higher than the intellectual validity of ideas; since in saying things patently more lofty, more searching, more universal, than what he says of that little blue flower, he might not have given us any comparable sensation nor (to turn from the reader to the maker) have found any trace of what was to inspire him and make us say in the same breath, This is Chateaubriand, and, This is beautiful. For perhaps the sole proof of the subservience of the noblest ideas to that mysterious thing, one's self, is that only when we meet with it is that high excitement at hand which makes our own words an enchantment to us, and makes others say, That is beautiful. (pp. 367-70)

Marcel Proust, "Chateaubriand" (1919), in his Marcel Proust on Art and Literature 1896-1919, *translated by Sylvia Townsend Warner (© 1958 by Meridian Books, Inc.; reprinted by permission of Georges Borchardt, Inc., as agents for the author), Meridian Books, 1958, pp. 367-70.*

MARIO PRAZ   (essay date 1930)

[Chateaubriand] invested incestuous love between brother and sister with poetic charm and sentimental dignity, elaborating certain events of his own life—though to what extent cannot be verified. In *Atala* he makes the lovers' passion culminate in the discovery of bonds of spiritual brotherhood, of 'amitié fraternelle', 'cette amitié fraternelle qui venait nous visiter et joindre son amour à notre amour' [that fraternal friendship which came to visit us and to join its love to our love].

Chateaubriand is also full of longing for the 'état de nature' idolized by the Encyclopédistes, in which he imagined it possible to realize his sensual ideal, notwithstanding certain theoretical remarks in the first preface of *Atala* [see excerpt above]. He speaks with an exile's regret of the 'mariages des premiers-nés des hommes, ces unions ineffables, alors que la soeur était l'épouse du frère, que l'amour et l'amitié fraternelle se confondaient dans le même coeur et que la pureté de l'une augmentait les délices de l'autre' [marriages of the first-born men, these ineffable unions, where the sister was married to the brother, where love and brotherly friendship were blended in the same heart and where the purity of the one was augmented by the delicacy of the other]. It is an absurd regret, because the relationship of lovers between brother and sister only fascinated him inasmuch as he felt it through the consciousness of sin; and since the possibility of the latter is lacking in the primitive natural state, that particular relationship could have no different savour from a relationship between strangers.

Not content with making Atala a quasi-sister, he shows her also as a virgin who has made vows of chastity, so that to the thrill of incest is added that of sacrilege. Moreover, this love kills Atala, 'la Vierge des dernières amours'; sexual pleasure is crowned with death. There is the same mingling of incest and sacrilege in *René,* when René, as sponsor of Amélie's monastic vows, hears from her lips the confession of her 'criminelle passion' and disturbs the ceremony by embracing her upon the bier of her symbolic death: 'Chaste épouse de Jésus-Christ, reçois mes derniers embrassements à travers les glaces du trépas et les profondeurs de l'éternité, qui te séparent déjà de ton frère' [Chaste wife of Jesus Christ, receive my final embrace through the glass of death and the profundities of eternity, that already separate you from your brother]. All the voluptuousness of incest, sacrilege, and death is condensed into this short phrase.

An idyllic background in the manner of Bernardin de Saint-Pierre, added to the charm of primitive Christianity, invests the turbid and sensual subject-matter of Chateaubriand with a halo of innocence. (pp. 111-12)

Mario Praz, ''The Shadow of the Divine Marquis,'' in his The Romantic Agony, *translated by Angus Davidson (translation © Oxford University Press 1970; reprinted by permission of Oxford University Press; originally published as* La carne, la morte e il diavolo nella letteratura romantica, *Soc. editrice ''La Cultura,'' 1930), second edition, Oxford University Press, London, 1970, pp. 95-196.**

RENÉ WELLEK (essay date 1955)

Chateaubriand's concepts of poetry and literary taste are really not so far from Madame de Staël's. As with her, his nearest models are Rousseau, Bernardin de Saint-Pierre, and Ossian. Rhythmic prose about man's (and woman's) yearning for infinity and the vanity of human existence is their concrete idea of the essence of true poetry. Like hers, his literary taste is circumscribed by the system of French classicism. Both make some allowance for what might liberalize it if it could assimilate Milton and parts of Shakespeare and Dante. Like her, Chateaubriand contributed to an increased feeling for history and to an understanding of the historical setting of literature. His most important contributions to criticism are suggestions about literature's relationship to the development of religion and sensibility. (p. 232)

[Chateaubriand's literary argument in *Le Génie du Christianisme*] consists of a confrontation of passages and figures from Greek and Latin poetry with analogous passages and figures from modern writers. It is a restatement of the quarrel between the ancients and moderns, with a bias in favor of the Christian moderns. But it is hard to see what could be the critical value of showing that Milton's Adam is more ''majestic and noble'' than Homer's Ulysses; that Lusignan in Voltaire's *Zaïre,* because he exhorts his daughter to martyrdom, is a more heroic father than Homer's Priam, who humbles himself before Achilles, the killer of his son, in asking for the body of Hector. . . . In most cases the passages and characters are not comparable critically, since sonship and motherhood, outside the context of a work of art, are no criteria of excellence. The standard imposed is inevitably quite external, applicable to a comparison of figures in life and history but not in literature. Literary success and greatness is in no way connected with the moral preference expressed. . . . As argument the whole scheme of these parallels seems mechanical and even puerile.

Nevertheless, Chateaubriand has genuine critical insights. He was apparently the first who interpreted French 17th-century literature not as a revival of classical antiquity but as a Christian literature, sharply set off from the decadent period of the unbelieving 18th century. Chateaubriand had a taste for what today we would call ''baroque,'' an insight into the tensions and conflicts between love and duty, body and soul, which seemed to him basically Christian even when dressed in the costume of classical antiquity. Thus Iphigénie in Racine's tragedy is a Christian girl who obeys the call of Heaven. Thus Phèdre is a ''Christian woman reproved, a sinner fallen alive into the hands of God.'' (pp. 232-33)

When Chateaubriand goes beyond parallels and abandons his purpose of disparaging classical mythology, he can give fresh interpretations of the great French writers of the past. Pascal

and Bossuet, La Bruyère and Massillon are his Christian heroes. Even Molière and La Fontaine are seen as touched by melancholy, by a recognition of the vanity of vanities which is the great theme of Chateaubriand's writings. The exaltation of the Christian classics of the 17th century serves, besides, to support the general thesis: without religion there can be no beauty or art. (pp. 233-34)

Chateaubriand also has a feeling for nature and a gift for description new at that time. He thought that his own feeling differed from that of antiquity and tried to establish its pedigree. Antiquity, he argues, did not know descriptive poetry in his sense, the poetry of solitude, of deserts, of the infinite skies in which man disappears before the grandeur of God. Ancient mythology of nature with its naiads and nymphs makes nature small and pretty, habitable, and merely human. Only with Christianity does there come a feeling for landscape in itself, apart from man. Though the attempt to trace this descriptive poetry back to the anchorites is fanciful, Chateaubriand succeeds in distinguishing stages of descriptive writing in modern literature: the 17th-century reaction against Renaissance pastoral, the British group beginning with Thomson, the French imitators of the English. He sets himself off from these contemporaries, such as Delille, who seem to him too minute practitioners of the Georgic vein, by claiming derivation from travelers and accounts of Jesuit missionaries in the 17th century and by appealing to Bernardin de Saint-Pierre, who ''owed his talent for describing scenes of solitude to Christianity.'' The thesis is pushed too far, but it adds a further item to the great issue of moderns versus ancients. (p. 234)

Chateaubriand, in a famous essay on Dussault . . . , advises us to ''abandon the petty and easy criticism of faults in favor of the great and difficult criticism of beauties.'' His own method is mostly that of quotation, appreciation, and confrontation, accompanied by occasional remarks on versification and the use of vowels and consonants. It is never that of a characterization of a single author or work, nor is it ever a speculative, theoretical argument. When he appeals to general principles, he can think only of the commonplaces of classicism. Thus the essay on Shakespeare . . . must be classed with a criticism of faults. In it Chateaubriand recognizes that Shakespeare had great historical merits in his time, that he has insight into human nature and depicts lively and impressive scenes, but despite this he insists that Shakespeare had no art. Like the earlier French and English critics of Shakespeare, Chateaubriand is completely blind to Shakespeare's constructive skill and insensitive to his verbal texture, which seems to him only bombast. Chateaubriand thus can argue that ''writing is an art, that art has genres and that every genre has rules.'' He thinks he can turn the tables on the admirers of Shakespeare's nature: ''Racine, in the whole excellence of his art, is more natural than Shakespeare; just as Apollo, in all his divinity, has more human forms than a crude Egyptian statue.''

All of Chateaubriand's critical pronouncements are thus full of the clichés of classicism. The *beau idéal* hides the ugly and low; beautiful nature must not imitate monsters; taste is the good sense of genius, and without it genius is only sublime folly; the rules even of the three unities, are valid at all times and places because they are founded in nature. These are the standards to which Chateaubriand constantly appeals in introducing, explaining, and defending his own works. . . . *Le Génie du Christianisme* might suggest a sympathy with the symbolic concept of poetry, but actually Chateaubriand allows only allegories of qualities and affections and has a most literal-minded conception of the allegorical and figurative meaning of the Bible.

The one point of theoretical innovation, beyond the not unconventional defense of the Christian marvelous, is the emphasis on the author's share in his own creation. Chateaubriand is convinced that great writers have "put their history into their work," that "they paint nothing so well as their own heart." Without quite identifying Milton and Satan, Chateaubriand suggests that Milton depicts his own spirit of perdition in Satan and that the loves of Adam and Eve reflect Milton's marital experiences. Virgil's sadness comes from his stuttering, his physical weakness, and disappointments in love. But this view is not imposed on everything, and the general scheme of classicism is never abandoned. (pp. 235-36)

His most sustained critical work is the *Essai sur la littérature anglaise*. . . . It is, in many ways, a disappointing book, full of lacunae and errors, heavily padded with digressions on Luther, Lammenais, Danton, and others. The discussion of the early periods is all second hand, a compilation from out-of-date English sources, without discernment and sense of proportion. The remarks on Chaucer and Spenser are grotesquely inadequate and erroneous. Actually only Shakespeare, Milton, and Byron are handled at any length and with any elaboration. The chapters on Shakespeare open promisingly. Chateaubriand recognizes that he "had measured Shakespeare with a classical spy glass." But that is a "microscope inapplicable to the observation of the whole." The section ends with a eulogy in which Shakespeare is ranked with the five or six *génies-dominateurs* or *génies-mères* of literary history, alongside Homer, Dante, and Rabelais, who are all now included in this new proclamation of tolerance. But in between, Chateaubriand reproduces, word for word, his criticism of thirty-five years before, and adds a disparagement of Shakespeare's comedy and his supposedly "ossianesque shadows" of women who cannot stand comparison with Racine's Esther. The point of view remains the same: romantic writers, e.g. Shakespeare and Dante, gain by being quoted in extracts, while the monuments of classical ages have the merit of "perfection of totality and the just proportion of its parts." Shakespeare's work, Chateaubriand concludes, lacks dignity, just as his life lacked it. He had no taste: the kind of taste which appears at very rare moments of the world's history, presumably mainly in the age of Louis XIV.

Milton was by far the closest of all English poets to Chateaubriand's heart and taste. He is quoted as a witness throughout the *Génie du Christianisme*. Late in life Chateaubriand published a complete translation of *Paradise Lost* into prose, and the *Essai* adds a fairly full description of Milton's other works. Chateaubriand had a surprisingly sympathetic attitude toward even the most criticized parts of *Paradise Lost:* he defends the last books as not inferior to the earlier ones, he praises even Sin and Death and saw the point of the artillery in heaven. He wrote two remarkable pages on the theology of *Paradise Lost* which distinguish the conflicting strands of Milton's ideas in the light of a good knowledge of theological and philosophical trends. (pp. 237-38)

Chateaubriand compares himself with Byron, both aristocrats, both carrying the "pageant of their bleeding heart" through Europe to the Orient. But Chateaubriand has to establish his priority and superiority. Byron is an ungrateful imitator; he strikes an insincere attitude; he lacks faith, always a sign of superficiality. Walter Scott is dismissed as the initiator of a false genre, who also remained on the surface of things. The

view that *Les Martyrs* is an epic probably for Chateaubriand obscured the fact that he had himself written something very like a historical romance. *Les Martyrs,* based on a multitude of sources painstakingly pieced together, annotated and defended, is, after all, a precursor of nothing better than *Quo Vadis?*

Chateaubriand's criticism thus never emancipates itself from the fixed canons of the rules and taste as formulated in French neoclassicism. In its methods it is still circumscribed by techniques of rhetorical comparisons or detailed comments on individual beauties. While it cannot be given a high place in a history of literary theory or of critical methods, it nevertheless reflects the shift of sensibility to which Chateaubriand's own creative writings are an eloquent testimony. While he hardly knew or cared for actual medieval literature (with the possible exception of Dante), his writings directed attention to the feudal past, to chivalry and to Gothic churches. While one cannot say that Chateaubriand was himself a serious historian of literature (the *Essai sur la littérature anglaise* is a mere compilation), his grasp of history in general, his strong sense of the flow of time, contributed to the awakening of the historical sense of the flow of time, contributed to the awakening of the historical sense in France. His emphasis on the Christian element in the French classics of the 17th century was apparently new and helped to establish them as the source of a permanent tradition even after adherence to strict neoclassical theory had weakened. His admiration for Milton and his very qualified interest in Shakespeare parallel Madame de Staël's more enthusiastic efforts on behalf of German literature. But most personally, Chateaubriand was one of the initiators of romantic aestheticism, not only in the attitude he took toward the beauties of Christianity, especially the Catholic ritual, but also in the fervent exaltation of the eternity of art and in the cult of the superiority and apartness of the genius. . . . Yet this seems doubtful today when the memory of the past and of great literature has weakened as never before and the "immortality" of even the greatest works seems precarious. The excesses of romantic aestheticism, its all-inclusive and therefore indefensible claims to the supremacy of art, of which Chateaubriand was one of the first proponents, have contributed to a reaction which has almost destroyed the legitimate position of literature and the arts in any scheme of human civilization. (pp. 238-40)

René Wellek, "Madame de Staël and Chateaubriand," in his A History of Modern Criticism: 1750-1950, The Romantic Age (copyright, 1955, by Yale University Press), Yale University Press, 1955, pp. 216-40.*

MORRIS BISHOP (essay date 1955)

Chateaubriand was a pure Romantic, in the larger sense of the word. In the smaller sense (an adherent of a certain French literary school, with its defined doctrines and aesthetic), he was not a member, but a great forerunner, like Rousseau. He opened the way to the proper Romantics by his idealization of the mysterious ego, by his poetic, emotional description of exotic nature, by his aesthetic Christianity, by his appreciation of the Middle Ages. He transformed French prose, revealing its powers of rendering sensuous meaning in harmonious cadences. He was and is a model for the student of prose style. (p. 5)

The young American of today, inclined to find Chateaubriand insufferably vain, ridiculous in his tragic pose, untrustworthy with facts, is apt to wonder why we esteem him so highly. The answer lies in the richness of his creative imagination, and especially in the magic of his style, which redeems every shortcoming. One can compare his style only to music. In his descriptions, as of the awe and mystery of American solitudes, he sought to transpose visual sensations into musical prose. There are passages which can be played on a flute, and others which seem to call for a full orchestra. The serious student should read aloud such paragraphs as that in *le Château de Combourg* beginning ''Les soirées d'automne et d'hiver . . .'' . . . or that in *René* beginning ''La solitude absolue . . .''. . . . Then, if he has any ear for the evocative harmonies of the French language, he will understand why Chateaubriand has been called, for a century and a half, the Enchanter. (p. 7)

> *Morris Bishop, ''Chateaubriand (1768-1848), in his* A Survey of French Literature: The Nineteenth and Twentieth Centuries *(copyright 1955, © 1965 by Harcourt Brace Jovanovich; reprinted by permission of the publisher), Harcourt Brace Jovanovich, 1955, pp. 5-23.*

ALBERT J. GEORGE (essay date 1964)

Chateaubriand, the contemporary of Xavier de Maistre and Mme de Staël, could boast of a higher order of talent, and he intended to remove *Atala* and *René* from the disrepute of popular short fiction by attaching them to the poetic forms of antiquity. However, he, too, struggled with the problem of a narrative heavily burdened by explicit sentimental moralizing. In the last analysis he did not, as he had hoped, create two fragments in the style of the *Iliad* and the *Odyssey* but, at least in *Atala,* produced a latter-day version of the sentimental *conte philosophique.* (p. 23)

Chateaubriand remained more French than neo-Greek. Following tradition, he fell back on the box-car structure so popular during the eighteenth century. The chronological arrangement, with peripatetic major characters in the fashion of the *conte philosophique,* permitted him to indulge a passion for painting exotic scenes. Since he grasped storytelling primarily in terms of *sensibilité,* he graduated the scenes according to what William Dean Howells called ''effectism,'' a steadily increasing charge of emotion infused into successive episodes that came to a climax in Atala's funeral. (p. 24)

Time has not treated parts of this story kindly, but the modern reader must remember that the wandering plot, the tearful Indians, and the coincidences did not constitute faults as Chateaubriand understood brief fiction. On the contrary, he needed them for the creation of scenes he could exploit. Since he conceived the story episodically, the transitions mattered little. Only slightly occupied with cause and effect, he intended to comment on human experience, not facts, and the structure he chose filled his requirements.

There is much in *Atala* that now seems to verge on the comic and the absurd. The logical-minded find it hard to accept Chateaubriand's determination to twist a pagan love story into a religious apology proving ''les harmonies de la religion avec les scènes de la nature et les passions du coeur humain'' [the harmonies of religion with scenes of nature and passions of the human heart]. The Indian lovers have the ardent temperament of the *fin du siècle,* with the vocabulary and delicacy of an age sophisticated in such matters. One may boggle at historical inaccuracies, wince at the ''miracles'' that occur opportunely, or balk at a conversion that takes place in the middle of a seduction. Father Aubrey's utopia comes from a long line of other paradises inhabited by ''good savages'' whose proximity to nature glorifies their primitiveness. The casual attitude toward probability, the ridiculous picture of the Mississippi, and the arranged ending all provide serious obstacles to the willing suspension of disbelief. Worst of all, the plight of the lovers helps little to understand the present; *Atala,* however delightful, exudes the color of a faded past.

Yet, despite manifold objections, partisans of *Atala* can summon strong arguments in its defense. During Chactas' monologue, Chateaubriand painted word pictures powerful enough to conceal his inaccuracies. His mastery of the language, his brilliant descriptions, overshadow the plot. And if the narrative structure is understood in the author's terms, if *Atala* is accepted as a poem, the ''faults'' disappear and the work increases in stature. Certainly Chateaubriand dazzled his contemporaries, and few subsequent writers have been able to match the evocative rhythms of his prose. (pp. 24-5)

The notion of an individual, separate and unique, of an inner world that functioned according to its own dynamics, remained unknown in short fiction until Chateaubriand published *René.* Still greatly influenced by eighteenth-century custom, he nevertheless indicated new worlds to explore as he shifted the focus of his narrative from what his hero did to how he felt and reacted. The artist's vision moved from outside to inside as Chateaubriand related the story of a young man's reaction to the discovery of his sister's incestuous passion for him. (pp. 25-6)

Whereas *Atala* was a story of frustrated love, *René* dealt with the powerful turbulences that rend a human being. Emotion was no longer merely stated but described in its genesis, development, and explosive effect on a human being. To do this, Chateaubriand relied on the form that had proved so successful with *Atala,* reusing the framework device and the first-person narrator who confessed his spiritual torments. Once again he turned to description to convey mood, although this time he was attempting to relate reaction to an event as well as the event itself. . . . *René,* like *Atala,* depended for dramatic tension on an unrevealed secret that precipitated the dénouement. (p. 26)

In *René* the emphasis falls on a personality that sums up the temper of a France deep in the shock of revolution. In *Atala* Chateaubriand had narrated almost flatly, his painted descriptions lending themselves to a shallow, exterior form of writing. In *René* he moved inside the protagonist to recreate an emotional history, to explain the pressures that warp a man's psyche. Although the action was set earlier, the hero mirrored contemporary concerns. An aristocrat, René saw his world crumble with the Ancien Régime, leaving his disenchanted and conscious of impermanence. He felt alienated from society, lonely with the loneliness of the insecure, unable to act because he lacked motive and direction to give life meaning. He *felt* the *mal du siècle,* the ennui of the young born old, the confused yearning of those passed by. René suffered an exaggerated form of the despair that faces every hypersensitive adolescent and, in this case, his incapacity to struggle out of his spiritual bewilderment matched that of a culture beset with similar difficulties. Since the past offered no guidance, his search for certainty only proved once again the theme of Ecclesiastes. Nature alone remained secure. René repeated every man's pursuit of a personal Holy Grail, and his geographical wanderings were but the exteriorization of mental anguish. (pp. 26-7)

His sister Amelia's passion for him served as the organizing principle for René's spiritual adventure; he symbolized the sensitive man who paraded his great suffering as a mark of genius. He reacted to some unknown original sin like the existential man lost in the void of his own being. His indecision was transformed into purpose by Amelia's acknowledgment of her illicit love. . . . He actually came to enjoy his suffering, to convert it into an occupation. Destiny could offer this great soul only the courtesy of a punishment for his humanity beyond that accorded ordinary mortals. *René* translates the theme of intellectual alienation into physical exile, a tragic atonement for the sin of a mysteriously imposed destiny.

In *Atala* the lush paintings had almost obscured the story, but in *René* Chateaubriand put his pictorial talent at the service of the plot. The usual scenes underline mood: ruins, stormy seas, the sadness of autumn—all hallmarks of the eighteenth century's enjoyment of grief and morbidity. The bells tolled to recall the message of Christianity and to speak of loneliness and salvation. In *Atala,* Chactas had confessed; now it was René's turn. At the end of the tale René, Chactas, and Father Souel returned to the village, the three figures symbolizing Chateaubriand's meaning: René as man's confusion and suffering; Chactas, blind wisdom; and the priest, the answer to the human predicament. René walked between the two older men, supported by unseeing faith. (pp. 27-8)

The romantics found [René] the perfect exemplar of their imagined predicament; he became the model for a public personality which they paraded as proof positive of their genius. René symbolized the major problem of these artists: how to find a self, given the hostility of society toward the different and the nonconforming. As a result, Father Souel's religion was watered down into religiosity; the introspection, the aversion to life, the mystery of a great destiny, served as patterns for Hernani and Antony. In the matter of form, Chateaubriand merely continued an eighteenth-century tradition, but his word-magic and the gigantic portrait of René greatly influenced a generation seeking the respectability of ancestry. Moreover, by his exploration of the private world of the mind, the insistence on what differentiated his hero from other people, he helped destroy the hitherto accepted conception of the universal man. The romantics would continue his exploration of the subconscious, developing new psychological understanding and constructing an image of man vastly different from that dear to the classicists. René thus achieved the ultimate compliment: later generations abstracted the hero from the tale, stripped him of his fictional world, then gave him the status of human being. (pp. 28-9)

> *Albert J. George, "Transition," in his* Short Fiction in France: 1800-1850 *(copyright © 1964 by Syracuse University Press), Syracuse University Press, 1964, pp. 17-52.**

CHARLES A. BRADY   (essay date 1968)

[Except] for Cooper and Bryant—and, to a certain extent, Freneau—the wilderness *mystique* [which pervades American literature from Cooper's Hawkeye to Faulkner's *The Bear*] took firmer and earlier root in Britain and the Continent than in America. (p. 20)

The great original fountainhead—and a very ornamental fountainhead he made, too—of [that] particular aspect of the yearning for *otherness* that is so inadequately labeled Romanticism, the first major artist to feel . . . nostalgia for America's "weeds

and the wilderness," was a certain Breton of noble blood. If James was to return to Europe, the most ecstatic of secular palmers, almost a century before that the Vicomte de Chateaubriand had come here every bit as ecstatically. Decades later, remembering the forests of New York State and the foaming plunge of Niagara in almost every capital in Europe, Chateaubriand helped father the forest *cultus* for Europe out of his seminal memories of the American wilderness. He did this, for his own lifetime, through his pioneer Indian romances, *Atala* and *Les Natchez,* the most unreadable of the world's famous books, the first of which antedates the first *Leatherstocking* by twenty-two years. These preposterously bad "great books" are now as dead as Ossian; and for much the same reason. Luckily for readers today, Chateaubriand committed the experiences that provide these books *données* to his *Voyage en Amérique* which, revised, was later incorporated in one of the very greatest books of its great age, his bronze-shod autobiography, *Mémoires d'Outre-Tombe,* which rolls like a Napoleonic gun-limber over sixty years of stirring event and remains, unaccountably, the least read of the last century's neglected masterpieces. (p. 21)

Chateaubriand was by no means the first French traveller to record his impressions of America—both Crèvecoeur and the Marquis de Chastellux had preceded him. Moreover, considered sheerly as historical documents, parts of both *Voyage en Amérique* and *Mémoires d'Outre-Tombe* are considerably suspect. . . .

[However, of] all early records of American travel it is far and away the most entrancing. . . . It is also virtually the ultimate romantic document. On the plane of the American forest's archetypal image, the *mystique* is here in the fullest possible sense as well as the countervailing tension of the frontier tamed, both dimensions expressed in irony, comedy and resonant historic generalization. The portion that concerns us, in our present context, might be described, in terms analogous to the Arthurian themes of Chrestien de Troies, as the Quest of the Chevalier Chateaubriand. It moves from forest to forest: from Merlin's and Nimue's mythical Broceliande, near which he grew up, to the forest primeval of the Five Nations which he did so much to stamp on the imagination of the world. . . .

Not only are [Chateaubriand's impressions of the United States] good in their own right, and for a period in regard to which notable travel record is hard to come by, but they even manage to anticipate certain points Alexis de Tocqueville would later make. (p. 22)

[*Mémoires d'Outre-Tombe*] is far from being a simple travel document. To begin with, Chateaubriand was the possessor of a powerful intellect and complex personality coupled with a rich, positively Proustian sensibility that constantly accreted new impressions in the manner of a coral reef. Throughout his *Mémoires* he looks before and after; memory echoes memory; parallel provokes parallel; lyricism invests shrewdness and shrewdness invests lyricism. It is a Wordsworthian method, very reminiscent of *The Prelude,* one that makes for continuous resonance, perspective, vista. Does it also make for credibility? Or is it, in its orotund way, but an early instance of what Theodore Roosevelt, in another context, would one day angrily denounce as "nature-faking"?

This is by no means an easy question to answer. Since the days of Mandeville and Marco Polo, "traveler" has been one of the accepted synonyms for "liar." The whole Florida sequence, for example, is worse than suspect. One may doubt if the author so much as set eyes on the Upper Mississippi. In fact, the researches of Monsieur Chinard indicate that these portions of the **Mémoires** are as much a poem as Coleridge's *Ancient Mariner* and, indeed, that they were composed in a way not at all unlike Coleridge's way in reference to that same fantasy of travel. . . . [One] must always make allowance in Chateaubriand for the presence of an artist who, like his friend Horace Vernet, liked to group historic events as a painter arranges the masses in his composition. (p. 23)

[The account of his foray with a Dutch guide from Albany into what would come to be thought of as Cooper country] is the real heart of his American journal; and the passage where the great operative image of the forest may be said to be working at its most powerfully suggestive. But not solely—no, like a double-exposure the counter-vailing image of advancing civilization shows through. It all begins with a superb scene of emblematic comedy that, by telescoping periods, counterpoints the continuing dilemma within the American experience: the confrontation between technologically civilized man and the primitivist demands of his imagination. Once across the Mohawk and into the deep woods that had never yet been felled, the young Frenchman, under the amazed eyes of his phlegmatic Dutch companion, was seized by a kind of "drunkenness of independence." He ran from tree to tree in a Rousseaustic delirium of absolute freedom, convinced that he and he alone—for who would count the Hollander?—existed in that platonic forest.

Then, very suddenly, the young Chateaubriand awoke from his dream. In the very heart of those seemingly trackless woods the two of them came upon a wooden shed full of half-naked Iroquois with crow's feathers in their hair earnestly dancing to the tune of *Madelon Friquet* scraped out on a pocket-fiddle by a little French dancing-master in powdered hair, apple-green coat and lace jabot. The master of ballet had been a *marmiton,* a scullion, for Rochambeau and now eked out a living by trading dancing-lessons for beaver-skins and bear-steaks. It was a minuet of demons; but it was palpably a minuet. The Chevalier had come face to face with Stone Age man and found him dancing to the music of an Orpheus of the Enlightenment. An illusion had been slain by the *instrument fatal* in the hand of M. Violet who insisted in referring to these charges of his as: "*Ces messieurs sauvages et ces dames sauvagesses.*" The Chevalier did not know whether to laugh or cry. (p. 26)

Before he closes his journal, Chateaubriand turns away from wilderness Arcadia to shrewd foreshadowings of what, in a few short years, was fated to be the world of *Chuzzlewit* and "Mrs. Trolopp," this latter inspired malaprop spelling being Chateaubriand's own. His somewhat extended extrapolations, most of them made from the vantage point of hindsight in 1822 and 1845, are not unlike Tocqueville's except that, in keeping with Chateaubriand's philosophic conservatism, they are more tinged with pessimism. (p. 29)

"*J'amenais avec moi,*" he writes in conclusion, "*non des Esquimaux des régions polaires, mais deux sauvages d'une espèce inconnue: Chactas et Atala.* I brought back with me no Eskimos from polar regions, but two savages of an unknown species: Chactas and Atala." It is far too modest a claim. Chateaubriand brought back also in his sea-chest the great image of the wilderness that, shot through as it was with a corrective irony, returned across the Atlantic to play its part in helping dominate one side of the American imagination. He carried back and forth, in addition, a much more dubious bequest, an inexhaustible supply of technicolor sunsets and cin-

ema dissolves. For the rest of his life, poet, ambassador, Foreign Minister, exile, the Chevalier exhibits an abiding nostalgia for the great cataract that flows forever in the very center of his American idyll. (p. 30)

> Charles A. Brady, "From Broceliande to the Forest Primeval: The New-World Quest of the Chevalier Chateaubriand," in Emerson Society Quarterly, *Vol. 42, 1968, pp. 17-31.*

ADDITIONAL BIBLIOGRAPHY

"Sketch of Chateaubriand." *American Literary Magazine* III, No. 1 (July 1848): 51-9.
> Obituary offering a biographical sketch which details Chateaubriand's visit to the United States.

Armstrong, Emma Kate. "Chateaubriand's America." *PMLA,* n.s. XV, No. 2 (1907): 345-70.
> Questions the verity of Chateaubriand's accounts of his American travels in *Voyage en Amérique* and *Mémoires d'outre-tombe.* Armstrong gives extensive, often humorous, examples of Chateaubriand's misconceptions of American life.

Barthes, Roland. "Chateaubriand: *Life of Rancé.*" In his *New Critical Essays,* translated by Richard Howard, pp. 41-54. New York: Hill and Wang, 1968.
> Examines *Life of Rancé* as a "book in which some of us may rediscover certain problems, which is to say, certain limits, of our own." Barthes applies a modern linguistic approach to the text and concludes that "this pious work of an old rhetorician . . . looming up out of that French Romanticism with which our modernity feels little affinity . . . can concern us, astonish us, fulfill us."

France, Anatole. "Chateaubriand." In his *The Latin Genius,* translated by Wilfrid S. Jackson, pp. 230-53. New York: Gabriel Wells, 1924.
> Biographical character studies of Chateaubriand and his sister Lucile. Highlighting the biographical resonances in Chateaubriand's writing, the critic asks, "How can we refuse to recognize Lucile in the *Amélie* of his *René?*"

Maurois, André. *Chateaubriand: Poet, Statesman, Lover.* Translated by Vera Fraser. New York: Harper & Brothers, 1938, 352 p.
> Biography detailing Chateaubriand's literary, political, and amorous achievements.

Porter, Charles A. "Chateaubriand's Classicism." *Yale French Studies* 38 (1967): 156-70.
> Illustrates Chateaubriand's classicism with quotes demonstrating his "firm belief that there are rules and principles to be sought out, developed, and followed." Despite his obvious Romanticism, the critic maintains, Chateaubriand valued above all "language and good taste."

Schaffer, Aaron. "References to Chateaubriand in an Unpublished Correspondence of Émile Deschamps." *Modern Philology* 52, No. 1 (August 1954): 23-8.*
> Cites references to Chateaubriand in the letters of "one of the founders of the French Romantic School," Émile Deschamps.

Switzer, Richard. "Chateaubriand's Sources in the *Voyage en Amérique.*" *Revue de Littérature Comparée* 42 (1968): 5-23.
> Detailed study of the source materials from which Chateaubriand derived *Voyage en Amérique.* The critic contends that although Chateaubriand integrated the works of other authors into his book, he put his unique mark on the material and actually plagiarized very little.

Switzer, Richard, ed. *Chateaubriand Today.* Madison: The University of Wisconsin Press, 1970, 296 p.

Twenty-seven essays in French and English, by various critics, on many aspects of Chateaubriand's life and work.

Walker, Thomas Capell. *Chateaubriand's Natural Scenery*. The Johns Hopkins Studies in Romance Literature, Extra Vol. XXI. Baltimore: The Johns Hopkins Press, 1946, 185 p.

Comprehensive analysis of Chateaubriand's descriptions of nature and landscape.

Whitridge, Arnold. ''Chateaubriand and Tocqueville: Impressions of the American Scene.'' *History Today* XIII, No. 8 (August 1963): 530-38.*

Compares the American writings of Chateaubriand with those of Alexis de Tocqueville, who was indirectly related to Chateaubriand. Tocqueville was the cousin and foster brother of Chateaubriand's nephews.

Charles Dickens

1812-1870

(Also wrote under the pseudonym of Boz) English novelist, short story writer, dramatist, poet, and essayist.

Since the publication of his first novel, Dickens has achieved popular and critical recognition to a degree rarely equalled in English letters. Almost all of his novels display, to varying degrees, his comic gift, his deep social concerns, and his extraordinary talent for creating unforgettable characters. Many of his creations, most notably Scrooge, have become familiar English literary stereotypes. And though he has sometimes been criticized for creating caricatures rather than characters, he has been defended as a master of imaginative vision, forging whole character types out of tiny eccentricities. Furthermore, the frequent early criticism that his works are "formless" is not accepted by most modern critics. Many now see Dickens's novels as vast and complex denunciations of a bourgeois society which, in his view, corrupted people from within as well as from without.

Dickens was the son of John Dickens, a minor government official who constantly lived beyond his means and was eventually sent to debtor's prison. This humiliation deeply troubled young Dickens, and even as an adult he was rarely able to speak of it. As a boy, he was forced to work in a factory for meager wages until his father was released from prison. Late in his teens, he learned shorthand and became a court reporter, which introduced him to journalism and aroused his contempt for politics. His early short stories and sketches, which were published in various London newspapers and magazines, were later collected to form his first book, *Sketches by Boz*. The book sold well and received generally favorable notices, setting the stage for a new, more unified series of fiction.

His next literary venture was *Posthumous Papers of the Pickwick Club*. By the time the fourth monthly installment was published, Dickens was the most popular author in England. His fame soon spread throughout the rest of the English-speaking world, and eventually to the Continent. It has never diminished. "The Pickwick Papers" are celebrations of individual character and full of the good-natured spirit of his humor. The most loosely structured of Dickens's novels, *Pickwick* proved to be well-suited for serial publication. Even as the structure of his novels grew more intricate, Dickens never abandoned this method of publication, for he cherished the constant contact with his readers through monthly or weekly installments. And the public returned his affection, lining up at bookstores for hours before a new number was distributed.

Success followed upon success for Dickens, and the number of his readers continued to grow during what is now regarded as his "early period," which includes the *Sketches, Pickwick, Oliver Twist, The Life and Adventures of Nicholas Nickleby,* and *The Old Curiosity Shop*. The last of these features one of his most famous and most sentimental creations, Little Nell. As well as inspiring public grief, Little Nell's death was seen by most of his contemporary critics as an example of pathos. However, later critics have viewed this scene as an example of Dickens's crude sentimentalism; it prompted Oscar Wilde to remark that "one must have a heart of stone to read the

death of Little Nell without laughing." But *The Old Curiosity Shop*, with a circulation of over 70,000, was Dickens's greatest early success.

In 1842, Dickens traveled to the United States, hoping to find an embodiment of his liberal political ideals. He returned to England deeply disappointed, dismayed by America's lack of support for an international copyright law, the practice of slavery, and at the vulgarity of the American people. His essay *American Notes for General Circulation* was seen as cranky and superficial. His next novel, *The Life and Adventures of Martin Chuzzlewit*, in which he satirized the American obsession with material possessions, was a popular book but a critical failure. Many critics see the novel as a turning point in Dickens's career, claiming that he realized the failure of the bourgeois ideal when he saw how deeply greed corrupted the human soul. Dickens was to become more and more concerned with avarice in what is called his "middle period," which began with *A Christmas Carol in Prose*.

An immensely popular work, *A Christmas Carol* chronicles the transformation of Ebenezer Scrooge from a miser to a generous being. Two other "Christmas books," *The Chimes* and *The Cricket on the Hearth*, soon followed. His next full-length novel, *Dealings with the Firm of Dombey and Son*, more tightly composed than any of his previous novels, delineates the dehumanizing power of wealth, pride, and commercial values. *Dombey and Son* was followed by the autobiographical *The Personal History of David Copperfield*, which gives its readers a glimpse into Dickens's childhood and signals a change in his art of narration, for it is the first of his novels to be narrated wholly in the first person.

In 1850, Dickens entered what critics call his "late period" with the powerfully pessimistic *Bleak House*. This novel portrays a society in decay while its institutions gain a frightening power and impersonality. The Chancery Court in *Bleak House* functions symbolically as a monolith which hangs threateningly over the heads of the novel's characters. Dickens was to continue for the rest of his career to use in each novel one particular institution to exhibit the overall decay of society. In *Little Dorrit*, the Marshalsea Prison is juxtaposed with the internal prison in each character's mind; in *Great Expectations*, Pip's inherent goodness is transformed into avarice by the prospect of inherited wealth; in Dickens's last completed novel, *Our Mutual Friend*, the dust piles represent wealth and deface the landscape of London. The only optimism in these late novels comes from individual initiative, which is often at odds with society.

While writing his last novels, Dickens experienced turmoil in his personal life. In 1858, he separated from his wife and formed a close relationship, the nature of which is still not known, with the actress Ellen Ternan. He also gave a great number of public readings from his works in both England and America; these left him exhausted. Many believe that increasing physical and mental strain led to the stroke Dickens suffered while working on *The Mystery of Edwin Drood*, which was left unfinished at his death. Many critics have attempted to use this work as a key to the understanding of Dickens and his works.

Despite the growing pessimism of his later years, Dickens never lost faith in the essential goodness of the human soul. Though many of his characters are unjustly crushed by forces outside their control, some are able to triumph over the negative forces of society and achieve happiness. And Dickens's sense of social justice never allows a villain to go unpunished. Perhaps his enormous popularity springs partly from the fact that he always values humanity above all of society's artificial creations. As Edgar Johnson stated: "The world he created shines with undying life, and the hearts of men still vibrate to his indignant anger, his love, his glorious laughter, and his triumphant faith in the dignity of man."

*PRINCIPAL WORKS

Sketches by Boz [as Boz]   (sketches and short stories) 1836
Posthumous Papers of the Pickwick Club [as Boz]   (novel) 1837
Oliver Twist   (novel)   1838
The Life and Adventures of Nicholas Nickleby   (novel) 1839
Barnaby Rudge   (novel)   1841
The Old Curiosity Shop   (novel)   1841
American Notes for General Circulation   (travel essay) 1842
A Christmas Carol in Prose   (short story)   1843
The Chimes   (short story)   1844
The Life and Adventures of Martin Chuzzlewit   (novel) 1844

The Cricket on the Hearth   (short story)   1845
Pictures from Italy   (travel essay)   1846
Dealings with the Firm of Dombey and Son   (novel)   1848
The Haunted Man, and The Ghost's Bargain   (short stories) 1848
The Personal History of David Copperfield   (novel)   1850
Bleak House   (novel)   1853
Hard Times for These Times   (novel)   1854
Little Dorrit   (novel)   1857
A Tale of Two Cities   (novel)   1859
Great Expectations   (novel)   1861
The Uncommercial Traveller   (sketches and short stories) 1861
Our Mutual Friend   (novel)   1865
No Thoroughfare [with Wilkie Collins]   (drama)   1867
The Mystery of Edwin Drood   (unfinished novel)   1870

*All of Dickens's novels were first published serially in magazines, usually over periods of from one to two years.

[T. H. LISTER]   (essay date 1838)

Mr. Charles Dickens, the author of ['**Sketches by Boz,**' '**The Pickwick Papers,**' '**The Life and Adventures of Nicholas Nickleby,**' and '**Oliver Twist**'], is the most popular writer of his day. Since the publication of the poems and novels of Sir Walter Scott, there has been no work the circulation of which has approached that of the '**Pickwick Papers.**' . . . They seem, at first sight, to be among the most evanescent of the literary *ephemerae* of their day—mere humorous specimens of the lightest kind of light reading, expressly calculated to be much sought and soon forgotten—. . . 'good nonsense,'—and nothing more. This is the view which many persons will take of Mr Dickens's writings—but this is not our deliberate view of them. We think him a very original writer—well entitled to his popularity—and not likely to lose it—and the truest and most spirited delineator of English life, amongst the middle and lower classes, since the days of Smollett and Fielding. He has remarkable powers of observation, and great skill in communicating what he has observed—a keen sense of the ludicrous—exuberant humour—and that mastery in the pathetic which, though it seems opposed to the gift of humour, is often found in conjunction with it. And to these qualities, an unaffected style, fluent, easy, spirited, and terse—a good deal of dramatic power—and great truthfulness and ability in description. We know no other English writer to whom he bears a marked resemblance. He sometimes imitates other writers, such as Fielding in his introductions, and Washington Irving in his detached tales, and thus exhibits his skill as a parodist. But his own manner is very distinct—and comparison with any other would not serve to illustrate and describe it. We would compare him rather with the painter Hogarth. What Hogarth was in painting, such very nearly is Mr Dickens in prose fiction. The same turn of mind—the same species of power displays itself strongly in each. Like Hogarth he takes a keen and practical view of life—is an able satirist—very successful in depicting the ludicrous side of human nature, and rendering its follies more apparent by humorous exaggeration—peculiarly skilful in his management of details, throwing in circumstances which serve not only to complete the picture before us, but to suggest indirectly antecedent events which cannot be brought before our eyes. Hogarth's cobweb over the poor-box, and the plan for paying off the national debt, hanging from the pocket of a prisoner in the Fleet, are strokes of satire very similar to some in the writings of Mr Dickens. It is fair, in making this comparison, to add, that it does not hold good throughout; and that Mr Dickens is exempt from two of Hogarth's least agreeable qualities—his cynicism and his coarseness. There is no misanthropy in his satire, and no coarseness in his descriptions—a merit enhanced by the nature of his subjects. His works are chiefly pictures of humble life—frequently of the humblest. The reader is led through scenes of poverty and crime, and all the characters are made to discourse in the appropriate language of their respective classes—and yet we recollect no passage which ought to cause pain to the most sensitive delicacy, if read aloud in female society.

We have said that his satire was not misanthropic. This is eminently true. One of the qualities we the most admire in him is his comprehensive spirit of humanity. The tendency of his writings is to make us practically benevolent—to excite our sympathy in behalf of the aggrieved and suffering in all classes; and especially in those who are most removed from observation. . . . His humanity is plain, practical, and manly. It is quite untainted with sentimentality. There is no mawkish wailing for ideal distresses—no morbid exaggeration of the evils incident to our lot—no disposition to excite unavailing discontent, or to turn our attention from remediable grievances to those which do not admit a remedy. Though he appeals much to our feelings, we can detect no instance in which he has employed the verbiage of spurious philanthropy.

He is equally exempt from the meretricious cant of spurious philosophy. He never endeavours to mislead our sympathies—to pervert plain notions of right and wrong—to make vice interesting in our eyes—and shake our confidence in those whose conduct is irreproachable, by dwelling on the hollowness of seeming virtue. His vicious characters are just what experience shows the average to be; and what the natural operation of those circumstances to which they have been exposed would lead us to expect. We are made to feel both what they are, and *why* they are what we find them. We find no monsters of unmitigated and unredeemable villany. . . . (pp. 75-8)

Good feeling and sound sense are shown in his application of ridicule. It is never levelled at poverty or misfortune; or at circumstances which can be rendered ludicrous only by their deviation from artificial forms; or by regarding them through the medium of a conventional standard. Residence in the regions of Bloomsbury, ill-dressed dinners, and ill-made liveries, are crimes which he suffers to go unlashed; but follies or abuses, such as would be admitted alike in every sphere of society to be fit objects for his satire, are hit with remarkable vigour and precision. Nor does he confine himself to such as are obvious; but elicits and illustrates absurdities, which, though at once acknowledged when displayed, are plausible, and comparatively unobserved. (p. 78)

The whole story of the action against Pickwick for breach of promise of marriage, from its ludicrous origin, to Pickwick's eventual release from prison, where he had been immured for refusal to pay the damages, is one of the most acute and pointed satires upon the state and administration of English law that ever appeared in the light and lively dress of fiction. The account of the trial is particularly good. . . . (p. 80)

The imprisonment of Pickwick affords an opportunity of depicting the interior of a debtor's prison, and the manifold evils of that system, towards the abolition of which much, we trust,

will have been effected by a statute of the past session. The picture is excellent, both in intention and execution, and as it bears strongly an air of truth, it is necessarily a painful one. (p. 82)

Mr Dickens is very successful as a delineator of those manners, habits, and peculiarities which are illustrative of particular classes and callings. He exhibits amusingly the peculiar turn of thought which belongs to each; and, as if he had been admitted behind the scenes, brings to light those artifices which members of a fraternity are careful to conceal from the world at large. (p. 84)

Mr Dickens's characters are sketched with a spirit and distinctness which rarely fail to convey immediately a clear impression of the person intended. They are, however, not complete and finished delineations, but rather outlines, very clearly and sharply traced, which the reader may fill up for himself; and they are calculated not so much to represent the actual truth as to suggest it. Analyses of disposition, and explanations of motives will not be found, and, we may add, will be little required. His plan is, not to describe his personages, but to make them speak and act,—and it is not easy to misunderstand them. These remarks are not applicable to *all* his characters. Some are too shadowy and undefined,—some not sufficiently true to nature; in some the representations consist of traits too trivial or too few; and some are spoiled by exaggeration and caricature. Pickwick's companions, Winkle, Snodgrass, and Tupman, are very uninteresting personages,—having peculiarities rather than characters—useless incumbrances, which the author seems to have admitted hastily among his *dramatis personae* without well knowing what to do with them. The swindler Jingle and his companion want reality; and the former talks a disjointed jargon, to which some likeness may be found in farces, but certainly none in actual life. The young ladies in the Pickwick Papers are nonentities. The blustering Dowler, and the Master of the Ceremonies at Bath, are mere caricatures. The medical students are coarsely and disagreeably drawn. Wardle, though a tolerably good country squire, is hardly a modern one; and it may be doubted if Mr Weller, senior, can be accepted as the representative of any thing more recent than the last generation of stage-coachmen.

On the other hand, there are many characters truly excellent. First stand Pickwick and his man Weller,—the modern Quixote and Sancho of Cockaigne. Pickwick is a most amiable and eccentric combination of irritability, benevolence, simplicity, shrewdness, folly, and good sense—frequently ridiculous, but never contemptible, and always inspiring a certain degree of respect even when placed in the most ludicrous situations, playing the part of butt and dupe. Weller is a character which we do not remember to have seen attempted before. He is a favourable, yet, in many respects, faithful representative of the Londoner of humble life,—rich in native humour, full of the confidence, and address, and knowledge of the world, which is given by circumstances to a dweller in cities, combined with many of the most attractive qualities of the English character,—such as writers love to show in the brave, frank, honest, light-hearted sailor. His legal characters, Sergeant Snubbin, Perker, Dodson, Fogg, and Pell, are touched, though slightly, yet all with spirit, and a strong appearance of truth. Greater skill in drawing characters is shown in **'Oliver Twist'** and **'Nicholas Nickleby,'** than in **'Pickwick.'** His Ralph Nickleby, and Mrs Nickleby, deserve to be noticed as peculiarly successful.

But Mr Dickens's forte perhaps lies less in drawing characters than in describing incidents. He seizes with great skill those circumstances which are capable of being graphically set before us; and makes his passing scenes distinctly present to the reader's mind. Ludicrous circumstances are those which he touches most happily; of which the Pickwick Papers afford many examples; such as the equestrian distresses of Pickwick and his companions, the pursuit of Jingle, and Pickwick's night adventures in the boarding-school garden,—incidents richly comic and worthy of Smollett; and which are narrated in Smollett's spirit, without his coarseness. His descriptions of scenery are also good, though in a minor degree; and among these the aspect of the town is perhaps better delineated than that of the country; and scenes which are of an unattractive kind with more force and effect than those which are susceptible of poetical embellishment. (pp. 84-6)

The 'Pickwick Papers' are, as the author admits in his preface, defective in plan, and want throughout that powerful aid which fiction derives from an interesting and well constructed plot. 'Nicholas Nickleby' appears to be commenced with more attention to this important requisite in novel-writing; and if the author will relieve the painful sombreness of his scenes with a sufficient portion of sunshine, it will deserve to exceed the popularity of Pickwick. But 'Oliver Twist,' a tale not yet completed, is calculated to give a more favourable impression of Mr Dickens's powers as a writer of fiction than any thing else which he has yet produced. There is more interest in the story, a plot better arranged, characters more skilfully and carefully drawn, without any diminution of spirit, and without that tone of humorous exaggeration which, however amusing, sometimes detracts too much from the truthfulness of many portions of the 'Pickwick Papers.' The scene is laid in the humblest life: its hero is a friendless, nameless, parish orphan, born in a workhouse; at a time when workhouses were not subjected, as now, to the control of a central superintending board, and when attention was comparatively little directed to the condition of the poor. (p. 86)

Unfinished as this tale still is, it is the best example which Mr Dickens has yet afforded of his power to produce a good novel; but it cannot be considered a conclusive one. The difficulties to which he is exposed in his present periodical mode of writing are, in some respects, greater than if he allowed himself a wider field, and gave his whole work to the public at once. But he would be subjected to a severer criticism if his fiction could be read continually—if his power of maintaining a sustained interest could be tested—if his work could be viewed as a connected whole, and its object, plan, consistency, and arrangement brought to the notice of the reader at once. This ordeal cannot be passed triumphantly without the aid of other qualities than necessarily belong to the most brilliant sketcher of detached scenes. We do not, however, mean to express a doubt that Mr Dickens can write with judgment as well as with spirit. His powers of observation and description are qualities rarer, and less capable of being acquired, than those which would enable him to combine the scattered portions of a tale into one consistent and harmonious whole. If he will endeavour to supply whatever may be effected by care and study—avoid imitation of other writers—keep nature steadily before his eyes—and check all disposition to exaggerate—we know no writer who seems likely to attain higher success in that rich and useful department of fiction which is founded on faithful representations of human character, as exemplified in the aspects of English life. (pp. 96-7)

[*T. H. Lister,*] *"Dickens' 'Tales',"* in The Edinburgh Review, *Vol. LXVIII, No. 137, October, 1838, pp. 75-97.*

FRASER'S MAGAZINE FOR TOWN AND COUNTRY (essay date 1840)

[In his preface to the **Pickwick Papers,** Dickens stated:]

> [If] it be objected to the Pickwick Papers, that they are a mere series of adventures, in which the scenes are ever changing, and the characters come and go like the men and women we encounter in the real world, he can only content himself with the reflection that they claim to be nothing else, and that the same objection has been made to the works of some of the greatest novelists in the English language. . . .

No critic worth reading objects to a "series of adventures in which the scenes are ever changing, and the characters come and go like the men and women we encounter in the real world." The writer who has the power of so delineating characters has indeed reached the highest point of dramatic and narrative art. What the critical reader of Boz's novels objects to is, that, whatever we may think of the *come-and-go* characters, that the *standing* characters are *not* like the men and the women of the real world. . . . [Beyond] supporting a character consistently through three or four caricature scenes, Mr. Dickens's power does not extend.

Let us, for example, take Mr. Pickwick himself. His first appearance is that of a vain, old fool, gravely occupied in the serious investigation of frivolous trifles. . . . (p. 382)

[Late in the novel, Mr. Pickwick becomes a noble, self-sacrificing character.] Mr. Pickwick with a countenance lighted up with smiles which the heart of no man, woman, or child, could resist! Is this the Mr. Pickwick of the fight with the cabman,—the hunt after the hat,—the drive to Dingley Dell,—the breakdown in the chase after Jingle,—the tender scene with his landlady,—the hiding in the boarding-school garden,—the wheelbarrow in the pound,—the double-bedded room, with the middle-aged lady . . .? [In] short, the Mr. Pickwick of Phiz from his first plate to the last? To borrow a favourite phrase of Sam Weller's, "*We* ray-ther think *not.*" The fact is, that Phiz is consistent in *his* conception of Mr. Pickwick throughout: he is the same idiotic lump of bland blockheadism, unrelieved by thought or feeling, from beginning to end. In the hands of Boz, he commences as a butt and ends as a hero.

In the other characters we have the same inconsistency. Winkle, a poor, unaccomplished, ungentlemanlike poltroon at first, is in the end a delicate and romantic lover, inspiring a handsome and interesting young lady with a refined attachment. Snodgrass, an ass of a poet, not fit to fill half-a-dozen lines of a review in the "Fraser Papers," turns out to be an honourable and sensible gentleman before the book concludes, and is duly rewarded with the hand of one of its favourite beauties. All this, certainly, is not, as the painters say, in keeping; and Mr. Dickens may perhaps now perceive that the objection to the Pickwick papers, as a whole, is not that "the characters come and go like the men and women we encounter in the real world," but that they do *not.* (pp. 390-91)

Mr. Pickwick begins as a *burlesque* man, who never was intended seriously as a representative of any thing that ever existed—sometimes well drawn, and sometimes ill drawn, as chance may be; whom the author makes an awkward effort to convert, at the end of his work, into a representative of a *real* man, acting upon *real* principles of honour and prudence. (p. 392)

In *Oliver Twist,* Mr. Dickens has just the same defect,—one which certainly cannot be urged against the great novelists. We do not wish to go at any great length into detail; but take the character of Mr. Brownlow. If, as the plates would lead us to believe, he is the magistrate who prevented Oliver Twist from being indentured to the master-sweep, he is described, on his first appearance, as being half blind and half childish; and, at all events, when introduced in his own name, he is a mere doting and dozing old fellow, who scarcely knows what he is doing; and such is the character which Cruikshank imparts to him throughout. Not so Boz. This dreamy and stupid old man displays not merely great goodness of heart, which certainly is not inconsistent with carelessness and abstraction, but what *is* inconsistent with these characteristics, unwearied zeal in tracing out the intricacies of a complicated plot, and determined activity in pursuing a murderer to his last haunt of refuge. . . . Or, again, is the Nance of the first volume the same Nance that we find in the third? (p. 394)

She talks the common slang of London, in its ordinary dialect, in the beginning of the novel; at the end no heroine that ever went mad in white satin talked more picked and perfumed sentences of sentimentality. (p. 395)

In *Nicholas Nickleby* the alteration of character is less striking, for the hero himself has no character at all, being but the walking thread-paper to convey the various threads of the story. Kate is no better; and the best-drawn characters in the book, Mantalini and Mrs. Nickleby, have only caricature parts to play; and, in preserving them, there is no great difficulty. In the other novels, Jingle and Sam Weller, Bumble and the Dodger, are, for the same reason, consistent throughout; but these are not the characters which people meet in common life. . . . In general we may remark that Boz's good-nature makes him improve his characters as he proceeds. Pickwick the ass becomes Pickwick the wise; Nance the naughty is converted into Nance the noble, and so on. In *Nicholas Nickleby* we have an exception. Squeers and Ralph Nickleby become worse and worse as the story proceeds; and here, too, the end of these worthies is not consistent with the beginning. Squeers at first is nothing more than an ignorant and wretched hound, making a livelihood for himself and his family by starving a miserable group of boys. The man has not intellect for any thing better or worse; and yet we find him at last an adept in disguising himself, in ferreting out hidden documents, in carrying through a difficult and entangled scheme of villany. Ralph Nickleby makes his appearance as a shrewd, selfish, hard-hearted usurer, intent on nothing but making and hoarding money; in the end we find him actuated by some silly feelings of spite or revenge, by which he cannot, under any circumstances, make a farthing, and which he would have looked upon as childish weaknesses that ought not to find their place in the bosom of a man of sense, and knowledge of the world. His committing suicide, and that out of remorse too, is perfectly out of character. (p. 396)

[When] Boz meddles with law, he is always unfortunate. It must have been a very queer jury that gave the plaintiff 700*l.* damages in the case of Bardell and Pickwick upon such evidence as is adduced in the report of the case. . . . The manner, too, in which Sam Weller contrives to get into the Fleet is much more ingenious than practical; and Mr. Pickwick's inability to discover the name of the person on whose suit his faithful follower was detained is rather remarkable. In *Oliver Twist* it is, no doubt, very satisfactory to the lovers of poetical justice that Fagin should be hanged, but the Old Bailey justice that consigned him to the gallows is somewhat peculiar. (pp. 396-97)

But for this, and many other slips in his stories and style, Boz has offered the adequate excuse, viz. the nature of his publication, in which every thing was to be postponed to the necessity of periodical appearance. . . . [The] necessity of filling a certain quantity of pages per month imposed upon the writer a great temptation to amplify trifling incidents, and to swell sentence after sentence with any sort of words that would occupy space. The very spirit of a penny-a-liner, for instance, breaks out in the prolix descriptions of the various walks through the streets of London, every turn in which is enumerated with the accuracy of a cabman. *Oliver Twist* and *Nicholas Nickleby* are stuffed with "passages that lead to nothing," merely to fill the necessary room. Now, in the separate monthly essays this was no harm,—on the contrary, it was of positive good to the main object, viz. the sale; but when we find them collected, they do not improve the sequence of the story, or advance the fame of the writer. . . .

But this is the only fault of Boz—if fault it can be called, to make hay while the sun shines. We wish him well; but talking of literature in any other light than that of a back trade, we do not like this novel-writing by scraps against time. . . . He has one great merit, independent of his undoubted powers of drollery, observation, and caricature,—he has not lent his pen to any thing that can give countenance to vice or degradation; and he has always espoused the cause of the humble, the persecuted, and the oppressed. This of itself would cover far more literary sins than Boz has to answer for; and, indeed, we do not remember any of importance enough to require covering at all. With this we bid not good *speed,* but good moderation of pace; and we trust that, since *Master Humphry* has set up *a clock,* he will henceforward take *time.* (p. 400)

"Charles Dickens and His Works," in Fraser's Magazine for Town and Country, *Vol. XXI, No. CXXIV, April, 1840, pp. 381-400.*

EDGAR ALLAN POE (essay date 1841)

[The plot of *The Old Curiosity Shop* is] the best which could have been constructed for the main object of the narrative. This object is the depicting of a fervent and dreamy love for the child on the part of the grandfather—such a love as would induce devotion to himself on the part of the orphan. We have thus the conception of a childhood, educated in utter ignorance of the world, filled with an affection which has been, through its brief existence, the sole source of its pleasures, and which has no part in the passion of a more mature youth for an object of its own age—we have the idea of this childhood, full of ardent hopes, leading by the hand, forth from the heated and wearying city, into the green fields, to seek for bread, the decrepid imbecillity of a doting and confiding old age, whose stern knowledge of man, and of the world it leaves behind, is now merged in the sole consciousness of receiving love and protection from that weakness it has loved and protected.

This conception is indeed most beautiful. It is simply and severely grand. The more fully we survey it, the more thoroughly are we convinced of the lofty character of that genius which gave it birth. That in its present simplicity of form, however, it was first entertained by Mr. Dickens, may well be doubted. That it was *not,* we are assured by the title which the tale bears. When in its commencement he called it "The Old Curiosity Shop," his design was far different from what we see it in its completion. It is evident that had he now to name the story he would not so term it; for the shop itself is a thing of an altogether collateral interest, and is spoken of merely in the beginning. (pp. 19-20)

But if the conception of this story deserves praise, its execution is beyond all—and here the subject naturally leads us from the generalisation which is the proper province of the critic, into details among which it is scarcely fitting that he should venture.

The Art of Mr. Dickens, although elaborate and great, seems only a happy modification of Nature. In this respect he differs remarkably from the author of *Night and Morning* [Bulwer-Lytton]. The latter, by excessive care and by patient reflection, aided by much rhetorical knowledge, and general information, has arrived at the capability of producing books which might be mistaken by ninety-nine readers out of a hundred for the genuine inspirations of genius. The former, by the promptings of the truest genius itself, has been brought to compose, and evidently without effort, works which have effected a long-sought consummation—which have rendered him the idol of the people, while defying and enchanting the critics. Mr. Bulwer, through art, has almost created a genius. Mr. Dickens, through genius, has perfected a standard from which Art itself will derive its essence, in rules.

When we speak in this manner of *The Old Curiosity Shop,* we speak with entire deliberation, and know quite well what it is we assert. We do not mean to say that it is perfect, as a whole—this could not well have been the case under the circumstances of its composition. But we know that, in all the higher elements which go to make up literary greatness, it is supremely excellent. We think, for instance, that the introduction of Nelly's brother (and here we address those who have read the work) is supererogatory—that the character of Quilp would have been more in keeping had he been confined to petty and grotesque acts of malice—that his death should have been made the *immediate* consequence of his attempt at revenge upon Kit; and that after matters had been put fairly in train for this poetical justice, he should not have perished by an accident inconsequential upon his villany. . . . Above all, we acknowledge that the death of Nelly is excessively painful—that it leaves a most distressing oppression of spirit upon the reader—and should, therefore, have been avoided.

But when we come to speak of the excellences of the tale these defects appear really insignificant. It embodies more *originality* in every point, but in character especially, than any single work within our knowledge. There is the grandfather—a truly profound conception; the gentle and lovely Nelly—we have discoursed of her before; Quilp, with mouth like that of the panting dog—(a bold idea which the engraver has neglected to embody) with his hilarious antics, his cowardice, and his very petty and spoilt-child-like malevolence. . . . There are other admirably drawn characters—but we note these for their remarkable originality, as well as for their wonderful keeping, and the glowing colors in which they are painted. We have heard some of them called caricatures—but the charge is grossly ill-founded. No critical principle is more firmly based in reason than that a certain amount of exaggeration is essential to the proper depicting of truth itself. We do not paint an object to be true, but to appear true to the beholder. Were we to copy nature with accuracy the object copied would seen unnatural. . . . Were these creations of Mr. Dickens' really caricatures they would not live in public estimation beyond the hour of their first survey. We regard them as *creations*—(that is to say as original combinations of character) only not all of the highest order, because the elements employed are not always of the highest. In the instances of Nelly, the grandfather, the Sexton,

and the man of the furnace, the force of the creative intellect could scarcely have been engaged with nobler material, and the result is that these personages belong to the most august regions of the *Ideal.*

In truth, the great feature of the *Curiosity Shop* is its chaste, vigorous, and glorious *imagination.* This is the one charm, all potent, which alone would suffice to compensate for a world more of error than Mr. Dickens ever committed. It is not only seen in the conception, and general handling of the story, or in the invention of character; but it pervades every sentence of the book. We recognise its prodigious influence in every inspired word. It is this which induces the reader who is at all ideal, to pause frequently, to re-read the occasionally quaint phrases, to muse in uncontrollable delight over thoughts which, while he wonders he has never hit upon them before, he yet admits that he never has encountered. In fact it is the wand of the enchanter.

Had we room to particularise, we would mention as points evincing most distinctly the ideality of the *Curiosity Shop*—the picture of the shop itself—the newly-born desire of the worldly old man for the peace of green fields—his whole character and conduct, in short—the schoolmaster, with his desolate fortunes, seeking affection in little children—the haunts of Quilp among the wharf-rats—. . . and, last and greatest, the stealthy approach of Nell to her death—her gradual sinking away on the journey to the village, so skilfully indicated rather than described—her pensive and prescient meditation—the fit of strange musing which came over her when the house *in which she was to die* first broke upon her sight—the description of this house, of the old church, and of the churchyard—every thing in rigid consonance with the one impression to be conveyed. . . . These concluding scenes are so drawn that human language, urged by human thought, could go no farther in the excitement of human feelings. And the pathos is of that best order which is relieved, in great measure, by ideality. Here the book has never been equalled,—never approached except in one instance, and that is in the case of the *Undine* of De La Motte Fouqué. (pp. 20-4)

Upon the whole we think the *Curiosity Shop* very much the best of the works of Mr. Dickens. It is scarcely possible to speak of it too well. It is in all respects a tale which will secure for its author the enthusiastic admiration of every man of genius. (p. 24)

Edgar Allan Poe, "'The Old Curiosity Shop'," in Graham's Magazine, *Vol. XVIII, No. 5, May, 1841 (and reprinted in* The Dickens Critics, *edited by George H. Ford and Lauriat Lane, Jr., Cornell University Press, 1961, pp. 19-24).*

THE ATHENAEUM   (essay date 1842)

[As to workmanship, we consider **'Barnaby Rudge'**] as better built than any of [Dickens's previous works]. It is true, that the Great Riots of '80, which professedly served for the foundation, are scarcely hinted at till the thirty-fifth chapter, which abruptly introduces the reader to Lord George Gordon. But this circumstance, instead of being a defect, is to the advantage of the story, and if not artistically contrived for the purpose, serves very happily to heighten the effect of the metropolitan tumults, and to point the moral of the tale. . . . [The novel] opens with peaceful and pastoral scenery—greenly and serenely, like the calm before a storm. Thus, the first chapter pleasantly plants us, not in Cato Street, but on the borders of

Epping Forest, at an ancient ruddy Elizabethan inn, with a Maypole for its sign—an antique porch, quaint chimneys, and "more gable ends than a lazy man would care to count on a sunny day." . . . And when the Riots do eventually break out,—when Newgate is in flames and Langdale's in a blaze, even these scenes, terrible as they are, scarcely come home to the feelings so impressively as the picture of the quaint hostel, late the abode of Peace and Plenty, with its pastoral Maypole dashed through the window, "like the bowsprit of a wrecked ship," and its pinioned proprietor, slow John, staring in a stupor at his staved barrels, shattered punch-bowls, and demolished furniture. For this powerful effect, as an intentional and not accidental contrast, we give Boz full credit; seeing how elaborately . . . he has fitted up the Bar—"the very snuggest, coziest, and completest bar that ever the wit of man devised,"—only to give the greater force to the profanation of poor Willet's sanctorum, and the smash of his household gods.

The Riots in the metropolis are graphically and historically described; and *some* of the fermenting elements which led to the outbreak are happily illustrated. For example, the vulgar ambition which urges upstarts such as Bubb Doddington, to "make a figure in the world, no matter how, but a figure they are resolved to make,"—the low craving for notoriety which leads a Billy Jones into a royal palace, or an Oxford from being the Pots at the Hog in the Pound, to become a state traitor. . . . But one essential character seems to us to be wanting,—a sample of the true sanctimonious bigot, the tyrannical fanatic, the persecutor of opinion, who would drive a slave trade in souls, and hold the conscience of his fellow-creatures in spiritual bondage. . . .

The noble grandfather of the Riots, Lord George Gordon, is drawn of course from traditional sketches, and Boz has treated the character in his usual charitable spirit. But we protest against calling the great Leader the misled—the designating of his wickedness as weakness, and the sheltering the misdeeds of this "poor crazy lord" under the plea of insanity. It is a common, but dangerous error to attribute all moral to mental obliquities—to mistake loose principles for unsettled reason—and to confound enthusiasm with fanaticism. (p. 77)

> *"Reviews: 'Barnaby Rudge',"* in The Athenaeum, No. 743, January 22, 1842, pp. 77-9.

THE NEW ENGLANDER (essay date 1843)

We have been greatly disappointed in the perusal of these **"American Notes."** We were well aware that there are some defects in our social organization, which might be hit off to advantage by a masterhand; and we had hoped that Mr. Dickens' keen perception of the ludicrous, would be exercised at our present expense, though for our ultimate profit. We should have thanked him for a humorous exhibition of our weak points of national character; but he seems either to have failed to apprehend them, or to have felt an unwonted reserve in making his "police reports." These Notes are barren of incident and anecdote, deficient in wit, and meagre even in respect to the most ordinary kind of information. They give no just conception of the physical aspect of the country of which they treat; much less do they introduce the reader to the homes and firesides of its inhabitants. . . . The little information to be gleaned from these two volumes, with few exceptions, might be gained much more advantageously from the map and gazetteer. The perusal of them has served chiefly to lower our estimate of the

man, and to fill us with contempt for such a compound of egotism, coxcombry, and cockneyism. . . .

The first two chapters of these Notes, descriptive of the departure and passage out, are, on the whole, rather entertaining, and exhibit more of that pleasantry which has hitherto characterized the productions of the author, than any of the succeeding chapters; though even here he sometimes fails in his attempts at wit. His description of the sensations produced by sea-sickness, have the merit of being intelligible, whatever may be thought of the taste of a writer who can expatiate on such a theme. (p. 67)

After a somewhat boisterous passage of eighteen days, Mr. Dickens arrived at Boston on Saturday, the 23d day of January, 1842, a day to be hereafter noted in every edition of the American Almanac. . . .

His first day in Boston was the Sabbath. Modestly declining a score of invitations to church, for want of "any change of clothes," he strolled abroad in his humble, unsanctified attire, to view the city. He seems to have been greatly amused with its "light, unsubstantial" appearance, as he is pleased to term it, notwithstanding the masses of Quincy granite by which he was surrounded, and the iron balconies that frown over the dark receding portals of stone. He was altogether amazed in walking the streets of a modern and growing city, not to find in every structure the solidity and grandeur of an Egyptian pyramid. The explanation of which is, that he missed the dense, dark atmosphere of London, and the vast cloud of smoke from bituminous coal, which hides the pure light of heaven from the natives of Cockaigne, and covers every thing with sooty stains. So to a man who had never been out of Pittsburg, Boston might seem as white, and airy, and unsubstantial, as it seemed to our author. (p. 69)

On the whole, however, he acknowledges that Boston is "a beautiful city." He speaks favorably of "the intellectual refinement and superiority" of the inhabitants, which he refers mainly, perhaps too much, "to the quiet influence of the university of Cambridge;" though it is unquestionably true that both the intellectual and moral influence of such an institution is always widely felt through the surrounding region: He speaks favorably of the American collegiate system, especially in respect to its liberal and practical nature; though nothing is more evident than that he knows very little on the subject. Mr. Dickens remained longer, we believe, in Boston than in any other city, and perhaps received more attention from literary men there than any where else. (p. 70)

On his journey to Washington, Mr. Dickens was particularly disgusted with the exuberant use of tobacco which he witnessed on all occasions. We heartily join him in his "counterblast" against the Stygian weed; yet we apprehend, that *his* practice of frequenting the *bar* was no less disgusting to some of his fellow travelers, than the use of tobacco on the part of others seems to have been to him. He could not go from New Haven to New York, without "exhausting the stock of bottled beer" on board the boat, and we believe that he even found a *bar* on board the little steamer between Springfield and Hartford. The habits of Mr. Dickens, in this respect, as our readers have already seen, need no inconsiderable reformation. (p. 77)

On Tuesday, the seventh of June, Mr. Dickens embarked in the packet ship George Washington, for his native land. The chapter describing the passage home is pleasantly written, and contains some important suggestions respecting the shipping of emigrants. It is followed by a chapter on slavery, embodying some facts, but lamentably deficient in argument and force. The chapter was written for the English market, and would probably have been different, had the author's scheme for an international copyright been successful.

The last chapter of the work contains some general remarks on the prominent features of American society, but none of them betray an accurate or philosophic mind. The topics discussed are some of them important, but they are dismissed with a few hasty, disconnected observations. (p. 79)

We regret that Mr. Dickens has published these volumes, for they bear the marks of hasty composition, evince no genius, add nothing to the author's reputation as a writer, and exhibit his moral character in a most undesirable light.

It remains that, in concluding this article, we present briefly the judgment which we have formed of Mr. Dickens as a writer. These Notes are by no means a favorable specimen of the talents of the author. They are very carelessly written, and the subject affords but little scope for the exercise of his peculiar powers. (p. 80)

"Dickens' Notes on America," in The New Englander, *Vol. I, No. I, January, 1843, pp. 64-84.*

THE NORTH AMERICAN REVIEW   (essay date 1843)

[All] American readers have read the [**"American Notes for General Circulation."**] They have been scattered over the country by the penny press, with the speed of rail-road and steam-boat. We believe they have been read with general approbation. Certainly they are pleasant reading, and highly characteristic of their author. Persons who expected from Dickens long disquisitions upon what are called American Institutions,—philosophical tirades upon the working of the republican machine of government,—or the future prospects of the world as affected by what we style the great experiment of self-government,—expected what they had no right to look for from the author of **"Pickwick."** Mr. Dickens had too much good sense to attempt a work for which he was unprepared by previous studies, habits of thought, and intellectual peculiarities; for which, had he possessed every needful prerequisite, his residence in the country was too short, and his opportunities of calm observation too limited and few. But he has a quick eye, from which nothing that comes within its range escapes; in his rapid passage from place to place, he would seize many characteristic points, and take in at a glance many amusing traits. Little incidents, that others would pass unnoticed, with him would be the germs of entertaining remark.

We had a right, therefore, to expect from him, not a didactic work, but a book full of graphic touches, good feeling, and pleasant observation; and in this expectation we have not been disappointed. Many of his strictures have given offence in various quarters. Some people seem to think, that if a fault of manners, or an inconvenience of social arrangements, or an awkward or disagreeable habit, is described by a traveller, it is described as something peculiar to them. Thus Dickens's humorous pictures of the discomforts of steam and canal boats, and stage coaches,—though all who have ever felt them, acknowledge the striking fidelity of his pencil,—are meant as satires upon American civilization in particular, and as if such things were found nowhere else; and not a little very excellent wrath has been expended upon him on that most gratuitous supposition. . . . It may be too,—we fancy it is,—the fact, that Dickens has never been much of a traveller. Probably his

previous wanderings had not extended far beyond the immortal journeyings of the Pickwickians; so that he could only have drawn comparisons, had he been disposed to do it at all, between the United States and England. We see nothing to complain of in the peculiarity of his book just touched upon; on the contrary, we are pleased to have, in their original freshness, the impressions made by our country on such a mind as his. With some of these we are far from agreeing. What he says of the absence of humor in the New England character, is directly opposed to the result of our own observations, and we can have no doubt, that he is here mistaken. In several minor matters of fact, he is also unquestionably wrong.

But these things hardly lessen the general interest, with which we read the book. The picture he draws of the character of the American newspaper press, darkly colored as it is, does not surpass the truth, when applied to a portion,—a very large portion, it must be confessed,—of the metropolitan papers. But he does not make sufficiently emphatic exceptions and distinctions; and, when he comes to speak of the universality of its evil influence, its omnipotence and omnipresence, his vigorous, startling, and almost terrific language is quite too unqualified. We have no faith in the existence of such a demoniac power, as that he describes. (pp. 227-29)

The style of this book is, like that of Dickens's other writings, free, graphic, and flowing. It has a rapid movement, as if he wrote as fast as his pen could be driven across the paper. . . . It abounds in touches of the poetical and imaginative. Striking expressions, brilliant descriptions, witty turns, and humorous sallies, are scattered in sparkling profusion over its animated pages. The sea-passages have attracted great and deserved admiration. The graver parts of the book,—such as the visit to the Blind Institution at South Boston, the affecting account of Laura Bridgman, and the forcible comments upon the solitary system of prison discipline in Philadelphia,—are written in a deep, earnest, fervent spirit, and come from a heart throbbing with the best sympathies of our nature. The tone of the book, throughout, is frank, honest, and manly. He has steered clear of all personalities, though he has not lost, through over-fastidiousness, any point of what he deems to be the truth. (pp. 230-31)

"Charles Dickens: 'American Notes for General Circulation'," in The North American Review, *Vol. LVI, No. CXVIII, January, 1843, pp. 212-37.*

THE ATHENAEUM   (essay date 1844)

We presume that **'Martin Chuzzlewit'** is to be regarded as an exposition of self-interest in some of its coarsest and most obvious workings. It is, in brief, the story of a Scrooge (no one who has read the **'Christmas Carol,'** can be at a loss for the allusion) told more diffusely—a story terminating in the repentance and conversion of the central egotist. Now, we are not without trust in human nature, nor a poetical faith in poetical justice: but we must confess that Grandfather Chuzzlewit is rather old to learn—very old to act the part he is described to have acted, when his heart is reformed—namely, lying *perdue* and, to all appearance, the imbecile tool of the arch-humbug of the tale till the fine morning when he breaks forth, hale, intelligent, and vigorous, to frown Vice into the dark corners of the world, and to treat, not to tempt modest Virtue, with a golden shower of competence and blessing! We submit, too, that were such transformation, and dramatic cunning, natural, the employment of deceit and artifice on Virtue's side, is too much like encountering a Pecksniff with his own weapons. . . . [The] device is of too low an order of morality, to be employed by a person so sound at heart as Mr. Dickens.

This first invention, then, strikes us as ill-considered; and it is not redeemed by any peculiar ingenuity or probability in the management of the incidents by which it is developed. There are smart hits by the thousand—capitally wrought up scenes—moments of serious suspense—but events and vicissitudes *reel* rather than march to a conclusion:—and as we come near the end, horrors and surprises are lavished with a vehemence, which disturbs rather than impresses us. We must, also, on every ground, protest against the American episode as an excrescence. Apart from the bad temper and prejudice pervading every line of it, the voyage and sojourn of Martin and his squire have a disagreeable and distracting effect—nor can the humours of the Pogram levee, nor the queer English, bribe us to forget the fault of moral taste which allowed these chapters a place in the work, nor the complete disregard of artistic craft in their management. . . .

In common with many another approved work of fiction, '**Martin Chuzzlewit**' has neither hero nor heroine: unless—as the author's preface seems to permit—we take Mr. Pecksniff for the former, and Mrs. Gamp (counting, of course, Mrs. Harris into the bargain,) for the latter. But then the author riots among his secondary characters. Tom Pinch is capital; in more than one sense, the best creature in the book. The sprightly and gamesome Mercy Pecksniff *goes off*, at the opening of the story, with the bounce and the froth of a bottle of ginger-beer; subsequently she sobers down into sadness and suffering, a little too amiably, we fear, for a damsel trained under such a professor of self-assertion as her father. (p. 665)

We had hoped to have found some improvement in the serious dialogue of Mr. Dickens; but here his taste and talent for amplification are in his way. He is too fond of propagating good sentiments in the form of harangues. There is an echo of stage pathos in many of his colloquies, where the briefest simplicity is the thing wanted. Emotion keeps no period; nor does affectionate feeling vent itself in sonorous expatiations. His style, too, continues more freakish and affected, on occasions, than a writer who has a European reputation should permit. The apostrophes and redundancies he indulges in, are tricks for the magazines, but have no place on the library shelf; and they are needless, since, when he writes without strain, Mr. Dickens uses language like a master of form and of colour. (p. 666)

"Reviews: 'Martin Chuzzlewit'," in The Athenaeum, *No. 873, July 20, 1844, pp. 665-66.*

THE EDINBURGH REVIEW (essay date 1845)

We do not know the earnestness to compare with [Dickens's] for the power of its manifestation and its uses. It is delightful to see it in his hands, and observe by what tenure he secures the popularity it has given him. Generous sympathies and kindest thoughts, are the constant renewal of his fame; and in such wise fashion as the little book before us [*Chimes*], he does homage for his title and his territory. A noble homage! Filling successive years with merciful charities; and giving to thousands of hearts new and just resolves.

This is the lesson of his *Chimes,* as of his delightful *Carol;* but urged with more intense purpose and a wider scope of application. What was there the individual lapse, is here the social wrong. Questions were handled there, to be settled with happy

decision. Questions are here brought to view, which cannot be dismissed when the book is laid aside. Condition of England questions; questions of starving labourer and struggling artizan; duties of the rich and pretences of the worldly; the cruelty of unequal laws; and the pressure of awful temptations on the unfriended, unassisted poor. Mighty theme for so slight an instrument! but the touch is exquisite, and the tone deeply true. (p. 181)

Could we note a distinction in the tale, from the general character of its author's writings, it would be that the impression of sadness predominates, when all is done. The comedy as well as tragedy seems to subserve that end; yet it must be taken along with the purpose in view. We have a hearty liking for the cheerful side of philosophy, and so it is certain has Mr Dickens: but there are social scenes and experiences, through which only tragedy itself may work out its kinder opposite. . . . Name this little tale what we will, it is a tragedy in effect. Inextricably interwoven, of course, are both pleasure and pain, in all the conditions of life in this world: crossing with not more vivid contrasts the obscure struggle of the weak and lowly, than with fierce alternations of light and dark traversing that little rule, that little sway, which is all the great and mighty have between the cradle and the grave. But whereas, in the former stories of Mr Dickens, even in the death of his little Nell, pleasure won the victory over pain, we may not flatter ourselves that it is so here. There is a gloom in the mind as we shut the book, which the last few happy pages have not cleared away; an uneasy sense of depression and oppression; a pitiful consciousness of human sin and sorrow; a feeling of some frightful extent of wrong, which we should somehow try to stay; as strong, but apparently as helpless, as that of the poor Frenchman at the bar of the Convention, who demanded of Robespierres and Henriots an immediate arrestment of the knaves and dastards of the world! (p. 183)

In so far as there is the machinery of a dream, the plan of the *Carol* is repeated in the **Chimes**. But there is a different spiritual agency, very nicely and naturally derived from the simple, solitary, friendless life of the hero of the tale. He is a poor old ticket-porter of London; stands in his vocation by the corner of an old church; and has listened to the chiming of its Bells so constantly, that, with nothing else to talk to or befriend him, he has made out for himself a kind of human, friendly, fellow voice in theirs, and is glad to think they speak to him, pity him, sympathize with him, encourage and help him. . . .

He is a delightfully drawn character, this unrepining, patient, humble drudge—this honest, childish-hearted, shabby-coated, simple, kindly old man. There is not a touch of selfishness, even in the few complaints his hard lot wrings from him. (p. 184)

May this wise little tale second the hearty wishes of its writer, and at the least contribute to the coming year that portion of happiness which waits always upon just intentions and kind thoughts. (p. 189)

" 'The Chimes', by Mr. Dickens," in The Edinburgh Review, *Vol. LXXXI, No. CLXIII, January, 1845, pp. 181-89.*

THE NORTH AMERICAN REVIEW (essay date 1849)

[*Dombey and Son* is a fresh creation of Dickens's] unexhausted mind, in which the old manner is reproduced to introduce new matter. Here, as in his other novels, the characters are every thing and the story nothing; but the characters are sufficiently original, various, and numerous to compensate for far greater defects of plot and design. Captain Cuttle, Bunsby, Sol Gills, Major Bagstock, Pinch, Toodle, Toots, Mrs. Chick, Susan Nipper, Lucretia Tox, Rob, the lady whose husband invested in the Peruvian mines, not to mention others, are personages whose acquaintance once made is never broken. The beauty and pathos of the work cluster around Paul and Florence, and in these exquisite creations Dickens has exceeded the previous promise of his powers. The defects of the novel are partly owing to the ingrained peculiarities of the author, and partly to his mode of publication. Every part he is compelled to make interesting and effective in itself, without due regard to the general impression of the whole, and accordingly he often overdoes his humorous scenes, and reduces events to incidents. Some of the characters, also, refer to persons with whom he has not sufficient imaginative sympathy to delineate vitally. Mr. Carker is hardly equal to the stereotyped villain of Mr. James, and Dombey and Edith are blocks of painted wood. The whole description of them is external, without any vision into their natures. The rich abundance of humor, pathos, and character, so profusely scattered over the work, can hardly blind the simplest reader to the fact that the author always fails when he departs from the landmarks of his genius, and attempts the delineation of persons whose natures have been essentially modified by fashion, by convention, by worldliness, by morbid sentiment and passion. Villains, autocrats, fashionable people, misanthropes, sentimentalists, and young ladies, are but faintly gifted with human nature as sketched by Mr. Dickens, for they lie altogether out of the sphere of his healthy and genial genius. (p. 405)

> *"Novels and Novelists: Charles Dickens,"* in The North American Review, *Vol. LXIX, No. CXXXXV, October, 1849, pp. 383-406.*

FRASER'S MAGAZINE (essay date 1850)

[*Pictures from Italy*] was the result of a Continental tour, and, we have no doubt, paid the expenses of the same. Like all that has ever come from that pen, it is pleasant, amiable, and readable; but still we are of opinion that such success as it had was due rather to the established reputation of the author than to the intrinsic merits of the book. . . . Dickens, we should suppose, is not profoundly versed either in old Latin or modern Italian, and he is too honest to pretend it; he has no sterling knowledge of art, and despises the spurious cant of connoisseurship, so his observation was necessarily confined to the *still life* of Italy; and his 'Pictures' are mere flower and fruit pieces. . . . (p. 703)

[*David Copperfield*] is, in our opinion, the best of all the author's fictions. The plot is better contrived, and the interest more sustained, than in any other. Here there is no sickly sentiment, no prolix description, and scarcely a trace of exaggerated passion. The author's taste has become gradually more and more refined; his style has got to be more easy, graceful, and natural. The principal groups are delineated as carefully as ever; but instead of the elaborate Dutch painting to which we had been accustomed in his backgrounds and accessories, we have now a single vigorous touch here and there, which is far more artistic and far more effective. His winds do not howl, nor his seas roar through whole chapters, as formerly; he has become better acquainted with his readers, and ventures to leave more to their imagination. This is the first time that the hero has been made to tell his own story,—

a plan which generally ensures something like epic unity for the tale. We have several reasons for suspecting that, here and there, under the name of David Copperfield, we have been favoured with passages from the personal history, adventures, and experience, of Charles Dickens. Indeed, this conclusion is in a manner forced upon us by the peculiar professions selected for the ideal character, who is first a newspaper reporter and then a famous novelist. There is, moreover, an air of reality pervading the whole book, to a degree never attained in any of his previous works, and which cannot be entirely attributed to the mere *form* of narration. (p. 704)

One of the finest passages to be found in this, or indeed any, book, is that description of the storm at Yarmouth, which flings the dead body of the seducer on the shore, to lie amid the wrecks of the home he had desolated. The power of the artist impresses such an air of reality upon it all, that we do not think of questioning the probability of such poetical justice.

We have said that in *David Copperfield* there was *scarcely* a trace of exaggerated passion. But for Rosa Dartle, we should have said there was *no* trace. Her character we must think unnatural, and her conduct melodramatic. A wound, even on a *woman's cheek,* inflicted by a child in a fit of passion, is not a sufficient cause to turn all the tenderness of that woman's nature to bitterness. (p. 706)

> *"Charles Dickens and 'David Copperfield',"* in Fraser's Magazine, *Vol. 42, No. CCLII, December, 1850, pp. 698-710.*

[DAVID MASSON] (essay date 1851)

As the popular novelists of the day, Dickens and Thackeray, and again, Thackeray and Dickens, divide the public attention. And as the public has learned thus to think of them together, so also, using its privilege of chatting and pronouncing judgments about whatever interests it, it has learned to set off the merits of the one against those of the other, and to throw as much light into the criticism of each as can be derived from the trick of contrast. . . . [We] think that, in this notion of contrast, the public has really got hold of a good thread for a critic to pursue, and we mean, as far as possible, throughout this paper, to avail ourselves of it.

It is admitted that both writers are as well represented in their last as in any of their previous productions. [**"David Copperfield,"**] according to the general voice of the critics, is one of the best of Mr. Dickens's stories, written with decidedly more care and effort than its immediate predecessors, as if the author had determined to shew the captious public that his genius was as fine and fresh as ever. And though we have heard ["The History of Pendennis"] described as a mere continuation of "Vanity Fair," and no advance upon it in point of excellence, we believe the general opinion to be that Mr. Thackeray has not discredited himself by his recent performance, but has rather increased his popularity. Moreover, no two stories are better calculated to illustrate, in the way of contrast, the characteristic peculiarities of their respective authors. The very spirit and philosophy of all Mr. Dickens's writings is that which we find expressed in the character and life of David Copperfield, so that, did we want to describe that spirit and philosophy in a single term, we should not be far wrong in calling it *Copperfieldism;* and, on the other hand, in no work has Mr. Thackeray exhibited so fully that caustic, thoroughly British, and yet truly original humour, with which he regards the world and its ways, as in his sketch of the Life and Adventures of

Mr. Arthur Pendennis. When we say "Pendennis" and **"Copperfield,"** therefore, it is really the same as if we said Thackeray and Dickens. And this facility of finding the two authors duly contrasted in the two stories, is increased by the fact that the stories are in some respects very similar. In both we have the life and education of a young man related, from his childhood and school-time to that terminus of all novels, the happy marriage-point; in the one, the life and education of the orphan child of a poor gentleman in Suffolk; in the other, the life and education of the only son of a West of England squire, with a long Cornish pedigree. In both, too, the hero becomes a literary man, so that the author, in following him, finds room for allusions to London literary life. . . . But however that may be, there can be no doubt that the general external similarity that there is between the two stories will serve to throw into relief their essential differences of style and spirit.

These differences are certainly very great. Although following exactly the same literary walk, and both great favourites with the public, there are perhaps no two writers so dissimilar as Mr. Dickens and Mr. Thackeray. To begin with a matter which, though in the order of strict science it comes last, as involving and depending on all the others,—the matter of style or language: here everybody must recognise a remarkable difference between the two authors. (pp. 57-9)

[Our] impression of the difference between the two authors in the matter of style is . . . that Mr. Thackeray is the more terse and idiomatic, and Mr. Dickens the more diffuse and luxuriant writer. Both seem to be easy penmen, and to have language very readily at their command; both also seem to convey their meaning as simply as they can, and to be careful, according to their notions of verbal accuracy; but in Mr. Dickens's sentences there is a leafiness, a tendency to words and images, for their own sake. . . . On the whole, if we had to choose passages at random, to be set before young scholars as examples of easy and vigorous English composition, we would take them rather from Thackeray than from Dickens. . . . Where Mr. Dickens is not exerting himself . . . in passages of mere equable narrative or description, where there is nothing to move or excite him, his style, as we have already said, seems to us more careless and languid than that of Mr. Thackeray; sometimes, indeed, a whole page is only redeemed from weakness by those little touches of wit and those humorous turns of conception which he knows so well how to sprinkle over it. It is due to Mr. Dickens to state, however, that in this respect his **"Copperfield"** is one of his most pleasing productions, and a decided improvement on its predecessor **"Dombey."** Not only is the spirit of the book more gentle and mellow, but the style is more continuous and careful, with fewer of those recurring tricks of expression, the dead remnants of former felicities, which constituted what was called his mannerism. Nor must we omit to remark also, that in passages where higher feeling is called into play, Mr. Dickens's style always rises into greater purity and vigour, the weakness and the superfluity disappearing before the concentrating force of passion, and the language often pouring itself forth in a clear and flowing song. (pp. 61-3)

Regarding the general intellectual calibre . . . of the two men, our impression is, that Thackeray's is the mind of closer and more compact, Dickens's the mind of looser, richer, and freer texture. . . . There is a general force of talent, a worldly shrewdness and sagacity, as well as a certain breadth of culture, latent in it, from which we argue that the writer would in any company make himself felt, if not as a man of energetic ac-

tivity, at least as a man of quiet brain and vigour. Mr. Dickens, too, is of course a man whose intellect would be remarkable anywhere; for no writer could rise to his degree of excellence in any department without much of that general force and fulness of mind which would have enabled him to excel in any other; perhaps, also, his natural versatility is greater than that of Mr. Thackeray; still we do not see in him that habitual knowingness, that close-grained solidity of view, that impressive strong sense, which we find in what Thackeray writes. Mr. Dickens may be the more pensive and meditative, but Mr. Thackeray is the more penetrating and reflective writer. . . . Neither, on the one hand, does Mr. Dickens deepen and elaborate his thoughts by special effort, which might be deemed unsuitable in a novel; nor, on the other hand, do all his thoughts on their first expression, carry with them that air of native weight which would belong, we imagine, to the opinions of Thackeray. . . . As Mr. Dickens's language, though loose and redundant in the tame and level passages, gathers itself up and acquires concentration and melody under the influence of passion or pathos, so his thought, ordinarily lax and unwrought, attains real pith and volume when his feelings are moved. For this, we repeat, is the prerogative of an essentially susceptible and poetic nature, that every part and faculty of it, judgment as well as fancy, does its best when the frenzy is upon it. (pp. 63-5)

Dickens is by far the more opinionative and aggressive, Thackeray by far the more acquiescent and unpolemical, writer. . . . To whatever cause the fact is to be attributed—whether to a native combativeness conjoined with great benevolence of disposition, or to external circumstances that have developed in him the habit of taking a side in all current controversies—we should say, without hesitation, that few men, dominated so decidedly by the artistic temperament, have shewn so obvious an inclination as Mr. Dickens to step beyond the province of the artist, and exercise the functions of the social and moral critic. . . . [Very] many of Mr. Dickens's judgments on practical matters are sound and excellent . . . ; on some points, however, and especially in those higher regions of speculative doctrine into which we have said that Mr. Dickens has not seldom ventured, we believe his sentiments to be defective. (pp. 65-67)

Mr. Thackeray, though more competent, according to our view of him, to appear in the character of a general critic or essayist, seems far more of a *pococurante* than Mr. Dickens. Whether it is that he is naturally disposed to take the world as he finds it, or that, having at some time or other had very unsatisfactory experience of the trade of trying to mend it, he has taken up *pococurantism* as a theory, we have no means of saying; but certain it is, that in the writings he has given forth since he became known as one of our most distinguished literary men, he has meddled far less with the external arrangements of society than Mr. Dickens, and made far fewer appearances as a controversialist or reformer. (p. 67)

To pass, however, to the consideration of what is after all the most conspicuous difference between the two novelists, namely, the essential difference between their styles of literary art, their peculiar faculties and tastes as descriptive and imaginative writers. Here it will assist us very much in our discriminations if we call to mind, by way of illustration, the leading distinctions of style and faculty in the kindred art of painting.

One evident source or reason of distinction, then, in the art of painting, is the outwardly-fixed variety of those objects which it may be the aim of the painter to seize. From this source arises first of all, the theoretical distinction of painters into two great classes—landscape-painters and figure-painters. The former, speaking generally, are those who seek to represent scenes of inanimate nature; portions, larger or smaller, of all that varied glory of form and colour that lies between the concave of sky and cloud above, and the plane of earth and sea beneath. The objects of the figure painter, on the other hand, are beings endowed with life, either singly or in groups. (pp. 68-9)

But, independent of these outwardly-determined distinctions, and helping greatly to complicate them, are others, having their origin not in the outer variety of nature, but in the spirit and form of thought of the painter. Taking rise in this source, for instance, is the important distinction between what may be called the Real, and what may be called the Ideal, (we beg Mr. Thackeray's pardon for the use of these two words, which we do not like any more than he, and would avoid if we could,) style or theory of art. In the real style of art, the aim is to produce pictures that shall impress by their close and truthful resemblance to something or other in real nature or life. . . . [In] the higher sense in which the word imagination is often used, as implying a rarer exercise of inventive power, it cannot be said that the real style of painting is so imaginative as that which we have called the ideal. In this style of art the conception or intention supplied by the painter bears a larger proportion to the matter outwardly given than in the other. A picture executed in this style strikes, not by recalling real scenes and occurrences, but by taking the mind out of itself into a region of higher possibilities, wherein objects shall be more glorious, and modes of action more transcendent, than any we see, and yet all shall seem in nature. . . . [Artists] who favour the ideal theory, usually work in the more ambitious departments of landscape or figure painting; and hence probably it is that the real style is sometimes, though perhaps not very happily, called Low Art, and the ideal style, High Art.

All this may be transferred with ease to the occupation of the literary artist, or writer of fiction. Thus, applying it to the particular case in view, it may be said, in the first place, with respect to our two novelists, that the artistic faculty of Dickens is more comprehensive, goes over a wider range of the whole field of art, than that of Thackeray. . . . The range of Thackeray, on the other hand, is more restricted. In the landscape department he can give you a quiet little bit of background, such as a park, a clump of trees, or the vicinity of a country-house, with a village seen in the sunset; a London street, also, by night or by day, is familiar to his eye; but, upon the whole, his scenes are laid in those more habitual places of resort, where the business or pleasure of aristocratic or middle-class society goes on. . . . And his choice of subjects from the life corresponds with this. Men and women as they are, and as they behave daily, especially in the charmed circles of rank, literature, and fashion, are the subjects of Mr. Thackeray's pencil. . . . (pp. 69-71)

On the whole it may be said that, while there are few things that Mr. Thackeray can do in the way of description which Mr. Dickens could not also do, there is a large region of objects and appearances familiar to the artistic activity of Mr. Dickens, where Mr. Thackeray would not find himself at home. And as Mr. Dickens's artistic range is thus wider than that of Mr. Thackeray, so also his style of art is the more elevated. Thackeray is essentially an artist of the real school; he belongs to what, in painting, would be called the school of low art. All that he portrays—scenes as well as characters—is within the limits, and rigidly true to the features, of real existence. In this

lies his particular merit. . . . Dickens, on the other hand, works more in the ideal. It is nonsense to say of his characters generally, intending the observation for praise, that they are life-like. They are nothing of the kind. . . . [Dickens's] characters are real only thus far, that they are transcendental renderings of certain hints furnished by nature. Seizing the notion of some oddity as seen in the real world, Mr. Dickens has run away with it into a kind of outer or ideal region, there to play with it and work it out at leisure as extravagantly as he might choose, without the least impediment from any facts except those of his own story. One result of this method is, that his characters do not present the mixture of good and bad in the same proportions as we find in nature. . . . It is different with Mr. Thackeray. The last words of his "Pendennis" are a petition for the charity of his readers in behalf of the principal personage of the story, on the ground that not having meant to represent him as a hero, but "only as a man and a brother," he has exposed his foibles rather too freely. . . . Now, while, according to Mr. Thackeray's style of art, this is perfectly proper, it does not follow that Mr. Dickens's method is wrong. The characters of Shakespeare are not, in any common sense, life-like. They are not portraits of existing men and women, though doubtless there are splendid specimens even of this kind of art among them; they are grand hyperbolic beings created by the breath of the poet himself out of hints taken from all that is most sublime in nature; they are humanity caught, as it were, and kept permanent in its highest and extremest mood, nay carried forth and compelled to think, speak, and act in conditions superior to that mood. . . . Art is called Art, says Goethe, precisely because it is *not* Nature; and even such a department of art as the modern novel is entitled to the benefit of this maxim. While, therefore, in Mr. Thackeray's style of delineation, the just ground of praise is, as he claims it to be, the verisimilitude of the fictions, it would be no fair ground of blame against Mr. Dickens, in *his* style of delineation, to say that his fictions are hyperbolic. A truer accusation against him, in this respect, would be that, in the exercise of the right of hyperbole, he does not always preserve harmony; that, in his romantic creations, he sometimes falls into the extravagant, and, in his comic creations, sometimes into the grotesque.

But, while Mr. Dickens is both more extensive in the range, and more poetic in the style of his art than Mr. Thackeray, the latter is, perhaps, within his own range and in his own style, the more careful artist. His stroke is truer and surer, and his attention to finish greater. (pp. 74-6)

It is by the originality and interest of its characters that a novel is chiefly judged. And certainly it is a high privilege, that which the novelist possesses, of calling into existence new imaginary beings; of adding, as it were, to that population of aerial men and women, the offspring of past genius, which hovers over the heads of the actual population of the world. . . . Mr. Dickens [is] decidedly the more poetical and ideal, and Mr. Thackeray [is] decidedly the more world-like and real in the style and tendency of his conceptions. (pp. 76-7)

But, after all, it is by the moral spirit and sentiment of a work of fiction, by that unity of view and aim which pervades it, and which is the result of all the author's natural convictions and endowments, all his experience of life, and all his intellectual conclusions on questions great and little—it is by this that the worth of a work of fiction, and its title to an honourable place in literature, ought ultimately to be tried. . . . It remains for us, therefore, to go somewhat deeper than we have hitherto done, in our discrimination of the spirit of Thackeray's, as compared with the spirit of Dickens's writings. Here also "Pendennis" and **"Copperfield"** shall form the chief ground of our remarks.

Into this important question, as between the two novelists, the public has already preceded us. Go into any circle where literary talk is common, or take up any popular critical periodical, and the same invariable dictum will meet you—that Dickens is the more genial, cheerful, kindly, and sentimental, and Thackeray the more harsh, acrid, pungent, and satirical writer. This is said everywhere. Sometimes the criticism even takes the form of partizanship. (p. 78)

In the first place, then, the question as between "the aspirations after sentimental perfection" of Mr. Dickens, and the "sardonic divings" of Mr. Thackeray, connects itself with what we have been saying as to the styles of the two authors. "Aspiration after sentimental perfection," in other words, the habit of representing objects in an ideal light, is a necessary ingredient in that poetic or romantic style of art which Mr. Dickens practises; and "sardonic diving," as the reviewer expresses it, is quite as necessary an ingredient in Mr. Thackeray's constitution as an artist of the real school. . . . As pearls neither grow in crimson caskets, nor get thither by their own exertions, and are yet justly admired when found there, so it is no valid objection to Mr. Dickens's writings, in his style of art, that they represent men and women ideally, and as they never existed, or have existed only by flashes and at moments; but, on the other hand, what we require of a writer like Mr. Thackeray is, that, whether in delineating the bad or the good, he shall not exceed the proportions of the real. Nor do we think that he has done so. . . . [While] a writer like Dickens may do good in one way, a writer like Thackeray may do good in another. Ask the waiters at the London clubs, if Mr. Thackeray's exposition of human nature as manifested in these institutions has not been of some service to them. Probably the reason why many readers do not like Mr. Thackeray's writings is, that they find them too personal in their allusions. So much the better. (pp. 80-1)

But whence arises this difference between the two writers? Why is Mr. Dickens, on the whole, genial, kindly, and romantic, and Mr. Thackeray, on the whole, caustic, shrewd, and satirical in his fictions? Clearly, the difference must arise from some radical difference in their ways of looking at the world, and in their conclusions as to the business and destinies of men in it.

Kindliness is the first principle of Mr. Dickens's philosophy, the sum and substance of his moral system. He does not, of course, exclude such things as pain and indignation from his catalogue of legitimate existences; indeed, as we have seen, few writers are capable of more honest bursts of indignation against what is glaringly wrong; still, in what may be called his speculative ethics, kindliness has the foremost place. (p. 81)

[This doctrine] is diffused through all Mr. Dickens's writings, and is affirmed again and again in express and very eloquent passages. Now, certainly, there is a fine and loveable spirit in the doctrine; and a man may be borne up by it in his airy imaginings, as Mr. Dickens is, (we might add the name of Mr. Leigh Hunt,) so cheerily and beautifully, that it were a barbarity to demur to it at the moment without serious provocation. Who can fail to see that only a benevolent heart, overflowing with faith in this doctrine, could have written the **"Christmas Chimes,"** or conceived those exquisite reminiscences of childhood which delight us in the early pages of

"Copperfield"? But when Mr. Dickens becomes aggressive in behalf of his doctrine, . . . then a word of remonstrance seems really necessary. Is the foregoing doctrine, then, so axiomatic and absolute that no one may, without moral ugliness of soul, impugn or limit it? For our part, we do not think so. We know men, and very noble men, too, who would *not* rather see a poor idiot happy in the sunlight than a wise man pining in a darkened jail; we know men, and very cheerful men, too, who do *not* find the pictures of the book of nature to be all in bright and glowing tints, nor the sounds of nature to be all pleasant songs. (p. 82)

[David Masson,] "Pendennis and Copperfield: Thackeray and Dickens," in The North British Review, Vol. XV, No. XXIX, May, 1851, pp. 57-89.*

[MARGARET OLIPHANT]   (essay date 1855)

[It is to the fact that Dickens] represents a class that he owes his speedy elevation to the top of the wave of popular favour. He is a man of very liberal sentiments—an assailer of constituted wrongs and authorities—one of the advocates in the plea of Poor *versus* Rich, to the progress of which he has lent no small aid in his day. But he is, notwithstanding, perhaps more distinctly than any other author of the time, a *class* writer, the historian and representative of one circle in the many ranks of our social scale. Despite their descents into the lowest class, and their occasional flights into the less familiar ground of fashion, it is the air and the breath of middle-class respectability which fills the books of Mr. Dickens. . . . Mr. Dickens' heroes are all young for a necessity. Their courage is of the order of courage which belongs to women. They are spotless in their thoughts, their intentions, and wishes. Into those dens of vice, and unknown mysteries, whither the lordly Pelham may penetrate without harm, and which Messrs. Pendennis and Warrington frequent, that they may see "life," David Copperfield could not enter without pollution. In the very heart and soul of him this young man is *respectable*. He is a great deal more; he is pure, a thoroughly refined and gentle-hearted boy; but his respectability is strong upon him. His comings and goings are within a lesser circle than are those of his contemporaries whose names we have mentioned. He cannot afford to defy the world's laugh, or to scorn it. . . . In the society of Mr. Dickens' admirable stories, there is no such thing as going to the Haunt of nights and coming from thence uninjured. There is no such thing possible or permissible in the class and society, which Mr. Dickens draws. . . . Mr. Dickens contents his genius in the sphere in which we suppose his lot to have been cast by nature, in the largest "order" of our community—the middle-class of England. Having identified himself with this portion of society, and devoted his powers to its illustration, this grateful public carries its novelist in its heart; and without denying in any way his claims to that higher genius which can give life and breath—the truth of nature, if not of conventional correctness—to every impersonation of its fellows, we cannot do justice to Mr. Dickens without recognising this, his first and greatest claim to our regard, as the historian of a class. . . . (pp. 451-52)

[This] class does not abound in picturesque situations, and sometimes the meaner vices grow and flourish where respectability and the strong grasp of appearances keep grosser sins away. But nowhere does the household hearth burn brighter—nowhere is the family love so warm—the natural bonds so strong; and this is the ground which Mr. Dickens occupies *par excellence*—the field of his triumphs, from which he may defy all his rivals without fear. (pp. 452-53)

Mr. Dickens is the favourite and spoiled child of the popular heart. There is a long ring of applause echoing after him wherever it pleases him to go; but for the sake of his great and well-deserved reputation, we think it would be well for Mr. Dickens to discover on which foundation it is that he stands most secure.

And in this volume before us, the latest work he has given to the world—*Hard Times*—we discover, not the author's full and many-toned conception of human life, its motives and its practices,—not the sweet and graceful fancy rejoicing in her own creations, nor the stronger and graver imagination following the fate of her complete idea, rather as a chronicler than a producer of the events which its natural character and qualities call forth,—but the petulant theory of a man in the world of his own making, where he has no fear of being contradicted, and is absolutely certain of having everything his own way. We have seldom seen a more lamentable *non sequitur* than *Hard Times*. A story written in direct illustration of some preconceived idea is seldom successful as a story. . . . [The] real object of the book is, to prove that the teaching of universal knowledge, the instruction in all the "ologies," the education which arbitrarily imposes fact and puts down fancy, is a system which makes very poor villains of our sons, and very wretched wives of our daughters, and that the perfectly opposite system of no education at all, save the natural growth of the sentiments and affections, produces angels, not only of goodness, but of wisdom and judicious courage almost unparalleled. (pp. 453-54)

The book is more palpably a *made* book than any of the many manufactured articles we have lately seen. It is neither born out of the natural fruition of a mind and fancy always astir—nor, after it has begun to be, do its characters and events proceed with the natural compulsion and impulse of life. If Mr. Dickens forgets himself now and then, and remembers the craft of which he is a master, by running into a natural exhibition of nature and life, he draws up immediately under the hard necessity of holding by his text and proving his theory. To say that the story was without character or without interest would not be true; but we are sure that every reader really admiring the fine genius of Mr. Dickens must, in the annoyance and regret with which he reads, have almost overlooked the inalienable gifts of the writer. (p. 454)

In his own sphere, no man living equals Mr. Dickens—and perhaps there is no modern writer of whom we can say so confidently that his great excellences are innate, and not acquired. Much as he moves us to laughter, we know that quite as skilfully, and often with great delicacy and tenderness, he can move us to tears. Nor do we fail to find noble sentiments and just views of human nature in these works of genius, which may take their place, as illustrations of our age and daily fashion of existence, on an equal platform with the highest productions of the same class in any period of our history. Mr. Dickens has won for himself what is more to the purpose than the approbation of criticism, an affectionate welcome in the households and homes of his country. . . . [We] would fain add a word of friendly counsel to the warm admiration we offer. The law of kindness has come to man under the very loftiest sanction, and kindness sublimated into charity, Love, is the pervading spirit of the Gospel;—yet there is such a thing as unwise kindness, injurious love, maudlin charity, a weak suffusion of universal benevolence which is good for nothing but pretty speeches, pretty pictures, pretty sentiments and actions. . . . What does Mr. Dickens mean by all the caressing condescension with which this powerful organ of his strokes down "the poor"—by all these small admirable moral histories, these truths and wonders diluted to the meanest capacity?—what by his admiration of the frightful little weedy arbours at Battersea or Greenwich, where his working man carries his family, and improves his Sunday by a pipe and a pint of beer? . . . In this nineteenth century, with all our boasts and our enlightenment, are a pipe and a pint of beer the utmost delights which Mr. Dickens can offer, in his day of leisure, to the workingman? The waiter in his white apron, with his tray of glasses, is he a better influence than the poor preacher?—and the beer-stains on the table in the arbour, and the long pipes, and the talk—are these things more good, more beautiful, more improving for the little Opuses, than even the miseries of church-going? It is an old, old system to set up pleasure as the only thing which makes life tolerable; but this, at the utmost, is only amusement, not pleasure. . . . Let Mr. Dickens think better of this grievous yet glorious mystery, this life which craves something more than relaxation. (pp. 465-66)

But to Mr. Dickens, in his purer and higher authorship, this censure does not reach; and we have nothing to say to the author of David Copperfield, of Tom Pinch, of a hundred other pleasant creations, but the hearty goodspeed which would drown the ravings of the equinox with its resounding echo, could every individual who joins in the wish, join in the utterance. A kinder audience no man ever had, and it becomes their favourite to use them well. (p. 466)

[*Margaret Oliphant,*] *"Charles Dickens," in* Blackwood's Edinburgh Magazine, *Vol. LXXVII, No. CCCCLXXIV, April, 1855, pp. 451-66.*

BLACKWOOD'S EDINBURGH MAGAZINE (essay date 1857)

[In his post-Pickwickian works Dickens] aspires not only to be a humourist, but an artist and a moralist; and in his later productions, which we shall talk of by-and-by, he aims at being, besides artist and moralist, politician, philosopher, and ultra-philanthropist. If we direct attention to his weakness in these latter characters, it is solely because he has for years past evinced more and more his tendency to abandon his strong point at humourist and comic writer, and to base his pretensions on grounds which we consider utterly false and unstable. For as a humourist we prefer Dickens to all living men—as artist, moralist, politician, philosopher, and ultra-philanthropist, we prefer many living men, women, and children to Dickens. It is because we so cordially recognised, and so keenly enjoyed, his genius in his earlier works, that we now protest against the newer phase he chooses to appear in. Formerly, his impulses came from within. What his unerring eye saw, as it glanced round the world, was represented in a medium of the richest humour. But gradually his old characteristics have slipt from him, supplanted by others totally different in origin and result. All his inspiration now seems to come from without. . . . A booby who aims at being thought a thinker, . . . [assures Dickens] that his great strength lies in "going to the heart of our deepest social problems;" and straightway Dickens, the genial Dickens, overflowing by nature with the most rampant hearty fun, addresses himself to the melancholy task, setting to work to illustrate some enigma which Thomas Carlyle perhaps, or some such congenial dreary spirit, after discussing it in two volumes octavo, has left rather darker than before. Another luminary tells him that it is the duty of a great popular writer to be a great moral teacher, and straightway a piece of staring morality is embroidered into the motley pattern. . . . The result of some such guidance as we have imagined here appears in *Bleak House* and *Little Dorrit,* as well as in great part of both *Dombey* and *Copperfield.*

In executing this piebald plan, the old natural, easy, unconscious Pickwickian style has given place to one to which all those epithets are totally inapplicable; and the characteristics of which, always to us unpleasant, are growing more prominent in every successive work. One of the most striking of these resembles a habit in which many favourite comic actors have indulged to the injury of their reputation—that of presuming on their favour with the audience in jests and drolleries altogether extraneous from their part in the drama. . . . [Dickens] indulges, to an extent quite unparalleled, his remarkable power of endowing all his personages with peculiar acts, tones, and gestures, and noting them minutely down. The effect of this upon a naturally-drawn character is to bring it frequently into the foreground, when, from its intrinsic or accidental insignificance, it has no business there; upon an unnatural one (whose spasms are all sure to be chronicled), to give it the look of motion without life, always unpleasant, sometimes shocking. . . . The personages of his stories, having once had particular qualities ascribed to them, are for ever exhibiting these attributes in a way which, were it ever done in real life, would render a knowledge of our species of very easy attainment, since everybody not absolutely idiotic would read everybody else's character; and it is for this reason, perhaps, that Dickens, in order that all the characters may not find each other out prematurely, finds it expedient to represent so many of them as of weak intellect; so that, besides a sprinkling of professional idiots, for whom he has a great liking, his pages are always garnished with a vast number of amateur fools, whose claims to the honours of fatuity are not clearly admitted by the author.

All these errors, which a true artist would only fall into by accident, and would secretly know them himself for blots, are so widely spread over Boz's later works, that it is only here and there that a scrap of his native youthful genius peeps almost doubtfully through the lavish uppergrowth of affectation; and when, at long intervals, we see a bit of the old rich natural humour, we groan over it as travellers who love wine groan over the scattered vines of Madeira. . . . We trace the first appearance of these weeds of his mind to *Chuzzlewit;* but there such brilliant flowers as the Gampia grandiflora, the Bailey Seedling, the Lupin, and the Transatlantic specimens, might well make us regardless of the surrounding patches of dockens and thistles, which have now, however, made head to such an alarming extent that we can't wait for the end of the wilderness of *Little Dorrit* before recording our earnest protest and deep lament; for in that wilderness we sit down and weep when we remember thee, O *Pickwick!*

The first broad general conclusion which we arrive at from reading this last book, so far as it has gone, is, that Dickens, with all his fertility of invention, has less constructiveness than falls to the lot of five novel-writers out of six, including all the worst. Even if, in the few remaining numbers, the joints of the story should be tightened up, and the different parts of the machinery made to work in something like harmony, yet that would not now retrieve the character of so aimless a work. A most cumbrous array of characters and scenes has been set in motion, and all for what? (pp. 495-97)

Mr. Dickens's blindest admirers will scarcely pretend that [*Little Dorrit*] is a work of art. But perhaps they will say that he has other grounds to build on besides art; and remembering how clear and vivid is the impression left by *Pickwick,* in which art certainly had little to do, we admit the justice of the reply. But if this is not a work of art, what is it? Is it a work of humour? (p. 498)

We suppose that all readers not deaf to reason on the subject of Dickens, will admit that [his current] style of writing, however long continued, will never constitute a work of humour. . . . Is it, then, a novel of character? (p. 499)

[In] the absence of incident, it is difficult to see how character can display itself. Hence arises another prime fault. In a great novel the incidents and characters work together for good, characters producing incident, incident calling forth traits of character, till in the very highest specimens the principal personages are scarcely fully developed before the end of the book. But here a character is minutely described on its first appearance, and henceforward it is a mere repetition, never developing or evolving itself in the least; and whole pages are taken up with the talk about nothing, of people who, if they talked about something, would not be worth listening to. (p. 500)

In Dickens's estimation, there is no such thing as insignificance. Throughout the book there is the same tendency apparent to exhaust every part of every subject, whether description, narration, or dialogue, the result being, of course, altogether inadequate to the power exercised, because the material is so worthless. It is like employing some vast machine that is meant for welding iron and cutting steel to macerate old rags.

A novel which, besides being destitute of well-considered plot, is not a novel of incident or character, can scarcely be a great picture of life; indeed, the number of puppets, dummies, and unnatural creations that grimace and jerk their way along the scenes, forbid it to be so considered. (p. 502)

If, then, this is not a work of any of the kinds we have mentioned, what is it? We really cannot tell? but we should imagine that Mr. Dickens, seeing his large canvass spread, remembering his successes, and feeling his power of work, conceives always an ambitious design of being at once a graphic storyteller, a social reformer, a limner of life, a great moral teacher, and a political satirist, and between all these stools, some of which have very weak legs, comes ignominiously to the ground, where he sits as complacently as if he were throned on Olympus.

What can be weaker in itself, to say nothing of the total want of art in connecting it with the story, than the intended satire on the Circumlocution Office? We don't in the least wish to stand up for the Circumlocution Office—curse the Circumlocution Office, say we. We know well the amount of insolence and ignorance to be found among Government officials of all departments. But the attempt to show it up in *Little Dorrit* is as inartificial as if he had cut half-a-dozen leading articles out of an Opposition newspaper, and stuck them in anyhow, anywhere. Besides, in all his attempts to embody political questions, Dickens has never shown a spark of original thought. . . . The next time Mr. Dickens dines out, the gentlemen on each side of him will probably be just as much entitled to a hearing on a political question as he is. We don't want him to be a politician, of whom there are plenty; we want him to be a humourist, and painter of passion and life, where he stands almost without a peer.

On reading over what we have written, we almost fear we have expressed ourselves with a little tinge of severity. But Dickens, dear Dickens, no offence—none! We have spoken to thee not in anger, but in sorrow—"not in drink, but in tears—not in words only, but in woes also." Can we bear that you, whom we ranked among the foremost men of all this world, should become a weaver of odds and ends into a pattern resembling nothing in heaven or earth, and which cannot even hold together? . . . We appeal from the author of **Bleak House** and **Little Dorrit** to the author of **Pickwick, The Old Curiosity Shop,** and the better parts of **Chuzzlewit.** Not in humour only are you dear to us, but in tragedy also, and in pathos we own your power. . . . [For] fancy and humour and pathos combined, there is that entire and perfect chrysolite the **Christmas Carol,** which we read aloud ever on a Christmas eve to an audience that ever still responds with weeping and with laughter. Remembering these benefits, ungrateful should we be beyond all measure of ingratitude, should we now write one word in spirit otherwise than of truest friendship of him who wrote so well in the brave days of old. . . . [If] you do not take our advice, and mean to go on building streets of Bleak Houses, and creating crowds of Little Dorrits, then we recommend you to inscribe on your next serial, "A Banter on the British Public. By Charles Dickens. In Twenty Parts." (pp. 502-03)

"Remonstrance with Dickens," in Blackwood's Edinburgh Magazine, *Vol. LXXXI, No. CCCCXCVIII, April, 1857, pp. 491-503.*

WALTER BAGEHOT (essay date 1858)

[Dickens's] range is very varied. He has attempted to describe every kind of scene in English life, from quite the lowest to almost the highest. He has not endeavoured to secure success by confining himself to a single path, nor wearied the public with repetitions of the subjects by the delineation of which he originally obtained fame. In his earlier works he never writes long without saying something well; something which no other man would have said; but even in them it is the characteristic of his power that it is apt to fail him at once; from masterly strength we pass without interval to almost infantine weakness,—something like disgust succeeds in a moment to an extreme admiration. Such is the natural fate of an unequal mind employing itself on a vast and various subject. (p. 171)

[Dickens] is utterly deficient in the faculty of reasoning. 'Mamma, what shall I think about?' said the small girl. 'My dear, don't think,' was the old-fashioned reply. We do not allege that in the strict theory of education this was a correct reply; modern writers think otherwise; but we wish some one would say it to Mr. Dickens. He is often troubled with the idea that he must reflect, and his reflections are perhaps the worst reading in the world. There is a sentimental confusion about them; we never find the consecutive precision of mature theory, or the cold distinctness of clear thought. Vivid facts stand out in his imagination; and a fresh illustrative style brings them home to the imagination of his readers; but his continuous philosophy utterly fails in the attempt to harmonise them,—to educe a theory or elaborate a precept from them. (pp. 171-72)

Nor has Mr. Dickens the easy and various sagacity which, as has been said, gives a unity to all which it touches. He has, indeed, a quality which is near allied to it in appearance. His shrewdness in some things, especially in traits and small things, is wonderful. His works are full of acute remarks on petty doings, and well exemplify the telling power of minute circumstantiality. But the minor species of perceptive sharpness is so different from diffused sagacity, that the two scarcely

ever are to be found in the same mind. . . . He excels in inventories of poor furniture, and is learned in pawnbrokers' tickets. But, although his creative power lives and works among the middle class and industrial section of English society, he has never painted the highest part of their daily intellectual life. He made, indeed, an attempt to paint specimens of the apt and able man of business in **Nicholas Nickleby;** but the Messrs. Cheeryble are among the stupidest of his characters. He forgot that breadth of platitude is rather different from breadth of sagacity. His delineations of middle-class life have in consequence a harshness and meanness which do not belong to that life in reality. He omits the relieving element. (pp. 172-73)

The *bizarrerie* of Mr. Dickens's genius is rendered more remarkable by the inordinate measure of his special excellences. The first of these is his power of observation in detail. . . . There are single pages containing telling minutiae which other people would have thought enough for a volume. Nor is his sensibility to external objects, though omnivorous, insensible to the artistic effect of each. There are scarcely anywhere such pictures of London as he draws. No writer has equally comprehended the artistic material which is given by its extent, its congregation of different elements, its mouldiness, its brilliancy.

Nor does his genius, though, from some idiosyncrasy of mind or accident of external situation, it is more especially directed to city life—at all stop at the city wall. He is especially at home in the picturesque and obvious parts of country life, particularly in the comfortable and (so to say) mouldering portion of it. (pp. 173-74)

Mr. Dickens has, however, no feeling analogous to the nature-worship of some other recent writers. There is nothing Wordsworthian in his bent; the interpreting inspiration (as that school speak) is not his. Nor has he the erudition in difficult names which has filled some pages in late novelists with mineralogy and botany. His descriptions of nature are fresh and superficial; they are not sermonic or scientific.

Nevertheless, it may be said that Mr. Dickens's genius is especially suited to the delineation of city life. London is like a newspaper. Everything is there, and everything is disconnected. . . . This is advantageous to Mr. Dickens's genius. His memory is full of instances of old buildings and curious people, and he does not care to piece them together. On the contrary, each scene, to his mind, is a separate scene,—each street a separate street. He has, too, the peculiar alertness of observation that is observable in those who live by it. He describes London like a special correspondent for posterity.

A second most wonderful special faculty which Mr. Dickens possesses is what we may call his *vivification* of character, or rather of characteristics. His marvellous power of observation has been exercised upon men and women even more than upon town or country; and the store of human detail, so to speak, in his books is endless and enormous. . . . He has a very peculiar power of taking hold of some particular traits, and making a character out of them. He is especially apt to incarnate particular professions in this way. Many of his people never speak without some allusion to their occupation. You cannot separate them from it. Nor does the writer ever separate them. What would Mr. Mould be if not an undertaker? . . . Accordingly, of necessity, such delineations become caricatures. We do not in general contrast them with reality; but as soon as we do, we are struck with the monstrous exaggerations which they present. You could no more fancy Sam Weller, or Mark Tapley, or the Artful Dodger really existing, walking about among common ordinary men and women, than you can fancy a talking duck or a writing bear. They are utterly beyond the pale of ordinary social intercourse. We suspect, indeed, that Mr. Dickens does not conceive his characters to himself as mixing in the society he mixes in. He sees people in the street, doing certain things, talking in a certain way, and his fancy petrifies them in the act. (pp. 175-77)

Some persons may think that this is not a very high species of delineative art. The idea of personifying traits and trades may seem to them poor and meagre. Anybody, they may fancy, can do that. But how would they do it? Whose fancy would not break down in a page,—in five lines? Who could carry on the vivification with zest and energy and humour for volume after volume? Endless fertility in laughter-causing detail is Mr. Dickens's most astonishing peculiarity. It requires a continuous and careful reading of his works to be aware of his enormous wealth. Writers have attained the greatest reputation for wit and humour, whose whole works do not contain so much of either as are to be found in a very few pages of his.

Mr. Dickens's humour is indeed very much a result of the two peculiarities of which we have been speaking. His power of detailed observation and his power of idealising individual traits of character—sometimes of one or other of them, sometimes of both of them together. His similes on matters of external observation are so admirable that everybody appreciates them, and it would be absurd to quote specimens of them; nor is it the sort of excellence which best bears to be paraded for the purposes of critical example. Its off-hand air and natural connection with the adjacent circumstances are inherent parts of its peculiar merit. Every reader of Mr. Dickens's works knows well what we mean. And who is not a reader of them?

But his peculiar humour is even more indebted to his habit of vivifying external traits, than to his power of external observation. He, as we have explained, expands traits into people; and it is a source of true humour to place these, when so expanded, in circumstances in which only people—that is complete human beings—can appropriately act. (pp. 180-81)

[It] is essential to remember, that however great may be and is the charm of such exaggerated personifications [as Mr. Pickwick], the best specimens of them are immensely less excellent, belong to an altogether lower range of intellectual achievements, than the real depiction of actual living men. It is amusing to read of beings *out of* the laws of morality, but it is more profoundly interesting, as well as more instructive, to read of those whose life in its moral conditions resembles our own. (p. 183)

There is one class of Mr. Dickens's pictures which may seem to form an exception to this criticism. It is the delineation of the outlaw, we might say the anti-law, world in ***Oliver Twist***. In one or two instances Mr. Dickens has been so fortunate as to hit on characteristics which, by his system of idealisation and continual repetition, might really be brought to look like a character. A man's trade or profession in regular life can only exhaust a very small portion of his nature; no approach is made to the essence of humanity by the exaggeration of the traits which typify a beadle or an undertaker. With the outlaw world it is somewhat different. The bare fact of a man belonging to that world is so important to his nature, that if it is artistically developed with coherent accessories, some approximation to a distinctly natural character will be almost inevitably made. (p. 184)

In the cases in which Mr. Dickens has attempted to make a long connected story, or to develop into scenes or incidents a plan in any degree elaborate, the result has been a complete failure. A certain consistency of genius seems necessary for the construction of a consecutive plot. An irregular mind naturally shows itself in incoherency of incident and aberration of character. The method in which Mr. Dickens's mind works, if we are correct in our criticism upon it, tends naturally to these blemishes. Caricatures are necessarily isolated; they are produced by the exaggeration of certain conspicuous traits and features; each being is enlarged on its greatest side; and we laugh at the grotesque grouping and the startling contrast. But the connection between human beings on which a plot depends is rather severed than elucidated by the enhancement of their diversities. (p. 186)

The defect of plot is heightened by Mr. Dickens's great, we might say complete, inability to make a love-story. A pair of lovers is by custom a necessity of narrative fiction, and writers who possess a great general range of mundane knowledge, and but little knowledge of the special sentimental subject, are often in amusing difficulties. The watchful reader observes the transition from the hearty description of well-known scenes, of prosaic streets, or journeys by wood and river, to the pale colours of ill-attempted poetry, to such sights as the novelist wishes he need not try to see. But few writers exhibit the difficulty in so aggravated a form as Mr. Dickens. Most men by taking thought can make a lay figure to look not so very unlike a young gentleman, and can compose a telling schedule of ladylike charms. Mr. Dickens has no power of doing either. The heroic character—we do not mean the form of character so called in life and action, but that which is hereditary in the heroes of novels—is not suited to his style of art. . . . [Most] men can make a tumble of blue eyes and fair hair and pearly teeth, that does very well for a young lady, at least for a good while; but Mr. Dickens will not, probably cannot, attain even to this humble measure of descriptive art. He vitiates the repose by broad humour, or disenchants the delicacy by an unctuous admiration.

This deficiency is probably nearly connected with one of Mr. Dickens's most remarkable excellences. No one can read Mr. Thackeray's writings without feeling that he is perpetually treading as close as he dare to the border-line that separates the world which may be described in books from the world which it is prohibited so to describe. . . . Mr. Dickens is chargeable with no such defect: he does not seem to feel the temptation. By what we may fairly call an instinctive purity of genius, he not only observes the conventional rules, but makes excursions into topics which no other novelist could safely handle, and by a felicitous instinct, deprives them of all impropriety. . . . At the same time it is difficult not to believe that this singular insensibility to the temptations to which many of the greatest novelists have succumbed is in some measure connected with his utter inaptitude for delineating the portion of life to which their art is specially inclined. He delineates neither the love-affairs which ought to be nor those which ought not to be.

Mr. Dickens's indisposition to 'make capital' out of the most commonly tempting part of human sentiment is the more remarkable because he certainly does not show the same indisposition in other cases. He has naturally great powers of pathos; his imagination is familiar with the common sorts of human suffering; and his marvellous conversancy with the detail of existence enables him to describe sick-beds and death-beds with an excellence very rarely seen in literature. . . . [But he] dwells on dismal scenes with a kind of fawning fondness; and he seems unwilling to leave them, long after his readers have had more than enough of them. He describes Mr. Dennis the hangman as having a professional fondness for his occupation: he has the same sort of fondness apparently for the profession of death-painter. The painful details he accumulates are a very serious drawback from the agreeableness of his writings. Dismal 'light literature' is the dismallest of reading. The reality of the police-reports is sufficiently bad, but a fictitious police-report would be the most disagreeable of conceivable compositions. Some portions of Mr. Dickens's books are liable to a good many of the same objections. They are squalid from noisome trivialities, and horrid with terrifying crime. (pp. 186-89)

Mr. Dickens's political opinions have subjected him to a good deal of criticism, and to some ridicule. He has shown, on many occasions, the desire—which we see so frequent among able and influential men—to start as a political reformer. . . . His is what we may call the 'sentimental radicalism;' and if we recur to the history of the time, we shall find that there would not originally have been any opprobrium attaching to such a name. The whole course of the legislation, and still more of the administration, of the first twenty years of the nineteenth century was marked by a harsh unfeelingness which is of all faults the most contrary to any with which we are chargeable now. . . . Mr. Dickens is an example both of the proper use and of the abuse of the sentiment. His earlier works have many excellent descriptions of the abuses which had descended to the present generation from others whose sympathy with pain was less tender. Nothing can be better than the description of the poor debtors' gaols in *Pickwick,* or of the old parochial authorities in *Oliver Twist.* No doubt these descriptions are caricatures, all his delineations are so; but the beneficial use of such art can hardly be better exemplified. . . . The contrast between the destitute condition of Job Trotter and Mr. Jingle and their former swindling triumph, is made comic by a rarer touch of unconscious art. Mr. Pickwick's warm heart takes so eager an interest in the misery of his old enemies, that our colder nature is tempted to smile. We endure the over-intensity, at any rate the unnecessary aggravation, of the surrounding misery; and we endure it willingly, because it brings out better than anything else could have done the half-comic intensity of a sympathetic nature.

It is painful to pass from these happy instances of well-used power to the glaring abuses of the same faculty in Mr. Dickens's later books. He began by describing really removable evils in a style which would induce all persons, however insensible, to remove them if they could; he has ended by describing the natural evils and inevitable pains of the present state of being in such a manner as must tend to excite discontent and repining. The result is aggravated, because Mr. Dickens never ceases to hint that these evils are removable, though he does not say by what means. (pp. 189-91)

We have throughout spoken of Mr. Dickens as he was, rather than as he is; or, to use a less discourteous phrase, and we hope a truer, of his early works rather than of those which are more recent. We could not do otherwise consistently with the true code of criticism. A man of great genius, who has written great and enduring works, must be judged mainly by them; and not by the inferior productions which, from the necessities of personal position, a fatal facility of composition, or other cause, he may pour forth at moments less favourable to his

powers. Those who are called on to review these inferior productions themselves, must speak of them in the terms they may deserve; but those who have the more pleasant task of estimating as a whole the genius of the writer, may confine their attention almost wholly to those happier efforts which illustrate that genius. We should not like to have to speak in detail of Mr. Dickens's later works, and we have not done so. There are, indeed, peculiar reasons why a genius constituted as his is (at least if we are correct in the view which we have taken of it) would not endure without injury during a long life the applause of the many, the temptations of composition, and the general excitement of existence. . . . The most characteristic part of his audience, the lower middle-class, were ready to receive with delight the least favourable productions of his genius. Human nature cannot endure this; it is too much to have to endure a coincident temptation both from within and from without. Mr. Dickens was too much inclined by natural disposition to lachrymose eloquence and exaggerated caricature. Such was the kind of writing which he wrote most easily. He found likewise that such was the kind of writing that was read most readily; and of course he wrote that kind. Who would have done otherwise? No critic is entitled to speak very harshly of such degeneracy, if he is not sure that he could have coped with difficulties so peculiar. If that rule is to be observed, who is there that will not be silent? No other Englishman has attained such a hold on the vast populace; it is little, therefore, to say that no other has surmounted its attendant temptations. (pp. 195-97)

> Walter Bagehot, ''Charles Dickens'' (1858), in his Literary Studies (reprinted by permission of the publisher, E. P. Dutton, Inc.), Dutton, 1911, pp. 164-97.

JAMES FITZJAMES STEPHEN (essay date 1859)

There are few more touching books in their way than the last of the *Waverly Novels.* The readers of *Castle Dangerous* and *Count Robert of Paris* can hardly fail to see in those dreary pages the reflection of a proud and honourable man redeeming what he looked upon as his honour at the expense of his genius. Sir Walter Scott's desperate efforts to pay his debts by extracting the very last ounce of metal from a mine which had long been substantially worked out, deserve the respect and enlist the sympathy which is the due of high spirit and unflinching courage. The novels, to be sure, are as bad as bad can be; but to pay debts is a higher duty than to write good novels, and as monuments of what can be done in that direction by a determined man, they are not without their interest and value. They have, moreover, the negative value of being only bad. They are not offensive or insulting. (p. 38)

In the *Tale of Two Cities,* Mr. Dickens has reached the *Castle Dangerous* stage without Sir Walter Scott's excuse; and instead of wholesome food ill-dressed, he has put before his readers dishes of which the quality is not disguised by the cooking. . . . It is a most curious production, whether it is considered in a literary, in a moral, or in an historical point of view. If it had not borne Mr. Dickens's name, it would in all probability have hardly met with a single reader; and if it has any popularity at all, it must derive it from the circumstance that it stands in the same relation to his other books as salad dressing stands in towards a complete salad. It is a bottle of the sauce in which *Pickwick* and *Nicholas Nickleby* were dressed, and to which they owed much of their popularity; and though it has stood open on the sideboard for a very long time, and has lost a good deal of its original flavour, the philosophic inquirer who is willing to go through the penance of tasting it will be, to a certain extent, repaid. He will have an opportunity of studying in its elements a system of cookery which procured for its ingenious inventor unparalleled popularity, and enabled him to infect the literature of his country with a disease which manifests itself in such repulsive symptoms that it has gone far to invert the familiar doctrines of the Latin Grammar about ingenuous arts, and to substitute for them the conviction that the principal results of a persistent devotion to literature are an incurable vulgarity of mind and of taste, and intolerable arrogance of temper. (pp. 38-9)

No portion of [Mr. Dickens's] popularity is due to intellectual excellence. The higher pleasures which novels are capable of giving are those which are derived from the development of a skilfully constructed plot, or the careful and moderate delineation of character; and neither of these are to be found in Mr. Dickens's works, nor has his influence over his contemporaries had the slightest tendency to promote the cultivation by others of the qualities which produce them. The two main sources of his popularity are his power of working upon the feelings by the coarsest stimulants, and his power of setting common occurrences in a grotesque and unexpected light. In his earlier works, the skill and vigour with which these operations were performed were so remarkable as to make it difficult to analyse the precise means by which the effect was produced on the mind of the reader. Now that familiarity has deprived his books of the gloss and freshness which they formerly possessed, the mechanism is laid bare; and the fact that the means by which the effect is produced are really mechanical has become painfully apparent. It would not, indeed, be matter of much difficulty to frame from such a book as the *Tale of Two Cities* regular recipes for grotesque and pathetic writing, by which any required quantity of the article might be produced with infallible certainty. The production of pathos is the simpler operation of the two. With a little practice and a good deal of determination, it would really be as easy to harrow up people's feelings as to poke the fire. The whole art is to take a melancholy subject, and rub the reader's nose in it, and this does not require any particular amount either of skill or knowledge. (p. 41)

To be grotesque is a rather more difficult trick than to be pathetic; but it is just as much a trick, capable of being learned and performed almost mechanically. One principal element of grotesqueness is unexpected incongruity; and inasmuch as most things are different from most other things, there is in nature a supply of this element of grotesqueness which is absolutely inexhaustible. Whenever Mr. Dickens writes a novel, he makes two or three comic characters just as he might cut a pig out of a piece of orange-peel. In the present story there are two comic characters, one of whom is amusing by reason of the facts that his name is Jerry Cruncher, that his hair sticks out like iron spikes, and that, having reproached his wife for "flopping down on her knees" to pray, he goes on for seventeen years speaking of praying as "flopping." If, instead of saying that his hair was like iron spikes, Mr. Dickens had said that his ears were like mutton-chops, or his nose like a Bologna sausage, the effect would have been much the same. . . . As there are many members in one body, Mr. Dickens may possibly live long enough to have a character for each of them, so that he may have one character identified by his eyebrows, another by his nostrils, and another by his toe-nails. No popularity can disguise the fact that this is the very lowest of low styles of art. (pp. 42-3)

One special piece of grotesqueness introduced by Mr. Dickens into his present tale is very curious. A good deal of the story relates to France, and many of the characters are French. Mr. Dickens accordingly makes them talk a language which, for a few sentences, is amusing enough, but which becomes intolerably tiresome and affected when it is spread over scores of pages. He translates every French word by its exact English equivalent. For example, "Voilà votre passeport" becomes "Behold your passport"—"Je viens de voir," "I come to see," &c. Apart from the bad taste of this, it shows a perfect ignorance of the nature and principles of language. (p. 43)

The moral tone of the *Tale of Two Cities* is not more wholesome than that of its predecessors, nor does it display any nearer approach to a solid knowledge of the subject-matter to which it refers. . . . The people, says Mr. Dickens, in effect, had been degraded by long and gross misgovernment, and acted like wild beasts in consequence. There is, no doubt, a great deal of truth in this view of the matter, but it is such very elementary truth that, unless a man had something new to say about it, it is hardly worth mentioning; and Mr. Dickens supports it by specific assertions which, if not absolutely false, are at any rate so selected as to convey an entirely false impression. It is a shameful thing for a popular writer to exaggerate the faults of the French aristocracy in a book which will naturally find its way to readers who know very little of the subject except what he chooses to tell them; but it is impossible not to feel that the melodramatic story which Mr. Dickens tells about the wicked Marquis who violates one of his serfs and murders another, is a grossly unfair representation of the state of society in France in the middle of the eighteenth century. (pp. 44-5)

England as well as France comes in for Mr. Dickens's favours. He takes a sort of pleasure, which appears to us insolent and unbecoming in the extreme, in drawing the attention of his readers exclusively to the bad and weak points in the history and character of their immediate ancestors. The grandfathers of the present generation were, according to him, a sort of savages, or very little better. They were cruel, bigoted, unjust, ill-governed, oppressed, and neglected in every possible way. The childish delight with which Mr. Dickens acts Jack Horner, and says What a good boy am I, in comparison with my benighted ancestors, is thoroughly contemptible. (p. 45)

*James Fitzjames Stephen, "'A Tale of Two Cities',"
in* The Saturday Review, *London, Vol. 8, No. 216,
December 17, 1859 (and reprinted in* The Dickens
Critics, *edited by George H. Ford and Lauriat Lane,
Jr., Cornell University Press, 1961, pp. 38-46).*

JOHN RUSKIN   (essay date 1860)

The essential value and truth of Dickens's writings have been unwisely lost sight of by many thoughtful persons merely because he presents his truth with some colour of caricature. Unwisely, because Dickens's caricature, though often gross, is never mistaken. Allowing for his manner of telling them, the things he tells us are always true. I wish that he could think it right to limit his brilliant exaggeration to works written only for public amusement; and when he takes up a subject of high national importance, such as that which he handled in *Hard Times,* that he would use severer and more accurate analysis. The usefulness of that work (to my mind, in several respects, the greatest he has written) is with many persons seriously diminished because Mr. Bounderby is a dramatic monster, instead of a characteristic example of a worldly master; and

Stephen Blackpool a dramatic perfection, instead of a characteristic example of an honest workman. But let us not lose the use of Dickens's wit and insight, because he chooses to speak in a circle of stage fire. He is entirely right in his main drift and purpose in every book he has written; and all of them, but especially **Hard Times,** should be studied with close and earnest care by persons interested in social questions. They will find much that is partial, and, because partial, apparently unjust; but if they examine all the evidence on the other side, which Dickens seems to overlook, it will appear, after all their trouble, that his view was the finally right one, grossly and sharply told. (pp. 47-8)

John Ruskin, "Unto this Last," in The Cornhill Magazine, *Vol. II, August, 1860 (and reprinted as "A Note on 'Hard Times'," in* The Dickens Critics, *edited by George H. Ford and Lauriat Lane, Jr., Cornell University Press, 1961, pp. 47-8).*

[EDWIN P. WHIPPLE] (essay date 1861)

The very title of this book ["**Great Expectations**"] indicates the confidence of conscious genius. In a new aspirant for public favor, such a title might have been a good device to attract attention; but the most famous novelist of the day, watched by jealous rivals and critics, could hardly have selected it, had he not inwardly felt the capacity to meet all the expectations he raised. We have read it, as we have read all Mr. Dickens's previous works, as it appeared in instalments, and can testify to the felicity with which expectation was excited and prolonged, and to the series of surprises which accompanied the unfolding of the plot of the story. In no other of his romances has the author succeeded so perfectly in at once stimulating and baffling the curiosity of his readers. He stirred the dullest minds to guess the secret of his mystery; but, so far as we have learned, the guesses of his most intelligent readers have been almost as wide of the mark as those of the least apprehensive. It has been all the more provoking to the former class, that each surprise was the result of art, and not of trick; for a rapid review of previous chapters has shown that the materials of a strictly logical development of the story were freely given. Even after the first, second, third, and even fourth of these surprises gave their pleasing electric shocks to intelligent curiosity, the *dénouement* was still hidden, though confidentially foretold. The plot of the romance is therefore universally admitted to be the best that Dickens has ever invented. Its leading events are, as we read the story consecutively, artistically necessary, yet, at the same time, the processes are artistically concealed. We follow the movement of a logic of passion and character, the real premises of which we detect only when we are startled by the conclusions.

The plot of "**Great Expectations**" is also noticeable as indicating, better than any of his previous stories, the individuality of Dickens's genius. Everybody must have discerned in the action of his mind two diverging tendencies, which, in this novel, are harmonized. He possesses a singularly wide, clear, and minute power of accurate observation, both of things and of persons; but his observation, keen and true to actualities as it independently is, is not a dominant faculty, and is opposed or controlled by the strong tendency of his disposition to pathetic or humorous idealization. Perhaps in "**The Old Curiosity Shop**" these qualities are best seen in their struggle and divergence, and the result is a magnificent juxtaposition of romantic tenderness, melodramatic improbabilities, and broad farce. The humorous characterization is joyously exaggerated

into caricature,—the serious characterization into romantic unreality. (pp. 380-81)

In "**Great Expectations**," on the contrary, Dickens seems to have attained the mastery of powers which formerly more or less mastered him. He has fairly discovered that he cannot, like Thackeray, narrate a story as if he were a mere looker-on, a mere "knowing" observer of what he describes and represents; and he has therefore taken observation simply as the basis of his plot and his characterization. . . . In "**Great Expectations**" there is shown a power of external observation finer and deeper even than Thackeray's; and yet, owing to the presence of other qualities, the general impression is not one of objective reality. The author palpably uses his observations as materials for his creative faculties to work upon; he does not record, but invents; and he produces something which is natural only under conditions prescribed by his own mind. He shapes, disposes, penetrates, colors, and contrives everything, and the whole action is a series of events which could have occurred only in his own brain, and which it is difficult to conceive of as actually "happening." And yet in none of his other works does he evince a shrewder insight into real life, and a clearer perception and knowledge of what is called "the world." The book is, indeed, an artistic creation, and not a mere succession of humorous and pathetic scenes, and demonstrates that Dickens is now in the prime, and not in the decline of his great powers.

The characters of the novel also show how deeply it has been meditated; for, though none of them may excite the personal interest which clings to Sam Weller or little Dombey, they are better fitted to each other and to the story in which they appear than is usual with Dickens. They all combine to produce that unity of impression which the work leaves on the mind. Individually they will rank among the most original of the author's creations. (pp. 381-82)

The style of the romance is rigorously close to things. The author is so engrossed with the objects before his mind, is so thoroughly in earnest, that he has fewer of those humorous caprices of expression in which formerly he was wont to wanton. Some of the old hilarity and play of fancy is gone, but we hardly miss it in our admiration of the effects produced by his almost stern devotion to the main idea of his work. There are passages of description and narrative in which we are hardly conscious of the words, in our clear apprehension of the objects and incidents they convey. The quotable epithets and phrases are less numerous than in "**Dombey & Son**" and "**David Copperfield**"; but the scenes and events impressed on the imagination are perhaps greater in number and more vivid in representation. The poetical element of the writer's genius, his modification of the forms, hues, and sounds of Nature by viewing them through the medium of an imagined mind, is especially prominent throughout the descriptions with which the work abounds. Nature is not only described, but individualized and humanized.

Altogether we take great joy in recording our conviction that "**Great Expectations**" is a masterpiece. . . . In our opinion, "**Great Expectations**" is a work which proves that we may expect from Dickens a series of romances far exceeding in power and artistic skill the productions which have already given him such a preëminence among the novelists of the age. (p. 382)

[Edwin P. Whipple,] "Reviews and Literary Notices: 'Great Expectations'," in The Atlantic Monthly, *Vol. VIII, No. XLVII, September, 1861, pp. 380-82.*

H. A. TAINE (essay date 1863-64)

[Dickens] has the painter in him, and the English painter. Never surely did a mind figure to itself with more exact detail or greater energy of the parts and tints of a picture. (p. 340)

An imagination so lucid and energetic cannot but animate inanimate objects without an effort. It provokes in the mind in which it works extraordinary emotions, and the author pours over the objects which he figures to himself, something of the ever-welling passion which overflows in him. Stones for him take a voice, white walls swell out into big phantoms, black wells yawn hideously and mysteriously in the darkness. . . . [In] this madness there is nothing vague or disorderly; imaginary objects are designed with outlines as precise and details as numerous as real objects, and the dream is equal to the truth.

There is, amongst others, a description of the night wind, quaint and powerful, which recalls certain pages of *Notre Dame de Paris.* The source of this description, as of all those of Dickens, is pure imagination. He does not, like Walter Scott, describe in order to give his reader a map, and to lay down the locality of his drama. He does not, like Lord Byron, describe from love of magnificent nature, and in order to display a splendid succession of grand pictures. He dreams neither of attaining exactness nor of selecting beauty. (pp. 340-41)

Dickens is a poet; he is as much at home in the imaginative world as in the actual. . . . Objects, with Dickens, take their hue from the thoughts of his characters. His imagination is so lively, that it carries everything with it in the path which it chooses. If the character is happy, the stones, flowers, and clouds must be happy too; if he is sad, nature must weep with him. Even to the ugly houses in the street, all speak. The style runs through a swarm of visions; it breaks out into the strangest oddities. Here is a young girl, pretty and good, who crosses Fountain Court and the low purlieus in search of her brother. What more simple? what even more vulgar? Dickens is carried away by it. To entertain her, he summons up birds, trees, houses, the fountain, the offices, law papers, and much besides. It is a folly, and it is all but an enchantment. . . . French taste, always measured, revolts against these affected strokes, these sickly prettinesses. And yet this affectation is natural; Dickens does not hunt after quaintnesses; they come to him. His excessive imagination is like a string too tightly stretched; it produces of itself, without any violent shock, sounds not otherwise heard.

We shall see how it is excited. Imagine a shop, no matter what shop, the most repulsive; that of a marine store dealer. Dickens sees the barometers, chronometers, telescopes, compasses, charts, maps, sextants, speaking trumpets, and so forth. He sees so many, sees them so clearly, they are crowded and crammed, they replace each other so forcibly in his brain, which they fill and litter. . . . (pp. 342-43)

The same faculty leads us to glory or throws us in a cell in a lunatic asylum. It is visionary imagination which forges the phantoms of the madman and creates the personages of an artist, and the classifications serving for the first may serve for the second. The imagination of Dickens is like that of monomaniacs. To plunge oneself into an idea, to be absorbed by it, to see nothing else, to repeat it under a hundred forms, to enlarge it, to carry it thus enlarged to the eye of the spectator, to dazzle and overwhelm him with it, to stamp it upon him so tenacious and impressive that he can never again tear it from his memory,—these are the great features of this imagination and style. In this, *David Copperfield* is a masterpiece. Never

did objects remain more visible and present to the memory of a reader than those which he describes. (pp. 343-44)

Dickens is admirable in the depicture of hallucinations. We see that he feels himself those of his characters, that he is engrossed by their ideas, that he enters into their madness. As an Englishman and a moralist, he has described remorse frequently. Perhaps it may be said that he makes a scarecrow of it, and that an artist is wrong to transform himself into an assistant of the policeman and the preacher. What of that? The portrait of Jonas Chuzzlewit is so terrible, that we may pardon it for being useful. Jonas, leaving his chamber secretly, has treacherously murdered his enemy, and thinks thenceforth to breathe in peace; but the recollection of the murder gradually disorganises his mind, like poison. He is no longer able to control his ideas; they bear him on with the fury of a terrified horse. (pp. 344-45)

Jonas is on the verge of madness. There are other characters quite mad. Dickens has drawn three or four portraits of madmen, very agreeable at first sight, but so true that they are in reality horrible. It needed an imagination like his, irregular, excessive, capable of fixed ideas, to exhibit the derangements of reason. Two especially there are, which make us laugh, and which make us shudder. Augustus, the gloomy maniac, who is on the point of marrying Miss Pecksniff; and poor Mr. Dick, half an idiot, half a monomaniac, who lives with Miss Trotwood. . . . [To] see the stupid smile, the vacant look, the foolish and uneasy physiognomy of these haggard old children who painfully involve idea in idea, and stumble at every step on the threshold of the truth which they cannot attain, is a faculty which Hoffmann alone has possessed in an equal degree with Dickens. The play of these shattered reasons is like the creaking of a dislocated door; it makes one sick to hear it. We find, if we like, a discordant burst of laughter, but we discover still more easily a groan and a lamentation, and we are terrified to gauge the lucidity, strangeness, exaltation, violence of imagination which has produced such creations, which has carried them on and sustained them unbendingly to the end, and which found itself in its proper sphere in imitating and producing their irrationality. (p. 346)

Dickens does not perceive great things; this is the second feature of his imagination. Enthusiasm seizes him in connection with everything, especially in connection with vulgar objects, a curiosity shop, a sign-post, a town-crier. He has vigour, he does not attain beauty. His instrument gives vibrating sounds, but not harmonious. If he is describing a house, he will draw it with geometrical clearness; he will put all its colours in relief, discover a face and thought in the shutters and the pipes; he will make a sort of human being out of the house, grimacing and forcible, which will chain our regard, and which we shall never forget; but he will not see the grandeur of the long monumental lines, the calm majesty of the broad shadows boldly divided by the white plaster, the cheerfulness of the light which covers them, and becomes palpable in the black niches in which it is poured, as though to rest and to sleep. (pp. 346-47)

[Dickens] has the feverish sensibility of a woman who laughs loudly, or melts into tears at the sudden shock of the slightest occurrence. This impassioned style is extremely potent, and to it may be attributed half the glory of Dickens. The majority of men have only weak emotions. . . . [We] are immersed for two hundred pages in a torrent of new emotions, contrary and increasing, which communicates its violence to the mind, which carries it away in digressions and falls, and only casts it on the bank enchanted and exhausted. It is an intoxication, and on a delicate soul the effect would be too forcible; but it suits the English public, and that public has justified it.

This sensibility can hardly have more than two issues—laughter and tears. There are others, but they are only reached by lofty eloquence; they are the path to sublimity, and we have seen that for Dickens this path is cut off. Yet there is no writer who knows better how to touch and melt; he makes us weep, absolutely shed tears; before reading him we did not know there was so much pity in the heart. (p. 349)

This same writer is the most railing, the most comic, the most jocose of English authors. And it is moreover a singular gaiety! It is the only kind which would harmonise with this impassioned sensibility. There is a laughter akin to tears. Satire is the sister of elegy: if the second pleads for the oppressed, the first combats the oppressors. Wounded by misfortunes and vices, Dickens avenges himself by ridicule. He does not paint, he punishes. Nothing could be more damaging than those long chapters of sustained irony, in which the sarcasm is pressed, line after line, more sanguinary and piercing in the chosen adversary. (p. 351)

Usually Dickens remains grave whilst drawing his caricatures. English wit consists in saying light jests in a solemn manner. Tone and ideas are then on contrast; every contrast makes a strong impression. Dickens loves to produce them, and his public to hear them.

If at times he forgets to castigate his neighbour, if he tries to sport, to amuse himself, he is no longer happy over it. The element of the English character is its want of happiness. The ardent and tenacious imagination of Dickens is impressed with things too firmly, to pass lightly and gaily over the surface. He leans, he penetrates, works into, hollows them out; all these violent actions are efforts, and all efforts are sufferings. To be happy, a man must be light-minded, as a Frenchman of the eighteenth century, or sensual, as an Italian of the sixteenth; a man must not get anxious about things, to enjoy them. Dickens does get anxious, and does not enjoy. (pp. 352-53)

Take away the grotesque characters, who are only introduced to fill up and to excite laughter, and you will find that all Dickens' characters belong to two classes—people who have feelings and emotions, and people who have none. He contrasts the souls which nature creates with those which society deforms. One of his last novels, **Hard Times**, is an abstract of all the rest. He there exalts instinct above reason, intuition of heart above positive science. . . . He satirises oppressive society; praises oppressed nature; and his elegiac genius, like his satirical genius, finds ready to his hand in the English world around him, the sphere which it needs for its development.

The first fruits of English society is hypocrisy. It ripens here under the double breath of religion and morality; we know their popularity and dominion across the Channel. In a country where it is scandalous to laugh on Sunday, where the gloomy Puritan has preserved something of his old rancour against happiness, where the critics of ancient history insert dissertations on the virtue of Nebuchadnezzar, it is natural that the appearance of morality should be serviceable. It is a needful coin: those who lack good money coin bad; and the more public opinion declares it precious, the more it is counterfeited. This vice is therefore English. Mr. Pecksniff is not found in France. His speech would disgust Frenchmen. If they have an affectation, it is not of virtue, but of vice: if they wish to succeed, they would be wrong to speak of their principles: they prefer to

confess their weaknesses; and if they have quacks, they are trumpeters of immorality. (pp. 358-59)

Tartuffe will speak of his hair-shirt and his discipline; Pecksniff, of his comfortable little parlour, of the charm of friendship, the beauties of nature. He will try to bring men together. He will be like a member of the Peace Society. He will develop the most touching considerations on the benefits and beauties of union among men. It will be impossible to hear him without being affected. Men are refined now-a-days, they have read much elegiac poetry; their sensibility is more active; they can no longer be deceived by the gross impudence of Tartuffe. This is why Mr. Pecksniff will use gestures of sublime long-suffering, smiles of ineffable compassion, starts, movements of recklessness, graces, tendernesses which will seduce the most reserved and charm the most delicate. The English in their Parliament, meetings, associations, public ceremonies, have learned the oratorical phraseology, the abstract terms, the style of political economy, of the newspaper and the prospectus. Pecksniff will talk like a prospectus. He will possess its obscurity, its wordiness, and its emphasis. He will seem to soar above the earth, in the region of pure ideas, in the bosom of truth. He will resemble an apostle, brought up in the *Times* office. (p. 360)

In contrast with [the] bad and factitious characters, produced by national institutions, you find good creatures such as nature made them; and first, children.

We have none in French literature. Racine's little Joas could only exist in a piece composed for the ladies' college of Saint Cyr; the little child speaks like a prince's son, with noble and acquired phrases, as if repeating his catechism. Now-a-days these portraits are only seen in France in New-year's books, written as models for good children. Dickens has painted his with special gratification; he did not think of edifying the public, and he has charmed it. All his children are of extreme sensibility; they love much, and they crave to be loved. . . . Poor little [David Copperfield] is every moment wounded by hard words. He dare not speak or move; he is afraid to kiss his mother; he feels himself weighed down, as by a leaden cloak, by the cold looks of the new master and mistress. . . . This incessant terror, hopeless and issueless, the spectacle of this wounded sensibility and stupefied intelligence, the long anxieties, the watches, the solitude of the poor imprisoned child, his passionate desire to kiss his mother or to weep on the breast of his nurse,—all this is sad to see. These children's griefs are as deep as the vexations of a man. It is the history of a frail plant, which was flourishing in a warm air, under a sweet sun, and which, suddenly transplanted to the snow, sheds its leaves and withers.

The common people are like the children, dependent, ill cultivated, akin to nature, and subject to oppression. That is to say, Dickens extols them. That is not new in France; the novels of Eugène Sue have given us more than one example, and the theme is as old as Rousseau; but in the hands of the English writer it has acquired a singular force. His heroes have admirable delicacy and devotion. They have nothing vulgar but their pronunciation; the rest is but nobility and generosity. . . . No one, according to Dickens, feels so strongly as they do the happiness of loving and being loved—the pure joys of domestic life. No one has so much compassion for those poor deformed and infirm creatures whom they so often bring into the world, and who seem only born to die. No one has a juster and more inflexible moral sense. I confess even that Dickens' heroes unfortunately resemble the indignant fathers of French melo-dramas. (pp. 363-64)

In reality, the novels of Dickens can all be reduced to one phrase, to wit: Be good, and love; there is genuine joy only in the emotions of the heart; sensibility is the whole man. . . . Believe that humanity, pity, forgiveness, are the finest things in man; believe that intimacy, expansion, tenderness, tears, are the finest things in the world. To live is nothing; to be powerful, learned, illustrious, is little; to be useful is not enough. He alone has lived and is a man who has wept at the remembrance of a benefit, given or received.

We do not believe that this contrast between the weak and the strong, or this outcry against society in favour of nature, are the caprice of an artist or the chance of the moment. When we penetrate deeply into the history of English genius, we find that its primitive foundation was impassioned sensibility, and that its natural expression was lyrical exaltation. Both were brought from Germany, and make up the literature existing before the Conquest. . . . Politics, business, and religion, like three powerful machines, have created a new man above the old. Stern dignity, self-command, the need of domination, harshness in dominion, strict morality, without compromise or pity, a taste for figures and dry calculation, a dislike of facts not palpable and ideas not useful, ignorance of the invisible world, scorn of the weaknesses and tendernesses of the heart,—such are the dispositions which the stream of facts and the ascendency of institutions tend to confirm in their souls. But poetry and domestic life prove that they have only half succeeded. The old sensibility, oppressed and perverted, still lives and works. The poet subsists under the Puritan, the trader, the statesman. The social man has not destroyed the natural man. This frozen crust, this unsociable pride, this rigid attitude, often cover a good and tender being. It is the English mask of a German head; and when a talented writer, often a writer of genius, reaches the sensibility which is bruised or buried by education and national institutions, he moves his reader in the most inner depths, and becomes the master of all hearts. (pp. 365-66)

> *H. A. Taine, "Book V: Modern Authors," in his* History of English Literature, Vol. II, *translated by H. Van Laun (originally published as* Histoire de la littérature anglaise, *L. Hachette et cie, 1863-64), Holt & Williams, 1871, pp. 337-542.**

[HENRY JAMES] (essay date 1865)

"Our Mutual Friend" is, to our perception, the poorest of Mr. Dickens's works. And it is poor with the poverty not of momentary embarrassment, but of permanent exhaustion. It is wanting in inspiration. For the last ten years it has seemed to us that Mr. Dickens has been unmistakably forcing himself. **"Bleak House"** was forced; **"Little Dorritt"** was labored; the present work is dug out as with a spade and pickaxe. Of course—to anticipate the usual argument—who but Dickens could have written it? Who, indeed? Who else would have established a lady in business in a novel on the admirably solid basis of her always putting on gloves and tieing a handkerchief round her head in moments of grief, and of her habitually addressing her family with "Peace! hold!" It is needless to say that Mrs. Reginald Wilfer is first and last the occasion of considerable true humor. . . . [But after we describe a dozen] happy examples of the humor which was exhaled from every line of Mr. Dickens's earlier writings, we shall have closed the list of the merits of the work before us. To say that the conduct of the story, with all its complications, betrays a long-practised hand, is to pay no compliment worthy the author. If this were, indeed, a compliment, we should be inclined to carry it further, and congratulate him on his success in what we should call the manufacture of fiction; for in so doing we should express a feeling that has attended us throughout the book. Seldom, we reflected, had we read a book so intensely *written,* so little seen, known, or felt.

In all Mr. Dickens's works the fantastic has been his great resource; and while his fancy was lively and vigorous it accomplished great things. But the fantastic, when the fancy is dead, is a very poor business. The movement of Mr. Dickens's fancy in Mrs. Wilfer and Mr. Boffin and Lady Tippins, and the Lammles and Miss Wren, and even in Eugene Wrayburn, is, to our mind, a movement lifeless, forced, mechanical. It is the letter of his old humor without the spirit. It is hardly too much to say that every character here put before us is a mere bundle of eccentricities, animated by no principle of nature whatever. . . . What do we get in return for accepting Miss Jenny Wren as a possible person? This young lady is the type of a certain class of characters of which Mr. Dickens has made a specialty, and with which he has been accustomed to draw alternate smiles and tears, according as he pressed one spring or another. But this is very cheap merriment and very cheap pathos. . . . Like all Mr. Dickens's pathetic characters, she is a little monster; she is deformed, unhealthy, unnatural; she belongs to the troop of hunchbacks, imbeciles, and precocious children who have carried on the sentimental business in all Mr. Dickens's novels; the little Nells, the Smikes, the Paul Dombeys.

Mr. Dickens goes as far out of the way for his wicked people as he does for his good ones. Rogue Riderhood, indeed, in the present story, is villanous with a sufficiently natural villany; he belongs to that quarter of society in which the author is most at his ease. But was there ever such wickedness as that of the Lammles and Mr. Fledgeby? Not that people have not been as mischievous as they; but was any one ever mischievous in that singular fashion? Did a couple of elegant swindlers ever take such particular pains to be aggressively inhuman?—for we can find no other word for the gratuitous distortions to which they are subjected. The word *humanity* strikes us as strangely discordant, in the midst of these pages; for, let us boldly declare it, there is no humanity here. . . . What a world were this world if the world of **"Our Mutual Friend"** were an honest reflection of it! But a community of eccentrics is impossible. Rules alone are consistent with each other; exceptions are inconsistent. Society is maintained by natural sense and natural feeling. We cannot conceive a society in which these principles are not in some manner represented. Where in these pages are the depositaries of that intelligence without which the movement of life would cease? Who represents nature? Accepting half of Mr. Dickens's persons as intentionally grotesque, where are those exemplars of sound humanity who should afford us the proper measure of their companions' variations? . . . If we might hazard a definition of [Dickens's] literary character, we should, accordingly, call him the greatest of superficial novelists. We are aware that this definition confines him to an inferior rank in the department of letters which he adorns; but we accept this consequence of our proposition. It were, in our opinion, an offence against humanity to place Mr. Dickens among the greatest novelists. For, to repeat what we have already intimated, he has created nothing but figure. He has added nothing to our understanding of human character. He is master of but two alternatives: he reconciles us to what is commonplace, and he reconciles us to what is odd. The value of the former service is questionable; and the manner in which Mr. Dickens performs it sometimes conveys a certain impression of charlatanism. The value of the latter service is incontestable, and here Mr. Dickens is an honest, an admirable artist. But what is the condition of the truly great novelist? For him there are no alternatives, for him there are no oddities, for him there is nothing outside of humanity. He cannot shirk it; it imposes itself upon him. For him alone, therefore, there is a true and a false; for him alone it is possible to be right, because it is possible to be wrong. Mr. Dickens is a great observer and a great humorist, but he is nothing of a philosopher. (pp. 786-87)

[Henry James,] "Literature: 'Our Mutual Friend'," in The Nation, Vol. 1, No. 25, December 21, 1865, pp. 786-87.

FRASER'S MAGAZINE (essay date 1870)

On the eighth of June, 1870, the busiest brain and busiest hand that ever guided pen over paper finished their appointed work, and that pen was laid aside for ever. Words of its inditing were sure of immediately reaching and being welcomed by a larger number of men and women than those of any other living writer—perhaps of any writer who has ever lived. . . .

For five-and-thirty years his keen observation and his exuberant and vivacious fancy had issued in an incessant bright stream of storytelling—a series of books readable beyond rivalry, describing his own time to itself in a new and striking style; heightening the familiar so as to give it an artistic impressiveness, enriching it with humour, softening it with sympathies, mingling shrewd sense with a fanciful picturesqueness so as to produce the most unexpected effects out of commonplace materials, and discovering many quaint and strange things lurking in the midst of everyday life. . . .

Perhaps of the many qualities that combined to produce his unrivalled success, not the highest but the most unmistakable and most telling is his constant flow of animal spirits—his vivacity, his clearness and *grip*. He excels in gay, voluble people. . . . He delights to put his persons in active motion, walking, cricketing, skating, dancing, playing blindman's buff, and what not, and he revels in a stagecoach journey. (p. 130)

In the ordinary intercourse of life his bright look, cheery grasp of hand, active and lively bearing, his tact and readiness in conversation, his hearty laugh, and ready sympathy, and his general *savoir faire*, made him, as will be easily conceived, widely popular. . . .

His fondness for all matters theatrical was well known. He was himself the very prince of amateur actors, and in his readings his remarkable mimetic powers enchanted countless audiences on both sides of the Atlantic. In fact, a story of his is like a drama for the fireside, furnished not only with situations and dialogue, but with appropriate scenery, gestures, action, by-play; the author, scene-painter, stage-manager, and moreover the whole company, tragic and comic, male and female, from 'stars' to 'supers,' being one and the same skilful individual.

The figures impress one rather as impersonations than as persons. But how telling they are, and what a list of dramatis personae is that of the *Theatre National Charles Dickens!* (p. 131)

In landscape and still life description he excelled, seizing with firm grasp the characteristics of a room, a house, a village, a

city, a wide prospect, any locality he selected for his scene. Many out-of-the-way nooks of London and bits of the rural scenery of England appear on his canvas with distinct outlines and effective colouring. In fact, he was an artist. He decided on the *effect* to be produced, chose his point of view, and worked on steadily in his own way. Keen observation of facts, humorous seizure and often grotesque exaggeration of the salient points, brilliant *quasi*-theatric expression of these; such was his method, instilled by nature, matured by steady practice. . . .

As to his literary style, that was his own—striking, brilliant, not seldom odd, sometimes awkward, yet even then with its own sort of tact. He was artful and skilful, but never attained, and never seems to have sought to attain, the kind of art which conceals itself; a certain care and elaboration were never absent; he took his aim carefully (he was in dress and in every other respect the opposite of a negligent man) and usually hit the mark. (p. 133)

He had a deep pity, a deep sympathy (and no idle or barren one) for the poor, and especially the hardworking poor. He could indicate and emphasise the absurdities of their manner and speech, their awkward gestures, bad grammar, inelegant pronunciation, without one touch to feed the contempt of the most cynical or the most ill-natured hearer; and he inculcated at every moment, directly or indirectly, the lesson of brotherly kindness. We have spoken of his high and unflagging animal spirits—a nature ever brisk, cheerful, and animated; yet withal, he is from first to last thoroughly innocent, and addresses himself at the gayest, without effort, *virginibus puerisque*. Neither has any satirist ever laughed at mankind so entirely without bitterness or ill nature.

The last seventy years in English literature form a period in which novel-writing has attained an unprecedented growth and influence. Now the most popular and most personally regarded novel-writer that ever handled pen is gone for ever, leaving no man like him in the world. (pp. 133-34)

He dies honoured and lamented by many nations of men; and his work remains after him. God bless him, and keep a grateful and loving memory of him in all our hearts! (p. 134)

"Charles Dickens," in Fraser's Magazine, Vol. II, No. VIII, July, 1870, pp. 130-34.

H. LAWRENNY (essay date 1870)

The Mystery of Edwin Drood may either be the subject of speculation as a novel, or of study as the last fragment from his fertile pen. In the first respect there are signs of a more carefully-designed intrigue than in most of his earlier works. (p. 2)

The Mystery of Edwin Drood, viewed as a fragment, shews little falling off from the writer's second-best works; the unfortunate cause of its fragmentary form lends it a peculiar interest. . . . The first thing that strikes a reader of Dickens is the absence of all familiar boundaries and landmarks: class distinctions are ignored or obliterated; different ages and sexes assume the prerogatives of their opposites; people transact incongruous business in impossible places; and with it all there is no apparent consciousness that the social order is confused and inverted. It is still more curious to watch this levelling tendency applied to matters of intellect. Dickens has a positive affection for lunatics, and with the exception of the favourites to whom he lends touches of his own imagination, a vast majority of his characters are born fools. In his queer world they fare none the worse for this; they cluster round one delusion or another, and defend it with just as much formality as if they were reasoning beings, and it almost seems as if, *caeteris paribus,* he preferred the thought that travelled by a crooked lane. The only light in this chaos is what falls from a few moral axioms concerning the duty to our neighbour, and these are of such universal application as to be rather indefinite. In such books as **Dombey** and **Martin Chuzzlewit** we seem lost in a millennium of illogical goodwill, in imagining which, no doubt, Dickens was principally influenced by his natural humour. . . . This is by no means a bad position for a humourist to occupy, for though we may have our doubts as to what makes Dickens's characters so much more laughable than life, it is something to have extracted the maximum of amusement out of innocent and even admirable eccentricities. (p. 3)

> *H. Lawrenny, "General Literature and Art: 'The Mystery of Edwin Drood'," in* The Academy, *Vol. 2, October 22, 1870, pp. 1-3.*

GEORGE HENRY LEWES (essay date 1872)

Dickens has proved his power by a popularity almost unexampled, embracing all classes. Surely it is a task for criticism to exhibit the sources of that power? If everything that has ever been alleged against the works be admitted, there still remains an immense success to be accounted for. It was not by their defects that these works were carried over Europe and America. . . . Other writers have been exaggerated, untrue, fantastic, and melodramatic; but they have gained so little notice that no one thinks of pointing out their defects. It is clear, therefore, that Dickens had powers which enabled him to triumph in spite of the weaknesses which clogged them; and it is worth inquiring what those powers were, and their relation to his undeniable defects.

I am not about to attempt such an inquiry, but simply to indicate two or three general points of view. It will be enough merely to mention in passing the primary cause of his success, his overflowing fun, because even uncompromising opponents admit it. (p. 58)

Great as Dickens is in fun, so great that Fielding and Smollett are small in comparison, he would have been only a passing amusement for the world had he not been gifted with an imagination of marvellous vividness, and an emotional, sympathetic nature capable of furnishing that imagination with elements of universal power. Of him it may be said with less exaggeration than of most poets, that he was of "imagination all compact"; if the other higher faculties were singularly deficient in him, this faculty was imperial. He was a seer of visions; and his visions were of objects at once familiar and potent. Psychologists will understand both the extent and the limitation of the remark, when I say that in no other pefectly sane mind (Blake, I believe, was not perfectly sane) have I observed vividness of imagination approaching so closely to hallucination. (pp. 58-9)

[Let] me say that I am very far indeed from wishing to imply any agreement in the common notion that "great wits to madness nearly are allied''; on the contrary, my studies have led to the conviction that nothing is less like genius than insanity, although some men of genius have had occasional attacks; and further, that I have never observed any trace of the insane temperament in Dickens's works, or life, they being indeed singularly free even from the eccentricities which often accompany exceptional powers; nevertheless, with all due lim-

itations, it is true that there is considerable light shed upon his works by the action of the imagination in hallucination. . . . When he imagined a street, a house, a room, a figure, he saw it not in the vague schematic way of ordinary imagination, but in the sharp definition of actual perception, all the salient details obtruding themselves on his attention. He, seeing it thus vividly, made us also see it; and believing in its reality however fantastic, he communicated something of his belief to us. He presented it in such relief tha. we ceased to think of it as a picture. So definite and insistent was the image, that even while knowing it was false we could not help, for a moment, being affected, as it were, by his hallucination.

This glorious energy of imagination is that which Dickens had in common with all great writers. It was this which made him a creator, and made his creations universally intelligible, no matter how fantastic and unreal. His types established themselves in the public mind like personal experiences. Their falsity was unnoticed in the blaze of their illumination. Every humbug seemed a Pecksniff, every nurse a Gamp, every jovial improvident a Micawber, every stinted serving-wench a Marchioness. Universal experiences became individualised in these types; an image and a name were given, and the image was so suggestive that it seemed to *express* all that it was found to *recall,* and Dickens was held to have depicted what his readers supplied. Against such power criticism was almost idle. . . . The imagination of the author laid hold of some well-marked physical trait, some peculiarity of aspect, speech, or manner which every one recognized at once; and the force with which this was presented made it occupy the mind to the exclusion of all critical doubts: only reflection could detect the incongruity. Think of what this implies! Think how little the mass of men are given to reflect on their impressions, and how their minds are for the most part occupied with sensations rather than ideas, and you will see why Dickens held an undisputed sway. . . . Dickens's figures are brought within the range of the reader's interests, and receive from these interests a sudden illumination, when they are the puppets of a drama every incident of which appeals to the sympathies. With a fine felicity of instinct he seized upon situations having an irresistible hold over the domestic affections and ordinary sympathies. He spoke in the mother-tongue of the heart, and was always sure of ready listeners. He painted the life he knew, the life every one knew; for if the scenes and manners were unlike those we were familiar with, the feelings and motives, the joys and griefs, the mistakes and efforts of the actors were universal, and therefore universally intelligible; so that even critical spectators who complained that these broadly painted pictures were artistic daubs, could not wholly resist their effective suggestiveness. (pp. 60-3)

Such were the sources of his power. To understand how it is that critics quite competent to recognise such power, and even so far amenable to it as to be moved and interested by the works in spite of all their drawbacks, should have forgotten this undenied power, and written or spoken of Dickens with mingled irritation and contempt, we must take into account two natural tendencies—the bias of opposition, and the bias of technical estimate.

The bias of opposition may be illustrated in a parallel case. Let us suppose a scientific book to be attracting the attention of Europe by the boldness, suggestiveness, and theoretic plausibility of its hypotheses; this work falls into the hands of a critic sufficiently grounded in the science treated to be aware that its writer, although gifted with great theoretic power and occasional insight into unexplored relations, is nevertheless pitiably ignorant of the elementary facts and principles of the science; the critic noticing the power, and the talent of lucid exposition, is yet perplexed and irritated at ignorance which is inexcusable, and a reckless twisting of known facts into impossible relations, which seems wilful. . . . [Can] this critic be expected to join in the chorus of admirers? and will he not rather be exasperated into an opposition which will lead him to undervalue the undeniable qualities in his insistence on the undeniable defects?

Something like this is the feeling produced by Dickens's works in many cultivated and critical readers. They see there human character and ordinary events portrayed with a mingled verisimilitude and falsity altogether unexampled. The drawing is so vivid yet so incorrect, or else is so blurred and formless, with such excess of *effort* (as of a showman beating on the drum) that the doubt arises how an observer so remarkably keen could make observations so remarkably false, and miss such very obvious facts. (pp. 63-4)

We all delight in imitation, and in the skill which represents one object in another medium; but the refinements of skill can only be appreciated by study. . . . [The] connoisseur no longer asks, What is painted? but How is it painted? The *what* may be a patch of meadow, the bend of a river, or a street boy munching bread and cheese, and yet give greater delight by its *how*, than another picture which represented the Andes, Niagara, or a Madonna and Child. When the critic observes technical skill in a picture, he pronounces the painter to be admirable, and is quite unmoved by any great subject badly painted. In like manner a great poet is estimated by the greatness of his execution of great conceptions, not by the greatness of his intention.

How easily the critic falls into the mistake of overvaluing technical skill, and not allowing for the primary condition, how easily he misjudges works by applying to them technical rules derived from the works of others, need not here be dwelt on. What I wish to indicate is the bias of technical estimate which, acting with that bias of opposition just noted, has caused the critics to overlook in Dickens the great artistic powers which are proved by his immense success; and to dwell only on those great artistic deficiences which exclude him from the class of exquisite writers. He worked in delf, not in porcelain. But his prodigal imagination created in delf forms which delighted thousands. He only touched common life, but he touched it to "fine issues"; and since we are all susceptible of being moved by pictures of children in droll and pathetic situations, and by pictures of common suffering and common joy, any writer who can paint such pictures with sufficient skill to awaken these emotions is powerful in proportion to the emotion stirred. That Dickens had this skill is undisputed; and if critical reflection shows that the means he employs are not such as will satisfy the technical estimate, and consequently that the pictures will not move the cultivated mind, nor give it the deep content which perfect Art continues to create, making the work a "joy for ever," we must still remember that in the present state of Literature, with hundreds daily exerting their utmost efforts to paint such pictures, it requires prodigious force and rare skill to impress images that will stir the universal heart. (pp. 67-8)

[While] on the one hand the critics seem to me to have been fully justified in denying him the possession of many technical excellencies, they have been thrown into unwise antagonism which has made them overlook or undervalue the great qualities which distinguished him; and that even on technical grounds

their criticism has been so far defective that it failed to recognise the supreme powers which ensured his triumph in spite of all defects. For the reader of cultivated taste there is little in his works beyond the stirring of their emotions—but what a large exception! We do not turn over the pages in search of thought, delicate psychological observation, grace of style, charm of composition; but we enjoy them like children at a play, laughing and crying at the images which pass before us. And this illustration suggests the explanation of how learned and thoughtful men can have been almost as much delighted with the works as ignorant and juvenile readers; how Lord Jeffrey could have been so affected by the presentation of Little Nell, which most critical readers pronounce maudlin and unreal. Persons unfamiliar with theatrical representations, consequently unable to criticise the acting, are stirred by the suggestions of the scenes presented; and hence a great philosopher, poet, or man of science, may be found applauding an actor whom every play-going apprentice despises as stagey and inartistic. (pp. 73-4)

George Henry Lewes, "Dickens in Relation to Criticism," in Fortnightly Review, *Vol. XVII, No. XCIX, February, 1872 (and reprinted in* The Dickens Critics, *edited by George H. Ford and Lauriat Lane, Jr., Cornell University Press, 1961, pp. 54-74).*

MATTHEW ARNOLD   (essay date 1881)

What a pleasure to have the opportunity of praising a work so sound, a work so rich in merit, as *David Copperfield*! . . . Of the contemporary rubbish which is shot so plentifully all around us, we can, indeed, hardly read too little. But to contemporary work so good as *David Copperfield,* we are in danger of perhaps not paying respect enough, of reading it (for who could help reading it?) too hastily, and then putting it aside for something else and forgetting it. What treasures of gaiety, invention, life, are in that book! what alertness and resource! what a soul of good nature and kindness governing the whole! Such is the admirable work which I am now going to call in evidence.

Intimately, indeed, did Dickens know the middle class; he was bone of its bone and flesh of its flesh. Intimately he knew its bringing up. With the hand of a master he has drawn for us a type of the teachers and trainers of its youth, a type of its places of education. Mr. Creakle and Salem House are immortal. The type itself, it is to be hoped, will perish; but the drawing of it which Dickens has given cannot die. (pp. 215-16)

Matthew Arnold, in his essay (originally published in "The Incompatibles" in Nineteenth Century, *Vol. 9, April, 1881), in* Charles Dickens: A Critical Anthology, *edited by Stephen Wall, Penguin Books, 1970, pp. 215-17.*

GEORGE GISSING   (essay date 1898)

So great a change has come over the theory and practice of fiction in the England of our times that we must needs treat of Dickens as, in many respects, antiquated. . . . Dickens suffers from a comparison with novelists, his peers, of a newer day, even with some who were strictly his contemporaries. We have now to ask ourselves in what other aspects his work differs markedly from the prevalent conception of the art of novel-writing. It will be seen, of course, that, theoretically, he had very little in common with our school of strict veracity, of realism—call it what you please; the school which, quite apart from extravagances, has directed fiction into a path it is likely to pursue for many a year to come. Hard words are spoken of him by young writers whose zeal outruns their discretion, and far outstrips their knowledge; from the advanced posts of modern criticism any stone is good enough to throw at a novelist who avows and glories in his moral purpose. . . . Endeavouring to judge Dickens as a man of his time, we must see in what spirit he approached his tasks; what he consciously sought to achieve in this pursuit of story-telling. One thing, assuredly, can never become old-fashioned in any disdainful sense; that is, sincerity of purpose. Novelists of today desire above everything to be recognized as sincere in their picturing of life. If Dickens prove to be no less honest, according to his lights, we must then glance at the reasons which remove him so far from us in his artistic design and execution. (pp. 78-9)

Here is the contradiction so irritating to Dickens's severer critics, the artistic generation of to-day. What!—they exclaim—a great writer, inspired with a thoroughly fine idea, is to stay his hand until he has made grave inquiry whether Messrs. Mudie's subscribers will approve it or not! The mere suggestion is infuriating. And this—they vociferate—is what Dickens was always doing. It may be true that he worked like a Trojan, but what is the use of work, meant to be artistic, carried on in hourly fear of Mrs. Grundy? Fingers are pointed to this, that, and the other Continental novelist; can you imagine *him* in such sorry plight? Why, nothing would have pleased him better than to know he was outraging public sentiment! In fact, it is only when one *does* so that one's work has a chance of being good.

All which may be true enough in relation to the speakers. As regards Dickens, it is irrelevant. Dickens had before him no such artistic ideal; he never desired freedom to offend his public. Sympathy with his readers was to him the very breath of life; the more complete that sympathy the better did he esteem his work. . . . Dickens could never have regarded it as within a story-teller's scope to attempt the conversion of his readers to a new view of literary morals. Against a political folly, or a social injustice, he would use every resource of his art, and see no reason to hesitate; for there was the certainty of the approval of all good folk. To write a novel in a spirit of antagonism to all but a very few of his countrymen would have seemed to him a sort of practical *bull;* is it not the law of novel-writing, first and foremost, that one shall aim at pleasing as many people as possible? (pp. 82-4)

When the readers of **Martin Chuzzlewit** fall off he is troubled, first and foremost, by the failure of popular sympathy. He asks himself, most anxiously, what the cause can be; and, with a touching deference to the voice of the crowd, is inclined to think that he has grown less interesting. For, observe, that Dickens never conceives himself, when he aims at popularity, as writing *down* to his audience. Of that he is wholly incapable; for that he has too much understanding of the conditions of literary success. . . . Dickens might alter his intention, might change his theme; but he never did so with the thought that he was condescending. In this respect a true democrat, he believed, probably without ever reflecting upon it, that the approved of the people was necessarily the supreme in art. At the same time, never man wrought more energetically to justify the people's choice.

How does this attitude of mind affect Dickens's veracity as an artist concerned with everyday life? In what degree, and in what directions, does he feel himself at liberty to disguise facts, to modify circumstances for the sake of giving pleasure or avoiding offence?

Our "realist" will hear of no such paltering with truth. Heedless of Pilate's question, he takes for granted that the truth can be got at, and that it is his plain duty to set it down without compromise; or, if less crude in his perceptions, he holds that truth, for the artist, is the impression produced on him, and that to convey this impression with entire sincerity is his sole reason for existing. To Dickens such a view of the artist's duty never presented itself. Art, for him, was art precisely because it was not nature. Even our realists may recognize this, and may grant that it is the business of art to select, to dispose—under penalties if the result be falsification. But Dickens went further; he had a moral purpose; the thing above all others scornfully forbidden in our schools of rigid art. (pp. 90-2)

Admitting his limits, accepting them even gladly, he was yet possessed with a sense of the absolute reality of everything he pictured forth. Had the word been in use he must necessarily have called himself a Realist. It is one of the biographical commonplaces concerning Dickens. Everyone knows how he excited himself over his writing, how he laughed and cried with his imaginary people, how he had all but made himself ill with grief over the deathbed of little Nell or of Paul Dombey. This means, of course, that his imagination worked with perfect freedom, had the fullest scope, without ever coming in conflict with the prepossessions of his public. Permission to write as Smollett and as Fielding wrote could in no way have advantaged Dickens. He was the born story-teller of a certain day, of a certain class. Again, he does not deem himself the creator of a world, but the laboriously faithful painter of that about him. He labours his utmost to preserve illusion. (pp. 94-5)

I never look into [*Our Mutual Friend*] without feeling a suspicion that Dickens originally meant Mr. Boffin to suffer a real change of character, to become in truth the miserly curmudgeon which we are told he only pretended to be. Careful reading of the chapters which bear on this point has confirmed my impression. . . . It may well have been that here again Dickens, face to face with an unpleasant bit of truth, felt his heart fail him. Again he may have asked, "Will it make people angry?" If so—on this I wish to insist—it was in no spirit of dishonest compliance that he changed his plan. To make people angry would have been to defeat his own prime purpose. Granting two possible Mr. Boffins: he who becomes a miser in reality, and he who, for a good purpose, acts the miser's part; how much better to choose the Mr. Boffin who will end in hearty laughter and overflowing benevolence!

Avoidance of the disagreeable, as a topic uncongenial to art—this is Dickens's principle. There results, necessarily, a rather serious omission from his picture of life. Writing once from Boulogne, and describing the pier as he saw it of an evening, he says, "I never did behold such specimens of the youth of my country, male and female, as pervade that place. They are really in their vulgarity and insolence quite disheartening.". . . But Dickens certainly had no need to visit Boulogne to study English "vulgarity and insolence;" it blared around him wherever he walked in London, and, had he wrought in another spirit, it must have taken a very large place in every one of his books. He avoided, or showed it only in such forms as amused rather than disgusted. (pp. 98-100)

Two examples dwell in my memory which show him in the mood for downright fact of the unpleasant sort. More might be discovered, but these, I think, would remain the noteworthy instances of "realism" in Dickens; moments when, for whatever reason, he saw fit to tell a harsh truth without any mitigation. One occurs in the short story of **Doctor Marigold.** We have seen that the figure of the Cheap Jack was ''refined and humoured;'' not so that of the Cheap Jack's wife, the brutal woman who ill-uses and all but kills her child. This picture is remorseless in everyday truth; no humour softens it, no arbitrary event checks the course of the woman's hateful cruelty. The second example is *George Silverman's Explanation,* another short story, which from beginning to end is written in a tone of uncompromising bitterness. Being told by Silverman himself, its consistent gloom is dramatically appropriate and skilful. Here we have a picture of pietistic virulence the like of which cannot be found elsewhere in Dickens; hard bare fact; never a smile to lighten the impression; no interference with the rigour of destiny. Anything but characteristic, this little story is still a notable instance of Dickens's power. Were the author unknown it would be attributed to some strenuous follower of our ''realistic'' school.

From his duty as he conceived it, of teaching a moral lesson, Dickens never departs. He has an unfailing sense of the high importance of his work from this point of view. . . . And his morality is of the simplest; a few plain ordinances serve for human guidance; to infringe them is to be marked for punishment more or less sensational; to follow the path of the just is to ensure a certain amount of prosperity, and reward unlimited in buoyancy of heart. The generality of readers like to see a scoundrel get his deserts, and Dickens, for the most part, gives them abundant satisfaction. No half measures. . . . Remorse alone, however poignant and enduring, would not seem an adequate penalty; we must see the proud lady, the sinful woman, literally brought low, down to the level of the poor wretch who was her accomplice. Ill-doers less conspicuous are let off with a punishment which can be viewed facetiously, but punished they are. It is all so satisfying; it so rounds off our conception of life. Nothing so abhorred by the multitude as a lack of finality in stories, a vagueness of conclusion which gives them the trouble of forming surmises.

Equally, of course, justice is tempered with mercy. Who would have the heart to demand rigour of the law for Mr. Jingle and Job Trotter? We see them all but starved to death in a debtors' prison, and that is enough; their conversion to honesty gives such scope for Mr. Pickwick's delightful goodness that nothing could be more in accord with the fitness of things. . . . Profoundly human, however crude to an age that cannot laugh and cry so readily. Good sound practical teaching, which will help the soul of man long after more pretentious work has returned to dust. (pp. 100-04)

It was not by computing the density of the common brain, by gauging the force of vulgar prejudice, that Charles Dickens rose to his supreme popularity. Nature made him the mouthpiece of his kind, in all that relates to simple emotions and homely thought. Who can more rightly be called an artist than he who gave form and substance to the ideal of goodness and purity, of honour, justice, mercy, whereby the dim multitudes falteringly seek to direct their steps? This was his task in life, to embody the better dreams of ordinary men; to fix them as bright realities, for weary eyes to look upon. He achieved it in the strength of a faultless sympathy; following the true instincts which it is so unjust—so unintelligent—to interpret as mere commercial shrewdness or dulness of artistic perception. (p. 105)

George Gissing, in his Charles Dickens: A Critical Study, *Dodd, Mead and Company, 1898 (and reprinted by Dodd, Mead, 1912), 318 p.*

G. K. CHESTERTON (essay date 1906)

Dickens in his cheapest cockney utilitarianism, was not only English, but unconsciously historic. Upon him descended the real tradition of ''Merry England,'' and not upon the pallid mediaevalists who thought they were reviving it. The Pre-Raphaelites, the Gothicists, the admirers of the Middle Ages, had in their subtlety and sadness the spirit of the present day. Dickens had in his buffoonery and bravery the spirit of the Middle Ages. He was much more mediaeval in his attacks on mediaevalism than they were in their defences of it. It was he who had the things of Chaucer, the love of large jokes and long stories and brown ale and all the white roads of England. Like Chaucer he loved story within story, every man telling a tale. Like Chaucer he saw something openly comic in men's motley trades. (p. 123)

In fighting for Christmas [Dickens] was fighting for the old European festival, Pagan and Christian, for that trinity of eating, drinking and praying which to moderns appears irreverent, for the holy day which is really a holiday. He had himself the most babyish ideas about the past. He supposed the Middle Ages to have consisted of tournaments and torture-chambers, he supposed himself to be a brisk man of the manufacturing age, almost a Utilitarian. But for all that he defended the mediaeval feast which was going out against the Utilitarianism which was coming in. He could only see all that was bad in mediaevalism. But he fought for all that was good in it. And he was all the more really in sympathy with the old strength and simplicity because he only knew that it was good and did not know that it was old. He cared as little for mediaevalism as the mediaevals did. He cared as much as they did for lustiness and virile laughter and sad tales of good lovers and pleasant tales of good livers. (p. 124)

[Dickens] imagined himself to be, if anything, a sort of cosmopolitan; at any rate to be a champion of the charms and merits of continental lands against the arrogance of our island. But he was in truth very much more a champion of the old and genuine England against that comparatively cosmopolitan England which we have all lived to see. And here again the supreme example is Christmas. Christmas is, as I have said, one of numberless old European feasts of which the essence is the combination of religion with merry-making. But among those feasts it is also especially and distinctively English in the style of its merry-making and even in the style of its religion. For the character of Christmas (as distinct, for instance, from the continental Easter) lies chiefly in two things; first on the terrestrial side the note of comfort rather than the note of brightness; and on the spiritual side, Christian charity rather than Christian ecstasy. (pp. 124-25)

This ideal of comfort belongs peculiarly to England; it belongs peculiarly to Christmas; above all, it belongs pre-eminently to Dickens. And it is astonishingly misunderstood. . . . Comfort, especially this vision of Christmas comfort, is the reverse of a gross or material thing. It is far more poetical, properly speaking, than the Garden of Epicurus. It is far more artistic than the Palace of Art. It is more artistic because it is based upon a contrast, a contrast between the fire and wine within the house and the winter and the roaring rains without. (pp. 125-26)

There is a current prejudice against fogs, and Dickens, perhaps, is their only poet. Considered hygienically, no doubt this may be more or less excusable. But, considered poetically, fog is not undeserving, it has a real significance. . . . Just as every lamp is a warm human moon, so every fog is a rich human nightfall. . . . Every rumble of a cart, every cry in the distance, marks the heart of humanity beating undaunted in the darkness. It is wholly human; man toiling in his own cloud. If real darkness is like the embrace of God, this is the dark embrace of man.

In such a sacred cloud the tale called **"The Christmas Carol"** begins, the first and most typical of all his Christmas tales. It is not irrelevant to dilate upon the geniality of this darkness, because it is characteristic of Dickens that his atmospheres are more important than his stories. The Christmas atmosphere is more important than Scrooge, or the ghosts either; in a sense, the background is more important than the figures. The same thing may be noticed in his dealings with that other atmosphere (besides that of good humour) which he excelled in creating, an atmosphere of mystery and wrong, such as that which gathers round Mrs. Clennam, rigid in her chair, or old Miss Havisham, ironically robed as a bride. Here again the atmosphere altogether eclipses the story, which often seems disappointing in comparison. The secrecy is sensational; the secret is tame. (pp. 128-29)

And as with his backgrounds of gloom, so with his backgrounds of good-will, in such tales as **"The Christmas Carol."** The tone of the tale is kept throughout in a happy monotony, though the tale is everywhere irregular and in some places weak. It has the same kind of artistic unity that belongs to a dream. A dream may begin with the end of the world and end with a tea-party; but either the end of the world will seem as trivial as a tea-party or that tea-party will be as terrible as the day of doom. The incidents change wildly; the story scarcely changes at all. **"The Christmas Carol"** is a kind of philanthropic dream, an enjoyable nightmare, in which the scenes shift bewilderingly and seem as miscellaneous as the pictures in a scrap-book, but in which there is one constant state of the soul, a state of rowdy benediction and a hunger for human faces. The beginning is about a winter day and a miser; yet the beginning is in no way bleak. The author starts with a kind of happy howl; he bangs on our door like a drunken carol singer; his style is festive and popular; he compares the snow and hail to philanthropists who "come down handsomely"; he compares the fog to unlimited beer. Scrooge is not really inhuman at the beginning any more than he is at the end. There is a heartiness in his inhospitable sentiments that is akin to humour and therefore to humanity; he is only a crusty old bachelor, and had (I strongly suspect) given away turkeys secretly all his life. The beauty and the real blessing of the story do not lie in the mechanical plot of it, the repentance of Scrooge, probable or improbable; they lie in the great furnace of real happiness that glows through Scrooge and everything around him; that great furnace, the heart of Dickens. Whether the Christmas visions would or would not convert Scrooge, they convert us. Whether or no the visions were evoked by real Spirits of the Past, Present, and Future, they were evoked by that truly exalted order of angels who are correctly called High Spirits. They are impelled and sustained by a quality which our contemporary artists ignore or almost deny, but which in a life decently lived is as normal and attainable as sleep, positive, passionate, conscious joy. The story sings from end to end like a happy man going home; and, like a happy and good man, when it cannot sing it yells. It is lyric and exclamatory, from the first exclamatory words of it. It is strictly a Christmas Carol. (pp. 130-31)

"The Chimes" is, like the **"Carol,"** an appeal for charity and mirth, but it is a stern and fighting appeal: if the other is a Christmas carol, this is a Christmas war-song. In it Dickens hurled himself with even more than his usual militant joy and scorn into an attack upon a cant, which he said made his blood boil. This cant was nothing more nor less than the whole tone taken by three-quarters of the political and economic world towards the poor. It was a vague and vulgar Benthamism with a rollicking Tory touch in it. It explained to the poor their duties with a cold and coarse philanthropy unendurable by any free man. It had also at its command a kind of brutal banter, a loud good humour which Dickens sketches savagely in Alderman Cute. He fell furiously on all their ideas: the cheap advice to live cheaply, the base advice to live basely, above all, the preposterous primary assumption that the rich are to advise the poor and not the poor the rich. There were and are hundreds of these benevolent bullies. Some say that the poor should give up having children, which means that they should give up their great virtue of sexual sanity. Some say that they should give up "treating" each other, which means that they should give up all that remains to them of the virtue of hospitality. Against all of this Dickens thundered very thoroughly in **"The Chimes."** (pp. 131-32)

Dickens had sympathy with the poor in the Greek and literal sense; he suffered with them mentally; for the things that irritated them were the things that irritated him. He did not pity the people, or even champion the people, or even merely love the people; in this matter he was the people. He alone in our literature is the voice not merely of the social substratum, but even of the subconsciousness of the substratum. He utters the secret anger of the humble. He says what the uneducated only think, or even only feel, about the educated. And in nothing is he so genuinely such a voice as in this fact of his fiercest mood being reserved for methods that are counted scientific and progressive. . . . The things the poor hate are the modern things, the rationalistic things—doctors, inspectors, poor law guardians, professional philanthropy. They never showed any reluctance to be helped by the old and corrupt monasteries. They will often die rather than be helped by the modern and efficient workhouse. Of all this anger, good or bad, Dickens is the voice of an accusing energy. When, in **"The Christmas Carol,"** Scrooge refers to the surplus population, the Spirit tells him, very justly, not to speak till he knows what the surplus is and where it is. The implication is severe but sound. (p. 133)

The third of his Christmas stories, **"The Cricket on the Hearth,"** calls for no extensive comment, though it is very characteristic. It has all the qualities which we have called dominant qualities in his Christmas sentiment. It has cosiness, that is the comfort that depends upon a discomfort surrounding it. It has a sympathy with the poor, and especially with the extravagance of the poor; with what may be called the temporary wealth of the poor. It has the sentiment of the hearth, that is, the sentiment of the open fire being the red heart of the room. That open fire is the veritable flame of England, still kept burning in the midst of a mean civilization of stoves. But everything that is valuable in **"The Cricket on the Hearth"** is perhaps as well expressed in the title as it is in the story. The tale itself, in spite of some of those inimitable things that Dickens never failed to say, is a little too comfortable to be quite convincing. **"The Christmas Carol"** is the conversion of an anti-Christmas character. **"The Chimes"** is a slaughter of anti-Christmas characters. **"The Cricket,"** perhaps, fails for lack of this crusading note. (pp. 134-35)

The actual tale of the carrier and his wife sounds somewhat sleepily in our ears; we cannot keep our attention fixed on it, though we are conscious of a kind of warmth from it as from a great wood fire. We know so well that everything will soon be all right that we do not suspect when the carrier suspects, and are not frightened when the gruff Tackleton growls. The sound of the festivities at the end come fainter on our ears than did the shout of the Cratchits or the bells of Trotty Veck. All the good figures that followed Scrooge when he came growling out of the fog fade into the fog again. (p. 135)

G. K. Chesterton, in his Charles Dickens: A Critical Study *(reprinted by permission of Miss D. E. Collins), Dodd, Mead & Company, 1906 (and reprinted as* Charles Dickens, *Methuen & Co Ltd, 1960, 224 p.)*

BERNARD SHAW (essay date 1914)

I read a good deal of [Dickens] in my childhood before I dreamt of asking whom a book was by. I was a good deal influenced by him. However, I must own that I do not find that cultivated young people in search of interesting novels, can stand Dickens nowadays.

The vogue of Little Nell and Paul Dombey persists only among those who are not likely to count for much in the making of the public opinion of the future; and from the technical literary point of view such slop work as *The Old Curiosity Shop* is indefensible. On the other hand, it you put *Little Dorrit* and *Our Mutual Friend* into the hands of an experienced man of the world who is deeply interested in social questions and behind the scenes in politics, he is startled by the penetration and accuracy of the study of English politics and the picture of governing class life which he finds there.

If Dickens's day as a sentimental romancer is over, his day as a prophet and social critic is only dawning. Thackeray's England is gone, Trollope's England is gone; and even Thackeray and Trollope mixed with their truth a considerable alloy of what the governing classes liked to imagine they were, and yet never quite succeeded in being. But Dickens's England, the England of Barnacle and Stiltstalking and Hamlet's Aunt, invaded and overwhelmed by Merdle and Veneering and Fledgeby, with Mr. Gradgrind theorising, and Mr. Bounderby bullying in the provinces, is revealing itself in every day's news, as the real England we live in. (pp. 150-51)

Strindberg himself has given us nothing more terrible in his picture of what our civilisation has made of women than Dickens's gallery of shrews and fools from Mrs. Raddle to Mrs. Gargery, from Mrs. Nickleby to Mrs. Wilfer. Dickens's prodigious command of the tricks by which grown-up children—as we all are more or less—can be made to laugh or cry concealed from his own generation the horror of the exposures he effected of our social rottenness.

His contemporaries perhaps understood "Dotheboys Hall" and Chancery as it is presented in *Bleak House.* They certainly did not grasp the horror of having Mr. Veneering in Parliament, or Mr. Sparkler at the Circumlocution Office. They laughed at Veneering and Sparkler, and did not notice that Dickens was laughing only with one side of his mouth, and was grimly prophetic with the other. . . .

I regard the books of Dickens's second period, from *Hard Times* to *Our Mutual Friend,* as of much greater importance than those of his first period. They can be read by thoughtful and cultivated adults as serious social history.

The earlier books are, no doubt, still delightful to simple folk, children, and Americans—who are still mostly villagers, even when they live in cities, but are at least literate, unlike our own villagers, who regard reading (perhaps wisely) as an eccentric, an unhealthy habit. The younger Dickens, for all his enormously entertaining character sketches and his incorruptible humanity and contempt for idolatry, is not guiltless of derisive ignorance and the sensationalism of the police intelligence. . . .

[The turning point which *Hard Times*] marks in his development from the satirist and reformer into the conscious and resolute prophet, and in the indulgence of his humour which, always riotous and extravagant, became utterly reckless when he realised that humanity is so grotesque that it cannot be caricatured. (p. 151)

Bernard Shaw, "On Dickens," in The Dickensian, *Vol. X, No. 6, June, 1914, pp. 150-51.*

GEORGE SANTAYANA (essay date 1921)

If Christendom should lose everything that is now in the melting-pot, human life would still remain amiable and quite adequately human. I draw this comforting assurance from the pages of Dickens. Who could not be happy in his world? Yet there is nothing essential to it which the most destructive revolution would be able to destroy. People would still be as different, as absurd, and as charming as are his characters; the springs of kindness and folly in their lives would not be dried up. Indeed, there is much in Dickens which communism, if it came, would only emphasize and render universal. Those schools, those poorhouses, those prisons, with those surviving shreds of family life in them, show us what in the coming age (with some sanitary improvements) would be the nursery and home of everybody. Everybody would be a waif, like Oliver Twist, like Smike, like Pip, and like David Copperfield. . . . (p. 58)

It is remarkable, in spite of his ardent simplicity and openness of heart, how insensible Dickens was to the greater themes of the human imagination—religion, science, politics, art. He was a waif himself, and utterly disinherited. For example, the terrible heritage of contentious religions which fills the world seems not to exist for him. In this matter he was like a sensitive child, with a most religious disposition, but no religious ideas. . . . The political background of Christendom is only, so to speak, an old faded back-drop for his stage; a castle, a frigate, a gallows, and a large female angel with white wings standing above an orphan by an open grave—a decoration which has to serve for all the melodramas in his theatre, intellectually so provincial and poor. Common life as it is lived was varied and lovable enough for Dickens, if only the pests and cruelties could be removed from it. Suffering wounded him, but not vulgarity; whatever pleased his senses and whatever shocked them filled his mind alike with romantic wonder, with the endless delight of observation. Vulgarity—and what can we relish, if we recoil at vulgarity?—was innocent and amusing; in fact, for the humorist, it was the spice of life. There was more piety in being human than in being pious. In reviving Christmas, Dickens transformed it from the celebration of a metaphysical mystery into a feast of overflowing simple kindness and good cheer. . . . Nor had Dickens any lively sense for fine art, classical tradition, science, or even the manners and feelings of the upper classes in his own time and country: in his novels we may almost say there is no army, no navy, no church, no sport, no distant travel, no daring adventure, no feeling for the watery wastes and the motley nations of the planet, and—luckily, with his notion of them—no lords and ladies. Even love of the traditional sort is hardly in Dickens's sphere—I mean the soldierly passion in which a rather rakish gallantry was sobered by devotion, and loyalty rested on pride. In Dickens love is sentimental or benevolent or merry or sneaking or canine; in his last book he was going to describe a love that was passionate and criminal; but love for him was never chivalrous, never poetical. (pp. 59-61)

I do not know whether it was Christian charity or naturalistic insight, or a mixture of both (for they are closely akin) that attracted Dickens particularly to the deformed, the half-witted, the abandoned, or those impeded or misunderstood by virtue of some singular inner consecration. The visible moral of these things, when brutal prejudice does not blind us to it, comes very near to true philosophy; one turn of the screw, one flash of reflection, and we have understood nature and human morality and the relation between them. (p. 63)

Dickens entered the theatre of this world by the stage door; the shabby little adventures of the actors in their private capacity replace for him the mock tragedies which they enact before a dreaming public. Mediocrity of circumstances and mediocrity of soul for ever return to the centre of his stage; a more wretched or a grander existence is sometimes broached, but the pendulum soon swings back, and we return, with the relief with which we put on our slippers after the most romantic excursion, to a golden mediocrity—to mutton and beer, and to love and babies in a suburban villa with one frowsy maid. Dickens is the poet of those acres of yellow brick streets which the traveller sees from the railway viaducts as he approaches London; they need a poet, and they deserve one, since a complete human life may very well be lived there. (pp. 64-5)

Having humility, that most liberating of sentiments, having a true vision of human existence and joy in that vision, Dickens had in a superlative degree the gift of humour, of mimicry, of unrestrained farce. He was the perfect comedian. When people say Dickens exaggerates, it seems to me they can have no eyes and no ears. They probably have only *notions* of what things and people are; they accept them conventionally, at their diplomatic value. . . . What displeases us in Dickens is that he does not spare us; he mimics things to the full; he dilates and exhausts and repeats; he wallows. He is too intent on the passing experience to look over his shoulder, and consider whether we have not already understood, and had enough. He is not thinking of us; he is obeying the impulse of the passion, the person, or the story he is enacting. This faculty, which renders him a consummate comedian, is just what alienated from him a later generation in which people of taste were aesthetes and virtuous people were higher snobs; they wanted a mincing art, and he gave them copious improvization, they wanted analysis and development, and he gave them absolute comedy. I must confess, though the fault is mine and not his, that sometimes his absoluteness is too much for me. When I come to the death of Little Nell, or to What the Waves were always Saying, or even to the incorrigible perversities of the pretty Dora, I skip. I can't take my liquor neat in such draughts, and my inner man says to Dickens, Please don't. But then I am a coward in so many ways! There are so many things in this world that I skip, as I skip the undiluted Dickens! (pp. 65-7)

It is usual to compare Dickens with Thackeray, which is like comparing the grape with the gooseberry; there are obvious points of resemblance, and the gooseberry has some superior qualities of its own; but you can't make red wine of it. The wine of Dickens is of the richest, the purest, the sweetest, the most fortifying to the blood; there is distilled in it, with the perfection of comedy, the perfection of morals. . . . Dickens was not one of those moralists who summon every man to do himself the greatest violence so that he may not offend them, nor defeat their ideals. Love of the good of others is something that shines in every page of Dickens with a truly celestial splendour. How entirely limpid is his sympathy with life—a sympathy uncontaminated by dogma or pedantry or snobbery or bias of any kind! How generous is this keen, light spirit, how pure this open heart! And yet, in spite of this extreme sensibility, not the least wobbling; no deviation from a just severity of judgement, from an uncompromising distinction between white and black. . . . I think Dickens is one of the best friends mankind has ever had. He has held the mirror up to nature, and of its reflected fragments has composed a fresh world, where the men and women differ from real people only in that they live in a literary medium, so that all ages and places may know them. And they are worth knowing, just as one's neighbours are, for their picturesque characters and their pathetic fates. Their names should be in every child's mouth; they ought to be adopted members of every household. Their stories cause the merriest and the sweetest chimes to ring in the fancy, without confusing our moral judgement or alienating our interest from the motley commonplaces of daily life. In every English-speaking home, in the four quarters of the globe, parents and children will do well to read Dickens aloud of a winter's evening; they will love winter, and one another, and God the better for it. What a wreath that will be of ever-fresh holly, thick with bright berries, to hang to this poet's memory—the very crown he would have chosen! (pp. 70-3)

> *George Santayana, "Dickens" (originally published in* The Dial, *Vol. LXXI, November, 1921), in his* Soliloquies in England and Later Soliloquies *(reprinted with the permission of Charles Scribner's Sons), Charles Scribner's Sons, 1924, pp. 58-73.*

ALDOUS HUXLEY (essay date 1931)

The case of Dickens is a strange one. The really monstrous emotional vulgarity, of which he is guilty now and then in all his books and almost continuously in *The Old Curiosity Shop,* is not the emotional vulgarity of one who simulates feelings which he does not have. It is evident, on the contrary, that Dickens felt most poignantly for and with his Little Nell; that he wept over her sufferings, piously revered her goodness and exulted in her joys. He had an overflowing heart; but the trouble was that it overflowed with such curious and even rather repellent secretions. (pp. 297-98)

One of Dickens's most striking peculiarities is that, whenever in his writing he becomes emotional, he ceases instantly to use his intelligence. The overflowing of his heart drowns his head and even dims his eyes; for, whenever he is in the melting mood, Dickens ceases to be able and probably ceases even to wish to see reality. His one and only desire on these occasions is just to overflow, nothing else. Which he does, with a vengeance and in an atrocious blank verse that is meant to be poetical prose and succeeds only in being the worst kind of fustian. (p. 299)

Mentally drowned and blinded by the sticky overflowings of his heart, Dickens was incapable, when moved, of re-creating, in terms of art, the reality which had moved him, was even, it would seem, unable to perceive that reality. Little Nelly's sufferings and death distressed him as, in real life, they would distress any normally constituted man; for the suffering and death of children raise the problem of evil in its most unanswerable form. It was Dickens's business as a writer to re-create in terms of his art this distressing reality. He failed. The history of Little Nell is distressing indeed, but not as Dickens presumably meant it to be distressing; it is distressing in its ineptitude and vulgar sentimentality.

A child, Ilusha, suffers and dies in Dostoevsky's *Brothers Karamazov*. Why is this history so agonizingly moving, when the tale of Little Nell leaves us not merely cold, but derisive? Comparing the two stories, we are instantly struck by the incomparably greater richness in factual detail of Dostoevsky's creation. Feeling did not prevent him from seeing and recording, or rather re-creating. All that happened round Ilusha's deathbed he saw, unerringly. The emotion-blinded Dickens noticed practically nothing of what went on in Little Nelly's neighbourhood during the child's last days. We are almost forced, indeed, to believe that he didn't want to see anything. He wanted to be unaware himself and he wanted his readers to be unaware of everything except Little Nell's sufferings on the one hand and her goodness and innocence on the other. . . . Thanks to Dickens's pathologically deliberate unawareness, Nell's virtues are marooned, as it were, in the midst of a boundless waste of unreality; isolated, they fade and die. Even her sufferings and death lack significance because of this isolation. Dickens's unawareness was the death of death itself. Unawareness, according to the ethics of Buddhism, is one of the deadly sins. The stupid are wicked. . . . Damned in the realm of conduct, the unaware are also damned aesthetically. Their art is bad; instead of creating, they murder. (pp. 300-02)

Aldous Huxley, "Vulgarity in Literature," in his Music at Night and Other Essays *(copyright 1931, 1959 by Aldous Huxley; reprinted by permission of Harper & Row, Publishers, Inc.; in Canada by Mrs. Laura Huxley and Chatto & Windus), Doubleday, Doran & Company, 1931, pp. 243-303.**

DAVID CECIL (essay date 1932)

[Dickens] is not only the most famous of the Victorian novelists, he is the most typical. If we are to see the distinguishing virtues and defects of his school at their clearest, we must examine Dickens.

This means, it must be admitted, that we see a great deal that is bad. The Victorian novelists are all unequal. But no Victorian novelist, no novelist of any period, is more sensationally unequal than Dickens. He cannot construct, for one thing. His books have no organic unity; they are full of detachable episodes, characters who serve no purpose in furthering the plot. Nor are these the least interesting characters; Mr. Micawber, Mrs. Gamp, Flora Finching, Mr. Crummles, Dickens' most brilliant figures, are given hardly anything to do; they are almost irrelevant to the action of the books in which they appear. We remember the story for them; but the story could perfectly well go on without them. Nor is this because there is not much story, because Dickens, like Tchekov, has eschewed the conventional plot in order to give freer play to his imagination. No, Dickens' books have only too much plot. More than any other novelist he is the slave of the formal conventions imposed on the novel by Fielding and Richardson: he cannot write a Christmas entertainment without erecting a whole structure of artificial intrigue, disguised lover, mistaken identity, long-lost heir, and all the rest of the hoary paraphernalia of romance, on which to hang it. But this structure is,

as it were, intermittent. After pages of humorous conversation Dickens will remember there should be a plot, and will plunge back for a paragraph or two into a jungle of elaborate intrigue; all the harder to follow from the fact that the fallible human memory has had to carry it unhelped through the long space of time since he let fall his thread. Very often he leaves a great many threads loose till the last chapter; and then finds there is not enough time to tie them up neatly. The main strands are knotted roughly together, the minor wisps are left hanging forlornly.

Again, he does not preserve unity of tone. His books are full of melodrama. This in itself is not a bad thing; and some of Dickens' melodrama is very effective. The murder of Nancy in *Oliver Twist,* Mr. Carker's last journey, haggard through the stormy night—these are masterpieces in their way. But they are melodrama. . . . They do not stir the emotions of pity and terror that they would awake if we came across them in real life. And they can only convince as long as they are not set against anything real. We can only believe in the limelight so long as we are not allowed to see the daylight. (pp. 37-9)

But his worst melodrama is less dreadful than his pathos. Pathos can be the most powerful of all the weapons in the novelist's arsenal. But it is far the most dangerous to handle. The reader must feel convinced that the story inevitably demands that a direct attack be made on his tender feelings. If he once suspects that his emotions are being exploited, his tears made to flow by a cold-blooded machination on the part of the author, he will be nauseated instead of being touched. The author must take the greatest care, therefore, first that the emotion he extracts from his pathetic situation is inevitably inherent in it; and secondly that he is not overstating it. . . . [Dickens] had a natural gift for homely pathos. But almost always he sins flagrantly against both the canons which govern its use. He overstates. He tries to wring an extra tear from the situation; he never lets it speak for itself. One would have thought the death of an innocent and virtuous child should be allowed to carry its own emotion; but Dickens cannot trust us to be moved by little Nell's departure from the world unassisted by church bells, falling snow at the window, and every other ready-made device for extracting our tears that a cheap rhetoric can provide. (pp. 39-40)

Finally Dickens often fails over his characters. His serious characters, with a few brilliant exceptions like David Copperfield, are the conventional virtuous and vicious dummies of melodrama. He cannot draw complex, educated or aristocratic types. And, what is more unfortunate, even in his memorable figures he shows sometimes an uncertain grasp of psychological essentials. He realizes personality with unparalleled vividness, but he does not understand the organic principles that underlie that personality. So that he can never be depended upon, not to make someone act out of character. (p. 41)

But if Dickens exhibits the Victorian defects in an extreme degree, so also does he exhibit the Victorian virtues. He may not construct his story well: but he tells it admirably; with his first sentence he engages our attention, and holds it to the end. He creates on the grand scale, covering a huge range of character and incident. Above all he has to the intensest degree possible that essential quality of the artist, creative imagination.

Of course, like that of every other artist, it has its limitations, its "range." The novelist's creative achievement is, as we have seen, born of the union of his experience and his imagination. But in any one writer there is only a certain proportion of his experience that can be so fertilized, only a certain proportion of what he has seen, felt and heard strikes deep enough into the foundations of his personality to fire his creative energy. (pp. 41-2)

Dickens is no exception to this rule. He was the child of poor middle-class parents, living mainly in and near London. And the range of his creative activity is, in the first place, limited to the world of his youth. All the vital part of his work is about it, all his living characters are members of it. As his own life in Border Scotland inspires Scott, so lower- and middle-class life in nineteenth-century London inspires Dickens. But—and here he parts company from Scott—it does not inspire him to give a realistic portrait of it. It is rather a jumping-off place for his fancy. . . . Dickens' stories may have the most realistic settings, their central figures be butchers and bakers and candlestick-makers in contemporary London. But butcher and baker and candlestick-maker and London are first of all characteristic of Dickens' world. And this means something not at all like the reality.

For his was a fantastic imagination. He was fascinated by the grotesque, by dwarfs and giants, by houses made of boats and bridecakes full of spiders, by names like Pumblechook and Gradgrind and Chuzzlewit. Any grotesque feature he noticed in the world came as grist to Dickens' mill. And such features as were not grotesque he tried to make so. This is how he modified his material; by accentuating its characteristic idiosyncrasies to a fantastic degree. . . . This is the second limitation of his range; it is confined to those aspects of life which are susceptible of fantastic treatment.

It is this which led to the old accusation made by Trollope fifty years ago and by less intelligent people since, that Dickens is exaggerated. Of course he is; it is the condition of his achievement. It would be as sensible to criticize a gothic gargoyle on the ground that it is an exaggerated representation of the human face as to criticize Mr. Pecksniff, for instance, on the ground that he is an exaggerated representation of a hypocrite. (pp. 42-4)

Dickens' London may be different from actual London, but it is just as real, its streets are of firm brick, its inhabitants genuine flesh and blood. For they have that essential vitality of creative art which is independent of mere verisimilitude. It does not matter that Dickens' world is not lifelike: it is alive.

Lower- and middle-class life in nineteenth-century London as seen from the angle of fantasy—this then is Dickens' range. And as long as he keeps within it his genius is always active. But it expresses itself especially in five ways. First of all in its actual appearance. Here indeed Dickens is not limited by the circumstances of his youth. Wherever they may take place, the settings of his stories have an extraordinary vividness. . . . The slums of *Oliver Twist,* the law-courts of *Bleak House,* the West End of *Little Dorrit,* the waterside of *Our Mutual Friend,* the suburbs whose privilege it was to provide a home for Mrs. Nickleby—all these form part of the same world, the world which is not London, but which London has stimulated Dickens' fancy to create. (pp. 44-5)

This power of realizing the actual setting never fails Dickens, even when everything else does. The plots of his dramas are often bad, the scenery is always admirable. . . .

It is as much a power of creating atmosphere as of actually describing appearance. And as such it is associated with Dickens' second distinction, his talent for horror. Dickens is one of the great masters of the macabre. It does not arise from character or situation; Dickens' figures of terror, Fagin, Bill Sykes, Jonas Chuzzlewit, Mr. Tulkinghorn, show Dickens at his most melodramatic and conventional, and the situations in which they are involved are as melodramtic and conventional as they are themselves. But they are shrouded in an atmosphere part sordidly realistic, part imaginatively eerie, of such sinister force as to shock the strongest nerves. We feel, as we read of them, both the ugly horror of a police-court report and the imaginative horror of a ghost story. (p. 48)

[Dickens' method of drawing characters] shows him once more as the typically Victorian. His great characters are all character parts. Mrs. Gamp and the rest of them are less intellectually conceived, their idiosyncrasies more emphatically insisted on even than those of the characters of Fielding or Scott or Smollett. As these were slightly caricatured, so are Dickens' figures startlingly caricatured. If they analyze them little, Dickens analyzes them less. . . . [As] Fielding and Scott and the others could fill their characters with an individuality beyond the power of meticulous realists, so much the more did Dickens.

It is here we come to the secret of Dickens' success. His was a fantastic genius. But fantasy, unless it is to be a mere ephemeral entertainment, must refer to reality: a good caricature is always a good likeness. Dickens' figures, for all that they are caricatures, derive their life from the fact that they do reveal, to an extraordinary degree, a certain aspect of real human nature—its individuality. As Trollope shows us living man in his social relations, and Dostoievski as a soul aspiring to God, so Dickens shows him as an individual. He had no special insight into the qualities which are characteristic of man as man; he had an acute discernment of those qualities which divide him from other men. In consequence he does not tell us much of the inner life; for it is in contrast with other men that individual characteristics reveal themselves most vividly. Nor has he much to tell us of human beings at the great crises of their lives, when individual differences are merged in common humanity. In those moments of death and despair when Tess or Meg Merrilies assume the sublime impersonal stature of man speaking for mankind, Dickens' characters dwindle to conventional mouthpieces of conventional sentiment. But his power to perceive the spark of individuality that resides in everybody, is unequaled. (pp. 52-3)

Yet they are none of them types. No two are the same; and there are an enormous number of them. Of all the crowded Victorian canvases his is the most crowded. His books are like mobs; huge, seething, chaotic mobs; but mobs in which there is no face like another, no voice but reveals in its lightest accents a unique unmistakable individuality.

Finally, over a character, setting and horror, quivers always the shadow of Dickens' poetry, the light of his humor. It may seem odd to speak of poetry in connection with a writer so mundane and so grotesque. Where should poetry find its home in novels so conspicuously unsuccessful in the romantic and the sentimental? But poetry is the expression of the imagination at its most intense activity: and such an intense imagination as that of Dickens cannot fail to generate it. It is an Elizabethan sort of poetry. Not, indeed, like the Elizabethans in their tragic or lyrical moods: Dickens' poetry is of a piece with the rest of his genius, fantastic. And it is akin to the Elizabethans on their fantastic side; the quips and cranks, part comic, part macabre, part beautiful, with which Webster and Tourneur and Ford have let their fancies play round the drama of life and death. It is this poetry which gives their force to Dickens' descriptions. The fog in **Bleak House** is a sort of poetic fantasy on a London fog. The sinister waterside of **Our Mutual Friend**, with its black shadows and murderous secrets, and the desolate marsh which struck a chill to the heart of the boy Pip at the beginning of **Great Expectations:**—each of these is a poetic fantasy on its subject.

It may be noticed that all three passages deal with the gloomy, the sordid and the sinister. Dickens' poetic imagination is not stimulated by the sweet and the sunshiny. If he does write about them, he falls into the same error as when he writes about sweet and sunshiny characters: he becomes sentimental and a little vulgar. . . . Dickens' genius needed something harsh to bite its powerful teeth on; it grinds the tender and delicate to atoms. (pp. 54-5)

Dickens' poetry is secondary to his humor. He is not a great poet. He is perhaps the greatest humorist that England has ever produced. All sane critics have felt it, and most have said it; to expatiate at any length on Dickens' humor is unnecessary. A man might as well praise a bird for having wings. But it is to be remarked that Dickens' humor is of two kinds, satiric humor and pure humor; and both are highly characteristic. Both, of course, are fantastic. But the satire, like the character-drawing, owes its force to the fact that the satire has reference to reality. The absurdity of Mrs. Leo Hunter, of the Veneering family rising so laboriously in the social scale, of the Circumlocution Office, type of all government offices, of the cultured society who entertained Martin Chuzzlewit on his visit to America, of Bumble and Buzfuz and Chadband, is wildly exaggerated. But the wildness of the exaggeration is only equaled by its effectiveness. Dickens hits with a bludgeon, but he always touches his victims' weak spot. Only he emphasizes the weak spot as much as possible in order to make it as ridiculous as possible. The caricaturist, drawing a man with a big nose, makes it as big as his foot; that is the convention of his art; and it is the convention of Dickens' art. . . . (pp. 56-7)

Satire, however, is only one-half of Dickens' humor, and not the most characteristic half. After all, there have been other satirists. Dickens' unique position as a humorist lies in his mastery of "pure" humor, jokes that are funny not for the satirical light they throw, but just in themselves.

> "'But the words she spoke of Mrs. Harris,'"
> says Mrs. Gamp, expatiating on the wickedness
> of Mrs. Prig, "'lambs could not forgive . . .
> nor worms forget.'"

> "'I wouldn't have believed it, Mr. Chuzzle-
> wit,' declares Mr. Pecksniff magnificently, 'if
> a Fiery Serpent had proclaimed it from the top
> of Salisbury Cathedral. I would have said that
> the Serpent lied. Such was my faith in Thomas
> Pinch, that I would have cast the falsehood back
> into the Serpent's teeth, and would have taken
> Thomas to my heart. But I am not a Serpent,
> sir, myself, I grieve to say, and no excuse or
> hope is left me.'"

> "'Rich folks may ride on camels,' says Mrs.
> Gamp again, 'but it ain't so easy for 'em to see
> out of a needle's eye.'"

The humor does not illustrate anything or tell us anything; one needs no extraneous information to see its point; it is simply, self-dependently, intoxicatingly funny.

Dickens, then, in his merits and in his defects, is the typical Victorian novelist. And he is so, because more than Thackeray or Trollope or Charlotte Brontë, he is open to the influences whence these particular merits and defects arise. The defects came from the immaturity of the novel form and the uninstructed taste of that middle class who formed the bulk of his readers. Dickens was himself by birth and instinct a member of that middle class, nor had he the intellectual power to discern its faults. Indeed, he was not an intellectual at all. He observed life; he had no power to analyze and co-ordinate his observations. . . . The actual facts of his own experience he realized extraordinarily vividly; like a child he made no generalization on them. He unquestioningly accepted the general ideas held in the world in which he found himself.

And this, in his circumstances, meant a very inadequate sort of idea. It was not just that Dickens grew up among the comparatively uneducated. So did Burns; but Burns grew up amid the uneducated of an ancient civilization, developed for centuries in close and stable connection with nature and the great primary institutions of human life, soaked in an instinctive tradition. But Dickens' world had no instinctive tradition. He was a man not of the country but of the town, the town of a new-born changing industrial society. He sprang from the swift rootless life of the London streets. And except for his genius he is the typical representative of such a world. He was an average nineteenth-century Cockney, only he had genius. (pp. 57-9)

Dickens' intellectual weakness meant that he had no sense of form. He could not impose order on the tumult of his inspiration; figures and scenes swam into his mind in a colored confusion, he just strung them together on any worn thread of clumsy conventional plot he could think of. Intellectual weakness, again, is the cause of his uncertain grasp of character. He sees his figures and he can make the reader see them too; but he cannot reason from their external personality to discover its determining elements. . . .

On the other hand it is because he was uneducated that he fails over so many types. He did not know any aristocrats or intellectuals, just as he did not know about the French Revolution or the English eighteenth century; so he could not write about them. But he did.

And here we come to the major cause of his failures. Because he was both unintellectual and uneducated, he fell into the novelist's first error—he wrote outside his range. (p. 60)

He is always bringing in all sorts of types outside his range, aristocrats like Sir Mulberry Hawk and Sir Leicester Dedlock, French revolutionaries like Madame Defarge; and since the conventions of his time taught him that some types, like the hero and the heroine for instance, were essential to a novel, one if not both of these waxwork, wearisome, impeccable dummies deforms his every book. One sin leads to another; in order to give them something to do, he is forced to construct a conventional plot. And of course his lack of education made this disastrous to him. For when his inspiration fails him he has no good tradition of story-telling to fall back on. His conventional melodrama and his sentiment are the conventional melodrama and sentiment of the Cockney, no better and no worse than those which burgeon in flamboyant lusciousness from six-penny novelettes and supercinemas today; and indeed very like them.

Yet the same cause which is responsible for his defects is also responsible for his merits. Not indeed for his actual creative power; this is a gift. But circumstances do condition the particular mode of its expression. No polish of conventional culture has rubbed the fine fresh edge off his primary perceptions as it rubbed off that of Fanny Burney's; the free lightening-play of his instinct was never hampered as that of George Eliot's grew to be by the conscientious, intellectual criticism to which she subjected it. With the Cockney's crudeness and vulgarity he has his zest for life, his warm heart and racy wit. Dickens' unselfconscious crudeness provides a saving grace even for his pathetic moments; they have not the lifelessness of an unreal and superficial culture, they have the emotional energy of spontaneous feelings which have never been drilled into restraint. (pp. 61-2)

Dickens is the great democrat of English literature. His every book is a crowd; and it is the crowd of a democracy, the exuberant, restless, disorganized, clamorous, motley crowd of Hampstead Heath on a Bank holiday, with its charabancs and cocoanut shies and skirling mouth-organs and beery conviviality, squalid and sunny, domestic and indelicate, sharp and sentimental, kindly and undignified.

It is clearly impossible that so flawed a talent should ever produce a book of any consistent merit. But certain aesthetic conditions suit it better than others; the picaresque form, for instance. *Pickwick* is far from being Dickens' best book, but it is the freest from his structural faults. For since it is avowedly a story of heterogeneous adventures only connected together by a central figure, it does not require that framework of conventional intrigue with which Dickens has felt it necessary to cumber up the more "orthodox" novels of *Bleak House* and *Great Expectations*. If you have little gift for form, the wisest thing to do is to write a book with as little form as possible. Again, he does best when he writes from a child's point of view. Children are instinctive, they have strong imaginations, vivid sensations; they see life as black or white, and bigger than reality, their enemies seem demons, their friends angels, their joys or sorrows absolute and eternal. They do not look at life with the eye of the intellectual or of the instructed observer; they are not ashamed of sentiment: in fact they see life very like Dickens. (pp. 64-5)

The first halves of *Great Expectations* and *David Copperfield* are among the profoundest pictures of childhood in English letters. Who that has read it can forget the vast sinister marsh of *Great Expectations,* with the convict rising like a giant of fairy-tale from its oozy banks; and the forge with its entrancing sparks; and kindly clumsy Joe Gargery and Mrs. Gargery, that comic ogress, as they appear to the wondering, acute six-year-old gaze of Pip?

But better still are the first one hundred and sixty pages of *David Copperfield,* the best Dickens ever wrote, one of the very best things in the whole of English. Here for once Dickens seems not only living, but lifelike; for though the world that he reveals is more exaggerated, lighted by brighter lights, darkened by sharper shadows than that of most grown-up people, it is exactly the world as it is seen through the eyes of a child. (pp. 65-6)

Indeed the whole episode of Mr. Creakle's school is an illustration of the inadequacy of mere realism. The school is unlike any modern school: and Dickens has taken no more trouble to make his description of it meticulously true to fact than he does anywhere else. But the essential features of school life, Steerforth's domination, David's devotion to him, Traddles' dislike of him; the cynical contempt of the pupils for the sy-

cophantic Mr. Creakle, their arrogant contempt for the kindly, feeble Mr. Mell, show an insight into the nature of boys beside which all the conscientious and free-spoken accuracy of later novelists [seems unreal]. (pp. 66-7)

But after one hundred and sixty pages David grows up; and with his childhood, Dickens' certainty of vision disappears. He still sees vividly and entertainingly, the rest of the book is crammed with good things: but the grasp on reality which marked its opening is there no more. Once again we are in the familiar Dickens world, where acute observation and brilliant fantasy and unctuous sentimentality and preposterous improbability tread on one another's heels. . . . And similarly cheap melodrama is the end of *Great Expectations.* It is always the way, always the reader endures the same series of impressions. He opens the book: easily, and irresistibly, in a paragraph, a line, a word, Dickens casts his spell; willingly we sink back on the strong wings of his imagination to be carried wherever he wishes. And then we are jolted and banged, now soaring to the central sun of the creative fancy, now falling with a bump on to a rock of ineptitude, now dragged through an oozing bog of false sentiment; till at the end we are only dazed. And when we close the book it remains in our memory, not as a clear, shapely whole, but as a gleaming chaos. Dickens is the most brilliant of all English novelists; but he is also one of the most imperfect. (pp. 68-9)

Creative imagination may not be the only quality necessary to the novelist, but it is the first quality. And no English novelist had it quite in the way Dickens had. Scott's imagination and Emily Brontë's were of a finer quality, Jane Austen's was more exactly articulated, but they none of them had an imagination at once so forceful, so varied and so self-dependent as Dickens. Indeed his best passages have the immediate irresistible force of music. Unassisted by verisimilitude or intellectual interest he sweeps us away, as Wagner does, by sheer dramatic intensity. This is why his popularity has not declined. Such intensity is not weakened by the lapse of time. Nor is Dickens' writing, even at his worst, ever wholly without it. His bad passages are more flagrantly faulty than those of Hardy or Scott; they are never so uninspired. The blaze of his towering imagination touches his most unreal scenes with a reflected light; bathed in its quivering glow the pasteboard figures seem for a moment to move, to be alive. (pp. 69-70)

> *David Cecil, "Charles Dickens" (originally given as a lecture at Oxford University between 1931-1932), in his* Early Victorian Novelists: Essays in Revaluation *(copyright 1935 by The Bobbs-Merrill Company, Inc.; copyright renewed © 1962 by David Cecil; used by permission of the publisher, The Bobbs-Merrill Company, Inc.; in Canada by Constable & Company Limited), Constable, 1934 (and reprinted by The Bobbs-Merrill Company, 1935), pp. 37-74.*

EDMUND WILSON (essay date 1939)

Of all the great English writers, Charles Dickens has received in his own country the scantiest serious attention from either biographers, scholars, or critics. He has become for the English middle class so much one of the articles of their creed—a familiar joke, a favorite dish, a Christmas ritual—that it is difficult for British pundits to see in him the great artist and social critic that he was. (p. 3)

Chesterton asserted that time would show that Dickens was not merely one of the Victorians, but incomparably the greatest

English writer of his time; and Shaw coupled his name with that of Shakespeare. It is the conviction of the present writer that both these judgments were justified. Dickens—though he cannot of course pretend to the rank where Shakespeare has few companions—was nevertheless the greatest dramatic writer that the English had had since Shakespeare, and he created the largest and most varied world. It is the purpose of this essay to show that we may find in Dickens' work today a complexity and a depth to which even Gissing and Shaw [see excerpts above] have hardly, it seems to me, done justice—an intellectual and artistic interest which makes Dickens loom very large in the whole perspective of the literature of the West. (pp. 4-5)

Of all the great Victorian writers, [Dickens] was probably the most antagonistic to the Victorian Age itself. He had grown up under the Regency and George IV; had been twenty-five at the accession of Victoria. His early novels are freshened by breezes from an England of coaching and village taverns, where the countryside lay just outside London; of an England where jokes and songs and hot brandy were always in order, where every city clerk aimed to dress finely and drink freely, to give an impression of open-handedness and gallantry. . . . When Little Nell and her grandfather on their wanderings spend a night in an iron foundry, it only has the effect of a sort of Nibelungen interlude, rather like one of those surprise grottoes that you float through when you take the little boat that threads the tunnel of the 'Old Mill' in an amusement park—a luridly lighted glimpse on the same level, in Dickens' novel, with the waxworks, the performing dogs, the dwarfs and giants, the village church. From this point it is impossible, as it was impossible for Dickens, to foresee the full-length industrial town depicted in *Hard Times*. (pp. 25-6)

But when Dickens begins to write novels again after his return from his American trip, a new kind of character appears in them, who, starting as an amusing buffoon, grows steadily more unpleasant and more formidable. On the threshold of *Martin Chuzzlewit* . . . , you find Pecksniff, the provincial architect; on the threshold of *Dombey and Son*. . . , you find Dombey, the big London merchant; and before you have got very far with the idyllic *David Copperfield* . . . , you find Murdstone, of Murdstone and Grimby, wine merchants. All these figures stand for the same thing. Dickens had at first imagined that he was pillorying abstract faults in the manner of the comedy of humors: Selfishness in *Chuzzlewit*, Pride in *Dombey*. But the truth was that he had already begun an indictment against a specific society: the self-important and moralizing middle class who had been making such rapid progress in England and coming down like a damper on the bright fires of English life—that is, on the spontaneity and gaiety, the frankness and independence, the instinctive human virtues, which Dickens admired and trusted. The new age had brought a new kind of virtues to cover up the flourishing vices of cold avarice and harsh exploitation; and Dickens detested these virtues. (pp. 26-7)

It is to be characteristic of Pecksniff, as it is of Dombey and Murdstone, that he does evil while pretending to do good. . . . Yet Pecksniff is still something of a pantomime comic whom it will be easy enough to unmask. Mr. Dombey is a more difficult problem. His virtues, as far as they go, are real: though he is stupid enough to let his business get into the hands of Carker, he does lead an exemplary life of a kind in the interests of the tradition of his house. He makes his wife and his children miserable in his devotion to his mercantile ideal, but that ideal

is at least for him serious. With Murdstone the ideal has turned sour: the respectable London merchant now represents something sinister. Murdstone is not funny like Pecksniff; he is not merely a buffoon who masquerades: he is a hypocrite who believes in himself. (p. 27)

In such a world of mercenary ruthlessness, always justified by rigorous morality, it is natural that the exploiter of others should wish to dissociate himself from the exploited, and to delegate the face-to-face encounters to someone else who is paid to take the odium. (pp. 27-8)

It is at the end of *Dombey and Son,* when the house of Dombey goes bankrupt, that Dickens for the first time expresses himself explicitly on the age that has come to remain:

> The world was very busy now, in sooth, and had a deal to say. It was an innocently credulous and a much ill-used world. It was a world in which there was no other sort of bankruptcy whatever. There were no conspicuous people in it, trading far and wide on rotten banks of religion, patriotism, virtue, honor. There was no amount worth mentioning of mere paper in circulation, on which anybody lived pretty handsomely, promising to pay great sums of goodness with no effects. There were no short-comings anywhere, in anything but money. The world was very angry indeed; and the people especially who, in a worse world, might have been supposed to be bankrupt traders themselves in shows and pretences, were observed to be mightily indignant.

And now—working always through the observed interrelations between highly individualized human beings rather than through political or economic analysis—Dickens sets out to trace an anatomy of that society. *Dombey* has been the first attempt; *Bleak House* . . . is to realize this intention to perfection; *Hard Times,* on a smaller scale, is to conduct the same kind of inquiry.

For this purpose Dickens invents a new literary *genre* (unless the whole mass of Balzac is to be taken as something of the sort): the novel of the social group. The young Dickens had summed up, developed and finally outgrown the two traditions in English fiction he had found: the picaresque tradition of Defoe, Fielding and Smollett, and the sentimental tradition of Goldsmith and Sterne. (pp. 29-30)

In *Bleak House,* the masterpiece of this middle period, Dickens discovers a new use of plot, which makes possible a tighter organization. (And we must remember that he is always working against the difficulties, of which he often complains, of writing for monthly instalments, where everything has to be planned beforehand and it is impossible, as he says, to 'try back' and change anything, once it has been printed.) He creates the detective story which is also a social fable. It is a *genre* which has lapsed since Dickens. (pp. 30-1)

Bleak House begins in the London fog, and the whole book is permeated with fog and rain. In *Dombey* the railway locomotive—first when Mr. Dombey takes his trip to Leamington, and later when it pulls into the station just at the moment of Dombey's arrival and runs over the fugitive Carker as he steps back to avoid his master—figures as a symbol of that progress of commerce which Dombey himself represents; in *Hard Times* the uncovered coal-pit into which Stephen Blackpool falls is a symbol for the abyss of the industrial system, which swallows up lives in its darkness. In *Bleak House* the fog stands for Chancery, and Chancery stands for the whole web of clotted antiquated institutions in which England stifles and decays. (pp. 31-2)

I go over the old ground of the symbolism, up to this point perfectly obvious, of a book which must be still, by the general public, one of the most read of Dickens' novels, because the people who like to talk about the symbols of Kafka and Mann and Joyce have been discouraged from looking for anything of the kind in Dickens, and usually have not read him, at least with mature minds. But even when we think we do know Dickens, we may be surprised to return to him and find in him a symbolism of a more complicated reference and a deeper implication than these metaphors that hang as emblems over the door. The Russians themselves, in this respect, appear to have learned from Dickens. (p. 32)

In *Little Dorit* and *Great Expectations,* there is . . . a great deal more psychological interest than in Dickens' previous books. We are told what the characters think and feel, and even something about how they change. And here we must enter into the central question of the psychology of Dickens' characters.

The world of the early Dickens is organized according to a dualism which is based—in its artistic derivation—on the values of melodrama: there are bad people and there are good people, there are comics and there are characters played straight. The only complexity of which Dickens is capable is to make one of his noxious characters become wholesome, one of his clowns turn into a serious person. The most conspicuous example of this process is the reform of Mr Dombey, who, as Taine says, 'turns into the best of fathers and spoils a fine novel.' But the reform of Scrooge in *A Christmas Carol* shows the phenomenon in its purest form.

We have come to take Scrooge so much for granted that he seems practically a piece of Christmas folklore; we no more inquire seriously into the mechanics of his transformation than we do into the transformation of the Beast in the fairy tale into the young prince that marries Beauty. Yet Scrooge represents a principle fundamental to the dynamics of Dickens' world and derived from his own emotional constitution. It was not merely that his passion for the theater had given him a taste for melodramatic contrasts; it was rather that the lack of balance between the opposite impulses of his nature had stimulated an appetite for melodrama. For emotionally Dickens *was* unstable. Allowing for the English restraint, which masks what the Russian expressiveness indulges and perhaps overexpresses, and for the pretenses of English biographers, he seems almost as unstable as Dostoevsky. He was capable of great hardness and cruelty, and not merely toward those whom he had cause to resent: people who patronized or intruded on him. . . . There is more of emotional reality behind Quilp in *The Old Curiosity Shop* than there is behind Little Nell. If Little Nell sounds bathetic today, Quilp has lost none of his fascination. He is ugly, malevolent, perverse; he delights in making mischief for its own sake; yet he exercises over the members of his household a power which is almost an attraction and which resembles what was known in Dickens' day as 'malicious animal magnetism.' Though Quilp is ceaselessly tormenting his wife and browbeating the boy who works for him, they never attempt to escape: they admire him; in a sense they love him. (pp. 51-2)

Shall we ask what Scrooge would actually be like if we were to follow him beyond the frame of the story? Unquestionably he would relapse when the merriment was over—if not while it was still going on—into moroseness, vindictiveness, suspicion. He would, that is to say, reveal himself as the victim of a manic-depressive cycle, and a very uncomfortable person.

This dualism runs all through Dickens. There has always to be a good and a bad of everything: each of the books has its counterbalancing values, and pairs of characters sometimes counterbalance each other from the casts of different books. There has to be a good manufacturer, Mr. Rouncewell, and a bad manufacturer, Mr. Bounderby; a bad old Jew, Fagin, and a good old Jew, Riah; an affable lawyer who is really unscrupulous, Vholes, and a kindly lawyer who pretends to be unfeeling, Jaggers. . . . (p. 53)

Dickens' difficulty in his middle period, and indeed more or less to the end, is to get good and bad together in one character. He had intended in *Dombey and Son* to make Walter Gay turn out badly, but hadn't been able to bring himself to put it through. . . . In *Great Expectations* we see Pip pass through a whole psychological cycle. At first, he is sympathetic, then by a more or less natural process he turns into something unsympathetic, then he becomes sympathetic again. Here the effects of both poverty and riches are seen from the inside in one person. This is for Dickens a great advance; and it is a development which, if carried far enough, would end by eliminating the familiar Dickens of the lively but limited stage characters, with their tag lines and their unvarying make-ups. (p. 54)

Three years had passed since *Great Expectations* before Dickens began another novel; he worked at it with what was for him extreme slowness, hesitation and difficulty; and the book shows the weariness, the fears and the definitive disappointments of this period.

This story, *Our Mutual Friend* . . . , like all these later books of Dickens, is more interesting to us today than it was to Dickens' public. It is a next number in the Dickens sequence quite worthy of its predecessors, a development out of what has gone before that is in certain ways quite different from the others. It may be said Dickens never really repeats himself: his thought makes a consistent progress, and his art, through the whole thirty-five years of his career, keeps going on to new materials and effects; so that his work has an interest and a meaning as a whole. The difficulty that Dickens found in writing *Our Mutual Friend* does not make itself felt as anything in the nature of an intellectual disintegration. On the contrary, the book compensates for its shortcomings by the display of an intellectual force which, though present in Dickens' work from the first, here appears in a phase of high tension and a condition of fine muscular training. The Dickens of the old eccentric 'Dickens characters' has here, as has often been noted, become pretty mechanical and sterile. . . . Also, the complex Dickens plot has come to seem rather tiresome and childish. But Dickens has here distilled the mood of his later years, dramatized the tragic discrepancies of his character, delivered his final judgment on the whole Victorian exploit, in a fashion so impressive that we realize how little the distractions of this period had the power to direct him from the prime purpose of his life: the serious exercise of his art.

As the fog is the symbol for *Bleak House* and the prison for *Little Dorrit,* so the dust-pile is the symbol for *Our Mutual Friend.* It dominates even the landscape of London, which has already been presented by Dickens under such a variety of aspects, but which now appears—though with Newgate looming over it as it did in **Barnaby Rudge**—under an aspect that is new: 'A gray dusty withered evening in London city has not a hopeful aspect,' he writes of the day when Bradley Headstone goes to pay his hopeless court to Lizzie Hexam. (pp. 61-2)

Dickens' line in his criticism of society is very clear in **Our Mutual Friend,** and it marks a new position on Dickens' part, as it results from a later phase of the century. Dickens has come at last to depair utterly of the prospering middle class. We have seen how he judged the morality of the merchants. In **Bleak House,** the ironmaster is a progressive and self-sustaining figure who is played off against parasites of various sorts; but in **Hard Times,** written immediately afterward, the later development of Rouncewell is dramatized in the exploiter Bounderby, a new kind of Victorian hypocrite, who pretends to be a self-made man. In **Little Dorrit,** the one set of characters who are comparatively healthy and cheerful still represent that middle-class home which has remained Dickens' touchstone of virtue; but even here there is a distinct change in Dickens' attitude. Mr. Meagles, the retired banker, with his wife and his beloved only daughter, become the prey of Henry Gowan, a well-connected young man of no fortune who manages to lead a futile life (the type has been well observed) between the social and artistic worlds without ever making anything of either. But the smugness and insularity, even the vulgarity, of the Meagleses is felt by Dickens as he has never felt it in connection with such people before. (p. 63)

[The] resentment is to get the upper hand. The Meagleses turn up now as the Podsnaps, that horrendous middle-class family, exponents of all the soundest British virtues, who, however, are quite at home in a social circle of sordid adventurers and phony *nouveaux riches,* and on whom Dickens visits a satire as brutal as themselves. Gone are the high spirits that made of Pecksniff an exhilarating figure of fun—gone with the Yoho! of the stagecoach on which Tom Pinch traveled to London. The Podsnaps, the Lammles, the Veneerings, the Fledgebys, are unpleasant as are no other characters in Dickens. . . . One of the ugliest scenes in Dickens is that in which Fledgeby ascribes his own characteristics to the gentle old Jew Riah and makes him the agent of his meanness and sharp-dealing. And not content with making Fledgeby a cur, Dickens himself shows a certain cruelty in having him ultimately thrashed by Lammle under circumstances of peculiar ignomiy and then having the little dolls' dressmaker apply plasters with pepper on them to his wounds. This incident betrays a kind of sadism which we never felt in Dickens' early work—when Nicholas Nickleby beat Squeers, for example—but which breaks out now and then in these later books in a disagreeable fashion.

If the middle class has here become a monster, the gentry have taken on an aspect more attractive than we have ever known them to wear as a class in any previous novel of Dickens. If an increase of satiric emphasis turns the Meagleses into the Podsnaps, so a shift from the satirical to the straight turns the frivolous and idle young man of good family, who has hitherto always been exhibited as more or less of a scoundrel—James Harthouse or Henry Gowan—into the sympathetic Eugene Wrayburn. Eugene and his friend Mortimer Lightwood, the little old dinerout named Twemlow, the only gentleman in the Veneerings' circle, and the Reverend Frank Milvey, 'expensively educated and wretchedly paid,' the Christian turned social worker, are the only representatives of the upper strata who are shown as having decent values; and they are all the remnants of an impoverished gentry. Outside these, you find the decent values—or what Dickens intends to be such—in an

impoverished proletariat and lower middle class: the modest clerk, the old Jew, the dolls' dressmaker, the dust-contractor's foreman, the old woman who minds children for a living. And the chief heroine is not Bella Wilfer, who has to be cured of her middle-class ideals, but Lizzie Hexam, the illiterate daughter of a Thames-side water-rat. Dickens has here, for the first time in his novels, taken his leading woman from the lowest class; and it will be the principal moral of **Our Mutual Friend** that Wrayburn will have the courage to marry Lizzie. (pp. 64-5)

Dickens has aligned himself in **Our Mutual Friend** with a new combination of forces. Shrinking from Podsnap and Veneering, he falls back on that aristocracy he had so savagely attacked in his youth, but to which, through his origins, he had always been closer than he had to the commercial classes. (p. 66)

There is, however, another element that plays an important rôle in the story: the proletarian who has educated himself to be a member of this middle class. Lizzie Hexam has a brother, whom she has induced to get an education and who, as soon as he has qualified himself to teach, drops his family even more callously than Pip did his; and the schoolmaster of Charley Hexam's school, another poor man who has advanced himself, is the villain of **Our Mutual Friend.** We are a long way here from the days when the villains and bad characters in Dickens, the Quilps and the Mrs. Gamps, could be so fascinating through their resourcefulness and vitality that, as G. K. Chesterton says, the reader is sorry at the end when they are finally banished from the scene and hopes that the discredited scoundrel will still open the door and stick his head in and make one more atrocious remark. Such figures are so much all of a piece of evil that they have almost a kind of innocence. But here Bradley Headstone has no innocence: he is perverted, tormented, confused. He represents a type which begins to appear in these latest novels of Dickens and which originally derives perhaps from those early theatrical villains, of the type of the elder Rudge or Monks in **Oliver Twist,** skulking figures with black looks and ravaged faces: a literary convention of which one would suppose it would be impossible to make anything plausible. Yet Dickens does finally succeed in giving these dark figures reality.

In Bradley Headstone's case, it is his very aspirations which have gone bad and turned the stiff and anxious schoolmaster into a murderer. . . . Bradley is the first murderer in Dickens who exhibits any complexity of character. And he is the first to present himself as a member of respectable Victorian society. There is a dreadful and convincing picture of the double life led by Headstone as he goes about his duties as a schoolmaster after he has decided to murder Eugene. In **Great Expectations** . . . Estella rejects the love of the hero. In **Our Mutual Friend,** Bella Wilfer rejects Rokesmith in much the same way—though less cruelly, and though she later marries him. But Rokesmith is a colorless character, and the real agonies of frustrated passion appear in **Our Mutual Friend** in the scene between Bradley and Lizzie. This is the kind of thing—the Carker and Edith Dombey kind of thing—that is likely to be bad in Dickens; but here it has a certain reality and a certain unpleasant power. Who can forget the tophatted schoolmaster striking his fist against the stone wall of the church?

The inference is, of course, that Bradley, if he had not been shipwrecked in this way, would have approximated as closely as possible to some sort of Murdstone or Gradgrind. But his death has a tragic symbolism which suggests a different kind of moral. In order to escape detection, he has disguised himself at the time of the murder as a disreputable waterside character who is known to have a grievance against Eugene. When the man finds out what has happened, he makes capital of it by blackmailing Bradley. Headstone finally tackles him on the edge of the deep lock of a canal, drags him into the water, and holds him under until he is drowned; but in doing so, he drowns himself. It is as if the illiterate ruffian whom he would now never be able to shake off has come to represent the brutish part of Bradley's own nature. Having failed to destroy Eugene, he destroys himself with the brute. (pp. 67-8)

> *Edmund Wilson, "Dickens: The Two Scrooges" (originally presented as a lecture at the University of Chicago in 1939), in his* The Wound and the Bow: Seven Studies in Literature *(reprinted by permission of Farrar, Straus & Giroux, Inc.; copyright © 1929, 1932, 1940, 1941 by Edmund Wilson; copyright renewed © 1966, 1968, 1970 by Edmund Wilson), Houghton Mifflin Company, 1941 (and reprinted by Farrar, Straus & Giroux, 1978, pp. 3-85).*

HUMPHRY HOUSE (essay date 1947)

The present lively interest in Dickens has in it an element never before prominent in all his hundred years of popularity—an interest in his mastery of the macabre and terrible in scene and character. His understanding of and power of describing evil and cruelty, fear and mania and guilt; his overburdening sense, in the crises, of the ultimate loneliness of human life—things like these are now seen to be among the causes of his enigmatic hold on people's hearts. He has worked as much beneath the surface as above it; and he was possibly not himself fully conscious of what he was putting into his books. . . . We now see more plainly that John Jasper may be any one of us; that the murderer is not far beneath the skin; that the thickness of a sheet of paper may divide the proud successful man of the world from the suicide or the lunatic. We have also lived again into what used to be dismissed as melodrama.

Lord Acton once wrote in a letter that Dickens "knows nothing of sin when it is not crime". Within the narrow limits of theological pigeon-holes this is true; the word "sin" hardly occurs in the novels; wickedness is not regarded as an offence agains a personal God. But if the judgment is that Dickens knows nothing of evil unless it is recognised and punishable by the law, it is quite false. The great black, ghastly gallows hanging over all, of which Dickens writes in the Preface to *Oliver Twist,* is not just the official retribution of society against those who break its rules; it is a symbol of the internal knowledge of guilt, the knowledge that makes Sikes wander back and forth in the country north of London, dogged not by fear of the police but by the phantom of Nancy, the knowledge that produces the last vision of her eyes which is the immediate cause of his death. . . . Dickens is continually dealing with the forms of evil which the absence or failure of love may breed, and with the more terrible effects of emotional greed, the exploitation of one person by another, which often overflows into cruelty and violence. His methods of dealing with these moral problems and the conflicts they involve are various, but they are always peculiar and oblique; they are rarely brought out openly on the main surface of the story; they are never analysed as the story goes along. They are sometimes displayed through a grotesque character in such a way that they become so sharp and hideous that it is hard to recognise their seriousness and truth. Such, for example, is Quilp's cruelty towards his

wife, which seems a fantastic travesty of human action if one overlooks Mrs. Quilp's one phrase:

> Quilp has such a way with him when he likes, that the best-looking woman here couldn't refuse him if I was dead.

That one sentence goes to the core of Quilp: for all his grotesque exterior he has in him a secret and serious human *power:* he is no figure of fun.

Except in such sudden phrases as these, Dickens's imagination usually concentrates through all the greater part of a story now on the black, now on the white, exclusively: the two don't interpenetrate. It is only in the portraits of boyhood and adolescence, such as those of Pip and the early Copperfield, that the medley of moral direction is really convincing. The adult characters for most of their course drive headstrong forward, virtuously or villainously or in some grotesque neutral zone where moral decisions do not have to be made. It is as if Dickens was afraid of attempting to portray the full complexity of an adult. Then, quite suddenly, a portentous thing happens. It is worth noticing first what does *not* happen. I cannot think of a single instance in which one of the good characters suddenly reveals a streak of evil: the Jarndyces and Cheerybles and Brownlows persevere infallible and unsullied to the end. The startling thing that *does* happen is that the villains suddenly reveal, if not a streak of good, a streak of vivid power, and then an immense depth of intricate, confused and pitiable humanity. Suddenly their awakened sense of guilt, their fears, remorse, regrets, and above all their terrible loneliness strike out like lightning from the complex plot. . . . Examples of this are Fagin, Sikes, Jonas Chuzzlewit, even Quilp: but for the moment let us look closely at Mr Carker in *Dombey and Son.*

Carker has most often been regarded as a typical villain out of melodrama. One critic at least has called his drive across France from Dijon to the coast a "masterpiece of melodrama". So persistent has this way of regarding it been that this same critic himself heightens the scene by speaking of Carker's "last journey through the *stormy* night". But Dickens makes no mention of any storm whatever; in fact he writes in quite a different mood of "a sigh of mountain air from the distant Jura, fading along the plain". It is nearer the truth to say that in this scene Carker shakes off the last suggestion of melodrama and becomes a figure of immense significance. (pp. 183-85)

It is only in the light of these great final scenes that Carker's character as shown earlier in the book becomes intelligible; it is then seen that he is not the motivelessly malignant villain of melodrama: he is a man of intellect, of great ambition and great sexual vitality; his worse flaws are self-centredness and vanity. It is exactly this sort of man who would be afflicted with a total blindness about what Edith Dombey, in a position, as he thinks, to satisfy both his ambition and his sexual desires, was really thinking and feeling. The final disclosure would have been bitter to Carker for many reasons, but bitterest perhaps because it showed him that he had been abysmally blind and *stupid;* yet he was too self-centred, intricate and cunning to allow reflection on his own stupidity to come uppermost in his tortured thoughts. There is much of Dickens himself in Mr. Carker: and it is startling to see the hopelessness of his wheels within wheels of thought: there is no solution but death.

One of the problems that face the critic of Dickens is to explain how this intimate understanding of morbid and near-morbid psychology links on to his apparent optimism, and above all to his humour. I think we can safely say that the countless scenes of gregarious and hearty happiness, which seem to us so unconvincing, seem so because they represent a revulsion from the abysses of evil, a strenous and ardent *wish* to achieve happiness, rather than the realisation of it. (pp. 186-87)

It is clear from the evidence of the novels alone that Dickens's acquaintance with evil was not just acquired *ab extra*, by reading the police-court reports (much as he loved them) and wandering about Seven Dials and the Waterside by night; it was acquired also by introspection. His own temptations and imaginings, isolated and heightened by the peculiar, narrowing, intense quality of his imagination, fed daily by the immense power which he felt himself to possess over others' personalities—these were the authentic sources of his great criminal characters. Their ultimate trembling loneliness, or hunted wanderings, or self-haunted hallucinations, or endless, destroying self-analysis, came also from himself. Our generation has come to recognise this by introspection, too. (p. 189)

Humphry House, "The Macabre Dickens" (originally presented as a B.B.C. Third Programme on June 3, 1947), in his All in Due Time: The Collected Essays and Broadcast Talks of Humphry House, *Rupert Hart-Davis, 1955, pp. 183-89.*

GRAHAM GREENE (essay date 1950)

The driest critic could not have quite blinkered his eyes to those sudden wide illuminations of comic genius that flap across the waste of words like sheet lightning [in *The Pickwick Papers*], but could he have foreseen the second novel [*Oliver Twist*], not a repetition of this great loose popular holdall, but a short melodrama, tight in construction, almost entirely lacking in broad comedy, and possessing only the sad twisted humour of the orphan's asylum?

Such a development was as inconceivable as the gradual transformation of that thick boggy prose into the delicate and exact poetic cadences, the music of memory, that so influenced Proust.

We are too inclined to take Dickens as a whole and to treat his juvenilia with the same kindness or harshness as his later work. *Oliver Twist* is still juvenilia—magnificent juvenilia: it is the first step on the road that led from *Pickwick* to *Great Expectations,* and we can condone the faults of taste in the early book the more readily if we recognize the distance Dickens had to travel. (pp. 102-03)

It is a mistake to think of *Oliver Twist* as a realistic story: only late in his career did Dickens learn to write realistically of human beings; at the beginning he invented life and we no more believe in the temporal existence of Fagin or Bill Sikes than we believe in the existence of that Giant whom Jack slew as he bellowed his Fee Fi Fo Fum. There were real Fagins and Bill Sikes and real Bumbles in the England of his day, but he had not drawn them, as he was later to draw the convict Magwitch; these characters in *Oliver Twist* are simply parts of one huge invented scene, what Dickens in his own preface called 'the cold wet shelterless midnight streets of London'. How the phrase goes echoing on through the books of Dickens until we meet it again so many years later in 'the weary western streets of London on a cold dusty spring night' which were so melancholy to Pip. But Pip was to be as real as the weary streets, while Oliver was as unrealistic as the cold wet midnight of which he formed a part. (p. 104)

We have most of us seen those nineteenth-century prints where the bodies of naked women form the face of a character, the Diplomat, the Miser, and the like. So the crouching figure of Fagin seems to form the mouth, Sikes with his bludgeon the jutting features, and the sad lost Oliver the eyes of one man, as lost as Oliver. (p. 105)

What strikes the attention most in this closed Fagin universe are the different levels of unreality. If, as one is inclined to believe, the creative writer perceives his world once and for all in childhood and adolescence, and his whole career is an effort to illustrate his private world in terms of the great public world we all share, we can understand why Fagin and Sikes in their most extreme exaggerations move us more than the benevolence of Mr. Brownlow or the sweetness of Mrs. Maylie—they touch with fear as others never really touch with love. It was not that the unhappy child, with his hurt pride and his sense of hopeless insecurity, had not encountered human goodness—he had simply failed to recognize it in those streets between Gadshill and Hungerford Market which had been as narrowly enclosed as Oliver Twist's. (p. 106)

This world of Dickens is a world without God; and as a substitute for the power and the glory of the omnipotent and omniscient are a few sentimental references to heaven, angels, the sweet faces of the dead, and Oliver saying, 'Heaven is a long way off, and they are too happy there to come down to the bedside of a poor boy.' In this Manichaean world we can believe in evil-doing, but goodness wilts into philanthropy, kindness, and those strange vague sicknesses into which Dickens's young women so frequently fall and which seem in his eyes a kind of badge of virtue, as though there were a merit in death.

But how instinctively Dickens's genius recognized the flaw and made a virture out of it. We cannot believe in the power of Mr. Brownlow, but nor did Dickens, and from his inability to believe in his own good character springs the real tension of his novel. The boy Oliver may not lodge in our brain like David Copperfield, and though many of Mr. Bumble's phrases have become and deserve to have become familiar quotations we can feel he was manufactured: he never breathes like Mr. Dorrit; yet Oliver's predicament, the nightmare fight between the darkness where the demons walk and the sunlight where ineffective goodness makes its last stand in a condemned world, will remain part of our imaginations forever. (pp. 108-09)

Graham Greene, "The Young Dickens" (1950), in his Collected Essays *(copyright 1951 © 1966, 1968, 1969 by Graham Greene; reprinted by permission of Viking Penguin Inc.; in Canada by Laurence Pollinger Ltd. for Graham Greene),* Viking Penguin, 1969, The Bodley Head, 1969, pp. 101-10.

V.S. PRITCHETT (essay date 1954)

Those who have written the best criticism of Dickens in the last twenty years are united in their belief that the serious and later Dickens is more important and has more meaning for the modern reader, than the comic Dickens; or, that, in any case, the comic Dickens has been overdone. I do not share this opinion, nor do I think that those intelligent readers who read for pleasure hold the opinion either. Dickens' reputation and achievement rests on his comic writing and above all on his comic sense of life. The comic world is a complete world in itself. . . . It is above all in the comic Dickens that we find the artist who has resolved, for a moment, the violent conflicts in his disorderly genius and who has found, what all the greatest artists have sought, the means of forgiving life. In these comic passages we find his poetry and a quality we can only call radiant. It is important to remember that, with the exception of *Edwin Drood*, where there is a change in prose style, the serious Dickens is *not* a realist. There are brilliantly funny things in *Edwin Drood,* but we notice how detachable they are from the realism of the background and the main story. The contrast between realism and fantasy becomes awkard in this book.

The early Dickens is, of course, soaked in Fielding, and Smollett. He can, at any period of his life, make use of their tradition when he wants to do so. The general, discursive, ironical tone of *Oliver Twist* is Fielding; the picaresque incident of *Pickwick* comes from him also. Sterne and the romantic movement have taught him the value of pathos, tears, changeableness, and the gestures against an unjust world. When I say that Fielding has had his effect, I refer to Fielding's Victorian novel *Amelia* rather than to the other novels. A very important difference is that Dickens is more violent than Fielding, yet far softer hearted— I mean violent in emotional temperament. Fielding's violence in *Jonathan Wild* is purely intellectual. We can explain this by saying that the sedate and abstract preconceptions of the eighteenth century have gone and that Man and Nature have been replaced by talkative men and women. There is also a class difference: the eighteenth-century writers were gentlemen or aspired to be men of the world of fashion. Dickens is plainly lower middle class—the most energetic, intelligent and insecure class of that society. Always on the defensive, they are the richest in fantasy life. They cannot afford the great passions, but demand to be judged by their dreams and sentiments. Oddity, being "characters," is their great solace. (pp. 309-11)

Another change, is that Dickens depends far more on *character* than on events, except perhaps in *Pickwick.* The horseplay is far less, the misadventures and knockabout have declined. The situations have become more subtle and depend on the characters themselves. Dickens' comedy is the comedy of people who *are* something, rather than the comedy of people who *do* something which leads to new plot, farces or messes. In the plot sense, Dickens stands still.

But the most important change is the dropping of sexual love. The ribald or sensual humor of the English tradition which puritanism did not really destroy, goes down before another enemy; the immense effort toward material progress which we call the industrial revolution or that great assertion of will which we call the Victorian age. Already in the eighteenth century there were many signs of a dichotomy: Hogarth contrasted *The Rake's Progress* with the story of *The Industrious Apprentice.* I need not go into the whole question of Victorianism and sex for it has often been done, except to say that the Victorian attitude is an aspect of the *violence* of Victorian society and Dickens was both a tender and a violent writer. Huge changes in the traditions of society produce their self-mutilations. It may well be that the violence, the rebellion, the histrionics, the egotism and fantasy of Dickens, all of which are manifest in his comedy just as they are in his social indignation, were deeply affected by a willful impatience with love. Of course, love has always been a stock comic subject: its illusions are irresistibly funny. . . . Against sex are built up the steadfast yet gentle defense of the sentiments, the drama of a black and white morality, and Dickens' personal feeling for power.

For the comic Dickens women are mainly of the insecure middle class, soured by marriage, capricious sluts, and termagants, a terrible sisterhood of scolds or frantic spinsters. This is essentially a boy's view derived from a nagging home, or from a boy's vanity. He was pretty enough and clever enough to want all attention for himself. Women are also fools, in his comedy, pettish in love, tiresome in childbirth, perpetually snuffling, continuously breeding. The hatred of children is another fundamental Victorian theme. Dickens is full of it and its natural daydream: the child-wife and the idealized child. What replaced the sane eighteenth-century attitude to sex in the comic writings of Dickens? I think probably the stress was put on another hunger—the hunger for food, drink and security, the jollity and good cheer. (pp. 311-13)

A more important change is in the *ground* or point of view of comedy. In the eighteenth century, this ground is the experience of the grown man. Even Sterne is a grown man. These writers are secure. In Dickens, the ground is the high visual sense and sharp ear of the experienced child who is insecure. The children of the Victorian age are precisely in the situation of the poor, and get much the same treatment: a huge, inevitable, sharp-witted and accusing class. Dickens' grotesque sense of physical appearance is the kind of sense the child has, and in the graver, later books, the sense that the writer is on his *own* and *alone* is very strong. He has grown up from the child *alone* into the man *alone.* (p. 313)

The gallery of Dickens' comic characters is so huge that it is hard to know where to begin. Dickens was a city. He was chiefly London, just as Joyce was Dublin. We can call Dickens' comedy gothic, a thing of saints, gargoyles, fantastic disorderly carvings. We can call it *mad.* A large number of his comic characters can be called *mad* because they live or speak as if they were *the only self in the world.* They live alone by some private idea. Mrs. Gamp lives by the fiction of the approval of her imaginary friend Mrs. Harris. Augustus Moddle lives by the fixed idea of a demon and by the profound psychological, even metaphysical truth that, in this life, everyone seems to belong to a person whom he calls "another." . . . These people are known to us because they are turned inside out: we know at once their inner life and the illusions they live by. An illusionist and a solitary himself, Dickens understands this immediately.

In Dickens, the comic characters who belong to what I call the *sane* tradition are comparatively few and they come notably early in his work. Mr. Pickwick, for example, is the standard unworldly, benevolent man of the eighteenth century. His chief troubles—the bedroom scene at Ipswich and the breach of promise case—seem to spring from being in an eighteenth-century situation with a nineteenth-century mind. If anyone gets into the wrong bedroom in the eighteenth century they either intend to do so or are prepared to fight their way out. Mr. Pickwick would never think of fighting and is genuinely shocked, as no eighteenth-century man could be, when his motives are impugned. Sam Weller is a sane character. But Tony Weller has the madness creeping on: the obsession with widows. (pp. 313-14)

It has been said that if the comic characters of Dickens are not exaggerations and caricatures, then at any rate, they are flat and static. They circle round in the strange dog basket of their minds, and never escape from their compulsions. But I cannot really agree that the compulsive pattern in these characters makes *all* of them static and flat. There is a considerable growth in Pecksniff. It is true that he certainly does not move forward and develop very far as a character in action in the manner of Iudushka or in the manner of Oblomov; unless we say that

Pecksniff begins by being a humbug and ends by becoming a villain. And we must admit that the comic or rather the fantastic characters are awkward when they have to act within the terms of a realistic, dramatic plot. They are essentially sedentary soliloquists, not people made for action.

The fact is that Dickens had a merely theatrical notion of evil. He thought bad men became evil men merely by becoming theatrical and non-comic; there is no need for Pecksniff to be a swindler; he is evil enough in rendering life meaningless. Yet there is a moment when Pecksniff does become permissibly evil and when his character shows a terrifying side. I am thinking of the scene when he proposes marriage of Mary Graham: a comic character dealing with a straight character. No metaphors now, no clowning, but smooth, persistent, planned and skillful tactics. Mr. Pecksniff is a cold hard libertine. He is capable of lust and violence and actually has courage in this scene. His courage makes him frightening and certainly shows a development in his character. (pp. 319-20)

How does Pecksniff compare with figures like Tartuffe or Iudushka? There can hardly be a correct analogy with Tartuffe simply because the theater has to simplify and intensify. Molière is more imaginative than Dickens in showing that Tartuffe not only gains his ends by pretending virture, but gets out of the attacks made on him, by grandiloquently confessing, knowing no one will believe him. Tartuffe, in other words, exploits vice as well as virtue. Since Tartuffe embodies the idea of hypocrisy he cannot be loved. Iudushka also surpasses Pecksniff because he is grimmer. He is comical because he is a bore. And he is also shown as self-corrupting. He bores himself. Dickens is certainly not as perceptive as the Russian writer, nor does Dickens rise to the heights that the Russian reaches in the scenes describing Iudushka's old age. Dickens had no real sense of the mind diseased. Closer to reality, facing the dreadful *fact* not the poetic fantasy of human solitude, the Russian sees the pathos indeed the tragedy of the egotist. Pecksniff goes out of his comedy with a speech and a gesture; Iudushka goes out of the squalid comedy with a scream of loss, pain, terror. (p. 321)

[There] is of course an anarchic and rebellious process continually going on against the pressure of society and the generalizations of Dickens are meant to reduce institutions to idiocy. He proceeds, in his usual way, to lift them off the ground, make them float absurdly in mid-air. The famous analysis of parliamentary government in *Bleak House* (which can be checked up in the acquiescent political comedies of Trollope) is an indignant lark. Dickens understood the art of calling people funny names and his ear for funny sounds is always splendid. The farce of the Circumlocution Office is not only funny itself, but, with deadly eye, Dickens sees that the place is not only a bureaucracy but is also a family stronghold. His comic genealogy of the Chuzzlewit family is not all of a piece. It satirizes many kinds of believers in genealogy. . . . Having run through the gamut of family snobbery he ends up with the superb statement of the outrageously common member of the family, that his grandfather was a nobleman called The Lord No Zoo. The generalizations about the Veneering Family have the same quality of irresponsible comic investigations, in depth.

When one reads the critics and hears this or that writer described as Dickensian, one very soon finds that this deeply important capacity for comic social generalization is missing. I rather think Wells was the last to have it—in the first part of *Tono-Bungay*. It has gone because the sense of the whole of a society has gone. The novel has become departmentalized. We now

talk of novels of private life, and novels of public life. In Dickens, on the contrary, the private imagination, comic, poetical and fantastic, was inseparable from the public imagination and the operation of conscience and rebellion. This amalgamation was possible, I think, because he felt from childhood the sense of being outside society, because he was a sort of showman, not because he was a social or political thinker with a program. (pp. 323-24)

V. S. Pritchett, "The Comic World of Dickens" (copyright © 1961 by V. S. Pritchett; reprinted by permission of Literistic, Ltd.), in The Listener, *Vol. LI, No. 1318, June 3, 1954 (and reprinted in* The Dickens Critics, *edited by George H. Ford and Lauriat Lane, Jr., Cornell University Press, 1961, pp. 309-24).*

KATHLEEN TILLOTSON   (essay date 1954)

Dombey and Son stands out from among Dickens's novels as the earliest example of responsible and successful planning; it has unity not only of action, but of design and feeling. It is also the first in which a pervasive uneasiness about contemporary society takes the place of an intermittent concern with specific social wrongs. (p. 157)

Whereas *Dombey* has its firm centre, of theme, character, and scene, Pecksniff and Martin divide the centre, the one static, but giving out vitality, the other progressing, but uninteresting. There is no scenic centre, and no coherent impression of period; no one would select *Chuzzlewit* as especially representative or reflective of the early eighteen-forties. We cannot mistake the earnestness of Dickens's moral and social concern to expose in Pecksniff a peculiarly English and contemporary vice, as distinct from remediable and specific abuses. But for various reasons the exposure is not complete—far less so than in the smaller scale figures of Chadband and Podsnap. Dickens had not grasped the difficulty of having a hypocrite bearing the weight of a main character—he can hardly stand the strain if he is only to be exhibited, never analysed. . . . Contrast the continued yet unstrained harnessing of the comedy to the 'general purpose and design' in *Dombey,* where the absurd is on the side of the angels. Toots and Susan Nipper and Captain Cuttle and Miss Tox, all, by their natures and their share in the action, supply continuous moral comment on the evil represented in Mr. Dombey; and they do so naturally and implicitly, without the copybook pointedness of Mark Tapley. (pp.161-63)

Not only the comedy, but all the characters and all the action are subordinated to Mr. Dombey. This is the first novel of Dickens to be dominated by a leading idea, embodied in a single character. He is the origin, centre, and continuum of the novel, as no previous character of Dickens's had been. Before this is demonstrated in relation to the structual unity of the book it will be necessary to look into this idea and character, and the other character upon whom they chiefly act. (p. 163)

In Mr. Dombey Dickens achieves the remarkable feat of making us aware of the hidden depths of a character, while keeping them largely hidden; his method respects Mr. Dombey's own proud reserve. The only times his thoughts are unrolled at length before us it is through the phantasmagoria of the railway journey, where Dickens can 'analyse' as it were panoramically with something of the picturesque freedoms of dream or allegory; and similarly again through the memories and visions called up when he roams through the silent house. Mr. Dombey has 'lonely thoughts, bred late at night in the sullen despondency and gloom of his retirement', but the reader is seldom admitted to them; yet he is often reminded, both by oblique reference and momentary pictures of that silent brooding presence, the shadow behind the figure which Mr. Dombey presents to the world, 'self-important, unbending, formal, austere'. What makes him interesting is the moral suspense: although Florence may serve partly as an externalized conscience, a troublesome and even hated reminder of the whole world of feeling that his pride has forsworn, she does so because something within him responds to her. Before Paul's birth, he had been merely indifferent; afterwards this indifference turns to uneasiness and resentment, which increase after Paul's death. But in this resentment there is an unadmitted sense of guilt, and even the seeds of repentance. (pp. 167-68)

Dombey and Son is also a plea for children; generally, for their right to be treated as individuals, instead of appendages and hindrances to parental ambition, and particularly, against the wrongs done to them in the name of education. It is a measure of this novel's largeness of scope that it is not often thought of as an exposure of misconceived schooling; but it is not less so than *Nicholas Nickleby* and penetrates into more protected places. While forwarding the general design Dickens has shown, incidentally and half-humorously but unmistakably, what is wrong with Dr. Blimber's academy; what the plight of the cherished rich man's child has in common with that of the foundling parish boy. Mr. Dombey's other educational mistake is more briefly but more angrily exposed: the committing of Robin Toodle to the mercies of the Charitable Grinders. And here he can venture to admit the twisting of a character by miseducation. (pp. 194-95)

But Dickens is not here concerned to attack specific abuses. He is not optimistic. In so far as *Dombey and Son* is a 'social' novel, its prevailing mood is one of deep disquiet about contemporary values, a suggestion that more is amiss with them than mere exposure and reform can hope to touch. Dickens had formerly presented the wealthly man as a benevolent fairy godmother or Father Christmas, in Mr. Brownlow, Abel Garland, or the Cheeryble brothers. There would be no place for such characters here. *Dombey and Son* suggests the gloom of wealth (more strongly even than Thackeray was to do) and its capacity to petrify or poison human relations, in the family and in society. (pp. 195-96)

Across the social picture are ruled the ruthless lines of the new order, symbolized in the railway. It links high and low, devastates Camden Town, uproots Stagg's Gardens, provides employment for Mr. Toodle, bears Mr. Dombey from grim past to grimmer future, and finally obliterates Carker. Its appearance on each of the four carefully spaced and placed occasions is emphasized by a volcanic upsurge in the style, by description much overflowing its narrative function. In these descriptions may be discerned the fascination of the new as well as the horror of the strange; but the tone is mainly that of dread. Twice the railway is used to highlight the darker thoughts of hero and villain, thoughts of fear and hate and death. The train is seen only as destructive, ruthless, an 'impetuous monster', a 'fiery devil'. There is no suggestion of hope, of social progress. This colouring of gloom and horror may derive from the over-riding mood of the novel; it may be a picturesque reflection of contemporary doubts; but more probably, from the evidence of the later novels, it represents a persistent shade in Dickens's own social view, which contains at least as much pessimism as optimism, and always more of the visionary than of the reformer.

The social criticism in *Dombey and Son* cannot be abstracted from the novel, and even such disengaging as is attempted here perhaps distorts it. It is pervasive, unformulated; not documentary in origin or usefulness; no purposeful journeys or reading of newspaper reports lie behind it, and it is not a convenient source for social historians. Partly for this reason, that it is inseparable, it assists instead of disturbing the firm unity of the design. (pp. 200-01)

> *Kathleen Tillotson, "Four Novels: 'Dombey and Son',"* in her *Novels of the Eighteen-Forties (reprinted by permission of Oxford University Press), Oxford University Press, Oxford, 1954, pp. 157-201.*

ANGUS WILSON (essay date 1961)

To examine the heroes and heroines of Dickens is to dwell on his weaknesses and failures. Only a strong conviction of Dickens's extraordinary greatness can make such an examination either worth while or decorous; since the literary critic, unlike the reviewer, can always choose his fields and should seek surely to appreciate rather than to disparage. Even in the weak field of his heroes and heroines, Dickens made remarkable advances, for though he matured—or, to use a less evaluating word, changed—late both as a man and as an artist, his immense energy drove him on through the vast field of his natural genius to attempt the conquest of the territory that lay beyond. The development of the heroes and heroines of his novels is indeed a reflection of this change or maturing, and a measure of his success in going beyond the great domain he had so easily mastered. (p. 3)

In general, the subject of Dickens's heroes has not received much attention from serious critics. Admirers have preferred to dwell on his excellencies; detractors had found more positive qualities to excite their antipathy. The child heroes and heroines brought tears to the eyes of contemporary readers, and have found equal portions of admiration and dislike in later times. There has been some general recognition that the now highly acclaimed late novels owe something of their declared superior merit to a greater depth in the portrayal of the heroes and the heroines.

I shall not here discuss the child heroes and heroines, except to suggest that as Dickens matured he found them inadequate centres for the complex social and moral structures he was trying to compose. The children too gained in realism by being removed from the centre. The peripheral Jo has a deeply moving realism that is not there in the necessarily falsely genteel Little Nell or Oliver. (pp. 3-4)

It is, however, the adult heroes and heroines with whom I am concerned. Let me first suggest the limitations which I believe hampered Dickens in successfully creating central fugures in his works, and then, by analysis of the development of the heroes and heroines through his novels, throw some light perhaps upon how far he overcame or could overcome these limitations.

The historical limitations of the Victorian novelists are too well known to be worth more than a mention. The happy ending is an unfortunate distortion in Dickens's work as it is in that of the other great Victorians, but, despite the change made to *Great Expectations,* it goes deeper than a mere capitulation to the whims of readers. With Dickens as with Thackeray, though for different reasons, the contemporary idea of domestic happiness as the resolution of, or perhaps more fairly one should say, the counterpoise to social evil, was a strongly held personal conviction. Even more vital to Dickens was the idea of pure love as the means of redemption of flawed, weak, or sinful men. Neither of these beliefs can properly take the weight that he imposed upon them; though the latter, at any rate, is not such a psychological falsity perhaps as many twentieth-century critics have thought. The main destructive effort of this exaggerated view of love as a moral solvent falls upon those characters in the novels who, under any view, could be regarded as heroes and heroines. . . . This censorship did, in fact, reduce the great Victorian novelists in the sexual sphere to a childish status beside their continental contemporaries. . . . [Great] Victorian novelists were forced at times to devices that are false, ridiculous, or blurred. And these faults occur too often at the moral heart of their work. In English fashion, and with reason, we may take pride in the degree to which our Victorian novelists achieved greatness in spite of this—but we can't efface it. No characters, of course, suffer so greatly as the heroes and heroines. Once again, however, I would suggest that Dickens had a special personal relationship to this sexual censorship—and that, while it sometimes led him into exceptionally absurd devices, it also produced a characteristically powerful effect. The sexual life of Charles Dickens, like that of most Victorians, has become a shop-soiled subject, but one may briefly say four things of it—he was a strongly sensual man, he had a deep social and emotional need for family life and love, he had a compensating claustrophobic dislike of the domestic scene, and he woke up to these contradictions in his sexual make-up very late. (pp. 4-5)

The contemporary censorship, in fact, went along with, rather than against, Dickens's natural inclinations. His submerged, but fierce, sensuality was to run some strange courses from the days of John Chester until it came to light in the diverging streams of Wrayburn and Headstone. Seduction withheld, deferred, foiled—at any rate never accomplished—produced many interesting and complex characters, who would not have been born in a fiction that reflected the real world where men are more resolute and women are weaker.

Perhaps even more important in its effect on his heroes and heroines than the imperfect view of love and the impossible view of sex that Dickens shared with his readers was the ambiguous view of Victorian society that he shared with so many of the artists and intellectuals of his age. Broadly speaking, one could say that the young Dickens aspired to a respectable middle-class radicalism attacking particular social evils, and ended as a middle-aged revolutionary with a peculiar hostility to the middle classes. Such an evolution in a man not given to intellectual self-analysis inevitably produced ambiguities in his portrayal of every social class at one time or another. And in no group of characters is this unconscious evolution with its accompanying contradictions more clearly displayed than in the young men who stand at the heroic centre of his books. This uneven course in his social opinions, now veering, now tacking, yet for all its changes moving in one final direction, affected his attitude to the future and to the past, to all classes, to education, to money, to ambition, to work, to play, to conformity, and to rebellion. This strange and complex pattern of life may be observed working out in various ways among his heroes and heroines.

Any account of Dickens must start with *Pickwick Papers,* the novel which announces an age of innocence before the course has begun. Perhaps Dickens never produced so satisfactory a hero as Mr. Pickwick again—a man who, like his author,

imperceptibly changes; but not from hope to despair, rather from nullity to positive goodness. None of the problems of Dickens are met in this book: Mr. Pickwick developed in the garden of Eden before the fall, the next step from him was to Oliver and Nell—children, at least, have their measure of original sin. Yet no article on Dickens's heroes should fail to salute the perfection of Mr. Pickwick before it goes on to the real story.

Apart from the children, the first group of heroes may be seen leading up to the self-portrait of David Copperfield. . . . Nicholas and Martin advance us a few steps: they are haters of hypocrisy, cant, and cruelty; sharp-tongued and humorous; hot-tempered; inclined to selfishness; a bit weak and spoilt; pale reflections, with their eye for the absurd, of the unintrospective young Dickens as he saw himself. Martin, with Jonas and Chevy Slyme for his relations, can hardly claim gentility; but Nicholas is a born gentleman of a somewhat ill-defined kind, although his uncle is a money-lender. The young, socially unsure Dickens had need not only of false gentility and of hatred of the aristocracy, he needed also a suffused and vague love of the past—a mark of the genteel. So Nicholas's first act, when he became a rich and prosperous merchant, was to buy his father's 'old house . . .'. (pp. 5-7)

It is something of the same undefined traditional gentility which so endears to David Copperfield Dr. Strong's vaguely traditional old school and the aroma of scholarship given off by his improbable dictionary. David is the culmination, in fact, of these purely genteel heroes for whom Pip was later to atone. Of course, being a self-portrait, David has more life, but, after childhood, it is a feeble ray. To begin with, who can believe that he is a novelist? Indeed, although he is said to be a model of hard work, we never have any sense of it except in his learning shorthand. Dickens was far too extrovert in those days to analyse the qualities in himself that made for his genius. It is notable that David is no more than 'advanced in fame and fortune', where Dickens was advanced in literary skill and imaginative power. It is also notable that after childhood, nothing happened to David himself except the passion of his love for Dora and the shock of her death—and these, which should be poignant, are somehow made less so by being smiled back upon through the tears as part of youth's folly and life's pageant. *David Copperfield* is technically a very fine novel of the sentimental education genre, but the mood of mellow, wise reflection is surely too easily held; and, when we think of Dickens's age at the time of its writing, held all too prematurely. (p. 7)

Nor is this smug, conformist quality of David helped by Agnes. A successful novelist guided by her 'deep wisdom' would surely become a smug, insensitive, comfortable old best seller of the worst kind. Agnes, indeed, is the first of the group of heroines who mark the least pleasing, most frumpy, and smug vision of ideal womanhood that he produced. Agnes, in fact, is betrayed by Esther Summerson, when Dickens in his next book so unwisely decided to speak through his heroine's voice. It is not surprising that this wise, womanly, housekeeping, moralizing, self-congratulating, busy little creature should have needed a good dose of childlikeness, a dose of Little Nell to keep her going when she reappears as Little Dorrit. If we cannot believe in the child-woman Little Dorrit, at least we are not worried as we are by Agnes or Esther Summerson about her complete lack of a physical body—a deficiency so great that Esther's smallpox-spoilt face jars us because she has no body upon which a head could rest.

But if nothing happens to David himself after Mr. Murdstone goes off the scene, something does happen in the novel, about which David (Dickens) uses language that suggests that there lies the real drama—as well he may, for with Steerforth's seduction of Em'ly, and indeed with Steerforth himself, we are at the beginning of all those twists and turns by which Dickens eventually transforms a somewhat stagy villain into a new sort of full-sized hero. From Steerforth to Eugene Wrayburn is the road of self-discovery. Of all the would-be seducers in Dickens's novels, James Steerforth alone gets his prey; yet he is the only one, until Wrayburn, whom Dickens seems to have wished to redeem. . . . If Dickens could have redeemed Steerforth he surely would have done so. And, indeed, he did; for Eugene Wrayburn is as much a redemption of Steerforth as Pip is a scapegoat for the falsities in David. On the whole, as I suggest, redemption through Wrayburn is a somewhat arbitrary business; but before that redemption came about, the figure of Steerforth had suffered under many guises and, in the course of his translation to hero, had borne witness to many changes in Dickens's social and moral outlook, had even assisted in the birth of a heroine more adequate to Dickens's mature outlook than either Little Nell or Agnes, or indeed the strange hybrid figure of Little Dorrit.

To trace these changes we should perhaps go back before Steerforth to earlier seductions in the novels. At the start the seducer is a cynical rake or libertine—John Chester or Sir Mulberry Hawk. He stands full square for the aristocratic dandy whom the middle-class radical Dickens detests as the source of outdated arbitrary power. . . . The seducer, then, up to *Dombey*, is a crude class symbol.

Dombey and Son brings us farther forward. Carker has some genuine sensuality, of the cold, calculating, rather epicene imitation-Byron kind that the early nineteenth century must often have bred. True, he is vulgar, hypocritical, and apparently subservient—but then, unlike Steerforth, he has to scheme and work for his living. Like Steerforth, his Byronic professional seducing spills over into other sorts of pleasure-loving—a somewhat ornately comfortable villa. There are four things in which Steerforth differs from him, apart from age: Steerforth despises the world, he puts other values above work, he sometimes wishes that he was not wasting his life, he has the vestige of a power to love or at any rate to want to be loved. It is not very much luggage, yet it proves enough to make the long journey to Eugene Wrayburn. Carker fails in his seduction, but then in Edith Dombey he has a much more difficult job than little Em'ly presents to Steerforth. . . . The female equivalent to the sort of professional minor Byronism that Steerforth and Harthouse and Gowan, no doubt, in his relations with Miss Wade, offer, is the minor, rather half-hearted coquetry that is touched on in Dolly Vardon, punished in Fanny Dorrit and Estella, and finally redeemed in Bella Wilfer. But Estella and Bella are more than coquettes, they are proud, frozen, unhappy women anxious to be free of desperate homes, they combine in fact the nearest approach that Dickens gets to a sensually alive woman with the proud cold beauties—Edith, Louisa, and Honoria. *Our Mutual Friend*, in fact, contains the developed hero and the most developed heroine in Dickens's fiction. The one has come a long journey from the seducer-villain; and the other, almost as long a journey from the coquette and the runaway wife. Even so they remain separate, each is reclaimed by a nullity, John Harmon and Lizzie Hexam. Yet in them Dickens had admitted to the saved a degree of sexual reality that argues well for the future.

We may leave Bella on one side; she has brought some frailty, some liveliness and some sexual warmth to Dickens's heroines; but she plays little part in the evolution of Dickens's social or moral outlook—it was not a woman's rôle to do so.

Eugene Wrayburn is a far more interesting case. His salvation is really immensely arbitrary. Even after he has left Lizzie for the last time before Headstone's murderous attack, he has not given up his ideas of seduction entirely—his father's voice tells him, 'You wouldn't marry for some money and some station, because you were frightfully likely to become bored. Are you less frightfully likely to become bored marrying for no money and no station?' It is indeed his rival's blows that save him. Yet we have seen that Steerforth had certain pleas to offer; Wrayburn offers all the same pleas and by this time they have become more urgent to Dickens. First, contempt for the World and for success—this, once hidden admiration, is now the centre of Dickens's moral values. . . . Loneliness, failure, pride, bitter rejection of all that made up Victorian progress and Victorian morality, a considered rejection of duty and hard work as moral ends, Dickens comes through to acceptance of these in the person of Eugene Wrayburn. And sensuality? Does he also redeem his own strong sensuality? This, I think, is less certain. The thin, calculated sensuality that runs from the Byronic Steerforth to the Yellow Book Wrayburn is not surely of the obsessive, tortured kind that we suspect in Dickens. Does not this real sensuality peep through in more sinister places? . . . The obsessive lust of Bradley Headstone finds no redemption. Yet as he rolls on the ground, after Charlie Hexam has left him, I believe that Dickens feels as strong a pity for him as David had felt for Steerforth. Would Dickens perhaps have left from here on another long pilgrimage deep into the holy places of his own soul? Can Jasper be the next strange step in that new pilgrimage? (pp. 7-11)

Angus Wilson, "The Heroes and Heroines of Dickens," in A Review of English Literature *(© Longmans, Green & Co. Ltd. 1961), Vol. 2, No. 3, July, 1961 (and reprinted in* Dickens and the Twentieth Century, *edited by John Gross and Gabriel Pearson, Routledge and Kegan Paul, 1962, pp.3-11).*

STEVEN MARCUS (essay date 1965)

Of all Dickens's novels, *The Old Curiosity Shop* is least likely to be read with sympathy today. The modern reader is inclined to believe that in this novel Dickens is most cruelly dated. Its very intensities—of sentiment, of the desire for moral and sexual purity, of the public indulgence of private sorrow—are those least suited to command the attention of the modern literary mind, as for similar reasons are Byron's personal lyrics. In both instances we tend to conclude that the writer has availed himself of a dying conventional form which he has simply used for pouring out his private emotions.

These strictures are in my view essentially correct—although nowadays they are come by too easily and seem slightly priggish. There is not much doubt that *The Old Curiosity Shop* is Dickens's least successful novel, a work in which he seems to have lost much of his intellectual control, abandoning himself to all that was weakest and least mature in his character as a writer. Yet it is interesting because it is a stage in the development of the mind of a novelist in whom the effort of growth was a regular source of power. And it is interesting because one can here observe with an especial clarity some of the conditions through which Dickens's imagination was moving toward enlargement. *The Old Curiosity Shop* was Dickens's fourth novel in as many years; in it he undertook to consider again certain matters that had recurred in his first three novels. He failed in this effort. Ten years later, in the final sections of *David Copperfield,* his command over his subject became nearly as uncertain as in this earlier work. In both books he was trying to bring to a satisfactory conclusion ideas he had previously dramatized; in both instances failure subsequently led him to abandon that kind of management of the theme. Like the second half of *David Copperfield, The Old Curiosity Shop* marks the end of a period in the history of Dickens's mind. (pp. 129-30)

The idyllic vision of life is one of the most primitive, which is to say that it is one of the most forceful and persistent, of literary conceptions. In Dickens's novels this vision continually reappears—though it undergoes much development—and each of his first three works contains an imagination of idyllic life. In *Pickwick Papers,* the representation of life at Dingley Dell is of this order. (p. 135)

[In *Oliver Twist* Dickens] displaces the recollection of harmony and pleasure further into the past, toward what has been forgotten, into unconscious memory, or into a metaphor of heaven. . . . At this point he appeared to be quite conscious of both the buried recollections from which this force of imagination springs, and of its circular character, the coherence of the transitory, idyllic, infantile past with the idyllic future that would recapitulate it.

In *Nicholas Nickleby,* this identification between idyllic past and idyllic future begins to be troubled by their very point of connection—death. In the discussion which begins after the telling of "The Five Sisters of York", a question is raised about the pain that accompanies any remembrance of "happiness which cannot be restored". An answer to this question is given in affirming the wish that memory should persist after death—"'memory, however sad, is the best and purest link between this world and a better'". . . . The faintly undecided reference in respect to the two "worlds" is one indication of an equivocal emotion whose presence began to be felt in the novel. (pp. 137-38)

When Dickens is at his best, no English writer of prose is better for range, variety, intensity of registration, directness and force, immediacy and compression; he is virtually unequalled. At his worst he is also unequalled; no writer of comparable genius has ever been so wayward. These extreme fluctuations are not confined to one novel as against another, or even to chapters or sections within a single novel; they happen in succeeding paragraphs and sentences, occasionally even in succeeding phrases.

In the face of such unusual irregularity the historic tendency of critics has been to understand Dickens by means of this very cleavage. The resulting image is of a radically divided sensibility, of two unrelated minds within one, each going its own autonomous way. There is no question of the substantial truth in this description. But it is my opinion that these two parts of Dickens's mind are also essentially related. Nothing in the development of Dickens's art is more [interesting] than the way in which one of them becomes accessible to the other, the way in which certain categories of feeling and conception which Dickens once could not manage at all come under the domination of his intellect. In order to understand the process of Dickens's growth as a novelist we must examine in some detail the internal conflict which was its precondition.

Dickens's inferior prose, generally speaking, is of two kinds. The first appears in characters like Nicholas Nickleby and has

always been recognized as melodramatic, which implies not only conventionality of idea but a deficiency of inwardness—for whatever reason, Dickens is keeping the character at arm's length. The second mode is sentimental; it too is conventionally inspired, but it appears as authentically inward in resonance, is delivered with impassioned sincerity, and is summoned for use in connection with the largest issues of moral conduct and religious belief. The continuous modifications Dickens wrought in his representation of the idyll, I think, reveal a typical development. Only the first attempt, the Christmas at Dingley Dell, is successful and convincing. In *Oliver Twist* and *Nicholas Nickleby,* though a considerable effort is made to assert its real possibility, the idyllic vision has become a poignantly felt need, but begins to seem remote, ambiguous and sentimental.

This incertitude comes to a climax in *The Old Curiosity Shop.* It begins with Nell and her grandfather, lost and forgotten in the solitude of London, and with Nell suffering under the change that has befallen them. . . .

She knows that they must escape from London and believes that in the country they will find "a return of the simple pleasures they had once enjoyed, a relief from the gloomy solitude in which she had lived, an escape from the heartless people by whom she has been surrounded . . . the restoration of the old man's health and peace, and a life of tranquil happiness". . . . She sets out, her grandfather's "guide and leader", and becomes a little picaresque girl, walking in no particular direction except away from London, and toward no particular destination except that region of existence she hopes to recover.

They move toward the country, which at first they simply believe embodies the past, in all its freedom, purity and openness. . . . But though they pass through scenes which recall the pastoral, agricultural past, they can find no place to stop, and are forced to move beyond the simple past toward the primitive and prehistoric. . . . [Their] asylum is a little lost village, "a very aged, ghostly place", within sight of the primeval heart of Britain, "the blue Welsh mountains far away". . . . And the ruin which is their final place of rest is of such antiquity as to be virtually outside of time and history. . . . In this place, lost and buried in the past, but by the same curious token liberated from society and history, Nell temporarily finds a home. To withdraw any further, to move beyond the primitive, is to leave existence itself—which Nell is also about to do.

In *The Old Curiosity Shop* the idyll does not celebrate recaptured joy and companionship: it celebrates peace, rest and tranquility. The strongest impulse with which the novel is charged is the desire to disengage itself from energy, the desire for inertia. The fatigue and steady decline of vitality which Nell suffers is merely one manifestation of this need. The idyll itself has been transformed into a Utopia of solitude, and Nell envisions happiness not in company or familial protection, but in the "fresh solitudes" she hopes to find in the country. . . . (pp. 139-42)

[In *The Old Curiosity Shop* Dickens's] prospect upon ideality has retired into impossibility and daydream. All Dickens's awareness of what he was doing notwithstanding, something was very wrong: how wrong we are continually reminded of by that prose which limps along in iambs, a prose prolonged here as nowhere else in Dickens's novels.

One cannot assume that Dickens's very idea—ill-founded and objectionable as it may seem—infallibly determined the novel's shortcomings. There is no iron law of nature or literature which proscribes success to any writing dedicated to the celebration of death. And it would be misguided to believe that there is some necessary connection between intellectual and literary distinction and the purposeful or non-purposeful affirmation of life. (pp. 143-44)

In *The Old Curiosity Shop,* [Dickens] tried to coerce all of reality into reflecting his condition of spirit. The England of this novel is nothing less than a vast necropolis. Those who are not yet in their graves soon will be—they are merely the living dead. Its first page introduces the idea of a man "condemned to lie, dead but conscious, in a noisy churchyard, and . . . no hope of rest for centuries to come". (p. 145)

In the *Old Curiosity Shop* Dickens was seized more strongly than ever with the idea of purity and seemed determined to reassure himself about something he was starting to doubt; that the child of grace was still an actuality and not a phantom from his memories of youth. To accomplish this he resorted to the radical polarities of representation which compose the shape of the book—the chief of which are the characterizations of Nell and Quilp.

Nell is purity incarnate. When she observes the Edwards sisters reunited and weeps with sympathy for their happiness and sorrow, Dickens remarks, "thank God that the innocent joys of others can strongly move us, and that we, even in our fallen nature, have one source of pure emotion which must be prized in Heaven". . . . "In our fallen nature"—never before had Dickens committed himself to this conventional expression, and he rarely did later on, but in the urgency of his need to assert Nell as the personification of absolute spirit it appeared to come naturally to hand. Quilp, her antithesis, is pure carnality. But he is more than her antithesis—he is her other half; and in this poetic disjunction of a single character into antagonistic parts, Dickens had descended again toward the deepest regions of his being. Quilp pursues Nell and her grandfather without any plausible external or ulterior motive—the law of his nature attracts him to them irresistibly. . . . To Nell, Quilp makes his appearance as a force whose purpose is to bring about not only her and her grandfather's corruption and ruin, but her death as well. And at this point *The Old Curiosity Shop* runs into a considerable difficulty, for the relation of Nell and Quilp reveals the irreconcilability of the crisis of feeling which the novel so precariously represents.

Nell is the spirit moving toward the peace of death, detached in her immaculateness from the source out of which spirit springs. Quilp, however, is that source; he is the flesh gone wild, and in a novel whose overpowering movement is toward death, he personifies the energy of life—life conceived as a perverse and destructive element, but life nonetheless. Vile as he is, no one has failed to remark that he is also genuinely, believably vivid and even gay. Despite his monstrous deformity and uncouthness, he is endowed with a creaturely wit and charm which he directs at women—and they, despite their repugnance and fear, are somehow compelled to respond. . . . He is a brilliantly refracted imagination of demonic, sexualized energy. He is always represented in the act of gratifying "that taste for doing something fantastic and monkey-like, which on all occasions had strong possession of him". Though he exists in an impetuous, dizzying and drunken rush of agitation, he is able to manipulate his wild force, and turn it to the domination of others. (pp. 151-53)

But whatever he is doing he must incessantly give off the remorseless, boundless vitality of desire which he embodies—

even when, as in the central, grotesque image of collocation, he sleeps in Nell's bed. . . . No doubt, like Richard III, he was born with teeth to bite the world. Consumed by a rapacious ecstasy, he is drawn toward Nell so that he may satisfy his instinctive craving to violate her. Nor does Dickens always unequivocally oppose his animality to her purity. Mrs Quilp, small, blond and sweet, is only a slightly varied image of Nell, and is drawn to Quilp because of her need to be violated. Dickens was here representing the truth of a dilemma which it seems in the nature of society to disregard: that the passion for purity becomes urgently felt only in proportion to the intensity of a passion for defiling it. I believe that Joyce had this in mind when he referred [in *Finnegans Wake*] to "the old cupiosity shape".

The resemblance between Quilp and Heathcliff should not go unremarked. Both of them are demons, alien spirits trapped in human form. Both seem to be embodiments of natural elements. Both are incomplete and seek complementary beings through whom their energies can be expressed. Both are consecrated to destruction and both are violently destroyed. (pp. 153-54)

But Quilp, a lower order of creature than Heathcliff, and a simpler one, remains closer to his origins; Dickens's conception of him also rises out of the movement toward the primitive past that characterizes Nell's journey. Indeed, Quilp comes directly from that past. He is, to begin with, a character from myth, and in this regard bears significant likeness to Caliban. One of Dickens's chief qualifications among the novelists of the nineteenth century was his extensive and operative familiarity with the folk-lore and mythology of England and Europe, and one of the strongest sympathies of his genius lay in its tendency to realize itself through these immemorial conceptions, as both Joyce and Eliot, with more organized deliberateness, were also to do. Quilp is a dwarf, and in the course of the novel he is called a goblin, demon, imp, ogre, Will o' the Wisp, savage, African chief, Chinese idol. He is further described as a panting dog, monkey, salamander, mole, weasel, hedgehog, bluebottle. Emerging from the realm of sleep, he resembles "a dismounted nightmare". . . . He has the strength, cunning, and audacity of his race, and turns them, as dwarfs usually do, against the civilization which has exiled him to existing in hidden places beneath the earth. For he is a subterranean creature, a Nibelung, and he suddenly materializes before Nell as if he has "risen out of the earth". . . . (p. 155)

The raging contrarieties of Quilp's sadism and masochism are the counterparts of the contradictory, sentimental emotions with which Dickens invested Nell. Sentimentality cannot here be adequately understood in its conventional definition: that it is an excessive and self-indulging effusion of sentiment, a response grotesquely disproportionate to the reality of a situation. (p. 159)

[A] large part of Dickens's sentimentality is not of the ordinary, maudlin quality we are most familiar with. Because his genius was fired by an especially abundant and intense energy, much of the sentimentality in his writings is of an unusually fierce order. We recognize a peculiar collapse and relaxation which always seems to characterize the ordinary forms of sentimentality, a certain foolishness, flabbiness and weakness. But with Dickens, all these components (none of which is lacking) frequently take on an intensity, a boldness, a sustained exertion of will which defy the kind of easy contempt we generally allow ourselves to feel towards the usual purveyor of sentimentality. Dickens was able to admit to sentimentality a greater quantity of the element of unpleasantness and pain than most who can be accused of this flaw. Here, indeed, is what makes Dickens's sentimentality often seem so extraordinary. Sentimentality, like self-pity, can be as amenable to the qualities of genius, both affective and intellectual, as any of our more primitive responses. (p. 160)

In *The Old Curiosity Shop* Dickens tended to regard Quilp and Nell as absolute and impenetrable essences and to drain the world outside them of all its vitality. The materially abundant reality of *Nicholas Nickleby* was replaced in this novel with a series of disjointed and rather inert abstractions—the ruined Arcadia, the old well, the graves, the road, the Shop itself, the Thames—none of which has the animation of the abstractions in *Oliver Twist*. In *The Old Curiosity Shop* society does not exist in any significant sense; the concentrated duality of Nell and Quilp has almost obliterated that middle ground. (p. 164)

> *Steven Marcus, in his* Dickens: From Pickwick to Dombey *(© Steven Marcus 1965; reprinted by permission of Basic Books, Inc., Publishers), Basic Books, Inc., Publishers, 1965, 389 p.*

F. R. LEAVIS   (essay date 1970)

Hard Times is not a difficult work; its intention and nature are pretty obvious. If, then, it is the masterpiece I take it for, why has it not had general recognition? . . . In the books and essays on Dickens, so far as I know them, it is passed over as a very minor thing; too slight and insignificant to distract us for more than a sentence or two from the works worth critical attention. Yet, if I am right, of all Dickens's works it is the one that, having the distinctive strength that makes him a major artist, has it in so compact a way, and with a concentrated significance so immediately clear and penetrating, as, one would have thought, to preclude the reader's failing to recognize that he had before him a completely serious, and, in its originality, a triumphantly successful, work of art.

The answer to the question asked above seems to me to bear on the traditional approach to the 'English novel'. For all the more sophisticated critical currency of the last decade or two, that approach still prevails, at any rate in the appreciation of the Victorian novelists. The business of the novelist, you gather, is to 'create a world', and the mark of the master is external abundance—he gives you lots of 'life'. The test of life in his characters (he must above all create 'living' characters) is that they go on living outside the book. Expectations as unexacting as these are not, when they encounter significance, grateful for it, and when it meets them in that insistent form where nothing is very engaging as 'life' unless its relevance is fully taken, miss it altogether. This is the only way in which I can account for the neglect suffered by Henry James's *The Europeans*, which may be classed with *Hard Times* as a moral fable—though one might have supposed that James would enjoy the advantage of being approached with expectations of subtlety and closely calculated relevance. (p. 187)

I need say no more by way of defining the moral fable than that in it the intention is peculiarly insistent, so that the representative signficance of everything in the fable—character, episode, and so on—is immediately apparent as we read. Intention might seem to be insistent enough in the opening of *Hard Times,* in that scene in Mr. Gradgrind's school. . . . [It] has no doubt been supposed that in *Hard Times* the satiric irony of the first two chapters is merely, in the large and genial

Dickensian way, thrown together with melodrama, pathos and humour—and that we are given these ingredients more abundantly and exuberantly elsewhere. Actually, the Dickensian vitality is there in its varied characteristic modes, which should—surely—here be the more immediately and perceptively responded to as the agents of a felt compelling signfiicance because they are free of anything that might be seen as redundance: the creative exuberance is controlled by a profound inspiration that informs, directs and limits.

The inspiration is what is given in the grim clinch of the title, *Hard Times*. Ordinarily what are recognized as Dickens's judgments about the world he lives in ('Dickens's social criticism') are casual and incidental—a matter of including among the ingredients of a book some indignant treatment of a particular abuse. But in *Hard Times* he is unmistakably possessed by a comprehensive vision, one in which the inhumanities of Victorian civilization are seen as fostered and sanctioned by a hard philosophy, the aggressive formulation of an inhumane spirit. The philosophy is represented by Thomas Gradgrind, Esquire, Member of Parliament for Coketown, who has brought up his children on the lines of the experiment recorded by John Stuart Mill as carried out on himself. What Gradgrind stands for is, though repellent, nevertheless respectable; his Utilitarianism is a theory sincerely held and there is intellectual disinterestedness in its application. But Gradgrind marries his eldest daughter to Josiah Bounderby, 'banker, merchant, manufacturer', about whom there is no disinterestedness whatever, and nothing to be respected. Bounderby is Victorian 'rugged individualism' in its grossest and most intransigent form. (p. 188)

[The success of *Hard Times*] is complete. It is conditioned partly by the fact that, from the opening chapters, we have been tuned for the reception of a highly conventional art—though it is a tuning that has no narrowly limiting effect. To describe at all cogently the means by which this responsiveness is set up would take a good deal of 'practical criticism' analysis—analysis that would reveal an extraordinary flexibility in the art of *Hard Times*. This can be seen very obviously in the dialogue. Some passages might come from an ordinary novel. Others have the ironic pointedness of the schoolroom scene in so insistent a form that we might be reading a work as stylized as Jonsonian comedy: Gradgrind's final exchange with Bitzer . . . is a supreme instance. Others again are 'literary', like the conversation between Grandgrind and Louisa on her flight home for refuge from Mr. James Harthouse's attentions.

To the question how the reconciling is done—there is much more diversity in *Hard Times* than these references to dialogue suggest—the answer can be given by pointing to the astonishing and irresistible richness of life that characterizes the book everywhere. It meets us everywhere, unstrained and natural, in the prose. Out of such prose a great variety of presentations can arise congenially with equal vividness. There they are, unquestionably 'real'. It goes back to an extraordinary energy of perception and registration in Dickens. . . . His flexibility is that of a richly poetic art of the word. He doesn't write 'poetic prose'; he writes with a poetic force of evocation, registering with the responsiveness of a genius of verbal expression what he so sharply sees and feels. In fact, by texture, imaginative mode, symbolic method, and the resulting concentration, *Hard Times* affects us as belonging with formally poetic works. (pp. 194-95)

There is no Hamlet in him, and he is quite unlike T. S. Eliot.

> The red-eyed scavengers are creeping
> From Kentish Town and Golders Green

—there is nothing of that in Dickens's reaction to life. He observes with gusto the humanness of humanity as exhibited in the urban (and suburban) scene. When he sees, as he sees so readily, the common manifestations of human kindness, and the essential virtues, asserting themselves in the midst of ugliness, squalor and banality, his warmly sympathetic response has no disgust to overcome. There is no suggestion, for instance, of recoil—or of distance-keeping—from the game-eyed, brandy-soaked, flabby-surfaced Mr. Sleary, who is successfully made to figure for us a humane, anti-Utilitarian positive. This is not sentimentality in Dickens, but genius. . . . (p. 195)

Sentimentality, as everyone knows, is to be found in Dickens's *oeuvre*. We have it in *Hard Times* (though not to any seriously damaging effect) in Stephen Blackpool, the good, victimized working-man, whose perfect patience under infliction we are expected to find supremely edifying and irresistibly touching as the agonies are piled on for his martyrdom. But Sissy Jupe is another matter. . . . The working of her influence in the Utilitarian home is conveyed with a fine tact, and we do really feel her as a growing potency. Dickens can even, with sufficient success, give her the stage for a victorious *tête-à-tête* with the well-bred and languid elegant, Mr. James Harthouse, in which she tells him that his duty is to leave Coketown and cease troubling Louisa with his attentions:

> She was not afraid of him, or in any way disconcerted; she seemed to have her mind entirely preoccupied with the occasion of her visit, and to have substituted that consideration for herself.

The victory of disinterestedness is convincing enough as one reads. (pp. 195-96)

The confutation of Utilitarianism by life is conducted with great subtlety. That the conditions for it are there in Mr. Gradgrind he betrays by his initial kindness, ungenial enough, but properly rebuked by Bounderby, to Sissy. 'Mr. Gradgrind', we are told, 'though hard enough, was by no means so rough a man as Mr. Bounderby. His character was not unkind, all things considered; it might have been very kind indeed if only he had made some mistake in the arithmetic that balanced it years ago.' The inadequacy of the calculus is starkly exposed when he brings it to bear on the problem of marriage in the consummate scene with his eldest daughter. . . . (pp. 196-97)

Criticism, of course, has its points to make against *Hard Times*. It can be said of Stephen Blackpool, not only that he is too good and qualifies too consistently for the martyr's halo, but that he invites an adaptation of the objection brought, from the negro point of view, against Uncle Tom, which was to the effect that he was a white man's good nigger. And certainly it doesn't need a working-class bias to produce the comment that when Dickens comes to the Trade Unions his understanding of the world he offers to deal with betrays a marked limitation. There were undoubtedly professional agitators, and Trade Union solidarity was undoubtedly often asserted at the expense of the individual's rights, but it is a score against a work so insistently typical in intention that it should give the representative rôle to the agitator, Slackbridge, and make Trade Unionism nothing better than the pardonable error of the misguided and oppressed, and, as such, an agent in the martyrdom of the good working man. (p. 205)

Just as Dickens has no glimpse of the part to be played by Trade Unionism in bettering the conditions he deplores, so, though he sees there are many places of worship in Coketown,

of various kinds of ugliness, he has no notion of the part played by the chapel in the life of nineteenth-century industrial England. The kind of self-respecting steadiness and conscientious restraint that he represents in Stephen did certainly exist on a large scale among the working-classes, and this is an important historical fact. But there would have been no such fact if those chapels described by Dickens had had no more relation to the life of Coketown than he shows them to have.

Again, his attitude to Trade Unionism is not the only expression of a lack of political understanding. Parliament for him is merely the 'national dust-yard', where the 'national dustmen' entertain one another 'with a great many noisy little fights among themselves', and appoint commissions which fill blue-books with dreary facts and futile statistics—of a kind that helps Gradgrind to 'prove that the Good Samaritan was a bad economist'.

Yet Dickens's understanding of Victorian civilization is adequate for his purpose; the justice and penetration of his criticism are unaffected. And his moral perception works in alliance with a clear insight into the English social structure. (p. 206)

[The] packed richness of *Hard Times* is almost incredibly varied. . . . The final stress may fall on Dickens's command of word, phrase, rhythm and image: in ease and range there is surely no greater master of English except Shakespeare. This comes back to saying that Dickens is a great poet: his endless resource in felicitously varied expression is an extraordinary responsiveness to life. His senses are charged with emotional energy, and his intelligence plays and flashes in the quickest and sharpest perception. That is, his mastery of 'style' is of the only kind that matters—which is not to say that he hasn't a conscious interest in what can be done with words; many of his felicities could plainly not have come if there had not been, in the background, a habit of such interest. Take this, for instance:

> He had reached the neutral ground upon the outskirts of the town, which was neither town nor country, but either spoiled. . . .

But he is no more a stylist than Shakespeare; and his mastery of expression is most fairly suggested by stressing, not his descriptive evocations (there are some magnificent ones in *Hard Times*—the varied *décor* of the action is made vividly present, you can feel the velvety dust trodden by Mrs. Sparsit in her stealth, and feel the imminent storm), but his strictly dramatic felicities. Perhaps, however, 'strictly' is not altogether a good pointer, since Dickens is a master of his chosen art, and his mastery shows itself in the way in which he moves between less direct forms of the dramatic and the direct rendering of speech. (pp. 206-07)

F. R. Leavis, " 'Hard Times': The World of Bentham," in Dickens the Novelist *by F. R. Leavis and Q. D. Leavis (copyright © 1970 F. R. Leavis and Q. D. Leavis; reprinted by permission of Pantheon Books, a Division of Random House, Inc.; in Canada by the Author's Literary Estate and Chatto & Windus Ltd.), Chatto & Windus, 1970 (and reprinted by Pantheon Books, 1971), pp. 187-212.*

HARVEY PETER SUCKSMITH   (essay date 1970)

Two major characteristics of Dickens's vision help to blend its different modes in a complex unity. One of these characteristics, the introverted quality of his vision, will be discussed in the next section. The other is a complex theme which dominates his vision and finds effective expression through the rhetoric of sympathy and irony.

This theme is a view of life as an ironic tragi-comedy of deception; often there is also a melodramatic element in this complex view. True, Dickens is less successful in blending the different elements of this vision in the earlier novels. In *Pickwick,* for example, deception is frequently explored as a comic—only occasionally as a tragic—idea, though the emergence of a tragi-comic vision largely accounts for the success of the episodes in the Fleet Prison. On the whole, Dickens shows increasing skill in combining the various elements of his vision as he matures. Thus, the compassionate and critical views of life embodied separately in Mr. Pickwick and Sam Weller are brought more closely together in *David Copperfield* and life, with its comedy and tragedy, pathos, and melodrama, is seen as a continuum of experience by being filtered through a single consciousness. The compassionate and ironic visions combine through the narrator's viewpoint as he looks back on his earlier naïvety and self-deception with feeling but also with the distance and hindsight which time provides. In *Great Expectations,* this complex kind of viewpoint is combined with a tightly organized plot which hinges on tragi-comic self-deception. The result is an extremely effective structural irony and pathos at the twists of fate find Pip sadly and searchingly wanting. And around Pip are grouped several characters with expectations, comic and tragic delusions, which also come to nothing.

On the other hand, the opening chapter of *Bleak House,* in which Dickens uses omniscient viewpoint, shows how intimately he learned to combine the various modes of vision in a view that has unity and yet does justice to different aspects of an experience. (pp. 325-26)

Dickens makes clear that the Court of Chancery is a mere charade of justice. The irony in the deliberate deception which is being practised is brought out in the description of the lawyers. They are 'players' in costume, 'making a pretence of equity with serious faces'. Their very wigs, which seek to impress the court with the majesty of justice, are only a ridiculous head-gear manufactured from the hair of goats and horses. Their parade of legal argument is a solemn mockery. This court of law is no more concerned with truth than with justice. The judge is preoccupied with maintaining a legal fiction rather than with acknowledging some awareness of a man he has helped to ruin. . . . [We] are even told that the court encourages 'trickery', 'evasion', and 'false pretences of all sorts'. 'Groping' and 'floundering' are an obvious consequence of deception. The fog symbolizes deception and self-deception as well as confusion. The presiding genius of deception and confusion is the Lord Chancellor, who wears 'a foggy glory round his head'; the word, 'glory', and the idea of a halo, normally associated with a very different context, are loaded with irony. (pp. 328-29)

The tragi-comic concept of Chancery is made clear enough in the final paragraph; elsewhere Dickens deliberately increases both the tragic and comic elements in his vision. In bringing Chancery's victims before our eyes, he deliberately emphasizes their wretched plight and shows us Chancery's effect on them, thus enlisting our pity for their tragically pathetic fates. To Chancery's toll of worn-out lunatics, he consciously adds the 'dead in every churchyard' and those reduced to 'slipshod heels and threadbare dress, borrowing and begging'. He goes further and shows us individual victims, the 'RUINED suitor from Shropshire', and 'a SALLOW Prisoner' who has unwittingly committed contempt of court through a legal technicality. On the other hand, the victims are comic as well as tragically pathetic figures. Some spectators linger in the court in the hope of getting a laugh out of the man from Shropshire's behaviour. . . . There is something cruelly absurd, too, about the predicament of the prisoner caught up in the Kafka-like idiocy of legal machinery. The comic situation also has a keen irony. Some of the victims are not only trapped in a web of deception but actively cling to it, trusting that the very court which has ruined them will somehow bring about their salvation in the end. The tragic and comic visions coalesce particularly well in the spectacle of Miss Flite. The poor little deluded woman, who has grown 'old' and 'mad' in the course of her obsession with Chancery and who never ceases to haunt the court 'from its sitting to its rising', is viewed with a conscious pathos and irony. (pp. 329-30)

A strong element of farce is mixed with the general comedy and satire. The lawyers' knockabout clowning with words and arguments is matched by the suitors' buffoonery; Miss Flite's 'documents', for example, consist of matches and lavender, the prisoner is in the habit of popping up, as absurdly as a jack-in-the-box, to try to purge his contempt, Gridley waits for his cue to pounce on the judge with his useless cry of protest. The farce reaches its climax at the end of the chapter when the judge forestalls Gridley by a dexterous disappearing act. Of course, this farce has direction. It implies that the whole proceedings are little better than a slapstick performance and thus helps to reinforce the impression of Chancery as a charade of deception.

An element of sensation is also merged in the over-all vision, for the account of Chancery's victims culminates in a scandalous suicide. Terror is increased through the addition of circumstantial detail, which lends immediacy, when Dickens substitutes [in his revision of the manuscript] 'blew his brains out at a coffee-house in Chancery Lane' for 'cut his throat'. All the same, there is also a suggestion of farce in Tom Jarndyce's final desperate act. Indeed, this is the tragedy of real life in which farce and melodrama play a part and hysterical laughter relieves our darkest distress and anxiety. Here, a kind of terror is also associated with a grim ironic comedy. (p. 330)

The way in which different modes are blended in a rich and complex over-all vision, here, points towards the achievement of Dickens's pupil, Dostoyevsky. . . . [Novels] like *Bleak House* and *Little Dorrit* are marvels of complexity and power. Moreover, a study of significant revisions in the manuscript of, say, *Bleak House,* together with the author's notes for this novel, now published in their entirety, shows how deliberately Dickens worked for this power and complexity at almost every phase of planning and execution. By examining the author's blueprint alongside his narrative practice, we catch glimpses of Dickens at the very moment when he is deliberately translating a complex vision, by means of a rhetoric itself complex, into the substance of a work of art.

Deception is a particularly fruitful theme for the novelist who wishes to give unity to his vision and, at the same time, wants to exploit the complexity and power which a combination of the various modes of vision and their associated effects offer him. Deception provides rich material for irony; but it does more than this. Deception may lead to tragedy and to comedy and so it is also liable to involve terror, pathos, and the other types of sympathy.

The tragi-comedy may be both public and private. A truly comprehensive vision will include both. Thus, in *Bleak House,* a single though not a simple scrutiny explores a world of comic delusion among the ruling class, in their social, political, judicial, and philanthropic aspects, whose result is the contemporary 'condition of England', a national tragedy signified by the ugly painful farce of Chancery, by the squalid Brickmaker's family, the illiterate Jo, and the pestilent slum of Tom-all-Alone's. (pp. 331-32)

The complex vision must find a rhetoric which will communicate it to the reader. This rhetoric is suggested by two notes, which indicate the pathos of Richard's tragedy and the structural irony at work in his fate: 'The two Wards, the subjects of the unhappy story of Jarndyce and Jarndyce' . . . ; 'The shadow of Miss Flite on Richard'. . . . It is those two words, 'unhappy' and 'shadow', which are so revealing and indicate the link between vision, structure, and a rhetoric of sympathy and irony.

Indeed, Dickens's notes reveal two instances in which both vision and rhetoric compelled him to modify original plans for the construction of *Bleak House.* Both concern the Dedlocks. Dickens's problem with the Dedlocks was that they had to fulfil a double function. The satirical vision required that, as typical members of the ruling class, they be anatomized with a cold irony, as they are in the early part of the novel. Yet the comprehensive vision, which sees the more private world of the Dedlocks in terms of a tragic irony and pathos, also required that, as individuals, they must be pitied as well as punished. While the novel was moving towards their catastrophe, then, a careful readjustment of sympathy towards the Dedlocks had to occur, if on the human level the reader was to be involved in their fate. The complexity of vision here is being built up throughout the course of their story.

The notes and manuscript show how conscious Dickens was of this process. The readjustment of sympathy towards Sir Leicester Dedlock, for instance, is held over in the memoranda for No. XVI, 'Sir Leicester? Very little. *reserve for next time. Hold him in'*, and begins in earnest in the following number. The outline for Chapter LIV carefully records a 'curtain' which, by emphasizing the husband's magnanimity as well as his distress, is calculated to earn our approval and awaken our pity: 'Sir Leicester swoons—compassionate and sorrowful. not angry.' This effect is deliberately strengthened by revisions in the manuscript. The human relationship between Sir Leicester and his wife is stressed. The verbal formula 'It is she', possibly a second thought, is repeated in a kind of counterpoint with the pronoun, 'he', thus subtly reflecting the concern for Lady Dedlock uppermost in her husband's mind. Yet the careful substitution in proof of 'almost to the exclusion of himself' for 'not himself' indicates the complexity of Sir Leicester's reaction to the shock, setting him up not as an unconvincing ideal of husbandly virtue but as an authentic human being whose genuine concern for another person is mixed with a little for himself in a moment of real crisis. . . . (pp. 332-33)

Does Dickens offer us a prospect of any enduring reality beyond delusion? True, in many novels, he fails to relate his view of love and goodness adequately to his vision of deception. Yet, in this respect, *Little Dorrit,* repeatedly described as his darkest novel, is also his most profoundly optimistic. The significance of the prison image is obviously the key to a full understanding of *Little Dorrit.* Society, as Dickens's notes confirm, 'Society like the Marshalsea' . . . is a prison. So is the world. Yet what does the prison symbol ultimately mean? To Trilling it represents the negation of the will, which paralyses the creative spirit. This is certainly one of its meanings but what Trilling's

argument overlooks is that the negation of the will is also the starting-point for spiritual progress towards enlightenment, a process in which Arthur Clennam is engaged.

Almost all the novel's major characters are incarcerated in a jail of deceit or self-deception. This idea helps to unify the novel and Dickens explores its tragic, melodramatic, and comic possibilities with irony and sympathy. Mrs. Clennam is shut up in the delusion of her narrow self-righteousness but a crippling guilt restricts her to her room. . . . William Dorrit's entire life is a prison of delusion. Fate gives him the wealth to realize his pretensions to gentility. Yet when fate exposes him to society as a former jailbird he reassumes the genteel posture of the Father of the Marshalsea. Life is, as it were, a delusion within an hallucination. Strip one veil of deception away and another veil hangs behind it.

Arthur Clennam is also imprisoned in a delusion, namely his stubborn belief that love is no longer for him. Significantly, it is in prison that the scales fall from his eyes, an enlightenment stressed symbolically by his deliverance from the Marshalsea. This conclusion to the second book brings out all the irony in William Dorrit's release from the Marshalsea which concluded the first book. Intended as parallel scenes, they stress that William Dorrit was not released from that other prison of delusion and indicate the full meaning of Arthur's deliverance. Significant also is the sense of alienation from society which Arthur and Amy experience and through which they move towards their union. When all the veils of delusion have been stripped away, love alone remains, the only ultimate, enduring human reality. Arthur and Amy's love must not be interpreted narrowly as primarily a sexual union. Amy Dorrit is shown as the epitome of womanly love in its widest aspects. . . . For once, the Victorian reticence about sexuality works for Dickens rather than against him. So does the Victorian emphasis on Amy's maternal qualities, since both are typical of the genuine archetype. True, Arthur's financial ruin rises out of an uncharacteristic act and his reluctance to marry Amy while she has wealth seems to us a curious Victorian notion about what is manly. Yet Dickens's deeply introverted feeling incorporates both of these as the stages of a ritual in a more profound vision. The sacred union of Amy and Arthur cannot take place while there are ties to the world. The final delusions of wealth and station, even as regards the decent soul, must be swept aside. Dickens consciously determined on a calm conclusion to the novel. In the notes, he writes: *'Very quiet conclusion'.* . . . Yet this is not simply a case of bringing the reader quietly out of the stress of the story and leaving him at peace. By an insertion in the corrected proofs, Dickens deliberately juxtaposes the sacred couple's serenity and the world's turmoil:

> They went QUIETLY down into the roaring streets, inseparable and blessed; and as they passed along in sunshine and in shade, the noisy and the eager, and the arrogant and the froward and the vain, fretted, and chafed, and made their usual uproar.

This conclusion is the nearest we get in Dickens's novels to T. S. Eliot's 'still point of the turning world'.

During the last two decades, scholars have noted discrepancies between the objective world of Victorian England and Dickens's picture of it. Thus, Humphry House [see excerpt above] claims that Dickens mixes different periods in his novels, confuses the regimes in workhouses under the old and new poor laws, exaggerates the inadequacy of workhouse dietaries, and evades certain ugly truths about crime and sanitation. . . . K. J. Fielding points out that Dickens renders less than justice to the Department of Practical Art in **Hard Times.** William O. Aydelotte even suggests that we should not look to Dickens and other social novelists, like Disraeli, Mrs. Gaskell, and Charles Kingsley, for a historically valid portrait of social and economic conditions in the England of Marx and Mills. Such fiction 'reflects principally not the times but the author'. Sheila M. Smith approaches the problem by distinguishing between a kind of fiction, like Reade's, which for all its strict adherence to the facts remains propaganda and a fiction, like Dickens's, which may get some of the facts wrong yet, through imagination, presents the essential truth of a situation. The special quality of the imaginative truth Dickens offers us may be defined, I believe, with great precision.

Dickens's vision is very largely an introverted one. . . . [The] imagination can create a vision of an eternal quality, such as the goodness of human affection, which has more value than the accuracy of historical facts. It is very easy to depreciate such an attitude, particularly from the extraverted standpoint. Since the terms 'introversion' and 'extraversion', 'introverted' and 'extraverted', are widely employed so loosely as to overrate or underrate the positive and negative aspects of these two basic attitudes to life, the terms are used here strictly according to C. G. Jung's definition in his classic work on the subject:

> Extraversion means an outward-turning of the libido [i.e. psychic energy]. With this concept I denote a manifest relatedness of subject to object in the sense of a positive movement of subjective interest towards the object. . . . Introversion means a turning inwards of the libido, whereby a negative relation of subject to object is expressed. Interest does not move towards the object, but recedes towards the subject. . . .

Whereas the extraverted attitude seeks its truth in external facts, the introverted attitude tries to find it in the eternal validity of the primordial images. The introverted attitude ventures into the world of external facts only to select what will confirm its subjective values and beliefs. (pp. 337-42)

In Dickens's hands, the rhetoric of sympathy and irony is well able to communicate this introverted vision of a spiritual universe pervading the material world. This vision is all the more impressive in that Dickens does not try to deny or weaken our immediate perception of the tangible world but renders it with a remarkable verisimilitude. The rhetoric of sympathy enables Dickens to explore and present the common bond between all things and to involve the reader in this process of viewing the world as a vital experience, to make him feel his identity with all creation. Not only is animism characteristic of the introverted vision but so also is the awareness of a force which permeates all things, a primitive identity. Yet to *be* all things not only means to sympathize with them in the sense of 'the sympathetic induction of emotion' or the *participation mystique,* it also offers the basis for the higher forms of sympathy. It is the foundation of mature love and compassion. The power which permeates all things is, in the final analysis, the loving joy which allows to all things their essential being. It is this delight in all creation which Garis would deny Dickens. Yet this delight reflects Dickens's (and the reader's) identity with life and energy of every kind, even pain and even evil. On the other hand, the ironic factor in Dickens's complex rhetoric helps to focus his introverted vision in two ways. First, struc-

tural irony recognizes the existence of a spiritual order at work in the universe and makes its presence felt. Secondly, by exploring the nature of appearance, by constantly tearing away veils of delusion, irony enables Dickens to shake our confidence in the value of many things in the material world. Since introversion withdraws value from objects, it can afford a critical view of the external world from a detached standpoint. The introverted vision is particularly useful, therefore, in examining extraverted forms and relationships. It has a deadly knack of exposing the superficiality of social institutions and social attitudes. This helps to explain the scathing manner in which Dickens's fiction hardly ever ceases to denounce society, Parliament, bureaucracy, courts of law, the legal, financial, and political worlds, workhouses, schools, and so on. In this respect, Dickens's vision is not necessarily reactionary. A complex rhetoric, which seeks a common identity between things and yet can simultaneously expose their spiritual bankruptcy, may afford a searching view of social life that has great positive value. Thus, Dickens frequently sums up an unhealthy state of society through an effective image, the fancy dress masquerade. He perceives an identity between the falseness of an empty society and its addiction to gaudy costumes and frivolous ceremonial. This is not a fanciful resemblance, it is a genuine 'correspondence'. . . . [In] the dust-heap symbol of *Our Mutual Friend,* Dickens intuitively finds an identity between the amassing of wealth and excrement, a genuine correspondence (as we know today) since the acquisition of gold is partly motivated by an anal complex. Yet through this symbol Dickens is also able to depreciate the acquisitive society with such a devastating irony because it exposes a gap between what is desirable and disgusting which corresponds to, and derives from, an ambivalent, infantile attitude towards excretion.

Introversion, together with a rhetoric which affords both detachment and an awareness of the mystical unity of things, enables Dickens to view his world from what can only be described as a cosmic standpoint. Such a standpoint entails all the complexity of a metaphysical vision which comprehends both benevolent and malevolent forces at work in the universe. (pp. 345-48)

[Dickens's] rhetoric of sympathy may stir within us that sense of compassionate involvement with mankind which, as in Balzac's *The Atheist's Mass,* surpasses the language of creeds. While his rhetoric of irony may offer us an almost pagan detachment, may even give play to those old gods whom we can sometimes hear laughing cruelly within ourselves at the fates of humankind. At its best, Dickens's vision is comprehensive and complex enough to take in our equal and contradictory passions for justice and for mercy. (pp. 356-57)

Harvey Peter Sucksmith, in his The Narrative Art of Charles Dickens: The Rhetoric of Sympathy and Irony in His Novels *(© Oxford University Press 1970; reprinted by permission of Oxford University Press), Oxford University Press, London, 1970, 374 p.*

ADDITIONAL BIBLIOGRAPHY

Belloc, Hilaire. "Dickens Revisited." *New Statesman* XXVIII, No. 717 (22 January 1927): 444-45.
    Criticizes Dickens's false sentiment and "gospel of kindliness," but recognizes his achievements in creating characters and class types. Belloc considers these to be even more remarkable in light of the fact that Dickens had "no tradition behind him, let alone

any systematic philosophy and religion, had no guide to keep him in touch with reality.''

"Charles Dickens." *Blackwood's Edinburgh Magazine* CIX, No. DCLXVIII (June 1871): 673-95.

Recounts all the traditional nineteenth-century criticisms of Dickens. The critic maintains that Dickens's dialogue is superficial but not elevated, that he cannot paint upper-class characters, and he too easily sinks into the grotesque.

Butt, John, and Tillotson, Kathleen. *Dickens at Work*. London: Methuen, 1957, 238 p.

Examines Dickens's novels in the light of their periodical publication. The critics state that Dickens followed in the tradition of the periodical essayist as well as that of Fielding and Smollett.

Chaplin, Charles. "The Birthday Dinner in London." *The Dickensian* LI, No. 315 (June 1955): 111-14.

A transcript of a speech in which Chaplin asks readers not to forget Dickens's critical attitude toward democracy. Chaplin believes that Dickens, were he alive today, would write eloquently about hypocrisy in western countries.

Cockshut, A.O.J. *The Imagination of Charles Dickens*. New York: New York University Press, 1962, 192 p.

Attempts to show that the "popular" and the "serious" Dickens cannot be separated—that he gained the depth and understanding necessary to his late novels through the use of melodrama and other popular devices. Cockshut identifies Dickens's major themes, and discusses their development throughout his career.

"Dickens and Daudet." *The Cornhill Magazine* 64, No. 382 (October 1891): 400-15.*

Compares the two writers in their choice of subject matter, delineation of character, and social concern for the lower classes. Dickens is seen to have a higher moral quality in his works.

Dyson, A. E. *The Inimitable Dickens: A Reading of the Novels*. London: MacMillan, 1970, 303 p.

An examination of the novels from *The Old Curiosity Shop* on, considering each as an organic whole. Dyson discounts both the notion that the novels are unstructured, and the idea that they are united, that each is "a snipped off length from the same rich cloth."

Eisenstein, Sergei. "Dickens, Griffith, and the Film Today." In his *Film Form: Essays in Film Theory*, pp. 195-255. Cleveland: The World Publishing Co., 1957.*

Discusses Dickens's use of atmosphere, his combination of visual and aural images, his use of the "close-up" to begin a novel, and his relationship with his audience. According to Eisenstein, an influential Russian movie director, these are all things which early filmmakers learned from Dickens.

Eliot, T. S. "Wilkie Collins and Dickens." In his *Selected Essays: 1917-1932*, pp. 373-82. New York: Harcourt, Brace and Co., 1932.*

Discusses literary affinities of Collins and Dickens, and emphasizes their fine use of melodrama.

Fielding, K. J. *Charles Dickens: A Critical Introduction*. New York: David McKay Co., 1958, 218 p.

A concise bio-critical account of Dickens's career. Fielding discusses the novels chronologically and often relates them to important biographical details.

Forster, John. *Forster's Life of Dickens*. Abridged and revised by George Gissing. London: Chapman & Hall, 1907, 349 p.

The standard biography for many years, written by Dickens's friend. Forster is often criticized for minimizing Dickens's other friendships and omitting crucial facts, but this book contains valuable primary source material.

Galsworthy, John. "Six Novelists in Profile: An Address." In his *Castles in Spain and Other Screeds*, pp. 203-35. New York: Charles Scribner's Sons, 1927.*

Points to Dickens as an example of the "born writer" who increases our knowledge of the natural world. Galsworthy claims,

though, that "no one would dream of going to Dickens to learn consciously the art of novel-writing."

Hardy, Barbara. "Work in Progress IV: Food and Ceremony in *Great Expectations*." *Essays in Criticism* XII, No. 4 (October 1963): 351-63.

Describes how Dickens attaches moral values to meals in *Great Expectations*. Meals, claims Hardy, "are not symbols but natural demonstrations."

Hardy, Barbara. *The Moral Art of Dickens*. New York: Oxford University Press, 1970, 155 p.

Centers on Dickens as a moral novelist. The first section discusses "the changing shape of his moral art;" the second examines form, character, and symbolism in *Pickwick Papers, Martin Chuzzlewit, David Copperfield*, and *Great Expectations*.

House, Humphry. *The Dickens World*. London: Oxford University Press, 1941, 231 p.

Examines both the internal world of Dickens's novels and the external world in which they were created. This important book claims that Dickens's works should not be used as reliable sources for history: "Dickens history is inseparable from Dickens reformism."

Jackson, T. A. *Charles Dickens: The Progress of a Radical*. New York: International Publishers, 1938, 302 p.

A Marxist approach to Dickens. Jackson's work, while being wholly accepted by very few, has been greatly influential.

Johnson, Edgar. "Dickens and the Bluenose Legislator." *The American Scholar* 17, No. 4 (Autumn 1948): 450-58.

Describes Dickens's 1836 pamphlet "Sunday under Three Heads," which attacks a strict bill to enforce the observance of the sabbath. Johnson contends that the pamphlet proves that Dickens "had already attained a defined social attitude."

Johnson, Edgar. *Charles Dickens: His Tragedy and Triumph*. 2 vols. New York: Simon & Schuster, 1952.

The definitive modern biography. Johnson makes use of much previously unavailable material.

Lasch, Christopher. Introduction to *American Notes*, by Charles Dickens, pp. vii-xii. Gloucester, Mass.: Peter Smith, 1968.

A short history of Dickens's first visit to the United States, which formed the background for *American Notes*.

Lukács, Georg. "The Historical Novel and the Crisis of Bourgeois Realism." In his *The Historical Novel*, translated by Hannah and Stanley Mitchell, pp. 171-250. London: Merlin Press, 1962.*

Claims that Dickens's characters grow "organically out of the age and its social events" in his "social" novels, such as *Little Dorrit* or *Dombey and Son*, but fail to do so in his historical novels, *Barnaby Rudge* and *A Tale of Two Cities*.

Miller, J. Hillis. *Charles Dickens: The World of His Novels*. Cambridge: Harvard University Press, 1958, 346 p.

Traces the development of Dickens's imagination. Miller proposes that Dickens tried to achieve a true picture of the city and city inhabitants by presenting the views of many diverse characters.

Miyoshi, Masao. "Broken Music: 1870." In his *The Divided Self: A Perspective on the Literature of the Victorians*, pp. 227-88. New York: New York University Press, 1936.*

An examination of Dickens's use of the split personality theme in *Our Mutual Friend*.

Moers, Ellen. "Dickens." In her *The Dandy: Brummell to Beerbohm*, pp. 215-50. New York: The Viking Press, 1960.

An entertaining description of Dickens's own dandyism and an account of how it appears in several of his characters.

Monod, Sylvère. *Dickens the Novelist*. Translated by Sylvère Monod. Norman: University of Oklahoma Press, 1967, 512 p.

A seminal work. Monod rejects the notion that Dickens was a negligent stylist and examines his manner of conceiving and writing novels.

Monod, Sylvère. "Some Stylistic Devices in *A Tale of Two Cities.*" In *Dickens the Craftsman: Strategies of Presentation,* edited by Robert B. Partlow, Jr., pp. 165-86. Carbondale: Southern Illinois University Press, 1970.
> A close examination of four stylistic devices: repetition, cumulative effects of vocabulary, images and comparisons, and the interplay between rhetoric and exhaltation, as Dickens uses them in *A Tale of Two Cities.*

Muir, Edwin. "The Dark Felicities of Charles Dickens." In his *Essays on Literature and Society,* rev. ed., pp. 206-14. Cambridge: Harvard University Press, 1965.
> Discusses how Dickens achieved a greater unity in his later novels, both in plot and character.

Needham, Gwendolyn B. "The Undisciplined Heart of David Copperfield." *Nineteenth-Century Fiction* 9, No. 2 (September 1954):81-107.
> A consideration of the theme of "the undisciplined heart" in *David Copperfield.*

O'Faoláin, Seán. "Charles Dickens and W. M. Thackeray." In *The English Novelists: A Survey of the Novel by Twenty Contemporary Novelists,* edited by Derek Verschoyle, pp. 139-52. London: Chatto & Windus, 1936.*
> Contends that Dickens is "sufficiently a master to be beyond criticism" as a reader's novelist, but that he does not influence contemporary writers.

Orwell, George. "Charles Dickens." In his *Critical Essays,* pp. 7-56. London: Secker and Warburg, 1946.
> Defines Dickens as a subversive, but ultimately bourgeois and limited writer. Orwell adds, however, that "the vagueness of his discontent is the mark of its permanence."

Quiller-Couch, Arthur. "Dickens." In his *Charles Dickens and Other Victorians,* pp. 3-99. New York: G. P. Putnam's Sons, 1925.
> A collection of Quiller-Couch's personal views on Dickens, commentaries on his works, and remarks on certain aspects of his oeuvre.

Saintsbury, George. "Dickens" and "Dickens (concluded)." In his *Corrected Impressions: Essays on Victorian Writers,* pp. 117-37. New York: Dodd, Mead and Co., 1895.
> States that Dickens's weaknesses only serve to illuminate his strengths—particularly his humor.

Stevenson, Lionel. "Dickens's Dark Novels, 1851-1857." *The Sewanee Review* 51, No. 3 (July-September 1943): 398-409.
> Discusses political, personal, and literary circumstances which contributed to Dickens's pessimistic outlook in *Bleak House, Hard Times,* and *Little Dorrit.*

Swinburne, Algernon Charles. *Charles Dickens.* London: Chatto & Windus, 1913, 84 p.
> A personal panegyric mixed with sharp critical commentary. This is a combination of two magazine articles.

Trilling, Lionel. "Little Dorrit." In *The Dickens Critics,* edited by George H. Ford and Lauriat Lane, Jr., pp. 279-93. Ithaca, N.Y.: Cornell University Press, 1961.
> Regards *Little Dorrit* as a work centering on "society in relation to the individual human will."

Wagenknecht, Edward. "White Magic." In his *Cavalcade of the English Novel: From Elizabeth to George VI,* pp. 213-33. New York: Henry Holt and Co., 1943.
> Brief overview stressing the spirit and faith in humanity expressed in Dickens's works.

Wagenknecht, Edward. *The Man Charles Dickens: A Victorian Portrait.* Rev. ed. Norman: University of Oklahoma Press, 1966, 269 p.
> A lengthy bio-critical analysis, containing insights on Dickens's work and character. Wagenknecht has been criticized for his handling of the Ellen Ternan episode.

Wilkinson, Ann Y. "*Bleak House:* From Faraday to Judgment Day." *ELH* 34, No. 2 (June 1967): 225-47.
> Examines the structure of *Bleak House* as a key to the novel's meaning.

Wilson, Angus. "Evil in the English Novel." *The Kenyon Review* XXIX, No. 2 (March 1967): 167-94.*
> Includes an analysis of the Döppelganger theme in Dickens. Wilson states that Jonas Chuzzlewit's dream "is a Döppelganger realization as considerable as anything in Dostoevsky."

Wilson, Angus. *The World of Charles Dickens.* New York: The Viking Press, 1970, 302 p.
> A profusely illustrated book, the text of which serves to illuminate the social and intellectual background of Dickens's time and its use in his novels.

Zweig, Stefan. "Dickens." In his *Three Masters: Balzac, Dickens, Dostoeffsky,* translated by Eden and Cedar Paul, pp. 51-95. New York: The Viking Press, 1930.
> Classifies Dickens as essentially part of the idyllic tradition and reviews his recurring themes.

Annette Freiin von Droste-Hülshoff

1797-1848

German poet and novella writer.

Droste-Hülshoff is considered Germany's greatest woman poet. Inspired by her love of nature and awareness of the supernatural, she wrote intimate and religious lyrics, epics, and ballads. Her poetry is often impressionistic, yet there are occasions of sharp clarity, when the poet keenly focuses her vision. While some critics attribute Droste-Hülshoff's shifts of focus to her myopic eyesight, others believe it was a conscious technique. Nearly all agree on the artistic merit of her poetry.

Droste-Hülshoff was the sickly daughter of an aristocratic Roman Catholic family, who from early childhood studied music and wrote verse. She was allowed to attend her brothers' private tutoring sessions, and excelled in languages and science. Her familiarity with biology and botany is evident in her fine observations of the natural world.

Droste-Hülshoff remained in her family home, leading essentially an invalid's existence. When she was in her thirties, she met Levin Schücking, a friend's son who was many years her junior and who shared her literary concerns. Many critics believe that Droste-Hülshoff wrote her most accomplished work during a stay at Meersburg where she and Schücking lived for a time with Droste-Hülshoff's sister. Soon after this interval, Schücking suddenly married. Droste-Hülshoff wrote little from that point on, and concentrated on dark, despairing themes.

One of Droste-Hülshoff's finest works is *Geistliches Jahr in Liedern auf alle Sonn- und Festtage,* which she began as a girl at her grandmother's request. These devotional verses, which commemorate Catholic holy days and festivals, express the poet's spiritual struggles. Although critics agree that Droste-Hülshoff's greatest achievement is her poetry, her novella *Die Judenbuche: Ein Sittengemalde aus dem gebirgichten Westfalen (The Jew's Beech Tree)* is most often the subject of critical discussion. Based on a true incident (of which her uncle had written a factual account), *Die Judenbuche* examines the social and psychological forces that cause the protagonist to commit murder. Vivid and concise, the story exhibits a keen psychological awareness that critics consider ahead of its time. It is regarded as one of the finest German *Stimmung* (atmosphere) novellas and an important exemplar of Poetic Realism.

Critics believe that Droste-Hülshoff's work is strengthened by her keen perception, which lends a sense of realism to both her poetry and prose. Yet, as Walter Silz remarked, although she "saw reality sharply . . . she was at her best only when she could see visions and dream dreams, when with rapt gaze she could discern and depict that inner landscape that to her was more real than reality." Like her contemporary, Emily Dickinson, Droste-Hülshoff made her small-scale world universal. Since her death, her reputation has continued to grow and she is widely regarded as the greatest woman writer of German literature.

PRINCIPAL WORKS

Dichtungen (poetry) 1838

Die Judenbuche: Ein Sittengemalde aus dem gebirgichten Westfalen (novella) 1842
[*The Jew's Beech Tree,* 1915]
Gedichte (poetry) 1844
Geistliches Jahr in Liedern auf alle Sonn- und Festtage (poetry) 1852
Samtliche Werke. 4 vols. (poetry and novella) 1925-30

E. K. BENNETT (essay date 1934)

[One] of the masterpieces of German Novellen literature is the Novelle of Annette von Droste-Hülshoff, *Die Judenbuche.* . . . Droste-Hülshoff's Novelle can be said to represent Poetic Realism in a form which is hardly surpassed by anyone except perhaps by Gottfried Keller. In the great period of Novellen literature [*Die Judenbuche*] is the first work which combines all those elements which constitute the distinctive type of the German Novelle; all that Goethe, Kleist and the Romantics had contributed to the creation of a new form: realism enriched by poetical depth and symbolical significance.

Annette von Droste-Hülshoff was in the first instance a lyrical poetess, whose descriptions of Westphalian landscape have a quality which no other German lyrical poetry possesses. . . . [*Die Judenbuche*] introduces a new factor in the Novelle of this period, a factor which is absent from the Novelle in its original form, namely the utilization of local colour as an important ingredient in the events that form the subject matter. It goes hand in hand with detailed nature description which occurs to a much greater extent in the Novellen of Adalbert Stifter and Theodor Storm. The more or less detailed elaboration of the setting—the Milieuschilderung—now becomes a permanent element in the Novelle. It is noticeable that the most important writers of this period—Droste-Hülshoff, Stifter, [Otto] Ludwig, Storm and Keller—nearly always make use of definitely localized settings for their stories—Westphalia, the Bohemian Forest, Thuringia, Schleswig-Holstein, Switzerland—and that the incidents and characters of the stories are so closely connected with the definite locality in which they are set, that their very existence appears to be conditioned by it. (pp. 129-30)

[In *Die Judenbuche,* a young peasant, Friedrich Mergel,] murders a Jew to whom he owes money and, having concealed his body under a beech tree in the forest, disappears from the neighbourhood. Twenty-eight years later he returns in disguise, and after living for some time in his native village hangs himself on a branch of the tree under which the body of his victim had been concealed. . . . [This story] is a piece of realistic literature far removed in style and intention from the abstracter methods of Goethe's later classicism. It is and purports to be 'eine Kriminalgeschichte' [a crime story] and the events which it relates are such as will hold the attention independently of any additions in the way of symbolization or Stimmung [atmosphere] which the poetess may add. The description of Friedrich Mergel's childhood, his drunken father and humiliated mother, the poaching and illegal traffic in timber, the midnight raids and scuffles—all these things have intrinsic interest. But the real 'Falke', to use Heyse's expression, is the tree itself; which has ceased to be merely a piece of scenery, and has become a symbol: a symbol of some more primitive conception of justice than the laws which the modern state has devised. The roots of the Judenbuche are in the Old Testament, in the days when the rule of an eye for an eye, a tooth for a tooth, was valid. Its branches overshadow the whole story with the sinister, long-enduring sense of retribution. After the death of their co-religionist, the Jews of the village bought the tree and carved into it with an axe a Hebrew inscription. This is printed in the text of the Novelle in Hebrew characters. At the end of the Novelle, when the dead body of the hero Friedrich Mergel is discovered hanging in the branches, the translation of the inscription is given: 'Wenn du dich diesem Orte nahest, so wird es dir ergehen, wie du mir getan hast' [When you approach this place, you will do to yourself what you have done to me]. The translation of the inscription at the very end—at least for those who are unable to read Hebrew—produces in the reader something in the nature of a thrill, in so far as it casts a light back upon the whole sequence of events and underlines, as it were, the real significance of the story. The same method, though infinitely more crude and sensational, is often employed by modern short-story writers—when they keep throughout the story a secret which only the last line reveals. But the Novelle does not as a rule descend to these melodramatic surprises at the end, which lie rather within the province of the short story. In the Novelle the Pointe or surprise or Wendepunkt, as it is variously called, is usually of a less sensational nature, and in [later Novellen] almost disappears.

One point is worth observing in the technique of the story: when Friedrich Mergel returns to his village after an absence of twenty-eight years, he gives himself out to be someone else—a cousin of his who had disappeared at the same time as himself—and is not recognized by the villagers as the murderer. The reader is not told whether he is Friedrich Mergel or not; indeed he is led to believe that it is the cousin, who relates what is in reality a fictitious account of Friedrich's death. So there is no possibility of psychological analysis—no account of the process of remorse which goes on within him and drives him to suicide. After living in the village for some time he disappears: by chance some time later the body is found, already half decayed, hanging in the tree—and with that discovery the reader is for the first time assured that it really was Friedrich who came back to the scene of his crime. By this means the poetess can produce her startling effect at the end.

A comparison of *Die Judenbuche* with two early Novellen . . .—Goethe's *Der Prokurator* and Tieck's *Der blonde Eckbert*—will show how the genre has developed from the original form, and what similarities it has retained. It is, to begin with, quite clear that *Die Judenbuche* is very much more akin to Tieck's Novelle than to Goethe's. Goethe's story is placed in a purely generalized setting—which indeed he calls Genoa, but takes no pains at all to describe; whereas *Die Judenbuche* depends for its particular effect upon the description of the exact locality, its people, customs and landscape. It has, however, this point of contact with *Der Prokurator* that it deals with a moral problem, that the principal character is in both instances a responsible moral being who recognizes the validity of moral laws and his or her own subjection to them. In Tieck's Novelle the characters are moved by blind impulse and instincts, and what they do and what befalls them is part of the unaccountable nature of the universe just as natural forces are. Both Tieck's and Droste-Hülshoff's Novellen are Stimmungsnovellen [atmosphere Novellen]—with this difference that in *Der blonde Eckbert* the Stimmung pervades the whole story, whereas in *Die Judenbuche* the Stimmung is a retrospective one—is not engendered until the end of the story when it flows back and envelopes the whole series of incidents in memory. Both the Romantic and the later Novellen owe a great deal to irrational elements; but in Droste-Hülshoff's work the irrational is not exploited for its own sake with the deliberateness which Tieck employs, but asserts itself as it were inevitably, as an ethical factor, appearing as the force which drives the murderer back to the scene of his crime and compels him to expiate it by a voluntary death. It may be pointed out that this irrational element is very much heightened by the fact that the reader is never told that the murderer has any stings of remorse, and that therefore he never sees the rational and logical steps which lead him to suicide. Unlike Tieck's Novelle, *Die Judenbuche* does not deal with a purely fantastic world but with the world of reality. It is again in essence a piece of gossip, raised to the level of literature, but with differences: (1) it is now a piece of village gossip, rather a sensational piece, it is true, and one which embodies an exceptional event; (2) it is not merely an incident and its effect upon a person or group of persons which is related, but the preliminary events which lead up to the central incident are also carefully recorded—the account of Friedrich's father and his first marriage; (3) something has been added by the poetess which may be called Stimmung or poetical vision or symbolical value, and this shifts the centre of interest from the mere events narrated . . . to the ethical content. (pp. 131-34)

E. K. Bennett, "The Novelle of Poetic Realism," in his A History of the German Novelle from Goethe to Thomas Mann, *Cambridge at the University Press, 1934, pp. 124-92.**

DORA M. SOLDNER   (essay date 1941)

[Annette von Droste-Hülshoff] is one of the most independent poets of her century, and can be listed with Post-Romanticism, which classification is best illustrated in her treatment of nature. (p. 38)

Annette's poetry is characterized by detailed nature-painting and a vigorous realism, at times impressionistic, but always individual. . . . The group of poems, *Heidebilder,* are the best examples of her treatment of nature. Her native Westphalia was her favorite theme and its heath and moore receive fine expression. *Die Lerche* might be entitled Nature's or Morning's Awakening. . . . [The] sun sends her rays upon the heath and with this the messenger of the day, the lark, awakes with her call to nature, which the poet depicts in original strokes of personification. First comes the awakening of the creatures, whose abode is in the plant sphere, and then follows—"die Kapelle des florbeflügelt Volk" [the band of flower-winged folk]. These stanzas are not a mere play on words; Annette finds the suitable tone and instrument for each creature, and now comes the call to those insects not gifted in music to play their part and with their response the herald, the lark, retires. Morning has glided into day. (p. 39)

[Annette's] poetry in the main lacks distinct and contrasting colors. She never has a colorful sea. . . . The general aspect is gray but when the spade is pushed down there are colors, possibly in the compact deposit. . . .

Instinkt does not belong to the *Heidebilder* but it is of interest to note that here Annette is occupied in botany and zoology. She is alone out in nature, round about her the grass, above her a bird and at her feet her faithful dog. Then thoughts come to her, as she says, whether healthy or pathological she does not know, and her reflections on plant life and animal instinct follow. (p. 42)

[The poem *Mondesnacht* from the *Letzte Gaben* group is an] example of detail-painting. The time just before the moon rises savors of the subdued so characteristic of Droste and is a good example of her choice of verbals suggesting the subdued, appealing to both the optic and the acoustic sense. . . . And when the moon has risen there is still a subdued verb effect, . . . as could only be the case in the moonlight. . . . The moon gives an indefinite and subdued effect as it would to the Romanticist, yet if we except the personal reflections in this poem, it is a recording of light and sound effects quite true to natural phenomena. (p. 43)

In treating the subject nature in Droste's poetry, one cannot overlook the ballad-poems, many of which are very indicative of that earthy or phenomenal mysteriousness, the so-called "episch-erdige" [earthy epic]. *Der Knabe im Moor* mirrors the terror of the moor as reflected in the imaginings of a school boy crossing it on his way home. The phantom is not an elfking or a demon; it really has no form, it dissolves in nature. The smoke hovers over the heath; this is caused by the burning of the surface of the moor to make it arable. The well-known folklore figures come to the boy's mind: such as the peat-digger, who sold his master's peat, Spinstress Lenore, who spun on Sundays and now suffers for it after death, and the

faithless fiddler who stole his fellow-musician's fee at the wedding. These all reflect the local superstitions as we learn from Droste's *Bilder aus Westphalen.* (p. 44)

In some of the *Zeitbilder,* for example in *Die Verbannten* and *Mein Beruf,* the poet uses nature as a framework for her thoughts. For Droste nature may create the mood but she does not use nature as a mirror of human sentiment or suffering. An expression of a mood is not an absolute necessity with her. (p. 45)

Aside from her early poems of an allegorical or phantastic type, Annette is realistic and presents a clear objective picture of nature, although her field is limited. A common usage is a nature milieu, which forms the background and creates the mood into which is woven the epic-lyric. At times she appears to revel in the dynamic of nature, a sort of all-encompassing force, frequently dissolving in a natural phenomenon. But whether it be the plastic or the "episch-erdige" it is boldly original. Intimate detailed nature-painting, "Naturkleinmalerei," if we may use this term, is her province and in it lies her fame. Her very heart beats with nature; she is veritably buried in it and we sense it with her. Her "red soil" never becomes a symbol; as for Eichendorf the forest becomes a symbol of the fatherland, a veritable green forest of freedom. Whether it be the rare personification of the sunrise in *Die Lerche* or the description of the environment in *Die Jagd* there is something plastic about it, making an appeal to a real conception. . . . Annette has no dreaming, no tittering and caressing violets, no pallid moonlight reveries. If the violet were as native to her as the heath and moor, she would probably have depicted it as objectively as Goethe. . . . (pp. 45-6)

Annette's treatment of nature best shows that she was little conscious of Romanticism, and if we ascribe her to Romanticism, we would have to speak of her as the fifth wheel in the movement, to use a part of the poet's own expression with relation to herself in family circles, who, being the "Fräulein" of the family, spoke of herself as "das fünfte Wagenrad." She was always "a daughter of the red soil" true to "Bei und zu Lande auf dem Land." (p. 46)

> *Dora M. Soldner, "Nature in Droste-Hülshoff's Poetry," in* The German Quarterly *(copyright © 1941 by the American Association of Teachers of German), Vol. XIV, No. 1, January, 1941, pp. 38-46.*

ADA M. KLETT   (essay date 1945)

A German reading Emily Dickinson cannot help recalling Annette von Droste-Hülshoff. In each a region became articulate, New England in Emily Dickinson, and Westphalia, which forms part of the homeland of Anglo-Saxons, in Annette von Droste. Being deeply rooted the two poets stood their ground in adversity. They drew their sustenance from the land of their fathers, northern lands with shut-in winters and glorious summers. As poets they stand alone in their respective times, Annette at the beginning, Emily at the end of the Victorian Age. They stood alone not so much because they lived secluded lives but rather because their fierce veracity made them shy of any decorum. (p. 37)

[The] sense of doom is more strongly prevalent in Annette's poetry, while the record of the soul's self-sufficiency under severest strain is Emily's outstanding achievement.

The theme of the soul's doom is treated by both poets and pervades their work. . . . [Annette's] cycle of religious poems,

The Year of Our Lord, . . . contains singularly forceful visions of the soul's anguish over personal guilt.

Most of the poems, each of which is based on the Gospel of a church holiday, take issue from a darkly oppressive or threatening thought contained in the text. The third poem begins with the line from Luke II, 48: "Behold, my Lord, I have sought Thee sorrowing." Where will she find Him? Not in her own heart, for it has lost its simple faith. She sought Him in nature, but she did not penetrate to the depths. So 'secular wisdom' [scientific knowledge?] was the only fruit. Though she feels that God is, this feeling arouses not joy, but fear. Her soul stands in self-chosen exile, alone in night and horror, sore to death. . . . The premonition of an early death, after a wasted life, is ever present—she will be cast out like the fig-tree doomed to wither. Yet she must go on voicing her doubt, impelled to fathom the unfathomable. This burden, of which the pious know nothing, weighs down her empty heart like a sharp-edged mass of rock which she cannot cast out. And the vision of doomsday comes to her, threatening, like a cosmic thunderstorm: "As when in stifling sultriness a dark mass of clouds blackens the night so that we implore God to send us cooling cloudbursts, with all their horrors: thus lies that nameless day in Thy eternity like a dark hot spot—but I make fast my eyes as with iron chains and stand pressing against the wall of the chasm lest I lose balance . . ." The depth of her anguish is reached in the two poems centered around Good Friday. . . . The poet is numbed in the presence of God. May He shatter His creation, for it cannot bear this day. Then there is ghastly suspense: what is it that approaches ominously? Is it eternal night? Is it a flood of light in blinding radiance? The song on Easter morn gives answer: Christ is arisen, life is given back to earth and men, the world rejoices. How can she join who remembers the agony of Christ? How can she silence her questioning: why did God make Him who was good suffer for our vast measure of sin? Yet for this one day God's holy book is almost open to her; she can forget damnation, can feel God as love. There is not one poem among these twenty-five from her early life, and none among the forty-seven which Annette added shortly before her death, that speaks of a loving God in radiant certainty of faith. Her womanly soul, so loving, generous, and forgiving, cries out for a God of love; but only in rare moments does she see Him thus. Integrity of mind forces her to abide by her tragic concept of the soul's doom in the presence of an uncompromising God.

If these religious poems, as poetry, are imperfect, and, as Annette states herself, are little suited to cheer or comfort a believing soul, they command our respect as the testimony of a valiant soul in terrifying struggle. Although a consciousness of personal guilt is the keynote of Annette's religious poetry this consciousness does not seem prompted by conventional theology. Definitely not fears instilled by the teachings of the church, but rather some deep-seated intuitive knowledge brought forth these anxious poems. We shall find this same theme of man's doom amidst cosmic forces recurrent in Annette's secular poetry.

We search in vain in Emily Dickinson's poetry for a comparable expression of the soul's cosmic doom. Anguish, suffering, dread, fear, agony, despair are voiced with intense poignancy; the word 'doom' occurs. Yet in every instance the unprotected soul takes a stand; its identity, 'the single hound', asserts itself somehow. The soul faces the foe. (pp. 40-2)

[Emily] sought danger, like her soldier who "invited death with bold attempt" because "to him, to live was doom." . . .

> I lived on dread; to those who know
> The stimulus there is
> In danger, other impetus
> Is numb and vital-less. . . .

Danger alone vitalizes; other stimuli leave one 'numb'. The state of being numbed by a blow dealt her soul recurs as a theme. It is experienced as a physical sensation in every nerve and accurately described as such. (p. 43)

In striking contrast to Emily's dynamic reaction to fright, though it numb the senses and make the soul tremble, Annette describes her experience of doom as a passive helplessness. (pp. 46-7)

Scents benumb [Annette], or the eerie atmosphere of a deserted quarry; or, while she walks in the dusk on the beach of Lake Constance whose

> Wave-nerve quivers to every touch
> Of a human foot as it treads the shore

she seems to herself like the foam underfoot, dissolving to formlessness. One might go on and on citing examples of poetic images that capture the peculiar spell cast upon her consciousness which produces 'a swimming sense'. Such gliding away of her self-control is in itself a frightening experience for one whose sense of moral and intellectual integrity is as strong as was Annette's. Moreover, the visions during these trance-like states are frequently haunting or torturing.

A recurrent theme is the inexorable passing of life, of young strength and health, and the threat of an end without fulfillment. The moaning lake by her side finds no peace:

> What are you about, uneasy lake
> Have you no share in blessed sleep? . . .
>
> O say, have you lived through so much, so much
> That it must return in your dreams of yore—

dreams of the passing of generations, age after age gone, their fleeting images buried on the bottom of the lake.

Or, as she walks over the high moors at dusk, the earth about her lies moaning like an ailing body, electric sparks in its shaggy hair of moss, and a cloud hangs heavy, a dark nightmare. She stumbles and finds herself lying among a mass of huge rocks piled up in heathen times to mark the grave of a hero. She presses her brow into the ground, 'greedily drinking sweet liquor of horror' (Wollüstig saugend an des Grauens Süsse)—an extraordinary line for any poet of her time to write—until something grips her with icy claws and her blood wells up, a glacier spring. Staring at the rock ceiling, listening to the wind with all her senses, she sees the burial of the hero, hears the dirge; she knows the urn stands close by, containing a wild heart in dust and ashes. In this poem she causes the spell to be broken by a call and a swaying light that approaches—her servant arrives and calmly opens an umbrella over her head. Such breaking of a mood, a favorite device of [Heinrich] Heine's, by the way, is also employed by Emily Dickinson at times. (pp. 47-8)

A bit of a real thing—. . . the servant's umbrella—helps [Annette] regain her grasp on reality which she was in danger of losing. This very means we find employed by Emily Dickinson. Both cling to small, familiar things, grateful to have a hold on reality. (p. 48)

No inner peace until death—this is also Annette's fate. However, while Emily builds up a hope for happiness beyond the grave . . . and thereby fortifies her divided self for utmost endurance, Annette has no such hope. She makes a valiant effort, but her strength of body and spirit fades away, slowly.

Even in an hour when she is joyously alive in the company of Schücking the thought of fleeting life and waning strength is with her. One sunny day in autumn they stop at an inn over-looking the Alps and Lake Constance. The host puts grapes before them, and she feels like saying to her young friend,

> O notice how the injured grape will shed
> Tears of pure blood that winter's frost is nearing.

At autumn's height she feels the blight of winter, her winter, nearing. The young life beside her knows no such apprehension. They watch a diving fowl on the lake:

> We both look down intently and in wonder:
> You smile and say, "It always reappears!"
> But I am thinking, "Always it goes under!" . . .

[There] is no escape from failure to fulfill her destiny. Ill and lonely she sees her fate foreshadowed in the death of a sky-lark. She watches it as it soars high toward the sun, jubilant, and suddenly falls down into the young grain, scorched, dying, silenced forever—a trenchant symbol of aspiration doomed. (p. 50)

> Ada M. Klett, "Doom and Fortitude: A Study of Poetic Metaphor in Annette von Droste-Hülshoff (1797-1848) and Emily Dickinson (1830-1886)," in Monatshefte (copyright © 1945 by the Board of Regents of the University of Wisconsin Systems), Vol. XXXVII, No. 1, January, 1945, pp. 37-54.*

SISTER M. ROSA, S.S.J.   (essay date 1948)

To the lyric quality of Elizabeth Barrett Browning and the novelistic gift of George Eliot [Annette von Droste-Hülshoff] united the German Romantic spirit.

The life of Annette von Droste-Hülshoff was without the highly emotional experiences peculiar to the other literary women of her time. She did not move in the political arena of a Madame de Staël, nor play the part of *une femme supérieure*. However, there is a virile note in her works that indicates a mine of unearthed energy. Unlike the two women Georges, Eliot and Sand, there was no domestic triangle in her life. Yet personal experience was thought by nineteenth century Romanticists to be a necessary element in the life of every portrayer of the gamut of human emotions.

If any comparison is to be made, it is with Elizabeth Barrett Browning, in that both women fell in love with a man many years younger than herself. With the English poetess this culminated in a happy marriage, but the German lyricist saw the man she loved lead another to the altar. Annette von Droste-Hülshoff spent her life in lonely spinsterhood. At first glance it was life apparently as peaceful as a lake unruffled by the tiniest ripple. Yet it was one of deep tragedy, which gave a minor tone to the poetic harmony. (p. 279)

Romanticism stood for what was the most personal and individual in things of the spirit, hence Annette von Droste-Hülshoff was representative of the movement in its purest form. The more mature fruits of her life and creative ability are seen in her poems. There her artistry is at its best and one literally walks through the vicissitudes of her life. She had tried out various methods and imitated several models until finally she arrived at her own. Although an early imitator of Goethe and

Schiller and the ballad-writer, Bürger, she rapidly outgrew them.

In her *Klänge aus dem Orient* she still shows an unconscious leaning on the master-mind of Freiligrath, so greatly was she impressed by his pen-pictures of the ocean and desert. Her best scenic description was the Westphalian heatherland with the call of the owl in the moor and other ghostlike figures with which superstition has peopled this solitude. She painted in Romantic colors this her native heath and was strengthened, like Antaeus of old, by every contact with mother earth.

The Scottish-English influence is apparent in *Der Graf von Tal.* With Lord Byron she considered her vocation as a poet to be a real martyrdom. What he said in his *Hebrew Melodies* she echoes, saying:

> Ja, Perlen fischt er und Jewele,
> Die kosten nichts—als seine Seele.
>
> Yes, pearls he fishes where oceans roll,
> They cost him nothing—but his soul.

Annette's real inspirational sources were nature, human existence, her own experiences of joy and sorrow and, finally, the historic past of Germany. Her Romantic interpretation of nature was both subjective and objective. Either she injected her own mood into nature or allowed the dormant to awaken.

The keeness of her observation was remarkable. She perceived the slightest flutter of insect wings, the fall of a berry, the crawling of a beetle among the weeds and even the gnawing of a caterpillar on a grapevine leaf. Atmospheric impressions worked powerfully on the poetess. She felt darkness like fine rain on her cheeks and an approaching storm she sensed in every nerve fiber. (pp. 284-85)

Walter shows Annette's own thoughts on renouncing the world and reflects her own nun-like existence. No answer is given to the question as to whether or not Walter will triumph over the inner struggle that arises at the thought of past wrongs he has suffered. As Annette was only twenty years of age when she wrote this epic, she shows an immaturity as compared to the splendid technique of later works.

Das Hospiz auf dem Groszen Sankt Bernhard was written ten years later. Her talent had become impressionistic and she filed down and chiseled away at the epic to produce the impression she desired. (p. 285)

The ruling idea of the poem is the power of Christian love for one's neighbor in contrast to the unfriendly forces of nature. Annette's religious susceptibility found an outlet in her description of the monastery and monks who dwelt in it. She paints with broad strokes the magnificent natural scenery, which was quite in accord with Romanticism. . . .

Die Schlacht im Loener Bruch is quite dependent on Lord Byron's pirate poetry and his attempts to portray "ruin in majesty" in heroes who were fallen angels. Woman-like, Annette von Droste-Hülshoff could not resist sympathizing with a character like Christian von Braunschweig, the rough, repellent figure of the Thirty Years' War. Although a historical personage she pictures him according to her own ideas.

However, the figure of Christian recedes into the background as the battle itself becomes the focal point of the epic. The description of the fight gave her a chance to sketch Westphalian landscape. Imitating Sir Walter Scott in his *Battle of Waterloo*, she makes clever use of this stage setting. As the epic progresses there is evidence of Lord Byron's *Corsair*, which results in a masterly production, such as no woman has ever equaled. (p. 286)

The fragment *Berta*, written in [Annette's] youth, shows the domination of the classical spirit of Schiller at the time of his collaboration with Goethe. The play is thrown on an Italian background, but with many references to "Helvetia's Alpine heights." The drama shows the Romantic conflict between art and life after the manner of Goethe's *Torquato Tasso*. There is also a didactic element in the conversation of the two sisters, Berta and Laurette, on life at the court and its danger to virtue. (p. 287)

Sister M. Rosa, S.S.J., "Romanticism in Annette von Droste-Hülshoff," in The Modern Language Journal, *Vol. XXXII, No. 4, April, 1948, pp. 279-87.*

WALTER SILZ (essay date 1948)

[Annette von Droste-Hülshoff's] capacity for revery, her power of abstraction from the present, was extraordinary. From the contemplation of ruined walls, of meteorites, of quarry rubble, her mind took off readily on a flight into the past, her ear opened to its spirit voices. . . . (p. 974)

The poem *Im Moose* is a remarkable example of her propensity to cast herself adrift from the present. Reclining in the darkening woods, she gets into a state of mental detachment that makes her feel already departed; like a disembodied spirit she ranges backward and forward through time, beholds herself as a child and then as an old woman, and finally, just before "coming to," sees herself, like vapor, being gently absorbed into the pores of the earth. . . .

Certainly [Annette] was, like Otto Ludwig, a poet of a decidedly visionary type. Already the child could be made distraught by the reality of things imagined; the young girl saw the objects of her longing with almost hallucinatory distinctness before her mind's eye. (p. 975)

Annette's best work is derived from this extraordinary vividness of inward vision. But she also produced work not so derived. There is a curious unevenness in the quality of her published writings. Some are the record of an inspired "Dichterin" [poetess], others the product of a "Schriftstellerin" [writer] who could write to order for any occasion from birthdays to public projects, or "do" a section on her native district for a "romantic and picturesque Germany" series. (p. 976)

Her best poetry, though essentially visionary, is not, of course, merely "unconscious" or "passive" in the making. There has gone into it, to begin with, a great deal of exact observation of reality. Annette was a person of exceptionally keen senses, especially of sight and of hearing. Her vocabulary reflects an extreme delicacy in the differentiation of sounds, and her almost microscopically minute vision has often been commented on. But these impressions of actuality had to be transmuted, in the mysterious depths of subconscious "work," into pictures suffused with the bright light of inward vision before they could be seen *again* and recorded, with Annette's prodigious powers of verbal expression, in all their vivid details of sight and sound and touch.

When there was a primary, real sense-impression, the vision could arise, even at a distance in place and time, as in the case of the brilliant *Heidebilder*, written in Meersburg. Where the primary sensory experience was lacking, the visualization was

inadequate, as in the *Hospiz auf dem großen St. Bernhard*, which is only incompletely realized and betrays its origin in hearsay and reading. Bookish, unauthentic provenience is apparent in Annette's early drama *Berta* and verse-epic *Walter*, and even in *Ledwina*, the novel-fragment which mirrors its young author and her morbid preoccupations.

The *Geistliches Jahr*, owing its inception to the wish of Annette's pious grandmother and its completion to the perseverance of Schlüter, is, as one might expect, only in part inspired and for the rest a dutifully executed work of edification. Even the moving record of the struggles of Annette's soul to surmount her critical reason and recover unquestioning faith, even the mastery of verse-form and language, do not make this great poetry, except in the few places where, beyond the verbal variation of ideas, the poet, having seen visions, could convey them in concrete detail, notably in *Am Feste Mariae Lichtmess*, in *Am 3. Sonntag nach Ostern*, and in *Gethsemane*.

The nightmare-like pictures of *Das Vermächtnis des Arztes*, the colorful historical frescoes and portraits of *Die Schlacht im Loener Bruch*, the dramatic succession of crucial scenes in *Die Judenbuche*, and the uncanny distinctness of things natural and supernatural in *Der Spiritus familiaris des Rosstäuschers*, accredit these works as the most authentic major products of Annette's genius. (pp. 977-78)

The core of Annette's poetic art is "Anschauung" [perception], primary and secondary, physical and mental. She possessed an extraordinary equipment for sensory perception: a hypersensitive ear, an all but prehensile eye, a skin-sense that reacted to subtle variations of atmosphere. . . .

Great virtuosity in sound-effects is reached in *Der Spiritus familiaris des Rosstäuschers*, especially in the description of the baleful creature in the vial. Annette's vocabulary for expressing sense-impressions, especially her arsenal of verbs that convey *sound* in all its gradations, is phenomenal; it exceeds that of any other poet of her time and is not matched before the era of Impressionism.

Her tactile sense, too, was exceptionally acute. She feels, or has her persons feel, the dew rising out of the ground in early morning . . . or the coolness seeping through her limbs. . . . With synaesthetic sensibility [in *Durchwachte Nacht*] she perceives the very darkness as a cool drizzle on her cheek. . . . (p. 979)

Concerning Annette's nearsightedness much has been written. First broached in the testimony of her friend Levin Schücking, and persuasively formulated by Richard M. Meyer, this matter of the limitation of Annette's physical vision has formed the traditional nucleus of discussions of her poetry ever since. It was easy to adduce examples of her minute description of near objects and of her "blurred distances" to bear out this point and neatly "characterize" this poet. More recently, it has become the fashion to replace this somewhat pathetic picture of the handicapped Annette by the portrait of Annette the pre-Impressionist: it was not limited vision, after all, but an astounding anticipation of Impressionistic technique that gave us her most brilliant descriptions.

Now every poet is more or less of an impressionist (small "i"), and the quality will inevitably be enhanced in a writer of such keen sensory receptiveness as Annette von Droste-Hülshoff. But it is, on the face of it, highly improbable that the works of an author that rise from such vivid *inner* vision as hers should be limited or impaired by a defect in personal

"Sehkraft" [strength of sight]. And if we look at her poems and tales without prejudice, we find the distance as clearly seen as the near view—when she wants it to be so seen.

The fact is that Annette's landscape is habitually that of her native heath, a land (especially in her time) of low, solitary moors and dense forests and mist-shrouded distances. Much that is misty and "out of focus" in her landscapes is simply Westphalian. Had she been native to a higher region where things are seen in clearer atmosphere, her backgrounds would have been different. (pp. 979-80)

Annette had a special predilection for the observation of small things: beetles, grasses, the moss on trees, the very infusoria in a glass of water. Partly this was . . . due to real scientific curiosity; partly, no doubt, to a feminine affection for what is small and "heimlich" [secret]; but in large part to a philosophical and religious conviction that small things are more valuable than great, and can do more to unlock the riddle of life and death with which her mind wrestled unceasingly. The exquisite miniatures in her poems, therefore—the beetle's golden armor, the sword-like blade of grass, the cricket stroking the rain off the "green glass" of its wings (*Die Vogelhütte*)—are not to be ascribed simply to defective eyesight, but to a particular devotion to these things.

Much that has been labelled myopic or Impressionistic in Annette's poetry is just good observation, imaginatively interpreted. A *locus classicus* for such discussions has been the quatrain in *Der Heidemann:*

> Man sieht des Hirten Pfeife glimmen
> Und vor ihm her die Herde schwimmen.
> Wie Proteus seine Robbenscharen
> Heimschwemmt im grauen Ozean.
>
> [One sees the pipe of the shepherd glimmer
> And before him swims the herd.
> As Proteus, gathering his robes about him,
> Swam home in the grey sea.]

Now the first two lines here are hardly even metaphorical, but simply a record of things seen in a swirling evening mist; the "schwimmen" is not far-fetched, but accurately descriptive of the progress of the sheep, whose backs and heads are visible above the ground-fog that hides the motion of their feet. The concept "schwimmen" does, however, then suggest a classical allusion of beautiful appropriateness, even to the Homeric grey common to fog and sea—an example on a small scale of the transition of the poet's eye from outward to inward vision, both utterly clear. (pp. 981-82)

Annette's descriptive style can be impressionistic-suggestive, or unsparingly realistic (as at the close of *Die Judenbuche*), or subjective-pathetic, or matter-of-fact (as in the *Bilder aus Westfalen*), but it is in every case distinctly pictorial. Every matter resolves itself for her into a series of pictures or scenes. Her lyrics, her ballads, her religious poetry at its best, her narratives in prose and verse, all share this quality of "Bildhaftigkeit." It is both her strength and her weakness, for the preternatural brightness of parts of her canvas only serves to heighten the obscurity of others, and one feels a certain lack of organizational power in her works, especially those of larger scope. *Die Schlacht im Loener Bruch,* for instance, is a sequence of sharply etched, brief, discrete pictures. We are taken first to one camp, then to the other, for an incident or a portrait; these are admirably vivid in themselves, but the work as a whole lacks a unifying "Gesamtidee" [central idea] and even a dominant figure, for Christian of Brunswick gives way to the young Count Tilly in the author's interest and affection; and some minor connections of the plot are never made clear. Annette's poetic imagination—again like Otto Ludwig's—seems on the whole to have furnished her with plastic individual scenes but not with the sustaining *nexus,* which was left to subsequent elaboration, so that her plot and structure are by no means faultless.

In the individual scenes of all her successful works, Annette evinces a marked "stage sense," that is, a power to visualize her persons' every movement and facial expression, and to hear their speech. And yet she lacked dramatic gift of any larger dimension; she could not construct a play, as her dismal failures in tragedy and comedy (*Berta* and *Perdu*) prove. The degree of dramatic force which she commanded is that inherent in the ballad. The isolated dramatic scenes, the "Sprunghaftigkeit" that leaves much connective matter in the dark for the sake of spotlighting the crucial points, the brief, tense dialogue, the suggestive background of nature and local history and the supernatural—all these earmarks of the folk-ballad are also characteristics of Annette's narrative art. Of her ballads proper, the best have a rudimentary dramatic structure of three "acts": exposition and preparation, clash of opponents, and dénouement; *Der Tod des Erzbischofs Engelbert von Köln* is an excellent example of this triadic arrangement—to which the equally undramatic Heine also was partial.

But, though she was a fine balladist, Annette's supreme distinction does not lie in her ballads, or even in those superlatively wrought pictures of her native heath that made her the northern peer of Lenau and Stifter. She saw reality sharply; but she was at her best only when she could see visions and dream dreams, when with rapt gaze she could discern and depict that inner landscape that to her was more real than reality. (pp. 982-83)

Walter Silz, "The Poetical Character of Annette von Droste-Hülshoff (1797-1848)," in PMLA, *63 (copyright © 1948 by the Modern Language Association of America; reprinted by permission of the Modern Language Association of America), Vol. LXIII, No. 3, September, 1948, pp. 973-83.*

WALTER SILZ (essay date 1954)

[Annette von Droste-Hülshoff] wrote only one Novelle, *Die Judenbuche,* but it is both a masterpiece of its genre and an early monument of Poetic Realism. (p. 36)

[In Friedrich Mergel, the hero of *Die Judenbuche,*] a whole lifetime is brought before us, from birth to death, fifty years and more—in fact, even the determinative conditions preceding his birth are clearly set forth. In other words, Annette has conquered a new field for the Novelle, a field traditionally reserved for the novel: the depiction of a personality in its entire scope and growth. . . . *Die Judenbuche* constitutes a modern enlargement of the Novelle which, by analogy to the great German tradition of the "Entwicklungsroman," the novel of development, might well be called an "Entwicklungsnovelle": though the conflict of a matured individual with society forms the climax of the story, we are shown the development of the hero up to this crisis, and on to his end. We see organically unfolding in him the qualities of character which will make him a mark for Fate. This prodigious condensation is made possible by a technique of scene-sequence, a series of dramatic pictures which give us glimpses of significant turning-points; a brilliant anticipation of the art of the cinema, illuminating only parts of the action and yet creating the illusion of continuity and completeness. (p. 37)

As a true realist, [Annette] aims at complete objectivity of report. She prefaces her story in an unusual way with a twelve-line poem which at once states her theme, sets a serious tone, and expresses her subjective attitude, which is one of sympathy, like Hauptmann's, for underprivileged and stunted lives. The poem, like the story itself in effect, is a preachment on the text: let the fortunate not cast stones. This sentiment of Christian charity contrasts strangely with the harsh Old Testament ethics later exemplified, yet both poem and story reflect a very modern awareness of the social factors—hereditary, environmental, educational—that determine character and ''guilt.''

Having thus as it were segregated her personal feelings in the introductory verses, the author maintains, in the story proper, an eminently objective and detached, even ironical, relation to her persons. (p. 38)

In her treatment of Nature, Annette employs, besides some lingering Romanticism, the more realistic manner of a newer age. She still senses the old irrational mystery of the ''Wald'' [forest]. . . . Yet Annette does not romanticize or humanize the crucial Beech . . . nor does she use it for lyrical ''Stimmung'' or atmosphere; she leaves it a real thing of Nature, even though the inscription on it has marked it with human significance.

Throughout the story, we are made aware of the natural background of every scene. But the description is never an end in itself, and is held to the utmost brevity. Nature has ''mood value'' but also functional importance in the human action. Man is still set in Nature, adjusted to it; but in a practical way. The forest, for example, is not the object of dreamy contemplation; it figures realistically as a means of livelihood for the villagers. (pp. 40-1)

[Throughout *Die Judenbuche*] we see the Romantic love of ''Naturstimmung'' [nature atmosphere] being tempered by a sober sense of fact. That the Nature here depicted is the author's familiar native heath is another element characteristic of Poetic Realism, for that movement was intimately linked with the development of regional art or ''Heimatkunst.''

Quite in the manner of Poetic Realism is the careful recording of the particulars of everyday living in cottage and castle, in field and forest—interiors as well as outdoor activities are vividly brought to view, but with the subtle artistic selection that distinguishes the Poetic Realist, and with the succinctness imposed by the restricted compass of the Novelle. Thus the former prosperity of the Mergel house is indicated by its chimney and extra-large window-panes; its deterioration by the neglected fence, the damaged roof, and the unweeded garden with its woody, unpruned rosebushes. . . . (pp. 41-2)

At the end of the story, Poetic Realism passes over into what a later period would have called outright Naturalism. Our noses assailed by the stench of putrefying human flesh, and our eyes by the sight of maggots at work in it. (p. 42)

With all her lucid realism, however, [Annette] has left an aura of mystery about her tale. In the sunlit village life there is at times a strange blurring of perception, not only of moral values but of actual happenings. . . . A good deal of the story runs underground, like a lost river; only parts of its course are in full view. Much of the psychological motivation is eliminated or ''covered'' by the fact that the returned Friedrich is taken

by the villagers to be Johannes, and deliberately lives the part which chance has assigned to him. We do not know what is going on in his mind, and the author could not tell us without giving away her plot; we get only surface manifestations—a furtive glance, a slashed spoon . . .—of the inner forces that drive this man to his doom. (pp. 42-3)

Annette's style, both in narrative and lyric, is distinctly pictorial: every matter resolves itself for her into a series of pictures or scenes. . . . It is her marvellous scene-technique that enables her to compress into a fifty-page Novelle the substance of a novel. (p. 43)

In the successive reworkings of her manuscript [Annette] eliminated—even to the point of eventual obscurity in some places—almost everything that did not bear directly on the development of her hero from birth to death, and she even considered prenatal influences. In her final revision, only the peasant-wedding scene and some of the doings in the ''Schloss'' [castle] (recorded with filial fondness) could strictly be called dispensable to the ideal ''leanness'' of the Novelle.

The carefully detailed picture of the young hero's ''Umwelt'' [environment] is Annette's most significant addition to her source. Her approach, through ever-narrowing circles of environment, is comparable to that of a motion-picture. It is plain from her prefatory poem that she means to deal with one of the obscure and under-privileged. She begins, indeed, with her hero's name and birthdate; but then, far from signalizing him as an extraordinary individual—as Kleist does in the opening sentence of *Michael Kohlhaas*—she depicts the social setting out of which grew this inconspicuous ''Menschenkind'' [man child] Friedrich Mergel. (pp. 46-7)

In less than four pages, Annette . . . [gives] us a complete and overwhelming picture of the suprapersonal forces that determine individual lives. It is clear that she means to ascribe a good part of her hero's guilt to social factors beyond his control. This is a new departure in the history of German fiction. It serves to remind us that we are here in the Post-Romantic age of Hegel and of new, collective, racial conceptions of history and morality that have supplanted the individualism of the ''Goethe-Zeit.'' The world of *Die Judenbuche* is a far cry from the age of Idealism and the moral freedom of Schiller's heroes; indeed, it anticipates by a half-century the social ethics of Naturalism. (pp. 47-8)

Die Judenbuche shows us the temptation and guilt of an entire community brought to a head in one of its members. Friedrich Mergel is no salient, heroic individual such as the previous literature knew, no Wallenstein or Guiskard challenging Fate, but an ordinary specimen of his kind, a man in whom good and bad are mixed, a product of the standards and prejudices of his time and place, who might have ''gone right'' as readily as wrong—for his nature, as well as his features, does not lack nobility. . . . He is conditioned by clan and community. Everything he does, up to the killing of the Jew, is within the *mores* of his group. . . . Only the actual slaying, as a private and individual deed, ''goes too far'' and makes Friedrich a marked man in the position of Manz and Marti in Keller's *Romeo und Julia,* the chance ''conductor'' of a crime that any fellow-citizen might have committed.

Beyond this persuasive exposition of the social determinants of right and wrong, however, *Die Judenbuche* adumbrates a larger, indeed a cosmic problem of Evil. The moral issue of the story is not so much one of Old Testament ethics (despite the fulfilment of the Hebrew inscription), nor so much one of

Fate in the Greek sense, as it is the demonstration of Man's moral frailty and defenselessness in a baffling and inimical world. For, when all is said and done, the punishment in this case does not fit the crime. Outwardly, Friedrich's suicide exemplifies the retributory justice of "an eye for an eye, a tooth for a tooth" which Aaron's widow invokes. Inwardly, it is a completely amoral solution, like the killing of a hunted animal. (pp. 49-50)

The stark cruelty of the ending of *Die Judenbuche* is predicated upon the savagery of life and of the dark forces that shape it. Friedrich's crime was unpremeditated and unwilled, it was not murder, but manslaughter in a quarrel, in hot blood, and human courts would normally have considered it cancelled by the passage of time (as in fact it was in Annette's source) as well as by the culprit's severe sufferings and present condition. For this deed, notwithstanding—with utter exclusion of the religious offices of confession and atonement—he is driven to suicide, thus adding to an ordinary crime a mortal sin—a conclusion that is surely amazing when considered as the work of a woman and a professed Catholic, and that makes sense only on the supposition that life is at its core irrational and beyond human understanding.

Annette's Novelle is thus an unusually characteristic example of the "Welt- und Kunstanschauung," the philosophical and artistic principles, of Poetic Realism. For though it is a "true story," presenting a complete and convincing picture of social facts and forces, the author does not stop at these in the manner of Determinism or of Existentialism; she imposes a pattern on them, she views them in relation to a higher and wider frame of reference: both her own metaphysical convictions and the sovereign powers of poetic re-creation that raise bare factuality to true reality. (pp. 50-1)

> *Walter Silz, "Droste-Hülshoff, 'Die Judenbuche' (1842)," in his* Realism and Reality: Studies in the German Novelle of Poetic Realism *(copyright 1954 The University of North Carolina Press), The University of North Carolina Press, 1954, pp. 36-51.*

BRIGITTE E. SCHATZKY (essay date 1961)

[Annette von Droste's *Das Geistliche Jahr in Liedern auf alle Sonn-und Festtage* is based] on the examination of conscience as the centre and exercise of the spiritual life, and confined to a rigid framework of prescribed Biblical texts and other Christian themes, the underlying emotion is that of contrition ("bittere Reue") and the soul's craving for God's grace. (p. 81)

[Annette von Droste's] microscopic gaze, which she was later to turn outwards to the world of nature, is trained mercilessly upon the minutest motions of the soul, cringing and writhing in ceaseless self-abasement. But real remorse presupposes real guilt, and for all her protestations about "sin," about "des Stolzes Klippen" [the proud cliffs] and "dieser Erde Freuden" [this joyful earth]—metaphors which rarely rise above the conventional—the first twenty-five cantos of *Das Geistliche Jahr* fail to carry conviction, and many subtle variations on Baroque and Romantic verse forms only serve to emphasize the basic poverty of experience. (p. 82)

[The] borderland between belief and doubt, between dreaming and waking was [Annette von Droste's] true realm—"unser Reich, was wir mit den Engländern und Schotten teilen" [our realm, which we share with the English and Scottish]. The kinship with English and Scottish literature is particularly evident in three long epic poems written after a period of stagnation. . . . The first, *Das Hospiz auf dem grossen Sankt Bernhard* . . . tells the old story of the St. Bernard dog who saves a boy from dying of cold and helps the good monks to recover the frozen body of his grandfather. It contains, amongst others, a macabre nocturnal scene in which the bodies in the morgue, where the old man and his grandson have sought shelter, seem to come alive. The theme is man in the grip of unknown and hostile powers, but neither the conventional paraphernalia of horror nor the inclemencies of an externally conceived landscape succeed in conveying the necessary sense of inevitability, especially as the terrors of the night are offset by the idyllic peace of the monastic life and the joys of motherhood. The language already betrays a characteristic angularity and pointed rhythmical quality, but there is no attempt to adapt it to the different moods of the action, thus giving the whole a faint monotony.

If *Das Hospiz* is indebted to Walter Scott, it is Byron's influence which is discernible in the next narrative poem, *Des Arztes Vermächtnis*. . . . The plot is clearly based on Schelling's *Die Letzten Worte des Pfarrers zu Drotning auf Seeland* published in 1802: a doctor is called out in the middle of the night to attend a dying man, member of a band of criminals living in the depths of the forest. He has to make the journey blindfold on horse-back, and after a night full of horrors is made to swear an oath not to divulge what he has seen to any living soul. On the homeward journey he witnesses in a condition of semi-consciousness the brutal murder of a woman whom he had met by the bedside of the wounded man, an experience which gradually undermines his sanity. . . . Identifying herself with the principal character, and as if she were herself sleep-walking, the poet follows him step by step into the regions of night and death, as, bereft of the protective power of his senses, he becomes the victim of a demonic power—"der Dunkle"—which is not entirely a figment of his fevered imagination. As in *Das Hospiz,* the horrors of the night give way to the beauteous calm of the morning, the hideous den in the forest to the peaceful dwelling in the valley. But the juxtaposition now spells a haunting sense of doubt. (pp. 83-4)

Wherever [Annette von Droste] uses traditional ghost story figures as agents of horror, it remains a matter of uncertainty whether these figures are real or illusory. Despite the poet's superior knowledge there remains the shudder of the mysterious unknown, a real sense of *Angst* lurks behind the "poetisches Gruseln" [poetic shudder] consciously aimed at.

For the setting of her third epic poem, *Die Schlacht am Loener Bruch* . . . Annette von Droste returned to her native Westphalia. The result is a heightening of the realistic quality as well as a deepening of the spiritual content. . . . [The] portrait of the hero and the magnificently ponderous battle scenes . . . are indeed without parallel in Annette von Droste's other work. The knightly valour of Christian von Braunschweig or Tilly's bold nocturnal ride through the ghostly forest to reconnoitre hard by the enemy camp seem like a wish-fulfilment of her own thwarted desires. Throughout nature plays a dominant part, not only in the many "Stimmungsbilder" [atmosphere pictures], but as an integral part of the action. The great battle itself is described like a natural phenomenon, unfolding like a thunderstorm from the earliest faint forebodings to the final clash of arms. . . . (pp. 84-5)

"Not like the poetry women usually write," remarked Charlotte Brontë about the work of her sister Emily. The same might be said in the case of Annette von Droste, who bears indeed a curious affinity to the English novelist. Almost exact contemporaries, they each created out of the depths of their imagination a stark, passionate world in contrast to their own quiet, circumscribed lives. Annette's *Wuthering Heights* was *Die Judenbuche* . . . , a sombre and powerful work . . . about a subject whose very stark simplicity fascinated and disturbed her. . . .

Sitting in the ordered tranquillity of her idyllic Rüschhaus, Annette von Droste found herself drawn into a world of disorder, depravity and evil. She is as far from revelling in her morbid theme as she is from moralizing about it, proceeding rather with reticence and caution, mindful of the limitations of human reason and of the obscure, unfathomable recesses of the mind. It is this, and not any superficial desire to mystify in the sense of a detective story, which accounts for the many question-marks in the narrative, the hidden clues, the apparently unconnected happenings, the atmosphere of semi-darkness, the many ambiguities in speech and action. Brief snatches of dialogue, swift questions and answers like the thrust-and-parry of a cross-examination serve to intensify the general sense of brooding fate rather than to elucidate the particular point under discussion. . . . (p. 85)

The character of Friedrick Mergel himself is shadowy and ambiguous. In her depiction of his strange double existence it is as though the author herself only half guessed at a pact with the devil. (p. 86)

Annette von Droste intended to incorporate *Die Judenbuche* into a larger work on Westphalia and the life and customs of its people. Though this was never realized, she continued to work along these lines, now inspired by Washington Irving's *Bracebridge Hall* to start on a kind of "Familiengemälde" [family portrait] in the form of a journal entitled *Bei und zu Lande auf dem Lande* . . . , now collaborating with Freiligrath and Schücking on their *Malerisches und romantisches Westfalen* (her contribution being subsequently published separately under the title of *Bilder aus Westfalen*). Interesting and attractive as these are—the former shot through with a sense of humour otherwise found only in Annette's letters, the latter written in a masterly prose style—these writings are at best only side-lines of her creative work, at worst distractions from and dissipations of her true talents. (p. 87)

The first complete edition of Annette von Droste's poetry . . . , *Gedichte von Annette Freiin von Droste-Hülshoff,* contains, it is true, a quantity of mediocre poems, especially among the *Gedichte vermischten Inhalts,* the group entitled *Scherz und Satire* and the so-called *Zeitbilder,* (written in the conservative-patriotic vein of her favourites Freiligrath and Geibel). At its best, however, it constitutes a break-through to a lyrical form of expression more spontaneous and direct than anything that had gone before. Not that it contains a great effusion of feeling, for it is characteristic of Annette von Droste that the precipitate of her deepest personal experience is found in her letters, not in her poetry. Even her few love poems—*Brennende Liebe, Die Schenke am See, An Levin Schücking*—are reticent in tone and heavy with a kind of subdued sadness.

Almost twenty of the Meersburg poems are ballads, in which the subjective element is of necessity least in evidence, especially where they are based on traditional models, as *Der Graf von Thal* and others. In atmosphere they have little of the sunny serenity of the place of their composition, being reminiscent rather of the earlier Rüschhaus ballads. . . . (pp. 89-90)

Der Fundator [is] perhaps the most successful of the ballads. The gradual building up of the ghostly atmosphere by means

of realistic, sensuous impressions from the world of nature—the blue haze and the vapours of the moon, the groaning of the toad, the rustling in the reeds, the "snoring" of the swans—link it with the finest part of the collection, the *Heidebilder.* As the title suggests, these once again take their inspiration from her native moorlands, and once again the intimate, "lyrical" note is absent. The language has none of the radiancy of Goethe's lyric poetry; the "spröde Rhythmik" [brittle rhythm] (as Wolfgang Kayser has aptly described it) seems harsh, even jerky when compared with his harmonious verse movements. In place of a musical appeal the verse often has the quality of speech, with a strong acoustic element (it ought properly to be read aloud). She uses words not for their associative symbolism or suggestive overtones, but in their basic, elemental sense and with a bold accuracy as though she were thereby able to conjure the world of natural phenomena. (p. 90)

The characteristic movement of [Annette von Droste's] verse is from a shadowy beyond to the clearly perceptible, from the incommensurate to the commensurate. . . . This is partly to be explained by Annette von Droste's extreme myopia which, while blurring distant objects, enabled her to see near-by ones with microscopic clarity. But fundamentally it answers her unconscious need to oppose the formless, the chaotic by clutching at the actual, the close-at-hand, to counterbalance her own deep-seated *Angst* by the most exact notation possible of the *données* of the world around her.

Not that she ever tried to "tame" nature in the *Biedermeier* sense of turning it into a well-kept garden of flowers and vegetables. At best the haven of house and garden is but a temporary refuge from the dark and sinister forces of nature at its most elemental. Even when the boy in *Der Knabe im Moor* has safely reached home after his perilous journey across the moor, the memory of what he has seen is all too real. . . . (p. 91)

[*Der Spiritus familiaris des Rosstäuschers* is] the last of her four epic poems. Based on one of the *Deutsche Sagen* of the brothers Grimm, it tells the story of a horse-dealer who, having through no fault of his own lost all he has, makes a pact with the devil. . . . In its preoccupation with the idea of guilt as it were overtaking man unawares and leading him to remorse and punishment, the poem seems to hark back to *Die Judenbuche.* But instead of the Old Testament fatalism of the *Novelle,* the final mood of the *Spiritus familiaris* is one of Christian redemption. . . . Though the horrors of death and putrefaction reach their highest point, they are depicted with a sensuous objectivity and sureness of touch which have their origin in a more positive, less somnambulistic *Weltanschauung.* . . . (pp. 92-3)

[Though Annette von Droste's posthumous collection, *Letzte Gaben,* is] again somewhat mixed in quality, it contains some of [her] finest poetry. . . . *Im Grase, Durchwachte Nacht* and *Mondesaufgang* are great lyric poems by any standards, combining as they do the experience of life as a harmonious whole with a more relaxed rhythm and a loosening up of conventional metric forms. The dominant atmosphere is no longer expressed in epithets such as "heiss," "schwer" or "dunkel" [hot, heavy, or dark], but by "süss," "tief" and "leise" [sweet, deep, and gentle], yet without loss to the characteristic sensory quality of the imagery. *Mondesaufgang* is at once more personal and more truly religious than the whole of *Das Geistliche Jahr:* a Wordsworthian "gentleness of heaven is on the sea," a "mildes Licht" which not only promises momentary shelter from the horrors of the night (viz. the lamp in *Der Knabe im Moor*), but banishes them altogether. (pp. 93-4)

[Annette von Droste's] was a lyre on which many notes were never struck. The note of humour, for instance, was deliberately suppressed. . . . The personal struggle for inner release never issues in a cry for freedom, as in the poetry of Emile Bronte. The struggle for political freedom taking place on her very doorstep found no echo in her work—except as an occasional protest delivered with all the indignation of her ''loyales Aristokratenblut'' [loyal aristocratic blood]. Unsustained by the discipline of the intellect, her work is occasionally obscure and contains much that is only second-rate. Yet if she did not fully exploit and develop her own capabilities, she never sacrificed her artistic integrity by attempting to go beyond them for the sake of effect or popularity. . . . (p. 94)

> *Brigitte E. Schatzky, ''Annette von Droste-Hülshoff,'' in* German Men of Letters: Twelve Literary Essays, Vol. 1, *edited by Alex Natan (© 1961 Oswald Wolff (Publishers) Ltd), Wolff, 1961, pp. 79-98.*

MARGARET MARE (essay date 1965)

[The epic form is not] one which gave full scope to Annette von Droste's genius. In spite of many fine passages, one is sometimes tempted to wish that she had used her material in another way.

What a wonderful poem *Das Hospiz auf dem grossen Sankt Bernhard* would have been if it had assumed the shape of a long ballad like *Der Spiritus familiaris des Rosstäuschers*, taking some half-dozen of the highlights of the tale and leaving the rest to flashbacks or the intelligence of the reader. . . . (p. 207)

[*Das Hospiz auf dem grossen Sankt Bernhard* is composed of] about 2,500 rhyming lines with four stresses, in which one can see the influence of Scott's epic poems. In the first canto in particular one can trace more of Scott, and indeed of many eighteenth-century poets, in the moralizing observations which intrude on the tale. . . . If, however, the reader perseveres, he will discover many passages in which Annette von Droste's realism and poetic mastery are already apparent. (pp. 207-08)

Significantly, the title first thought of for the poem was 'Barry, der Hund vom St Bernhard', underlining the thought which often occupied Annette: the sureness, if not superiority of an animal's instinct (compare the later poem *Instinkt*) to anything of which man is capable (über menschliches Können und Wollen). Certainly Barry is just as much a real dog as 'shaggy Tremm', lying half asleep beside his mistress in *Instinkt*. . . . He behaves like any other dog when he allows little Henri to play with him in the monastery, but on the terrible search for old Benoit he is wiser and braver than the humans. . . . (p. 210)

The virtuosity of language in *Des Arztes Vermächtnis* [, Annette von Droste's second epic, represents a] great advance on *Das Hospiz*. . . . There is hardly a weak line in the whole poem, and the tension never slackens. . . . Annette herself stated that the aim of the poem was to show 'the annihilating influence of horrible, uncanny (des Schauerlichen) and incomprehensible happenings on a human being, whose soul is by its nature open to the extraordinary, but is made incapable of bearing this by his innocence and kindliness'. (p. 215)

There is nothing of the spirit world in Annette von Droste's third long poem, *Die Schlacht im Loener Bruch*. . . . It is firmly based on exhaustive historical researches. . . . (p. 216)

The description of the battle which ends the poem is a *tour de force* of history made visual. Annette had acquainted herself with every detail of seventeenth-century weapons and equipment, and the names come pouring out, but so naturally woven into the texture of the verse that there is no hint of pedantry. It is as if the poet were posted on a hill surveying the battlefield and reporting the fight in ten pages of closely packed description. (p. 220)

If *Die Schlacht im Loener Bruch* had been published anonymously, it would have been difficult to guess a woman's hand behind it. Annette's style, so sparing of adjectives and with many terse sentences of noun and verb, is admirably suited to such a subject. One cannot think of any contemporary verse description of a battle coming anywhere near its realism and sweep. To equal it one needs to turn to the prose of Stendhal and Thackeray. (p. 221)

In Annette von Droste's poetry, . . . images and symbols are a great enrichment. Sometimes they may enhance the visual effect of the poetry in our mind's eye; at others they pull us up short, as we read in tranced enjoyment, and make us stop to think what message this often obscure poetess is trying to convey to us.

In the nature of things there is more symbolism in *Das Geistliche Jahr* than in the rest of Annette von Droste's poetry, though a large proportion of it is that common to most religious verse. What is noteworthy is that she does not in general use the jargon of initiates of her own sect but expresses herself in terms accessible to those of other persuasions. She was obviously more familiar with the Bible than are many Roman Catholics— perhaps an outcome of the Gallitzin tradition—as well as with great devotional writings like the *Imitation of Christ*. Hence Annette used symbols common to other Christian writers: smoking flax, a broken reed, Lot's wife standing as a warning to others, the rainbow, gall, honey, straining at a gnat and swallowing a camel, the pearl of great price, the mote and the beam, smoke to denote transitoriness, God as light while sinners sit in darkness, doubters struggling through morasses and deep chasms or the 'slough of despond'. Just as frequently occur symbols more suggestive of the mystics than Bible phraseology: in the *Spiritus familiaris des Rosstäuschers* grace is equated to angels' wings, the dragon represents sin and condemnation; grace is also a torch. . . . These are all figures of speech well known to us, but Annette contrives to use them so that they rarely strike us as religious clichés but come fresh to the eye and ear. Sometimes she would take a familiar parable and make a completely individual application of it. In the gospel for the *First Sunday after Trinity*, for instance, she herself is one of the unwilling guests of the man who made a great supper. . . . (pp. 223-24)

Even more individual than this twisting of a Bible text to her own needs is Annette's use of symbols which have a peculiar significance for her. 'Blood' has nothing to do with its religious connotation of redemption by vicarious sacrifice. Perhaps Droste-Hülshoff would agree with Mephistopheles in calling it 'ein ganz besondrer Saft' [a whole, special juice], for to her it means something real and intensely felt. The idea of blood does not arouse in her physical disgust, since in *Brennende Liebe* . . . she tells how she cherished the handkerchief used to staunch the blood of a lover who had cut himself when hacking berries for her from a shrub—to us a notion even more repulsive than the keepsake of human hair dear to the Victorians. The bloody token signifies to Annette 'Sein Blut und meine brennende Lieb' [your blood and my burning love]. Even in the early oriental poems she states that all she has said, done, and written is with her 'Herzens flammendes Blut' [heart's flaming blood]. . . . (p. 225)

In several poems Droste-Hülshoff castigates the insincerity and heartlessness she sees in many aspects of contemporary life. She herself knows that her poetic mission was given her 'by the grace of God' and that it was her duty, as a real person, to enter the lists against the rottenness behind much fair seeming, for which she uses the image of the phosphorescent light on decayed wood, flowers covering the bog, and a *bloodless meteor*—a symbol for the spirit or mind—extinguished in a swamp. . . . After enumerating all the false objectives of contemporary literature in her address *An die Schriftstellerinnen in Deutschland und Frankreich* . . . , she adjures them: 'Kniet vor des Blutes gnadenvoller Spende', by which she means they are to 'tend the sacred fire entrusted to them'. (pp. 226-27)

[Annette von Droste's poetic style was] one of the most original in German literature. The conventional were shocked at the dialect forms and words abounding in her poems, but, although they demand a special glossary even for Germans, no one would nowadays deny the naturalness they impart. . . . Annette was very quick to pick up dialects, so, after living in Meersburg, an occasional Swabian word crops up. . . . Sometimes she invents a High German word based on a Low German original, as when in *Dichters Naturgefühl,* she calls the waterfilled ruts made by wheels in the soggy ground 'Wassertruhen' (L. G. Wassertrone). She is also not afraid of colloquialisms. . . . (p. 238)

Sometimes, however, Annette von Droste went to the other extreme and indulged in learned or archaic words. French was a *sine qua non* for the aristocrat, so the use of French words was not an affectation on her part. . . . Nor did Italian come amiss: tempi passati. There are also a number of words and allusions testifying to Annette's wide reading and classical education. . . . Annette's hobby of fossil collecting and the botanical interests of her father and sister provide a great many unusual words: all the geological terms of the *Mergelgrube* and the frequently used Asbest and Lava; the botanical datura, Dionaea, oculi christi, Naphthablüten (this is also a remedy; Annette's constant dealings with doctors and homoeopaths made her free of their jargon). Indeed, scientifically observed facts are often behind much of her striking imagery. . . . Only very rarely did Annette von Droste resort to medieval allusions picked up from Lassberg, or to the language of romanticism. In one of the religious poems she speaks, however, of drinking the refreshing draught of faith 'aus dem heil'gen Gral' [from the Holy Grail] and in *Der Graf von Thal,* the one poem smacking of romanticism, she uses Kemnate (ladies' bower) and Minstrel. When she speaks in *Am Turme* of the life of a woman being 'fein und klar' [delicate and bright], a favourite epithet of the romantics culled from the folk-song, she is ironical. Annette was more inclined to go back to eighteenth-century poetic diction than to that of the period just preceding her own. (pp. 239-40)

All these, however, are the striking but less usual features of Annette von Droste's diction. There are also a number of more ordinary words particularly characteristic of her style. She is constantly preoccupied with thoughts of decay, and words such as morsch, vermorscht, Moder, Schemen, Tod, Verwesung [rotten, mouldering, mould, delusion, death, putrefication], are used both metaphorically and literally. One of her favourite words is *wüst*, used with every possible shade of meaning from the colloquial 'ugly, bad' to 'wild, waste, dissolute' of literary language. She is extremely fond of words with an *i* sound. . . .

But her range of all onomatopaeic words is tremendous. Two contradictory features in Annette von Droste's style can probably be explained by her extreme short-sight. Levin Schücking wrote to his fiancée, Luise von Gall, about Annette: 'nearby she can see the infusoria in a drop of water, but five or six paces away hardly anything'. This accounts for the exactitude of her descriptions of every movement of small insects or of each blade of the grass in which she loved to lie. . . . (p. 240)

Droste-Hülshoff uses several devices for emphasis. She frequently arrests the reader's attention by beginning a poem with a question . . . , notably in the Schücking poems. . . . In two of the religious poems, *Am Neujahrstag* . . . and that for the *Monday in Holy Week* . . . the question develops into a dialogue with the human soul. [We can see how Annette von Droste] analysed the shifting of words to be emphasized, even separable prefixes, out of their normal position to the beginning of a line, or how she draws attention to them by an irregular stress. These devices are, of course, common to all poets, but they are particularly marked in Annette von Droste's verse. . . . [There] are probably fewer attributive adjectives in her poems than in those of any other German poet. In general the preponderance of nouns and verbs lends her style movement and incisiveness. . . . The most individual of all Annette von Droste's devices to give weight to what she is saying is repetition, . . . [as] in the poem for the *Second Sunday in Advent* . . . : 'ich seh es flammen, aber bleich, ach bleich!'; again, the doctor's nervous tension in the robbers' den, as he listens for every sound, is expressed by 'Ich lauschte, lauschte, lauschte' (*Des Arztes Vermächtnis* . . .).

It is only after reading the poetry of Annette von Droste's contemporaries that a modern is struck by her realism. She shrinks from nothing that a twentieth-century poet would say, except as regards the erotic and cloacal. Count Isenburg, who has murdered the Archbishop of Cologne [in *Der Tod des Erzbischofs Engelbert Köln*], is broken on the wheel and his corpse left to be devoured by crows and maggots. A particularly horrible touch is given by his wife's scaring off the ravens with her kerchief. . . . All Annette von Droste's realism was not, of course, of this repulsive kind. We have noted again and again that she never sees nature, human or inanimate, through a romantic haze, but is always aware of the little details which give people, animals, and objects the stamp of reality. (pp. 241-43)

Hardly a poet does not resort to personification, but with Annette von Droste it is more than usually frequent, particularly at the start of a poem. . . . Annette's *tour de force* of personification is *Die Lerche,* since the whole of that delightful poem is built up of it. The rising sun is a young princess, while the lark is a herald and all the flowers are courtiers assisting at her toilet. . . . Some of the insects form an orchestra to delight the princess, while others are merchants bringing her jewels and finery. It is brilliantly done. Each insect, though metamorphosed, moves and sounds as it does in reality. (pp. 243-45)

To the eye, turning over the pages of Annette's works, the majority of the poems seem to be written in verses of a conventional pattern, but reading them out loud reveals the broken rhythms which split the lines into units of sense where no nuance of meaning is lost. There is hardly a verse in all Annette von Droste's output in which the stresses are completely regular. (p. 247)

What is notably absent in Annette von Droste's poetry are free rhythms, which seems surprising when so many turns of phrase make one realize that she knew and loved Goethe's poetry. Her clinging to conventional verse-forms reminds one of the great Russian poets, who found them no hindrance to the expression of every nuance of poetic emotion. The only unrhymed verses written by Annette von Droste were the *Klänge aus dem Orient* and the two early ballads *Der Barmekiden Untergang* and *Bajazeth,* where she was deliberately writing pastiche of oriental poetry. (p. 248)

The greatest metrical variety is to be found in the *Heidebilder,* poem cycles like *Ein Sommertagstraum* and *Volksglauben in den Pyrenäen,* and, above all, *Das Geistliche Jahr.* What is most notable about the religious lyrics is how few of them are in the least like hymns, though all of them have verses of equal length and similar metre. Even the poem for the *Saturday in Holy Week* . . . , which takes the form of a litany with 'O Herr erhalt uns', 'O Herr verschon uns', and so forth, at the end of every verse does not immediately suggest melodies in use for the litany type of hymn. . . . (p. 249)

Some critics, while conceding to Annette von Droste's verse great visual beauty, are uncertain as to its musical quality. If we look again at such poems as *Der Weiher,* we can have no doubt that Annette could write verse which delights the ear. When her lines cease to flow freely, it betokens a pause for thought, a hesitation until the right word has been found, which imparts depth and naturalness to her poetry. The effect of this is not inharmonious. (p. 251)

It is not surprising that [*Ledwina,* Annette von Droste's early novel,] remained a fragment. . . . Annette was as yet incapable of sublimating her experiences into the language of art, and they had therefore to remain unspoken. Like most youthful novels *Ledwina* could not extricate itself from autobiography. (p. 252)

The fascination of *Ledwina* lies both in the insight it affords into the young Annette and in the glimpses of the family life of Hülshoff or Bökendorf. One feels sure that the conversation of Ledwina, her brother and sisters and the neighbours who spend a day with them allow us to eavesdrop on a German country house of the period. What strikes one most is how much the talk turned on personalities, in the absence of many happenings, or on abstract questions. Their discussion of the loyalty of old family servants and the calm assumption that these will always be ready to sacrifice their life for their employers makes strange reading. One is relieved to note that Ledwina was really distressed to think that an old man might have got the pneumonia that killed him by going out to sweep a path for her in the snow and that she took the drowning of his son, while lighting a rider along the dangerous river bank,

more hardly than did the rest of the family. The two strands in the *Ledwina* fragment do not seem quite to join. Annette had not been able to make up her mind whether she wished to write a description of manners and society or a psychological novel, where nature and people were regarded through the eyes of Ledwina's sensibility. (pp. 252-53)

> *Margaret Mare, in her* Annette von Droste-Hülshoff, *with translations by Ursula Prideaux (reprinted by permission; © 1965 by Margaret Mare), Methuen and Co., Ltd, 1965, 322 p.*

ADDITIONAL BIBLIOGRAPHY

Chick, Edson. "Voices in Discord: Some Observations on *Die Judenbuche.*" *The German Quarterly* XLII, No. 2 (March 1969): 147-57.
> Examines conflicting critical interpretations of *Die Judenbuche.* Chick argues that Droste-Hülshoff's world view in this novella is more similar to "the Victorian atheist morality of Ibsen's plays" than many critics have supposed.

Coenen, Frederic E. "The 'Idee' in Annette von Droste-Hülshoff's *Die Judenbuche.*" *The German Quarterly* XII, No. 4 (November 1939): 204-09.
> Asserts that in *Die Judenbuche* Droste-Hülshoff betrayed a bias toward upper-class society.

Flygt, Sten G. "'Durchwachte Nacht': A Structural Analysis of Annette von Droste-Hülshoff's Poem." *The Journal of English and Germanic Philology* LV, No. 2 (April 1956): 257-74.
> A detailed examination emphasizing the visual imagery and aural effects of "Durchwachte Nacht". This essay also offers an interpretation of the child figure in the poem.

Hallamore, Joyce. "The Reflected Self in Annette von Droste's Work: A Challenge to Self-Discovery." *Monatshefte* XLI, No. 1 (Spring 1969): 58-74.
> Views Droste-Hülshoff's artistic activity as a process of self-confrontation and self-exploration.

Suttner, Christa. "A Note on the Droste-Image and 'Das Spiegelbild'." *The German Quarterly* XL, No. 4 (November 1967): 623-29.
> Claims that Droste-Hülshoff was aware of contemporary philosophical and psychological theories, as evidenced in "Das Spiegelbild" by her recognition of the power of the unconscious.

Thomas, L.H.C. "*Die Judenbuche* by Annette von Droste-Hülshoff." *The Modern Language Review* LIV, No. 1 (January 1959): 56-65.
> Attempts to clarify *Die Judenbuche* by examining Droste-Hülshoff's plans and drafts for the story, and by reviewing the factual account of the incident on which the novella was based which was written by her uncle.

Eugene Field

1850-1895

American poet, journalist, short story writer, and essayist.

The creator of the newspaper feature column, Field was among the first journalists to incorporate personal observations and viewpoints in his writing for journals. His articles varied from satirical attacks on the nouveau riche to translations of Horace, but he is best remembered for the children's verse that he often included in his column. In such poems as "Dutch Lullaby" (known as "Wynken, Blynken and Nod") and "Little Boy Blue," Field captured the child's world.

Field's mother died when he was six, and he was taken from St. Louis, his birthplace, to Amherst, Massachusetts. There he was raised by Mary Field French, a cousin to whom he later dedicated *A Little Book of Western Verse*. While Field grew up in the East, his loyalties belonged wholly to the West, in whose development he saw the future of the United States.

After being expelled from three colleges, reportedly for his practical jokes, Field spent his inheritance touring Europe. Returning to St. Louis, he became an apprentice journalist, and soon gained a reputation as a witty writer. He worked at various newspapers in the West and Midwest, finally settling in Chicago, where he wrote for the *Daily News*. Field's most popular contributions were his "Odds and Ends" column in the Denver *Tribune* (later collected and published in *The Tribune Primer*), and "Sharps and Flats," his column in the Chicago *Daily News* (collected and published as *Culture's Garland*).

Field's work reflects his personal and often sentimental creative intent. His devotion to his wife is evident in "Lover's Lane, St. Jo.," his love of animals inspired "The Bench-Legged Fyce" and "O Had I Wings Like a Dove," his interest in Horace informed *The Love Affairs of a Bibliomaniac*, and his fondness for children is evoked in his whimsical stories and verse. These, and all his writings, establish Field as a writer of warmth and humor, and, in the words of his brother, Roswell Martin Field, "a gentle singer of the faithful and the good."

The Writings in Prose and Verse of Eugene Field (essays, short stories, and poetry) 1898-1901

PRINCIPAL WORKS

The Tribune Primer (poetry, short stories, essays) 1882
Culture's Garland (poetry, short stories, essays) 1887
A Little Book of Profitable Tales (poetry and short stories) 1889
A Little Book of Western Verse (poetry) 1889
Echoes from the Sabine Farm [with Roswell Field] (poetry) 1892
A Second Book of Verse (poetry) 1892
With Trumpet and Drum (poetry) 1892
The Holy Cross and Other Tales (short stories and poetry) 1893
Love-Songs of Childhood (poetry) 1894
Lullaby Land (poetry) 1894
An Auto-Analysis (autobiography) 1896
The Love Affairs of a Bibliomaniac (essays) 1896

JULIAN HAWTHORNE (essay date 1887)

The name of Eugene Field, of the Chicago "Daily News," though heard for the first time only a few years ago, is already a famous and a favorite name in journalism. He . . . bears the reputation of a humorist: but his humor is not of the conventional order; it has a wider and a loftier scope. He has a gentle yet intrepid heart, a penetrating but broad intellect, and a pen that is at once trenchant and kindly, sensible and imaginative. He is the author of some of the purest and most charming fairy-tales that have been written since Hans Christian Anderson's time. He has produced poems whose effortless art and tender pathos have brought them to the knowledge of perhaps half the newspaper readers of America; and, withal, he has poured out genuine and spontaneous fun. . . . Yet, in all his jesting, he has never jested heedlessly or cruelly. If he has laughed at what is foolish, he has honored what is good: if he has unsparingly satirized what is absurd or unworthy in our civilization, he has always reverenced what is sacred and holy in our nature. His is no common mind and we have as yet seen but a small arc of its complete circle. No man born on this continent is a more robust American than he; no man scents a sham more unerringly, or abominates it more effectively; no man's ideal of American literature is higher or sounder. And though circumstances have hitherto confined his contributions to that literature within comparatively narrow limits, yet he has given ample indications of vigorous powers and a catholic range. (pp. vii-viii)

> *Julian Hawthorne, in his preface to* Culture's Garland: Being Memoranda of the Gradual Rise of Literature, Art, Music and Society in Chicago, and Other Western Ganglia *by Eugene Field (copyright 1887 by Ticknor & Company), Ticknor and Company, 1887, pp. vii-ix.*

THE CRITIC   (essay date 1890)

Mr. Field's genius is a peculiar one; his talents are many, and his cleverness is unbounded. One gets all three in **'A Little Book of Profitable Tales,'** and at least two in **'A Little Book of Western Verse'**—which two, the reader will decide for himself. Both of these books are worth buying, reading and keeping. There is nothing just like them in English literature. The prose volume contains twenty-one original and delightful child stories; the verse volume is full of exquisite lullabies, pathetic child-verses, quaint and curious renderings of Horace, and several Western dialect rhymes which abound in wit and hilarity. . . .

[For] all the pathos of **'Little Boy Blue,'** the fun of **'Casey's Table d'Hôte,'** the exquisite fancy of **'Wynken Blynken, and Nod,'** and the keen cleverness of the Horace skits,—for all these excellent things, we still give our preference to **'A Little Book of Profitable Tales,'**—and to those tales which are written for a child's delight. Mr. Field shows a rare faculty in the choice of his topics: just a glance at the titles of these tales gives one a thrill of pleasure. **'The Symbol and the Saint,' 'The Divell's Chrystmasse,' 'Margaret: A Pearl,' 'The Fairies of Pesth,' 'The Robin and the Violet,'**—what a host of happy fancies come trooping up as we read them! Many of these tiny romances are for Christmas-time, and what happy Christmas-times little Mary French Field must have had,—she to whom her father has dedicated this book! Bravo, Mr. Field! This book is worth a thousand of the volumes written every year for children. A good child story is a good story for grown-up people, and each of these is of that kind.

> *"Two Worthy Little Books," in* The Critic, *n.s. Vol. XIV, No. 356, October 25, 1890, p. 201.*

HARPER'S NEW MONTHLY MAGAZINE   (essay date 1891)

Mr. Field has tried his clever hand in a good many ways, and [his *Little Book of Western Verse*] consists largely, perhaps too largely, of proofs of what he can do in each; if there had been more unity of direction he might have gone farther. We confess to the same misgiving about the pieces in mining-camp "dialect" that we feel concerning the pieces in archaic English; they seem to us written by a somewhat remote and exterior witness. . . . Not that Mr. Field does not do other kinds of things very well: the poems that relate to children are full of unaffected tenderness, and have now and then a keen pathos that comes from the heart and goes to it. (p. 966)

> *"Editor's Study," in* Harper's New Monthly Magazine, *Vol. LXXXII, No. CCCCXCII, May, 1891, pp. 964-68.**

THE CRITIC   (essay date 1893)

Mr. Eugene Field is a very popular writer of a somewhat peculiar style of prose and of many and various varieties of verse. . . . Mr. Field's gifts are a knowledge of the business of amusing people, an appreciation of what is pathetic or comic in the lives and manners of mankind about him, and a happy faculty of being able to adapt the more striking of his experiences, real or imaginary, to the requirements of his compositions in verse. Besides these, he has an accurate ear for rhymes, a fair notion of the mechanism of different verse-forms, and a facility in writing which enables him to keep pace with the fleetest Pegasus that may be entered in the race-track of poetry from time to time. . . . Of lullabies Mr. Field has about exhausted the stock. Many of them are tender and musical, and would, we are sure, induce slumber. But it is in the unfenced domain of comic and curious rhyme that the genial and versatile versifier moves about most gracefully, and holds his audience in a vise of risible rapture. We do not mean to jest with the Jester, nor to grow thin in practising our feeble fancy in flights of humor. We are fond—very fond—of many of Mr. Field's ingenious and ofttimes genuine verses. His first collection of **"A Little Book of Western Verse"** proved him to be a writer who can touch the hearts of his readers, and his work now as then is stamped with individuality.

This **"Second Book of Verse"** is inferior in quality to its elder brother, but it is almost certain to be as widely read and as generally admired. The most conspicuous faults in Mr. Field's verse seem to be the overdoing of a few of the commonplace metres, the occasional errors of taste in some of his humorous and harmless allusions, and the artificially pathetic verse written of children. The last-mentioned is noticeable more especially in the charming little volume entitled **"With Trumpet and Drum."** It is as a writer for children that we like Mr. Field quite as well as when he is making us weep with laughter; yet we are sure that there are many things in **"With Trumpet and Drum"** that are either inappropriate for little folk or cannot be comprehended by them.

Gladly one commends these new volumes. In them are some things almost doggerel, others almost poetry. Verse is what Mr. Field modestly and rightly calls his work; and there be many poets who might rejoice to do something as good.

> *"Mr. Eugene Field's New Verse," in* The Critic, *n.s. Vol. XIX, No. 584, April 29, 1893, p. 269.*

WILLIAM MORTON PAYNE   (essay date 1893)

Mr. Eugene Field's **"Second Book of Verse"** marks a distinct improvement upon his first. The workmanship is more careful, there are fewer infelicities of diction, and fewer lapses from good taste. Mr. Field's verse never reaches a high level of seriousness, and the more serious its aim, the more apparent is the artificiality both of sentiment and expression. A possible exception to this dictum is offered by the best of his lyrics of childhood. In these the sentiment is genuine, and the expression less strained than elsewhere. But Mr. Field's successes are achieved upon the lower, although by no means unworthy, planes of the humorous dialect ballad, the reminiscence of travel, and the song of the antiquarian or bibliomaniac. In the first of these categories **"Modjesky as Cameel"** occupies a high place. It is one of several dialect poems of the West that are quite as good as Mr. Harte's work in similar vein. Of the humorous travel-sketches **"Carlsbad"** is quite our favorite. Probably the gem of the entire collection is the fancy entitled **"Dibdin's Ghost,"** a poem that must reach the heart of every lover of rare books. (pp. 282-83)

Mr. Field's songs of childhood occupy so distinctive a place in his work as a whole that he has collected the best of them into a special volume, **"With Trumpet and Drum."** To furnish forth this charming volume both of his collections of verse have been drawn upon, and we are given such delightful pieces as **"The Sugar-Plum Tree," "Buttercup, Poppy, Forget-me-not,"** and **"Wynken, Blynken, and Nod."** As the writer of these lyrics Mr. Field has a secure place in the hearts of his readers, whatever they may think of the familiar license with which he has handled his Horace, or of the verbal vulgarisms to which he has chosen to give currency in many of his verses addressed to a maturer public. (p. 283)

> *William Morton Payne, "Recent Books of Poetry: 'Second Book of Verse',"* in The Dial *(copyright, 1893, by The Dial Publishing Company, Inc.), Vol. XIV, No. 165, May 1, 1893, pp. 282-83.**

THE ATLANTIC MONTHLY   (essay date 1893)

The newspapers have made Mr. Field's work very familiar, yet one cannot pass his *Second Book of Verse* without some mention of its Americanism, so purely of the type that will please those English cousins of ours who are unwilling to believe that any American can speak without the direct aid of his nose. Indeed, there could be no possibility of mistaking Mr. Field's work for anything but that of an American, and one to whom the West is almost as much of the world as he cares to recognize, except in European journeys undertaken for the strictly utilitarian purpose of dispelling dyspepsia and recovering from overwork. Nevertheless, it must be said that there is in Mr. Field's work a robust nonchalance, a broad vein of humor, a perfectly outspoken vulgarity,—if so harsh a word must be used,—which command a certain sort of liking from nearly all classes of readers, and wins a large number of lovers of free and easy verse completely to his side. (p. 416)

> *"Some Recent American Verse,"* in The Atlantic Monthly, *Vol. LXXII, No. CCCCXXXI, September, 1893, pp. 414-19.**

THE NATION   (essay date 1894)

[Mr. Field's *The Holy Cross, and Other Tales*] is attractively printed, with hints at the archaic which suit very well the matter of parts of the text; two or three of the stories dealing with folklore, and with that kind of aloofness from today which makes appropriate the use of such phrases as "It is to tell of," "Naught recked he," "Great marvel had he to this thing," "A full evil cat," "A monster ribald dog pup," "Now wit ye well," and so on, now like William Morris, and anon like Pepys, and again after Brander Matthews. Occasionally the grammar is a trifle archaic also, as, "whereby not only you and me but even the Jew shall be redeemed to Paradise." From this the note changes to the ultra-gushing or free-sugar style, thick with roses, angels, and birds, and lastly we have the American-humorist style—a manner for every mood. Personally we own to a preference over all the rest for **"Daniel and**

the Devil" and for **"Félice and Petit Poulain."** In these the fun and the fancy of Mr. Field leave their high-water mark, and flow along that middle way wherein he walks most safely. The one is less strained than the over-humorous **"Methuselah";** the other, a charming sketch of a French horse carried off to do duty for the Prussians, is free from the pulpiness of certain other pages. There is, however, a genuineness about even the long comings of Mr. Field which disarms irritation. It is not that affectation injures his writings; what we remark is, that lush expression does not befit a tranquilly poetic feeling, nor publicity a humor meant for the table. (p. 488)

> *"Recent Novels: 'The Holy Cross, and Other Tales',"* in The Nation, *Vol. LVIII, No. 1513, June 28, 1894, pp. 488-89.**

CATHOLIC WORLD   (essay date 1895)

Two of America's greatest poets possessed [the] heavenly gift of human assimilation; and Eugene Field, whose place in the temple of fame is now a matter of warm logomachy, was endowed with it in much greater proportion than either Longfellow or Holmes.

It may not be consolatory to the thinkers of fine thoughts to know, but it is undeniable nevertheless, that the poems which live are those which reach the million. In especial the children's poems. We do not know the poets' names, very often. Of all the songs we sung when we were toddling babies, not one gives the slightest clue to the author's identity. Eugene Field's poems bid fair to make a break in this long record of undeserved oblivion. There are songs of his destined to live when "Locksley Hall" will have vanished into the smoke of the past; for they are songs of the hearth and the domestic circle, and which touch the fountains of human affection without having to make any artesian well to get there.

And yet it would not be correct to say that Eugene Field was one of the great and the gifted in the art of poetical expression. He occupied a position somewhat akin to that of Hogarth in English art—telling us truths and interpreting for us feelings by so simple a process that the great masters looked upon it all as mere charlatanism. It is wrong to deny that Eugene Field had the poet's gift beyond the power to rhyme and put a bit of homespun human sentiment together. His inclination mostly led him to the latter form of poetical work; but he could on occasion take higher flights, as any one can easily find by looking through *A Little Book of Western Verse,* the last published volume of his collections. Some of his adaptations of Horace are especially happy, and would have been fine but for the irrepressible tendency of the poet to make fun where he should only be cheerful and witty. His imitations of old English, too, show some clever work. . . . (p. 423)

Field, in fine, was a peculiarly American institution, fully and gracefully vindicating the claims of the American character to a peculiar and well-defined national humor. (p. 424)

> *"Talk about New Books: 'A Little Book of Western Verse',"* in Catholic World *(copyright 1895 by The Missionary Society of St. Paul the Apostle in the State of New York), Vol. LXII, No. 367, October, 1895, pp. 422-24.*

EDMUND CLARENCE STEDMAN   (essay date 1895)

In paying a tribute to the mingled mirth and tenderness of Eugene Field—the poet of whose going the West may say,

"He took our daylight with him"—one of his fellow journalists has written that he was a jester, but not of the kind that Shakespeare drew in Yorick. He was not only,—so the writer implied,—the maker of jibes and fantastic devices, but the bard of friendship and affection, of melodious lyrical conceits. . . . (p. ix)

For my own part, I would select Yorick as the very forecast, in imaginative literature, of our various Eugene. Surely Shakespeare conceived the "mad rogue" of Elsinore as made up of grave and gay, of wit and gentleness, and not as a mere clown or "jig maker." (p. x)

Of all moderns . . . here or in the old world, Eugene Field seems to be most like the survival, or revival, of the ideal jester of knightly times; as if Yorick himself were incarnated, or as if a superior bearer of the bauble at the court of Italy, or of France, or of English King Hal, had come to life again— as much out of time as Twain's Yankee at the Court of Arthur; but not out of place,—for he fitted himself as aptly to his folk and region as Puck to the fays and mortals of a wood near Athens. In the days of divine sovereignty, the jester, we see, was by all odds the wise man of the palace; the real fools were those he made his butt—the foppish pages, the obsequious courtiers, the swaggering guardsmen, the insolent nobles, and not seldom majesty itself. (p. xi)

Field "caught on" to his time—a complex American, with the obstreperous *bizarrerie* of the frontier and the artistic delicacy of our oldest culture always at odds within him—but he was, above all, a child of nature, a frolic incarnate, and just as he would have been in any time or country. (p. xii)

Eugene Field was so mixed a compound that it will always be impossible quite to decide whether he was wont to judge critically of either his own conduct or his literary creations. As to the latter, he put the worst and the best side by side, and apparently cared alike for both. That he did much beneath his standard, fine and true at times,—is unquestionable, and many a set of verses went the rounds that harmed his reputation. On the whole, I think this was due to the fact that he got his stated income as a newspaper poet and jester, and had to furnish his score of "Sharps and Flats" with more or less regularity. For all this, he certainly has left pieces, compact of the rarer elements, sufficient in number to preserve for him a unique place among America's most original characters, scholarly wits, and poets of brightest fancy. Yorick is no more! But his genius will need no chance upturning of his grave-turf for its remembrance. When all is sifted, its fame is more likely to strengthen than to decline. (pp. xx-xxi)

> *Edmund Clarence Stedman, "Introduction" (originally contributed to the "Souvenir Book" of the N.Y. Hebrew Fair, December, 1895), in* The Writings in Prose and Verse of Eugene Field: The Holy Cross and Other Tales, *by Eugene Field, Charles Scribner's Sons, 1914, pp. ix-xxi.*

THE NATION   (essay date 1896)

The prose essays of which ['**The Love Affairs of a Bibliomaniac'**] consists are written in what may be called the mock-serious manner, one of the varieties of English humor which are part of the literary inheritance of the race. . . . In the '**Love Affairs of a Bibliomaniac'** we have all the machinery of this style—an imaginary friend of the author's, with a full account of his habits and character, extracts from his poems, and statements of his opinions; invented authors, fictitious quotations,

and nonsense made to masquerade as fact. Of course, these things are greatly matters of taste, but for ourselves we confess to liking good nonsense quite as well as sense; and if a great deal of it is apt to weary, Mr. Field could plead that his book was a very little one. Some of the humor is overdone, and part of the success of the volume is due, no doubt, to the fact that Chicago is as yet still proud with the pride of an overgrown village in the fact that it counts among its inhabitants persons who can write something which other people call literature, and which will be "written up" in the newspapers, and, best of all, be sold at wholesale and retail, just as pork is. The pride of locality has puffed out the sails of many a reputation less deserving than that of Mr. Field.

We have liked best the account of the physical effects produced by the respiration of books. . . . If the humor were throughout as natural and unforced as in these passages, Mr. Field would have written a classic. A melancholy interest attaches to the volume, as the author died almost in writing its last lines.

> *"Notes: 'The Love Affairs of a Bibliomaniac',"* in The Nation, *Vol. LXII, No. 1602, March 12, 1896, p. 224.*

LOUIS J. BLOCK   (essay date 1896)

[We would not say that Eugene Field's] work is deficient in finish, or that it is lacking in thought; but only that in whatever he does we find preëminent that generosity, that *bonhomie*, which is the man. Whenever we open one of his books, we find, in addition to the story or the poem or the oddity which is the product of a humor always alert, the genial personality of the author rising before us and thus enhancing the gift which his hands are bearing to us. (p. 333)

The humanity of Mr. Field has brought him safely through waters where many another vessel has gone to pieces. The dialect story or poem, if it be more than a mere curiosity or a scientific disclosure of an out-of-the-way phase of life, must reveal some trait that touches the universal heart. Mr. Field has fairly done this in his best efforts of the kind, although he would doubtless have agreed with the critic who classed the dialect effusions among writings of his that he estimated at the lowest rate.

It is always an interesting thing to watch the growth of a writer, to find him becoming gradually cognizant of where his main strength lies, and winning a mastery more and more sufficient of that strength. Mr. Roswell M. Field, in his touching memorial of his brother . . . , speaks of the deepening insight and enlarging sympathy manifest in the later years of Eugene Field's life. In [*The Holy Cross and Other Tales*], one sees this conscious command of the instrument which he has selected for his use. The motives in these stories are more home-like, the fancy is better held in check, the humor is delicate as anywhere in Field's efforts. The author is evidently making his way to the doing successfully of what he can do best. The actualities of life impress him more, the whimsicalities have in them something besides their strangeness and oddity. He is on the threshold of the book which contains so much of his sincerest thought and feeling, the **"Love Affairs of a Bibliomaniac."** . . .

The poetry of Eugene Field contains his truest contribution to the thought and art of his day; whether we consider his disclosures of the pleasures and weaknesses of the bibliophile, in which he was so immersed and which he knew so well, or whether we read his renderings of Horace into a modernity at times perhaps somewhat too insistent, we touch the truest chord of the poet's nature; and when we come to his songs of the intimate life of home and childhood, we are aware of a gift unique and tender. Whatever technical deficiencies we may find, or however a false note in some of the best known of these verses may offend our ear, we are quick to overlook it in the simplicity and genuineness of the feeling. (p. 334)

> *Louis J. Block, "Eugene Field," in* The Dial *(copyright, 1896, by The Dial Publishing Company, Inc.), Vol. XX, No. 239, June 1, 1896, pp. 333-35.*

THE ATLANTIC MONTHLY (essay date 1896)

Perhaps the most surprising characteristic of the short tales and sketches, to those who knew of Field only as a Western newspaper wit, is the old fashion of their sentiment and form. The story of the Holy Cross . . . is exactly in the tone of outworn romanticism of the early decades of the century. It recalls Chateaubriand, but without his ardency, or at least without the breath of adventure that permeates the first attempts in a given literary mode. Such pieces as **"The Oak-Tree and the Ivy,"** of which there are a great number in [*A Little Book of Profitable Tales, The Holy Cross,* and *The Second Book of Tales*], . . . are so much akin to the profitable tales which one remembers from sleepy Sunday afternoons over the godless imitators of Hans Andersen that one feels a humorous desire to charge the author with plagiarizing his own nursery books. Tale after tale, again, is written in a sort of sham-archaic diction which Field invented for himself, and which, used as it is for the most divergent purposes without a corresponding change of key, ends by giving a distressingly artificial effect. Answering to this lack of modernity in form is a still more curious persistence of old-fashioned sentiment. (p. 265)

It is only fair to add that sometimes this homeliness of sentiment, so far from being insipid, acts as a tremendous reinforcement. In such a sketch as **"The Little Yaller Baby,"** for example, the elements of pathos, though as familiar as maternity, are as poignant as the presence of death. If Field had written a dozen things like that one, he would deserve a place among those who, having known the eternal secrets of the heart, stand outside time, and of whom it is impertinent to inquire whether their work is old or new. But this intense entering into a human situation is very rare with him. Pathos his tales often have, but it is the pathos of reminiscence, the pathos of the popular song which depends upon the manipulation of a few chords warranted by long service to produce a melting effect; sincerity they have, but it is the sincerity of a mind not thoroughly awake, of an imagination not quite vitally quickened.

This lack of tenseness in Field's prose work shows itself in two striking ways, significant enough of the conditions under which he labored to deserve mention. The first is his poverty, or at least his unwarrantable repetition, of motive. The note which he struck so tenderly and resonantly in the poem by which almost alone his name is widely known, **"Little Boy Blue,"** the tragedy of childhood led away from its toys and its prattle by the shadowy hand of death, reappears again and again, in less and less persuasive adumbrations, until one's sense of delicacy is outraged, and one is forced to cry out against what has come to seem little better than cant. This is, alas, only one instance out of many; almost every striking tale or poem . . . is flanked by two, three, or half a dozen weak

replicas. The second way in which Field's lack of self-criticism and of artistic strenuousness shows itself is in his wanton marring of carefully prepared effects for the sake of introducing some bit of irrelevant humor which has struck his predatory journalistic eye. (p. 266)

It is pleasant to turn from the prose to the verse, for here we come upon bits of well-nigh flawless workmanship, and upon something that approaches supreme perception. The verse divides itself loosely under five heads: rollicking jingles, the aim of which is to raise a laugh at any cost; serious or semi-serious poems of a reflective sort; translations, both serious and flippant; dramatic poems, usually in dialect; and the inimitable "poems of childhood." The jingles are supreme in their irresponsible and delightful class. Such delectable titles as **"The Schnellest Zug," "Plaint of the Missouri 'Coon,"** and **"The Two Little Skeezucks"** only faintly suggest the joy that is in them. The author has thrown himself into these happy-go-lucky trifles with a whimsical gusto. . . . At callous moments we can find fault with them: we can see that they are too long, that their nonsense is not always so weirdly inspired as we had thought it. But for the most part we submit ourselves to their tyranny, and are left with only a titillation of fun in the roots of our hair and an unspeakable gratitude in the region of the risibles.

The reflective poems, including the more serious of the translations, are much less successful. There are, to be sure, a few pieces which command respect for their sincerity and tenderness, such for example as the famous **"Little Boy Blue"** and **Contentment,"** which latter has a note of quiet nobility thoroughly fine. Usually, however, Field had not the power to speak of old things with a new voice. Here, even more than in his prose, the lack of magnetic correspondence between substance and style is apparent. The thought does not indue itself with expression by any inner willfulness. There is a sameness of style which in the end amounts to a drone. His lack of subtlety in the perception of style is especially noteworthy in the translations. (pp. 266-67)

Closely connected with this latency of the stylistic sense is the tendency to introduce types, and not individuals, which makes the dramatic verse of Field so essentially undramatic. The pieces which deal with the life of the Western mining-camp, **"Red Hoss Mountain,"** as well as many others written in the same good-natured thumping seven-foot lines, come beyond all chance of question from the same mouth. This is not to say that they are therefore failures. By no means. . . . It is only to say that the magical touch which could lift these bundles of quizzical humors into imaginative reality . . . is hopelessly to seek.

With the same pleasure that one turns from Field's prose to his verse one turns again to that best portion of his verse which deals with child life; for here the most guarded critic can forget his qualms, and yield himself whole-heartedly to a new and naïve fascination. The reputation which some of the more serious of these child poems have achieved is not, to my thinking, wholly deserved. There is in them just a hint of stock sentiment, at the minimum in such direct and concrete things as **"Little Boy Blue,"** at the maximum in such self-conscious ones as **"The Dead Babe."** It is in the lighter, more fanciful and rollicking of the verses that the author strikes a vein thoroughly fresh and charming. . . . Always excepting Stevenson's *Child's Garden of Verse*, I know of no work, save perhaps that of Field's own friend Riley, which gives us the atmosphere of the young mind as faithfully as the delightful boyish soliloquy called **"Seein' Things at Night."** . . . Strangely enough, too, in the handling of these sympathetic little subjects, many of the technical limitations of the poet's gift which we have noticed are refined quite away. Elsewhere his sense of style is dull or non-existent; here the diction springs new as a flower out of rich deposits of nursery tradition, and the tune . . . leaps and lingers and bickers and swirls like the spirit of water. . . . It is no small thing to voice the joys and woes of one whole stage of the earthly journey, however short, especially when that stage is full of the most enormous little psychic adventures. This Field has done. He has written the Canterbury Pilgrimage of infancy. (pp. 267-68)

But Field did not pretend to be an artist; one can imagine the droll repudiation he would have made of the title. Yet at rare moments and in dealing with a few subjects he had the artist's touch. Moreover, it is not difficult to see that in the last years of his life his sense of the beauty and value of creative art rapidly deepened. . . . Yet if this rare touch had never come to him, he would still have been, from many points of view, an engaging and suggestive figure. (p. 268)

> *"Eugene Field and His Work," in* The Atlantic Monthly *(copyright © 1896, by The Atlantic Monthly Company, Boston, Mass.), Vol. LXXVIII, No. CCCCLXVI, August, 1896, pp. 265-69.*

THE NATION   (essay date 1896)

Mr. Field began by writing some very amusing caricatures of Chicago life and manners. **"Culture's Garland"** is very broad humor, but we defy any one to read the account of the literary folding-bedstead or the poems of Sappho without laughing, and for ourselves we are inclined to think that laughter, and not solemn laudation, would be to Mr. Field's shade the most refreshing tribute. When critics enter Journalia, the true divisional line between which country and Bohemia is often difficult to trace, they should remember that it is a land, as Mr. Field would have said, "to mirth devote," and that to the author of **"Casey's Tabble dote"** the more tragic life was, the more of a ridiculous jumble it became. . . .

Mr. Field's talent was distinctly imitative; he is a literary mimic, as dozens of poems show, a caricaturist, as others prove (some of his caricature Chaucerian verse is often laughable), and does not object on occasion to lower flights, when, if the humor strikes him, he will cheerfully grin at his audience through a horse-collar. He was a great practical joker, as the true journalist often is. His pathos, which is as genuine as his humor, is also quite as loose. It is good, bad, and indifferent. On the other hand, one or two of the allegories are quite as good as many of Hans Andersen's. His children's poems reek of the nursery, and often drop into genuine baby talk. Many of them are just the sort of doggerel which a gifted nurse might be able to compose. Whether they can hold their place as literature may be doubted, but then we are not sure that we know exactly what literature is, or will be. To make Mr. Field a solemn classic is a pious effort on the part of his publishers, to which every one who loves a joke will wish godspeed.

> *"The Writings in Prose and Verse of Eugene Field," in* The Nation, *Vol. 63, No. 1626, August 27, 1896, p. 165.*

THE SATURDAY REVIEW   (essay date 1898)

[We have read Eugene Field's] songs of **"Lullaby-Land"** with pleasure, with admiration, and occasionally with enthusiasm, but . . . we cannot pretend that they have subjugated us with that fascination which they appeared to have exercised in Indiana and Illinois. Eugene Field had a real metrical gift, and a choice of diction that was sometimes exquisitely tuned to the nonsensical symbolism he affected. (p. 499)

It will be acknowledged that [his poems] are instances of the very sublime of "Georgy-porgey, ride in coachey-poachey" language; and that, indeed, is what they all amount to. Eugene Field caught, with an admirable knack that was quite his own, the turn of that coaxing nonsense which cuddling mothers murmur when they want their too bright-eyed charges to put on sleep. He mixed this with something of Edward Lear, something of Hans Andersen, and he produced a very pretty manufacture of his own. We like him least when he makes faces at us over the children's head, and talks of "attenuate" sprites or speaks of a red hen's feathers as "foliage of vermilion hue." We like him best when he gives himself up most completely to the crowing music of infancy. We advise our readers to add **"Lullaby-Land"** to their nursery library, and we can promise them that they will discover in it one poem which is as good as the best in this class that was ever written. It is called **"Wynken, Blynken and Nod."** . . . (pp. 499-500)

> *"Lullaby-Land," in* The Saturday Review, *London, Vol. 86, No. 2215, April 9, 1898, pp. 499-500.*

COLIN BARCLAY MATHESON   (essay date 1901)

Field contributed [to the Chicago Daily News] a column of paragraphs, entitled *Sharps and Flats*, revealing an untiring pen, an unflagging humour and a shrewd philosophy, which caused him to be the most widely quoted of his class in the newspaper world. . . .

Humour is the conspicuous note in the larger portion of the comment . . . ; paradox and parody make up the majority of the verse; and as for the latter it is doubtful whether the author of *Love Songs of Childhood* has gained any further reputation as a poet by the fugitive pieces now presented to the reading public [in *Sharps and Flats*]. Of the political squibs, which formed so large a part of his daily column, a goodly share have been included, and there are many delicious bits of satire as pertinent now as when they were first written. (p. 72)

It is a little early to determine Eugene Field's place in permanent literature. His remarkable and far-reaching personality still holds sway among the many living who knew and admired him, and his songs of childhood, the rhythm of **"Wynken, Blynken and Nod"** sing of a subject so suggestively sweet and tender as to decry the rudeness of the critic who might probe into the art of the lullaby. . . . *Sharps and Flats* are necessarily fragmentary, yet they indicate the range of Field's capabilities and prove him a generous humourist, a keen observer and a shrewd philosopher. (p. 73)

> *Colin Barclay Matheson, " 'Sharps and Flats'," in* The Bookman, *New York (copyright, 1901, by George H. Doran Company), Vol. XIII, March, 1901, pp. 72-3.*

A. ST. JOHN ADCOCK   (essay date 1911)

[**"The Poems of Eugene Field"**] is a book of poetry that, whether it satisfies] the petty canons of the merely critical or not, will certainly move, delight, and sway the affections of men. They do not aim at giving themselves a superficial air of distinction by indulging in scholarly exercises on classical themes that were natural and fitting to their own day, but are artificial and out of date in such a day as this; they have not the finicking, effeminate airs that make so much modern poetry minor poetry and keep it so; but they have sentiment, humour, fancy, melody, and they carry these graces as a man should—manfully; they have a vigour and frank masculine quality, a strong tonic, morning message that is better worth singing than are many twilight maunderings that are perhaps more cunningly phrased. They draw their inspiration from the common life of common day; the joy and sadness in them are the joy and sadness of ordinary, healthy humanity; the beauty and tenderness of childhood, the hopes and dreams of youth, the strife, endurance, heroism, and wise disillusion of manhood and womanhood; and they have the charity and breadth of outlook that come to a man who has lived and lived long enough to know that his own world is never the only one. . . .

Some of the poems included seem to me a little trivial, some a little commonplace, but nobody will judge the book by these. There are delightfully humorous ballads and narrative poems that amply atone for them, and more than all there is a wealth of that poetry about children, quaint, fantastic, humorous, and touched with simple pathos, in the writing of which Eugene Field has scarcely a living rival. There is the same exquisite note of pathos in many of the poems of older life, such as **"Gettin' On,"** or **"Lizzie,"** or **"Telka,"** and the same winsome, whimsical humour; but always you go back for the best things to such inimitable child-poems as **"Wynken, Blynken, and Nod,"** **"At the Door,"** **"Father's Letter,"** **"The Grandsire,"** **"Little Homer's Slate,"** **"Little Boy Blue,"** **"The Rock-a-by-Lady,"** **"The Dinkey Bird,"** **"Googly-Goo,"** **"Little-Oh-Dear,"** and a score of others so familiar that one feels it is needless to quote them. . . . (p. 138)

Eugene Field is essentially the poet of the family and the fireside. (p. 139)

> *A. St. John Adcock, "For the Human Man," in* The Bookman, *London, Vol. XL, No. 237, June, 1911, pp. 138-9.*

FRED LEWIS PATTEE   (essay date 1925)

Eugene Field wrote [**"Love Affairs of a Bibliomaniac"**] not at all for the market-place; he wrote it, as all real books have been written, for himself and the gods. . . . [From] end to end of his book there is not a morbid note, not a caustic word, not a single outburst of bitterness. If you seek Eugene Field you will find him here. I know not where else. (p. 272)

Sad perplexity has Field's little book brought to librarians. It has been skied remote in the zero corner of the stacks catalogued as "bibliography"; it has been classified as "essays," as "narrative," even as "humor." No one, so far as I have known, has given it its real place; it is autobiography. The soul of the book, like the soul of every genuine book, is autobiographic. By a thousand unconscious touches Field has painted his own portrait, he has psychoanalyzed his own soul and revealed it conclusively as undamaged. (p. 274)

To escape from [the world] to Eugene Field's little book, wholesome as mountain air, human in its emotions as the men of the elder world, unhurried, cheerful, courageous; facing the quick-coming dark without whining or shudder—to escape to this was like finding an atoll in a South Seas storm and running safely within where the palm-trees make a tiny horizon of beauty and all is peace save the angry roar of the baffled ocean without. (pp. 283-84)

> *Fred Lewis Pattee, "In the Hospital Ward," in his* Tradition and Jazz *(copyright, 1925, The Century Company; copyright renewed, 1953, by Ethel B. Gorrell), The Century Company, 1925 (and reprinted by Books for Libraries Press, 1968; distributed by Arno Press, Inc.), pp. 256-89.* *

RICA BRENNER   (essay date 1933)

It is well to acknowledge at the outset that Eugene Field was not a great poet and that no one of his poems is a great poem. No note of apology, however, need accompany that statement. For, though denied a place among the great, Field was not without significance. A generation younger than the New England group of poets, he represented not only a time but a part of American life that they could never have represented. . . . [The America that Field interpreted] was fresher, less intellectualized; one with feelings more easily stirred, one interested in people and in gossip rather more than in social movements and philosophy. Moreover, Field was one of the forerunners of much of our current American verse. . . . Through him can be traced that school of writing which has developed in many ways: in those of the sentimentalist, the humorist, the "wisecracker," the topical rhymester, the self-analyst who draws his own portrait for the delight of his readers. (p. 321)

[Of Field's] quantity of verse, probably but few poems will find a long lasting place in American poetry. But the poems, both those destined to be remembered and those destined to be forgotten, reveal not only the poet Field, but also the early forms of much of our current lighter verse. . . .

The force of Field's simple emotional appeal came from a certainty of technique developed through study of the older poets. He had read Herrick, Suckling, and Skelton for variety of verse form. His reading of foreign poets resulted in translations, like those of the French poet Beranger and, particularly, those of Horace.

If, in the case of the latter, a classicist might object on the ground of accuracy, still, written as they might have been had Horace, himself, used the American idiom, the poems have unquestionably caught the spirit and tone of the Latin poet. . . . (p. 336)

The ability to catch the essential spirit of another writer and to modify it with a humorous touch is suggested by **"The Human Lad,"** a parody of Isaac Watts. . . . (p. 337)

Field's technical skill is apparent both in his metrics and in his rhymes. A glance through his collected works is sufficient to show the variety of his verse forms; and these are unerringly and gracefully handled. Almost any poem, taken at random, shows his rhyming facility. . . . One finds no false, no tortured rhymes in Field's verse. Those perfectly obvious mispronunciations necessary for rhyme, which are to be found and in great numbers, are used for the sake of humor. (pp. 337-38)

In adhering to [his] principle of self-expression, Field showed one curious manifestation. A strange duality existed in his choice of diction: a use of forms of speech with an archaic flavor that linked him to the poets of the past, and a use of current idiom that connected him with the poets that were to write in the future. The poems written in archaic diction reflected his interest in the medieval. Sometimes the device was employed primarily for the purpose of humor, as in **"A Proper**

Trewe Idyll of Camelot.'' But frequently it was used to convey the spirit of the past: something more than quaint spelling, odd words, and age-flavored figures. (p. 339)

"Marthy's Younkit" is one of Field's Red Hoss Mountain poems. These, written in dialect, give pictures of the Colorado of his time. Highly sentimentalized pictures these may be, pictures wherein the portraits are far from life-like. But they give the spirit that has come to be accepted as that of the West, a spirit made up of humor, rough actions, and tender feelings; a spirit new, and fresh, young in attitude and outlook. . . . (p. 341)

Field's use of the rich material of the Coloradan scene, alone, would mark him as an essentially American writer. But his Americanism consisted of something more than this; it embraced both his subject matter and his point of view. There was, to be sure, in Field's writing some influence of books and of various literatures; but even this influence was modified by the life about him, in which he was by turn enthusiastic observer and active participant. (pp. 341-42)

Field's humor is, for the most part, the humor of the incongruous. "A Proper Trewe Idyll of Camelot," for example, projects against the medieval past the phrases and incidents of what was Field's present; "The Conversazzhyony" presents a contrast between the ambition for sophistication and an unsophisticated background; in "The Delectable Ballad of the Waller Lot" the contrast lies between the simple incident and its epic telling. The humor may, as in "Mr. Dana of the New York Sun," be derived from some incident which helps point the jester's finger at mankind. Or it may be touched with irony, as it is in "An Imitation of Dr. Watts.". . . (p. 344)

Field's poetry reveals swift play of feeling. From one extreme to another, from bright humor to deep pathos, he varied; and in this variability, he suggested the uncontrolled emotions of a child. Always he retained something of the childish spirit. This spirit entered into his verse and made him preëminently a poet of children and of childhood. (pp. 344-45)

Of all his poems of childhood it is, indeed, the lullabies which seem to express Field's deepest feelings. (p. 346)

The road to sleep—to glamor and to surcease from care—was the road that Field constantly sought. For him it led to the past, to the security of childhood. So he sought it through his pranks, his boyish enthusiasms, his wistful clinging to youth. His very poetry was his groping effort to recapture it. (p. 347)

> Rica Brenner, "Eugene Field," in his Twelve American Poets Before 1900 (copyright 1933 by Harcourt Brace Jovanovich, Inc.; copyright 1961 by Rica Brenner; reprinted by permission of Harcourt Brace Jovanovich, Inc.), Harcourt Brace Jovanovich, 1933 (and reprinted by Books for Libraries Press, 1968; distributed by Arno Press, Inc.), pp. 321-47.

JOHN T. FLANAGAN (essay date 1945)

As a satirist Field had a real and well defined gift. Possibly not in the great tradition of Swift and Cervantes, probably because he lacked their passionate warmth, he yet could flick the peccadilloes of his time with deft asperity. . . . Field detested pretension, but he also saw its value to the satirist and he did not neglect it. Probably satire was his richest ore. Unfortunately, his earliest samples were often crude, and after he had learned how to polish his work he utilized less frequently the satirical gift in which he had proved his proficiency.

The sentimentality which distinguishes much of his later work seems fraudulent today. In other words, Field deliberately cultivated the sentimental because he was convinced of its literary value. Thus his many poems on Christmas, on domestic devotion, on the delicacy and joys of childhood are more than a little factitious, concocted for the market somewhat as a poet laureate celebrates a royal anniversary. (p. 169)

Pertinent and clever as some of the thrusts at Potter Palmer, George Pullman, Colonel McVicker are [in *Culture's Garland*], they are hardly good-humored joking. . . . Some of the most incisive satire in the book concerns the pretenders to culture, but it is not good-natured. (p. 170)

Much of Field's contemporary reputation was the result of his ability to produce humorous verse, verse which exemplified such time-honored devices as puns, quibbles, extravagant rhymes, false simplicity, and surprising epithets. . . . [In some of Field's poems] the cleverness is all verbal, a tendency which remained with [him]. He liked to toy with words, to employ them in various combinations and forms. Hence his interest in dialect and particularly in imitations of old English style. Tales like "The Cyclopeedy" and "The Little Yaller Baby" gain much of their effect from the Pike County idiom employed; "The Divell's Chrystmasse" illustrates Field's conception of mediaeval English. Usually his language was extremely simple, as in the well known poem "The Little Peach," but by the time he came to write *The Love Affairs of a Bibliomaniac* he had learned the language as well as the charm of bibliophily. But simple or erudite, Field's style was deliberately calculated to achieve an effect, and he was usually enough of an artist to succeed. (pp. 170-71)

Like Poe, Eugene Field was a meticulous and cunning workman, and again like Poe, he deliberately contrived his effects. . . . Within a certain range Field was versatile. He seemed unwilling or unable to write anything requiring sustained effort. His poems and tales—and again the parallel with Poe comes to mind—are consistently short, deft, and carefully planned. Certainly within a brief compass he secured a variety of results. The broad humor of his early western verse, often based on dialectal eccentricities, is one example, although it is often pallidly imitative of Bret Harte. Another is his Horatian poetry, parodies and elaborations rather than translations. A third group includes the imitations of old English style, with the labored archaisms, the floridness, the inverted syntax. And finally there is the verse written purely for entertainment and relying obviously on word play and nonsense. . . .

[Field's] verse is generally simple in form, quatrains, six-line stanzas, rhyming alternately, with a succession of tetrameter and trimeter lines. (p. 171)

When *A Little Book of Western Verse* appeared . . . Field, perhaps a little doubtful of its reception, provided a wistful salutation: "Go, little book; and if an one would speak thee ill, let him bethink him that thou art the child of one who loves thee well." Today such a *bon voyage* makes the reader ponder. For the book carried a miscellaneous and ill-assorted cargo. Here are various lullabies, imitations of Horace and Beranger, poems like "Krinken" and "The Little Peach" that were to achieve celebrity almost immediately, dialectal exercises like "The Conversazzhyony" which showed little originality, and verse quite as banal as most of Edgar Guest. The next half dozen years saw books pour from the pen of Eugene Field, but *A Little Book of Western Verse* still reveals best of all the breadth, the merit, and the flaws in the author's poetic gift.

Some growth is visible, to be sure, and such feeble newspaper verse as his poem in reminiscence of work on the "St. Joe Gazette" had few later parallels. But the limited range of subjects, the small emotional appeal, the simplicity of language (varied only by his later toying with archaic style), and the conventional verse forms were indicated from the beginning. . . .

Today Field's name appears on a dozen and more title pages but the quantity of genuinely meritorious work is small indeed. A handful of children's poems, a few tales, several satires and imitations survive after a full half century. Little enough to insure his reputation for another fifty years, little enough to preserve his name when his personality has faded completely from the minds of adulators! (p. 172)

> *John T. Flanagan, "Eugene Field after Fifty Years,"* in The University of Kansas City Review *(copyright University of Kansas City, 1945), Vol XI, No. 3, Spring, 1945, pp. 167-72.*

ROBERT A. DAY (essay date 1951)

If Eugene Field is remembered at all today, it is as the author of **"Little Boy Blue," "Wynken, Blinken, and Nod,"** and a few other children's poems. . . . He produced an enormous quantity of satiric prose paragraphs and sketches, which gained him much of his reputation as a wit and humorist and which have qualities that his verse never had: vigor, spice, and a sometimes exquisite and often clever sense of what can be done with the right word in the right place. The most important aspect of these sketches and squibs, however, is their purpose; for the majority of them are pungent topical satire. (p. 466)

Culture's Garland is subtitled "Memoranda of the Gradual Rise of Literature, Art, Music and Society in Chicago and Other Western Ganglia." . . . The task of making adequate illustrative comment on the volume is a difficult one. Field's fancy was inexhaustible, and he approached his game from many paths. Perhaps the device he uses most frequently is the imitation of a bit of cultural news. Sometimes the "news" in the item is entirely apocryphal; sometimes Field deals with the imaginary sayings and doings of real Chicagoans . . . ; again he writes bogus book reviews and literary notes. (p. 468)

The humor is heavy-handed; there is not the slightest doubt of what the satirist is getting at. . . . However slapdash the writing may be, it shows that Field was capable of a vigor and energy which he did not demonstrate in the poems and fairy-tales.

Perhaps the most striking characteristic of *Culture's Garland* is the astonishing number and variety of the devices Field uses to start off his sketches. In his pose as slightly bewildered or deadpan recorder of events or as passionate defender of Chicago culture, he deals with dramatic performances, opera, new books, the visits of literary notables, the reactions of Chicagoans to Eastern or European culture, various activities of Chicago cultural or literary groups, and the bons mots or adventures of the local *cognoscenti*. One trick to which he was particularly addicted was the writing of atrocious verse which he ascribed to various celebrities, local or otherwise. . . . (p. 469)

[Field's work] flicks at a multitude of stupidities, and with no light hand. It is vigorous, but uneven; it runs the gamut of wit from clumsy puns to ironical understatement. It is completely merciless, and the effect Field's biographers say it had can be deduced from its complete lack of ambiguity. Moreover, Field

often displays in it a talent for burlesque and parody, as in his imitation of Midwestern journalistic "high style." . . . He knows how to use words when he is willing to exercise his ability; his vocabulary is sizable. And it is impossible not to be convinced of Field's sincerity, even though it is hard to decide how deeply his convictions ran. (p. 473)

[In *The Love Affairs of a Bibliomaniac*], in the translations of Horace, and in the imitations of Chaucer's English, a great deal of the dilettante appears; Field seems to be a lover of books, rather than of what is in them. His Horatian poems do not differ materially in quality from those of his brother; they are no neater or more appealing; they are only somewhat more audacious and slangy. Cleverness is there, but not much intellect. This, too, is a fault of his fairy tales. They have a certain elegance and charm of diction, but on the whole they are merely a feebler version of such Oscar Wilde tales as "The Nightingale and the Rose." Of his poetry it is unnecessary to speak; it is merely meretricious. (pp. 474-75)

[Field] had a most modest view of all his work, thought his satire his best effort, and felt almost a terror—at least a complete incapacity—at coping with things as they are. On the other hand, his satire is often couched in tones of realism so blunt as to be in bad taste. (p. 476)

Historically, Field's work furnishes a commentary on one phase of America's cultural development, and gives a detailed picture of the hobbledehoy age of Chicago. As literature it is amusing, though of poor quality, and it is vigorous. It is in some respects a reflection of the tradition of American humor. . . . It reflects talent, if not genius, brilliant manipulation of words and phrases at times, and an amazing display of inventiveness and variety. . . . (p. 478)

> *Robert A. Day, "The Birth and Death of a Satirist: Eugene Field and Chicago's Growing Pains," in* American Literature *(reprinted by permission of the Publisher; copyright © 1951, copyright renewed © 1979, by Duke University Press, Durham, North Carolina), Vol. XXII, No. 4, January, 1951, pp. 466-78.*

EARL C. KUBICEK (essay date 1974)

Eugene Field is probably more favored by the elderly than the youth of today for he wrote during that mellow Indian Summer of the last century, an age which, if not of complete faith, was at least one of reasonable credulity.

Faith in Santa Claus, in elves, and in dickey-birds is not for today. This simple faith has been replaced by one born of a cynicism bred in lurid tales of death and personal destruction. In these tenderness and simplicity of spirit have little part.

Far removed from this pragmatic world is the kind of tender faith expressed by Field in his **"Hushaby Song."** . . .

As a children's poet, Eugene Field will live on if only in the hearts of those who are "young at heart." He is the poet who has the power to rekindle the spark of childhood in everyone. He brings back the glow of eternal tenderness, of gentleness, and of love. He is the Homer of childhood. . . .

While his songs of childhood will ever remain a monument to his memory, keeping it ever green, his other writings, penned over the years, mark him for posterity as having that gentle sweetness of a kindly man. His verses have the warmth, the sympathy that reawakens the inner springs of memory in their readership.

At his death a friend penned a message that well bespeaks the thoughts uppermost in the minds of those that love Field's works:

> Sleep well, dear poet of the heart!
>   In dreamless rest by cares unbroken;
> Thy mission fulfilled, in peace depart,
>   Thy message to the world is spoken.

(p. 19)

Earl C. Kubicek, "Eugene Field: Poet Laureate of Childhood," in American Book Collector, *Vol. 25, No. 2, November-December, 1974, pp. 12-19.*

ADDITIONAL BIBLIOGRAPHY

Conrow, Robert. In his *Field Days: The Life, Times, & Reputation of Eugene Field*. New York: Charles Scribner's Sons, 1974, 244 p.
> Biographical study, tracing not only the personal life of Field, but also the political and cultural climate of Chicago during his career.

Dennis, Charles H. In his *Eugene Field's Creative Years*. New York: Doubleday, Page & Co., 1924, 339 p.
> A cultural study of Field's era, discussing the social impact of his writing.

Field, Roswell Martin. "Eugene Field: A Memory" (1896). In *The Writings in Prose and Verse of Eugene Field: "A Little Book of Western Verse,"* by Eugene Field, pp. ix-xlvii. New York: Charles Scribner's Sons, 1899.
> A loving tribute by Field's brother.

Ticknor, Caroline. "Eugene Field's First Book." In her *Glimpses of Authors*, pp. 224-42. Boston: Houghton Mifflin Co., 1922.
> Explores the events leading up to the publication of *Culture's Garland,* including Field's personal thoughts regarding the book.

Jakob Ludwig Karl Grimm

1785-1863

Wilhelm Karl Grimm

1786-1859

German philologists and collectors of folk tales.

World renowned for their charming *Kinder-und Hausmärchen (Grimm's Fairy Tales)*, the brothers Grimm celebrated the richness of the German literary tradition. They are distinguished as well for their scholarly studies in the field of philology. In their efforts, they brought to light the richness of Germany's medieval language, literature, and culture.

Throughout their lives, the brothers shared a close intellectual and emotional relationship. Both studied law at Marburg University in Kassel and both were distracted from their studies by their interest in medieval German literature. After graduation, they travelled to Göttingen, where Jakob received a professorship and an appointment as librarian, and Wilhelm a position as Jakob's assistant. In 1837, when the King of Hanover objected to their political convictions, they were discharged from their duties. They later accepted teaching positions at the Berlin Academy of Sciences, where both lectured on German politics, literature, and folklore.

The partnership of the brothers was invaluable. Each complemented the other, Jakob being more scientific and scholarly, and Wilhelm more poetic. Although their most memorable works are the pieces done in collaboration, their individual efforts are also significant.

Jakob's *Deutsche Grammatik* marks the beginning of the systematic study of philology in Germany. In this work, he developed "Grimm's Law," predicated on his investigation of the German language and its origins. His *Deutsche Mythologie (Teutonic Mythology)*, a collection of the folk stories of Germany, offered the world an account of Germany's colorful mythic past. *Deutsche Mythologie* credits folklore and myth-telling as valuable art forms, which are important to a country's identity. Later, Jakob and Wilhelm collected and reprinted these folk tales.

Jakob's success was due in part to Wilhelm, who edited and transcribed his brother's work. Wilhelm also published works of his own, such as the investigative studies of German tales of heroism and mystery in *Die deutschen Heldensage* and *Über deutsche Runen*. These works were of cultural significance, for, like the works of Jakob, they reveal the faded brilliance of Germany's past.

The collaborative efforts of the brothers Grimm were their greatest works, combining Jakob's skill as a grammarian with Wilhelm's sensitivity as a man of letters. The most outstanding of their cooperative projects are *Deutsches Wörterbuch*, a German dictionary, which they began and which is recognized as comparable in importance to the *Oxford English Dictionary*, and *Grimm's Fairy Tales*, the most famous collection of folk tales. This was a compilation which the brothers transcribed

from stories recounted by peasants in the German countryside. Through this method, the Grimms hoped to preserve the oral tradition of folklore. They attributed the bulk of their findings to Frau Viehmann, a German peasant whose "Memory kept a firm hold of all sagas." The brothers were devoted to precise recreations rather than haphazard revisions. Their work was originally intended for the student of folklore rather than for the entertainment of children. Still, the fairy tales became immediately popular with children, and remain among the most famous works of children's literature.

The brothers Grimm remain an integral part of Germany's literary, philological, and historical past. In their efforts to define their literary heritage, the brothers reflect the Romantic spirit. Unfortunately for English-speaking students, many of the Grimms's scholarly contributions remain untranslated. Nonetheless, their fairy tales have provided folklore scholars with valuable information regarding the art of story-telling, and children of every age with fantasy and delight.

PRINCIPAL WORKS

Altdänische Heldenlieder [by Wilhelm Grimm]   (songs) 1811

Über den altdeutschen Meistergesang [by Jakob Grimm] (essay)   1811

Kinder-und Hausmärchen [by Jakob and Wilhelm Grimm] (fairy tales)   1812-15

   [*German Popular Stories*, 1824-26; also published as *Grimm's Fairy Tales*, 1872; *Fairy Tales*, 1900; and *Household Tales*, 1906]

Deutsche Sagen [by Jakob and Wilhelm Grimm]   (literary history)   1816

Deutsche Grammatik [by Jakob Grimm]   (grammar book) 1819-37

Über deutsche Runen [by Wilhelm Grimm]   (folklore) 1821

Die deutschen Heldensage [by Wilhelm Grimm]   (folklore) 1829

Deutsche Mythologie [by Jakob Grimm]   (folklore)   1835-54

   [*Teutonic Mythology*, 1882-88]

*Deutsches Wörterbuch [by Jakob and Wilhelm Grimm, editors]   (dictionary)   1838-1961

Geschichte der deutschen Sprache [by Jakob Grimm] (history)   1848

*This work was completed by Hildebrand, Wiegand, and others.

EDGAR TAYLOR   (essay date 1823)

[The rich collection of tales from the Brothers Grimm] is very interesting in a literary point of view, as affording a new proof of the wide and early diffusion of [the] gay creations of the imagination, apparently flowing from some great and mysterious fountain head, whence Calmuck, Russian, Celt, Scandinavian, and German, in their various ramifications, have imbibed their earliest lessons of moral instruction. (p. xvi)

The result of their labours ought to be peculiarly interesting to English readers, inasmuch as many of their national tales are proved to be of the highest Northern antiquity, and common to the parallel classes of society in countries whose populations have been long and widely disjointed. (p. xvii)

The sports and songs of children, to which MM. Grimm have directed considerable attention, often excite surprise at their striking resemblance to the usages of our own country. We wish, with Leucadia Doblado, speaking of Spanish popular sports, "that antiquarians were a more jovial and volatile race, and that some one would trace up these amusements to their common source," if such a thing were possible, or at any rate would point out their affinities. (p. xviii)

The valuable notes and dissertations added by MM. to their work, have principally for their object to establish the connexion between many . . . traditions and the ancient mythological fables of the Scandinavian and Teutonic nations. "In these popular stories," they are sanguine enough to believe, "is concealed the pure and primitive mythology of the Teutons, which has been considered as lost for ever; and they are convinced, that if such researches are continued in the different districts of Germany, the traditions of this nature which are

now neglected, will change into treasures of incredible worth, and assist in affording a new basis for the study of the origin of their ancient poetical fictions." On these points their illustrations, though sometimes overstrained, are often highly interesting and satisfactory. Perhaps more attention might have been directed to illustrate the singular admixture of oriental incidents of fairy and romance with the ruder features of Northern fable; and particularly to inform us how far the well-known vehicles of the lighter southern fictions were current at an early period in Germany. It often seems difficult to account for the currency, among the peasantry on the shores of the Baltic and the forests of the Hartz, of fictions which would seem to belong to the Entertainments of the Arabians, yet involved in legends referable to the highest Teutonic origin. (pp. xix-xx)

Among the most pleasing of the German tales are those in which animals support the leading characters. They are perhaps more venerable in their origin than the heroic and fairy tales. They are not only amusing by their playful and dramatic character, but instructive by the purity of their morality. None bear more strongly the impress of a remote Eastern original, both in their principles and their form of conveying instruction. Justice always prevails, active talent is every where successful, the amiable and generous qualities are brought forward to excite the sympathies of the reader, and in the end are constantly rewarded by triumph over lawless power. It will be observed as a peculiarity of the German fables, that they introduce even inanimate objects among their actors, a circumstance sometimes attended with considerable effect. Even the sun, the moon, and the winds form part of the *dramatis personae*. (pp. xxi-xxii)

Edgar Taylor, "Preface" (1823), in Popular Stories *by Jacob Grimm and Wilhelm Grimm, edited by Edgar Taylor, Chatto & Windus, 1920, pp. xv-xxiv.*

JAKOB GRIMM and WILHELM GRIMM   (essay date 1859?)

Our first aim in collecting these stories has been exactness and truth. We have added nothing of our own, have embellished no incident or feature of the story, but have given its substance just as we ourselves received it. It will, of course, be understood that the mode of telling and carrying out of particular details is principally due to us, but we have striven to retain everything that we knew to be characteristic, that in this respect also we might leave the collection the many-sidedness of nature. For the rest, every one engaged on a work of this kind will know that this cannot be looked on as a careless or indifferent method of collection, but that, on the contrary, a care and skill which can only be gained by time are required to distinguish the version of the story which is simpler, purer and yet more complete in itself, from the falsified one. Whenever we found that varying stories completed each other, and that no contradictory parts had to be cut out before they could be joined together, we have given them as one, but when they differed, we have given the preference to that which was the better, and have kept the other for the notes. (p. iv)

Jakob Grimm and Wilhelm Grimm, "Preface" (1859?), in their Household Tales, Vol. I, *edited and translated by Margaret Hunt, G. Bell & Sons, Ltd., 1910, pp. iii-v.*

THE CHRISTIAN EXAMINER   (essay date 1864)

Jakob and Wilhelm Grimm till but lately were the acknowledged patriarchs of German letters. . . . One in scholarship, one in love, their lives and their work were alike blended. But to recognize the spirit in which they labored in more to us here over the seas, than to commemorate the fame they won. (p. 233)

The investigations of Wilhelm Grimm were devoted chiefly to the poetry of the Middle Age, of which he published many specimens with many commentaries, remarkable alike for their profound learning and their poetic insight. Jakob took a wider flight. To develop the intellectual life of the German people, as it showed itself in their language and literature, in their law and customs and faith, and in their relations to other nations, was the task he selected and did so much to accomplish. . . . Till he came upon the stage, there was little knowledge of the beauty, and less appreciation of the importance, of the early German age. . . . Scrupulous and polished to the minutest details, Wilhelm worked out with indefatigable care the smaller subjects he selected. Restless, vigorous, anxious rather to collect than to analyze, Jakob swept over many fields for the material he mastered. To what extent the results he attained are permanent, it is useless to speculate. He was not in any degree a master of form; and it is the perfect form only which survives. . . . The works of Jakob Grimm are mines of facts, but the thought he pursues is too often buried in the mass of details he accumulates. Impatient of general conclusions, of speculations which intoxicate, but do not enrich the mind, he liked best, as he himself expresses it, to seek the universal truth in the particular fact. (pp. 234-35)

In the finer poetical sense with which they penetrated the subjects they studied, the brothers Grimm stand in striking contrast with the scholars of their age. They fled from abstractions as from a ghost of doom. Life with its earthly meaning, and as it were its bodily form in the symbolism of domestic customs and public law, in the very words even in which this symbolism was expressed,—life as it was lived, and not imagined, poetic often, but always real, full of beauty, but fuller of thought,— that was their study. In their historical representation of the sagas there is little reflection, and no invention. They borrowed from the romantic school in which they were educated nothing but its hatred of logic.

In his *Deutsche Grammatik* Jakob Grimm undertook a minute analysis of the grammatical forms of all branches of the German language. . . . (p. 235)

[The] origin and character of the tribes to which are to be traced the early dialects of Germany were reserved for his *Geschichte der deutschen Sprache,* in which he showed that it is through the Thracians that the Greeks and Romans connect themselves with the Germans,—that the Thracians have an affinity with the Getae, who are identical with the Goths,—that the Scythians are not Mongols, as Niebuhr affirmed, but composed of various races, the most important living an affinity with the Germans. And it is in this investigation that he developed with so much success the operation of the laws of the displacement of consonants and the modifications of vowels by which words of Indo-Germanic origin, as the Sanscrit, Latin, and Greek, are modified in the German dialects. (p. 236)

In the [*Deutsche*] *Mythologie,* the *Rechtsalterthümer,* and the *Weisthümer* [Jakob Grimm] develops with the same vast learning and the same poetic sympathy the religious conceptions and the domestic customs of the primitive races and the Middle Age. . . .

Vast, however, as had been their previous labors, it is in the *German Dictionary* that the singular industry and learning of the brothers Grimm are brought to bear with the most practical

results on the German language. . . . It remains a splendid *torso.* Nothing, writes Jakob Grimm, marks more clearly the distinction between the ancient and modern time, than the conception of a dictionary (*Wörterbuch*). (p. 237)

The works to which we have alluded are addressed for the most part, and in the first instance, to the narrow circle of the learned. *The Household Stories and Fairy Tales* carry the name of the brothers Grimm across the seas to many lands. There was a certain childlike freshness, a touch of perpetual youth, in these men, which drew them irresistibly to the childlike ages and the youthful thought,—which opened to them the poetry and the wisdom of a long-forgotten world. This courtly notion, they said, that whole centuries are pervaded by a barbarism, deep and obstinate, contradicts at once the benevolence of God and the experience of man. In the worst ages there is a light as of heaven, if we will but open our eyes to it. The gradual development of their language in the course of its history they did not fail to recognize and describe, but they loved best to linger over its sensuous fulness in the epochs of its formation. Yet we cannot but smile at the enthusiasm which led Jakob Grimm to regret that the Germans were ever subjected to the influence of the Roman civilization, or to be willing to sacrifice for the lost fragments of Ulfilas the whole poetry of the thirteenth century.

The first edition of the *Kinder- und Hausmährchen* . . . was the work of both brothers. The subsequent editions owed their increasing charm to the delicate taste and the scrupulous care of Wilhelm. The tales which they contain are the last relics of that mythical world which has lived through so many ages of diverse culture and a hostile religion,—taken down from the mouths of the peasants with all the *naïveté* with which they were told, with that wholly natural credulity of an ignorant but believing people from which alone the true fairy-tale can spring. To lift men out of themselves, to flatter their wishes, to make them forget the conditions to which they are chained, was, according to Goethe, the office and the charm of the genuine *Mährchen.* But myths of that sort are a growth, not an invention. You cannot write fairy-tales, you can only collect them. Especially important, therefore, is the distinction which, as Gervinus remarks, the brothers Grimm were the first to make in Germany between the creations of the people and those of the poet. As with the Greeks, the great epics of the Germans are of popular origin, of gradual development.

Still full of many plans,—his *Grammatik* to be finished, a work upon German morals to be written, another upon *Dorfweisthümer* nearly done,—indefatigable in carrying forward the *Dictionary,*—the years sat lightly upon Jacob Grimm. (pp. 238-39)

"The Brothers Grimm," in The Christian Examiner, *Vol. 77, September, 1864, pp. 232-39.*

THE NORTH AMERICAN REVIEW   (essay date 1865)

The name of Jacob Grimm has long been known as that of one of the most eminent representatives of erudition and of science produced by our century. His [*Deutsche Grammatik*], although it has done but little for learners of the German language, has not failed of even grander results, and has since the day of its publication been prized as one of the most valued guides to linguistical and ethnological researches of every kind. Of late years his colossal enterprise, the ponderous Thesaurus of his language [*Deutsches Wörterbuch*], has again brought out his name conspicuously among the *savants* of Europe, and carried it far beyond the limits of his country, not only wherever the German is read or spoken, but as far as there are lexicographers to profit from the lessons of a master in a science of which he is one of the originators. (p. 390)

[The first great work of Jacob Grimm] was the first volume of his **"German Grammar"** *(Deutsche Grammatik . . .),* which was destined to be a colossus of four thick octavos, and compared with which all his previous publications dwindled into secondary rank. It was in its scope and execution a grammar in a sense in which none had been seen before; and it has justly been said of it, that it for the first time demonstrated to the learned world what a language is. Its method was a complete revolution in the science of grammar,—the substitution of a natural and comparative process, in lieu of the former *a priori* rules, which had scarcely varied since the time of the grammarians of Alexandria and Rome. All the languages of Germanic origin were here considered as dialects of one, and not only were they subjected to a minute comparison of their sounds and forms, with a view to determining the law of their transition from one into the other, but the different epochs of each of them were also examined with scrupulous care, so as to bring out completely their history and the successive phases of their organic life. And in the execution of this plan the author not only communicated the results of his researches to his readers, but he worked as it were before their eyes, and never drew his generalizations until he had first adduced long lists of examples, all of which were derived from and credited to authentic sources. The book, it is true, became thus somewhat ponderous and unpractical; but of what consequence is this in labors of the sort? Its scientific method and exactness won it, from the outset, an authority which placed it on a level with the Comparative Anatomy of Cuvier. The plan on which Grimm's work is Grimm's work is executed must doubtless be attributed to his invention, although the movement to which it belongs goes back as far as the commencement of the century. (pp. 400-01)

[In his great work on the legal antiquities of Germany, *Deutsche Rechtsalterthümer,*] he again astonished the world of letters by demonstrating how closely the history of a nation's jurisprudence is linked to that of its manners and customs, and to its archaeology. The author here disclosed vestiges of law from sources in which no one had ever looked for them before; and his book diffused an effulgence of light on the Germanic manners of the Middle Age, which extended its beneficent rays to other nations even. (p. 401)

His study on the syntax [in the last volume of his **"Grammar"**] extends only to the end of the simple proposition, without as much as touching on the complex, in which so many and so serious difficulties are involved. He seems to have deferred the completion of it until it was too late or inconvenient to accomplish it. His **"Grammar"**, however, is nevertheless a splendid and an admirable work, and in spite of this defect we doubt if there is another one to rival it in any language. During this same period he published his edition of the text of the old popular favorite **"Renard the Fox"** *(Reinhart Fuchs . . .),* accompanied, as in other instances, by a valuable dissertation on the origin, the development and specific character, of the legends in which animals figure as interlocutors, and on the necessity of distinguishing them from the common fable, with which they had been improperly confounded.

[The last fruit of his labors] at Göttinger is one of those to which we may justly point as one of the great pillars of his vast celebrity. It is his equally original, thorough, and acute **"German Mythology"** *(Deutsche Mythologie).* . . . This work,

although not strictly a comparative mythology in the wide sense of the term, is yet one which far transcends the limits of the nation to which it properly refers, and derives light from a variety of sources more or less remotely related to its own. Its characteristic feature is the introduction of the popular element, which, up to this time, had been excluded from researchers of the kind; and its information is derived almost entirely from the traditional superstitions of past and present times. . . . It is from [the] vast mine of popular lore, which up to his day had lain unexplored by any one, that Grimm derived a multitude of myths, which to most of his readers were as novel as they are intrinsically curious and significant; and it is on this account that his **"Mythology"** from the day of its appearance became not only the model for subsequent researches of the kind, but also an invaluable guide for the exploration of other national myths more or less akin. (pp. 404-06)

[The] most important original work from [Jacob's] pen while at Berlin is his **"History of the German Language"** *(Geschichte der deutschen Sprache).* . . . This work linked itself essentially to the author's **"Grammar"**, and is in a certain sense the complement of it. The title, however, does not give us a correct idea of its character; for it is so far from tracing the development of the language to the entire extent of its history, that it scarcely passes beyond the limits of its antiquities. But these it treats with a thoroughness and exactness rarely to be met with and unsurpassed in any scientific department. All the old dialects of the German, the Gothic, the Scandinavian, the High and Low German subdivisions, &c., are here once more subjected to a close examination of their characteristic law of development, and compared not only with each other and with the kindred idioms of Indo-European descent, but even with those less related idioms geographically contiguous to them, as, for example, with the Finnish. Grimm had here again a patriotic end in view. His object was to determine with the utmost possible exactness the limits of the Germanic race and of the nations which constituted it, and to demonstrate their original identity. The work has, therefore, an immense scientific value; and although offering but little interest to the general reader, it will yet hereafter be looked upon as an indispensable introduction, not only to the history of Germany, but also to that of the barbaric invasions which buried the old Roman empire. (pp. 414-15)

[The first complete volume of the great Lexicon (*Deutsches Wörterbuch*)] embraces in its vocabulary the German language as represented by the authors of the nation for the last three centuries, commencing with Luther and ending with Goethe; that is to say, it professes to be a complete Thesaurus of the third period of the language, which Jacob in his Grammar has designated as the Modern High German. The Old and Middle High German had necessarily to be excluded from the alphabetical order of the words, but they are nevertheless respectably represented, not only in the etymological researches, but also in the quotations introduced to elucidate or define the words employed by the writers of a later date. The citations from authors are numerous, and well calculated to bring out the meanings of the word which they are intended to illustrate, while the etymological researches are such in every sense as we might expect from two great philologians who in this department stood unrivalled. The definitions are mostly in German, but under the most important words generally also, as the prospectus promised, in Latin, or in some modern language. The plan is as unique as it is comprehensive; and the work will doubtless prove an invaluable mine to the scholar and the future author of the nation, however unpalatable and comparatively useless it may be to those who are too indolent or ignorant to use it. "It appears to me," says Jacob in a letter to Adolph Regnier, "to be the first time that in the case of a modern idiom an attempt is made to make one's self master of the entire living language, by comprising in it those expressions even which it has lost in the course of the last centuries. With a view to this end, abundance and exactness of citations are indispensable. Our aim should not be to interdict the use of words to the writers of the present or of future time, but to make it easier for them to reintroduce some of those now out of date. Our object, therefore, was first of all to open a complete archive of the language, as it actually exists and has existed during the time in question, let the practical use that shall be made of it be what it may. If the work shall be continued and completed as we have commenced it, the trite complaint about the dryness of lexicons will entirely disappear." (p. 416)

[In all his writings Jacob] Grimm exhibits certain peculiarities of style which distinguish him from all other authors of his nation, with the sole exception of his brother William. Both of them show themselves accomplished writers, when in the midst of their philological technicalities they find some narrative to relate or some popular legend to record. Their *Hausmärchen* are masterpieces in the department of literature to which they belong, and never has literature succeeded so completely in imitating and reproducing the naïve simplicity of the popular mind. But Jacob has a certain manly independence and originality of style and thought peculiar to himself, and stands, in this respect, far above his brother. (pp. 420-21)

We have thus far considered Grimm chiefly as a scholar, a man of science, and a writer. If it be true that the style constitutes the man, then he who placed himself at the head of an extensive school like that of the Germanists must, in respect to his personality, have been a man not only of the primitive Teutonic force, but also one of the rarest and profoundest endowments both of the intellect and of the heart. And such he was in every sense, combining as he did the most delicate poetical sensibility with the thoroughness, exactness, and comprehension of the man of science, while the nobility and strength of his character were displayed in his devotion to his country and his nation, to honor and the truth. (p. 421)

With Grimm Germany lost one of the last representatives of the great generation of men, which rendered it illustrious in literature, science, and art, and which will be respected for centuries as one of the brightest mirrors of its individuality and history. (p. 422)

"Jacob Grimm," in The North American Review, *Vol. C, No. CCVII, April, 1865, pp. 390-422.*

JOHN RUSKIN (essay date 1868)

[Grimms' *Fairy Tales*] are in many respects common, imperfect, vulgar; but their vulgarity is of a wholesome and harmless kind. It is not, for instance, graceful English, to say that a thought "popped into Catherine's head;" but it nevertheless is far better, as an initiation into literary style, that a child should be told this than that "a subject attracted Catherine's attention." And in genuine forms of minor tradition, a rude and more or less illiterate tone will always be discernible; for all the best fairy tales have owned their birth, and the greater part of their power, to narrowness of social circumstances; they belong properly to districts in which walled cities are surrounded by bright and unblemished country, and in which a healthy and bustling town life, not highly refined, is relieved

by, and contrasted with, the calm enchantment of pastoral and woodland scenery, either under humble cultivation by peasant masters, or left in its natural solitude. Under conditions of this kind the imagination is enough excited to invent instinctively, (and rejoice in the invention of) spiritual forms of wildness and beauty, while yet it is restrained and made cheerful by the familiar accidents and relations of town life, mingling always in its fancy humorous and vulgar circumstances with pathetic ones, and never so much impressed with its supernatural phantasies as to be in danger of retaining them as any part of its religious faith. The good spirit descends gradually from an angel into a fairy, and the demon shrinks into a playful grotesque of diminutive malevolence, while yet both keep an accredited and vital influence upon the character and mind. But the language in which such ideas will be usually clothed must necessarily partake of their narrowness; and art is systematically incognizant of them, having only strength under the conditions which awake them to express itself in an irregular and gross grotesque, fit only for external architectural decoration. (pp. xi-xiii)

John Ruskin, "Introduction" (1868), in Popular Stories *by Jacob Grimm and Wilhelm Grimm, edited by Edgar Taylor, Chatto & Windus, 1920, pp. v-xiv.*

(essay date 1886)

The **"Kinder und Hausmärchen"** of the Brothers Grimm is a world-renowned book. Every collector of stories has borrowed from its treasures,—hundreds of artists have illustrated it,—plays have been founded on many of the tales,—and learned essays of deep research have been written upon it by men of literary eminence.

The Brothers Grimm themselves thus speak of their work:

We may see, not seldom, when some heaven-directed storm has beaten to the earth a whole field of ripening corn, one little spot unscathed, where yet a few ears of corn stand upright, protected by the hedge of bushes which grow beside them. The warm sun shines on them day by day, and unnoticed and forgotten they ripen and are fit for the sickle, which comes not to reap them that they may be stored in some huge granary. They remain till they are full ripe, and then the hand of some poor woman plucks and binds them together and carries them home to store them up more carefully than a whole sheaf, for perchance they will have to serve for all the winter, and she cannot tell how long beyond.

Thus does it appear to us when we consider how little is left of all that bloomed in earlier days,—how even that little is well-nigh lost, save for the popular ballads, a few legends and traditions, and these innocent Household Stories. The fire-side hearth and chimney-corner; the observance of high-days and holy-days; the solitude of the still forest-glade; above all, untroubled fancy; these have been the hedges which have kept intact the field of legendary lore and handed it down from age to age.

"Preface," in Household Stories *by the Brothers Grimm, George Routledge and Sons, 1886, p. v.*

THE CRITIC   (essay date 1894)

[Pick up old Jacob Grimm!] A breath as from some real, delicious world of ferns and greenery and leafiness, and of real women and children, blows freshly in one's face and stirs the roots of one's hair as with currents that flash from magnetic fingers. It was not in vain that the wonderful brethren went "poking about" in 1812-19 in Hesse and Hanan and gathered from cow-herds' wives as their Scheherezade the incomparable bouquet of "house tales" and fairy-lore now known as *Grimms' Tales*. All the world soon rang with the strange music of the new Oberon's horn, and its notes were such that, wild as it was, and enchanting as Hungarian music under the fingers of Liszt it instantly caught the popular ear and became intelligible to all singing and understanding creatures. . . . One cares not whether or not these tales are found in "Pentamerone" or Perrault, in Strapparola or the "Gesta Romanorum": as the Grimms tell them, they are as new as if they had never been told before, and, different from the Celtic art romances, they are full of meaning. The elaborate literary atmosphere, the air of court life which haunts and hangs around the Gaelic romantic creations is as apart from the atmosphere of the Teutonic fairy-tale as the Tannhäuser-legend in Wagner's hands is distinct from the precious original germ from which it sprang. The Celtic poem-story rather resembles the Middle-High-German court-epic with its complicated ceremonial, unreality and phantom splendor. As a test, read one of each sort to an intelligent child, and see the result.

"Fairy Tales: 'Grimms' Fairy-Tales'," in The Critic, *n.s. Vol. 22, No. 652, August 18, 1894, p. 104.*

G. P. GOOCH   (essay date 1913)

['**Kinder-und Hausmärchen**'] made the name of Grimm a household word throughout Germany. The brothers accomplished for the fairytale what Arnim and Brentano had done for the Volkslied. Herder had remarked that a collection of children's stories would be a Christmas present for the young people of the future. His forecast was fulfilled; but the main object of the work was to reveal the national wealth. The brothers strongly disapproved of the liberties which Arnim and Brentano took with their precious material. 'They care nothing for a close, historical investigation,' wrote Jacob to Wilhelm in 1809; 'they are not content to leave the old as it is, but insist on transporting it to our own time, to which it does not belong.' With their childlike natures and delight in folk-poetry the Grimms were ideal interpreters of the fairy-tale to the modern world. More than any other part of the romantic output the '**Märchen**' became part of the life of the German nation. The collection of German sagas which followed ['**Deutsche Sagen**'] was less successful. Most were already in print, though a few were added from oral tradition. A strange mixture of Christian and heathen elements, of magic and history, they were of the utmost value as a revelation of the popular mind. [Jacob] Grimm declared that the earliest history of every people was the Folk-Saga, which was always epic. He agreed with Arnim's dictum that epics composed themselves, and with the paradox of Novalis that there was more truth in the tales of the poets than in the chronicles. The Romanticists grasped the cardinal truth that the historian had to reconstruct the life and achievements of the peoples. History had neglected sagas and ballads because they contained no 'facts.' These views were powerfully expressed in the essay, '**Thoughts on Myth, Epic and History**'; but Grimm's teaching was not without grave flaws. He attributed to the sagas more historical substance than they possessed.

In his devotion to folk poetry he was unjust to other and later types. The conscious is reckoned inferior to the unconscious, individual work to the spontaneous creations of the community. He loved to regard mediaeval literature, like mediaeval cathedrals, as the anonymous expression of the soul of a people.

The repetition and development of the romanticist views of early literature led to a sharp criticism by August Schlegel, who ridiculed the contention that epics and folk-songs write themselves. That we do not know the author is no proof that they grew alone. The saga and the heroic lay were the common property, not the common product of their age. 'When we see a lofty tower rising above the habitations of men, we know that many hands brought stones for its construction; but the stones are not the tower. That is the work of the architect.' Without nature there is no life; but without art there is no form. All poetry is the combination of nature and art. Schlegel laughed at their reverence for the unimportant, their enthusiasm for old wives' fables and nursery rhymes. In the latter criticism there lurks something of the arrogance of the *Aufklärung;* but the essay as a whole came like a keen, cool breeze. The indictment extended to Grimm's etymology. The study of old German literature, he declared, could only succeed if based on exact grammatical knowledge. Grimm felt the justice of the criticism and began to turn to grammatical studies. Rask, whose Icelandic grammar he had praised on its appearance in 1811, had said that philology should not so much decree how words should be formed as describe how they had been formed and altered. This principle found a ready response in Grimm, who entertained the same reverence for language as for folk-poetry. The grammarian must be the student, not the teacher of language. Writing in the noonday of the *Aufklärung,* Adelung despised dialects, and constrained the language with bit and bridle. Others urged the expulsion of certain words and the alteration of many more. The attack on ancient forms was as repugnant to Grimm as an outrage on morals. The production of a bald uniformity was like the method of the Terrorists in the French Revolution; and the fabrication of new words was a sin. It was the wrinkles and warts that gave the incommunicable stamp of home, as on a familiar face. In place of learned pedantry and levelling reform he offered historical grammar, which taught respect for every living element. (pp. 56-7)

The purpose of [Jacob Grimm's '**Deutsche Grammatik**'] was to reveal the operation of law in language as in history; and the key could only be recovered by careful comparison of all Teutonic languages and dialects. His chief thesis was that all the families of Germany speech were closely related and that the present forms were unintelligible without a reference to the oldest. He made full use of the work of his predecessors, above all of Hickes and Rask and, in another field, of Bopp; but he introduced the comparative method into Teutonic philology. In the purely German territory he had to lay the foundations himself; and an architectural whole appeared where there had been nothing but isolated details. The book gave far more than its title suggested for it was in truth a history of the Teutonic languages. Grimm's masterpiece formed one of the instruments by which historical science has ever since made its advance. The most competent of judges, Benecke, declared that he did not know whether most to admire the author's insight or knowledge. His old critic Schlegel, hastened to express his congratulations. (p. 58)

The work was out of print in a year, and in 1820 its author began to rewrite it. He made new and important discoveries as he worked, and the printed sheets were revised by Lachmann. The arrangement of material was improved, and the second edition was in many respects a new work. The most important addition was the statement of **'Grimm's Law,'** or the explanation of the change of letters. There were laws of sound. No words could be traced to a common origin unless the differences in their sounds could be explained by a law of variation. In this way the relations of peoples could be recovered, and some knowledge of the early life of humanity be obtained. Three further volumes of the **'Grammatik'** were published, the latest attacking the problems of syntax. When the publisher inquired whether Grimm preferred to complete or to revise his work, he chose the latter. Though incomplete, it is beyond comparison the most important work ever devoted to German philology. No one had ever penetrated so deep into the innermost recesses of language and seized its intimate relation to life. In becoming a philologist Grimm did not cease to be a poet. His creative insight is continually flashing light on dark places. Adelung had asked what sense there could be in giving a sex to lifeless things and abstract conceptions. Grimm answers by trying to retrace the path along which primitive fancy moved. In its early forms language is concrete and pictorial; in its later, abstract and intellectual. This view of the transition from the sensible to the rational was a weighty contribution to the history of mankind.

Between the first two and the last two volumes of the **'Grammatik'** Grimm published his marvellous work on Legal Antiquities, a picture of early German life from a particular angle. The differences he had shown to exist between the early and later stages of literature and language existed equally in the realm of law and religion. . . . He was especially interested in symbolic actions, the forms in which conceptions expressed themselves. In an early essay on Poetry in Law, he had declared that they had grown in one bed. The poet and the judge alike uttered the common thoughts. He was unjustly accused of failing to treat the subject historically or to trace the gradual transformation of institutions. . . . He confined himself to the sensible, the visible, the pictorial element, the customs and uses, the actions and forms which an unlettered age demanded. His chief authorities were the so-called Weistümer, or dooms, and early literature and legend. No jurist could have written the book, for no jurist possessed the requisite knowledge of the languages and literatures of the mediaeval Teutonic world. While Eichhorn desired to discuss the foundations of modern law and practice, Grimm never troubled himself about later developments. Every usage possessed its importance as an expression of the folk-spirit.

The book was hailed with delight by the jurists of Germany. Savigny rejoiced in the brilliant development given to his own teaching. Eichhorn was warm in his praise, without realising to the full extent its creative character. Michelet gave intense satisfaction to the modest author by building his own 'Symbolic Origins of French Law' on its foundations. Grimm truly declared that his book was a work of suggestion. Its suggestiveness is still unexhausted nearly a century after its appearance, and its influence may be traced in every subsequent writer on early Teutonic law. (pp. 58-9)

A further aspect of early Teutonic life was explored in the **'German Mythology.'** . . . 'In my books,' declared Grimm in the preface, 'I have tried to show that the language of our ancestors was not rough and wild but fine and harmonious; that they did not live in hordes but were free, moral and observant of law. I now desire to exhibit their hearts full of belief, to recall their magnificent if imperfect conceptions of higher

beings.' Literature, sagas, fairy-tales, customs, language were made to yield their contribution, and a mass of oral matter was collected. The old world revived with its brilliant colouring and fantastic shapes. The stage was crowded with gods, swan-maidens, nixies, cobolds, elfs, dwarfs and giants. Mythology being a creation of the poetical spirit, the talent of Grimm was peculiarly fitted to deal with it. . . . The **'German Mythology'** took its place among the classics of European scholarship. But though it is often regarded as his most perfect work, and though its vitality and insight are marvellous, it is not without serious faults. The picture of Teutonic civilisation is too rosy, and he credits early times with many customs and beliefs of subsequent growth. (p. 60)

[Grimm's **'History of the German Language'**] was rather a series of dissertations than a connected narrative, and may almost be described as an appendix to the Grammar. . . . The researches of Zeuss had interested him in ethnography; and though parts of the work are fantastic and some of its identifications of early tribes incorrect, the attempt to throw the light of philology on ethnology and culture was not without importance. (pp. 60-1)

[Wilhelm Grimm's] greatest achievement was his study of the German heroic saga. His scope was far narrower than that of his brother. It was his instinct rather to select a limited territory and to examine every corner of it with loving care than to roam over immense tracts of country. He lacked the creative genius of Jacob; but he was the more exact and careful worker. The relations of the brothers form one of the idylls in the history of scholarship, and they remain associated in the memory as they appear in the frontispiece of the Dictionary. They loved the German people, and their love has been richly repaid. They rank immediately after Goethe and Schiller among the spiritual influences which have made Germans all over the world conscious of their unity. (p. 61)

> *G. P. Gooch, "Jacob Grimm," in his* History and Historians in the Nineteenth Century *(copyright, 1913 Longmans, Green & Company; reprinted by permission of the Literary Estate of G. P. Gooch), Longmans, Green, 1913 (and reprinted by Peter Smith, 1949, pp. 54-63).*

W. P. KER (essay date 1915)

[The ***Kinder- und Hausmärchen,***] the best known of their books, seems to have come to [the brothers Grimm] almost without thinking. Folk tales could be picked up anywhere in Hesse, at their very doors. They were left to Wilhelm Grimm to comment and illustrate, while Jacob kept them in mind for his ***Mythology*** later. Wilhelm shared in many other works of that time; particularly in that lone first volume of the ***Elder Edda*** where in translation of the old Northern poems (beginning with Völund's Lay and going down to the Death-ride of Brynhild) is shown the same skill of narrative style as in the popular tales. Jacob by himself about the same time published one of the pleasantest of all his collections, the little volume of Spanish ballads, ***Silva de romances viejos***—which shows that he could occasionally wander away from his old German forests. (p. 226)

The brothers Grimm have a place in the history of the Romantic School, but they are not subject to every vanity of that creature. They had not much taste for romantic excursions and inventions; their temper is just the opposite of that empty romantic craving, like the hunger of lean kine, which sent the poets and novelists ranging over the Universe in search of subjects, properties, and local colour. (p. 229)

For every student it must be of interest to follow the record of so great a learner and teacher, so enthusiastic and so painstaking. And by the way it may be interesting to compare the opinions of Jacob Grimm with those of his great contemporary Hegel. The men resemble one another in their vast ideals and their capacity for taking pains; and Hegel was, further, himself a student of literary history and especially of poetry. At first we may be inclined to say that he and Jacob Grimm divide the range of poetry between them; Hegel's poets are the tragedians, while for Grimm dramatic poetry is something like the devil; it is that mode of human thought most different from Nature-poetry, from the inspired original epic of the golden heroic age. Hegel speaks slightingly of the *Nibelungen* (though he respects Ossian); he looks like a champion of the classics against the barbarism of the North. But he is much more liberal than he sometimes appears, and more in agreement with the tastes of the brothers Grimm. He is fond of ballads; he names Fauriel's collection of Romaic popular songs; he has higher praise for the Arabian poems of the "Ignorance"; the Cid is one of his heroes; and his descriptions of the heroic age and of the age of chivalry show his talent as an abstractor of quintessence, as well as his sympathy with the literary fashions of his time, even with the Romantic School. (pp. 232-33)

Grimm's large additions to positive science seem at times like the result of chance. They came as a precipitate from the most extraordinary vague vapour of ideas—a strange enthusiastic religion, the worship of an imaginary golden age. In details, the work of Jacob Grimm is sometimes as extravagant as the derivation of *cheval* from *equus:* Plato's *Cratylus* is no more antiquated in Philology than some of the early papers of Jacob Grimm. But the cloud of his fancies and aspirations had fire and life in it; and the history of Jacob Grimm, his progress and his conquests, is a demonstration of the power of that great god *Wish* whom Jacob Grimm was the first to name. The moral seems to be *Fay ce que voudras,* when that counsel is rightly understood. It was never intended for any but honourable persons, and of such was Jacob Grimm, and Wilhelm his brother. (p. 233)

> *W. P. Ker, "Jacob Grimm" (originally an address presented to the Philological Society on May 7, 1915), in his* Collected Essays of W. P. Ker, Vol. II, *edited by Charles Whibley, Macmillan and Co., Limited, 1925, pp. 222-33.*

PADRAIC COLUM   (essay date 1944)

"Household Tales," almost the first, have remained the most popular of the collections of European folk-tales. To the great German pioneers and to the many who followed them in various European countries, all imaginative and studious men, we owe a deep debt of gratitude. They brought us lore that will always be an entertainment for us; they brought us, too, an account of our forefathers' ways which we should be mindful of. The people who told and who listened to the traditional stories lived under emperors, monarchs, viceroys; they spoke diverse languages; they lived on mountains and in valleys, in forests and dales. But they were at one in their love for certain things—for human good nature, for enterprise, wisdom and devotion, for the genius through which men are drawn to the far-off and the superior—the Golden Tree, the Water of Life, the Matchless Maiden.

We have another past besides the past that history tells us about, a past which is in us, in individuals, more livingly than the recorded past. It is a past in which men slowly arrived at self-consciousness while building up the community, the arts and the laws. Today we have advanced poets and novelists who are trying to find means to suggest the unrecorded past in our memories and in our attitudes and so give their work another dimension. Well, it is this long past, the past that merges with the time when men were comradely with the animals and personalized the powers of nature that comes over to us in these and in other traditional stories. With it certain things are restored to our imagination. Wilhelm Grimm who knew much more about the inwardness of these stories than the philologists and the historians of culture who were to comment on them was aware of "fragments of belief dating back to most ancient times, in which spiritual things are expressed in a figurative manner." "The mythic element," he told us, "resembles small pieces of a shattered jewel which are lying strewn on the ground all overgrown with grass and flowers, and can only be discovered by the most far-seeing eye." "Their signification has long been lost, but it is still felt," he says, "and imparts value to the story." It is this felt but hidden value that makes a connection between certain subtle modern works and these old-world fairy tales. (pp. xiii-xiv)

> *Padraic Colum, "Introduction" (reprinted by permission of the Literary Estate of Padraic Colum),* The Complete Grimm's Fairy Tales *by Jacob Grimm and Wilhelm Grimm, translated by Margaret Hunt and James Stern, Pantheon Books, 1944 (and reprinted by Pantheon Books, 1974, pp. vii-xiv).*

JOSEPH CAMPBELL   (essay date 1944)

The special distinction of the work of Jacob and Wilhelm Grimm . . . was its scholarly regard for the sources. Earlier collectors had felt free to manipulate folk materials; the Grimms were concerned to let the speech of the people break directly into print. Among the Romantics of the generation just preceding, folk poetry had been venerated profoundly. Novalis had pronounced the folk tale, the primary and highest poetical creation of man. . . . Sir Walter Scott had collected and studied the balladry of the Scottish border. Wordsworth had sung of the Reaper. Yet no one before the Grimms had really acquiesced to the irregularities, the boorishness, the simplicity, of the folk talk. Anthologists had arranged, restored, and tempered; poets had built new masterpieces out of the rich raw material. But an essentially ethnographical approach, no one had so much as conceived.

The remarkable fact is that the Grimm brothers never *developed* their idea; they began with it full blown, as young students hardly out of law school. . . . [While assisting Clemens Brentano and Ludwig Achim von Arnim with their collection of folk songs, *Des Knaben Wunderhorn,* the Brothers Grimm were, at the same time] seeking out, deciphering, and beginning to edit, manuscripts from the Middle Ages. The book of fairy tales represented only a fraction of their immediate project. (pp. 834-35)

> *Joseph Campbell, "Folkloristic Commentary" (reprinted by permission of Russell & Volkening, Inc, as agents for the author), in* The Complete Grimm's Fairy Tales *by Jacob Grimm and Wilhelm Grimm, translated by Margaret Hunt and James Stern, Pantheon Books, 1944 (and reprinted by Pantheon Books, 1974, pp. 833-62).**

W. H. AUDEN (essay date 1952)

Many deplorable features of modern life, irrationalism, nationalism, idolization of mass-feeling and mass-opinion, may be traced back to the Romantic reaction against the Enlightenment and its Polite Learning; but that same reaction is also responsible for the work of Jacob and Wilhelm Grimm who, with their successors, made the fairy story a part of general education, a deed which few will regret. (p. 198)

There are quite a number of people who disapprove of fairy tales for children, and on various grounds. Let us take the most reasonable first: those who claim that the fairy tale as we know it from Grimm and Andersen is not viable in modern culture. Such tales, they argue, developed in a feudally organized society which believed in magic, and are irrelevant to an industrialized democracy like our own. Luckily the test of viability is a simple one. If a tale is enjoyed by the reader, or audience, it is viable; if he finds it boring or incomprehensible, it is not. (p. 199)

The second charge against fairy tales is that they harm the child by frightening him or arousing his sadistic impulses. To prove the latter, one would have to show in a controlled experiment that children who have read fairy stories were more often guilty of cruelty than those who had not. Aggressive, destructive, sadistic impulses every child has and, on the whole, their symbolic verbal discharge seems to be rather a safety valve than an incitement to overt action. . . .

Lastly there are the people who object to fairy stories on the grounds that they are not objectively true, that giants, witches, two-headed dragons, magic carpets, etc., do not exist; and that, instead of indulging his fantasies in fairy tales, the child should be taught how to adopt to reality by studying history and mechanics. I find such people, I must confess, so unsympathetic and peculiar that I do not know how to argue with them. If their case were sound, the world should be full of Don Quixote-like madmen attempting to fly from New York to Philadelphia on a broomstick or covering a telephone with kisses in the belief that it was their enchanted girl friend. (p. 200)

A fairy story, as distinct from a merry tale, or an animal story, is a serious tale with a human hero and a happy ending. The progression of its hero is the reverse of the tragic hero's: at the beginning he is either socially obscure or despised as being stupid or untalented, lacking in the heroic virtues, but at the end, he has surprised everyone by demonstrating his heroism and winning fame, riches, and love. Though ultimately he succeeds, he does not do so without a struggle in which his success is in doubt, for opposed to him are not only natural difficulties like glass mountains, or barriers of flame, but also hostile wicked powers, step-mothers, jealous brothers and witches. In many cases, indeed, he would fail were he not assisted by friendly powers who give him instructions or perform tasks for him which he cannot do himself; that is, in addition to his own powers, he needs luck, but this luck is not fortuitous but dependent upon his character and his actions. The tale ends with the establishment of justice; not only are the good rewarded but also the evil are punished.

Take, for example, **"The Water of Life."** Three brothers set out in turn on a difficult quest to find the water of life to restore the King, their sick father, to health. Each one meets a dwarf who asks him where he is going. The two elder give rude answers and are punished by being imprisoned in ravines. The third brother gives a courteous answer and is rewarded by being told where the water of life is and how to appease the lions

who guard it, but is warned to leave before the clock strikes twelve. He reaches the enchanted castle, where he finds a princess who tells him to return in a year and marry her. At this point he almost fails because he falls asleep and only just manages to escape as the clock strikes twelve and the iron door shuts, carrying away a piece of his heel. On the way home he again meets the dwarf and begs him to release his brothers, which he does with a warning that they have bad hearts. The brothers steal the water of life from him and substitute salt water so that his father condemns him to be secretly shot. The huntsman entrusted with the task has not the heart to do it, and lets the young prince go away into the forest. Now begins a second quest for the Princess. She has built a golden road to test her suitors. Whoever rides straight up it is to be admitted, whoever rides to the side is not. When the two elder brothers come to it, they think "it would be a sin and a shame to ride over that" and so fail the test. At the end of the year, the exiled brother rides thither but is so preoccupied with thinking of the Princess that he never notices the golden road and rides straight up. They are married, the King learns how the elder brothers had betrayed the Prince, and they, to escape punishment, put to sea and never come back.

The hero is in the third or inferior position. (The youngest son inherits least.) There are two quests, each involving a test which the hero passes and his brothers fail.

The first test is the encounter with the dwarf. The elder brothers disregard him a) because he looks like the last person on earth who could help them; b) they are impatient and thinking only of their success; and c) what is wrong with their concentration on their task is, firstly, over-self-confidence in their own powers and, secondly, the selfishness of their motive. They do not really love their father but want him to reward them.

The hero, on the other hand, is a) humble enough; b) cares enough for his father's recovery; and c) has a loving disposition toward all men, so that he asks the dwarf for assistance and gets it.

The second test of the golden road is a reversal of the first: the right thing to do this time is to take no notice of it. The brothers who dismissed the dwarf notice the road because of its worldly value, which is more to them than any Princess, while the hero, who paid attention to the dwarf, ignores the road because he is truly in love. (pp. 201-02)

If such a tale is not history, what is it about? Broadly speaking, and in most cases, the fairy tale is a dramatic projection in symbolic images of the life of the psyche, and it can travel from one country to another, one culture to another culture, whenever what it has to say holds good for human nature in both, despite their differences. Insofar as the myth is valid, the events of the story and its basic images will appeal irrespective of the artistic value of their narration; a genuine myth, like the Chaplin clown, can always be recognized by the fact that its appeal cuts across all differences between highbrow and lowbrow tastes. Further, no one conscious analysis can exhaust its meaning, There is no harm, however, if this is realized, in trying to give one.

Thus reading **"The Water of Life,"** it occurs to me that the two quests, for the water which heals the old sick King and the Princess through marriage with whom the new life will come into being are one and the same, though it is only by first trying to restore the past that one comes to discover one's future path. (p. 203)

The Grimm brothers were the first men to attempt to record folk tales exactly as they were told by the folk themselves without concessions to bourgeois prudery or cultured literary canon, an example which, in the case of prudery, at least, has not been followed, I am sorry to say, by their translators. (p. 204)

> W. H. Auden, "Grimm and Andersen" (originally published as his introduction to Tales of Grimm and Andersen, edited by Frederick Jacobi, Jr., Modern Library, 1952), in his Foreword and Afterwords, edited by Edward Mendelson (copyright © 1973 by W. H. Auden; reprinted by permission of Random House, Inc.), Random House, 1973, pp. 198-208.*

RENÉ WELLEK (essay date 1955)

[Jakob Grimm,] who was the greater scholar of the two, formulated the more extreme view of natural poetry as composing itself, quite unconsciously, far in the dim past and as gradually deteriorating with the distance from the divine source of Revelation, the childhood of mankind, which shone for him in the bright light of paradisaical reminiscence. Wilhelm Grimm . . . , had a greater trust in human nature and was prepared to admit that even contemporary poets can and should achieve "nature." Wilhelm was the more artistic of the two brothers: he translated verse very well and to him we owe, apparently, the stylistic form of the fairy tales. Jakob, who wrote in a terse and often crabbed style, had hardly any interest in modern literature. He lived completely in the past, among the Teutonic myths, the *Nibelungen,* the *Edda,* fairy tales, legends, fables, everything that seemed to him ancient and Germanic. But though his writings are permeated by a fervent pan-Teutonic patriotism, one must beware of thinking him ignorant or uninterested in other nations. Jakob studied and admired folk poetry wherever he found it. . . . (pp. 283-84)

While many of Jakob's early reviews and articles define his general position, the correspondence with Arnim gives the clearest statement. There is, Jakob Grimm asserts, an eternal distinction between nature poetry and art poetry. They are so different that they cannot exist simultaneously. Ancient nature poetry is based on myth, and our standard of judging it must be whether the poetry is more or less faithful to this basis. Grimm expressly chides those who would make aesthetic distinctions in the study of Old Germanic poetry: whatever is to be studied is the myth and the myth itself makes a totality dependent on its time, which thus can be recognized even from misshapen and dead forms. The historian of nature poetry must explain and describe the different shapes in which the myth appeared and trace it back as far as possible to its origins. History, in the sense of factual truth, seems to Grimm always subordinated to myth and poetry, but great historical events are necessary as a stimulus to the creation of heroic myth. (p. 284)

The exact way this original poetry composed itself remains, however, quite mysterious. Collective creation is pushed so far into the past that the origins of poetry and myth become fused and we are brought up against something ultimate whose source is Divine Revelation. The whole process since then has been one of decay, in exact parallel to the history of language, which Grimm conceives of as decaying from its pristine stage by shedding cases, verbal forms, suffixes, and so on. Only in 1893 did Otto Jespersen succeed in reversing this view by arguing for progress in language toward simplicity and lack of inflection. . . . The epic, fairy tales, local legends, folk songs,

even animal fables are thus looked at as hallowed relics of the divine youth, the golden age of humanity. Grimm argued vigorously for considering the *Renard* stories as remains of a genuine old epic cycle of primitive antiquity when men lived with animals and recognized their human features as a matter of course. Grimm stresses the folk element in the Renard stories, deriving the name from the Germanic *Reginhald* (adviser); he fails to see the satirical, ironical, and definitely clerical tone of the early medieval versions. (pp. 285-86)

Grimm is always cool to art poetry. In reflections occasioned by a trip to Italy (1844) he condemns all Italian literature as artificial. The contents of Dante are dead, Petrarch is a derivative of the troubadours, Ariosto ridicules the ancient epic, Tasso is a sentimentalist. Only Boccaccio, presumably because he is nearest to the people, finds favor in Grimm's eyes. (p. 286)

Wilhelm Grimm shares in most respects his brother's views and tastes. His discussion of the origin of Old Germanic poetry . . . also asserts that history and poetry were originally the same and that the two together made the epic. . . . Wilhelm Grimm sets off very sharply (far too sharply, we would say today) [The *Nibelungenlied,*] which is completely indigenous and shows no foreign trait, against the courtly poetry of the time, which does not "directly concern the essence of genuinely German poetry." It was the product of a class, and since national poetry was then still alive, it was not merely art poetry but "mannered" poetry, "completely outside the spirit of the nation."

But Wilhelm, in spite of these pronouncements, has more understanding for art poetry than his brother, and has a greater trust in the continuity of human creativeness. While Jakob deplores even his brother's translations from the *Edda* and the Danish ballads and resigns himself to the fact that ancient poetry is completely irrecoverable, except to the historical scholar, Wilhelm defends modernizations and adaptations and even grants that the distinction between nature and art poetry need not be completely rigid. (pp. 286-87)

In most details the general structure of the Grimms has since crumbled. The reaction against their views has gone far. Much evidence has been accumulated to show that a great deal of what they considered folk literature is the composition of a single author in the Western tradition and not unacquainted with antiquity. The *Nibelungen,* the *Edda,* even *Beowulf,* are neither primitive nor purely Teutonic. The *chansons de geste* have been shown to be monkish compositions. Folk songs, fairy tales, and chapbooks are frequently quite late in origin, traceable even to specific authors and full of the devices and traditions of artificial poetry. . . . Granted the exaggeration of [the Grimms'] position, there is much in it that is basically sound. Medieval poetry has ultimate roots in folk poetry and folk traditions. Scholars are even coming back to the view that the courtly love lyric has its origins in folk forms. Myth is almost palpably discernible behind much poetry even of modern times, and the "archetypal patterns," derived from Jung and expounded by Maud Bodkin, do not differ substantially from what the Grimms meant by myth. While the dichotomy of natural and artificial poetry is indefensible if it implies different aesthetic standards, undoubtedly folk poetry does have its own specific ways of creation and specific problems of transmission and social setting, which are very different from those of written literature and can still be observed today in many countries. The study of oral literature is an indispensable part of literary scholarship. The Grimms were wrong only in pushing it too far into the past and thus preventing clear discriminations between myth and actual poetry. Finally, nobody need sympathize with their very influential dislike for the tradition of complex learned poetry of the West. (pp. 287-88)

*René Wellek, "The Younger German Romantics,"
in his* A History of Modern Criticism, 1750-1950
*(copyright, 1955, by Yale University Press), Yale
University Press, 1955, pp. 279-97.**

ARLAND USSHER and CARL von METZRADT
(essay date 1957)

What is the real significance of the stepmother—that ever-recurring personage in the folk-tales, always depicted as fair without and foul within? There is evidently more here than the natural dislike of the interloper—the rival in the father's affections; the position of real stepmothers is always delicate, but they are not necessarily for that reason either beautiful or wicked. Moreover a man making a second marriage is generally at an age of mature judgment and presumably not without some care of providing a good mother for his children. Into the Sophoclean dooms of the Freudian incest-patterns one forbears to enter; beyond suggesting, perhaps, that we see and dislike in the Stepmother the image of *the Parent,* cut loose from custom and consanguinity and (as it were) objectified—we vent upon her the resentment of the Undivided Principle in us against this world of division and suffering into which we are flung. But it will be preferable to follow tracks less well-trodden by the dismal psychological determinism of today. Is there perhaps a danger and a fallacy lurking in that "mature and considered choice" of the father? Is it not the very type of the human "freewill," which begins by oppressing and tormenting the children-instincts—that rational will which is a portion of the eternal order inserted in the temporal, and which, till it has learned a divine acceptance, can only be a demoniacal destroyer, a literal thorn in the living flesh—that "ideal" which our civilisation has found to be such a perfect marriage-bed? Is the Stepmother the archetypal example of the Second Thought—often fallaciously held to be the best: the Second Chance—supposed to correct the first: the *esprit de l'escalier*—almost always too perfect to be "right"? Adam, according to the Cabbalistic tradition, had two wives: Eve, who ate of the Forbidden Fruit and became a human sinner, and Lilith, who did *not* eat of it—refusing childbearing—and became a demon. And though Lilith in the legend was Adam's *first* wife, the pattern is the same; every man who comes into the world is wived by these two women, the productive and the sterile one, the sinner through love and the sinner through pride, the body and the brain—the pair who perhaps re-appear in the figures of Martha and Mary, raised to a new innocence, and the order of higher and lower inverted. This lengthy preamble was necessary if we are to understand the story of *Sneewittchen* ["**Snow-White**"] pursued by the unrelenting hate of the Stepmother-Queen, as was Virgil's Aeneas by the Queen of the Gods. At the outset we are shown two contrasting pictures—a Mother who looks out of a window and, a little later, a Stepmother who looks into a mirror. The Mother has pricked her finger in sewing, the usual *three* blood-drops fall on the snow, and she wishes for a daughter as white as the snow, as red as the blood, as black as the window-frame: the very colours of a new Dawn on the margin of Night and Day. Her wish is granted, but—as generally happens with wishes—at a price; the Mother loses her life, and the Stepmother soon after reigns in her stead—the spirit of Night continues to make itself felt, but now banefully, as it were on the other side of reality, like a mental image from which vital meaning has departed. The King, in re-mar-

rying, calls on the Past, which was a true mother to the Present, but—like all who make the attempt to fix what should be fugitive—he only succeeds in calling up a vampire-like semblance. The Princess reaches that climacteric of childhood the seventh year, and is "fair as the day"; when the Stepmother, who has the habit of asking questions of her mirror (as if to suggest that her existence is only a mental or "ideal" one), receives the disturbing reply that Snow-White is a thousand times fairer than she. The Queen orders a huntsman to take the child away and destroy her, but to bring back the lungs and liver; the huntsman however—smitten with pity—lets her go free in the forest, and hoodwinks the Queen by bringing her the liver and lungs of a beast, which the wicked woman greedily devours. There is here a suggestion that the forms of the Past, in trying to draw posthumous life from the Present, can only absorb bestial and bestialising elements, as we have seen in various regressive or reactionary movements of our time—their communion, or community-spirit, is that of the Black Mass which is always parodying the White, and often enough does so in what is called "good faith." Snow-White, wandering in the labyrinthine ways of her threatened but growing life, happens upon a hut owned by seven dwarfs, diggers for gold and metals, who receive her kindly; it is the Flight into Egypt, that land of mystery and gold, where all treasures are delved after and guarded for the future. And now begins a series of renewed attempts on her life by the wicked Queen, for the mirror of the rational self—of the abstract mind's "speculation"—reveals to her that the young Princess is alive and where she is hidden; with the patience of blind and narrow wills, she comes to the door of the hut three times in the garb of a pedlar. The first time, she comes selling laces, and, offering to lace Snow-White's bodice for her, she tightens it until the girl falls as if dead. On the second occasion she sells her a poisoned comb, with which she insists on combing her head; the poison works upon the Princess, who again falls in a deep swoon. After both these attempts, Snow-White is revived by the seven dwarfs, who return like the seven planets in the sky at every sundown. But the Queen, whose malice is as persistent as the Princess's simplicity, comes a third time, and now she sells her an apple of which one half is poisoned; being tempted with this, the rosy half, the girl eats and falls dead—in earnest at last, as it seems. The manner of the three temptations is here to be noted; the Princess's emotional self is assaulted through the constriction of the ribbon, her cerebral self through the comb, her volitional self—traditionally seated in the belly—through the apple. But only the apple is fatal to her—as it was to Eve; for only the falsification of the instincts and the will can work deep change or injury in the human being. Now indeed the ministrations of the good dwarfs are unavailing; the kindly genii of Nature cannot help the person in whom the poison of the "Stepmother" has entered—in whom self-will has been planted. But because they are loath to consign her body to the earth, they preserve it in a glass-coffin on the hillside, and there they watch by Sneewittchen in turn, and she is mourned by the owl, the raven and the dove—the symbolic birds of antiquity. A king's son, in passing by, espies the fair tenant of the glass-coffin, instantly falls in love and by his entreaties obtains it from the dwarfs; the same crystal and mental consciousness which betrayed the beauty of the Present to the false Stepmother—the ghost of the Past—now reveals her to the true lover—the genius of the future. The coffin is transported to the palace; in mid-route the fatal apple's core is jolted from Snow-White's throat; and—miracle!—she returns to life, for it is the Redemption and Resurrection of the Spring, and the winter-curse of the eaten Eden-apple is lifted. The wedding follows with the customary celerity, and the wicked Queen—"forgetting nothing and learning nothing"—cannot keep away; she comes to the festivity, there to meet her doom—she must dance in red-hot slippers till she falls, a Kali dancing down the firebrands, for so-called "free agency" cannot escape from Action's own pitiless logic. The seven good dwarfs seem to have been forgotten in the general rejoicing; but it could not be otherwise, for the seven-day round of the week must continue, though it carries all man's holidays. In the pride of the mature culture, when the Mind has found and espoused its Image, the rude ancestral shapes that piety saw around the cradle fade from sight. Beauty, however, remains eternally disquieting, like a temptation—a Second Marriage of the world, which cannot be thought of without the magic glass; the kindly shadows of unselfconscious things have but retreated a little from the human glare and heat—and at sundown they return. (pp. 9-12)

The story of *The Juniper-Tree*—both by its perfection of form and richness of symbolism is surely the greatest of all fairy-tales. It conforms—almost—to the Classical unities of place and number of personages, and the characters fall naturally into a significant pattern, repeating the ancient hierarchies of chess and playing-cards. Further, its central theme, the Tree whose berries are eaten by the mother, whose roots are fertilised by the bones of the son, whose leaves and branches—in a Pentecostal wind and flame—engender the sweet-singing bird, combines in a familiar symbolism all the elements of man's story. The evergreen juniper is—it is scarcely necessary to say—the tree of Juno, the Great Goddess, linked (long ages before the discovery of the beverage of Geneva) with the generative rhythms of the woman; it is the German *Wach*holder or *Queck*holder—the awakening, quicking, rejuvenating tree. It is under the dark tree, amidst the gleaming snow, that the mother in the tale stands paring an apple; and, as she cuts her finger and the blood-drops fall on the snow, she prays—like the mother in *Sneewittchen*—for a child that shall be white and red, cold as beauty and radiant as life, like the snow and the blood. It is felt that she prays to the tree—to the universal Life that rises in the unity of desire and bends and fruits in the duality of good and evil. Her prayer is heard and, as the year increases, the germinal life within her increases, and she partakes of the berries of the tree as in the archetypal Communion, the intermixture of perishable things, and as she eats them her separate life dwindles, and she dies after giving birth to a son—that son who is to reverse the vegetative process by himself being eaten, as it were, and re-quickened by the Tree. The wife is buried beneath the tree, like the invisible world buried in the tomb of the visible, and in due course the husband marries again—as man, losing innocence, enters the second great phase, the phase of law and rationalism. By this second marriage the father has a daughter, Marlenchen—his son however has no name in the story, for, like the ineffable God of the Old Testament, he is no more than the destined heir, and he has not yet received a character. The father is man, wived by Eternity and Time as if balanced between two darknesses, but possessing a little patch of light in each—the two beams of spiritual and corporeal vision; but the daughter seems to us the more real of the two, as the things of sense, though further from us than the creations of the mind, seem to have more content and solidity. The stepmother is jealous of the son—the father's link with the buried and unseen Other—as Matter, not content with giving birth to her own children, wages perpetual war against the children of Mind: those "spirits of the twilight," as a German phrase describes the angels. Jealousy, indeed, is the passion which is inseparable from Life, Life which is always

at a disadvantage against the Eternity of the non-living (Kierkegaard's "in the wrong before God"), Life which—in passing—is always *losing* something; Life is forever poisoned by the attempt to "live up to" the static perfection which is Death. So one day Marlenchen begs her mother for an apple, and the mother takes her to a heavy-lidded chest to give it to her; but she bethinks herself, and bidding the girl wait, tells her that her brother too must have one when he returns from school. She offers him the apple as soon as he enters, looking at him with a strange look; he accepts in surprise and bewilderment, but as he bends over the chest to take it she slams down the lid, severing his head from his shoulders. It is the Eden legend, which formed the first panel, so to speak, of our triptych—the story of the Mother—here repeated as a prologue in the second—the story of the Son, as the Son of Man himself was tempted. The apple is the German *übel* (ill) as *melos* is *malus*; it is most probably connected with Apollo, the fallen Lucifer—the self-enclosed circle of Day; the apple, as has been said, brought discord by Adam, by Paris, by Newton (it may be added, by Cézanne)—it is the fabled fruit which was fair without, ashes within. It is by assimilation to the environment through the act of nutrition that hereditary virtue is in the first place mixed and adulterated; the son, tired of abstract studies in the "school," wishes to make sensuous contact with his world—as did the modern "Faustian" man at the commencement of the Renaissance-era—and thus slips into the power of the stepmother—the mechanicism of civilisation. In the gesture of grasping the promised fruit he literally "loses his head"—the ancestral balance of intuitive wisdom. To return to our narrative, the artful woman replaces the boy's head on the trunk, ties a handkerchief around the neck, and sits him on a chair with the apple in his hand; then she tells Marlenchen to go to him and ask him for the apple he holds, and to cuff him if he refuses it to her. She does so and the head falls off, but the mother soothes her for this seeming catastrophe, bidding her tell no one and she will make black-puddings of her brother for the father's evening meal; she cuts him into strips which she throws upon the pan, and the uncomprehending Marlenchen salts them with her tears. We note here that the natural sense (personified by Marlenchen) are raised by the conviction of guilt to the grace which intuition (or the son) enjoys by birthright; for pity is only divine if it is activated by a sense of mystical guilt and remorse, and Christ—the sinless—feels not pity but love. Remorse is the salt of our daily bread, of the materialised substance of God, like the seas that circle the earth, like the unresting blood in our frames; it is through remorse that we know nostalgia, as from the blood comes consciousness—blood, it might be said, itself implies blood-guiltiness. At evening the father returns, and the black-puddings are served up to him for his dinner; and, in spite of his anxiety at the absence of his son, he is surprised to feel his spirits rising while he devours this Saturnian feast. Marlenchen however will not be comforted, and, as soon as the "abendmahl" is over, she collects the bones of the murdered brother, ties them in her best scarf, and lays them under the sacred tree—another Joseph of Arimathaea, another Isis collecting the limbs of Horus. And as she rests beneath the tree, her sorrow turns to a strange joy, the tree is stirred and agitated and breaks into flames at its top, and out of the flames rises a brightly-coloured bird—like a Phoenix out of the ashes, like the divine voice from the burning bush. The conception of the child took place in midwinter, but the birth of the bird of the Spirit occurs—it is emphasised—in bright sunshine; Christmas and Whitsun are festivals of the earth and the sun, the imprisoned and the liberated light, but Easter—the great movable feast of the calendar—is the festival of the mutable moon, forever appearing and vanishing between earth and heaven, like the male-principle in our story between the rival spouses—or like the vacillating Peter in Leonardo's Last Supper, between Judas and John. And now the bird flies to a goldsmith's, a cobbler's and a miller's—where twenty millers are at work, as it were the commoners in this soul's-pageant; and outside the door of each she sings a song, known in various forms to the folk-literatures of most countries—"My mother she killed me, my father he ate me." We remember that in all folklore the goldsmith is the artistic man, the cobbler the logical—usually indeed the village-atheist; whereas the miller is commonly the rogue—he represents in fact the man of Will, his grinding-stone is the cruel weight of the Ego, and the mill is the prototype of the factory of our industrialism. All are charmed by the bird's song, and—in childish fashion—beg her to "do it again"; this she will do only in return for gifts—a golden chain, a pair of red shoes, and lastly the millstone, which she thrusts her neck through and carries away as lightly as if it were a ruff, as Will is borne by the pure-souled. One sees the three stages in the assimilation of a new truth—the aesthetic sentimental appeal of the ring, the utilitarian servicability of the shoes, the irresistible compelling weight of the stone. The bird, returning with these acquisitions, sings before the door of the father's house; the father, running out, receives the chain around his neck—Marlenchen, following, receives the shoes, in which she leaps and dances—and the stepmother, who experiences the supernatural brightness of the day as a burning anguish, rushes from the house in her turn, only to be flattened by the millstone amid more smoke and flames. Then the whole strange dream—which, one is made to feel, Marlenchen dreamt beneath the Juniper Tree—dissolves, and the resuscitated son stands once again among his family; only the evil stepmother has vanished. It is that reintegration of personality which Christianity symbolises under the Resurrection of the Body, when this natural universe shall shrivel away in flames—that End of the World which each religion has conceived after its fashion, but which will always remain a mystery for materialistic science. The family return into the house, and sit down again merrily to table. The story seems unfinished; for to *this* story there really *is* no ending except the words of the doxology—"World without end." The Pagan triad of Mother, Father and Child has changed into the Christian triad of Father, Son and Maid, and the unholy Stepmother who mediated the change was but Illusion. It was necessary that Guilt should come that its daughter, the healing Pity, should also come, and the new trinity—more human and more divine—be born. Being has sent out Becoming like a branch, and the join between them is Nothing. The Past—which, closed upon itself, was the sinister apple-chest, the "Abyss" of mystics—has opened a new dimension into the Future, and the Present is a mere logical-mathematic scission. (pp. 37-41)

> *Arland Ussher and Carl von Metzradt, "The Magic Crystal" and "The Greatest Fairy-Tale," in their* Enter These Enchanted Woods: An Interpretation of Grimm's Fairy Tales, *second edition, The Dolmen Press, 1957, pp. 9-12, 37-41.*

FRANCIS P. MAGOUN, JR.   (essay date 1960)

Kinder- und Hausmärchen (Folk Tales for Children and the Home), as gathered and brought out in its more or less cannonical form by Jacob and Wilhelm Grimm . . . and often loosely and inaccurately referred to as **"Grimms' Fairy Tales,"** is a collection of eighteenth-century and earlier German folk tales, in part taken from contemporary oral tradition, in part from older printed sources. As finally presented by the Grimms, these appear in a straightforward, somewhat unadorned though by no means barren style, while a certain matter-of-factness and chattiness colors the whole. . . . [This collection, Wilhelm Grimm's final achievement, is] one of the noblest monuments of German prose.

Originally composed by intelligent, keen-witted German peasant folk and told for mutual entertainment by grown-ups for grown-ups, these famous folk tales are, contrary to popular notion, not essentially for younger children, to whom, in fact, only a few are likely to appeal. A limited number, perhaps some twenty or thirty commonly included in almost innumerable select translations especially designed for children, have, to be sure, achieved notable success among children; yet because of its false emphasis, the Grimms subsequently regretted using the word *Kinder* in their title. . . . *German Folk Tales* . . . quite exactly describes the contents, disposes of the misleading emphasis on "children," and leads to no ambiguity since there are no other genuine German folk tales outside of the Grimms' collection. The tales will, as a whole, appeal essentially to grown-ups with a taste for a good story well told. In the diction, style, and development of the various narratives there is nothing childish or juvenile, still less anything mannered or from the point of view of the original teller anything archaic. (pp. vii-viii)

> *Francis P. Magoun, Jr., in his foreword to* The Grimms' German Folk Tales *by Jacob Grimm and Wilhelm Grimm, translated by Francis P. Magoun, Jr. and Alexander H. Krappe (copyright © 1960 by Southern Illinois University Press; reprinted by permission of Southern Illinois University Press), Southern Illinois University Press, 1960, pp. vii-viii.*

ELIZABETH BOWEN   (essay date 1963)

From Grimm's Law to Grimms' Fairy Tales seems a far cry. There might seem, even, a contrariety between them, but on closer analysis there is not. The 210 fairy and folk tales collected by Jacob and Wilhelm Grimm bore the title **"Kinder- und Hausmärchen"** (in English, **"Nursery and Household Tales"**). (p. 112)

Success was immediate—for good reason—and the success was encircled by wide sensation. For the *literati*, the brothers were revolutionaries. How so? Why, in the manner of the telling. Here came tales still warm from the lips that told them. Here was the insubordinate, uncalculated beauty of the vernacular. Old, old, their origins lost in time, these tales had renewed their youth and recharged their batteries onward from generation to generation—their eager hearers having become vivid tellers, passing them on. Word-of-mouth tales, transmitted as word-of-mouth; tales unchastened (this is very important) by refining "literary" taste, tales which bore no stamp given them by the Grimms themselves.

The brothers wrote down these stories—that is to say transcribed them. They did not write them—insofar as one means, when one speaks of "writing" that an act of imaginative invention has taken place. They found these tales, thereby rescuing many from the oblivion into which they might have fallen. Having found them, they presented them to the world. And what a gift! For the brothers, the giving was joy enough, personal "self-expression" they never sought.

The Grimms' criteria in the choosing of the stories was authenticity. They used no tales of which the (regional) origin could not be traced. Working together, they brought to a fine point an instinct which protected them from the specious. And Jacob brought also, to the selection, the developed faculties of the philologist. The vocabulary in which a tale was clothed, when it came to him, could in itself be a guarantee. Fairy tales for children contained more of the original soul of old Germany than anything else the Grimm brothers could find.

In insisting on this direct presentation, or transcription, the Grimms, with their interlocked, offbeat genius, fell foul of many of their contemporaries in the early 19th-century phase of the German Romantic movement. They seemed anti-esthetic. Stylishness and refinement they seemed to scorn. (pp. 112-13)

Some of the tales, it was true, had been disinterred from volumes or manuscripts in those time-darkened libraries which added a further dimension to Jacob's youth. But the main stream of them, the majority, had been transcribed direct from the lips of tellers native to the regions the tales haunted. One great source had been Frau Katerina Viehmann, tailor's wife in a village not far from Cassel. With delight, the student brothers frequented her home. "She recounts her stories," reported Wilhelm, "thoughtfully, accurately, with uncommon vividness. . . . Much was recorded in this way, and its fidelity is unmistakable. Anyone believing that traditional materials are falsified and carelessly preserved, and hence cannot survive for a long period, should hear how close she always keeps to her story and how zealous she is for its accuracy; never does she alter any part in repetition, and she corrects a mistake herself, immediately she notices it. Among people who follow the old ways of life without change, attachment to inherited patterns is stronger than we, impatient for variety, can realize." . . .

The Grimm brothers, I learn, were among those who have pointed out that folk tales are "monstrous, irrational and unnatural." And that goes for fairy tales, we may take it? The 210 released by the brothers Grimm, I refuse to discuss in scholarly terms. They hold me too close—I like them too well. Here is a boisterous, lusty, quick-witted world, with thickets of mysticism shot through by beauty.

Its inhabitants are children, robbers, huntsmen, discharged soldiers, tailors, peasants, fishermen, cowherds, goatherds and goose girls, kings and queens, and princes and princesses, malevolent witches and kind enchantresses, wicked stepmothers, tricky serving maids, horrid boys, ingenious little girls and inspired simpletons, giants, Tom Thumbs, good dwarfs and disagreeable gnomes. Its fauna consists of lions, bears, wolves, foxes, cats and, of course, dogs, also hares and mice—there appear to be no badgers and no tigers. There is almost every variety of bird, with the exception of blackbirds and peacocks. Frogs play a considerable part. Sole and herring are the more prominent fish. In a group to themselves are dragons and griffins.

The flora is headed by roses, which act dramatically. There are sinister lilies, and many innocent wildflowers. Fruit, particularly apples, is abundant, delicious and charged with magic. You cannot be too careful as to what you eat, what you promise to a stranger, or what you wish.

Much of the landscape consists of forests, and these are trackless, moody and very deep. Glittering and dangerous glass mountains may soar up into existence at any moment. Rivers are slippery customers; any ocean, you should think twice before embarking upon. Wherever a heath occurs, it is strewn with rock; glades are seldom not jewel-brilliant with flowers. Architecture is represented by castles, hung inside with crystal chandeliers, which appear or disappear at will; horrible, incarcerating towers; intensely snug little houses in forest clearings; occasional churches and humble fishermen's huts.

Few dooms in this perilous world are permanent, it is consoling to remember. The prey of devouring carnivores, bolted whole, can be rescued alive from the brute's interior. Dismembered persons, pieced together again, walk away smiling. Birds, bears, lions and hideous monsters may at any time reassume human form. A maiden deserted, owing to a spell, by her dear lover almost invariably reclaims him. Only really evil schemers come to bad ends, and very excruciating *those* are. . . .

Yes, this world of the tales is a blend of coziness and bloodthirstiness, of slapstick comedy, coarse-grained good sense and inadvertent, ethereal beauty. **"The Girl Without Hands," "The Singing, Soaring Lark," "Frederick and Catherine" "Clever Elsie," "The Shoes That Were Danced to Pieces," "The Six Servants," "Donkey Cabbages," "The Devil's Sooty Brother," "The Young Giant."** . . . Where must one now stop and where next turn?

These are tales for all ages. They are tales for all. For children, they have the particular virtue of making sense. Everything that a child feels should happen *does* happen. In one if not another of these stories, rough justice rules—but may not justice be rough? Transformations, disguises fall into line with an infant's sense of the trickiness of the world. And, above all, here the extraordinary is the beautiful. Why not? Should beauty ever grow ordinary, what a sad affair! (p. 113)

> *Elizabeth Bowen, "Enchanted Centenary of the Brothers Grimm," in* The New York Times Magazine *(© 1963 by The New York Times Company; reprinted by permission), September 8, 1963, pp. 28-9, 112-13.*

MURRAY B. PEPPARD (essay date 1971)

[Next to the Bible, *The Children's and Household Tales* of the Brothers Grimm] is the most widely read book in Germany, and has become a household book in many lands and languages. All over the world it is the family book of fairy tales, the first and often the only book to come to mind when one thinks of such tales. The very definition of a fairy tale for many is "a tale like a story from *Grimms' Fairy Tales*" . . . Not only have the tales been a source of joy and wonderful entertainment for children, but they have also served as the basis for learned investigations into folklore, thereby providing source material for many scholars.

It is ironic that this gift to the world had its origins in the Grimms' patriotic fervor. . . . The brothers presented the book to their nation as an encouraging reminder of its spiritual history at a time when Germany was about to rise with renewed courage from its days of defeat and despair; in fact, so much of what they wrote is suffused with this love of their country and its cuture. (pp. 39-40)

Jacob and Wilhelm were, however, not just responding to an upsurge of patriotic enthusiasm; they also had serious pedagogical purposes in mind. Their wish to revive and give new value to a genre that had fallen into disrepute is one of their lasting achievements. *Grimms' Fairy Tales* have become international property in part because of the educational value of the tales, a value which the Grimms were among the first to see. (p. 40)

The appeal of the stories, their obvious quality, and the summons to preserve such tales before they were lost forever urged the [Grimms] on. The principle of collecting living folk culture in its original form without seriously altering the texts was now becoming firmly established in their minds. (p. 45)

The brothers' interest in the oral traditions of the "folk," or common people, was intimately connected with their already profound concern with the national past. Their study of folklore was part and parcel of their work in medieval literature and history. They had the same attitude toward the fairy tales and folk tales that they had toward the written documents from Germany's history. Work on *Reynard the Fox (Reinhart Fuchs)*, the famous medieval beast epic, had been started by Jacob [who was soon aided by Wilhelm]. Both brothers felt that popular, oral tradition could be used to reinforce the lessons learned from literary documents. Wilhelm had already expressed his high opinion of fairy tales in the preface to his Danish ballads: "In the fairy tales a world of magic is opened up before us, one which still exists among us in secret forests, in underground caves, and in the deepest sea, and it is still visible to children. These fairy tales deserve more attention than they have been given up to now, not only because of their poetry, which has its own special charm and which, gives everyone who has heard them in childhood a golden rule and happy memories for life, but also because they belong to our national poetic heritage since it can be proved that they have existed among the people . . . for several centuries." (pp. 47-8)

The brothers did not use organic and botanical metaphors by accident, but very deliberately chose them in describing the processes of the creation of folk literature. Jacob believed that the fairy fale "has preserved most purely the nature of early epic poetry and has transmitted a whole element of it down to our present times. It is a poetry which belongs to the childhood of the race—and therefore children take to it so readily." But by being closer to the origins of mankind, the tales were also closer to their Creator; for the religious core of the fairy tales was as important to the Grimms as any other aspect. Their piety extended to the pagan past—they were not narrow in their Christianity—and wherever they thought they had found a faith men once lived by, they adopted an attitude of reverence. (pp. 48-9)

Their sense of the sanctity of what had been inherited made them annoyed with those who . . . tampered with the texts of songs or tales. "The wonderful last echoes of ancient myths" which they believed they heard in the fairy tales they did not wish to see deflected in any way. . . .

[The Brothers Grimm] brought to bear all their knowledge in whatever special aspcct of thcir rcsearch thcy wcre working on at any time. Their efforts were always harmonious parts of one grand, total attempt to rediscover the nation's past. Once they had conceived the notion that the fairy tales go back to a common mythical heritage at the dawn of time, it was not hard to envision a comprehensive myth (*Urmythus*) that served as a core for all later developments. The mythical component they believed to be the heart of all ancient poetry. (p. 49)

Murray B. Peppard, in his Paths through the Forest: A Biography of the Brothers Grimm *(copyright © 1971 by Murray B. Peppard; reprinted by permission*

of Holt, Rinehart and Winston, Publishers), Holt, Rinehart and Winston, 1971, 266 p.

BRUNO BETTELHEIM (essay date 1976)

[In **"Brother and Sister"**], like many other fairy tales which feature the adventures of two siblings, the protagonists represent the disparate natures of id, ego, and superego; and the main message is that these must be integrated for human happiness. This type of fairy tale presents the necessity of integrating the personality in a different way than "The Queen Bee"—here the nefarious doings of an "evil spirit" turn one sibling into an animal, while the other remains human. It is hard to conceive of a more vivid, succinct, and immediately convincing image of our contradictory propensities. Even the earliest philosophers viewed man as having both an animal and a human nature.

During much of our life, when we have not succeeded in achieving or maintaining inner integration, these two aspects of our psyche war against each other. When we are young, whatever we feel at the moment fills our entire existence. Becoming aware that he feels two ways about something at the same time—for example, when the child wants to grab the cookie, but also wants to obey Mother's order not to—confuses the child. Understanding this duality requires a cognizance of inner processes which is greatly facilitated by fairy tales illustrating our dual nature.

Such fairy tales begin with an original lack of differentiation between the two siblings: they live together and feel alike; in short, they are inseparable. But then, at a certain moment in growing up, one of them begins an animal existence, and the other does not. At the end of the tale the animal is changed back into his human form; the two are reunited, never to be separated again. This is the fairy tale's symbolic way of rendering the essentials of human personality development: the child's personality is at first undifferentiated; then id, ego, and superego develop out of the undifferentiated stage. In a process of maturation these must be integrated, despite opposite pulls.

In the Brothers Grimm's story **"Brother and Sister,"** "Little brother took his little sister by the hand and said . . . 'Come, we will go forth together out into the wide world'" to escape from a home which had become a depriving one. "They walked the whole day over meadows, fields and rocky expanses; and when it rained, little sister said: 'Heaven and our hearts are weeping together.'"

Here, as in many fairy tales, being pushed out of the home stands for having to become oneself. Self-realization requires leaving the orbit of the home, an excruciating painful experience fraught with many psychological dangers. This developmental process is inescapable, the pain of it is symbolized by the children's unhappiness about being forced to leave home. The psychological risks in the process, as always in fairy stories, are represented by the dangers the hero encounters on his travels. In this story the brother represents the endangered aspect of an essentially inseparable unity, and the sister, as symbol of motherly care once one has become alienated from home, is the rescuer.

The fairy tale leaves no doubt in the child's mind that the pain must be endured and the risky chances taken, since one must achieve one's personal identity; and, despite all anxieties, there is no question about the happy ending. While not every child can or will inherit a kingdom, the child who understands and makes his own the message of the fairy tale will find the true home of his inner self; he will become master over its vast realm by knowing his mind, so it will serve him well. (pp. 78-9)

[The] brother and sister come to a spring from which brother wants to drink; but sister, who is not carried away by her id (instinctual pressures), understands that the water is murmuring: "Who drinks of me becomes a tiger." Because of her entreaties, her brother abstains from drinking despite the promptings of his thirst.

The sister, representing the higher mental functions (the ego and superego), warns her brother, who—id-dominated—is ready to permit himself to be carried away by his wish for immediate gratification (of his thirst), no matter what the cost of doing so. But should the brother give in to the pressure of the id, he would become asocial, as violent as a tiger. . . .

But as the pressure of the id (brother's thirst) increases, it overpowers the restraints of ego and superego: the sister's admonitions lose the power to control, and as brother drinks from the spring, he turns into a fawn.

Sister promises that she will never leave her fawn-brother. She symbolizes ego control, since, despite her thirst, she was able to abstain from drinking. She unties her golden garter and fastens it around the fawn's neck, and plucks some rushes and weaves these into a soft leash which she fastens to the little animal. Only a very positive personal tie—the golden garter—can make us forgo giving in to our asocial desires and lead us on to a higher humanity. (p. 80)

But until we have achieved full personality integration, our id (our instinctual pressures, our animal nature) lives in uneasy peace with our ego (our rationality). The fairy tale tells how when the animal instincts are strongly aroused, rational controls lose the power to restrain. After the sister and fawn-brother have lived happily for some time in the wilderness, the king of the country arranges for a big hunt. When the fawn hears the blowing of horns, the barking of the hounds, and the merry shouting of the hunters, he says to his sister, "Let me out to join the hunt; I can't stand it any longer," and begs so long that at last she consents.

The first day of the hunt all goes well, and at nightfall the deer-brother returns to his sister and the safety of their little hut. The next morning he hears again the tempting noises of the hunt and becomes restless, demanding to be let out. Toward the end of the day he is slightly wounded in the leg and manages to limp home, but this time the deer, with his golden collar, is observed by one of the hunters, who reports it to the king. The king recognizes the meaning of the garter, and he orders that on the next day the deer is to be pursued and caught, but not to be hurt.

At home, sister takes care of brother's wound. The following day, despite her tears and entreaties, the deer forces her to let him out again. In the evening not only the fawn but the king too comes to the hut. Captivated by the girl's beauty, the king asks her to marry him; she agrees, provided the fawn will live with them.

For a long time they all live happily together. But, as so often in fairy tales, three repetitions of the same ordeal—the three days the deer was being hunted—are not sufficient for the final resolution. While brother has undergone his ordeal which could become his initiation to a higher form of existence, the sister has not.

All goes well until one day, when the king is out hunting, the queen gives birth to a boy. (p. 81)

Like all important transformations, [childbirth] is fraught with great dangers. . . . These dangers are given body in this story by a witch stepmother, who, after the child has been born, insinuates herself into the queen's life by assuming the form of her lady-in-waiting. She entices the queen, who is sick from childbirth, to take a bath—where she causes the queen to suffocate. The witch then has her own ugly daughter take the queen's place in the royal bed.

At midnight the queen reappears in the nursery to take her child into her arms and nurse him; nor does she forget to take care of the roebuck. . . . After some time has passed, the queen begins to talk during her midnight visits with her child, and says,

> "How is my child? How is my deer?
> Twice shall I come, then nevermore."

The nursemaid tells this to the king, who sits up the following night to watch the same thing happen, with the difference that the queen says that she will come only once more. The third night, when the queen says that she'll never come again, the king no longer restrains himself and calls her his beloved wife, at which she comes back to life.

As there were three repetitions of the brother trying to drink from a brook, and of the deer running out to join the hunt, so there were three visits by the dead queen to her child during which she spoke the verses. But the queen's being restored to life and reunited with her king still leaves her brother in his animal form. Only after justice has been meted out and the witch is burned to ashes does the fawn regain his human form, and "sister and brother lived happily together until their end." (p. 82)

The real issue of **"Brother and Sister"** is that the animalistic tendencies in man, as represented by the deer, and the asocial ones, symbolized by the witch, are done away with; and this permits the human qualities to blossom. The discrepancy in human nature indicated by the sister's and fawn-brother's existence is resolved through human integration as brother and sister are reunited in their human forms.

In the story's ending, two strands of thought are combined: integration of the disparate aspects of our personality can be gained only after the asocial, destructive, and unjust have been done away with; and this cannot be achieved until we have reached full maturity, as symbolized by sister's giving birth to a child and developing mothering attitudes. The story also suggests the two great upheavals in life: leaving the parental home, and creating one's own family. These are the two periods of life when we are most vulnerable to disintegration, because an old way of life has to be given up and a new one achieved. In the first of these two turning points, brother gets temporarily swept away; in the second, the sister.

While no inner evolution is spelled out, its nature is implied: what redeems us as human beings and restores us to our humanity is solicitude for those whom we love. The queen, on her nocturnal visits, does not try to satisfy any of her own desires, but worries about others who depend on her: her child and her deer. This shows that she has successfully made the transition from wife to mother, and thus she is reborn to a higher stage of existence. The contrast between the brother's giving in to the proddings of his instinctual desires and the sisters ego and superego motivated concern for her obligations to others clearly indicates what the battle for integration and victory in it consist of. (pp. 82-3)

> *Bruno Bettelheim, "'Brother and Sister': Unifying Our Dual Nature," in his* The Uses of Enchantment: The Meaning and Importance of Fairy Tales *(copyright ©, 1976 by Bruno Bettelheim; reprinted by permission of Alfred A. Knopf, Inc.), Knopf, 1976, pp. 78-83.*

RALPH MANHEIM   (essay date 1977)

Some students of folklore have found fault with the Grimm brothers for "Improving" on the tales they collected. The Grimms themselves claimed to have taken down the stories faithfully. Of course they improved on the spoken word; some storytellers are fluent, others hem and haw, and from the storytelling point of view there would seem to be no point in recording their hemming and hawing. But at the same time the Grimms *were* astonishingly faithful, undeterred by the irrational or unseemly. . . . [The greatest mark of the Grimms' genius is that] they make us hear the voices of the individual storytellers, and much more clearly I am sure than if they had been two tape recorders. In the German text the human voice takes on a wide variety of tones—mysterious, elegiac, hushed-and-frightened, poetic, whimsical, rowdy, solemnly or mock-solemnly moralizing, and so on. But everywhere—or almost—it is a natural human voice, speaking as someone might speak, and seldom if ever do we hear anything resembling the never-never, good-nursery, fairytale style prevalent in the English translations of these and other folk tales. (p. 1)

> *Ralph Manheim, in his preface to* Grimms' Tales for Young and Old: The Complete Stories *by Jacob Grimm and Wilhelm Grimm, translated by Ralph Manheim (translation copyright © 1977 by Ralph Manheim; reprinted by permission of Doubleday & Company, Inc.), Doubleday, 1977, pp. 1-2.*

ROBERT HARBISON   (essay date 1980)

When Jacob and Wilhelm Grimm began collecting what appeared first . . . as the *Kinder-und Hausmärchen* they saw themselves recovering bits of the national or racial memory strewn about within easy reach but uncared for, not visionaries like Chateaubriand but compilers, or at most naturalists gifted with a sharper eye for the disappearing species hidden in the hedgerows. They present their collection as the first truly scientific in German, meaning that variants have been carefully compared, that the source is often verbal, transcribed in the dialect of the speaker not affected-naïve diction concocted by themselves, and that the apparent crudities of the original are not smoothed away. Such abdication before qualities sensed in folk products is revolutionary for its investment in uncorrected spontaneity, but it wasn't as easy to escape one's educated self as the Grimms believed. Collection is an anti-instinctive and critical procedure, even without their unformulated rules for what makes one story better than others, because a proximity not usual in nature allows comparison of stories after their selection. Fixing on a printed form traduces oral tradition further by putting a stop to the succession of versions in which a story is never the same twice, but always improving and decaying, until suddenly immobilized into literature.

Besides this they exercised more conscious influence by conflation, whereby incidents from different versions were combined if they did not conflict and duplications relegated to notes, resulting in a richer growth than occurred in nature, an approximation of the density of conscious art. An earlier generation could prefer Ossian and Gothick to the real thing or scrupulous recoveries, because they were more elegant and less gross, more obviously emotive and to an eighteenth-century sense coherent, than medieval or pre-medieval works themselves. In spite of their preference for the authentic fragment over the imposed continuity the Grimms overlaid the nostalgia which offended them in Ossian on their versions of the fairy tales, supplying an equivalent of the mists of time or haze of distance prominent in Macpherson and Chateaubriand and absent from true folk products.

One of the best of the tales, *Brüderchen und Schwesterchen,* which inspired the comforting mythic frontispiece to the first volume of the 1819 edition, only comes into its own because it symbolizes what for us fairy tales are about. The brother and sister leave home like many other pairs and enter in the forest a life of deepening strangeness, whose pull the boy is less able to resist, finally drinking from the third of the brooks which warn her in whispers while calling to his thirst. This disaster initiates one of the Grimms' most beautiful idylls, for to hold the deer he has turned into she binds him with her belt and finds them a house in the woods, where life continues till disrupted by his enthusiasm for the hunters' horns. It is a visionary union of rude vigor and domesticity, of reassimilation to wild origins, return to childhood and sympathy with animals.

Because it matches Romantic notions of life in the woods so well one suspects that much of the feeling is interpolated by the Grimms, but the closest one can come to verifying their sources is to summon a Russian parallel, where the brother drinks from the hoofprints of the beasts he is successively threatened with becoming, and stumbles into the king's garden without passing through a house in the woods, the great pivot on which the Grimms' version turns.

The pattern is the same, its meaning different, but fairy tales disconcert us most by how little they care about their meaning in our sense of the word, discarding or retaining it by chance. That this story is "about" wildness and civilization, a welcome idea to us, seems finally illicit, and perhaps precious because alien to the circumstances in which we find it. Such fondness for its own settings, as in spite of its spareness the Grimms' language often conveys, jars with the most inalienable formal principles of the tales, the old geometry of threes and the familiar unraveling which retraces the same steps in reverse order, like a series of gates one must pass through both coming and going in order to gain credit. Left to itself a fairy tale never feels the burden of its past but returns to former haunts as a train passes through stations, fulfilling obligations and impervious to sentiment on hearing names long familiar, the romance of such journeys an imagination of those who see the names as surprises prepared for them by the night, who like the characters have the power of forgetting instantly what the kind old man has said. (pp. 130 31)

> *Robert Harbison, "Romantic Localism: Folk Styles," in his* Deliberate Regression *(copyright ©1980 by Robert Harbison; reprinted by permission of Alfred A. Knopf, Inc.), Knopf, 1980, pp. 115-47.**

ADDITIONAL BIBLIOGRAPHY

Carsch, Henry. "Witchcraft and Spirit Possession in Grimm's Fairy Tales." *Journal of Popular Culture* II, No. 4 (Spring 1969): 627-48.

Discusses the use of the supernatural in Grimm's fairy tales, and the psychological dimensions they assume.

Michaelis-Jena, Ruth. "Oral Tradition and the Brothers Grimm." *Folklore* 82 (Winter 1971): 265-75.
Explains the Grimms's interest in collecting folk tales, the preparatory steps they took to achieve their goals, and the methods they used in compiling the tales.

Rubenstein, Ben. "The Meaning of the Cinderella Story in the Development of a Little Girl." *The American Imago* 12, No. 2 (Summer 1955): 197-205.
Discusses specific psychological themes which attract children to "Cinderella." The author recounts his own daughter's identification with the story, and observes how her reaction to it reflects "both obvious and disguised wishes and defenses."

Victor Marie Hugo

1802-1885

French novelist, poet, dramatist, and critic.

Hugo is considered one of the leaders of the Romantic movement in French literature, as well as its most prolific and versatile author. Although chiefly known outside France for the novels *Les misérables* and *Notre Dame de Paris (The Hunchback of Notre Dame)*, he is renowned in his own country primarily for his contributions as a Romantic poet. In his lifetime, Hugo also received considerable acclaim for his extensive dramatic output, but critical opinion of his theatrical work has waned in this century and his plays retain significance only in scholarly circles. Regardless of the endurance of his individual works, Hugo remains an outstanding symbol of liberty and humanitarianism in France.

Born into a military family, Hugo traveled extensively during his childhood until, at age twelve, his parents separated. He settled in Paris with his mother, attended school, and attained literary recognition at a young age. At the age of twenty, Hugo founded a prominent literary magazine, *Le conservateur littéraire*, and published his first volume of poetry, *Odes et poésies diverses*. This earned him a pension from Louis XVIII and enabled him to marry his childhood sweetheart, Adèle Foucher. His home became a center of intellectual activity and he counted among his devoted friends Charles Sainte-Beuve and Théophile Gautier. During this period, Hugo wrote several novels and volumes of poetry which express the exoticism and youthful vigor which foreshadow his Romantic tendencies.

Hugo's dramatic work began with the publication of the controversial preface to his lengthy and unstageable verse-drama, *Cromwell*. This preface sought to establish a new set of dramatic principles which were to become the manifesto of the Romantic movement. Hugo demanded a new form of verse drama which abandoned the formal rules of classical tragedy. These precepts were put to the test in 1830, with the Comédie française's turbulent production of Hugo's *Hernani*. Its debut was referred to as the "battle of *Hernani*" because of censorship difficulties and the heated reaction of the theater goers. Champions of literary classicism found themselves suddenly at odds with proponents of a new dramatic freedom.

In 1831, Hugo's first great novel, *The Hunchback of Notre Dame,* was published. Its emotional power and sentimentality served as a vehicle for Hugo's social concepts; he believed that although all men are equal, the poor remain society's underlings. His evocation of basic human rights and needs met with resounding international acclaim.

While Hugo's literary life flourished, his personal life deteriorated. Adèle Hugo fell in love with his best friend, Sainte-Beuve, and Hugo, devastated by his wife's infidelity, found solace in a number of romantic liaisons. He maintained a gallant exterior—possibly because of his professional tie to Sainte-Beuve—and, though Hugo and his wife lived thereafter in a state of platonic affection, the pain of her defection cast a melancholy tone on his later work.

In 1841, Hugo was elected to the Académie française and four years later was made a peer. The number of his publications

diminished not only because of the demands of his new position, but also because of his grief at the death of his daughter Léopoldine, in 1843. He devoted himself to politics; then, distressed by Louis Napoléon's dictatorial ambitions, he fled to Belgium in 1851. His first poetical work in exile, *Les châtiments,* was a political indictment of Louis Napoléon. Tiring of overtly political topics, he next explored the metaphysical aspects of death and life in *Les contemplations*. His use of symbol and metaphor to give new, sometimes obscure, meaning to poetic language, along with his often highly personal and reflective work, influenced the later Symbolist poets.

After publishing several volumes of poetry while still in exile, Hugo returned to an unfinished novel he had begun much earlier. The finished work, *Les misérables*, was an overwhelming success. Hugo considered it a religious epic of his beloved Paris. For many readers, the excitement of its narrative overcomes its tendency for digression and melodrama, and critics praise the novel's theme of the search for justice and its realistic character development. *Les misérables* has remained Hugo's most memorable work and is considered to be a recreation of the endless human battle against evil as well as proof of Hugo's own social concerns.

Upon his return to France, Hugo was publicly acclaimed. Though nominated for a public office, Hugo took little further interest in national affairs. His final years were marked by personal loss and, though he continued to write prolifically, he became increasingly detached from the world around him. He died a national hero. Though he lay in state under the Arc de Triomphe and was buried in the Panthéon, his body was transported in the hearse of a poor man, in accordance with his last request.

Though critical opinion of Hugo's work diminished shortly after his death, modern critics consider him an outstanding poet whose technical virtuousity advanced French poetry. Hugo's reputation as a prose writer has waned in this century, but his work has proved a dominant force in French letters and he is remembered as an artist of great popularity and importance. Charles Baudelaire said of Hugo, "No artist is more universal than he."

PRINCIPAL WORKS

Odes et poésies diverses   (poetry)   1822
Han d'Islande   (novel)   1823
  [*Hans of Iceland*, 1845]
Bug-Jargal   (novel)   1826
  [*The Slave King*, 1833]
Cromwell [first publication]   (drama)   1827
  [*Cromwell*, 1900]
Le dernier jour d'un condamné   (novel)   1829
  [*The Last Day of a Condemned*, 1840]
Les orientales   (poetry)   1829
  [*Eastern Lyrics*, 1879]
Hernani   (drama)   1830
  [*Hernani*, 1833]
Les feuilles d'automne   (poetry)   1831
Marion de Lorme   (drama)   1831
  [*The King's Edict*, 1872; also published as *Marion de Lorme*, 1934]
Notre Dame de Paris   (novel)   1831
  [*The Hunchback of Notre Dame*, 1833]
Le roi s'amuse   (drama)   1832
  [*The King's Fool*, 1841]
Lucrèce Borgia   (drama)   1833
  [*Lucretia Borgia*, 1842]
Ruy Blas   (drama)   1838
  [*Ruy Blas*, 1861]
Les burgraves   (drama)   1843
Les châtiments   (poetry)   1853
Les contemplations   (poetry)   1856
La légende des siècles. 3 vols.   (poetry)   1859-83
  [*The Legend of the Centuries*, 1894]
Les misérables   (novel)   1862
  [*Les Misérables*, 1862; also published as *The Wretched*, 1863]
William Shakespeare   (criticism)   1864
  [*William Shakespeare*, 1864]
Les travailleurs de la mer   (novel)   1866
  [*The Toilers of the Sea*, 1866]
L'homme qui rit   (novel)   1869
  [*The Man Who Laughs*, 1869; also published as *By Order of the King*, 1870]
Quatre-vingt treize   (novel)   1874
  [*Ninety-three*, 1874]
Choses vues   (essays)   1887
  [*Things Seen*, 1887]

THE NEW MONTHLY MAGAZINE   (essay date 1823)

Han d'Islande is the most extraordinary and *ultra* horrible production of a disordered imagination that has ever frozen the blood and blanched the cheeks of romance readers. The writer, whose "seething," or rather madly boiling brains, have thrown off this monstrous abortion, is M. Hugo, whose poetical effusions ("Odes et Poesies sacrées") are in considerable repute here. By this publication he may claim the merit, if merit it be, of having outstripped all his competitors in the race of terror. . . . For the benefit of those who may be amateurs of the horrible, we shall attempt some account of this singular production. The scene is laid in Norway; the reader, on opening the first volume, finds himself in "that lugubrious house, consecrated, by public piety and social foresight, to the reception of unknown corpses;" in common *parlance*, the *Morgue* at Drontheim. . . . We have gone into more than usual detail upon this work; first, because the author, M. Hugo, enjoys no inconsiderable reputation as a writer; and secondly, because he is one of the most distinguished members of a society that has been for some time established here, called *La Societé des Bonnes Lettres*, in contradistinction to those who cultivate the *Belles Lettres*. These *soi-disant* reformers profess it to be their intention to restore literature to that moral and classical dignity which invested it under Louis XIV. *Han d'Islande* offers a remarkable proof of the absurdity of their efforts, or the insincerity of their professions. (pp. 174-75)

> *"Foreign Publications, with Critical Remarks: 'Han d'islande',"* in The New Monthly Magazine, *Vol. IX, No. XXVIII, April 1, 1823, pp. 174-75.*

THE FOREIGN QUARTERLY REVIEW   (essay date 1828)

[In "**Cromwell**"] there is a leaven of ingenuity and good sense, that raises up the otherwise torpid and heavy mass into something which forms really almost as palatable fare as critic could desire. It will not be expected that we should give any detailed account of a preface of sixty-four octavo pages. The author is a romanticist. He conceives that there have existed three great and distinct ages of poetry, each adapted to, and created by, a corresponding state of society. These three are, the ages of the ode, the epos, and the drama. The primitive, or what the ancients called the fabulous time, is lyrical; the time of the ancients, epic; and that of the moderns, dramatic. The ode sings eternity, the epos solemnizes history, the drama paints life. . . . "**Cromwell**" is less a drama than a historical romance in dialogue; and yet it is so dramatic in spirit, that we feel angry it should not be so also in body; and so amusing without being perfectly dramatic, that we regret being constantly reminded that it was the author's intention to concoct a drama. The story relates to a double conspiracy among the cavaliers and round-heads against the protector. In the first act, the conspirators of both factions meet in a tavern, and the plan of the royalist plot is developed, together with the characters of the personages who are engaged in it. (pp. 715-16)

When the reader is informed that this "drama" is about four times longer than an ordinary tragedy, he will perceive that we can only have given a very faint outline even of the more remarkable incidents; and if we could afford room for a few specimens, we are convinced he would agree with us in lamenting, that where there are all the materials both of a tale and a drama, the work of M. Victor Hugo should be neither the one nor the other. (pp. 717-18)

"Critical Sketches: 'Cromwell, Drame'," in The Foreign Quarterly Review, *Vol. II, No. IV, June, 1828, pp. 715-19.*

THE FOREIGN QUARTERLY REVIEW (essay date 1829)

The poetry of Hugo has appeared in various forms at various times: the reader has now, however, all the trouble of collection saved him, by the appearance of a beautiful and complete edition, in which he has arranged it in a new order, and put the last hand of the author to many pieces with which time had led him to be dissatisfied. The two first volumes are entitled "Odes et Ballades," the third is named "Les Orientales;" over these three our approbation is very unequally divided.

The first volume of Odes is almost entirely political, that is to say, each celebrates some national event. It is generally agreed that this is a most difficult style of composition; to try it is to enter the lists with Pindar and Horace, and to tread upon the failures of a whole catacomb of extinct poet-laureates and triumphal bards. Perhaps, therefore, our small relish for this portion of M. Hugo's labours may be, first, our repugnance to his subjects in particular, and next to the whole class of laureate hymns. . . . [The] loyalty of Hugo, as shown in his poems, is of a kind which does not flourish in England. . . . (pp. 206-07)

The titles alone of these political hymns, such as the "**Birth of the Duke of Bordeaux**," the "**Funeral of Louis XVII.**" &c., will show the writer's loyal inclinations; but it is only a perusal of them that can make the reader understand the extraordinary *unction* with which he treats such topics—an unction least to be expected from the son of a general of the Revolution and the Empire, himself a *quondam* page of King Joseph. We are sorry for this turn of the poet's enthusiasm, not merely because such notions are inconsistent with free and enlightened monarchical institutions; but because they shut against the author a most copious source of noble inspiration. (p. 208)

Although we have freely expressed our dislike to the outpourings of M. Hugo's political devotion, we are far from denying that even these pieces are in many instances written in a strain of real, though misguided, enthusiasm, and that in the midst of an exaggeration incidental to the celebration of public events, many thoughts of great beauty are to be found. (p. 209)

A much pleasanter part of our task awaits us: we take up the second volume, which contains the odes of fancy, and the odes of personal experience. In this division, and in the manner in which the author discusses the arrangements of his poems, the reader will detect an imitation of Wordsworth's preface to his collected poems. These two divisions of the work, as well as the ballads forming the latter portion of the second volume, cannot be read without the highest gratification by any one susceptible of the pleasures of the imagination. There may be failures among so numerous a collection; there may be parts of comparative flatness; there may even be conceits which to some may appear cold; but in general every lover of poetry must dwell with delight on the harmony of their tone, calm and peaceful as a summer's evening—on the delicate tenderness of the affections they develope—on the amiable play of the imagination in which the author dresses up the objects of his regard, whether they be simply the golden dreams of former happiness, or the more real charms of existing loveliness. The poet here is in his true character—pensive and wayward, sensitive and contemplative, alive to the brilliancy of the world,

easily affected by the recollections of the past, desponding for the future, but showing in his pride and his high-mettled fierceness the unbroken spirit of youth, and in fact proving that his melancholy and his sorrow are rather the reaction of an overwrought temperament than the bitterness of the heart, torn and bruised by a life of care and sad experience. (p. 210)

Of the many poems in these volumes of the tender and sentimental class, our favourite is the piece which bears the title of "**Her Name.**" It is a most elegant specimen of amorous eloquence. (p. 211)

[The *Orientales*] are treated in somewhat of an Eastern spirit; at least as far as gaiety and lightness of heart are peculiar to the East. The shepherd in the Arcadia is said to pipe as if he would never grow old; it is the character of such Eastern writings as we are acquainted with, that their poets sing as if death had no terrors, and as if men had no souls. This species of reckless hilarity is conspicuous in the *Orientales* of M. Hugo, though on the whole we think he has rather hit the tone of Moorish song than that of the genuine East. . . . Byron is immortalized in Paris, perhaps even more for his supposed sacrifices to Greek liberty, than as a poet of stupendous talents. We must not therefore be astonished to find a considerable part of the *Orientales* occupied by Greek topics, and the reflection of Lord Byron's genius upon them. Canaris, the captain of the fireship, is generally the poet's hero: he celebrates his exploits repeatedly, and on occasion of a false rumour of his death, he writes the singular piece called *Les Têtes du Serail*. (p. 216)

Le Feu du Ciel is another singular poem. The cloud charged with pestilential fire passes along the sky under celestial guidance: it stops over each region over which it arrives: a general sketch is given of its appearance—a sort of bird's-eye view—at the end of which a voice from the clouds demands whether it is *here* the vengeance is to fall?—the answer is negatived until the land of the cities of Sodom and Gomorrah comes into view. . . .

Some of these passing sketches—the plan of which, not to be profane, reminded us of that ingenious device of the pantomimes in which the tour of Europe is performed by persons sitting in the pit—are executed with considerable vigour. (p. 217)

The claims of Hugo as a romancer will be more easily admitted than as a poet:—whether it be that the standard is higher, or that the readers and judges of poetry are more fastidious than the admirers of the romance or novel—the modern epopoea. His productions in this branch possess those striking features which arrest the attention of the most regardless persons; while the more cautious examiner cannot fail to detect the evidences of a powerful imagination. He forsakes the beaten path, and adds the charm of novelty to the attractions of moving accidents, extraordinary character, and vividly described scenery. The English writer to whom we should most unreluctantly compare the author of *Han d'Islande*, is Maturin;—this would be but slender justice, however; for with Maturin's power of working upon the passion of fear, and of conceiving situations of great horror, he possesses a taste and a knowledge of art which save him from overstepping the mark, and, consequently, producing sensations of a nature entirely opposed to those intended. (p. 218)

Bug-Jargal is an episode from the history of the insurrection of the negro slaves of Haïti. It is remarkable, like *Han d'Islande,* for the vigour with which its scenes are supported, and the boldness with which its characters are drawn; while the framework of description is even more accurately and vividly set before the mental eye than in the Norwegian romance. Works of fiction, in which negro slaves have been principal figures, have been not unfrequent in England; so that Bug-Jargal would not be the novelty in our own country that it appeared to the French: neither are the forms in which the black character show themselves in M. Hugo's conceptions extremely unlike the forms in which our own writers have represented them. We have read before of a noble self-denial in a virtuous negro—of deep passion, heroic courage, and a readiness to make the most painful sacrifices: these are in fact, the qualities of a hero, and heroes have been painted black before Bug-Jargal. The grotesque cruelty, the undignified tyranny, the ridiculous aping of European vice and folly in Biassou, another of the principal rebel leaders, are drawn in the most striking colours: neither, perhaps, does this complexion of atrocity meet us with the air of novelty, because, being drawn from nature, a copy has been attempted before. . . . In addition to the serious interest of Bug-Jargal, the author has contrived to turn a tolerable vein of ridicule upon the democratic mania of the times to which the rebellion of the blacks is to be attributed. He does not spare the philanthropic whites, who preached the wild doctrines of equality till they began to take effect, and who then showed the extraordinary want of analogy observable between the words of the mouth and the rules of man's conduct. (pp. 228-29)

["**The Last Day of a Prisoner condemned to Death,**"] is the supposed record of the thoughts that agitate the breast of a person in this awful position, together with a description of the few but important incidents which occur to the inmate of a solitary dungeon. It is an affecting picture, and too beautifully drawn to resemble closely the coarseness of nature. It is the last day of a malefactor—but that malefactor is Victor Hugo, a man, assuredly, who would not commit murder, and whom no just tribunal would condemn;—it is the last day of a man of a fine imagination, of a tender and amiable disposition—in short, of a gentleman and a poet. . . . We have seen that Hugo loves to transgress a little beyond the limits prescribed by persons of taste to the decently horrible, but we must say that it is not in his last work that we should look for his offences of this nature. The pleasure arising from contemplating the workmanship of the weapon diverts the mind from considering its deadly purposes. The play of the writer's fancy divides the attention of the reader of the "**Dernier Jour,**" and relieves the painfulness of sympathy. . . . It is a strange thing for a man to set himself to paint a dungeon *en beau*—and yet this is the task of M. Hugo; he has reduced the awful interval between judgment and doom to a kind of metaphysical experiment. The author rather says to himself, what is such a person likely to think of under the circumstances? than sets himself energetically to conceive and to pourtray all the horrors or all the apathy of the dungeon. In short, the "**Dernier Jour**" is the waking dream of a poet, who chooses to fancy himself condemned to death. (pp. 233-34)

> *"Victor Hugo's Poems and Novels," in* The Foreign Quarterly Review, *Vol. IV, No. VII, April, 1829, pp. 205-35.*

BLACKWOOD'S EDINBURGH MAGAZINE   (essay date 1829)

"*Dernier jour d'un condamné*" is a very extraordinary and powerful production,—over-wrought certainly, but it is the exaggeration of truth, not the extravagance of affectation. To this story, or transcript of the reflections of a criminal condemned to death, he prefixes a little comedy by way of preface,

in which the doctrines of the opponents of his style are introduced and ridiculed with that happy piquant levity, in which he is as successful as the generality of his countrymen. . . .

Remorse, as the author afterwards justly observes in the course of his book, visits the mind of a criminal more frequently before than after his condemnation—once condemned, the horrible contemplation of death is all in all. There may be remorse in his sensations, but he knows it not—distinguishes it not as remorse—he thinks of his punishment, not of his crime.

But what is most new throughout this French book, is the perception of the true poetical connexion between visible external things, and internal feelings and emotions. Hitherto we find French writers giving us merely a highly finished picture of external things, and apparently insensible of the thoughts which lie wrapped up in them, but which come forth, when genius places them in such a situation, that they seem to speak to the occasion. (p. 208)

Throughout this little book, the wanderings of the tortured imagination of the condemned man are traced and described with great power and truth, and the minute circumstances which make up the details of the misery of a creature in so wretched a situation, are drawn with a curious fidelity, which makes us start back from the picture as from a horrible reality. Yet after all, M. Hugo's criminal is a poor creature, with womanish nerves, and womanish sensibility, with whom we stern English could have but small sympathy; and though he claims and receives our pity, we cannot avoid mingling it with some contempt. (pp. 208-09)

Some passages in Mr. Hugo's romance hint that it has a political object, and that a desire to induce the abolition of the punishment of death has been the motive for writing it. If such be indeed the author's view, the means and the end are about equally extravagant. To attempt a reform in the law by writing a romance, seems an exploit rather more worthy of the Knight of la Mancha, than of a sane man in this age, when the Schoolmaster and sober reason are said to have so much to do with the affairs of men; and the notion that no crime, however atrocious, should be punished with death, is certainly more appropriate to the dreams of a romance-writer, than the deliberate judgment of a politician. It is not, however, to be wondered at, that he who makes a romance the vehicle of his politics, should form his politics after the dictates of romance. (p. 209)

> *J., "French Literature," in* Blackwood's Edinburgh Magazine, *Vol. XXVI, No. CLV, August, 1829, pp. 205-10.**

THE FOREIGN QUARTERLY REVIEW   (essay date 1830)

A dramatic work which bears the name of Victor Hugo—which had been announced as likely to bring to issue the great contest between the adherents of the classic and romantic schools, and which since its appearance has been made alternately the subject of eulogium or abuse, grave criticism and parody—may safely be assumed as deserving of notice. The name of its author is a guarantee. Whatever system of literary opinions he may adopt, he will follow it fairly up to its results; there will be no compromises with the view of gaining over a party; no shrinking from the exhibition of those startling points of the system which may shock the prejudices of his countrymen; no mere attempt to dress up with a more modern colouring of sentiment or expression themes of which the groundwork is substantially old and hackneyed. What Victor Hugo does, we feel a conviction beforehand that he will to the best of his ability do thoroughly. (p. 455)

[*Hernani*] is one which, while it sparkles with poetical beauties, both of situation and expression, is very far indeed from realizing that ideal of a French tragedy, which we have sketched in the outset. The study of Spanish History and Poetry, and the inspiration of Calderon and the Romancero General have, indeed, enabled the author to spread over the still life of his play, and over some of the lesser shades of character, a Spanish colouring; the principle of Castilian honour, which seems to be the hinge upon which the piece turns, is exhibited in striking and varied lights; and the details of manners seem accurately and naturally filled up. But the play, we fear, errs grievously against the weightier matters of the law;—the laws of historical truth, and of universal nature.

The character of Charles the Vth., as exhibited in this drama, revolts against all our recollections of the past, and all our conceptions of the probable. (p. 470)

But the character seems not less objectionable in general truth and consistency, than in historical fidelity. If the light and frivolous adventure could graduate into the ambitious and cautious politician, at least the steps would be obvious, and the reasons of the change satisfactory and palpable. But in the Charles of Victor Hugo, these inconsistent qualities are made to exist at the same moment; the monarch, who is risking his life in a midnight love adventure, is at the same time pursuing his ambitious designs upon the empire; struggling for that eminence which he himself describes as the possession of half the world. M. Hugo may assure himself that not even in the wide circuit of the romantic, far less within the confines of nature, is there room at once in the heart for two such passions. (p. 471)

It would almost appear as if M. Hugo thought that inconsistency in one character might be palliated by a greater inconsistency in another, as some painters relieve one shadow against another still darker. Else, how are we to account for those contradictions which deform the characters of Hernani and Ruy Gomez; how explain the process by which the long-cherished vengeance of the former is cast from him, like a worn-out mantle, at a word from the emperor; or the latter suddenly converted from a warm-hearted, impetuous, honourable nobleman, into a cold and remorseless monster. Doubtless, hatred may yield to generosity; but the accumulated wrongs of his father and himself; his vows of vengeance, so often and even so unnecessarily repeated, attested by oaths, recalled to his recollection by fresh taunts and outrages, can hardly be conceived as so suddenly effaced from Hernani's mind even by the theatrical clemency of Charles. Still less can the character of Ruy Gomez be explained upon any consistent principle; it is a "formless infinite" of contending qualities. The conversion of the lively, talkative and apparently kind-hearted nobleman into the brutal fiend, reminds us of nothing but some scene in a pantomime, where Pantaloon sinks suddenly, and all at once the devil rises in his stead.

If therefore any character in the drama has any pretension to consistency it must be that of Donna Sol; and here something like unity has been preserved. (pp. 471-72)

We have left ourselves no room, even if we were inclined, to enter into minute criticism of this drama. The diction, which has been clamorously applauded and condemned in France, seems to us a decided improvement on the ordinary style of the French school. The awkward or harsh lines, the occasional coarseness of expression, which are so easily laid hold of and remembered, might with the labour of a few hours be effaced, while there would remain a vast preponderance of passages, finely conceived, and expressed in a language and versification in a high degree nervous, pliant, and poetical. Of the beauties of the calmer parts of the play some of the short specimens we have already extracted will give an idea; in many others of a more passionate character, there is a rapidity and condensation, a laconic brevity of expression, which approaches to the sublime. In fine, we cannot better compare M. Hugo's drama than to one of those gothic castles, amidst which he has placed his scenes; it is vast and striking from the magnitude of its outline, varied from the accumulation of materials it contains, powerful from the wild strength which has been employed, or rather wasted in its construction; but, like it, incoherent in its plan, and mixed in its architecture; with pillars where it is impossible to trace any connection between the capital and the base, shapeless chambers, where meanness sits side by side with magnificence, and dark and winding passages, which terminate after all in a prospect of a dead wall, or an empty court yard. (pp. 472-73)

> *"Victor Hugo's 'Hernani',"* in The Foreign Quarterly Review, *Vol. VI, No. XII, October, 1830, pp. 455-73.*

THE EDINBURGH REVIEW   (essay date 1833)

[Victor Hugo,] though still young, has already distinguished himself in almost every walk of imaginative literature;—disputing the prize of lyric poetry with Lamartine, in his **Odes,** his **Orientales,** and **Feuilles d d'Automne;** occupying one of the most eminent positions on the stage, by his **Cromwell, Hernani, Marion de l'Orme, Le Roi s'amuse,** and **Lucrece Borgia;** and indisputably at the head of romance, since the publication of his **Notre Dame de Paris.** Supcrior to his contemporaries in creative imagination,—being in fact the only one of them who seems to see his way with some clearness, or to possess the power of inventing, brooding over, and working out with patience one leading view—superior to them even in that particular in which their strength lies, mere *power* of painting and description; he is yet more visibly elevated above their sphere of inspiration by the purer spirit with which his works, as a whole, have been animated, the generous sympathy for goodness and devotion of every kind which he evinces, and the absence of those querulous doubts, those contradictory and self-neutralizing views by which in their works the reader is harassed. In many respects, indeed, he might be referred to as being 'among them, but not of them,'—an exception from, rather than an illustration of, the spirit of his time. Still, unfortunately, he remains connected with it by sufficient ties to identify him as one of those who have written during a century of confusion; nay, whose own example, however unconsciously, may have tended to increase the perplexity. And comparing his earlier tales—**Han d'Islande,** and **Bug-Jargal,** in which, amidst all the horrors in which they deal, a spirit of humanity, a fine sensibility to virtue and nobleness, always left the mind something to repose upon with satisfaction,—with his later works,—particularly his Dramas of **Le Roi s'amuse,** and **Lucrece Borgia,** in which scarcely any humane or generous emotion leavens the mass of licentiousness, incest, and murder, in which they deal,—we regret to think that instead of disengaging himself more and more from evil influences of his day, they seem rather to be acquiring a firmer hold over his mind;—as if the moral barometer has begun to sink at last under the pressure of the loaded atmosphere which surrounded it, and the index which once pointed to calm and sunshine, were now likely to waver for a time between deluge and storm.

We trust, however, this anticipation may not be realized. It is not for a man of Hugo's great and varied talent, to copy the mock misanthropy, and distrust of goodness, which we regret to see so generally affected by La Jeune France. It is never a pleasing sight to see misanthropy, the painful privilege of age, invading the province of youth;—to see the heart wrinkle before the brow. But it is doubly disagreeable, when we have reason to suspect that the author is not a whit more sincere in his misanthropy than in anything else; and that this mask, like any other, is merely put on for the sake of effect. Nature herself forbade to Victor Hugo the gloomy walk of indifference, callousness, or cynicism, and pointed out to him the sunny path of enthusiasm, hope, and sympathy, as that alone where he ought to wander. (pp. 346-48)

[*Notre Dame de Paris*] is in a strain of a higher mood than any he had previously attempted. The idea, we have seen it mentioned, is taken from the *Gitanilla* of Cervantes. The resemblance, however, is something like that between the rivers in Macedon and Monmouth: there are gipsies in both—nothing more. Here the author has brought his antiquarian learning to bear with effect, not . . . overlaying his story with erudition, but vivifying the dry bones of history by the warmth and brilliancy of his fancy; while an extraordinary effect of unity is given to the whole, by making the whole movement of the tale emanate from and revolve round the gipsy heroine Esmiralda, and concentrate itself about the venerable terrors of *Notre Dame*. There is a play of Calderon's which bears the title '*El Mayor Encanto Amore*,'—Love is the greatest of Enchantments. This sentence seems to us to embody the leading idea of the work. Love makes the learned archdeacon forget his studies, his clerical character, his reputation for sanctity, to court the favour of a volatile Bohemian. Love for this same Parisian Fenella softens the human savage Quasimodo—the dumb one-eyed bell-ringer of *Notre Dame*—and transforms him into a 'delicate monster,'—a devoted humble worshipper of the Bohemian;—while she, who is the cynosure of neighbouring eyes, the object of adoration to these singular lovers, is herself hopelessly attached in turn to a giddy-pated captain of the guard, who can afford to love no one but himself. The charm of the romance unquestionably lies in the conception of the character of Quasimodo, and in the singular art by which the monster, who first awakens our terror or disgust, comes at last, when his mind, like Cymon's, begins to expand and refine under the passion of love, to be an object of our pity and admiration. Frollo, the archdeacon, on whose character the author seems to have bestowed much pains, is, on the contrary, a complete failure. Esmiralda herself, a sort of Marion L'Escaut in character, is a very beautiful creation. There is exquisite pathos in that scene where she is brought in to exhibit in presence of him to whom her heart has attached itself, and of his intended bride; and in that where she again catches his eye on the balcony as she passes to execution, as well as in the heart-rending scene where the Penitent, who had betrayed her into the hands of justice, discovers her to be his own daughter. In power Hugo is never deficient; but certainly nothing in any of his former works is to be compared to his description of Notre Dame, and the mysterious adaptation, and pre-established harmony, as it were, which seemed to exist between it and its monstrous child Quasimodo;—of the attack of the Truands (the Alsatians of Paris) upon the cathedral, and their repulse by the superhuman exertions of the bell-ringer;—and finally of that awful scene

where the archdeacon, gazing down from the tower of *Notre Dame* upon the execution of his victim in the square beneath, is seized by Quasimodo—who has now relapsed into the savage, since the destruction of the only being to whom his heart had opened—and hurled from a height of two hundred feet 'plumb down' upon the pavement below. This description is terrible beyond conception. Every motion, every struggle of the wretched priest, every clutch of his nails, every heave of the breast, as he clings to the projecting spout which has arrested his fall; then the gradual bending of the spout itself beneath his weight; the crowd shouting beneath, the monster above him—weeping;—(for he had loved the priest, and only the fury of disappointed attachment had urged him to this crime;)—the victim balancing himself over the gulf, his last convulsive effort ere he resigns his hold, even the revolutions of his body as he descends, his striking on the roof, from which he glides off like a tile detached by the wind, and then the final crash and rebound upon the pavement—all are portrayed with the most horrible minuteness and reality. (pp. 352-54)

"French Literature—Recent Novelists," in The Edinburgh Review, *Vol. LVII, No. CXVI, July, 1833, pp. 330-57.**

THE LONDON REVIEW   (essay date 1835-36)

[With M. Victor Hugo, imagination] is all in all: Imagination alone conceives and executes. From the peculiar turn of his mind, combined with the unfortunate influences of our age, an age little favourable to the production of works destined for immortality, Reason has but a small share in M. Hugo's creations. We find in them no thoughts susceptible of being applied to conduct; nothing, or next to nothing, of real life; no philosophy—no ethics—no attempt to improve or to criticize his age, either by intelligent and searching inquiry, by sympathy, or by satire; no plan, no purpose; no opinions—for we cannot give that name to the commonplaces, whether serious or light, which have served him as a mere ground to embroider verse and prose upon. We find nothing, in short, of that which, in a literary production, speaks more particularly to the Reason. As little is there of taste, or critical perception and discernment. Being, as we conceive, even originally, deficient in these qualities, M. Hugo has, besides, erected contempt of criticism into a system: no uncommon case with those writers who have cultivated but half their mind, and who, when there is an excellence which they cannot reach, invent a theory to prove that they can do without it, or that they are to be most especially admired for not having it. M. Hugo writes from his fancy alone, to a nation whose literature is peculiarly addressed to the practical understanding—and in a language which excels chiefly in expressing the kind of ideas which correspond to such a literature. (pp. 395-96)

M. Victor Hugo has written numerous plays and romances; most of them (perhaps all, except **Hans d'Islande** and **Bug-Jargal**) less from inclination or choice, than from domestic necessities, and the burthens of a numerous family, which constrained him to devote himself to a lucrative kind of literature. . . . These plays and romances represent almost exclusively M. Victor Hugo; and not even M. Hugo complete, or in a natural state, but M. Hugo with his imagination on the rack—with feelings and passions drawn from the head alone—under the feverish excitement of nocturnal labours—laughing without gaiety, weeping without tenderness, ranting without enthusiasm, putting to the torture, not the passions of the human soul, to wring from them undiscovered secrets, but the French language, to extort from it unusual combinations and striking effects of style. Or else, perhaps, M. Hugo exhaling through the lips of his heroes his own annoyances: his dissatisfaction with the public, who always hesitate before they admire him, and whom he sometimes astonishes, but never moves; the obstacles he has had to overcome before arriving at his still contested reputation; his hopes, his disappointments, and the incredible illusions of his isolated existence. Those who know the author may be interested or amused by tracing his own character through the personages whom he has invented; but those who, with the immense majority of the public, are not privately acquainted with him, cannot understand, or know what to think of, those personages; finding neither in themselves, nor in their experience of others, any clue to the comprehension of them. They look upon them with curiosity; in the first place because these monsters are not destitute of a certain originality and strength; and next because they are (many of them) represented in a brilliantly decorated theatre, which keeps the eyes occupied while the mind sleeps; and (to do M. Hugo justice) because they occasionally exhibit something not wholly unlike sensibility and passion, laughter and tears. You can see at times, in these contorted visages, some slight relationship and resemblance to the human countenance.

The truth is that Imagination, even Imagination by itself, can counterfeit, so as to deceive a blunt perception, the other faculties of the mind; sensibility, passion, and even reason itself. A writer who has but imagination and memory can construct, from the recollections of his reading, a scene of passion, though he neither understand the passions of others, nor perhaps have any genuine or accurate consciousness of his own. He will put into the mouth of a mother, or a mistress, a language similar to that spoken by such characters in the best works of the kind; he will throw in a kind of sensibility, which, if not examined very closely, looks natural enough; he will weep with propriety, will deliver himself of jests which will pass with the careless or the uncultivated for genuine comedy; he will hit by accident, from having read something of a similar kind, upon some rational observations which may be mistaken for the produce of his own reason. All this we find in the dramatic writings of M. Victor Hugo. His lovers show a semblance of love; those who are supposed to weep, look as if their eyes were moistened; his laughers look sufficiently different from those who cry: it would be exaggeration to pretend that all his various personages are radically false and impossible. But we do not hesitate to affirm that none of the sentiments which he puts into their mouths come from the source from whence a great poet draws his resources: his sensibility comes not from the heart, nor his passionate scenes from a soul capable of feeling the passions which he bestows upon others; his mirth comes not from a vivid joyous perception of ridicule, nor his tears from the physical commotion which even imaginary suffering causes to a sensitive organization; and the reasonable things which are said, come not from that instinctive insight, fortified by reflection and experience, which is termed Reason.

The most remarkable creations of this imagination rushing on in the dark, with the uncertainty, but also with the sometimes successful temerity of one who wanders without a guide, are Didier in the drama of **Marion Delorme;** Hernani in the piece so called; and above all, Esmeralda and Quasimodo in the justly-admired romance of **Notre Dame de Paris.** (pp. 397-99)

M. Hugo's writings appear in more favourable colours when remembered than when actually read. In that gentle and pleasing impression which a book leaves on the memory, the ex-

aggerations disappear, the asperities are softened down, the superfluities retrenched, the excesses of an ill-regulated imagination are blotted out, and the overdrawn figures (for they are all overdrawn, even when the original conception is in nature) are replaced by genuine and simple ones. Seen from a distance, in the dim light of recollection, Esmeralda and Quasimodo are beautiful creations of a romantic fancy, and are certainly the two happiest conceptions of M. Victor Hugo, but when examined closely, in the book itself, they offend the judicious reader by the flood of details—false, exaggerated, ridiculous—with which the genuine traits of nature are overlaid. Esmeralda, when she is intended to be simple, is too often silly. Quasimodo plays the Corydon; and his ugliness, already so repulsive in the simplest sketch, becomes a very caricature of hideousness in the minuteness beyond measure with which it is depicted by the author. Those glimpses, few and far between, of eternal truth, which alone leave any impression on the memory, are lost in the profuse detail of mere outward circumstance and got-up sensibility and passion. (p. 401)

[M. Victor Hugo] has made no impression upon his age; the only feeling he has excited in it is curiosity. We see him, not at the head of any opinion, either affirmative or negative, but taking his cue from all opinions in succession; using them as the commonplaces of the moment, to make the temporary fortune of a volume. Instead of taking the lead of his age, either by identifying himself with its tendencies, or by keeping himself apart from it, and endeavouring, either by doing something himself, or by criticising what others do, to impress upon it a direction of his own—he seems to float on its surface, gathering up all the things which he hears said in it into his memory, and reproducing them with his imagination; seizing upon the fashion, the conceit, the ephemeral taste of the moment, and attaching a book to it, either in verse or prose, which lives as long as a fashion, a conceit, or a passing taste; like leaves flung upon a stream formed by a sudden shower, which will float no farther than the stream, and no longer than the shower. M. Hugo is, as indeed he says himself, the *écho sonore* of what passes on the surface of his times—but not the intelligent observer of what is going on below the surface; never leading, but always led; the *laureate*, first of royalty, and afterwards of the people, but never the poet of either. He sings for royalty, unbidden; he sings for the people, and the people never can make out what he would have with them. He is never the creator, the master of an idea; but makes himself, with profuse demonstrations of self-esteem, the humble servant and mouthpiece of any foreign idea which may help to sell one or two editions of one of his works. By his memory he keeps himself *au courant* of everything; by his imagination he can put on all tones and all opinions; but whoever has these two qualities, however brilliant in their kind, for sole stock, instead of leading anybody, always arrives *after* all the rest of the world. (pp. 403-04)

The real strength of M. Victor Hugo lies in description—the child of memory and fancy: memory, which recalls and arranges the objects; fancy, which colours them. His is not, indeed, the description which we admire in the ancient epics—simple and summary, telling every thing with a few touches, and making us feel the spirit of an object rather than placing before us its details; that description, more philosophical than mechanical, which sets the mind framing pictures for itself, instead of presenting it with an outline ready filled up. M. Hugo's is, on the contrary, the minute, mechanical sort of description, characteristic of a declining literature; more resembling a plan than a landscape; representing objects, not with the roundness of forms and fusion of colours which belong to visible nature, but with the violent contrasts of colour, the asperities, the angularities, and the exaggerated proportions, which objects have when viewed under the microscope. In this style of description, however, M. Hugo excels. Few poets, either in the present or in past ages, have been gifted with so eminent a talent for making the reader see, as it were with his bodily eyes, pictures painted by means of words. (pp. 408-09)

In lyric poetry, which depends for effect upon images and bold transitions, M. Victor Hugo has written some pieces which will live. An ode consists generally of a common thought, enveloped in brilliant language; this thought may be compared to a *cocoon*, round which, itself coarse and of no value, the poet spins his rich tissue of dazzling and harmonious verse. The Ode therefore is a style of composition admirably suited to a poet whose own stock of ideas is but slender, and who is rather a decorator of thoughts than a thinker. There are no more beautiful odes in the French language than the two or three finest of M. Victor Hugo. There, all the riches of his purely *external* talent have a free field for displaying themselves: his bold and distinct imagery; his sentences replete with melody; his words so felicitously arranged as almost to pass for thoughts; his abundance of strokes for unexpected effect, that piquant but equivocal beauty, the peculiar ornament of lyric poetry—in which we are left in doubt whether it is the idea, or only the turn of expression which strikes us—ingenious combinations, which please but do not instruct. It is here that the natural infirmity of a poet who has but an imagination and a memory, does not prevent him from attaining the perfection of the *genre*. (pp. 409-10)

Some impartial readers, and ourselves among the number, prefer M. Hugo's prose to his verse. It is not so much because his prose is more perfect in itself, measured by the degree of perfection which in the French language is required of every work which is destined to live; but because the faults of M. Hugo are more supportable in prose, and his rare excellencies have freer scope. The rules of French verse are of excessive strictness; but as that strictness has not prevented the production of *chefs-d'oeuvre*, and has even, according to the most far-seeing critics, powerfully contributed to it, by crushing mediocrity, and keeping writers of eminence constantly on their guard against moments of carelessness—it cannot be expected that a country which possesses finished performances should be satisfied with imperfect ones, or should indulge a poet of the nineteenth century with a dispensation from the rules to which those of the seventeenth have submitted. Now, M. Hugo's metrical productions (except some of his odes, which have attained all the excellence belonging to that class of compositions) swarm with faults in the midst of their beauties. The good verses are drowned by the bad ones: he constantly stuffs in unnecessary words for the sake of the rhyme; the first verse of a couplet serves continually but to introduce the second. And this display of the mere springs and wheels of poetry, which it is the glory of a great writer to conceal, M. Hugo not only practises in almost all his pieces, but, what is worse, justifies in all his prefaces. His prose, therefore, is more generally relished than his verse; because in prose there is no need of expletives or other surplusage, to usher in a striking passage; and where the rocks and quicksands are least frequent, shipwrecks are rarest.

Many pages in M. Hugo's prose works are of the best school of French literature; correct and powerful; faithful to the genius of the language, and yet enriching it by novelty; boldly and energetically turned, brilliant without tinsel, original without quaintness, melodious without effeminacy; written sometimes with a mistaken, but with an honest, active, and ever present, sentiment of *propriety* in style. (pp. 410-11)

D.N., "Victor Hugo," in The London Review, *Vol. II, July-January, 1835-36, pp. 389-417.*

[J. W. CROCKER]   (essay date 1836)

Victor Hugo our readers will recollect as the author of ***Marion de Lorme, Le Roi s'amuse,*** and ***Lucrèce Borgia,*** three of the worst in point of moral, and of the best in point of talent, of the dramas we have so often referred to. His novels are (except one) of an earlier date, and exhibit little, in our opinion, of the vices or merits of his dramas. They do not belong to our subject, for they do not affect to describe the manners of the day. ***Hans d'Island*** is a Norwegian, and ***Bug Jargal*** a West-Indian tale; ***Notre Dame de Paris*** carries us back to the reign of Louis XI; and is an imitation of Sir Walter Scott—whom, *soit dit en passant,* it resembles as *Goose Gibby* in his helmet and buff coat might resemble the noble chivalry of Lord Evandale. But Hugo's last romance, ***Le dernier jour d'un Condamné,*** belongs to recent days. We have nothing to object to it, except the depraved taste which the author shows in himself, and imputes to the French public, by drawing out into a volume the agonies of a dying wretch. (p. 77)

We suspect, from the prefaces and notices which he is apt to affix to his works, that M. Hugo is somewhat sore to even the gentlest touches of criticism. This story is preceded by what he calls 'A *comedy* on the subject of a *tragedy,*'—a dramatic scene, in which a mixed company discuss the merit of the author and his works. The object of this modest little comedy is to sneer at the old *régime* and manners of France, and to exalt the superiority, generally, of the present era, and particularly of its greatest ornament,—M. Victor Hugo. We regret, however, to be obliged to say, that if this scene recalls the idea of [Molière's] *Critique de l'Ecole des Femmes,* it also again reminds us of *Goose Gibby,* and convinces us that M. Hugo is about as formidable a rival to Molière as to Walter Scott. But we notice this little piece chiefly for the defence which the personage who plays the character of the sound and enlightened critic makes for the painful and odious subject of the work. 'Its object,' says the apologist, 'is to contribute to the abolition of capital punishments.' 'But,' replies an objector, 'I do not see how that purpose is fulfilled, for he tells us nothing about the man, but that he is condemned; nothing is hinted of the alleged crime, nor its circumstances—nor whether the man be innocent or guilty—nor his rank in life—nor his character—nor, in short, any of the motives which could influence our judgment as to the expediency or justice of the punishment.' 'Oh no,' answers the apologist, 'to be sure—there lies the author's chief merit. Those incidental circumstances would have diverted the attention of the reader from the *abstract principle*. If the author had told you whether the crime was great or small, and the man innocent or guilty, it would have disturbed the logical consideration of the philosophic theory.' . . . [The] fact is, that there is not a line in the book which leads to any general thoughts on the subject; on the contrary, the whole narrative is so occupied—by the description of the judges, the jury, the prisoner, the gaolers, the fellow-convicts, the cart, the guillotine—(all of which could be better related by any one else rather than the unhappy sufferer, who over and over again confesses that he was in a stupid vertigo, and incapable even of thinking)—that we have never read any accounts, real or fictitious, of the last moments of a criminal, which brought so little to our minds—not merely the abstract expediency of capital punishment, but even the simple idea of death. The truth, we have no doubt, is, that M. Victor Hugo wanted to dash off a book suited to the depraved taste of the times, and hit upon *le dernier jour d'un Condamné*, as a piquant subject: but when he had finished his story, he perceived that it was at once odious and idle, equally destitute of interest or instruction; and the *metaphysical apology* was then introduced to cover the feebleness and inanity of the original performance. We must, however, do M. V. Hugo the justice to add, that although in his **Notre Dame de Paris** there are some scenes rather too free, yet, in his other novels, and especially in the **Dernier Jour d'un Condamné,** there is nothing offensive to decency. (pp. 77-9)

[J. W. Crocker,] *"French Novels," in* The Quarterly Review, *Vol. LVI, No. CXI, April, 1836, pp. 65-131.**

THE FOREIGN QUARTERLY REVIEW   (essay date 1836)

[In **"Mary Tudor"**] many beauties are more than counterbalanced by innumerable defects; resembling in this most of the other productions of its remarkable author, who, being gifted with more warmth of imagination than discrimination and judgment, allows himself to be carried away by the former in a far greater degree than would be expected in one who aspires to the first rank among dramatic writers. But, whatever may be the literary merit, and some it undoubtedly possesses, whatever may be the stage effect of the tragedy in question, what idea should be formed of it with respect to that loftiness of purpose, that ennobling end, which ought to characterize every dramatic production? What moral instruction is to be found contained in **"Mary Tudor"**? None: certainly none,—a case unfortunately too general with the tragedies of this author.

The imaginary amours and crimes of a queen are the subject of the tragedy. The former are of no interest to any one, and where is any moral instruction to be found in the latter? The least consideration will convince us that the only effect produced by this and similar dramas of Victor Hugo's is that of creating in the minds of the spectators a profound disgust and contempt for man and life itself. Every circumstance appears in the blackest colours, every fact is represented in the worst light, and every action is attributed to the worst motives. No string which returns a cheerful and spirit-stirring sound is touched by our author; his touch awakens only those whose mournful and lugubrious resonance discourages and depresses the mind; he either does not or will not see that a never-ceasing repetition of the same strain generates not only ennui, but an extreme indifference, in the auditors, whose attention it will be almost impossible afterwards to arouse: in the same manner as opium, when administered in too large quantities to the Orientals, renders them stupid and insensible, nothing but an increase of the dose being able to produce in them the desired effect. By continually touching a string which should be struck not only seldom but with great judgment, the author has deprived himself of one great source of producing stage-effect; he has to a certain degree annihilated his terror-exciting power. Nor will it be irrelevant to point out to our readers how often Victor Hugo is in open contradiction with his own principles, or rather to show how totally void he is of any, and how determined never to acknowledge them. (pp. 425-26)

[Victor Hugo] does not appear to us, either in the tragedy before us or in the greater part of his other productions, to have

fulfilled the duty or attained the end which we conceive is to be expected from the dramatic poet, or which should constitute his chief stimulus and highest ambition; that the path he pursues, though occasionally strewed with flowers, is decidedly a wrong one; and that, though one of momentary brilliancy, his will not prove a lasting fame. (p. 427)

" 'Marie Tudor'," in The Foreign Quarterly Review, *Vol. XVII, No. XXXIII, July, 1836, pp. 417-27.*

FRANCES TROLLOPE   (essay date 1836)

I have never mentioned [Victor Hugo] or his works to any person of good moral feeling and cultivated mind, who did not appear to shrink from according him even the degree of reputation that those who are received as authority among our own critics have been disposed to allow him. I might say, that of him France seems to be ashamed. (p. 96)

There is so much meretricious glitter in the works of Victor Hugo,—nay, so much real brightness now and then,—that I expected to find at least the younger and less reflecting part of the population warm in their admiration of him.

His clinging fondness for scenes of vice and horror, and his utter contempt for all that time has stamped as good in taste or feeling, might, I thought, arise from the unsettled spirit of the times; and if so, he could not fail of receiving the meed of sympathy and praise from those who had themselves set that spirit at work.

But it is not so. The wild vigour of some of his descriptions is acknowledged; but that is all of praise that I ever heard bestowed upon Victor Hugo's theatrical productions in his native land.

The startling, bold, and stirring incidents of his disgusting dramas must and will excite a certain degree of attention when seen for the first time, and it is evidently the interest of managers to bring forward whatever is most likely to produce this effect. . . .

The romance of **"Notre Dame de Paris"** is ever cited as Victor Hugo's best work, excepting some early lyrical pieces of which we know nothing. But even this, though there are passages of extraordinary descriptive power in it, is always alluded to with much more of contempt than admiration. . . . (p. 97)

[Such] productions as Victor Hugo's are calculated to do great injury to human nature. They would teach us to believe that all our gentlest and best affections can only lead to crime and infamy. There is not, I truly believe, a single pure, innocent, and holy thought to be found throughout his writings: Sin is the muse he invokes—he would

> Take off the rose
> From the fair forehead of an innocent love,
> And set a blister there.

Horror is his handmaid; and "thousands of liveried *monsters* lackey him," to furnish the portraits with which it is the occupation of his life to disgust the world.

Can there, think you, be a stronger proof of a diseased intellect among the *décousu* part of the world, than that they not only admire this man's hideous extravagances, but that they actually believe him to be . . . at least they say so . . . a second Shakspeare! . . . A Shakspeare!

To chastise as he deserves an author who may be said to defy mankind by the libels he has put forth on the whole race, requires a stouter and a keener weapon than any a woman can wield; but when they prate of Shakspeare, I feel that it is our turn to speak. How much of gratitude and love does every woman owe to him! He, who has entered deeper into her heart than ever mortal did before or since his day, how has he painted her?—As Portia, Juliet, Constance, Hermione;—as Cordelia, Volumnia, Isabella, Desdemona, Imogene!

Then turn and see for what we have to thank our modern painter. Who are his heroines?—Lucrèce Borgia, Marion de Lorme, Blanche, Maguelonne, with I know not how many more of the same stamp; besides his novel heroine, whom Mr. Henry Lytton Bulwer calls "the most delicate female ever drawn by the pen of romance"—The Esmeralda! . . . whose sole accomplishments are dancing and singing in the streets, and who . . . delicate creature! . . . being caught up by a horseman in a midnight brawl, throws her arms round his neck, swears he is very handsome, and thenceforward shows the delicate tenderness of her nature by pertinaciously doting upon him, without any other return or encouragement whatever than an insulting caress bestowed upon her one night when he was drunk . . . "delicate female!"

But this is all too bad to dwell upon. It is, however, in my estimation, a positive duty, when mentioning the works of Victor Hugo, to record a protest against their tone and tendency. . . . (pp. 98-99)

I will introduce M. Hugo in **"Le Roi s'amuse,"** which, from the circumstance (the happiest, I was assured, that ever befell the author) of its being withdrawn by authority from the Théâtre Français, has become infinitely more celebrated than any other he has written. . . .

The first glorious moment of being forbidden at the Français appears almost to have turned the lucky author's brain. His preface to **"Le Roi s'amuse,"** among many other symptoms of insanity, has the following:—

> The first emotion of the author was one of unbelief. . . . The deed was so arbitrary as to seem incredible . . . he could not give credit to such a stretch of insolence and folly. . . . The minister had indeed, in the exercise of his divine right of minister, made the order. . . . The minister had taken from him his play, his right, his property; there was but one thing left—namely, to throw him, the poet, into the Bastile.
>
> Has there indeed, then, been such a thing as the revolution of July? . . . What could be the motive of such a proceeding? It seems that our censors find their morality offended by 'Le Roi s'amuse;' the name alone of the author should have been a sufficient refutation of the charge (!!!) . . .
>
> (p. 100)

I wish much that some one would collect and publish in a separate volume all M. Victor Hugo's prefaces; I would purchase it instantly, and it would be a fund of almost inexhaustible amusement. (pp. 100-01)

[The plot of **"Le Roi s'amuse"**] is beyond doubt what may be called "a tragic situation," and I confess it does seem very hard-hearted to laugh at it: but the *pas* that divides the sublime

from the ridiculous is not distinctly seen, and there is something vulgar and ludicrous, both in the position and language of the parties, which quite destroys the pathetic effect. (pp. 102-03)

[The story] is very shocking; but it is not tragedy,—and it is not poetry. Yet it is what we are told has heaved the earth from under Racine! . . .

Racine has not produced dramas from ordinary life; it was not his object to do so, nor is it the end he has attained. It is the tragedy of heroes and demigods that he has given us, and not of cut-purses, buffoons, and street-walkers.

If the language of Racine be poetry, that of M. Hugo is not; and wherever the one is admired, the other must of necessity be valueless. (p. 103)

It would be much less difficult, I conceive, so strongly to excite the imagination by the majestic eloquence of Racine's verses as to make you conscious of fellow-feeling with his sublime personages, than to debase your very heart and soul so thoroughly as to enable you to fancy that you have any thing in common with the corrupt creations of Victor Hugo.

But even were it otherwise—were the scenes imagined by this new Shakspeare more like the real villany of human nature than those of the noble writer he is said to have set aside, I should still deny that this furnished any good reason for bringing such scenes upon the stage. Why should we make a pastime of looking upon vulgar vice? Why should the lowest passions of our nature be for ever brought out in parade before us?

It is not and it cannot be for good.

The same reasoning might lead us to turn from the cultured garden, its marble terraces, its velvet lawns, its flowers and fruits of every clime, that we might take our pleasure in a bog—and for all consolation be told, when we slip and flounder about in its loathsome slime, that it is more natural. (pp. 104-05)

> *Frances Trollope, "Victor Hugo—Racine," in her* Paris and the Parisians in 1835, *Harper & Brothers, 1836, pp. 96-105.**

ALEXANDER SERGEYEVICH PUSHKIN (essay date 1837)

Of all great foreign authors Milton was the most unfortunate as far as France was concerned. . . . How was he presented by Victor Hugo, [a] favourite of the Parisian public? Maybe readers have forgotten . . . *Cromwell* and are therefore unable to judge of the absurdity of Victor Hugo's pictures. Let us bring [it] before the judgement of any educated and right-thinking person. (pp. 453-54)

We will not try to follow in the halting steps of the dull and monstrous play; we only want to show our readers how it presents Milton, who, still unknown as a poet, is famed throughout Europe as a political writer for his embittered and overbearing eloquence. (p. 454)

In a scene having neither historical truth nor dramatic probability, in a meaningless parody of the ceremonial followed at the coronation of the Kings of England, the chief parts are played by Milton and one of the court jesters. Milton advocates a republic, the jester takes up the gage of a royalist knight. . . .

It is as such a pathetic madman and insignificant windbag that Milton is portrayed by a man who probably did not realize himself what he was doing when he insulted that mighty spirit!

In the course of the whole tragedy Milton hears nothing except taunts and curses; but it is true that he himself does not once utter a sensible word. He is an old buffoon whom everybody despises and to whom nobody pays the slightest attention.

No, Mr. Hugo! That is not what John Milton was like, the friend and champion of Cromwell, the austere fanatic, the stern author of the *Eikonoklastes* and of *Defensio populi*. He who addressed to Cromwell his famous and prophetic sonnet, 'Cromwell, our chief of men', would not have spoken to him in this language. He, who 'though fall'n on evil days . . . and evil tongues', in poverty, persecuted and blind, retained an inflexibility of soul and dictated *Paradise Lost,* could not have been made a laughing-stock by the dissolute Rochester and by the court jesters.

If Mr. Hugo, himself being a poet (albeit a second-rate one), understood Milton so badly, anyone can guess what happened to Cromwell under his pen, for whom he had no sympathy whatsoever! But that does not concern us here. Let us pass from the uneven and crude works of Victor Hugo and his ugly tragedies. . . . (pp. 456-57)

> *Alexander Sergeyevich Pushkin, "On Milton and Chateaubriand's Translation of 'Paradise Lost'" (originally published under a different title in Sovremennik, Vol. 6, 1837), in his Pushkin on Literature, edited and translated by Tatiana Wolff (© 1971 by Tatiana Wolff), Methuen & Co Ltd, 1971, pp. 452-63.**

THE NEW MONTHLY MAGAZINE   (essay date 1856)

These **"Contemplations"** might have a motto prefixed from one of Campbell's lyrics—

> In the silence of twilight's *contemplative* hour,
> I have mused in a sorrowful mood.

The themes are sorrow-laden; and tones of lamentation, and semi-tones of keen anguish and demi-semi-tones of blank despair, occur with oppressive frequency. The poet had ever a kindness for *il penseroso*. As he has grown an older, he has grown too a sadder man. His path is not as the shining light, that shineth more and more unto the perfect day. We are rather reminded of twilight merging into eve, and eve saddening (in Coleridge's phrase) into night.

As the eye glances over the pages of the second of these volumes, containing M. Hugo's latest poems, written at intervals during the past twelve years, it is continually lighting on words of a gloomy cast, pertaining to the night side of nature, and the woes of poor humanity. (p. 213)

Passages of deep tenderness and touching affection—nay, whole poems of this character—are largely interfused; but shades of the prison-house close them in; everywhere we are haunted by Time the Skeleton and Death the Shadow; and, as in the home appointed for all living, the worms seem already to feed sweetly upon us, the worms are under us, and the worms cover us. . . . At times, indeed, the utterly desponding and dejected poet expresses himself like a man who has no hope, and is without God in the world. . . . And certainly the tone in which he literally upbraids his Maker, for taking away that which He had given, for commissioning death to visit the work of His own hands, is audacious to the full extent of French audacity. (pp. 213-15)

> *"Victor Hugo: 'Les contemplations',"* in The New Monthly Magazine, *Vol. CVIII, No. CCCCXXX, October, 1856, pp. 213-17.*

CHARLES BAUDELAIRE   (essay date 1861)

Today when we glance over the recent poetry of Victor Hugo, we see that he has remained what he was, a thoughtful wanderer, a solitary man, yet in love with life, a contemplative and inquiring mind. But it is no longer in the wooded and flowering outskirts of the great city, on the rough embankments of the Seine, in paths swarming with children that he sets his feet and eyes to wander. Like Demosthenes, he talks with the wind and the waves; formerly he roamed alone in places seething with human life; today he walks in solitudes peopled with his thoughts. And so he is perhaps even greater and more remarkable. The colors of his dreams have taken on a solemn hue and his voice has grown deeper in rivaling that of the Ocean. But there as here, he still seems to us like a statue of Meditation in movement. (p. 236)

In the days, already so distant, . . . happy days when men of letters formed a society sorely missed by its survivors, who will never again find its equal, Victor Hugo was the one to whom everyone turned, seeking the watchword. Never was royalty more legitimate, more natural, more acclaimed by gratitude, more confirmed by the impotence of rebellion. When one recalls what French poetry was before he appeared, and what a rejuvenation it has undergone since he came; when one imagines how insignificant it would have been without him, how many mysterious and profound sentiments that have been given expression would have remained unvoiced, how many intellects he has discovered, how many men made famous by him would have remained obscure, it is impossible not to consider him as one of those rare, providential minds who bring about the salvation of all men in the literary order, as others do in the moral order and still others in the political order. (p. 237)

Victor Hugo was, from the outset, the man who was best endowed and most obviously chosen to express in poetry what I shall call *the mystery of life.* Nature which lies before us, no matter where we turn, and which envelops us like a mystery, shows herself under several simultaneous aspects, each of which, to the extent that it is more intelligible, more perceptible to us, is reflected more intensely in our hearts: form, attitude and movement, light and color, sound and harmony. The music of Victor Hugo's verses is adapted to the profound harmonies of nature; as a sculptor, he carves into his stanzas the unforgettable form of things; as a painter, he illuminates them with the right color. And the three impressions penetrate the reader's mind simultaneously, as if they came directly from nature. From this triple impression comes *the morality of things.* No artist is more universal than he, more suited to put himself in contact with the forces of universal life, more inclined to bathe ceaselessly in nature. Not only does he express precisely and translate literally what is clearly and distinctly visible, but he expresses with an *indispensable obscurity* what is obscure and vaguely revealed. His works abound in extraordinary features of the kind which we could call *tours de force,* if we did not know that they are essentially natural to him. The poetry of Victor Hugo can translate for the human soul not only the most direct pleasures that it draws from visible nature but also the most fleeting, the most complicated, the most moral (I am purposely using the word moral) sensations which are transmitted to it by visible substance, by inanimate or what is called inanimate nature; it can translate not only the form of substance exterior to man, vegetable or mineral, but also its aspect, its expression, its sadness, its tenderness, its exultant joy, its repulsive hate, its charm or its horror; in short, in other words, all that is human in every imaginable thing and also all that is divine, sacred, or diabolic. (pp. 237-38)

From his ability to absorb the life around him, unique in its amplitude, as well as from his powerful faculty of meditation, Victor Hugo has become a very extraordinary poetic character, questioning, mysterious, and, like nature itself, vast and detailed, serene and agitated. Voltaire did not see mystery in anything, or at least in very few things. But Victor Hugo does not cut the Gordian knot of things with Voltaire's military dispatch; his keenly perceptive senses reveal abysses to him: he sees mystery everywhere. . . .

Victor Hugo possesses not only greatness but universality. How varied is his repertory and, although always *one* and compact, how many-sided it is! (p. 240)

[His] genius is without limits. Here we are dazzled, enchanted, and enveloped as if by life itself. The transparent air, the domed sky, the outline of a tree, the gaze of an animal, the silhouette of a house are painted in his books with the brush of an accomplished landscapist. In everything he puts the palpitation of life. (p. 241)

As for love, war, family pleasures, the sorrows of the poor, national splendors, all that which is peculiar to man and which constitutes the domain of the genre painter and of the history painter, what have we seen that is richer and more concrete than the lyrical poetry of Victor Hugo? If space allowed, this would doubtless be the occasion to analyze the moral atmosphere which hovers and moves through his poems and which derives very obviously from the author's own temperament. It seems to me that it is unmistakably characterized by a love which makes no distinction between what is very strong and what is very weak, and that the attraction exercised over the poet by these two extremes stems from a single source, which is the very strength, the primordial vigor with which he is endowed. . . . On the other hand, but through a different tendency, whose source is, however, the same, the poet always shows warm compassion for all that is weak, lonely, sorrowful, for all that is fatherless: a paternal attraction. The man of strength, who senses a brother in all that is strong, sees his children in all that has need of protection or consolation. It is from strength itself and from the certainty that it gives to one who possesses it that the spirit of justice and of charity is derived. Thus in the poems of Victor Hugo there constantly occur those notes of love for fallen women, for the poor who are crushed in the cogwheels of society, for the animals that are martyrs of our gluttony and despotism. (p. 242)

The excessive, the immense are the natural domain of Victor Hugo; he moves in it as if in his native atmosphere. The genius which he has always displayed in painting *all the monstrosity* surrounding man is truly prodigious. But it is especially in recent years that he has experienced the metaphysical influence emanating from all these things; the curiosity of an Oedipus obsessed by innumerable Sphinxes. . . . The suggestive contemplation of the heavens occupies an immense and dominant place in the most recent works of the poet. (p. 243)

In the hands of a poet other than Victor Hugo, such themes and such subjects could too easily have taken on a didactic form, which is the greatest enemy of true poetry. To recount in verse *known* laws governing the movement of the moral or

sidereal world is to describe what has been discovered and what falls completely under the scientist's telescope or compass; it is to confine oneself to tasks pertaining to science, to encroach on its functions, and to encumber its traditional language with the superfluous and, in this case, dangerous embellishment of rhyme; but to give oneself up to all the reveries suggested by the infinite spectacle of life on earth and in the heavens is the legitimate right of anyone, consequently of the poet who is empowered to translate into a magnificent language, other than prose and music, the eternal conjectures of inquiring humanity. In describing what is, the poet is degraded and descends to the level of the professor; in recounting the possible he remains faithful to his function; he is a collective soul who questions, who weeps, who hopes and who sometimes finds the answer. (p. 245)

Charles Baudelaire, "Reflections on Some of My Contemporaries: Victor Hugo" (originally published under a different title in La revue fantaisiste, *1861), in his* Baudelaire As a Literary Critic, *edited and translated by Lois Boe Hyslop and Francis E. Hyslop, Jr. (copyright © 1964 by The Pennsylvania State University), The Pennsylvania State University Press, University Park, 1964, pp. 233-47.*

CHARLES BAUDELAIRE (essay date 1862)

[*Les Misérables*] is a book of charity, that is to say a book intended to excite, to stimulate a charitable spirit; it is a book that raises questions, that poses complex social problems, agonizing and terrible in nature, that says to the reader's conscience: "Well, what do you think about this? What is your conclusion?" (p. 285)

It is quite evident that in *Les Misérables* the author wanted to create living abstractions, ideal figures, each of which, representing one of the principal types necessary to the development of his thesis, was raised to epic heights. It is a novel constructed in the manner of a poem in which each character is an exception only through the exaggerated manner in which he represents a *generality*. The way in which Victor Hugo has conceived and constructed this novel and the way in which he has cast the rich elements usually employed in special works (the lyric sense, the epic sense, and the philosophical sense) into an indefinable amalgam in order to make a new Corinthian metal, confirms once again the fatality which led him as a young man to partially transform the ancient ode and ancient tragedy into the poems and dramas that we know.

Thus Monseigneur Bienvenu represents hyperbolic charity, endless faith in self-sacrifice, absolute confidence in Charity considered as the most perfect means of moral instruction. In the painting of this type there are observations and touches of wonderful delicacy. It is apparent that the author took delight in perfecting this angelic model. (pp. 285-86)

Valjean is the naïve, innocent brute; he is the ignorant proletarian, guilty of an offense we would all doubtless excuse (the theft of a loaf of bread), but which, legally punished, casts him into the school of Evil, that is to say into Prison. There, his intelligence is developed and sharpened in the oppressive thoughts of imprisonment. At length he leaves, cunning, formidable, dangerous. He has repaid the Bishop's hospitality with a second theft, but the latter saves him by a white lie, convinced that Pardon and Charity are the only lights that can dissipate all the darkness. (pp. 286-87)

Les Misérables is then a book of charity, an astounding call to order of a society too enamored of itself and too little concerned with the immortal law of brotherhood; a plea for the *wretched* (those who *suffer* from poverty and are degraded by it), uttered by the most eloquent lips of our day. In spite of any possible intentional deception or any unconscious bias in the manner— in the eyes of strict philosophy—in which the terms of the problem are stated, we believe, just as does the author, that *books such as this are never useless.*

Victor Hugo is for *Man,* and yet he is not against God. He trusts in God, and yet he is not against Man.

He spurns the frenzy of rebellious Atheism, and yet he does not approve the bloodthirsty gluttony of the Molochs and the Teutatès.

He believes that Man is born good, and yet even in the face of the constant disasters that befall him he does not accuse God of cruelty and malice.

I believe that even for those who find in orthodox doctrine, in pure Catholic theory, an explanation, if not complete, at least more comprehensive, of all the disturbing mysteries of life, Victor Hugo's new book should be *Bienvenu* [welcome] (in keeping with the name of the bishop whose triumphant charity it relates); it is a book to be applauded and to be appreciated. (p. 289)

> *Charles Baudelaire, " 'Les misérables' " (originally published under a different title in* Le boulevard, *April, 1862), in his* Baudelaire As a Literary Critic, *edited and translated by Lois Boe Hyslop and Francis E. Hyslop, Jr. (copyright © 1964 by The Pennsylvania State University), The Pennsylvania State University Press, University Park, 1964, pp. 280-89.*

THE ATLANTIC MONTHLY   (essay date 1862)

Every resource of bookselling ingenuity has been exhausted in order to make every human being who can read think that the salvation of his body and soul depends on his reading "Les Misérables." . . .

The French bookseller also piqued the curiosity of the universal public by a story that Victor Hugo wrote "Les Misérables" twenty-five years ago, but, being bound to give a certain French publisher all his works after his first celebrated novel, he would not delight the world with this product of his genius until he had forced the said publisher into a compliance with his terms. . . .

"Fantine" [the first of five novels under the general title of "Les Misérables"] comes before us as an attempt both to include and to supersede the Christian religion. . . . [We] may venture to affirm that Christendom is not the beginning of which *Hugoism* is the complement and end. We think that the revelation made by the publisher of "Les Misérables" sadly interferes with the revelation made by Victor Hugo. Saint Paul may be inferior to Saint Hugo, but everybody will admit that Saint Paul would not have hesitated a second in deciding, in the publication of *his* epistles, between the good of mankind and his own remuneration. . . . At last a book-selling Barnum appears, pays the price, and a morality which utterly eclipses that of Saint Paul is given to an expectant world.

This morality . . . is represented by Bishop Myriel. The character is drawn with great force, and is full both of direct and subtle satire on the worldliness of ordinary churchmen. (p. 124)

[From a] bare abstract, the story does not seem to promise much pleasure to novel-readers, yet it is all alive with the fiery genius of Victor Hugo, and the whole representation is so intense and vivid that it is impossible to escape from the fascination it exerts over the mind. Few who take the book up will leave it until they have read it through. It is morbid to a degree that no eminent English author, not even Lord Byron, ever approached; but its morbid elements are so combined with sentiments abstractly Christian that it is calculated to wield a more pernicious influence than Byron ever exerted. Its tendency is to weaken that abhorrence of crime which is the great shield of most of the virtue which society possesses, and it does this by attempting to prove that society itself is responsible for crimes it cannot prevent, but can only punish. To legislators, to Magdalen societies, to prison-reformers, it may suggest many useful hints; but, considered as a passionate romance, appealing to the sympathies of the ordinary readers of novels, it will do infinitely more harm than good. The bigotries of virtue are better than the charities of vice. On the whole, therefore, we think that Victor Hugo, when he stood out twenty-five years for his price, did a service to the human race. The great value of his new gospel consisted in its *not* being published. We wish that another quarter of a century had elapsed before it found a bookseller capable of venturing on so reckless a speculation. (p. 125)

> *"Reviews and Literary Notices: 'Les Misérables',"* in The Atlantic Monthly *(copyright © 1862, by The Atlantic Monthly Company, Boston, Mass.), Vol. X, No. LVII, July, 1862, pp. 124-25.*

[G. H. LEWES]   (essay date 1862)

[As] the present critic does not feel much sympathy with Victor Hugo's works, in spite of their very remarkable qualities, and their transcendant picturesqueness, he is desirous, while paying every deserved tribute to genius, to state in a few words the reason why this poet is not, and cannot be, loved with the love bestowed on great writers. (p. 172)

[Wherein] lies his great defect? If we say that it lies in a radical insincerity, we shall express our conviction in language which may appear at variance with our recognition of his seriousness as an artist; yet a word or two of explanation may clear away the seeming contradiction. The perfectly sincere artist not only loves his Art, but above all things loves it as the splendour of truth: an artist is insincere, in our sense of the word, in proportion as he prefers "effects" to truth, in proportion as he uses all his cunning in dressing up phantasms which will arrest the incurious eye, rather than in patiently, lovingly, laboriously, striving to express the actual visions of his own soul, confident that whatever is truly felt by him will be felt as true by others; or supremely careless whether all the world fails to recognise its truth, so that his own soul affirms it. Far be it from us, in wantonness of speech, even to hint that Victor Hugo is insincere, in the ordinary meaning of that word. But we are deeply convinced of his having the insincerity which weakens imperfect artists, and which betrays itself by their eyes being intently fixed on the *public* rather than on their *work;* so that instead of painting the vision they see, *as* they really see it, they paint what they imagine the public will expect to see, or will most applaud. In its lowest form this insincerity becomes claptrap. In every form it is untruth—sometimes the untruth of conventional "idealism," sometimes the untruth of insidious flattery of popular prejudice.

There can be no doubt that Victor Hugo is a very effective writer. He produces a succession of pictures which startle the most incurious; and such is the vigour of his imagination, that he not unfrequently kindles the imagination of his readers. But he rarely touches the deeper chords of their minds, and never with more than a passing breath. Hence we are startled, but not moved; we admire—we do not love. No great heart is felt to be throbbing through his works; no serene mind is raying out its effulgence. We think him immensely clever, and rather silly; bold, original, and bombastic; swaggering and blasphemous, even among swaggering and blaspheming Frenchmen. . . . It is the same with his style—a style glittering with imagery, pointed with epigrams, but never at the service of truth, nor ever expressing immortal phrases. One cannot say that, considered as mere style, it is not rich and rare; but it charms us no more than the exquisite jewels which glitter on some tawdry image of the Madonna. As a man, Victor Hugo seems to us moved by generous and noble sentiments, and his verses show an exquisite tenderness towards children. We remember many offensive passages in his writings, but no page that is base or mean. Nevertheless he repels all our sympathy by an abiding untruthfulness in conception and presentation. (pp. 172-73)

Esmeralda and Quasimodo are wonderful creations; but they are wholly *un*human, and only flatter the picturesque imagination. In Victor Hugo's last romance, **'Les Misérables,'** we miss the creative genius which gives so great a charm, and has given so immense a popularity, to **'Notre Dame de Paris;'** nor do we find that ''years have brought the philosophic mind,'' or added any chords to the lyre. (p. 175)

'Fantine' opens with an elaborated—we cannot say elaborate—picture of a bishop-saint. No less than one hundred and sixty-five pages are devoted to the presentation of his character; and, to our surprise, no sooner is the character presented, than, after serving the author in one scene, and giving one incident to the story, it disappears for ever. In constructive art this is as great a mistake as if the portico of the Parthenon were the entrance to a shed; and this objection would equally apply if the picture were as admirable as it is ambitious; if the portico *were* that of a Parthenon, instead of being a lath-and-plaster imitation. We have intimated that we consider this portrait a failure, although it is lovingly painted, and some of its touches are really touching. It fails because it is not true. The bishop is meant to be good, and is only ''goody.'' His humanity is sacrificed to unreal sentiment of the ''goody'' order. Few artists seem to be great enough—that is, courageously truthful enough—to paint good men. They shrink from truth, take out the human heart such as nature makes it, and replace it by an impossible ideal of passionless morality. Afraid to represent goodness as it really exists, amid human infirmities and humorous weaknesses which challenge sympathy and secure our love even out of the very pity and laughter they provoke, the imperfect artist hopes to achieve his aim by a representation of transcendant virtue. The virtue is transcendant because it springs from moral *maxims,* instead of from *feelings;* from abstractions, instead of from complex individualities. (pp. 175-76)

So much for the general want of truth. Descending to the details, we find many defects. The author's besetting sin of antithesis obliges him to intimate that his saint was formerly a sinner; as it obliges him, when painting a model of female chastity, to take her from the streets. *C'est de rigueur.* Nevertheless, after the sinner has become a saint, and especially after he has become a bishop, it is trespassing too far on our credulity

to make this bishop listen placidly to a long tirade of blasphemy and cynicism from the mouth of a senator seated at the dinner-table with him. (p. 176)

Victor Hugo seldom does things by halves. Having made his heroine take to the streets, he makes her one of those wretched creatures who flaunt in beggarly finery, and strive to deaden memory by drink. . . .

The subject is undoubtedly a fine one, if treated in a true and sympathetic style. No more harrowing picture can be thought of than that of a mother forced into sin, dragged into degradation, in order to feed and educate her child; a picture full of pathos, full of the actual tragedy of social life, full of lessons. But to bring out this piteousness, and to call forth our deepest sympathies with the victim, while giving rise to serious thoughts respecting the social condition which creates such a tragedy, it is above all things necessary that the writer be thoroughly sincere, severely true; passionate, it may be; vehemently indignant; but never for one moment false and sentimental; never by one phrase of misplaced rhetoric diverting our sympathies from the truth. It is the besetting sin of most French writers to be incapable of trusting to the truth; and Victor Hugo is eminently French. They appeal to our sympathies on grounds which make it impossible for us to respond. Victor Hugo in the present instance wishes to rouse sympathy with the wretched Fantine. The simple statement of her story would certainly have roused it. We could not think of a mother's agony hurrying her into sin, without feeling deeply moved. But Victor Hugo is not contented with the simple story. He makes Fantine degraded as well as wretched; he intensifies her prostitution by every art of his powerful style; and having painted a brawling, flaunting street-walker, he audaciously calls upon us to accept her as a model of chastity and purity! Instead of appealing to our pity for the woman and the mother, he insults our understandings by demanding our belief in her modesty. (p. 179)

The preface forbids our regarding the work simply as a novel. According to the jargon of the day, ''it has a social idea.'' And what is that idea? Apparently this: Society is to blame for tolerating prisons where innocent but unfortunate men enter, to quit them hardened ruffians. Society is to blame for not acknowledging that wretched women take to the streets to prove their virtue. We can make out no other teaching.

Victor Hugo is an artist, and only a moralist in so far as art is indissolubly bound up with moral influences. It is as an artist, therefore, that we chiefly consider him here. We have already intimated our general appreciation of his merits and demerits, and may rapidly express the little we have to say regarding **'Les Misérables.'** There is here no character, in the high dramatic sense; none of the great dramatist's ventriloquism. The figures are all figures of puppets, and constantly betray their strings. We are throughout unpleasantly aware of the clever showman's presence. . . . The writing is throughout elaborate, coloured, polished; the rhetoric is often brilliant; the epigrams are incisive; the turns of phrase are original and felicitous. But the rhetoric is not eloquence; the brilliancy is mere glitter; the epigrams are seldom wise. In one word, it is not the strong, healthy, inspiring eloquence of a serious and beautiful mind, but rather the turbulent and factitious power of a strong talent loosened from all control: a debauch of diction, not a draught from Helicon. (pp. 181-82)

[*G. H. Lewes,*] *''Victor Hugo's Last Romance,'' in* Blackwood's Magazine, *Vol. XCII, No. DLXII, August, 1862, pp. 172-82.*

ECLECTIC MAGAZINE   (essay date 1862)

It is impossible to mention without some disappointment the last work of a great writer, entitled *Les Misérables*. This romance, which was intended to throw light on important social questions, and to avenge the cause of the poverty-stricken and neglected, is so overcrowded with exaggerated and occasionally revolting detail, that its greater beauties can scarcely be seen on account of the unnatural and unpleasant setting. . . . The same tendency toward the monstrous and unnatural which has been betrayed by Bulwer Lytton in his more advanced years seems now to be manifested by M. Victor Hugo, though, unlike the author of *A Strange Story*, it is comparatively easy to trace the development of this wild and mystical *penchant* in the mental and literary history of the accomplished Frenchman. A knowledge of the standard literature of every country is so undoubtedly important to those who would form a clear and unbiased judgment on the merits and defects of its current literature, that we can plead no excuse for occasional retrospection, deeming that a longer notice than usual of the career of a writer who, like M. Victor Hugo, has exercised an important influence on the spirit and poetry of his times, can not be unacceptable to our readers, but will form the most appropriate introduction to his new and somewhat startling romance. (p. 489)

"Literature of Victor Hugo," in Eclectic Magazine, *Vol. LVII, No. 4, December, 1862, pp. 489-94.*

THE NEW ENGLANDER   (essay date 1864)

[We have before us] five books, **Fantine, Cosette, Marius, l'Idylle rue Plumet, Jean Valjean,** forming a long series of essays enshrined as it were in different novels, each distinct, and yet connected like the acts of a drama [to form **"Les Miserables"**]. The first book—**Fantine,** although the title is hardly appropriate—the character after whom it is named playing in it but a subordinate part,—has been the most read, and deservedly so. As a work of art, it is superior to the others. It presents us in three large pictures, whose subjects are the Bishop, the Convict, the Grisette, three fine studies, carefully drawn, with bold outlines, and of so vigorous a conception that we cannot help recognizing in them a master's hand. (pp. 458-59)

M. Hugo wields a powerful pen, no doubt; he gives us at times Miltonic sketches, but he allows too often his imagination to run away with his common sense; and in these cases he actually practices imposition upon the good-natured reader. He lures him with false promises, captivates his attention, wins his sympathies, and, suddenly, for no reasonable cause whatever, without there being the least necessity for it, he tears off the mask of the endeared image and shows him a monster so steeped in vice, that he must needs lose all hopes of him. Again and again is the reader thus startled, and his sympathies violently wrecked against these strange stage effects of M. Hugo's composition. We look in vain for any plausible reason that the author may have had, in making his hero so determined a villain. It is obvious from the first that he wishes to secure our sympathy with the convict; he is the embodiment of his darling theme—oppressed humanity. For this purpose his subject should have been a more redeemable character, and it is useless to say that the unexpected conduct of the convict, in robbing the bishop, makes it very hard for us to believe in his sudden reformation, and still harder to accept the astonishing deeds of heroism, and charity, and self-abnegation which he is made to perform in subsequent situations. The whole career of *Jean*

Valjean presents a series of impossible cases, of strange incongruities, and stands in continuous antagonism with the principles of truth and honor which ought to be every honest man's line of conduct. *Jean Valjean* is made a saint in one sense, and in another a convict. We cannot make the two agree. . . . The novel, it is true, commands a wide field of operations, and has a right to all the vast resources of imagination and sentiment, to the multiplied expressions of all human passions, and the endless ramifications of fancy, but its boundaries should still be art. It should work upon our emotions without imparting pain, should interest the heart, and yet keep entire the liberty of the mind; it should allow us to preserve amidst the deepest impressions, the empire of our contemplative faculties. But **"Les Miserables"** does not fulfill any of these conditions. The more we advance in the work, the more we feel our sympathy with the convict to abate. We suspect all along that the author is pulling at all the wires of his far reaching imagination to force his hero upon our admiration.

Fantine is no less an abortion than *Jean Valjean*. It is impossible to inclose within the same being two such incompatible things as exquisite purity of heart and moral degradation. M. Hugo, it is well known, is found of strong contrasts; antithesis is his hobby; but however well it may serve his purposes at times, he cannot employ it always, and especially in spite of all reason and common sense. M. Hugo may declaim in his most grandiloquent rhetoric that the more Fantine sinks in the mire, the purer she arises from it, but we do not believe it. (pp. 462-64)

Marius is another living contradiction, besides being a kind of namby pamby, milk and water creation. M. Hugo in vain attempts to force him upon our interest by lending him the most extravagant qualities of disinterestedness and honor; such qualities are totally incompatible with so sluggish a nature as his is represented to be. How can we possibly couple the total indifference which, in his earlier years, he manifests towards a father of whose existence he is aware,—and whom, from mere reports, he casts from him,—with that excess of filial devotion that causes him to sacrifice subsequently all feelings of love and humanity to a false supposition? (pp. 464-65)

The love of Eponine for Marius, is another far-fetched antithesis. The fig cannot be culled on the thornbush, no more than such disinterested affection and chivalrous sentiments as those with which our author would fain endow the wretched prostitute, could be found amidst beings born and raised in the very bosom of vice and crime. There are fluids that will not mix, and M. Hugo endeavors in vain to fuse vice with virtue, purity with degradation, baseness with elevation;—they cannot mingle. His gorgeous phraseology and deceptive imagery rob us for a moment of our power of reflection, and we look for a while with awe and wonder upon these strange creations that seem to move before us so life-like and vivid; but the instant we put our hand upon them, to test their humanity, they vanish as so many optical illusions. This constant adherence to antithesis, this mad worship of the contraries which characterize all of M. Hugo's productions—poetical as well as prose—carry him repeatedly beyond all historic reality and human truth. Thus are his characters generally false. He does not look upon the world like a man that has lived and remembers facts, but as a hermit, who, in his self-imposed solitude, judges of things according to his *a priori* conceptions. (p. 465)

One principle defect in this vast panorama, **"Les Miserables,"** so varied in situations, characters, and groupings, so dazzling in color, so impressive as to its motive, is the want of perspective. All is foreground, no soft middle tints shading off smoothly into a vague and suggestive distance. (p. 467)

To describe the little scamp Gavroche, M. Hugo enters into an endless digression, and gives us the history of Paris in its "atom," as he calls it, and to draw M. Mabeuf, who is truly a charming creation, full of life and truth, he stops the narrative to give us a delightful description of the character of an old and unsophisticated bibliomaniac. These two sketches, among his best, perhaps, and most original, are entirely out of place; they would be accepted with delight anywhere else, but here they only make confusion. Again, we would like to see the accessory *personae* at a greater distance, in a less decided attitude, and adding as it were by their feebler outlines to the more vigorous conception of the fearful figures. These have no other relief but what is given them by the dark background formed by the fearful *Thenardier* band. Gloomy enough is the picture of the cavern of evil in which reign such monsters as *Babet, Gueulemer, Claquesous,* and *Montparnasse.*

That such really exist is sufficiently proved by the sad police records of the great capitals of Europe, but to attribute their moral degradation solely to ignorance, is taking rather an over indulgent view of what constitutes vice and crime. There is besides the darkness of ignorance in which men fall into sin, the spirit of defiance that rebels against the law. The angels that made war in heaven did not sin through ignorance, but through defiance, and the fearful deeds perpetrated on earth are more often the results of rebellion than of ignorance. M. Hugo's reflections as to the existence of such a state of things are most unsatisfactory, and his philosophy is altogether illogical. (pp. 467-68)

The interest of the spectator increases, we admit, as he passes from one to the other of the stirring chapters contained in the first book, *Fantine,* and follows the strange fortunes of its hero convict. Towards the end of the volume all his interest centres upon the unfortunate M. Madeleine, who, victim of his heroic sacrifice, is cast again a reprobate upon the world, and doomed to affront again the direful perils of a convict's life. Eager to learn the fate of the poor wanderer, he opens anxiously the second volume, *Cosette,* when lo! he finds himself upon entirely new ground—the plain of Waterloo! He turns page after page to look for M. Madeleine again, *Jean Valjean,* but in vain. Nineteen chapters of history separate him from him. The introduction of the scoundrel Thenardier, robbing the dead and wounded after the battle, is hardly a sufficient reason for so elaborate a digression. But the reader, thus cheated out of his just expectations, shall be compensated for his disappointment. M. Hugo's powerful brush sweeps over the memorable battle ground, and with a few magic touches calls up before our astonished eyes all the immortal martyrs of the great tyrant's ambition. . . . Waterloo, under his nervous pen, becomes a new battle ground, and like his immortal statue of Mirabeau, which in former years he carved out so grandly from its marble block of history, appears in such magnificent grandeur that we must needs stoop to its magnitude. But it is not in its place in the **"Miserables;"** as a study by itself it would have been entitled to much praise; but forced as it is into the picture, cutting off its connecting links, it loses much of its merits. Besides, the author's ungovernable mania to strike at sudden and startling effects, leaves a blot upon it for which its finer qualities will hardly atone. (pp. 469-70)

[In] supposing even M. Hugo to be an honest and sincere socialist, what good, we ask, can such a work as **"Les Miserables"** do to his cause? It cannot materially contribute to the reformation of society. Society is human nature taken collectively, and to expect a revolution in society would be to expect a revolution in human nature; nor will it be likely to effect a change of heart in the police agents. The case of Saint Jean Valjean is not that of convicts in general, and the watchfulness of the police cannot be too great in regard to such individuals; it will neither encourage criminals, should they happen upon the book, to reform and follow in the footsteps of the model presented to them, for Jean Valjean's sad experiences in the practice of virtue are sufficient to repel the best intentioned. The whole work has a vulgarizing effect; its plot and the management of the same tend to increase if possible the already bitter feeling that exists between the two inevitable antagonisms in society, the rich and the poor. It seems to say to the first: You shall always have the rich against you; and to the rich, You shall always have the poor against you. The multitude, it is true, can only be impressed by the outward, by forcible and vivid images, yet might these images be as well of an elevating as of a vulgarizing character. Let them be pictures of noble deeds, of generous actions, of heroic virtues, of courageous suffering, of contentment in humble life, and resignation under affliction. Such imprints left upon the soul would serve to awaken the dormant principles of the good and the beautiful among the masses, and raise them more effectually above the commonplaceness of their condition than the feverish and far-fetched contrasts of the sensational school, by which they are kept in such constant excitement. But it is more than probable that such better books would not yield their authors five hundred thousand francs! Alas! we are much afraid that M. Hugo, in the composition of his great novel, had less a socialistic than a pecuniary interest at heart. But letting alone all uncharitable suppositions, we still object to the work as a work of art. It is a picture without centre and background, its most insignificant details are worked up with a painful minuteness, and it is interlarded with a number of lengthy digressions which, despite their actual merits, lose all their worth for being out of place. . . . Yet do we allow to M. Hugo genius, most of his productions have in them that principle which insures life; pearls of the finest quality are generally found in them, buried it is true under heaps of rubbish, but pearls nevertheless—diamonds set in diamonds, regardless of squandered riches, which might have been used to far better purpose. M. Hugo is an excellent miner; he has dug diligently the secret depths of literature and collected much gold and precious gems, but when he has obtained the treasure he does not always know what to do with it, or how to bring it into the service of high art. While he is so skillful an artist that he gives to the most inconceivable figures an appearance of life that startles us, he renders himself guilty of debaucheries of colors equaled only by those of Rubens. Like that tremendous colorist, he revels in all the extremes of brilliancy, and forces his subjects upon our imagination by the magnificence of their vestments. (pp. 476-78)

He has given us, at various intervals, startling novels, during whose perusal we are alternately applauding with all our heart, or throwing the book away in disgust; beautiful pages of poesy where the *grandiose* and sublime are so linked with the trivial that we are at a loss to tell which is which, or in a short epigrammatic form the results of his graver studies, as in **"Literature et Philosophie Mêleés,"** which present us a bewildering maze of intricate thoughts and ideas that only serve to confuse our own. The very quality that constitutes his glory is also the one that is fatal to its highest manifestation; his force spends itself equally upon the majestic and the trivial. . . .

As to the philosophic tendency of M. Hugo's works, they are of less importance than they are generally supposed to be. (p. 478)

[We look in vain in **"Les Miserables"**] for any powerful dominant idea, pervading the whole and resolving itself into a determinate form. It seems from beginning to end, and throughout all its characters, plots and counterplots, but a painful endeavor on the part of the author to incarnate his favorite system, to draw sweetness from bitterness, such as he has himself revealed it to us when he laid bare the machinery of his **"Lucrezia Borgia."**

"Take," says he, "the most hideous moral deformity, place it where it is most appalling, in the heart of a woman, and then mix with this moral deformity a pure sentiment, the purest that woman can feel, maternal love, and you will have a monster that will excite your pity even to tears; the deformed soul will appear beautiful, the moral deformity will be purified by maternal love." But M. Hugo can never convince us with such *a priori* conceptions. We all know what constitutes maternal love; there must exist a certain amount of spirituality in that sentiment, otherwise it is nothing but a brute's instinct. The wild beast loves its offspring, but that does not redeem its ferocious nature. (pp. 479-80)

"Victor Hugo and 'Les Miserables'," in The New Englander, *Vol. XXIII, No. LXXXVIII, July, 1864, pp. 454-81.*

[G. H. LEWES] (essay date 1866)

Les Travailleurs de la Mer has qualities which will variously affect the reader. There is a certain gorgeous enormity, a daring inflation about it which cannot be met elsewhere; and if the splendour is barbaric, it is undeniably splendid. Page after page, and chapter after chapter may be mere fireworks which blaze and pass away; but as fireworks, the prodigality is amazing: Bengal lights follow upon Roman candles; rockets climb luminous and hissing, and descend in sprays of varied colour; Catherine-wheels whirl and squibs spurt, suddenly bursting out in a fresh place, when you imagine the tumult is subsiding. I cannot say that such writing is to my taste, but I know it throws many readers into raptures.

Unless the reader greatly cares for rhetoric which has more imagery than sense, and for a certain poetical mode of looking at things which is quite as much capricious as poetical, and will seldom bear the steady light of reflection, he will not rank this novel among his favourites, because the story and characters are subordinated to the rhetoric; and although the great nodes in the fable are chosen with the admirable instinct of the picturesque by which Victor Hugo in all his works forcibly impresses the imagination of the public, yet his mastery over human nature is by no means comparable to his mastery over the picturesque, and the passionate interest of the story is feeble. . . . [The] Infinite certainly has the part of protagonist in this work, under the forms of the Abyss, the Unknown, Night, the Shadows, and Immensity, so fatiguingly familiar to all Victor Hugo's readers. And when these are the actors, human beings may shrink into neglected corners, or make their appearance only to be dwarfed by the comparison.

This is a mode of treatment which so evidently issues from the author's peculiar genius that we have no right to complain of it, though we have a perfect right to express our preference for another mode of treatment. He has given us a poetical vision of the sea, which is more like an apocalypse than the vision of a healthy mind; but at any rate it is what he sees. He presents us with that; whether we can see with him or not is our concern, not his. I confess I cannot. Fond as I am of the sea, in all its aspects, and of submarine life in all its varieties, I never feel myself looking with his eyes. There is a certain large felicity of style which every now and then stirs me with a poetic thrill, but I never find myself dwelling on the pictures and finding out fresh beauties as the attention is prolonged. (p. 31)

[When] so considerable a writer gives us a novel, we are bound in very respect to him to criticise it as literature, and not to let it pass with the half-contemptuous tolerance usually awarded to novels. If, as we have seen, the plot is mainly for the sake of the writing, we are bound to look a little closely into the writing. I willingly allow that the writing is often singularly felicitous, if it is also often singularly faulty, and even absurd. He has no sobriety; little respect for truth; no solicitude about sense: a sonorous phrase, or a startling image, exercises a spell over him which he is unable to resist. People are apt to consider that when a writer departs widely from commonplace he is powerful, and that when he presents images of grandiose unreality he is imaginative. But it is not so. Real power is plastic; a fine imagination sees vividly and truly. The difference between the aimless wanderings of reverie, and the concentrated, regulated, orderly movements of thought, may be tested by any one in his own experience. It is easy to let the mind wander capriciously amid the evanescent suggestions of reverie, and difficult to fix the thought upon the true relations of things. If the reader who has been delighted with the *brio* of one of Victor Hugo's descriptions, and astounded at its wealth of images, will only think of the thing described, and ask himself whether it has become more vivid to him—whether through these images he has learned to see it with a keener and a nobler vision, or finds himself in any way enriched, he will be able to estimate aright the value of this prodigal rhetoric. Unless the poet "lends a precious seeing to the eye," he has used his arts in vain. Now, in my opinion, Victor Hugo rarely sees things truly; he sees them fantastically, and expresses them hyperbolically. Hence it is, that although he keeps us in a constant state of amazement at his ingenuity and cleverness, we never lay down the book enriched by an enlarged faculty of vision. (p. 46)

[G. H. Lewes,] "Victor Hugo's New Novel," in The Fortnightly Review *(reprinted by permission of Contemporary Review Company Limited), Vol. V, No. XXV, May 15, 1866, pp. 30-46.*

THÉOPHILE GAUTIER (essay date 1867)

"Hernani" no longer needs its veteran guard, for no one thinks nowadays of attacking it. The public has followed the example set by Don Carlos; it has forgiven the rebel and restored all his titles. Hernani is now John of Aragon, grand master of Avis, Duke of Segorba and Duke of Cardona, Marquis of Monroy, Count Albatera; Donna Sol's arms cling round his neck above the collar of the Golden Fleece, and but for the imprudent pact entered into with Ruy Gomez, he would be perfectly happy.

But it was not so of yore, and night after night Hernani had to blow his horn to summon his mountain hawks, that not infrequently bore away in their talons a Classicist scalp as a token of victory. Certain lines were stormed and restormed like redoubts that two armies fight for with equal obstinacy.

One evening the Romanticists triumphed with a passage that the enemy captured the next night, and from which it had to be driven. What a din there was! What shouts! What hoots! What hisses! What bursts of bravos! What thunders of applause! The leaders of the contending parties insulted each other like the heroes of Homer before they came to blows, and at times, I am bound to confess, they were not more courteous than Achilles and Agamemnon. But the winged words flew up to the top of the house and attention was quickly recalled to the stage.

We would come out at the close of the performance worn out and breathless; elated when the evening had been a fortunate one for us, cursing the Philistines when we had suffered a reverse; and until every man had regained his home, the echoes of night gave back fragments of Hernani's monologue or of Don Carlos'; for one and all we knew the play by heart, and even now, if need were, I could do the prompting from memory.

To the generation of that day "Hernani" was what the "Cid" had been to Corneille's contemporaries. Whoever was young, valiant, in love, or poetical, was filled with the breath of it. The fine heroical and Castilian exaggeration, the splendid Spanish pomposity, the language at once so proud and haughty in its familiarity, the images so dazzlingly strange intoxicated us, made us ecstatic, and turned our heads with their entrancing poetry. Undoubtedly the author of "Hernani" has written plays as beautiful, as complete, and perhaps even more dramatic than that one, but none of them fascinated us to such an extent. (pp. 157-59)

Time has gone by, the public has become educated little by little, and the very things that revolted it before, now are taken as a matter of course. The supposed defects have turned into beauties, and men are surprised to find themselves shedding tears over passages they laughed at, and becoming enthusiastic over others that they once hissed. The prophet did not go to the mountain, but, contrary to the Islamic legend, the mountain drew near to him.

With the lapse of time the work itself has gained a magnificent patina, the violent colouring has toned down, the harsh touches have become softened, and the fierce impasto has disappeared as under a golden varnish that softens and warms at one and the same time. It exhibits the sober richness, the masterly and broad touch seen in those portraits by Titian in which the painter to Charles V has depicted a great personage, with his coat of arms in one corner of the canvas. (pp. 159-60)

It gives one the liveliest pleasure to see, after having had to endure so many melodramas and vaudevilles, this work of genius, with its characters larger than life, its mighty passions, its mad lyricism, and its action which seems to be a legend drawn from the "Romancero" and put upon the stage like that of the Cid Campeador. And especially is it delightful to listen to that beautiful, richly coloured verse, so poetic, so firm and yielding, lending itself to the rapid familiarity of the dialogue, in the course of which the retorts cross like sword-blades and strike fire, or again soaring with the wings of an eagle or a dove in moments of reverie and of love.

As the great monologue of Don Carlos before the tomb of Charlemagne was being spoken, I seemed to be ascending a stair, every step of which was a verse, leading to the top of a cathedral spire, from which the world appeared to me as in a Gothic woodcut of a cosmography, with pointed steeples, crenelated towers, palaces, garden walls, carved roofs, zig-zagging ramparts, bombards set on their carriages, spirals of smoke, and in the background a swarming population. The poet excels in such lofty, wide views of the ideas, the appearance, or the politics of an epoch. (pp. 161-62)

> *Théophile Gautier, "The Revival of 'Hernani'" (1867), in his* The Works of Théophile Gautier: A History of Romanticism, *Vol. 16, edited and translated by F. C. de Sumichrast (translation copyright, 1902, by George D. Sproul), The Jenson Society, 1906, pp. 156-62.*

THE NATION (essay date 1869)

From the falling off which his two subsequent novels show, Victor Hugo no doubt reached his high-water mark in **"Les Misérables,"** which, after all deductions have been made, is a remarkable and, perhaps, a great work. It certainly goes deep and has made an impression on many classes of readers that will not soon be effaced—not pre-eminently as a novel, though it has many excellences in this respect, but on account of its vast energy, its lyrical fire, its splendid descriptive passages, and a sort of epic swing and intensity throughout. But neither of **"The Man who Laughs"** nor of its immediate predecessor, **"The Toilers of the Sea,"** can as much be said. They both have, indeed, something of the sort of lurid moral grandeur that characterized **"Les Misérables,"** but they possess far less interest as stories, and show a hardening and intensifying of those peculiarities of Victor Hugo's mind and manner that make the reading of his novels, even the best of them, to some persons a kind of literary torture. His stiff and stilted dialogues; the jerky, abrupt, galvanic movements of his characters, his morbid craving for the monstrous; his epileptic tendency; his violation of dramatic law; his want of humor; his contortions when his invention fails him, and a certain incongruity that is like false time in music—these faults and deficiencies, prominent enough in all of his works, are at times painfully so in **"The Man who Laughs."** (p. 509)

Most American readers, we imagine, will feel the want of humor more than anything else, because in English literature humor has a functional importance like the juices and lubricating liquids in the animal organism, and because, also, in this work Hugo essays its introduction in no small measure. This want is noticeable in the author's inability to enter into or to understand certain facts and conditions of life, or certain occurrences, like the prizefight which he describes, but it is conspicuous in the manner in which he perpetually confounds the grotesque with the hideous. The former it is impossible for him to portray. He invariably pushes it so far that it becomes the monstrous, the abnormal, and excites our disgust rather than our laughter. His hero, Gwynplaine, he would have us believe, was the most comic, mirth-provoking object the sun ever shone upon, and yet he repeatedly describes him as a gnome, a hydra, a full-blown monster. . . .

Neither do we think Victor Hugo any more successful in portraying the passion of love in this work than in depicting the emotion of mirth. Few readers, we fear, will be touched by the spectacle of the billing and cooing of Gwynplaine and Dea. The conception, as it lay in the author's mind, of this frail, sightless girl loving this noble but fate-smitten being is no doubt very praiseworthy. We sympathize thoroughly with the purpose and aspiration of the artist in contrasting the two figures, and in granting to Gwynplaine the one ray of heaven's sunlight in his sepulchral life—the satisfaction of being loved by a woman, and a woman to whom his hideous deformity could have no existence—as, indeed, we may say we sympathize with the theoretical artist throughout the book; but from the working out of the passion we get no pleasure. It is indeed even nauseating. He gives the endearing expressions of the lovers, divested of all those little graces, those arch and playful moods, those cunning indirections, those soft tones and ways, etc., which mark the talk of lovers, and the result is a mere bandying of epithets. . . .

The only character in the book that has any degree of reality, or is at all dramatically shown us, is Ursus—a gusty, crusty old quacksalver and native philosopher, full of wit, necromantic lore, and practical benevolence, who simulates the bear while really he is the lamb—a type of character which Hugo draws easily and personates admirably. (p. 510)

For the rest, there are graphic descriptions of character, but the article itself is not there. We are treated to a reminiscence or an analysis, and not to an actual, living creation; the author's own personality monopolizes most of the attention; there is no doubting what manner of man he is; and if he would or could draw a little to one side, and give these figures a chance to act and speak for themselves, most of his readers would be a deal better satisfied. . . .

Whatever may be Victor Hugo's merits as a writer—and they are many and great in certain directions—it becomes more and more apparent that he is not *par excellence* a novelist. His quality is lyrical rather than creative. Especially does he lack that continence and equability necessary to the artist who would average and reproduce nature and life. We feel at all times a want of good flesh and blood—of something that moves otherwise than by sudden leaps and starts, like a jumping-jack or the images of a puppet-show. (p. 511)

> "'The Man Who Laughs'," in The Nation, *Vol. IX,*
> *No. 232, December 9, 1869, pp. 509-11.*

HENRY JAMES (essay date 1874)

A new work from Victor Hugo may be considered a literary event of some magnitude. If the magnitude of the event, indeed, were measured by that of the work in chapters, books, and volumes, we should need one of the author's own mouth-filling epithets to qualify it. The present performance ['**Quatrevingt-treize**'] is apparently but a fragment—the first *"récit"* of a romance destined to embody on a vast scale the history of a single year. Like all the author's novels, it abounds in subdivisions and minor headings, which serve as a kind of mechanical symbolism of his passion for the moral enormous. It is nevertheless complete enough to give us a solid reminder of his strangely commingled strength and weakness. The '**Misérables**,' we suppose, may have been called a great triumph; but we doubt if its successors—the '**Travailleurs de la Mer**' and '**L'Homme qui Rit**'—found many readers who were constant to the end. The verdict on the present work, however, so far as it has been pronounced, has been eminently favorable, and we are assured that M. Hugo has rekindled his smoldering torch at the pure flame of inspiration. The reader, indeed, has only to open the volume at hazard to find that M. Hugo is himself again with a vengeance. . . . [The] author has not flinched from his chosen path, and . . . he walks escorted between the sublime and the ridiculous as resolutely as his own most epic heroes. In truth, at M. Hugo's venerable age, and with one's forehead aching with laurels, it is not to be expected that one should ever drop a glance at the swarm of nameless satirists; but the moral of the matter is that the luxurious cul-

tivation of his own peculiar manner, for which our author continues remarkable, seems now not only the natural thing, but on the whole the sagacious one. If you are sure of your strength, the lesson seems to read, cleave to your ideal, however arrogant, however perverted, however indifferent to the ideals of others, and in the end even the fastidious will accept you. We confess to a conservative taste in literary matters— to a relish for brevity, for conciseness, for elegance, for perfection of form. M. Hugo's manner is as diffuse as that of the young woman in the fairy tale who talked diamonds and pearls would alone have a right to be, and as shapeless and formless as if it were twenty times the "grande improvisation" which is his definition of the French Revolution. His prolixity, moreover, has the further defect of giving one a nearly intolerable impression of conceit; few great rhetoricians have the air of listening so reverently to their own grandiloquence. And yet we frankly admit that the effect of these volumes has been to make us submit to the inevitable, and philosophically accept the author whose shoulders sustain so heavy a load of error. (pp. 138-40)

[In '**Quatrevingt-treize**'] M. Hugo has chosen a subject in which his imagination may revel at its ease; his inordinate relish for the huge and the horrible may feast its fill upon the spectacle of the French Revolution. One might have wondered indeed that he should not long ago have made it his own; but he has shown the instinct of the genuine epicure in such matters in keeping it in reserve. . . . If anything were wanted to prove that, as a philosopher, M. Hugo has nothing of the smallest consequence to say, the extraordinary intellectual levity with which he faces the unsolved problems of his theme would amply suffice. He has not attempted, however, to give us a picture of the whole Revolution, but, choosing a salient episode, has dramatized with characteristic vividness the sanguinary strife of the Royalists of Brittany and the Republican troops. As a story, M. Hugo's work as yet is meagre; it has no hero, no heroine, no central figure, none of the germs of a regular drama. The hero properly is the Republican army, the heroine the fanatical horde of the Vendéans. We are shifted from place to place, hurried through deserts of declamation and oceans of paradox, tossed, breathless, from a bewildering antithesis to an astounding "situation" with all that energy to which, from of old, M. Hugo's readers have received notice that they must accommodate their intellectual pace. (pp. 140-41)

[The] story is chiefly a compound of blood and gunpowder, of long descriptions, geographical and genealogical, which are frequently mere strings of proper names drawn out through pages, and of infinite discourse on things in general by M. Hugo. The only really charming element in the work is the occasional apparition of three little children, whose adventures indeed are the *nodus* of the action. Very charming it is, and lighted up with the author's brightest poetry. With a genius at once powerful and eccentric, like M. Hugo, if one has great disappointments, one has great compensations. A writer in whom the poetic heat is so intense that he must be sublime under all circumstances and at any cost, makes many a strange alliance and produces many a monstrosity; but every now and then it befalls him to flash his lantern upon an object which, as one may say, receives transfiguration gracefully. (pp. 142-43)

The whole work is a mine of quotations—nuggets of substantial gold and strange secretions of the mere overflow of verbiage. M. Hugo's pretension is to say many things in the grand manner—to fling down every proposition like a ringing medal stamped with his own image. Hence, for the reader, an intolerable sense of effort and tension; he seems to witness the very contortions of ingenuity. But, as we say, the contortions are often those of the inspired sybil, and the poet utters something worth hearing. We care little for the Marquis de Lantenac and less for the terrible Cimourdain; but the author's great sense of the sad and tragic has rarely been exercised more effectively than in the figures of Michelle Fléchard, the poor stupid starving peasant-mother of the three children, and of Tellemarch, the philosophic beggar who gives her shelter in her desperate quest. Here the author deals with the really human and not with the mechanical and monstrous, aping the human. . . . Expressed with perfect frankness, the leading idea of **'Quatrevingt-treize'** seems to us to be that the horrible—the horrible in crime and suffering and folly, in blood and fire and tears—is a delightful subject for the embroidery of fiction. After this there is no denying that M. Hugo is really fond of horrors. He is an old man; he has written much and seen much; he may be supposed to know his own mind; yet he dives into this sea of blood for the pearl of picturesqueness with a truly amazing freshness of appetite. If we were inclined to interpret things rigidly, we might find a very sombre meaning in the strange complacency with which his imagination contemplates the most atrocious details of his subject. His fellow-countrymen lately took occasion to remind the world forcibly that they were of the same stock as their ancestors, and that when once they had warmed to the work again they could burn and kill on the same extensive scale. One would have said that, to a reflective mind, it might have seemed that the blood-stains and ashes of French history had, for some years to come, better be consigned to obscurity. The sublimely clear conscience with which M. Hugo drags them into the light proves, to say the least, an inordinate share of national vanity. To say, in combination with this, that we have enjoyed the work, may seem but an admission that we have been passing through an atmosphere of corrupting paradox. But what we have enjoyed is neither Cimourdain nor Marat, nor the woman-shootings of the Royalists, nor the ambulant guillotine of the Republicans. It is M. Hugo himself as a whole, the extraordinary genius that shines through the dusky confusion of repulsive theme and erratic treatment. It is the great possibilities of his style and the great tendencies of his imagination. The latter sometimes leads him astray; but when it leads him aright he is great. (pp. 143-44)

> Henry James, "Victor Hugo's 'Ninety-Three'," in The Nation, *Vol. XVIII, No. 239, April 9, 1874 (and reprinted in his* Literary Reviews and Essays: On American, English, and French Literature, *edited by Albert Mordell, Twayne, 1957, pp. 138-44).*

ROBERT LOUIS STEVENSON (essay date 1874)

Victor Hugo's romances occupy an important position in the history of literature; many innovations, timidly made elsewhere, have in them been carried boldly out to their last consequences; much that was indefinite in literary tendencies has attained to definite maturity; many things have come to a point and been distinguished one from the other: and it is only in the last romance of all, *Quatre Vingt Treize,* that this culmination is most perfect. (p. 13)

The moral end that the author had before him in the conception of *Notre Dame de Paris* was (he tells us) to "denounce" the external fatality that hangs over men in the form of foolish and inflexible superstition. To speak plainly, this moral purpose seems to have mighty little to do with the artistic conception; moreover it is very questionably handled, while the artistic conception is developed with the most consummate success. Old Paris lives for us with newness of life: we have ever before our eyes the city cut into three by the two arms of the river, the boat-shaped island "moored" by five bridges to the different shores, and the two unequal towns on either hand. We forget all that enumeration of palaces and churches and convents which occupies so many pages of admirable description, and the thoughtless reader might be inclined to conclude from this, that they were pages thrown away; but this is not so: we forget, indeed, the details, as we forget or do not see the different layers of paint on a completed picture; but the thing desired has been accomplished, and we carry away with us a sense of the "Gothic profile" of the city, of the "surprising forest of pinnacles and towers and belfries," and we know not what of rich and intricate and quaint. And throughout, Notre Dame has been held up over Paris by a height far greater than that of its twin towers: the Cathedral is present to us from the first page to the last; the title has given us the clue, and already in the Palace of Justice the story begins to attach itself to that central building by character after character. It is purely an effect of mirage; Notre Dame does not, in reality, thus dominate and stand out above the city. . . . [But] it is an effect that permeates and possesses the whole book with astonishing consistency and strength. And then, Hugo has peopled this Gothic city, and, above all, this Gothic church, with a race of men even more distinctly Gothic than their surroundings. We know this generation already: we have seen them clustered about the worn capitals of pillars, or craning forth over the churchleads with the open mouths of gargoyles. About them all there is that sort of stiff quaint unreality, that conjunction of the grotesque, and even of a certain bourgeois snugness, with passionate contortion and horror, that is so characteristic of Gothic art. Esmeralda is somewhat an exception; she and the goat traverse the story like two children who have wandered in a dream. The finest moment of the book is when these two share with the two other leading characters, Dom Claude and Quasimodo, the chill shelter of the old cathedral. It is here that we touch most intimately the generative artistic idea of the romance: are they not all four taken out of some quaint moulding, illustrative of the Beatitudes, or the Ten Commandments, or the seven deadly sins? What is Quasimodo but an animated gargoyle? What is the whole book but the reanimation of Gothic art?

It is curious that in this, the earliest of the five great romances, there should be so little of that extravagance that latterly we have come almost to identify with the author's manner. Yet even here we are distressed by words, thoughts, and incidents that defy belief and alienate the sympathies. (pp. 21-3)

In spite of the horror and misery that pervade all of his later work, there is in it much less of actual melodrama than here, and rarely, I should say never, that sort of brutality, that useless insufferable violence to the feelings, which is the last distinction between melodrama and true tragedy. Now, in *Notre Dame,* the whole story of Esmeralda's passion for the worthless archer is unpleasant enough; but when she betrays herself in her last hiding-place, herself and her wretched mother, by calling out to this sordid hero who has long since forgotten her—well, that is just one of those things that readers will not forgive; they do not like it, and they are quite right; life is hard enough for poor mortals, without having it indefinitely embittered for them by bad art.

We look in vain for any similar blemish in *Les Misérables.* Here, on the other hand, there is perhaps the nearest approach to literary restraint that Hugo has ever made: there is here certainly the ripest and most easy development of his powers. It is the moral intention of this great novel to awaken us a little, if it may be—for such awakenings are unpleasant—to the great cost of this society that we enjoy and profit by, to the labour and sweat of those who support the litter, civilisation, in which we ourselves are so smoothly carried forward. People are all glad to shut their eyes; and it gives them a very simple pleasure when they can forget that our laws commit a million individual injustices, to be once roughly just in the general; that the bread that we eat, and the quiet of the family, and all that embellishes life and makes it worth having, have to be purchased by death—by the death of animals, and the deaths of men wearied out with labour, and the deaths of those criminals called tyrants and revolutionaries, and the deaths of those revolutionaries called criminals. It is to something of all this that Victor Hugo wishes to open men's eyes in *Les Misérables;* and this moral lesson is worked out in masterly coincidence with the artistic effect. The deadly weight of civilisation to those who are below presses sensibly on our shoulders as we read. A sort of mocking indignation grows upon us as we find Society rejecting, again and again, the services of the most serviceable; setting Jean Valjean to pick oakum, casting Galileo into prison, even crucifying Christ. There is a haunting and horrible sense of insecurity about the book. The terror we thus feel is a terror for the machinery of law, that we can hear tearing, in the dark, good and bad between its formidable wheels with the iron stolidity of all machinery, human or divine. (pp. 23-4)

With so gloomy a design this great work is still full of life and light and love. The portrait of the good Bishop is one of the most agreeable things in modern literature. The whole scene at Montfermeil is full of the charm that Hugo knows so well how to throw about children. . . . Take it for all in all, there are few books in the world that can be compared with it. There is as much calm and serenity as Hugo has ever attained to; the melodramatic coarsenesses that disfigured *Notre Dame* are no longer present. There is certainly much that is painfully improbable; and again, the story itself is a little too well constructed; it produces on us the effect of a puzzle, and we grow incredulous as we find that every character fits again and again into the plot, and is, like the child's cube, serviceable on six faces; things are not so well arranged in life as all that comes to. Some of the digressions, also, seem out of place, and do nothing but interrupt and irritate. But when all is said, the book remains of masterly conception and of masterly development, full of pathos, full of truth, full of a high eloquence. (p. 25)

[And in *Les Travailleurs de la Mer*] once more the artistic effect and the moral lesson are worked out together, and are, indeed, one. Gilliat, alone upon the reef at his herculean task, offers a type of human industry in the midst of the vague "diffusion of forces into the illimitable," and the visionary development of "wasted labour" in the sea, and the winds, and the clouds. No character was ever thrown into such strange relief as Gilliat. The great circle of sea-birds that come wonderingly around him on the night of his arrival, strikes at once the note of his pre-eminence and isolation. He fills the whole reef with his indefatigable toil; this solitary spot in the ocean rings with the clamour of his anvil; we see him as he comes and goes, thrown out sharply against the clear background of the sea. And yet his isolation is not to be compared with the isolation of Robinson Crusoe, for example; indeed, no two books could be

more instructive to set side by side than *Les Travailleurs* and this other of the old days before art had learnt to occupy itself with what lies outside of human will. Crusoe was one sole centre of interest in the midst of a nature utterly dead and utterly unrealised by the artist; but this is not how we feel with Gilliat; we feel that he is opposed by a "dark coalition of forces," that an "immense animosity" surrounds him; we are the witnesses of the terrible warfare that he wages with "the silent inclemency of phenomena going their own way, and the great general law, implacable and passive:" "a conspiracy of the indifference of things" is against him. There is not one interest on the reef, but two. (p. 26)

But in *Les Travailleurs,* with all its strength, with all its eloquence, with all the beauty and fitness of its main situations, we cannot conceal from ourselves that there is a thread of something that will not bear calm scrutiny. There is much that is disquieting about the storm, admirably as it begins. I am very doubtful whether it would be possible to keep the boat from foundering in such circumstances, by any amount of breakwater and broken rock. I do not understand the way in which the waves are spoken of, and prefer just to take it as a loose way of speaking, and pass on. And lastly, how does it happen that the sea was quite calm next day? Is this great hurricane a piece of scene-painting after all? And when we have forgiven Gilliat's prodigies of strength (although, in soberness, he reminds us more of Porthos in the Vicomte de Bragelonne than is quite desirable), what is to be said to his suicide, and how are we to condemn in adequate terms that unprincipled avidity after effect, which tells us that the sloop disappeared over the horizon, and the head under the water, at one and the same moment? Monsieur Hugo may say what he will, but we know very well that they did not; a thing like that raises up a despairing spirit of opposition in a man's readers; they give him the lie fiercely, as they read. (p. 27)

In *L'Homme qui Rit,* it was Hugo's object to "denounce" (as he would say himself) the aristocratic principle as it was exhibited in England; and this purpose, somewhat more unmitigatedly satiric than that of the two last, must answer for much that is unpleasant in the book. The repulsiveness of the scheme of the story, and the manner in which it is bound up with impossibilities and absurdities, discourage the reader at the outset, and it needs an effort to take it as seriously as it deserves. And yet when we judge it deliberately, it will be seen that, here again, the story is admirably adapted to the moral. The constructive ingenuity exhibited throughout is almost morbid. (p. 28)

There is here a quality in the narration more intimate and particular than is general with Hugo; but it must be owned, on the other hand, that the book is wordy, and even, now and then, a little wearisome. Ursus and his wolf are pleasant enough companions; but the former is nearly as much an abstract type as the latter. There is a beginning, also, of an abuse of conventional conversation, such as may be quite pardonable in the drama where needs must, but is without excuse in the romance. (p. 29)

Romance is a language in which many persons learn to speak with a certain appearance of fluency; but there are few who can ever bend it to any practical need, few who can ever be said to express themselves in it. It has become abundantly plain in the foregoing examination that Victor Hugo occupies a high place among those few. He has always a perfect command over his stories; and we see that they are constructed with a high regard to some ulterior purpose, and that every situation is informed with moral significance and grandeur. Of no other man can the same thing be said in the same degree. His romances are not to be confused with "the novel with a purpose" as familiar to the English reader: this is generally the model of incompetence; and we see the moral clumsily forced into every hole and corner of the story, or thrown externally over it like a carpet over a railing. Now the moral significance, with Hugo, is of the essence of the romance; it is the organising principle. (pp. 32-3)

Having thus learned to subordinate his story to an idea, to make his art speak, he went on to teach it to say things heretofore unaccustomed. . . . There is no hero in *Notre Dame:* in *Les Misérables* it is an old man: in *L'Homme qui Rit* it is a monster: in *Quatre Vingt Treize* it is the Revolution. Those elements that only began to show themselves timidly, as adjuncts, in the novels of Walter Scott, have usurped ever more and more of the canvas; until we find the whole interest of one of Hugo's romances centring around matter that Fielding would have banished from his altogether, as being out of the field of fiction. . . . [For] Hugo, man is no longer an isolated spirit without antecedent or relation here below, but a being involved in the action and reaction of natural forces, himself a centre of such action and reaction; or an unit in a great multitude, chased hither and thither by epidemic terrors and aspirations, and, in all seriousness, blown about by every wind of doctrine. (pp. 33-4)

[*Notre Dame, Les Misérables, Quatre Vingt Treize, L'Homme qui Rit,* and *Les Travailleurs*] would have made a very great fame for any writer, and yet they are but one façade of the monument that Victor Hugo has erected to his genius. Everywhere we find somewhat the same greatness, somewhat the same infirmities. In his poems and plays there are the same unaccountable protervities that have already astonished us in the romances. There, too, is the same feverish strength, welding the fiery iron of his idea under forge-hammer repetitions— an emphasis that is somehow akin to weakness—a strength that is a little epileptic. He stands so far above all his contemporaries, and so incomparably excels them in richness, breadth, variety, and moral earnestness, that we almost feel as if he had a sort of right to fall oftener and more heavily than others; but this does not reconcile us to seeing him profit by the privilege so freely. We like to have, in our great men, something that is above question; we like to place an implicit faith in them, and see them always on the platform of their greatness; and this, unhappily, cannot be with Hugo. . . . If we look back, yet once, upon these five romances, we see blemishes such as we can lay to the charge of no other man in the number of the famous; but to what other man can we attribute such sweeping innovations, such a new and significant presentment of the life of man, such an amount, if we merely think of the amount, of equally consummate performance? (p. 35)

Robert Louis Stevenson, "Victor Hugo's Romances" (originally published as an unsigned essay in The Cornhill Magazine, *Vol. XXX, No. 176, August, 1874), in his* The Essays of Robert Louis Stevenson, *Macdonald, 1950, pp. 13-35.*

THÉOPHILE GAUTIER (essay date 1874)

While the genius of other masters becomes bent, weak, and wrinkled with years, age seems to add new strength, new vigour, and fresh beauty to that of Hugo. He grows old in lion fashion; his brow, furrowed with august wrinkles, bears a longer and thicker mane, more formidably wild than of yore. His brazen talons have grown, and his yellow eyes resemble suns in a cavern. When he roars, all animals remain dumb. He may also be compared to the oak that o'ertops the forest; the huge, rugged trunk sends out in every direction branches as thick as ordinary trees and curiously twisted; its deep-plunging roots draw sap from the heart of the earth, and its head almost touches the high heavens. At night the stars shine through its mass of foliage, and in the morning it is alive with the song of birds. It resists heat and cold, wind, rain, and thunder; the very strokes of the lightning merely add a splendid grimness to its beauty.

In the **"Contemplations"** the part entitled **"Of Yore"** is bright as the dawn, and that called **"To-Day"** is richly coloured like the sunset. While the edge of the horizon is lighted up with a blaze of gold, topaz, and purple, cold violet shadows grow at the extremities; there is more darkness in the work, and through the obscurity the sunbeams flash like lightnings. More intense black brings out the well placed lights, and each sparkling point flames in dread fashion like a cabalistic microcosm. The poet's saddened soul seeks deep, mysterious, sombre expressions. . . . (pp. 347-48)

Regret has often been expressed that France possesses no epic poem. . . . Now, however, if we do not yet possess a regular epic poem in twelve or twenty-four cantos, Victor Hugo has at least given us the small change of one in the **"Legend of the Ages,"** a currency struck with the effigies of every epoch and of every civilisation upon medals of gold of the purest metal. The two volumes comprise, as a matter of fact, a dozen epic poems, concentrated, rapid, and condensing in a small space the aspect, the colour, and the character of an age or of a country.

As one reads the **"Legend of the Ages"** one seems to be wandering in a vast cloister, a sort of *Campo Santo* of poetry, the walls of which are covered with frescoes painted by a marvellous artist who is familiar with every style, and who, according to the subject he has chosen, passes from the almost Byzantine stiffness of Orcagna to the Titanic boldness of Michael Angelo, representing with equal skill knights in plate amour and nude giants swelling their invincible muscles. Each picture gives one the living, lifelike, deep impression of a vanished age. (pp. 348-49)

The **"Legend of the Ages,"** in the mind of the author, is but a partial cartoon of a colossal fresco which the poet means to complete, unless the mysterious breath extinguishes his lamp in the middle of his work; for here below no man can be sure of completing what he has begun. The subject is man, or humanity rather, traversing the various environments due to barbarism or relative civilisation, and constantly progressing from darkness to light. This thought is not expressed in philosophical and declamatory fashion; it springs from the very essence of things. Although the work is unfinished, it is nevertheless a complete whole. Each period is represented by an important and characteristic picture, and one that is always absolutely perfect in itself. (pp. 349-50)

Perhaps the most striking and splendid passage in the whole book is that which forms the opening part of **"Ratbert."** Of all poets Victor Hugo alone was capable of writing it. (pp. 353-54)

There is no one who knows the worth of names as well as Victor Hugo; he always manages to discover strange, sonorous, characteristic ones that mark the bearer and remain ineffaceably imprinted in the memory. (p. 354)

Théophile Gautier, "The Progress of French Poetry Since 1830" (originally published under a different title in Histoire du romantisme, Charpentier, 1874), *in his* The Works of Théophile Gautier: A History of Romanticism, *Vol. 16,* edited and translated by F. C. de Sumichrast (translation copyright, 1902, by George D. Sproul), The Jenson Society, 1906, pp. 233-360.*

T. S. PERRY (essay date 1875)

[In *Han d'Islande* and *Bug-Jargal*] it is easier to recognize the familiar Victor Hugo than it is in his first poems. As for the stories, they are enormous absurdities; the plots are as wild as those of the maddest pantomimes, but without a trace of humor. . . . [If *Han d'Islande*] were merely an outburst of boyish folly which the author had afterwards outgrown, it would be unfair to give it any prominence in a discussion of Hugo's characteristics. But unfortunately we find in this novel the very same qualities which distinguish much of his subsequent work, as we shall presently show. He here made his first attempt to attract by what was merely horrible, and having made his odious idol with the teeth of a wolf, the glowing eyes of a tiger, the appetites of a cannibal, and the general appearance of a cannibal's idol, he seems to forget that to himself is due the credit of inventing the monster, and he is the first to fall down and worship it. Slighter similarities to his later work may be observed; the epigrammatic antitheses of the conversation, the ardor of the descriptions, have now, although in more brilliant colors, become familiar to us all. It shows, too, another peculiarity of Hugo, namely, the slight claim he makes upon his reader's imagination; he never gives it the least chance to spread its wings, he is beforehand with his inventions. This fact probably has something to do with his popularity, but it cannot wholly explain it.

What is then the reason of Hugo's popularity? It is not every writer who will be read if he chooses dead-houses and dusky caverns for his stage, hangmen and hybrid demons for his *dramatis personae,* murder and arson for his incidents, even if he rattles his thunder continuously and turns down his gas till it burns blue. There must be something more than an appeal to traits surviving from the habits of our man-eating ancestors, which has won Hugo readers. What more especially distinguishes him is the ingenuity with which he puts into the mouths of his characters not what is best said, much less what any human beings would be likely to say, but, rather, what is perhaps the brightest thing they could say, what most forcibly strikes the reader. It is easy to understand how naturally a man would be led, by such brilliancy as that of which Hugo feels himself the possessor, to ascribe undue value to his own unusual merits. Whatever he may have to express, he cannot help knowing that he expresses it well. He never stumbles, nor hesitates for a word, is never awkward, is never dull. If in the greatest genius there were not qualities which escaped definition, he would be one of the greatest of geniuses; as it is, he has all the gifts the fairies could give him, and he has never been troubled by distrust of himself. His many volumes of poems are good examples of his skill and often of his imagination. . . . With regard to his plays, however, it is possible for us to be fairer judges. We know what the power of these plays is, how in even the most diluted translations and with incompetent actors they have the power of making the spectator hold his breath, or grow pale in eager uncertainty over the fate of some brilliant character in great danger of losing his life. But it is another matter when we ask, Do these plays mirror

life? Are they full of instruction? Do they give lofty delight? Do we read them over and over to learn how one more great man regards the joys and sufferings and passions of human life? Far from it: they are written for the few hours during which we sit in the theatre; they are meant to fascinate us by a clever plot which shall introduce all manner of stage machinery, the familiar stock characters, especially black-browed assassins, and by means of clever contrasts and brilliant antitheses cajole us into a feeling of surprise, which, if we are not careful, we are likely to mistake for admiration. Admiration of a certain sort it may be, of course. We are grateful to any one who is a real master of the art of amusing us; it would be unjust to wrap ourselves up in disdain immediately after being thrilled and fascinated by one of his plays, to say, He is not Shakespeare, and so pass him by with contempt. But when, on the other hand, it is claimed in his behalf, by himself as well as by others, that this is the true voice for which the world has long been waiting, that here we have the spirit of the nineteenth century, it is well that such important claims should be carefully weighed. And if, moreover, we are told that we should not condemn him, because all who have introduced reforms which were admired by later generations have been abused by their contemporaries, we need not give up at once and acknowledge ourselves beaten, because there is another general remark of equal truth, that not all reforms are wise or sure of the approbation of posterity. . . . To take *Ruy Blas,* which is perhaps the most familiar to us on this side of the water, seems so absurd as to be almost unfair. To undertake to show that this play,—its fantastic Don Salluste, who is so angry with the queen and so grim in his vengeance; the queen, so melancholy in her royalty; and its hero, who becomes prime minister by simply changing his clothes,—to undertake to show that this contains any picture of life as it exists anywhere, except on the stage of a theatre, seems an impossible thing. Such characters are not human beings; they are animated scenery. The play is not written to set forth the relations between different men and women, but these are introduced to give zest to the mechanism of the play. . . . To make a list of all the impossibilities in the play would be idle; it nowhere comes near the ground of probability. The mirror is not held up to nature, but to the most ingenious inventions for making dramatic performances interesting. It is sheer melodrama, and to enjoy it we have to lay aside all criticism and devote ourselves merely to looking. . . . (pp. 168-70)

Broad contrasts, antitheses, ingenious invention always taking the place of what is probable, and the horrible held up for our admiration, these are some of the qualities most noticeable in Victor Hugo. That he is vigorous in drawing his scenes no one can deny. In his plays he manages his stage-effects admirably; he keeps the threads of the drama in his hands, and only brings matters to a solution when that will be most impressive. He well knows how to please his audience. He never steps aside to show any complexities of character in his dramatis personae, because they never have any; they are simply embodiments of some picturesque passion. . . . Every one is there for a specific purpose. . . . Victor Hugo complies with the first duty of a writer—he is interesting; but it would be as unwise to give him too much praise for that as, in view of the fact that the first duty of men is to be carefully washed, to lavish approbation on a man because he is clean. (p. 171)

[*Notre Dame de Paris*] shows very clearly almost the same qualities as those which are to be found in the plays. It is a novel which any one will read with great interest the first time he takes it in his hands, but one to which he will return with less enthusiasm after he has once followed the different victims in their excursions to the gallows, and has feverishly turned over the leaves to find out whether this time the characters are actually going to suffer a violent death; but having once solved this problem, its repetition leaves him cold. What is most noticeable is the curious collection of mediaeval properties the author has industriously accumulated. He puts before us the picture of Paris of the fifteenth century after a manner which is half pre-Raphaelitism and half scene-painting. To be sure, there is to be noticed, perhaps, the influence of the author's romantic affection for the architecture of the cathedral, but there is no serious effort to show us human nature, the real heart of man, amid the surroundings the author draws. . . . The characters, too, are all painted in but one color each: the archdeacon is all fiery, unholy passion, Esmeralda is love for the captain's uniform, the captain is frivolity, and Jehan Frollo is the Gavroche of his century; and when they talk they express either Victor Hugo's epigrams, their prevailing passion, or some bit of archaeology,—never a bit of human nature. It is again a success in melodrama that the author has made, but it is interesting melodrama, with incidental bits of eloquence, and all so filled with enthusiasm that one is almost ashamed of being critical and irresponsive to the author's fire. It requires some effort to resist the unholy fascination the book exercises. (pp. 171-72)

[However,] *Notre Dame de Paris,* with all its picturesqueness, almost pales before the equal vividness of the pathos in *Les Misérables.* There is no mediocrity in it. The whole is distinctly conceived in the author's mind, and it is set before the reader with uniform distinctness; there is not a dull tint, not an uncertain line in the whole book; even more than that, there is hardly a page which is devoid of thrilling interest. . . . Hugo remains true to his old fashion of mingling the horrible with what is beautiful, the tragic with the comic, and then giving us the combination as a true picture of life. From beginning to end the book is a direct appeal to the feelings. Nothing is hinted, everything is painted in the most striking colors. But what is the upshot of it all? We see the familiar monotonous characters, this time people of the present century, but as truly vehicles of a single passion as the illustrative dramatis personae of *Notre Dame de Paris.* . . . [Hugo] knows better than any writer of the time how to excite physical horror, and it is in general to his ability to excite sympathetical physical sensations that nine tenths of his success is due. . . . Hugo is so clever a writer that he does not fail to interest his readers, indeed almost every reader; but the means he employs never rise above this direct appeal to the simpler feelings. He is sure of a large audience; his bait tempts the multitude. (pp. 172-73)

Hugo remains monotonous whatever be the new soil in which he is working. He brings down the green curtain after the loudest explosion of all, and in [*Les Travailleurs de la Mer*], just as the ship conveying the happy bride and bridegroom disappears beneath the horizon, the head of the disconsolate rival, who had stationed himself on a rock of the sea-shore, is covered by the rising tide. It is by detecting such failures to be impressive as this that one may perhaps best learn to see the insincerity of his methods. In itself this coincidence is no absurder than many of those which are devised to lend brilliancy to his books, but it is more likely to cause a smile than many others. What makes the whole scene ridiculous is the total lack of connection between a woman's refusing one man, accepting and marrying another, and the state of the tides. It is not a poetical effect, it is as purely a theatrical trick as the use of the trapdoor to cause sudden disappearances. . . .

With his flow of words he confounds his hearers, and then he wins their suffrages; he knows no world but the one he is at the time creating, and his frenzy carries all away, for a time at least. . . .

He can draw an almost irresistible picture of some emotion, he can make a sensation, but having accomplished that one end, he rests contented for the time, and when he turns to anything new it is to perform the same tricks with different material. In short, in novels as in plays he is a perfect master of melodrama; he puts all his wonderful talent to but one purpose, and he makes a more taking show than any one else can, but there he stops. If emotion were all that is to be asked in life, and rather crude, physical emotion at that, criticism would be idle and there would be nothing to do but to give assent to all that Hugo's admirers claim for him. But there is something more which we have the right to claim of genius: that it should teach us not merely to thrill and shiver, but to know the heart of man; that it should regard life not as a combination of startling incidents, but as a problem in which thrilling scenes and dangers play but a small part. (p. 174)

T. S. Perry, "Victor Hugo," in The Atlantic Monthly, *Vol. XXXVI, No. CCXIV, August, 1875, pp. 167-74.*

HENRY JAMES   (essay date 1877)

Victor Hugo's new volumes [in his series **'Légende des Siècles'**] are as characteristic as might have been expected—as violent and extravagant in their faults, and in their fine passages as full of imaginative beauty. Apropos of the sense of humor, the absence of this quality is certainly Victor Hugo's great defect— the only limitation (it must be confessed it is a very serious one) to his imaginative power. . . . This "nouvelle série" of the **'Légende des Siècles'** is not a continuation of the first group of poems which appeared under this name: it is rather a return to the same ground, the various categories under which the first poems appeared being supplied with new recruits. These categories are too numerous to be mentioned here; they stretch from the creation of the world to the current year of grace. It is an immense plan, and shows on the author's part not only an extraordinary wealth of imagination, but a remarkable degree of research. It is true that Victor Hugo's researches are often rather pedantically exhibited; no poet was ever so fond of queer proper names, dragged together from dusty corners of history and legend, and strung together rhythmically—often with a great deal of ingenuity. He is too fond of emulating Homer's catalogue of the ships. But he has what the French call an extraordinary *scent* for picturesque subjects. . . . These volumes contain the usual proportion of fulsome adulation of Paris and of the bloodiest chapters in its history—that narrow Gallomania which makes us so often wonder at times, not whether the author is, after all, a great poet, but whether he is not very positively and decidedly a small poet. But, outside of this, this new series of what is probably his capital work contains plenty of proofs of his greatness—passages and touches of extraordinary beauty. (pp. 136-37)

Henry James, "Hugo's 'Légende des siècles'" (originally published in The Nation, *Vol. XXIV, No. 618, May 3, 1877), in his* Literary Reviews and Essays: On American, English, and French Literature, *edited by Albert Mordell, Twayne Publishers, 1957, pp. 136-38.*

ALFRED TENNYSON   (essay date 1877)

[*The following is Alfred Tennyson's poem, "To Victor Hugo."*]

Victor in Poesy, Victor in Romance,
Cloud-weaver of phantasmal hopes and fears,
French of the French, and Lord of human tears;
Child-lover; Bard whose fame-lit laurels glance
Darkening the wreaths of all that would advance,
Beyond our strait, their claim to be thy peers;
Weird Titan by thy winter weight of years
As yet unbroken, Stormy voice of France!
Who dost not love our England—so they say;
I know not—England, France, all man to be
Will make one people ere man's race be run:
And I, desiring that diviner day,
Yield thee full thanks for thy full courtesy
To younger England in the boy my son.

> *Alfred Tennyson, "To Victor Hugo," in* The Nineteenth Century, *Vol. I, No. IV, June, 1877, p. 547.*

GEORGE SAINTSBURY (essay date 1881)

[In *Les Quatre Vents de l'Esprit,* the] "Four Winds of the Spirit"—satire, drama, lyric, epic—give the author a subject of the kind certain to put him in the right vein as to general treatment. A fanciful critic seeking for picturesque analogies could find few better for Victor Hugo himself than the image of a "rushing mighty wind." The peculiar faculty of carrying his readers off with him which he possesses, the impetuous indifference with which he attacks every subject that presents itself, the very mechanical and technical structure and sound of his verse lend themselves equally to the simile. The work by which under the four heads the poet has by turns illustrated his conception and his mastery of the four modes of poetry is very miscellaneous in kind (at least in the satiric and lyrical sections), but for the most part has a pervading unison of sentiment—that of the well-known Hugonian perfectibilism. (p. 40)

The first division of the book is on the whole by far the weakest; despite the *Châtiments,* it may be doubted whether satire is the poet's forte, unless one is prepared to concede (which I certainly do not concede) that indignation and a faculty of expression combined suffice to make a satirist. Among the defects which sane criticism must note in Victor Hugo, an insufficient sense of humour and a certain incapacity to appreciate the proportions of things must be counted, and both these are terrible drawbacks to successful satire. The satirist has no need of the vague and the vast, the special regions in which this poet's genius delights to expatiate. He must be cool, and M. Victor Hugo is never cool; dispassionate, and M. Victor Hugo is never dispassionate; able to guard himself at all points while he attacks others, and M. Victor Hugo is always laying his flanks open to the archers. . . . It is positively painful to an admirer of the greatest poet of the last half-century to find him still harping on the trumpery Brussels business, when a few dozen ragamuffins, overcome with faro and zeal, threw or did not throw a handful or so of pebbles at his windows. The piece "**Muse, un nommé Ségur**" is in every way inferior to the poem on the same subject in *L'Année Terrible,* of which it seems to have been a first and very properly withdrawn draft. . . . But even in this, the only unsatisfactory part of the book (I shall not have to make a single other uncomplimentary criticism), the splendid and imperishable literary workmanship which makes Victor Hugo what he is, appears everywhere, and more than reconciles the reader. (pp. 40-1)

To feel the full *ivresse de Victor Hugo* [intoxication of Victor Hugo], the peculiar excitement which makes the blood (com-

pounded of water and ink) of veteran writers run quicker, and tears rise to eyes which are bleared by the perusal of ten thousand volumes of dull prose and duller verse, the means used to produce the picture, and not merely the picture itself, must be studied till they can be instantaneously appreciated. The even and almost stealthy flow of the first line, diversified by no specially sounding syllable, and with a hardly noticeable caesura; the swell and crash of the second, the very contrast of form and cadence in the members of the last half of it, all enter into the total effect, and must all be appreciated if the full pleasure that the couplet can give is to be felt. . . . Of course there are persons for whom *Les Quatre Vents de l'Esprit* will have an additional zest because the author is a republican, an anti-formalist and anti-dogmatist, if not exactly an antichristian, a holder of wild and impracticable social theories, an egotist, a patriot almost absurdly *borné* in his patriotism. But there are other persons, and perhaps a greater number, to whom all these characteristics, or some of them, are *per se* unmitigatedly distasteful and absurd. . . . It has been well said of Victor Hugo that no poet, when he has once got a grip of his reader, has a greater power of transporting. Whether that grip is ever fixed or not, is of course very much the reader's own affair. . . . A certain amount of good-will and of natural aptitude must be contributed by those who trust themselves to this Chariot of the Four Winds. But those who have made the voyage will hardly forget it, and will tread the lower earth in future with fuller and gladder memories and with loftier thoughts. (pp. 52-3)

> *George Saintsbury, "'The Four Winds of the Spirit'," in* The Fortnightly Review *(reprinted by permission of Contemporary Review Company Limited), Vol. XXX, July, 1881, pp. 40-53.*

BRANDER MATTHEWS (essay date 1881)

All Victor Hugo's plays are the work of his youth (he was not forty when the '**Burgraves**' was acted), and they are thus free from the measureless emphasis which is the besetting sin of his later work. And unfortunately Hugo has not obeyed Goethe's behest, to beware of taking "the faults of our youth into our old age; for old age brings with it its own defects." This is just what Hugo has done. No author of his years and fame has ever changed so little since he first came forward. There has been extension, of course; but there has not been growth. So, although Hugo stopped short his dramatic production, we may doubt whether the future would have had any surprise in store for us. (pp. 40-1)

If one seeks proof that Hugo is not a great dramatic poet of the race and lineage of Shakspere, but rather a supremely clever playwright, an artificer of dramas, not because the drama was in him and must out, but because the stage offered the best market and the most laurels, one has only to consider '**Marie Tudor,**' or '**Angelo.**' No great dramatic poet, no one who was truly a dramatic poet, could have written such stuff. In spite of all their cleverness, they are unworthy of a poet who has any sense of life. That these plays are so inferior to the metrical dramas goes to show that Hugo needs the restraint of verse, and that he is at his best when working under the limitations of the Alexandrine,—limitations, which, as I have said, are fatal to dramatic poetry of the highest rank. Putting this and that together, I find that Hugo's plays are melodramas, written by a poet, and not poetic plays written by a dramatic poet. . . . Hugo's plays are not poetic in conception, however poetic they may be in verbal clothing. Neither the plots nor the personages are poetic in conception. The plot is melodramatic, but the best of melodramas because of its simplicity and strength, and because it is the work of a man of heavier mental endowment than often takes to melodrama. Nor are the characters more poetic than the situations: they are not saturated with the spirit of poesy, and lifted up by the breath of the music. Most of Hugo's people, especially the tragic, are drawn in outline in monochrome: they are impersonations of a single impulse. Miss Baillie wrote a series of Plays for the Passions: Hugo gives a passion apiece to each of his people, and lets them fight it out. Put one of Hugo's villains, the Don Salluste of **'Ruy Blas,'** say,—a sharp silhouette, all black,—and set it by the side of Iago, and note the rounded and life-like complexity of Shakspere's traitor. Or compare Hugo's characters with Molière's, and see how thin their substance seems, how petty their natures, in spite of all their swelling speech. They have not the muscle and the marrow, they have not the light and the air, of Molière's poetically conceived creatures.

Melodramatic as situations and characters are, however, the best of Hugo's plays are still poetic, in appearance at least. This is because Victor Hugo is a great poet, although not a great dramatic poet. It is because his plays, while they are melodramas in structure, are the work of an artist in words. The melodramatist, when he has once constructed the play, calls on the poet to write it; for in Hugo are two men,—a melodramatist doubled by a lyric poet. The joints of the plot are hidden, and the hollowness of the characters is cloaked, by the ample folds of a poetic diction of unrivalled richness. It is the splendor of this lyric speech which blinds us at first to the lack of inner and vital poetry in the structure it decks so royally. Although, therefore, his plays are immensely effective in performance, and his characters wear at times the externals of poetic conception, Victor Hugo is not that rare thing, a great dramatic poet,—a thing so rare, indeed, that the world as yet has seen but a scant halfscore.

There is no need to say here that Victor Hugo's glory does not depend on his dramas, nor, indeed, upon his work in any single department of literature. His genius has, turn by turn, tried almost every kind of writing, and on whatsoever it tried it has left its mark. He is a master-singer of lyrics and a master-maker of satires. The song is as pure as the spring at the hillside, and the satire is as scorching as the steel when it flows from the crucible. He is mighty in romance, and moving in history; giving us in **'Notre Dame de Paris'** historical romance, and in the **'History of a Crime'** romantic history. Even in criticism and philosophy he has done his stint of labor. But his best work is not merely literary. Literature is too small to hold him, and the finest of him is outside of it. The best part of him has got out of literature into life. . . . Beyond and above Hugo's great genius is his great heart. He is the poet of the proletarian and of the people; he is the poet of the poor and the weak and the suffering; he is the poet of the over-worked woman and of the little child; he is the friend of the down-trodden and the outcast; and his is the truly Christian charity which droppeth like the gentle dew from heaven. (pp. 41-4)

> *Brander Matthews, "Victor Hugo" (1881), in his* French Dramatists of the Nineteenth Century, *revised edition, Charles Scribner's Sons, 1901 (and reprinted by Benjamin Blom, 1968), pp. 15-45.*

THE SATURDAY REVIEW   (essay date 1885)

No recent illness of any Frenchman has excited anything like the feeling which [Hugo's fatal illness] has called forth, and all parties have united in a manner, unfortunately less common in France than elsewhere, to mourn the greatest of living Frenchmen, the last very great man whom France has to boast. . . .

What we have to do here is to estimate briefly, but as sufficiently as possible, the literary value of a career not often paralleled as regards acknowledged literary supremacy and mixture of literary with practical influence. (p. 708)

No one that we ever heard of in France or England, except Mr. Swinburne, took Victor Hugo very seriously as a politician; no one could be perverted or even scandalized by his peculiar form of theistic free thought in religion, except very feeble persons; no one, except persons still feebler, was likely to go to him as an authority on fact, an arbiter of criticism, or a witness to be taken unreservedly on points of private likes and dislikes. He was a poet, and nothing but a poet, whether he wrote verse or prose.

It is much more the proper appreciation of his poetical merits than the proper discarding or minimizing of his defects which ought to be urged on English readers. Victor Hugo's prose was remarkable, his drama more remarkable, his poetry proper most remarkable of all. But it is very much to be doubted whether the average English reader has ever appreciated the point of view from which these three great bodies of literature, in an ascending order, challenge and deserve the admiration of critics. It is even to be doubted whether in these days of glib talking about literature, and French literature especially, many critics even are quite in case to appreciate. . . . The Alexandrine of Victor Hugo is not more beautiful than his lyrical measures; but it is probably safe to say that no one who does not appreciate it can appreciate them. What Victor Hugo did before all as a poet (putting aside for the moment his innovation of subjects, stage arrangements, and the like) was to rediscover the secret of crashing sound in French verse. Since the death of Corneille French poetry had rippled; Victor Hugo taught it once more the movement and the music of the wave. In his lyrical pieces, the limitation which even he was not able quite to destroy of French metre to the iambus made his earlier verse to some uninstructed ears perhaps approach the verse of Lamartine or of Chénier. Only a complete ignorance of the very rudiments of the matter could confuse his Alexandrines with theirs or with any Alexandrines of any poet from Racine downwards. Victor Hugo is not to be scanned by couplets; he is to be scanned by verse paragraphs or *tirades* of irregular length, where the rhymes simply mark the breaking of each wave, each successive wave, till the paragraph finishes with the *fluctus decumanus*. Until some little initiation in this has been gone through, the admiration of even reasonable Hugolâtres for Hugo must always seem a mystery and an affectation. The Englishman who founds his knowledge of French on a few yellow novels, a translation or two, some second-hand stories about Gautier's waistcoat and Cyrano de Bergerac's nose, the faculty of wading through a column of *faits divers* and *nouvelles à la main* without always missing the point, and perhaps a little more of the same kind, will never understand Hugo all his life long. . . . We forget who it was who first spoke of the *ivresse de Victor Hugo* [the critic perhaps refers to the excerpt above by George Saintsbury], but no other phrase properly expresses the effect of his work when it is once comprehended, and, unlike most intoxications, it does not bring about any subsequent disgust.

It is, no doubt, a result of the peculiarities which bring about this strange and unique effect (for no other writer that we can think of produces exactly or nearly the same complete forget-fulness of anything but the music and the swing of the verse, the rush and sweep of the language) that Victor Hugo has, independently of the personal faults and the faults of matter alluded to and dismissed above, some purely literary weak-nesses which mar his work. No prose book of his, with the possible exception of the *Travailleurs de la mer,* can be said to have the solid plan and the complete working out necessary to perfect prose. They are rhapsodies like, in different ways, *Han d'Islande* and *William Shakespeare,* chronicles like *Notre Dame de Paris,* congeries of beauties and defects like nearly all the later novels. In the same way his warmest admirers admit that his plays show a singular inability or unwillingness on the part of so fertile and poetical a genius to submit to the not very difficult or recondite laws of dramatic presentation, a constant contempt of the simplest arts of the playwright, an invincible confusion of the epic and the drama, the poem and the play. Even his poems proper do not escape a just as well as an unjust censure. The common cant that the later volumes are unfit to rank with the earlier is foolish enough, for as a matter of fact much of the matter of the later dates from the time of the earlier, the earlier themselves contain much in-equality, and nothing that the author has ever written excels the finest part of *Les quatre vents de l'esprit* and some of the other recent issues. But it has never been Victor Hugo's strong point to introduce the law of measure into his work; to be conscious of what there is not to say, to practise economy and reserve. His poetical quality is of quite another sort, and the wise go and will go to him for it, just as they go to the other great poets each for his own secret. That he is, on the whole, the greatest poet of France we make no doubt whatever. That he is, also, among the great poets of the world, we hesitate no more to pronounce. And the denial of such a place to him can only come from the old and undying blunder of asking from a man something which is not his to give, but some one else's. It is Victor Hugo's function to transport—at one time by pathos, at another by terror, at a third by mere splendour and glory of verse and of language which excites no ideas and appeals to no feelings but simple and unmixed admiration. The man who compares him with Shakspeare is absurd, for to the two great qualities of universality and unerringness which dis-tinguished Shakspeare he has less claim than many smaller men. It is scarcely less absurd to compare him with others. But Victor Hugo is Victor Hugo (the formula, if not the ap-plication, comes from no mean critic), and whoso cannot taste Victor Hugo is shut out from one of the fullest and most intense of literary pleasures. (pp. 708-09)

"Victor Hugo," in The Saturday Review, London, *Vol. 59, No. 1544, May 30, 1885, pp. 708-09.*

M.O.W. OLIPHANT   (essay date 1885)

[The] great mass of the work which Victor Hugo has left behind him can be separated from the polemics of his troubled age and fiery temper. It is not in any sense a peaceful literature. Conflict is its very inspiration. The struggle of human misery with all the confusing and overbearing forces of life; of poverty with the requirements and oppressions of wealth; of the small with the great; of the people with tyrants; of Man with Fate: these are his subjects, and he is never an impartial historian. He is on the side of the weak in every combat, the partisan of the oppressed. But this does not detract from his work when his opponents are the oppressors of the past, or the still more subtle, veiled, and unassailable forces of Destiny. The poet's

region is there: he is born, if not to set right the times, which are out of joint, at least to read to the world the high and often terrible lesson of the ages. But it vulgarizes his work when he is seen, tooth and nail, in violent personal conflict with foemen unworthy of his steel, embalming in poetry the trivial or the uncompleted incidents of contemporary warfare. (pp. 11-12)

Hugo has enough and to spare for all subjects that occurred to him. A sunset, a landscape, a love song, alternate in his pages with a philosophical discussion or a brief and brilliant scene snatched from history, from contemporary life, from his own inner existence, all clothed in the noblest verse of which the French language is capable. His power over that language is boundless, the wealth of an utterance which never pauses for a word, which disregards all rules yet glorifies them, which is ready for every suggestion and finds nothing too terrible, noth-ing too tender, for the tongue which, at his bidding, leaps into blazing eloquence, or rolls in clouds and thunder, or murmurs with the accent of a dove. Never had there been so great a gamut, a compass so extended. (p. 17)

It is impossible, or almost impossible, to convey through the medium of translation the melody and beauty of lyrical poetry from one language to another; it is even difficult for a foreigner to appreciate fully, though well acquainted with the language, that finer soul of verse which is dearest to the native ear. And we do not venture to attempt to explain and describe the in-describable. But yet there are many of Victor Hugo's most striking poems which might be translated with at least an ap-proximate success. For that in which he is perhaps at his best is the delineation of a sudden scene, an incident in which human nature is seen at its highest or lowest, a spark struck out of the darkness in which history leaves the mass of humankind. (p. 18)

It is not, however, upon his poetry, either in the form of drama, lyric, or narrative, that his fame out of France, or at least in England, is founded. There is no more usual deliverance of superficial criticism in this country than that which declares French poetry in general to be either nought—which is still a not uncommon notion—or at least not great enough to be worth the study which alone could make it comprehensible. There are many good people who dare to say this yet live, audacious, and unconscious of their folly. We have now, however, to consider Victor Hugo on a ground which no one ventures to dispute. The great Romances—for which we should like to invent another name—which we cannot call novels, and which are too majestic even for the title of romance, though that means something more than the corresponding word in English—are in their kind and period the greatest works produced in his time. We are glad that we are not called upon to make any comparison of the Frenchman with our own beloved romancer, the master of all fiction in England, the name most dear in literature. Scott's noble, sober, temperate, and modest genius is in all things different from the tempestuous, fantastic, and splendid imagination—the nature fiery, violent, yet profound—of his successor in the field. That Hugo penetrates deeper, that the depths of that abyss of which he is so fond lie open before him, and that nothing in Scott gives the terrific impression which the dark and surging mass of vitality, misery, and crime lurking in the backgrounds of Paris both mediaeval and actual, conveys to us, we readily admit. (pp. 19-20)

"Notre Dame de Paris," with all its strange learning and won-derful panoramic effects, is not like the work of a young man, or a first essay in the art of fiction. Yet [Hugo] was scarcely twenty-eight when it was written. It has nothing of the frank reality and open-air life of Scott. Its extreme elaboration and detail resemble more the work of Manzoni in the "Promessi Sposi," and it has evidently been the model, conscious or unconscious, of "Romola." George Eliot, who was not, so far as we are aware, a disciple of Hugo, bears more resemblance to him than any other writer of historical romance. Scott has no object but that of telling his manful delightful story of times which charm him by their picturesqueness, which have seized upon his imagination in all their glory of arms and adventure, and with that advantage of distance which makes the past the true land of romance. Manzoni has no story to tell, nor spontaneous impulse like that of our great romancist, but the distinct and carefully worked out purpose of elucidating the Middle Ages in Italy, and laying before us the conditions of life in that departed condition of affairs. Victor Hugo adds something to both. He has his tale to tell, but the tale is a parable—he has his revelation to make, his old world to light up with a lurid illumination, which does not diffuse itself over the landscape, but lights up here and there with miraculous Rembrandt effects against the background of a world of shadows. With him there is meaning in everything, and the common struggle and conflict of humanity at large with the forces that oppress and enslave is never lost sight of, even when his principal object is to trace out some individual struggle against those awful powers of fate which have been the subject of so many dramas, and have affected the imagination of so many poets. (p. 20)

Victor Hugo makes no historical portraits. The group of beings round whose hapless feet he draws the coils of fate are all offsprings of his fancy. The dancing girl of the streets, an image most probably borrowed from the "Precioza" of Cervantes—if among such sovereigns of poetic inspiration there could ever be any question of borrowing—the frightful spectre of the priest, the deformed and formidable monster Quasimodo, with his hideous body and faithful soul, all linked together in fatal fortuitous combination, belong to the imagination alone. The *beau capitaine* has a certain footing on the solid earth, and is, indeed, a remorseless picture of the young libertine, handsome and heartless and beloved, with whom fiction is but too familiar. But all these figures are primitive, in the elementary stage of existence; they have no defence of character, of individual life or thought against the constraining force of the fatality which grasps them, and which they cannot escape. Even the girl, who is the image of purity and innocence amid all those sombre and terrible scenes, is pure only till temptation really touches her, and has in herself no protest against sin, but only against that to which she has no inclination. The priest in his vile soul has no pretence of a higher feeling. The passion that rages in him has no right to be called love; for it is the basest and most gross of animal desires. (p. 21)

According to his own explanation, it is the struggle of human nature with superstition which Victor Hugo has set himself to demonstrate in this book. But it is much more. Superstition is the feeblest of the forces in it. The condemnation of the hapless girl as a sorceress is little more than the framework of the drama. The sudden commotion of the fierce yet easily diverted crowd, the merciless apparition of Tristan L'Hermite and his soldiers, and the various scenes about the gibbet give but a superficial support to this theory. The picture is really more dark and fatal, less temporary and chronological. With greater reason it might be said that the *motif* of the sombre strain is that which plays so little part in ancient tragedy, but which is so great an actor in the modern. . . . The drama is, in fact, deeper and of far wider significance than the author claims for

it. It is the errings and mistakes of the half-enlightened human creature, "moving about in worlds not realized," stumbling into paths discovered too late to be fatal, half seeing, not understanding, till time brings the terrible explanation. Superstition has not much more to do with it than has the grand shadow under which all is enacted: that magnificent Notre Dame which it is scarcely possible to think of, standing there, the central figure in the scene, as an inanimate thing.

This was Victor Hugo's *coup d'essai* in fiction, and it stands by itself a work, so far as we know, without parallel—a piece of mediaeval life and of universal tragedy, vivid, terrible, appalling. (p. 22)

There is no tenderness in **"Notre Dame."** Love itself is a delirium, and pity is so qualified with horror that there is no softness in it. But when we come to the **"Misérables,"** all is pity and tenderness, and a compassion which melts the heart. To turn from Claude Frollo, and find ourselves suddenly in the presence of Bishop Myriel, is a change for which we can find no words. In the gloomy world, wherein the dark priest of Notre Dame represents religion, there is no repentance or power of betterment, nor healing touch of sympathy, but only fierce remorse and execration and terror. But when the great romancist begins his second chapter of human history and fate, the altered atmosphere makes itself felt in a moment. (p. 23)

The **"Misérables"** is the story of [the] struggle in the soul and life of the rescued criminal, but it is also the story of the world that lies behind and around him. Again, that swarming, tumultuous Paris, with its suffering multitudes, its chaos of discordant elements, and the great stream of life that carries on all those contradictions and anomalies. No city was ever so overflowing with the sound of a multitude; every roof hides a little secondary conflict; everywhere there are the tokens of the struggle, not with the law only and its rigid rules, but of the nobler with the baser, of mercy with judgment. . . . Nothing is omitted in this wonderful book. If its chief subject is in the depths, it rises also to the serenest heights of imagination. It is the epic of the miserable; but since that great change which in the late twilight, among the wild freedom of the open moors, we saw taking place in the soul of the miserable convict, it becomes also the romance of the happy. For that is the turning-point—not Javert and his needless pursuit, but the fact that Jean Valjean becomes the père Madeleine—the repentant, the sorrowful who has obtained mercy. There are many indications of vice, such as were indispensable to the subject; and there are also, as unfortunately in all Victor Hugo's works, much wild talk and rhapsodies which to the innocent may sound like blasphemy. But withal, the **"Misérables"** is the greatest of religious romances: a noble, modern, nineteenth-century legend of the saints.

The **"Travailleurs de la Mer"** is more strictly and formally true to the author's declared purpose. It is the struggle of Man with the forces of Nature in a clearer sense than the **"Misérables"** represents the struggle with Society. The fantastic character of that conflict, and of the devilish being with which it is made, is within the privileges of art, though not perhaps according to the laws of probability. . . . The concentration of the struggle with brute force, and the hideous, unreasoning will which seems to confront man in his attempts to subjugate the earth, and resist him to the death, in a malignant creature, is in this point of view quite justifiable. But here again the subject widens, and the larger atmosphere of humanity comes in. Gilliat's death struggle is not with the pieuvre, nor with the winds and seas, over which the resources and expedients of humanity (in his case naturally strained to extravagance) are always victorious in the end; but with a thing much slighter and much greater—a trifling thing, not worth counting in the history of the race—yet not to be overcome by those forces which can move mountains, or touched by the lever even which could upset the earth. It is the heart of another human creature, the foolish impulse of another's inclination, which is the object, unconquerable by any giant, and against which, with all his strength and patience and boundless resource, this conqueror of the seas is brought to shipwreck and destruction. (pp. 24-5)

[Hugo's] former works were full of night effects, strong contrasts of light and shade: but here the sky and horizon have all the largeness, the breadth and space which belong to the sea. The scene is larger, but it is less peopled, the actors in the drama are few, for a great part of the work Gilliat alone holds by himself the human side of the struggle, and all the uncertainty of incident and surroundings, which in the former works were so endless and varied, are here entirely laid aside. It is an epic rather than a tragedy, yet the most tragic epic: the story of our life. (p. 27)

We may permit ourselves to take the privilege of selection, and omit the next of his works, the **"Homme qui Rit."** The book is an embodiment of all that is offensive in Hugo—extravagance, false taste, false rhetoric, and a choice of the painful, the horrible, and the grotesque, which in itself is a vice. He was weary of exile, of sorrow, of long waiting for the good to come, when he had this nightmare. His next great work of fiction was produced under happier auspices. It was intended to have been followed by two others, in which the story of the Revolution should have been repeated and summed up; but this intention was never carried out. As a matter of fact, a sequel to the portion of the work already before us would be little possible, since two of the chief personages, and these the typical leaders of the Revolution, had demonstrated the poetical impossibility of the undertaking by their tragic end.

In **"Quatre-vingt-treize"** we come back from the stillness of the island, the concentration of life within the surroundings of the seas, once more to the crowds and heat and conflict of tumultuous existence, into the bitter misery of civil war, and that desperate struggle for mastery which had not yet found a solution in Bonaparte. No scene in Victor Hugo's works is more characteristic than the scene in the ship with the cannon which has broken loose. The blind and fatal thing, simulating the struggles of a creature that has life and some sort of intelligence, is such a symbol as is dear to him. It is like the pieuvre, it is like Javert, an irresponsible instrument of evil; malign, yet innocent; striving to murder, yet without guilt. Its bounds and plunges are so many details in his parable—the man who stands with his life in his hands opposed to that threatening, redoubtable, lifeless monster, is man incarnate against the powers of destiny. (pp. 27-8)

[The charm of the sombre volumes of **"Quatre-vingt-treize"** is] also the charm of the poet's old age—the wonderful group of children which appears in the midst of all the fire and flame, the conflict of passions and elements. There is no chapter of the life of childhood in literature known to us which we could place beside the chapter entitled "Le Massacre de St. Barthélemy." The men outside may be types and symbols, the children live and breathe. . . . The little group altogether fills our eyes as we read with the moisture of delight, with something of that unspeakable tenderness, compassion, adoration, which

is in the eyes of the writer. These little beings are in all the freshness of the inarticulate, creatures conceived, not described; fresh from the hand of God, not sullied by the touch of that reverent yet playful beholder through whom we see the blossoming of their unconscious life. Their seriousness, their busy-ness, their tremendous discoveries, their absorption in the little world about them, and indifference to all that passes outside; the masculine energy of René-Jean and Gros-Alain; the finer dreamer, twenty months old, not yet sufficiently entered in life to give her full attention to it—form such a picture as neither poet nor painter had dreamed of. The atmosphere about them is half heaven, half morning—the little comedy of their existence is full of a pathos which is at once heartrending and delightful. Amid all the wonders of Hugo's genius, this is perhaps the most wonderful of all. (pp. 30-1)

> *M.O.W. Oliphant, "Victor Hugo," in* Contemporary Review, *Vol. XLVIII, July, 1885, pp. 10-32.*

ALGERNON CHARLES SWINBURNE (essay date 1886)

In the spring of 1616 the greatest Englishman of all time passed away with no public homage or notice, and the first tributes paid to his memory were prefixed to the miserably garbled and inaccurate edition of his works which was issued seven years later by a brace of players under the patronage of a brace of peers. In the spring of 1885 the greatest Frenchman of all time has passed away amid such universal anguish and passion of regret as never before accompanied the death of the greatest among poets. The contrast is of course not wholly due to the incalculable progress of humanity during the two hundred and sixty-nine years which divide the date of our mourning from the date of Shakespeare's death: nor even to the vast superiority of Frenchmen to Englishmen in the quality of generous, just, and reasonable gratitude for the very highest of all benefits that man can confer on mankind. For the greatest poet of this century has been more than . . . a force of indirect and gradual beneficence as every great writer must needs be. His spiritual service has been in its inmost essence, in its highest development, the service of a healer and a comforter, the work of a redeemer and a prophet. Above all other apostles who have brought us each the glad tidings of his peculiar gospel, the free gifts of his special inspiration, has this one deserved to be called by the most beautiful and tender of all human titles—the son of consolation. His burning wrath and scorn unquenchable were fed with light and heat from the inexhaustible dayspring of his love—a fountain of everlasting and unconsuming fire. We know of no such great poet so good, of no such good man so great in genius: not though Milton and Shelley, our greatest lyric singer and our single epic poet, remain with us for signs and examples of devotion as heroic and self-sacrifice as pure. And therefore it is but simply reasonable that not those alone should mourn for him who have been reared and nurtured on the fruits of his creative spirit: that those also whom he wrought and fought for, but who know him only as their champion and their friend—they that cannot even read him, but remember how he laboured in their cause, that their children might fare otherwise than they—should bear no unequal part in the burden of this infinite and worldwide sorrow.

For us, who from childhood upwards have fostered and fortified whatever of good was born in us—all capacity of spiritual work, all seed of human sympathy, all powers of hope and faith, all passions and aspirations found loyal to the service of duty and of love—with the bread of his deathless word and the wine of his immortal song, the one thing possible to do in this first hour of bitterness and stupefaction at the sense of a loss not possible yet to realize is not to declaim his praise or parade our lamentation in modulated effects or efforts of panegyric or of dirge: it is to reckon up once more the standing account of our all but incalculable debt. (pp. 1-2)

Poet, dramatist, novelist, historian, philosopher, and patriot, the spiritual sovereign of the nineteenth century was before all things and above all things a poet. Throughout all the various and ambitious attempts of his marvellous boyhood—criticism, drama, satire, elegy, epigram, and romance—the dominant vein is poetic. His example will stand for ever as the crowning disproof of the doubtless more than plausible opinion that the most amazing precocity of power is a sign of ensuing impotence and premature decay. There was never a more brilliant boy than Victor Hugo: but there has never been a greater man. (p. 3)

[*Cromwell* is] a work sufficient of itself to establish the author's fame for all ages in which poetry and thought, passion and humour, subtle truth of character, stately perfection of structure, facile force of dialogue and splendid eloquence of style, continue to be admired and enjoyed. (p. 5)

The Cromwell of Hugo is as far from the faultless monster of Carlyle's creation and adoration as from the all but unredeemed villain of royalist and Hibernian tradition: he is a great and terrible poetic figure, imbued throughout with active life and harmonized throughout by imaginative intuition: a patriot and a tyrant, a dissembler and a believer, a practical humourist and a national hero. (p. 9)

[*Les Orientales* is] the most musical and many-coloured volume of verse that ever had glorified the language. From *Le Feu du Ciel* to *Sara la Baigneuse,* from the thunder-peals of exterminating judgment to the flute-notes of innocent girlish luxury in the sense of loveliness and life, the inexhaustible range of his triumph expands and culminates and extends. Shelley has left us no more exquisite and miraculous piece of lyrical craftsmanship than *Les Djinns;* none perhaps so rich in variety of modulation, so perfect in rise and growth and relapse and reiterance of music. (p. 10)

And here, like Shelley, was Hugo already the poet of freedom, a champion of the sacred right and the holy duty of resistance. (p. 11)

[Of *Hernani*'s] dramatic and poetic quality what praise could be uttered that must not before this have been repeated at least some myriads of times? But if there be any mortal to whom the heroic scene of the portraits, the majestic and august monologue of Charles the Fifth at the tomb of Charles the Great, the terrible beauty, the vivid pathos, the bitter sweetness of the close, convey no sense of genius and utter no message of delight, we can only say that it would simply be natural, consistent, and proper for such a critic to recognize in Shakespeare a barbarian, and a Philistine in Milton.

Nevertheless, if we are to obey the perhaps rather childish impulse of preference and selection among the highest works of the highest among poets, I will avow that to my personal instinct or apprehension *Marion de Lorme* seems a yet more perfect and pathetic masterpiece than even *Hernani* itself. (p. 14)

In one point it seems to me that this immortal masterpiece may perhaps be reasonably placed, with *Le Roi s'amuse* and *Ruy Blas,* in triune supremacy at the head of Victor Hugo's plays. The wide range of poetic abilities, the harmonious variety of congregated powers, displayed in these three great tragedies

through almost infinite variations of terror and pity and humour and sublime surprise, will seem to some readers, whose reverence is no less grateful for other gifts of the same great hand, unequalled at least till the advent in his eighty-first year of *Torquemada.* (p. 15)

From the *Autumn Leaves* to the *Songs of the Twilight,* and again from the *Inner Voices* to the *Sunbeams and Shadows,* the continuous jet of lyric song through a space of ten fertile years was so rich in serene and various beauty that the one thing notable in a flying review of its radiant course is the general equality of loveliness in form and colour, which is relieved and heightened at intervals by some especial example of a beauty more profound or more sublime. (p. 16)

The year after *Notre-Dame de Paris* and *Les Feuilles d'Automne* appeared one of the great crowning tragedies of all time, *Le Roi s'amuse.* As the key-note of *Marion de Lorme* had been redemption by expiation, so the key-note of this play is expiation by retribution. The simplicity, originality, and straightforwardness of the terrible means through which this austere conception is worked out would give moral and dramatic value to a work less rich in the tenderest and sublimest poetry, less imbued with the purest fire of pathetic passion. After the magnificent pleading of the Marquis de Nangis in the preceding play, it must have seemed impossible that the poet should without a touch of repetition or reiterance be able again to confront a young king with an old servant, pour forth again the denunciation and appeal of a breaking heart, clothe again the haughtiness of honour, the loyalty of grief, the sanctity of indignation, in words that shine like lightning and verses that thunder like the sea. But the veteran interceding for a nephew's life is a less tragic figure than he who comes to ask account for a daughter's honour. Hugo never merely repeats himself: his miraculous fertility and force of utterance were not more indefatigable and inexhaustible than the fountains of thought and emotion which fed that eloquence with fire. (pp. 21-2)

Lucrèce Borgia, the first-born of [Hugo's tragedies in prose], is also the most perfect in structure as well as the most sublime in subject. The plots of all three are equally pure inventions of tragic fancy: Gennaro and Fabiano, the heroic son of the Borgia and the caitiff lover of the Tudor, are of course as utterly unknown to history as is the self-devotion of the actress Tisbe. It is more important to remark and more useful to remember that the mastery of terror and pity, the command of all passions and all powers that may subserve the purpose of tragedy, is equally triumphant and infallible in them all. . . . [The] exquisite and melodious libretto of *La Esmeralda,* which should be carefully and lovingly studied by all who would appreciate the all but superhuman versatility and dexterity of metrical accomplishment which would have sufficed to make a lesser poet famous among his peers for ever, but may almost escape notice in the splendour of Victor Hugo's other and sublimer qualities. . . . No one that I know of has ever been absurd enough to make identity in tone of thought or feeling, in quality of spirit or of style, the ground for a comparison of Hugo with Shakespeare: they are of course as widely different as are their respective countries and their respective times: but never since the death of Shakespeare had there been so perfect and harmonious a fusion of the highest comedy with the deepest tragedy as in the five many-voiced and many-coloured acts of *Ruy Blas.* (pp. 26-7)

There are not, even in the whole work of Victor Hugo, many pages of deeper and more pathetic interest than those which explain to us 'what exile is.' Each of the three prefaces to the three volumes of his *Actes et Paroles* is rich in living eloquence, in splendid epigram and description, narrative and satire and study of men and things: but the second, it seems to me, would still be first in attraction, if it had no other claim than this, that it contains the record of the death of Captain Harvey. No reverence for innocent and heroic suffering, no abhorrence of triumphant and execrable crime, can impede or interfere with our sense of the incalculable profit, the measureless addition to his glory and our gain, resulting from Victor Hugo's exile of nineteen years and nine months. Greater already than all other poets of his time together, these years were to make him greater than any but the very greatest of all time. . . . The main facts recorded in the pages of *Napoléon le Petit* and *L'Histoire d'un Crime* are simple, flagrant, palpable, indisputable. The man who takes any other view of them than is expressed in these two books must be prepared to impugn and to confute the principle that perjury, robbery, and murder are crimes. But, we are told, the perpetual vehemence of incessant imprecation, the stormy insistence of unremitting obloquy, which accompanies every chapter, illuminates every page, underlines every sentence of the narrative, must needs impair the confidence of an impartial reader in the trustworthiness of a chronicle and a commentary written throughout as in characters of flaming fire. (pp. 35-7)

But, valuable and precious as all such readers will always hold these two books of immediate and implacable history, they will not, I presume, be rated among the more important labours of their author's literary life. (p. 37)

There is not, it seems to me, in all this marvellous life, to which wellnigh every year brought its additional aureole of glory, a point more important, a date more memorable, than the publication of the *Châtiments*. Between the prologue *Night* and the epilogue *Light* the ninety-eight poems that roll and break and lighten and thunder like waves of a visible sea fulfil the choir of their crescent and refluent harmonies with hardly less depth and change and strength of music, with no less living force and with no less passionate unity, than the waters on whose shores they were written. Two poems, the third and the sixth, in the first of the seven books into which the collection is divided, may be taken as immediate and sufficient instances of the two different keys in which the entire book is written; of the two styles, one bitterly and keenly realistic, keeping scornfully close to shameful fact—one higher in flight and wider in range of outlook, soaring strongly to the very summits of lyric passion—which alternate in terrible and sublime antiphony throughout the living pages of this imperishable record. A second Juvenal might have drawn for us with not less of angry fidelity and superb disgust the ludicrous and loathsome inmates of the den infested by holy hirelings of the clerical press: no Roman satirist could have sung, no Roman lyrist could have thundered, such a poem as that which has blasted for ever the name and the memory of the prostitute archbishop Sibour. . . . But it would be necessary to dwell on every poem, to pause at every page, if adequate justice were to be done to this or indeed to any of the volumes of verse published from this time forth by Victor Hugo. . . . In the second book, the appeal '**To the People**,' with a threefold cry for burden, calling on the buried Lazarus to rise again in words that seem to reverberate from stanza to stanza like peal upon peal of living thunder, prolonged in steadfast cadence from height to height across the hollows of a range of mountains, is one of the most wonderful symphonies of tragic and triumphant verse that ever shook the hearts of its hearers with rapture of rage and pity. The first and the two last stanzas seem to me absolutely un-

surpassed and unsurpassable for pathetic majesty of music. (pp. 38-40)

If ever a more superb structure of lyric verse was devised by the brain of man, it must have been, I am very certain, in a language utterly unknown to me. Every line, every pause, every note of it should be studied and restudied by those who would thoroughly understand the lyrical capacity of Hugo's at its very highest point of power, in the fullest sweetness of its strength.

About the next poem—'**Souvenir de la nuit du 4**'—others may try, if they please, to write, if they can; I can only confess that I cannot. Nothing so intolerable in its pathos, I should think, was ever written. (p. 42)

The close of the fourth poem in the third book is a nobler protest than ever has been uttered or ever can be uttered in prose against the servile sophism of a false democracy which affirms or allows that a people has the divine right of voting itself into bondage. There is nothing grander in Juvenal, and nothing more true. (pp. 43-4)

The sixth and seventh poems in this book are each a superb example of its kind; the verses on an interview between Abd-el-Kader and Bonaparte are worthy of a place among the earlier *Orientales* for simplicity and fullness of effect in lyric tone and colour; and satire could hardly give a finer and completer little study than that of the worthy tradesman who for love of his own strong-box would give his vote for a very Phalaris to reign over him, and put up with the brazen bull for love of the golden calf: an epigram which sums up an epoch. The indignant poem of *Joyeuse Vie,* with its terrible photographs of subterranean toil and want, is answered by the not less terrible though ringing and radiant song of *L'empereur s'amuse;* and this again by the four solemn stanzas in which a whole world of desolate suffering is condensed and realized. . . . *A Night's Lodging,* the last poem of the fourth book, is perhaps the very finest and most perfect example of imaginative and tragic satire that exists: if this rank be due to a poem at once the most vivid in presentation, the most sublime in scorn, the most intense and absolute in condensed expression of abhorrence and in assured expression of belief. (pp. 44-5)

The Caravan, a magnificent picture, is also a magnificent allegory and a magnificent hymn. The poem following sums up in twenty-six lines a whole world of terror and of tempest hurtling and wailing round the wreck of a boat by night. It is followed by a superb appeal against the infliction of death on rascals whose reptile blood would dishonour and defile the scaffold: and this again by an admonition to their chief not to put his trust in the chance of a high place of infamy among the more genuinely imperial hellhounds of historic record. . . . Then, in the later editions of the book, came the great and terrible poem on the life and death of the miscreant marshal who gave the watchword of massacre in the streets of Paris, and died by the visitation of disease before the walls of Sebastopol. There is hardly a more splendid passage of its kind in all the *Légende des Siècles* than the description of the departure of the fleet in order of battle from Constantinople for the Crimea; nor a loftier passage of more pathetic austerity in all this book of *Châtiments* than the final address of the poet to the miserable soul, disembodied at length after long and loathsome suffering, of the murderer and traitor who had earned no soldier's death.

And then come those majestic 'last words' which will ring for ever in the ears of men till manhood as well as poetry has ceased to have honour among mankind. And then comes a poem so great that I hardly dare venture to attempt a word in its praise. We cannot choose but think, as we read or repeat it, that 'such music was never made' since the morning stars sang together, and all the sons of God shouted for joy. This epilogue of a book so bitterly and inflexibly tragic begins as with a peal of golden bells, or an outbreak of all April in one choir of sunbright song; proceeds in a graver note of deep and trustful exultation and yearning towards the future; subsides again into something of a more subdued key, while the poet pleads for his faith in a God of righteousness with the righteous who are ready to despair; and rises from that tone of awe-stricken and earnest pleading to such a height and rapture of inspiration as no Hebrew psalmist or prophet ever soared beyond in his divinest passion of aspiring trust and worship. It is simply impossible that a human tongue should utter, a human hand should write, anything of more supreme and transcendent beauty than the last ten stanzas of the fourth division of this poem. The passionate and fervent accumulation of sublimities, of marvellous images and of infinite appeal, leaves the sense too dazzled, the soul too entranced and exalted, to appreciate at first or in full the miraculous beauty of the language, the superhuman sweetness of the song. (pp. 53-6)

[The *Contemplations* is] the book of which he said that if the title did not sound somewhat pretentious it might be called 'the memoirs of a soul.' No book had ever in it more infinite and exquisite variety; no concert ever diversified and united such inexhaustible melodies with such unsurpassable harmonies. The note of fatherhood was never touched more tenderly than in the opening verses of gentle counsel, whose cadence is fresher and softer than the lapse of rippling water or the sense of falling dew: the picture of the poet's two little daughters in the twilight garden might defy all painters to translate it: the spirit, force, and fun of the controversial poems, overflowing at once with good humour, with serious thought, and with kindly indignation, give life and charm to the obsolete questions of wrangling schools and pedants; and the last of them, on the divine and creative power of speech, is at once profound and sublime enough to grapple easily and thoroughly with so high and deep a subject. The songs of childish loves and boyish fancies are unequalled by any other poet's known to me for their union of purity and gentleness with a touch of dawning ardour and a hint of shy delight: *Lise, La Coccinelle, Vieille chanson du jeune temps,* are such sweet miracles of simple perfection as we hardly find except in the old songs of unknown great poets who died and left no name. (p. 58)

If nothing were left of Hugo but the sixth book of the *Contemplations,* it would yet be indisputable among those who know anything of poetry that he was among the foremost in the front rank of the greatest poets of all time. Here, did space allow, it would be necessary for criticism with any pretence to adequacy to say something of every poem in turn, to pause for observation of some beauty beyond reach of others at every successive page. In the first poem a sublime humility finds such expression as should make manifest to the dullest eye not clouded by malevolence and insolent conceit that when this greatest of modern poets asserts in his own person the high prerogative and assumes for his own spirit the high office of humanity, to confront the darkest problem and to challenge the utmost force of intangible and invisible injustice as of visible and tangible iniquity, of all imaginable as of all actual evil, of superhuman indifference as well as of human wrongdoing, it is no merely personal claim that he puts forward, no vainly egotistic arrogance that he displays; but the right of a reasonable conscience and the duty of a righteous faith, common to all

men alike in whom intelligence of right and wrong, perception of duty or conception of conscience, can be said to exist at all. If there be any truth in the notion of any difference between evil and good more serious than the conventional and convenient fabrications of doctrine and assumption, then assuredly the meanest of his creatures in whom the perception of this difference was not utterly extinct would have a right to denounce an omnipotent evil-doer as justly amenable to the sentence inflicted by the thunders of his own unrighteous judgment. How profound and intense was the disbelief of Victor Hugo in the rule or in the existence of any such superhuman malefactor could not be better shown than by the almost polemical passion of his prophetic testimony to that need for faith in a central conscience and a central will on which he has insisted again and again as a crowning and indispensable requisite for moral and spiritual life. From the sublime daring, the self-confidence born of self-devotion, which finds lyrical utterance in the majestic verses headed *Ibo,* through the humble and haughty earnestness of remonstrance and appeal—'humble to God, haughty to man'—which pervades the next three poems, the meditative and studious imagination of the poet passes into the fuller light and larger air of thought which imbues and informs with immortal life every line of the great religious poem called *Pleurs dans la nuit.* In this he touches the highest point of poetic meditation, as in the epilogue to the *Châtiments,* written four months earlier, he had touched the highest point of poetic rapture, possible to the most ardent of believers in his faith and the most unapproachable master of his art. Where all is so lofty in its coherence of construction, so perfect in its harmony of composition, it seems presumptuous to indicate any special miracle of inspired workmanship: yet, as Hugo in his various notes on mediaeval architecture was wont to select for exceptional attention and peculiar eloquence of praise this or that part or point of some superb and harmonious building, so am I tempted to dwell for a moment on the sublime imagination, the pathetic passion, of the verses which render into music the idea of a terrene and material purgatory, with its dungeons of flint and cells of clay wherein the spirit imprisoned and imbedded may envy the life and covet the suffering of the meanest animal that toils on earth; and to set beside this wonderful passage that other which even in a poem so thoroughly imbued with hope and faith finds place and voice for expression of the old mysterious and fantastic horror of the grave, more perfect than ever any mediaeval painter or sculptor could achieve. (pp. 66-8)

Last comes the magnificent and rapturous hymn of universal redemption from suffering as from sin, the prophetic vision of evil absorbed by good, and the very worst of spirits transfigured into the likeness of the very best, in which the daring and indomitable faith of the seer finds dauntless and supreme expression in choral harmonies of unlimited and illimitable hope. The epilogue which dedicates the book to the daughter whose grave was now forbidden ground to her father—so long wont to keep there the autumnal anniversary of his mourning—is the very crown and flower of the immortal work which it inscribes, if we may say so, rather to the presence than to the memory of the dead. (p. 72)

As the key-note of *Notre-Dame de Paris* was doom—the human doom of suffering to be nobly or ignobly endured—so the key-note of its author's next romance [*Les Misérables*] was redemption by acceptance of suffering and discharge of duty in absolute and entire obedience to the utmost exaction of conscience when it calls for atonement, of love when it calls for sacrifice of all that makes life more endurable than death. (p. 73)

Two years after *Les Misérables* appeared the magnificent book of meditations on the mission of art in the world, on the duty of human thought towards humanity, inscribed by Victor Hugo with the name of William Shakespeare. To allow that it throws more light on the greatest genius of our own century than on the greatest genius of the age of Shakespeare is not to admit that it is not rich in valuable and noble contemplations or suggestions on the immediate subject of Shakespeare's work; witness the admirably thoughtful and earnest remarks on Macbeth, the admirably passionate and pathetic reflections on Lear. The splendid eloquence and the heroic enthusiasm of Victor Hugo never found more noble and sustained expression than in this volume—the spontaneous and inevitable expansion of a projected preface to his son's incomparable translation of Shakespeare. . . . The miraculous dexterity of touch [in *Chansons des Rues et des Bois*], the dazzling mastery of metre, the infinite fertility in variations on the same air of frolic and thoughtful fancy, would not apparently allow the judges of the moment to perceive or to appreciate the higher and deeper qualities displayed in this volume of lyric idyls. The prologue is a superb example of the power peculiar to its author above all other poets; the power of seizing on some old symbol or image which may have been in poetic use ever since verse dawned upon the brain of man, and informing it again as with life, and transforming it anew as by fire. (pp. 73-4)

[The] *Souvenir des vieilles guerres* is one of Hugo's most pathetic and characteristic studies of homely and heroic life. The dialogue which follows, between the irony of scepticism and the enthusiasm of reason, on the progressive ascension of mankind, is at once sublime and subdued in the fervent tranquillity of its final tone: and the next poem, on the so-called 'great age' and its dwarf of a Caesar with the sun for a periwig, has in it a whole volume of history and of satire condensed into nine stanzas of four lines of five syllables apiece. (p. 76)

[None of his five great romances] is to me personally a treasure of greater price than *Les Travailleurs de la Mer*. The splendid energy of the book makes the superhuman energy of the hero seem not only possible but natural, and his triumph over all physical impossibilities not only natural but inevitable. . . . Victor Hugo's acquaintance with navigation or other sciences may or may not have been as imperfect as Shakespeare's acquaintance with geography and natural history; the knowledge of such a man's ignorance or inaccuracy in detail is in either case of exactly equal importance: and the importance of such knowledge is for all men of sense and candour exactly equivalent to zero. (p. 78)

In the first division [of *Les Quatre Vents de l'Esprit*], the book of satire, every page bears witness that the hand which wrote the *Châtiments* had neither lost its strength nor forgotten its cunning; it is full of keen sense, of wise wrath, of brilliant reason and of merciful equity. The double drama which follows is one of the deepest and sweetest and richest in various effect among the masterpieces of its author. In *Margarita* we breathe again the same fresh air of heroic mountain-ranges and woodlands inviolable, of winds and flowers and all fair things and thoughts, which blows through all the brighter and more gracious interludes of the *Légende des Siècles:* the figures of Gallus, the libertine by philosophy, and Gunich, the philosopher of profligacy,—the former a true man and true lover at heart, the latter a cynic and a courtier to the core—are as fresh in their novelty as the figures of noble old age and noble young

love are fresh in their renewal and reimpression of types familiar to all hearts since the sunrise of *Hernani*. The tragedy which follows this little romantic comedy is but the more penetrative and piercing in its pathos and its terror for its bitter and burning vein of realism and of humour. The lyric book is a casket of jewels rich enough to outweigh the whole wealth of many a poet. (pp. 88-9)

[*Torquemada* is] one of the greatest masterpieces of the master poet of our century. The construction of this tragedy is absolutely original and unique: free and full of change as the wildest and loosest and roughest of dramatic structures ever flung together, and left to crumble or cohere at the pleasure of accident or of luck, by the rudest of primaeval playwrights: but perfect in harmonious unity of spirit, in symmetry or symphony of part with part, as the most finished and flawless creation of Sophocles or of Phidias. . . . The young lovers are two of the loveliest figures, Torquemada is one of the sublimest, in all the illimitable world of dramatic imagination. The intensity of interest, anxiety, and terror, which grows by such rapid and subtle stages of development up to the thunderstroke of royal decision at the close of the first act, is exchanged in the second for an even deeper and higher kind of emotion. The confrontation of the hermit with the inquisitor, magnificent enough already in its singleness of effect, is at once transfigured and completed by the apparition of the tremendous figure whose very name is tragedy, whose very shadow sufficed for the central and the crowning terror which darkened the stage of *Lucrèce Borgia*. (pp. 97-8)

[Among] all Hugo's romantic and tragic poems of mediaeval history or legend the two greatest are in my mind *Eviradnus* and *Ratbert*. I cannot think it would be rash to assert that the loveliest love-song in the world, the purest and keenest rapture of lyric fancy, the sweetest and clearest note of dancing or dreaming music, is that which rings for ever in the ear. . . . (p. 115)

[But if *Ratbert*] be the highest poem of all for passion and pathos and fire of terrible emotion, the highest in sheer sublimity of imagination is to my mind *Zim-Zizimi*. Again and again, in reading it for the first time, one thinks that surely now the utmost height is reached, the utmost faculty revealed, that can be possible for a spirit clothed only with human powers, armed only with human speech. (p. 117)

It is noticeable that the master of modern poets should have in the tone and colour of his genius more even of the Hebrew than the Greek. In his love of light and freedom, reason and justice, he is not of Jerusalem, but of Athens; but in the bent of his imagination, in the form and colour of his dreams, in the scope and sweep of his wide-winged spiritual flight, he is nearer akin to the great insurgent prophets of deliverance and restoration than to any poet of Athens except only their kinsman Æschylus. (pp. 120-21)

Among the many good things which seem, for the lovers of poetry, to have come out of one and so great an evil as the long exile of Hugo from his country, there is none better or greater than the spiritual inhalation of breeze and brine into the very heart of his genius, the miraculous impregnation of his solitary Muse by the sea-wind. This influence could not naturally but combine with the lifelong influence of all noble sympathies to attract his admiration and his pity towards the poor folk of the shore, and to produce from that sense of compassion for obscurer sorrows and brotherhood with humbler heroism than his own such work as the poem which describes the charity of a fisherman's wife towards the children of her dead neighbour. It has all the beautiful precision and accurate propriety of detail which distinguish the finest idyls of Theocritus or Tennyson, with a fervour of pathetic and imaginative emotion which Theocritus never attained, and which Tennyson has attained but once. All the horror of death, all the trouble and mystery of darkness, seem as we read to pass into our fancy with the breath of pervading night, and to vanish with the husband's entrance at sunrise before the smile with which the wife draws back the curtains of the cradle. (pp. 127-28)

It is more than fifty years since *Les Orientales* rose radiant upon the world of letters, and the hand which gave them to mankind has lost so little of its cunning that we are wellnigh tempted to doubt whether then, for all its skill and sureness of touch, it had quite the same strength and might of magnificent craftsmanship as now. There was fire as well as music on the lips of the young man, but the ardour of the old man's song seems even deeper and keener than the passion of his past. The fervent and majestic verses . . . strike at starting the note of measureless pity and immeasurable indignation which rings throughout the main part of the fifth and last volume almost louder and fuller, if possible, than it was wont. All Victor Hugo, we may say, is in this book; it is as one of those ardent evening skies in which sunrise and sunset seem one in the flush of overarching colour which glows back from the west to the east with reverberating bloom and fervour of rose-blossom and fire. There is life enough in it, enough of the breath and spirit and life-blood of living thought, to vivify a whole generation of punier souls and feebler hearts with the heat of his fourscore years. It may be doubted whether there ever lived a poet and leader of men to whom these glorious verses would be so closely applicable as to their writer. (p. 132)

It is held unseemly to speak of the living as we speak of the dead; when Victor Hugo has joined the company of his equals, but apparently not till then, it will seem strange to regard the giver of all the gifts we have received from him with less than love that deepens into worship, than worship that brightens into love. (p. 147)

> *Algernon Charles Swinburne, in his* A Study of Victor Hugo, *Chatto & Windus, 1886 (and reprinted by Kennikat Press, 1970), 148 p.*

ALGERNON CHARLES SWINBURNE (essay date 1887)

[In *Choses Vues,*] the posthumous volume which gives us the register of [Hugo's] opinions and experiences, personal and political, during many years of life, there are many notes and memoranda of high and serious interest. There is nothing unimportant to the student of a great character and a transcendent genius even in the slightest entries; even in the most questionable inferences from history or tradition, in the most untenable inductions or deductions from experience or from theory. His vivid and varied power of intelligence is not more generally manifest than the single-hearted fervour of his confidence, the passionate and childlike spontaneity of his charitable or indignant sympathies. This book alone would suffice to prove that the greatest writer born in the nineteenth century had wit enough for a cynic combined with enthusiasm enough for an apostle. At its very opening the summary sketch of Talleyrand is a model at once of historic and humorous analysis. . . . A paltry sputter of Parisian discontent in 1839 gave occasion for one among many proofs of Victor Hugo's quiet intrepidity and

observant presence of mind, and for one among a thousand instances of the graphic and incisive power of realism which the most passionate, imaginative, and sublime of modern poets could display at will in his description of actual and often of homely or prosaic incidents. (pp. 342-43)

The record of the incident which suggested one of the most famous chapters in [*Les Misérables*] is as vivid and pathetic as it is characteristic and illustrative of that genius of beneficence which was so great a component part of the moral and intellectual faculty of Victor Hugo. Again we may be reminded of a chapter in the same volume of his second great masterpiece in prose fiction, when we read the singularly lucid record of a dream bearing date four months after the accidental death of the Duke of Orleans. This record has all the tragic truthfulness of incoherence, all the vivid confusion of significant with fantastic details, which we recognise in the immortal and incomparable vision of Jean Valjean on the eve of his first great act of self immolation. And the hand which could thus carve the outlines of the dark and chisel the features of a shadow could also transcribe or portray with the realism of a professional reporter the talk of kings and ministers, the interior of palaces and prisons, the record of political and of criminal trials, anecdotes, studies, sketches, epigrams, reflections, revolutions, deliberations, intercessions, observations, and appeals. Two characters were always more especially his, whatever other part he might be called upon by circumstances to combine with them: the student's and the mediator's. All his logic, all his reason, all his conscience, had been resolved by nature into a single quality or instinct, the principle or the impulse of universal and immitigable charity. All his argument on matters of social controversy is based on the radical and imprescriptible assumption that no counter consideration can be valid, that no other principle exists. All moral evil must in his judgment be regarded as disease, to be healed or allayed by a process of criminal sanitation; unless indeed it be merely the consequence of social inequalities, the upshot of legal iniquities, the result of systematic dereliction on the part of the world at large. The blackest traitor and seller of blood, the most hideous assassin or infanticide, holds his life by a right as inviolable as that of the most innocent child or the most virtuous man alive. (p. 344)

That Victor Hugo, when he pleased, could be as great and as mere a naturalist, in the pure and genuine sense of the term, as the most absolute devotee of photographic realism, a single instance in this single book would amply suffice to show. The study "after nature" of a girl then living with a painter would have kindled the admiration of Balzac and the envy of a meaner artist. There are touches in it that remind us of Esther Gobseck, and others that remind us of Doll Tearsheet. The reality of the animal under either phase, cynical or sentimental in self-devotion or self-exposure, must be recognisable by the veriest novice in that field of scientific research. . . .

Few sections of [*Choses Vues*] are more remarkable than that which narrates the detection and trial of a spy before a tribunal of the exiles whose bread he had eaten and whose trust he had betrayed. And in this narrative there is nothing more noteworthy than the combination of practical sense and theoretical dogmatism in the counsels of Victor Hugo himself. Not to spare the rascal's life would have been sheer madness; there could have been no rational reply to the argument from expediency. But to the argument from principle, that there must be no such thing as a sentence of capital punishment, no more against a spy than against a parricide, it does seem singular that no voice should have replied, No more? Most certainly not; if anything, less. But what man on earth could dream of asking for more?

There are many lessons, direct and indirect, to be derived from the study of this book; but the crowning moral of it all is given at the close, as the final result and summary of all its author's manifold experiences. That there is but one thing under heaven to which a man should bow—genius; and but one thing to which a man should kneel—goodness. And while reverence endures for either, the veneration of all time will cherish the memory of Victor Hugo. (p. 346)

> *Algernon Charles Swinburne, "Victor Hugo: 'Choses Vues',' in* The Fortnightly Review *(reprinted by permission of Contemporary Review Company Limited), Vol. XLII, September, 1887, pp. 342-46.*

EDWARD DOWDEN   (essay date 1897)

To say that Hugo was the greatest lyric poet of France is to say too little; the claim that he was the greatest lyric poet of all literature might be urged. The power and magnitude of his song result from the fact that in it what is personal and what is impersonal are fused in one; his soul echoed orchestrally the orchestrations of nature and of humanity. . . . And thus if his poetry is not great by virtue of his own ideas, it becomes great as a reverberation of the sensations, the passions, and the thoughts of the world. He did not soar tranquilly aloft and alone; he was always a combatant in the world and wave of men, or borne joyously upon the flood. (pp. 377-78)

[In *Les Feuilles d'Automne*] Hugo is a master of his instrument, and does not need to display his miracles of skill; he is freer from faults than in the poetry of later years, but not therefore more to be admired. His noblest triumphs were almost inevitably accompanied by the excesses of his audacity. Here the lyrism is that of memory and of the heart—intimate, tender, grave, with a feeling for the hearth and home, a sensibility to the tranquillising influences of nature, a charity for humankind, a faith in God, a hope of immortality. (p. 379)

The best pages in [his last works] are perhaps equal to the best in any of their author's writings; the pages which force antithesis, pile up synonyms, develop commonplaces in endless variations, the pages which are hieratic, prophetic, apocalyptic, put a strain upon the loyalty of our admiration. The last legend of Hugo's imagination was the Hugo legend: if theism was his faith, autotheism was his superstition. Yet it is easy to restore our loyalty, and to rediscover the greatest lyric poet, the greatest master of poetic counterpoint that France has known. (pp. 382-83)

> *Edward Dowden, "Poetry of the Romantic School," in his* A History of French Literature *(copyright, 1897, by D. Appleton and Company) D. Appleton, 1897 (and reprinted by D. Appleton, 1900), pp. 363-95.**

EDMUND GOSSE   (essay date 1902)

To the nineteenth century in France [Victor Hugo] was what Voltaire had been to the eighteenth. That is to say, an absolutely momentous power, extending so far in so many directions as to pass outside the bounds of convenient definition. To ask whether Hugo had any influence on letters in his own country is like asking whether, if the Atlantic Ocean were let into the Great Sahara, it would have any influence there. In the first place, he was original to a quite extraordinary degree. It is

difficult to point to any modern writer, at least any writer of the last two centuries, who owes so little to preceding forms of expression as Hugo does. He cultivated a sort of graceful fealty of Vergil, which was rather like the tribute of a dish of fruit which some great chieftain may think it courteous to send once a year to a nominal head of his clan; but as a matter of fact, Victor Hugo owed little or nothing to Vergil. In his own country he had been preceded in his revolution against the prevailing languor of poetry by Chateaubriand, by Lamartine, by Vigny, but when the moment came and the age was ripe; it was the trumpet-note of Hugo's celebrated formula, and not the voices of his elders, that broke down the walls of the classical Jericho. (p. 629)

There are many reasons, which even an Anglo-Saxon can appreciate, for the amazing vogue of Hugo. He has had thousands of imitators, but not one of them has contrived to give anything of the Hugonian impression of life in its fulness. Hugo sees everything enormous and distended, exuberant and colossal, but he preserves alongside of this dangerous tendency a sense of harmony, almost of logic, which prevents it from being too obviously preposterous. We are prepared to laugh, but something makes us grow serious as we listen; the smile dies away and we kindle with admiration, terror and joy. It is the evidence of splendid vitality which carries us on, which drags us unwillingly in the train of Victor Hugo, which induces us to throw up our hands and resign ourselves to this tremendous and astounding tide of energy. If he seemed to force the note, or, as people say, "worked himself up," we could easily turn from him with a smile, with a shrug. But that is impossible. The spontaneity of the man is irresistible. The fountain of his song leaps and gushes and flows forth in all directions; we can but sail upon it. It takes us out of sight of shore, it tosses us on that luminous and buoyant ocean which is the personal genius of Victor Hugo. (pp. 629-30)

Victor Hugo, if he had not many original reflections, made up for them in the prodigality and fulness of his sensations, and he possessed the gift of translating these into language of the most transcendent eloquence. But our race is easily suspicious of oratorical effects, and the tumultuous rhapsodies which enchanted the French were apt to leave us cold and wary. When a foreign poet of excessive genius shouts like a tempest and moans like an organ, when his cadences attempt to compete with oceans and battlefields and whirlwinds, the Anglo-Saxon world is unsympathetic and adopts the attitude of a doubting Thomas. If Victor Hugo had been a more pensive and a more ingenious writer, he might have exercised a considerable influence in English literature. But it would have been at the cost of much wider influence in his own.

While we deny that Victor Hugo was an intellectual or reflecting poet, in the sense that Browning was, we must not exaggerate his neglect of mental apparatus. . . . His writings are full of evidences of genuine and assiduous literary labor; he read immensely, and he digested what he read. The results of all this literature did not appear, of course, until they had passed into the poet's personal nature and become part of himself. In some remarkable lines which he wrote on his seventy-eighth birthday, Victor Hugo remarked that "every man who writes writes a book, and that book is himself." But that book, even when a Hugo writes it, is the product of a thousand previous thoughts and expressions, tinged through and through with the color of the mind which has assimilated them.

One approaches the study of Victor Hugo with a kind of timidity—so vast is he, so multiform; like the century which he illustrated, so crowded. His voice seems to carry the very accent of the sea, that mysterious sound that can never be interpreted. But in stringing together these few reflections on the occasion of his centenary, I have tried at least to bear in mind the claim which he put forward for himself: that, in the tumult of opinion, in the rage of party, in the midst of all the passion and hatred and fury through which he labored, his voice was always that of a man worthy of esteem. Heroic, dignified, with a serene gesture that embraced the world, Victor Hugo stands up in the midst of the nineteenth century as one of its largest and noblest figures. (p. 634)

> Edmund Gosse, "The Influence of Victor Hugo," in The Cosmopolitan, *Vol. 32, No. 6, April, 1902, pp. 627-34.*

G. K. CHESTERTON   (essay date 1902)

[Victor Hugo] represented two great revolutions, the first artistic and the second political. The artistic revolution was that connected with the word romanticism: the political revolution was that connected with the word democracy. And the great difficulty involved in properly appreciating him lies in this, that both romanticism and democracy have conquered and therefore become commonplace. They have been so triumphant as to become invisible: just as existence itself is triumphant and invisible. (p. 37)

It is the custom among certain literary men of this era to sneer at the novels of Hugo, chiefly on the ground that they are sensational; as if all art were not sensationalism and the whole artistic temperament best definable as the temperament which is sensational or receptive of sensations. But the novels of Victor Hugo have one very actual and direct claim upon the attention of everybody. They are, in one sense, the most interesting of all novels. The reason is that Hugo is typically a mystic, a man who finds a meaning in everything. We all know what are the uninteresting, the inevitably uninteresting parts of fiction; we all know what parts of a novel to skip. We skip the long description of the country where the hero was born, with its flat sandy wastes, made ragged with fir trees and tumbling towards the West into low discoloured hills. (pp. 38-9)

Now the greatest and boldest tribute that can be paid to Hugo, the greatest and boldest, perhaps, that can be paid to any novelist, may be stated in the form that it is not safe to skip these passages in a novel by Victor Hugo. In other novelists all these details are dead; in Hugo they are all alive. . . . [There] is not a dull line in Hugo. (p. 39)

The description of the room of the Duchess in *L'Homme Qui Rit* is really a riot of a kind of bestial mysticism and of evil sanctities, such as might have filled some forgotten Phallic temple. This is the first and most admirable thing about Hugo as a novelist—that he is always interesting, and interesting for the best and most impressive reason, that in everything, however small, he is interested. Those parts of a novel, scenery, minutiae, explanations, which in most novelists are the most tedious, in him are almost the most fascinating. . . . For to him there is neither a large thing nor a small one; he has abolished the meanest and most absurd of all human words, the word "insignificant": he knows that it is impossible for anything to signify nothing.

Thus in what is, as a work of art, perhaps his most successful novel, *Notre Dame de Paris,* the sumptuous and fantastic details

of Gothic architecture are practically almost as alive as the people that pass underneath them. . . . In *Les Misérables,* as in *Notre Dame,* Paris is almost the chief character of the novel. In *L'Homme Qui Rit* the best description is that of two very weird and fierce and inscrutable things—the sea, and the English aristocracy according to Victor Hugo. In *Les Travailleurs de la Mer* he spends a vast deal of trouble on the reality of the cuttle-fish, and very little on the possibility or probability of the gentleman who fights with him. Hugo is not a successful novelist according to the conception that a novelist must understand human nature. He does not even pretend to understand human nature; he is a poet, and boasts of understanding nothing; he glories in an astounded and uplifted ignorance. Human nature to Hugo was a spontaneous and unbegotten and thrilling thing, a thing like the lightning and the burst of song among the birds. He did not profess to have vivisected man in the modern manner. Man was to him an awful thing, a thing to fly from, as he must have been to the animals in Eden.

The manifest theatricality and vanity of Victor Hugo have undoubtedly interfered with his appreciation by English readers, for we English people have thoroughly embedded in our minds the idea that vanity is a morbid and fantastic thing, developed by a high degree of hyper-civilization. We think this although every one of us has constantly noticed vanity in a child of three. We think this although every one of us knows that savages are vainer than civilized men, and that even the bonnets of Bond Street are not more elaborately feathered than the headdresses of the Cannibal Islands. The truth is that Hugo represents all the ultimate and fundamental things—love, fury, pity, worship, hatred, and consequently, among other things, vanity. (pp. 39-41)

Anyone who has ever watched a child for the first five years of its life will know that when the human soul first awakens to the immensities of mere existence, the first thing it does is to begin to act a part. In that first movement of the child we see the great part of the literary and political history of Victor Hugo. He had in all things an innocent arrogance, he had, if a paradoxical but accurate phrase may be employed, an utterly unconscious self-consciousness. And this quality fitted him supremely to be the expression of France in the nineteenth century; for France, having renewed her youth in that century, was really young. She had not only the fire and anger and hope of youth, she had also that more obvious and more painful characteristic of youth, its cleverness. *Quatre-Vingt-Treize,* the great novel of the Revolution, was not the most successful, perhaps; it was possibly the most Hugo-esque of the works of Hugo; for Hugo was supremely at one with the spirit of the Revolution, and his novel, like the Revolution itself, was one mass of epigrams. (p. 42)

The second of the misunderstandings which interfere with the general appreciation of Victor Hugo is the misunderstanding of his idea of Republicanism or democracy. He appears at the first glance, from our point of view, a furious poet and an ineffectual politician, who was exiled from his country by the decision of a Bonapartist majority of his countrymen. He never ceased from calling down curses on the majority which was the basis of his own political creed, he never ceased from clamouring and praying for the rule of the very people whose decision had set him upon a lonely rock in the Channel. (pp. 43-4)

Hugo stood for the fact that democracy isolated the citizen fully as much as the ancient religions isolated the soul. He resisted the rule of the Third Napoleon because he saw that it had the supreme and final mark of the rule of the tyrant, the fact that it relied on the masses. As if a million of the images of God could by any possibility become a mass. He made his appeal to the individual, as every poet must do, and asked the solitary citizen to act as if he were really not only the only human being on the earth, but the only sentient being in the universe. He realised the obvious and simple truth, so often neglected, that if the individual is nothing, then the race is nothing—for the plain mathematical reason that a hundred times nought is nought. Therefore his sublimest figure, his type of humanity, was not either a king or a republican, but a man on a desert island. (p. 44)

> G. K. Chesterton, "Victor Hugo" (originally published in Pall Mall Magazine, 1902), in his A Handful of Authors: Essays on Books & Writers, edited by Dorothy Collins (reprinted by permission of the Estate of G. K. Chesterton), Sheed and Ward, Inc., 1953, pp. 36-44.

CLAYTON M. HAMILTON (essay date 1903)

Victor Hugo was born one of the chief lyrists of all time; but a great lyric poet may or may not succeed when he bends his energies to composition for the theater. Goethe tried it, and failed; Schiller attempted it, and succeeded. But Hugo was more than a mere poet. He was born also with the instincts of a novelist, with an extraordinary mastery of thrilling incident, a keen eye for picturesque effect, a grasp on the more obtrusive aspects of human character, and an instinctive feeling for the antithesis between the beautiful and the ugly, the grotesque and the sublime. There was something intensely theatrical in Victor Hugo's personality, and a vein of staginess recurs incessantly throughout his work. It would seem, therefore, that when this great artist, possessing at once a gift for the lyrical, the novelistic, and the theatrical, turned his attention seriously and conscientiously to dramatic composition he would inevitably produce plays worthy to be ranked near to those of Shakespeare and of Molière. But this Victor Hugo failed to accomplish.

The secret of this failure appears to be that in Victor Hugo the dramatist the talents of the lyric poet are but imperfectly united with those of the theatric novelist. His plays are either too lyrical or too mechanical, too theatric or too poetic. In *Les Burgraves* the dramatist is lost in the poet, and in *Marie Tudor* the dignified poet of the theater is shrouded in the garb of the hack playwright. Either Hugo's claptrap cankers his poetry, or his poetry runs away with his theatrical cleverness. In none of his pieces are these two talents wedded with perfect harmony. This, it seems to me, is the chief reason why we cannot consider him as a worthy compeer of Sophocles and Molière, Shakespeare and Ibsen. (pp. 169-70)

From the very beginning, Hugo was an ardent romanticist. He was a born leader, and it was but natural that the young revolutionary poets of the day should rally around him. The walls of classicism were crumbling to decay when Hugo, flushed with the fervor of youthful energy, sounded the summons to assault and flaunted the banner of literary freedom. (p. 170)

The *Preface to Cromwell* is one of the ablest critical manifestoes ever published; and after reading it, we naturally look forward to a work of unusual excellence in the drama itself. In this, however, we are disappointed. Hugo planned the play for Talma, who died before it was finished; and, despairing of having his piece adequately acted, the author completed it in a desultory

manner, allowing his poetry to lead him astray into labyrinthine bypaths, almost entirely ruining the theatrical effectiveness of the drama. The piece, as we have it, is at least three times too long; but if we laboriously dissect it, we can find in it elements which, if carefully sifted, might be made into an acting play. The figure of the humorous Rochester is the best-drawn character in the piece. . . . Throughout the almost interminable drama are scattered many excellent scenes. The diverse pictures of the Cavalier and the Puritan conspirators in the first act are full of spirit, although the poet's treatment of the Puritans degenerates into caricature. . . . Many of the scenes of the play are pictorially effective; much of the humor is spontaneous, and several passages ring with a note of lyric eloquence.

In spite of these excellences, however, *Cromwell* is a gigantic failure. Its main intrigue is buried under an avalanche of extraneous stuff; and, in spite of its extraordinary length, the play fails to give the impression of breadth of scope. (pp. 171-72)

Considered as a reflection of history, *Cromwell* is but a laughable caricature. . . . Ambitious, hypocritical, and cruel, bloody, unscrupulous, and vain, Hugo's Cromwell struts and frets his many hours upon the stage armed in the theatric panoply of a colossal villain; but he bears no more resemblance to the Cromwell of history than Hamlet to Hercules. (p. 172)

[*Hernani*] is probably more widely known than any other of Victor Hugo's dramatic compositions; but yet after all, if examined closely, it appears to be hardly more than what Goethe called it—"an absurd production." Picturesqueness and moving force it has in abundance; and in spite of the fact that the life which it depicts is utterly unreal, it is imbued throughout with an interesting theatricism. The repartee of the first act is clever; and the exposition is terse, direct, and rapid. The love scenes are rendered with a great deal of lyric fervor, and Hugo's great poetic power makes their passionate ardor very moving. The vein of sardonic humor which runs through Don Carlos during the first three acts is also interesting.

But the play has faults of construction and of characterization heavy enough to outweigh all of these excellences. . . . The melodramatic effectiveness of the picture scene—which, in many ways, is the best situation in the play—is simply worked to death. It is claptrap pure and simple, and even the harmony of Hugo's verse cannot drown the creaking of its mechanism. (p. 173)

Hernani is a cheap melodrama disguised in a garb of gorgeous verse. The plot is always arbitrary, and often ridiculous; and the characters, except perhaps Don Carlos, are tediously wooden. The catastrophe of this play never seems inevitable, and whatever pathos it has arises from the beautiful color of its verse rather than from the expression of human emotions by living characters. . . .

As a drama, *Hernani* is much inferior to its contemporary, *Marion Delorme*. I am inclined to think that the latter is the greatest of all Hugo's plays; at any rate, it shows a remarkable superiority to its predecessors on the boards. Unlike *Cromwell*, it possesses great dramatic unity; and unlike *Hernani*, its plot is no longer evidently arbitrary. Its characters, moreover, are finely drawn. (p. 174)

Marion Delorme has many merits besides its character-drawing. A jovial humor hovers about the person of Saverny and pervades the whole drama, while not infrequently the tragic passages of the play rise to heights of poetic eloquence. . . .

This play unites perhaps better than any other of Hugo's the elements of humor and tragic passion, and admirably embodies the principles expressed in the *Preface to Cromwell*. (p. 175)

[Considered as a work of art, *Le Roi s'Amuse*] is hardly less successful than *Marion Delorme*. The light and easy wit which scintillated throughout the earlier piece still flits through the somber mazes of the latter. To this is united a vast fund of tragic pathos; and there can be no doubt that the lyric fluency of Hugo's dramatic verse finds its climax in this play. (p. 176)

This play, together with *Marion Delorme,* represents the climax of Hugo's dramatic power. The chief characters are drawn with a careful attention to detail, the incidents are plotted with a skill which fixes the reader's interest throughout, and the progress of the action is apparently inevitable. The woe of Triboulet seems all the more poignant when we reflect that he has wrought his own misery. The bitter irony of the jester's existence and his deep-seated misanthropy are powerfully reconciled with that worshipful affection for his daughter through which he is to be stricken to the heart. Triboulet resembles a work of Gothic art, in which the grotesque is blended with the sublime. *Le Roi s'Amuse* is a perfectly moral play, and Hugo's defense of it in his preface is well founded. . . .

From poetic elevation, Hugo descends, in his prose plays, to mechanical theatricism. Divested of the glamour of his engaging verse, his dramatic muse appears nothing but a gaunt, though well-articulated, skeleton. Hugo's prose pieces give us plots without characters, and daggers and poison without life. Thrilling they often are, but they fail to touch the springs of aesthetic emotion. Considered even from the standpoint of construction, they are markedly inferior to the plays in verse. In his prose melodramas Hugo's expositions become bald and conventional, he overworks his dramatic effects, and his curtain-falls become painfully theatrical. (p. 177)

Lucrèce Borgia is a frank melodrama, divested of every glimpse of poetry. Many features of the piece, especially the dramatic irony of the passages between Lucrèce and Gennaro, are a little overworked. In the last act, however, Hugo demonstrates a tremendous mastery of pure *situation*, with aiding pictorial accessories. The characterization is poor throughout the play; and the piece fails to touch the heart, like *Marion Delorme* and *Le Roi s'Amuse*. In fact, it is the most *unhuman* of Hugo's dramas. (p. 178)

Marie Tudor, Hugo's next melodrama, hardly shows an advance over its immediate predecessor. The exposition is very arbitrary. There is more humor, however, in Joshua, the turnkey, than in the other characters of the prose dramas; and the second act is notable for the tempestuous passion of the queen. The last two acts are skillfully plotted; and the concluding scene represents at its highest Hugo's extraordinary command of suspense. . . .

Hugo prided himself upon the historical accuracy of his dramas; and in his notes to *Marie Tudor* he has cited a formidable array of historical archives which he consulted before writing his piece. But while in *Marie Tudor* he may have held rigorously to the facts of history, he has failed entirely to seize its truth. The atmosphere of the drama is totally foreign to the England of the Tudors, and the queen herself is a more distorted caricature than even the same author's Cromwell. As an historical drama, *Marie Tudor* is all but ridiculous; but yet, considered as melodrama pure and simple, it is not devoid of many excellent qualities. After it is once well under way, the action

rushes on with tempestuous energy, and grips the reader's attention with an inexorable clutch. (p. 179)

[I am inclined to prefer *Angelo, Tyran de Padoue,*] to the other prose plays of Hugo. Its exposition is very much better; its characters are more skillfully drawn; and while the element of humor is still lacking, it possesses moments of genuine pathos. The scenic machinery is well managed, and the element of suspense is often admirably employed. This melodrama has at once the most complicated and the most skillfully handled plot of all Hugo's plays. It is interesting throughout, and is a triumph of clever intrigue. It also contains more poetry than Hugo's other prose plays.

From the preface to *Angelo* we learn, what we should hardly otherwise have supposed, that Hugo attempted in this melodrama to give a philosophical study of social conditions. . . . *Angelo* is extremely interesting, but it is not profound. (p. 180)

Ruy Blas is one of the very best of Hugo's plays, although I cannot but consider it inferior to *Marion Delorme* and *Le Roi s'Amuse*. The exposition is rapid, the plot is energetically developed; the characters are carefully distinguished, and in the happy-go-lucky figure of Don César we have a pleasing return to Hugo's early humor. . . . The preface to *Ruy Blas* opens with Hugo's famous division of the theatrical audience into the crowd, who demand action; the women, who crave passion; and the thinkers, who exact the study of character. He then proceeds to define the fundamental law of the drama, deducing it from these diverse demands of the spectators. Passing on to the consideration of *Ruy Blas* in particular, and looking at it from the historical and the universal points of view, the author attempts to read into it several grand conceptions which the ordinary reader would never discover. (p. 181)

Considered from the standpoint of the theater, [*Les Burgraves*] is unquestionably the poorest of Hugo's plays; while, looked at merely as a poem, it is one of the most serenely beautiful of his works. It represents, as Hugo says in his preface, the struggle of the mediaeval Titans against the mediaeval Jupiter, of the Burgraves against the Emperor. The poet took Æschylus for his model, but hardly succeeded in catching the majestic austerity of the master.

The exposition of this dramatic poem is exceedingly obscure, and the greater part of the first act is incomprehensible at the first reading. It contains, however, a beautiful scene between the young lovers, Otbert and Régina, which glows with much of [the] lyric fervor that was met with in *Marion Delorme*. (p. 182)

Otbert and Régina are the only human figures in the play. Both the Emperor and the Burgraves are altogether too statuesque for true dramatic purposes. In his attempt to give them the heroic proportions and the somber austerity of marble monuments, the poet has failed to endow his chief characters with life. Guanhumara is a mere personification of fatality, and the Emperor, of providence. Hugo attempted too much in endeavoring to link the epic and the dramatic interest of this play, and did not succeed in his purpose. (pp. 182-83)

[The interest of Hugo's last play, *Torquemada,*] is twofold. It consists of a good play, buried beneath a good epic poem. Whatever genuine theatrical interest it possesses is centered in the love tragedy of Don Sanche and Doña Rosa; but these characters are completely forgotten during the second and third acts, while the drama is lost in the epic. At bottom *Torquemada* is a good play; but, like *Cromwell*, it could not be produced in the theater without many alterations. While, poetically, the piece is an organic whole, it does not possess dramatic unity. (p. 184)

The plays of Victor Hugo practically represent the work of a single decade of his life, for *Torquemada* [written when he was about eighty years old] merely echoes the dramatic triumphs of his youth. It is but natural, therefore, that they should possess an evident sameness in tone. A single motive seems to be at the root of all of his dramatic pieces, and this motive is one which we should naturally expect in the work of a poet essentially lyrical. . . . Ingenious in device, thrilling in situation, picturesque in setting, his plays glow with a gaudy complexity which dazzles the eye, arrests the attention, and rivets the interest. Hugo's dramas have all of the multifarious immensity of a Gothic cathedral; and his incessant use of antithesis, both in his construction and in his detail, lends a striking power to his work.

But yet, in spite of his excellences, Victor Hugo lacks the essential qualifications of a great dramatic poet. He has given us no lifelike picture of his own, or indeed of any other, times. . . . His plots invariably condition his characters, and the characters themselves are never true to nature. For the most part they embody but a single passion, and this reigning trait is commonly of an unusual nature. (pp. 184-85)

Hugo's poetic gift, as exhibited in his dramas, is a matter of words rather than of conceptions. In writing his scenes he uses his faculty as poet, but in conceiving them he employs his talent as melodramatic novelist. (p. 185)

But even though Victor Hugo may not be a supremely great dramatist, we cannot take leave of his plays without some passing tribute to the poet and the man. Although he has left us no single monument of dramatic art, we could ill afford to lose the vari-colored splendor of his plays and the lyric eloquence of his most beautiful scenes. And then we must not forget the priceless service which he rendered to the theater of his country in emancipating it from the shackles of emasculated classicism. (p. 186)

> *Clayton M. Hamilton, "The Plays of Victor Hugo,"* in The Sewanee Review *(reprinted by permission of the editor; 1903 by The University of the South), Vol. XI, No. 2, April, 1903, pp. 169-86.*

GEORGE MOORE   (essay date 1917)

Hugo is not perverse, nor even personal. Reading him was like being in church with a strident-voiced preacher shouting from out of a terribly sonorous pulpit. **"Les Orientales. . . ."** An East of painted cardboard, tin daggers, and a military band playing the Turkish patrol in the Palais Royal. . . . The verse is grand, noble, tremendous; I liked it, I admired it, but it did not—I repeat the phrase—awake a voice of conscience within me; and even the structure of the verse was too much in the style of public buildings to please me. Of **"Les Feuilles d'Au-tomne"** and **"Les Chants du Crépuscule"** I remember nothing. Ten lines, fifty lines of **"Les Légendes des Siècles,"** and I always think that it is the greatest poetry I have ever read, but after a few pages the book is laid down and forgotten. Having composed more verses than any man that ever lived, Hugo can only be taken in the smallest doses; if you repeat any passage to a friend across a *café* table, you are both appalled by the splendour of the imagery, by the thunder of the syllables. (pp. 59-60)

But I never read through a volume without feeling that Hugo's genius is more German than French and perhaps that is why the poem is better than the volume, the story better than the poem. . . . [**"La Fête Chez Thérèse"**] is an admirable picture of mediaeval life, but we never really enjoy it except when the newspapers quote it. Humanitarianism is especially German, and of all his treatment of God: arm in arm he romps Him round the universe—two immortalities, it is true, but of the two Hugo prefers his own. His delight in little children is perhaps still more unbearable, for while telling their innocence he watches them curiously, and as soon as the song is over, and the crowd disperses, he entices them down a by-way.

The first time I read of *une bouche d'ombre* I was astonished, nor did the second or third repetition produce a change in my mood of mind; but sooner or later it was impossible to avoid conviction, that of the two "the rosy fingers of the dawn," although some three thousand years older, is younger, truer, and more beautiful. Homer's similes can never grow old; *une bouche d'ombre* was old the first time it was said. It is the birthplace and the grave of Hugo's genius. (pp. 60-1)

Hugo—how impossible it is to speak of French literature without referring to him. Let these, however, be concluding words that he thought he could by saying everything, and, saying everything twenty times over, for ever render impossible the rehearsal of another great poet. And the net result of Hugo's ambition is that nobody reads him except when the journalists quote him in the newspapers. . . . (p. 70)

> *George Moore, in a chapter in his* Confessions of a Young Man, *edited by George Moore (copyright © 1959, Capricorn Books, G. P. Putnam's Sons; reprinted by permission of the Literary Estate of George Moore), William Heinemann, 1917 (and reprinted by Capricorn Books, 1959, pp. 56-81).*

C. E. VAUGHAN   (essay date 1926)

[Primarily] Hugo is a poet; and it must now be our task to indicate the relation of his poetry to the idea which has hitherto been traced in his Drama and Romance. (pp. 424-25)

In political poetry, Hugo stands as much alone as in the writing of Romance. No poet, except Juvenal, has attempted a task resembling that which he has performed: and Juvenal, supreme as he is, could hardly claim to have struck so deep a chord as is struck in the volumes mentioned above. The poetry of Hugo in this department may be compared, indeed, with the romances written by himself before and during the period of his exile. The idea which underlies it is identical: the treatment is, fundamentally, the same. In the poetry, as in the romances, there is a conflict; here, as there, all the light is on one side, nothing but darkness on the other. Of course the difference of form involves to a certain extent, a modification in the treatment of the idea. There can be no question here of the completeness which is given to the representation of society in *Les Misérables,* of nature in *Les Travailleurs de la mer.* But, what is lost in completeness is more than compensated by the greater appropriateness of the setting in which the conception is put forth. *Les Misérables* claims to give a portraiture of society, as it always tends to be, as it actually was after the fall of the Empire and the Revolution of 1830 in modern France. (p. 425)

Satire and invective—which is a more direct, and therefore in worthy hands a nobler, form of satire—have never gone deeper and higher than in *L'expiation* and *La vision de Dante* on the one hand, and in *Le Te Deum du I*er *Janvier* and *Le Jour des* *rois* upon the other. The poet of conflict was never more in his element than when crusading against tyranny and superstition. The spirit of Voltaire might seem to walk the earth again; but of Voltaire raised and widened by the influence of the two movements, revolutionary and romantic, that since his death had renovated the world. The satire of Hugo—to use the word in a wider sense than above—is not less, but more, direct and uncompromising than that of Voltaire himself.

Nor is it only in the bare fact of writing satire that Hugo shows himself pre-eminently the poet of conflict. The specific form which his satire takes exhibits still more plainly the same tendency at work. Other satirists have branded what was unrighteous and contemptible. Hugo alone has confronted successful wickedness with the purity and justice which it had trampled under foot. No part of his satire is more characteristic, no part is more essential, than such poems as that on the child shot on the 4th of December, and the Hymn of those transported in *Les Châtiments,* or *Le Crapaud* and *Les pauvres gens* in *La Legénde des Siècles.* (p. 426)

In satire, as in Drama and Romance, conflict is the idea which underlies all that Hugo has produced. The idea is, as has been seen, carried a stage further, because it is worked out more consistently in satire than in Romance: but in both it is fundamentally the same.

In turning to Hugo's poetry of nature, we are, at first sight, met with a singular deviation from the conception which has so far been traced through the various divisions of his work. Occasionally, indeed, as in the *Toilers of the Sea,* man may be represented in the act of struggling with nature. But far more generally the very reverse of this is done. Nature is not commonly portrayed as the antagonist who wrestles with man, but as the superior who disdainfully mocks, or disdainfully instructs him. . . . (p. 427)

[What] induces Hugo to put nature above man, and by consequence instinct above reason, is zeal for the progress which, by so doing he seems to set aside, but which, only if set aside for the moment, could in his view be permanently ensured. The conflict is stayed for the instant, and in this region, that it may be fought more relentlessly in other fields. Man is bidden throw himself on the sustaining power of nature that from her breast he may drink fresh strength for the war which he is to wage with man and, when occasion calls, with nature.

The form which this conception takes in Hugo is either more or less explicit. In the earlier volumes of poetry it is less so, and its full scope is hardly recognised by the poet himself. It is true, indeed, that even here to him, as to Wordsworth, nature is greater and richer than man. What is wanting here, and what is present in the later poems, is the thought that what nature has to give to man is specifically combative energy and power of resistance. (p. 429)

In the poems written after the beginning of his exile all is changed. Nature is still the source of truth, but she is the source also of action, for men. And this implies an essential change in the conception of truth itself. It is no longer sought with groping steps, but with some measure of assurance. There is a certainty in the note which nature, as the organ of truth, gives out through the second volume of *Les Contemplations* and *La Legénde des Siècles* which is wanting, as the titles might indicate, to the poems contained in *Les Chants de Crépuscule* and *Les rayons et les ombres. Pensar, dudar*—to think is to doubt,—the title of one among the greatest of Hugo's early poems, might be taken to give the keynote of the earlier period:

to think is to believe and do is the fundamental conception of his later writings. And if there is a mystical strain about the later, which was absent or but seldom present in the earlier, poems, that is no contradiction but rather a confirmation of what has been said. (p. 430)

To Hugo it is the storm and tempest, the strength and fury which seem the essential thing in nature. In themselves they are indifferent; they inspire the horror of the storm-wind and the malignity of the Devil-fish in the *Toilers of the Sea* as much as the Lion of Androcles, and the waves that console the exile or the forests that rebuke the bandit in *Les Châtiments.* But, when swept into the circle of human life even at their wildest, even at what appears to be their worst, they may be an essential element in the mysterious "formation of the law of progress." And at certain crucial moments of history, to have committed himself trustfully to their rushing tide has been necessary to man that he may be saved from himself, and exchange the exhausted soil of an old world for the rich life of a new. Thus, it might be said, at the Christian era, man threw himself on nature, and received the gift of love: at the Renaissance, he threw himself on nature and received a new conception of God, and a new sense of life and knowledge; at the Revolution, he threw himself on nature, and received freedom. The second of these periods, under a grand figure, forms the subject of *Le Satyre,* which, if we are to take any one poem, gives probably the most complete and splendid expression to the genius of Hugo.

To describe that poem would be an impossible and, it may be supposed, a superfluous task. It affords, in truth, an apt symbol to represent the "new birth" which, in the language of Michelet, "discovered nature and re-discovered man," and which, it might be added, brought religion, as Socrates brought philosophy, down from heaven to earth, snatching it from the hand of a priestly caste to make it the common possession of mankind. But what most concerns us at the present moment to remark is the faith with which, in this poem, Hugo trusts himself to the undisciplined powers which start from the depth of nature to play their part in the changed order of the world. (p. 431)

[In the Drama,] the struggle was within the character of the individual: in Romance it was between the individual and the world without. Here the battlefield is still wider. The struggle is in nature; and nature is but that writ large which in man is written small; man therefore is ranged with nature in the fight which, in detail always, on a large scale at the turning-points of history, is being waged against the powers of darkness. Man and nature are associated, almost identified: together they fill the whole circle of life; and they in turn are filled with the spirit of conflict. And, to enlarge the stage of action still further, that against which the conflict lies is either kept out of sight or but darkly shadowed forth. . . . It is the application of the idea of conflict to history and nature, and the harmonisation of man, as of history, with nature that gives so wide a reach to the best of what Hugo has written on these two subjects. He is a great political poet, and he is a great poet of nature; and he is one because he is the other. The reflection of man in nature, and of nature into man, the recognition of the same law of conflict working out to the same end in both man and nature, opens out a possibility of wider issues, and a more intense life, in his treatment of either subject. . . . The humanisation of nature, the penetration of her forms with the idea of conflict, has for its result to raise the vitality of nature to the highest point which it can reach. Bird and beast, even wind and wave, become instinct with the life, and combative energy, which we are apt to regard as the property of man alone. To nature may be applied the figure which, in one of the poems in *La Légende des Siècles,* represents Hugo's conception of history. The outer coating of the blind wall that fronts man melts away; and the whole tissue behind, which he had taken for inanimate and dead, is seen to be built up from countless myriads of souls in ceaseless activity to weave "the web of being spun," in some cases blindly, in others with full consciousness. (pp. 432-33)

His conception of life does not stop with the component parts, but is extended to the whole. Each part of nature may have a separate life: but there is a life, a personality for the whole which, in his view, is still more essential. "If the world had no individual life, man, who has it, would be greater than the world"; or again, "I believe in nothing apart from God":—this thought lies at the root of Hugo's way of conceiving nature. . . . It is the chief work of his later years to have bridged the gulf between man and nature, and to have fused both from end to end with the idea of God, a living and loving God, who works both through man and nature, indifferently in the tempest and the calm. (pp. 433-34)

> *C. E. Vaughan, "Goethe and Hugo," in* John Rylands Library Bulletin, *Vol. 10, No. 2, July, 1926, pp. 407-34.**

JOSEPH WARREN BEACH (essay date 1932)

[It is not in the story proper of "Les Misérables"] that one should look for the serious significance of Victor Hugo; it is in the political history with which the private chronicle is so richly interlarded, it is in the social comment, the philosophy. And indeed no good story-teller ever took out so much time to work up a background of general historical and social interest. Whole books, many chapters long, are devoted solely to this background material: one entire book to the battle of Waterloo, another to a sociological study of the Paris street urchin, another to the history and description of the sewers of Paris. Two books are devoted to an account of a convent of the Bernadines and to the general theory of convent life. There are entire books in which there is nothing but general discussion, and during which the story simply waits. And there are scattered through the novel many more chapters wholly devoted to general background and theorizing, not to speak of the incidental passages in the course of the action in which the author instructs the reader what to think about it all.

As for the background material, it is brilliantly served up, and tends, in the long run, to give the book in review a sort of monumental solidity and grandeur. But in so far as it is a substitute for the serious close-up presentation of human nature—the ordinary business of good fiction—it serves simply to deceive both author and reader into supposing that the book is on a higher intellectual level than it really is. As a study of human nature it is not at all on a high level intellectually. The historical and philosophical digressions are for the most part a turning aside from the particular case at issue, an evasion of the problem of fiction. And while they are interesting enough in their own right, and full of information, they are, after all, only a kind of high-class journalism.

The style of Hugo is the style of high-class journalism, or more exactly that of the clever parliamentarian of the romantic period. It is self-conscious and complacent. It is sentimentally effusive where the occasion calls for pathos. It is given to

rhetorical repetition in the manner of Dickens and rhetorical question in the manner of De Quincey. It is witty, antithetical, bobastic, pathetic, figurative, grandiloquent, and makes an English reader think of Macaulay and Carlyle and De Quincey and Frank Crane and Fra Elbertus all rolled into one. And it is that kind of style which has the effect, very often, of diverting attention from the characters, the subject, on to the author himself. (pp. 59-60)

So then we have, in "Les Misérables," on the one side an exciting story, and on the other a series of dissertations on history, sociology, psychology, etc. But that would seem to imply that there was no relation between Hugo's story and his philosophy. Whereas it is clear that the whole story was constructed with a view to proving a thesis. Hugo tells us most explicitly what was his thesis in "Les Misérables":

> The book which the reader has under his eyes at this moment, is nothing, from one end to the other, in the whole and in the details, whatever may be the interruptions, the exceptions and the failures, but the march forward from evil to good, from the unjust to the just, the false to the true, from night to day, from appetite to conscience, from decay to life, from bestiality to the sense of duty, from hell to heaven, from nothingness to God. Point of departure: matter. Goal: the spirit. A hydra at the beginning, an angel at the end.

This evolution from evil to good, social, moral, religious, is to be seen in operation, according to his design, not merely in the individual characters—the bishop, the convict, the street urchin, the political revolutionary—but likewise in the whole state and body politic. What the "socialists" of Hugo's time were seeking, he says, is "the end of oppression . . . the end of the sword, work for man, instruction for the child, social sweetness for woman, liberty, equality, fraternity, bread for all, ideas for all, the Edenizing of the world—in short, Progress." (pp. 61-2)

It is clear that Hugo is a romantic humanitarian. And one may not be so down on romanticism and humanitarianism as Professor Babbitt to realize that Hugo's humanitarianism is rather sentimental, exaggerated, and naïve. But as an artist, what is the matter with him is not merely that he has a sentimental philosophy, but that he has constructed his fable to be a simple vehicle for this philosophy, and that human nature is considered exclusively as a means of proving a theory. The good bishop is in every respect an ideal figure of Christian virtue. Long before one has finished the fourteen chapters which make up the first book, and which are entirely given over to an account of the character of Monseigneur Bienvenu, one realizes that one has to do here not with that art whose aim is to present human nature as the author knows it from experience. (p. 63)

The fault of "Les Misérables" is not that a philosophy of life is implied in the action, and is breathed forth by the characters—that is sometimes true of novels of a finer grain, like "Anna Karenina," "Vanity Fair," "Kristin Lavransdatter," or "Manhattan Transfer"—it is that in "Les Misérables" the fable is artificially constructed, the philosophy is forced, and the characters are but puppets in a pantomime. (p. 64)

> *Joseph Warren Beach, "Philosophy: Hugo," in his* The Twentieth Century Novel: Studies in Technique *(© 1932, renewed 1960; adapted by permission of*

*Prentice-Hall, Inc., Englewood Cliffs, New Jersey),
Appleton-Century-Crofts, Inc., 1932, pp. 55-64.*

ELLIOTT M. GRANT (essay date 1945)

Victor Hugo was something more than an important figure in literary history, a prose-writer of distinction and a poet of high renown. He was quite simply a great man. Not a perfect man, be it clearly understood, for like other mortals he had his defects. But his noble qualities stand forth in sharp outline. He was courageous and steadfast, devoted to great ideals, sincere and ardent in his convictions, progressive in his outlook, charitable and humane. (p. 334)

His vitality was incredible, his nature at once exuberant and simple. The amount of work he turned out in his mature years as well as in his youth amazes posterity no less than his contemporaries. (p. 335)

Superior to many of his critics, to Montalembert, or Veuillot, or Thiers, he was one of the forward-looking men of his time, inspired by a genuine idealism without which it is surely difficult to achieve grandeur. (p. 336)

Every generation indulges in [a quest for pure poetry], redefines tragedy, novel, or lyric, and in its enthusiasm outlaws much if not all, of what has gone before. Posterity is not obliged to share these prejudices. Let us not then be afraid to assert that poems like **"Aymerillot," "La Rose de l'Infante," "Les Pauvres Gens"** are magnificent specimens of heroic poetry for which no apologies need be made. Let us recognize that the eloquent satire of *Les Châtiments* was not only sincere but justified. Let us realize that freedom and liberty were more than abstractions for Victor Hugo, that they represented great realities, and that when he upheld these ideals he was speaking of eternal truths and eternal values. (pp. 336-37)

But the essence of Hugo's genius, . . . is by no means limited to eloquence and rhetoric. We need only recall that poems like **"Nuits de juin"** and **"Spectacle rassurant"** in *Les Rayons et les ombres* or **"Crépuscule"** in *Les Contemplations* are quite the opposite of the rhetorical. In such poems Hugo excels in simplicity. . . . His poems on childhood are a reflection of that same inward and spiritual grace. The touching lines on his daughter's death are expressed in the language of the common man.

From a simple and direct rendition of the mystery of the universe Hugo passed frequently to a vision of things in which the great enigma of human fate is suggested in accents quite unknown to the other Romantic poets. (p. 337)

[The ideas expressed in Hugo's later poems] are rarely the product of close, deductive reasoning, but rather the result of Hugo's capacity for spontaneous insight and prophecy. They are nonetheless interesting in their metaphysical implications and nonetheless beautiful.

What diverse talent, what inexhaustible inspiration, what power of language and imagery Hugo's poetry reveals! Not only does he express as Baudelaire said long ago, "the mystery of life," but "no artist is more universal than he, more apt to put himself in contact with the forces of universal life, more disposed to bathe himself incessantly in nature" [see excerpt above]. And Baudelaire recognized too, his extraordinary virtuosity in the manipulation of language, his capacity for "cutting out, in his stanzas, the unforgettable shape of things," and for "illuminating them with their proper color." (pp. 338-39)

Conscious throughout his career of the importance of style, Victor Hugo sought to achieve the maximum of literary beauty. In 1834 he declared:

> Beautiful expression embellishes thought and preserves it. It is at once an adornment and an armor. Style clothing an idea is like enamel covering a tooth.

> Design! Design! That is the first law of all art. And do not think that this law diminishes liberty or nature in any way.

To this ideal he remained faithful as long as he could wield a pen, without, however, falling into the limitations of Art for Art's sake, and without diluting in any marked degree the sincerity and the spontaneity of his inspiration. For whenever he wrote, as he continually said, he felt exalted.

His prose is both melodious and balanced, infinitely colorful and varied, but solidly constructed. All the elements of his composition: the novel in its entirety, the chapter, the paragraph, the sentence, the individual word, received his most careful attention. Nor was the immensity of his vocabulary a barrier to this meticulous care. He felt no need to limit himself to achieve a definite effect. Economy he considered synonymous with sterility. Words tumbled and poured from his pen, but they were not uncontrolled. Somehow the novelist maintained complete mastery. His power over the written word was little short of miraculous. (pp. 339-40)

That Victor Hugo did not have a highly original mind and that he was not a philosopher in the sense that Descartes, Condillac, and Kant were philosophers can readily be admitted. He was nevertheless an intelligent as well as a gifted man. The critical articles he wrote for the *Muse française*, the *Préface de Cromwell,* and the preface to *Hernani,* some of the pages of *Littérature et philosophie mêlées,* sections of his *William Shakespeare,* reveal a keen literary perception. He did not develop, like Hippolyte Taine or Brunetière, a complex critical system, but his reactions were frequently penetrating and sound. (p. 341)

[His philosophical ideas] are stimulating and interesting. From a rather conventional orthodoxy in his youth, he moved with greater maturity through a provisional skepticism to the elaboration of a complex set of beliefs. The double nature of man, the notion of the vitality of the whole universe, the benevolent existence of an all-wise Deity, the doctrine of metempsychosis, the moral progress of humanity, and the immortality of the soul are some of the concepts which he defined in poetic lines of great beauty. All of these ideas were in circulation before his day, but he made them his own and he expressed them as only a very talented poet could. Sections of **"Le Satyre,"** of **"Ce que dit la bouche d'ombre,"** and **"Les Mages,"** of *La Fin de Satan* and *Dieu* easily compete with the best philosophical poems of the Western World.

His political beliefs were not original either, but were sincerely, skillfully, and provocatively expressed. Throughout his life he was a great humanitarian, believing with all his mind and heart that the lot of the common man could and should be improved. (p. 342)

Victor Hugo was extraordinarily representative of his age. The nineteenth century, which he almost spanned, was traversed by a certain number of conflicts: romanticism versus classicism, science versus religion, Church versus State, monarchy versus republic, useful art versus Art for Art's sake. All are reflected in varying degrees in Victor Hugo's work and career.

If the nineteenth century had any positive belief it was that democracy and science would usher in the millennium; democracy would give men liberty; science would give them comfort. Poverty, tyranny, and war would be abolished. Victor Hugo shared that belief and became one of its most eloquent exponents. The seventeenth century is commonly called in France "The Century of Louis the Great"; the eighteenth, "The Century of Voltaire"; the nineteenth is far too complex to be summed up in the person of one man, but if we attempted to do so, we should undoubtedly have to call it "The Century of Victor Hugo." (p. 343)

> *Elliott M. Grant, in his* The Career of Victor Hugo *(copyright © 1945, copyright renewed © 1973, by the President and Fellows of Harvard College; excerpted by permission), Cambridge, Mass.: Harvard University Press, 1945, 365 p.*

V. S. PRITCHETT   (essay date 1947)

"Hugo began life as a mature man and is only now entering on adolescence." The words of Vigny's referred to Hugo's life when he was twenty-seven, not to his work, but they come back when we read *Notre Dame de Paris* and *Les Misérables.* There are the dreams we dream no longer, powerful frescoes without intimacy. They belong to the volcanic periods of life—so apt to return—when the unconscious erupts, when the superego pronounces, when the monstrous and the ideal hog or transfigure our natures, when the self is still molten and has not been hardened into unproductive habit. In Hugo, it never became hardened. He spread into journalism and epic. Content to impersonate medieval history in *Notre Dame de Paris,* Hugo became universal history, man, justice, natural and spiritual law, the Infinite by the time he came to the 2900 pages of *Les Misérables.* It has been said that, like Balzac, he had too much confidence in his own genius. So had all the Romantics. The criticism is useless: take away excess from Hugo and the genius vanishes. . . . [We] can nowadays recognize, by general psychological aid and the torture chambers of contemporary history, the monstrous side of a book like *Notre Dame de Paris,* but have disconnected it from the ideal. We can recognize horror and grotesque, and even respond to the rhetoric of darkness; we are unable to credit the rhetoric of light. We are too absorbed in the rediscovery of evil. For Hugo, the black and white artist, one could not exist without the other. He was a primitive in that respect—or a commercial.

In *Notre Dame de Paris* Hugo's dreams are magnified in outline, microscopic in detail. They are true but are made magical by the enlargement of pictorial close-up, not by grandiloquent fading. . . . If we object that Hugo's world is rhetorical, his skepticism, irony and wit give the rhetoric earth to stand on. Quasimodo is put to the torture in a ferocious scene, but it follows a trial which is based on the stock stagy comedy of deaf prisoner at odds with deaf judge. The novel is a romance, but its parts exist in equilibrium. Interwoven with the tragedians—Quasimodo, the girl, the lusting priest—is the pedestrian Gringoire who has been quick to make his peace with the world, like some Shakespearean clown. He grows before our eyes, as all the characters grow. Beginning as a bore, he becomes the nervous smile on the face of that practical pusillanimity which we call the common experience and the instinct to survive. (pp. 353-55)

Hugo was the impresario of a split personality. Out of the depths came the monsters created by chastity: lust, cruelty, jealousy, violence, maiming, murder, in pursuit of the inno-cent, the loving and the merciful. The black and white view is relieved by the courage of the priest's feckless brother and the skepticism of Gringoire, the whole is made workable by poetic and pictorial instinct. It has often been pointed out that Hugo had the eye that sees for itself. Where Balzac described things out of descriptive gluttony, so that parts of his novels are an undiscriminating buyer's catalogue; where Scott describes out of antiquarian zeal, Hugo brings things to life by implicating them with persons in the action in rapid "takes." In this sense, *Notre Dame de Paris* was the perfect film script. Every stone plays its part. (pp. 355-56)

Hugo's simplification of the inner life are required by a superb sense of the theatre. He works entirely within its terms. One can see where he was trained. He works by stage scenes. The scene before Notre Dame is a stage set. He has the art of placing a situation, opposing an obstacle, creating a new situation, reversing it, doubling and redoubling. . . . He is rich in dramatic irony. There is a purely stage scene where Louis IX inspects at length the construction of a wooden cage in which a prisoner is wailing for mercy. The king does not notice the prisoner because, in his avarice, he is too interested in the cost of the wood. Yet when another prisoner appeals for mercy the king lets him off out of whim. Fate rules us all, the Wheel of Fortune is a trickster. Hugo's whole method as a novelist is contained in these dramatic ironies and reversals, but he applies it in such a variety of ways and at so many levels that we do not notice the mechanics of it. (pp. 356-57)

The fact that Hugo's characters are larger than life as individuals and are only life-size when they are part of a crowd—judges, soldiers, beggars, populace—does not mean, of course, that they are not individual and recognizable, or even that they are either allegorical or caricature. There are no unconvincing or sentimentalized characters in *Notre Dame* or *Les Misérables,* as there are in Scott. (The two novelists are not really comparable; it would be more sensible to call Hugo "incurious Dostoevsky" rather than "inferior Scott." Hugo was simply too extroverted to know how morbid the sources of some of his ideas were; he merely knew that they drove his brother mad, not himself.) If *Les Misérables* is a lesser and more ambitious work than *Notre Dame,* this is partly because it is humorless and has little comedy. But Hugo's genius was for the creation of simple and recognizable myth. The huge success of *Les Misérables* as a didactic work on behalf of the poor and oppressed is due to its poetic and myth-enlarged view of human nature—intermingled with that fundamental regard for human cunning which a popular culture seems to call for. . . . Myth and theatre, rather than fact and dogma, are what have made Quasimodo, Valjean, Javert universal in popular esteem. It is remarkable that the eight hundred superfluous pages of digression did not wreck the book. (pp. 358-59)

> *V. S. Pritchett, "Hugo's Impersonations," in his* The Living Novel and Later Appreciations *(copyright 1947, © 1964 and renewed 1975 by V. S. Pritchett; reprinted by permission of Random House, Inc.; in Canada by Literistic, Ltd.), revised edition, Random House, 1964, pp. 353-59.*

RENÉ WELLEK   (essay date 1955)

[*William Shakespeare,*] Hugo's major work of criticism in later years, is an extremely exasperating series of incoherent, flamboyant meditations full of incredible verbiage and ecstatic rhetoric. As a book on Shakespeare it can be easily dismissed, since only a small part is concerned with Shakespeare at all and since the information on Shakespeare's life and times is grossly uncritical and even fantastically wrong. The occasional comments on the plays can also be ignored, as it is hard to see what is meant by saying oracularly and solemnly that "Macbeth *is* hunger" or "Othello *is* Night." The lack of critical spirit, the complete negation of discrimination is proclaimed complacently by the author himself. "Genius is an entity like nature and must, like her, be accepted purely and simply. We must take or leave a mountain." (pp. 256-57)

But among all the welter of names, exhortations, declamations against stupid critics, persecutors of poets, and so on, there are a few pages which show a remarkable insight into a mythic concept of poetry and anticipate the Jungian view of literature as a creation of "archetypal patterns." Hugo calls them "types," "Adams" which he well distinguishes from mere universals. "A type does not reproduce any man in particular . . . it sums up and concentrates under one human form a whole family of characters and minds. A type does not abbreviate, it condenses. It is not one, it is everybody." . . .

Hugo's conceptions of imagination and the history of poetry fit in with this view of art as a re-creation of the very deepest patterns of humanity. Imagination is the great "plunger into the deep," the reconciler of everything with everything. There is thus no progress in art. Decadence and renaissance are meaningless terms: there is no rise and no fall in art. Contraries do not exclude each other. Everything mirrors everything. (p. 257)

Hugo has such a tremendous desire for synthesis, for reconciliation, that he finally abolishes all barriers and ends in what must be described as grandiose confusion. (pp. 257-58)

No doubt he was not a good practical critic, for he had no patience, no power of analysis, and little discrimination. One can hardly imagine that a theory of literature could be built on his pronouncements, for they lack system and continuity. But granting all the faults of loose phrasing and rash generalization, Hugo, of all the French writers of the time, seems to have by far the profoundest insights into the nature of poetry. He found many striking formulas for central problems: the internal order of a work of art, the identity of form and content, the union of the opposites, the transformation of the ugly and grotesque in a higher synthesis. Moreover, his later view of "types" or patterns is of far greater consequence than the battle against the rules and unities, which had been long since decided in other countries. Even as a polemicist Hugo was extremely important, at least in France: the rejection of the rules and the abolition of the old distinctions of genres and levels of style were a historical necessity which made the development of modern literature possible. (p. 258)

> *René Wellek, "Stendhal and Hugo," in his* A History of Modern Criticism: 1750-1950, The Romantic Age *(copyright, 1955, by Yale University Press), Yale University Press, 1955, pp. 241-58.**

WOLFGANG KAYSER (essay date 1957)

[In the preface to *Cromwell,*] Victor Hugo treated the grotesque as the hallmark of all art created since antiquity, including that of the Middle Ages: "Here, then, is a principle unknown to antiquity, a new type of poetry. . . . This type is the grotesque." Hugo derived his knowledge of the concept from German Romanticism through translations and especially through the writings of the philosopher Victor Cousin. But Hugo enlarged its scope and considerably increased its meaning and importance.

To the new "principle" of the grotesque belongs a new artistic genre—that of comedy. At first glance, this connection between the grotesque and comedy appears to hark back to the traditional identification of the grotesque with *comique, ridicule,* and *bouffon.* Hugo acknowledged this antecedent but considered it merely as one aspect of the grotesque, the other being the deformed and the horrible: "The grotesque . . . is everywhere; on the one hand it creates what is deformed and horrible, on the other what is comic and farcical." . . . The preface to *Cromwell* leaves some doubt as to whether Hugo regarded both aspects as necessary for the grotesque, since some of the illustrations he furnishes are exclusively comic and burlesque. Yet he certainly considered the monstrous and horrible traits to be most essential, as is shown by the large number of examples he furnishes. (pp. 56-7)

But, with the comically farcical and the monstrously horrible, the grotesque is by no means exhausted for Victor Hugo, who places it in the vicinity of the ugly which, unlike the one type of beauty, exists in a thousand different shapes. This reflection tends to make the concept diffuse; when Hugo proceeds to study the "origin and evolution of the grotesque" in literature, art, and customs since antiquity he seems, at times, to admit of no limits whatsoever. But Hugo's illustrations raise still another basic problem. Can a single, isolated figure (such as a dwarf) or object (such as a gargoyle) be clearly regarded as grotesque? Are physical ugliness and deformity sufficient to render things grotesque? For if that were the case, the grotesque would belong among the esthetic categories determined by their external appearance, such as blank verse, Alexandrine, first-person narrative, and a five-act play. Occasionally, Hugo seems to use it in that sense. But the reader who often does not want to decide too quickly, who should like to make the answer depend on the context, and on the place and function it assigns to the individual object, takes the grotesque more seriously. Only in context, as part of a larger structure or as a vehicle of meaning, does the individual form become expressive and does it belong to the grotesque. (pp. 57-8)

As soon as [Hugo] proceeds from specific illustrations to general considerations, he abandons the structural point of view. He even goes beyond the grotesque as an entity by assigning to it a function within a larger whole. He takes it to be one pole of a tension whose opposite pole is constituted by the sublime. He thus ceases to think of the grotesque as the only characteristic feature of modern art and comes to look at it as a contrasting device. He defines art as a means of creating a harmonious relation between them. According to him, naïve popular literature occasionally reveals "with admirable instinct this mystery of modern art; antiquity could not have produced *La Belle et la Bête*." Among the artists, however, Hugo finds only one to have succeeded in combining "the sublime with the grotesque, the terrible with the burlesque, and tragedy with comedy" in drama, the highest form of art: Shakespeare, "the greatest poet of the modern age."

The true depth of the grotesque is revealed only by its confrontation with its opposite, the sublime. For just as the sublime (in contrast with the beautiful) guides our view toward a loftier, supernatural world, the ridiculously distorted and monstrously horrible ingredients of the grotesque point to an inhuman, nocturnal, and abysmal realm. Hugo's language justifies this interpretation of the grotesque, even though he himself did not actually furnish it. (p. 58)

Victor Hugo is fond of using the contrast between the purely spiritual and the *bête humaine* in order to characterize the tension between the sublime and the grotesque. He probably does this essentially in order to indicate that inhuman forces have invaded the familiar world. The precision of this formulation is somewhat impaired, however, by the examples which Hugo cites. At the same time a new element, which Hugo mistakenly sought to include in his formula, emerges. If Caesar is afraid of falling from his triumphal chariot, and Socrates, on the morning of his death, interrupts a conversation about the immortality of the soul with the request to sacrifice a cock to Aesculapius, Hugo would compel one to regard Caesar's fright and Socrates' distraction as grotesque, which apparently they are not. For here the *bête humaine* is nothing else than ordinary human nature. Hugo's examples are grotesque only insofar as they exemplify a certain form of contradiction or contrast. Nothing that is inherently sublime or grotesque is fused in a "beautiful" or "dramatic" structure; rather the grotesque consists in the very contrast that ominously permits of no reconciliation. To recognize and reveal such a construct of opposites is somewhat diabolic; the order is destroyed and an abyss opened where we thought to rest on firm ground. At this point the proximity to, and difference from, the comic are made obvious. The comic innocuously annihilates greatness and dignity, especially if they are wrongly assumed. It effects the annihilation by placing us on the secure level of reality. The grotesque totally destroys the order and deprives us of our foothold. (pp. 58-9)

> *Wolfgang Kayser, "The Grotesque in the Age of Romanticism," in his* The Grotesque in Art and Literature, *translated by Ulrich Weisstein (translation copyright © 1963 by Indiana University Press; originally published as* Das Groteske, seine Gestaltung in Malerei und Dichtung, *Gerhard Stalling Verlag, 1957), Indiana University Press, 1963, pp. 48-99.**

PATRICIA A. WARD (essay date 1975)

Despite the hatred for certain aspects of medieval society he expressed in the 1870s, Hugo the creative artist with extraordinary powers of memory and imagination could never totally relinquish his Romantic vision of the Middle Ages. (pp. 105-06)

Hugo's attraction to Dante, the great emperors, the burgraves, and the chevaliers can . . . be attributed to his personality. The "Ego Hugo" in all its roles—*mage, visionnaire, prophète, homme politique, exilé*—found aspects of itself in these heroic figures which could not be rejected in the poet's later years despite his gradual conviction that the Middle Ages as a whole were scarcely illuminated by any form of human progress. Inheriting, then, the popular conception of the medieval period which existed during the pre-Romantic and Romantic periods and, in turn, helping mold that taste, Hugo rejected the concept of a homogeneous, ideal Christian medieval era. He personalized and transformed certain elements of Romantic medievalism.

Medieval motif serves as a touchstone for an understanding of Hugo's gradual perception of the concept of historical change and the portrayal of this change in literary form. Before *Notre Dame,* the Middle Ages were a distant, exotic past, reflected in the conventional images and formal experiments of the *Ballades.* But with his novel of fifteenth-century Paris, Hugo documented and tried to recapture the color of a waning era. He did not, however, produce a totally integrated novel, for there

is a dichotomy between the poetic reality of the medieval atmosphere and the melodramatic plot.

With *Le Rhin* and *Les Burgraves,* history (now a term implying both recorded history and legend) became much more than a distant moment to be recaptured. Hugo envisioned the dynamism within the Middle Ages as the struggle between the forces that would unify or disrupt civilization. He projected this antithetical conflict into the mythic figures of Barbarossa and Job, but given the historical conflict in *Les Burgraves,* there is a dichotomy in the literary form. Conscious that his interpretation of the past could influence his contemporaries, Hugo created a drama that functions on two levels, as a melodrama geared to the popular audience and as a series of poetic arias which would convey his political ideas by means of a rhetoric of images.

By means of the epic scope of *La Légende des Siècles,* Hugo conveyed both the dynamic conflict within the Middle Ages and the movement of history from the past toward an apocalyptic future. The historical distance between the medieval past and the empire of Napoléon III is again apparent when the Middle Ages serve as an allegory of contemporary injustice. But in those cases in which Hugo allows the past to speak for itself through its symbolic figures, as in "L'Aigle du casque," he creates narrative poetry which exists in and for itself as a self-contained rhythmic whole. The distance between the medieval past and the present finally disappears on the fictive level in *Quatrevingt-treize* where Hugo recreates a moment in time when man thinks he is destroying the past and creating a new future. The Tourgue exists finally as a battered symbol of the Middle Ages which are now a memory. (pp. 106-07)

> *Patricia A. Ward, in her* The Medievalism of Victor Hugo *(copyright © 1975 by The Pennsylvania State University), The Pennsylvania State University Press, University Park, 1975, 134 p.*

ADDITIONAL BIBLIOGRAPHY

Baring, Maurice. "Goethe and Victor Hugo: A Comparison." *The National Review* XXXIV, No. 204 (February 1900): 901-13.*
> Maintains that Goethe was a "thinker" and Hugo a "seer".

Brandes, George. "Lyric Poetry: Lamartine and Hugo." In his *The Reaction in France.* Main Currents in Nineteenth Century Literature, vol. III, pp. 198-221. New York: Boni & Liveright, London: William Heinemann, 1924.*
> A discussion of Hugo's place in literary history.

Duclaux, Madame. *Victor Hugo.* New York: Holt, Rinehart and Winston, 1921, 268 p.
> Praises Hugo's graceful prose in *Notre Dame de Paris* and *Les misérables.*

Ellis, Havelock. "Victor Hugo." *The Fortnightly Review* LXXII, No. 422 (February 1902): 217-27.
> A biographical study of Hugo.

Grant, Richard B. *The Perilous Quest: Image, Myth, and Prophecy in the Narratives of Victor Hugo.* Durham, N.C.: Duke University Press, 1968, 253 p.
> Follows the development of Hugo's literary motifs.

Guérard, Albert Leon. "Romantic Humanitarianism." In his *French Prophets of Yesterday: A Study of Religious Thought under the Second Empire,* pp. 118-58. New York: D. Appleton & Co., 1913.*
> Discusses the pessimism of Hugo's work.

Hooker, Kenneth Ward. *The Fortunes of Victor Hugo in England.* New York: Columbia University Press, 1938, 353 p.
 A compilation of British critical reception to Hugo's work.

Josephson, Matthew. *Victor Hugo: A Realistic Biography of the Great Romantic.* Garden City, N.Y.: Doubleday, Doran & Co., 1942, 514 p.
 A detailed, incisive biography. Josephson considers Hugo ''one of the greatest exemplars of the sedentary, meditative type of man, turning from his study to service in public life.''

Marzials, Frank T. *Life of Victor Hugo.* London: Walter Scott, 1888, 224 p.
 General biographical study.

Maurois, André. *Olympio: The Life of Victor Hugo.* Translated by Gerard Hopkins. New York: Harper & Brothers, 1956, 498 p.
 The definitive biography. Maurois calls Hugo the greatest of all French poets and adds that ''we need to know the story of his life if we are to understand his tormented genius to the full.''

Poulet, Georges. ''Hugo.'' In his *The Interior Distance,* translated by Elliott Coleman, pp. 153-81. Baltimore: The Johns Hopkins Press, 1959.*
 An analysis of Hugo's concept of time as manifested in his poetry.

Nikolai Mikhailovich Karamzin

1766-1826

(Also transliterated as Nikolay; also Mikhaylovich; also Karamsin, Karamzín) Russian historian, short story writer, poet, essayist, and translator.

Karamzin was the most important Russian writer of his generation and the leader of the Russian Sentimentalist movement. Influenced by Jean Jacques Rousseau, Samuel Richardson, and other European eighteenth-century writers, his works established Sentimentalism as the predominant literary school of his day and influenced such later literary movements as Russian Romanticism and psychological realism. Karamzin was also influential in his linguistic reforms. He introduced French syntax and cultural terms, eliminated many Slavonic words, and based his writing on the spoken language of the gentry, thereby transforming the Russian literary language.

Educated in Moscow, Karamzin developed an early appreciation for French, English, and German literatures. He also became involved with Russian Freemasonry and such writers as Vasili Petrov and Nikolai Novikov. The emotional piety central to the Freemason movement and the influence of European literature are obvious in Karamzin's early publications. These include translations of Gotthold Lessing, William Shakespeare, and others. In 1789, Karamzin left Moscow and traveled through Germany, Switzerland, France, and England. Eighteen months later he returned to Russia and founded the literary journal *Moskovsky zhurnal* in which he began the serial publication of his *Pis'ma Russkogo puteshestvennika (Travels from Moscow through Prussia, Germany, Switzerland, France, and England);* he called this work the "mirror of my soul." Influenced by Laurence Sterne's *Sentimental Journey* and characterized by an intense subjectivity, these letters brought Karamzin immediate recognition and established him as a leading literary figure in Russia. However, in 1803, when *Travels from Moscow* appeared in English, it was poorly received. Critics considered the work derivative, overly sentimental, and inferior to previous works of travel literature.

"Bednaya Liza" (*Poor Liza*), Karamzin's best-known tale, portrays the seduction, betrayal, and suicide of a young woman. The story was well-received throughout Europe and became the central work of the Russian Sentimentalist movement. After publishing numerous short stories, poems, and essays throughout the 1790s, Karamzin founded *Vestnik Evropy* in 1801, and it became the most successful and influential political and literary review of its day.

In 1804, after being appointed official historian of the Russian Empire by Czar Alexander I, Karamzin abandoned the editorship of *Vestnik Evropy* and devoted himself exclusively to his most important work, the monumental history *Istoriya gosudarstva Rossiiskogo,* commonly referred to in English as *History of the Russian State.* The work was extremely popular and when, in 1818, the first eight volumes appeared, they sold out in less than a month. Karamzin spent the rest of his life working on his history, which was still incomplete at the time of his death. Considered to be the first comprehensive study of Russian history, *History of the Russian State* impressed contemporaries with its eloquent epic quality and was hailed as

the greatest achievement in Russian prose that had yet appeared. Although it influenced many great nineteenth-century Russian writers, *History of the Russian State* is now appreciated primarily as a work of literature rather than scholarship and is criticized for its narrow historical perspective, didacticism, and blind advocacy of autocracy.

Although he and the Russian pre-Romantic movement have been largely ignored by modern critics, Karamzin is now generally recognized as an important innovator who ushered in a new era in Russian literature. Through his efforts, the scope of Russian literary techniques, genres, and themes was substantially expanded and prose fiction became an important branch of Russian literature. His most significant and lasting contribution, however, was his reform of the literary language of his country, which has influenced all of subsequent Russian prose.

PRINCIPAL WORKS

"Bednaya Liza" (short story) 1792; published in journal *Moskovsky zhurnal*
[*Poor Liza,* 1803]
"Poeziia" (poetry) 1792; published in journal *Moskovsky zhurnal*

"Ostrov Borngol'm" (short story) 1793; published in
    journal *Moskovsky zhurnal*
    ["The Island of Bornholm" published in *Selected Prose
    of N. M. Karamzin*, 1969]
Pis'ma Russkogo puteshestvennika (fictional letters) 1801
    [*Travels from Moscow through Prussia, Germany,
    Switzerland, France, and England*, 1803; also published
    as *Letters of a Russian Traveler: 1789-1790*, 1957]
Sochineniia Karamzina. 8 vols. (short stories, essays, and
    poems) 1803-04
*Istoriya gosudarstva Rossiiskogo. 12 vols. (history)
    1818-29
Selected Prose of N. M. Karamzin (short stories and
    essays) 1969

*These works are collectively referred to in English as *History of the
Russian State*.

ANTI-JACOBIN REVIEW (essay date 1804)

[It is evident in Karamzin's *Travels from Moscow, through
Prussia, Germany, Switzerland, France, and England*] that his
letters are written on the spur of the moment, without previous
reflection or study, the sentiments flowing warm from the
heart, and intended only for the ear and the bosom of friendship.
In a word, Mr. K. certainly sat down to write what he thought,
and not, like most modern travellers and tourists, to think what
he should write. On this account, we have followed him, with
pleasure, and with interest, through scenes not naturally calculated to excite either; and have attended with pleasure to the
genuine effusions of his youthful heart, even where we smiled
at his simplicity, or censured his judgment. Through the first
volume, indeed, strong marks of an untutored, though not
uninformed, mind, are constantly visible; and a mawkish strain
of *sentimentality*, and *universal philanthropy*, could scarcely
fail to excite disgust, were not the sentiment checked by the
conviction that it proceeds not from affectation, but is the result
of studies, improperly directed, operating upon a lively fancy
and an ardent imagination. (p. 23)

When his mind shall have been more matured, and his judgment
corrected, by study and observation, his talents will appear to
much greater advantage, and enable him to instruct those readers whom he now only seeks to amuse. (p. 37)

> "Original Criticism: 'Travels from Moscow, through
> Prussia, Germany, Switzerland, France, and En-
> gland'," in Anti-Jacobin Review, Vol. XVII, No.
> LXVI, January, 1804, pp. 23-37.

[HENRY BROUGHAM] (essay date 1804)

The effusions of Mr. Nicolai Karamsin in his *Travels from
Moscow through Prussia, Germany, Switzerland, France, and
England* appear to us, we will confess, to vary far below the
writings of those travellers whom we have been accustomed
to follow, and abound so copiously in all their faults, with
such a universal want of their good qualities that nothing but
the rarity of a Russian work, and the amusing badness of the
author's head, could have induced us to exempt this book from
our quarterly catalogue.

Mr. Karamsin, it is proper to premise, is of that gentle class
of travelers who may be termed purely sentimental; who wander over a great track of country in order to put forth feelings
which might be excited and indulged in equal variety within
the four corners of any given chamber; and who, possessing
the faculty of attaching peculiar emotions to the observation
of the most ordinary occurrences, carefully treasure up the
remembrance of such trifling objects as have happened, according to the capricious movements of their fancy, to connect
themselves with the workings of their souls, while they studiously neglect the most important events, and shut their eyes
to those grand spectacles which are interesting to all the rest
of the world.

It is a first principle with these sentient beings, to refer every
thing to themselves, and to consider their own concerns as the
objects upon which all eyes have turned. The optics of most
men, indeed, diminish the magnitude of external objects in
proportion to their difference. But in this tribe, the sphere of
distinct vision is of infinitely small extent. They hardly perceive
what is not almost touching them, and *that*, they see magnified
in a wonderful manner. . . . If they ever think of anything
beyond their own sights and smiles, it is only to form the most
ridiculous judgements of men and things, according to the
standard of the first impression. . . . The world must be admitted to a share in their emotions; and volumes are thus made
up of dull epistles, which could only have interested such
friends as might wish to ascertain the fact of the writer's welfare
during his absence. An apology for inserting every trivial occurrence, is easily found in the example of those professed
tales of fiction, which, abounding in uncommon incidents, are
assimilated to the narratives of real life by an admixture of
ordinary circumstances; and whole chapters are filled with trifles which happen to be true, because the same trifles, if wrought
up in romance, with a multitude of striking passages, would
communicate to the whole an air of probability. (pp. 321-22)

We think the concluding remark of this author extremely judicious. After saying that his letters contain a true mirror of
his soul, his thoughts, and his waking dreams, he asks, 'What
is more interesting to a man than his own dear self? But perhaps
others too will be amused with my sketches; perhaps—that,
however, is their concern, and not mine.' (p. 328)

> [Henry Brougham,] "Karamsin's Travels in Eu-
> rope," in The Edinburgh Review, Vol. III, No. VI,
> January, 1804, pp. 321-28.

V. G. BELINSKY (essay date 1834-36)

Karamzin was endowed by nature with a musical ear for language and a faculty for facile and eloquent expression; consequently, it was not difficult for him to remodel the language. . . . Probably Karamzin strove to write the language
the way it was spoken. In this respect he was to blame for
having neglected the idiom of the Russian language, for not
having lent an ear to the vernacular of the common people and
generally for not having made a study of native sources. But
he rectified this mistake in his *History*. Karamzin set before
himself the aim of *developing in the Russian public a reading
habit*. I ask you: can the vocation of an artist lend itself to a
premeditated aim, no matter how splendid that aim may be?
More: may an artist debase himself, bend, so to speak, to the
public which does not reach above his knees and is therefore
incapable of understanding him! Let us presume that it is permissible; then another question crops up: can he in such a case

remain an artist in his creations? Undoubtedly not. The person who converses with a child becomes a child himself for the moment. Karamzin wrote for children, and wrote childish-fashion; is it surprising that these children forgot him when they grew up, and in their turn passed his works over to their children? . . . [Who] is to blame that *Poor Liza* is now being laughed at as much as it was once cried over? You can say what you like, messieurs Karamzin admirers, but I would rather read the stories of Baron Brambeus than *Poor Liza* or *Natalia the Boyar's Daughter*! New times, new customs! Karamzin's stories inculcated a desire for reading, and many people learned to read from them; then let us be grateful to their author; but let us leave them in peace, even tear them out of the hands of our children, for they will cause considerable mischief: they will corrupt their feeling with false sentimentality.

Apart from this Karamzin's works lose much of their value in our days because he was rarely *sincere* and *natural* in them. . . . [You] will scarcely find a well-meaning simpleton these days who believes that Karamzin's copious torrents of tears flowed from his heart and soul and were not the favourite coquetry of his talent, the habitual stilts of his authorship. (pp. 48-9)

[Did] he accomplish as much as he could, or less? I reply emphatically: *less*. He undertook a journey: what a splendid opportunity he had of unfolding before the eyes of his compatriots the great and alluring picture of the fruits of centuries of education, the progress of civilization and social organization of the noble members of the human race! . . . And what did he do instead? What are his *Letters of a Russian Traveller* filled with? We learn from them, for the most part, where he dined, where he supped, what dishes were served him and how much the tavern keeper charged him; we learn how Mr. B— paid court to Madame N— and how a squirrel scratched his nose; how the sun rose above a Swiss village through which a shepherd girl with a bouquet of roses pinned to her breast was driving a cow. . . . Did he have to travel so far to see this? . . . Because he had not prepared himself properly for the journey he was not sufficiently learned. But, despite this, the triviality of his *Letters of a Russian Traveller* was due more to his personal character than to insufficient information. He was not quite conversant with Russia's requirements in the intellectual field. Of his verses little need be said: they are the same phrases but in rhyme. There, as everywhere else, Karamzin is a reformer of the language, but certainly not a poet. (pp. 50-1)

In justice to him it should be said that his works, where he has not been carried away by sentimentality and is sincere, are pervaded by a warm candour; that is especially evident in the passages where he speaks of Russia. Yes, he loved the good, he loved his country and served it to the best of his ability; his name is immortal, but his works, with the exception of his *History,* have died and will never be resurrected. . . .

The History of the Russian State is Karamzin's most important exploit; there he is mirrored with all his faults and merits. . . . [One] cannot deny that his study was a prodigious feat. Its chief fault consists in his view of things and events, often childish and always, at any rate, unmanly; in vociferous rhetorics and a misplaced desire to be didactic and edifying where the facts speak for themselves; in a partiality for the heroes of his narrative which does credit to the author's heart but not to his intelligence. Its chief merit consists in interesting narrative and skilful presentation of events, not infrequently in artistic delineation of characters and, above all, in style, in which he decidedly excels. Nothing has yet been written in our country

that would resemble it in this respect. Karamzin's style in *The History of the Russian State* is pre-eminently a Russian style; it can only be compared to the verses of Pushkin's *Boris Godunov*. It is nothing like the style the author has used in his minor works; for there the author has drawn on native sources, is permeated with the spirit of historical monuments; here his style, with the exception of the first four volumes which are for the most part mere rhetorical flourish but in which the language is nevertheless remarkably well-finished, is dignified, majestic and vigorous, and frequently becomes truly eloquent. In brief, according to the expression of one of our critics, *The History of the Russian State* is a monument to our language against which Time will break his scythe. I repeat: the name of Karamzin is immortal, but his works, with the exception of his *History,* are already dead and will never be resurrected! (pp. 51-2)

> *V. G. Belinsky, "Literary Reveries" (1834-36), in his* Selected Philosophical Works *(originally published as Izbraniye filosophskiye socheneniye,* State Publishers of Political Literature, 1941), *Foreign Languages Publishing House, 1956, pp. 3-103.**

C. E. TURNER   (essay date 1877)

No one now, we presume, would shed a tear over the loves of Erastus and Louisa [in Karamsin's *Poor Louisa*]. The plot and characterisation of the tale have a strange poverty of invention; the ideas and language assigned to the heroine and her mother are altogether out of harmony with their position in life, and beyond an effeminate gracefulness of style there is nothing in the story calculated to please or to attract. The novelist, however, must not be blamed for thus idealising his characters, since anything like a realistic description of life was quite foreign to the ideas which then prevailed as to the true province of fiction, and a romancist was expected to adorn the conversation of his personages, and to make it as far removed as possible from the language of ordinary men. The peasant girl, accordingly, talks and weeps like a heroine, and it is precisely those high-flown and sentimental tirades, which offend us as being so unnatural and so lachrymose, that most pleased his readers. She at least belonged to their own country, and however idealised was not altogether removed from the actualities of contemporary life, and Karamsin, by his choice of subject alone, gave a fatal blow to the classical novel. . . . The power of love that destroys all social distinctions and makes the humble Louisa the equal of Erastus, the squire's son, however a hackneyed theme to us, had never before been exposed with such eloquence; and any defects of local or individual colouring were amply redeemed by the idea of wide humanity which forms the basis of the story. (p. 190)

From Karamsin's *Letters of a Russian Traveller,* better than from any other of his works, we are able to form an accurate estimate of his early disposition and tastes. They most clearly evince his thirst for information, his sympathy with all that contributes to the healthy development of individual or national character, his ready powers of keen observation, his facility in familiarising his readers with the scenery, life, and habits of strange countries, and above all his passionate and devoted love of everything Russian. And if the letters are too often concerned with trivialities, and if the judgments pronounced on the society and institutions of foreign lands are at times superficial, we must remember that they are addressed to private friends of the writer, and are the production of a young and inexperienced traveller. (p. 192)

Like all the writers of his age, [in his **History of Russia** Karamsin] divides his subjects into epochs, without apparently suspecting the artificial and arbitrary character of such a division, or perceiving that he thereby destroys the continuity of history. The sections are severally distinguished by the name of some prince, as if the reign of each separate prince marked a distinct period in the historical development of Russia into one united and absolute monarchy. . . . The whole work is written to enforce the justice of these divisions; and instead of correcting and modifying theories by historical investigations, the events of the past are studied only so far as they can be made to serve as evidence in favour of a preconceived doctrine. The external phases of society are painted in bright and captivating colours, and it is seldom that the annals of a country have been related in a more pleasing style; but the inner signification of a fact is constantly sacrificed to the outer and accidental shape which that fact assumed. For this reason, many of the great characters in Russian history as delineated by Karamsin are instructive and edifying sketches rather than true and faithful portraitures. They are drawn melodramatically and not historically, being made to figure either as heroic models of virtue or as warning examples of unrestrained wickedness. (p. 194)

The *History* is written throughout with a picturesqueness of fancy and a brilliancy of rhetoric that render it one of the most fascinating works in Russian literature of the eighteenth century. The rhetoric is even pushed to an excess, and by its constant employment the author prevents the reader from being able to make any true distinction in the relative importance of historical events, since they are all alike described in the same dignified and oratorical language. . . . The *History* of Karamsin has necessarily lost much of its value in our days, though we must still admire the ease and vivacity of its style, and above all the honourable, if exaggerated, patriotism with which its pages are inspired. (pp. 194-95)

> *C. E. Turner, "Studies in Russian Literature: Karamsin," in* Fraser's Magazine, *Vol. 16, No. XCII, August, 1877, pp. 186-95.*

D. S. MIRSKY (essay date 1927)

Karamzín's object was to make literary Russian less like the old ecclesiastical languages, Slavonic and Latin, and more like French, the new language of polite society and secular knowledge. . . . His reform was successful and immediately accepted by the majority of writers, but it was by no means an unmixed blessing to the language. It only substituted one foreign model for another. It even increased the distance between the written and the spoken language. . . . By reforming the language as he did, Karamzín contributed to widen the gap between the educated classes and the people, and between new and old Russia. The reform was anti-democratic (in this a true child of the eighteenth century) and anti-national (in this still more so). But whatever we may say against it, it was victorious and facilitated the coming of an age of *classical* poetry: the ultimate justification of Karamzín's language is that it became the language of Púshkin. (pp. 59-60)

The intrinsic value of Karamzín's literary work does not today strike us as great. He was not a creative mind. He was an interpreter, a schoolmaster, an importer of foreign wealth. Besides being the most cultured mind, he was the most elegant writer of his age. Never had Russian prose sought so much to enchant and fascinate. . . .

All Karamzín's early work bears the stamp of the New Sensibility. It is the work of a man who has first discovered in his feelings an infinite source of interest and pleasure. He announces the good news of Sensibility: that happiness consists in making the best use of our spontaneous impulses, and that to be happy we must have confidence in our feelings, for they are *natural,* and Nature is good. But Karamzín's Rousseauism is tempered by an innate mediocrity (in the unabusive Aristotelian sense of the term). An elegant moderation and a cultured urbanity are the constant characteristics of his writings. And to remind us that we are still up to the ears in the eighteenth century, his Sensibility is never divorced from an intellect that judges at least as keenly as it feels. (p. 61)

Karamzín was the first Russian author to give prose fiction a degree of attention and artistic finish that raised it to the rank of literature. But apart from this the merits of his tales and novels are small. His later stories, *A Knight of Our Times* and *The Sensitive Man and the Cold Man,* are superior to the rest, for they display a genuine originality of psychological observation and sentimental analysis.

Karamzín's poetry is imitative, but important, like the rest of his work, as the indication of a new period. He was the first in Russia for whom poetry was a means of expressing his "inner life." . . .

[His *The History of the Russian State*] is remarkable for its outspoken criticism of the Russian monarchs of the eighteenth century, from Peter to Paul. From a literary point of view, its vigorous clarity of argument, unblurred by rhetoric and sentimentality, make it the writer's masterpiece. (p. 62)

[However,] Karamzín's historical outlook is narrow and crippled by the essentially eighteenth-century character of his mind. He concentrated almost exclusively on the political actions of Russian sovereigns and practically overlooked the Russian people. His judgment of the rulers is often sentimentally moralistic, and his basic idea of the virtues of autocracy distorts his reading of individual facts.

But these defects have their redeeming points. By forcing on the reader a consistent view of Russian history as a whole, Karamzín helped to understand its essential unity. By taking a moralistic view of the behavior of sovereigns, he was able to condemn their selfish or tyrannical policies. By concentrating on the actions of princes, he added dramatic value to his work: the parts that struck the readers' imagination most powerfully were precisely those stories of individual monarchs, founded no doubt on solid fact, but arranged and unified with the consummate skill of a dramatist. (p. 63)

The style of the *History* is rhetorical and sustainedly eloquent. It is a compromise with the literary conservatives, who forgave Karamzín all his early sins for having written the *History*. But in the main it is a development of the essentially French eighteenth-century style of the younger Karamzín. Abstract and sentimental, it avoids, or rather misses, all historical and local color. The choice of words is calculated to universalize and humanize, not to individualize, Old Russia, and the monotonously rounded cadences convey an idea of the continuousness, but not of the complexity, of history. Contemporaries liked his style. A few critics found fault with its stiltedness and sentimentality, but on the whole the age was fascinated by it and recognized it as the greatest achievement of Russian prose. (pp. 63-4)

> *D. S. Mirsky, "The Age of Classicism," in his* A History of Russian Literature from the Earliest Times

to the Death of Dostoyevsky (1881) *(copyright 1926, 1927, 1949 © 1958 by Alfred A. Knopf, Inc.; reprinted by permission of the publisher), Knopf, 1927 (and reprinted in his* A History of Russian Literature Comprising "A History of Russian Literature" and "Contemporary Russian Literature," *edited by Francis J. Whitfield, Knopf, 1955, pp. 40-70).*

LEON STILMAN   (essay date 1957)

Of Karamzin's creative writing, especially in his short stories . . . , we may sum up its quality with the statement that it belongs to that period of lachrymose, virtuously self-complacent, and decorous sensibility which is especially alien to the twentieth-century reader. His poetry is smooth and graceful in a rather colorless way and his [*History of the Russian State*], which impressed his contemporaries with its eloquence and its epic grandeur, has long become obsolete both as a product of scholarship and as a literary work. The latter is what it was primarily intended to be, for historiography in Karamzin's day was not clearly differentiated from belles-lettres. But among his works there is one book which is still eminently readable: his *Letters of a Russian Traveler,* a vivid picture of the Western Europe of the end of the eighteenth century as seen by a young Russian, remarkably well-read, perceptive, and intelligent, a sentimental traveler who had at least as much sense as he had sensibility. (pp. 4-5)

No manuscript of the *Letters* has survived . . . and whatever can be said of the history of the text is conjectural. It may be asserted, however, that the *Letters* were not actual "letters," but a literary work: a travel book in epistolary form, very probably based on notes taken, or perhaps on a journal kept during the journey, and certainly supplemented by materials borrowed from various written sources.

The fiction of an actual correspondence with friends is maintained quite consistently, especially in the earlier sections of the book; later, however, it is less convincing, and occasionally it is abandoned. But even though the epistolary form of the *Letters* is fictitious, Karamzin does introduce into his book a genuine note of privacy and intimacy. . . . (p. 20)

Karamzin greatly admired Sterne, and there are, in the *Letters,* references not only to *A Sentimental Journey,* but also to *Tristram Shandy.* But if a few passages in Karamzin's book are reminiscent of Sterne's manner . . . , these passages are not evidence of any kinship, nor even of any serious influence. Karamzin's sentimentality was not that of the *Sentimental Journey,* and Karamzin would not have been able to ride for any length of time Sterne's vehicle, a vehicle kept in balance only by its own swift and digressive motion. . . .

[All of the] information and documentation is interwoven in Karamzin's book with the incidental and the private, with the movements, the moods, and the emotions of the traveler. . . .

The variegated materials of which the *Letters* are made up are blended, quite successfully, quite gracefully, into a vivid and kaleidoscopic whole. In the concluding paragraphs of his book Karamzin describes it as a "mirror of his soul"; this sentimental cliché is not an altogether accurate description, for the "mirror" reflects a good deal of the outside world, not to mention borrowed documentation. But there certainly is some introspection in the *Letters,* if not especially profound introspection, and there is a good deal of the sentimentalist's awareness of his own sensibility, with an almost narcissistic enjoyment of the contemplation of the delicacy and beauty of his own emotions, the predominant one being pleasurable melancholy. (p. 22)

[Karamzin's] was largely a cultivated sensibility, and it received much of its nourishment from literary sources. It was not merely pretense or imitation: like many of his contemporaries, Karamzin moved, first cautiously, then with greater assurance, into the new areas of emotional experience discovered by various preromantic pioneers. . . . [Thus,] Karamzin did not seem to be capable of any very intense response to the beauties of nature unless they were properly certified by the authority of poetry. There is in the *Letters* this rather naive admission: "Spring would not be so beautiful for me had not Thomson and Kleist described for me all its beauties." (p. 23)

Karamzin's limitations—and there were many—were largely those of his age. For he was a man of his age, civilized and well-informed, interesting in his very limitations and shortcomings, because they belonged to and reflected an epoch in the history of European culture. (p. 26)

> *Leon Stilman, in his introduction to* Letters of a Russian Traveler: 1789-1790 *by N. M. Karamzin, edited and translated by Florence Jonas (copyright © 1957 Columbia University Press; reprinted by permission of the publisher), Columbia University Press, 1957, pp. 3-26.*

HORACE W. DEWEY   (essay date 1958)

Today, almost one hundred and fifty years after it was written, the *History of the Russian State* still makes excellent reading. It is not hard to understand why it has become a classic and a landmark in Russian historical writing. However, sentimentality is certainly not its predominant mood. In Karamzin's mature years—the years which he devoted to writing the *History of the Russian State*—he had largely forsaken the "cult of feeling" and had eradicated other traces of Western influence from his work. The sentimentalism which survives in Karamzin's history appears to serve different ends from the sentimentalism which filled his earlier essays and fiction.

The first important sentimental passage in the *History of the Russian State* concerns the early Slavs. Karamzin presents them as fair-haired, sun-bronzed people, endowed as a folk with admirable qualities. (pp. 41-2)

[Those passages depicting the Slavs] appear to fuse two familiar sentimental themes: the idealization of national antiquity and the Rousseauist glorification of "natural man". In this case, to be sure, it is not simply the noble savage, but rather the noble *Slavic* savage, who is portrayed. (p. 43)

Karamzin's sentimentalism extended beyond his narrative style. It guided him in his treatment of sources as well. . . . [He] always followed the sources which best fit the sentimental narrative. . . . It is to his great credit as a historian that he did not seek to suppress the other sources—those which conflict, in whole or in part, with the versions which he prefers. However, he does feel obliged to "explain" the opposing sources in some instances, and on other occasions he denounces them outright. (p. 46)

Karamzin had a combination of motives in writing his history. For one thing, he wished to enlighten and to educate. He felt that most Russians did not know their own national history, and he wanted his history to be accessible to the widest possible circle of readers. It had therefore to be "readable". Sentimentalism as a method had proved tremendously successful in his earlier fictional works; why should he not employ it, where suitable, to arouse readers' emotions and sympathies in historical writings as well? The simplicity and one-sidedness which are inherent in the sentimental approach to history also have didactic advantages. With this approach Karamzin effectively achieved what today would be termed a "single effect" in literature, and it undoubtedly had a stronger effect on his readers—at least, on his less-sophisticated readers—than a more objective analysis of events could have had.

Karamzin's historical sentimentalism was a highly moral sentimentalism. (p. 49)

[He] was a patriot. He was also a political conservative in the true sense, and believed in unlimited monarchy as the only suitable form of government for Russia. Some of his sentimentalized accounts of Russian historical events fully support his patriotic and monarchistic leanings. As a patriot, he sought to instill in his readers a pride in their national antiquity with such passages as those describing the ancient Slavs. As a monarchist, he could be expected to take a viewpoint which favored benevolent autocracy wherever possible. Such a viewpoint is most apparent in passages like that which explains the Tsar's motives for introducing the legislation which brought serfdom to Russia. It may have led him to attribute Ivan the Terrible's latter-day excesses to grief and derangement brought on by an external event (Anastasia's death), rather than to evils which others would claim are inherent in autocracy. One may even suspect an autocratic rationale for Karamzin's hostility to Boris Godunov in the Uglič tragedy: of the conflicting evidence here, would a convinced monarchist not prefer that which favored the legitimate heir over the opportunist and usurper?

Though not the dominant element, sentimentalism does play an important part in the *History of the Russian State*. It undoubtedly contributed to the popularity of Russian national historical studies. It also seems clear that Karamzin used sentimentalism to support patriotic and monarchistic views, in addition to achieving an artistic presentation of his subject. (pp. 49-50)

Horace W. Dewey, "Sentimentalism in the Historical Writings of N. M. Karamzin," in American Contributions to the Fourth International Congress of Slavicists, Moscow, September 1958 *(© Mouton & Co., Publishers), Mouton Publishers, The Hague, 1958, pp. 41-50.*

RICHARD PIPES   (essay date 1959)

The quality which first strikes the reader of the *Memoir on Ancient and Modern Russia* is the violence of its criticism. It is true that Karamzin concedes Alexander's good intentions, but in the exposition of the policies themselves it is difficult to find anything except charges of ignorance, stupidity, and uncontrollable vanity. Even the chance approval of some minor government actions actually reflects contempt: so insignificant are they compared to the failures. The whole work is filled with the spirit of anger and of scorn. In this respect it is a document without precedent in Russian history: never before had a Russian subject dared to address his monarch in similar terms. Karamzin spoke out not as a dispassionate observer, but as a living conscience of his nation, as a prophet.

This quality determined the style and to some extent even the content of his work. Written hastily, with a sense of urgency, it abounds in minor errors and inaccuracies. Though it opens with major stylistic chords, which resound with all the rich

tones demanded by the age of weighty subjects, most of the narrative is composed in a conversational style, which in certain parts (e.g. the section dealing with finance) acquires an almost stenographic brevity. (pp. 75-6)

To what extent was Karamzin's criticism sound? He certainly tended to underestimate the complexities of practical government, and dismissed as superfluous features of political life without which administration was inconceivable: a tendency particularly striking in his discussion of political institutions. In certain parts of his analysis he was handicapped by the secrecy with which the government surrounded some of its reforms. . . . He was at his best in the discussion of the financial and legal reforms; these sections are factually correct (save for some trivial inaccuracies) and original in conception. The sections dealing with foreign policy and political institutions suffer from the author's ignorance of the vital documents, and are less convincing, yet they too, broadly speaking, are justified. The least satisfactory part of the criticism is that devoted to the serf question; here Karamzin reveals a complete lack of social conscience, and twists the evidence to suit his arguments. But this part does at least have the merit of pointing out certain connotations of a landless emancipation of which the government was not fully cognizant. In the balance of things, his criticism thus comes out well.

Karamzin is far less convincing as a constructive than as a destructive critic. He has an extremely naive conception of administrative procedure, and rejects nearly all attempts to reform the governmental apparatus on the correct but irrelevant grounds that states are run by men and not by institutions. He is blind to the need of a soundly planned system of political institutions, and his positive suggestions are, for all practical purposes, quite useless. (pp. 83-4)

Richard Pipes, "The Background and Growth of Karamzin's Political Ideas Down to 1810," in his Karamzin's Memoir on Ancient and Modern Russia: A Translation and Analysis *(copyright © 1959 by the President and Fellows of Harvard College; excerpted by permission), Cambridge, Mass.: Harvard University Press, 1959, pp. 3-92.*

HENRY M. NEBEL, JR.   (essay date 1962)

By placing the center of poetry in man's emotions, and making the poet, himself, a fashioner of these impressions, Karamzin took a giant step toward romantic art, whose depth and variety depend upon the poet's curiosity and originality. . . . However, this sensuous approach to art produces a new burden: if reality depends upon the individual creative ego, it will differ from poet to poet and, indeed, from moment to moment for a single poet. An unstable, relativistic world is the result. Karamzin early recognized that a Pandora's box had been opened; in a letter of May 31, 1789 (*Letters of a Russian Traveler*), he curses that "restlessness of the human heart which draws us from object to object; . . . which attunes our fancy to dreams and drives us to search for happiness in the uncertain future". Curse it he may but accept it he must for this "restlessness" is provoked by that excruciating sensitivity of the sentimentalist which, in turn, provides opportunities for the insights and visions of his, and succeeding, poetic generations. (p. 85)

[Karamzin] had been influenced to a large degree by classicism; he admired the rational approach to art while, at the same time, attacking it. This ambivalence creates a tension, a hesitancy to accept the new standards at full value and a reluctance to retreat to the past. The result is a moderation which, in its own way, is a fine testimony to his literary insight and judgment. At the turn of the century, an intelligent counterbalance to classicism was needed to allow a new synthesis to emerge. Karamzin provided this quite effectively. (p. 86)

["Poetry"] is a rather clear formulation of an aesthetic creed to which Karamzin remained remarkably faithful throughout his life. This poem also illustrates an interesting aspect of his creative life: he was neither an original nor a profound intellect but he possessed a flair for the systematic and coherent exposition of others' ideas. In his poetry and prose, he adapted these concepts, simplifying, and popularizing them for his Russian readers. In "Poetry", Karamzin turned to [Johann Gottfried-von] Herder and the Abbé Batteux, reworking their ideas to these ends. (pp. 86-7)

The real significance of this poem lies in its acceptance of the emotional nature of poetry. This was dictated, partly, by Batteux's theory of taste, partly, by Karamzin's reaction to classical poetry, and, partly, by the development of lyrical genres in Russia. In a sense, Karamzin simply refurbishes the ancient Parthenon with more contemporary images. However, in so doing he modified the understanding of the poetic process and freed the poet to explore his own psyche, catalogue his reactions to nature, and analyze his knowledge of man. . . . [For Karamzin,] the poet ceases to be a court singer, precariously dependent on a patron's capricious indulgence; instead, the poet begins to assume the romantic mantle of prophet or high priest, mysteriously in contact with Divine Mysteries. (p. 91)

In "Poetry" the poetic process is conceived as an intuitive response to the world. In the nineties, Karamzin considerably modifies this view. Already in his polemical essay of 1793, **"Nećto o naukax, iskusstvax i prosvesĉenii" ("Something on the Sciences, Arts, and Enlightenment")**, Karamzin indicates that even before the poetic "song" breaks forth another process occurs within the individual: the mind sets order to "innumerable ideas or emotional concepts, which are nothing but direct reflections of objects carried in the soul without order. . . ." Later, in the poem, **"Gifts"**, Karamzin expands upon the mind's function. . . . The authority of emotional judgment and emotional standards is considerably curtailed. A diarchy of reason and feeling is hypothesized, acting in unity to be sure but acting together and not independently. This concept is a stage beyond classical aesthetics where reason was the dominant and dominating factor and a stage before romantic aesthetics with its unfettered emotional reign. (pp. 92-3)

Karamzin's concept of the poet was also revised during [the 1790s] but more directly in a romantic direction. In "Poetry" the artist reacts intuitively to man and the world, imitating the order and proportion found in nature. In the nineties, poetry still remains an imitation of nature but the poetic process now becomes an imitation of the entire creative power of nature, a recreation of nature's sights and sounds and truths. The poet is directly, sensuously related to the world, a man who understands "all its most mysterious bonds". Thus, the distinction between the creative energy of nature and the creative energy of the poet is effaced. The poet now becomes a creator, one with God, producing or reproducing a world in every poem. . . .

[However, talent] and knowledge are not enough to create art. What is necessary is a "tender heart", a capability to feel others' sufferings and an ability to express this experience in print.

Further, if one wants to be an author, one must ask "*What sort of a person am I?* [Karamzin's italics] because you want to paint the portrait of the soul and heart." Here is the core of sensibility: the individual ego, in describing itself, transcends the ephemeral and attains the eternal realm of art. This emphasis on the poet and his personal experience is found in Karamzin's own poetry, if in a very conventional form. Nonetheless, the lyrical ego and its many moods are vital to his writings. (p. 94)

If Karamzin's theories were ahead of his times, they were also ahead of his own poetic practice. According to his poetics, the poet concentrates on the "self" and on his emotional life. It is true that Karamzin does this in his own poetry but the thematic similarity, the restricted imagination, and conventional treatment make much of it monotonous, pale, and trite. This should not obscure his value, however. (p. 98)

The major portion of Karamzin's poetic production in the early nineties consisted of love lyrics, personal lyrics, and some anacreontic verse. The latter genre well illustrates Karamzin's shift of focus. . . . [With this genre he] describes his personal life, the pin-pricks of fate, the failures in literature and love, and the exquisite delights of sentimental suffering. Karamzin's anacreontic poems are dark and melancholic, not quite the normal mood of the genre. (pp. 98-9)

The lyrical poem is a personal revelation and, yet, if it lives as art it has to transcend the personal and become a universal statement on life. . . . In reading Karamzin's lyrical verse, a stereotyped image of the poet arises, and, across the span of centuries, it is difficult to be moved by the poet's account of his emotional adventures. . . . Unfortunately, the conventional image of the "belle âme" dominates these poems and, in a real sense, prevents Karamzin from discussing his shared intimacies frankly, directly, and truthfully. If he had done so, such poetry would still, perhaps, appeal to us. Instead, the poet emerges as a man closely bound to a select circle of friends, nervously enthusiastic about nature, and deeply possessed by melancholy. The revelation is personal to be sure but, somehow, petty and repetitious. (pp. 100-01)

In discussing discordant personal events, Karamzin fails to go beyond description to an analysis of cause and effect. The simple description dominates this poetry, whose images, epithets, and themes are uniformly similar. (p. 101)

Karamzin reveals the transitional role and moderation of his sentimentalism in his poetry. His poetic principles differ from certain concepts of classicism, but they are not an outright refutation or rejection of them. Indeed, it is difficult to construct a consistently sentimental aesthetic credo from Karamzin's poetry and critical essays because of the patently contradictory ideas that continually intrude. However, this difficulty itself creates an insight into the essential nature of his sentimentalism. Karamzin recognized that antinomies could exist in his own poetry, since it was an emotional, even intuitive, response to his experiential world and, furthermore, the purpose of poetry was not to "reconcile ideas" but to "affect and amuse". (p. 114)

One fundamental aesthetic principle emerges from these varying and often contradictory views: The sentimental poet must exercise extreme care in order to present the "pleasant things of life. . . ." He must carefully avoid that which might violate his reader's sensitivity. Realism, violent passions other than those canonized by sentimental authorities, harsh satire, primitive nature, sensuality, and much more do not find their way into Karamzin's poetry. One must return to the idyllic tradition for the clearest formulation of a similar aesthetic principle. . . . The idyll deliberately avoided the coarse and the vulgar, e.g., exact descriptions of the "sordid occupations of the shepherds. . . ." For the most part, it was precisely this tradition which guided Karamzin in his choice of subject matter, the resolution of theme, and the manner of presentation. (p. 116)

Karamzin's tales are a slim but significant contribution to Russian literary developments. (p. 121)

While ["**Poor Liza**"] may be too sentimental and simple for the contemporary reader, it represents an extremely important stage in the development of Russian fiction. (p. 122)

Karamzin eliminates the innumerable adventures both physical and psychological of the older novel forms and considerably condenses the drawn out intrigues of the English novel. In this latter respect, "**Poor Liza**" concerns a contemporary event, a minor domestic tragedy, which like [Goethe's *The Sorrows of Young Werther*] ends in suicide. As in the English novel, the obstacle to the success of this love is the social barrier separating the lovers. But it is only mentioned briefly by Karamzin. . . . [The] onus for Erastus' actions remains with him alone. He is "weak and giddy" and his boredom arises from his egotistical pursuit of "worldly amusement". Erastus is simply a weak creature. Finally, Karamzin refuses to condemn Erastus too harshly and suggests in his conclusion that both Liza and her lover have been reconciled in heaven. It is the same plea for tolerance and humanity heard in *Werther*, [and in Samuel Richardson's] *Pamela,* and *Clarissa.* (p. 125)

The characters of Liza and her mother are defined by Karamzin's sentimental aesthetics and should not be interpreted as a democratic defense of the superiority of the peasantry. Karamzin does not reproduce reality in these personalities. . . . Liza is in the tradition of the idyllic heroines: a delicate and refined creature who thrives on a pure love. . . .

[Erastus'] superficiality makes him unable to understand the depth of Liza's love. He pursues his own pleasures quite wittingly, and unwittingly, becomes the instrument of his "shepherdess'" destruction. His idealistic dream of a "passionate friendship" and an idyllic pastoral life with Liza is revealed for what it is, the vain illusion of an unrealistic, selfish youth. . . . Although indebted to the pastoral tradition for his plot and certain literary devices, Karamzin criticizes in the person of Erastus the unreality of arcadian life. (p. 127)

The clarity and musicality of Karamzin's prose style, which proved so attractive to his contemporaries, is well exemplified in this tale. (p. 128)

[To] create prose that was "pleasant to hear", Karamzin emphasized the sentence's rhythm and balance, its melody and intonation, all of which provided a harmonious accompaniment to the concrete semantic meaning. (p. 130)

[The] harmony and musicality is augmented by such poetic devices as alliteration, assonance, and parallelism. . . . It is actually a type of "poeticized" prose, the effect of which is achieved through these devices. (p. 131)

"**Marfa posadnica**" ("**Marfa the Mayoress**") . . . marks the origin of the Russian historical novel. . . .

The significance of "**Marfa the Mayoress**" lies in its suggested historicity. Karamzin realizes the experimental value of the tale "based on one of the most important happenings of Russian History" and assures his readers that "all the chief events are historically accurate". The characters also correspond to a large degree to their historical models. (p. 138)

To bolster this illusion of historical validity, Karamzin uses several conventional literary devices. The most important is that of an "ancient manuscript" which "chance had placed" in Karamzin's hands. . . . Karamzin, as editor of the manuscript has retained the basic text, only changing "obscure and unintelligible words". Consequently, the narrative retains many historical terms, suggesting the intimacy of the putative author with the place, period, and people concerned. . . .

Finally, an historical "atmosphere" is created by allowing the various characters to make constant references to past historical events. Karamzin uses these references to suggest the continuity of history to the reader and to justify the actions of his characters. . . .

Karamzin, however, is aware that this tale diverges from historical truth. He is not only writing an "historical tale" but also a highly imaginative story (**skazka**) and, hence, has taken certain liberties with real events. (p. 139)

["**Sierra Morena**"] differs considerably from Karamzin's other tales. (p. 148)

The narrator's sudden love, Elvira's retreat into a nunnery, and Alonso's suicide are typical elements of the sentimental tale. The narrator is a type of *belle âme,* emotionally sensitive, melancholy, and disgusted with the vanity and philistinism of the world. . . .

[Karamzin] created several different types of tales during his brief literary career, the love tale ("**Poor Liza**"), the historical tale ("**Marfa the Mayoress**"), and the romantic tale ("**Island of Bornholm**"). Despite their variety, a definite uniformity in theme, characters, and method of treatment can be noted in these tales, and, as in his poetry, this uniformity reveals those sentimental aesthetic standards which directed and controlled his prose. (pp. 149-50)

Consequently, the exposition of "common passions", most notably, that of love, and the delineation of ordinary humans, are central to Karamzin's thematics and characterizations. "Common passions" and ordinary people may be Karamzin's aim, but, on reading his tales, it becomes clear that the characters are extraordinary and their passions, uncommon. . . . Karamzin so idealizes [love] that it is difficult for his characters to achieve, and for his readers to believe. Much the same can be said of Karamzin's characters. To facilitate the identification of the reader with them, Karamzin selects his heroes and heroines chiefly from the middle level of the nobility. . . . However, these people are not typical representatives of their social class. They are either deeply sensitive or capable of recognizing, and reacting to, sentimentality and, in so doing, reflect Karamzin's sentimental views rather than their own unique personalities. (p. 150)

Karamzin consistently uses certain literary devices to create the impression of reality. The most important of these is the unique position of the narrator in the tales. He is the reader's personal friend, who is recounting a truthful incident. The narrator insists that this tale is true, not an invention or figment of the imagination. . . . The intimate relation between the narrator and the reader would preclude any deviation from the truth, since the reader has entered the circle of "beloved friends" ("**Island of Bornholm**") to whom all falsehood is repugnant. In maintaining this fiction of a circle of friends, the narration takes on all the aspects of a conversation, where the narrator occasionally pauses to express a personal reaction to the events. . . .

The impression of reality is deepened by Karamzin's use of local color. (p. 151)

He is not actually interested in reproducing a specific site exactly, but in his own subjective reactions to it. Consequently, his descriptive passages are highly colored, introducing the emotions of the author and setting the mood of the story. In the same fashion, Karamzin tries to create an illusion of reality by presenting ''common passions'', ordinary people, the ''sad truth'', and so on. But these tales are little more than a faltering step in the direction of realism. . . . The characters, their problems and the solutions are all filtered through the prism of Karamzin's aesthetic selectivity. (pp. 151-52)

Despite the frequent triviality of his prose and poetry, Karamzin significantly influenced Russian literary developments. Although indebted in a large measure to the classical aesthetic tradition, Karamzin represents one of the most important forces in the last years of the eighteenth century working to alter the long-dominant classical style and to replace the heroic ideals of classicism with the more democratic humanistic ideals of sentimentalism. (p. 171)

[He] lavishes the same solicitude on the peasants and the noble class and accords them the same respect that the classical dramatists and epic-writers had reserved for the upper aristocracy. . . .

[He] honors the peasant, like Tolstoj, as a ''hero of the spirit'', a being whose inner harmony can not be destroyed by the evils of any political or social system. (p. 172)

If Western sentimentalism in the eighteenth century is associated with an increased political and social respect for the individual and the growth of democratic ideals, then Karamzin's sentimentalism represents a defense of spiritual liberty, the primacy of the emotions, and the freedom of the imagination. It is apolitical and extremely individualistic. (pp. 172-73)

To find suitable means for expressing his sentimental ideas, Karamzin was forced to introduce new prose and poetic genres, which he found in Western literature, or to develop genres, which already existed in Russian literature, along different lines. It is not an unfair generalization to say that Karamzin created the Russian short story in many varieties. The love tale with its more realistic treatment of material taken from Russian life was one of his major contributions. Another, quite different in intent if not in style and theme, was the tale of ''alarum and terror''. **''The Island of Bornholm''** is the first Russian Gothic tale and it contains many of the elements and themes which became standard equipment in the romantic period. . . . (pp. 174-75)

The historical tale, developed by Karamzin on the basis of earlier Russian experiments, is no less important. **''Marfa the Mayoress''** attempts to unravel the knot of the past and deal objectively with emotionally-charged issues of political freedom and political tyranny. . . . Karamzin attempts to illume an entire historical period on many different levels, and this first, feeble step leads eventually to the most consummate of all historical ''tales'', *War and Peace*. (p. 175)

Henry M. Nebel, Jr., in his N. M. Karamzin: A Russian Sentimentalist *(originally a thesis presented at Columbia University in 1962; © copyright 1967, Mouton & Co., Publishers; excerpted by the editors of this book and not by the author), Mouton Publishers, The Hague, 1967, 190 p.*

A. G. CROSS (essay date 1971)

[*Letters of a Russian Traveler*] is Karamzin's outstanding literary achievement in the eighteenth century and the work, which, together with **''Poor Liza,''** ensured his contemporary success and popularity. (p. 66)

[In *Letters*] Karamzin reveals considerable skill in sustaining the illusion of a real correspondence. . . . The epistolary form allows him to change swiftly from one subject to another, to describe, philosophize, rhapsodize, to insert touching sentimental scenes and anecdotes, to alternate nature descriptions with conversations en route, to be melancholic, reflective, flippant, ironic. He succeeds in capturing the feeling of immediacy and freshness he seeks. (pp. 68-9)

Letters is essentially a work in four parts, which correspond to the principal countries Karamzin visited. Linking these parts and giving unity to the whole is the figure of the traveler himself. Each of the four countries has a particular center of interest for Karamzin: Germany—writers and scholars; Switzerland—Arcadian simplicity; France—epitomized in Paris, the home of culture and the social graces; England—national enlightenment, public and political institutions. This interest in turn dictates a diversity of manner and style. (p. 71)

Karamzin's interest in Paris and London, which he calls the two highlights of his journey, leads to an obvious difference between the various parts of *Letters*. In Germany and Switzerland Karamzin had been a sentimental *traveler*, journeying from place to place in search of entertainment for the heart and mind; in Paris and London he becomes a temporary resident with time to describe at leisure and in great detail historical buildings, places, and streets. He makes excursions to surrounding places of interest, but his narrative is more sedate and predictable. His letters on England are the least sentimental in the work; they are a cautious and considered investigation into manners and institutions with an emphasis on the imperfections in the parliamentary system and electoral procedure. (p. 81)

Karamzin emphasized the personal factor in his aesthetic judgments, but behind them stood the authority of an age. His subjective responses reflect the *Zeitgeist* of the late eighteenth century and his ''I'' is not to be divorced from the ''we,'' the European men of feeling. Karamzin's originality lies precisely in the skill and panache with which he purveyed European tastes and fashions to a Russian audience. Undoubtedly it was the overtly sentimental tone of *Letters* which guaranteed its success and it is interesting to examine in some detail Karamzin as a representative sentimental man, the product of both natural inclination and pronounced literary influence, a person in whom it is sometimes difficult to separate genuine response from expected response, true feeling from sentimental fiction. . . .

At the center of the sentimental mystique was the cult of the feeling heart [or sensibility]. . . . It is in his propaganda for the naturally virtuous heart, which confers both infinite bliss and infinite sorrow on its possessor, that Karamzin is linked with Sterne, Rousseau, and Goethe as the most eloquent apologists of the age of feeling. . . . Karamzin, no less than they, praises sensibility and its riches. The heart assures men of the existence of an afterlife, when reason is powerless to help; sensibility is the key to all deeds of philanthropy, compassion and magnanimity, which in their turn enraptured the man of feeling. (p. 87)

A literature devoted to nuances of feeling and meaning and lyrical description could not have been successful without a fine instrument—"the new style," invariably associated with the name of Karamzin. (p. 89)

His new style was first and foremost a syntactical revolution; he strove for clarity, simplicity, logic, based on a philosophy of language, on a clear understanding of what to say and how best to say it. (p. 90)

The letter is an excellent example of Karamzin's mastery of his chosen method, of his ability to marry content and style. Yet the abuses to which his style lay open, its mannerisms and artificiality are evident. In the sense that Karamzin called Sterne "original, inimitable" he too was unique in Russian literature; few of his contemporaries had his feeling for language and harmony or the technical accomplishments to go beyond facile imitation of sentimental words and attitudes. (p. 92)

The contribution *Letters of a Russian Traveler* made to Russian literature was varied and considerable. Although its contemporary appeal is attributable first and foremost to the transitory vogue of sentimentalism—it was both the first and best example of a Russian sentimental journey—it possesses more durable qualities. The first Russian prose work of extended length to be consistently readable and entertaining, *Letters* provided its readers with abundant information on European culture. It is a work marked by an often naïve enthusiasm, but this is found alongside passages based on acute and critical observation. (pp. 92-3)

Reacting strongly against the principal prose form of pseudo-classicism—the interminable adventure novel with its involved and fantastic plot, incredible coincidences and puppet-like characters, Karamzin sought simplicity and naturalness [in his short stories], a world peopled by recognizable men and women, experiencing the joys and sadnesses of life, such as might, theoretically at least, befall anyone at any time in any estate. Literature was not to be divorced from life; it was part of life. In Russia Karamzin's stories were the first to establish this link and **"Poor Liza"** is the outstanding tribute to his success. (p. 96)

[Although his predecessors] anticipated scenes, attitudes, even turns of phrase which Karamzin was to incorporate into his own work, they lacked the command of language and form, which were the basic and essential components of his undoubted revolution in Russian prose. (pp. 96-7)

[Karamzin's fiction] has a diversity and richness largely obscured by the fame and/or notoriety of **"Poor Liza."** Establishing prose as a worthy medium of artistic expression, Karamzin left distinctive Russian examples of stories popular in contemporary western literature. His range embraces the sentimental peasant story, the Gothic tale, the *conte moral*, the historical tale, the psychological character-sketch, a would-be *Bildungsroman*. There is a development from the story with few characters and virtually devoid of plot toward the major form of the novel. In this development, as well as in other respects, **"Julia"** is the pivotal work. The unfinished **"A Knight of Our Time"** represents the limit of this trend in fictional terms, although his monumental *History of the Russian State* might be seen as its logical culmination. No longer obliged to assert the "truth" of his work, he assumes the *persona* of the responsible historian, but brings to his task his artistic talents

for a lively depiction of events, a sentimental-psychological interest in character, and an exacting attention to style. (pp. 137-38)

All his stories are united by his interest in the psychology of characters, in the depiction of their emotions: **"Poor Liza"** and **"A Knight of Our Time"** differ in the artistic means he employs to reveal character. Karamzin's stories show, at one end of the scale, his close contacts with pseudoclassicism and at the other, his anticipation of further developments in nineteenth-century fiction through romanticism to realism. (p. 138)

With Karamzin's increasing emphasis [in his later stories] on the portrayal of man in society and a truer understanding of the complexity of personality there is a subsequent loss of other characteristic features of his earlier tales, principally their lyricism. This lyricism comes from the sentimental poeticization of the beauties of the emotions and of nature and the carefully devised syntactical structure which supports it. In the depiction of character lyricism tends to replace analysis; in nature descriptions the particular detail which would arrest or detract is rejected for the general which merges into the overall picture. (p. 139)

Although the Russian coloring in his stories is relatively superficial, there is little doubt that Karamzin emphasized the "Russianness" of his work from the beginning. . . . His was a "Russianness" which the reading public he addressed, and was partly responsible for creating, was prepared to accept, for his approach was by talented assimilation of European literary example—content, form, and style—and not by its rejection. (pp. 139-40)

Karamzin's fiction, when judged in its entirety, faithfully mirrors his development and reveals him as an author of considerable talent and attainment. His work was a necessary and important prelude to the emergence of the great Russian novel of the nineteenth century and a direct springboard to the romantic fiction of Beztuzhev-Marlinskii and to the prose of Pushkin. Karamzin brought to Russian fiction a clear sense of form, an exact, supple style, a gallery of pale but well-delineated characters, including glimpses of the idealized Russian women of the later Russian novel, the beginnings of psychological analysis, and a feeling for nature. (p. 142)

A. G. Cross, in his N. M. Karamzin: A Study of His Literary Career, 1783-1803 *(copyright © 1971 by Southern Illinois University Press; reprinted by permission of Southern Illinois University Press), Southern Illinois University Press, 1971, 306 p.*

ROGER B. ANDERSON   (essay date 1973)

The biography of N. M. Karamzin, Russia's most influential sentimentalist of the late eighteenth century, indicates that he went through a spiritually trying period in the mid 1790's. His correspondence of the time suggests a deep sense of personal loneliness and lack of purpose in life. (p. 204)

Karamzin's prose fiction from this period is equally expressive of his pessimistic turn, both in its thematic choices and in its production of appropriately morose moods. Earlier Karamzinian tales like **"Natalia the Boyar's Daughter"** [**"Natalija bojarskaja doč'"**] . . . or **"The Beautiful Princess and the Fortunate Dwarf"** [**"Prekrasnaja carevna i sčastlivoj karla"**] . . . emphasize a sense of emotional stability within which positive characters are rewarded by eventual happiness. . . . In tales like **"Bornholm Island"** [**"Ostrov Borngol'm"**] . . . and **"Sierra**

Morena'' ["Sierra-Morena"] . . . , however, that stability definitely breaks down. Good characters come to irrevocably bad ends and there reigns a fatalistic sense of fortuitous human waste. The metaphysical vision of life here is, at best, estranged from man's desire to live by his natural feelings. At the worst, fate is overtly hostile to him.

"Bornholm Island" is particularly interesting as an indication of Karamzin's changed *Weltanschauung*. It captures in microcosm the essence of his movement from positive hope (present in his early prose) to the newer vision of life as alienated from the ideals of noble sentiment and moral justice. . . . Of special importance in "Bornholm Island" is Karamzin's use of the narrator device. The teller of this tale is not only responsible for relating its sequential events; he provides a richly lyrical medium of suggestion through which Karamzin realizes the full emotional potential of his theme. (p. 205)

The narrator, through his rich gifts of lyricism, builds the scanty facts of the tale into an extensive chain of subjective associations, moody nature descriptions, and personal speculations on what he learns about life. The rhythm of his swelling subjectivity does more than accentuate his adventures. His agitated thoughts and personalized descriptions organize those events into the overall production of his private tone poem. The work is a chronicle of the narrator's changing world view as much as it is a recounting of events in other people's lives. . . . The narrator's perception of places and characters, his subjective descriptions of locale, and the general direction of his accumulated moods, combine to constitute the compositional center of the work. Fabulous events serve as a convenient narrative frame on which Karamzin, through his narrator, weaves the work's lyrical cloth.

The component parts of Karamzin's tone poem in prose are, first, the narrator's intimacy and his general tendency to conjure associations between what he sees and his own fertile imagination. Second, Karamzin orchestrates his narrator's subjective moods with numerous nature descriptions. These reinforce his moods and heighten their emotional potential. Third, the motif of the narrator's sea voyage itself, with its alternation between the safety of the ship and the hostile power of the sea, serves to restate poetically the central theme of the work. On each of these levels Karamzin develops several examples of a single movement from hopefulness to gloom. These accumulate and develop into a consistent statement on the theme of life's instability. (pp. 206-07)

The effectiveness of the narrator's account of faith's dissolution in the course of his adventures is greatly enhanced by his refusal to explain what he learns about the lovers from his host. It is, he says, too disturbing and painful for him to discuss. The secret not only piques the reader's curiosity but it drives home once more the fact that there is no explaining consciousness in the story. The narrator portrays his own distraught response to the pitfalls of life, but he cannot square them with any overall purpose or meaning. The reader's feelings of disquiet at the unsolved enigma creates in him a sense of helpless disorder which besets the narrator to a far greater degree. The ending is thus consistent, both with the basic theme of instability, and with the emotional perspective and limited cognition implicit in the narrator's point of view. (p. 213)

The lyrical composition of "Bornholm Island" concentrates the reader's attention primarily on the evolution of the narrator's subjective view of life. He is an emotional presence in the story, and his ordering of events and descriptions reflects the alteration of his own vision. That change is delicately chronicled in his growing disenchantment with hope and the increasing evidence of some hostile force in life which defeats man at each turn (e.g. in the lovers he meets singly, the master of the castle as well as his own perception of nature's mutability and the incessant symbol of the sea's dark power).

The grim, unrelenting hostility which invades all levels of "Bornholm Island" evokes a radically different tone from that of the earlier stories Karamzin wrote. These reflect his own confidence in the high ideals of personal virtue and honest feeling as workable alternatives to life's vicissitudes. His own faltering confidence in the mid 90's leads him to develop the more romantic poetics of anxiety in this tale. The success with which Karamzin transmutes that personal change into a polished union of theme, narrative perspective, and compositional structure, reveals the prodigious talent and sensitivity he brought to the literary craft. (p. 214)

> Roger B. Anderson, "Karamzin's 'Bornholm Island': Its Narrator and Its Meaning," in Orbis Litterarum, Vol. XXVIII, No. 3, 1973, pp. 204-15.

RUDOLF NEUHÄUSER   (essay date 1974)

[It was] not so much in his poetry, as in his prose where Karamzin's concept of the world emerged clearly as a complex and contradictory one. On the one hand, he seemed to accept the Rousseau'an idea of man's inherent goodness, and the parallel thought—typical for the 18th century deist—of nature as the benevolent source of material perfection, the depository of divine goodness; on the other hand, he noticed time and again the inroads of evil, the inexplicable onsets of melancholy, unhappiness, and despair. (p. 177)

Karamzin's famous story *Poor Liza* illustrated well the basic problem, the precarious balance between good and evil, with which Karamzin came to grapple in the early 1790's [during his spiritual crisis]. The conflict arose out of the failure of the hero to remain true to his love. Karamzin stressed the narrow borderline between good intention based on a good and kind heart and the temptation to deviate from the proper path. (p. 179)

If one can draw a conclusion concerning the causes of the tragedy [presented in this story, it is] . . . that the Rousseau'an concept of human goodness must have seemed to Karamzin somewhat naive and utopian. . . . [The lovers'] idyllic sentimental happiness was not of long duration. Liza's inborn goodness, her education through nature, did not protect her, nor did it work for Erast who succumbed to voluptuousness. Karamzin underlined the morally negative influence of the civilization of the city as reflected in Erast who—though basically good—could not escape being marred for life by pleasures that were associated with society and the city. Again Karamzin seemed to stress the inescapable fact that good and evil existed both together, in one and the same person. This complex understanding of our human existence transcended the conventions of sentimental literature and reached what is understood here as preromantic.

Two of Karamzin's prose stories, both dated 1793, exhibited strong romantic features. They were *The Island of Bornholm* and *Sierra Morena*. (p. 180)

The well-known *Song* of the novella *The Island of Bornholm* . . . stated clearly that man was *not* responsible for the passions that nature had given him. Most often it was rather human law that produced unhappiness through a conflict with nature as Karamzin pointed out quite in the Rousseau'an spirit. (p. 181)

In his exposition of this theme Karamzin proved a master at eliciting a mood of melancholy, especially in his descriptions of the sea. The key terms were *gloomy, terrifying, frightful* which appeared in all descriptive scenes. The descriptions increased in intensity as the story proceeded. . . . The climax came when the traveller walked into the garden at night and discovered a woman . . . locked up in a cave, suffering and slowly dying. This climax was followed by a philosophic inquiry as to how man could be led to destroy human life, i.e. to be harsher to those of his own kind than nature was to living beings. The writer provided no answer. He ended this passage with a question, "Creator! Why did you give people the fatal power to make one another and oneself unhappy?" This sentence seems to sum up the basic problem Karamzin was grappling with, the problem of the origin, power, and the role of evil in this world. . . . As in *Poor Liza*, it was not so much the human soul or mind which was the source of evil, but rather evil arose out of a combination of various factors, natural inclinations which contradicted human laws, the negative influence of civilization, and a combination of unhappy circumstances for which only the word *fate* seems to be the appropriate term.

Sierra Morena restated the topic in an even more sharply defined context. . . . Again the writer stated facts, but did not offer a solution, he did not even seem to be aware of a potential resolution. The style of the tale was characterized by romantic features, the awareness of unresolvable conflicts expressed in the polarity of terms chosen by the author. . . . In both tales we can see elements of the Gothic novel, especially in the medieval setting of Bornholm, the dreams of the narrator in the castle, the mysterious, not fully explained events. In *Sierra Morena* the exotic element, the stylistic features of "southern style" were predominant. As in *The Island of Bornholm* scenes of nature were woven into the texture of the story. They established the mood and linked the characters to the larger context of life, i.e. emotional, sensual life as springing from nature that was a constant influence on their actions. (pp. 182-84)

It seems reasonable to assume that Karamzin's spiritual crisis began soon after his return from abroad, i.e. between 1790 and 1791, and increased in intensity until spring 1793 . . . , when he sought refuge in a return to the sentimental concepts of his early youth.

The short essay *What Does an Author Need?* was the earliest statement of Karamzin's withdrawal to more conservative views.

Karamzin retained the Rousseau'an premise of literature as an intimate confession and "a portrait of the soul and heart," but linked it to a central concept of sentimentalism. Literature ought to deal with the refined, it should depict beauty, harmony, and pleasant emotional impressions. In a manner typical for the sentimentalist, Karamzin now identified the aesthetically appealing with the morally good and demanded that a writer had to be a good person in order to write good literature. The author had to have "a passion towards the good, an unlimited desire for the common weal."

It is obvious that strict adherence to such precepts would rule out a work like *The Island of Bornholm,* in which Karamzin presented the reader with a portrait of human suffering and illicit passion, and protested against conventional morality.

Karamzin's second essay, written immediately after *What Does an Author Need?* went further and deeper. The title already

indicated his concern, *Something about Learning, the Arts and Enlightenment*. Karamzin took issue with Rousseau's condemnation of learning as a source of evil in civilization. He defended human progress as based on increasing enlightenment and the benefits resulting from it. Learning . . . was defined as the cognition of Nature and man. (pp. 184-85)

Karamzin regarded Nature as the depository of the divine, as the source of knowledge and goodness. In the simplifying manner of sentimentalism he assumed that there existed a straight, irreversible evolution from primitive learning to the complex and elaborate forms of knowledge of later ages. . . .

Karamzin took issue with Rousseau's concept of human happiness in nature preceding the establishment of civilized society, and categorically denied that there ever was such a golden age at the dawn of civilization. Human morals must have evolved from lower to higher forms parallel to the evolution of enlightenment.

Karamzin then defined the source of evil as a *lack of education*, i.e. enlightenment, and *idleness* which lead to a passion for luxury and result in moral depravity. He reaffirmed that true enlightenment, based on a study of Nature and man, could not but lead to moral improvement and social order. In the simplistic manner of the sentimentalist he concluded that the beauty of Nature was identical with moral perfection. Nature revealed its beauty to the sensitive observer. This led to the elevation and refinement of the soul and human emotional responses. The result was order, harmony, and moral perfection. (p. 186)

[The] presence of evil in the world which contradicted man's basic goodness and inclination towards virtuous actions presented Karamzin with a problem that he was unable to resolve. All of the characters of the works [written in the early 1790's] . . . were basically good, kind-hearted, and yet ended in unhappiness. Evil in one form or another entered their hearts and brought about their destruction. One way out of this dilemma was the escape into an irrational denial of the purpose of life, the denial of divine providence, of the meaningfulness of virtue, religion, and, in the last consequence, of God. . . . Having denied himself this escape, which would have entailed a revolt against society and its fundamental beliefs in Russia at that time . . . , he faced a second alternative, or escape, in the direction of the advice he had already stated in *Something on Learning*. . . . The second alternative was based on a quiet acceptance of God's providence, even if we cannot temporarily explain events in its light ("We will not demand an account of eternal wisdom in its dark ways"), a renewed emphasis on friendship as the foundation of a virtuous life, a renewed stress on a withdrawal to nature and a reaffirmation of the healing effects of Nature. . . . (p. 190)

Karamzin's advice to the poet was to withdraw from society and reflect on sentiments, morals, and nature. . . . This attitude represented a return to the concepts and images of sentimental aestheticism. (p. 191)

> *Rudolf Neuhäuser, "Russian Preromantic Writing,"* in his Towards the Romantic Age: Essays on Sentimental and Preromantic Literature in Russia *(© 1974 by Martinus Nijhoff), Martinus Nijhoff, 1974, pp. 169-236.**

J. G. GARRARD (essay date 1975)

The appeal of "**Poor Liza**" rests in large part upon the delicate tracing of emotions that it contains. There is no doubt that

Karamzin was the first Russian writer capable of portraying erotic emotion successfully. Comparisons of his descriptions with those in the fiction of earlier writers, for example, Fëdor Emin, show the enormous distance that Karamzin had travelled.

One of the most important features of Karamzin's portrayal of characters undergoing strong emotion is their concrete and visual quality. Karamzin is able to give a picture of a woman in love. One of the ways he does this is by the use of physical gesture. When Erast first visits the cottage, Liza is nearly overcome with embarrassment and pleasure. Karamzin illustrates this by showing Liza's actions: she "looked down at her left sleeve and picked at it with her right hand." . . . (pp. 43-4)

Unlike the characters of the earlier romances, Karamzin's do not howl and bemoan their lot at great length; they protest and expostulate, but in general are much more restrained. Karamzin is also very good on the subtle change that takes place in the relationship of Erast and Liza after they have made love for the first time, although he cannot resist having Liza's loss of innocence accompanied by thunder and lightning. . . . The effect of the seduction and Liza's own belated sense of guilt is to remove the atmosphere of innocent eroticism which both had been enjoying and pretending could last forever. Giving the reader a perhaps superfluous and not very subtle explanation of the changed attitude of Erast, the narrator remarks that "The satisfaction of *all* desires is the most dangerous temptation of love." . . . (p. 44)

There is some strong writing towards the end of the story just before Liza's suicide. Demonstrating genuine psychological insight, Karamzin shows Liza coming to the sudden decision to kill herself when her aimless wandering brings her to the pond near the Simonov Monastery. . . . [Her] wandering and sudden arrival at a place which has profound significance for her, calling up memories of her past with Erast, . . . looks forward to the suicide of Anna Karenina, which in similar fashion is triggered by her arrival at the railroad station.

And yet when all this has been said, and one has listed the not inconsiderable merits of the story, one is still faced with a problem. What went wrong?

A large part of our difficulty in appreciating the story no doubt lies in the modern conception of human beings. Since the Romantic period we have been taught that man is a battleground between the forces of good and evil, and this Manichaean approach prevents us from having much faith in the possibility of pure and naive innocence: it is not "true to life". On the other hand, it is important to realize that there is nothing implicit in the events themselves that would make Karamzin's story sentimental and therefore unpalatable. The seduction and abandonment of a naive peasant girl is certainly not the stuff of modern fiction, but it is as good a plot as any other for the time Karamzin was writing. The bare bones of the plot of [*The Sorrows of Young Werther*] might seem equally unpromising and yet Goethe was able to produce a novel from them that can still be read with genuine aesthetic pleasure.

The crucial difference between *Werther* and "Poor Liza" lies not in the plot, not in the "what", but in the "how", that is, in narrative technique, in the manner in which the story is told. Goethe has Werther tell his own story in the form of letters to a friend in such a way as to convey Werther's feelings and yet at the same time reveal other aspects of his predicament of which he (Werther) is unaware. (pp. 44-5)

Karamzin chose to narrate "Poor Liza" in the third person by an apparently omniscient narrator, who sympathizes openly and directly with Liza. Unlike Goethe, Karamzin does not make clear enough to his reader the difference between his own views and those of his narrator. Hence, as in his early piece "Eugene and Julia" although to a lesser degree, one misses an intellectual or ethical voice on this story. Left with the narrator as his sole guide, the reader is bound to feel that he has understood the events and characters of the story more fully than, or even quite differently, from the author. (p. 46)

It requires considerable skill for an author employing this manner of narration to distinguish between himself and his narrating *persona* (who is telling the story in the third person) and also to maintain the necessary aesthetic distance; otherwise, he risks succumbing to the temptation of authorial partisanship.

This is Karamzin's problem in "Poor Liza." . . . [The] narrator immediately steps into the foreground and from his opening confessional remarks one is led to expect that what follows will be something along the lines of a first-person narrative, a recollection of some crucial episode in the narrator's life, presumably involving Liza. Had Karamzin continued with a straight first-person narrative, he might have produced a quite different story, one in which the author's feelings were submerged and his sympathies more subtly concealed, as indeed is the case with his later sketch "My Confession" ("Moja ispoved'"). (pp. 47-8)

Logically, the narrator of "Poor Liza" must either be omniscient—simply telling a story—or else he must be talking about events and characters that he knew—as a witness or participant; he can as it were tell and show at the same time, but he will not be omniscient. Karamzin begins by talking to us as a first-person narrator, but then he switches to omniscient narration and in the course of the story shows us events actually taking place and "goes inside" his characters in a way that the *persona* he establishes at the beginning of the story could not possibly do. After all, these events are supposed to have taken place thirty years previously. First we are led to believe that the narrator probably took part in the events, and then it becomes clear that he had no part in them whatsoever. We are ready to consider the narrator the central figure in the story, but then he turns out not to be. Furthermore, he is not fully realized as a narrator and we are disturbed by his effusiveness: why does he feel so strongly about the fate of "poor" Liza?

It is only at the very end of the tale that Karamzin through his narrator attempts to resolve some of these problems. The narrator tells us that he is a friend of Erast's and that Erast had told him the whole story shortly before he died one year previously. Erast, we are informed, had been tormented by his guilt in the suicide of Liza and had never forgotten her or forgiven himself. This belated effort to frame the story and create an epic situation for the narrator is not very convincing and can only serve to frustrate the reader, making him feel that he has been cheated.

Liza is seen through the eyes of an admiring narrator, who never knew her. If we follow the frame of the story, he is looking back at her through the eyes of the repentant Erast. It is not surprising then that through this double veil of emotion and repentance we do not get anything approaching an objective view of Liza, who remains a pale and cloying figure. . . . Significantly, because the narrator is less emotionally involved with Erast, he is able to see him more objectively, with the result that Erast is a more successful character than Liza. He is certainly more interesting and more important for the future development of Russian literature. Erast is really an early harbinger of the superfluous men who populate the works of Puškin, Lermontov, Turgenev, and Gončarov. . . . Erast pays for his mistake just as much as Liza, since the rest of his life is supposedly spent in unhappy recollection. If there is a tragic figure in the story, it is Erast. . . . (pp. 48-9)

Karamzin suspends intellectual and ethical judgment with Liza, but not with Erast, who becomes a more successful character. The narrator explicitly states that Erast believed that he had found in Liza a "shepherdess" like those he had read about. . . . Hence Erast is acting out a romance, transferring to real life impressions he has gained from books. The whole story therefore becomes a rather severe comment on the romances, verse idylls and pastorals that were so popular at the time both in Russia and elsewhere. There had been many attacks on the romances in Russian literature, but Karamzin does not choose the typical satirical approach, except briefly and gently in the passage just quoted. Instead he tries to show that tragedy can result if a man lives according to the romances and does not pay due attention to the actual feelings of those people he meets. (p. 50)

Karamzin's narrative approach results from his aims and views of literature's function. His emotionally-charged adjectives, rhetorical questions and laments are introduced first, in order to demonstrate his own sensibility, and secondly, to guide his readers and show them the sort of response and attitude expected from them. Karamzin represents a turning point in the history of Russian literature, but it would be a mistake to think that he simply turned neoclassicism upside down. He is as didactic as his predecessors, but has an emotional message that he wishes to convey. . . .

Karamzin's tales were a false start [towards the development of Russian prose fiction], but a start nevertheless deserving a place in the sun. **"Poor Liza"** was written at the beginning of Karamzin's career and it is incorrect to regard it, as is often done, as a fair representation of his work in this genre. . . . His later stories, beginning with **"The Island of Bornholm"** (**"Ostrov Borngol'm"**) and especially the tales he published in his second journal, *Messenger of Europe (Vestnik Evropy)* merit further study. They demonstrate more completely Karamzin's mature style and narrative technique. They might well help us to get a fairer measure of his achievement. (pp. 54-5)

> *J. G. Garrard, "Poor Erast, or Point of View in Karamzin," in* Essays on Karamzin: Russian Man-of-Letters, Political Thinker, Historian, 1766-1826, *edited by J. L. Black (© copyright 1975 Mouton & Co. N.V., Publishers), Mouton Publishers, 1975, pp. 40-55.*

J. L. BLACK (essay date 1975)

[The] political stimuli behind Karamzin's move into historical writing were the military and intellectual uncertainties of the French revolutionary era which, he said, posed a serious threat to the security and welfare of all Russians. . . . Hence, the immediate goal of [his *History of the Russian State*] was to neutralize the social effects of the Revolution on his homeland. Motivated above all by patriotism, Karamzin endeavoured to persuade the emperor to act solely for the happiness of Russians and, simultaneously, to convince Russians that they must accept the existing autocratic system. . . . Politically eclectic, Karamzin saw no contradiction in his aim, for he assumed that Russia's autocratic government was synonymous with both security and the general welfare. (p. 100)

The great writer rarely spoke of contemporary affairs in the *History,* and so his misgivings about matters of the present were revealed mainly through the nature of his general scheme for Russian history. Nevertheless, his frank treatment of Ivan IV's sordid reign could only mean that he had in mind Russia's future as much as its past. Before describing the terrors of *oprichnina* and cognate events, he warned that 'evil passions rage in centuries of civil enlightenment as well' and so that readers could not miss his meaning, he added in a footnote, 'see the history of the French Revolution!' . . .

The starting point for Karamzin's division of Russian history into distinct eras was the assumption that a unified and strong state was the ultimate goal of all peoples. It followed, then, that the degree to which such a polity was attained reflected the greatness of the people represented by it. In order to best serve a plan based on this world view, the *History* seemingly was an examination of the progressive evolution of a primitive society to a sophisticated autocratic one, represented in a pendulum-like pattern of times of strength, decline, and then resurgence to a stronger, more highly developed form. . . .

More precisely, the manner in which the *History* was planned resembled a philosophy of historical progress that Karamzin himself had outlined in 1793: 'the centuries serve as a kind of staircase to rationality, on which reason reaches perfection, sometimes slowly.' (p. 102)

Major shifts in the degree and location of central authority dictated Karamzin's periodization. For that reason, the *History* was often described as a fragmented survey, with too little connection between epochs. In reality, he developed two somewhat opposing pictures of the evolution of Russian state and society. At first glance, the work gives an impression of sharp changes in governmental forms and very little evidence of historical progress. But a closer look reveals the gradual flowering of a modern state, with each stage in its history serving as a precedent for the next. The former tendency resulted from the author's desire to present a particularly political point of view, the latter tendency was a product of his vast knowledge of Russian history. (p. 104)

Throughout the *History,* Karamzin analysed different forms of government as they were tested under Russian circumstances and found all except autocracy to be unsuitable for his fatherland. Autocracy, he said, was 'one of the greatest political creations,' and had been the means for Russian survival in the face of seemingly insurmountable odds. This theme provided him with criteria for stressing some events while ignoring others, and for judging individual monarchs and long-term phenomena. (p. 105)

In his opinion, it was primarily due to Tatar rule that Russian nationalism was stimulated enough to allow for the leadership of Moscow and ultimately the achievement of autocracy. The concept that autocracy and Russian nationalism were inseparable phenomena remained an invariable component of the *History.* . . .

Karamzin treated the Tatar epoch as an advantageous one for Russia because it was only through alien domination that Russians could be made to see the absolute necessity of autocracy and, at the same time, be provided with the means to attain it. The major obstacles to autocracy had been the ancient right of the people to participate in government and the strength of the *boyar* class. In order to best present his hypothesis that the people chose autocracy for themselves, Karamzin had to blame the disappearance of such privileges on a non-Russian force. Thus, it was a consequence of Tatar rule that the *veche* system and the influence of the *boyars* declined until there was no longer in Russia 'any legal way to oppose the prince.' Since such institutions 'were natural only in small states' anyway, he contended that just as 'Rome was saved by a Dictator,' Russia was saved by autocracy. (p. 110)

Characterizing all Russian history before Ivan III as a time of chaos and weakness, Karamzin gave prominence to the growing prestige of Russia among European nations. It was at this point that evolutionary trends seemed to be forgotten and the achievement of autocracy was represented as an accomplishment of Ivan alone. According to the *History,* Ivan was given a free hand by God 'to decide the fate of peoples,' whereas all other rulers had been responsible for their own actions, the results of which 'depended upon God.' On this premise, Karamzin was able to excuse all of Ivan's reprehensible actions on the ground that they benefited the autocratic edifice. (p. 111)

Crediting autocracy with the 'final' victory over the Tatars, he even made an analogy between Ivan and Moses, who had freed the Israelites from the Egyptian pharaohs. (p. 112)

Karamzin's scheme, centring as it did around the evolution and necessity of autocracy in Russia, appeared to be very similar to the traditional ideas disseminated by his predecessors. It was his stress on the role of the people as an integral and contributing part of the state that made his scheme original and modern.

He made it clear that autocracy carried with it certain obligations on the part of the ruler to govern in the best interests of the entire nation, and often spoke of the people as the most consistently reliable force in the state during times of emergency. Assigning to them a constructive role in the evolution of the state, Karamzin commented that 'there is no government which does not need the love of the people for its success.' . . . As a matter of fact, he proclaimed in no uncertain terms that the fate of each prince hinged upon the degree of love or hatred felt for them by the Russian people. . . .

As the politically determined history unfolded, there also emerged an effective characterization of Russian princes which enabled Karamzin to impress upon readers his image of the ideal ruler and of the ideal citizen. In the main, his image-making was intended for the edification of tsars and statesmen because, in spite of references to other, more general factors in the historical process, in practice he seldom wavered from a conviction that the prince was always the most important activator of historical progress. (p. 118)

The dual element of the *History,* expressed in the parallel notions that history had to be interesting and, secondly, to be dedicated 'solely to truth,' was well illustrated in its foreword. Here [Karamzin] gave pre-eminence to the entertainment value of history. The greatest talent for an historian to have, he said, was the ability 'to depict events' and to enliven the narrative. In the same foreword, however, he also insisted that historical writing 'did not tolerate fictions' and that criticism had to be exacting and strict. . . .

The fusion of truth and artistry remained one of Karamzin's objectives throughout the text of the *History,* although emphasis on the former was far more evident in his early days of historical writing than later. (p. 124)

As the *History* progressed, Karamzin's differentiation between truth and conjecture became less well defined. Indeed, he gradually developed a belief in their complementary character. . . .

[However, in] spite of the literary manner in which the *History* was written, and the subordination of it to a general, didactic scheme, there still can be no doubt that Karamzin remained fully conscious of the scholarly demands of historical studies. (p. 125)

[His] expressed aim in writing the *History* was more complex and modern than that of his predecessors, most of whom held an exclusively utilitarian concept of history. In contrast to them, Karamzin claimed that he wanted to 'unify what has been handed down to us by centuries, into a clear and coherent system . . . ,' and to describe everything 'that goes into the civil being of man.' (p. 126)

Karamzin's view on historical writing was a synthesis of several major influences. His highly literary presentation, moral judgements, and above all, pragmatism, were the products of eighteenth-century practices, while the emphasis on gradual, organic evolution of political institutions and social relations were of more recent origin. Overshadowing all other considerations, however, was his belief in the instructive nature of literature. The formative factor in Karamzin's ideas on the national historical process had been the course of events in France during his own lifetime. The image, in his mind, of the great French nation fallen to a level of barbarism obligated him, as a sage, to make an effort to forestall similar developments in Russia. The aim of the *History* therefore was to instill in readers his own conviction that, for the time being at least, stability and order were essential for the well-being of all Russians. (pp. 127-28)

> *J. L. Black, in his* Nicholas Karamzin and Russian Society in the Nineteenth Century: A Study in Russian Political and Historical Thought *(© copyright 1975 by University of Toronto Press), University of Toronto Press, 1975, 264 p.*

ADDITIONAL BIBLIOGRAPHY

Anderson, Roger B., "Karamzin's *Letters of a Russian Traveller:* An Education in Western Sentimentalism." In *Essays on Karamzin: Russian Man-of-Letters, Political Thinker, Historian, 1766-1826,* edited by J. L. Black, pp. 22-39. The Hague: Mouton, 1975.
    An examination of Karamzin's use of sentimental narrative technique in *Letters of a Russian Traveller.*

Black, J. L. "The Soviets and the Anniversary of N. M. Karamzin." *The New Review: A Journal of East European History* VIII, No. 3 (September 1968): 139-47.
    Discusses Soviet interpretation and censorship of Karamzin's works.

Cross, Anthony [G]. "Karamzin Studies: For the Bicentenary of the Birth of N. M. Karamzin (1766-1966)." *The Slavonic and East European Review* XLV, No. 104 (January 1967): 1-11.
    A comprehensive listing and analysis of critical studies, primarily Russian, of Karamzin's work. Cross provides valuable information on available twentieth-century Russian criticism.

Cross, Anthony [G]. "Problems of Form and Literary Influence in the Poetry of Karamzin." *Slavic Review* XXVII, No. 1 (March 1968): 39-48.
    A study of Karamzin's poetic technique.

Cross, [Anthony] G. "Karamzin in English: A Review Article." *Canadian Slavic Studies* III, No. 4 (Winter 1969): 716-27.

An invaluable guide to English translations and critical studies of Karamzin's works.

Cross, [Anthony] G. "N. M. Karamzin's 'Messenger of Europe' (*Vestnik Yevropy*), 1802-3." *Forum for Modern Language Studies* V, No. 1 (January 1969): 1-25.
    Explores the political and literary philosophies set forth in Karamzin's journal *Vestnik Yevropy* and chronicles the articles which appeared throughout its duration.

McGrew, R. E. "Notes on the Princely Role in Karamzin's *Istorija gosudarstva Rossijskogo*." *The American Slavic and East European Review* XVIII, No. 1 (February 1959): 12-24.
    An analysis of Karamzin's interpretation of Russian history, with particular emphasis on his treatment of the ruler's role, in *Istoriya gosudarstva Rossiiskogo*.

Slonim, Marc. "The New Era." In his *The Epic of Russian Literature: From Its Origins through Tolstoy,* pp. 49-64. New York: Oxford University Press, 1964.*
    Discusses Karamzin's influence on Russian literature.

Edward Lear

1812-1888

(Also wrote under the pseudonym of Derry Down Derry) English poet, songwriter, and short story writer.

While he attained some prominence as a landscape artist, Edward Lear is better known as one of the foremost nonsense writers in the English language. Lear's poems, limericks, and stories, purportedly for children, received critical acclaim and were popular with every age group. Many critics believe that Lear, through the characters in his best-known work, *Book of Nonsense,* attempted to challenge Victorian conventions. Victorian society is symbolized in the poetry by the omnipresent, judgmental "they," who hover throughout his work. Poignantly, "they" also represent the social world from which Lear felt painfully isolated.

Born into a family of twenty-one children, Lear was raised by his oldest sister after his father was sent to debtor's prison. Mrs. Lear ignored the needs of her large family, and devoted herself instead to the daily preparation of a six-course meal for her husband. Lear's lifelong depression stemmed from his parents' neglect, and was deepened by his struggle with epilepsy. Some critics feel that his humorous writings resulted from an overwhelming desire for love and acceptance.

At the age of fifteen, Lear took a job as an ornithological artist. Later, he was hired to sketch the Earl of Derby's private zoo at Knowsley, and created his *Book of Nonsense* for the Earl's grandchildren. When published, the book "swept England like a delightful species of plague," according to one critic. Lear's genius is generally considered to be most apparent in the short poems of this book. Its resounding success has been attributed to the fact that Lear's characters are so very human, unlike the virtuous heroes of Victorian fiction. Lear wrote to make children happy, and his work reflects his natural affinity for them.

Though Lear became increasingly popular in England, the climate did not agree with his delicate health. The Earl of Derby financed his voyage to Rome, where he resided for ten years. He traveled extensively throughout Europe during this time, and supported himself by giving drawing lessons. After his return to England, he instructed Queen Victoria in sketching. The watercolor landscape sketches Lear produced while in Europe are considered outstanding for their topographical and geographical accuracy. The travel diaries accompanying much of Lear's artwork are acknowledged as interesting, but not as the best indication of his literary prowess. Today, most interest in Lear's artwork is centered on the nonsensical drawings he created to accompany his poetry. Though Lear's self-portraits depict a homely and unlovable man, the jubilant whimsy of the animal and vegetable creatures in his drawings anticipates the similar drawings of the twentieth-century humorist James Thurber.

The work of Lear's later years is marked by an attitude of increasing despair. Unlike his earlier limericks, which he had popularized in *Book of Nonsense,* Lear's final poems, such as "The Courtship of the Yonghy-Bonghy Bò," poignantly reflect his increasing alienation from formal Victorian society. They are technically accomplished works, which indicate in

their melodious word play the influence of Lear's close friend, Alfred, Lord Tennyson.

In the twentieth century, Lear's work is highly esteemed. His nonsensical writings, often compared with those of Lewis Carroll, are generally considered to be the more lyrical and poetic. Recent poets such as Ogden Nash have emulated Lear's style, but their efforts, while considered commendable, have confirmed critics' views of Lear as the superior poet of nonsense.

PRINCIPAL WORKS

Illustrations of the Family of Psittacidae (drawings) 1832
Book of Nonsense [as Derry Down Derry] (poetry) 1846; also published as *A Book of Nonsense* [enlarged edition] 1861
Illustrated Excursions in Italy (travel essay) 1846
Nonsense Songs, Stories, Botany and Alphabets (poetry and short stories) 1871
More Nonsense, Pictures, Rhymes, Botany, etc. (poetry and short stories) 1872
Laughable Lyrics (poetry) 1877
Letters of Edward Lear (letters) 1907
Later Letters of Edward Lear (letters) 1911
Queery Leary Nonsense (poetry and short stories) 1911

The Collected Nonsense Songs of Edward Lear   (songs)
1947
The Complete Nonsense of Edward Lear   (poetry, short
stories, and songs)   1947

THE ATHENAEUM   (essay date 1846)

[Lear's *Illustrated Excursions in Italy*] is a welcome, because
a well-written, and well illustrated tour; equally calculated to
recall with satisfaction the beauties of the interesting country
through which it passes, and to form a pleasant companion to
the scenes themselves. The author, be he artist or *littérateur*—
professional or amateur,—has performed his task with dili-
gence of examination and taste in selection. . . . A second
volume is made dependent on the reception of the first;—and
if the author bring to it the ability displayed in this, it will be
welcome.

> *"New Publications: Lear's 'Illustrated Excursions
> in Italy',"* in The Athenaeum, No. 922, October 31,
> 1846, p. 1120.

THE SPECTATOR   (essay date 1870)

Mr. Lear has followed up his delightful **"Book of Nonsense"**
by a new one, called **"Nonsense Songs, Stories, Botany and
Alphabets,"** which contains many great triumphs of the scientific feeling for nonsense, and we are disposed to say,—
though this is somewhat rash, without the co-operation of a
jury of children,—some decided failures also. The old **"Book
of Nonsense"** contained no failures. . . . In the **"Book of Nonsense"** Mr. Lear never went beyond the limits of true nonsense.
His delightful rhymes and delightful pictures defied sense—
which is just what nonsense ought to do,—but the defiance
was in itself at once acknowledgment and rebellion. What we
want from Nonsense is exactly this,—a gay rebellion against
sense. But there is no relief to the mind unless there be enough
sense in the nonsense to make the nonsense visible, just as,

> Glowing embers through the room
> Teach light to counterfeit a gloom."

Thus nothing can be more admirable than Mr. Lear's Nonsense
Botany. His picture of "the Bottleforkia Spoonifolia" is one
which would make Dr. Hooker roar; the thing looks so like a
new botanical genius, with its bottle-shaped calyx, and fork-
shaped stamcus, and spoon-shaped leaves, and sounds so like
a true genus as well. So again, the "Manypeeplia Upsidownia"
is so delicious a caricature of the fuchsia that we are not sure
it would not engender a new sense of humour in that pendulous
plant, and make its petals quiver with suppressed mirth. The
"Piggiwiggia Pyramidalls" might at a little distance betray a
Campanula into something like recognition of kindred; and as
for the "Plumbunnia Nutritiosa," it is a sort of gigantic straw-
berry with a mottled and darker colour, and the same sort of
leafy calyx. The nonsense botany is genuine nonsense,—extravagant enough to make the most prosaic man laugh; but yet
nonsensical precisely because it recognizes the laws of sense,
and directly traverses them. . . . If you suddenly substitute a
flat no-meaning where the law of association led them to expect
meaning, children will laugh, often almost hysterically. But
the question is not so much 'Will a child laugh at this?' as 'Is
it the sort of nonsense at which it ought to laugh?' And we

can't think it is. There is not the trace of that gaiety and
elasticity of feeling in the author which is the *sine quâ non* of
all good nonsense. (pp. 1505-06)

All nonsense should be audacious and capricious defiance of
sense, but never go far enough from sense to lose the feeling
of the delightful freedom which is implied in the rebellion.
Mr. Lear is a little too fond of inventing absurd words or using
existing words in an absurd sense. The discovery of "The Co-
operative Cauliflower" by the four little children who explore
the world, is not a bad idea, and perhaps there is enough ghost
of suggestion to be nonsensical about the statement that the
Co-operative Cauliflower arose and hurried off "in a somewhat
plumdomphious manner towards the setting sun;" but when
the children promise a testimonial to Lionel "as an earnest
token of their sincere and grateful *in*fection," the Malapropism
has no particular fun as being out of character with the story;
and so, too, of the statement that "they cooked their provisions
in the most translucent and satisfactory manner," and that after
stuffing their rhinoceros, they placed it outside their father's
door as a "Diaphanous Doorscraper." We can't laugh at this,
and we doubt if children could. Anything that gives to nonsense
the air of far-fetchedness destroys its exhilarating character. It
must bubble up from a real spirit of extravagance and joyous
rebellion against sense, or it is not true nonsense. The sense
of effort destroys its true character as nonsense altogether.
Nonsense written for the sake of nonsense is not good, and
has a tendency to become gibberish; nonsense written for the
sake of defying sense, and in the mood which exults in defying
sense, is one of the most delightful of the many forms in which
human liberty asserts itself. The lower animals are capable of
plenty of sense, but only just touch the verge of nonsense. A
retriever who runs off with your boot to express her delight
that you are going to put it on, reaches indeed the very verge,
but hardly passes it. An animal capable of true nonsense, as
distinguished from mere high spirits, would be the equal of
man. And in spite of little failures here and there, the ideal of
nonsense is attained by Mr. Lear, who, in this respect, may
be said to stand at the very summit of the human race. (p. 1506)

> *"The Science of Nonsense,"* in The Spectator (©
> 1870 by The Spectator), Vol. 43, No. 2216, Decem-
> ber 17, 1870, pp. 1505-06.

THE SATURDAY REVIEW   (essay date 1870)

Take it altogether, [*Nonsense Songs, Stories, Botany and Alphabets*] is a very comical little book, and ought to be most
welcome among all young folk, almost down to the baby. We
should not quite recommend, however, any one to read it at
one sitting, or he might find in it a certain sameness. Opened
by chance, it will always afford a laugh. The "Nonsense Botany," to our poor judgment, is a great improvement on serious
botany, and much more readily understood. We would venture
to commend it to the consideration of the Senate of the University of London, as a subject for their matriculation examination.

> *" 'Nonsense Songs, &c.',"* in The Saturday Review,
> London, Vol. 791, No. 30, December 30, 1870, p.
> 814.

SIDNEY COLVIN   (essay date 1872)

A stout, jovial book of *More Nonsense,* by Mr. Edward Lear,
transcends criticism as usual. We may just indicate the interest

of the preface, in which the author explains the genesis of this class of composition; we may point out the great felicity of some of the new botanical figures and names—"Nastycreechia Krorluppia," "Stunnia Dinnerbellia," and the rest; we may protest, with deference, against the absence of the charms of rhyme in the alliterative pieces at the end of the volume; and then leave the reader to his unmolested entertainment. (p. 24)

Sidney Colvin, "'More Nonsense: Pictures, Rhymes, Botany, &c.'," in The Academy, *No. 40, January 15, 1872, pp. 23-4.*

THE SPECTATOR   (essay date 1876)

We are not able to appreciate *Laughable Lyrics,* . . . the author's "fourth book of nonsense," as it is called in the advertisement. The "first book" was published as much as thirty years ago, and made a decided success. "The young lady of Sweden who went by the railway to Weedon," and other distinguished personages, were then introduced to the public. To go on writing good nonsense for so long a period must be far more difficult than to go on writing good sense. So the volume before us would seem to show, but it may be that it is our critical faculty and not the author's vein of fancy that is at fault. The best thing, perhaps, is **"The Akond of Swat."** . . . (p. 1516)

"Current Literature: Christmas and Gift Books," in The Spectator *(© 1876 by* The Spectator*), No. 2527, December 2, 1876, pp. 1516-17.**

THE SATURDAY REVIEW   (essay date 1876)

No one sets forth nonsense, and the poetry of it, "with such a pencil, such a pen," as Mr. Lear. *Laughable Lyrics* . . . is his fourth work of this kind, and it is worthy of its predecessors. Mr. Lear's great quality is one which he shares with Milton, and Scott, and Æschylus. He uses the sonorous names of remote, and indeed undiscovered, regions with majestic effect. What lines these are, for example:—

> When awful darkness and silence reign
> Over the great Gromboolian plain.

What a sense that conveys of vastness and space, tenanted by fabulous monsters! . . . **"The Cummerbund"** is Mr. Lear's best piece, and is notable for the masterly ease with which he introduces foreign yet melodious words, full of music and suggesting sweet strange passages of colour. . . . The nonsense-botany and the alphabets are as good, or better, than ever; but, with the meloobious lapse of the graver and grander lyrics in our ears, we cannot linger even over the drawing of "Queeriflora Babyoides."

"Christmas Books," in The Saturday Review, *London, Vol. 42, No. 1102, December 9, 1876, p. 734.**

EDWARD LEAR   (essay date 1879)

[*The following is Edward Lear's poem, "How Pleasant to Know Mr. Lear".*]

> "How pleasant to know Mr. Lear!"
>   Who has written such volumes of stuff!
> Some think him ill-tempered and queer,
>   But a few think him pleasant enough.

> His mind is concrete and fastidious,
>   His nose is remarkably big;
> His visage is more or less hideous,
>   His beard it resembles a wig.

> He has ears, and two eyes, and ten fingers,
>   Leastways if you reckon two thumbs;
> Long ago he was one of the singers,
>   But now he is one of the dumbs.

> He sits in a beautiful parlour,
>   With hundreds of books on the wall,
> He drinks a great deal of Marsala,
>   But never gets tipsy at all. (p. 393)

> He has many friends, lay men and clerical,
>   Old Foss is the name of his cat;
> His body is perfectly spherical,
>   He weareth a runcible hat.

> When he walks in waterproof white,
>   The children run after him so!
> Calling out, "He's come out in his night-
>   Gown, that crazy old Englishman, oh!"

> He weeps by the side of the ocean,
>   He weeps on the top of the hill;
> He purchases pancakes and lotion,
>   And chocolate shrimps from the mill.

> He reads, but he cannot speak Spanish,
>   He cannot abide ginger beer:
> Ere the days of his pilgrimage vanish,
>   How pleasant to know Mr. Lear! (p. 394)

Edward Lear, "How Pleasant to Know Mr. Lear," (1879) in his Nonsense Books *(copyright 1888, by Roberts Brothers), Roberts Brothers, 1891, (and reprinted by Little, Brown, and Company, 1930, pp. 393-94).*

THE SPECTATOR   (essay date 1887)

Among the writers who have striven with varying success during the last thirty or forty years to awaken the merriment of the "rising generation" of the time being, Mr. Edward Lear occupies the first place in seniority, if not in merit. The parent of modern nonsense-writers, he is distinguished from all his followers and imitators by the superior consistency with which he has adhered to his aim,—that of amusing his readers by fantastic absurdities, as void of vulgarity or cynicism as they are incapable of being made to harbour any symbolical meaning. He "never deviates into sense;" but those who appreciate him never feel the need of such deviation. He has a genius for coining absurd names and words, which, even when they are suggested by the exigencies of his metre, have a ludicrous appropriateness to the matter in hand. His verse is, with the exception of a certain number of cockney rhymes, wonderfully flowing and even melodious—or, as he would say, *meloobious*—while to all these qualifications for his task must finally be added the happy gift of pictorial expression, enabling him to double, any, often to quadruple, the laughable effect of his text by an inexhaustible profusion of the quaintest designs. Generally speaking, these designs are, as it were, an idealisation of the efforts of a clever child; but now and then—as in the case of the nonsense-botany—Mr. Lear reminds us what a genuine and graceful artist he really is. . . .

A noticeable feature about ["**The Book of Nonsense**"], and one which we think is peculiar to it, is the harsh treatment which the eccentricities of the inhabitants of certain towns appear to have met with at the hands of their fellow-residents. No less than three people are "smashed,"—the Old Man of Whitehaven "who danced a quadrille with a Raven;" the Old Person of Buda; and the Old Man with a gong "who bumped at it all the day long," though in the last-named case we admit that there was considerable provocation. Before quitting the first "**Nonsense-Book,**" we would point out that it contains one or two forms that are interesting,—*e.g.,* "scroobious," which we take to be a Portmanteau word, and "spickle-speck-led," a favourite form of reduplication with Mr. Lear, and of which the best specimen occurs in his last book, "He tinkledy-binkledy-winkled the bell." . . . ["**Nonsense Songs, Stories, Botany, and Alphabets**"] shows Mr. Lear in the maturity of sweet desipience, and will perhaps remain the favourite volume of the four to grown-up readers. The nonsense-songs are all good, and "**The Story of the Four Little Children who went Round the World**" is the most exquisite piece of imaginative absurdity that the present writer is acquainted with. (p. 1251)

[In "**More Nonsense, Pictures, Rhymes, Botany, and Alphabets**"] Mr. Lear takes occasion in an entertaining preface to repudiate the charge of harbouring any ulterior motive beyond that of "Nonsense pure and absolute" in any of his verses or pictures, and tells a delightful anecdote illustrative of the "persistently absurd report" that the Earl of Derby was the author of the first book of "Nonsense." In this volume he reverts once more to the familiar form adopted in his original efforts, and with little falling-off. It is to be remarked that the third division is styled "Twenty-six Nonsense Rhymes and Pictures," although there is no more rhyme than reason in any of the set. . . .

[In "**Laughable Lyrics**,"] the] last of Mr. Lear's books, we meet not only with familiar words, but personages and places,—old friends like the Jumblies, the Yonghy-Bonghy-Bo, the Quangle Wangle, the hills of the Chankly Bore, and the great Gromboolian plain, as well as new creations, such as the Dong with a Luminous Nose, whose story is a sort of nonsense-version of the love of Nausicaa for Ulysses, only that the sexes are inverted. In these verses, graceful fancy is so subtly interwoven with nonsense as almost to beguile us into feeling a real interest in Mr. Lear's absurd creations. (p. 1252)

> *"Lear's Nonsense-Books," in* The Spectator *(© 1887 by The Spectator), No. 3090, September 17, 1887, pp. 1251-52.*

[EDWARD STRACHEY] (essay date 1888)

The late Mr. Edward Lear was the creator of a new and important kind of that Nonsense for the honours of which the pen and the pencil contend; and at the same time he fixed the name of Nonsense to the Art, while giving a kind of concreteness to the things named, by his *Books of Nonsense, Nonsense Songs, Nonsense Botany, Nonsense Cookery,* and so on. With the dreamy sensitive temperament of the man of genius, and a complete disregard of material interests, he was in all things a conscientious lover of hard work—'whatsoever his hand found to do, he did it with his might.' . . . [He] composed song music, some of which at least (for we fear that some has been lost, as he could not write down what he played) will live, married to the immortal verse of his friend, the great poet [Tennyson] whose poems he was never weary of illustrating with his brush

or pencil: he illustrated books of Natural History: and the Journals of his travels are graphic in every sense. But for all these things he is known to comparatively few, though the audience and the beholders may be select and fit. To men, women, and children everywhere, he is known as one of our great humorists: for though his *Books of Nonsense* were made for children, grown men and women, if they have not quite lost in worldliness the hearts of children, delight in them no less than these, and return to them again and again with ever fresh pleasure. (pp. 357-58)

[Though Mr. Lear] modestly puts from himself the merit of inventing the illustrated verse with which he has filled so many pages, none but a humorist could have poured out such a flood of laughable absurdities. . . . Not less laughable are the illustrations of "**The Owl and the Pussy Cat**," "**The Duck and the Kangaroo**," "**The travels of the Four Children**," and so many more stories than we have space to enumerate. But in nothing does the humour of Mr. Lear's pen and pencil express itself more strikingly than in the two series of his *Nonsense Botany*. The botanical names are all epigrammatic. And *Barkia Howlaloudia,* like a snap-dragon of dog's heads; *Arthbroomia Rigida,* a sort of thistle; *Nasticreechia Krorluppia,* like a stem of catkins; the *Bassia Palealensis,* the *Shoebootia Utilis,* and all the rest; are not mere grotesque distortions, but natural representations of dogs and caterpillars, hearth-brooms, bottles, and boots, severally combined into such life-like imitations of actual flowers, that the botanist who would not wish to be able to add them to his herbarium must be as dry as his own *hortus siccus.* . . . Humour is a thing of genius, and of necessity original in each particular from which it takes. If we could call up him who left half-told—or indeed untold—the story of 'Pigrogromitus and the Vapians passing the equinoctial of Queubus,' we should find no resemblance to that of the 'Jumblies who went to sea in a sieve:' nor among the old men and young ladies throughout Lear's Nonsense-Books do we meet any counterparts of Shakspeare's Hermit of Prague and the niece of King Gorborduc. Yet we almost venture to say that the 'fooling' of the one is hardly less 'gracious' than that of the other. In each creation some touch of art which escapes analysis makes the grotesquely impossible, a living, flesh-and-blood reality. Like Sir Thomas Browne, we quote the Latin father and say, *Credo quia impossibile est.* Tables and chairs and fire-irons, ducks and kangaroos, and a host of nondescript creatures, such as the Quangle-Wangle, the Dong, and the Yonghy Bonghy Bo, are endowed with human sentiment and moral life; and all their little hopes and fears and frailties are so natural in their absurdity, that the incongruity of thoughts and images is carried to the utmost height of humour. (pp. 359-60)

[As] Charles Lamb reaches the top of his Nonsense in the 'Essay on Roast Pig,' so we think does Mr. Lear in his song of "**The Courtship of the Yonghy Bonghy Bo.**" (p. 361)

And though we have not the least reason for suggesting that there might have been somewhere an actual Lady Jingly sitting among her milk-white hens of Dorking on a heap of stones, yet we cannot but have a feeling, that the good old bachelor-poet was putting something of his own life into the tragi-comedy of the Yonghy Bonghy Bo, and so giving it a pathos and an interest which make us seem to feel a real sympathy with the absurd hero, 'though he's such a Hoddy Doddy.' (p. 363)

Mr. Lear's letters were not like those of Lamb, elaborate literary compositions of Fine Art Nonsense. But they were always funny. . . .

The good and kind old man is gone: he was content to go, he said. But he has left a rich fund of harmless gaiety to those boys and girls he loved so well, and in their name we lay this wreath upon his grave. (p. 365)

> [Edward Strachey,] "Nonsense as a Fine Art," in The Quarterly Review, Vol. CXLVI, No. CCCXXXIV, October, 1888, pp. 335-65.*

THE SATURDAY REVIEW   (essay date 1889)

Nonsensical books must not for a moment be confounded with the immortal *Book of Nonsense* and its supplements. If there flourishes in the United Kingdom a man or woman of a greater age than four years who has no knowledge whatever of the *Book of Nonsense,* that individual is much to be pitied. A striking contrast may be observed by contemplating the enormous mass of merriment and wisdom which Mr. Lear's inimitable volumes of avowed nonsense have added to the gaiety of these islands, and then casting a horrified eye over [works] . . . which pretend to lay before the cultivated public the results of peculiar and esoteric wisdom. (p. 388)

> "Nonsensical Books," in The Saturday Review, London, Vol. LXVIII, No. 1771, October 5, 1889, pp. 388-89.*

EDWARD STRACHEY   (essay date 1894)

Edward Lear first openly gave Nonsense its due place and honour when he called what he wrote pure and absolute Nonsense, and gave the affix of "Nonsense" to every kind of subject; and while we may say, as Johnson did of Goldsmith, that there was hardly a subject which he did not handle, we may add with Johnson, that there was none that he did not adorn by his handling. . . . His visit to India supplied him with matter for what I might call Nonsense Philology and Nonsense Politics; and even since his death I have been able to add two new forms of his Nonsense, an **"Eclogue"** with the true classical ring, or **"The Heraldic Blazon of Foss the Cat"**; the music to which he set the **"Pelican Chorus"** and the **"Yonghy Bonghy Bò"** is worthy of the words to which it is wedded; and those who remember the humourous melancholy with which the old man sat down at the piano to play and sing those songs, will give his Nonsense Music a place too.

But "pure and absolute" as Edward Lear declared his Nonsense to be, he was no mere buffoon. His own sketch of his life . . . , fully confirmed by all that he has left behind him, shows him to have been a conscientious lover of hard work. . . . And while it is true that, without all this preparation, the *Books of Nonsense* could not have been written, it is true also that they are only the outcome and overflow of a life which was no less serious and noble than genial and loving. Like Shakespeare, he understood that all merriment should be held "within the limit of becoming mirth," and this limit he found for himself in his fondness for children,—"he loved to see little folks merry,"—and in that habit of doing conscientious and finished work which characterises the true artist. (pp. 10-11)

> Edward Strachey, "Introduction" (1894), in Nonsense Omnibus by Edward Lear, Frederick Warne & Co., Ltd., 1943, pp. 9-16.

G. K. CHESTERTON   (essay date 1908)

Many who remember the admirable poem in which Mr. Edward Lear professed to describe his own personality [see excerpt above] will probably prefer it to a longer account of him in prose. It is not supremely important to know where Edward Lear was born, or what were his views on politics; but the information conveyed in the line—

> He weareth a runcible hat

is really solid and important. It was also essential to appreciate the distinction involved in the words—

> He reads, but he cannot speak Spanish,
> He cannot abide Ginger Beer.

And, after reading the poem, we were all quite ready to agree in concluding the verse:—

> Ere the days of his pilgrimage vanish
> How pleasant to know Mr. Lear.

I, for one, am prepared to believe in the eternal and spiritual Edward Lear against all shows of this world and all phantoms of the flesh. I believe that "his body *was* perfectly spherical", and that he did verily and in truth wear a runcible hat. I will have no Modernism on this subject; or indeed on any other. Perhaps there was a sensible Edward Lear who wrote letters and criticised current affairs. But the great Edward Lear, the serious Edward Lear, was the silly one. (p. 120)

[The] solid mid-Victorian lives led by Lewis Carroll and Edward Lear had a great deal to do with their creating themselves kings of the remote empire of unreason. The simplicity and rationality of that race attracted the fairies. They had a basis, moral and material, on which the bizarre pagodas could be built. It is too little remembered that if you want to reach nonsense you must go through sense.

Of course there was a difference of degree in the two cases and even, perhaps, a difference of kind. Edward Lear in his letters is not subtle, but he is exhilarating. Mr. Dodgson, in his private utterances, was neither exhilarating nor subtle. But they were both very good examples of the well-informed Englishman of the mid-Victorian time. And the chief mark of the well-informed Englishman of that time was that he was an ill-informed Englishman. It is impossible to read Lear's letters without feeling how insulated and provincial were the best English minds during a certain period. Here is a man of genius, a good Greek scholar, a traveller of experience, a man priding himself on the liberality of his mind; and yet he criticises all things not English as if they were indefensible eccentricities in an English village. . . . He breaks out, as Thackeray did, into pages of denunciation of the life of a monastery; though he does not (as Thackeray did) actually propose that monastic vows should be legally forbidden, like human sacrifice. But he does fly into a furious and sustained passion against a system which is, after all, a voluntary system, while it never occurs to him to make any protest against the dominance of the English aristocracy, which is not voluntary—except on the part of the aristocrats. . . . Like all the English of his strange time he could have seen that the Irish were a priest-led people; but could not have seen that the English are a squire-led people. And it is surely more manly to follow the leaders of your own philosophy than merely to follow the owners of your own farms. Such are at least the letters of Edward Lear; full of broad English fun, full of splendid English high spirits. But the very broadness of the fun only illustrates the narrowness of the outlook. Even the high spirits only show the low political education. Everything that is English is liberal; especially the illiberal aristocracy. (pp. 121-22)

To say this is of course to leave out of the real Edward Lear a great mass of real humour, of real liberality, and knowledge of the world. Nevertheless, if we drop the real Edward Lear and turn to the unreal one—oh, bless him, how much more real he is! The mystical Edward Lear, the one who wore the runcible hat, is one of the great masters of English literature. . . . And when we delight (as we certainly do when reading his letters) in the heartiness, the good fellowship, the Dickensian camaraderie of that fine old English world, we may add with enthusiasm the line, as if we were shouting it all together in a chorus—

He cannot *abide* Ginger Beer!

But the Lear of the nonsense world still remains a sort of super-Lear, a being far more transcendental and awful.

For the truth is that Edward Lear was greater than Lewis Carroll; at least, he could do what Lewis Carroll could not do. Lewis Carroll's nonsense was merely mathematical and logical. Edward Lear's nonsense was emotional and poetical. The long rolling lines of Lear have the feeling of fine poetry in them, which does not exist in the excellent poem of "Jabberwocky". (pp. 123-24)

> *G. K. Chesterton, "How Pleasant to Know Mr. Lear" (originally published in* The Nation, *1908), in his* A Handful of Authors: Essays on Books & Writers, *edited by Dorothy Collins (copyright 1953 by Sheed and Ward, Inc.; reprinted with permission from Andrews and McMeel, Inc.), Sheed and Ward, Inc., 1953, pp. 120-24.*

THE LIVING AGE (essay date 1912)

[Lear's **"Later Letters"**] is a delightful book and an intimate book. It takes us into the inner circle of the friendships of the eccentric and lovable man whose name it bears, and reveals the hopes and opinions and troubles of the "dirty Landscape painter," as it amused the author of **"The Book of Nonsense"** to call himself. (p. 54)

In one sense the book is disappointing; for in its 400 pages we have found scarcely a story that can be termed new or a witticism worth remembering, unless it be the translation of the famous answer to the question, Is life worth living? . . . Nor in the course of this lifelong correspondence with a Cabinet Minister is there any contribution to political history. The nearest approach to an indiscretion to which Carlingford could be goaded by the pinpricks of Lear's vehement denunciations of Gladstone's later manner is the admission that "in foreign affairs I sigh for Palmerston." The main interest of the book, then, is purely personal—the self-revelation of the fascinating and versatile individuality of the author, artist, and musician, Edward Lear. It is a sufficiently absorbing and interesting one. Through the medium of these whimsical letters of his with their quaint conceits, their outspoken comments on men and affairs, their humorous turns and verbal witticisms—for Lear was the most inveterate of punsters—the artist portrays himself.

He describes his travels and troubles, his work and plans, his mode of life, his financial difficulties, his visitors, and his views upon men in extraordinary detail. He could suck humor out of what would have been to most artists an unforgivable offence. . . .

But, above all, this paradox emerged from the perusal of these letters: the Father of Nonsense took himself very seriously, and, in spite of his devotion to frivolity, worked exceedingly

hard and conscientiously throughout his long life of seventy-six years. (p. 55)

> *"Edward Lear," in* The Living Age *(copyright 1912, by the Living Age Co.), Vol. 272, January, 1912, pp. 54-6.*

AFFABLE HAWK [pseudonym of J. C. Squires] (essay date 1923)

The merit of Lear, and the secret of his survival, lie in his nonsense being lyrical and entirely absurd. It is untinctured by irony or by criticism. It is difficult for us, who have seen pure nonsense so often exploited since, to realise how original he was. Lewis Carroll was intellectual compared with him. . . .

Like Lewis Carroll, Edward Lear was active in other pursuits than the one by which he endeared himself to his own and later generations. Lewis Carroll was a mathematician; Edward Lear an artist. His letters throw more light on him as an artist and a man than as a discoverer of a new spring of humour, though they are often illustrated by delightful nonsense pictures and are full of a queer delicious go-as-you-please drollery, too. . . .

He was sensitive, indeed, to beauty in all directions. There is a strong feeling for beauty in his somewhat unduly literal landscapes; but where he responded to it most was, the reader of his letters expects, in kind, radiantly young men, who understood sadness and isolation, not intimately, but well enough to appreciate the advances of sensitive affection.

> *Affable Hawk [pseudonym of J. C. Squires], "Current Literature: Books in General," in* New Statesman *(© 1923 The Statesman Publishing Co. Ltd.), Vol. XXI, No. 527, May 19, 1923, p. 172.*

ALDOUS HUXLEY (essay date 1923)

There are few writers whose works I care to read more than once, and one of them is certainly Edward Lear. Nonsense, like poetry, to which it is closely allied, like philosophic speculation, like every product of the imagination, is an assertion of man's spiritual freedom in spite of all the oppression of circumstance. As long as it remains possible for the human mind to invent the Quangle Wangle and the Fimble Fowl, to wander at will over the Great Gromboolian Plain and the hills of the Chankly Bore, the victory is ours. The existence of nonsense is the nearest approach to a proof of that unprovable article of faith, whose truth we must all assume or perish miserably: that life is worth living. It is when circumstances combine to prove, with syllogistic cogency, that life is not worth living that I turn to Lear and find comfort and refreshment. I read him and I perceive that it is a good thing to be alive; for I am free, with Lear, to be as inconsequent as I like.

Lear is a genuine poet. For what is his nonsense except the poetical imagination a little twisted out of its course? Lear had the true poet's feeling for words—words in themselves, precious and melodious, like phrases of music; personal as human beings. Marlowe talks of entertaining divine Zenocrate; Milton of the leaves that fall in Vallombrosa; Lear of the Fimble Fowl with a corkscrew leg, of runcible spoons, of things meloobious and genteel. Lewis Carroll wrote nonsense by exaggerating sense—a too logical logic. His coinages of words are intellectual. Lear, more characteristically a poet, wrote nonsense that is an excess of imagination, coined words for the sake of their colour and sound alone. His is the purer nonsense, because more poetical. Change the key ever so little and the **"Dong**

with a Luminous Nose'' would be one of the most memorable romantic poems of the nineteenth century. (pp. 161-62)

Lear's genius is at its best in the Nonsense Rhymes, or Limericks, as a later generation has learned to call them. In these I like to think of him not merely as a poet and a draughtsman—and how unique an artist the recent efforts of Mr. Nash to rival him have only affirmed—but also as a profound social philosopher. No study of Lear would be complete without at least a few remarks on "They" of the Nonsense Rhymes. "They" are the world, the man in the street; "They" are what the leader-writers in the twopenny press would call all Right-Thinking Men and Women; "They" are Public Opinion. The Nonsense Rhymes are, for the most part, nothing more nor less than episodes selected from the history of that eternal struggle between the genius or the eccentric and his fellow-beings. . . . [It] raises the whole question of punishment and of the relation between society and the individual.

When "They" are not offensive, they content themselves with being foolishly inquisitive. Thus, "They" ask the Old Man of the Wrekin whether his boots are made of leather. "They" pester the Old Man in a Tree with imbecile questions about the Bee which so horribly bored him. In these encounters the geniuses and the eccentrics often get the better of the gross and heavy-witted public. (pp. 163-64)

The sort of people "They" like do the stupidest things, have the vulgarest accomplishments. Of the Old Person of Filey his acquaintance was wont to speak highly because he danced perfectly well to the sound of a bell. And the people of Shoreham adored that fellow-citizen of theirs whose habits were marked by decorum and who bought an umbrella and sate in the cellar. Naturally; it was only to be expected. (p. 166)

> *Aldous Huxley, "Edward Lear," in his* On the Margin: Notes and Essays *(copyright, 1923, 1951 by Aldous Huxley; reprinted by permission of Harper & Row, Publishers, Inc; in Canada by Laura Huxley and Chatto and Windus), George H. Doran, 1923, pp. 161-66.*

CLARENCE DAY, JR.   (essay date 1936)

If a crown were awarded to the greatest love story, there might be many candidates, but surely only one would seem preeminent to a competent jury. Most of the famous love stories are entirely too smoky, too turgid. Abélard and Héloïse, Paolo and Francesca, Tristan and Iseult—none has the clear note of beauty. No, the noblest and best of such tales was written by a Victorian, a troubadour disguised as a jester—the good Edward Lear.

The characters in his drama are, first, Handel Jones, Esquire, who is the head of Handel Jones & Company, a great English firm. Second, his wife, Lady Jingly Jones, who does not like her husband. Third, a small, lonely hermit, with the heart of a Romeo or Leander, whose musical and mysterious name is the Yonghy-Bonghy-Bò.

An uninspired writer would either begin with the woes of the Joneses, or else he would have the third person appear in their home and plant complications. But why describe the old familiar details of an unhappy marriage? As well describe the spots in each case of measles—they are always the same. And why dwell on the complications of a triangle? That is quite as banal to free spirits, in spite of the ever-fresh interest taken in them by prisoners.

Edward Lear, being a man of genius, omits the whole business. He begins by introducing us, not to the husband and wife, but to the true hero, the Other Man. And where does he ingeniously place him? Why, far off in the wilds. We are made to feel at first as though he were utterly alone in the world. He sets him before us so simply that we are attracted at once. . . . (p. 86)

When Ibsen wrote the "Doll's House" his fame spread round the world. But long before the "Doll's House" was written, Lear gave us this sequel. Ibsen's play ended with Nora's going out of the door to achieve independence. Lear shows us what she did with it, nothing: except to wreck one more life. But the Bò had so beautiful a spirit that he hardly seems wrecked, as he sails away into the sunset, singing that longing farewell.

And then in the last scene of all, we are given a glimpse of the woman. As the Bò disappears on the ocean, Lear turns back our eyes and shows us that small huddled figure alone on her stones, weeping into a jug without a handle, among the incurious hens. (p. 89)

> *Clarence Day, Jr., "The Sequel to Ibsen's 'A Doll's House'," in his* After All *(copyright by Katharine B. Duy 1910, 1912, 1914, 1915, 1916, 1917, 1918, 1919, 1920, 1921, 1922, 1923, 1924, 1925, 1927, 1931, 1933, 1934, 1935, 1936; reprinted by permission of Alfred A. Knopf, Inc.), Knopf, 1936 (and reprinted as "The Greatest Love Story in the World," in* The Yale Review Anthology, *edited by Wilbur Cross and Helen MacAfee, Yale University Press, 1942, pp. 86-9).*

ANGUS DAVIDSON   (essay date 1938)

[In] Lear's nonsense-world it is not his drawings, but his poems, which take first place. . . . [Here] he invented something entirely new. In his poems, pure and absolute nonsense as they are, he yet found a vehicle for the expression of his deepest feelings, paradoxical though this may seem: and this is the often unsuspected secret of their peculiar power to move others. . . . [Behind the sense of rhythm in his poems] there lies the emotional force that is an essential quality of all true poetry, a force that is derived from life itself. Even in some of the limericks, light-hearted as they are, there is, if one chooses to think of it, a foundation of human experience. Is not the story of the *Old Man of Thermopylae, who never did anything properly:*

> But they said, "If you choose to boil Eggs in your Shoes,
>   You shall never remain in Thermopylae"

—sadly true to life? . . . What a world of implication there is in Lear's 'they!' 'They' are the force of public opinion, the dreary voice of human mediocrity: 'they' are perpetually interfering with the liberty of the individual: 'they' gossip, 'they' condemn, 'they' are inquisitive and conventional and almost always uncharitable. The only people 'they' really approve of are people like the *Old Man of Hong Kong, who never did anything wrong.* . . . (pp. 195-96)

But it is, of course, in some of the later and longer poems that the moving, personal quality of Lear's emotional force can be most strongly felt. Though his method of expressing his own deepest feelings was to make fun of them, the emotion is none the less real: it is perhaps the more poignant. Who is the Yonghy-Bonghy-Bò but Lear himself, living poor and solitary on the Mediterranean shore? . . . **'My Aged Uncle Arly,'** too, the last and saddest of all the poems, written during one of the illnesses that darkened the last two years of his life, is filled with the forlorn sense of desolation and failure that possessed him. Many of these longer poems were written in his moments of most hopeless despondency; and almost all of them have an echo of deep sadness that sounds beneath the gaiety of their surface. Whimsical humour is closely allied with tears: and Lear is yet another instance of this, of the classic pathos of the clown, the tragi-comedy of Punch.

It is a strange world that he created, a world in which fire-irons and nutcrackers, tables and chairs, owls, kangaroos, pelicans, and such unlikely creatures as the Dong with the Luminous Nose, Mr. and Mrs. Discobbolos, the Pobble and the Jumblies, are all endowed with human life and feelings and weaknesses, and so convincingly portrayed that their adventures and characters seem a perfectly natural part of their own extraordinary ambience. Lear's great gift is that he can transport his reader into this world and make him accept its values, and it is in the incongruity of taking such values seriously that much of the humour lies. Yet 'pure' nonsense such as Lear's is more than a mere absence of sense: it has an absolute value of its own; it enriches life with a new kind of wisdom; it is a true child of the imagination, and its native realm is poetry. In this respect Lear is greater than Carroll—not so much because he invented something new, from which the younger man learned much, but because he was a greater poet. (pp. 196-98)

Lear was a master of the art of inventing words. What could be more expressive than 'stamping our feet with a *flumpy* sound'? 'The great Gromboolian plain' has all the mystery and melancholy of the limitless steppe: and when he speaks of scenery as 'pomskizillious and gromphibberous,' of people as 'omblomphious,' of a hat, or a cat, or a spoon, as 'runcible,' of a bird as 'scroobious,' these epithets, even if they have no precise meaning, give a vivid colour, a marked character, to the nouns which follow them. These are words created for the quality of their *sound*. It amused him also, in his letters, to invent new and absurd spellings for real words. (p. 199)

Lear, clearly, was much influenced by Tennyson—more than merely to the extent of using his metres (the **'Yonghy-Bonghy-Bò,'** for instance, is in the metre of 'Row us out from Desenzano'; **'My Aged Uncle Arly'** in that of 'The Lady of Shalott'; **'Calico Pie'** in that of 'Sweet and Low,' etc.). But he did not burlesque him: his poetry, rather, is in the nature of a burlesque of bad romantic poetry of the popular kind. While good poetry confines the reader to the poet's own point of view at the moment, bad poetry, by the use of vague images, allows the reader to interpret it in his own way and in accordance with his own associations. Lear suggests very often the kind of effect attained by this use of vague images: yet his own images are always perfectly clear and conscious. His poetry might be called the 'reductio ad absurdum' of Romanticism. It is here that he has some slight resemblance to the Surrealists, who have claimed him as one of themselves. . . . [However,] Lear's writing is intended to be absurd, whereas that of the Surrealists is not. Lear's effects are deliberate, carefully thought out, selective: there is about him none of the conscious, and self-conscious, irresponsibility that is one of the principal dogmas of the Surrealists. Lear might well have been parodying them in anticipation when he wrote **'Mrs. Jaypher'** and added the direction that the poem 'is to be read sententiously and with grave importance.' . . . (pp. 200-01)

But, even without Mrs. Jaypher, posterity has already many causes of gratitude to the 'dirty landscape-painter' who produced not only a number of excellent landscapes (which pos-

terity has already well-nigh forgotten) but created a whole new and fantastic world for the delight of all ages of humanity. For, though made for children, it is not only to children that Lear's world is open. Children are more readily at home in a world of pure imagination: in a grown-up, perhaps, the entry to it demands an act of faith such as that made by Alice when she tried to go and meet the Red Queen—of starting in the opposite direction. It is an act of faith worth making, and generously rewarded. (pp. 201-02)

Angus Davidson, in his Edward Lear: Landscape Painter and Nonsense Poet (1812-1888) *(copyright 1938), J. Murray, 1938 (and reprinted by Kennikat Press, 1968), 280 p.*

W. H. AUDEN (essay date 1939)

[*The following is W. H. Auden's poem "Edward Lear."*]

Left by his friend to breakfast alone on the white
Italian shore, his Terrible Demon arose
Over his shoulder; he wept to himself in the night,
A dirty landscape-painter who hated his nose.

The legions of cruel inquisitive They
Were so many and big like dogs: he was upset
By Germans and boats; affection was miles away:
But guided by tears he successfully reached his Regret.

How prodigious the welcome was. Flowers took his hat
And bore him off to introduce him to the tongs;
The demon's false nose made the table laugh; a cat
Soon had him waltzing madly, let him squeeze her hand;
Words pushed him to the piano to sing comic songs;

And children swarmed to him like settlers. He became a land.

W. H. Auden, "Edward Lear" (1939; copyright 1940 and renewed 1968 by W. H. Auden; reprinted by permission of Random House, Inc.; in Canada by Faber and Faber, Ltd.), in Collected Poems, *edited by Edward Mendelson, Random House, 1976, Faber and Faber, 1976, p. 149.*

S. A. NOCK (essay date 1941)

Among the many writers of nonsense, Edward Lear seems to have been unique in writing in nonsense his emotional biography. We have known for some time that a good many of his nonsense poems are not, by any stretch of risibility, funny; but we have not understood very well why they are as effective as they are. . . .

Lear found in nonsense the vehicle of expression which other writers of nonsense neither found nor needed; and in that form he wrote about himself. . . . Lear, furthermore, had the gift of writing verse of such beautiful sound that it carries one along with it, sense or nonsense. (p. 68)

Not least among his accomplishments was Lear's ability to inspire his reader to continue on in imagination for himself in the regions and among the characters he only vaguely suggests. It is an ability shared by a number of poets of the "romantic" periods, and one which is quickly appreciated when the realms of imagination are also realms of sense or what sounds like sense. Lear alone, apparently, carried his readers to lands of nonsense, and there left them inspired to continue on their way.

Why Lear used nonsense as he did, why it was his special vehicle of expression, is a question that may be answered to some degree at least by studying his life. His power to suggest, and his gift of music we can only be thankful for. (p. 69)

Because he was so happily at home among children, because he could think like a child, he was able to delight children with his "nonsenses". Lear was able to think like a child, perhaps because he had never had much opportunity to exercise his imagination as a child; perhaps because in his lonely childhood he had only his thoughts for company and had never forgotten them; and perhaps because his own timidity and feeling of insecurity among adults made him more sympathetic than most men to the childish way of thinking. In any case, in his verses he wrote about such things as delight children, and in his illustrations he gave them pictures such as they tried to draw themselves, but could not.

It is in these illustrations that we see Lear's complete sympathy with children. If a child with his childish imagination were a competent draftsman, he might draw pictures like Edward Lear's. Certainly a competent draftsman, like Lear, who could think [like] a child, could draw pictures immediately appealing to children. In Lear's drawings we have the childish point of view, the childish disproportion of elements, the childish omission of everything except what is absolutely essential. Perhaps, however, what is most important is that in these drawings there is the same serene madness which pervades childish attempts at art. (p. 72)

Children's drawings are all out of proportion; limbs and features are stuck on in most surprising places; the actions of people and animals are quite fantastic; and yet there is consistency. As far as representation of the world may go, children's drawings are utterly mad; but they are, at the same time, serene. . . .

This serene madness is characteristic of Lear. His characters have the preposterous appearance of children's characters, and the assured rightness in their strange environment. The principal difference is that Lear knew exactly what he wanted to do and made his characters do exactly as he planned.

One is never in doubt about one of Lear's characters. One always knows what he is doing and how he feels when he is doing it. The frown which adorned the face of the old person of Down; the expression of amazement on the face of the old man in a casement; the expressiveness of countenance and posture in the old man who sat on a chair till he died of despair—all these are the work of the capable draftsman. . . .

On the other hand, because Lear was in his time, and according to some, for all time, the supreme artist in nonsense, he delighted adults as well as children. Because his childish drawings are so extremely expressive; because his versification is so finely managed; because his vocabulary is so stimulating and so inevitable, Edward Lear charms the sophisticated quite as much as he charms the child. All who relish accuracy in choice of words, exquisite modulation of English verse, and complete and satisfying expression of ideas are delighted with Edward Lear. Perhaps he is expressing for them as they would express it themselves if they could, delight in things childish and secure. (p. 73)

Probably for most artists, whatever public they work for, there is still one ultimate public who must be satisfied and usually never is: the artist himself. John Milton had to write *Paradise Lost, Paradise Regained,* and *Samson Agonistes* before he could

drop his pen "with calm of mind, all passion spent". Lear, since he was an honest man and an honest artist, knew his shortcomings, and for the same reason, appreciated his "nonsenses". They satisfied him as they satisfied children and delighted adults. Here was his medium of expression, the medium by which he could reach the audience he most desired to reach, children and Edward Lear. (p. 74)

His mind roamed as well as his body. Of course in his limericks he had to use geographical names from all over the world; but in those nonsense poems which are self-expressive rather than amusing the characters are always roaming. Some of them at the end of their wanderings find happiness, some do not. Even in the "nonsenses" which he wrote for his youthful friends, the characters are everlastingly on the go. They don't belong anywhere, except perhaps the Jumblies. (pp. 75-6)

[Perhaps] Lear was seeking not so much a wife as a mother, and was more or less unconsciously repelled from a woman who would be for him a wife rather than a mother. Certainly his bachelorhood increased his loneliness, his isolation from his fellows; and that it affected him deeply, we may see from some of his poems.

The Owl and the Pussy-cat are happy because they married, and at the end of their wanderings they can dance by the light of the moon. The Jumblies are happy because their relationship is one of intimate and perfect fellowship: it is the Jumblies, and not individual members of the clan, who go gallivanting about the world and return happy and successful. The personages in Lear's poems who enjoy companionship such as he never found are the happy ones.

On the other hand, the Yonghy-Bonghy-Bò, who seeks in vain to marry the Lady Jingly Jones, sails away on his turtle into the setting sun in utter despair. Perhaps Edward Lear never proposed to his love, as did the Yonghy-Bonghy-Bò, only to be rejected; but perhaps Edward Lear feared that if he did propose he would be rejected. . . .

Even more than the Yonghy-Bonghy-Bò, the Dong arouses our sympathy. He fell in love with a Jumbly girl who came to his shores with the other Jumblies. From her he learned the Jumbly songs, and to her he became utterly devoted. Then with her own kind she departed and left the Dong alone to lament her going. (p. 76)

We can hardly find out surely what Edward Lear was thinking about when he wrote about the Dong. But we can remember that the man who wrote thus was one who was, and felt himself to be, different from his fellows; who realized that nonsense, and not his serious profession, was his genuine art; who loved but saw the one he loved content with her own kind rather than with him; and who nearsightedly followed a disastrous nose. He it was who wrote most musically about the Dong, whose love departed from him to remain with her own kind, who squeaked on his pipe as he darkling followed his enormous nose. . . .

Lear was the first and, in some respects, the greatest of the three famous British writers of nonsense. Like Lewis Carroll and W. S. Gilbert, he was a master of versification and vocabulary: he could invariably find or invent the precise word. Like W. S. Gilbert, he had facility in inventing geography and inhabitants of strange places. Lear's geography is more comprehensive and more detailed; and Lear carried his countries from poem to poem, with the same flora and fauna. (p. 77)

Both Gilbert and Carroll, with their sharp, bright descriptions, make their characters clear and definite personalities; and the illustrations by Tenniel and Gilbert further distinguish the individuals as definitely recognizable individuals. Lear is vague. Of the Jumblies, we know that their heads were green and their hands were blue, and that they could sing and sail in a sieve. His pictures of them are equally uninforming: they are merely little people that look like a lot of Edward Lear's other little people. (pp. 77-8)

We have a pretty good idea of the Owl and the Pussy-cat because we have seen owls and pussy-cats; we even have a pretty fair idea of the Yonghy-Bonghy-Bò; but they stand out unusually clear among Lear's creations, most of which are like dream figures.

On the other hand, these dream-like, uncertain, undefined creatures, although they lack the realistic detail of the Duchess or the Red Queen, have still such definite personalities that their fates are of considerable importance to the sympathetic reader. Unhuman as they are, they are not inhuman. . . .

There is very little to be said for the esthetic effects of Lear's limericks. The limerick does not lend itself to music. Some of the poems, however, are as musical as any lyrics in the language, and they are the best known, with the exception of the Dong, of all Lear's works. (p. 78)

Lear was a composer of music: not the prolific composer of very good music, but the occasional composer of satisfactory music. His settings to some of his own poems are perhaps the best he ever wrote, and permit us to guess that he wrote his poems with an ear very attentive to musical possibilities. (p. 79)

There is a vagueness in Lear's poems which entrances and leads on the reader, which induces the reader to call up in his own mind the details of the landscape only suggested. Somehow or other, the lands where the Jumblies live are among the most mysterious of poetic realms. Why it is so, one might argue indefinitely: whether the mystery lies in choice of words, or in sound of syllables. (p. 80)

Lear has done in nonsense what Milton did in the epic, what Collins did in pastoral poetry, what Coleridge did in a realm of imagination nobody else has quite reached: he has sung his readers into fairyland of one sort or another, given him a few directions with large gestures, and inspired him to go on.

In other words, whereas Carroll, Gilbert, and others present to the reader a complete, and in some cases almost documented picture or act which the reader may accept and understand, Lear does hardly more than stir the reader to go adventuring for himself. Lewis Carroll did for a moment offer his readers opportunity to go on their own adventures when he wrote *Jabberwocky;* but in the conversation of Humpty Dumpty he very soon afterwards gave complete maps and charts, together with all necessary detailed information. The reader of Edward Lear must go out and meet for himself the Dong and the Yonghy-Bonghy-Bò. If he will, he may become one of "those who watch at that midnight hour From Hall or Terrace or lofty Tower;" and with them he may cry, "The Dong! The Dong!" But first he has to find his way to them.

In short, Edward Lear has written the beginnings of poems; and in so doing he has permitted the reader to become part of his "scheme of things entire." He has made of his reader a fellow adventurer, a creator, and consequently a vastly more sympathetic individual than he might be in the company of Lewis Carroll or W. S. Gilbert. Nobody wants to get acquainted with Gentle Alice Brown; nobody has a great desire to meet the Walrus and the Carpenter; but the Dong, and the Yonghy-Bonghy-Bò, and the Jumblies—like Edward Lear himself, they would be welcome anywhere the important things of life are not very important, and where beauty and gentleness are in all things. (p. 81)

S. A. Nock, "Lacrimae Nugarum: Edward Lear of the Nonsense Verses," in The Sewanee Review *(reprinted by permission of the editor; 1941 by The University of the South), Vol. XLIX, No. 1, Winter, 1941, pp. 68-81.*

HOLBROOK JACKSON   (essay date 1947)

Lear was no ordinary writer turning out humorous books for a living, nor were those books his only productions; on the contrary his nonsense began as the sideline of a professional life devoted to the illustration of books, mainly ornithological, and the pursuit of the picturesque for those landscapes which were latterly his main source of revenue. At the same time nonsense was not merely an occasional, still less an idle occupation. What appeared to begin and end in the casual amusement of children was actually a method of amusing, or, better, diverting himself. His excursions into the realm of nonsense were certainly occasional but the occasions were so frequent as to pervade the whole of his life, ultimately becoming a continuous as well as a formal medium of expression. Nonsense was the safety-valve of his consciousness responding to most of his approaches to himself and his environment. It became ultimately a world in itself specially created by him as a refuge from the trials and irritations of life: ill-health, lack of means, and, above all, an over-strung sensibility. (pp. ix-x)

There was something preposterous about Edward Lear, amiably preposterous. He might have stepped out of one of his own nonsense books, and he seemed to know it and to make the most of it. He pokes fun at himself even when he is serious, and his letters dance with caricatures of his own plump figure, high-domed brow, and bushy whiskers. (p. xi)

[His] nonsense drawings and their attendant verse and prose reveal an invincible boyishness. On one side Lear was as old as the rocks he painted, on another as young as the children he loved or the child he awoke in the adults who loved him. This plump, bewhiskered man with high-domed brow, small, spectacled eyes and loose-fitting clothes was ineradicably childlike, although he must have looked what he would have called an 'old cove' nearly all his life. But in spite of that there was something of him that would not grow up: his peter-pantheism was no pose. (p. xiii)

Lear's nonsense is no mere tissue of quips and jokes. It is a thing in itself in a world of its own, with its own physiography and natural history; a world in which the nature of things has been changed, whilst retaining its own logical and consistent idiom. He expresses a nonsensical condition which is peculiar to himself and necessary to his serenity, and it may be that this fantastic world gratifies for him a desire which we all share to some extent, probably more than we are willing to admit, and which he seems to share, by anticipation, with the surrealists of our own time. (p. xxiii)

Lear is an adept at the game of monkeying with words. Like Rabelais and Swift and Joyce he has a genius for fantastic verbal adventures, but often they do little more than play tricks with established spelling. The more familiar the words the more he is tempted to tamper with them. The habit is ingrained, the result not alone of a natural love of the whimsical and an indomitable sense of fun, but it is also, as he himself is aware, an instinctive effort to bridge a gap between idea and expression. . . .

It is natural that Lear should have fallen, as we should now believe, into the then widespread vogue of punning. But he is no slavish imitator of Lamb and Hood. Even his puns have a style of their own which often trips over the boundaries of humour into his own rightful realm of nonsense. (p. xxiv)

But as he is not content with being a punster, he quickly enters into the fun of any verbal trick new or old, and when Charles Dickens popularises Wellerisms, Lear becomes an easy convert to that once fashionable kind of humour: 'On the whole, as the morbid and mucilaginous monkey said when he climbed up to the top of the Palm-tree and found no fruit there, one can't depend upon dates.' (p. xxv)

Phonetic spelling plays a considerable part in many of his nonsense words, and often a complete effect is obtained by this process as in 'yott' (yacht), 'rox' (rocks), 'korn' (corn), and 'toppix' (topics). (pp. xxv-xxvi)

It is none of these verbal adventures, however, that reveal Edward Lear at his best as a word-maker. In the examples I have given he is doing little more than amusing himself and his friends by following a fashion of the moment for that sort of thing, although his success indicates both a natural gift for word-building and a need for that kind of expression. His inventiveness is extraordinary and what nearly always begins as fun often ends in an extension of the boundaries of expression. His imagination is always at its best when it has some concrete form or idea for its objective. This is proved by the nomenclature of his nonsense creatures. In this realm he has only one peer—Lewis Carroll. But where the creator of *Alice* has some half dozen masterpieces to his credit such as the *Jabberwock, Bandersnatch, Snark* and *Boojum,* Lear has a whole zooful of distinguished creatures many of which, like the *Pobble* and the *Quangle Wangle,* have become common objects of the popular imagination. (pp. xxvi-xxvii)

> *Holbrook Jackson, "Edward Lear: Laureate of Nonsense," in* The Complete Nonsense of Edward Lear *by Edward Lear, edited by Holbrook Jackson (reprinted by permission of Faber and Faber Ltd.), Faber and Faber, 1947 (and reprinted by Dover Publications, Inc., 1951, pp. ix-xxviii).*

C. M. BOWRA   (essay date 1949)

Like Poe, [Edward Lear] was a prey to melancholy and a haunting sense of failure, and, like Poe, he transmuted his misery into melodies in which the music of words is much more important than their sense. He is a master of glowing rhythms. His nonsense poems bewitch the ear, and compared with him even Lewis Carroll has no more than a logical or mathematical elegance. Nor are Lear's subjects entirely alien to a Romantic taste. He too has a predilection for remote places and unusual happenings, even something like Wordsworth's interest in a primitive simplicity of life. Are not most elements of Romantic poetry to be found in the strange situation of the Yonghy-Bonghy-Bò? . . . The accomplishment [in the tale of the Yonghy-Bonghy-Bò] is perhaps greater than anything in Poe, but the methods are the same as Poe's, from the ingeniously interrelated rhymes to the emphatic repetitions, and their origin in Lear's personal history bears some resemblance to the sources of Poe's inspiration. . . . In his emotions and his

methods, Lear bears a startling resemblance to some of the Romantic poets, and his unprecedented art raises awkward questions about their achievement.

Lear's nonsense poetry is literally a *reductio ad absurdum* of Romantic methods, and especially of the belief in vagueness. He differs from his grave models not in his means but in his end. He wished to write nonsense, and with the insight of genius saw that the Romantic technique was perfectly suited to it. With him the Romantic indefiniteness passes beautifully into absurdity, and his own inchoate sorrows vanish in the divine light of nonsense. He has indeed his own kind of imagination which is accompanied by a special insight. By transforming his state into that of the Yonghy-Bonghy-Bò or the Quangle Wangle Quee or the Dong with the Luminous Nose, he both invents enchanting figures of fancy and is able to have a clearer insight into his own troubles by placing them in an unexpected perspective. Lear showed how close the Romantic vagueness was to nonsense, and exploited it for his own purposes. The result is outside all literary canons, but none the less miraculous and magical. Lear chose his means deliberately in a full knowledge of their worth. (pp. 278-80)

> *C. M. Bowra, "The Romantic Achievement," in his* The Romantic Imagination *(copyright 1949 by the President and Fellows of Harvard College; copyright renewed © 1977 by the Estates Bursar as Executor of Cecil Maurice Bowra; excerpted by permission), Cambridge, Mass.: Harvard University Press, 1949, pp. 271-94.**

PETER QUENNELL   (essay date 1952)

In all the best of [Lear's] incomparable productions, there presently emerges an uncouth and lonely figure—a Dong or a Pobble or a Yonghy-Bonghy-Bo—who strays across the dream-landscape with an air of romantic disenchantment, bound on some endless quest or impelled by the recollection of some mysterious sorrow. . . . It is difficult to avoid the conclusion that this figure is Lear himself, or bears the same relation to Lear that Childe Harold bore to Byron, a symbol of his disillusionment, a projection of his own interior restlessness. Among the poems that I personally enjoy most, there is only one on which the romantic shadow does not fall. Uncle Arly comes to a lugubrious end; the Pobble's excursion terminates in disaster; and Yonghy-Bonghy-Bo, irremediably crossed in love, bids a Byronic farewell to the pleasant coast he had inhabited. . . . The Owl and the Pussy-Cat provide a lyrical exception. Their journey alone—a journey is usually hinted at or described in Edward Lear's poems: he was himself an inveterate traveller, and incurably explorative—winds up with lover's meeting and with the marriage of true minds, as the ill-assorted yet harmonious pair dance hand-in-hand down a shimmering beach beneath the tropic moonlight. Otherwise the note of frustration prevails—attenuated and subtilised by the climate of the dream-world, yet none the less perceptible; for our waking thoughts are bound to invade our dreams, and there is no lasting escape, even in fantasy, from the painful stresses and strains of everyday experience. (pp. 98-9)

It is by his verses that Edward Lear will always be remembered, for nowhere else does the peculiar quality of his imagination—mocking yet plaintive, ludicrous yet elegiac—reveal itself so clearly; but among his most fascinating products is his *Nonsense Botany.* For some tastes it may be a little too whimsical; but the whimsicality of the effect is redeemed by its breathtaking extravagance. One is reminded of Bosch or Breughel, of witches' sabbaths and Temptations of St. Anthony, in which *homunculi* creep out of eggs, half-human fishes crawl with legs on dry land, and sinister domestic utensils peer with glassy orbs from crevices. The inspiration is the same. How strangely different the handling of it! The moral influence of the Victorian age, disinfecting, refining, has extended even to the land of nightmares; yet the innocence of the symbolism and the prosaic neatness of the draughtsmanship make Lear's botanical specimens still more odd and terrifying. A plant blossoms in a slug, the *Sophtsluggia Glutinosa.* Delicate stems are garlanded with boots and shoes, or burst into pigs and fiddles, blue-bottles, combs, knives and forks, buns, tea-kettles and barking dogs. *Pollybirdia Singularis* (of which the petals are formed of five impassive parakeets), *Cockatooca Superba* and *Manypeeplia Upsidownia* are exotics that would not be out of place in the man-eating vegetation of an Amazonian jungle. (pp. 100-01)

[His] sense of the strangeness of life (which he could scarcely hope to express in the meticulous representation of foreign birds and landscapes) escaped and overflowed into his nonsense verse and pictures; and it was the mixture of adult perplexity and childish sensibility that gave his imaginative escapades their special grace and brilliance. (p. 101)

> Peter Quennell, "Edward Lear," in his Singular Preference: Portraits & Essays *(reprinted by permission of Curtis Brown Ltd as agents for the author; in Canada by William Collins Sons & Co Ltd),* Collins, 1952, pp. 95-101.

CLIFTON FADIMAN (essay date 1955)

Whatever Lear did that was of his time is dead. When he created a time and space of his own choosing, he got a handhold on immortality. Of all his contemporaries Lear venerated Tennyson most. (p. 411)

The central note of Lear's nonsense (and Carroll's too) is rebellion, even subversion. All of Lear's songs are songs of escape. Many of the limericks are too:

> There was an Old Person of Ischia,
> Whose conduct grew friskier and
>   friskier;
>   He danced hornpipes and jigs,
>   And ate thousands of figs,
> That lively old Person of Ischia.

The Ischian is Lear's expression of impatience with the restraints normal experience imposes on us. The Ischian conduct is organized defiance, but a defiance that is clearly not intended to be taken seriously or to lead to action on the part of the reader. (In such a case Lear would have been writing satire.) Nonsense is harmless; its appeal is not to the strongly reasoning mind, but merely to that deep fund of impatient emotion in us which is always, no matter how censored or throttled, craving to upset routine, defy the rules, and escape from the dull wisdom of our superiors. Here lies its great appeal to children; and here also lies its appeal to the children concealed within the grownups. The greatest men—in fact *especially* the greatest—feel this appeal precisely because their lives are spent in organizing experience, in subduing the mad stuff of living to orderly forms. Lincoln loved nonsense, he escaped through it. William Pitt put it profoundly: "Don't tell me of a man's being able to talk sense; everyone can talk sense. Can he talk nonsense?"

But the comic spirit is not irresponsible. It is wise and balanced; it knows that defiance of reality often entails punishment. (Only the genuine lunatic escapes completely.) Accordingly most of Lear's limericks are the product of a tension between his gleeful try at kicking over the traces and his rueful knowledge that it can't really be done. The typical Lear limerick is both funny and catastrophic, as the finest comedies somehow involve someone's discomfiture. (pp. 418-19)

All thoughtful admirers of Lear agree that while he is funny, he is seldom *purely* funny. There is almost always an undertone either of punishment (*Alice in Wonderland,* too, is full of it) or of sadness. The punishment is not a "real" punishment, but an absurd one; therefore it does not make us uncomfortable; but it is there all the same. (p. 419)

> Clifton Fadiman, "How Pleasant to Know Mr. Lear!" in his Party of One: The Selected Writings of Clifton Fadiman *(copyright © 1955 by Clifton Fadiman; reprinted by permission of Harper & Row, Publishers, Inc.),* World Publishing Co., 1955, pp. 411-22.

WILLIAM JAY SMITH (essay date 1959)

Recently, when friends of mine were to depart on an ocean voyage with their children, aged three, seven, and ten, I presented them all with a copy of *The Complete Nonsense Book* of Edward Lear. . . . Surely no book is better calculated to dispel the moments of tedium, disorientation, and malaise that we experience at sea, when the last bit of land dips out of sight, when familiar objects are stored away in our minds, and the roll of the ship provides us with rhythms to which we must somehow respond. Since the publication of his first book of nonsense in 1846, Edward Lear has meant home and hearth to English-speaking children everywhere: he has offered them a room that is never locked, a world accessible to all who need not be reminded that life can be pleasant and gay. My friends' children delighted in the poems of Lear as children always will. One of the limericks appealed to them instantly—and I like to picture them there, beating it out as they pounded up and down the deck:

> There was an Old Man with a gong,
> Who bumped at it all the day long;
> But they called out, 'O law! you're a horrid old bore!'
> So they smashed that Old Man with a gong.

"So they *smashed* that Old Man . . ." How children love to come down on the word *smashed* as they must in the last line. Nonsensical the limerick certainly is, and violent, too; unhealthful, it is not. It is clean, wonderful fun, and reveals its author's profound understanding of the child's world.

The song, the sound—that is always the best part of a poem for children. The sense will follow. (pp. 105-06)

Lear himself always remained something of a child; being a painter and a poet, he could remember vividly what childhood is like and could speak to children in their own language. He could invent, as they do, words that suggest far more than they mean—"ombliferous," "borascible"—words which delight with their sound. Because with sound he was always ahead of sense, he leapt ahead as children do, but he left no doubt that the sense would follow. Words have meaning but their meaning is multiple, a fact which we as adults, bound by our dictionary distinctions, can easily forget. When the Co-operative Cauliflower advances "in a somewhat plumdomphious manner" towards the setting sun, supported by his Waterwagtails and his "two superincumbent confidential cucumbers," the children contemplate him "with mingled affection and disgust," as well they might. Things are multitudinous and mingled, they are preposterous and parallel, but they are never blurred.

Lear remembers that in the child's world things *happen:* they happen not once but many times over, and in rapid succession. In that world, the child's arrow, like that of Zeno, never reaches its mark because it must traverse a series of moments in time, and each moment is eternal. The child wants the assurance of things happening; every minute must be replete with action. Darkness and fear settle down only when his unconscious mind is unable to summon up a series of actions and events to hold them off; when he cannot, his defenses are down, terror moves in, and he becomes its real and tangible victim. The objects, animals, and characters in that delightful sequence of Lear's verse, *Teapots and Quails,* are in continual motion: they sail, jig, drive, hop, fly, roll, poke, and jump. Everyone in Lear's nonsense drawings, as in his verse, is moving: people are falling, running, throwing out their two hands behind them or in front, one foot is always in the air. People swing from ropes, hop into trees, fly, ride—no one is still. When characters do remain in place, they become, by the very fact, ridiculous. . . . Household objects are unhappy only because they must stay put. And so what do they do about it? Like the table and the chair, the poker and the tongs, they go for a walk or a ride.

Things are in motion, things are happening, and violent things indeed. A man leaves the door ajar and some very large rats come in to devour his clothes; an old woman threatens to burn her grandchild; men fall into the river, the sea, the broth; a man locks his wife in a box; a wife bakes her husband in a stew; a man tumbles from his horse and is split asunder; another fans off his niece's head. All this removed from its context and the gusto given it by rhythm and rhyme sounds terrifying. But there is nothing alarming or wrong or dangerous in it simply because everything is made to happen in the way children expect it to: unconditioned by logic and unimpeded by moral consequence. The delight is in the happening—as it is at the circus, where the air is filled with marvels and where the child imagines that he tames the roaring lion and flies with the aerialist on the trapeze. (pp. 107-08)

The world [Lear] presents is upside-down, top-heavy, topsy-turvy as it is in a dream—or in the carnival, which is the child's dream in action. It is also inside-out: the poems and stories present the happenings of an inner world, justified and illumined by human emotion.

So they smashed that Old Man with a gong. The lines reverberate in the memory as Edward Lear intended; and the limerick, when recited, is followed by a familiar sound, which is that of children laughing. Was there ever one more wonderful at any time and in any land? (p. 109)

> *William Jay Smith, "'So They Smashed That Old Man . . .'" (originally published in* The Horn Book Magazine, *Vol. XXXV, No. 4, August, 1959), in his* The Streaks of the Tulip: Selected Criticism *(copyright © 1954, 1955, 1957, 1958, 1959, 1960, 1961, 1962, 1963, 1964, 1965, 1966, 1967, 1968, 1969, 1970, 1972 by William Jay Smith; reprinted by permission of the author), Delacorte Press, 1972, pp. 105-09.*

JOANNA RICHARDSON (essay date 1965)

What is the secret of [Lear's] immortality? Where is the charm of Lear? It lies (as it always does with poets) in his love of words: their cadences, their very look on the page, their mystery, their endless, exciting power of avocation. Lear played delightedly with language; and if, at times, he deliberately misused it (where else have we heard 'a promiscuous oration'?), even his misuse seems to have a meaning. When the Queen's English proved to be restricting or inadequate, he simply invented a word for his purpose:

> There was an old person of Grange.
> Whose manners were scroobious and strange. . . .

Far be it from us to observe that Lear applies the identical epithet to a snake. Runcible is an adjective which is cheerfully accorded to a spoon, a raven and a hat. But what does that matter? It is a word, like many others in Lear, which gives us unique, indescribable delight.

Lear coined a vocabulary, and he did so with gusto. I think it is in his gusto that he differs most from Carroll. One never feels with Lear that his nonsense is an intellectual recreation; one never has the sense of contrivance. We can almost hear him pottering round his garden at San Remo, spontaneously christening his plants Sophtsluggia Glutinosa, or Minspysia Deliciosa. We can hear the limericks tossed off the moment the first line is given. And yet what art, deliberate or natural, lies behind those apparently casual verses! Lear is the master of the incompatible, the wildly impossible. . . . He is master, too, of the totally unexpected: of the line which catches the reader unawares. (pp. 34-5)

Lear understands every kind of humour: the humour of words and the humour of situation; he can be dry, rumbustious, zany, slapstick, and, sometimes, macabre. Occasionally he anticipates—and parodies in advance—the 'automatic writing', the irrational inspiration of the Surrealists. . . . But the magic of Lear cannot really be analysed. (p. 35)

Lear is often compared with his contemporary in nonsense, Lewis Carroll; but a world divides them. Carroll approached his nonsense by way of logic and mathematics, Lear approached it through his painting and through poetry, and—which is most important—through life itself. Lear was intensely human—and his humanity, warm and honest and spongetanious, cannot fail to be endearing. (p. 36)

> *Joanna Richardson, in her* Edward Lear *(© Profile Books Ltd. 1965), British Council, 1965, 39 p.*

ALISON WHITE (essay date 1966)

In the limericks Lear's drawings supplied the wit which his slack, repetitive last lines never attempted. As pictured, the serpentining nose of his first old man [in his *Book of Nonsense*], looped and knotted, is not at all too long: it serves some children as a jump-rope. (If a nose is said to be too long, the question is, 'Too long for what?') One of large-nosed Lear's old men used his proboscis to support a light when he fished at night. Another turned his into a trumpet. On the nose of a third 'Most birds of the air could repose.' And as for chins, when a chin is called too sharp, is it not ideal for playing the harp? (As in the instance of a 'Young Lady whose chin / Resembled the point of a pin.')

Lear's antic personages not only compensate for their deformities and afflictions, but they also defy the world by goings-on that the etiquette books could never have thought to proscribe. One of them runs up and down in his Grandmother's gown. A second gets smashed for bumping at a gong all the day long. A curtseying old lady twirls round and round till she sinks into the ground. In bygone days England had its share of eccentrics. As the Beatles age, we may see their like again. Eccentrics have grown scarce. If . . . humour rises from the mechanization of life, it may be that automation has pre-empted eccentricity and transferred it to the mixmasters and univacs. Still, Lear, thou shouldst have been living at that hour of recent history when a certain Old Person from Moscow on a table did thump with his shoe, at one of mankind's most august assemblages. (pp. 281-82)

Death is a leading topic of Lear's limericks. Death has long been seen as comical. The skull maintains its grin. Graveyards are for whistlers as well as sleepers. Gallows wit will long outlive the institution of capital punishment. And lovers of limericks must laugh until they weep. Like all wise mourners they must weep until they laugh—over the Old Man of Madras who was killed by the length of the ears of the creamcoloured ass he rode upon; or, more understandably, over the old man killed by the conduct of his children. Here, too, are the baked people, the choked people, the smashed people. The comic violence is that of our frenetic film cartoons. Lear's limericks must have brought into Victorian parlours welcome release of licensed rudeness. And the ultimate rudeness is violent death. Also, in his limericks Lear, like all of us, is trying to get used to death, to dull its sting. (pp. 283-84)

I have looked into the limericks for Lear's inner world because, of all his poems, they are by far the most spontaneous. They must have emerged from his subconscious virtually unedited. Not nearly all of them are alarming or dire. Some convey the deep charm he must have had, according to children and others who flocked about him, and also according to the young Queen Victoria, who greatly enjoyed her art lessons with Mr. Lear. Is there not the Edward Lear hypnotic charm working through an old man who hoped to smile a 'horrible Cow' into submission? . . .

So, with his beard full of birds, in a society whose bonnet was full of bees, we leave Lear among the limericks. I have explored these to the neglect of more subtle poems. One is the saga of the Jumblies, which, were it less delirious, could be a noble contribution to heroic literature. Edward Lear had genius. His creations have a strange dignity. It is perhaps only by the—for us—fortunate circumstance of the poet's despair and self-deprecation that his intense poetic phantasms should have emerged humbly as owls and pussycats, ducks and kangaroos. They form an indispensable part of English poetry; and because of them the days of Lear's pilgrimage are unlikely to vanish. (p. 285)

Alison White, "With Birds in His Beard" (copyright © 1966 Saturday Review; all rights reserved; reprinted by permission of the publisher and the author), in Saturday Review, *Vol. XLIX, No. 3, January 15, 1966 (and reprinted in* Only Connect: Readings on Children's Literature, *edited by Sheila Egoff, G. T. Stubbs, L. F. Ashley, Oxford University Press, 1969, pp. 279-85).*

VIVIEN NOAKES (essay date 1968)

Nonsense is a universe of words. Lear was unusually aware of the sounds words make and he would analyse them phonetically. . . . With his strong musical sense he would mull over the words and phrases he heard, so that Díghi Dóghi Dà reappears twenty years later as the Yonghy-Bonghy-Bò, and Mr & Mrs Discobbolos are named after the Grecian sculpture a cast of which still stands in the Royal Academy Schools. He would use words incongruously as in 'The Cummerbund', and he liked rounded words like promiscuous and pusillanimous which he used out of their place as meaningless, musical adjectives. (p. 224)

One of the characteristics of pure nonsense is detachment—neither the writer nor the reader is to be involved with the characters. To establish this Lear showed quite clearly by his drawings that the hero, even when human, is not for a moment to be treated seriously, and he created imaginary characters like the Quangle Wangle and the Pobble. Once this detachment has been established it is quite acceptable and not at all distressing to find a man being baked in an oven or coiled up like a length of elastic. . . . But though in the limericks, which are pure nonsense, violence and distortion leave us unmoved, in the nonsense songs they begin to bother the reader for here the detachment is no longer complete.

Lear's nonsense falls into three overlapping groups. The first, begun at Knowsley or even earlier and going all through the rest of his life, comes under the original classification of the happy and inconsequential. Here are the limericks, the botany, the cookery, the alphabets and the nonsense he put into letters to amuse his friends. Humour, though not an essential ingredient of nonsense, is often found in this group, but in the other two it gradually diminishes.

In the second group are stories, in both prose and verse, nearly always of wandering and travel, and either with happy endings—'The Owl and the Pussy-cat', 'The Duck and the Kangaroo'—or sad endings which don't worry us for they are pure nonsense—'The Story of the Seven Families from the Lake Pipple-popple'.

Between this and the third group the unhappiness becomes disturbing, for the detachment is beginning to break down. (pp. 224-25)

By the time we have reached the third group the detachment has gone. Here are verses which express Lear's deep personal feelings, written no longer for children but for himself, songs like 'The Pelican Chorus'. . . . (p. 225)

[They] are songs of wandering, but now the emphasis is on looking back to a time of happiness that has gone for ever, or wandering grief-stricken like Demeter in search of Persephone, seeking someone who in Lear's songs will never return. In fact, his development as a nonsense writer is increasingly away from pure nonsense into sad and moving poetry. (p. 227)

Vivien Noakes, in her Edward Lear: The Life of a Wanderer *(copyright © 1968 by Vivien Noakes; reprinted by permission of Bolt & Watson Ltd), Collins, 1968 (and reprinted by Houghton Mifflin Company, 1969), 359 p.*

EDMUND MILLER (essay date 1973)

One method of approach to Edward Lear's nonsense songs, what might be called the traditional method if there were anything like a body of Lear criticism, is to regard the songs as nearly perfect confections of romantic poetry, to see them as self-contained descriptions of life in the green world. Aldous Huxley suggests, "Change the key ever so little and 'The Dong With a Luminous Nose' would be one of the most memorable romantic poems of the nineteenth century" [see excerpt above].

The "ever so little" is very significant. Lear's green world is not a Forest of Arden where bad people reform. It is a world where there are for the most part no people of any kind, no real human beings. The central characters of the songs do have a lot of human characteristics, but they meet few people and even few other humanoid animals, animals not in the dramatis personae at the very beginning of a poem. And the people—and whatnot—they do meet are always types from a very limited range. (p. 5)

In fact, the key to the romantic charm Lear's songs do have seems to be to a large extent the result of the melancholy apartness of the characters from any kind of traditionally organized society. The typical concern of the few central characters of a song is romantic relationship with each other. Romantic longing is a motif. The courtship of the Yonghy-Bonghy-Bò is the sort of thing we find. The Jumblies and the Dong are looking and looking, always looking. But the ultimate situation for a Lear nonsense song is the marriage of two green-world creatures who would be bitter enemies in the real world—or at least incompatible there. The strange couples Lear habitually establishes place especially strong emphasis on the need for love in his green world. Not only is marriage everywhere in the green world, but the most unlikely marriages are everywhere. The kangaroo lies down with the duck; the spider is a friend to the fly. But Lear's theme is not simply that all creatures love one another in his dehumanized green world. His moral is narrower, less traditional. He seems to be saying something like: This perverse relationship between two animals is the only one left and the only one available because these are the only two creatures about in the naked landscape of the green world, in the cardboard world painted a solid, flat, unrelieved pea-green.

"The Owl and the Pussycat," Lear's most famous poem, is the one that most clearly adopts this point of view. At the beginning of the poem Owl and Pussycat go out to sea, setting themselves apart from the normal world by the very color of their boat—pea-green: green, suggesting the green world for which they are searching, but frivolous pea-green, making clear that the search is not serious comedy, not real romance. But the romance elements of the story are numerous and clear. Owl and Pussycat take food and money with them as if to establish themselves in a little society apart from the world (of course their provisions are parodic). . . . [However, it] becomes horribly clear that there is great emptiness someplace in the universe. But the green world cannot be the place of this emptiness because it is before the reader's eyes in all the reality of verbalization—insistent, repetitious verbalization. The world of the poem must be real because the reader believes in it enough to read about it. The world of the poem has an immediate if tenuous reality, so the emptiness is turned away from the green world of the poem onto the normal world that has no part in the poem. Horrible loneliness may throw the central characters of a Lear song together, but the characters are no longer lonely in the world and marriage they have. This is their escape. In **"Mr. and Mrs. Discobbolos,"** Mr. Discobbolos sees the danger of the empty social forms of the normal world as being so great that he finds death preferable for himself and his whole family. The joy of the green world is that fragile. (pp. 5-6)

But "melancholy desolation" and escape to the green world are only part of Lear's theme. A second approach can fruitfully be taken to Lear's nonsense songs. They need to be understood as a body of literature peculiarly stamped by their author's personality. . . . Lear's psychological peculiarities, while irrelevant to an appreciation of the fun of his nonsense, cannot be regarded as merely his own personal business, because they are what his nonsense is about, what it presents under comic disguises. The limericks have for a long time been recognized as presenting a picture of Lear as a man with a narrow range of rather explicit obsessions—noses, beards, eating, growth, age. But many a nonsense song, as has not been widely noted, goes even further and plays with an obsession to suggest a thesis about it—that is, works out a complete theme through comic disguise.

Consider **"The Pobble Who Has No Toes."** "Who has no toes" is a persistent refrain, almost a Homeric epithet. The Pobble cannot so much as be mentioned without the central fact of his life's being mentioned too. His toelessness becomes terribly, metaphysically important. And the cold but perceptive *they,* the hard-headed people of the world who figure so prominently in Lear's nonsense, see from the beginning that the Pobble is bound to lose his toes, that losing his toes is going to be the theme of the Pobble's life. . . . When he sets out to seek the world in the immemorial fashion of youth, specifically to swim the Bristol Channel, he protects his toes by wrapping up his nose in scarlet flannel. The suggestion of sexual displacement becomes at this point inescapable. The male genitalia are at the root of the Pobble's problem. The color is, as usual in Lear, explicit. The Pobble's nose has a long, symbolic tradition behind it. The point is that by choosing to make his poem about Freudian displacement and comic disguise—that is, by having his character express his concern about his toes by doing something to his nose—Lear tells his reader to speculate that maybe Pobble and poet are concerned about neither toes nor nose, but about sexual potency and the possibility of castration. (pp. 6-7)

Lear lends himself to sexual explication rather readily. His very favorite word, *runcible,* for example, can be taken as pure nonsense and a charming irrelevance whenever it occurs. But there is such a thing as a runcible spoon, a kind of fork with two short blunt prongs and one long, curved, pointed one—a virtual sculpture of the male genitalia, something never far from Lear's mind. (p. 7)

Where this kind of analysis ultimately leads, however, is another issue. Where it leads immediately is to the Dong with the luminous nose. Sometimes in Lear's nonsense songs the comic disguise and sexual displacement work beautifully, as in **"The Owl and the Pussycat,"** and sometimes they work well, as in **"The Pobble Who Has No Toes."** . . . But sometimes Lear's obsessions just get in the way. **"The Dong With a Luminous Nose"** simply does not hold up as romantic melancholy. Lear here straps on the artificial apparatus right before the reader's eyes:

> And he wove him a wondrous Nose,—
> A Nose as strange as a Nose could be!
> Of vast proportions and painted red,
> And tied with cords to the back of his head.
> —In a hollow rounded space it ended
> With a luminous Lamp within suspended,
> All fenced about
> With a bandage stout
> To prevent the wind from blowing it out;—
> And with holes all round to send the light,
> In gleaming rays on the dismal night.

You would have to have the wit of a six-year-old not to laugh at this. But you are not laughing in the spirit of the poem. You cannot laugh with the Dong—because the poet does not recognize phallic worship when he participates in it. The comic character here is the poet himself. And you are embarrassed for him because he does not realize how funny he is.

What keeps **"The Dong With a Luminous Nose"** from being one of the memorable romantic poems of the nineteenth century is its gaucherie. The theory of the green world cannot explain the unfunny and the embarrassingly ludicrous in Lear. Serious attention to Lear's sexual obsessions is helpful in understanding all his poetry. It is necessary for understanding why some of his poems are failures or partial failures, why some of his poems are ridiculous, rather than sublime, nonsense. (pp. 7-8)

> *Edmund Miller, "Two Approaches to Edward Lear's Nonsense Songs," in* The Victorian Newsletter *(reprinted by permission of* The Victorian Newsletter*), No. 44, Fall, 1973, pp. 5-8.*

JOHN LEHMANN (essay date 1977)

Lear's nonsense poetry, by the comic absurdity of its statement, has given delight to countless thousands of readers, adults as well as the children for whom it was originally written; and one feels inclined to leave it at that. All nonsense, whether by Lear or Carroll or any one of their numerous modern successors, is a parody or standing-on-its-head of the strict and rational world in which we have to live, and so momentarily releases us from its chains. The argument doesn't make sense: it is in fact non-sense. (p. 51)

However comic, fantastic and inconsequential the limericks are, they would be far less so in their total effect without the drawings with which Lear regularly accompanied them: it is in the combination that his unique genius lies. (p. 54)

Sometimes, one feels, Lear may have had to keep a very close censorship on the emotions that welled up from his subconscious. And sometimes in his verses, too, one finds him approaching the wilder shores of surrealism. . . . (p. 58)

Some time in the 1860s, after his wanderings in Calabria, Greece and Albania and the Holy Land were over, Lear began to write a different kind of nonsense poetry, more ambitious and more original than the limericks—those songs for which he is most cherished and most lovingly remembered. They are a kind of transposed Romantic poetry, written with remarkable skill, with a sense of rhythmic architecture and word music that recalls the masters, especially his beloved Tennyson. They are not parodies, for they have an undertone of deep feeling that hints at the troubles of Lear's own emotional life, but a new mixture: one revels in the inconsequential play of the imagination while one responds to the counterpointing sadness and heartbreak. His invented places, 'the Hills of the Chankly Bore' and 'the great Gromboolian plain', have a resonance as profound as that of Shelley's 'wild Carmanian waste' and 'lone Chorasmian shore'. The result is that, if you succumb to the incantation, if you don't pull yourself up and examine the sense, you are almost ready to accept the poems in which they appear as examples of the great Romantic tradition. (p. 62)

[It] seems likely that the first of all to be written was the one that is probably still the greatest favourite, **'The Owl and the Pussy-cat'**. . . . Nothing could be more light-heartedly nonsensical and captivating, nor could a happier end be devised. . . . (pp. 62-3)

One feels that this song must have come out of a particularly happy moment in Lear's life. The same mood permeates **'The Duck and the Kangaroo'**, and **'The Jumblies'** with its magical chorus. . . . Like the Owl and the Pussy-cat and the Duck and the Kangaroo, and even Mr. Daddy Long-legs and Mr. Floppy Fly (who appear to have been the first of Lear's creatures to reach the 'great Gromboolian plain'), the Jumblies found solace and fulfilment in a long voyage beyond the limits of the known world (even though they came back, unlike the little creatures of **'Calico Pie'**). One cannot help feeling that Lear himself, forever setting forth upon yet another long journey, had a dream of pushing out one day beyond the names in the atlas.

When we come to the songs in . . . *Laughable Lyrics,* a new note makes itself heard. It is true that in **'The Pobble Who Has No Toes'** and **'The Quangle Wangle's Hat'** the happy mood of 'all's well that ends well' reappears; but through the nonsensical trappings and absurd *dramatis personae* (and the equally absurd drawings which accompany them) of **'The Courtship of the Yonghy-Bonghy-Bò'** and **'The Dong with a luminous Nose'**, one is aware of a theme of personal sadness and desolation, at moments so strong that one is on the verge of tears in the midst of one's laughter. Is it far-fetched to see, in the proposal of the Yonghy-Bonghy-Bò and Lady Jingly Jones's reply, a parable of Lear's own failure to find the perfect person to love and live with him? . . . (pp. 63-4)

'The Dong' is the most richly orchestrated of the songs in [*Laughable Lyrics*], perhaps the most richly orchestrated of all Lear's songs, and the one in which he shows his poetic skill at its highest by creating a menacing, doom-laden atmosphere by a combination of verbal effects and sonorous images of wild nature worthy of Tennyson himself. . . . This macabre Romantic fantasia is the dark pendant to **'The Jumblies'**, using the same chorus but this time to emphasize the Dong's desolation and sense of abandonment. To balance the heightened emotional mood, Lear invents the most ludicrous of all his nonsense creatures, the most fearsome and at the same time the funniest emanation from his subconscious of his sense of personal physical repulsiveness. . . . (p. 66)

It is pointless to regret that a man so sensitive to the music of words, and with such poetic skill at his command, never wrote a poem to which laughter is not an essential part of our reaction. **'The Dong with a luminous Nose'** is likely to last as long, and will continue to bewitch our imagination as powerfully, as any poem of serious intent; unless in the future we were ever to reach a stage where we were born grown up, without having known the wonder-world of childhood where even the Pobble who has no Toes and the Quangle-Wangle are possible. (p. 67)

> *John Lehmann, in his* Edward Lear and His World *(copyright © 1977 John Lehmann; reprinted with the permission of Charles Scribner's Sons), Charles Scribner's Sons, 1977, 128 p.*

ADDITIONAL BIBLIOGRAPHY

Baring, Maurice. "Edward Lear." In his *Punch and Judy and Other Essays*, pp. 255-60. Garden City, N.Y.: Doubleday, Page & Co., 1924.
    An analysis of Lear's correspondence.

Boynton, H. W. "Everyman in His Humor." *Putnam's Monthly and the Reader* V, No. 4 (January 1909): 490-91.

A review of Lear's correspondence. Boynton finds the letters both enlightening and delightful.

Cammaerts, Emile. *The Poetry of Nonsense*. London: Routledge, 1925, 86 p.*
 A theoretical analysis of the genesis of nonsense. Lear's nonsense is called "wildly obvious and absurd."

Hark, Ina Rae. *Edward Lear*. Boston: Twayne, 1982, 161 p.
 A biographical and critical study.

Johnson, Burges. "Recognizing a Professor When You See One." In his *Professor at Bay*, pp. 141-48. New York: G. P. Putnam's Sons, 1937.
 Sees Lear as a bemused commentator on human foibles.

MacCarthy, Desmond. "Thurber and Lear." In his *Memories*, pp. 157-61. London: Macgibbon & Kee, 1953.*
 A comparison of the humor of James Thurber and Lear.

Malcolm, Ian. "Edward Lear." *The Living Age* CCLVI, No. 3320 (22 February 1908): 469-75.
 An appreciative look at Lear's career.

Orwell, George, "Nonsense Poetry." In his *In Front of Your Nose: 1945-1950*. The Collected Essays, Journalism and Letters of George Orwell, edited by Sonia Orwell and Ian Angus, vol. IV, pp. 44-8. London: Secker & Warburg, 1968.*

A study of nonsense poetry. Orwell calls Lear "one of the first writers to deal in pure fantasy . . . without any satirical purposes."

Partridge, Eric. "The Nonsense Words of Edward Lear and Lewis Carroll." In his *Here, There and Everywhere: Essays Upon Language*, pp. 162-88. London: Hamish Hamilton, 1950.*
 An elaborate study of nonsensical dialogue in Carroll's and Lear's work.

Prickett, Stephen. "Consensus and Nonsense: Lear and Carroll." In his *Victorian Fantasy*, pp. 114-49. Bloomington: Indiana University Press, 1979.*
 An analysis of Lear's limericks in a romantic context.

Rother, James. "Modernism and the Nonsense Style." *Contemporary Literature* XV, No. 2 (Spring 1974): 187-202.*
 A contemporary survey of the nonsensical writings of Lear and Carroll.

Sewell, Elizabeth. *The Field of Nonsense*. London: Chatto & Windus, 1952, 198 p.*
 A technical study of nonsensical writing. Sewell calls Lear's nonsense "simple, concrete, descriptive, and unconversational."

Utter, Robert Palfrey. "Lear's Characters." In his *Pearls and Pepper*, pp. 172-77. New Haven: Yale University Press, 1924.
 Studies the mysterious "they" of Lear's limericks. Utter maintains that "they" are the voice of proper, Victorian social consciousness.

Frederick Marryat

1792-1848

English novelist and editor.

Marryat wrote novels which reflect his own life as an English sea captain. Unlike his precursor, Tobias Smollett, and his successor, Joseph Conrad, who loved the sea, Marryat loved the sailor's life without developing a similar love of the ocean. It was rather the naval experience itself which intrigued and amused him. While his books enjoyed immense popularity in their day, Marryat is now chiefly remembered for his later writings for children, which have endured as works of universal appeal.

Marryat displayed an early interest in the sea and joined the navy at age fourteen. He kept elaborate logs for many years before publishing his first novel, *The Adventures of a Naval Officer; or, Scenes and Adventures in the Life of Frank Mildmay*. After its popular reception, Marryat resigned from the navy in 1830 and became, in his words, "a working man of letters." He took to writing with the same enthusiasm he had had for his naval career, but his creative fervor was fueled by financial need more than by the desire for artistic expression. In the 1830s, he wrote prolifically. From 1832 to 1835 Marryat edited the *Metropolitan Magazine*, where five of his most important novels appeared in serial form: *Newton Forster, Peter Simple, Mr. Midshipman Easy, Jacob Faithful*, and *Japhet in Search of a Father*. While *Peter Simple* and *Mr. Midshipman Easy* are still respected as examples of entertaining sea novels, *Jacob Faithful* and *Japhet in Search of a Father* mark a transition to more diverse subject matter. As Marryat said, "In *Jacob Faithful* we quitted the salt water for the fresh. From the wherry we shall now step on to shore."

Marryat was popular on both sides of the Atlantic. During the run of *Japhet in Search of a Father* in the *Metropolitan Magazine*, an American ship met a British vessel, and signalled a message. It did not indicate any form of distress. The Americans, instead, inquired whether Japhet had yet found his father. Marryat himself lived in the United States from 1837 to 1839. His insights into American manners and society were compiled in *A Diary in America, with Remarks on Its Institutions*, a work that annoyed most critics, who felt that Marryat's harsh criticism of American society was unwarranted. The book was burned, and Marryat hung in effigy. However, the diary is now considered by social historians to be an insightful view of Jacksonian democracy.

In 1839, Marryat retired to his country home in Langham, England, where he wrote a series of children's books. *Masterman Ready; or, The Wreck of the Pacific*, his first juvenile work, is often compared to Daniel Defoe's *Robinson Crusoe*. While he presented strong moral messages in these novels, Marryat did not patronize his readers. His loose, objective, style and occasionally grotesque humor is particularly noteworthy in light of the sentimental trend in children's literature at that time. Subsequent works, notably *The Children of the New Forest*, are still considered excellent renderings of the exuberance of youth. When Marryat died in 1848, he was at work on another juvenile novel, *The Little Savage*, which was completed by his son Frank.

Critics have called Marryat's nature decidedly "*un*artistic." He took little pride in his literary skills and asserted that authorship was only a profession, stating, "I should like to disengage myself from the fraternity of authors and be known in future only as a good officer and sea man." Despite this disclaimer, Marryat is considered responsible for instilling realism and humor into the sea novel. Conrad said of him, "His novels are not the outcome of his art, but of his character, like the deeds that make up his record of naval service."

PRINCIPAL WORKS

The Adventures of a Naval Officer; or, Scenes and Adventures in the Life of Frank Mildmay   (novel)   1829
The King's Own   (novel)   1830
Newton Forster   (novel)   1832
Jacob Faithful   (novel)   1834
Peter Simple   (novel)   1834
Japhet in Search of a Father   (novel)   1836
Mr. Midshipman Easy   (novel)   1836
Snarleyyow; or, The Dog Fiend   (novel)   1837
A Diary in America, with Remarks on Its Institutions   (travel essay)   1839

Masterman Ready; or, The Wreck of the Pacific   (novel) 1841-42
Joseph Rushbrook; or, The Poacher   (novel)   1842
Percival Keene   (novel)   1842
The Children of the New Forest   (novel)   1847
*The Little Savage   (novel)   1848-49

*This work was completed by Frank Marryat.

THE EDINBURGH REVIEW   (essay date 1839)

In the spring of 1837, Captain Marryat was looking out for new combinations of human nature. Having exhausted the old world, he bethought him of the new. The puerilities and contradictions of former travellers to the United States, had only provoked and puzzled him. He resolved, therefore, to take the case into his own hands. . . . [Marryat explains:] 'I did not sail across the Atlantic to ascertain whether the Americans eat their dinners with two-prong iron, or three-prong silver forks. My object was to examine and ascertain *what were the effects of a democratic form of government and climate upon a people which, with all its foreign admixture, may still be considered as English.'*

These are brave words. The misfortune is, that they have nothing to do, or next to nothing, with [*A Diary in America, with Remarks on Its Institutions*], beyond shining in the introduction. They belong to an 'all hail hereafter.' In the last paragraph of the last volume, the reader learns for the first time, from the author, (what, to be sure, he had previously discovered for himself,) that, 'in justice to the Americans,' he must suspend his judgment for the present; for that 'an examination into American society and government, and the working out of the problem, are still to be executed.' The announcement, it must be confessed, comes rather late. We never before encountered an introduction, written, as it were, for the express purpose of leading its readers to expect an entertainment of an entirely opposite description to what the author had provided for them. The contrast between the magnificent feast to which we were asked with all this ceremony, and the light repast which is actually served up, can produce only surprise and mortification, the worse for being gratuitous. Both author and reader lose so much by it, that we sincerely hope we may never meet with an experiment of the kind again. From the same cause, another ridicule attaches to the *Diary* and *Remarks* in their present shape. Their pretension to philosophical superiority over former publications on the United States, is absolutely ludicrous. (pp. 123-24)

The book which Captain Marryat has given us, is therefore not only not the book, but it is not even a part of the book, which he had promised. While he has not performed a tittle of his undertaking, may it not happen, nevertheless, that he has established the converse, and proved that the undertaking is one which he never can perform? This, we think, Captain Marryat has done—at least it is a point on which, slightly as he has approached his subject, he has thrown as much light as a reasonable person could desire. Sundry generalizations of human nature and democracy, are interspersed amongst the anecdotes. They are coarse and rash, and can conciliate no confidence towards him as a philosopher. Passing on to his anecdotes, the greater part of them have much less the air of sober history than of petulant and facetious caricature. (pp. 124-25)

Captain Marryat, as every body knows, is sailor and novelist by profession. Both his old callings stand in the way of his new one. He may be right in saying, 'After all, there is nothing like being a captain!' Nevertheless, a life at sea is a sorry preparation for judging of life ashore. Every thing seems to suffer there 'some sea change.' Upon the great faculties and qualities which it quickens, it also impresses a form and colour of its own. No landsman can have been on board a ship a week, without coming to the conclusion that a sensible house-dog is more like the people he has left at home, than most of his new companions; and that it would be nearly as capable of solving problems on national character. The talents and habits of a novelist, are scarcely less unfavourable. A habitual story-teller prefers invention to description. He delights in sailing before the wind, and letting his humour take its course. He writes for effect; at one and the same time stiffening his characters into arbitrary consistency, and throwing both persons and things into contrasts beyond what exists in nature. (p. 125)

[That] a commentator on a people should visit them for the purpose of observing them for himself, and should resolve, as soon as he had got there, on avoiding them as much as possible, is to take more trouble than the breathing of their air, or the looking at the mere outsides of their existence, can possibly be worth. . . . The solitary grandeur of the quarterdeck, and the silent musings of the study, have their charms; and a passionate longing to fly from the haunts of men, to 'ocean prairies and wild forests,' is doubtless very fine. But the romance of spleen and sentiment on this occasion, was unfortunately in contradiction with the very object of his journey. If we are to believe Captain Marryat's own account of his moodiness, abstraction, and estrangements, he did not afford himself a chance with the Americans. (pp. 126-27)

Captain Marryat very unnecessarily narrowed his sphere of observation; and . . . what he did observe must have fallen into a crucible ill adapted to the furnishing scientific tests of truth. The levity with which the book is written, is also often disagreeably out of keeping with its professed object, and very embarrassing besides. . . . If Captain Marryat has been compelled, by his wilfulness and exclusiveness, to piece out his argument with insufficient evidence, and with the odds and ends of silly stories, the necessity, instead of being an excuse, is a serious aggravation. . . .

An analysis of human nature being the talisman by which Captain Marryat is to work his wonders—the discovery of what it means will enable us to divine what sort of treasures we are to expect from it. His first and principal point is the identity of human nature. (p. 127)

Perfectibility is no part of Captain Marryat's creed. Quite the contrary. Human nature, it appears, is so far to be presumed against, that at every stage of society experiments for raising the average of its virtues, especially its severe ones, are fallacies which must end in failure. (p. 128)

A theory of the uniformity of human nature, which should leave things as they are, would at least let us know the worst; but, according to Captain Marryat, a process of deterioration, which it is impossible to resist, is a part of the uniformity. It was a favourite speculation of earlier ages, that the earth was to wear out, and that its productions were in a course of gradual decay. A credulous assent to the virtues of barbarians, and to the wisdom of our ancestors, was in harmony with this opinion; but Captain Marryat's view of the principle of population is much more desolate. He takes away from us the hope for future generations. (p. 129)

Many men might collect materials for a house who could not build one. This, however, is not Captain Marryat's case. He is scarcely better fitted for the humbler than for the higher office. The *Diary* and remarks abundantly exemplify his mode of verifying facts, and of applying them. On this point it would be useless to wait for further evidence. There is such a want of range and precision in his personal observations—so little of sceptical sagacity in his scrutiny of the information of others—so wide a departure in his statements, here and there, from the severity of historical narrative, that a cloud of uncertainty is necessarily thrown over the whole. His imagination is plainly at times at its old tricks—forgetting the difference of the object on which he is now engaged. (p. 136)

Captain Marryat's information is not in a state to hold a stout battle against any communications from third persons, however extraordinary. He has a weak point, besides, in not having the heart to reject any thing which came in the shape of a good story. His means of information, too, being so confined, he had to make the most of what he got. (p. 146)

We are afraid Captain Marryat will not think that we are entitled to ask a favour of him. But, as his own fame is as much concerned in it as our personal gratification, we venture, in conclusion, to suggest to him the desirableness of his returning to his ancient track of original and humorous composition. There he must always amuse. But we much question, on considering the lighter parts of the present volumes, whether he could ever write a good book of ordinary travels. The only descriptions of scenery which he has introduced, are of waterfalls: they are poor and tawdry. His descriptions of manners, which in one sense are so much better, are in another worse. Besides being intemperate and capricious, they frequently too much resemble the trifling of a schoolboy, who cannot help running away from his business, to laugh over an idle story, or play with a tricksy word as a kitten with its tail. A grave and philosophical subject, we are sure, he could never fathom. It is a pity that he should not rest content with the goodly heritage that nature has assigned to him. His lot was marked out by the original diversity of human talents; and its boundary has since been still more strongly drawn by the division of intellectual labour which that diversity creates. It lies in a pleasant land. (pp. 148-49)

> *"'A Diary in America, with Remarks on Its Institutions',"* in The Edinburgh Review, *Vol. LXX, No. CXLI, October, 1839, pp. 123-49.*

[EDGAR ALLAN POE] (essay date 1841)

[Captain Marryat's **"Diary in America"**] is the most extraordinary national libel, which the press of England, fertile in such productions, has yet given to the world. Among the ephemeral tribe of tourists, whom business, or curiosity, or the pestilent itch of scribbling, has attracted to this country during the last forty years, we have to complain of much misrepresentation—of many erroneous inferences and ill-natured remarks; but in none have we discovered such a bitter feeling of hostility to America—such a settled predetermination to revile our manners, character and institutions, as in the work before us. The splenetic effusions of Capt. Marryatt's predecessors in the line of American travel are mildness itself, compared with that style of scurrilous and indiscriminate vituperation which he has thought proper to adopt. He threatens us with a continuation of his calumnies; and we might exclaim, though not with equal consternation, like Macbeth, when the

magic glass disclosed to his startled vision the long line of the "blood-boltered Banquo,"

> Another!
> What! will the line stretch out to the crack of doom?

If our author has fallen into any mistakes; if his reasoning is inconsequential, and his assertions unwarranted by an accurate induction of facts, he has debarred himself from the plea of ignorance and incapacity; because he sets out with such lofty pretensions, and modestly professes to have founded his remarks on a most extensive examination of American society, and a philosophical analysis of human nature. The blunders of other English travellers he attributes, among other things, to their "being more active in examining the interior of houses than the public path, from which they should have drawn their conclusions;" as if the domestic habits of a people were not an essential element in the estimate of national manners and morals. In his survey of the United States, he has, accordingly, taken special care to avoid this important field of observation, and takes great credit to himself for not having violated the rites of hospitality. Another fruitful source of error in his predecessors, he supposes to be their habit of considering the Americans as one nation, when in fact they are more properly an assemblage of nations, cemented together under a general form of government. (p. 253)

Believing that the malcontents of Europe have been encouraged in their projects of revolution by the living example of our success, he labors to represent our republic as tainted with anarchy, corruption—in short, with every moral and political evil. For this purpose, he magnifies every act of dishonesty or lawless violence committed in our country, and would fain infer that they are of daily and general occurrence: to impeach our moral purity, he rakes up, with malignant assiduity, from the repositories of slander, every scandalous tale that time had consigned to oblivion: to establish the profligacy of our public men, and the venality of our elections, he records, as from the oracles of truth, every foul imputation bandied by an infuriated press in the heat of a party contest. . . .

Capt. Marryatt was a willing instrument in the dirty work of defaming a whole people. . . .

With all his contempt for our homely thrift and imputed cupidity, the gallant captain has shown himself a profound adept in the art of book-making as a source of emolument; and the motive of providing materials for that gainful trade, though unavowed, was, we suspect, not the least operative in producing his visit to this country.

Many . . . passages might be culled from his **"Diary"** were it necessary, to prove that, in consequence of our author's political bias, his mind was tinged with the most bitter prejudices against the people and government of this country. (p. 255)

Capt. Marryatt is unquestionably a man of talents and education. He is favorably known to the laughing and the sentimental world as an author of considerable celebrity in one department of literature. Though not remarkable for their refinement, and sometimes of equivocal moral tendency, his romances certainly evince considerable invention and an extensive knowledge of mankind, and have often furnished an agreeable amusement to our hours of idleness. In his delineations of fictitious characters, his leading fault is a disposition to "overstep the modesty of nature"—to present a caricature instead of a likeness; and perhaps we are indebted to this habit for some of the exaggerations of the present work. Indeed, he seems incapable of those master strokes, those discriminating touches, which give verisimilitude to the portrait, and excels principally in those rough sketches that strike us only from their grotesque extravagance. But a criticism of his efforts in this branch of composition is foreign from our purpose. Public opinion, the great arbiter of literary fame, has already assigned them their appropriate rank in the republic of letters, and it is not our province to confirm or reverse its immutable decrees. We suspect, however, that the present work will not add to our author's reputation. Like an enchanter, whose spell has been broken, he seems bereft of his peculiar powers, when he abandons the magic region of romance. The graphic description, the sprightly narrative, the humorous sallies, which embellish his fictions, find no counterpart in his **"Diary"**. The relation of his personal adventures forms an inconsiderable part of the work; but, meagre and lifeless as that account is, it affords a much more favorable specimen of our author's talents and feelings, than the indiscriminate calumny, the crude and superficial speculations, which constitute the staple of these volumes. There are certainly some shrewd and just observations interspersed through these voluminous disquisitions, but they are scarcely of sufficient value to repay the labor of extracting them from the libellous matter in which they lie embedded. The style of Capt. Marryatt, though not remarkable for vigor or elegance, is always easy, lucid and unambitious. His wit is by no means brilliant or refined; and the anecdotes, culled for the entertainment of his readers, bespeak no great delicacy of taste or acuteness of observation.

The most amusing part of our author's **"Diary"** is the narrative of his excursion through the lakes to the Mississippi. When he leaves the haunts of men and plunges into the vast inland seas and verdant prairies of our western valley, he seems to recover some of that raciness and elasticity which characterized his former publications. While describing his journey through those immense solitudes, where nature has lavished her richest treasures of beauty and fertility, he discards, for a time, his political reasonings, and reposes from the work of defamation. Yet even there, on the verge of civilization, he finds occasion to vent his animosity against this country. The breach of faith towards the Sioux Indians, imputed by him to the American government, and its agents, is, if it really occurred, highly reprehensible. So far as his account of this transaction is founded on personal knowledge, we are willing to believe that Capt. Marryatt asserts what he believes to be true; but he may have misunderstood the affair, or been misinformed; and, in point of justice, we are bound to suspend our judgment, till the parties accused have been heard in their defence. (p. 256)

In his report of the sayings and conversations of Americans, the surprising uniformity of the language, which our author puts into the mouths of his interlocutors, gives rise to the suspicion that he was more indebted to his invention than to his memory for these precious morsels of slang and vulgarity. It is evident that he has imitated the vulgar patois to be found in Sam Slick and Jack Downing, as if it was the universal language of this country. . . . What would be the indignation of Capt. Marryatt, if an American traveller, with a candor or sagacity equal to his own, were to describe the rude dialect of Devonshire or Cornwall, or even the cockney phrase of London, as the universal English tongue? It is to the writings of its literary men, and the conversation of its polite and cultivated circles, that a traveller, disposed to act with fairness, would look to ascertain the peculiar language of any country. . . .

It seems to have stirred up our traveller's bile, that some foolish and ignorant persons had arrogated to this country a superiority over England in purity of language. Such an opinion, in that sense, is not prevalent among our intelligent and well-informed men; but we certainly do maintain that the English tongue is spoken with correctness and propriety by our educated classes,— and that, in consequence of the roving character of our population, and the constant intercourse between all orders of men, resulting from our representative system, it is less debased by provincialisms than in England. (p. 257)

To entitle Capt. Marryatt to pronounce with such an air of confidence on American character, he should have spent years in this country; have mingled with us familiarly in public and private; and frequented not only the society of towns and cities, but the hospitable dwellings of our rural population. By his own acknowledgment, he shunned designedly the invitations proffered to him by the courtesy of our citizens. His observations were circumscribed, in a great measure, to the inhabitants of towns and cities; to the company at a few fashionable watering-places; and to the motley throng, who crowd our hotels, mail-coaches and steamboats. He had scarcely a glimpse of that numerous and intelligent class, who are engaged in tillage. We cannot discover from his **"Diary"** that he visited any part of that immense tract, embraced in the limits of the southern and south-western states, except Western Virginia; and he must therefore have known nothing of that lawless and barbarous region, as he describes it, but from the report of others. Though many men of worth and intelligence are found in our cities, their population consists chiefly of needy adventurers in pursuit of gain, of a lawless rabble, and of a numerous body of discontented and turbulent emigrants, the very refuse of Europe. There are said to be forty thousand Irish in New York alone. In such an assemblage of heterogeneous materials, it is not surprising that vice should predominate; and indeed, according to Capt. Marryatt's own hypothesis, nothing can be more demoralizing than to pack men in masses within a narrow space. The same causes are at work in the cities of Europe, and with results, if we may judge from our author's opinion, equally disastrous to the interests of virtue. (p. 258)

Capt. Marryatt must have had a very slight and imperfect acquaintance [with our country dwellers] when he promulgated his severe and unqualified strictures on American morals. His time was spent chiefly in hotels, stages and steamboats, and it is therefore not at all remarkable that he should have charged intemperance on us as a national vice; for it is to such places that the votaries of the bottle usually resort for the gratification of their ruling propensity. Though we are a migratory people, thousands nevertheless traverse the United States annually with their own conveniences for travelling; and hence the bulk of those, who avail themselves of public conveyances, are by no means the *elite* of our population. It is notorious to every man at all conversant with such matters, that there is a class of people who hang very loosely on society, and who, having no regular occupation or permanent abiding place, infest all our great thoroughfares in considerable numbers. The habits and manners of such men are surely no fair index of American character. . . . Little did we think, that a simple traveller, with no higher credentials than a captain's commission in the British navy, and coming here apparently on a mere excursion of curiosity or amusement, was big with the fate of empires; and was preparing to arrest, by a stroke of his pen, the fearful progress of revolution.

The gallant captain avers that he should not have uttered this libel against the United States but in defence of his own country; the logic of which ingenious apology amounts to this, that the vilification of his neighbor is the most conclusive argument of his own purity. (pp. 258-59)

In his indictment against the moral character of the Americans, Capt. Marryatt charges them "with a disregard to truth," . . . with dishonesty, . . . with ingratitude to public men, with intemperance, . . . and with various other peccadilloes too tedious to recapitulate. We plead not guilty, and demand the proof. . . .

Some of our author's aspersions are so coarse and scurrilous, that we find it difficult to restrain our indignation—to confine our language within the bounds prescribed by dignity and decorum. But we disdain to retort those dirty missiles, which he has hurled at us in such profusion, and mindful rather of what is due to ourselves than to him, will discuss his foul and scandalous charges with calmness and moderation. With that remarkable respect for decency and justice, which forms the distinguishing feature of his book, our author observes, that "what the Americans have been so often taxed with, is but too prevalent among us—a disregard of truth." When, and by whom, we ask, were the Americans ever before taxed with mendacity as a national vice? (p. 259)

We now close our analysis of this extraordinary publication. It embraces many minute topics of vituperation and calumny, which we have been compelled to overlook; but we have endeavored to discuss its main points as fully as our limits would permit, refraining, if possible, from the use of intemperate language. We do not charge Capt. Marryatt with wilful misrepresentation; but we believe he came here, possessed of inveterate prejudices, laboring under a political calenture, which disqualified him for the task of fair and candid examination; and that, to increase his mental obliquity, the real or supposed ill-treatment which he encountered during his stay in the United States, left behind a soreness, a rankling spirit of resentment, which has given a tincture of bitterness to all his remarks and speculations. . . . We might be well justified in inquiring whether one, who deals his foul charges right and left with such remorseless severity, is himself of spotless manners and character. But we have no taste for private scandal, or public defamation, and we forbear therefore from the ungracious task of investigating Capt. Marryatt's personal merits. The internal evidence of this work, however, authorizes us to say, that he is a man of gross perceptions, and vulgar propensities; for none but a person of that description, would have polluted his pages with those vulgarisms and ribald anecdotes, which he must have picked up in the dissolute society of steamboats and hotels. His declarations, that "he came over to America well-inclined towards the people," and that "he expected to find them more virtuous and moral than his own," we must pronounce disingenuous, and designed to give greater effect to his work; nor do we believe, that any impartial man can read this **"Diary,"** without coming to a similar conclusion. (p. 275)

[Edgar Allan Poe,] *"Capt. Marryat, and His Diary,"* in Southern Literary Messenger, *Vol. VII, No. 4, April, 1841, pp. 253-76.*

C. WHITEHEAD (essay date 1848)

It would be unprofitable to dwell upon the genius of Marryat as a novelist. His merits lie upon the surface, and are obvious to every man, woman, and child, who take up one of his works and find themselves unable to lay it down again. He tells plainly and straight-forwardly a story, tolerably well constructed, of diversified incidents, alive with uncommon characters, and, as

his experience was large and had been acquired over a wide expanse, he had always something to tell which would excite curiosity or rivet attention. He had one quality in common with great men, and in which men of finer genius than himself have been deficient—a thorough manliness of heart and soul, which, by clearly showing him what he was able to accomplish, preserved him against the perpetration of that sublime nonsense and drivelling cant which now-a-days often pass for fine writing and fine sentiment. **"Peter Simple"** has been pronounced his best novel; but we confess we like **"Jacob Faithful"** at least as well; although we think it would have been better if the Dominie had been mitigated, who is rather an extravagance than an original, and if that passage had been discarded in which the parish-boy tells us he read Tacitus and Horace at a charity-school.

His **"Diary in America"** gave great offence on the other side of the Atlantic. We do not know whether the captain ever regretted it, but it was an ill-advised publication, and was certain, from its tone as well as its matter, to wound deeply a gallant and sensitive people, who, say what some few of them may to the contrary, are anxious to stand well in the estimation of the mother-country. But that this work was written with malice prepense against the Americans we cannot believe. . . . (pp. 542-43)

C. Whitehead, *"Memoir of Captain Marryat, R. N., C. B.,"* in The Living Age *(copyright 1848, by the Living Age Co.), Vol. XIX, No. 238, December 9, 1848, pp. 540-43.*

JOSEPH CONRAD (essay date 1898)

It is by his irresistible power to reach the adventurous side in the character, not only of his own, but of all nations, that Marryat is largely human. He is the enslaver of youth, not by the literary artifices of presentation, but by the natural glamour of his own temperament. To his young heroes the beginning of life is a splendid and warlike lark, ending at last in inheritance and marriage. His novels are not the outcome of his art, but of his character, like the deeds that make up his record of naval service. To the artist his work is interesting as a completely successful expression of an unartistic nature. It is absolutely amazing to us, as the disclosure of the spirit animating the stirring time when the nineteenth century was young. There is an air of fable about it. Its loss would be irreparable, like the curtailment of national story or the loss of an historical document. It is the beginning and the embodiment of an inspiring tradition.

To this writer of the sea the sea was not an element. It was a stage, where was displayed an exhibition of valour, and of such achievement as the world had never seen before. The greatness of that achievement cannot be pronounced imaginary, since its reality has affected the destinies of nations; nevertheless, in its grandeur it has all the remoteness of an ideal. History preserves the skeleton of facts and, here and there, a figure or a name; but it is in Marryat's novels that we find the mass of the nameless, that we see them in the flesh, that we obtain a glimpse of the everyday life and an insight into the spirit animating the crowd of obscure men who knew how to build for their country such a shining monument of memories.

Marryat is really a writer of the Service. What sets him apart is his fidelity. His pen serves his country as well as did his professional skill and his renowned courage. His figures move about between water and sky, and the water and the sky are there only to frame the deeds of the Service. His novels, like amphibious creatures, live on the sea and frequent the shore, where they flounder deplorably. The loves and the hates of his boys are as primitive as their virtues and their vices. . . . His morality is honourable and conventional. There is cruelty in his fun and he can invent puns in the midst of carnage. His naïveties are perpetrated in a lurid light. There is an endless variety of types, all surface, with hard edges, with memorable eccentricities of outline, with a childish and heroic effect in the drawing. They do not belong to life; they belong exclusively to the Service. And yet they live; there is a truth in them, the truth of their time; a headlong, reckless audacity, an intimacy with violence, an unthinking fearlessness, and an exuberance of vitality which only years of war and victories can give. His adventures are enthralling; the rapidity of his action fascinates; his method is crude, his sentimentality, obviously incidental, is often factitious. His greatness is undeniable.

It is undeniable. To a multitude of readers the navy of to-day is Marryat's navy still. He has created a priceless legend. If he be not immortal, yet he will last long enough for the highest ambition, because he has dealt manfully with an inspiring phase in the history of that Service on which the life of his country depends. The tradition of the great past he has fixed in his pages will be cherished for ever as the guarantee of the future. (pp. 73-5)

> *Joseph Conrad, "Tales of the Sea" (originally published in* Outlook, *Vol. 60, October 1, 1898), in his* Notes on Life & Letters, *J. M. Dent & Sons Ltd., 1921, pp. 73-8.*

A. A. MILNE   (essay date 1920)

Having read lately an appreciation of that almost forgotten author Marryat, and having seen in the shilling box of a second-hand bookseller a few days afterwards a copy of *Masterman Ready,* I went in and bought the same. I had read it as a child, and remembered vaguely that it combined desert-island adventure with a high moral tone; jam and powder in the usual proportions. Reading it again, I found that the powder was even more thickly spread than I had expected; hardly a page but carried with it a valuable lesson for the young; yet this particular jam (guava and cocoanut) has such an irresistible attraction for me that I swallowed it all without a struggle, and was left with a renewed craving for more and yet more desert-island stories. Having, unfortunately, no others at hand, the only satisfaction I can give myself is to write about them.

I would say first that, even if an author is writing for children (as was Marryat), and even if morality can best be implanted in the young mind with a watering of fiction, yet a desert-island story is the last story which should be used for this purpose. For a desert-island is a child's escape from real life and its many lessons. Ask yourself why you longed for a desert-island when you were young, and you will find the answer to be that you did what you liked there, ate what you liked, and carried through your own adventures. It is the "Family" which spoils *The Swiss Family Robinson,* just as it is the Seagrave family which nearly wrecks *Masterman Ready.* What is the good of imagining yourself (as every boy does) "Alone in the Pacific" if you are not going to be alone? Well, perhaps we do not wish to be quite alone; but certainly to have more than two on an island is to overcrowd it, and our companion must be of a like age and disposition.

For this reason parents spoil any island for a healthy-minded boy. He may love his father and mother as fondly as even they could wish, but he does not want to take them bathing in the lagoon with him—still less to have them on the shore, telling him that there are too many sharks this morning and that it is quite time he came out. (pp. 24-5)

I am not saying that a boy would really be happy for long, whether on a desert-island or elsewhere, without his father and mother. Indeed it is doubtful if he could even survive, happily or unhappily. Possibly William Seagrave could have managed it. William was only twelve, but he talked like this: "I agree with you, Ready. Indeed I have been thinking the same thing for many days past. . . . I wish the savages would come on again, for the sooner they come the sooner the affair will be decided." A boy who can talk like this at twelve is capable of finding the bread-fruit tree for himself. But William is an exception. I claim no such independence for the ordinary boy; I only say that the ordinary boy, however dependent on his parents, does like to pretend that he is capable of doing without them, wherefore he gives them no leading part in the imaginary adventures which he pursues so ardently. (pp. 25-6)

Masterman Ready seems to me, then, to be the work of a father, not of an understanding writer for boys. Marryat wrote it for his own children, towards whom he had responsibilities; not for other people's children, for whom he would only be concerned to provide entertainment. But even if the book was meant for no wider circle than the home, one would still feel that the moral teaching was overdone. It should be possible to be edifying without losing one's sense of humour. (p. 26)

However, the story is the thing. As long as a desert-island book contains certain ingredients, I do not mind if other superfluous matter creeps in. Our demands—we of the elect who adore desert-islands—are simple. The castaways must build themselves a hut with the aid of a bag of nails saved from the wreck; they must catch turtles by turning them over on their backs; they must find the bread-fruit tree and have adventures with sharks. (p. 27)

This is the story which we want, and we cannot have too many of them. Should you ever see any of us with our noses over the shilling box and an eager light in our eyes, you may be sure that we are on the track of another one. (p. 28)

> *A. A. Milne, "The Robinson Tradition," in his* If I May *(reprinted by permission of Curtis Brown, Ltd.; copyright © 1920, 1948 by A. A. Milne), E. P. Dutton & Company, 1920, pp. 24-8.*

J. C. SQUIRE   (essay date 1921)

If there is in the English language a book of the adventurous kind more full of exciting fights and escapes, freer from dull pages, more diversified, more amusing, and, I may add, better written [than *Midshipman Easy*], I do not know it. It may certainly be argued that the adventures are very crowded, that luck unduly favours the hero, and that the good characters are exceptionally good; but it is as realistic as a book of the sort could be, and if nothing is to happen in novels that could not happen in normal life, we should have a tedious time of it. The characters are slight, and some of them are caricatures; but that is bound to be so if incident is what a writer is mainly concerned with, and Marryat seems to me to give as good pictures of his people as is conformable with the nature, pace, and rapid change of his story. As an inventor of good incident not even the Stevenson of *Treasure Island,* not even, I think, Dumas, could beat him at his best. And in *Midshipman Easy* he was at his best all the time. (pp. 224-25)

The epigrammatic economy of the style is preserved throughout the book. There is no straining after phrases. Marryat scatters freely little *mots* like, ''A man who is able and willing to pay a large tavern bill will always find followers—that is to the tavern''; but these always arise directly out of the narrative— are never (as it were) stuck on. There is none of that terrible sermonising which adds immeasurably to the tedium of Henty and W.H.G. Kingston, and is, no doubt, supposed to be ''good for boys.'' Marryat closes his discussions like this: ''Here an argument ensued upon love, which we shall not trouble the reader with, as it was not very profound, both sides knowing very little on the subject.'' But we can stand more talk from Marryat's heroes than from those of any writer of mere ''books for boys.'' For instance, Jack's philosophisings about the rights of man, the ratiocinations by which he consoles himself in the most uncomfortable predicaments are done with delicious lightness. (p. 228)

I am not sufficiently acquainted with the biography of Marryat to know if there is evidence that he had read Voltaire. But his mode of narration is most obviously derived from Voltaire, and the relations between Easy *père* and Jack were, I should say, almost unquestionably suggested by those between Dr. Pangloss and Candide. It is a far cry from the subversive sceptic of Ferney to the English post captain; but stranger connections have been established.

Marryat is unduly neglected. *Midshipman Easy* is beyond doubt his masterpiece; but *Peter Simple* runs it very hard. These and *Poor Jack* and the *Pirate* and the *Three Cutters* certainly seem to me as works of art, as stories, and as pictures of life. . . . Yet [Smollett's] *Peregrine Pickle* and *Roderick Random,* little though they may be read, are treated as classics in all textbooks, whilst Marryat usually has to be contented with a paragraph or a mere ''mention'' in a list. Is it because his books interest boys and are therefore supposed to be fit for no one else? Perhaps he would be taken a little more seriously in this age of propaganda if the fact were recalled that he consciously (though not excessively) worked with a purpose. He desired not only to write amusing and exciting books, but to expose the brutalities and injustices of the Old Navy; and, just as the effects of Mr. Galsworthy's *Justice* were, by ministerial admission, immediately evident in prison legislation, so Marryat's *The King's Own* led to changes in naval administration, as the Admiralty frankly acknowledged. (pp. 229-31)

> J. C. Squire, '' 'Midshipman Easy','' in his Life and Letters *(copyright, 1921, by George H. Doran Company; copyright renewed © 1948 by J. C. Squire), Doran, 1921, pp. 224-31.*

MICHAEL SADLEIR   (essay date 1924)

Marryat's works are utterly the man himself. Although at times he made deliberate attempts to assume a literary as opposed to a natural personality, he never succeeded. Actuality and the rough and tumble of daily happening soon shook him from the elegance of authorship into the fighting attitude of one determined to face life and master it. (p. 783)

Marryat has remained a ''juvenile'' and is now losing his hold even on boys and girls. Perhaps the opportunity of bringing him once more into the parlor may be seized. The nursery casts

him out because he knew not wireless nor aeroplanes; the library will do well to take him in, because he studied men and tramped life's highways and sailed her seas in wind and sunshine, and knew to fill his pages with fresh air and color them with health and make them musical with words.

For it is as a stylist that Marryat first claims the notice of the modern reader. His easy, rakish mastery of words, which swings his narrative along with something of the graceful swagger that must have distinguished his beloved frigates, carries the mind right back to Fielding and to Smollett, for between their day and the eighteen-thirties was little enough of word-economy or of the writing that sought point and humor and let elegance go hang.

A Marryat anthologist would remark, for honorable inclusion in his collected extracts, the superb opening paragraphs of **"Mr. Midshipman Easy"** (perhaps the only ones in literature that read the better for the puns that they contain); and the first two pages of **"Snarleyyow,"** a book published years later. This same anthologist would take care to secure examples of Marryat's engaging tendency to break off, to wink at the reader in a sort of breathless undertone, to confess the troubles or the shifts of authorship, gaily to boast, pertly to moralize, and then without change of countenance to take up his story once again and go rollicking on.

Sometimes his love of mischievous inconsequence leads him to interpose several pages of saucy irrelevance. The reflections on the incompatibility of fat and of ambition; the warnings to ardent readers that he himself is corpulent and dull and not at all a dashing spark like Bulwer-Lytton; that he is bored with authorship and bites his pens and stimulates his genius with brandy, are slapstick comedy of first-rate quality, and are among the brightest passages in **"Newton Forster."**

Even at moments of grandiose description, Marryat's pace and litheness do not desert him. (pp. 784-85)

With his sinister characters Marryat has been known to fumble. Vanslyperken is good; but Schriften in **"The Phantom Ship"** has a very tedious and persistent villainy, that cannot be forgiven even to a being partly supernatural. Perhaps this failure and that success have a significance beyond their individual application. **"The Phantom Ship"** is a serious attempt at a romance of terror; **"Snarleyyow"** is rather a parody of the same *genre.* Marryat, who went through life sneering at beliefs he was ashamed to share but cared not to deny, could ridicule his superstitions but could not ennoble them. It is characteristic of the man, and part of his appeal to this self-conscious age of ours, that he most felt what he most seemed to mock.

A sense of the ridiculous being so large an element in Marryat's power of observation, it is not surprising that, like Dickens, he is no novelist of heroines. Drunken old women or wantons he can draw, with fun and kindliness—almost with affection. But before young girls of gentle breeding he stands fatuously conventional. His sentimentality that can detect the lovable behind the seemingly grotesque, can only smirk and moralize, confronted with the candor and serenity of girlhood. Only Amine in **"The Phantom Ship"** and Poor Jack's Bessy in her final chapters are of all his heroines anything but pretty dolls. But Bessy is a child of poverty and Amine a Dutch miser's daughter. They are not English virgins of the upper class, so that to them are permitted enterprise and strong emotion that would be thought unfeminine or worse in the sheltered damsels of the England Marryat knew. (pp. 786-87)

The blemishes, when all are told, are not so serious. His heroines are pretty dolls. This has been said and tentatively explained. His younger heroes have at times a precocity and an insensitive conceit that are an irritation. . . . [However, that] young Tom Beazeley in **"Jacob Faithful,"** and Timothy in **"Japhet"** should be so wise, so impudent, and so successful is probably good realism; the vagrant life of those early days must have taught resource if it taught nothing else. In the same way the little girls in **"Poor Jack"**—one a milliner at fourteen, the other housewife at nine—likely have parallels to-day that live unchronicled.

More damaging to Marryat's reputation as a man of sense is his evident delight in those Admirable (but priggish) Crichtons who frequently befriend, champion, and humbly admire the cheeky boys jaunting across the world in their unthinking teens. Mesty, the negro worshipper of young Jack Easy; O'Brien in **"Peter Simple"**; Anderson in **"Poor Jack"**—here, indeed, are a trio of horrible perfections. Their creation and the relish with which it is achieved, imply that Marryat, like many another jovial good liver, was at no time indisposed to preach morality and preach it with pomposity. (pp. 787-88)

That he is fond of punning and of knockabout will endear him to a public greater than that which is distraught by such innocuous amusements. The rest of Marryat is sheer delight.

One may go to him for cynical good sense; for knowledge of the world; for gaiety and laughter; for swift, uproarious pantomime; for plots that ripple easily to their end or swirl over rocks or slide dangerously between steep banks; for vivid pictures of a vanished world; for agile, simple English. He offers all of these and more. (pp. 788-89)

Michael Sadleir, "Captain Marryat," in The Yale Review *(© 1924 by Yale University; reprinted by permission of the editors), Vol. XIII, No. 4, July, 1924, pp. 774-89.*

GEORGE SAINTSBURY (essay date 1928)

Marryat's ships are queer old hulks without so much as a steam—much less an oil—engine of the most rudimentary kind in them, and without any screws to hand except those one drives with screwdrivers. Instead of sinking each other not so much at sight as out of sight, they come close together and the crews indulge in vulgar 'rags' on each others' decks. The separation of classes is awful: and there is actually flogging of those who don't and, which is worse, of those who do deserve it. There is much too much rum drunk: though, by the way, Marryat himself is not very partial to rum. There is not so much as mention of a submarine or an aircraft-carrier. Turning to land matters, the boys fight at school—a disgusting habit. The girls, when they are ladies, are much too submissive to the men, and when they are not, display in the treatment of them the same undue 'class'—feelings which offended before. The technique is lamentable: and though there can hardly be said to be a deficiency of 'pattern', it isn't the pattern we want and like. The 'values' are wrong.

All which, without any apologies to those who may have uttered it or who may have been influenced by it, is simply rubbish.

There might be some small danger in attempting to cure it, get rid of it, or turn it to useful stuff, by pointing out that even were all of it true, the books provide most interesting and trustworthy illustration of that wonderful naval effort which

for a quarter of a century played *Britannia contra mundum;* made it possible for the Army to win the last round of that game, and as long as history is history will be a more and more notable part of our English record. . . . Marryat's novel-romance-stories are good novel-romance-stories—very good sometimes; never or hardly ever very bad. And he is a good novelist-romancer-story-teller, though for the reason given in the last few words, and perhaps for others, to be called so with certain qualifications and limitations.

The most important of these others we may perhaps take at once.

There are several touchstones, dividing lines of good and bad, or whatever term be preferred—which affect novels; but there is one of pre-eminent importance though common to the other kinds of 'fiction' or creations in the lower depth, that is to say drama, poetry which is not *merely* poetry, and (some would add) history. The question which best applies this test is, 'Are the people in this story live people, and are the things done what live people would do?' If the answer is 'Yes', the book is saved offhand: though it may be placed in lower or higher divisions of the Heaven of human creations. If 'No', it must be shut out, though of course again there are several—indeed many—mansions in the corresponding Inferno. (pp. 38-9)

[*Frank Mildmay*] has a peculiar interest of its own *as* a first book. Critics with a fair knowledge of general literary history, to back a pretty long experience of books coming fresh from the press, know, or ought to know, some classifying points about these latter. If there are any instances of an utterly bad beginning turning to a good ending here I do not know them. Beginnings as yet characterless may turn to splendid after-developments. Milton is almost one of these, and Shelley and Tennyson are quite two. Uncomfortably numerous, especially in novel-writing, are those which seem to shew a certain promise, never to be fulfilled. Innumerable, of course, are those which—what shall one say?—are like the beginnings of Milton and Shelley and Tennyson but are not in the least degree followed by followings similar to theirs. But *Frank Mildmay* belongs to none of these classes. It is a piece of quite genuine and (though it may be rash to say this when one was not present at its actual first appearance and did not read it till one was familiar with some at least of its best successors) obvious novice or apprentice work. The writer has both experience and invention of life; he can tell a story; and he can make if not characters, character-*parts*. But there is a sort of coarseness in him which may worsen into brutality, and a roughness which may draw near to ruffianism; though he can tell a story, he does not know how to manage it; he tries other things that he cannot manage, and he leaves the reader with rather a bad taste in his mouth.

Now Marryat evidently saw this, set to work to correct it, and did to a very great extent succeed. (pp. 42-3)

Of praising and, what is not always the same thing, enjoying *Mr. Midshipman Easy,* there will, I hope, be no end with me till I myself end. . . . It seems to me almost perfect of its kind. In the words of an old friend of mine on something else 'there is nothing to omit and nothing to deplore'. It is amusing all through, and there is also in it, and blowing over it all through, something which, if not 'better than amusement', is unfortunately not always found where amusement is—a thoroughly clean, healthy, manly and gentlemanly spirit. (p. 44)

The general public, I believe, have generally preferred *Peter Simple,* and the preference has got itself registered after the usual vague manner in the form of stock descriptions of it as his 'best' book. Far be it from me to say a word against Peter as a whole. . . . But I should like the whole or almost the whole Privilege business (the incident of the wicked uncle's being checkmated in the matter of O'Brien's appointment is good) removed—and if, as it probably would, it took Peter's papa with it I should not mind. With this removal I should have nothing but praise left for it, though I should never like Peter quite so well as Jack and though he ought not to have had that fatal conversation with the man on the taffrail. For when one turns to the rest one is almost ashamed at having found any fault at all. (pp. 44-5)

I believe *Jacob Faithful* has some pretensions to be at the top of the competition among Marryat's novels for favour of the 'best' kind. . . . It has sometimes been charged against Marryat that, when he had no actual fighting to season and light up his books, he was too apt to take to melodrama. We certainly here start with spontaneous combustion and end with a man saved from shooting when the order to fire is all but given; while, earlier than the middle, we have the hero chucked overboard with every chance of being knocked on the head if he tried to get on board again. But none of these incidents is allowed too big a place; and in particular Marryat was wiser than Dickens in not attempting any elaborate defence of the spontaneous combustion business.

Again, it may have been—and to go farther, probably has been—said that Marryat had better have left women out altogether, or kept himself to 'Susan on my knee' and the . . . 'young lady very nicely dressed' who got Peter sent on board. He obviously had the traditional sailors' limitations in his knowledge of them; though, oddly enough, he knew or imagined originals suggesting good working up, such as the prophetess in *Japhet*, . . . and that Eugenia in *Frank Mildmay* who, proper or improper, is so far in advance of her rather ruffianly lover. But Agnes and Céleste in his two chief books and Minnie in *Percival Keene* are little more than outline; the heroine, if you can call her so, of *The King's Own* is even less; and as for Poor Jack's first love, Janet Wilson, who makes a fool of him and nearly prevents him from making a happy man of himself, she is simply spoken of, and never seen at all. Bessy in this last book and Sarah here are pleasant sensible girls and no doubt made capital wives, but that is all. (pp. 46-7)

The rest of the book requires no extensive criticism in detail, but should have a little, such criticism being, not as some moderns do vainly seem to think, an impertinent intrusion, but a comely salute and performance of ushership. Jacob himself, one sometimes fancies, is that not infrequent and nearly always interesting *persona* in which the author puts a good deal of himself, or his own idea of himself, with characteristics strikingly different to disguise this. (p. 47)

Snarley-yow, or the Dog-Fiend, is of course inferior as literature to [*Peter Simple, Jacob Faithful, Japhet in Search of a Father,* and *Mr. Midshipman Easy*]. . . . It is almost throughout an example of what the Greek rhetoricians called *rhyparography*—coarse writing, or at least writing about coarse stuff which sometimes, as in the dog's-tail business, becomes disgusting. It sometimes also outrages probability if not possibility, in more than one detail as well as the total effect of the attempt of Vanslyperken's greater fiend of a mother to murder Smallbones. Its history (not an unimportant item) is more than once queer.

And yet, somehow or other, readers—even readers who are not fond of rhyparography, who cannot help reading critically,

and to whom it is not even new—find themselves reading it again with interest from cover to cover. That this reading is to some extent, as in the case of *Poor Jack,* bribed by the interspersion of the songs, may be true. Some of these songs are of the very best of their kind. (p. 48)

However, the songs come mostly . . . early in the book, and their absence, though it would certainly lessen, would not destroy the pleasure it gives. The secret of this pleasure is that the man *can tell.*

Besides his display of the mysterious and invaluable gift so often displayed by the spinsters and the knitters in the sun, and so often missing in gentlemen who are acquainted with the very latest theories of novel-technique, there is something else to be noted in this book which is not quite so fully present in the quartet of 'firsts' themselves—at least in the two best of them, for both *Jacob* and *Japhet* have something. This is, if not exactly plot, something like plot—an end proposed, forwarded, and reached. (p. 49)

In *Snarley-yow* things are completely different. . . . The interwoven fates of this hell-hound and his more disgusting if less terrible master seize you at once, hold you throughout and only let you go when the fiend and the scoundrel have ceased kicking at their several yardarms. The re-appearances of Snarley-yow are extremely well managed, and combined with those of Smallbones in a really ingenious manner, while the humours of the crew and the Dutch widow are adjusted as relieving touches quite *secundum artem*. In everything but quality of substance it really would not be extravagant to call this Marryat's best book—from some modern points of view it probably is.

Of Marryat as a short story-teller—his performances as such belong mainly to the period before his American journey—it is difficult to say much. I do not remember anything of his in this way which pleases me more than the story, in *The Pasha of Many Tales,* of the wind which was so strong that it blew a drowning man in ricochets from the crest of one wave to that of another, till the last landed him on the keel of a capsized boat and he was saved. There is really a great deal there that you can recommend to a friend: the great deal consisting of things of the most different kind, from the enormous audacity of the conception to the picture, not in the least impossible to the imagination, of its carrying out in fact. (pp. 49-50)

The *Diary in America* is a very curious book, though perhaps not, to the general reader, a very interesting one. . . . In the first place, it is not a 'Diary' in the usual sense at all. . . . But for its immense length, and a kind of pillar-to-post wandering of treatment which is rather irritating—to which must be added a constant bickering with Harriet Martineau which is more irritating still—the book would be both pleasant and instructive.

From the American book, one sees or seems to see—what indeed the unamiable reader may say might be seen or seem to be seen about other people—that Marryat had desires, ambitions, 'inklings', or whatever you like to call them, which his defects of education and the character of his early experience made it impossible for him to carry out. There is certainly no need to be unhappy about this from the selfish point of view: for no alteration of the scheme of things in this direction could possibly have given us anything better than *Mr. Midshipman Easy* and *Peter Simple;* or could even possibly have given us *them,* while it might probably have given nothing at all. But it is interesting to find him so little of a Captain Cutwater, with no ideas in his head except those connected with regions bounded by rudder, bowsprit, topgallant mast, and keel, prodigal of delight though the ideas actually connected with that region may have been to us. (pp. 50-1)

[*The Phantom Ship*] has interested different people rather differently. I have myself never been able, either when I first read it in midway of life or now, to enjoy it much. I have no objection to its *diablerie,* or magic or whatever you may call its furbishing up the Legend of Vanderdecken. I admit that Amine the heroine is not merely the most ambitious but the most heroine-like of all Marryat's heroines. Her fate in the Inquisition does not of itself make me dislike the book; for though I have no foolish contempt for happy endings I grant that unhappy ones can be made effective. But it seems to me on the whole *heavy,* and destitute of the 'liveness' of which we have talked. At the same time it *is* interesting as further evidence of what was said above in connection with the *Diary* itself—that there was always more or less a kind of 'quest' in Marryat, or at least a temptation to questing. It is not his only historical novel or romance, for *Snarley-yow* had been that in a way; but it is his only romance in the sense in which that term is more generally used.

In *Poor Jack* he returned in another sense to England, home, and if not beauty such as he had found in America, the life on river if not on sea, which he knew so well and could tell of so vividly; while here as in *Snarley-yow* he was rather prodigal of capital verse of the kind which some call doggerel, but which can be famously good *of* its kind. The ruffian is not very good; Marryat was never good at ruffians except when he didn't mean to make them such; but nearly all the rest is excellent.

I am rather afraid of getting myself regarded as, if not a quack of anti-modernity, a hopeless crank of it, when I say that I put down *Masterman Ready* almost with Marryat's best work and certainly as a most remarkable example of his extraordinary *naturalezza* when he had his hand thoroughly 'in'. 'Why! the thing is a mere suggestion from the *Swiss Family Robinson!'* says the enemy. Of course it is: and that is part, though very far indeed from the whole, of the beauty of it. . . . [*The Swiss Family Robinson*] is as dull as ditchwater and as heavy as Mr. Jingle's baggage. *Masterman Ready* is bright and light, and all that it according to any reasonable specification ought to be. Once more we may say that the sea has still been a refresher of such powers as he had.

Percival Keene . . . has had hard measure in some competent quarters, but I have always had a certain kindness for it. Not for the hero, in whom we must, I fear, allow an unpleasant lapse or even relapse into something like the character of Frank Mildmay. . . . [There] is not much virtue about Percival. He discovers precociously, and more than precociously works on, his illegitimate relationship to his captain; he himself has more than a touch of Frank Mildmay's bad blood; he is even snob enough to avoid, as below him, when he is rising in the service, a rather charming aunt—who as a girl has comforted and petted him as a child; and when we leave him with a very nice wife, 'the name and arms of Delmar' and eight thousand a year which he has not exactly stolen but worked himself into—we can't give him the other tag about *meruit* and *ferat.* But the book—the last but one of Marryat's mainly sea-books—recovers much of the freshness and liveness of his best efforts; the explosion of the schoolmaster at the beginning puts one—especially if one has known much of 'education' from the inside—into a good humour, and there is an excellent sailor man named Cross who comes in just after and continues till the very end. . . . When I read this book again after some half-century's interval

it was at once quite familiar and quite fresh. The fighting is plentiful and excellent. (pp. 51-3)

[*Joseph Rushbrook or The Poacher*] is not a good book, and those 'vital spirits' which we have noted in its author's best work not merely begin to 'fail' here, but, with the exception of a few flashes, fail altogether. Interest of course is not wanting to a particular kind of reader—that rather inhuman kind who may be called the critical student. For him it is worth while to compare the book with *Percival Keene,* also a work of the declining years. For that too goes back to the sea: and on the sea Marryat could never be wholly dead; in *The Poacher* he is almost wholly so. Everybody knows, of course, or should know, that mere improbabilities, nay sheer impossibilities, need matter of themselves little or nothing in a novel. You do not only forgive them but you hardly notice them till you are familiar with the book and have leisure to attend to its minor details. But, in order to make you thus inattentive or thus forgiving at first, there must be the driving power which is only conferred or infused by very interesting incident or very live character. And as in life so in literature, the character need not be, though it may be, intricate and problematical. It must be *live,* according to its own scheme and schedule of liveness. Dukes and cooks, fairies and charwomen, saints and sinners, bookmen and illiterates, they can all be made to live, and they must be so made if the book is to live itself.

Unfortunately Marryat's last sea-book, *The Privateersman,* cannot be so well spoken of. . . . Marryat had saddled himself with the too often crushing handicap-weight of autobiography in some of his best books, and had come in a winner. Here it is altogether too much for him. Few things are odder in the differential calculus of novel criticism than the way in which the autobiographical form ceases to be drama and becomes mere *recit.* It has become so here, and though there is adventure, fighting, and so forth all through the book, it communicates no liveness. If it does not displace *The Poacher* from that uncomfortable position of 'last' which racing reports (I never quite knew why: does anybody bet on it?) cruelly and specially publish it is because it attempts less. (pp. 54-5)

As for *The Pirate and the Three Cutters* little more than mention is required. It has no great positive faults like the two just noticed, but its melodrama in the *Pirate* is a sort of enlarged replica of the pirate episode in *Percival Keene* and its farce in the *Cutters* is mainly Marryat's second or third best fun. I would rather read it again, though I have just done so, than either the *Poacher* or the *Privateersman,* but that is about all I can say. . . .

[This] examination may have shown that Marryat was something more than a mere retailer of naval yarns, though his sea stories are far above all his others and at the very top of their own kind. (p. 55)

Of plot he was no master: and oddly enough from one point of view, less so from another, there is more of it in his worst book, *The Poacher,* than anywhere else. The beginning and the end are here really, or at least might be, connected. But the middle is mere packing, not weaving. It is at the best strung by the chase after Joey, whose successive adventures might have happened to half a dozen different persons. His characters, too, are almost entirely external—sometimes actually labelled or ticketed by catch-words. The one most curious exception to this has been touched on more than once: but not the least part of its curiosity has yet to be noticed—that it is a sort of anticipation in reverse, failure, refusal, or whatever you like to call it, of one of the most modern of novel personages. Eugenia in

Frank Mildmay, Aramathea Judd (in a slightly different order), the two Nancys in *Snarley-yow* and *The Poacher,* are all no better than they should be, though Aramathea, as far as we are allowed to know, was spiritually rather than bodily improper. The other three are more elaborate, but the dealings with them are uncertain and insufficient. If Marryat had been a modern novelist he would have combined them all, added to the combination a good deal of what he has actually given Mary in *Jacob,* but also added a great deal else. Whether it would have been a success in the hands of a modern novelist one cannot say, and it is not necessary to guess; that it would certainly not have been a success in any such hands as Marryat has shown is certain, and so he was no doubt wise not to try. What he could do with those hands he has also shown us: and 'while it was day', to borrow not the least great of phrases, he succeeded.

The character was, as admitted, always what is called external character and what has just been said practically implies that: but it was external character that was wanted. So . . . , requisite of description the picturesque, if not out of place, would have been superfluous—a distinction by no means without a difference. Marryat has done some fair description of the regulation sort in his two diaries, and there are some striking bits elsewhere—especially that of the death trap in the desolate island in *Frank Mildmay* where the dog saves its master at the price of its own life, and at the same time shows the cause of former fatalities by mistaking the wet moss overhanging a cliff-edge for solid turf. But of that very different kind of description which deals with action he is a wonderful master. (pp. 57-8)

His funny talk is too often merely punny: and though puns are much better things than it is the fashion to think now, and has been the fashion to think before, you can have too much of them, and they do vary in merit. Nor is his 'society' talk very good; nor some other kinds. But when he has got, as remarked before, his hand in, he 'can do it'. (pp. 58-9)

If my memory does not deceive me, the light-of-love hero in [Honoré d'Urfé's] *Astrée,* reproached for adding a new lady to his list of beloveds, retorts that a particular place or niche was vacant in his heart and that this lady exactly fitted it. Now it seems to me that a hundred years ago a particular place was vacant in the hearts or heads of good novel-lovers and that Marryat just fitted it.

That should be enough to say. (p. 59)

> *George Saintsbury, in his introduction to* Jacob Faithful *by Frederick Marryat, Constable & Co., 1928 (and reprinted as "A Study of Marryat," in his* A Last Vintage: Essays and Papers, *edited by John W. Oliver, Arthur Melville Clark, and Augustus Muir, Methuen & Co. Ltd., 1950, pp. 38-59).*

VIRGINIA WOOLF (essay date 1935)

[*Peter Simple* and *Jacob Faithful*] are quite capable of being read, though nobody is going to pretend that they are among the masterpieces. They have not struck out any immortal scene or character; they are far from marking an epoch in the history of the novel. The critic with an eye for pedigree can trace the influence of Defoe, Fielding, and Smollett naturally asserting itself in their straightforward pages. It may well be that we are drawn to them for reasons that seem far enough from literature. The sun on the cornfield; the gull following the plough; the simple speech of country people leaning over gates, breeds the desire to cast the skin of a century and revert to those simpler

days. But no living writer, try though he may, can bring the past back again, because no living writer can bring back the ordinary day. He sees it through a glass, sentimentally, romantically; it is either too pretty or too brutal; it lacks ordinariness. But the world of 1806 was to Captain Marryat what the world of 1935 is to us at this moment, a middling sort of a place, where there is nothing particular to stare at in the street or to listen to in the language. So to Captain Marryat there was nothing out of the way in a sailor with a pigtail or in a bumboat woman volleying hoarse English. Therefore the world of 1806 is real to us and ordinary, yet sharp-edged and peculiar. And when the delight of looking at a day that was the ordinary day a century ago is exhausted, we are kept reading by the fact that our critical faculties enjoy whetting themselves upon a book which is not among the classics. When the artist's imagination is working at high pressure it leaves very little trace of his effort; we have to go gingerly on tip-toe among the invisible joins and complete marriages that take place in those high regions. Here it is easier going. Here in these cruder books we get closer to the art of fiction; we see the bones and the muscles and the arteries clearly marked. It is a good exercise in criticism to follow a sound craftsman, not marvellously but sufficiently endowed at his work. And as we read *Peter Simple* and *Jacob Faithful* there can be no doubt that Captain Marryat had in embryo at least most of the gifts that go to make a master. . . . [For] pages at a time he writes that terse springy prose which is the natural speech of a school of writers trained to the business of moving a large company briskly from one incident to another over the solid earth. Further, he can create a world; he has the power to set us in the midst of ships and men and sea and sky all vivid, credible, authentic, as we are made suddenly aware when Peter quotes a letter from home and the other side of the scene appears; the solid land, England, the England of Jane Austen, with its parsonages, its country houses, its young women staying at home, its young men gone to sea; and for a moment the two worlds, that are so opposite and yet so closely allied, come together. But perhaps the Captain's greatest gift was his power of drawing character. His pages are full of marked faces. There is Captain Kearney, the magnificent liar; and Captain Horton, who lay in bed all day long; and Mr. Chucks, and Mrs. Trotter who cadges eleven pairs of cotton stockings—they are all drawn vigorously, decisively, from the living face, just as the Captain's pen, we are told, used to dash off caricatures upon a sheet of notepaper.

With all these qualities, then, what was there stunted in his equipment? Why does the attention slip and the eye merely register printed words? One reason, of course, is that there are no heights in this level world. Violent and agitated as it is, as full of fights and escapes as Captain Marryat's private log, yet there comes a sense of monotony; the same emotion is repeated; we never feel that we are approaching anything; the end is never a consummation. Again, emphatic and trenchant as his characters are, not one of them rounds and fills to his full size, because some of the elements that go to make character are lacking. . . . The intenser emotions of the human race are kept out. Love is banished; and when love is banished, other valuable emotions that are allied to her are apt to go too. Humour has to have a dash of passion in it; death has to have something that makes us ponder. But here there is a kind of bright hardness. Though he has a curious love of what is physically disgusting—the face of a child nibbled by fish, a woman's body bloated with gin—he is sexually not so much chaste as prudish, and his morality has the glib slickness of a schoolmaster preaching down to small boys. In short, after a fine burst of pleasure there comes a time when the spell that Captain Marryat lays upon us wears thin, and we see through the veil of fiction facts—facts, it is true, that are interesting in themselves; facts about yawls and jolly boats and how boats going into action are "fitted to pull with grummets upon iron thole pins"; but their interest is another kind of interest, and as much out of harmony with imagination as a bedroom cupboard is with the dream of someone waking from sleep. (pp. 40-4)

> *Virginia Woolf, "The Captain's Death Bed" (1935), in her* The Captain's Death Bed and Other Essays *(copyright 1950, 1978 by Harcourt Brace Jovanovich, Inc.; reprinted by permission of the publisher; in Canada by the Author's Literary Estate and The Hogarth Press), Harcourt Brace Jovanovich, 1950, pp. 37-47.*

EDWARD WAGENKNECHT   (essay date 1943)

[It is not] sexual irregularity that troubles us in Marryat's heroes. . . . [His] morality as a novelist was very proper; it was even prudish. But it takes a strong stomach to relish his appetite for physical horrors, and the calculating selfishness and hardness of his young men is more repulsive than lust alone can be. (p. 204)

In a way, the degradations to which Marryat's heroes are submitted in the course of his narratives seem to have little effect on their characters. We are so absorbed by "the poetry of circumstance," to borrow a distinction of Stevenson's, that "the poetry of conduct" quite passes us by. But we should feel more comfortable about Marryat himself if he could give some indication of knowing that not all is quite as it should be.

The first book is the most objectionable from this point of view. *The Naval Officer, or Scenes and Adventures in the Life of Frank Mildmay* . . . is sometimes judged as having fallen between the two schools of fiction and autobiographical memoir. But nobody capable of enjoying Marryat at all can fail to relish *Peter Simple, Jacob Faithful* . . . , and *Mr. Midshipman Easy*. . . . The last named would deserve immortality if only for the unmarried wet-nurse whom Dr. Middleton brings to Mrs. Easy. When the latter objects to receiving into her house an unmarried woman who has borne a child, the offender drops a curtsey and explains that "if you please, ma'am, it was a very little one."

In *Peter Simple* the theme is the growth to manhood, through naval service, of the fool of the family; in *Easy* we have the contrast between naval discipline and the theories of liberty and equality with which the hero's father has indoctrinated him. Jacob Faithful does not join the navy; he is a waterman on the Thames. It would be too much to say that all the incidents in these books are quite convincing. But they are nearly all vastly entertaining. (pp. 204-05)

Marryat attempts little in the way of elaborate plot-structure or detailed characterization; his own judgment of himself was that his mind was like a kaleidoscope except that there was no regularity in it. He could always make the particular incident sufficiently absorbing to prevent our worrying too much about its relationship to the general design, and the idiosyncrasies of his characters sufficiently vivid to take our minds off the moot matter of their general reality.

What he has in the way of philosophy is conventional and superimposed. He moralizes about Jacob Faithful's resentment against his benefactor, Mr. Drummond, who had discharged

him for an alleged fault, and he believes that the adventures of that hero in general go to show that "There is no such thing in the world as independence, unless in a savage state. In society we are all mutually dependent upon each other." But nobody ever remembers any of that in connection with *Jacob Faithful,* and the book would be quite what it is if the idea had never crossed Marryat's mind.

His heroines are generally lay-figures, but in Mary Stapleton, of *Jacob Faithful,* he did go in for psychology. Mary has inherited frivolity and love of adventure from a recreant mother, and she does not learn how to control herself until she has nearly destroyed the man she sincerely loves. (pp. 205-06)

In general, however, if we are to maintain Marryat's claim to a place among the English novelists, it must rest, as Sadleir has rested it first of all on his style, "his easy, rakish mastery of words," [see excerpt above] and then, as has already been suggested, on his ability to resurrect a vivid, buried world. (p. 206)

> *Edward Wagenknecht, "From Scott to Dickens," in his* Cavalcade of the English Novel: From Elizabeth to George VI *(copyright © 1943 by Henry Holt and Company, Inc.; copyright renewed, 1971, by Edward Wagenknecht; reprinted by permission of the author), Holt, Rinehart and Winston, 1948, pp. 173-212.**

JOHN SEELYE   (essay date 1976)

The castaway story, one of the most popular Victorian genres for children, originates with *Robinson Crusoe,* but Wyss's *Swiss Family Robinson* added a significant variation to the type early on, and it is to that tradition that Captain Marryat's *Masterman Ready* belongs. We must acknowledge, however, one more influence, that of Thomas Day's *Sandford and Merton,* whose titular characters are the literary ancestors of the awful Seagrave brothers, William and Tommy, who are another example of that hardy perennial pair, the Good and the Bad Boy. Like Day's, Marryat's boys are pedagogical devices, but what was radical and innovative in *Sandford and Merton* has rather a reactionary tone in *Masterman Ready.*

With Mark Twain's, our interest if not our sympathy flies to the Bad Boy, in this case the most lively character in the book. Master Tommy, like a miserable medieval page, exists solely for the purpose of being punished—he is a literary whipping boy. Yet it should be pointed out that no one but himself hurts Master Tommy, whose punishments always emerge from the circumstances of his misdeeds—a distinctly Calvinistic version of dramatic irony in which the final course of a meal of greed is a just dessert of wormwood and gall. Day's little Merton likewise suffers for the sake of truth, but Merton at least improves during the course of instruction while Tommy ends up in the Army, feeding his face forever. And as for his brother, William is as impossibly *good* as Tommy is bad; his one misdeed is undertaken to please his mother, and the folly of it he immediately perceives with a piously unpleasant writhing.

On Captain Marryat's behalf, however, it can be said that this sort of thing is not typical of his books for boys, the best of which—like *Mr. Midshipman Easy*—were written for adults and are therefore much less self-consciously moral and didactic. One wonders, indeed, how *Masterman Ready* gained its popularity, for it lacks the subtle use of adversity for the sake of verisimilitude and suspense that characterizes *Robinson Crusoe* and the warm sense of family that irradiates Wyss's great book. . . . In attending to details so as to "adhere to the probable, or even the possible,'' Marryat overlooked the Larger Realism. For all its zoological inaccuracy, *Swiss Family Robinson* remains greatly alive, while **Masterman Ready** has the interest and excitement of a Victorian daguerreotype in which a family assumes Anglo-Saxon attitudes of impossible rigor that would give cramps to a normal human being. (pp. v-vi)

Still, some interesting realignments are taking place in Marryat's contribution to the castaway genre. Wyss's classic is totally family-centered, the pastor and his wife providing a strong core of morality, instruction, and affection. But in Marryat's book there is a secondary force at work, manifested in saintly Old Ready, which tends to reduce the importance of Mr. and Mrs. Seagrave. (p. vii)

Old Ready the sailor is the only interesting character in the book, a clean old man who plays both mother and father, being something of an androgyne, a seagoing Tiresius of forethought if not foresight. A celebration of the loyal Heart-of-Oak Jack Tar familiar to the readers of Marryat's sea-stories, Ready is a sentimentalized (which is to say a Christianized) version of the type. . . . Ready's own story takes up the slack at the middle of the book in an interlude typical of the Sunday-School pamphlet literature of the day, a dreary descendent of the spiritual autobiographies which provided a central strand in *Robinson Crusoe*. This tale within the tale puts an indelible didactic stamp on Ready, a tattoo in which the ideas of Mother, Christ, and Repentance are inextricable.

Ready is in effect a Good Governess figure, but in his relationship with William he exercises a decidedly masculine role, one most flattering to the boy reader, for William is entrusted with duties and confidences worthy of an older man, even further reducing the role of Mr. Seagrave. Ready's customary precaution is responsible for the almost total lack of suspense in the narrative, and his moral perfection, his absolute inability to make a mistake, are detractions also. But in the tutorial companionship between the Good Old Man and the Good Boy we see foreshadowed not only those metaphorical castaways, Jim and Huck—another pair in whom moral virtue transcends social bounds—but also Long John Silver and Jim Hawkins. Indeed, Stevenson's version is virtually a parody of Marryat,

Long John the very antithesis of Old Ready, and Jim a curiously amoral version of the Good Bad Boy, whose misdeeds always turn out all right. In sum, **Masterman Ready** is one of those unfortunate books which, like Master Tommy himself, are chiefly valuable as a demonstration of the superiority of others. (pp. vii-viii)

> *John Seelye, in his preface to* Masterman Ready *by Frederick Marryat, Garland Publishing Inc., 1976, pp. v-viii.*

ADDITIONAL BIBLIOGRAPHY

Ford, Ford Madox. *The English Novel from the Earliest Days to the Death of Joseph Conrad*. New York: Lippincott, 1929, 140 p.*
  Praises *Peter Simple* and calls Marryat ''the greatest of English novelists.''

Hughes, Kenneth J. ''Marryat's *Settlers in Canada* and the White Commonwealth.'' *Journal of Canadian Fiction* III, No. 4 (Winter 1975): 69-73.
  A historical study of Marryat's *Settlers in Canada*.

Lloyd, Christopher. *Captain Marryat and the Old Navy*. London: Longmans, Green, & Co., 1939, 286 p.
  A biographical account of Marryat's naval experience.

Marryat, Florence. *Life and Letters of Captain Marryat*. 2 vols. New York: D. Appleton & Co., 1872.
  A collection of sketches and correspondence by Marryat's contemporaries, compiled by his daughter.

McGrath, M. ''A Century of Marryat.'' *The Nineteenth Century* CVI, No. 632 (October 1929): 545-55.
  A retrospective look at Marryat's literary career.

Poe, Edgar Allan. ''Frederick Marryat.'' In his *The Complete Works of Edgar Allan Poe, Vol. VI*, pp. 520-25. New York: Colonial Press, 1876.
  A negative review of *Joseph Rushbrook*. Poe calls its English slovenly and its events improbable.

Warner, Oliver. *Captain Marryat: A Rediscovery*. London: Constable, 1953, 210 p.
  A well-written, informative biography.

Herman Melville

1819-1891

American novelist, short story writer, and poet.

Melville is one of the major American literary figures of the nineteenth century and is best known for *Moby-Dick; or, The Whale*, his complex metaphysical novel of the quest for the white whale. Virtually unrecognized at the time of his death, Melville is now praised for his rich rhythmical prose and complex symbolism. A master of both the realistic and allegorical narrative, Melville was also an incisive social critic and philosopher who strove to penetrate the ambiguities of life and to define the individual's relation to society and the universe.

Born and raised in New York, Melville had a relatively comfortable childhood until his father's business failure and early death. Melville ended his formal education at age twelve to help support his family. He worked in the family fur business and as a bank clerk, and taught at various schools until, in 1839, he sailed as a cabin boy aboard a merchant ship bound for Liverpool. This experience, shocking in its revelation of squalor and human cruelty, inspired his fourth novel, *Redburn: His First Voyage*. Melville's later journey to the South Seas, begun aboard the whaling ship *Acushnet*, proved to be his most important experience, and provided the background for his greatest works. Finding the conditions unbearable aboard the *Acushnet*, Melville abandoned ship in the Marquesas and spent several months in captivity among a tribe of cannibalistic Polynesians. He finally escaped to a passing whaling vessel. Again appalled by the conditions at sea, Melville joined in a mutiny and was briefly imprisoned in Tahiti. He then moved on to Hawaii, and later returned to New York aboard a U.S. naval vessel.

Melville had not previously contemplated a literary career, but at the urging of family and friends he began to write of his remarkable journeys. His first novels, *Typee: A Peep at Polynesian Life* and its sequel, *Omoo: A Narrative of Adventures in the South Seas*, are fictionalized versions of his experiences and were popular with a reading public who had thrilled to the travel narrative of Richard Henry Dana, Jr. in his *Two Years Before the Mast*. Immediately successful, these novels made Melville famous as the "man who lived among the cannibals," a reputation that he was never able to overcome, and which interfered with the appreciation of his later works. Although they were generally praised for their excitement, romance, and splendid descriptions of the South Seas, *Typee* and *Omoo* infuriated members of the Christian missionary community, who resented Melville's negative portrayal of them.

Melville's mature voice begins to emerge in *Mardi: And a Voyage Thither*. He was growing restless with the adventure narrative, and was increasingly drawn to explore philosophical and metaphysical questions in his novels. Although *Mardi* begins as an adventure story, it becomes a combination of philosophical allegory and satire, and anticipates both *Moby-Dick* and *Pierre; or, The Ambiguities* in its symbolical levels of meaning, exploration of metaphysical problems, and use of a questing hero. *Mardi* represents an important step in Melville's artistic development, yet its publication marked the beginning of the decline in his popularity. Discouraged by the novel's

poor reception and in need of money, Melville temporarily returned to the travel narrative and produced *Redburn* and *White-Jacket; or, The World in a Man-of-War*.

Like *Mardi*, *Moby-Dick* was begun as another realistic narrative based on Melville's experience at sea. However, as he wrote, Ahab's quest for the white whale took on epic proportions. The whale has been variously interpreted as God, evil, good, and, perhaps most accurately, a symbol of the ambiguity of nature. Both the influence of William Shakespeare, whose plays Melville was reading as he composed *Moby-Dick*, and his friendship with Nathaniel Hawthorne, to whom he dedicated the novel, had a significant effect on the rhythmic prose and complex levels of meaning found in the work. Although Melville's contemporaries gave it little notice, *Moby-Dick* has been studied more intensively in the twentieth century than any other American novel and is now considered one of the greatest novels of all time.

Emotionally exhausted following the publication of *Moby-Dick* and desperate for recognition, Melville immediately began work on *Pierre*, a pessimistic novel which is considered the most autobiographical of his works. His popularity, already seriously damaged by the publication of *Moby-Dick*, was completely destroyed by *Pierre;* the reading public, who preferred the entertainment of *Typee* and *Omoo*, was confused by the novel's metaphysical questionings and offended by its theme of incest. Despite considerable flaws, however, *Pierre* is now noted as a predecessor of the modern psychological novel.

Melville continued writing prose through the 1850s, despite the critical and popular failure of *Pierre* and *Moby-Dick*. He published numerous short stories in periodicals and collected six of his best in *The Piazza Tales*. This volume includes "Benito Cereno," which is generally considered his finest short story. *The Confidence-Man: His Masquerade*, published the following year, is an allegorical satire on mid-nineteenth-century American life, and was Melville's last novel published during his life. *Billy Budd*, left in manuscript at his death and considered one of his finest novels, was not published until 1924.

Melville's poetry has been overshadowed by *Moby-Dick* and his other prose works and has only recently received critical attention. He began writing poetry in 1860, although his first collection, *Battle-Pieces and Aspects of the War*, was not published until 1866. That year he also became a customs official in New York, a post he held for twenty years. Melville continued writing poetry which was privately printed towards the end of his life in *Timoleon* and *John Marr and Other Sailors*. *Clarel: A Poem and Pilgrimage in the Holy Land*, a book-length philosophical poem based on his journey in 1857 to Jerusalem, treats questions of politics and religion.

At the time of his death, Melville was unknown and unappreciated, and his accomplishments were not recognized for nearly a generation. The tremendous revival of interest in his work began in the 1920s, following the publication of Raymond Weaver's biography, *Herman Melville: Mariner and Mystic*, and constitutes a dramatic reversal nearly unprecedented in American literary history. Melville's works, particularly *Moby-Dick*, have been the subject of innumerable interpretations and the body of Melville criticism, already immense, continues to grow. Melville is now recognized as one of America's greatest writers and *Moby-Dick* is widely acclaimed as a work of genius.

(See also *Dictionary of Literary Biography, Vol. 3: Antebellum Writers in New York and the South*.)

PRINCIPAL WORKS

Typee: A Peep at Polynesian Life   (novel)   1846
Omoo: A Narrative of Adventures in the South Seas   (novel) 1847
Mardi: And a Voyage Thither   (novel)   1849
Redburn: His First Voyage   (novel)   1849
White-Jacket; or, The World in a Man-of-War   (novel) 1850
Moby-Dick; or, The Whale   (novel)   1851; also published as *The Whale*, 1851
Pierre; or, The Ambiguities   (novel)   1852
Israel Potter: His Fifty Years in Exile   (novel)   1855
The Piazza Tales   (short stories)   1856
The Confidence-Man: His Masquerade   (novel)   1857
Battle-Pieces and Aspects of the War   (poetry)   1866
Clarel: A Poem and Pilgrimage in the Holy Land   (poetry) 1876
John Marr and Other Sailors   (poetry)   1888
Timoleon   (poetry)   1891
Billy Budd and Other Prose Pieces   (novel and short stories)   1924

NATHANIEL HAWTHORNE   (essay date 1846)

[Herman Melville's *'Typee, or a Peep at Polynesian Life'*, is] a very remarkable work. . . . The book is lightly but vigorously written; and we are acquainted with no work that gives a freer and more effective picture of barbarian life, in that unadulterated state of which there are now so few specimens remaining. The gentleness of disposition that seems akin to the delicious climate, is shown in contrast with traits of savage fierceness. . . . [The author] has that freedom of view—it would be too harsh to call it laxity of principle—which renders him tolerant of codes of morals that may be little in accordance with our own; a spirit proper enough to a young and adventurous sailor, and which makes his book the more wholesome to our staid landsmen. The narrative is skilfully managed, and in a literary point of view, the execution of the work is worthy of the novelty and interest of its subject. (p. 329)

> *Nathaniel Hawthorne, in an excerpt from "Hawthorne's Contributions to 'The Salem Adviser'" by Randall Stewart (originally published in* The Salem Adviser, *March 25, 1846), in* American Literature *(reprinted by permission of the Publisher; copyright 1934 by Duke University Press, Durham, North Carolina), Vol. V, 1933-34, pp. 328-29.*

WILLIAM OLAND BOURNE   (essay date 1846)

An apotheosis of barbarism! A panegyric on cannibal delights! An apostrophe to the spirit of savage felicity! Such are the exclamations instinctively springing from our lips as we close [*Typee: a Residence in the Marquesas*]. . . . (p. 85)

The author seems to possess a cultivated taste and a fair education, but a deficient reading, and to this latter cause we assign many of his errors of general fact, as well as gross misstatements concerning the missionaries. With a lively imagination and a good and often graceful description, together with a somewhat happy strain of narrative, he has written an attractive history of personal adventure and unwilling *abandon* among the happy and sequestered Typees. (p. 86)

[We] remark of the book generally: 1. It is filled with the most palpable and absurd contradictions; 2. These contradictions are so carelessly put together as to occur in consecutive paragraphs; 3. It is throughout laudatory of the innocence and freedom from care of the barbarians of the South Seas, particularly the Marquesans; 4. It compares their condition with civilized society as being the more desirable of the two; 5. It either excuses and wilfully palliates the cannibalism and savage vices of the Polynesians, or is guilty of as great a crime in such a writer, that of ignorance of his subject; and, 6. It is redundant with bitter charges against the missionaries, piles obloquy upon their labor and its results, and broadly accuses them of being the cause of the vice, misery, destitution, and unhappiness of the Polynesians wherever they have penetrated. (pp. 87-8)

We are inclined to doubt seriously whether our author ever saw the Marquesas; or if he did, whether he ever resided among the Typees; or, if he did, whether this book is not a sort of romantic satire at the expense of the poor savages. . . .

The worst feature of the book is the undisguised attempt to decry the missionary work in its every feature. . . .

[The author] looks at the savage life with a captivated eye, and seals his approbation with a constant phrenzy to be freed from this happy vale—being in almost daily fear of finding himself hashed in the most approved style of Typee epicurean rites, or tenderly roasted and served up in calabashes for 'the regal and noble Mehevi' and his chiefs!

We have borne with the pretensions of this book as though it were a narrative of real events. It may be, and likely is, though somewhat highly colored. But whether true or false, the real or pseudonymic author deserves a pointed and severe rebuke for his flagrant outrages against civilization, and particularly the missionary work. The abuse he heaps upon the latter belongs to the vagabonds, fugitives, convicts, and deserters of every grade—and there let it rest. (p. 88)

> *William Oland Bourne, in an extract from "'Typee':*
> *The Traducers of Missions" (originally an unsigned*
> *essay in* Christian Parlor Magazine, *Vol. III, July,*
> *1846 (and reprinted in* Melville: The Critical Heri-
> tage, *edited by Watson G. Branch, Routledge & Ke-*
> *gan Paul, 1974, pp. 85-9).*

WALT WHITMAN   (essay date 1847)

Omoo, the new work . . . by Mr. Melville, author of *Typee,* affords two well printed volumes of the most readable sort of reading. The question whether these stories be authentic or not has, of course, not so much to do with their interest. One can revel in such richly good natured style, if nothing else. We therefore recommend this 'narrative of adventures in the south seas,' as thorough entertainment—not so light as to be tossed aside for its flippancy, nor so profound as to be tiresome. (p. 95)

> *Walt Whitman, in an extract from his essay (origi-*
> *nally unsigned), in* Daily Eagle, *May 5, 1847 (and*
> *reprinted in* Melville: The Critical Heritage, *edited*
> *by Watson G. Branch, Routledge & Kegan Paul,*
> *1974, pp. 95-6).*

HORACE GREELEY   (essay date 1847)

Omoo, by Herman Melville, is replete alike with the merits and the faults of its forerunner, *Typee.* All of us were mistaken who thought the fascination of *Typee* owing mainly to its subject, or rather to the novel and primitive state of human existence it described. *Omoo* dispels all such illusions and proves the author a born genius, with few superiors either as a narrator, a describer, or a humorist. Few living men could have invested such scenes, incidents and persons as figure in *Omoo* with anything like the charm they wear in Melville's graphic pages; the adventures narrated might have occurred to any one, as others equally exciting have done to thousands of voyagers in the South Seas; but who has ever before described any so well? *Typee* and *Omoo,* doubtless in the main true narratives, are worthy to rank in interest with *Robinson Crusoe* and in vivacity with the best of Stephens's *Travels.*—Yet they are unmistakably defective if not positively diseased in moral tone, and will very fairly be condemned as dangerous reading for those of immature intellects and unsettled principles. Not that you can often put your finger on a passage positively offensive; but the *tone* is bad, and incidents of the most objectionable character are depicted with a racy lightness which would once have been admired but will now be justly condemned. A *penchant* for bad liquors is everywhere boldly proclaimed, while a hankering after loose company not always of the masculine order, is but

thinly disguised and perpetually protruding itself throughout the work. This is to be deplored not alone for the author's sake, nor even for that of the large class which it will deter from perusing his adventures. We regret it still more because it will prevent his lucid and apparently candid testimony with regard to the value, the effect and the defects of the Missionary labors among the South Sea Islanders from having its due weight with those most deeply interested. (pp. 121-22)

> *Horace Greeley, "'Omoo'," in* Weekly Tribune,
> New York, *June 23, 1847 (and reprinted in* Melville:
> The Critical Heritage, *edited by Watson G. Branch,*
> *Routledge & Kegan Paul, 1974, pp. 121-22).*

GEORGE WASHINGTON PECK   (essay date 1847)

The reckless spirit which betrays itself on every page of [*Omoo*]— the cool, sneering wit, and the perfect want of *heart* everywhere manifested in it, make it repel, almost as much as its voluptuous scenery-painting and its sketchy outlines of stories attract. (p. 124)

[Melville] makes always a striking picture, and, as we skim rapidly over one after another, it does not always occur to us at first to question the truth of the details. But when we come to look at them through a second reading, these details are seen to be thrown in with such a bold disregard of naturalness and congruity as one could never put on who was painting from the actual. . . . (p. 125)

[We] wish not to have this sort of writing forced upon us under any other than its own proper name. It is mere frothy, sketchy outlining, that will bear the test of comparison with nature as little as would scene painting or the pictures on French paper hangings. If Typee were to tell his stories as he does, in the witness box, he would be a poor lawyer who could not make it evident to a jury that they would not stand sifting; his readiness and flippancy might make a brief impression while he was giving his evidence in chief, but it would take no very rigid cross-examination to bring him into discredit. (pp. 125-26)

[Control] and discipline of the fancy seems to us just wherein [Melville] fails. He has all the confidence of genius, all its reckless abandonment, but little of its power. He has written a very attractive and readable book, but there are few among those who have an eye for nature and a lively fancy, but who could write as good a one if they had the hardihood—if they could as easily throw off all fear of making the judicious grieve. Were he put to his confession, there is no doubt but he would own that, in drawing pictures, he does not rigidly adhere to a fixed image, something that he has seen or remembers; that he does not endeavor to present his first landscape in a clear, strong, rich light, but often, as his narrative grows road weary, lets it throw the bridle rein of strict veracity on the neck of his fancy, and relieve itself by an occasional canter. (p. 127)

But let us thank the author for the good he has given us. . . . (p. 128)

We do most heartily envy the man who could write such a book as *Omoo,* for nothing disturbs his serenity in the least; he is always in a good humor with himself, well pleased with what he writes, satisfied with his powers, and hence never dull. It must be owned he has some ground for complacency. He exhibits, on almost every page, the original ability to be an imaginative writer of the highest order. Some of his bits of description are very fine, and that in the highest and most poetic way. . . .

. . . It is an ably written book; so good, in fact, (in point of ability . . .)—that we are not pleased with it because it is not better. The author has shown himself so very capable of using a great style, and comes, at times, so near excellence, that we feel disposed to quarrel with him for never exactly reaching it. He is bold and self-contained; no cold timidity chills the glow of his fancy. Why does he not, before abandoning himself to the current of Thought, push out till he comes over the great channel of Truth? Or, not to speak in a parable, why does he not imitate the great describers, and give us pictures that will bear dissection, characters true to themselves, and a style that moves everywhere with the same peculiar measure? (pp. 128-29)

> *George Washington Peck, "'Omoo',"* in American Review, *Vol. VI, July, 1847 (and reprinted in* Melville: The Critical Heritage, *edited by Watson G. Branch, Routledge & Kegan Paul, 1974, pp. 123-32).*

BENTLEY'S MISCELLANY   (essay date 1849)

For feeling in its ordinary shapes [Mr. Melville] has no toleration, and he thinks, not altogether perhaps without reason, that the world also is growing weary of it. He endeavours, therefore [in his new novel **"Mardi"**], to imitate one of the most striking processes of civilisation, and to build up for fancy a distant home in the ocean. In the development of this design he is guilty of great extravagance; but while floating between heaven and earth, creating archipelagos in the clouds, and peopling them with races stranger and more fantastical than

> —The cannibals that each other eat;
> The Anthropophagi, and men whose heads
> Do grow beneath their shoulders,

he contrives to inspire us with an interest in his creations, to excite our passions, to astonish us with the wild grandeur of his landscapes, and to excite in us a strong desire to dream on with him indefinitely. (pp. 439-40)

[From the details of the novel's plot] it is easy to perceive how much excitement and pleasure may be extracted. Yet the story is the least part of the work, which consists of an infinite number of episodes and digressions, descriptions and speculations, theories and commentaries sometimes immeasurably fantastical. Occasionally the author determines to display his learning, when vanity gets the upper hand of him, bewilders his judgment, and makes us laugh heartily at the weakness of human nature. (pp. 440-41)

We have no objection to a writer's setting down his opinion on all possible subjects, and therefore we would rather encourage this intellectual gambolling, especially when it is done in jest, and no offence in the world is meant; but we have some dislike to meeting with ideas in so thick a haze that we are unable to perceive distinctly which is which, except where . . . something so exceedingly delicate is to be shadowed forth, that the more opaque the veil the better. In such passages an author's skill is put to the test. (p. 441)

Mr. Melville abjures all connection with [the] rules and principles [of art]. His cardinal notion is, that provided you effect your purpose, awaken interest, and excite admiration, it signifies very little by what means your design is accomplished. He occasionally, therefore, soars into verse, occasionally sinks

to the ordinary level of prose, but habitually operates through a medium which is neither the one nor the other, but a singular compound of both, which tolerates the bold licences of the former and the minuteness and voluminousness of the latter.

It must be allowed, however, that the subject being given, it would not be easy to find a style better fitted for recommending it to the reader. The thing to be achieved is no less than the reconciling of the mind to the creation of an Utopia in the unknown latitudes of the Pacific, to call into existence imaginary tribes and nations, to describe fabulous manners; and to glass them so distinctly in the fancy that they will appear to have been implanted there by memory. This was obviously to be effected either by the exaggeration of ideas, or by exaggeration of language, or by both. . . . Nothing was left . . . but to give to strange thoughts and ideas a strange utterance, and by churning up language, as the gods in the Indian fable churned the ocean, to create in the reader a sense of bewilderment and dizziness, which must put to flight all wish to revert to a simple phraseology.

To follow the fugitives from the deck of the Arcturion, from the time they drop their boat into the ocean till the last of them is swept from our view in a cloud of spray, is to move through a gorgeous dream, where the scenes change so rapidly, where danger and strife and plunder alternate with tranquillity and ease and serenity, and where the most stupendous of the known phenomena of nature are exaggerated infinitely by the insatiable appetite of human fancy. (pp. 441-42)

Everywhere there is freshness, originality, or a new way of treating old things. . . . [Mr. Melville] deals with materials very different from those of the ordinary novelist and romance writer; wild and fabulous he is, and full of Utopian fantasies. But in his company we at least escape from those vapid pictures of society which, differently brushed up and varnished, have been presented to us a thousand times before. **"Mardi"** is a book by itself, which the reader will probably like very much or detest altogether, according to the measure of his own imagination. In us it has excited, on the whole, very pleasurable sensations. (p. 442)

> *"Literature of the Month: 'Mardi, and the Voyage Thither',"* in Bentley's Miscellany, *Vol. XXV, April, 1849, pp. 439-42.*

GEORGE RIPLEY   (essay date 1849)

We have seldom found our reading faculty so near exhaustion, or our good nature as critics so severely exercised, as in an attempt to get through this new work [*Mardi*] by the author of the fascinating *Typee* and *Omoo*. If we had never heard of Mr. Melville before, we should soon have laid aside his book, as a monstrous compound of Carlyle, Jean-Paul, and Sterne, with now and then a touch of Ossian thrown in; but remembering our admiration of his former charming productions, we were unable to believe that the two volumes could contain so little of the peculiar excellence of an old favorite, and only mock us with a constant sense of disappointment.

Typee and *Omoo* were written under the immediate inspiration of personal experience.—The vivid impressions which the author had received from his residence among those fairy Edens of the Sea had not faded from his mind. He describes what he saw and felt, with the careless hilarity of a sailor, relating a long yarn to his shipmates in the forecastle. . . . [He] talks on in his riotous, rollicking manner, always saucy, often swaggering, but ever revealing the soul of a poet and the eye of a painter. . . . (pp. 161-62)

The present work aims at a much higher mark but fails to reach it. It professes to be a work of imagination, founded on Polynesian adventures, and for a portion of the first volume maintains that character with tolerable success. . . . There are passages in this part of the work, which, taken as separate pictures, display unrivaled beauty and power—the same simple, unaffected grace—the same deep joy in all the rare and precious things of nature—and the same easy command of forcible, picturesque language, which in his former productions called forth such a gush of admiration, even from the most hidebound reviewer.

But the scene changes after we arrive at 'Mardi' and the main plot of the book (such as it is) begins to open.

We are then presented with a tissue of conceits, fancifully strung about the personages of the tale, expressed in language that is equally intolerable for its affectation and its obscurity. The story has no movement, no proportions, no ultimate end; and unless it is a huge allegory—bits of which peep out here and there—winding its unwieldy length along, like some monster of the deep, no significance or point. We become weary with the shapeless rhapsody, and wonder at the audacity of the writer which could attempt such an experiment with the long suffering of his readers.

We should not think it worth while to express ourselves so unambiguously on the character of this work, if we did not recognize in Mr. Melville a writer not only of rare promise, but of excellent performance. He has failed by leaving his sphere, which is that of graphic, poetical narration, and launching out into the dim, shadowy, spectral, Mardian region of mystic speculation and wizard fancies. Even the language of this work is a hybrid between poetry and prose.—Every page abounds in lines which might be dovetailed into a regular poem without any change in the rhythm. It can easily be read aloud so that the nicest ear could not distinguish it from heroic verse. Let the author return to the transparent narration of his own adventures, in the pure, imaginative prose, which he handles with such graceful facility, and he will be everywhere welcomed as one of the most delightful of American writers. (pp. 162-63)

George Ripley, '''Mardi','' in Tribune, *New York, May 10, 1849 (and reprinted in* Melville: The Critical Heritage, *edited by Watson G. Branch, Routledge & Kegan Paul, 1974, pp. 161-63).*

THE SPECTATOR   (essay date 1849)

[Mr. Melville's *Redburn his First Voyage*] is even more remarkable than his stories "founded on fact" descriptive of native scenery and life in the islands of the Pacific. In *Typee* and *Omoo* there was novelty and interest of subject. Everything was fresh and vigorous in the manners of the people, the character of the country and its vegetation; there were rapidity, variety, and adventure in the story, with enough of nautical character to introduce the element of contrast. In *Redburn his First Voyage* there are none of these sources of attraction; yet, with the exception of some chapters descriptive of commonplace things, the book is very readable and attractive. . . . *Redburn,* though merely the narrative of a voyage from New York to Liverpool and back, with a description of the characters of officers and crew, is . . . a book both of information and

interest. We get a good idea of life at sea, as it appears at first to the boy novice and afterwards to the more experienced seaman. The hardships and privations of the crew, the petty tyranny, the pettier greatness, with the tricks and frauds practised in a common merchant-vessel on the raw hands, are well exhibited, without exaggeration. . . .

The plan of the book is well designed to bring out its matter effectively; though the position and reputed character of Redburn as "the son of a gentleman," contrived apparently for the sake of contrast and the display of a quiet humour, is not always consistently maintained. . . . The idea of throwing a simple and innocent-minded lad, just fresh from home, into the midst of the roughness, rudeness, and startling novelty of a ship, may be found in [Frederick Marryat's] *Peter Simple;* but the circumstances of poor Redburn are so different from those of the well-connected midshipman, and the nautical incidents and characters have so little in common, that the story has the effect of originality. The quiet humour arising from the contrast between the frame of mind of the boy and his position and circumstances, as well as the sharp reflections his freshness and home education induce him to make, bear some resemblance in point of style to Marryat; but it may arise from the nature of the subject.

There is nothing very striking in the incidents of **Redburn**—nothing, in fact, beyond the common probabilities of the merchant service in almost every vessel that sails between Great Britain and America: the characters, or something like them, may doubtless be met in almost every ship that leaves harbour. Nor does Mr. Melville aim at effect by melodramatic exaggeration, except once in an episodical trip to London: on the contrary, he indicates several things, leaving the filling up to the reader's imagination, instead of painting scenes in detail, that a vulgar writer would certainly have done. The interest of **Redburn** arises from its quiet naturalness. It reads like a "true story"—as if it had all taken place. (p. 1020)

''Herman Melville's 'Redburn','' in The Spectator *(© 1849 by The Spectator), Vol. 22, No. 1113, October 27, 1849, pp. 1020-21.*

[EVERT A. DUYCKINCK]   (essay date 1850)

The keen sense of outward life, mingled with the growing weight of reflection which cheers or burdens the inner man, observable in Mr. Melville's later volumes, keep us company in [**White Jacket**]. It is this union of culture and experience, of thought and observation, the sharp breeze of the forecastle alternating with the mellow stillness of the library, books and work imparting to each other mutual life, which distinguishes the narratives of the author of **Typee** from all other productions of their class. He is not a bookish sailor or a tar among books; each character is separate and perfect in its integrity, but he is all the better sailor for the duty and decision which books teach, all the better reader for the independence and sharpness of observation incidental to the objective life of the sea. It is very seldom that you can get at the latter from this point of view. . . . To have the fancy and the fact united is rare in any walk, almost unknown on the sea. Hence to Herman Melville, whose mind swarms with tender, poetic, or humorous fancies, the ship is a new world, now first conquered. No one has so occupied it. Sailors have been described and well described, as sailors, and there has been a deal of brilliant and justly admired nautical writing, from the quarter-deck; but the sailor as a man, seen with a genial philosophy and seen from the forecastle, has been reserved for our author. The effect is novel and startling. . . .

[It] is a sound humanitarian lesson which he teaches, or rather that life teaches, which he records. There is no sentimentality, no effort to elevate the "people" or degrade the commodores; his characters are not thrust out of their ordinary positions or range of ideas; he does not sew any finery upon them, but they are all heroes nevertheless, interesting while they are on the stage, one and all, as genuine Shakspearean, that is human personages. . . .

Herman Melville tests all his characters by their manhood. His book is thoroughly American and democratic. There is no patronage in his exhibition of a sailor, any more than in his portraits of captains and commodores. He gives all fair play in an impartial spirit. There is no railing, no scolding; he never loses his temper when he hits hardest. A quaint, satirical, yet genial humor is his grand destructive weapon. It would be a most dangerous one (for what is there which cannot be shaken with ridicule?), were it not for the poetic element by which it is elevated. Let our author treasure this as his choicest possession, for without it his humor would soon degenerate into a sneer, than which there is nothing sadder, more fatal. In regarding, too, the spirit of things, may he not fall into the error of undervaluing their forms, lest he get into a bewildering, barren, and void scepticism! (p. 271)

> [*Evert A. Duyckinck,*] *"Mr. Melville's 'White Jacket',"* in The Literary World, *Vol. VI, No. 163, March 16, 1850, pp. 271-72.*

HERMAN MELVILLE   (essay date 1851)

What's the use of elaborating what, in its very essence, is so short-lived as a modern book? Though I wrote the Gospels in this century, I should die in the gutter. . . . What "reputation" H. M. has is horrible. Think of it! To go down to posterity is bad enough, any way; but to go down as a "man who lived among the cannibals"! When I speak of posterity, in reference to myself, I only mean the babies who will probably be born in the moment immediately ensuing upon my giving up the ghost. I shall go down to some of them, in all likelihood. "Typee" will be given to them, perhaps, with their gingerbread. I have come to regard this matter of Fame as the most transparent of all vanities. . . . I did not think of Fame, a year ago, as I do now. My development has been all within a few years past. I am like one of those seeds taken out of the Egyptian Pyramids, which, after being three thousand years a seed and nothing but a seed, being planted in English soil, it developed itself, grew to greenness, and then fell to mould. So I. Until I was twenty-five, I had no development at all. From my twenty-fifth year I date my life. Three weeks have scarcely passed, at any time between then and now, that I have not unfolded within myself. But I feel that I am now come to the inmost leaf of the bulb, and that shortly the flower must fall to the mould. (pp. 129-30)

> *Herman Melville, in his letter to Nathaniel Hawthorne on June 1, 1851, in* The Letters of Herman Melville, *edited by Merrell R. Davis and William H. Gilman (© 1960 by Yale University Press, Inc.), Yale University Press, 1960, pp. 126-31.*

[HENRY F. CHORLEY]   (essay date 1851)

[*The Whale,* by Herman Melville,] is an ill-compounded mixture of romance and matter-of-fact. The idea of a connected and collected story has obviously visited and abandoned its writer again and again in the course of composition. The style of his tale is in places disfigured by mad (rather than bad) English; and its catastrophe is hastily, weakly, and obscurely managed. (p. 1112)

Frantic though [the novel's plot] seems to be, it might possibly have been accepted as the motive and purpose of an *extravaganza* had its author been consistent with himself. . . . There is a time for everything in imaginative literature;—and, according to its order, a place—for rant as well as for reserve; but the rant must be good, honest, shameless rant, without flaw or misgiving. . . . Ravings and scraps of useful knowledge flung together salad-wise make a dish in which there may be much surprise, but in which there is little savour. The real secret of this patchiness in the present case is disclosed in Mr. Melville's appendix; which contains . . . an assortment of curious quotations . . . suggesting the idea that a substantial work on the subject may have been originally contemplated. Either Mr. Melville's purpose must have changed, or his power must have fallen short. The result is, at all events, a most provoking book,—neither so utterly extravagant as to be entirely comfortable, nor so instructively complete as to take place among documents on the subject of the Great Fish, his capabilities, his home and his capture. Our author must be henceforth numbered in the company of the incorrigibles who occasionally tantalize us with indications of genius, while they constantly summon us to endure monstrosities, carelessnesses, and other such harassing manifestations of bad taste as daring or disordered ingenuity can devise. (pp. 1112-13)

Mr. Melville has to thank himself only if his horrors and his heroics are flung aside by the general reader, as so much trash belonging to the worst school of Bedlam literature,—since he seems not so much unable to learn as disdainful of learning the craft of an artist. (p. 1113)

> [*Henry F. Chorley,*] *"Reviews: 'The Whale',"* in The Athenaeum, *No. 1252, October 25, 1851, pp. 1112-13.*

[GEORGE RIPLEY]   (essay date 1851)

[In] point of richness and variety of incident, originality of conception, and splendor of description, [Herman Melville's *Moby Dick; or, The Whale*] surpasses any of the former productions of this highly successful author. . . . [On the slight framework of the novel's plot], the author has constructed a romance, a tragedy, and a natural history, not without numerous gratuitous suggestions on psychology, ethics, and theology. Beneath the whole story, the subtle, imaginative reader may perhaps find a pregnant allegory, intended to illustrate the mystery of human life. Certain it is that the rapid, pointed hints which are often thrown out, with the keenness and velocity of a harpoon, penetrate deep into the heart of things, showing that the genius of the author for moral analysis is scarcely surpassed by his wizard power of description.

In the course of the narrative the habits of the whale are fully and ably described. Frequent graphic and instructive sketches of the fishery, of sealife in a whaling vessel, and of the manners and customs of strange nations are interspersed with excellent artistic effect among the thrilling scenes of the story. The various processes of procuring oil are explained with the minute, painstaking fidelity of a statistical record, contrasting strangely with the weird, phantom-like character of the plot, and of some of the leading personages, who present a no less unearthly appearance than the witches in *Macbeth*. These sudden and decided transitions form a striking feature of the volume. Difficult of management, in the highest degree, they are wrought with consummate skill. To a less gifted author, they would inevitably have proved fatal. He has not only deftly avoided their dangers, but made them an element of great power. They constantly pique the attention of the reader, keeping curiosity alive, and presenting the combined charm of surprise and alternation.

The introductory chapters of the volume . . . are pervaded with a fine vein of comic humor, and reveal a succession of portraitures, in which the lineaments of nature shine forth, through a good deal of perverse, intentional exaggeration. . . . Nothing can be better than the description of the owners of the vessel, Captain Peleg and Captain Bildad, whose acquaintance we make before the commencement of the voyage. The character of Captain Ahab also opens upon us with wonderful power. He exercises a wild, bewildering fascination by his dark and mysterious nature, which is not at all diminished when we obtain a clearer insight into his strange history. Indeed, all the members of the ship's company . . . stand before us in the strongest individual relief, presenting a unique picture gallery, which every artist must despair of rivaling.

> [*George Ripley,*] *"Literary Notices: 'Moby-Dick',"* *in* Harper's New Monthly Magazine, *Vol. IV, No. XIX, December, 1851, p. 137.*

[EVERT A. DUYCKINCK]   (essay date 1852)

The purpose of Mr. Melville's [**"Pierre; or, the Ambiguities"**], though vaguely hinted, rather than directly stated, seems to be to illustrate the possible antagonism of a sense of duty, conceived in the heat and impetuosity of youth, to all the recognised laws of social morality; and to exhibit a conflict between the virtues. (p. 118)

The pivot of the story is the pretended marriage of Pierre with his sister, in order to conceal her illegitimacy and protect his father's memory. . . . Apart from the very obvious way of gaining the same object at an infinitely smaller cost, is it natural that a loving youth should cast away the affection of his mother and his betrothed and the attachment of home to hide a dim stain upon his father's memory and to enjoy the love of an equivocal sister? Pierre not only acts thus absurdly, but pretends to act from a sense of duty. He is battling for Truth and Right, and the first thing he does in behalf of Truth is to proclaim to the whole world a falsehood, and the next thing he does is to commit in behalf of Right, a half a dozen most foul wrongs. . . . In a word, Pierre is a psychological curiosity, a moral and intellectual phenomenon; Isabel, a *lusus naturae*; Lucy, an incomprehensible woman; and the rest not of the earth nor, we may venture to state, of heaven. The object of the author, perhaps, has been, not to delineate life and character as they are or may possibly be, but as they are not and cannot be. We must receive the book, then, as an eccentricity of the imagination.

The most immoral *moral* of the story, if it has any moral at all, seems to be the impracticability of virtue; a leering demoniacal spectre of an idea seems to be speering at us through the dim obscure of this dark book, and mocking us with this dismal falsehood. (pp. 118-19)

In commenting upon the vagueness of the book, the uncertainty of its aim, the indefiniteness of its characters, and want of

distinctness in its pictures, we are perhaps only proclaiming ourselves as the discoverers of a literary mare's nest; this vagueness, as the title of the **"Ambiguities"** seems to indicate, having been possibly intended by the author, and the work meant as a problem of impossible solution, to set critics and readers a woolgathering. It is alone intelligible as an unintelligibility. . . .

All the male characters of the book have a certain robust, animal force and untamed energy, which carry them through their melodramatic parts—no slight duty—with an effect sure to bring down the applause of the excitable and impulsive. Mr. Melville can think clearly, and write with distinctness and force—in a style of simplicity and purity. Why, then, does he allow his mind to run riot amid remote analogies, where the chain of association is invisible to mortal minds? Why does he give us incoherencies of thought, in infelicities of language? (p. 119)

The author of **"Pierre; or, the Ambiguities;"** the writer of a mystic romance, in which are conjured up unreal nightmare-conceptions, a confused phantasmagoria of distorted fancies and conceits, ghostly abstractions and fitful shadows, is certainly but a spectre of the substantial author of **"Omoo"** and **"Typee,"** the jovial and hearty narrator of the traveller's tale of incident and adventure. . . . If this novel indicates a chaotic state of authorship,—and we can distinguish fragmentary elements of beauty—out of which is to rise a future temple of order, grace, and proportion, in which the genius of Mr. Melville is to enshrine itself, we will be happy to worship there; but let its foundation be firmly based on *terra firma*, or, if in the heavens, let us not trust our common sense to the flight of any waxen pinion. We would rejoice to meet Mr. Melville again in the hale company of sturdy sailors, men of flesh and blood, and, strengthened by the wholesome air of the outside world, whether it be land-breeze or sea-breeze, listen to his narrative of a traveller's tale, in which he has few equals in power and felicity. (pp. 119-20)

> [*Evert A. Duyckinck,*] *"'Pierre; or the Ambiguities',"* *in* The Literary World, *Vol. XI, August 21, 1852, pp. 118-20.*

THE CHRISTIAN EXAMINER   (essay date 1855)

[Mr. Melville's **"Israel Potter: His Fifty Years of Exile"**] scarcely sustains the reputation which he won by the earlier productions of his pen. In them he entered upon a comparatively uncultivated field. . . . But in his later works (and especially in the volume before us) he has dealt with another and very different class of characters, and placed them in circumstances very different from those which gave interest to his earlier volumes; and here his success has been much less apparent. **"Israel Potter,"** indeed, notwithstanding some fine passages and some skilful descriptions, is rather heavy reading. Its style is, in the main, flowing and graceful, and its tone genial and healthy; and yet the author fails to interest us very much in the fortunes of his hero. His character, in truth, lacks those elements which arrest and enchain the reader's sympathies; and, at the best, it is only a feeble delineation of a very commonplace person. Nor are the other characters portrayed with greater skill. In our author's delineation, Dr. Franklin's homely wisdom and shrewd philosophy degenerate into ridiculous cant and officious imbecility; and the portraiture of Paul Jones seems almost equally infelicitous. There are, however, some vigorous descriptions of the exploits of this remarkable man on the coasts of Scotland

and Ireland, which constitute, perhaps, the ablest and most interesting part of the volume. But from this praise we would exclude the account of the battle between the Bon Homme Richard and the Serapis. A battle so sanguinary and brutal in its whole character cannot form an attractive episode in a work of high art; and it is to be regretted that Mr. Melville should have dwelt so minutely upon its details. (pp. 470-71)

> *"Notices of Recent Publications: 'Israel Potter: His Fifty Years of Exile',"* in The Christian Examiner, *Vol. 58, No. CLXXXIX, May, 1855, pp. 470-71.*

TRIBUNE   (essay date 1856)

[In *The Piazza Tales*] we find the peculiar traits of the author's genius, though in a [less] decided form, than in most of his previous compositions. They show something of the boldness of invention, brilliancy of imagination, and quaintness of expression which usually mark his writings, with not a little of the apparent perversity and self-will, which serve as a foil to their various excellences. **'Bartleby,'** the scrivener, is the most original story in the volume, and as a curious study of human nature, possesses unquestionable merit. **'Benito Cereno,'** and **'The Encantadas,'** are fresh specimens of Mr. Melville's sea-romances, but cannot be regarded as improvements on his former popular productions in that kind. **'The Lightning-Rod Man'** and **'The Bell Tower,'** which complete the contents of the volume, are ingenious rhapsodies.

> *"'The Piazza Tales',"* in Tribune, New York, *June 23, 1856 (and reprinted in* Melville: The Critical Heritage, *edited by Watson G. Branch, Routledge & Kegan Paul, 1974, p. 357).*

WESTMINSTER AND FOREIGN QUARTERLY REVIEW (essay date 1857)

We are not among those who have had faith in Herman Melville's South Pacific travels so much as in his strength of imagination. The *Confidence-Man* shows him in a new character—that of a satirist, and a very keen, somewhat bitter, observer. . . . It required close knowledge of the world, and of the Yankee world, to write such a book and make the satire acute and telling, and the scenes not too improbable for the faith given to fiction. Perhaps the moral is the gullibility of the great Republic, when taken on its own tack. At all events, it is a wide enough moral to have numerous applications, and sends minor shafts to right and left. Several capital anecdotes are told, and well told; but we are conscious of a certain hardness in the book, from the absence of humour, where so much humanity is shuffled into close neighbourhood. And with the absence of humour, too, there is an absence of kindliness. The view of human nature is severe and sombre. . . . A moneyless man and a heartless man are not good exponents of our state. Mr. Melville has delineated with passable correctness, but he has forgotten to infuse the colours that exist in nature. The fault may lie in the uniqueness of the construction. Spread over a larger canvas, and taking in more of the innumerable sides of humanity, the picture might have been as accurate, the satire as sharp, and the author would not have laid himself open to the charge of harshness. Few Americans write so powerfully as Mr. Melville, or in better English. . . . [The *Confidence-Man*] is a remarkable work, and will add to his reputation. (pp. 385-86)

> *"The 'Confidence-Man',"* in Westminster and Foreign Quarterly Review, *n.s. Vol. XII, July, 1857 (and*

> *reprinted in* Melville: The Critical Heritage, *edited by Watson G. Branch, Routledge & Kegan Paul, 1974, pp. 385-86).*

THE ATLANTIC MONTHLY   (essay date 1867)

[Mr. Melville's collection of poetry titled **Battle-Pieces and Aspects of the War**] possesses the negative virtues of originality in such degree that it not only reminds you of no poetry you have read, but of no life you have known. Is it possible—you ask yourself, after running over all these celebrative, inscriptive, and memorial verses—that there has really been a great war, with battles fought by men and bewailed by women? Or is it only that Mr. Melville's inner consciousness has been perturbed, and filled with the phantasms of enlistments, marches, fights in the air, parenthetic bulletin-boards, and tortured humanity shedding, not words and blood, but words alone? . . .

Mr. Melville's skill is so great that we fear he has not often felt the things of which he writes, since with all his skill he fails to move us. In some respects we find his poems admirable. He treats events as realistically as one can to whom they seem to have presented themselves as dreams; but at last they remain vagaries, and are none the more substantial because they have a modern speech and motion. . . .

With certain moods or abstractions of the common mind during the war, Mr. Melville's faculty is well fitted to deal: the unrest, the strangeness and solitude, to which the first sense of the great danger reduced all souls, are reflected in his verse, and whatever purely mystic aspect occurrences had seems to have been felt by this poet, so little capable of giving their positive likeness. . . .

[The] book is full of pictures of many kinds,—often good,—though all with an heroic quality of remoteness, separating our weak human feelings from them by trackless distances. (p. 252)

A tender and subtle music is felt in many of the verses, and the eccentric metres are gracefully managed. . . . [However, the] persons in Mr. Melville's poetry seem as widely removed as he from our actual life. If all the Rebels were as pleasingly impalpable as those the poet portrays, we could forgive them without a pang, and admit them to Congress without a test-oath of any kind. (pp. 252-53)

> *"Reviews and Literary Notices: 'Battle-Pieces and Aspects of the War',"* in The Atlantic Monthly *(copyright © 1867, by The Atlantic Monthly Company, Boston, Mass.), Vol. XIX, No. CXII, February, 1867, pp. 252-53.*

[EDMUND CLARENCE STEDMAN]   (essay date 1876)

[Mr. Melville's *Clarel*] is no less hazardous than ambitious. A narrative poem of such a length demands all the charms of verse, the strength and interest of plot, the picturesqueness of episode, and the beauty of sentimental or reflective digression which the author's art is capable of creating; and even then it may lack the subtle spell which chains the reader to its perusal. *Clarel,* we must frankly confess, is something of a puzzle, both in design and execution. (p. 399)

[There is] no plot in the work; but neither do the theological doubts, questions, and disputations indulged in by the characters, and those whom they meet, have any logical course or lead to any distinct conclusions. The reader soon becomes hopelessly bewildered, and fatigues himself vainly in the effort to give personality to speakers who constantly evade it, and connection to scenes which perversely hold themselves separate from each other. The verse, frequently flowing for a few lines with a smooth, agreeable current, seems to foam and chafe against unmanageable words like a brook in a stony glen: there are fragments of fresh, musical lyrics, suggestive both of Hafiz and of William Blake; there are passages so rough, distorted, and commonplace withal, that the reader impatiently shuts the book. It is, in this respect, a medley such as we have rarely perused,—a mixture of skill and awkwardness, thought and aimless fancy, plan shattered by whim and melody broken by discords. It is difficult to see how any one capable of writing such excellent brief passages should also write such astonishingly poor ones—or the reverse.

The descriptive portions of the poem are often bold, clear, and suggestive of the actual scenes. We might make a collection of admirable lines and couplets, which have the ring and sparkle of true poetry. On the other hand it would be equally easy to multiply passages . . . the sense of which is only reached with difficulty. . . . (p. 400)

There is a vein of earnestness in Mr. Melville's poem, singularly at variance with the carelessness of the execution; but this only increases the impression of confusion which it makes. (pp. 401-02)

> [*Edmund Clarence Stedman,*] *"'Clarel',"* in Tribune, *New York, June 16, 1876 (and reprinted in* Melville: The Critical Heritage, *edited by Watson G. Branch, Routledge & Kegan Paul, 1974, pp. 399-402).*

H. S. SALT   (essay date 1889)

The chief characteristic of Herman Melville's writings is [the] attempted union of the practical with the ideal. Commencing with a basis of solid fact, he loves to build up a fantastic structure, which is finally lost in the cloudland of metaphysical speculation. He is at his best, as in *Typee,* when the mystic element is kept in check, and made subservient to the clear development of the story; or when, as in certain passages of *Mardi* and *Moby Dick,* the two qualities are for the time harmoniously blended. . . .

The tone of Melville's books is altogether frank and healthy, though of direct ethical teaching there is little or no trace, except on the subject of humanity, on which he expresses himself with strong and genuine feeling. (p. 416)

That Melville, in spite of his early transcendental tendencies and final lapse into the 'illimitable inane,' possessed strong powers of observation, a solid grasp of facts, and a keen sense of humour, will not be denied by any one who is acquainted with his writings. . . . His literary power, as evidenced in *Typee* and his other early volumes, is also unmistakable, his descriptions being at one time rapid, concentrated, and vigorous, according to the nature of his subject, at another time dreamy, suggestive, and picturesque. The fall from the masthead in *White Jacket* is a swift and subtle piece of writing of which George Meredith might be proud; the death of the white whale in *Moby Dick* rises to a sort of epic grandeur and intensity. . . . (pp. 416-17)

[It] is a cause for regret that the author of *Typee* and *Mardi* should have fallen to a great extent out of notice, and should be familiar only to a small circle of admirers, instead of enjoying the wide reputation to which his undoubted genius entitles him. (p. 417)

> *H. S. Salt, "Herman Melville," in* Scottish Art Review, *Vol. II, November, 1889 (and reprinted in* Melville: The Critical Heritage, *edited by Watson G. Branch, Routledge & Kegan Paul, 1974, pp. 413-17).*

RICHARD HENRY STODDARD   (essay date 1891)

There was a wealth of imagination in the mind of Mr. Melville, but it was an untrained imagination, and a world of the stuff out of which poetry is made, but no poetry, which is creation and not chaos. He saw like a poet, felt like a poet, thought like a poet, but he never attained any proficiency in verse, which was not among his natural gifts. His vocabulary was large, fluent, eloquent, but it was excessive, inaccurate and unliterary. He wrote too easily, and at too great length, his pen sometimes running away with him, and from his readers. There were strange, dark, mysterious elements in his nature, as there were in Hawthorne's, but he never learned to control them, as Hawthorne did from the beginning, and never turned their possibilities into actualities. (p. 272)

> *Richard Henry Stoddard, "Mr. Stoddard on Herman Melville," in* The Critic (© The Critic 1891), *n.s. Vol. XVI, No. 411, November 14, 1891, pp. 272-73.*

W. CLARK RUSSELL   (essay date 1892)

Until Richard H. Dana and Herman Melville wrote, the commercial sailor of Great Britain and the United States was without representation in literature. Dana and Melville were Americans. They were the first to lift the hatch and show the world what passes in a ship's forecastle; how men live down in that gloomy cave, how and what they eat, and where they sleep; what pleasures they take, what their sorrows and wrongs are; how they are used when they quit their black sea-parlors in response to the boatswain's silver summons to work on deck by day or by night. These secrets of the deep Dana and Melville disclosed. By doing so, they . . . expanded American literature immeasurably beyond the degree to which English literature had been expanded by, say, the works of two-thirds of the poets named in [Samuel Johnson's "Lives of the Poets"], or by the whole series of [Sir Walter Scott's] Waverley novels, or by half the fiction, together with much of the philosophy, theology, poetry, and history, that has been published since the death of Charles Dickens. . . .

Dana and Melville created a world, not by the discovery, but by the interpretation of it. They gave us a full view of the life led by tens of thousands of men whose very existence, until these wizards arose, had been as vague to the general land intelligence as the shadows of clouds moving under the brightness of stars. (p. 138)

Melville wrote out of his heart and out of wide and perhaps bitter experience; he enlarged our knowledge of the life of the deep by adding many descriptions to those which Dana had already given. His "South Seaman" is typical. Dana sighted her, but Melville lived in her. His books are now but little read. When he died the other day . . . , men who could give you the names of fifty living American poets and perhaps a hundred living American novelists owned that they had never heard of Herman Melville. . . . Famous he was; now he is neglected; yet his name and works will not die. He is a great figure in shadow; but the shadow is not that of oblivion. (p. 142)

Americans! honor your Dana and your Melville. Greater geniuses your literature has produced, but none who have done work so memorable in the history of their native letters. (p. 149)

W. Clark Russell, "A Claim for American Literature," in The North American Review, *Vol. CLIV, No. CCCCXXII, January, 1892, pp. 138-49.**

FRANK JEWETT MATHER, JR.   (essay date 1919)

Melville, in prose, for he was also no mean poet, had three styles, like an old master. The swift lucidity, picturesqueness, and sympathy of **"Typee"** and **"Omoo"** have alone captured posterity. Melville lives by his *juvenalia*. **"Redburn"** and **"White Jacket"** are straightforward manly narratives, less colorful than their predecessors. They have not stood the competition with Dana's quite similar "Two Years Before the Mast." They are not quite as solid as that classic, but their chief fault was merely in being later. Then Melville developed a reflective, mystical, and very personal style, probably influenced by Carlyle, which the public has from the first eschewed. It asserts itself first in the strange allegory, **"Mardi, and a Voyage Thither,"** . . . it pervaded **"Pierre, or the Ambiguities"** . . . and other later books. **"Moby Dick"** shows an extraordinary blend of the first and the last style—the pictorial and the orphic; is Melville's most characteristic and, I think, his greatest book. (pp. 156-57)

[It is] less opinion than pictures which counts in **"Typee,"** and the pictures are so vivid because there is no condescension in the observer's attitude. Melville was one of the earliest literary travelers to see in barbarians anything but queer folk. He intuitively understood them, caught their point of view, respected and often admired it. Thus **"Typee"** in a peculiar sense is written from the inside. The ready tolerance that Melville had learned in the forecastle had not blunted the gentleman in him, but had prepared him to be the ideal spectator of a beautiful life that has forever passed. As having distinctly saved a vanishing charm for posterity, **"Typee"** is perhaps Melville's most important book. (p. 158)

Among underworld romances it is strange that [**"Omoo"**] has not taken the high place which on its merits it deserves. The style, as in the case of **"Typee,"** had doubtless profited through Melville's habit of telling these yarns to friends. There is a clarity which tends to fade in the later and more consciously literary works. I don't know that any American writer has had a better eye than Melville. He is not merely a capital storyteller, but a most trenchant picture maker. In a few just strokes, without pretentiousness or faltering, he achieves his sketch. (p. 159)

[**"Moby Dick"** and **"Mardi, and a Voyage Thither"**] are companion pieces: **"Mardi"** is a survey of the universe in the guise of an imaginary voyage of discovery, **"Moby Dick"** is a real voyage skilfully used to illustrate the cosmos; **"Mardi"** is a celestial adventure, **"Moby Dick"** an infernal. **"Mardi"** is highly general—the quest of a mysterious damsel, Zillah, a sort of Beatrice, a type of divine wisdom; **"Moby Dick"** is specific, the insanely vengeful pursuit of the dreaded white whale. The people of **"Mardi"** are all abstractions, those of **"Moby Dick"** among the most vivid known to fiction. **"Mardi"** was far the most ambitious effort of Melville's, and it failed. Personally I like to read in it; for its idealism tinged with a

sane Rabelaisianism, for its wit and rare pictorial quality, for the strange songs of Yoomy, which, undetachable, are both quaintly effective in their context, and often foreshadow oddly our modern free verse. It is often plethoric and over-written, it drops out of the Polynesian form in which it is conceived, and becomes too overt preaching and satire. It justifies the Bacchic philosopher Babbalanja's aphorism—"Genius is full of trash"; but it is also full of wisdom and fine thinking. It represents an intellectual effort that would supply a small library, and I suppose it is fated to remain unread. Perhaps its trouble is its inconclusiveness. (pp. 160-61)

"Moby Dick" has the tremendous advantage of its concreteness. Captain Ahab's mad quest of the white whale imposes itself as real, and progressively enlists and appalls the imagination. . . . The style still has the freshness and delicate power of **"Typee,"** but is subtler. (pp. 161-62)

But **"Moby Dick"** is more than what it undisputedly is, the greatest whaling novel. It is an extraordinary work in morals and general comment. In the discursive tradition of Fielding and the anatomist of melancholy, Melville finds a suggestion or a symbol in each event and fearlessly pursues the line of association. . . . It is the interplay of fact and application that makes the unique character of the book. As for the Christian fathers the visible world was merely a similitude or foreshadowing of the eternal world, so for Melville the voyage of the Pequod betokens our moral life in the largest sense. (pp. 162-63)

The preachments are the essence. The effect of the book rests on the blend of fact, fancy, and profound reflection, upon a brilliant intermingling of sheer artistry and moralizing at large. . . . So while no one is obliged to like **"Moby Dick"**—there are those who would hold against Dante his moralizing and against Rabelais his broad humor—let such as do love this rich and towering fabrique adore it whole-heartedly—from stem to stern, athwart ships and from maintruck to keelson. (pp. 163-64)

[**"Pierre, or the Ambiguities"**] is repellent and overwrought, yet powerful. . . . The moral that one must somewhat bend to things as they are is almost commonplace. The demonstration is powerful, but without much sequence; reflection and satire burgeon over the mishaps of the luckless brother and sister, as if the red, red rose and the briar should finally conceal the twin tombs of the ballad lovers. Yet as a literary curiosity **"Pierre"** is worth reading. . . . (p. 164)

[Of his verse,] nothing except **"Battle Pieces"** . . . was even intended for the public. . . . Melville had rather the soul of a poet than great poetical capacity, or facility, but there is power and probity in his feelings that atone for halting verse and occasional makeshift rhyme. He is too original a figure in American poetry ever to be quite forgotten. (pp. 165-66)

Of those who have actually perused the four books and two volumes of **"Clarel"** I am presumably the only survivor. Yet there are in **"Clarel"** vividness, humor, irony, and mind-stuff sufficient to stock the entire imagist school; only the blend was never quite right and the fashion of the poem has passed. . . . There are charming lyrics, sharp and well-seen descriptions. The problem of faith and doubt is turned over in every sense, the bearing of both on public and private morals is constantly adumbrated often with prophetic intuition. . . . Melville admits all the doubts, but *quand même* lets the individual hold his modicum of faith in humanity and a God, and his hope in immortality. . . . With its patent *longueurs* and lapses **"Clarel"** is about all America has to show for the poetical stirring of the deeper theological waters which marked the age of Matthew Arnold, Clough, Tennyson, and Browning. And we need not be ashamed of our representation. (pp. 167-68)

[Melville] seemed written out at thirty-two, when most authors are just beginning to strike their gait. Yet it should not be forgotten that not even the most neglected works of his are negligible for a reader who values rich idiosyncrasy. "**Pierre**" is perhaps the only positively ill-done book, and it is stuffed with memorable aphorisms. Amid the somewhat dreary wastes of "**The Confidence Man**" are numerous tidbits of irony and wit. "**Israel Potter**" contains the best account of a seafight in American fiction. But it is undeniable that after "**Moby Dick**" Melville never conceived a good book—"**White Jacket**" was a hangover; his inventive processes became uncertain and fluctuating, the moralist in him eclipsed the man of letters. The extraordinary artistry, the ineffable magic of words so frequent in his beginnings becomes intermittent and rare. The new sententiousness and oracular eloquence never quite fulfill themselves. (pp. 168-69)

If Melville relatively failed in the synthesis he sought, he left the evidence of its possibility in "**Moby Dick.**" In sheer capacity to feel most American writers look pale beside him. . . . At his best he commanded a witchery of words beyond any American save only Edgar Allan Poe. He combined in an extraordinary degree impressionistic delicacy and precision with emotional and mental vigor, and withal robust humor; he was both drastic and refined, straightforward and deeply mystical, precious, and delightfully homely. . . . [He was] the most personally alluring of American men of letters. . . . (p. 169)

> *Frank Jewett Mather, Jr., "Herman Melville" (reprinted by permission of Frank Jewett Mather, III), in* Review, *Vol. I, August, 1919, (and reprinted in* The Recognition of Herman Melville: Selected Criticism since 1846, *edited by Hershel Parker, University of Michigan Press, 1967, pp. 155-69).*

D. H. LAWRENCE (essay date 1923)

The greatest seer and poet of the sea for me is Melville. His vision is more real than Swinburne's, because he doesn't personify the sea, and far sounder than Joseph Conrad's, because Melville doesn't sentimentalize the ocean and the sea's unfortunates. (p. 131)

Melville at his best invariably wrote from a sort of dream-self, so that events which he relates as actual fact have indeed a far deeper reference to his own soul, his own inner life.

So in *Typee* when he tells of his entry into the valley of the dread cannibals of Nukuheva. Down this narrow, steep, horrible dark gorge he slides and struggles as we struggle in a dream, or in the act of birth, to emerge in the green Eden of the Golden Age, the valley of the cannibal savages. This is a bit of birth-myth, or re-birth myth, on Melville's part—unconscious, no doubt, because his running underconsciousness was always mystical and symbolical. He wasn't aware that he was being mystical. (p. 134)

Herman found in Typee the paradise he was looking for. It is true, the Marquesans were "immoral," but he rather liked that. Morality was too white a trick to take him in. (p. 135).

Plenty to eat, needing no clothes to wear, sunny, happy people, sweet water to swim in: everything a man can want. Then why wasn't he happy along with the savages?

Because he wasn't.

He grizzled in secret, and wanted to escape. (pp. 135-36)

The truth of the matter is, one cannot go back. Some men can: renegade. But Melville couldn't go back: and Gauguin couldn't really go back: and I know now that I could never go back. Back towards the past, savage life. One cannot go back. (p. 136)

The book that follows on from *Typee* is *Omoo.*

Omoo is a fascinating book: picaresque, rascally, roving. . . . It is good reading.

Perhaps Melville is at his best, his happiest, in *Omoo.* For once he is really reckless. For once he takes life as it comes. For once he is the gallant rascally epicurean, eating the world like a snipe, dirt and all baked into one *bonne bouche.*

For once he is really careless, roving with that scamp, Doctor Long Ghost. For once he is careless of his actions, careless of his morals, careless of his ideals: ironic, as the epicurean must be. The deep irony of your real scamp: your real epicurean of the moment. (p. 140)

.   .   .   .   .

[*Moby Dick*] is a great book.

At first you are put off by the style. It reads like journalism. It seems spurious. You feel Melville is trying to put something over you. It won't do.

And Melville really is a bit sententious: aware of himself, self-conscious, putting something over even himself. But then it's not easy to get into the swing of a piece of deep mysticism when you just set out with a story.

Nobody can be more clownish, more clumsy and sententiously in bad taste, than Herman Melville, even in a great book like *Moby Dick.* He preaches and holds forth because he's not sure of himself. And he holds forth, often, so amateurishly. (pp. 145-46)

But he was a deep, great artist, even if he was rather a sententious man. He was a real American in that he always felt his audience in front of him. But when he ceases to be American, when he forgets all audience, and gives us his sheer apprehension of the world, then he is wonderful, his book commands a stillness in the soul, an awe. (p. 146)

As a soul history, it makes one angry. As a sea yarn, it is marvellous: there is always something a bit over the mark, in sea yarns. Should be. Then again the masking up of actual seaman's experience with sonorous mysticism sometimes gets on one's nerves. And again, as a revelation of destiny the book is too deep even for sorrow. Profound beyond feeling. (pp. 148-49)

Melville manages to keep it a real whaling ship, on a real cruise, in spite of all fantastics. A wonderful, wonderful voyage. And a beauty that is so surpassing only because of the author's awful flounderings in mystical waters. He wanted to get metaphysically deep. And he got deeper than metaphysics. It is a surpassingly beautiful book. With an awful meaning. And bad jolts. (p. 150)

[*Moby Dick* is] the greatest book of the sea ever written. It moves awe in the soul.

The terrible fatality.

Fatality.

Doom. (pp. 159-60)

Doom of what?

Doom of our white day. We are doomed, doomed. And the doom is in America. The doom of our white day. . . .

Melville knew. He knew his race was doomed. His white soul, doomed. His great white epoch, doomed. Himself, doomed. The idealist, doomed. The spirit, doomed. . . .

What then is Moby Dick?—He is the deepest blood-being of the white race. He is our deepest blood-nature.

And he is hunted, hunted, hunted by the maniacal fanaticism of our white mental consciousness. We want to hunt him down. To subject him to our will. And in this maniacal conscious hunt of ourselves we get dark races and pale to help us, red, yellow, and black, east and west, Quaker and fire-worshipper, we get them all to help us in this ghastly maniacal hunt which is our doom and our suicide.

The last phallic being of the white man. Hunted into the death of upper consciousness and the ideal will. Our blood-self subjected to our will. Our blood-consciousness sapped by a parasitic mental or ideal consciousness. (p. 160)

> *D. H. Lawrence, "Herman Melville's 'Typee' and 'Omoo'" and "Herman Melville's 'Moby Dick',"* in his Studies in Classic American Literature *(copyright 1923 by Thomas Seltzer Inc.; copyright renewed 1951 by Frieda Lawrence; copyright renewed 1961 by the Estate of the late Mrs. Frieda Lawrence: reprinted by permission of Viking Penguin Inc.), Thomas Seltzer Inc., 1923, William Heinemann Ltd., 1924 (and reprinted by Viking Press, 1964, pp. 131-43, 145-61).*

JOHN FREEMAN (essay date 1926)

Melville began by being a writer of simple direct prose, reminding one partly of Defoe and partly of Borrow, and he became a writer of eloquent elaborated prose wantoning in its strength and movement as his whales wanton in water. . . . He was not an irregular innovating genius who overthrows idols and breaks up a language in order to build and make anew: he used the things he loved, for they possessed his mind. But he was able to use them because of his own genius, and one of the chief gifts of that genius was his ear for rhythm. (p. 170)

He depended, for his impression on his reader, less upon picture than upon music, and his chief influence over our minds is felt, not when he is presenting something for us to see, but when he is vibrating with rhythms that stimulate our feelings. His appeal is emotional; his own imagination awakes him to an emotional response, and he writes as one who composes by playing music, seeking to match the unheard melody by rhythms that shall prolong and repeat the author's apprehension of the inward air. Vivid epithet and swift succession of comparison and image would not achieve his purpose, as he grew in consciousness of it and of his own capacity. (p. 171)

It need not be suggested—for that would be foolish—that Melville wrought consciously to effect all that analysis might reveal; the unconscious mind, stealing silently between the eyes and the pen, suggests, offers, presses and overwhelms the conscious mind, and makes it less an equal than a servant. This is the character of genius, that what is unconscious and infinite intercepts the hand of the conscious, and writes in its

own unaccountable way out of another vision and another energy than the author is clearly aware of.

Nor can it be maintained that Melville wrote consistently with the same happy sureness, or even throughout a single book. There is more of this perfection in *Moby-Dick* than elsewhere, but there is something of it in several of the books—in *Mardi* and *Pierre*; and it is because this perfection is not casual but truly characteristic that he must be called a great prose writer. Too often he is at the mercy of a bad genius, who tempts him to use all his gifts save one—restraint; and thus his lavish latinisms, his fond compound words, his Biblical allusions, his large metaphors and easy movements—all may be used, but restraint is lacking and the result is ornate, or heavy, or slow, or extravagant, and merely unreadable. His very virtues need support from the withheld Virtue, but given that support all his great powers of mind are fused into beauty of speech; and the marvels of *Moby-Dick* leap out on almost every page. . . . To admit that Melville did not always write greatly is easy, but it must be acknowledged first that he was nevertheless among the greatest of modern imaginative writers of prose. (pp. 176-77)

[However, no] one can read his work extensively without noticing the almost complete absence of women and his almost complete silence about sex. A cold nature his assuredly was not, and passages in *Pierre* have a power so unholy that one reads shrinkingly. But excepting *Pierre* and one or two of the lesser books, and also *Clarel* among the poems, there is scarce a hint that Melville was aware of what it is that teases, exalts, ennobles and destroys men. The sharpest sexual passion anywhere in his work, and it is an all but solitary instance, is incestuous. Was it perhaps the upgathered impulses of his puritanic heritage that warred with his natural passion and made out of that strife a silence, a desolation? Of all modern imaginative writers Melville is the least obviously troubled by the struggle that Blake seraphically viewed as a part and an image of spiritual life. Here, indeed, the analogy between Blake and Melville suddenly fails. For Blake, as for other mystics, the sexual strife was a rehearsal of the unending vaster conflict between the forces of man and God, Time and Eternity; but Melville saw it as something only to be annulled. Save for the abundance of masculine passion expressed in other books and other ways, and the normality revealed in nearly all of them, it might have seemed that he was deficient in humanity; but against this all his writing, and all his life so far as it is recorded, is clear evidence. (pp. 180-81)

His gift of lucid, easy narrative, his early adherence to faithful description, his use of rich resources of experience, his strangely modern psychology, his delightful skill in portraiture, his volubility in dialogue— . . . against these must be set his comparative failure in invention, his disdain of a particular range of emotions the most urgent if not the most powerful of all, his extravagance and his unresisted tendency to philosophize. But to pursue this ledger method does not help us, and it leaves unnoticed Melville's grand faculty, the faculty which stations him uniquely among modern imaginative writers. He was a myth-maker, a creator, a poet in the essential meaning of the word, and all his best powers were fused in one vital imagination, *Moby-Dick*. It is as purely a creation as *Paradise Lost*, born of the same mythopoetic faculty, and making of the myth, in the old heroic way, a parable as well. This *making* power is the supreme power in the imaginative arts. . . . [Melville] was capable of the darkest and deepest analytic psychology, as *Pierre* showed, but he was more splendidly endowed with the energy of creation. It was a gift with spiritual affiliations, not always found among imaginative writers, in the strength of which he could look at heaven and earth and the heart of man and behold everything in an eternal light, as a conflict between infinite and irreconcilable desires. He was a poet in whose vision the world existed as imagination, and existed thus more vividly than in the common sensuous apprehension.

Turning to the possible classification of his work in the old way, it is clear that Melville followed the full romantic tradition. He disdained every curbing and extravagated with absolute wilfulness, being tempted by the richness and wildness of life rather than by its order and discipline. He brooded upon a vast, lava-like grandeur, still smoking heat, with passion and sorrow hanging huge above, cloud-like; and for all his wide difference in theme he is as romantic as Scott and Dickens in England, or Poe and Hawthorne in America. His chief failure, *Pierre,* shows his allegiance as plainly as his chief success; and failure, indeed, is often as eloquent as success in explaining a writer's qualities. Melville is as unlike any classic, architectural writer as Emily Brontë is unlike Jane Austen. Irregularity and vehemence allure him; they are as weapons used to affront the forbidding mysteries of the heart of man and the ways of God; they are the natural expression of his aspiring, sombre spirit. (pp. 182-84)

Little audacity, indeed, is wanted to [express], in concluding, the assertion . . . that Melville is the most powerful of all the great American writers. (p. 187)

> *John Freeman, in his* Herman Melville *(© 1926 by The Macmillan Company), Macmillan, 1926, 200 p.*

WILLIAM FAULKNER   (essay date 1927)

I think that the book which I put down with the unqualified thought "I wish I had written that" is *Moby Dick.* The Greek-like simplicity of it: a man of forceful character driven by his somber nature and his bleak heritage, bent on his own destruction and dragging his immediate world down with him with a despotic and utter disregard of them as individuals; the fine point to which the various natures caught [and passive as though with a foreknowledge of unalterable doom] in the fatality of his blind course are swept—a sort of Golgotha of the heart become immutable as bronze in the sonority of its plunging ruin; all timeless phase: the sea. And the symbol of their doom: a White Whale. There's a death for a man, now; none of your patient pasturage for little grazing beasts you can't even see with the naked eye. There's magic in the very word. A White Whale. White is a grand word, like a crash of massed trumpets; and leviathan himself has a kind of placid blundering majesty in his name. And then put them together!!! A death for Achilles, and the divine maidens of Patmos to mourn him, to harp white-handed sorrow on their golden hair.

> *William Faulkner, "Moby-Dick, 'Golgotha of the Heart'" in* Books—Chicago Tribune, *copyright, 1927, Chicago Tribune; used with permission), July 6, 1927 (and reprinted in* The Merrill Studies in Moby Dick, *edited by Howard P. Vincent, Charles E. Merrill Publishing Company, 1969, p. 162).*

E. M. FORSTER   (essay date 1927)

Moby Dick is an easy book, as long as we read it as a yarn or an account of whaling interspersed with snatches of poetry. But as soon as we catch the song in it, it grows difficult and immensely important. Narrowed and hardened into words the spiritual theme of *Moby Dick* is as follows: a battle against evil conducted too long or in the wrong way. The White Whale is evil, and Captain Ahab is warped by constant pursuit until his knight-errantry turns into revenge. . . . The idea of a contest we may retain: all action is a battle, the only happiness is peace. But contest between what? We get false if we say that it is between good and evil or between two unreconciled evils. The essential in *Moby Dick,* its prophetic song, flows athwart the action and the surface morality like an undercurrent. It lies outside words. (pp. 199-200)

The extraordinary nature of the book appears in two of its early incidents—the sermon about Jonah and the friendship with Queequeg.

The sermon has nothing to do with Christianity. It asks for endurance or loyalty without hope of reward. (p. 201)

Immediately after the sermon, Ishmael makes a passionate alliance with the cannibal Queequeg, and it looks for a moment that the book is to be a saga of blood-brotherhood. But human relationships mean little to Melville, and after a grotesque and violent entry, Queequeg is almost forgotten. Almost—not quite. Towards the end he falls ill and a coffin is made for him which he does not occupy, as he recovers. It is this coffin, serving as a life-buoy, that saves Ishmael from the final whirlpool, and this again is no coincidence, but an unformulated connection that sprang up in Melville's mind. *Moby Dick* is full of meanings: its meaning is a different problem. It is wrong to turn the Delight or the coffin into symbols, because even if the symbolism is correct, it silences the book. Nothing can be stated about *Moby Dick* except that it is a contest. The rest is song.

It is to his conception of evil that Melville's work owes much of its strength. . . . Evil to most novelists is either sexual and social or is something very vague for which a special style with implications of poetry is thought suitable. . . . For a real villain we must turn to a story of Melville's called *Billy Budd.*

It is a short story, but must be mentioned because of the light it throws on his other work. . . . The hero, a young sailor, has goodness. . . . He is not aggressive himself. It is the light within him that irritates and explodes. On the surface he is a pleasant, merry, rather insensitive lad, whose perfect physique is marred by one slight defect, a stammer, which finally destroys him. . . . Claggart, one of the petty officers, at once sees in him the enemy—his own enemy, for Claggart is evil. It is again the contest between Ahab and Moby Dick, though the parts are more clearly assigned, and we are further from prophecy and nearer to morality and common sense. But not much nearer. Claggart is not like any other villain. (pp. 202-05)

Billy Budd is a remote unearthly episode, but it is a song not without words, and should be read both for its own beauty and as an introduction to more difficult works. Evil is labelled and personified instead of slipping over the ocean and round the world, and Melville's mind can be observed more easily. . . . He has not got that tiresome little receptacle, a conscience, which is often such a nuisance in serious writers and so contracts their effects—the conscience of Hawthorne or of Mark Rutherford. Melville—after the initial roughness of his realism—reaches straight back into the universal, to a blackness and sadness so transcending our own that they are undistinguishable from glory. He says, "in certain moods no man can weigh this world without throwing in a something somehow like Original Sin to strike the uneven balance.'' He threw it in, that undefinable something, the balance righted itself, and he gave us harmony and temporary salvation. (p. 206)

> *E. M. Forster, ''Prophecy,'' in his* Aspects of the Novel *(copyright 1927 by Harcourt Brace Jovanovich, Inc.; copyright 1955 by E. M. Forster; reprinted by permission of the publisher; in Canada by Edward Arnold Ltd. in connection with Kings College, Cambridge and The Society of Authors as the literary representatives of E. M. Forster's Estate), Harcourt Brace Jovanovich, 1927, pp. 181-212.* *

VAN WYCK BROOKS   (essay date 1927)

Eleven years was . . . virtually the whole span of Melville's literary life; and never, surely, in so short a time has a mind undergone a more singular transformation. As we survey [his] books in conjunction it becomes clearer than ever that ''**Moby-Dick**'' is Melville's one masterpiece; but none of them is entirely negligible, and all, to say the least, throw some light on the history and the quality of their author's mind. We can understand as we read them successively why it was that Melville seemed to his contemporaries such an enigma. The whole tendency of his work was, in the first place, an implicit assault on the doctrine of progress as the nineteenth century conceived it. He never hesitated to say that he had found the civilized white man ''the most ferocious animal on the face of the earth.'' He pictured the savages of the South Seas not as the rudimentary Europeans that people liked to think them, but as the masters of an art of living in many ways incomparably superior to ours. Such things were hard to forgive; and harder still, in a hopeful age, was the note of tragic scepticism that reverberated through his work. (pp. 172-73)

''**Moby-Dick**'' is his one supreme achievement, it is because here, and here alone, the subjective and objective elements in his mind approach some sort of equilibrium. ''**Redburn**'' and ''**White Jacket**,'' like ''**Typee**'' and ''**Omoo**,'' are simple chronicles. Nothing could be better of its kind than the first of these books, the ''sailor-boy confessions and reminiscences of the son of a gentleman in the merchant service.'' . . . [Here] we find that delight in health and physical beauty which is one of the bonds between Melville and Walt Whitman. ''**Moby-Dick**'' is full of this delight. (pp. 174-75)

Of ''**White Jacket**'' not . . . much can be said. It tells us more about Melville himself, but it is not so good a book. . . . [The] book itself, competent as it is, is as much inferior to ''**Redburn**'' as ''**Omoo**'' is to ''**Typee**.'' It is a loose exposition rather than a well-knit narrative; but it deserves to live, side by side with ''Two Years Before the Mast,'' as the record of an aspect of life that will never have such another chronicler. (pp. 176-77)

''**The Confidence Man**'' is an abortion: it is broken off in the middle, apparently, but not before the author has lost the thread of his original idea. . . . [The] satire is lost in a fog of undirected verbiage; but how bright is the scene when, at moments, the fog lifts, and how admirable is the vision that we seem to see laboring to be born in its baffled author's brain! . . . [We] can see that Melville intended to satirize the follies and illusions of humanity while conveying, at the same time, the gist of his own philosophy. But he had lost command of his medium; and the book remains, interesting indeed, but the product of a premature artistic senility.

Aside from ''**Moby-Dick**,'' ''**Mardi**'' and ''**Pierre**'' are Melville's most ambitious books. They seem to me, however—except for the latter chapters of ''**Pierre**''—rather the products of his reading than of any intense personal experience. . . . As a simple romance, perhaps, [''**Mardi**''] was begun; but having opened as the story of the pursuit of the girl Yillah, it presently turns into the most complicated and chaotic allegory that ever drifted through a human mind. The lost maiden may symbolize either truth or happiness—but indeed the question matters very little. . . . [Neither] the ostensible nor the concealed meaning is presented with sufficient force to hold our attention long. In form the work is a more or less direct imitation of the fourth and fifth books of Rabelais. . . . (pp. 177-80)

Melville was a natural, an unconscious artist; and such men fall an easy prey to the most casual influences. . . . In ''**Moby-Dick**'' Melville achieved a style that is at once highly personal and a palingenesis of the grave and splendid prose of the seventeenth century. (p. 181)

It seems to me now less chaotic than it seemed at first. . . . It seemed to me intolerable that he had not removed the chapters on whales in general, on whaling, pitchpoling, ambergris, the try-works, etc., and published them separately: they were glorious, but I could not believe that they had been deliberately introduced to retard the action. It struck me that the action should have been retarded as it were within the story. I do not feel this now. The book is an epic, and an epic requires ballast. . . . This freight of inanimate or partially inanimate material gives ''**Moby-Dick**'' its bottom, its body, in the vintner's phrase; and I am sure that Melville knew exactly what he was about.

It is only when we have grasped the nature of the book that we begin to see how cunning is its craftsmanship throughout. . . . [Glance] for a moment at the single episode of Father Mapple's sermon in the Whaleman's Chapel. Why is it that, once read, this episode seems to have built itself permanently into the tissues of our imagination? It is because of the skill with which Melville has excluded from our minds every irrelevant detail. (pp. 196-97)

[This episode] shows with what deliberate art Melville has ensnared his readers. To turn now to the work as a whole, how carefully, with what prevision, he had built up the general scheme: the pitch of the book, the mystery of the White Whale, the character of Captain Ahab. . . . [We] have the note of the saga; and this is consistently sustained by a dozen different means. Take the portraits of the three mates, Starbuck, Stubb, and Flask, ''momentous men'' all, and the three fantastic harpooneers, the cannibal Queequeg, Tashtego, the Gay Head Indian, and the gigantic Negro, Daggoo. By a process of simplification that heightens their effect without removing it from reality, Melville invests these characters with a semblance as of Homer's minor heroes. . . . (pp. 198-99)

No less extraordinary is the development of the legend of ''**Moby-Dick**,'' of the sense of impending fatality. Towards the end it may be thought that Melville strains a point or two in order to produce this latter effect. I am thinking especially of the chapter in which the sea-hawk darts away with Ahab's hat; but the chapters on the ''candles'' and the needle are open to the same objection. . . . Machinery of this kind is much more in place in works like ''The Ancient Mariner'' that frankly embody supernatural elements. But consider, at the outset of the book, the apparition of Elijah. Consider that astonishing chapter on the whiteness of the whale. . . . The fabulous whale torments our imagination till we, like Gabriel, think of him as "no less a being than the Shaker God incarnated"; and all this, be it noted, without a word of direct description on Melville's part. Until he reveals himself just before the chase, we see Moby-Dick solely through the consequences of his actions and the eyes of superstitious men. (pp. 200-02)

[All] this fantasy of "Moby-Dick" has behind it everywhere a substantial fabric of fact: that is why, at the most extravagant moments, we accept every detail as veracious. (p. 203)

How admirable again, in the character of Captain Ahab, is Melville's power of construction! . . . It can fairly be said that by the time the chase begins, Ahab is as mighty and terrible a figure in our minds as Moby-Dick himself. The two fabulous characters have grown, by similar means, side by side. (pp. 203-04)

"Moby-Dick" is our sole American epic, no less an epic for being written in prose; and has it been observed that it revives in a sense the theme of the most ancient epic of the English-speaking peoples? Grendel in "Beowulf" might almost be described as the prototype of the White Whale. Was not Grendel also the symbol of "all that most maddens and torments, all that stirs up the lees of things, all truth with malice in it, all that cracks the sinews and cakes the brain, all the subtle demonisms of life and thought, all evil—visibly personified"? (p. 205)

> *Van Wyck Brooks, "Notes on Herman Melville," in his* Emerson and Others *(copyright, 1927 E. P. Dutton & Company; copyright renewed © 1954 by Van Wyck Brooks; reprinted by permission of the publisher, E. P. Dutton, Inc.), Dutton, 1927, pp. 171-205.*

VERNON LOUIS PARRINGTON (essay date 1927)

Set down beside the austere Bryant and the plebeian Greeley, Herman Melville seems grotesquely out of company; and yet such proximities may suggest, better perhaps than words, an explanation of the futility of his dreams and the irony of the bitter penance of his days. Lifelong he was lacerated by the coldly moral in his environment, and harassed by the crudely practical; and without forcing the comparison, one may feel that Bryant and Greeley embodied in nobler form the twin forces that seized upon his bold and rich nature, and bound it to the rocks to be fed on by eagles. Like Jacob he wrestled all night with an angel, yet got no blessing from the touched thigh. Instead, his free spirit was tormented and his adventurous heart seared with fire. Far more truly than of DeQuincey might one say of Melville: *Eccovi*, this little child has been in hell! All the powers of darkness fought over him, all the devils plagued him. They drove him down into the gloom of his tormented soul, and if they did not conquer, they left him maimed and stricken. The golden dreams of transcendental faith, that buoyed up Emerson and gave hope to Thoreau, turned to ashes in his mouth; the white gleams of mysticism that now and then lighted up his path died out and left him in darkness. Life could not meet the demands he made on it, certainly not life in America in the eighteen-fifties; the malady lay deeper than Greeley thought—it lay in the futility of life itself; and so after pursuing his vain dreams to the ends of the seas, the rebellious transcendentalist withdrew within himself while awaiting annihilation. (p. 258)

There is no simple clue to his mystery, no common pass-key to unlock his mind. . . . An arch romantic, he vainly sought to erect his romantic dreams as a defense against reality, and suffered disaster. In love with the ideal, and pursuing it in a wild adventure into the South Seas—his magic realm of Poictesme—yet "not so much bound to any haven ahead as rushing from all havens astern," he found there only disenchantment. (p. 259)

An Ishmael Melville unhappily conceived himself to be, an outcast and wanderer on the earth because man is an outcast and wanderer, to whom Nirvana is the only comfort and hope. (p. 261)

The stages in Melville's progress towards Nirvana are sufficiently marked by the four books, *Typee, Mardi, Moby Dick,* and *Pierre.* The first is his answer to the French romantic Utopia of man in a state of nature. That the rankling wounds in man's heart are poisoned, if not originally inflicted, by social institutions, he was partly convinced, and he felt a lively concern lest western civilization should bring its futile restlessness to the simple island people. (pp. 261-62)

Mardi is a vast welter of satire and idealism, formless and wild, which in turn was no more than prologue to *Moby Dick.* This colossal book, fierce as *Gulliver,* broad as Rabelais, with its *saeva indignatio* that laughs as it rends life, is the great confession of his defeat. (p. 262)

After *Moby Dick,* what remained but to put the external world of experience aside and turn in upon his own thwarted hopes to analyze them? *Pierre, or the Ambiguities* is his spiritual autobiography, the confession of a stricken soul. In the inconsequential matter of plot, a story of incest and murder and suicide, in its deeper purpose, it is a wild fierce tale of mortal passions, that traces the *élan* of mystical idealism to the buried depths of procreative instinct. . . . In *Mardi* the search for Yillah had been carried on under the watchful eye of Hautia, the temptress. . . . In *Pierre* Hautia reappears as Isabel, likewise a child of Heaven and Earth, who is set over against Lucy—the pure daughter of Heaven alone; and this dark Isabel robed in the midnight of her hair, by appealing unconsciously to Pierre's noblest impulses, draws him from the safe orbit of the Gansevoort moralities [those epitomized by Melville's mother, Maria Gansevoort], and makes of him "the fool of Truth, the fool of Virtue, the fool of Fate." Isabel is wild, unquestioning, mysterious passion, untouched by any Hebraisms; and this half-sister of his blood, this lovely embodiment of his star-crossed dreams, drives him unwittingly to destruction. Pierre learns at last that the vision brings poison in its kisses. . . . The dream is man's final ironical curse; Yillah and Hautia and Lucy and Isabel—changing embodiments of the same mystical idealism—bring death to their lovers—this is the conclusion of *Pierre.* . . . (p. 263)

That Melville was the spiritual child of [Jean Jacques Rousseau], that the consuming nostalgia he suffered from was mortal, the most casual acquaintance with his passionate rebellions should make clear; and that his pessimism was a natural end and outcome of his transcendental speculations, once those speculations had come to intimate contact with life, is perhaps equally clear. . . . But transcendentalism in the forecastle of the whaler *Acushnet,* transcendentalism that drove fiercely into the blood-red sunsets of dwarfing seas, transcendentalism in the hot and passionate heart of a man whose vast dreams outran his feet—this was something very different from the gentle mysticism of cooler natures and unembittered hearts where no Promethean fires were raging. (p. 264)

Like all the transcendentalists Melville was a democrat, but his democracy sprang rather from his sympathies than from his philosophy. It was a democracy learned rather from Ecclesiastes than from Emerson; it sprang from his pessimism rather than from any transcendental faith in the divinity of man. He knew only too well how weak and foolish are the children of Adam; but in presence of the common fate to which the indifferent years hurry us, how stupid and callous are the social distinctions that society erects! Why should not life be a leveler, as well as death? His experience before the mast had taught him sympathy for the common man; he regarded quizzically the ways of the exploiting few and the sufferings of the exploited many; and he smiled ironically at the neat little classification that divides the human animal into sinners and saints. He was as comprehensive a democrat as Whitman, of the same all-embracing school that denied the common social and ethical categories of excellence; but alienated from his fellows, not drawn to them as Whitman was. It was not a sense of social aloofness that held him apart, but the isolation of loneliness. (p. 265)

Such a man would not so much turn critic as embody criticism. His life—even more than Emerson's—laid upon America was a yardstick to measure the shortcomings of a professed civilization. . . . Perhaps it was well enough that his generation could not comprehend his devastating speculations, and called him mad; or it would have cried out to crucify this maligner of all the tribal fetishes. (p. 266)

> *Vernon Louis Parrington, "Some Contributions of New England," in his* Main Currents in American Thought, an Interpretation of American Literature from the Beginnings to 1920: The Romantic Revolution in America, 1800-1860, Vol. 2 *(copyright 1927 by Harcourt Brace Jovanovich, Inc.; copyright 1955 by Vernon L. Parrington, Jr., Louise P. Tucker, Elizabeth P. Thomas; reprinted by permission of the publisher), Harcourt Brace Jovanovich, 1930 (and reprinted by Harcourt Brace Jovanovich, 1958), pp. 238-67.**

PERCY H. BOYNTON (essay date 1927)

[Melville's *Typee* and *Omoo*] and particularly *Typee,* are an extraordinary achievement for a man in the middle twenties. He seemed able without apparent effort to put character and action on the printed page, life and color so simply and so vividly presented that they have never been surpassed for these islands. Together the books offer a picture of South Sea life of a sort to allure the fancy of any victim of a driving northern civilization. . . . (p. 32)

[*Mardi*] is the work in which Melville, retaining all his feeling for the sea and the poetry thereof, passed over into the realm of allegory from which he was never to return. (p. 35)

From *Mardi* to *White Jacket* was a natural step for Melville, and it was taken very quickly. . . . Like *Typee* and *Omoo* it is based on fact; like *Mardi* it is filled with allegory; and like the coming *Moby Dick* it is cyclopedic in its information. It is the chronicle of a voyage with no superimposed plot. The frigate "Neversink" becomes what Mardi was, a microcosm of the world. The book is compounded of meditation, myth, and maxim. . . . (p. 37)

There are fine characters and characterizations in the book. Jack Chase, first captain of the top, is a splendidly picturesque figure. There are thrilling episodes told with masterly skill; but

through them all, now and then subordinated but never forgotten, the "one proper object" is pursued—to picture "the world in a man-of-war." And this world is freighted with passengers, who though fate ridden, are yet the possessors of free will. (p. 38)

[In *White Jacket*] allegory was united with fact as well as with romance. But as yet Melville had not resorted to the richest of all his materials—whalers, whales, and whaling. (p. 39)

In the critic's experience of adventuring among masterpieces there can be only a few to equal the thrill of sailing the high seas with Captain Ahab. . . . Like most other colossal stories, *Moby Dick* has its offering to submit to every degree of literary acumen. On the surface it is the tale of Captain Ahab, long ago maimed in an encounter with the terror of the South Seas, of his consuming hatred for the monster, and of the voyage for revenge which ends in fatal conflict with the foe. (p. 40)

However great it is as a literal whaling adventure—and there is nothing better of the sort in literature—it is greater as a story of life that is only incidentally told in terms of whales and whalers. This is the story of Eve and of Prometheus, the perennial story of man's struggle for spiritual victory in the midst of a world of harassing circumstance, and in the midst of a world where fate opposes the individual in the form of his own thwarting self. (p. 41)

Moby Dick is as didactic in its sustained and applied metaphors as in its carefully documented chapters on cetology, the lore of the whale. The ocean is the boundless truth, the land is the threatening reef of human error. The whiteness of the great whale figures forth the ghostly mystery of infinitude. Human life is the product of the Loom of Time, whereof the warp is necessity, the shuttle-driven thread, free-will, and chance, the stroke of the staff that drives the woof-thread to its horizontal place. The whale itself is symbol of all property and all privilege. Melville takes no chances at having these elements misunderstood or overlooked. He expounds them at length and recurs to them incessantly. If it be a sin to write prose allegory, never man sinned as Melville. (p. 42)

Yet, regardless of the secondary purpose of *Moby Dick,* the story as a story is superbly successful. In spite of a thousand digressions the whole tale moves with a grim ruthlessness to its tragic outcome. Captain Ahab is more than an incarnate spirit of revenge. He is a terribly human being. He has none of the actuality of the fiction types in whom one may recognize contemptible or detestable acquaintances; but he is undeniably real with the reality of a Richard or an Oedipus. . . . As the end comes near he is eager to joust with death. He carries the reader with him as he carries his crew; and leaves a vast silence behind him. (p. 43)

> *Percy H. Boynton, "Herman Melville," in his* More Contemporary Americans *(reprinted by permission of The University of Chicago Press; copyright 1927 by The University of Chicago),* University of Chicago Press, 1927, pp. 29-50.

JOHN ERSKINE (essay date 1928)

Moby Dick is not a novel, but a poem. Though written in prose it has the power of a great epic—that is, it gathers up our emotions around a central figure, a central incident, and one central mood. (p. 223)

To call the book a poem is not a fantastic apology for it. We are beginning to realize that more than one American writer of the early periods left us so-called novels which make the effect of poetry—Cooper's *Deerslayer* is an illustration. But *Moby Dick* leads them all in the vastness of the impression it makes. In moments of enthusiasm we like to say that it is the greatest of sea stories. While we read, the ocean, all the oceans, seem to spread around us. In that immense space a handful of men hunt for one particular whale, one fish out of all the seas, and, terrible thought! we begin to understand that the great whale is hunting for one man on that one ship. Nothing can keep them apart. Here perhaps is an image of fate simpler and more awful than we can find in ancient story. Not peculiarly American, of course—rather a universal image. The American pictures in the book belong to the shore, to the ports of time and space from which these mariners come. On the sea the characters resolve into human nature, the horizons melt into infinity. (p. 224)

Obviously a story of this kind can succeed only if it overwhelms us with the sense of terror and grandeur. The realistic portions of the book . . . serve as unexpected aids to this effect. Melville wants to repeat the idea of the whale in many moods and variations, as one would repeat a musical theme, until it becomes a sort of obsession with the reader. . . . If the book is long, it is so because Melville needed room to suggest these terrors and store them up in us. In this preparation he is an artist of the greatest skill. (pp. 225-26)

[When] we say that this story is a poem rather than a novel, we mean that its art consists not in reproducing pictures of the outside of life, such as we can call faithful, but rather in preparing our minds for an effect of emotion, so that at the end there will be a powerful catharsis, or release of feeling. From this point of view he would be a bold critic who would call the book too long, or would attempt to abbreviate. No detail is lost in the ultimate effect. Where Melville learned the skill to choose these details and to produce that effect, we don't know. The book is an inspiration of genius. (p. 230)

Many a poet through the centuries has turned to the sea as to one aspect of nature which seems to resist men's moralizing tendency. . . . The shores keep the wreck of civilizations, and are scarred by human history; the waters are now as they were at the dawn of creation. Morally so, as well as physically. . . . But the awful stretch of waters in their normal state, rolling beyond eyesight, almost beyond reach of thought—this, few poets have rendered. (pp. 232-33)

Something of this awful grandeur Melville has incorporated in his book, and it is his success in conveying this mood to the reader which sets him apart from other writers. The whale is the image of the sea, if you choose, of this mysterious and terrible space, but the sea is the image of nothing but itself, and after the last page is read, the picture which remains with us is of the undisturbed waters below which Ahab, the monster and the strong ship have disappeared for ever. Melville repeats this image of the vastness of the sea, playing variations on it, but letting us forget it in no part of the story. (p. 233)

Melville makes a curious kind of circle out of the three ideas of the sea, the captain's madness, and the whale. The image of the wide waters, dwelt on continuously, becomes terrible, even though the whale were not there. It expresses the horror of space. (p. 234)

Completing the circle of the three ideas, space, madness and monster, Melville uses the theme of growing insanity and increasing efficiency to fix our attention more surely on the whale. He tells us, and we see for ourselves as we read, that

the whale haunting Captain Ahab's mind serves to bring out a strange unity in his character. . . . When he enters the boat for his last chase of his enemy, he is no longer like most of us, a divided or incomplete personality; he is united within himself. His body and his soul, as Melville says, are one, alike maimed, if you choose, but equally steeled to an effort which can hardly be explained in ordinary terms of motives and causes, but which provides complete expression of the man's whole life.

In another sense, also, the whale, even before we meet it, is made to engulf the other interests of the book. It is a white whale. Melville calls attention to the importance of this ghostly animal in a magnificent chapter, one of the most splendid in our literature. . . . He suggests that the whiteness itself, the absence of color, or the presence of all colors, brings to some sensitive instinct in our heart the thought of space and emptiness; annihilation; death itself. And he raises one terrific question which colors the rest of the book for us—whether nature, if we could look at it with entirely clear vision, would not prove to be altogether white—that is, might it not prove to be an infinite emptiness? (pp. 235-36)

> *John Erskine, "'Moby Dick'," in his* The Delight of Great Books *(copyright 1928, 1935 by John Erskine; copyright renewed © 1955 by Helen Worden Erskine), The Bobbs-Merrill Company, 1928 (and reprinted by World Publishing Co., 1941, pp. 223-40).*

LEWIS MUMFORD (essay date 1929)

[Herman Melville] shares with Walt Whitman, I think, the distinction of being the greatest imaginative writer that America has produced: his epic, *Moby-Dick,* is one of the supreme poetic monuments of the English language: and in depth of experience and religious insight there is scarcely any one in the nineteenth century, with the exception of Dostoyevsky, who can be placed beside him. (p. 4)

[*Typee,* Melville's first novel,] belongs to the morning of the imagination. . . . It is direct, fresh, free from self-consciousness, like the healthy youth who experienced these adventures and sat down to write about them. That quality is precious and irretrievable. (p. 71)

Typee communicates its own simple health and manly confidence: its keenness, its straightforwardness, its hearty appetite for life. It is written with that skill which disarms skill, with the clarity beside which a more deliberate artifice would be clumsy. (p. 72)

Melville sets out to teach us nothing: but at every step we follow eagerly and find ourselves making notes, instituting comparisons, seeing the world in fresh perspective. *Typee* is a magic mirror. In *Typee* we grasp the secret of youth, and hold the world up to its clear surface: for the first time, perhaps, we note its unhealthy complexion, its fat paunch, its jaded smile, its fatuous anxieties, its lack of even animal repose. (p. 73)

Omoo is a description of Melville's life from the day he escaped the Typees to his signing up for another whaling voyage off the coast of Japan. . . . The narrative itself is done in the direct, vigorous, rapid style of *Typee:* if anything, there is more humour in it, and Melville gave himself greater liberties in using the material and embroidering it. . . . The relatively unromantic, if outlandish, quality of these later adventures, with the exception of the mutiny of the Julia's crew, made him rely more heavily upon his own skill: and although the main incidents are probably accurate, all the characters are focussed with a slight distortion, through Melville's sense of the comic. . . . (pp. 81-2)

Omoo was a rambling book: it had in a formal sense neither beginning nor end; but it had something of the bright immediacy of a sketchbook filled with graphic notes that might be worked into a finished picture. . . . [Melville] never overloaded *Omoo:* he knew where to skip and where to elaborate: he is a writer who knows that one wants everything in a travel book except the tedium and fatigue of actuality. . . . More and more, his speech cleansed itself of affectations: the direct, vigorous lingo of the sea, with all its Elizabethan locutions, was doubtless a sound influence in this part of his development. . . . (pp. 84-5)

In *Typee* and *Omoo,* Melville had that superb aplomb—formed by an athleticism, an inner poise, a dexterity of hand, a sharpness of eye—which we call Greek because for a little while the Attic peoples experienced it as a community; the attitude which Whitman valued as the sign and seal of the new American. Melville is appreciative; he is humorous; but he is neither a professional funny man nor a syrupy preserver of glamour. His aplomb never deserts him. He is always in command. That trait is the key to his early literary success; it explains the effortless accuracy of his descriptions. Such poise, such aplomb, such confidence, rest on the nicest sort of spiritual and physiological interplay: blood and muscle form a part of it as well as mental serenity. We have seen this balance in our own day, embodied in a young man who flew to Europe alone. The gesture surrounding this act was the same precious essence that *Typee* and *Omoo* give us in the form of art. I have called this quality youth; but it is what the Athenians called virtue; and as soon as we depart from it we are hoary with sin, and there is no health in us. (p. 85)

[*Mardi*] is not a perfect book; but it has something in it that defies death; and that something is the presence of Melville himself, now arriving at maturity, a traveller who has gone to the ends of the earth, and has not left his head smugly at home—a vehement, clear-witted, copious, steady-eyed, jocose, untamable man. The poise and completeness of *Typee* is gone: much as we prize youth, the cost of continuing that balance, without a fresh integration, is arrested development; and Melville went on. *Mardi* has all the promise of imperfection. (p. 93)

[Melville] had no intention of merely amusing his public with a less literal *Omoo. Mardi* is the world, and Yillah is not a maiden but the spiritual life, who was brought to Mardi and given a home there, but treacherously treated by the fates. . . . [The] tropical isles are a counterpart of the Western world, and in a thousand wild metaphors and noble tropes, all the triumphs and follies of our civilization parade again before the mind, clearer because of the disguise, more immediate because they are so distant. Evil has entered Melville's paradise; evil, that "chronic malady of the universe" which, "checked in one place, breaks forth in another," and the knowledge of good and evil is the beginning of his own sad wisdom. (p. 96)

In the guise of king, poet, philosopher, Melville became a philosophic commentator, retelling the story of Europe and Christianity and faith and doubt and religion and science, exploring time, delivering himself through his dreams, disclosing, in Babbalanja's demonic inner man, Azzageddi, his own ultimate perceptions. It is almost impossible to convey the

vastness, the variety, the genuine wealth of these pictures. (p. 97)

In *Mardi* Melville keeps ideas in the air like a juggler's balls; the images pass and repass, making in those agile hands a single pattern. Satire is only one of the moods of *Mardi:* poetic reverie, as in the chapter on Dreams, and philosophic reflection, thread their ways in and out of these scattered islands of sense. (p. 99)

Mardi is strong enough as a satire and a criticism of life to stand a frank admission of its weaknesses; and I shall not try to conceal them. The book starts out to be one thing; it presently becomes another; and before *Mardi* is entirely explored it becomes a third: the adventure, the strange scenes and personages, the philosophic reflection, the satire, all accrete together rather than form a single intermingled whole. (p. 101)

The satire at its best achieves its end by a delicate parody of actuality, as in the scene where Melville takes off a session of the United States Congress; but sometimes Melville's invention flags, and he repeats actual history, with altered names, instead of distorting, magnifying, transposing. Verbally, his touch is almost as uncertain: at times he drops into obvious metres, only to rise into passages of prose that have far greater claim to be set off as verse than any of Yoomy's stanzas. . . . These are all faults; and not little ones; but what means infinitely more is the fact that a brave, vigorous spirit presides over *Mardi,* appraising all the evil and injustice and superstition and ugliness in the world—as they masquerade under the guise of religion and patriotism and economic prudence and political necessity. In *Mardi,* one begins to feel Melville's range, and his depth.

In this satiric fantasy, Melville had not the sure touch he later achieved in *Moby-Dick:* but for all that, his thoughts exploded in a succession of great rockets and Roman candles and flag-bombs; and the spectacle was a dazzling and beautiful one. Such wit, such humour, such starry intelligence, such wide knowledge, such resolute diving, were not known in American literature before; and they are rare enough in any literature. Much though we value Melville's great American contemporaries, he had something to give in *Mardi* that is beyond their reach. (pp. 101-02)

Mardi performed a more important work for its author than it did for its immediate readers: it disclosed to him the nature of his own demon—that deeper other half whom Babbalanja called Azzageddi. (p. 102)

From Azzageddi's mouth the deepest perceptions of Melville's spirit came forth first, in the form of jests and demonic laughter. Azzageddi was free in the only unqualified sense of freedom: he was irresponsible. . . . He was Melville, shorn of everything that might make him circumspect and limited, a skeleton facing the world with its ultimate grin. Azzageddi brought Melville to his supreme triumph in *Moby-Dick,* and plunged him into temporary disaster in *Pierre;* for he worked out of the bottomless parts of Melville's unconscious, and when he was given free line, he might haul up anything out of those depths—a chest of gold or a green corpse or a white whale. His appearance in *Mardi* was the first sign of Melville's maturity; and the attempt of the world to castigate and repress Azzageddi was excellent proof that Melville had found within himself something worth the saying. *Mardi* was Melville's spiritual *Omoo.* It gave him the courage to be an intellectual rover, and to scorn the easy domesticities in which thought reposes, and snores. . . .

Melville was plainly aware of the fact that he was now acquiring a new language, not a new set of weaknesses: his inward eye was now keeping pace in its growth with his outward one: he was at last achieving that genuine bi-focal vision wherein "matter" and "spirit" united to give depth and perspective to the world which only through joint effort do they effectually behold. Already, he had eternity in his eye. (p. 104)

White-Jacket was the sort of book that Melville could hardly have attempted until he was sure of his capacities as a writer. Although there is more than one adventurous passage in *White-Jacket,* it is full of sober description and realistic criticism; and it depends for its interest on Melville's own strength of character, his shrewd, quick insight, and his easy, seamanlike way of taking the world, rather than on the glamour of his adventures. (p. 114)

White-Jacket shows, I think, a greater art and control over the material than any of Melville's earlier books: in *Typee* the art is gracefully unconscious: in *White-Jacket* it is deliberate. . . . At thirty he had mastery: he could take the dull routine of the man-of-war and make every part of it live, from the maintop to the hold: he could take a hundred dispersed threads and weave them into a solid pattern. (pp. 114-15)

In *White-Jacket,* Melville's power of invention appears only a few times; but when it does, it is magnificent. The chapters on the Surgeon of the Fleet and his operation show Melville's satire at its acutest. . . . (p. 115)

The satire is perfect; and it is perfect because, at the broadest extreme of caricature, it does not lose sight of the pathetic reality underneath. Melville did not waste breath dissecting the obvious impostors and charlatans; for all but the simple can escape them. It is the man in command, the man we admire, respect, put all our confidence in, that Melville so skilfully opened up. No one has done a better job of it: Cuticle and his operation must be put alongside the best passages in Molière. (p. 116)

In *White-Jacket* his powers did not widen; but they gained firmness and control. . . . The prose of *White-Jacket* is an advance on all his previous writing; it has a richness of texture, a variety of rhythm, a decisiveness of phrase that his earlier work had only promised and that *Mardi* itself had not quite fulfilled. (p. 117)

White-Jacket is a portrait gallery: but it is more than that: it is one of the best all-round characterizations and criticisms of a powerful human institution that the century produced. Melville dealt with the effect of regimentation, with the relation of superior to underling, with the accidents and mischances and the oridinary routine of a man-of-war's life, in such a fashion that he included other institutions as well: the human truths and relationships would remain, though all the navies of the world were scrapped next week. . . . Apart from *Moby-Dick,* *White-Jacket* is, I think, Melville's fullest achievement: and it is the best reasoned and seasoned of all his factual narratives. (pp. 117-18)

Moby-Dick is a story of the sea, and the sea is life, "whose waters of deep woe are brackish with the salt of human tears." *Moby-Dick* is the story of the eternal Narcissus in man, gazing into all rivers and oceans to grasp the unfathomable phantom of life—perishing in the illusive waters. *Moby-Dick* is a portrait of the whale and a presentation of the demonic energies in the universe that harass and frustrate and extinguish the spirit of man. We must gather our own strength together if we are to penetrate *Moby-Dick;* no other fable, except perhaps Dante's, demands that we open so many doors and turn so many secret keys; for, finally, *Moby-Dick* is a labyrinth, and that labyrinth is the universe. (p. 158)

[The] central figure is the whale, and the whale stands for the universe. (p. 161)

When the whale enters, the narrative for the first time pauses; and, in the pause, one discovers that the story and the people are secondary matters, while something more wide and reaching comes into the fable. (p. 162)

[The] physical pursuit of the whale is only a part of the story: the more one learns about such a creature, the more widely do its relations ramify, not merely in its own world, but in man's: and the higher the significance of the hunt itself. [The] passages about the whale and the methods of whaling, about its dignity and adventure, [the] comments upon the science of cetology— all these things are not uncouth interruptions in the narrative; they are profoundly part of it. . . . [The] universal, symbolic aspect of the story, and its direct, scientific, practical aspect move in and out like the threads of a complicated pattern: one modifies the other, and is by turns figure and background. The physical expanse of the book, its deliberateness of movement, its slow undulations, are necessary, like the long swells and the wide expanse of the ocean itself, to give a feeling of immensity, immensity and power. (p. 164)

The whale is no phantom symbol; and this stage is no pasteboard stage. If this is not the universe, the full universe, that Melville embodies under these symbols, no one in our time has had inkling of a fuller one. *Moby-Dick* is an imaginative synthesis; and every aspect of reality belongs to it, one plane modifying the other and creating the modelled whole. (p. 171)

Moby-Dick is a poetic epic. Typographically, *Moby-Dick* conforms to prose, and there are long passages, whole chapters, which are wholly in the mood of prose: but in spirit and in actual rhythm, *Moby-Dick* again and again rises to polyphonic verse. . . . His prose is prose: hard, sinewy, compact; and his poetry is poetry, vivid, surging, volcanic, creating its own form in the very pattern of the emotional state itself, soaring, towering, losing all respect for the smaller conventions of veracity, when the inner triumph itself must be announced. It is in the very rhythm of his language that Ahab's mood, and all the devious symbols of *Moby-Dick* are sustained and made credible: by no other method could the deeper half of the tale have been written. In these poetic passages, the phrases are intensified, stylized, stripped of their habitual associations. If occasionally, as with Shakespeare, the thought itself is borne down by the weight of the gold that decorates it, this is only a similar proof of Melville's immense power of expression. (pp. 181-82)

Moby-Dick is a symphony; every resource of language and thought, fantasy, description, philosophy, natural history, drama, broken rhythms, blank verse, imagery, symbol, is utilized to sustain and expand the great theme. The conception of *Moby-Dick* organically demands the expressive interrelation, for a single total effect, of a hundred different pieces: . . . not a stroke is introduced that has not a meaning for the myth as a whole. (p. 182)

Melville's instrumentation is unsurpassed in the writing of the last century: one must go to a Beethoven or a Wagner for an exhibition of similar powers: one will not find it among the works of literature. (pp. 182-83)

What is the meaning of *Moby-Dick*? There is not one meaning; there are many; but in its simplest terms, *Moby-Dick* is, necessarily, a story of the sea and its ways, as the *Odyssey* is a story of strange adventure, and *War and Peace* a story of battles and domestic life. (p. 183)

But *Moby-Dick,* admirable as it is as a narrative of maritime adventure, is far more than that: it is, fundamentally, a parable on the mystery of evil and the accidental malice of the universe. The white whale stands for the brute energies of existence, blind, fatal, overpowering, while Ahab is the spirit of man, small and feeble, but purposeful, that pits its puniness against this might, and its purpose against the blank senselessness of power. (p. 184)

[The] white whale is the symbol of that persistent force of destruction, that meaningless force, which now figures as the outpouring of a volcano or the atmospheric disruption of a tornado or again as the mere aimless dissipation of unused energy into an unavailable void. . . . The whole tale of the West, in mind and action . . . , is a tale of this effort to combat the whale—to ward off his blows, to counteract his aimless thrusts, to create a purpose that will offset the empty malice of Moby-Dick. (p. 185)

Ahab has more humanity than the gods he defies: indeed, he has more power, because he is conscious of the power he wields, and applies it deliberately, whereas Moby-Dick's power only seems deliberate because it cuts across the directed aims of Ahab himself. And in one sense, Ahab achieves victory: he vanquishes in himself that which would retreat from Moby-Dick and acquiesce in his insensate energies and his brutal sway. His end is tragic: evil engulfs him. But in battling against evil, with power instead of love, Ahab himself, in A. E.'s phrase, becomes the image of the thing he hates: he has lost his humanity in the very act of vindicating it. . . .

[That] evil Ahab seeks to strike is the sum of one's enemies. He does not bow down to it and accept it: therein lie his heroism and virtue: but he fights it with its own weapons and therein lies his madness. All the things that Ahab despises when he is about to attack the whale, the love and loyalty of Pip, the memory of his wife and child, the sextant of science, the inner sense of calm, which makes all external struggle futile, are the very things that would redeem him and make him victorious. (pp. 185-86)

[There] is another meaning in Ahab's struggle with Moby-Dick. He represents, not as in the first parable, an heroic power that misconceives its mission and misapplies itself: here he rather stands for human purpose in its highest expression. His pursuit is "futile" because it wrecks the boat and brings home no oil and causes material loss and extinguishes many human lives; but in another sense, it is not futile at all, but is the only significant part of the voyage, since oil is burned and ships eventually break up and men die. . . . [There] is no struggle so permanent and so humanly satisfactory as Ahab's struggle with the white whale. In that defeat, in that succession of defeats, is the only pledge of man's ultimate victory, and the only final preventive of emptiness, boredom, and suicide. (pp. 189-90)

In *Moby-Dick* Melville achieved the deep integrity of that double vision which sees with both eyes-the scientific eye of actuality, and the illumined eye of imagination and dream. (p. 194)

Melville was not without his weaknesses, and they rose to the surface in his new book, *Pierre, or, The Ambiguities. Moby-*

Dick had disintegrated him: by some interior electrolysis, its sanative salt was broken up into its poisonous elements. In this disintegration, *Pierre* rises at times as high as *Moby-Dick,* and sinks lower than any of Melville's other books. (p. 196)

There is a sense in which *Pierre* is an abortive complement to *Moby-Dick. Moby-Dick,* great fable that it is, contains a good part of human life under one figure or another; but it does not contain everything. I would claim much for it; I would claim much for Melville's work as a whole; but there is still a great segment that remained unexplored till Melville wrote *Pierre,* and that, to the end, he never satisfactorily penetrated or freely brooded upon.

All Melville's books about the sea have the one anomaly and defect of the sea from the central, human point of view: one-half of the race, woman, is left out of it. Melville's world, all too literally, is a man-of-war's world. . . . The whales dally in *Moby-Dick* and beget offspring; but all the trouble, beauty, madness, delight of human love, all that vast range of experience from the mere touch of the flesh to the most enduring spiritual loyalty, all that is absent. One looks for some understanding of woman's lot and woman's life in *Moby-Dick;* and one looks in vain. One looks for it again in *Pierre,* and one is disappointed, although its ambiguities are concerned with nothing else. With experience of woman in every relationship, sweetheart, wife, mother, matron, he described her in only one aspect—that of the remote and idealized mistress of romantic courtship. (pp. 200-01)

[The] story of *Pierre,* hard to accept in bald summary, is no less difficult to accept in detail. The plot is forced: the situations are undeveloped: the dominant colours are as crude as the lithograph advertisements of a melodrama, although there are subordinate parts which are as delicately graded as a landscape by Corot. There is no passage between the various planes of action and mood, as there is in *Moby-Dick:* Melville slips from prose into poetry, from realism into fantasy, from the mood of high tragedy into that of the penny dreadful.

For the moment, Melville had lost the power to fuse these discordant elements, to reject what could not be fully absorbed: he was at the mercy of his material. All that lives with a vital unity in *Moby-Dick* has become a corpse in *Pierre:* there is life in the dead decomposing members, but it does not pertain to the body as a whole. The fragments of *Pierre* are sometimes marvellous, as the broken leg or arm of a great piece of sculpture may be: but the whole is lost. From the moment the story opens to the fatal lines that bring it to a close, one is in an atmosphere of unreality. I do not mean that the facts are untrue to life; I mean that the work as a whole is untrue to the imagination. (p. 206)

The style itself is witness to this psychal disruption, quite as much as the fable. *Pierre* is quarried out of the same quarry as *Moby-Dick;* but whereas there the texture is even and firm, here it is full of flaws and intrusive granulations. (p. 207)

In language, *Pierre* is just the opposite of [*Moby Dick*]: from the first pages, it is perfervid and poetical in a mawkish way. With the disclosure of the two lovers, Pierre and Lucy, in the opening chapter, the style becomes a perfumed silk, taken from an Elizabethan chamber romance. . . . In style, Melville had suddenly lost both taste and discretion. He opened on a note that could not be carried through. Lovers may indeed once have used such silly rhetoric, but it would take a more careful hand than Melville's to persuade us that the rest of the world adopted these affectations: when scene after scene is conducted in the same tone, the style becomes tedious, intolerable, ridiculous. . . . Occasionally, by some happy concentration of emotion, Melville either drops these flabby phrases or permits the reader to forget them, and there are passages which, when read as poetry, are almost as fine as Whitman's verses. But these intervals of good writing do not overcome the main impression; and the main impression is of hectic and overwrought language. (pp. 207-08)

What did Melville consciously set himself to do when he wrote *Pierre*? He sought, I think, to arrive at the same sort of psychological truth that he had achieved, in metaphysics, in *Moby-Dick*. (p. 211)

As concerns his psychological purpose. . . , *Pierre* for all its weaknesses will stand comparison with the pioneer works of its period. *Pierre* is one of the first novels in which the self is treated as anything but a unit, whose parts consist of the same material, with the grain, as it were, running the same way. Pierre's double relation towards his father's image and towards his mother's actual presence, his mixed attitudes towards Lucy and Isabel, the conflict between his latent interests and his actions and rationalizations, all these things are presented with remarkable penetration: if there is slag at the entrance of this mine, there is a vein of exceptionally rich ore running through it. (p. 212)

Israel Potter has suffered, like all Melville's later books, from the apathy of criticism, quite as much as from its own weaknesses. . . . Not merely does *Israel Potter* contain, as Mr. F. J. Mather, Jr., has remarked, one of the best accounts of a sea-fight in history [see excerpt above]; not merely is its portrait of John Paul Jones a far more illuminating study of that great shark of the seas than Cooper's picture in *The Pilot;* but it is one of the few works of American fiction that deal with patriotic episodes in a generous, straight-forward way. Melville took a crude, bald narrative and poured life into it: he took a smudgy woodcut and made a living picture out of it, building up the background, creating incident and character where none had existed before, projecting every figure into the third dimension. (p. 241)

Israel Potter is many removes from Melville at his best; but it would be absurd to throw it out of the Melville canon. It has some of the fine qualities of his art, the mixture of tradition and fresh experience, the purification and heightening of actuality, with a loss of realism and a gain in reality: what it chiefly lacks is centrality. It is Melville *manqué*—but still Melville. His poorest work was many degrees above mediocrity. (p. 242)

["**Benito Cereno**"] marked the culmination of Melville's power as a short-story writer, as *Moby-Dick* marked his triumph as an epic poet. (p. 244)

[The] interplay of character, the cross-motives, the suspense, the central mystery, are all admirably done: in contrast to some of Melville's more prosy sketches, there is not a feeble touch in the whole narrative. (p. 245)

As in *The Encantadas*, the writing itself was distinguished: it had a special office of its own to perform, and did not, as in *Typee* and *Redburn*, serve merely as carriage for the story. (p. 246)

The fable of *The Confidence Man* is plain as far as it goes: there is nothing obscure or difficult in the symbolism; but it has the abrupt and scanty appearance of a Manx cat. In the individual sections, the writing is always competent; and some-

times far more than that: but the story moves as torpidly and sinuously as the muddy Mississippi itself. . . . (p. 253)

When one regards *The Confidence Man* in its true light, not as a novel, but as a companion volume to *Gulliver's Travels,* its whole aspect changes: its turbid, tedious, meandering quality remains: but there are rapids of dangerous and exhilarating satire. . . . *The Confidence Man* may be considered as Melville's own masquerade; his own bitter plea for support, money, confidence. Indeed, a Mississippi steamboat whose passengers quote Zimmermann, Hume, Francis Bacon, Rabelais, Jeremiah, Jeremy Taylor, Diogenes, and Timon could scarcely be anything but Melville's own heavily laden soul, all its characters and incidents being part of that long soliloquy in which Melville struggled with a cankerous mood that threatened to remove, not merely the clothes, but the epidermis, no, the very bowels of his fellow creatures.

The passionate defiance was gone: a more savage, relentless humour took its place, a humour that stabbed and punctured with intent to kill. (pp. 253-54)

[In his long narrative poem *Clarel,*] Melville's insight no longer shrivelled and blasted the very constitution of man, as in *The Confidence Man;* but it pierced, perhaps, even deeper. (pp. 312-13)

When one examines the mood of *Clarel* and the conclusions of one of the pilgrims, Mortmain, the Swede. . . , one becomes conscious of the exceptional maturity of Melville's social observation. (p. 314)

[Melville] did not in *Clarel* take refuge in any of the cheap opiates of his time: his scepticisms are as inexorable, as thoroughgoing, as they had been in the most devastating pages of *The Confidence Man;* but, with all this dubiety, there is a difference in the mood; and though *Clarel* pictures the thoughts of men unfrocked in faith, and shows them wandering over many arid deserts and picking their way through the broken streets of many ruined towns, something solid, the beginnings of a new faith, kept Melville himself from slipping into hopeless indifference or even more hopeless despair. (p. 319)

[Why, with all its] virtues of thought, is *Clarel* necessarily Melville's most neglected book? The capital difficulty, I think, is inherent in its very conception as a narrative poem: it is impossible to carry through so many pages the quick sympathies and empathies that it is in the nature of verse to give. . . . Melville's eight-syllabled lines in *Clarel* are monotonous, vary the rhyme scheme as he will; they are made even more tedious by the stale poetic airs that accompanied it. (pp. 320-21)

[In] *Clarel* he was too frequently the victim of his uncertain taste. He tags adjectives on to nouns to eke out the line; he uses, all too frequently, words like fane and sward and rue and twain and nigh, and, with unforgivable recurrence, he rhymes elf and self; above all, not relying on his ear for more subtle quantities, he fills out lines with redundant words or phrases—or clips them off. This clumsiness in detail adds to the clumsiness of conception: what might have been vivid prose became dull verse. . . . Mid all this poetizing there remains, of course, a little poetry: lines that lift out of the grey pages like a sudden sea gull from the monotonous surface of the ocean; there are even whole passages, in particular the Dirge that comes toward the end, which are veritably moving. But although the materials for intense feeling or vivid imagism are present, they are spoiled in the mixing. All this acute observation of men, things, places, seems to clog Melville's spirit: when he achieves victory, it is a victory of thought: an idea becomes pregnant and a dozen good lines are born. But the detail over-rides the general impression . . . : the movement is slow: the aim is dispersed. There is a story and a climax in *Clarel;* but we do not feel them in passage. (pp. 321-22)

[Because] Melville did not find harmonious form for his intuitions, we are deprived of a good part of them, and those that remain we must pick, like precious shards, from the refuse heap of the poem. He was a true poet; but formal verse was not his medium; and the relentless probity of his mind, the keen reaching into the heart of a dilemma, lacked in these lengthy verses an appropriate vehicle. (p. 322)

Melville's last poems gain by comparison with his earlier work: but his prose inevitably loses a little. One does not miss his lack of energy in a quatrain; it is plain and perceptible even in a short novel. . . . The immediateness of the old narratives was gone. *Billy Budd,* his final novel, is not a full-bodied story: there is statement, commentary, illustration, just statement, wise commentary, apt illustration: what is lacking is an independent and living creation. (p. 353)

[The] story itself takes place on the sea, but the sea itself is missing, and even the principal characters are not primarily men: they are actors and symbols. The story gains something by this concentration, perhaps: it is stripped for action, and even Melville's deliberate digressions do not halt it. Each of the characters has a Platonic clarity of form. (pp. 353-54)

Billy Budd is the story of three men in the British Navy: it is also the story of the world, the spirit, and the devil. . . . Good and evil exist in the nature of things, each forever itself, each doomed to war with the other. In the working out of human institutions, evil has a place as well as the good. . . . These are the fundamental ambiguities of life: so long as evil exists, the agents that intercept it will also be evil, whilst we accept the world's conditions: the universal articles of war on which our civilizations rest. Rascality may be punished; but beauty and innocence will suffer in that process far more. There is no comfort, in the perpetual Calvary of the spirit, to find a thief nailed on either side. Melville had been harried by these paradoxes in *Pierre.* At last he was reconciled. He accepted the situation as a tragic necessity; and to meet that tragedy bravely was to find peace, the ultimate peace of resignation, even in an incongruous world. As Melville's own end approached, he cried out with Billy Budd: God bless Captain Vere! (pp. 356-57)

Lewis Mumford, in his Herman Melville *(copyright, 1929, by Harcourt Brace Jovanovich, Inc.; copyright renewed © 1956 by Lewis Mumford; reprinted by permission of the author), Harcourt Brace Jovanovich, 1929, 377 p.*

GRANVILLE HICKS (essay date 1935)

To what extent [Melville's] first voyage had revealed to him the evil in the world *Redburn* shows, just as *White Jacket* suggests how inevitably a ship symbolized for him the world of men. What more natural than that, for his supreme effort, his great symphonic development of his chosen theme, he should find in the *Pequod* of Nantucket the epitome of the world, in its captain the titanic protagonist of a cosmic drama, and in a great white whale the perfect symbol of blind, unreasoning evil? What had been for him the world of reality, what would remain to the end—as *Billy Budd* shows—the most vivid setting for his allegories that his experience had revealed or his imag-

ination could conceive, gave him in *Moby Dick* a flawless metaphor.

Melville attacked his problems in *Moby Dick* so courageously and resourcefully that one marvels at the failure of the book to impress and influence the generation after the war. But the explanation is simple: after the war men were wrestling with the problem of evil as it presented itself in concrete economic phenomena. Melville's problem was real enough, but the terms in which he stated it were irrelevant. This explains, in part, why *Moby Dick,* with all its virtues, is not comparable to the great metaphysical epics of the past, which have made room for all the principal varieties of experience in their eras. It is impossible to suppose that Melville—or anyone else living in mid-nineteenth century America—could have been a Lucretius or a Dante, and the mere fact that he could conceive of writing an epic is itself magnificent. There is every reason to be thankful that, in this era of intellectual expansion, there was one writer who could find terms, whatever they were, for the expression of his vision of the universe. (pp. 7-8)

Granville Hicks, "Heritage," in his The Great Tradition: An Interpretation of American Literature since the Civil War *(copyright © 1933, 1935 by Macmillan Publishing Co., Inc.; originally published in 1933 by The Macmillan Company, New York; new material in the revised edition copyright ©1969 by Granville Hicks; reprinted by permission of Russell & Volkening, Inc., as agent for the author), revised edition, Macmillan, 1935, Quadrangle Books, 1969, pp. 1-31.**

CONRAD AIKEN (essay date 1937)

Without any question the greatest book which has come out of New England, and one of the very greatest works of prose fiction ever written in any language, [*Moby Dick*] is also the final and perfect finial to the Puritan's desperate three-century-long struggle with the problem of evil. Hunted from consciousness into the unconscious, and in effect beyond space and time, magnificently sublimated so that it becomes not one issue but all issues, a superb and almost unanalyzable matrix of universal symbolism, the white whale is the Puritan's central dream of delight and terror, the all-hating and all-loving, all-creating and all-destroying implacable god, whose magnetism none can escape, and who must be faced and fought with on the frontier of awareness with the last shred of one's moral courage and one's moral despair. Man against God? Is the principle of things, at last, to be seen as essentially evil? And redeemable only by war *à l'outrance?* Impossible, at any rate, to surrender; one's freedom to feel toward it what one will, whether hatred or love, must be preciously preserved. One must grapple with it, and alone, and in darkness, no matter whether it lead to a death throe or to an all-consuming love. (p. 91)

Conrad Aiken, "Literature in Massachusetts" (originally published as "Literature," in Massachusetts: A Guide to Its Places and People *by the Federal Writers' Project of the Works Progress Administration for the State of Massachusetts, Houghton Mifflin, 1937), in his* Collected Criticism *(copyright © 1935, 1939, 1940, 1942, 1951, 1958 by Conrad Aiken; reprinted by permission of Brandt & Brandt Literary Agents, Inc.), Oxford University Press, New York, 1968, pp. 82-93.**

YVOR WINTERS (essay date 1938)

The symbolism of *Moby Dick* is based on the antithesis of the sea and the land: the land represents the known, the mastered, in human experience; the sea, the half-known, the obscure region of instinct, uncritical feeling, danger, and terror. (p. 53)

The relationship of man to the known and to the half known, however, is not a simple and static one; he cannot merely stay on land, or he will perish of imperception, but must venture on the sea, without losing his relationship to the land; we have, in brief, the relationship of principle to perception, or, in other words, the problem of judgment. (p. 56)

[After the *Pequod* sets] sail, the mates are introduced and described. They represent various levels of normal human attitudes toward physical and spiritual danger, the highest being that of Starbuck, the first mate, who represents the critical intelligence. . . . Starbuck's desperate effort to turn Ahab from his purpose, and, after his failure, his submission to Ahab, is thus a major crisis in the book; it represents the unsuccessful rebellion of sanity and morality against a dominant madness.

Ahab himself has lost a leg to Moby Dick, the white whale, on a previous voyage, and has set out on this voyage with the secret intention of vengeance, in spite of the fact that he owes a primary allegiance to the interests of his owners. As the whale represents death and evil, Ahab's ivory leg represents the death that has become a part of the living man as a result of his struggle with evil; it is the numb wisdom which is the fruit of experience. (pp. 62-3)

Fedallah, Ahab's harpooneer, who guides and advises him in the direction of his undoing, and who, according to Melville's own suggestion, may be some kind of emanation from Ahab himself, is perhaps the sinning mind as it shows itself distinct from the whole man. . . . The crew regard Fedallah as the devil in disguise, and he appears in general to be offered as a manifestation of pure evil. (p. 65)

But predestined or otherwise, it is with Ahab the sinner that the book is concerned; his sin, in the minor sense, is monomaniac vengeance; in the major, the will to destroy the spirit of evil itself, an intention blasphemous because beyond human powers and infringing upon the purposes of God. (pp. 65-6)

The symbolism of the whale is part of the symbolism of the sea. The sea is the realm of the half-known, at once of perception and of peril; it is infested by subtle and malignant creatures, bent on destruction; it is governed by tremendous, destructive, and unpredictable forces, the storms, calms, currents, tides, depths, and distances, amid which one can preserve oneself by virtue only of the greatest skill, and then but precariously and from moment to moment. Of all the creatures in the sea, the whale is the greatest, the most intelligent, and the most dangerous. . . . It is thus naturally, in a general way, the symbol of evil and of death, and this symbolism is developed from beginning to end of the book carefully and elaborately. . . . [One] is familiarized in great detail with the structure, size, and functions of the animal, as well as with his habits, and with the stupendous medium in which he moves. Probably no other book exists which so impresses us at once with the vastness of the physical universe and with the vastness of the idea of the universe. The allegory is incalculably strengthened by this sense of vastness and power, and by the detailed reality through which it is established. . . . [We] see how the idea of the whale is imbedded in all nature, for his physical form is repeatedly suggested in rocks, in mountains, and in stars.

This general symbolism is concentrated in Moby Dick, the White Whale, who is especially intelligent, malignant, and powerful. . . . In an earlier encounter, he had bitten off Ahab's leg; Ahab is bent on vengeance. This intense desire for revenge is a sin; and in Ahab's case the sin is heightened by the conviction that a power greater and more malignant than any proper to mere animal nature is acting in or through the whale: he is convinced of the true existence of the "demonism of the world." He thus endeavors to step outside of the limitations of man and revenge himself upon the permanent order of the universe. . . . (pp. 66-8)

The most extensive elucidation and defense of the notion of the demonism of Moby Dick, as well as of "the demonism of the world," occurs in the chapter on the whiteness of the whale, equally one of the most astonishing pieces of rhetoric and one of the most appalling specimens of metaphysical argument in all literature. . . . (pp. 68-9)

Through elaborate and magnificent physical description we are made to realize the tremendousness of the whale and of his medium; through exposition of this nature, we are shown his spiritual significance. It is not that one object stands for another, as a bare allegorical formula; the relationship is more fully and subtly developed in the book than one can develop it in summary. The possibility that the physical and the spiritual are one and the same, according to the terms employed, is established; and one is convinced, with Ahab, for the time being, of the probability in this instance. Or if one is not, one is brought to an understanding of Ahab's conviction; so that his entire course of action becomes in its spiritual effect, what it was for him in literal fact, a defiance of the divine order. (pp. 70-1)

[*Moby Dick*] is beyond a cavil one of the most carefully and successfully constructed of all the major works of literature; to find it careless, redundant, or in any sense romantic, as even its professed admirers are prone to do, is merely to misread the book and to be ignorant of the history leading up to it.

The book is less a novel than an epic poem. The plot is too immediately interpenetrated with idea to lend itself easily to the manner of the novelist. The language in which it is written is closer to the poetry of *Paradise Lost* or of *Hamlet* than it is to the prose of the realistic novelist. (p. 73)

[However,] the epic hero is normally a successful figure, and not a tragical one; Ahab, on the other hand, obeys the traditional law of tragedy, and destroys himself through allowing himself to be dominated by an heroic vice: he is another Coriolanus, but in dimensions epical, in the quality of his mind and of his sin metaphysical, and in his motivating ideas Calvinistical. One should note that Melville, in writing a tragic instead of a traditionally heroic epic, displayed a thorough understanding of his material: the Calvinistic view led to sin and catastrophe, not to triumph, although at times to sin and catastrophe on an inspired and heroic scale. . . . (pp. 74-5)

The book, then, partakes in some measure of the qualities of a novel and of a tragic drama; but essentially it is an epic poem. Form and subject are wedded with a success equal to that observable in Milton, Vergil, or Shakespeare.

The book is not only a great epic; it is profoundly an American epic. . . . In its physical events, *Moby Dick* is a narration of exploration and heroic adventure; it is thus typical of the United States of the nineteenth century, by land as well as by sea. . . . (p. 75)

[The greatest works of Melville, aside from *Moby Dick*], are *Benito Cereno, The Encantadas,* and *Billy Budd.* These works, in the matter of style, are essentially prose; *The Encantadas* contains traces of the style of *Moby Dick,* along with traces of its subject-matter, but the rhetoric is subdued in structure and in feeling. In *Benito Cereno,* and in the other later works, there is scarcely a trace of the style of *Moby Dick;* we have the style of a novelist, and in *Benito Cereno* especially this style occurs in a form both classical and austere. (pp. 76-7)

The morality of slavery is not an issue in [*Benito Cereno*]; the issue is this, that through a series of acts of performance and of negligence, the fundamental evil of a group of men, evil which normally should have been kept in abeyance, was freed to act. The story is a portrait of that evil in action, as shown in the negroes, and of the effect of the action, as shown in Cereno. It is appalling in its completeness, in its subtle horror, and in its silky quiet. (p. 77)

Melville's descriptive power in [*The Encantadas*] is at its best; the islands in all their barren and archaic horror are realized unforgettably. (p. 78)

[Despite] the difference in plot and in subject matter, the idea of [*Pierre*] is the same as that governing *Moby Dick,* but with a shift in emphasis: it is the relationship of principle to perception, and the difficulty of adjusting principle to perception in such a manner as to permit a judgment which shall be a valid motive to action. . . . In *Pierre* and in *The Confidence Man* alike it is assumed that valid judgment is impossible, for every event, every fact, every person, is too fluid, too unbounded to be known. . . . (p. 79)

Pierre acts—he surely cannot be accused of moral paralysis—but he acts hastily and on unsound principles; he is convinced that the world is one of moral confusion, and he proceeds in confusion; intellectually, if not emotionally, he is satisfied with confusion; and for the time being his author is at one with him in this respect. (p. 80)

There are in the plot of *Pierre,* two situations in particular, the two central issues of the book, which are intended to illustrate the ambiguity of all supposed morality. One is the double image of his father: that of the father remembered and represented by the portrait painted after his marriage; and that of the young rake who begot Isabel, whose existence was suddenly disclosed to Pierre, and who is represented by the portrait painted when he was visiting Isabel's mother. Between the extremes of the two portraits Pierre's judgment of his father blurs and shifts and cannot be fixed; it is this difficulty that disturbed Pierre to the extent that he precipitately projected himself into the relationship with Isabel. This relationship provides the second ambiguity, for though at the time of his action Pierre believed that he was acting wholly for moral and generous reasons, he discovered immediately after acting that he was the victim of an incestuous passion for Isabel, so that he learns to distrust his own motives. At the conclusion of the book, the author confronts the reader with a final ambiguity, the problem of judging Pierre. . . . (p. 81)

[The morality of *Pierre* is] that the final truth is absolute ambiguity, and that nothing can be judged. . . . [The] essence of Pierre is that he can judge nothing and that all his actions derive from confusion and end in it. It is small wonder that a book composed in this temporary twilight should have been so unsatisfactory as a whole and in detail; for a work of art, like each detail comprising it, is by definition a judgment. The prose of Pierre is excited and inflated; it contains brilliant

passages, but in the main is a bad compromise between the prose of *Moby Dick* and the prose of the novelist.

The theme of *The Confidence Man* is identical; the details of the action are very different. The action takes place on a Mississippi River steamer, aboard which a confidence man, a scoundrel of metaphysical abilities and curiosity, operates partly for profit and partly for malicious enjoyment. (p. 82)

In each avatar, the Confidence Man tries to beguile his fellow-travelers into feeling enough confidence in him to give him money; that is, to form a judgment on which they are willing to act. It should be noted, of course, that if they do so, they are hoodwinked. The word *confidence* recurs repeatedly, and is the key-word of the allegory. (p. 83)

The Confidence Man is unsatisfactory as philosophy and is tediously repetitious as narrative; but the prose, unlike that of *Pierre,* is crisp and hard, and in a few passages the comment is brilliant. . . .

Melville was in a kind of moral limbo when he wrote these books, however, and they are essentially unsatisfactory, though they display greater intellectual activity than such works as *White Jacket, Typee,* and *Omoo,* works which within their limits are successful. (p. 85)

In the final masterpiece, *Billy Budd,* the most profound of the later works, if not the best written—the prose, unfortunately, shows a little structural awkwardness, the result of thirty years of disuse—the problem posed in *Pierre* and *The Confidence Man* received its answer. . . .

The captain, Vere, is able to fathom the situation; from the standpoint of purely private morality, he sympathizes with Billy. But Billy, in striking Claggart under these conditions committed a capital crime, and in killing him committed another, facts which Billy knew perfectly; to free him would establish at least a precedent for freeing the whole matter of criminal justice in the navy to the caprices of private judgment; the men would be likely to take advantage of it, to the damage of discipline. There had, moreover, been serious riots in the navy but a short time before. Vere can see only one solution to the situation: to act according to established principle, which supports public order, and, for the margin of difference between established principle and the facts of the particular situation, to accept it as private tragedy. (p. 86)

[The solution] of this story, and as a matter of general principle, is at once unanswerable, dignified, and profound; the characterization of Vere and of Claggart represents an insight worthy to be the final achievement of so long and so great a life. (p. 87)

Yvor Winters, "Herman Melville, and the Problems of Moral Navigation," in his Maule's Curse: Seven Studies in the History of American Obscurantism *(© 1938, by New Directions; copyright renewed © 1965 by Yvor Winters; reprinted by permission of Ohio University Press, Athens), New Directions, 1938 (and reprinted in his* In Defense of Reason, The Swallow Press, *1947, pp. 53-89).*

F. O. MATTHIESSEN (essay date 1941)

At the time of Melville's death, Richard Henry Stoddard, one of his few professed defenders, felt obliged to state that 'his vocabulary was large, fluent, eloquent, but it was excessive, inaccurate, and unliterary' [see excerpt above]. Some just application can be found for all the first five adjectives, for the fourth and fifth especially in *Pierre*; but the reaction of the modern reader to the last is that the Melville of *Mardi,* and, on occasion, even of *Moby-Dick*, could all too easily fall into the 'literary.' Stoddard's conventional standards betray themselves in his further remark that Melville's early books made him 'famous among his countrymen, who, less literary in their tastes and demands than at present, were easily captivated by stories of maritime life.' Actually Melville had felt himself constrained by just such genteel demands. In *White Jacket,* for instance, he said that his aim was to be a chronicler of the navy exactly as it was, of what might become obsolete, 'withholding nothing, inventing nothing.' Yet he found that he quickly reached the limits that were permitted him. When he wanted to present the scene of a flogging, the captain's abusive epithet had to be left blank, with the note, 'The phrase here used I have never seen either written or printed and should not like to be the first person to introduce it to the public.' His own modesty joined again with the taboos of his age when he came to probe the daily life of the men, for he skirted the subject with remote allusions to the *Oedipus* and to Shelley's *Cenci*. . . . (pp. 421-22)

His liberation in *Moby-Dick* through the agency of Shakespeare was almost an unconscious reflex. . . . In his effort to endow the whaling industry with a mythology befitting a fundamental activity of man in his struggle to subdue nature, he came into possession of the primitive energies latent in words. He had already begun to realize in the dream-passages of *Mardi* that meaning had more than just a level of sense, that the arrangement of words in patterns of sound and rhythm enabled them to create feelings and tones that could not be included in a logical or scientific statement. But he did not find a valuable clue to how to express the hidden life of men, which had become his compelling absorption, until he encountered the unexampled vitality of Shakespeare's language. (p. 423)

The most important effect of Shakespeare's use of language was to give Melville a range of vocabulary for expressing passion far beyond any that he had previously possessed. The voices of many characters help to intensify Ahab's. For instance, as he talks to the blacksmith about forging his harpoon, he finds the old man 'too calmly, sanely woeful . . . I am impatient of all misery . . . that is not mad.' This seems to have drawn upon the mood of Laertes' violent entrance, 'That drop of blood that's calm proclaims me bastard'; or since it has been remarked that 'Ahab has that that's bloody on his mind,' it probably links more closely to Hamlet's 'My thoughts be bloody, or be nothing worth.' (p. 425)

In view of Shakespeare's power over him, it is not surprising that in 'The Quarter Deck,' in the first long declaration from Ahab to the crew, Melville broke at times into what is virtually blank verse, and can be printed as such:

But look ye, Starbuck, what is said in heat,
That thing unsays itself. There are men
From whom warm words are small indignity.
I meant not to incense thee. Let it go.
Look! see yonder Turkish cheeks of spotted tawn—
Living, breathing pictures painted by the sun.
The pagan leopards—the unrecking and
Unworshipping things, that live; and seek and give—
No reasons for the torrid life they feel!

That division into lines has been made without alteration of a syllable, and though there are some clumsy sequences, there

is no denying the essential pattern. . . . The danger of such unconsciously compelled verse is always evident. As it wavers and breaks down again into ejaculatory prose, it seems never to have belonged to the speaker, to have been at best a ventriloquist's trick. The weakness is similar in those speeches of Ahab's that show obvious allusions to a series of Shakespearean characters. The sum of the parts does not make a greater whole; each one distracts attention to itself and interferes with the singleness of Ahab's development. (p. 426)

In Melville's case the accident of reading Shakespeare had been a catalytic agent, indispensable in releasing his work from limited reporting to the expression of profound natural forces. Lear's Fool had taught him what Starbuck was to remark about poor Pip, that even the exalted words of a lunatic could penetrate to the heavenly mysteries. But Melville came into full possession of his own idiom, not when he was half following Shakespeare, but when he had grasped the truth of the passage in *The Winter's Tale* that 'The art itself is nature,' when, writing out of his own primary energy, he could end his description of [Ahab] in language that suggests Shakespeare's, but is not an imitation of it: 'But Ahab, my captain, still moves before me in all his Nantucket grimness and shagginess; and in this episode touching emperors and kings, I must not conceal that I have only to do with a poor old whale-hunter like him; and, therefore, all outward majestical trappings and housings are denied me. Oh, Ahab! what shall be grand in thee, it must needs be plucked at from the skies, and dived for in the deep, and featured in the unbodied air!' (p. 428)

In driving through to his conception of a tragic hero who should be dependent upon neither rank nor costume, Melville showed his grasp of the kind of art 'that nature makes.' . . . His practice of tragedy, though it gained force from Shakespeare, had real freedom; it did not base itself upon Shakespeare, but upon man and nature as Melville knew them. Therefore, he was able to handle, in his greatest scenes, a kind of diction that depended upon no source, and that could, as Lawrence noted, convey something 'almost superhuman or inhuman, bigger than life' [see excerpt above]. . . . [Another] example of how Melville had learned under Shakespeare's tutelage to master, at times, a dramatic speech that does not encroach upon verse, but draws upon a magnificent variety and flow of language, is Ahab's defiance of fire:

> Oh! thou clear spirit of clear fire, whom on these seas I as Persian once did worship, till in the sacramental act so burned by thee, that to this hour I bear the scar; I now know thee, thou clear spirit, and I now know that thy right worship is defiance. To neither love nor reverence will thou be kind; and e'en for hate thou canst but kill; and all are killed. No fearless fool now fronts thee. I own thy speechless, placeless power; but to the last gasp of my earthquake life will dispute its unconditional, unintegral mastery in me. In the midst of the personified impersonal, a personality stands here. Though but a point at best; whenceso'er I came; whereso'er I go; yet while I earthly live, the queenly personality lives in me, and feels her royal rights. But war is pain, and hate is woe. Come in thy lowest form of love, and I will kneel and kiss thee; but at thy highest, come as mere supernal power; and though thou launchest navies of full-freighted worlds, there's that in here that

still remains indifferent. Oh, thou clear spirit,
of thy fire thou madest me, and like a true child
of fire, I breathe it back to thee.

The full meaning of that speech can be apprehended only in
its context in the tumultuous suddenness of the storm, and in
relation to Ahab's diabolic bond with the fire-worshipping Parsee. Even in that context it is by no means clear exactly how
much Melville meant to imply in making Ahab regard the fire
as his father, and presently go on to say: 'But thou art my fiery
father; my sweet mother, I know not. Oh, cruel! what hast
thou done with her? There lies my puzzle.' Immersed in primitive forces in *Moby-Dick,* Melville soon learned that—as he
made Ishmael remark concerning 'the gliding great demon of
the seas of life'—there were 'subterranean' levels deeper than
his understanding could explain or fathom. But whatever the
latent radiations of intuition in this passage they emanate from
a core of articulated thought. Here, if Emerson's prejudice
against the novel had only allowed him to see it, was the proof
that the dialect of mid-nineteenth-century America could rise
to dramatic heights. That does not mean that any American
ever spoke like this, any more than Elizabethans talked like
Lear; but it does mean that the progressions of Melville's prose
are now based on a sense of speech rhythm, and not on anybody
else's verse. The elaborate diction should not mislead us into
thinking that the words have been chosen recklessly, or merely
because they sounded well. For they are combined in a vital
rhetoric, and thereby build up a defense of one of the chief
doctrines of the age, the splendor of the single personality. . . .
The resources of the isolated man, his courage and his staggering indifference to anything outside himself, have seldom
been exalted so high.

The verbal resources demonstrate that Melville has now mastered Shakespeare's mature secret of how to make language
itself dramatic. He has learned to depend more and more upon
verbs of action, which lend their dynamic pressure to both
movement and meaning. (pp. 429-30)

But Melville's new ripeness of power should not be thought
of solely in relation to his drama. It is just as apparent in his
narrative, as can be suggested very briefly by one of his many
Biblical allusions, which for once he makes not for solemnity
but to heighten humor. He is just finishing his chapter on 'The
Tail': 'Dissect him how I may, then, I but go skin deep; I
know him not, and never will. But if I know not even the tail
of this whale, how understand his head? much more, how
comprehend his face, when face he has none? Thou shalt see
my back parts, my tail, he seems to say, but my face shall not
be seen. But I cannot completely make out his back parts; and
hint what he will about his face, I say again he has no face.'

The effect of that burlesque is to magnify rather than to lessen
his theme, not to blaspheme Jehovah, but to add majesty to
the whale. Melville's inner sureness was now such that it freed
his language from the constrictions that had limited *White Jacket.*
He had regained and reinforced the gusto of *Typee* on a level
of greater complexity. Whether or not he consciously intended
to symbolize sex in the elemental energies of fire or of the
white whale, when he wanted to deal with the subject directly
he did not resort to guarded hints, but handled very simply the
Whitmanesque comradeship between Ishmael and Queequeg.
In 'The Cassock' he could also write a chapter about the heroic
phallus of the whale. (p. 431)

F. O. Matthiessen, *"The Revenger's Tragedy,"* in
his *American Renaissance: Art and Expression in the
Age of Emerson and Whitman* (copyright 1941 by

*Oxford University Press, Inc.; reprinted by permis-
sion), Oxford University Press, New York, 1941, pp.
396-466.*

WILLIAM ELLERY SEDGWICK   (essay date 1942)

The tragedy of mind is a version of the great universal drama
of being, in which the mind plays the crucial role, a role fairly
shrouded in ambiguities. Between the mind and the heart of
man there is a fatal conflict, of which the heart is invariably
the innocent victim. (p. 57)

In Melville's view of life, a great man combines a great heart
with a great mind. Both are integral parts of his greatness. The
trouble begins, as Melville also perceived, in that their respective exigencies lead them in opposite directions. . . . [The]
dualism of human nature is such that where it would glorify
it brings ruin. At the centre of the destruction which it wreaks
is the death of the heart. . . . Herein lies the mainspring and
conclusion of the tragedy of mind. The great man, the fairest
possible semblance of humanity, is impelled to achieve a noble
and impossible ideal, and in the very effort to achieve this ideal
destroys the fairest semblance of humanity. He brings death
within and without. Thus it was with Taji [in *Mardi*], whose
two oldest companions were killed by the avengers' arrows
intended for him. [In *Moby Dick*] Captain Ahab, already maimed,
dies cut off from the crew of his ship, who were also the victims
of the heroic, indeed the superhuman, exertion of his humanity.
Pierre, like Hamlet, royally endowed with the attributes of
human nature, is determined to shoulder all the claims of human
nature. And, like Taji, he brings death on the only two persons
who cling to him and dies himself at his own hands.

Mardi is the first of Melville's tragedies. . . . The world of
Mardi is "the world of mind." Not only does it contemplate
this world; but its allegory is of the mind's way of seeing and
ordering experience. Nevertheless, throughout the book, Melville is constantly making shift to allow for man's physical and
sensuous nature. The mental character of the book is offset by
a lavish sensuousness of decor unparalleled in Melville's writings. (pp. 58-9)

[In *Mardi*] Melville takes on the full weight of what it is to be
a man and struggles to embrace in a noble synthesis all the
mixed elements in man's nature. The form proposed for this
synthesis is the pursuit of truth. . . .

Mardi has force, yet it fails of the force which we are entitled
to expect of tragedy, of whatever kind, and the reason for this
failure is not far to seek. To say that the weakness lies in the
unreality of Yillah or any of the characters only touches the
surface of what is wanting. It presents an image of harmonious
being. Yet the image is partial. More important, it is incomplete
as an exertion of being or consciousness. . . . It has all the
lopsidedness of precocity. It has brilliance without warmth. It
is emotionally immature. Underneath the intellectual juggling,
there are the tensions of profoundly serious intellectual aspirations, and we feel the reality of the mind in the throes of its
noble importunity after the truth, but the realities of life and
being which Melville identified with the heart—these are not
there. (p. 60)

The tragic necessity that the mind is under to reach for the
infinite is present in *Mardi*. But the tragedy of mind involves
another victim of the mind's aspirations than the mind itself.
Without this victim the tragic force is less than it should be
by more than a half. Before Melville could imbue tragedy with

the force which tragedy requires, he would have to command pity. He would have to realize the realities of the heart's attachments, or, in Keats's phrase, "the holyness of the Heart's affections." (p. 61)

In *Moby Dick,* as in Shakespeare's tragedies, there is a solid, crowded foreground of material things and of human characters and actions. Yet this solid ground will suddenly seem to give under our feet, so that we feel ourselves hung momentarily over the abyss. We owe this sensation to the fact that solidity has been sacrificed to transparency for the sake of a more immediate view into the ultimate. Shakespeare was satisfied to leave the mysterious background of life to random probings or to inference. Melville could not. He was bound by many diverse considerations—by his inherited and his temperamental Calvinism, by the American pioneer in him as well as the Puritan—to confront the truth as directly and comprehensively as possible. In *Moby Dick* the mysterious background truth looms in the foreground of palpable facts. It articulates itself in those facts and by so doing it confers upon them something of an apocalyptic scale and intensity foreign to Shakespeare's prevailing naturalism. (p. 86)

[It] would appear that Melville aimed to strike a balance between Dante and Shakespeare. Certainly, there are two actions in the book which although they mesh are distinct from one another, one of which is Shakespearean, the other Dantesque. The Shakespearean or outward tragic action includes Ahab's conflict with forces outside himself and, also, the bitter, agonizing self-conflict which follows on its heels. All the other characters are caught up in this action, but it centers in Ahab. The other action, the Dantesque, lies entirely with Ishmael, who, let me say for the moment, stands to Ahab as the shadow to the object which casts it. Pushing a paradox, I shall call this action passive as well as inward—inward, that is, with respect to the book as a whole. Like the action that extends from first to last in the *Divine Comedy,* it is the action of man's comprehension slowly completing itself. (pp. 87-8)

The richness of *Moby Dick* consists in its combination of [a] deep insight with a young athletic and sensuous spirituality that manifests itself constantly in the fullness of its vision of things. . . . Melville was with the best of [American writers] for his vivid visualizations. To this freshness he adds a wholeness of vision which is not found elsewhere in American literature, and which might be summed up roughly by adding Hawthorne's human interiors to Thoreau's nature. The best American trait in *Moby Dick* finally distinguishes it from all other American books. It is this: with the same absence of bookishness that we recognize in Thoreau's description of the Maine woods, Melville saw anew and represented in *Moby Dick* the matter of the world's oldest books. With the same penetrating freshness with which Thoreau looked about him on Mount Katahdin, Melville looked into the oldest and darkest recesses in the human soul, which open backward beyond our individualities, beyond the different generations into the dim beginnings of the race. (pp. 95-6)

Ahab, the White Whale, the sea—these are Melville's greatest creations in *Moby Dick.* Ahab is the hero, but the White Whale is the central character. The sea embraces them both and brings them face to face with one another. Here is a trinity, a three in one.

Ahab is more than a whaling captain; he is man. He is man sentient, speculative, purposive, religious, standing his full human stature against the immense mystery of creation. His antagonist, Moby Dick, is that immense mystery. (p. 97)

Moby Dick stands for the mystery of creation which confronts and challenges the mind of man at the same time that it lies ambushed in the process of his own consciousness. He is significant of the massive inertia in things, and of the blind beauty and violence of nature—all that ignores or twists or betrays or otherwise does outrage to man's purposes.

In the third place there is the sea, perhaps the most wonderful of Melville's symbols. The sea is the element of truth as also of man's greatness and infinite aspirations. It is the ubiquitous hide-out of Moby Dick. It leads away from all definitions, all traditional sanctities, all securities. (p. 98)

Ahab's soul and his religious sense refers us back to the main view that Melville takes of his hero, the view on which his tragedy hinges. That is, Ahab is the grand human thing itself. He will not abate one inch of his whole high broad human form. He will not renounce his speculative intellect. Neither, on the other hand, will he abase himself by denying his spiritual nature. His soul is part of his royal crown of a man. (pp. 103-04)

Ahab is a king by natural right. Like Lear he is mad—with the madness of vital truth. His madness is the final expression of his nobility. It is the furthest thrust of his sea instinct. . . . Ahab's madness springs from an excess of humanity. The truth upon which he has concentrated all his energies and sacrificed all that is kind to man's mortality has a profound and universal import for man. The moral and spiritual universe, all that is cherished and cherishable by men, is at stake in it. . . . Ahab's great heart is stretched to bursting under the ceaseless effort of his mind to lay hold of it. (p. 108)

Ahab pursues the truth as the champion of man, leaving behind him all traditional conclusions, all common assumptions, all codes and creeds and articles of faith. (p. 109)

While the story of Ahab's pursuit of Moby Dick goes forward to its end, a drama of inner conflict is unfolded. A victim of his own nature, a victim of the tragedy of mind, Ahab would have been torn asunder . . . under any circumstances. His tragedy is far more bitter and more terrible because, finally, his own hand is raised against himself. His monomania has all but possessed itself of his noble madness. Therefore, his humanity is all but hideously perverted as well as otherwise maimed. Viewed outwardly, Ahab is like a figure in an old morality play, standing between a good and a bad angel and each suing for his soul. Starbuck is his good angel. His bad angel is Fedallah, "tall and swart, with one white tooth evilly protruding." But the drama of inner conflict I speak of is deeper; it is the struggle of Ahab's humanity—stout even in this extremity—to free itself from the fell clutches of his evil monomania. (pp. 112-13)

Melville's idealism responded to Ahab—was, of course, projected in Ahab. Yet he stopped short of Ahab. He stopped short of the point where idealism, embittered, turns against humanity, and where preoccupation with the ultimate truth breaks with those realities, apart from which it has no human significance. True to the considerations which prompted them in the first place, his idealism and preoccupation with truth remained not a negation but an affirmation of life. What is the truth? he asked in *Moby Dick,* the whole force of his nature bent to the question. The question, however, did not lead to a vanishing point. It was, to change the image, a lever applied with great force, that heaved up its own only possible answer, the truth of what it is to be alive. It is an act of being.

Moby Dick is a representation of life like *Hamlet* or *King Lear,* but with a difference. . . . Melville is more present and pressing in his masterpiece than Shakespeare is in any of his plays. His subjective being is constantly taking over, by identifying itself with, the forms of his objective seeing. Or, returning to a point of similarity between *Hamlet* and *Moby Dick,* in each the range and variety of vision depends essentially on an inward balance and the most inclusive and exacting self-possession on the part of their respective authors. But in *Hamlet* this balance and self-possession is something achieved outside the scope of the play. In *Moby Dick,* on the other hand, Melville's exertion to keep his balance, upon the loss of which his vision would crumble, goes on in the book. All that he discovers as he perseveres is felt like so many threats in as many contending directions to his keeping his all-important balance. It appears, then, that to call *Moby Dick* an act of being is not so much to praise it as to characterize it accurately. (pp. 131-32)

The mention of Starbuck, however, calls attention to the weakness of *Moby Dick* as a representation of life, a weakness which is all the more apparent when we compare it with any one of Shakespeare's tragedies. In Starbuck we see where the wholeness of its humanity is wanting. He is simply a counterpiece. For when he described Starbuck Melville's imagination failed him, and it failed him because his sympathies did not lie in the direction of such characters. His failure, so apparent in Starbuck, was not confined to him. In the whole book only Queequeg is a lovable character, and that, in view of the effect that Melville aimed at, is a serious defect. Melville's failure even reaches to Ahab, where it is most serious. Ahab's heart struggles to restore itself to human ties, without which it must perish. We know this, but we seldom feel it. A character that in many respects can stand comparison with King Lear, Ahab is not poignant like King Lear. The "soft feeling of the human" is not there, at any rate not in the right proportion for his heroic stature. His tragedy inspires terror as does no work in the language outside of Shakespeare. But it fails to inspire pity. (pp. 133-34)

Pierre was the only book of Melville's maturity as ambitious as *Moby Dick.* . . . Different as is the foreground of fact in *Pierre* from the foreground in its predecessor, the speculative background is much the same, and it was there, in the speculative background, that Melville's momentum, coming out of *Moby Dick,* drove him to place his main interest. Accordingly, for all the realistic notation of psychological truths in *Pierre,* another spirit so impregnates and usurps the characters and their actions that in the final impression of the book its realistic features are all but lost sight of. The characters and their actions are less human actualities than they are so many mathematical quantities used in psychological equations. (pp. 144-45)

There is nothing genial in the desperate philosophy in *Pierre.* In contrast to *Moby Dick,* the mood has grown taut; it shows the constriction that comes from insecurity within; it is wild more than wayward. It becomes hysterical. We feel that it issues from intolerable tensions and uncertainties—that it is the expression of a grief-stricken man. (p. 156)

[Whereas] with Ahab thought has the body of action, with young Pierre action rapidly becomes thought. The same difference appears in the character of the symbols. Always holding on to his awareness of the outside world, the visible world of experience, Melville's symbols in *Moby Dick* have a rounded organic life of their own. In *Pierre,* on the other hand, the main symbols are felt as the coinages of Melville's mind, and instead of adding to each other's significance, they collide with

and block one another, or collapse within themselves, frittering their force away in a multiplicity of intellectual refinements. Again, in the style of *Moby Dick,* as in the mood, there is the resilience of a consciousness in free and full possession of itself. . . . Admittedly, in *Pierre* Melville wrote in several different styles by intention, but there is not the same security on Melville's part with reference to his different intentions as there is in *Moby Dick* with reference to the whole. There are some very fine passages in the book, with a peculiar tenor and urgency of their own. But we virtually never feel the force of a consciousness that is constantly reviving and invigorating its inner sources by drawing on the outside world of tangible objects. (p. 159)

Pierre is but a shadow to Melville, and Melville, in the grip of his idealism, the upshot of his radical protestantism, has lost all communication with the visible world of experience, and its restorative perspectives in which men are united in physical action, in love, in worship and the pursuit of truth. . . . Melville himself has become one with Ahab and like Ahab his humanity is wounded and like Ahab he trains murderous guns inboard. He hates the common human nature which he shares. Of all the paradoxes in which we see Melville caught up, the most terrible is this, that his love of virtue and truth—and of virtue as set forth in the New Testament—has brought him to Ahab's extremity. Such is his love of virtue that he hates men for being unworthy and abusing it, and his hate goes beyond men to the unscrutable laws of the universe for betraying virtue to the ignoble uses of men. . . . [While] doubting all things earthly, he has lost hold of intuitions of some things heavenly. His human integrity has been wounded, the wound is hate, Ahab's quenchless feud is his.

Melville saw in *Hamlet* the tragedy of youthful idealism and he repeated it in *Pierre,* identifying himself with his hero and, at the same time, adding to its other aspect or other dimension, as Shakespeare had done before him, that other aspect or dimension being the tragedy of mind. (pp. 166-67)

The last tragic realization of all is that the mind in the noble pursuit of truth comes only to a true sense of itself as the only reality, and that reality is the principle of destruction. . . . The element of doubt which he found in *Hamlet,* Melville pushed to the ultimate. But giving skepticism a new body, as it were, he could find no refuge in it. (p. 172)

William Ellery Sedgwick, in his Herman Melville: The Tragedy of Mind, *edited by Sarah Cabot Sedgwick (1942; copyright © 1944, copyright renewed © 1972, by the President and Fellows of Harvard College; excerpted by permission), Cambridge, Mass.: Harvard University Press, 1945, 255 p.*

ROBERT PENN WARREN   (essay date 1945)

It is ordinarily said that [Melville] did not master the craft of verse. Few of his poems are finished. Fine lines, exciting images, and bursts of eloquence often appear, but they appear side by side with limping lines, inexpressive images, and passages of bombast. In a way, he is a poet of shreds and patches. (pp. 184-85)

[However, if] we examine the poems under the title **"Fruit of Travel Long Ago,"** in the *Timoleon* volume of 1891, we see that the verse here is fluent and competent. In his belated poetic apprenticeship, he was capable of writing verse which is respectable by the conventional standards of the time. But the effects which he could achieve within this verse did not satisfy him. (p. 185)

Perhaps the violences, the distortions, the wrenchings in the versification of some of the poems are to be interpreted as the result not of mere ineptitude but of a conscious effort to develop a nervous, dramatic, masculine style. (p. 186)

[If we turn] to **"In a Bye-Canal,"** we may observe that the poem is broken not only by a shift in rhythm but also by a shift in tone. . . . Probably no one would argue that the disparate elements in this poem have been assimilated. . . . But I think that one may be well entitled to argue that the confusions of temper in this poem are not merely the result of ineptitude but are the result of an attempt to create a poetry of some vibrancy, range of reference, and richness of tone. (p. 187)

It must be admitted that Melville did not learn his craft. But the point is that the craft he did not learn was not the same craft which some of his more highly advertised contemporaries did learn with such glibness of tongue and complacency of spirit. Even behind some of Melville's failures we can catch the shadow of the poem which might have been. And if his poetry is, on the whole, a poetry of shreds and patches, many of the patches are of a massy and kingly fabric—no product of the local cotton mills. (p. 189)

[In **"The Conflict of Convictions"** there are] ideas which relate to Melville's concern with the fundamental ironical dualities of existence: will against necessity, action against ideas, youth against age, the changelessness of man's heart against the concept of moral progress, the bad doer against the good deed, the bad result against the good act, ignorance against fate, etc. These ideas appear again and again, as in **"The March into Virginia."** . . . Youth, action, will, ignorance—all appear in heroic and dynamic form as manifestations of . . . the spirit which had informed **Moby Dick.** But in these poems the commitment is nicely balanced, and even as we find the praise of the dynamic and heroic we find them cast against the backdrop of age, idea, necessity, wisdom, fate. . . . All bear their "fated" parts. All move toward death or toward the moment of wisdom when they will stand, as **"The March into Virginia"** puts it, "enlightened by the volleyed glare." (pp. 190-91)

"Secession, like Slavery, is against Destiny," Melville wrote in the prose Supplement to **Battle-Pieces.** For to him, if history was fate (the "foulest crime" was inherited and was fixed by geographical accident upon its perpetrators), it might also prove to be redemption. In **Mardi** . . . Melville exclaims: "Time— all-healing Time—Time, great philanthropist! Time must befriend these thralls." Melville, like Hardy, whom he resembles in so many respects and with whose war poems his own war poems share so much in tone and attitude, proclaimed that he was neither an optimist nor a pessimist, and in some of his own work we find a kind of guarded meliorism, like Hardy's, which manifests itself in the terms of destiny, fate, time, that is, in the historical process.

The historical process, however, does not appear always as this mechanism of meliorism. Sometimes the resolution it offers is of another sort, a sort similar to the elegiac calm of the natural process: the act is always poised on the verge of history, the passion, even at the moment of greatest intensity, is always about to become legend, the moral issue is always about to disappear into time and leave only the human figures, shadowy now, fixed in attitudes of the struggle. (pp. 194-95)

Nature and history proved the chief terms of resolution in **Battle-Pieces.** . . . It is actually in the terms of nature and

history that the attitude which characterizes **Clarel** first begins to make itself felt. Mr. Sedgwick has defined Melville's attitude as the result of a "religious conversion to life" [see excerpt above]. In it he renounced the quest for the "uncreated good," the individualistic idealism of **Moby Dick,** the "radical Protestantism." Mr. Sedgwick continues: "Behind **Clarel** lies the recognition that for ripeness, there must be receptivity; that from the point of view of the total consciousness it is not more blessed to give than to receive. One receives in order to be received into life and fulfilled by life. . . . Melville's act was toward humanity, not away from it. He renounced all the prerogatives of individuality in order to enter into the destiny which binds all human beings in one great spiritual and emotional organism. He abdicated his independence so as to be incorporated into the mystical body of humanity." There is the affirmation at the end of **Clarel:**

> But through such strange illusions have they passed
> Who in life's pilgrimage have baffled striven—
> Even death may prove unreal at the last,
> And stoics be astounded into heaven.
>
> Then keep thy heart, though yet but ill-resigned—
> Clarel, thy heart, the issues there but mind;
> That like the crocus budding through the snow—
> That like a swimmer rising from the deep—
> That like a burning secret which doth go
> Even from the bosom that would hoard and keep;
> Emerge thou mayst from the last whelming sea,
> And prove that death but routs life into victory.

Or we find the same attitude expressed by the comforting spirit which appears at the end of **"The Lake":**

> She ceased and nearer slid, and hung
> In dewy guise; then softlier sung:
> "Since light and shade are equal set,
> And all revolves, nor more ye know;
> Ah, why should tears the pale cheek fret
> For aught that waneth here below.
> Let go, Let go!"
>
> With that, her warm lips thrilled me through,
> She kissed me while her chaplet cold
> Its rootlets brushed against my brow
> With all their humid clinging mould.
> She vanished, leaving fragrant breath
> And warmth and chill of wedded life and death.

And when, in the light of these poems we look back upon **"The Maldive Shark"** we see its deeper significance. As the pilot fish may find a haven in the serrated teeth of the shark, so man, if he learns the last wisdom, may find an "asylum in the jaws of the Fates."

This end product of Melville's experience has, in the passage which I have already quoted from Mr. Sedgwick, been amply defined. What I wish to emphasize is the fact that there is an astonishing continuity between the early poems, especially **Battle-Pieces,** and **Clarel.** Under the terms of nature and history, the religious attitude of **Clarel** and **"The Lake"** is already being defined. (pp. 196-98)

Robert Penn Warren, "Melville the Poet" (1945), in his Selected Essays *(copyright © 1958 by Robert Penn Warren; reprinted by permission of Random House, Inc.), Random House, 1958, pp. 184-98.*

W. SOMERSET MAUGHAM (essay date 1948)

Whatever reservations one may make, Melville wrote English uncommonly well. His style reached its perfection in *Moby Dick*. Sometimes, of course, the manner he had acquired led him to rhetorical extravagance, but at its best it has a copious magnificence, a sonority, a grandeur, an eloquence that no modern writer, so far as I know, has achieved. It does indeed often recall the majestic phrase of Sir Thomas Browne and the stately period of Milton. . . . [There is an] ingenuity with which Melville wove into the elaborate pattern of his prose the ordinary nautical terms used by sailor men in the course of their daily work. The effect is to bring a note of realism, the savor of the fresh salt of the sea, to the somber symphony which is the unique novel of *Moby Dick*. (pp. 227-28)

Why have the commentators assumed that Moby Dick is a symbol of evil?. . . . Melville looked upon the natural man as good. Why should the White Whale not represent goodness rather than evil? Splendid in beauty, vast in size, great in strength, he swims the seas in freedom. Captain Ahab with his insane pride is pitiless, harsh, cruel and revengeful; *he* is Evil; and when the final encounter comes and Ahab with his crew of "mongrel renegades, castaways and cannibals" are destroyed, and the White Whale, imperturbable, justice having been done, goes his mysterious way, evil has been vanquished and good at last triumphed. Or if you want another interpretation . . . you might take Ahab with his dark wickedness for Satan and the White Whale for his Creator. Then when God, though wounded to the death, has destroyed the Evil One Ishmael, man, is left to float on the "soft and dirge-like main" with nothing more to hope or fear, alone with his unconquerable soul.

Fortunately *Moby Dick* may be read, and read with passionate interest, without a thought of what allegorical significance it may or may not have. I cannot repeat too often that a novel is to be read not for instruction or edification but for intelligent enjoyment. . . . (p. 230)

Some critics have accused Melville of lacking invention, but I think without reason. It is true that he invented more convincingly when he had a substratum of experience to sustain him; but then so do most novelists, and when he had this his imagination worked freely and with power. . . . [When] Melville has action to describe he does it magnificently, with great force, and his somewhat formal manner of writing curiously enhances the thrilling effect. The early chapters, when the scene is laid in New Bedford, are intensely real and at the same time enchantingly romantic. They beautifully prepare the mind for what is to come after. But of course it is the sinister and gigantic figure of Captain Ahab that pervades the book and gives it its emotional quality. I can think of no creature of fiction that approaches his stature. You must go to the Greek dramatists for anything like that sense of doom with which everything that you are told about him fills you, and to Shakespeare to find beings of such terrible power. It is because Herman Melville created him that, notwithstanding all the reservations one may make, *Moby Dick* is a great, a very great book. (p. 232)

W. Somerset Maugham, "Herman Melville and 'Moby Dick'," in his Great Novelists and Their Novels: Essays on the Ten Greatest Novels of the World, and the Men and Women Who Wrote Them *(copyright, 1948, by W. Somerset Maugham; copyright renewed © 1976 by Alan Frank Searle), The John C. Winston Company, 1948, pp. 211-32.*

ALEXANDER COWIE (essay date 1948)

Melville's achievement, if viewed impartially, must be accounted enormous. . . . [Precisely where] the true estimate of Melville lies no one can say. But it is sure that after the last critic has barked and the last devotee has lit his candle, Melville's greatness as a writer will endure solidly in the candid record of time. He was a writer rare in gifts and unpredictable in performance. Even his most fervid admirers would not call him "the faultless artist." He could be discursive, quixotic, bombastic, even incoherent. . . . And Melville realized his fallibility. He may have been conscious of his great powers, but he did not look for perfection. He took himself as he was ("It is too late to make any improvements now," says Ishmael) and tried to give true expression to his inmost self. On the whole he succeeded in his aim: as much as any writer, perhaps, he wrote the books he wanted to write. The various phases of his temperament and experience found expression in his books. He would not seek a popular leverage and sustain it for profit against the instincts of his nature. . . . He had in mind a work of greater dimensions. And there was a time when he gathered up all the diverse elements of Herman Melville and housed them permanently—in *Moby-Dick*. Here, for once at least, was harmony of all the parts. Here all Melville's styles—the playful, the ironical, the saturnine, the forthright, the tragic, the Promethean—were fused together and worked with each other to support the colossal epic of Melville's imagining. The unity of *Moby-Dick* is readily perceptible to one who reads it entire, and yet the book has been widely used in detached quotation. Preceded by a collection of passages on whaling *Moby-Dick* has itself become an anthology of great prose. Removed from its context each passage loses a little of beauty and power, but each contains enough of the essence of Melville to suggest the great whole of which it is a part. So with the valedictory to the dying whale:

> It was far down the afternoon; and when all the spearings of the crimson fight were done: and floating in the lovely sunset sea and sky, sun and whale both stilly died together; then, such a sweetness and such plaintiveness, such inwreathing orisons curled up in that rosy air, that it almost seemed as if far over from the deep green convent valleys of the Manilla isles, the Spanish land-breeze, wantonly turned sailor, had gone to sea, freighted with these vesper hymns.

> Soothed again, but only soothed to deeper gloom, Ahab, who had sterned off from the whale, sat intently watching his final wanings from the now tranquil boat. For that strange spectacle observable in all sperm whales dying—the turning sunward of the head, and so expiring—that strange spectacle, beheld of such a placid evening, somehow to Ahab conveyed a wondrousness unknown before.

> "He turns and turns him to it,—how slowly, but how steadfastly, his homage-rendering and invoking brow, with his last dying motions. He too worships fire; most faithful, broad, baronial vassal of the sun!—Oh that these too-favouring eyes should see these too-favouring sights. Look! here, far water-locked; beyond all hum of human weal or woe; in these most candid and impartial seas; where to traditions no rocks fur-

nish tablets; where for long Chinese ages the billows have still rolled on speechless and unspoken to, as stars that shine upon the Niger's unknown source; here, too, life dies sunward full of faith. . . .

This is, perhaps, great writing, but what makes it so is scarcely capable of analysis. Certainly Melville would not be the man to explain. His instincts were against textual criticism or commentary. Great texts were to be reverenced and used, not analyzed. He hoped for no additions to the text of Shakespeare, he once exclaimed, ''lest the commentators arise, and settling upon his sacred text, like unto locusts, devour it clean up, leaving never a dot over an I.'' As for his own text, it invites analysis for biographical and historical purposes, but the real secret of its power and magic must remain, like the sea, forever inscrutable. (pp. 409-11)

> *Alexander Cowie, ''Herman Melville,'' in his* The Rise of the American Novel *(copyright 1948, 1951, by American Book Company; reprinted by permission of D. C. Heath and Company), American Book, 1948 (and reprinted by American Book, 1951), pp. 363-411.*

RICHARD CHASE   (essay date 1949)

[It] is misleading to assume that after 1852 Melville was plunged into impotent despair, blind cynicism, and ''morbidity.'' It has too often and too easily been assumed that since Melville himself was poor, unhappy, and unhealthy after 1852, and especially during the 1853-1856 period, everything he wrote was injured by excessive introspection and pessimism. On the contrary, a look at such writings as *The Lightning-Rod Man, The Tartarus of Maids, Bartleby the Scrivener, Benito Cereno, The Fiddler, Jimmy Rose, I and My Chimney, Israel Potter, The Confidence Man,* and *The Encantadas* gives us the impression of a man carefully probing new areas of experience and seeking out new styles. Most of the short stories have faults of taste and conception, but *Benito Cereno* is surely one of the best of short stories, *Israel Potter* is a superior light novel, and *The Confidence Man* is a striking achievement of the moral intelligence, and a work, furthermore, which conditions our final idea of Melville more deeply than any single book except *Moby-Dick.* (pp. 142-43)

Bartleby is a starkly simple tale told with great economy of metaphor and symbol, for Melville is preeminently interested in simplicity—a kind of simplicity at once nakedly tragic and wistfully comic. The story is relieved of the clashing commotion and weight of *Moby-Dick* and *Pierre* largely because the central figure has no will. *Moby-Dick* and *Pierre* take their inner dynamism from compulsively violent assertions of will, building up slowly to an apocalyptic crescendo; *Bartleby* proceeds in reverse, toward a gradually encroaching silence. (p. 144)

On the aesthetic principles of unity, coherence, and style, *Benito Cereno* is one of the best single pieces Melville wrote. The mood of the story is fully achieved and maintained to perfection. Melville's characteristic contrasts of light and dark are resolved into a gray monotone occasionally illumined by flashes of fire. . . . Heroic actions, such as those in *Moby-Dick,* are absent; in *Benito Cereno* all is muted and somnambulant. (pp. 150-51)

The central figure remains in a twilit stage of consciousness. Benito Cereno is ''withdrawn.'' His spiritless passivity is stirred into action only in the form of sudden vague attempts at communicating with Captain Delano, attempts which are not always distinguishable from nervous starts and twitches. (p. 151)

The mood of withdrawal . . . is a literary style in which Melville wrote some of his best prose. It is perhaps a peculiarly American style. In Melville, it is a twofold mood, varying from the infinitely moving lyricism of certain passages in *Moby-Dick* and *Benito Cereno* to a kind of closely knit textural style reproducing the complexity of subdued psychic experience. The lyrical mood carries us away from living experience toward the condition of sleep or death; the textural mood carries us back toward the sense of life. (p. 152)

Those who think Melville's sensibility is merely imprecise and his language mere vague rhetoric will do well to ponder how wonderfully poised is the universe evoked by [*Benito Cereno*]. It is a universe poised upon a present that continually merges with the opulent debris of a dying past and reaches into a vacant and terrifying future. It is a universe in which consciousness is poised between the rich texture of concrete fact existing in time [and a void]. . . . It is a phantasmal world wonderfully conditioned by circumstance and yet trembling with the possibility of entirely unmotivated and irresponsible events, which may happen, as the cats-paw comes, ''unheralded, unfollowed''—a world poised between necessity and chance, between reason and madness. . . . And it is a universe poised between speech and silence, communication and isolation, a universe almost intolerably rich in associable human experience but a universe, nevertheless, in which men must try to communicate with each other with half-formed, half-intended gestures—a universe in which consciousness is completely involved and yet completely alienated. To present a universe thus delicately at rest within the tensions of its own disequilibrium is an *intellectual* feat which disarms all talk of Melville's being merely a ''natural'' genius. (p. 156)

Like *Bartleby,* which presents the parallel relationship of Bartleby and his employer, *Benito Cereno* shows the limited grasp on life of the successful American gentleman. . . . Captain Delano is that familiar fictional American—the man of energy and good will bewildered by the European scene. For though Captain Delano eventually comes through to an equivocal happy ending, he is nearly lost in the miasma of ancient sin, chaos, and decay, an enigmatic world of ruined summer-houses in desolate gardens, of deserted chateaux and rotting balustrades—a savage forest of equivocations, treacheries, and uncommunicated talk among doomed men. The suffering of Don Benito, a son of the old culture, has given him spiritual light, but the ordeal has been fatal. Captain Delano, unacquainted with the further ranges of human experience, lives on. But plainly Melville is guessing that the accomplishment of the New World will be abortive if the American remains ignorant of the Old World's spiritual depths. . . . The American, in so far as he is like Captain Delano, remains spiritually unfulfilled because he cannot decisively ''withdraw.'' (pp. 158-59)

The Paradise of Bachelors and the Tartarus of Maids is remarkable for its sexual symbolism. (p. 159)

[The] second section of the story is one of the most uncompromising allegorizations of biological processes on record. Occasionally, it is *too* uncompromising, for Melville does not always find symbols which adequately transmute the brute facts into viable material, so that some of the symbols are monstrous, that is, half symbol, half fact. This is, of course, reprehensible in any work of art, though the half-symbols in this story have at least the psychological validity that they are like the half-symbols of dreams. (pp. 159-60)

The remarkable story called *Cock-a-Doodle-Doo* deals with the artist's need for the sense of power and the guilt-feelings which accompany it. (p. 163)

This story presents us with two pictures of Melville: the dejected and sickly man with certain neurasthenic symptoms who becomes joyful and strong after listening to the cock; and, on the other hand, Merrymusk, who is also buoyed up by the spiritual joy of the cock's song but over whom the cock gains a frightening ascendancy which somehow brings about his death. . . . The idea of madness is indicated by certain obsessive ideas (train wrecks, trains crawling over each other, the earth looking like raw flesh), but more importantly by the single obsessive, slowly intensifying cry of the cock, which (the narrator discovers by inquiry) no one can hear except the central figures of the story. The effect of the song of the cock, as it rises to its finally intolerable intensity, is ambivalent. The golden-voiced cock, a hieratic symbol of sheer power subdued to a majestic form, sings with the very rhythm of universal life. Since power subdued to form is a rudimentary definition of art, it is perfectly natural that the cock should fill the narrator of the story with joy—a joy which is not simply "happiness," but a displacement of vision which changes the narrator's whole perception of life. That is the ambivalent voice at its lower intensity. At its higher intensity the voice is a pure unconditioned affirmation of force, changing as the pitch rises into a hymn of destruction which the Merrymusks listen to with rapt acquiescence while it slowly kills them. (pp. 165-66)

[The] upshot of the story is an acceptance of "gladness" at the lower level of ecstasy: the narrator will sing "COCK-A-DOODLE-DOO!" This new resolution and new independence we cannot suppose a poor compromise or a superficiality in a writer who has faced so terrible a collaboration as that between the cock and Merrymusk. The artist who has had this vision is justified in indicating, through the death of Merrymusk, that the Merrymusk aspect of his personality does not point the direction which that personality will take; that, in fact, the creative artist's personality will be continually reborn out of the continual dying away of Merrymusk. (pp. 166-67)

Israel Potter is a distinctly American book. The rapidly shifting scenes and the often inconsequential adventurousness, commented upon by a humorous or oracular muse, remind one of Melville's earliest novels. But *Israel Potter* is, perhaps, more beguiling than most of these. There are somber depths in the book, but they are less oppressive than in *Typee*. The self-conscious erudition, the rather heavy heartiness, the sometimes awkward language, the slightly oafish philosophizing of *Omoo* and *Mardi* Melville has pretty much purged by the time he arrives at *Israel Potter*. His style has become more mature, lighter, more sunny and open. It has achieved the nimbleness and efficiency which will animate *The Confidence Man,* though in that book it will gain a toughness and satirical edge unknown to *Israel Potter*. (p. 176)

The interest of *Israel Potter* is threefold: for the lively story itself, for its embodiment of certain of Melville's lifelong themes, and for the portraits of three American figures who are half historical and half legendary: Franklin, John Paul Jones, and Ethan Allen. As Melville re-creates him during the time of his embassy to the French, Franklin is a strange combination of the Magian and the practical man, with rather more of the Magian, in the sense of wizard or medicine man, in him than one might expect. Melville's attitude is humorously hostile. He makes his Franklin stand halfway between such fabulous

zanies as Babbalanja in *Mardi* and that marvelous figure he was yet to create, the confidence man. (p. 178)

There is another American type who has a sterner and more heroic poetry than Potter. John Paul Jones, "a rather small, elastic, swarthy man," flashes upon the scene with the barbarous civility of "a disinherited Indian Chief in European clothes." (p. 180)

As Melville pictures him, there is much of the Promethean spirit in John Paul Jones. But Jones is, in Melville's final estimation, more an Ahab than a Bulkington. . . . This was precisely Melville's deepest fear about the American character: that it would turn out to be inorganic, unstable, possessed by an enormous impatience which would lead it to plunge violently into undertakings for which it was unprepared. (p. 182)

In Melville's portrait of Ethan Allen we have the American character stabilized, principled, and organic. Yet, as with Bulkington and Melville's other Handsome Sailor, we are not sure what, beyond a wonderful promise, the character of Ethan Allen is—whether it is a miracle out of time and context or whether, after all, it implies a stabilized, principled, and organic American society which we think cannot exist only because we do not yet understand our own culture well enough. This is the tantalizing question the character of Melville's Ethan Allen leaves us with. It is, at any rate, a wonderful enough character so far as we see it. . . . Courteous, haughty, his whole mien bespeaking his experience and mastery of every dark and every exalted emotion, alternately pacific and ferocious, the flower of man's spiritual agony in the New World, Allen is the "true American." (pp. 182-83)

One reason for the general underestimation of *The Confidence Man* is the failure to see that, like *Israel Potter*, it is a book of folklore, that it examines the American character as it manifests itself in folk ideals. The confidence man is one of the most extraordinary figures in American literature. Melville was aiming very high when he created this character, and it has not yet been seen, I believe, how well he succeeded. If he succeeded, he did so because by the time of *The Confidence Man* . . . his satiric vision of American life had attained its full clarity and he was ready to make his one definite adverse statement. Earlier, in *Moby-Dick,* he had achieved the fullness of his lyric-epic comprehension of the American spirit. But his work would have been less complete without what one is tempted to call his second-best book, in which he was able to display a ripe satirical intelligence in a style unique among his writings for its leanness, nimbleness, and jaunty vigor. (p. 185)

The book is carefully planned. It has the unity of any episodic work, the unity of the pervading themes. It has the dramatic unity of a dialectical movement of ideas. It is unified by the character of the confidence man, which, though it is a portmanteau character and tends to merge and then separate itself from other characters in the book, can be meaningfully summed up. . . .

The Confidence Man is a supreme achievement. More than any of his other writings it establishes Melville's claim to moral intelligence; it is an intellectual act of the greatest force and authority. (p. 206)

Richard Chase, in his Herman Melville: A Critical Study *(reprinted by permission of Macmillan Publishing Co., Inc.; copyright 1949 by Richard Chase; renewed 1977 by Frances W. Chase), Macmillan, 1949, 305 p.*

NATHALIA WRIGHT (essay date 1949)

In all that Melville wrote he was no nearer saying what he had to say at the end than he was at the beginning. His effect, like Shakespeare's, is one of extension rather than of volume. One receives the impression of spaces and distances, of approaches and retreats, of vistas opened but not entered upon. One is always traveling but never arrives. (p. 173)

Above all, one is made to feel that what has been left unsaid is unspeakably vaster than what has been said. The super-abundance of material appals him, and he is driven at last to think of all truth as voiceless and of the question as more final than any answer. "God keep me from ever completing anything," cries Ishmael. "This whole book is a draught—nay, but the draught of a draught."

Had Melville's inspiration been any less inclusive or had his achievement been any more definitive, the irregularities of his thought and his style would be intolerable. As it is, these irregularities are nothing else than the "careful disorderliness" which he declared to be for some enterprises the true method. Not definition is its aim, but suggestion; not keen analysis but bold juxtaposition, contrasts and paradoxes, catalogues and citations, reflections, reminiscences, and reverberations. (pp. 173-74)

To this desire to extend the scope of his work, to this fear of appearing final, all Melville's rhetorical devices and all his voluminous sources are subservient. So indiscriminately are they introduced and associated that they tend at last to lose their separate identities. They are but fragments of a boundless creation, undistinguished otherwise in the hands of its creator. Of them all, however, no single one so far extends the bounds of what Melville wrote as the Bible. However he alluded to it he was assured of a contrast with his immediate material: between the common and the great, the present and the past, the natural and the supernatural. And though each is a contrast achieved by many other means as well, only this one enabled him to make them all simultaneously, at once magnifying his characters and their affairs, establishing for the briefest moment a background of antiquity, and suggesting the presence of yet another, unseen world beyond the vast scene which meets the eye.

Originally and essentially, of course, all Melville's material is simple and commonplace, becoming transformed through a marvelous imagination. Viewed strictly in the light of fact his characters are of limited powers and lowly station. Yet as their lives unfold in passion and in problem, they seem to be super-men, inhabiting a world one degree larger than life. The effect is deliberate, and it is deliberately more than the general exaggeration of his pen. (pp. 174-75)

This effect of magnitude in Melville's characters is achieved largely by figurative language, since his imagery contains references to so many great personages of history and literature. Side by side with the nameless crews of his ships walk Henry VIII, Charlemagne, Xerxes, Apis, Ammon, Jove, Perseus, Prometheus, Mohammed, Faust, Hamlet, Beelzebub, Abraham. With many of them Melville briefly compared his own characters. . . . The Bible, in fact, provides genealogies to ennoble the meanest of men, for all, it asserts in various accounts, are descendants of the Jehovah-created Adam, of the sons of God who intermarried with the daughters of men, of the patriarch Noah, and spiritually of the New Testament Father. Melville cited them all.

More important than this casual imagery, though, is the deeper relationship which is made to exist between some of these personages and Melville's characters, whereby the patterns of their lives are both clarified and given significance. Some of them are named for the great, and thus the parallel moves with them. (pp. 175-76)

Appropriately are they called. For these same characters . . . wrestle with problems which have preoccupied heroes, sages, prophets, and gods. (p. 176)

The speech of these people, too, is appropriate, containing some of the most magnificent of stylistic echoes from the seventeenth century, the Elizabethans, the Anglo-Saxons, the authors of the Bible. . . . [All] add eloquence to pretentiousness. Like the Teutonic war song of Yoomy and the Shakespearean ranting of Pierre, these words, whether spoken by or about Melville's characters, make each of them seem less and less like a single individual, more and more like Everyman.

It is in just this conception of character, in fact, that the intricate connections between Melville's religious thought, his use of the Bible, and the entire Romantic school to which he belonged are most clearly revealed. Quite likely its belief in the dignity and the possibility of the individual more than all else commended Christianity to him. For this he held to be the great value, the field on which all conflicts were fought, the divinity shaping every end. Man, by the very fact of his being, could be neither common nor insignificant, and often the darkest of skin and the most primitive of mind held closest communion with the heart of the universe.

But it was significantly the Calvinistic and the Lockean elements of this Christian individualism to which he subscribed, not the apostolic or the medieval. It was, in fact, a sublime egotism, at least as much Satanic as theistic, and to no small degree political. Hence all Melville's characters have something in common with the Renaissance and with the Byronic hero. And hence all those in the Bible on whom he depended most to magnify his own were carefully chosen: the ambitious Ahab rather than the repentant David, the rebellious Jonah and the lonely Jeremiah rather than the priestly Isaiah, the aspiring but not the obedient Jesus. For all this is more than magnitude; this is the assault upon the bastions of heaven.

Nor do these characters come alone to Melville's pages. The ancient past to which most of them belong, and which inevitably accompanies them, towers up everywhere, a presence of which he was constantly aware. And again, since none of the scenes of his narratives is older than the eighteenth century, it is largely a figurative method he adopted. (pp. 177-78)

[In] the last analysis Melville considered all recorded history but a fraction of the past, and the cultivated intellect only a part of consciousness. The unexplored regions of the individual and of the racial mind, reaching back into prehistoric mists, beckoned him. Hence he was constantly adding an extra dimension to his scene by suggesting the existence of an invisible world. (p. 182)

In all that he wrote, in fact, the line between the seen and the unseen is almost indistinguishable. So vast is the universe he depicted that its outermost reaches are well nigh beyond perception: the stars which are to Taji worlds on worlds, the mysterious submarine life at which the men of the *Pequod* peer as they sail through the great armada of whales. Reality merges imperceptibly into unreality. Rather significantly, *Typee* and *Omoo* were followed by *Mardi,* which begins like them as a realistic tale of the sea. But once launched in their boats from the *Arcturion,* Jarl and Taji sail gradually but completely out of the natural world into the "world of mind," on which the wanderer gazes, it is added, with more wonder than Balboa in the Aztec glades.

No less casually and utterly do Ahab, Pierre, and Billy Budd move farther and farther from all that is objective until at last the outward circumstances of their lives mean nothing and the inner significance is everything. Vast as the universe is about them, that within themselves is yet vaster and more mysterious. (pp. 182-83)

Dreams and portents, hypersensitive natures, and miraculous events—these outline Melville's invisible world. (p. 183)

[In] his belief in the existence of [a] world beyond the world of sense Melville has often been called, and even called himself, Platonic. Like the Platonists, he did believe truth resided in the unseen world of ideas and conceptions rather than in the world of material manifestations. But in his essentially romantic conception of this invisible sphere he was closer to the Hebrews than to the Greeks. Order, rhetoric, and logic did not represent the primal truth to him as did elemental and undisciplined energy. (p. 184)

[Strangeness and terror are the chief characteristics] of the unseen to Melville. "Though in many of its aspects this visible world seems formed in love," asserts Ishmael, "the invisible spheres were formed in fright." Of the invisible terrors the sea, with the mysterious creatures that pass through it, is the symbol, while the earth is the symbol of the known world. . . .

As the sea and the land thus alternate as symbols in his scenes, so the calm and the storm alternate on Melville's sea. For though calmness is sweet and agreeable, the motionless ship is destined to decay. In the rack of the storm it leaps forward, drawing fire from heaven, approaching its goal according as it courts disaster. At the heart of the storm, in the midst of the Great Mutiny, Melville's seekers of truth find and worship it. (p. 185)

Nothing less than a spirit touching good and evil was adequate to preside over the universe [Melville] envisaged. Even in his earliest voyages he found that the green valley of the Typee was, like the Garden of Eden, but a small plot of the earth. And to the end, side by side in the Maldive sea, swam the pilot fish and the white shark, as long before the white whale swam ahead of Ahab while the beckoning breezes blew softly from the green shore. The law which could hang a criminal could also hang the purest of the pure, and that without shattering the universe, but only dyeing its vast sky a deeper rose. (p. 187)

It is significant that Melville's persistent image for truth . . . is of something hidden. Ultimate reality exists at the core of this complex universe, at the very heart of its vast reaches, indeed well-nigh impossible to attain for the superficies which surround it. . . . Speaking of his own twenty-fifth birthday, Melville wrote to Hawthorne: "Three weeks have scarcely passed, at any time between then and now, that I have not unfolded within myself. But I feel that I am now come to the inmost leaf of the bulb, and that shortly the flower must fall to the mould" [see excerpt above].

So all Melville's art and all the vast scene it reared are not ends in themselves but means to an end. All his borrowings and all his conjurings are but approximations. They are circumferences of the center, cerements around the mummy, an-

techambers to the throne room, husks about the kernel. Not truth itself is his culminating vision, but "cunning glimpses," "occasional flashings-forth," "short, quick probings at the very axis of reality"; symbolic and fragmentary manifestations of the one absolute, which is in the last analysis inviolable. (pp. 187-88)

> *Nathalia Wright, in her* Melville's Use of the Bible *(reprinted by permission of the author; copyright 1949 by Duke University Press, Durham, North Carolina; copyright renewed © 1976 by Nathalia Wright), Duke University Press, 1949 (and reprinted by Octagon Books, 1969, 209 p.).*

W. H. AUDEN (essay date 1950)

To understand the romantic conception of the relation between objective and subjective experience, *Moby Dick* is perhaps the best work to study. . . .

If we omit the White Whale itself, the whole book is an elaborate synecdoche, i.e., it takes a particular way of life, that of whale-fishing, which men actually lead to earn their livelihood and of which Melville had first-hand experience and makes it a case of any man's life in general. (p. 58)

For example:

(1) Whalemen kill for their living. So in one way or another must we all.

(2) The proprietors of the *Pequod* are Quakers, i.e., they profess the purest doctrine of non-violence, yet see no incongruity in this; . . . . So always in every life, except that of the saint or the villain, there is a vast difference between what a man professes and how he acts.

(3) The crew are involved in each other's actions and characters. So every world is a world of social relations.

(4) In their attitude towards their job of killing whales, they reveal their different characters. Thus Starbuck is a professional who takes no risks unless he has to and will have no man in his boat who is not afraid of the whale. Stubb is a reckless gambler who enjoys risks. Flask follows the fish just for the fun of it.

In so far as the book is this, any other form of activity or society which Melville happened to know well would have served his purpose. (p. 59)

[In] his treatment of the White Whale, Melville uses symbols in the real sense.

A symbol is felt to be such before any possible meaning is consciously recognized; i.e., an object or event which is felt to be more important than the reason can immediately explain is symbolic. Secondly, a symbolic correspondence is never one to one but always multiple, and different persons perceive different meanings. Thus to Ahab 'All visible objects, man, are but pasteboard masks. To me the white whale is that wall shoved near to me. Sometimes I think there's naught beyond. I see in him outrageous strength with an insatiable malice sinewing it. That inscrutable thing is chiefly what I hate.' . . .

To Melville-Ishmael it is neither evil nor good but simply numinous, a declaration of the power and majesty of God which transcends any human standards of ethics. To Starbuck it signifies death or his fatal relation to his captain, the duty which tells him he cannot depart his office to obey, intending open war, yet to have a touch of pity. (p. 61)

Ishmael cannot properly be called a member of the crew; for, from the moment that he steps on board, he only speaks or is spoken to once more when after his first ducking (baptism) he makes his will, i.e., consciously accepts the absolute finality of his commitment. From then on, he becomes simply the recording consciousness, the senses and the mind through which we experience everything.

This suggests that if we are identified with him then, we should also identify ourselves with him during the prologue when he does have a certain personal existence. (p. 98)

Ishmael is a white man and a Presbyterian: Queequeg is a South-Sea Islander and a Pagan, formerly a cannibal. The Christian world is the world of consciousness, i.e., the ethically superior world which knows the truth, both the artistic and scientific truths and the moral truth that one should love one's neighbour as oneself.

The pagan world is the unconscious world, which does not know the truth. The cannibalism it practises is a symbol of self-love, of treating one's neighbour as existing solely for one's own advantage. Queequeg left his island in order to become conscious of the truth, only to discover that those who are conscious of it do not obey it, and so has decided to live as a pagan in the Christian world.

Ishmael, like us, has two preconceived notions:

(1) That men who are not white are ugly, i.e., in a physical sense, aesthetically inferior. (pp. 99-100)

(2) That pagans cannot obey the Christian commandment to love one's neighbour as oneself, because they have never heard the Word of the true God, i.e., they are ethically inferior.

Ishmael is disabused of both notions. He admits that Queequeg is beautiful, and that he loves his neighbour, in fact, more than most Christians. . . . He is a doer of the Word who has never heard the Word.

By accepting Queequeg—the symbolic act of acceptance is his joining in the worship of Queequeg's idol—Ishmael proves himself worthy of the voyage. (p. 100)

The voyage of the *Pequod* is one voyage for Ishmael and with him us, and another for the rest of the crew.

For us the voyage signifies the exploration of the self and the world, of potential essences. . . .

For the rest of the crew, however, it is not the voyage of self-inspection before the act, but the act of historical existence itself. They learn nothing about themselves, but they are changed before our eyes, and reveal themselves unwittingly in what they say and do. (p. 103)

Queequeg, Tashtego and Dagoo form a trio related to and contrasted with the white trio Starbuck, Stubb, and Flask, i.e., the three untormented by the problems of consciousness and the three who in different ways fail to live up to the challenge of consciousness.

Queequeg and Fedallah are opposites in their relation to Christianity. I.e., Queequeg is the unconscious Christian, Fedallah is the unconscious anti-Christian, the tempter of Ahab. In the Biblical story of Ahab, the Lord sends a lying spirit to entice him to his death. Such is Fedallah, who is Ahab's shadow and makes the *Macbeth*-like prophecies which finally persuade Ahab that he will succeed in killing the White Whale and survive. Fedallah alone, though he has not suffered Ahab's catastrophe,

intuitively shares Ahab's attitude. Like Ahab he is a fire-worshipper. (p. 105)

[That Ahab's loss of a leg to Moby Dick] is a castration symbol is emphasized by the story of how shortly before the present voyage he was found insensible in the street 'by some unknown, and seemingly inexplicable, unimaginable casualty, his ivory limb having been so violently displaced that it had stakewise smitten, and all but pierced his groin.' It is possible to attach too much importance to this as also to the sexual symbolism of the Whale as being at once the *vagina dentata* and the Beast with two backs or the parents-in-bed. The point is that the sexual symbolism is in its turn symbolic of the aesthetic, i.e., the Oedipus fantasy is a representation in aesthetic terms of the fantasy of being a self-originating god, i.e., of the ego (Father) begetting itself on the self (Mother), and castration is the ultimate symbol of aesthetic weakness, of not being an aesthetic hero.

Ahab, then, the exceptional hero, suffers a tragic fall in the Greek sense, he is reduced to being lower than the average. In a Greek story this would be a punishment by the gods for hubris, and would come at the end of the book. Here, however, it comes before the book starts, so we must take it differently. How should Ahab react? Repent of his past pride? Perhaps, but the important thing is the future. What is the catastrophe telling him to become? . . . (pp. 115-16)

He neither says, 'I am justly punished' if he has been guilty nor 'Though He slay me yet will I trust in Him' but 'Thou art guilty and shalt be punished'. His nature or self certainly does not wish to go rushing off in his aged maimed state round the world chasing a whale. It wants, as he himself admits, peace, family and, above all, happiness. It is as if, knowing that this is also what God wills him to become, he, his ego, defiantly wills to be always at every moment miserable. His extra wounding of himself, mentioned above, may well have been, at least unconsciously, not an accident, but a goading of himself to remember his vow. (p. 116)

[Ahab's whole life] is one of taking up defiantly a cross he is not required to take up. Consequently, the normal reactions to pleasure and pain are reversed for him. Painful situations like the typhoon he welcomes, pleasant and happy ones like the calm day he regards as temptations. This is a counterfeit version of the saints' acceptance of suffering and distrust of pleasure. The aesthetic hero reacts normally, in that it is pleasure that tempts him to do wrong, and if he is doing wrong, suffering will dissuade him. . . . The Religious Hero, however, is related in exactly the opposite way, and if his god be his own defiant will, it is pain that tempts him further, and pleasure that could save him.

In the same way Queequeg is a saint, but he is not the Christ incarnate, the second Adam, for, though he goes down with the rest of the crew, he does not suffer uniquely as an individual. For Melville's treatment of the Religious Hero and the Devil or the negative Religious Hero in their absolute form, we must now turn to his last work, ***Billy Budd***.

If, when we finish reading ***Billy Budd***, we are left with questions which we feel have been raised but not answered, if so to speak the equation has not come out to a finite number, as in a work of art it should, this is not due to any lack of talent on Melville's part, but to the insolubility of the religious paradox in aesthetic terms. (pp. 118-19)

The Passion of Billy Budd is convincing, but fails in [certain respects] . . . , and the ways in which [Melville] fails are interesting for the light they throw on the romantic conception of life. Like many other romantics Melville seems to hold:

(1) That innocence and sinlessness are identical, or rather perhaps that only the innocent, i.e., those who have never known the law, can be sinless. Once a man becomes conscious, he becomes a sinner. As long as he is not conscious of guilt, what he does is not sin. . . . Thus when Billy Budd first appears he is the Prelapsarian Adam. . . . (p. 120)

(2) That the unconscious and innocent are marked by great physical beauty, and therefore that the beautiful are sinless. This is true for Billy Budd as it was for Bulkington and Queequeg.

If the story were to be simply the story of the Fall, i.e., the story of how the Devil (Claggart) tempted Adam (Budd) into the knowledge of good and evil, this would not matter, but Melville wants Budd also to be the Second Adam, the sinless victim who suffers voluntarily for the sins of the whole world. But in order to be that he must know what sin is, or else his suffering is not redemptive, but only one more sin on our part. Further, as long as Billy Budd is only the Prelapsarian Adam, our nostalgic image of what we would still be if we had not fallen, his beauty is a perfectly adequate symbol but the moment he becomes the Second Adam, the saving example whom we all should follow, this beauty becomes an illegitimate aesthetic advantage. The flaw of the stammer will not quite do, for this is only an aesthetic weakness, not a deliberate abandonment of advantages. It succeeds in making Billy Budd the innocent who 'as a sheep before the shearer is dumb so openeth he not his mouth', but it makes his dumbness against his will not with it. We can never look like that, any more than, once we have become conscious, we can go back to unconsciousness, so how can we imitate his example? He becomes an aesthetic hero to admire from a distance. Melville seems to have been aware that something must happen to Billy to change him from the unconscious Adam into the conscious Christ but, in terms of his fable, he cannot make this explicit and the decisive transition has to take place off-stage in the final interview between Billy and Captain Vere. (pp. 120-21)

Just as the bias in Melville's treatment of Billy Budd is a tendency to identify consciousness and sin, so he makes Claggart identify innocence with love; 'To be nothing more than innocent', he sneers on seeing Billy Budd. This is no doubt what the serpent says to Adam, but is not what he says to himself, which is rather 'To be nothing more than loving'. (p. 122)

In *Billy Budd,* the opposition is not strength/weakness, but innocence/guilt-consciousness, i.e., Claggart wishes to annihilate the difference either by becoming innocent himself or by acquiring an accomplice in guilt. If this is expressed sexually, the magic act must necessarily be homosexual, for the wish is for identity in innocence or in guilt, and identity demands the same sex.

Claggart, as the Devil, cannot, of course, admit a sexual desire, for that would be an admission of loneliness which pride cannot admit. Either he must corrupt innocence through an underling or if that is not possible he must annihilate it, which he does. (pp. 122-23)

> *W. H. Auden, in his* The Enchafèd Flood: Or the Romantic Iconography of the Sea *(copyright 1950 by The Rectors and Visitors of the University of Virginia; reprinted by permission of Random House,* Inc.), Random House, 1950 (and reprinted by Faber and Faber, 1951, 126 p.).*

NEWTON ARVIN   (essay date 1950)

[It] is idle to look for great depths or difficulties in [*Typee* and *Omoo*]; to do so would be to miss their special quality of spontaneity and youthfulness. Yet there are intimations of complexity in them, and in a purely literary sense, easy though they seem, they are curiously many-faceted. (p. 79)

Already in these early, experimental books, with varying degrees of success, Melville knows how to cover a gamut of painterly and emotional effects that ranges all the way from the broad and serene to the wild, the grim, and even the grotesque. And indeed it is evident that these contrasts of tone and feeling, especially marked in *Typee,* are conscious and artful, not merely inadvertent, and that they express a native feeling for structure and style that already suggests how much farther Melville may go as an imaginative writer than any of the narrators he is emulating. *Two Years Before the Mast* is a greater book than either *Typee* or *Omoo,* in its strong, sustained austerity of style as well as in its grandeur of feeling; but Melville's books are the unmistakable products of a far more complex and ductile mind than Dana's, and potentially, of course, of a richer creative power. Dana's great book suggests no artistic mode beyond itself; *Typee* and *Omoo* hint constantly at the freer and more plastic form of fiction. (p. 83)

[Compared] with the billows of almost demoniac humor on which *Moby Dick* is so incredibly sustained, the humor of *Typee* and even of *Omoo* seems gentle and rather tame. Yet one feels at once that it is the expression of a genuinely humorous fancy. . . . One feels this youthful humor chiefly . . . in the individual characters in whom both books abound, and who are treated with a freedom far closer to fiction than to mere reminiscence. . . . [In] the period when he was writing *Typee* and *Omoo,* it was mostly the amusing, even lovable oddities and humors of human character that engaged him, not its darknesses and depravities. (pp. 85-6)

His instincts had guided him rightly when they sent him wandering into the young Pacific world, and they guided him rightly when they drove him away from it again and back to civilized society, to resume a burden he had temporarily laid down—the burden of consciousness, of the full and anguished consciousness of modern man. (p. 88)

Month by month, one imagines, as he was writing *Typee* and surely *Omoo,* the need was growing on him to descend deeper and deeper into [the] obscure and questionable regions of the mind, and to move on, as a writer, from the manner of an American Gautier or Kinglake to a larger, bolder, more complex, and more symbolic manner that would be capable of rendering the richness and the fullness of his maturing thought. (p. 89)

What he did, as a result, when he came to write *Mardi,* was to grope his way forward toward a new manner by writing alternately in several manners, no one of them quite the right one. (p. 90)

[The] most remarkable thing about the book is Melville's attempt to endue it with the enchantment of the exotic and also with the grandeur of the legendary and mythical by using, throughout, the imagery of Polynesian life. It was an effort that deserved to succeed better than it did: Melville, after all, was the first Western writer of genius who had lived in the

South Seas himself, and he was the first of the actual travelers to go beyond mere narrative and to aim at converting his remembered impressions into serious, ambitious, and poetic fiction. (p. 92)

Beyond all this, however, Melville was feeling his way forward, rather timidly and fumblingly, to a genuinely mythopoeic form by investing his narrative with something of the quality of Polynesian legend and myth. The attempt was on the whole an abortive one, but the important thing is that he made it. . . . [It] must be confessed that, in all this, *Mardi* remains a sketch, a promise, an intimation, and not a consummated achievement. (pp. 93-4)

[Doubtless] it is with a momentary flash of self-criticism that he remarks in *Mardi* itself: "Genius is full of trash." If *Mardi* is a mixture of trash and genuineness, however, it is the sort of mixture of which only genius is capable. The unalloyed metal still remained to be run into the molds. (p. 100)

[What] he did when he went on to write *Redburn* and *White-Jacket* had superficially the air of a return upon himself, a lapse back to the vein he had already worked in *Typee* and *Omoo*, the vein not of metaphysical allegory but of unpretentious reminiscent narrative, vibrating again between the poles of literal autobiography and free fictional improvisation. . . . *Redburn* and *White-Jacket*, though they have lost the youthful charm of the earlier books, are denser in substance, richer in feeling, tauter, more complex, more connotative in texture and imagery. Whatever imperfections they may have, they give us the clear sense that the man who wrote them was again on his own track.

The prose, for one thing, is that of a much more mature person and more expert writer. One easily sees how much ground Melville has gained, partly as a result of writing *Mardi*. . . . (p. 101)

The sense of symbol in *Redburn* is unmistakably more acute than in anything of Melville's that preceded *Mardi,* and moreover there are two or three points in the book at which one sees Melville moving toward an even franker and more direct form of symbolism, one which he himself would doubtless have called "allegorical.". . . (pp. 107-08)

In its richness of emotion and variety of tone, *Redburn* generally is the most likable of Melville's secondary books; and it is only because he was so rebelliously conscious how much higher he was capable of going that Melville could have spoken of it contemptuously as "beggarly *Redburn*."

Taken as a whole, *White-Jacket* . . . is something of a drop in quality after *Redburn*. . . . (pp. 109-10)

Hitherto he had intuitively succeeded in finding pretty much the true balance between narrative and factuality, between the imaginative and the informative, and in *White-Jacket* he continues to alternate the two—but now in what seems a relatively perfunctory and even wearied manner. The current of personal narrative is simply not full enough or strong enough to buoy up and float along the solid and sometimes rather lumpish blocks of straight exposition and description. . . . (pp. 110-11)

The book suffers too, more than the earlier books had done, from the humanitarian note that dominates it as it dominates no other work of Melville's. . . . *White-Jacket* is not a novel, to be sure, but it is not a mere pamphlet either; it is an imaginative work of a very special and precarious sort, and it would

have gained incalculably if Melville had made his protests far less insistent and less explicit, and if he had dramatized them much more. . . . Melville dilutes the force of his protest partly by his repetitions of the shocking image and partly by his detailed comments on the evil. His moral passion, as so often happens, had asserted itself overaggressively at the expense of his inventive and dramatic gift. (pp. 111-12)

[Morally speaking,] *White-Jacket* has a higher *relievo* and a more complex truth than *Redburn*. . . . The stage in *White-Jacket* is occupied by a much more richly representative cast of characters. . . . Melville, as he wrote the book, had at least for the time recovered from the despairing mood of *Mardi* and from the largely resentful mood of *Redburn*. (p. 119)

To speak of the structure and the texture of *Moby Dick* is to embark upon a series of paradoxes that are soberly truthful and precise. . . . [Not] many imaginative works have so strong and strict a unity, and not many are composed of such various and even discordant materials; few great novels have been comparably concrete, factual, and prosaic, and few of course have been so large and comprehensive in their generality, so poetic both in their surface fabric and in their central nature. In form alone *Moby Dick* is unique in its period. . . . (p. 151)

If one must look for analogies that will do a little to express the effect *Moby Dick* has on us in form—and they can do no more than that at the very most—it is not to tragedy that one should turn but to heroic poetry, to the epic. (p. 156)

In sober fact, of course, the book is not a heroic poem but a work of its own age; yet it genuinely helps to define the formal quality of *Moby Dick* if one says that what he feels in its spacious narrative movement is not unlike what he feels in the narrative movement of the *Iliad,* of the *Odyssey,* and even of the more "literary" poems that derive from them, the *Aeneid,* the *Lusiads.* . . . [The] movement forward, as in all such poems, is not from climax to climax in the sharp dramatic sense, but from one wave-crest to another, from one chase or encounter to another, from cruising-ground to cruising-ground, from departure to arrival, from storm to calm. It is in short an undulant, not a peaked and valleyed [narrative] line, and as a result the book has an epiclike pattern that, at least in quality, cannot be mistaken. . . . (p. 157)

Meanwhile the principle of variety is observed and its effect achieved not in pitch only but in pace and key also. For surely what the descriptive and expository chapters on whales and whaling do is partly to slow down the tempo and partly to provide for a change of key. They suggest the passages of deliberate quietness and even dullness in all very large poems, and they are placed and spaced with beautiful compositional tact. . . . (p. 158)

In the strictest sense Melville had no great model for the introduction of these magnificent non-narrative chapters; they sprang from his own creative feeling for composition and chiaroscuro. . . . In its formal wholeness, indeed, as one has to repeat, *Moby Dick* is unprecedented and unique. No great poet has ever, before or since, brought zoology and poetry together in an even comparable way. (pp. 158-59)

Certainly nothing could be more eloquent of the incandescence out of which *Moby Dick* was written than the variety and the idiosyncrasy of the metaphors with which it is animated; nothing, perhaps, except the equally extraordinary resourcefulness and inventiveness of Melville's language. For this there is nothing in his earlier books to prepare us fully, though there are hints of it in the best passages of *Redburn* and *White-Jacket*. In general, however, the diction in those books is the current diction of good prose in Melville's time; it has a hardly definable personal quality. Now, in *Moby Dick,* it takes on abruptly an idiosyncrasy of the most unmistakable sort; it is a question now of Melvillean language in the same intense and special sense in which one speaks of Virgilian language, of Shakespearean, or Miltonic. It is a creation, verbally speaking; a great artifice; a particular characterizing idiom; without it the book would not exist. (p. 162)

The moral meanings of *Moby Dick,* though of course they transcend its oneiric meanings and exist in a sense on another plane, are by no means independent of them: on the contrary, the unity of the book is so masterly that only by artifice can we disentangle its various strands of significance. From the oneiric point of view Ahab is the suffering and neurotic self, lamed by early experience so vitally that it can devote itself only to destructive ends and find rest only in self-annihilation. (p. 175)

Ahab is not only the sick self; he is, for his time and place, the noblest and most complete embodiment of the tragic hero. He is modern man, and particularly American man, in his role as "free" and "independent" Individual, as self-sustaining and self-assertive Ego, of forcible will and unbending purpose all compact, inflexible, unpitying, and fell, but enlarged by both his vices and his strength to dimensions of legendary grandeur. (p. 176)

He has ceased to be anything but an Ego; a noble Ego, to be sure; a heroic one; but *that* rather than a Self. He is no longer a free mind: his thought has become the slave of his insane purpose. He is no longer emotionally free: his heart has become the slave of his consuming hate. Nor is he any longer morally free: his conscience too has allowed itself to be deadened and stupefied by the compulsive quest for Moby Dick. (p. 177)

It is partly his momentary gleams of insight, nevertheless, that preserve Ahab's tragic stature even in his perdition. He has penetrated to one of the fatal truths about himself when he uses the phrase, "against all natural lovings and longings." His ideal man would have "no heart at all," and he himself has striven with terrible success to destroy his own great native capacity for love. (p. 178)

In our identification with Ahab we have undergone the double movement of aggression and submission, of self-assertion and self-surrender, that is the secret of the tragic release, and we are freed by it. (p. 179)

Deep as are the psychological meanings, and serious as are the moral meanings, of *Moby Dick,* they by no means exhaust between them the richness of its interest or the scope of its significance. In the end, as one reflects on the book, one is aware that one must reckon with the most comprehensive of all its qualities, the quality that can only be called mythic. (p. 182)

[Nowhere] is Melville's myth-making power at work in a more truly primordial sense than in the creation of the White Whale himself.

Here chiefly, in the aggrandizement of a huge and fearsome animal to deiform proportions, does Melville surpass all other poets of his century in the rejuvenation of myth. On this ground he is quite incomparable; no other writer of the century can be set beside him. (p. 184)

The White Whale is a grandiose mythic presentation of what is godlike in the cosmos as this could be intuited by a painfully meditative and passionately honest poetic mind in the heart of the American nineteenth century. Moby Dick is an Animal God such as only the imagination of that century in the Western world could have conceived and projected; a god in Nature, not beyond it; an immanent god in some sense, not a transcendent one; an emergent deity, not an Absolute; a deity that embodies the physical vastness of the cosmos in space and time as astronomy and geology have exhibited it; a deity that represents not transcendent purpose and conscious design but *mana;* energy; power—the half-conscious, half-unconscious power of blind, restless, perhaps purposeless, but always overbearing and unconquerable force. (p. 189)

Critically speaking, and from the point of view of poetic value, almost nothing Melville later did is comparable to his one very great book. Much that he later did has so real an interest, and has incited so much commentary, as to blur and becloud the fact that it is work not only on a lower level but on a level that is lower by several wide degrees. (pp. 217-18)

Pierre itself, taken as a whole and considered on strictly literary grounds, is one of the most painfully ill-conditioned books ever to be produced by a first-rate mind. . . . [And yet] it must be said at once that *Pierre*'s badness is an active and positive, not a merely negative one; it is the badness of misdirected and even perverted powers, but not of deficiency or deadness. (p. 219)

[It] is evident that *Pierre* is the work of a man who has acquired a terrible knowledge of human motives, a terrible insight into all the concealed and unapparent regions of human nature, and the association there of the most passionate love with the most murderous hate. If Melville's constructive and expressive power, when he wrote *Pierre,* had been equal to this knowledge, the book would have been the great book it so signally fails to be. Even as it is, Melville's expressive power by no means wholly deserts him. (p. 224)

The experience of writing *Pierre* had demonstrated to Melville himself how utterly uncharacteristic and inexpressive for him that conventional novelistic form was: he never returned to it. . . . [After completing *Pierre,* for] the first time, and if only because it takes less breath, he tries his hand at the short tale. . . . (p. 231)

["**Benito Cereno**" of the *Piazza Tales* is unduly] celebrated, surely. For neither the conception nor the actual composition and texture of "**Benito**" are of anything like the brilliance that has been repeatedly attributed to them. The story is an artistic miscarriage, with moments of undeniable power. (p. 238)

Much praise has been lavished on the art with which an atmosphere of sinister foreboding and malign uncertainty is evoked and maintained through all the earlier parts of the tale. It is hard to see why. There are a few fine touches in the very first paragraphs . . . , but even in these first pages the rhythms of the prose are slow, torpid, and stiff-limbed; and they remain so, with a few moments of relief, throughout. Nor is the famous "atmosphere" of "**Benito**" created swiftly, boldly, and hypnotically, as Melville at his highest pitch might have created it; on the contrary, it is "built up" tediously and wastefully through the accumulation of incident upon incident, detail upon detail, as if to overwhelm the dullest-witted and most resistant reader. (p. 239)

In all the intangible senses, moreover, the substance of "**Benito Cereno**" is weak and disappointing. A greater portentousness of moral meaning is constantly suggested than is ever actually present. Of moral meaning, indeed, there is singularly little. (p. 240)

It is true that **"The Encantadas"** is only a loosely organized series of sketches, with no very intense unity among them, rather than a completely fused whole; that one or two of these sketches, the fourth and fifth, are hardly more than pedestrian; and that the eighth sketch, the story of the Chola widow, Hunilla, touching though its subject is, is written in a manner so forcedly and self-consciously pathetic that not even its substance redeems it from the lachrymose. It remains true that nowhere in Melville are there grander images of utter desolation than those evoked, in the first three sketches, of the uninhabited and uninhabitable islands, the Galápagos. . . . [In] these first three wonderful sketches Melville's deepest, most despairing sense of abandonment and sterility is expressed. . . . [The] ninth sketch, **"Hood's Isle and the Hermit Oberlus,"** is as dismally convincing, in its dramatization of pure deviltry, the delight in degradation for its own sake, as **"Benito Cereno"** is unconvincing. (p. 241)

There is an extraordinary harmony of image and feeling, of matter and meaning, in the best passages of **"The Encantadas"**: it is only because the piece as a whole is so loosely and unequally formed that it falls short, as it does, of the highest effect. A few months earlier Melville had written the solitary tale of this period in which the substance seems wholly adequate to the mold, the embodiment wholly adequate to the meaning. This is **"Bartleby."** . . . Very little that Melville elsewhere wrote succeeds in suggesting quite so much, with means so simple and even stark, as **"Bartleby"** does. In nothing else that he wrote did he achieve, by the accumulation of details in themselves commonplace, prosaic, and humdrum, a total effect of such strangeness and even madness as this. It reminds one of no other American story, certainly no other of Melville's time. . . . (pp. 241-42)

When he wrote *The Confidence Man* Melville's purely plastic power, his fictive and dramatic power, was at too low an ebb for him to give a rich imaginative embodiment to the things he wished to say; and *The Confidence Man* is not a great allegorical satire because it is not a living narrative. (p. 249)

The Confidence Man is meager and monotonous. . . . It is a series of conversations rather than an action, and though there is now and then a certain life in these conversations, on the whole they keep recurring to the same theme too compulsively, with too few variations, to be anything but unendurably repetitious. (p. 250)

The Confidence Man is one of the most *infidel* books ever written by an American; one of the most completely nihilistic, morally and metaphysically. . . . [It] might have been a work of great and bitter intensity . . . if, in the first place, Melville had not forgotten that blackness itself, unless it is to lose all its painterly value as blackness, needs some small area of light as a set-off. . . . Yet the real failure of *The Confidence Man* lies not so much in its monotone of blackness, as in the fact that, for the most part, that blackness is only a deep and dreary shade of gray. The actual effect of the book imaginatively is, after all, not terror but tameness; what in fact it expresses, except at rare moments, is not a passion of bitterness but a dull despondency of mistrust and disbelief. . . . What had happened to Melville that he could not imagine chicaneries more imposing than these?

The answer can only be that, in losing for the moment his last shred of confidence in both nature and man, he had lost his

sense of the tragic. What was left was hardly more than psychoneurotic suspiciousness. This had not been true when he wrote *Moby Dick:* he had been capable, at that time, of imagining and embodying human error in association with human greatness, as he had been capable, in the figure of Fedallah, of dramatizing the principle of pure evil. He had had the capacity, too, to perceive in nature both the diabolic and the deific. He had had, in short, a vision of tragic grandeur. He had lost it by the time he came to write *The Confidence Man;* an obsession with littleness and falsity had taken its place. . . . (pp. 250-52)

[Though] it has gone largely unread and very little criticized, Melville's work as a poet has far too marked and masculine a character to be neglected or forgotten. Except for Whitman, the best of whose work was done when the Civil War was over, Melville strikes one now as much the most interesting writer who was publishing verse in this country during those arid decades of the decline. It is true that poetry was a kind of afterthought for Melville, that he is primarily a prose writer, like Hardy or Meredith, and that when he writes verse one feels at once it is a prose writer who is at work. In a serious sense, indeed, his verse strikes one as more prosaic than much of his prose. This was not the result of inattention, however, but of a more or less conscious design: if Melville's poems have a strongly prosaic quality, this is their distinction, not their defect. (p. 262)

Quite as far from the conventionally poetic as his language is Melville's highly idiosyncratic imagery. One has to make a simple distinction here between the purely pictorial imagery, the imagery given by the subjects themselves, and the true metaphors. The pictorial imagery of *Battle-Pieces,* for example, is of course the imagery of war, and here it is not too much to say that Melville is the first poet in English to realize the meaning of modern technological warfare, and to render it, grimly and unromantically, in his work. (p. 267)

[His] deepest, most instinctive apprehension of the war was . . . a radical and ambiguous emotion of mingled horror and elatedness, of terrified jubilation. It was the appalled consciousness of looking on at some wild but splendid convulsion in the natural world; some sudden and shocking eruption, upon the smiling scene, of elemental forces of destruction and re-creation. (p. 268)

Battle-Pieces makes it clear that the war had roused Melville, for the time at least, from the mood of disbelief and apathy into which he had fallen in the 'fifties, and given him an invigorating sense of participation in the emotions of his countrymen generally. The long poem, *Clarel,* is much more a product, from this purely historical point of view, of the mood of reaction, letdown, and anxiety into which, like other writers, Melville fell in the rather squalid years that followed the war. . . . In general *Clarel* is an extraordinary work, a very full and rich expression of Melville's later intellectual life, and one regrets that its uninviting form and its extreme length—it is perhaps twice as long as *Paradise Lost*—seem destined permanently to keep it from being much read.

Yet it belongs to a literary type that is rare in American literature even now, and we can hardly afford to undervalue it. . . . [Its] narrative line is, as it ought to be, of the most tenuous: what counts is not the action—there is the least possible of that—but the drama of thought and argument that, however indecisively, is enacted among a group of strongly characterized and contrasted people, thrown together by the chances of travel. (pp. 269-70)

[It] would be easy to exaggerate and throw out of focus the purely stylistic crudities of *Clarel.* At the worst they are far from fatal blemishes in a poem of which the interest is so great as this poem's is. To the reader with a vigorous enough taste to accept [the] clumsier mannerisms the form and language of *Clarel* will in other ways seem admirably suited to its intention. . . . [The] fact is that, when he wrote *Clarel,* Melville's linguistic and compositional powers were passing through a kind of autumnal rejuvenescence. (p. 271)

[There] can be few poets anywhere, since Camoëns, more genuinely seagoing than Melville is in [*John Marr and Other Sailors*]. *John Marr* smells of salt air and seaweed, it reverberates with the uproar of storms at sea, as very little poetry in English or perhaps any modern language does. For most poets to whom the sea has been a profound symbol—for Heine, for Whitman, for Rimbaud—it has been the sea mainly as a landsman would know it and feel it, the sea as envisaged from the shore or in fancy, a symbol of freedom, of liberation, of infinitude. Melville is a rare case of a serious poet who has also been a sailor before the mast, and the sea exists in his verse with a kind of cruel, bitter, but still salubrious reality with which it exists in few of the others. (p. 278)

Many of the poems in the last collection Melville printed, *Timoleon,* seem weaker, tamer, and more conventional than those in either *Battle-Pieces* or *John Marr.* . . . They abound in palaces, villas, and gardens, in statues and paintings, in temples, cathedrals, and pyramids. Only occasionally does this imagery of the *sehenswürdig* really glow with a metaphorical luminousness, but it does so, at the least, in **"Pisa's Leaning Tower"** (with its metaphor of suicide), in the extraordinary Venetian poem, **"In a Bye-Canal,"** and in the familiar little exercise in the style of Landor, **"The Ravaged Villa."** For the rest, *Timoleon* would be memorable if only for the now well-known and certainly remarkable poem, **"After the Pleasure Party."** . . . (pp. 279-80)

Everyone has felt [*Billy Budd, Foretopman*] to be the work of a man on the last verge of mortal existence who wishes to take his departure with a word of acceptance and reconciliation on his lips. (p. 292)

[The real feeling of *Billy Budd*] is very deep and very affecting; it triumphs even over the stiff-jointed prose, the torpidity of the movement, the excess of commentary, and Melville's failure to quicken any of the scenes with a full dramatic life. In spite of these blemishes of form and manner, the persons in *Billy Budd* and the moral drama they enact have too much largeness, as well as too much subtlety, in their poetic representativeness, not to leave a permanent stamp on the imagination. (p. 294)

> *Newton Arvin, in his* Herman Melville *(copyright, 1950, by William Sloane Associates, Inc.; abridged by permission of William Morrow & Company, Inc.),* Sloane, 1950, 316 p.

EDWARD WAGENKNECHT   (essay date 1952)

[*Typee, A Romance of the South Seas*] is generally placed in the Rousseau tradition of the "noble savage." This is not strictly accurate. (p. 60)

Melville did admire wholeheartedly the mental and physical health of the islanders, their excellent dispositions, and their freedom from the vices of civilization, but he saw these things not as the spontaneous productions of "nature," but as the achievements of a social order which they had made, and which was right for them. He is very clear that when the whites and the people of the South Seas come together, the latter do not corrupt but are corrupted. It was on this ground that he threw down the gauntlet by manifesting an imperfect sympathy for the missionaries, who, as he saw it, brought to the South Seas a religion too austere for its people to understand, and who all too often served as an entering wedge for imperialistic aggression. . . . But this noble indignation never tempted him to believe that a white man might solve his problems by "going native," as we may see by his unfriendly portrait of one Lem Hardy, who had done just that, as well as in his own determination to escape from the Pacific paradise—Fayaway and all—at the earliest possible moment. (p. 61)

The continuation of the story in *Omoo, A Narrative of Aventures in the South Seas* is less exotic in its materials and more prosaic in its tone. Being confined on suspicion of mutiny is less uplifting and enjoyable than bathing with naked girls, and Melville's description of it is correspondingly less stimulating. But the author's attitude toward his materials has changed also; this time he has got less of the spirit of youth into his book. Nevertheless, Dr. Long Ghost, once a gentleman, is a vivid character in the Smollett tradition, and there are memorable vignettes of Mrs. Bell, the Haughty Youth, and others. (p. 62)

White-Jacket; or The World in a Man-of-War, is hardly a novel; it is an account of life on a battleship, notable chiefly for its attacks upon flogging and on war itself. (pp. 63-4)

Perhaps the most memorable single figure in *White-Jacket* is the surgeon Cadwallader Cuticle, who kills a sailor by an unnecessary operation, first divesting himself "of nearly all inorganic appurtenances." This is comedy in the Swiftian manner. His name and contemporary records combine to attest that this horrible creature came not from Melville's experiences in the navy but from his own imagination and from Smollett.

Mardi, Moby-Dick, and (save that it is not a story of the sea), *Pierre* . . . comprise a second group among Melville's fictions. This affinity appears in the metaphysical complexities and allegorical suggestions contained in all three. . . .

Mardi represents Melville's first attempt to break away from the simple, direct narratives with which he had begun. . . . (p. 64)

The manner of [Taji's] journey recalls Rabelais; the style is often suggestive of Sir Thomas Browne. But though the ostensible setting remains the South Seas, the ideas involved belong to a much more sophisticated milieu—Melville's own literary and social and political world of New York society.

Yillah herself has been variously interpreted. She is opposed to Hautia, the lady of sensuality and pride, and it seems clear that at least two ideas are involved in her. On one level of meaning, in an anti-ascetic book, she is placed over against both lust and a febrile Platonism; Taji's relationship with her is both physical and spiritual and therefore altogether satisfying. And on another level she is evidently truth, and the value of life itself is bound up with the search for her.

Moby-Dick seems far more coherent than *Mardi,* but its meaning is no less controversial. As fiction, it tells the story of Captain Ahab's attempt to revenge himself upon the Great White Whale that had swallowed his leg. But what *is* Ahab, and what *is* the Whale? . . . It is clear that to Ahab the Whale symbolizes everything malevolent or intransigent in the world and, on occasion at least, everything that runs counter to the will of Ahab. (pp. 66-7)

In the ordinary sense of the term, *Moby-Dick* is hardly a novel. Melville never mastered the common technique of fiction; he hardly attempted to do so except in *Pierre*. It was upon this ground that contemporary critics condemned the story of the Whale; we accept it today because we believe that the book is great enough to create its own category, at the same time creating the taste by which it is understood. . . .

Of plot there is hardly enough to make a good short story; the mood is frequently that of the epic or saga, the method that of the Elizabethan drama. (p. 68)

New readers of Melville are often tempted to tell themselves that the man is a stippler, that an accumulating effect is beyond him. Now, there is much evidence to show that Melville as fictionist was bound to the episodic method. *Moby-Dick* itself is divided into 135 chapters, some of them less than a page in length. Yet it not only has its climax, in Ahab's fatal encounter with the Whale, but when it comes at last, it is one of the most thrilling things in American literature.

The third, and in a sense climactic, book of the group, *Pierre; or, The Ambiguities,* has often gone strangely uncomprehended even during the Melville revival. (p. 69)

The allegorists have tortured *Pierre* less than either *Mardi* or *Moby-Dick;* those who must have an allegory here find Pierre as Melville's own spiritual being, his father as God, his mother as the World, Lucy as "the simple objective inclination" of his mind, Isabel as the "introspective tendency" of his mind, and Glen Stanly as his public self. The contrast between Lucy and Isabel repeats the pattern already employed in *Mardi,* where Yillah was opposed to Hautia. Unlike Hautia, Isabel is not evil, but hers are the "Songs of Experience" to set over against Lucy's "Songs of Innocence." Isabel does, however, embody the fascination which the tragic side of life held for Melville, and, unlike the ever-virginal Lucy, she embraces the dark, fertile, life-giving qualities of passion. The suggestion of incest . . . may have been intended to suggest introversion and all its dangers, but it also served admirably to indicate the puzzles of moral ambiguity into which Pierre is thrust, and possibly to illuminate the bad judgment which contributes so importantly to his destruction. (pp. 70-1)

> *Edward Wagenknecht, "The Ambiguities of Herman Melville," in his* Cavalcade of the American Novel *(copyright © 1952 by Henry Holt and Company, Inc.; copyright renewed © 1980 by Edward Wagenknecht; reprinted by permission of the author), Holt, Rinehart and Winston, 1952, pp. 58-81.*

ALBERT CAMUS (essay date 1952)

[Melville's] admirable books are among those exceptional works that can be read in different ways, which are at the same time both obvious and obscure, as dark as the noonday sun and as clear as deep water. The wise man and the child can both draw sustenance from them. The story of captain Ahab, for example, . . . can doubtless be read as the fatal passion of a character gone mad with grief and loneliness. But it can also be seen as one of the most overwhelming myths ever invented on the subject of the struggle of man against evil, depicting the irresistible logic that finally leads the just man to take up arms first against creation and the creator, then against his fellows and against himself. Let us have no doubt about it: if it is true

that talent recreates life, while genius has the additional gift of crowning it with myths, Melville is first and foremost a creator of myths.

I will add that these myths, contrary to what people say of them, are clear. They are obscure only insofar as the root of all suffering and all greatness lies buried in the darkness of the earth. . . . But it seems to me . . . that Melville never wrote anything but the same book, which he began again and again. This single book is the story of a voyage, inspired first of all solely by the joyful curiosity of youth (*Typee, Omoo,* etc.), then later inhabited by an increasingly wild and burning anguish. *Mardi* is the first magnificent story in which Melville begins the quest that nothing can appease, and in which, finally, "pursuers and pursued fly across a boundless ocean." . . . *Moby Dick* simply carries the great themes of *Mardi* to perfection. But since artistic perfection is inadequate to quench the kind of thirst with which we are confronted here, Melville will start once again, in *Pierre: or the Ambiguities,* that unsuccessful masterpiece, to depict the quest of genius and misfortune whose sneering failure he will consecrate in the course of a long journey on the Mississippi that forms the theme of *The Confidence Man.*

This constantly rewritten book, this unwearying peregrination in the archipelago of dreams and bodies, on an ocean "whose every wave is a soul," this Odyssey beneath an empty sky, makes Melville the Homer of the Pacific. But we must add immediately that his Ulysses never returns to Ithaca. The country in which Melville approaches death, that he immortalizes in *Billy Budd,* is a desert island. In allowing the young sailor, a figure of beauty and innocence whom he dearly loves, to be condemned to death, Captain Vere submits his heart to the law. And at the same time, with this flawless story that can be ranked with certain Greek tragedies, the aging Melville tells us of his acceptance for the first time of the sacrifice of beauty and innocence so that order may be maintained and the ship of men may continue to move forward toward an unknown horizon. Has he truly found the peace and final resting place that earlier he had said could not be found in the Mardi archipelago? Or are we, on the contrary, faced with a final shipwreck that Melville in his despair asked of the gods? "One cannot blaspheme and live," he had cried out. At the height of consent, isn't *Billy Budd* the worst blasphemy? (pp. 289-92)

[But this] should not mislead anyone as to Melville's real genius and the sovereignty of his art. It bursts with health, strength, explosions of humor, and human laughter. . . . [Spiritual] experience is balanced by expression and invention, and constantly finds flesh and blood in them. Like the greatest artists, Melville constructed his symbols out of concrete things, not from the material of dreams. The creator of myths partakes of genius only insofar as he inscribes these myths in the denseness of reality and not in the fleeting clouds of the imagination. . . . [In] Melville the symbol emerges from reality, the image is born of what is seen. . . . Melville's lyricism, which reminds us of Shakespeare's, makes use of the four elements. He mingles the Bible with the sea, the music of the waves with that of the spheres, the poetry of the days with the grandeur of the Atlantic. He is inexhaustible. . . . (pp. 292-93)

We find in [Melville's works] revolt and acceptance, unconquerable and endless love, the passion for beauty, language of the highest order—in short, genius. (p. 294)

> *Albert Camus, "Herman Melville" (originally published as "Herman Melville," in* Les écrivains cé-

lèbres, Vol. III, *edited by Raymond Queneau and A. J. Arberry, L. Mazenod, 1952), in* Lyrical and Critical Essays, *edited by Philip Thody, translated by Ellen Conroy Kennedy (copyright © 1967 by Hamish Hamilton, Ltd. and Alfred A. Knopf, Inc.; and © 1968 by Alfred A. Knopf, Inc.; reprinted by permission of the publisher), Knopf, 1968, pp. 288-94.*

LAWRANCE THOMPSON (essay date 1952)

Melville did not completely rebel against his Calvinistic heritage until after he had written and published his first two travel-narratives, **Typee** and **Omoo.** Even during his writing of **Mardi,** when the struggle between his beliefs and his doubts reached a crisis, he still managed to salvage a modified assertion of mystical religious affirmation, short-lived, because it did not satisfy and sustain him. (pp. 4-5)

[One] might fear that Melville's concept of the Calvinistic God might gradually have become so repulsive that he might have move through doubt and skepticism to a denial of the existence of God. This final step he never took. As it happened, however, Melville actually experimented with several different kinds of resolution, without achieving any lasting comfort or consolation. Mystically inclined, he preferred or wanted to think of God as that benevolent and personal source of Truth, to whom each individual could talk directly; and this attitude was an important part of his Protestant heritage. Nevertheless, while writing **Mardi,** he seemed to toy with the wavering and unpleasant suspicion that God could not possibly be what Melville wanted him to be. As a result, the asserted affirmation in the tableau-conclusion of **Mardi** was merely an assertion: it lacked conviction. (p. 5)

Melville arrived at a highly ironic conclusion: believing more firmly than ever in the God of John Calvin, he began to resent and hate the attributes of God, particularly the seemingly tyrannous harshness and cruelty and malice of God. Thus, instead of losing faith in his Calvinistic God, Melville made a scapegoat of him, and blamed God for having caused so many human beings to rebel. . . . Melville came to view God as the source from whom all evils flow, in short, the "Original Sinner," divinely depraved. (pp. 5-6)

Melville's spiritual idiom . . . controlled and determined his artistic idiom. The tensions of Melville's peculiar and inverted religious beliefs prompted him to give them outlet in some kind of literary expression, and yet he hesitated to express himself frankly. He knew very well that his contemporary reading public was too deeply committed to Christian beliefs in the goodness of God to tolerate any open assertions as to the malice and evil of God. (p. 6)

Still craving the satisfaction of giving literary vent to his secret and heretical beliefs, Melville gradually formulated a complex variety of stylistic and structural methods for expressing himself in such a way as to protect himself from heresy hunters. . . . [He] ingeniously arranged to pretend, in the telling, that no matter how much he indulged in occasional religious doubts and questionings, his ultimate goal was to praise and honor the orthodox Christian viewpoint. This pretense was very convenient for purposes of sarcasm and satire and irony, because the pretense gave the illusion of proceeding in a direction exactly opposite from the anti-Christian direction of the story itself, the plot itself. Within this flexible formula of sustained irony, Melville achieved ample elbowroom for playing with innumerable artistic devices for defensive concealment, subterfuge, deception, hoodwinking, ridicule. (pp. 6-7)

Absorbing and intricate as Melville's literary art proves to be, and praiseworthy as that intricacy certainly is, the disturbing fact remains that a comparison between his artistically expressed range of vision and that of other celebrated literary figures (James, for example) reveals that Melville's range was limited by his inability to achieve some mature and working reconciliation of his confused inner conflicts; that Melville's art dramatizes, more vividly than anything else, a kind of arrested development. Spellbound by his own disillusionments, he became stranded in the narcissistic shallows and miseries of those disillusionments.

Melville seemed compelled to devote most of his art to the emblematic telling and retelling of his spiritual autobiography, with the main emphasis on disillusionment. (p. 419)

[He] mistakenly employed his skepticism and agnosticism merely as destructive weapons to bludgeon the idealism of others, and particularly Christian idealism. At the same time, ironically, he chose to remain an idealist, without realizing the idealistic nature of his choice: proceeding on the immature and childish notion that because an object is not white it must be black, he clung to a religious idealism which was merely an inversion of that secondhand Calvinistic idealism which he had intended to discard. We must proceed cautiously, here as elsewhere. Melville seems to me to have been correct in his notion that the Calvinistic concept of God was in some ways an ugly and unacceptable concept of God, which did not encourage anyone to love God so much as to fear God. When he chose to turn his back on that concept, however, he faced a considerable variety of substitute choices, as he certainly knew; but from . . . **Mardi** we may gather that he actually proceeded to make several different choices at one and the same time. Gradually, however, his "progress" through the inferno of his disillusionment brought him only deeper into an inner inferno, which seems to me to have been a quaintly childish oversimplification: if the Calvinistic God did not inspire love, that God must inspire hate. If He was not white, He was black. (p. 422)

It would be easy enough to insist that Melville never did quarrel with God; that he merely quarreled with the Calvinists for having created such an outrageous concept of God. The evidence, here, is very strong. Melville did devote much time and space to attacking the Calvinistic concept of God. But again there were numerous and different ways of attacking the concept, and Melville had plenty of company, in his own day, in America. . . . For deeply religious people . . . the ugliest tenets of Calvinistic dogma (the basic concepts of Original Sin and Innate Depravity) became merely discarded pieces of theological furniture. Instead of merely discarding this furniture, however, Melville devoted the best part of his life to kicking that discarded furniture to pieces. Why?

Because his responses to life were what they were, he needed a scapegoat: someone to blame. Having started with hating Christians because they were not sufficiently Christian, he proceeded to hate Christians because they were Christians. When that scapegoat failed to satisfy him, he went on to hate the Calvinistic concept of God, and then proceeded to hate God. It never seemed to occur to him that he had merely declared his independence from the ideal of Calvinism in order to pledge his allegiance to an inverted form of that same ideal. (pp. 422-23)

Finally, we may quite easily summarize the essential element in the general range of Melville's vision, because that element remained so constant throughout so much of his later life. . . . [The] general range of Melville's vision is somewhat disappointing (not nearly so exciting and fascinating as the infinite variety of his devices for representing it) because that vision narrows down to the sharp focus of a misanthropic notion that the world was put together wrong, and that God was to blame. The gist of it is that simple. He spent his life not merely in sneering at the gullibility of human beings who disagreed with him but also in sneering at God, accusing God, upbraiding God, blaming God, and (as he thought) quarreling with God. The turn which his life had taken translated him from a transcendentalist and a mystic into an inverted transcendentalist, an inverted mystic. To this extent, then, he was consistent, in spite of all his concomitant inconsistencies, to the very end of his life. Like his own Captain Ahab, he remained a defiant rebel, even in the face of death. (pp. 424-25)

> *Lawrance Thompson, in his* Melville's Quarrel with God *(copyright 1952, © renewed 1980 by Princeton University Press; excerpts reprinted by permission of Princeton University Press), Princeton University Press, 1952, 474 p.*

R.W.B. LEWIS (essay date 1955)

Melville took the loss of innocence and the world's betrayal of hope as the supreme challenge to understanding and to art. He wanted not to accept that betrayal; and for a while he kept going back over the ground of his experience as if to prove the betrayal untrue or avoidable. That illusory effort is part of the meaning of *Redburn* and most of the meaning of *Pierre* and *Clarel*. But in the course of his deeply vexed odyssey, Melville found the resources for coming to terms with his losses: terms of extraordinarily creative tension in *Moby-Dick* and terms of luminous resolution in *Billy Budd*. His resources were moral and intellectual ones, but they were available to him only as he discovered the artistic resources. Experience fulfilled and explained itself for Melville only and finally in language. (pp. 129-30)

What Melville thought at the end, when he saw everything he had said, was, curiously enough, a dialectically heightened value in something he had supposed irretrievably destroyed. He found a new conviction about the saving strength of the Adamic personality. When this conviction became articulate in *Billy Budd*, the American hero as Adam became the hero as Christ and entered, once and for all, into the dimension of myth. (p. 130)

Moby-Dick, for all its humor, is, of course, a novel ablaze with anger. Yet it is the humor, or what the humor represents, that makes us fully aware of the scope of the anger.

What had been a mere rustle of resentment over a world false to the promises of hope had grown, by 1851, into a fury of disenchantment: Adam gone mad with disillusion. *Moby-Dick* manages to give very clear voice to that fury. . . . Melville had discovered how to establish an attitude toward his own sense of outrage or, inversely, how to establish his outrage in relation to a comprehensive and in some ways traditional attitude. The relation expresses itself in *Moby-Dick* in the actual dramatic relation between frenzied Ahab and far-seeing Ishmael; and psychologizing critics might tell us that what happens in the novel is the "splitting-off" of a personality first introduced as Ishmael into fragments of itself—one still called Ishmael, others called Ahab and Starbuck and Pip and so on. But we can regard the achievement in terms of the materials of

narrative. From this viewpoint, it may be argued that the success of *Moby-Dick* and the clarity of its anger are due to Melville's peculiar, yet skilful, exploitation of the legacy of European literature—and "the tradition" which that literature has made manifest.

The legacy was the greatest of Melville's resources as, in his own way and according to his own needs, he gradually came into possession of it. The anger in *Moby-Dick* becomes resonant in the tension it creates with the legacy and the tradition. And, conversely, it is the tradition which—in the choral voice of Ishmael and for what it is worth within the ironic frame of the novel—transvaluates the values implicit in the anger. (pp. 138-39)

[Melville] belongs to the company of gifted romantics from Blake and Baudelaire to Thomas Mann, who have supposed that art is somehow the flower of evil and that the power through which the shaping imagination is raised to greatness may also be a power which destroys the artist; for it is the strength derived from the knowledge of evil—not the detached study, but perhaps a very descent into the abyss. At some stage or other, Melville felt, art had to keep an appointment with wickedness. He believed with Hawthorne that, in order to achieve moral maturity, the individual had to engage evil and suffer the consequences; and he added the conviction that, in order to compose a mature work of literature, the artist had to enter without flinching into the "spheres of fright." (p. 140)

Moby-Dick is an elaborate pattern of countercommentaries, the supreme instance of the dialectical novel—a novel of tension without resolution. Ishmael's meditation, which transfigures the anger and sees beyond the sickness and the evil, is only one major voice in the dramatic conversation; and not until *Billy Budd* does this voice become transcendent and victorious. In *Moby-Dick*, Melville adopted a unique and off-beat traditionalism—a steadily ambiguous re-rendering of the old forms and fables once unequivocally rejected by the hopeful—in order to recount the total blasting of the vision of innocence. He went beyond a spurious artistic originality to give narrative birth to the conflict with evil: that evil against which a spurious and illusory innocence must shatter itself. In doing so, he not only achieved a sounder originality but moved a great step toward perceiving a more durable innocence. In *Pierre*, the following year, Melville faltered and went back once more over the old dreary ground of disillusion; but in *Billy Budd*, he was to come home. (p. 146)

Billy Budd is, of course, unmistakably the product of aged serenity; its author has unmistakably got beyond his anger or discovered the key to it. . . . It is woeful, but wisely, no longer madly. Its hero is sacrificially hanged at sea, but its author has come home, like Odysseus.

In Melville's last work, the New World's representative hero and his representative adventure receive a kind of sanctification. . . . *Billy Budd* helps us to see that the action so described is one grounded in the pressures and counterpressures not of any world but of the New World. It is the action of the soul in general as shaped under a New World perspective. Melville's achievement was double: he brought myth into contemporary life, and he elevated that life into myth—at once transcending and reaffirming the sense of life indicated by the party of Hope. (p. 147)

Melville exposed anew the danger of innocence and its inevitable tragedy; but in the tragedy he rediscovered a heightened value in the innocence.

Melville's achievement, as in *Moby-Dick,* was an artistic achievement, and it may be measured by the failure of *Pierre,* more than three decades earlier. For the action fumbled with in *Pierre* is essentially the same as that of *Billy Budd.* (p. 148)

The symbolic distance accomplished in *Moby-Dick* narrows fatally in *Pierre;* and if ever there was a case of symbolic suicide in literature, it is Melville's in the indiscriminate destruction in the concluding pages of *Pierre.* The myth which had been an ambiguous source of strength in *Moby-Dick* has now overwhelmed the life. And so in *Clarel,* Melville's next extensive piece of writing, we are not surprised to find an imagination winding its way through a maze of wasteland imagery, quite explicitly lamenting the bewildering and painful loss of Eden.

The recovery in *Billy Budd* is astonishing. The entire story moves firmly in the direction of a transcendent cheerfulness: transcendent, and so neither bumptious nor noisy; a serene and radiant gladness. The climax is prepared with considerable artistry by a series of devices which, though handled somewhat stiffly by a rusty creative talent, do their work nonetheless. The intent of all of them is to bring into being and to identify the hero and his role and then to institute the magical process of transfiguration. Billy appears as another Adam: thrust (like Redburn and Pierre) into a world for which his purity altogether unfits him. (p. 149)

Billy is the type of scapegoat hero, by whose sacrifice the sins of his world are taken away: in this case, the world of the H.M.S. "Indomitable" and the British navy, a world threatened by a mutiny which could destroy it. Melville brought to bear upon such a hero and his traditional fate an imagination of mythic capabilities: I mean an imagination able to detect the intersection of divine, supernatural power and human experience; an imagination which could suggest the theology of life without betraying the limits of literature. (p. 151)

It is this, I suggest, which accounts for something that might otherwise bother us in the *novella:* the apparent absence of impressive change—not in the world but in the character of Billy Budd. We expect our tragic heroes to change and to reveal (like Donatello) a dimensionally increased understanding of man's ways or of God's ways to man. Billy is as innocent, as guileless, as trusting, as *loving,* when he hangs from the yardarm as when he is taken off the "Rights of Man." What seems like failure, in this respect and on Melville's part, is exactly the heart of the accomplishment. For the change effected in the story has to do with the *reader,* as representative of the onlooking world: with the perception forced on him of the indestructible and in some sense the absolute value of "the pristine virtues." The perception is aroused by exposing the Christlike nature of innocence and love, which is to raise those qualities to a higher power—to their highest power. Humanly speaking, those qualities are fatal; but they alone can save the world. (pp. 151-52)

> R. W. B. Lewis, "Melville: The Apotheosis of Adam,"
> *in his* The American Adam: Innocence, Tragedy and
> Tradition in the Nineteenth Century *(reprinted by
> permission of The University of Chicago Press;* ©
> *The University of Chicago, 1955), University of Chi-
> cago Press, 1955 (and reprinted by The University
> of Chicago Press, 1959, pp. 127-55).*

ROBERT E. SPILLER   (essay date 1955)

If in Emerson and Thoreau the soul of the infant Republic had found its first affirmation and in Poe and Hawthorne its agony

and its tragic voice, the times were ready by 1850 for a literary masterwork which would cry out with a timeless world cry of both faith and despair. Only of such stuff is great literature made, and of such were *Moby-Dick* [and Whitman's *Leaves of Grass*]. (p. 89)

In the popular mind their moods and messages seem to be in violent contrast. Melville's voice is the voice of irony and despair, his ultimate faith is in the certainty of evil, if faith can be said to have at all transcended his cosmic doubt. He seems the Devil's advocate in contrast to Whitman's voice crying out for confidence in life, in the future, and in the common goodness of humanity. Melville seems philosophically to link with Poe and Hawthorne; Whitman, with Emerson and Thoreau. But the contrast is illusory. . . . *Leaves of Grass* except for the blatantly assertive "Song of Myself," is a deeply sad tribute to man's weakness in the midst of cosmic splendor. *Moby-Dick,* like all great tragedy, purges the emotions of their violence and gives its lone survivor the steady eye of experience with which to look out upon the world. (p. 90)

Melville was throughout his life a dual personality; he could live on two levels of consciousness and be fully and keenly alive on both at the same moment. The experience is a common one, of being caught up by an emotional situation and at the same time being critically aware of what is happening, but seldom is it made so articulate as in Melville's autobiographical romances. The suicidal lonely youth and the happy and favored brother who was off to glorious adventures were both there waving from the rail. And they collaborated later to make the novel *Redburn* a narrative of what happened and an extraordinarily accurate revelation of the inner conflict of adolescence. Even in this, one of Melville's lesser works, the artist could step into the breach and make the voyage of Redburn a symbol of the first meeting of youthful dreams with the hard facts of experience. The same process, far more intricate and involved, created *Mardi, Moby-Dick,* and *Pierre,* where passion and understanding reached their maximum intensity while the artist Melville retained control and direction of both. (p. 92)

Melville's art builds up to and away from the tragic epic *Moby-Dick.* It would present a confused and meaningless pattern without that central peak; with that focus it is an aesthetic and interrelated whole.

So concentrated is the vision of this great book that it could be called merely a battle between the mad captain Ahab of the whaler *Pequod* and the mightiest of whales, the "white" monster Moby-Dick. (p. 95)

Saturated in the lore and facts of the art of whaling, [Melville] packed his novel so that it breathed sea air and reeked of boiling whale blubber; deeply moved by the problem of free man confronting his own destiny, he made his captain one of the company of Titans who defy both God and Nature. Fact became symbol and incident acquired universal meaning. . . . (p. 97)

[Melville's] skepticism and his symbolism can both be traced back to his earlier works; but the real preparation for *Moby-Dick* was the loose-jointed, humorous, serious, satiric, poetic allegory *Mardi.* The voyage of Taji through the islands of an infinite archipelago in quest of the maiden Yillah is a rather obvious symbolic study of man's fruitless search for a vague ideal of beauty or self-completion, and the various islands provide a handy device for reviewing all the ways in which man has tried to reconcile his insatiable desires to the laws of God and Nature. At the end, Taji is still searching, as was his creator. *Moby-Dick* had to be a romance of moral inquiry and it had to be the allegory that Melville feared it might become.

Once he had determined to allow Ahab to ask the ultimate questions, he could give his imagination and his artistry full freedom to mold a gigantic work. The nature of good and evil, the power of the will to defy fate, the validity of those insights which contradict the apparent laws of experience, the eternal conflict of God and Nature in which man is caught—these are the issues that are raised by Ahab's defiance. In the person of Ahab, whom he conceived in total tragic abandon, he could ask questions that had no answers; in Ishmael he could stand by and allow reason to speculate on the events. Because he supplied no one formula of interpretation, he left his readers the same freedom he gained for himself—the ability to move back and forth between fact and meaning on the bridge of symbolism. (pp. 97-8)

[In the next novel, *Pierre*,] he experimented with a literary method that might help him resolve the "ambiguities" of his own heart, but this time he chose one of total subjectivity. Because Pierre cannot escape from his author, he cannot finally ask his questions clearly. The most searching of all Melville's novels threatens alternately to become pure philosophy and pure melodrama. In **The Confidence-Man**, the short tales like **"Benito Cereno"** and **"Bartleby, the Scrivener,"** and the poems—particularly the long and philosophical *Clarel*—he weaves rational webs of increasing subtlety and complexity, but is held by his growing skepticism from ever stating his case clearly. Finally, in **Billy Budd** . . . , he returned to his central problem of man's moral dilemma, in the character of the boy-sailor caught fairly between the laws of man and the laws of God. . . . Like Johnson's *Rasselas*, Melville's speculations led only to a conclusion in which nothing is concluded, but, as in all great art, the reader may form his own answer in the clear and simple presentation of the problem that Melville here at last achieves; but what his own answer is or was, no one can know. (pp. 98-9)

> Robert E. Spiller, "Romantic Crisis: Melville, Whitman," in his The Cycle of American Literature: An Essay in Historical Criticism *(reprinted with permission of Macmillan Publishing Co., Inc.; © 1955 by Macmillan Publishing Co., Inc.), Macmillan, 1955, pp. 89-110.**

ALFRED KAZIN   (essay date 1956)

Moby-Dick is not only a very big book; it is also a peculiarly full and rich one, and from the very opening it conveys a sense of abundance, of high creative power, that exhilarates and enlarges the imagination. This quality is felt immediately in the style, which is remarkably easy, natural and "American," yet always literary, and which swells in power until it takes on some of the roaring and uncontainable rhythms with which Melville audibly describes the sea. (p. 52)

It is [the] constant sense of power that constitutes the book's appeal to us, that explains its hold on our attention. *Moby-Dick* is one of those books that try to bring in as much of life as a writer can get both hands on. Melville even tries to create an image of life itself as a ceaseless creation. The book is written with a personal force of style, a passionate learning, a steady insight into our forgotten connections with the primitive. It sweeps everything before it; it gives us the happiness that only great vigor inspires.

If we start by opening ourselves to this abundance and force, by welcoming not merely the story itself, but the manner in which it speaks to us, we shall recognize in this restlessness, this richness, this persistent atmosphere of magnitude, the essential image on which the book is founded. For *Moby-Dick* is not so much a book *about* Captain Ahab's quest for the whale as it is an experience *of* that quest. This is only to say, what we say of any true poem, that we cannot reduce its essential substance to a subject, that we should not intellectualize and summarize it, but that we should recognize that its very force and beauty lie in the way it is conceived and written, in the qualities that flow from its being a unique entity.

In these terms, *Moby-Dick* seems to be far more of a poem than it is a novel, and since it is a narrative, to be an epic, a long poem on an heroic theme, rather than the kind of realistic fiction that we know today. . . . [What] distinguishes *Moby-Dick* from modern prose fiction, what ties it up with the older, more formal kind of narrative that was once written in verse, is the fact that Melville is not interested in the meanness, the literal truthfulness, the representative slice of life, that we think of as the essence of modern realism. His book has the true poetic emphasis in that the whole story is constantly being meditated and unravelled through a single mind. (pp. 52-3)

[It is the] emphasis on Ishmael's personal vision, on the richness and ambiguity of all events as the sceptical, fervent, experience-scarred mind of Ishmael feels and thinks them, that gives us, from the beginning, the new kind of book that *Moby-Dick* is. It is a book which is neither a saga, though it deals in large natural forces, nor a *classical* epic, for we feel too strongly the individual who wrote it. It is a book that is at once primitive, fatalistic, and merciless, like the very oldest books, and yet peculiarly personal, like so many twentieth-century novels, in its significant emphasis on the subjective individual consciousness. The book grows out of a single word, "I." . . .

The power behind this "I" is poetical in the sense that everything comes to us through a constant intervention of language instead of being presented flatly. Melville does not wish, as so many contemporary writers do, to reproduce ordinary life and conventional speech. He seeks the marvellous and the fabulous aspects that life wears in secret. He exuberantly sees the world through language—things exist as his words for them—and much of the exceptional beauty of the book lies in the unusual incidence of passages that, in the most surprising contexts, are so piercing in their poetic intensity. But the most remarkable feat of language in the book is Melville's ability to make us see that man is not a blank slate passively open to events, but a mind that constantly seeks meaning in everything it encounters. (p. 53)

With the entry of Ahab a harsh new rhythm enters the book, and from now on two rhythms—one reflective, the other forceful—alternate to show us the world in which man's thinking and man's doing each follows its own law. Ishmael's thought consciously extends itself to get behind the world of appearances; he wants to see and to understand everything. Ahab's drive is to *prove*, not to discover; the world that tortures Ishmael by its horrid vacancy has tempted Ahab into thinking that he can make it over. . . . As Ishmael is all rumination, so Ahab is all will. Both are thinkers, the difference being that Ishmael thinks as a bystander, has identified his own state with man's utter unimportance in nature. Ahab, by contrast, actively seeks the whale in order to assert man's supremacy over what swims before him as "the monomaniac incarnation" of a superior power. . . . (p. 55)

But Ahab is not just a fanatic who leads the whole crew to their destruction; he is a hero of thought who is trying, by terrible force, to reassert man's place in nature. And it is the struggle that Ahab incarnates that makes him so magnificent a *voice*, thundering in Shakespearean rhetoric, storming at the gates of the inhuman, silent world. Ahab is trying to give man, in one awful, final assertion that his will *does* mean something, a feeling of relatedness with his world. (p. 56)

[By] the end of the book Ahab abandons all his human ties and becomes a complete fanatic. But Melville has no doubt—nor should we!—that Ahab's quest is *humanly* understandable. And the quest itself supplies the book with its technical *raison d'être*. For it leads us through all the seas and around the whole world; it brings us past ships of every nation. Always it is Ahab's drive that makes up the *passion* of **Moby-Dick**. . . . And this passion may be defined as a passion of longing, of hope, of striving: a passion that starts from the deepest loneliness that man can know. It is the great cry of man who feels himself exiled from his "birthright, the merry May-day gods of old," who looks for a new god "to enthrone . . . again in the now egotistical sky; in the now unhaunted hill." The cry is Ahab's—"Who's to doom, when the judge himself is dragged to the bar?"

Behind Ahab's cry is the fear that man's covenant with God has been broken, that there is no purpose to our existence. The *Pequod* is condemned by Ahab to sail up and down the world in search of—a symbol. But this search, mad as it seems to Starbuck the first mate, who is a Christian, nevertheless represents Ahab's real humanity. For the ancient covenant is never quite broken so long as man still thirsts for it. And because Ahab, as Melville intended him to, represents the aristocracy of intellect in our democracy, because he seeks to transcend the limitations that good conventional men like Starbuck, philistine materialists like Stubb, and unthinking fools like Flask want to impose on everybody else, Ahab speaks for the humanity that belongs to man's imaginative vision of himself.

Yet with all this, we must not forget that Ahab's quest takes place, unceasingly, in a very practical world of whaling, as part of the barbaric and yet highly necessary struggle by man to support himself physically in nature. It is this that gives the book its primitive vitality, its burning authenticity. For **Moby-Dick,** it must be emphasized, is not simply a symbolic fable; nor, as we have already seen, can it possibly be construed as simply a "sea story." . . . **Moby-Dick** is a representation of the passionate mind speaking, for its metaphysical concerns, out of the very midst of life. . . . Melville insists that our thinking is *not* swallowed up by practical concerns, that man constantly searches for a reality equal to his inner life of thought—and it is his ability to show this in the midst of a brutal, dirty whaling voyage that makes **Moby-Dick** such an astonishing book. Just as Ahab is a hero, so **Moby-Dick** itself is a heroic book. What concerns Melville is not merely the heroism that gets expressed in physical action, but the heroism of thought itself as it rises above its seeming insignificance and proclaims, in the very teeth of a seemingly hostile and malevolent creation, that man's voice *is* heard for something against the watery waste and the deep, that man's thought has an echo in the universe.

This is the quest. But what makes **Moby-Dick** so fascinating, and in a sense even uncanny, is that the issue is always in doubt, and remains so to the end. . . . [In] the struggle between man's effort to find meaning in nature, and the indifference of nature itself, which simply eludes him . . . , Melville often

portrays the struggle from the side of nature itself. He sees the whale's view of things far more than he does Ahab's: and Moby Dick's milk white head, the tail feathers of the sea birds streaming from his back like pennons, are described with a rapture that is like the adoration of a god. . . . In Melville's final vision of the whale, it is not fair but it is entirely *just* that the whale should destroy the ship, that man should be caught up on the beast. . . . What Melville does is to speak for the whirlwind, for the watery waste, for the sharks.

It is this that gives **Moby-Dick** its awful and crushing power. It is a unique gift. (pp. 56-7)

> Alfred Kazin, "Introduction" (copyright 1956 by Alfred Kazin; reprinted by permission of Houghton Mifflin Company), in Moby-Dick; or The Whale by Herman Melville, edited by Alfred Kazin, Houghton Mifflin, 1956 (and reprinted in Discussions of "Moby-Dick," edited by Milton R. Stern, D. C. Heath and Company, 1968, pp. 52-9).

MARIUS BEWLEY (essay date 1959)

Apart from his actual works we do not know very much about the state of Melville's mind, and in attributing to him a profound disillusionment with American democracy I am looking ahead to that appalling picture of the American mind and heart he has given us in **The Confidence Man**. . . . Melville was not a political writer in the sense that Cooper was, but the profound disillusionment that fills his later books strikes one as being, partly at least, political in character. The rift in American experience, which Cooper, Hawthorne, and James dealt with pragmatically, was approached more directly by Melville, who, undercutting these proximate tensions, struck at the metaphysical heart of the dilemma. Yet, paradoxically, what finally confronted him was not a polarity between good and evil, corresponding to the polarity of the others' tensions, but a tragic confusion in which good and evil were indistinguishable. . . . [The] very texture of the American universe revealed the way it had been betrayed by God. Democracy existed only in ruthless competition, and God, who alone might have redeemed it, was unequal to the task: that, if anything, seems to be the meaning of the final chapter of **The Confidence Man**.

But before that stage had been reached, Melville made a tremendous effort, in **Moby Dick,** to introduce order into his moral universe, and to establish a polarity between good and evil without which he could not give form either to his experience or to his art. In terms of this one book he succeeded magnificently; but in **Pierre** and **The Confidence Man** the distinction he had made in his great masterpiece could not be sustained, and a pursuit of the knowledge of good and evil was replaced by a suffocating sense of the ambiguity which he formally and cynically seemed to formulate and preach as the ultimate knowable moral truth. In other words, moral action (which is to say, *human* action) became an impossibility. With no metaphysical poles of good and evil, and no dialectical pattern on the pragmatic levels of life to guide them, Melville's heroes became incapable of development or progression. They became the passive victims of their situation in life, trapped in the endless unfolding of moral ambiguities whose total significance was to drain all possible meaning from life. (pp. 190-91)

Moby Dick is . . . Melville's great attempt to create order in a universe in which a break-down of the polarity between good and evil is threatened. This threat comes from Ahab, whose hatred of creation is the symptom, or perhaps the consequence, of that democratic disillusionment with the universe— . . . that resentment of the spirit's betrayal of matter, and of God's betrayal of the world. In so far as Melville's own thought is to be equated with any particular person's, it is with Ishmael's. Ishmael represents Melville's resistance against the temptation to follow Ahab which was so powerful for him; he represents Melville's hold on the world of reality and of nature. But as Melville plunged almost immediately into the writing of *Pierre* when he had finished *Moby Dick,* the sanity and grace that had shaped the earlier of the two books was to vanish for good. (pp. 210-11)

[*Moby Dick*] represents a high point of form in the American novel. The structural tensions that Cooper, Hawthorne, and James employed were elevated here to a metaphysical level, and the struggle between good and evil not only became the form of the action, but the very terms themselves were newly carved out of the ambiguous element of the American experience by the creative fiat of the artist. . . . [However Melville] proved incapable of sustaining the elaborately achieved form of *Moby Dick* in his later work. (p. 211)

[It] was through their sense of the European experience that Cooper, Hawthorne, and James avoided that provincial formlessness that overtook Melville after *Moby Dick.* In *Pierre* Melville wrote:

> Deep, Deep, and still deep and deeper must we go, if we would find out the heart of a man; descending into which is as descending a spiral stair in a shaft, without any end, and where the endlessness is only concealed by the spiralness of the stair and the blackness of the shaft.

It is usual to speak of this as illustrating Melville's interest in the unconscious. Perhaps it does; but the image itself suggests even more powerfully Melville's retreat from the real world. The task that he proposes here with so much earnestness is both vague and infinite in Santayana's sense, and pursued to the end which the image itself proposes—or, to be more accurate, pursued through its endlessness and indetermination— would terminate in a negation of consciousness itself, an attempt to stretch a measurable meaning to infinity, and to escape the limits of the rational and the real. But one can escape from them only into nothingness. (p. 216)

Melville lost touch with [the] polarity he had created in *Moby Dick* the possibility of a moral action began to recede from him, and as a consequence, an element of formlessness entered his novels. If there is motion at all, it is circular and descending, and as the terminus of departure is a world of shifting and ambiguous forms about which there is little certainty for Pierre, so the terminus of arrival is lost sight of 'among the empty eternities'.

In its own way *The Confidence Man* continues the same process of negation that we have glanced at in *Pierre,* but focused so emphatically against an American democratic background that it reveals for us, as nothing had before, how profoundly American were the roots of Melville's despair. . . . It is less a criticism than a denial of life, and Melville succeeds, with a skill he had never exhibited in *Pierre,* in lifting the lid of the sarcophagus that rests in the central room—to reveal that no body is there. The one certain fact about the confidence man is that he does not exist. He is appearance drained of all reality. Lift any one of the masks that pass in succession before one; one encounters only vacancy. . . . The book as a whole is a practical commentary on Melville's exploration of the Amer-

ican heart, 'descending into which is as descending a spiral stair in a shaft, without any end, and where the endlessness is only concealed by the spiralness of the stair and the blackness of the shaft'. As such a descent, in Melville's view, has no end, the final sentence of the book, which has puzzled so many critics, was inevitable: 'Something further may follow of this Masquerade.' (pp. 217-18)

Despite its repetitive monotony, which was inevitable when we consider the endless circling theme of *The Confidence Man,* the novel is executed with a good deal of incisive energy, and in its peculiar way it is tightly and effectively organized. And its meaning is realized in its form. But it is the form of death, and not the form of life. (p. 219)

Marius Bewley, "Melville," in his The Eccentric Design: Form in the Classic American Novel (reprinted by permission of the publisher), Columbia University Press, 1959, (and reprinted by Columbia University Press, 1963, pp. 187-219).

J. B. PRIESTLEY (essay date 1960)

[Melville] is a morbid, ambiguous, unfinished character; one half of him a belated Elizabethan genius, the other half an untalented, cranky, pseudo-philosophic, mock-profound type, familiar enough in or near New York throughout this age. Though we include him here among the novelists, simply because he is generally accepted as one, he is not really a novelist. Not even his sea stories, including the posthumous, powerful but overpraised *Billy Budd,* are those of a novelist; *Typee* and *Omoo* are romanticised travel books; *Mardi,* though some of its writing has a new power, is an unsuccessful attempt to turn the travelogue into philosophical fiction; *The Confidence Man* is a good idea bungled through inadequate technique; and *Pierre,* though it anticipates some of our newest fiction by rebellious inverts, reads as if a Jacobean tragedian, a [John] Ford or a [Cyril] Tourneur, had tried to collaborate with the young editor of a mid-nineteenth-century college magazine. What remains, like a whale among halibut and turbot, is *Moby Dick.* And where *Moby Dick* is weak, it is worse than the average goodish novel. We do not always know who is telling the story; there is too much information, breaking the narrative, about whales and whaling (probably because Melville originally intended it to be a semi-documentary book); the best characters are not kept steadily in our sight; there is too much eloquence for its own sake, too many salutations "to the possibilities of the immense Remote, the Wild, the Watery, the Unshored". But where it is strong, it is better than a good novel. It moves into another dimension. It takes on the quality of dramatic and epic poetry. (p. 237)

In spite of Hawthorne's influence, to which we probably owe Melville's more ambitious redrafting of the book, *Moby Dick* is not allegorical, in Hawthorne's familiar manner, but truly symbolical, which means that a single inner meaning cannot be attributed to it. The whale itself is entirely evil only in the mind of Captain Ahab, the figure on humanity's quarter-deck, the will that drives the ship on its tragic quest, the mind in its complete self-dependence, in its ruthless opposition to the whale as a force of Nature, in its appalling *hubris.* The whale is neither good nor evil. It is the mighty Other or Opposite, what we leave when we split totality and claim half as our own before demanding the whole again, Nature as against Man, the unconscious as against consciousness, the feminine as against the masculine principle; and the more we separate ourselves from it, challenge it, hunt it and hope to destroy it, the more powerful, menacing, and finally destructive it becomes. In the rich but unbalanced and neurotic nature of Melville, like the age to which he belongs, there is no reconciling element, no principle of integration; he cannot help seeing life in terms of the opposites, of a Manichean conflict; and his tragic story of Captain Ahab and the *Pequod* and the White Whale (all colours except black are contained in white), with its epic grandeur and flashing poetry of phrase, is his deepest and truest account of himself and his time. (p. 238)

> *J. B. Priestley, "Mostly before 1914," in his* Literature and Western Man *(copyright © 1960 by J. B. Priestley; reprinted by permission of the author), Harper & Row, Publishers, Inc., 1960, pp. 236-69.**

JOYCE CAROL OATES (essay date 1962)

Like Shakespeare, Melville is obsessed with the fragmentary and deceiving nature of "reality"; unlike Shakespeare, he is obsessed as well with the relationship of man to God. Melville's God can take any shape, being magically and evilly empowered—He is a primitive God, related to or actually contained in a beast; He is an intellectual God, existing only in the imagination of man; He is a God of all that is antihuman, perhaps the Devil himself. Melville felt most passionately about the role of the artist, that highest type of man—here is the statement he makes after having read Hawthorne:

> There is the grand truth about Nathaniel Hawthorne. He says No! in thunder; but the Devil himself cannot make him say *yes*.
>
> (pp. 61-2)

[The] naysaying Melville seems impossible to reconcile with the general tone of his last work, *Billy Budd*—that strange, exhausted, flawed tragedy, a work of fiction only partway imagined, in which Melville's powerful rhetoric tries vainly to do the work of his imagination. The problem of *Billy Budd*—its role as a "testament of acceptance" or a pure, dispassionate rejection of the accidental or humanly manipulated injustice of life—is a critical problem that, on the level of an assumed antithesis in its conception, will never be solved. . . . But the problem of the place of *Billy Budd* in Melville's work and the more general, and less obvious, problem of Melville's attitude toward art, life, and nature are not insoluble, at least not unapproachable, if the current critical appeal to Melville—usually as the basis upon which to work out more general phases of American literature—is recognized as not consistent in Melville himself, and, in fact, not borne out by his later major writings.

The "No! in thunder" describes well a youthful climate of mind found in such an early work as *White Jacket*. . . . (pp. 62-3)

The "infinite background" of *White Jacket* is the ocean of a romanticism that is, somehow, always pure in spite of its experience with, and frequent obsession with, the forces of "evil." It must not be considered a romanticism that would eclipse a vision of evil such as Melville has already expressed as early as *Typee,* but rather a romanticism that sees past the existential to the essential, beyond the immediate suffering in man to his capacity for new experience, new roles, an invasion into the universe, perhaps even a masculine victory. The tone of *White Jacket,* for all its social protest, is one of an irrepressible optimism: the optimism that grows out of a faith in one's self and in the solidarity of man as a species, without which the "no" one cries against the devil would be meaningless.

The most famous naysayer of American literature, Captain Ahab, inhabit a world of an "infinite background," which is intolerably hidden from him by the masks of physical reality. Yet it is a temptation to him because he wills it to be so; the nightmare of *Moby Dick* (the annihilation of man by an utterly devastating nature) is not without redemption for us because we are made to understand continually that the quest, whether literal or metaphysical, need not be taken. Man chooses this struggle. The doom that overturns upon the human constituents of the drama is a doom that they, as willful human beings, insist upon: for Ahab does insist upon his doom. (pp. 63-4)

Ahab's monomania does not exclude a recognition of his confusing role in the drama—is he Ahab, or is "Ahab" someone else? What is his identity? Does he exist as an autonomous being or is he merely the acting-out of a decree of another will? His consciousness of his own futility, at times, suggests that he is a tragic hero of a new type—one who knowingly and willingly chooses his "fate," however mistaken this may seem to others. He is a romantic hero, in relation to the white whale as Milton's Satan is to God, an alternately raging, alternating despairing rebel against the supreme order. The human victim within such a tautology is a victim who demands disaster; we feel that if the personified universe did not destroy him he would have to destroy himself. (p. 65)

Pierre is the tale of a quest on land that, like Ahab's on sea, is to lead to a confrontation of "truth" and a definition of the self measured by this truth—ideally; it should lead to a victory and a rejection of the conventional world of social and physical and psychological arrangements. The movement in the novel is away from the appearance of things to the penetration of a supposed reality; it is a concern for the definition of this reality, a qualification of truth by endless ambiguities in the self as well as in the world. Thus the novel seems a psychological fantasy, where the will of the hero creates events in the way in which an author creates. . . . So far as Pierre's rejection of appearance is sincere, and even so far as his gradual awareness of the ambiguity within his own heart is considered in terms of a real dichotomy between good and evil, Pierre belongs to the sphere of the pre-Adamic figure turned Adamic and fallen, in turn changed to the Faustian figure somewhat akin to Ahab—that is, a man involved in a real struggle with appearance and reality, good and evil, God and Satan. (pp. 66-7)

From the ambiguity of his small cloistered world to the ambiguity of the outer world and, finally, to the ambiguity of his own "pure" and unquestioned motives, Pierre is led to the discovery of a world of lies. It is not only a world that tells lies but a world that has been committed—created—in lies. The questioning of Pierre's own motives in protecting Isabel provides one of the most interesting of the novel's ambiguities, for even the motif of incest will not serve as an adequate explanation of sorts for the conflict of the novel. While it can be assumed that the gradual awareness of an incestous desire for his "sister" comes to Pierre to typify both the ambiguity of the world and his own corrupted purity, the incest-motif might not be the concern or fear of the protagonist at all, but rather its opposite: he is really afraid of a healthy and normal love relationship. (p. 68)

The climate of a swollen, pretentious rhetoric at the beginning of the novel gives way—as nature gives way abruptly to the city—to the statement of nihilism that Pierre offers, partly to rationalize his passion for Isabel, partly as a judgment upon life. He says of Virtue and Vice: "a nothing is the substance, it casts one shadow one way, and another the other way; and these two shadows cast from one nothing; these, seems to me, are Virtue and Vice." . . . Considered in the light of the latter part of the novel, the much-criticized rhetoric of the beginning is justified; it is the "nothing," the sickly, sweet, distorted pastoralism of nature and of human relationships that are to be investigated and found hollow. (p. 69)

[*Pierre*] marks the beginning of the apparent Timonism of *The Confidence-Man,* which is a continuation of the theme of *Pierre;* and it marks also, though the relationships may appear puzzling, the beginning of that climate of mind that can give us, without incongruity, the work *Billy Budd.* (p. 71)

The Confidence-Man is centrally flawed in that its "comedy of action" dissolves backward into a comedy of speculation, to reverse Melville's stated intention. So the work, concerned with philosophical problems, does not always translate itself into art but remains conversation, vaguely dialectical, at its worst accumulative and concentric.

It will help to think of *The Confidence-Man* as a series of tales of a perhaps feigned Manichean dualism, about which the confidence-man dreams a long and complicated dream. The atmosphere of the dream, so much more strident than in *Pierre,* allows the confidence-man a certain omnipotence—the power of assuming and rejecting identity, or the various forms of his central identity; he is, then, in the unique position of an author. If the tales constitute a dream, at their core we find the atmosphere of a fallen world and the peculiar desire on the part of the protagonist to posit faith and test it, perhaps a secret desire for this faith to triumph. . . . When the confidence-man is defeated, Christianity itself is defeated, for it is no longer innocent. The loss of the confidence-man is a token of the hypocrisy of Christianity itself—like the life preserver examined in the concluding pages of the novel, it "looks so perfect—sounds so hollow." The confidence-man is the hero of this world, and the measure of his odd heroism is not his own confidence or cunning but rather the vulnerability of the world that he can easily seduce. (pp. 71-2)

The confidence-man cannot be understood except as the embodiment of an idea. He posits himself as the diabolical agent seeking to lure and betray an unsuspecting "good," and while it is certainly going too far to suggest that the confidence-man really represents Christian value in discord with a secular world, it is assuming too much to see him as an agent of the Devil—or the devil himself—as if this were the extent of the problem Melville sees. . . . Melville surely had some aspects of Milton's Satan in mind, however, in creating his confidence-man: he is equated with the Devil "gulling Eve"; he is associated with snake imagery—he "writhes"; he exercises a hypnotic fascination upon his victims and, in an ironic reversal, he is suggested as the creature who charms man (as opposed to the usual snake-charming human being). But Milton's Satan recognizes a belief—however despised—in the Christian myth that the confidence-man would not be prepared to make. Satan is doomed to defeat within a vast hierarchical tautology, while the confidence-man's problem is more complicated, more resourceful, than the usual struggle between good and evil, between God and the Devil with the earth as the stage; at bottom it is a concern obsessed with the sheer burden of defining this struggle. (pp. 74-5)

The education of the confidence-man progresses in proportion to the degree of complexity and cynicism expressed by the people he meets—though, since the novel does have the persistent atmosphere of a dream, one feels that the confidence-

man already possesses whatever knowledge is revealed to him. The "cold prism" of the transcendental intellect is more than a match for the confidence-man's charm. . . . He is educated not to the truth of transcendentalism, or to its finer ethics, but rather to the essential cruelty and inhumanity, even the triteness, of the transcendental ethic when it has been enticed down to the level of the particular.

There is a fault in assuming that, given two apparently antithetical points of view, one must necessarily be right and the other wrong. Melville's intention is to display of hollowness, the inadequacy, of both points of view: the truth that will not be comforted, the "no trust" world, the grave beneath the flowers, the transcendental ethic, the discomforting reality that underlies appearance—and, against this, the world of professed Christianity, the faith in charity, in confidence. The confidence-man's defeat at the hands of the transcendentalist disciple is a token of the ultimate defeat of the surface confidence of the heart by the irrefragable reality that underlies it—the grave beneath. (pp. 77-8)

After his symbolic defeat by the transcendentalist, the confidence-man begins to move away from us. . . . We have at the end not only a confidence-man who does not believe in confidence, but a Christian who does not believe in Christianity—who is, therefore, not a Christian. . . . The final movement is a movement into darkness: it is not the triumph of evil over good but rather the negation of struggle, the disintegration into an underlying nihilism that has resulted, within the novel, from the long series of negations that constitute the confidence-man's experience. . . . It is important to see, though the observation may appear odd, that for the force of evil as well as the force of good the struggle must be sustained, the disintegration into nihilism must be resisted. On the more immediate level, without confidence in man, in society, one falls into despair; and the condition of man is a shuttling movement between the illusory contentment of charity and the confrontation of the truth that will not be comforted—that is, despair. (pp. 79-80)

In *Billy Budd,* the quest theme of Melville has run its course. We have no Adamic-turned-Faustian hero, a superman of sorts like Ahab, Pierre, and the confidence-man; we have instead individuals like Billy and Vere and Claggart, one-dimensional, almost passive role-takers in a triangle of archetypal scope.

The problem of *Billy Budd,* then, stems from the disintegration of the quest and from the acceptance of death as not evil—which leads romantically to the sailor's apotheosis in the folklore of his time, and classically to the acceptance of social necessity, of forms and order. But the intent of the work may well transcend this compatible dichotomy to suggest an acceptance of impending death, of annihilation, in somewhat Nirvanic terms, for the work is "angry," or represents part of a "quarrel" only if death is taken, as it conventionally is, to be at least painful and frightening. The terror of the white whale, infinity pressing back upon its perceiver (or creator), becomes here the transcendental dissolving of considerations of good and evil, of struggle, of life itself. (p. 81)

The experience of Vere is in broad terms that of the father who manipulates the figure of innocence into the transcendent Nirvana of nonexperience and nonidentity that he himself will earn, after a time, but that he has reached only after this experience—which invariably wounds—in the painful world of appearances, of good and evil, of constant struggle, and, most perniciously, of unnatural, repressed lusts. For a writer whose aim is to penetrate into a "basic truth," the sustainment of any two points of view will suggest, in the end, the mockery of assigning to one of two antithetical views a positiveness worthy of one's faith—worthy of one's life. The quest ends, ideally, in the negation and not in the compromise or resolution of tension in Melville's irreconcilable world of opposites; it is at once a transcendence and an annihilation, no longer an image of romantic diffusion as in *White Jacket,* surely not an image of the vicious and self-consuming pessimism of *Pierre*. (p. 82)

Nineteenth-century in his conception of the forms of fiction and of "characterization," Melville is strikingly contemporary in his conception of the internal tensions that comprise a work. In a sense he is not a writer of "fiction" at all, but a writer of ideas who is using the means of fiction; let us speculate that he used fiction because of its essential ambiguity, its "muteness," and because of the possibility of his hiding behind its disguises. Just as he dares to do no more than hint at the homosexual perversion of sailors in *White Jacket* and *Billy Budd,* so, in mid-nineteenth-century America he can do no more than hint at the blankness behind the age-old negotiable forms of virtue and vice, good and evil, God and the Devil. (p. 83)

> Joyce Carol Oates, "Melville and the Tragedy of Nihilism" (originally published in Texas Studies in Literature and Language, *Spring, Vol. IV, No. 1, 1962), in her* The Edge of Impossibility: Tragic Forms in Literature *(copyright © 1972 by Joyce Carol Oates; reprinted by permission of the publisher, Vanguard Press, Inc.), Vanguard Press, 1972, pp. 59-83.*

WARNER BERTHOFF (essay date 1962)

Of all Melville's work it was *Moby-Dick* which, in its magnitude and boldness of design, laid the heaviest tribute upon his descriptive powers, and most strenuously tested his ambition to seek out the deeper logic of fact and appearance. It is of course his masterpiece. And one great factor in his accomplishment in *Moby-Dick* is the grandeur and animation of the settings, which in turn do not merely illustrate the book's action and themes but actively create them. The larger part of the narrative is simply the patiently detailed yet consistently high-spirited setting out of a scene sufficiently vast and prodigious to contain the central drama and justify its intensity. Melville's job is to create for us the huge "world" he means dramatically to exploit. . . . The narrative, in the large, is nothing less than a confession *à fond* of the several "worlds" human existence marvelously moves through—and in this multiform context Ahab himself is in some danger of becoming only an incidental marvel, one among many, and a rather mechanical one at that. At a certain date in our acquaintance with the book *Moby-Dick* we are no longer in doubt about the outcome; nor can we still be entirely surprised or astounded by the more highly wrought individual passages, of meditation, description, comedy, bravura declamation, analogy-running, or whatever, though we continue to be charmed by them. What does still lay claim on us then, and perhaps more powerfully than ever, is the imaginative coherence and embrace of the whole. The correspondences, the insistent illusion of a universe brimful of consenting and conspiring phenomena ceaselessly interacting, prove to be not forced but in the nature of the revealed materials. (pp. 78-9)

[By] "setting" I mean something more than the environment or material occasion within which the drama is played out. I mean rather that whole context, as the narrative establishes it, out of which the action rises—a context of idea and feeling as well as of observation and description; I mean all that in the convenient language of recent criticism may be called the "world" of behavior peculiar to an author's vision of existence. In *Moby-Dick* four distinct "worlds" may be defined, and all are fundamental to the import of the novel as Melville built it up.

(1) With the narrative beginning ashore and staying ashore for twenty-odd chapters, the first "world" put before us is that of the dry land, or at least the thronged edges of it: New York, New Bedford, Nantucket, and the streets, chapels, inns, and offices to be met on the way to the sea. . . . It is, successively, a dream-tormented world of unsatisfied yearnings, a "stepmother" world, a "wolfish" world, a world which "pays dividends" to sharp practice, a finished and unameliorable world of frost, death, teeth-chattering, and the sorrows of the orphaned, and of poverty and hard bargaining; a world finally (as even in the intensifying rush of the book's closing movement the figures of the carpenter and blacksmith do not let us forget) which is continually casting away the human wrecks and derelicts it has stripped and ruined.

(2) It is, in short, the world of men, whose "permanent constitutional condition," we are told, is "sordidness." The next broad context which the narrative begins to build up is also a world of men, but here Melville develops a different emphasis. For this is the self-sufficient world of the quaint, rare, old, noble, trophy-garnished, battle-worn, cannibalistic, melancholy *Pequod*. . . . (pp. 79-80)

[The] ship is shown to be a virtual city of the races and talents of men. From the first we are encouraged to think of her as a paradigm of the marvelous hive of corporate human life (though Melville does not impose that symbolism on the whole novel)— she is at once a parliament, guildhall, factory, and fortress, and goes "ballasted with utilities" like the world-renewing Ark itself. . . . [The] long succession of passages describing the crew at its jobs makes up a "song for occupations" as comprehensive and ecstatic as Whitman's. Conversely we find Melville turning back to the general routine of common earthly labor for descriptive metaphors, invoking the whole range of its trades, tools, and artifacts in aid of his exposition. Such effects, we must agree, are wonderfully natural in *Moby-Dick*. For merely to describe one feature of the whale's anatomy or of the practical business of stripping it down is to give an impression of surveying no small part of the fantastic material apparatus by which ordinary civilized life if maintained. (p. 81)

(3) The men of the *Pequod* and their exploits are the practical measure also of the next "world" we can discern in *Moby-Dick,* the non-human world of the sea and the indifferent elements. (p. 84)

[The] great expanse of the sea . . . dwarfs the most extravagant human pretensions; "two thirds of the fair world it yet covers." Its vastness corresponds ambiguously to the grandeur of Ahab's design—corresponds ironically, of course, insofar as it is literally immeasurable, and wholly indifferent to the character and purposes of men. Its very mildness is tormenting; the haunting descriptions of its moments of sun-burnished serenity, prairie-meadow loveliness, or moonlit quietness are invariably shaded by undertones of another sort, so that the stillness is "preternatural," the beauties are "appalling" and "unearthly," "all space" is felt to be "vacating itself of life," and the mild billows support only such a "formless, chance-like apparition of life" as the giant squid. Prolonged exposure to these weird, uncivil spheres of being, in "exile from Christendom and civilization," reduces men (rather, "restores" them, Melville pointedly writes) to a condition of "savagery." And Ishmael apart, the virtues-in-trade of the men of the *Pequod* are chiefly savage virtues. Their splendor is a primitive splendor that suits their character as great warriors, hunters, migratory navigators, efficient agents all of the hive-disciplined assault on nature. . . . (pp. 85-6)

(4) In the nature of their trade's incessant conflict with the non-human elements, the whalemen are also described as peculiarly subject to superstition and legend-making; the book comes naturally by its solid foothold in folklore. . . . And it is particularly through Ishmael's thoughtful and excited narrative witness that the free passage of our attention is secured into the final, furthest "world" set out in *Moby-Dick*—the world of "inscrutable" things, unknown depths, unanswerable questions, "ungraspable phantoms," "pyramidical silences," hieroglyphic riddles, "celestial thoughts" which are "to reason absurd and frantic," "bodiless" agents, "sourceless primogenitures" and fatherless specters; a world that communicates to men only in signs, portents, and equivocal omens, and seems intelligible only to madmen like Ahab or Pip, yet is felt at times to control human destinies to the last detail. (p. 86)

In *Moby-Dick* [these] various "worlds" which compose the book's setting (and so much of its substance) are not made to cohere philosophically, or allegorically. They need every lodgment in common fact that Melville can manage to give them. They satisfy us as they satisfy our sense of reality. Yet in the descriptive mass of the narrative, subtlety does appeal to subtlety, and Melville, as he builds up and inquires into the contexts that activate his impressive story, and in the process enlarges that very sense of reality, magnificently justifies the challenge he throws out to his reader: that "without imagination no man can follow another into these halls." (p. 89)

Critics of prose fiction who are concerned with the element of characterization are not likely to offer Melville's narratives as typical evidence. The "novel of character" (if such a thing exists) is not the kind of undertaking we think of him as engaged in. . . . Yet how roundly, in his best work, Melville's characters occupy the space allotted them; and how easily our imagination opens out to them, how securely they stay in mind. . . . Very much the same imaginative freedom and extravagance that we [observe] . . . in Melville's settings, and the same truth-abiding search after some vital measure of the common order of earthly existence, direct his rendering of character. . . . (pp. 90-1)

What is perhaps most revealing about Melville's presentation of his characters is his curiosity about them. Why *are* they what they palpably are? . . . What circumstance and breeding lie back of them? Through what conditioning have their present features emerged? And what now might they do? What characteristic event is still reserved for them?

For it is not, strictly speaking, in the moral types they exemplify that Melville's characters have their vitality—though most Melville criticism would have us think so—but in the openmindedness, the unremitting inquisitive fascination, of his absorption with them. He is not, at his most effective, a moral fabulist or allegorist but a recorder of life-histories. What his imagination responds to most quickeningly are certain kinds of men ("some men") in whom the conditions of the life of the world ("this world") materialize with beautiful or terrible directness. (pp. 91-2)

Several of his characters, particularly in the early books and in those narrative passages that come nearest allegory, do simply embody some abstract moral concept or category of being. But these characters are usually the least satisfactory in themselves; we only tolerate them for the sake of the story, the elsewhere-secured alignment of forces—Fedallah is a fair example. When the character too perfectly represents something foreknown, or something independent of his participation in it, we not only find it hard to believe in him and his behavior, but we may also find it hard to be seriously interested in the idea he is supposed to enforce. (p. 93)

What is at the heart of Melville's treatment of his characters . . . is not a philosophy of fate, chance, and free will in the actions of men (though he maneuvers such terms with great freedom and power) but a moral apprehension of the lifelong course of existence natural to the human individual; and it is precisely from the response of the individual actor to the materializing fatality of this course—through his awareness of it as a person, and therefore through his free struggle as a person with the necessities of his history as a creature—that the distinctive Melvillean drama opens out.

Neither the bare assertion of free individuality nor the bare denial of it satisfied Melville's practical sense of the form of men's lives. Their accumulating hostage, his longer narratives demonstrate, is not to any single accident or scheme of fate but to the common sequences of time and change, which are, first, accidental, and, second, irreversible. It is in just this understanding of the common pathos of the careers of men that Melville's characterizations are richest. What each man shares with his kind, in Melville's narrative view, is the plastic capacity to be acted upon and to act in response, a capacity for variation and change within his own life-cycle and the frame of his mortality. (pp. 96-7)

The two attempts at full-scale dramatic characterization in Melville's work are Ahab and Pierre. It may seem unnecessary to remark that the first is on the whole the more effective. Yet if anything comes near to spoiling *Moby-Dick* it is the presentation of Ahab as a personal agent in the drama; and if anything comes near to saving *Pierre* it is the presentation of the unfolding inward nature, capable of passional action and change, of its otherwise preposterous hero (who is hardly more preposterous, however, than the type of the free-born young male, on the edge of manhood, in actual life). The characterization of Ahab can succeed because *Moby-Dick* as a whole does not depend on it. Its strength is borrowed from the strength of the whole recital of which it is a part (including the brazenly suspenseful plot of the hunt after a fabulous creature). Its chief artistic virtue is its consistency with what is elsewhere revealed, defined, and rehearsed in this extraordinary book. The characterization of the young Pierre, on the other hand, is in certain ways a more thoughtful and potentially a more interesting undertaking; but there is little else in the book capable of supporting it, or of bringing the crude formal conventions it is encased by back into living reality. (pp. 108-09)

Mad from the beginning, Ahab makes a strange and awesome figure but not, in the main, one arousing tragic pity and fear. The sublimity of his posture and the astonishing energy of his "monomania" are skillfully indicated. . . . The role Ahab is given to play is in earnest of Melville's drive and ambition in the book. But the characterization itself is static in conception, and contrived and mechanical in the actual working out. Ahab acts most of the time in a trance of calculating madness; or, to put it in another way, he stays monotonously within the mold established for him. . . . Yet there are moments of genuine poignancy in the presentation of Ahab that enrich the whole book, most notably the touching interlude of Chapter 132, ''The Symphony,'' in which for once he steps briefly out of his appointed role and questions it, in Starbuck's presence, from his ''own proper, natural heart.'' (pp. 110-11)

With Ahab Melville projected, and brought off, a great effect; with the hero of *Pierre* he aimed at nothing less than the ''sacred truth.'' The imaginative strength of this disordered book is in its oddly angled but deeply measured insight into the common pathos of human becoming; and as it pursues this excellent subject, as it tries to define the developing action of the human soul's natural history, I think it moves rather closer to the specific dimension of tragedy than does *Moby-Dick*. It falls very short, of course—but only by a technical incompetence so extraordinary as to be of no real technical interest. The characterization of Pierre is subordinated (as it should be) to the shifting display of passion and motive within him, a display that registers more impressively than would seem possible, given the preposterousness of the story. Where this characterization is most effective, it is as largely explanatory and descriptive, rather than dramatic, as that of Ahab. And it is even more impersonal. (p. 111)

[It] is when Melville's concern is not with the substance of Pierre's thought but with the mysterious process of his arriving at it and being acted upon by it that the writing most successfully rescues itself from bombast and from emblem-mongering. At such moments the narrative is likely to back off from the plot, and view altogether impersonally, and analytically, its announced subject, that ''maturer and larger interior development'' promised in Pierre. (p. 113)

Melville is most likely to write well in *Pierre* when he is most analytic. . . . There is little use in trying to imagine how the book as a whole might have been salvaged. It is enough to say that the protracted characterization *Pierre* is mainly built upon is, potentially, as compatible with the illimitable art of prose fiction as are the analytic meditations of a Proust. . . . Both Melville and Proust were concerned to anatomize the behavior of individual human persons in the light of certain profounder necessities of human nature; and both grounded their inquiries in more or less systematic conceptions of what, morally, their findings must finally amount to. Of course this method of characterization will be most successful when the analysis and exposition are firmly in the service of some serious and absorbing *story,* such as in their major work both these writers did have to tell. (p. 114)

Melville's work stands, in the main, well apart from what were becoming the major conventions of the nineteenth-century novel, and his use of first-person narration is a leading aspect of its irregularity. The types of fiction he most often chose to start from where not the dramatic or the ''well-made'' novel, nor the novel of character or of manners, nor even the ''romance,'' but the personal adventure-chronicle, the recital, the confession, in all of which the interposing of a narrator's voice tends to become the chief formal precipitant of interest and of significance. (p. 115)

The Melvillean narrator acts and is acted upon, being a character in his own recital. (Indeed in the five books before *Moby-Dick* there are scarcely any other developed characters; there are only sketches, types, more or less distinctive examples of the conditions of life being described.) But more especially he *tells*—recalls, considers, meditates, emphasizes, explains. He acts, that is, primarily in his formal role, coming to life through his own narrative voice. A certain degree of absorbed passivity

and reflective detachment marks off the Melvillean narrator from the Romantic hero of passion and energy or from the type of the quester after experience. His character, as recording witness, is to remain radically open to experience without being radically changed by it; he is to identify and judge matters wihout equivocation, yet not show himself too overridingly anxious to impose his outlook upon them. . . . Thus, the role given the narrator in Melville's chronicles is determined, we may say, not only by the situation and actions being rendered but by the very job of rendering them. Certainly Melville used his narrators to convey his own thought and feeling; what should be emphasized is that he was at the same time subjecting his reckless personal bent toward declamatory self-expression to the formal discipline of a naturally suitable working method. (pp. 120-21)

Melville had an impressive flair, as a writer, for direct, unmediated assertion, but when he attempted to make it the whole basis and instrument of his exposition, as in *Pierre,* it could go outrageously to waste. In *Moby-Dick,* on the other hand, the plain procedures of narrative recollection, the tangible gathering up of past events into the present sequences of a recital, are the means, practically, of his success; through them the most prodigious and terrific phenomena are subdued to the masterable logic of human time and human understanding. All other characters in the book exist only within the action of the story, and are wholly subject, as we see them, to its course of happenings. The narrator, however, exists to tell the whole story out, and therefore moves above it and around it, as well as through it, in relative freedom. The result is that the leading gestures of the work as a whole, and the pattern of experience displayed in it, are never quite the same as what its staged events add up to—or would add up to if presented dramatically only. At least a double focus is established; we see things as they are in the immediate passion of human effort, but also as they appear to detached observation in the mere succession of their occurrence. (p. 122)

The authority his name and work still have for us testifies, of course, to the gravity of his themes and the amplitude of his address to them, yet the virtue that finally holds us to [Melville] as a writer is specifically a literary virtue. It is an exertion of mastery over certain elected forms of prose narration. So the leading question for criticism is not, what did Melville think, or, what system of understanding can be assembled from his successive books (matters, after all, of plain record; we need only to read him carefully), but rather, what is the nature of the example he presents of the work of imaginative creation, and of that process of free conversion by which thought, feeling, observation, fact, judgment, vision, are fixed into the abiding forms of his art.

More simply: within the chosen directions of his work, what virtue shows itself and works itself out? With Melville, it is [his] exceptional persistence and tenacity in imaginative definition that seems to me the distinguishing thing. (pp. 205-06)

[The] decisive immediate virtue in Melville's prose is the insistent thrust forward it develops toward an entire explicitness, an unstinting exactness. This virtue, as we find it, is not limited to special operations like encyclopedic description or the analysis of character. Rather it is generic and constitutional. It marks his simplest rendering of physical objects and actions; it equally animates the moral and psychological probings of his most strenuously ambitious work. After a thirty-year interval it is as strong as ever in *Billy Budd,* though much else has gone by the board. Scarcely a sentence in Melville's best writing is not stamped with its urgency: an odd adjective; a defining participle; an unexpected sequence of verbs; circuitous and often distracting parentheses; imputations from all points of the compass as to cause and origin, category and probability, special feature and general law—all aimed at discovering the precise and entire mode of existence of the matter at hand. Without this virtue the ingratiating mannerisms of Melville's ordinary style would largely have gone to waste (though it is also a cause of tendiousness and overwriting). . . . Like so many of the major Americans he is an explainer, and his narratives are often most satisfactory (contrary to textbook dogmas) when most directly explanatory. His art, not always under control, is in keeping this will-to-explain in the service of his prime narrative objects—their definition, their clarification. And what he was moved to say of them he did find the words for—with a thoroughness and consistency, I think, that are matched by no other of our prose masters except the undistractible Emerson. This seems to me the prime truth about Melville as a writer. (pp. 208-09)

Warner Berthoff, in his The Example of Melville *(copyright © 1962 by Princeton University Press; excerpts reprinted by permission of Princeton University Press), Princeton University Press, 1962, 218 p.*

LESLIE A. FIEDLER   (essay date 1966)

Moby Dick can be read . . . not only as an account of a whale-hunt, but also as a love story, perhaps the greatest love story in our fiction, cast in the peculiar American form of innocent homosexuality. . . .

In *Moby Dick,* the redemptive love of man and man is represented by the tie which binds Ishmael to Queequeg, while the commitment to death is portrayed in the link which joins Ahab to Fedallah; but the two relationships are disturbingly alike: both between males, one white and one colored. Indeed, the very darkness of Queequeg betrays a doubt about the angelic companion, oddly confuses him with the Satanic one. Melville is more conscious than he seems at first glance of the ambiguous nature of the love which he celebrates in *Moby Dick,* and which, beginning with the encounter of Ishmael and Queequeg, grows ever more general and inclusive, but never less suspect, as the story unfolds. (p. 370)

It will not do to sentimentalize or Christianize Melville's pagan concept of love. It is not *caritas* which he celebrates; and his symbol for the redeeming passion is Priapus rather than the cross. Perhaps it is least misleading to think of the love which redeems Ishmael as Platonic, in the authentic historical sense of the word. Rising from the particular object to the universal, it remains suspect nonetheless. . . . Genteel or orthodox advocates of love should look hard at Melville's text before deciding to applaud the conquest of death he celebrates in *Moby Dick.* Yet it is love in the fullest sense which that book makes its center; not a brutal or casual relationship, but one which develops on the pattern of a marriage: achieving in the course of a single voyage the shape of a whole lifetime shared, and symbolizing a spiritual education. (p. 372)

When Ahab enters the book, however, the theme of love and marriage is pushed into the background, from which it emerges (in the unforeseen posthumous consummation of the relationship between Ishmael and Queequeg) only after Ahab has destroyed himself and the whole shipboard world he has subverted. Ishmael himself has been bent temporarily to Ahab's

will, totally committed to the fulfillment of his monomaniac quest until the moment of his sperm-squeezing conversion; but he can do nothing even at that point, remains still the spectator he has become from the moment of Ahab's ascendancy over him. But as a spectator and Ahab's man, he has no longer any use for Queequeg, who is also converted into an accomplice to the blasphemous hunt.

Corresponding to the gothic mood of *Moby Dick* after the voyage has begun is another relationship between a white man and a colored one, a quite different projection of the commitment of the ego to a life of impulse and instinct. In Ishmael, the heart of Western white civilization reaches out to the uncorrupted sources of natural life; in Ahab, the head of Western man turns to the same sources in search of power and fear. Queequeg's counterpart is Fedallah, the Parsee, who becomes Ahab's harpooner. He and his crew, however, are not signed on to the *Pequod,* but smuggled aboard, bootlegged on a commercial voyage by a madman; and once the ship is at sea, they rise out of the hold like nightmares. (p. 377)

It is not . . . until the first lowering that Fedallah and his tiger-yellow cohorts make a daylight appearance. . . . [Once] the figure of Fedallah "tall and swart . . . with one white tooth evilly protruding from its steellike lips" has hissed "Ready" to Ahab, he and his crew are handled in terms of peculiarly Melvillean melodrama:

> But what it was that inscrutable Ahab said to that tiger-yellow crew of his—these were words best omitted here; for you live under the blessed light of the evangelical land. Only the infidel sharks in the audacious sea may give ear to such words, when, with tornado brow, and eyes of red murder, and foam-glued lips, Ahab leaped after his prey.

The style, overstated, hysterical, a little ridiculous, dismays the modern reader, as do the stock descriptions of Ahab as the gothic hero-villain. Indeed, the whole relationship of Ahab to Fedallah is rendered in precisely so artificial and unconvincing a mode, from their first lowering to Ahab's last sight of the Parsee tangled in the harpoons on Moby Dick's back. . . .

Yet the Parsee stands at the center of the whole machinery of signs and portents and prophecies, which lend the book its characteristically Satanic tone. In him is made manifest the spirit of Ahab's quest, all that impels "the rushing *Pequod,* freighted with savages, and laden with fire, and burning a corpse, and plunging into that blackness of darkness," and makes her "the material counterpart of her monomanic commander's soul." (p. 378)

Without the Parsee to make explicit his damnation, Ahab is merely crazy, *Moby Dick* meaningless. But Melville does not really know how to handle him; for he is not a "character" at all, in the sense that Ishmael is a character—or even Queequeg. He possesses not literal reality but representative truth, and should be understood as a conventional device for portraying inwardness, a projected nightmare. Even Ahab, with his Machiavellian posturing, his rhetoric half out of Byron, half out of the Elizabethans, is almost equally absurd when understood literally. Though in the purely novelistic scenes with Starbuck, he must be taken as a genuine protagonist, with a mind and a past, in his relationship with Fedallah, he has no more mind than Moby Dick; for, like the whale, he is a projection: an emblem of the head itself, cut off from the heart and driven toward its own destruction in its sultanic loneliness. But he is also Faust, as the Parsee is also the Devil, both of them archetypes as well as projections. Certainly, Ahab lives a Faustian life: a ''godlike ungodly old man'' pressing on beyond all limits to penetrate the ultimate mysteries in despite of God himself; and certainly, he dies a Faustian death, howling defiance to the end. . . . (p. 379)

Such a life and such a death Melville can render, however rhetorically, at least without embarrassment; but the compact with the Devil upon which they both depend for their meanings, and for whose sake, indeed, he has invented Fedallah, he cannot bring himself to portray. Only obliquely through the comic comments of Stubb and Flask, do we come to suspect that the bargain which makes Ahab a Faust has already been struck. . . . If the point of such evasions is not a simple failure of nerve, but a desire to undercut ironically the whole Faustian myth, why is Fedallah in the action to begin with, and why do his Macbethian predictions so precisely and tantalizingly come true? What sort of double game is Melville playing with the very myth which lies at the center of his work? The second American Faust, like the first, was written by a man who did not know whether he believed in the Devil, and was embarrassed by the machinery of gothicism, which he was unable to abandon. Yet finally *Moby Dick* triumphs over the shoddiness of its gothic devices, as it triumphs over the naïveté and parochialism of its ''Western'' love story by deeply mythicizing both its components, and thus liberating them from novelistic restrictions and the implicit judgment of realism: by becoming, in short, the most improbable of all epic poems.

In the latter part of *Moby Dick,* even Queequeg is gradually transformed from a character into a myth, though he never quite loses his status as a fully realized protagonist—never seems, like Fedallah, *merely* what he stands for. (pp. 379-80)

Controller of life and death, Queequeg's own existence is in his power; and indeed, he is shown at one point as simply refusing to die, though a fever has brought him almost to his ''endless end.'' Recalling, Ishmael tells us, some uncompleted obligations, the harpooner returns to life, after everyone has given him up, but not before he has made his own coffin from ''some heathenish . . . lumber . . . cut from the original groves of the Lackaday Islands.'' On this coffin, after his recovery, Queequeg spends long hours copying the signs from his body, which not only stand for his identity, but constitute as well ''a mystical treatise on the art of attaining truth.'' For a little while, this wonderously engraved coffin serves as his sea-bag; then, at Queequeg's own hint, it is converted into a life-buoy to replace one that has been lost. (pp. 380-81)

Of all the ship's accoutrements, only the coffin-lifebuoy survives . . . after Moby Dick has rammed the *Pequod*. . . . The coffin-lifebuoy is not, however, the only symbolic analogue for Queequeg the savior in the complex pattern of the book. Wherever the choice is made of a seeming death which is really life, a suicidal plunge which eventuates in a resurrection, the holy marriage with Queequeg is being analogically repeated. Queequeg, who represents Oceania, the watery area of the world, is equated with the sea and with the whale who inhabits its depths. This, of course, to say, with *Ishmael's* sea and *Ishmael's* whale; for Ahab's version of both are quite different, and are associated with the Satanic Fedallah. The descent into either (as opposed to the assault upon either), like the love-union with the dark savage (as opposed to the pact with him), signifies a life-giving immersion in nature or the id, a death and rebirth. That is why such erotic terminology is used to describe both the innards of the whale and the depths of the

sea: the vestibule of the whale called ''the bridal chamber of his mouth''; the bottom of the sea referred to as ''the very pelvis of the world.'' (pp. 381-82)

The romance of Ishmael (even as the tragedy of Ahab) is finally seen against a dream landscape, where time has not yet come into existence; and where the acts of men are motivated not by psychology but by mythic patterns, set thousands of years before America was discovered.

It is with Jonah that Melville identifies Ishamel, the archetypal runaway; but his name further complicates the identification, making him an Ishmael who is a Jonah: an outcast son who is cast into the depths and brought forth again by the God whom he is fleeing. What Ishmael saw in his plunge into the depths we are not directly told; but we assume that his experience must have been like that of Jonah, to whom wisdom came in the belly of the whale. . . .

Ishmael interprets his glimpse into the world of natural immortality, where life is endlessly renewed by physical generation, as a guarantee that there is a renewal of the spirit, too, in human ''dalliance and delight,'' which is all the immortality man can ever achieve. For this natural renewal of the soul, the Holy Marriage of Males, immune to the spiritual death, implicit in freshly marriage with women, is an alternative symbol. (p. 382)

Infinitely rich in significance, the descent into the depths is a theme in the oldest epic literature of our civilization; but it represents only one half of the archetypal adventures of the epic hero, who must not only disappear into the sea and rise again, but must also slay the dragon of the deep. Ishmael is, then, but one part of the split epic hero (and surely his splitting is a sign in itself of the divided state of the psyche in modern life), whose other part is Ahab. In the case of the latter, too, there is a tension established between the primary suggestion of the name Ahab, a wicked king whose blood was licked by dogs, and the secondary mythical association with Perseus and St. George: deliverers both and slayers of monsters. Ahab, however, saves no one, not even himself. He is the hero who is lost, even as Ishmael is the coward who is saved; for in Melville's scheme, the warrior who attacks the ravening beast goes down to death, while the prophet who runs away is preserved alive. Though like Ishmael Ahab seeks the whale ''in the heart of quickest perils,'' he seeks him not to plunge into his jaws and be swallowed up but to attack and destroy him. (pp. 383-84)

But why is Ahab doomed, the once heroic act of Perseus become in him an analogue of the Faustian bargain with the Devil? What does it mean to kill the monster anyway? As rich in significance as the baptismal descent, the battle with the dragon can be interpreted as the victory of light over storm and darkness; an attack of the son against the father; a destruction of whatever is dark, repressive, and authoritarian in the psyche itself; a combat with the Devil or with God or with an inscrutable being who may be either; an assault on the irrational in nature and an attempt to resolve the world's mysteries by liquidating them. For Melville, such an onslaught is suspect in several ways. Not only does he sense a kind of Oedipal guilt in Ahab's frenzy against the ''fiery father,'' in whose despite he seeks to hunt down the whale, but perceives that in him the struggle against the monstrous becomes the struggle against a Calvinist God, whom Ahab confuses with the traditional figure of the Devil!

Is not Moby Dick, after all, identified with Leviathan himself; and is not Leviathan the immortal symbol of the inscrutability of the created world, a mystery not to be resolved until the end of days? Is not that lower inscrutability, moreover, a type of the higher, of the ultimate mystery of the divine? Melville, for whom in *Moby Dick* the precepts of the New Testament are irrelevant, and who put in Christ's place a Polynesian harpoon, could not close his ears to the Old Testament challenge: "Canst thou catch Leviathan with a hook?" And does not the man who tries, does not Ahab become, in his alienation, his sultanism, his pride, blasphemy, and diabolism, finally more monstrous than the beast he hunts? When, on the last day, they confront each other, which is the Monster, Moby Dick in his "gentle joyousness," his "mighty mildness of repose," or Ahab screaming his mad defiance?

In complete contempt of the three-thousand-year-old pattern of myth, Melville permits the dragon-slayer to be slain, the dragon to escape alive; but it is hard to tell whether he really stands the legend on its head, allows evil to survive and heroism to perish. Only Ahab believes that the whale represents evil, and Ahab is both crazy and damned. Yet no child can abide the ending as it stands—in the book which parents and librarians alike expect them to enjoy; and in the comic-book version, revised for their special benefit, Moby Dick goes down with Ahab, whose death becomes merely the heroic price he pays for victory. For simple minds, the salvation of Ishmael is not enough; they cannot project their dreams of glory upon so passive a sufferer: the fugitive from life cast up after a three-day chase, which both represents and parodies the immersion of Jonah as a type of Christ's burial and resurrection.

Ahab lost and Ishmael saved, the destroyer destroyed and the lover preserved by the symbolic body of his beloved: it is not finally quite so obvious and pat. Though Ahab and Ishmael are opposites, they are also one—two halves of a single epic hero; and only in their essential unity is the final unity of the book to be found. What Melville disjoined, in a typically American stratagem of duplicity, the reader must re-unite. In *Moby Dick,* the king-god-culture hero, who kills and is redeemed, is split into an active older brother and a passive younger, different sons of the same terrible father, who move, as it were, through separate works of art: the first through a belated horror tragedy, the latter through a nineteenth-century *Bildungsroman.* Yet though the agent in the first is projected as a finally rejected "he," and the witness in the second as a beloved "I," even structurally their two actions become one. The tragic play is encysted, enclosed in a comic narrative frame, on a model suggested, perhaps, by the Book of Job; though in Job, the chief protagonist is the same in the drama and frame-story. In *Moby Dick,* the protagonist of the frame-story is Ishmael, who becomes the trapped spectator of the drama of Ahab's fall, experiencing the catharsis of which Ahab is incapable. The heart, that is to say, witnessing the mad self-destruction of the head is itself purged and redeemed. (pp. 384-86)

Leslie A. Fiedler, "The Failure of Sentiment and the Evasion of Love," in his Love and Death in the American Novel *(copyright © 1960, 1966 by Leslie A. Fiedler; reprinted with permission of Stein and Day Publishers), revised edition, Stein and Day, 1966, pp. 337-90.**

WILLIAM BYSSHE STEIN (essay date 1970)

A flippant observation by Randall Jarrell, "Melville is a great poet only in the prose of *Moby-Dick,*" helps to place the neglect of the latter's poetic achievement in perspective. Not living up to the lyrical expectations heralded by the language of the novel, it is looked upon as the labored output of an exhausted talent. This opinion is perfectly appropriate if the technical qualities are appraised in accordance with the virtuosity of the great nineteenth-century poets. Then Melville's verse has to be adjudged crude and unpolished. Its hobbled metrics, its stumbling rimes, its contorted language: none of these would make sense to an ear conditioned by the cadences of Shelley, Byron, Keats, Tennyson, Arnold, or even Longfellow (underrated though he is). But since we are concerned with the reaction to Melville's poetry after the revival of his literary reputation in the 1920's, it would seem that his critics have been strangely delinquent. . . . It is common knowledge that Melville chose to write as he did. . . . Very consciously he set out to give embodiment to unmitigated experience, to events and emotions consistent with the nature of existence. Or put another way, he undertook to de-romanticize the idealistic view of human destiny that colors the traditions of English and American poetry during the nineteenth century. Thus he exalted the temporal over the eternal, the empirical over the mystical, the flesh over the spirit. The more he wrote poetry the more he became convinced that the measured euphony of verse belied experiental reality, and as a consequence he finally settled upon ugly discordance and incongruity—in meter, rime, image, symbol, and language—as the indices of truth in the finite world. Thus his poetry has to be judged in terms of his realization of a revolutionary method: no other standard has valid application. (pp. 3-4)

[In] *Battle-Pieces* he first realizes that orthodox poetics cannot be accommodated to his vision of life. Extremely disturbed by the irrational animosities awakened by the Civil War, he sets out to etch a verbal picture of the conflict that will objectively display the impact of the warfare upon individuals from both sides, the military participants and the civilians. While forced by convention to pay tribute to loyalist patriotism, he equally lauds the bravery and fortitude of the contending forces—his gesture of justice and pity for all. But only the latter two sentiments really have meaning for Melville. The former virtues are tainted by the circumstances of the struggle, by the conversion of man into a puppet of his own technological ingenuity, a thing controlled by the things of destruction, from cannons to ironclad ships. Once this aspect of Melville's outlook obtrudes, the historical moment loses its significance, for the horror of war evolves into the horror of human nature in war. . . . (pp. 4-5)

"The Portent," the introductory poem of *Battle-Pieces,* is a parodic masterpiece that foreshadows the subtle techniques of Melville's late creative activity. Actually written in honor of the revolutionist John Brown, it is revolutionary in conception and execution, an exquisitely controlled mechanism of irony which dramatizes the stagnation of Christian love. . . . (p. 7)

More often than not, Melville's experiments in rhythmical atonality do not succeed [in *Battle-Pieces*] probably as a consequence of his own uncertainty about the method. In the longer poems there are frequent lapses in figurative language, an addiction to the commonplace in image and analogy that is tasteless and trite. Such flaws occur mostly when Melville shackles his thought in rigid metrical forms which force compromises in acuity of expression. This is to say that he writes most cogently when he disregards conventional mechanics and allows his thought to find its own mold. Then his perceptions evolve with thorny sharpness, couched in a diction and rhythm pregnant with the immediate realities of the subject, not affected or strained, not wishy-washy or insincere. Nevertheless, given the climate of opinion when he composed *Battle-Pieces,* his performance is quite extraordinary, providing a glimpse of war that can be compared only to Goya's paintings of military carnage. No such candor nor integrity about war had ever before governed the composition of poetry—not excluding Walt Whitman's.

Unlike *Battle-Pieces,* Melville's *Clarel* is essentially a personal creation, a product of psychological necessity. It represents a deliberate attempt to face up to a crippling pessimism about the basic corruption of human nature—an outlook far darker than any articulated by the most fanatical Calvinist. The various personas in the poem think out, feel out, and act out all the problems inherent in this plight, providing him with an arsenal of defense mechanisms. Though nothing is finally resolved, Melville does empty himself of the most virulent emotional and spiritual poisons. . . . [The] poem argues that ideas per se have no permanent validity, especially as applied to human acts. In their impact upon the mind they take the coloring of an individual's complex conditioning, and as a consequence every expression or implementation of a belief assumes the form of an unconscious prejudice. In short, it is impossible to view reality objectively, except to the extent that the laws of nature are immutable. This knowledge shapes the philosophy of Melville's old age, providing him a belated reconciliation with the treacheries of existence.

The riming iambic tetrameter is the norm measure for the six hundred odd pages of *Clarel,* and not even the most beguiling sophistries can justify Melville's stubborn allegiance to this monotonous pattern of verse. Since it is not easily adaptable to the subtleties of metaphysical discouse, Melville is betrayed into countless infelicities of execution: grotesque inversions, tortured ellipses, banal rimes, expedient archaisms, distorted word forms, and limping rhythms. These flaws unite to convey the effect of a bewildering prosiness that defies categorization. Stiff, stuffy, and stultifying, the style is out of key with the subject of the poem. (pp. 9-11)

Melville's late poetry [found in *John Marr and Other Sailors, Timoleon,* and the two manuscript collections, *Weeds and Wildings, with A Rose or Two* and *Marquis de Grandvin*] flowers out of the rich soil of emotional and spiritual contentment. It is written in a mood of quiet exultation. Even though his recurrent subjects are still disaster, death, defeat, suffering, and frustration, they are treated with a resilient irony. The old bugaboo of dualism no longer haunts his mind, and he revels in the exposure of Manichean fancies and fantasies. While he is not at peace with the aspirations of his times, he is at peace with the wisdom of old age. Thus what he has to say, he says with candor, simplicity, and probity. Speaking through innumerable personas—old and young, male and female, ancient and modern, biblical and legendary, historical and mythological—Melville rarely distorts objective truth, even where subjective feeling is deeply rooted. For the most part he cultivates an ironic detachment from his subject matter, adapting his rhetoric to the peculiarities of individual situation and sensibility (especially in the handling of his own recollections of experience). However, on occasions there are clumsy, disconcerting lapses in imaginative expression, a seemingly inexplicable recourse to folksy archaisms, trite figures, and gushing colloquialisms. But these breaches of poetic decorum are consistent with his deceptive employment of grating literalities, and are an indication of his desire to underscore the crudeness of ordinary existence. And it is in this sense that Melville changes the definition of poetry, at least as understood by his contemporaries. He refuses to be governed by the traditional conventions of prosody, diction, form, and theme. Apparently he is convinced that his vision of reality, as strictly defined by personal interests, associations, and memories, has to be articulated in a harsh, forthright manner, without undue concern with sublime thoughts or idealistic fancies (a far cry from the great white whale of creative aspiration so familiar to most of his readers). Nevertheless Melville still retains an early habit of composition. He delights in the pleasure of ulteriority, of saying one thing and meaning another, of saying one thing in terms of another. In effect, his metaphors work deep beneath the surface of his poems, always requiring close analysis. (pp. 12-13)

[The poems in *John Marr and Other Sailors*] are all matter-of-fact in situation, with many of them characterized by sudden shifts in style and tone and by unexpected dislocations of syntax and meter. This sort of originality (or perverseness) is apt to stagger or poison the judgment of the critic. But if it is taken for granted that Melville is in rebellion against the romantic subjectivity of so much nineteenth-century verse, then his achievement has to be measured by other standards of appreciation or excellence. As even a cursory reading discloses, the poems are bizarre impressions of things-as-they-are in the contingent universe. Generally speaking, they project the radical limitations of finite existence, the pathos and bathos of the human condition when observed with disinterested eyes. The world of John Marr and the other sailors reflects the cold neutrality of nature, the setting of life in which the absence of God is as self-evident as the inevitability of suffering and death. This fact inspires literally hundreds of chortling blasphemies on the absurdity of belief in a supernatural power. A kind of Freudian in his old age, Melville also relates the basic insecurity of experience to unsuspected psychosexual anxieties and disturbances which are induced by the frustrations of hope and desire. Moreover, he couches these insights in patterns of mythic imagery which embrace the now commonly recognized archetypes of the unconscious. In short, his relentless focus on the inherent disorder of things coincides with his antipoetic rhetorical practices.

Timoleon complements the vision of *John Marr and Other Sailors.* This volume of poems catalogues the human subterfuges which down through time have been employed to build up defenses for the ego against the marauding forces of historical contingency. According to Melville, the instinctual appetites provide escapes from reality no less delusory than infatuations with the importance of art, science, religion, philosophy, and politics. Surveying the rise and decline of the great civilizations of the past, he is unable to arrive at any significant distinction between the self-reliance and the self-deception of prideful cultural attainments, either material or intellectual. As Melville finally resolves this paradox in the terminal poem of the collection, he concludes that in the face of ultimate oblivion the grandest human aspirations are a waste of energy and ingenuity. For him there is nothing that can order the blundering course of history and of life. This outlook on the futility of existence determines the execution of the poems. Less startling and contorted in formal organization and more traditional in diction and imagery, though by no means without crusty innovations in perceptual detail, he relies chiefly upon the play of irony and wit in conveying his thought. Except in the few instances where he tacitly exalts the transcendent value of artistic creation, he invariably undercuts literal meaning through tonal incongruities produced by his analogies. Such discordances are his substitute for the wrenchings of form and language in *John Marr and Other Sailors*. From this point of view, then, *Timoleon* captures Melville in his conservative moments of poetic experimentation.

The manuscript collections, *Weeds and Wildings, with A Rose or Two* and *Marquis de Grandvin,* offer a reinterpretation of the terrors of time, and once again Melville's rhetoric is carefully molded into angular and twisted, if not grotesque, expressional forms. However, he tempers the cynicism and pessimism of the two previous collections. Now he posits a formula of reconciliation: the revival of Dionysian worship. No longer dismayed by the defects of mortality, he insists that the unchanging cycle of the year in its rhythm of birth, death, and rebirth attests the continuity of existence, though not of individual organisms. Cosmic becoming is viewed as an eternal succession of rounds in which the same reality is made, unmade, and remade. On this basis Melville argues that the preoccupation of advanced civilizations with historical determinism obviates a genuine psychological adjustment to the contingent manifestations of time, to the inevitable disillusionments of finitude. In accordance with this logic he ridicules the nineteenth-century obsession with evolutionary political, economic, social, and moral progress—the delusion that human effort can transform the world into a paradise. He also finds the linear timetable of Christian salvation incompatible with the cyclical scheme of things. These negative attitudes culminate in his buoyant consecration of the fecund energies of nature and the sexual gustos of man. Needless to say, Melville has to resort to indirection in order to convey most of these iconoclastic sentiments. On the one hand, he affects all sorts of bumpkin poses so that he can slyly poke fun at the self-deceptions lurking behind the pompous ideals of Victorian culture. On the other, he masks his celebration of Dionysian freedom in a torrent of hilarious puns, euphemisms, and double entendres. In effect, both *Weeds and Wildings* and *Marquis de Grandvin* reveal that Melville has finally resolved the agonizing moral and emotional conflicts of his middle years. This fact is evident not only in the themes of the poems but also in the manner of their execution: what he has to say, he says the way he wants to—be damned tradition! (pp. 13-15)

> *William Bysshe Stein, in his* The Poetry of Melville's Late Years: Time, History, Myth, and Religion *(reprinted by permission of the State University of New York Press; © 1970 by The Research Foundation of State University of New York), State University of New York Press, 1970, 275 p.*

R. BRUCE BICKLEY, JR.   (essay date 1975)

Melville's success with the short story in his own time certainly owed a good deal to his ability to work within the popular magazine forms of the travel sketch (**"The Encantadas"**), the gothic story or tale of mystery with a "solution" at the end (**"Benito Cereno"** and **"The Bell-Tower"**), the Romantic confessional (**"I and My Chimney"** and **"The Piazza"**), and the familiar essay or character sketch (**"Bartleby," "Jimmy Rose,"** or **"The Apple-Tree Table"**). Yet in the short fiction there was little sacrifice of intellectual integrity, for Melville had discovered ways of concealing larger philosophical (and sometimes ribaldly comical) issues below the more overtly magazinish surface of his stories. At the same time, he found in the compression and discipline that the short story required a new artistic strength. (pp. 21-2)

In his short tales Melville, in a sense, harnessed the declamatory pyrotechnics of *Mardi, Moby-Dick,* and *Pierre,* carefully

releasing his imaginative energies through, and around, a collection of ironic personae. Thus Melville anticipates the twentieth century and the vogue of ironic narrator-heroes like Prufrock, Meursault, and Jake Barnes: the "real" stories that he tells, more often than not, are about his narrators' anxieties and insecurities, or their failures of vision—sometimes comically rendered, sometimes pathetically or even tragically revealed. (p. 22)

The intellectual, perceptual, or psychological inadequacies of Melville's first-person narrators, and their imperfect understanding of themselves, make their stories complex. At the same time these characters, like Tommo, Redburn, and Ishmael, come to life as identifiably "real" people because of their human limitations. In addition, there is the familiar Melvillean paradox that complicates the problem of what his narrators can know and, therefore, of what the reader can learn from them. (p. 23)

[In] writing his short stories [Melville] consulted Irving and Hawthorne, and with some frequency. Irving's presence is chiefly felt in the narrative technique of **"Bartleby"** and Hawthorne's in the story's metaphysical dimensions. Also, both writers appear to have contributed considerably to Melville's method of characterization. (p. 27)

The rhetorical design and narrative strategy of several of Melville's tales parallel Irving's, and Crayon and his storytelling acquaintances are, it would appear, models for at least five of Melville's short story protagonists. It seems that Irving's example reinforced Melville's own best tendencies in first-person narration. . . . The basic similarities between Irving's and Melville's tales are in matters of narrative perspective. Essentially, the "bachelor" is the controlling consciousness in Irving, as he was in Melville's novels and would continue to be, with some interesting variations, in his tales. . . . Prone to sentiment, both real and affected, and even to mild neurosis, Irving's sketchers often ironically reveal more about themselves than about the external reality they pretend to describe.

Melville, following up his instincts and earlier narrative strategies, modifies and expands the Crayonesque prototype in his magazine works. . . . [He] deemphasizes Irving's often cumbersome framing devices and allows his narrators to tell their own stories. Compared to Irving's, his method is at once more dramatic and rhetorically demanding of the reader: it multiplies the possibilities for irony, making the narrator's moods and attitudes an emotional and intellectual grid through or around which the reader must, in Jamesian terms, "see."

These patterns are at work in **"Bartleby."** The lawyer-narrator is a Crayonesque sketcher who enjoys storytelling. . . . Conservative, and himself a sentimentalist, the lawyer anticipates the narrative personae in several stories, **"I and My Chimney," "Jimmy Rose,"** and **"The Paradise of Bachelors."** He insists on telling his reader about Bartleby, who was the "strangest" scrivener he ever saw. However, in acknowledging at the outset the difficulty of the task he has set for himself, for "no materials exist, for a full and satisfactory biography of this man," the narrator hints at one of the central ironies of the story: he will never succeed in "characterizing" Bartleby. The scrivener's personality, inner drives, and sensibilities will remain relatively unknown quantities to the narrator. The lawyer's character sketch is, in effect, a series of attempts to align or harmonize his clerk with something he himself knows or can respond to, and these attempts continually fail. Although the lawyer never realizes it, the "chief character . . . to be presented" will not be Bartleby, but himself. (pp. 28-30)

As a nay-sayer, Bartleby is philosophically reminiscent of, and perhaps to some extent based upon, those protagonists in Hawthorne's gloomier short fiction whom critics have viewed as portraits of the artist, and in whose alienation is symbolized Hawthorne's own skeptical retreat. . . . Philosophically, in **"Bartleby"** and, with varying emphases, in later stories as well, Melville seems to have confronted anew the implications of Hawthorne's perception of "blackness." In this first story, however, he defined the ultimate extension of a Hawthornean world-view: a self-willed death. Bartleby . . . finally capitulates to the suffering he has experienced and to his skepticism about the possibilities for human understanding and love. (pp. 32-3)

Representing those who would "prefer not" to commit themselves to a meaningless way of life, he is a stoical study in what Melville terms in his story "passive resistance"; but through him Melville also warns humanity against a self-destructive surrender to a vision of blackness. (p. 34)

The rhythmic pattern of events prior to Bartleby's inevitable dismissal makes up the story's essential form: from the introductory self-portrait to the page-long "sequel" concerning the scrivener's earlier work in the Dead Letter Office occur approximately a dozen confrontations between the employer and his clerk. Melville's structure is rhetorically quite effective. It enables him to exhibit several distinctive responses to the enigma of Bartleby, none of which succeeds in revealing his character. Thus the levels of available meaning are multiplied, and the reader is left free to identify with any, or none, of the lawyer's emotional and mental reactions to his scrivener. Melville would find this method useful later, in the encounters of narrators and "original" characters in **"The Fiddler," "The Lightning-Rod Man,"** and **"Benito Cereno,"** for example. Melville's rhetorical strategy dictates that no interpretation of Bartleby offered by the lawyer could ever be complete, for the scrivener is a phenomenon totally alien to the narrator's experience and sensibilities. Yet the story raises an even larger rhetorical question. The lawyer may have his limitations, but does not Melville also suggest that Bartleby is incapable of giving enough of his own self to deserve even that charity which his employer extends? Where does the moral or ethical emphasis of the tale rest, finally? In the best Ishmaelian tradition, Melville offers no neat answers. (pp. 35-6)

[Surely there are] significant meanings latent in Bartleby's insistent use of the word "prefer." . . . During one of their encounters the narrator tested the extent of his scrivener's perversity by asking him to run an errand to the Post Office (probably the last place, if the rumor is correct, that Bartleby would ever want to go). The scrivener gives his standard reply, "I would prefer not to." "You *will* not?" demands the lawyer; "I *prefer* not," answers Bartleby. . . . The lawyer, characteristically, offers no meaningful interpretive commentary on this crucial distinction, but for the modern reader the sequence is an intriguing prefiguration of the existential dilemma. In **"Bartleby"** Melville portrays not only an obsessive Hawthornean vision of blackness, but also an image of one man's confrontation with what he feels to be the meaninglessness of the universe. Ahab had spoken of an "unreasoning force," inexorably in control of all nature, that denies man both identity and power. There is no possibility of meaningful action, Bartleby seems to say, and it is certain that man cannot successfully will anything. Perhaps the only tenable stance is merely to *prefer* to do something; this gives one at least a temporary hedge against fate, and somehow it is not quite so painful if one's "preferences" are denied. (p. 42)

["**Jimmy Rose**"] bears a certain structural resemblance to **"Bartleby."** It, too, is a character sketch in the form of a familiar essay; the narrator, William Ford, spends several pages describing his own surroundings and chatting about his likes and dislikes before he introduces his announced subject, the "gentle Jimmy Rose." Melville's point is, again, that Ford, like the lawyer in **"Bartleby,"** is in many ways the real subject of his own sketch. Philosophically, **"Jimmy Rose"** is a minor work, but rhetorically the story is a carefully rendered satire on the limits of human perception and self-knowledge. (p. 45)

Melville uses imagery in his story to help develop character and meaning. Jimmy's introduction comes at the end of a page-long rhapsody on the faded rose- and peacock-patterned Louis XVI wallpaper in the Fords' parlor—a room which the sentimental and old-fashioned narrator refuses to let his wife and daughters remodel. He loves to dwell upon the "real elegance," albeit rather dimmed, and the "sweet engaging pensiveness" of the peacocks in the room, but chiefly he associates the parlor with Jimmy Rose. From this point on the tale has a twofold development: as Ford entrenches himself in memories of Jimmy's social success and abrupt decline and reminds the reader that through it all Jimmy's carmine cheeks never lost their glow, he not only succeeds in evoking Jimmy himself but also reveals his own attraction for the gilt-edged showiness and social artificialities of the past. (p. 47)

Jimmy *was* vain and aritifical, but Ford could not let himself admit it. To do so would mean to acknowledge the shallowness in his own character and his reluctance, if not inability, to adjust to the modern world.

The chatty, informal narrator of **"I and My Chimney"** . . . is another of Melville's genial sentimentalists. Like Ford in **"Jimmy Rose,"** he is restless in a marriage to a youthful wife who is impatient with his idiosyncrasies, he worships the past, and he defends his old age and old-fashioned tastes with a stubborn, if not at times a blind, tenacity. (pp. 48-9)

Melville's digressive and improvisatory mode keeps **"I and My Chimney"** in constant motion, and as a stylistic and verbal performance it is equal to anything in the Melville canon. In punnning on the chimney's shape and size, the surgical operations it has undergone, and its position relative to the narrator, to say nothing of its power to hatch the wife's eggs, Melville toys with his nineteenth-century audience even more boldly than he had in describing Carlo's "hand-organ" in *Redburn,* or the whale's "grandissimus" in *Moby-Dick.* . . .

The chimney, like the whale, is a seemingly endless source of anecdote, as well as meaning. Following up his instincts in narrative portraiture, Melville develops in his tale the comic possibilities of human reflexes and involuntary gesture, as characters react to the chimney or are affected by it. (p. 52)

Amidst the punning and the comic anecdotes, the narrator's chimney assumes important philosophical dimensions in the story. In making proud claims for his chimney's impressiveness as the "grand seignior" and "king" in the house, and for its massiveness and majesty, as well as its mystery, the narrator is romantically celebrating himself. By worshiping the chimney, serving it, sentimentally communing with it, and defending it from harassment and possible destruction, he is simultaneously preserving his own identity. And yet the chimney represents more than the protagonist's own personality. It becomes a complex symbol for humanity as a whole—man's spirit, his inviolable soul, his masculinity, as well as his stubborn egotism and whimsical idosyncrasies.

Melville's choice as narrator of a likable old hearty who has a penchant for sentiment and for philosophy also helps to expand the implications of the story. The protagonists's "indolent" habit of meditation, as he and his chimney "smoke and philosophize together," makes the expository form of the story appear natural. Finally, the narrator's digressions on old age, integrity, and man's quest for identity and fulfillment convey the tragicomic nature of life itself. (p. 54)

The ironic narrative strategies of "**The Lightning-Rod Man**" . . . and "**The Apple-Tree Table**" . . . are especially telling indicators of the ways in which Melville's literary imagination shaped the complex world he saw. Philosophically, the stories echo the enigmatic questions that *Moby-Dick* had raised, for his two protagonists explore events which have theological as well as metaphysical overtones. . . . In a way the two stories form contrasting halves of an allegorical diptych on religious orthodoxy, and the two slightly manic narrators are psychologically kin. The first story portrays Calvinistic fatalism ironically, and in the second the narrator's uncertainty about Providence's role in human affairs also has ironic implications. In both works the Melvillean stance seems, finally, to be one of tentative compromise: the Unknown is, after all, unknowable, and both narrators—although one of them does not realize it— are denied the truth.

The two characters in the allegorical "**Lightning-Rod Man**" are humorously exaggerated mouthpieces for opposing theological positions. The story can be viewed as a double-edged satire, directed primarily against the cringing and pessimistic salesman who fears lest God's wrath strike him at any moment, but also against the overly devout narrator, who perhaps too readily accepts the Almighty's plan for him. (p. 67)

Melville aims his satirical thrusts first of all at nineteenth-century Calvinistic Christianity, at those ministers who use warnings of doom and damnation as rhetorical leverage on unbelievers. But he also levels an ironic blow at the narrator's own beliefs. Melville does not imply that the narrator's confidence and his stance "at ease in the hands of my God" is the only tenable religious attitude. (pp. 69-70)

["**The Apple-Tree Table**"] is a delightful piece of improvisation and narrative self-portraiture, characteristically Melvillean in its emphasis on comic gesture and reflex response. At the same time, the story raises the kinds of complex questions that disturbed Melville all of his life: what does nature symbolize, and what sway do the Devil and God have over events? Of more significance, perhaps, is the fact that the story subtly satirizes those who presume to have the answers to these questions. (p. 71)

The rhetorical strategy of the tale holds the key to its meaning. The subtitle of the story, "**Original Spiritual Manifestations**," implies that its real subject will be the spiritual significance of a physical object, but of course what is finally made "manifest" may be one thing to the narrator and something else to the reader. For in facing the mysteriously ticking table the protagonist not only must confront his own inner self but also his more public self, as head of his family. The narrative rhythm of the story is based primarily upon a series of reverses that occur in the narrator's inner and outer behavior towards the table. Behind these reverses—some of which the protagonist recognizes and some of which he does not—speaks Melville's ironic voice. The narrator is revealed as the victim, although to a large degree a sympathetic one, of his own unredeemable contradictoriness. (pp. 71-2)

["**The Bell-Tower**" and "**Benito Cereno**"] are anomalies among Melville's magazine works. Temporarily abandoning the Crayonesque self-portraying narrator, Melville chooses instead the third-person, limited-omniscient voice. Melville's technique in his two tales is essentially Poe's classic method in the so-called detective stories. Like "Murders in the Rue Morgue," the two stories are designed as elaborate riddles in detection, and their solution reveals that inhuman forces of annihilation have been at work; as in Poe, the last several pages of "**The Bell-Tower**" and "**Benito Cereno**" provide explanations of the preceding mysterious events and at least partially clear up ambiguities. (p. 95)

In "**The Bell-Tower**" Melville's commitment to an allegorical formula imposes certain structural restraints on his narrative, denying him sufficient latitude for improvisation in theme and character. "**Benito Cereno**," however, is one of Melville's most rhetorically effective tales. Through limited omniscient narration Melville hints at the real condition of things aboard the *San Dominick,* while portraying Delano's confused quest for the truth. The imagery, furthermore, adds to the rhetorical power of his story. It intensifies the atmosphere of the tale, and, in a more subtle way, it helps to give external form to the horror and violence that have ravaged Don Benito's soul. (pp. 95-6)

In recreating his source materials as art [in "**Benito Cereno**"], Melville worked a variation on his characteristic rhetorical mode, first-person ironic narration. He sought a method for hinting at Delano's incomplete view of reality, yet at the same time he wanted to preserve the immediacy and familiarity of the first-person technique, which had proven itself artistically seaworthy in his previous writings. What he settled on was a limited-omniscient narrator, one privileged to enter Delano's mind alone, but also permitted to draw partially aside the masks that conceal the identities of Babo and Cereno. Melville conceived his tale as an interior psychological portrait of the American captain, counterpointed by an alternately increasing and decreasing atmospheric pressure of suspense as Delano wavers between uneasiness and restored confidence. (p. 101)

[The tale] moves with a studied uncertainty towards its climax, as the narrator explores Delano's subjective responses to Cereno and to the scenes which shape and reshape themselves before his eyes. (p. 102)

Another Melvillean "bachelor," good-natured Delano is naively confident about the world, and about his own God-given potentialities as a leader of men of will and benefactor of those weaker than himself. Out of his naiveté arises both a sense of superiority and a conviction that one is treated as he treats others. But Delano is also perceptually obtuse: he is unwilling and unable to allow his intuitive glimpses of the truth to overturn his preconceived notions about reality and human nature. . . . Too thorough an understanding of reality can precipitate dangerous reflex actions; in Delano's obtuseness lies his salvation, and, for the moment at least, Don Benito's as well. (pp. 102-03)

Melville's narrative method carefully prepares the reader for the culminating irony of the story. In spite of what they have experienced together, Delano understands as little about Cereno's spiritual and psychological state at the end as he did at the beginning of their relationship. To the last Delano remains an innocent, for even after learning of Babo's atrocities he fails to see why the broken-spirited Don Benito cannot forget the past. (pp. 103-04)

The imagery of "**Benito Cereno**" counterpoints Delano's interior monologue: Melville's images establish and reinforce mood, while they also symbolize the disintegrated psyche of the Spanish captain. In its basic form the tale is a meditation upon the texture of reality. For Delano reality is a flux of ambiguous images, but for Benito the images of reality are static, their meaning horribly apparent. . . . Motifs of ambiguity and unreality dominate Delano's field of vision and probably the reader's as well, his first time through the tale; at the same time, images of physical deterioration, brutality, and death inject into the tale's ambiguousness a disquieting sense of pending violence and destruction. It is these images of decay and physical violence that come to represent the tormented consciousness of Don Benito. (pp. 104-05)

Motifs of decay, brutality, and death . . . augment the threatening quality of the atmosphere [of the *San Dominick*], but they also help to generate additional levels of meaning in the story. The Negroes aboard the *San Dominick* are compared to the Black Friars, the Dominicans who conducted the Inquisition; mastering both the mind and the body of Cereno, they even extract "false confessions" from him, for Delano's benefit. Cereno's vessel, furthermore, is likened to the monastery to which Charles V of Spain retired, and it serves as a fitting symbol of the faded glory and strength of the Spanish empire. Melville's story thus becomes a kind of allegory on the confrontation of primitive Africa, civilized Europe, and naive America, and on the destruction and spiritual loss attendant upon political and religious upheaval. (p. 106)

[In "**The Encantadas**" Melville returns] to the familiar ground of the travel narrative, and it is not surprising that the guide-figure in the sketches is philosophically reminiscent of the Ishmael of *Moby-Dick* days. (p. 109)

The major tension in the sketches . . . is that between the stark reality of the Galápagos and their baffling unreality and supernatural quality. What the senses tell the observer about the islands is insufficient, we find, for the "archipelago of aridities" leaves its most meaningful impressions at a deeper level: in the psyche. Melville's narrator-observer closes Sketch First with the somewhat embarrassed admission that the Encantadas had affected him mentally, for they had, absurd to say, made him a believer in enchantments. (p. 111)

For Melville the Galápagos Islands are a world to themselves, but a world under Satan's dominion. Sketches First through Tenth are permeated by images of heat, aridity, and destruction by fire—motifs appropriate to the organically and spiritually dead landscape of hell. (p. 112)

Nothing living can endure long on the Galápagos, Melville suggests. . . . In what is probably the most striking single image in the sketches, Melville describes the unchangeable desolation of these lands: "Like split Syrian gourds left withering in the sun, they are cracked by an everlasting drought beneath a torrid sky.". . .

Images of enchantment and unreality comprise the second descriptive pattern in the sketches. Baffling winds and calms and unaccountable currents give the Enchanted Isles their name, and the anecdote of the *Essex,* as well as the stories of Oberlus and Hunilla, include allusions to the bewitching forces at work in the archipelago. (p. 113)

In the third unifying imagery pattern Melville focuses upon the character and experiences of the human habitants of the archipelago. Here the opposing tensions in the sketches are es-

pecially noticeable. At the upper end of the islands' scale of humanity is Hunilla, who triumphed heroically over the degradation that she was forced to undergo; at the lower end is the Dog King of Charles Isle, and, more particularly, the hermit Oberlus, to whom degradation and depravity came naturally. Somewhere in the middle of the scale are the buccaneers, those free and roving cavalier souls who sought out the islands as a "bower of ease." (p. 114)

The final and most important motif in the sketches is the symbol of the tortoise. This reptile is the central force for resolving the major tensions in the sketches: those between degradation and triumph, between life and death, and between the real and the supernatural. With the tortoise, "The Encantadas" synthesize as art and as philosophy.

In the first place, the tortoise is a symbol of the eternal punishment which is the isles' peculiar curse. . . . [The] tortoises seem "the victims of a penal, or malignant, or perhaps a downright diabolical enchanter." (p. 118)

At the same time, however, the tortoise represents the Hunilla-like qualities of heroic triumph and endurance. . . . What other creature lives as long as the Encantadas tortoise, Melville asks, and "What other bodily being possesses such a citadel wherein to resist the assaults of Time?" . . . Yet it is this very quality of ageless endurance which reminds the narrator, even during "scenes of social merriment," of his own ephemeral existence. Like the figure of Hunilla, the turtle symbolizes the power of the life force, even as it makes one aware of his own proximity to death.

Finally, the tortoise is a complex synthesis of the basic dialectic in "**The Encantadas**": the contrast between reality and unreality. As a symbol of reality, Melville explains in "**Two Sides to a Tortoise**," the tortoise has its "melancholy" side and its "bright side." The tortoise may appear grim and monstrous, and so reality, too, has its evil half. But still one cannot deny the tortoise his virtues, or life its blessings. (p. 119)

Like the whale, the tortoise remains larger than all of the meanings man can find for it; so, too, the Encantadas. (p. 120)

In experimenting with short fiction in the middle 1850's, Melville found new artistic strength. Obliged by the form of the magazine tale to compress and focus his creative powers, he saw more clearly than he had before the effect of discipline on craftsmanship. As a result, there is very little wasted motion in the magazine stories, and some of the tales reveal a verbal facility unrivalled anywhere in his works. The onesided conversations in "**Bartleby,**" the comic interaction of characters in "**I and My Chimney**" and "**The Apple-Tree Table,**" or the imagistic art of "**The Encantadas**" and "**The Piazza**" constitute some of Melville's very best writing; in terms of originality and inventiveness, the short fiction is as rich as *Mardi* or *Moby-Dick.* . . . [Many] of the tales convey the same sense of exuberance and delight in literary creation that we find in Taji's and Ishmael's greatest improvisational moments.

Yet it is the relationship between vision and technique in the short stories that makes them among Melville's most significant literary achievements. Invariably, in the short tales, Melville puts human personality and reflexes at the center of art. It is a character's comic, pathetic, melodramatic, or even neurotic response to experience, or his failure to respond at all to the things around him, that forms the immediate world of Melville's tales. The other world of his short fiction is the reader's. The distance between these two worlds varies in each story, but there is always a noticeable degree of separation, and hence irony. (pp. 131-32)

The ironic mode was essentially a subversive one, Melville realized. Employing a narrator as a potentially false guide for the reader was artistically perilous, but in the short tales Melville mastered the technique, often using it more subtly than had Poe or Irving, in fact. Behind the persona of a methodical Wall Street lawyer, or an indolent old hearty before his fireplace, or a well-intentioned sea captain, Melville tested the platitudes and assumptions of his reading public; yet always, as he had in the great novels, he revealed a higher order of truth or reality in place of man's conventionalisms. (p. 132)

> *R. Bruce Bickley, Jr., in his* The Method of Melville's Short Fiction *(reprinted by permission of the Publisher; copyright © 1969, 1975 by Duke University Press, Durham, North Carolina), Duke University Press, 1975, 142 p.*

JOHN UPDIKE   (essay date 1982)

"Pierre" proved to be . . . grindingly, ludicrously bad. It is doubtful if elsewhere in the history of literature two books as good and bad as "Moby-Dick" and "Pierre" have been written back to back. The action of "Pierre" is hysterical, the style is frenzied and volatile, the characters are jerked to and fro by some unexplained rage of the author's. . . .

Whereas in "Moby-Dick" the figure of Ahab takes all the madness upon himself, here it belongs to the author; where the basic chase action of the earlier book carries us through all the elaborations, digressions, and explosions of authorial wit, in "Pierre" the white whale never surfaces but slides as an unsighted horror beneath the clashing, improbable waves. When Pierre receives the news that he has a bastard sister, and reacts by swooning and vowing to love and protect her "through all," Melville wonders in print at so violent a reaction to "a piece of intelligence which, in the natural course of things, many amiable gentlemen, both young and old, have been known to receive with a momentary feeling of surprise, and then a little curiosity to know more, and at last an entire unconcern." Throughout the book, we long for that amiable gentleman, that representative of mundane orderly and elastic society. Instead, the book runs a constant fever, and seems especially unreal in the Arcadian setting of its first half. . . . Melville was, in truth, at sea on land. The domestic and social arrangements he imagines are as gothic and moldering as those in Poe. . . . (p. 124)

Where "Pierre" does burn through to reality is in the evocation, in the city part of the novel, of the menace of poverty and the ordeal of writing. (p. 125)

The stories of "The Piazza Tales" are, with "Moby-Dick," "Typee," and "Billy Budd," the most widely read of Melville's work. They evince a competence, even a mastery, that Melville chose not to exercise much. "I would prefer not to," Bartleby famously says, and there is in all these tales a certain reserve, a toning down into brown and sombre colors the sunny colors and brilliant blacks of the earlier work, a desolation hauntingly figured forth by the eerie slave-seized ship of "Benito Cereno" and the cinderlike islands of "The Encantadas." The style, though a triumphant recovery from the hectic tropes of "Pierre," is not quite the assured, playful, precociously fluent, and eagerly pitched voice of the sea novels. It is a slightly *chastened* style, with something a bit abrasive and latently aggressive about it. However admirable, these tales are not exactly comfortable; their surfaces are not seductive

and limpid, like those of Hawthorne's tales. How uncomfortable Melville was will burst forth in "The Confidence-Man," which has the texture of gnashing teeth; but before grappling with it we might linger a moment upon "Israel Potter," the one book of Melville's quite out of print, and yet a charming one, and one indicating how entertainingly Melville could perform when bound to the constraints of a brisk professional intent.

Like "Benito Cereno" and "Billy Budd," "Israel Potter" is based upon a document. . . . In the footsteps of this bizarre, not very consequential memoir, Melville trots along amiably, elaborating, poeticizing, inventing portraits of such eminences as Ben Franklin, John Paul Jones, and Ethan Allen, and giving us a vivid notion of our country's patriotic pantheon while its deities were not many decades in the grave. Though caustic in places, the book has something of its hero's naïve patriotism and that innocence of an Edenic America lost forever with the eighteen-fifties. "Israel Potter" is notable for containing the one sketch in all post-Polynesian Melville of a woman perceived as an inviting sexual object. . . . "Israel Potter" also holds a number of matchless descriptions of battles at sea, Olympian in their mood and startling in their playful poetry. . . . (pp. 132, 134-35)

No writer, not even Dickens, invents from whole cloth; but Melville was especially an embroiderer, who needed the ready-made fabric of either his own recalled adventures or an account of someone else's to get his needle flying. His sense of truth held him stubbornly close to the actual; he was, in a style we can recognize as modern, both bookish and autobiographical. (p. 135)

Memories of [a] Mississippi trip and of his unhappy family and dismal youth may have contributed to the dire pessimism of "The Confidence-Man." This crabbed and inert work has attracted much learned comment and appreciation in recent decades, second in this respect only to "Moby-Dick," and no doubt there is much to be said for it: it yields many evidences of ingenuity to academic analysis, and does anticipate an apocalyptic vein of American fiction, from the later Twain to Nathanael West to yesterday's black humorists. Black the book is, and humorous its intent; but appreciation should begin with the acknowledgment that it is suffocatingly difficult to read. . . . Where "Pierre" is at least a bad novel, "The Confidence-Man" is no novel at all; it is a series of farfetched but rather joyless conversations upon the theme of trust, or confidence. . . . [By] mid-excursion Melville seems to forget his trickster theme and permits his shifty central figure to stay in one costume and to indulge in a parade of haranguing dialogues. . . . The objective of swindling has sunk within some murkier purpose satisfied, it seems, by sheer discourse. The novel, with hardly a female character though many women must have ridden the riverboats, strikes me as the most homosexual of Melville's works; men are trying to "get at" each other with a merciless, adhesive nagging. The action is all verbal and takes place in a sensory vacuum; almost no attempt is made to render the boat itself or the river and its banks real—how far a fall is here from the sea sense the early books give us! Melville's style has dismissed the voluptuousness that excited and even scandalized his first readers, and ranges from sharp and dry to monstrous. . . . (pp. 137-38)

However, the theme, of confidence, is a mighty one. . . . [It] is worth a satire or a tragedy, neither of which Melville was well equipped to write. (p. 138)

We have, perhaps, more tolerance for the awkwardness and obliquity that damned his verse with contemporary reviewers; but even the most sympathetic reader now cannot but be struck by a feeling of deliberate and stubborn effort in the poems, an effect of *muttering* quite unlike the full-throated ease of the prose. Like another novelist turned poet out of disgust, Hardy, Melville moves us with his effort to thrust honesty and complex insight toward us through the resistant slats of metre and rhyme. Whereas Whitman and Dickinson turned their backs on the ornate variety of Victorian verse forms and created individual prosodies, Melville set himself to school with traditional metrics, wielding the stanzas of English balladry with frequent archaism of diction and striking a resolute music of iron and wood. . . . A massive work of over eighteen thousand lines in rhyming tetrameter, [**"Clarel"**] is an epic of doubt, scored for a dozen male voices and set, as it were, amid the menacing wrinkles of Moby Dick's brow. (pp. 141-42)

The characters, as in **"The Confidence-Man,"** represent a cross-section, but they are more leisurely and tolerantly drawn. . . . The poetry can be comically awkward, with its rhyming inversions . . . [and] its innocent flatness. . . . But it can also be quite lively, its desert imagery compulsively shot through with memories of the sea. . . . Compared with that of **"Pierre"** and **"The Confidence-Man,"** the air of **"Clarel"** breathes with relief; there is still pain in the topic, but less in the writing. Melville is here engaged in his favorite pastime—woolgathering upon absolute matters in an atmosphere of male companionship. The characters are not quite rounded, but, like sets of facts, they are seen in different lights, as the controlling mind restlessly moves. (pp. 142, 145)

[**"Billy Budd"**] combines Melville's preoccupations in a beautifully calm, enigmatic fashion. Like Shakespeare's "Tempest," it seems to sum up, and takes us beneath the troubled waves. Billy at the end lies full fathom five, and oozy weeds about him twist. The message of **"Billy Budd"** is no more consoling, really, than that of Father Mapple's sermon in **"Moby-Dick;"** that is, a counterfeit Christ legend is shown in the coining, and Billy goes to death blessing his condemner as credulous men everywhere go down to doom praising God. (p. 145)

> *John Updike, "Reflections: Melville's Withdrawal"*
> *(© 1982 by John Updike), in* The New Yorker *Vol.*
> *LVIII, No. 12, May 10, 1982, pp. 120-47.*

ADDITIONAL BIBLIOGRAPHY

Allen, Gay Wilson. *Melville and His World.* New York: Viking, 1971, 144 p.
  An excellent biography which includes many interesting photographs and paintings of Melville, his family, and his assorted residences. Maps of Melville's voyages and pictures of the islands he visited are also included.

Beebe, Maurice; Hayford, Harrison; and Roper, Gordon. "Criticism of Herman Melville: A Selected Checklist." *Modern Fiction Studies* VIII, No. 3 (Autumn 1962): 312-46.
  A useful list of scholarly and critical discussions of Melville's work.

Blackmur, R. P. "The Craft of Herman Melville: A Putative Statement." In his *The Expense of Greatness*, pp. 139-66. Gloucester: Peter Smith, 1940.
  Disputes the merit and influence of Melville's literary style. Blackmur contends that "Melville never influenced the direction of the art of fiction. . . . He added nothing to the novel as a form, and his work nowhere showed conspicuous mastery of the formal devices of fiction which he used."

Braswell, William. *Melville's Religious Thought: An Essay in Interpretation.* New York: Octagon Books, 1973, 154 p.
  Discusses the background and influences central to Melville's religious disillusionment and analyzes the treatment of religious themes throughout his works.

Canby, Henry Seidel. "Hawthorne and Melville." In his *Classic Americans: A Study of Eminent American Writers from Irving to Whitman with an Introductory Survey of the Colonial Background of Our National Literature*, pp. 226-62. New York: Russell & Russell, 1959.*
  Explores the parallels between Melville and Hawthorne.

Franklin, H. Bruce. *The Wake of the Gods: Melville's Mythology.* Stanford: Stanford University Press, 1963, 236 p.
  Studies the importance of mythology to the structure and meaning of Melville's works.

Hetherington, Hugh W. *Melville's Reviewers: British and American, 1846-1891.* Chapel Hill: The University of North Carolina Press, 1961, 304 p.
  A thorough account of British and American critical response to Melville's works during the years 1846-1891.

Hillway, Tyrus, and Mansfield, Luther S., eds. *"Moby-Dick" Centennial Essays.* Dallas: Southern Methodist University Press, 1953, 182 p.
  A collection honoring Melville's centennial which includes essays by Randall Stewart, Tyrus Hillway, and Hugh Hetherington.

Homans, George C. "The Dark Angel: The Tragedy of Herman Melville." *The New England Quarterly* V, No. 4 (October 1932): 699-730.
  Treats *Mardi, Moby-Dick,* and *Pierre* as an intellectual tragedy in three acts.

Howard, Leon. *Herman Melville: A Biography.* Berkeley: University of California Press, 1951, 354 p.
  A biography that aims "to place the basic facts of Melville's life in their proper physical, historical, intellectual, and literary contexts."

Levin, Harry. *The Power of Blackness: Hawthorne, Poe, Melville.* New York: Knopf, 1970, 263 p.*
  A study of darkness as a unifying theme and its manifestation in the works of Hawthorne, Poe, and Melville.

Metcalf, Eleanor Melville. *Herman Melville: Cycle and Epicycle.* Cambridge: Harvard University Press, 1953, 311 p.
  A biography by Melville's oldest grandchild which draws heavily upon family correspondence and previously unpublished diary entries. Says Metcalf: "This family had no more distinction than many another; yet their letters may perform a unique service in providing the intimate social scene in which a man of genius lived and moved, but failed to find his being."

Miller, James E., Jr. *A Reader's Guide to Herman Melville.* New York: Octagon Books, 1973, 266 p.
  A critical survey which focuses on recurrent patterns of meaning in Melville's work.

Olson, Charles. *Call Me Ishmael.* New York: Grove Press, 1958, 119 p.
  Demonstrates the influence of Shakespeare's plays upon *Moby-Dick.*

Parker, Hershel, ed. *The Recognition of Herman Melville: Selected Criticism since 1846.* Ann Arbor: The University of Michigan Press, 1967, 364 p.
  A comprehensive selection of criticism which traces the recognition of Melville as an important American writer.

Parker, Hershel, and Hayford, Harrison, eds. *"Moby-Dick" as Doubloon: Essays and Extracts (1851-1970).* New York: Norton, 1970, 388 p.

A collection which "displays the range of approaches, interpretations and judgments of the first century-and-a-quarter of *Moby-Dick* criticism."

Pullin, Faith, ed. *New Perspectives on Melville*. Kent, Ohio: The Kent State University Press, 1978, 314 p.

A collection reflecting recent interpretations of Melville's work which includes essays by such critics as Richard H. Brodhead, Larzer Ziff, and Q. D. Leavis.

Springer, Haskell, ed. *The Merrill Studies in "Billy Budd."* Columbus, Ohio: Charles E. Merrill, 1970, 142 p.

A selection of critical essays on *Billy Budd* "chosen for their historical importance, representative viewpoints, or creative insights."

Stern, Milton R. *The Fine Hammered Steel of Herman Melville*. Urbana: University of Illinois Press, 1968, 255 p.

A complex analysis of Melville's thematic and perceptual development in *Typee, Mardi, Pierre,* and *Billy Budd.*

Trilling, Lionel. "'Bartleby the Scrivener: A Story of Wall Street'." In his *Prefaces to the Experience of Literature,* pp. 74-8. New York: Harcourt Brace Jovanovich, 1967.

A brief interpretation of Bartleby's relationship to social order and the significance of his answer "I prefer not to."

Untermeyer, Louis. "Herman Melville." In his *Makers of the Modern World,* pp. 47-59. New York: Simon and Schuster, 1955.

A concise overview of Melville's life, literary career, and critical reception.

Vincent, Howard P. *The Trying-Out of "Moby-Dick."* Boston: Houghton Mifflin Co., 1949, 400 p.

A chapter-by-chapter analysis which "combines a study of the whaling sources of *Moby-Dick* with an account of its composition, and suggestions concerning interpretation and meaning."

Vincent, Howard P., ed. *The Merrill Studies in "Moby-Dick."* Columbus, Ohio: Charles E. Merrill Publishing Co., 1969, 163 p.

A collection of essays on *Moby-Dick* ranging from contemporary reviews to modern appraisals.

Weaver, Raymond M. *Herman Melville: Mariner and Mystic*. New York: George H. Doran Co., 1921, 399 p.

The biography central to the Melville revival of the 1920s. This work was extremely influential in establishing Melville's reputation as an author of world importance.

Adam Mickiewicz

1798-1855

Polish poet, dramatist, and novelist.

Founder of the Romantic movement in Polish literature, Mickiewicz, with his sentimental, patriotic, and expressive verse, was the voice of the nineteenth-century Polish émigrés. In such pieces as *Dziady (Forefathers' Eve)* and *Pan Tadeusz; Czyli, ostatni zajazd na Litwie (Master Thaddeus; or, The Last Foray in Lithuania),* he reflected his fervent nationalism and concern for the liberation of his homeland, qualities which continue to distinguish him as Poland's national bard.

Born in the Lithuanian region of Poland, Mickiewicz was raised as a member of the petit Polish nobility during one of the darkest periods of Poland's history, the Napoleonic Wars. His works evoke the memories of Napoleon's defeat and the turmoil which ensued in Poland. He wrote in the style of the classicists in his early work, incorporating the ideas of the Enlightenment. While a student at Wilno University, he founded and played an active role in an organization called the Philomaths, whose goal was to encourage "learning as a means for social progress and freedom." His *Oda do Młodości (Ode to Youth),* written to the Philomaths, best expresses the ideals of the fellowship, stressing "friendship, unity, and love for liberty." However, the Russian government accused the Philomaths of political conspiracy and, in 1823, arrested several of its members. Mickiewicz was jailed and exiled to Russia in 1824, never again to return home. While in exile, he watched with grief and disgust as his homeland fell into the hands of Russia. Out of this experience grew Mickiewicz's resolve to write poetry which would celebrate Poland, sing of its greatness, and inspire all Poles to restore their country's independence.

Although his four-year stay in Russia was an unhappy one, it proved to be a significant factor in his writing career. His pieces reflect not only his suffering, but also his close association with such prominent European authors as Alexander Pushkin, Nikolay Alexeyevich Polevoi, Ivan Ivanovich Kozlov, Zygmunt Krasiński, and Juliusz Słowacki. He traveled to the Crimea and brilliantly evoked its exotic beauty in *Sonety krymskie (Sonnets from the Crimea).* While there, he read the works of Johann Wolfgang von Goethe, Sir Walter Scott, and Lord Byron, whose literary styles influenced his own. After receiving permission in 1829 to leave Russia, Mickiewicz traveled to Rome, where he experienced a religious awakening. The most characteristic piece written as a result of his newfound fervor is *Księgi Narodu polskiego i Pielgrzymstwa polskiego (The Books of the Polish Nation and the Polish Pilgrimage),* composed in the style of the Gospel and intended to comfort and instill hope in his desperate people. Mickiewicz reminded his readers of a "justice on high," and assured them that Poland would someday win its liberation.

In 1840, after he had settled in France, a position was created especially for him. He was made professor of Slavonic Studies at the Collège de France. Four years later, however, Mickiewicz was dismissed on charges that his lectures contained subversive political doctrines. It was at this time, too, that he came under the influence of Andrew Towiański, whose mys-

tical beliefs Mickiewicz adopted. According to P. A. Vyazemsky, he "created a dreamy and nonsensical teaching about some sort of Napoleonic Messianism." In 1847, he broke with Towiański, unable to endure the "spiritual terrorism, moral exhibitionism, and torturing of the souls of the 'brethren'." A year later, inspired by the cause to liberate Poland, Mickiewicz founded *La tribune des peuples,* a newspaper written in French which was devoted to perpetuating the ideals of freedom and social progress which were fermenting in the contemporary political atmosphere. The journal was banned by the French government shortly after its debut.

Published in *Poezje, I,* Mickiewicz's *Ballady i romanse,* a collection of ballads and romances, marked the beginning of Polish Romanticism. *Master Thaddeus,* a statement of his devotion to Poland, and *Forefathers' Eve,* a celebration of the past as well as the most important work of the Polish theater, won Mickiewicz renown as an outstanding writer and brilliant scholar. In these works, Mickiewicz combined mystical, prophetic, folkloristic, and religious elements which, in the words of Ernest J. Simmons, "captured in bright, deathless verse the full image and ultimate aspirations of his people." Yet, in the prime of his literary career, Mickiewicz renounced literary endeavors, choosing instead an active political life. Thus, the last twenty years of his life were devoted to living out, rather than writing about, his political beliefs. At the outbreak of the Crimean War, Mickiewicz was in Constantinople organizing forces against Tsarist Russia. It was there that he died, attempting to secure his country's freedom.

Mickiewicz was a patriot, above all else. His patriotism is most notably expressed in *Forefathers' Eve*, his love for the homeland in *Master Thaddeus*, his search for justice in *Konrad Wallenrod (Conrad Wallenrod)*, and his hope for the future of Poland in *The Books of the Polish Nation*. Critics generally praise Mickiewicz as an author whose talents equal those of Goethe, Friedrich Schiller, and Victor Hugo, and he has been called "the Polish Byron." Through his work, he brought Poland into the sphere of European literature. He was acclaimed by E. J. Dillon as "the most patriotic of poets and the most poetic of Polish patriots."

PRINCIPAL WORKS

Do Joachim Lelewela (poetry) 1822
*Poezje, I (poetry and drama) 1822
**Poezje, II (poetry and drama) 1823
Sonety (poetry) 1826
 [*Sonnets*, 1917]
Sonety krymskie (poetry) 1826; published in *Sonety*
 [*Sonnets from the Crimea*, 1917]
Oda do Młodości (poetry) 1827
 [*Ode to Youth*, n.d.]
Trzech Budrysów (ballad) 1827-28 (?)
 [*The Three Sons of Budrys*, 1835]
Farys (poetry) 1828
 [*The Faris*, 1831]
Konrad Wallenrod (novel) 1828
 [*Conrad Wallenrod*, 1841]
Do Matki Polki (poetry) 1830
 [*To a Polish Mother*, 1833]
Dziady, III (drama) 1832
 [*Forefathers' Eve*, 1926; also published as *The Ancestors*, n.d.]
Księgi Narodu polskiego i Pielgrzymstwa polskiego (poetry) 1832
 [*The Books of the Polish Nation and the Polish Pilgrimage*, 1925]
Pan Tadeusz; Czyli, ostatni zajazd na Litwie (poetry) 1834
 [*Master Thaddeus; or, The Last Foray in Lithuania*, 1917]
Drames polonais. Les confédérés de Bar; Jacques Jasiński; ou, Les deux Polognes (unfinished drama) 1867
Forefathers' Eve, Parts One, Two and Three (drama) 1944-46
Poems by Adam Mickiewicz (poetry) 1944
Adam Mickiewicz: Selected Poetry and Prose (poetry and prose) 1955
Adam Mickiewicz: Selected Poems (poetry) 1956
Adam Mickiewicz: New Selected Poems (poetry) 1957

*This work includes the poetry *Ballady i romanse*.

**This work includes Parts II and IV of the drama *Dziady*.

THE ATHENAEUM (essay date 1829)

The name of the poet Adam Mickiewicz is one at the mention of which the heart of every Pole will vibrate with quicker pulsations, and the effect which his poems produce on his countrymen, as may be imagined, is in no degree lessened by the darkness and mystery which hang over his fate. . . . As far as the poet is concerned, Mickiewicz belongs to the new German school, and often displays his intimate acquaintance with German poetry. He is particularly celebrated for his tales and romances, which possess a charm of great originality. In his diction, he permits himself great license, and is often bold and novel. Many important words have been borrowed by him from the oriental tongues, and become naturalized. At the same time there are critics who object to his want of correctness and purity, and who rank his lyrics no higher than those of a [Piotr] Kochanouski.

> "Mickiewicz, the Polish Poet," in The Athenaeum, No. 97, September, 1829, p. 553.

THE ATHENAEUM (essay date 1834)

[Adam Mickiewicz is] a Polish poet, who, like many of his countrymen, possessed much genius and little discretion. . . . French and German translations [of *The Books and the Pilgrimage of the Polish Nation*] have already appeared, which may be taken as a proof of the esteem in which the work is held by our continental brethren. It certainly contains some vivid description and bold declamation, but, unfortunately, the style being an imitation, and in many places, indeed, a mere parody on Scripture, it is not likely to suit the taste of a British public. (pp. 47-8)

> "Our Library Table: 'The Books and the Pilgrimage of the Polish Nation'," in The Athenaeum, No. 325, January 18, 1834, pp. 47-8.*

L'ÉMANCIPATION (essay date 1834)

[*Books of the Polish Pilgrimage*] possesses a character of seriousness and originality which is striking and moving. It is not written in that polite, cute, and capricious style to which we have been accustomed by today's literature; it is not made up of those thoughts, often gracious, yet often no less mad and airy, which are to be found in the pretty tales now enjoying such success; the *Pilgrimage* is written in a simple and serious style like that of the Gospels. It is bathed in that majestic poetry, grand in its simplicity, of which the Holy Scriptures have given us an example. For the cause of Poland, we needed an epic as noble as herself, and the poet has risen to the level of his mission: he has not been afraid to touch upon the vast problem of the future; he has positioned himself with daring between past and future . . . (p. 291)

One cannot, however, hide the fact that many people will find the book about the pilgrims written too exclusively for Poland. But is not the cause of Poland the cause of humanity? Can one not grasp this from the fear aroused in absolute monarchs by the unfortunate proscripts? . . .

If, then, you have a generous and understanding soul, if your heart has bled as you thought of unfortunate Poland, if you wept at the fall of Warsaw, and if, glimpsing but an instant the future, you have cried: "The day will come!"—then read the *Books of the Polish Pilgrimage;* you will understand it. If you believe in God and in liberty, read the *Books of the Polish Pilgrimage*. But if you have remained cold in the reflection of a burning capital, if upon seeing a nation crushed you have said, "They are only rebels . . . ," if you fear the future—

then step back; for you will profane the **Books of the Polish Pilgrimage**. (p. 292)

A. D., in his extract from "A Note on Mickiewicz in the Belgian Press" by Gustave Charlier, translated by J. Robert Loy (originally published in an article in L'émancipation, *March 10, 1834), in* Adam Mickiewicz in World Literature, *edited by Wacław Lednicki, University of California Press, 1956, pp. 291-92.*

ALEKSANDER PUSHKIN (essay date 1834)

[The following is Aleksander Pushkin's poem "He Lived among Us."]

He lived among us,
Among a tribe foreign to him.
He did not harbor malice against us in his soul, and we
Loved him. Peaceful, benevolent,
He attended our gatherings. With him
We shared both pure dreams
And songs. (He was inspired from above
And looked upon life from on high.) Frequently
He spoke of future times,
When nations, having forgotten their quarrels,
Will unite in one great family.
Greedily we listened to the poet. He
Left us for the West—our blessings
Went with him. But now
Our peaceful guest has become our enemy—
And he fills his poems with poison
To please the tempestuous mob.
From afar there comes to us
The voice of the angered poet,
The well-known voice! O God! Grant
Peace to his embittered and troubled soul.

Aleksander Pushkin, "He Lived among Us" (1834), in Pushkin's "Bronze Horseman": The Story of a Masterpiece *by Wacław Lednicki (reprinted by permission of the University of California Press), University of California Press, 1955, p. 152.*

STANISLAS KOZMIAN (essay date 1838)

The appearance of [Adam Mickiewicz] in ordinary times, though hailed with admiration, would have been only like a brief angel-visit without a message from heaven,—like lightning unfollowed by thunder. But the rise and progress of his genius, falling as they did within the verge of a great era, must necessarily impress upon our minds the justness of Bacon's remark, that great men are like great mountains, which reflect the first rays of the coming sun. From the very nature of his mission he belongs not to the class of those who spring up from the very womb of the eruption to stem and direct the current, but of those who alight on earth carried on the wings of the faintly-heard sound of distant convulsions,—who are born to shadow forth coming events, to foretell or suffer, to be prophets or martyrs, as fortune may determine. To display the extent of his powers and consequent influence is here impossible: all that can be done is to enumerate his works, pointing as we go to the golden thread which runs throughout them. It is enough to say, that modern Polish literature, however interesting and diversified, would lose its crowning excellen-

cies, its connecting link, were the name of Mickiewicz obliterated. . . .

To detail the wanderings of the poet and improvisatore, (for Mickiewicz unites both characters,) would lead us too far: let me endeavour to show him as an author—as a benefactor to his country. (p. 534)

[In '**Grażyna**'] the poet himself casts off the gossamer clothing of imagination for the armour of well-marked purpose—exchanges Poland scarcely awakened and still dreaming among its dim old fables, for Poland devoting herself for the union of her dismembered race, and the combination of their strength against their common enemy. . . . How the Polish poet dealt with [Dziady, or the Feast of the Dead, in '**Dziady**',] and with what magnificent touches of feeling and fancy he ennobled it, it is easier to conceive than explain. . . . ['**Konrad Wallenrod**',] which appears mysterious to historians, and is related as a miraculous event in the old chronicles, presented no difficulties to the imagination of the poet. His Konrad Wallenrod is a Lithuanian, who has sworn the ruin of his country's foes. The Poles caught at once the whole range of the poet's conception. While they enthusiastically admired the beauty of particular images in the transcendent sublimity of the narrative, they recognized its deeper purpose. Konrad Wallenrod became the watchword of the national conspiracies. . . . ['**Farys**' is] a short piece of poetry, which sums up the poetical vision of Mickiewicz. . . .

Mickiewicz was exiled into Russia for his participation in the secret societies of Wilna. But though condemned as a traitor, he was received, both in Moscow and in St. Petersburgh, with a warm and admiring welcome; foremost in which were the aristocracy of Russia. Such manifestations not being peculiarly acceptable to the police, they ordered him into the Crimea, over the ruins of which, as Gaszynski says, "he strewed diamonds." Indeed, his '**Crimean Sonnets**' are the offspring of his happiest inspiration. . . . The third canto of '**Dziady**' was his first poetic composition after [Mickiewicz's religious] metamorphosis. . . . '**Squire Taddeus**' is a voluminous poem founded upon a tale from the annals of the feuds of the Polish nobles. Its images, its descriptions, remind us of the best days of his genius: but it is a record of the past, without any moral for the future—a meed to the valour of the dead, without a word for the living;—the lyrist is lost in the historian—the poet in the mystic. . . . To analyze his merits coolly is not easy for our national love. Endowed with more of Byron's imagination than of Goethe's searching philosophy, we find that he combines, in a remarkable degree, the faculties of both—the imagery of the east with the contemplativeness of the west. (p. 535)

Stanislas Kozmian, "Literature of the Nineteenth Century," in The Athenaeum, *No. 561, July 28, 1838, pp. 532-36.**

THE FOREIGN QUARTERLY REVIEW (essay date 1838)

The writings of Mickiewicz abound in passionate and patriotic sentiments, the evident results of his own peculiar temperament, darkened by melancholy; his sarcasm is brilliant and severe: and the moody spirit that pervades his compositions is relieved and set off by great powers of poetry and sweetness. (p. 146)

"Polish Poetry," in The Foreign Quarterly Review, *Vol. XXII, No. XLIII, October, 1838, pp. 135-53.**

[S. B. GNOROWSKI]   (essay date 1840)

Mickiewicz must be considered in a twofold aspect. In one view, as an apostle and martyr of that fervent patriotism which impels with irresistible power his countrymen to struggle to preserve the national existence; in the other, as the deliverer of national genius from school trammels, directing its course in the independent track of Homer and Shakespeare. (p. 182)

[**"Sir Thaddeus" ("Pan Tadeusz")**] does not aim at one grand catastrophe, nor contain any conspicuous character, but presents a masterly picture of the ancient habits of the nobility, and of their patriotic exertions since the partition; describing the impenetrable primitive forests of Poland with their countless inhabitants; her exuberant corn-fields, and even her very kitchen gardens. It is in our opinion the most successful attempt at *Georgics* ever made; and Poles, when they read it, wonder how they can have trodden amongst such beautiful objects for centuries, and been so little alive to them. It has been criticised for its want of any direct moral, but the censurers forget that the highest morality of man, considered as an esthetic being, is to look upon all creation as a temple of beauty. After having revivied the poetic and historical traditions of his country, and pointed out its natural beauties with a Byronian imagination, though deeply imbued with religious sentiment and philosophic faith, he composed a work of lamentation, of retribution and justice, of consolation and hope, which in proud modesty he entitled **"A Book."** It consists of two parts. The one called **"The Acts of the Polish Nation since the beginning of the World to its Crucifixion,"** is a synthetic and theosophic history of Poland in Biblical phraseology. As our national taste is completely opposed to the application of Scripture to politics, and as great disgust has been excited in Paris by the efforts in this shape by the Abbé Lammenais, we shall not extract from this first portion.

The second is a series of precepts and parables addressed to the Polish pilgrim, and these display the poet's great power of lyric composition, his knowledge of his art; and the soul of a patriot, and a believer, energetic, but resigned, sympathising and persuasive. Counsels, intreaties, threats, consolation, hope, all are to be found in this second part. Some of the parables are keen satires upon the men and affairs of the present day. (pp. 183-84)

[*S. B. Gnorowski,*] *"Polish Literature," in* The Foreign Quarterly Review, *Vol. XXV, No. XLIX, April, 1840, pp. 159-88.*

[WILLIAM H. BARNES]   (essay date 1864)

It is high time that the claims of such really remarkable poets as Mickiewicz . . . were at least laid before the English reader. Were we but superficially acquainted with the masterpieces of Polish literature, we should not need the excitement of an insurrection to turn our thoughts towards, and remind us of the continued existence of, that unfortunate nation. It should be borne in mind that the Poles do not die when the newspapers cease to write about them. That unintelligent sympathy, which is ready to burst out in England whenever the Poles throw down the gauntlet to one or other of their oppressors, would then be changed into an intelligent admiration of a people which in its century of bonds has produced so remarkable a literature. Just as Vesuvius resorts to periodical eruptions to save itself from falling quite out of the world's memory, so does the

indifference of Europe drive Poland to insurrection, that men may at least talk of her for a time.

Whether it really be the difficulty of the language, or not rather the want of interest taken in Poland in repose, combined with a general disbelief in the existence of a Polish literature, which keeps the very [name of Mickiewicz] a dead secret to the outside world, it is a fact which is much to be regretted. If we are thereby the losers, the Poles, on the other hand, gain by the intense fervour with which their poets address themselves to the narrow circle of their own countrymen. I shall not easily forget the enthusiasm with which a Polish lady remarked to me one day, "Nous avons Mickiewicz—*à nous,"* as much as to say, "We have him all to ourselves. To you he is nothing, but to us he makes up for everything else." While an Italian or German poet is to a certain extent the common property of all nations, the Pole is conscious that his song will be unheeded by the world at large; and hence that intense nationality which characterizes Polish poetry. (pp. 198-99)

Byron, almost alone of Englishmen, knew and appreciated Mickiewicz; and it is much to be regretted that the time which he devoted at Venice to translations from the Armenian was not spent in rendering some portion of his friend's poems into English. (p. 199)

[*William H. Barnes,*] *" 'Resurrecturis': A Poem from the Polish of Sigmund Krasinski," in* Macmillan's Magazine, *Vol. 10, No. 57, July, 1864, pp. 198-203.**

[WILLIAM R. MORFILL]   (essay date 1879)

Of all the writings of Mickiewicz, his lyrical pieces strike us as the most beautiful, and show the language in its strength and grace. His works are but little known except to his own countrymen, and there was both pathos and irony in the expression used by a Polish lady to a foreigner, "Nous avons notre Mickiewicz à nous.". . . His ballads are full of interest; their colouring is entirely national, treating of Lithuanian superstitions. . . . (p. 375)

[Mickiewicz's *Crimean Sonnets*] are exquisitely-finished compositions; the three most beautiful, in our opinion, are **"The Storm," "Bakche-Sarai,"** and **"The Grave of the Countess Potocka."** The last two pieces are written on the Palace of the Khans of the Crimea, and the story of the Polish captive detained there, which forms the subject of Pushkin's fine poem "Bakchi Saraiski Fontan" (The Fountain of Bakchisarai). In **"Konrad Wallenrod,"** a narrative poem detailing the battles of the Prussian knights with the heathen Lithuanians, Mickiewicz disguised under a thin veil a representation of the sanguinary passages of arms and burning hatred which had characterised the long feuds of the Russians and Poles. . . . Almost every style of metre is employed in it with equal facility; the few songs interspersed are models of consummate grace and finish. (p. 376)

One of the longest and most celebrated pieces of Mickiewicz is his *Pan Tadeusz,* by many considered to be his *chef d'oeuvre.* . . . The poem is full of local colouring, and is worth hundreds of the productions of the Polish poets, while under the influence of the so-called classical school and the rhetorical teaching of the Jesuits. To Mickiewicz it was a labour of love to describe the habits and scenes of his native country, Lithuania, which he was never to revisit. (p. 378)

[William R. Morfill,] "Polish Literature," in The Westminster Review, n.s. Vol. LV, No. II, April 1, 1879, pp. 359-86.*

E. J. DILLON (essay date 1890)

[Mickiewicz,] whose niche in the temple of poetry is beside those of Schiller, Byron, Hugo, is in his writings no less than in his actions a Pole of the Poles. Now there are no two peoples more different from each other in temperament and character than Englishmen and Poles, between whom there is a psychological gulf to the full as wide and deep as that which separates the inhabitants of Scotland from the Baboos of Bengal. And as Mickiewicz was the most patriotic of poets and the most poetic of Polish patriots, the circumstance that to Englishmen he is still but an unpronounceable name needs no further explanation. The most accurate characteristic of his life and work has, to my thinking, been given by the poet himself in one of his best-known works [*The Ancestors (Dziady)*], in which it is said of another person, "Whether thou castest thyself into hell or shinest from the heights of heaven, thou art brilliant as a sun-lit cloud, erring but sublime, wotting not whither thou driftest, and knowing not what thou dost." (p. 202)

[*Konrad Wallenrod*] is descriptive of an episode in the secular Wars between the Teutonic Order and Pagan Lithuania, the sands of whose national existence were fast running out. (p. 209)

It requires no rare gift of penetration to see that in this poem the Lithuanians are merely another name for Poles, and the Teutonic Order is Russia in thin disguise. This would have sufficed to wreck the poem in Russia, had it not been for the apparently candid preface, in which the author takes credit to himself for having selected a theme which allows him to depict only passions that are long since extinct, instead of awakening those that still slumber in the breasts of his countrymen. The censors, in consequence, allowed the poem to be published, with the exception of one line:—

> Treason's the last strong weapon of the slave.
>
> (p. 210)

[Mickiewicz's fantastic poem, *Master Thaddeus*,] is an imposing picture of Poland at the end of the eighteenth century, at the winding up of an epoch, the final scene of a long and chequered national existence. Nature and civilisation are there vividly depicted with that inimitable art which is the nearest approach to creative power. The period chosen was in many respects unique: the types and forms of one age were in process of disintegration, and those of the new epoch were as yet in the womb of the future; passion struggled with passion, patriotism was grafted on piety or selfishness, self-sacrifice and heroism throve side by side with cruelty and baseness. (p. 212)

[The thread of the story] is closely interwoven with the most fateful events of the world's history. The individual will of the *dramatis personae* is, as it were, wrapped up in that of the guiding spirit of the universe; and so our interest, at first claimed by the living and doing of everyday men and women, is at last centred in the destiny of nations, the mission of humanity. While Goethe's [*Hermann und Dorothea*] lacks tragical motive, *Master Thaddeus* possesses a sufficiently absorbing one in a blood debt which in the end is wiped out by sorrow and repentance, self-sacrifice, and patriotism. Such action as there is in the Polish poem centres in the love of Thaddeus, a manly, noble-minded youth, with nothing of the hero in his composition. The success of his suit is the conclusion of the plot, which interests the reader far less than the story of the loves of Hermann and Dorothea. But the plot is merely the peg on which are hung artistic beauties of which *Master Thaddeus* is a marvellous mosaic; delightful pictures of daily life in time of peace such as charm all intelligent lovers of Wordsworth; glowing descriptions of the morning freshness fluttering through the trembling foliage of dewy bushes and towering trees and waking up the slumbering songbirds; the lisping of children and the innocent chatter of men and women who are but older children, as they jog cheerfully onwards on the highways of life; the weaving of looms, the turning of spindles accompanying long tales told on winter nights; then again the clang of arms, the roar of cannon, the groans of the dying, soon absorbed by the eternal silence of the dead. *Hermann und Dorothea* is perhaps more classical, follows straight lines more thoroughly, is less realistic, and at the same time less romantic, inasmuch as it admits to a much lesser extent the humorous element than the masterpiece of Mickiewicz, who, as a rule, rarely delights us with a glimpse of the play of human passion, unless when wholly consecrated to the service of Poland or humanity.

This latter tendency is equally palpable in *Grażyna,* a charming little poem. . . . (pp. 212-13)

A much larger poem is *The Ancestors* . . . , in which the manners and customs of the "good old times" are portrayed to the life; it deserves an article to itself, and it is perhaps better to dismiss it with a passing allusion than by an imperfect analysis to run the risk of giving a false, because a one-sided impression. (p. 213)

Mickiewicz was the poet of recollection rather than of hope, a painter of the irrevocable past rather than a moulder of the plastic future. His works might be fitly termed "Songs after Sunset." Like ivy they cling to the hallowed old ruins of a bygone age which are as likely to be restored to their pristine splendour as the Palace of Persepolis or the Temple of Jerusalem. Patriotism informed his verse as it still inspires the gorgeous canvases of the Polish painter Matejko; but it inspires without wholly absorbing; and every theme he treats, however exclusively Polish it may seem, has always the deep and far-reaching significance which lies at the root of all true poetry. Mickiewicz was an enthusiastic adept of the romantic school; and yet we find much in his works that favorably distinguishes him from the majority of romantic poets. His poetry is not of the whining and puling description so common among his contemporaries; it avoids wire-drawn sentimentality, is manly, healthy, sustained by deep conviction, directed to a noble purpose. He knew nothing of the sickly introversion that plays such a large part in so-called art for art. If his creations do not prove eternal, the reason lies less in the execution than in the materials in which he worked—the languages of certain Slavonic peoples constituting, as it were, the fading water-colours of literary painting. The language and diction of Mickiewicz are lost to the majority even of such enlightened foreigners as read Goethe, Calderon, and Bellman in the originals. It is well, however, to know that there is something, nay, very much to lose; that the music of his verse is intoxicating. The harmonious blending of thought, imagery and style in the poet's best work bears witness to his exquisite sense of just proportion. (p. 216)

E. J. Dillon, "Mickiewicz: The National Poet of Poland," in The Fortnightly Review (reprinted by permission of Contemporary Review Company Limited), Vol. XLVIII, August 1, 1890, pp. 202-17.

W. R. MORFILL (essay date 1895)

It is much to be regretted that, in consequence of the neglect of the Polish language among the English and French, the writings of this really great poet [Mickiewicz] are so little known. . . .

[Mickiewicz] occupies the position of the representative poet of his nation. In his writings whatsoever is Polish, and especially Lithuanian, finds an echo. He was the first great romantic poet of his country, who could tell the world of her traditions, her scenery, her customs, and her aspirations. In "**Konrad Wallenrod**" and "**Grażyna**" he poetises some pages of her history; in "**Pan Tadeusz**" he gives us a picture of extraordinary power of the condition of society in Poland at the time of the Napoleonic invasion of Russia in 1812. . . .

[Mickiewicz's poem "**The Sailor**" ("*Zeglarz*") is] a striking piece, in which the vague, unsatisfied impulses of life are described with extraordinary power. The poet pictures himself as alone upon the ocean; he cannot advance, he cannot retreat, nor dare he abandon the guidance of his frail vessel! It is now all tempest, but it was calm and hopeful when he set out. The immortal "**Ode to Youth**," of course, comes in for its proper share of praise. "Without heart, without soul, we are but a people of skeletons. Youth! lend me thy wings!" (p. 334)

["**Farys**" is a] fiery poem in which the author represents himself as hurried on through the desert, passing on his way the whitened bones of those who have perished before him. It is a fine Oriental study, with a subtle inner meaning. . . . All the sonnets of Mickiewicz are beautiful, but especially those on localities in the Crimea, which he composed when visiting that romantic part of Europe just before he finally left Russia. Of the "**Pan Tadeusz**" of Mickiewicz, confessedly his finest work, M. Toporski [the popular Polish critic] says . . . that it is the greatest epic of the century. This is, perhaps, exaggerated praise, although we must remember that it is not easy to point to any great epics of quite modern times. "**Pan Tadeusz**" is, in our opinion, rather a charming idyllic poem. It is a delightful picture of Lithuanian life, told in the most harmonious verse. . . . Here are to be found some of the most wonderful forest and cloud-pictures. . . . Every kind of forest tree is described by Mickiewicz with the minutest accuracy. He has all the vigour of a Wordsworth or a Shelley. He reminds us especially of the latter. And then the splendid cloud-pictures, parallels to which are only to be found in Shelley, or in the beautiful lines in which the broken Anthony addresses his page Eros in Shakspere's great tragedy! This idyllic poem, as we prefer to consider it, contains a charming love-story. All goes at the end

Merry as a marriage-bell;

and the news comes of the arrival of the great conqueror, at whose feet of clay the Poles have so often prostrated themselves. (pp. 334-35)

W. R. Morfill, "The Polish Poet Mickiewicz," in The Academy, No. 1225, October 26, 1895, pp. 334-35.

GEORGE RAPALL NOYES (essay date 1930)

[More] important than the praises of the finest literary critics is the enthusiastic affection cherished for *Pan Tadeusz* by the great body of the Polish people. Perhaps no poem of any other European nation is so truly national and in the best sense of the word popular. Almost every Pole who has read anything

more than the newspaper is familiar with the contents of *Pan Tadeusz*. No play of Shakespeare, no long poem of Milton or Wordsworth or Tennyson, is so well known or so well beloved by the English people as is *Pan Tadeusz* by the Poles. To find a work equally well known one might turn to Defoe's prosaic tale of adventure, *Robinson Crusoe;* to find a work so beloved would be hardly possible. (pp. ix-x)

In the work of Mickiewicz as a whole two characteristics predominate: a great intensity of feeling, which sometimes sinks into sentimentality, and at others rises into lyric fervour; and a wonderful truth, not only to the general impressions of his experience, but to the actual concrete facts of it, even to such trifles as the names of persons and places. Thus *The Forefathers*, despite all its fantastic elements, reproduces many incidents in which the poet himself was concerned. Furthermore, in certain works, as in his early tale *Grażyna*, Mickiewicz had shown a wonderful ability suddenly to detach himself from passing currents of emotion and to rise into regions of Olympian calm, giving to his work a classic, rounded completeness worthy of Grecian art. All these aspects of his genius are present in *Pan Tadeusz*. Echoes of the poet's personal emotion are heard in Jacek's tale of his passion for Eva: and an ardent love of country permeates the poem and breaks out again and again with lyric force. On the other hand the book is faithful to reality in its picture of Lithuanian manners and customs; the great romantic poet is at the same time the first realistic novelist of Poland. Minor details beyond number are introduced from the writer's personal recollections. . . . Through the whole book runs a humour not often found elsewhere in Mickiewicz; the reports of the debates in Jankiel's tavern and in Dobrzyn hamlet are masterly in their blending of kindly pleasantry with photographic fidelity to truth. The poet sees the ludicrous side of the Warden, the Chamberlain, the Seneschal, and the other Don Quixotes who fill his pages, and yet he loves them with the most tender affection. In his descriptions of external nature—of the Lithuanian forests or of the scene around Soplicowo on the moonlight night just before the foray—Mickiewicz shows a genius for throwing a glamour of poetic beauty over the face of common things such as has never been surpassed. Finally, the whole poem is perfect in its proportions; from its homely beginning, with pictures of rural simplicity and old-fashioned hospitality, it swells into rustic grandeur in the panorama of the hunt, and at last reaches the most poignant tragedy in the scene about the death-bed of Jacek Soplica: then, lest the impression should be one of total sadness, the narrative concludes with the magnificent epilogue of the last two books, full of hopes of rescue for Poland, full of gaiety and courage. A large epic calm pervades the whole. The age-long conflict between Pole and "Muscovite" is the theme of the epic, but the tone is not that of passionate hatred and revolt such as fills *The Forefathers;* human kindliness breathes through the whole work; not indignation and rebellion, but faith, hope, and love are at its foundation. (pp. xv-xvi)

George Rapall Noyes, in his introduction to Pan Tadeusz by Adam Mickiewicz, translated by George Rapall Noyes (reprinted from Everyman's Library by permission of J M Dent & Sons Ltd), second edition, Dent, 1930, pp. ix-xxi.

JULIAN KRZYZANOWSKI (essay date 1930)

[Mickiewicz's] *Ode to Youth*, now one of the favourite poems of Polish young people, is among the most far-sighted products of his inspiration. It forms a link between the old and new worlds of the ideas of the eighteenth-century thinkers, and of those of the first quarter of the succeeding century. In similes full of rhetorical power the poet denounces egotism, as an element of social life leading to death, and glorifies the commonwealth as being the supreme ideal of mankind. The realization of this sublime ideal, flying high above the earth, may sometimes demand not only strength and endeavour on the part of the fighters, but even their self-sacrifice; they must not retreat, for even the defeat of the noble brings nearer the realization of human happiness. But what is to be done if the goal seems too distant and the forces too weak? The young poet here brings to the path of enlightened thought the Romantic belief in the value of irrational elements within the human soul. It is Enthusiasm and Belief that help Man in the most difficult moments, and that enable him to overcome all the obstacles he may meet on his way. Only a man in full control of all his soul's forces can carry out all his aims, on behalf of his fellow-creatures, on behalf of humanity.

Mickiewicz, who well knew the idealistic philosophy and poetry of Schiller, explained his thoughts on the subject with all the splendour of his enthusiastic soul and with all the power of a youthful fervour unknown to the more sceptical German master. Both this enthusiasm and this belief in the importance of irrational forces of the human soul are the true evidence of Mickiewicz's Romanticism, though the poem was given a carefully classical form, and though the poet's first official or rather public Romantic utterance was to be postponed until . . . after he had written his *Ode*. . . . (pp. 44-5)

[Mickiewicz's] ballads are crowded with "goblins, ghouls and human vampires, spectres, hags and howling wer-wolves, and all other evil spirits". In introducing all these apparitions the young poet followed the fashion of the time as one can occasionally notice in his *Romanticism*. This statement, however, does not imply that he was but an imitator. Certainly he was not. He tried to create his own imaginary world after the patterns of Polish and Lithuanian folk-lore, and he succeeded. (p. 47)

On the whole, the *Ballads* were a successful achievement, for they established not only Mickiewicz's renown amongst the young writers of his period, but they also became a model for the future. For the writer himself they were only the first stage in his literary career. He soon decided to climb higher, and he did so in his second volume, published in the next year. . . . It contained three works of greater value than the *Ballads, i.e.* two parts of a dramatic poem, *The Forefathers' Eve (Dziady)*, and a story in verse called *Grażyna*. (p. 51)

In dealing with both earlier parts of *The Forefathers' Eve* as a whole, one must point out that there is the same strange mixture of realistic observation and fancifulness which appears in *Ballads and Romances;* the first of these factors undoubtedly prevails, for the poet was skilful enough to rely upon his own inner life, the experience of which he dared to raise to the heights of true and great art.

Passing to the last of Mickiewicz's early works, *Grażyna,* one feels a little surprise, for this short tale recalls rather the academic and classical productions of the poet's predecessors than his own Romantic pictures. Particularly striking is the fact that it lacks all the fantastic element and that love does not play any part in its plot. Yet one finds no difficulty in showing that it has embodied elements already met in Mickiewicz's *Ballads*. The poet here gives voice to his Romantic inclination for the past and, at the same time, to his personal love of

heroism in the human soul. As in the *Legend of Lake Switez,* he represents in his *Grażyna* an ancient heroine, who preferred to die rather than to live in dishonour. (p. 55)

The most important [feature of Mickiewicz's youthful poetry] is the fact that the poet is entirely conscious of what he is doing. He does not grope his way; his steps are quite sure. He has firm views on man in his attitude to the world. He wants to develop the whole individuality of man, particlarly his emotional powers, for they are the key to the problems that man finds on his way. . . . [Already] in his first work one can discover the nuclei of the ideas that will often be met in Mickiewicz's later works.

On the other hand, the young writer distinctly expresses here his views upon the poet's duties towards the subjects he intends to treat. He breaks away from the limits of the classical poetics; it is not the ancient poet's example that matters, but the modern writer's personal attitude to life is the deciding value of his art. He shall not be bound by poetic recipes, but he shall express in his own way all he sees around him. This was a Romantic revolt against the routine, and, like each revolt, it could succeed, provided the bold theory were accompanied by actual practice. And this had been done in Mickiewicz's works. He discovered a new world of the human soul, and a new world of human life, untouched by the Polish poets of earlier periods, and he proved himself able to demonstrate it in an unfading halo of beauty. This fact was sufficient to secure for him a victory. (pp. 56-7)

In his short cycle [*Crimean Sonnets*], containing eighteen carefully polished pearls of poetry, Mickiewicz showed not only his love for beauty, but also his ability to paint in words. All the charms of southern nature, the immense meadows, covered with grass and flowers, the calm and motionless surface of the sea, the many-coloured gardens, the mountains in the sunshine and moonlight, live in his sonnets. He notices the slightest and most delicate shadows and lights, murmurs and melodies; no colour can escape his keen eye, no voice his sensitive ear. Since an analogous seventeenth-century cycle of poems, the Latin *Sylviludia* by Casimir Sarbiewski, no other Polish poet has produced such a fine wealth of impressions inspired by Nature, in such a perfect form, as did Mickiewicz in his sonnets.

But it is their Oriental tincture that contributes to their special charm. Mickiewicz, interested in Oriental poetry, added to his observations the results of his studies; he is very careful in rendering the "local colour" of the Crimea; we meet, then, in his work with very interesting comparisons and metaphors from the Persian and Arabian mythologies, with some striking particulars of the Oriental habits and beliefs, and finally with many Oriental ideas. He even daringly tries to imitate the Oriental method of thinking and expressing himself. (pp. 60-1)

At the same time Mickiewicz does not forget the question which was inevitable with all Romantics, the question of the poet's personality. His *Crimean Sonnets* have much to tell us about the author's feelings and thoughts, about his anxieties and hopes for the future. His homesickness and feeling of abandonment, his inner struggles, his feigned calmness and Byronic solitude, found fine expression in this cycle. All these elements combined to form a perfect work of art, and the author was quite aware of what he had done. Consequently the last sonnet of the sequence is full of proud consciousness that his work is a little collection of poetic jewels. Mickiewicz, whose characteristic feature was modesty, does not here conceal his ambitious claim for the laurels which he deserved. (pp. 61-2)

The *Crimean Sonnets,* perfect as they are, never evoked such attention as the following work [*Conrad Wallenrod*]. . . . (p. 62)

Conrad Wallenrod is the first of Mickiewicz's works in which there appears a universal man, a representative of his community, a man who is ready to save his fellow-men at the cost of his own happiness. His formula runs: "Joy did not dwell in his house, when his fatherland knew only sorrow." This ideal, founded on the Romantic appreciation of the individualistic and the heroic, from this moment on was to become a cornerstone of Polish national life for the whole period of Romanticism and afterwards until our own days. One must understand its roots, its origin, but—at the same time—one cannot help noticing that it was mere poetry blended with politics, a natural product of a life where there was no room for political ideas, except in the realm of dreams and poetry. (p. 69)

Conrad Wallenrod exerted a strong influence on Polish youth, though an impartial onlooker might prefer the view that both the rising and the poem were results of the spirit of the age, the first being its political, the latter its poetic manifestation. This statement explains the fact that *Conrad Wallenrod* was accepted by readers with enthusiasm, and that even many of Mickiewicz's antagonists, the classicist poets, bowed their heads and acknowledged his superiority. (pp. 69-70)

[When reading Mickiewicz's *Pan Tadeusz*], one feels its Homeric spirit; it is apparent even in the Polish poet's standpoint. According to the rules of classical poetry the epic poet should take his subject from a remote epoch, in order to avoid any partiality, any personal tincture of the facts which he is going to relate. Mickiewicz obeyed this rule, bestowing on his poem an epic objectivism and impartiality, and although in several lyric passages he gave voice to his personal opinions and feelings, he was then concerned with the character of the period rather than with its personalities. In other words, in *Pan Tadeusz* both these elements, classical calm and impartiality, romantic vividness and lyric emotions, are perfectly balanced.

The moment itself, chosen by the poet, facilitated his epic task. The period which he had described, though not distant in time, was in reality of a forgotten past. Old Polish life, unchanging through long centuries, was over at the moment when the Napoleonic wars came to Poland. Napoleon's defeat but accelerated the new policy of the powers in possession of the dismembered country who seized the opportunity to abolish the remnants of Polish institutions. The poet skilfully accentuated these facts in the very title of his poem. It runs: *Master Thaddeus or the Last Foray (Zaiazd) in Lithuania.* (pp. 83-4)

[The] characteristics of old Polish life, represented in Mickiewicz's epic as decaying fast, allowed the poet to keep his epic calm and granted the poem the merit of being a perfect picture of old customs and habits. One must wonder at the subtle intuition which led him to choose such a characteristic and exceptional moment in Poland's past in which the old mode of life suddenly ceased to exist.

The plot of *Pan Tadeusz* is rather simple and to a certain degree commonplace. At the same time it is closely connected with Polish national history, (p. 85)

Generally speaking, one can call [*Pan Tadeusz*] a rich store, an encyclopaedia of old-Polish life and habits. In its twelve cantos Mickiewicz brought together the great mass of all the peculiarities of Polish life at the end of the eighteenth century. The old castles, the manor-houses and the inns, the garments and the arms, the tools—in short, the whole of the material outfit presents itself perfectly in the poem. Mickiewicz's descriptions, exact and minute, combine both Homer's picturesqueness and Sir Walter Scott's accuracy. All these details combine to give a long series of lively pictures portraying the occupations and entertainments of the epoch, like hunting, dancing, etc.

Among the most interesting elements of the poem are its descriptions of Nature. Mickiewicz, who has excelled already as a painter of Nature in his earlier *Crimean Sonnets,* is here at his very best. From the first lines of the poem he drew hundreds of pictures recalling the Polish landscape with striking fidelity and unique beauty; the dawns, sunrises and sunsets, the sights of the fields and forests, appear and reappear incessantly and change Lithuania into a wonderland. It is hardly possible to quote here many examples of the poet's admirable painting in words; it is sufficient to remark that under his fairy pen each detail, even the commonest one, becomes a part of something perfect in its beauty. . . . It is noteworthy that the details spoken of cannot be regarded as an additional or occasional decoration; though they do not belong to the plot, and live their independent life, they contribute to the whole of Poland's life of the period.

Finally one must mention the innumerable gallery of characters in the poem. The most interesting amongst them [is] Jacek, with its many features of profound suffering, self-sacrifice and moral conscience. . . . Around him Mickiewicz grouped a crowd of less profound but very characteristic men and women, the latter however being in a striking minority. Judge Soplica, his visitors and tenants, such as the old Chamberlain representing the nobility, and Assessor, Regent and Woiski, representatives of the middle gentry, the two old stewards, Gerwazy and Protazy, as well as a number of half-peasants, half-gentry, form the whole of the little community, representing the most peculiar traits of the nation. Each personality has his own method of thinking and expressing himself by means of gestures and speech. The poet not only was very careful to reproduce their special features; at the same time he surrounded them with a very quaint air of humour. He did not conceal the ridiculous in their characters—most of them are odd and strange worshippers of the past, in their ridiculous obstinacy which bids them reject all that seems modern; at the same time, however, he succeeded in pointing out their moral value, their human virtues; thanks to this method of treating them, the reader cannot help admiring or even loving them, despite all their faults.

Looking back on the whole of Mickiewicz's last poetical achievement, one must stress the marvellous harmony of various *motifs* in *Pan Tadeusz.* The tragic colours of Jacek's history, the merry finale of joy produced by the reawakened national hopes, the poet's benign smile at the sight of the eccentric characters, the clear and bright air of a fairy-tale—all these elements combine to intensify the impression of a masterpiece of uncommon artistic merit. (pp. 90-1)

There is no other Polish poet whose importance in national life can be compared to that of Mickiewicz, for though Polish literature in its earlier periods produced many high-class writers, yet none of them reached the rank of a genius. They expressed the spirit of their times in a manner more or less exact, but their horizons were limited. None of them was able to render the Polish life and character in their permanent landmarks, to show their universal human value; it was Mickiewicz who created a series of perfect pictures, universal in their character and, at the same time, entirely Polish in their essence. Let us remember his great epic achievement, *Master Thaddeus,* with its Homeric dignity and perfect beauty, or his *Forefathers' Eve,* with its picture of a modern Prometheus fighting against oppression, as his predecessors did, and yet entirely Polish in his most profound sense, for he expressed the modern attitude of a man, an individual, towards this nation.

At the same time Mickiewicz was the first great personality in Polish literature, a personality which found its full expression in its artistic works. . . . In his youthful *Ballads* he discovered the poet's principal duty, the duty of expressing the entire man, all his rational and irrational movements of soul; in his *Conrad Wallenrod* he blended the problems of an individual with those of the nation; in his *Books of the Polish Nation* he established the relation between a nation and humanity. Rich and many-sided in its outward aspects, his work is—at the same time—entirely uniform. The reader everywhere feels the poet's spirit forming the basis of all his literary achievements. Everywhere he meets with the poet's love of life and liberty, his high appreciation of the heroic, his looking for the heroic even in the commonest everyday affairs. His love of the natural and the supernatural, of the common and of the sublime, form a perfect whole; he reminds us of a powerful oak with its roots deeply in the earth and its crest in the blue skies. No wonder, then, that the poet's individuality which gave his works this unity could not but exert a profound influence on his contemporaries and successors. All his brother-poets grew in his benign shade, and one of them, Z. Krasinski, expressed perfectly their attitude towards him, saying that "he was milk and honey to them, that they were all his offspring". (pp. 103-05)

> *Julian Krzyzanowski, "Adam Mickiewicz," in his* Polish Romantic Literature *(reprinted by permission of George Allen & Unwin Ltd), Allen & Unwin, 1930, pp. 41-105.*

VLADISLAV KHODASEVICH (essay date 1939?)

[Mickiewicz] is not just poetry, but somehow indissolubly bound up with prayer and with Poland, that is, with the church, that Polish church in the Milyutin Lane where mother and I used to go on Sundays. I had never seen Mickiewicz or Poland, they cannot be seen, no more than God, but they are where God is behind the low grille upholstered in red velvet, in the rumbling of the organ, in the smoke of the incense, and in the golden light of the slanting rays of the sun, falling from somewhere at the side onto the altar. The altar was for me the portal, or even the beginning, of "the other world," where I had been before I was, and where I shall be when I am no longer.

God—Poland—Mickiewicz: something invisible and incomprehensible but familiar. And inseparable from each other. (pp. 153-54)

> *Vladislav Khodasevich, "Vladislav Khodasevich on 'Pan Tadeusz'" (1939?), translated by Gleb Struve, in* Adam Mickiewicz in World Literature, *edited by Wacław Lednicki (copyright © 1956 by The Regents of the University of California; reprinted by permission of the University of California Press), University of California Press, 1956, pp. 153-58.*

MANFRED KRIDL (essay date 1951)

The language of Mickiewicz is marked by simplicity raised to the highest level of poetic art. He relies mainly on elementary words, those already in existence for centuries, homely words that every Pole can understand. He avoids neologisms and even artificiality in his language; he does not devise new and difficult and amazing combinations; he shows none of the linguistic virtuosity characteristic of Słowacki, Norwid, and Malczewski. Yet out of this simple, colloquial material he builds a style not only incomparably clear, clean, and precise; not only infallible in its designation of both material objects and psychological processes; but full of amazing force, light, color, epic exactness, and emotional dynamics. This he does by his unerring choice of words, by their application and localization—their apt association with other words and adjustment to them—by their rhythmic accent and cadence.

These basic properties are in all the masterpieces of Mickiewicz: in the dreams and visions of *The Forefathers' Eve,* the epic descriptions and characterizations of *Pan Tadeusz,* and the purely emotional utterances of the lyric poems. Even his most abstract images, his boldest flights far above the earth into the unknown, he expresses in a concrete, solid, and precise style. Even his most romantic passions and conceptions are free from any romantic verbosity, vagueness, obscurity, or carelessness. (p. 23)

[*The Forefathers' Eve* depicts] an image of concrete reality, although, naturally, "poetized." It presents authentic incidents and even quotes authentic names. It is an epic narrative full of concrete, realistic episodes and details, although certainly with a lyric undercurrent. (pp. 23-4)

[The language is] devoid of any real, earthy element; it employs pure emotions, abstracts, symbols, colors. (p. 24)

At the opposite extreme is his purely epic style, applied throughout *Pan Tadeusz,* except in some lyric invocations and digressions. This is rich in objective values. Because of them, everything depicted in this poem possesses the undeniable and overwhelming quality of truth . . . and fidelity to reality. Mickiewicz treats with . . . Homeric carefulness and love of detail both great and small subjects, even very common things, mean and base phenomena of life, such as food and drink. Nature and the life of animals occupy an important place in the whole picture because men live in nature and nature in them. Every detail is, so to speak, autonomous and as if treated apart, and yet deeply involved in the whole picture. People live in themselves, and they live in other things, through them and for them. This penetrating insight of the poet, his all-embracing poetic attitude, his understanding of nature and human beings, enabled him to create a work that is both highly individual, original, specifically Polish, and at the same time universal, close to every human soul, independent of nationality.

Polish versification attained in Mickiewicz's works one of the highest degrees of perfection. Its general aspect is analogous to that of the language; that is, there are no amazing novelties in his meter, rhythm, and rhyme, no "discoveries" or revolutionary trends against tradition. On the contrary, many of the metrical forms used by him had been known in earlier Polish poetry. And yet his verse is really new and highly original because it is endowed with new force and light, new rhythmical movement, disposition of main and secondary accents, stressing the value of significant words by rhymes, and so on. In this respect his was a mastery hitherto unknown in Polish poetry. One would be inclined to speak, in connection with him, of an absolute mastery of verse in all its aspects. He could be, and really was, sometimes, unsuccessful in structure, could compose his works of heterogeneous elements, could introduce into them components motivated by extraliterary reasons, but his mastery of versification was indeed marked by an unprecedented certainty and infallibility—it does not know hesitation, mistake, or stumbling. . . . Mickiewicz's verse is the traditional Polish syllabic. In this general framework there is a great variety of metrical and rhythmical forms, depending not only on the number of syllables, but on the differentiation of accents, the use of caesura, and of *enjambements.* (pp. 24-5)

Mickiewicz's rhymes are relatively simple and easy; at any rate, they do not distinguish themselves by any special refinement or virtuosity. . . . Yet they achieve in a perfect way their natural task, which is the unification of verses in a structural and sonorous whole, the stressing of significant and important words—or rather investing the words with significance and importance by virtue of rhymes—the emphasizing of accents, collaboration with rhythm in creating "sounding" pauses and borders and in rhythmical repetition. These qualities are, *mutatis, mutandis,* shown in all his mature works. (p. 25)

The importance of Adam Mickiewicz in the history of Polish poetry cannot be overestimated. He was the first Polish poet of true genius, surpassing all former poets of his nation, including Jan Kochanowski, the great Polish poet of the Renaissance, by the range and wealth of his talent, by the scope and extent of his creative work, by his significance in Slavic and Western European literature, and by the influence which he gained. Romanticism sometimes limited his poetry to forms of expression that reflected only temporary trends. On the other hand, his frequent treatment of specifically Polish problems, close to the heart of every Pole, is apt to limit the appeal of his work to foreigners. But the greatness and universality of Mickiewicz lie in the fact that he created, beyond the limits of romanticism, works of permanent and general value, and that in some of his works he endowed Polish problems and Polish life with a universal meaning. Owing to his works, Polish literature gained a high place among Slavic literatures and entered the orbit of world literature. (p. 33)

> *Manfred Kridl, "Adam Mickiewicz," in* Adam Mickiewicz, Poet of Poland: A Symposium, *edited by Manfred Kridl (copyright 1951 by Columbia University Press; reprinted by permission of the Literary Estate of Manfred Kridl), Columbia University Press, 1951, pp. 11-34.*

CZESŁAW MIŁOSZ (essay date 1951)

Mickiewicz has been more than often described as the chief representative of the Polish romantic school. His manifestoes, his tumultuous life, his political activities, and his role as national prophet were in complete accord with the ideas of the romantic poet. At the beginning of his literary career he revolted against the French classicism then dominating the Polish literary scene and published a volume, *Ballads and Romances,* which was labeled by the Polish admirers of Delille as "monstrous and barbarous." In defiance of the classical unities still accepted by Polish dramatists, he wrote his great poetic drama, *The Forefathers' Eve,* which, when staged by Wyspiański, a pioneer among directors of the twentieth century, showed his infallible instinct for effective theatrical detail.

Nevertheless, Mickiewicz does not quite belong to European romanticism. . . . By saying that Mickiewicz cannot be classified as entirely romantic in his technique, I wish to stress the elements in his poetry that make him dear to the new poets writing in Polish. Unfortunately, that quality of his is inaccessible to readers who can judge of him only by English translations. English translations of his poems, so far as I can pronounce an opinion, have a very definite late romantic or Victorian touch.

The work of Mickiewicz has its roots in the literature of the eighteenth century and in the philosophy of the Enlightenment. . . . Among his first literary works were a translation of a brief excerpt from Voltaire's satiric epic *La Pucelle* and a poem of his own entitled *The Potato*—"a poem with a subject," in this case the discovery of America by Columbus and the blessing of introducing the potato to European agriculture. The poem expresses the author's sympathy for the American Revolution and, in somewhat veiled allusions, prophesies the victory of the ideals of freedom. These first poems were constructed in a "rationalistic" and "artificial" manner. (pp. 58-9)

[Mickiewicz was] a sort of prophet who opened a new era by breaking the rules of the dry, slavish classicism which had repressed Polish national feeling. He introduced folk beliefs, folk customs, and legends into his poems. He became *the* national poet, not afraid of expressing contemporary emotions and more widely read than any of the "classicists" who used allegories taken from antiquity and incomprehensible to unschooled readers. (pp. 59-60)

[It] is important to remember that the one word "romantic" does not cover all the elements in the poetry of Mickiewicz.

The style of Mickiewicz is manly and simple. He knew how to use conventional phrasing and, without straying beyond its limits, how to transform it into something completely new. That is not easy. Many poets maintain their standards only at the price of being unconventional, and drop into dullness as soon as they venture to use traditional methods. Through a slight retouching of words, a genuine poet is able to invest a commonplace sentence with charm. But genuine poets are rare, and there are periods of history when such an operation is impossible, because the use of a "common style" is then beyond the reach of even the great poets.

Mickiewicz attains his effects by fusing a classical ("dry") control with a free flow of images; his style is natural, not because he does not care about the method of expressing what he wants to say, but because his effort is hidden. He does not appear learned nor does he give the impression of being a master. (p. 60)

The equilibrium attained by Mickiewicz suggests the thesis that the richest periods in art are the transitional periods, the periods when a certain way of feeling and thinking is broken but still exists as a basis for a new effort. Such a thesis would be risky, but it may be accepted in a modified form: that stability does not exist in art; that from the youth of a certain trend to its old age is only one step; that the mature years are no more than an imperceptible moment.

Mickiewicz's work is not homogeneous. It is full of pulsations, of different tendencies, succeeding each other. The first phase was purely classicist. The second—that of *Ballads and Romances*—was a revolt. What is often overlooked is that the ballads are not so sincere and naive as they have seemed to be. Mickiewicz's approach to folk superstitions and legends is sympathetic and half serious, but his simplicity is a device. He made use, however indirectly, of popular songs. . . . Mickiewicz transformed those popular songs into poems which derive their simple charm from a contrast between the conscious aim of the artist and the apparently primitive quatrain: he knew how to suspend his belief or disbelief, while his imitators . . . tried to be as naive as their subject matter. Of course, he believed in nymphs and miraculous metamorphoses no more than Ovid did. His preoccupation with such subjects was for him a way to show his conviction that through the "wisdom of the heart" of humble people we are nearer to the mystery of the world. But he was not a folk artist: his obvious enjoyment in imitating a folk credulity creates a world *als ob,* a country of fairy tale. What is puzzling is his tone, rather deep, solemn, and religious: he betrays his detachment from the subject through the general character of his structure. We later find the same puzzle in his novel in verse, *Pan Tadeusz.* Some critics have accused the heroes of that poem of being petty, egotistic, and interested only in hunting, drinking and quarreling. Mickiewicz never tells the reader that he judges them severely; ergo, he approves their way of life. Of course, such an accusation can only recoil on the critic. Mickiewicz does not judge his characters, because he enjoys them as they are: they are not great figures or examples for mankind, but they are very human, average people, noisy and goodhearted, and a little stupid, seen from a remote time and place. (pp. 60-2)

Before Mickiewicz attained a quiet tone in his epic, he went through divergent modes of expression. Some parts of *The Forefathers' Eve* and *Farys* are marked by a turbulent tone far removed from that of either his earlier or his later writings. Other parts of *The Forefathers' Eve* such as scenes of political depravity and a long digression descriptive of Tsarist Russia that ends the drama, rank among the scanty examples of poetry that combines strength with political insight. . . . No poet of France or England is so politically terrifying [as Mickiewicz]. He has suffered and he has seen his people suffer—that is the explanation. Characteristically, in his most poignant poems he presents or paints rather than makes a direct appeal.

The concreteness of Mickiewicz's language contributes to the ambivalence of the poem *Grażyna*. It would be a well-known type of romantic story in verse were it not for the steadiness of its lines, which have a metallic ring. (p. 62)

Mickiewicz did not embellish his lines; [his poetry] is not poetical—it is an observation, or, which in art is the same, a discovery. (pp. 62-3)

Poland has never had a great novel which could be compared with Stendhal's *The Charterhouse of Parma,* Tolstoy's *War and Peace,* or Fielding's *Tom Jones.* To be quite honest, Poland has produced very few good novels at all, but her masterpiece is a poem having, in addition, all the features of a good novel. I say "in addition" as if such a quality could be deducted from a poem. Since it cannot be done, we have to define *Pan Tadeusz* as an epic poem with characters who survive no less than do Sancho Panza or Gargantua.

Pan Tadeusz is virtually unknown to non-Slavic nations—and no wonder, for translated into prose it loses its balance. Once the atmosphere given by the meter is destroyed, the actors move either too quickly or too slowly—the effect is that of an opera recited without music. The joy which a Polish reader derives from the poem is similar to that which one has from

watching a perfect theatrical performance. What matters is not that reality has been more or less successfully imitated or parodied, but the mere movement of actors who pretended to be somebody else; or, to be more exact, it is the joy of watching a ballet: the apparent freedom of dancers is limited by the regular pace of Mickiewicz's verse. (pp. 63-4)

Poland's most popular poem is humorous, realistic, and merry, despite the fact that it was written in one of the several black moments of Poland's history, after the unsuccessful uprising of 1831. Such moments are not especially propitious for calm and objective literature, which we are inclined to associate with a golden age or with periods of buoyant growth. Mickiewicz wrote *Pan Tadeusz* in a spirit of contradiction, at more or less the same time that he wrote *The Books of the Polish Nation and of the Polish Pilgrims,* a prophetic, passionate prose tract by a political *émigré*. He did it, I suppose, because he always had before his eyes the dream of a golden age—that of antiquity, or the Polish golden age of the sixteenth century. In *Pan Tadeusz* he is one of the few really "civilized" poets. Let us hope that the adjective has not yet lost its meaning. (p. 64)

Czesław Miłosz, "Mickiewicz and Modern Poetry," in Adam Mickiewicz, Poet of Poland: A Symposium, *edited by Manfred Kridl (copyright 1951 by Columbia University Press; reprinted by permission of the Literary Estate of Manfred Kridl), Columbia University Press, 1951, pp. 57-65.*

MANFRED KRIDL   (essay date 1951)

["**Kartofa**" **(The Potato)** is a little poem from Mickiewicz and] is a mixture of serious and humorous elements, sometimes approaching parody, sometimes—historiosophy. The very beginning is a travesty of the classic "argument" (a summary in verse); as the poet is starting to praise various plants, a potato cries out from the stove and suggests to him the subject of the poem: the glorification of the potato and of all that led to its discovery. The poet, ashamed and repenting, changes his subject and recites a parody of an apostrophe, not to the Muse, but to the potato, asking it to inspire him and promising to immortalize its beauty and its "inner" qualities. (p. 242)

The poem is written in a classic style full of long comparisons, inversions, periphrases, artificially constructed sentences, replete with pomp, rhetoric, and mythology. Within this general character of poetic language the poet frequently achieves vivid descriptions, humorous images, and rhetorical force. He does not shrink, however, from using colloquial expressions and even dialect, which provides his language with a special flavor. In general, he is here a faithful disciple of Polish and foreign classicists, but a disciple who already shows originality and invention. (pp. 244-45)

Manfred Kridl, "Mickiewicz on America and the American Potato," in Adam Mickiewicz, Poet of Poland: A Symposium, *edited by Manfred Kridl (copyright 1951 by Columbia University Press; reprinted by permission of the Literary Estate of Manfred Kridl), Columbia University Press, 1951, pp. 242-45.*

WIKTOR WEINTRAUB   (essay date 1954)

[The style of the poems of Mickiewicz's student-years] is that of eighteenth century mock-heroic poetry: solemn Classical paraphrases used for fun together with apostrophes to figures of the Classical Olympus, sharp juxtaposition of vocabulary from two different lexical levels, the solemn, poetic, and the slangy, colloquial.

If we had to judge Mickiewicz by these poems exclusively, we would say: a vigorous, jovial youth, a nice fellow, but hardly anything more. (p. 22)

[Mickiewicz] assumed a pose of delicate mockery and couched the poem in an extremely elaborate style verging on parody. Complicated paraphrases, rare and unexpected metonymies give the poem the character of a stylistic exercise in imitating and exaggerating the characteristic devices of Trembecki's style. . . .

In a more ambitious undertaking, a 'little poem in four cantos,' *The Potato* . . . , we find a mock-heroic treatment, an elaborate Classical style, and anti-clerical notes. The poem was never finished. (p. 23)

The poet's friends, when the first canto [of *The Potato*] was read at one of their meetings, praised it highly for its concise style and rich vocabulary. But in spite of a certain incontestable technical mastery, the style is artificial, conventional, rhetorical, and the poet's treatment of diverse motifs is proof of a still very immature imagination. But the poem is an interesting example of the lofty symbolic meaning America had acquired for young Mickiewicz. Later on, allusions to America would appear in Mickiewicz's poetry rarely and only fleetingly, as in his poem *To a Polish Mother* and in his *Books of the Polish Nation,* but they would always have a similar emotional connotation. (p. 25)

The mock-heroic note sounds also in a short didactic poem, *The Draughts.* The poem was written . . . in the form of an epistle to a friend to whom the poet was explaining the rules of the game treating the figures in the typical mock-solemn way as fighting 'knights' and describing their 'deeds' with the conventional apparatus of heroic poetry. Later on Mickiewicz added to this epistle an elegiac ending, reminiscences of games played with his beloved Maryla, and published the rather disparate whole in the first volume of his poetry. (pp. 25-6)

[From] the very beginning we can detect in the young Mickiewicz a clear and very sincere note of deep idealism. It found its strongest expression in his programme poems written for the Society. One such poem, known usually by its first line, *Sullen clouds have disappeared from the fair sky,* he read at a meeting of the Society as early as 1818. The other, *The Song of the Philaretians* . . . , was written in 1820. . . .

A similar spirit of enthusiasm is expressed in Mickiewicz's most ambitious and best known early Classical work, his *Ode to Youth.* (p. 26)

Ode to Youth is the first poem by Mickiewicz which can be reckoned as great poetry. It is great not simply because it is good poetry but also because its spiritual content has a mark of greatness. And in spite of its general character, it is, in a way, a personal poem. The image of flight was to become a distinguishing feature of Mickiewicz's poetry. It would appear often with connotations of rapture, of a striving after ideals, a feeling of his own greatness. The idea of revolutionary changes as repetitions of God's act of creation will also recur in Mickiewicz's poetry. (p. 28)

[The poem *To Joachim Lelewel*] contains some memorable, pithy, gnomic expressions but, taken as a whole, it cannot claim any higher literary values. It is conventional in its expression and sometimes verges on pomposity.

It is not without interest, since it gives us insight into Mickiewicz's ideas at an important turning point. (p. 29)

The Lilies is not only the only ballad based on an authentic folk poem, but also the one in which Mickiewicz went the farthest in creating the primitive folklore-like poetic style. Comparison between the poem and its' folklore source shows us some of the characteristic features of Mickiewicz's balladry. (p. 36)

[With] *The Lilies* Mickiewicz went furthest in the direction of stylistic primitivism. The ballad is written in extremely simple and short sentences, avoids metaphors, makes use of some of the expressions of folksongs. We find in it also frequent repetitions of lines and even of whole passages.

Another attempt at primitivism, this time not so much stylistic as psychological, is to be found in *Father's Return.* . . .

Both in *Father's Return* and in *The Lilies* Mickiewicz avoided metaphoric language. But in other ballads he tried to create a poetic medium by means of saturating the verses with unexpected, fresh metaphors. Thus, we find in the ballads a considerable stylistic diversity, to a certain extent deliberate, but to a certain extent the mark of insecurity in a new poetic idiom, the mark of groping and experiment. (p. 38)

One of Mickiewicz's humorous ballads, *Mrs. Twardowski,* is among his best. The protagonist, the sorcerer Twardowski, is a Polish counterpart of Dr. Faustus. The story is a popular, international story of a bad wife who proves too much even for the devil. . . . Mickiewicz's version is a gay extravaganza told in a racy colorful language and with a madly paced action. One event chases another, one more improbable than the other. We are introduced into a mad, drunken, topsy-turvy world where any improbable thing can become reality, except the devil's conjugal life with Mrs. Twardowski. The frequent use of exclamations, idiomatic expressions, of some Latin words as well as words humorously twisted, enhances the general impression of hilarious grotesquerie. *Mrs. Twardowski* is the gayest thing Mickiewicz ever wrote. (p. 39)

Among the most interesting of the ballads is *Alpujarra* included in the epic tale *Konrad Wallenrod.* It is a ballad of a new type, following in content the Spanish *romances fronterizos,* the ballads of the Moorish wars. (p. 41)

A swift pace, a vividly convened mood of horror and tragic events, fresh and expressive language make of *Alpujarra* (in spite of some of the conventional features of the 'Romanticism of horror') one of the best of Mickiewicz's ballads. . . .

[*The Three Budryses* and *The Watch*] are simple stories, free of any supernatural elements. In both of them the principle of composition is the same. The action is built up in such a way that the culminating dramatic effect, a sudden twist, comes at the very end. This sudden, abrupt end, a kind of *pointe,* has in the first ballad a humorous, in the other a tragic coloring. (p. 42)

Both ballads are in praise of love and youth, and in both of them we have to deal with sensuous love, free of any Romantic overtones. In both we have a great economy of poetic means: simple, straightforward, muscular language, swift pace of action. They are remarkable for their directness of effect and precision of wording.

They are a new venture in the history of Polish prosody. (p. 43)

All in all, Mickiewicz wrote no more than twenty ballads. But their variety is surprising. With regard to these ballads we can observe one of Mickiewicz's most characteristic features. He very seldom repeats himself. Even within the limits of a single genre he tries different approaches, different stylistic possibilities.

As to their literary value, Mickiewicz's ballads are very uneven. Two of them, however, are the best Polish literature has ever attained in the field of balladry. But even they could hardly give us a just idea of Mickiewicz's real stature. His greatness lies elsewhere. (p. 45)

[The epic poem] *Grażyna* is a curious blend of Romantic and Classical elements. The mysteriousness in the unfolding of the plot, the night as a steady background which we are never allowed to forget, the care taken in recreating an exotic and at the same time primitive world—all that belongs to the Romantic repertory. The mysterious black knight is a typically Romantic cliché. But there is no intrusion of the lyrical 'I' of the poet. It is true that some scenes are presented as if they were seen through the eyes of an unspecified observer. But the few remarks of this 'observer' are of no consequence. The epic distance is sustained all through the poem and with it, the unity of style: traditional, with marked Classical elements, full of dignity and poise. (p. 54)

The Epilogue [in *Grażyna*] strikes us today as superfluous, spoiling the general impression of the poem. Its main purpose is to fill some gaps in the story. The trouble, is, however, that we do not feel that the gaps need to be filled. For a modern reader, with the rich tradition behind him of Romantic poetic tales that often make far bolder use of the devices of fragmentary technique of narration, such an additional elucidation seems to be quite superfluous. (pp. 54-5)

Grażyna is not without major blemishes. The plot of the poem is very clumsy and the psychology of its characters rudimentary. But in one respect, in the creation of a noble epic diction, it is already a great triumph. While in the ballads there is still a lot of groping and a good deal of mannerism, a master fully in possession of his tools is already evident in this poem. (p. 55)

Forefathers' Eve can be judged as a whole, as an attempt at creating a new type of drama which would grow out of the presentation of the rites of *dziady*. As such it is a failure. The poet did not succeed in welding together into one whole the story of the unhappy love affair and the presentation of the rites. (pp. 67-8)

[The fragments of *Forefathers' Eve* are loose], of different subject matter, and of different value. Part Two is a little, fantastic spectacle, mixing the elements of folklore, of Rococo and of the 'Romanticism of horror', full of charm in spite of a certain stylistic ambiguity, evocative, but decidedly a minor work. Part Four is a powerful lyrical work slightly spoiled at the end by a mechanical intrusion of alien elements, but in spite of all that, bearing an indelible mark of greatness, a splendid love poem, the first of Mickiewicz's masterpieces. (p. 68)

[Mickiewicz's erotic love poetry, entitled *Crimean Sonnets*,] has stylistic unity to a considerable degree, its style being virile and straightforward. The first impression is often that of the poet expressing himself in the simplest and most natural way. However, this impression of simplicity is to a large extent deceptive. As careful reading reveals, the simplicity does not preclude either subtle stylistic effects, or considerable stylistic variety. In fact, we have to deal here with a fine craftsman, conscious of his tools, and with an extraordinarily fine feeling for language. (p. 88)

[The] reader of *Konrad Wallenrod* has to swallow a lot of conventional and rather clumsy matter, both in the delineation of character and, above all, in the building up of the plot. Wallenrod with his gloomy mask and sardonic smile has about him very much of the Byronic cliché. As for the plot, . . . Mickiewicz did not have a light hand at building up a coherent story. . . . The action often degenerates into a hotch-potch of conventional and carelessly motivated elements. . . .

Moreover, the poem has other, more serious, blemishes, eating deep into its poetic texture. Mickiewicz intended to write a poem dealing with the moral aspect of politics, a poem about a man who, when he had no other choice left, saved his nation by means of treason, bringing havoc on his enemy and himself. The poem extolled such a 'patriotic treason' as heroic, and had clear political implications. Its message was manifest: the physical superiority of the oppressor is no excuse for abandoning the fight for freedom. (p. 122)

Mickiewicz's *Wallenrod* brought something new. First of all, never before had the claims been so all-embracing. Here, the poet asserted his rights to national leadership. And never before had these claims been expressed with such power and passion.

The poem began a development which is the distinctive feature of Polish Romantic literature, that of patriotic poetry with claims to national leadership. Some of the greatest works of Polish Romanticism are in this line. It was a supreme school of exalted patriotism, if rather dubious as a school of political wisdom. The important point, however, is that in the climate of exalted national feelings, and in the absence of institutions that could provide natural political leadership, these claims of the poets were widely accepted as legitimate. The subsequent development of poetry, Mickiewicz's poetry included, could not but be influenced by such a situation.

In order to bring out prominently the message of the poem, Mickiewicz dealt very freely with historical data. At the time of the historical Wallenrod's rule, Lithuania had already been in union with Poland and was, at least officially, Christian. In Mickiewicz's poem Lithuania is still pagan and has to bear alone the burden of wars against the Order. (pp. 127-28)

The 'Roman' lyrics are quite different in character [than Mickiewicz's other poetry]: far simpler, quite straightforward, and conveying the feeling of a deep, personal religious experience. There are five of them: *To M. Ł. on the Day of Taking Her Holy Communion, The Master of Masters, Evening Discourse, Reason and Faith,* and *Sages.* What first of all characterizes them is their bitter denunciation of reason. There was in Mickiewicz a kind of inborn, deep-seated irrationalism. It had found its expression in the introductory ballad to his first volume of poetry, *Romanticism.* Now it obtained a religious sanction. . . .

[In] *The Sages,* the rationalists, *esprits forts,* are represented as stern hangmen, repeating in their souls the act of the crucifixion of Christ, intent upon the murder of God. Their cruel endeavors, however, end in a failure: 'God lives, He died only in the spirit of the sages' (*Bóg żyje, tylko umarł w mędrców duchu*).

The same note is struck again in the poem *Reason and Faith.* (p. 140)

[Here] we come across the most personal, the distinctive note of this poetry. Mickiewicz was a very proud man. He was proud by nature, and he was proud because he was conscious of being a great, inspired poet, the spiritual leader of his nation. He knew that in order to attain the state of Grace he must humble himself before God, and was firmly resolved to do it. But here was the main paradox of his religious life. His religious certainty became the source of a new pride, greater than ever. He was not only an inspired poet who knew the right way, but, from now on, his spiritual leadership in his nation received, in his eyes, a supernatural sanction. From now on, his religious life was to be marked by a desperate struggle between pride and humility. It would be the main problem of *Forefathers' Eve, Part Three,* as well as of the spiritual life of the main protagonist of *Pan Tadeusz,* Jacek Soplica. (p. 141)

[*Reason and Faith*] is in praise of humility. But it is a peculiar kind of humility. The head which is bent before God is not an ordinary head; it is powerful, shining with wisdom. And the act of humility surrounds this head with the halo of a prophet. It becomes the testimony of God's covenant with the afflicted nation, the source of consolation for the afflicted. One can hardly go further in the way of spiritual pride.

The predominant note of these stanzas is that of a triumphant acceptance. But things were not as simple as that for Mickiewicz. We find an illuminating counterpart to the feelings expressed in *Reason and Faith* in the little poem *To M.Ł. on the Day of Taking Her Holy Communion*. . . . The belief that the human soul communicates in dreams with the supernatural world, and that dreams reveal the true character of one's spiritual life, which was to play such an important part in *Forefathers' Eve, Part Three,* had found its expression in this poem. (pp. 141-42)

Evening Discourse is the most personal and the most direct of all Mickiewicz's 'Roman' lyrical poems. Its verse structure is distinguished by a certain defiant carelessness. The poem is divided into three parts. The first, three stanzas long, is written in *ottava rima*, the last stanza having one supernumerary line; the second part, written in *sestina rima*, is composed of two stanzas; one *sestina rima* forms part three. (p. 142)

[It] is treated in a very personal way. Thanks mostly to a bold usage of colloquialisms, the prevailing impression is not that of awe but of great intimacy, as if someone were able to span a deep precipice with a bridge. One is conscious of the presence of the precipice, but one feels safe. (p. 143)

[*Evening Discourse*] is one of the summits of Polish religious poetry. It conveys with great directness and force the peculiar religious experience of oneness with God. The background of sin and remorse gives the poem a third dimension, that of depth. There is always a dramatic element in Mickiewicz's religious poetry. It is true that in *Evening Discourse* the conflict is dissolved in tears of relief and happiness; nevertheless, it looms largely in the background as an obstacle which the poet once had to overcome.

The Master of Masters is a poem of a quite different character. What strikes one first when reading it is the majestic quality of its sweeping imagery. The artist as a creator and thus, a god-like creature, was one of the favorite ideas of the Romantics. Mickiewicz worked it in the opposite direction. It is God who is in his creation the greatest artist, 'the master of masters.' The idea is expressed in the first three stanzas in an imagery which has Mickiewicz's straightforwardness and con-ciseness, and is full of grandeur—a splendid 'cosmic' imagery. Each stanza ends on the same note: people fail to recognize 'the master of masters' in spite of the greatness and splendor of his work. . . .

We find in this poem the same ambiguity in the treatment of pride and humility which is the distinctive mark of Mickiewicz's other religious poems. He humbles himself before God, but it is the humility of an otherwise extremely proud man. (p. 144)

[*Forefathers' Eve, Part Three*] is the most baffling and difficult of all Mickiewicz's works. It is a mystical work, but most of its scenes are written in a full-blooded realistic style. In fact, one can enjoy its poetry to a large extent without being aware of its mystical implications. It mixes realistic scenes from a recent past, scenes concerning people most of whom were still living at the time the drama was written, with mystical visions. It is a drama, but an unfinished drama containing only the prologue and first act. . . . Were it not a work overbrimming with superb poetry it would be a literary curiosity. But such as it is, it is a work of daring originality, exploring hitherto unexplored regions of human experience, a queer and sublime masterpiece. (p. 152)

Part Three as it is has a very loose construction and no dramatic action in the traditional sense of the word. Only the first three scenes, dealing with what may be called 'Konrad's drama,' have a unity of action and form a close sequence. In the original manuscript they formed one scene. The other scenes are disconnected, and their order seems to be arbitrary. (pp. 178-79)

The drama has, broadly speaking, two different subjects. One of them is the drama of the spiritual leader of the nation revolting against God, the other is the tragedy of the persecuted nation, presented not through a continuous action but in a series of loose historical tableaux. The two subjects, different as they are, form one in the light of Mickiewicz's mystical doctrine. If Konrad is one with his nation, if he is the nation incarnate, then what happens to the nation becomes the essence of his spiritual life, and, at the same time, his spiritual story becomes the epitome of national history. This idea, queer and abstruse as it may seem, found followers other than Mickiewicz in Polish Romantic literature. (p. 179)

Mickiewicz is extremely free in dealing with the requirements of dramatic technique, not only in the sense that his drama dissolves into a sequence of loose scenes of different character but also in the sense that a particular scene may dissolve into a short narrative poem . . . , or into pure lyricism. . . . Twice the drama is transformed into music-drama. As a drama of a loose, 'open' form, mixing freely sublime and grotesque elements and having at its center a hero who rebels against the limitations of the human condition, Part Three belongs to the progeny of Goethe's *Faust*. But it is a highly original variety of the species. On the one hand it gravitates toward drama-*reportage*, as exemplified by *Les Soirées de Neuilly*, and on the other toward the medieval mystery drama. The two conceptions of the drama seem to be very far apart, reflecting two ideas of the theater having little in common. But in the light of Mickiewicz's ideas the cross between drama-*reportage* and the mystery play is not as incongruous as it might seem. If the sufferings of the nation are a re-enactment of the drama of Christ, then the scenes of *reportage* describing these sufferings become a modern version of the Passion.

The stylistic range of the drama is immense. The style can be not only sublime . . . , or grotesque, . . . it can render splendidly . . . casual, every-day talk. . . . There is, however, a basic stylistic unity, underlying the vast diversity. Except for long stretches of . . . abstruse allegory, and for the last scene, where the poet's inspiration obviously slackened, the style of the drama is marvellously direct, precise, fresh and full of an emotional charge.

These stylistic qualities reflect the drama's basic unity, which is strongly felt by the reader in spite of a superficial disparity of single parts, although difficult to define. Perhaps the best approximate description would be to say that a national spirit of prophecy pervades the entire drama. A great drama, involving not only the destiny of a whole nation but the forces of Good and Evil as well, unfolds before our eyes. We see now one facet of the drama, now another. There is no continuity between the scenes. Their choice seems arbitrary. Nevertheless, we feel them to be different facets of the same drama, and Mickiewicz has managed to convey a sense of the tremendous spiritual importance of the drama. (pp. 179-80)

[Each poem of *The Digression*] forms a whole. Occasionally, the poet refers to occurrences in previous poems, and the sequence has a certain order. The first poem bears the title *The Road to Russia*. The title is somewhat misleading. The poem in fact deals with the first impressions of Russia gathered during the trip to St. Petersburg. The title of the second poem is: *The Suburbs of the Capital*. The third bears the title *St. Petersburg* and gives a general impression of the capital. The three following poems also have St. Petersburg for background. Their titles give a rather accurate idea of their subjects. The title of the fourth is *The Monument of Peter the Great,* of the fifth, *The Review of the Army*. The sixth has a double title: *The Day Preceding the St. Petersburg Flood of 1824* and *Oleszkiewicz*. It introduces the mystic Oleszkiewicz as a man who predicted the forthcoming inundation.

There is in all these poems a severe choice of detail. Only those symbolic details relevant for a judgment of Russia and its government are used and the descriptive passages are interspersed with comments on Russia and her destiny. The descriptions serve as foundations on which generalizations about Russia are built, as food for thought. The whole *Digression* is an appraisal of Russia.

This appraisal is expressed not only, and not even primarily, in what the poet has to say explicitly about Russia. It is suggested primarily through consistent imagery, endowed with great evocative force and emotional charge. This imagery not only gives the poems their marked stylistic unity, but its unusual expressiveness also forces upon the reader the poet's vision of Russia. (pp. 182-83)

The Digression is not a travelogue but a poem in which the poet does not feel bound by the chronological sequence of his actual travel impressions [through Russia] but arranges his material in the way that best suits his aims. (p. 187)

[It] seems probable that the *Digression* was planned as a sort of introduction to the second act of [*Forefathers' Eve*], providing it with a historical background. As it is, it is an independent poetic work in its own right, a vivid, expressive and biting satire on Russia in general and St. Petersburg in particular. The satire is rooted in concrete observation, and thus vivid and plastic. These observations are integrated into a coherent vision of the Russian world.

The satire is passionate, but free from any chauvinistic note, not merely because Mickiewicz introduces a representative of 'the other Russia,' but, above all, because he judges Russia against a set of general values and avoids the easy temptation of playing off his own nation against the Russians. Moreover, the general tenor of his criticism strikingly resembles some ideas current in the Russia of that time. The idea that the Russian people have no genuine history, for example, resembles the theory pronounced by Chaadaev in his *Philosophical Letters*. . . . (pp. 189-90)

[Also] a certain parallelism between the thought of Mickiewicz and that of the Russian Slavophils exists, and there is a quaint irony in this parallelism. . . . [There] are few points of contact between Mickiewicz's poetry and Russian literature in spite of Mickiewicz's long stay in Russia. Of all Mickiewicz's poems the *Digression* is the most anti-Russian, and yet proves to be at the same time the most Russian in its inspiration. (p. 190)

The *Digression* ends with a lyrical apostrophe, written in nine four-line stanzas, *To Muscovite Friends (Do przyjaciól Moskali)*. The word *Moskal* (Muscovite) has a markedly derogatory meaning in modern Polish. '*Przyjaciel Moskal'*—'a Muscovite friend,' produces the effect of an oxymoron, a friend belonging to an enemy nation. This conflict in the title is the subject of the poem. (p. 191)

Complex feelings entered into the composition of this poem. Mickiewicz wanted to make it clear that if he, who had been so friendly with Russians, raised his voice against Russia, it did not mean that he had changed, that he betrayed these friendships: some of them might have changed but not he. He was determined not to allow his poem to look like a justification. The harsh note of the last stanza might dispel any such suspicion. But passionate fighter against Russia though he was, he still tried to preserve the treasure of his Russian friendships. He made conditions. His Russian friends must be at one with him in the fight against tsardom. (p. 192)

In *Pan Tadeusz* the plot is far more complicated [than in *Grazyna* or *Wallenrod*]. In addition to the main action, rich in development, there are also several secondary plots, and everything is worked together into a highly complicated structure. . . . Yet in spite of all complications, the action forms an adroitly contrived, well-balanced whole. It is true, that careful reading might disclose several minor inconsistencies and loose ends, some of them the vestiges of abandoned plans . . . but they are of minor importance and do not spoil the impression of a well-contrived whole. The plots are, indeed, so fitting and well formed that *Pan Tadeusz* can be read with pleasure in prose translation. Certainly, the reader of such a translation loses a good deal, the entire splendid poetic texture, in fact the greatest charm of the poem, but what remains is an interesting novel with a rich, vivid, and well constructed plan of action. (pp. 223-24)

The poet seldom describes his characters, and when he does so, the descriptions are always summary; but he has an extremely keen eye for their gestures, and he knows splendidly the art of fixing the peculiar quality of a specific gesture with an apt and precise formula. (p. 244)

Some of the gestures described are mechanical tics; yet Mickiewicz's characters are far removed from the automata, produced by some of the novelists of Sterne's school, who go through the same trick over and over again, mechanically. Much of our enjoyment is derived from the fact that we can easily visualize the poem's characters in various and usually vivid gestures. Moreover, the overall impression of enhanced vitality derives to a large extent from the great visualized mobility of its human world. Nowhere is this more clear than in the battle scenes. (p. 245)

Pan Tadeusz has a wide emotional range, from pathos to sheer fun. Most often, however, we move in a middle region, that of a quiet and even narration, tinged with discreet and tender humor. Passage from one emotional state into another is easy, even nonchalant. It is a far cry from *Pan Tadeusz* to the wayward lyrical composition of such Romantic poems as Byron's *Don Juan.* Nevertheless, in the considerable easing of the rules of narrative composition, in the off-hand passages from one situation and one mood into another, there is in the poem something of their inheritance.

The vocabulary of the poem is extremely rich, far richer than that of any other poem by Mickiewicz. In the evocation of old Polish life the specific terms connected with various spheres of that life play an important part, and the poet uses them in profusion. (pp. 258-59)

Generally speaking . . . , the verse of *Pan Tadeusz,* in spite of its appearance of primitiveness, proves to be an unusually flexible and rich poetic instrument. In the usual narrative passages, it is as inconspicuous as possible, the more so since the poet makes frequent use of enjambement, and since, generally speaking, the division into sentences often does not tally with the metrical pattern. Thus, the metrical pattern often plays the part of a discreet accompaniment, relegated to the background. (p. 260)

[Some of the passages in the epilogue to *Pan Tadeusz,* published after his death,] belong with the purest lyrical poetry Mickiewicz ever wrote.

The epilogue bears witness to Mickiewicz's growing disillusionment and depression. The poem, we learn from it, became for its creator, a means of refuge into 'the land of childhood' (*kraj lat dzieciecych*), 'holy and pure as first love.' It was, as we might call it to-day, an escape. It is strange to think that the sunny, optimistic last books of *Pan Tadeusz* were written by an unhappy man, fighting despair. (p. 262)

The poem, we read further on, is idyllic, simple, and the poet would consider it his greatest reward to find readers among simple people, 'under thatched roofs,' along with folk-songs or Brodziński's idyll *Wieslaw*—another surprise, since it was precisely Brodziński whom Mickiewicz had singled out for ridicule in *Forefathers' Eve, Part Three* (the Warsaw drawing room scene) for his advocacy of idyllic poetry as the most in keeping with the Slavic spirit ('We Slavs like idylls').

In fact, it is a far cry from *Forefathers' Eve, Part Three* to *Pan Tadeusz.* It is true that certain scenes of the dramatic poem (the first scene, and some part of the satirical scenes) in a way proclaimed the new style, simpler, more straightforward, more realistic in its attempts to reproduce the everyday idiom. But the ethos of *Forefathers' Eve, Part Three* had very little in common with that of *Pan Tadeusz.* There was nothing in this passionate, mystical poem that foreshadowed the apotheosis of everyday life and common people, the realistic savor of the *minutiae* of life and the calm optimism, which are the essence of *Pan Tadeusz.* With supreme boldness, bordering on insanity, the poet explored in *Forefathers's Eve* the extreme regions of the ultra-Romantic idea of the poet as superman, a creator equal to God. *Pan Tadeusz* marks the overcoming of Romanticism by Mickiewicz, and the poem's 'Romantic' figure is represented condescendingly as a crank, whereas the acceptance of

everyday life in its seemingly most trivial phenomena is preached as supreme wisdom. To be sure, the life which the poet thus praises, is seen through a nostalgic haze. It is so very precious and beautiful, because it is the lost paradise of childhood, because it is no longer there. Nevertheless, it is significant that this beauty is seen in terms of the everyday life of common, simple people.

It is small wonder that *Pan Tadeusz* met with a mixed reception among the poet's contemporaries. Mickiewicz's great competitor, Slowacki, is representative in this respect. In a beautiful passage of his poem *Beniowski* he hailed it as a splendid evocation of the past, but in another place he expressed his displeasure at the poem's 'piggishness' (*wieprzowatość*). For him it was somehow too much down-to-earth.

It was this so-called 'piggishness,' however, and the great naturalness of diction which made it easy for people to accept *Pan Tadeusz,* nay, to hail it, in fact, as the national Polish epic poem, the masterpiece of Polish literature, when an anti-Romantic 'positivistic' tide set in. . . . This attitude has remained. . . . Whereas the tribute paid to other great poems of the Romantic period was often a kind of lip service, and out of proportion to the real popularity of the poems, the appeal of *Pan Tadeusz* has proved to be both very wide and lasting. (pp. 263-64)

In *Forefathers' Eve, Part Three* and in the [*Books of the Polish Nation and of the Polish Pilgrimage* Mickiewicz] spoke with the authority of a man who had assumed the role of a national leader, a prophet of national liberation. (p. 282)

[Such] an attitude, with all the idolatry it implies, does Mickiewicz's poetry harm. It distracts people from the literary value of Mickiewicz's work . . . , places in the center of our attention the most questionable facet of that work, Mickiewicz's doctrine of national Messianism. And it presents a onesided and distorted picture of his poetry. How to reconcile the love sonnets with the lofty image of a prophet? And if the sonnets can be dismissed as a passing deviation, how to account for *Pan Tadeusz* with its rich realism of detail? And what about the jovial, broad smile of the fables? There is a basic misunderstanding in such a 'prophetic' approach to Mickiewicz. Mickiewicz was able to express the 'prophetic' side of his nature with such compelling power only because he was, first of all, a great poet, a man with an extremely fine sense of the possibilities of language and with a remarkably wide range of expression. He was able to express a good many other things as well.

The richness and variety of his poetry is amazing. It is not very impressive in bulk. The poet's creative period lasted no longer than fourteen years, and during that time Mickiewicz wrote only intermittently. Thus, his entire poetic output, including poems and fragments published posthumously, can easily be contained in a little more than a thousand pages of average size. He never repeated himself, however. From the purely formal point of view, his work seems like a series of bold experiments in style. Once the poet masters one medium of expression, he does not repeat his performance but tries his hand at a new one: the traditional, Classical style, the popular idiom of the ballads, two poetic tales, each of them couched in a different style, the ornamental, Oriental style of the *Crimean Sonnets,* the vivid, rustic style of the fables, the biblical prose of the *Books,* the bold attempt at creating a new drama, partaking of the nature of a libretto, a mystery play and a drama-*reportage,* the unique blend of realistic and idyllic elements in *Pan Tadeusz,* and, finally, the utter simplicity and bareness of the Lausanne lyrics. The variety is truly dazzling.

This stylistic variety is the expression of an extraordinarily wide amplitude of spiritual experience. Mickiewicz is a unique writer, some of whose poems invoke and hear comparison with the poetry of Saint John of the Cross while others are written in the vein of La Fontaine. He is of the race of great rebels, and yet, in *Pan Tadeusz,* he could express *la joie de vivre,* a sheer delight in the minutiae of every day life with a freshness of feeling hardly ever matched elsewhere.

There is a certain unity underlying this rich variety. It cannot be explained simply in terms of the period-style, by saying that Mickiewicz was a Romantic poet. Surely, as the author of *Ballads and Romances,* he was a standard-bearer of the Polish Romantic movement, and in *Forefathers' Eve, Part Three,* he explored some of the vertiginous uttermost regions of the Romantic idea of the poet as superman. *Pan Tadeusz,* however, cannot be labelled Romantic without stretching the meaning of the word to such an extent that it becomes almost empty.

The unity is of a different kind, personal and more elusive. It is the unity of a rich, passionate nature, ebullient, tormented, pressing headlong in one direction or another, but always virile, noble, and deeply sincere. In this variety there is also a fine logic of inner development, from the conventional idiom of the student's poems, through the headlong leap into the Romantic world, culminating in the sublime metaphysical revolt of 'the Improvisation,' to the mellow acceptance of common life, full of good humor in *Pan Tadeusz,* and the bare austerity of the last lyrical poems. Thus, Mickiewicz is not only the writer of a number of great poems. Taken as a whole, his work is an expression of a unique and fascinating personality. (pp. 282-84)

Wiktor Weintraub, in his The Poetry of Adam Mickiewicz *(copyright 1954 by Mouton & Co., Publishers; reprinted by permission of Wiktor Weintraub), Mouton Publishers, 1954, 302 p. (revised by the author for this publication).*

ZBIGNIEW FOLEJEWSKI   (essay date 1956)

Wherever there are Poles, at home in Poland or in exile, wherever the Polish word is written or spoken, the name of Adam Mickiewicz is frequently called on, in literary works, in political articles and speeches, and—perhaps most important of all—in everyday conversation. (p. 11)

[One] of the secrets of Mickiewicz's never ceasing appeal is the fact that his poetry never limits itself to any narrow pattern of lyricism, epic or drama, nor of classicism, romanticism or realism. His works are all this and more, too; they are simple enough and complex enough to fascinate every reader, to touch some string in everyone. They simply are universally human. Everyone finds in them something of his own, his dreams and hopes, his victories and defeats. For the same reason Mickiewicz belongs not only to the Polish people but to every admirer of poetry. (p. 13)

Through all the works of the poet, there flows a stream of poetic and human conviction, a rare synthesis of the most intimate individual lyricism and broad, "democratic", epic simplicity. In his time Mickiewicz voiced a Romantic protest against the taste of the literary law-makers. But it was more than purely Romantic individualism; the secret of his poetic

victory lies in the fact that he broke with abstract artificial patterns and concerned himself with what really concerned living people. This apparently esoteric Romantic poet did not hesitate to introduce into literature the common, everyday, thematic and linguistic elements that are the flesh and blood of everyday living. Although he was an individualist, unafraid to stand alone against the whole world, he was at the same time able to reflect the spirit of the common people. From the commonplace elements of everyday life he created his own convincing poetic reality. He demonstrated that poetry is not a fireworks display of elaborate metaphors and adornments. On the contrary, such common and allegedly "vulgar" things as planting potatoes or preparing and eating soup do have an important place in poetry. For they are *human* things, and we all know, although we sometimes seem to forget it, that the closer art is to everyday human problems, the more resonance it finds in human hearts and minds. The poet's genius is essentially the artistic selection and refraction of elements taken from reality. (pp. 16-17)

Zbigniew Folejewski, "Mickiewicz and the Poles in the West," (originally a lecture delivered at the University of Buffalo on August 4, 1955), in Mickiewicz and the West: A Symposium, *edited by B. R. Bugelski (copyright 1956 by the University of Buffalo, now State University of New York at Buffalo), University of Buffalo, 1959, pp. 11-17.*

EDWARD STANKIEWICZ   (essay date 1975)

One "idea" that Mickiewicz might have encountered in his reading of Romantic philosophy and esthetics had to do with the different values assigned to the senses of sight and hearing, with the latter recognized as the sense fundamentally related to the art of poetry and having a direct connection with the language of emotion. But even if we ignore the philosophical background that might have prompted Mickiewicz to weigh the relative merits of sight and sound, we cannot fail to notice that some of his poems explore poetically this opposition and assign priority to hearing and sound. Nowhere is this opposition more consistently expoited than in the *Crimean Sonnets,* which are both thematically and compositionally organized around it. This opposition does not, to be sure, figure by itself, but on the contrary is intertwined with a number of other semantic equivalences and oppositions which together lend to the *Sonnets* their richness of meanings and their peculiar resonance and brilliance of color. (p. 494)

The eighteen poems which make up the cycle of the *Crimean Sonnets* are a travelogue that can be broken up into four clearly articulated stages or parts. Part one, which includes Sonnets II, III, IV ("Cisza morska" ["Silent Sea"], **"Żegluga"** ["Navigation"], **"Burza"** ["Storm"]), is the description of a sea voyage; part two, which includes Sonnets VI, VII, VIII, IX ("Bakczysaraj", **"Bakczysaraj w nocy"** ["Bakczysaraj at Night"], **"Grób Potockiej"** ["Tomb of Mrs. Potocki"], "Mogiły haremu" ["Harem's Graves"]), pictures the ruins of the once powerful Moslem world and the tombs of the women of the harem; part three consists of Sonnets XI, XII, XIII ("Ałuszta w nocy" ["Ałuszta at Night"], "Ałuszta w dzień" ["Ałuszta at Day"], "Czatyrdah") and confronts us with a view of the Crimean mountains; part four, which includes Sonnets XV, XVI (**"Droga nad przepaścic w Czufut-Kale"** ["Road along the Precipice in Czufut-Kale"], **"Góra Kikineis"** ["Hill in Kikineis"]), gives a description of precipices, while Sonnet

XVII ("**Ruiny zamku w Bałakławie**" ["**Ruins of the Castle in Bałakławie**"]), resumes and concludes the motive of decay that is first introduced in Sonnet VI.

Each of the individual sonnets announces the basic character of the part it belongs to in its title or in its opening lines. (pp. 494-95)

The above thirteen sonnets constitute the descriptive core of an external, physical voyage which advances progressively, and as if vertically, from sea to land and high mountains, to descend again via treacherous canyons to the open sea. This descriptive core of the journey is embraced within a frame which opens with Sonnet I ("**Stepy akermańskie**" ["**Akerman Steppes**"]), and concludes with Sonnet XVIII ("**Ajudah**"). The two enclosing sonnets mirror asymmetrically the progress of the entire journey: the description of the steppe given in Sonnet I precedes the voyage by sea, and the opening vista of the sea of Sonnet XVIII is placed at the end of the journey by land.

Inserted between the four basic parts of the descriptive, dynamic cycle are Sonnets V ("**Widok gór ze stepów Kozłowa**" ["**Sight of the Hills from the Kozłowa Steppes**"]), X ("**Bajdary**"), and XIV ("**Pielgrzym**" ["**Pilgrim**"]), which link the various sections of the cycle and constitute their contemplative, reflexive, and partly stationary counterpart. In Sonnet V the Pilgrim comes face to face with his guide and the new, mysterious world that opens before him, and brings forth his awestruck exclamation *Aa!*, an exclamation which breaks and spills over the confines of the fourteen lines of the sonnet. In Sonnet X we see the poet in quest of a momentary rest from the fast-moving, kaleidoscopic impressions of an alien land. . . . Sonnet XIV sharpens the poet's awareness of the contrast between the immediate landscape . . . and his distant beloved homeland. . . . (pp. 495-96)

The contrast between the immediate and remote, between the present and past, which is explicitly stated in this sonnet, runs like a persistent strain through the other, descriptive parts of the cycle as well. Thus external images alternate with memories which rise like a Hydra from the depth of the mind . . . , the passivity of the landscape looms against the restlessness of the poet's heart, and the shifting scenery gives rise to thoughts on permanence and inner values. The progressive journey in space is thus at each point stalled by a retrospective journey in time, and under the surface of the outer, exotic world flows an undercurrent of the poet's innermost longings and aspirations. This continuous tension between a forward and backward movement is dramatically announced at the very outset of the journey (in Sonnet I), which is interrupted by the exclamation "Stójmy!" [Let's wait!] and which is resumed in the final line with the words "Jedźmy! nikt nie woła" [Let's go! No one is calling us], a movement that comes to a halt only in the last poem (XVIII) when the harvest of the poet's songs pushes the "Hydra of memories" and the tribulations of passion back into the deep. . . . (p. 496)

The incessant interplay of contrapuntal elements gives to the *Sonnets* a unique rhythm in which each poem is charged with its own, internal conflicts, and serves simultaneously as a link in the compositional structure of the entire cycle. Such a double, metaphoric and constructive function is also imparted to separate parts of the poems, and even to individual metaphors. A salient example is the opening stanza of Sonnet I, in which the metaphors pertaining to land and sea . . . anticipate metonymically the overall structure of the sonnets with their fundamental opposition and movement between land and sea. The erotic metaphors employed in the description of night in Sonnet VII ("**Bakczysaraj w nocy**") anticipate in a similar manner the description of the graves given in Sonnet IX ("**Mogiły haremu**"), with the difference that the idyllic picture of love in the harem of nature given in the former . . . acquires elegiac and tragic notes in the description of the harem of man in the latter. . . . (p. 497)

The metaphoric language of the *Sonnets* is thus never random, but evokes associations and references which radiate beyond their immediate context and lend depth and unity to the entire structure.

The contrast between an external, sensuous world and an inner, spiritual world is highlighted in the *Sonnets* by the tension between visual and auditory impressions, by the opposition between a passive, registering eye and an active, "curious" ear. . . . And as the cycle of the *Sonnets* unfolds, it becomes apparent that the external journey is but a continuing flow of transient visual images, whereas the contrapuntal internal journey is attuned to a world of sound, and vibrates to the voice of emotion, and especially to the sounds of the poet's native tongue.

The contrast between seeing and hearing is established at the very outset and organizes the entire composition of Sonnet I. (pp. 497-98)

The opposition of sight and hearing re-emerges in Sonnet VI, where it is presented within the framework of an empty, silent domain . . . and a voice that calls in the wilderness. . . . All that remains and is worthwhile, the poet seems to say, amidst the ruins of a once colorful world . . . is a crying fountain which laments its own permanence and the passing of power and glory. The description of Bakczysaraj at night, given in Sonnet VII, is nothing but a string of polychromatic images . . . which concludes with the vision of a deserted and silent sky. . . . By contrast, Sonnet VIII resumes in the tercets the motive of sound, extolling the power of the native language . . . and of song which will secure the immortality of the Polish captive woman and of the poet who, like her, may find his lonesome grave in a faraway land. The tombs of the harem are seen (in Sonnet IX) only through the eyes of Mirza, who translates the world around him into visual terms: death is a dark womb . . . ; the cold turban over tombs shimmers in the garden . . . ; the beauty of the odalisques is hidden from the eye of the unfaithful . . . , the look of the stranger stains the tombs. . . . The accumulation of visual impressions reaches a culminating point in "**Bajdary**" (Sonnet X), where the poet becomes dizzy with the whirl of images . . . , and when the mirage of forests, valleys and rocks . . . is refracted from his burning eye . . . like from a broken mirror. . . . He seeks peace then in the roar of the waves, and hopes to find forgetfulness by reaching out and embracing the onrushing sea.

The description of the mountains given in Sonnets XI, XII, and XIII is almost totally visual, and picks up the chain of images that was initiated in Sonnet VII, adding only new color and intensity to their sequence. In Sonnet XI we are confronted with fields of golden shafts . . . , with multi-colored butterflies . . . , naked rocks . . . , and an ominous sea in whose depths the light plays, like in the eyes of a tiger. . . . This sea is thus far more foreboding than the sea of Sonnet II ("**Cisza morska**"), which stands metaphorically for the poet's soul and in whose depths there sleeps a "Hydra of memories". It is a hostile and threatening sea which holds in store storms for the land of man . . . , and is reminiscent of the transcendental evil embodied in Blake's tiger. . . . The poet reaches a point of momentary rest in Sonnet XII under the cover of darkness, when "the lamp of the world is extinguished". . . . It is only then that the fragrant air begins to play, like the music of flowers . . . and "to speak to the heart in a voice that is concealed from the ear". . . . But the hope for peace is short-lived: like an oriental odalisque, night caresses the poet to sleep only to awaken him soon with a flood of golden light and glaring meteors, just like an oriental odalisque who wakes up to new caresses with sparkling eyes. . . . The sensual eroticism of the oriental night is matched in Sonnet XIII by a picture of trembling submissiveness of the Moslem man . . . in front of the mighty peak, Czatyrdah, which sits eternally immobile and mute . . . between heaven and earth. Small and humble oriental man has no access to God and his universe, and it is only Czatyrdah, the *padishah* and *drogman* (interpreter) of creation that translates for him the incomprehensible language in which God speaks to his children. . . . In Sonnet XIV the poet takes leave of this world of brilliance and opulence . . . to return in memory to his native land which resounds with rustling forests . . . and where everything speaks to his beloved of his lasting devotion. . . . (pp. 499-500)

In Sonnets XV and XVI the poet turns the floor over again to Mirza whose oriental hyperboles and literary allusions depict a world of wonder and peril and whose description is interrupted by such exclamations as "Tam nie patrz" [Don't look there] . . . , "ręką nie wskazuj" [Don't point with your hand] . . . , "Spojrzyj w przepaść" [Wait at the precipice] . . . , "Czy widzisz" [Can you see] . . . , "Patrzaj" [Look]. . . . Sonnet XVII completes the picture of isolation and ruin which began to unfold before us in Sonnet VI. To this picture the last sonnet opposes the poet's spiritual progress and the affirmation of the power of sound, which finds its ultimate expression in "immortal songs".

The opposition between sight and sound, the eye and the ear, which runs like a red thread through the **Crimean Sonnets,** is by no means limited to this work alone. Beginning with Mickiewicz's juvenile, largely programmatic poetry and ending with some of his latest works, we find him often extolling the power of sound (in particular of the spoken word), and rejecting the superficial, confining, and deceptive qualities of the eye. The motto from Hamlet ("Methinks I see . . . Where?—In my mind's eyes"), placed at the beginning of **Romantyczność** and the concluding lines of the poem, are characteristic, in a paradigmatic way, of the poet's identification of the visual, observable world with "dead truths" . . . , and of his equation of spiritual, "live truths" . . . with the voice of emotion and with language, even though language itself (in line with Romantic persuasion) is incapable of expressing the innermost stirrings of the soul. Primary in his conception remains the rejection of the eye as an organ which can cope only with the world of external, superficial appearances, but which cannot penetrate the essence of things. . . . The distrust of the eye as a limiting, purely external organ is also expressed in some later works of Mickiewicz. In **Rosmowa wieczorna** the poet tells us that his innermost feelings must remain hidden from the eye of his fellow citizens . . . , but can sometimes be conveyed, even though imperfectly, by means of words. . . . The contrast between an indifferent, superficial eye and the compassionate, speaking heart (or soul) recurs again in the exquisite lyrical poems of the Lausanne period. (pp. 500-01)

Edward Stankiewicz, "Sound and Sight in the 'Sonety krymskie' of Adam Mickiewicz," in For Wiktor

Weintraub: Essays in Polish Literature, Language, and History Presented on the Occasion of His 65th Birthday, *edited by Victor Erlich and others (© copyright 1975 in The Netherlands), Mouton Publishers, 1975, pp. 493-503.*

ADDITIONAL BIBLIOGRAPHY

Fagin, Helen N. "Adam Mickiewicz: Poland's National Romantic Poet." *South Atlantic Bulletin* XLII, No. 4 (November 1977): 103-13.
  Discusses the quality and content of Mickiewicz's poetry in light of his personal convictions and political situation.

Gardner, Mary Monica. "Adam Mickiewicz: Poland's National Poet." *The Dublin Review* 143 (October 1908): 360-75.
  Studies Mickiewicz's fervent nationalism and its effect on his work.

Gardner, Monica M. *Adam Mickiewicz: The National Poet of Poland.* New York: E. P. Dutton, 1911, 317 p.
  Sketches the significant events of Mickiewicz's life and discusses his literary works. The author states that her purpose is "to awaken in any English heart some interest or sympathy, not merely for [Mickiewicz], but still more for the sufferings, struggles and ideals of the great and heroic nation of whom he was a devoted son."

Giergielewicz, Mieczyslaw. "Sound and Sight in the *Sonety krymskie* of Adam Mickiewicz." In *For Wiktor Weintraub: Essays in Polish Literature, Language, and History Presented on the Occasion of His 65th Birthday,* edited by Victor Erlich, Roman Jackson, Czesław Miłosz, Riccardo Picchio, Alexander M. Schenker, and Edward Stankiewicz, pp. 493-503. The Hague: Mouton, 1975.
  Explores the religious symbolism of *The Crimean Sonnets,* particularly the Catholic elements employed in *Forefathers' Eve.*

Helsztynski, Stanislaw, ed. *Adam Mickiewicz, 1798-1855: Selected Poetry & Prose, Centenary Commemorative Edition.* Warsaw: Polonia, 1955, 192 p.
  A selection of laudatory prefaces, letters, and addresses, as well as English translations of the bulk of Mickiewicz's work, collected for the centenary celebration of "Poland's greatest man of letters."

Krzyżanowski, J[ulian]. "Mickiewicz and Pushkin." *The Slavonic Review* VI, No. 18 (March 1928): pp. 635-45.*
  Examines the relationship between Mickiewicz and Pushkin, and how each influenced the other's life and work.

Krzyżanowski, Julian. "James Fenimore Cooper and Adam Mickiewicz: A Stylistic Device from Prison Lore." *International Journal of Slavic Linguistics and Poets* IV (1961): 75-83.*
  Compares Cooper's *The Spy* to Mickiewicz's *To a Polish Mother.*

Lechon, Jan. "Mickiewicz Yesterday and Today." *Bulletin of the Polish Institute of Arts and Sciences in America* III, Nos. 3, 4 (April-June 1945): 472-78.
  Analyzes Mickiewicz as an author whose works influenced those of his own era, and future generations as well.

Lednicki, Wacław. "Adam Mickiewicz: Poland's Romantic Ambassador to the Court of Realism." In his *Bits of Table Talk on Pushkin, Mickiewicz, Goethe, Turgenev and Sienkiewicz,* pp. 111-31. The Hague: Martinus Nijhoff, 1956.
  Regards Mickiewicz as a powerful author who sought to solve Poland's political problems by "aiming at the depths of the human heart," considering "the heart superior to the mind," and opposing "irrationalism to rationalism."

Lednicki, Wacław. "Ex Oriente Lux (Mickiewicz and Pushkin)." In his *Bits of Table Talk on Pushkin, Mickiewicz, Goethe, Turgenev and Sienkiewicz,* pp. 157-79. The Hague: Martinus Nijhoff, 1956.*

Examines the use of exotic, or "Oriental," imagery in the works of Mickiewicz and Pushkin.

Miłosz, Czesław. "Adam Mickiewicz." *The Russian Review* 14, No. 4 (October 1955): 322-31.
A presentation of "the main problems raised by Mickiewicz's works today, particularly in the Polish People's Democracy."

Struve, Gleb. "Mickiewicz in Russia." *Slavonic and East European Review* XXVI, No. 66 (November 1947): 126-43.
Focuses on Mickiewicz's reputation in Russia and his importance to European literature.

Weintraub, Wiktor. "Mickiewicz's *Forefathers*." In *Forefathers*, by Adam Mickiewicz, translated by Count Potocki of Montalk, pp. viii-xxii. London: The Polish Cultural Foundation, 1968.
Critical introduction to *Forefathers* by one of the leading Mickiewicz scholars.

Welsh, David. *Adam Mickiewicz*. New York: Twayne, 1966, 165 p.
An analytical study of Mickiewicz's life and work.

Windakiewicz, St. "The Anglomania of Mickiewicz." Translated by M. P. *The Slavonic Review* VIII, No. 22 (June 1929): 131-39.
Studies the effect that Mickiewicz's interest in the English language and its authors had on his work. Windakiewicz believes Mickiewicz's "Britanomania" provides "the first strong link between Polish literature and that of the British Isles."

Alexander (Sergeyevich) Pushkin

1799-1837

(Also transliterated as Aleksandr, Alexandre, Aleksanndr; also Sergeivich, Sergeevich, Sergieevich, Sergeivitch, Sergeyeivich, Sergyeevich, Sergîeevich, Sergèyevich, Serguéevitch; also Pushchkin, Púshkin, Pouchkin, Poushkin, Púskin, Pùshkin, Puškin) Russian poet, dramatist, short story writer, novelist, essayist, and critic.

Pushkin is as significant to Russian culture as William Shakespeare is to English, or Johann Wolfgang von Goethe to German. Emphasizing the simplicity and beauty of his native tongue, he transformed the Russian literary language, and helped Russian literature to escape from the domination of eighteenth-century European classicism. Pushkin absorbed many of the structural and stylistic characteristics of European authors (notably François Voltaire, Lord Byron, Shakespeare, and Sir Walter Scott), recasting them in a uniquely Russian mold. Pushkin's work exhibits a universality which Fedor Dostoevski proclaimed as the essence of the Russian people and Russian art.

Pushkin was proud of his aristocratic ancestors, particularly his maternal great-grandfather, Abram Petrovich Hannibal, a Moorish noble who was kidnapped, taken to Russia, and made a ward of Peter the Great. As a child, Pushkin was closest to his grandmother and to his nurse, Arina, who told him fairy tales and folk legends which he later incorporated into his writings. At twelve Pushkin was sent to the government lycée at Tsarskoe Selo, where he read much—especially French literature—and wrote prolifically. When Pushkin recited his poem *Recollections at Tsarskoe Selo* at the lycée examinations in 1815, Gavriil Romanovich Derzhavin, the leading poet of the time, was so moved that he wanted to embrace the young student.

After graduation Pushkin obtained a sinecure in St. Petersburg. There he alternated between periods of dissipation and intense writing, and finished his first full-length piece, *Ruslan i Lyudmila (Ruslan and Lyudmila)* in 1820. This *poema*, or verse narrative, was based on folklore and stylistically influenced by Voltaire, Evariste Parny, and André Chenier, as was much of his early work. Just before its publication, however, Alexander I exiled Pushkin to southern Russia for his allegedly "revolutionary" verse. Censorship remained a lifelong problem for Pushkin; even after Nicholas I appointed himself his personal censor, he was under strict observation, forbidden to travel freely or leave Russia. Pushkin despaired: "The devil prompted my being born in Russia with a soul and with talent."

Pushkin was productive during his four-year southern exile, however, writing, among other works, *Kavkazski plennik (The Captive of the Caucasus)*, *Bakhchisaraiski fontan (The Bakchesarian Fountain: A Tale of the Tauride)*, and *Tsygany (The Gipsies)*. These are romantic *poemas* which reflect the influence of Byron, whom Pushkin read during this period. Byronism is evident, too, in *Yevgeny Onegin (Eugene Onegin)*, which Pushkin began in 1823 and completed in 1831. Critics agree that this "novel-in-verse" is Pushkin's masterpiece, representing, according to V. G. Belinsky, "an encyclopedia of

Courtesy of Prints and Photographs Division, Library of Congress

Russian life." In addition to its pure, expressive language, which is the hallmark of Pushkin's style, the work features character types that appear frequently in later Russian fiction: the "superfluous man," represented by Onegin, and the idealized Russian woman, characterized by Tatiana.

Eugene Onegin inaugurated a new Russian genre, as did *Boris Godunov (Boris Godunoff)*, a historical drama based on Shakespeare, which Pushkin hoped would break the influence of the French classical style that had long dominated Russian theater. Although *Boris Godunoff* was completed in 1825, censors prevented it from being published until 1831, and it was not performed until 1870. A further innovation in Russian theater is represented by Pushkin's "Little Tragedies," four one-act plays in blank verse which emphasize character development. *Pir vo vremya chumy (A Feast in the City of the Plague)*, for example, which was adapted from John Wilson's *The City of the Plague*, is considered one of the first Russian dramas of psychological realism. *Medny vsadnik (The Bronze Horseman)*, a later poem, was inspired partially by the poetry of Adam Mickiewicz, the Polish nationalist whom Pushkin met while in exile. In this work, Pushkin juxtaposes the omnipotence of Peter the Great with the helplessness of the character Eugene, who is symbolic of the masses sacrificed for the construction of St. Petersburg and the glory of imperial Russia.

407

Later in his career, Pushkin devoted himself to writing short stories and novellas. These reflect his belief that prose should be simple and unembellished, in the style of Nikolai Mikhailovich Karamzin, whom he admired. Ivan Belkin, the narrator and central character of a series of loosely related short stories titled *Povesti Belkina (The Tales of Ivan Belkin)*, was a prototype for the realistically depicted Russian character, and his matter-of-fact style of narration became a model for Russian fictional prose. The influence of Scott is obvious in Pushkin's fiction, particularly in *Kapitanskaya dochka (The Captain's Daughter; or, The Generosity of the Russian Usurper Pugatscheff)*, but his own pure style transcends imitation. Here, as in all of his writing, Pushkin exemplifies George Saintsbury's comment: "When a man of genius steals, he always makes the thefts his own."

Pushkin was killed in 1837 by a French officer in a duel over Nathalia Pushkin, his young wife. Mourned then as Russia's national poet, Pushkin remains in the minds of many critics the greatest and most influential of Russian authors. Yet Pushkin is rarely read in foreign countries. Critics attribute this to the fact that his superlative style virtually defies translation. Although foreign readers may not be directly acquainted with Pushkin's works, his influence is evident in the more widely-known books of Dostoevski, Leo Tolstoy, Ivan Turgenev, and Nikolai Gogol, each of whom acknowledged his debt to Pushkin. Pushkin has also touched Russian music: both the operas *Boris Godunov* by Modest Mussorgsky and *Eugene Onegin* by Peter Illyich Tchaikovsky are based on his works. His impact on Russian culture is immense. Alexander Herzen said of him: "As soon as he appeared he became necessary; as though Russian literature could never again dispense with him. The other Russian poets are read and admired; Pushkin is in the hands of every civilized Russian, who reads him again and again all his life long."

PRINCIPAL WORKS

Ruslan i Lyudmila (poetry) 1820
  [*Ruslan and Lyudmila* published in *Tales and Legends of Old Russia*, 1926]
Kavkazski plennik (poetry) 1822
  [*The Captive of the Caucasus*, 1890]
Bakhchisaraiski fontan (poetry) 1824
  [*The Bak-chesarian Fountain: A Tale of the Tauride*, 1849]
Stansy (poetry) 1826
Bratya razboiniki (poetry) 1827
Graf Nulin (poetry) 1827
  [*Count Nulin* published in *Three Comic Poems: Alexander Pushkin*, 1974]
Tsygany (poetry) 1827
  [*The Gipsies* published in *Translations from Pushkin in Memory of the Hundredth Anniversary of the Poet's Birthday*, 1899]
Poltava (poetry) 1829
  [*Poltava* published in *Russian Lyrics in English Verse*, 1887]
Boris Godunov [first publication] (drama) 1831
  [*Boris Godunoff* published in *Translations from Pushkin in Memory of the Hundredth Anniversary of the Poet's Birthday*, 1899]
Motsart i Saleri [first publication] (drama) 1831
  [*Mozart and Salieri* published in *Translations from Pushkin in Memory of the Hundredth Anniversary of the Poet's Birthday*, 1899]

Povesti Belkina (short stories) 1831
  [*The Tales of Ivan Belkin*, 1954]
Pir vo vremya chumy [first publication] (drama) 1832
  [*A Feast in the City of the Plague*, 1927; also published as *A Feast during the Plague* in *Little Tragedies*, 1965]
Domik v Kolomne (poetry) 1833
  [*The Little House in Kolomna* published in journal *Slavonic and East European Review*, 1933]
Yevgeny Onegin (novel) 1833
  [*Eugene Onéguine*, 1881; also published as *Eugene Onegin*, 1937]
Pikovaya dama (novella) 1834
  [*The Queen of Spades*, 1850]
Skazi (fairy tales) 1834
Istoriya Pugacheva (history) 1835
Kapitanskaya dochka (novella) 1836
  [*The Captain's Daughter; or, The Generosity of the Russian Usurper Pugatscheff*, 1846]
Puteshestvie v Arzrum (travel essay) 1836
  [*A Journey to Arzrum*, 1974]
Skupoi rytsar [first publication] (drama) 1836
  [*The Avaricious Knight*, 1933; also published as *The Covetous Knight* in *The Poems, Prose and Plays of Alexander Pushkin*, 1936]
Arap Petra Velikogo (unfinished novel) 1837
  [*The Moor of Peter the Great* published in *Russian Romance*, 1875; also published as *The Negro of Peter the Great*, 1924]
Istoriya sela Goryukhina (unfinished novel) 1837
  [*History of the Village of Goryukhina* published in *The Queen of Spades and Other Stories*, 1892]
Medny vsadnik (unfinished poetry) 1837
  [*The Bronze Cavalier* published in *Translations from Pushkin in Honor of the Hundredth Anniversary of the Poet's Birthday*, 1899; also published as *The Bronze Horseman* in *Russian Poems*, 1929]
Kammeny gost [first publication] (drama) 1839
  [*The Statue Guest* published in *Translations from Pushkin in Honor of the Hundredth Anniversary of the Poet's Birthday*, 1899; also published as *The Stone Guest* in *The Poems, Prose and Plays of Alexander Pushkin*, 1936]
Dubrovski (unfinished novel) 1841
  [*Dubrovsky* published in *The Prose Tales of A. Pushkin*, 1894]
Rusalka (unfinished drama) 1841
  [*The Water Nymph*, 192?]
Table Talk (essays) 1857
Poems by Alexander Pushkin (poetry) 1888
The Poems, Prose and Plays of Alexander Pushkin (poetry, drama, short stories, and novellas) 1936
Pushkin's Poems (poetry) 1945
Polnoe sobranie sochienii. 16 vols. (poetry, drama, short stories, novellas, novels, essays, criticism, and letters) 1937-49
The Letters of Alexander Pushkin. 2 vols. (letters) 1963
The Critical Prose of Alexander Pushkin (criticism) 1969
Pushkin on Literature (letters, journals, and essays) 1971

*These works are collectively referred to as "Little Tragedies."

THE NEW MONTHLY MAGAZINE AND LITERARY JOURNAL
(essay date 1824)

The young poet, Puschkin, has completed a new production ["**Fountain of Baktschissarai**"], which, though of no great extent, surpasses, in the unanimous opinion of the critics, all his former productions. . . . Puschkin is a literary phenomenon, endowed by nature with all the qualifications of an excellent poet; he has begun his career in a manner in which many would be happy to conclude. . . . [Up] to this time, when he is scarcely twenty-five years of age, he has composed, besides a number of charming little pieces which have been received with great approbation by the literary journals, three more considerable poems, which are real ornaments of the Russian Parnassus; and what is a particular merit in these days of translation, they are quite original. The first of them is "**Russlan and Ljudmilla.**" . . . The subject of the poem (in six cantos) is the carrying off of the Princess Ljudmilla by the magician Tschernomor, and her deliverance to her husband Russlan, a valiant knight. The plan is admirable, the execution masterly, and, notwithstanding the numerous characters introduced, and the episodes and events which cross each other, the narrative is rapid, the characters well drawn, the descriptions animated, and the language excellent. Russlan was soon succeeded by "**Kaw Koskoi Plennik**" ["**The Prisoner of the Caucasus**"], a smaller, though not less excellent poem; which describes the rude manners of the banditti of Caucasus, their mode of life, and the peculiarity of the country and its inhabitants, in the most lively colours. . . . Puschkin's new poem, the "**Fountain of Baktschissarai**," is in many respects superior to his former productions. (pp. 545-46)

> *"Foreign Varieties: Russia," in* The New Monthly Magazine and Literary Journal, *n.s. Vol. XII, No. XLVIII, December 1, 1824, pp. 545-46.*

PETER VYAZEMSKY   (essay date 1824)

A Conversation between the Publisher and a Classicist from the Vyborg Side or Vasilev Island:

CLASSICIST: Is it true that young Pushkin is printing a third new poem, a poem, that is, in the romantic sense of the word—I don't know what to call it in our terms.

PUBLISHER: Yes, he has sent *The Fountain of Bakhchisarai* which is being printed here now.

CLASSICIST: One cannot help regretting that he writes so much; he'll soon write himself out.

PUBLISHER: Prophecies are confirmed by events; one needs time to check them; and meanwhile I will note that if he writes a lot in comparison to our poets, who write almost nothing, he writes little in comparison with his other European colleagues. Byron, Walter Scott, and a number of others write tirelessly and are read tirelessly.

CLASSICIST: You expect to shut the mouths of the critics and their objections by exhibiting these two Britons! In vain! We are not of timid nature. It is impossible to judge a writer's talent by the predilection for him of the superstitious mass of readers. They are capricious, they often pay no attention to the most worthy writers. . . . I would like to know about the content of Pushkin's so-called poem. I confess that from the title I don't understand what can be suitable for a poem here. I understand that one can write stanzas, even an ode, *to a fountain.* . . .

PUBLISHER: A legend well-known in the Crimea even today serves as the basis for the poem. It is told that Khan Kerim-Girey abducted the beautiful Pototsky and kept her in the Bakhchisarai harem; it is even supposed that he was married to her. . . . [Our] poet did very well in assimilating the Bakhchisarai legend to poetry and enriching it with realistic fictions, and even better that he used both elements with perfect artistry. The local color is preserved in the narration with all possible vividness and freshness. There is an eastern stamp on the tableaux, in the emotions themselves, and in the style. In the opinion of judges whose verdict can be considered final in our literature, in the new work the poet showed signs of a talent which is maturing more and more. . . . Pushkin's story is lively and interesting. There is a lot of movement in the poem. Into a rather tight frame he has put action full not of a multitude of characters and a chain of different adventures, but of artistry—with which the poet was able to depict and add nuances to the main characters of his narration. *Action* depends, so to speak, on the *activity* of talent: style lends its wings or slows its motion with weights. The interest of the reader is maintained from beginning to end in Pushkin's work. —One cannot achieve this secret except with allurement of style.

> *Peter Vyazemsky, "In Place of a Foreword to 'The Fountain of Bakhchsarai'" (1824), in* The Critical Prose of Alexander Pushkin: With Critical Essays by Four Russian Romantic Poets *by Alexander Pushkin, edited and translated by Carl R. Proffer (translation copyright © 1969 by Indiana University Press), Indiana University Press, 1969, pp. 258-65.*

[J. G. COCHRANE]   (essay date 1827)

Romantic poems, in the manner of those of Lord Byron, have for some time past been greatly in vogue in Russia. The youthful Poushkin . . . was the first who attempted this species in his **Captive of Caucasus;** and he has since published several others, all of which exhibit the same faults and the same beauties. An easy, harmonious, and mellifluous versification, and natural and poetical descriptions, form his beauties; the want of plan and *ensemble,* the monotony of sentiments, and the repetition of some favourite expressions, constitute his faults. The best of his productions, in our opinion, is his poem of **Ludmila,** the subject of which is taken from the fabulous traditions of the reign of Vladimir, the Russian Charlemagne. Poushkin, in this instance, had only the unfortunate example of a celebrated author to guide him—an example, which like a beacon, warned him of the dangers he had to shun. It is much to be regretted that he has not applied himself more to this truly national species of composition, and that his ambition was not excited to become the Russian Ariosto. (p. 625)

> [J. G. Cochrane,] *"Russian Literature," in* The Foreign Quarterly Review, *Vol. I, No. II, November, 1827, pp. 595-631.**

IVAN KIREEVSKY   (essay date 1828)

Accounting for the pleasure works of art give us is both an indispensable requirement of, and one of the highest gratifications for, the educated mind: why then has so little been said about Pushkin? Why have his best works been left unexamined, and why do we hear, instead of analysis and judgment, only fatuous exclamations: "Pushkin is a poet! Pushkin is a real poet! *Onegin* is a superb poem! *The Gypsies* is a masterly work," and so forth? Why has no one so far ventured to define the over-all nature of his poetry, to appraise its merits and faults, and to determine what rank our poet has succeeded in acquiring among the leading poets of his time? (p. 3)

When speaking about Pushkin . . . it is difficult to express one's opinion resolutely; it is difficult to bring the diversity of his works into focus and to find a general criterion for the nature of his poetry, which has taken on so many different shapes. For, excepting the beauty and originality of their poetic language, what traces of common origin do we find in *Ruslan and Liudmila, The Prisoner of the Caucasus, Onegin, The Gypsies,* and so forth? Not only is each of these narrative poems different from the others in its plot development and in its manner of narration *(la manière),* but some of them differ in their very nature, reflecting diverse views of the world by the poet, so much so that in translation it would be easy to take them for works, not of one, but of several authors. The light humor—a child of gaiety and wit—which in *Ruslan and Liudmila* dresses all objects in sparkling colors, is no longer to be encountered in the poet's other works. In *Onegin,* its place is taken by scathing mockery—an echo of a skepticism of the heart. Good-natured gaiety has here changed into a dismal coldness which regards all objects through the dark veil of doubt, conveys its observations through caricature, and creates only in order to revel in the imminent destruction of its creature. In *The Prisoner of Caucasus,* on the other hand, we find neither the trust in fate which vivified *Ruslan,* nor the contempt for human beings that we remark in *Onegin.* Here we see a soul embittered by treason and loss, yet one that has still not betrayed itself, nor lost the freshness of its former sensations; one still faithful to its sacred inclinations. It is a soul maimed but not conquered by fate; the outcome of the struggle is still a question of the future. In the narrative poem *The Gypsies,* the nature of the poetry is again unique, different from Pushkin's other narrative poems, and the same can be said about almost every one of his major works.

Yet after a careful perusal of Pushkin's works, from *Ruslan and Liudmila* to chapter five of *Onegin,* [In a footnote the translator states: Only five chapters had been published at the time Kireevsky was writing his review.] we find that his poetry—with all its meandering course—has had three periods of development, each of which differs sharply from the others. We shall attempt to define the distinctive feature and content of each of these, and then draw broad conclusions about Pushkin's poetry in general. (pp. 4-5)

I would call the first period of Pushkin's poetry, that including *Ruslan* and some minor lyrics, the period of the *Italian-French school.* The sweetness of Parny, the ingenuous, light wit, the delicacy, the purity of form, which are all characteristic of French poetry in general, have here been united with the splendor, lively exuberance, and freedom of Ariosto. (p. 5)

While in his subsequent works Pushkin was to endow almost all the creatures of his imagination with the individuality of his own character and way of thinking, here he often appears a *poet inventor.* He does not seek to convey to us his own special view of the world, of fate, life, and man; he simply creates for us a new fate, a new life, a new individual world, and populates it with beings that are new and disparate, belonging exclusively to his creative imagination. This is the reason why no other poem of his has the same completeness and congruity which we remark in *Ruslan.* This is why each canto, each scene, each digression has its own distinctive, full existence; why each part is woven into the pattern of the whole creation so indispensably that nothing could be added or sub-

tracted without utter loss of harmony. . . . This is why the author, correlating the parts with the whole, carefully avoids anything pathetic which might stir up the reader's soul. For strong feelings are incompatible with the comically miraculous; they agree only with the majestically marvelous. Charm alone can lure us into the realm of magic; and if in the midst of enchanting impossibility something affects us in all seriousness, making us revert to ourselves, then good-bye to our faith in the improbable! Miraculous specters are scattered to the winds and the whole world of the fantastic collapses, disappears, the way a motley dream is interrupted when something among its concoctions reminds us of reality. The Finn's story, if it had a different ending, would destroy the effect of the whole poem. . . . In general one can say that even if an exacting criticism should find weak, uneven passages in *Ruslan and Liudmila,* still it will detect nothing superfluous or irrelevant in it. Chivalry, love, sorcery, feasts, war, mermaids— all the poetry of an enchanted world—were here combined in one creation, and despite the motley parts, everything is well-proportioned, harmonious, *congruous.* (pp. 5-6)

If in *Ruslan and Liudmila* Pushkin was exclusively a *poet* faithfully and unfalteringly transmitting the impulses of his fancy, in *The Prisoner of the Caucasus* he appears as a *poet-philosopher* who in his poetry tries to depict the doubts of his reason and thus gives all objects the general color of his individual views, often forsaking the objects in order to dwell in the realm of abstract thinking. What he presents, in *The Prisoner, Onegin,* and other works, are no longer sorcerers with their miracles, nor unconquerable heroes or enchanted gardens; rather, his subject is real life and the human being of our time, with his emptiness, insignificance, and dullness. Unlike Goethe, however, he does not seek to elevate his object by revealing both the poetry in ordinary life and a full reflection of all mankind in contemporary man; rather, like Byron, he sees only contradiction in the whole world, only betrayed hope, so that one could call almost every one of his heroes *disillusioned.*

It is not only in his view of life and man that Pushkin concurs with the bard of *The Giaour:* he also resembles him in other aspects of his poetry. The manner of presentation is the same; so is the tone and the form of his poems; there is the same vagueness with regard to the whole and the same detailed explicitness in the parts; the structure is the same; and even the characters in most cases are so similar that at first glance one would take them for immigrant aliens who have journeyed from Byron's world into Pushkin's creations.

Nevertheless, despite such similarity to the British poet, we find in *Onegin,* in *The Gypsies,* in *The Prisoner,* and in other works so much original beauty belonging exclusively to our poet, such guileless freshness of feeling, such veracity of description, such subtlety in observation and naturalness in presentation, such originality in language, and, finally so much that is purely Russian that even in this period of his poetry he cannot be called a mere imitator. . . . It is evident to those who have looked into the souls of both poets that Pushkin did not meet Byron accidentally, but borrowed from him, or more accurately, unwittingly submitted to his influence. Byron's lyre had to reverberate in his epoch, for it was itself the voice of its epoch. One of two antagonistic tendencies of our time gained expression in it. Is it surprising that it did not sound for Pushkin in vain? Only perhaps he yielded too much to its influence. Had he retained more originality, at least in the exterior form of his poems, he would have invested them with even greater excellence.

Byron's influence was manifested first of all in *The Prisoner of the Caucasus.* Here the marks of similarity mentioned above are particularly evident. The structure of the poem demonstrates, however, that this was Pushkin's first attempt in this particular manner: for the descriptions of the Circassians, their way of life, customs, games, and so forth—which fill the first canto—arrest the action to no end, snap the thread of interest, and do not accord with the tone of the poem as a whole. It is one's impression that the poem has not one, but two unblended subject matters, each appearing separately and diverting attention and feeling in two different directions. But by what merits is this important fault redeemed! What poesy pervades all the episodes! What freshness, what power of feeling! What veracity of lively descriptions! No other work by Pushkin offers so many faults and so many beauties.

Just as great—or perhaps an even greater—similarity to Byron appears in *The Fountain at Bakhchisarai,* but here a more skillful execution reveals the greater maturity of the poet. . . . All the digressions and interruptions are tied together by one prevalent feeling; everything strives to produce one principal impression. An apparent irregularity in narration is an invariable criterion of the Byronic manner; but this irregularity is only seeming, for the dissonant presentation of objects reverberates in the soul as a harmonious train of sensations. (pp. 8-9)

How naturally and harmoniously are eastern voluptuousness and sensuality here blended with the strongest outbursts of southern passion! The contrast between the luxurious description of the harem and the gravity of the principal action betrays the author of *Ruslan.* He has descended to earth from the immortal world of enchantment, but he has not lost his sense of enthralling sensuality even in the midst of conflicting passions and misfortunes. His art of poetry in *The Fountain* could be compared with the Oriental peri who, although bereft of paradise, has retained her unearthly beauty: her aspect is thoughtful and grave, but through the affected coldness a strong agitation of her spirit is perceptible. (p. 9)

The poem of Pushkin's which is furthest from Byron is *The Robber Brothers,* despite the fact that by its subject matter, episodes, descriptions, and all other elements it must be called a replica of *The Prisoner of Chillon.* It is more a caricature than an imitation of Byron. Bonnivard and his brothers suffered "For the God their foes denied"; and however cruel their torment may be, there is an element of poetry in it which commands our sympathy. On the other hand, Pushkin's detailed description of the sufferings of the captured robbers engenders only revulsion—a feeling similar to what we experience at the sight of the torment of a criminal justly sentenced to death. It can be asserted that there is nothing poetic in this poem beyond the introductory stanzas and the charming versification—which latter is always and everywhere a mark of Pushkin.

This charming versification is seen above all in *The Gypsies,* where the mastery of versecraft has reached its highest degree of perfection and art has assumed the appearance of free casualness. Here it seems that each sound has poured forth from the soul unconstrained, and everything is pure, complete, and free, despite the fact that each line—except perhaps two or three in the whole poem—has received the ultimate in polish.

Does the content, however, have the same merit as the form? We see a nomadic, semibarbaric people which knows no laws, despises luxury and civilization, and loves freedom above all.

Yet this people is familiar with sentiments characteristic of the most refined community: the memory of a former love and a nostalgia for the inconstant Mariula fill the old gypsy's whole life. But, while the gypsies experience exclusive, lasting love, they do not recognize jealousy; Aleko's feelings are incomprehensible to them. One might assume that the author wished to represent a golden age, in which people were just without laws, in which passions never trespassed beyond proper limits, in which all was free but nothing disturbed the general harmony, and inner perfection was the result, not of an arduous education, but of the happy innocence of a natural integrity. Such an idea could have great poetic merit. But here, unfortunately, the fair sex destroys all the enchantment, and while the gypsies' love is *"drudgery and anguish,"* their wives are like the moon which "serenely strays, / On all creation gently pouring / Her undiscriminating rays." Is this feminine imperfection compatible with the perfection of the tribe? The gypsies either do not form permanent, exclusive attachments, or if they do they are jealous of their inconstant wives; in the latter case revenge and other passions cannot be alien to them. If such is the case, then Aleko cannot seem strange and incomprehensible to them, then European manners differ from theirs only by the advantages of education, and then they represent, not a golden age, but simply a semibarbaric people which is not bound by laws and is poor and wretched, just like the actual gypsies of Bessarabia. And then the whole poem contradicts itself. (pp. 9-10)

But there is a quality in *The Gypsies* which redeems in a way the disorder of the subject matter. This quality is the poet's greater originality. The author of "A Review of Literature in 1827" correctly observed that this poem reveals a struggle between Byron's idealism and the Russian poet's nationally oriented paintings. Indeed, take the description of gypsy life separately, regard Zemfira's father, not as a gypsy, but simply as an old man with no reference to his nationality, consider the passage about Ovid: the completeness of creation, developed in all details and inspired by an originality, will prove to you that Pushkin had already sensed the power of his independent talent, free of foreign influences.

All the faults of *The Gypsies* are functions of these two discordant tendencies: one original and one Byronic. Therefore the very imperfection of the poem is a guarantee of the poet's future progress.

A striving for an independent brand of poetry is even more manifest in *Eugene Onegin,* although not in its first chapters where Byron's influence is obvious, nor in the manner of narration which derives from *Don Juan* and *Beppo,* nor even in the character of Onegin himself, which is of the same kind as that of Childe Harold. But the further the poet moves from his main hero, abandoning himself to collateral descriptions, the more independent and national he becomes.

The time of Childe Harolds, thank God, has not yet come for our fatherland: young Russia has not partaken of the life of western states and our people, as a personality, is not getting old under the weight of others' experiences. A brilliant career is still open to Russian activity; all kinds of art, all branches of knowledge still remain to be mastered by our fatherland. Hope is still given to us: what is the disillusioned Childe Harold's business among us?

Let us examine which qualities the British flower transplanted into Russian soil has retained and which it has lost.

The British poet's most cherished vision is an extraordinary, lofty creature. Not a paucity, but a superabundance of inner strength makes this creature unsympathetic to his environment. An immortal idea dwells in his heart day and night, consuming all his being and poisoning all his pleasures. Whatever shape it takes—haughty contempt for mankind, nagging sense of guilt, gloomy despair, or insatiable yearning for oblivion—this idea is all-embracing and everlasting. What is it if not an instinctive, constant striving for the better, a nostalgia for an unattainable perfection? (pp. 12-13)

On the other hand, Onegin is an entirely ordinary and insignificant being. He is also indifferent to his environment; not despair, however, but an inability to love made him cold. His youth also passed in a whirlpool of amusement and dissipation, but he was not carried away by turbulent passion and an insatiable soul; rather he led a fashionable fop's empty, indifferent life on the parquet floor of the salon. He also quit the world and people; not, however, in order to seek scope for his agitated thoughts in solitude, but because he was equally bored everywhere,

> Because he yawned with equal gloom
> In any style of drawing room.

He does not lead a special inner life which rises above the lives of other people, and he despises mankind merely because he is unable to respect it. There is nothing more common than this breed of people, and there could not be less poetry in such a character.

This is, then, the Childe Harold of our fatherland: praise be to the poet that he did not present us with the real one. For, as we have already said, the time for Childe Harolds has not come to Russia, and we pray to God that it never will.

It seems that Pushkin himself felt the emptiness of his hero and for this reason did not anywhere in the novel try to bring him close to his readers. He gave him no definite physiognomy; he represented, not one person, but a whole class of people in his portrait: Onegin's description may fit a thousand different characters. (p. 13)

As far as *Eugene Onegin* in general is concerned, we have no right to judge the plot by its beginning, although we can hardly imagine the possibility of a well-composed, complete, fertile plan emerging after such a beginning. Still, who can discern the limits of possibility for such poets as Pushkin? It is their prerogative to amaze their critics at all times.

The faults of *Onegin* are in essence the last homage Pushkin paid to the British poet. The narrative's innumerable merits—Lensky, Tatiana, Olga, St. Petersburg, the countryside, the dream, the winter, the letter, and so forth—are our poet's inalienable property. It is in these that he clearly reveals the innate tendency of his genius. These signs of original creation in *The Gypsies* and in *Onegin,* coupled with the one scene we know from *Boris Godunov,* [In a footnote the translator states: Kireevsky is referring to the monastery scene which had been published in *Moskovsky restnik* 1 (1827).] constitute, though they do not exhaust, the third period in the development of his poetry, which could be called the *period of Russo-Pushkinian poetry.* Its essential features are: a pictorial vividness, a certain abandon, a singular pensiveness, and, finally, an ineffable quality, comprehensible only to the Russian heart: for what can you call the feeling with which the melodies of Russian songs are imbued, to which the Russian people most frequently resort, and which can be regarded as the center of its spiritual life?

In this period of Pushkin's development one particularly notices an ability to be absorbed in the environment and in the passing moment. This same ability is the foundation of the Russian character: it is at the very inception of all the virtues and failings of the Russian people. From this ability emanate courage, lightness of heart, intractability of momentary impulses, generosity, intemperance, vehemence, perspicuity, geniality, and so on and so forth. (pp. 13-14)

The above-mentioned scene from *Boris Godunov* particularly manifests Pushkin's maturity. The art which in such a narrow frame represents the spirit of the epoch, monastic life, Pimen's character, the state of contemporary affairs, and the beginning of the dramatic action; the special, tragically serene atmosphere that involes the chronicler's life and presence for us; the new, striking manner in which the poet acquaints us with Grishka; and finally the inimitable, poetic, precise language: all this taken together makes us expect of this tragedy—let us say it boldly—something *magnificent.*

Pushkin was born to be a dramatist. He is too many-sided, too objective to be a lyric poet. One can observe in each of his poetic tales an instinctive urge to endow each separate part with individual life—an urge injurious to the whole in epic creations but necessary and invaluable to the dramatist. . . .

Few are selected by fate to enjoy the affection of their contemporaries during their lifetime. Pushkin belongs to their number, which reveals to us still another important quality in the nature of his poetry: a *congruence with his time.*

It is not enough to be a poet in order to be a national poet: it is also necessary to have been raised, as it were, in the midst of the nation's life and to have shared in the fatherland's hopes, aspirations, and passions—in short to live its life and to express it spontaneously while expressing oneself. Such a lucky attainment may be a rare accident: but are beauty, intelligence, insight—all the qualities with which man captivates man—not just as accidental? And are these latter qualities any more substantial than the capacity to reflect a nation's life in oneself? (p. 15)

Ivan Kireevsky, "On the Nature of Pushkin's Poetry" (originally published as "Nechto o kharaktere poezii Pushkina," in Moskovsky vestnik, *Vol. 8, 1828), in* Literature and National Identity: Nineteenth-Century Russian Critical Essays, *edited and translated by Paul Debreczeny and Jesse Zeldin (reprinted by permission of University of Nebraska Press; translation © 1970 by the University of Nebraska Press),* University of Nebraska Press, *1970, pp. 3-16.*

ALEXANDER PUSHKIN   (essay date 1830)

The study of Shakespeare, Karamzin, and our old chronicles gave me the idea of clothing in dramatic forms one of the most dramatic epochs of modern history. Not disturbed by any other influence [in writing *Boris Godunov*], I imitated Shakespeare in his broad and free depiction of characters, in the simple and careless combination of plots; I followed Karamzin in the clear development of events; I tried to guess the way of thinking and the language of the time from the chronicles. Rich sources! Whether I was able to make the best use of them, I don't know—but at least my labors were zealous and conscientious. (p. 99)

I frankly confess that the failure of my drama would distress me, for I am firmly convinced that national laws of the Shakespearean drama are appropriate for our theater—not the court convention of Racine's tragedies—and that every unsuccessful experiment can delay the reform of our stage. [In a footnote the translator states: Pushkin means that Shakespeare's plays were English in spirit and enjoyed by people from many classes (not just courtiers).] . . .

I will proceed to explanations of a few particulars. The line which I have used (iambic pentameter) is ordinarily accepted by the English and Germans. . . . I have preserved the caesura of French pentameter in the second foot, and I think, erred in this, by voluntarily depriving my line of the variety peculiar to it. There are coarse jokes, scenes of the commonfolk. It is good if the poet can avoid them (the poet should not be vulgar of his own free will), but if not, he has no need of trying to replace them with something else.

Finding in history one of my ancestors who played an important role in this unfortunate epoch, I introduced him onto the stage without thinking about the delicacy of propriety, *con amore*—but without any aristocratic haughtiness. Of all my imitations of Byron, aristocratic haughtiness was the most ridiculous. The new gentry makes up our aristocracy; the ancient gentry has gone into decline, its rights have been equalized with the rights of other classes, the great estates have been splintered, destroyed, and no one, not even the descendants themselves etc. In the eyes of the judicious rabble, belonging to the old aristocracy does not present any advantages, and an isolated show of respect for the glory of one's ancestors can only draw censure for eccentricity or senseless imitation of foreigners. (p. 100)

> *Alexander Pushkin, in an extract from "Drafts of a Preface to 'Boris Godunov'" (1829-30), in his* The Critical Prose of Alexander Pushkin: With Critical Essays by Four Russian Romantic Poets, *edited and translated by Carl R. Proffer (translation copyright © 1969 by Indiana University Press), Indiana University Press, 1969, pp. 98-101.*

ALEXANDER PUSHKIN   (essay date 1830)

Being a Russian writer, I have always considered it a duty to follow current literature, and I have always read criticisms which I occasioned with particular attention. I honestly admit that praise touched me as a clear and apparently sincere sign of good-will and friendliness. I dare say that reading the most hostile critiques I always tried to enter into my critic's way of thinking and follow his judgments without refuting them with egotistic impatience, but wishing to agree to them with all possible authorial self-effacement. Unfortunately, I noticed that for the most part we did not understand each other. As for critical articles written with the sole aim of offending me in any way possible, I will say only that they angered me very much, at least in the first moments, and that therefore their writers may be content, assured that their labors were not lost. If during sixteen years of my life as an author I never answered a single criticism (I'm not talking about the abuse), this occurred, of course, not from scorn. (pp. 101-02)

I haven't answered my critics because I lacked the desire, good humor, or pedantry either, nor because I supposed these critics had no influence on the reading public. But, I confess, I was ashamed to repeat banal or grade-school truths to refute them, to discourse on grammar, rhetoric, and the alphabet, and, what is most embarrassing of all, to justify myself where there were no accusations, to say pompously:

Et moi je vous soutiens que mes vers sont très bons
[I maintain that my verse is very good]

[attributed in a footnote to Molière's *Misanthrope*] or, for lack of anything to do, to go squabble before the public and try to make it laugh (for which I have not the slightest proclivity). For example, one of my critics—a good and well-intentioned man, incidentally—analyzing *Poltava,* I think, presented a few excerpts and in place of any criticism, asserted that such verses in themselves "poorly recommend themselves." What could I answer him to this? And almost all of his comrades behaved the same way. Our critics usually say: this is good because it is excellent, but that is bad because it is rotten. There is no way you will lure them out of this position. (pp. 102-03)

In general *Ruslan and Ludmila* was received favorably. . . . No one even noticed that it is cold. They accused it of immorality for a few slightly sensual descriptions, for verses which I deleted in the second edition:

> Oh, terrible sight! The decrepit wizard
> Caresses with a wrinkled hand, etc.

for the introduction to I don't remember which canto:

> In vain you have hidden in the shadow, etc.

and for the parody of *Twelve Sleeping Maidens* [a poem by Vasily Zhukovsky]; for the latter I could well be reproved for a lack of esthetic feeling. It was inexcusable (especially at my age) to parody a pure, poetic creation to please the rabble. (p. 103)

A Prisoner of the Caucasus was the first unsuccessful study of a character whom it was difficult for me to cope with; thanks to a few elegiac and descriptive verses, it was received better than anything else I have written. But Nikolai and Alexander Raevsky and I laughed to our hearts' content at it.

The Fountain of Bakhchisarai is weaker than the *Prisoner* and, like it, echoes the reading of Byron, over whom I had gone out of my mind. The scene of Zarema with Maria has dramatic merit. I don't think it was criticized. A. Raevsky roared at the following verses:

> Often in fateful battles
> He would raise his saber—and with a swing
> Suddenly remained motionless,
> Look madly around,
> Turned pale, etc.

Young writers in general do not know how to depict the physical movements of passions. Their heroes always tremble, laugh wildly, gnash their teeth, and so forth. All this is ridiculous, like a melodrama. (p. 104)

Our critics left me at peace for a long time. This does them honor: I was far from being in favorable circumstances. From habit they kept supposing I was a very young man. As I recall, the first hostile articles began to appear after the publication of the fourth and fifth cantos of *Eugene Onegin*. The critique of these chapters printed in the *Athenaeum* suprised me by its good tone, good style, and the strangeness of its quibbles. The most ordinary rhetorical figures and tropes stopped the critic: can one say "the glass bubbles" instead of "the wine bubbles in the glass," "the fireplace smokes" instead of "steam comes out of the fireplace"? Aren't "jealous suspicion" and "faithless ice" too bold? (pp. 104-05)

A few cases of poetic license: the accusative and not the genitive case after the negative particle . . . caused my critic great consternation. Most of all he was irritated by the line:

> *Ljudskuju molv' i konskij top*
> [People's talk and horses' clattering]

"Do we who have learned from the old grammars express ourselves like this, can one mangle the Russian language like this?" . . . *Molv'* [talk] is an indigenous Russian word. *Top* [clatter] instead of *topot* is just as often used as *sip* [hiss] instead of *sipen'e*. (As in the old Russian poem: "He let out a hiss [*sip*] like a snake.") . . .

Besides, this entire line is not mine, but was taken whole from a Russian folk-tale. . . . The study of ancient songs, folk-tales, etc. is essential for a complete knowledge of the qualities of the Russian language. It is in vain that our critics scorn them. (pp. 105-06)

The spoken language of the simple folk (who don't read foreign books and, thank God, don't express their thoughts in French as we do) is also worth the deepest studies. Alfieri studied Italian in a Florentine bazaar; it wouldn't be bad for us to occasionally listen to the Moscow candle-mongers. They speak an amazingly pure and correct language. . . .

The omitted stanzas [in *Eugene Onegin*] repeatedly gave rise to reproaches. There is no reason to be surprised that there are stanzas which I could not or did not want to print in *Eugene Onegin*. But, being omitted, they interrupt the connection of the story, and therefore the place where they belonged is designated. It would have been better to replace these stanzas with other ones or to rewrite and fuse together the ones which I did keep. But sorry, I'm too lazy for that. I humbly confess also that there are two omitted stanzas in *Don Juan*. (p. 107)

Count Nulin caused me a great deal of trouble. It was found (if I may say it) obscene—in the journals, of course—in society it was favorably received—and none of the journalists wanted to stand up for it. A young man dares to enter a young woman's bedroom at night and gets a slap in the face from her! How awful! How dare one write such repulsive filth? The author asks what Petersburg ladies would have done in Natalya Pavlovna's place: what impudence! Apropos of my poor tale (written, be it said in passing, in the most sober and decent manner), all of classical antiquity and all of European literature was raised against me! (pp. 112-13)

These critics found a strange way to judge the degree of morality of any poem. One of them has a 15-year old niece, another has a 15-year old female acquaintance—and everything which by the determination of their parents they are still not permitted to read is declared indecent, immoral, and obscene etc.! As if literature exists only for 16-year old girls. The prudent instructor probably doesn't let them—or even their brothers—have the complete collected works of a single classical poet, especially an ancient one. Readers, selected passages, and such like are published for that. But the public is not a 15-year old maiden and not a 13-year old boy. It, thank God, can safely read itself the tales of the good La Fontaine and the eclogues of the good Virgil, and everything that the critics themselves read when by themselves, if our critics read anything besides the galley-proofs of their own journals. (p. 113)

Poltava had no success. It probably wasn't worth it; but I was spoiled by the reception given my earlier—and much weaker—works; besides, it is a completely original work, and I will bet on that.

Our critics tried to explain the reason for my failure to me—and here's how.

First, they informed me that no one had ever seen a woman fall in love with an old man, and that therefore Maria's love for the old hetman (N.B. proven historically) could not exist. . . . I couldn't be satisfied by this explanation; love is the most capricious passion. I won't even speak of ugliness and stupidity, which are daily preferred to youth, intellect, and beauty. Remember the mythological legends of Ovid's *Metamorphoses*—Leda, Filira, Pasiphaë, Pygmalion—and admit that all these fictions are not foreign to poetry. And Othello, the old Negro who captivated Desdemona with the stories of his travels and battles? . . . And Myrrha, who inspired the Italian with one of his best tragedies? . . .

Maria (or Matrena), they told me, was carried away by vanity, but not love: it is a great honor for the daughter of a supreme judge to be the concubine of a hetman! Next they told me that my Mazeppa was an "evil and stupid old man." That I depicted Mazeppa as evil I confess: I do not find him good, especially at the moment when he is arranging for the execution of the father of the girl whom he has seduced. And the stupidity of a man shows up either in his acts or in his words: in my poem Mazeppa acts exactly as in history, and his speeches explain his historical character. (pp. 115-16)

In *The Messenger of Europe* it was noted that the title of the poem was erroneous, and that I probably didn't call it Mazeppa so as not to recall Byron. Correct, but there was another reason for this too—the epigraph. Thus, in the manuscript *The Fountain of Bakhchisarai* was called *The Harem*, but the melancholy epigraph (which is, of course, better than the whole poem) seduced me.

However, apropos of *Poltava* the critics referred to Byron's *Mazeppa*—but how they understood that! Byron knew Mazeppa only from Voltaire's *History of Charles XII*. He was struck only by the picture of a man attached to a wild horse and plunging across the steppes. A poetic picture, of course, and then look what he made of it. But don't try to find either Mazeppa or Charles there—or the dark, hateful, tormenting character who appears in almost all Byron's works, but who (to the misfortune of one of my critics), as if on purpose, is not in *Mazeppa*. Byron didn't even think about them; he exhibited a row of pictures, one more striking than the next—and that's all. (p. 117)

Alexander Pushkin, "Refutations of Criticisms" (1830), in his The Critical Prose of Alexander Pushkin: With Critical Essays by Four Russian Romantic Poets, *edited and translated by Carl R. Proffer (translation copyright © 1969 by Indiana University Press), Indiana University Press, 1969, pp. 101-21.*

[WILLIAM HENRY LEEDS] (essay date 1832)

By many of his countrymen, Pushkin has been styled the Russian Byron—an appellation too flattering, if meant to imply poetical powers and energy equal to those of the English bard; and more correct, perhaps, than complimentary, if intended merely to characterize that external resemblance of form and manner which he will be found to bear to the latter. We do not mean to say that he is such a direct imitator as to forfeit all originality; far from it: but he has undoubtedly looked at Byron as a model. It is upon him that he has formed his style and his mode of treating his subjects, more particularly in his narrative poems. . . . Although we could wish that Pushkin did not remind us quite so much of Byron, we consider his productions as affording evidence of indisputable genius and power; they exhibit many masterly touches, much vigour of hand, and not a few beauties and traits of detail, together with that peculiar hue which is derived from the language in which they are expressed. As far as the nature and structure of two such very different idioms will admit, his style is evidently Byronic; his narrative at once graphic and lyrical; now rapid and condensed, rather hinting at than clearly expressing events and circumstances; now again dwelling minutely, but poetically, upon particulars, and giving them great prominency and relief. His narratives themselves, withal, are little more than fragmentary episodes; insulated scenes and situations; single groups, which are rescued from insipidity, or rather we ought to say, invested with life, spirit and effect, by the skill with which they are worked up, and by mastery of execution; so that the apparent scantiness of the subject in some degree increases our admiration, by reminding us how very simple are the materials to which the poet has had recourse. At the same time, we must acknowledge a feeling of dissatisfaction at finding him invariably confining himself to subjects which admit not of prolonged interest, and exercising his talent upon brief sketches, in preference to applying it to some theme that would afford him ampler scope. . . . Exquisite as may be the workmanship of a mere piece of *bijouterie,* it can hardly make that impression upon us which would be produced by a similar piece of design on a larger scale; or at least, however admirable in itself, it claims our regard by qualities very remotely, if at all, allied to grandeur, or indicative of power. Like the "Giaour," "The Siege of Corinth," "Mazeppa," and Byron's other productions of that class, those of the Russian poet have nothing of the epic in their composition; as little do they belong either to the ballad or poetical legend, or to the versified tale or romance. They rather partake of a dramatic character, the more striking parts being generally given in the form of monologue or dialogue; while the narrative portion exhibits, not unfrequently, a strong tendency to lyrical description, and indulges in the abrupt transitions, the free, incitated step, together with the vivid energy, both of idea and expression, which distinguish the genius of the lyre. This species of poetry, therefore, cannot with propriety, nor, indeed, without injustice, be classed with that superior order of poetic narrative which professes to give us a systematic whole, constructed according to a regular plan, and hinging upon one grand action or event, yet admitting of a variety of accesory parts and undercurrents of episode. To do so would be trying it by a standard to which it is unequal. (pp. 398-99)

The present bias of poetry seems to tend alternately to the two opposite antagonistic poles of highly impassioned feeling and deep meditation; or to the sportive, the comic and the satiric. Here again, too, we find Pushkin an emulous follower of Byron, for like him he has attempted to display the versatility of his muse by undertaking a satiric narrative; but with far less success, his **"Onaegin"** being unquestionably very inferior to "Beppo" and "Juan." He appears to greater advantage in the picturesque, romantic and impassioned styles, than in that which depends for effect upon humorous *persiflage,* or unsparing, tranchant causticity. With some touches of pleasantry, and occasional traits of lighter satire, **"Onaegin"** has none of that rich poignancy, or of that sparkling point, which distinguish those two productions of Byron; added to which, while the manners and frivolities depicted in his poem are un-English enough to be destitute of that interest arising from our acquaintance with the originals, they are not so very remote as to strike by their novelty and singularity. Neither does the

Russian "Beppo"—if we may so term it—possess aught corresponding with the attraction of the unusual and fanciful compound rhymes which of themselves tend materially to heighten the humour of the subject, and impart to it an additional zest. In fact, the poem of **"Onaegin"** is rather remarkable for the quiet easiness, than for the vivacity of its narrative; nor does it make any pretensions to that facetiousness for the nonce which forms so prominent a characteristic of Byron's petulant muse. (pp. 400-01)

[Pushkin's] earlier compositions, some of which were produced while he was at the Tzarskoselo Lyceum, and at about the age of fourteen, are for the most part short lyrical and amatory effusions, together with some few imitations of the ancient poets. Among these, or at least in the general collection of his fugitive pieces, which comprises several of a much later date than what we have mentioned, there are several which display considerable poetic fancy and feeling, and afford indications of a true poetical temperament. His **"Epistle to Ovid,"** the **"Triumph of Bacchus," "Anacreon's Grave,"** the **"Rusalka"** (in ancient Slavonian mythology, a spirit combining the powers of a water-nixe and a wood-nymph), may be mentioned as possessing more interest than the generality. When he essays the loftier species of ode, as that on Napoleon, he disappoints us: here he is far inferior to Lomonosov and Derzhavin, and instead of displaying any thing equal to their vigour of imagination and boldness of lyric flight, or approaching the *verba ardentia* and the *fulmina* of their poetic language, he hardly rises to what may be thought the ordinary level of the subject. (p. 402)

[Puskin's real poetical career] is to be dated from the appearance of his **"Ruslan and Liudmila."** . . . [This little romance] is marked by a graceful easiness and equability of style, a skill in the narrative, and a degree of sportive yet tempered pleasantry in many of the incidents, that certainly do not betray the hand of a novice. . . . The incidents have no more pretension to probability than those of an Arabian Night's tale; nevertheless, although the invention itself may, like that of many of those oriental fictions, seem a mere tissue of puerile and grotesque caprices, the poet has, independently of the charm by which curiosity is attracted and fascinated, thrown in many a touch of real nature, and withal there is an admixture of shrewd good sense enveloped in the enigmas that seem to set reason at defiance. (pp. 402-03)

[Pushkin's subsequent works have scarcely any thing in common with **"Ruslan and Liudmila"**]. Instead of exhibiting, like that, a connected story, however simple or brief, they are, almost all of them, planless fragments without any regular succession of incidents, mere *situations,* in which the poet confines himself to a single point of time, and the delineation of one or two characters. The transition from **"Ruslan and Liudmila,"** to its immediate successor, the **"Prisoner of the Caucasus,"** is striking enough: instead of amusing us by fantastic and sportive images, and by indulging in such satiric pleasantries as those where he describes the amorous advances of the no longer blooming Naina to the lover she had formerly rejected, and the unceremonious manner in which Liudmila treats the redoubtable Tchernomore, the poet endeavours to interest us by the workings of the feelings alone, and the emotions of the human heart. The reader must not ask us for the story, or we shall be compelled to reply in the words of the knife-grinder to the Friend of Humanity:—"Story! God bless you, I have none to tell, Sir." (p. 404)

[Pushkin] is considerably indebted to Byron: in the poem of which we are speaking, and in a considerable portion of his

"**Poltava**" the resemblance between them is, indeed, too striking to be overlooked, even were we not in some measure prepared to expect it by previous report. Had Byron written in Russian, he would hardly have expressed his thoughts otherwise. We must, however, be understood *cum grano salis,* lest, our words being taken too literally, it should be inferred that Pushkin is a plagiarist: our remark goes no further than to express hyperbolically, since we cannot do so with precision, that parallelism of style which exists between the two. Whatever is his subject, Byron, in truth, goes considerably beyond his Russian compeer, if the term be allowable; not only is there greater depth in him, and a far greater command of language, which enables him to mould it to his will on every occasion, but he possesses withal, in an extraordinary degree, the art of suggesting a deeper meaning where he appears to suppress his ideas within himself, and that not because he cannot find expressions sufficiently forcible, but because he has defined it so completely, that further explicitness would rather weaken the effect, by destroying that degree of mystery which impresses the matter on our minds far more powerfully than even the clearest words. Something of this mystery and reticence of diction is affected by Pushkin; we ought, perhaps, to say that he has carried it still further, since his extreme conciseness of description and narration not unfrequently both disappoints us, and leaves us in a disagreeable uncertainty as to whether we have rightly comprehended the particulars so vaguely hinted at. Neither can we avoid entertaining a suspicion, that some of the more than Spartan laconisms which occur in his poems have been resorted to, not so much on account of their particular merit or beauty, as from the inability to fill up these chasms in the details to his own satisfaction. More than one instance of the kind is to be met with in the "**Prisoner of the Caucasus,**" but no where is it more striking than in the passage which contains the catastrophe itself. Here, instead of Byronic *compression* and condensation of ideas, there is rather a total *supression* of them, a vacancy and baldness that certainly are not redeemed by any superior poetical graces of language. How very different from such meagreness in the very part where we expect the writer to throw in his greatest force, is the beautiful stanza in the Bride of Abydos, which informs us of Zuleika's death. The event itself is rather indicated by concomitant circumstances than expressed in words; but how vivid, picturesque, and forcible are the images employed to denote it, and which impart to it such a powerfully pathetic effect! (pp. 405-06)

The "**Fountain of Baktchiasarai,**" [Pushkin's] next production, is somewhat more animated in its subject, and less meagre in its outline. (p. 406)

If in its reckless impetuosity, Zarema's character seems to bear a considerable resemblance to that of Byron's Gulnare, it is exhibited under different and almost opposite circumstances, she being as jealous to continue the favoured slave of her lord, as the other is abhorrent of doing so. . . . Upon the whole, the "**Fountain of Baktchisarai**" is superior to the "**Prisoner of the Caucasus,**" and added, not undeservedly, to the poet's reputation. (p. 408)

The chief attraction of [Pushkin's next poem, "**Tzigani,**" or "**The Gipseys**"] consists in the freshness of the colouring of the descriptive parts, and in the bold, although slight and hasty, manner in which the character of Aleko, and that of Zemfira's father are touched. The form, too, is more dramatic than that of any other of Pushkin's poems, a very considerable portion of it being entirely in a dialogue, with the names of the inter-

locutors prefixed to their speeches; owing to which the whole becomes in some degree a sort of lengthened idyl, composed of description, narrative, and dialogue intermixed. We may further remark, that the poet seems to have intended to convey something like a moral lesson, by showing us in the person of Aleko, the workings of a moody mind, which, impatient of the restraints and habits of civilized life, is willing to purchase an exemption from them, even though it be by foregoing all those advantages which more than counterbalance the partial and incidental vexations attendant upon society even in its most favourable forms. Many of the reflections seem to countenance such a conjecture, for they point at the comparative happiness enjoyed by the free rover, who acknowledges no laws, and that of the social state, which, if it seems to have more alloy, has at the same time greater value and utility. Considered in this point of view, the "*Tzigani*" acquires an importance which redeems the seeming triviality of the subject, and heightens the intrinsic beauty of the poetry itself. (pp. 409-10)

Both in its general design and execution we consider ["**Poltava,**" Puskin's latest poetic narrative,] superior to Pushkin's other compositions of the same class, although it does not appear to have been received with quite so much applause as his earlier ones. It certainly possesses more stirring interest; nor is it less attractive to us, from our having previously formed some poetical acquaintance with its hero, through Byron's ["**Mazeppa**"]. . . . As here exhibited, there is undoubtedly quite as much of the extraordinary attached to him, as in the poem of the English bard; in both, the story must be admitted to make considerable demands upon our credence, nor are there many who will be able to persuade themselves that Mazeppa, the hetman grown grey in battle, should be as fascinating in the eyes of Maria, as Mazeppa, the stripling page, is in those of Theresa. In either legend there is, perhaps, far more of 'romance' than of 'reality;' in Byron's, indeed, not as regards the lady, but as respects the horse adventure, which seems too much for mortal frame to have endured; while, in Pushkin's, the devotion of the youthful heroine for her aged lover appears to be quite as much beyond the imitation of her sex. (pp. 415-16)

The style of ["**Poltava**"] exhibits greater vivacity and variety of colouring, more graphic force and richness; and there is a passionate energy of expression in many of the passages that bespeaks a bolder hand. There is more dramatic spirit thrown into the dialogue, more skill evinced in the general management of the subject, more power in the details. Neither is there that indistinctness of outline of which we have complained in some of his other productions. Upon the whole, we are inclined to think that Pushkin has as yet hardly done himself justice, having employed his pen in too limited a field, and in desultory poetical skirmishes, instead of exerting it in some achievement that would call forth his powers. He has "fleshed" his weapons, let him now use them strenuously; he has done enough for mere popularity, it behoves him to do something for enduring fame; for unless he can produce something of sounder stamina than he has hitherto done, he will rather be an instance of early promise than of great actual performance; and although he may just at present happen to be conspicuous, because there are so few others in the field, he must ultimately be content to take his place among the *poetae minores* of his country. (p. 416)

[*William Henry Leeds,*] *"Pushkin and Rilaeev," in* Foreign Quarterly Review, *Vol. IX, No. XVIII, May, 1832, pp. 398-418.**

ALEXANDER PUSHKIN　(essay date 1836)

[The following is Alexander Pushkin's poem "Unto Myself I Reared a Monument."]

　Exegi monumentum
Unto myself I reared a monument not builded
By hands; a track thereto the people's feet will tread;
Not Alexander's shaft is lofty as my pillar
　　That proudly lifts its splendid head.

Not wholly shall I die—but in the lyre my spirit
Shall, incorruptible and bodiless, survive—
And I shall know renown as long as under heaven
　　One poet yet remains alive.

The rumor of my fame will seep through vasty Russia,
And all its peoples speak this name, whose light shall reign
Alike for haughty Slav, and Finn, and savage Tungus,
　　And Kalmuck riders of the plain.

I shall be loved, and long the people will remember
The kindly thoughts I stirred—my music's brightest crown,
How in this cruel age I celebrated freedom,
　　And begged for ruth toward those cast down.

Oh, Muse, as ever, now obey your God's commandments,
Of insult unafraid, to praise and slander cool,
Demanding no reward, sing on, but in your wisdom
　　Be silent when you meet a fool.

> *Alexander Pushkin, "Unto Myself I Reared a Monument" (1836), translated by Babette Deutsch, in his* The Poems, Prose and Plays of Alexander Pushkin, *edited by Avrahm Yarmolinsky (copyright 1936 and renewed 1964 by Random House, Inc.; reprinted by permission of Random House, Inc.),* The Modern Library, *1962, p. 88.*

V. G. BELINSKY　(essay date 1844)

We confess: it is not without a certain diffidence that we embark upon the critical examination of such a poem as *Eugene Onegin*. Indeed, that diffidence is justified by numerous reasons. *Onegin* is Pushkin's sincerest work, the darling of his fantasy, and few works can be cited in which the individuality of the poet is mirrored so fully, brightly and clearly as that of Pushkin in *Onegin*. Here we have his whole life, his soul, his love; here we have his emotions, conceptions and ideals. To appraise such a work means appraising the poet in the whole range of his creative activity. Apart from the aesthetic merits of *Onegin,* this poem possesses great historical and social significance for us Russians. From this point of view even that which the critics could justifiably point out in *Onegin* as being weak and obsolete is filled with deep significance and great interest. (p. 211)

We first of all see *Onegin* as a poetical picture of Russian society, taken during one of the most interesting moments of its development. From this angle, *Eugene Onegin* is a *historical* poem in the full sense of the word, though it does not contain a single historical personage. The historical merit of the poem is all the greater that it was the first and brilliant attempt of its kind to be undertaken in Russia. Pushkin here is not simply and only a poet, but a representative of a newly-awakened social consciousness: that is immeasurable merit! Russian poetry before Pushkin was merely an intelligent and adept tyro

of the European muse—hence all the works of Russian poetry prior to Pushkin somehow more resembled sketches and copies rather than the free productions of original inspiration. . . . With the advent of Pushkin Russian poetry, from the timid tyro, became a talented and experienced master. Naturally, this did not occur suddenly, for nothing is done suddenly. In his poems *Ruslan and Ludmila* and *The Robber Brothers* Pushkin, like his predecessors, was no more than a pupil,—not, like them, in poetry alone, but also in his efforts at poetical presentation of Russian reality. It is to this pupilage we owe the fact that there is so little of Russia and so much of Italy in his *Ruslan and Ludmila* and that his *Robber Brothers* so much resembles a vociferous melodrama. Pushkin has a Russian ballad, *The Bridegroom,* written in 1825, in which there appeared the first chapter of *Onegin*. This ballad, both in form and matter, is permeated to the core with the Russian spirit, and a thousand times more truly than of *Ruslan and Ludmila* one can say of it:

> A Russian savour here is floating!
>
> (pp. 212-13)

[That Eugene Onegin] is not generally recognized as a national work is due to the oddly rooted opinion that a Russian man in a frock coat or a Russian woman in a corset are no longer Russians, and that the Russian spirit should be sought only among the *zipoons* [coats worn by peasants], bast sandals, corn brandy and souerkraut. (p. 216)

[It] is time men realized that a Russian poet, on the contrary, can reveal himself as a genuinely national poet only by depicting in his works the life of educated society: for, in order to discover the national elements in a life half-muffled in forms that were originally alien to it, the poet must needs be endowed with great talent and be national at heart. . . . A great national poet is able to make both the gentleman and the peasant speak each in his own way. And if a work the subject matter of which is taken from the life of educated society does not merit the name of a national work, it is obviously worthless as a work of art, since it is untrue to the spirit of the reality it purports to portray. (pp. 220-221)

[The determination of Pushkin in Eugene Onegin] to present the moral aspect of Russia's most Europeanized social estate is clear enough proof that he was and deeply felt himself to be a national poet. He understood that the day of the epic poem had long since passed, and that in order to portray modern society, in which the prose of life had so deeply invaded the poetry of life, a romance was needed and not an epic poem. He took this life as he found it, without subducing merely its poetical moments; took it with all its frigidity, its prose and its banality. Such a bold design would have been less surprising had the romance been conceived in prose; but to write such a romance in verse at a time when there was not a single worthwhile romance in the Russian language written in prose, was a feat of daring vindicated by its enormous success and is undeniable evidence of the poet's genius. . . . The form of the romaunt, such as *Onegin,* was created by Byron; at least, the style of narrative, the mixture of prose and poetry in depicting reality, digressions, the poet's soliloquizing, and, especially, that too palpable intrusion of the poet's person in his own work—all that belongs to Byron. Of course, to adopt someone else's new form for your own matter is not quite the same thing as inventing it yourself; nevertheless, in comparing Pushkin's *Onegin* to Byron's *Don Juan, Childe Harold* and *Beppo,* all that they will be found to have in common are form and treatment. Not only the content but the spirit of Byron's poems

preclude all possibility of any essential similarity being established between them and *Onegin.* Byron wrote about Europe for Europe; that subjective spirit, so deep and mighty, that personality so colossal, proud and unbending aspired not so much to depict contemporary mankind as to pronounce upon its past and present history. We repeat: we need not look for a shadow of resemblance. Pushkin wrote about Russia for Russia—and the token of his great and original talent lies in the fact that Pushkin, true to his nature, a nature so diametrically opposite to that of Byron, and to his artistic instinct, was far from letting himself be tempted to create anything Byronic when writing his Russian romance. . . . He was not concerned in trying to take after Byron—he was concerned in trying to be himself, to do justice to the reality, untried and untouched before him, which flowed to his pen. That is why his *Onegin* is a supremely original and national Russian creation. (pp. 221-22)

Many have held and still hold that there is no plot [in *Eugene Onegin*], since the story has no denouement. Indeed, we have here no deaths (neither from consumption nor the dagger) and no weddings—that sanctioned consummation of all novels, stories and plays, especially Russian. And then how many incongruities! While Tatiana was a girl Onegin was left cold to her passionate confession; but when she became a woman he fell madly in love with her without being sure whether she loved him. Unnatural, quite unnatural! And what an unmoral character that man is: he coldly reads a homily to the infatuated girl instead of promptly falling in love with her himself, and then, obtaining in due form the parental blessings, leading the maid to the altar and becoming the happiest man in the world. And then again: Onegin kills poor Lensky for nothing at all—that young poet with golden hopes and rainbow dreams—and does not even shed a tear over him, or at least utter a pathetic speech containing a mention of bloody spectres and so on. Such, or very nearly such, was and still is the opinion pronounced on *Onegin* by many "gentle readers"—at any rate we have had occasion to hear many such opinions that once used to exasperate us but now merely amuse. (p. 226)

[Onegin] is certainly no monster or profligate, though he was certainly not a paragon of virtue. It was one of Pushkin's great merits that he disestablished the vogue of monsters of vice and heroes of virtue, depicting instead just ordinary people. (p. 227)

[The defects of *Onegin*] may be expressed in a single word—"obsolete"; but is the poet to blame that things in Russia move so swiftly? and is it not the poet's great merit that he was able with such fidelity to grasp the reality of the given moment in the life of society? If nothing in *Onegin* were to strike us now as being obsolete or backward of our times, it would be an obvious sign that the poem lacks truth, that it has depicted an imagined society and not a society that really existed: in that case, what kind of poem would it have been and would it have been worth talking about? . . . (pp. 229-230)

The higher circle of society at that time was so isolated from the other circles that people who did not belong to it spoke of it as people throughout Europe before Columbus spoke of the antipodes and Atlantides. Onegin, as a result, was set down as an unmoral man from the very first lines of the romance. This opinion of him has not entirely disappeared to this day. We remember how warmly many readers expressed their indignation at Onegin being glad of his uncle's illness and smarting under the necessity of posing as a sorrowing relation—

> You sigh, and think with furrowed brow—
> 'Why can't the devil take you now?'

Many deprecate it even now. This shows what an important work, in all respects, *Onegin* was for the Russian public, and how happy was Pushkin's choice of a society man for the hero of his romance. A feature of men of society is a lack of hypocrisy, as coarse and stupid as it is amiable and creditable. (p. 231)

[Onegin's] uncle was a stranger to him in every way. Indeed, what could there be in common between Onegin, who already—

> In time-worn halls and those that just
> Had been refurnished, yawn he must,

and the respectable squire, in the seclusion of his village

> . . . where the old man berated
> His housekeeper for forty years,
> Killed flies, and snugly rusticated. . . .

It will be said: he is his benefactor. Why his benefactor, when Onegin was the lawful heir to his estate? The benefactor in this case is not his uncle, but the law, the right of inheritance. Can you imagine the position of a man who is constrained to play the role of distressed, compassionate and affectionate relative at the deathbed of an utter stranger? It will be said: who obliged him to play such a base role? What do you mean, who? A feeling of delicacy, humanity. If you are unable for any reason to avoid the necessity of entertaining a man whose company you find irksome and boring, are you not obliged to be polite and even affable, though in your heart of hearts you may send him to the devil? That Onegin's words betray a kind of mocking lightness is merely evidence of intellect and candour, for an absence of stiff and heavy solemnity in the expression of ordinary and everyday relations is a sign of intellect. In people of polite society it is not even intellect, but more often a mannerism, and a very clever mannerism at that. With people of the middle circles, on the contrary, the manner is one of showing off a profusion of diverse deep feelings on every important, *in their opinion,* occasion. (pp. 232-33)

[It] requires a noble courage to be the first to speak one's true mind. And how many such truths are uttered in *Onegin*! Many of them today are neither new nor even very deep; but had not Pushkin uttered them *twenty* years ago they would now be both new and deep. And it is therefore to Pushkin's great credit that he was the first to give utterance to these now outworn and undeep truths. He could have delivered himself of more positive and more deep truths, but his work would then have lacked veracity: it would have been a description but not a mirror of Russian life. Genius never anticipates his time, but always merely divines its to everybody else invisible substance and meaning.

Most of the public utterly denied a heart and soul in Onegin, whom they regarded as a cold, callous man and an egoist by nature. There can be no more mistaken and crooked view of a man. Nay more: many amiably believed and still believe that the poet himself wished to depict Onegin as a cold egoist. That amounts to having eyes and seeing nothing. Society life did not kill Onegin's feelings, but merely cooled them to barren passions and idle pleasures. Remember the stanzas in which the poet describes his acquaintance with Onegin:

> The *beau monde*'s burdensome conventions
> I too had dropped, and found him then—
> As bored as I with vain inventions—
> The most congenial of men.

His way of dreaming, willy-nilly
His sharp intelligence and chilly,
I liked, and his peculiar pose;
I was embittered, he morose. . . .

Recalling in the soft sweet air
Many a distant love-affair—
The pleasures relished, triumphs thwarted,
Like prisoners released in sleep
To roam the forests, green and deep,
We were in reverie transported,
And carried to that region where
All life before us still lay fair.

The least these verses reveal to us is that Onegin was neither cold, nor dry, nor callous, that poesy lived in his soul, and that he was in fact not of the ordinary run of men. His way of dreaming, willy-nilly, the carefree and emotional contemplation of the beauties of nature and recollection of the loves and romances of bygone days—all this speaks more of feeling and poesy than of coldness and dryness. The fact is that Onegin was not addicted to day-dreaming, he felt more than he spoke, and did not bare his heart to everyone. An embittered mind is also the symptom of a higher nature, for a man with an embittered mind is usually displeased not only with other men, but with himself. (pp. 235-37)

Onegin's proud coldness and heartless hauteur are a result of the sheer incapacity of many readers to understand the character created with such fidelity by the poet. But we shall not stop at this and shall get to the bottom of the whole matter. . . .

[Why] upbraid him thus severely?
Is it because we like to sit
Upon the judgment-seat, or merely
Because rash ardour and quick wit
Are found absurd or else offensive
By those whose parts are not extensive?
Is it because intelligence
Loves elbow-room and thrusts us hence?
Or is it stupidity malicious—
And trifles of importance to
Important folk, and is it true
That only mediocrity
Befits and pleases you and me? . . .

These verses are the key to the mystery of Onegin's charater. Onegin is neither Melmoth nor Childe Harold, neither demon, parody, modern craze, genius, nor great man, but simply "a decent chap—like you or me" and all the world. The poet rightly calls the habit of looking everywhere for geniuses and extraordinary men a shabby mode. We repeat: Onegin is a good chap, though an uncommon man. He is not fit to be a genius, and does not aim at being a great man, but idleness and life's triviality gall him; he does not even know what he wants, what he is after; but he does know, and only too well, that he does not want what smug mediocrity is so content and delighted with. (pp. 239-41)

The romance ends with Tatiana's rebuff, and the reader takes his leave of Onegin at the bitterest moment of his life. . . . But what is this? Where is the romance? Where is the idea? And what sort of romance is it that has no end? We believe that there are romances the very idea of which consists precisely in the fact that they have no ending, because there are events in real life that have no denouement, there is existence without aim, creatures difficult to define, baffling to everybody, even to themselves, in short, what the French call *les êtres manqués*

les existences avortées. These creatures are often richly endowed with moral excellence and powers of the soul; they promise much, fulfill little, or nothing at all. This does not depend upon them, it is Fate, which is latent in the reality that surrounds them like the air and from which it is beyond the strength of man to free himself. Another poet [Lermontov in *A Hero of Our Time*] gave us another Onegin under the name of Pechorin: Pushkin's Onegin gave himself up with a sort of self-abnegation to ennui; Lermontov's Pechorin grapples in mortal combat with life from which he wishes to wrest his dole; the ways are different, but the results are the same: both romances close without an ending, like the lives and activities of the men who wrote them. . . . (pp. 254-55)

Onegin's is a real character in the sense that it has nothing dreamful and fantastic about it, that he could be happy or unhappy only in reality and through reality. In Lensky Pushkin has depicted a character which is the complete opposite of Onegin's, a character utterly abstract, utterly alien to reality. (p. 255)

Lensky was a romanticist both by nature and the spirit of the times. Needless to say, this was a creature who embraced all that was beautiful and sublime, a soul that was pure and noble. At the same time "his heart though fond was ignorant," he was for ever talking about life without ever having known it. Reality had no effect upon him: his joys and sorrows were the creatures of his imagination. (p. 256)

He had a great deal of good in him, but the best in him was that he was young and that he died in time to save his reputation. His was not one of those natures for whom to live means to develop and go forward. He was, we repeat, a *romanticist,* and nothing more.

Had he remained alive Pushkin would have found no other use for him than to spread throughout a whole chapter what he had so fully said of him in a single stanza. Men like Lensky, for all their undeniable merits, have this weak point that they either degenerate into utter philistines or perpetually remain true to original type. . . . For ever wrapt up in self, considering themselves the centre of the universe, they look placidly upon what is going on in the world and asseverate that happiness lies within us, that our souls should aspire to the starry heights of dreams and we should not dwell on the futilities of this world, where reign hunger, and want, and. . . . The Lenskys have not died out yet; they have merely degenerated. (p. 258)

It is Pushkin's great merit that he was the first, in his romance . . . to reveal to us in the persons of Onegin and Lensky its principal, *i.e.,* male, side; perhaps still greater is our poet's merit in that he was the first to give us, in the person of Tatiana, a poetical delineation of Russian womanhood. (p. 259)

[It is by no means easy] to define Tatiana's character. Tatiana's nature is not complex, but it is deep and strong. Tatiana lacked those painful contradictions which are inherent in over-complex natures; Tatiana is made, as it were, out of one whole piece without any complements or admixtures. Her whole life is steeped in that integrity and unity which, in the world of art, constitutes the highest merit of a work of art. A passionately infatuated, simple village girl, later the society lady of fashion, Tatiana is always the same in all conditions of life. (p. 270)

[Idealists] think they are filled with passions, feelings and lofty aspirations, whereas the fact of the matter is that their imagination is developed to the detriment of all their other faculties, pre-eminently that of reason. They possess feeling, but more of sentimentality and still more a proclivity and capacity for contemplating their sensations and eternally discussing them. They have wit, but not their own—it is conned and bookish, and therefore frequently full of glitter and always void of sense. (p. 272)

Tatiana did not escape the sad fate of falling into the . . . category of ideal maids. True, we said that she represents a great exception in the world of like phenomena—and we do not retract what we have said. Tatiana excites warm sympathy and not derision—not because she bore no resemblance to the "ideal maids," but because her deep and passionate nature overshadowed whatever there was in her of this ideality's ludicrous and vulgar traits, and Tatiana remained inartificially simple within the very artificiality and deformity of the mould in which her environment had cast her. One the one hand—

> Tanya with simple faith defended
> The people's lore of days gone by;
> She knew what dreams and cards portended,
> And the moon might signify.
> She quaked at omens; all around her
> Were signs and warnings to confound her—
> Her heart assailed, where'er she went,
> By some obscure presentiment.

On the other, Tatiana liked to roam the fields,

> There, wistful-eyed, behold her stand,
> With a French volume in her hand.

This amazing mixture of crude, vulgar prejudices with a passion for French books and a veneration for the profound work of *Martin Zadeka* is possible only in a Russian woman. (pp. 276-77)

[The] real Onegin did not exist for Tatiana—it was not given to her to understand or know the real one; hence she must needs endow him with qualities borrowed from books instead of from life, because life, too, Tatiana was unable to understand or know. Why did she love to imagine herself as Julie, Clarissa and Delphine? Because she understood and knew herself as little as she did Onegin. We repeat: a creature passionate, deeply emotional and at the same time undeveloped, closely locked up in the dark vacancy of her intellectual being, Tatiana, as an individuality, appears before us in the shape not of a graceful Greek statue wherein all the inbeing is so transparently and saliently reflected in outward beauty, but of an Egyptian statue, immobile, heavy and bound. But for the books she would have been an utterly inarticulate creature and her burning parched tongue would not have found a single live and passionate word with which to relieve the stress of her emotions. (pp. 278-79)

Tatiana's conversation with her nurse is a marvel of artistic perfection! It is a complete drama imbued with profound truth. It portrays with remarkable fidelity the *Russian young lady* in the tumult of her overmastering passion. Repressed feeling always breaks through to the surface, especially in the early period of a new and unexperienced passion. To whom should she open her heart?—her sister?—but she would *misunderstand* her. Her nurse would not understand her at all; precisely because of this Tatiana reveals her secret, or rather does not conceal her secret from her nurse. (p. 280)

In the words of the nurse, simple and popular, without triviality and vulgarity, we are given a complete and vivid picture of the inner domestic life of the people, its view on the relations of the sexes, on love and marriage. . . . And this the great

poet accomplishes by a single dash, cursorily, in passing! How fine are those well-natured simple-hearted lines:

> What notions! You may find it blameless,
> But in my youth no one engaged
> In talk of love. It was thought shameless—
> My mother-in-law would have raged.

What a pity that so many of our poets who are so preoccupied with nationality, fall short of precisely this kind of nationality, and accomplish no more than a garish triviality. . . . (pp. 280-81)

[In her second meeting with Onegin,] Tatiana's essence is fully expressed. In this meeting is expressed everything that constitutes the essence of a Russian woman with a deep nature developed by society—everything: ardent passion, the sincerity of simple and deep-felt emotions, the purity and sanctity of the naive impulses of a noble nature, moralizing, injured vanity and outraged virtue masking a servile fear of the world's opinion, the cunning syllogism of the mind and conventional morals that paralyze the generous impulses of the heart. . . . (pp. 288-89)

The underlying idea of Tatiana's reproaches [in her final speech] consists in her conviction that Onegin had not loved her then merely because there had been no lure of temptation for him; whereas now it was the thirst for scandalous repute which brought him to her feet. . . . This whole conception betrays an obvious fear for her reputation. . . .

> "Why do you pay me these attentions?
> Because society's conventions,
> Deferring to my wealth and rank,
> Have given my prestige? Be frank!
> Because my husband's decoration,
> A soldier's, wins us friends at court,
> And all would relish the report
> That I had stained my reputation—
> I would give you in society
> A pleasant notoriety? . . ."

(p. 290)

These lines reveal a trembling fear lest her good name be blemished in society, whereas the next lines provide undeniable evidence of a profound contempt for high society. . . . What a contradiction! And saddest of all, both are equally true of Tatiana. . . .

> "To me, Onegin, all these splendours,
> The tinsel of unwelcomed days,
> The homage that the gay world tenders
> My handsome house and my soirées—
> To me all this is naught. . . ."

(pp. 290-91)

We repeat: these words are as unfeigned and sincere as the preceding. Tatiana does not like society, and would gladly relinquish it for the peace of the country; but as long as she is in society its opinion will always be her idol and fear of its judgment will always be her virtue. . . .

> "*I love you* (why should I dissemble?)
> *But I became another's wife;*
> *I shall be true to him through life.*"

This last verse is remarkable—truly *finis coronat opus*! This reply could serve as an example of the classical *sublime* with the reply of Medea: *moi!* and old Horace's *qu'il mourût*. Here is the true boast of feminine virtue! But I *became* another's

wife—precisely *became* and *not gave myself*! Eternal fidelity—
to whom and *in what*? Fidelity to relations which are a desecration to feelings and to the chasteness of femininity, for there
are certain relations, which, unsanctified by love, are supremely immoral. . . . But with us these things somehow get
on well together: poetry and life, love and marriages of convenience, the life of the heart and strict execution of outward
obligations which are all too often inwardly violated. . . . A
woman's life is chiefly centred in the life of the heart: for her
to love means to live, and to sacrifice means to love. It was
for this role nature created Tatiana; but society remade her. . . .
Tatiana typifies Russian womanhood. . . . The enthusiastic
idealists who have studied life from Marlinsky's stories demand
that the ordinary woman should scorn society's opinion. That
is a falsehood: a woman cannot despise society's opinion, but
she can forego it modestly, without phrases and self-praise, if
she be aware of the greatness of her sacrifice, the weight of
the obloquy she is bringing down upon herself in obeying
another sublime law—the law of her nature, and her nature is
love and self-abnegation.

Thus, in the person of Onegin, Lensky and Tatiana Pushkin
has portrayed Russian society in one of the phases of its in-
choation and development—and how truly, with what fidelity,
fullness and artistry he has shown it to us! We say nothing of
the multitude of episodic portraits and silhouettes included in
the poem which complete the picture of Russian higher and
middle society; we say nothing of the scenes of rural balls and
city fêtes. . . . We would merely remark that the personality
of the poet, so fully and vividly reflected in this poem, is at
one and the same time superb and humane and eminently artistic. He is everywhere discernible as a man who in body and
soul belongs to the fundamental principle that comprises the
substance of the class which he portrays; in short, you see
everywhere the Russian landed gentry. . . . In this class he
attacks everything that is opposed to humanity; but the principle
of class is to him an eternal truth. . . . Hence his very satire
contains so much affection, and his very negation so often
resembles approbation and admiration. . . . (pp. 291-93)

Onegin was written in the course of several years, and the poet
therefore developed together with his poem, each new chapter
of which was more interesting and mature than its predecessors.
And the last two chapters differ sharply from the first six: they
bear obvious signs of a higher and maturer stage in the poet's
artistic growth. . . . In the last two chapters we are at a loss
what to select for praise, since everything in them is excellent;
however, the first half of chapter seven (the description of
spring, reminiscences of Lensky, Tatiana's visit to Onegin's
deserted house) stands out amid the deep and wistful fragrance
that pervades the exquisite lines. . . . The poet's digressions
from his narrative and his disquisitions are filled with ineffable
grace, sincerity, emotion, intellect and wit; the individuality
of the poet here is so loving, so humane. He has succeeded in
this poem in touching on so much and hinting at so much that
belongs exclusively to the world of Russian nature, to the world
of Russian society! *Onegin* could be called an encyclopedia of
Russian life, and a supremely national work. No wonder that
this poem was so enthusiastically received by the public and
exercised such a profound influence on contemporary and subsequent Russian literature! And its influence on the ways of
society? It was an act of consciousness for Russian society,
almost the first, but nevertheless great step forward for it! It
was a gigantean stride, after which there could no longer be
any question of standing still. . . . Time may flow and bring
with it new exigencies and new ideas, Russian society may

grow and excel *Onegin:* but however far it advances it will
always love this poem and bring a grateful and affectionate
gaze to rest upon it. . . . (pp. 293-94)

> *V. G. Belinsky, "The Works of Alexander Pushkin:
> 'Eugene Onegin' " (originally published under a dif-
> ferent title in* Otechestvenniye zapiski, *1844), in his*
> Selected Philosophical Works, *Foreign Languages
> Publishing House, 1956, pp. 211-98.*

THOMAS B. SHAW (essay date 1845)

Púshkin is undoubtedly one of that small number of names
which have become incorporated and identified with the literature of [Russia]; at once the type and the expression of that
country's nationality—one of that small but illustrious band,
whose writings have become part of the very household language of their native land—whose lightest words may be incessantly heard from the lips of all classes; and whose expressions may be said, like those of Shakespeare, of Molière,
and of Cervantes, to have become the natural forms embodying
the ideas which they have expressed, and in expressing, consecrated. In a word, Pushkin is undeniably and essentially the
great national poet of Russia. (p. 657)

["**Ruslán and Liudmíla**"] may be said to have been the very
first embodiment of Russian fancy, at least the first such embodiment exhibited under a form sufficiently European to enable readers who were not Russians to appreciate and admire. . . . [Its] appearance must be considered as giving the
finishing blow to the worn-out classicism which characterizes
all the poetical language of the eighteenth century. (p. 662)

[Púshkin's next work, "**Prisoner of the Caucasus**" is] a romantic poem, which breathes the very freshness of the mountain breeze, and must be considered as the perfect embodiment,
in verse, of the sublime region from whence it takes its title. . . .

Between the first of these two remarkable poems ("**Ruslán and
Liudmíla**") and the second—"**The Prisoner of the Caucasus**,"
the mind of Púshkin had undergone a most remarkable transformation. . . . In the earlier work all is studied, elaborated,
carefully and scientifically *composed;* worked out from the
quarry of memory, chiselled by the imagination, and polished
by a studious and somewhat pedantic taste: while the imagery,
the passion, and the characters of the later production are modelled immediately from Nature herself. The reader perceives
that the young artist has now reached the first phase of his
development, and has thrown aside the rule and compass of
precedents and books, and feels himself sufficiently strong of
hand and steady of eye to look face to face upon the unveiled
goddess herself, and with reverent skill to copy her sublime
lineaments. (p. 663)

[In "**The Fountain of Bakhtchisarái**"] we may remark the first
decided essay made by the poet towards delineating and contrasting, in an artistic manner, the characters of human personages. The dramatic opposition between the two principal
characters of the tale, Maria and Zarema, is well conceived
and most skilfully executed. . . . The powers of dramatic delineation which may be seen, as it were, in embryo in this
work, were to be still further developed in Púshkin's next
production ["**The Gipsies**"]. . . . [It] is difficult to select what
is most admirable in this exquisite little work—the completeness and distinctness of the descriptions of external nature—
the artful introduction of various allusions, (particularly in one
most charming passage, indicating Ovid's exile in the beautiful

country which is the scene of the drama,) or the intense interest which the poet has known how to infuse into what would appear at first sight a subject simple even to meagreness. Poets of many nations have endeavoured, with various qualifications, and with no less various degrees of success, to represent the picturesque and striking features of the nomad life and wild superstitions of the gipsy race; none however, it may be safely asserted, have ever produced a picture more true or more poetical than is to be found in the production of Púshkin. . . . It is at this period that Púshkin began the composition of his poem entitled **"Evgénii Oniégin."** . . . This work, in its outline, its plan, in the general tone of thought pervading it, and in certain other *external* circumstances, bears a kind of fallacious resemblance to the inimitable production of Lord Byron [*Don Juan*], a circumstance which leads superficial readers into the error (unjust in the highest degree to Púshkin's originality) of considering it as an imitation of the Don. It is a species of satire upon society, (and Russian fashionable society in particular,) embodied in an easy wandering verse something like that of Byron; and so far, perhaps, the comparison between the two poems holds good. Púshkin's *plot* has the advantage of being (though sufficiently slight in construction, it must be confessed) considerably more compact and interesting than the irregular narration which serves Byron to string together the bitter beads of his satirical rosary; but, at the same time, the aim and scope of the English satirist is infinitely more vast and comprehensive. The Russian has also none of the terrible and deeply-thrilling pictures of passion and of war which so strangely and powerfully contrast with the bitter sneer and gay irony forming the basis of the Don; but, on the other hand, the interest of the reader (scattered, in Byron's work, upon the various, unconnected, and somewhat monotonous outlines of female characters in Julia, Haidée, Gulbeyas, &c.,) is in **"Evgénii Oniégin"** most powerfully concentrated upon the heroine, Tatiana—one of the most exquisite tributes that poetry has ever paid to the nobility of woman. (pp. 665-66)

["Evgenii Oniégin"] must be considered as the fullest and most complete embodiment that exists in Russian literature, of the nationality of the country. It will be found to be the expression of those apparently discordant elements the union of which composes that hard riddle—the Russian character. A passage of Púshkin's dedication will not incorrectly exhibit the variety of its tone:—

> Accept this heap of motley traits,
> Half gay, half sad, half false, half real,
> Half every-day, yet half ideal,
> The careless fruit of idle days,
> Of sleepless nights; slight inspirations
> Of unripe years, of wasted art—
> The reason's frigid observations,
> And sad conclusions of the heart.
>
> (p. 666)

It is almost unnecessary to state that there is no resemblance whatever between [Púshkin's **"Poltava"** and Byron's "Mazépa"]. While the production of Byron is rather an admirable development of certain incidents, either entirely invented by the poet, or only slightly suggested by passages of the old Kazak Hetman's biography, the *Mazépa* of Púshkin is a most spirited and faithful version of the real history of the romantic life of the hero. . . . (p. 667)

["Bóris Godunóff" is] a dramatic picture full of spirit, of passion, of character, and of life; and some of the personages, particularly those of the pretender Dimitri, and the heroine

Marina, are sketched with a vigorous and flowing pencil. The *form* of this play is ostensibly Shakspearian; but it appears to us to resemble less the works of Shakespeare himself, than some of the more successful imitations of the great dramatist's manner—as, for instance, some parts of the Wallenstein. As to the language and versification, it is in blank verse, and the style is considered by Russians as admirable for ease and flexibility. (p. 668)

Thomas B. Shaw, "Púshkin, the Russian Poet," in Blackwood's Edinburgh Magazine, *Vol. LVII, No. CCCLVI, June, 1845, pp. 657-78.*

ALEXANDER IVANOVICH HERZEN (essay date 1851)

People have supposed that they see in Pushkin an imitator of Byron. The English poet has, in fact, exerted a great influence on the Russian poet. No one can form a close intimacy with a strong and sympathetic character, without retaining traces of its influence, and having his own mind ripened in its warmth. The confirmation of that which is hidden in the heart, the confirmation which is received in every echo from a mind which is dear to us, gives us new strength. But the difference between this natural influence and imitation is great. After the first poems of Pushkin, in which the influence of Byron was clearly pronounced, had appeared, he became in each new production more and more original; and though full of admiration for the great English poet, he was neither his dependent nor his parasite, neither *traduttore* nor *traditore*. Pushkin and Byron diverge widely towards the end of their career; and this for a very simple reason. Byron was thoroughly English, and Pushkin thoroughly Russian—a Russian of the epoch of St. Petersburg. He had experienced all the pain incident to high culture; but he had preserved a faith in the future which the poet of the West no longer possessed. Byron, with all his grand and free individuality, from isolating himself in his independence, and gradually wrapping himself up in pride and in a haughty and sceptical philosophy, became more and more gloomy and implacable. He saw no near future; oppressed by bitter thoughts, disgusted with the world, he devotes himself to a people of Slavo-Hellenic barbarians, whom he mistakes for the Greeks of the ancient world. Pushkin, on the contrary, becomes more and more calm; he dives into the study of Russian history, gathers materials for a monograph of Pugatsheff, composes a historical drama entitled *Boris Godunoff,* and has a firm faith in the happy future of Russia." (pp. 376-77)

Onegin is a Russian; he is nowhere else possible but in Russia, where he is indigenous, and you meet him every where. Onegin is an idler because he has never found any calling; he is superfluous in the sphere in which he lives, without having the energy of character to leave it. He is a man who tries life till death, and would fain try death, to see if it is not better than life. He has commenced every thing, without persevering in any; he has thought the more the less he has done; he is old at twenty, and, when beginning to be old, becomes young again through love. He has constantly, like all of us, expected something, because no one can be foolish enough to believe in the duration of the actual state of things in Russia; but nothing has come, and life declines. The character of Onegin is so national, that you meet him in all the novels and poems which have had any fame in Russian literature; not because he has been copied, but because he is every where to be met with in Russia, even in one's own heart. . . .

The young Russian meets no living interest in the world of servility and petty ambition. And yet it is this society in which he is condemned to live; for the *people* are still too far removed. Fashionable society is at least composed of beings as degraded as himself, while he has nothing in common with the people. The traditions of the upper and lower classes have been so completely severed by Peter I., that there is no human force capable of uniting them, at least at present. Nothing is left but isolation or struggle; and we have not sufficient moral strength either for the one or the other. Thus we become like Onegin if we do not perish in the public-houses or in the casemates of a fortress. In contrast to Onegin, Pushkin has drawn Wladimir Lenski, another victim of Russian life, the opposite of Onegin. This is acute by the side of chronic suffering. . . . . . . Pushkin has delineated the character of Lenski with that tenderness which men preserve for their youth, for the recollections of that time when they were so full of hope, of purity, of ignorance. Lenski is the last outcry of Onegin's conscience; for he is Onegin himself, his ideal of youth. The poet saw that such a man had nothing to do in Russia; he kills him by the hand of Onegin—of Onegin who loved him, and who, pointing at him, intended not to hurt him. Pushkin himself was frightened by this tragic end; he hastens to comfort the reader by describing the commonplace life which awaited the young poet. (pp. 378-79)

> *Alexander Ivanovich Herzen, in his excerpt in "Russian Literature and Alexander Pushkin" (originally published under a different title in his* Du developpment des idées révolutionnaires en Russie, *Nice, 1851), in* National Review, *No. XIV, October, 1858, pp. 361-82.*

THE NATIONAL REVIEW (essay date 1858)

[Pushkin's] life as a poet presents three periods, distinguished from each other by the character of his poetical activity and the class of subjects on which he wrote. The first period begins with his poetical essays at the Lyceum, and ends with *Ruslan and Ljudmila;* its general character being that youthful wildness and excitement, of which, as we have seen, he was himself fully aware. The second period is characterised by a tone of disappointment, scepticism, and at the same time a leaning towards social revolutions; it begins with the *Prisoner in the Caucasus,* and terminates with *Eugene Onegin.* The third period finally shows us the accomplished artist, who has retired from the struggles of political life; and to it belong all the productions of his later years, among others the epic poem *Poltawa.* . . . His first models in poetry were Dershawin and Shukowski, whom he regarded as his teachers. He expressed his admiration for them in many verses, particularly in the *Recollections of Tsarskoe-selo;* but nevertheless he soon outstripped them. He afterwards felt the influence of Batushkoff and Kriloff, two other Russian authors of that age. From the first he adopted the plastic form of thought and verse which we inherit from the old classic poets; and adopted it with so much success, that, without being acquainted with the Greek language, he wrote several poems, *The Muse* and others, which are really Hellenic. From the second he borrowed the national element; and developed it so fully, that even at this early period he proved himself a thoroughly national poet in *The Drowned* and several other poems. Later he became the most national of the national school.

Russian influences, however, were not the only ones that wrought upon him. He himself, in his *Priests of Parnassus,* enumerates his favourite writers, chiefly from the French school of the eighteenth century, above all Voltaire and Parni. . . . He ac-

knowledged his debt to these poets in a number of poems, in which again he frequently surpassed his models, as, for instance, in his *Proserpine,* suggested by Parni's *Les Déguisements de Vénus,* but greatly surpassing it in beauty. All his poems written about that time have a tone of forced mirth and voluptuousness; and although he freed himself more and more from the influence which these writers exerted over him, its traces were long visible, and are even discernible in some of his later productions. . . . He bade [the French school of the eighteenth century] farewell, however, in his first larger poem, *Ruslan and Ljudmila,* a tale in verse in the manner of Ariosto's *Orlando Furioso.* . . . By its bold neglect of the traditional rules [this poem] gave birth to a sharp contest between the young and old generation; and while it drew down on him the severest criticism of the elder school, it secured for him the most enthusiastic admiration of the young, and the flattering attention of all. (pp. 373-75)

[Pushkin was] so much influenced by Lord Byron that the second phase of his literary life may be said to have been entirely determined by him. . . . His *Prisoner in the Caucasus* begins the series of poems written at that time. Several larger poems belong to it, as *The Fountain of Bachtshisarai, The Robber-Brothers, The Bohemians,* and others; all of which betray strong traces of an intimate acquaintance with Byron. They have a similar form; their heroes and heroines resemble those of Lord Byron's poems; the gloomy colouring, the mysterious connection between guilt and fate, are the same. Nevertheless we do not at all believe that Pushkin was a mere imitator of Byron. Even in the above-mentioned poems, which bear the strongest resemblance to their models, we find this marked difference, that Byron took his subjects from a foreign world, where the power of imagination had to supply the place of actual observation, while Pushkin took them from places and a society with which he was thoroughly familiar, and consequently was enabled to give them a distinctly local tone and colour. This is particularly striking in the *Bohemians,* where the "Tabor" and the restless life of the poetical vagrants are delineated with masterly effect. The realistic element which is prominent in Pushkin's heroes offers a strong contrast to the idealistic vagueness with which the Manfreds, Conrads, Giaours, &c. of Byron are designed. (p. 376)

[The second] period of Pushkin's poetical activity closed with *Eugene Onegin,* the greatest and most remarkable of his works. This poem satisfactorily proves that his imitation of Byron was merely a *phase* of his literary development, from which he stepped forth into entire artistic independence and nationality. (p. 377)

Onegin is an image of his nation and his time, an image in which the poet's own characteristics are blended with a general type of character; and this, besides its poetical value, gives this work a lasting historical significance. We find a similar significance in Goethe's *Faust,* in Byron's *Don Juan* and *Childe Harold;* and we find it again in a novel of George Sand's, *Horace.* These four creations show us the different historical developments of modern society within little more than half a century, each with a peculiar national colouring of its own.

Faust is the child of the "Sturm- und Drangperiode," the spirit of mankind awakening to a new intellectual life, and eager to gratify every restless craving of a vigorous but undisciplined national character. He is the spirit of the German people; which is apt to grasp far beyond its reach at a shadowy ideal, at an abstract perfection, while the present slips from its hands and leaves it to the torment of a life divided between lofty dreams and low realities. Childe Harold and Don Juan represent a somewhat later stage, as well as a different national phase of the same history,—the bitter disappointment, namely, caused by the shipwreck of those yearnings of which Faust was the representative. Through all, however, nobler elements may be seen,—admiration for the beautiful in art and nature, and a fundamental hatred of tyranny; while the peculiar English element shines forth in the proud and independent individuality which, in the face of the whole world, remains itself and unchanged. [Onegin] is the contemporaneous character in Russia, what man must inevitably become under the most complete and energetic despotism of modern times. His political and social yearnings have been nipped in the bud; he knows only, by his own instincts, so much of a nobler existence as is necessary to make him the more miserable in his own; life to him is an immense void, and society an agglomeration of vicious and contemptible materials. He is Russian in his weak yielding to circumstances, and in his dread of the opinion of that same society which he so utterly despises. Horace, lastly, may, as a characteristic image of contemporaneous humanity, range with the first-named masterpieces. He stands, undoubtedly, on the last step of the scale we have been descending. He is the type of that *bourgeois* character which has comfortably settled down on the world which the "Himmelsstürmer" strove in vain to regenerate, which the Childe Harolds left in despair and disgust, and on which the Onegins die from weariness and *ennui*. He has no real passion, no real suffering, no real genius, no real aristocratic force. He makes himself beloved because it flatters his vanity to conquer; . . . he aspires to nothing save imitating the aristocracy and being admitted to its charmed circle. (pp. 379-80)

The historical drama *Boris Godunoff* is ranked by some critics next to *Onegin*. It is indeed full of poetical beauties; but might rather be considered as a series of dramatic scenes than as a complete drama, and seems unfit for performance on the stage. The historical point of view is taken from the Russian history by Karamsin. Owing to the deficiences of this book, and the inadequate knowledge of Russian history which had at that time been attained, Pushkin's historical conception of the principal characters—Godunoff and the false Demetrius—is wrong; but there are beautiful details of perfect national colouring, full of fidelity to ancient life, which give to this composition its chief value.

Far higher, as a dramatic work of art, do we place the *Stone Guest*, which we rank with *Onegin* as the two finest gems of Pushkin's poetry. The subject is, with some variation, the well-known story of the Stone Guest from Mozart's *Don Juan;* but how much more poetical! The characters of Don Juan, Laura, and Donna Anna are conceived with a profound knowledge of the human heart, and the delineation is perfect. The whole has a character of finished simplicity that may with perfect propriety be called classic.

Most perfect, from the poetical as well as the pscyhological point of view, is also the fragment *Mozart and Salieri,* where the contrast between the childlike carelessness of genius, which receives its inspirations freely and unsolicited, and the bitter anguish of mere intellect longing for the denied gift, is admirably delineated. . . . Russia had in Pushkin a poet,—a truly national poet,—standing in an exactly similar relation to his country and to his people to that in which Byron and Goethe stood to theirs. (p. 381)

"Russian Literature and Alexander Pushkin," in The National Review, *No. XIV, October, 1858, pp. 361-82.*

FYODOR DOSTOYEVSKY   (essay date 1880)

Pushkin is an extraordinary phenomenon, and, perhaps, the unique phenomenon of the Russian spirit, said Gogol. I will add, "and a prophetic phenomenon." Yes, in his appearing there is contained for all us Russians something incontestably prophetic. Pushkin arrives exactly at the beginning of our true self-consciousness, which had only just begun to exist a whole century after Peter's reforms, and Pushkin's coming mightily aids us in our dark way by a new guiding light. In this sense Pushkin is a presage and a prophecy.

I divide the activity of our great poet into three periods. I speak now not as a literary critic. I dwell on Pushkin's creative activity only to elucidate my conception of his prophetic significance to us, and the meaning I give the word prophecy. I would, however, observe in passing that the periods of Pushkin's activity do not seem to me to be marked off from each other by firm boundaries. The beginning of *Eugène Onyegin*, for instance, in my opinion belongs still to the first period, while *Onyegin* ends in the second period when Pushkin had already found his ideals in his native land, had taken them to his heart, and cherished them in his loving and clairvoyant soul. It is said that in his first period Pushkin imitated European poets, Parny and André Chénier, and above all, Byron. Without doubt the poets of Europe had a great influence upon the development of his genius, and they maintained their influence all through his life. Nevertheless, even the very earliest poems of Pushkin were not mere imitations, and in them the extraordinary independence of his genius was expressed. In an imitation there never appears such individual suffering and such depths of self-consciousness as Pushkin displayed, for instance, in *The Gipsies,* a poem which I ascribe in its entirety to his first period; not to mention the creative force and impetuosity which would never have been so evident had his work been only imitation. Already, in the character of Aleko, the hero of *The Gipsies,* is exhibited a powerful, profound, and purely Russian idea, later to be expressed in harmonious perfection in Onyegin, where almost the same Aleko appears not in a fantastic light, but as tangible, real, and comprehensible. In Aleko Pushkin had already discovered, and portrayed with genius, the unhappy wanderer in his native land, the Russian sufferer of history, whose appearance in our society, uprooted from among the people, was a historic necessity. The type is true and perfectly rendered, it is an eternal type, long since settled in our Russian land. These homeless Russian wanderers are wandering still, and the time will be long before they disappear. If they in our day no longer go to gipsy camps to seek their universal ideals in the wild life of the Gipsies and their consolation away from the confused and pointless life of our Russian intellectuals, in the bosom of nature, they launch into Socialism, which did not exist in Aleko's day, they march with a new faith into another field, and they work zealously, believing, like Aleko, that they will by their fantastic occupations obtain their aims and happiness, not for themselves alone, but for all mankind. For the Russian wanderer can find his own peace only in the happiness of all men; he will not be more cheaply satisfied, at least while it is still a matter of theory. It is the same Russian man who appears at a different time. (pp. 47-9)

[In *The Gipsies*] already is whispered the Russian solution of the question, "the accursed question," in accordance with the faith and justice of the people. "Humble yourself, proud man, and first of all break down your pride. Humble yourself, idle man, and first of all labour on your native land"—that is the solution according to the wisdom and justice of the people.

"Truth is not outside thee, but *in* thyself. Find thyself in thyself, subdue thyself to thyself, be master of thyself and thou wilt see the truth. Not in things is this truth, not outside thee or abroad, but first of all in thine own labour upon thyself. If thou conquer and subdue thyself, then thou wilt be freer than thou hast ever dreamed, and thou wilt begin a great work and make others free, and thou wilt see happiness, for thy life will be fulfilled and thou wilt at the last understand thy people and its sacred truth. Not with the Gipsies nor elsewhere is universal harmony, if thou thyself art first unworthy of her, malicious and proud, and thou dost demand life as a gift, not even thinking, that man must pay for her." This solution of the question is strongly foreshadowed in Pushkin's poem. Still more clearly is it expressed in *Eugène Onyegin,* which is not a fantastic, but a tangible and realistic poem, in which the real Russian life is embodied with a creative power and a perfection such as had not been before Pushkin and perhaps never after him. (pp. 51-2)

[At the beginning of the poem, Eugène] is still half a coxcomb and a man of the world; he had lived too little to be utterly disappointed in life. But he is already visited and disturbed by

> The demon lord of hidden weariness.

In a remote place, in the heart of his mother country, he is of course an exile in a foreign land. He does not know what to do and is somehow conscious of his own quest. Afterwards, wandering over his native country and over foreign lands, he, beyond doubt clever and sincere, feels himself among strangers, still more a stranger to himself. (pp. 52-3)

Tatiana is different. She is a strong character, strongly standing on her own ground. She is deeper than Onyegin and certainly wiser than he. With a noble instinct she divines where and what is truth, and her thought finds expression in the finale of the poem. Perhaps Pushkin would even have done better to call his poem *Tatiana,* and not *Onyegin,* for she is indubitably the chief character. She is positive and not negative, a type of positive beauty, the apotheosis of the Russian woman, and the poet destined her to express the idea of his poem in the famous scene of the final meeting of Tatiana with Onyegin. One may even say that so beautiful or positive a type of the Russian woman has never been created since in our literature, save perhaps the figure of Liza in Turgeniev's *A Nest of Gentlefolk.* But because of his way of looking down upon people, Onyegin did not even understand Tatiana when he met her for the first time, in a remote place, under the guise of a pure, innocent girl, who was at first so shy of him. He could not see the completeness and perfection of the poor girl, and perhaps he really took her for a "moral embryo." She, the embryo! She, after her letter to Onyegin! If there is a moral embryo in the poem, it is he himself, Onyegin, beyond all debate. (pp. 53-4)

In the immortal lines of the romance the poet represented [Tatiana] coming to see the house of the man who is so wonderful and still so incomprehensible to her. I do not speak of the unattainable artistic beauty and profundity of the lines. She is in his study; she looks at his books and possessions; she tries through them to understand his soul, to solve her enigma, and "the moral embryo" at last pauses thoughtfully, with a foreboding that her riddle is solved, and gently whispers:

> Perhaps he is only a parody?

Yes, she had to whisper this; she had divined him. Later long afterwards in Petersburg, when they meet again, she knows him perfectly. (p. 55)

[Onegin] has no root at all, he is a blade of grass, borne on the wind. She is otherwise: even in her despair, in the painful consciousness that her life has been ruined, she still has something solid and unshakable upon which her soul may bear. There are the memories of her childhood, the reminiscences of her country, her remote village, in which her pure and humble life had begun: it is

> the woven shade,
> Of branches that o'erhang her nurse's grave.

Oh, these memories and the pictures of the past are most precious to her now; these alone are left to her, but they do save her soul from final despair. And this is not a little but rather much, for there is here a whole foundation, unshakable and indestructible. Here is contact with her own land, with her own people, and with their sanctities. And he—what has he and what is he? Nothing, that she should follow him out of compassion, to amuse him, to give him a moment's gift of a mirage of happiness out of the infinite pity of her love, knowing well beforehand that to-morrow he would look on his happiness with mockery. No, these are deep, firm souls, which cannot deliberately give their sanctities to dishonour, even from infinite compassion. No, Tatiana could not follow Onyegin.

Thus in *Onyegin,* that immortal and unequalled poem, Pushkin was revealed as a great national writer, unlike any before him. In one stroke, with the extreme of exactness and insight, he defined the very inmost essence of our high society that stands above the people. He defined the type of the Russian wanderer before our day and in our day; he was the first to divine him, with the flair of genius, to divine his destiny in history and his enormous significance in our destiny to be. Side by side he placed a type of positive and indubitable beauty in the person of a Russian woman. Besides, of course, he was the first Russian writer to show us, in his other works of that period, a whole gallery of positively beautiful Russian types, finding them in the Russian people. The paramount beauty of these lies in their truth, their tangible and indubitable truth. It is impossible to deny them, they stand as though sculptured. I would remind you again. I speak not as a literary critic, and therefore do not intend to elucidate my idea by a particular and detailed literary discussion of these works of the poet's genius. Concerning the type of the Russian monkish chronicler, for instance, a whole book might be written to show the importance and meaning for us of this lofty Russian figure, discovered by Pushkin in the Russian land, portrayed and sculptured by him, and now eternally set before us in its humble, exalted, indubitable spiritual beauty, as the evidence of that mighty spirit of national life which can send forth from itself figures of such certain loveliness. This type is now given; he exists, he cannot be disputed; it cannot be said that he is only the poet's fancy and ideal. You yourself see and agree: Yes, he exists, therefore the spirit of the nation which created him exists also, therefore the vital power of this spirit exists and is mighty and vast. Throughout Pushkin sounds a belief in the Russian character, in its spiritual might; and if there is belief, there is hope also, the great hope for the man of Russia. . . . [No] single Russian writer, before or after him, did ever associate himself so intimately and fraternally with his people as Pushkin. (pp. 59-61)

All these treasures of art and artistic insight are left by our great poet as it were a landmark for the writers who should come after him, for future labourers in the same field. One may say positively that if Pushkin had not existed, there would not have been the gifted writers who came after him. At least they would not have displayed themselves with such power and clarity, in spite of the great gifts with which they have succeeded in expressing themselves in our day. But not in poetry alone, not in artistic creation alone: if Pushkin had not existed, there would not have been expressed with the irresistible force with which it appeared after him (not in all writers, but in a chosen few), our belief in our Russian individuality, our now conscious faith in the people's powers, and finally the belief in our future individual destiny among the family of European nations. This achievement of Pushkin's is particularly displayed if one examines what I call the third period of his activity.

I repeat, there are no fixed divisions between the periods. Some of the works of even the third period might have been written at the very beginning of the poet's artistic activity, for Pushkin was always a complete whole, as it were a perfect organism carrying within itself at once every one of its principles, not receiving them from beyond. The beyond only awakened in him that which was already in the depths of his soul. But this organism developed and the phases of this development could really be marked and defined, each of them by its peculiar character and the regular generation of one phase from another. Thus to the third period can be assigned those of his works in which universal ideas were pre-eminently reflected, in which the poetic conceptions of other nations were mirrored and their genius re-embodied. Some of these appeared after Pushkin's death. And in this period the poet reveals something almost miraculous, never seen or heard at any time or in any nation before. There had been in the literatures of Europe men of colossal artistic genius—a Shakespeare, a Cervantes, a Schiller. But show me one of these great geniuses who possessed such a capacity for universal sympathy as our Pushkin. This capacity, the pre-eminent capacity of our nation, he shares with our nation, and by that above all he is our national poet. The greatest of European poets could never so powerfully embody in themselves the genius of a foreign, even a neighbouring, people, its spirit in all its hidden depth, and all its yearning after its appointed end, as Pushkin could. On the contrary, when they turned to foreign nations European poets most often made them one with their own people, and understood them after their own fashion. Even Shakespeare's Italians, for instance, are almost always Englishmen. Pushkin alone of all world poets possessed the capacity of fully identifying himself with another nationality. . . . How profound and fantastic is the imagination in the poem **"A Feast in Time of Plague."** But in this fantastic imagination is the genius of England; and in the hero's wonderful song about the plague, and in Mary's song,

> Our children's voices in the noisy school
> Were heard. . . .

These are English songs; this is the yearning of the British genius, its lament, its painful presentiment of its future. Remember the strange lines:

> Once as I wandered through the valley wild. . . .

It is almost a literal transposition of the first three pages of a strange mystical book written in prose by an old English sectarian—but is it only a transposition? In the sad and rapturous music of these verses is the very soul of Northern Protestantism, of the English heresiarch, of the illimitable mystic with his dull, sombre, invincible aspiration, and the impetuous power of his mystical dreaming. . . . [Pushkin is] in my opinion a prophetic phenomenon, because . . . because herein was ex-

pressed the national spirit of his poetry, the national spirit in its future development, the national spirit of our future, which is already implicit in the present, and it was expressed prophetically. For what is the power of the spirit of Russian nationality if not its aspiration after the final goal of universality and omni-humanity? No sooner had he become a completely national poet, no sooner had he come into contact with the national power, than he already anticipated the great future of that power. In this he was a seer, in this a prophet. (pp. 61-5)

[Beyond] all doubt, the destiny of a Russian is pan-European and universal. To become a true Russian, to become a Russian fully, (in the end of all, I repeat) means only to become the brother of all men, to become, if you will, a universal man. All our slavophilism and Westernism is only a great misunderstanding, even though historically necessary. To a true Russian, Europe and the destiny of all the mighty Aryan family is as dear as Russia herself, as the destiny of his own native country, because our destiny is universality, won not by the sword, but by the strength of brotherhood and our fraternal aspiration to reunite mankind. (p. 66)

I say that to this universal, omni-human union the heart of Russia, perhaps more than all other nations, is chiefly predestined; I see its traces in our history, our men of genius, in the artistic genius of Pushkin. . . . He surely could contain the genius of foreign lands in his soul as his own. In art at least, in artistic creation, he undeniably revealed this universality of the aspiration of the Russian spirit, and therein is a great promise. If our thought is a dream, then in Pushkin at least this dream has solid foundation. Had he lived longer, he would perhaps have revealed great and immortal embodiments of the Russian soul, which would then have been intelligible to our European brethren; he would have attracted them much more and closer than they are attracted now, perhaps he would have succeeded in explaining to them all the truth of our aspirations; and they would understand us more than they do now, they would have begun to have insight into us, and would have ceased to look at us so suspiciously and presumptuously as they still do. Had Pushkin lived longer, then among us too there would perhaps be fewer misunderstandings and quarrels than we see now. But God saw otherwise. Pushkin died in the full maturity of his powers, and undeniably bore away with him a great secret into the grave. And now we, without him, are seeking to divine his secret. (pp. 67-8)

> *Fyodor Dostoyevsky, "On the Unveiling of the Push-kin Memorial," (originally The Pushkin Address delivered in 1880 in Moscow), in* Pages from the Journal of an Author, *translated by S. S. Koteliansky and J. Middleton Murry, George Allen and Unwin, Ltd., 1916, pp. 47-68.*

PRINCE KROPOTKIN   (essay date 1901)

[Apart] from his very latest productions in the dramatic style, there is in whatever Púshkin wrote none of the depth and elevation of ideas which characterised Goethe and Schiller, Shelley, Byron, and Browning, Victor Hugo and Barbier. The beauty of form, the happy ways of expression, the incomparable command of verse and rhyme, are his main points—not the beauty of his *ideas*. And what we look for in poetry is always the higher inspiration, the noble ideas which can help to make us better. In reading Púshkin's verses the Russian reader is continually brought to exclaim: "How beautifully this has been told! It could not, it ought not, to be told in a different way.'' In this beauty of form Púshkin is inferior to none of the greatest poets. (p. 40)

It is extremely interesting to compare Púshkin with Schiller, in their lyrics. Leaving aside the greatness and the variety of subjects touched upon by Schiller, and comparing only those pieces of poetry in which both poets speak of themselves, one feels at once that Schiller's personality is infinitely superior, in depth of thought and philosophical comprehension of life, to that of the bright, somewhat spoiled and rather superficial child that Púshkin was. But, at the same time, the individuality of Púshkin is more deeply impressed upon his writings than that of Schiller upon his. Púshkin was full of vital intensity, and his own self is reflected in everything he wrote; a human heart, full of fire, is throbbing intensely in all his verses. This heart is far less sympathetic than that of Schiller, but it is more intimately revealed to the reader. In his best lyrics Schiller did not find either a better expression of feeling, or a greater variety of expression, than Púshkin did. In that respect the Russian poet decidedly stands by the side of Goethe. (pp. 40-1)

The main force of Púshkin was in his lyric poetry, and the chief note of his lyrics was love. The terrible contradictions between the ideal and the real, from which deeper minds, like those of Goethe, or Byron, or Heine, have suffered, were strange to him. Púshkin was of a more superficial nature. It must also be said that a West-European poet has an inheritance which the Russian has not. Every country of Western Europe has passed through periods of great national struggle, during which the great questions of human development were at stake. Great political conflicts have produced deep passions and resulted in tragical situations; but in Russia the great struggles and the religious movements which took place in the seventeenth century, and under Pugatchóff in the eighteenth, were uprisings of peasants, in which the educated classes took no part. The intellectual horizon of a Russian poet is thus necessarily limited. There is, however, something in human nature which always lives and appeals to every mind. This is love, and Púshkin, in his lyric poetry, represented love under so many aspects, in such beautiful forms, and with such a variety of shades, as one finds in no other poet. Besides, he often gave to love an expression so refined, so high, that his higher comprehension of love left as deep a stamp upon subsequent Russian literature as Goethe's refined types of women left in the world's literature. After Púshkin had written, in was impossible for Russian poets to speak of love in a lower sense than he did. (p. 45)

Altogether, Púshkin's force was not in his elevating or freedom-inspiring influence. His epicureanism, his education received from French *emigrés,* and his life amidst the high and frivolous classes of St. Petersburg society, prevented him from taking to heart the great problems which were already ripening in Russian life. This is why, towards the end of his short life, he was no longer in touch with those of his readers who felt that to glorify the military power of Russia, after the armies of Nicholas I. had crushed Poland, was not worthy of a poet; and that to describe the attractions of a St. Petersburg winter-season for a rich and idle gentleman was not to describe Russian life, in which the horrors of serfdom and absolutism were being felt more and more heavily.

Púshkin's real force was in his having created in a few years the Russian literary language, and having freed literature from the theatrical, pompous style which was formerly considered necessary in whatever was printed in black and white. He was great in his stupendous powers of poetical creation: in his

capacity of taking the commonest things of everyday life, or the commonest feelings of the most ordinary person, and of so relating them that the reader lived them through; and, on the other side, constructing out of the scantiest materials, and calling to life, a whole historical epoch—a power of creation which, of those coming after him, only Tolstóy has to the same extent. Púshkin's power was next in his profound realism—that realism, understood in its best sense, which he was the first to introduce in Russia, and which . . . became afterwards characteristic of the whole of Russian literature. (p. 46)

Towards the end of his very short life a note of deeper comprehension of human affairs began to appear in Púshkin's writings. He had had enough of the life of the higher classes; and, when he began to write a history of the great peasant uprising which took place under Pugatchóff during the reigh of Catherine II., he began also to understand and to feel the inner springs of the life of the Russian peasant-class. National life appeared to him under a much broader aspect than before. But at this stage of the development of his genius his career came to a premature end. (p. 47)

Prince Kropotkin, "Pushkin; Lermontoff" (originally a lecture delivered at the Lowell Institute in March, 1901), in his Ideals and Realities in Russian Literature *(copyright, 1905, by McClure, Phillips & Co.; copyright, 1915, by Alfred A. Knopf; reprinted by permission of the publisher), Knopf, 1915, pp. 39-66.**

VLADISLAV KHODASEVICH   (essay date 1922)

It was not until eighty-one years after his death that Pushkin's *Gavriliad* was printed without abridgment or condensation. The poem was under edict, and only a very few read it in its entirety. (p. 24)

The Gavriliad was under edict for two reasons: it was declared, in the first place, blasphemous and, in the second, obscene. Well, yes, of course this is not a book for children or young girls. But even its blasphemy and obscenity must be subjected to a reexamination.

The time of the composition of ***The Gavriliad,*** 1821, relates wholly to the so-called "Kishinev" period of Pushkin's life. This in itself tells us much. No matter how sad the great poet may have been in those days, no matter how many times he compared himself with Ovid "dragging out a miserable existence in days of darkness" on the shores of the Dunai, it is nonetheless indisputable that this sadness and gloom did not wholly correspond to his view of life at that time. One does not require any particular wisdom to see how this was so. It is quite natural and psychologically logical that, in his hours of contemplation and solitude, Pushkin thought deeply about his lot in life, exile, and that he remembered all that he had left in the north and that he had lost so short a time before, when he had parted with the Raevskys, and this saddened him. But in addition to the elegiac Pushkin there also existed another one: the friend of Vsevolozhsky and Yurev, the member of the Green Lamp, the indefatigable "Cricket" of Arzamas, the follower of Bacchus and Aphrodite. For this Pushkin, Kishinev, with its noise, its merrymaking, its mischief, its beautiful Jewesses, its proud Moldavians, its "well-shaven cuckolded husbands," the duels, and all the rest—this presented him a broad and gay field of activity. . . . And as if this were not enough, remember that he was twenty-two years old, the time of burning joy in life and youth! For, wise from the cradle though he was, Pushkin from his earliest days was young in a way that no other Russian ever was; in this, as in everything, he surpassed all.

It was in such spiritual moods that *The Gavriliad* evolved, and it reflected these moods. This was inevitable. The boundless joy and ecstacy which grew from the observation of such a vivid, splendid, and thoroughly hearty world had to issue forth from him. The Bible, which Pushkin was reading at that time, furnished him with a subject which would transport the future reader into the brightest and most luxuriant provinces that have been dreamed of by mankind. The picture could simultaneously unfold on three planes: on earth in torrid Palestine, not entirely on earth in the initial Paradise, and entirely beyond earth in the heavens. This possibility must have been a great temptation to Pushkin, for it gave limitless scope to his ecstatic contemplation of the world.

In addition, the Bible furnished the poet with the narrative of his tale and with rich pictorial material. Pushkin fixed the spirit of his future creation by means of his own life, and I would say that it is really the spirit of the Renaissance. Yes, in the beginning of the nineteenth century there was a moment in Russia when the greatest of her artists, with no "stylization" and without imitating, but naturally and effortlessly, on the sole basis of his internal needs, brought back to life the Renaissance itself. It is for this reason that *The Gavriliad* occupies a unique place in Russian literature.

Among the outstanding characteristics of the Italian Renaissance were its pagan joy in life, its acceptance of the world with "demonic" delight, and the way it reworked Biblical Christian themes. This is generally known. The greatest masters of the Renaissance, if they were not actually pagans, were at any rate not Christians in the way that this had been understood before them and, to a significant degree, was understood after them. It would appear that the Venetian artists exceeded all others in this regard—a circumstance which did not evade the attention of contemporaries and even the Catholic Church, insofar, at any rate, as they and the Church itself were not infected with the same spirit. At that time, too, there was talk about the blasphemousness of works of art intended for the most part for the Church, and indeed at times the matter reached a very serious turn: Veronese, for his overly magnificent and joyous depiction of Biblical occurrences, had to answer before a court of the Inquisition. The explanations which he gave to the court are magnificent. He allowed no motives for what he had done besides the purely artistic, and he gave no justifications except aesthetic ones. (pp. 25-7)

But no matter how remarkable Veronese's explanations were, he all the same did not say or did not want to say the main thing. For if he had, he would have told the clerics that in adorning the personages of the Bible in the elegant clothing of Venetian patricians, or in having some soldiers gorge themselves on tasty food without paying any attention to the presence of Christ, he was not merely succumbing to a desire for strong artistic effects, but was rather doing something much more complicated. He would have said that the world in which he, Veronese, was then living was so dear to him, so beautiful, that he would not want to part with this world even for the sake of the most sacred places and the most sacred moments. He would have said that indeed the very house of the Lord would not please him if it was not at all similar to Venice. (p. 27)

[There are] a number of deep differences between the paintings of Veronese and Pushkin's long poem. First of all, there is not a shade of the jest and mischief, unquestionable in *The Gavriliad*, in Veronese. Veronese limited himself to the free reworking of a Biblical theme, while Pushkin's reworking moved directly counter to the tenets of the Christian faith. Their approach to the theme, however, was essentially the same, for it grew out of one and the same feeling—exaltation at the world surrounding them. Both artists did not wish to take leave of their earthly passions. And if Veronese made Christ a Venetian, then Pushkin with the same artistic care made all the heavenly personages of *The Gavriliad* Kishinevtsy. (p. 28)

In 1822, and even before that, Pushkin was a nonbeliever, and a short time after that he considered himself to be an outright "atheist." Of all the manifestations of his atheism, however, that which shows in *The Gavriliad* is the weakest and least dangerous in essence, although, of course, it is the sharpest in form. It is too light, gay, and unserious to be dangerous. It is careless and lacks any demonism. Its sting is superficial and non-lethal. The Lyceum poems of Pushkin are really more dangerous than *The Gavriliad*, for it was necessary to possess real "faithlessness" to write them. If one examines *The Gavriliad* closely, then one sees, through the shell of blasphemy, the tender radiance of love for the world, for the earth, and such tenderness before life and beauty that one finally has to ask, is not this love itself a religious love?

There has been immeasurably less written about *The Gavriliad* than about the other creations of Pushkin. The poem still waits for a full and complete examination, and it seems to me that someday the figure of Mary will occupy her proper place in the ranks of Pushkin's ideal women. Through all the improper and untoward occurrences which play themselves out around her and in which she herself takes part, Mary passes unstained and pure. So great was Pushkin's reverence before the sacredness of beauty that in his poem Mary radiates innocence through sin itself.

Of course, the story of *The Gavriliad* is not for children or innocent girls. But for anyone whose view can penetrate a little more deeply than the outward plot, all the indelicacies of the poem are cleansed by the clear flame of beauty which burns evenly almost from the first line to the last. (p. 29)

> *Vladislav Khodasevich, "Vladislav Khodasevich on Pushkin" (originally published under a different title in his* Stat'i o russkoi poezii, 1922), in *The Completion of Russian Literature: A Cento, edited and translated by Andrew Field (copyright © 1971 by Andrew Field; reprinted with the permission of Atheneum, New York), Atheneum, 1971, pp. 24-9.*

ALEXANDR SLONIMSKY   (essay date 1922)

Pushkin had an intense interest in the intimate rhythm of ordinary life, both of his time and in the past, which was finally to play an important part in his transition from poetry to prose. (p. 42)

Against the background of everyday customs [however,] the ominous figures of his romantic heroes and criminals clearly stand out—they are in sharp contrast to "normal life." The antithesis of strong individual will against ordinary life is given in *The Bronze Horseman,* in the opposition of Peter the Great and the poor clerk Eugene. This antithesis becomes a characteristic compositional form for Pushkin after 1830.

In the *Tales of Belkin* and *The Captain's Daughter* . . . ordinary life predominates, but still the adventurous and heroic element takes the fore. This is achieved in both cases because the story is narrated not by the author but by a narrator of a very ordinary sort. This is how Pushkin contrives to use simple speech even about unsimple occurrences. "The Shot" is narrated by a Lieutenant I.T.L. *The Captain's Daughter* is narrated in the form of a memoir. Thus the criminality of characters such as Pugachev and Shvabrin can be accepted because we see it through the prism of the patriarchal and noble feelings of Pyotr Andreevich Grinev. . . . On the other hand, in *Dubrovsky* and *The Queen of Spades* . . . the heroic element is dominant. At the center are the heroic figures of Dubrovsky and Hermann. Here the narrative is conducted by the author himself, and thus the heroic nature of the central figures is not obscured by another narrator. (pp. 42-3)

The fantastic *fabula* of *The Queen of Spades* gives it a special position among Pushkin's narrative works. The fantastic is usually introduced by Pushkin in connection with some realistic justification (Tatiana's dream, the dream of the undertaker, Eugene's delirium). In *The Queen of Spades* we have three fantastic moments: the story of Tomsky (Chapter I), the vision of Hermann (Chapter 5), and the miraculous win (Chapter 6). But only the final moment—the win—is purely fantastic. (p. 43)

Tomsky's story holds the center of the first chapter; the conversations about cards serve as a framework for it. The mystery of the story contrasts with the casual and ironic attitude of the listeners. "'Mere chance!' said one of the guests. 'A fairy tale,' remarked Hermann. 'Perhaps there were trick cards?' joined in a third.'" The end of this chapter underscores this conclusion: "The young people drained their glasses and went their separate ways." Tomsky's story is first taken as an old anecdote. Returning to the theme of the miraculous cards at the end of the second chapter, the author uses precisely the word "anecdote": "The anecdote of the three cards had had a strong effect upon his imagination." (pp. 43-4)

The final scene returns us to the tale's point of departure—to the card table. The sixth chapter has the same framework of card conversation as the first. The theme of the magic cards is also at the center of this chapter; but the anecdote of the first chapter has here turned into an actual event. This difference underscores by contrast the attitude of all the other characters to the anecdote and the miraculous gambling performance of Hermann. In the beginning there was indifference and natural skepticism (a fairy tale, chance); now there is strained attention. . . . What was in the beginning an anecdote and a fairy tale becomes the source of real catastrophes (the death of the Countess, the love tragedy of Liza, and the madness of Hermann).

In the description of Hermann's vision the fantastic is mingled with the realistic. The appearance of the ghost seems to be fantastic because the cards which the Countess names actually later prove to be the winning cards. But just at that point, before the description of the apparition, another cause is given. "Hermann was quite out of sorts all day. Eating in a solitary tavern, he, contrary to his ordinary custom, drank a lot of wine. And this wine inflamed his imagination still more." In this way an explanation for Hermann's apparition as a simple hallucination is prepared. (pp. 44-5)

This same coincidence of realistic and fantastic motivation occurs in the discovery of the secret of the three cards. These three cards are first revealed to him by the ghost of the Countess: "Three, seven, ace in succession will win for you." This apparition is described in the fifth chapter, but earlier—in Chapter

2—there is a concealed hint about these same cards in the concentrated contemplations of Hermann. . . . [A] notion of the grouping of three is dominant in connection with the idea of three cards: "three faithful cards . . . three faithful cards . . ." This notion is to be found in the triple scheme: "Calculation, calmness, and industry: those are my three faithful cards . . ." To this there are added references to seven: "eighty-seven years . . . a week [seven days] . . ." Then the two numbers are placed next to each other: "treble . . . increase, seven times over . . ." This is the exact order in which the cards are named in the vision: three, seven. There needs to be added only the final ace. The determination of the first two cards takes place in a dual way: extrinsically on the part of the Countess and internally on the part of Hermann. So, along with a clearly fantastic explanation, there is a hint of a possible psychological explanation. (pp. 45-6)

The particular significance of the three cards is shown in the rhythmic quality of Hermann's thoughts. The theme of the three cards inevitably brings to mind a three-stressed speech pattern, sometimes passing into a perfect dactyl.

> *Chtó esli stáraya grafínya*
> *Otkróet mné svoiu taínu?*
> *íli naznáchit mné*
> *étu tri vérnye kárty?*
>
> [Whát if the áged old Cóuntess
> shóws me the sécret or
> indicates sómehow to
> mé those thrée fáithful cards?]

The dactyl stands out sharply in the words of the Countess: "*Troika, semerka, i tuz* [Three, seven, ace] . . ." The repetitive stresses of this dactyl in the beginning of the sixth chapter (immediately after the apparition) take on a magic character. "The three, seven (pause) ace soon overshadowed the image of the dead old woman in Hermann's imagination. . . . The magic dactyl becomes, as it were, Hermann's leitmotif, and it furnishes the end of the tale: "*Gérmann soshyól s umá. . . . Troíka, semérka, túz! Trokía, semérka, dáma!* . . . [Hermann has gone out of his mind. . . . Three, seven, ace! Three, seven, queen! . . .]"

The ground for the burst into madness on the ace is laid with amazing precision. The ace occupies a special place among the three cards. The particular position of the ace is seemingly underscored by its peculiar rhythmic positioning—it destroys the correctness of the dactyl meter: "*Troíka, semérka,* (pause) *túz.*" The break at the ace reflects Hermann's behavior. (pp. 46-7)

The Napoleonic, superhuman element within Hermann prompts his win with the three and the seven. The normal human element within him comes forward with his breakdown on the ace. It is in the final moment of the tale that Hermann's magic strength is first revealed; that is, the fantastic element intrudes upon the realistic and psychological plane. The fantastic wins, but reality at once has its revenge: awkwardness and human distraction interfere with the complete victory of Hermann's magic power. "He could not believe his own eyes and was unable to understand how he could have failed." Hermann perishes because of the tragic contradiction between his magic power, of which he himself is unaware, and the common aspect of his personality.

The fantastic element in *The Queen of Spades* plays itself out in harmony with the background of time past. The action occurs in the 1830s—that is, in a setting which was contemporary with Pushkin. But behind this contemporary plane we are shown what things were like sixty years ago—that is, in the 1770s. This sense of the past is well suited to the figure of Hermann. The past seems closer to him, more comprehensible than the contemporary. . . . One scholar considers the detailed description of the Countess's bedroom in the third chapter to be an artistic mistake because Hermann could not have observed all this in this moment of such great strain. But precisely this strained expectation of a miracle is closely connected in Hermann's mind with his sharpened sense of the past. Hermann's magic is constantly accompanied by the motif of "olden times." The detailed description of the antiques and the old furniture is the best correspondent that could be imagined to Hermann's departure into the fantastic.

The most intricate compositional tasks are resolved in *The Queen of Spades* with the ease and simplicity of genius. Even the rhythm of speech serves the demands of composition. The final blending of the two narrative modes, the real and the fantastic, into the single effect of the triumph and downfall of Hermann's magic power produces a strong impression of almost musical polyphony. (pp. 47-9)

> Alexandr Slonimsky, "Alexandr Slonimsky on Pushkin" (originally published under a different title in Pushkinsky sbornik pamyati, edited by S. A. Vengerov, 1922), in The Complection of Russian Literature: A Cento, edited and translated by Andrew Field (copyright © 1971 by Andrew Field; reprinted with the permission of Atheneum, New York), Atheneum, 1971, pp. 42-9.

VLADISLAV KHODASEVICH (essay date 1922)

[The] poet, by the very nature of his craft, cannot set less than two problems for himself, for poetry itself contains at least two forms of content: the logical and the aural.

One of the most amazing characteristics of Pushkin's poetry and, perhaps, one of the secrets of its well-known harmoniousness, lies in an unusual balance with which the poet resolves the two parallel problems. The evenness with which he divides his attention between them, and the exhaustive fullness with which he resolves them simultaneously, are amazing. In a piece the purport of which is the blessings of a peaceful, domestic, laboring life, one finds depicted with equal attention the kind house spirits, to whom the poem is addressed, the prayerful humility of the inhabitant of the house, and finally, the manor itself, with its forest, garden, time-worn fence, noisy maples and green slope of hills. The goals of a lyricist, who transmits his own spontaneous feeling, and those of a folklorist or a painter, are resolved each separately, with complete fullness. At the same time and with equal force, three different feelings are evoked in the reader. The three planes of the picture lend it a stereoscopic depth.

Such series of parallel goals can be discovered in any of Pushkin's works, but nowhere does his mastery in solving his problems attain such heights as in the long narrative poems. Here one is amazed not only by the mastery in resolving the problems, but also by their quantity. One can draw up a long list of themes which receive a full and deep elaboration, for example, in *The Bronze Horseman*. First of all, it is a national tragedy in the narrow definition of the word: here is depicted, as has often been pointed out, the collision of Petrine autocracy with the inherent love of freedom in the masses. This tragedy

acquires a special significance if one looks at the rebellion of poor Evgeny as a protest of the personality against coercion by the state, as a collision of private and common interests. This tragedy will receive a special shade of meaning if one would remember that it is indeed Pushkin's Peter that sees Petersburg as a window to Europe. Here will be lanced a part of that most damned question, the name of which is: Europe and us. But it is not to be forgotten that *The Bronze Horseman* is at the same time an answer to the Polish events of 1831, that the rebellion of Evgeny against Peter is the mutiny of Poland against Russia. Finally, . . . *The Bronze Horseman* is one of the links in the chain of Pushkin's Petersburg tales, which depict the collision of man with demons. However, the aims of this long poem are far from being exhausted by what has already been said. He who will see in it a guileless tale of the broken hopes of love of an insignificant man will be correct, as would be he who would single out from the poem its descriptive side and underscore in it the marvelous description of Petersburg, prosperous at first, then "surfacing like the Triton" from the waves of the flood, which in itself is described with documentary precision. Finally, we would be incorrect if we were not to give the *Introduction* to the poem its due, as an example of sparkling polemic against Mickiewicz. (pp. 61-2)

To the objects of his imagined world [Pushkin] lends the same fullness of existence, the same relief, the same multidimensional and polychromatic qualities which are possessed by objects in the real world. For this reason to each of his works one can apply a whole series of criteria that are also applicable to objects which surround us. Just as the artist, the geometrician, the botanist, and the physicist reveal in one and the same object different sets of qualities, so too in the works of Pushkin different people with equal reason find different things. Pushkin is indeed a *creator*, for the life created by his thought is full and diversified. There is something miraculous in the genesis of this life. But there is nothing miraculous, or even surprising, in the fact that, having once appeared, the world created by Pushkin finds a fate of its own, its own independently flowing history. (pp. 62-3)

Pushkin has been and is interpreted in varying ways. But the multiplicity of interpretations is, so to speak, the professional risk of geniuses—and one must confess that in recent times the unexpectedness of opinions expressed about Pushkin becomes particularly striking. True, much of what is said is correct and perceptive, but many things astound one by their distance from the spontaneous and unbiased impression that one receives from the works of the poet. And finally, much goes directly against the grain of the incontestable clarity of Pushkin's text. (p. 63)

[If] the face of a great writer unavoidably changes in the eyes of changing generations, then in our days, and, furthermore, in reference to the endlessly polymorphous Pushkin, this change will come about with exceptional force. Our history has made such a leap that between yesterday and today there has appeared a void of some sort, which is psychologically painful as an open wound. And everything around us has changed: not only the political system and all social interrelations, but also the outer forms, the very rhythm, system, daily aspects, and style of life. We have new customs, mores, clothes, even, if you like, fashions. The Petersburg in which we shall go home tonight is not the Petersburg of the not-so-long-ago. The world which surrounds us has become a different one. (p. 64)

And thus, in application to Pushkin's legacy, one must draw certain conclusions from the conditions which have arisen. It is not only that Pushkin's works will undergo a series of changes in the consciousness of the readers. I have . . . spoken of these changes as distinct evidence of the fact that Pushkin is already, so to speak, detached from his own time and has entered the open sea of history, where it is his fate, like that of Sophocles or Dante, to be covered with a growth of interpretations and commentaries. But something else will also happen. (p. 65)

Already many do not hear Pushkin as we hear him, because from the roar of the last six years their ears have become a bit deaf. They are forced to translate Pushkin into the language of their own sensations, which are dulled by the heart-rending dramas of the cinema. Already many of Pushkin's images say less to them than they say to us, for they do not see clearly the world from which these images are drawn, in contact to which these images were born. And here again these people are not renegades, not degenerates: they are simply new people. (p. 66)

Much in Pushkin is almost incomprehensible to some of the younger poets, for the reason, by the way, that they are not always familiar enough with all that surrounds Pushkin; because the spirit and the style of his epoch are alien to them, and they have not come into contact with any remnants of his era. The same thing should be said of the language. Perhaps they even follow Pushkin's exhortation to learn the language from Moscow's women bakers of liturgical breads—but they themselves no longer speak the same language. Many shades of Pushkin's lexicon, so meaningful to us, to them are no more than archaisms. (pp. 66-7)

The Revolution brought much that is good. But we all know that together with the war it brought an as-yet-unseen bitterness and coarsening in all, without exception, strata of Russian people. . . . [No] matter how we should strain toward the preservation of culture, a time of temporary decline and tarnishing of culture lies ahead. Together with culture the image of Pushkin will also tarnish. . . .

The historical rupture with the previous, Pushkinian epoch, will forever move Pushkin away into the depths of history. That closeness to Pushkin within which we grew up shall never again repeat itself . . . (p. 68)

Time drives the crowd of people, who hurry to climb up on the stage of history, in order to play their role . . . and relinquish their place to others who are already shoving from behind. Making noise and crowding around, the mass shakes the tripod of the poet. We throw out our most valuable possessions, our love for Pushkin, like a handful of sweet-smelling grass, into the fire of the tripod. And it will burn.

Moved back into the "smoke of centuries," Pushkin will arise in gigantic stature. National pride in him will flow into indestructible bronze forms—but that spontaneous closeness, that heart-felt tenderness with which *we* loved Pushkin will never be known to coming generations. They will not be granted this joy. They will never see the face of Pushkin as we have seen it. This mysterious face, the face of a demigod, will change, in the very manner that it sometimes seems the bronze face of a statue changes. . . . Perhaps they will solve the riddles that we did not solve. But much of what was seen and loved by *us* they will never see. (p. 69)

Vladislav Khodasevich, "The Shaken Tripod,"
translated by Joel Stern (© 1974 by Ardis Publishers;
originally published under a different title in Epokha,
1922), in Modern Russian Poets on Poetry, *edited*
by Carl R. Proffer, Ardis, 1976, pp. 61-71.

D. S. MIRSKY   (essay date 1926)

In the life-work of Pushkin *Evgeni Onegin* occupies a central place. . . . No other single poem of his contains such an abundance of beautiful poetry. This poetry is in his freest and most spontaneous manner. It is genial and hospitable, entirely devoid of what in much of his later work seeemed to his contemporaries, and may still seem to us, a defiant *odi profanum vulgus*, a jealous wall erected against the reader's ecstasies. Even more than his lyrics *Evgeni Onegin* produces the impression of admitting the reader into the poet's innermost intimacy. (p. 137)

[In *Onegin*] the apparent freedom and expansiveness of the style is kept in control by the unapparent but ubiquitous forces of discipline. The two great elements of Poetry—the fertility of the creative impulse and the steadiness of critical inhibition—were united in Pushkin in a perfect harmony, and this harmony is perhaps nowhere more happily balanced than in *Evgeni Onegin.* (p. 138)

The novel is written in octosyllabics, in a peculiar 14-line stanza, the rhyming pattern of which is a b a b c c d d e f f e h h, a, c and e being double and b, d, f and h single rhymes. The Letters of Tatiana to Onegin in the third and of Onegin to Tatiana in the eighth chapter are in unstanzaed octosyllabics. The third chapter contains a short story (eighteen lines) in a folklore measure. A few of the stanzas are incomplete. (p. 140)

Evgeni Onegin, then, is a "novel in verse." It proceeds from *Don Juan* avowedly and candidly. The idea of writing a loosely constructed tale of modern life in stanzaed verse, in a mixed style of grave and gay, and admitting sentimental or humorous digressions ad libitum, with a free use made of Sternian ways of toying with the plot and playing with the narrative illusion, was suggested to Pushkin by Byron. The direct influence of Sterne (of whom Pushkin was a great admirer) is also indubitable. But the differences between Pushkin's novel and its models is far greater than the resemblance, and, when all is said and done, *Evgeni Onegin* is the most original of all Pushkin's writings (except *The Bronze Horseman*). The principal differences between *Onegin* and *Don Juan* are three: firstly, it is not satirical; secondly, it is the picture of contemporary Russian life in the exact frames of a given time and place, free from all semi-romantic Sevilles and Harems; thirdly, it is a complete whole with a beginning, a middle, and an end, and the ultimate impression produced by it is not conditioned by the cumulative effect of the individual parts, but by the thread of plot that holds them together. (pp. 140-41).

Evgeni Onegin is like a living growth: the same throughout, and yet different. We recognize in the eighth chapter the style of the first as we recognize a familiar face, changed by age. The difference is great and yet the essential proportions are the same. It is a face of unique beauty.

The genealogy of Pushkin's manner in *Evgeni Onegin* is complicated and includes many foreign ancestors. The initial French groundwork is always recognizable. It is thoroughly Russian, so Russian as even to be incapable of reproduction in any other tongue. But it is the Russian of an age that spoke French as well as and oftener than Russian. Pushkin never disclaimed this French flavour of his Russian. He alludes to it often, humorously and affectionately. He does not omit to mention, before quoting it, that Tatiana'a letter to Onegin was written in French, and that his translation of the "original" is only "the pale copy of a living picture" or Weber's *Freischütz* "played by the fingers of timid schoolgirls." It is amusing to retranslate it: it can easily be done word for word. (p. 147)

But the triumph, the pure quintessence of the style, is in the first chapter. Here it reaches its greatest freedom and expansive force. It bubbles and plays like a fountain in the sun. Its sparkling lightness has been compared to a newly uncorked champagne bottle, and its exhilarating effect can be likened to nothing but champagne. The lyrical digressions especially, so spontaneous, so effortless, so divinely light, give that effect of creation out of the void which is not elsewhere to be found in Pushkin. The flawless perfection of the craftsmanship is all the more striking as it is quite concealed and can produce nothing but the effect of absolutely spontaneous improvisation on the lay reader. The youthful exuberance of this first unfettered flight is somewhat sobered down in the later chapters. But the essential lightness and spontaneity of the style remains. The story is told spaciously and freely. It moves in an atmosphere of pure yet earthly and unromantic poetry, where humour and feeling form a blend of exquisite mellowness. The scene is laid with detailed and perfect realism, which is only sublimated by the light touch of the poetic wand. There are scenes almost verging on broad comedy; as the picture of the provincial ball at the Larins'; but humorously transfused sentiment is the main tone of the central chapters (from the second to the sixth). The note of tragedy is first sounded in the sixth chapter when Onegin, instead of showing himself a "man of honour and understanding," proves to be a "playball of prejudice," and with incredible but inevitable levity accepts Lensky's challenge. In the closing scene of the chapter—the death of Lensky—the style rises to the intense pathos and high moral earnestness of tragedy, but never for a moment does this make the lightness and transparency of the poetical atmosphere heavier or dimmer. In the eighth chapter the style is still the same, but the note of tragedy and of retaliation grows. It extends even over the sad smile of the closing stanzas. There is no emphasis, no underlining; understatment is always the trusty instrument of Pushkin. And yet the sentiment of the inevitable, of the operation of Karma, of Paradise missed, makes this last chapter of the boisterously begun poem one of the most tragically coloured of all his works. It is a discreet and homely sort of tragedy, a tragedy in the minor key. The eighth chapter of *Onegin* left a profound impress on the subsequent destinies of Russian literature. Of all Pushkin's situations the parting of Onegin and Tatiana is the one that bore the most abundant posthumous fruit. It is the egg out of which Turgenev hatched all his endings, and its progeny can be traced through the whole of Russian narrative literature of the nineteenth century, from its first born, the great novel of Lermontov, to its distant collateral descendants, the tales of Chekhov.

Altogether the influence of *Evgeni Onegin* on Russian literature was greater than that of all the rest of Pushkin's works put together. It is the real ancester of the main line of Russian fiction. For it was as a novel not as a poem that it was most fruitful. Its poetic manner was often imitated, without fruitful originality if not without success. But the setting, the "argument," and the characters of *Evgeni Onegin* are as authentic a "source" as can be discovered in the History of Literature. Pushkin's picture of Russian provincial life laid its impress on all the main line of Russian novelists from Lermontov to Chekhov. The characters of Onegin and Tatiana were the direct ancestors, the authentic Adam and Eve of the Mankind that inhabits Russian fiction. And the muffled, unhappy ending, as I have already said, became the standard ending of all Russian novels. Turgenev in particular is saturated with the fable, though not with the manner, of Pushkin's great novel in verse. (pp. 148-50)

The characters of *Evgeni Onegin* are the least classical productions of Pushkin's workshop. They are very largely achieved by "suggestion" and "atmosphere." They are essentially lyrical. They are irreducibly individual, but this individuality of theirs is not achieved by the objective methods of Tolstoy, Dostoyevsky, or Proust, not by the actions or words that are ascribed to them, but by what the poet himself says of them and by the way he says it. Their unity is one of atmosphere, and in this respect it is again Turgenev who is the truest disciple of Pushkin (or rather of the author of *Onegin*). It is essentially irrelevant to look for pscyhological consistency in the personalities of Onegin or of Tatiana, for their portraits are not achieved by objective psychological methods. Contemporary criticism, for instance, not without good grounds noticed an inconsistency between the Tatiana of the eighth and of the previous chapters. We do not, as a rule, remark this, however familiar we may be with the poem, and even the more familiar we are the less we see the inconsistency. Our Tatiana is the rural Tatiana of the early chapters plus the married Tatiana, and we see each half-Tatiana in terms of the whole Tatiana. Still, psychologically and logically speaking, the gulf between the two is very real, and it is bridged by no psychological bridgework, only by a poet's arbitrary *sic iubeo*. We have obeyed the poet, but we have done so because we have been fascinated by his lyrical power, not because we have weighed the objective evidence as we have been allowed to do in the case of a very similar transformation, that of Tolstoy's Natasha. In this sense *Evgeni Onegin* is evidently lyrical and subjective and to return to what we began with, it is the ripest and fullest expression of Pushkin's early, lyrical, and subjective manner. This manner, by the time the Novel was being finished, had long given way, in all his other works, to a new manner, impersonal and objective, which had already brought and was yet to bring to light, other and very different sides of his multiform genius. (pp. 150-52)

The first expression on a larger scale of Pushkin's turn towards objectivity and self-restriction is the tragedy of *Boris Godunov*. . . . *Boris Godunov* is a premeditated and experimental work, written not so much for the subject as for the literary form. (p. 153)

During his first year at Mikhaylovskoye Pushkin, we know from his letters, gave much of his time to the reading of history, in particular of Karamzin, and of Shakespeare. *Boris Godunov* is the result of these readings. The subject is taken from the *History* of Karamzin and the treatment from the histories of Shakespeare. "I tried to imitate Shakespeare in his broad painting of character," said Pushkin, but he imitated him in more than that: in the choice of blank verse, in the occasional introduction of prose dialogue, in the mixture of grave and gay, in the decided contempt for at least two of the unities: the scene changes very often (twenty-five times during the whole play) and the time stretches out over a space of seven years, from 1598 to 1605. Only the unity of action is fully preserved. (p. 156)

[*Boris Godunov* is] a drama of expiation, and the thread of "crime and punishment" is kept up from beginning to end of the play. The idea of Boris's guilt is taken bodily from Karamzin, and the treatment of it, as in Karamzin, is mainly melodramatic and rhetorical. The idea of tragic poetic justice was a main idea of Pushkin's, and no one more than he felt those secret forces that move the moral universe. But in his really original and free-born works the idea is treated differently, more tragically, more impersonally, and less sentimentally. In the *Gypsies,* in *Onegin,* in *Mozart and Salieri,* it is just touched on in a climax of infinite pregnancy. In the *Stone Guest* it is treated with a rapid concision and terseness which leave no place for sentimental moralizing. In *Boris Godunov* it is not free-born, it is imposed by a preconceived idea of foreign origin (Karamzin), and this sentimental treatment of the tragic situation is the original sin of the play.

It must be confessed that, apart from this original sin, we are in a singularly bad position to be as enthusiastic about *Boris Godunov* as its first hearers were. The play loses if compared with Shakespeare, it loses if compared with Pushkin's own little tragedies of 1830, it loses (it must be confessed) when compared with the great musical drama Musorgsky built up with its partial help. It is on the other hand too closely connected with its posthumous progeny, the numerous historical dramas written since 1860. The consistent mediocrity of these plays casts a disagreeable reflection on their common ancestor. Another point which is more evident now than it was in 1826 is that the great poet of Petrine Russia (for all his genealogical sympathies) could not assimilate the spirit of Old Muscovy. This is especially apparent in the conventional diction of the metrical dialogue; and all the more apparent since in his later (European) dramas he succeeded in creating a style of dramatic diction infinitely superior and more vigorous, and also because it was precisely this conventional and inadequate diction that the later dramatists perpetuated when they did not debase it. The metre is also inadequate, monotonous and stiff, and again the comparison with the Little Tragedies is not to the advantage of the earlier play—a slight change of the metrical pattern (absence of compulsory caesura after the second foot) made the stiff and lifeless verse of *Godunov* one of the richest and most pregnant metres of the Russian language. It is like the change from *Gorboduc* to *Anthony and Cleopatra.* (pp. 158-59)

But though we cannot share the enthusiasm of the first hearers of *Boris Godunov,* . . . it is still a work by Pushkin and abounds in merits of the highest order. The construction, though not strictly dramatic, is masterly, and gives signal proof of that artistic economy which was gradually becoming his most outstanding characteristic: there is not a scene too much. . . . If the tone of the metrical dialogue and the poet's view of the high classes of Muscovite society do to a certain extent jar on our excessively developed sense of historical colour—for after all it was through the sentimentally magnificent rhetoric of Karamzin that Pushkin saw old Muscovy—the popular scenes still retain their original charm, and the prose dialogue, always verging on the comic, is wonderful without reserve. The mass-scenes are admirably managed, and it is no wonder that Musorgsky chose the play for the material of his "popular drama" (though the last scene of his opera—the lynching of Khrushchov—is an addition of his own). The comic parts are on the whole best, and the scene in the tavern near the Lithuanian frontier with the two vagabond monks (the broadest and the best of Pushkin's hints to Musorgsky) is a glorious masterpiece. The scene between the Patriarch and the Abbot who comes to report to him the escape of an obscure novice, who is to become the Impostor, is marked by a fine, incisive, Swiftean irony. The scene where the news of the appearance of a Pseudo-Demetrius is broken to the criminal Tsar Boris is remarkable for an irony of a sterner and grimmer kind, and the scene at the fountain between the Impostor and his Polish fiancée, Marina Mniszek, is an excellent piece of dramatized emotional reasoning. Finally the climax of the play, the death of Boris, with its paradoxical and transient katharsis, followed in the

next scene by the tragic end of his innocent family, is a conception of rare and audacious originality, dictated though it may have been by historical tradition. The closing scene of the massacre (behind the scenes—no blood flows on the stage; here at least Racine had the better of Shakespeare) of the boy Tsar Theodore and of his mother moves the reader (perhaps for the only time in the play) to "pity and terror." (pp. 160-61)

[What] Pushkin did not achieve in *Boris Godunov,* he achieved in the four miniature plays written in Boldino in the autumn of 1830, *The Covetous Knight, Mozart and Salieri, The Stone Guest,* and *The Feast during the Plague.* They are known as the Little Tragedies, a name given to them by Pushkin himself. . . . The form of the miniature drama seems to have been suggested to Pushkin by the "diminutive dramas" of Barry Cornwall, an author for whom, like Pushkin, so many of his contemporaries had an admiration that we have not inherited. But unlike *Boris Godunov,* the Little Tragedies are not primarily experiments in form. They are "dramatic investigations" of character and situation. They were not intended to revolutionize the Russian stage, but just to embody certain dramatic situations that had occured to their author. They belong to a more intimate and "esoteric" category than the earlier tragedy. Only two of them (*Mozart and Salieri* and *The Feast during the Plague*) were published immediately after their completion. *The Covetous Knight* appeared (anonymously) in 1836; *The Stone Guest* only after the poet's death.

The Tragedies are associated with English influences. The hint came from Barry Cornwall; *The Covetous Knight* bears the sub-heading "from Chenstone's tragi-comedy *The Cavetous* (sic) *Knight*" . . . ; *The Feast during the Plague* is a (fairly exact) translation of a scene from John Wilson's *The City of the Plague,* to which are only added two original songs. The metre of the Tragedies is blank verse of a kind much more akin to the English dramatic variety as represented in Shakespeare's later plays, and entirely free from the stiffness and monotony of the same metre as used in *Boris Godunov.* (pp. 162-63)

[The longest of the *Little Tragedies*] is *The Stone Guest,* a variation on the eternal theme of Don Juan. Pushkin probably did not know Tirso de Molina's play, and his only "sources" were Molière and the libretto of Mozart's *Don Giovanni. The Stone Guest* has more than once been proclaimed Pushkin's masterpiece, and it is certainly one of the serious candidates for that title. It is admirable and perfect from what ever standpoint it be viewed. The style and the diction solve the seemingly insoluble problem of writing realistic and humorous Russian dialogue representative of foreign speech. It is the only Russian work of imaginative literature where the realistic dialogue of foreign rogues and adventurers has not the intolerable taste of translated vulgarity. This problem, I believe, is peculiar to the Russian language, but it is none the less real. It has never been solved since Pushkin. The construction of the play is a marvel of nicety, economy, and inevitable logic. The situation is borrowed, but it is treated with a sureness of touch and a skill that do not belong to the originals. It is constructed with the precision of a mathematical formula, and the combination of this mathematical terseness with the live and vibrating flexibility of the dialogue produces a unique effect. It is also one of the most impressive and ultimate expressions of Pushkin's fundamental idea of inherent Nemesis. The romantic conceit of the original legend becomes in Pushkin's hands the inevitable working of a moral law. (pp. 163-64)

[*Mozart and Salieri*] is founded on a tradition which charges the composer Salieri with having poisoned Mozart out of envy.

Another anecdote reports that at the first night of *Don Giovanni* Salieri, alone in the audience, hissed and walked out of the theatre. Pushkin remarked of these two traditions that the man who was capable of hissing *Don Giovanni* was fully capable of poisoning the author. The play originally bore the name of *Envy.* But Pushkin does not make Salieri a vulgar envier. He has devoted all his life to the service of music and achieved much, but now Mozart has come who, without trouble, without labour, merely by the unjust gift of the gods, has created music that casts into the outer darkness all Salieri's achievement. . . . The play is largely a monologue and once again the exposition is so packed and condensed that it is impossible to give a résumé of it. For passionate reasoning Pushkin never surpassed the monologues of Salieri, and the tragedy, like **The Guest,** has claims to be considered his masterpiece. (pp. 165-66)

The Covetous Knight is less severely constructed: it consists of three almost loosely connected scenes. In the first and the third, where the principal person is the Covetous Baron's thriftless son, the dialogue rivals that of **The Stone Guest.** . . . It is the most *magnificent,* the most poetically saturated, the most ''Elizabethan'' creation of Pushkin, and this magnificence and this saturation are arrived at without his for a moment departing from the fundamental characteristics of his style—the absence of metaphor and imagery. They are arrived at by the mere concrete, emotional, and logical value of the words, by the pregnant flexibility of the blank verse, and by the perfect distribution of the vowels and consonants. (pp. 166-67)

The Feast during the Plague is on the face of it the least original of the Little Tragedies. It is merely a translation of a scene from Wilson's play. It is the custom with Russian critics to expand on the infinite superiority of the translation to the original. This is nonsense. Wilson's play and the special scene are by no means contemptible. Pushkin's translation is almost word for word; the conscious alterations are very few; there are, on the other hand, several obvious misunderstandings of the English text. And still **The Feast during the Plague** is one of the great masterpieces of Pushkin and takes an infinitely greater place in Russian Literature than that held by Wilson's play in English Literature. There is of course the terrible handicap of perfection in verse and diction. At the time he wrote *The Feast* Pushkin was simply incapable of writing a line without imparting to it the absolute pefection he had attained. Then there is the choice of the scene, where to begin and where to end it. But even this would not make *The Feast* a great masterpiece were it not for the two songs, which, though vaguely suggested by *The City of the Plague,* are in substance quite original. They give to the Little Tragedy that magical touch which lifts it above mere efficient craftsmanship. The first of them has an English (or rather Lowland Scottish setting) and English names (Jenny and Edmund). It is the song of a girl awaiting death from the plague and imploring her lover not to approach her body when she dies, and to pay her grave a visit when the pestilence is over. It is one of Pushkin's sweetest and most piercing lyrics. . . . The other song is very different. It is a **Hymn in Honour of the Plague,** a grim and haunting poem, one of the most highly strung in the whole of Pushkin's poetry. It was particularly popular and frequently quoted in the days . . . when Symbolism, the cult of the Dark and Nietzschean individualism, were the order of the day. (pp. 167-69)

One is apt to abuse the adjective ''unique'' in speaking of Pushkin, but **Rusalka** [Pushkin's unfinished drama] is unique in a stricter sense than any other of Pushkin's works. Of course, it has ''sources,'' the principal of which is *Das Donau-*

weibchen, a Viennese romantic *opéra-comique.* But its uniqueness is not so much in its originality (which however is perhaps greater than that of any other poem of Pushkin's) as in its inimitability. In it is created a world which did not survive, a world of Russian Romance which, however incompatible these two words may seem, is both unmistakably Russian and undoubtedly Romantic. It is at the same time distinctly Realistic and, in so far as we can judge of the potential whole from the torso we have, it would have been as genuine a tragedy as Pushkin ever attempted. (pp. 169-70)

In **Rusalka** Pushkin certainly reaches one of his highest summits, for, whatever he may have made of the continuation, the existing part is saturated with a poetry where Romance, tragic truth, and Russian raciness appear in a blend of infinitely complex *bouquet* and which opens infinitely receding vistas of suggestiveness. The blank verse is, if possible, of an even higher quality than in the other tragedies. It is all transfused with a mellow maturity and softness, without the slightest trace of debility or laxity. But such descriptive terms convey no impression to the reader. And one can only feel a tantalizing pity for those who are prevented from tasting of it. . . .

After the comic scenes in **Boris Godunov** Pushkin never returned to prose comedy. But there exists a little sketch, **The Almanach-Monger** which shows that he might have achieved great things in this direction. **The Almanach-Monger** is an incisive and unkind skit of a type of Grub Street parasite that was one of the pests of the time. (p. 171)

[As a prose writer Pushkin is, to a certain extent,] the pupil of Karamzin; he inherited most of his vocabulary and his mannerism of ending sentences with an adjective—an obvious Gallicism. He has a great concern for the good balance of a sentence, but he is careful to make its rhythm always strictly prosaic. His prose is curiously free from rhetorical cadence. His real masters were the French. In that which has always been regarded by them as the crowning virtue of prose, a neat exactness of expression, Pushkin's prose has never been equalled by any subsequent Russian writer. But Pushkin's literary prose (as distinct from that of his letters) has not that appearance of ease and freedom which his verse has in **Onegin** and in the dialogue of the **Little Tragedies.** It is obviously canalized. It produces the effect of being premeditated, of following an external rule, in short, of being what in our modern literary jargon we call ''stylized,'' that is, drawn to a foreign pattern. In reading Pushkin's prose one always feels its form, one is always conscious of ''the resistance of the material'' and though the spectacle, at which one unintermittently assists, of the material being victoriously applied to the writer's purpose, is one of the highest artistic enjoyments obtainable, the higher level is never reached (as it always is in Pushkin's verse) where all awareness of effort and resistance disappears and perfection seems to be the result of a natural, unpremeditated growth. (p. 174)

Recent students of Pushkin's prose have discovered in it unmistakable traces of his familiarity with verse. It appears to be articulated into short cola approximately of the length of an octosyllabic line. But these cola, though due to the constant practice of that line, are organized along lines not only entirely different, but studiously obliterative of every trace of their metrical origin. Pushkin was very careful to avoid all similarity between the movement of prose and verse, and in his work the two are as distinct as were Latin verse and Latin (pre-Livian) prose. In this respect Pushkin went counter to the general tendencies of his, and of the following age which found expression in the rhythmical and ornamental prose of Bestuzhev, Welt-mann, Odoevsky, and above all of Gogol. To contemporaries his prose seemed reactionary, as it was in certain respects (persistent structural Gallicisms and certain details of vocabulary). But the practice of later Russian prose is allied to Pushkin, through the intermediary of Lermontov and not to Gogol. Pushkin's mannerisms and idiosyncrasies were not inherited by his successors but the general will to keep prose as far as possible from poetry dominates all the second half of the nineteenth century. (p. 175)

[*The Nigger of Peter the Great*] owes its existence to Pushkin's desire to write a historical novel, and its subject to the romantic interest he took in the person of his black great-grandfather. However, he was imperfectly acquainted with the details of "Hannibal's" life and the novel is not founded on facts. The first chapter which deals with the Nigger's life in Paris, his success in French society, and his love affair with a French Countess, is admirable and displays almost all the best qualities of Pushkin's prose. The story of the Countess's giving birth to a black child on the eve of Hannibal's departure for Russia and of the way it was replaced by a white one in order not to disturb the unsuspecting Count is particularly good. It is reminiscent of the French novelists of the eighteenth century rather than of Scott. But the following chapters are over-encumbered with historical colour and all the antiquarianism dear to the heart of Sir Walter. There is good reason to believe that it was precisely this that caused Pushkin to leave off in the beginning, for in his latter work he never revived the manner.

Tales by Belkin are five short and rapidly told stories—*The Shot, The Snowstorm, The Stationmaster, The Undertaker* and *The Peasant Gentlewoman.* They are ascribed by the author to one Ivan Petrovich Belkin. . . . This mask was necessary to Pushkin for two reasons. The *Tales* were an experimental work; he was not quite sure of its good reception by the public, and wanted an *alias.* On the other hand the simplicity and naïvety of their alleged narrator was a justification of the self-effacement and studied naïvety of their real author, which Pushkin thought essential to the good story-teller. (pp. 177-78)

Pushkin attached a great importance to the *Tales.* . . . They were meant as "exemplary novels," as models for the future story-teller of the right way to tell a story. They are absolutely barren of all ornament. Their style is studiously simple. They contain no psychology, no reflections, no irrelevant descriptions, and very little conversation. They are all action—real stories. At the same time they are free from the nervous concentration of *The Queen of Spades.* The narrative is leisurely and moves on without haste, without omission. . . . [Pushkin] had deliberately eliminated from [the stories] every element of interest except that of sheer narrative. The subjects were mere anecdotes, sometimes disturbingly naïve and openly puerile. Their conscious triviality embarrassed the critics of the Thirties who had not yet freed themselves from the grand style of French Classicism and were already infected by the pretensions of German Idealism. They continued to embarrass the critics through the nineteenth century, and only by degrees (partly owing to a growing spirit of idolatry) did they come to be acknowledged as masterpieces. This they certainly are, and not because of the deep hidden meanings which imaginative criticism has of late discovered in them, but because they show a perfect adaptation of means to end and a highly developed art of narrative. As perfect narrative constructions they are unsurpassed (except by Pushkin himself and by Leskov) in the whole range of Russian literature. They are anecdotes. (pp. 178-79)

The *Tales* were evidently written originally without any idea of Belkin, who came as an afterthought. But when he came, Pushkin was not satisfied with the silhouette of him given in the preface, and Ivan Petrovich soon expanded into a living and pathetically humorous figure. This happened in the *History of the Manor of Goryukhino*. . . . [Belkin decides] to write a history of his estate the Manor of Goryukhino. The preface (together with the earlier preface) presents Ivan Petrovich Belkin as one of the most delightfully humourous figures in Russian literature. His portrait by Pushkin is perhaps the first in date to display that blend of fun and sympathy which is characteristic of modern humour. The *History* itself is at once a parody of the *Russian History* of Polevoy (Pushkin's journalistic enemy and in history an unintelligent, self-confident, and ignorant imitator of Niebuhr), and a keen and concentrated Swiftian satire on the social system based on serfdom. (pp. 179-80)

[Pushkin left] numerous fragments and unfinished stories in various stages of completion, from *A Russian Pelham,* of which only the plan and a few opening lines survive, to *Dubrovsky,* consisting of eighteen complete chapters and a detailed summary of what was to follow. This last story which occupied Pushkin in the winter of 1832-1833 is closely allied in manner to *Tales by Belkin.* It is melodramatic in subject and exceedingly simple in style. . . . The story is perfectly thrilling and, were it not for its unfinished state, it would be the best story of incident in the language. But unlike *Tales by Belkin* it has more besides. It has a very definite social background and gives a forcible and ruthless picture of Russian rural conditions under Catherine II. The two great noblemen, Troekurov and Vereysky, both bullies, but the one an uncouth country lord, the other covered with a Parisian veneer, are evocative of the medieval environment. They are both, and especially Troekurov, powerful creations of character and important figures in Pushkin's portrait gallery. The hero Dubrovsky is of course conventional; he is the noble brigand of romantic tradition. There is in him a noble and bracing "theatricality", often found in French and English novelists and absent from later Russian literature. But that Pushkin was capable of grimmer effects is proved by the terrible and ruthless scene of the burning of Dubrovsky's house with the drunken law-officers in it, which might have been conceived by a contemporary novelist writing of the Civil War.

The remaining fragments are of very varied nature. *A Russian Pelham* was planned as a vast biographical and social novel. *Roslavlev,* the story of an heroic girl during Napoleon's invasion, and the beginning of a novel in letters, were to be novels à *thèse* abounding in discussions on social, political, and moral subjects. The novel in letters especially stands halfway between Pushkin's imaginative and journalistic prose.

The most interesting *membra disjecta* of Pushkin's prose are those which he intended to form the framework of the epic fragment on *Cleopatra,* originally written in 1825. The picturesquely horrible theme of that poem needed a pretext to be introduced into a novel, and Pushkin attempted numerous ways of doing so. One of his plans was to introduce it into a story of Roman life. He began what is perhaps the piece of prose that is most frequently known by heart to his admirers. It begins "Caesar was travelling", and shows him in his most "Latin" and Caesar-like aspect. Finally Pushkin adopted the device of introducing the poem as the performance of a wandering Italian improvisatore given at an artistic house in St Petersburg. These three chapters (entitled *The Egyptian Nights*) are very remarkable, particularly for the figure of Charsky, the aristocrat-poet, who is ashamed of his genius because it makes him a ridiculous figure in society. It is a striking study of the psychology of the Snob, or to use a less offensive and more contemporary word, of the Dandy. It would have pleased Stendhal. There is good ground to believe, as is currently assumed, that Charsky is a projection of Pushkin himself, though emphasized and accentuated for purposes of "psychic cure."

The only stories completed by Pushkin after *Tales by Belkin* were *Kirjali, The Queen of Spades,* and *The Captain's Daughter.* They are unequal in length and importance. *Kirjali* is merely a well-told anecdote of the life of a famous Moldavian brig-and—a reminiscence of Bessarabian days. *The Queen of Spades* and *The Captain's Daughter* are, together, Pushkin's most important achievement in prose. They are mutually complementary and representative of two opposed tendencies in his developed prose manner. The former is a short story, pointing towards E.T.A. Hoffmann and Edgar Allan Poe—the latter an almost Waverley novel of broad narrative painting. Both display that compact terseness which is the essence of Pushkin's prose, but they display it in very different ways. *The Queen of Spades* is nervously compact like a compressed spring. *The Captain's Daughter* in an ever greater degree than *Tales by Belkin* progresses in a calm and homely manner, leisurely epical even when it dwells on the horrors of the great Jacquerie that is its historical setting. (pp. 179-83)

The *Queen of Spades* is beyond doubt Pushkin's masterpiece in prose. Its cold and concentrated glamour has exercised a most powerful effect on romantic readers, among others on Dostoyevsky. But it is essentially a glorified anecdote, or *novella,* and the "glamour" is everywhere tempered by a no less cold and essentially "classical" irony.

The Queen of Spades contains a little over 10,000 words; *The Captain's Daughter* about 45,000, and there is more elbowroom in it and less tension. . . . It is avowedly due to the influence of Scott, and the last chapter has a rather close parallel in the Kew Gardens scene of [Lodovico Ariosto's] *The Heart of Midlothian.* But the story is far more concise and compact than any one of the Northern Ariosto's. It is quite free from all antiquarianism, description, and bric-a-brac. Pushkin's customary virtues of under-statement and economy of means are displayed fully. The story is told in the first person, and its tone in many cases is reminiscent rather of Fielding or the Abbé Prevost than of Scott, whose influence amounts to the manner of treating the past as if it were the present and to a scrupulous regard for historical truth. The story is neatly constructed but without too great an elaboration of plot, and combines the elements of a novel of adventure and of a family novel. As in *Dubrovsky* and unlike *Tales by Belkin* the interest is divided between the narrative development, the painting of manners, and the drawing of character. Captain Mironov himself and his wife are masterpieces of the very highest order. Comical and seemingly trivial, though honest and kind-hearted in time of peace, the Mironovs rise to a noble courage in the face of emergency and meet death at the hands of the rebels with calm and simple heroism. This unpretending heroism was a new and novel departure in portrait painting and, together with the figure of Belkin, those of the Mironovs are among the most decisive fountainheads of subsequent Russian realism. Another very notable character is the hero's servant, Savelyich, at once servile and despotic with his master and heroic when emergency claims him. The rebel leader, Pugachev, is surrounded with a romantic glamour in the true tradition of the Russian robber folk-songs, and in spite of his lack of historical

truth he is one of the most popular and national of Pushkin's creations.

The Captain's Daughter was not, like *Boris Godunov* and *Tales by Belkin,* a premeditated experiment in form. It was almost the chance by-product of the historical studies the author had entered on since 1832. The direct product of these stories, of which the novel was an offshoot, was Pushkin's only completed, historical work *The History of the Pugachev Rebellion. . . . The History* is, all said and done, a masterpiece and, though modern historians have tried to discredit it as insufficiently attentive to social conditions, such disparagement only proves a lack of historical perspective in these historians. All Pushkin's training and literary past conditioned his exposition of history as the history of individuals and individual actions. But he by no means loses sight of the social background and social mainsprings of the Rebellion, though his classicism prevented him from presenting it in the generalized and abstract terms of "mass movement" and "class struggle". If *The History* has a fault, it is a fault of information: owing to the lack of material Pushkin did not give the right proportions to the various individual movements constituting the rebellion and concentrated too much on the army of Pugachev himself, at the expense of the numerous armies that operated under less conspicuous leaders. But he does not idealize Pugachev in *The History* as he does in the novel, and he clearly sees him as the plaything of his environment. But whatever it may be as history, as literature *The History of the Pugachev Rebellion* is a masterpiece. . . . In this respect Pushkin approaches Voltaire, though his outlook is far wider and more "modern" than Voltaire's.

The other historical *opus magnum* of Pushkin, *The History of Peter the Great,* remained practically uncommenced. The notes intended for it often reveal to us the depth of Pushkin's historical insight, but they do not allow us to guess what form it would have taken had it been written.

Closely allied to *The History of Pugachev* is Pushkin's only work of travel, *A Voyage to Arzrum. . . .* It shows his prose style at its tersest and nudest, and considered in this light is one of his most characteristic productions. But apart from these formal works, Pushkin has left us another very different kind of historical writing. These are the anecdotes collected by him under the title of *Table Talk* (the title is in English). . . . [Pushkin] was a true child of the eighteenth century in his love of pointed stories and of every kind of anecdote. The most interesting series of these are those told him by Mlle Zagryazhsky, a grand aunt of his wife's, who was the daughter of Elizabeth's favorite Razumovsky and was young in 1760. These stories are particularly admirable for the way in which the speech and very accent of the old lady are reproduced—a considerably less "literary" and schoolmastered language than Pushkin's formal prose—and with close affinities to his letters.

Pushkin's letters, quite apart from their importance for the biographer, are as admirable as literature and as worth reading as anything he wrote. (pp. 186-89)

The age produced several letter-writers of the first order. . . . But Pushkin is as obviously first among them as he is among the poets, and in the whole range of Russian Literature his letters are as *facile principes* as are his poems. The prose of his letters is very different from that of his journalistic writings and of his stories. It is as free and racy as the other is formal and severe. The ease and sparkling brilliancy of his letters is akin much more to the verse of *Onegin* than to the prose of

The Queen of Spades. As with *Onegin,* reading them is like drinking Champagne. There is no emotional talk in them (the only sentiments given vent to are anger and impatience), but they are full of wit both in the lower and more modern and in the higher and older meaning. The most interesting and characteristic are those written to his literary friends, Vyazemsky, Bestuzhev, Pletnev. They are almost untranslatable in such a masterly manner does he avail himself of the particular expressive means of the Russian language and so saturated are they with contemporary allusion. The letters dealing with literary facts are full of excellent criticism and are an inexhaustible mine to the literary historian. Somewhat less topical and more translatable are his letters to his wife, which are also curiously free from all emotionalism, and which are perhaps his highest achievement in the written use of the free, colloquial, unliterary language of good society.

Many of his letters are in French, and, though of course they cannot present as much interest from the literary point of view, they contain much that we would hate to miss in our general conception of Pushkin. Their variety is as great as that of the Russian letters (if not greater). They range from the mischievously frivolous and impertinent letters to Mme. Kern (his only extant love-letters) to the grave and serious discussion of problems of the highest national and historical importance in his letters to his old friend, Chaadayev, on the occasion of that remarkable man's famous and parodoxical *Philosophical Letters*. (pp. 190-91)

> *D. S. Mirsky, in his* Pushkin *(reprinted by permission of Routledge & Kegan Paul Ltd), G. Routledge & Sons, Ltd., 1926, 266 p.*

MAURICE BARING (essay date 1932)

Pushkin is to the Russians not only the most poetical of poets; he is what Goethe is to the Germans; what Dante is to the Italians; what Shakespeare is to the English—the incarnation of their national ideal; and the Russians, moreover, rank him with Shakespeare, Dante and Goethe among the greatest poets of the world. To the foreign reader, reading his work in Russian, this claim does not seem exaggerated; indeed, all that can be said against it is that the pubblic opinion of the world has not allowed the claim, in spite of not knowing the Russian language, whereas public opinion of the world has done this in the case of Shakespeare, Dante and Goethe, however little they have known English, Italian or German. (p. 146)

[The] consensus of the world, *orbis terrarum,* has said, "Although we cannot understand English, Italian and German, we are convinced by what we have heard and by what we have read in translation, that Shakespeare, Dante and Goethe are among the very greatest poets of the world. We are not convinced that the same is true about Racine; we are not sure the French even make that claim, and we are not convinced that it is true about Pushkin, although we are told the Russians do make that claim."

This may be so because the translations of Pushkin's work are few and inadequate, or it may be so because the world is right by instinct; and that, as great a poet as Pushkin is, he may not be in the same rank as the very greatest of all.

And there I will leave the question; I only know that when you do read Pushkin in Russian it is impossible to admire a poet more, or to think of anyone who has ever written better. (pp. 146-47)

[Pushkin's] earliest work was influenced by the French and the Eighteenth Century. His earliest work was like a classical ballet. But from the moment Pushkin began to write at all, he wrote well. From the very start the beauty of his poetry arises from his use of words, from the perfect manipulation of his vocabulary, and from his always using just the right word and never the wrong word; from a sudden juxtaposition of nouns and epithets, from changes of rhythm and a magical use of alliteration and rhymes. He treated the language as a great orchestrator writes an orchestral score, and as a great conductor interprets the lights and shadows and renders the musical values of the score.

He has no recourse to imagery or metaphor in these early poems; he is just a supreme master of his vehicle, a lord of language. (p. 149)

Later on he was influenced by three foreign poets—André Chénier, Byron and Shakespeare. He next turned to narrative poems.

He wrote these when he was between the ages of twenty-one and twenty-three; they are Byronic in subject; one of them is called the **"Prisoner of the Caucasus,"** and the other the **"Fountain of Bakhchisaray":** Byronic titles, both of them. They are Byronic too in the manner of their presentation: fragmentary, abrupt and full of transitions; but the style is not at all Byronic. (pp. 149-50)

Compared with [Byron's] verse, Pushkin's verse in artfulness and closeness of utterance is like that of Pope; it is as if you set beside the lines of [Byron] . . . , lines like these:

> Muse! at that name thy sacred sorrows shed,
> Those tears eternal, that embalm the dead:
> Call round her tomb each object of desire,
> Each purer frame inform'd with purer fire:
> Bid her be all that cheers or softens life,
> The tender sister, daughter, friend and wife:
> Bid her be all that makes mankind adore;
> Then view this Marble, and be vain no more!
> Yet still her charms in breathing paint engage;
> Her modest cheek shall warm a future age.
> Beauty, frail flow'r that every season fears,
> Blooms in thy colours for a thousand years.

The secret of the beauty of Pushkin's verse is like that of Pope's. It arises neither from a singing quality, nor from suggestive imagery, but it is the result of consummate mastery over the instrument that is being played.

During this same period, that of his youth, Pushkin wrote a number of beautiful lyrics; but it was later in his maturity, from the time he was twenty-four until he was thirty-one, that his greatest work was produced: and of this work his masterpiece, his most important achievement, was a narrative poem in verse called **"Evgenie Oniegin."** It was suggested to him by Byron's "Beppo": the idea of writing something modern and in accordance with the spirit of the age; but it differs from "Beppo" and from "Don Juan" in that it is a complete story artfully constructed.

It is in fact a novel. Evgenie Oniegin is the name of the hero.

It is the first Russian novel, and as a novel it has never been surpassed. (pp. 150-51)

[**"Evgenie Oniegin"**] is told with lightness, ease and certainty of touch; there is not a bad line in it. It passes easily from grave to gay, from brilliance to seriousness, from wit to pathos.

The characters are parents of a whole host of characters in Russian fiction; the heroine Tatiana is the most charming character in Russian literature, as real as Elizabeth Bennet in *Pride and Prejudice*. as lively as Sophia Western, as beautifully true as Shakespeare's Imogen.

The chief quality of this novel in verse is its realism. It is poetical, and yet it neither Bowdlerises nor idealises. Besides this great work, Pushkin wrote several other masterpieces, as well as a flow of lyrics. . . . Besides these he wrote a long drama, **Boris Godounov**—a Shakespearean chronicle play. It shows little instinct or care for stage-craft: it is disjointed and without a definite beginning and end. . . . It is neither an artistic nor a dramatic whole: it is material for a drama rather than a drama. The drama has not been written by Pushkin. But the material is magnificent. The scenes are as vivid and the characters are as living as any in Shakespeare, and in some of the speeches Pushkin reaches not only his own but a universal high-water mark. (pp. 152-53)

It is in his short poems that [Pushkin's] variety and versatility are most apparent. Swinburne says that nothing about Byron is more striking than the scope and range of his power. The same thing is true about Pushkin in a still higher degree.

It is astonishing. (pp. 153-54)

The best-known and perhaps the greatest of his short poems is **"The Prophet,"** inspired by Ezekiel. No translation can give any idea of the beauty of the sonorous syllables, and the deadly sure and subtle rhythm. . . . (p. 155)

If what Goethe says is true, that all good poetry is occasional or ought to be occasional, then Pushkin is certainly one of the greatest poets of the world, for nearly all his lyrics are occasional.

His most interesting poems and his most poignant lyrics were the fruits of the most poignant situations of his life. . . . [He], more than any other Russian poet, perhaps more than any of the world's poets, combined and fused into one the dream and the business.

He is always a realist, always he writes of everyday life, of what everybody has seen and felt, and what everybody can feel and understand; and yet he invests the prose of everyday life with poetry, without veiling it in fantastic webs and stuffs of fancy or metaphor, without idealising it; he touches the facts and sights of life, and their poetry, the poetry that is in them, not the poetry that people weave about them, is revealed. Every phase of life is open to him. He is at home everywhere: a universal man, a citizen of the world.

Once more we wonder at the prodigality and infinite variety, or, if you like, the economy of Providence.

The son of a fell-monger at Stratford becomes the greatest dramatic poet of the world; the offspring of a line of Sussex Troy squires embodies the most fantastic dreams ever woven by the mind of man in soaring lyrical notes of song; a penniless and friendless Corsican lieutenant conquers Europe by his military genius; and Pushkin, a St. Petersburg aristocrat, a Government official, and a man-about-town in the dullest and most conventional period of Russian history, transforms the Russian language by setting it free from conventional bondage, and reveals to the world and to the Russians themselves the poetry of their language, of their landscape, and of the life that is around them, in words which become their most precious inheritance, respected even by the Bolsheviks.

Truly, "the wind bloweth where it listeth." (pp. 156-58)

Maurice Baring, "Pushkin," in his Lost Lectures or The Fruits of Experience *(copyright 1932 by Maurice Baring and renewed © 1960 by Sir William Gosselin Trower; reprinted by permission of Alfred A. Knopf, Inc.; in Canada by the Trustees of the Maurice Baring Will Trust), Knopf, 1932, pp. 141-58.*

EDMUND WILSON   (essay date 1937)

[Evgeni Onegin] really belongs among those figures of fiction who have a meaning beyond their national frontiers for a whole age of Western society. The English Hamlet was as real, and as Russian, to the Russians of the generations that preceded the Revolution as any character in Russian literature. Let us receive Evgeni Onegin as a creation equally real for us.

It has always been difficult for Westerners—except perhaps for the Germans, who seem to have translated him more successfully than anyone else—to believe in the greatness of Pushkin. We have always left him out of account. . . . Carlyle, in *Heroes and Hero Worship,* described Russia as a 'great dumb monster,' not yet matured to the point where it finds utterance through the 'voice of genius.' Turgenev struggled vainly with Flaubert to make him recognize Pushkin's excellence; and even Renan was so ignorant of Russian literature that it was possible for him to declare on Turgenev's death that Russia had at last found her voice. Matthew Arnold, in writing about Tolstoy, remarked complacently that 'the crown of literature is poetry' and that the Russians had not yet had a great poet; and T. S. Eliot, not long ago, in a discussion of the importance of Greek and Latin, was insisting on the inferior educational value of what he regarded as a merely modern literature like Russian, because 'half a dozen great novelists'—I quote from memory— 'do not make a culture.' Even today we tend to say to ourselves, 'If Pushkin is really as good as the Russians think he is, why has he never taken his place in world literature as Dante and Goethe have, and as Tolstoy and Dostoevsky have?'

The truth is that Pushkin *has* come through into world literature—he has come through by way of the Russian novel. Unlike most of the poets of his period, he had the real dramatic imagination, and his influence permeates Russian fiction—and theater and opera as well. Reading Pushkin for the first time, for a foreigner who has already read later Russian writers, is like coming for the first time to Voltaire after an acquaintance with later French literature: he feels that he is tasting the pure essence of something which he has found before only in combination with other elements. It is a spirit whose presence he has felt and with whom in a sense he is already familiar, but whom he now first confronts in person.

For the rest, it is true that the poetry of Pushkin is particularly difficult to translate. It is difficult for the same reason that Dante is difficult: because it says so much in so few words, so clearly and yet so concisely, and the words themselves and their place in the line have become so much more important than in the case of more facile or rhetorical writers. It would require a translator himself a poet of the first order to reproduce Pushkin's peculiar combination of intensity, compression and perfect ease. (pp. 31-3)

[Failing] any adequate translation, we have tended, if we have thought about Pushkin at all, to associate him vaguely with Byronism: we have heard that *Evgeni Onegin* is an imitation of *Don Juan*. But this comparison is very misleading. Pushkin was a great artist: he derived as much from André Chénier as from Byron. *Don Juan* is diffuse and incoherent, sometimes brilliant, sometimes silly. . . . Byron's achievement, certainly quite remarkable, is to have raised the drunken monologue to a literary form. But the achievement of Pushkin is quite different. He had, to be sure, learned certain things from Byron—for example, the tone of easy negligence with which *Evgeni Onegin* begins and the habit of personal digression; but both of these devices in Pushkin are made to contribute to a general design. *Evgeni Onegin* is the opposite of *Don Juan* in being a work of unwavering concentration. Pushkin's 'novel in verse' came out of Pushkin's deepest self-knowledge and was given form by a long and exacting discipline. The poet had adopted a compact speech and a complicated stanza-form as different as possible from Byron's doggerel. . . . (pp. 33-4)

One can convey a much more accurate impression of what Pushkin's actual writing is like by comparing him to Keats than to Byron. There are passages in *Evgeni Onegin,* such as those that introduce the seasons, which have a felicity and a fullness of detail not unlike Keats's *Ode to Autumn*—or, better perhaps, the opening of *The Eve of St. Agnes,* which resembles them more closely in form. . . . (p. 34)

[Pushkin] can make us see and hear things as Keats can, but his range is very much greater: he can give us the effect in a few lines of anything from the opening of a bottle of champagne or the loading and cocking of pistols for a duel to the spinning and skipping of a ballet girl—who 'flies like fluff from Aeolus' breath'—or the falling of the first flakes of snow. And as soon as we put *The Eve of St. Agnes* (published in 1820) beside *Evgeni Onegin,* it seems to us that Keats is weakened by an element of the conventionally romantic, of the mere storybook picturesque. But Pushkin can dispense with all that: here everything is sharp and real. No detail of country life is too homely, no phase of city life too worldly, for him to master it by the beauty of his verse. Artistically, he has outstripped his time; and neither Tennyson in *In Memoriam* nor Baudelaire in *Les Fleurs du Mal* was ever to surpass Pushkin in making poetry of classical precision and firmness out of a world realistically observed. (p. 35)

To have written a novel in verse, and a novel of contemporary manners, which was also a great poem was Pushkin's unprecedented feat—a feat which, though anticipated on a smaller scale by the tales in verse of Crabbe and several times later attempted by nineteenth-century poets, was never to be repeated. . . . Pushkin's genius, as Maurice Baring has said [see excerpt above], has more in common with the genius of Jane Austen than with the general tradition of the nineteenth-century novel. It is classical in its even tone of comedy which is at the same time so much more serious than the tragedies of Byron ever are, in its polishing of the clear and rounded lens which focuses the complex of human relations.

But Pushkin is much more vigorous than Jane Austen: the compression and rigor of the verse cause the characters to seem to start out of the stanzas. And he deals with more violent emotions. *Evgeni Onegin* is occupied with Byronism in a different way than that of deriving from Byron: it is among other things an objective study of Byronism. Both in the poem itself and in a letter that Pushkin wrote while he was working on it, he makes significant criticisms of Byron. 'What a man this Shakespeare is!' he exclaims. 'I can't get over it. How small the tragic Byron seems beside him! . . .' And in *Evgeni Onegin,* he speaks of Byron's 'hopeless egoism.' Pushkin has been working away from his early romantic lyricism toward a Shakespearean dramatization of life, and now he is to embody in

objective creations, to show involved in a balanced conflict, the currents of the age which have passed through him. Evgeni Onegin is presented quite differently from any of the romantic heroes of Byron or Chateaubriand or Musset: When Byron dropped the attitudes of Childe Harold, the best he could do with Don Juan was to give him the innocence of Candide. Evgeni differs ever from his immediate successor and kinsman, Lermontov's Hero of Our Time—because Lermontov, though he tells his story with the distinctive Russian realism absent in the other romantic writers, is really involved to a considerable degree with the attitudes of his hero; whereas Pushkin, in showing us Evgeni, neither exalts him in the perverse romantic way nor yet, in exposing his weakness, hands him over to conventional morality. There is, I think, but one creation of the early nineteenth century who is comparable to Evgeni Onegin: Stendhal's Julien Sorel; and the poem is less akin to anything produced by the romantic poets than it is to *Le Rouge et le Noir* and *Madame Bovary.* (pp. 36-7)

The truth about Evgeni's fatal weakness [is driven home for the first time in Tatyana's final speech]: he has never been able to judge for himself of the intrinsic value of anything; all his values are social values; he has had enough independence, he has been enough superior to his associates, to be dissatisfied with the life of society, but, even in his disaffection, he has only been able to react into the disaffected attitude that is fashionable; his misanthropy itself has been developed in terms of what people will think of him, and, even trying to escape to the country, he has brought with him the standards of society. He had had enough sense of real values to know that there was something in Tatyana, something noble about her passion for him, to recognize in his heart that it was she who was the true unquiet brooding spirit, the true rebel against the conventions, where his quarrel with the world had been half a pose; but he had not had quite enough to love her just as she was: he had only been able to shoot Lensky.

Pushkin has put into the relations between his three central characters a number of implications. In one sense, they may be said to represent three intellectual currents of the time: Evgeni is Byronism turning worldly and dry; Lensky, with his Schiller and Kant, German romantic idealism; Tatyana, that Rousseauist Nature which was making itself heard in romantic poetry, speaking a new language and asserting a new kind of rights. And from another point of view they represent different tendencies in Russia itself: both Evgeni and Lensky are half foreigners, they think in terms of the cultures of the West, whereas Tatyana, who has spent her whole life on the wild old feudal estate, is for Pushkin the real Russia. Tatyana, like Pushkin, who said he owed so much to the stories of his Russian nurse, has always loved old wives' tales and is full of country superstitions. Before the fatal Saint's-Day party and after her conversation with Onegin, she has an ominous dream. . . . [She] sees Onegin stab Lensky. It is the sensitive though naïve Russian spirit, always aware of the hidden realities, with which Tolstoy and Dostoevsky were later on still attempting to make contact in their reaction against Western Civilization. Yet with Pushkin, as Gide says of Dostoevsky, the symbols are perfectly embodied in the characters; they never deform the human being or convert him into an uninteresting abstraction. *Evgeni Onegin* has been popular because it has for generations been read by young Russians as a story—a story in which the eternal reasoning male is brought up against the eternal instinctive woman—like Elizabeth Bennet and Mr. Darcy; and in which the modest heroine—who, besides, is Cinderalla and will end up expensively dressed and with the highest social position—gets morally all the best of it.

But there is still another aspect which the characters in *Evgeni Onegin* present. Pushkin speaks, at the end, of the years which have elapsed since he first saw Evgeni dimly, before the 'free novel' which was to shape itself could be discerned 'through the magic crystal.' This magic crystal was Pushkin's own mind, which figures in the poem in a peculiar way. The poet, when he talks about himself, is not willful and egoistic like Byron; his digressions, unlike Byron's or Sterne's, always contribute to the story: they will begin by sounding like asides, in which the author is merely growing garrulous on the subject of some personal experience, but they will eventually turn out to merge into the experience of one of his characters, which he has been filling-in in this indirect way. Yet the crystal sphere is always there: it is inside it that we see the drama. Pushkin, throughout this period, had been tending to get away from his early subjective lyricism and to produce a more objective kind of art. After *Evgeni Onegin,* he was to write principally stories in prose. And in *Evgeni Onegin* it is almost as if we had watched the process—as we can see in the life-cell the nucleus splitting up into its separate nuclei and each concentrating its filaments and particles about it—by which the several elements of his character, the several strands of his experience, have taken symmetry about the foci of distinct characters. Pushkin had finally transfused himself into a dramatic work of art as none other of his romantic generation had done—for his serenity, his perfect balance of tenderness for human beings with unrelenting respect for reality, show a rarer quality of mind than Stendhal's. (pp. 44-6)

Pushkin, who had done for the Russian language what Dante had done for Italian and who had laid the foundations of Russian fiction, had, in opposing the natural humanity of Tatyana to the social values of Evgeni, set a theme which was to be developed through the whole of Russian art and thought, and to give it its peculiar power. Lenin, like Tolstoy, could only have been possible in a world where this contrast was acutely felt. Tatyana, left by Pushkin with the last word, was actually to remain triumphant. (p. 47)

· · · · ·

In *The Bronze Horseman,* as in *Evgeni Onegin,* we can see very clearly the process by which the creations which Pushkin in the beginning has identified more or less with himself become detached from the author, turn into sharply outlined characters and dramatize the impulse which engendered them in a purely objective way. The original intention of Pushkin had been to continue *Evgeni Onegin.* In this sequel Evgeni was to have played some role in connection with the Decembrist revolt of 1825, in consequence of which so many of Pushkin's friends had been executed or sent to Siberia. He wrote this tenth canto in cipher and then, still fearing that it might get him into trouble, burned most of the manuscript. Then he embarked on an entirely new poem in the same stanza-form as *Evgeni Onegin* and with a hero whose first name was still Evgeni, but whose family name was different and who was in fact a quite different person. The new Evgeni is the descendant of an illustrious old boyar family—Pushkin begins with a long genealogy—whose possessions and credit have terribly dwindled. . . . The situation of the new Evgeni was a caricature of Pushkin's own. He himself was the descendant of boyars—the early Pushkins had been among the electors of the first Romanov—and now he found himself a socially insignificant person in a *haut monde*

where neither his ancient blood nor his genius as a poet was much respected. (pp. 48-9)

And, as Pushkin begins to develop his real theme, the new Evgeni evolves entirely out of the *Evgeni Onegin* frame. Pushkin drops the genealogy, the *vers de société* stanza-form, the amusing man-of-the-world digressions. . . . At the beginning of *Evgeni Onegin,* we see Evgeni, the Petersburg dandy, returning home after a night of gaiety just as the common people of the capital are getting up and going about their tasks. The new Evgeni is now one of these common people: Pushkin has dropped even the literary avocations which he gave him in his original version. And he has made out of Evgeni's collision with the power and pride of St. Petersburg a poem which has been put by Russian critics beside the longer masterpiece that preceded it—which has indeed been described by D. S. Mirsky as probably the greatest Russian poem ever written.

It would be impossible to reproduce in English the peculiar poetic merits of *The Bronze Horseman.* The terseness and compactness of Pushkin's style, which constitute one of the chief difficulties of translating him, reach a point in this poem where, as Mirsky says, 'the words and their combinations' are 'charged to breaking-point with all the weight of meaning they can bear.' The two terrific themes of violence: the oppressive power of the city, made solid in stone and metal, the liquid force and fury of the flood, are embodied in language of a density and energy which are hardly to be found in English outside the first books of *Paradise Lost* (pp. 49-50)

[This] tale in verse is certainly one of the most enlightening things ever written about Russia by a Russian. It is not only in the portrayal of chaos, the resounding accents of power, that Pushkin is comparable to Milton. Pushkin's poor clerk Evgeni, too, is defying Eternal Order. But his defiance no longer appears under the aspect of a theological struggle; it is the great theme of the nineteenth century: the struggle of the individual with society—the theme of which, in terms of the bourgeois world, the great artistic presentation is in Ibsen. But Pushkin had dramatized it in terms of a society partly modernized and yet basically and belatedly feudal. . . . [Evgeni] is the pettiest of *petits bourgeois;* with his two chairs and his pot of cabbage soup, he has been reduced practically to a working-class level. The distance between him and the Statue, and what the Statue represents, is immense. He will be crushed, and his protest will never be heard—or rather, it would never have been heard if it had not been transmitted by Pushkin, whose poet's vocation it was to hear and to give a voice to the voiceless. (pp. 50-1)

Edmund Wilson, "In Honor of Pushkin" (1937), in his The Triple Thinkers: Twelve Essays on Literary Subjects *(reprinted by permission of Farrar, Straus & Giroux, Inc.; copyright Edmund Wilson 1938, 1948; copyright renewed 1956, 1971 by Edmund Wilson and 1976 by Elena Wilson, executrix of the Estate of Edmund Wilson), revised edition, Oxford University Press, New York, 1948 (and reprinted by Noonday, 1976), pp. 31-52.*

M.M. BAKHTIN (essay date 1940)

[Recent] types of stylistic analysis to a greater or lesser degree are remote from those peculiarities that define the novel as a genre, and they are also remote from the specific conditions under which the word lives in the novel. They all take a novelist's language and style not as the language and style of a *novel* but merely as the expression of a specific individual artistic personality, or as the style of a particular literary school or finally as a phenomenon common to poetic language in general. (p. 42)

The differences between the novel (and certain forms close to it) and all other genres—*poetic* genres in the narrow sense—are so fundamental, so categorical, that all attempts to impose on the novel the concepts and norms of *poetic* imagery are doomed to fail. Although the novel does contain poetic imagery in the narrow sense (primarily in the author's direct discourse), it is of secondary importance for the novel. What is more, this direct imagery often acquires in the novel quite special functions that are not direct. Here, for example, is how Pushkin characterizes Lensky's poetry [in *Evgenij Onegin*]:

> He sang love, he was obedient to love,
> And his song was as clear
> As the thoughts of a simple maid,
> As an infant's dream, as the moon. . . .

(a development of the final comparison follows).

The poetic images (specifically the metaphoric comparisons) representing Lensky's "song" do not here have any direct poetic significance at all. They cannot be understood as the direct poetic images of Pushkin himself (although formally, of course, the characterization is that of the author). Here Lensky's "song" is characterizing itself, in its own language, in its own poetic manner. Pushkin's direct characterization of Lensky's "song"—which we find as well in the novel—sounds completely different . . . :

> Thus he wrote gloomily and *languidly*. . . .

In the four lines cited by us above it is Lensky's song itself, his voice, his poetic style that sounds, but it is permeated with the parodic and ironic accents of the author; that is the reason why it need not be distinguished from authorial speech by compositional or grammatical means. What we have before us is in fact an *image* of Lensky's song, but not an image in the narrow sense; it is rather a *novelistic* image: the image of another's . . . language, in the given instance the image of another's poetic style (sentimental and romantic). The poetic metaphors in these lines ("as an infant's dream," "as the moon" and others) in no way function here as the *primary means of representation* (as they would function in a direct, "serious" song written by Lensky himself); rather they themselves have here become the object of representation, or more precisely of a representation that is parodied and stylized. (pp. 43-4)

Another example from *Onegin* . . . :

> He who has lived and thought can never
> Look on mankind without disdain;
> He who has felt is haunted ever
> By days that will not come again;
> No more for him enchantment's semblance,
> On him the serpent of remembrance
> Feeds, and remorse corrodes his heart.

One might think that we had before us a direct poetic maxim of the author himself. But these ensuing lines:

> All this is likely to impart
> An added charm to conversation

(spoken by the posited author to Onegin) already give an objective coloration to this maxim. Although it is part of authorial speech, it is structured in a realm where Onegin's voice and

Onegin's style hold sway. We once again have an example of the novelistic image of another's style. But it is structured somewhat differently. All the images in this excerpt become in turn the object of representation: they are represented as Onegin's style, Onegin's world view. In this respect they are similar to the images in Lensky's song. But unlike Lensky's song these images, being the object of representation, at the same time represent themselves, or more precisely they express the thought of the author, since the author agrees with this maxim to a certain extent, while nevertheless seeing the limitations and insufficiency of the Onegin-Byronic world view and style. Thus the author (that is, the direct authorial word we are postulating) is considerably closer to Onegin's "language" than to the "language" of Lensky: he is no longer merely outside it but in it as well; he not only represents this "language" but to a considerable extent he himself speaks in this "language." . . . The image of another's language and outlook on the world . . . simultaneously represented *and* representing, is extremely typical of the novel; the greatest novelistic images (for example, the figure of Don Quixote) belong precisely to this type. These descriptive and expressive means that are direct and poetic (in the narrow sense) retain their direct significance when they are incorporated into such a figure, but at the same time they are "qualified" and "externalized," shown as something historically relative, delimited and incomplete—in the novel they, so to speak, criticize themselves.

They both illuminate the world and are themselves illuminated. Just as all there is to know about a man is not exhausted by his situation in life, so all there is to know about the world is not exhausted by a particular discourse about it; every available style is restricted, there are protocols that must be observed.

The author represents Onegin's "language" (a period-bound language associated with a particular world view) as an image that speaks, and that is therefore preconditioned . . . . Therefore, the author is far from neutral in his relationship to this image: to a certain extent he even polemicizes with this language, argues with it, agrees with it (although with conditions), interrogates it, eavesdrops on it, but also ridicules it, parodically exaggerates it and so forth. . . . [All] essentially novelistic images share this quality: they are internally dialogized images—of the languages, styles, world views of another (all of which are inseparable from their concrete linguistic and stylistic embodiment). The reigning theories of poetic imagery are completely powerless to analyze these complex internally dialogized images of whole languages.

Analyzing *Onegin,* it is possible to establish without much trouble that in addition to the images of Onegin's language and Lensky's language there exists yet another complex language-image, a highly profound one, associated with Tatiana. At the heart of this image is a distinctive internally dialogized combination of the language of a "provincial miss"—dreamy, sentimental, Richardsonian—with the folk language of fairy tales and stories from everyday life told to her by her nurse, together with peasant songs, fortune telling and so forth. What is limited, almost comical, old-fashioned in Tatiana's language is combined with the boundless, serious and direct truth of the language of the folk. The author not only represents this language but is also in fact speaking in it. Considerable sections of the novel are presented in Tatiana's voice-zone (this zone, as is the case with zones of all other characters, is not set off from authorial speech in any formally compositional or syntactical way; it is a zone demarcated purely in terms of style).

In addition to the character-zones, which take up a considerable portion of authorial speech in the novel, we also find in *Onegin* individual parodic stylizations of the languages associated with various literary schools and genres of the time (such as a parody on the neoclassical epic formulaic opening, parodic epitaphs, etc.). And the author's lyrical digressions themselves are by no means free of parodically stylized or parodically polemicizing elements, which to a certain degree enter into the zones of the characters as well. Thus, from a stylistic point of view, the lyrical digressions in the novel are categorically distinct from the direct lyrics of Pushkin. The former are not lyrics, they are the novelistic image of lyrics (and of the poet as lyricist). As a result, under careful analysis almost the entire novel breaks down into images of languages that are connected to one another and with the author via their own characteristic dialogical relationships. These languages are, in the main, the period-bound, generic and common everyday varieties of the epoch's literary language, a language that is in itself ever evolving and in process of renewal. All these languages, with all the direct expressive means at their disposal, themselves become the object of representation, are presented as images of whole languages, characteristically typical images, highly limited and sometimes almost comical. But at the same time these represented languages themselves do the work of representing to a significant degree. The author participates in the novel (he is omnipresent in it) with *almost no direct language of his own.* The language of the novel is a *system* of languages that mutually and ideologically interanimate each other. It is impossible to describe and analyze it as a single unitary language. (pp. 44-7)

It is impossible to lay out the languages of the novel on a single plane, to stretch them out along a single line. It is a system of intersecting planes. In *Onegin,* there is scarcely a word that appears as Pushkin's direct word, in the unconditional sense that would for instance be true of his lyrics or romantic poems. Therefore, there is no unitary language or style in the novel. But at the same time there does exist a center of language (a verbal-ideological center) for the novel. The author (as creator of the novelistic whole) cannot be found at any one of the novel's language levels: he is to be found at the center of organization where all levels intersect. The different levels are to varying degrees distant from this authorial center.

Belinsky called Pushkin's novel "an encyclopedia of Russian life" [see excerpt above]. But this is no inert encyclopedia that merely catalogues the things of everyday life. Here Russian life speaks in all its voices, in all the languages and styles of the era. Literary language is not represented in the novel as a unitary, completely finished-off and indisputable language—it is represented precisely as a living mix of varied and opposing voices . . . developing and renewing itself. (pp. 48-9)

The stylistic structure of *Evgenij Onegin* is typical of all authentic novels. To a greater or lesser extent, every novel is a dialogized system made up of the images of "languages," styles and consciousnesses that are concrete and inseparable from language. Language in the novel not only represents, but itself serves as the object of representation. Novelistic discourse is always criticizing itself. (p. 49)

M. M. Bakhtin, "From the Prehistory of Novelistic Discourse" (originally a lecture delivered at the Gorky Institute of World Literature, October 14, 1940), in his The Dialogic Imagination, *edited by Michael Holquist, translated by Caryl Emerson and Michael Holquist (translation copyright © 1981 by the University of Texas Press; originally published as* Voprosy literatury i estetiki, State Publishers of Literature, 1975), University of Texas Press, 1981, pp. 41-83.*

IVAR SPECTOR (essay date 1943)

A careful study of Pushkin's works in the light of their historical background and development reveals the fact that, with few exceptions, his songs were those of an unusually gifted bard rather than of a poet; or to employ an appropriate Ukrainian term he was a *Kobzar,* albeit of noble rank. A *Kobzar* (bard), broadly speaking, is a national singer, while a poet is universal. In other words, a *Kobzar* is closer to his own people than a poet, who, for the most part, is a citizen of the world. We speak of national poets when we really mean bards (*Kobzars*). A case in point is Lermontov, known as the Russian Byron, who is a true poet, "poet of eternity," yet he has never occupied the same place as Pushkin in the hearts of the Russian people. For Pushkin, being a *Kobzar par excellence,* has been more intimately related to the Russian people than any other poet in Russian literature. His truth is precisely the truth of the Russians. . . . On the one hand, his work reveals a passion for all that is new, and on the other, an unswerving devotion to the old, particularly to Russian folklore and ballads. (p. 29)

Pushkin has done more for the Russian language than Shakespeare for the English. As Peter the Great, in the span of one short life, sought to bridge the gap created by the Mongolian invasions, Pushkin cherished the same dream for Russian literature and the Russian language. He found it a rough uncut diamond with great potentialities, and he left it a polished medium of expression unsurpassed by other modern languages. Even into the foreign words he borrowed, he breathed a new spirit. In the Russian language he was able to give expression to the pent-up thoughts and emotions of a previous generation as well as of his own contemporaries. He gave wings to the Russian language in poetry. (p. 30)

[Pushkin's] influence is clearly discernible throughout the entire period, many ideas being directly traceable to him. For instance, his *Eugene Onegin,* a novel in verse, provided the pattern for all subsequent novelists in Russia. His *Dubrovsky* forms an excellent background for Turgenev's *Memoirs of a Sportsman.* Tolstoy's *War and Peace* was patterned after Pushkin's *The Captain's Daughter,* while *The Queen of Spades* by Pushkin may have inspired Dostoyevsky's *Crime and Punishment.* To be sure, Dostoyevsky always acknowledged his indebtedness to Pushkin. For it was he who made the *Kobzar* famous by evincing his admiration for Pushkin's *The Prophet.* (p. 31)

Ivar Spector, "Alexander Sergeyevitch Pushkin" (originally a lecture delivered at the University of Washington during the academic years 1931-42), in his The Golden Age of Russian Literature *(copyright 1939, 1943 by Ivar Spector), revised edition, The Caxton Printers, Ltd., 1943, pp. 24-32.*

EDMUND WILSON (essay date 1943)

[The] great fountainhead of Russian literature is Pushkin. From him [Turgenev, Chekhov, Tolstoy, and Dostoevsky] in more or less degree derive. . . .

The Russians are in the habit of comparing Pushkin with Mozart, and this is perhaps the nearest one can come to a simple comparison. Pushkin does, through both his career and his qualities, somewhat recall Mozart: he is able to express through an art that is felicitous and formal a feeling that is passionate and exquisite; he has a wide range of moods and emotions, yet he handles them all with precision; and . . . he achieved in the poetry of his time a similar preëminence to Mozart's in music. (p. 16)

The poets that overlapped the [eighteenth and nineteenth centuries] or were born in the early eighteen hundreds, who lived in the stimulating disturbing time between the old world and the new, tend, in the very disorder of their lives, to repeat the same evolution. They are precocious, they soon make themselves masters of their art; they do personal and original work, and they are likely to try their hands at several genres: they die before their time, of disease or dissipation or the results of reckless living. . . . Byron, Keats, Shelley, Heine, Poe, Musset—here the earliest date (Byron's birth) is 1788 and the latest (Musset's death) 1857, with all these writers except the tough Heine dying in their twenties or thirties or forties (as Mozart died at thirty-five). (pp. 16-17)

Now, though Goethe is of course the figure who dominates the perilous swing out of the past into the modern world, Pushkin . . . is the great figure of this short-lived group. Unlikely though it may seem, he had something in common with every one of the writers named above. He is the universal poet of that moment. Pushkin's cultural roots and branches reach out about him in every direction; he studied Latin and Greek, and he made a beginning with Hebrew; he digested the age of Voltaire and derived from it all that he needed; he tried his hand at translating Wordsworth, exploited Barry Cornwall by borrowing the form of the Englishman's *Dramatic Scenes,* and he achieved a perspective on Byron which few of the European romantics had, by a careful reading of Shakespeare, from whom he learned what he required for his chronicle play, *Boris Godunov,* he established with the Polish poet Mickiewicz one of those intimate literary relationships, half-competitive, half-coöperative, that are likely to be so profitable to both parties, and he exchanged, for Prosper Mérimée's pioneer work in learning Russian and translating him and Gogol into French, translations which improved the originals, of Mérimée's forged Slavic folk-songs: and in the field of Russian culture itself, he retold the Russian fairy stories as perhaps the fairy stories of no other nation have ever been retold; he acted as literary godfather to Gogol, giving him the cues to his artistic development and supplying him with the themes of *Dead Souls* and *The Inspector General;* bequeathed to the Russian composers enough subjects for ballets and operas to last all the rest of the century, and sowed the seeds of a Russian realism united with a fine sensibility that has been flourishing ever since. Pushkin had a mastery of language as remarkable certainly as that of any other nineteenth-century poet; and, with this, a kind of genius which none of the other poets had, and few of the novelists to the same degree: the genius for dramatic projection.

In this rare combination of qualities, it seems to me that Pushkin is the only modern poet in the class of Shakespeare and Dante. . . . The scale of Pushkin's work is different because his life-span is different. Just as the subject of Shakespeare is the full experience of a man who is young and passes through middle age and finally grows old, and as Dante's whole project depends for its force on a discipline in organizing experience through self-discipline and an ultimate aloof contemplation hardly attainable before late middle age (Dante died at fifty-six, as soon as his poem was finished); so Pushkin, incongruously

situated in the Russia of the Decembrist uprising, where he had felt all his life at the back of his neck the pressure of a remorseless paw, found a way to make his fate itself both the measure and the theme of his work, with a dignity, an objectivity, a clear and pure vision of human situations which remove him completely from the category of the self-dramatizing romantic poets. (pp. 17-19)

[Pushkin] is one of the few writers who never seem to fall—from the point where he has outgrown his early models—into formulas of expression. He finds a special shape and a special style for every successive subject; and, even without looking for the moment at his dramatic and narrative poems, one is amazed at the variety of his range. You have lyrics in regular quatrains that are as pointed and spare as Greek epigrams or as forceful and repercussive as the *Concord Hymn,* and you have lyrics in broken accents: soliloquies that rise out of sleep or trail off in unspoken longings—where the modulated meter follows the thought; you have the balladry and jingling of folksongs, and you have set-pieces like *To a Magnate* . . . (in the meter and rhyme scheme of Boileau's epistles) of a rhetorical solidity and brilliance that equals anything in Pope or the Romans; you have droll little ribaldries like the *Tsar Nikita,* informal discursive poems like *Autumn* that are like going to visit Pushkin for a week-end in the country, and forgings of fierce energetic language, now metallic and unmalleable, now molten and flowing, like *The Upas Tree* and *The Prophet.* You have, finally, dramatic lyrics like *The Fiends* and *Winter Evening,* for which it is hard to find phrases or comparisons because they are as purely and intensely Pushkin as *Furi et Aureli, comites Catulli* is purely and intensely Catullus or *Sweeney among the Nightingales* Eliot.

As for the texture of Pushkin's language and its marvelous adaptation to whatever it describes, one is helpless to give any idea of it without direct quotation from his poetry; but a passage . . . may be mentioned in which the patterns and motifs must be obvious even to readers who do not know Russian. (pp. 19-20)

[A] charming example is in *The Tale of the Tsar Saltan,* when the brave little prince, adrift with his mother, begins his appeal to the sea: . . .

> "O thou, my sea, my sea!
> So indolent and free" . . .

[In Russian,] the v's alternate with *l*'s, and the soft *l*'s alternate with hard *l*'s. The rhyme words—*sea* and *free*—are identical except for this difference in the *l*'s. Pushkin here uses metonymically the word for *wave* for *sea*; and the whole effect is smooth and undulating like the movement of a gentle swell. (pp. 21-2)

It is characteristic of Pushkin that [this passage should owe its] vividness primarily to the representation of *movement.* Movement is a specialty of Pushkin's. He can do sounds, landscapes, personalities, and all the other things, too; but there is probably no other poet since Virgil, with his serpents, his limping Cyclops, his wheel of Ixion, and his armies moving off, who has this sense so completely developed as Pushkin; and the control of the consistency and pace of the hexameter can never give the freedom for such effects that Pushkin finds in his rapider meters. The flood in *The Bronze Horseman,* the ballet-girl in *Evgeni Onegin,* the hawk that drops on the chicken-yard in *Ruslan and Lyudmila,* the cat in *Count Nulin* creeping up and pouncing on a mouse—Pushkin is full of such pictures of actions that seem as we read to take place before our eyes without the intervention of language.

This natural instinct for movement is shown in another way in the poet's command of the movement of his verse and the movement of his play or his story. I have spoken in an earlier note of the timing of Russian fiction. The timing in Pushkin is perfect. He never for a moment bores you, yet—touching on nothing, however briefly, without some telling descriptive stroke—he covers an immense amount of ground. The one hundred and seventy pages of *Onegin* take us through as much of life as many Victorian novels, and give us the feeling of having lived it more intimately. (pp. 22-3)

The events that resulted in Pushkin's death make one of the queerest and most disquieting stories in the whole of literary history—a story perhaps more dramatic than anything Pushkin ever invented; and it would provide one of the most fascinating problems for which literature affords the opportunity, to try to explain Pushkin's writing and these happenings in terms of one another. I am by no means prepared to undertake the explanation, but I am certain that, as Pushkin perfects his art, as he sharpens the profile of his style and intensifies his concentration on human personalities and relations, he is reflecting ever more clearly the internal and external conflicts in which he finds his spirit involved. Aleko [in *The Gypsies*], who flees to the gypsies from the organized social world, but finds himself eventually driven to commit among them the same kind of crime that has originally made him an outlaw, and so becomes outlawed by the gypsies themselves; the clerk of *The Bronze Horseman*, who loses all he has in the flood and yet pays for his rebellion with madness; the young guardsman in *The Little House in Kolomna* who dresses as a woman and works as a cook . . .—all are the images of Pushkin's false position between the old nobility and the new, between the life of society and the life of art, between the tsardom and the instincts of modern thought, between marriage and the man for himself.

Yet in these dramas the whole situation is usually seen so much in the round, the presentation of opposing forces is so little obscured by animus, that it becomes almost impossible to say that the poet is on either side. In *Onegin* the clever but sterile Evgeni envies the stupid Lensky for his idealism, his poetic aspirations and his capacity for love, and manages to kill him in a duel; in *Mozart and Salieri* the academic composer envies the genius and poisons him. Both themes are plainly the reflections of something that has been deeply experienced by Pushkin and on which he might have brooded with bitterness; yet he handles them in such a way that there is never any melodrama involved: Lensky is extremely sincere, but foolish and perhaps a bad poet; Salieri is a villain, but he states his point of view with so much conviction and dignity that we almost come to respect him. The emotion that we get from reading Pushkin is something outside the picture: it is an emotion, half-comic, half-poignant, at contemplating the nature of things. He gives us the picture created by art—and this is to a considerable extent true even of his personal poetry—and refrains from other comment. . . . (pp. 25-6)

We always feel, thus, in reading Pushkin, that there is something behind and beyond, something we can only guess at; and this makes his peculiar fascination—a fascination which has something in common with the inexhaustible interest of Shakespeare, who seems to be giving us his sonnets and *Hamlet* and *Lear* and the rest as the moods and dreams of some drama the actuality of which we never touch.

Others abide our question. Thou art free.
We ask and ask: Thou smilest and art still . . .

Pushkin smiles, but he is never free in the sense that Shakespeare in the end is free, and he has always in relation to his art a seriousness and an anxiety of one who knows the night is coming. As his mind grows in clarity and power, the prison of the world grips him tighter; and his final involvement and defiance and defeat are themselves a projection of the drama which is always still behind and beyond. (pp. 26-7)

> *Edmund Wilson, "Pushkin" (1943), in his* A Window on Russia: For the Use of Foreign Readers *(reprinted by permission of Farrar, Straus and Giroux; copyright © 1943, 1944, 1952, 1957, 1965, 1967, 1969, 1970, 1971, 1972 by Edmund Wilson; copyright renewed 1971, 1972 by Edmund Wilson), Farrar, Straus and Giroux, 1972, pp. 15-27.*

JANKO LAVRIN   (essay date 1947)

It has almost become a custom to refer to [Pushkin] as the Mozart of European poetry. Trite though this comparison may be, it still holds good. Pushkin's lucidity and dancing ease are "Mozartian" in the best sense of the word. No matter how deep and painful his inner experiences, he usually expresses them in the simplest manner imaginable. It does not take long, however, to discover that this simplicity is complexity crystallised and transmuted—by a kind of verbal alchemy—into poetic forms, the very perfection of which gives the impression of spontaneity. (pp. 65-6)

In discussing Pushkin one is struck by the difficulty of finding a definition which would cover all his works. A classicist, a romantic and a realist in turns, he defies any attempts at being reduced to a single literary school or to any specified "ism." Yet his supremacy in Russian poetry, from Lomonosov onwards, remains unchallenged. Lomonosov had introduced into Russian prosody the regular tonic metre (prevalent also in German) as being the most suitable poetic medium in so far as his native tongue was concerned. Pushkin brought that medium to the height of flexibility and perfection. Parallel with that there was a less conspicuous trend modelled on the rhythm of the folk-song or even more frequently of the pseudo-folk-song, which created a tradition of its own and reached its climax in the work of Alexander Koltsov . . . and Nikolay Nekrasov. . . . This trend, too, found in Pushkin one of its exponents, although in the bulk of his poetry he adhered to Lomonosov's principle. He even adopted the simple four-footed iambic, advocated by Lomonosov, as his favourite metre. But whatever metre he used, he entirely abolished the declamatory eighteenth-century manner and imparted to his poems a new inflection, a new texture, and above all a conversational ease, combined with a short-hand realism the dynamic condensation of which carries one far beyond mere visual effects even in his descriptive verse. Take the beginning of his poem *The Avalanche,* in which he records one of his Caucasian impressions:

> Beaten by jagged rocks to steam,
> Before me pours the boiling stream;
> Above my head the eagles scream,
>   The pine-wood speaks,
> And through the mist there faintly gleam
>   The mountain-peaks.

Only six brief rhythmic lines, and the picture is complete—not in its repose, but in its sweeping flux or movement which evokes corresponding emotions in the reader. (pp. 77-8)

[Pushkin] was destined to play a double rôle as a poet: while completing the eighteenth-century currents, he at the same time led the way to modern Russian literature. Having paid due tribute to the conventional poetry of the previous age, as well as to the intimately personal verses of the romantics (who deliberately confused the various *genres* and insisted on originality at the expense of convention), he eventually superseded both schools. He even had a brief spell of Ossianism, and this at a time when Voltaire and Parny were among his chief influences. From the French, he learned above all technical neatness, lucidity and that gay if often malicious wit which found a corresponding echo in his own nature. (pp. 80-1)

He certainly struck [in *Ruslan and Ludmila*] a new path in Russian poetry. Everything in this poem was new to Pushkin's contemporaries: the verse, the wit, and even the fairy-tale element with its ingeniously interwoven echoes of Voltaire, Ariosto, Wieland's *Oberon* and of the Russian chap-books. There is a hint in it of the folk-sagas or *byliny,* notably those of the Kiev cycle with Prince Vladimir and his heroes in the centre, but the spirit of the poem is still that of an eighteenth-century romance. . . . (p. 84)

Some of Pushkin's expressions were so "ungenteel" that they aroused much anger among the traditionalists. . . . In spite of the polemics it provoked, *Ruslan and Ludmila* became something of a milestone and inaugurated the most brilliant period, a veritable Golden Age, in Russian poetry. In addition it was a step forward in the process of democratising poetry, without lowering its highest standards. It certainly provided a link between literature and the people, even if its folk-quality, its "Russianness," was still purely decorative and external. (pp. 85-6)

[The period of Pushkin's exile in southern Russia] was responsible for his Byronic interlude, so important for his development as a poet. A complementary influence was that of the French poet, André Chénier, whose short, wonderfully balanced "anthological" manner appealed to Pushkin even during his romantic period. (p. 86)

It can hardly be said that [the egotistical hero of *The Prisoner in the Caucasus*], who is nearer to Chateaubriad's René than to Byron's vigorous adventurers, is as concrete as are the majority of figures created by Pushkin. He is a shadow rather than a three-dimensional character, but this itself may have been due to Pushkin's intention "to depict in him that indifference to life and to its pleasures, that premature mental old age which is so salient a feature in the youths of the nineteenth century," as he confessed in a letter to his former schoolfellow V. P. Gorchakov. Besides, the centre of gravity of this romantic poem lies more in the realistic background (as distinct from Byron's fanciful East) than in the love-drama. Pushkin's pictures of the mountaineers' manners and ways of life are surprisingly concrete. Nor does he sentimentalise their primitiveness, but shows them as they are: reckless, hardy and cruel. (pp. 88-9)

[Pushkin's *Gipsies*] marks his tendency to free himself from Byron and romanticism. It is a very dramatic tale and at the same time so condensed that Prosper Mérimée, who translated it into French and published it together with his own *Carmen* . . . , said: *Pas un mot à retrancher, et cependant tout est simple, naturel* [Not a single word could be taken out, and yet the whole of it is simple and natural]. (pp. 90-1)

[*The Gipsies*] unmasks the Byronic hero by revealing his inner blind-alley. Whatever Aleko may stand for, he personifies the bankruptcy of romantic self-centredness . . . and even more the inability of a civilised man to run away from civilisation, "back to nature" or, for that matter, "back" to anything. Such a flight or regression is always forced and therefore insincere, unreal. Pushkin, who was at the height of the civilisation of his time, knew something about this, and said it as powerfully as he could. (p. 93)

Pushkin took from Byron the new pattern of poetic narrative with its fragmentary character, its lyrical tonality and its romantic themes. But having done this he went his own way, dictated to him by that interest in external reality which gradually led him to *Onegin* and later to prose. With the completion of *The Gipsies* he shed his own Byronic period, but not entirely. Some of its elements, duly modified, lingered on in his work. Nor did he discard the structural pattern of the Byronic tale in verse, but perfected it instead. (pp. 94-5)

His sprightly *conte* in verse, *Count Nulin* . . . , unites the influences of both Byron and Shakespeare, while yet remaining thoroughly Pushkinian. It is a subtle parody of *The Rape of Lucrece* (in a realistic Russian setting), told with the humorous verve reminiscent of *Beppo*. (p. 96)

[Pushkin's] chief title to glory is however his lyrical poetry. . . . His favourite metre was the iambic, but he could put into the regularity of any metre an astonishing variety of rhythm and music. (pp. 97-8)

[Pushkin was] capable, during the process of creation, of turning a theme into something which had nothing in common with the starting-point itself. His *Legend* about the medieval quixotic knight who had devoted his life to the worship of the Madonna is a proof. From the recently examined drafts it is clear that Pushkin first chose the theme in a frivolous or even cynical mood, and intended to treat it as a joke. But during the process of writing all the dross fell off, and finally the poem became an apotheosis of the eternal feminine as understood by a medieval worshipper of the Holy Virgin. Pushkin himself was neither a philosopher in a narrow sense nor a religious seeker, but he had a profound sense of values which usually came to his rescue. (pp. 103-04)

[*Poltava* is] divided between personal fates and passions (Mazepa-Maria) on the one hand and the problem of the historical destiny of Russia (Peter-Charles XII) on the other. "Strong characters, and the profoundly tragic shadow hovering over all the horrors—this was what appealed to me," Pushkin said in a letter. "I wrote *Poltava* in a few days; but for that, I would have given it up." The strong characters, Peter and Mazepa, stand out also as the two contrasts. While Mazepa's passions and ambitions are those of a great egoist, Peter represents the idea of the State, which is also his principal passion. In spite of a certain lack of unity between its two themes, this poem yet marks one of the summits of Pushkin's creative power. Impersonal, terse, and metallic in its diction, it is the nearest approach to what might have been worked out into a great national epic, had Pushkin not been in such a hurry to finish it in "a few days."

In contrast with *Poltava, The Bronze Horseman* is all of a piece. . . . Among the literary influences that may have affected Pushkin in this case were two poems by his Polish friend

Adam Mickiewicz: one of them, *The Monument of Peter the Great*, prophesied the symbolic downfall of the statue, while the other—*Oleszkiewicz*—gave a picture of the eve of the flood in 1824. Pushkin made the flood the starting-point of his poem, and the triumph (not the downfall) of Peter's monument its climax. The poem thus became a realistic-symbolic masterpiece the like of which had never before appeared in Russian. (pp. 109-11)

[It was in the spirit of Russian folklore that Pushkin wrote] his *Skazki* or *Fairy-Tales* in verse. (p. 117)

Only one of these tales—the one about the parson and his workman (stylised like doggerel for the people)—was due entirely, and *The Tale of Tsar Saltan* partly, to the stories which Pushkin heard from [his childhood nurse, Arina]. *The Tale of the Dead Princess* was based on the Grimm brothers' *Snow White (Schneewittchen)*. So was *The Tale of the Fisherman*. The source of *The Golden Cockerel*, on the other hand, was the legend of the Arab astrologer in Washington Irving's *The Alhambra*. . . . (pp. 117-18)

Attempts at adapting motifs from borrowed fairy-tales to the Russian tone and spirit had been made, before Pushkin, by Zhukovsky. But in contrast to Zhukovsky's purely conventional Russian garb, Pushkin succeeded in bringing his own *skazki* so close to the people's style and favour that his *Tale of the Fisherman,* for example, became a genuine Russian folk-tale and was later registered by Afanasyev as such. It matters little whether Pushkin took his themes from the Brothers Grimm or from Irving. The important thing is that he knew how to turn them into masterpieces which the Russian people could regard as their own and even include in the treasury of their lore. Here, if anywhere, Pushkin took the literary language out of Karamzin's drawing-room and imbued it with a new vitality coming from the people, thereby enlarging the scope of his literary achievements. But if we want to see Pushkin's genius in all its broadness and maturity we must go to his principal work—*Evgeny Onegin*. (p. 118)

Here, if anywhere, Pushkin showed all his descriptive and plastic power, as well as his capacity for rendering character by means of suggestive lyrical "atmosphere." It was through *Onegin* that he squared his accounts with Byron and the romantic movement. Having started his "novel" at the height of his own Byronic period, Pushkin gradually pronounced in it a double verdict on romanticism. Tatyana's summing up of Onegin as a parody was one of them, while the other was indicated in Pushkin's bantering attitude towards Lensky (a product of the German romantic movement . . .). Further, *Evgeny Onegin* expresses Pushkin's philosophy of the acceptance of life, a philosophy not so much of happiness as of a balanced serenity on the part of a man who has learned both the value and the price of things in our bewildering world. (p. 139)

[Pushkin's interest in Shakespeare—coupled with his] study of Russian history—resulted in the first Shakespearean play of merit in Russian literature: *Boris Godunov*. (p. 140)

[It] would be wrong to see in *Boris Godunov* only a psychological theme. The play, with its variety of scenes and characters, develops on two planes. One of them is psychological, and the other—broadly speaking—political. The first is represented by the inner drama of Boris, while the second merges with the historical background. The play has been described as a social-political tragedy, and Pushkin himself wrote . . . "I look upon him (Boris) from a political standpoint without paying attention to the poetic side."

Boris Godunov is certainly less brilliant with regard to its "poetic side" than Schiller's *Demetrius,* for example. It is also less agitated, less rich in passion than Shakespeare's plays. But this toning down was due to Pushkin's tendency to make his characters speak as simply and naturally as they would in real life. "Convincingness of situations and naturalness of the dialogue"—this was what Pushkin demanded from a play, and he kept to this rule even at the risk of appearing bald in comparison with his chief model, Shakespeare. The five-footed iambic line used by him made a return to the solemn declamatory Alexandrine quite impossible. Several scenes are in ordinary conversational prose. And instead of the strict unity of time and place there is a fairly loose sequence of episodes, each of them as it were with its own climax.

In spite of the title it is not Godunov but Dimitry who dominates the stage and provides the focus unifying the play. From a dramatic standpoint Dimitry is the most articulate of all the characters presented. While Godunov necessarily remains in one prevailing mood, Dimitry is shown in a variety of moods, although he has no definite political line except that of dexterously exploiting the circumstances. (pp. 151-52)

Having taken from Shakespeare what he needed, [Pushkin] intensified thereby his own peculiar realism in art, in spite of the fact that he considered the play a "romantic drama." Besides, the period presented was itself as "romantic" as its protagonists, and so a free composition, in the manner of a chronicle-play, suited Pushkin's task very well indeed. Yet he combined his artistic freedom with the most rigorous artistic economy. Language, style, character-drawing, the colour of the epoch—all were reduced to their bare essentials. As a result they gained in intensity. Even those characters who appear only once (the monk Pimen, for instance) are alive and memorable.

In one respect Pushkin anticipated even the Ibsenian drama: by transferring Boris's tragic guilt into the past and showing on the stage only the Tsar's psychological reactions to it, with the "atmosphere" of approaching Nemesis hovering over all his doings. The kaleidoscopic variety of the scenes—from the comic one on the Lithuanian frontier to the tragic pathos of Boris's death (reminiscent of the death of Henry IV)—is thus worked out, in spite of its seeming looseness, according to a definite pattern. (pp. 153-54)

If in *Boris Godunov* [Pushkin] made Shakespeare his starting-point, he turned in [his **"little tragedies"**] to themes and characters previously worked out by some other poets or dramatists. And again he made use of them not in order to repeat what had already been said, but to show them in a new light, and from a new angle. (p. 160)

Other themes were to deal with passions or obsessions of general human significance, and Pushkin was not deterred by the fact that they had already been treated by a number of important European authors before him. On the contrary, it was through such general themes that he hoped to affiliate all the more closely his native literature with the literary tradition of the West, while showing at the same time the themes themselves in a new and original light.

He must already have contemplated something similar in his brilliant *Scene from Faust*. Pushkin's Faust is not a titanic character but a paranoiac, utterly disappointed with his new knowledge and more depressed by his regained youth than he had been by his old age before his deal with Mephistopheles. As if reluctant to compete with Goethe on his own ground,

Pushkin turned to such traditional motives as avarice (*The Miser Knight*), carnal lust (*The Stone Guest*), and envy (*Mozart and Salieri*), which he endeavoured to show as far as possible from an original angle, and with the greatest artistic discipline at his disposal. (pp. 161-62)

[In] spite of the brevity of his **"little tragedies,"** Pushkin succeeded in avoiding the schematised presentation of characters according to the pseudo-classic canon, which demands that each character should embody one feature only. He endowed them instead with several contradictory features and with something of that inner complexity which he had learned from "our father Shakespeare." (p. 164)

[In *Mozart and Salieri*, Pushkin] showed above all the contrast as well as the eternal antagonism between genius and mere talent. . . . Pushkin's Salieri is an industrious craftsman, fanatically devoted to music and at the same time devoid of true creative power. So he is doomed to remain a solemn plodder who cannot grasp how it is that the greatest creative genius should have been bestowed on the carefree, childishly irresponsible "idle frivoller" Mozart, and not upon himself as a reward for all his zeal and toil. He listens with amazement to Mozart's music, but the more he is compelled to admire it the more he feels the smart of some injustice which is beyond man's ken. On this plane, Salieri's attitude transcends mere envy; it is tragic and at the same time unanswerable. (p. 165)

[Salieri] is presented by Pushkin as a Hamlet-like character, and his tortuous complexity comes out during his conversation with the transparently simple Moazart. Salieri hates through admiration, and admires through hatred. While listening to the "frivoller's" music, he realises more than ever before that its perfection is like God's Grace—something which cannot be imitated; and that Mozart is, quite *undeservedly,* in a different category from Salieri himself and hundreds of other hard-working musicians. (pp. 167-68)

[This] **"little tragedy"** ends on a note of Hamlet-like doubt. No problems have been solved by it. But they have been powerfully stated, or at least suggested. And this is what art is for. (p. 170)

[In prose too Pushkin] proved to be a pioneer, and was largely responsible for the character of modern Russian prose, which he imbued with the same "naked beauty" as his poems. (pp. 182-83)

Pushkin adopted from the outset a deliberate matter-of-fact conciseness, which he raised to the highest artistic level. Although primarily a poet, he would never confuse the methods of poetry with those of prose. Using the latter as a medium entitled to its own laws, he emancipated it from all "poetic" propensities in the name of an intimate and homely realism. And if he was not the first to introduce the "little man" into Russian fiction (Karamzin had forestalled him in this), he yet democratised and at the same time vitalised Russian literary language by including in it a number of idioms and inflections taken from the people's speech. In this manner he not only raised the level of Russian prose but also enlarged its basis. (p. 184)

[The five stories contained in *Tales of Belkin*] are not commonly regarded as masterpieces, although they aroused little attention when first published: their art was too much of the kind that conceals art. Like Scott in his *Tales of My Landlord*, Pushkin, too, here ingeniously put between himself and the reader a supposed narrator, Belkin, whose personal tone and inflection

are preserved. Belkin takes the reader in turns to the Russian country house, the post-coach station, the suburban artisans' quarter and to army circles, often evincing that sense of humour which is the more effective by being or rather by appearing unconscious. Pushkin was thus able to exercise his own humour or parody in an indirect manner. (pp. 185-86)

Linked with these stories is Pushkin's unfinished satire on the serf-system, *A History of the Village Goryukhino,* since once again the supposed narrator (or in this case the compiler) is Belkin. . . . The mixture of *naïveté* and "unconscious" satire with which Belkin unfolds the annals of a village victimised by the brutality of the system only strengthens the final effect. (p. 187)

Another example of a romantic theme handled with even greater realistic terseness is *The Queen of Spades* . . . , a story which makes one think of Hoffman, but rewritten in the lucid, compact prose of Voltaire, Stendhal or Mérimée. . . . This Petersburgian *novella* is, apart from *The Gipsies,* the most condensed work Pushkin ever wrote. If there is such a thing as dynamic dryness, we find it here. Yet both the story and its background—the atmosphere of the 'twenties,—are for this very reason all the more effective. (p. 188)

Among Pushkin's minor works and fragments *A Romance in Letters* . . . is of particular interest to English readers. It is done in the epistolary form as created by Richardson, to whose *Clarissa Harlowe* Pushkin refers. In it he tackles the social problem to which he attached great importance at the time: the historical rôle, the tasks and prospects of his own class. (p. 194)

A Russian Pelham, of which only the plan is known, reminds one again of English literature: this time of the well-known but hardly outstanding novel by Bulwer Lytton. The title does not necessarily mean that Pushkin was anxious to imitate the English novelist. What he wanted to do was to write a novel of adventure, as if designed to counteract Bulgarin's vulgar *Ivan Vyzhigin.* . . . As far as one can gauge, Pushkin's work was to have been also a social novel of manners. . . . (p. 195)

Finally, a place of honour in Russian prose is allotted to Pushkin's critical notes, articles, and most particularly his letters. In criticism he showed a literary knowledge which was no less astonishing than his discrimination. His judgments, while always to the point, are full of wit and of that almost clairvoyant common sense which was an inalienable feature of his intelligence. The same applies to his letters, the bubbling humour and spontaneity of which are unsurpassed in Russian literature. (p. 196)

[Pushkin's influence upon Russian prose was far-reaching.] His *Tales of Belkin,* for instance, relegated Karamzin's stories to an irrevocable past as regards style and manner. But while enlarging the base of Russian literary language Pushkin also widened the social base of literature itself by introducing into it a great variety of characters: from Peter the Great and Catherine II to the unassuming Mironov and the humble "little man," all of whom he treated with the same care and the same artistic sympathy. Gogol's *Greatcoat* and Dostoevsky's *Poor Folk* came largely out of Pushkin's *Post-Stage Master,* and the rôle played by the first of these stories in the development of the "natural school" championed by Belinsky is known to every student of Russian literature. The strongest influence on Russian fiction—at least in its thematic aspects—was exercised, however, by *Evgeny Onegin.* (p. 203)

Pushkin introduced his own equivalent of the Childe Harold type to Russian readers at a time when a number of ambitious but frustrated youths were a fact of Russian life. So this uprooted hero was soon adopted under the unromantic label of the "superfluous man," and gradually became the staple character of Russian realism. In Aleko [of *The Gipsies*] we saw him being stripped of his romantic halo. In Onegin he was shown as a product of artificial Petersburg society and therefore hardly entitled to be more than a parody. He became tragic, however, in Lermontov's Pechorin, the chief character in the novel *A Hero of our Time*. Pechorin is a further stage of the uprooted Onegin-type. He is an exceptionally strong and gifted individual, but frustrated by the atmosphere of the "leaden regime" which he is compelled to endure. (p. 204)

After Lermontov's Pechorin, the "superfluous man" began to invade Russian literature not as a fictitious but as a real product of Russian life. Beltov in Herzen's novel *Whose Fault* was a variety of the same character towards the end of the 'forties. Tentetnikov in the second part of Gogol's *Dead Souls* was another, and he led straight to the hero of Goncharov's masterpiece *Oblomov*. (pp. 204-05)

In Dostoevsky's works the "superfluous man" became the "underworld man" who, in his social and spiritual uprootedness, analysed away not only his own self but the whole of existence, like Raskolnikov in *Crime and Punishment*, Stavrogin in *The Possessed* and Ivan in *The Brothers Karamazov*. Pushkin's *Post-Stage Master*, on the other hand, was responsible, via Gogol's *Greatcoat*, for the gallery of the "insulted and injured" in Dostoevsky's novels, from *Poor Folk* onwards. It is known that the initial idea for his novel *A Raw Youth* was taken by Dostoevsky from the monologue in Pushkin's *The Miser Knight*. *The Idiot* was partly inspired by the *Legend* beginning with the line "Once there lived a poor knight" which is quoted in the novel. Also the irrational "Petersburg" flavour of *The Queen of Spades* left a strong mark in Dostoevsky's novels. (pp. 205-06)

Pictures of Russian country life, such as those in *Onegin,* were continued, and on a broad scale, by Turgenev, Goncharov, Tolstoy and scores of others. Turgenev was a past-master at depicting the autumnal moods of the decaying gentry. Goncharov found his proper medium in characteristic small touches, in *Kleinmalerei;* whereas Tolstoy preferred a full-blooded realism tempered by psychological analysis. As for the "Russian house's annals" type of narrative, it came into its own in Sergey Aksakov's *Family Chronicle*, partly in Tolstoy's *War and Peace*, and in *Anna Karenina*. (pp. 206-07)

A special mention should be made of the thematic importance of Pushkin's works, beginning with *Evgeny Onegin*. The Tatyana-Onegin motive (the meeting of a strong woman with a weak "superfluous" man) set an indelible stamp upon the whole of Russian fiction after Pushkin. It is particularly conspicuous in Turgenev's *Rudin* and in Goncharov's *Oblomov* as well as in his *Precipice*. (p. 207)

An unheroic hero, an unexciting and somewhat loose plot, and especially an inconclusive ending, typical of *Onegin,* became adopted almost as a canon by Russian authors whose distaste for the escapist romance (with wedding bells and other blessings at the end) was notorious. Also personal digressions, so frequent in Pushkin's works, penetrated to some extent into Russian fiction, to begin with Gogol's *Dead Souls* . . . , the idea for which had been suggested by Pushkin himself.

But while speaking of the thematic importance of Pushkin's works we cannot possibly by-pass his *History of the Village Goryukhino*. The influence of this fragment was quite out of

proportion to its size, especially from the 'forties onwards, when the realism of the "natural school" with its indictments was in the ascendant. The bugbear was of course serfdom. (p. 208)

Less pronounced was Pushkin's influence upon the development of Russian drama. His *Boris Godunov,* from which he expected a reform of the theatre, not only had to wait six years for permission to be published but was at first considered unsuitable for the stage. True enough, but putting an end to pseudo-classic plays in Russian literature *Boris Godunov* helped to clear the ground for realism on the stage, but the latter received a stronger impetus from Gogol's satirical comedy of manners *The Inspector General*. . . . (p. 210)

On the other hand, Pushkin's work as a whole came to dominate the Russian stage through music, since there is hardly a Russian composer of note who has not found at least some inspiration in Pushkin. This refers not only to his lyrics but to all his works, most of which provided suitable material for operas and ballets. (p. 211)

All this is only a further proof that Pushkin can be looked upon not only as a great poet and author but also as one of those cultural forces the vitality of which is bound to "live and move eternally," as Belinsky said. It was through him that Russian literature received its focus and at the same time that direction in which the soul of his nation can look for its true image and self-expression. The whole of Russian literature after Pushkin has been above all a process of this kind, and some of its results have been so striking as to astonish the world. (pp. 212-13)

> *Janko Lavrin, in his* Pushkin and Russian Literature, *Hodder & Stoughton, 1947 (and reprinted by Russell & Russell, 1969), 226 p.*

HENRY GIFFORD (essay date 1949)

[John Wilson's *The City of the Plague*] shows the defects that Richard Garnett observed in Wilson: "want of restraining judgment and symmetrical proportion." . . . But there was something to salvage; and Puškin found a focus in the one scene that he selected [and loosely translated as *Feast in Time of Plague*]. "The fundamental idea," said Belinskij, "is an orgy in time of plague, an orgy of 'despair, the more terrible, the gayer. A truly tragic idea!'" That is the pathos of Wilson's drama, summed up by Puškin in the last two lines of the song he wrote for the Master of Revels: "We drink the breath of a rose-maiden, it may be, full of the plague!"

Puškin did not translate the whole of Act I, scene 4. He took it to the departure of the Priest, after which the duel links it up with the main plot. But the two hundred-odd lines that Puškin followed form an episode independently, and as a dramatic scene they need little alteration. (p. 40)

The impression that Puškin's scene gives is of something more coherent and distinct than the original. This is largely due to the superior style, which we shall examine later. But there are certain changes Puškin has made in the action. These come in the final episode, when the Priest enters and rebukes the revelers. In the first place, his recognition of Walsingham is more dramatic. He seems suddenly to find him among the others. Then, after the Priest's appeal to Walsingham that he should abandon the revels, Puškin has cut out fifteen lines that only weaken the action: in them the Priest is interrupted by profane comments from the young man, Walsingham pleads for respect to the Priest's grey hairs, and the Priest reiterates his appeal.

Instead, Puškin's version passes immediately to Walsingham's distressed reply. The struggle between Walsingham and the Priest is more definite. Again, when the Priest mentions Walsingham's dead wife, in Puškin's version Walsingham, rather than remind him of his oath never to speak her name, actually calls on him to swear now for the first time. Walsingham apostrophizes her in heaven; the comment of the "Female Voice," merely cynical as Wilson wrote it—

> The fit is on him.
> Fool! thus to rave about a buried wife!—

is softened to: "He is mad: he raves about his buried wife," which perhaps shows more horror than scorn. . . . All this passage is an example of how Puškin, by slight changes of perspective, organizes the scene to bring out the characters more individually and movingly. And by breaking off at that point, he makes us more aware of Walsingham as the central figure in the scene. It is Walsingham who represents, by the conflict in his own mind, the dilemma of all his companions.

The other significant change that Puškin made can be seen by comparing his songs with those of Wilson. Songs are introduced in various other scenes of the drama; and on the whole their effect is adventitious. They merely decorate, without forwarding the action. (pp. 40-1)

Mary Gray's song in the original runs to sixteen four-line stanzas, and it is written in the Scots dialect:

> I walk'd by mysel ower the sweet braes o' Yarrow,
> When the earth wi' the gowans o' July was drest;
> But the sang o' the bonny burn sounded like sorrow,
> Round ilka house cauld as a last simmer's nest.

For these, Puškin substituted five eight-line stanzas in trochaics instead of amphibrachs. The greater compactness of this arrangement allows him to develop his thought by clear-cut stages, whereas Wilson's song practically stands still, repeating the initial contrast between the summer landscape, which recalls happier days, and the silent houses and fields. (p. 42)

Puškin's song begins with the contrast between the prosperity of former days and the present stillness; but he gives it a greater point by describing each state in a different verse. The opening lines recall the pastoral note of Wilson's poem: "Time was, when our countryside bloomed in peace" . . . lines which have the ring (though not the meter) of Russian folk song. There follow two images from Wilson's poem—the church and the school—and the stanza is completed by a couplet describing harvest in the "bright field." The second stanza turns to the present dereliction: "all is still, the graveyard alone is not empty nor silent." Puškin has made the plague contemporary; and his third stanza, developing the idea of the "fifty brown hillocks," describes the graves crowding together like a frightened flock. This leads naturally to the entirely new thought of the fourth stanza: if the singer is doomed to an early grave, let her lover not come near. In the fifth stanza she bids him leave the village, and visit her "poor dust" only when the plague is past. It is clear that this expansion of Wilson's idea greatly improves the poem. What was before merely decorative, a pleasant echo of other Scots dirges like "The Flowers of the Forest," has become real and painful because of Jenny's love and self-sacrifice.

The second song, the celebrated **"Hymn to the Plague,"** owes little to Wilson except its underlying idea, and even that has been deepened and stripped of its rather silly bravado. Puškin retains the iambic meter, but he avoids the rhyming couplets of Wilson, using a more varied scheme—*aabcbc*—with feminine rhymes in the third and fifth lines. . . . [Wilson's fifth stanza] opens with the words:

> To thee, O Plague! I pour my song,
> Since thou art come I wish thee long!

It is the plague that "strikes the lawyer 'mid his lies" and "the priest 'mid his hypocrisies," sets gold free from the miser, and the widow from her old dotard. Each verse has the refrain which probably suggested to Puškin the last two lines of his song:

> Then, leaning on this snow-white breast,
> I sing the praises of the Pest!
> If me thou would'st this night destroy,
> Come, smite me in the arms of Joy,

though Puškin has made his lines pathetic rather than defiant.

Puškin's poem has, for a start, formal beauties that were beyond Wilson. The first three of its six stanzas develop one idea—a comparison of the plague with winter; and as, at the onset of winter, men feast by the crackling fire, so should they do to celebrate the reign of that "dread empress, the Plague." . . . Then, in the last three stanzas, Puškin takes up the thought which is expressed in Wilson's refrain, and penetrates below all the hectic extravagance of the original to the underlying human truth, which Wilson had no more than hinted, if even that, to the "inexplicable delights" that a mortal heart finds in all things that are threatened with doom. Battle has its joy, the precipice, the storm at sea, and the desert whirlwind—and so has the plague. "Then—glory to thee, Plague!" It is hedonism, but altogether different from that in Wilson's last stanza. It is rather the willing acceptance of fate, "the truly tragic idea" that Belinskij admired. (pp. 42-4)

It remains to indicate briefly the high poetic quality of Puškin's translation. . . . [When] we compare any passage of Wilson's verse with Puškin's rendering, it becomes plain how greatly the language has been improved. Let us examine a few lines which occur after Louisa has fainted on seeing the dead cart go by. . . . Louisa, recovering, says:

> I saw a horrid demon in my dream!
> With sable visage and white-glaring eyes,
> He beckoned on me to ascend a cart
> Filled with dead bodies, muttering all the while
> An unknown language of most dreadful sounds.
> What matters it? I see it was a dream.
> —Pray, did the dead-cart pass?

It may be interesting to give here the literal translation of Puškin's words:

> A terrible demon appeared in dream to me:
> All black, white-eyed. . . . He called me into his cart.
> In it lay dead men—and they muttered a terrible
> Unknown speech. . . . Tell me: was this in my dream?
> Did the cart go by?

Perhaps the most striking thing here is the directness of Puškin's style. Wilson uses a pretentious vocabulary: "with sable visage," "he beckoned on me to ascend a cart." Puškin goes straight to the sense: he has no interest in "period" diction. So elsewhere we see "that jovial wassailer" becomes "the reveler". . . . Then we see that Puškin has misunderstood the subject of "muttering"—surely it was the demon and not the dead bodies! But only a poet would make such a mistake, and it puts new life into the description. Finally, he improves on

Wilson by making Louisa's uncertainty more hesitant: "Tell me: was this in my dream?"

Throughout, we observe that Puškin discards the many otiose adjectives in Wilson's verse. For example, "the dim dull yellow of that Scottish hair" becomes simply "the yellow." Again,

> Amid the churchyard darkness as I stood
> Beside a dire interment, circled round
> By the white ghastly faces of despair. . . .

is reduced to this: "amid the horror of a lamenting funeral, amid pale faces I pray in the churchyard." (pp. 44-6)

It may be said, then, that Puškin virtually recreated Wilson's scene by making numerous minor changes in phrasing and even in structure, by transforming the two songs, and by steeping the whole in the pure element of his style. The *Feast in Time of Plague* cannot be detached from the other "little tragedies." Here, perhaps, we may quote the words of Carlyle: "Wilson seems to me always by far the most *gifted* of our literary men either then or still. And yet intrinsically he has written nothing that can endure. The central gift was wanting." But this one fragment of Wilson's, from a work thrown off in his youth and then forgotten, will endure because Puškin, in whom the central gift was not wanting, could make up its deficiencies. (p. 46)

Henry Gifford, "Puškin's 'Feast in Time of Plague' and Its Original," The American Slavic and East European Review, *Vol. VIII, 1949, pp. 37-46.**

MARC SLONIM (essay date 1950)

[No convincing proof for Pushkin's poetic genius] can be offered in English, French, or German translations, for, with a few rare exceptions, they are rather disappointing and to non-Russians do not justify the reputation Pushkin enjoys in Russia. Hardly anything in these translations is striking or particularly beautiful, and the European or American reader has to take for granted that Pushkin was a marvelous poet. (p. 81)

To the general difficulties inherent in translating poetry, Pushkin adds some special ones. One of the main characteristics of his poetry is its perfect marriage of sound and meaning. Pushkin's poems do not merely follow Arnold's definition in presenting the best words in the best order. They endow the plainest, almost trivial words with poetic meaning. The simplicity and naturalness of Pushkin's lines turn into platitudes in translations, because the latter fail to convey their musical lucidity, their freshness and melodious quality. Pushkin had the magic power of extracting poetic resonance from colloquialisms, of instilling emotional intensity into the simplest sentences, of expressing profound thought in easy and concise statements. What is called the perfection of Pushkin's form is the complete coalescence of sound, rhythm, image, and meaning. Another aspect is Pushkin's clarity and directness of style, as well as his ability to obtain unobtrusive enduring effects—with economy, sober directness, and a sense of measure and balance; these do not exclude subtlety and a wide range of technical devices, which the poet—an astonishing master of versification—used with superb craftsmanship. He also had the gift of giving the same word—placing it in another context or qualifying it by varying the epithets or enhancing it by a diversified rhythmic and melodical movement—a solemn, an intimate, or a pensive value, according to the inner spirit of the individual poem. A poem by Pushkin in Russian creates the impression that what he says could never be said otherwise, that each word

fits perfectly, serving as a necessary part of a whole, and that no other words could ever assume a similar function. And still these words are, for the most part, the plain words we use in our daily talk.

With Pushkin the Russian modern literary style was born, which was undoubtedly a phenomenon of national importance. He liberated Russian literature from the heavy legacy of Church-Slavonic, as well as from the artificial mannerisms prevailing at the beginning of the nineteenth century. His was not the language of any particular class (although he knew how to employ the linguistic mannerisms of each social group and was fully aware of the differences between them) but that of contemporary Russia—alive, rich, expressive, blending popular colloquialisms with the achievements of literary evolution. The entire development of Russian letters in the eighteenth century and at the beginning of the nineteenth was in the direction of a fusion of folklore and literary tradition, but only Pushkin succeeded in accomplishing this task. (pp. 81-2)

The role played by Pushkin in this process explains the importance of one of his first (but not best) poems, *Russlan and Liudmila*. . . . Despite all its weaknesses, *Russlan and Liudmila* marked the beginning of a new way of writing—free, lively, and colloquial. At the same time by its opposition to the remnants of Classicism and its distinct avoidance of sentimentality or the Romantic 'poetry of horror,' it inaugurated a new literary and stylistic movement. (p. 83)

[Pushkin's lyrical, subjective poetry has] two distinct features that give it its inimitable character. First of all, these intensely emotional lines are never vague or misty. The imagery, the rhythm, and the melodious movement of each stanza are perfectly amalgamated with the actual idea, reflecting the activity of a lucid and penetrating mind. Whether they capture a fleeting mood, unfold an image, or express a thought, they are plastic, precise, unmistakably clear even in their conciseness, and all this without sacrificing the slightest nuance or relapsing into academic aloofness. Secondly, whatever the actual theme of these lyrics may be, even the most despairing ones, they are filled with potent vitality, with a sense of life that accepts reality and masters it. . . . [Even the] pensive lyrics never stress despair and are balanced by a positive attitude toward reality. But Pushkin's 'healthy optimism' is no mere acceptance of reality. He does not shut his eyes to the horrors and contradictions of life; he is extremely conscious of death, pain, injustice; and he does not attempt to hide anything or to play with illusions—but his attachment to the earth and his desire of experiencing everything, of living life fully in every way, give his poems intensity and power. . . . Pushkin also wrote a score of sensual and erotic poems in a pagan and Epicurean tone. But sensuality and eroticism are no more than a facet of his Apollonian genius. His delight in life embraces the subtle joys of the mind, the exaltation of spirituality, the simple pleasures of nature, as well as the raptures of the flesh and the voluptuousness of love. A coined phrase labels Pushkin's poetry as 'sunny,' and a bright and warm light as of midday does illumine his poems. However, such a definition is too constrained, for Pushkin also knew how to explore and present the nocturnal and ambiguous side of life. (p. 84)

Pushkin's poetry in its emphasis on the dignity of man is profoundly humanistic. It extols man—in all his aspects. Man, freedom, action, love, art, are for Pushkin the true values.

This supreme poet reveals himself as both human and humane, not only in his serious works but also in his light ones. Abhorring anything flat, stilted, and dull, he attacked pretentiousness, academic solemnity, and artificiality, in both life and literature. He wrote biting epigrams, which made him many enemies; blasphemous facetiae (such as his **'Gabrieliad,'** . . . in which the Virgin Mary is seduced by the Serpent, the Archangel Gabriel, and the Holy Ghost, all in one day), rather indecent but decidedly droll; erotic poems (such as **'Czar Nikita'** and **'Count Nulin'** . . . , the latter a version of *The Rape of Lucrece*). . . . These poems had a definite literary and psychological importance. They were weapons with which Pushkin fought against the rigidity of established forms and canons, demolishing the restrictions of Classicism and effecting a reunion of life and literature. This was one of his main aims— to bring art down to earth, to make poetry realistic, alive, capable equally of creating laughter or treating serious problems. . . .

It was with precisely [the intent] of bringing realism to art that Pushkin began his long novel in verse, *Eugene Oneghin*. . . . (p. 85)

Eugene Oneghin, like all of Pushkin's poems, has a diversity of elements, a peculiar structure: the narrative is interrupted by long lyrical passages devoted to the poet's personal feelings or memories; the author converses with the reader, discusses his own work, indulges in intimate confessions or jests, and, in general, creates an atmosphere of ease and intimacy. While the lyrical passages of the poem are subtle and suggestive, the pictures of Russian autumn and winter, the countryside, or Moscow society are among the highest achievements of Russian descriptive art. . . .

Begun as a mere fanciful imitation of the Romantic pattern, this light novel turned out to be a serious and realistic representation of Russian life, with social and psychological portraits of Pushkin's contemporaries which assumed the proportions of all-Russian types. (p. 86)

[Reading *Eugene Oneghin*, Pushkin's contemporaries] were most impressed by two things: that a simple plot taken from every-day life and deliberately devoid of exciting adventures could provide enough material for a long poem, and that the author's purpose had been fulfilled through the great variety of poetic devices, with such clarity, freshness, *brio*, humor, and feeling. (p. 88)

When Pushkin was twenty-two he wrote a few poems 'under the sign of Byron.' The influence of the English poet was, however, superficial and evanescent. Pushkin was too lucid, too fond of reason, logic, and reality, and far too fond of balance and measure in art to become a true disciple of the author of 'The Corsair' and 'Manfred.' Nevertheless Byron's influence, mitigated by these tendencies of Pushkin, is apparent in certain early poems, such as *The Caucasian Captive*. . . . And in *The Gypsies* . . . [a] Byronic hero, Aleko, while fleeing the 'thralldom of the stifling city,' joins a band of wandering gypsies and falls in love with Zemphira—a beautiful daughter of the 'prophetic tribe'—but fails in his attempts to lead a romantically free life. After Aleko kills Zemphira, who has betrayed him, and her lover, he is rejected by the chief of the gypsies. 'Leave us, proud man,' the old man tells him. 'You are not born for a free life; you look but for your own fancy, you are wicked and bold—whereas we are kind and peaceful; no need have we of bloodshed and groans.' This juxtaposition of the 'noble savage' to the forceful intellectual is far from the Byronic idealization of the 'dark hero.' The simplicity and kindness of the gypsies (somewhat in the Russian tradition) triumph over the evil sophistication of the city dweller.

In his fragmentary **'The Brigand Brothers'** . . . and the delightful **'Fountain of Bahchisarai'** . . . , which evokes a vision of Tartar khans and their harems and wives captured in battle, the Byronic influence has been assimilated to such an extent as to appear completely transformed. Despite the ardor and tempestuousness of his own temperament, Pushkin disliked exaggeration in art and carefully avoided the unbelievable or supernatural in his non-folkloristic poems. The protagonists of his most Romantic works are far from being mysterious or wild: they are simply disenchanted souls like the Caucasian captive whose aloofness from life is the result of precocious experiences that have seared his heart. Pushkin's attitude to this sort of hero changes rapidly: at first he treats him seriously (the Caucasian captive, or Aleko in *The Gypsies*), then, more critical of this representative of a prematurely aged generation, he makes him the target of satire and parody (Eugene Oneghin).

Pushkin's departure from the Romantic pattern marks his liberation from Byronic influence. By 1825, when he was fully aware of Byron's affectations and other faults, he reproaches the English poet for making each of his heroes merely the personification of some one trait of his own personality: one of his pride, a second of his scorn, a third of his melancholy— 'thus out of a sombre, energetic and full character Byron has created several insignificant ones.' (pp. 88-9)

Pushkin's chief debt to Romanticism was the idea of freedom. He wrote in the forms adopted by the school—the novel, the short story, historical chronicle, drama, light verse—and he evinced a certain interest in dramatic situations and in the clash of strong emotions. He utilized freely the Romantic blend of diverse elements—serious, comic, sublime, ironic—in the same work. He also voiced repeatedly that supreme longing for things beyond reality that is the essence of Romanticism, but he could never accept the Romantic lack of proportion and haphazard, whimsical, and fantastic way of writing. His style, therefore, scarcely touched by Romanticism, is pure, sober, classically perfect; its richness never lapses into luxuriance, its originality never becomes a prose. (pp. 89-90)

Pushkin was convinced that a true poet was a sounding board responsive to the voices of contemporary life. He wanted the poet to be actively interested in the ideas and events of his time. A series of his poems on political themes proves that he put this theory into practice. He was also of the opinion that a free, independent writer was bound to produce works of social and moral significance. In his justly proud poem **'A Monument I Reared'** [see excerpt above] . . . , he foretells his future fame and explains why his name will be cherished by the people, over all of great Russia: 'Because I awakened kind feeling with my lyre, because in my ruthless age I glorified freedom and called for mercy for the vanquished.' These lines are no mere generalities. Pushkin had a definite political stand and he was the poet of freedom. . . . Throughout his life Pushkin remained a Westernizer and a liberal. He belonged to the progressive tradition of the educated nobility, which owed its beginnings to Peter the Great, and he therefore attached prime importance to the reforms initiated by the Great Czar. (pp. 91-2)

Pushkin condones the oppression and violence Peter had used in order to lead Russia toward the West, and he hails his will power indomitable energy, and grandiose vision. . . . Pushkin was the first Russian poet who consciously accepted the Empire and the St. Petersburg period of Russian history. And he was also the first rhapsodist of the new capital, of that beautiful and fantastic metropolis. . . . (p. 92)

Pushkin knew the price the common man had to pay for the splendor of this artificial and proud capital. It was a price paid by the Russian people for the consolidation and expansion of the Empire, for its military conquests, and for its glorious position among other nations. He was fully aware of the fundamental conflict between the fate of an individual and the destiny of the State: the individual longings for peace and happiness were crushed by the merciless progress of the nation. This tragic and universal paradox is the theme of *The Bronze Horseman,* which, in my opinion, is the most beautiful and haunting of Pushkin's poems, written in vigorous, sweeping, and supple verse. (p. 93)

The prologue of the poem is a miniature epic of the city's creation. The narrative shifts to a later day and describes the flood of 1824—hostile nature in elemental revolt against the works of man. During the flood the hero of the poem, Eugene, a minor official, loses all his dreams of happiness—his betrothed, his home, and all his belongings. Overwhelmed by the horror of the catastrophe, his mind becomes unhinged. In a fit of frenzy he threatens Peter, the Bronze Horseman, the cause of all his ills, the cruel builder of this unreal city that defies God and nature. The Bronze Horseman and horse leap down from the pedestal and pursue the offender through the empty streets of a silent city. Wherever Eugene turns he hears at his heels hoofs thundering over the reverberating pavement.

The symbolism of the poem is all too obvious. The Bronze Horseman 'on the height, at the very edge of the abyss, with his bridle of iron, has made Russia rear'—and none can tell which way he will go. In his flight over cliffs and precipices many lives will inevitably be sacrificed. But the acceptance, and even the justification, of this historic necessity does not prevent Pushkin from feeling sympathy and compassion for the victims. The Eugene of this poem is portrayed as a lonely 'little man' whose misfortune, misery, and madness affect us deeply. The lot of the 'little man' was to become one of the main themes of Russian literature, from Gogol (directly influenced by Pushkin) and Dostoevsky to Chekhov and the Soviet writers.

One of the most striking features of *The Bronze Horseman* is the portrayal of Eugene's madness, which is so vivid that the grim pursuit of the minor official by an equestrian statue becomes a reality. In this romantic fusion of realism and fantasy, devoid of exaggeration, Pushkin is again a forerunner of Gogol and Dostoevsky. The delirium of his hero is depicted by Pushkin in a simple, succinct, matter-of-fact manner.

He used the same device in his prose. His short stories, told in an efficient, brisk style free of adornment or grandiloquence (they are on a par with those of Mérimée and Stendhal), often treat romantic or fantastic situations in a soberly rational way (*The Coffin-Maker* has a ghastly nightmare after a celebration, the *Queen of Spades* brings about the ruin of Hermann, a gambler with *Übermensch* notions, and so on). The economy of artistic devices and the directness of the style make alive and concrete the episodes and characters in Pushkin's short stories and novelettes. They were the most important phenomenon in Russian prose since Karamzin, but they are far removed from the affected sentimentality and artificiality of the author of *Poor Liza.* Here again he is a pioneer, leaving the posterity perfect specimens of the short story (*The Shot, The Blizzard*), the novelette (*The Queen of Spades*), and the short historical novel (*The Captain's Daughter*). (pp. 93-4)

In *Boris Godunov,* that romantic tragedy in which the Byronic influence is definitely supplanted by the Shakespearean, the reader is engrossed not only by the masterful characterization, the swiftly moving plot, and the suspense, but also by the vision of the hidden springs of Russian history and by the interpretation of the national psychology. The true hero of the tragedy is the people, but they are silent when the boyars, after their murders and uprisings, announce their new Czar—none other than Dimitri, the mock pretender. It is a silence pregnant with symbolic significance: sooner or later the people will make themselves heard—at first clamorously, as during the Pugachev rebellion, but the day will inevitably come when it will be in an articulate voice. Pushkin dreamt of education through freedom and tolerance, enabling the Russian people to take the place that was rightly theirs. He well knew the merits and deficiencies of the Russian national character; he nurtured no illusions, admitting that a Russian revolt was always senseless and cruel, but at the same time he could not help but feel and think as a typical representative of Russia. (pp. 94-5)

Pushkin's national awareness, his feeling for Russia as a unit, did not affect his fundamental liberalism. He suffered from political oppression and exposed the evils of the autocratic regime. What was more, he never lapsed into chauvinism, and combined his national pride and patriotism with a strong leaning towards Western Europe. This combination formed one of the many complexities of the Pushkin phenomenon in Russian culture. His self-assertion as a Russian was coincident with his acceptance and assimilation of the Western legacy. (p. 95)

'I love Europe with all my heart,' said Pushkin, and he displayed his love and his intuitive understanding of Europe in his poems and dramatic pieces, which involve Scotland (*A Feast during the Plague*), Spain (*The Stone Guest,* dealing with Don Juan), Italy (*Angelo* and numerous lyrics), the Balkans (*Songs of the Western Slavs*), and which range in time from the Middle Ages (*The Covetous Knight*) to the eighteenth century (*Mozart and Salieri*) and Pushkin's own day (his lyrical poems). In his translations or 'imitations' he rendered the spirit of various periods and countries in the most striking fashion. He so absorbed the spirit of various forms of European civilization that he was right in proclaiming himself as much a Westerner as a Russian. He was at once a national and a European writer without ever being inconsistent, for in this, as in so many other things, Pushkin presented a oneness, an organic unity seldom found among great poets. According to Dostoevsky [see excerpt above], his universality was not only the main feature of Pushkin's work and mentality, but it made him the most typical representative of the Russian spirit in so far as the latter always tends to transform the national into the universal.

Whatever this universality may be, one fact remains certain: Pushkin's work, for all its unmistakably national flavor, is part and parcel of world literature. It was Pushkin who won for Russian letters a place in European art, and this came about at the very moment Russian literature acquired, also through Pushkin, an awareness of its national peculiarities and asserted its formal and spiritual individuality. The whole importance of Pushkin's role is contained in this statement. The curious part of it is that Pushkin himself was conscious of what he was doing and had set precise objectives for himself and for his fellow writers. Despite all the romantic aura about his conception of the poet as the beloved child of the Muses and the inspired disciple of the gods, Pushkin acted as a man of great intellectual power and understanding. (pp. 96-7)

Pushkin was one of the few great writers who won true fame during their lives. His contemporaries acclaimed his genius.

The 'School' of Pushkin included practically all the poets of his period, and even such original writers as Lermontov could not entirely escape his influence. The national significance of Pushkin's work, however, became fully apparent only after his death, when the growth of his popularity assumed extraordinary proportions; he became the symbol of national and artistic perfection. 'He is an astounding and perhaps a unique phenomenon of the Russian spirit,' proclaimed Gogol, 'He embodies what the Russian may become two hundred years hence.'

The founder of the modern Russian literary language, who fulfilled the hopes of the past and opened the roads for further development, Pushkin appealed equally to realists like Nekrassov, to idealistic esthetes like Fet, to the symbolists of the 'nineties like Bruissov, or to the Soviet poets who still strive to imitate his clarity, directness, and simplicity and willingly employ his metric forms. Although anti-Pushkin revolts took place in the 'sixties and in 1920, it is safe to say that all Russian poetry of the last hundred years advanced under the aegis of Pushkin and can never shed his spell. He determined its development, established its standards, formulated its idiom, and even shaped its main forms.

His influence upon Russian prose was no less profound. He laid the foundations of Russian realism in the short story, in the novel, in the historical narrative, and in the drama, not counting his contributions to the essay and literary criticism. Gogol considered himself his disciple; Dostoevsky worshiped him with a kind of superstitious awe; Leo Tolstoy advised young writers to take Pushkin's short stories as models and spoke of their lasting and beneficial effect on his own prose; Chekhov and Gorky placed Pushkin above all other Russian writers—even as Soviet poets and novelists do today. (pp. 106-07)

> Marc Slonim, "Pushkin," *in his* The Epic of Russian Literature from Its Origins through Tolstoy *(copyright 1950 by Oxford University Press, Inc.; renewed 1977 by Tatiana Slonim; reprinted by permission of the publisher), Oxford University Press, New York, 1950, pp. 81-107.*

TATIANA A. WOLFF (essay date 1952)

[Pushkin's] use of dramatic scenes to mark the significant moments of the action in the *Gypsies,* the breaking of the romantic framework of *Poltava* in order to include national epic material, an interest in the part played by the crowd in history, particularly when in conflict with its rulers, were all pointers in the direction of *Boris Godunov.* Pushkin turned to drama to express his conception of tragedy; to the intensity and directness which it alone could provide in dealing with the conflict of man with man, of the individual with the crowd, and of that within a man's own soul. And in turning to drama he turned to Shakespeare. (p. 94)

Boris Godunov deals with the problem of usurpation and civil war, a problem as relevant to Pushkin's contemporaries as to Shakespeare's. Pushkin lived in a Europe of revolution and dynastic change. At the very time of writing, the radical elements of the Russian aristocracy were preparing their final plans for the December rising, the aim of which was to force the new Tsar to grant a constitution. The historical period chosen by Pushkin for his tragedy also resembles that of Shakespeare's history plays. Boris's accession to the throne, following the murder of the rightful heir in the preceding reign, was the prelude to a series of usurpations, known as the 'Time of Troubles', which bridged the gap between the dynasties of Rurik and Romanov; events which can be compared to the murders, usurpations and wars of the Houses of York and Lancaster. (pp. 94-5)

The tragedy does not trace Boris's rise to power, but shows him in the first scene on the brink of realizing his high ambitions. Having cleared the way to the throne Boris proclaims that he has decided to renounce the world, and he then retires to a monastery. The people of Moscow, led by the Patriarch and clergy, flock to him to beg him to accept the crown. . . . Finally Boris yields to the prayers of the Church and the cries of the people, and in a speech filled with humility prays that he may prove worthy of the task he accepts.

This episode provides a good example of Pushkin's use of Shakespearian material. The situation on the surface is almost exactly parallel to Richard III's devotions, which start at precisely the same moment as the Lord Mayor and Buckingham begin to exhort the people of London to cry "Long live King Richard!". There is the same false humility, the same sudden decision to forsake the world, followed by a gradual compliance with the wish of the populace. Fundamentally, however, the attitude of the two kings to religious observances is completely different. They both use them as a mask for their true intentions, but whereas Richard throws the prayer-book over his shoulder when it has served its purpose, Boris, having a religious and even superstitious nature, continues to seek in the Church comfort for his troubled spirit.

Once Boris is enthroned the play moves quickly forward in time, to the moment when external circumstances will reawaken his guilty conscience; for Boris, like Richard, has ascended the throne over the body of a murdered child. That fact seals his fate: that poison in his soul brings him to his downfall. Six years have passed. A Pretender appears and incarnates the secret fears that have long been tormenting Boris. His spirit is exhausted, and he cannot summon the energy and courage needed to meet the situation. (p. 95)

Pushkin shows [Boris] weakened and despairing, supporting with difficulty the burden of kingship. This was an aspect of kingship Shakespeare often stressed—the human frailty beneath the robes of state, with its consciousness of responsibility, its ever-present fear of treachery. Boris had feigned at first this desire to retreat from the world and from rule, but it is with deep conviction that he now exclaims

> How heavy art thou, crown of Monomakh!
>
> (pp. 95-6)

It is in the comic scenes of *Boris Godunov* that the other Shakespearian parallels are to be found. They do not form a subplot but are directly connected with the main action. Here in a frontier inn are found Russian counterparts to Falstaff's companions, mendicants, drinking down all they collect in alms for their monastery, whose speech varies from proverbial jingles to pious Old Slavonic as the occasion demands. The situation they are involved in is delightful, and, although it has no direct parallel in Shakespeare, is written in the Shakespearian comic manner. In this scene Pushkin, having caught the spirit of Shakespeare's humour, has adapted it to a Russian setting with complete success. (p. 97)

The other comic relief is provided by the foreign mercenaries recruited by the Pretender in Poland. They include a Frenchman and a German, who mix their native tongues with their inadequate Russian, and engage in vituperation very similar to that of their prototypes, the Captains Fluellen, Gower, Macmorris and Jamy.

Finally, an important part is played in the tragedy by the crowd, the common people: at times easily swayed from anger to pity, as is the Roman mob in *Julius Caesar,* or silent and obstinate, as in *Richard III;* ignorant, as in *Coriolanus,* or humorous, as its representatives in *Henry IV* and *Henry V.* It symbolizes the shifting foundations on which autocracy rests. In the first draft, the play ended with the crowd, typically compliant, shouting "Long live Tsar Dmitri!" But Pushkin changed this ending and gave it a deeper significance. In the play as it now stands, at the proclamation "Long live Tsar Dmitri!", "The People are silent". This silence is an ominous portent of the fate which awaits the Pretender, a fate similar to that which has struck down the House of Godunov. It is the result of the crowd's horror at the fresh crimes perpetrated in the name of lawful succession.

Unlike most of Shakespeare's plays, *Boris Godunov* closes on a hopeless note. There is no harmony or order at the end; the tragedy has not been an expiation which leads to peace. Instead of the trumpets of the victors, the last sounds are the cries of Boris's family as the Tsarevich is slain: a new usurper has replaced the old, and once more he has reached his throne over the body of a murdered child. (pp. 97-8)

In style and structure, *Boris Godunov* also owes much to Shakespeare: in the use of blank verse, in the mingling of verse and prose, with prose used chiefly in the comic scenes and blank verse in the tragic, often with rhymed endings for closing emphasis; in the long period of time the play covers; and in the constant change of scene from court to monastery, from patriarch's palace to frontier tavern, and from public square to battlefield, with corresponding transitions of mood from tragedy to comedy, and from calmness and serenity to storm and anguish. (p. 98)

Boris Godunov was not the only play Pushkin wrote under the impetus of his admiration for Shakespeare; but it was his only attempt to write a tragedy in the purely Shakespearian manner. In the *Little Tragedies* Shakespeare's influence is felt in the spirit of the whole, in single phrases or incidents, or in the development of character. In them Pushkin at times reaches Shakespearian heights, and transmutes his material with Shakespearian fire. . . .

In *Boris Godunov* Pushkin was concerned with the interaction of the people's fate with that of single personalities; in the *Little Tragedies,* or *Dramatic Scenes* as they were called after those of Barry Cornwall to which they owed their form, Pushkin is concerned only with the fate of individuals. Whereas in *Boris Godunov* he had aimed at breadth in his development of character, in these plays he aimed at depth; where previously he had concentrated largely on unique historical figures, he now concentrated on universal types, consumed by some over-riding passion.

The Covetous Knight, the first of these plays, has for its theme the passion for wealth. . . . To understand Pushkin's intention in this play one should read it in the light of his criticism of *The Merchant of Venice,* in which he contrasts the dramatic methods of Shakespeare and Molière. Molière when creating a miser was conscious only of his miserliness, and presented him as a man whose one abiding and all-embracing passion was gold. Shakespeare, on the other hand, in Shylock showed a man compact of many passions, of vindictiveness, pride and avarice.

Pushkin, following Shakespeare's example, saw his covetous knight as a complex character, whose love of gold is complementary to his love of power, the power which that gold bestows. He desires not so much the tangible products of wealth, but the knowledge that the power to obtain such possession lies in his cellars. He worships gold because it raises him above his fellow-men and allows him to contemplate the vast estates and palaces that could be his. So Shylock seeks wealth because it is the one thing which gives him self-confidence against the hate and the disdain of the Venetians. Further, in *The Covetous Knight* the type of miserly Jew is separated from the character of the avaricious knight; and the cringing shiftiness of the one is opposed to the cruel yet magnificent vision of the other. Written in blank verse more mature and flexible than that of *Boris Godunov,* the play in its short span rises to great intensity of feeling. (p. 101)

The last work which Pushkin wrote under Shakespeare's influence, and the last in which he used dramatic form, was his part translation, part adaptation of *Measure for Measure.* . . . He had started with the intention of simply translating *Measure for Measure,* but that proved cramping to his creative powers, and so he decided to change the whole into a narrative poem with a few dramatic scenes. For this he freely translated the five scenes which lie at the core of the play and relate directly to the conflict that divides the soul of Angelo, and to the ordeal that tests Isabella's chastity. . . .

Concentrating on the psychological problem of Angelo's dualism, Pushkin discarded all extraneous elements. He linked together the dramatic centres he translated with narrative verse, in which he epitomized all the rest of the action that was relevant to his theme. When actually translating he kept fairly close to the original, although throughout he shows a tendency to condense. He followed the main plot closely, with only a few slight alterations, such as changing the scene to Italy, making the Duke older, and Mariana the deserted wife of Angelo. The poem is interesting as an example of Pushkin's use of Shakespearian material for his creative needs, but it lacks the strength and originality of the *Little Tragedies;* and shows that Pushkin was nearer realizing the spirit and power of Shakespearian composition when he was creating independently than when translating, however freely, and constrained by an original. (p. 102)

The theatre which Pushkin wished to reform was both well ahead of, and far behind, that in which Shakespeare worked and for which he wrote. The technical possibilities were infinitely wider and more elaborate; the stage could be adapted to every kind of pageant, spectacle and dance, with fountains, horses and flamboyant scenery. But this varied apparatus was cumbrous, and it broke down when a play like *Boris Godunov,* in which there were endless changes of scene, required staging. The result was that the play was immediately declared unsuitable for the stage, on the grounds that the scene-shifters would be exhausted by having to move so many sets, and a myth arose, that proved as tenacious as it was unjustified, that *Boris Godunov* was unactable—all this being quite apart from the censorship difficulties [the play encountered]. (pp. 102-03)

Shakespeare was a man of the theatre at a time when it was at the height of achievement and vitality. He was well versed in all the technical details that go to make a successful play, and was fully acquainted with the demands of his critical public. His aim was to expand, transcend and deepen, but not to reform. Pushkin was the leader of a band of reformers, wishing to replace the existing form of drama with one they considered more suitable and compact of great possibilities; and it was a very uphill fight against tradition, prejudice and conservatism.

In his adaptation of Shakespearian drama to the Russian stage Pushkin at one point found himself under the influence of two contradictory tendencies. He lived in the age of Scott and consequently wanted to combine with the Shakespearian drama of universal humanity the romantic drama of historical reality. But he realized that excessive historical realism was limiting to great tragedy, binding it by a fear of anachronism and a too great concentration on insignificant detail. Speaking of the *Little Tragedies* Dostoevsky said that Pushkin was more universal than Shakespeare because he could create characters true to whichever country or period he chose, whereas Shakespeare's Romans and Italians always remained Englishmen [see excerpt above]. Dostoevsky is here judging Shakespeare's art by the standards of nineteenth-century realism; not understanding that, just as in his own novels time and place are irrelevant to the central core of the action and thought, so in Shakespeare's plays a more complete universality is achieved by his comparative indifference to historical detail. (p. 103)

Most of his contemporaries were carried away by one or other of the great literary influences of the time; Pushkin assimilated them all and yet throughout remained original, and true to his own genius. Byron, Shakespeare and Scott each contributed to his literary development. He learned from them himself, he encouraged others to learn from them; but he showed his contemporaries by his example that to learn is not to imitate but to assimilate, to mould, to select and to adapt. He never lost his critical faculty in a welter of enthusiasm. His exclamation that Byron and Scott were "food for the soul" and "Read Shakespeare, that is my refrain!" were expressions not of empty adulation but of a great intellectual vitality, which enabled him to imbue himself with the spirit of one writer after another, take all he could from each, and then return to his own writing enriched by new experience, and with a widened literary horizon. (p. 104)

> *Tatiana A. Wolff, "Shakespeare's Influence on Pushkin's Dramatic Work," in* Shakespeare Survey: An Annual Survey of Shakespearian Study & Production, Vol. 5, *edited by Allardyce Nicoll, Cambridge at the University Press, 1952, pp. 93-105.**

WACŁAW LEDNICKI (essay date 1955)

The theme "I love thee, Peter's creation" almost entirely fills the Introduction [to *The Bronze Horseman*], which is developed in the style of the panegyric ode. From this point of view *The Bronze Horseman* concludes a whole series of panegyric poems started by poets of the times of Elizabeth and Catherine which glorified both the city of Peter and the reforms of the great Emperor. Such was the first reaction of Russian literature to that new event which occurred in the life of the Empire. (p. 43)

[There is in St. Petersburg] the pathos of space. There is also the tranquillity of an achieved victory. A hundred thousand victims were necessary for its construction; swamp and river had to be overcome. . . . Hence Antsiferov, an expert and apologist of Petersburg, correctly named it a city of struggle and victory. But it was also a visible symbol of growing imperialism. It rose on foreign land, and, having established itself there, it seeks to defend the fatherland of which it became the intentional capital, a capital created *ad hoc;* its purpose is to threaten the enemy, further and further expanding the boundaries of the imperialism it represents. It is the city-symbol of

triumphant imperialism. Such is the essential content of the Introduction of Pushkin's poem. It synthesizes the panegyrics of the poet's predecessors. (pp. 43-4)

[The whole group of poets who had previously written about St. Petersburg] glorified the reforms of Peter the Great and his capital, hardly touching on the tragic split which these reforms caused in Russian civilization. They made light of the obstacles which lay on Russia's path to Europeanization, naïvely believing in the possibility of leaping the barrier erected by the centuries of Russia's entirely isolated historical life. This naïve faith was justified by the fact that this whole group of poets represented the enthusiasm of collaborators and followers of Peter, people who themselves were pioneers of the Europeanization of Russia in the realm of humanistic culture. There was no room for doubt and fear in the hearts of these men who were absorbed in the promulgation of these reforms. (p. 46)

Although born in Moscow, Pushkin did not like the old capital: he was a child of Petersburg. Probably his life would have been quite different and certainly happier if, after his marriage, he had remained in Moscow instead of settling in Tsarskoe Selo and then in Petersburg. His private letters contain many derogatory remarks about Moscow, but at times Pushkin was aware of his duty as a great national poet to the historical capital of Russia. So, in several stanzas of the ninth chapter of *Eugene Onegin,* he paid his tribute to Moscow and to its glorious role in 1812. (p. 47)

[This] theme of the juxtaposition of Moscow and Petersburg has not disappeared from the pages of Russian literature. The two classic formulations of this juxtaposition are those of Gogol, in his "Petersburg Notes of 1836," and of Herzen, in his "Moscow and Petersburg". . . . The juxtaposition of Moscow and Petersburg becomes almost a permanent theme in Tolstoy's great novels, and Dostoevsky will insist that Petersburg is "the most theoretical and intentional city in the world."

The Introduction of Pushkin's poem, I repeat once again, is a brilliant synthesis of an optimistic conception of Petersburg—the capital of triumphant imperialism. *The Bronze Horseman,* however, does not end with the Introduction. After it comes the tragic tale of the flood and of the misfortune of Eugene, his protest and his ruin. The poet shows us Petersburg inundated by a terrible flood, under an overcast sky full of whirling clouds pregnant with storm. It is a Petersburg lashed by wind and rain—grim, sullen, tragic. One of the variants of the Introduction contains a statement of this shifting image of the capital which by contrast stands out against the background of the optimistic eulogy in the opening lines of the poem:

> It was a fearful time . . .
> I will tell of it, friends,
> And let my words be
> An eternal tale of specters
> And not a legend of ill-omened years.
>
> (p. 48)

There are several such gloomy images of Petersburg in Pushkin's works. Here is how he describes the "romantic castle of the Maltese knight," "a crowned knave," in his **"Ode to Freedom"** . . . :

> When on the gloomy Neva
> The stars of midnight twinkle,
> And quiet sleep
> Descends on the unconcerned head,

A pensive bard looks
Upon the tyrant's deserted monument,
Sleeping menacingly midst the fog,
And upon the palace abandoned to oblivion.

(pp. 48-9)

There are other such depictions. In *The Negro of Peter the Great* he speaks of the founding of the city, of the first victories of human will over the opposing elements. In *Eugene Onegin* he stresses a genre picture of an early Petersburg morning; he paints with the delicacy of a watercolor the elegance of a Petersburg ball. In *The Little House in Kolomna* he reproduces the boredom of the capital's sleepy suburbs. (p. 49)

The true poem of Petersburg, however, is *The Bronze Horseman.* Here the Petersburg theme is clearly developed, even though in a dualistic manner.

The Introduction indeed synthesizes the panegyric works of the eighteenth century (as well as the poetic formulations of Batyushkov, Prince Vyazemsky, and Shevyrev). . . . On the other hand, however, *The Bronze Horseman* discloses the tragic secret of the existence of the Northern capital, and, moreover, it conceals in itself, as it were, a prophecy of its future fate.

In the Introduction, Peter is shown to us in the shape of a god against the background of chaos. He is the embodiment of a tragic, superhuman will of fate, of the law of history. The poet calls him a "master of destiny." Petersburg is the magical, miraculous result of this will. And this will remains alive in the city. In the poem, Peter's statue is conceived on a mythological plane. This terrible deity protects his city and subdues the elements. Proudly he opposes the incursions of the Neva's billows; he endures in his haughty attitude, set upon an unattainable summit. Effortlessly he triumphs over the rebellious elements. On the day after the flood the dawn reddens the "quiet capital" and the great devastation caused by the flood is bathed in purple. The old order is restored, optimistic faith triumphs henceforth: the future of the city is secure under the guardianship of the bronze giant. (pp. 49-50)

[Antisferov wrote that Pushkin was the last bard of the "bright side of St. Petersburg."] But was not Pushkin at the same time the first singer of the gloomy, sullen, and tragic side of Petersburg? For not everything in *The Bronze Horseman* is encouraging and exalting. Its optimistic tone is disturbed by the story of Eugene. The pitiable end of the "poor" hero's dreams of happiness and the equally pitiable end of his life are silent negations of the very right to optimism. And precisely the contrast between Peter and Eugene, that is, between the rights and interests of the capital and the Empire on the one hand and the personal rights and interests of the anonymous individual on the other, acquires a great significance here. The greater the contrast and the smaller the victim of the "miracle-creator," the more eloquent becomes the negation of the right to optimism, the more pathetic the entire poem. And here I wish to direct attention to a profoundly arresting episode at the end of *The Bronze Horseman* in which the proud and threatening "master of destiny," the bronze giant, leaves his elevated site. What compels him to do this? The protest of an infinitesimally small man, the trampled victim of Peter's *raison d'état,* who, having lost all of his tiny lot of human happiness, raises a protest in the name of *his* own *raison d'état.* This little man went mad from sorrow and threatened the "thaumaturgic" malefactor. And at that moment the malefactor set out in pursuit. He set out in pursuit because the little man himself was frightened of his threat and began to flee. How tragically roars

and thunders this gallop of the giant as he rushes at night on a bronze horse across the stone pavements of the empty Petersburg streets after the fleeing, physically and morally tattered, "poor" Eugene! He was not stirred from his stance by unbridled natural elements, nor by the threat of God's anger and punishment. On the contrary, he was moved by the voice of a weak man, the protest of a human heart tormented to the point of madness. And after this fleeing, beating heart galloped the Tsar. . . . The fact that this gallop of the threatening Tsar is only a hallucination of Eguene's mind seized by madness does not weaken the impressiveness and the symbolic meaning of this fantastic chase. (pp. 51-2)

Soon, however, order reigned also in this realm. Eugene perished and was buried; Peter once again stood on his lofty crag. Nevertheless, a crack is made in the smooth surface of panegyrism. The poet enabled us to look behind the brilliant façade of the "Northern Palmyra" and to perceive there elements of a tragic disorder. In this way the poem offers a dualistically conceived Petersburg, and, thus, it marks a transition in the history of this theme in Russian belles-lettres.

It is worth our while to dwell on still another feature in Pushkin's stylization of this theme: its fantastical coloring. It is significant that Pushkin in general was inclined to localize fantastical elements within the frames of a Petersburg landscape. We find such examples in *The Queen of Spades,* in the story *The Little House on Vasilievsky Island*—written by V. P. Titov as he heard it from Pushkin,—and, finally, in *The Bronze Horseman.* The specific climatic conditions of Petersburg, the particular suggestiveness of its white nights, the abundance of water in the immense river and in the numerous canals which intersect the city, and, finally, the very foundation of the capital on the perilous quagmire which had sucked in countless sacrifices of labor and human lives, creating in this way a tragedy in the gaping subsoil—all this made up a special atmosphere suitable for the development of all kinds of fantastic legends or tales. (p. 52)

For a long time literature did not at all react to this aspect of the city. Pushkin was the first to feel and show this fantastical aspect of Petersburg, just as the English impressionists first put London fogs on painters' canvases. In this respect, therefore, *The Bronze Horseman* was a poem of revelation. True, Gogol's Petersburg stories were written almost at the same time, and some of them were published before *The Bronze Horseman.* . . . *The Overcoat,* written in 1839 and published in 1842, shows an obvious dependence on *The Bronze Horseman.* We may say, then, that Gogol, from the chronological point of view, shares with Pushkin the credit for that fantastical stylization of Petersburg.

And indeed, precisely in this critical period literary works begin to appear which bring a somewhat decadent perception of Petersburg. This is the dualistic Petersburg of Gogol, uniting "oppressive prose" with "charming fantasy," "fantastic banality" with "deceitful illusiveness." This is the Petersburg in which instead of the "Bronze Horseman" there appears a mysterious "stranger" representing the eternal feminine element of Russia and of its capital. This approach to Petersburg denies any kind of Petersburg Messianism so typical for Pushkin. This is the "Miasma" of Polonsky, a poem containing a threat of the terrible revenge of the victims whose body and blood became the foundation of the capital. (pp. 52-3)

The threat of elements which will devastate this new Sodom and Gomorrah appears in the *Russian Nights* of Prince V. F.

Odoevsky. The poetry of Lermontov severely judges Petersburg, giving at the same time a marvelous sketch of the romantic landscape of Petersburg and a subtle feeling for the unusual sinfulness of this city. The apocalyptical poems of Pecherin proclaimed the final damnation of the capital. M. Dmitriev develops the theme of the tragic end of the "underwater city." Nekrasov writes about the "physiology" of Petersburg. Finally came Garshin and Korolenko, and Dostoevsky with his weird fantasticalness, with his obsession for the Petersburg landscape, with his visions of Petersburg's decay and annihilation. (p. 53)

There is no doubt that it was *The Bronze Horseman* which from the beginning was the point of departure for all [the subsequent] poetry and literature connected with Petersburg. This literature of the second half of the nineteenth century predominantly contains motifs of antipathy, criticism, shame, skepticism, and, ultimately, fear of the capital, a capital opposed by almost the entire Russian society of the epoch of decadence and decline. Strange then was the fate of "poor" Eugene's protest. This protest, taken up by successive generations of the Russian intellectual elite, or, as they are called today, "clerks," was transformed finally into something so great and powerful that the "bronze giant" was no longer able to cope with it. He had lost his mythological significance, and, along with it, his creative strength was exhausted.

How does it happen, however, that Pushkin, who was the last of the Russian poets to glorify the triumph of Petersburg, was at the same time the first who felt its tragic side? Do we owe this to his particular historical and artistic intuition? Much is to be said in favor of this belief, but this was not the only factor, essential though it may have been. First, the birth of this tragic perception of Petersburg was accompanied by the beginning of the actual decline of this city. . . . The mournful episode of Radishchev might be considered a preamble to the Decembrist Insurrection of 1825. And in between occurred the Napoleonic Wars, which also diminished the prestige of Petersburg: the victory over Napoleon was engraved in the imaginations of the Russian people as a national, not an autocratic, deed, and Moscow became the symbol of this deed. So, to use Antsiferov's formula, "the God of history abandoned Petersburg." (pp. 54-5)

Secondly, one ought to take into account the influence of foreign literature. In this realm Mickiewicz played the decisive role. He was the first [in his poem *Digression*] to oppose so distinctly, so manifestly, the cult of Petersburg. He criticized this cult and showed Pushkin the picture of a satirized capital, disclosing the sinful elements in the history of the "Northern Babylon." In the crystal of Mickiewicz's poetry the "eternal gate" was transformed into the "gate of tears." Mickiewicz developed this conception of Petersburg as a city which revealed the wretchedness of Russian civilization and at the same time its tragedy. His Petersburg was, furthermore, a symbol of militarism, exploitation, slavery, parasitism, and debasement. Finally, Mickiewicz made an apocalyptic prophecy of the fall of the "Assyrian throne" and the devastation of the "city of Babylon." (pp. 55-6)

[There] can be no doubt that—in some degree under the influence of Mickiewicz—Pushkin did not confine himself in his poem to songs of triumph and laudation, but also presented a picture of Petersburg as a capital of tragic imperialism. And therefore, *mutatis mutandis*, Mickiewicz's vision of Petersburg as an ingredient in the poetic content of *The Bronze Horseman* became in the final analysis a factor destroying the integrity

of the "Northern Palmyra" in Russian poetry and literature. Mickiewicz's *Digression* penetrated Pushkin's poem like a kind of Trojan Horse, and it disaggregated the triumphant essence of this poem, which was intended to be a citadel of Russian national poetry. Pushkin himself was, perhaps, not aware of the secret effects of this invasion when he opened the gates of his poem to Mickiewicz's gifts. (p. 56)

> *Wacław Lednicki, in his* Pushkin's 'Bronze Horseman': The Story of a Masterpiece *(reprinted by permission of the University of California Press), University of California Press, 1955, 163 p.*

J. THOMAS SHAW (essay date 1958)

[*The Letters of Alexander Pushkin*] are in a real sense literary creations, in that, like everything he wrote, they reflect his artistic conscience and were composed often with rough drafts and variants, like his creative works. (p. 40)

About three-fourths of the letters are written in Russian, and the remainder are in French, the language of polite society and the court. . . . Pushkin's French is the slightly formal conventional language of the French-speaking Russian aristocracy. He was at home in these conventions, and he uses them with charm, flexibility, and power, and with a breadth of range and effects. But the intimate, homely, familiar letters are all in Russian, and Russian was the language of his personal correspondence on matters of life and literature. His French possesses a slightly old-fashioned charm, the reflection of a society that is no more. His Russian is still fresh and immediate.

Pushkin's correspondence falls into two main categories, with an appropriate style and form for each. One group is composed of the official letters, addressed to governmental functionaries, including two tsars. (p. 41)

The official letters are correct, formal, and impersonal in tone, following the official amenities, but noteworthy in their brevity, severity in form, and lack of flattery, fulsomeness, or subservience. In Pushkin's personal crises, their conciseness verges upon dryness. He often takes full advantage of the conventional formal opening and complimentary close to cover up his actual feelings. (pp. 41-2)

[Pushkin's] real quality is shown in the personal and personal-literary correspondence. The personal letters are like the lyrics in their saturation, their succinctness, and the immediacy of their presentation of thought and feeling. Though his letters are never lyrical—Pushkin's prose, epistolary or otherwise, is never "poetic"—they may be compared with the lyrics in their revelation of his thought, feeling, and development. And he often permits them to reflect much more of the momentary, the individual, and the private than the poetry and prose fiction.

The letters have a broad variety in style and expressiveness. They range from the burning, mad passion of the love letters to Mme. Kern, to the coldly insulting hatred of those to Heeckeren; from warm, friendly banter to scintillating brilliance; from colloquial everyday prose to gravely respectful or even severe utterance; from "spleen," or melancholy, to rapture; from blunt pain-spokenness to formal correctness; from direct statement to wit, humor, and parody. Pushkin thought that the "first task of a man of intelligence is to know whom he is dealing with": the intellectual, social, and literary level and tastes of his correspondents and also his own relationships with them are implicit, not only in the substance, but also in the tone and style of the letters.

But with all their variety, the letters have basic qualities in common. One of them is an extreme brevity and tight construction. The average length is less than four hundred words, and a great portion of them consist of only one paragraph. Pushkin comes immediately to the point, makes terse comments on each of the principal topics of the letter being answered or on matters of mutual interest at the moment, and concludes crisply. The beginning may be striking and effective—an announcement, a literary allusion, a folk expression; and the conclusion is often similarly striking and pithy. He moves from one topic to another with little or no transition; the thread of connection is provided by the successive points of the letter being answered or by a relationship between one topic and the next, suggested to him by it. He uses juxtaposition to indicate relationships, and a new paragraph to indicate a basic change in thought or tone or a break in rhythm. (pp. 42-3)

No English author has used such a naked, saturated style as that of Pushkin's formal prose or his letters. His sentence structure is stark in its simplicity: it is based on the brief simple clause, made up predominantly of noun and verb, with few adjectives and sparing use of subordinate clauses. The result is a dynamic style characterized by immediacy, swiftness, and impatient nervousness, and by abrupt sentences which, in rapid rhythm, point toward an idea, without bothering to spell it out in detail. His terseness often approaches the telegraphic, as he gives only the main heads of his judgments, leaving amplification and further discussion for later "leisure." The expression of feeling is curt and even severe; it never spills over into sentimentality or mawkishness. . . . At the same time, the prose is flexible, moving easily, from one letter to another or within a single letter, to the expression of a wide range of tone and of ideas and emotions. Pushkin's style in the letters shows finish—not that of "literariness" or an effort at smoothness or gracefulness or elegance, but that of an artistic consciousness for which the curve of expression and the rhythm of phrase are a part of the thing expressed. And the effect is one of ease and unconstraint.

Pushkin's letters to his personal friends who are also men of letters—such as Vyazemsky—sparkle with fireworks which are not to be found elsewhere in his works. His comments, always brief and pointed, here tend toward the pithy, witty, aphoristic phrase. . . . The letters are saturated with literary allusions and with quotations, often from Pushkin's own works, and not infrequently used ironically. He often twists quotations or allusions to make a particular application. He seldom cites the exact or full title of a work, including his own but substitutes a key word or the name of a character. Humor, recognition, and even criticism are often present in the form of the citation as well as in the direct comment. There are relatively few figures of speech, but when they appear they tend to be more striking and pungent than in his formal works; he found publishing a journal in Russia "all the same thing as *honey-bucketing* . . . ; to clean up Russian literature means to clean out privies. . . ." (pp. 43-4)

The vocabulary of the Russian letters has a wide variety, from the ordinary language of his time and class, to the literary language, to the use of antiquated or high-flown words for the sake of parody, to homely folk expressions. Few of the words and expressions used by him have become archaic. (p. 45)

There is a continuing play of irony, usually on what the over-practical or unpoetic man would think or do. At first glance it may sometimes appear to be cynicism and to have been meant to be taken at face value—and indeed not only Pushkin's ac-

quaintances, but scholars and critics to this day, seem often to miss the point. . . . Occasionally the irony is elusive and may be completely missed unless one senses the smile in the tone of the passage or catches the allusion: ". . . console me; that is the sacred duty of friendship (that sacred feeling)." Pushkin sometimes covers genuine feeling with ironic hyperbole, which he may have meant to be misinterpreted: "First love is always a matter of sentiment: the sillier it is, the more delightful memories it leaves. The second, do you see, is an affair of voluptuousness. . . . Natalia . . . is my one hundred thirteenth love. . . ." (p. 46)

With all the stylistic variety of the letters, their most characteristic qualities remain frankness, simplicity, and sincerity. Love is presented, not in terms of subjective perception of the emotion, but the qualities of the beloved and his experience with her. . . . Pushkin's letters are masterful in all their varied types and styles, but they are most appealing when, with the sincerity and simplicity peculiar to himself he for a moment reveals himself, in order to share a particular feeling or experience with a loved one. (pp. 47-8)

> *J. Thomas Shaw, "Introduction" (1958), in* The Letters of Alexander Pushkin *by Alexander Pushkin, translated by J. Thomas Shaw (copyright © 1967 by the University of Wisconsin Press; reprinted by permission of the publisher), University of Wisconsin Press, 1967, pp. 5-47.*

ERNEST J. SIMMONS (essay date 1965)

Though writing in the nineteenth century, the qualities of [Pushkin's] mind and art were formed largely by the eighteenth. That is to say, he was a classicist in his literary tastes, in his sense of form, and in his habits of thought and feeling. The special intellectual essence which we associate with the classical approach to life and art—nothing over much, a preference for the reality of things, and an intense dislike of excess and insincerity—characterized not only the manner in which he wrote, but also the themes he selected. Unlike such great writers of fiction as Balzac and Dostoevsky, who by becoming emotionally involved at times in the life they observed and in the men and women they created and to this extent distorted the realistic image of their milieu, Pushkin's artistic detachment enabled him to remain quite objective even when there could be no doubt of his social sympathies or prejudices. Irony appealed to him more than direct criticism, subtle satire more than forthright denunciation. Like Tolstoy, his breeding as a member of the gentry colored his whole outlook on life, but unlike Tolstoy, his "six-hundred-year-old ancestry" never turned him into a conscience-stricken nobleman. (p. 24)

The beginning of Pushkin's transition from romanticism to realism may be discerned . . . in the exquisite dramatic narrative poem, *The Gypsies,* in which both strains are curiously mingled. (p. 25)

In *The Gypsies* an effective concentration on descriptive details of setting and action in order to achieve verisimilitude and convey atmosphere strikes an entirely new realistic note in Russian literature. Some notion of these effects may be obtained from a literal, unrhymed rendering of a few of the opening lines, however much violence it may do to the poetic beauty of the original:

> The gypsies in a noisy crowd
> Wander over Bessarabia.
> Today they spend the night
> In tattered tents by a river bank.

Like freedom their camp is joyous,
And they sleep peacefully under the sky.
Between the cart wheels,
Half-covered by rugs,
A fire burns; a family round it
Prepares supper; in the open field
Horses graze; before a tent
A tame bear lies untied.

(pp. 25-6)

Pushkin's classical realism eschewed overt philosophizing. The only major Russian author who resembled him in this respect was Chekhov, a fact recognized by Doctor Zhivago many years later. For Pasternak's hero prefers the modest reticence of Pushkin and Chekhov who, unlike Dostoevsky or Tolstoy, thought it pretentious and presumptuous to indulge in speculation on the ultimate purpose of mankind. . . .

Pushkin had hardly finished *The Gypsies* when he took another step in the direction of realism. He had discovered Shakespeare, and with that innovating boldness which was a distinctive trait of his genius, he decided to write a historical tragedy that would end the long neoclassical tradition of Racine in the Russian theater and, hopefully, start a new trend in native drama. (p. 27)

The play, of course, is *Boris Godunov,* and though it has failings as a historical tragedy in blank verse, Shakespeare's full-blooded realism is reflected in the best of the characterizations, in the mob scenes where the dialogue so naturally suits the lowly speakers, and especially in the comic scene of the two miscreant monks in the inn at the Lithuanian border. (p. 28)

[Pushkin liked to regard *Eugene Onegin*] as a novel and actually divided it into chapters instead of cantos. . . . [If] one cares to accept Pushkin's odd but meaningful description of *Eugene Onegin,* containing much of his finest verse, one may regard it as the first Russian realistic novel, for it possesses the ordinary surface features of the genre: characters, a plot with well-marked beginning, middle, and end, and a treatment of the precise content of life in given circumstances. (p. 29)

Onegin is the first convincing full-length characterization in Russian literature. Pushkin, however, does not employ fine-spun analysis to bring out the complexities of his nature or to explain the motivation of his feelings, a technique which he must have observed in Rousseau's *Nouvelle Héloïse* and Richardson's novels. Though the limitations of a novel in verse may have rendered such an approach peculiarly difficult, it was also alien to Pushkin's classical temperament and the objectivity and restraint which were touchstones of his art. The indirect realistic method he used was very much his own. The total image of Onegin emerges from an artistically contrived mosaic of impressions—the furnishings of his room, his toilet articles, the books in his study with special passages marked by the imprint of his fingernail, his actions and statements as they affected others, and their reactions to him. Later Turgenev learned much from this method. (pp. 30-1)

[There] can be no question that Pushkin's depiction of the country existence of the middle gentry and the city life of its more socially prominent members is realistically perfect and extraordinarily effective. . . . One is fascinated not only by his uncanny selection of precise detail, but also by his amazing re-creation of the moral, emotional, and spiritual pattern, the moods and feelings, and the inner rhythm of this order of society. (p. 33)

Pushkin's first completed effort in prose fiction, *Tales of Belkin* . . . , was a conscious experiment in artistic form and narrative approach at a time when both seemed inconsequential to Russian writers of fiction. (p. 37)

[Pushkin's narrative method was] conscientiously pruned of all the conventional ornaments of fiction writing. The stories are told in an extremely simple, direct style, with a paucity of description, dialogue, and authorial reflection or analysis. They are largely action stories, and in this type, Pushkin believed, nothing should be allowed to get between the reader and the forward progress of the action. (p. 38)

It occurred to Pushkin to continue the development of Belkin, the ficticious narrator of the *Tales,* and in *The History of the Village of Goryukhino* he turns him, even in that incomplete portrayal, into a memorable character—a shy, lovable, wryly humorous individual with timid ambitions to be an author. With the aid of old records he has discovered, he sets out to write the history of Goryukhino, the village in which his estate is situated. Actually this is an amusing parody of *The History of the Russian People* by Pushkin's literary enemy Nikolai Polevoi, and at the same time an effective satire on the whole structure of serfdom. Behind Belkin's distorted historical account of the village and its inhabitants, reflecting the pomposity of pseudo-scholarship in his comic legalistic reverence for forms and titles, looms the somber reality of the ruination of the peasants because of the steward's calculated repressions. (pp. 39-40)

In *Dubrovsky* the tensions growing out of a different social situation are treated. . . . Pushkin finished only about half of this novel which is one of his best examples of sheer storytelling ability. There is perhaps more Scott-like romance than realism in the melodramatic action of a tale that involves the vow of young Dubrovsky to avenge his father's death. . . . But the plausibility of these romantic adventures is secured by a realistically conceived picture of the social milieu in which they take place—expansive daily life on huge landed estates, the absolute power of their owners over law courts and all who are socially inferior, and the stark horror of the murder of the drunken officer of the law in Dubrovsky's flaming manor house. Though the hero, young Dubrovsky, is the pure stuff of old-fashioned romance, the characterizations of Troekurov and the sinister Vereisky are among Pushkin's best and are harbingers of the great realistic portraits to come in Russian fiction.

Pushkin's zeal for experimentation in prose as well as in poetry, an important service in this early stage of Russian literature, continued during the last few years of his life when he wrote more prose than verse. Another such experiment, the long short story, *The Queen of Spades* . . . , was his most popular contribution to fiction during his lifetime. E.T.A. Hoffmann's tales of the supernatural may well have suggested the plot-line of *The Queen of Spades,* where the ghost of the old countess conveys to Herman the mysterious secret that will enable him to win at cards, but there is nothing of the German's romanticism in Pushkin's narrative manner. A carefully designed pattern of realistic effects compels a suspension of disbelief in the central supernatural device, and the swiftly moving action is heightened by a taut, terse, unadorned prose that subtly contrives an atmosphere of utter credibility. (pp. 40-1)

Nothing remotely resembling *The Queen of Spades* had appeared in Russian literature before Pushkin, and though its total artistic impact, more one of manner than of substance, was never successfully duplicated, the story greatly impressed and obviously influenced such writers as Gogol in *The Portrait* and Dostoevsky in *The Gambler*. (p. 41)

[The] works of Walter Scott were in Pushkin's mind, especially *The Heart of Midlothian*, in his final effort at fiction—the historical novel **The Captain's Daughter**. . . . Like everything he wrote, however, this novel also bears the stamp of Pushkin's originality. It is shorter and more compact that Scott's novels, and it is centered as much on the history of two families, the Grinevs and the Mironovs, as on the re-creation of the historical past. Though Pushkin is exact about historical details and local color, with his usual sense of measure he does not overwhelm the reader with an elaborate superstructure of antiquarian research. His interest is concentrated more on the manners and morals of people than on the dress and loose ornament of history. Perhaps this is why he succeeds so brilliantly in such portrayals as the comically henpecked Captain Mironov. . . . (pp. 41-2)

Pushkin has been criticized in **The Captain's Daughter** for allowing the interest in events to predominate over the interest in details of feeling. This is essentially true, particularly in young Grinev's love for Captain Mironov's daughter which hardly rises above the banality of Scott's treatment of affairs of the heart. But this criticism could also be applied, with only few exceptions, to the whole development of fiction in the West and in Russia from Cervantes to Pushkin. . . . In the chronicling of action, events were an end rather than a means in determining why characters acted or felt as they did. The analysis of feelings by Richardson and Rousseau and their imitators was too dominated by the cult of sensibility to become an effective instrument for probing the multifaceted aspects of human behavior.

In this respect it cannot be said that Pushkin contributed anything startlingly new to the novel. But in other ways—plot-making, situations, narrative methods, characterization, and prose style—he tremendously advanced the whole conception of Russian realism. That is, the life of the landed gentry which he described seemed to readers to be life as it is, free from the bookish stereotyped conventions and artificialities of the efforts of his native predecessors and contemporaries. And this achievement, as well as the finest characters he created, significantly influenced the subsequent development of Russian realism. (pp. 42-3)

> Ernest J. Simmons, ''Pushkin—The Poet As Novelist,'' in his Introduction to Russian Realism (copyright © 1965 by Indiana University Press), Indiana University Press, 1965, pp. 3-43.

JOHN BAYLEY (essay date 1971)

[Romance, unparodied, is in full flow in **Poltava,** though] it is not the melodramatic travelogue of Byron but the 'storied romance' of Scott. The poem does not exploit the weaknesses of romantic material and construct a brilliant variation on them. Instead it takes all the ingredients of the historical romance soberly and seriously, pares them down and rearranges their proportions to create a remarkable specimen of an otherwise undistinguished genre. (pp. 107-08)

Pushkin does not . . . use history as many of his contemporaries did—as Byron, for example, had done in *Marino Faliero*, where the executed Doge becomes an early champion of the liberties of the people and, inevitably, a projection of one of Byron's images of himself. In his poem *Voynarovsky* Ryleev

presented Mazepa as an honourable and patriotic leader, seeking to preserve the Ukraine from the despotic centralism of Peter, and tragically compelled to realise his aim through the aid of a foriegn interventionist. . . . As a sympathetic friend of Ryleev Pushkin admired *Voynarovsky*, and noted that an incident from it suggested the plot for his own **Poltava**. But he felt that both Byron and Ryleev had painted a false picture of the historical Mazepa—Byron because he had based his poem on a paragraph out of Voltaire's *History of Charles XII*.

The idea suggested to Pushkin was the tragic fate of Mazepa's opponent Kochubey, his wife driven mad by their daughter's infatuation for their political enemy. It is as melodramatic a theme as Byron's poetic treatment of the apocryphal nightmare of Mazepa's youth, bound to a wild horse by the jealous husband of the Polish noblewoman he had loved. Byron's tale is told by the old Mazepa to Charles after their defeat at the battle of Poltava, and without any mention of the historical and biographical background which Pushkin had carefully studied. Both begin with the idea of 'wild tale', but where Byron's had nothing more to offer, Pushkin's can expand into the sober dimension of historical narrative. (p. 112)

[Pushkin's] technique in **Poltava** is not to mix the elements of romance and heroic history but carefully to compartmentalise them. There is a danger, clearly, that one will show up the other and that history will discredit romance as (in the view of some of his contemporaries) the accurate study of Circassian life revealed the insubstantial nature of the Captive, or that of the Gipsies, Aleko's. Pushkin avoids this by making his private characters in **Poltava** as convincing as the public ones—as Gukovsky says, they are not 'lyric emanations but independent strengths and objective realities'. Whereas Scott's heroine might be one of his own female readers taken on a trip to the past. . . , Pushkin's Mariya belongs to her environment. Her infatuation with the aged Mazepa is not romantically typical but peculiar, almost monstrous; it isolates her in its own reality.

Isolated thus, she is ignorant of everything else in the poem, knowing and caring as little of what is happening as an actual girl of her historical situation would have done, and this separates her romance with Mazepa from what he is doing in the Ukraine. When the two themes meet she vanishes, and it is a misfortune that Pushkin succumbed to the demands of romantic atmosphere and brought her back at the end of the poem, where she acquires that quasi-supernatural freedom of action enjoyed by heroines of the period, who suddenly pop up, in wilderness or ruin, to confront their betrayers with mad laughter. Her mother receives this privilege earlier on, when she materialises before her daughter on the eve of her husband's execution and pleads with her to intercede with Mazepa and save him. But this is dramatically justified, for Mariya's stupefied exclamation '*Kakoy otets? Kakaya kazn?*' ('What father? What execution?') is the last touch, and the best, in the build-up of the kind of heroine she should be. Her words are as pregnant, as psychologically revealing, as—in Racine's *Andromaque*—Hermione's cry to Oreste, whom she has ordered to kill the man she loves: '*Qui te l'a dit?*' But after this the tension collapses and Mariya becomes merely a period heroine. . . .

> God, God! . . . Today! My poor father! And
> the girl fell back on the couch as a cold corpse
> falls.

(pp. 114-15)

Kireevsky, in an article which Pushkin himself thought perceptive, drew attention to the division between the heroic and the romantic themes [in *Poltava*]. I have suggested that if we are aware of the models Pushkin chose, and perceive what he made of them, this division is not a weakness, for both themes can enhance each other and acquire their own separate reality, as do the private and public scenes in a Shakespeare history. The real crack in the poem is perhaps not between history and romance but between two kinds of romance—which both Scott and Byron habitually mix—the modern melodrama and the traditional tragic ballad. The latter should work by distance: its heroine should be seen clearly but from far off, and Pushkin correctly and beautifully employs one of its devices in the last lines of the poem. . . .

> Only the blind Ukrainian bard, at times when
> he plays the hetman's songs before the village
> people, recalls in passing to the young Cossacks
> the name of the erring girl.

That frames Mariya, and is proper to our ignorance of the girl who, like a sleepwalker, brings disgrace upon her father without knowing or caring until it is too late. As in a ballad there should be no explanation; her relations with parents and lover should be guessed at, not known; while her mother, too, should properly be seen like the old wife in a ballad, scheming in the bedchamber and urging her husband to avenge the wrong. But Pushkin also makes us see mother and daughter through the painfully powerful lens of modern melodrama. (pp. 118-19)

Belinsky, we must remember, thought Mariya an admirable character, more energetically *narodnaya* even than Tatyana in *Evgeny Onegin,* and there is nothing romantically languorous about her passion for the old hetman and her possessive jealousy. Does Mazepa return her feelings? We are not told directly. He is *mrachny*, obscure and devious, deep-set in guile. He has something of the depth of a Shakespeare portrait—to Belinsky the poem smelt of the Renaissance—and he also suggests qualities which we shall find in their proper naturalistic setting in Pushkin's creation of Pugachev. We can see why he is as dangerous as a force of nature, and why he inspires devotion. He can be all things to all men the more effectively because even his calculation has something irresponsible about it; his collectedness hides a coiled spring of impulse and unreason. He schemes—'he does not decide in a hurry what can and what can't be done'—and yet the exercise of power is not for him a process of cold logic. (p. 119)

Mazepa has no country and freedom means nothing to him: he cannot love. His self is in the part he plays; his reality in his wrongs and his ability to avenge them.

Pushkin referred critics who objected that Mariya's love for Mazepa was implausible and unnatural to Desdemona and her 'blackamoor'. *Boris Godunov* shows how he had studied Shakespeare's dramatic method, and *Andzhelo* and the *Little Tragedies* show his deep interest in Shakespearean portraiture, an interest also seen in *Poltava*. The reference to *Othello* is significant. It is only a guess, certainly, but the heroic atmosphere of the play, and the dramatic contrast between its two great protagonists, might have entered Pushkin's mind. It is the tragedy of Othello to play a part unsuited to him: he should lead us into 'the stately tent of war' not to an intrigue in a marriage chamber; and yet the tented field is always in the background of the action and the decisions proper to it fatally determine the domestic issue. *Poltava* too makes war the background of love, and though the two have little dramatic interplay the dark figure of Mazepa is set against the brilliant Peter, duped by Mazepa as Othello by Iago. Duped, Peter betrays his loyal

servants and the tragic consequence is the death of Iskra and Kochubey. It is an aspect of Pushkin's separations that the political failure of Peter, which resulted in the execution of the loyal pair and the triumph of Mazepa's plot in the Ukraine, does not diminish the glory of his victory and his god-like stature on the field of Poltava; yet it remains a shadow in the poem, a question mark in blood which suggests the equivocal relationship of the Tsar and his antagonist, not on the battlefield but in the dark background of power and intrigue. (pp. 120-21)

[Great art] takes men as the measure of the historical process, and sees public consequences in their private weaknesses and desires; the motivation of Kochubey and Mazepa is as psychologically revealing as that of Brutus and Cassius. Kochubey is Mazepa's old friend and comrade; he does not denounce him to the Tsar out of public spirit but to revenge the disgrace of his daughter, and he finds a particular satisfaction in the hope that Mazepa will suffer at the hands of the public executioner in Moscow for the private wrong he has done. To gain one's ends indirectly is the supreme reward of power politics, and when the plot miscarries the final bitterness of Kochubey is to find himself in the position in which he hoped to place Mazepa. The undeclared motive behind the true denunciation has only strengthened the hetman's position, and Kochubey must die as an apparent traitor, without a chance of clearing his name and with his daughter's shame (as he feels it) still unavenged.

Despite his motives Kochubey in his last hours has a nobility denied to Mazepa, whose motives, like Iago's, lack any spontaneity of simple passion. On the night before the battle he tells his henchman Orlik the reason for his hatred of Peter—the quarrel long ago in Astrakhan when Peter had seized him by his moustaches. . . . Critics professed to find the use of the word *moustaches* low and ridiculous in a heroic context, and Pushkin replied, straight-faced, that for a Pole or Little Russian to have his moustaches pulled was as deadly an insult as tugging a Muscovite by his beard (he did not mention Peter's decree against beards). In fact he removes any real suggestion of the trivial by the subtlety with which he compounds Mazepa's psychology. His motives and their declaration, like Iago's, give the impression of having been thought up, cherished: they are a part of his general deviousness and the self-exculpation that makes him persuade Mariya—when he has already decided her father must die—into a confession that his life is dearer to her than her father's. (pp. 121-22)

Lyricism, [in *Poltava*], does not exist for its own picturesque sake but as a part of the same linkage of revealing imagery. . . .

> Silent is the Ukrainian night. Clear is the sky.
> The stars shine. The air has no will to master
> its own drowsiness. The leaves of the silvery
> poplars hardly stir.

These phrases of tranquil beauty are twice repeated: the night and stars seen by the condemned Kochubey from his prison cell, and then by Mazepa as he walks in his garden outside. . . . Night, stars, and trees are seen by Kochubey for the last time; they are seen in and for themselves, objects of total tranquillity. But for Mazepa they are voluble and alive, a part of his own vigilant and unquiet consciousness. The trees are like a tribunal, and the open summer night a stifling prison. Like Clarence and Macbeth he sees nature populated by accusing spirits and symbols of judgement.

Imagery exerts a dramatic leverage throughout the action of *Poltava*, but its operation is objective and formal: the characters do not have the acoustic individuality which we can detect even in the spare dialogue of *The Gipsies*. There we can hear the voice of Aleko dissociating himself from the Gipsies' permissiveness—the tone of *'Ya ne takov'* ('I am not that kind of man') catches the sullen conviction of his personal right to jealousy and revenge—while a simple and unselfconscious resignation is in the old man's voice as he describes his desertion by Zemphira's mother. . . . The spoken drama of Poltava is developed in appropriately impersonal tones; in Kochubey's vindictive monologue, in Mazepa's last formal utterance on the eve of battle, in the blank incomprehension of Mariya's *'Kakoy otets?'* ('What father?'), most of all in Peter's sudden cry on the field of Poltava *'Za delo, s bogom!'* ('To the business, with God's aid!'). In this brief and rapid sweep of history Pushkin is right not to bring us close enough to hear his characters' voices. . . . The historical narrative of *Poltava* is not brought close, in the painstaking romantic fashion, but distanced; and its figures are all the more meaningful historically because they are not dressed out in the attempted intimacy of local colour.

The battle is the set piece and climax of *Poltava,* and yet the best of the poem is over before it. A battle scene does not suit Pushkin's instinct for precision. The duel between Onegin and Lensky in *Evgeny Onegin* can be seen in every detail and followed in the exactest sequence; but a panorama of bayonets, regiments and cannon smoke allows no opportunity for the accuracy that follows events each moment viewed with the eye. Stendhal observed that since poetry must generalise it cannot describe what really happens in a battle, which is seen by a number of excited and isolated eyewitnesses. . . . Pushkin's generalisations do a conventional job, in a mode in which convention is at a disadvantage. (pp. 123-25)

Poltava sees history in terms of personality, *The Bronze Horseman* in terms of historical determinism, though such a generalisation does little to indicate the remarkable difference in 'feel' between the two poems. . . . With *Poltava* we know at once what sort of poem we are dealing with—a romantic and recreative poem, the opening taste of which subtly corresponds to the coniness in the idea of recreation. There is a world of difference between Kochubey, 'in his habit as he lived', and Peter at the beginning of *The Bronze Horseman*. . . .

> On a shore of desolate waves stood *he*, full of
> high thoughts, and gazed into the distance. . . .

In the first draft of the poem Peter was named, placed as a person in the past like Kochubey. In the final version there is only *he*, almost *it*—history personified, as in *Poltava* he was war personified. . . . The superhuman size of Peter is common to both poems, but in *Poltava* it is only incidental. In *The Bronze Horseman* Peter is the vast *kumir*, the image of the poem as of the city and destiny.

Yet Peter had been very much a personality, and one studied by Pushkin with always increasing fascination; his extraordinary nature, his omnivorous interests and colossal energy, were aspects of a god who might none the less be represented in all his humanity. Just before *Poltava*, Pushkin had begun a historical novel about Peter, *The Negro of Peter the Great*. . . . (pp. 127-28)

Belinsky says it would have been a great novel, but we may doubt this, and so clearly did Pushkin, for he wrote no more than a few chapters. Lively enough when it is dealing with Gannibal's adventures in France, the writing becomes flat and almost embarrassed when the action returns to Russia: it is the

only occasion in Pushkin when an air of unnaturalness creeps in, as if the author were an *enfant terrible* constrained to behave with dull decorum in the presence of a feared and respected father. (p. 128)

The most important of the sources [for *The Bronze Horseman*] was Mickiewicz's poem, *Forefathers' Eve*. . . . Konrad Wallenrod of *Forefathers' Eve* is Mickiewicz himself, and the *Digression* in the poem describes the journey of the exile to the capital and what he sees there. It is a satire, the vigour of which only partially redeems its crudity, but circulating in secret among the Petersburg intelligentsia it created a sensation, and there is some evidence that Pushkin thought of translating it. Everything about the poem must have outraged his aesthetic sense, but like the grit in the oyster it worked in him until the final casting of the pearl. . . . *The Bronze Horseman* is not a reply to Mickiewicz's poem, but it might not have been written without it.

In both poems Falconet's great bronze statue of Peter the Great is a symbol of the city and of the autocrat who built it. For Mickiewicz the statue is an occasion for homily; for Pushkin it is the central feature of a tragic tale, a tale based on accounts of the great Petersburg flood of 1824. (pp. 130-31)

Such a sculpture is as subject as poetry and other art may be to the interpretation of the audience; and the point is of some importance, because it is by exploiting the enigma that Pushkin's poem achieves its dispassion and its universalising force. . . .

> Terrible was he in the surrounding gloom! What
> thought was in his brow! What strength was
> hidden in him! And in this steed what fire!
> Where are you galloping, proud horse, and where
> do your hoofs fall? O mighty master of fate!
> Was it not thus, aloft on the very edge of the
> abyss, that you reined up Russia with your iron
> curb? . . .

As in *Poltava* Peter is both splendid and terrible, but now the epic simplicity of the hero on the battlefield has given place to a vision that is shot through and through with deliberate equivocation. 'Where are you galloping proud horse? And where do your hoofs fall?' Where indeed. The aesthetic and the political are cunningly blended, for the poet's open admiration is for the statue, whose qualities *qua* statue are never lost sight of. (pp. 132-33)

Symbolism of Peter and Russia as rider and horse, explicit in Mickiewicz and indeed more than a trifle grotesque when we begin to follow up all the permutations of the relation, is in Pushkin equally explicit but uninsistent. The statue remains a statue, for the really important contrast is not between the possibilities of interpretation suggested by the romantic dynamism of its design, but between the rhetoric that this design inspires, and the actual and solid presence of the bronze figure in the darkness. . . .

> . . . and him who motionless held his bronze
> head aloft in the darkness.

The heavy lines are decisive. Where Mickiewicz, through Konrad and his friend the bard, engages in homiletics about freedom and tyranny, justice and injustice, Pushkin converts all to drama and to the dramatic confrontation of his two protagonists, statue and clerk. Through the crazed mind of his hero Evgeny is already running the fantasy of the bronze horseman, and the responses that the statue might evoke, and yet the poem all the time keeps steadily before us the giant unresponsiveness and immobility of the thing. It is as indifferent to what we make of it as—outside the mad climax in his own mind—it is heedless of Evgeny himself. (p. 133)

[In *The Bronze Horseman*] Pushkin is not celebrating the capital in a straightforward sense. Instead he enlists the reader as 'one of us', one of *les Nôtres,* the *beau monde* of Peter's city, to whom it is life and nature itself. Even the figure of Peter is drawn into this participatory intimacy: it is here—most unexpectedly—that he becomes briefly but completely human to our imagination, whereas in *The Negro of Peter the Great* he had remained wooden. Here he too is one of us, the charmed circle of the poet's genius, and with gigantic relish he acts his part as destiny's executor, brooding in the soughing forest by the deserted shore, ignoring with us the insect traces of the wretched Finn. (p. 135)

[We] feel a complete solidarity with this Peter. It seems a privilege to be partners in crime, one of his family, and to participate in the building of the new city before which (and again we hear the undercurrent of hilarity beneath the resounding phrase) the old capital of Moscow will appear like a dowager in purple widow's weeds before a new Empress. (p. 136)

[*The Bronze Horseman*] achieves its profound and universal political meaning through having no truck with the liberal ideals and assumptions of its time. By a curious irony this could only happen with a poet as cosmopolitan and European in his outlook as Pushkin was. The 'defence' of Petersburg would be nothing if it were the mere defensiveness and xenophobia characteristic of many Russian authors, not excluding Dostoevsky, and commonplace in the provincial and proletarian ethos of Soviet writing. Only a poet with Pushkin's instinctively European outlook could have written a masterpiece as universal and yet as deeply and subtly nationalistic as *The Bronze Horseman.* The greatest political poem of the nineteenth century rests on the paradox which Pushkin threw off with typical lightness and accuracy in that comment in his letters—'Of course I despise my fatherland from head to foot. However it makes me angry when a foreigner shares my feeling'—a paradox which Tolstoy would have understood, and which relates to his own great creative division between war and peace, the pride of the flesh and the logic of pacifism.

Pushkin's hero Evgeny is naturally the opposite of Konrad Wallenrod. He is indifferent alike to the injustices of the present and the glory of the past. He would rather not be poor, and he is honest enough to wish he had more brains, but he will work hard to make up for these things and for the rewards of a happy married life with his Parasha. . . . Unobtrusively he should give the impression of being a sensible straightforward young Russian, as opposed to all these modish and romantic young Europeans and Poles. But Pushkin avoids any combativeness in the contract by being as cursory and noncommittal about him as he can. (pp. 140-41)

In *The Bronze Horseman* we see the combination [of Pushkin's creative and reflective sides] at its most masterly. The Prologue: genial, personal, appealing; the Tale: the climax and masterwork of Pushkin's 'opposites'. . . . [The] fable of the poem is used to secure a total objectivity, exploring a theme in ways quite different from anything Pushkin himself wrote in poem or letter. The bronze statue and the Petersburg flood are the most distanced and the most elaborately treated of these fable materials. (p. 150)

More than any other comparable work of the modern literary imagination *The Bronze Horseman* includes the experience of modern man, urban animation and urban solitude, the images of which are more vivid and more haunting even than those of the statue and Evgeny, power and the personal fate. They are proffered with no persistence and no sign of deliberate attempt—the positive in Pushkin's 'opposites' seems unaware of the negative leverage, and the solitude of the tale is equally unconscious of the gaiety and acceptance of the Prologue. In its 'abyss of space' every object in the poem denies its fellows. . . . Pushkin in *The Bronze Horseman,* it seems to me, gives us modernity in poetry before it has come to give this characteristically modern representation of itself.

In the world of the poem nothing comes out of the past but power, in the shape of the bronze statue, and in the inhuman world it has created life is sustained as Evgeny in his madness sustains it. . . . The irony of the poem's comprehensiveness is that 'all human life is there' but appears only in its absence, the absence even of human speech, for the removal of Evgeny's dreaming soliloquy means that he utters only five words in the poem: . . .

> Lowering he stood before the proud effigy and clenching his teeth, clenching his fists, as if possessed by some black force, he whispered, trembling with fury: 'All right then, miracle-builder!—you've got it coming to you! . . .'

The solitary madman has found his voice and established a kind of human contact. And the effigy, who ignored the waves that were inundating his capital, now seems abruptly to react as one human being to another. . . .

> It seemed to him that—lit with a flicker of rage—the face of the dread Tsar was slowly turning . . .

Evgeny has two human contacts in the poem, with the heroine we never see, and with the statue itself. Parasha and Peter are not present in human form but in places, the local habitations of Evgeny's day-dream and his nightmare. . . .

> . . . almost by the gulf itself is an unpainted fence and a willow and a shabby little house: there they are, the widow and her daughter, his Parasha, his dream . . .

Yet there is no explicit contrast between the unpainted fence, the little house and the willow, and Peter's square and monument, with its vast rock and iron railing. And Evgeny has no further contact with the statue. If he passed the square in his deranged wanderings he would remove his cap without raising his eyes. But his body is found on the island where the cottage, like a black bush, has been washed up by the flood. In the final lines of the poem the brief sentences interrupt the rhythm, placing a full stop in the centre of almost every line; after the sonorous onomatopoeia of the charging horseman the effect is almost like Shakespearean prose following on the rhetoric of verse. No only is the rhythm prosaic; it dies away into the mutter of the last line, with its feminine ending: . . .

> By the threshold my madman was found and in that very place his cold corpse was buried, out of charity.

—an ending which contrasts more obviously with the two triumphant concluding syllables of the Prologue's demand: . . .

Let the Finnish waves forget their old enmity
and bondage, and let them not disturb with their
vain rancour Peter's eternal sleep!

And that is all. Lear does not die with Cordelia in his arms.
Peter is exalted and Evgeny laid low, and each epiphany seems
unconscious of the other. Yet the needs of tragedy are fulfilled,
and we are moved, as only the greatest art can move us, that
in a poem of absence, of utter separation, Evgeny's body should
be found where it is. Characteristically the tragic dismissal is
buried far back in the poem when the flood subsides, the people
walk in the streets again 'with cold unfeeling', and 'everything
returned to its former order' (*V poryadok prezhny vce voshlo*),
a line that twins and locks into place the last line of the Prologue: *pechalen budet moy rasskaz.* But one thing has not
returned. Tragedy is human, and the corpse of Evgeny is left
by its own free and final will outside the prison of power.

The Bronze Horseman is the most remarkable of nineteenth-
century poems in that it achieves the goal which the most
ambitious of them set themselves without recourse to any structure of mythology or meditation, legend or symbol. It does
not—like *Faust* or *Prometheus Unbound*—create a world of
its own to image man's condition and the forces that determine
it. It brings the past into the present, using history and fantasy
to give a yet sharper reality to an actual place and event. It is
the last wholly comprehensive work of literature to present
itself to us in the form of a poem, and to make that form not
the *chose préservée* that for Valéry poetry in the nineteenth
century had necessarily become, but a medium that is meaningful on the same terms as the novels that came after it. (pp.
162-64)

> *John Bayley, in his* Pushkin: A Comparative Com-
> mentary *(© Cambridge University Press 1971),
> Cambridge at the University Press, 1971, 369 p.*

V. S. PRITCHETT (essay date 1979)

It is said that among foreigners only the Baltic Germans can
see Pushkin's genius as a lyrical poet at once. The rest of us
who have no Russian and read his poetry in English or French
translation echo the remark made by Flaubert to Turgenev—
'Il est plat, votre poète'; it expresses our polite embarrassment
before a mystery. To the dramatic poet-novelist in *Eugene
Onegin,* to the prose tales and above all to his marvellous
letters, we do respond. In the last we hear the natural voice of
the man that goes leaping along beside the cooler voice of the
conscious artist and we at once see why the Russians think
him the greatest of their letter writers. He is there before us. . . .
We see the courtier trapped by the Court; we see the rake who
wears his nails long and who looks like a monkey, the aristocrat
of two aristocracies: the Court and Art; the patriot who, like
the Spanish Cid, is struggling with a false king. Pushkin had
the art of appearing suddenly dishevelled or elegant, out of the
very hour he was living. He is as concise as impulse itself. He
is as clear as ice, as blinding as snow. (p. 77)

Pushkin has the appetite for life and, more important from a
letter-writer's point of view, a genius for playing with it, for
changing his tone, for leaving some things sardonically unsaid
and others spoken bluntly. He is entranced by his laughing
mastery of all kinds of style from the drily formal, the eloquent,
the witty to the hotly argued and tenderly felt. He enjoyed
rewriting. He was a keen tester of phrase. Each sentence rings
like a true coin. For the moment he is all ours and we, on
hearing him, are all his. (p. 78)

[Pushkin] takes it for granted that he is known and that we
know what it is to be a man. He is modest. He is expressive
but neither tortuous nor exhibitionist. His stress is not on the
egotist's 'I' because he is multifarious. He writes rather as the
messenger or familiar of a human being called Pushkin who,
though perpetually in some sort of scandal or trouble, is like
a swimmer who knows how to survive in a storm of his own
making and who will make no fuss if he sinks. The appetite
for life is not simply a matter of extroversion; it is inseparable
from the appetite for putting it into words. (p. 79)

He is inhabited by a genius that guarantees his integrity; but
his is not a mad genius: it is sane, orderly, generous, serene
in feeling. It is impossible to imagine ourselves trusting the
judgment or good sense of a Dostoevsky or a Tolstoy. Egotism
distorts them. Pushkin one entirely trusts. He is so open. His
follies expose the corruption of the society he lived in, rather
than falsity in himself. (pp. 79-80)

[Both] as a man and an artist, Pushkin got what was vivid and
valuable in his life and work from venturing; not from change
itself, but from the capacity to make it. His vitality jumps out
in every sentence. For one who scattered his life in storms and
comedies, he is astonishing for a fundamental seriousness. And
what he read! Byron, Shakespeare, Corneille, Goethe, Scott
and Voltaire, of course. Racine to quarrel with and Mme de
Staël to defend. He hated German metaphysics. But he knew
enough about Addison and Steele and the system of patronage
in English literature. He could recall lines from the low characters of Fielding. He treats literature as a form of action.
(p. 81)

When we turn to Pushkin's prose tales, the common opinion
is that he writes in frozen, formal, well-corseted style that seals
the subjects from the outside air. (p. 83)

On the surface *The Queen of Spades* or *The Stationmaster* are
no more than skilful anecdotes in an antique setting. . . . They
emerge from 'old papers', hearsay or after-dinner talk, in the
conventional manner, and a tale like *The Stationmaster* looks
at first sight like a simple reversal of the Prodigal Son story,
as it might be retold by Maupassant. On a second reading one
sees that this is not so. At the end we do not give a shrewd
grin at the expense of the poor stationmaster's mistaken belief
that his daughter's 'fall' will be a moral disaster, when it has
turned out to be a most respectable success. Indeed, the success
is not the sort of paradox enjoyed by a man of the world, but
is humanly moving. We see a life unexpectedly surviving the
clever or stupid misunderstanding of experience, and compassion cuts the claws of irony. In the last lines of the flat ending,
life, doubting life, assimilates not only father and daughter,
but the narrator himself. The 'closed' end is really open. The
same may be said of the far richer *Queen of Spades,* where the
terse picture of a society and an obsession with meaningless
luck can be read on several levels and where the curious Russian
gift of exact portraiture-by-accident or devastating miniature
puts an indelible glitter on the people. The story melts into the
interests of other lives.

Pushkin was a constant literary collector, but he changed what
he collected. He is an example of the writer who shocks old
subjects into life by a gay and intelligent search for new means.
It is interesting that the incident in *The Captain's Daughter*
where the girl goes on a journey to the Empress to plead for
the life of her betrothed was taken from the *Heart of Midlothian,* yet with what new dramatic ease or innocence of eye! The
economy and the impudent bravura of these tales are shapely,

but the sense of the open, passing hour is always there and it will pervade all the great Russian novels that follow. (pp. 84-5)

> *V. S. Pritchett, "Alexander Pushkin: Founding Father," in his* The Myth Makers: Literary Essays *(copyright © 1979 by V. S. Pritchett; reprinted by permission of Random House, Inc.), Random House, 1979, pp. 77-88.*

ADDITIONAL BIBLIOGRAPHY

Baring, Maurice. "The New Age: Pushkin." In his *An Outline of Russian Literature*, pp. 30-100. New York: Henry Holt and Company, 1915.
  Biographical-critical essay affirming Pushkin's place as the national poet of Russia.

Bayley, John. "The Russian Background." In his *Tolstoy and the Novel*, pp. 9-30. London: Chatto & Windus, 1966.*
  Examines Pushkin's influence on Tolstoy and compares the major themes of each author.

Blok, Alexander. "On the Mission of the Poet." In *Modern Russian Poets on Poetry*, edited by Carl R. Proffer, translated by Alexander Golubov, Jane Gary Harris, David Lapeza, Angela Livingstone, and Joel Stern, pp. 71-80. Ann Arbor: Ardis, 1976.
  An exploration of the poet's role, underscored by thoughts on Pushkin's life and poetry.

Brasol, Boris. *The Mighty Three: Poushkin, Gogol, Dostoievsky; A Critical Trilogy*. New York: William Farquhar Payson, 1934, 295 p.*
  Studies of Pushkin and two of his literary descendants.

Cross, S. H., and Simmons, Ernest J., eds. *Centennial Essays for Pushkin*. New York: Russell & Russell, 1937, 226 p.
  Essays addressing various aspects of Pushkin's life and literature.

Debreczeny, Paul. "Poetry and Prose in *The Queen of Spades*." *Canadian-American Slavic Studies* 11, No. 1 (Spring 1977): 91-113.
  Detailed study of the symbolic structure of *The Queen of Spades*.

Freeborn, Richard. "*Eugene Onegin*." In his *The Rise of the Russian Novel: Studies in the Russian Novel from "Eugene Onegin" to "War and Peace"*, pp. 10-38. Cambridge: Cambridge at the University Press, 1973.
  A critical analysis of Pushkin's "novel in verse," with commentary on Pushkin's authorial presence in the novel, and the importance of the characters Onegin and Tatyana.

Gibian, George. "Love by the Book: Pushkin, Stendhal, Flaubert." *Comparative Literature* VIII, No. 2 (Spring 1956): 97-109.*
  Contends that the protagonists of *Eugene Onegin, Le Rouge et le Noir*, and *Madame Bovary* form their concepts of love through literature. The critic demonstrates that "Pushkin uses his characters' reading as a cogent means of defining Onegin, Tatyana, and her parents in relation to each other."

Gide, André. "Preface to *The Queen of Spades*." In his *Pretexts: Reflections on Literature and Morality*, edited by Justin O'Brien, translated by Angelo P. Bertocci, Jeffrey J. Carre, Justin O'Brien, and Blanche A. Price, pp. 275-77. London: Secker & Warburg, 1959.
  Brief appreciation of the "clarity, balance, harmony" of Pushkin's work.

Greene, Militsa. "Pushkin and Sir Walter Scott." *Forum for Modern Language Studies* I, No. 1 (January 1965): 207-15.*
  Examines the essential differences and parallels between Pushkin and Scott.

Gregg, Richard. "A Scapegoat for All Seasons: The Unity and Shape of *The Tales of Belkin*." *Slavic Review* 30, No. 4 (December 1971): 748-61.
  Studies the figure of Ivan Belkin and discusses the common themes uniting "his" tales.

Johnson, D.J.L. "Pushkin and Serbian Tradition." *The Slavonic and East European Review* 34 (1955-56): 388-407.
  Investigates Serbian folk sources of two poems contained in Pushkin's "Songs of the Western Slavs."

Keefer, Lubov. "Pushkin and Goethe." *Modern Language Notes* LVI, No. 1 (January 1941): 24-34.*
  Discusses the influence of German writers—particularly Goethe—on Pushkin's work.

Lavrin, Janko. "Alexander Pushkin." In his *Russian Writers: Their Lives and Literature*, pp. 33-54. New York: D. Van Nostrand Company, Inc., 1954.
  A laudatory overview.

Lednicki, Wacław. *Bits of Table Talk on Pushkin, Mickiewicz, Goethe, Turgenev, and Sienkiewicz*. The Hague: Martinus Nijhoff, 1956, 263 p.*
  Comparative studies of five authors. There are references to Pushkin throughout, in addition to specific essays discussing Pushkin's prose pieces, his tale "The Snowstorm," and his poems "Monument" and "Tazit."

Maloff, Nicholas. "Musorgskii's *Boris Godunov*: Pushkin's Drama Resurrected." *Canadian Slavonic Papers* XIX, No. 1 (March 1977): 1-15.*
  Examines the similarities and differences between the text of Pushkin's *Boris Godunov* and the libretto of Modest Musorgskii's opera of the same name. The critic also discusses Musorgskii's musical interpretation of the drama.

Nabokov, Vladimir. "Pushkin and Gannibal: A Footnote." *Encounter* XIX, No. 1 (July 1962): 11-26.
  Sketches the mysterious origin and unusual life of Abram Gannibal, Pushkin's African maternal great-grandfather.

Poggioli, Renato. "The Masters of the Past: Pushkin." In his *The Poets of Russia: 1890-1930*, pp. 14-26. Cambridge: Harvard University Press, 1960.
  Biographical appreciation of the "greatest of all poets."

Posin, J. A. "Pushkin and Onegin as Viewed by Two Generations." In *Slavic Studies*, edited by Alexander Kaun and Ernest J. Simmons, pp. 132-45. Ithaca, N.Y.: Cornell University Press, 1943.
  Examines *Onegin* criticism written by the early Russian critics V. G. Belinsky and Dmitri Pisarev. While the article focuses on the methods of the two critics, the juxtaposition of their views on Pushkin is valuable.

Pushkin, Aleksandr. *Eugene Onegin: A Novel in Verse*. 4 Vols. Bollingen Series LXXII, translated with commentary by Vladimir Nabokov. New York: Pantheon Books, 1964.
  Contains detailed commentary on *Eugene Onegin* by Vladimir Nabokov. Volumes 2 and 3 of this four-volume edition are devoted to Nabokov's analysis, which Anthony Burgess termed "a massive act of copulation with scholarship."

Schmidgall, Gary. "Peter Ilyich Tchaikovsky: *Eugene Onegin*." In his *Literature as Opera*, pp. 217-46. New York: Oxford University Press, 1977.*
  Contrasts Pushkin's conception of *Eugene Onegin* with Tchaikovsky's interpretation of the story in his opera of the same name. The critic argues that Tchaikovsky's opera is a too serious, literal, and emotional rendering of the story, which Pushkin meant as a romantic *satire* of romanticism.

Simmons, Ernest J. *Pushkin*. Cambridge: Harvard University Press, 1937, 485 p.
  Authoritative biography by a noted Pushkin scholar.

Troyat, Henri. *Pushkin*, translated by Nancy Amphoux. Garden City, N.Y.: Doubleday & Company, Inc., 1970, 655 p.
  Well-illustrated and annotated biography.

Whittier, John Greenleaf. "Alexander Pushkin." In his *Whittier on Writers and Writing: The Uncollected Critical Writings of John Green-*

leaf Whittier, edited by Edwin Harrison Cady and Harry Hayden Clark, pp. 118-20. Syracuse: Syracuse University Press, 1950.

> A non-critical article alluding to Pushkin's "negro" descent, "for the purpose of exposing the utter folly and injustice of the common prejudice against the colored race in this country."

Woll, Josephine. "'Mozart and Salieri' and the Concept of Tragedy." *Canadian-American Slavic Studies* 10, No. 2 (Summer 1976): 250-63.

> A study of Pushkin's use of the tragic tradition in developing the new form of tragedy he created in "Mozart and Salieri."

Wreath, Patrick J., and Wreath, April I. "Alexander Pushkin: A Bibliography of Criticism in English." *Canadian-American Slavic Studies* 10, No. 2 (Summer 1976): 279-304.

> Lists essays and books published in English between 1920 and 1975, in addition to selected reviews of books about Pushkin.

Yarmolinsky, Avrahm. Introduction to *The Works of Alexander Pushkin: Lyrics, Narrative Poems, Folk Tales, Plays, Prose,* edited by Avrahm Yarmolinsky, pp. 11-48. New York: Random House, 1936.

> Detailed biographical essay.

Donatien Alphonse François, Comte de Sade

1740-1814

French novelist, short story writer, dramatist, and essayist.

To many, the Marquis de Sade is a French author whose erotic and licentious writings lent his name to the concept of sadism. However, he is considered by some critics to be a forerunner of Romanticism and a precursor of Freudian psychology. Unlike other authors of the Enlightenment, Sade rejected the concept that reason and rational behavior should be the goals of humankind and advocated complete anarchy. And while philosophers such as Jean-Jacques Rousseau viewed nature as a positive force, Sade saw it only as a collection of warring impulses. Sade's value as a writer is not considered as significant as his comment on the nature of human cruelty. He is a figure of literary notoriety who thought the unthinkable and recorded it in writing that was then, and is often now, considered unprintable.

Sade was born into a wealthy, titled family. However, despite the financial comforts he was afforded, Sade received little parental attention and his early feelings of alienation are thought to have stemmed from this neglect. Accounts of his temperamental childhood indicate the development of his deranged personality. Sade's many amorous encounters with women later were thought to be attempts to compensate for his failure to win his mother's love. After one year at a military academy, Sade enlisted as a soldier in the French army and served in the Seven Years' War. Upon leaving the military profession, Sade returned to his parents' home. Disturbed by his depraved lifestyle, Sade's parents decided that an arranged marriage would provide stability. However, shortly after his marriage, Sade was jailed on counts of criminal debauchery and sexual offenses. This, the first of repeated incarcerations, had little effect on him, and he continued to lead a life of flagrant immorality. In his writings, Sade claimed that his violent actions against society were committed in an attempt to negate any concept of ultimate morality.

In 1768, Sade's increasing madness resulted in a violent and brutal attack on a prostitute for which he was again jailed. A similar incident in Marseille led to Sade's condemnation to death. His mother arranged for his escape to Italy; however, on his return, he was again jailed. While in prison, Sade wrote his atheistic manifesto, *Dialogue entre un prêtre et un moribund (Dialogue between a Priest and a Dying Man)*. This account of a priest's death-bed conversion questions why God, after creating a human nature which is inherently corrupt, should test humanity by endowing humankind with freedom of choice. In this work, the priest ultimately succumbs to the pleasures of amorality and libertinage.

Sade was later transferred to the Bastille, where he began *Les 120 journées de Sodome, ou l'école du libertinage (The 120 Days of Sodom; or, The Romance of the School for Libertinage)*, a vast work which illuminates the psychopathology of sex. Though he wrote prolifically, his stay in prison disturbed his already fragile mental balance and he was transferred to the insane asylum of Charenton. In 1789, Sade was freed under the aegis of the French Revolution. He wrote plays for the Comedie Française, held public office, and attempted to publish his

works, but he was again arrested and jailed; this time for "moderatism." In poor health and virtually destitute upon his release, Sade sold several works, but their sales did not ease his financial difficulties. Napoleon's police kept Sade under surveillance and seized his manuscripts. He was arrested for writing *Justine, ou les malheurs de la vertu (Justine; or, The Misfortunes of Virtue)*, a work in which obscenity is used to define Sade's concept of immorality. *Justine* is the story of a young woman whose horrifying experiences, according to Sade, belie the omnipotence or existence of God. Once again, he was confined to Charenton, where he died insane. He had spent twenty-seven years of his life in prison.

In 1956, a trial was held in Paris to judge whether Sade's works should still be considered as obscene and as dangerous as they had been in the nineteenth century, when reading *Justine* was said to destroy both body and soul. Though eventually published in France, Sade's work is still banned in England.

Sade's vision evokes, with frightening aptness, a Godless universe, one that knows no higher law than that of a chaotic and ultimately cruel Nature. The obscenity of his work reveals its philosophical intentions: its graphic depictions of immorality were intended to liberate Sade from the rules of church, state, and any restraining conventions. Though certainly not considered a major writer, Sade created a fictional world of incomparable horror and depravity, in which some critics find a terrifying indication of man's innate brutality.

PRINCIPAL WORKS

Justine, ou les malheurs de la vertu (novel) 1791
[*Justine; or, The Misfortunes of Virtue*, 1931; also
published as *Justine; or, Good Conduct Well Chastised*,
1953]
La philosophie dans le boudoir (novel) 1795
[*The Bedroom Philosophers*, 1953; also published as
Philosophy in the Bedroom, 1965]
Juliette, ou les prospérités du vice (novel) 1797
[*The Story of Juliette; or, Vice Amply Rewarded*, 1965]
La nouvelle Justine (novel) 1797
[*The New Justine*, 1956]
Les crimes de l'amour (short stories) 1800
[*The Crimes of Love*, 1964; also published as *The Crimes
of Passion*, 1965]
*Les 120 journées de Sodome, ou l'école du libertinage
(unfinished novel) 1904
[*The 120 Days of Sodom; or, The Romance of the School
for Libertinage*, 1954]
**Dialogue entre un prêtre et un moribund (novel) 1926
[*Dialogue between a Priest and a Dying Man*, 1927]

*This work was written in 1785.

**This work was written in 1782.

MARQUIS de SADE (essay date 1800)

I must reply to the reproach leveled at me when *Aline et Valcour* was published. My brush, 'twas said, was too vivid. I depict vice with too hateful a countenance. Would anyone care to know why? I have no wish to make vice seem attractive. Unlike Crébillon and Dorat, I have not set myself the dangerous goal of enticing women to love characters who deceive them; on the contrary, I want them to loathe these characters. 'Tis the only way whereby one can avoid being duped by them. And, in order to succeed in that purpose, I painted that hero who treads the path of vice with features so frightful that they will most assuredly not inspire either pity or love. In so doing, I dare say, I am become more moral than those who believe they have license to embellish them. The pernicious works by these authors are like those fruits from America beneath whose highly polished skins there lurk the seeds of death. This betrayal of Nature, the motive of which 'tis not incumbent upon us to reveal, is not done for man. Never, I say it again, never shall I portray crime other than clothed in the colors of hell. I wish people to see crime laid bare, I want them to fear it and detest it, and I know no other way to achieve this end than to paint it in all its horror. Woe unto those who surround it with roses! their views are far less pure, and I shall never emulate them. Given which, let no one any longer ascribe to me the authorship of *J . . . . .* [*Justine*]; I have never written any such works, and I surely never shall. They are naught but imbeciles or evildoers who, despite the authenticity of my denials, can still suspect me of being the author of that work, and I shall henceforth use as my sole arm against their calumnies the most sovereign contempt. (pp. 115-16)

Marquis de Sade, ''Reflections on the Novel'' (originally published as ''Idée sur les romans,'' in his Les crimes de l'amour, *Massé, 1800), in* The Marquis de Sade: The 120 Days of Sodom and Other Writings, *edited and translated by Austryn Wainhouse and Richard Seaver (reprinted by permission of Grove Press, Inc.; copyright © 1966 by Austryn Wainhouse and Richard Seaver), Grove Press, 1966, pp. 91-116.*

VILLETERQUE (essay date 1800)

A detestable book by a man suspected of having written one even more horrible. I do not know, nor do I wish to know, to what extent this suspicion has any foundation in fact. A journalist has the right to pass judgment on books, and not the right to make accusations. I shall go even further: he ought to feel sorry for him over whose head there hovers so terrible a suspicion, until such time as, having been found guilty, he is denounced for public execration.

In a piece entitled **"Reflections on the Novel"** [see excerpt above], which serves as a preface to *Les Crimes de l'Amour,* the author raises three questions, which he proposes to answer: Why is this kind of literary work called a ''novel''? Amongst what people did the novel originate, and what are the most famous examples history has to offer? And, finally, what are the rules one must follow if one wishes to succeed in writing well?

I shall not bother with the first two questions, which have been discussed frequently and in sufficient detail by others, except to remark that the author, in discussing these first two questions, makes a great show of his erudition, which is actually riddled with errors, and prates on irrelevantly about them at great length. I shall move on to what he calls, with respect to the novel, ''perfecting the art of writing.''

''It is not,'' says the author, ''by making virtue triumph that we arouse interest. This is no wise essential in the novel. Nor is it even the rule most likely to arouse interest on the part of the reader. For when virtue triumphs, the world being in joint and things as they ought to be, our tears cease to flow even, as it were, before they have begun. But if, after severe trials and tribulations, we finally witness 'virtue overwhelmed by vice,' our hearts are inevitably rent asunder and, the work having moved us deeply, it must indubitably arouse the interest which alone can assure a writer of his laurels.''

Is this not tantamount to reducing into principles the plot of the infamous work which the author disclaims [*Justine*]? Do we not run the risk, by simply repudiating and disassociating ourselves from the notoriety connected with the execrable form of this work, do we not run the risk of seeming to embrace its basic premises, which in the final analysis are none other than to portray ''virtue overwhelmed by vice''?

Why else would anyone paint scenes in which crime reigns triumphant? Such scenes awaken evil tendencies in the wicked; from the virtuous man, who is ever steadfast in his principles, they provoke cries of indignation; and in him whose heart is willing but whose flesh is weak, they incite despondent tears. These horrible portraits of crime do not even serve the purpose of rendering crime more odious; therefore, they are both useless and dangerous. These calamitous principles are so patently false that even those persons who subscribe to them in private disown them in public. (pp. 117-18)

I was unable to read these four volumes, full of the most revolting atrocities, without a feeling of indignation. Nor does the author's style in any wise compensate the reader for the disgust inspired by the stories themselves. In the present work, that style is pitiful, constantly lacking in any sense of proportion, teeming with sentences in bad taste, filled with contradictions and trivial reflections. Now and then, in a few pages, one finds a smattering of reflections which are reasonable and based upon principles of justice, but 'tis as though they were tacked onto the work as an afterthought. One feels they do not relate at all to anything which has preceded or to anything that follows.

Nor should the reader believe for a moment that a single crime for every story is sufficient for the author, for such is not the case; he crams them in: 'tis a tissue of horrors. (pp. 118-19)

You who write novels, 'tis no longer in the world around you, in the realm of reality whose events either trouble or embellish life, nor is it any longer in the more complete and perfect understanding of the human heart, that you must look for your subjects. Rather must you delve into the history of poisoning, debauchery, and murder, and draw therefrom. And you must portray villains as being happy—all for the greater glory and encouragement of virtue.

Rousseau, Voltaire, Marmontel, Fielding, Richardson, et al., you have not written novels. You have painted customs, you should have painted crimes. You make virtue appear attractive by proving to us that virtue alone is the way to happiness. You are all wrong. You should show us "virtue overwhelmed by vice"; 'tis thus one instructs and holds the reader's interest. (p. 119)

> Villeterque, *"Villeterque's Review of 'Les crimes de l'amour'"* (originally published under a different title in Le journal des arts, des sciences, et de la littérature, *Vol. IX, No. 90, October 22, 1800), in* The Marquis de Sade: The 120 Days of Sodom and Other Writings, *edited and translated by Austryn Wainhouse and Richard Seaver (reprinted by permission of Grove Press, Inc.; copyright © 1966 by Austryn Wainhouse and Richard Seaver), Grove Press, 1966, pp. 117-20.*

D.-A.-F. de SADE (essay date 1803)

From the stupid account Villeterque gave *Les Crimes de l'Amour* [see excerpt above], 'tis obvious he has not read the book. If he had, he would never have put words into my mouth that have never even crossed my mind; nor would he quote out of context isolated phrases—which someone no doubt dictated to him—in order that, by twisting them to fit his purpose, he might give them a meaning they were never intended to have.

And yet, without having read the book (as I have just shown), Villeterque begins by labeling my work DETESTABLE and by CHARITABLY declaring that this DETESTABLE *work comes from the hand of a man suspected of having penned one even more* HORRIBLE.

At this point, I challenge Villeterque to do two things he cannot refuse me: 1) To publish not isolated, truncated, and mutilated phrases, but complete passages which prove my book to be DETESTABLE, although those who have read it are in agreement that it is, on the contrary, a work solidly based upon a refined and heightened sense of morality. 2) I challenge him

to prove that I am the author of that even more HORRIBLE book. (pp. 121-22)

I state and affirm that I have never written any *immoral books,* and that I never shall. I repeat it again here, not for the sake of the hack writer Villeterque—'twould be seeming to ascribe too much weight to his opinion—but for the sake of the public, whose judgment I respect as much as I despise Villeterque's. (p. 122)

In my **"Reflections on the Novel,"** Villeterque-the-ignoramus assures us that I am guilty of an infinite number of errors, despite all my seeming erudition. Here again should the charge not be backed up by proof? But in order to recognize errors of *erudition,* one must have a smattering of erudition oneself, and Villeterque, who is soon going to demonstrate that he does not have even a nodding acquaintance with scholarly works, is far from possessing the erudition it would require to prove my errors. Therefore he limits himself to declaring that I commit them, without having the courage to specify what they are. (p. 123)

Yes, learned and profound *Vile stercus,* I have said before and I say again that the study of the great masters has proven to me that 'twas not through the constant triumph of virtue that a writer could claim to hold the public's interest in a novel or a tragedy; that this rule, whether it applies to Nature herself or to the works of Aristotle or those of any of our poets, is one whereunto all men must conform for the common weal, without its being absolutely essential in a dramatic work of whatever kind. But what I am expounding here are not my own principles; I am inventing nothing new: read my works and you will see not only that what I am saying here is but the result of the impact upon me of a close study of the great masters, but also that I have not even adhered to this maxim, however excellent or wise I deem it to be. For, in the final analysis, what are the two principal mainsprings of dramatic art? Have all the authors worthy of the name not declared that they are *terror* and *pity*? Now, what can provoke *terror* if not the portrayal of crime triumphant, and what can cause *pity* better than the depiction of virtue a prey to misfortune? One therefore has either to forego interest or submit to these principles. That Villeterque is not widely enough read to appreciate the truth of this statement, so be it, this will be a source of surprise to no one. It is useless to be familiar with the rules of any art when one's only ambition is to write soporific bedtime stories, or to copy some insipid tales out of *A Thousand and One Nights* with a view toward proudly passing them off as one's own. But if Villeterque-the-plagiarist is unaware of these principles, for the simple reason that he is unaware of practically everything, at least he does not dispute them. (p. 124)

I prove that without bringing virtue into the picture, it is impossible to write any dramatic work worthy of the name; I offer this truth, since I believe and affirm that indignation, anger, and tears must be the result of the insults whereof virtue is the object and the misfortunes wherewith it is afflicted. And from this, if one is to believe Villeterque, it follows that I am the author of that execrable book wherein one finds the exact opposite of everything I set forth and profess! Yes, quite the exact opposite, for the author of that work appears to make vice triumph over virtue only out of spite . . . or out of libertinage. A perfidious scheme, from which he has no doubt not deemed it necessary to derive the least dramatic interest, whilst the models I cite have always taken the opposite tack, and whilst I, insofar as my poor powers have enabled me to emulate these masters, have depicted vice in my works only in those colors most likely to make it forever detested; and if upon occasion I have allowed vice some modicum of triumph over virtue, it was never for any other reason than to make virtue appear more interesting or more beautiful. My taking the opposite tack from that taken by the author of the book in question does not mean, therefore, that I accept or sanction that author's principles. Since I loathe these principles and shun them in my works, I therefore cannot have adopted them. And Villeterque-the-irresponsible, who imagines he will prove my guilt by in fact citing the very evidence which exonerates me from it, is in consequence naught but a cowardly *slanderer*, whom it behooves us to unmask.

"But, pray tell, what is the purpose of all these scenes of crime triumphant?" asks the hack. The purpose, Villeterque, is to have them act as a foil for the opposite scenes, and that in itself is quite enough to prove their usefulness. Furthermore, where precisely does crime emerge triumphant in those stories you attacked so *stupidly* and with such *effrontery*? (pp. 125-26)

In *Florville et Courval*, does the hand of fate allow crime to triumph? All the characters who involuntarily perpetrate these crimes are but the pawns of that fate wherewith the Greeks endowed their gods. Do we not daily witness the same events as the misfortunes of Oedipus and his family? (p. 127)

Finally, in *Eugénie de Franval,* does the monster I painted not run himself through with his own sword?

Villeterque . . . Villeterque-the-hack, where in the name of all that is holy does crime emerge victorious in my stories? Ah! the truth of the matter is that the only thing I see triumphing here is your own ignorance and your cowardly desire to slander.

Now, I ask my *reprehensible censor* upon what grounds he dares to describe such a work as "a compilation of revolting atrocities," when none of his reproaches proves to be well founded? And once having proved that much, what remains of the criticism leveled by that inept *phrase-maker*? Nothing but satire without a trace of wit, of criticism without the slightest discernment, and of spleen without provocation—all because Villeterque is a fool, and from fools there never stems aught but foolish things. I contradict myself, the pedagogue Villeterque goes on to say, whenever I put into the mouth of one of my protagonists thoughts in any wise contrary to those enunciated in my preface. Loathsome ignoramus: have you not yet learned that every character in any dramatic work must employ a language in keeping with his character, and that, when he does, 'tis the fictional personage who is speaking and not the author? and that, in such an instance, 'tis indeed common that the character, inspired by the role he is playing, says things completely contrary to what the author may say when he himself is speaking? . . . Ah, Monsieur Villeterque, what a fool you are! This is one truth concerning which both I and my characters will always be in complete agreement whenever we have the occasion to exchange views regarding your prosaic existence. But what a show of weakness on my part! Must I then resort to reason when 'tis contempt that is called for? And, indeed, what more does a lout deserve, one who dares to say to him who at every turn has castigated vice: "Show me some villains who are happy, 'tis what is required for one to perfect one's art: the author of *Les Crimes de l'Amour* will prove it to you!" No, Villeterque, I neither claimed nor proved any such thing; and in my defense I appeal from your stupidity to the enlightenment of the public. I said quite the contrary, Villeterque, and my works are constructed upon the opposite bases. (pp. 127-28)

Ah! Villeterque, I have somewhere written that when one aspires to write without having the good fortune to be endowed with any talent for it, it would be infinitely preferable to fashion ladies' dancing pumps or boots; at the time I wrote these words, I did not realize they were meant for you. Follow that advice, my good fellow, pray do; you may perhaps turn out to be a tolerable good shoemaker, but as sure as I'm alive you will never be anything but a wretched writer. (p. 129)

D.-A.-F. de Sade, "The Author of 'Les crimes de l'amour' to Villeterque, Hack Writer" (originally published as a pamphlet by Massé, 1803), in The Marquis de Sade: The 120 Days of Sodom and Other Writings, *edited and translated by Austryn Wainhouse and Richard Seaver (reprinted by permission of Grove Press, Inc.; copyright © 1966 by Austryn Wainhouse and Richard Seaver), Grove Press, 1966, pp. 121-32.*

J. K. HUYSMANS (essay date 1884)

[Sadism, a] strange and ill-defined condition cannot in fact arise in the mind of an unbeliever. It does not consist simply in riotous indulgence of the flesh, stimulated by bloody acts of cruelty, for in that case it would be nothing more than a deviation of the genetic instincts, a case of satyriasis developed to its fullest extent; it consists first and foremost in a sacrilegious manifestation, in a moral rebellion, in a spiritual debauch, in a wholly idealistic, wholly Christian aberration. There is also something in it of joy tempered by fear, a joy analogous to the wicked delight of disobedient children playing with forbidden things for no other reason than that their parents have expressly forbidden them to go near them.

The truth of the matter is that if it did not involve sacrilege, sadism would have no *raison d'être;* on the other hand, since sacrilege depends on the existence of a religion, it cannot be deliberately and effectively committed except by a believer, for a man would derive no satisfaction whatever from profaning a faith that was unimportant or unknown to him.

The strength of sadism then, the attraction it offers, lies entirely in the forbidden pleasure of transferring to Satan the homage and the prayers that should go to God; it lies in the flouting of the precepts of Catholicism, which the sadist actually observes in topsy-turvy fashion when, in order to offend Christ the more grievously, he commits the sins Christ most expressly proscribed—profanation of holy things and carnal debauch.

In point of fact, this vice to which the Marquis de Sade had given his name was as old as the Church itself; the eighteenth century, when it was particularly rife, had simply revived, by an ordinary atavistic process, the impious practices of the witches' sabbath or medieval times—to go no further back in history. (p. 162)

[An] outpouring of foul-mouthed jests and degrading insults was to be seen in the works of the Marquis de Sade, who spiced his frightful sensualities with sacrilegious profanities. He would rail at Heaven, invoke Lucifer, call God an abject scoundrel, a crazy idiot, spit on the sacrament of communion, do his best in fact to besmirch with vile obscenities a Divinity he hoped would damn him, at the same time declaring, as a further act of defiance, that that Divinity did not exist. (p. 163)

J. K. Huysmans, in a chapter from his novel Against Nature, *translated by Robert Baldick (translation copyright © 1959 by the Estate of Robert Baldick; reprinted by permission of Penguin Books Ltd; orig-*

inally published as À rebours, *G. Charpentier, 1884), Penguin Books Inc., 1959, pp. 144-65.*

EDGELL RICKWORD (essay date 1926)

Sade places his positive value on the destructive impulses because, he would say, they ensure a swifter return to Nature of the raw material of which it is in need, breaking down the more complex organisms into simpler ones. But this seems to be a value derived from sensibility alone, for there is no reason to believe that the energy pent up in the body of a man is abstracted from Nature; rather, the more complex organizations enable more energy to be expended, mass for mass, than simpler ones. If the end of existence is the running down of this primordial, universal movement to zero-level, stillness; then for this a poet would seem to be more effective than the same weight of maggots.

The illogical judgement is a clue to temperament. In spite of Sade's appearance of being a sensationist, a pursuer of whatever may excite or stimulate the nerves, his implacable hostility to the object of passion shows that he is actually seeking to annihilate the concept of perception. Freud suggests in 'Beyond the Pleasure-Principle' that when an organism ostensibly seeks pleasure, its desire is a release from the pressure of, physically, the sexual glands, metaphysically, the world of phenomenon . . . a womb-like state in which there would be no differentiation between the subject and the concept, such as would exist in Sade's cosmos with the cessation of the individual consciousness. (pp. 217-18)

In the phantasmal world of Sade's romances the moral platitude is elaborated and illustrated with the audacity and inventiveness of the dream-power. The futility of virtue, its fatal contradiction by the actual workings of the world of matter, which makes it a source of pain and disappointment to those who try to carry out its ludicrous code, and the fact that this virtue is, after all, only a roundabout way of getting what we want, persuade him that it is better to yield directly to impulse, no matter what the consequences to others. (p. 218)

> *Edgell Rickword, "Notes for a Study of Sade" (originally published in* The Calendar of Letters *Vol. 2, No. 12, February, 1926), in his* Essays and Opinions: 1921-1931, *edited by Alan Young (copyright © Edgell Rickword 1920, 1921, 1922, 1923, 1924, 1925, 1926, 1927, 1928, 1929, 1930, 1931, 1974; reprinted by permission), Carcanet Press, 1974, pp. 213-22.*

MARIO PRAZ (essay date 1930)

Let us give Sade his due, as having been the first to expose, in all its crudity, the mechanism of *homo sensualis,* let us even assign him a place of honour as a psycho-pathologist and admit his influence on a whole century of literature; but courage (to give a nobler name to what most people would call shamelessness) does not suffice to give originality to a thought, nor does the hurried jotting down of all the cruel fantasies which obsess the mind suffice to give a work mastery of style. It is true that the Surrealists, who have now made themselves the champions of Sade's greatness, hold a curious theory on the subject of 'automatic writing', as being the only kind of writing to reveal the whole man, without hypocrisy or changes of mind; but this theory of untrammelled self-expression is precisely an extreme application of that very romanticism which, being so open to Sade's influence, is on that account the least fitted to

judge him dispassionately. The most elementary qualities of a writer—let us not say, of a writer of genius—are lacking in Sade. . . . [His] whole merit lies in having left documents illustrative of the mythological, infantile phase of psycho-pathology: he gives, in the form of a fantastic tale, the first systematized account of sexual perversions.

Was Sade a 'surromantique'? No, but he was certainly a sinister force in the Romantic Movement, a familiar spirit whispering in the ear of the 'mauvais maîtres' and the 'poètes maudits'; actually he did nothing more than give a name to an impulse which exists in every man, an impulse mysterious as the very forces of life and death with which it is inextricably connected. (pp. xvii-xviii)

[The Marquis de Sade]—and here was his originality—reversed the convenient ethical theory of [Darles de Montighy's] *Thérèse philosophe,* which was actually the same as that of Jean-Jacques [Rousseau]. 'Everything is good, everything is the work of God' becomes in him 'Everything is evil, everything is the work of Satan'. It is therefore necessary to practise vice because it conforms to the laws of nature (Rousseau's 'les plus pures lois de la nature'!) which insists upon destruction. Evil is the axis of the universe. . . . (p. 104)

The Marquis de Sade empties his world of all psychological content except the pleasures of destruction and transgression, and moves in an opaque atmosphere of mere matter, in which his characters are degraded to the status of instruments for provoking the so-called divine ecstasy of destruction. . . . [The] butcheries of Sade are hardly different from experiments in a chemical laboratory. . . . The cycle of possible chemical disaggregations which constitute his tortures is soon exhausted, because, as Proust remarks, nothing is more limited than pleasure and vice, and—to make a play upon words—it may be said that the vicious man moves always in the same vicious circle. The sense of the infinite, banished from human relationships by the suppression of any spiritual meaning, takes refuge in a sort of cosmic satanism. . . . (pp. 106-07)

[There] is a *reductio ad absurdum* of Sade's 'philosophy', since, if it is admitted that Nature's aim is destruction and that no act of destruction can irritate or insult her . . . , the supreme insult which can be had upon her, and from which the sadist should legitimately derive the greatest pleasure of transgression, would be precisely—the practice of virtue! And the supreme joy of sadism should in fact be the joy of remorse and expiation: from Gilles de Rais to Dostoievsky the parabola of vice is always identical. (pp. 107-08)

[The persecutions] of Justine, developing on a physical plane, offer no more spiritual interest than a series of chemical experiments. (p. 108)

> *Mario Praz, "Preface to the First Edition" and "The Shadow of the Divine Marquis," in his* The Romantic Agony, *translated by Angus Davidson (translation © Oxford University Press 1970; reprinted by permission of Oxford University Press; originally published as* La carne, la morte e il diavolo nella letteratura romantica, *Soc. editrice "La Cultura", 1930), second edition, Oxford University Press, London, 1970, pp. xv-xxiii, 95-196.*

MAURICE BLANCHOT (essay date 1949)

Today, when the writings of Henry Miller cause us to quake and quail, who would dare to compete with Sade's licentiousness? Yes, the claim can be made: we have here the most scandalous work ever written. Is this not reason enough for us to turn our attention to it? What! You mean to say we have here the opportunity to acquaint ourselves with a work beyond which no other writer, at any time, has ever managed to venture; we have, so to speak, a veritable absolute in our hands, in this relative world of letters, and we make no attempt to question or consult it? You mean to say it does not occur to us to ask *why* it is unique, why it cannot be exceeded, what there is about it which is so outrageous, so eternally too strong for man to stomach? Curious neglect. But can it be that the purity of the scandal is solely dependent upon this neglect? When one considers the precautions that history has taken to make a prodigious enigma out of Sade, when one thinks of those twenty-seven years behind bars, of that fettered and forbidden existence, when the sequestration affects not only a man's life but his afterlife—so much so that the condemnation of his work to seclusion seems to condemn him as well, still alive, to some eternal prison—then one is led to wonder whether the censors and judges who claim to immure Sade are not actually serving him instead, are not fulfilling the most fervent wishes of his libertinage, he who always aspired to the solitude of the earth's entrails, to the mystery of a subterranean and reclusive existence. In a dozen different ways, Sade formulated the idea that man's wildest excesses call for secrecy, for the obscurity of the farthest depths, the inviolable solitude of a cell. (pp. 37-8)

Luckily, Sade defends himself rather well. Not only his work but his thinking remains impenetrable—and this in spite of the fact that both abound in detailed theories, which he expounds and repeats over and over again with disconcerting patience, and in spite of the fact that he reasons with impeccable clarity and not inconsiderable logic. He has a penchant—and even a passion—for systems. He expounds and affirms and offers proof; he comes back to the same problem a hundred times over (and a hundred is a conservative figure), he studies it from every angle, he considers every possible objection and answers them all, then manages to come up with some further objections and replies to them as well. And since what he says is usually simple enough, since his language is rich but precise and firm, it would seem that nothing should be more simple in dealing with Sade than to elucidate the ideology which, in his case, is inseparable from passion. And yet, what *is* the gist of Sade's thought? What in fact *did* he say? What is the scheme, the order of this system? Where does it begin and where does it end? Is there, indeed, more than the shadow of a system in the probing of this mind, so obsessed as it is with reason? And why is it that so many well co-ordinated principles fail to form the solid whole which they ought to and which, at least on the surface, they in fact seem to? That too remains unclear. Such is the first peculiar characteristic of Sade: his theories and ideas are constantly generating and unleashing irrational forces to which they are bound. (p. 39)

Sade's stated principles—what we may term his basic philosophy—appears to be simplicity itself. This philosophy is one of self-interest, of absolute egoism: Each of us must do exactly as he pleases, each of us is bound by one law alone, that of his own pleasure. This morality is based upon the primary fact of absolute solitude. Sade has stated it, and repeated it, in every conceivable form: Nature wills that we be born alone, there is no real contact or relationship possible between one person and another. The only rule of conduct for me to follow, therefore, is to prefer whatever affects me pleasurably and, conversely, to hold as naught anything which, as a result of

my preferences, may cause harm to others. The greatest pain inflicted on others is of less account than my own pleasure. Little do I care if the price I have to pay for my least delight is an awesome accumulation of atrocious crimes, for pleasure flatters me, it is within, while the effects of crime, being outside me, do not affect me.

These principles are clear. We find them reiterated and developed in a thousand ways through some twenty volumes. Sade never tires of them. What he infinitely enjoys is to square them against the prevailing theories of the time, the theories of man's equality before Nature and the law. He then proposes this kind of reasoning: Since all men are equal in the eyes of Nature, I therefore have the right, because of this identity, not to sacrifice myself for the preservation of others, their ruin being indispensable to my happiness. Or else he will propound a kind of Declaration of the Rights of Eroticism, with this axiom—equally valid for men and women alike—as a fundamental precept: Give yourself to whomsoever desires you, take from whomever you please. "What evil do I do, what crime do I commit when, upon meeting some lovely creature, I say: 'Avail me of that part of you which can give me a moment's satisfaction and, if you wish, make full use of that part of mine which may prove agreeable to you'?" To Sade, such propositions seem irrefutable. For pages on end he invokes the equality of individuals and the reciprocity of rights, without ever realizing that his arguments, far from being buttressed by these lofty principles, are becoming meaningless because of them. (p. 40)

Sade discerned clearly that, at the time he was writing, power was a social category, that it was part and parcel of the organization of society such as it existed both before and after the Revolution. But he also believes that power (like solitude, moreover) is not merely a state but a choice and a conquest, and that only he is so powerful who by his own will and energy knows how to make himself so. Actually, Sade's heroes are recruited from two opposing milieux: from among the highest and the lowest, from among the mighty of the world and, at the opposite pole, fished up from the sewers and cesspools of the lower depths. (p. 42)

[Equality,] inequality; freedom to oppress, revolt against the oppressor; these are merely provisional arguments by which Sadean man, depending on his position in the social hierarchy, asserts his right to power. Actually, the distinction between those who require crime in order to survive and those for whom crime is the sole source of pleasure, will soon vanish. (p. 43)

Now, what happens? A few men have become powerful. Some were bequeathed power by birth, but they have also demonstrated that they deserve it by the way in which they have accrued it and enjoyed it. Others have risen to power, and the sign of their success is that, once having resorted to crime to acquire power, they use it to acquire the freedom to commit any crime whatsoever. Such then is Sade's world: a few people who have reached the pinnacle, and around them an infinite, nameless dust, an anonymous mass of creatures which has neither rights nor power. Let us see what now happens to the rule of absolute egoism. I do whatever I please, says Sade's hero, all I know, all I recognize is my own pleasure, and to make certain I get it I torture and kill. You threaten me with a like fate the day I shall happen to meet someone whose happiness is dependent on torturing and killing me. But I have acquired power precisely in order to raise myself above this threat. Whenever Sade comes up with answers such as these, we can feel ourselves slipping toward an area of his thought which is sustained solely by the obscure forces which lurk therein. (pp. 43-4)

There can be no doubt that Sade is profoundly convinced of at least this: that the man of absolute egoism can never fall upon evil days; better, that he will, without exception, be forever happy, and happy to the highest degree. A mad idea? Perhaps. But with Sade the idea is allied to forces so violent that they finally render irrefutable, in his eyes, the ideas they support. In actual fact, the translation of this conviction into doctrine is not at all that simple. Sade resorts to several solutions, he tries them endlessly, although none can really ever satisfy him. The first is strictly verbal: it consists in repudiating the social contract which, according to Sade, is the safeguard of the weak and, theoretically, constitutes a grave menace for the powerful. (p. 45)

[Although] the heroes of his books are constantly drawn into close alliance with one another by the conventions which determine the limits of their power and superimpose order on chaos, the possibility of betrayal is forever present: between accomplices there is a constantly mounting tension, so much so that they ultimately feel themselves less bound by the oath that unites them than by the mutual need to violate this oath. (p. 47)

For Sade, sovereign man is impervious to evil because no one can do him any harm. He is a man possessed of every passion, and his passions are slaked by any and every thing. . . . The absolute egoist is he who is able to transform everything disagreeable into something likable, everything repugnant into something attractive. Like the bedroom philosopher, he declares: "I love everything, I enjoy everything, my desire is to commingle all kinds and contraries." (p. 50)

[To] the integral man, who is at his fullest, there is no possible evil. If he injures others, the result is voluptuous; injury endured at their hands is sheer delight. Virtue pleases him because Virtue is weak and he crushes it; Vice pleases him because he finds pleasure in the chaos that results from it, even though it be at his expense. If he lives, there is no circumstance, no event that he cannot turn into happiness. And if he dies, he finds an even greater happiness in his death, and in the knowledge of his destruction he sees the crowning achievement of a life whose sole justification lay in the need to destroy. He is therefore inaccessible to others. He is impervious to all attacks, nothing can rob him of his power to be himself and to enjoy himself. That is the primary meaning of his solitude. Even if he in his turn seemingly becomes a victim and a thrall, the violence of the passions he knows how to slake in any situation assures him of his sovereignty and makes him feel that in any circumstance, in life as in death, he remains omnipotent. It is for this reason that, despite the analogy of the descriptions, it seems only fair to leave to Sacher-Masoch the paternity of masochism, and the paternity of sadism to Sade. The pleasure Sade's heroes find in degradation never lessens their self-possession, and abjection adds to their stature. Shame, remorse, a penchant for punishment—all such feelings are foreign to them. (pp. 51-2)

Sade's heroes draw their sustenance from the deaths they cause, and there are times when, dreaming of everlasting life, he dreams of a death he can inflict eternally. The result is that the executioner and the victim, set eternally face to face, find themselves endowed equally with the same power, with the same divine attribute of eternity. It would be impossible to claim that such a contradiction does not exist in Sade's work.

But even more often he attempts to by-pass it by the use of arguments that give us a much clearer and more profound picture of the world that is his. . . . It may well be that the criminal is inextricably bound to and involved with the person he murders. But the libertine who, as he immolates his victim, feels only the need to sacrifice a thousand others, seems strangely free of all involvement with him. In his eyes, the victim does not of itself exist, he is not a distinct individual but a mere sign, which is indefinitely replaceable in a vast erotic equation. When we read statements such as this: "Nothing is so amusing, nothing so stimulates and excites the brain as do large numbers," we comprehend more fully why Sade utilizes the concept of equality so often to buttress his arguments. To declare that all men are equal is equivalent to saying that no one is worth more than any other, all are interchangeable, each is only a unit, a cipher in an infinite progression. For the Unique Person, all men are equal in their nothingness, and the Unique One, by reducing them to nothing, simply clarifies and demonstrates this nothingness.

That is what makes Sade's world so strange. Scenes of savagery are followed by more scenes of savagery. The repetition is as extraordinary as it is endless. . . . What is especially striking is the fact that the world in which the Unique One lives and moves and has his being is a desert; the creatures he encounters there are less than things, less than shades. And when he torments and destroys them he is not wresting away their lives but verifying their nothingness, establishing his authority over their non-existence, and from this he derives his greatest satisfaction. (pp. 54-5)

[Whenever] Sade's heroes exclaim: "Ah, the lovely corpse!" and wax ecstatic at the insensibility of death, they have generally begun their careers as murderers, and it is the effects of this capacity for aggression that they are striving to prolong beyond the grave. It is undeniable that what characterizes Sade's world is not the desire to become one with the cadaver's immobilized and petrified existence, nor is it the attempt to slip into the passivity of a form representing the absence of forms, of a wholly real reality, shielded and protected from life's uncertainties and yet incarnating the very essence of irreality. Quite the contrary: the center of Sade's world is the urgent need for sovereignty to assert itself by an enormous negation. This negation, which cannot be satisfied or adequately demonstrated on the plane of the particular, requires large quantities, for it is basically intended to transcend the plane of human existence. It is in vain that Sadean man imposes himself on others by his power to destroy them: if he gives the impression of never being dependent on them, even in the situation where he finds himself obliged to annihilate them—if he invariably seems capable of doing without them, it is because he has placed himself on a plane where he and they no longer have anything in common, and he has done this by setting himself such goals and lending his projects a scope which infinitely transcends man and his puny existence. (p. 56)

Clearly, with Sade the criminal instinct stems from a nostalgic, transcendental vision which the miserable practical possibilities are forever debasing and dishonoring. The most glorious crime which this poor world is capable of providing is a wretched nothing which makes the libertine blush with shame. (pp. 56-7)

Sade's originality seems to us to reside in his extremely firm claim to found man's sovereignty upon a transcendent power of negation, a power which in no wise depends upon the objects it destroys and which, in order to destroy them, does not even presuppose their previous existence because, at the instant it destroys them, it has already previously, and without exception, considered them as nothing. A dialectic such as this finds both its best example and, perhaps, its justification, in the stance Sade's Omnipotent One assumes with respect to divine omnipotence. . . .

Sade's is not a cold-blooded atheism. The moment the name of God is interjected into even the mildest discussion or plot, the language is instantly ignited, the tone becomes haranguing and the words are infused with and overwhelmed by hate. It is surely not in the scenes of luxury and lust that Sade's passion is revealed; but whenever the Unique One finds the slightest vestige of God in his path, then are the violence and scorn and heat of pride and the vertigo of power and desire immediately awakened. (p. 58)

Sadean man denies man, and this negation is achieved through the intermediary of the notion of God. He temporarily makes himself God, so that there before him men are reduced to nothing and discover the nothingness of a being before God. . . .

Sade's man, who has taken unto himself the power to set himself above men—the power which men madly yield to God—never for a moment forgets that this power is completely negative. To be God can have only one meaning: to crush man, to reduce creation to nothing. (p. 59)

[If] Sade's most tempestuous passions are unleashed by things religious, by the name of God and by his priests, whom Sade terms "God-makers," it is because the terms *God* and *religion* embody virtually every form of his hatred. In God, he hates the nothingness of man, who has fashioned such a master for himself, and the thought of this nothingness irritates and inflames him to such an extent that all he can do is join forces with God to sanction this nothingness. And he also hates God's omnipotence, in which he recognizes what should properly belong to him, and God becomes the figure and embodiment of his infinite hate. And finally, what he hates in God is God's poverty, the nullity of an existence which, however much it may posit itself as existence and creation, is nothing, for what is great, what is everything, is the spirit of destruction.

This spirit of destruction, in Sade's system, is identified with Nature. . . . "Nature" is one of those words Sade, like so many eighteenth-century authors, delighted in writing. It is in the name of Nature that he wages his battle against God and against everything that God stands for, especially morality. There is no need to emphasize this point: Sade emphasizes it over and over again; his material on the subject is truly staggering. According to him, this Nature is first of all universal life, and for hundreds and hundreds of pages his whole philosophy consists in reiterating that immoral instincts are good, since they are the facts of Nature, and the first and last appeal must be to Nature. In other words, no morality: the fact reigns. But subsequently, bothered by the equal value he sees himself obliged to accord both to good and evil instincts and impulses, he attempts to establish a new scale of values with crime at the summit. . . . Sade was perfectly well aware of the fact that to annihilate everything is not to annihilate the world, for the world is not only universal affirmation but universal destruction as well, and can be represented alike by the totality of being and the totality of non-being. It is for this reason that the struggle with Nature represents, in man's history, a far more advanced dialectical stage than his struggle with God. We can safely state, without fear of unduly modernizing Sade's thought, that he was one of the first thinkers of his century to have

recognized and incorporated into his world view the notion of transcendence: since the notion of nothingness, of non-being, belongs to the world, one cannot conceive of the world's non-being except from within a totality, which is still the world.

If crime is the spirit of Nature, there is no crime against Nature and, consequently, there is no crime possible. Sade states this, at times with the most profound satisfaction, and then again with the deepest resentment and rage. For to deny the possibility of crime allows him to deny morality and God and all human values; but to deny crime is also to renounce the spirit of negation, to admit that this spirit can suppress itself. (pp. 61-4)

Sade, having discovered that in man negation was power, claimed to base man's future on negation carried to the extreme. To reach this ultimate limit, he dreamed up—borrowing from the vocabulary of his time—a principle which, by its very ambiguity, represents a most ingenious choice. This principle is: Energy. Energy is, actually, a completely equivocal notion. It is both a reserve of forces and an expenditure of forces, both potential and kinetic, an affirmation which can only be wrought by means of negation, and it is the power which is destruction. Furthermore, it is both fact and law, axiom and value.

One thing quite striking is that Sade, in a universe full of effervescence and passion, suppresses desire and deems it suspect rather than emphasizing it and raising it to the highest level of importance. The reason he does so is that desire denies solitude and leads to a dangerous acknowledgment of the world of others. But when Saint-Fond declares:

> My passions, concentrated on a single point, resemble the rays of a sun assembled by a magnifying glass: they immediately set fire to whatever object they find in their way,

we can see very clearly why "destruction" and "power" may appear synonymous, without the destroyed object deriving the slightest value from this operation. This principle has another advantage: it assigns man a future without saddling him with any feeling of indebtedness to any transcendental concept. For this all honor is due Sade. He has claimed to overthrow the morality of Good, but despite a few provocative affirmations he has been very careful not to replace it with a Gospel of Evil. (pp. 64-5)

Sade was clearly aware of the fact that the supremacy of energetic man, insofar as he achieves this supremacy by identifying himself with the spirit of negation, is a paradoxical situation. The integral man, who asserts himself completely, is also completely destroyed. He is the man of all passions, and he is without feeling. First he destroyed himself as man, then as God, and then as Nature; thus did he become the Unique Being. Now he is all-powerful, for the negation in him has vanquished everything. To describe his formation, Sade resorts to an extremely curious concept to which he gives the classical name: *apathy.*

Apathy is the spirit of negation applied to the man who has chosen to make himself supreme. In a way, it is both the cause and the principle of energy. Sade, it would seem, reasons about as follows: the individual of today represents a certain quantum of force; generally he squanders and disperses his forces, by estranging them, to the benefit of those simulacra which parade under the names of "other people," "God," or "ideals." Through this dispersal, he makes the mistake of exhausting his possibilities, by wasting them, but what is worse, of basing his conduct on weakness, for if he expends himself on behalf of others it is because he believes he needs them as a crutch to lean upon. (pp. 66-7)

One of the most surprising aspects of Sade and his fate is that, although scandal has no better symbol than he, all that is daring and scandalous in his thinking has for so long remained unknown. There is no need to list and classify the themes he discovered—themes which the most adventurous minds of future centuries will apply themselves to developing and reaffirming. We have touched upon them in passing, and even so we have limited ourselves to depicting the main elements of his thought by stressing the basic doctrine. . . . In Sade there is also something of the traditional moralist, and it would be a simple matter to make a collection of his maxims which would make those of La Rochefoucauld seem weak and hesitant by comparison. Sade is often accused of having written badly, and, in fact, he often did write in extreme haste and with a prolixity that tries the patience. But he is also capable of a strange humor, his style reveals an icy joviality and, in its extravagance, a kind of cold innocence. . . . What is more, Sade's doctrine is presented as the theory of that depravity, a blueprint of his personal penchant, a doctrine which attempts to transpose the most repugnant anomaly into a complete *Weltanschauung*. For the first time, philosophy is openly conceived of as being the product of an illness, and it has the effrontery to present as a logical and universal theory a system the sole guarantee for which is the personal preferences of an aberrant individual.

This again is one of Sade's most important and original contributions. One may safely say that Sade performed his own psychoanalysis by writing a text wherein he consigns everything which relates to his obsessions and wherein, too, he seeks to discover what logic and what coherence his remarks reveal. But, what is more, he was the first to demonstrate, and demonstrate proudly, that from a certain personal and even monstrous form of behavior there could rightfully be derived a world view significant enough so that some eminent thinkers concerned only with the human condition were to do nothing more than to reaffirm its chief perspectives and provide added proof of its validity. (pp. 69-70)

First of all, what was he exactly? A monstrous exception, absolutely outside the pale of humanity. . . . [Examining Sade's thought closely, we see] that, amidst all its teeming contradictions, there emerges, on the problem which Sade's name illustrates, insights more significant than anything the most learned and illuminated minds have come up with on the subject to this day. We do not say that this philosophy is viable. But it does show that between the normal man who imprisons the sadistic man in an impasse, and the sadist who turns the impasse into a way out, it is the latter who is closer to the truth, who knows more about the logic of his situation and has the more profound understanding of it, and it is he who is in a position to be able to help the normal man to self-understanding, by helping him to modify the bases of all comprehension. (pp. 71-2)

> *Maurice Blanchot, "Sade," in* The Marquis de Sade: The Complete "Justine," "Philosophy in the Bedroom," *and Other Writings* by Marquis de Sade, *edited and translated by Richard Seaver and Austryn Wainhouse (reprinted by permission of Grove Press, Inc.; translation © 1955 by Richard Seaver and Austryn Wainhouse; originally published as* Lautreamont et Sade, *Editions de Minuit, 1949), Grove Press, 1965, pp. 37-72.*

ALBERT CAMUS   (essay date 1951)

[Sade] is exalted as the philosopher in chains and the first theoretician of absolute rebellion. He might well have been. In prison, dreams have no limits and reality is no curb. Intelligence in chains loses in lucidity what it gains in intensity. The only logic known to Sade was the logic of his feelings. He did not create a philosophy, but pursued a monstrous dream of revenge. Only the dream turned out to be prophetic. His desperate demand for freedom led Sade into the kingdom of servitude; his inordinate thirst for a form of life he could never attain was assuaged in the successive frenzies of a dream of universal destruction. In this way, at least, Sade is our contemporary. (pp. 36-7)

Is Sade an atheist? He says so, and we believe him, before going to prison, in his *Dialogue between a Priest and a Dying Man;* and from then on we are dumbfounded by his passion for sacrilege. One of his cruelest characters, Saint-Fond, does not in any sense deny God. He is content to develop a gnostic theory of a wicked demiurge and to draw the proper conclusions from it. Saint-Fond, it is said, is not Sade. No, of course not. A character is never the author who created him. It is quite likely, however, that an author may be all his characters simultaneously. Now, all Sade's atheists suppose, in principle, the nonexistence of God for the obvious reason that His existence would imply that He was indifferent, wicked, or cruel. Sade's greatest work ends with a demonstration of the stupidity and spite of the divinity. (p. 37)

The idea of God which Sade conceives for himself is, therefore, of a criminal divinity who oppresses and denies mankind. That murder is an attribute of the divinity is quite evident, according to Sade, from the history of religions. Why, then, should man be virtuous? Sade's first step as a prisoner is to jump to the most extreme conclusions. If God kills and repudiates mankind, there is nothing to stop one from killing and repudiating one's fellow men. This irritable challenge in no way resembles the tranquil negation that is still to be found in the *Dialogue* of 1782. The man who exclaims: "I have nothing, I give nothing," and who concludes: "Virtue and vice are indistinguishable in the tomb," is neither happy nor tranquil. The concept of God is the only thing, according to him, "which he cannot forgive man." . . . A double rebellion—against the order of the universe and against himself—is henceforth going to be the guiding principle of Sade's reasoning. In that these two forms of rebellion are contradictory except in the disturbed mind of a victim of persecution, his reasoning is always either ambiguous or legitimate according to whether it is considered in the light of topic or in an attempt at compassion.

He therefore denies man and his morality because God denies them. But he denies God even though He has served as his accomplice and guarantor up to now. For what reason? Because of the strongest instinct to be found in one who is condemned by the hatred of mankind to live behind prison walls: the sexual instinct. What is this instinct? On the one hand, it is the ultimate expression of nature, and, on the other, the blind force that demands the total subjection of human beings, even at the price of their destruction. Sade denies God in the name of nature—the ideological concepts of his time presented it in mechanistic form—and he makes nature a power bent on destruction. For him, nature is sex; his logic leads him to a lawless universe where the only master is the inordinate energy of desire. . . . The long arguments by which Sade's heroes demonstrate that nature has need of crime, that it must destroy in order to create, and that we help nature create from the moment we destroy it ourselves, are only aimed at establishing absolute freedom for the prisoner, Sade, who is too unjustly punished not to long for the explosion that will blow everything to pieces. In this respect he goes against his times: the freedom he demands is not one of principles, but of instincts.

Sade dreamed, no doubt, of a universal republic, whose scheme he reveals through his wise reformer, Zamé. He shows us, by this means, that one of the purposes of rebellion is to liberate the whole world, in that, as the movement accelerates, rebellion is less and less willing to accept limitations. But everything about him contradicts this pious dream. He is no friend of humanity, he hates philanthropists. The equality of which he sometimes speaks is a mathematical concept: the equivalence of the objects that comprise the human race, the abject equality of the victims. Real fulfillment, for the man who allows absolutely free rein to his desires and who must dominate everything, lies in hatred. (pp. 37-9)

He rejects, with exceptional perspicacity for his times, the presumptuous alliance of freedom with virtue. Freedom, particularly when it is a prisoner's dream, cannot endure limitations. It must sanction crime or it is no longer freedom. On this essential point Sade never varies. This man who never preached anything but contradictions only achieves coherence—and of a most complete kind—when he talks of capital punishment. An addict of refined ways of execution, a theoretician of sexual crime, he was never able to tolerate legal crime. . . .

But his hatred for the death penalty is at first no more than a hatred for men who are sufficiently convinced of their own virtue to dare to inflict capital punishment, when they themselves are criminals. You cannot simultaneously choose crime for yourself and punishment for others. You must open the prison gates or give an impossible proof of your own innocence. From the moment you accept murder, even if only once, you must allow it universally. (p. 40)

The universal republic could be a dream for Sade, but never a temptation. In politics his real position is cynicism. In his *Society of the Friends of Crime* he declares himself ostensibly in favor of the government and its laws, which he meanwhile has every intention of violating. It is the same impulse that makes the lowest form of criminal vote for conservative candidates. The plan that Sade had in mind assures the benevolent neutrality of the authorities. The republic of crime cannot, for the moment at least, be universal. It must pretend to obey the law. In a world that knows no other rule than murder, beneath a criminal heaven, and in the name of a criminal nature, however, Sade, in reality, obeys no other law than that of inexhaustible desire. But to desire without limit is the equivalent of being desired without limit. License to destroy supposes that you yourself can be destroyed. Therefore you must struggle and dominate. The law of this world is nothing but the law of force; its driving force, the will to power. (p. 41)

For Sade, the law of power implies barred gates, castles with seven circumvallations from which it is impossible to escape, and where a society founded on desire and crime functions unimpeded, according to the rules of an implacable system. The most unbridled rebellion, insistence on complete freedom, lead to the total subjection of the majority. For Sade, man's emancipation is consummated in these strongholds of debauchery where a kind of bureaucracy of vice rules over the life and death of the men and women who have committed themselves forever to the hell of their desires. (p. 42)

Sade, as was the custom of his period, constructed ideal societies. But, contrary to the custom of his period, he codifies the natural wickedness of mankind. He meticulously constructs a citadel of force and hatred, pioneer that he is, even to the point of calculating mathematically the amount of the freedom he succeeded in destroying. . . .

If that were all, Sade would be worthy only of the interest that attaches to all misunderstood pioneers. But once the drawbridge is up, life in the castle must go on. No matter how meticulous the system, it cannot foresee every eventuality. It can destroy, but it cannot create. The masters of these tortured communities do not find the satisfaction they so desperately desire. Sade often evokes the "pleasant habit of crime." Nothing here, however, seems very pleasant—more like the fury of a man in chains. The point, in fact, is to enjoy oneself, and the maximum of enjoyment coincides with the maximum of destruction. (p. 43)

What part, in this universe, could pleasure play or the exquisite joy of acquiescent and accomplice bodies? In it we find an impossible quest for escape from despair—a quest that finishes, nevertheless, in a desperate race from servitude to servitude and from prison to prison. If only nature is real and if, in nature, only desire and destruction are legitimate, then, in that all humanity does not suffice to assuage the thirst for blood, the path of destruction must lead to universal annihilation. We must become, according to Sade's formula, nature's executioner. But even that position is not achieved too easily. When the accounts are closed, when all the victims are massacred, the executioners are left face to face in the deserted castle. Something is still missing. The tortured bodies return, in their elements, to nature and will be born again. (p. 44)

[The] greatest degree of destruction coincides with the greatest degree of affirmation. The masters throw themselves on one another, and Sade's work, dedicated to the glory of libertinism, ends by being "strewn with corpses of libertines struck down at the height of their powers." The most powerful, the one who will survive, is the solitary, the Unique, whose glorification Sade has undertaken—in other words, himself. At last he reigns supreme, master and God. But at the moment of his greatest victory the dream vanishes. The Unique turns back toward the prisoner whose unbounded imagination gave birth to him, and they become one. He is in fact alone, imprisoned in a bloodstained Bastille, entirely constructed around a still unsatisfied, and henceforth undirected, desire for pleasure. He has only triumphed in a dream and those ten volumes crammed with philosophy and atrocities recapitulate an unhappy form of asceticism, an illusory advance from the total no to the absolute yes, an acquiescence in death at last, which transfigures the assassination of everything and everyone into a collective suicide. (p. 45)

Sade's success in our day is explained by the dream that he had in common with contemporary thought: the demand for total freedom, and dehumanization coldly planned by the intelligence. The reduction of man to an object of experiment, the rule that specifies the solution between the will to power and man as an object, the sealed laboratory that is the scene of this monstrous experiment, are lessons which the theoreticians of power will discover again when they come to organizing the age of slavery.

Two centuries ahead of time and on a reduced scale, Sade extolled totalitarian societies in the name of unbridled freedom—which, in reality, rebellion does not demand. The history and the tragedy of our times really begin with him. He only believed that a society founded on freedom of crime must coincide with freedom of morals, as though servitude had its limits. Our times have limited themselves to blending, in a curious manner, his dream of a universal republic and his technique of degradation. Finally, what he hated most, legal murder, has availed itself of the discoveries that he wanted to put to the service of instinctive murder. Crime, which he wanted to be the exotic and delicious fruit of unbridled vice, is no more today than the dismal habit of a police-controlled morality. Such are the surprises of literature. (pp. 46-7)

> Albert Camus, ''Metaphysical Rebellion,'' in his The Rebel: An Essay on Man in Revolt, edited and translated by Anthony Bower (translation © 1956 Alfred A. Knopf, Inc.; reprinted by permission of Alfred A. Knopf, Inc.; originally published as L'homme révolté, Gallimard, 1951), revised edition, Vintage Books, 1960, pp. 23-104.*

SIMONE de BEAUVOIR (essay date 1952)

From adolescence to prison, Sade had certainly known the insistent, if not obsessive, pangs of desire. There is, on the other hand, an experience which he seems never to have known: that of emotional intoxication. Never in his stories does sensual pleasure appear as self-forgetfulness, swooning, or abandon. Compare, for example, Rousseau's outpourings with the frenzied blasphemies of a Noirceuil or a Dolmancé, or the flutters of the Mother Superior in Diderot's La Religieuse with the brutal pleasures of Sade's tribades. The male aggression of the Sadist hero is never softened by the usual transformation of the body into flesh. He never, for an instant, loses himself in his animal nature; he remains so lucid, so cerebral, that philosophic discourse, far from dampening his ardor, acts as an aphrodisiac. We see how desire and pleasure explode in furious attacks upon this cold, tense body, proof against all enchantment. They do not constitute a living experience within the framework of the subject's psychophysiological unity. Instead, they blast him, like some kind of bodily accident.

As a result of this immoderateness, the sexual act creates the illusion of sovereign pleasure which gives it its incomparable value in Sade's eyes; for all his sadism strove to compensate for the absence of one necessary element which he lacked. The state of emotional intoxication allows one to grasp existence in one's self and in the other, as both subjectivity and passivity. . . . The curse which weighed upon Sade—and which only his childhood could explain—was this 'autism' which prevented him from ever forgetting himself or being genuinely aware of the reality of the other person. Had he been cold by nature, no problem would ever have arisen; but his instincts drove him toward outside objects with which he was incapable of uniting, so that he was forced to invent singular methods for taking them by force. (pp. 24-5)

Sade knew, as we have seen, that the infliction of pleasure may be an aggressive act, and his tyranny sometimes took on this character, but it did not satisfy him. To begin with, he shrinks from the kind of equality which is created by mutual pleasure. . . . 'The idea of seeing another person experience the same pleasure reduces one to a kind of equality which spoils the unutterable charms that come from despotism.' And he declares, more categorically, 'Any enjoyment is weakened when shared.' (p. 25)

The libertine 'would really deserve pity if he acted upon an inert, unfeeling object.' That is why the contortions and moans of the victim are necessary to the torturer's happiness, which explains why Verneuil made his wife wear a kind of headgear that amplified her screams. In his revolt, the tortured object asserts himself as my fellow creature, and through his intervention I achieve the synthesis of spirit and flesh which was first denied me.

If the aim is both to escape from one's self and to discover the reality of other existences, there is yet another way open; to have one's flesh mortified by others. (pp. 25-6)

His heroes amuse themselves by deflowering little girls. This bloody and sacrilegious violence tickled Sade's fancy. But even when they are initiating virgins, they often treat them as boys rather than make them bleed. More than one of Sade's characters feels a deep disgust for women's 'fronts'. Others are more eclectic in taste, but their preferences are clear. Sade never sang that part of the female body so joyously celebrated in The Arabian Nights. (pp. 26-7)

[In Sade's novels, women's] wickedness makes a striking contrast with the traditional gentleness of their sex. When they overcome their natural abjection by committing crime, they demonstrate much more brilliantly than any man that no situation can dampen the ardor of a bold spirit. But if, in imagination, they become first-rate martinets, it is because they are, in reality, born victims.

The contempt and disgust which Sade really felt for these servile, tearful, mystified, and passive creatures runs all through his work. (p. 27)

It is impossible to tell to what extent women were anything but surrogates and toys for Sade. It may be said, however, that his sexual character was essentially anal. This is confirmed by Sade's attachment to money. Trouble involving embezzlement of inheritances played an enormous role in his life. (p. 28)

Sade's coprophilia has still another meaning. 'If it is the dirty element that gives pleasure in the act of lust, then the dirtier it is, the more pleasurable it is bound to be.' Among the most obvious sexual attractions, Sade includes old age, ugliness, and bad odors. His linking of eroticism with vileness is as original as his linking it with cruelty, and can be explained in like manner. Beauty is too simple. We grasp it by an intellectual evaluation which does not free consciousness from its solitude or the body from its indifference, whereas vileness is debasing. The man who has relations with filth, like the man who wounds or is wounded, fulfills himself as flesh. It is in its misery and humiliation that the flesh becomes a gulf in which consciousness is swallowed up and where separate individuals are united. Only by being beaten, penetrated, and befouled could Sade succeed in destroying its obsessive presence.

He was not, however, masochistic in the ordinary sense of the word. He sneers bitterly at men who become slaves to women. . . . Sade's world is essentially rational and practical. The objects, whether material or human, which serve his pleasure are tools which have no mystery, and he clearly sees humiliation as a haughty ruse. Saint-Fond, for example, says, 'The humiliation of certain acts of debauchery serves as a pretext for pride.' And Sade elsewhere says of the libertine that 'the degradation which characterizes the state into which you plunge him by punishing him pleases, amuses, and delights him. Deep down he enjoys having gone so far as to deserve being treated in such a way.' (pp. 28-9)

[We] can perceive the significance of Sade's cruelty and masochism. This man, who combined a violent temperament—though quickly exhausted, it would seem—with an emotional 'apartness' almost pathological in character, sought a substitute for anxiety in the infliction of suffering or pain. The meaning of his cruelty is very complex. In the first place, it seems to be the extreme and immediate fulfillment of the instinct of coitus, its total assumption. It asserts the radical separation of the other object from the sovereign subject. It aims at the jealous destruction of what cannot be greedily assimilated. But above all, rather than crowning the orgasm impulsively, it tends to induce it by premeditation. . . . Sade also gained insight into himself as passive flesh. He slaked his thirst for self-punishment and accepted the guilt to which he had been doomed. And this enabled him to revert immediately from humility to pride through the medium of defiance. In the completely sadistic scene, the individual gives vent to his nature, fully aware that it is evil and aggressively assuming it as such. He merges vengeance and transgression and transforms the latter into glory.

There is one act which stands as the most extreme conclusion of both cruelty and masochism, for the subject asserts himself in it, in a very special way, as tyrant and criminal; I am speaking of murder. It has often been maintained that murder was the supreme end of sexuality in Sade. (pp. 30-1)

There is, no doubt, something vertiginous in the transition from life to death; and the sadist, fascinated by the conflicts between consciousness and the flesh, readily pictures himself as the agent of so radical a transformation. But though he may occasionally carry out this singular experiment, it cannot possibly afford him the supreme satisfaction. The freedom that one hoped to tyrannize to the point of annihilation has, in being destroyed, slipped away from the world in which tyranny had a hold on it. If Sade's heroes commit endless massacres, it is because none of them gives full satisfaction. (p. 31)

Blangis strangles his partners with the very fury of orgasm, and there is despair in the rage wherein desire is extinguished without satisfaction. His premeditated pleasures are less wild and more complex. (pp. 31-2)

Sadistic crime can never be adequate to its animating purpose. The victim is never more than a symbol; the subject possesses himself only as an imago, and their relationship is merely the parody of the drama which would really set them at grips in their incommunicable intimacy. (pp. 33-4)

The moment of plotting the act is an exceptional moment for the libertine because he can then be unaware of the inevitable fact, that reality will give him the lie. And if narration plays a primary role in Sadistic orgies and easily awakens senses upon which flesh-and-blood objects cease to act, the reason is that these objects can be wholly attained only in their absence. Actually there is only one way of finding satisfaction in the phantoms created by debauchery, and that is to accede to their very unreality. In choosing eroticism, Sade chose the make-believe. It was only in the imaginary that Sade could live with any certitude and without risk of disappointment. He repeated the idea throughout his work. (p. 34)

Sade had always spun stories for himself around his debauches; and the reality which served as a frame of reference for his fantasies may have given them a certain density, yet it also cramped them by its resistance. The opacity of things blurs their significance, which is the very quality which words preserve. Even a child is aware that crude drawings are more obscene than the organs and gestures which they represent, because the intention to defile is asserted in all its purity. Blasphemy is the easiest and surest of sacrilegious acts. Sade's heroes talked on and on indefatigably. . . .

Literature enabled Sade to unleash and fix his dreams and also to transcend the contradictions implied by any demonic system. Better still, it is itself a demonic act since it exhibits criminal visions in an aggressive way. That is what gives it its incomparable value. Anyone misunderstands Sade who finds it paradoxical that a 'solitary' should have engaged in such a passionate effort to communicate. He had nothing of the misanthrope who prefers the company of animals and virgin forests to his own kind. Cut off from others, he was haunted by their inaccessible presence. (p. 35)

It is both natural and striking that Sade's favorite form was parody. He did not try to set up a new universe. He contented himself with ridiculing, by the manner in which he imitated it, the one imposed upon him. He pretended to believe in the vain fancies that inhabited it; innocence, kindness, devotion, generosity and chastity. When he unctously depicted virtue in *Aline et Valcour,* in *Justine,* or in *Les Crimes de l'Amour,* he was not being merely prudent. The 'veils' in which he swathed Justine were more than a literary device. In order to derive amusement from harassing virtue, one must credit it with a certain reality. Defending his tales against the charge of immorality, Sade hypocritically wrote, 'Who can flatter himself that he has put virtue in a favorable light if the features of the vice surrounding it are not strongly emphasized?' But he meant the very opposite: how is vice to be made thrilling if the reader is not first taken in by the illusion of good? Fooling people is even more delicious than shocking them. And Sade, in spinning his sugary, roundabout phrases, tasted the keen pleasures of mystification. Unfortunately, he generally amuses himself more than he does us. His style has often the same coldness and the same insipidity as the edifying tales he transposed. . . . (pp. 36-7)

Sade was the precursor of the novel of horror, but he was too deeply rationalistic to lose himself in fantasy. When he abandons himself to the extravagances of his imagination, one does not know which to admire the most, his epic vehemence or his irony. The wonder is that the irony is subtle enough to redeem his ravings. It lends, on the contrary, a dry, poetic quality which saves them from incredibility. This somber humor which can, at times, turn on itself, is more than a mere technique. With his shame and pride, his truth and crime, Sade was the very spirit of contentiousness. It is when he plays the buffoon that he is really most serious, and when he is most outrageously dishonest, that he is most sincere. His extravagance often masks ingenuous truths, while he launches the most flagrant enormities in the form of sober and deliberate arguments; he uses all kinds of tricks to avoid being pinned down; and that is how he attains his end, which is to disturb us. (p. 37)

It was, paradoxically, the very necessity of Sade's work which imposed upon it its aesthetic limits. He did not have the perspective essential to an artist. He lacked the detachment necessary to confront reality and recreate it. He did not confront himself; he contented himself with projecting his fantasies. His accounts have the unreality, the false precision, and the monotony of schizophrenic reveries. He relates them for his own pleasure, and he is unconcerned about imposing them upon the reader. We do not feel in them the stubborn resistance of the real world or the more poignant resistance that Sade encountered in the depths of his own heart. Caves, underground passageways, mysterious castles, all the props of the Gothic novel take on a particular meaning in his work. They symbolize the isolation of the image. Perception echoes data's totality and, consequently, the obstacles which the data contain. The image is perfectly submissive and pliant. We find in it only what we put into it. (pp. 37-8)

Not only do the orgies, to which he invites us, take place in no particular time or locality, but—what is more serious—no living people are brought into play. The victims are frozen in their tearful abjection, and the torturers in their frenzies. Instead of giving them lifelike density, Sade merely daydreams about them. Remorse and disgust are unknown to them; at most they have occasional feelings of satiety. . . . If a story like Poe's 'The Pit and the Pendulum' is so full of anguish, it is because we grasp the situation from within the subject; we see Sade's heroes only from without. They are as artificial and move in a world as arbitrary as that of Florian's shepherds. That is why these perverse bucolics have the austerity of a nudist colony.

The debauches which Sade describes in such great detail systematically exhaust the anatomical possibilities of the human body but they do not reveal uncommon emotional complexes. Nevertheless, though he failed to endow them with aesthetic truth, Sade adumbrated forms of sexual behavior unknown until then, particularly those which unite mother-hatred, frigidity, intellectuality, 'passive sodomy,' and cruelty. No one has emphasized with more vigor and link between the imagination and what we call vice; and he gives us from time to time, insights of surprising depth into the relation of sexuality to existence. (pp. 38-9)

From a literary point of view, the commonplace-ridden speeches with which he intersperses his debauches finally rob them of all life and all verisimilitude. Here, too, it is not so much the reader to whom Sade is talking, but himself. His wearisome repetitions are tantamount to a purification rite whose repetition is as natural to him as regular confession is to a good Catholic. Sade does not give us the work of a free man. He makes us participate in his efforts of liberation. But it is precisely for this reason that he holds our attention. His endeavor is more genuine that the instruments it employs. Had Sade been satisfied with the determinism he professed, he should have repudiated all his moral anxieties. But these asserted themselves with a clarity that no logic could obscure. Over and above the facile excuses which he sets forth so tediously, he persists in questioning himself, in attacking. It is owing to this headstrong sincerity that, though not a consummate artist or a coherent philosopher, he deserves to be hailed as a great moralist. (pp. 40-1)

In the solitude of his prison cells, Sade lived through an ethical darkness similar to the intellectual night in which Descartes wrapped himself. He emerged with no revelation, but at least he disputed all the easy answers. If ever we hope to transcend the separateness of individuals, we may do so only on condition that we be aware of its existence. Otherwise, promises of happiness and justice conceal the worst dangers. Sade drained to the dregs the moment of selfishness, injustice, and misery, and he insisted upon its truth. The supreme value of his testimony is the fact that it disturbs us. It forces us to re-examine thoroughly the basic problem which haunts our age in different forms: the true relation between man and man. (p. 61)

Simone de Beauvoir, "Must We Burn Sade?" translated by Annette Michelson (originally published as "Faut-il-bruler Sade?" in Les temps modernes, *December, 1951 and January, 1952; translation © by*

Paul Dinnage 1962), in The Marquis de Sade, *edited by Paul Dinnage, John Calder (Publishers) Ltd.; 1962 (and reprinted by New English Library, 1972, pp. 7-61).*

EDMUND WILSON (essay date 1952)

[Let] us not try to disguise the congenital, the compulsive and inveterate sadism of the life and works of the Marquis de Sade. What, then, is he worth to the world? More than you might expect. His difficulties with his own aberrations made him interested in those of other people, and he brought to this whole so long outlawed subject a certain scientific point of view. He always likes to document himself, and he will tell you in a note that, fantastic though some hair-raising episode may sound, it is based on an actual case that recently came to light in a certain provincial city. He compiled—in *Les 120 Journées de Sodome*—the first systematic catalogue of sexual abnormalities, to the number of six hundred, for he discriminated many nuances; he anticipated Freud in perceiving that sexual constitution was determined at an early age and that a sexual element was present in all family relationships; and he had also the anthropological approach, for he was constantly invoking travel books to show that there is no sort of practice that is not somewhere the accepted thing. He was something of a scientist, something of a philosopher, something of a man of letters, and—if you can stand him at all—he is not without interest in any of these roles. He has even at moments some merit as a writer. Sade's cardinal defect as a novelist was his infantile inability to transpose his erotic fantasies into terms of the real world. The horrors that are perpetrated by his characters are made to take place in a kind of void: they rarely have any of the consequences that they would in actual life, and that they did, to his sorrow, for Sade himself. . . . But what is most striking about Sade is that, wordy and repetitious, implausible and disgusting though he tends to be, he gives expression to human malignance in a characteristically extreme and abstract eighteenth-century way that makes it forever impossible not to recognize the part it plays in all fields of human activity.

With the Surrealists and in some other quarters, the appeal of the horrific Marquis has been that of an upsetter of conventions and a purveyor of violent thrills. But there have been other reasons lately for the interest in Sade and for the curious forms it has sometimes taken. In Europe, since the Second World War, the professional intellectual has found himself under a frightening pressure: he has had to try in some way to accommodate—morally, intellectually—in the world that has been conceived by the ordinary educated man, the murderous devices for large-scale murder, for suffocating, burning or blowing up one's enemies, that the professedly Christian countries have lately been going in for as heartily as the Odin-worshipping Nazis, the Emperor-worshipping Japanese, or the officially atheist Russians; and here is a writer, the Marquis de Sade, of whom one knows that he always insisted that such things were perfectly normal and who tried to reason about them. The atrocities he loves to describe do not today seem as outrageous as they did before. . . . The result of consulting the work of a professional diabolic to find some way of coming to terms with the forces of destruction that threaten one is, thus, to be moved to attempt to tailor for this diabolic an aspect more acceptable and "human"—that is to say, less psychopathic. The Marquis accepted these forces; he had evolved a code of behavior, a proposed set of legislative reforms, a whole system of philosophy based on them. May he not, then, have made some sense? May he not have been an excellent, if embittered, man, who desired to save his own soul, to procure the welfare of the human race?

Now, the Marquis did not make sense; he did not love the human race. But he does have his definite importance in the history of Western thought, and there is a gap if we leave him out. . . . [In the politico-philosophical field,] the Marquis appears as the opposite pole to Rousseau, and if we do not allow him his place, the picture remains incomplete. To the rebellious but ingenuous mind of Rousseau, it came as a revelation that men were "naturally" good and that it was only institutions that had led them astray. To Sade, also non-conformist, also biassed by abnormality, it seemed obvious that crimes and perversions were prompted by tendencies that we had in common with all the rest of "Nature," and that the error of institutions was their effort to censor these tendencies. The logic of Sade, of course, reduces the argument from Nature to absurdity, but then so does the logic of Rousseau. We want to put to them both the same question: Are not our moral and legal codes also the products of natural instincts? But it was difficult still in that age to conceive of man as an animal with certain superior faculties, in the light of which he tries to discipline his so diverse natural instincts for purposes he strongly feels but is unable to formulate definitively (as they tried to do with everything in the eighteenth century) since he never can see to the end of them; and in the meantime the Rousseauist doctrine was in need of a correction, a contradiction, that it got with a vengeance in Sade. . . . [The] Marquis de Sade still stands as a reminder that the lust for cruelty, the appetite for destruction, are powerful motivations that must be recognized for what they are.

But, except for the Surrealist, the connoisseur of horrors, the relisher of sensations for their own sake, it is difficult to see how Sade can meet any other need. He tends only toward annihilation. Though he justifes himself by appealing to Nature, he also turns against Nature for having made him what he is: "Is it a being so contemptible, so odious as this that has given me life for no other purpose than to make me take pleasure in what injures my kind?" Nor does he shrink from destroying himself, for, like his characters, he is what is called today masochistic as well as what is called sadistic. . . . One of Sade's most extraordinary scenes is that in *La Nouvelle Justine* in which the misanthropic chemist encountered on Etna explains that he has mastered a method for producing artificial eruptions, and expresses a strong desire to devastate the whole of Sicily. He will be watching from a mountain, he says, and copulating with the goats. He will not even have to depend on another human being for the pleasure of indulging his lust. The last interest that ties him to others will have been repudiated. Now, grotesque though this scene may sound, it is quite close to recent states of mind. It is probable that the fascination at present exerted by Sade is due partly to the vertiginous excitement of a destructiveness that is ultimately self-destructive. (pp. 167-71)

To encourage this impulse is the ultimate blasphemy—far more terrible than the Voltairean jeering at theology or the Byronic defiance of law—and it is Sade's queer unique distinction to have declared it with the ultimate audacity.

In Sade's will, one of the most effective things he wrote, he invoked complete oblivion. . . . But we have not been able to forget him. We have never been able to shake him off, because we know that he is not entirely mad, not entirely out of touch with reality—that, nauseous and "hipped" though he is, he is

harping on something that is sometimes felt by other human beings who seem to be sane. Let us hope that his moment is passing. (pp. 171-72)

Edmund Wilson, "The Vogue of the Marquis de Sade" (originally published in The New Yorker, *Vol. XXVIII, No. 35, October 18, 1952), in his* The Bit between My Teeth: A Literary Chronicle of 1950-1965 *(reprinted by permission of Farrar, Straus and Giroux, Inc.; copyright © 1952 by Edmund Wilson; copyright renewed © 1980 by Helen Miranda Wilson), Farrar, Straus and Giroux, 1952, pp. 158-73.*

GEOFFREY GORER (essay date 1963)

[Sade] has no graces of style at all: he abounds in clichés of every sort, and one would have to search hard to find an original metaphor or simile; he writes at such speed that his syntax is frequently inextricably convoluted; and his books have a tendency to proliferate like cancers, burgeoning monstrously, with constant additions but, as far as the evidence of the surviving manuscripts is a guide, with no cuts at all. He writes really badly most of the time, somewhat in the same way as Dickens or Balzac write really badly most of the time; and on one level at least he can be compared to these two writers, and put on a par with the greatest prose writers of any country. In his most typical novels he has created a world of his own as personal and as hallucinating as that of any other great writer: de Sade leaves his unmistakable imprint on the page as clearly as Dickens or Dostoievsky, Balzac or Proust. He is a great creator; and in literature, this is so rare a quality that, when it occurs, the presence or absence of the lesser graces hardly matter at all.

The world which de Sade depicts has not the extent or variety of the worlds of Dickens and Balzac; he is not impressed by the variability of human environments at all, and of human characters only in so far as their hidden desires and lusts differ. Despite some surface realism, the world he depicts is not an external world at all; it is the internal world of the deep and primitive unconscious, the wishes which human beings have to suppress and forget on their path from infancy to civilized adulthood made real and life-like, acted out on a model of the contemporary world. . . . Unaided, de Sade saw into the deepest abysses of his own soul and recognized the horrors that he found there; he placed these horrors on paper with only such disguise as a semblance to reality demanded, apparently thinking that his readers would have as great courage as he had in recognizing the deepest truths about themselves; and he created a world, or a hell, where all wishes could be realized, where every fantasy of love and hate could be made real, where one received only such punishment as one desired, and where the will, the intellect, the passions and the lusts held undisputed sway. It is a world of unparalleled sombre majesty, of terror and horror unapproached by the Gothic writers of the eighteenth and nineteenth, or pulp writers of the twentieth century. It is the appalling creation of a writer of genius. (pp. 215-17)

If it is made abundantly clear that nothing that can be said about de Sade's character explains the fact that he wrote his books, it is possible to get some notion of the sort of person who wrote them.

The first clear fact about de Sade is that, in the language dear to the students of delinquency, he came from a broken home. (pp. 217-18)

If de Sade were just a neurotic, this lack could be made to explain a good deal of his subsequent behaviour and attitudes. One would say that he never forgave the mother who abandoned him, and was always trying to take his revenge on maternal figures; and at the same time his ideal of sexual attraction was the cruel woman who hurt, humiliated, and abandoned all who loved her. (p. 218)

Probably too much weight should not be placed on the fact that an eighteenth-century author writes as a woman in the first person; the example of Richardson, for whom de Sade had so great an admiration, made the practice a very general one. Even in the nineteenth century such popular authors as Dickens and Wilkie Collins wrote large sections of some novels as their heroines in a winsome and wincing style. My impression is, however, that when authors write any sizable section of their books in the first person of the sex which is not their own they tend to portray, without much disguise, their ideal of the other sex. I do not therefore think it significant that part of de Sade's novels should be written as if recounted and experienced by women; but I do think it revealing that he did *not* write in the first person when describing the misfortunes of Justine. (p. 219)

[Numbers] had a permanent fascination for de Sade; when his mind was nearly unbalanced in the despair and uncertainty of the first years of what seemed like life-long imprisonment, his ideas of reference were founded on the belief of a hidden numerical code, the crazy numerology of the "signals"; and the formal neatness of pattern which distinguishes so much of his work (in particular *Les 120 Journées de Sodome*) depends on numerical symmetry. Typically, too, he was always turning people into things, at least in fantasy, by reducing them to corpses; and his preferred phrase for the forced participants and victims in debauchery is "objets de luxure"—*objects* for lust. (p. 224)

In my re-reading of part of de Sade's work, I have been continually impressed with the strength of his conscience, with the severity of his super-ego, to use a psychoanalytic term that has deeper overtones than the common phrase. Even at his most perverse, even in the great misanthropy and blasphemy of *Les 120 Journées,* even when he is saying with the greatest elaboration the written word has ever witnessed: "Evil, be Thou my Good," he is never in the slightest doubt of what is good, what evil. He is no moral imbecile, not even an amoralist like so many of the writers (and people) of the eighteenth century in France. (pp. 226-27)

Morally, de Sade was caught in an inextricable dilemma. He could only get adequate relief from his painful sexual tension in situations of subordination or superordination, of playing despot or playing victim; and he did not believe that his sexual constitution was uncommon. But when he was not sexually excited, he was one of the most impassioned partisans of equality between and freedom for all people of either sex. Nearly all his speculative writing is an attempt to reconcile these two contradictory demands. (p. 227)

Why did de Sade so persistently over-rate [his own theatrical productions], so continuously press for their performance? Why did he think of himself as a playwright, rather than as a novelist? Besides his clandestine publications and manuscripts, and the semi-disavowed first version of *Justine,* he had openly published *Aline et Valcour*—a novel of considerable, if unrecognized, merits—and *Les Crimes de l'amour;* these works are serious and worthy of being taken seriously, whereas his plays are not; but de Sade never seems to have suspected this disparity.

I should like to suggest that the reason for de Sade's continuous preoccupation with the theatre, and his failure to recognize his own incapacity as a dramatist, lies in the fact that, on a fairly abstract level, there is a close connection between theatricality and true Sadism. What does a successful playwright or actor do? By his skills, he commands the emotions of his audience, makes them laugh or cry, shudder or exult, as he plans; he produces visible and audible changes in the people who are under his spell. But, in a crude and concrete way, this is precisely what a sadist wishes to do to his victims; in a great number of cases one might say that the sadist is acting out a play with an audience of one. (pp. 229-30)

If I am right in thinking that some sort of theatricality or dramatic ritual was a constant component in de Sade's sexual sado-masochism, then it perhaps becomes understandable why he could never admit his incapacity as a professional dramatist. If he could have been a successful playwright, then he would have been able to achieve in a socially acceptable way many of the pleasures which he could otherwise obtain only from dangerously unsocial acts.

As a man (as opposed to the writer), de Sade is important as a paradigm. Except in his honesty, and his easy access to his deepest unconscious, there is no reason to think him unique. . . . [A] psychoanalytic explanation of de Sade's failure as a dramatist might well be that his repressions were not strong enough, that he "acted out" too much.

Another interpretation seems to me possible. It seems possible that the mysterious drive for creativity is very primitive in some individuals—recall the reported responses of the infant Mozart to the first hearing of a trumpet; and that, when this drive for creativity is thwarted, either by technical incapacity or public indifference, there is a "back-formation" to more direct sado-masochism. I suggest that sado-masochism may be, in some cases, a substitute for creativity, rather than that creativity is purely a sublimation of repressed infantile drives. (pp. 230-31)

De Sade would be an important precursor of contemporary political science if he had done nothing more than raise the question of the connection between an individual's lusts and his political beliefs and actions. (p. 231)

De Sade's stringent egalitarian morality made him decide that all people who seek or acquire power were evil; the political aspects of his work could be viewed as a gleeful documentation of Acton's famous apothegm that "All power tends to corrupt; absolute power corrupts absolutely"; and he portrays the corruption of power in the most concrete, revolting and gory detail. . . . Since he lacked the psychological concept of the unconscious, de Sade could only illustrate the hidden desires of power-holders by writing as if they were fully acted out; but with that proviso apart, no European writer, to my knowledge, has penetrated more deeply into the destructive motives of those who seek or hold power. What he ignored was the desire to make restitution which, on an unconscious level, can counterbalance the desire to apply severe sanctions; and consequently he could not conceive the possibility of a good, or tolerable, government; when he abandoned the hope of Utopia he really fell back on complete anarchy. (pp. 232-33)

Psychologically one of the most important aspects of de Sade's thinking is the question which he raises of the connection of the will and the emotions. The will is perhaps the major casualty of contemporary psychological systems; it is a concept which plays at best a minor rôle in psychoanalytic thought, and none at all in the different behaviourist or gestalt or to-pological systems. For de Sade the will ranks with the imagination and the lusts as the determinants of human behaviour.

In de Sade's implicit psychology, the lusts are innate, dependent on constitution only; people are born with a certain physique and with certain tastes through which alone they can get complete gratification. . . .

De Sade uses the concept of imagination to link together a number of psychological activities which modern psychology keeps separate. (p. 233)

[Sadism] could be defined as the pleasure derived from the activity of the will; and the most obvious link between active and passive algolagnia, between clinical sadism and clinical masochism, is that the situation is under the control of the person taking his or her pleasure, that the other participants are fulfilling the will of the pleasure-seeker, whether they do this by submitting to or inflicting ill treatment. It is because he linked the will and the passions, the head and the genitals, that de Sade made his unique contribution to the literature of psychology and the psychology of literature. (p. 235)

> *Geoffrey Gorer, in his* The Life and Ideas of the Marquis de Sade *(reprinted by permission of W. W. Norton & Company, Inc.; in Canada by Harold Ober Associates Inc., as agent for the author; copyright © 1962, 1963 by Geoffrey Gorer), Norton, 1963, 250 p.*

LESTER G. CROCKER   (essay date 1963)

Sadism is a dark pool formed by those streams of eighteenth-century philosophy which flow into it. There is nothing in Sade's nihilism which, in essence or in embryo, is not also found in the writings [of Rousseau, Diderot, Voltaire, and Pascal]. The differences are great; but they are differences of degree, thoroughness, universality, consistency. Sade unifies the disparate elements of seventeenth- and eighteenth-century nihilistic thinking into a powerful revolutionary system and carries it ruthlessly to the most extreme conclusions possible.

Two mainstreams of thought empty into the sadian pool: the idea that pleasure is the sole value in a wholly natural and valueless world; and the idea that man must escape contingency (anguish, insecurity) by an affirmation of his own being. The sexual torture and murder associated with Sade's name are, in fact, the ultimate, exacerbated expression of these earlier findings. These two major propositions are synthesized through Sade's general concept of sex, which also had ample precedents. The major propositions are supported by a congeries of minor propositions, all of which the reader will recognize. Sade's originality lies in his discovery of the all-pervasiveness of the sexual libido, in addition to its previously recognized connection with aggression, and in the synthesis of these facts into a total nihilistic philosophy. (pp. 398-99)

Sade was the first to construct theoretically and to realize graphically, in the concreteness of literary character and actions, a complete system of nihilism with all its implications, ramifications, and consequences. If we look backward, we can picture Sade collecting the dispersed heritage of more than two thousand years of the revolt of instinct against culture, and igniting it with the spark that made it flame. If we look forward, we can picture his fame and his work glowing and smoldering under the cover of bourgeois smugness and cant, a beacon to misguided rebels of many kinds. (pp. 399-400)

[Sade agrees] with those eighteenth-century formalists of Natural Law theory who held that positive law does not create justice, right or wrong. For him, however, what matters is that the law tries to resolve the conflict between personal interest and general interest in favor of the latter. Since the sole value he admits is personal interest, the law is, *ipso facto*, unjust. . . . Sade's philosophy leads, as is obvious, to a dream of the *Uebermensch* [superman]. It leads also to the gratuitous act, to the absurd act which Lautréamont and the surrealists were to flaunt. Juliette, for instance, converted to the philosophy of nihilism, goes out into the street, to shoot the first person who happens to pass by. There are innumerable other episodes, absurd in their motive and in the immolation, except that they produce perverse pleasure. (pp. 411-12)

Conscience, for Sade, is purely a matter of conditioning. Since there are no objective moral judgments or universal values, it is possible to manipulate the nervous system so as to form a conscience that would torment us each time we did not commit what is known as a crime, if it were conducive to our satisfaction. It is possible to feel sorry that one has done too much evil, or not enough. . . .

The upshot of Sade's nihilism is the proclamation of anarchy. The present mixture of good and evil leads to confusion; but in a social order in which evil only is esteemed, there is a clear road. In a society of vice and evil, there will be no unhappiness due to fear, remorse, laws, and conventions. Every man will do his own justice, and all, abandoned to nature, will be led better than by the stupidities of criminal law. (p. 412)

It is an error to consider [Sade's] view of sex outside of its true place as a coherent element of his philosophy. His importance in this regard lies not only in his studies of the abnormal, although his description of six hundred kinds of perversions, in *Sodome et Gomorrhe*, was a notable feat. His attitude toward the sexual impulse and experience was an attitude toward men, society, and life. His rejection of the human being as end, rather than means, signifies his denial of man as a moral or spiritual being. This stand is crystallized in the sexual use and abuse of men and women. Sex thus becomes the focus of the Sadian revolt, doubtless because it is the primary energy and vitality of the life force and of the will to power and possession. (pp. 413-14)

Sade has no concept whatsoever of love, of the human function of Eros; and none of the mediating function of sexual experience in creating unity and exalting the human person. The three elements in his philosophy are absolute freedom of all sexual impulses, the culmination of these impulses in crime, and the justification of nihilism. (p. 414)

One of Sade's perceptions is that our pleasures and passions, especially those derived from crimes, are forms of sexual energy and satisfaction. . . . Theft is especially considered by Sade from the sexual viewpoint. Murder, however, is the greatest stimulus, above all, as we have seen, when the victim is innocent and when it is preceded by torture and sexual abuse. Death, the ultimate truth and act of life, can be experienced subjectively only once. But if one can die only once, he can kill several times and thus enjoy the "ecstasy of death." (pp. 414-15)

[Sade] wanted to strip the idol of love of its hypocrisies, and restore it to what he thought was its true status as animal pleasure, not pure and lovely, not even merely bestial, but inherently and necessarily cruel. This was for him one way of uncovering the true man, man the animal, beneath the self-imposed halo of a being made in the image of God. He wanted to study man not only as he shows himself, but in all the horrible forms his passions may lead him to take. If Sade is repulsive, it is because men can also be repulsive, as many in our own time know only too well. (pp. 416-17)

Unlike other radical moralists of the eighteenth century such as La Mettrie and Diderot, Sade did not make sexual freedom a *terminus ad quo*. He made the sex impulses basic to all human behavior, basic to its many disguised forms. He realized that the vitalities in human life are destructive—his error being to make them entirely so. He understood the intimate relation of sex to the aggressive instincts, to the power drive in all its forms. . . . The sexual climax, Sade wrote, is "a kind of rage." Sex, then, is the blind impulse which demands the total possession of beings, even at the price of their destruction. Control of the sexual instinct, Sade knew, implies control of the other, the destructive instinct. Freedom for the one means freedom also for the other. . . . Thus the sexual activity of man becomes ultimately, in his mind, the nucleus of a philosophy of life. (p. 417)

The seeds of eighteenth-century nihilism blossom in the incarnadine flowers of Sade's rebellion. Sade embraces the absurd, demands the absolutes, and returns to Pascal—but without God. He rejoins the Augustinian-Calvinist-Jansenist doctrine of man's total depravity, but accepts it joyously and exploits it. There is no election for salvation, but there is the election of the happy here on earth. The only grace is power. (p. 418)

Sade disturbed profoundly the consciences of his contemporaries and of the later generations. They tried to bury him, like decent, respectable people; but they have had to deal with him. What he brought to light about human nature and the human condition could never be buried again. . . . In the Kafkaesque trial which modern man has had to undergo, he is a star witness. (pp. 418-19)

The theme of Sade's most important novels—the Justine-Juliette series—is, as we see, precisely the denial of the *philosophes'* greatest attempt to unite nature and reason, their rationalization that virtue inevitably produces happiness, and that the wicked man, despite his prosperity, is secretly uneasy and unhappy. Sade himself took the alternative course and carried the self-interest psychology to an ultimate conclusion that destroyed the basis of ethics.

That Sade foretold the course of the crisis of Western civilization is obvious. (p. 420)

Sade speaks with loudest voice to our own time, and through our own time, for it is our age that has had to live the truths he revealed, to live through the night he uncovered. (p. 421)

The philosophy of nihilism is a nonviable one, and it annuls itself. Although Sade showed courage in uncovering truths about human nature, the philosophical system he draws from those truths is false and untenable, as well as dangerous to human life. It is riddled by a fatal inner contradiction. To be consistent in the absurd, one should not try to justify his acts. True nihilism, if it were possible, would require no valuation of right and wrong: but even the nihilist (precisely as Diderot had said) must argue that nihilism is "right." Sade is constantly "justifying." . . . What is natural and instinctual is characterized as "legitimate," "good," "sacred." Sade's nihilism is a principle, a belief in what is right. A consistent nihilist must say that it is indifferent whether one is a nihilist or not, since there is no way to judge his acts or another's. He cannot

say nihilism is "true," or that if it is, its truth is a reason to adopt it. This fundamental contradiction is again obvious when Sade declares that the greatest pleasure (*jouissance*) comes from the greatest crimes. (pp. 424-25)

Nihilism, then, is untenable, since value judgments cannot be avoided. For Sade, in fact, value is egoistic pleasure, a solid, irrefutable value. But by setting up this value, he at once opens the door to going beyond the absurd. We see this in his frequent statements that only the types of pleasure he enjoys (sex and destruction) are real, or that they are *better* than other types of pleasure. (p. 425)

A second inconsistency which occurs time and again in Sade's books lies in the fact that on the one hand he deifies nature and justifies all impulses in her name, and on the other hand, he declares that man is not bound by nature, but may defy her as he wishes. (pp. 425-26)

Still a third inconsistency is Sade's view on lack of human communication. "All creatures are born isolated and without any need of each other." But if one can confirm his being and enjoy only by making victims of others, if—to follow Simone de Beauvoir's modern analysis [see excerpt above]—one can satisfy the need to overcome isolation only by possession of the other—then obviously men do need each other and do enjoy enterprises in common. (p. 427)

The holocaust and the apocalypse—these are the termini of nihilism. In his ever-mounting frustration and furious crises of excitement, the Sadian nihilist desires finally to exterminate the human race and to pulverize the universe itself. Murder, as Sade has made clear, allows nature to create new life. (p. 428)

To the extent in which Sade has revealed the truth about man, he is the answer to all those in the eighteenth century who praised "natural man" and said that society has corrupted him by creating an artificial man to war with him. Sade's man, as we now know, is indeed what men would be *naturally*, if "artificial" pressures were not exerted to restrain them, that is, if men could live outside of a culture. The essential weakness in Sade's nihilism is, as Rousseau understood, that the so-called "artificial" is *natural* to men living in any possible social community. In carrying to its final limit the eighteenth-century reduction of man to the natural, Sade admitted only those aspects of human nature which were precisely the opposite of the ones admitted by optimists like Shaftesbury—those aspects which we have in common with animals. His assumption is that what is most vile is most sincere and natural. He denies that pity, sympathy, justice, the surpassing of self, and the demand for limit are natural, whereas in fact they constitute a large part of the initial adjective in the phrase, "human nature." The only *human* dimension he allows is the unique capacity for evil. (pp. 428-29)

Man, insofar as he is an organism, is superior to many things in nature, but does not transcend them. He is superior to *all* other known things, in his attainment of an intellectual level of abstraction, a psychological level of self-consciousness, a moral level of ethical judgment. And in these attainments he does truly transcend nature. Modern man, having passed the stage of myth, is deprived of external guidance and support, and must shift for himself. If he were to be left only to the nature he does not transcend, there would be no hope. Sadism, Nazism, or the surrender to inert despair (as in Samuel Beckett), would be his inevitable lot. But because of the other part, the human part of his nature, he can project an image of himself as he would like to be, and casting his net around the stars, pull himself up to them. (p. 429)

Lester G. Crocker, "The Nihilist Dissolution," in his Nature and Culture: Ethical Thought in the French Enlightenment *(© 1963 by The Johns Hopkins Press), The Johns Hopkins University Press, 1963, pp. 326-429.**

RAYMOND GIRAUD   (essay date 1965)

I first read *Justine* many years ago. It was one of those quick furtive readings of forbidden books, rapidly ransacked for erotic morsels to titillate the adolescent imagination. Scanned for those purposes, the book was a disappointment. Now I read it again and, though I still fail to be sensually excited or even profoundly shocked, I have a strong feeling that this is a remarkable work despite its many crudities and considerable intellectual confusion.

The absence of a thrill of horror might seem at first a bit puzzling. Even though other works of Sade are more lavish in detail, the first *Justine* is still an exceedingly distasteful story. . . . The reader is spared some of the most disturbing of sadistic pleasures, like coprophilia, incest and murder, but he can not fairly complain of having been cheated. But the sad fact is that sadism has become commonplace both within and outside of literature. Obviously there are vast quantities of sleazy subliterary writing, enormously successful in appealing to readers at every conceivable social and educational level and offering among their chief pleasures the spectacle of violence, the sensations procured by vicariously participating in the infliction of pain and indignity on the human body and spirit. The reader who denounces Sade, but finds nothing wrong with *No Orchids for Miss Blandish* or Mickey Spillane's and Ian Fleming's fictions is either a hypocrite or a victim of self-deception.

Such books, however, are only the lower fringe of literature. They deserve to be mentioned not for their merits, but because of the truly frightening fact that they are read *for fun*. We must view in a totally different spirit those novels containing "sadistic" characters and actions as a serious revelation of social reality, of what once was called human nature. Never the less, even though these are books we do *not* denounce, they inevitably blunt the shock a mid-twentieth century reader might experience in opening a book of Sade's.

Of some importance too, I suspect, is the eternal rivalry of fact and fiction. Sade himself, though he called the novelist a "man of nature" created by nature to be her painter, also remarked that in his time there was no individual who had not suffered more misfortunes in four or five years than the most famed novelist could depict in a whole century. The novel of terror, he maintained, was an inevitable product of a time of troubles, a time, moreover, when enlightened men could be aware of how much man had been a wolf to man. Today extraordinarily cruel revelations indeed are required to match the horrors we read about each morning in our daily papers. Would it be a tribute to Sade's genius or a commentary on our insensibility to reality if we were as much affected by the sexual fantasies an obese middle-aged man wrote in prison as by the unspeakable atrocities committed in the name of "freedom," "Christianity" or "the Southern way of life"? (pp. 39-40)

Had Sade been able to—had he wished to—communicate Justine's experience of pain, that aspect of the book might have been far more moving than it is. But, paradoxically perhaps, because it is from Justine's point of view that the story is narrated, her consciousness, her sensations are never probed very deeply. Her waking hours are nightmarish (the word is Sade's own), but hers are not the kind of nightmares that are more vivid, more surreal, than reality itself. The sympathy of the reader is curtailed by the fact that, by accepting her point of view, he becomes not so much a participant in her sufferings as a spectator of her tormentors' sufferings. For it is they who are the true heroes of the book. And what more intimate view can one get of them than the image mirrored in the eyes of their victim? . . .

Justine's innocence has spared her the special subtler kinds of suffering that come from doubt, guilt, remorse, even pleasure. Sade had read Laclos and was far from unaware of the delight a libertine can take in undermining virtue. In Justine, however, he chose to portray absolute incorruptibility.

Another aspect of Justine that makes her torments easier for us to bear is that she is never troubled very long by them. What she goes through in any one incident would put most of us in the hospital for weeks, might drive us mad; but Justine is usually up and about in no time, often forgets her pain immediately. (p. 41)

Time means nothing to Justine. Days or years go by and she is unchanged. Even at the end of the book, when her sister rescues her from the police, she makes an instantaneous recovery: "In the hands of her sister Justine was soon herself again, and her recent experiences were rapidly being blotted out of her mind." Once again the slate is being wiped clean. Is not pity wasted on such a girl? Nature herself, impatient with Justine's stubborn indestructibility, both moral and physical, will now have to take a hand in the action to bring the book to an end.

It is clear that Justine's misfortunes are not what gives this account its interest. What, however, of the villains of the piece: the homosexual Bressac, who murders his rich aunt; the experimental surgeon, Dr. Rodin, who whips children and plans to lay bare his own daughter's veins in the interest of science; Gernande, the Gargantuan eater who bleeds his wife every fourth day? Dreadful as these and all the others are, it is they to whom Sade directs our attention and for whom he begs our understanding. True, we see them best at an inauspicious moment through the eyes of their suffering victim Justine, but it is precisely only she who can observe them unmasked in the throes of their frenzies. Through her they reveal themselves to the reader as they really are. Sade's portrait of his heroine does not convince us of his proclaimed dedication to truth and plausibility (*vraisemblance*). But his heroes—or anti-heroes—are the real truth of his story.

It is hard to say what Sade wanted most to tell his reader through the behavior of these men. What is most conspicuous is his tremendous eagerness to catalogue their vices, to pile up the innumerable repetitious and hyperbolic practices that bring them pleasure. (p. 42)

Like Voltaire, Sade was educated by Jesuits and like him too he became a man of the Enlightenment. It is by no accident that his heroes are usually identified as "philosophers" and that Justine's objections to their practices are attributed to her unphilosophic attitude. . . . He was in his own words a "fanatical" atheist. And so are all his heroes. Only the victims, the weak, like Justine, believe in worshipping God and that "the foundation of this worship is virtue." (pp. 42-3)

Gernande and the other anti-heroes of the novel clutch for their "happiness," such as it is, at the cost of another's suffering, if need be. They have the strength of Nature, brute force, at their command and are totally and unhypocritically selfish in exploiting it. But it seems clear that this "strength" is resorted to because of what, in another context, might be called weakness.

The sadistic hero also accepts the duality of good and evil; he refers to crime and corruption, to his own "mad lust," his "perversion," "brutality," "ferocity." He refutes a categorical morality and then reestablishes it by incorporating its very terms in his own language. Curiously too in this world of corruption in which everyone Justine meets is a monster of depravity, all of them, doctors, judges, priests, following their own "nature" and yet also freely deciding not to swim against the stream, each one feels the need to keep his vices secret. For all these rationally defended natural acts are carried out behind locked doors, stone walls and moats, in buried dungeons and remote castles. Sade presents a world in which everyone (except Justine) is doing more or less the same thing, but must hide what he does from everyone else.

There is more than one reason for the secrecy. The sadistic lover must possess his victim absolutely. His pleasure is selfish and not altruistic; the victim must not be permitted to escape; there must be no possibility of interference. (pp. 44, 47)

It is an inescapable fact, however, that although Sade himself retired with lackeys, prostitutes and maid-servants to his castle or his "petite maison" outside of Paris, he opened up the landscape of these secret places in his books. They are not realistic representations of his own experiences, but they have the ring of authenticity. The episodic structure of the book, its simple, straightforward, stylized language, the quasi-philosophic arguments, Justine's unnatural invulnerability to physical damage at the hands of Sade's heroes: all these factors may cushion the shock, as may some of the external circumstances I briefly reviewed at the outset. Sade's principal revelation, however, as I have come to see it, is not the physical abuses suffered by Justine, but the embarrassing spectacle of what the sadist himself undergoes. I submit that it took some courage on Sade's part to reveal in such minute detail these mirror images of himself in pursuit of "happiness," hitherto witnessed only by paid prostitutes and servants behind closed doors. These are revelations, too, that could be resented by others, who might prefer to keep the door shut. (p. 47)

Raymond Giraud, "The First 'Justine'," in Yale French Studies *(copyright © Yale French Studies 1965), December, 1965, pp. 39-47.*

PIERRE KLOSSOWSKI (essay date 1965)

In Sade's work the uneasy conscience of the debauched libertine represents a transitional state of mind between the conscience of social man and the atheistic conscience of the philosopher of Nature. It offers at one and the same time those negative elements which Sadian thought, in its dialectical movement, makes great efforts to eliminate, and the positive elements which will make it possible to move beyond this intermediary state of mind in order to get to the atheistic and asocial philosophy of Nature and a moral system based on the idea of Nature as perpetual motion.

The libertine's conscience maintains a negative relationship with God on one hand and with his neighbor on the other. Both, the notion of God and the notion of his neighbor, are indispensable to him. The relationship with God is negative because the libertine's conscience, as we find it in Sade, is not atheistic in a cold-blooded way; rather its atheism is the result of effervescence and therefore of resentment; his atheism is only a form of sacrilege. (p. 61)

At times the atheism which is affected by the libertine conscience, and the wrong which it projects doing, are meant to be provocations addressed to the absent God as though scandalous provocations were a way of forcing that God to manifest his existence. . . . The conscience of the debauched Sadist keeps its claim on free will and uses its moral categories, all the while maintaining a belief in its ability to do evil. The conscience of the debauched libertine, according to Sade's description, not only appears to be in complete opposition to atheism but also has a counsinship with the analysis of Evil for Evil's sake which we find in Saint Augustine's *Confessions.*

Such a conscience is consequently susceptible to elaborating an entire destructive theology centered about the religion of a Supreme Being of Wickedness, the only Supreme Being that Saint-Fond, the exemplar of the great libertine and debauched lord, is willing to profess. This religion of evil is not yet ready to deny crime as the philosophy of perpetual motion does, but prefers to admit it as an outflow from the existence of an infernal God. Nor is it the refutation of the dogma found in the first version of *Justine,* that the innocent must be sacrificed for the salvation of the guilty. (pp. 61-2)

The libertine conscience also needs to establish an equally negative relationship with its neighbor: "I am happy with the evil I do to others as God is happy with the evil he does to me." The libertine's enjoyment comes from the fact of the continuous opposition between this idea and the notion of love for one's neighbor. He makes use of this opposition in establishing his theory of *pleasure through comparison.* (p. 64)

[The] conscience of the debauched libertine, though it turns them upside down, is content to remain with those moral categories which the atheist conscience will condemn as structures forged by the weak. But, out of their need for comparisons, the strong put their own strength on trial. By making a comparison of his condition with that of the unfortunate, the fortunate man makes a fatal identification with him. In tormenting the object of his lust in order to derive pleasure from his suffering, and by seeing in the suffering of another his own suffering, he will also see his own punishment. . . . The debauched man remains attached to the victim of his lust and to the individuality of that victim whose sufferings he would like to prolong "beyond the bounds of eternity—if eternity has any." The true atheist, to the degree that he really exists, attaches himself to no object; caught in nature's perpetual motion, he obeys his impulses, looking upon others as no more than nature's slag. The conscience of the debauched libertine cannot give up its all too human aspirations; perhaps only the stoic atheist would be capable of doing so. The libertine's conscience remains obsessed not only by his neighbor as victim, but also by death. (pp. 64-5)

In this phase his conscience none the less betrays a murky need for expiation—an expiation which, if his need could be elucidated, would have no other direction than that of self-liquidation, a freeing of the self by the self. These are the positive particulars of his conscience. The degree to which he seeks expiation is the degree to which his conscience represents one of the moments of Sade's own conscience. (p. 65)

Saint-Fond reveals still another characteristic trait of the libertine conscience: pride in his situation, scorn for his fellow man, and, finally, a hatred, mixed with fear, of "that vile lowlife known as the people." All the elements of this haughty attitude go hand in glove with the exercise of humiliating debaucheries, most of which are planned to deliver a shock to popular morality: "Only minds organized like ours know how well the humiliation imposed by certain wanton acts serves as pride's nourishment." In effect, what the popular or, better, the bourgeois mentality would be incapable either of admitting or of understanding is that those who are supposed to be the guardians of the social order should, by their voluntary degradation, challenge that order and, in so doing, overturn all social values. But in this humiliation—even though it is only a fiction for the Sadian libertine—there is also manifest a desire for voluntary debasement and, in that need, an indication of the libertine's belief that his superior social position gives him special rights. Chief among these rights is his right to revise the notion of what man is. It is an *experimental right,* one which could not be extended to the common run of mortals without danger. It is precisely the exercise of this *right to conduct forbidden experiments* which, born from the libertine conscience, will form one of the fundamental commitments of the Sadian conscience. (pp. 65-6)

For Sade *the substitution of Nature in a state of perpetual motion* for God signifies, not the arrival of a happier era for humanity, but only the beginning of tragedy—the tragedy being man's open and conscious acceptance of the change. (p. 66)

We become the public at a strange spectacle where Sade insults Nature as he used to insult God; he discovers in Nature the traits of that God who created the greatest number of men with the aim of making them run the risk of eternal tortures "even though it would have conformed more with goodness and with reason and justice to create only stones and plants rather than to shape men whose conduct could only bring endless chastisements." (p. 67)

Sade will push materialistic atheism to a point where it will be invested with the form of a truly transcendental fatalism. We see an example of this in the *System of Nature* set forth by the Pope in his long discussion with Juliette. Here Sade's thought determinedly gets away from its human condition in order to attempt integration with a mythical cosmogony—the only chance it has, apparently, of getting away from the trial where it stands as much accused as it was at the beginning of its efforts. In vain Sade seeks a judge who will acquit him, and does this even though he has withdrawn the judge's competence in the realm of human morality.

Sade first of all admits of the existence of an original and eternal Nature who exists outside the realm of the three kingdoms of species and of creatures [the animal, vegetable, and mineral]. "Were Nature to find herself subject to other laws, the creatures who are the result of her present laws would no longer exist." Nature would still exist, though under different laws. (p. 69)

[We] see the dimensions of the path which Sadian man has traversed from his theology of a Being supreme in its wickedness to this conception of Nature. We saw him at first accepting the existence of God in order to declare God guilty and to take advantage of God's everlasting guilt; later we saw him confusing this God with a no less ferocious Nature, but still keeping himself on the side of moral categories. But the satanization of Nature was only preparing for the liquidation of moral categories. The conception of a Nature which aspires to recapture her highest potential signifies in effect the dehumanization of

Sade's thought—a dehumanization which now takes on the form of a singular metaphysics. If Sade, in contradistinction to what he habitually affirms, now goes so far as to consider man entirely distinct from Nature, it is primarily in order to emphasize better a profound lack of harmony between the notion of the human being and the notion of the universe. Eager to reclaim his own rights, he is also eager to explain that the extent of Nature's efforts must be measured in direct proportion to that lack of harmony. In Sade's attempt we might also see his will to separate himself from man by imposing on himself the categorical imperative of a cosmic situation which demands the annihilation of all that is human. Without doubt, what Sade is trying to do is declare his separation from a Nature which is the slave of her own laws—and to do so without Nature's knowing about it. . . . Sade soars directly into myth. The philosophy of his century no longer suffices once it becomes a question of resolving the problem raised by cruelty. As we have just seen, he would like to *integrate* cruelty into a universal system where it would be brought to its pure state by recovering its cosmic function. Henceforth, passions—from the *simple* passions to the *complicated* ones—have a transcendental significance: if man believes he is satisfying himself in being obedient to them, he is in reality only satisfying an aspiration which goes beyond his person. . . . Let us for a moment compare the principle of life and death, which will determine Sade's new position on the problem of destruction, with Freud's death instinct. Freud, opposing this instinct to that of Eros—the life instinct—uses the two notions as the basis for his ontological theory. While Freud only envisages life at the organic level, Sade—much more the metaphysician despite appearances to the contrary—admits of no difference between life at the organic and inorganic level; he detaches himself from all considerations which relate to the species and to the social milieu in order to offer a single principle:

> The principle of life in all beings is no other than the death principle; we receive them both and nourish them both at the same time. At that moment we call death, everything appears to dissolve; we believe this because of the excessive difference which is then visible in this portion of matter which no longer seems alive. But this death is only imaginary; it exists only figuratively and has no reality. . . .

Corruption, putrefaction, dissolution, exhaustion, and annihilation: these are aspects of life's phenomena which will have a meaning for Sade that is as moral as it is physical. Only motion is real; creatures are nothing but motion's changing phases. . . . Sadian man—having accepted the notion of a Nature which is no more shrewd in wickedness than the Supreme Being, no more voracious than the Minotaur, but rather enslaved from the start by her own laws and the first among the universe's victims—will arrive at a point where he considers himself a microcosm of Nature, suffering, like Nature, from his own activity. That activity, rather than allowing Nature to achieve her highest potential, allows her only to create, to destroy, to create anew, along with her creatures, in a cycle which proves her impotence. . . . Just as Nature creates obstacles for herself by her will to create, Sadian man creates his neighbor out of a will to create himself. He seems to do this out of a need to destroy the other. Yet he had once aspired to a break with this necessity; through his aspiration towards innocence he had admitted the existence of others and given them reality. Still he remained saddled with the necessity of destroying; and since he wished to prolong the existence of others, he became guilty at that very moment because he had decided to prolong the others' existence only in order to destroy them. Like Nature, which always and simultaneously aspires to and renounces its highest potential, Sadian man faces the question of whether he can renounce others and be prepared to destroy.

If comparison with the unfortunate—a comparison which remains indispensable if the libertine is to know happiness—presupposes the existence of his neighbor, the first step to be taken in the direction of a renaturalization of cruelty will be to deny the reality of his neighbor and to rid the notion of neighbor of its meaning. In implying the neighbor's existence, the pleasure of comparison implies evil. Love of neighbor, the chimera which haunted Sade, is converted by the libertine conscience into a love-hatred of the neighbor. Here the libertine makes a mistake, for love-hatred of his neighbor, while it helps liquidate the reality of the other, liquidates his own reality.

How can Sadian man ever give up his object, which is the other, and accept destruction in all its purity, as he must do if he is faithful to his idea of a Nature freed from the need of creating? To do so, he must renounce, not just the other, but also his individual condition as a self.

In apparently solipsistic terms, a quantity of statements made by Sade's characters imply a doctrine whose conclusions are thoroughly opposed. Under the guise of a *Nature aspiring to its highest potential,* the doctrine takes absolute and sovereign desire as its principle. But in the name of this principle, it establishes between the self and the other a negative reciprocity. . . . (pp. 70-4)

The moral nihilism which tends to suppress awareness of oneself and the other on the level of acts, but which implies no fewer contradictions on Sade's part, appears here as the last consequence of his atheism. In effect Sade could not limit himself to denying the existence of a personal God, the principle of a self who is responsible and who is the guarantor of Sade's own selfhood and privacy; he must also attack him. Just as we saw him attacking the principle of the conservation and propagation of the species, we see him now making an issue of the normative principle of individuation in order to give free scope to the erosive forces he has described: the perversions and abnormalities which indicate the emergence within the individual of a sensitive polymorphism by which conscious individuation has been accomplished within individuals. But far from being satisfied with describing those abnormalities, he lends them the eloquence of his spokesmen who refute the existence of a God, guarantor of the norms, in order to plead, in the language of those very norms, the cause of the abnormalities they bear. (p. 75)

The practise of apathy, as it is suggested by Sade's characters, presupposed that what we call *soul, conscience, sensitivity, heart,* are only miscellaneous structures brought about by a concentration of the same driving forces. Under pressure from the world of others, these forces can transform the faculties into intimidating influences; but just as readily, when under pressure from our own inner drives, they can become subsersive influences; in either instance, their reaction is immediate. What remains constant is the fact that our own inner forces intimidate us at the very moment that they make insurgents out of us. . . . How can this practise of apathy become a viable method for the achievement of "voluptuous toughness"? Nothing would seem more contradictory in Sade than this break with others when the result of the abolition of our duties towards others and their consequent exclusion from our sensitivity is translated

clearly and constantly by acts which, because of their violence, need the other—acts which by their very nature reëstablish the reality of the other and of myself.

If the other is no longer anything for me, and if I am nothing for the other, how can these acts be performed since, in effect, they would turn out to be the acts of a nothing on a nothing?

In order that this nothing never again be filled by my reality and the reality of the other, through the presence either of enjoyment or of remorse, I must disappear in an endless reiteration of acts which I run the danger of regretting because, when they are suspended, the reality of the other imposes itself on me once again. (pp. 76-8)

What is the purpose behind this reiteration of similar acts which is dictated by the moral attitude of apathy? Sade clearly understood the difficulty even in those moments when he was unable to resolve the dilemma: the enjoyment which negative contact with the other procures for me should be anticipated quite as much as remorse. Remorse here is only the other side of enjoyment, and the two are only different forms of behavior which have their sources in the same drives. . . . Thus the moral principle of apathy, which provokes the greatest disturbance in the drives, tried to create a coincidence of the disturbance with an equally strong wariness designed to guarantee the purity of the disturbance. If the habit of apathy is to render the individual capable of doing in cold blood acts which would have brought remorse when done in a moment of frenzy, a similar process could be found for vice; with the result that virtue would never have a chance to make us remorseful. "In virtue's name you will no longer conceive of repenting, because you will have grown accustomed to doing evil in answer to virtue's reappearance and in order to do evil no longer you would prevent her from ever appearing . . . .".

Could this be the solution to the dialectical drama visible in the Sadian conscience? The answer depends on an answer to a more difficult question: Can the conscience of Sadian man accept any solution? To get beyond the notion of evil, which is always conditioned by the degree of reality he accords to others, we have seen Sadian man carry the exaltation of the ego to its height; yet the height of this exaltation was supposed to be found in apathy where the ego abolished itself simultaneously with the other, where enjoyment disassociated itself from destruction, and where destruction identified itself with desire in its pure form. In this way, the Sadian conscience reproduces in its own operations the perpetual motion of nature which creates but which, in creating, sets up obstacles for herself. The only way she recovers her liberty, even momentarily, is by destroying her own works. (pp. 78-9)

Pierre Klossowski, "A Destructive Philosophy," in Yale French Studies *(copyright © Yale French Studies 1965), December, 1965, pp. 61-79.*

IHAB HASSAN   (essay date 1971)

Paradox and duplicity riddle Sade's ideas as well as his life. His ideas are not seminal but they have the partial truth of excess, of release. They constitute a dubious myth of consciousness. (p. 30)

Sade speaks for the novelist and pretends to explore the business of fiction. He asks that the full ambiguity of man's nature be recognized; he rejects the sentimental and didactic rhetoric that dominate the novel. But we insult Sade's intelligence when we take him at his word. His concern is neither art nor nature but dreamful liberty. He finds that liberty in evil. The plot of his monomyth requires villainy to remain in ascendance till the parodic resolution. (pp. 30-1)

Everywhere, Sade focuses on the energy of evil. He varies the background: now it is the Huguenot wars of France, now eighteenth-century England (Fielding appears in one of the tales as an honest magistrate), now Spain during a Moorish invasion. But it is obvious that Sade has little interest in place, time, or person, in the concrete reality of things of human character. His myth of the battle between Vice and Virtue always takes the form of a game of sexual permutations. The necessary rules of the game define its morality. (p. 31)

[*Dialogue Between a Priest and a Dying Man*] states this "morality" more explicitly. God, according to Sade, is a superfluous hypothesis; and the Redeemer of Christianity is "the most vulgar of tricksters and the most arrant of all imposters." The Marquis glibly invokes cultural and religious relativism to bolster the arguments of his dying man. The only constant is Nature, and Nature is indifferent to what men call vice or virtue. It is simply a process of death and regeneration in which nothing is ever lost. Men are part of Nature and subject to instinctual necessity; they have no freedom to choose. "We are the pawns of an irresistible force, and never for an instant is it within our power to do anything but make the best of our lot and forge ahead along the path that has been traced for us." The dying man ends by persuading the priest; and, needless to say, both join in an orgy with six women kept on hand for the funereal occasion.

The personal argument is hidden. Sade attacks God in the name of Nature. The idea of Christian Divinity repels him because it rests on piety and tradition, and it often serves the advantage of corrupt men. But the true cause of his revolt against Deity is double: he needs the erotic release of transgression against authority—in blasphemy, in desecration—and he resents any power that might qualify the omnipotence of the Self. (p. 32)

Crime, at any rate, is merely one aspect of libertinage, the politics of human freedom. This is the lesson of *Philosophy in the Bedroom*. . . . The book is a manifesto ringing as loud as Marx's: "Voluptuaries of all ages, of every sex, it is to you only that I offer this work. . . . It is only by sacrificing everything to the senses' pleasure that . . . this poor creature who goes under the name of Man, may be able to sow a smattering of roses atop the thorny path of life." It is also a catechism of libertinage relieved, with deadly regularity, by practice orgies and computerized perversions. Like all Sade's works, the book is repetitious. But it is also grotesquely comic in parts, a parodic novel of manners which insists on the complaisancies of the drawing room, the school room, and the bedroom.

The assertion of Dolmancé throughout the seven dialogues is hard to miss: the end of libertinage is pleasure. . . . [For] Sade no other selves exist; the world is full only of sources of pain or pleasure. Dolmancé is therefore consistent when he says of man: "Victim he is, without doubt, when he bends before the blows of ill fortune; but criminal, never." For crime presupposes the existence of others. Since each one of us is alone and for himself in the world, cruelty to others is, from one's own point of view, a matter of profound indifference—unless it can be made a source of orgasm. . . . [However,] the benefits of cruelty are not exhausted in orgasm, Dolmancé insists; cruelty is also "the energy in a man civilization has not yet altogether corrupted: therefore it is a *virtue*, not a *vice* [italics

mind]." Sade revives the terms which he has raged to obliterate. (pp. 32-4)

Virtue and Vice are locked in eternal combat, though Vice seems to hold the upper hand. Sade poses as a naturalist who lives beyond good and evil. Yet his constant use of such terms as "degrade," "deprave," "debauch," and "pervert" indicates that his world is anything but morally neutral. It is a world in which *transgression* is real and *sacrilege* dear. "Oh, Satan!" Dolmancé cries, "one and unique god of my soul, inspire thou in me something yet more, present further perversions to my smoking heart, and then shalt thou see how I shall plunge myself into them all." Can we wonder that he, like all Sade's villains, constantly applies religious imagery to sexual functions? Furthermore, Sade's world is one in which Nature must remain sterile. Copulation thrives, procreation never. (p. 34)

[The] world of Sade is a prison of consciousness. The power of Vice and Virtue, the vitality of Nature, vanish in the dungeon of the Self. In the moment of orgasm, the Sadian Self seeks desperately to become something other than itself. Yet it cannot; it ends by incarcerating the world with itself. As a despot in its dungeon, the Self cannot tolerate pleasure in anyone else. It induces pain in order to assimilate others to its unique existence. . . .

[*Justine: Or Good Conduct Well Chastised*,] the most cherished of Sade's works, is a parody of picaresque, gothic, and sentimental fiction. . . . It pushes the fantasies of Sade one step farther toward outrage without altering their content; it merely varies the format by accretion of horrors. (p. 35)

The special effect of *Justine* derives precisely from its two correlative fantasies: the omnipotence of the Sadian tyrant-villain and the abjectness of his victim-heroine. The fantasies are sustained by various devices. Justine, for instance, insists on calling her tormentors "monster," "tyrant," "tiger"; she inflates their powers as well as their organs. For like Sade himself, she is eternally complicit in her victimization. . . . As for Sade's villains, they must all enjoy the advantages of power, wealth, or high birth. Their black eyes glint, their white teeth sparkle, their members beggar description. (pp. 37-8)

The consummation of the Sadian will is in death; the limits of an omnipotent consciousness are murder and suicide. We should not be surprised, therefore, if the villains of *Justine* serve Thanatos reverently. . . . The ultimate revenge of man who can neither kill God nor can, like God, create, is to kill His creatures. This is why, in the end, Sade must arbitrarily kill off his own fictional creations. Justine, who has survived all hazards and finally earned her peace, is suddenly transfixed by a thunderbolt as she stands idly in her room. The bolt goes through her breast, heart, and belly. Thus the Marquis succeeds where all his villains have failed: he murders Justine. . . . No ideas mar the onanistic intentions of [*The 120 Days of Sodom*]. Such exclamations as "Oh, incredible refinement of libertinage!" recur in order to seduce the author more than his readers. . . . Sade, the pornographer, speaks out frankly, speaks even truly, but even as a pornographer he speaks mainly to pleasure himself.

This is why the form of *The 120 Days* is reflexive; it can only mirror, or rather echo, itself. (pp. 38-9)

The pattern of the work justifies the rubric of anti-form in another sense: it is purely arithmetical. With demented ingenuity, Sade reduces his fantasy to an equation. There are four master libertines, four wives who are their daughters, four women historians, four duennas, eight fuckers, eight young girls, eight young boys, and six female cooks and scullery maids. The book is divided into four parts; the orgy lasts seventeen weeks, or 120 days. All the arrangements of this mathematical ménage are specified meticulously, the number of wines and dishes, the number of lashes for each punishment. The statutes which govern the progress of the orgy are as clear as they are inflexible; the schedule for the whole period is fixed. . . . Number and ratio, we see, rule the form of this game directed by an autoerotic computer. Sade's fiction is truly a dream of logic. In this, he prefigures the parodic dream of Beckett.

But the work is not only abstract, it is also hermetic. Nothing, absolutely nothing, must penetrate the Fortress of Silling where the action takes place, except the mind. That castle, situated somewhere on an impossible peak in the Black Forest, is impregnable because it lies within the skull. (pp. 39-40)

[The Sadian self] finds its consummation in death, and this is nowhere more obvious than in the apocalypse of *The 120 Days* where the final authority rests with Thanatos. The first sections are dominated by cloacal fantasies; the human organism is conceived not as energy but as waste. Behind the scatological comedy and the delights of Sodom, scarcely disguised, appears the hatred of life. At Silling, the life and fecal economies of the community unite under a strict control. No birth is permitted, and elimination is reduced; therefore, life is hindered from self-renewal. Lower forms of organization, like excrement, are valued above higher forms, like food. At Silling, entropy is dominant, and annihilation the ultimate goal. (p. 41)

We see at last the sad equation of Sade: man is orgasm, and orgasm is death. Prisoner of his consciousness, he tries to escape through the language of macabre onanism. His visions mortify, desiccate the body, and open in the flesh an abyss wherein consciousness is swallowed. The Sadian self, seeking desperately to become another, sinks back into itself. Its only release is in death. . . .

We see Sade, almost, as the first avant-gardist, the daemon of Romanticism and of Gothic fiction, a Surrealist before our time, and a herald of anti-literature. We imagine him as a precursor to Darwin, Freud, and Nietzsche, and as a forerunner of the anarchists, Max Stirner and Bakunin. We feel his genius in Dachau, Belsen, and Auschwitz, and in all apocalyptic politics. We accept him, at the same time, as an apostle of pornotopia, a child of the Enlightenment, and an example of metaphysical rebellion. This is all to say that we still struggle to see Sade clearly through his outrageous myth. Yet there is no doubt that his spirit moves in our culture, and defines, more than an aspect of pathology, a crucial element of our consciousness. (p. 42)

Sade's contribution to literary history does not exhaust itself in romantic decadence. It depends, rather, on his effort to supplant the sentimental novel, and to give Gothic fiction new authority. During his own lifetime, the morality of the bourgeois novel spends itself; revolutionary thought demands new values. Sade calls hell to the rescue, thinking thus to redeem the reality of fiction. He even assumes a larger task which he never quite realizes: the creation of the modern novel. (p. 43)

The very form of Sade's work qualifies for the term anti-literature. The conventions of Gothic fiction, the picaresque novel, the novel of manners, the philosophic dialogue, and utopian pornography make their perfunctory appearance in that

work. But the function of form as control or realization of a human impulse is denied, for Sade's impulses defy all satisfaction. . . . Sade outshines the common pornographer. His works are almost wholly independent of time, place, and person, and their autistic purpose is single. Without full comprehension of his role in Western thought, Sade may thus be the first to wrench the imagination free from history, to invert the will of art, and to set language against itself.

He may also be the first to limn the modern consciousness within its void. He wants to restore man to nature, to the force of instincts. He perceives, with a rigor akin to Freudian determinism, the bizarre equivalences of mind and body, fantasy and flesh, in the pursuit of love. He has an intuition of the primal horde, the taboo against incest, the Oedipal drama we re-enact continually with our fathers and mothers, brothers and sisters. He knows that dreams extend the meaning of our waking life, and employs them in his stories accordingly. Above all, Sade complicates for us, in a tragic and irrevocable way, the image of life-giving Eros by revealing the long shadow Thanatos casts upon it. He understands that violence is a condition of vitality, and that nature revels in destruction; he brings the Enlightenment to an end. Yet he never loses the sense that love always lurks where death rules. (pp. 45-6)

In the end, however, Sade limits his relevance to us because he demands to be taken only on his own terms. The Sadian self permits no encounter, no negotiation. It solves the problem of evil by converting all pain, whether inflicted or received, into a source of personal pleasure. Sade can therefore experience orgasm when he hears that he has been burned in effigy. (p. 46)

The imagination of Sade is inflamed by crime because all its energies are committed to transgression. Vice defies Virtue, against God stands the Devil. But this Manicheanism is superficial. Sade denies God vehemently, and ends by identifying himself with Omnipotence. The dialectic of transgression moves toward infinity. . . . The true spirit of the Sadian self is priapic and continuous denial. This leads it *finally* to deny itself by invoking a void which may engulf even its own omnipotence. The consciousness of Sade, raised to the highest level, is anti-consciousness as his work is anti-literature. The mind and the language, caught in hatred, seek release from their own forms into a silence commensurate with outrageous vision.

There is a paradox in the attempt of the Divine Marquis to write anything, as there is a further paradox in my attempt to write about his writings. But paradoxes betray the limits of logic rather than of reality. The works of Sade prefigure the destructive element of our world, and the claims he makes upon us are hard, perhaps impossible, to meet. Yet we dare no longer ignore these claims. There can be no life for men until Sade is answered. (pp. 46-7)

> *Ihab Hassan, "Sade: The Prison of Consciousness" (1971), in his* The Dismemberment of "Orpheus": Toward a Post Modern Literature *(copyright © 1971, 1982 by Ihab Hassan; all rights reserved), second edition, The University of Wisconsin Press, 1982, pp. 24-47.*

NANCY K. MILLER (essay date 1976)

Justine apparently obeys the conventions of fictional organization as they prevail in the eighteenth-century novel: a first-person account of suffering virtue. And not any virtue, but that eminently popular and vulnerable commodity, exemplary femininity via the metonymy of virginity. From the beginning, however, the reader can anticipate not only *Perversion* with a capital "P" as Sollers defines it, "la pensée théorique elle-même," but a concretization of the phenomenon by a *conversion* of establishment values, where positivity is marked with a negative sign, and negativity with a positive one.

The title itself serves as the first "signpost" directing the calvary to come; and the English translation, *Justine or Good Conduct Well Chastised,* points even more clearly to the reversal of canonical and positive itineraries, the sagas of virtue well rewarded. (p. 216)

Justine subverts every quest for happiness undertaken by a virginal heroine in the fictional universe of the eighteenth-century novel, although it is a parody that elicits no laughter.

The novel opens with the all-purpose eighteenth-century celebration of the truth as guiding light. . . . It is a rule of thumb that authenticity serves as license to mutilate the maxim, to promulgate the implausible and/or unacceptable. In the eighteenth-century novel, "fact" is often stranger than fiction.

The opposition of Vice to Virtue is first concretized in the characters of Justine and Juliette; as the title of the novel indicates, it is Justine's destiny that has been granted primacy. Nonetheless, Juliette's function is crucial to the structure of the novel; not merely as the dark-haired vicious foil to Justine's blond virtue, but as a point of narrative suture. Juliette solicits Justine's tale of woe. Juliette's dizzying rise, the author informs us, begins with the successive and successful exchange of her "pristine fruits." Hyperbolic courtesan, she sleeps her way to the top. Justine, on the other hand, like the virtuous heroine of the sentimental novel, is mortified by and rejects the prospect of such prosperity attained at the cost of purity. (pp. 216-17)

It has been said that in eighteenth-century fiction, chastity attracts rape as the sacred invites sacrilege. And what figure is more vulnerable to sexual catastrophe than a destitute, friendless, virginal and virtuous orphan? (p. 217)

Justine's source of attraction comes, on the contrary, not from her ripeness (after all she is only twelve years old at the start) but from her greenness. Or to choose a less gustatory metaphor from the catalogue of descriptive clichés of femininity, she is the bud and not the rose. Her fragility, her delicacy, the essence of positive femininity in the eighteenth-century novel, provide the measure of her potential for suffering: she is not robust enough for comedy. The occasion of Justine's first trial, the one with which *her* narrative opens, clearly establishes the pathetic-erotic pattern of her trials to come. . . . Like the sentimental heroine, Justine prefers death to dishonor. Such is not her destiny, however; consistently she is condemned to that fate worse than death. (pp. 218-19)

From the beginning, Justine is concerned with assuring the reader as to the authenticity of her suffering and alienation. . . . Thus, in conformity with the role of the victim, Justine submits, protests and regrets. Yet there are those who find complicity, or at least an index of ambiguity in her claims to pure disgust. (p. 219)

The problem posed by Justine's version of the facts, it seems to me, is less a function of psychological reliability than narrational liability. As subject and object of a scatalogical destiny, Justine must account for the repertory of sexual experiments and experiences in which she is a reluctant participant. Moreover, since the Sadian erotic involves at least as much sexual discourse as sexual intercourse, Justine's role as narrator

compels her to relay and relate to the reader the text of her oppression—the libertine's credo. (pp. 219-20)

Still, Justine does admit to knowledge of the dynamics of feminine wiles which she generally claims to ignore or despise. . . . Yet does that make her less of a victim and more to the point, does it undermine her credibility as reporter at the scene of the crime? (pp. 220-21)

The sexual reliability of narrative voice, however, is only one area of critical attack on Justine's believability as a character. Justine has often been accused of mental and physical retardation: "Whatever befalls her, Justine is unprepared for it, experience teaches her nothing, her soul remains ignorant, her body more ignorant still." But this sort of criticism proceeds from the assumption that Justine is a character with the potential for development associated with the traditional psychological novel, where according to the famous Jamesian formulation, character determines incident and incident illustrates character in an interlocking system of exchange. Justine above all must carry the weight of the author's counter-demonstration as articulated in the dedication. From the title she is presented as suffering virtue itself. (p. 221)

[The] problem in Sade's text is to close the credibility gap between subject and object of narration, to justify the *instance* of narration. By this I mean that a situation must be created from which this kind of narration could plausibly be generated. Thus for Justine to speak for herself, and at length, a captive is granted an audience. . . .

I suggest that Sade's novel belongs to that form of literary production defined by Todorov in his essay "Les hommes-récits." In this kind of literature (exemplified by the *A Thousand and One Nights*), action is privileged at the expense of character, what counts is the verb and not the subject (or in our case, the object) of the verb. In such an a-psychological mode, a character is no more than his own story, an "homme-récit," he is what happens. As a result, tautology replaces causality: thus, Justine is a victim because she is victimized; she is victimized because she is a victim. . . .

But the added dimension to Justine's suffering as the exemplary victim in a universe where eros is inseparable from logos, is that she must also record and play-back. (p. 222)

[Although] Justine is denied the satisfaction of even a superficial linear progression—she goes in circles despite her desire to reach the south of France, and at the end of practically every adventure finds herself back where she started with the only and minimal difference that time has passed and things are worse—the fiction of her wanderings is at last brought to a close. And to my mind, the final installment of the trials of suffering virtue crystallizes the problems of narrativity and credibility in the text as I have sketched them out until this point. My hypothesis is that at the end of the novel, the disparity between the code and the message, the mimesis of the quest and its subversion, is unequivocally confirmed.

It is Saint-Florent, Justine's first violator, who orchestrates Justine's last torture, her final incarnation as hyperbolic victim. (pp. 222-23)

The scene begins with the familiar permutations of postures available to four libertine men and one female victim; nothing unusual for Justine. What is new is the preparation for immolation that she must undergo to satisfy Saint-Florent, whose specialty consists in deflowering virgins. (p. 223)

[The] fact of Justine's being sewn up, restored to her virginal space, just as previously her wounds were healed to leave no traces, means that her story as *souffre-douleur* is potentially endless, despite the conclusion of the novel, beyond the terminus of the printed page. Curiously, this also means that in the final analysis, Justine's virginity can be reproduced as artificially as Juliette's was at the beginning of her career—which undermines, once again, the sanctity of virginity—and to return to another point of departure, the reader may recall that Justine's first venture on the job-market was to approach her mother's seamstress. (p. 224)

[The] very last paragraph of the novel takes up the terms of the dedication, evoking the tears shed over the misfortunes of virtue, apologizing again for the "heavy brushstrokes," and praising the mysteries of divine providence and its ultimate rewards. The novel stops having come full circle. But then the obvious question: what kind of circle has been described? Which brings me at last to my title and conclusion, the circle of my own text.

While the vicious circle is an expression of common parlance, a glance at the dictionary is still informative. One finds three definitions in Webster's Third New International; all three pertain to different aspects of the novel. The first, "a chain of circumstances constituting a situation in which the process of solving one difficulty creates a new problem involving increased difficulty in the original situation," applies to the automatic conversion process that controls Justine's interaction: she asks for help and is betrayed by her protector, she extends a helping hand and is victimized by her beneficiary—whatever she does, she makes matters worse. The third, "a chain of abnormal processes in which a primary disorder leads to a second which in turn aggravates the first one," characterizes the chain reaction of disasters set in motion by her first sexual encounter. . . . The second, "an argument or definition that is valueless because it overtly or covertly assumes as true something which is to be proved or defined," describes the author's discourse as demonstrated by the identity of his assumptions and conclusions.

Indeed, when as readers we arrive at the end of the road, and we measure the distance traveled, we realize that like Justine we have gone around in circles. The narrative has ended; there seems to have been a story with a beginning, a middle and an end, an innocent heroine, villains, an unfortunate destiny and a moral—in other words structural conformity with the eighteenth century's house of fiction. (pp. 224-25)

Under the Sadian sign of perversion, the linear logic of before/after, now/then, why/because, the logic of memoir as history, proves to be vicious. What Justine as narrator registered as chronology was in fact stasis and progression repetition. Justine's text is but a pretext for a sexual combinatory whose permutations are infinite. It is not surprising, then, that Justine and Juliette should be revived for a final version a few years later. Vicious circle where circle of virtue spirals into circle of vice, there is no way or reason to stop until the author or his reader is exhausted. (p. 226)

Nancy K. Miller, "'Justine', or, the Vicious Circle," in Studies in Eighteenth-Century Culture, Vol. 5, *edited by Ronald C. Rosbottom (copyright 1976 American Studies for Eighteenth-Century Studies), University of Wisconsin Press, 1976, pp. 215-28.*

HERBERT JOSEPHS (essay date 1977)

In Sade's writings, we are able to recognize at least two contrasting figures of woman that in turn dominated his imagination; these figures have been identified schematically by Maurice Tourne as the mythical figures of Penelope and Circe. Circe, represented in the Sadean corpus most fully by Léonore of **Aline et Valcour** and by Juliette, is the fascinating libertine adventuress whose proclivities to pleasure are more violent than even those of the male libertines who crowd the pages of Sade's fiction; she has broken out of her historically determined enslavement to emerge as emblematic of her creator's rebellious energies. . . . She was conceivable, however, only together with the previous destruction of the cult of an earlier image of woman, that of the enslaved female object. Indeed, most of the "metaphysical chimeras" assaulted by Sade were expressed in the figure of Penelope. She was the conventionally passive and eternally devoted feminine ideal of literature and society, the martyred victim who combatted the philosophical temptations offered by her suitors with silent suffering, with an inviolable attachment to chastity and faith. (p. 100)

But the deepest urges of Sade's imagination seem often to crave satisfaction in the possession and perversion of some mysterious condition of innocence or purity attached to this latter form, the pure and virginal female persona of his fiction. And since this troubling figure is inevitably subjected to calumny and vilification, it seems justifiable to discern in Sade one of the more transparent literary illustrations of "protesting too much." . . . [She is] not the only woman portrayed by Sade; eventually she will be most completely understood only in a broader context that should include her destructive sisters, the Juliettes of Sade's fiction. And although Sade did perceive her as the bearer of prejudices and metaphysical values that enslave the truly human in our destinies, she will be treated here less as the symbolic obstacle to social reform than as an obsessional presence which the author was striving to exorcise. It is her persistent reappearances in his fiction which serve perhaps best to uncover the tortured world of the marquis de Sade. She is the beautiful creature from whom all anger has been first purged and then cast into the shape of a libertine monster. With her unassailable innocence, she is proud and passively defiant. She brings into play in her creator's imagination the grotesque coupling of an urge toward degradation with an awed fascination for a creature that comes to resemble, especially in her consecrated cultural form, a sacred object of taboo. Possessing the appeal of the incestuous object, she simultaneously compels and forbids transgression. It is her inevitable defilement that constitutes for Sade a singularly perverse act of deference. (pp. 100-01)

Until the emergence of the female libertine, the figure of woman that provides the characteristic atmosphere for Sade's fiction is the haunting image of feminine virtue. Only with her immolation, Sade would invite us to believe, is the regeneration of a moribund society possible. The familiar targets of his relentless acts of violence, both verbal and physical, are the mother, the devoted spouse, and the innocent maiden. She is both protected and disdained by law and custom, and she is the object simultaneously of contempt and veneration. In her maternal guise, she is the moral, religious, and even artistic ideal of the civilization that imprisoned the marquis. (p. 101)

That Sade feared women is more immediately apparent than that he envied and venerated them. . . . Yet, the ritual recurrence of certain motifs involving women in his writings testifies to his endlessly renewed attempts to express and to master the dilemma of the dominion exercised over his imagination by the female and by her virtually preconscious symbolic attributes. The intensity with which Sade attempted to sever all bonds between sexuality and a sense of the taboo suggests that these bonds were never undone in his imagination, and although the libertine philosopher strained to persuade himself that there is nothing either dangerous or sacred about sexual activity, his writings reveal the contrary.

Few facts are more incontrovertible in Sade's fiction than the unequivocal horror which his heroes express for the female genitals. (p. 102)

The prodigious taste of the Sadean hero for buggering both the male and female permits, as a stimulant to ecstasy, the obliteration of sexual differences which seems magically to avert a primitive horror provoked in the libertine's imagination by the female genitalia. . . . [The] female victim of the Sadean dragon remains somehow untouched by the indecent; the holy figure of woman is preserved intact. Combining caresses with invectives, celebrating and degrading his innocent victim simultaneously, Rodin is driven by antagonistic impulses to the pure and the impure. (p. 103)

The obsessive desecrations and sacrilege, then, imply the presence in Sade's fiction of the sacred. Likewise, the public display of copulation in its more perverse forms, expressed principally in the *Cent Vingt Journées de Sodome* and in *La Philosphie dans le boudoir* are the attempts of a feverish imagination to disguise a sexual puritanism of dimensions as awesome as his heroes' phallic endowment. Whatever particular private fears Sade may have experienced in his erotic imaginings are submerged in a more generalized orgiastic frenzy that is not unlike the festive atmosphere of a liberation ritual. What Sade communicates profoundly to his reader, however, through his momentous outbreaks of violence is the fearsome intuition of an abyss that lies waiting on the far side of the forbidden. And finally, it is woman, the fusion of purity and fertility, of natural creation and of the permanent denial of desire, who calls forth Sade's abominations. He experiences her with yearnings and rage, with a combination of awe and disgust. (pp. 103-04)

It has been generally observed that no matter how frequently and diversely Justine may be possessed, what she represents remains intact. Long after defloration, she can present herself to Bandole with the healed appearances of a reconstructed virginity. For we encounter in Sade's fiction a form of innocence unlike the characteristic inexperience of the Enlightenment ingenue, that intellectual or moral innocence that eventually would be left behind, one hoped, in the wake of socializing experience. . . . Sade's fictional women must be assimilated into the basic movement of transgression which commands his destiny. The ambivalences of this attitude are reflected in the mixture of euphemism and sacrilege, of contemporary sentimentalism and libertine values that provides the hybrid tones of his fiction. It contributes to a narrative atmosphere in which the religious awe characteristic of the Gothic is interwoven with the licentious devices of enlightened thinking. (pp. 104-05)

Perhaps the simplest narrative strategy employed by Sade to dramatize the conflict of the pure and the sensual currents of human feeling is the division of the feminine figure into two opposing functions, one corresponding to the desirable, sexually motivated creature and the other a representative of the stable values of tradition. This doubling tendency was, of course, a familiar convention of fiction and it appears in modified forms even in such relatively contemporary works as *Le Diable amoureux* (1722) and *Les Liaisons dangereuses* (1782). In Sade we discover it not solely in the opposition of Justine and Juliette

but also in the principal female figures of *La Philosophie dans le boudoir* and in *Eugénie de Franval*. In each of these works, we have a daughter proselytized and then indoctrinated into the "plus beaux systèmes du libertinage," and a mother who embodies the conventional attitudes to love and sex, in short, the object to be tortured since she cannot be perverted. In these fictional patterns we can recognize the familiar passive moral conscience and, dwelling alongside it, the shadow figure that resides more generally in dreams, jungles, or in the prisons of mind and society. In Sade's fiction, the two female functions of holiness and of impurity behave like detachable fictions split off from the self; their clash represents not so much a struggle by the author to integrate conflicting urges in the Jekyll and Hyde manner as a compulsion to uncover the perverse from behind the mask of the pure. (pp. 105-06)

If one were to heed Sade's explicit teachings most directly, the portrait of the marquis that emerges is that of a frenzied libertine striving methodically to empty the universe of metaphysics and to convert pleasure into the highest value of a coherent hedonist doctrine. Sometimes the Sadean sexual venture assumes the decidedly revolutionary guise . . . of a desire to liberate mankind from all the constraints of prohibition and taboo. For if it is true that the feminine figure of innocence and/or of conventional morality stimulates within Sade's libidinous hero feelings of terror that derive from veneration, Sade does appear throughout to be attempting a determined escape from a sense of the forbidden. . . . One of the more paradoxical absurdities of the Sadean libertine is that of an enlightened imagination reenergized by the phenomenon of evil. Fundamental to those moral doctrines of materialist naturalism that were inherited by Sade and selectively developed by him is the credo of meaninglessness—the meaninglessness of evil and the emptiness of all the spiritual values and forms that had structured life for his predecessors. Yet, the pursuit of pleasure for Sade's libertine hero and heroine, by their own admission, can be satisfied only by the most heinous of crimes and the most satanic of blasphemies. Pleasure, to put it simply, depends for Sade upon the possibility of evil, to which, however, he denies any existence. It is to the restoration of the sacred and its taboos, therefore, all destroyed by the rationalism that he professed, that his energies must frequently be directed. (pp. 106-07)

Sade's characters behave most often as if they must torture woman for the sin of not having adequately realized the illusory values that have been traditionally associated with her image; they must desecrate her likeness for having revealed herself to be an imperfect incarnation of some distant purity. Each painful reminder of the absence of purity seems to provoke an ever deeper and more vindictive anguish. It is especially to the symbolic maternal figure that the feverish antagonism of Sade is directed. Her principal crime is to have participated in the sexual nature of humanity and betrayed those mysteriously divine origins which he ascribes to her and which she continues to reflect in the cultural values associated with her.

The mother is necessarily a denial of the purity she represents as a result of her fusion with the prohibited and the unattainable. Hatred for the mother in Sade carries in its wake an unrelieved hostility to the notion of the propagation of the species as well as a rigorous denial of the mother's dominant role in procreation. . . . [In] a passage drawn from the *Cent Vingt Journées de Sodome,* we find the almost archetypal playing out of the peculiarly Sadean anger for the mother: the awkward insistence that detesting one's mother, the most intense of all human aversions, is a sentiment placed in us by Nature; the satire of sentiments of gratitude for an "animal" who enjoyed to excess the act of procreation; the brutal violation of the maiden, all the more indefinably beautiful because, weeping, she defends the memory of her devoted mother. With all these familiar elements assembled in preparation for an orgy of defiance, we are offered the image, of legendary proportions, of the outraged and aroused duc de Blangis, frustrated, blaspheming, and in an ultimate menacing gesture, directing his enormous penis at the skies. Sade's unveiled disturbance at the thought of a mother enjoying sexual intercourse to the exclusion of all maternal concerns is psychologically transparent; it is exacerbated in his imagination by the mother's role as denied object of his own desire and, consequently, as the symbolic form signalling the condemnation of all desire. (pp. 107-08)

Perhaps the most startling expression which Sade gave to this compulsion to uncover the truth of sexual desire from beneath the modest appearances of feminine *pudeur* occurs in *La Philosophie dans le boudoir*. Mme de Mistival is introduced into the dialogues, it would seem, solely for her value as a representative of the poisonous virtue of conventional values and of the puritan mentality; it is she who, predictably, is made to carry the symbolic burden of the despised taboo against erotic pleasure. Her sudden appearance and victimization reveal the deepest intentions of a work that has the appearances of the inverted ritual of an initiation or puberty ceremony. By cancelling the traditional delay between sexual maturity and sexual activity, the dialogues seem to be inspired by the desire to remove the condition of transgression from the erotic life. The haunting phantoms of woman are to be exorcized by repeated acts of collective hysteria which must culminate in the violent desexualizing of the mother-scapegoat. (pp. 109-10)

While one could select virtually at random illustrations in Sade's writings of the haunted transgressor seeking to pervert innocence, the antagonistic drives expressed in these acts of awe and desecration are present most dramatically in Sade's treatment of the religious myth of the Virgin mother. Sade's invective is directed, as we might anticipate, at the *impurity* of the mother of Christ. Mary is referred to almost invariably as the "putain céleste [holy whore]." She is the perverted image of sacred woman in that she was diverted by the pleasures of sex from her more appropriate concerns with the generation of a Savior. The myth of the Virgin mother, then, is revealed as another variant on the infantile fantasy, expressed so transparently by Sade, that denies sexual intercourse to the mother. This fantasy occurs in Sade as the obverse of the author's attempts to defile the image of the Virgin. (p. 111)

[The myriad acts of transgression in Sade] reveal a tendency endemic to the libertine temperament during the closing stages of the movement of Enlightenment, the ambiguous impulse to outrage and destroy the most cherished of the inherited values. The figure of purity, mother or maiden, who alone was able to incorporate the many moral and religious delusions of a vanishing age, could no longer command the belief of the intellectual. It did, however, continue to beguile him especially because of its promise to save love from the insipid experience of mechanical copulations. . . . [And if] the supreme pleasure of love lies in wrongdoing, the possibilities logically remaining for transgression in the valueless world of Sade's universe were few. For whom, after all, does Sade repeat without quarter the sacrileges addressed to vacant heavens? His outpourings of accumulated hatred seem to be provoked whenever he realizes that he will not succeed in outraging the nonexistent or in

desecrating what he could not hold sacred. His iconoclasm betrays itself as the prisoner's impotence, in sex undoubtedly as well as in cosmic rebellion.

Sade occasionally acknowledged the frustration that inevitably attended his challenges to the divine. . . . The ritual application of the vocabulary of the divine and the holy to the excremental functions and the sexual organs also finds its explanation here. In *La Philosophie dans le boudoir* Sade admitted that although the profanation that results from the sacrilegious juxtaposition of the foul and the obscene with the language of the sacred can serve no meaningful purpose, such profanation represented at least a small victory for the pride of man humiliated by centuries of enslavement. But more important, it alone could serve the demands of his imagination. (pp. 112-13)

Sade's aspirations turned inside out rejoin those of Rousseau by identifying fulfillment only in the realm of "that which is not." For Sade, such imaginative fulfillment had to be sought not by voluntary withdrawal from the affairs of men to the silent world within, but rather, from the solitude of confinement, in the dream of mad assaults upon woman. He belongs to our race not only through having established a fraternity of the monstrous residing in the hidden corners of the psyche, through the maidens and mothers that he assaults but, as Lacan has suggested, through those whom he also spares and preserves for the memory of the sacred. (p. 113)

> Herbert Josephs, "Sade and Woman: Exorcising the Awe of the Sacred" (reprinted by permission of the author) in Studies in Burke and His Time, *Vol. 18, No. 2, Spring, 1977, pp. 99-113.*

RONALD HAYMAN (essay date 1978)

[That Sade] found relief by writing is unremarkable. In his situation [in prison], nothing could have been more natural than the urge to pour words over every available scrap of paper. But if what he wrote had not been important, it would not be disturbing 200 years later. He did not choose to turn his attention inwards: he had no option. His achievement is that before the Romantic movement had been launched, he succeeded in making solipsism look like omniscience.

His [*Dialogue entre un prêtre et un moribond*] is the story of a death-bed conversion, but it is the priest who is converted. (p. 124)

The priest is unable to explain why God, after creating a corrupted nature, should have wanted to test humanity by giving it freedom of choice. He must have been able to see into the future, and if he wanted us to resist temptation, why did he choose not to make us stronger? As it is, we are all driven by irresistible forces, victims of our own inclinations. Our virtues and our vices are equally necessary to Nature, who skilfully holds the balance between them. The best incentive to virtuous behaviour is not intimidation but reason. Ethics depend entirely on the principle of trying to make other people as happy as we wish to be ourselves. The dying man would therefore like to make the priest as happy as he intends to be himself in his final minutes. (pp. 124-25)

The priest's change of heart is totally unrealistic, and so is the vigour the dying man displays in arguing and in making love. But the dialogue belongs to the convention by which literature—obliged, in self-defence, to prove itself morally useful—had been combining the arts of oratory and fable. (p. 125)

The *Dialogue* contains the seeds of all his subsequent fiction. The crucial experience, I suspect, was the discovery of how much pleasure was to be had from writing out his fantasy about an orgy involving a priest, a dying man and six beautiful women. Erotic daydream draws freely, if tenuously, on memories of physical contact; the act of writing, the appearance of words on paper, not only stabilizes the imaginary action but helps to elaborate it. In becoming less cerebral, the experience becomes more orderly. Even if the words will never be read, they are hostages to space outside the mind. They have a tangible, if two-dimensional existence, and they systematize the action, discipline it, commit it tidily to a sequence or a scheme. A description of a woman's body, for instance, may be based on a merging of memory with desire, anthologizing any number of appetizing features, but it must be self-consistent. (pp. 128-29)

120 journées is not a healthy, wholesome or balanced book, but if Sade is recognized as the patriarch of modern nihilism, it must also be acknowledged that it was not mere *ennui* that was alienating him. It could be said of all his decadent descendants that their aggressions against humanity were, in origin, defensive, and that they were defending themselves against pain, psychological or physical or both. It seems that Sade did much of the preliminary work for *120 journées* when he was in both kinds of pain. (p. 131)

120 journées is a diabolically ingenious machine which simultaneously inverts the reality of Sade's situation and subverts the morality that justified it. He described his four debauched heroes as 'champions'; they were for him what Beckett calls 'vice-existers'. They even gave him a flattering mirror-image of his own isolation. To enjoy flagellation, perversion and sexual excess, they imprison their victims in a Gothic castle which is remote and inaccessible enough to guarantee freedom from society's interference. What Sade accepted involuntarily they chose.

Realistic criteria are almost as irrelevant as they were to the *Dialogue*. Having total power over their victims, the libertines would not need to explain anything, but the narrative is replete with explanations. Subtitled *L'Ecole de libertinage,* the novel reverses the tradition of the moral fable, while illustrating Sade's dictum that to be erotic it is essential to articulate crime in language. It is not merely that words were his only means of representing actions: what was revolutionary about the book was its uninhibited exploration of the space between sensation and formulation. Unlike animals, we seldom enjoy a sensation without describing it to ourselves. Awareness of pleasure or pain is always impure, contaminated by words, even when they remain unspoken. At the same time, verbalization extends the pleasure or the pain. Once words have been let in, the imagination cannot be kept out. . . . A play-within-a-play tends to focus attention on the relationship between action and audience by offering an onstage simulacrum of it; stories-within-a-story can question the relationship between fiction and reader in a similarly provocative way. Sade's four libertines have recruited four experienced ex-prostitutes to reminisce about unsavoury episodes. The function of these stories is to revive the libertines' appetite for new orgies.

Without any grounds for expecting the book to be published, Sade was visualizing a male reader, and writing with one eye on his erectile tissue. We are obviously intended to follow the example of the libertines, who continually interrupt the storytelling in order to act out something that has been directly or indirectly suggested. Even if we do not follow suit, the deft

alternation between the two levels of narrative not only reminds us of the medium but forces us to re-examine the connection between word and sensation, image and action.

One of the stock arguments against describing the sexual act is that it is always the same. Sade's structure is based on the conviction that it is not: an enormously extended set of variations moves progressively away from the original theme. This was not merely a stratagem for avoiding repetition: it was a logical development from the assumption that to the connoisseur of sexual pleasure, diversification is essential. For the libertine who has the means of gratifying every desire, the problem is how to save the appetite from becoming jaded. . . . Sade's narrative method was wedded to his immoralism. Analysis and classification lead naturally to diversification, which will inevitably carry us further and further from the norms. One of his deadliest insights is expressed in one of his pithiest epigrams: 'The true way of enlarging and multiplying one's desires is to wish to impose limits on them.' This also explains the principle by which the book was written. (pp. 133-35)

He also did well to make the libertines formulate strict rules for themselves and their victims. The subject matter is potentially anarchic. The sexual excesses and the coprophilia break down all the barriers erected by hygiene and by civilization. Some of the libertines' rules go directly against the old rules. Religious piety is severely punished. . . .

But if Sade had finished the novel, he might have found himself needing to modify his style, as if he were progressively introducing discord into a classical symphony. The 120 days are spread over four winter months, November to February, and each of the story-tellers is on duty for a month. We know that the criminality will increase steadily, both in the main narrative and in the storytellers' stories, so the mounting disorderliness of the behaviour creates a disturbing, almost disrupting, pressure within the geometrically orderly framework. Between bouts of progressively outrageous self-indulgence, the libertines are mouthpieces for Sade's philosophizing. (p. 135)

The Duc de Blangis regards man as a machine in the hands of nature, and he boasts that he has been faithful to the principles he formed in his youth. 'They taught me that virtue was empty, a nothing . . . only vice was made so that man could experience that moral and physical vibration, source of the most exquisite pleasures . . . So I have nothing to hold me back except the laws . . . My money and my credit put me above the vulgar plagues which should attack only the people.' Properly regarded, the laws are valuable because they stand between desire and its attainment, and there is no satisfaction to be had if desires are attained too easily. As Sade makes Durcet, the financier, put it: 'Happiness consists not in consummation but in desire, in shattering the restrictions imposed as obstacles to it.' Living at the opposite pole of deprivation from his characters—having unlimited opportunities for desire and none for consummation—Sade led them to conclusions from which he could take comfort. They find it very frustrating to have pleasure so readily available. 'I swear,' says Durcet on the eighth day, 'that ever since I have been here, my sperm has not flowed for what is here. It is things which are not here that make me come.' The principle of negation had never been stated more simply or more powerfully. Here is a rationale for rejecting reality in favour of the imaginary alternative, denying what is present for the sake of what is not. Sade is squashing his characters into incapacity for enjoyment of immediate action. Implicitly sexual activity is being negated and fantasy invested with the energy taken from it, as if thought and language were the only valid components in the experience of sex. (pp. 136-37)

For the sadist, one of the greatest disadvantages of solitude is that he cannot feel superior to anyone else. Sade put his dissatisfaction into the mouth of Durcet: 'What we are lacking is comparison . . . I need the satisfaction of seeing someone who is suffering from not having what I have . . . Happiness will never exist without inequality. It is like the man who does not understand the value of health until he is ill. The greatest sensual pleasure in the world is watching the tears of those overwhelmed with misery.' . . . One of the reasons Sade needed his fiction was that it enabled him to feel superior to his characters. He also used them as a device for remodelling his memories of earlier experiences. (pp. 137-38)

The acid internal logic of *La Philosophie dans le boudoir* is partly distilled from the harshness of the surrounding circumstances, and the book is quite unlike *Justine* in its references to current events. Though written in dialogue, it is less like a play than a novel or a moral tale, but the tension is always entertainingly theatrical and despite inconsistencies, contradictions and absurdities, Sade comes surprisingly close to synthesizing the libertine philosophy of his earlier fiction with the ideas he had championed in his political speeches. A radical pamphlet, which may have been written separately, is interpolated into the dialogue, and the characters find it easy to reconcile the substance of it with their orgiastic behaviour. (p. 141)

The arguments against the existence of God are in line with those of *Dialogue entre un prêtre et un moribund* but the statement is more forceful. God is 'an inconsistent and barbarous being, creating today a world he disapproves of tomorrow . . . a feeble being who can never make men do what he wants . . . If he had made them good enough, they would have been incapable of doing evil, and only then would the work be worthy of a God.' Eugénie's conversion is as unrealistically rapid as the Priest's in the *Dialogue*. She immediately renounces this feeble God. Though still handicapped by the impossibility of breaking free from the categories of good and evil, virtue and vice, Sade makes the point, as in *Aline et Valcour,* that norms have varied from one century to another and one country to another. What is new is his anti-authoritarian insistence that citizens of a republic should have no need of the religious dogma which has been a tool of monarchical autocracy. (pp. 198-99)

Though not alone in wanting to set up Nature as a god and to dispense with priestly appeasers of conscience, Sade was almost alone in refusing to pretend that Nature was moralistic. Still relying on La Mettrie's premiss that Nature must want us to indulge the impulses she has implanted, he goes on to make suggestions for reforming the legal system. He was right to insist that the death of monarchy must lead to changes in manners: in a society based on liberty and equality there should be fewer legal prohibitions, fewer actions which are branded as crimes. Capital punishment should be abolished. Even murderers, he suggests, should be treated as Louis XV treated Charolais: 'I grant you pardon,' said the King, 'but I will also pardon whoever kills you.'

Nor should stealing be regarded as a crime, according to *La Philosophie*. It breeds courage, skill and tact—virtues useful to a republican society, and it tends towards a more even distribution of wealth. Is it not unjust that the man who has nothing should be forced by the law to respect the man who has everything? A social contract to respect property is a weapon of the strong against the weak.

Rape does less harm than theft, because nothing is taken away. Nature's intention is that women should belong to all men. Exclusive ownership is as bad as slavery, and no woman should have the right to reject any man who makes advances. If men were not entitled to compel submission, why would Nature have given them superior strength? Love is anti-social, serving only the happiness of two people. Women, like roadside fountains, are there for everybody.

The separation of sensation from emotion was essential to the underlying equation of liberty with libertinism. Love had to be discredited. 'What is the base of this sentiment? Desire. What are its consequences? Madness . . . The aim is to possess the object. Well, let us try to succeed, but prudently. Let us enjoy it when we have it, and console ourselves when we fail. All men and all women are alike . . . nothing is more deceptive than this intoxication which so upsets our senses as to make us think that we do not see, do not exist, except through this madly adored object.' The libertine is concerned only with his physical sensations. Eugénie has no interest in raising a family. Childbirth is not only bad for the figure, it reduces sensitivity. (pp. 199-200)

As in *120 journées,* the plot's movement towards bloodshed reflects a fundamental ambivalence towards the immoralists. It cannot be evil to strip away superstitions, prejudices and inhibitions when they stand in the way of harmless physical pleasures, but Sade compulsively develops his narrative to culminate in evil-doing that cannot fail to alienate his readers. (pp. 200-01)

In *Juliette* Sade reverts to the first person, but with this narrator there is no need for circumlocution. The novel is nearly as long as *War and Peace,* though the main strain on the reader is the progressive brutality. Like Eugénie in *La Philosophie,* we must be liberated not only from shame and inhibition but from the scruples that make us condemn violence. Action and argument work like battering rams to break down three ancient doors—Christianity, truthfulness and chastity. Dismissing the idea of love, one of Sade's libertines quotes Voltaire's definition of it as imagination's embroidery on nature's homespun.

In fictional defences of conventional morality, virtue is either rewarded—in this world or the next—or presented as its own reward. A clear conscience and the prospect of heaven are offered as enticements for rationing the body to a small fraction of the pleasures for which it is equipped. But even the fiercest enemies of promiscuity, like Richardson, are prone to ambivalence. (p. 204)

If punishment in actuality could be as grossly disproportionate to crime as [Sade's] imprisonment had been, the whole system must be rotten, and the revolution had failed to overturn it because France was ignoring the warning of *La Philosophie:* Frenchmen were not making the 'one more effort' it would have taken to abolish God. If the old hierarchy was merely being replaced by another one, with God still at the apex, justice would still be dispensed in public according to an unacceptable scale of values. The only trustworthy judges were the most sensitive parts of the body.

But why did Sade need so much brutality? Why not simply write hymns of praise to the orgasm, indulging his preference for anal intercourse by implanting similar tastes in his heroes? He was still using literature as a means of unpicking the past, inverting reality. In reality, he did not want the blood of the Montreuils; in fantasy, his thirst for vengeance was unquenchable. In theory he could prove that any action, however base, was natural and therefore did not need to be justified; in practice he could not shake off the compulsion to infiltrate self-justification into everything he wrote. Addiction to the habit had merely made him more skilful in designing elaborate superstructures.

Unlike Baudelaire, he seldom used the word evil, not because he disbelieved in evil but because he believed it to be all-pervasive. So what effect could his writing have? If it did harm, it would only be helping Nature to achieve her purposes, though, in his ambivalence, he could not help trying to persuade himself that it would do good by demystifying, disabusing the credulous victims of hypocrisy—the majority that was so willingly deceived. The public must be taught, for instance, that churchmen are not motivated by altruism. Of all the priests and monks in his fiction, there is scarcely one who does not use religion as a cloak for lechery. (pp. 204-05)

It makes more sense to condemn [*Juliette*] as propaganda than as pornography. Sade is less interested in arousing us sexually than he was in *120 journées,* and more interested in convincing us. He knows that, unlike Eugénie, we are not going to be converted by a single discourse, but if he can make us read on he is making us his accomplices, at least to the extent of acquiescing in a flow of events which we will be unable to stop. Like Juliette, we are receiving lessons in apathy. Her first comes from the Mother Superior, who advises her to hold back from interfering in other people's sufferings. A quick-witted pupil, she immediately points out that apathy will lead to criminality.

To survive the assault course of horror Sade presents, we may—without becoming criminals—cultivate a certain apathy that will remain with us. This danger is increased by his usual strategy of dividing the narrative into two levels: as in *120 journées,* the interruptions illustrate the aphrodisiac effect the chronicle of crime is having on the listeners. 'We soon lit the fire of the passions from the torch of philosophy.' Once again, words are leading to actions within the narrative, and this makes it more difficult to treat the whole fictional world of crime as if it were merely verbal. In the same way that the Jesuits encouraged children to emulate the saints, Sade structures his stories on the way student libertines emulate virtuoso sinners. The pattern of *La Philosophie* is developed. (p. 206)

In *Juliette,* more obviously than in any novel since *120 journées,* Sade enjoyed his absolute power over characters who themselves had absolute power over an unlimited supply of victims. Instead of identifying with the victim, as in so many of the intervening fictions, he was writing from the libertine's blinkered viewpoint. . . . The victim becomes a depersonalized representative of a submissive Nature. (p. 207)

When, in the second half of the novel, Sade sends his characters out on their travels, his object is to fortify private experience with a semblance of cosmic validity, but he fails to make the world seem real. The narrative technique is the accomplice of action and argument in their campaign to devalue external reality: nothing is given any solidity in its own right. He does even less than in *Aline et Valcour* to make landscape or objects into felt presences. The word *Nature* keeps recurring, but if natural scenery is described, it is only in terms of its effects on the imagination. . . .

Sade is aware that he is arrogating the right to remodel Nature according to the momentary needs of his narrative. His aesthetic assumptions are as solipsistic as his imaginative premiss. (p. 208)

Implicitly the novel is giving divine status to the imagination, while relegating Nature to an inferior position, but at the same time the libertines are challenging Nature to revenge herself for the outrages they perpetrate against her. She gives no sign of wanting to, but in all the philosophizing the possibility that she may be unconcerned about human behaviour comes to the surface only twice: Noirceuil, who has defined crime as something that conflicts with natural laws, recognizes that nothing can conceivably 'outrage a Nature which is ceaselessly in flux'. But within a page he is talking of 'Nature's learned hand', which generates order out of chaos, and reasserts the equilibrium by implanting the same destructive instincts in men as she has in the animals. We get the other glimpse of the possibility when Sade makes the Pope declare: 'Mankind has no relationship to Nature; nor has Nature to man.' This was an extraordinarily advanced position to adopt, even momentarily, in the eighteenth century, and it should not surprise us that Sade's pontiff immediately retreats into talking as if creatures 'do well by Nature' if they destroy each other. Nature abhors propagation, he maintains, and delights in destruction. The cruelty that leads to murder is a disposition received from Nature. . . .

Objects and actions are devalued in relation to sensations and fantasies. Even works of art—products of the imagination—are assessed according to their effects on the imagination of the characters. In the Uffizi Gallery the paintings and sculptures are exciting only if they are provocative. (p. 209)

There was nothing unusual about Sade's pride in calling himself a libertine. What was exceptional was his obstinacy in refusing to dichotomize theory and practice, ideas and sensations. . . . [He] was a pre-Romantic individualist, though he was also typical of his period in so far as he believed in the possibility of using his experience to evolve categorizations which would have a general validity. No pervert has ever been a more avid cataloguer. His *120 journées de Sodome* was intended as a comprehensive listing of the destructive sexual passions. He also had an extraordinary talent for self-analysis and it is only prejudice and historical myopia that has denied him his importance as an originator of the alienated art in which case-history is inseparable from oeuvre: Sade, Baudelaire, de Nerval, Lautréamont, Rimbaud, Artaud, Genet. . . . As an artist, of course, Sade cannot be placed on the same level as Baudelaire, de Nerval or Rimbaud, but in all these French *poètes maudits* the rebellion against the conventional language was inextricable from a rebellion against conventional morality and the idea of God, while the thirst for beauty and intensity of experience was imbued with a death-wish. What matters is to penetrate, at whatever cost, to the unknown. (pp. 232-33)

Ronald Hayman, in his De Sade: A Critical Biography *(copyright © 1978 by Ronald Hayman; reprinted by permission of Harper & Row, Publishers, Inc.), Thomas Y. Crowell Co., Inc., 1978, 252 p.*

ADDITIONAL BIBLIOGRAPHY

Barthes, Roland. "Sade I." In his *Sade, Fourier, Loyola,* translated by Richard Miller, pp. 15-37. New York: Farrar, Straus, Giroux: 1976.
  A study of Sade's erotic code.

Brissenden, R. F. "*La philosophie dans le boudoir:* Or, a Young Lady's Entrance into the World." In his *Virtue in Distress: Studies in the Novel of Sentiment from Richardson to Sade,* pp. 268-93. New York: Barnes & Noble, 1974.

    A psychological study of Sade's personality as manifested in *La philosophie dans le boudoir.*

Bryan, C.D.B. "Sade: Chronicles of a Misanthrope." *The New Republic* 153, No. 18 (30 October 1965): 20-3.

    A modern view of Sade's work. Bryan says that Sade "carves up the mind."

Hampshire, Stuart. "Sade." In his *Modern Writers and Other Essays,* pp. 56-62. London: Chatto & Windus, 1969.

    States that Sade's starting points for his philosophy were angry atheism and thorough determinism.

Harari, Josue V. "De Sade's Narrative: Ill-logical or Illogical." *Genre* VII, No. 1 (March 1974): 112-31.

    A technical analysis of Sade's narrative style.

Thomas, Donald. *The Marquis de Sade.* London: Weidenfeld & Nicolson, 1976, 214 p.

    An informative, detailed biographical study.

Weightman, John. "King Phallus." *The New York Review of Books* V, No. 2 (26 August 1965): 249-55.

    A study of Sade's work as proof that he was mentally ill.

William Gilmore Simms

1806-1870

American novelist, short story writer, essayist, editor, dramatist, poet, biographer, and historian.

Simms was an early advocate for the establishment of a national, and, more particularly, a Southern fiction. Although he wrote in numerous genres and considered himself primarily a poet, Simms is best known for his colorful, romantic novels which depict various aspects of Southern life, from the Revolutionary War to the Civil War. His subject matter, themes, and characters are distinctly Southern, and Simms is credited with contributing to the legend of the Old South that writers continue to draw upon today.

Born in Charleston to a family of some wealth but little social status, Simms spent most of his youth reading novels and listening to his grandmother's tales of her experiences in South Carolina during the Revolutionary War. He was convinced at an early age of the historical importance of the South's contribution, both politically and culturally, to the formation of the country. Simms lived in and around Charleston all of his life, except for a short stay with his father in the frontier country of Mississippi. This trip furnished Simms with a first-hand view of the Indian and colonial life which later enlivened the pages of *The Yemassee, The Cassique of Kiawah*, and *The Wigwam and the Cabin*. One of Simms's greatest sorrows was the slow acceptance of his work in the South, where he was snubbed long after his literary reputation was established in the North and abroad. It was not until after his second marriage to the daughter of a wealthy plantation owner that he received the acknowledgment he felt due him. At Woodlands, his wife's plantation, Simms entertained extensively, and his hospitality was renowned in both the North and South. He knew the most promising Southern writers of the time and encouraged them by publishing their works in several literary journals which he edited and contributed to himself.

During the quiet years at Woodlands between 1836 and 1861, Simms wrote most of his major works. Left to his leisurely brooding, Simms might have learned to refine his writing, which is often criticized for being uneven in quality. Unfortunately, the Civil War shattered Simms's pleasant, reflective life. As tension grew between the North and South, Simms became an increasingly adamant advocate of the Southern cause. In *The Sword and the Distaff; or, "Fair, Fat, and Forty,"* later published as *Woodcraft; or, Hawks about the Dovecote*, he attempted to answer Harriet Beecher Stowe's *Uncle Tom's Cabin*, and, in his nonfiction, he blatantly criticized the North. Simms's strong secessionist views alienated some of his friends in the North, thus closing many publishing doors. By 1865 the war was over, Woodlands was burned, his wife was dead, and Simms, impoverished, was forced to make a living for himself and his six remaining children. His last works show the strain of his economic and personal struggles. They were hurriedly written without heart or reflection, and most were serialized; these works have never been collected. Simms died poor, overworked, and in relative obscurity.

All of Simms's novels are characterized by hasty production with little or no revision. They contain many events piled, at

times indiscriminately, one on top of the other; however, Simms's vibrancy shines through, particularly in his presentation of characters from the lower classes. The best of Simms's work can be divided into three groups: the colonial romances, the border romances, and the Revolutionary romances. Simms preferred to call these works romances rather than novels because, as he stated, a novel is "confined to the felicitous narration of common and daily occurring events," whereas a romance "does not insist upon what is known, or even what is probable. It grasps at the possible." There is an obvious tension, however, between romance and realism in Simms's works, evident in the scenes of violence throughout his novels. These scenes were criticized by contemporaries as sensational, morbid, and in poor taste. Modern critics, however, applaud Simms's vivid portrayal of violence.

There is speculation as to which group of romances represents Simms's best work. Of the colonial romances, *The Yemassee* is best known. It is universally praised for its realistic portrayal of Indians, who, unlike James Fenimore Cooper's idealized "noble savages," are shown to be heir to the same evils and virtues as white men.

With the border romances, *Guy Rivers, Richard Hurdis; or, The Avenger of Blood, Border Beagles, Beauchampe; or, The Kentucky Tragedy*, and *Charlemont; or, The Pride of the Vil-*

lage, Simms introduced American readers to the unruly border country. In these works, which contain some of his most violent and disturbing scenes, Simms ventured into the psychological novel. Critics disagree about his success. The majority believe that Simms's forte lies in his genius for fast-paced action, and that his dallying with the inner functions of the mind and heart merely displays his tendency towards melodrama.

The seven Revolutionary romances, which include *The Partisan, Katharine Walton; or, The Rebel of Dorchester*, and *Woodcraft*, are generally considered Simms's best efforts. In them, he creates his most memorable character, Captain Porgy, who has been called an American Falstaff. This comparison has drawn both favorable and unfavorable criticism, but William P. Trent, Simms's biographer, maintains that Porgy is not strictly based on Shakespeare's character but is rather a fictionalization of Simms himself—robust, gentlemanly, and abidingly Southern.

In some respects, Simms was a casualty of the Civil War, since the writing of Southern authors was generally suppressed after the Yankee victory. Although most critics agree that Simms has been unduly neglected, they acknowledge that his careless writing, heavy reliance on stock characters, and tendency towards melodrama are valid reasons for his present reputation. Nevertheless, Simms remains a notable, though minor, figure in the development of Southern fiction. J. V. Ridgely defines him as "a maker of myths about the South's past, present and future during the important period when the area was seeking its identity."

(See also *Dictionary of Literary Biography, Vol. 3: Antebellum Writers in New York and the South*.)

PRINCIPAL WORKS

Martin Faber (novel) 1833
Guy Rivers (novel) 1834
The Partisan (novel) 1835
The Yemassee (novel) 1835
Mellichampe (novel) 1836
Richard Hurdis; or, The Avenger of Blood (novel) 1838
Border Beagles (novel) 1840
Confession; or, The Blind Heart (novel) 1841
The Kinsmen; or, The Black Riders of the Congaree (novel) 1841; also published as *The Scout*, 1854
Beauchampe; or, The Kentucky Tragedy (novel) 1842
Donna Florida (poetry) 1843
The Wigwam and the Cabin (short stories) 1845
Katharine Walton; or, The Rebel of Dorchester (novel) 1851
Norman Maurice: The Man of the People [first publication] (drama) 1851
The Sword and the Distaff; or, "Fair, Fat, and Forty" (novel) 1852; also published as *Woodcraft; or, Hawks about the Dovecote*, 1854
The Forayers; or, The Raid of the Dog-Days (novel) 1855
Michael Bonham; or, The Fall of Bexar (drama) 1855
Charlemont; or, The Pride of the Village (novel) 1856
Eutaw: A Sequel to The Forayers; or, The Raid of the Dog-Days (novel) 1856
The Cassique of Kiawah (novel) 1859
Voltmeier; or, The Mountain Men (novel) 1869

AMERICAN MONTHLY MAGAZINE (essay date 1834)

We discover, when we have closed [Mr. Simms's *Guy Rivers*], that we have been reading a moral treatise; that we have been learning the process by which the heart of man lapses into sin; that we have seen the channels of that heart laid open; that we have studied the progress, the dominion, and the consequences of evil; and, though the novel be not concluded with a pompous "Go thou and do likewise," we fail not to make the application, and rise up convinced of having seated ourselves merely to be entertained. . . . There is more acquaintance, displayed in these two volumes, with secret springs of human action, with the traits of character that make men heroes or villains, accordingly as they are moulded into good or evil by the influence of education, than in all the novels Cooper ever has written, or will ever write. A work full of a dark and terrible interest, it chains down our faculties as we read; yet in the most exciting scenes, we pause to admire the justice of the arguments, the correctness of observation which has given rise to such a tale. With much that reminds us of *Martin Faber,* it is wholly original, and as far superior to that clever little work, as a finished painting must be superior to a sketch by the same pencil. (p. 297)

The scene of action is laid in the gold regions of Georgia, a district which is described with no less graphic force, than the characters whom we meet therein are justly conceived, and vividly portrayed. (p. 298)

[It is] in depicting character that the author of *Guy Rivers* is most happy, and we have a dozen different personages playing their intricate and deep-laid parts with a propriety, such as we rarely meet with in fictitious composition. Every word tends to the identity of their characters, every action springs naturally from the sentiments, the nature of the actor, and conduces to the development of the heart and principles of each no less than to the main action of the tale. . . . *Guy Rivers* is a book which could have been written by no hand but that of one who had read the heart and studied the essence of man, in varied circumstance, and in all its hundred lights and shadows; who had observed shrewdly, reflected deeply. . . . *Guy Rivers* is in fact a novel of mind, Cooper's nay Scott's novels of matter! (p. 302)

One remark we must make in conclusion. . . . Mr. Simms is the only author of our country who has been truly happy in his females. We know not why it is, but not one of all our many and talented writers has produced a female personage that could for an instant be compared with Katharine Walton, Lucy Monro, or Ellen, the victim of our flagitious hero. All other novel heroines are mere boarding-school misses when compared to these highly wrought creations. . . . (p. 304)

> *"'Guy Rivers—A Tale of Georgia'," in* American Monthly Magazine, *Vol. III, No. V, July, 1834, pp. 295-304.*

AMERICAN MONTHLY MAGAZINE (essay date 1835)

[We] have no hesitation in declaring our opinion, that the *Yemassee* is by far the best representation of the peculiarities of [the Indian] race, that has ever been published. It is beginning to be pretty generally admitted, that the Indians of Cooper, beautiful and striking as they are, if considered as creations, are quite incorrect as portraits; and we know that by our officers and frontiers-men they are considered as mere works of fancy. (p. 174)

[In the *Yemassee,* we] do not find [the Indians] acting at one instant as creatures of impulse and of nature, and at another, as civilized men—all is in keeping, and all is beautiful. Indeed, in no respect has this author more wonderfully improved, since the publication of *Guy Rivers,* than in the truth, identity, and distinctness of his characters. In the former, all the personages talked, and thought, nearly in the same style; here each is clearly conceived, and boldly drawn—all stand out, in groups, or in single figures, boldly relieved, and correct in their smallest details. . . . The style, too, is much improved. Mr. Simms is given to neologism—somewhat too much so for our taste, as we hold that our language is even now too copious—and in *Guy Rivers* he had indulged himself too largely in this respect; besides which, his meanings were, at times, a little obscure, from his usage of familiar words in unfamiliar senses, and of oddly-constructed phrases; this is, however, by no means so often the case in the *Yemassee.* On the contrary, the language is strong, rich, and melodious, and in many instances, we meet whole pages of what we can call by no other name than poetry—exquisite, true poetry. (p. 175)

We have no hesitation in placing [the *Yemassee*] above any romance of native production on a native subject. There are faults—several, but trifling, faults—both of manner and matter in the work before us; but the thoughts and style are equally original—the first are generally unexceptionable, and if the latter were fully equal to them, we know few writers of fiction, whom we could unhesitatingly prefer to the author of the *Yemassee.* (p. 181)

> *"'The Yemassee',"* in American Monthly Magazine, *Vol. V, No. III, May, 1835, pp. 171-81.*

THE SOUTHERN LITERARY JOURNAL   (essay date 1836)

As a novel, we think [*The Partisan*] a decided improvement upon Simms's previous works. It contains no one incident that we would willingly have passed over. . . .

As an observer nothing escapes Simms's remark. In this respect, we think he possesses all the minuteness of Irving, with much more of his power. If for instance he passes through our swamps—nothing is omited to make the picture perfect. There you find Dr. Oakenburgh, encountering the huge mockasin snake—Porgy like a true epicure, crawls after the *soupy* terrapin, or perchance, levels his rifle at the stately stag, browsing upon the green herbage of its boggy soil. Does he leaves this and approach the river, you find the breeze freshened as it sweeps on its upward course from the ocean. These are a few of the little items which in our opinion, show that the author sketches with the pencil of a painter. They bespeak his aptitude for the species of literature he has undertaken, and constitutes the chief merits of the novelist. (p. 358)

> *"'The Partisan: A Tale of the Revolution',"* in The Southern Literary Journal *(copyright 1836 by the Department of English, University of North Carolina at Chapel Hill), Vol. 1, No. 5, January, 1836, pp. 347-58.*

[EDGAR ALLAN POE]   (essay date 1836)

There is very little plot or connexion in [**"The Partisan"**]; and Mr. Simms has evidently aimed at neither. Indeed we hardly know what to think of the work at all. Perhaps, with some hesitation, we may call it an historical novel. . . . Whether the idea ever entered the mind of Mr. Simms that his very

laudable design . . . might have been better carried into effect by a work of a character *purely* historical, we, of course, have no opportunity of deciding. To ourselves, every succeeding page of **"The Partisan"** rendered the supposition more plausible. The interweaving fact with fiction is at all times hazardous, and presupposes on the part of general readers that degree of intimate acquaintance with fact which should never be presupposed. In the present instance, the author has failed, so we think, in confining either his truth or his fable within its legitimate, individual domain. Nor do we at all wonder at his failure in performing what no novelist whatever has hitherto performed. . . .

The history of the march of Gates' army, his foolhardiness, and consequent humiliating discomfiture by Cornwallis, are as well told as any details of a like nature can be told, in language exceedingly confused, ill-arranged, and ungrammatical. (p. 118)

Of the numerous personages who figure in the book, some are really excellent—some horrible. The historical characters are, without exception, well drawn. The portraits of Cornwallis, Gates, and Marion, are vivid realities—those of De Kalb and the Claverhouse-like Tarleton positively unsurpassed by any similar delineations within our knowledge. The fictitious existences in **"The Partisan"** will not bear examination. [Major Robert] Singleton is about as much of a non-entity as most other heroes of our acquaintance. . . . Goggle is another miserable addition to the list of those anomalies so swarming in fiction, who are represented as having vicious principles, for no other reason than because they have ugly faces. Of the females we can hardly speak in a more favorable manner. Bella, the innkeeper's daughter is, we suppose, very much like an innkeeper's daughter. . . . Emily, Singleton's sister, is not what we would wish her. Too much stress is laid upon the interesting features of the consumption which destroys her; and the whole chapter of abrupt sentimentality, in which we are introduced to her sepulchre before having notice of her death, is in the very worst style of times *un peu passés.* Katharine Walton is somewhat better than either of the ladies above mentioned. In the beginning of the book, however, we are disgusted with that excessive prudishness which will not admit of a lover's hand resting for a moment upon her own—in the conclusion, we are provoked to a smile when she throws herself into the arms of the same lover, without even waiting for his consent.

One personage, a Mr. Porgy, we have not mentioned in his proper place among the *dramatis personae,* because we think he deserves a separate paragraph of animadversion. This man is a most insufferable bore; and had we, by accident, opened the book when about to read it for the first time, at any one of his manifold absurdities, we should most probably have thrown aside **"The Partisan"** in disgust. . . . He is a very silly compound of gluttony, slang, belly, and balderdash philosophy, never opening his mouth for a single minute at a time, without making us feel miserable all over. The rude and unqualified oaths with which he seasons his language deserve to be seriously reprehended. (p. 119)

Mr. Simms' English is bad—shockingly bad. This is no mere assertion on our parts—we proceed to prove it. "Guilt," says our author, ... "must always *despair its charm* in the presence of the true avenger"—what is the meaning of this sentence?—after much reflection we are unable to determine. . . . [At a later point] we are told—"She breathed more freely released from his embrace, and he then gazed upon her with a *painful sort of pleasure,* her look was so clear, so dazzling, so spiritual, so *unnaturally life-like.*" The attempt at paradox has here led Mr. Simms into error. The *painful sort of pleasure* we may suffer to pass; but *life* is the most natural thing in the world, and to call any object unnaturally life-like is as much a bull proper as to style it artificially natural. . . . We are at a loss, too, to understand what is intended . . . by "a look so pure, so bright, so fond, so becoming of heaven, yet so hopeless of earth." Becoming heaven, not *of* heaven, we presume should be the phrase—but even thus the sentence is unintelligible. (pp. 119-20)

One or two other faults we are forced to find. The old affectation of beginning a chapter abruptly has been held worthy of adoption by our novelist. He has even thought himself justifiable in imitating this silly practice in its most reprehensible form—we mean the form habitual with Bulwer and D'Israeli, and which not even their undoubted and indubitable genius could render any thing but despicable—that of commencing with an "*And,*" a "*But,*" or some other conjunction thus rendering the initial sentence of the chapter in question, a continuation of the final sentence of the chapter preceding. . . .

Instances of bad taste—villainously bad taste—occur frequently in the book. Of these the most reprehensible are to be found in a love for that mere *physique* of the horrible. . . . [We] are entertained with the minutest details of a murder committed by a maniac, Frampton, on the person of Sergeant Hastings. The madman suffocates the soldier by thrusting his head in the mud of a morass—and the yells of the murderer, and the kicks of the sufferer, are dwelt upon by Mr. Simms with that species of delight with which we have seen many a ragged urchin spin a cockchafer upon a needle. (p. 120)

In spite, however, of its manifest and manifold blunders and impertinences, **"The Partisan"** is no ordinary work. Its historical details are replete with interest. The concluding scenes are well drawn. Some passages descriptive of swamp scenery are exquisite. Mr. Simms has evidently the eye of a painter. Perhaps, in sober truth, he would succeed better in sketching a landscape than he has done in writing a novel. (p. 121)

> *[Edgar Allan Poe,]* "*'The Partisan',*" in Southern Literary Messenger, *Vol. II, No. 3, January, 1836, pp. 117-22.*

SOUTHERN LITERARY MESSENGER   (essay date 1844)

After two careful perusals, we commend **"Donna Florida"** to our readers, because its perusal will well repay them, because it has beauty and humor; because it is a continuous poem, with variety of incident and delineations of character. (p. 18)

The metre and style of the Poem are borrowed from [Lord Byron's] "Don Juan," which the author thinks unfortunate. All poems are likely, in these respects, to resemble others that have been written; yet the more celebrated and unique the model, the more will the imitation suffer from the contrast. But the author has not borrowed his thoughts, nor his subject from Byron. It is true that the waywardness of his reflections, and the *mélange* of pathos, humor and sober thought are copied after the Noble Bard, and there are many points of resemblance, many concurrent ideas; but the delineations of character are the author's own. Still the poem suffers greatly from the contrast with its original, in every respect, but one. It discards, with one or two slight exceptions, the impurity of its model. (pp. 18-19)

With a few critical remarks, we will dismiss the Poem. The digressions are, to use the author's own words, "too long and too artificial, for the success of a composition, which, forbearing personal sarcasm and domestic satire, makes no appeal to those vulgar tastes, which delight in nothing half so much." The reflections are often just and well-timed; but sometimes the author, we suppose, gives place to humor rather than to his true sentiments. In some passages, the good and bad in human nature are well contrasted, as in the case of woman. Sometimes, too little attention is paid to perfecting the rhyme and metre. (pp. 21-2)

> "*'Donna Florida',*" in Southern Literary Messenger, *Vol. X, No. 1, January, 1844, pp. 18-22.*

THE NORTH AMERICAN REVIEW   (essay date 1846)

[Mr. Simms] means to be understood as setting up for an original, patriotic, native American writer; but we are convinced that every judicious reader will set him down as uncommonly deficient in the first elements of originality. He has put on the cast-off garments of the British novelists, merely endeavouring to give them an American fit. . . . (pp. 357-58)

The style of Mr. Simms . . . is deficient in grace, picturesqueness, and point. It shows a mind seldom able to seize the characteristic features of the object he undertakes to describe, and of course his descriptions generally fail of arresting the reader's attention by any beauty or felicity of touch. His characters are vaguely conceived, and either faintly or coarsely drawn. The dramatic parts are but bungling imitations of nature, with little sprightliness or wit, and laboring under a heavy load of words.

This author, as if to carry out more completely the contradiction between his statements of principle and his practice in the matter of originality, published a poem, . . . [*Donna Florida*], in palpable imitation of [Byron's] *Don Juan,*—a dull travesty of a most reprehensible model. (p. 358)

The Wigwam and the Cabin [however] is a collection of masterly efforts; and judged by themselves, and without the magnifying effect of comparison with the infinitesimal smallness of the works in their neighbourhood, there is a degree of talent shown in these tales and sketches, which entitles them to a place in the not very high department of literature to which they belong. There is much in them that is characteristic, much that fixes attention and remains in the memory; and something that gives us a real insight into the forms of life and the relations of society, which are the central point around which they turn. But for the heavy dissertations which preface some of the stories, as if they were set up at the opening pages for the sake of warning off the trespassing reader, they would be interesting and attractive; and he who has once fairly got over these stumblingblocks at the threshold will go on with pleased attention to the end. (pp. 359-60)

"The Snake of the Cabin" is a tale of vulgar villany, well told, but not superior in material to criminal reports which may be read daily in the newspapers. One of the best pieces in the collection is the story of Oakatibbé, or the Choctaw Samson. Besides its merits as a specimen of narrative fiction, it deserves the attention of the philosopher for the weighty observations it contains on the general subject of civilizing and reclaiming the savage tribes. (pp. 368-69)

The Views and Reviews in American History, Literature, and Fiction are a collection of articles, contributed "to the periodical literature of the country in the last fifteen years.'' . . . These papers contain but little valuable criticism; they unfold no principle of beauty, and illustrate no point in the philosophy of literature and art. They breathe an extravagant nationality, equally at war with good taste and generous progress in liberal culture. That the writer is wrong in all this, we have no doubt; that he fails to see the bearings of the great theme of a national literature is most certain. (p. 376)

"Simms's Stories and Reviews," in The North American Review, *Vol. LXIII, No. CXXXIII, October, 1846, pp. 357-81.*

EDGAR ALLAN POE (essay date 1846)

The "bad taste" of [Mr. Simms's] *Border Beagles* was more particularly apparent in *The Partisan, The Yemassee,* and one or two other of the author's earlier works, and displayed itself most offensively in a certain fondness for the purely disgusting or repulsive, where the intention was or should have been merely the horrible. The writer evinced a strange propensity for minute details of human and brute suffering, and even indulged at times in more unequivocal obscenities. His English, too, was, in his efforts, exceedingly objectionable—verbose, involute, and not unfrequently ungrammatical. He was especially given to pet words, of which we remember at present only "hug," "coil," and the compound "old-time," and introduced them upon all occasions. Neither was he at this period particularly dexterous in the conduct of his stories. His improvement, however, was rapid at all these points, although, on the two first counts of our indictment, there is still abundant room for improvement. But whatever may have been his early defects, or whatever are his present errors, there can be no doubt that from the very beginning he gave evidence of genius, and that of no common order. . . . The "intrinsic value" consisted first of a very vigorous imagination in the conception of the story; secondly, in artistic skill manifested in its conduct; thirdly, in general vigor, life, movement—the whole resulting in deep interest on the part of the reader. These high qualities Mr. Simms has carried with him in his subsequent books; and they are qualities which, above all others, the fresh and vigorous intellect of America should and does esteem. It may be said, upon the whole, that while there are several of our native writers who excel the author of *Martin Faber* at particular *points,* there is, nevertheless, not one who surpasses him in the aggregate of the higher excellences of fiction. (pp. 131-32)

All the tales in [*The Wigwam and the Cabin*] have merit, and the first has merit of a very peculiar kind. *Grayling, or Murder Will Out,* is the title. (p. 132)

It is really an admirable tale, nobly conceived, and skillfully carried into execution—the best ghost story ever written *by an American*—for we presume that this is the ultimate extent of commendation to which we, as an humble American, dare go. (p. 133)

Edgar Allan Poe, "Simms's 'The Wigwam and the Cabin'" (1846), in The Shock of Recognition: The Development of Literature in the United States Recorded by the Men Who Made It, *edited by Edmund Wilson (copyright © 1955 by Edmund Wilson), Farrar, Straus and Cudahy, 1955, pp. 130-33.*

THE LITERARY WORLD (essay date 1851)

[In Mr. Simms' *Norman Maurice*] the characters are immediate and actual—a leading politician, an attorney, a duelist, a widow in Philadelphia, a client, a servant girl, &e. As if to try the experiment at greatest risk, and in its whole force, the author has not employed prose as the language of his *dramatis personae,* but blank verse. In this, we think, he has shown art and judgment. If he had given us nothing but prose, and with that, of course, only such prose as can be heard any day, the whole tone of the piece would have been let down, and the question could have been fairly asked, Why does Mr. Simms occupy our time with transcripts of mere commonplace, when he announces a drama? This damning question he has avoided by elevating the subject, the characters, and the entire atmosphere, with the aid of skilfully delivered verse—a happy medium between slow-footed prose and the remoter elegancies of pure fancy. The omission of characters of a degraded or vulgar cast has saved him from the absurdity of mis-employing the blank measure in mouths unworthy of it: although, as it is, there are some scenes so familiar and matter of course, that it requires some indulgence to pass them by without a smile. (p. 223)

"Mr. Simms's 'Norman Maurice'," in The Literary World, *Vol. IX, No. 242, September 20, 1851, pp. 223-24.*

[PAUL HAMILTON HAYNE] (essay date 1857)

We unhesitatingly say that Mr. Simms' **"Norman Maurice"** is one of the boldest literary ventures on record. (p. 242)

[The play] is pathetic, and true to nature, crowded with genial philosophies, and broad, vigorous characterizations. In a word, it is an impressive tragedy, equally fufilling the conditions of the picturesque and the imaginative, but all through the drama we find ourselves exclaiming—"IF out of *such* material, so crude, harsh, ponderous and rugged, the poet has been able to fashion so striking a creation, what might he not have done with material more plastic?" It is as if one stood before a statue carved with art and labor, out of some rough, uncouth granite, here and there so *intractible in the grain,* as sometimes by its *inherent defects* to mar the fair proportions of the otherwise perfect figure. (p. 253)

[Still, in] the hands of the author, an unpromising subject has been wrought into a work vivid in action, just in sentiment, and compact of imaginative life. The faults are inherent in the theme. We know the personages of the play too well, and are inclined to greet them with undue familiarity. Sometimes we are impelled to smile where properly we should feel bound to weep.

There are so many ideas necessarily low and sordid, connected with the scenes through which Maurice, the lawyer and politician, *must* pass in his way to place and power, that no genius—not the genius of Shakspeare himself—could have *completely* harmonized them with the proprieties of High Art. Therefore, let the dramatist—bent upon writing tragedy—hereafter beware of contemporary *American* topics. That a man of peculiar versatility of powers, and an imagination as bold as original, should have treated one of this class of subjects with a large share of success, proves little beyond the fact, that to the poet roused to all his energies, and really determined to conquer and to create the *Possible* in art, becomes soon converted into the form and substance of actual and vital performance. (p. 254)

[Paul Hamilton Hayne,] "The Dramatic Poems of Wm. Gilmore Simms," in Russell's Magazine, *Vol. II, No. 3, December, 1857, pp. 240-59.*

SOUTHERN LITERARY MESSENGER   (essay date 1859)

It should always be kept in view that dramatic development is one of the main aims of [Mr. Simms]; he expends almost as much attention on his incidents and the plot generally as upon the historical colouring and the delineation of character. In this . . . he differs very greatly from the present school of writers, who, with extremely rare exceptions, concentrate all their faculties upon characterization, or the philosophic monologue of which Mr. Thackeray is so great a master. . . . Having selected for his field of operation, the hurrying and changeful scene of the Revolutionary era, Mr. Simms avails himself of every advantage attaching to the period and its modes of life; he embodies all the passion and humour and excitement of the tragedy or the tragi-comedy; he rides with his troopers on the nocturnal foray; burrows with Marion and his men in the swamps of the Santee, and catches everywhere the rush and roar of the contest, the entire spirit and meaning of the drama. So strong is this characteristic in some of these books that the reader is almost oppressed with the thronging incident, the plot within plot, the never resting advance of the narrative. A very fertile and active imagination seems ever at work, planning, devising, scheming, without cessation or sense of fatigue. The amount of dramatic interest thus communicated to the narrative is extraordinary. . . . Cooper has made the sweeping world of the prairie and the sea his own; Mr. Simms holds in fee simple, as complete, the tangled jungle, the river gliding beneath gigantic cypresses festooned with drooping moss, and stretching out their "knees" like spectres in the moonlight; the lagoon, the hidden camp, the mysterious expanse of verdure, into which no eye can pierce, and which the imagination peoples with strange weird figures, scarcely more weird and uncouth than the real forms, occupying the concealed depths. . . . [In all the scenes of this region,] Mr. Simms displays a fertility of invention and vigour of description which entitle him to the praise of an original writer of the first class.

In more conventional society he is not so vivid or picturesque,—which of course arises in a measure from the nature of "convention"; uniformity, and absence of strong emotion; but also from his evident dislike for the *stereotyped*, and commonplace. What is called "good society," most certainly affords the utmost enjoyment to a cultivated person—but it is a very bad theme for the novelist or rather romancer. . . . The dull uniformity of the drawing-room wearies him; he longs for character, incident, adventure, humour and passion—for scenes and personages less trimmed and pruned to the conventional standard. He seeks these in the field and forest, and likes them best for their nearer approach to nature. Mr. Simms handles his polite ladies and gentlemen very gracefully, however. The pictures of Charleston life and society in *Katharine Walton* are pleasant and well executed, but they lack the fresh odour of the forest, the animation of the open air life which we long to get back to. (pp. 356-58)

We hazard nothing in saying that in delicate delineation of woman, and the passion of "heroic love" . . . Mr. Simms is surpassed by no writer since the days of Walter Scott. . . . There is about the characters and emotions of the young ladies delineated by Mr. Simms a purity, freshness, and artless goodness which is extremely delightful. They are by no means mere pretty pieces of inane perfection such as it is the present fashion among the feebler body of writers, to contrast with their female plotters, and designing *intriguantes:*—whose characters possess no strength, and who are good and weak-minded, because in the estimation of those writers, to be pure is necessarily to be feeble. They are living, breathing women, of strong char-acters, ardent feelings, and determined natures, which prove them to be heroines indeed in time of peril. . . . It is the delicacy and fidelity to nature displayed in these pictures that charm the reader. The old "innocence of love" rests like a rosy atmosphere upon the figures; a sweet and soothing emotion arises in the heart of the reader; he recognizes the purely ideal, and the warmly real, blending as they blend in life, and forming the perfect picture of true, womanly love. Mr. Simms delineates *the lady* with exquisite fidelity and fineness of touch. All the emotions, sympathies, impulses, and modes of thought and action, which characterize the "high-bred" woman are caught and reflected by the artist with unfailing accuracy. Katharine Walton, Flora Middleton, and the heroine in **Mellichampe,** with many others are especial instances of this. (p. 359)

[We] doubt if Mr. Simms in any other character which he has ever drawn, has reached so high a point of originality, and creative excellence [as in Captain Porgy]. . . . [He] is one of the most admirably conceived and clearly defined creations of modern literature. With a rare tact and skill, akin to that which the supreme master of the dramatic art, has exhibited with such affluent power in his wonderful conception of *Falstaff*, the historian of Captain Porgy and his achievments, has made his hero both weak and strong—both unworthy of admiration, and strangely attractive. We cannot respect Captain Porgy, but we are compelled to love him. There is something irresistibly fascinating about the fat soldier—his utterances possess an attraction greater than that of the wittiest and most brilliant of his associates. The strange blending of pathos and humour is in all his discourse; the keen worldly wisdom: the quick eye for "provant" as says Captain Dalgetty; the ease with which he passes from a feast to a foray, and then from the foray where many a brave fellow has bit the dust, back to his feast again— all this goes to make up a picture of strange interest, which enlists all the sympathies of the reader. The worthy Captain, as we have said, is a sort of epic giant. He will not be killed off. *Falstaff* was compelled to die at last, but Porgy flourishes still in imperishable vigor. (p. 364)

"William Gilmore Simms, Esq.," in Southern Literary Messenger, Vol. XXVIII, No. 21, May, 1859, pp. 355-70.

THE NORTH AMERICAN REVIEW   (essay date 1859)

"The Cassique of Kiawah" is the most recent in the series of novels that Mr. Simms has given to the public, and in artistic skill and vivid narrative is hardly inferior to the best of its predecessors. . . .

He has evidently a thorough mastery of the resources of the English language; yet we do not always approve his selection of words; and, while his sentences are usually well constructed, and often with peculiar skill, they sometimes betray extreme carelessness. In higher qualities, also, we find him irregular; yet we recognize in his writings, in a superlative degree, the power of picturesque description, the imaginative conception of character, the nice delineation of its delicate shades, the ability to deal with subtile and violent passions, and the skilful arrangement and development of intricate plots. (p. 559)

[It is obvious that the] contrast in the interests of the brothers [in **"The Cassique of Kiawah"**], and the likeness and unlikeness of their characters which their common blood and different position would generate, must needs furnish a skilful writer with many scenes of the intensest dramatic interest, and that the proper unravelling of such a skein would call for no slight exertion of genius.

We must say, that, in our opinion, Mr. Simms has achieved this difficult task with remarkable success. The proprieties of characters and position are everywhere preserved, and all the violent contrasts that face us at the outset are perfectly harmonized in the consummation. (p. 561)

> *"Critical Notices: Simms's 'Cassique of Kiawah',"* in The North American Review, Vol. LXXXIX, No. CLXXV, October, 1859, pp. 559-61.

DEBOW'S REVIEW   (essay date 1860)

Although Mr. Simms has attained eminent distinction as an historian and poet, yet will his more durable fame rest mainly on his fictitious works. . . .

[His genius] is purely and essentially Southern; it is ever redolent of the perfume of the jessamine, fragrant orange groves, and forests of perpetual verdure; it tells of the genial clime, where flowers ever blossom, and the song-bird ceases not its lay. . . . (p. 707)

[Mr. Simms never descends] from his elevation, to drag the skirts of his high office through the unclean byways of inferior motive and unrefined passion. Never indulging in seductive appeals to vitiated tastes—never stooping to gratify groundless proclivities. . . . His genius is familiar with all the phases and modifications of thought and feeling, perceives with intuitive quickness the motives of action, and by a broad and rapid generalization arrives at a true knowledge of psychical laws, and the invariable principles of human conduct.

With conceptive and creative faculties of the rarest order; with an invention bold, vigorous, fertile, discriminating; with a power of analysis and fervor of passion that resolve and reduce to its constituents the masses and combinations that come under their influence—his endowment realizes a happy combination of philosophic force with poetic grace, speculative refinement with imaginative sensibility. In propriety of sentiment, delicacy of feeling, harmony of design, vigor of execution, correctness of delineation, warmth of coloring, picturesqueness of description, and beauty of narration, the novels of Mr. Simms are beautiful productions of high art. . . . (p. 709)

[The] quality of his poetry partakes somewhat of the characteristics of the Lake school, in its preference for the delineation of ordinary objects, and the narration of commonplace events, finding books in running brooks, sermons in stones, and good in every thing; uniting to the contemplativeness of Wordsworth, and the dreamy reverie of Coleridge, much of the gorgeous power of Southey, and the purely ethereal and intellectual beauty of Shelley, all heightened and adorned by the large benevolence, the trusting faith, the gentle sympathies, the sweet, spiritual graces, and deep, soul-informing sensibilities, that make the divine, poet gift, the sovereignest of the world's throned powers.

Of Simms, the historian, it were supererogation to speak—the high commendation his **"History of South Carolina"** has gained, and the honors it has borne away at the Olympic festivals of his native State. Correct, luminous, picturesque, graphic, and condensed, it tells the story of the ancient common wealth, from lisping infancy to manhood's full meridian. . . . The only regret felt by the Southern reader, in rising from the perusal

of Mr. Simms' **"History,"** is, that it were not more full on the subject of the proprietary era of South Carolina. (p. 711)

Mr. Simms is yet in the meridian of his faculties—time, alone, can complete the fulness of his fame; and as the dawn was bright and full of promise, and the noon illumined by the splendors of performance, the evening will catch the accumulated radiance, and plant among the fixed lights, the constellation that glitters to his genius. (p. 712)

> *"William Gilmore Simms,"* in Debow's Review, n.s. Vol. IV, No. 6, December, 1860, pp. 702-12.

JAMES WOOD DAVIDSON   (essay date 1869)

The tendency of [Mr. Simms's] mind has been from the subjective to the objective; from the inner life to the outer; from motives and their analyses to deeds and events. *Martin Faber* presents to us subtle analyses of inner action, evolved through events; but we see that the author keeps in view his hero's motive nature. Gradually, in subsequent books, Mr. Simms has left out of view more and more the inner man, and has given us the outer with increasing vividness and power. And, further yet, many of his fictions thrust forward events—*events,* rather than *deeds*—to the exclusion of almost everything else. We lose sight of the man—the hero—himself as well as his motives in the dizzying whirl of events. In doing this, Mr. Simms has determined for himself a position not held in the same degree by any other writer of fiction, North, South, or British. In that wielding of events, that sacrificing of characters to situations, he stands unsurpassed—to a great extent unapproached. [In America] the contest for first place in general merit, or in the balance of merits (including quantity), lies between our author and Cooper. In characterization and in polish, Cooper has the advantage; while in the energy of action, variety of situations, and perhaps in literal truthfulness of delineation—I mean the absence of fanciful and impossible personages—Mr. Simms has clearly the advantage.

In general results—take both for all in all, quantity, versatility, and quality—it may be reasonably questioned whether Mr. Simms has an equal in America. I believe he has not. In general value to his sphere of literature he is *facile princeps* both North and South. (p. 515)

As a poet also Mr. Simms has written a great deal—more than any other Southern writer.

It would be pleasant for me to record my conviction that he stands as high in this department of letters as he does in that of prose fiction; but the conviction is wanting, and I cannot make the record. . . .

Atalantis is perhaps the best of [Mr. Simms's] narrative poems. The story is an impossible one of a Nereid, a sea-monster, and a Spanish knight—a fairy fiction of passible merit as a story. It is told mainly in blank verse. The interest of the narrative is meagre, far removed as it is from human sympathies and from the heart-life of mankind in general. Its success when published was moderate, but fully equal to its merits. There are in it some passages of true poetry, and numbers of detached thoughts that are very fine. (p. 518)

If *The Cassique of Accabee* were given in good prose, the effect would be better than as it is; and the story—a love legend of Indian life and Indian passion in the long ago—would stand properly upon its merits; stand, I mean, unencumbered with the detriment of second-rate versification. That it is a romance, and not a poem, is abundantly apparent at every step in the perusal; and, at the conclusion, one naturally wonders why it has been put into verses or stanzas at all. (pp. 518-19)

The City of the Silent is apparently the least ambitious of all these more elaborate poems; certainly the most successful. It is a grave theme, in its nature poetical, handled with earnestness, and full of thought. (p. 519)

The grand difficulty with our author's poems, considered in general, is comprised in a generality; a generality, however, that will impress any one who reads the volumes themselves. That difficulty pertains to both manner and matter. It is that they are *prosaic;* excellent things, mainly of them, in their way, but not poetically excellent. They evince thought, information, reading, and a sense of beauty, and even imagination and fancy; but they are *prosaic* for all that.

The author's mind seems often to be *genial* enough; but when giving utterance for others, he manifests a want of *congeniality,* and that want is painfully manifest at every step. It arises from a too absorbing ego-personal character of mind. The poet can not forget, can not sufficiently ignore, himself.

Besides the prosaic, one finds too much of what may be called the commonplace. This element appears more in the choice of subject—rather in the subjects chosen—than in the style. But it is fatal in both. (p. 521)

As a writer of dramas Mr. Simms has been more successful, I am disposed to say, than in any other branch of the art poetic. His two dramas—*Norman Maurice* and *Michael Bonham*—are vigorous productions. They are, as the design evidently was that they should be, popular. The scenes are striking, and are such as tell upon an auditory; but there is too much speechmaking—too much stumping—especially in *Norman Maurice.* The style in general is too diffuse, too full and hurried, and the language is verbose, turgid, and popular; but in these features, it must be confessed, it is true to nature. *Michael Bonham* is better in most of these respects; but there is a strong family likeness in all respects between these brother tragedies. For representation on the stage—a Western stage—they may pass pretty well, but for the closet they will not do. (p. 525)

> *James Wood Davidson, "William Gilmore Simms, LL.D.," in his* The Living Writers of the South, *Carleton, Publisher, 1869, pp. 508-26.*

RUFUS WILMOT GRISWOLD   (essay date 1870)

Mr. Simms writes at times with great power. His descriptions of persons and places are often graphic. His characters have marked and generally well-sustained individuality, and some of them, particularly of the Indian and negro races, are eminently original. His novels are interesting, but the interest arises more from situation than from character. Our attention is engrossed by actions, but we feel little sympathy with the actors. He gives us too much of ruffianism. The coarseness and villany of many of his characters has no attraction in works of the imagination. If true to nature, which may be doubted, it is not true to nature as we love to contemplate it, and it serves no good purpose in literature. It may be regarded as the chief fault of Mr. Simms, that he does not discriminate between what is irredeemably base and revolting, and what by the hand of art may be made subservient to the exhibition of beauty, which should be the prime aim of the writer of poetical and romantic fiction. . . .

Mr. Simms's paintings of southern border scenery are vivid and natural; but he has little repose. He delights in action, whether of men or of the elements, and is most successful in strife, storm, and tumult. (p. 504)

The shorter stories of Mr. Simms are his best works. They have unity, completeness, and strength, and though not written with elegance, are comparatively free from redundancies and weighty offences against taste. The collection entitled *The Wigwam and the Cabin,* is deeply interesting, and on many accounts must be regarded as a valuable contribution to our literature. Of his reviews I think less favourably, not agreeing with what is peculiar in his principles as a critic; but they are elaborate and have uniformly an air of independence and integrity.

By his skill in analysis, his knowledge of the movements of character and the secret springs of action, his sympathy with what is true and honourable, his acquaintance with history and letters, and his broad field of observation, with a certain philosophical tone of judging of men and measures by other than local and temporary standards, and the unwearied industry by which in various departments he is constantly exhibiting these resources, Mr. Simms is entitled to a large share of public attention. (p. 505)

> *Rufus Wilmot Griswold, "William Gilmore Simms," in his* The Prose Writers of America: With a Survey of the History, Condition, and Prospects of American Literature, *revised edition, Porter & Coates, 1870, pp. 503-17.*

VERNON LOUIS PARRINGTON   (essay date 1927)

In taste and temperament Simms was a pronounced realist, but his career took shape from a generation given to every romantic excess. His genius, in consequence, was always at cross purposes with the popular taste. His realism turned naturally to low-life adventure; his upper-class romance became stilted and posturing, and his love of action degenerated into swashbuckling. (p. 126)

Little as he is known to later readers Simms is by far the most virile and interesting figure of the Old South. . . . He poured out his material copiously, lavishly, with overrunning measure. His stories flow as generously as his Jamaica rum. He is a veritable geyser of invention, an abundant sea of salty speech. He has no sense of restraint; he does not stop to prune the tangle of his imagination; he refuses to strip the plot of extraneous incident to hasten its action. He is as episodic as Dickens at his worst, piling up action and multiplying threads till the story bogs down. The major plot is always struggling from hummock to hummock in the endless swamp where his characters slip in and out, rarely getting to firm ground, yet never quite submerged. Prodigal of adventure and loving action, clumsy as the natural man when confronted with sentiment, he is an American Fielding with a dash of Smollett. He is at ease only out of doors, in the fields and swamps and highways; there his speech becomes racy, and there the rich poetry of his nature, which somehow rarely got into his verse, comes to abundant and spontaneous expression. When he enters the drawing-room his stilted language betrays his lack of ease. . . . But let him come upon a happy-go-lucky blackguard and he loves him as Fielding would have loved him. . . . Like Fielding also is his criterion of morality. A frank and generous nature is his infallible test of worth, and if his patriotism led him to bestow a large share of generosity on the patriots, and a correspondingly meager share on the Loyalists and British, he was but exercising an ancient prerogative of the romancer. (pp. 127-28)

Simms was a loving student of older English literature and drew much of his water from excellent wells. A happy instinct led him back to the robust time of Elizabeth and those masculine playwrights whose ample natures were so like his own. Shakespeare may be reckoned his particular master—especially the prose of Shakespeare with its Cheapside colloquialisms and racy idiomatic rhythms. No better training school could be desired, and his loving apprenticeship to the older vernacular serves to explain the source of Simms's greatest literary virtue. From long familiarity with the Elizabethans he derived his mastery of English idiom that sets him widely apart from most other contemporary Americans. In easy outpouring of picturesque speech, of the lithe and muscular idiom of the old literature, he was without a rival in his generation. . . . Later critics have been singularly obtuse in their failure to do justice to his rich linguistic equipment. Quite too much comment has been devoted to his careless slips in rhetorical construction, and quite too little to his command of masculine English prose. It is absurd to couple him with Cooper in sinning against good writing. They are as unlike as two men could well be. Simms is incomparably the greater master of racy prose, as he is much the richer nature. The only contemporary indeed who approaches him is Melville in *Moby Dick*. He is careless and slovenly enough in all conscience; when he goes on a rampage he mouths his lines like any town crier. But though he keeps a sharp eye on the groundlings, though he is often preposterous, he is rarely wooden, never feeble.

The Elizabethan influence comes out strikingly in the character of Lieutenant Porgy. . . . [He is] the most amusing and substantial comic character in our early fiction. . . . In battle he is an avalanche of patriotic valor, and in his deference to the weak and dependent, in his free-handed generosity that encumbers him with penniless hangers-on, he is model of southern chivalry. But in the far greater matters of the belly, he is strikingly Falstaffian. (pp. 130-31)

The two major themes with which [Simms's] romances deal, as has been often pointed out, are the frontier and the Revolution; but the intimate connection between them has not been so commonly remarked. In much of his better work the two themes blend into one. The conditions of civil war in the South thrust into sharp relief the cultural and psychological frontier that clung to the outskirts of the plantations—the ragged edges of a society that kept the poor whites submerged and bred a numerous progeny of coarse and primitive creatures, little better than social outcasts. . . . With his strong bias towards realism Simms refused to romanticize what was inherently unlovely. . . . The frontier . . . is rarely absent from [Simms's] stories, and it is [his] picaresque interpretation that sets him so sharply off from Cooper. . . . Cooper's frontier existed only in his imagination. When he came face to face with the reality, as in the case of old Aaron Thousandacres and his lawless brood, he hated it too frankly to portray it justly. (pp. 132-33)

The picaresque note is frankly emphasized in Simms's Revolutionary tales. All the swamp-suckers and rapscallions found their heaven-sent opportunity in the disorders of civil war. No realist could write about the Revolution in South Carolina without noting the flocks of buzzards gathering to fall upon the carrion. (p. 133)

[In] dealing with the Indians [Simms] entered a domain preempted by the romantic, and his picaresque realism suffered a disastrous rivalry. . . . *The Yemassee* is heavily marked by the frontier psychology. It was unfortunate, perhaps, that Simms did not follow Cooper's example and plunge into the wilderness, leaving behind him the squatter and settler with their sordid prose. Instead, his Indians are encompassed by a dark background of civilization, and their tragic destiny is poignantly dramatized in the fate of young Occonestoga, besotted with the white man's rum, and doomed to a destruction far less poetic than befalls Uncas fighting his hereditary foes. Nevertheless a wealth of romantic material is crowded into the volume, enough to serve Cooper for half a dozen tales. In simplifying his plots to the uncomplicated problem of flight and pursuit, the latter gains in dramatic swiftness of movement, but he loses in abundance of accompanying action—the sense of cross purposes and many-sided activities, which *The Yemassee* so richly suggests. The latter is an elaborately carved and heavily freighted Spanish bark that is left far astern by the trim Yankee clipper ship; yet its cargo of the gold of the Indies is far richer. (p. 135)

> Vernon Louis Parrington, ''Adventures in 'Belles-Lettres','' *in his* Main Currents in American Thought, an Interpretation of American Literature from the Beginnings to 1920: The Romantic Revolution in America, 1800-1860, Vol. 2 *(copyright 1927 by Harcourt Brace Jovanovich, Inc.; copyright 1955 by Vernon L. Parrington, Jr., Louise P. Tucker, Elizabeth P. Thomas; reprinted by permission of the publisher), Harcourt Brace Jovanovich, 1930 (and reprinted by Harcourt Brace Jovanovich, 1958), pp. 109-36.*

ARTHUR HOBSON QUINN   (essay date 1936)

[*Confession; or, The Blind Heart*] is carried on in one tone—a bit monotonous, but still powerful. One reason it is better than many others of Simms' novels lies in the absence of conversation; the characters of Edward Clifford, his uncle and aunt are quite real. (p. 115)

[The] combination of the supernatural with the story of crime is represented often in Simms' shorter narratives. The earlier ones included in *Carl Werner* . . . , being based largely on ''monkish legends,'' are not as effective as those published . . . in *The Wigwam and the Cabin*. ''Grayling, or Murder Will Out'' is a well constructed supernatural story in which the appearance of a murdered man leads James Grayling, a boy, to the discovery and apprehension of his assassin by the heightening of mental and emotional processes which may account for his supposed vision of his murdered friend, the Major. ''The Giant's Coffin'' contains a strong climax in which an epileptic buries alive a man he hates; in his efforts to escape from his living grave, the victim cuts off his left hand which was caught and crushed in the fall of the rocky lid of the ''coffin,'' only to drown ultimately by the rising of the river. It is a gruesome but powerful scene. (p. 116)

Of Simms' historical novels, the largest group are devoted to the Revolution. . . . [In *The Partisan*], Gates' defeat at Camden is described with the skill Simms usually showed when fighting was to be portrayed, and while there is little fighting under Marion's leadership, the life in his camp in the swamps is vividly drawn. Simms attempts to lighten the story with humor through a character, Lieutenant Porgy, who appears in several of the novels, but humor is not Simms' forte. . . . Much better drawn is the Tory spy, Blonay, the half-breed son of an Indian and a witch, who takes an even greater share of attention in the sequel, *Mellichampe*. . . . The way in which this disfigured being, ignorant and half-savage, tracks Lieutenant Humphries, whose troop had trampled Blonay's mother to death, and the mixture of greed and of a queer sense of gratitude toward Janet Berkeley, the heroine of *Mellichampe,* makes Blonay unforgettable. . . . It was [his] inability, except in a few cases, to carry a character or a motive through to its logical end, which prevented Simms from being a great novelist. This is illustrated in one of the best of the novels of the Revolution, *Katharine Walton*. . . . [The] weakness of *Katharine Walton* does not lie, as is usually stated, in his inability to represent the social life of Charleston after Katharine has been taken there. The interplay of Whig and Tory society is used suitably enough to provide occasions for carrying on the plot, for the conveying of information from Singleton to Kate and to Major Proctor. . . . The scenes in the city are a welcome relief from the rather tiresome descriptions of Porgy and his gastronomic feats. But the change of the chief interest from Singleton to the British officer Proctor midway in the book is unfortunate, first because Singleton is more interesting and second because Proctor's escape and desertion of the British cause after he kills Vaughn do not form a climax by which an American can be thrilled as he is, for example, by the rescue of Walton in *The Partisan*. Walton's execution at the end of *Katharine Walton* is tragic, but the book seems hurried; the last paragraph, in which Simms steps into the novel to defend his historical accuracy, is unforgivable. The central characters are all spirited people, however. . . . (pp. 117-18)

[*Woodcraft*], first published as *The Sword and the Distaff* . . . , pictures the conditions in Charleston and its neighborhood at the close of the Revolution. Mrs. Everleigh . . . is as refreshing in her direct and natural language as Simms' usual heroines are unnatural, probably because she is fighting for her rights. Most interesting is the realistic description of the economic and social results of the Revolution, the thin line that divided plenty from ruin, and the portrayal of a class of citizens like Lieutenant Porgy who returned to a small plantation to find literally nothing on which to live. . . .

[In *The Forayers*] and its sequel *Eutaw* . . . , Simms repeated the formula of his romances of the Revolution, in the strife of Whig and Tory, and again, as was natural, the evil or abnormal characters are best portrayed. The lovers, Sinclair and St. Julien, and the heroines, Carrie Sinclair and Bertha Travis, remain mere names. But the old Tory father, Colonel Sinclair, the double traitor Captain Travis and, best of all, the half-mad girl, Nellie Floyd, who dogs the steps of Inglehardt's Tory band to persuade her brother to leave them, are the actors we remember. The battle of Eutaw is pictured with the skill Simms always showed in the description of conflict. (p. 119)

Simms' excursions into Spanish history, *Pelayo; a Story of the Goth* . . . and its sequel *Count Julian* . . . , are filled with conventional figures of early Spanish history. . . . Simms knew little about Spanish character, early or late, though he read industriously, and *Vasconselos* . . . , which belongs evidently to an earlier period of composition, while based on some research, is far inferior to [Robert Montgomery] Bird's romance of Mexico, so far as understanding of the mingled motives which animated the Spanish conquerors is concerned. De Soto is a caricature and Philip de Vasconselos, the Portuguese hero, is conventional. The relations of Olivia de Alvaro and her uncle are revolting rather than tragic, and the few bright spots are the tourneys and the battles. The Indians do not approach the level of those in *The Yemassee,* and the novel gives an impression of haste and carelessness. (p. 121)

Simms did his poorest work in the "border romances." . . . [The] stories are sheer melodrama, for the characters talk in a language certainly never spoken by human beings. Even more serious is a fault not peculiar to Simms, but rather to romance. He can establish a sense of danger to Hurdis [in *Richard Hurdis*] in a confederacy which spreads all over the South, and which Hurdis is defying apparently to his certain death; yet the confederacy collapses at one cavalry charge. A reader has the sense of irritation that comes in fiction when his apprehension has been awakened unjustifiably. Simms has been criticized unjustly, however, for the way his heroes are convicted, upon the slightest evidence, of murder, for he knew that justice was administered in that way on the frontier. Perhaps, after all, the material was not so good for fiction, for when life is illogical a novelist must treat it as Bret Harte knew how to do, but as Simms did not. He should have found his heroes among the men of the frontier and not built them upon a pattern created by Walter Scott. (pp. 121-22)

> *Arthur Hobson Quinn, "The Development of Idealistic Romance," in his* American Fiction: An Historical and Critical Survey *(© 1936, renewed 1963; adapted by permission of Prentice-Hall, Inc., Englewood Cliffs, N.J.), Appleton-Century-Crofts, 1936, pp. 102-31.**

EDD WINFIELD PARKS (essay date 1936)

Simms as poet was typically Southern. He preferred the occasional subject, preferred to write at white heat while men were stirred mightily by some immediate event.

In that was his fatal flaw, poetically. Brief and subjective lyric poems can be dashed off, in spite of all that critics may say, and some of them are surprisingly good; long poems even of the romantic type require a sustained thought—an effort which the Southerner grounded in the tenets of inspirational romanticism was unwilling to give to fiction or verse, but which he gave unsparingly to political theory. Simms shared this attitude, with the result that his long poems contain vivid and stirring passages, but mainly they contain a facile correctness which rarely attains distinction. Although his poetic masters were Byron and Wordsworth, his mind was more like Dryden's. But he lacked Dryden's severe genius; he could expand an idea much more easily than he could prune back the luxuriant growth of his fancy. (pp. xcii-xciii)

Simms managed to smother some really excellent work under the weight of too much mediocrity. This bulky inequality is enough to explain why casual readers have passed him by, but it does not explain why the anthologists or, even more, his biographer [William P. Trent], have paid so little attention to separating the good from the bad. For Simms could write powerfully, if not perfectly: in the rank undergrowth of words in **"The Edge of the Swamp"** there is caught a miasmic atmosphere redolent with local color; in many short poems the man's mental vitality more than compensates for his lack of artistry. That he lacked utterly the faculty of self-criticism was best revealed when he expanded and sadly vitiated his finest poem, until it lost the grandeur and finality of the first version: **"The Lost Pleiad"** is an orchestrated expression of the transiency of the most stable objects, a poem which cuts through the conventionalities of that over-used subject and gives to it a lasting freshness and significance.

Simms was a man of positive defects and flaws. These are obvious enough, but their obviousness has for too long obscured his equally positive merits and achievements. From his entire poetic work only a small volume of excellent poems could be selected, but that volume would entitle Simms to rank with the better American poets. (p. xciii)

Edd Winfield Parks, "Southern Poets: Introduction," in Southern Poets, *edited by Edd Winfield Parks, (copyright, 1936, by American Book Company; reprinted by permission of D. C. Heath & Company),* American Book, *1936, pp. xvii-cxxx.**

CARL VAN DOREN (essay date 1940)

Cooper's closest rival—in some respects his superior—among the romancers of his school of romance was William Gilmore Simms. . . . (p. 50)

A born story-teller, like Cooper, Simms was as casual as Cooper in regard to structure, but he was too rapid to be dull and he revealed to Americans a new section of their adventurous frontier. (p. 51)

Having succeeded with the matters of the Frontier and the Settlement [in *Guy Rivers* and *The Yemassee*], Simms now turned to the Revolution and wrote *The Partisan* . . . , designed as the first member of a trilogy which should properly celebrate those valorous times. He later wavered in his scheme, and though he finally called *Mellichampe* . . . and *Katherine Walton* . . . the other members of his trilogy, he grouped round them four more novels that have obvious marks of kinship [*The Scout, The Sword and the Distaff,* later known as *Woodcraft, The Forayers,* and *Eutaw*]. . . . Of these *The Scout* is perhaps the poorest, because of the large admixture of Simms's cardinal defect, horrible melodrama; *Woodcraft* is on many grounds the best, by reason of its close-built plot and the high spirits with which it tells of the pranks and courtship, after the war, of Captain Porgy, the most truly comic character ever created by this school of American romance. But neither of these two works is quite representative of the series; neither has quite the dignity which Simms imparted to his work when he was most under the spell of the Carolina tradition. . . . [Unfortunately, Simms] had a tendency to overload his tales with solid blocks of fact derived from his wide researches, forgetting, in his passionate antiquarianism, his own belief that "the chief value of history consists in its proper employment for the purposes of art"; or, rather, he was too much thrilled by bare events to perceive that they needed to be colored into fiction if they were to fit his narratives. Simms never took his art as a mere technical enterprise. He held that "modern romance is the substitute which the people of the present day offer for the ancient epic," and his heart beat to be another Homer. . . . The defect of Simms was that he relied too much upon one plot for each of his tales—a partisan and a loyalist contending for the hand of the same girl—and that he repeated certain stock scenes and personages again and again. His virtue was not only that he handled the actual warfare [in the depiction of the Revolution] with interest and power but that he managed to multiply episodes with huge fecundity. (pp. 52-3)

If Simms is more sanguinary than Cooper, he is quite as sentimental. His women, though Nelly Floyd in *Eutaw* is pathetic and mysterious, and Matiwan in *The Yemassee* is nearly as tragic as formal romance can make her, are almost all fragile and colorless. Even more than Cooper, Simms was tediously old-school toward his women. He was also too often condescending toward his common men. Yet it was chiefly with his

common men, rather than with his wooden gentlemen, that he was most successful. (p. 54)

Simms was at his best in dealing with the matter of the Revolution; he was less happy with the Frontier. Perhaps the earlier frontier had been intrinsically more dignified than the one which Simms had observed along the Mississippi and which had a contemporary comic hero in the very real David Crockett. Certainly Cooper's frontier, lying deeper under the shadow of the past, had been romanticized more than Simms's. Simms grew more melodramatic, rather than more realistic, the further he ventured from the regions of law and order. [*Richard Hurdis, Border Beagles, Beauchampe,* and its sequel *Charlemont*] . . . are amazingly sensational—bloody and tearful and barbarously ornate. Nor was Simms happier when he abandoned native for foreign history, as in [*Pelayo, The Damsel of Darien, Count Julian,* and *Vasconselos*]. . . . He constantly turned aside to put his pen to the service of the distracted times through which he lived. As the agitation which led to civil war grew more heated, he plunged into stormy apologetics for the grounds and virtues of slavery, as passionately conservative as Dr. Johnson or Sir Walter Scott. Just on the eve of the struggle Simms produced a romance of seventeenth-century Carolina, *The Cassique of Kiawah* . . . , a stirring, varied story which, however generally neglected, must be ranked with his best books. . . . By nature a realist, with a flair for picaresque audacity, [Simms] let himself be limited by a romantic tradition which did not seem to him to justify and call for his natural gifts. It was more or less in spite of his conscious aims that he now and then wrote about striking characters and situations through vivid pages in simple, nervous, racy language. (pp. 54-5)

Carl Van Doren, "Romances of Adventure," in his The American Novel: 1789-1939 *(reprinted with permission of Macmillan Publishing Co., Inc.; copyright 1921, 1940 by Macmillan Publishing Co., Inc.; renewed 1949 by Carl Van Doren; renewed © 1968 by Anne Van Doren Ross, Barbara Van Doren Klaw and Margaret Van Doren Bevans), revised edition, Macmillan, 1940, pp. 43-57.**

J. ALLEN MORRIS (essay date 1942)

Many readers are familiar with one or two of Simms's short stories—"**Grayling**," perhaps, or "**Sharp Snaffles**"—and a few readers have read the thirteen stories in *The Wigwam and the Cabin;* but these represent only a small part of the canon of his stories. He wrote at least fifty-nine stories, a considerable number for a pioneer writer working in the period before the American short story achieved a recognized position as a literary form.

Though Simms wrote some very good stories, and though he produced almost as many stories and tales as did his gifted friend and contemporary, Edgar Allan Poe, his unique and significant contribution to American literature has been overlooked because reliable information about his stories is very difficult to obtain. (p. 20)

Simms was the first important American writer to use the Negro as a character in a short story. . . . [Since his Negro characters] are distinctly individualized portraits rather than type characters, they represent a very real contribution to Southern literature. (p. 29)

A study of Simms's use of Negro dialect shows that it is much less faulty than is generally thought. As a matter of fact, it is remarkably—almost scientifically—correct. . . . In thus making use of Negro dialect for the improvement of his characterization, Simms is the forerunner of a long line of Southern writers of stories about Negroes.

Probably his best story of Negro life is **"The Lazy Crow."** In addition to its inherent value as a good story, **"The Lazy Crow"** is important because it shows that Simms recognized the literary value of Negro superstitions that he learned from a first-hand acquaintance with the superstitious Negroes of the antebellum South; and because it shows that he was sufficiently capable as a story writer to be able to use these superstitions as literary materials in building his story. (pp. 29-30)

In his stories of pioneer life Simms draws some excellent pictures of pioneer men, women, and children. These stories are more valuable for their settings and characters than for their plots. In them he presents a colorful collection of individuals; yet, like the pilgrims in Chaucer's *Canterbury Tales,* they represent types while remaining individuals. Though the quality of these stories is very uneven, the stories themselves are not uninteresting. The majority of them can be read today without difficulty and even with pleasure if one likes stories of adventure and red-blooded action. The best stories are those drawn from Simms's own experiences.

The wide variety of characters, individualized but suggesting types, offers a collection of men, women, and children sufficiently well drawn to constitute a literary cross section of life in America before the Civil War. His excellent portraiture of Southern people, especially of "striking and original characters drawn from the humbler walks of life," is one of his chief claims to literary attention and study. (p. 32)

Steeped in the legends and history of the South, observant and inventive, Simms was a writer with a strong, vivid imagination and an immense fertility. (p. 34)

A careful study of the entire body of [his] stories indicates that William Gilmore Simms, as a writer of short stories, should rank high as an early American pioneer story writer. (p. 35)

> *J. Allen Morris, "The Stories of William Gilmore Simms," in* American Literature *(reprinted by permission of the Publisher; copyright © 1942 by Duke University Press, Durham, North Carolina), Vol. XIV, March, 1942, pp. 20-35.*

VAN WYCK BROOKS (essay date 1944)

[Simms was the] greatest by far, save Poe alone, of all the Southern writers. . . . (p. 299)

In his romances Simms excelled in picturing . . . forest scenes where the partisan leader Marion and his fellow-guerrillas had carried on their warfare in the Revolution. For his best tales, the series including *The Partisan, The Forayers, Woodcraft,* portrayed the Revolution in South Carolina. . . . They were authentic historically. Simms took pains with his documentation, and he represented truthfully the courageous young lieutenants who started up with their squads on every side. . . . There were fine scenes too in all these tales of the old colonial plantation-life and the rivalry of the Anglo-Saxon and the Huguenot magnates who largely divided the rule of the region between them, while among a great variety of episodes and characters one figure, Captain Porgy, kept reappearing. . . . A berserker in battle, a wit and buffoon, a *bon vivant* and gourmet, a philosophical humorist and great reader, this living relic as it were of the days of Queen Elizabeth reflected Simms's own full-flowing nature. *Woodcraft,* the finest of these books,

a tale of the days that followed the war, was certainly the best historical novel that was written in the South, or anywhere else, for that matter, at the time, in the country. Here Simms's talent for the picaresque and his feeling for comedy came to the fore in the episodes finally involving Captain Porgy and the blackguards and outlaws who swarmed through the state, brought to the front by the war. These types had a peculiar appeal for Simms's realistic eye, and in fact it was his realism that kept the work of Simms alive when readers lost their taste for other romancers. (pp. 313-14)

> *Van Wyck Brooks, "Charleston and the Southwest: Simms," in his* The World of Washington Irving *(copyright, 1944, by Van Wyck Brooks; copyright renewed © 1972 by Gladys Brooks; reprinted by permission of the publisher, E. P. Dutton, Inc.), Dutton, 1944, pp. 291-314.*

ALEXANDER COWIE (essay date 1948)

As in Cooper, the Indians [in Simms's works] are treated with moderate sympathy bred of the author's conviction that their worst traits have been brought out by association with white people. Yet a writer of romance cannot regard the aborigines mainly as sociological problems; consequently although Simms often evokes admiration for their better qualities, he does not shrink from describing most gruesome results of their cunning and cruelty. Their ultimate defeat he accepts philosophically as dictated by destiny. Simms's portrayal of Indian character is probably closer to reality than Cooper's, for he had better sources of information. He exposes for example the popular fallacy that Indians are uniformly stoical by showing that they frequently shed tears. In general it was his aim to show both their virtues and their defects in due proportion. (pp. 232-33)

Simms handled the Revolutionary romance well, but not supremely well. In expository and background material he frequently overshot the mark of thoroughness, and he trespassed on the reader's patience by introducing quantities of technical military detail relating to military matters. Moreover, seen as a whole, the Revolutionary romances lack a good focus of the reader's hopes and affections. Generals Marion and Greene are admirable men, and there are fictitious juvenile heroes aplenty, as well as a host of splendid minor characters, but there is no single character comparable in power and interest to Natty Bumppo in the Leatherstocking series. Nor could the exciting plots of his stories wholly conceal the slipshod style into which Simms was often betrayed by the speed of his production. Yet most of the Revolutionary tales are avowedly stories "of events, rather than of persons," and regarded as stories of adventure they are still among the most readable in the history of the American novel. (pp. 234-35)

[Simms's] border story, *Beauchampe* . . . , a "tale of passion," is unrelated in its action to the preceding [border romances, *Guy Rivers, Richard Hurdis,* and *Border Beagles*], but although it showed Simms tending toward the psychological novel it is equally sensational. . . . In his narrative Simms is apparently concerned to keep close to the facts in the case, but the result is a story exhibiting the most sustained emotional tension of any that Simms ever wrote. *Beauchampe* (with *Charlemont*) has been disparaged as "salacious" and "barbarously ornate," but although lacking in restraint and crude in artistry, it has a good deal of power, and it is more than mere melodrama (if by melodrama we mean thrills for the sake of thrills), for Simms was sincerely interested in the social problem involved. Less can be said for *Confession; or the Blind Heart* . . . , which is a pretentious and over-written "domestic story" based upon the motif of jealousy. . . . Simms had a good general understanding of human passions, but when, deliberately rejecting incident, he made it his business to "analyze the heart . . . in its obliquities and perversities," he was less successful than in handling the more tangible problems that fill his border and Revolutionary romances. Psychology was not Simms's forte. (pp. 235-36)

Sex may have been tabooed in the fiction of Simms's time, but murder was not, and Simms made the most of it. The theme of crime is prominent in a number of his books. There was nothing he preferred to a good gory crime replete with all its ghastly details. Some of his stories so reeked with blood that even Poe was revolted [see excerpt above]. It is true, however, that Poe's horrors were slightly more refined. Moreover, except in **Martin Faber,** Simms showed much less interest in the *detection* of crime than Poe. In fact in **Beauchampe** he amusingly satirizes the writers who waste time on the "dreary details" connected with the solution of a murder case. On the other hand, Simms, more than Poe, was interested in the social implications of crime. He gave voice to theories of crime which, although they did not wholly excuse the offender, at least showed to what extent social conditions may favor the growth of crime. In **Guy Rivers** he made much of this theme. Rivers is no common illiterate thug but an intelligent robber (once a lawyer) with a turn for philosophy; and he is quite capable of showing that his antisocial acts were in part provoked by society through "favoritism and prejudice." (pp. 240-41)

Deeply as Simms was interested in political and social issues as well as literary theory, he is now remembered chiefly as a story-teller. As such he relied upon a relatively simple equipment, which he handled well. Like Cooper, he painted his characters in primary colors, leaving the subtle shades to the romance-writers of the last decade of the century. He relied on range and variety rather than depth of characterization. . . . The regions described were in their way just as terrifying and sordid as the Georgia, North Carolina, and Mississippi described with latter-day realism by Caldwell, Wolfe, Faulkner, and others. When readers shuddered at the recurrence of brutality and violent death in Simms's novels, especially the border romances, Simms replied by pointing out the factual basis of his stories. Yet the fact remains that his weakness was a love for melodrama. (pp. 244-45)

Probably the reason why Simms encountered the charge of being too "gloomy and savage" is that although he was on the side of right living, he was not rich in the vein of ready moralizing that characterized the domestic novel of his time. Moreover though capable of strong indignation at political chicanery and literary skulduggery, he was not keenly sensitive to those economic problems which have formed the basis of so many modern novels of the South. (p. 245)

Historically Simms is important as complementary to Cooper. Between them they surveyed most of the Atlantic seaboard from Maine to Florida and many points inland. They were both writers of immense vigor and range, with corresponding defects in the treatment of detail. In the historical romance they found a medium which called out their best powers and was kind to their weaknesses. (p. 246)

Alexander Cowie, "Contemporaries and Immediate Followers of Cooper, II," in his The Rise of the American Novel *(copyright 1948, 1951 by American Book Company; reprinted by permission of D. C.*

*Heath & Company), American Book, 1948 (and reprinted by American Book, 1951), pp. 228-75.**

JAY B. HUBBELL   (essay date 1954)

At his best Simms is as good as Cooper, but he sometimes forgets that his readers' primary interest is not in South Carolina history but in men and women undergoing exciting adventures. Unlike Scott and Cooper, he often fails to keep his leading character at the front of the stage. (p. 588)

The pattern of historical romance gave full play to Simms's love of incident and of picturesque border fighters, but it did not permit full play to his bent toward realism, which was strong. . . . For nobility of character Simms had as high regard as any other writer, but he felt it his duty to picture men and women as they are. To those who objected to the oaths which he placed in the mouths of some of his characters he replied that he could not alter for the better the backwoodsman's vocabulary. To those who objected to his realistic treatment of certain characters in the first of the Revolutionary Romances, he replied: "The low characters predominate in the '**Partisan,**' and they predominate in all warfare, and in all times of warfare, foreign and domestic. They predominate in all imbodied armies that the world has ever known." As the Border Romances show, Simms saw as clearly as William Faulkner or Robert Penn Warren the strain of violence in Southern life—in life in all lands, for that matter—the strain of violence and disorder which sentimental readers and writers have always been disposed to ignore. (pp. 589-90)

In addition to his historical romances, Simms wrote several novels and short stories which . . . he characterized as "the moral imaginative." [To this category belong **Martin Faber, Carl Werner, Confession, Castle Dismal** and many of the short stories in **The Wigwam and the Cabin**.]. (p. 591)

[Simms said of these works]: "The attempt is made to analyze the heart in some of its obliquities and perversities; to follow its toils, pursue its phases, and to trace, if possible, the secret of its self-deceptions, its self-baffling inconsistencies, its seemingly wilful warfare with reason and the sober experience." . . . Perhaps the reading public was right in preferring Simms the romancer to Simms the psychological novelist of crime and introspection, but that does not excuse students of the American novel from grossly neglecting his many attempts at psychological fiction. He deserves recognition along with Hawthorne and Poe as a forerunner of Henry James and William Faulkner and Robert Penn Warren. (p. 592)

If Simms lacked genius such as Poe had, he certainly had talent and industry. In his best books one is impressed by his fertility of invention, his power, his variety, and by the sense of reality in them. In their individual scenes his Revolutionary Romances often seem as effective as Cooper's in the Leather-Stocking Tales. He failed, however, to create any one great character comparable to Cooper's best. What was it that Simms lacked? Perhaps it was a keener sense of style and literary form and a passion for perfection such as Poe and Hawthorne had. Simms, like Hawthorne, owed much initially to [Scott's] Waverley romances, but he did not, like the author of *The Scarlet Letter,* work out his own individual pattern of historical romance, one that at once best suited his own gifts and the materials he wished to present. Similarly, when Simms ventured into the domain of [the gothic psychological novel of] William Godwin and Charles Brockden Brown, he did not develop an individual artistic medium which suited his talents, as Poe did. Simms wrote some of the best short stories of his time, but again they suffer from comparison with those of Poe, Hawthorne, and Irving. Simms had something of the power and intensity of Melville, but in him we miss the conjunction of time, writer, and theme which enabled Melville to produce a masterpiece in *Moby-Dick*. (p. 597)

> *Jay B. Hubbell, "William Gilmore Simms," in his* The South in American Literature: 1607-1900 *(reprinted by permission of the Publisher; copyright 1954 by Duke University Press, Durham, North Carolina), Duke University Press, 1954, pp. 572-602.*

C. HUGH HOLMAN   (essay date 1962)

In [*The Yemassee*], despite its tendency to present slavery as an ideal institution, Simms was dealing with an aspect of the Southern experience that was harmonious with the broad pattern of the national experience, with one of the great matters of American tragic romance, the conflict of Indian and white cultures, the pain and injustice with which civilization hacks its path into the American wilderness, the suffering and the tragic grandeur of being one of a fated folk overwhelmed by the onrushing wave of history. It is in this moment of his extinction that the Indian has made his greatest claim upon our literary interests. It is that fated, admirable, almost-Hemingwayesque pitting of honor, courage, and pride upon the conscious, desperate, and last battle which may be said to epitomize a recurring aspect of our national past and our character. With all its flaws of imitation, of carelessness, of haste, of infelicity of style, of strained coincidence and huddled action, *The Yemassee* achieved its author's expressed purpose of creating an American epic and speaking truthfully and powerfully to a resonant chord in the American spirit. But in the 1850s Simms seemed able no longer to speak forcefully to his readers as fellow Americans. (p. 129)

[Intense] defensive anger can and often does vitalize the pages of [Simms's later novels; his] skill with low-life characters finds in their pages a full and rewarding play; his ability to sketch violent action with great excitement and power is often well employed. Yet the ultimate purport and the final impact of these works is obviously and unmistakably local, defensive, and finally trivial. The author of *The Yemassee* was a young man with something compelling to say to his nation, with a vision of the nature of its reduplicating experience to communicate, and with a generous admiration for courage and integrity in friend and foe alike. In that novel he wrote of Carolina history as an American; in the Revolutionary romances of the 1850s he wrote of American history as a Carolinian. (p. 134)

The answer to Simms's failure to grow, to the increasing insularity of his subject matter and the increasing triviality of his purposes in art, to his failure to mature as a serious artist during that period when American art was reaching its first maturity is both simpler and more compelling than most of the critics have thought. . . . A closed mind does not grow, and its product is the self-absorptive triviality into which Simms's talent tended to fall; for he was a victim of the intellectual blockade, the *cordon intellectuale* by which the South guarded its endangered pride. For that blockade shut out from him, by centering his attention on other things, that growth of mind and interest that might have made him properly a part of [the American literary Renaissance]. . . . (pp. 136-37)

> *C. Hugh Holman, "William Gilmore Simms and the 'American Renaissance'," in* The Mississippi Quarterly, *Vol. XV, No. 3, Summer, 1962, pp. 126-37.*

J. V. RIDGELY   (essay date 1962)

To Simms "the South" was infinitely more than a geographical designation for a group of states; the words stood for a nation within a nation—an area with a heroic past, a unique social structure, and a potentiality for an ideal future. These passionately held beliefs permeated all his best work. . . . (p. 19)

Through the dozens of tales which he devoted to . . . [the South] moves a cast which includes nearly every type of person who played any vital role in the South during three centuries—a diverse crowd unmatched in scope in the writings of any other ante-bellum Southern author. Over this welter of historical detail and this packed gallery of characters Simms exercised control through regular attention to a central organizing principle—the South as a unique social structure. (p. 25)

Like other theorists of an ordered society, Simms was most concerned with the leader class. . . . They represented tradition and continuity, and their innate sense of justice and order was to prove invaluable to the culture to which they were now devoting their own futures. Members of this native aristocracy appear regularly in Simms's fiction, and many readers are apt to condemn them as simply the counterparts of the lords and ladies of romantic fiction or to scoff at what they take to be Simms's toadying to the ruling circles of Charleston. But to adopt such an attitude is to miss what Simms actually reveals about his upper-level society. For he is highly critical of failure among its members, and he makes fundamental conflicts within the group a central theme of several of the Revolutionary tales. The right to power can be forfeited, Simms constantly reminds his readers, by a leader's refusal or inability to recognize concomitant responsibility. The world of the colonial and Revolutionary periods was not yet stabilized, and only those who continued to meet the challenge of disorder deserved to retain any hereditary rights. It may be urged that some of the younger nobles and most of the heroines are overly idealized in manners and in personal appearance, but such external portraiture was a romantic convention of fiction from which Simms could not easily free himself. Wooden his leaders often are—but they are not, the close reader will observe, wooden idols.

The second class of society, as Simms reconstructed it fictionally, was naturally the most varied. It was an amorphous group, with each member seeking his own proper place; but it also had responsibilities to the classes above and below it. . . . [Symbolically, the frontiersman, scout, or borderer] stood for the recent native product of the forest, clearing, and swamp—just as the hero was the type formed by the settled and more stable city and plantation culture, with its European heritage. The scout often was, as Simms directly termed him, a "natural noble"; and it was he who, with more education and polishing, would be welcomed by the upper ranks of a future day.

In Simms, the scout and the young noble represent halves of a developing type—the ideal Southern leader; only their close interrelationship could bring each to the full development of his latent capabilities. (pp. 26-7)

Within the lowest class, the unalterable position of the slaves was ordained. . . . They had to continue, throughout foreseeable time, acting as the tillers and harvesters of the soil, as the cooks, the gardeners, and the house and body servants. But in his fiction, in contrast to his polemical journalistic defenses of the South's "peculiar institution," Simms ordinarily made this point obliquely by emphasizing a mutual affection between master and slave and by always asserting what he took to be the resultant benefits of the system to the Negro. As for the other dwellers on this bottom level—outlaws, squatters, Indians, poor-whites—Simms's position was just as adamant. If they could not be improved by training and led to perform socially useful functions, they would be driven out. (pp. 27-8)

It must be noted, finally, that Simms throughout all his fiction portrayed Southern society as in the process of *becoming*. It had been born in colonial days and it grew up in the clashes of the Revolution; but that "heroic" time was not in itself the Golden Age, however applicable its lessons might be for the present. The Golden Age still loomed ahead; unlike some other Southern apologists, Simms did not make the claim—at least in his romances—that total perfection was already a Southern accomplishment. It is true that in the world of practical affairs he became, as war loomed, increasingly shrill and dogmatic; but in the realm of his imagination he took care to portray the disparities, the tensions, and the violence out of which order would one day evolve. It was a strange dream, and it was to prove a tragically delusive one; but whatever power the fiction of Simms still has arises entirely from his commitment to it. (p. 28)

All of the weaknesses of the popular romance as a genre are manifest in Simms's books—but so are its strengths. He was incurably careless in overall structure and in diction, and he worked to irritating excess the nick-of-time appearance of the rescuing agent. But he often managed his suspense with effect that can still be felt; and he did adapt old literary conventions to the special conditions of Southern life. Most importantly, clinging to his concept of the romance as the "modern epic," he did develop a unique controlling theme: the rise of the South through harsh trials to status as a new nation. If, because of his need to win a wide readership, he never entirely freed himself from formulas which had succeeded so many times before, he nonetheless perceived in the romance the possibility of seriously rendering the tensions and aspirations of American life. (pp. 36-7)

Simms's standard was that of decorum; each figure had to be presented according to his or her "quality." The heroine could never be seen in her nightgown or the hero too deep in his cups; the low person, on the other hand, could be surprised in acts that would be shameful in the higher classes. Every member of the cast had necessarily to appear and to act in the way in which society at large generally observed him. (p. 39)

Much has been written about the accuracy of Simms's portrait of the Indian and about his retelling of the Yemassee War [in *The Yemassee*]. But it would be an error to suppose that his main interest was in authenticity, despite his quick summation of the end of the conflict in his final chapter and his flaunting of historical sources in his footnotes. For the book's major theme is what the colonists and the Indians signify in terms of a growing civilization in the South, and he exercises fully the romancer's privilege (which he argues for in his preface) to weave the facts of history into a wholly fictional main plot. (p. 52)

For the stoic courage which Sanutee and Matiwan show, Simms allows human sympathy; but he does not permit us to be carried away into approval of the Indian cause. Though the natives

have had a prior claim to the land, their reign as "the nation" is necessarily finished; unlike the Negroes, they cannot even be absorbed into the white society. (p. 53)

Because the Indian problem is in the process of being resolved in *The Yemassee*, Simms does not here suggest more than a broad outline of the colony's social structure. But there are, nonetheless, representatives of each part of his threefold system: leader, middle class, and lower order. Gentry comes into the book in the person of an actual Englishman of rank, Governor Craven—or Gabriel Harrison. . . . (p. 54)

Simms also gives some attention to another type of potential leader who was to become increasingly prominent in his later fiction—the youth who, though qualified by innate worth and intelligence to assume high rank, needs to be purged of head-strongness through extreme trials. In *The Yemassee* such a man is Hugh Grayson. . . .

This portrait is a foreshadowing of a whole gallery of young Southern heroes yet to come. Their fieriness of character Simms saw as both a virtue and a potential menace, but the trait seemed to him inherent in the Southern nature. (p. 55)

[It is the type of woman represented by the character of Mrs. Granger], Simms urges, that society must have in its middle classes: a woman strong, adaptable, and not too sensitive—one willing to accept responsibility when required . . . but otherwise content to remain in her secondary station. (p. 57)

There remains, in our survey of the social orders represented in *The Yemassee*, the third and lowest class. The renegade or outcast is melodramatically present in the persons of Richard Chorley and his piratical crew. . . .

Simms was sly enough to insert a testimonial to the slave system in Hector, the body servant of Harrison. Hector's functions (aside from muddling the plot) are dual: he provides in speech and action traditional comic relief; and, in a scene in which Harrison attempts to give him his freedom, he allows Simms an opening for the earliest direct defense of slavery in his fiction. (p. 58)

Simms's view of border society as it is expressed in *Richard Hurdis* comes to this: The new lands can have real value only when the borderers are ready to develop them with the future of man in mind. The land must not be wasted or despoiled—or society will die along with it. That is why the scout, who is in harmony with the wild, is a "natural noble" to Simms; that is why the self-seeking outlaw, the wanderer, and the squatter are types who must fall before the carriers of civilization. *Richard Hurdis* has all of Simms's common flaws. But, almost intuitively, he touched upon a theme—the fate of the virgin wilderness—which has remained a powerful one in American writing. And by relating it to his objective of a structured society, he achieved what was, in many ways, the most significantly Southern romance he had yet composed. (p. 79)

[In *Confession; or, The Blind Heart*, Simms ventures into the realm of the] "psychological novel"; and like all of Simms's other struggles to compose in the contemporary, domestic vein, it is the stillborn child of dogged determination alone. (p. 85)

Clifford, as Simms renders him, is not an understandably jealous man but a novelistic contrivance; and, with our realization of this fact, the whole ponderous structure collapses. It is not a tragedy of character, because Clifford has none; the protagonist is an automaton wound up and set to walking a straight course to the brink. It is theatricality without being drama. (p. 86)

The immediate source of *Beauchampe* was a notorious murder case of the 1820's—one that has passed into literature as "the Kentucky tragedy." (p. 87)

The facts behind the real-life case were confused enough, and it matters little whether Simms was striving for accuracy in his own retelling. For his story fails simply as story. The main characters are analyzed incessantly but unconvincingly, and they are too simply conceived to bear the implications of the plot itself. Here was a ready-made instance of savagery suddenly springing out of Southern society, involving overtones of border politics, of chicanery in office, of immorality hiding behind the mask of respectability—and Simms failed to come to grips with these complexities. He was unable to relate these real, bloody events to the kind of civilization he had described in other works; he could not shape the factual materials into anything of his own.

Fundamentally, this is the reason all Simms's psychological novels miscarry and why the Revolutionary romances are more often successful. In his novels he was too close to surface minutiae, too insistent that he had his details correct to be able to see that they lacked the one element that could make them right: imaginative recasting into the artificial world of fiction. In the Revolutionary tales, on the other hand, he had begun with a general theme—the war as a heroic period that had helped to mold the Southern character—and he had unfolded it through representative or symbolic types. (pp. 87-8)

[Simms's] repeated mention of loyalty to one's own soil [in *Katharine Walton*] is a measure of how intensely Simms was coming to identify his Revolutionary patriots with rebellious South Carolinians of the 1850's; once again his state should stand against all tyranny from without. His preface to *Katharine Walton* specifically announces his awareness of the example of the past. With "a natural feeling of pride and satisfaction," he gazed back over what he had already done for Southern fiction. (pp. 95-6)

It was with this renewed sense of his past achievements—of his discovery of a vitally useful "myth of the South"—that Simms undertook the three works which form the most carefully wrought segment of the Revolutionary romances [*Woodcraft, The Forayers,* and *Eutaw*]. (p. 96)

In *Woodcraft* Simms made his reply to [Harriet Beecher Stowe's *Uncle Tom's Cabin*] both explicit and implicit. Most explicit, of course, was the presentation of Porgy as solicitous master. This portrayal was clear-cut, and many Southern readers would have echoed [James Henry] Hammond's judgment that Simms had "admirably defended our 'Institution.'" If this were all that the romance accomplished, it could easily be relegated to a place among the countless tracts of Southern apologists. And yet in this book Simms also managed to present a view of the South as a responsible society, one misunderstood and misrepresented by the North. No mere defensive tract-writer, he endeavored to give a positive dramatic rendering of a region which, he argued, had been the victim of ignorant abolitionists. In carrying out this aim, he produced what is his most coherent and cogent single work of fiction. (p. 104)

[The concept of a natural aristocracy presented in *The Forayers* and *Eutaw*]—of a social framework flexible enough to allow the individual of fundamental worth to rise, no matter what his origins—is not novel in Simms's fiction. . . . What is dis-

tinctive here is that the principle is developed in numerous explicit bits of action; throughout all the gradations of society Simms shows change in operation—the new order in the actual process of becoming. (p. 111)

[The] problem of the person who sets himself outside established law, who accepts no responsibility for his behavior, long obsessed Simms. In story after story he returned to the type and exposed as many of its facets as convention allowed him to. Partly, Simms depicted such dark rogues to gratify the tastes of his readers; but on a more serious thematic level they were intended to symbolize the result of a social order in disruption. They were to be expected in the South Carolina of the Revolutionary period; they were equally to be watched for in the raw Alabama settlements of *Richard Hurdis.* But they could not survive indefinitely; when the community structure became solidified, such terrorists would have to depart.

What would insure the downfall of the marauder, [*The Forayers* and *Eutaw*] suggest, was to be the extension of education in its broadest sense—the inculcation in all ranks of a belief in the necessity for finding one's rightful place. Learning had to be made available to all—not only so that the "natural noble" might rise but also so that those of inferior capabilities might be made conscious of their duties. For too long a time, Simms intimates, education had been the prerogative of the wealthy; in an ideal South every man must at least have the chance to develop his mind as far as possible. (pp. 114-15)

The grand movement from *The Partisan* through *Eutaw* had been from despair to hope, from military defeat to a South triumphant in arms. Simms had portrayed all levels of society and he had interconnected them by one central theme: the responsibility of each to all in the establishment of a lasting system. The "epic" period was over; now it was time for physical rebuilding, for the growth of the nation within a nation. It was time, in other words, for Simms's contemporary South to make its appearance on the stage of world history as a potentially ideal social order. (p. 118)

[Simms's romantic legend about the Old South was] to provide a powerful stimulus to such writers of the South as William Faulkner and Robert Penn Warren. This is not a suggestion that these authors have drawn directly from knowledge of Simms's work. But surely Simms's portraits of the old aristocrat, the common-sensical frontiersman, the young hothead, the self-seeking poor white, helped to fix these archetypal figures in the Southern consciousness. Certainly better than any other creative writer of his era and region he managed to capture the essence of the Old South dream. (p. 130)

J. V. Ridgely, in his William Gilmore Simms *(copyright © 1962 by Twayne Publishers, Inc.; reprinted with the permission of Twayne Publishers, a Division of G. K. Hall & Co., Boston), Twayne, 1962, 144 p.*

THOMAS L. McHANEY (essay date 1973)

Simms wrote too hastily, as he himself repeatedly recognized. The literary fashions of the day were against his natural bent. He rarely transcended the conventions of form and style which he had inherited from Cooper, Scott, and others. Invariably, he hobbled his romances with the obligatory love interest, stilted dialogue and all. But he wrote with intense and determined honesty within the boundaries he accepted and he found ways to include into his romantic novels good solid chunks of the raw humor, the violence, and the realism of the frontier. (p. 180)

Simms parallels and improves upon Cooper in *The Yemassee,* perhaps one reason the novel has received so much attention. His Indians are well-imagined . . . , though a little precipitous, and the portraits of Sanutee and Matiwan are justly admired. Also worthy of admiration, however, are fine examples of a kind of unflinching realism that doesn't appear in American writing until much, much later. (p. 183)

[*The Cassique of Kiawah*] has been neglected at the expense of *The Yemassee.* Yet it is a far more even book and the story more compellingly told. In it, Simms works the backwoods and the frontier vernacular at great length. He displays a rich imagination in the creation of character and event; he skillfully works abrupt shifts in time and scene; and he resists the convention—which Hawthorne could not escape—of making the dark, romantic heroine lose her love and life in a conflict with the saintly blonde, no small triumph in American fiction of the period. (p. 184)

It is true that *Cassique,* like Simms's tales of South Carolina in the Revolution, superficially seemed to merit the charge of too narrow a provincialism in its own day, but the detail which possibly put off readers in the nineteenth century should not matter now any more than it does in *Moby-Dick.* (p. 185)

Richard Hurdis represents another experiment by Simms. Like *Martin Faber,* it is a first-person narrative, but in a different form and tone from the confessional tale. The device, in this case, does not always work, especially whenever Richard must reveal events . . . beyond his experience, but Simms deserves credit for the attempt; Melville and Hawthorne, in *Moby-Dick* and *Blithedale Romance,* were not able to solve the problem any better technically, though their failures were not quite so obvious as Simms's. (p. 186)

Simms was exploring new ground [with these novels], and however badly he was often doing it, he still opened up material and methods for writers to come and helped to prepare an audience for them, if only by confronting his readers with [gruesome, though realistic scenes] in what they supposed were romantic novels in the old style. (p. 187)

Most of the handy phrases by which Simms has been described are obviously incomplete. He was a bigger and tougher writer than he has been given credit for being. . . . Simms had more experience of the rawness, unpredictability, violence, and varied tragedy of human existence than any major American writer until we get to Twain and Crane. He lost parents, wives, children, home, library, estate, "country," fortune and fame, but something in him never gave in to these circumstances, and perhaps what would not give in to them, would not . . . or could not use them fully for artistic purposes either. He seems, artistically, never to have driven life into a corner. He never fully expressed its tragedies or its joys or created a character with the fullness of strength and spirit which he himself must have understood and possessed. (pp. 189-90)

Thomas L. McHaney, "William Gilmore Simms," in The Chief Glory of Every People: Essays on Classic American Writers, *edited by Matthew J. Bruccoli (copyright © 1973 by Southern Illinois University Press; reprinted by permission of Southern Illinois University Press), Southern Illinois University Press, 1973, pp. 173-90.*

CHARLES S. WATSON (essay date 1976)

The influence of drama on Simms's fictional technique appears particularly in his characterization. The psychology found in Elizabethan and Restoration plays influenced Simms's presentation of the humors and passions. (p. 112)

Parallels between Shakespearean scenes and characters and Simms's are numerous and demonstrate the influence. Porgy is likened to Falstaff in the Revolutionary novels. He has a big belly and in *Katharine Walton* calls for a drink from Lance Frampton much as Falstaff does from Prince Hal in *Henry IV, Part 1.* The wild, Macbeth-like imagination is seen in *Richard Hurdis* in the visions of Pickett. In *Border Beagles,* Horsey the Shakespearean actor, is full of dramatic poesy, like Pistol. A favorite quote from Shakespeare was "Othello's occupation's gone," which Simms used in *Woodcraft.* Othello is a source for the jealous husband in *Confession.*

Simms's knowledge of drama influenced his fundamental fictional theory as seen in his comparison of the drama to the romance in the preface to *The Yemassee.* Simms wrote that the standards are much the same for the drama and the romance. The action of both occurs in "a narrow space of time"; both require the "same unities of plan, of purpose and harmony of parts." Simms's writing and attending plays also must have contributed to his handling of exciting theatrical climax, evident in the siege of the Block House in *The Yemassee.* (pp. 112-13)

Simms composed plays from a very early age to almost the end of his life. Although he succeeded much better in fiction, he showed progress in dramaturgy. (p. 115)

Michael Bonham [Simms's only performed play] is most significant for its political purpose, which demonstrates the Southern response on the stage to the anti-slavery movement. It is inaccurate to think that the Southern stage responded to the anti-slavery movement only through burlesques of such abolition plays as *Uncle Tom's Cabin.* In this play by Simms, the dramatist took the offensive by advocating the balancing of sectional power by the annexation of Texas. (pp. 125-26)

Simms wrote his best play, *Norman Maurice; or, The Man of the People,* in 1847. Its political purpose is to advocate admission of slave states from the West. It has another aim also. In *Norman Maurice,* Simms presents his concept of the good political leader. He portrays his qualities of courage against tyranny and his ability to follow his own counsel. The work is also interesting for the colloquial dialogue of its contemporary characters in blank verse. Simms thus tries to do what Maxwell Anderson attempted later in such a play as *Winterset* when he attempted to combine natural speech and poetry. (p. 129)

What makes [*Norman Maurice*] exceptional is that it goes beyond a mere political purpose to deal with a provocative subject, the nature of the good political leader, one that has concerned thinkers from Plato to Machiavelli, from Shakespeare to Shaw. (p. 137)

[*Norman Maurice*] is the best play of the most skilled and important writer to compose for the Charleston stage, William Gilmore Simms. (p. 142)

Charles S. Watson, "William Gilmore Simms," in his Antebellum Charleston Dramatists *(copyright © 1976 by The University of Alabama Press), University of Alabama Press, 1976, pp. 110-42.*

ADDITIONAL BIBLIOGRAPHY

Eaton, Clement. "The Romantic Mind: William Gilmore Simms." In his *The Mind of the Old South*, pp. 181-201. Baton Rouge: Louisiana State University Press, 1964.
> A consideration of Simms's literature, as well as his politics, as representative of the spirit of the Old South.

Erskine, John. "William Gilmore Simms." In his *Leading American Novelists*, pp. 131-77. New York: Henry Holt, 1910.*
> A comparison of James Fenimore Cooper and Simms. Erskine finds Cooper's work to be superior to Simms's in both imagination and form.

Guilds, John C. "The Literary Criticism of William Gilmore Simms." *The South Carolina Review* 2, No. 1 (November 1969): 49-56.
> An overview of Simms as a critic.

Hetherington, Hugh W. *Cavalier of Old South Carolina: William Gilmore Simms's Captain Porgy*. Chapel Hill: The University of North Carolina Press, 1966, 373 p.
> A detailed study of the relationship between Porgy and Falstaff. This book also includes large excerpts from Simms's seven Revolutionary romances.

Keiser, Albert. "Simms' Romantic Naturalism." In his *The Indian in American Literature*. New York: Oxford University Press, 1933, pp. 154-74.
> A discussion of Simms's portrayal of the American Indian.

Parks, Edd Winfield. *William Gilmore Simms as Literary Critic*. Athens: University of Georgia Press, 1961, 152 p.
> Discusses the importance of Simms's work as a literary critic.

Shillingsburg, Miriam J. "Politics and Art: Towards Seeing Simms as a Whole." *Southern Literary Journal* VII, No. 2 (Spring 1975): 133-48.
> Assesses the various interpretations by recent critics of Simms's writing, politics, and personal life.

Trent, William P. *William Gilmore Simms*. New York: Houghton, Mifflin and Co., 1892, 351 p.
> The authoritative biography of Simms.

Anne Louise Germaine Necker, Baronne de Staël-Holstein
1766-1817

French critic, novelist, historian, and playwright.

Madame de Staël is credited with inculcating the theories of Romanticism into French literary and political thought. Her belief that critical judgment is relative and based on a sense of history sharply altered the French literary attitudes of her time. In her *De la littérature considérée dans ses rapports avec les institutions sociales (The Influence of Literature upon Society)*, Mme. de Staël delineated the distinction between the classical literature of southern Europe, and northern Europe's Romantic literature. Though her fiction is considered mediocre, her historical and critical works influenced a generation of writers.

The daughter of Louis XVI's minister of finance, Mme. de Staël was raised in Paris. Her intellectual and literary interests were encouraged by her parents, whose literary salon included such notables as Edward Gibbon, Denis Diderot, and Friedrich Grimm. She was married in 1786 to the Swedish ambassador in Paris, Eric de Staël-Holstein. Though Mme. de Staël had begun to write at fifteen, it was not until she published *Lettres sur les ouvrages et le caractère de J. J. Rousseau (Letters on the Works and Character of J. J. Rousseau)* that she became known as a theorist. Published just before the outbreak of the French Revolution, the book advocated liberal thinking and the ideas of the Enlightenment as antidotes to the then current political crisis. During the Revolution, her husband's political immunity enabled Mme. de Staël to remain in France and arrange the escape of numerous refugees. Ultimately, however, she was forced to flee to Switzerland.

Upon her return to Paris in 1797, Mme. de Staël began what many critics consider to be the most brilliant segment of her career. She published several important political and literary essays, notably *De l'influence des passions (A Treatise on the Influence of the Passions upon the Happiness of Individuals and Nations)*, a document of European Romanticism. The French painter and author Benjamin Constant, who was one of her lovers, first exposed Mme. de Staël to the German philosophy that influenced this work.

By 1800, her political and literary concepts had become more defined, as evidenced in *The Influence of Literature upon Society*. The book's thesis states that a literary work must reflect the moral and historical reality, or *Zeitgeist*, of the country in which it is created. Her novels of this period, *Delphine* and *Corinne; ou, L'Italie (Corinne; or, Italy)*, are limited illustrations of Mme. de Staël's literary concepts. Critics view the misunderstood heroines of these books as fictional self-portraits which reflect Mme. de Staël's desire for a loving and secure personal life.

Mme. de Staël was considered as powerful in the political realm as she was in the literary world. Napoleon viewed her as a personal enemy; when she formed a liberal opposition to his political aims, he banished her to Switzerland. During her ten-year exile, she visited Germany and was inspired to write *De l'Allemagne (Germany)*, a serious study of the *Sturm und Drang* (Storm and Stress) movement. The work introduced German Romanticism in France, and inspired new modes of

Courtesy of Prints and Photographs Division: Library of Congress

thought and expression. Mme. de Staël idealized Germany and saw its culture as a model for French intellectual development. Napoleon, however, found *Germany* subversive, and he ordered its proof sheets to be destroyed. Mme. de Staël again left France, and traveled to England. After the publication of *Germany* in England in 1813, she returned to Paris and attempted to establish a literary salon, but she died within a few years.

The clarity and objectivity of Mme. de Staël's literary theories proved a strong influence on writers to follow, notably Charles Augustin Sainte-Beuve and Victor Hugo. She awakened an interest in foreign literature and sought to transform the aging spirit of classicism into the new currents of Romanticism. Contemporary critics consider her responsible for the Europeanization of modern thought.

PRINCIPAL WORKS

Lettres sur les ouvrages et le caractère de J. J. Rousseau (essays) 1788
   [*Letters on the Works and Character of J. J. Rousseau*, 1789]
De l'influence des passions (essays) 1796
   [*A Treatise on the Influence of the Passions upon the Happiness of Individuals and Nations*, 1798]

[SYDNEY SMITH] (essay date 1803)

This dismal trash [*Delphine*], which has nearly dislocated the jaws of every critic among us with gaping, has so alarmed Bonaparte, that he has seized the whole impression, sent Madame de Staël out of Paris, and, for aught we know, sleeps in a nightcap of steel, and dagger proof blankets. To us it appears rather an attack against the Ten Commandments, than the government of Bonaparte, and calculated not so much to enforce the rights of the Bourbons, as the benefits of adultery, murder, and a great number of other vices, which have been somehow or other strangely neglected in this country, and too much so (according to the apparent opinion of Madame de Staël) even in France.

It happens, however, fortunately enough, that her book is as dull as it could have been if her intentions had been good; for wit, dexterity, and the pleasant energies of the mind, seldom rank themselves on the side of virtue and social order; while vice is spiritual, eloquent and alert, ever choice in expression, happy in allusion, and judicious in arrangement. (p. 172)

Making every allowance for reading this book in a translation, and in a very bad translation, we cannot but deem it a heavy performance. The incidents are vulgar; the characters vulgar too, except those of Delphine and Madame de Vernon. Madame de Staël has not the artifice to hide what is coming. In travelling through a flat country, or a flat book, we see our road before us for half the distance we are going. There are no agreeable sinuosities, and no speculation whether we are to ascend next, or descend; what new sight we are to enjoy, or to which side we are to bend. Leonce is robbed and half murdered; the apothecary of the place is certain he will not live: we were absolutely certain that he would live, and could predict to an hour the time of his recovery. In the same manner, we could have prophesied every event of the book a whole volume before its occurrence.

This novel is a perfect *Alexandrian*. The two last volumes are redundant, and drag their wounded length: It should certainly have terminated where the interest ceases, at the death of Madame de Vernon; but, instead of this, the scene-shifters come and pick up the dead bodies, wash the stage, sweep it, and do every thing which the timely fall of the curtain should have

excluded from the sight, and left to the imagination of the audience. (p. 173)

[Sydney Smith,] *"Madame de Staël's 'Delphine',"*
in The Edinburgh Review, *Vol. II, No. III, April,
1803, pp. 172-77.*

THE EDINBURGH REVIEW (essay date 1807)

The plan of [*Corinne; ou, L'Italie*], if not altogether new, is at least very different from that of an ordinary novel. The object of Madame de Staël has been, to intermix, with the incidents of a fictitious narrative, the description of whatever was to be found in Italy most worthy of attention, while that country remained in full enjoyment of the noble patrimony which it inherited from past ages. This attempt, therefore, is in some respects the same with that of Barthelemi, in the Travels of the Younger Anacharsis. It must, however, be admitted, that the union of the true with the imaginary is much more skillfully effected in the work before us than in that of the French academician. . . . The narrative of Madame de Staël is as lively and affecting as her descriptions are picturesque and beautiful; so that each of them, by itself, could maintain a high place in the species of composition to which it belongs. The conception of the story is also in a high degree original; the difference of national character is the force that sets all in motion; and it is Great Britain and Italy, the extremes of civilized Europe, that are personified and contrasted in the hero and heroine of this romantic tale. (p. 183)

Much is said through the whole book, of the effect of climate; and the sun of Italy is never mentioned but with an enthusiasm, that we believe arises from the author having really felt all that she describes. We are persuaded, however, that she has ascribed too much to physical causes, and that she does not sufficiently allow for the circumstances, moral and political, by which they are often overruled. The climate of Italy is not probably very different now from what it was in ancient times; and yet, what a difference between the ancient Romans and the modern Italians? We are persuaded we shall not, even by Mad. de Staël, be accused of any immoderate partiality in favour of our countrymen, when we say that an Englishman bears a much greater resemblance to a Roman, than an Italian of the present day. Here, therefore, the possession of liberty and laws, and, above all, the superiority which a man derives from having a share in the government of his country, has, in opposition to climate and situation, produced a greater resemblance of character, than the latter was able to do, when counteracted by the former.

On the whole, notwithstanding some such imperfections as we have now pointed out; notwithstanding also, that in the analysis of feeling, which is usually managed with great skill, some fanciful reflections now and then occur,—some false refinements, and some sentiments brought from too great a distance, we can have no hesitation to say, that those blemishes are very inconsiderable, compared with the general execution of the work—with the imagination, the feeling, and the eloquence displayed in it. (pp. 193-94)

From the history and fate of the amiable and accomplished Corinna, the reader may learn to watch over a passion which, if left to itself, may become one of the worst distempers of the mind, blasting and consuming even the noblest faculties. One may learn, too, the necessity of conforming to those rules that restrain the intercourse of the sexes, and that are not to be rashly dispensed with, even where no immediate danger is apprehended.

The example of Lord Nelvil is calculated to show the danger of irresolution, especially when the interest of another is concerned; and to remind us, that a man, by the fear of doing what is not perfectly correct, may be led, if he is not on his guard, to the commission of what is highly criminal. The fear of impropriety might have been consulted, when the mutual attachment of Corinna and himself was in its commencement; but it was mere selfishness and want of feeling to be afterwards guided by such a fear, in opposition to the best sentiments of the heart, and one of the greatest and most imperious of all moral obligations. (pp. 194-95)

> *"Madame de Staël—'Corinne',"* in The Edinburgh Review, *Vol. II, No. XXI, October, 1807, pp. 183-95.*

JAMES MACKINTOSH   (essay date 1808)

—'Corinne,' first volume.—I have not yet received the original; and I can no longer refrain even from a translation.

"It is, as has been said, a tour in Italy, mixed with a novel. The tour is full of picture and feeling, and of observations on national character, so refined, that scarcely any one else could have made them, and not very many will comprehend or feel them. What an admirable French character is D'Erfeuil! so free from exaggeration, that the French critics say the author, notwithstanding her prejudices, has made him better than her favourite Oswald. Nothing could more strongly prove the fidelity of her picture, and the lowness of their moral standard. She paints Ancona, and, above all, Rome, in the liveliest colours. She alone seems to feel that she *inhabited* the eternal city. It must be owned that there is some repetition, or at least monotony, in her reflections on the monuments of antiquity. The sentiment inspired by one is so like that produced by another, that she ought to have contented herself with fewer strokes, and to have given specimens rather than an enumeration. The attempt to vary them must display more ingenuity than genius. It leads to a littleness of manner, destructive of gravity and tenderness.

In the character of Corinne, Madame de Staël draws an imaginary self—what she is, what she had the power of being, and what she can easily imagine that she might have become. Purity, which her sentiments and principles teach her to love; talents and accomplishments, which her energetic genius might easily have acquired; uncommon scenes and incidents fitted for her extraordinary mind; and even beauty, which her fancy contemplates so constantly, that she can scarcely suppose it to be foreign to herself, and which, in the enthusiasm of invention, she bestows on this adorned as well as improved self,—these seem to be the materials out of which she has formed Corinne, and the mode in which she has reconciled it to her knowledge of her own character.

13th.—Second and third volumes of 'Corinne.' I swallow Corinne slowly, that I may taste every drop. I prolong my enjoyment, and really dread the termination. Other travellers had told us of the absence of public amusements at Rome, and of the want of conversation among an indolent nobility; but, before Madame de Staël, no one has considered this as the profound tranquillity and death-like silence, which the feelings require in a place, where we go to meditate on the great events of which it was once the scene, in a magnificent museum of the monuments of ancient times. (pp. 405-06)

15th.—Fourth and fifth volumes of 'Corinne.' Farewell Corinne! powerful and extraordinary book; full of faults so obvious, as not to be worth enumerating; but of which a single sentence has excited more feeling, and exercised more reason, than the faultless models of elegance.

To animadvert on the defects of the story is lost labour. It is a slight vehicle of idea and sentiment. The whole object of an incident is obtained, when it serves as a pretext for a reflection or an impassioned word. Yet even here there are scenes which show what she could have done, if she had been at leisure from thought. The prayer of the two sisters at their father's tomb, the opposition of their characters, is capable of great interest, if it had been well laboured. The grand defect is the want of repose—too much and too ingenious reflection—too uniform an ardour of feeling. The understanding is fatigued; the heart ceases to feel.

The minute philosophy of passion and character has so much been the object of my pursuit, that I love it even in excess. But I must own that it has one material inconvenience. The observations founded upon it may be true in some instances, without being generally so. Of the small and numerous springs which are the subject of observation, some may be most powerful at one time, others at another. There is constantly a disposition to generalise, which is always in danger of being wrong. It may be safe to assert, that a subtle ramification of feeling is natural; but it is always unsafe to deny that an equally subtle ramification of the same feeling, in an opposite direction, may not be equally natural.

There are, sometimes, as much truth and exactness in Madame de Staël's descriptions, as in those of most cold observers. Her picture of stagnation, mediocrity and dulness; of torpor, animated only by envy; of mental superiority, dreaded and hated without even being comprehended; and of intellect, gradually extinguished by the azotic atmosphere of stupidity is *so* true! The unjust estimate of England, which this Northumbrian picture might have occasioned, how admirably is it corrected by the observation of Oswald, and even of poor Corinne, on their second journeys! and how, by a few reflections in the last journey to Italy, does this singular woman reduce to the level of truth the exaggerated praise bestowed by her first enthusiasm on the Italians!

How general is the tendency of these times towards religious sentiment! Madame de Staël may not, perhaps, ever be able calmly to believe the dogmas of any sect. She seems prepared, by turns, to adopt the feelings of all sects. Twenty years ago the state of opinion seemed to indicate an almost total destruction of religion in Europe. Ten years ago the state of political events appeared to show a more advanced stage in the progress towards such a destruction. The reaction has begun everywhere. A mystical philosophy prevails in Germany; a poetical religion is patronised by men of genius in France. It is adopted in some measure by Madame de Staël, who finds it even by the help of her reason in the nature of man, if she cannot so deeply perceive it in the nature of things. (pp. 406-08)

> *James Mackintosh, in his journal entry on June 11, 1808, in his* Memoirs of the Life of the Right Honourable Sir James Mackintosh, *Vol. I, edited by Robert James Mackintosh, Edward Moxon, 1835, pp. 405-09.*

THE MONTHLY ANTHOLOGY   (essay date 1808)

Corinna is a novel engrafted on a journey and description of Italy, and the licentious fashion of blending fancy and reality is more innocent and justifiable in this kind of work than in any other. Of the advantages, which it possesses, Madame de Stael has availed herself in the ablest manner. The description of the interesting and magnificent objects of Rome, the disquisitions on Italian society, and the progress of the novel, are most ingeniously mingled, and by being alternately brought forward, prevent the most fastidious reader from tiring. (p. 466)

The persons of the novel are few in number, but these few are sketched with that delicate and minute observation of character, which belongs to her sex; while the contrasts arising from different tempers and education, and the effects of the passions, are developed with all the force and skill produced by a profound knowledge of the human heart. . . . Corinna is the fair monster of the work: she is a character out of nature; so at least she will be generally, and so she had better be considered: yet she has enough of humanity in her composition, a sufficient portion of the faculty of inspiring and suffering emotion, to excite, even in the generality of readers, an interest beyond that of a mere heroine of romance.

The incidents are many of them striking and novel; and in the present state of literature, this is one of the rarest kinds of merit. . . . The style is eloquent; and the thoughts are many of them singularly just, beautiful and original.

The intimate knowledge, which is discovered of the character of different nations, is a remarkable feature of this work; and it is hard to say which is delineated most accurately, the French, the Italian or the English. (p. 467)

The work is not without its faults; and those, who are fonder of the chaff than the grain, may select them. But there is one obliquity of sentiment, which becomes the more remarkable, as it exercises a fatal influence over the conduct of her hero. Madame de Stael was extremely fond of her father, and has attempted in a book, she published, containing his posthumous works, to sublimate this affection, into a mysterious, metaphysical passion, which exposed her to severe reprehension from the French criticks. If she had persuaded the world in this respect, she could only acquire credence for singularity; yet, by a kind of perversity, she has made this indefensible principle a governing motive in her new work. Peculiar circumstances may modify the affections unnaturally in a few individuals: will Madame de Stael make an unfortunate exception a general rule? . . .

The *improvisations* of *Corinna* will be less admired than any other part of the work. That, which she makes at the capital, is eloquent, and would be beautiful in Italian verse, but is too florid for prose. The last, which is recited at Florence, must be excepted; it is affecting and sublime. He, who can read it without emotion, would do well never to leave the bounds of demonstration to wander among the fields of literature. (p. 468)

> *"Observations on Madame de Staël's 'Corinna',"* in The Monthly Anthology, *September, 1808, pp. 465-70.*

THE EDINBURGH REVIEW   (essay date 1813)

[Madame de Staël's] novels bear testimony to the extraordinary accuracy and minuteness of her observation of human character, and to her thorough knowledge of those dark and secret workings of the heart, by which misery is so often elaborated from the pure elements of the affections. Her knowledge, however, we must say, seems to be more of evil than of good. The predominating sentiment in her fictions is, Despair of human happiness and human virtue; and their interest is founded almost entirely on the inherent and almost inevitable heartlessness of polished man. The impression which they leave upon the mind, therefore, though powerfully pathetic, is both painful and humiliating; at the same time that it proceeds, we are inclined to believe, upon the double error of supposing that the bulk of intelligent people are as selfish as those victims of fashion and philosophy from whom her characters are selected; and that a sensibility to unkindness can survive the extinction of all kindly emotions. [*De la littérature considérée dans ses rapports avec les institutions sociales*], however, exhibits the fairest specimen which we have yet seen of the systematizing spirit of the author, as well as of the moral enthusiasm by which she seems to be possessed.

The professed object of this work is show that all the peculiarities in the literature of different ages and countries, may be explained by a reference to the condition of society, and the political and religious institutions of each;—and at the same time, to point out in what way the progress of letters has in its turn modified and affected the government and religion of those nations among whom they have flourished. All this, however, is bottomed upon the more fundamental and favourite proposition, that *there is a progress,* to produce these effects— that letters and intelligence are in a state of constant, universal, and irresistible advancement—in other words, that human nature is tending, by a slow and interminable progression, to a state of perfection. This fascinating idea seems to have been kept constantly in view by Mad. de Staël, from the beginning to the end of the work before us;—and though we conceive it to have been pursued with far too sanguine and assured a spirit, and to have led in this way to most of what is rash and questionable in her conclusions, it is impossible to doubt that it has also helped her to many explanations that are equally solid and ingenious, and thrown a light upon many phenomena that would otherwise have appeared very dark and unaccountable.

In the range which she here takes, indeed, she has need of all the lights and all the aids that can present themselves;—for her work contains a critique and a theory of all the literature and philosophy in the world, from the days of Homer to the tenth year of the French Revolution. . . . To go through all this with any tolerable success, and without committing any very gross and ridiculous blunders, evidently required, in the first place, a greater allowance of learning than has often fallen to the lot of persons of the learned gender, who lay a pretty bold claim to distinction, upon the ground of their learning alone; and, in the next place, an extent of general knowledge, and a power and comprehensiveness of thinking, that has still more rarely been the ornament of great scholars. Mad. de Staël may be surpassed, perhaps, in scholarship, (so far as relates to accuracy at least, if not extent), by some—and in sound philosophy by others. But there are few indeed who can boast of having so much of both; and no one, so far as we know, who has applied the one to the elucidation of the other with so much judgment, boldness, and success. (pp. 3-5)

She observes, with great truth, that much of the guilt and the misery which are vulgarly imputed to great talents, really arise from not having talent enough,—and that the only certain cure for the errors which are produced by superficial thinking, is to be found in thinking more deeply:—At the same time it ought not to be forgotten, that all men have not the capacity of thinking deeply—and that the most general cultivation of literature will not invest every one with talents of the first order. If there be a degree of intelligence, therefore, that is more unfavourable to the interests of morality and just opinion, than an utter want of intelligence, it may be presumed, that, in very enlightened times, this will be the portion of the greater multitude,—or at least that nations and individuals will have to pass through this troubled and dangerous sphere, in their way to the loftier and purer regions of perfect understanding. The better answer therefore probably is, that it is not intelligence that does the mischief in any case whatsoever, but the presumption that sometimes accompanies the lower degrees of it; and which is best disjoined from them, by making the higher degrees more attainable. (pp. 6-7)

[It is impossible] that we can now find room to say any thing of her exposition of German or of French literature—and still less of her anticipations of the change which the establishment of a Republican government in the last of those countries is likely to produce,—or of the hints and cautions with which, in contemplation of that event, she thinks it necessary to provide her countrymen. These are perhaps the most curious parts of the work:—But we cannot enter upon them at present;—and indeed, in what we have already said, we have so far exceeded the limits to which we always wish to confine ourselves, that we do not very well know what apology to make to our readers—except merely, that we are not without hope, that the miscellaneous nature of the subject, by which we have been insensibly drawn into this great prolixity, may have carried them also along, with as moderate a share of fatigue as we have ourselves experienced. (pp. 49-50)

> *" 'De la littérature considérée dans ses rapports avec les institutions sociales',"* in The Edinburgh Review, *Vol. XXI, No. XLI, February, 1813, pp. 1-50.*

THE EDINBURGH REVIEW (essay date 1813)

The voice of Europe has already applauded the genius of a national painter in the author of **Corinne.** But it was there aided by the power of a pathetic fiction—by the variety and opposition of national character—and by the charm of a country which unites beauty to renown. In the work before us [**De l'Allemagne**], she has thrown off the aid of fiction. She delineates a less poetical character, and a country more interesting by expectation than by recollection.

But it is not the less certain that it is the most vigorous effort of her genius, and probably the most elaborate and masculine production of the faculties of woman. What woman indeed, and (we may add) how many men, could have preserved all the grace and brilliancy of Parisian society in analyzing its nature—explained the most abstruse metaphysical theories of Germany precisely, yet perspicuously and agreeably—and combined the eloquence which inspires exalted sentiments of virtue, with the enviable talent of gently indicating the defects of men or of nations, by the skilfully softened touches of a polite and merciful pleasantry? (p. 205)

The work is divided into four parts.—On Germany and German manners.—On literature and the arts.—On philosophy and morals.—On religion and enthusiasm.

The first is the most perfect in its kind; belongs the most entirely to the genius of the writer; and affords the best example of the talent for painting nations which we have attempted to describe.

It seems also, as far as foreign critics can presume to decide, to be in the most finished style of any composition of the author, and more securely to bid defiance to that minute criticism which, in other works, her genius rather disdained than propitiated. (p. 207)

The society and manners of Germany are continually illustrated by comparison or contrast with those of France. Some passages and chapters on this subject, together with the author's brilliant preface to the thoughts of the Prince de Ligne, may be considered as the first contributions towards a theory of the talent (if we must not say of the art) of conversation, which affords so considerable a part of the most liberal enjoyments of refined life. (p. 210)

The second, and most generally amusing, as well as the largest part of this work, is an animated sketch of the literary history of Germany, with criticisms on the most celebrated German poets and poems, interspersed with reflections equally original and beautiful, tending to cultivate a comprehensive taste in the fine arts, and to ingraft the love of virtue on the sense of beauty. (pp. 213-14)

The Third Part of this work is the most singular. An account of metaphysical systems by a woman, is a novelty in the history of the human mind: whatever may be thought of its success in some of the parts, it must be regarded on the whole as the boldest effort of the female intellect. It must, however, not be forgotten, that it is a contribution rather to the history of human nature, than to that of speculation; and that it considers the source, spirit, and moral influence of metaphysical opinions, more than their truth or falsehood. 'Metaphysics are at least the gymnastics of the understanding.' The commonplace clamour of mediocrity will naturally be excited by the sex, and even by the genius of the author. Every example of vivacity and grace, every exertion of fancy, every display of eloquence, every effusion of sensibility, will be cited as a presumption against the depth of her researches, and the accuracy of her statements. On such principles, the evidence against her, would doubtless be conclusive. But dullness is not accuracy;—ingenious and elegant writers are not therefore superficial; and those who are best acquainted with the philosophical revolutions of Germany, will be most astonished at the general correctness of this short, clear, and agreeable exposition. (p. 220)

The subject of the Fourth Part, is the state of Religion, and the nature of all those disinterested and exalted sentiments which are here comprehended under the name of Enthusiasm. A contemplative people like the Germans, have in their character the principle which disposes men to religion. (p. 221)

[This work], which for variety of knowledge, flexibility of power, elevation of view, and comprehension of mind, is unequalled among the works of women; and which, in the union of the graces of society and literature with the genius of philosophy, is not surpassed by many among those of men.

To affect any tenderness in pointing out the defects or faults of such a work, would be an absurd assumption of superiority. It has no need of mercy. The most obvious and general objection will be, that the Germans are too much praised. But every writer must be allowed to value his subject somewhat higher than the spectator. Unless the German feelings had been adopted, they could not have been forcibly represented.

It will also be found, that the objection is more apparent than real. M. de Staël is indeed the most generous of critics; but she almost always speaks the whole truth to intelligent ears;

though she often hints the unfavourable parts of it so gently and politely, that they may escape the notice of a hasty reader, and be scarcely perceived by a gross understanding. A careful reader, who brings together all the observations intentionally scattered over various parts of the book, will find sufficient justice (though administered in mercy) in whatever respects manners or literature. It is on subjects of philosophy that the admiration will perhaps justly be considered as more undistinguishing. Something of the wonder excited by novelty in language and opinion still influences her mind. (pp. 225-26)

In this as in the other writings of M. de Staël, the reader (or at least the lazy English reader) is apt to be wearied by too constant a demand upon his admiration. It seems to be her literary system, that the pauses of eloquence must be filled up by ingenuity. Nothing plain and unornamented is left in composition. But we desire a plain groundwork, from which wit or eloquence is to arise, when the occasion calls them forth. The effect would be often greater if the talent were less. The natural power of interesting scenes or events over the heart, is somewhat disturbed by too uniform a colour of sentiment, and by the constant pursuit of uncommon reflections or ingenious turns. The eye is dazzled by unvaried brilliancy. We long for the grateful vicissitude of repose.

In the statement of facts and reasonings, no style is more clear than that of M. de Staël. What is so lively must indeed be clear. But in the expression of sentiment she has been often thought to use vague language. In expressing either intense degrees, or delicate shades, or intricate combinations of feeling, the common reader will seldom understand that of which he has never been conscious; and the writer placed on the extreme frontiers of human nature, is in danger of mistaking chimeras for realities, or of failing in a struggle to express what language does not afford the means of describing. There is also a vagueness incident to the language of feeling, which is not so properly a defect, as a quality which distinguishes it from the language of thought. Very often in poetry, and sometimes in eloquence, it is the office of words, not so much to denote a succession of separate ideas, as, like musical sounds, to inspire a series of emotions, or to produce a durable tone of sentiment. The terms perspicuity and precision, which denote the relations of language to intellectual discernment, are inapplicable to it when employed as the mere vehicle of a succession of feelings. A series of words may, in this manner be very expressive, where few of them singly convey a precise meaning: And men of greater intellect than susceptibility in such passages as those of M. de Staël, where eloquence is employed chiefly to inspire feeling, unjustly charge their own defects to that deep, moral, and poetical sensibility with which they are unable to sympathize. (pp. 226-27)

"'De l'Allemagne'," in The Edinburgh Review, Vol. XXII, No. XLIII, October, 1813, pp. 198-238.

BLACKWOOD'S EDINBURGH MAGAZINE (essay date 1837)

No one can exceed Madame de Staël in the expression of the sentiment or poetry of nature, or the development of the varied and storied associations which historical scenes or monuments never fail to awaken in the cultivated mind; but in the delineation of the actual features she exhibits, or the painting of the various and gorgeous scenery or objects she presents, she is greatly inferior to the author of the Genius of Christianity. She speaks emotion to the heart, not pictures to the eye. (p. 717)

Corinne is not to be regarded as a novel. Boarding-school girls, and youths just fledged from college, may admire it as such, and dwell with admiration on the sorrows of the heroine and the faithlessness of Lord Nelvil; but considered in that view it has glaring faults, both in respect of fancy, probability, and story, and will bear no comparison either with the great novels of Sir Walter Scott, or the secondary productions of his numerous imitators. The real view in which to regard it is as a picture of Italy; its inhabitants, feelings, and recollections; its cloudless skies and glassy seas; its forest-clad hills and sunny vales; its umbrageous groves and mouldering forms; its heart-inspiring ruins and deathless scenes. As such it is superior to any work on that subject which has appeared in any European language. Nowhere else shall we find so rich and glowing an intermixture of sentiment with description; of deep feeling for the beauty of art, with a correct perception of its leading principles; of historical lore with poetical fancy; of ardour in the cause of social amelioration, with charity to the individuals who, under unfortunate institutions, are chained to a life of indolence and pleasure. Beneath the glowing sun and azure skies of Italy she has imbibed the real modern Italian spirit: she exhibits in the mouth of her heroine all that devotion to art, that rapturous regard to antiquity, that *insouciance* in ordinary life, and constant *besoin* of fresh excitement by which that remarkable people are distinguished from any other at present in Europe. She paints them as they really are; living on the recollection of the past, feeding on the glories of their double set of illustrious ancestors; at times exulting in the recollection of the legions which subdued the world, at others recurring with pride to the glorious though brief days of modern art. . . . (p. 718)

Not less vividly has she portrayed, in the language, feelings, and character of her heroine, the singular intermixture with these animating recollections of all the frivolity which has rendered impossible, without a fresh impregnation of northern vigour, the regeneration of Italian society. We see in her pages, as we witness in real life, talents the most commanding, beauty the most fascinating, graces the most captivating, devoted to no other object but the excitement of a transient passion; infidelity itself subjected to certain restraints, and boasting of its fidelity to one attachment; whole classes of society incessantly occupied with no other object but the gratification of vanity, the thraldom of attachment, or the imperious demands of beauty, and the strongest propensity of cultivated life, the *besoin d'aimer,* influencing, for the best part of their lives, the higher classes of both sexes. In such representation there would probably be nothing in the hands of an ordinary writer but frivolous or possibly pernicious details; but by Madame de Staël it is touched on so gently, so strongly intermingled with sentiment, and traced so naturally to its ultimate and disastrous effects, that the picture becomes not merely characteristic of manners, but purifying in its tendency.

The *Dix Années d'Exil,* though abounding with fewer splendid and enchanting passages, is written in a higher strain, and devoted to more elevated objects than the Italian novel. . . . [In her migrations] through Tyrol, Poland, Russia, and Sweden, to avoid [Napoleon's] persecution during the years which preceded the Russian war, we have the noblest picture of the elevated feelings which, during this period of general oppression, were rising up in the nations which yet preserved a shadow of independence, as well as of the heroic stand made by Alexander and his brave subjects against the memorable invasion which ultimately proved their oppressor's ruin. These are animating themes; and though not in general inclined to dwell on description, or enrich her work with picturesque narrative, the scenery of the north had wakened profound emotions in her heart which appear in many touches and reflections of no ordinary sublimity. (pp. 718-19)

Madame de Staël does not paint the features of the scene, but in a few words she portrays the emotion which she experienced on beholding it, and contrives by these few words to awaken it in her readers. . . . (p. 719)

[Madame de Staël is superior] in rousing the varied emotions dependent on historical recollections or melancholy impressions. It is remarkable that, though she is a southern writer, and has thrown into *Corinne* all her own rapture at the sun and the recollections of Italy, yet it is with a northern eye that she views the scenes it presents—it is not with the living, but the mighty dead, that she holds communion—the chords she loves to strike are those melancholy ones which vibrate more strongly in a northern than a southern heart. (p. 726)

> *"Modern French Classics: Madame de Staël and Chateaubriand,"* in Blackwood's Edinburgh Magazine, *Vol. XLI, No. CCLX, June, 1837, pp. 715-26.**

JANE T. LOMAX (essay date 1842)

There is no name among the authoresses of her own land, whose celebrity has been more widely extended than that of Madame de Staël; and, without being exempt from the imperfections which sully the works of many among the famous authors of France, we discover in hers, less to censure, and more to admire. Her faults, exaggeration of feeling, and a confirmed confidence in her own opinions, amounting almost to prejudice, are those into which a strong and self-relying mind, united to an ardent disposition, would be likely to fall. In her graver compositions where her real sentiments are apparently expressed, without the incumbrance of fiction, there is much which the generous critic would fain pass over in the "charity of silence;" but though there may be found opinions too bitter, and theories too bold, to become a woman's pen, these are decked in a drapery so graceful, we half forget to blame the impulse from which they sprang. Whatever may be their defects, her writings must always stand in favorable contrast with the style of "George Sand," and the too long list of her imitators. There is something too, that excites our sympathy in Madame de Staël's proud struggle for intellectual freedom, her battling with the persecutions, which, whether merited or not, left dark records on the disposition no oppression could subdue, and lingered to shadow and to haunt the heart they had striven in vain to humble. (pp. 231-32)

She excels in that philosophizing sort of composition which combines the reflection of the German, with the worldly tact of the French author. Her genius is thoughtful, rather than imaginative, and more successful in depicting scenes and persons as they actually exist, than in portraying them as they might be. Her fictitious characters are too unreal; her loftiest inspiration deserts her at the threshold of fancy. The plots of her novels are generally improbable, sometimes impossible, and her personages, while reasoning most eloquently, frequently act most unreasonably. She had no talent for grasping the life-like in trifles; while seeking to disclose the concealed springs of conduct, she neglected the trivial events, the light-spoken words, which convey more vivid and accurate impressions than many lines of profound portrayal. The features in her portraits are painted from humanity, but they lack the slight

touches which give the expression of life. There is always some one delineation on which the writer seems to have lavished peculiar care; some being whose more than ordinary beauty atones for any deficiency in the other actors in the novel. If, in the detail of common occurrences, and the working out of her plots, Madame de Staël sometimes falters, her success in recording the flow of feeling, and the troubled history of the heart's world, has seldom been excelled. It is a rare thing for a woman to fail in depicting the gentler attributes of human nature; she has such deep sympathy with their power, so much knowledge of their influence, and partakes so largely of the *rein menschlich,* that she has only to recall the traces which experience has written on her own life, and she finds a key to the emotions of others. In the picturing of her own sex in its most intellectual form, Madame de Staël has been particularly fortunate. Perhaps even there, she is too ideal; even Corinne, the high, the gifted, and the beautiful, the "martyr'd saint of lovers," is more of the heroine than the woman, yet so lovely in her dream-like loftiness, we can scarcely wish to lose that beauty in one more earthly. . . . Madame de Staël never surpassed the grace of that portrait, the glowing delineation of the conflict between a proud and solitary soul, (whose very superiority made it lonely,) with the shackling forms and prejudices of society; the imprudence of daring a war so unequal; the wretchedness of final submission; its grief and its despair; with the ever-recurring contrast, in the sufferer's thoughts, of what she was, with what she had been; of the immortality intellect might have won her, and the trial that love had brought. . . .

Perhaps no one ever finished the last exquisite pages of *Corinne,* without a feeling of disappointment, that a character so rarely gifted, whose aspirations were noble, and the moral of whose destiny might have been made so beautiful, should descend from a station but "a little lower than the angels," to become a mere love-sick heroine. The transition is emblematic of the mind which depicted it, and evinces how strangely the lofty and the frivolous mingled in the writer's fancies. (p. 232)

"Toutes les grandes pensées, viennent du coeur" [All great thoughts come from the heart], was the saying of Vauvenargue; and Madame de Staël is an example of its truth. She is never so eloquent as when she writes from the dictates of ardent feeling, and gives free way to the enthusiasm inseparable from ambitious genius. There were times when the trials of her destiny brought gentler emotions than the bitter ones they were calculated to excite in a spirit too conscious of superiority to be long submissive—when the sadness which gives wisdom was with her, and when, in the fervor of inspiration and the exercise of intellect, she forgot all of grief but its holiness. . . .

Madame de Staël's dramatic writings are not favorable specimens of her powers. Though unfettered by the restraints of rhyme, they possess the artificial style and stiffness which distinguish French productions of that character; they need the naturalness, the *je ne sais quoi* of reality. . . . [Her] genius is exclusive, rather than universal. She is loftiest, when, looking on the world with calm, philosophic gaze, she paints life in all its earnestness and sublimity, and scans sadly, yet kindly, the troubled depths of the heart, and reveals the workings of passion, or the sorrows of feeling. The gift of *"many-sidedness"* is one rarely if ever possessed by a woman. The nature of her existence, in a manner, prevents it; she is apart from excitements of a general character, and, moving in a sphere comparatively contracted, she seldom experiences vivid and permanent interest beyond it. Her inspiration is the consequence of ardent emotion oftener than the result of profound reflection; she dwells among the charms of thought and love, and her genius is brightest and truest, when, with reverence, it draws aside the temple's veil, and teaches us the deep mysteries within our own hearts. . . .

The works of Madame de Staël are not calculated to convey any important or original instruction; for they appeal more to taste and intellect than to the judgment. They seem to have been composed less for universal approval than for self-satisfaction, and are the channel for sentiments too bold and stirring to be still, and for feelings whose deepest enthusiasm found no resting place in the allurements of common life, and no satisfaction in its aims. . . .

If her pages leave us no dazzling lesson, they at least lead us to reflect with profounder earnestness on the nature and the destiny of our moral being, and we recall their writer as one who taught us something of that self-knowledge whose end is wisdom. We remember her, when experience realizes and brings back to us some of the striking truisms she scattered so lavishly; the spell of romance which her genius has woven will long linger to bind young hearts with its intellectual beauty. (p. 233)

> *Jane T. Lomax, "Madame de Staël," in* Southern Literary Messenger, *Vol. VIII, No. 3, March, 1842, pp. 231-33.*

C. A. SAINTE-BEUVE (essay date 1856)

Connected by paternal descent with the party of reform, Mme. de Staël is saved from one-sidedness by having received her education and passed her first youth in the drawing-rooms of the old school. The personages among whom she grew up, and who smiled on her precocious efforts, all belong to the most intellectual circle of the latest years of the bygone time. . . . If she made herself conspicuous on her first appearance by a slight excess of animation and sentiment, criticised by certain envious aristocrats, it was because she was destined, wherever she went, to carry the same impulsive, unstudied manner. Even while she remained in that tranquil circle, her life was one of its most decided ornaments; and she was to continue, under a less formal and grandiose aspect, that succession of *salons* which had rendered the old French society illustrious. There lingered then with Mme. de Staël just enough of the style and charm of former days; but she was not tenacious of this heritage, for, like most geniuses, and more eminently than any other, she was distinguished by the universality of her intelligence, her need of change and renewal, her vast capacity for love. (pp. 152-53)

[The] existence of Mme. de Staël, in its entirety, seems a mighty empire, which, like that other conqueror, her contemporary and her oppressor, she strove unceasingly to extend and complete. But hers is no material struggle. Her tireless activity does not covet and annex province after province, and realm after realm. It is the domain of her mind that she is ever extending; it is the multiplicity of lofty ideas, profound sentiments, and enviable relations, which she endeavors to organize within and around her. Yes; throughout the whole of her potent life, by virtue of her ready sympathy and her impetuous curiosity, she aspired to hold a vast court, to sway a growing empire of intellect and affection, where nothing graceful or valuable should be overlooked; where all the grades of talent, birth, patriotism, beauty, should receive due homage beneath her eye; where, like an empress of thought, she could enclose every appanage within her free domains. (pp. 154-55)

The predominant characteristic of Mme. de Staël, the main unity of all the contrasts of her character, the swift, keen spirit which circulated through every member of that vast assemblage, and vivified the whole, was, beyond a doubt, a genius for conversation, for sudden improvisation, springing, all divine, from the unfailing fountain of her soul. This, properly speaking, constituted her *life*—a magical word, which she employs very frequently, and which he who would speak of her must use with equal freedom. . . . [The] writings of Mme. de Staël long continued to show traces of her conversational habits. There are marks of negligence, roughnesses of language, a certain hastiness allowable in conversation, but conspicuous in composition, which remind us that she has changed her form of expression for one which demands increased care. . . . [Her works] through the very imperfection of many of their details, their rapid succession of thoughts, and the sweep of their movement, become in many cases all the better transcript of her subtile thought, her panting and agitated soul; while, as a poem and a work of art, the romance of *Corinne* alone would constitute an immortal monument. Artist of a high order by virtue of *Corinne,* Mme. de Staël remains eminent also in other departments—as a politician, a moralist, a critic, and an author of memoirs. It is her life in its unity and variety, the fragrance of her soul arising through her works, yet circling round and pervading all the circumstances of their composition. . . . (pp. 155-57)

The *Letters on Jean Jacques* are a tribute of gratitude to her admired and favorite author, the one to whom Mme. de Staël was most intimately related. Others there are who are careful to conceal, and either fail to mention, or mention only to criticise, the literary parents who gave them birth. She, at the very outset of her career, acknowledges with noble candor the name of him from whom her inspiration is derived, from whose hands she has received the torch, from whom has flowed in upon her a vast wave of noble speech, like that for which Dante blessed Virgil of old. In literature, as in life, Mme. de Staël had her filial passion. The *Letters on Jean Jacques* are a hymn, but a hymn full of earnest thought, and varied by delicate observation—a hymn even then masculine and lofty in its tone, wherein we recognize Corinne after her descent from the capitol. All the future productions of Mme. de Staël, of whatever character,—romantic moral, political,—are foreshadowed in this rapid and harmonious eulogium on those of Rousseau, as the great musical work already complete in the mind of the composer is indicated in the overture. (pp. 166-67)

[The *Essay on Fiction*] foreshadows all the poetry of *Delphine.* Grieved at the aspect of the real, the imagination of Mme. de Staël fondly betakes itself to better and fairer creations, or, at least, to sorrows the memory and tale of which move to softer tears. At the same time it is for the genuine romance of nature, for the analysis and dramatization of human passions, that Mme. de Staël is specially distinguished among fictitious writers. She will have no mythology, no allegory, no fantastic, supernatural, or fairy element, no obtrusive philosophical aim. . . . [We] find, in the *Essay on Fiction,* that airy rapidity of movement, that wealth of vivid, apt, and suggestive words, those delicious touches of feeling which we get only from Mme. de Staël, and in which, properly speaking, the peculiarly poetic and dreamy melody of her style consists. When she speaks thus, there are tears even in the most brilliant notes of her voice. The more insignificant the thought, the more striking the accent, as, for instance, "In this life which we must pass, rather than feel." . . . (pp. 175-76)

But this kind of inspired sentimentalism, this mysterious reflection thrown from the depths of the heart, irradiates throughout the book *On the Influence of the Passions,* and imparts to it an indefinable charm, which, for certain pensive natures, at certain periods of life, is unsurpassed by the influence of anything else that can be read, even by the sadness of Ossian or Oberman. The earlier pages of the book are, moreover, remarkable from a political point of view. In fact, the author, who has treated at length only of the influence of the passions on individual happiness, designed to investigate, in a second part, the influence of these same motives on the happiness of society, and the main questions preliminary to this vast inquiry, are raised and touched upon in an eloquent introduction. (pp. 176-77)

The design of the author of *Delphine* was to produce a moral and analytical romance,—passionate, but perfectly true to nature. For my own part, delicious as I find its every page, I prefer a less natural, less realistic tale, such a one as Mme. de Staël herself foreshadowed in her *Essay on Fiction*. . . . [Its] epistolary form entails too much of formality and literary method. One of the disadvantages of a novel in the form of letters is, that the personages are obliged at the very outset to assume a tone too entirely in harmony with their supposed characters. . . . But allowing for this error of form in *Delphine,* what delicacy and passion in the whole book! what overflowing sensibility! what subtile discrimination of character! Apropos of its characters, the world of that day could not refrain from seeking portraits among them. I do not myself think that complete portraits are often drawn by novelists of fertile imagination. They merely copy more or less of the leading traits, and these soon become transformed, and attain a new development. The author and creator of the characters alone could indicate the secret, sinuous line where invention joins memory. (pp. 208-10)

And yet, when all has been said in its justification, it must be confessed that *Delphine* is a disquieting book; but the disquiet to which we would not expose perfect innocence is often only a salutary stimulus to feeling in souls that were being fast usurped by stern realities and a dreary disenchantment. Blessed be the disquiet that tends to revive within us youth's tender feelings and capacity for self-devotion! (p. 220)

Corinne is what Mme. de Staël aspired to be, and what (save for the difference caused by an artificial grouping and arrangement of life) she really was. Not merely does she share with Corinne the capitol and the triumph. With her she will also die of sorrow. (p. 236)

One of the most charming portions of *Corinne*—all the more so in that it is unstudied—is the conversational wit so often introduced by the Count d'Erfeuil, and pervading the reflections on French society. Mme. de Staël ridicules that society, and the excessive levity of its tone, but at such times she has more of it than she suspects; and, as often happens, she disdains what are perhaps her best sayings.

As in *Delphine,* we have portraits. Mme. d'Arbigny, the calculating Frenchwoman and universal manager, is one of them. Like Mme. de Vernon, she was identified in private whispers, and people also knew of what slightly incongruous elements the noble figure of Oswald was composed, while they believed in the perfect veracity of the parting scene, and well nigh remembered Corinne's anguish during her lover's absence.

But though *Corinne* abounds in conversations and pictures of society, Mme. de Staël cannot be accused of any lack of strength

and consistency of style in this book, nor of haste in the arrangement of her thoughts. As regards the general execution of the work, she has entirely laid aside her conversational brilliancy and habit of written impersonation, as indeed she sometimes did when standing (*stans pede in uno*) and leaning against an angle of the chimney. If there are still imperfections of form, they are rare accidents. I have seen noted in pencil in a copy of *Corinne* a prodigious number of *buts,* which give an air of monotony to the earlier pages. But on the whole a watchful care presides over the details of this monument of her powers. The writer has attained to art, sustained dignity, and rhythm. (pp. 237-38)

[The work on Germany] may seem to us of to-day incomplete in its historic portions. Public opinion has shown of late a growing sense of its defects. But aside from the honor of having made a beginning, of which no one else was then capable . . . I do not think there is to be found elsewhere any vivid picture of the birth of German genius, of that brilliant age of poetry which may be called the age of Göthe, since German poetry of a high order would almost seem to have been born and died with that great man. It lived but a single patriarchal life, and all since has been decomposition and decay. In her view of Germany, Mme. de Staël laid great stress upon the subject of philosophy, and on an order of ideas differing from those of the French ideologists, although in so doing she found herself sufficiently far removed from the doctrines of her own youth. And here we must not fail to note the revelation of a growing care for the moral tone of her writings. No work appears to her sufficiently moral which does not help to perfect the soul in some direction. (pp. 238-39)

> C. A. Sainte-Beuve, "Madame de Staël," in his Portraits of Celebrated Women, *translated by H. W. Preston (originally published as* Portraits de femmes, *Didier, 1856), third edition, Roberts Brothers, 1895, pp. 151-248.*

GEORGE BRANDES   (essay date 1872)

De la Littérature considérée dans ses Rapports avec les Institutions Sociales [is] a work which, from its general purport, must be classified as belonging to that great body of writings in which, ever since the days of the Renaissance, the relative merits of ancient and modern literature have been discussed. . . . [Mme. de Staël] believes in the capacity of humanity to improve, and in the gradual perfecting of social institutions, and on this belief grounds her assurance that literature will contain a steadily increasing treasure of experience and insight. At this stage of her development there is no question of any profound and systematic literary psychology; she calmly, for instance, excludes imagination from the list of faculties which are capable of development—why?—because in spite of all her enthusiasm for Ossian, she cannot deny that Homer's is the fuller, richer, poetry. The merit of her book, however, does not depend upon what it proves, but upon what it proclaims and urges, namely the necessity for a new literature, new science, and a new religion. She draws attention to the literature of England and Germany, to the Icelandic sagas, and the old Scandinavian epics; but Ossian is to her the great type of all that is splendid in the poetry of the North. She loves his seriousness and melancholy, for, she says, "melancholy poetry is the poetry which accords best with philosophy." (pp. 92-3)

[The fundamental idea of *De la Littérature*] is, that free social conditions must inevitably lead to a new development of literature, that it would be absurd if a society which had won political liberty for itself were to own only a literature shackled by rules. (p. 93)

The spiritless, resigned motto of *Delphine:* "A man should be able to defy public opinion, a woman to submit to it," almost betrays its authoress, Madame de Staël's mother. The actual story harmonises with the motto, but the spirit of the book and the very fact of its publication contradict it. For the book is a justification of divorce, and it appeared in the same year that Napoleon concluded the Concordat with the Pope; it attacked indissoluble wedlock and the religious sacrament of marriage, at the very moment when the marriage laws were being made more stringent, and a portion of its old power was being restored to the Church.

The book answers to its motto in so far that it teaches, through the fate of its heroine, that if a woman, even after a generous and prolonged sacrifice of her own well-being, transgress the rules of society, though it may be only to prevent the ruin of her lover, she is lost. It contradicts its motto in so far that the crying injustice of such a fate speaks more powerfully than any declamation, of the imperfection of the social organism and of the preposterousness of that power to coerce and make unhappy, which man's short-sightedness and pusillanimity have entrusted to the antiquated institutions under the pressure of which Delphine is crushed. She is depicted from the very first as a superior being, pure, benevolent, spirited, elevated by the very fact of her purity above the pharisaical morality of society. (pp. 96-7)

[The] book makes protest throughout against the great mass of received opinions, the prejudices with which most men are clad as it were in a coat of triple mail, the beliefs which must not even be approached, because the very ground around them is holy within a circumference of so and so many square miles. It cannot be too plainly asserted that, in this particular, *Delphine* is a more vigorous, remarkable work than most of the other productions of the Emigrant Literature. (p. 101)

The breach between society and the individual depicted in *Delphine* is entirely in the spirit of the Emigrant Literature. The same bold revolt followed by the same despair in view of the uselessness of the struggle, is to be found throughout the whole group of writings. In the present case the revolt is a spirited, desperate attempt to hold fast one of the gains of the Revolution at the moment when it is being wrested away by the reaction. The despair is due to the sorrowful feeling that no remonstrance will avail, that the retrograde movement must run its course, must exceed all reasonable limits, before a better condition of things can be looked for. Was a woman's novel likely to prevail against an autocrat's compact with a Pope! (pp. 102-03)

The temperamental foundation upon which Mme. de Staël built was genuinely feminine. The final ideal of this undeniably ambitious woman was a purely personal, purely idyllic one— happiness in love. It is upon this that her two great novels, *Delphine* and *Corinne,* turn; the improbability of finding it in marriage as ordained by society, and the impossibility of finding it outside marriage, are her fundamental ideas; and the perpetual conflict between domestic happiness and noble ambitions or free love, is merely the expression of her constant complaint, that neither genius nor passion is compatible with that domestic happiness which is her heart's eternal desire. In her books the woman only seeks the path of fame when she has been disappointed in all her dearest hopes. (p. 114)

Corinne, ou l'Italie is Mme. de Staël's best tale. In Italy, that natural paradise, her eyes were opened to the charms of nature. She no longer preferred the gutters of Paris to the Lake of Nemi. And it was in this country, where a square yard of such a place, for instance, as the Forum, has a grander history than the whole Russian empire, that her modern, rebellious, melancholy soul opened to the influence of history, the influence of antiquity with its simple, austere calm. . . . Corinne is, in the world of fiction, like a prophecy of what Elizabeth Barrett Browning was to be in the world of reality. One thinks of Corinne when one reads that Italian inscription upon a house in Florence: "Here lived Elizabeth Barrett Browning, whose poems are a golden thread binding Italy to England." (p. 124)

In Corinne the authoress has depicted for us her own ideal. She has borrowed the chief characteristics of her heroine from her own individuality. Corinne is not, like Delphine, the woman who is confined to the sphere of private life; she is the woman who has overstepped the allotted limits, the poetess whose name is upon all lips. . . . Mme. de Staël has endowed Corinne with her own culture. It is expressly stated that it was her knowledge of the literatures and understanding of the characters of foreign nations that gave Corinne so high a place in the literary ranks of her own country; her charm as a poet lay in her combination of the southern gift of colour with the northern gift of observation. Employing all these borrowed characteristics, and inventing many others, the authoress has, it is to be observed, succeeded in producing a distinctly Italian type of female character.

Mme. de Staël's literary activity divides itself, as it were, into two activities—a masculine and a feminine, the expression of thoughts and the dwelling upon emotions. We can trace this duality in *Corinne.* The book has, unquestionably, more merit as an effort of the intellect than as a work of creative imagination. A peculiar fervour and a certain tenderness in the treatment of the emotions betray that the author is a woman. Psychology is still in such a backward condition that as yet only the merest attempt has been made to define the characteristic qualities of woman's mind, of woman's soul, as distinguished from man's; when the day comes for making the attempt in good earnest, Mme. de Staël's works will be one of the most valuable sources of enlightenment.

The woman's hand is, perhaps, most perceptible in the delineation of the hero. The authoress supplies us with the reasons for each of his distinguishing qualities. His sense of honour is explained by his distinguished birth, his melancholy by his English "spleen" and by his unhappy relations with the father whom he worshipped. . . . (pp. 127-29)

One might call *Corinne* a work on national prejudices. Oswald represents all those of England; his travelling companion, Count d'Erfeuil, all those of France; and it is against the prejudices of these two nations, at that time the most powerful and the most self-reliant in Europe, that the heroine does battle with her whole soul. It is no cold-blooded, impersonal warfare, for Corinne's future depends upon whether she can succeed in freeing Oswald from his national prejudices to such an extent as to enable him to be happy with a woman like herself, whose life conflicts at every turn with the English conception of what is becoming in woman. But while she is attempting to widen Oswald's view of life and to impart pliancy to his rigid mind, which always starts back again into its accustomed grooves, she is at the same time carrying on the education of the reader. Mme. de Staël continues in the domain of the emotions the task with which we have seen her occupied in the domain of thought. She sketches the first outlines of *national* psychology, shows how there is a colouring of nationality even in men's most private, personal feelings. Her countrymen were then, much in the manner of the Germans of to-day, attempting to blot out the national colours of neighbouring countries in the complacent persuasion that they themselves had a monopoly of civilisation. Her inmost desire is to show them that their conception of life is but one among many conceptions that are equally justifiable, some of them possibly more justifiable. (p. 135)

The strongly opposed and long suppressed book [*De l'Allemagne*] on Germany is the most mature production of Mme. de Staël's culture and intellect. It is the first of her longer works in which she so entirely loses herself in her subject as to have apparently forgotten her own personality. In it she gives up describing herself, and only appears to the extent that she gives an account of her travels in Germany and reproduces her conversations with the most remarkable men of that country. (p. 164)

She never wearies of praising the integrity and truthfulness of the German men, and only very occasionally does she hint at a pretty general lack of refinement and tact. We feel that their conversation often wearied her, but for this she blames the social customs and the language. It is impossible, she says, to express one's self neatly in a language in which one's meaning as a rule only becomes intelligible at the end of the sentence, in which, consequently, the interruptions which give life to a conversation are almost impossible, it being also impossible always to reserve the pith of the sentence for the end. (p. 165)

Mme. de Staël was necessarily much impressed by the intellectual life of Germany. In her own country everything had stiffened into rule and custom. There, a decrepit poetry and philosophy were at the point of death; here, everything was in a state of fermentation, full of new movement, life, and hope. (pp. 166-67)

The next great contrast with French intellectual life that struck Mme. de Staël was the prevailing idealism of German literature. The philosophy which had reigned in France during the last half of the eighteenth century was one which derived all human ideas and thoughts from the impressions of the senses, which, consequently, asserted the human mind to be dependent upon and conditioned by its material surroundings. It was certainly not in Mme. de Staël's power to estimate the nature and the bearing of this philosophy, but, like a genuine child of the new century, she loathed it. She judged it like a woman, with her heart rather than her head, and ascribed to it all the materialism she objected to in French morals, and all the servile submission to authority she objected to in French men. . . . The ethics of Kant and Fichte and the poetry of Schiller proclaimed exactly that sovereignty of the spirit in which she had believed all her life. These great thinkers demonstrated, that inspired poet in each of his poems proved, the spirit's independence of the world of matter, its power to rise above it, to rule it, to remould it. They expressed the most cherished convictions of her heart; and it was in her enthusiasm for these doctrines, for German high-mindedness and loftiness of aspiration, that she set to work to write her book *De l'Allemagne* (as Tacitus in his day had written *De Germania*), for the purpose of placing before her fellow-countrymen a great example of moral purity and intellectual vigour.

Mme. de Staël had always looked upon enthusiasm as a saving power. She had said in *Corinne* that she only recognised two really distinct classes of men—those who are capable of enthusiasm and those who despise enthusiasts. It seemed to her that in the Germany of that day she had found the native land of enthusiasm, the country in which it was a religion, where it was more highly honoured than anywhere else on earth. Hence it is that she ends her book with a dissertation on enthusiasm. But this belief in enthusiasm, in the power of imagination and the purely spiritual faculties, led her to many rash and narrow conclusions. In her delight in the philosophic idealism of Germany, she treats experimental natural science with the most naïve superiority—is of opinion that it leads to nothing but a mechanical accumulation of facts. (pp. 167-68)

The Romantic doctrine of the all-importance of imagination won her approbation, but the Romanticists' conception of the nature of imagination was incomprehensible to her. They started from the hypothesis that at the foundation of everything lay a perpetually producing imagination, a species of juggling imagination, which with divine irony perpetually destroyed its own creations as the sea engulfs its own billows; and they held that the poet, that creator on a small scale, should take up the same ironical position towards the creatures of his imagining, towards his whole work, and deliberately destroy the illusion of it. (p. 181)

Like all the authors involved in the first reaction against the eighteenth century, she became as time went on more and more positively religious. The philosophical ideas of the revolutionary times were gradually effaced in her mind, and their place was supplied by ever more serious attempts to imbue herself with the new pious ideas of the day. She, who in her youth had eagerly controverted Chateaubriand's theory of the superiority of Christian subjects in art, now becomes a convert to his aesthetic views. She accepts unreservedly the Romanticist doctrine that modern poetry and art must build upon Christianity, as the antique had built upon the Greco-Roman mythology; and, living, listening, talking herself into ever greater certainty that the eighteenth century was completely astray, and constantly meeting men who have returned to the pious belief of the past, she finally herself comes to believe that idealism in philosophy, which to her, as a woman, is the good principle, and inspiration in poetry, which to her, as an authoress, is the saving, emancipating principle, must necessarily restore its authority to revealed religion, seeing that sensationalism, the principles of which in both philosophy and art are antipathetic to her, has opposed religion as an enemy. Thus it is that in her book on Germany she actually comes to range herself on the side of that passionate, prejudiced, and often painfully narrow reaction against the eighteenth-century spirit of intellectual liberty, which had broken out on the other side of the Rhine, and was to reach its climax in France itself. (pp. 181-82)

George Brandes, in his Main Currents in Nineteenth Century Literature: The Emigrant Literature, Vol. I, *translated by Diana White and Mary Morison (originally published as* Hovedstrømninger i det 19de aahundredes litteratur, *1872),* Heinemann Ltd., *1901 (and reprinted by Boni & Liveright, Inc., 1924), 198 p.**

S. G. TALLENTYRE [pseudonym of EVELYN BEATRICE HALL] (essay date 1901)

[Madame de Staël's] works are personal in an extraordinary degree. It is "I," "me," "my," always. The most famous of her books are full of appeal, of insistence that the world should admire, not German literature or a heroine of romance, but Anne Germaine Necker de Staël-Holstein.

"Delphine" is not immoral French fiction half so much as it is a brilliant girl's passionate cry for enjoyment—the outburst of a very young heart that could not yet quite believe that "we were not sent into the world to be happy, but to be right."

"Corinne," that "chef-d'oeuvre of the youth of her talent," is a picture of Italy photographed upon a most poetic heart. Corinne crowned at the Capitol, Corinne with her lyre, her beautiful sentiments, and her passionate grief, has all the ardour and genius and the lack of stern, cool common-sense of the real Corinne, Madame de Staël. The authoress always wrote, as it were, with the blood of her heart. Her cousin calls **"Delphine"** the book "where she has said everything." Her genius and weakness alike consisted in this. She always said everything. She put down what she felt at the moment. She never paused to reflect what effect the record of those feelings would have on other minds. She never corrected or thought over what she had written. . . . If her feelings were always changing, they were not the less acute feelings for the time. **"Corinne"** and **"Delphine"** will never altogether die, because when they were written they came straight from the heart of the woman who wrote them, and abound in those touches of nature which make all men kin. The supreme achievement of Madame's talent was doubtless **"De l'Allemagne"**. (pp. 130-32)

If her **"Dix Années d'Exil"** revealed a great deal more of her own character than it did of Napoleon's, yet not the less, with her intuitive genius, she had her infidel a thousand times upon the hip.

Her **"Essay on Literature,"** which has been called "the greatest of all the literary productions of women," abounds in fine aphorisms, and has all the splendid dash and vigour which were pre-eminently the de Staël's.

There are few writers who have such quick-flowing grace of expression, and at once such warmth, such spirit, such passion, and such tenderness. (p. 132)

All her thoughts have thus the softness of pearls or the sparkle of diamonds. They are exquisite gems for ornament, if they are not gold for use.

Whatever be the judgment of future generations upon the talent of Madame de Staël, the woman herself is immortal. . . .

The other Salonières made their Salons their world. It was only this one who attempted to make the world her Salon. (p. 133)

> S. G. Tallentyre [*pseudonym of Evelyn Beatrice Hall*], *"Madame de Staël," in her* The Women of the Salons and Other French Portraits, *Longmans, Green, and Co., 1901 (and reprinted by G. P. Putnam's Sons, 1926), pp. 111-33.*

IRVING BABBITT (essay date 1912)

It has been said that the rôle of Madame de Staël was to understand and make others understand, that of Chateaubriand to feel and teach others to feel; which is only another way of saying that Chateaubriand is more intimately related to romanticism than Madame de Staël. . . . Her style is of that age; it lacks, however, the epigrammatic neatness of the eighteenth century before Rousseau, and though not always free from the sentimentality and declamation that the late eighteenth century had caught from Rousseau at his worst, it lacks the imaginative freshness and warmth of coloring of Rousseau at his best. It

has its own merits as a medium for conveying ideas, but it is deficient in both the old art and the new poetry.

Madame de Staël belongs no less decisively to the Old Régime in preferring society to nature and solitude. Napoleon, in his ten years' duel with her, discovered that he could inflict sufficient torment simply by keeping her at a distance from Paris. (p. 5)

In spite of her excess of understanding, her love of the drawing-room and her comparative coolness towards nature, Madame de Staël is nevertheless a disciple of Rousseau. We merely need to define carefully this discipleship. She might have said, though in a somewhat different sense from Rousseau, that "her heart and her head did not seem to belong to the same individual." . . . [The] element that Madame de Staël conceived to be common to Rousseau and herself and at the same time to distinguish the Germans, manifests itself especially in the power of "enthusiasm." She is, then, not only temperamentally an enthusiast, but also an enthusiast by the direct influence of Rousseau as well as by the Rousseauism that she received from Germany. (p. 6)

[For] Madame de Staël as for Rousseau, virtue is a mere process of emotional expansion, related to the region of impulse below the reason rather than to the region of insight above it. (p. 7)

It would not, however, be entirely fair to Madame de Staël to see in her conception of morality a mere Rousseauistic intoxication. The two ruling passions of her life were hatred of Napoleon and love for her father, and as she grew older she showed herself more and more not merely the daughter but the disciple of Necker. Both her rationalism and her emotionalism were tempered by the traditional views of morality and religion of the Swiss protestant. In her political thinking again, both on her own account and as a follower of her father, she departed from Rousseau in putting her chief emphasis on liberty. (p. 8)

Rousseauistic enthusiasm remains after all the essential aspect of Madame de Staël's genius. She differs however from many of the posterity of Jean-Jacques in being intellectually as well as emotionally expansive. In so far as she desired only expansiveness and refused either an inner or an outer check, she was unbalanced and did not escape the Nemesis that pursues every form of lack of balance, especially, perhaps, lack of emotional balance. Yet it may be said in her behalf that the half-truths on which she insisted were the half-truths that the age needed to hear, and that the excess by which she erred was—in spite of the charges of masculinity brought against her by her contemporaries—the excess of the feminine virtues. She really had the largeness and generosity of outlook that her theory required, and hers was above all a magnificently hospitable nature. (p. 9)

Any one who conceives of life as expansively as did Madame de Staël, comes inevitably to be interested less in form than in expression. The partisan of form is fastidious and exclusive, whether his sense of form rests on a living intuition or on the acceptance of certain traditional standards. Now Madame de Staël almost entirely lacked the living intuition of form and had repudiated the traditional standards. She was led by her interest in expression to exalt the variable element in literature, to see it not absolutely but relatively; above all, as we have seen, to look on it as the expression of society and therefore as changing with it. (p. 10)

The use of the historical method in the book on **"Literature"** is much obscured by the utterly unhistorical conception of perfectibility, that faith in a mechanical and rectilinear advance of the human race which so many people still hold naïvely, imagining themselves to be evolutionists. Madame de Staël assumes the superiority of Roman over Greek philosophy simply because it comes later. . . .

We find in the **"Literature,"** along with many other passages that anticipate at least faintly the "Germany," the first form of the celebrated distinction between the two literatures, that of the North and that of the South (she does not however as yet apply to the former the epithet romantic). (p. 11)

Her **"Germany"** bears the marks not only of her travels in Italy, Austria, and Germany during the ten years that had elapsed since the publication of the **"Literature"** but also of important personal influences. We are told that the proper rule to follow in accounting for the ideas of a woman is, *Cherchez l'homme;* and we cannot entirely neglect this rule even in the case of Madame de Staël, the most intellectual of modern women. . . . [She] not only gave undue attention to certain German romantic writers, but inclined to romanticize Germany in general. (p. 12)

This legend of an idyllic Germany, a land of sentimental dreamers and philosophers who refused to interest themselves in anything less than the universe, survived in France to some extent until the rude awakening of 1870. To this nation of noble enthusiasts Madame de Staël opposes the drily analytical French. . . . The German is not, like the Frenchman, imprisoned in the uninspired understanding (*Verstand*), but dwells in the region of the imaginative and synthetic reason (*Vernunft*). The psychological elements of the opposition thus worked up into a fine metaphysical distinction, are already manifest in the quarrel between Rousseau the enthusiast, and Voltaire the mocking analyst. We are simply witnessing the international triumph of Rousseau over Voltaire. The closing pages of the "Germany" in which she exalts enthusiasm as the distinctive German virtue and at the same time warns the French against the spirit of cold reasoning and calculation are, as she herself says, the summing up of her whole work. They are also, we are told, the pages that give the best idea of her actual conversation.

Madame de Staël is really arguing against a social order the ultimate refinements of which were necessary, as we have seen, for her own happiness. In her whole attack on French society, its artificiality and conventionalism and its abuse of ridicule, in her charge that the spirit of imitation had killed spontaneity and enthusiasm, she simply repeats, often less tellingly, the arguments of Rousseau. . . . A certain conception of decorum, a "certain factitious grandeur not made for the human heart," as Rousseau had put it, always stood in the way of naturalness. (pp. 13-15)

This idea of decorum, as Rousseau had already pointed out, had been especially fatal to naturalness in the drama. . . . "We rarely escape," says Madame de Staël in turn, "from a certain conventional nature which gives the same coloring to ancient as to modern manners, to crime as to virtue, to murder as to gallantry." The pathway of escape from this pale conventionality is a more thorough study of history. (p. 15)

The weapon with which society punishes those who depart from its notions of decorum and good taste is ridicule. . . . The whole error arises from confounding taste in the literary with taste in the society sense. Madame de Staël therefore makes her main attack on "good taste," and its tendency to be merely negative and restrictive. Taste in the literary sense should get beyond petty fault-finding, based on rules and formal requirements, and become generous and comprehensive and appreciative. Taste in poetry derives from nature and like it should be creative. The principles of this taste are therefore entirely different from those that depend on social relations. (p. 16)

Though Madame de Staël is interested in differences rather than identities, the differences that interest her most after all are not so much those between individuals as those between nationalities. To the claims of the French and the classicist to possess a monopoly of good taste, what she really opposes are the claims of national taste. . . . Few persons have been more preoccupied than she with questions of national psychology. In **"Corinne,"** for example, we have not merely the conflict and interplay of different characters, but of different civilizations; and as usual the French do not show to advantage in contrast with other nationalities. (p. 18)

Her conception of the relation of nationalities to one another simply reproduces on a larger scale the Rousseauistic conception of the proper relation of individuals. Each nationality is to be spontaneous and original and self-assertive, and at the same time infinitely open and hospitable to other national originalities. Nationalism in short is to be tempered by cosmopolitanism, and both are to be but diverse aspects of Rousseauistic enthusiasm. The first law for nationalities as for individuals is not to imitate but to be themselves. Thus Madame de Staël is indifferent to the work of Wieland because it seems to her less a native German product than a reflection of French taste (*l'originalité nationale vaut mieux*). Having, however, made sure of its own originality each nation is then to complete itself by foreign borrowings. (pp. 18-19)

Madame de Staël thus appears as the ideal cosmpolitan, as the person who has perhaps done more than anyone else to help forward the comparative study of literature as we now understand it. But is there not something utopian in the whole conception, is there any adequate counterpoise to the inordinate emphasis that is placed on the centrifugal elements of originality and self-expression? When individual or national differences are pushed beyond a certain point what comes into play is not sympathy but antipathy. Madame de Staël admits that her cosmopolitanism is only for the few. (pp. 19-20)

Possibly the most important chapter in the **"Germany"** is that in which Madame de Staël takes up again her distinction between the literature of the South and that of the North and definitely describes the two traditions as classic and romantic, thus giving international currency to the application that the Schlegels had made of these epithets to two distinct literary schools. Classic had always passed as the norm of perfection. But Madame de Staël refuses to discuss the relative superiority of classic and romantic taste. "It is enough to show," she says, turning determinist for the moment, "that this diversity of tastes derives not only from accidental causes, but also from the primitive sources of imagination and thought." . . . In true Rousseauistic fashion we are to advance by looking backward, we are to progress by reverting to origins; only in this way can we escape from the artificial and the imitative and recover the spontaneous and the original. Our choice is not between classic poetry and romantic poetry, "but between the imitation of the one and the inspiration of the other." (pp. 21-2)

The chief Rousseauist venom of the whole point of view is found in the elimination of the aristocratic and selective element from the standard of taste, and in the assumption that the proper judges of poetry are the illiterate. (p. 23)

Madame de Staël, to judge from her choice of examples, seems to be in some confusion as to the nature of popular poetry. (pp. 23-4)

[The] procedure of the Rousseauist is always to get rid of law or discipline on the ground that it is artificial or conventional, and to set up in its stead some enthusiasm or sympathy. Madame de Staël and the romanticists were strong in their attacks on formalism, but in discarding the idea of law itself along with the conventionalities in which it had got embedded they were almost incredibly weak. (p. 28)

The unit of Madame de Staël's thinking, it should be observed, is the nation and not the race. The nation as she conceives it, though she is not specially clear or consistent on this point, is not so much a mere product of environment as a sort of spiritual entity, a body of men united by common memories and achievements and aspiring to common ends. (p. 30)

> *Irving Babbitt, "Madame de Staël," in his* The Masters of Modern French Criticism *(copyright © 1912 by Irving Babbitt; renewal copyright © 1940 by Edward S. Babbitt and Edward S. Babbitt, Jr.; reprinted by permission of Edward S. Babbitt), Houghton Mifflin, 1912 (and reprinted by Farrar, Straus and Company, 1963), pp. 1-33.*

GEORGE SAINTSBURY (essay date 1917)

There are many *worse* books than **Delphine.** It is excellently written; there is no bad blood in it; there is no intentional licentiousness; on the contrary, there are the most desperate attempts to live up to a New Morality by no means entirely of the Higgins kind. But there is an absence of humour which is perfectly devastating: and there is a presence of the most disastrous atmosphere of sham sentiment, sham morality, sham almost everything, that can be imagined. It was hinted in the last volume that Madame de Staël's lover, Benjamin Constant, shows in one way the Nemesis of Sensibility; so does she herself in another. But the difference! In *Adolphe* a coal from the altar of true passion has touched lips in themselves polluted enough, and the result is what it always is in such, alas! rare cases, whether the lips were polluted or not. In **Delphine** there is a desperate pother to strike some sort of light and get some sort of heat; but the steel is naught, the flint is clay, the tinder is mouldy, and the wood is damp and rotten. (p. 3)

In fact, to get any appropriate metaphorical description of it one has to change the terminology altogether. In a very great line Mr. Kipling has spoken of a metaphorical ship—

> With a drogue of dead convictions to keep her
>   head to gale.

Madame de Staël has cast off not only that drogue, but even the other and perhaps commoner floating ballast and steadier of dead *conventions,* and is trying to beat up against the gale by help of all sorts of jury-masts and extemporised try-sails of other new conventions that are mostly blowing out of the bolt-ropes. . . . In **Delphine** there is not a glimmer of amusement from first to last, and the whole story is compact (if that word were not totally inapplicable) of windbags of sentiment, copy-book headings, and the strangest husks of neo-classic type-worship, stock character, and hollow generalisation. (pp. 3-4)

[The thing] is perhaps worth reading once (nothing but the sternest voice of duty could have made me read it twice) because of the existence of **Corinne,** and because also of the undoubted fact that, here as there, though much more surpris-

ingly, a woman of unusual ability was drawing a picture of what she would have liked to be—if not of what she actually thought herself. . . . That Delphine makes a frantic fool of herself for a lover whose attractions can only make male readers shrug their shoulders—for though we are *told* that Léonce is clever, brave, charming, and what not, we see nothing of it in speech or action—may be matter of taste; but that her heroine's part should seem to any woman one worth playing is indeed wonderful. (pp. 6-7)

Between **Delphine** and **Corinne** Madame de Staël had, in the fullest sense of a banal phrase, "seen a great deal of the world." She had lost the illusions which the Duessa Revolution usually spreads among clever but not wise persons at her first appearance, and had *not* left her bones, as too many such persons do, in the *pieuvre*-caves which the monster keeps ready. (pp. 7-8)

A critical reader of **Corinne** must remember all this, and he must remember something else, though the reminder has been thought to saviour of brutality. (p. 8)

Delphine had been dull, absurd, preposterous; **Corinne,** if it has dull patches, saves them from being intolerable. If its sentiment is extravagant, it is never exactly preposterous or exactly absurd; for the truth and reality of passion which are absent from the other book are actually present here, though sometimes in unintentional masquerade.

In fact, **Corinne,** though the sisterhood of the two books is obvious enough, has almost, though not quite, all the faults of **Delphine** removed and some merits added, of which in the earlier novel there is not the slightest trace. (p. 9)

The story of **Corinne,** though not extraordinarily "accidented" and, as will be seen, adulterated, or at least mixed, with a good many things that are not story at all, is fairly solid, much more so than that of **Delphine.** (p. 11)

[And yet] I should be sorry for any one who regards **Corinne** as merely a tedious and not at all brief subject for laughter. One solid claim which it possesses has been, and is still for a moment, definitely postponed; but in another point there is, if not exactly a defence, an immense counterpoise to the faults and follies just mentioned. Corinne to far too great an extent, and Oswald to an extent nearly but not quite fatal, are loaded . . . with a mass of corporal and spiritual wiglomeration (as Mr. Carlyle used expressively and succinctly to call it) in costume and fashion and sentiment and action and speech. But when we have stripped this off, *manet res*—reality of truth and fact and nature.

There should be no doubt of this in Corinne's own case. It has been said from the very first that she is, as Delphine had been, if not what her creatress was, what she would have liked to be. The ideal in the former case was more than questionable, and the execution was very bad. Here the ideal is far from flawless, but it is greatly improved, and the execution is improved far more than in proportion. Corinne is not "a reasonable woman"; but reason, though very heartily to be welcomed on its rare occurrences in that division of humanity, when it does not exclude other things more to be welcomed still, is very decidedly not to be preferred to the other things themselves. Corinne has these—or most of them. She is beautiful; she is amiable; she is unselfish; without the slightest touch of prudery she has the true as well as the technical chastity; and she is really the victim of inauspicious stars, and of the misconduct of other people—the questionable wisdom of her own father; the folly of Nelvil's; the wilfulness in the bad sense, and the weakness of will in the good, of her lover; the sour virtue and *borné* temperament of Lady Edgermond. (pp. 16-17)

To say that it is in great part a "guide-book novel," as indeed its second title honestly declares, may seem nowadays a doubtful testimonial. It is not really so. For it was, with certain exceptions in German, the *first* "guide-book" novel: and though some of those exceptions may have shown greater literary genius than Madame de Staël's, the Germans, though they have, in certain lines, had no superiors as producers of tales, have never produced a good novel yet. Moreover, the guide-book element is a great set-off to the novel. It is not—or at any rate it is not necessarily—liable to the objections to "purpose," for it is ornamental and not structural. It takes a new and important and almost illimitably fresh province of nature and of art, which is a part of nature, to be its appanage. (p. 18)

[Madame de Staël] sees, or helps to see, the "sensibility" novel out, with forcible demonstration of the inconveniences of its theory. She helps to see the aesthetic novel—or the novel highly seasoned and even sandwiched with aesthetics—in. She manages to create at least one character to whom the epithets of "noble" and "pathetic" can hardly be refused; and at least one other to which that of "only too natural," if with an exceptional and faulty kind of nature, must be accorded. . . . [She] preserves the tradition of the great *philosophe* group by showing that the writer of novels can also be the author of serious and valuable literature of another kind. (p. 19)

> George Saintsbury, *"Madame de Staël and Chateaubriand,"* in his A History of the French Novel (to the Close of the 19th Century): From 1800 to 1900, Vol. II *(reprinted by permission of the author), Macmillan and Co., Limited, 1917 (and reprinted by Russell & Russell, Inc., 1964, pp. 1-38).**

ALBERT THIBAUDET (essay date 1936)

All Mme. de Staël's books were talked before they were written. No one found more inspiration in others than did she, and yet the problem of her "sources" would never be posed, for they were superseded by innumerable streams, by a watercourse at ground level, by the reflections of men and the passage of their words. (p. 41)

Mme. de Staël, was the first model of the career of a great writer defined by the amenities of a *salon*.

Her books of criticism could be more aptly called manifestos. Hers was a passionate intelligence and, to flower, her ideas required the heat of enthusiasm. Since in addition she spoke and made others speak of the events and the ideas of the moment, since she lived in the present, since Jacques Necker's daughter aspired to be the comptroller general of ideas in France as long as she lived there, and since all this in her was governed by genius, she was able to write two manifestos of great compass, *Littérature* and *L'Allemagne*. The full title of the first, *De la Littérature considérée dans ses rapports avec les institutions sociales,* in itself marks a date. Such a title, the promises of which were virtually all kept, carried the idea and the method of Montesquieu into literature, prepared the way for an *Esprit des lois* of literature. Although its style is labored, congested, and heavy, exactly the opposite of Montesquieu's, the modern reader makes his way to the end of Mme. de Staël's book with considerably less effort than to the end of the *Esprit des lois*. He is kept interested by the movement of a conversation. The

first part, which deals with the past, is often venturesome or challengeable, even absurd, Mme. de Staël having read little and knowing books principally through the people who talked about them. But the second part introduces us into the heart of the literary consciousness of that generation of 1789, into the problems that were posed to them. (pp. 41-2)

The greatest injustice that could be committed toward *L'Allemagne* would be to judge it on itself, to demand of it inherent and lasting truths and beauties. It must be judged (and it was also from this point of view that Napoleon judged it) as a manifesto, for its capacity to excite, and as we judge Voltaire's *Lettres anglaises*. Friedrich Schiller said that he found more flashes than light in it, and we may add that the fire contained even more motive power than flashes. What was that motive power?

It is not to be found in the first part, *De l'Allemagne et des moeurs des allemands*. The Germans have never liked Mme. de Staël's convention of the German spirit or the platitudes that it has engendered. But the three other parts—*De la Littérature et des arts, La Philosophie et la morale, La Religion et l'enthousiasme*—though they abound in errors and trivialities, created or brought to light for the French a land of romanticism, or a climate of romanticism. That literary and philosophical Germany was to remain the Germany of literary and philosophical romanticism. (p. 44)

Delphine is the first society novel, written by a woman who lived at the center of society. When one has the key to the novel, *Delphine* can still imbue one's reading of it with something of the interest that the public of 1802 took in it. In contrast, though *Delphine* takes place from 1790 to 1792, in the midst of events that were already pitting one France against another, there is only a meaningless portrayal of political feelings and events. The length of the often languishing letters, the confusion of characters and adventures, the heavy and abstract style are all discouraging. It is remarkable, however, that Mme. de Staël's own letters, of which her cousin, Mme. Necker de Saussure, said that for fire and spirit they did not match her talk, are diametrically opposite in form to the artificial letters of *Delphine;* they leap out in spontaneity, disorder, vehemence, immediate sincerity, turmoil, and inaccuracy. The epistolary form, which was not natural to the author, certainly spoiled *Delphine*.

Equally deserving of being read, *Corinne* is of better workmanship. It was long considered Mme. de Staël's great book, and, from a certain decorative point of view, this opinion can be supported. The paths of her genius cross in it. . . . Just as, in *Delphine,* she had written the first novel that could be called "un Coeur de femme," so in *Corinne* she wrote the first "cosmopolis," the first novel of that cosmopolitan life that she lived and that made Geneva a way station for Britons and Frenchmen on the road to Italy. Geneva itself is absent from it, but the spirit of Geneva is in it.

Two subjects, but perfectly fused: this novel of cosmopolitan life and the novel of the woman of genius. (pp. 46-7)

Corinne ou l'Italie could also be "Corinne ou la Poésie." Unfortunately nothing is more lacking from Mme. de Staël's book than poetry. The granddaughter of Brandenburgers, Corinne travels in Italy in order to be educated, to "profit"; French by culture, she travels there in order to talk in the country and about it. But she does not travel in order to feel: a feeling for nature and a taste for the arts are foreign to her. She would have traded the Bay of Naples, she says, for a quarter of an hour of conversation. But for her the interest of the place is precisely the quarter of an hour of written conversation that it can suggest. Between the sensual sweep of the shore, the very lines of which the prose of *Les Martyrs* embraces, and the Neopolitan poetry of Lamartine, Corinne spreads out only a desert of ideas. Mme. de Staël has defined the genius of a woman as the splendid mourning of happiness. *Corinne,* in a certain way, is the thinking mourning of poetry. (pp. 47-8)

Corinne established the prestige of cosmopolitan life and of the international dialogue of ideas. It added to Europe's civilization. Corinne at the Cape of Miseno, inspired by that invented Plato at the Cape of Sunium of Abbé Jean-Jacques Barthélemy, belongs for us to the ingenuity of an Empire clock. But for thirty years, in Chateaubriand's circle, the friends of Mme. Récamier gathered beneath that portrait by François Gérard; an idealized Germaine, abandoned to enthusiastic prophecy, personified the grip of the mind and of letters on that romantic generation, and one is reminded of those altar paintings, with their two levels, in which the circle of the earth is dominated by the circle of glory. Perhaps all the poetry of *Corinne* has retreated from that name and that presence. But she remains, and she will endure. (p. 48)

> *Albert Thibaudet, "Madame de Staël," in his* French Literature from 1795 to Our Era, *translated by Charles Lam Markmann (translation copyright © 1967 by Harper & Row Publishers, Inc.; reprinted by permission of Harper & Row, Publishers, Inc.; originally published as* Histoire de la littérature française de 1789 à nos jours, *Stock, 1936), Funk & Wagnalls, 1968, pp. 41-9.*

MARY M. COLUM (essay date 1937)

[Madame de Staël] represented the strong currents of the eighteenth century that were passing away, as well as the new currents of the nineteenth century that were just setting in. From the side of the eighteenth century her mind had been formed by the Encyclopedia and the Encyclopedists, above all by Diderot, Voltaire, Rousseau and Helvetius—in fact, it may be said that the general tendencies of their thought became fused in her enfranchised and strongly intuitive intellect so that something new and prophetic of the new forces came out of it.

On the negative side these general tendencies were a desire to break away from the authority of tradition, from old forms of government, old social stratification, from the classical school in literature and from organized religion. On the positive side they stood for a belief in reason, in progress, in the continuous development of the mind and of the arts. They stood for joy in the delights of the senses, in the present time and in the passing moment. (p. 80)

In her book *De la Littérature* she had already criticized the shackled condition of French drama and poetry, which she declared had lost vigor under the domination of the salons; their endeavor to conform to the spirit of good society had placed grace and taste before originality and power. . . . French literature had stood in the same place too long, and this chiefly because of continual imitation of the masterpieces, both its own and the ancient Greek and Roman. Nothing in life ought to be stationary, and when art does not *change* it becomes petrified. Life had *changed;* the Revolution had altered the foundations of society, and now on the threshold of the nine-

teenth century, she perceived that a new sort of life was coming into being, and this new sort of life needed a new sort of literature. She offered to her countrymen as the type of this innovation the literature that was being produced in Germany, with its originality, its individuality, its free form, its philosophic depth, its independence of social conventions: this was what she called the literature of the North, modern literature, in contra-distinction to the literature of the South, classical literature. (pp. 82-4)

[Madame de Staël] is the originator of a school of social criticism which, especially in America, has had a noteworthy influence on life and literature. Her thesis that literature is an expression of society is also the thesis of every social and sociological critic since her time.

As a social critic Madame de Staël was the most stirring and the most original of the train of those who are her descendants. Like all social critics she had serious limitations on the purely literary and aesthetic side, which have to be taken into account in all applications of her theories, particularly her early theories as expressed in *De la Littérature*. She understood best the sort of writing that was the expression of society and thought that all literature was neither more nor less than this. In spite of her ardent espousal of the poetic theories of Herder she appears to have got little out of poetry except its intellectual and emotional content, a weakness of all social critics since her time, including the Americans. The poetic utterance itself, the apprehension of the form, all that really made the process of poetry different from the process of poetic, or imaginative, or lyrical prose, she seemed either constitutionally incapable of grasping, or, it may be, she was determined to measure all writing by the eighteenth-century standards of reason and logic. (pp. 86-7)

[However much Goethe and Schiller admired her,] they did not think she really understood their poetry. Her theory of literature as an expression of society works very well when applied to memoirs, diaries, certain kinds of drama and fiction; it was to work very well when applied to the new form of writing that was coming in and which, to some extent, she practised herself—the novel. Applied to literature of other types, the highly imaginative or the deeply philosophic, or to most types of poetry, it creaks ominously. To state its defects, however, is not to deny the great influence of the challenge that it gave, or to limit the enduring influence her own explanation of it has had on literary thought. It stirred new writers to the study of the actual life around them with the object of expressing this life and this society in literature, it started off whole movements in technique, especially in prose. But like all literary doctrines its limitations became clearly visible when applied wholesale to literature by too literal minds, which happened almost immediately. Her theory . . . explains some traits in all kinds of literature including the ancient Greek; it explained almost completely that new form of literature that was coming in—the novel—as well as the new drama of contemporary life; she herself showed that it could be applied with revealing results even to the sort of drama that was going out, the classical theatre of Racine.

But, after all, the work that was to have the most thrilling influence on her immediate successors was her book on Germany for which all her early work was a preparation and which represented the highest flight of her mind. (pp. 87-8)

Her comparison of the simplicity of Greek civilization, where men carried the action of the soul outwards, personifying nature and ideas, with the modern tendency towards continually turning the mind inwards, influenced people to take this complex modernity of mind more and more into account; so this had the effect of increasing the mood of introspection and subjectivism. Romantic literature, she believed, was the only type of literature natural to this modern mood, because it alone had, according to her conception, the potentiality of growth and renewal.

Through her power to foresee the trend that civilization and literature were taking, she was able to define in advance the character of the prose and poetry that were to be dominant in Europe for the next century. The qualities she saw in this new literature, "the sorrowful sentiment of the incompleteness of human destiny, melancholy, reverie, mysticism, the sense of the enigma of life," became the qualities pursued by the new writers. She pointed out the main defects of French literature: that in type, form, and content it belonged to a civilization that had become obsolete; that besides being a reflection of the Greek, it had been developed too much according to the demands of good society. The brilliant company that had congregated in the salons required above all a form of writing that could be easily read and understood. Profundity, the power of meditation, of brooding on life, all had been sacrificed to grace and good taste, qualities which ended in sterility, lack of fervor and monotony. (pp. 90-1)

What she actually succeeded in bringing about was a fusion of the qualities of the Teutonic and the Latin literatures, a fusion not entirely relished by some of her French critics: she has indeed been accused by them of diverting the national literature from its native direction. But, like Lessing, she affected profoundly the minds of the writers who came after her, and this in spite of a curious moralizing tone in her criticism, which belonged to her Genevan background rather than to the country she was addressing. Her emancipated literary ideas were frequently interlarded with such assertions as, that it was not in the power of a poet to draw forth a tragic effect from an incident which admitted the smallest tendency to an immoral principle, or that "literary criticism is not infrequently, indeed, a sort of treatise on morality," and she was sure that "perfect virtue" is the *beau idéal* of the intellectual world.

The main defect, however, in her criticism is her attitude to poetry. Schiller, indeed, went so far as to say "of what we call poetry, she has no perception." Yet, as a good disciple of Herder, she asserted the primacy of lyric poetry—that song on the wing that he said all real poetry was, and that all early poetry had been. She re-stated Herder's remarks about poetry, perhaps without really comprehending them; she even put forward the strange statement, very strange in a champion of lyricism, "poetry is, of all the arts, that which belongs closest to reason." Still, in spite of such limitations, she, more than any of the other critics up to her time, made ideas and literatures seem the common possession of all men and of all countries; she led the European spirit across national frontiers, even though she was not able to lead it across class frontiers. The new writers took as guide-posts watchwords and talismanic phrases drawn from her books. (pp. 92-4)

Mary M. Colum, "De Staël Brings the New Ideas to France" (1937), in her From These Roots: The Ideas That Have Made Modern Literature *(copyright 1937, 1944, copyright renewed © 1965 by Columbia University Press; reprinted by permission of the publisher),* Columbia University Press, 1944 *(and reprinted by Kennikat Press, Inc., 1967), pp. 78-97.*

RENÉ WELLEK (essay date 1955)

De la Littérature is much inferior to *De l'Allemagne*. Its program is, however, excellent; it attempts to show the "influence of religion, manners, and laws on literature, and what the influence is of literature on religion, manners, and laws." She thus resumes a subject treated before by Dubos, Marmontel, the Scotch sociologists, and Herder, and she does so resolutely by putting the central historical question on the title page. Unfortunately the book does not come up to the expectations raised by its program. Much of it has hardly anything to do with literature but is just one more survey of Western history in the speculative manner beloved by the 18th century. Much else is nothing but abstract declamation about virtue, glory, liberty, and happiness, fuzzy and pompous and so empty of concrete content that it is difficult to summarize. Yet there is a kernel of literary theory in the book; her conception of poetry stands out very clearly. It is in essence the conception of the early Diderot: poetry is emotion, sensibility, pathos, melancholy, sweet sorrow, somber reflection. . . . Passages which seem to defend the novel of manners (as she had done before in her *Essai sur les fictions*, . . . in which she disparaged the marvelous in fiction) are also a recommendation of sensibility, of a Rousseauistic analysis of emotions. Even her new defense of the supernatural, of witches and ghosts in Shakespeare, is prompted by her desire for emotional upheavals: for the effects of terror and awe and the thrills of the horrible.

This emotionalist theory is combined, rather incongruously, with a belief in perfectibility, a frantic faith in progress, which clashes oddly with her taste for melancholy and her admiration for Ossian. Madame de Staël displays the double point of view . . . [of] Warton, Hurd, and Blair, in so obvious a juxtaposition that its contradictoriness would seem apparent. In theory, Madame de Staël tries to preserve a division between the arts of imagination, which are not progressive, and the inventions, sciences, politics, morals, and even sensibility, shown especially in the improved position of women, which are progressing steadily and uninterruptedly. But the two beliefs, the primitivistic applicable to poetry and the intellectualistic applicable to social life, cannot be kept separate by her. In spite of compliments to the earliest writers for their pictures of manners and nature Madame de Staël cannot help seeing the history of literature as a constant progress of refinement, of sensibility and pathos, leading up directly to Rousseau and Young. (pp. 220-21)

Details in Madame de Staël's literary history are often vague, wrong, or simply absent. Her discussion of Greek literature is almost grotesque. The Greeks were supposed to lack a "more moral philosophy," a "profounder sensibility." There is no moral conclusion in Aeschylus. Plato lacks method and propounds a bizarre metaphysics. The Greek historians trace only events and neglect characters and causes. The main offense of the Greeks is the low status granted to women: Telemachus ordering Penelope to be silent must have conjured the vision of some man giving the same order to Madame de Staël. Latin literature is treated with more sympathy and knowledge, but medieval writings seem hardly known to her at all. (pp. 221-22)

Shakespeare, whom she discusses in some detail, must also conform to her preconceptions. He is the great melancholiac, a master of pathos. His deviation from the rules is defended by the familiar argument that they are merely local, temporal rules which Shakespeare need not have kept. But she admits that he also violates the eternal principles of taste: his mixture of the tragic and comic and his display of horrors are condemned as genuine faults. Madame de Staël tolerates the marvelous in Shakespeare, if it is emotionally effective, but she thinks that *Macbeth* would be better without the witches, even though she gives them an allegorical interpretation. She has, however, no appreciation of Shakespeare's comedy. Falstaff is called a "popular caricature."

Restoration comedy is judged almost as Lamb judged it later. It seems to her completely divorced from English reality. English audiences, she asserts, enjoy Congreve as fairy tales, as fantastic images of a world which is not theirs. Such an art seems to her very inferior to Molière's, which requires life in a genuine society. (p. 222)

Thus admiration for the vein of pathos and sensibility in English 18th-century literature (which includes her favorite Ossian) goes well with her taste in French letters. She admired Racine and Fénelon for their delicacy, but she goes into throes of ecstasy only at Voltaire's *Tancrède,* which produces emotions greater than Racine, "all kinds of rapture [*volupté*] of the soul." . . . Setting on fire is her main view of the function of literature: it is emotionalist and rhetorical, but also moralistic and utilitarian. The masterpieces of literature produce an agitating transport of admiration in us. "Virtue becomes an involuntary impulse, a movement which passes into the blood."

At this stage Madame de Staël has no means of distinguishing between imaginative literature and eloquence. She hesitates about the value of verse and clearly favors the impassioned prose of Rousseau above all other forms of style. Yet she cannot distinguish between such writing and the eloquence of an advocate or even a conversation. When she discusses the future of literature—she was writing under the Republic, just at the beginning of the rise of Napoleon—she sees its effects as eminently social and practical. . . . She believes that conviction and sincerity are a guarantee of truth, that sentiment cannot err. Thus she manages to combine an ardent faith in progress and republicanism with a sense of melancholy about human life, which to her is both sad and delicious. When she specifically refers to the traditional genres, tragedy, epic, and lyric, she recognizes that the decay of taste and manners was brought about by the Revolution. But very timidly she recommends only such innovations for the French stage as would allow it to move in the direction of historical tragedy. In poetry she sympathizes with Delille, Fontanes, and Saint-Lambert, the imitators of English descriptive poetry; for the novel she wants poetic prose in the style of Rousseau or Bernardin de Saint-Pierre, or a feminine novel of sensibility. Literature must have a social effect. Its emotions must lead us to virtue, meaning Republican virtue, enlightenment, liberalism. It is not difficult to relate this effect to her critical terms: virtue is for her emotion, enlightenment is sympathy, liberalism, primarily a feeling of the heart. (pp. 223-24)

[*De l'Allemagne*] cannot be judged as primarily a work of literary criticism. It is the picture of a whole nation, a sketch of national psychology and sociology, and also something of a personal travel book. The discussion of literature in a narrow sense takes up about a third of the book and is constantly pursued with a view toward a general characterization of the nation and interspersed with personal impressions.

From our point of view these parts are greatly superior, as poetics and criticism, to *De la Littérature.* The vague rhetoric, the factual ignorance are gone. The bulk of the book conveys solid information on the texts known to Madame de Staël,

whatever her lapses and gaps in knowledge may be from the point of view of a modern student of German literature. (pp. 224-25)

[Madame de Staël] has kept her emotionalist conception of poetry. She shows no sympathy for the symbolist view of poetry, or even for a mystical view, as an access to a higher reality, though there are a few traces of these doctrines in the book. On several occasions she alludes unfavorably to the teachings of the "new school" of the German romantics, especially to the Schlegels' exaltation of objectivity and irony, to their disparagement of tears as an effect of literature, to their minimizing of mere subject matter, and to their general intolerance. (p. 226)

Madame de Staël did not change her basic view of literature and poetry: *De l'Allemagne* is completely continuous with *De la Littérature.* But she had greatly improved as a literary critic, especially in analyzing and characterizing individual works of art. "The animated description of masterpieces" is her critical ideal, an ideal that she achieves rather often. (p. 227)

[Her] sympathy for German literature is always tempered by her almost instinctive adherence to the principles of French taste. She does not hold them rigidly; she draws comfort from the distinction between eternal and temporal principles and is quite ready to give up the rules. But the eternal principles are constantly interpreted as following closely the specific taste of French neo-classicism. She seems frequently of two minds. Granting certain irregular beauties, she deplores bad taste and extravagancies. She would like to have it both ways: German literature more regular, more tasteful, and French literature less circumscribed by rigid conventions, freer to indulge in flights of imagination. She hopes that Frenchmen would be more "religious," Germans a little "more worldly."

But this desire for a reconciliation on middle ground, for a harmonious European spirit, is counteracted by her other wish that each nation should express its national character as clearly and freely as possible. (p. 229)

Her exposition of the contrast between the classical and the romantic culminates in her avowal of preference for romantic literature because it alone can be improved, "because, having its roots in our own soil, it alone can grow and revive; it expresses our religion; it recalls our history." The literature of the ancients is with us a transplanted literature: romantic or chivalrous literature is indigenous.

Her conception of the epic is completely primitivistic, Ossianic. "An epic poem is almost never the work of a single man and the ages themselves, so to speak, work at it . . . the characters of an epic poem must represent the original character of a nation." Madame de Staël finds the differences of national taste most pronounced in the drama. She can say that "nothing would be more absurd than wanting to impose the same system on all nations." But she does not really keep her own advice and makes concrete proposals for the liberalizing of the French system, criticizing German plays for their lack of conformity to French standards. She shares Johnson's and Schlegel's views on the unities. Only the unity of action is indispensable; change of place and extension of time are allowed if they increase the emotion and make the illusion stronger. She disapproves of the uniform solemnity of French alexandrines, obviously preferring prose, and she recommends historical tragedy as the natural tendency of the century, the main remedy against the threatening sterility of French drama. Yet she constantly disclaims recommending the adoption of German principles and can be very severe on German lapses from taste. (pp. 229-30)

De l'Allemagne contributed importantly to that "world literature" which Goethe envisaged later as a synthesis of the European spirit. The very limitations of Madame de Staël's taste and sympathy enhanced the effect of her book. Her literary theory hardly went beyond Rousseauistic emotionalism. Her taste is mildly preromantic, in favor of historical tragedy, descriptive poetry, and the novel of sensibility. . . .

[Nothing] can diminish the merit of the book. It really made a breach in the Chinese wall between the countries. It was enormously important for the spread of the term and concept of the "romantic." It was an early step in the history of French emancipation from the tenets of neoclassicism and a manifesto of the new literary cosmopolitanism. (p. 231)

> *René Wellek, "Madame de Staël and Chateaubriand," in his* A History of Modern Criticism, 1750-1950 *(copyright, 1955, by Yale University Press), Yale University Press, 1955, pp. 216-40.**

JANET TODD (essay date 1980)

[*Delphine*] is an epistolary novel, written when third-person narration had carried the day. The oppositions in period and form are paralleled by oppositions in the novel, which in turn account for the strange tension of writing and acting. The book presents the story of an unconventional, superior woman who pursues a passion opposed by the conventional, inferior society which ultimately defeats her. But another story is told beside the first—of an unconventional, superior woman who both desires and fears to be conventional and inferior, who internalizes society's conventions and opposes them at the same time. The novel is then both revolutionary and reactionary, in keeping with the two periods it inhabits. Its dual nature is intimated again in its women: Delphine, the seemingly unconventional, is kept from convention by women who are themselves either sincerely or hypocritically conventional.

In her own account and the accounts of friends, Delphine combines sensibility and grace, genius and beauty. Indeed in her virtues she is almost supernatural, an angel among mortals; a dying friend clutches at her to intercede before God and she plays the priest éclat at two death scenes. (pp. 227-28)

Conventional society—almost a character in this novel—is unappreciative, even contemptuous, of such youthful goodness, and Delphine at first returns the feelings; she has, she believes, the qualities for autonomy—for happiness within the self without social approval. Yet her rejection is superficial, a verbal repulse that carries only moderate conviction, and, when society seduces with more subtlety, she responds ambiguously. Although she scorns many of society's cruder values—female stupidity and the inexpiable sexual sin for women, for example—she is drawn to its ideal of sacrifical femininity, of the woman's subservience to the man she loves, however spectacular her own gifts and accomplishments may be. And she yearns for passion, whose social dynamics require the woman to repudiate her autonomous self. . . . The ambivalence and

fatedness of Delphine's passionate pursuit is represented in Leonce, who is object of a passion that is both conventional in its subjection of the woman and unconventional in its illegal intensity. While he seems to free Delphine from social constraint, he is also the embodiment of constraint—he is perfect but for one fault, an excessive concern for honor, reputation, and public opinion. Answering Delphine's deep social need for loving and being loved, then, he also functions as society's revenge on the woman who insisted she scorned its power. (pp. 228-29)

Delphine is ultimately an ambiguous novel, built on antithesis as well as single thesis. The struggle of an independent, superior woman for her love against the institutions of society, it is also the suffering of a divided soul pulled toward independence on one side and love and society on the other. In her preface, Staël suggested that events of her book had little importance in themselves and were intended more as occasions for emotional display. Yet it is less in these passions alone than in the dialectic of events and expressed passions that the poignancy of the novel lies. In this dialectic the ultimate opposition appears to be not vice and virtue, society and love, or even Delphine and Leonce against the rest, but Delphine and her female friends against Leonce and the social image of woman he implies. The politics of revolution and reaction is, then, not merely a context of the book but also an ironic commentary on it. The Bastille has fallen and men have been forced through the gates, in much the same way as women in this novel leave their social prison through female friends. And yet women remain imprisoned in the image of the prison, an image which the book's rhetoric does much to sustain. Like many sufferers from the old regime, Delphine edges her way toward an unwelcome freedom. But, despite female friendship, she ends her life with Leonce alone, reinstated in a cell she has voluntarily entered. (pp. 244-45)

> *Janet Todd, "Political Friendship," in her* Women's Friendship in Literature *(copyright © 1980 Columbia University Press; reprinted by permission of the publisher), Columbia University Press, 1980, pp. 191-245.**

ADDITIONAL BIBLIOGRAPHY

Andrews, Wayne. *Germaine: A Portrait of Madame de Staël.* New York: Atheneum, 1963, 237 p.
    A modern view of the life of Madame de Staël.

Blennerhassett, Lady Charlotte. *Madame de Staël: Her Friends and Her Influence in Politics and Literature.* 3 vols. Translated by J. E. Cumming. London: Chapman and Hall, 1889.
    The definitive biography of Madame de Staël.

Goldsmith, Margaret. *Madame de Staël: Portrait of a Liberal in the Revolutionary Age.* London: Longmans, Green, 1938, 276 p.
    An analysis of Madame de Staël's political concepts.

Herold, J. Christopher. *Mistress to an Age: A Life of Madame de Staël.* New York: Bobbs-Merrill, 1958, 500 p.
    A detailed biographical study.

Harriet (Elizabeth) Beecher Stowe

1811-1896

(Also wrote under the pseudonym of Christopher Crowfield)
American novelist and essayist.

Referred to as the "Crusader in Crinoline" by one reviewer, Stowe stirred the conscience of the nation and the world with her famous novel, *Uncle Tom's Cabin; or, Life among the Lowly*. Its strong humanitarian tone and antislavery theme made *Uncle Tom's Cabin* one of the most popular and profoundly influential novels of the nineteenth century.

Stowe was raised in Litchfield, Connecticut, in a home with strong Puritan values. The daughter, sister, and wife of outstanding pulpit orators and Calvinist preachers, she developed a strict moral and spiritual code which influenced all her writings. She later rebelled against the harshness of her faith and converted to Episcopalianism. Still, the moral earnestness of her youth is evident in the antislavery novels, which she described as "works of religion." Stowe considered herself "an instrument of the Holy Spirit."

In order to supplement her preacher husband's meager wages, Stowe contributed short stories and sketches to several magazines, often using the pseudonym Christopher Crowfield. In 1842, she collected several of her magazine pieces and published them as *The Mayflower; or, Sketches of Scenes and Characters among the Descendants of the Puritans*. These stories presage Stowe's later work, for they are didactic in tone, and describe America and its people.

Uncle Tom's Cabin, originally serialized in an abolitionist magazine, *The National Era*, was inspired by a visit to Kentucky. The people Stowe met there, as well as the scenes and events she experienced are easily recognizable. The success the novel achieved was phenomenal: never before in America was a piece so widely read, adapted, and debated. Never before had an author received such diverse attention. In the North she was praised by some, but criticized by abolitionists for being too lenient; in the South she was reviled. The South charged her with slander, and a number of "anti-Tom" novels appeared as a challenge to the book. But Stowe defended herself and her masterpiece with *A Key to Uncle Tom's Cabin: Presenting the Original Facts and Documents upon Which the Story Is Founded*, in which she confronted her antagonists with court records, newspapers, laws, and letters in order to substantiate her message. The timing of the novel was also a part of its success, for it was published during the height of the abolitionist movement and after the passage of the Fugitive Slave Act of 1850. The opposing tensions reached a climax within a decade, with the outbreak of the Civil War. Stowe's contribution to the rising political turmoil was commented on by Abraham Lincoln, who said, "So this is the little woman who brought on this big war." Her second antislavery novel, *Dred: A Tale of the Great Dismal Swamp*, did not achieve the fame of *Uncle Tom's Cabin*, but is important in tracing Stowe's stylistic development and her continuing concern for the plight of the slaves.

With the exception of *Agnes of Sorrento* and *Sunny Memories of Foreign Lands*, Stowe's later works reflect her youth, her family, and life in the United States. Her use of local scenery

and dialect, particularly in *Oldtown Folks*, anticipates Mark Twain's *The Adventures of Huckleberry Finn*. *The Minister's Wooing*, an exposé of the parodox and irony in the Calvinist religion, has been compared to Nathaniel Hawthorne's *The Scarlet Letter* and has established her as an important New England novelist. However, her reputation in England diminished after she wrote "The True Story of Lady Byron's Life" for the *Atlantic Monthly*. Although harshly criticized for boldly exposing Lord Byron's moral delinquency, Stowe continued her defense of Lady Byron in *Lady Byron Vindicated: A History of the Byron Controversy, from Its Beginning in 1816 to the Present Time*. Later the charges she made were proven correct, and Stowe regained her popular reputation abroad.

Despite her prolific output, Stowe is mainly remembered for one novel, *Uncle Tom's Cabin*. It is a remarkable work of literary and historical significance. Some critics suggest that Stowe reinforced negative conceptions of blacks in expressing her beliefs. In the mid-twentieth century, some have interpreted Uncle Tom as a servile and complacent character and little more than a negative stereotype. The term "Uncle Tom," therefore, carries a strongly pejorative connotation. However, most critics feel that Stowe's failure to present a realistic depiction of blacks was due to her didactic purpose and not to any racist sentiment. While Stowe is regarded as a significant literary figure, through the impact of her writing she has also come to be regarded as a force in American history.

(See also *Dictionary of Literary Biography, Vol. 1: The American Renaissance in New England.*)

PRINCIPAL WORKS

A New England Sketch   (short story)   1833
The Mayflower; or, Sketches of Scenes and Characters among the Descendants of the Puritans   (short stories) 1843
Uncle Tom's Cabin; or, Life among the Lowly   (novel) 1852
A Key to Uncle Tom's Cabin: Presenting the Original Facts and Documents upon Which the Story Is Founded (essays)   1853
Sunny Memories of Foreign Lands   (travel essay)   1854
Dred: A Tale of the Great Dismal Swamp   (novel)   1856
The Minister's Wooing   (novel)   1859
Agnes of Sorrento   (novel)   1862
The Pearl of Orr's Island: A Story of the Coast of Maine (novel)   1862
Oldtown Folks   (novel)   1869
Lady Byron Vindicated: A History of the Byron Controversy, from Its Beginning in 1816 to the Present Time   (essay) 1870
Sam Lawson's Oldtown Fireside Stories   (short stories) 1872
Poganuc People: Their Loves and Lives   (novel)   1878

HARRIET BEECHER STOWE   (essay date 1852)

The writer has often been inquired of, by correspondents from different parts of the country, whether this narrative is a true one; and to these inquiries she will give one general answer.

The separate incidents that compose the narrative are, to a very great extent, authentic, occurring, many of them, either under her own observation or that of her personal friends. She or her friends have observed characters the counterpart of almost all that are here introduced; and many of the sayings are word for word as heard herself, or reported to her.

The personal appearance of Eliza, the characters ascribed to her, are sketches drawn from life. The incorruptible fidelity, piety, and honesty of Uncle Tom had more than one development, to her personal knowledge. Some of the most deeply tragic and romantic, some of the most terrible incidents, have also their parallel in reality. (p. 502)

The author hopes she has done justice to that nobility, generosity, and humanity, which in many cases characterize individuals at the South. Such instances save us from utter despair of our kind. But, she asks any person, who knows the world, are such characters *common,* anywhere?

For many years of her life, the author avoided all reading upon or allusion to the subject of slavery, considering it as too painful to be inquired into, and one which advancing light and civilization would certainly live down. But, since the legislative act of 1850, when she heard, with perfect surprise and consternation, Christian and humane people actually recommending the remanding escaped fugitives into slavery, as a duty

binding on good citizens,—when she heard, on all hands, from kind, compassionate, and estimable people, in the free states of the North, deliberations and discussions as to what Christian duty could be on this head,—she could only think, These men and Christians cannot know what slavery is; if they did, such a question could never be open for discussion. And from this arose a desire to exhibit it in a *living dramatic reality*. She has endeavored to show it fairly, in its best and its worst phases. In its *best* aspect, she has, perhaps, been successful; but, oh! who shall say what yet remains untold in that valley and shadow of death, that lies the other side?

To you, generous, noble-minded men and women, of the South,—you, whose virtue, and magnanimity, and purity of character, are the greater for the severer trial it has encountered,—to you is her appeal. Have you not, in your own secret souls, in your own private conversings, felt that there are woes and evils, in this accursed system, far beyond what are here shadowed, or can be shadowed? Can it be otherwise? Is *man* ever a creature to be trusted with wholly irresponsible power? (pp. 504-05)

The writer has given only a faint shadow, a dim picture, of the anguish and despair that are, at this very moment, riving thousands of hearts, shattering thousands of families, and driving a helpless and sensitive race to frenzy and despair. There are those living who know the mothers whom this accursed traffic has driven to the murder of their children; and themselves seeking in death a shelter from woes more dreaded than death. Nothing of tragedy can be written, can be spoken, can be conceived, that equals the frightful reality of scenes daily and hourly acting on our shores, beneath the shadow of American law, and the shadow of the cross of Christ. (pp. 505-06)

This is an age of the world when nations are trembling and convulsed. A mighty influence is abroad, surging and heaving the world, as with an earthquake. And is America safe? Every nation that carries in its bosom great and unredressed injustice has in it the elements of this last convulsion.

For what is this mighty influence thus rousing in all nations and languages those groanings that cannot be uttered, for man's freedom and equality?

O, Church of Christ, read the signs of the times! Is not this power the spirit of HIM whose kingdom is yet to come, and whose will to be done on earth as it is in heaven? (p. 510)

A day of grace is yet held out to us. Both North and South have been guilty before God; and the *Christian Church* has a heavy account to answer. Not by combining together, to protect injustice and cruelty, and making a common capital of sin, is this Union to be saved,—but by repentance, justice, and mercy; for, not surer is the eternal law by which the millstone sinks in the ocean, than that stronger law, by which injustice and cruelty shall bring on nations the wrath of Almighty God! (pp. 510-11)

> *Harriet Beecher Stowe, "Concluding Remarks," in her* Uncle Tom's Cabin; or, Life Among the Lowly, *J. P. Jewett & Company, 1852 (and reprinted by Collier—Macmillan, 1962, pp. 502-11).*

THE LITERARY WORLD   (essay date 1852)

Mrs. Stowe, abandoning her husband's hose, has seized upon that of the abolition engine and is playing away a full stream upon Southern people and Southern institutions generally. How to treat her book [*Uncle Tom's Cabin*] is our difficulty at present, for as a lengthy abolition tract, we desire no acquaintance with it, as a political affair it is entirely out of our province, its descriptions of the white and the colored races as they exist below ''Mason's and Dixon's'' are too nearly antipodical to reality to entitle it to much usefulness as an ethnological essay, and finally when warm weather is coming rapidly in, a novel, with heroes and heroines exclusively African, and winding up by the introduction of a colored lady whom a white gentleman of birth, respectability, and wealth has taken to wife, thereby setting a laudable example to the rising generation of amalgamationists, is rather too potent and decidedly odorous for our—perhaps fastidious—taste. . . .

[*Uncle Tom's Cabin*], despite its subject and the mode of handling it, has many good points, and we are disposed to do full justice to them; but unlike the fair author,—being somewhat indisposed to all amalgamation,—we will not serve up the ludicrous and the revolting together. . . .

Mrs. Stowe is evidently intended by nature for an humorous writer, and an occasional dash of wit and fun prove that her forte is rather farce than comedy and tragedy or political economy. . . .

The episode of Eva St. Clair is truly beautiful and affecting—nay, for humor and pathos, a gem—and causes us the more to regret that such scenes should be introduced but to gild a pill of abolition gun-cotton, and to persuade innocent women and ignorant men to swallow it as good, honest medicine. The negro dialogue has been very generally commended, and we are willing to confess that the author knows quite as much about it as she does of slaves and slavery, but unfortunately very little of either. . . .

With the incidents of the book—always excepting the episode of Eva—we have small wish to meddle. They are revolting and unjust, inasmuch as atrocities that may have been committed by some depraved wretch devoid of human feeling, are here set down and pictured forth, as if such things were of common and daily occurrence.

We can assure Mrs. Stowe that Planters are neither in the habit of severing families, selling infants, or whipping their best hands to death. (p. 291)

We cannot but regret the gusto with which our authoress describes all the incidents concerning the running off of the various negroes, first feigning a series of horrible persecutions in order to enlist the reader's feelings in their escape, and their accustoming us to scenes of violence, shooting down of pursuers, &c., in the very spirit of the late Pennsylvania massacre.

Slavery is bad enough, but for Heaven's sake, Mrs. Stowe! wife of one clergyman, daughter of another, and sister to half a dozen, respect the cloud of black cloth with which you are surrounded, and if you *will* write of such matters, give us plain unvarnished truth, and strive to advise us in our trouble—not to preach up bloodshed and massacre, for, by our present ''Manual for Runaways,'' you but rivet the chains of those whom we firmly believe you honestly and truly desire to serve. . . .

On the eve of closing a book capable of producing infinite mischief—for it lacks neither wit nor talent, only truth—she very naturally appeals again to ''the generous, noble-minded men and women of the South,'' you whose virtue, and purity, and magnanimity of character, &c., &c.

Modesty! thy name is Beecher. (p. 292)

> ''*'Colored' Views*,'' *in* The Literary World, *Vol. X, No. 17, April 24, 1852, pp. 291-92.*

THE WESTMINSTER AND FOREIGN QUARTERLY REVIEW
(essay date 1852)

[In ''**Uncle Tom's Cabin**'' Mrs. Stowe] has hit the nail on the head, not only as a *littérateur*, but as an abolitionist. No senator in Congress, no editor in a leading article, can come round the subject and round the reader, and into the heart of both so effectively, as this book—so superior is dramatic representation (where it can be employed) to the sharpest weapons of logic and the loudest thunders of oratory. To its employment in the present instance many objections will be made; but slavery, besides being an abstract theory of human relations, and as such debateable, is a concrete reality of human life, and, as such, dramatizable. . . . As one of the ''peculiar institutions'' of the luxurious South, [slavery] had become positively picturesque. In the North, it had become a question of law and logic, to be settled by the policeman and the parson with their fugitive-warrants and passages of ''holy writ.'' How was this to be remedied? By representing it as a question of humanity, by reproducing the forgotten or concealed realities of the system—thereby dispelling the haze of romance which in the course of years gathers about the most hideous corruptions, and transferring it, if possible, to the side of righteousness and truth. Such has been the aim of ''**Uncle Tom's Cabin;**'' and it is due to the author to say, that she has achieved her difficult and delicate task without falling into either vulgarity or exaggeration—the two dangers most imminent in the treatment of such a subject. . . . [''**Uncle Tom**''] is not exclusively a book of horrors; and it cannot be accused of presenting a one-sided picture: it is remarkable rather for its breadth of view, its variety of character and incident, its genial charity—tracing the evils of the system rather to its essential nature than to accidental circumstances, and showing that its worst features sometimes grow out of the mildest conditions in which it can possibly exist. (pp. 282-83)

> ''*Contemporary Literature of America*,'' *in* The Westminster and Foreign Quarterly Review, *Vol. LVIII, No. CXIII, July 1, 1852, pp. 272-87.**

CHARLES DICKENS   (essay date 1852)

I have read [*Uncle Tom's Cabin*] with the deepest interest and sympathy, and admire, more than I can express to you, both the generous feeling which inspired it, and the admirable power with which it is executed.

If I might suggest a fault in what has so charmed me, it would be that you go too far and seek to prove too much. The wrongs and atrocities of slavery are, God knows! case enough. I doubt there being any warrant for making out the African race to be a great race, or for supposing the future destinies of the world to lie in that direction; and I think this extreme championship likely to repel some useful sympathy and support.

Your book is worthy of any head and any heart that ever inspired a book. I am much your debtor, and I thank you most fervently and sincerely.

> *Charles Dickens, in his letter to Harriet Beecher Stowe on July 17, 1852, in* Uncle Tom's Cabin; or, Life Among the Lowly *by Harriet Beecher Stowe,*

F. E. Longley's, 1881 (and reprinted by Collier—Macmillan, 1962, p. 24).

THE LIBERATOR   (essay date 1852)

I am an Abolitionist heart and soul, and though I revere the spirit of the authoress, still, on reading *Uncle Tom's Cabin*, I look on her as the worst enemy of a good cause. . . .

I fear the book will raise the jests of the profane, and the sneers of those whom we want most to bring to our party. . . .

The book, which might have done worlds of good in other hands, will sink to the sewer of literature in penny numbers, and will be turned to the worst of instead of to the best purposes. If this book be really a faithful record of what slavery is in America, and of what slaves are, let slavery remain and work out its own cure.

"'Uncle Tom's Cabin'," in The Liberator, *Vol. XXII, No. 43, October 22, 1852, p. 170.*

SOUTHERN LITERARY MESSENGER   (essay date 1852)

[*Uncle Tom's Cabin*] is a fiction—professedly a fiction; but, unlike other works of the same type, its purpose is not amusement, but proselytism. (p. 721)

We have examined the production of Mrs. Harriet Beecher Stowe, which we purpose to review, and we discover it to belong to [this] class, and to be one of the most reprehensible specimens of the tribe. We own that we approach the criticism of the work with peculiar sensations of both reluctance and repugnance. We take no pleasure in the contact with either folly or vice; and we are unwilling to handle the scandalous libel in the manner in which it deserves to be treated, in consideration of its being the effusion of one of that sex, whose natural position entitles them to all forbearance and courtesy, and which, in all ordinary cases, should be shielded even from just severity, by that protecting mantle which the name and thought of woman cast over even the erring and offending members of the sex. But higher interests are involved: the rule that every one bearing the name and appearance of a lady, should receive the delicate gallantry and considerate tenderness which are due to a lady, is not absolutely without exception. If she deliberately steps beyond the hallowed precints—the enchanted circle—which encompass her as with the halo of divinity, she has wantonly forfeited her privilege of immunity as she has irretrievable lost our regard, and the harshness which she may provoke is invited by her own folly and impropriety. . . . We will endeavor, then, as far as possible, to forget Mrs. Harriet Beecher Stowe, and the individuality of her authorship, and will strive to concentrate our attention and our reprehension on her book. . . . (pp. 721-22)

We have said that *Uncle Tom's Cabin* is a fiction. It is a fiction throughout; a fiction in form; a fiction in its facts; a fiction in its representations and coloring; a fiction in its statements; a fiction in its sentiments, a fiction in its morals, a fiction in its religion; a fiction in its inferences; a fiction equally with regard to the subjects it is designed to expound, and with respect to the manner of their exposition. It is a fiction, not for the sake of more effectually communicating truth; but for the purpose of more effectually disseminating a slander. It is a fictitious or fanciful representation for the sake of producing fictitious or false impressions. Fiction is its form and falsehood is its end. (p. 722)

[In *Uncle Tom's Cabin,* the vice of] depraved application of fiction and its desolating consequences, may be readily detected. Every fact is distorted, every incident discolored, in order to awaken rancorous hatred and malignant jealousies between the citizens of the same republic, the fellow countrymen whose interests and happiness are linked with the perpetuity of a common union, and with the prosperity of a common government. With the hope of expediting or achieving the attainment of a fanatical, and in great measure, merely speculative idea, of substituting the real thraldom of free labor for the imaginary hardships of slavery—the hydra of dissension is evoked by the diabolical spells of falsehood, misrepresentation, and conscious sophistry. What censure shall we pass upon a book, calculated, if not designed, to produce such a result? What condemnation upon an effort to revive all the evils of civil discord—to resuscitate all the dangers of disunion—allayed with such difficulty, and but recently lulled into partial quiescence by the efforts of the sages and the patriotic forbearance of the States of the Confederacy? What language shall we employ when such a scheme is presented, as the *beau ideal* of sublimated virtue, under the deceptive form of literary amusement, and is seriously offered as the recreation of our intellectual leisure? (pp. 722-23)

[Though] we condescend to give more attention to *Uncle Tom's Cabin* than we think such a work or such an attack entitled to on its own score, we will not prolong our disagreeable duty so far as to follow it through all the mazes of its misrepresentation—through all the loathsome labyrinths of imaginary cruelty and crime, in which its prurient fancy loves to roam. So far as a false statement can be rectified by positive denial,—so far as misrepresentation can be corrected by direct, abundant, unquestionable proof of the error, this service has been already adequately rendered by the newspapers and periodical literature of the South. We have intimated our belief, that both the negation and the refutation are useless, for our adversaries are as deaf and as poisonous too, as the blind adder. But this service has already been fully rendered. It would, then, be a work of supererogation to repeat the profitless labor, to trace the separate threads of delusion which enter into the tissue of deception, and to exhibit the false dyes and the tangles of fiction which aid in the composition of the web. It would seem almost a hopeless waste of time to show how the truth which has been so scantily employed, has been prostituted to base uses, and made to minister to the general falsehood; how human sympathies have been operated on to encourage and sanctify most unholy practices: how every commandment of the decalogue and all the precepts of the Gospel have been violated in order to extend the sanctification of the higher-law, to every crime denounced and condemned by laws, human and divine. Unfortunately for the cause of the South, the evidence for or against her, is neither weighed nor regarded: the defence is rejected without consideration, and all slanders are cordially received, not because they are known or proved to be true, but because they are wished to be so; and harmonise with preconceived and malicious prejudices. We have not the ear of the court; our witnesses are distrusted and discredited, and in most cases, they are not even granted a hearing; but the case is presumed to be against us, and by a summary process a verdict of guilty is rendered, without any regard to the real merits of the cause, but in compliance with the fanatical complicity of the jurors. Why is this? and what is the court before which we are required to plead?

Assuredly, there is no necessity to convince the slave owners, or the residents in the Southern States, that the condition of society, the *status* of the slave, the incidents and accidents of slavery, the practices or even the rights of masters, are exhibited in a false light, and are falsely stated in *Uncle Tom's Cabin;* and that, by whatever jugglery or sorcery the result is obtained, the picture, with all its ostensible desire of truthful delineation, is distorted and discolored, and presents at one time a caricature, at another a total misrepresentation of things amongst us. It is not to Southern men that it is necessary to address any argument on a topic like this. They are already aware of the grossness of the slander by their own observation and experience. No, the tribunal to which our defence must be addressed, is the public sentiment of the North and of Europe. In both latitudes, the case is already prejudged and decided against us; in both, popular ignorance and popular fanaticism, and a servile press have predetermined the question. . . . The ignorant and unreflecting outcry of those whose social condition is infinitely below that of our slaves, is eagerly caught up by the myriad serfs of the dominant cottonocracy; is reechoed from all points of the horizon; and is believed to be the language of truth because it is the clamor of a multitude. A better class stimulates and repeats the defamation, because their interests are supposed to accord with the perpetuation of ignorance and the propagation of delusion on this subject; and because it is a cheap expenditure of philanthropy to melt in sentimental sorrow over remote and imaginary evils, while neglecting the ever present ills and pressing afflictions in their own vicinage. Such a tone of sentiment among both the educated and the illiterate classes in those communities where literature is a trade and the mercenary principles of Grub street constitute the morality of all intellectual avocations, generates a literary atmosphere which is fatal to the dissemination of unpopular truths, and which gives singular vitality and longevity to error, by pandering to the popular desire for its circulation and confirmation. In this manner, we may understand both the cause of the thousands of copies of *Uncle Tom's Cabin,* which have been sold at the North and in England, and also the extreme difficulty, not to say absolute impossibility, of securing a dispassionate hearing for our defence, or of introducing the antidote where the poison has spread. There is no obduracy so impracticable—no deafness so incurable—as that Pharisaical self-sanctification and half-conscious hypocrisy, which gilds its own deliberate delusions with the false colors of an extravagant morality, and denounces all dissent from its own fanatical prejudices, as callous vice and irremediable sin. The whole phalanx of Abolition literature, in all its phases and degrees, is fully imbued with this self-righteous spirit; and its influence, under all forms—in fiction and in song—in sermon and in essay—in political harangue as in newspaper twaddle— is completely turned against us: and an aggregation of hostile tendencies is brought to bear upon us so as to deny to our complaints, our recriminations, or our apologies, either consideration or respect. (pp. 723-24)

It is a natural and inevitable consequence of [the] silly and fatal indifference to the high claims of a native and domestic literature, that the South is now left at the mercy of every witling and scribbler who panders to immediate profit or passing popularity, by harping on a string in unison with the prevailing fanaticism. It is a necessary result of the same long continued imprudence, that no defence can be heard, no refutation of vile slander regarded in the courts of literature, which comes from a land whose literary claims have been disparaged and crushed by its own blind recklessness and meanness. In *Uncle Tom's Cabin,* there is certainly neither extraordinary genius nor remarkable strength: the attack is unquestionably a weak one: there is only that semblance of genius which springs

from intense fanaticism and an earnest purpose; and that plausibility which is due to concentrated energy and a narrow one-sided exposition of human afflictions: yet, though so slight be the merits of the book, the only criticism in reply which could pretend to any general efficiency in arresting the current of the virtual slander—and then by no means an adequate one—must be sought beyond the Atlantic, and gathered from the columns of the *London Times*. The South has benumbed the hearts and palsied the arms of her natural and willing defenders: she has dismantled her towers, and suppressed her fortresses of all efficient garrison, and she is now exposed, unarmed and unprotected, to all the treacherous stratagems and pitiless malice of her inveterate and interested enemies. She has invited and merited her own fate: she has wooed the slander which she is almost powerless to repel: she has offered a premium to vituperation and imposed a grave penalty on every attempt to redress the indignity to which she has subjected her citizens. (p. 725)

[We have] endeavored to estimate this inflammatory publication with all possible sobriety and coolness: we have tempered our indignation as nearly as might be to philosophic impartiality: we have conceded all that is or could be asked in favor of *Uncle Tom's Cabin;* and yet we find, that even if its facts were true, they would not support the inference which the work is designed to convey, much less justify the practices which it is intended to enforce. A libel is a libel still, notwithstanding the truth of its allegations, because it is calculated to disturb the peace of societies, and to destroy the harmony of any community. The ignorance of the libeller of the import or tendencies of his own language will remove neither the penalty nor the guilt, because the injury inflicted is not diminished thereby, and the public danger is not mitigated by the plea of folly. When, then, *Uncle Tom's Cabin* employs representations of Southern slavery, even if supposed to be true, which are calculated not merely to wound and outrage the feelings of Southerners, which would be comparatively a slight offence, but to pander to malignant prejudices, to disseminate throughout the Union dissensions and hostilities, and to circulate scandal abroad throughout the world, neither sincerity nor ignorance would afford any palliation for the rash, foolish, and criminal procedure. It is a caution frequently given to children, not to meddle with edge-tools, and if weak women or other persons of mature years but immature discretion, venture to engage in seditious pursuits, knowing the aim but ignorant of the character of the means, they must pay the penalty. (p. 730)

Almost every page [of *Uncle Tom's Cabin*] shows that however it may revel in the altitudes of an ideal perfection, the practices inculcated and the cause espoused by it, are at variance with all law, order, and government, with solemn oaths and established obligations, with the well-being of society, and with the perpetuity of the Union. Is either simplicity or fanaticism any excuse for that mole-eyed blindness, which fancies it sees afar off the duty of an organized crusade to conquer a disputed point of morals or social economy, and yet cannot behold the ever present obligation to perform those common duties of life which lie at the foundation of all social and political communion? Is it not either wilful hypocrisy or deliberate perversity, when a solitary crotchet of sentimental morality is conceived to transcend all the commandments of the decalogue, all the prescriptions of the Bible, and all the laws of man? Yet all this is done,—purposely, systematically, continually, and malignantly done in that immaculate encyclopaedia of fictitious crimes—*Uncle Tom's Cabin.* The commandment inscribed by the finger of God on the tablets of stone which Moses bore to the Israelites as the everlasting will of Jehovah, burns in our eyes in characters of flame while perusing this intricate tissue of deception. THOU SHALT NOT BEAR FALSE WITNESS AGAINST THY NEIGHBOUR.

This, however, is by no means the sole violation of the Decalogue which is committed by the book, but it is the most prominent. Of the others we have scarcely the patience, and we have very little inclination to speak. Yet all the commandments relative to the duties of mankind to each other are frequently and systematically contravened, with the significant exception of that against adultery, which was not a very delicate prescription for a lady to handle, although she does assiduously endeavor to assert its habitual disregard in the South by slave-owners towards their female slaves. (pp. 730-31)

The essence of murder according to the laws of all nations and the public sentiment of all periods lies in the taking, contrary to law, and with malice prepense, the life of a rational fellow-creature. Unless the definition be altered entirely and the moral principles of mankind be changed, murder is distinctly prescribed and applauded both by the precept and example of this book.

There is one sin which is justly regarded as the most despicable and debasing in the catalogue of crimes—the sin of perjury. Yet this is deliberately commended by this new missionary of the higher law.

It has always been esteemed the duty of good men and the pride of patriots to obey the solemn laws and uphold the institutions of their country. The whole tenor of these would-be immaculate volumes is directed to the subversion of both.

The Bible is either blasphemously mocked by the infidel, or reverently received by the Christian: but here with professions of more than Christian sanctity, its doctrines are distorted or disavowed, and its ministers maligned.

It is easy for even sincere fanaticism to run ignorantly and precipitately into the practice or palliation of crime; but in this instance the fanaticism clothes itself with the raiment of a pretended impartiality, and feigns justice the better to effectuate iniquity. There is an obvious discord between the professions and the purposes, the sentimentalism and the precepts of *Uncle Tom's Cabin,* which can scarcely permit us to withhold from it the charge of deliberate hypocrisy. (pp. 730-31)

We dismiss *Uncle Tom's Cabin* with the conviction and declaration that every holier purpose of our nature is misguided, every charitable sympathy betrayed, every loftier sentiment polluted, every moral purpose wrenched to wrong, and every patriotic feeling outraged, by its criminal prostitution of the high functions of the imagination to the pernicious intrigues of sectional animosity, and to the petty calumnies of wilful slander. (p. 731)

> *"'Uncle Tom's Cabin',"* in Southern Literary Messenger, Vol. XVIII, No. 12, December, 1852, pp. 721-31.

GEORGE SAND   (essay date 1852)

To review a book, the very morrow after its appearance, in the very journal where it has just been published, is doubtless contrary to usage, but in [the case of **"Uncle Tom's Cabin"**] it is the most disinterested homage that can be rendered, since the immense success attained by this work at its publication does not need to be set forth.

This book is in all hands and in all journals. It has, and will have, editions in every form; people devour it, they cover it with tears. It is no longer permissible to those who can read not to have read it, and one mourns that there are so many souls condemned never to read it,—helots of poverty, slaves through ignorance, for whom society has been unable as yet to solve the double problem of uniting the food of the body with the food of the soul.

It is not, then, it cannot be, an officious and needless task to review this book of Mrs. Stowe. We repeat, it is a homage, and never did a generous and pure work merit one more tender and spontaneous. She is far from us; we do not know her who has penetrated our hearts with emotions so sad and yet so sweet. Let us thank her the more. Let the gentle voice of woman, the generous voice of man, with the voices of little children, so adorably glorified in this book, and those of the oppressed of this old world, let them cross the seas and hasten to say to her that she is esteemed and beloved!

If the best eulogy which one can make of the author is to love her, the truest that one can make of the book is to love its very faults. It has faults,—we need not pass them in silence, we need not evade the discussion of them,—but you need not be disturbed about them, you who are rallied on the tears you have shed over the fortunes of the poor victims in a narrative so simple and true.

These defects exist only in relation to the conventional rules of art, which never have been and never will be absolute. If its judges, possessed with the love of what they call "artistic work," find unskilful treatment in the book, look well at them to see if their eyes are dry when they are reading this or that chapter. (p. 33)

Therefore it is that this book, defective according to the rules of the modern French romance, intensely interests everybody and triumphs over all criticisms in the discussions it causes in domestic circles.

For this book is essentially domestic and of the family,—this book, with its long discussions, its minute details, its portraits carefully studied. Mothers of families, young girls, little children, servants even, can read and understand them, and men themselves, even the most superior, cannot disdain them. We do not say that the success of the book is because its great merits redeem its faults; we say its success is because of these very alleged faults. (p. 34)

Mrs. Stowe is all instinct; it is the very reason that she appears to some not to have talent. Has she not talent? What is talent? Nothing, doubtless, compared to genius; but has she genius? I cannot say that she has talent as one understands it in the world of letters, but she has genius, as humanity feels the need of genius,—the genius of goodness, not that of the man of letters, but of the saint. Yes,—a saint! Thrice holy the soul which thus loves, blesses, and consoles the martyrs. Pure, penetrating, and profound the spirit which thus fathoms the recesses of the human soul. Noble, generous, and great the heart which embraces in her pity, in her love, an entire race, trodden down in blood and mire under the whip of ruffians and the maledictions of the impious. . . .

In matters of art there is but one rule, to paint and to move. And where shall we find creations more complete, types more vivid, situations more touching, more original, than in **"Uncle Tom."** . . .

What hand has ever drawn a type more fascinating and admirable than St. Clare—this exceptional nature, noble, generous, and loving, but too soft and too nonchalant to be really great? Is it not man himself, human nature itself, with its innate virtues, its good aspirations, and its deplorable failures?—this charming master who loves and is beloved, who thinks and reasons, but concludes nothing! (p. 35)

The life and death of a little child and of a negro slave!—that is the whole book! This negro and this child are two saints of heaven! The affection that unites them, the respect of these two perfect ones for each other, is the only love-story, the only passion of the drama. I know not what other genius but that of sanctity itself could shed over this affection and this situation a charm so powerful and so sustained. (p. 36)

Children are the true heroes of Mrs. Stowe's works. Her soul, the most motherly that could be, has conceived of these little creatures in a halo of grace. George Shelby, the little Harry, the cousin of Eva, the regretted babe of the little wife of the Senator, and Topsy, the poor diabolic, excellent Topsy,—all the children that one sees, and even those that one does not see in this romance, but of whom one has only a few words from their desolate mothers, seem to us a world of little angels, white and black, where any mother may recognize some darling of her own, source of her joys and tears. In taking form in the spirit of Mrs. Stowe, these children, without ceasing to be children, assume ideal graces, and come at last to interest us more than the personages of an ordinary love-story.

Women, too, are here judged and painted with a master hand; not merely mothers who are sublime, but women who are not mothers either in heart or in fact, and whose infirmities are treated with indulgence or with rigor. By the side of the methodical Miss Ophelia, who ends by learning that duty is good for nothing without love, Marie St. Clare is a frightfully truthful portrait. One shudders in thinking that she exists, that she is everywhere, that each of us has met her and seen her, perhaps, not far from us, for it is only necessary that this charming creature should have slaves to torture, and we should see her revealed complete through her vapors and her nervous complaints.

The saints also have their claw! it is that of the lion. She buries it deep in the conscience, and a little of burning indignation and of terrible sarcasm does not, after all, misbecome this Harriet Stowe, this woman so gentle, so humane, so religious, and full of evangelical unction. Ah! yes, she is a very good woman, but not what we derisively call "goody good." Hers is a heart strong and courageous, which in blessing the unhappy and applauding the faithful, tending the feeble and succoring the irresolute, does not hesitate to bind to the pillory the hardened tyrant, to show to the world his deformity.

She is, in the true spirit of the word, consecrated. Her fervent Christianity sings the praise of the martyr, but permits no man the right to perpetuate the wrong. She denounces that strange perversion of Scripture which tolerates the iniquity of the oppressor because it gives opportunity for the virtues of the victims. She calls on God himself, and threatens in his name; she shows us human law on one side, and God on the other!

Let no one say that, because she exhorts to patient endurance of wrong, she justifies those who do the wrong. Read the beautiful page where George Harris, the white slave, embraces for the first time the shores of a free territory, and presses to his heart wife and child, who at last are *his own*. What a beautiful picture, that! What a large heart-throb! what a trium-

phant protest of the eternal and inalienable right of man to liberty!

Honor and respect to you, Mrs. Stowe! Some day your recompense, which is already recorded in heaven, will come also in this world. (pp. 36-7)

> *George Sand, in an extract from her letter to Harriet Beecher Stowe on December 17, 1852, in* Uncle Tom's Cabin; or, Life Among the Lowly *by Harriet Beecher Stowe, F. E. Longley's, 1881 (and reprinted by Collier—Macmillan, 1962, pp. 33-7).*

[CHARLES F. BRIGGS]   (essay date 1853)

[The success achieved by *Uncle Tom's Cabin*] does not, by any means, argue that [it] is superior to all other books; but it is an unmistakable indication that it is a live book, and that it will continue to live when many other books which have been pronounced immortal, shall be dead and buried in an oblivion, from which there is no resurrection.

Uncle Tom is not only a miracle of itself, but it announces the commencement of a miraculous Era in the literary world. (p. 98)

Not the least remarkable among the phenomena that have attended the publication of *Uncle Tom* has been the numerous works written expressly to counteract the impressions which the book was supposed likely to make. This is something entirely new in literature. It is one of the most striking testimonials to the intrinsic merit of the work that it should be thought necessary to neutralize its influence by issuing other romances to prove that *Uncle Tom* is a fiction. Nothing of the kind was ever before deemed necessary. . . . *Uncle Tom* had scarcely seen the light when dozens of steel pens were set at work to prove him an impostor, and his author an ignoramus. . . .

The chances were a thousand to one against the success of the book. And yet it has succeeded beyond all other books that were ever written. And the cause is obvious; but, because it was obvious and lay upon the surface, it has been overlooked, there being an opinion among most men that truth must lie a long way out of reach. (p. 100)

[*Uncle Tom's Cabin*] is a live book, and it talks to its readers as if it were alive. It first awakens their attention, arrests their thoughts, touches their sympathies, rouses their curiosity, and creates such an interest in the story it is telling, that they cannot let it drop until the whole story is told. And this is done, not because it is a tale of slavery, but in spite of it. . . . It is the conummate art of the story teller that has given popularity to *Uncle Tom's Cabin,* and nothing else. The anti-slavery sentiment obtruded by the author in her own person, upon the notice of the reader, must be felt by every one, to be the great blemish of the book; and it is one of the proofs of its great merits as a romance, that it has succeeded in spite of this defect. If Mrs. Stowe would permit some judicious friend to run his pen through these excrescences, and to obliterate a flippant attempt at Picwickian humor, here and there, *Uncle Tom's Cabin* would be a nearly perfect work of art, and would deserve to be placed by the side of the greatest romances the world has known. . . . In all the great requisites of a romance it is decidedly superior to any other production of an American pen.

There are not, in *Uncle Tom's Cabin,* any of the delicacies of language which impart so great a charm to the writings of Irving and Hawthorne, nor any descriptions of scenery such as abound in the romances of Cooper, nor any thing like the bewildering sensuousness of Typee Melville; but there are broader, deeper, higher and holier sympathies than can be found in our other romances; finer delineations of character, a wider scope of observation, a more purely American spirit, and a more vigorous narrative faculty. We can name no novel, after [Fielding's] *Tom Jones,* that is superior to **Uncle Tom** in constructive ability. The interest of the narrative begins in the first page and is continued with consummate skill to the last. . . . Mrs. Stowe, like Fielding, seizes upon the attention at the outset, and never lets it go for a moment until the end. (pp. 100-01)

In no other American book that we have read, are there so many well-delineated American characters; the greater part of them are wholly new in fiction. The mischievous little imp Topsy, is a sort of infantine Caliban, and all the other darkies are delineated with wonderful skill and freedom; and each page of the book is like a cartoon of charcoal sketches. It has been objected to **Uncle Tom,** that all the whites are impossibly wicked, and all the blacks are impossibly good. But nothing could be further from the truth than such an assertion; the most amiable of the characters are some of the slave owners, while the most degraded and vile are, of course, the slaves. There is no partisanship apparent in the narrative proper, and if the author did not, occasionally, address the reader in her own person, greatly to her own prejudice, we should hardly suspect her of anti-slavery leanings. (p. 101)

Mrs. Stowe's book gives a much more agreeable picture of Southern slavery than any of the works we have seen which profess to give the right side of the tapestry. A desire to degrade America surely cannot be the reason why the representation of dramatic scenes in **Uncle Tom** have proved so attractive in our own theatres. For our part, we think that the actual effect of Mrs. Stowe's romance will be to create a much more indulgent and forgiving spirit towards the people of the South than has prevailed in England heretofore. (p. 102)

> [*Charles F. Briggs,*] *"Uncle Tomitudes," in* Putnam's Monthly Magazine, *Vol. I, No. I, January, 1853, pp. 97-102.*

SOUTHERN QUARTERLY REVIEW   (essay date 1853)

Most painful it is to us to comment upon a work [like **"Uncle Tom's Cabin"**]. What though "our withers be unwrung!" Does slander cease to be painful because it is gross? Is it enough for us to know that these obscene and degrading scenes are false as the spirit of mischief which dictated them? and can we, therefore, indifferently see these loathsome rakings of a foul fancy passed as current coin upon the world, which receives them as sketches of American life by an American citizen? We cannot; and loathsome as is the task; little as we hope to be heard in any community where such a work can be received and accredited, and where the very fact of such reception proves at once that our case is prejudged; yet will we speak and sift the argument of this fair lady, who so protests against vice that we might think her, like that "noble sister of Publicola," that "moon of Rome"

> Chaste as the icicle
> That's cruded by the frost from purest snow,
> And hangs on Dian's temple,

were it not that her too vivid imagination, going so far ahead of facts, shows too clearly, that not now, for the first time, does it travel the muddy road. Some hints from the unfortunately fashionable reading of the day—some flashes from the

French school of romance—some inspirations from the Sues and the Dumas', have evidently suggested the tenor of her pages.

The literary taste of our day (i.e. the second-rate literary taste; the fashionable novel-reading taste) demands excitement. Nothing can be spiced too high. Incident, incident, and that of the vilest kind, crowds the pages of those novels which are now unfortunately all the vogue. . . . For such tastes, Mrs. Stowe has catered well. Her facts are remarkable facts—very. (pp. 82-3)

[The readers of **"Uncle Tom's Cabin"** will find in it] one mass of gross misrepresentation and ridiculous blundering. The authoress is so ignorant of Southern life and slave institutions, that she does not know how very far she leaves behind her, the track of probability. . . . Mrs. Stowe has wandered almost as far from the possible [as the "Mother Goose" fairy tale]. If she has not given us moons of green cheese, she has given what is just as far from God's creation, a nation of men without heart, without soul, without intellect; a nation, too, (strange incongruity!) of cultivated human beings, so ignorant of right and wrong, so dead to all morality, that it were an insult to Deity, to believe in their existence. So anomalous a creation was never sent by God upon this earth, and satan or Mrs. Stowe must claim the honour of the invention. (pp. 115-16)

Mrs. Stowe, in spite of experience, in spite of science, determines that the negro is intellectually the white man's equal. She "has lived on the frontiers of a slave State," "she has the testimony of missionaries," &c., and "her deductions, with regard to the capabilities of the race, are encouraging in the highest degree." Bravo! Mrs. Stowe! Your deductions are bold things, and override sense and reason with wonderful facility. Perhaps they would become a little more amenable to ordinary reasoning, if, instead of living "on the frontiers of a slave State," you should see fit to carry your experience, not theoretically, but practically, into the heart of one; or still better, perhaps, avoiding the contaminating system, to explore at once the negro nature in its negro home, and behold in native majesty the *undegraded* negro nature. In native and in naked majesty, the lords of the wild might probably suggest more appreciable arguments, for difference of race, than any to which Mrs. Stowe has chosen to hearken. The negro alone has, of all races of men, remained entirely without all shadow of civilization. It is a mere quibble to talk of his want of opportunities and instruction. (p. 116)

> *L.S.M., "'Uncle Tom's Cabin'," in* Southern Quarterly Review, *n.s. Vol. VII, No. XIII, January, 1853, pp. 81-120.*

THE LIBERATOR   (essay date 1853)

We have not reviewed **Uncle Tom's Cabin,** chiefly because we felt our views of the tendency and nature of that work to be so hostile, that we could scarcely judge of it in a proper critical manner.—We believe it to possess a certain melo-dramatic power, equal in pathos to the 'Green Bushes' at the Adelphi, and in incident to a popular novel something between the style of Eugene Sue and George Reynolds. But we believe it also to be devoid of truth, principle and reality, and that its tendencies are highly mischievous, and detrimental to the interest of mankind. In saying this, we entirely acquit its authoress, Mrs. Stowe, of any evil desire, any wicked feeling, or intended falsehood. That lady, for all we know, may be a most excellent, as she is undoubtedly a very talented person. We fully give her credit for good motives; we doubt not that she believes herself entrusted with a mission, as much as ever did any 'eminent female.' . . . We can imagine her to be endowed with an awful sense of womanhood, and to make—if ever she condescended to such task, since the second edition of her book was sold—about the worst dumplings that were ever placed upon a dirty table-cloth in a slovenly parlor. . . . The book is false in fact, as the fine ladies are false in sentiment. . . .

We do not admit that the state of the negro slave is anything like what it is pictured to be in *Uncle Tom's Cabin,* in any case. There may be solitary cases approaching it in abomination. But the Americans, abolitionists or not, shall and will get rid of slavery as they please themselves, and every thing done in England, either sentimentally or not, only adds force to opposition. Mrs. Stowe has libelled her countrymen; let them look to that. England need not back her with Holy-well-street ignorance and Exeter Hall cant. If she do, she will sow the wind and reap the whirlwind.

"The 'Uncle Tom's Cabin' Mania," in The Liberator, *Vol. XXIII, No. 3, January 21, 1853, p. 9.*

ECLECTIC REVIEW   (essay date 1853)

['**The Key to Uncle Tom's Cabin**'] is a marvellous book, more so if possible than '**Uncle Tom's Cabin**' itself. We have read it with deep emotion, and hasten to apprize our readers of its character. . . . Wherever this book is read a profound conviction will be induced that [Mrs. Stowe] has understated rather than otherwise her case. Indeed, our pervading feeling now is one of astonishment at the self-control she must have exercised. The facts which came in her way are stated without elaboration. There is no appearance of effort, no accumulation of epithets in her portraiture of the slave system. The *thing* is shown in its daily working. Its actual life is unfolded, and all the licence she gives herself is in the appeals—so truly woman-like and noble-hearted—by which she seeks to arouse the sympathies of her white readers on behalf of a down-trodden race. We have never met with a work in which so little of human infirmity mingled with unsparing denunciations of a vicious system. The *manner* of the work always amazed us, but now that the '**Key**' is before us, it does so in a tenfold degree. . . . There has been nothing like it in the history of book-making, and it appears to us as philosophical as it is Christian-like to recognise in such case the special agency of Heaven. The inspiration of genius may do much, but we are free to acknowledge that in the spirit and style of '**Uncle Tom's Cabin,**' we trace a higher range of influence than is ordinarily exercised. At any rate the book is the expression of genius ardent even to passion, yet controlled in its utmost excitement by knowledge and sound judgment. (pp. 600-01)

Of the artistic skill of '**Uncle Tom's Cabin,**' there cannot be two opinions. 'But the work,' we are told, 'had a purpose entirely transcending the artistic one, and accordingly encounters at the hands of the public demands not usually made on fictitious works. It is *treated* as a reality, sifted, tried, and tested as a reality; and therefore as a reality it may be proper that it should be defended.' So far from being, as its opponents have alleged, a mere fancy picture, it is 'more perhaps than any other work of fiction that ever was written, a collection and arrangement of real incidents, of actions really performed, of words and expressions really uttered, grouped together with reference to a general result. . . . The writer acknowledges that the book is a very inadequate representation of slavery; and it is so, necessarily, for this reason—that slavery, in some

of its workings, is too dreadful for the purposes of art. A work which should represent it strictly as it is would be a work which could not be read; and all works which ever mean to give pleasure must draw a veil somewhere, or they cannot succeed.'

Such is Mrs. Stowe's introductory statement, and now that we have read her '**Key,**' we are fully assured of its truthfulness. (p. 602)

[We] tender Mrs. Stowe our unfeigned thanks for the service she has rendered. It is unnecessary to recommend her volume. It will be read by thousands, and if we may judge from our own experience, its impression will be deep and painful beyond expression. 'How long, O Lord, how long?' is the inquiry which arises to our lips. May early repentance and prompt reparation avert the evils which impend over America. There is a dark cloud looming in her sky, and unless she humble herself, and abandon her wickedness, the storm will burst upon her with terrible fury. In the meantime our duty is obvious. No religious fellowship must be had with them, whatever their name or standing, who are partakers of her wickedness. The slave-holder must be to us as the drunkard, the swearer, the unchaste. The times of ignorance are passed. The crime of the system is now manifest, and he who still adheres to it must be treated as any other incorrigible offender. (p. 617)

"'Key to Uncle Tom's Cabin'," in Eclectic Review, *n.s. Vol. IV, May, 1853, pp. 600-17.*

G[EORGE] F[REDERICK] H[OLMES]   (essay date 1853)

Mrs. Stowe obtrudes herself again upon our notice, and, though we have no predilections for the disgusting office of castigating such offences as hers, and rebuking the incendiary publications of a woman, yet the character of the present attack, and the bad eminence which she and her books have both won, render a prompt notice of the present encyclopaedia of slander even more necessary than any reply to her previous fiction. Her second appearance on the stage of civil dissension and social polemics is much changed from what it was at the time when her first revelations were given to the world. She was then an obscure Yankee school-mistress, eaten up with fanaticism, festering with the malignant virus of abolitionism, self-sanctified by the virtues of a Pharisaic religion, devoted to the assertion of woman's rights, and an enthusiastic believer in many neoteric heresies, but she was comparatively harmless, as being almost entirely unknown. She has now, by a rapid ascent and at a single dash, risen to unequalled celebrity and notoriety; and, though we believe with Dryden, that

Short is the date of all immoderate fame;

yet, at the present moment, she can give currency to her treacherous doctrines and her big budget of scandal by the prestige of unprecedented success. That success has been attained less by the imaginary merits of the fiction, though these have obtained unmeasured commendation, than by the inherent vices of the work. Its unblushing falsehood was its chief passport to popular acceptance. But, however acquired, she has certainly won a brilliant vantage-ground for the repetition of her assault upon the South. (p. 321)

["**Uncle Tom's Cabin**"] was a fiction designed as an embodiment of the truth—but possessing all the characteristics of fiction, and many that do not legitimately belong even to romance. ["**A Key to Uncle Tom's Cabin**"] is professedly a compilation of facts for the purpose of sustaining the allegations of imagination, and of proving the reality to be worse than conjecture. The first was an intricate involution and convo-lution of fictions for the insinuation of slander; the second is a distortion of the facts and mutilation of the records, for the sake of giving substance to the scandalous fancy, and redu-plicating the falsehood of the representation. "Uncle Tom's Cabin" is represented in the present work as "a mosaic of facts"—and "The Key" is now supplied to give access to the quarry from which the facts were taken. We think the desig-nation of a fictitious mosaic of facts equally applicable to both romances, for the fancy, which was displayed before in false colouring and perverse arrangement, is now exercised in the congenial task of false representation and misinterpretation. (p. 322)

It is a horrible thought that a woman should write or a lady read such productions as those by which her celebrity has been acquired. Are scenes of license and impurity, and ideas of loathsome depravity and habitual prostitution to be made the cherished topics of the female pen, and the familiar staple of domestic consideration or promiscuous conversation? Is the mind of woman to be tainted, seduced, contaminated, and her heart disenchanted of its native purity of sentiment, by the unblushing perusal, the free discussion, and the frequent med-itation of such thinly veiled pictures of corruption? Can a lady of stainless mind read such works without a blush of confusion, or a man think of their being habitually read by ladies without shame and repugnance? It is sufficiently disgraceful that a woman should be the instrument in disseminating the vile stream of contagion; but it is intolerable that Southern women should defile themselves by bringing the putrid waters to their lips? . . . Grant that every accusation brought by Mrs. Stowe is perfectly true, that every vice alleged occurs as she has rep-resented, the pollution of such literature to the mind and heart of woman is not less—but perhaps even more to be appre-hended. . . . If Mrs. Stowe will chronicle or imagine the in-cidents of debauchery, let us hope that women—and especially Southern women, will not be found poring over her pages. . . . The Stowe-ic philosophy is a fatal contamination to woman. (pp. 322-23)

[It] is not the falsehood of any particular facts that we would now object to, it is the general, and uniform fallacy or sophistry of their interpretation which is fatal to the credibility of the whole work. We wish we had the time to examine . . . the perverse ingenuity with which she conceals every thing that conflicts with her predetermined misconstruction, and distorts to wrong everything that admits of such misuse in the pliant hand of fanaticism. (p. 327)

Mrs. Stowe's demonstration of deceit is suggestive, not so much in consequence of what it alleges, as in consequence of what it omits; not from the cogency and profundity of the argument, but from the depth of the error and the intricacy of the endless web of sophistry which it reveals. (p. 329)

G[eorge] F[rederick] H[olmes], "'A Key to Uncle Tom's Cabin'," in Southern Literary Messenger, Vol. XIX, No. 6, June, 1853, pp. 321-30.

[WILLIAM GILMORE SIMMS] (essay date 1853)

[A Key to Uncle Tom's Cabin] opens more wards than those of slavery. It equally applies to the condition of society in all parts of the world. It makes the simple, but sufficient mistake, of charging upon an institution, what are the defects and vices of humanity at large; and, as we anticipated, claims to establish a case against the slave States, by the accumulation of in-stances, drawn from an interminable tract of time, and from the occurrences, in new conditions of society, scattered over a thousand miles of territory. This was the vital error in the plan of Mrs. Stowe's novel. Having resolved against the in-stitution of slavery, her business was chiefly to find out what-ever facts might be made to bear against it. It did not matter, in her sight, or make any difference to the argument, that the crimes she showed, as taking place in the slave States, were of continual occurrence in the free; or that the sum total of crime, according to all experience, was infinitely greater in the free than in the slave communities. . . . Such small difficulties offer no embarrassment to a woman-reasoner, whose process of thought is wholly sensuous. "I hate slavery," says the good lady, "and I see crime"—her conclusion is immediate. The one grows out of the other; and here is the sort of record which she has kept, and which she fondly fancies, is to make out the case against us. The good lady gives little heed to the non sequitur. Her key is shaken triumphantly before our eyes. We fancy we hear her chucklings. She evidently regards the ar-gument as triumphant, and the history complete. (pp. 214-15)

Mrs. Stowe's generalizations and assumptions are not drawn from her facts. Her facts, on the contrary, have been sought to establish her assumptions. This is always a dangerous mode of argumentation. So far as the mind of the person arguing is concerned, the argument is decided before it is discussed. The case is determined long before she hears the evidence. The mind, thus under bias, is incapable of right-reasoning. The will stands in the way of the thought. The fact, whatever it be, is only valued so long as it seems to sustain the assumption. If it makes at all against it, it is dismissed with contempt or anger. To this sort of treatment, our author subjects the statements and opinions of all sorts of questioners who come in conflict with her decision. She readily listens to all, however worthless or silly, which go to sustain her. Every old woman's story of private griefs, fancied wrongs and foolish fancies, is greedily seized upon, and held up with exultation, if it speaks for her bias. But, for the other side, she has no ears. The testimony of the clergy in behalf of the slave States, she treats with contempt. In their case, she accounts for their opposition by assuming their baseness. The Bible authority is regarded with just as little reverence. But the day has gone by in New-England when the Bible was authority. Here is her Bible—the key before us. This is the book of Stowe. Here is the true inspi-ration. The divine truths which she only acknowledges, are all here written down, and in a style which is particularly impos-ing—to the writer. (p. 216)

The attempt to establish a moral argument through the medium of fictitious narrative, is, per se, a vicious abuse of art and argument. The thing cannot be done conscientiously. (pp. 216-17)

[Mrs. Stowe] has made a collection of all the crimes that have taken place in the slave States from the beginning of the slave trade. Here they are, a portion at least, in this formidable key, massed together in all their putrescence. . . . Now, suppose we admit all her facts—and we have not the slightest doubt that the most of them are true—what do they establish? Literally nothing, beyond the facts themselves! Do they establish her case against slavery? Not a bit of it. For this purpose, they are not worth the paper upon which they are written. (pp. 217-18)

The wholeness of truth is its supreme essence. It is the ce-menting property of facts. The absence of this element from Mrs. Stowe's volumes is their fatal defect, considered in the nature of evidence, and upon a moral issue. (p. 219)

[The] mood of Mrs. Stowe very frequently, throughout her books, prompts her to inflict a sting upon the people of her own precincts who have been too christian to be philanthropic, and who have not sufficiently sympathized with her in the crusade against the South. For all that class of Yankees who think kindly of the South, and are willing to keep hands off from her in anger, she has the most unqualified loathing. Hence, many of her scenes and some of her personages. In these it is difficult to say which she prefers most to victimize, Southron or Yankee. The case of Legree, himself, is one of this sort; and it is curious to note that, in her anxiety to do a little stabbing and poisoning among her own people while slashing away at the South, *she makes Legree, himself, a Yankee,* born in puritan cradle, and swathed from the first in that native sheepskin which is found so frequently to unfold, only for the development of a full grown wolf. Legree, born a Yankee, bred a Yankee, and monstrous even for a Yankee, is not to be received as representing the people of the South. We have only to shake our skirts and be free of the filthy creature. He is not one of us, and we are not answerable for his doings. If the purpose was to render us thus responsible, the author has mistaken her process. But she has made another mistake in connection with this subject. The idea of such a portrait of monstrosity as she has drawn of Legree, and such delineations of horror as he is made to exhibit, is that these shall represent the usual workings and results of slavery, and show what society in the South must be held responsible for. But here again our author blunders as an artist. (pp. 226-27)

Thus, through all her labours, a merely passing inspection, such as ours, will suffice to show, it will be seen, that her art fails to sustain her moral, and convicts itself, where most she labours to convict us. She has wrought out her argument only by distorting the fact, suppressing the fact, *supplying* the fact, in false conclusions from what is imperfectly known, and, altogether, making such a jumble of fragmentary truths with full fledged falsehoods, that to those who examine the work, without prejudice, the conviction is inevitable that she has wrought more in malice than in sorrow. Seeing, she resolved not to see, and hearing, not to understand. She will only hear what she pleases,—what will justify her previous resolution, that slavery is a foul thing which it is her mission to subdue and destroy. It is amusing, turning to "the key" before us, to see from what a variety of sources she has drawn, or sought to draw, the aliment on which she loves to feed. (pp. 227-28)

[As] the painter, finding nowhere in nature any model of that which he wished to make, took a beauty here and a beauty there—borrowed from this woman an eye, from that a mouth, from another a nose, from a fourth a chin, or cheek, or forehead; hair from a fifth, and complexion from a sixth;—so good Mrs. Stowe, not aiming at the beautiful, but at the ugly and the odious, for her ideal, borrows an ugly fact here, and a brutal fact there, and a dirty fact in a third place, and so on,—picking up, now in North and South-Carolina, now in Georgia and Virginia, now in Alabama and Louisiana, until she has completed her fanciful portrait of the whole;—and the result is a Mosaic monster! (pp. 228-29)

[*William Gilmore Simms,*] *"Stowe's 'Key to Uncle Tom's Cabin',"* in The Southern Quarterly Review, *n.s. Vol. VIII, No. XV, July, 1853, pp. 214-54.*

[SAMUEL WARREN]   (essay date 1853)

[Let] us say for ourselves, that though our silence, and that of one or two quarterly contemporaries, may have excited notice,

both in America and this country, we have been by no means indifferent spectators of the reception which this singularly-successful book [*Uncle Tom's Cabin*] has met with; regarding it as one of those sudden phenomena in literature, demanding, even, a deliberate consideration of cause and effect. We apprehend no one will doubt that, to excite such attention and emotion among all classes of readers, in both hemispheres, as this work has excited, it must possess *something* remarkable; and what that is, it will be our endeavour to determine. . . . We shall judge *Uncle Tom's Cabin* by its own intrinsic merits or demerits—occasionally looking for the light which [Mrs. Stowe] has thought proper to reflect upon it from its companion volume [*The Key to Uncle Tom's Cabin*]. (pp. 394-95)

Uncle Tom's Cabin is a remarkable book, unquestionably; and, upon the whole, we are not surprised at its prodigious success, even as a mere literary performance; but whether, after all, it will have any direct effect upon the dreadful INSTITUTION at which it is aimed, may be regarded as problematical. Of one thing we are persuaded—that its author, as she has displayed in this work undoubted genius, in some respects of a higher order than any American predecessor or contemporary, is also a woman of unaffected and profound piety, and an ardent friend of the unhappy black. Every word in her pages issues glistening and warm from the mint of woman's love and sympathy, refined and purified by Christianity. We never saw in any other work, so many and such sudden irresistible appeals to the reader's heart—appeals which, moreover, only a wife and a mother could make. One's heart throbs, and one's eyes are suffused with tears without a moment's notice, and without anything like effort or preparation on the writer's part. We are, on the contrary, soothed in our spontaneous emotion by a conviction of the writer's utter artlessness; and when once a gifted woman has satisfied her most captious reader that such is the case, she thenceforth leads him on, with an air of loving and tender triumph, a willing captive to the last. There are, indeed, scenes and touches in this book which no living writer, that we know of, can surpass, and perhaps none even equal. (p. 395)

Let us speak first, and in only general terms, of the literary characteristics of the author, as displayed in her work.

Mrs. Stowe is unquestionably a woman of GENIUS; and that is a word which we always use charily: regarding genius as a thing *per se*—different from talent, in its highest development, altogether, and in kind. . . . Now, we imagine that no person or genius can read *Uncle Tom's Cabin,* and not feel in glowing contact with genius—generally gentle and tender, but capable of rising, with its theme, into very high regions of dramatic power. This Mrs. Stowe has done several times in the work before us—exhibiting a passion, an intensity, a subtle delicacy of perception, a melting tenderness, which are as far out of the reach of mere talent, however well trained and experienced, as the prismatic colours are out of the reach of the born blind. But the genius of Mrs. Stowe is of that kind which instinctively addresses itself to the Affections. . . . With the one she can exhibit an exquisite tenderness and sympathy; watching the other, however, with stern but calm scrutiny, and delineating both with a truth and simplicity, in the one case touching, in the other really *terrible*. (pp. 395-96)

She has endeavoured to show [slavery] fairly in its best and its worst phases. In its *best* aspect, she has perhaps been successful; but oh! who shall say what yet remains untold in that *valley and shadow of death* that lies on the other side? . . . . . "The writer has only given a faint shadow—a dim picture—

of the anguish and despair that are at this very moment riving thousands of hearts, shattering thousands of families, and driving a helpless and sensitive race to frenzy and despair'' [see excerpt above by Harriet Beecher Stowe]. . . .

Occasionally, also, Mrs. Stowe displays a fine perception of external nature—irradiating her inanimate scenes with the rich hues of imagination. At these, however, she generally looks through a sort of solemn religious medium. (p. 396)

Character is often drawn by our author with delicate discrimination; and, at the same time, she almost as often exhibits a poverty and crudeness in dealing with such subjects, which would be surprising, but that it is evidently referrible to haste and inattention. Her mind, too, is so intent upon the great, noble, and holy purpose of her book, that she often does not give herself time to develop or mature her own happiest conceptions. The momentary exigencies of her story require the introduction of an additional figure; on which, having paused for a moment to call up the image of one before her mind's eye, she forthwith gives a few strokes, possibly intending, at a future time, to complete and retouch them; but that future time never comes, for she has got into new scenes, and moves on, crowded with new characters and associations. In this respect her book may be compared to the *studio* of a great painter, where the visitor sees some pictures in all the splendour of their completeness, and others in various stages of incompleteness—some exhibiting the master's hand, and others that of a hasty and unskilled workman; all which may, perhaps, be visibly accounted for by the painter's being absorbed by some masterpiece, itself, however, only approaching completeness. We feel bound, nevertheless, to express our opinion that an additional solution of the matter is to be found in her probably limited range of observation of actual life, at all events of such life as Europeans can appreciate. In delineating the character of slaves and the ''slave-trader, kidnapper, negro-catcher, negro-whipper,'' as she herself groups them, she handles her pencil with the confident ease of a master. (pp. 397-98)

While the pathos of Mrs. Stowe is deep and pure, her *humour and satire* are genuine and racy, but quiet. Gloomy as is the prevalent tone of her work, her reader's feelings are discreetly relieved by many little touches of quaint dry drollery. (p. 398)

There are, however, many indications throughout the work of the writer's humorous powers being checked and restrained, either purposely or unconsciously, as if from a severe sense of the purpose with which she writes—as though before her mind's eye was ever the bleeding heart of the negro. We have an indistinct recollection of more than one disposition, or rather juxta-position, of persons and incidents most suggestive of *fun:* but they are suddenly discarded, the reader breathlessly following the grave and ardent writer, over whose pale countenance the smile had but furtively flickered for an instant, like a glance of moonlight on a gloomy sea. (p. 399)

[Mrs. Stowe's] dialogue is almost always admirable; brief, lively, pointed, and characteristic—that is, when she does not, so to speak, crowd too much sail upon it, in her intense anxiety to be didactic and hortatory on the great subject on which her eyes are ever fixed. When she yields to the promptings of her own power over character and expression, she exhibits high dramatic capabilities. She perceives a fine *situation* with the unerring intuition of genius, and inspires her characters with fitting sentiments, conferring upon them appropriate eloquence. Akin to this is the easy strength of her narrative. She hurries her reader along with her, breathless. The flight and

pursuit of poor Eliza and her child—the incidents selected to heighten the interest in their fate—the introduction of Marks and Tom Loker, and their interview with Haley—their encounter at the rocky pass with George and his wife and child, are, in parts, worthy of the pencil of Sir Walter Scott: but, it must be added, that that consummate master of his art would never have drawn up suddenly in his exciting course, to interpolate drivelling allusions to Austria and the Hungarians, Poland, Ireland, and England—or tame and even irritating moralisings at the very crisis of the adventure, as is but too often the case with Mrs. Stowe. But this very fault, and a serious one to a reader of fiction it is, must be referred to a cause infinitely and eternally honourable to the author—her pure and noble purpose in writing the book. With our eye fixed on that purpose, we will forgive her five times as many faults of style and arrangement as she is fairly chargeable with. (pp. 400-01)

It is evident that the writings of one English author at least of the present day have made a deep impression on Mrs. Stowe. This is Mr. Dickens, with whom, indeed, she has much in common; but he must not attribute it to mere gallantry, if we express our opinion that there are parts of *Uncle Tom's Cabin* which he never can surpass, which he never has surpassed. She probes human nature every whit as tenderly and truly as he; her sympathies are as keen and subtle, her spirit is as generous, as his; her perception of the humorous as quick and vivid as his own. She shows also his—so to speak—structural faults; which, in a general way, we may indicate by saying, that condensation and directness of course would greatly improve the compositions of both. . . . It occurs to us, that had Mr. Dickens passed his life among the same scenes as Mrs. Stowe, making allowance for certain special circumstances affecting the latter, he would have produced a work very similar, in both its faults and excellencies, to *Uncle Tom's Cabin*. (p. 401)

[A considerable portion of Mrs. Stowe's defective workmanship] consists of preaching—always, doubtless, perfectly orthodox and evangelical, but smacking too strongly—will she forgive us?—of the *conventicle* twang. . . . [Doubtless] she knows that portion of the American public for which she chiefly writes, and what kind and amount of *hard-hitting,* so to speak, is necessary to make an impression on sensibilities enclosed in rhinoceros hide. We do not say that it is so; but we suppose that Mrs. Stowe has classes of hard people in view, and knew the rough force requisite to hit home.

All these, however, and other similar little matters which might be mentioned, are mere motes in sunbeams, when regarded by the eye of a just and generous criticism. . . . The book had a purpose entirely transcending artistic purpose, and accordingly encounters, at the hands of the public, demands not usually made on fictitious works. It is treated as a reality—sifted, tried, and tested as a reality; and, therefore, as a reality it may be proper that it should be defended. . . . It is a very inadequate representation of slavery, and necessarily so, for this reason—that slavery, in some of its workings, is too dreadful for the purpose of art. (pp. 402-03)

The tale opens with a very skilfully contrived scene, the object being to arrest attention, without plunging into horrors which might at first shock a reader, and render him incredulous; and yet it is very startling to a European not familiar with slavery. . . . [In the] introductory dialogue we meet with new and fearful phraseology, as applied to human beings. Mrs. Stowe, with much tact, contrives, by a word or two, to excite the reader's interest in Tom long before he comes on the scene. . . . [The whole of the] introductory scene is highly creditable to

Mrs. Stowe's powers: it is graphic and dramatic, character and incident being hit off with a quiet strength, auguring well for the rest of her performance. She has not overdrawn Haley. She has given us quite enough to startle and disgust us with—the *system,* more than the individual, and has at the same time relieved the reader's mind by a just perceptible strain of drollery and piquant satire. . . . The first few chapters of this work will satisfy the most fastidious reader that he is sitting down before the production of a great artist. . . . From the first to the end of the eighth chapter, including also the tenth, we are conducted, indeed, "from gay to grave, from lively to severe;" the lights and shadows of negro life are brought before us with equal vividness and distinctness, by scenes most happily contrived, without a tinge of exaggeration, or a disfiguring touch of coarseness. (pp. 404-05)

Taken as a *literary* whole, *Uncle Tom's Cabin* is a work standing before the critical eye in large proportions, but somewhat irregularly and inartificially disposed; exhibiting, here and there, minor and easily removable marks of haste, and inexperienced workmanship. It would have been easy to contrive incidents, and that without deranging her general scheme, which would have kept curiosity on the stretch from first to last, and secured a sort of poetical justice, which might have satisfied the minds of many of her readers. . . . (p. 422)

The main defect of the construction of her work as a "story"— for such she terms it—is, its want of connectedness. The reader is hurried incessantly from side to side of the dividing line between the fortunes of Uncle Tom, and those of George and Eliza Harris, with the episodical incidents depending on them; coming to each with sympathies attuned to the *other;* which, again, as soon as they have begun to be attracted to the new object, are suddenly dissociated, to address themselves to the one which they had but recently quitted so abruptly.

With all its defects, however, this book is an instrument worthy of contributing to effect a grand purpose, to attack and subvert A SYSTEM; the only condition, in this view, being, that it is founded, not upon exaggeration and misrepresentation, but upon TRUTH. . . . [*A Key to Uncle Tom's Cabin*] is, in fact, simply a series of *Proofs and Illustrations* of the truth of her representations. We have examined this *Key* to the *Cabin* with some attention, and are of opinion that its alleged *facts* are such as must be *answered;* or those whose accusations provoked its publication, will have succeeded in only placing a professed Fiction upon the solid basis of Fact. No one who reads this *Key* will tolerate being simply told, that *Uncle Tom's Cabin* is founded on falsehood. . . . This volume, in a word, we commend to the serious consideration of every reflecting European and American reader of *Uncle Tom's Cabin.* (pp. 422-23)

[The] Christian statesman, the enlightened politician, in either hemisphere, is bound, we think, to deal with the existence of this book, and the extensive effects produced by it, as a signal FACT. Great as are its literary merits, they are by no means sufficient, of themselves, to account for the universal attention which it has excited. . . .

Harriet Beecher Stowe, be it known a century hence, that we are ashamed of neither yourself, nor our reception of your book; that one not of the least important names of the present century is your own—already, and though you should never write another book. We doubt, indeed, whether you ever will do so— whether, at least, it will, or can be, a great book; for this one embodies your life-long experiences, heart-yearnings, and long-cherished thoughts. Your whole soul is wrapped up in its single noble purpose; so, *Sis faemina Unius Libri.* (p. 423)

[Samuel Warren,] "'Uncle Tom's Cabin'," in Blackwood's Edinburgh Magazine, *Vol. LXXIV, No. CCCCLVI, October, 1853, pp. 391-423.*

ECLECTIC REVIEW (essay date 1854)

['**Sunny Memories of Foreign Lands**' is] sure to be extensively read. The name of Mrs. Stowe guarantees this. The unprecedented popularity of '**Uncle Tom's Cabin**' has rendered it familiar to all classes of our countrymen, and has naturally awakened an intense desire to know all that can be learnt respecting the author. The extraordinary qualities of that work have commanded universal admiration. . . . The sensation created by this work is wholly unprecedented, and stands out as one of the distinctive features of our day. When, therefore, it was first announced that Mrs. Stowe was engaged in the preparation of a work descriptive of her visit to 'the old country,' few readers failed to anticipate intense pleasure in its perusal. This feeling will not be disappointed. We have read the volumes before us with more than ordinary satisfaction. They are very much what we anticipated, and we can honestly and warmly recommend them to our readers. (p. 327)

The work consists of familiar letters, written during her residence in Europe to friends and relations in America. As a literary composition it is, therefore, open to some exception; and there is a minuteness of personal detail in some of the letters which might have been advantageously dispensed with. Mrs. Stowe will do well to retrench these matters in subsequent editions of her work, and this may be easily done without affecting its general character. . . . We take her volumes, however, as they are; and without doubt or hesitancy affirm that we have rarely been more gratified than in their perusal. From some of her judgments we dissent. Her criticisms naturally partake, in many cases, of the complexion of the American mind, but there is a geniality and warm-heartedness combined with a rich vein of shrewd sense and intelligent refinement throughout her work, which would counterbalance far more weighty faults than she has fallen into. . . . [It would] be the height of folly to regard her volumes as the calm exposition of an unbiassed observer. They make no pretensions to anything of the kind. She describes what she saw, acknowledges the kindness she received, and institutes comparisons between her own and the mother country, in the most cordial and cheering spirit. We take, therefore, her volumes for what they profess to be, and look to other writers for an impartial and searching analysis of our character and habits. (pp. 328-29)

Her volumes are enriched with numerous illustrations, and will be perused with intense delight by large numbers of our countrymen. We part from them with regret. Unlike our ordinary experience, we were sorry to arrive at their close. We wished that she had gone on writing, and shall be glad to renew our acquaintance with her at the earliest possible moment. (p. 341)

"'Sunny Memories of Foreign Lands'," in Eclectic Review, *n.s. Vol. VIII, September, 1854, pp. 327-41.*

THE EDINBURGH REVIEW (essay date 1855)

The sale of '**Uncle Tom's Cabin**' is the most marvellous literary phenomenon that the world has witnessed. (p. 293)

Its moral influence, though it has not been as wonderful as its literary popularity, has been remarkable. In the form of a novel it is really a political pamphlet. It is an attack on the Fugitive

Slave Law of America, and though it has not effected the repeal of that law, it has rendered its complete execution impossible. (p. 294)

['**Uncle Tom**'] is a purely American work. When it first appeared in the columns of a newspaper, the author looked only to a narrow local circulation. When it was reprinted, the American market only was thought of. Mrs. Stowe did not address herself, like Washington Irving, or Prescott, or Wheaton, to an European public. She wrote only for Americans, and writing for them she poured out her sympathy with the weak and the humble, her indignation against the oppressor, her obedience to justice, and her adoration of liberty, in words as bold and as uncompromising as any that were ever uttered by Milton, or Fox, or Wilberforce. She does not discuss the highest principles of human conduct, she assumes them: she takes for granted that they are not only known to her readers, but professed by them. If '**Uncle Tom**' were still only in manuscript, and it had been shown to us, with the information that an American lady intended to publish it in America, we should have said, 'The readers for whom that book is intended, must enjoy a high civilisation and great moral and intellectual cultivation. They must be religious, just, and humane. If they form part of an empire tainted by slavery, they must be impatient of the disgrace, and alarmed by the sin.' And the result would have more than justified us, as it has more than justified Mrs. Stowe.

We must admit, however, that Mrs. Stowe, writing from personal observation, draws a dark picture of the influence of slavery, and of the slave trade, on a portion of her countrymen who take part in active political life. (pp. 304-05)

[Mrs. Stowe's] pictures carry with them the excitement of novelty as well as the weight of truth. This authoress has put into our hands a telescope, by which the coloured races are brought so near to us, that we can see them in their labours and in their sports, in their sufferings and in their enjoyments, in their insecure happiness—if any state that is insecure deserves to be called happiness—in their terrors, and in their despair. We do not wonder at the crowds that have been collected by a spectacle so strange without being surprising, so unlike any thing that ever was seen before and yet so obviously real.

Next in importance to the attractiveness of the subject is the attractiveness of the moral colouring with which Mrs. Stowe has lighted it up. The reader always sympathises with the writer, and always feels himself the better for doing so. It is difficult for a poet not to paint himself while he thinks that it is describing only the creatures of his imagination. No one can read 'Amelia,' or 'Persuasion,' without seeing who sat for the principal character. We rise from 'Don Quixote' as well acquainted with Cervantes as with the knight of the rueful countenance. This is peculiarly the case with Mrs. Stowe; as her work is as much a piece of rhetoric as of poetry—in fact, is more so,— she is more anxious to persuade than she is to please. The moral, which is absent from most poems, and, where it exists, is generally so concealed as to be discovered only on reflection, is prominently exhibited in every chapter of '**Uncle Tom.**' Now it has been admitted from the times of Aristotle . . . that the speaker whom you believe to be sincere, and with whose feelings you sympathise, has already half persuaded you. '**Uncle Tom**' possesses . . . [this] means of influence, and . . . in its highest excellence. It is obviously an honest book. Some of the critics of Mrs. Stowe accuse her of having over-coloured her pictures. Admitting her to have done so, no candid reader

can think that she has done so intentionally. There is nothing exaggerated or artificial in her loathing of cruelty, in her indignation at oppression, or in her scorn of the wretched sophistry with which they are palliated or even defended. Her descriptions and her declamation are as much the relief of a mind which seeks vent for the sense of misery and wrong, as they are among the means by which that misery and wrong may be mitigated. And the reader can no more refuse to her his sympathy than he can his confidence. She has both the loftier and the humbler virtues. She is bold, high-minded, and enthusiastic; she is kind, tender, and affectionate; and over her character is spread a tint of piety which softens, refines, and harmonises the whole. New Englander as she is, there is nothing austere or ascetic, or menacing in her religion. It is a religion of hope and of love, not of fear or of denunciation. Present assistance and future reward are constantly promised: temptation and punishment are kept out of sight. Our Saviour appears in every page: the existence of Satan is almost ignored, except, indeed, when she makes the negroes assign to him the duty of taking the slave traders who tear children from their parents. 'Lor, if the Devil don't get them, what he good for?' No sectarian doctrine, no sectarian feeling intrudes. If we did not know that '**Uncle Tom**' has been prohibited by the Pope, we should have supposed that there was no form of Christian faith in which it would not find grateful admirers. (pp. 313-14)

When we give the first place, among the causes of '**Uncle Tom**'s' popularity, to its subject, we speak of its European popularity. We believe that the principal cause of its American popularity, was its religious colour. In the New England States there is a general dislike, or rather a general dread, of works of fiction. Among Puritans, the fear of evil predominates over the hope of good. Any source of pleasure, which may also be a source of mischief, is prohibited. They think it safer, perhaps easier, to be abstinent than to be temperate. Novels give much amusement, and good novels give some instruction; but the reading, even of good novels, is easily carried to an excess which is always injurious to the mind, and often to the character. A total abstinence, therefore, from novel reading pervades New England. . . . Even in this country in some classes, particularly among the Dissenters, novel reading is forbidden; and here, as in America, '**Uncle Tom**' is excepted from the general prohibition. It is difficult for those who have not been subjected to this ascetic interdiction of works of imagination, to estimate adequately the effect of such a story on minds to which the intoxicating stimulus of fiction was unknown. It must have been to them like light given to those blind from birth,—the revelation of a new sense.

We have shown how much of the popularity of '**Uncle Tom**' arises from its appealing to our sympathies. We fear that we must add that much of that popularity arises from its also appealing to our antipathies. The anti-slavery feeling in America is less diffused than it is in Europe, but it is more intense. Scarcely any man can proclaim himself an abolitionist without having to make a considerable sacrifice of popularity, perhaps of fortune. Even those who stop short of abolition, but are unfavourable to the extension of slavery into territories as yet free from it, have to play a losing game—a contest which strongly tasks the temper and the charity of the player; which may bind him closely to his own cause, but is certain to embitter him against that of his opponents; which may make him love his friends, but cannot fail to make him hate his enemies. To men in this state of mind '**Uncle Tom**' was a god-send. Mrs. Stowe came like a heavenly auxiliary, like the divine Twins at the battle of the Lake Regillus, or St. Jago in the van of

Cortez, using weapons such as they had never thought of, wielded with a skill which they did not possess. She showered on the supporters of the Fugitive Slave Law and of the extension of slavery, invective, ridicule, contempt, and defiance, with arrows winged by genius, and barbed, and pointed, and poisoned by truth. The anti-slavery party would have been more than men if they had not welcomed with enthusiasm such an ally,—if they had not deified the amazon who, if she had not led them to victory, at least had given them revenge.

The evil passions which 'Uncle Tom' gratified in England were not hatred or vengeance, but national jealousy and national vanity. We have long been tired of hearing America boast that she is the freest and the most enlightened country that the world has ever seen. Mrs. Stowe taught us how to prove that democrats may be tyrants, that an aristocracy of caste is more oppressive than an aristocracy of station; and, above all, that a clergy supported by their flocks is ready to pervert the fundamental principles of Christianity to suit the interests or the prejudices of their paymasters. (pp. 315-16)

Another source of the popularity of 'Uncle Tom' is its naturalness. It has no plot, no *peripateia*. The fortunes of the different *dramatis personae* move on in separate lines, little influencing one another, without the elaborate entanglement and clever unravellings to which we are accustomed in fiction. The events are connected rather by time than by causation. In few incidents does the hand of the inventor betray itself. In general, however, the illusion of reality is admirably kept up. Scene after scene follows, without effort, without dulness, and without exaggeration, in which every character acts and talks as we expected him to do. One of the elements of the naturalness of the story is the absence of love: that is, of love between unmarried persons, for of conjugal love, of parental love, and of religious love, there is abundance. Mrs. Stowe is to be added to the very small list of great poets who have attempted to interest the reader without the aid of a pair of lovers. That the attempt is an arduous one may be inferred from its rarity, and that rarity gives to 'Uncle Tom' a double advantage. The ordinary reader observes the absence of one of the badges of fiction: the critic admires the genius and the courage of the writer who has dared to compose a novel making no use of the material which is supposed to be the staple of novel writing. (p. 317)

We have said that the actors in 'Uncle Tom' act and talk as we expect them to do. To recur, however, to a classification on which we ventured when reviewing Thackeray's novels,—the characters are generally simple: that is to say, characters to whom only a few qualities are given, all of which combine to lead their possessor into one line of conduct.

Uncle Tom, for instance, is simply perfect. Not a particle of human infirmity is allowed to profane his excellence. He is pious, affectionate, brave, honest, intelligent, confiding, humble,—in short, he is composed of every Christian virtue and grace without alloy. Eva is also perfect. Her whole character is formed of youthful love and piety. Marie is another simple character. She is made up merely of intense selfishness and weak intelligence. Haley, Harris, Eliza, Legree,—in short, each of the *dramatis personae,* except Ophelia, St. Clare, and Topsy, is coloured with an uniform tint. Those who are wicked have no virtues, those who are good have no vices. This certainly impairs the naturalness which we have mentioned as one of Mrs. Stowe's merits. (pp. 317-18)

But though this mono-chromatic colouring—this absence of shade where there is light, and of light where there is shade—

is an artistic defect, we are not sure that it may not have contributed to the popularity of the work. (p. 318)

The 'Key to Uncle Tom's Cabin,' is too long. The portion of it which shows that American slavery and the American slave trade can produce real events similar to those related in 'Uncle Tom,' was scarcely necessary. Such events are, as we have already remarked, the inevitable incidents to the system, nor is the production of a real counterpart for every story in 'Uncle Tom,' a complete defence of Mrs. Stowe against the charge of misrepresentation.

With respect to the internal slave trade of America, we do not believe misrepresentation to be possible. Every part of it is so utterly hateful, that its horrors cannot be exaggerated. But with respect to the treatment of slaves by their owners, while employed in their houses or in their fields, we think it possible that 'Uncle Tom' may produce a false impression, not by describing events that do not happen, but by leading us to think that they happen habitually. It is probable, we hope that it is true, that there are twenty Shelbys for one Legree. Evil affects the imagination so much more pungently, and dwells so much more in the memory, than good, that if we run through a list of the railway accidents of a year, we are inclined for an instant to suppose railways to be the most dangerous means of travelling, instead of being, as they are, the safest. So after reading Mrs. Stowe, we forget the Shelbys, and remember only the Legrees. If Mrs. Stowe be accused, as perhaps she may fairly be, of producing this exaggerated impression, she cannot defend herself by proving, as she does triumphantly, that Legrees exist.

The great value of the 'Key' consists in the specimens which it gives of the legislation of the Slave States, and of the arguments by which it is defended. (pp. 321-22)

> *"Slavery in the United States," in* The Edinburgh Review, *Vol. CI, No. CCVI, April, 1855, pp. 293-331.*

THE NORTH AMERICAN REVIEW (essay date 1855)

Though we recollected many of the pieces in ["**The Mayflower, and Miscellaneous Writings**"], and they had made us think the better of the magazines in which they originally appeared, they yet had not separately produced upon us the impression which together they now make with regard to their writer. As we read them in their collective form, we perceive that [Harriet Beecher Stowe's] world-famous tale was not the miraculous outblooming of a genius that had previously given no sign, but that in the "**Miscellaneous Writings**" of earlier years there had been the distinct presage of high and enduring reputation. There are among them specimens of character-painting and of dialogue, of the ludicrous and the pathetic, which are hardly surpassed in their kind by corresponding passages in "**Uncle Tom's Cabin**." (pp. 276-77)

> *"Mrs. Stowe's 'Mayflower'," in* The North American Review, *Vol. LXXXI, No. CLXVIII, July, 1855, pp. 276-77.*

[G. P. FISHER] (essay date 1856)

The splendid success of her previous work ["**Uncle Tom's Cabin**"] has not deterred [Harriet Beecher Stowe] from testing her strength again in the same field of literary effort. That she has not been intimidated by her own fame, is a sign that she takes up her pen from a better impulse than the desire of distinction. With ambition for a motive, she would have shrunk from competing with a rival so formidable as herself. (p. 515)

["**Dred**"] lacks a firm unity, and after the death of Nina, the interest of the reader rapidly declines. What follows seems to have been written for the purpose of dealing blows at different parties without much regard to the progress of the tale. In both her works, the author has shown more skill in the delineation of individual character than in the management of the plot. So slender is the thread that connects the different parts with one another, that "**Dred**" might be better styled a series of sketches pertaining to slave-life. The hero himself does not take hold on the sympathies of the reader. There is terrible power which we have never so much felt before, in the Hebrew prophets whom he personates; but he excites for himself no profound feeling. His part in the book reminds us of a criticism of Hazlitt on the Indian in Campbell's Gertrude. "He vanishes," says Hazlitt, "and returns after long intervals, like the periodical revolutions of the planets. He unexpectedly appears just in the nick of time, after years of absence, without any known reason but the convenience of the author and the astonishment of the reader; as if nature were a machine constructed on a principle of complete contrast, to produce a theatrical effect." . . . Mrs. Stowe has written, it is plain, under the consciousness that the justness of her picture of slavery would be disputed. Her desire to guard against this censure, has cramped her pen and marred the simplicity and power of her story. She goes after historical facts to make the narrative probable. . . . [The] author, at a single stroke, destroys her own creation, and wantonly disenchants the reader. [The facts and arguments within the story], as well as the appendix, are out of place. If they must appear at all, to vindicate the credit of the book, let them come by themselves, in a separate publication. We are displeased with the author when she lifts her forefinger and begins to argue; because she violates the law on which her own success depends. She puts us on a work of investigation at the moment when she would move our passions. And she will not suffer us to regard her characters as real beings—so quickly does she commence to dissect them. The author has not been able to suppress her indignation at the iniquities of slavery, and the champions of slavery. Her feeling is impatient of the circuitous channel afforded by the story, and demands a quicker outlet. It breaks forth in sharp assertions or satirical hints. If the deepest tone in "**Uncle Tom**" was sympathy with the suffering slave, the deepest tone in "**Dred**" is antipathy to the oppressive master. In the concluding portion of the book especially, the author is not cool enough to give naturalness to the action of the characters and the movement of the plot. Indeed, this part of the book, it must be said, is composed in a slovenly manner and betrays the haste of the writer. The characters have their fortunes fixed by a summary decision, without permitting the reader to note the steps of their progress. (pp. 517-19)

As a work of Art, as a passionate and moving story, we judge "**Dred**" to be inferior to "**Uncle Tom's Cabin.**" Yet we meet with passages and with characters which are hardly surpassed in the earlier tale. Aunt Milly's account of her life—what is there in Uncle Tom, more pathetic? Old Tiff, with his disinterested devotion to "dese y'er chil'en" is a truly original conception. His nobleness of heart so mixes with his droll manners that we admire and are amused at once. (p. 519)

Old Tiff will stand next to Uncle Tom in the heart of every reader of these wonderful tales. Other characters in "**Dred**," are also finely drawn. Aunt Nesbit, though bordering on a

caricature, is a humorous conception. So is Mr. Jekyl, who appears in his theology, which is sketched at length, to be a pretty consistent Edwardean. Clayton makes a poor figure in comparison with St. Clare. But Nina—what shall we say of Nina? A creature whose noble nature develops, and crowding away the weeds on the surface, forms a strong, lovely woman. Her death—not the death of Dred—but the death of Nina, with the light of beauty on her brow, and the light of faith in her soul, is the tragical event of the story.

As an exposition of the slave system, this work is much *above* "**Uncle Tom's Cabin.**" The author has evidently applied herself to the study of American slavery, in all its parts. We do not believe that she has given an unfair representation of society in the Southern states. The slaveholders cannot complain that she has treated them with injustice. . . . That humane and Christian men are found among the masters, Mrs. Stowe has taken pains to show. The difficulties which impede this class in their attempts to do good, are clearly set forth. The laws stand in their way. The jealousy of the body of the community and the dread of whatever tends to cultivate the intelligence of the negro, are a still stronger obstacle. The slaveholders have a hard but sound logic. (pp. 521-22)

Mrs. Stowe's book affords an appalling view of the hindrances which an effort for the emancipation of the slaves would have to encounter. The condition of a benevolent master is seen to be full of embarrassment. . . . We can easily conceive that the impression of "**Dred**" on some minds will be contrary to that which the author intends to make. (pp. 522-23)

Of the character of the negroes, Mrs. Stowe has given, as all confess, a graphic delineation. Few of the slaves have the marked traits which would qualify them to play a prominent part in a story. Hence, her books may give the idea that the slaves are higher, intellectually, than they are. . . . The characteristics of the negro, both constitutional and acquired, are faithfully depicted by Mrs. Stowe, and her views are confirmed by authentic statements from Southern writers. (p. 523)

Much has been said about the religious tendencies and temper of Mrs. Stowe's novel. "**Dred**" is charged, we see, in one of the religious newspapers, with "a contempt for orthodox religion." . . . We hold it to be the best service which Mrs. Stowe has rendered, that she has shown the power of the Gospel to elevate and sustain the humblest souls; and this she has done to myriads who would never have been reached by the Gospel in any other way. The divine beauty of religion has rarely been taught with better effect than on the pages of "**Dred**" and "**Uncle Tom.**" This excellence prevents the satire on counterfeit types of religion, from doing harm. (p. 525)

There are other points suggested in the perusal of "**Dred**," on which we should be glad to speak. We must leave the book, with these imperfect comments, but not without expressing our satisfaction in the fact that freedom has found a friend so able and devoted, as the author of these volumes. (p. 526)

[G. P. Fisher,] "Mrs. Stowe's New Novel," in The New Englander, *Vol. XIV, No. LVI*, November, 1856, pp. 515-26.

DUBLIN UNIVERSITY MAGAZINE (essay date 1856)

[Mrs. Stowe] is a character-monger—she excels in *situation*, but her pieces want *action*. The *denouement* of the story may come of itself, but her characters do not work it out. They rise into their places in every scene as the puppets in a show, and talk and behave most naturally while on the stage—but they sink again, and are no more seen 'till they rise in a new situation. Whatever plot there is, works itself out as well without them as with them. [*Dred*] is a drama with a rapid succession of scenes, but not divided into acts.

This want of plot was a fault in Uncle Tom. . . . There is nothing to bring the characters together before the curtain falls. . . . Of all the unities of the drama there is only one which cannot be dispensed with—the unity of interest; this unity *Uncle Tom* wants. It is not therefore a novel, for a novel must obey this law of the drama—but a narrative of events skilfully told, and enlivened by a gallery of portraits taken from life and fitted to the narrative.

Dred has the same extraordinary merits as a narrative, and defects as a drama, as *Uncle Tom*—in an even exaggerated form. The chief characters in both are duplicates, with some disguise and a few additions. Nature has moulded in Mrs. Stowe's mind a certain stock of characters in pairs and then broken the mould. (pp. 676-77)

The plot in *Dred* is even less skilfully handled than in *Uncle Tom*. The story is so unfinished that we look on it as a cartoon or a key to the coming *Dred*. . . .

Dred is not a novel, although it is advertised "at all the libraries." It is a political pamphlet to suit the age. . . . Never before has a novel dealt such blows on a giant evil. (p. 678)

Mrs. Stowe has thrown herself with all her heart and mind and soul and strength into the cause of abolitionism. The novel is only a thin veil thrown over her real purpose: Abolitionism is the theme of every chapter. She is too true an artist to accumulate horrors on horrors; the joys of slave life are told as well as the sorrows. But amid the wildest mirth, amid the most peaceful scenes of content, Mrs. Stowe never forgets her purpose; "*Surgit amari aliquid;*"—the end of that mirth is always heaviness. (p. 679)

> "*Slavery,*" in Dublin University Magazine, *Vol. XLVIII, No. CCLXXXVIII, December, 1856, pp. 675-90.**

THE IRISH QUARTERLY REVIEW (essay date 1856)

"**Dred,**" in proportion, is undoubtedly nearer to [Mrs. Beecher Stowe's "**Uncle Tom's Cabin**"], than "Shirley," or ["Villette"] is to "Jane Eyre;" but, notwithstanding, . . . we feel, if the authoress does not, that the riches of the mine have been pretty well worked out by the laborer, and that, in all human probability, the lower she goes the less she will get. This, perhaps, was to be expected; one cannot be an intellectual prodigal without suffering by the excessive expenditure, especially when a particular region is chosen, and a particular object is pertinaciously kept in view. When Thomas Campbell was asked to write a poem similar in style and metre to his "Pleasures of Hope," his answer was, "No; a man may make a single plunge and bring up a pearl, but he may dive a hundred times after, and find nothing but oyster shells to reward him for his pains." This was not Mrs. Beecher Stowe's view of her own capability, and it could hardly be expected that it could. Enthusiastic as she is as an abolitionist, and successful as she has been as a novelist, either motive might have swayed her to re-enter the lists, but with both to actuate her, impression was impossible. (pp. 776-77)

We know not what time it may have taken to compose "**Uncle Tom's Cabin;**" but it is abundantly evident that its successor has been written in too great a hurry; and although, in this instance, we could not go so far as to say that Mrs. Stowe's "easy writing is d—d hard reading," still the fact of undue haste is not less patent, and we have a right to complain that we are thereby deprived of a very sensible pleasure which we resent as an unnecessary loss. In the first place, the authoress had no story to tell; she had an essay to write, and she has thrown it into the form of desultory dialogues, with interlocutors, the greater number of whom are thoroughly uninteresting, and by far too large a number of them coarse, vulgar, and revolting in the extreme. In the second place, the characters, such as they are, do nothing *but* talk; they have the *vox et proterea* gift to an alarming extent; but when they come to act, they are as barren of fruit as a fig tree in December. Dred, the hero of the book, in name, is a half-maddened mystic, who lives in the dismal swamp, threatens his tyrants in scriptural language, and is shot down, we are not told how, but certainly without striking a stroke in his own defence, or that of any body else. Nina is allowed to live, until she becomes interesting, and then she is carried off by cholera, as Mercutio is by the sword of Tybalt, just when we particularly wish her not to die. Her gay, bluff, good-hearted old uncle, is finished off in the same manner; and although Harry and Clayton survive, they are so sketchy and imperfect as *actors,* that we hardly care a button whether they live or die. The villain of the book, Tom Gordon, outrages all our notions of poetical justice, by being allowed to lynch, whip, tar-and-feather, ravish, rob, exterminate, and commit such like atrocities, without a single hair of his guilty head being the worse of it. He may be getting drunk and blaspheming to this very hour, for aught we know, as when Mrs. Stowe dropped him, he was as prosperous as any slave-holding scoundrel could well be. We have certainly the consolation to hear that "Tiff" survives and prospers, and we are glad of it, inasmuch as we think that he and "Milly" are the only two characters worth a maravedi in the whole list. We might probably include "Tomtit" only that Tom evaporates like the rest, in order to make room for casuists and preachers, who, like almost all the other white people introduced, have little to recommend them but the ability to say much and do nothing.

What we regret particularly to learn from the book, are two disheartening facts; namely, that slavery, as an institution, is fixed and likely to be permanent; and that religion, properly so called, is at the very lowest ebb in the southern states of the American union. . . . We suppose that Mrs. Stowe has chosen the least disinterested as examples, but we cannot wonder that the whites are as black as sin can make them, when their spiritual affairs are directed by such men; and it is utterly hopeless to suppose that the blot of slavery can ever be removed, when each sect is afraid of giving its rival sect an advantage by counselling its removal from the national banner. If we required any additional illustrations of the danger which "the Bible let loose" is capable of doing, Mrs. Stowe's "**Dred,**" affords a series of "notes and comments," which Christians of all creeds would do well to ponder over, and which we cannot but hope will have a salutary effect, if anything can. (pp. 777-79)

> "*Novels of the Day,*" in The Irish Quarterly Review, *Vol. VI, No. XXIV, December, 1856, pp. 766-79.**

SOUTHERN LITERARY MESSENGER (essay date 1858)

[The] Beechers defy both natural and artificial methods of

classification, and can be ranked only in the catalogue of American curiosities. As we direct travellers to a hot spring or a mammoth cave, as the peculiarity of American nature, so we point out to him the Beecher family as the freak of American humanity. (p. 284)

Now, though it has been shrewdly suspected, that if the quality called Beecher were analyzed, it would be found to be identical with other forms of human depravity, yet as long as it passes for something better, its possessors are allowed immunities denied to the rest of the world. They can trample on conventionalities, say and do what others would be condemned for saying and doing, and all this is looked upon as only the characteristic manifestation of an elementary substance. (p. 284)

Mrs. Stowe appeared before the American public as the authoress of *Uncle Tom's Cabin*—she visited Europe, and on her return published two volumes of adjectives, which were sold and read as another work from the authoress of *Uncle Tom's Cabin;* and just as Thomas Campbell complained that he was never recognized in any other capacity than that of Author of the *Pleasures of Hope,* it seemed probable that Mrs. Stowe would be known to futurity, only as the patroness of poor Uncle Tom. "**Life among the Lowly**" was made the measure by which all subsequent publications of like kind should be guaged, and it was supposed that even its authoress, a modern Cervantes, would be unable again to produce anything which should quite come up to its standard. In defiance of this opinion, and no doubt with the triple intention of replenishing her purse, furthering moral reform, and reminding the world that she is mentally alive, Mrs. Stowe has issued another work [*Dred*], published simultaneously in three countries.

Instead of avoiding comparisons by aiming at a different target, with true Beecherly boldness she again selects the subject of slavery, and brings out of the Dismal Swamp some spirited sketches founded on the South Carolina insurrection, the Cincinnati slave case, and the attack on Mr. Sumner.

These are surnamed *Dred,* for no other reason than that it is a novel and attractive name. In fact, Dred is the most uninteresting and unnatural character in the book, and no more the hero than Mr. Edward Clayton, a man dubbed idealist because he followed his conscience rather than his interest, or Miss Nina, a singular combination of coquetry and practical philosophy, a rainbow with a pot of money at the end,—or best of all, Old Tiff, a negro who had possessed such extreme veneration for the "F.F.V.'s," that only the hard experience of age, and a residence in New England, could convince him that character was equivalent to family, and that as a lady could not marry all the generations back, it was best for her to look at the man himself rather than his ancestors.

In their portraiture of Southern life, we do not criticise the lights and shades of Mrs. Stowe's work. Let us rather look at its literary merits and moral character, at it, as the work of a popular authoress and Christian lady.

While *Uncle Tom* may be said to contain the pith of her genius, *Dred* is not wanting in the lively wit, drama and argument, which marked its predecessor. At the same time there is frequently discernible in it, a want of that delicacy always so pleasing in female writers, and of a reverence for sacred things no less essential to literary refinement than to consistent Christianity. Indeed, one of the most prominent features of the work is a constant bordering on profanity, and such frequent use of irreverent expressions as leads us to inquire into the nature of Mrs. Stowe's philanthropic zeal.

Is she engaged in a crusade against sin, or against slavery?

If against *sin,* what is accomplished, when, in destroying one form of evil she builds up another, and lends her influence at once to overturn oppression and encourage profanity? One would almost conclude that, in her view, slavery was the only synonym for guilt, and that she thought it no wrong to break the third specific commandment, to enforce the great general law of love.

The only apology for these expressions must be, that they are necessary to the effectiveness of her picture of Southern wrongs. But is profanity any more a *sina-qua-non* to *Dred* than cotton to the North, or negroes to the South?

The "shalt not" is as strict against profanity as against oppression, and the only plea for it is one that our anthoress denies to the South, that of expediency. (pp. 284-85)

From one identified with the tribe of Levi, as a daughter, sister, and wife, we could not have anticipated such libellous reflections on the American ministry as *Dred* contains. (p. 285)

[There] are accusations of the brethren as well as of the clergy. . . .

Of all the persons mentioned as lay professors of Christianity, not one is consistent save Tomtit, "who jined the church and did beautiful." The clear starched Aunt Nesbit, the barbarous Zekyl, are the examples of orthodox Christianity; while all genuine goodness is vested in Clayton, Nina, and non-professing Christians.

At once, to decide the matter for the scrupulous, *Dred* was advertised as a novel. It is, however, perused by anti-fictionists, who read *Uncle Tom* because it was true, and read *Dred* because they read *Uncle Tom,* though one tithe of the profanity it contained would interdict the work of any of the old novelists from our puritan homes.

Mrs. Stowe says, "In a book, it is contact with the personality of the author that improves you—a real book always makes you think that there is more in the writer than he has said."

We beg pardon for hoping that there is nothing unexpressed in *Dred,* and that its authoress, like the Queen of Sheba, "has no more spirit in her." . . .

We envy not the authoress who, in the deliberation of retirement, can fill her pen with unrefined expressions; we fear for the Christianity that can trifle with the use of profaneness; we do not acknowledge the patriotism which, in a foreign country, can quietly sit under the mutilated flag of our country.

Were she a woman, we should blush for the sex—luckily she is only a Beecher. (p. 286)

"Mrs. Stowe and 'Dred'," in Southern Literary Messenger, *n.s. Vol. VI, October, 1858, pp. 284-86.*

[HENRY JAMES]   (essay date 1859)

It has always seemed to us that the anti-Slavery element in the two former novels of Mrs. Stowe stood in the way of a full appreciation of her remarkable genius, at least in her own country. It was so easy to account for the unexampled popularity of "**Uncle Tom**," by attributing it to a cheap sympathy with sentimental philanthropy! . . . We had the advantage of reading that extraordinary book in Europe, long after the whirl of excitement produced by its publication had subsided, in the seclusion of distance, and with a judgement undisturbed by those political sympathies which it is impossible, perhaps unwise, to avoid at home. We felt then, and believe now, that the secret of Mrs. Stowe's power lay in that same genius, by which the great successes in creative literature have always been achieved—the genius that instinctively goes right to the organic elements of human nature, whether under a white skin or a black, and which disregards as trivial the conventional and factitious notions which make so large a part both of our thinking and feeling. . . . [The] creative faculty of Mrs. Stowe, like that of Cervantes in "Don Quixote" and of Fielding in "Joseph Andrews," overpowered the narrow specialty of her design, and expanded a local and temporary theme with the cosmopolitism of genius. . . .

There can be no stronger proof of the greatness of her genius, of her possessing that conceptive faculty which belongs to the higher order of imagination, than the avidity with which **"Uncle Tom"** was read at the South. It settled the point that this book was true to human nature, even if not minutely so to plantation life. . . .

It is a great satisfaction to us that in the **"Minister's Wooing"** she has chosen her theme and laid her scene amid New England habits and traditions. There is no other writer who is capable of perpetuating for us, in a work of art, a style of thought and manners which railways and newspapers will soon render as palaeozoic as the mastodon or the saurians. Thus far the story has fully justified our hopes. The leading characters are all fresh and individual creations . . . and all these are characters new to literature. And the scene is laid just far enough away to give proper tone and perspective.

We think we find in the story the promise of an interest as unhackneyed as it will be intense. There is room for the play of all the passions and interests that make up the great tragi-comedy of life, while all the scenery and accessories will be those which familiarity has made dear to us. We are a little afraid of Colonel Burr, to be sure, it is so hard to make a historical personage fulfill the conditions demanded by the novel of everyday life. He is almost sure to fall below our traditional conception of him, or to rise above the natural and easy level of character necessary to *keeping*, into the vague or the melodramatic. Moreover, we do not want a novel of society from Mrs. Stowe; she is quite too good to be wasted in that way, and her tread is much more firm on the turf of the "dooryard" or the pasture, and the sanded floor of the farm house, than on the velvet of the *salon*. . . .

In the materials of character already present in the story, there is scope for Mrs. Stowe's humor, pathos, clear moral sense, and quick eye for the scenery of life. We do not believe that there is any one who, by birth, breeding and natural capacity, has had the opportunity to know New England as well as she, or who has the peculiar genius so to profit by the knowledge.

> [Henry James,] *"Mrs. Stowe's New Novel," in* New York Tribune, *June 13, 1859, p. 5.*

THE DUBLIN REVIEW   (essay date 1860)

Like an old painting, ["**The Minister's Wooing**"] is not drawn for effect, it is a natural expression of the writer's soul; and we approach the consideration of it, therefore, with the diffidence and respect; because it is not of a mere tale that we have

to speak, nor yet is it a mere production of the imagination, nor yet a mere picture of the actual life the authoress seeks to portray, or of the historic personages she brings on the scene; our task is deeper, and higher, and more important; we have to deal with a high, and noble, and immortal being, whose life gives to the book its animation, and whose musical plaintiveness runs throughout it, mostly below the surface, but often openly betraying itself.

Let us speak the word boldly. The writer of this story is, unconsciously it may be, but nevertheless really, athirst after what alone can satisfy her, but which as yet, to judge from this book, she knows not as it is—the Catholic religion! (p. 190)

This story is none of our every day sickly sentimental unrealities; on the contrary, its very reality and freshness constitute its charm; and it is full of bright and cleverly-drawn scenes. (p. 191)

Of the whole volume it may be said, in the words of the fellow-countryman of the authoress [Longfellow], it is full of—

> . . . . the throngs
> Of the poet's songs,
> Memories of pleasures, and pains, and wrongs,
> The sound of winged words.
>
> This is the cry
> Of souls, that high
> On toiling, beating pinions fly,
> Seeking a warmer clime.
>
> (p. 206)

We do not say, however, that the book is faultless. There is that absence of the due appreciation of supernatural grace, which is so constantly found in Protestant writings; and, as might be expected, there is an undue exaltation of the natural. (p. 224)

If her book contains a few mistakes about Catholic practice or doctrine, there is no wilful, no unkind misrepresentation. We have not gone into all these mistakes, nor explained every point we could have desired to explain. But we cannot allow ourselves to conclude without expressing the earnest prayer of our heart, that the truth in all its divine beauty may one day, and that day an early one, shine in its fulness upon a heart so calculated to appreciate it, and to expand still more largely under the influences of its beams of heavenly love. Such is the best parting-wish we can offer to one who, if it were only as the poor negro's friend, must ever command our earnest sympathy. (pp. 227-28)

> *"'The Minister's Wooing'," in* The Dublin Review, *Vol. XLVII, No. XCV, May, 1860, pp. 190-228.*

[J. R. DENNETT]   (essay date 1869)

[Harriet Beecher Stowe's book, **"Oldtown Folks"**,] though it is called a novel, is better to be described as a series of pictures of life as seen from the kitchen, and best-room, and barnyard, and meadow, and wood-lot of a Massachusetts parsonage of the pre-locomotive days. So far as it is a novel, **"Oldtown Folks"** cannot be said to call for remark except from those whose duty it may be to point out defects of literary workmanship. Such persons will discover matter for fault-finding throughout the book. There is none of Mrs. Stowe's books that we know in which she has not failed as completely in the creation of character as she has succeeded decidedly in depicting typical Massachusetts men and women who—embodied in this and that individual person—have been under her observation ever since she began to observe, and whom she puts before us as she has seen the outside of them, and not as she has tried to imagine them. . . . [In] this story, nothing could be much better in its way than Mrs. Stowe's picture of the village do-nothing, Sam Lawson—whose do-nothingness is perhaps a little too much insisted upon—a being with whom every observer who knows New England villages is perfectly familiar in one or another incarnation of him, and whose traits lie upon the surface crying to be drawn. But no 'prentice hand would do much worse work than Mrs. Stowe's picture of Horace Holyoke. The entirely needless mistake is made, too, of putting the whole story into the mouth of this person, who has a deal too much to do to look like a man in his own place in the story without having it imposed on him to think and talk like a man about men's and women's acts and thoughts and feelings. While he is young he is not a boy but a little dreamy female, and as he grows on to the age and past it when the human character becomes distinctively—and with an obvious as well as a real distinctiveness—male or female, he becomes a more or less unsuccessful simulacrum of a man, except when he is a more or less unfeminine woman. Mr. Avery, on the other hand, who is minister rather than man, Mrs. Stowe gets on with reasonably well; she knows the ministerial type so far as a spectator can; and so she does well, too, with Mr. Jonathan Rossiter, who is not man so much as he is a schoolmaster of the old New England academy sort. Harry Percival, however, who is nothing New Englandish, but is to serve as the chief male figure of the novel, is destitute of sex or personality—a vaguely outlined prig.

In **"Oldtown Folks"** we not only have no male personages with a real existence of their own as individual men, but we have no such personages at all, whether male or female. (p. 437)

> [*J. R. Dennett,*] *"Mrs. Stowe's 'Oldtown Folks',"* in The Nation (*copyright 1869* The Nation *magazine,* The Nation Associates, Inc.), *Vol. VIII, No. 205, June 3, 1869, pp. 437-38.*

HENRY JAMES   (essay date 1875)

It would be rather awkward to attempt to tell what Mrs. Stowe's [*We and Our Neighbors; or, The Records of an Unfashionable Street: A Sequel to "My Wife and I"*] is about. . . . Mr. Henderson's dinner is one of the principal events of the book, and Mrs. Stowe's second manner, as we may call it, comes out strongly in the description of it. (pp. 242-43)

There are a great many . . . people, of whose identity we have no very confident impression, inasmuch as they never do anything but talk—and that chiefly about plumbing, carpet-laying, and other cognate topics. We cannot perhaps give chapter and verse for the discussion of these particular points, but the reader remains in an atmosphere of dense back-stairs detail which makes him feel as if he were reading an interminable file of tradesmen's bills. There is in particular a Mrs. Wouvermans, an aunt of . . . [Eva], who pervades the volume like a keeper of an intelligence office, or a female canvasser for sewing-machines. This lady, we know, is intended to be very unpleasant, but would it not have been possible to vary a little, for the relief of the reader, the form of her importunity? . . . [None] of Mrs. Stowe's ladies and gentlemen open their mouths without uttering some amazing vulgarism, and if we were to believe her report of the matter, the language used by good society in New York is a singular amalgam of the rural Yankee

dialect (so happily reproduced by Mrs. Stowe in some of her tales), the jargon of the Southern negroes, and the style of the paragraphs in the *Home Journal* about such-and-such a lady's "German." (p. 244)

> *Henry James, " 'We and Our Neighbors: Records of an Unfashionable Street' by Harriet Beecher Stowe" (originally published in* The Nation, *June 22, 1875), in his* Literary Reviews and Essays: On American, English, and French Literature, *edited by Albert Mordell (copyright, 1957, by Albert Mordell; reprinted with the permission of Twayne Publishers, a Division of G. K. Hall & Co., Boston), Twayne, 1957, pp. 242-44.*

OLIVER WENDELL HOLMES   (essay date 1882)

[*The following are Oliver Wendell Holmes's poems, "At the Summit," and "The World's Homage."*]

"At the Summit"

Sister, we bid you welcome,—we who stand
    On the high table-land;
We who have climbed life's slippery Alpine slope,
And rest, still leaning on the staff of hope,
Looking along the silent Mer de Glace,
Leading our footsteps where the dark crevasse
Yawns in the frozen sea we all must pass,—
    Sister, we clasp your hand!

Rest with us in the hour that Heaven has lent
    Before the swift descent.
Look! the warm sunbeams kiss the glittering ice;
See! next the snow-drift blooms the edelweiss;
The mated eagles fan the frosty air;
Life, beauty, love, around us everywhere,
And, in their time, the darkening hours that bear
    Sweet memories, peace, content.

Thrice welcome! shining names our missals show
    Amid their rubrics' glow,
But search the blazoned record's starry line,
What halo's radiance fills the page like thine?
Thou who by some celestial clue couldst find
The way to all the hearts of all mankind,
On thee, already canonized, enshrined,
    What more can Heaven bestow!

"The World's Homage"

If every tongue that speaks her praise
For whom I shape my tinkling phrase
    Were summoned to the table,
The vocal chorus that would meet
Of mingling accents harsh or sweet,
From every land and tribe, would beat
    The polyglots at Babel.

Briton and Frenchman, Swede and Dane,
Turk, Spaniard, Tartar of Ukraine,
    Hidalgo, Cossack, Cadi,
High Dutchman and Low Dutchman, too,
The Russian serf, the Polish Jew,
Arab, Armenian, and Mantchoo,
    Would shout, "We know the lady!"

Know her! Who knows not Uncle Tom
And her he learned his gospel from
　　Has never heard of Moses;
Full well the brave black hand we know
That gave to freedom's grasp the hoe
That killed the weed that used to grow
　　Among the Southern roses.

When Archimedes, long ago,
Spoke out so grandly, "*dos pou sto*—
　　Give me a place to stand on,
I'll move your planet for you, now,"—
He little dreamed or fancied how
The *sto* at last should find its *pou*
　　For woman's faith to land on.

Her lever was the wand of art,
Her fulcrum was the human heart,
　　Whence all unfailing aid is;
She moved the earth! Its thunders pealed,
Its mountains shook, its temples reeled,
The blood-red fountains were unsealed,
　　And Moloch sunk to Hades.

All through the conflict, up and down
Marched Uncle Tom and Old John Brown,
　　One ghost, one form ideal;
And which was false and which was true,
And which was mightier of the two,
The wisest sibyl never knew,
　　For both alike were real.

Sister, the holy maid does well
Who counts her beads in convent cell,
　　Where pale devotion lingers;
But she who serves the sufferer's needs,
Whose prayers are spelt in loving deeds,
May trust the Lord will count her beads
　　As well as human fingers.

When Truth herself was Slavery's slave,
Thy hand the prisoned suppliant gave
　　The rainbow wings of fiction.
And Truth who soared descends to-day
Bearing an angel's wreath away,
Its lilies at thy feet to lay
　　With Heaven's own benediction.

　　　　　　　　　　　　　　　(pp. 272-73)

> *Oliver Wendell Holmes, "Two Poems to Harriet Beecher Stowe on Her Seventieth Birthday" (1882), in* The Complete Poetical Works of Oliver Wendell Holmes, *Houghton, Mifflin and Company, 1895, pp. 272-73.*

SARAH ORNE JEWETT　(essay date 1889)

. . . I have been reading the beginning of **"The Pearl of Orr's Island"** and finding it just as clear and perfectly original and strong as it seemed to me in my thirteenth or fourteenth year, when I read it first. I never shall forget the exquisite flavor and reality of delight that it gave me. . . . It is classical—historical—anything you like to say, if you can give it high praise enough. I haven't read it for ten years at least, but *there it is!* Alas, that she couldn't finish it in the same noble key of simplicity and harmony; but a poor writer is at the mercy of much unconscious opposition. You must throw everything and everybody aside at times, but a woman made like Mrs. Stowe

cannot bring herself to that cold selfishness of the moment for one's work's sake, and the recompense for her loss is a divine touch here and there in an incomplete piece of work. I felt at the funeral that none of us could really know and feel the greatness of the moment, but it has seemed to grow more great to me ever since. (pp. 46-7)

> *Sarah Orne Jewett, in her letter to Mrs. Fields on July 5, 1889, in* Letters of Sarah Orne Jewett, *edited by Annie Fields (copyright, 1911, by Houghton Mifflin Company; reprinted by permission of Houghton Mifflin Company), Houghton Mifflin, 1911, pp. 46-8.*

HENRY JAMES　(essay date 1913)

There was, . . . I think, for that triumphant work [*Uncle Tom's Cabin*] no classified condition; it was for no sort of reader as distinct from any other sort, save indeed for Northern as differing from Southern: it knew the large felicity of gathering in alike the small and the simple and the big and the wise, and had above all the extraordinary fortune of finding itself, for an immense number of people, much less a book than a state of vision, of feeling and of consciousness, in which they didn't sit and read and appraise and pass the time, but walked and talked and laughed and cried and, in a manner of which Mrs. Stowe was the irresistible cause, generally conducted themselves. Appreciation and judgment, the whole impression, were thus an effect for which there had been no process—any process so related having in other cases *had* to be at some point or other critical; nothing in the guise of a written book, therefore, a book printed, published, sold, bought and "noticed," probably ever reached its mark, the mark of exciting interest, without having at least groped for that goal *as* a book or by the exposure of some literary side. . . . If the amount of life represented in such a work is measurable by the ease with which representation is taken up and carried further, carried even violently furthest, the fate of Mrs. Stowe's picture was conclusive: it simply sat down wherever it lighted and made itself, so to speak, at home; thither multitudes flocked afresh and there, in each case, it rose to its height again and went, with all its vivacity and good faith, through all its motions. (pp. 159-60)

> *Henry James, in his* A Small Boy and Others *(copyright © 1913 by Charles Scribner's Sons; copyright renewed © 1941 by Henry James; reprinted with the permission of Charles Scribner's Sons), Charles Scribner's Sons, 1913, 419 p.**

GAMALIEL BRADFORD　(essay date 1918)

[Mrs. Stowe's] stories, all her stories in greater or less degree, are founded on an extensive study of character and manners. This is true of her Southern novels, and they show that she had made good use of her opportunities in collecting material, both consciously and unconsciously. It is far more true of her New England books; and the fine and varied insight of **"The Minister's Wooing,"** **"The Pearl of Orr's Island,"** especially of **"Oldtown Folks,"** has hardly been surpassed since. In this line it must be remembered that Mrs. Stowe was an originator, for Hawthorne's work was entirely different in spirit. If Miss Jewett, Mrs. Freeman, and Miss Alice Brown have developed some sides more effectively, Mrs. Stowe deserves credit for having set the great example. (pp. 123-24)

[She] was filled with an overwhelming zeal to convey to others what beliefs she had. It is here that she differs from the notable writers who have succeeded her. They, for the most part, observe and report life as it is, from scientific and artistic curiosity. But to Mrs. Stowe every heart is a text and every tragedy a fearful example. (pp. 124-25)

And as her observation and material were affected by her missionary spirit, so her artistic methods were affected even more. Everywhere the illustration of human truth is a secondary object; the first is to produce an effect—naturally, a moral effect. Now, in literature the subordination of truth to effect, no matter for what purpose, is melodrama. Dumas and the thousands like him arrange effective incident merely to amuse, to startle and excite the reader; Mrs. Stowe arranges it to jolt the reader into the path of virtue. (p. 125)

> Gamaliel Bradford, "Harriet Beecher Stowe," (originally published in The Atlantic Monthly, Vol. 122, No. 1, July, 1918), in his Portraits of American Women (copyright, 1919 by Gamaliel Bradford; copyright renewed 1947 by Helen T. Bradford; reprinted by permission of Houghton Mifflin Company), Houghton Mifflin, 1919, pp. 99-300.

CONSTANCE MAYFIELD ROURKE   (essay date 1927)

[Carelessly combined as it seems, *Uncle Tom's Cabin*] has structure, with a free flow of narrative, and a wealth of invention. Slender as had been her observation of slavery, [Stowe] used every touch of it, acquiring the basic gift of the creative artist, that of deriving the essential from the fragmentary, of judging the whole piece by the small bit of pattern. It has become the custom to belittle *Uncle Tom's Cabin* as a work which was always over-colored, which never had a place outside the turbid sphere of propaganda, and is now outdated. But propaganda sole and simple it is not; it declares no platform, and is unconcerned with measures; what it offers is a sweeping picture and an outcry. Battered though it has become through the overplus of excitement which has attended its career, defective though it is in certain essentials, it still has qualities which lift it above its contemporary position as a tract, qualities which should dismiss the easy, usual charge of exaggeration. Obviously the book lacks a genuine realism; but perhaps it should not be judged as realism at all. Obviously it lacks the hardiness and purity of view which belong to great writing; its emotion is never free, but intensive, indrawn, morbid, sentimental if one chooses, running an unchecked course which seemed created by hysteria. But the unbroken force of that emotion produced breadth; in its expansions and uncalculating balances, its flowing absorption in large sequences of action and its loose combinations of interwoven fates, the story at least brings to mind what is meant by the epical scale; it has above all that affecting movement toward unknown goals over long distances which becomes the irresistible theme of the greater narrative, rendered here with pathos because the adventure is never free, but always curtailed or fatefully driven. Diminish it as one may by stressing its sentimentalities or juxtaposing against it gentler glimpses of slavery, there is no denying that *Uncle Tom's Cabin* presents an elementary human condition with all its stark humiliations and compulsions, the straits of mind and body and feeling to which man can reduce man. Viewed at a distance, apart from its inevitable association with a cause, its worth becomes that of the typical or prototypical; subtract it from literary history, and a certain evaluation of human experience would be gone. (pp. 104-05)

Out of the stilted pathos of the main story [of *Dred*] arises a bold and terrible fantasy—pure fantasy—which outstrips the obvious theme. Fear runs through the narrative, never quite like a passion, always a little suppressed; demonism haunts it. An impenetrable thick growth of cypress and wild vine and blasted trees in a deep swamp makes a wilderness where hunted negroes find sanctuary, from which emerges the figure of Dred, who cries in eerie places at dawn and sweeps down upon the huddled revivalism of a negro camp-meeting with something of the terror of the Hebraic God. . . . [Out] of Dred's wailing utterances, his shouts of the fallen star called wormwood, of sharp sickles and ripe grapes, came an unmistakable foreboding of the black chaos of war. At the same time Mrs. Stowe fought her inheritance; like a sharp and acrid theme through the book runs an attack on Calvinistic doctrine and the Calvinistic ministry—an attack so bitter as to draw comments from its adherents on all sides, though few of Mrs. Stowe's contemporaries, it seems, were in a position to recognize its implications or the sources of her rancor. (p. 115)

[The opening chapters of *The Pearl of Orr's Island*] are idyllic, fluent, yet hardly soft; within them humor rises easily, humor of a native tang . . . ; this prelude is a little gold and silvery perhaps, but its unexalted perceptions might have gone far toward establishing the tradition of a simple realism if they had been carried steadily onward. Mrs. Stowe had written these passages as a sudden venture after the turmoil of producing *Uncle Tom's Cabin,* as if in their freshness and clarity she had found a natural harbor. Here, perhaps, was something of the sweet and tranquil mood into which she had drifted as a child among the green hills of Litchfield, a serene emotion which had naturally belonged to her. But now she destroyed this mood; as she continued her story she transformed it into a buttress for the new faith which she had struggled so often to maintain; her tale became a dull and exaggerated glorification of a death glimpsed without terror. . . . And once more the old enemy Calvinism was demolished; the novel became an argument. (pp. 120-21)

[*Oldtown Folks*] summed up the many-sided warfare of a lifetime. Its pages were crowded with ministerial characters, whose harshness of essential temperament were limned, whose marrying habits were freely discoursed upon; among other circumstances Mrs. Stowe pointed out the trials of their wives, who more frequently than not died under the strain; one of these stern apostles was married three times, like Lyman Beecher [Stowe's father]. . . . Filled to the brim with lively notations of people and places, this book remains the richest and raciest of Mrs. Stowe's novels; and ironically enough, its background was drawn in the main from the homely reminiscences of Calvin Stowe [her husband]. (p. 135)

[Undoubtedly] *Lady Byron Vindicated* was a feminist document, the wild offshoot of a sturdy movement; Mrs. Stowe's strained syllables were part of the feminist vocabulary of the day. With her extraordinary talent for slipping blindly into a public drama without knowledge or perception of its outcome, once more she found herself abreast of a momentous agitation. (p. 141)

> Constance Mayfield Rourke, "Harriet Beecher Stowe," in her Trumpets of Jubilee (copyright © 1927 by Harcourt Brace Jovanovich, Inc.; copyright renewed © 1958 by Alice D. Fore; reprinted by permission of the publisher), Harcourt Brace Jovanovich, 1927, pp. 87-148.

STARK YOUNG (essay date 1933)

As literary effort "Uncle Tom's Cabin" is mere period trash; which means something that would in any epoch have been trash, but that is trash rendered in the style of a certain epoch, in this case the mid-nineteenth century, a slightly belated American version of the English manner of that day. . . .

With Mrs. Stowe it is more a lack of literary talent than—shall we say?—brains or experience and observation, for she had been thrown in contact with slavery and knew much about Southern varieties of slave and family and plantation life or incident. She has seen plenty of blacks but cannot make them talk. Her ear is impossible; she has no sense of their rhythm or vividness. She has no knowledge of their African past and appears to picture African families as living hearths of devotion, despite the fact that many slaves were sold to the traders by their own kin and tribesmen. Her main character, Uncle Tom, she intends as a vehicle that will convey to us the Negro goodness; but she makes him only a dummy. The special goodness characteristic of his kind, with its own spontaneity, simplicity, innocence, animality and beauty, eludes her. All she can do with her material is to superimpose her own ideas, rule the figures of her story into definite types in the argument and plod onward very seriously and with a curious elaboration.

What, then, can be the point about this epochal book? For it cannot be true that a book can make such a stir in the world as did "Uncle Tom's Cabin" and have no virtues. Apart from the topicalities and incidental appeal of the subject, the problem analyzes itself down to simple terms:

The argument is scrupulously divided, fair to both sides. I should be astonished after reading the book to think how poignantly it struck the North and how it enraged the South, if I had not had a chance during the World War to see what passion, prejudice and the force of issues do to people's minds. As far as individuals themselves go, man to man, the people in the North get quite as much dressing down from Mrs. Stowe as the Southerners do; you could not imagine—save at your peril and the threat of even more of those infinite, boring scenes where the points are to be established—a greater show of justice in the debate. On one ground only the Southern indignation can be justified. It did not appear to Mrs. Stowe, but it was a real ground: she settles the matter too easily. Plenty of Southern people did not believe in slavery, but they knew no ready solution for the problem. Mrs. Stowe in just getting the slaves free, happy and whole, sails a bit head-on. . . . On this ground her smooth and holy solutions were rightly irritating. Otherwise her blows are equally distributed, whether on Northern conscience or on Southern property and pride. (pp. 212-13)

Technically her book is led to choosing two themes which are indisputable and which have human interest with a bang. The two defects that are inherent in slavery and that compose these themes are, first, slavery could lead to the separation of families, a hideous inhumanity that nobody could deny. . . . The other defect inherent was that the prosperity of the slave depended on the master into whose hands he fell, which cannot be denied either. . . .

[For] an emotional finale to her argument and exhortation, Mrs. Stowe resorts to a pathological case in selling Tom to a man whose pleasures lead him into destroying what cost him fifteen hundred dollars, a situation too lavish to be common even among the brutal slaveholding men down the river. Nevertheless it fits the argument. And it is the best part of the book as fiction. The Gothic novel helps the writer at this point toward

effects of terror, and there is something savory enough in this mad figure torturing, drinking, killing, whatever the expense and the probability. Good raw horror, mystery and sanctity have after all their literary rights. (p. 213)

> *Stark Young, "Uncle Tom's Measure" (reprinted by permission of the Literary Estate of Stark Young), in* The New Republic, *Vol. 76, No. 983, October 4, 1933, pp. 212-13.*

ARTHUR HOBSON QUINN (essay date 1936)

[Harriet Beecher Stowe] began, so far as her novels are concerned, with an idealistic treatment of the Negro. . . . Viewed critically now, [*Uncle Tom's Cabin*] seems poor art. The characters are, from nearly all points of view, either black or white. Uncle Tim, Eva, Topsy, Eliza, are by any critical standard, absurdities, and if Legree and Loker seem overdrawn to us now, it can be imagined how the South looked upon them in 1852. . . . Yet when a novel has become an historical landmark and when a sophisticated audience is thrilled by the play when well presented after half a century, it is necessary to inquire the reason for its great human appeal. This lies in Mrs. Stowe's choice of one of the most dramatic of all themes, the spectacle of one human being under the absolute power of another. Two elements are necessary in order to secure that dramatic interest to the greatest degree. The two human beings must be as much alike, mentally, morally, and spiritually, as possible, in order to make the situation tragic, and the cruelty must be intense. Mrs. Stowe was forced, therefore, to select individuals from the white race that were much lower than the average and choose slaves that were much higher. She was also obliged to put the cruelty on with a brush. This she did, consciously or not, and the result was success. (pp. 159-60)

[Turning] to New England life, which she knew better than slavery, she produced her best novel, *The Minister's Wooing,* a story laid some time after the Revolution. Aaron Burr is brought in as a dangerous but fascinating person, but the interest of the book lies not in its history but in the study of human beings like Mary Scudder, in the throes of intense spiritual struggle. If her agony at the thought of her sailor lover, lost forever because he was not a member of her church, seems now unnatural, it was then stark reality, and was based on the experience of Mrs. Stowe's sister. The clergyman, Samuel Hopkins, is also a real person; not only was his sermon against the slave trade drawn from her own father's stock, but it is embedded in narrative which proved Mrs. Stowe's right to be called a master. She could not help the didactic tone which is never absent from her stories. She came from the ministerial class, she married into it, and the generations who had pondered over motives natural and supernatural speak in some of the finest passages in the book. (pp. 160-61)

[*Agnes of Sorrento*] is filled with the conventional Italian figures which bear no relation to actuality, and it marks no progress. Much better was *The Pearl of Orr's Island,* which was in her mind in 1852, but which was not published until 1862; it is a good example of her virtues and defects as a novelist. At times it is exquisite in its depiction of the spiritual intensity of Mara Pennel, the little girl whose parents die and leave her to be brought up by her grandparents. The boy and girl life of Mara and "Moses," who is rescued from drowning and who is of Spanish descent, is real; her complete absorption in him, while it makes her ideal rather than real, is also artistically done. She is, of course, too much of an angel, but her visions of eternal life while she waits for the inevitable approach of death by tuberculosis are not only absolutely true to life, under such circumstances, but are also written in a style for which Mrs. Stowe need make no apology. (pp. 161-62)

Mrs. Stowe went out of her field in a social satire, *Pink and White Tyranny*. . . . There is a fair revelation of a selfish woman's ability to ruin her husband's life, but Mrs. Stowe did not understand that a novelist cannot create society in its more exclusive forms by simply stating that her characters belong to it. (pp. 162-63)

Mrs. Stowe's position in our fiction will probably be determined by a book which is far from being her best work. But just because she was one of the greatest social and moral forces of her time, she could hardly hope to be one of its greatest artists. When the moral teacher was colored by the instinct for the supernatural and held in check by the power of an objective artist, New England gave us a Hawthorne; when the moral teacher overshadowed even the supernatural, and the artist remained subjective, New England produced Mrs. Stowe. (p. 163)

> *Arthur Hobson Quinn, "The Transition of Realism,"*
> *in his* American Fiction: An Historical and Critical
> Survey *(© 1936, renewed 1963; adapted by permission of Prentice-Hall, Inc., Englewood Cliffs, N.J.),*
> Appleton-Century-Crofts, 1936, pp. 159-205.*

ELIZABETH BOWEN   (essay date 1942)

Authoress of a best seller that made history, Mrs. Beecher Stowe would appear to owe much to the unhappiness of her youth. It is from the ranks of ill-adjusted people that crusaders most often emerge. If *Uncle Tom's Cabin* is not a work of art, it is the explosion of a remarkable temperament. Her humane indignation was real enough. But, with that sublime unscrupulousness to be found in even the minor artist, she cashed in on a real abuse to express her own passions—passions which a blameless, indigent marriage, motherhood, and one or two female friendships had not, so far, released. (p. 91)

> *Elizabeth Bowen, "Success Story," in* The Observer
> *(reprinted by permission of The Observer Limited),*
> *1942 (and reprinted in her* Collected Impressions,
> *Alfred A. Knopf, 1950, pp. 91-3).*

CHARLES HOWELL FOSTER   (essay date 1948)

In *The Minister's Wooing,* Mrs. Stowe balanced the dark aspects of New England religion and life against her conviction that "Never was there a community where the roots of common life shot down so deeply, and were so intensely grappled around things sublime and eternal. The founders . . . turned their backs on the whole glory of the visible to found . . . a republic of which the God of Heaven and Earth should be the sovereign power. . . . In a community thus unworldly must have arisen a mode of thought, energetic, original, and sublime." This defense of New England civilization has its origin, partially at least, in Mrs. Stowe's reappraisal of Puritanism during her European journey. In the same weeks in which she gradually realized the aesthetic limitation of Puritanism, she came to realize its social contribution. The rough verses commemorating eighteen thousand Covenanters slain between 1661 and 1688 inspired her to defend "the world's benefactors and reformers," who, in being "without form or comeliness," were a trial to our virtue. (p. 497)

Mrs. Stowe's mature evaluation of Puritanism may be

traced to her first encounter with the Old World, but her embodiment of that evaluation in character and incident in *The Minister's Wooing* had its primary source in the appeal of her father, Lyman Beecher, age seventy-eight, for help from his children in preparing his autobiography. (pp. 499-500)

The degree to which Mrs. Stowe made conscious and calculated use of her father's *Autobiography* it is impossible to determine in many instances. But the *Autobiography* must still be regarded as the primary source for many of the personalities and striking details of the picture of Puritanism in *The Minister's Wooing.* . . . The major revelation derived from comparison of the *Autobiography* with *The Minister's Wooing* concerns Mary Scudder, who in losing a lover at sea has been identified in the past with Catharine Beecher in life. In terms of Mrs. Stowe's use of the *Autobiography* or of her own memories, however, Mary Scudder's story was only in bare outline that of Catharine. Mary's character was in all likelihood modeled on that of Mrs. Stowe's mother, Roxana Foote Beecher. Mary as a New England nun embodying all the Puritan virtues was like Roxana in instance after instance. (pp. 501-02)

At the center of *The Minister's Wooing* Mrs. Stowe thus placed in a fictionalized portrait of her mother the clearest vindication of Puritanism furnished by her father's *Autobiography.* (p. 504)

The event which caused [the] diverse materials to germinate rapidly in Mrs. Stowe's mind and imagination was, of course, the death of Henry Ellis Stowe in the summer of 1857. . . . In composing *The Minister's Wooing,* Mrs. Stowe could give semilyrical expression to her own inner crisis and by imaginative extension she could find the release countless men and women have found in writing themselves out of their anguish. (pp. 512-13)

[In] the period of her grief equivalent to that in which Catharine had imagined herself following her lost friend rebelliously to hell, Mrs. Stowe could write placidly of a perfect reconciliation to sorrow that made it blessedness. (p. 514)

In [her] firm faith in God, and in Henry's salvation, Mrs. Stowe felt no need to reject the Calvinism which had shaped all of her basic intellectual and emotional attitudes. . . . It was as one well aware of the beautiful possibilities of reconciliation that Mrs. Stowe wrote *The Minister's Wooing,* and she did not even fundamentally question Calvinistic views concerning the eternal punishment of evil. (p. 516)

> *Charles Howell Foster, "The Genesis of Harriet Beecher Stowe's 'The Minister's Wooing',"in* The
> New England Quarterly *(copyright 1948 by The New England Quarterly), Vol. XXI, No. 4, December, 1948, pp. 493-517.*

ALEXANDER COWIE   (essay date 1948)

The virtues of *Uncle Tom's Cabin* as a novel arise from Mrs. Stowe's humanity, her ardent imagination, and her ability to finger detail sensitively; its faults are mainly attributable to the author's unwillingness to let the objective facts speak for themselves and to her always inadequate control of structure. The changing locale of the action made breaks in the narrative which Mrs. Stowe spliced with so little skill that the whole structure seems to sprawl. This, however, was common enough in American fiction before the time of Howells and James. More serious is the violence done to the story by Mrs. Stowe's doctrinaire method. Time and again she interrupts the narrative to press home a moral which the action itself has spelled in large enough letters. Her apostrophes to the reader, though precedented in Dickens's similar exhortations, do not strengthen the novel. Most serious of all is her tendency to sacrifice character to moral crusade. A few of the minor characters, Sam, for example, seem almost wholly real. Most of the others have a basic strength which is impaired in varying degree as they become the pawns of propaganda. Uncle Tom's simple affectionate nature, his manifold troubles, and even his zeal for salvation make for reality, but he is occasionally drafted crudely into the service of Mrs. Stowe's Christian war. . . . Tom's forgiveness of his enemies, though factually credible, is too facile. So with the other characters: they suffer loss of realism when touched by the saintliness of Eva and Tom or when used as a vehicle for polemic. Topsy's diablerie is described with a good deal of vraisemblance, but her reform, though slow, seems a mechanical dispensation. The amiable but vacillating St. Clare is at first a splendidly drawn character, but Mrs. Stowe, who has foreordained his conversion, finally makes him utter religious sentiments that ring as hollowly as his earlier opinions on slavery (pro and con) had sounded genuine. The worst of all the characters is the hypocritical Mrs. St. Clare, who is merely a vessel into which Mrs. Stowe pours her contempt for the selfish and unthinking proponents of slavery. Even Legree, chief of the sinners in the hands of an angry Mrs. Stowe, is more real than Mrs. St. Clare. Yet though a number of real elements went into Legree's characterization (including his Vermont background), the whole synthesis seems spurious. He is as wicked as Uncle Tom is saintly.

As for sentimentalism, it was a demand of the times. There is in *Uncle Tom* more sighing, sobbing, weeping, and "earnest" exhortation, more talk of angels and glory, than goes down with readers accustomed to the emotional understatement of many twentieth-century writers. . . . Yet the fifties were a decade of sentimentality in life as in literature, and what now seems mawkish (in Dickens as well as Mrs. Stowe) was then regarded as real pathos. Moreover, Mrs. Stowe's tears were no mere substitute for real emotion, for she had what few contemporary purveyors of sobs had, namely, a tremendous intensity of purpose and an unquestioned sincerity. For this reason *Uncle Tom's Cabin* has lived on as a serious, though artistically defective, book while T. S. Arthur's *Ten Nights in a Bar-Room* has been laughed into the museum. . . . Mrs. Stowe's warm humanity so well covered the technical defects of the book that the response to it was almost wholly emotional. Seldom has a novel subsisted so largely on sheer sincerity and integrity. . . . [In her *A Key to Uncle Tom's Cabin*] Mrs. Stowe reveals her enormous industry; yet though critics subjected it to close scrutiny, the public was less interested in sources than in results and it continued to prove its devotion to *Uncle Tom's Cabin* as an irresistible story on a great theme. (pp. 450-52)

Dred is structurally ineffective in that Dred's story is not successfully united with Nina's. Yet there is no character in *Uncle Tom's Cabin* at once so appealing and so real as Nina Gordon, and her death, briefly described, is more tragic to modern readers than Eva's carefully ordered demise. Old Tiff is just as lovable as Uncle Tom, and he is not laid under such fearfully holy requirements. The story as a whole is not so intense as *Uncle Tom's Cabin,* but it is more comprehensive and it is well grounded. Its more objective treatment was approved by Harriet Martineau, who believed that *Dred* would do endless good "by suddenly splitting open Southern life, for everybody to look into." (p. 453)

[In *The Minister's Wooing* Mrs. Stowe] is less the prophet or protagonist than the chronicler. Here if ever she should prove how far she was an artist. The action is a simple one involving the hand of a girl unconsciously in love with a young man of uncertain spiritual state and at the same time governed by an admiration for a minister to such an extent that under the influence of her ambitious mother she is persuaded to plight her hand (thinking that the heart would follow) in accordance with the whisper of "duty." Intimations that the report of the young man's death by drowning may have been exaggerated are anxiously weighed in the reader's mind against the fearful blow the minister would suffer if he lost his betrothed. Ultimately, without very great sacrifice of plausibility, Mrs. Stowe manages to evolve that happy ending which was the tacit demand of so many novel readers of the period. For this story Mrs. Stowe did not have to "get up" very much of her materials. . . . For modern readers the book doubtless contains too much parleying on theology and a too obvious championship of right living. (pp. 454-55)

[*The Pearl of Orr's Island*] is a mixture of idyll and tragedy experienced by the families of sea-captains and fishing folk on the coast of Maine. It was originally designed to be a sketch of the childhood of the chief characters, but Mrs. Stowe later decided to extend it to a full-length story. She did not succeed in welding together its two parts, but she did succeed in investing the book with genuine New England data. (p. 455)

[*Agnes of Sorrento*] is one of the few stories in which Mrs. Stowe wholly forsook New England scenery and characters. The story is more continuously "romantic" than was usual with Mrs. Stowe. . . . In tone *Agnes of Sorrento* has much in common with the sentimental romance. . . . Coincidence and melodrama are freely drawn upon to whip up a plot far more exciting superficially than those of most of Mrs. Stowe's other stories. The religious ferment of the times (which Mrs. Stowe compares with a Wesleyan revival) gives body to the book. (p. 456)

Beyond an ability to release honest feeling Mrs. Stowe had very few of the attributes of a first-rate writer. . . . She was often repetitious and literal. Her defective knowledge of sentence-structure and syntax occasionally brought her to such an impasse that "it sometimes needed the combined skill of all the proofreaders and the assistant editor to extricate her." . . . [She] was at home only in New England. Without apparent effort she could set down descriptions of New England scenes that wear the face of reality. . . . Yet except for those scenes which had sunk into her mind through "unconscious observation" she was not skilful at conveying a feeling of locale. With good right it was complained that *Dred* did not reveal a thorough acquaintance with North Carolina. She never gave a comprehensive picture of actual working conditions on a plantation in the far South, nor will her New Orleans settings compare in richness with those of Cable or Tourgée or even De Forest. She was fond of dramatic crises in action; but coldly examined, most of them, including the famous ice-cake episode of Eliza, seem amateurish in technique; only the author's contagious excitement carried them off. In short Mrs. Stowe had very little to go on except a store of honest experience as an enlightened daughter of Puritanism and a simple eloquence in expressing her love of humanity. (pp. 460-61)

Mrs. Stowe's literary career was, then, a curious one. If she had stopped writing in 1859 (after *The Minister's Wooing*) she would have left undone no book which is valued today by any but special devotees. The first of her two themes, slavery, was removed by history; the second, the New England heritage, was discounted as time went on. She continued to mint genuine coin but the collectors gradually lost interest: they cared only for the early issues. Perhaps Mrs. Stowe was prone to insist upon too large a proportion of the gold of truth; she never learned the formulas of those alloys which have the greatest currency and are able to withstand the attrition of years. Her honest, naive studies of contemporary social life could not match those of Mary J. Holmes and Augusta Jane Evans Wilson and a number of other artful practitioners of the novel of manners who had learned how dearly the public loves the truth if it is so bundled up in sentiment as to be unrecognizable. Her reputation, therefore, rests mainly upon one book, *Uncle Tom's Cabin,* which even today glows with much of that emotional fire which at first concealed the blurred lines of Mrs. Stowe's imperfect art. (p. 463)

> Alexander Cowie, "Experiment and Tradition," in his The Rise of the American Novel (copyright, 1948, by American Book Company; copyright, 1951, by American Book Company; reprinted by permission of D. C. Heath and Company), American Book, 1948 (and reprinted by American Book, 1951), pp. 447-504.*

JAMES BALDWIN   (essay date 1949)

Uncle Tom's Cabin is a very bad novel, having, in its self-righteous, virtuous sentimentality, much in common with *Little Women.* Sentimentality, the ostentatious parading of excessive and spurious emotion, is the mark of dishonesty, the inability to feel; the wet eyes of the sentimentalist betray his aversion to experience, his fear of life, his arid heart; and it is always, therefore, the signal of secret and violent inhumanity, the mask of cruelty. *Uncle Tom's Cabin*—like its multitudinous, hard-boiled descendants—is a catalogue of violence. This is explained by the nature of Mrs. Stowe's subject matter, her laudable determination to flinch from nothing in presenting the complete picture; an explanation which falters only if we pause to ask whether or not her picture is indeed complete; and what constriction or failure of perception forced her to do so depend on the description of brutality—unmotivated, senseless—and to leave unanswered and unnoticed the only important question: what it was, after all, that moved her people to such deeds.

But this, let us say, was beyond Mrs. Stowe's powers; she was not so much a novelist as an impassioned pamphleteer; her book was not intended to do anything more than prove that slavery was wrong; was, in fact, perfectly horrible. This makes material for a pamphlet but it is hardly enough for a novel. . . . (pp. 578-79)

It is [the] power of revelation which is the business of the novelist, [the] journey toward a more vast reality which must take precedence over all other claims. . . . Both *Gentleman's Agreement* and *The Postman Always Rings Twice* exemplify [the] terror of the human being, the determination to cut him down to size. And in *Uncle Tom's Cabin* we may find foreshadowing of both: the formula created by the necessity to find a lie more palatable than the truth has been handed down and memorized and persists yet with a terrible power.

It is interesting to consider . . . the method [Mrs. Stowe] used to solve the problem of writing about a black man at all. Apart from her lively procession of field-hands, house-niggers, Chloe, Topsy, etc.—who are the stock, lovable figures presenting no problem—she has only three other Negroes in the book. These

are the important ones and two of them [George and Eliza], may be dismissed immediately, since we have only the author's word that they are Negro and they are, in all other respects, as white as she can make them. . . . The figure from whom the novel takes its name, Uncle Tom, who is a figure of controversy yet, is jet-black, wooly-haired, illiterate; and he is phenomenally forbearing. He has to be; he is black; only through this forbearance can he survive or triumph. . . . The virtuous rage of Mrs. Stowe is motivated by nothing so temporal as a concern for the relationship of men to one another—or, even, as she would have claimed, by a concern for their relationship to God—but merely by a panic of being hurled into the flames, of being caught in traffic with the devil. She embraced this merciless doctrine with all her heart, bargaining shamelessly before the throne of grace: God and salvation becoming her personal property, purchased with the coin of her virtue. Here, black equates with evil and white with grace; if, being mindful of the necessity of good works, she could not cast out the blacks—a wretched, huddled mass, apparently, claiming, like an obsession, her inner eye—she could not embrace them either without purifying them of sin. She must cover their intimidating nakedness, robe them in white, the garments of salvation; only thus could she herself be delivered from ever-present sin. . . . Tom, therefore, her only black man, has been robbed of his humanity and divested of his sex. It is the price for that darkness with which he has been branded.

Uncle Tom's Cabin, then, is activated by what might be called a theological terror, the terror of damnation; and the spirit that breathes in this book, hot, self-righteous, fearful, is not different from that spirit of medieval times which sought to exorcize evil by burning witches; and is not different from that terror which activates a lynch mob. (pp. 580-81)

> James Baldwin, "Everybody's Protest Novel" in Partisan Review (copyright © 1949 by Partisan Review, Inc., copyright © reassigned 1955 to James Baldwin), Vol. 16, No. 6, June, 1949, pp. 578-85.

EDWARD WAGENKNECHT   (essay date 1952)

One of the domestic sentimentalists, Harriet Beecher Stowe, must have separate and more respectful treatment, for her *Uncle Tom's Cabin* . . . was the most sensational event in the world history of the novel, and it made its author the most famous American woman of her time. (p. 91)

Over *Uncle Tom's Cabin* the critical battle still rages. But there is general agreement on Mrs. Stowe's gifts as a storyteller, her vivid power of invention, her ability to "build" a book. (p. 93)

But attempts are still made to discredit the novel on the ground that Mrs. Stowe did not know slavery well enough to be able to write about it. This view can be strongly defended. . . . Mrs. Stowe, as Lowell perceived, had the mind of a romancer. Divination, intuition—not scholarship nor exact historical knowledge—are the hallmarks of such a mind. And when we come to characterization, the coarseness and obviousness—in a realistic sense, the glaring unreality—of many of Mrs. Stowe's personages is quite clear, but their tremendous vitality as powerful types of human myth or fantasy is even clearer. The epic-like rhythm of the book has impressed many critics. . . . (p. 94)

Dred is much more literary than its predecessor; pigmentation aside, its hero would have felt quite at home in the world of *Old Mortality.* It should be added that *Uncle Tom's Cabin* itself became a source for *Dred:* Old Tiff is almost Uncle Tom; Harry is nearly George Harris; Tomtit is a mild, masculine Topsy.

But the author's mood is much less conciliatory than it was in her first novel. This time she is out to show the bad influence of slavery not only upon the slaves but also upon their masters. Miscegenation she takes boldly in her stride, for Harry, the faithful steward, is his master's son by a slave woman. She warns the South that there is a day of reckoning coming. In place of the Christian pacifism of Uncle Tom, we now have the Old Testament militarism of Denmark Vesey's son, who takes to the swamps, whence he proposes to strike boldly as the avenger.

In the heroine of *Dred,* Nina Gordon, we get the first striking example of Mrs. Stowe's strange tenderness for the fashionable, frivolous girl. Nina's development, through the love of a wise man and sudden, cruel contact with the world's evil, is beautifully done up to a point. Unfortunately Mrs. Stowe did not know where to stop. A girl of courage and fine humanity did not satisfy her; she had to have a saint; and this is about as convincing as it had been to make Topsy, in her ultimate phase, a missionary to Africa! Worse, having accomplished this, Mrs. Stowe turns about and slays the girl, with typical Victorian sadism, as she had already slain Little Eva and was to slay Mara, of *The Pearl of Orr's Island,* and even the hapless infant at the beginning of *My Wife and I.* And when she killed Nina, she came close to killing the book. (p. 95)

Mrs. Stowe represents the Novel as Evangel. Even *Uncle Tom's Cabin* was more than an antislavery tract. Slavery is used to introduce universal problems: a mother's struggle for her child, the cruelty of the strong and the helplessness of the weak, the terror of all mankind in the face of death. (p. 100)

Mrs. Stowe was no bigot and no prude. No bigot could have presented the skeptical St. Clare so sympathetically, or given Clayton, the ideal young hero of *Dred,* so little orthodoxy. No prude could have responded to George Sand and Madame de Staël and George Eliot as Mrs. Stowe did; in an age when it was notoriously improper for a woman to speak out in meeting upon any subject, no prude could have spoken as Mrs. Stowe spoke—of miscegenation, of incest, of every other terrible thing that needed to be spoken of in the name of the Kingdom of God. George Sand called Mrs. Stowe a saint [see excerpt above]. If she was, she wore her halo at a slightly rakish angle; it was not for nothing that Leonard Bacon said his country was inhabited by "saints, sinners, and Beechers."

The most powerful preachers of the Christian faith in Mrs. Stowe's fiction are two Negro women—Candace, who comforts Mrs. Marvyn when she believes her son lost and damned, and the slave Milly, in *Dred.* Chapter XVI of that novel, which is Milly's account of how it became possible for her to forgive and befriend the heartless mistress who had sold her children, is as powerful a presentation of the Gospel as American literature has achieved. (pp. 100-01)

In Mrs. Stowe's pages, women are the true spiritual guides. She never bowed down to the clergy. She was the daughter, the wife, the mother of a clergyman, and the sister of seven clergymen—she understood that breed only too well. But the insight of a Christian mother—ah! that is the norm by which she tests everything. (p. 101)

I have said nothing of the best known of all Mrs. Stowe's religionists, Evangeline St. Clare. It is difficult to be fair to Little Eva in this day and age: she belongs to the period of

Paul Dombey and Little Nell. But though one may doubt with John Erskine [see excerpt above] that even Eva could have redeemed Topsy, the distinction Mrs. Stowe is making between the powerlessness of Miss Ophelia, who tried to do her duty by the little imp while fundamentally despising her, and the power of Eva, who loved as Jesus loved, is perfectly sound; neither could one ask for a truer piece of insight on her part that her keen perception of the difference between the New England abolitionist who would free the Negro yet hates to touch him, and the Southerner, who enslaves him, but lives with him, and, in a sense, loves and understands him.

In the Preface to *Oldtown Folks,* the narrator, Horace Holyoke, disdains both teaching and preaching, and presents himself as "the observer and reporter, seeing much, doubting much, questioning much, and believing with all my heart in only a very few things." He has tried to make his mind "as still and passive as a looking-glass or a mountain lake, and then to give . . . merely the images reflected there." In view of the excellence achieved, this pronouncement gives Mrs. Stowe's critics an excellent opportunity to observe how much better a writer she might have been had she everywhere steered clear of didacticism.

Whether she really would have been we shall never know. As she is, she flatters few of our contemporary prejudices, and she pays the price for her refusal. . . . She lived in a world of confusion, fatigue, and cloudy abstraction, and she suffered at times from a Messianic complex. But she had the root of the matter in her, as a writer and as a woman. Her contemporaries paid her no more than her due, and posterity neglects her at its peril. (pp. 101-02)

> Edward Wagenknecht, "Mrs. Stowe and Some Contemporaries," in his Cavalcade of the American Novel (copyright © 1952 by Henry Holt and Company, Inc.: copyright renewed © 1980 by Edward Wagenknecht; reprinted by permission of the author), Holt, Rinehart and Winston, 1952, pp. 82-108.*

RUTH SUCKOW (essay date 1953)

There are obvious reasons for [*Oldtown Folks's*] present neglect. It is a Victorian-type novel, loosely constructed, with dips into sentimentality. The richly racy Yankee speech is often given dialect spelling, hard to read, and tending to provincialize a book not intrinsically provincial. Some of the issues are theological, of a kind which have long seemed virtually obsolete. But the over-all reason for *Oldtown Folks* falling into obscurity is simply, I think, that the fame of *Uncle Tom's Cabin* has tended to swallow up everything else that Mrs. Stowe wrote. (p. 315)

Oldtown Folks should be restored to the American reading list as a historical novel of the years immediately following the Revolution. The local and regional setting carries on the historical interest. . . .

It is the novel among her later books with New England setting for which Mrs. Stowe herself said that she had "reserved the cream." The "regional" stories of later New England writers, Sarah Orne Jewett, for example, although now held in higher literary esteem than those of Mrs. Stowe, seem to me a bit prettified alongside the vigor of *Oldtown Folks.*

Oldtown Folks has claim to be read as a religious novel. Its concerns go deeper than theology. To write a novel definitely religious in meaning, and to reveal its fundamental ideas through people and situations intensely real in themselves, not by way of symbol or allegory, and not distorted to prove a sectarian point, is even more rare than to write a historical novel which never seems labored or pompous. Yet *Oldtown Folks* accomplishes this almost impossible feat in the art and practice of fiction. . . .

It can at least be said that behind the writing of Harriet Beecher Stowe lay wider actual experience of the Pilgrim-Puritan religion in America than that possessed by Hawthorne. (p. 316)

The social vigor of Mrs. Stowe's Oldtown, the religious center of which was the austere yet fervent meeting-house, as the kitchen of the Deacon Badger home with its glowing fireplace, abundant cooking, and broad hospitality was a human center, is scarcely present in Hawthorne's view of New England. It is not merely a question of two kinds of writing—say, roughly, romance and realism—but of the need for the novel which has slipped off the American reading list to complement, round out, and turn fresh light on the great novels which have been retained. (p. 317)

It has seemed feasible to try to get at the substance of *Oldtown Folks* by way of its characters, the people who make it a novel and not a tract or treatise; even though in the space allotted I can do scant justice to their rich variety. Since the historical element is so strong throughout, these characters may be viewed through a rapid survey of the religious generations passing through the story. *Oldtown Folks* is not chronological in method, however. It is told through a narrator, Horace Holyoke, who begins his memoirs in childhood—when his father dies, and he and his mother come to live with his grandparents, Deacon and Mrs. Badger—and who is an elderly gentleman at the end of the book. By this technical means, effectively used, the author has been able to portray the life not only of a person and a family but of an entire community and in and through this community to trace changes in religious thought and form, while still the great issue remains man's relationship to the Eternal. (p. 318)

[The] characters of *Oldtown Folks,* while sharply set in time and place—as all human life is set, whatever the particular setting may be—are treated as eternal souls. Here lies my most compelling reason for affirming that *Oldtown Folks* is needed in a contemporary consideration of literature—why I have been bold to call the novel an American classic, which we cannot afford to let slip into obscurity. (p. 325)

> *Ruth Suckow,"An Almost Lost American Classic," in* College English *(copyright © 1953 by the National Council of Teachers of English; reprinted by permission of the publisher), Vol. 14, No. 6, March, 1953, pp. 315-25.*

CHARLES H. FOSTER   (essay date 1954)

Lady Byron Vindicated deserves our respect not only as a courageous statement of fact but as an interpretation of Byron. Harriet postulated not a moral monster but a sick man. (p. 225)

Harriet, of course, had been reading Byron's poems critically since that day in her childhood when she asked what he could possibly have meant by "One I never loved enough to hate." With the master clue confirmed by Lady Byron, she now demonstrated what no critic had dared to demonstrate before, the significance of the incest theme in "Manfred," "Cain," and other poems, and she indicated for the first time that those moments when Byron cast himself on the world's sympathy

as the nobly misunderstood were parts of an intentional program of deception, calculated to put the blame for the failure of his marriage on the already overburdened shoulders of his wife. Of the later and greater Byron of *Don Juan,* Harriet was unappreciative, but though the world shouted her down, she had inaugurated the modern study of one of the major romantic poets. (p. 226)

We may often wish to smile at *Pink and White Tyranny* for its crude diatribe, but it has the large virtue of attacking those aspects of the Gilded Age deserving satire. Harriet's primary target was the newly rich like Dick Follingsbee, "one of those shoddy upstarts, not at all our sort of folks . . . a vulgar sharper, who has made his money out of our country by dishonest contracts during the war." Follingsbee glows with the bright colors of decay. His wife, an unscrupulous social climber, lives for show and, taking her cue from cheap French novels, carries on a tepid amour with her interior decorator, Charlie Ferrola. Harriet's description of Charlie shows her awareness of the essential decadence of that world given as the prize of virtue by Horatio Alger to his Ragged Dicks and Tattered Toms. . . . (pp. 227-28)

In *My Wife and I* Harriet again drew the contrast between the old and new aristocracy. (p. 229)

Harriet here dealt . . . with the "woman question" currently agitating America. As the American woman who had made the most conspicuous public success in her generation, Harriet, we might suppose, would have encouraged any reform giving new freedom and a greater measure of equality to women, but she insisted that the woman question must be answered in a Christian spirit with the proper reverence for marriage as a sacrament. In Audacia Dangyereyes, she expressed her disapproval of Victoria Woodhull, Tennie Claflin, Elizabeth Cady Stanton, Susan Anthony, and other female reformers, who seemed to her to be running true reform into the ground. (pp. 230-31)

We and Our Neighbors is a disappointing sequel to *My Wife and I,* giving the impression again and again that Harriet wrote a long book because she did not have time for a short one. The neighbors are potentially interesting but Harriet dealt with them, apparently, only when she remembered her title. Her primary concern was that profound attraction for the Catholic Church, which she had indicated thirteen years before in *Agnes of Sorrento.* (p. 232)

With *We and Our Neighbors,* Harriet came to a weak conclusion in her fictionalizing of the Gilded Age, but in her three novels she had still managed, not only to make perceptive comments, but to record a significant change in American life, the migration of New Englanders to New York and their increasing involvement in a world hostile to the traditional assumptions and practices of the Puritan village world. She here opened a new literary frontier, blazing the way hurriedly and sometimes crudely for later writers such as Howells, Henry James, and John P. Marquand.

In *Poganuc People,* Harriet concluded her career, as she had begun it in "**A New England Sketch,**" with a fictionalizing of Lyman Beecher; and, though she now described her father in his Litchfield ministry rather than in his youthful Yankee cleverness, there is an interesting similarity between these portraits forty-five years apart. In both, she was primarily interested, not in the Puritan clergyman, but in the warm and generous human being. (p. 233)

Perhaps Harriet was led into this generous tribute by the feeling that she had not been quite fair to Lyman Beecher in fictionalizing him as Mr. Avery in Jonathan Rossiter's letter in *Oldtown Folks*. But I think we are justified in suspecting deeper reasons and in supposing that here once again, as in all her best books, we have an attempt to encompass a spiritual and intellectual situation through "symbolic action." (pp. 234-35)

Her final novel, however, is much more than a consoling dream. As in her previous books, Harriet registered not simply inner concern but her realistic and humorous awareness of New England life and history. By supposing the Episcopal Church was of recent origin at Poganuc Center in 1811 (it had been actually established at Litchfield in 1745), she was able to concentrate history and demonstrate in brief compass the various causes which had made Yankees "sign off" to Anglicanism and thereby strengthen the Democratic hand in its destruction of the theocracy. (pp. 236-37)

[The] final claim for Harriet Beecher Stowe must rest on her ability to give us a balanced and immediate sense of the vital and complex Puritan past. It was here that she made a permanently significant contribution to American culture, for it is only as Puritan New England comes to life in our imaginations and our emotions as well as in our understandings that we can discover how "usable" a past we actually possess. A study such as I have written is no substitute for *The Minister's Wooing, The Pearl of Orr's Island, Oldtown Folks, Oldtown Fireside Stories,* and *Poganuc People.* Harriet Beecher Stowe gives us something far better than an interpretation; she gives us at a single remove in the world of imagination a deep and moving and often beautiful experience. Reading her novels we are likely to discover that we have surprising sympathies with the intellectuality, the moral boldness, the intense soul-searching, the warm and vital humor and humanity of New England Puritanism. We are likely to discover a new source of refreshment in a return to our intellectual and spiritual roots in the New England village. (pp. 242-43)

> *Charles H. Foster, in his* The Rungless Ladder: Harriet Beecher Stowe and New England Puritanism *(reprinted by permission of the Publisher; copyright 1954 by Duke University Press, Durham, North Carolina), Duke University Press, 1954, 278 p.*

KENNETH S. LYNN (essay date 1961)

Uniting reality with fantasy, Mrs. Stowe [in *Uncle Tom's Cabin*] applied the standard, throat-catching examples of homely infelicity on which the sentimental novelists had battened for years to the one area of American experience where the sorrow could not be over-dreamed. Striking to the very heart of the slave's nightmare—and of the white South's guilt—she centered her novel on the helpless instability of the Negro's home life. In so doing she also tapped the richest emotional lode in the history of the American sentimental novel. Thus *Uncle Tom's Cabin* is the greatest tear-jerker of them all, but it is a tear-jerker with a difference: it did not permit its audience to escape reality. Instead, the novel's sentimentalism continually calls attention to the monstrous actuality which existed under the very noses of its readers. Mrs. Stowe aroused emotions not for emotion's sake alone—as the sentimental novelists notoriously did— but in order to facilitate the moral regeneration of an entire nation. Mrs. Stowe was deeply serious—a sentimentalist with a vengeance—and the clichés she invokes in *Uncle Tom's Cabin* are not an opiate, but a goad.

Throughout the book the horror of slavery is brought home to the reader in scenes of domestic anarchy . . . , while the moral degradation of the loathsome Legree is measured by the broken-down, ill-kept dwelling where he has set up housekeeping with his mulatto mistress—and explained by the fact that as a young man he had not had the moral guidance of a mother! Thus do the most time-hallowed situations of the sentimental tradition give form to a tragic story.

Mrs. Stowe's exploitation of the sentimental conventions was brilliantly conceived and brilliantly executed; yet her use of these conventions is not the heart of her novel's vitality. *Uncle Tom's Cabin* is not merely a historical curiosity which sold half a million copies in the United States (and a million in Great Britain) in its first five years, stirred up the North, enraged the South, elicited numerous novelistic "answers" and started, as Lincoln half-jokingly said, the Civil War. It is also an unforgettable piece of American writing, and what makes it so is the penetrating and uncompromising realism of its portrayals of American character. If the plot of the novel and much of its diction derive from the sentimental tradition, only a small percentage of the characters do; for the most part, the dramatis personae of *Uncle Tom's Cabin*—black and white, Northern and Southern—are shockingly believable, no matter how factitious the dramatic situations may be in which they are placed. Augustine St. Clare, for example, is put through the paces of a deathbed act which may have moved nineteenth-century readers to tears but which strikes us today as hackneyed from beginning to end. . . . The personality of St. Clare, however, is so extraordinarily interesting, and so persuasively real, that the saccharine phoniness of his final scene simply washes off our memory of him. When we come away from *Uncle Tom's Cabin,* we cannot but recall its most celebrated sentimental scenes—Eliza fleeing across the ice, Uncle Tom and Little Eva talking about Christ, the death of Little Eva, and so on—for these histrionic moments are marvelous specimens of a confectionery art. But what really lives in our minds are the people we have met. Those critics who label *Uncle Tom's Cabin* good propaganda but bad art simply cannot have given sufficient time to the novel to meet its inhabitants. If they should ever linger over it long enough to take in the shrewdness, the energy, the truly Balzacian variousness of Mrs. Stowe's characterizations, they would surely cease to perpetuate one of the most unjust clichés in all of American criticism.

The Negroes in the novel constitute an amazing achievement. To be sure, some of them are comic stereotypes out of the minstrel shows, and one or two come perilously close to the "beautiful quadroon" type, but the majority are human beings, with all the individual differences one finds among the white people in the novel. The key to Mrs. Stowe's understanding of the Negro personality is her awareness of the destruction that the "peculiar institution" was wreaking on the slave's humanity. (pp. x-xi)

[No] American author before Mrs. Stowe had realized that the comic inefficiency of a Black Sam could constitute a studied insult to the white man's intelligence or comprehended that the unremitting gentleness of Uncle Tom was the most stirring defiance of all. In the age of Martin Luther King we can appreciate more fully than before the genius of such comprehension. She had an instinct, too, for the consolations that humor offered to the slave. The backstairs persiflage of the servants in the St. Clare household is at once funny and pathetic, a combination which has since become familiar to us in the Negro humor of a number of later writers, but which has rarely been handled more deftly. (p. xii)

Although Mrs. Stowe's studies of white character are no more powerful than her Negro portraits, they are more subtly drawn. . . . Although the New England spinster is one of the recurrent characters in American literature, never has she been "done" with more devastatingly accurate comic effect than Mrs. Stowe's Ophelia. (pp. xii-xiii)

[In] an era when American literature was still romantic and the great Balzac had a significant following only among the young and the unpublished, Mrs. Stowe had produced a work that throbbed with the spirit of realism. Instead of depicting Nature and the Self, she had portrayed character and society. . . . It is breath-taking enough to realize that an inexperienced writer, the author of a modest volume of stories and sketches entitled *The Mayflower* . . . , could bring to the sentimental novel such an unprecedented seriousness of purpose as to turn an escapist genre into an instrument of social upheaval. By the early 1850's, the greatest geniuses of American writing, Hawthorne and Melville, were taking drastic liberties with the formulas of the romance; *Uncle Tom's Cabin,* at its vital best, simply transcended them. (p. xv)

> *Kenneth S. Lynn, "Introduction" (1961), in* Uncle Tom's Cabin; or, Life Among the Lowly *by Harriet Beecher Stowe (copyright © 1962 by the President and Fellows of Harvard College; excerpted by permission), Cambridge, Mass.: Harvard University Press, 1962, pp. vii-xxiv.*

EDMUND WILSON (essay date 1962)

[To expose oneself in maturity to *Uncle Tom's Cabin* may] prove a startling experience. It is a much more impressive work than one has ever been allowed to suspect. The first thing that strikes one about it is a certain eruptive force. . . . Out of a background of undistinguished narrative, inelegantly and carelessly written, the characters leap into being with a vitality that is all the more striking for the ineptitude of the prose that presents them. These characters—like those of Dickens, at least in his early phase—express themselves a good deal better than the author expresses herself. The Shelbys and George Harris and Eliza and Aunt Chloe and Uncle Tom project themselves out of the void. They come before us arguing and struggling, like real people who cannot be quiet. (pp. 5-6)

What is most unexpected is that, the farther one reads in *Uncle Tom,* the more one becomes aware that a critical mind is at work, which has the complex situation in a very firm grip and which, no matter how vehement the characters become, is controlling and coördinating their interrelations. Though there is much that is exciting in *Uncle Tom's Cabin,* it is never the crude melodrama of the decadent phase of the play; and though we find some old-fashioned moralizing and a couple of Dickensian deathbeds, there is a good deal less sentimentality than we may have been prepared for by our memories of the once celebrated stage apotheosis. . . . We may even be surprised to discover that the novel is by no means an indictment drawn up by New England against the South. Mrs. Stowe has, on the contrary, been careful to contrive her story in such a way that the Southern states and New England shall be shown as involved to an equal degree in the kidnapping into slavery of the Negroes and the subsequent maltreatment of them, and that the emphasis shall all be laid on the impracticability of slavery as a permanent institution. The author, if anything, leans over backwards in trying to make it plain that the New Englanders are as much to blame as the South and to exhibit the Southerners in a favorable light. . . . (pp. 6-7)

One of the strongest things in the novel is the role played by Uncle Tom—another value that was debased in the play. The Quakers who shelter Eliza are, of course, presented as Christians; but not one of the other white groups that figure in *Uncle Tom's Cabin* is living in accordance with the principles of the religion they all profess. It is only the black Uncle Tom who has taken the white man's religion seriously and who—standing up bravely, in the final scene, for the dignity of his own soul but at the same time pardoning Simon Legree—attempts to live up to it literally. The sharp irony as well as the pathos is that the recompense he wins from the Christians, as he is gradually put through their mill, is to be separated from his family and exiled; tormented, imprisoned and done to death. (pp. 9-10)

Mrs. Stowe had got rid of Calvinism; she had dramatized the teaching of Jesus. Yet her God was still a God of Justice rather than a God of Love. Her pity runs to sentimentality, which is to say that it sometimes seems false; but she is never an obnoxious moralist: her judgment of men is quite sober and her judgment of ideas quite sound. (p. 58)

> *Edmund Wilson. "Harriet Beecher Stowe" (originally published in a different version as "No! No! My Soul An't Yours, Mas'r!" in* The New Yorker, *Vol. XXIV, No. 40, November 27, 1948), in his* Patriotic Gore: Studies in the Literature of the American Civil War *(reprinted by permission of Farrar, Straus & Giroux, Inc.; copyright © 1962 by Edmund Wilson), Oxford University Press, New York, 1962, pp. 3-58.*

LESLIE A. FIEDLER (essay date 1966)

The greatest of all novels of sentimental protest is . . . dedicated not to the problem of drink but to that of slavery, though its author was a total abstainer, who would appear at literary luncheons only if promised that no wine would be served. The novel, of course, is Harriet Beecher Stowe's *Uncle Tom's Cabin.* . . . It is an astonishingly various and complex book, simplified in the folk mind, which has remembered in its place the dramatic version in which Mrs. Stowe had no hand and which she saw, secretly, only once.

In *Uncle Tom's Cabin,* there are two contrasting studies of marriage: one between an opportunistic, morally lax husband and an enduring Christian wife; another between a hypochondriacal, self-pitying shrew—an acute but cruel caricature of the Southern lady—and a gentle, enduring husband. The latter relationship between the St. Clares, who are mother and father to Little Eva, is from a purely novelistic point of view the most skillfully executed section of the book; but it is scarcely remembered by *Uncle Tom's* admirers. No more do the really erotic episodes stick in the collective memory of America: neither Legree's passionate relationship with the half-mad slave girl, Cassy, nor his breathless, ultimately frustrated attempt to violate the fifteen-year-old quadroon, Emmeline. The story of the decline of Cassy from a protected Creole childhood, in which she is scarcely aware that she is a Negro, through her lush bondage to a chivalrous white New Orleans lover, in which she is scarcely aware she is a slave, to the point where she is pawed publicly in the slave market and degraded to the level of becoming Legree's unwilling mistress is fictional material of real interest; merely sketched in by Mrs. Stowe, it has recently been worked out in great detail by R. P. Warren in *Band of Angels.* Yet it fades from the mind even just after we have read *Uncle Tom.* It is not essential to the book which became part of our childhood. Of the complex novel created by Mrs. Stowe (or God!), America has chosen to preserve only the child's book.

Though we *know* Emmeline and Cassy are cowering in the attic at the moment that Quimbo and Sambo under Legree's direction are beating Uncle Tom to death, it is only the latter scene which we *feel*. We respond to the suffering and the triumph and the distressingly tearful arrival, just too late, of Marse George, the boy who has loved and remembered Tom and who is our surrogate in the book. All the conventional loves and romances of the book slip away, precisely because they are conventional, but also because they are irrelevant: the boy-girl all-white love of Eva and her cousin Henrique; and even, though it is a unifying thread joining the first volume of the novel to the second, the separation, the individual flights, and the joyous reunion in Canada of Eliza and George. We remember Eliza and the bloodhound, Eliza on the ice; we have to check the text to discover what happened to her after she left the floes behind, to remember that with her husband she emigrated to Liberia! Poor George—his existence is fictional only, not mythic. Unlettered Negroes to this day will speak of a pious compromiser of their own race, who urges Christian forbearance rather than militancy, as a "Tom" or "Uncle Tom"; it has become a standard term of contempt. But no one speaks of the advocate of force who challenges him as a "George," though Mrs. Stowe's protagonist of that name was a very model for the righteous use of force against force.

Only Uncle Tom and Topsy and Little Eva have archetypal stature; only the loves of the black man for the little white girl, of the white girl for the black, of the white boy for the slave live the lives of myths. Mrs. Stowe's laudable effort to establish a counter-stereotype to the image of the black rapist that haunts the mind of the South was a failure. We do not remember the turncoat puritan Legree squeezing the virginal breast of Emmeline, eyeing her lustfully; he is frozen forever, the last enduring myth of the book, in his role of slave-driver, at his purest moment of passion, himself the slave of his need to destroy the Christian slave Tom: "There was one hesitating pause, one irresolute relenting thrill, and the spirit of evil came back with sevenfold vehemence; and Legree, foaming with rage, smote his victim to the ground." It is at this moment that Legree seems the archetypal Seducer, ready for the final violation which the reader has all along feared and awaited with equal fervor.

For all the false rhetoric of Mrs. Stowe's description, that blow has an impact as wide in its significance as the assault of Lovelace, the attack of Cain; in it, the white man seals his guilt against the black, confesses his complicity in an act at once predestined and free. This is the moment that stays with us always, balanced against the counter-moment in which George grasps the hand of the dying Tom—*too late*, for Mrs. Stowe cannot help telling the truth—and weeps. The fact of brutality, the hope of forgiveness and mutual love: these are the twin images of guilt and reconciliation that represent for the popular mind of America the truth of slavery. How oddly they undercut the scenes of separated families, of baffled mother-love, at which Mrs. Stowe worked so hard—feeling perhaps that to her bourgeois readers slavery would stand condemned only if it were proved an offense against the sacred family and the suffering mother.

The chief pleasures of *Uncle Tom's Cabin* are, however, rooted not in the moral indignation of the reformer but in the more devious titillations of the sadist; not love but death is Mrs. Stowe's true Muse. For its potential readers, the death of Uncle Tom, the death of Little Eva, the almost-death of Eliza are the big scenes of *Uncle Tom's Cabin*, for they find in the fact and

in the threat of death the thrill once provided by the fact or threat of sexual violation. Death is the supreme rapist who threatens when all other Seducers have been banished to the semi-pornographic pulps. And it is the sexless child who comes to seem his proper victim, after the nubile Maiden is considered too ambiguous and dangerous a subject for polite literature. (pp. 264-66)

Little Eva seemed the answer to a particularly vexing genteel dilemma. To save the female for polite readers who wanted women but not sex was not an easy matter. The only safe woman is a dead woman; but even she, if young and beautiful, is only half safe, as any American knows, recalling the necrophilia of Edgar Allan Poe. The only *safe*, safe female is a pre-adolescent girl dying or dead. But this, of course, is Little Eva, the pre-pubescent corpse as heroine, model for all the protagonists of a literature at once juvenile and genteelly gothic.

Though the essential theme of the novel is, as we have come to see, love, it has never been forbidden the spice of death; and in its beginnings, it presented both in one, though both in terms of a fully adult world. In the earliest bourgeois fiction, we remember, the reader was permitted to assist at the last moments of the betrayed woman, no more excluded from the deathbed than from the marriage bed or the couch of sexual betrayal. In the later, more genteel stages of the novel, however, when it was no longer considered permissible to witness female sexual immorality, the reader was banned from the bedrooms of mature women even at the moment of their deaths. He had to content himself with the spectacle of the immaculate child winning her father to God by her courage in the face of a premature end.

Little Eva is the classic case in America, melting the obdurate though kindly St. Clare from skepticism to faith. What an orgy of approved pathos such scenes provided in the hands of a master like Harriet Beecher Stowe. . . .

> "Dear papa," said the child, with a last effort, throwing her arms about his neck. In a moment they dropped again; and, as St. Clare raised his head, he saw a spasm of mortal agony pass over the face—she struggled for breath, and threw up her little hands.
>
> "O God, this is dreadful," he said, turning away in agony, and wringing Tom's hand. . . . "O, Tom, my boy, it is killing me!" . . .
>
> The child lay panting on her pillows, as one exhausted—the large clear eyes rolled up and fixed. Ah, what said those eyes, that spoke so much of heaven? Earth was past, and earthly pain; but so solemn, so mysterious, was the triumphant brightness of that face, that it checked even the sobs of sorrow. . . .
>
> The bed was draped in white; and there, beneath the drooping angel-figure, lay a little sleeping form—sleeping never to waken!

If there seems something grotesque in such a rigging of the scene, so naked a relish of the stiffening white body between the whiter sheets; if we find an especially queasy voyeurism in this insistence on entering the boudoirs of immature girls, it is perhaps the fault of our post-Freudian imaginations, incapable of responding sentimentally rather than analytically to such images. The bed we know is the place of deflowering as well as dying, and in the bridal bed, a young girl, still virgin, dies to be replaced by the woman, mourning forever the white thing she once was. At least, so an age of innocence dreamed the event; they did not have to *understand* what they dreamed. With no sense of indecorum, they penetrated, behind Mrs. Stowe, the bedroom of the Pure Young Thing and participated in the kill. (pp. 267-68)

It is the unendurable happy ending, as the white slip of a thing too good for this world prepares to leave it for the next, while readers and parents, lovers all, sob into their handkerchiefs. The Good Good Girl, blond, asexual goddess of nursery or orphanage or old plantation house ("Always dressed in white," Mrs. Stowe writes of Eva, "she seemed to move like a shadow through all sorts of places, without contracting spot or stain; and there was not a corner or nook . . . where those fairy footsteps had not glided, and that visionary golden head, with its deep blue eyes, fleeted along"), must die not only so we may weep—and tears are, for the sentimentalist, the true baptism of the heart—but also because there is nothing else for her to do. There lies before the Little Evas of the world no course of action which would not sully them; allowed to grow up, Little Eva could only become—since she is forbidden the nunnery by the Protestant ethos and the role of the old maid is in our culture hopelessly comic—wife, mother, or widow, tinged no matter how slightly with the stain of sexuality, *suffered* perhaps rather than sought, but, in any case, *there!* (p. 269)

Leslie A. Fiedler, "Good Good Girls and Good Bad Boys: 'Clarissa' As a Juvenile," in his Love and Death in the American Novel (copyright © 1960, 1966 by Leslie A. Fiedler; reprinted with permission of Stein and Day Publishers), revised edition, Stein and Day, 1966, pp. 259-90.*

ALICE C. CROZIER (essay date 1969)

[Stowe's] novels are historical in that they record contemporary events in the manner of the providential historian and in that they consequently propound arguments for the proper solution to contemporary problems in the context of the historical commitment of the nation to its covenant with God. . . .

Artistically too the novels are historical; that is, they belong to the tradition of the historical romance in the manner of Scott and his American followers, Cooper, Simms, Kennedy, Cooke, and others. Mrs. Stowe's use of some of the conventions of the historical romance is often as different from her models as is her imitation of the providential history or the clerical Jeremiad, but only if we appreciate her artistry in the practice of the genre can we evaluate her achievement even as a polemicist, much less as a novelist. (p. 55)

[Scott's] double use of descriptive background to verify events and to stir the reader's poetic imagination is one of the skills which Mrs. Stowe, who could recite Scott's novels by the chapter, learned from the great romancer.

A good example of her use of this technique comes early in *Uncle Tom's Cabin,* in the famous episode of Eliza crossing the ice on the Ohio River in her flight from Marks and Loker. (p. 56)

[The] reader is brought into the episode in such a way that it becomes his own experience. The camera, as it were, follows Eliza; we see the ice up close, we see her bleeding feet. We are close enough to hear the ice creak as she jumps onto it. We see and hear and feel what she does and, in this specific sense, we not only believe in her flight, we are also able to

identify with her during it. This is precisely the function of verisimilitude in the historical romance: not only to convince us of the tale but to include us, imaginatively, in its sights and sounds and drama. . . . It is undoubtedly this sort of scene painting, which Mrs. Stowe learned from Scott, which creates the impression that the novel is not fiction but a documentary. The vitality of the novel's settings and incidental descriptions is the source of much of its power. Like Scott, she achieves not only credibility but, further, an imaginative reality more potent than mere factual realism.

Our sense of place is deepened by descriptions which include not only physical features of the land but also the mood and style of the life there. As might be expected from her New England background, Mrs. Stowe does a particularly sensitive rendering of a Vermont village. (pp. 57-8)

It is not a description of white steeples and quaint eccentrics, but is rather a beautifully lucid glimpse into the heart of that stillness in a New England village which the casual visitor might mistake for inactivity. It alludes to a regional past and way of life deftly and truthfully. Once again the reader recognizes authenticity, and, if he does not recognize it, he feels that he is learning the truth. (pp. 58-9)

Mrs. Stowe's early and devoted familiarity with the Waverly novels, in addition to stimulating what proved to be a great talent for setting and description, led to her ease in handling a large cast of characters, especially minor characters, to further verify and enliven the action of a plot. In *Uncle Tom's Cabin; or, Life Among the Lowly,* the role of minor characters and incidents is of major significance. (p. 60)

The variety of the Negro characters in the novel and the deftness with which they are drawn is more remarkable still in that, with the occasional exception, Negro characters are absent from American fiction before the Civil War. *Uncle Tom's Cabin* includes a great many Negroes, clearly characterized and quite different from each other, whose cumulative presence complements and extends the large cast of white characters and vastly enhances the effect of a comprehensive national dramatis personae. (p. 62)

Some people object that the slaves in *Uncle Tom's Cabin* are minstrel show darkies. This is a misleading criticism. First, as is evident in the preceding passage, they are not all alike, and they quarrel in a way far too serious for the mirth of old Jim Crow. Second, to the extent that the Negro characters in the novel are stereotypes, they are certainly no more so than the whites. If Sam and Andy's prank on Haley is minstrel stuff, then Haley is surely a stage villain and Shelby and St. Clare are stereotypes of the Southern planter. (p. 64)

It was one of the conventions of the American historical novel that the story should be presented on a split-level stage. The upper part is allotted to respectable more or less upper class characters who speak perfect and often pompous English, who dress in the fashionable equivalent of buckles and brocades, and whose education has made them familiar with European tastes and ideas. On the lower stage are enacted the scenes which concern those characters called lowly: servants, or, more often, rustics of some sort—farmers, woodsmen, sailors. (p. 68)

Because of the particular way in which the low life scenes and characters of historical romance had come to be treated in America, the portrayal of "life among the lowly" in *Uncle Tom's Cabin* was especially disturbing. Although Mrs. Stowe retains the stock low life figures and situations to some extent, she introduces a new and startling variation on the conventions by often making these characters and scenes deal entirely, or mainly, with the slaves. In just the places where the American reader had come to expect the especially native product, he found a native he had, in literature at least, overlooked. We must put ourselves in the position of Mrs. Stowe's readers then, and remember the popularity of the genre and the power of its conventions, if we are to understand the extraordinary drama she created for her audience. (p. 71)

There are several kinds of dialect in the novel. The most unusual for the time was that of the slaves, but Haley, Marks and Loker speak a tough river slang, the Canadian Quakers are given a very pure 'thee' and 'thou' language, and the preachers in the novel sound their clerical jargon with a vividness that only a woman who was daughter, wife, sister and mother of ministers could command. Indeed all the characters in the book are given, to a greater or lesser extent, a typical way of speaking. Thus the convention of the double stage found in earlier American historical romances is further modified. Although the cast of characters ranges geographically, racially, and socially through a very wide spectrum, the stage is continuous and the use of dialect and special idiom in characterization is not reserved for the low life characters alone. In this respect, the double stage is abandoned entirely and with it the self-conscious decorum of the polite characters. The Shelbys and St. Clares are every bit as native in word and deed as are the traders, servants and field hands. (pp. 71-2)

[When Mrs. Stowe] used comic, low life scenes to portray not backwoods rustics or homespun patriots, but slave cabins and slave quarters, the planter's kitchen or the auction warehouse— she showed herself worthy of Lincoln's greeting: "So you're the little lady who started this big war."

It is easy for us to forget, dazzled as we are by the masterpieces of the 1850s, that the American reader of the mid-century had read far more historical romance, American and English, than he had read of whalers, Walden Pond or the Salem Custom House. Mrs. Stowe's audience, although most of them could probably not recite Scott's novels as she could, were far more familiar with them and their American variants than with any other form of fiction. When we think of Mrs. Stowe's predecessors in the genre in America, we can recognize in her first novel the sources of its power to move and persuade its audience. We can also appreciate that, from the merely artistic point of view, *Uncle Tom's Cabin* is an achievement of great subtlety and originality. (pp. 72-3)

Alice C. Crozier, in her The Novels of Harriet Beecher Stowe *(copyright © 1969 by Oxford University Press, Inc.; reprinted by permission of Oxford University Press, Inc.), Oxford University Press, New York, 1969, 235 p.*

JOHN R. ADAMS   (essay date 1974)

The outline of *Uncle Tom's Cabin* is unmistakably clear and so overwhelmingly persuasive that readers accept the book as both imaginatively convincing and historically accurate. The remarkable feature of this success is that the plot is largely accidental, for the contract under which the story was written prohibited any foreshadowing of its conclusion. It was first designed as a loosely connected series of sketches on the sins of slavery . . . but it grew to ten months at the demand of its readers and terminated when it threatened to become too long for a two-volume hard-cover novel. Mrs. Stowe pictured it

scene by scene, not always in chronological order . . . , with this framework filled in by a vivid imagination or from memory, current reading, and information solicited from relatives and friends. The superb organization of this material, necessarily unconscious, has puzzled analysis to this day. She never understood it herself, contenting herself with the ultimate explanation that "God wrote it."

Her other nine novels without exception are damaged by thin plots, eccentric changes of emphasis, digressions, or other structural weaknesses. Her second, *Dred: A Tale of the Great Dismal Swamp,* falls apart midway, losing whatever momentum might have been generated. The reason, as she explained, was the physical attack by a Southern upon a Northern United States senator, which produced a sarcastic editorial comment in *Dred* and, more importantly for the novel, an abiding rage which altered the tone of the story, the balance of characters, and the message to be conveyed. (p. 51)

Among her serial novels the pressure of weekly deadlines, which had interrupted *Uncle Tom's Cabin* on several occasions, was disastrous to the unity of *The Pearl of Orr's Island*. . . . Less than disastrous to *My Wife and I* (which had less to promise from the beginning) were vital changes induced by the distasteful feminist agitation of Victoria Woodhull. . . .

Mrs. Stowe's four New England novels are on all counts her best (except, of course, the incomparable *Uncle Tom's Cabin*). They have been studied repeatedly for theme, less for construction. The theme changes little, for Mrs. Stowe's religious doctrines were firmly set by the time she wrote *The Minister's Wooing*. . . . The structure varied more from book to book, depending on external conditions. Some differences among them are almost self-explanatory. *The Pearl of Orr's Island,* the earliest planned, . . . was projected as rich in local color though slight in plot: the presumed loss of a lover at sea, with his safe return, not to happy reunion but to the pathetic death of his sweetheart. How well this might ever have been integrated with the landscape sketches, the rural society, and the domestic emotional distress is problematical. As finally completed, the inherent deficiencies in structure are obvious. (p. 52)

The plot [of *The Minister's Wooing*] is scanty, though Mrs. Stowe gave her heroine three suitors instead of the usual two competitors. The wholly spiritual Dr. Hopkins, at forty, is twice Mary Scudder's age, an impractical theological genius such as Mrs. Stowe knew in her own family. Aaron Burr's intentions, strictly dishonorable, combine the wickedness of Byronism with the political trickery imputed to him by his Federalist opponents. James Marvyn, Mary's childhood sweetheart and the obvious winner, has been reported drowned, but heaven is with him and he returns home, barely in time (in the final installment, naturally) to save the girl from self-sacrificing matrimony. The plot is one of the less important elements of the book. More enjoyable to readers are the spirited and closely observed scenes of village life—quilting bees, dressmaking sessions, preparations for weddings, and the like. Most important to Mrs. Stowe were the messages, neither completely new nor soon to be abandoned: (1) Slavery is demoralizing to the North; (2) Calvinism endangers righteousness; (3) Women are more responsible than men; (4) humble people who speak in dialect are closer to elementary truth than educated theorists. Notably the two wisest persons in the story are Miss Prissy, a gossipy dressmaker, and Candace, an Amazonian Negress of prophetic insight and practical wisdom who exerts overall influence second only to that of the saintly heroine.

Among Mrs. Stowe's five early novels only *Agnes of Sorrento* . . . is a complete or almost complete failure. The reason is not lack of structure but rather superfluous stiff framework and equally wooden substance. As a derivative of Walter Scott at his most solemn, with transference of New England theological conflicts to Renaissance Italy, it seldom gets off the ground. (pp. 52-3)

When completed [*Oldtown Folks*] was acclaimed, though not without reservations, as her major work and still holds that position. . . . [The] central characters are static. Neither Horace Holyoke with his visions nor his sweetheart, the orphan waif, Tina, are absorbingly interesting types, and Ellery Davenport is no more than a slightly improved fictional duplication of Aaron Burr, his supposed cousin. Certain new elements in plotting, including the seduction of one trusting maiden and a foolish marriage by another, complicate rather than advance the action. The minor characters, representing the whole scope of village and country life, contribute little to forwarding the action. The planned digressions—discussions of theology and genre pictures of rural customs—are the true substance of the book. . . . *Oldtown Folks* is thus a mixture of purposes and styles, carefully composed in its details and carelessly diffuse as a whole. *Poganuc People* . . . , Mrs. Stowe's last New England novel, has neither the weaknesses nor strength of *Oldtown Folks*. . . . The plot is extraneous, but the victory of the sensitive girl over her stubborn father is the story of Harriet Beecher's own escape from sex discrimination and ideological subservience into the freedom of maturity. (p. 53)

> John R. Adams, "Structure and Theme in the Novels of Harriet Beecher Stowe," in American Transcendental Quarterly (copyright 1974 by Kenneth Walter Cameron), No. 24, Part 1, Fall, 1974, pp. 50-5.

ADDITIONAL BIBLIOGRAPHY

Adams, John R. *Harriet Beecher Stowe*. New York: Twayne, 1963, 172 p.
  Examines Stowe's work, describing her technique "not only in *Uncle Tom's Cabin* but in her later, more representative and characteristic books."

Burns, Wayne, and Sutcliffe, Emerson Grant. "*Uncle Tom* and Charles Reade." *American Literature* XVII, No. IV (January 1946): 334-47.*
  Traces the influence of *Uncle Tom's Cabin* and *The Key* on the works of other authors, particularly *It's Never Too Late to Mend* by Charles Reade.

Drummond, Andrew L. "New England Puritanism in Fiction." *The London Quarterly and Holburn Review* CLXXI (January 1946): 19-34.*
  Studies Stowe's regional novels, and how she, along with several contemporaries, sought "to revive the dying interest in New England traditions."

Erskine, John. "Harriet Beecher Stowe." In his *Leading American Novelists*, pp. 275-323. New York: Henry Holt, 1910.
  Recounts the life and works of Stowe, highlighting her literary style and humanitarian values.

Fiedler, Leslie A. *The Inadvertent Epic: From "Uncle Tom's Cabin" to "Roots."* Toronto: Canadian Broadcasting Corporation, 1979, 85 p.*
  Scrutinizes American popular classics which Barry Hayne defines in the preface as embodying a "feminine, pro-society, domestic

and familial" myth, rather than the prevalent "male, subversive, anti-family" one. Fiedler uses *Uncle Tom's Cabin* as a basis and continual reference point for his discussion of works from D. W. Griffith's film *The Birth of a Nation* to Alex Haley's *Roots*.

Fields, Annie. "Days with Mrs. Stowe." In her *Authors and Friends*, pp. 157-226. Cambridge, Mass.: The Riverside Press, 1896.
  A personal portrait by Stowe's friend and biographer.

Furnas, J. C. *Goodbye to Uncle Tom*. New York: William Sloane Associates, 1956, 435 p.
  Questions the accuracy and tone of Stowe's depiction of blacks in *Uncle Tom's Cabin*, and examines how her well-intended novel actually deepened the rift between North and South. Furnas asserts that Stowe's work fostered misconceptions of black culture, which it continues to perpetuate.

Gilbertson, Catherine. *Harriet Beecher Stowe*. New York: D. Appleton, 1937, 330 p.
  Biography which attempts an objective portrait somewhere between the affectionate accounts of Stowe's friends and the colder judgment of critics.

Haley, Alex. "In 'Uncle Tom' Are Our Guilt and Hope." *New York Times Magazine* (1 March 1964): 23-4.
  An interesting discussion of the development of the pejorative term "Uncle Tom." Says Haley: "It is a deep irony that, a century later, the very name of Mrs. Stowe's hero is the worst insult the slaves' descendants can hurl at one another out of their frustrations in seeking what other Americans take for granted."

Hildreth, Margaret Holbrook. *Harriet Beecher Stowe: A Bibliography*. Hamden, Conn.: Archon Books, 1976, 257 p.
  A bibliography of published works by and about Stowe.

Howe, Julia Ward. "Harriet Beecher Stowe." *The Reader Magazine* 5, No. 5 (April 1905): 613-17.
  A personal look at Stowe's moral and spiritual integrity and its effect on her "slave stories."

"Pro-Slavery Literature." *The Liberator* XXII, No. 45 (5 November 1852): 179.*
  Briefly reviews books and pamphlets refuting the antislavery stance of *Uncle Tom's Cabin*.

Lowell, James Russell. *New Letters of James Russell Lowell*. Edited by M. A. De Wolfe Howe. New York: Harper & Row, 1932. 364 p.
  Contains a letter dated September 15, 1869, to Edmund Quincy, condemning the subject matter and scandalous nature of Stowe's *Lady Byron Vindicated*.

Maurice, Arthur Bartlett. "Famous Novels and Their Contemporary Critics: *Uncle Tom's Cabin*." *The Bookman* XVII (March-August 1903): 23-30.
  Offers excerpts of contemporary criticism—negative and positive—of *Uncle Tom's Cabin*.

Mott, Frank Luther. "'This Iliad of the Blacks'." In his *Golden Multitudes: The Story of Best Sellers in the United States*, pp. 114-22. New York: Macmillan, 1947.
  Brief description of the inception of *Uncle Tom's Cabin*, and its critical reception.

Pattee, Fred Lewis. "The Novel That Precipitated a War." In his *The Feminine Fifties*, pp. 130-45. New York: D. Appleton, 1940.
  A discussion of the historical climate in which *Uncle Tom's Cabin* was created.

Stowe, Charles Edward. *Life of Harriet Beecher Stowe: Compiled from Her Letters and Journals*. Cambridge, Mass.: The Riverside Press, 1890.
  A detailed biography by Stowe's son, including many family letters and documents.

Stowe, Lyman Beecher. *Saints, Sinners, and Beechers*. Indianapolis: Bobbs-Merrill, 1934, 172 p.

A well-illustrated family history.

Wagenknecht, Edward. *Harriet Beecher Stowe: The Known and the Unknown*. New York: Oxford University Press, 1965, 267 p.

A sympathetic biography of Stowe which the author calls "a psychograph, or 'portrait', or character study."

Whicher, George H. "Literature and Conflict." In *Literary History of the United States: History,* rev. ed., edited by Robert E. Spiller,

Willard Thorp, Thomas H. Johnson, Henry Seidel Canby, and Richard M. Ludwig, pp. 563-86. New York: Macmillan, 1963.

A literary and historical overview.

Wilson, Forrest. *Crusader in Crinoline: The Life of Harriet Beecher Stowe*. New York: Lippincott, 1941, 706 p.

A definitive biography.

Royall Tyler

1757-1826

(Born William Clark Tyler; also wrote under the pseudonyms of Spondee and Dr. Updike Underhill) American dramatist, novelist, journalist, and poet.

Though he is not an outstanding literary figure, Tyler is considered important to the development of the American theater. He is especially remembered for *The Contrast*, the first comedy professionally produced in the United States. With the main character Jonathan, who is naïve, gawky, and endowed with a native honesty, Tyler introduced the "Yankee type" that reappears in various guises throughout American literature. Through Jonathan, Tyler expressed his own patriotic beliefs and endorsed the moral and religious ideals of the emerging nation.

As an undergraduate, Tyler was active in student military groups which supported the Revolutionary War and he later became a distinguished major in the army. After the war, he received his law degree from Harvard and joined the firm of John Adams. Tyler, despite his interest in literature, placed his legal practice above all else. He employed his professional expertise in the suppression of Shays' Rebellion in New York and became renowned for his brilliant lectures on the uprising. He was later elected state's attorney for Windham County, Vermont, became a justice on the bench of the Vermont Supreme Court, and eventually was appointed Chief Justice.

Throughout his career as a jurist, Tyler continued to write. His talent as a playwright was first recognized by Thomas Wignell, a popular comedian whom Tyler met in New York. With Wignell's encouragement, Tyler, within five weeks, wrote *The Contrast,* which was produced immediately with Wignell playing the lead role. Some critics attribute the overwhelming success of this first production to Wignell's acting ability. Others, however, recognize Tyler's ability to depict local dialects, situations, and character types which shine in spite of the play's didactic tone. To preserve his dignity as a lawyer, Tyler transferred the manuscript and copyright to Wignell, who ascribed *The Contrast* to "A Citizen of the United States." Nonetheless, the identity of the author was common knowledge, and he enjoyed his literary fame.

Tyler wrote didactic works which point out the follies of upper-class society and emphasize the importance of virtuous lives. *May Day in Town; or, New York in an Uproar,* a play in the same style as *The Contrast,* and the novel *The Algerine Captive; or, The Life and Adventures of Doctor Updike Underhill: Six Years Prisoner among the Algerines* both stress moral lessons but, at the same time, reflect Tyler's concern with problems of the day; he wanted particularly to emphasize the need for American art forms. Tyler's last four plays, *The Origin of the Feast of Purim, Joseph and His Brethren, The Judgement of Solomon,* and *The Island of Barrataria,* were published posthumously as *Four Plays by Royall Tyler,* but were never produced; however, they are considered important reflections of Tyler's character and beliefs.

Another of Tyler's endeavors was a newspaper column written in partnership with Joseph Dennie. As "Colon and Spondee," the two contributed prose, verse, and reviews of plays and

books to *The Farmers' Weekly Museum,* a newspaper with a Federalist outlook. But Tyler's good fortune and popularity soon came to an end; he lost his position as a judge, his eldest son died, and his property was divided among his creditors. He attempted to re-establish a private legal practice, but died of cancer and left his family impoverished.

Tyler's literary contribution is small, but he is acknowledged by historians as the first native American to have professionally produced a comedy. Jonathan, the protagonist of *The Contrast,* cited as the archetypal Yankee personality in literature, is believed to be the prototype for the legendary "Uncle Sam." For his patriotic, humorous works, Tyler is a noted figure of American drama.

PRINCIPAL WORKS

The Contrast (drama) 1787
May Day in Town; or, New York in an Uproar [first publication] (drama) 1787
The Algerine Captive; or, The Life and Adventures of Doctor Updike Underhill: Six Years Prisoner among the Algerines [as Dr. Updike Underhill] (novel) 1797
The Georgia Spec; or, Land in the Moon [first publication] (drama) 1797
The Yankey in London (fictional letters) 1809

The Chestnut Tree (poetry) 1931
Four Plays by Royall Tyler [first publication] (drama) 1941
The Verse of Royall Tyler (poetry) 1967
The Prose of Royall Tyler (essays) 1972

*This work was written in 1824.

CANDOUR (essay date 1787)

[*The Contrast*] is certainly the production of a man of genius, and nothing can be more praise-worthy than the sentiments of the play throughout. They are the effusions of an honest patriot heart expressed with energy and eloquence. The characters are drawn with spirit, particularly Charlotte's; the dialogue is easy, sprightly, and often witty, but wants the pruning knife very much. The author has made frequent use of soliloquies, but I must own, I think, injudiciously; Maria's song and her reflections after it, are pretty, but certainly misplaced. . . . That part of her speech which respects Dimple, might be retained; she may very well be supposed to talk on so material a subject to her own happiness, even when alone, and her feelings, upon a marriage with a man she has every reason to despise and abhor, are very well painted. Col. Manly's advice to America, tho' excellent, is yet liable to the same blame, and perhaps greater. A man can never be supposed in conversation with himself, to point out examples of imitation to his countrymen: at the same time the thoughts are so just, that I should be sorry they were left out entirely, and I think they might be introduced with greater propriety, in the conversation with Dimple.

I cannot help wishing the author had given a scene between Dimple and Maria. The affronting coldness of Dimple's manner might have interested us for Maria, and would in some degree have supplied the greatest defect of the play, the want of interest and plot. We might then have been more easily reconciled to the sudden affection and declaration of love between Manly and Maria, which cannot fail, as the play now is, to hurt our opinion of both. The author's great attention to the unity of time, which he has indeed very well preserved, has in some degree produced this sudden attachment.

Jessamy is a closer imitation of his master than is natural, and his language in general is too good for a servant; the character would have produced a better effect if he had been more awkward in his imitation. The satire of the play is in general just, but the ridicule of Lord Chesterfield's letters, should be well considered. (pp. 24-5)

To point out the many beauties of the play, tho' an agreeable, would be an unnecessary task, the unceasing plaudits of the audience did them ample justice, and it cannot fail, if judiciously curtailed, being a great favorite. . . . Upon the whole the defects of the play are so much overbalanced by its merits, that I have made no scruple of mentioning those which occurred to me, and I have done so the rather, because I think in general they may be easily remedied, and that the piece, particularly when considered as the first performance, does the greatest credit to the author, and must give pleasure to the spectator. (p. 25)

> Candour, "Royall Tyler's 'The Contrast'" (originally published in The Daily Advertiser, April 18, 1787), in The American Theatre as Seen by Its Critics 1752-1934, edited by Montrose J. Moses and John Mason Brown, W. W. Norton Inc., 1934, pp. 24-5.

MONTHLY ANTHOLOGY AND BOSTON REVIEW (essay date 1810)

[*The Yankey in London*] is a very useless addition to the almost innumerable books of travels, which crowd the shelves of libraries. (p. 50)

There is a degree of smartness and some humour in this writer, that would induce us to think he might do better. The fault of his work is, that it gives nothing new, nothing but what a man, with some knowledge of English history, and the habit of reading English newspapers and magazines, might write in this country. (pp. 57-8)

> "'The Yankey in London'," in Monthly Anthology and Boston Review, Vol. XIII, January, 1810, pp. 50-8.

WILLIAM DUNLAP (essay date 1832)

"The Contrast" ranks first in point of time of all American plays, which had been performed by players. It is extremely deficient in plot, dialogue, or incident, but has some marking in the characters, and in that of *Jonathan* . . . a degree of humour, and knowledge of what is termed Yankee dialect, which . . . was relished by an audience gratified by the appearance of home manufacture—a feeling which was soon exchanged for a most discouraging predilection for foreign articles, and contempt for every literary home-made effort. . . . [The publication of the play] was coldly received in the closet: yet Jonathan the First has, perhaps, not been surpassed by any of his successors. He was the principal character, perhaps, strictly speaking, the only character. (pp. 71-2)

[The] first efforts of our dramatists were strictly local. Mr. Tyler, in his **"Contrast,"** and some later writers for the stage, seem to have thought, that a Yankee character, a Jonathan, stamped the piece as American, forgetting that a clown is not the type of the nation he belongs to. (p. 85)

> William Dunlap, in his A History of the American Theatre, J. & J. Harper, 1832, 420 p.*

ORAL SUMNER COAD (essay date 1917)

The first American comedy worthy of the name was **"The Contrast."** . . . It contains a well-defined and skilfully managed plot of considerable interest. The play contrasts the affected, Europeanized American with the sincere and sterling home-bred citizen.

Royall Tyler's distinct contribution to our drama was a new humorous character, the Yankee. His *Jonathan* was the progenitor of a long and honorable line of stage Yankees, commonly glorying in the baptismal name of their ancestor, and all inheriting his ignorance and gawkiness, his shrewdness and honesty, his dialect and "darnations." Dialect had occasionally been employed before in American plays, [Andrew Burton's] "The Disappointment" for instance, but Tyler's *Jonathan* was the first attempt to create humor by exploiting provincialism.

For our purpose **"The Contrast"** is noteworthy primarily as the earliest sentimental play to be written in this country. As such it was the shower which preceded the deluge. Tyler's model, of course, was the emotional comedy of England, which had been so conspicuous on the British stage throughout the century, and which had also gained a large following in the New World. The purpose of English sentimental comedy was twofold: to correct morals and to arouse the feelings to a high pitch of activity. The former aim was generally accomplished by the reformation of a rake, as in Cibber's "Careless Husband" (1704) and Kelly's "School for Wives" (1773); the latter by the reuniting of long-lost brothers and sisters, or parents and children, and by the distress and final happiness of lovers. . . . (pp. 133-35)

Apparently Tyler studied diligently in the English school of sensibility, for "The Contrast" is entirely orthodox. There is a rascal of the name of *Dimple* who must be exposed. There is a hero, *Col. Manly*, and a heroine, *Maria*, whose happiness is balked for a time by a headstrong father. The lovers are as thorough a pair of sentimentalists as writer ever invented. Their sense of delicacy is awe-inspiring. Ridiculed by their gay and thoughtless acquaintance, they pursue unperturbed the path of solemn rectitude which leadeth unto matrimony. The curtain descends on the triumph of sentimentality and the discomfiture of the frivolous and still unmated scoffers. (pp. 135-36)

> *Oral Sumner Coad, "The Original Plays," in his* William Dunlap: A Study of His Life and Works and of His Place in Contemporary Culture *(copyright 1917 by The Dunlap Society; reprinted by permission of the Literary Estate of Oral Sumner Coad), The Dunlap Society, 1917 (and reprinted by Russell & Russell, Inc., 1962), pp. 129-92.**

ARTHUR HOBSON QUINN   (essay date 1923)

To those who have had an opportunity to see [*The Contrast*] there can be little surprise at its success. The play reads well, but in the hands of a competent company the old comedy actually comes to life upon the stage. Tyler wrote it in three weeks, but he had before him good models and he had a natural talent for conversation. From the very beginning Charlotte and Letitia, the frivolous girls of the period, wake a quick interest in audiences who recognize the essential permanence of the types Tyler satirizes. (p. 66)

[It] is not the plot which makes *The Contrast* significant. It is the character portrayal, and above all it is the way in which it meets the test of drama, namely, that it shall act better than it reads. (p. 70)

Four manuscript dramas remain by which we may judge of Tyler's work. *The Island of Barrataria* [sic] is an amusing farce in three acts, based upon Chapters 44, 45, 47, 49, 51 and 53 of the Second Part of *Don Quixote*. Sancho Panza becomes Governor of Barataria, and despite his ravenous hunger, he is forced through the rigor of form and precedent to postpone his dinner until he has presided at a court of law. Tyler takes the opportunity to satirize the proceedings of his own profession by contrasting the verbiage of the lawyers and the shrewd common-sense with which Sancho decides the cases. One of these provides a love story, partly of Tyler's own invention, which forms the subplot of the farce. Tyler quickens the action, allowing Sancho only one day of rule, and he selects cleverly from the narrative, the most dramatic incidents. The farce reads as though it would act well, though it seems doubtful that it saw the stage. . . . The three "sacred dramas," *The Origin of the Feast of Purim, or The Destinies of Haman and Mordecai, Joseph and His Brethren,* and *The Judgement of Solomon* are written in blank verse of a flexible and at times distinguished

quality. The characters of Esther, of Joseph, and of Zernah and Maachah, the two mothers in *The Judgement of Solomon,* are well conceived. (pp. 72-3)

[*The Algerine Captive*] is amusing, especially the early portion, which satirizes the medical profession of [Tyler's] day. He was a voluminous writer of essays and verse of a humorous character, and his *Yankey in London* . . . is an interesting series of letters which were supposed to be written from London to his friends. Tyler's dramatic sense is shown in both these imaginary experiences, which deceived the readers of his day. The remainder of Tyler's career lies outside our special interest. (p. 73)

> *Arthur Hobson Quinn, "The Coming of Comedy," in his* A History of the American Drama: From the Beginning to the Civil War *(copyright 1923, 1943, 1951 by Arthur Hobson Quinn; copyright renewed © 1970 by Arthur Hobson Quinn, Jr.; reprinted by permission of the Literary Estate of Arthur Hobson Quinn), second edition, F. S. Crofts & Co., 1943 (and reprinted by Appleton-Century-Crofts, Inc., 1951, pp. 61-73).**

ALLAN GATES HALLINE   (essay date 1935)

The Contrast is an outgrowth of the period in which it was written. The nationalistic forces which had brought about the Revolution and carried it to a successful conclusion were now struggling to consolidate themselves in some permanent form; the concept of national unity reached its culmination in the drafting of the Constitution. This, coincidentally enough, was in 1787. Close as it is to the Revolution, *The Contrast* exhibits little of the belligerent spirit; it is neither wrathful nor malicious; it is scarcely anti-Anglican; but it is essentially nationalistic; the assumption which lies back of its central attitudes is the intrinsic worth of American as opposed to European culture; it is in its own sphere a spiritual Declaration of Independence. In the words of Manly: "But, if our country has its errors in common with other countries, I am proud to say America—I mean the United States—has displayed virtues and achievements which modern nations may admire, but of which they have seldom set us the example." It is not, however, possible to regard this nationalism either as relentlessly felt or as perfectly applied in view of the fact that Tyler fashions part of his play after a foreign model, Sheridan's *School for Scandal;* but even though Tyler made a well-nigh necessary concession with respect to the means he employed, yet his nationalistic intent is not therefore invalidated.

Other nationalistic currents find expression in the play, e.g., the contemporary reverence for Washington, the high esteem for Lafayette, the movement for confidence in the federal currency, the agitation for aid to the disabled veterans. Suggested by the foregoing and in view of Manly's strictures on the Grecians, who divided and fell, the nationalism of the play appears to be Federalistic; like other plays of the period, particularly *André* by Dunlap, *The Contrast* reflects, in a mild way, the philosophy of the Hamiltonian Federalists with respect to strong union. (p. 5)

Since Jonathan has been traditionally spoken of as the conspicuous contribution of the play, it must not be casually supposed that he furnishes the contrast to Dimple; obviously, Manly is the proponent of the American view. A second misconception should be guarded against: that of not taking Manly seriously. . . . Though the modern temper and modern drama shun the obviously moralistic, yet in 1787 the theatregoer was more receptive to sentiment and the technique of the drama was less highly developed than it is today.

We have, then, inner moral worth and essential respect of others as it reveals itself in opposition to external accomplishment of manners and comparative disregard of one's fellowmen—especially fellow-women. Though the nationalism of the play is not malevolent, . . . yet little care is taken to distinguish the variety from the species, i.e., the offensive pseudo-Chesterfieldian from the European. That such inattention is dramatic rather than malicious is suggested by the presence of Jonathan himself, who is as ridiculous as Dimple is odious. But inattention it remains, and one thus tends to regard *The Contrast* as a nationalistic document rather than a completely disinterested evaluation of Anglo-American cultural relationships.

Tyler gives the first dramatic presentation of the concept of American cultural self-consciousness and self-sufficiency which developed over and above the antagonism to foreign culture incidental to the more comprehensive, more intense spirit of hostility that lay back of the Revolution itself. (pp. 5-6)

In *The Contrast* not only do we see the reception accorded to a particular type of foreign culture, but we glimpse other aspects of contemporary American society as well, particularly that of New York. Though in no sense a comprehensive or thorough study of social life, yet Tyler's play contains representations, at once suggestive in detail and authentic in import, of current dress, entertainment, manners, sentiments, morals, and character. (pp. 6-7)

It is remarkable that a man so little trained dramatically as Tyler should write a play so sharp in its characterization, so effective in dramatic presentation, and so significant culturally. (p. 7)

> *Allan Gates Halline, "Royall Tyler (1757-1826),"* in American Plays, *edited by Allan Gates Halline (copyright 1935 by American Book Company; reprinted by permission of D. C. Heath & Company),* American Book, *1935, pp. 1-40.*

ARTHUR H. NETHERCOT (essay date 1941)

[To some degree,] recognition of the dramatic background of Tyler's comedy has increased, but this recognition has scarcely kept pace with the appreciation of the interest and effectiveness of [*The Contrast*] as a play. . . .

[An] examination of the play itself indicates that, if anything, Tyler knew the rules [of the drama] *too* well and followed them *too* closely to produce a really natural and original work. The play could scarcely have been written with as little study and preparation as critics have implied. (p. 436)

Undoubtedly, so far as structure is concerned, *The Contrast* is mostly an exemplification of the rules. It is divided into the conventional five acts, and it adheres to the dramatic unities. The plot is completely conventional, and clues to its future development are so obviously "planted" that there is no real suspense—the audience, if it is dramatically intelligent at all, knows at once what is going to be the outcome. (p. 437)

In characterization, too, Tyler has obviously been going to school to the accepted models. Almost without exception his characters are drawn according to the still prevailing comic technique of the "humors." In conformity with these principles many of the names, such as Colonel Manly, Dimple, Van

Rough, and Jonathan, give an immediate clue as to their possessors' dominating qualities. Nor does Tyler endeavor to conceal his master in this technique, for in the lesson on laughter given by Jessamy to Jonathan in Act V, scene i, Jessamy informs his pupil: ". . . this is a piece, written by Ben Jonson, which I have set to my master's gamut." (pp. 437-38)

In view of the many common features of situation, character, and point of view shared by *The Contrast* and at least a half-dozen well-known English comedies of the eighteenth century, the student today may well hesitate to accept the implication of [several critics] that the author of the "first American comedy" was almost completely unversed in the theory and literature of the drama. (p. 446)

> *Arthur H. Nethercot, "The Dramatic Background of Royall Tyler's 'The Contrast',"* in American Literature *(reprinted by permission of the Publisher; copyright © 1941 by Duke University Press, Durham, North Carolina), Vol. XII, January, 1941, pp. 435-46.*

GEORGE FLOYD NEWBROUGH (essay date 1941)

[*The Island of Barrataria, The Origin of the Feast of Purim; or, The Destinies of Haman O Mordecai; Joseph and His Brethren,* and *The Judgement of Solomon*], apart from their intrinsic worth, are valuable for the light they throw on an important pioneer figure as well as on the standards of the age.

In spite of his limited reputation at present, it cannot be doubted that Tyler was an important influence in his day. . . . *The Contrast,* his first play, was a surprising success for the time. . . . *The Algerine Captive,* a picaresque novel purporting to be autobiographical, . . . was the first American work of fiction to be reproduced in England. . . . (p. vii)

The Contrast, with its humor, its Americanism, its vivid caricature of the New England Yankee, measures up as a worthy first specimen of its genre to appear on the American stage. Colonel Manly, the Hero, succeeded, despite his pompous diction, in exposing foreign affectation in favor of simple native worth; and Jonathan, "waiter" to Colonel Manly, constituted an object lesson on the dramatic possibilities of native character types—possibilities which a little later were neglected by the first American novelists. Delightful in his Yankee talk sixty years before Hosea Biglow and refreshing in his independence and naturalness, remaining only his homespun self even when he tries to court or laugh by rule, Jonathan turns out to be the first American stage Yankee.

Other plays by Tyler which appear to have had successful runs but which are no longer extant, are: *May Day in Town, or New York in an Uproar* . . . ; *A Georgia Spec, or Land in the Moon* . . . ; *The Farm House, or The Female Duellists,* a farce, apparently an alteration of Kemble's play of the same name; *The Doctor in Spite of Himself,* an adaptation of Molière.

The Algerine Captive deals, like *The Contrast,* with native manners and customs. In the preface the author insists that in American letters two things are primarily wanted: "that we write our own books of amusement, and that they exhibit our own manners," and proposes to "display a portrait of New England manners, hitherto unattempted." The first half of the fictitious narrative especially is in line with this proposal, even if out of line with the title, for we often sense the author's first-hand impressions, as in his satiric accounts of the country medical practitioner or in his description of the college at Cambridge as an antiquated place where the instructors teach the dead languages simply because "they must teach their pupils what they know, not what they do not know."

Though Tyler is not often so explicit concerning his aims as in the preface just referred to, it is obvious that he had serious aims and that they extended over a wide range of style, form, and content. In a long poem, *The Chestnut Tree,* he sees in fancy a future critic smiling at his verse because of "The formal phrase, the bald still style;" yet simplicity and naturalness are also to be found in Tyler's works. His verse, in fact, is generally simple and sprightly; and the Algerine captive, Doctor Updike Underhill, is as unaffected as that other Yankee, Jonathan, in *The Contrast*—which is to say, about as unaffected as anyone, even a Yankee, can be. (pp. vii-viii)

> George Floyd Newbrough, "Royall Tyler," in Four Plays *by Royall Tyler, edited by Arthur Wallace Peach and George Floyd Newbrough (copyright © 1941 by Arthur Wallace Peach; reprinted by permission of Indiana University Press), Princeton University Press, 1941 (and reprinted in* America's Lost Plays: Four Plays, *Vol. 15, Barrett H. Clark, General Editor, Indiana University Press, 1965, pp. vii-viii).*

CONSTANCE ROURKE (essay date 1941)

The Contrast was produced against a background of momentous national events, and it was recognized at once as a national achievement. When it was published in 1790, Washington headed the list of subscribers.

The theme was nationalistic, the picture social. In the simple story, "contrast" was satirically established between the English and the American character, with triumphant virtue on the American side. On the whole, the portraiture along these main lines was colorless: the play came to genuine life with the entrance of the minor figure of Jonathan, a Yankee. (pp. 115-16)

Jonathan in *The Contrast* was a national symbol, and he sprang into life almost full blown. Not even a prose sketch picturing the Yankee had preceded Tyler's play. Perhaps an improvisation of Yankee ways and Yankee speech had been poured into the delineations of some of the Revolutionary plays in their impromptu performances: Tyler must have seen some of them. But the most likely progenitor of his Jonathan was "Yankee Doodle." Some of Jonathan's talk has the flavor of this ballad, for which new stanzas were continually being improvised, which had already become the most widespread national song. . . . His origin was not literary. Like the jigging tune of "Yankee Doodle" and its innumerable story-telling verses, he derived from the folk.

His sudden emergence full length in *The Contrast* had its oddities. In other literatures such figures had most often been established slowly, in ballads and folk-plays. When they have become tangible, writers have discovered them and they have moved into literature. . . . The Yankee had leapt full blown into "Yankee Doodle," thence into a full-length play, and from a localism became a national folk-figure. The theater itself had followed this boldly syncopated course as it had moved from a minor to a major place in the national life, out of the sphere of private enjoyment to become suddenly—even with a rush—a public possession. (pp. 117-18)

[*The Contrast*] was simple, naive, even primitive in its fable and its handling. But it had momentum, even now it reads and

acts more than passably well because it is so direct and because of the character of Jonathan. . . . There is no precise unraveling of [Tyler's] approaches to [Jonathan's] portrayal; yet the character is drawn not only with accuracy but with pride and gusto. In a quiet obscure fashion the Yankee had materialized, had succeeded in impressing himself upon Tyler and others; for the play would not have been an immediate success if it had not stirred the sense of recognition in its audiences. This, the liveliest, the most positive American character in the portraiture of the stage had emerged from the life of the folk and had come from New England; still further this Yankee was already a magnified symbol of the American. . . . A few other native folk-characters were being sketched on the stage, the backwoodsman, the Negro, the wandering Irishman who came here and never seemed to settle down, but their portraiture was slight and was long to remain so. The Yankee was the dominating figure. American characters from many backgrounds were being pictured on the stage, in increasing numbers, but they were usually pegs upon which ideas were hung: they failed to come to life. Slightly drawn as were the backwoodsman, the Negro, the Irishman, they usually captured more stirring bits of speech and song than did the merchants or lawyers or young men about town who were the formal heroes of the plays. But Jonathan exceeded them all in living qualities. In *The Contrast* he all but blotted out the other people in the play.

Tyler had by no means finished either with the stage or with the Yankee when he wrote *The Contrast.* His literary career suggests many things regarding the American imagination and the forces acting upon it in this era. For Tyler an obscure and complicated inner life had developed which no doubt in some fashion conditioned everything he wrote. What he did and failed to do was set within its framework. (pp. 119-21)

Immediately after the success of *The Contrast,* Tyler had dashed off another comedy, *May Day in New York,* a sprightly panoramic piece with the theme of moving day which poured upon the stage motley groups of characters. This play was produced but was not a success. (p. 121)

Tyler achieved polished prose, neat verses and satire with the best of them. Yet on his long and lonely trips, during his hardly less solitary sojourns at home, he carried on writing of quite a different order, related in freshness and sometimes in theme to *The Contrast.* He wrote or adapted a number of plays, among them one that satirized a notable American trait, the passion for wild speculation. It was called *The Georgia Spec; or Land in the Moon,* and it had to do with land speculation at Yazoo. A journalistic piece, it could hardly have enjoyed a long life, but it was given a number of performances in Boston and New York. Tyler's other plays were equally short-lived. (p. 122)

[All Tyler's] efforts represented, in a sense, fragments of [himself]. His main concern lay with the Yankee, with Yankee life in its already varied forms. He never matched the success of *The Contrast,* but he studiously and affectionately worked on the essential Jonathan in the midst of his many other preoccupations. . . . Cast in the form of an autobiography, [*The Algerine Captive*] persuasively seems an actual record. His *Yankee in London* likewise seems a precise account of fact and was generally taken for one when it was anonymously published. . . . The humor is keen, the style silvery-sharp: the little book is close to being a minor classic. (pp. 123-24)

The first portrayal in American letters belonged to Tyler. Whatever his political theory, whatever the morose inner strains that seemed to separate him from a full life, he somehow kept his warm perception of common folk in New England, and he had cleaved out a primary work. (p. 124)

> Constance Rourke, "The Rise of Theatricals" (1941), in her The Roots of American Culture and Other Essays, edited by Van Wyck Brooks (copyright 1942 by Harcourt Brace Jovanovich, Inc.; copyright renewed © 1970 by Alice D. Fore; reprinted by permission of the publisher), Harcourt Brace Jovanovich, 1942, pp. 60-160.*

ALEXANDER COWIE (essay date 1948)

The quality of Royall Tyler's writing is a sufficient reminder that even in the early days of the national literature it was not axiomatic that we should produce crude and naive fiction. Disadvantages there were, but after all much depended on the individual writer. With the rich legacy of English literature to draw upon—and beyond that, the wealth of the classics—no new writer needed to begin with the A B C's of his craft. . . . With Tyler, as with most literary figures of his time, writing was an avocation, but he brought to it such talents that he earned a permanent, if modest, niche in American literary annals. A dramatist, he wrote our first American comedy, *The Contrast* . . . , a play as enjoyable to witness even today as the average twentieth-century production. An essayist and poet, he collaborated with Joseph Dennie in a series of humorous papers, *Colon and Spondee,* which are now neglected not so much because of any lack of inherent merit as because of their topical nature. A novelist, he wrote one extended narrative, *The Algerine Captive* . . . , which, however deficient in the elements that make for popularity among readers in quest of "heart-thrills," was the work of one of the most interesting minds of his day. *The Algerine Captive* is picaresque in framework—being a narrative stitched together by road and maritime episode—and alternately satirical and humanitarian in tone. (p. 60)

Notwithstanding the power and the probable veracity of Tyler's presentation of Algerian oppression, the literary values of [*The Algerine Captive*] lie closer to home, and they are found largely in the earlier chapters. His true weapon as a satirist was not the howitzer but the rifle, and he excelled in puncturing follies and affectations which had come under his own observation or had long been familiar to him through reading. The targets of his satire were not new—education, medical quackery, duelling, social life—but it is a delight to observe his expert marksmanship. (p. 63)

Tyler's claim to priority as a delineator of New England manners can be pretty well substantiated, for those domestic books which preceded *The Algerine Captive* glanced no more than obliquely at many things that Tyler confronted intimately. It must be added—what is true of many early English and American "novels"—that his tale is really no novel in a modern sense. . . . [It] is picaresque in pattern, but it does not achieve even [the] flimsy semblance of a rounded plot. Yet a novelist cannot live by plot alone; indeed his longevity depends more on other elements, especially the author's reflection of that general life of which the "action" purports to be a concrete example. Quite as important also is the author's ability to give memorable expression to those ideas, images, and emotions which form the raw material of fiction. In maturity of observation and in command of language, Tyler was far superior to the average popular novelist, whose book generally rendered up its final value as soon as certain arbitrarily withheld facts were divulged in the ultimate chapter. It is Tyler's finished

prose—swift, well-balanced, allusive but comparatively unembellished—which lends interest to his satire of what were inevitably temporary problems.

This is not to imply that *The Algerine Captive* is a great book. It has been unduly neglected by historians of literature . . . , but it can never claim a place of first importance. It possesses weight, but not *sufficient* weight. It is witty and apposite, but it lacks [general significance]. . . . Placed in his own period, Tyler appears to advantage, but forced into comparison with first-rank writers, he would inevitably diminish in stature. He was a good man of letters—not a towering genius. (pp. 67-8)

> Alexander Cowie, "Early Satire and Realism: Gilbert Imlay, Hugh Henry Brackenridge, Royall Tyler," in his The Rise of the American Novel (copyright 1948, 1951, by American Book Company; and reprinted by permission of D. C. Heath and Company), American Book, 1948 (and reprinted by American Book, 1951), pp. 38-68.*

ROGER B. STEIN (essay date 1965)

[*The Contrast*] has long been acknowledged as the first sophisticated attempt by an American dramatist to come to terms with the question of our national identity. . . . In fact the play suggests a whole range of questions to which Americans have been peculiarly sensitive, from the reference in the title to the contrast between European manners and American morals, between, at the extremes, a corrupt experience and a foolish innocence, to the less fully developed themes of the noble savage, the morality of art, the business ethic of the main chance, or the need for American fiscal responsibility. What has been generally either overlooked or misunderstood heretofore is the extent to which *The Contrast* is thematically concerned with questions of language; for *The Contrast* is a sensitive register and indeed a dramatic statement of "the question of our speech" at a crucial juncture of American literary history.

Because they have failed to recognize the linguistic orientation of *The Contrast,* previous critics have failed to see the real strengths and weaknesses of the play and either overvalued it as one of the first American dramas and a useful "document," or undervalued it as merely a provincial copy of Sheridan. The play deserves even more attention than it has hitherto received from historians concerned with tracing the transition from classic to romantic in American letters, but finally *The Contrast* must stand or fall as a work of art on its own dramatic merits and not on its usefulness to the student of American cultural chauvinism, the student of literary influences, or the intellectual historian. To take the play seriously as drama is to see that all three of these critical concerns are treated by Tyler first and last as problems of speech.

To begin with the play's chauvinism. The overt intention of the play has always been clear, for it is insisted upon from the opening command of the prologue, "Exult each patriot heart!—this night is shewn / A piece, which we may fairly call our own," to the conclusion. . . . Within the context of the drawing-room comedy, Tyler asserts the superiority of American life in a variety of ways. It is never far below the surface and often . . . it is painfully insisted upon. But assertions and statements are not inherently dramatic, for drama is concerned essentially with conflict. The critical problem which the chauvinism of the play raises is whether American values are ever seriously questioned. Do these values emerge through dramatic encounter or is the play essentially dogmatic and propagandistic? (pp. 454-56)

If indeed the latter is the case, then the play does lack dramatic validity for modern readers, for [the general] critical view implies that we can no longer give assent to the central impulse of the drama but can only appreciate it condescendingly as an historical document. The weakness of all these criticisms, though, is that they fail to consider the dramatic lines themselves with sufficient care. They find the plot weak, characterization stereotyped (except perhaps Jonathan), and yet neglect the speech itself, the dialogue, where Tyler's real strength—and indeed any dramatist's—lies.

This becomes a special problem when one reflects on the question of Tyler's dramatic sources. . . . Even though Tyler had probably never before seen a play performed on the stage, he was certainly no provincial; he had a sophisticated background in the literature of his time and had undoubtedly more than a passing familiarity with contemporary dramatic modes. (pp. 457-58)

[The] central critical problem of the play is that of dialogue. Both the earlier criticism, which finds the dramatic weakness in the gap between the play's moral and national ideal and its dependence upon dialogue, and the genesis of the play, in an English mode that exploited the possibilities of dialogue perhaps more than the drama ever had before, point us in this direction. (p. 459)

[If Henry James] was correct that the quality, authenticity, and security of speech is the supreme measure of the integrity of our existence, then Tyler in *The Contrast* projects us into a troubled world indeed; for rather than accepting unquestioningly the speech of his characters, at almost every turn of the play he indicates the variety in quality of speech, questions its authenticity, and shows it to be a very insecure medium at best. The characters speak not as one integral American chorus but contrapuntally, with the scenes arranged constantly to juxtapose characters and speech patterns. . . . Such contrasts occur also within the speech of individuals. . . . (pp. 459-60)

[Furthermore,] the contrasts often serve to question the authenticity of patterns of speech. The first half of the play abounds in situations which tend to isolate speech from character and action, driving a wedge between the speech and the speaker. Speech becomes thus not a function of the speaker but a mask behind which the speaker lurks. (p. 460)

[In] the world of *The Contrast* there is no security in speech. Words are constantly shifting in meaning. Jonathan's malapropisms are simple but powerful suggestions of this: Jessamy's "gallantry" becomes Jonathan's "girl huntry"; . . . the former's "poignancy of penetration" becomes the latter's "pugnancy of tribulation." . . . The "Holy Ground" turns out to be not a religious precinct as Jonathan expects, "a place where folks go to meeting," . . . but the rendezvous of harlots. This particular linguistic shift is developed later as Tyler turns religious language into bawdy play when Jonathan tells Jenny in the seduction scene that "all my tunes go to meeting tunes, save one, and I count you won't altogether like that 'ere." . . . Later Jonathan is taught by Jessamy that "grace" refers to the body, not to theology. . . . Jonathan himself joins in the linguistic game by suggesting to Jessamy that there is a semantic difference between "kiss" and "buss." . . . In fact it is Jonathan who has earlier posed the central, if finally unanswered question of the play: "What the dogs need of all this outlandish lingo?" (pp. 461-62)

Tyler's delight in word play and his ear for sound are keen. Maria and her father's discussion about the seriousness of marriage turns on the different meanings they give to the word "cost": financial for Van Rough, sentimental for Maria. . . . Charlotte tries to coax her brother into sharing her views by linguistic legerdemain. . . . The balanced diction which Tyler employs here is used again and again, with subtle differences between the lighter balance of Charlotte's sentences and the more ponderous, Johnsonian balance of Manly's. At times characters seem to be carried away by the sheer poetry of sound. . . . The pattern of banter, the repetitions and inversions of words, the gradual movement towards perfect rhyme and meter, are further testimony to Tyler's linguistic skill. The cumulative effect of all this attention to language should indicate the seriousness of Tyler's investigation of "the question of our speech" through the care and self-consciousness which he devoted to the writing of this play.

Finally, we must return to the central problem of the play, the relation of Tyler's investigation of speech to those moral and national concerns which give the play its dramatic structure. Looked at in these terms, the linguistic drama has much broader implications. In the first half of the play, Tyler developed skillfully a drama which depends almost entirely upon dialogue, upon linguistic shifts; but the dramatic situation which dialogue establishes led him to an impasse, and the only way out was through abandoning the satiric drama of dialogue and turning to a more conventional sentimental resolution of conflict in terms of plot. If the result is finally unsatisfying, the failure is an important one, not just a case of ineptness. It is a failure in which Tyler expresses the literary dilemma of his age and which he passes on as a legacy to later generations of American writers like Cooper, Twain, and Hemingway: the difficulty of finding an adequate American speech, a distinct native idiom.

In the first half of *The Contrast* the real drama centers on the different voices contending for dominance. Commanding his muse to display her powers on native themes in the prologue, Tyler searches as well amid the babble of his characters' speeches for a native voice and subjects each of the carefully distinguished voices to the severest scrutiny, satirizing the patterns of diction of all of his characters and showing their weaknesses with a satiric strength which shadows Sheridan, if it does not equal the master. The problem is that Tyler's critique is so sweeping that it threatens to destroy his avowed purpose, to establish in the play a national ideal. (pp. 462-64)

[If] one puts aside for a moment the nationalistic impulse behind [*The Contrast*] which leads Tyler to organize character and action to move towards what seems to us a rather trite and obvious triumph of American probity, virtue, honor over a corrupted Europeanized world of fashion, there is another and more ambiguous kind of drama in the play, a drama of language itself in search of honesty. Looked at in these terms, all of the characters seem to be wearing verbal masks. Honesty of thought and feeling is hidden behind a façade of artificial language, and the formal hero and heroine are no less tainted than the villain. Manly clearly does not provide us with a standard of American speech, even though he provides the moral standard of the drama.

The characters who do speak with most distinctly native voices are unsatisfying in a different way and further complicate the picture. (pp. 467-68)

[The character of Jonathan] has been singled out deservedly as Tyler's major contribution to our literature. As the prototype of the stage Yankee, Jonathan's richness as a character is unquestionable. His vitality and the broadly comic scenes between him and Jessamy, bring out what the *Pennsylvania Journal* called at the time "the pernicious maxims of the Chesterfieldian system, of all others the most dangerous to the peace of society," by pitting Jessamy's world against Jonathan's ignorance coupled with honesty, his clumsiness coupled with an instinctive feeling for the morally clean. While the prig Manly lectures to us on the superiority of probity, virtue, honor, Jonathan conveys the idea through dramatic encounter. The same may be said for the scene where Jonathan and Jenny discuss the theater. As a comic scene based upon the stock eighteenth-century situation of the country bumpkin faced with the complex sophisticated world of the city, the scene is a good one of its type, English or American. It also has value as a social document, a register of provincial attitudes towards the theater.

Furthermore, if one examines this scene in context and especially with its sequel, it emerges as much more centrally related to the issues of the play than critics . . . have assumed. . . . Tyler is able to suggest through the dramatic metaphor both the strength and the limits of the world of art by eliciting from his audience contrasting responses. . . . (pp. 468-69)

Tyler's skill resides in eliciting [two] reactions from the audience but forcing us to keep the two separate: for if we should condemn Jonathan's theatrical failure to seduce Jenny, we would be forced to approve the rake . . . and if we should approve of Jonathan's moral attitude towards the theater as the "devil's drawing-room," . . . we would be in the embarrassing position of having to condemn Tyler and *The Contrast* itself. The comic richness of Jonathan gives Tyler the double perspective which he needs but does not fully find in any other character except Charlotte. He can praise the world of masks and theatrical artifice and yet at the same time condemn those who would transform the values of art into values by which to live, without falling into either pompous moralizing or a corrupt aestheticism.

Unfortunately, from the point of view of language Jonathan offers no solution to the dramatist's dilemma. Jonathan's salty New Englandisms add flavor to the drama, but they by no means provide us with that standard of honest speech for which the play is in search. Dialect here, as in Tyler's English models, is a source of humor. We share the other characters' condescending attitude toward it. . . . Jonathan's language in general is clearly labeled as provincial; it does not become for Tyler a standard of speech for the new nation. Basically we are called upon to laugh at Jonathan, not with him.

And beyond this, Tyler the sophisticated language-manipulating dramatist, even pokes fun at the moralists. A close examination of Jonathan's diction shows it to be a corrupted version of Puritan theology. His "tarnal" this and "tarnal" that, his Biblical allusions, his perception of the character of Joseph Surface—"he talked as sober and as pious as a minister; but like some ministers that I know, he was a sly tike in his heart for all that" . . .—are in their various ways implicit and explicit condemnations of a traditional American moral standard. Not only does Jonathan provide us with no approved linguistic standard in the drama; the direction in which the character moves and which Tyler exploits for its comic possibilities seems to laugh out of the theater any residual Puritan morality at the same time it mocks the Chesterfieldian cant of ambrosia and flames. The only alternative to this seems to be the very tearful and grave sentimentalism which Tyler satirizes elsewhere in the play, the moral sententiousness to which the

comedy of Jonathan is such a healthy antidote. Thus the very richness of Jonathan threatens to turn the drama into a linguistic nightmare and in certain ways to threaten the moral assumptions upon which the play is based. Tyler's exuberant treatment of Jonathan almost leads him to a dramatic impasse.

Almost, but not quite, for after we have had our fun, have been exposed to the drama of dialogue, of contending voices seeking for precedence and each in its turn satirized by the sophisticated dramatist, Tyler turns more directly in the concluding scenes of the play to the moral and national task at hand. Linguistic drama is exchanged for plot situation, and a correct if rather tiresome and predictable sentimental conclusion is achieved. Manly gets his girl, Dimple is shuttled off into the wings, and Charlotte makes a quasi-religious recantation. The sophisticated comedy of manners where dialogue is plot becomes another American moral fable. Manly has the last words and the moral American hero triumphs not only over Dimple but over a vital American speech as well.

The "question of our speech" which *The Contrast* raises is not resolved and in these terms the conclusion is at best ambiguous. The dilemma which Tyler was unable to resolve here and later was passed on to later writers to struggle with well on into the nineteenth century. (pp. 469-72)

> *Roger B. Stein, "Royall Tyler and the Question of Our Speech," in* The New England Quarterly *(copyright 1965 by* The New England Quarterly*), Vol. XXXVIII, No. 4, December, 1965, pp. 454-74.*

JACK B. MOORE (essay date 1966)

Royall Tyler's success as a dramatist has long overshadowed his other contributions to American literature. His achievement in *The Contrast* is great, for the play is not only the first social comedy by an American performed by a professional company, but perhaps more significantly it is a genuinely funny play whose humor still has vitality. . . . Tyler's novel *The Algerine Captive* is second only to *The Contrast* as an intrinsically worthwhile attempt to establish a truly native literature.

In stylistic purity and the clarity with which Tyler investigates and dramatizes American manners, the book stands alone in our earliest fiction. (p. v)

The Algerine Captive purports to be in form an autobiography or history. Insistence is made throughout that its author is Dr. Updike Underhill, and all the apparatus of the book—its dedication, for example—corroborates this pretense. Many of the early novels presented themselves as "true revelations" or "lamentable and true histories" partly for verisimilitude and partly—in America especially—to overcome the moral and social bias against reading fiction. The putative author is following tradition when he insists that his story is "founded on FACT," and that in relating his mother's dream he will "only relate facts, and leave the reader to his own comments." The novel is to a degree factual, being based upon experiences of Tyler's uncle and some childhood experiences of Tyler himself. However, the autobiographic framework is also a skillfully employed satiric mask for Tyler. In the Algerian sequence for example, Updike and his Mohammedan interrogator Mollah argue the merits of the Bible and Alcoran. The dialogue quite clearly enables the reader to see Updike's provincial inflexibility in maintaining the unique rightness of his religion and holy book. But within the body of the novel, Updike himself remains absolutely unconvinced: Tyler's mask never drops.

The book is not rigidly historical or autobiographical, however, and perhaps its form could be more meaningfully described as an anatomy. As such it is characterized by satiric ridicule of false learning of one sort or another, including impractical education and quack medicine; digressive exposition; stylized characterizations; and forum discussions. Tyler's satire is gentle and humane, but none the less sure. (pp. vii-viii)

What criticism exists on Tyler's book usually attacks its structure, but contemporary readers should not be bothered by its seeming looseness. . . . (p. x)

[Tyler] includes one of the earliest examples in fiction of Yankee bumpkin letterwriting, combining comic dialect spelling with the traditional, neo-classic attack on dueling. . . . (p. xii)

Some critics feel that the book breaks in two [when Updike sails from the South as a ship's doctor]. Prior to the sailing, the book has been basically comic and regionally American. Its quacks and pedants have been natives, its discussions blandly innocent or comically ridiculous, as when four New England doctors diagnose a drunk jockey who has fallen senseless: one orders the windows and doors shut and declines an opinion since he has left "Pringle on contusions" home; the second prognosticates a compound fracture, calls for a half-dose of opium and trepanning instruments; the third orders brown paper dipped in rum and cobwebs; the fourth tells a joke and then prays. But as Updike leaves America eventually to become an Algerian captive, the book stops being gently satiric. Tyler selects as a pivotal transitional experience Updike's landing at London where he finds nothing comic, only dirt and depravity and "a motley race, in whose mongrel veins runs the blood of all nations." As Liverpool was to Melville's Redburn, so is London to Underhill. Life thereafter is no longer jocular and safe. (pp. xiii-xiv)

[When Updike sails aboard a slower ship ironically called "Sympathy,"] the book's tonal shift is reflected in the now no longer humanely satiric dialogue: one mate says about the slaves, "What signifies . . . the lives of the black devils; they love to die. You cannot please them better, than by chucking them into the water." In this section as elsewhere Tyler carefully avoids the then current vice of literary sentimentality. (p. xv)

In its clean, crisp prose style, its accurate regional satire, its portrayal of American manners, its depiction of Updike's growing-up, its final insistence upon ways the emergent country must be careful to take if it was to triumph in its earliest trials, *The Algerine Captive* is a highly interesting if partially flawed book. Its miscellaneous chapters—so typical of the grab-bag anatomy form—on Algerian history, government, revenue, on the life of "Mahomet," might have been made less dully encyclopedic. Yet for such an early American novel and such an early attempt to render native character, the book's deficiencies are slight. *The Algerine Captive* remains an example of its author's skill in developing an American literature native in content and intrinsically valuable in performance. (p. xvii)

> *Jack B. Moore, "Introduction" (1966), in* The Algerine Captive; or, The Life and Adventures of Doctor Updike Underhill, Six Years a Prisoner among the Algerines *by Royall Tyler, Scholars' Facsimiles & Reprints, 1967, pp. v-xvii.*

WALTER J. MESERVE (essay date 1977)

The Contrast lacks much of a plot and tends to be a talky play with little action, but it has many compensating strengths.

Though imitative of the eighteenth-century British sentimental comedy, it is relieved by an originality in thought and in character presentation which distinguishes this play above all other comedies in eighteenth-century America. Structurally, it follows the traditional five-act pattern, while, in keeping with its thesis of "contrast," each act divides into two scenes which provide contrast in form as well as in content. Tyler was both well read and talented, and the play shows his familiarity with traditional dramatic techniques, idiosyncratic language, and literature of the period.

Basically, the play satisfied all the demands of the theatre audience of 1787. The prologue—"Exult each patriot heart!"—characterizations of Jonathan and Colonel Manly, the dialect, the issues, and the final line of the play—all emphasize the new nationalism. Although they may be caricatures, the characters' distinctive qualities delight the reader and viewer. . . . Finally, there is the satire which American audiences had always enjoyed: satire on fashion, theatre, the English, and gossip. Additionally, to enliven the play there were songs, while superimposed on all elements was contrast—contrast between the people of England and those of America, between affectation and straightforwardness, between city and country, between hypocrisy and sincerity, and between foreign fraud and native worth. (pp. 98-9)

Tyler went on to write other plays but never with the skill or appeal which *The Contrast* showed in sufficient quantity to give him an immediate reputation. (p. 100)

> *Walter J. Meserve, "Early Dramatists of the New Republic," in his* An Emerging Entertainment: The Drama of the American People to 1828 *(copyright © 1977 by Indiana University Press), Indiana University Press, 1977, pp. 92-125.*

DONALD T. SIEBERT, JR. (essay date 1978)

[*The Contrast* is the result of Tyler's] "bold attempt" to create a truly original comedy within the formal context of seventeenth-and eighteenth-century English drama, and if his attempt was in many respects the failure which he hints it might be, he still deserves more critical applause for what he succeeded in doing than he has yet received. (p. 5)

[Tyler's] play certainly owes its formal identity to the tradition, but as it takes shape by calling on most of the conventional devices and expectations, it declares, as it were, its independence of that tradition.

First of all, the play identifies itself essentially as a laughing, rather than a weeping or sentimental comedy. The play does present a sentimental heroine, the modest and grave Maria, and finally matches her up with that type of noble sentiments, Colonel Manly; nevertheless, laughter achieved by almost every device of the comedy of manners is dominant. On the other hand, the often extremely staid sentiments, though clearly threatened by the element of laughter, are not finally undercut. This conflict between sentiment and humor, or even farce that often evokes a horse-laughter of which Lord Chesterfield would scarcely approve, is admittedly a real problem. Manly's first speech, for instance, strains to achieve a sententious dignity which even Parson Weems might have disowned with embarrassment. . . . One can hardly believe that Tyler intended such language to be heard without smiling, especially in the spirited atmosphere generated by Manly's rattling sister. . . . [Both] the laughter of free-wheeling comedy and the dignity of noble sentiment co-exist in the play. The laughter may be dominant, yet it does not invalidate the seriousness of the straight-faced preaching. That in itself marks *The Contrast* as beyond the ordinary in dramatic history.

Most of all the play presents itself as a rollicking comedy of manners, more like those libertine plays of the Restoration period than those more decent ones written later by Goldsmith or Sheridan. This wantonness makes the juxtaposition of laughter and sentiment all the more unusual. . . . [In] this respect Tyler was being particularly audacious, almost as though he were pretending ignorance of all the moral reforms generally observed on the English stage during the course of the eighteenth century—and this in a young country where the theater itself was almost officially regarded with suspicion.

Admittedly, Tyler acquits himself of profaneness and indecency to a large extent by the weight of his moral instruction, and so heavy, or heavy-handed, is this element that critics have even identified *The Contrast* as a sentimental play. Yet such a judgment is surprising, for there appears to be a bit more spicy material in the play than would be needed to relieve the blandness of the moral repast. (pp. 5-6)

Although Tyler may be gently satirizing his character's affectations, it would be wrong to think that he is satirizing the malicious practice of twisting the poor playwright's words. Rather he is playing a game with his audience. Charlotte's sporting with the word "monosyllable" is, after all, Tyler's. We are expected to laugh at the bawdiness, to enjoy the dramatic irony, and yet if we entertain any puritanical suspicion of the theater, to feel somewhat uncomfortable at the same time. Should the pious object to such talk, Tyler could reply that any salacious interpretation of the passage depends entirely upon the listener. . . . Tyler is safe. He is getting away with daring language among some rather provincially timid theatergoers. He has surprised his audience; he is testing their reactions.

In a larger sense, however, Tyler is testing his audience. . . . [He] is alerting them against being too facile in their judgments, or . . . the joke will be on them. (p. 8)

The Contrast seems designed to encourage that independence of spirit that perhaps too often it takes time out to preach. The moral is implicit in the structure just as much as it is explicit in the set speeches of the sentimental characters. It is an independence observed in the artist's use of his inherited tradition, and it is an independence of judgment which he encourages in his audience. What we have is a play which seems to challenge every expectation. It assumes the form of a Restoration comedy of manners and yet finally praises those very qualities a Restoration comedy ridicules: all those dowdy things like provincialism, plain talk and dress, humorless morality. Yet it refuses to be typed as a sentimental comedy either. If those dowdy qualities seem to be praised, they are laughed at, too, for the play is hardly the work of a grim-faced moralist. Quite simply, *The Contrast* seems to play fast and loose with any number of traditions and assumptions. (pp. 8-9)

The purpose of *The Contrast* is therefore not to lavish praise on American innocence while exposing and condemning European corruption and polish. Rather, the play reveals the contrast between Americans who are themselves and those who try to be something they are not, between dowdy virtue and supposedly fashionable deceit and selfishness, between independence and servility. It seeks to give Americans an uncompromising look at themselves for the purpose of taking stock. This sense of self-examination is emphasized by Tyler's repeated efforts to remind his audience that they are inside a playhouse, that somehow the play's meaning and significance involve them. They are on the stage in a performance being presented by a fellow American, as of course Tyler identifies himself. In a way the true hero is not Manly but the author, who was able to use the materials of European drama in new and unexpected ways and to make thereby his own declaration of literary independence. I am hardly saying that Tyler's transformation of these materials was masterful. It is doubtful to what degree one can make a traditional comedy of manners into something new, at least without the strain showing. Perhaps licentious comedy and high-minded didacticism are finally immiscible. Still, Tyler's effort itself is significant. We may say that if an author's purpose is to urge his audience to examine themselves honestly, to determine for themselves what manners, fashions, and values they will be known by, above all to ground their new political liberty on an *independence of spirit*, he can do no better than to set them a "bold example." (p. 10)

Donald T. Siebert, Jr., "Royall Tyler's Bold Example: 'The Contrast' and the English Comedy of Manners," in Early American Literature (copyrighted, 1978, by the University of Massachusetts), Vol. XIII, No. 1, Spring, 1978, pp. 3-11.

ADDITIONAL BIBLIOGRAPHY

Havens, Daniel F. "Enter Jonathan." In his *The Columbian Muse of Comedy: The Development of a Native Tradition in Early American Social Comedy, 1787-1845*, pp. 83-96. Carbondale and Edwardsville: Southern Illinois University Press, 1973.*
    Examines the similarities and differences in Richard Sheridan's *School for Scandal* and Tyler's *The Contrast*. This study also traces the development of the character Jonathan, the prototype for the "Yankee character," from Tyler's pen to the present.

Killheffer, Marie. "A Comparison of the Dialect of *The Biglow Papers* with the Dialect of Four Yankee Plays." *American Speech* III, No. 3 (February 1928): 222-36.*
    Traces James Russell Lowell's use of native American dialect in *The Biglow Papers* to Tyler's plays.

Leary, Lewis. "Royall Tyler: First Gentleman of the American Theater." In his *Soundings: Some Early American Writers*, pp. 8-51. Athens: University of Georgia Press, 1970.
    Analyzes *The Contrast* and provides some bibliographical information on Tyler.

Péladeau, Marius B. "Royall Tyler's *Other* Plays." *The New England Quarterly* XL, No. 1 (March 1967): 48-60.
    Discusses Tyler's unpublished and unsuccessful plays.

Tanselle, G. Thomas. *Royall Tyler*. Cambridge: Harvard University Press, 1967, 281 p.
    The definitive biography and bibliography for the Tyler student.

Jean Marie Mathias Philippe Auguste, Comte de Villiers de l'Isle-Adam

1838-1889

French dramatist, novelist, short story writer, and poet.

Villiers's wild and imaginative works form an important bridge between the French schools of Romanticism and Symbolism. His hero Axël is seen by Edmund Wilson as the embodiment of the Symbolist hero; Villiers also influenced such important French writers as Joris-Karl Huysmans and Stéphane Mallarmé. However, his uncompromising idealism was out of step with bourgeois tastes, and the public's vehement rejection of his works placed him in a state of appalling poverty. Villiers was possessed of a romantic sensibility, believing that materialism was the bane of society, and he treated monetary interest with vicious sarcasm. His *Contes cruels (Cruel Tales)* are the best example of his talent for sarcasm, but his masterpiece, *Axël*, demonstrates his belief in an ideal world. The central characters, Axël and Sara, reject their religion and their treasure, and finally their lives in idealistic pursuit. "As for living," exclaims Axël, "our servants will do that for us."

Much of Villiers's best work is lost, because he often wrote on scraps of paper, and was fond of reciting his tales, but rarely committed them to writing. His literary executors, Huysmans and Mallarmé, apparently neglected their duty, since little posthumous work appeared. A marvelous raconteur, Villiers displayed wit in conversation that was unrivaled in literary France; when Oscar Wilde arrived in Paris, he was compared to Villiers. Villiers's humor lives today in the *Cruel Tales*, in his parodies of bourgeois life, *Tribulat Bonhomet*, and in *L'Ève future*, a satiric attack on science. *L'Ève future* concerns a beautiful, intelligent woman whose only fault is that she is an automaton whose personality reflects only what her lover wishes her to be. As soon as he ceases to believe that she is real, she disintegrates. Thus Villiers summed up his attitude toward science.

Villiers began his career with attempts at poetry. Critics now consider his poems to be weak, but acknowledge that they show flashes of the genius that would appear in his later dramas and short stories. Though the dramas are often criticized as ornate and overwritten, Villiers's blending of ironic social criticism with a passionate plea for his own extreme idealism was praised throughout the last century. He combined his diverse philosophical and literary influences with remarkable grace. Charles Baudelaire's influence is evident in the mystification and refinement found in Villiers's works, and his interest in the macabre and the grotesque was probably inspired by the works of E.T.A. Hoffmann and Edgar Allan Poe, both of whom he greatly admired. Richard Wagner, with whom Villiers formed a tenuous friendship, was a major source of his notions of idealistic grandeur. Villiers's combination of Catholicism, occultism, and Hegelianism add an ethereal quality to his works, which vivifies their idealism and strengthens their ironic touch.

Villiers's plays were rarely performed, and were poorly received. He died the uncompromising idealist that he had been throughout his life. Few people heard his distinct voice, but his mastery over powerful ideas and his ability to express them in a direct, concise style mark Villiers as a provocative literary figure.

PRINCIPAL WORKS

Deux essais de poésie (poetry) 1858
Premières poésies (poetry) 1859
Isis (unfinished novel) 1862
Elën (drama) 1866
Morgane (drama) 1866
Claire Lenoir, étude physiologique (short story) 1867
   [*Claire Lenoir*, 1925]
La révolte (drama) 1870
   [*The Revolt* published in *The Revolt and The Escape*, 1910]
L'evasion (drama) 1871
   [*The Escape* published in *The Revolt and The Escape*, 1910]
Arazël (prose poem) 1878
Le nouveau monde (drama) 1880
Contes cruels (short stories) 1883
   [*Sardonic Tales*, 1927; also published as *Cruel Tales*, 1963]
Akëdysséril (prose poem) 1886
L'Ève future (novel) 1886
Tribulat Bonhomet (short stories) 1887
Histoires insolites (short stories) 1888
Nouveaux contes cruels (short stories) 1888

Axël (drama) 1890
  [*Axël*, 1925]
Chez les passants (essays and satire) 1890
Propos d'au delà (short stories and unfinished novel)
  1893

J.—K. HUYSMANS (essay date 1884)

[The] cerebral clinic where, vivisecting in a stifling atmosphere, this spiritual surgeon [Poe] became, as soon as his attention wandered, the prey of his imagination, which sprayed about him, like delicious miasmas, angelic, dream-like apparitions, was for Des Esseintes a source of indefatigable conjectures; but now that his neurosis had grown worse, there were days when reading these works exhausted him. . . .

He therefore had to hold himself in check and only rarely indulge in these formidable elixirs, just as he could no longer visit with impunity his red entrance-hall and feast his eyes on the horrors of Odilon Redon and the tortures of Jan Luyken.

And yet, when he was in this frame of mind, almost anything he read seemed insipid after these terrible philtres imported from America. He would therefore turn to Villiers de l'Isle-Adam, in whose scattered writings he discovered observations just as unorthodox, vibrations just as spasmodic, but which, except perhaps in *Claire Lenoir*, did not convey such an overwhelming sense of horror. (p. 192)

Claire Lenoir was the first of a series of stories linked together by the generic title of *Histoires moroses*. Against a background of abstruse speculations borrowed from old Hegel, there moved two deranged individuals, a Doctor Tribulat Bonhomet who was pompous and puerile, and a Claire Lenoir who was droll and sinister, with blue spectacles as big and round as five-franc pieces covering her almost lifeless eyes.

This story concerned a commonplace case of adultery, but ended on a note of indescribable terror when Bonhomet, uncovering the pupils of Claire's eyes as she lay on her deathbed, and probing them with monstrous instruments, saw clearly reflected on the retina a picture of the husband brandishing at arm's length the severed head of the lover and, like a Kanaka, howling a triumphant war-chant.

Based on the more or less valid observation that, until decomposition sets in, the eyes of certain animals, oxen for instance, preserve like photographic plates the image of the people and things lying at the moment of death within the range of their last look, the tale obviously owed a great deal to those of Edgar Allan Poe, from which it derived its wealth of punctilious detail and its horrific atmosphere.

The same was true of *L'Intersigne,* which had later been incorporated in the *Contes cruels,* a collection of stories of indisputable talent which also included *Véra,* a tale Des Esseintes regarded as a little masterpiece.

Here the hallucination was endowed with an exquisite tenderness; there was nothing here of the American author's gloomy mirages, but a well-nigh heavenly vision of sweetness and warmth, which in an identical style formed the antithesis of Poe's Beatrices and Ligeias, those pale, unhappy phantoms engendered by the inexorable nightmare of black opium.

This story too brought into play the operations of the will, but it no longer showed it undermined and brought low by fear; on the contrary, it studied its intoxication under the influence of a conviction which had become an obsession, and it also demonstrated its power, which was so great that it could saturate the atmosphere and impose its beliefs on surrounding objects.

Another book of Villiers', *Isis,* he considered remarkable for different reasons. The philosophical lumber that littered *Claire Lenoir* also cluttered up this book, which contained an incredible hotch-potch of vague, verbose observations on the one hand and reminiscences of hoary melodramas on the other—oubliettes, daggers, rope-ladders, in fact all the romantic bric-à-brac that would reappear, looking just as old-fashioned, in Villiers' *Elën* and *Morgane.* . . . (pp. 193-94)

The heroine of this book, a Marquise Tullia Fabriana, who was supposed to have assimilated the Chaldean learning of Poe's women and the diplomatic sagacity of Stendhal's San-severina-Taxis, not content with all this, had also assumed the enigmatic expression of a Bradamante crossed with an antique Circe. These incompatible mixtures gave rise to a smoky vapour in which philosophical and literary influences jostled each other around, without managing to sort themselves out in the author's mind by the time he began writing the prolegomena to this work, which was intended to fill no less than seven volumes.

But there was another side to Villiers' personality, altogether clearer and sharper, marked by grim humour and ferocious banter; when this side was uppermost, the result was not one of Poe's paradoxical mystifications, but a lugubriously comic jeering similar to Swift's bitter raillery. A whole series of tales, *Les Demoiselles de Bienfilâtre, L'Affichage céleste, La Machine à gloire* and *Le plus beau dîner du monde* revealed a singularly inventive and satirical sense of humour. All the filthiness of contemporary utilitarian ideas, all the money-grubbing ignominy of the age were glorified in stories whose pungent irony sent Des Esseintes into raptures of delight.

In this realm of biting, poker-faced satire, no other book existed in France. (p. 194)

> *J.-K. Huysmans, in a chapter from his novel* Against Nature, *translated by Robert Baldick (translation copyright © 1959 the Estate of Robert Baldick; reprinted by permission of Penguin Books Ltd; originally published as* À rebours, *G. Charpentier, 1884), Penguin Books Inc., 1959, pp. 178-200.**

THE ATHENAEUM (essay date 1889)

['**Eve Future**' is in many respects Villiers's most idiosyncratic production.] The new Eve is an artificial woman, constructed out of a variety of materials by [Thomas] Edison, and so wonderfully made by her American creator that by means of electricity she walks, speaks, sings, and performs several other human functions. An idea so suggestive, if not original, afforded full scope for De l'Isle-Adam's lively imagination and bitter irony. It permitted him to freely indulge his wonted raillery against the demoralizing effects of modern civilization and its accompanying scientific discoveries. The Edisonian Eve has been invested with all the charms calculated to fascinate the susceptible Adams of this age, and is enabled to utter from the depths of her phonographic bosom words of wisdom and sentences of divine poesy, all carefully culled from the leading poets and whispered into the prepared receptacle by her creator.

This automatic woman needs only a soul to render her perfect; and this one thing needful, the one thing her American maker could not supply, she does ultimately come into possession of. The inspiration of a soul is, indeed, the mainspring of the story, and the way in which the spiritual element subdues the material, the master touch of the *raconteur.*

Any criticism of De l'Isle-Adam's writings here would be unnecessary, but if the enthusiastic opinions of his surviving contemporaries may be only partially accepted, his place in the literature of this century will be a lofty one. Much of his best work is apparently lost, having been left not merely un-printed, but even unwritten, lingering only in the memories of those friends to whom he recited it. He lived in a world of mystery and fiction—so much so that many doubted the reality of the misery and ills he did endure, yet accepted his legends for truth.

J.H.I., "Villiers de l'Isle-Adam," in The Athe-naeum, *No. 3228, September 7, 1889, p. 321.*

ANATOLE FRANCE   (essay date 1891)

[Villiers] belonged to that family of neo-Catholics whose com-mon father is Chateaubriand, and which produced Barbey d'Aurévilly, Baudelaire, and more recently M. Joséphin Pé-ladan. What they enjoyed above all things in religion were the charm of sin and the greatness of sacrilege. Their sensualism revelled in the dogmas which added to luxury the supreme luxury of damning themselves. (pp. 121-22)

Like the rest of them, Villiers de l'Isle-Adam was a great mystical dilettante. His piety was terribly impious. He indulged in terrific irony. He died, and left us without regret. "I am going to rest," he said. He left the world without ever having tasted what are called the good things of this life. Poverty held him in its grip, and his best friends, his most ardent admirers, could never tear him from what seemed a part of his na-ture. . . . Villiers, in thought, lived always in enchanted gar-dens, in marvellous palaces, in subterranean chambers full of the treasures of Asia, glittering with the gaze of royal sapphires and hieratic virgins. This unhappy man lived in fortunate lands of which the happy of this world have not the remotest con-ception. He was a seer; his dull eyes looked within and saw dazzling visions. He wandered through life as in a dream; not seeing what we see, and beholding that which is not permitted to us. Weighed down as we are, we have no right to complain. He knew how to turn the dull round of life into an ever-renewed rapture. He scattered purple and gold in abundance over mean café tables smelling of beer and tobacco. (pp. 122-23)

Must we see in Villiers de l'Isle-Adam nothing but a mind teeming with hallucinations? Far from it. If this waking dreamer carried away with him the secret of his most beautiful dreams, if he has not told us all he saw in that long dream whereof his life consisted, he has at any rate written enough to leave us some idea of the original wealth of his imagination. He was an eccentric writer; and his formless, illegible, scattered, lost manuscripts were recovered in all directions. Somnambulists are possessed of faculties that we cannot understand. Villiers would recover at night, in the gutters, the vanished pages of his masterpieces. (pp. 124-25)

This must be said, to the confusion of those that ignored him while he lived: Villiers is a writer, and a writer in the greatest of styles. When he does not cumber his sentences with inci-dences of too deep a meaning, when he does not over-prolong

his obscure irony, when he renounces the pleasure of aston-ishing himself, he is a writer of magnificent prose, full of harmony and brilliance.

His drama, the *Nouveau monde,* contained dialogues of incom-parable fragrance, purity, and distinction. The collection which he called *Contes cruels* contains pages full of beauty. (pp. 125-26)

Villiers, profoundly musical and full of Wagner, filled his prose with expressive sonority and intimate melody. Besides, he loved the art of writing with all his heart. There is no love without superstition. He believed in the virtue of words. For him certain words, like the Scandinavian runes, had a secret power. That is typical of a good artisan of words. There lives no true writer without this weakness.

With all his marvellous gifts, Villiers never won the favour of the public, and I fear that his books, even after his death, are read only by a very limited number. They are full of a cruel irony. It is this very irony, often painful and obscure, which is the impediment. His chuckle, still ringing in the ears of all who knew Villiers, that short sharp chuckle of his may be found in all that he wrote, and lends a grimace to his purest thoughts. This visionary extended mockery beyond the per-missible, and even the conceivable. He mingled it curiously with his philosophic contemplations, his pious ecstasies and his sublimest meditations. (pp. 126-27)

Anatole France, "Villiers de l'Isle-Adam," in his On Life & Letters, third series, *translated by D. B. Stewart (originally published as* La vie litteraire, *Vol. III, Calmann Levy, 1891), John Lane Company, 1922, pp. 121-29.*

THE ATHENAEUM   (essay date 1893)

[The **'Nouveaux Contes cruels'**] consist of eight stories which were published in a volume under that title in the author's lifetime, followed by five stories, an article, and a letter, of which the stories had previously appeared in newspapers only. The article, which had been refused by the *Figaro,* and the letter, which is new, are worthless. But the first four of the five new stories are excellent examples of the art of a great master. The whole of Villiers de l'Isle-Adam's stories were written for money—little money, alas!—to enable him to live while he was doing more serious work. But his stories may be remembered, while his more serious work is, we fear, already forgotten. He is, perhaps, the greatest writer of the modern French novelette, except Catulle Mendès, and, though cynical in his disappointment and bitterness, he is less perversely cruel and wilfully wicked than his brother poet.

"'Nouveaux contes cruels'," in The Athenaeum, *No. 3422, May 27, 1893, p. 667.*

W. B. YEATS   (essay date 1894)

Thirty thousand francs and enthusiastic actors have been found to produce the **'Axel'** of . . . Villiers De L'isle Adam. On February the 26th a crowded audience of artists and men of letters listened, and on the whole with enthusiasm, from two o'clock until ten minutes to seven to this drama, which is written in prose as elevated as poetry, and in which all the characters are symbols and all the events allegories. It is noth-ing to the point that the general public have since shown that they will have none of **'Axel,'** and that the critics have denounced it in almost the same words as those in which they denounce in this country the work of Dr. Ibsen, and that they have called the younger generation both morbid and gloomy. (p. 15)

[In the last scene of '**Axel**' the lovers complete their] fourfold renunciation—of the cloister, of the active life of the world, of the labouring life of the intellect, of the passionate life of love. The infinite is alone worth attaining, and the infinite is the possession of the dead. Such appears to be the moral. Seldom has utmost pessimism found a more magnificent expression.

The final test of the value of any work of art to our particular needs, is when we place it in the hierarchy of those recollections which are our standards and our beacons. At the head of mine are a certain night scene long ago, when I heard the wind blowing in a bed of reeds by the border of a little lake, a Japanese picture of cranes flying through a blue sky, and a line or two out of Homer. I do not place any part of '**Axel**' with these perfect things, but still there are lines of the adept Janus, of the Medusa Sara, which are near them in my hierarchy. Indeed the play throughout gives a noble utterance to those sad thoughts which come to the most merry of us, and thereby robs them of half their bitterness. . . . In a decade when the comic paper and the burlesque are the only things sure to awaken enthusiasm, a grim and difficult play by its mere grimness and difficulty is a return to better traditions, it brings us a little nearer the heroic age.

I hear that there is a chance of '**Axel**' being performed in London; if so, I would suggest that the second and third acts be enormously reduced in length. The second act especially dragged greatly. The situation is exceedingly dramatic, and with much of the dialogue left out would be very powerful. The third act, though very interesting, to anyone familiar with the problems and philosophy it deals with, must inevitably as it stands bore and bewilder the natural man, with no sufficient counterbalancing advantage. There was no question of the dramatic power of the other acts. Even the hostile critics have admitted this. The imaginative drama must inevitably make many mistakes before it is in possession of the stage again, for it is so essentially different to the old melodrama and the new realism, that it must learn its powers and limitations for itself. It must also fail many times before it wins the day, for though we cannot hope to ever again see the public as interested in sheer poetry, as the audiences were who tolerated so great a poet, so poor a dramatist as Chapman, it must make its hearers learn to understand eloquent and beautiful dialogues, and to admire them for their own sake and not as a mere pendent to the action. For this reason its very mistakes when they are of the kind made by the promoters of '**Axel**' help to change the public mind in the right direction, by reminding it very forcibly that the actor should be also a reverent reciter of majestic words. (pp. 15-16)

> *W. B. Yeats, "A Symbolical Drama in Paris" (reprinted by permission of Michael and Anne Yeats), in* The Bookman, *London, Vol. VI, No. 31, April, 1894, pp. 14-16.*

REMY de GOURMONT (essay date 1896)

Some take pleasure, an awkward testimony of a piously troubled admiration, in saying and even in basing a paradoxical study on the saying: "Villiers de L'Isle-Adam was neither of his country nor time." This seems preposterous, for a superior man, a great writer is, in fine, by his very genius, one of the syntheses of his race and epoch, the representative of a momentary humanity, the brain and mouth of a whole tribe and not a fugitive monster. Like Chateaubriand, his brother in race and fame, Villiers was the man of the moment, and of a solemn moment. . . . Villiers belonged to his time to such a degree that all his masterpieces are dreams solidly based on science and modern metaphysics, like *l'Eve Future* or *Tribulat Bonhomet,* that enormous, admirable and tragic piece of buffoonery, where all the gifts of the dreamer, ironist and philosopher come to converge, so as to form perhaps the most original creation of the century.

This point cleared, we declare that Villiers, being of prodigious complexity, naturally lends himself to contradictory interpretations. He was everything, a new Goethe, but if less conscious and less perfect, keener, more artful, more mysterious, more human, and more familiar. He is always among us and in us, by his work and by the influence of his work, which exultantly goes through the best of the writers and artists of the actual hour. He has reopened the gates of the beyond, closed with what a crash we remember, and through these gates a whole generation was hurled to infinity. . . . Villiers exercised these two functions for us: he was the exorcist of the real and the porter of the ideal.

Complex, but we may see a double spirit in him. There were two essentially dissimilar writers in him, the romanticist and the ironist. The romanticist was the first to come to birth and the last to die: *Elen* and *Morgane; Akedysseril* and *Axel.* Villiers, the ironist, author of *Tribulat Bonhomet,* is intermediate between these two romantic phases; *l'Eve future* should be described as a mixture of these two so diverse elements, for the book with its overwhelming irony is also a book of love.

Villiers at once realized himself by fancy and irony, making his fancy ironic, when life disgusted him even with fancy. No one has been more subjective. His characters are created with particles of his soul, raised, in the same way as a mystery, to the state of authentic, complete souls. If it is a dialogue, he will cause a certain character to utter philosophies quite above his normal understanding of things. In *Axel,* the abbess speaks of hell as Villiers might have spoken of Hegelianism, whose deceptions he learned towards the end, after having accepted its large certitudes in the beginning: "It is done! the child already experiences the ravishment and intoxications of Hell!" He experienced them: as a Baudelairian, he loved blasphemy for its occult effects, the immense risk of a pleasure taken at the expense of God himself. Sacrilege is in acts, blasphemy in words. He believed in words more than in realities, which are but the tangible shadows of words, for it is quite evident, and by a very simple syllogism, that if there is no thought in the absence of words, no more is there matter in the absence of thought. (pp. 91-4)

Without going as far as Berkeley's pure negations, which nevertheless are but the extreme logic of subjective idealism, he admitted in his conception of life, on the same plan, the Interior and the Exterior, Spirit and Matter, with a very visible tendency to give the first term domination over the second. For him the idea of *progress* was never anything but a subject for jest, together with the nonsense of the humanitarian positivists who teach, reversed mythology, that terrestrial paradise, a superstition if we assign it the past, becomes the sole legitimate hope if we place it in the future.

On the contrary, he makes a protagonist (Edison doubtless) say in a short fragment of an old manuscript of *l'Eve future:*

''We are in the ripe age of Humanity, that is all! Soon will come the senility and decrepitude of this strange polyp, and the evolution accomplished, his mortal return to the mysterious laboratory where all the Ghosts eternally work their experiments, by grace of *some unquestionable necessity.*''

And in this last word, Villiers mocks his belief in God. Was he Christian? He became one towards the end of his life: thus he knew all the forms of intellectual intoxication. (pp. 97-8)

> Remy de Gourmont, ''Villiers de L'Isle-Adam,'' in his The Book of Masks, translated by Jack Lewis (originally published as Le livre des masques: Portraits symbolistes, Vol. I, Mercure de France, 1896), John W. Luce & Co., 1921 (and reprinted by Books for Libraries Press, 1967; distributed by Arno Press, Inc.), pp. 91-100.

ARTHUR SYMONS (essay date 1899)

Axël is the Symbolist drama in all its uncompromising conflict with the ''modesty'' of nature and the limitations of the stage. It is the drama of the soul, and, at the same time, it is the most pictorial of dramas. I should define its manner as a kind of spiritual romanticism. The earlier dramas, *Elën, Morgane,* are fixed at somewhat the same point in space; *La Révolte,* which seems to anticipate *The Doll's House,* shows us an aristocratic Ibsen, touching reality with a certain disdain, certainly with far less skill, certainly with far more beauty. But *Axël,* meditated over during a lifetime, must certainly be taken as Villiers' ideal of his own idealism.

The action takes place, it is true, in this century, but it takes place in corners of the world into which the modern spirit has not passed. . . . The characters, Axël d'Auërsperg, Eve Sara Emmanuèle de Maupers, Maître Janus, the Archidiacre, the Commandeur Kaspar d'Auërsperg, are at once more and less than human beings: they are the types of different ideals, and they are clothed with just enough humanity to give form to what would otherwise remain disembodied spirit. The religious ideal, the occult ideal, the worldly ideal, the passionate ideal, are all presented, one after the other, in these dazzling and profound pages. Axël is the disdainful choice from among them, the disdainful rejection of life itself, of the whole illusion of life, ''since infinity alone is not a deception.'' And Sara? Sara is a superb part of that life which is rejected, which she herself comes, not without reluctance, to reject. In that motionless figure during the whole of the first act, silent but for a single ''No,'' and leaping into a moment's violent action as the act closes, she is the haughtiest woman in literature. But she is a woman; and she desires life, finding it in Axël. Pride, and the woman's devotion to the man, aid her to take the last, cold step with Axël, in that transcendental giving up of life at the moment when life becomes ideal.

And the play is written throughout with a curious solemnity, a particular kind of eloquence, which makes no attempt to imitate the level of the speech of everyday, but which is a sort of ideal language, in which beauty is aimed at as exclusively as if it were written in verse. The modern drama, under the democratic influence of Ibsen, the positive influence of Dumas *fils,* has limited itself to the expression of temperaments in the one case, of theoretic intelligences in the other, in as nearly as possible the words which the average man would use for the statement of his emotions and ideas. . . . [It] is evident that the average man can articulate only a small enough part of what he obscurely feels or thinks; and the theory of Realism

is that his emotions and ideas are to be given only in so far as the words at his own command can give them. Villiers, choosing to concern himself only with exceptional characters, and with them only in the absolute, invents for them a more elaborate and a more magnificent speech than they would naturally employ, the speech of their thoughts, of their dreams.

And it is a world thought or dreamt in some more fortunate atmosphere than that in which we live, that Villiers has created for the final achievement of his abstract ideas. (pp. 44-7)

The ideal, to Villiers, being the real, spiritual beauty being the essential beauty, and material beauty its reflection or its revelation, it is with a sort of fury that he attacks the materialising forces of the world: science, progress, the worldly emphasis on ''facts,'' on what is ''positive,'' ''serious,'' ''respectable.'' Satire, with him, is the revenge of beauty upon ugliness, the persecution of the ugly. It is not merely social satire, it is a satire on the material universe by one who believes in a spiritual universe. Thus it is the only laughter of our time which is fundamental, as fundamental as that of Swift or Rabelais. And this lacerating laughter of the idealist is never surer in its aim than when it turns the arms of science against itself, as in the vast buffoonery of *L'Eve Future.* A Parisian wit sharpened to a fineness of irony, such as only wit which is also philosophy can attain, brings in another method of attack; humour, which is almost English, another; while again satire becomes tragic, fantastic, *macabre.* In those enigmatic ''tales of the grotesque and arabesque'' [the *Contes Cruels*], in which Villiers rivals Poe on his own ground, there is for the most part a multiplicity of meaning which is, as it is meant to be, disconcerting. I should not like to say how far Villiers does not, sometimes, believe in his own magic.

It is characteristic of him, at all events, that he employs what we call the supernatural alike in his works of pure idealism and in his works of sheer satire. (pp. 48-9)

There is, in everything Villiers wrote, a strangeness, certainly both instinctive and deliberate, which seems to me to be the natural consequence of that intellectual pride which . . . was at the basis of his character. He hated every kind of mediocrity; therefore, he chose to analyse exceptional souls, to construct exceptional stories, to invent splendid names, and to evoke singular landscapes. It was part of his curiosity in souls to prefer the complex to the simple, the perverse to the straightforward, the ambiguous to either. His heroes are incarnations of spiritual pride, and their tragedies are the shock of spirit against matter, the invasion of spirit by matter, the temptation of spirit by spiritual evil. . . . And his heroines, when they are not, like *L'Eve Future,* the vitalised mechanism of an Edison, have the solemnity of dead people, and a hieratic speech. . . . And their voice is always like the voice of Elën: ''I listened attentively to the sound of her voice; it was taciturn, subdued, like the murmur of the river Lethe, flowing through the region of shadows.'' They have the immortal weariness of beauty; they are enigmas to themselves; they desire, and know not why they refrain; they do good and evil with the lifting of an eyelid, and are innocent and guilty of all the sins of the earth.

And these strange inhabitants move in as strange a world. They are the princes and *châtelaines* of ancient castles, lost in the depths of the Black Forest; they are the last descendants of a great race, about to come to an end; students of magic, who have the sharp and swift swords of the soldier; enigmatic courtesans, at the table of strange feasts. . . . And we see them always at the moment of a crisis, before the two ways of a decision, hesitating in the entanglements of a great temptation. And this casuist of souls will drag forth some horribly stunted or horribly overgrown soul from under its obscure covering, setting it to dance naked before our eyes. He has no mercy on those who have no mercy on themselves.

In the sense in which that word is ordinarily used, Villiers has no pathos. This is enough to explain why he can never, in the phrase he would have disliked so greatly, "touch the popular heart." His mind is too abstract to contain pity, and it is in his lack of pity that he seems to put himself outside humanity. (pp. 49-52)

Contempt, noble as it may be, anger, righteous though it may be, cannot be indulged in without a certain lack of sympathy; and lack of sympathy comes from a lack of patient understanding. It is certain that the destiny of the greater part of the human race is either infinitely pathetic or infinitely ridiculous. Under which aspect, then, shall that destiny and those obscure fractions of humanity be considered? Villers was too sincere an idealist, too absolute in his idealism, to hesitate. "As for living," he cries, in that splendid phrase of *Axël,* "our servants will do that for us!" . . . In this haughtiness towards life, in this disdain of ordinary human motives and ordinary human beings, there is at once the distinction and the weakness of Villiers. (pp. 53-4)

> *Arthur Symons, "Villiers de L'Isle-Adam," in* The Fortnightly Review *(reprinted by permission of Contemporary Review Company Limi ed), Vol. LXVI, August, 1899 (and reprinted in his* The Symbolist Movement in Literature, *E. P. Dutton and Company, 1908, pp. 37-58).*

THE BOOKMAN   (essay date 1901)

Villiers de l'Isle Adam's **"Revolt,"** written nearly a decade before "The Doll's House," will never take its place, and this for several reasons. First, Ibsen is a master of stagecraft, while, for stage purposes, **"The Revolt"** is about as badly contrived as possible. Then Nora is to the majority of persons a far more conceivable woman, on first acquaintance, than Elisabeth, who will be pronounced too "high-falutin'." Elisabeth appeals to a narrower world, numerically speaking, and the greater one may sympathise with Felix, and laugh at his romantic wife's failure. Yet a little more stage-craft, and **"The Revolt"** would have been by far the finer play. It is higher in conception than Ibsen's, because of the poetry at its source and all along its course; and because of its universal application. "The Doll's House" is a dramatised tract in favour of the feminist movement. **"The Revolt"** is not the tragedy of a wife who has been tyrannised over; it is the tragedy of every soul that, in the name of duty, undertakes the lower task, while with a clear eye seeing the higher. (pp. 184-85)

> *"Ibsen Forestalled," in* The Bookman, *London, Vol. XX, No. 120, September, 1901, pp. 184-85**

JAMES HUNEKER   (essay date 1905)

His life long, Villiers traversed the darkness which encompasses with the sure, swift step of a nyctalops, one who can pierce with his glance the deepest obscurity. So it is that in his plays and stories we are conscious of the great mystery of life and death hemming us about. Sometimes this atmosphere is morbidly oppressive, sometimes it is relieved by gay, ma-

niacal bursts of laughter. Again it lifts and reveals the mild heavens streaked with menacing irony. There is a lugubrious undercurrent in the buffooncries of Villiers. . . . This poet slew his soul by his evocation of terror.

He is a mystic, a spiritual romantic, and only a realist in his sardonic pictures of Paris life, tiny cabinet pictures, etchings, bitten out with the *aqua fortis* of his ghastly irony. There is the irony, a mask behind which pity, sympathy, lurk; Shakespeare wore this mask at times. And there is the irony that withers, that blasts. This is Villiers.

Axël is both difficult and illuminative reading. It is in four acts with nine scenes. Each act or part is respectively entitled: The Religious World, The Tragic World, The Occult World, The Passional World. The poet had not known Wagner and his Tetralogy for naught. Sara is a superb creation—but not on the boards, in the disillusioning, depoetizing, troubled, and malarial air of the stage! It was a mistake to play *Axël* in Paris. Its solemn act of rejection of life at the moment "when life becomes ideal" is hardly fitting for the theatre. A drama to be played by poets before a parterre of poets! (pp. 356-57)

[Villiers lived and died] a stranger in a strange world. His plays may be better appreciated some day. If Ibsen profited by *The Revolt,* then the seed of Villiers has not been sown in vain. Nothing reveals Ibsen's mastery of the dramatic form so completely as his treatment of the woman who revolts and leaves her home, when compared to Villiers's handling of the same idea. Elizabeth goes away in despair, but to return. Nora departs, and the curtain quickly severs us from her future, her "miracle" speech being a faint prophecy that may be expanded some day into a fulfilment. Villiers was perhaps the pioneer; though revolting women abound in Dumas, abound in the Bible, for that matter; but the specific woman who puts up the shutters of the shop, and declares the dissolution of the matrimonial firm, is the creation of Villiers. Ibsen developed the idea, and, great artist that he is, made of it a formal drama of beauty and dramatic significance—which *The Revolt* is not. There are many loose psychologic ends left untied by the Frenchman, and his conclusion is dramatically ineffectual.

What is the value of such a life, what its meanings? may be asked by the curious impertinents. Why select for study the character and career of a half-mad mystic? Simply because Villiers is a poet and not a politician. It is because Villiers is Villiers that he interests the student of literature and humanity. And the bravery, the incomparable bravery, of the man who like Childe Roland blew his slug-horn, dauntless to the last! In his *Azrael* he uses as a motto Hassan-ben-Sabbah's "O Death! those who are about to live, salute thee." All the soul of Villiers de l'Isle Adam is in that magnificently defiant challenge! (pp. 365-66)

> *James Huneker, "Villiers de l'Isle Adam," in his* Iconoclasts: A Book of Dramatists, *Charles Scribner's Sons, 1905 (and reprinted by Charles Scribner's Sons, 1921), pp. 350-65.*

ARNOLD WHITRIDGE   (essay date 1922)

The visible world, with all its ramifications of duty and obligation, simply did not exist, as far as [Villiers] was concerned. If he never experienced the yearning of the normal man to leave his mark behind him, it was because the unseen world was infinitely more vivid. From the moment he set foot in Paris he repudiated the boundaries between this world and the next. Other men have attempted his attitude of serene detachment but they have rarely succeeded. Only Villiers could ask himself with perfect sincerity, "A quoi bon agir pour un instant?" (pp. 82-3)

Villiers' faith in the saving grace of blue blood is the key to one-half of his work. The pride of "being" and the pride of "becoming," as Arthur Symons puts it, "are the two ultimate contradictions set before every idealist." To Villiers' mind there was no question as to which of the two states was the more desirable. He gloried in his nobility because it was inherent and beyond the power of man to imitate or to achieve. From this belief naturally followed a contempt for the bourgeois world he saw around him, which found its best expression in that masterpiece of irony, *Tribulat Bonhommet.*

Villiers acknowledged *Tribulat Bonhommet* to be his favorite creation. He intended him to be "l'archétype de son siècle," the greatest Philistine ever conceived of by the mind of man. . . . He is the incarnation of common sense rendered detestable. Villiers not only kept adding fresh chapters to *Tribulat Bonhommet* all his life, but he even sought refuge in personifying him whenever he found himself in unsympathetic surroundings. Sometimes it was persiflage, sometimes it was bitter mockery, but the Bonhommet mood was always one of contempt for materialism. But Villiers was more than a great satirist. If his high lineage accounted for a certain impatience with the mob it was also responsible for a very real yearning toward perfection. While the one half of him was mocking at the pitiful efforts of society to raise its head out of the welter of materialism, the other half was always ready to acclaim the slightest indications of idealism. (pp. 85-7)

Some one has defined the symbolist movement in literature as a revolt against the tyranny of fact. Villiers de l'Isle-Adam was more than usually susceptible to this particular form of tyranny, and it is not surprising that he should have gravitated to the group of ardent spirits who had sworn to achieve its downfall. Founding their society in 1866 as a protest against the sterility of nineteenth-century romanticism, the young poets, who modestly christened themselves the Parnassians, welcomed Villiers with open arms. The cry of art for art's sake was perhaps not as original as they imagined, but that it was a sincere cry cannot be questioned. (pp. 87-8)

In this association for the infusion of backbone into romanticism, for this was really what it was, Villiers de l'Isle-Adam played a prominent part. As a poet he gained little distinction, but as a raconteur and a musician he was unrivalled. . . . [It] was as a talker that he especially excelled. All of the *Contes Cruels* and many of his other books were talked before they were written. That was Villiers' usual method of composition. (pp. 88-9)

A dreamer and mocker—it is not often that the two types go together—but in Villiers de l'Isle-Adam irony and idealism are continually treading on each other's heels. In *Tribulat Bonhommet* and the *Contes Cruels* the mockery is uppermost, but Villiers is never persistently bitter. Even Bonhommet is offset by the gentle figure of Claire Lenoir, and the tales, satirical as they are, would have been far more savage in the hands of a Swift or a Voltaire. Take, for instance, *Les Trois Filles de Milton* in the volume of *Nouveaux Contes Cruels*. Villiers has seized the pathos of the inspired poet driving his starving daughters to the breaking-point, but he does not subject their misery to the microscope. (p. 90)

The wounds of society are laid open, but there is no sprinkling of acid to make the victim squirm.

To be really embittered an author must be a man of the world, a questionable distinction which Villiers never attained. (p. 91)

Undoubtedly Villiers' masterpiece was *Axël,* though it was by no means suited to the stage. The mixture of mysticism and romanticism, of beautiful heroines escaping from nunneries, of castles in the middle of dark forests, and heroes dabbling in transcendental philosophy—all this he has poured into the dramatic mould. To be sure, he has not been able to convey all that he has thought, but underlying the twisted thread of narrative we get the impression of will-power dominating everything else. There is no new doctrine of philosophy in *Axël,* for Villiers' genius did not tend to the systematic development of any one field of thought. As a young man he had steeped himself in the German philosophers, and the clumsy nuggets brought to light by Hegel are reproduced in the beautiful setting of Villiers' yearning idealism. (pp. 95-6)

The gleanings from Hegel and Kant, however, do not represent the total of Villiers' debt to Germany. His romantic imagery must have been at least partly inspired by Wagner, whose genius he was one of the first to acclaim, and with whose theories of art he was always in complete sympathy. (p. 96)

> *Arnold Whitridge, "Villiers de l'Isle-Adam" (originally published in* Cornhill Magazine, *Vol. LIII, No. 314, August, 1922), in his* Critical Ventures in Modern French Literature *(copyright © 1924 by Charles Scribner's Sons: reprinted with the permission of Charles Scribner's Sons), Charles Scribner's Sons, 1924, pp. 71-101.*

RENÉ LALOU (essay date 1922)

A militant idealism, far removed from the sham, insipid idealism of Octave Feuillet's novels—such is also the dominant trait of Villiers de L'Isle-Adam's works; but here, however attractive the figure of the writer, his production deserves to remain in the foreground, its author's personal tastes being retained only as a thread permitting a more living study of these luxuriant, harmonious books.

Seen with the perspective afforded by the passing of thirty years, Villiers' work presents itself then as an ample symphony a few easily discernible motives of which ensure the supple unity. For they themselves all derive from a unique and fundamental concord which—stripping it for an instant of its multiple power of sonorous creations—the critic might formulate in these three affirmations: Breton, gentleman and Catholic.

The last two terms of this definition eliminate the memory of the Breton Renan with whom Villiers, in fact, shares only the love of soaring revery. They permit a comparison with Chateaubriand of whom Villiers is truly the successor. Their differences are sufficiently justified by the unfolding between them of the Romanticism of which one was the first, the other the last great prose-writer—a haughty, disabused Romanticism which is, perhaps, merely a borrowed attitude for Chateaubriand but which penetrated Villiers' soul—an ideal to which he lent all the refinement of his genius before burying it under the crypts at Auërsperg. (pp. 55-6)

Axël is not only Villiers de l'Isle-Adam's most characteristic and complete work. It is also the last expression of European Romanticism, the Faust of the expiring nineteenth century. However, between Goethe and Villiers, Wagner has intervened. Many a passage in the *Contes* shows how much the great musician's triumph had appealed to Villiers' imagination. . . . The gigantic proportions of the works which provoked the enthusiastic exodus of pilgrims towards his Bavarian shrine, emphasized still further the scope of such a victory. *Axël* keeps a gleam of this inspiration. Axël and Sara, having like the heroes of the *Tetralogy* undergone the ordeal of love and of gold, die, as Tristan and Isolde would die if they dared render eternal their ecstasy in the second act; but in his esoteric masterpiece Villiers is not crushed by this comparison with the master of philter and ring. His work remains intensely personal. The antithesis between Axël who embodies all he loves and Kaspar in whom all he detests lives again, the parallelism confronting the hero and the heroine who renounce, the ineffable serenity of the final scene where the lovers, freed from their corporeal vestments, recover their souls which are but one soul, purified—these motifs of the supreme symphony, a glorification of the Dream to such a degree that the mind is unable to decide whether it be "inhuman or superhuman," have been heard ringing throughout Villiers' work. . . . We know that Villiers felt doubts as to the ending of *Axël,* fearing it would not satisfy the orthodox mind. Whether or not these conscientious scruples are justified, from the point of view of Art such a finale is a worthy crown for the work of him who wrote: "I deign to punish the gulfs—with my wings alone." (pp. 59-60)

> *René Lalou, "The Anti-Naturalistic Reaction," in his* Contemporary French Literature, *translated by William Aspenwall Bradley (translation copyright 1924 and renewed 1952, by Alfred A. Knopf, Inc.; reprinted by permission of the publisher; originally published as* Histoire de la litterature française contemporaine, *G. Cres et cie, 1922), Knopf, 1924, pp. 52-79.**

EDMUND WILSON (essay date 1931)

Villiers de l'Isle-Adam's **"Axel"** . . . is a sort of long dramatic poem in prose, which, as it was the last thing Villiers wrote, sums up and gives final expression to his peculiar idealism. (p. 259)

It will easily be seen that this super-dreamer of Villiers's is the type of all the heroes of the Symbolists, of our day as well as of his: Pater's contemplative, inactive Marius [in "Marius the Epicurean"], the exquisitely sensitive young men of his "Imaginary Portraits"; Laforgue's Lohengrin, who, the night of his wedding, shrinking from union with his Elsa, turns his back on her and embraces his pillow begging it to carry him away—his Salome, "the victim of having tried, like all of us, to live in the factitious instead of in the honest everyday"; the Hamlet of Mallarmé's posthumous drama, "Igitur," who is the only character in the play and does nothing but soliloquize. And above all, Huysman's Des Esseintes [in "A Rebours"], who set the fashion for so many other personalities, fictitious and real, of the end of the century: the neurotic nobleman who arranges for himself an existence which will completely insulate him from the world and facilitate the cultivation of refined and bizarre sensations; who sleeps by day and stays up at night and whose favorite reading is Silver Latin and the Symbolists. Des Esseintes is living up to the ideal of Axel and Sara when, having set out to visit London—excited by the novels of Dickens—he turns back at the railroad station: he has already driven in a cab through a foggy day in Paris, visited Galignani's English book-store, dined at an English restaurant on oxtail soup, haddock, beefsteak and ale—and as he remembers that he has left his tooth-brush, it occurs to him that on

a former occasion he had been sadly disappointed by a visit to Holland and that the real London cannot possibly come up to the one he has just been imagining. . . . [If] we compare Villiers's point of view with the point of view of the Romantics, we see plainly the fundamental difference between Symbolism and Romanticism.

The later movement, as I have already said, was an antidote to nineteenth-century Naturalism, as the earlier had been an antidote to the neo-classicism of the seventeenth and eighteenth centuries: Symbolism corresponds to Romanticism, and is in fact an outgrowth from it. But whereas it was characteristic of the Romantics to seek experience for its own sake—love, travel, politics—to try the possibilities of life; the Symbolists, though they also hate formulas, though they also discard conventions, carry on their experimentation in the field of literature alone; and though they, too, are essentially explorers, explore only the possibilities of imagination and thought. (pp. 264-65)

> *Edmund Wilson, "Axel and Rimbaud," in his* Axel's Castle: A Study in the Imaginative Literature of 1870-1930 *(copyright 1931 by Charles Scribner's Sons; renewal copyright © 1959 by Edmund Wilson; reprinted with the permission of Charles Scribner's Sons), Charles Scribner's Sons, 1931, pp. 257-98.**

VINCENT O'SULLIVAN (essay date 1940)

[Villiers] was a man who laboured his prose, wrote slowly as a rule, and kept his proofs long by him, altering and mending. . . . His greatest fault is an abuse of emphasis, together with a continual straining to write in an unusual and artificial way. The first projection of his thought in words did not satisfy him by any means. Nothing would do him till he had displaced the clauses, scattered the words, spread a light haze of obscurity. Great trouble indeed he gave himself, and too often with an ill result. (p. 25)

But it was for these very faults that he was admired by the Symbolists, who hailed him as one of their masters. Some of them carried their master's peculiarities so far that they were almost unreadable in their day and generation, and are now quite so. Never in France was such an orgy of "art" writing, generally difficult and often unintelligible, as in the eighteen-eighties. (p. 26)

Those stories of his which are the best in substance, which, it is easy to see, really took him by the throat while he was writing them, are also the most well written. In *La Torture par l'Espérance,* for example, he does not go into divagations concerning politics or theology or Hegelism or anything else: he is too absorbed by his story for that kind of amusement. This is surely one of the greatest short stories of its kind, the terror kind, ever written. It is as concentrated as any of Merimée's; every word tells, and every word in it is needed. The "motto" or epigraph is from Edgar Allan Poe, and some have seen in the story the inspiration of *The Pit and the Pendulum,* just as many are given to talk loosely about Poe and Villiers being in the same category. Villiers admired Poe, partly no doubt because Baudelaire and Mallarmé admired him; I think he may have desired to write like Poe if he could. But he could not; his personality was too marked. No two men more unlike than Poe and Villiers both as men and as artists ever existed. As artist Villiers never deals in physical horror; his effects are cerebral. Fear, which dominates in some of Poe's best stories, is totally absent from those of Villiers. Arrogance, often present in stories by Villiers, is totally absent from Poe's.

How Poe affected Villiers, it seems to me, was in leading him to exhibitions of scientific and mechanical erudition which most readers have not the power to control. . . . The fact is that neither Poe nor Villiers had any education in science worth speaking of during their youth, and their after lives were not such as give an opportunity for exact study of abstruse subjects. (pp. 26-7)

About the only other resemblance between Poe and Villiers is that although they both bring women fairly often into their tales they leave them mere shadows, "out of space, out of time,"— Poe always, and Villiers too always, except when the woman is there as a target for his scorn and irony. It is so in *Les Demoiselles Malfilatre* and *Les Amies de Pension,* two stories turning on the same theme—a theme awkward to set forth in a family magazine. . . . So it is too with some other stories, and with the wife of the English nobleman in his novel *L'Eve Future,* to whom is opposed in contrast the woman manufactured in a laboratory—the machine. And so it is with the woman in *Le Meilleur Amour.* This is the last story he wrote and one of his best. As has been said, in his best stories his style is at its best, and it is at its best in this story in which the reader hardly notices the style, so subdued it is to its matter. While it remains distinctly Villiers' style, while nobody else could have written just like that, it brings back a remembrance of Flaubert's perfect style in *Un Coeur Simple.* (pp. 27-8)

Tribulat Bonhommet is not comic, nor is Villiers ever comic. He has no sense of the comic, no humour, though like many humourless persons he thought he had and attempted it on occasion. The character may have been suggested to him in its rudiments by Henri Monnier's *M. Prudhomme* and Ludovic Halévy's *M. Cardinal,* both characters that have the real stuff of the comic in them. Villiers may have thought he was creating a figure somewhat akin. But *Bonhommet* does not move to laughter. He is uncanny, insidious, furtive, incalculable, who gives the impression of a charlatan doctor, very dangerous, and he commits some atrocious acts. All this would come out plainer if *Bonhommet* were developed as a human being and not as a figure of parable. But as it is oftenest with Villiers, he cannot go far in creating a human being, and *Bonhommet* accordingly is a grotesque, abstract, and almost mechanical expounder of all the theories, beliefs, and philosophies which Villiers especially loathed:—Voltairian deism, Atheism, latest scientific discoveries, Progress,—in which last both Villiers and Baudelaire saw something more than the word implies. The doctor believes also in democracy, and admired a republican form of government. Against all that Villiers sets up barrages in the shape of disputants who present the Christian, or rather Catholic, and royalist side. The book would be in danger of becoming somewhat tedious if it did not contain the extraordinary episode of *Claire Lenoir,* where again the genius of Villiers is at flood-tide.

Many of what are called his stories are not stories in any proper sense. They are mere frames set up to enable Villiers to put across his ideas on politics, social reform, or what not. Thus, the piece called, *Maitre Pied,* is a satire on Parliamentary government and popular elections. . . . (p. 30)

In the same way, he has now and then set up a frame to enable him to speak in an oblique fashion of himself. In no piece of his writings I know does he complain directly of his misfortunes, his hard luck. But at times he has taken advantage of a fictitious situation and character to put forward what amounts to a proud yet vehement defence of his life, explaining his poverty, continued ill-success, and the unpopularity of what

he writes. He sees very well what awaits him in such conditions; in that very sketch just named, *Maitre Pied,* he sets it forth in harrowing and unflinching terms.

But it is in the long speech he puts into the mouth of Milton in *Les Filles de Milton* that this kind of oblique defence of himself is most amply presented. The story was found in rather an unfinished state after the death of Villiers by Remy de Gourmont who pieced it together and published it, saying that it had been the intention of Villiers to study seriously the life of Milton. If Villiers had done so he would have ended perhaps by throwing the whole thing in the fire, it is so full of errors. (pp. 30-1)

The story reads like the scenario of a play, and perhaps Villiers intended to make a play of it. Play or story, it is of little significance. There have been novels and dramas which in spite of errors and anachronisms have vivified history. But Villiers' story shews too much unfamiliarity with the materials of Milton's life; the blunders are of a kind to neutralize it even as a fantastic picture of Milton's household. All the same, it should not be rejected from any collection of Villiers' stories and sketches, because it contains the passage spoken by Milton wherein Villiers sets forth in unmistakable terms the disappointments, poverty, humiliations, and long agony of his own life. (p. 32)

Vincent O'Sullivan, "The Tales and Stories of Villiers de l'Isle-Adam," in The Dublin Magazine, *Vol. XV, No. 2, April-June, 1940, pp. 25-34.*

MELVIN J. FRIEDMAN (essay date 1959)

Axel, in an important sense, is the literary application of the formula for the synthesis of the arts set down in Wagner's treatise *Opera and Drama.* Villiers de l'Isle-Adam was another in the long succession of Symbolist writers who turned to the German composer for inspiration. He shared the opinion of his contemporaries who fashioned an ideal Wagner—making him over into a literary figure who had inadvertently wandered into music.

Turning to *Axel,* one is struck by a series of "fin de siècle" effects which have been forced into a form casually resembling a play. It is divided into four sections each of which is referrred to as a "monde": monde religieux, monde tragique, monde occulte, and monde passionnel. Indeed each division of the work is a *world* or a distinct way of observing the universe. One has the impression that *Axel* has four beginnings and ends. The world of religion seems to have little connection with the tragic world; neither is closely connected with the occult. (p. 237)

The plan of *Axel* makes for four separate "tableaux" or panels. The fourth part, the world of passion, is, however, the drama in miniature. The first three divisions, resembling a Renaissance triptych, are balanced by the fourth which not only embraces their three conceptions of the world but is actually something more.

Sara is the introspective type of the Symbolist heroine. She is not unlike Mallarmé's Hérodiade, Laforgue's Andromeda. She dominates the first section of the work and shares the spotlight with Axel in the fourth division. She is bathed in narcissism; she would probably make an appropriate and appealing subject for Picasso's *Girl before a Mirror.* Sara is filled with all the lyricism and poetic appeal of the woman infatuated with herself. (pp. 237-38)

Axel is the male counterpart of Sara. We encounter him earlier in Lautréamont and Rimbaud among the Symbolists. But he even goes beyond his models and becomes virtually a universal type. In the same way that Hamlet is the man of indecision, Don Quixote the man of imaginative escape, Oblomov the man of inactivity, so Axel is the man of renunciation. . . .

But this is not the entire story. Axel possesses an ambivalence which drives him on the one hand toward perfection, on the other toward self-denial, rejection. He manages to reconcile the extremes of his character by suicide. He has known absolute wealth, he has spent a chaste evening of "love" with Sara. He has never put the newly-discovered treasure to practical use nor has he consummated his liaison with Sara. But the dream for Axel is of more consequence than the reality. (p. 238)

There is nothing, thus far, very new about *Axel*. The principal characters have numerous prototypes in Symbolist literature. The theme of renunciation is as old as the Greeks. The Faust and Wagner influences are found everywhere during this period.

Villiers' handling of his material, the form he gives it constitute his contribution. One would naturally expect *Axel* to have been written in verse: the subject lends itself so appropriately to poetic treatment. . . .

Yet, curiously enough, *Axel* is written in prose. Edmund Wilson effectively calls it "a sort of long dramatic poem in prose."

Unfortunately, Villiers de l'Isle-Adam has left us no literary testament, no justification for anything he wrote. The only explanation we can offer is that *Axel* was written at a time when the "genre tranché" was no longer regarded as sacred. The Symbolists indeed favored the mixing of several literary forms in a single work. It was not considered at all heretical to write poetic prose or prose poetry, or to compromise prose with poetry in a manner suggestive of the breakdown of the classical distinction between the two.

But *Axel* is untraditional in quite another way. It seems to lack all the essential ingredients of drama. Its character development, painfully labored, the progress of the situation, extended to the infinite, beg comparison with the novel. Certain speeches in the final act—Sara's long discourse on escape, Axel's justification for suicide—are some three pages in length. They seem pronounced for no dramatic purpose. In fact, one is never aware of the presence of an auditor. (p. 239)

This almost complete rejection of an exterior dimension sets the stage for Villiers' play. When reading *Axel* one is almost oblivious to anything occurring outside the minds of Axel and Sara. This is peculiarly the case in the final section when the unpronounced is so much more important than what the characters actually say. Their words are only a thin disguise for hidden, unexpressed meaning. Villiers sets up a kind of dramatic periphery more artfully than the proponents of the expressionist theatre—of whom he is a natural precursor. (pp. 239-40)

To return to our earlier question: why Villiers' choice of prose as a medium? In the first place, poetry would probably add to the artificiality of the speech, make it more unreal than it is now. One of the strengths of Villiers' style is its fluid quality, its avoidance of any set patterns or formulas. The alexandrines of Racine, especially effective in Phaedra's death speech, would seem somewhat stilted coming from Axel's "fin de siècle" 19th century lips. In the second place, the effect of the present syntax, although bizarre with its frequent circumlocutions, is

provocative enough to elicit the reader's patronage, indeed to involve him personally in Axel's "ennui."

We have, then, with *Axel* the case of a work obviously destined for poetry—in terms of the subject of the play and the writer's distinguished career as a poet—handed over to prose. Villiers compromises poetry with prose as he does drama with fiction. Good Symbolist that he is, Villiers de l'Isle-Adam seems intent on breaking down the barriers between the various forms of literature; he even wanders into another art, music, for many of his effects. The myth of the "genre tranché" might be said to be finally destroyed for French literature with the appearance of *Axel* in 1890. (p. 240)

Villiers de l'Isle-Adam would not have wanted our sympathy or even our admiration. He avoided his contemporaries because he could scarcely forget what he believed to be his natural superiority to others; he enjoyed the relatively unique distinction of being able to date his ancestry back to the Middle Ages. It is then a curiosity of literary history that his posthumously published play should have had so wide an influence. Although he didn't allow himself Stendhal's snobbery by dedicating *Axel* to the "happy few," we can feel certain that he would have been horrified if his play were ever widely known and appreciated. [Edmund Wilson's] *Axel's Castle* began the *Lazare veni foras*. A new English translation might complete the task of rousing *Axel* from its undeserved anonymity. (p. 243)

Melvin J. Friedman, "A Revaluation of 'Axel'," in Modern Drama *(copyright © 1959, University of Toronto, Graduate Centre for Study of Drama; with the permission of* Modern Drama*), Vol. 1, No. 4, February, 1959, pp. 236-43.*

A. W. RAITT (essay date 1963)

At first sight, the **Cruel Tales** betray little of [Villiers's] fantastic and tormented existence. The sumptuousness of their style, the richness of their settings, the apparent remoteness from any confessional element, even the resoundingly aristocratic name of their author, could easily give the impression that they were the pastime of some elegant and moneyed amateur—and that is no doubt how Villiers would have liked them to be read. But their coruscating surface only partly hides the drama of Villiers's life. Permanently at odds with the spirit of the age in which he lived, Villiers delights in denouncing its idols, but his bitter irony does not stay on a level of abstract expostulation; many of his tales are the fruit of his own most humiliating experiences. The unfortunate young genius in **'Two Augurs'**, for instance, has had a career exactly parallel to Villiers's own, and the publisher who refuses his works is identifiable as Émile de Girardin, one of the pundits of the Second Empire press. Similarly, most of the characters of **'Sombre Tale, Sombre Teller'** can be unmasked as dramatists and actors whose facile successes had, in Villiers's view, made the public impervious to the philosophical drama which he had striven in vain to create on the Parisian stage. (p. vi)

Villiers the individual is equally present in the more romantic and emotive tales. The fascination with gold which he had inherited from his father is memorably evoked in the rhythmic prose of **'Occult Memories.'** . . . In **'The Sign'**, despite the reminiscences of Poe's 'Fall of the House of Usher', one is conscious that Villiers is thinking of his uncle, a country priest in Brittany with whom he had frequently stayed in his youth. It can be deduced from Villiers's correspondence that the heroine of **'Maryelle'**, with her startling ideas on fidelity preserved in inconstancy, was in fact one of his mistresses. **'The Eleventh-Hour Guest'** is none other than Villiers in disguise; he may never have gone so far as to play the hangman himself, but it is well attested that he had a morbid obsession with public executions. The furious misogyny of **'The Unknown Woman'** reflects the innumerable disappointments of his search for an impossible ideal in love. One may even detect in **'Sentimentality'** and **'Sombre Tale, Sombre Teller'** another private worry which appears to have disturbed him at intervals throughout his career: the fear that the constant practice of literary mimetism would eventually destroy his capacity for feeling spontaneous personal emotion. It is certain too that he saw himself as the melancholy hero of **'Véra'**, as the mysteriously doomed **'Duke of Portland'** (a highly romanticized interpretation of the oddities by which the Fifth Duke had made himself notorious in Villiers's time), even as the aspirant Magus in **'The Messenger'.**

Were it not for these constant reminders of a vibrant human personality beneath the often impassive presentation, the philosophic intentions of the *Cruel Tales* might risk turning them into abstract allegories. For Villiers was deeply committed in the struggle of ideas which dominated French intellectual life in the latter part of the nineteenth century, and almost all his stories have some ulterior purpose in the conflict between scientism and positivism on the one hand and idealism, whether Christian or not, on the other. . . . Villiers was fascinated by the intervention in human affairs of mysterious, otherworldly forces, the existence of which in his work is a constant challenge to the assumptions of materialism—the materialism which excites him to those angry and derisive onslaughts which form the basis of so many of his stories. The objects of these attacks include attachment to money in **'Celestial Publicity'** and **'Virginia and Paul'**, faith in political panaceas in **'Vox Populi'**, the commercialization of art in **'Two Augurs'**, the supposed virtues of the bourgeoisie in **'The Brigands'**, and the arrogance of science in **'Doctor Tristan's Treatment'.** This combination of vision and satire in the *Cruel Tales* is one of the hallmarks of Villiers's work.

Villiers's individuality stands out more clearly if one compares him with some other famous French short-story writers. He has none of the cosy picturesqueness of Daudet; apart from a brief but evocative sketch of the Breton countryside in **'The Sign'** and one or two striking townscapes, such as the one which opens **'The Desire to be a Man'** or the one which he ingeniously satirizes in **'The Very Image'**, he takes little interest in description. Nor has he Maupassant's gift for the realistic delineation of character—on the rare occasions where his primary aim is psychological dissection, as in **'Antonie'**, **'The Eleventh-Hour Guest'**, or **'Maryelle'**, he proceeds much more in the manner of Poe's case-histories of lurid abnormalities. Indeed, he sometimes even eschews the sharp narrative outlines associated with the French short story as practised by Mérimée and Maupassant: **'Vox Populi'** and **'Occult Memories'** are as much prose poems as they are tales. That he has an astonishing talent for suspenseful anecdote is undeniable—he was an outstanding *raconteur* in conversation, and stories such as **'Véra'** and **'The Sign'** are as masterful in the gradual unfolding of their plot as anything any of his rivals wrote. But it is rare for him to tell a story simply for its own sake—**'Queen Ysabeau'** is perhaps the only example in this collection, and it is not one of the best.

One is thus less struck by the impression of manual dexterity conveyed by so many short-story writers from Mérimée on-

wards than by the essential strangeness of Villiers's tales. He deliberately and invariably tries to disturb his readers, either by transporting them to the distant realms of his own prolific imagination, as in **'The Messenger'**, or by making them see their world through the distorting prism of his unorthodox view of it, as in those fantasies like **'Celestial Publicity'** where he insidiously extols some fictitious but plausible invention in order to reveal the ridicule inherent in modern habits of mind. That is why one is nearly always obliged to think twice before one can be sure one has penetrated to the hidden meaning of Villiers's stories; they do not immediately offer up all their secrets as do most tales, but contain shifting and unsuspected depths of irony and meditation. For the same reason, they do not pall on rereading, since their attraction lies in a background of subtle intentions and not in the meretricious thrill of a surprise ending (even though they often supply that too). (pp. vi-x)

The style as much as the subject-matter is made to contribute to this disorientation of the reader. Villiers detested prosaic realism and continually sought to make his writing as unusual, as individual, as surprising as he could, whether in the mock-heroics of **'Doctor Tristan's Treatment'**, with its sudden glimpses of unwonted perspectives through the fog of verbiage, or in the sustained and elevated harmonies of **'The Sign'**. Rare words, curious inversions, unlikely juxtapositions, complex and involuted clauses, cunningly calculated poetic rhythms, a multiplicity of typographical devices, abrupt changes of tone—all is designed to make one feel that here is something new, something unique. . . . Sometimes, it is true, this striving for solemn effect can degenerate into self-conscious posturing, in which the style and the subject-matter seem to have lost contact with each other, as happens in **'The Messenger'**, where Villiers sacrifices to a frigid Parnassian splendour. Sometimes, too, he overworks the trick of parodying the exaggerations of his opponents, and the pseudo-scientific pieces are liable to become wearisome with their relentless exploitation of a single joke. But at its best Villiers's style has extraordinary power and beauty—a beauty which has drawn tribute from authors as diverse as Mallarmé, Valéry, Barrès, and Yeats.

These qualities yield a volume of short stories quite unlike any other, whether it be by Poe, Mérimée, Maupassant, Chekhov, Katherine Mansfield, or Somerset Maugham. Villiers's understanding of character may be less convincing than theirs, his evocation of atmosphere less absorbing, his technical skill less perfect. But he has something which is uniquely his and which no other short-story writer can match: his genius for imparting simultaneously emotional excitement and intellectual stimulation. A French critic, urged to read the works of some new author who was said to have exceptional talents for description, plot, psychology, and style, asked simply: 'Yes, but has he a *voice*?' In Villiers's case, there can be no doubt about the answer. He has a voice which is unmistakably his own and which rings out as powerfully today as it did when he first raised it in protest against the abuses and errors of his time. (pp. x-xi)

A. W. Raitt, "Introduction" (© Oxford University Press 1963; reprinted by permission of Oxford University Press), in Cruel Tales *by Villiers de l'Isle-Adam, translated by Robert Baldick, Oxford University Press, London, 1963, pp. v-ix.*

MARILYN GADDIS ROSE (essay date 1968)

What [*Axel*] is is an amalgam of Romantic and Symbolist drama. Long recognized, although unread, as the epitome of

Symbolist drama, it elaborates upon the tenets and clichés of Symbolism at such length that it nearly becomes too explicit to be Symbolistic. We soon realize that its Symbolist elements are those which carry over from Romanticism, with, to be sure, an increased accentuation of the morbid escapist orientation particularly associated with Symbolism, and that its expansive exploitation of these elements is more typical of Romanticism than of Symbolism. (pp. 174-75)

Axel manifests the cultivation of mystery dear to both Romantics and Symbolists. Its language has the high degree of plasticity associated with the Parnassian modifications of Romantic diction. The dialogue is only intermittently in what Eliot has called the dramatic voice. That is, we rarely hear characters speaking *to* each other *in front of us.* (Villiers seldom has more than two speakers on stage.) Rather, we hear them as they alternate discursive monologues and lyrical apostrophes. These alternating speeches, a literal speaking *à tour de rôle*, resemble neither those of ambiguous Chekhovian dialogue where A is too distracted by C to listen to B nor the communication breakdown of Absurdist dialogue where it is evident that A and B cannot hear each other. Instead, in its discursive moments the dialogue of *Axel* is similar to the extensive expositional dialogue of traditional dramas from *Oedipus Rex* to *The Wild Duck* (to name a play of the mid-1880's which has fared better with modern repertory than *Axel*); such expositional dialogue is of course present in the plays of Hugo and Dumas père. In its lyrical moments the dialogue of *Axel* is like that in Maeterlinck's plays or in Mallarmé's fragment *Hérodiade*, where the characters cannot hear one another because they speak from different planes of existence. Villiers' stage directions are novelistic commentary. . . . Villiers' descriptive directions probably have their most nearly kindred counterpart in Hardy's *The Dynasts*. They are part of the play and provide information and interpretation which the dialogue and stage movement cannot convey. This technique, carried over from the novel, is in no way restricted to Romantic writers—Shaw, O'Neill, and Hardy are post-Naturalist—but it is antipathetic to Symbolism which was posited upon suggestion, allusion, and mystery and which was in fact singularly unsuccessful in producing prose equal to its poetry. (p. 175)

Villiers's religiosity and mystical leanings, his flirtation with the occult, his respect for Catholicism gave him a conviction in the beyond, a nearly sincere contempt for the temporal. *Axel* demonstrates this sincere conviction and equivocal contempt. But the play does demonstrate; its characters say that words are "virtual" and proceed to explain them, debate them, repeat them. And in the end we have had, to oversimplify somewhat, a Romantic expansion of a Romantic-Symbolist dictum.

Yet like its mage Master Janus, *Axel* looks forward at the same time it looks back. It might be unwarranted to speak of "influence" with a play known so largely by hearsay. The fact remains that *Axel* opened paths which subsequent writers have discovered to be their ways also. Sara, the active protagonist, is the affective component of the spirit; she is a Baudelairian embodiment whose intellect can be reached only through the senses. . . . Her magnetism comes partly from her twenty-three years of virginity. Villiers, as we deduce from his depiction of the dazzling novice in the title story of *L'Amour suprême* . . . , found sex appeal in chastity. Sara's passion is all the more seductive for having been cloistered. She is a quasi-Christian counterpart of the Hérodiade of his friend Mallarmé. . . . Axel, the passive protagonist, axis of the world which Sara substantiates, is one more renunciatory *fin-de-siècle*

hero. Since he is the intellectual component of the spirit, his senses can be reached only after the sensory stimuli have been spiritually metamorphosed by passing through other characters. Like Gide's André Walter in the confessional novel of the same name or Julian Green's first-person narrators in "Christine" and "Les Clefs de la Mort," he is content to know life secondhand and despite his protestations of vital impulses to Master Janus, when given opportunities for living, Axel rejects them. (pp. 176-77)

Together Sara and Axel form one mind. . . . They are still heroine *and* hero, but Villiers' manipulation of them as if they were one person whose schizophrenia would be resolved in the confrontation and union of self in death recalls Lenormand's manipulation of Lui and Elle in *Les Râtés,* perhaps even Synge's manipulation of blind Martin and Mary Doul in *The Well of the Saints* or Beckett's disposition of blind Dan and lame Maddy Rooney in *All That Fall.* Sara and Axel are counterpoised against foils before they are counterpoised against each other, for the dialogue, while incorporating narratives, lyrics, and liturgy, is, in the final analysis, an extended debate on the nature of reality with the axis of the debate doing a quarter turn for each act. (p. 177)

The dialogue has to be a debate with a shifting axis because each act puts on stage liturgy representing shifting planes of secularity. In Act I we have a quasi-orthodox mass with a sermon and the interrupted marriage of a bride of Christ. In Act II we have a ritual of secular honor: a duel. In Act III we witness a rejection of the preparatory rites of hermeticism. In Act IV, after Sara pulls apart the winter-blooming rose which lay upon her dagger in Rosicrucian steadfastness, her overtures have a cadence suggesting litanies to Venus, and her expectations make sexual consummation sound as ecstatically fulfilling as Bacchic rites. When Axel dissuades her, she joins him in a suicidal Eucharist. Drama as liturgy had not been a novel concept since Nietzsche's *The Birth of Tragedy* in 1872. . . . We are now accustomed to drama which allusively imitates types of liturgy, e.g., Yeats's Noh-type plays, Genet's Black Masses. But liturgy in drama is still unusual; the mass in Eliot's *The Murder in the Cathedral* and the exorcism and office for the dead in Albee's *Who's Afraid of Virginia Woolf?* prove that the contexts for staged liturgy must still be as special as that in *Axel* to be tolerable.

Villiers, however, was as little concerned with being tolerable as Brecht was or Genet and Leroi Jones are. *Axel* shows that Villiers has contempt for the audience. He prevents audience participation by taking up irrelevant concepts, by indulging in time-consuming arguments, and by presenting only antipathetic characters, *all* of whom have a flaw which makes them repugnant. Axel's misanthropy, which goes so deep as to imply criticism of God's Plan, is the final lashing of spectators who cannot not be human. These harangues may differ in degree from the bestial suppositions of Weiss's *Marat-Sade,* but the kinship is unmistakable. In looking ahead to Weiss (who was looking back to Sade) *Axel* illustrates in small the function it performs in Western drama: its legendary impact is representatively that of the two literary periods which it brings together.

And *Axel* is the new product which a creative synthesis should be. It is more than what it summed up and prefigured. It is probably the most deliberately typological drama in Western literature. All of its dramatic elements have counterparts and come into the play like counterpoised leitmotifs. As we turn our attention directly to the play, we see how this structural repetition makes a whole of the old and new in *Axel.* (pp. 177-78)

Through all four acts, we notice that Axel hardly stirs. The others have come to him. And, although Master Janus may have planned the intersection, Axel controls the plot. All characters who confront him must ultimately do what he pleases. In the context of the play his egocentricity is justified. He is the human Tau, the axle around whom other men turn. (pp. 178-79)

As a literary monument, *Axel* was the last glow of the first generation of Symbolists, those reared on Romanticism and trained in Parnassianism. But it was a glow that, whatever the filtering lanterns, illuminated works that were to come. At the axis of the world it revealed spirit and love—and death. (pp. 183-84)

> *Marilyn Gaddis Rose, "'Axel': Play and Hearsay," in* Comparative Drama *(© copyright 1968, by the Editors of* Comparative Drama*), Vol. 2, No. 3, Fall, 1968, pp. 173-84.*

IVOR A. ARNOLD (essay date 1972)

The intent of the fiction of Villiers de l'Isle-Adam is pre-eminently moral and the prose is couched in a didactic mode highly charged with the tension of Idealism and disenchantment in perpetual conflict. Villiers' typical expressivity is a dense, polysyllabic, "traditional" rhetoric, frequently modified and tautened,—and at times rendered violent—by disjunctive forms and highly convoluted syntax. His style ranges from peroration to irony (often grounded in banality, cliché, and deliberate ambiguity) to passionate near-incoherence. Although meaning is often enhanced with conventional symbolism, the texture of the rhetoric is generally excessively ratiocinative, tending to obscure meaning with complex syntactic figures and intricate hypotaxis, and moreover prone to high affective tension and multiple and unexpected shifts of register and style-type.

Within this general texture there is a highly significant occurrence of image-patterns, dominated by conceits and "visions" and heavy with ornaments of the occult: the horrendous, the transfigured, the ritualistic. The "visions" often take "painterly" form, dynamically composed into fluid, "arrested", emblematic, or "open-formed" tableaux, with a predilection for mixtures of the sensual and apocalyptic in the major "canvases."

Of the two major image-types, the conceit is the more conventional. This is usually densely arranged with mixtures of opposites or of logical illogicalities, the latter form functioning psychologically in place of the more direct paradox, noticeably rare in Villiers. There is a loose relationship of form and concept: fanciful flights of the imagination often lead to excessive elaboration and an obscuring of the original motivation. Conceits that pertain to love tend to be more conventional and stress the mortality of earthly experience; mystical conceits stress sensuality and reflect Villiers' obsession with occult "correspondences", expressed in esoteric symbolism, cabalistic paraphernalia, blazoning and, occasionally, enigma.

Visions are projected in alternating, interpenetrating and/or multi-focal planes which, especially in the more massive instances, eschew synthesis. The effect is very frequently combined with stock "gothic" properties to create melodramatic tension: luminous distortions, macabre symbolism, images of decay and decomposition, and a feeling of the play of super-natural forces. The total effect of massiveness and intricacy stems from the desire for completeness of impression and richness of affective impact, without regard for the norms of *mesure,* coherence and balance of a classical tradition. (pp. 142-43)

Villiers de l'Isle-Adam has been characterized in Lansonian terms as a *"romantique attarde"*. But in the Villieresque strings of style characteristics there is a textual convergence with baroque style-sets too pronounced to be obscured by a ready allusion to the broad concept of Romanticism. And to assert simply that the Romantics had their own peculiar forms of violence and excessiveness, together with temperaments akin both to Villiers and to many baroque writers, is to underestimate the conclusive stylistic evidence of Villiers' image-technique as a basic indicator to his style. (pp. 143-44)

> *Ivor A. Arnold, "Villiers de l'Isle-Adam: Image-Technique in the Shorter Fiction," in* Orbis Litterarum*, Vol. XXVII, No. 2, 1972, pp. 122-44.*

ADDITIONAL BIBLIOGRAPHY

Albertson, L. Ludwig, and Rose, Marilyn Gaddis. "Villiers' Axël: What's in a Name?" *Romance Notes* XIX, No. 3 (Spring 1979): 321-26.
> Claims that Villiers used two Scandinavian works, Adam Oehlenschläger's *Axel og Valborg* and Esaias Tegnér's *Axel,* as sources for his *Axël.*

Arnold, Ivor. "Villiers de l'Isle-Adam and *écriture artiste.*" *The French Review* XLVII, No. 5 (April 1974): 874-81.
> Describes how Villiers made use of Jules and Edmond de Goncourt's prose technique, applying Impressionist theories of form and light to prose.

Conroy, William T., Jr. *Villiers de l'Isle-Adam.* Boston: Twayne Publishers, 1978, 167 p.
> A mostly biographical study, incorporating critical comments on all of Villiers's works.

du Pontavice de Heussey, Robert. *Villiers de l'Isle-Adam: His Life and Works.* Translated by Lady Mary Loyd. London: William Heinemann, 1894, 286 p.
> A chatty biography by Villiers's nephew, with several interesting anecdotes.

Knapp, Bettina. "Adam/Axel/Alchemy." *L'Esprit Créateur* XVIII, No. 2 (Summer 1978): 24-41.
> Examines *Axel* in the light of alchemical transformation, and discusses the theme of rebirth.

Parks, Lloyd. "The Influence of Villiers de l'Isle-Adam on W. B. Yeats." *Nineteenth-Century French Studies* VI, Nos. 3-4 (Spring-Summer 1978): 258-76.*
> Describes how Yeats was attracted to Villiers's *Axel* as a heroic and symbolic model for his vision of the Irish theater.

Raitt, A. W. "Villiers de l'Isle-Adam in 1870." *French Studies* XIII, No. 4 (October 1959): 332-48.
> Describes Villiers's flight from Germany at the outbreak of the Franco-Prussian War, and his falsified war reports for Paris journals.

Rose, Marilyn Gaddis. "Entropy and Redundancy in Decadent Style: Translating Villiers de l'Isle-Adam." *Sub-Stance,* No. 16 (1977): 144-48.
> Claims that Villiers is "a, if not the, quintessential decadent," and contends that the use of redundancy in decadent writing is a device to create a feeling of entropy.

Appendix

THE EXCERPTS IN NCLC, VOLUME 3, WERE REPRINTED FROM THE FOLLOWING PERIODICALS:

The Academy
The Academy and Literature
American Book Collector
American Literature
American Monthly Magazine
American Quarterly Review
American Review
The American Slavic and East European
    Review
American Transcendental Quarterly
Anti-Jacobin Review
The Athenaeum
The Atlantic Monthly
Bentley's Miscellany
Blackwood's Edinburgh Magazine
The Bookman, *London*
The Bookman, *New York*
Catholic World
Chicago Tribune
The Christian Examiner
Christian Parlor Magazine
College English
Comparative Drama
Contemporary Review
The Cornhill Magazine
The Cosmopolitan
The Critic, *London*
The Critic, *New York*
The Daily Advertiser
Daily Eagle
Debow's Review
The Dial
The Dickensian
The Dublin Magazine
The Dublin Review
The Dublin University Magazine
Early American Literature
Eclectic Magazine
The Eclectic Review
The Edinburgh Review
Éire-Ireland
Emerson Society Quarterly

The Foreign Quarterly Review
The Fortnightly Review
Fraser's Magazine
Fraser's Magazine for Town and Country
The German Quarterly
Graham's Magazine
Harper's Bazar
Harper's New Monthly Magazine
Hispanic Review
The Horn Book Magazine
The Hudson Review
The Irish Quarterly Review
John Rylands Library Bulletin
The Liberator
Lippincott's Magazine of Popular Literature
    and Science
The Listener
The Literary World
The Living Age
London Magazine
The London Review
Macmillan's Magazine
The Mississippi Quarterly
Modern Drama
The Modern Language Journal
Monatshefte
The Monitor
The Monthly Anthology
Monthly Anthology and Boston Review
The Monthly Review
The Nation
The National Review
The New England Quarterly
The New Englander
The New Monthly Magazine
The New Monthly Magazine and Literary
    Journal
The New Republic
New Statesman
The New York Times Magazine
New York Tribune
The New Yorker

The Nineteenth Century
Nineteenth-Century Fiction
The North American Review
The North British Review
The Observer
Orbis Litterarum
Outlook
Pall Mall Magazine
Partisan Review
PMLA
Putnam's Monthly Magazine
The Quarterly Review
Review
A Review of English Literature
Russell's Magazine
The Salem Advertiser
Saturday Review
The Saturday Review, *London*
The Saturday Review of Literature
Scottish Art Review
The Sewanee Review
Shakespeare Survey
The Southern Literary Journal
Southern Literary Messenger
The Southern Quarterly Review
The Spectator
Studies in Burke and His Time
Texas Studies in Literature and Language
The Times
Tribune, *New York*
The University of Kansas City Review
University of Toronto Quarterly
University Review
The Victorian Newsletter
Weekly Tribune, *New York*
The Westminster and Foreign Quarterly
    Review
The Westminster Review
Yale French Studies
The Yale Review

THE EXCERPTS IN NCLC, VOLUME 3, WERE REPRINTED FROM THE FOLLOWING BOOKS:

Aiken, Conrad. Collected Criticism. *Oxford University Press, 1968.*

Aiken, Conrad. Introduction to Massachusetts: A Guide to Its Places and People, *by the Federal Writers' Project of the Works in Progress Administration for the State of Massachusetts. Houghton Mifflin, 1937.*

American Contributions to the Fourth International Congress of Slavicists, Moscow, September, 1958. *Mouton Publishers, 1958.*

Arnold, Matthew. Essays Literary & Critical. *E. P. Dutton Co., 1906.*

Arvin, Newton. Herman Melville. *Sloane, 1950.*

Auden, W. H. The Enchafèd Flood: Or the Romantic Iconography of the Sea. *Random House, 1950, Faber and Faber, 1951.*

Auden, W. H. Forewords and Afterwords. *Edited by Edward Mendelson. Random House, 1973.*

Auden, W. H. Collected Poems. *Edward Mendelson, ed. Random House, 1976, Faber and Faber, 1976.*

Babbitt, Irving. The Masters of Modern French Criticism. *Houghton Mifflin, 1912, Farrar, Straus and Company, 1963.*

Bagehot, Walter. Literary Studies. *Dutton, 1911.*

Bakhtin, M. M. The Dialogic Imagination. *Edited by Michael Holquist. Translated by Caryl Emerson and Michael Holquist. University of Texas Press, 1981.*

Baring, Maurice. Lost Lectures or The Fruits of Experience. *Knopf, 1932.*

Baudelaire, Charles. Baudelaire As a Literary Critic. *Edited and translated by Lois Boe Hyslop and Francis E. Hyslop, Jr. The Pennsylvania State University Press, 1964.*

Bayley, John. Pushkin: A Comparative Commentary. *Cambridge at the University Press, 1971.*

Beach, Joseph Warren. The Twentieth-Century Novel: Studies in Technique. *Appleton-Century-Crofts, Inc., 1932.*

Beauvoir, Simone de. The Marquis de Sade. *Edited by Paul Dinnage. Translated by Annette Michelson. John Calder (Publishers), Ltd., 1962, New English Library, 1972.*

Beddoes, Thomas Lovell, The Brides' Tragedy. *F. C. & J. Rivington, 1822.*

Beddoes, Thomas Lovell. Death's Jest Book. *William Pickering, 1850.*

Beddoes, Thomas Lovell. The Works of Thomas Lovell Beddoes. *Edited by H. W. Donner. Oxford University Press, 1935.*

Belinsky, V. G. Selected Philosophical Works. *Foreign Languages Publishing House, 1956.*

Bell, Aubrey F. G. Portuguese Literature. *Oxford University Press, 1970.*

Bennett, Arnold. Books and Persons: Being Comments on a Past Epoch, 1908-1911. *Doran, 1917.*

Bennett, E. K. A History of the German Novelle from Goethe to Thomas Mann. *Cambridge at the University Press, 1934.*

Berthoff, Warner. The Example of Melville. *Princeton University Press, 1962.*

Bettelheim, Bruno. The Uses of Enchantment: The Meaning and Importance of Fairy Tales. *Knopf, 1976.*

Bewley, Marius. The Eccentric Design: Form in the Classic American Novel. *Columbia University Press, 1963.*

Bickley, R. Bruce, Jr. The Method of Melville's Short Fiction. *Duke University Press, 1975.*

Bishop, Morris. A Survey of French Literature: The Nineteenth and Twentieth Centuries. *Harcourt Brace Jovanovich, 1955.*

Black, J. L. Nicholas Karamzin and Russian Society in the Nineteenth Century: A Study in Russian Political and Historical Thought. *University of Toronto Press, 1975.*

Black, J. L., ed. Essays on Karamzin: Russian Man-of-Letters, Political Thinker, Historian, 1766-1826. *Mouton Publishers, 1975.*

Bloom, Harold. The Visionary Company: A Reading of English Romantic Poetry. *Rev. ed Cornell University Press, 1971.*

Bowen, Elizabeth. Collected Impressions. *Alfred A. Knopf, 1950.*

Bowra, C. M. The Romantic Imagination. *Harvard University Press, 1949.*

Boynton, Percy H. More Contemporary Americans. *University of Chicago Press, 1927.*

Bradford, Gamaliel. Portraits of American Women. *Houghton Mifflin, 1919.*

Branch, Watson G., ed. Melville: The Critical Heritage. *Routledge & Kegan Paul, 1974.*

Brandes, George. Main Currents in Nineteenth Century Literature: The Emigrant Literature, Vol. I. *Translated by Diane White and Mary Morison. Heinemann Ltd., 1901, Boni & Liveright, Inc., 1924.*

Brenan, Gerald The Literature of the Spanish People from Roman Times to the Present Day. *Cambridge at the University Press, 1951.*

Brenner, Rica. Twelve American Poets Before 1900. *Harcourt Brace Jovanovich, 1933, Books for Libraries Press, 1968.*

Brooks, Van Wyck. Emerson and Others. *Dutton, 1927.*

Brooks, Van Wyck. The World of Washington Irving. *Dutton, 1944.*

Brophy, Brigid; Levey, Michael; and Osborne, Charles. Fifty Works of English Literature We Could Do Without. *Stein and Day, 1968.*

Bruccoli, Matthew J., ed. The Chief Glory of Every People: Essays on Classic American Writers. *Southern Illinois University Press, 1973.*

Bugelski, B. R., ed. Mickiewicz and the West: A Symposium. *University of Buffalo, 1959.*

Camus, Albert. The Rebel: An Essay on Man in Revolt. *Edited and translated by Anthony Bower. Rev. ed. Vintage Books, 1960.*

Casey, Daniel J., and Rhodes, Robert E., eds. Views of the Irish Peasantry: 1800-1916. *Archon Books (The Shoe String Press, Inc.), 1977.*

Cecil, David. Early Victorian Novelists: Essays in Revaluation. *Constable, 1934, Bobbs-Merrill, 1935.*

Chase, Richard. Herman Melville: A Critical Study. *Macmillan, 1949.*

Chateaubriand, François René de. The Memoirs of François René, Vicomte de Chateaubriand, Sometime Ambassador to England, Vol. I. *Translated by Alexander Teixeira de Mattos. G. P. Putnam's Sons, 1902.*

Chateaubriand, F. A. Preface to Atala: Or the Love and Constancy of Two Strangers in the Desert. *Edited by William Leonard Schwartz. Translated by Caleb Bingham. Stanford University Press, 1930.*

Chesnutt, Margaret. Studies in the Short Stories of William Carleton. *Acta Universitatis Gothoburgensis, 1976.*

Chesterton, G. K. A Handful of Authors: Essays on Books & Writers. *Edited by Dorothy Collins. Sheed and Ward, Inc., 1953.*

Chesterton, G. K. Charles Dickens: A Critical Study. *Dodd, Mead & Company, 1906; also published as* Charles Dickens. *Methuen & Co Ltd, 1960.*

Clark, Barrett H., ed. America's Lost Plays: Four Plays, Vol. 15. *Indiana University Press, 1965.*

Coad, Oral Sumner. William Dunlap: A Study of His Life and Works and of His Place in Contemporary Culture. *The Dunlap Society, 1917, Russell & Russell, Inc., 1962.*

Colum, Mary M. From These Roots: The Ideas That Have Made Modern Literature. *Columbia University Press, 1944, Kennikat Press, Inc., 1967.*

Colum, Padraic. Introduction to The Complete Grimm's Fairy Tales, *by Jacob Grimm and Wilhelm Grimm. Pantheon Books, 1974.*

Conrad, Joseph. Notes on Life & Letters. *J. M. Dent & Sons Ltd., 1921.*

Cowie, Alexander. The Rise of the American Novel. *American Book, 1951.*

Crocker, Lester G. Nature and Culture: Ethical Thought in the French Enlightenment. *The Johns Hopkins University Press, 1963.*

Cross, A. G. N. M. Karamzin: A Study of His Literary Career, 1783-1803. *Southern Illinois University Press, 1971.*

Crozier, Alice C. The Novels of Harriet Beecher Stowe. *Oxford University Press, 1969.*

Davidson, Angus. Edward Lear: Landscape Painter and Nonsense Poet. *J. Murray, 1938.*

Davidson, James Wood. The Living Writers of the South. *Carleton, Publisher, 1869.*

Davis, Merrell R., and Gilman, William H., eds. The Letters of Herman Melville. *Yale University Press, 1960.*

Davis, Thomas. Essays Literary and Historical. *W. Tempest, Dundalgan Press, 1914.*

Day, Clarence, Jr. After All. *Knopf, 1936.*

Debreczeny, Paul, and Zeldin, Jesse, eds. Literature and National Identity: Nineteenth-Century Russian Critical Essays. *Translated by Paul Debreczeny and Jesse Zeldin. University of Nebraska Press, 1970.*

Donner, H. W., ed. The Browning Box or the Life and Works of Thomas Lovell Beddoes as Reflected in Letters by His Friends and Admirers. *Oxford University Press, 1935.*

Donner, H. W. Introduction to Plays and Poems of Thomas Lovell Beddoes, *by Thomas Lovell Beddoes. Edited by H. W. Donner. Routledge and Kegan Paul Ltd, 1950.*

Dostoyevsky, Fyodor. Pages from the Journal of an Author. *Translated by S. S. Koteliansky and J. Middleton Murry. George Allen and Unwin Ltd., 1916.*

Dowden, Edward. A History of French Literature. *D. Appleton, 1900.*

Dukes, Ashley. The Youngest Drama: Studies of Fifty Dramatists. *Ernest Benn, Limited, 1923.*

Dunlap, William. A History of the American Theatre. *J. & J. Harper, 1832.*

Erlich, Victor, & others, eds. For Wiktor Weintraub: Essays in Polish Literature, Language, and History Presented on the Occasion of His 65th Birthday. *Mouton Publishers, 1975.*

Erskine, John. The Delight of Great Books. *The Bobbs-Merrill Company, 1928, World Publishing Co., 1941.*

Fadiman, Clifton. Party of One: The Selected Writings of Clifton Fadiman. *World Publishing Co., 1955.*

Fiedler, Leslie A. Love and Death in the American Novel. *Rev. ed. Stein and Day, 1966.*

Field, Andrew, ed. The Complection of Russian Literature: A Cento. *Atheneum, 1971.*

Flanagan, Thomas. The Irish Novelists: 1800-1850. *Columbia University Press, 1959.*

Ford, George H., and Lane, Lauriat, Jr., eds. The Dickens Critics. *Cornell University Press, 1961.*

Forster, E. M. Aspects of the Novel. *Harcourt Brace Jovanovich, 1927.*

Foster, Charles H. The Rungless Ladder: Harriet Beecher Stowe and New England Puritanism. *Duke University Press, 1954.*

France, Anatole. On Life & Letters, third series. *Translated by D. B. Stewart. John Lane Company, 1922.*

Freeman, John. Herman Melville. *Macmillan, 1926.*

Gaskell, E. C. The Life of Charlotte Brontë. *Dutton, 1957.*

Gassner, John. The Theatre in Our Times: A Survey of the Men, Materials and Movements in the Modern Theatre. *Crown, 1954.*

Gautier, Théophile. The Works of Théophile Gautier: A History of Romanticism, Vol. 16. *Edited and translated by F. C. de Sumichrast. The Jenson Society, 1906.*

George, Albert J. Short Fiction in France: 1800-1850. *Syracuse University Press, 1964.*

Gissing, George. Charles Dickens: A Critical Study. *Dodd, Mead, 1912.*

Gooch, G. P. History and Historians in the Nineteenth Century. *Longmans, Green, 1913, Peter Smith, 1949.*

Gorer, Geoffrey. The Life and Ideas of the Marquis de Sade. *Norton, 1963.*

Gosse, Edmund. Introduction to The Poetical Works of Thomas Lovell Beddoes, Vol. 1, *by Thomas Lovell Beddoes. J. M. Dent and Co., 1890.*

Gourmont, Remy de. The Book of Masks. *Translated by Jack Lewis. John W. Luce & Co., 1921, Books for Libraries Press, 1967.*

Grant, Elliott M. The Career of Victor Hugo. *Harvard University Press, 1945.*

Greene, Graham. Collected Essays. *Viking Penguin, 1969, The Bodley Head, 1969.*

Gregor, Ian, ed. The Brontës: A Collection of Critical Essays. *Prentice-Hall, Inc., 1970.*

Grimm, Jakob, and Grimm, Wilhelm. Preface to Household Tales, Vol. I, *by Jakob Grimm and Wilhelm Grimm. Edited and translated by Margaret Hunt. G. Bell & Sons, Ltd., 1910.*

Griswold, Rufus Wilmont. The Prose Writers of America: With a Survey of the History, Condition, and Prospects of American Literature. *Rev. ed. Porter & Coates, 1870.*

Gross, John, and Pearson, Gabriel, eds. Dickens and the Twentieth Century. *Routledge and Kegan Paul, 1962.*

Gwynn, Stephen. Irish Literature and Drama in the English Language: A Short History. *Thomas Nelson, 1936.*

Halline, Allan Gates, ed. American Plays. *American Book, 1935.*

Harbison, Robert. Deliberate Regression. *Knopf, 1980.*

Hassan, Ihab. The Dismemberment of "Orpheus": Toward a Post Modern Literature. *2d ed. The University of Wisconsin Press, 1982.*

Hawthorne, Julian. Preface to Culture's Garland: Being Memoranda of the Gradual Rise of Literature, Art, Music and Society in Chicago, and Other Western Ganglia, *by Eugene Field. Ticknor and Company, 1887.*

Hayman, Ronald. De Sade: A Critical Biography. *Thomas Y. Crowell, Inc., 1978.*

Heath-Stubbs, John. The Darkling Plain: A Study of the Later Fortunes of Romanticism in English Poetry from George Darley to W. B. Yeats. *Eyre & Spottiswoode, 1950.*

Hicks, Granville. The Great Tradition: An Interpretation of American Literature Since the Civil War. *Rev. ed. Macmillan, 1935, Quadrangle Books, 1969.*

Holmes, Oliver Wendell. The Complete Poetical Works of Oliver Wendell Holmes. *Houghton, Mifflin and Company, 1895.*

House, Humphry. All in Due Time: The Collected Essays and Broadcast Talks of Humphry House. *Rupert Hart-Davis, 1955.*

Preface to Household Stories, *by the Brothers Grimm. George Routledge and Sons, 1886.*

Hubbell, Jay B. The South in American Literature: 1607-1900. *Duke University Press, 1954.*

Huneker, James. Iconoclasts: A Book of Dramatists. *Charles Scribner's Sons, 1921.*

Huxley, Aldous. On the Margin: Notes and Essays. *Doran, 1923.*

Huxley, Aldous. Music at Night and Other Essays. *Doubleday, Doran & Company, 1931.*

Huysmans, J. K. Against Nature. *Translated by Robert Baldick. Penguin Books Inc., 1959.*

Jackson, Holbrook. The Complete Nonsense of Edward Lear. *Faber and Faber, 1947.*

James, Henry. A Small Boy and Others. *Charles Scribner's Sons, 1913.*

James, Henry. Literary Reviews and Essays: On American, English, and French Literature. *Edited by Albert Mordell. Twayne, 1957.*

Jewett, Sarah Orne. Letters of Sarah Orne Jewett. *Edited by Annie Fields. Houghton Mifflin, 1911.*

Kayser, Wolfgang. The Grotesque in Art and Literature. *Translated by Ulrich Weisstein. Indiana University Press, 1963.*

Kazin, Alfred. Introduction to Moby-Dick; or, The Whale, *by Herman Melville. Edited by Alfred Kazin. Houghton Mifflin, 1956.*

Ker, W. P. Collected Essays of W. P. Ker, Vol. II. *Edited by Charles Whibley. Macmillan and Co., Limited, 1925.*

Kridl, Manfred, ed. Adam Mickiewicz, Poet of Poland: A Symposium. *Columbia University Press, 1951.*

Kropotkin, Prince. Ideals and Realities in Russian Literature. *Knopf, 1915.*

Krzyzanowski, Julian. Polish Romantic Literature. *Allen & Unwin, 1930.*

Kulp-Hill, Kathleen. Rosalía de Castro. *Twayne, 1977.*

Lalou, René. Contemporary French Literature. *Translated by William Aspenwall Bradley. Knopf, 1924.*

Lamm, Martin. Modern Drama. *Translated by Karin Elliot. Basil Blackwell, 1952.*

Lavrin, Janko. Pushkin and Russian Literature. *Hodder & Stoughton, 1947, Russell & Russell, 1969.*

Lawrence, D. H. Studies in Classic American Literature. *Thomas Seltzer Inc., 1923, William Heinemann Ltd., 1924, Viking Press, 1964.*

Lear, Edward. Nonsense Books. *Robert Brothers, 1891.*

Leavis, F. R., and Leavis, Q. D. Dickens the Novelist. *Chatto & Windus, 1970, Pantheon Books, 1971.*

Lednicki, Wacław. Pushkin's "Bronze Horseman": The Story of a Masterpiece. *University of California Press, 1955.*

Lednicki, Wacław, ed. Adam Mickiewicz in World Literature. *Translated by J. Robert Loy. University of California Press, 1956.*

Lehmann, John. Edward Lear and His World. *Charles Scribner's Sons, 1977.*

Lewis, R.W.B. The American Adam: Innocence, Tragedy and Tradition in the Nineteenth Century. *University of Chicago Press, 1959.*

Lewisohn, Ludwig. The Modern Drama: An Essay in Interpretation. *B. W. Huebsch, 1915.*

Lynn, Kenneth S. Introduction to Uncle Tom's Cabin; or, Life Among the Lowly, *by Harriet Beecher Stowe. Harvard University Press, 1962.*

MacKintosh, James, ed. Memoirs of the Life of the Right Honourable Sir James MacKintosh, Vol. I. *Edward Moxon, 1835.*

Magoun, Francis P., Jr. Foreword to The Grimms' German Folk Tales, *by Jacob Grimm and Wilhelm Grimm. Translated by Francis P. Magoun, Jr. and Alexander H. Krappe. Southern Illinois University Press, 1960.*

Manheim, Ralph. Preface to Grimms' Tales for Young and Old: The Complete Stories, *by Jacob Grimm and Wilhelm Grimm. Translated by Ralph Manheim. Doubleday, 1977.*

Marcus, Steven. Dickens: From Pickwick to Dombey. *Basic Books, Inc., Publishers, 1965.*

Mare, Margaret. Annette von Droste-Hülshoff. *Methuen and Co., Ltd, 1965.*

Martin, Robert Bernard. The Accents of Persuasion: Charlotte Brontë's Novels. *Faber and Faber, 1966.*

Matthews, Brander. French Dramatists of the Nineteenth Century. *Rev. ed. Charles Scribner's Sons, 1901, Benjamin Blom, 1968.*

Matthiessen, F. O. American Renaissance: Art and Expression in the Age of Emerson and Whitman. *Oxford University Press, 1941.*

Maugham, W. Somerset. Great Novelists and Their Novels: Essays on the Ten Greatest Novels of the World, and the Men and Women Who Wrote Them. *The John C. Winston Company, 1948.*

Meserve, Walter J. An Emerging Entertainment: The Drama of the American People to 1828. *Indiana University Press, 1977.*

Milne, A. A. If I May. *E. P. Dutton & Company, 1920.*

Mirsky, D. S. Pushkin. *G. Routledge & Sons, Ltd., 1926.*

Mirsky, D. S. A History of Russian Literature from the Earliest Times to the Death of Dostoyevsky. *Knopf, 1927.*

Mirsky, D. S. A History of Russian Literature Comprising "A History of Russian Literature" and "Contemporary Russian Literature." *Edited by Francis J. Whitfield. Knopf, 1955.*

Moore, George. Confessions of a Young Man. *Edited by George Moore. William Heinemann, 1917, Capricorn Books, 1959.*

Moore, Jack B. Introduction to *The Algerine Captive; or, The Life and Adventures of Doctor Updike Underhill, Six Years a Prisoner among the Algerines, *by Royall Tyler. Scholars' Facsimiles & Reprints, 1967.*

Moses, Montrose J., and Brown, John Mason, eds. The American Theatre as Seen by Its Critics 1752-1934. *Norton, 1934.*

Mumford, Lewis. Herman Melville. *Harcourt Brace Jovanovich, 1929.*

Natan, Alex, ed. German Men of Letters: Twelve Literary Essays, Vol. I. *Wolff, 1961.*

Nebel, Henry M., Jr. N. M. Karamzin: A Russian Sentimentalist. *Mouton Publishers, 1967.*

Neuhäuser, Rudolf. Towards the Romantic Age: Essays on Sentimental and Preromantic Literature in Russia. *Martinus Nijhoff, 1974.*

Noakes, Vivien. Edward Lear: The Life of a Wanderer. *Collins, 1968.*

Noyes, George Rapall. Introduction to *Pan Tadeusz, *by Adam Mickiewicz. Translated by George Rapall Noyes. 2d ed. Dent, 1930.*

Oates, Joyce Carol. The Edge of Impossibility: Tragic Forms in Literature. *Vanguard Press, 1972.*

O'Connor, Frank. A Short History of Irish Literature: A Backward Look. *G. P. Putnam's Sons, 1967.*

O'Donoghue, David J. The Life of William Carleton: Being His Autobiography and Letters; and an Account of His Life and Writings, from the Point at which the Autobiography Breaks Off, Vol. II. *Downey & Co., 1896.*

Parker, Hershel, ed. The Recognition of Herman Melville: Selected Criticism since 1846. *University of Michigan Press, 1967.*

Parks, Edd Winfield. Introduction to *Southern Poets. Edited by Edd Winfield Parks. American Book, 1936.*

Parrington, Vernon Louis. Main Currents in American Thought, an Interpretation of American Literature from the Beginnings to 1920: The Romantic Revolution in America, 1800-1860, Vol. 2. *Harcourt Brace Jovanovich, 1958.*

Pattee, Fred Lewis. Tradition and Jazz. *The Century Company, 1925, Books for Libraries Press, 1968.*

Peppard, Murray B. Paths through the Forest: A Biography of the Brothers Grimm. *Holt, Rinehart and Winston, 1971.*

Pipes, Richard. Karamzin's Memoir on Ancient and Modern Russia: A Translation and Analysis. *Harvard University Press, 1959.*

Praz, Mario. The Romantic Agony. *Translated by Angus Davidson. 2d ed. Oxford University Press, 1970.*

Priestley, J. B. Literature and Western Man. *Harper & Row, Publishers, Inc., 1960.*

Pritchett, V. S. The Living Novel and Later Appreciations. *Rev. ed. Random House, 1964.*

Pritchett, V. S. The Myth Makers: Literary Essays. *Random House, 1979.*

Proffer, Carl R., ed. Modern Russian Poets on Poetry. *Ardis, 1976.*

Proust, Marcel. Marcel Proust on Art and Literature 1896-1919. *Translated by Sylvia Townsend Warner. Meridian Books, 1958.*

Pushkin, Alexander. The Poems, Prose and Plays of Alexander Pushkin. *Edited by Avrahm Yarmolinsky. The Modern Library, 1962.*

Pushkin, Alexander. The Critical Prose of Alexander Pushkin: With Critical Essays by Four Russian Romantic Poets. *Edited and translated by Carl R. Proffer. Indiana University Press, 1969.*

Pushkin, Alexander Sergeyevich. Pushkin on Literature. *Edited and translated by Tatiana Wolff. Methuen & Co Ltd, 1971.*

Quennell, Peter. Singular Preference: Portraits & Essays. *Collins, 1952.*

Quinn, Arthur Hobson. American Fiction: An Historical and Critical Survey. *Appleton-Century-Crofts, 1936.*

Quinn, Arthur Hobson. A History of the American Drama: From the Beginning to the Civil War. *2d ed. F. S. Crofts & Co., 1943, Appleton-Century-Crofts, Inc., 1951.*

Rafroidi, Patrick, and Brown, Terence, eds. The Irish Short Story. *Colin Smythe Ltd., 1979.*

Raitt, A. W. Introduction to Cruel Tales, *by Villiers de l'Isle-Adam. Translated by Robert Baldick. Oxford University Press, 1963.*

Rathburn, R. C., and Steinmann, M., eds. From Austen to Conrad. *University of Minnesota Press, 1958.*

Richardson, Joanna. Edward Lear. *British Council, 1965.*

Rickword, Edgell. Essays and Opinions: 1921-1931. *Edited by Alan Young. Carcanet Press, 1974.*

Ridgely, J. V. William Gilmore Simms. *Twayne, 1962.*

Roscoe, William Caldwell. Poems and Essays, Vol. II. *Edited by Richard Holt Hutton. Chapman and Hall, 1860.*

Rourke, Constance Mayfield. Trumpets of Jubilee. *Harcourt Brace Jovanovich, 1927.*

Rourke, Constance. The Roots of American Culture and Other Essays. *Edited by Van Wyck Brooks. Harcourt Brace Jovanovich, 1942.*

Sade, Marquis de. The Marquis de Sade: The Complete ''Justine,'' ''Philosophy in the Bedroom,'' and Other Writings. *Edited and translated by Richard Seaver and Austryn Wainhouse. Grove Press, 1965.*

Sade, Marquis de. The Marquis de Sade: ''The 120 Days of Sodom'' and Other Writings. *Edited and translated by Austryn Wainhouse and Richard Seaver. Grove Press, 1966.*

Sainte-Beuve, C. A. Portraits of Celebrated Women. *Translated by H. W. Preston. 3d ed. Robert Brothers, 1895.*

Sainte-Beuve, C. A. Causeries du Lundi (April, 1850-July, 1850), Vol. II. *Translated by E. J. Trechmann. George Routledge & Sons, Limited, 1911.*

Saintsbury, George. A History of Nineteenth Century Literature (1780-1895). *Macmillan, 1896.*

Saintsbury, George. A History of the French Novel (to the Close of the 19th Century): From 1800 to 1900, Vol. II. *Macmillan and Co., Limited, 1917, Russell & Russell, Inc., 1964.*

Saintsbury, George. A Last Vintage: Essays and Papers. *Edited by John W. Oliver; Arthur Melville Clark; and Augustus Muir. Methuen & Co. Ltd., 1950.*

Saintsbury, George. Introduction to Jacob Faithful, *by Frederick Marryat. Constable & Co., 1928.*

Santayana, George. Soliloquies in England and Later Soliloquies. Charles Scribner's Sons, 1924.

Sedgwick, William Ellery. Herman Melville: The Tragedy of Mind. Edited by Sarah Cabot Sedgwick. Harvard University Press, 1945.

Seelye, John. Preface to Masterman Ready, by Frederick Marryat. Garland Publishing Inc., 1976.

Shaw, J. Thomas. Introduction to The Letters of Alexander Pushkin, by Alexander Pushkin. Translated by J. Thomas Shaw. The University of Wisconsin Press, 1967.

Sherry, Norman. Charlotte and Emily Brontë. Evans Brothers, 1969, Arco Publishing Company, Inc., 1970.

Silz, Walter. Realism and Reality: Studies in the German Novelle of Poetic Realism. The University of North Carolina Press, 1954.

Simmons, Ernest J. Introduction to Russian Realism. Indiana University Press, 1965.

Slonim, Marc. The Epic of Russian Literature from Its Origins through Tolstoy. Oxford University Press, 1950.

Snow, Royall H. Thomas Lovell Beddoes: Eccentric & Poet. Covici, Friede, 1928.

Spector, Ivar. The Golden Age of Russian Literature. Rev. ed. The Caxton Printers, Ltd., 1943.

Spiller, Robert E. The Cycle of American Literature: An Essay in Historical Criticism. Macmillan, 1955.

Squire, J. C. Life and Letters. Doran, 1921.

Stein, William Bysshe. The Poetry of Melville's Late Years: Time, History, Myth, and Religion. State University of New York Press, 1970.

Stern, Milton R., ed. Discussions of "Moby-Dick." D. C. Heath and Company, 1968.

Stevenson, Robert Louis. The Essays of Robert Louis Stevenson. Macdonald, 1950.

Stilman, Leon. Introduction to Letters of a Russian Traveler: 1789-1790, by N. M. Karamzin. Edited and translated by Florence Jonas. Columbia University Press, 1957.

Stowe, Harriet Beecher. Epilogue to Uncle Tom's Cabin; or, Life Among the Lowly. F. E. Longley's, 1881, Collier-Macmillan, 1962.

Strachey, Edward. Introduction to Nonsense Omnibus, by Edward Lear. Frederick Warne & Co., 1943.

Strachey, Lytton. Literary Essays. Harcourt Brace and Company, 1949.

Strachey, Lytton. A Century of the Essay: British and American. Edited by David Daiches. Harcourt Brace and Company, 1951.

Sucksmith, Harvey Peter. The Narrative Art of Charles Dickens: The Rhetoric of Sympathy and Irony in His Novels. Oxford University Press, 1970.

Swinburne, Algernon Charles. A Study of Victor Hugo. Chatto & Windus, 1886, Kennikat Press, 1970.

Symons, Arthur. The Symbolist Movement in Literature. E. P. Dutton and Company, 1908.

Taine, H. A. History of English Literature, Vol. II. Translated by H. Van Laun. Holt & Williams, 1871.

Tallentyre, S. G. [pseudonym of Evelyn Beatrice Hall]. The Women of the Salons and Other French Portraits. Longmans, Green, and Co., 1901, G. P. Putnam's Sons, 1926.

Taylor, Edgar. Preface to Popular Stories, by Jacob Grimm and Wilhelm Grimm. Edited by Edgar Taylor. Chatto & Windus, 1920.

Thibaudet, Albert. French Literature from 1795 to Our Era. Translated by Charles Lam Markmann. Funk & Wagnalls, 1968.

Thody, Philip, ed. Lyrical and Critical Essays. Translated by Ellen Conroy Kennedy. Knopf, 1968.

Thompson, Francis. Literary Criticisms: Newly Discovered and Collected. Edited by Rev. Terrence L. Connolly, S. J. E. P. Dutton and Company, Inc., 1948.

Thompson, Lawrance. Melville's Quarrel with God. *Princeton University Press, 1952.*

Tillotson, Kathleen. Novels of the Eighteen-Forties. *Oxford University Press, 1954.*

Todd, Janet. Women's Friendship in Literature. *Columbia University Press, 1980.*

Trollope, Frances. Paris and the Parisians in 1835. *Harper & Brothers, 1836.*

Tyler, Royall. Four Plays. *Edited by Arthur Wallace Peach and George Floyd Newbrough. Princeton University Press, 1941.*

Ussher, Arland, and Von Metzradt, Carl. Enter These Enchanted Woods: An Interpretation of Grimm's Fairy Tales. *2d ed. The Dolmen Press, 1957.*

Van Doren, Carl. The American Novel: 1789-1939. *Rev. ed. Macmillan, 1940.*

Vincent, Howard P., ed. The Merrill Studies in Moby Dick. *Charles E. Merrill Publishing Company, 1969.*

Wagenknecht, Edward. Cavalcade of the English Novel: From Elizabeth to George VI. *Holt, Rinehart and Winston, 1948.*

Wagenknecht, Edward. Cavalcade of the American Novel. *Holt, Rinehart and Winston, 1952.*

Walkley, A. B. Drama and Life. *Methuen & Co., 1907.*

Wall, Stephen, ed. Charles Dickens: A Critical Anthology. *Penguin Books, 1970.*

Ward, Patricia A. The Medievalism of Victor Hugo. *The Pennsylvania State University Press, 1975.*

Warren, L. A. Modern Spanish Literature: A Comprehensive Survey of the Novelists, Poets, Dramatists and Essayists from the Eighteenth Century to the Present Day, Vol. II. *Brentano's Ltd, 1929.*

Warren, Robert Penn. Selected Essays. *Random House, 1958.*

Watson, Charles S. Antebellum Charleston Dramatists. *University of Alabama Press, 1976.*

Waxman, Samuel Montefiore. Antoine and the Théâtre-Libre. *Harvard University Press, 1926.*

Weintraub, Wiktor. The Poetry of Adam Mickiewicz. *Mouton Publishers, 1954.*

Wellek, René. A History of Modern Criticism: 1750-1950, The Romantic Age. *Yale University Press, 1955.*

Whitridge, Arnold. Critical Ventures in Modern French Literature. *Charles Scribner's Sons, 1924.*

Wilson, Edmund. Axel's Castle: A Study in the Imaginative Literature of 1870-1930. *Charles Scribner's Sons, 1931.*

Wilson, Edmund. The Wound and the Bow: Seven Studies in Literature. *Houghton Mifflin Company, 1941, Farrar, Straus & Giroux, 1978.*

Wilson, Edmund. The Triple Thinkers: Twelve Essays on Literary Subjects. *Rev. ed. Oxford University Press, 1948, Noonday, 1976.*

Wilson, Edmund. The Bit between My Teeth: A Literary Chronicle of 1950-1965. *Farrar, Straus and Giroux, 1952.*

Wilson, Edmund. Patriotic Gore: Studies in the Literature of the American Civil War. *Oxford University Press, 1962.*

Wilson, Edmund. A Window on Russia: For the Use of Foreign Readers. *Farrar, Straus and Giroux, 1972.*

Wilson, Edmund, ed. The Shock of Recognition: The Development of Literature in the United States Recorded by the Men Who Made It. *Farrar, Straus and Cudahy, 1955.*

Winters, Yvor. Maule's Curse: Seven Studies in the History of American Obscurantism. *New Directions, 1938.*

Winters, Yvor. In Defense of Reason. *The Swallow Press, 1947.*

Wood, Butler, ed. Charlotte Brontë, 1816-1916: A Centenary Memorial. *Dutton, 1918.*

Woolf, Virginia. The Common Reader. *Harcourt Brace Jovanovich, 1925.*

Woolf, Virginia. The Captain's Death Bed and Other Essays. *Harcourt Brace Jovanovich, 1950.*

Wright, Nathalia. Melville's Use of the Bible. *Duke University Press, 1949, Octagon Books, 1969.*

Yeats, W. B. Introduction to Stories from Carleton, *by William Carleton. Edited by Ernest Rhys. Walter Scott, 1889, Lemma Publishing Corporation, 1973.*

Yeats, W. B. Introduction to Representative Irish Tales. *Edited by W. B. Yeats. Humanities Press, 1979.*

ISBN 0-8103-5803-4

90000>
9 780810 358034